SOCIAL PSYCHOLOGY

Eighth Canadian Edition

DAVID G. MYERS
HOPE COLLEGE

JEAN M. TWENGE
SAN DIEGO STATE UNIVERSITY

CHRISTIAN H. JORDAN
WILFRID LAURIER UNIVERSITY

STEVEN M. SMITH
SAINT MARY'S UNIVERSITY

Social Psychology
Eighth Canadian Edition

ISBN-13: 978-1-26-032701-4
ISBN-10: 1-26-032701-9

1 2 3 4 5 6 7 8 9 10 M 27 26 25 24 23 22 21

Printed and bound in Canada.

Director of Product, Canada: *Rhondda McNabb*
Portfolio Manager: *Alex Campbell*
Marketing Manager: *Patti Rozakos*
Senior Manager, Content & Product Development: *Denise Foote*
Content Developer: *Veronica Saroli*
Portfolio Associate: *Tatiana Sevciuc*
Supervising Editor: *Jack Whelan*
Permissions Editor: *Marnie Lamb*
Copy Editor: *Laurel Sparrow*
Production Coordinator: *Jason Stubner*
Cover and Interior Design: *Liz Harasymczuk*
Cover Image: *SHSPhotography/Getty Images*
Page Layout: *MPS Limited*
Printer: *Marquis*

About the Authors

Source: ©David Myers.

David G. Myers, since receiving his PhD from the University of Iowa, has spent his career at Michigan's Hope College, where he is a professor of psychology and has taught dozens of social psychology sections. Hope College students have invited him to be their commencement speaker and named him "outstanding professor."

Dr. Myers also communicates psychology science to the general public. His writings have appeared in four dozen magazines, from *Today's Education* to *Scientific American.* His 17 books include *The Pursuit of Happiness* and *Intuition: Its Powers and Perils.*

His research and writings have been recognized for the Gordon Allport Prize, for an "honored scientist" award from the Federation of Associations in the Brain and Behavioral Sciences, and for the Award for Distinguished Service on Behalf of Personality–Social Psychology.

Source: ©Sandy Huffaker, Jr.

Jean Twenge has drawn on her research in her books for a broader audience, *iGen: Why Today's Super-Connected Kids Are Growing Up Less Rebellious, More Tolerant, Less Happy—And Completely Unprepared for Adulthood* (2017) and *Generation Me: Why Today's Young Americans Are More Confident, Assertive, Entitled—And More Miserable Than Ever Before* (2nd ed., 2014). An article by Dr. Twenge in *The Atlantic* was nominated for a National Magazine Award. She frequently gives talks and seminars on generational differences to audiences such as college faculty and staff, parent–teacher groups, military personnel, camp directors, and corporate executives.

Dr. Twenge grew up in Minnesota and Texas. She holds a BA and MA from the University of Chicago and a PhD from the University of Michigan. She completed a postdoctoral research fellowship in social psychology at Case Western Reserve University. She lives in San Diego with her husband and three daughters.

Source: ©Christian Jordan.

Christian H. Jordan is a professor and associate chair of the psychology department at Wilfrid Laurier University. He teaches lecture courses and seminars in social psychology and research methods at both the undergraduate and graduate levels.

Dr. Jordan is also an active researcher, studying self-esteem, narcissism, and self-enhancement processes. His work has been published in a number of scholarly handbooks and journals, including the *Journal of Personality and Social Psychology, Journal of Personality,* and *Journal of Experimental Psychology.* He has also written popular instructional pieces on how to effectively read journal articles and how to conduct and report persuasive psychology experiments. He is currently an associate editor of the *Journal of Personality* and has served as associate editor of *Self & Identity.*

In his spare time, Dr. Jordan spends time with his family and friends, reads, listens to music, drinks craft beer, and exercises. He enjoys cycling during the summer months. Christian and Lynne Jordan have two sons, Grayson and Hayden, and a daughter, Reilly, whom they lost to leukemia.

Source: ©Steven M. Smith.

Steven M. Smith is a professor of psychology and the associate vice-president academic and enrolment management at Saint Mary's University in Halifax. He completed his BA (honours) at Bishop's University in Lennoxville, Quebec, and his MA and PhD in social psychology at Queen's University in Kingston, Ontario. Dr. Smith regularly teaches courses in social behaviour, attitudes and persuasion, and psychology and law. His lectures are well received, and he been awarded a lifetime service award for major contributions to students from the Saint Mary's University Student Association.

Dr. Smith is an active researcher and is dedicated to applying his theoretical work to real-world concerns. His research has been supported by the Social Sciences and Humanities Research Council, the Canadian Institutes of Health Research, the Nova Scotia Health Research Foundation, the Nova Scotia Gaming Foundation, and a number of private organizations. His work has appeared in journals such as the *Journal of Applied Psychology, Law & Human Behavior, Journal of Personality and Social Psychology, Personality and Social Psychology Bulletin, Social Psychology and Personality Science,* and *Psychophysiology.*

Dr. Smith has lent his expertise to a number of community organizations, advising on communication and social marketing issues. He has also served as an expert witness at criminal trials. His wife, Isabel, is a clinical developmental psychologist, and together they have two fantastic but heavily analyzed children, Sydney and Dylan.

Brief Contents

Preface		**xi**
CHAPTER 1	Introducing the Science and Methods of Social Psychology	1
Part One	Social Thinking	29
CHAPTER 2	The Self in a Social World	30
CHAPTER 3	Social Beliefs and Judgments	73
CHAPTER 4	Behaviour and Attitudes	115
Part Two	Social Influence	147
CHAPTER 5	Persuasion	148
CHAPTER 6	Conformity	192
CHAPTER 7	Group Influence	224
Part Three	Social Relations	265
CHAPTER 8	Altruism: Helping Others	266
CHAPTER 9	Aggression: Hurting Others	300
CHAPTER 10	Attraction and Intimacy: Liking and Loving Others	341
CHAPTER 11	Prejudice	383
CHAPTER 12	Conflict and Peacemaking	426

References RE-1
Chapter Sources CS-1
Glossary GL-1
Name Index NI-1
Subject Index SI-1

Table of Contents

Preface xi

CHAPTER 1

Introducing the Science and Methods of Social Psychology 1

What Is Social Psychology? 2
How Much of Our Social World Is Just in Our Heads? 3
If You Were Ordered to Be Cruel, Would You Comply? 3
Would You Help Others? Or Help Yourself? 3

What Are the Major Themes of Social Psychology? 4
We Construct Our Social Reality 4
Our Social Intuitions Are Often Powerful but Sometimes Perilous 5
Social Influences Shape Our Behaviour 6
Personal Attitudes and Dispositions Also Shape Behaviour 6
Social Behaviour Is Biologically Rooted 7
Relating to Others Is a Basic Need 7
Social Psychology's Principles Are Applicable in Everyday Life 8

How Do Values Affect Social Psychology? 8
Obvious Ways in Which Values Enter Social Psychology 8
Not-So-Obvious Ways in Which Values Enter Social Psychology 9

Is Social Psychology Merely Common Sense? 11
Common Sense, Revisited 13

Research Methods: How Do We Do Social Psychology? 15
Forming and Testing Hypotheses 15
Correlational Research: Detecting Natural Associations 17
Experimental Research: Searching for Cause and Effect 21
Generalizing From Laboratory to Life 26

Summing Up 27

Part One

Social Thinking 29

CHAPTER 2

The Self in a Social World 30

Spotlights and Illusions: What Do They Teach Us About Ourselves? 31

Self-Concept: Who Am I? 34
At the Centre of Our Worlds: Our Sense of Self 34
Social Comparisons 34
Self and Culture 37
Self-Knowledge 43

What Is the Nature and Motivating Power of Self-Esteem? 46
Self-Esteem Motivation 47
The Trade-Off of Low vs. High Self-Esteem 50
Self-Efficacy 52

What Is Self-Serving Bias? 53
Explaining Positive and Negative Events 54
Can We All Be Better Than Average? 55
Unrealistic Optimism 58
False Consensus and Uniqueness 59
Temporal Comparison 60
Explaining Self-Serving Bias 61

How Do People Manage Their Self-Presentation? 62
Self-Handicapping 62
Impression Management 63
Doubting Our Ability in Social Situations 65
Overpersonalizing Situations 66

What Does It Mean to Have Perceived Self-Control? 67
Learned Helplessness Versus Self-Determination 68

Summing Up 70

CHAPTER 3

Social Beliefs and Judgments 73

How Do We Judge Our Social Worlds, Consciously and Unconsciously? 74

Priming 74
Intuitive Judgments 76
Overconfidence 78
Heuristics: Mental Shortcuts 83
Counterfactual Thinking 86
Illusory Thinking 87
Mood and Judgment 89

How Do We Perceive Our Social Worlds? 91

Perceiving and Interpreting Events 91
Belief Perseverance 93
Constructing Memories of Ourselves and Our Worlds 94

How Do We Explain Our Social Worlds? 98

Attributing Causality: To the Person or the Situation? 98
The Fundamental Attribution Error 100
Why Do We Make the Attribution Error? 102
Why Do We Study Attribution Errors? 106

How Do Our Social Beliefs Matter? 106

Teacher Expectations and Student Performance 107
Getting From Others What We Expect 108

What Can We Conclude About Social Beliefs and Judgments? 110

Summing Up 112

CHAPTER 4

Behaviour and Attitudes 115

How Well Do Our Attitudes Predict Our Behaviours? 116

Are We All Hypocrites? 116
When Attitudes Predict Behaviour 117

When Does Our Behaviour Affect Our Attitudes? 121

Role-Playing 122
When Saying Becomes Believing 124
The Foot-in-the-Door Phenomenon 125
Low-Ball Technique 126
Door-in-the-Face Technique 127
Immoral and Moral Acts 128
Social Movements 130

Why Does Our Behaviour Affect Our Attitudes? 131

Self-Presentation: Impression Management 131
Self-Justification: Cognitive Dissonance 132
Self-Perception 136
Comparing the Theories 141

Summing Up 144

Part Two

Social Influence 147

CHAPTER 5

Persuasion 148

What Paths Lead to Persuasion? 150

The Central Route and the Peripheral Route 151
Different Routes for Different Purposes 152

What Are the Elements of Persuasion? 152

Who Says? The Communicator 152
What Is Said? The Message Content 156
How Is It Said? The Channel of Communication 164
To Whom Is It Said? The Audience 169

Extreme Persuasion: How Do Cults Indoctrinate? 173

Group Indoctrination Tactics 173
Attitudes Follow Behaviour 174
Persuasive Elements 175
Group Effects 176

Persuasion and Climate Change: How Do We Address Global Warming? 178

Psychology and Climate Change 178
New Technologies 181
Reducing Consumption 181

How Can Persuasion Be Resisted? 183

Attitude Strength 183
Information-Processing Biases 183
Reactance 185
Strengthening Personal Commitment 185
Inoculation Programs 186
Implications of Attitude Inoculation 189

Summing Up 190

CHAPTER 6

Conformity 192

What Is Conformity? 193

What Are the Classic Conformity and Obedience Studies? 194

Sherif's Studies of Norm Formation 194
Asch's Studies of Group Pressure 197
Milgram's Obedience Studies 199
What Breeds Obedience? 201
Reflections on the Classic Studies 204

What Predicts Conformity? 209

Group Size 209
Unanimity 210
Cohesion 210
Status 211
Public Response 211
No Prior Commitment 212

Why Conform? 213

Who Conforms? 215

Personality 215
Culture 217
Gender 217
Social Roles 218

Do We Ever Want to Be Different? 219

Reactance 219
Asserting Uniqueness 221

Summing Up 222

CHAPTER 7

Group Influence 224

What Is a Group? 225

Social Facilitation: How Are We Affected by the Presence of Others? 226

The Mere Presence of Others 226
Crowding: The Presence of Many Others 229
Why Are We Aroused in the Presence of Others? 230

Social Loafing: Do Individuals Exert Less Effort in a Group? 231

Many Hands Make Light Work 232
Social Loafing in Everyday Life 233

Deindividuation: When Do People Lose Their Sense of Self in Groups? 236

Doing Together What We Would Not Do Alone 236
Diminished Self-Awareness 241

Group Polarization: Do Groups Intensify Our Opinions? 241

The Case of the "Risky Shift" 242
Impact of Group Discussion on Individuals' Opinions 243
Explaining Polarization 245

Groupthink: Do Groups Hinder or Assist Good Decisions? 248

Symptoms of Groupthink 249
Critiquing Groupthink 252
Preventing Groupthink 252
Group Problem Solving 253

Leadership: How Do Leaders Shape the Group's Actions? 256

Task Leadership and Social Leadership 256
Transactional Leadership 257
Transformational Leadership 257

The Influence of the Minority: How Do Individuals Influence the Group? 258

Consistency 259
Self-Confidence 259
Defections From the Majority 260
Group Influences in Juries 260

Summing Up 262

Part Three

Social Relations 265

CHAPTER 8

Altruism: Helping Others 266

Why Do We Help? 269

Social Exchange 269
Social Norms 273
Evolutionary Psychology 276
Comparing and Evaluating Theories of Altruism 278

When Will We Help? 282

Number of Bystanders 282
Helping When Someone Else Does 289
Time Pressures 289
Similarity to the Victim 290

Who Helps? 291
Personality Traits 291
Gender 291

How Can We Increase Helping? 292
Reduce Ambiguity, Increase Responsibility 292
Guilt and Concern for Self-Image 293
Socializing Prosocial Behaviour 294
Postscript: The Kitty Genovese Case Revisited 297
What to Do When You Need Help 298
Conclusions 298

Summing Up 299

CHAPTER 9

Aggression: Hurting Others 300

What Is Aggression? 301

What Are Some Theories of Aggression? 303
Aggression as a Biological Phenomenon 304
Aggression as a Response to Frustration 309
Aggression as Learned Social Behaviour 312

What Are Some Influences on Aggression? 315
Aversive Incidents 315
Arousal 316
Aggression Cues 318
Media Influences: Pornography and Sexual Violence 319
Media Influences: Television, Movies, and the Internet 322
Another Media Influence: Video Games 327
Group Influences 332

How Can Aggression Be Reduced? 335
Catharsis? 335
A Social Learning Approach 336
Culture Change and World Violence 338

Summing Up 338

CHAPTER 10

Attraction and Intimacy: Liking and Loving Others 341

What Leads to Friendship and Attraction? 345
Proximity 345
Physical Attractiveness 349
Similarity Versus Complementarity 359
Liking Those Who Like Us 362
Relationship Rewards 364

What Is Love? 365
Passionate Love 366
Companionate Love 369

What Enables Close Relationships? 371
Attachment 371
Equity 375
Self-Disclosure 376

How Do Relationships End? 378
Divorce 379
The Detachment Process 380

Summing Up 381

CHAPTER 11

Prejudice 383

What Is the Nature and Power of Prejudice? 384
Defining *Prejudice* 384
Prejudice: Implicit and Explicit 386
Racial Prejudice 387
Gender-Based Prejudice 390
LGBT Prejudice 392

What Are the Social Sources of Prejudice? 394
Social Inequalities: Unequal Status and Prejudice 394
Socialization 395
Institutional Supports 399

What Are the Motivational Sources of Prejudice? 400
Frustration and Aggression: The Scapegoat Theory 400
Social Identity Theory: Feeling Superior to Others 401
Motivation to Avoid Prejudice 405

What Are the Cognitive Sources of Prejudice? 406
Categorization: Classifying People Into Groups 406
Distinctiveness: Perceiving People Who Stand Out 408
Attributions: Is It a Just World? 412
Motivation to See the World as Just 413

What Are the Consequences of Prejudice? 415
Self-Perpetuating Prejudgments 415
Discrimination's Impact: The Self-Fulfilling Prophecy 416
Stereotype Threat 417
Do Stereotypes Bias Judgments of Individuals? 419

Summing Up 423

CHAPTER 12

Conflict and Peacemaking 426

What Creates Conflict? 427
Social Dilemmas 427
Competition 434
Perceived Injustice 436
Misperception 437

How Can Peace Be Achieved? 441
Contact 441
Cooperation 446
Communication 453
Conciliation 458

Summing Up 460

References RE-1

Chapter Sources CS-1

Glossary GL-1

Name Index NI-1

Subject Index SI-1

Preface

Welcome to the Eighth Canadian Edition of *Social Psychology.* We (Steven Smith and Christian Jordan) were excited to write this new edition but also knew it would be a challenge. We are thrilled to be working with David Myers and Jean Twenge. Both are known for their excellent books, which are solidly scientific and warmly human, factually rigorous, and intellectually provocative. Their texts are simply the best.

We continue to meet the challenge of creating a comprehensive Canadian social psychology text. How does one select the material for inclusion in a "reasonably comprehensive" introduction to one's discipline—a text long enough to allow rich narrative (to weave a story) but crisp enough not to overwhelm? Further, what Canadian content will most capture the imaginations of Canadian students? We have sought to present theories and findings that are not too esoteric but that capture the fundamental concepts of the field in a scientifically rigorous manner. In doing so, we have sought to balance classic findings with significant current Canadian research. We think you will find that as the book emphasizes the Canadian context, it also has a strong research focus presented in an understandable and engaging style.

Organization

The book opens with a single chapter that includes our methods of inquiry. The chapter also warns students about how findings can seem obvious—once you know them—and how social psychologists' own values permeate the discipline. The intent is to give students just enough background to prepare them for what follows.

The book then unfolds around its definition of social psychology: the scientific study of how people *think about* (Part One), *influence* (Part Two), and *relate to* (Part Three) one another.

Part One, on *social thinking,* examines how we view ourselves and others. It assesses the accuracy of our impressions, intuitions, and explanations; and it examines the relation of our behaviour and our attitudes.

Part Two explores *social influence.* In this edition, we begin by discussing how social influence can shape attitudes—that is, how persuasion occurs. This structure allows instructors to focus on attitude formation and change in a unit that covers Chapter 5, Chapter 6, and Chapter 7. We continue to examine social influence by examining the nature of persuasion, conformity, and group influence.

Part Three considers the attitudinal and behavioural manifestations of both negative and positive *social relations.* It flows from altruism to aggression and attraction to prejudice. Notably, in this edition we have condensed the material on prejudice into one chapter, but still highlight both the causes and consequences of prejudice in Chapter 11. Complementing this focus on relations between different social groups, we have expanded coverage of research on conflict and peacemaking so that it has its own, comprehensive coverage in Chapter 12. Applications of social psychology are interwoven throughout every chapter.

This book also has a multicultural emphasis that we seek to stress in every chapter. All authors are creatures of their cultures, and we are no exceptions. Yet by reading the world's social psychology literature, by corresponding with researchers worldwide, and by examining Canada's extensive research on the many cultures represented in this country, we have sought to present a multicultural text to a Canadian audience. The book's focus remains the *fundamental principles of social thinking, social influence, and social relations as revealed by careful empirical research.* However, hoping to broaden our awareness of the human family, we aim to illustrate these principles multiculturally.

To assist readers, we have organized chapters into three to six readable-length sections. Each begins with a preview and ends with a summary that highlights the organization and key concepts.

We have sought, paragraph by paragraph, to craft the most engaging and effective book possible. The definitions of key terms appear both in the text and in the Glossary.

Highlights of the Eighth Canadian Edition

- **Current research.** The text is updated throughout, with more than 750 new citations, to include the most cutting-edge research in social psychology. The latest findings on automatic processing, evolutionary psychology, video games and aggression, perceptions of media bias, counter-arguments and attitude inoculation, culture and helping strangers, motivational sources of prejudice, and misperceptions of out-groups are just some of the examples of updated research in this new edition.
- **Application of social psychology.** Social psychology is a very applied discipline. Yet sometimes there is a gap between the research described on the page and how it might roll out in real life—the connection can be a bit abstract. In this edition of the text, we have tried hard to bridge that gap. Chapters feature a set of insights or a hands-on activity that applies the science you are learning to the real world and teaches you how to apply what you have learned to your everyday life.
- **Additional coverage of gender.** Research on gender continues to evolve. Gender is examined by a number of different researchers in a number of different contexts. As such, it seems that gender is less a subfield of social psychology and more a very important variable that is studied in many contexts. Given this evolution, gender is covered throughout the book in many subsections.
- **Additional coverage of social cognitive neuroscience.** New developments in brain imaging and recording have provided a number of new insights in the field. These findings make a substantial contribution to a number of chapters.
- **Strong pedagogy.** Readers benefit from features designed to engage interest while encouraging understanding of core concepts. Pedagogical elements include section previews; numerous photos, figures, and tables; a running glossary; Focus On boxes highlighting applied concepts; The Inside Story vignettes, written by leading researchers; a summary of each major section within the text; the Summing Up sections moved to the end of each chapter, to become a resource for students reviewing for exams; and an index that highlights coverage of concepts such as culture, ethics, gender, law and justice, and sexuality.
- **Relevant examples.** Drawn from the arts, business, sports, and current events, the text's examples appeal to students from a variety of majors and academic backgrounds.

What's New in the Eighth Canadian Edition

Highlights of new and updated material in the Eighth Canadian Edition include the following.

Chapter 1: Introducing the Science and Methods of Social Psychology

- Revised chapter opener
- New discussion of correlation and causation

- New activity exploring potential causes for correlations
- Updated and recent research incorporated throughout the chapter

Chapter 2: The Self in a Social World

- New studies and examples about social comparison on Facebook
- Studies showing that individualism is on the rise globally
- New studies on how narcissism develops and how it impacts leadership
- New study and example of online "humblebragging" as a self-presentation strategy
- Self-control research reports on when failures of self-control most likely appear and when they do not, and how self-control exertion leading to self-control failure may be a uniquely Western occurrence

Chapter 3: Social Beliefs and Judgments

- Current research on partisanship leading to trust or distrust in news media
- New priming research with a new figure and a subliminal-exposure example
- Example of how embodied cognition can be social and positive
- New overconfidence research on how people can change their opinions
- New confirmation bias research on "ideological echo chambers"
- Updated statistics on transportation safety as related to the availability heuristic
- New example about fake news as related to belief perseverance

Chapter 4: Behaviour and Attitudes

- Updated chapter opening
- Revised Activity box that asks readers to explore how they can understand, use, and defeat compliance tactics
- Updated coverage of topic
- New research in multiple sections

Chapter 5: Persuasion

- Revised chapter opener
- Activity box that asks readers to deconstruct ads and understand the principles underlying their construction
- New research and recent studies
- New explanations and current examples for elements of persuasion

Chapter 6: Conformity

- Revised chapter and section openers
- Updates of conformity and obedience examples
- Activity box that asks readers to reflect on personal experiences of conformity
- Enhanced discussion of conformity issues in online contexts
- Discussion on conformity in hazing and "frosh week" situations

Chapter 7: Group Influence

- Revised chapter and section openers
- Enhanced discussion of group polarization on the Internet and in politics

- Revised Activity asking readers to reflect on their own experience of group influence
- Updated and recent research incorporated throughout the chapter

Chapter 8: Altruism: Helping Others

- Revised chapter and section openers
- Updated and recent research incorporated throughout the chapter
- Revised Activity box that asks readers to consider their definition of *altruism* as experienced by them
- Updated discussion of the iconic Kitty Genovese case that launched this line of research
- Discussion of how the reader can encourage people to help in an emergency situation

Chapter 9: Aggression: Hurting Others

- Analysis of studies confirming that alcohol consumption is associated with higher levels of aggression especially among men
- New studies on testosterone and alcohol
- New studies with examples of relative deprivation
- Added examples of aggressive cues related to anger
- Reporting on 130 studies across 10 countries showing laws restricting firearm sales producing reductions in gun-related crimes
- Research showing the connection between sexually explicit/violent movie watching and dating sexual violence; how pornography viewing makes people more likely to be sexually aggressive
- Research showing evidence of the link between violent video games and aggression and fewer prosocial acts
- Research showing how aggressive behaviour spreads in social groups through modelling
- New examples of how to reduce aggression

Chapter 10: Attraction and Intimacy: Liking and Loving Others

- Research showing how mere exposure by reading can change attitudes
- Study showing that too much exposure can have a negative effect
- Discussion and research example about online dating sites using similarity as a basis for matching
- Studies showing how passionate love involves the same brain reward pathways as addictions to substances
- Research revealing how anxiously attached people can become anxiously attached to their smartphones
- Research showing that couples report more relationship satisfaction when their partner understands their perspective in a disagreement

Chapter 11: Prejudice

- Previously separate chapters on the sources and consequences of prejudice have been combined into a single, comprehensive chapter
- Added examples of prejudice in politics

- Example of how strong beliefs can exaggerate reality
- Added discussion of criticisms of the Implicit Association Test (IAT)
- Updated statistics on racial prejudice, hate crime incidents, and White nationalist views
- Many new examples of favouritism in employment discrimination
- New reporting on implicit-bias training for police and in the political arena
- New reporting on hostile and benevolent sexism
- Discussion and statistics on job discrimination against gay and transgender people
- New discussion on consequences of homophobia and transphobia
- Added research study showing that individuals differ in own-race bias

Chapter 12: Conflict and Peacemaking

- Material previously in a module has been considerably expanded to form this new chapter, with relevant material incorporated from prior prejudice chapters
- Research showing how threats (terrorist bombings, pandemic diseases) can increase competition
- New political polarization research in "Mirror-Image Perceptions" section
- Study showing that highlighting genetic differences between ethnic groups contributes to violence risk, while learning about genetic similarities helps foster peace
- Research showing that, when at an impasse, simply going for a walk and experiencing movement synchrony can help engender cooperation

Features

In addition to the authors' renowned engaging and personal writing style, which reflects their enthusiasm for the subject, *Social Psychology,* Eighth Canadian Edition, also offers pedagogical elements designed to help students get the most out of the text.

Section Previews

These previews introduce each major section within a chapter, bringing forward the concepts and issues to be discussed in the ensuing pages.

> **How Well Do Our Attitudes Predict Our Behaviours?**
>
> *To what extent, and under what conditions, do attitudes drive our outward actions? Why were social psychologists at first surprised by a seemingly small connection between attitudes and actions?*

Key Terms

Key terms are defined in the text and Glossary.

Quotations

Found throughout the text, quotations from philosophers, writers, and scientists highlight how social psychological concepts relate to many aspects of everyday society.

> *"The past is to be respected and acknowledged, but not to be worshipped. It is our future in which we will find our greatness."*
>
> Pierre Elliott Trudeau, *Canadian Museum of History Library*
>
> Ross and Wilson (2002) also observe that we perceive positive past selves as psychologically closer in time and negative past selves as more distant. Students who recall being popular in high school report that high school feels more recent ("It seems like yesterday!") than those who recall high school as a more socially awkward time ("It's ancient history"). This tendency extends to our social groups: German but not Canadian students felt as though the Holocaust had occurred in the more distant past when they read about German atrocities committed at that time (Peetz, Gunn, & Wilson, 2010).

The Inside Story

In their own words, prominent social psychologists explain the motives and methods behind the studies conducted in their areas of expertise. These vignettes give students a first-hand account of studies cited in the text.

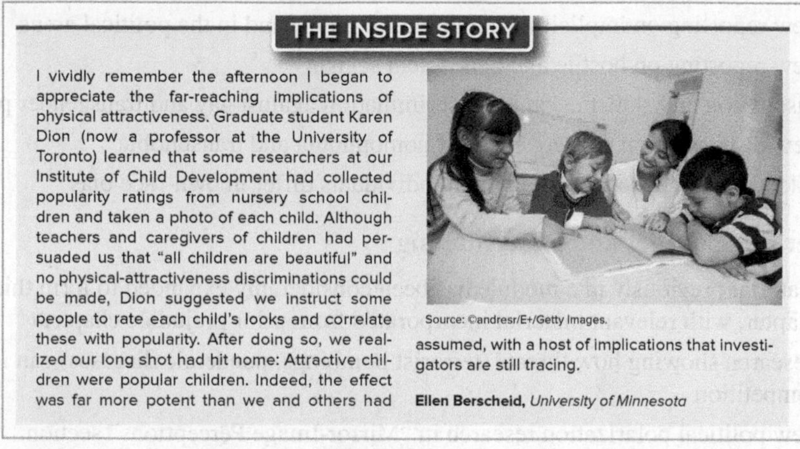

THE INSIDE STORY

I vividly remember the afternoon I began to appreciate the far-reaching implications of physical attractiveness. Graduate student Karen Dion (now a professor at the University of Toronto) learned that some researchers at our Institute of Child Development had collected popularity ratings from nursery school children and taken a photo of each child. Although teachers and caregivers of children had persuaded us that "all children are beautiful" and no physical-attractiveness discriminations could be made, Dion suggested we instruct some people to rate each child's looks and correlate these with popularity. After doing so, we realized our long shot had hit home: Attractive children were popular children. Indeed, the effect was far more potent than we and others had assumed, with a host of implications that investigators are still tracing.

Source: ©andresr/E+/Getty Images.

Ellen Berscheid, *University of Minnesota*

Focus On

In these boxes, a point–counterpoint approach to issues encourages students to apply the concepts of social psychology to their real-world experience.

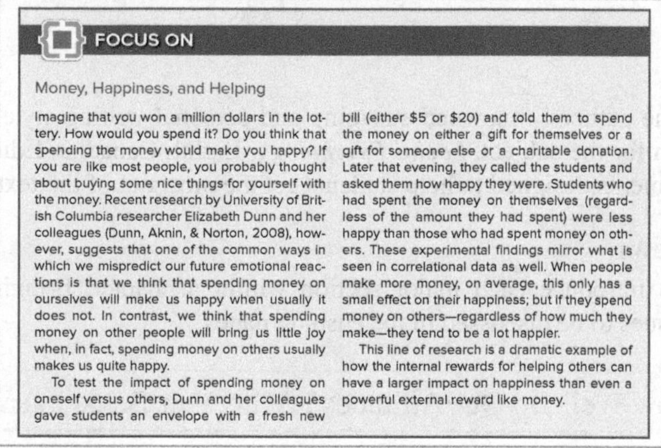

FOCUS ON

Money, Happiness, and Helping

Imagine that you won a million dollars in the lottery. How would you spend it? Do you think that spending the money would make you happy? If you are like most people, you probably thought about buying some nice things for yourself with the money. Recent research by University of British Columbia researcher Elizabeth Dunn and her colleagues (Dunn, Aknin, & Norton, 2008), however, suggests that one of the common ways in which we mispredict our future emotional reactions is that we think that spending money on ourselves will make us happy when usually it does not. In contrast, we think that spending money on other people will bring us little joy when, in fact, spending money on others usually makes us quite happy.

To test the impact of spending money on oneself versus others, Dunn and her colleagues gave students an envelope with a fresh new bill (either $5 or $20) and told them to spend the money on either a gift for themselves or a gift for someone else or a charitable donation. Later that evening, they called the students and asked them how happy they were. Students who had spent the money on themselves (regardless of the amount they had spent) were less happy than those who had spent money on others. These experimental findings mirror what is seen in correlational data as well. When people make more money, on average, this only has a small effect on their happiness; but if they spend money on others—regardless of how much they make—they tend to be a lot happier.

This line of research is a dramatic example of how the internal rewards for helping others can have a larger impact on happiness than even a powerful external reward like money.

Applying Social Psychology

As we noted above, most chapters have a hands-on Activity box that applies the science you are learning to the real world and teaches you how to apply what you have learned to your everyday life.

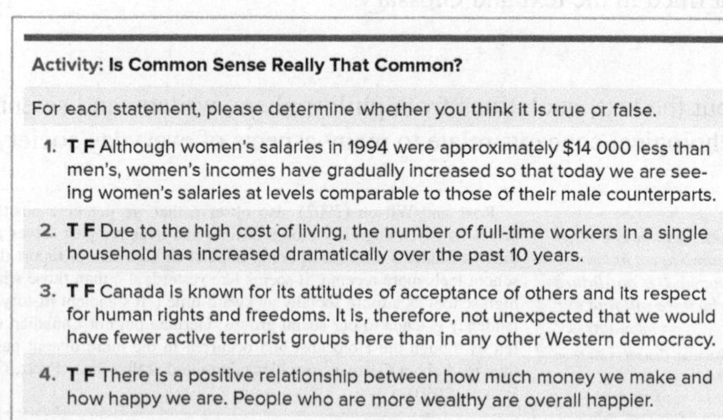

Activity: Is Common Sense Really That Common?

For each statement, please determine whether you think it is true or false.

1. **T F** Although women's salaries in 1994 were approximately $14 000 less than men's, women's incomes have gradually increased so that today we are seeing women's salaries at levels comparable to those of their male counterparts.
2. **T F** Due to the high cost of living, the number of full-time workers in a single household has increased dramatically over the past 10 years.
3. **T F** Canada is known for its attitudes of acceptance of others and its respect for human rights and freedoms. It is, therefore, not unexpected that we would have fewer active terrorist groups here than in any other Western democracy.
4. **T F** There is a positive relationship between how much money we make and how happy we are. People who are more wealthy are overall happier.

Summing Up

Found at the end of each major section within a chapter, this feature summarizes key concepts and draws connections between important issues.

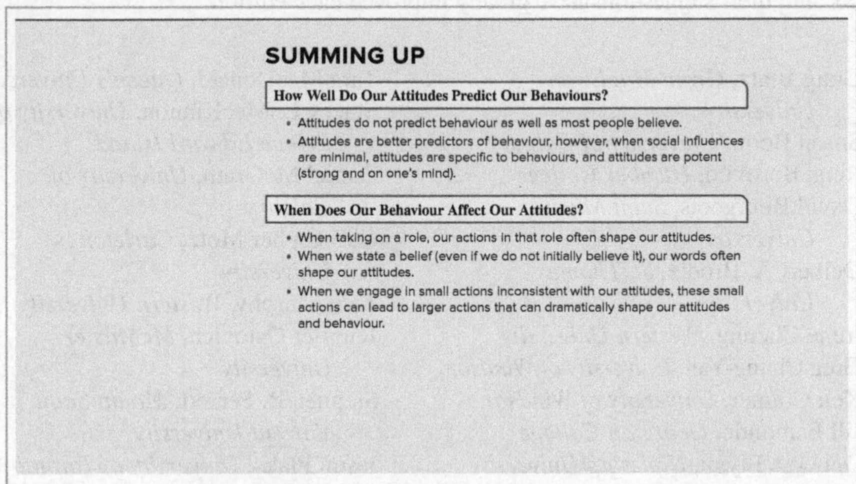

SUMMING UP

How Well Do Our Attitudes Predict Our Behaviours?

- Attitudes do not predict behaviour as well as most people believe.
- Attitudes are better predictors of behaviour, however, when social influences are minimal, attitudes are specific to behaviours, and attitudes are potent (strong and on one's mind).

When Does Our Behaviour Affect Our Attitudes?

- When taking on a role, our actions in that role often shape our attitudes.
- When we state a belief (even if we do not initially believe it), our words often shape our attitudes.
- When we engage in small actions inconsistent with our attitudes, these small actions can lead to larger actions that can dramatically shape our attitudes and behaviour.

In Appreciation

We would like to thank the many people, past and present, who helped us in writing and revising this book. The following Canadian scholars provided thoughtful and thorough reviews, and their suggestions have greatly improved each edition:

Craig Blatz, *Grant MacEwan University*
Susan Boon, *University of Calgary*
Rena Borovilo, *Humber College*
David Bourgeois, *Saint Mary's University*
Delbert A. Brodie, *St. Thomas University*
Irene Cheung, *Western University*
Greg Chung-Yan, *University of Windsor*
Ken Cramer, *University of Windsor*
Jill Esmonde, *Georgian College*
Deborah Flynn, *Nipissing University*
Ken Fowler, *Memorial University of Newfoundland*
James Gibson, *University of Victoria*
Gerald Goldberg, *York University*
Naomi Grant, *Mount Royal University*
Stephanie Hancock, *University of Lethbridge*
Gabriella Ilie, *University of Toronto Scarborough*
Linda Jessup, *University of Waterloo*
Erika Koch, *St. Francis Xavier University*
Diane Lachapelle, *University of New Brunswick*
Stephen Livingstone, *University of Toronto*
Christine Lomore, *St. Francis Xavier University*
Tara MacDonald, *Queen's University*
Stacey L. MacKinnon, *University of Prince Edward Island*
Daniel McGrath, *University of Calgary*
Christopher Motz, *Carleton University*
Tom Murphy, *Western University*
Jennifer Ostovich, *McMaster University*
Stephen B. Perrott, *Mount Saint Vincent University*
Jason Plaks, *University of Toronto St. George*
Kelley Robinson, *University of Manitoba*
Stanley Sadava, *Brock University*
Saba Safdar, *University of Guelph*
Rodney Schmaltz, *University of Alberta*
Kelly Schwartz, *University of Calgary*
Monika Stelzl, *St. Thomas University*
Mahin Tavakoli, *Carleton University*
Warren Thorngate, *Carleton University*
Susan Weir, *University of Regina*
Anne E. Wilson, *Wilfrid Laurier University*

We also want to thank the editorial staff at McGraw Hill for their excellent work. Alex Campbell followed the vision for the new edition of the text. Veronica Saroli provided editorial feedback and assistance throughout the development of the manuscript. Jack Whelan provided excellent help in guiding the book through the final changes needed for publication.

Christian Jordan
Wilfrid Laurier University
Waterloo, ON N2L 3C5
Email: cjordan@wlu.ca

Steven M. Smith
Saint Mary's University
Halifax, NS B3H 3C3
Email: steven.smith@smu.ca

Award-Winning Technology

McGraw Hill Connect® is an award-winning digital teaching and learning solution that empowers students to achieve better outcomes and enables instructors to improve efficiency with course management. Within Connect, students have access to SmartBook®, McGraw Hill's adaptive learning and reading resource. SmartBook prompts students with questions based on the material they are studying. By assessing individual answers, SmartBook learns what each student knows and identifies which topics they need to practise, giving each student a personalized learning experience and path to success.

Connect's key features also include analytics and reporting, simple assignment management, smart grading, the opportunity to post your own resources, and the Connect Instructor Library, a repository for additional resources to improve student engagement in and out of the classroom.

Instructor Resources for Myers, *Social Psychology,* Eighth Canadian Edition

- Instructor's Manual
- Test Bank
- Microsoft® PowerPoint® Presentations
- Practice Tests

Power of Process

New to the Eighth Canadian Edition, Power of Process for *Social Psychology* helps students improve critical-thinking skills and allows instructors to assess these skills efficiently and effectively in an online environment. Available through Connect, preloaded journal articles are available for instructors to assign. Using a scaffolded framework such as understanding, synthesizing, and analyzing, Power of Process moves students toward higher-level thinking and analysis.

Writing Assignments

The Writing Assignment tool delivers a learning experience to help students improve their written communication skills and conceptual understanding. As an instructor you can assign, monitor, grade, and provide feedback on writing more efficiently and effectively.

Test Builder

Available within Connect, Test Builder is a cloud-based tool that enables instructors to format tests that can be printed or administered within a Learning Management System. Test Builder offers a modern, streamlined interface for easy content configuration that matches course needs, without requiring a download.

Test Builder allows you to:

- access all test bank content from a particular title
- easily pinpoint the most relevant content through robust filtering options
- manipulate the order of questions or scramble questions and/or answers
- pin questions to a specific location within a test
- choose the layout and spacing
- add instructions and configure default settings

Test Builder provides a secure interface for better protection of content and allows for just-in-time updates to flow directly into assessments.

connect + proctorio

Remote Proctoring & Browser-Locking Capabilities

New remote proctoring and browser-locking capabilities, hosted by Proctorio within Connect, provide control of the assessment environment by enabling security options and verifying the identity of the student.

Seamlessly integrated within Connect, these services allow instructors to control students' assessment experience by restricting browser activity, recording students' activity, and verifying students are doing their own work.

Instant and detailed reporting gives instructors an at-a-glance view of potential academic integrity concerns, thereby avoiding personal bias and supporting evidence-based claims.

CHAPTER 1

Introducing the Science and Methods of Social Psychology

Source: ©denis_pc/iStock/360/Getty Images.

CHAPTER OUTLINE

What Is Social Psychology?

What Are the Major Themes of Social Psychology?

How Do Values Affect Social Psychology?

Is Social Psychology Merely Common Sense?

Research Methods: How Do We Do Social Psychology?

With the number of blended families these days, the following scenario should be easy to imagine. Indeed, you may have lived it!

Your mother has remarried. Your stepfather has a child, a few years younger than you, who complains about chores, their new room, your pets—everything. Even worse, your new stepsibling goes to the same school as you and wants to follow you everywhere.

Although you are only reasonably popular, you manage to get invited to the "party of the year" being thrown by the coolest kid in school, the one you've had your eye on for months. Your new sibling wants to come. "No way," you respond.

You arrive at the party, things are going great, and just when you are about to make your move on your crush, an interloper shows up in a borrowed limo, dressed to kill, music blaring. The new arrival grabs all of the attention, including that of your crush, who now has no time for you. As the two of them leave together in the limo, you suddenly realize that the intruder is your stepsibling!

Does this story sound even vaguely familiar? If so, it might be because this is simply a retelling of a classic folk tale ("Cinderella") but told from the perspective of one of the wicked stepsisters. Isn't it interesting that the person you root for changes depending on the perspective being taken? That is the power of the situation and the power of perspective.

The French philosopher–novelist Jean-Paul Sartre (1946) would have had no problem accepting the Cinderella premise. We humans are, he believed, "first of all beings in a situation, we cannot be distinguished from our situations, for they form us and decide our possibilities" (pp. 59–60).

What Is Social Psychology?

What are the parameters of social psychology?

social psychology The scientific study of how people think about, influence, and relate to one another.

Social psychology is a science that studies the influences of our situations, with special attention to how we view and affect one another. More precisely, it is the scientific study of how people think about, influence, and relate to one another (Figure 1–1).

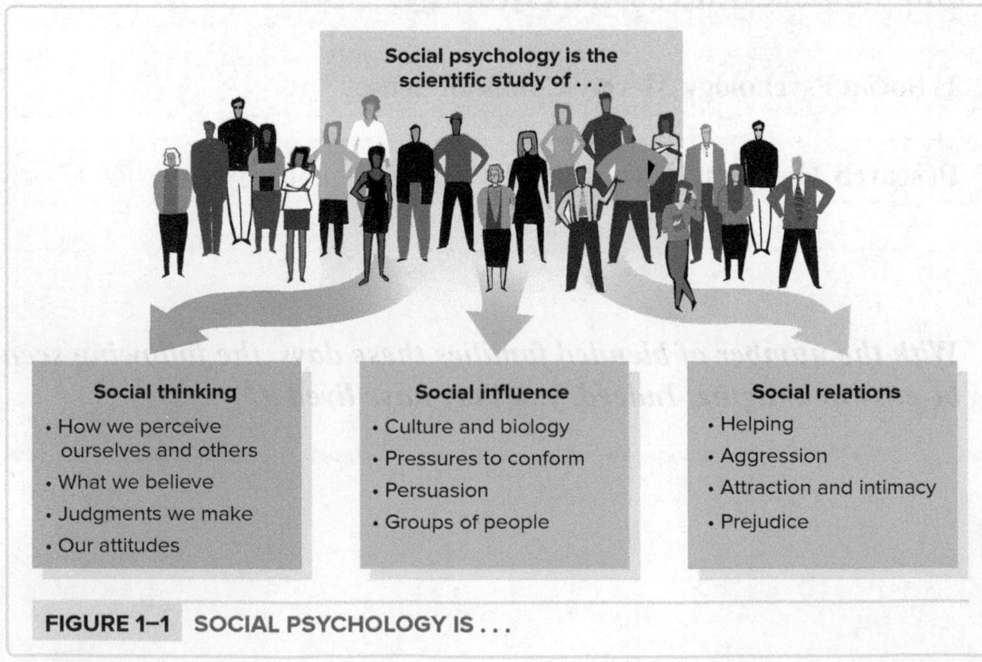

Social psychology is the scientific study of . . .
Social thinking
• How we perceive ourselves and others
• What we believe
• Judgments we make
• Our attitudes
Social influence
• Culture and biology
• Pressures to conform
• Persuasion
• Groups of people
Social relations
• Helping
• Aggression
• Attraction and intimacy
• Prejudice

FIGURE 1–1 SOCIAL PSYCHOLOGY IS . . .

Social psychology lies at psychology's boundaries with sociology. Compared with sociology (the study of people in groups and societies), social psychology focuses more on individuals, employing methods that more often use experimentation. Compared with personality psychology, social psychology focuses less on differences among individuals and more on how individuals, in general, view and affect one another.

Social psychology is still a relatively young science. Indeed, the first social psychology experiments were performed just over a century ago (1898), and the first social psychology texts did not appear until around 1900, in France, Italy, and Germany (Smith, 2005). Not until the 1930s did social psychology assume its current form. And not until the Second World War did it begin to emerge as the vibrant field it is today.

Social psychology studies our thinking, influence, and relationships by asking questions that have intrigued us all. Here are some examples.

How Much of Our Social World Is Just in Our Heads?

As we saw with the story that opened this chapter, our social behaviour varies not just with the objective situation but with how we construe it. Social beliefs can be self-fulfilling. For example, happily married people will attribute their spouse's grumpy "Can you *please* put that where it belongs?" to something external ("It must have been a frustrating day"). Unhappily married people will attribute the same remark to a mean disposition ("Wow, that's rude!") and may, therefore, respond with a counterattack. Moreover, expecting hostility from their spouse, they may behave resentfully, thereby eliciting the hostility they expect.

If You Were Ordered to Be Cruel, Would You Comply?

Sadly, history is filled with unconscionable acts of genocide: in Nazi Germany, in Rwanda, in Sudan, in Syria, and even in Canada, against Indigenous peoples. These unspeakable acts occurred because thousands of people followed orders. In Germany, *people* put the prisoners on trains, *people* herded them into crowded "showers," and *people* poisoned them with gas. How could ordinary people engage in such horrific actions? To investigate this, Stanley Milgram (1974) set up a situation where people were ordered to administer increasing levels of electric shock to someone who was having difficulty learning a series of words. As we will see in Chapter 6, the experimental results were quite disturbing.

A memorial to Robert Dziekanski, who died at the Vancouver International Airport after he was tasered by authorities. He became confused and agitated after a long flight and could not understand authorities as they tried to deal with his behaviour. Police tasered him, and, tragically, he died. Social psychologists ask these questions: Could such an incident have been avoided if rules allowed more flexible responses to altercations with authorities? Did the police officers' pre-existing biases influence their actions?

Source: The Canadian Press/Jonathan Hayward.

Would You Help Others? Or Help Yourself?

As bags of cash tumbled from an armoured truck on a fall day in 1987, $2 million was scattered along a Toronto, Ontario, street. The motorists who stopped to help returned $100 000. Judging from what disappeared, however, many more stopped to help themselves. When similar incidents occurred in San Francisco, California, and Columbus, Ohio, the results were the same: passersby grabbed most of the money (Bowen, 1988). Yet several videos of 2020 Black Lives Matter protests show BLM protesters caring for and rescuing injured counter-protesters.

Throughout this book, sources for information are cited parenthetically and then fully provided in the References section at the end of the book.

What situations trigger people to be helpful or greedy? Do some cultural contexts—perhaps villages and small towns—breed greater helpfulness?

A common thread runs through these questions: They all deal with how people view and affect one another. And that is what social psychology is all about. Social psychologists study attitudes and beliefs, conformity and independence, love and hate.

What Are the Major Themes of Social Psychology?

What are social psychology's big lessons—its overarching themes?

What concepts are on social psychology's list of central ideas? What themes, or fundamental principles, will be worth remembering long after you have forgotten most of the details? At a broad level, the fundamental principles of social psychology can be captured by a classic statement by one of its founders, Kurt Lewin, who said, "behaviour is a function of the person and the situation" (1952). From this general principle, we have developed a short list of "great ideas we ought never to forget," each of which we will unpack in chapters to come (Figure 1–2).

We Construct Our Social Reality

We humans have an irresistible urge to explain behaviour, to attribute it to some cause, and, therefore, to make it seem orderly, predictable, and controllable. You and I may

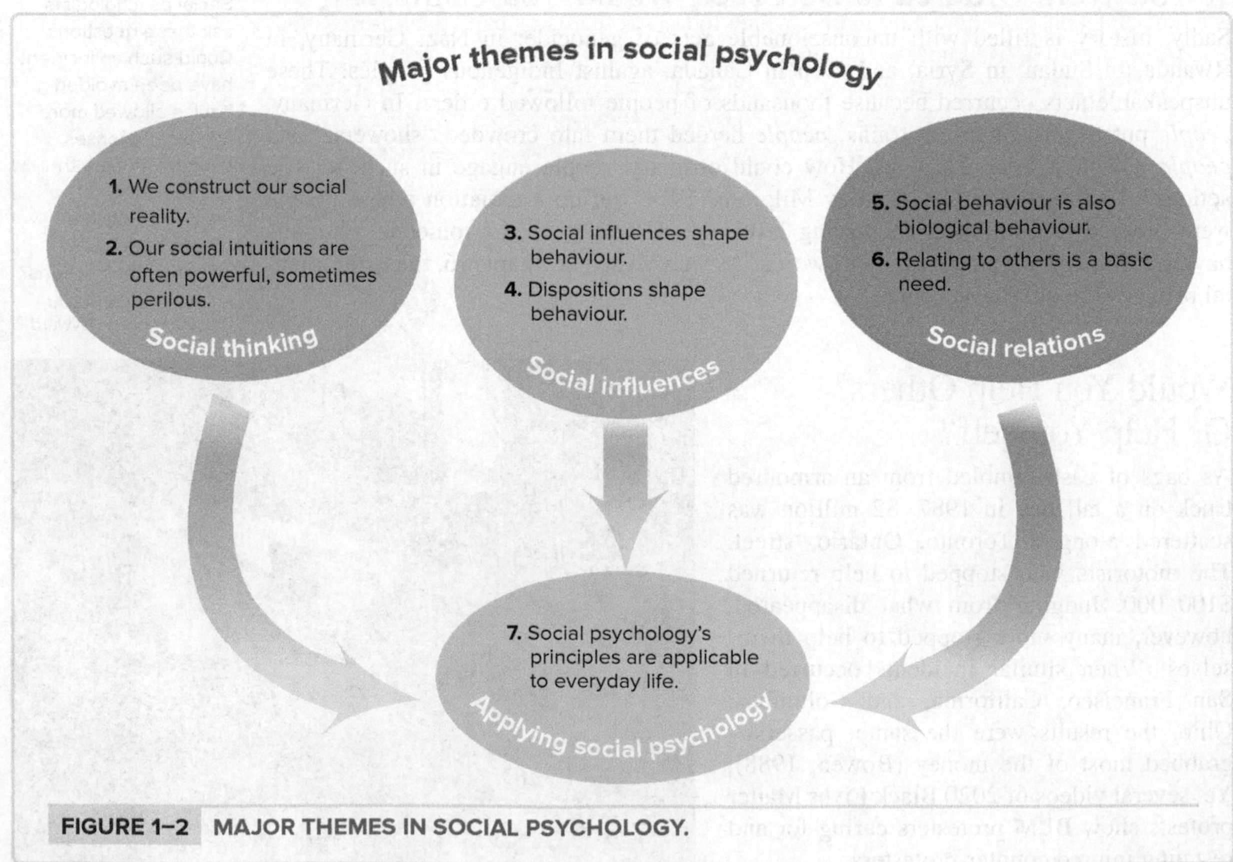

FIGURE 1–2 MAJOR THEMES IN SOCIAL PSYCHOLOGY.

react differently to similar situations because we think differently. Your perception of the world you live in and the experiences you have depends on whether you are Cinderella or her stepsister.

In a way, we are all intuitive scientists. We explain people's behaviour, usually with enough speed and accuracy to suit our daily needs. When someone's behaviour is consistent and distinctive, we attribute their behaviour to their personality. For example, if we observe someone who makes repeated snide comments, we may infer that that person has a nasty disposition and then we might try to avoid the person.

Our beliefs about ourselves also matter. Do we have an optimistic outlook? Do we see ourselves as in control of things? Do we view ourselves as relatively superior or inferior? Our answers influence our emotions and actions. How we construe the world, and ourselves, matters.

Our Social Intuitions Are Often Powerful but Sometimes Perilous

Our intuitions shape our fears (Is flying dangerous?), impressions (Can I trust them?), and relationships (Do they like me?). Intuitions influence leaders in times of crisis; gamblers at the table; eyewitnesses in front of a lineup of suspects; jurors in their assessments of guilt; and human resources professionals when assessing applicants. Such intuitions are commonplace.

Indeed, psychological science reveals a fascinating nonconscious mind—an intuitive backstage mind—that we often don't realize is guiding our thoughts and behaviour. As we will see, studies of automatic processing, implicit memory, heuristics, spontaneous trait inference, instant emotions, and nonverbal communication unveil our intuitive capacities. Thinking, memory, and attitudes all operate on two levels—one conscious and deliberate, the other nonconscious and automatic—which today's researchers call "dual processing." We know more than we know we know.

Intuitions are powerful, but they are also perilous. We misperceive others, and we often fail to appreciate how our expectations shape our evaluations. Even our intuitions about ourselves often err. We intuitively trust our memories more than we should. We misread our own minds: In experiments, subjects have denied being affected by things that did influence them. We mispredict our own feelings: how bad we'll feel a year from now if we lose our job, our relationship, or even a *hand*! Similarly, we are bad at predicting how good we'll feel a year from now if we win the lottery or get that job we want. And we often mispredict our own future: When buying clothes, people approaching middle age will still buy snug clothing, claiming, "I can lose this weight"; rarely does anyone say, more realistically, "I'd better buy a relatively loose fit."

Our social intuitions, then, are noteworthy for both their power and their perils. For example, during the 2016 U.S. presidential election, many people liked Donald Trump because his off-the-cuff responses and snap decisions made him seem more "authentic." But people mistake authenticity for truthfulness and competence when, in fact, the opposite is often true (Leary, 2016). Trump's presidency, constantly peppered by scandal, protests, and more recently the widespread death and economic issues related to the COVID-19 pandemic, has shown the impact of this flawed logic. Indeed, Niccolò Machiavelli wrote almost 500 years ago in his famous work *The Prince* (1532) that people's tendency toward uncritically believing what they are told, their instinct for self-preservation, and their desire to be part of a group could be used by a leader (or aspiring leader) to manipulate the populace to support them.

By reminding us of intuition's gifts and alerting us to its pitfalls, social psychologists aim to fortify our thinking. In most situations, "fast and frugal" snap judgments serve us well enough. But in others, where accuracy matters—as when needing to fear the right things and spend our resources accordingly—we had best restrain our impulsive intuitions with critical thinking.

Social Influences Shape Our Behaviour

We are, as Aristotle long ago observed, social animals. We speak and think in words we learned from others. We long to connect, to belong, to live in a society, and to be well thought of. For example, Matthias Mehl and James Pennebaker (2003) quantified their students' social behaviour by inviting them to wear recording devices. Once every 12 minutes during their waking hours, the device would record for 30 seconds. Although the observation period covered only weekdays (including class time), almost 30 percent of their time was spent talking. Relationships are a large part of being human.

As social creatures, we respond to our immediate contexts. Sometimes, the power of a social situation leads us to act in ways that depart from our espoused attitudes. Indeed, powerful situations sometimes overwhelm good intentions, inducing people to unspeakable cruelty: Under Nazi influence, many otherwise decent people became instruments of the Holocaust; over a period of hundreds of years across the Americas, governments implicitly and explicitly condoned colonization of the continent and the genocide of countless Indigenous peoples. Other situations may elicit great generosity and compassion: The 2010 earthquake in Haiti, the 2011 tsunami in Japan, the 2016 fires in Fort McMurray, Alberta, the 2018 hurricane that devastated Puerto Rico, and the 2020 COVID-19 pandemic inspired unprecedented generosity from Canadians across the country (and indeed around the world).

Your culture helps define your situation; your standards regarding promptness, frankness, and clothing vary with your culture. Here are some examples:

- Whether you prefer a slimmer or larger body type depends on when and where in the world you live.
- Whether you define social justice as equality (all receive the same) or as equity (those who earn more receive more) depends on whether your ideology has been shaped more by socialism or by capitalism.
- Whether you tend to be expressive or reserved, casual or formal, hinges partly on your culture and your ethnicity.
- Whether you focus primarily on yourself—your personal needs, desires, and morality—or on your family, clan, and communal groups depends on how much you are a product of modern Western individualism.
- How you perceive your social situation can depend on your social networks—the more time you spend on Facebook and other social networking sites can increase envy and depression (Tandoc et al., 2015).
- In some countries, whether or not you wear a mask during a respiratory virus pandemic depends on your political orientation.

Social psychologist Hazel Markus (2005) summed it up: "People are, above all, malleable." Said differently, we adapt to our social context. Our behaviour, then, is shaped by external forces.

Personal Attitudes and Dispositions Also Shape Behaviour

Internal forces also matter. We are not passive tumbleweeds, blown this way and that by the social winds. Our inner attitudes affect our behaviour. Our political attitudes influence our voting behaviour. Our attitudes toward smoking influence our susceptibility to peer pressure to smoke. Our attitudes toward poor people influence our willingness to support them. (As we will see, attitudes also follow behaviour, which leads us to believe strongly in those things for which we have committed ourselves or for which we have suffered.)

Personality dispositions also affect behaviour. Facing the same situation, different people may react differently. Emerging from years of political imprisonment, one person exudes bitterness and seeks revenge. Another, such as South Africa's Nelson Mandela, seeks reconciliation and unity with former enemies.

Social Behaviour Is Biologically Rooted

Twenty-first-century social psychology is providing us with ever-growing insights into our behaviour's biological foundations. Many of our social behaviours reflect a deep biological wisdom.

Nature and nurture together form who we are. Biology and experience together create us. As evolutionary psychologists remind us, our inherited human nature predisposes us to behave in ways that helped our ancestors survive and reproduce. We carry the genes of those whose traits enabled them and their children to survive and reproduce. Thus, evolutionary psychologists ask how natural selection might predispose our actions and reactions when we are dating and mating, hating and hurting, caring and sharing. Nature also endows us with an enormous capacity to learn and to adapt to varied environments. We are sensitive and responsive to our social context.

If every psychological event (every thought, every emotion, every behaviour) is simultaneously a biological event, then we can also examine the neurobiology that underlies social behaviour. What brain areas enable our experiences of love and contempt, of helping and aggression, of perception and belief? How do mind and behaviour function together as one coordinated system? What does the timing of brain events reveal about how we process information? Such questions are asked by those in **social neuroscience** (Cacioppo et al., 2010; Klein et al., 2010).

social neuroscience An integration of biological and social perspectives that explores the neural and psychological bases of social and emotional behaviours.

Social neuroscientists do not reduce complex social behaviours, such as helping and hurting, to simple neural or molecular mechanisms. Their point is this: To understand social behaviour, we must consider both under-the-skin (biological) and between-skins (social) influences. Mind and body are one grand system. Stress hormones affect how we feel and act. Social ostracism elevates blood pressure. Social support strengthens the disease-fighting immune system.

We are bio-psycho-social organisms: We reflect the interplay of our biological, psychological, and social influences. And that is why today's psychologists study behaviour from these different levels of analysis.

Relating to Others Is a Basic Need

We want to fit in with others, and our relationship with others can be an important source of stress and pain as well as joy and comfort. Kip Williams and his colleagues (Williams, 2002; Williams, Cheung, & Choi, 2000; Williams & Zadro, 2001) have shown that feeling left out can have dramatic effects on how people feel about themselves. They had university students play a simple computer game in which each player was represented by a cartoon figure on the screen and the figures passed a ball to one another. When confederates of the experimenter passed the ball to one another and left the real participants out of the action, the participants felt miserable and reported steep drops in their self-esteem. Apparently, even university students can feel the pain that many schoolchildren experience when they are not included. Acts of aggression and prejudice inflict this sort of pain.

For some, this type of seclusion and ostracism plays out constantly in our everyday lives. For example, Indigenous students who leave their home to go to university often feel ostracized by the system due to the fundamental differences of living in solitary versus community settings. There are misconceptions that all Indigenous students have funded university education, creating a divide between not only their own communities but their university peers (Hardes, 2006). Similarly, due to government regulations about how an Indigenous person obtains "status" (which can differ wildly from what a band defines as someone being a "member" of that band), many Indigenous people in Canada have their status denied by the government (Council of Ontario Universities, 2013). They are denied their identity.

Of course, relating to others is not all pain. When others help, when we form romantic relationships, and when we promote harmony between groups, interpersonal relations can be an important source of joy and comfort. In fact, according to Mark Leary and Roy Baumeister (2000), our relationships with others form the basis of our self-esteem. They argue that our self-esteem is nothing more than a reading of how accepted we feel by others. In this view, relating to others is a basic need that shapes all of our social actions.

"You can never foretell what any [person] will do, but you can say with precision what an average number will be up to. Individuals may vary, but percentages remain constant."

Sherlock Holmes, in Sir Arthur Conan Doyle's *A Study in Scarlet*, 1887

Social Psychology's Principles Are Applicable in Everyday Life

Social psychology has the potential to illuminate our lives, to make visible the subtle forces that guide our thinking and acting. It also offers many ideas about how to know ourselves better, how to win friends and influence people, how to transform closed fists into open arms.

Scholars are also applying social psychological insights to other disciplines. Principles of social thinking, social influence, and social relations have implications for human health and well-being, for judicial procedures and juror decisions in courtrooms, and for the encouragement of behaviours that will enable an environmentally sustainable human future.

As but one perspective on human existence, psychological science does not seek to engage life's ultimate questions: What is the meaning of human life? What should be our purpose? What is our ultimate destiny? But social psychology does give us a method for asking and answering some exceedingly interesting and important questions. Social psychology is all about life—your life: your beliefs, your attitudes, your relationships.

How Do Values Affect Social Psychology?

Social psychologists' values penetrate their work in ways both obvious and subtle. What are these ways?

Social psychology is less a collection of findings than a set of strategies for answering questions. In science, as in courts of law, personal opinions are inadmissible. When ideas are put on trial, evidence determines the verdict. But are social psychologists really this objective? Because they are human beings, don't their values—their personal convictions about what is desirable and about how people ought to behave—seep into their work? And, if so, can social psychology really be scientific?

Obvious Ways in Which Values Enter Social Psychology

Values enter the picture with our choice of research topics. These choices typically reflect social history (Kagan, 2009). It was no accident that the study of prejudice flourished during the 1940s as fascism raged in Europe; that the 1950s, a time of look-alike fashions and rows of identical suburban homes, gave us studies of conformity; that the 1960s saw interest in aggression increase with riots and rising crime rates; that the 1970s feminist movement helped stimulate a wave of research on gender and sexism; that the 1980s offered a resurgence of attention to psychological aspects of the arms race; that the 1990s were marked by heightened interest in how people respond to cultural diversity; and that the 2000s saw substantial research on extremism and terrorism. Undoubtedly, as social media's impact on society, the widespread acceptance of conspiracy theories (such as the anti-vaccination movement), and political polarization continue to grow in Western democracies, those will become topics of significant focus in the field. Social psychology reflects social history (Kagan, 2009).

Values differ not only across time but also across cultures. In Europe, people take pride in their nationalities. The Scots are self-consciously distinct from the English; and the Austrians from the Germans. Consequently, Europe has given us a major theory of "social identity," whereas North American social psychologists have focused more on individuals—how one person thinks about others, is influenced by them, and relates to them (Fiske, 2004; Tajfel, 1981; Turner, 1987). Australian social psychologists have drawn theories and methods from both Europe and North America (Feather, 2005). Values also influence the types of people attracted to various disciplines (Campbell, 1975a; Moynihan, 1979). Have you noticed differences in students attracted to the humanities, the natural sciences, or the social sciences?

Finally, values obviously enter the picture as the object of social–psychological analysis. Social psychologists investigate how values form, why they change, and how they influence attitudes and actions. None of this, however, tells us which values are "right."

Not-So-Obvious Ways in Which Values Enter Social Psychology

We less often recognize the subtler ways in which value commitments masquerade as objective truth. Consider these not-so-obvious ways in which values enter social psychology and related areas.

The subjective aspects of science

Scientists and philosophers now agree: Science is not purely objective. Scientists do not simply read the book of nature. Rather, they interpret nature, using their own mental categories. In our daily lives, too, we view the world through the lens of our preconceptions.

> ***"Science does not simply describe and explain nature; it is part of the interplay between nature and ourselves; it describes nature as exposed to our method of questioning."***
>
> Werner Heisenberg, *Physics and Philosophy*, 1958

While reading these words, if you have normal sight, you have been unaware that you are also looking at your nose. Your mind blocks from awareness something that is there, if only you were predisposed to perceive it. This tendency to prejudge reality based on our expectations is a basic fact about the human mind.

Because scholars at work in any given area often share a common viewpoint or come from the same **culture**, their assumptions may go unchallenged. What we take for granted—the shared beliefs that European social psychologists call our **social representations** (Augoustinos & Innes, 1990; Moscovici, 1988, 2001)—are our most important but often most unexamined convictions. Sometimes, however, someone from outside the camp will also call attention to these assumptions.

culture The enduring behaviours, ideas, attitudes, traditions, products, and institutions shared by a large group of people and transmitted from one generation to the next.

social representations Socially shared beliefs; widely held ideas and values, including our assumptions and cultural ideologies. Our social representations help us make sense of our world.

During the 1980s, feminists exposed some of social psychology's unexamined assumptions, criticizing the ideas of scientists who favoured a biological interpretation of gender differences in social behaviour (Unger, 1985). Socialist thinkers called attention to the inherent support for the benefit of competition and individualism—for example, the assumptions that conformity is bad and that individual rewards are good. These groups, of course, make their own assumptions, as critics of "political correctness" are fond of noting. Social psychologist Lee Jussim (2005), for example, argues that progressive social psychologists sometimes feel compelled to deny group differences and to assume that stereotypes of group difference are never rooted in actual group differences but that perceived differences are just the result of racism.

In Chapter 3, we will see more ways in which our preconceptions guide our interpretations. What's crucial for our behaviour is less the situation-as-it-is than the situation-as-we-construe-it.

The hidden values in psychological concepts

Implicit in our understanding that psychology is not objective is the realization that psychologists' own values play an important part in the theories and judgments they support. Psychologists refer to people as mature or immature, as well-adjusted or poorly adjusted, as mentally healthy or mentally ill. They talk as if they were stating facts, when really they are making value judgments. Here are some examples:

- *Forming concepts.* Hidden values even seep into psychology's research-based concepts. Pretend you have taken a personality test and the psychologist, after scoring your answers, announces, "You scored high in self-esteem. You are low in anxiety. And you have exceptional ego-strength." "Ah," you think, "I suspected as much, but it feels good to know that." Now another psychologist gives you a similar test. For some peculiar reason, this test asks some of the same questions. Afterwards, the psychologist informs you that you seem defensive, for you scored high in "repressiveness." You wonder, "How could this be? The other psychologist said such nice things about me." It could be because all these labels describe the same set of responses (a tendency to say nice things about oneself and not to acknowledge problems). Shall we call it high self-esteem or defensiveness? The label reflects a value judgment.
- *Labelling.* Value judgments are often hidden within our social–psychological language—but that is also true of everyday language. Here are some examples:
    - Whether we label someone engaged in guerrilla warfare a "terrorist" or a "freedom fighter" depends on our view of the cause.
    - Edward Cornwallis was (and still is) a "hero" to many descendants of British settlers in Canada for his work establishing the British colonies. But he is seen as a murderer for his actions to eliminate Indigenous peoples.
    - Whether we view wartime civilian deaths as "war crimes" or as "collateral damage" affects our acceptance of the deaths.
    - Whether we call public assistance "welfare" or "aid to the needy" reflects our political views.
    - When "they" exalt their country and people, it is nationalism; when "we" do it, it is patriotism.
    - Whether Donald Trump is a "racist misogynist" or an "authentic straight-shooter" depends on your place on the political spectrum (as does whether or not you will wear a mask to slow disease spread).
- "Brainwashing" is bad but "social influence" is good.
- Whether wearing hijab is "oppression of women" or "expression of religious devotion" depends on your interpretation of the Islamic faith.
- *Naturalistic fallacy.* A seductive error for those who work in the social sciences is sliding from a description of *what is* into a prescription of *what ought to be.* Philosophers call this the **naturalistic fallacy**. The gulf between "is" and "ought to be," between scientific description and ethical prescription, remains as wide today as when philosopher David Hume pointed it out 200 years ago. No survey of human behaviour—say, of sexual practices—logically dictates what is "right" behaviour. If most people don't do something, that does not make it wrong. If most people do it, that does not make it right. We inject our values whenever we move from objective statements of fact to prescriptive statements of what ought to be.

naturalistic fallacy The error of defining what is good in terms of what is observable: For example, what's typical is normal; what's normal is good.

Hidden (and not-so-hidden) values seep into psychological advice. They permeate popular psychology books that offer guidance on living and loving.

Source: ©Rawpixel.com /Shutterstock.

As these examples indicate, values lie hidden within our cultural definitions of mental health, our psychological advice for living, our concepts, and our psychological labels. Throughout this book, we will call your attention to additional examples of hidden values. The point is never that the implicit values are necessarily bad. The point is that scientific interpretation, even at the level of labelling a phenomenon, is a human activity. It is, therefore, natural and inevitable that prior beliefs and values will influence what social psychologists think and write.

Should we dismiss science because it has its subjective side? Quite the contrary: The realization that human thinking always involves interpretation is precisely why we need researchers with varying biases to undertake scientific analysis. By constantly checking our beliefs against the facts, as best we know them, we check and retrain our biases. Systematic observation and experimentation help us clean the lens through which we see reality.

Is Social Psychology Merely Common Sense?

Is social psychology simply common sense? Do social psychology's theories provide new insight into the human condition? Or do they only describe the obvious?

Many of the conclusions presented in this book will probably have already occurred to you, for social psychology is all around you. We constantly observe people thinking about, influencing, and relating to one another. Much of our thinking aims to discern and explain relationships among social events. It pays to discern what that facial expression predicts, how to get someone to do something, or whether to regard another person as friend or foe. For centuries, philosophers, novelists, and poets have observed and commented on social behaviour, often with keen insight.

Does this mean that social psychology is only common sense but using fancy words? We wouldn't have written this book if we thought so. Nevertheless, it must be acknowledged that social psychology faces two contradictory criticisms: first, that it is trivial because it documents the obvious; second, that it is dangerous because its findings could be used to manipulate people.

We will explore the second criticism in Chapter 5. For the moment, let's examine the first objection. Pause your reading here, and complete the activity on the next page before coming back here to read further.

> ***"A first-rate theory predicts; a second-rate theory forbids; and a third-rate theory explains after the event."***
>
> Aleksander Isaakovich Kitaigorodskii, 1975

Do social psychology and the other social sciences simply formalize what any amateur already knows intuitively? Writer Cullen Murphy (1990) thought so: "Day after day social scientists go out into the world. Day after day they discover that people's behaviour is pretty much what you'd expect."

But why did you give the answers you did to the questions above? For example, let's look at number 4. Does this make sense to you? Does money buy happiness? When we ask our classes this question, the opinions split. Some say "no" but many say "yes." But ask a different question—"Would a *little* more money make you a *little* happier?"—and most of us will say "yes." There is, we believe, a connection between wealth and well-being. That belief feeds what Juliet Schor (1998) has called the "cycle of work and spend"—working more to buy more. According to a 1990 Gallup poll, one in two women, two in three men, and four in five people earning more than $75 000 a year in the United States would like to be rich—although, to that half of the world's population who live on less than $2 a day, an income of $75 000 means they are already fabulously wealthy (Shah, 2005).

Materialism surged during the 1970s and 1980s. The most dramatic evidence came from a large-scale annual survey of nearly a quarter million students entering university. The proportion considering it either highly desirable or crucial that they become economically affluent rose from 39 percent in 1970 to 74 percent in 2005. Those proportions virtually flipped with those who considered cultivating a significant belief system to be very

Activity: Is Common Sense Really That Common?

For each statement, please determine whether you think it is true or false.

1. **T F** Although women's salaries in 1994 were approximately $14 000 less than men's, women's incomes have gradually increased so that today we are seeing women's salaries at levels comparable to those of their male counterparts.
2. **T F** Due to the high cost of living, the number of full-time workers in a single household has increased dramatically over the past 10 years.
3. **T F** Canada is known for its attitudes of acceptance of others and its respect for human rights and freedoms. It is, therefore, not unexpected that we would have fewer active terrorist groups here than in any other Western democracy.
4. **T F** There is a positive relationship between how much money we make and how happy we are. People who are more wealthy are overall happier.
5. **T F** Manitobans are likely to say they have more in common with people in Nova Scotia than with Americans just south of them in North Dakota.
6. **T F** Nine out of every ten Canadians strongly or somewhat support "having more women in elected office to achieve a well-functioning political system."
7. **T F** Most of us have quite accurate insight into the factors that influence our moods.
8. **T F** Most people rate themselves as worse than average on socially desirable characteristics.
9. **T F** Memory is like a storage chest in the brain into which we deposit material and from which we can withdraw it later if needed. Occasionally, something gets lost from the chest, and then we say we have forgotten it.
10. **T F** The greater the reward promised for an activity, the more we will come to enjoy the activity.

How did you do? Go to the end of the chapter to find out.

important. More recently, a survey of over 25 000 Canadian university students found that they expected a starting salary of over $50 000, and that most expected their salary to increase by 70 percent in the first five years (Schweitzer & Lyons, 2019).

> ***"Whoever said money can't buy happiness isn't spending it right."***
>
> Lexus advertisement, quoted by Booth (2019)

Does consumption, indeed, enable "the good life"? Does being well-off produce—or at least correlate with—psychological well-being? Would people be happier if they could exchange a simple lifestyle for one with palatial surroundings, Alpine ski vacations, and executive-class travel? Would they be happier if they won the lottery and could choose any indulgence? Social psychological theory and evidence offer some answers.

We can observe the traffic between wealth and well-being by asking, first, if rich nations are happier. There is, indeed, some correlation between national wealth and well-being (measured as self-reported happiness and life satisfaction). Scandinavians have been mostly prosperous and satisfied; Bulgarians are neither. But 1990s data revealed that once nations reached about $10 000 GNP per person, which was roughly the economic level of Ireland before 1990, higher levels of national wealth were not predictive of increased well-being. Better to be Irish than Bulgarian. But happiness was about the same for an average Irish person, or an average Belgian, Canadian, or Norwegian—with more than double the Irish purchasing power (Inglehart, 1990).

We can ask, second, whether within any given nation rich people are happier. In poor countries—where low income more often threatens basic human needs—being relatively well-off does predict greater well-being (Howell & Howell, 2008). In affluent countries, where most can afford life's necessities, affluence still matters—partly because people with more money perceive more control in their lives (Johnson & Krueger, 2006). But compared with poor countries, income matters little. Once a comfortable income level is reached, more and more money provides diminishing long-term returns. World values researcher Ronald Inglehart (1990, p. 242) found the income–happiness correlation to be "surprisingly weak."

Even the super-rich—for example, those on the Forbes 100 list—have reported only slightly greater happiness than average (Diener, Horwitz, & Emmons, 1985). And winning a major lottery seems not to elevate well-being enduringly (Brickman, Coates, & Janoff-Bulman, 1978). Such jolts of joy have "a short half-life," noted Richard Ryan (1999).

It is further striking that individuals who strive most for wealth tend to live with lower well-being, a finding that "comes through very strongly in every culture I've looked at," reported Richard Ryan (1999). Seek extrinsic goals—wealth, beauty, popularity—and you may find anxiety, depression, and psychosomatic ills (Eckersley, 2005; Sheldon et al., 2004). Those who instead strive for intrinsic goals, such as "intimacy, personal growth, and contribution to the community," experience a higher quality of life, concluded Tim Kasser (2000; Kasser & Ahuvia, 2002; see also Chen et al., 2014).

Common Sense, Revisited

One problem with common sense is that we invoke it after we know the facts. Events are far more "obvious" and predictable in hindsight than beforehand. Experiments reveal that when people learn the outcome of an experiment, that outcome suddenly seems unsurprising—certainly less surprising than it is to people who are simply told about the experimental procedure and the possible outcomes (Slovic & Fischhoff, 1977). Likewise, in everyday life, we often do not expect something to happen until it does. We *then* suddenly see clearly the forces that brought it about, and we feel unsurprised.

On June 23, 2012, a section of the roof parking lot at the Algo Centre Mall in Elliot Lake, Ontario, collapsed onto shoppers and employees, killing two people and injuring more than 20 more. The media and residents of Elliot Lake strongly criticized the mall's owners as well as the structural engineer who had inspected the structure prior to its collapse. Couldn't more have been done to avoid the death and destruction in this case? Maybe. However, given what we know about the hindsight bias, is the extent of the criticism fair? We often think we knew what we actually did not. As the philosopher–theologian Søren Kierkegaard put it, "Life is lived forwards, but understood backwards."

If this **hindsight bias** (also called the *I-knew-it-all-along phenomenon*) is pervasive, you may now be feeling that you already knew about it. Indeed, almost any conceivable result of a psychological experiment can seem like common sense—*after* you know the result.

hindsight bias The tendency to exaggerate, after learning an outcome, one's ability to have foreseen how something turned out; also known as the *I-knew-it-all-along phenomenon.*

You can demonstrate this phenomenon yourself (e.g., see Hom & Van Nuland, 2019). Take a group of people and tell half of them one psychological finding; tell the other half the opposite result. For example, tell half the group this:

> Social psychologists have found that, whether choosing friends or falling in love, we are most attracted to people whose traits are different from our own. There seems to be wisdom in the old saying, "Opposites attract."

Tell the other half this:

> Social psychologists have found that, whether choosing friends or falling in love, we are most attracted to people whose traits are similar to our own. There seems to be wisdom in the old saying, "Birds of a feather flock together."

Ask each group of people to explain the result given to that group. Then ask each group to indicate whether the finding is "surprising" or "not surprising." Virtually everyone will find whichever result they were given "not surprising."

Indeed, we can draw upon our stockpile of proverbs to make almost any result seem to make sense. If a social psychologist reports that separation intensifies romantic attraction, Joe Public responds, "You get paid for this? Everybody knows that 'absence makes the heart grow fonder.'" If, however, it turns out that separation weakens attraction, Judy Public may say, "My grandmother could have told you 'out of sight, out of mind.'"

The hindsight bias creates a problem for many psychology students. Sometimes, results are genuinely surprising (for example, that Olympic *bronze* medallists take more joy in their achievement than do *silver* medallists, something you might notice when watching Canadian athletes at the Olympic Games Tokyo 2020 [postponed to the summer of 2021 because of COVID-19] as they win their many bronze medals).

Consider the last time you failed a test (or had a car accident, or experienced some other negative outcome). Why did it happen? Is there something you could have done to avoid it? Considering what you now know about the hindsight bias, and counterfactual thinking, how accurate do you think your judgments are in terms of how you could have changed the outcome?

But trained professionals are not immune to this either—mental health professionals said they were more likely to predict a specific outcome for a patient (e.g., likelihood of self-harm; likelihood of harming others) if they knew the outcome in advance, than when they did not; and these are people who have been trained to understand the role of hindsight bias in decision making (Beltrani et al., 2018). Even with knowledge, these biases can be difficult to overcome.

> ***"It is easy to be wise after the event."***
>
> Sherlock Holmes, in Sir Arthur Conan Doyle's "The Problem of Thor Bridge," 1922

Fundamentally, people are not very good at identifying the causes of their failure, and when they try to (and make mistakes) it can actually inhibit later performance (Petrocelli, Seta, & Seta, 2013; Petrocelli et al., 2011). For example, you might think you failed your test because you were out drinking, but if the real cause was that you did not read the material, simply not drinking the night before the next test will not solve your problem.

We sometimes blame ourselves for "stupid mistakes"—perhaps for not having handled a person or a situation better. Looking back on the event, we see how we should have handled it. "I should have known how busy I would be at the end of the semester and started that paper earlier." But sometimes we are too hard on ourselves. We forget that what is obvious to us now was not nearly as obvious at the time. Physicians who are told both a patient's symptoms and the cause of death (as determined by an autopsy) sometimes wonder how an incorrect diagnosis could have been made. Other physicians, given only the symptoms, don't find the diagnosis nearly as obvious (Dawson et al., 1988). Indeed, this even extends to judgments of defendants in criminal trials—jurors who know that a crime victim died were more likely to say the defendant should have foreseen the outcome (Evelo & Greene, 2013).

So what do we conclude—that common sense is usually wrong? Sometimes it is. Until science dethroned the common-sense view, centuries of daily experience assured people that the sun revolved around the earth. Medical experience assured doctors that bleeding was an effective treatment for typhoid fever, until someone in the middle of the last century bothered to experiment by dividing patients into two groups: one group was bled while the other was given mere bed rest.

Other times, conventional wisdom is right, or it falls on both sides of an issue: Does happiness come from knowing the truth or from preserving illusions? From being with others or from living in peaceful solitude? No matter what we find, there will be someone who foresaw it. But which of the many competing ideas best fits reality?

The point is not that common sense is predictably wrong. Rather, common sense usually is right *after the fact.* We, therefore, easily deceive ourselves into thinking that we know and knew more than we do and did. And this is precisely why we need science—to help us sift reality from illusion and genuine predictions from easy hindsight.

Research Methods: How Do We Do Social Psychology?

How does social psychology try to accomplish its goals?

We have considered some of the intriguing questions that social psychology seeks to answer. We have also seen the ways in which subjective, often unconscious, processes influence the work that social psychologists do. Now let's consider the scientific methods that make social psychology a science.

We are all amateur social psychologists. People-watching is a universal hobby: in parks, on the street, at school. As we observe people, we form ideas about how humans think about, influence, and relate to one another. Professional social psychologists do the same, only more systematically (by forming theories) and painstakingly (often with experiments that create miniature social dramas to pin down cause and effect).

> ***"Nothing has such power to broaden the mind as the ability to investigate systematically and truly all that comes under thy observation in life."***
>
> Marcus Aurelius, *Meditations*

In their quest for insight, social psychologists propose theories that organize their observations and imply testable hypotheses and practical predictions. To test a hypothesis, social psychologists may do research that predicts behaviour using correlational studies, often conducted in natural settings. Or they may seek to explain behaviour by conducting experiments that manipulate one or more factors under controlled conditions. Once they have conducted a research study, they explore ways to apply their findings to people's everyday lives.

Forming and Testing Hypotheses

Social psychologists have a hard time thinking of anything more fascinating than human existence. As we wrestle with human nature to pin down its secrets, we organize our ideas and findings into theories. A **theory** is an integrated set of principles that explain and predict observed events. Theories are a scientific shorthand.

In everyday conversation, "theory" often means "less than fact"—a middle rung on a confidence ladder from guess to theory to fact. Thus, people may, for example, dismiss Charles Darwin's theory of evolution as "just a theory." Indeed, noted Alan Leshner (2005), "Evolution *is* only a theory, but so is gravity." People often respond that gravity is a fact—but the fact is that your keys fall to the ground when dropped. Gravity is the theoretical explanation that accounts for this observed fact.

To a scientist, facts and theories are apples and oranges. Facts are agreed-upon statements that we observe. Theories are ideas that summarize and explain facts. "Science is built up with facts, as a house is with stones," wrote French scientist Jules Henri Poincaré (1905), "but a collection of facts is no more a science than a heap of stones is a house."

> **theory** An integrated set of principles that explain and predict observed events.
>
> **hypotheses** Testable propositions that describe relationships that may exist between events.

Theories not only summarize; they also imply testable predictions, called **hypotheses**. Hypotheses serve several purposes. First, they allow us to test the theory on which they are based. By making specific predictions, a theory puts its money where its mouth is. Second, predictions give direction to research. Any scientific field will mature more rapidly if its researchers have a sense of direction. Theoretical predictions suggest new areas for research; they send investigators looking for things they might never have thought of. Third, the predictive feature of good theories can also make them practical. What, for example, would be of greater practical value today than a theory of aggression that would predict when to expect aggression and how to control it?

When testing our theories with specific hypotheses, however, we must always translate variables that are described at the theoretical level into the specific variables that we are going to observe. This process, called *operationalization,* is often as much an art as a science.

Consider how this works. Say we observe that people who loot, taunt, or attack others (i.e., exhibit extreme violence) often do so in crowds. We might, therefore, theorize that the presence of others in a crowd leads to extreme violence. Let's play with this idea for a moment. In order to test this hypothesis, we need to translate our theoretical variable *crowd* into a meaningful example of it that we will observe. In this case, maybe we would operationalize this variable as 20 strangers together in a relatively small room, even though this definition of *crowd* would probably be different from the crowds we originally observed. The crucial question for this study would be this: Does our operational variable of *crowd* represent what we mean theoretically by a crowd? The answer to that question determines whether our operational variable is a *valid* measure of our theoretical variable. If we can accept it as valid, then we can go on to test our hypothesis. If we can't accept it as valid, then the proposed research will not tell us much about our theory, and we should develop a new operationalization. What do you think of this operationalization of *crowd*? Could you do better? Good social psychology requires both following the principles of science and developing tests of theories that creatively capture the essence of the theory being tested.

If we are going to test our hypothesis, however, we also need to operationalize extreme violence. What if we asked individuals in "crowds" to administer punishing shocks to a hapless victim without knowing which one of the group was actually shocking the victim? Would these individuals administer stronger shocks than individuals acting alone, as our theory predicts? In this example, administering punishing shocks would be the operational variable of our concept of extreme violence. To be a good operationalization, we would need to believe that it is a valid measure of violence; we would also need to believe that by using this measure, differences in violence could emerge and we would get basically the same results if we did the study over again. That is, we would need to believe that it is a *reliable* measure. If this measure of violence sometimes showed violence and other times didn't, we might very well miss our effect.

When we test our theories, we necessarily must make observations; and when we make observations, we have to decide what we are going to observe. This process of deciding on our observations, called operationalization (as mentioned above) is how science puts its theories to the test. A good operationalization captures the essence of the theoretical concept—that is, it is valid—and it does so sensitively and consistently—that is, reliably—so that tests of the theory can be observed.

You will note throughout the text, however, that quite regularly more than one theory can explain what we know about a given phenomenon. Not only must we test our own theory, but science often proceeds by testing between two theories. How do we conclude that one theory is better than another? A good theory accomplishes the following:

- It effectively summarizes many observations.
- It makes clear predictions that we can use to do the following:
  - Confirm or modify the theory.
  - Generate new exploration.
  - Suggest practical applications.

When we discard theories, usually it's not because they have been proven false. Rather, like old cars, they get replaced by newer, better models.

Source: ©Sheila Fitzgerald/ Shutterstock.com.

Correlational Research: Detecting Natural Associations

Let's go backstage now and take a brief look at how social psychology is done. This glimpse behind the scenes will be just enough, we trust, for you to appreciate findings discussed later and to think critically about everyday social events.

Social–psychological research varies by location. It can take place in the laboratory (a controlled situation) or it can be **field research** (everyday situations). And it varies by method: **correlational research** (asking whether two or more factors are naturally associated) or **experimental research** (manipulating some factor to see its effect on another). If you want to be a critical reader of psychological research reported in newspapers and magazines, you need to understand the difference between correlational and experimental research.

field research Research done in natural, real-life settings outside the laboratory.

correlational research The study of the naturally occurring relationships among variables.

experimental research Studies that seek clues to cause–effect relationships by manipulating one or more factors (independent variables) while controlling others (holding them constant).

Today's psychologists often relate personal and social factors to human health. Soft drink companies have long argued that weight-conscious consumers could help control their weight by drinking diet soft drinks. Sharon Fowler and her colleagues (see Fowler et al., 2005) found that consuming regular soft drinks was correlated with obesity—the more you drink, the more likely you are to be obese. Given soft drinks' high sugar content, perhaps this finding was not surprising. However, what surprised the researchers even more was that consuming *diet* soft drinks was even *more* strongly related to obesity rates.

As shown in Figure 1–3, the risk of becoming obese is higher in every consumption category for diet soda drinkers over regular soda drinkers.

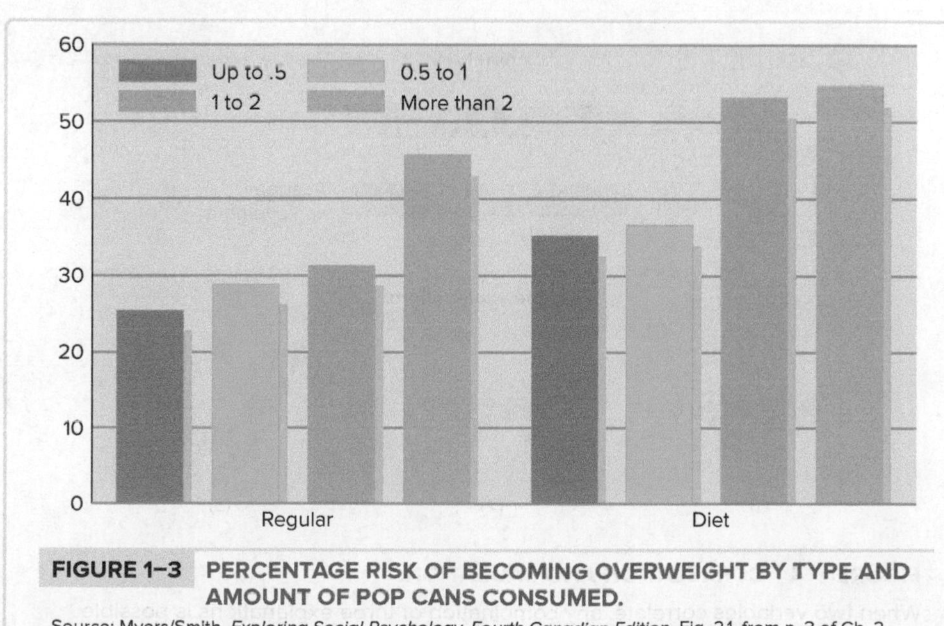

FIGURE 1–3 PERCENTAGE RISK OF BECOMING OVERWEIGHT BY TYPE AND AMOUNT OF POP CANS CONSUMED.
Source: Myers/Smith, *Exploring Social Psychology, Fourth Canadian Edition*, Fig. 2.1, from p. 3 of Ch. 2.

Why? Could it be that drinking diet soda causes weight to increase? Should obese people who drink diet soft drinks switch to regular soft drinks to lose weight? What are some of the alternative explanations for this effect?

Correlation versus causation

The diet cola–weight gain question illustrates the most irresistible thinking error made by both amateur and professional social psychologists: When two things go together, it is very tempting to conclude that one is causing the other. Correlational research, therefore, allows us to predict, but it cannot tell us whether changing one variable will cause changes in another.

Below are a number of potential reasons that drinking diet soft drinks is related to weight gain. Now, for each of the explanations below, evaluate the extent to which you believe this explanation is true (i.e., correct) and also why you think the way you do.

1. There is a direct and causal relationship because there is an as yet unknown property of artificial sweeteners that triggers hunger and causes people to eat more.
2. Drinking diet sodas is causally related to weight gain but reversed: People who are overweight drink diet soft drinks in an attempt to lose weight, but it is too late. Thus the effect is causal, but in the reverse direction (i.e., being overweight causes the drinking of diet soft drinks).
3. There is a third variable involved; thus, there is no causal relationship. People who drink diet colas are less likely to consume good drinks (e.g., milk, green tea) and good foods (e.g., fruits, vegetables) that can help control weight gain.

Now that you have thought this through, ask your friends what they think. Do they agree or disagree with you? Why?

The correlation–causation confusion is behind much muddled thinking in popular psychology. Consider another very real correlation: between self-esteem and academic achievement. Children with high self-esteem tend also to have high academic achievement. (As with any correlation, we can also state this the other way around: High achievers tend to have high self-esteem.) Why do you suppose this is? (See Figure 1–4 for a representation of three possible scenarios.)

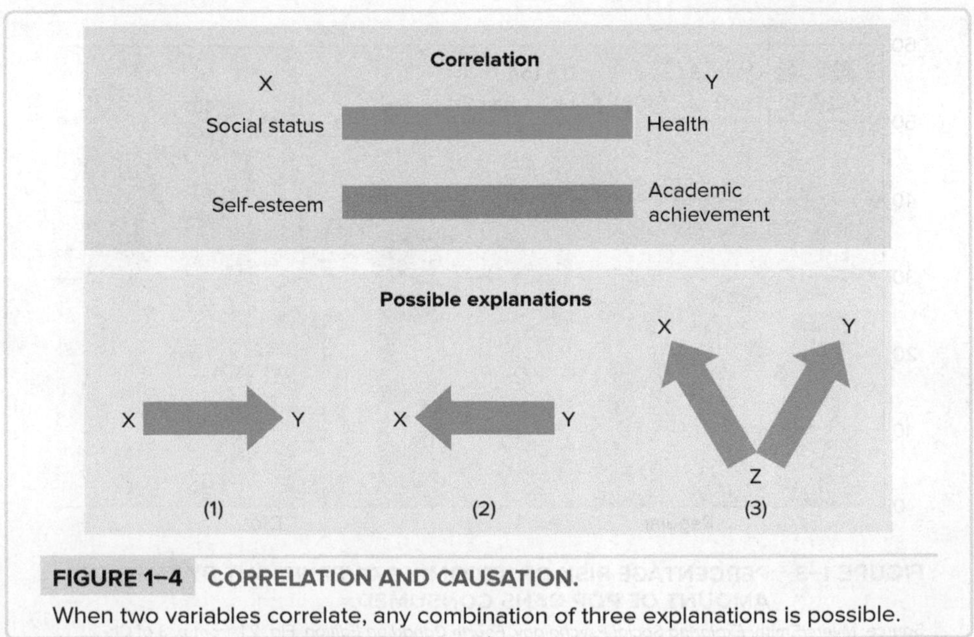

FIGURE 1–4 CORRELATION AND CAUSATION.
When two variables correlate, any combination of three explanations is possible.

Some people believe a "healthy self-concept" contributes to achievement. Thus, boosting a child's self-image may also boost school achievement. But others, including psychologists William Damon (1995), Robyn Dawes (1994), Mark Leary (1998), and Martin Seligman (1994), doubt that self-esteem is really "the armor that protects kids" from underachievement (or drug abuse and delinquency). Perhaps it's the other way around: Perhaps problems and failures cause low self-esteem. Perhaps self-esteem often reflects the reality of how things are going for us. Perhaps self-esteem grows from hard-won achievements. Do well, and you will feel good about yourself; goof off and fail, and you will feel like a dolt. A study of 635 Norwegian schoolchildren suggests that a string of gold stars beside one's name on the spelling chart and constant praise from an admiring teacher can boost a child's self-esteem (Skaalvik & Hagtvet, 1990). Or, perhaps, as in a study of nearly 6000 German Grade 7 students, the traffic between self-esteem and academic achievement runs both ways (Trautwein & Lüdtke, 2006).

It's also possible that self-esteem and achievement correlate because both are linked to underlying intelligence and family social status. That possibility was raised in two studies: one, of 1600 young men; another, of 715 teenagers (Bachman & O'Malley, 1977; Maruyama, Rubin, & Kingbury, 1981). When the researchers statistically removed the effect of intelligence and family status, the correlation between self-esteem and achievement evaporated.

Correlations quantify, with a coefficient known as *r*, the degree of relationship between two factors: from −1.0 (as one factor score goes up, the other goes down), through 0, to +1.0 (the two factors' scores rise and fall together). Scores on self-esteem and depression tests correlate negatively (*r* is about −0.6). The intelligence scores of identical twins correlate positively (*r* is about +0.08). The strength of correlational research is that it tends to occur in real-world settings in which we can examine factors such as race, gender, and social status (factors that we cannot manipulate in the laboratory). Its great disadvantage lies in the ambiguity of the results. The point is so important that even if it fails to impress people the first 25 times they hear it, it is worth repeating: Knowing that two variables change together (correlate) enables us to predict one when we know the other, but correlation does not specify cause and effect.

The correlation does not equal causation issue is why we see so many competing health claims in the media. We hear one day that flax seeds are "linked" to increased lifespan but we hear the next day that flax is "linked" to cancer. Both can be true because of any one of the reasons cited above (for fun, go through the soft drink example again, but replace "diet soft drinks" with "flax seed"). Always be dubious of what you hear in the media. Think critically in order to understand what conclusions you can and should draw.

When correlational research is extended over time, it is called longitudinal research. Longitudinal research can begin to sort out cause and effect because we know that some things happen before others. Causes always happen before effects, so if we know that children almost always have a healthy positive self-image before they start to show more achievement than their peers, then we can rule out that it is achievement that causes a healthy positive self-image. Advanced correlational techniques can suggest cause–effect relations. *Time-lagged* correlations reveal the sequence of events (for example, by indicating whether changed achievement more often precedes or follows changed self-esteem). Researchers can also use statistical techniques that extract the influence of "confounded" variables, as when the correlation between self-esteem and achievement disappeared after extracting intelligence and family status.

Survey research

How do we measure such variables in the population? One way is by surveying representative samples of people. Survey researchers obtain a representative group by taking a **random sample**—one in which every person in the population being studied has an equal chance of inclusion. With this

random sample Survey procedure in which every person in the population being studied has an equal chance of inclusion.

procedure, any subgroup of people—red-haired people, for example—will tend to be represented in the survey to the extent that they are represented in the total population.

It is an amazing fact that whether we survey people in a city or in a whole country, 1200 randomly selected participants will enable us to be 95 percent confident of describing the entire population with an error margin of 3 percentage points or less. Imagine a huge jar filled with beans, 50 percent red and 50 percent white. Randomly sample 1200 of these, and you will be 95 percent certain to draw out between 47 percent and 53 percent red beans—regardless of whether the jar contains 10 000 beans or 100 million beans. If we think of the red beans as supporters of one political party and the white beans as supporters of the other party, we can understand why polls taken just before national elections have diverged from election results by an average of less than 2 percent. As a few drops of blood can speak for the whole body, so can a random sample speak for a population.

Bear in mind that polls do not literally *predict* voting; they only *describe* public opinion and voting intentions as of the moment they are taken. Both can shift. For example, in the 2011 Canadian federal election, surveys just two days before the election (LISPOP, 2011) suggested that the Liberal Party would get as many seats as the New Democratic Party (NDP); but clearly the NDP was gaining momentum and ended up capturing many more seats than the Liberals. In the 2015 and 2019 Canadian federal elections, despite being "too close to call" just prior to the election, the Liberals won both (albeit with a minority in 2019) (CBC, 2015a, 2019). Similarly, in the 2016 U.S. election, polls consistently had Hillary Clinton in the lead, but Donald Trump won a significant majority of the needed electoral college votes (despite that Clinton won the popular vote by nearly 3 million votes). At the time of this writing, Joe Biden has a commanding lead over Donald Trump in the 2020 presidential race. Did it hold?

To evaluate surveys, we must also bear in mind four potentially biasing influences: unrepresentative samples, the order and timing of the questions, the response options, and the wording of the questions.

Unrepresentative samples

How closely the sample represents the population under study matters greatly. In 1984, columnist Ann Landers accepted a letter writer's challenge to poll her readers on the question of whether women find affection more important than sex. Her question was this: "Would you be content to be held close and treated tenderly and forget about 'the act'?" Of the more than 100 000 women who replied, 72 percent said "yes." An avalanche of worldwide publicity followed. In response to critics, Landers (1985, p. 45) granted that "the sampling may not be representative of all American women. But it does provide honest—valuable—insights from a cross-section of the public. This is because my column is read by people from every walk of life, approximately 70 million of them." Still, one wonders, are the 70 million readers representative of the entire population? And are the 1 in 700 readers who participated representative of the 699 in 700 who did not?

Order and timing of questions

Given a representative sample, we must also contend with other sources of bias, such as the order in which we ask questions. Emily Grise and her colleagues at McGill University found results that all travel groups should be aware of—depending on when and how questions are asked, and the season in which they are asked, travellers reported more positive or more negative travel experiences. When prompted to consider their own commutes on a "warm and sunny" day, responses about their travels were much more positive than if prompted to consider "cold and snowy" conditions (Grise et al., 2019).

Response bias and social desirability

Consider, too, the dramatic effects of the response options. When Joop van der Plight and his colleagues (1987) asked English voters what percentage of Britain's energy they wished came from nuclear power, the average preference was 41 percent. They asked others what percentage they wished came from (1) nuclear, (2) coal, and (3) other sources. Their average preference for nuclear power was 21 percent.

It is not just the response options, however, that can bias people's responses. Sometimes people don't want to admit their true actions and beliefs either to the experimenter or sometimes even to themselves. Questions about prejudice often show very low levels of reported prejudice by the respondents. Yet systematic experiments demonstrate that prejudice is all too common. Why the difference in findings? People may not want to admit on a survey or even to themselves that they harbour some feelings of prejudice. This tendency for people to say what they want others to hear or what they want to believe about themselves is called *social desirability.* Social psychologists have developed new methods of measuring people's beliefs without their knowing that their beliefs are being measured. These *implicit measures* are often used when concerns about social desirability arise.

Wording of the questions

Given a representative sample, we must also contend with other sources of bias, such as the wording of questions. For example, one poll found that people favoured cutting "foreign aid" yet opposed cutting funding "to help hungry people in other nations" (Simon, 1996). Even subtle changes in the tone of a question can have large effects (Schuman & Kalton, 1985). Thus, it is not surprising that politicians in Ottawa and Quebec have fought bitterly about the wording of referendum questions about Quebec sovereignty. Federalists have long charged that the Parti Québécois purposely has devised questions that are unclear and designed to elicit a "yes" vote in favour of sovereignty. In the 1995 election, Quebec residents voted on this question (Gall, Millette, & Lambert, 2015): "Do you agree that Quebec should become sovereign, after having made a formal offer to Canada for a new economic and political partnership, within the scope of the Bill respecting the future of Quebec and the agreement signed on June 12, 1995?" Did this question affect the outcome of the election? It certainly might have, because even when people say they feel strongly about an issue, a question's form and wording may affect their answer (Krosnick & Schuman, 1988). Survey researchers must be sensitive to subtle—and not so subtle—biases.

Knowledge of the issues, however, can sometimes interact with the wording of the question to influence responses. Consider a study conducted by Darin Lehman of the University of British Columbia and his colleagues (Lehman et al., 1992). They had students read a number of newspaper clippings preceding a provincial election. Some of the articles sided with the New Democratic Party (NDP), while others sided with the Social Credit Party (SCP)—the two main rivals in the election. After the students had read the articles, Lehman and his colleagues asked the students in one condition to respond to a series of questions about how fair the articles were to the NDP. The students in the other condition were asked to respond to nearly the same questions, except that they rated how fair the articles were to the SCP. The questions tended to lead students to see bias against one party over the other. Did the wording of the question affect all students equally? No. It primarily affected students who were less knowledgeable about the issues in the election. These students saw more bias against the NDP when the questions were about the NDP and more bias against the SCP when the questions were about the SCP. More knowledgeable students, on the other hand, were unaffected by the wording of the question.

Experimental Research: Searching for Cause and Effect

The difficulty of discerning cause and effect among naturally correlated events prompts most social psychologists to create laboratory simulations of everyday processes whenever this is feasible and ethical.

independent variables Experimental factors that a researcher manipulates.

Control: Manipulating variables

Social psychologists experiment by constructing social situations that simulate important features of our daily lives. By varying just one or two factors at a time—called **independent variables**—the experimenter pinpoints how changes in the one or two things affect us. The experiment enables the social psychologist to discover principles of social thinking, social influence, and social relations. Social psychologists experiment to understand and predict human behaviour.

It is important that we understand the distinction between correlation and experimental research (see Figure 1–5). Historically, social psychologists have used the experimental method in about three-quarters of their research studies (Higbee, Millard, & Folkman, 1982), and in two out of three studies, the setting has been a research laboratory (Adair, Dushenko, & Lindsay, 1985). To illustrate the laboratory experiment, consider two experiments that typify research from upcoming chapters on prejudice and aggression. Each suggests possible cause–effect explanations of correlational findings.

Correlational and experimental studies of prejudice against the obese

The first experiment concerns prejudice against people who are obese. People often perceive the obese as slow, lazy, and sloppy (Ryckman et al., 1989). Do such attitudes spawn discrimination? In hopes of finding out, Steven Gortmaker and his colleagues (1993) studied 370 obese 16- to 24-year-olds. When they restudied them seven years later, two-thirds of the women were still obese, and these women were less likely to be married and earning high salaries than a comparison group of some 5000 other women. Even after correcting for any differences in aptitude test scores, race, and parental income, the obese women's incomes were $7000 a year below average. *Note:* Obesity correlated with marital status and income.

Correcting for certain other factors makes it look as though discrimination might explain the correlation between obesity and lower status, but we can't be sure. (Can you think of other possibilities?) Enter social psychologists Mark Snyder and Julie Haugen (1994, 1995). They asked 76 University of Minnesota male students to have a getting-acquainted phone conversation with one of 76 women students. Each man was shown a photo *said* to picture his conversational partner. Half were shown an obese woman (not the actual partner); the other half were shown a normal-weight woman. Whom the men were shown—a normal-weight or an overweight woman—was the independent variable.

In one part of the experiment, the men were asked to form an impression of the women's traits. Later analysis of just the women's side of the conversation revealed that when

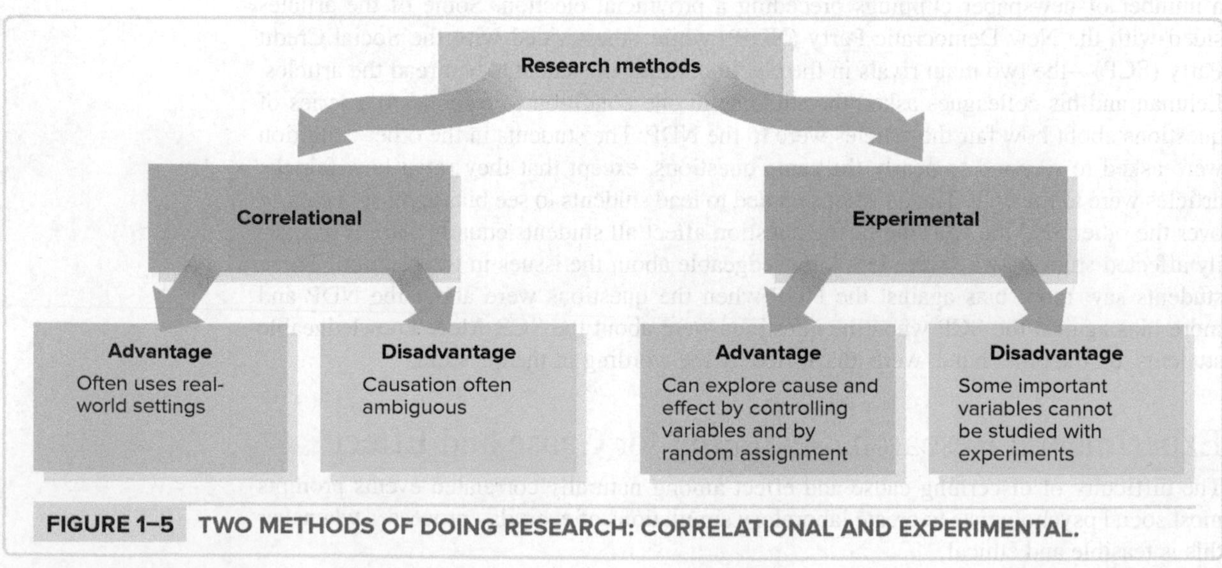

FIGURE 1–5 TWO METHODS OF DOING RESEARCH: CORRELATIONAL AND EXPERIMENTAL.

women were being evaluated, the men spoke less warmly and happily if the women were presumed to be obese. Clearly, the men's beliefs induced the men to behave in a way that led their supposedly obese partners to confirm the idea that such women are undesirable. Prejudice and discrimination were having an effect.

Does viewing violence on TV or in other media lead to imitation? Experiments suggest that it does, especially among children.

Source: ©Peter Byron/ Science Source.

Correlational and experimental studies of TV violence viewing

As a second example of how an experiment can clarify causation, consider the correlation between television viewing and children's behaviour. Children who watch many violent television programs tend to be more aggressive than those who watch few. This suggests that children might be learning from what they see on the screen. But, as we hope you now recognize, this is a correlational finding. There are at least two other cause–effect interpretations that do not implicate television as the cause of the children's aggression. (What are they?)

Social psychologists have, therefore, brought television viewing into the laboratory, where they control the amount of violence the children see. By exposing children to violent and nonviolent programs, researchers can observe how the amount of violence affects behaviour. Chris Boyatzis and his colleagues (1995) showed some elementary schoolchildren, but not others, an episode of the 1990s' most popular—and violent—children's television program, *Power Rangers.* Immediately after viewing the episode, the viewers committed seven times as many aggressive acts per two-minute interval as the nonviewers. We call the observed aggressive acts the **dependent variable**. Such experiments indicate that television can be one cause of children's aggressive behaviour.

dependent variable The variable being measured, so called because it may *depend* on manipulations of the independent variable.

random assignment The process of assigning participants to the conditions of an experiment such that all persons have the same chance of being in a given condition.

So far we have seen that the logic of experimentation is simple: By creating and controlling a miniature reality, we can vary one factor and then another and discover how these factors, separately or in combination, affect people. Now let's go a little deeper and see how an experiment is done.

Every social–psychological experiment has two essential ingredients. We have just considered one: *control.* We manipulate one or two independent variables while trying to hold everything else constant. The other ingredient is *random assignment.*

Random assignment: The great equalizer

Recall that we were reluctant, on the basis of a correlation, to assume that obesity *caused* lower status (via discrimination) or that viewing violence *caused* aggressiveness (see Table 1–1 for more examples). A survey researcher might measure and statistically extract other possibly pertinent factors and see if the correlations survive. But researchers can never control for all of the factors that might distinguish obese from non-obese, and violence viewers from nonviewers. Maybe violence viewers differ in education, culture, or intelligence, or in dozens of ways the researcher hasn't considered.

In one fell swoop, **random assignment** eliminates all such extraneous factors. With random assignment, each person has an equal chance of viewing the violence or the nonviolence. Thus, the people in both groups would, in every conceivable way—family status, intelligence, education, initial aggressiveness—average about the same. Highly intelligent people, for example, are equally likely to appear in both groups. Because random

TABLE 1-1 Recognizing Correlations and Experimental Research.

	Can participants be randomly assigned to condition?	Independent variable	Dependent variable
Are early maturing children more confident?	No → Correlational		
Do students learn more in online or classroom courses?	Yes → Experimental	Take class online or in classroom	Learning
Do school grades predict vocational success?	No → Correlational		
Does playing violent video games increase aggressiveness?	Yes → Experimental	Play violent or nonviolent game	Aggressiveness
Do people find comedy funnier when alone or with others?	(you answer)		
Do higher-income people have higher self-esteem?	(you answer)		

assignment creates equivalent groups, any later aggression difference between the two groups must have something to do with the only way they differ—whether or not they viewed violence (Figure 1–6).

Note the distinction between random *assignment* in experiments and random *sampling* in surveys. Random assignment helps us infer cause and effect. Random sampling helps us generalize to a population.

observational research methods Where individuals are observed in natural settings, often without awareness, in order to provide the opportunity for objective analysis of behaviour.

Unfortunately, true experimental manipulation is not always possible. Some situations (such as cases of child welfare) do not allow for random assignment or for direct manipulations of independent variables. For example, one cannot randomly assign children to be brought up by "alcoholic" versus "not alcoholic" parents to see what impact a substance-abusing parent has on a child's welfare (Foster & McCombs-Thornton, 2013). That would be unethical (see below). So, some researchers need to try to make causal inferences using **observational research methods** where

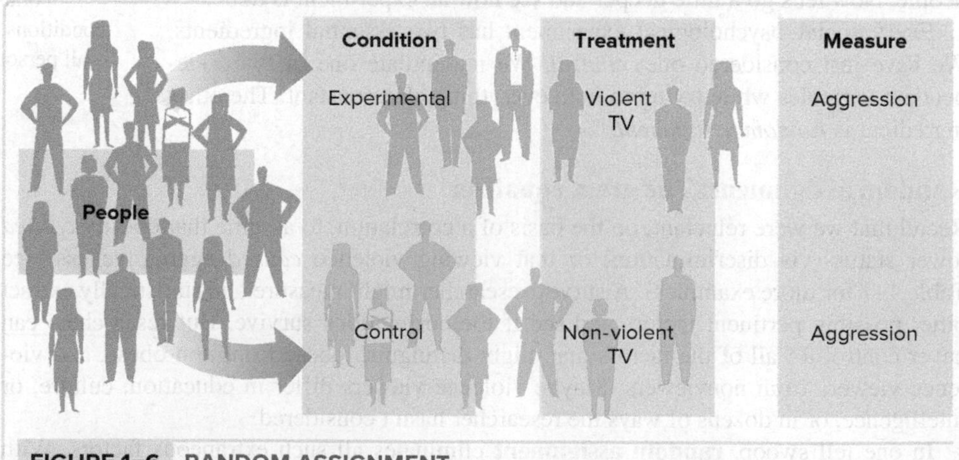

FIGURE 1–6 RANDOM ASSIGNMENT.

Experiments randomly assign people either to a condition that receives the experimental treatment or to a control condition that does not. This gives the researcher confidence that any later difference is somehow caused by the treatment.

individuals are observed in natural settings, often without awareness, in order to provide the opportunity for objective analysis of behaviour. Observational researchers use sophisticated statistical analysis techniques to make inferences about cause and effect where a true experiment is not possible.

The ethics of experimentation

Our television example illustrates why some experiments are ethically sensitive. Social psychologists would not, over long time periods, expose one group of children to brutal violence. Rather, they briefly alter people's social experience and note the effects. Sometimes, the experimental treatment is a harmless, perhaps even enjoyable, experience to which people give their knowing consent. Sometimes, however, researchers find themselves operating in a grey area between the harmless and the risky.

Social psychologists often venture into that ethical grey area when they design experiments that engage intense thoughts and emotions. Experiments need not have what Elliot Aronson, Marilynn Brewer, and Merrill Carlsmith (1985) called **mundane realism**. That is, laboratory behaviour (for example, delivering electric shocks as part of an experiment on aggression) need not be literally the same as everyday behaviour. For many researchers, that sort of realism is, indeed, mundane—not important. But the experiment *should* have **experimental realism**—it should absorb and involve the participants. Experimenters do not want their people consciously play-acting; they want to engage real psychological processes. Forcing people to choose whether to give intense or mild electric shock to someone else can, for example, be a realistic measure of aggression. It functionally simulates real aggression.

mundane realism Degree to which an experiment is superficially similar to everyday situations.

experimental realism Degree to which an experiment absorbs and involves its participants.

demand characteristics Cues in an experiment that tell the participant what behaviour is expected.

Achieving experimental realism sometimes requires deceiving people with a plausible cover story. If the person in the next room actually is not receiving the shocks, the experimenter does not want the participants to know this. That would destroy the experimental realism. Thus, about one-third of social–psychological studies (though a decreasing number) have required deception (Korn & Nicks, 1993; Vitelli, 1988).

Experimenters also seek to hide their predictions lest the participants, in their eagerness to be "good subjects," merely do what's expected or, in an ornery mood, do the opposite. In subtle ways, the experimenter's words, tone of voice, and gestures may call forth desired responses. To minimize such **demand characteristics**—cues that seem to "demand" certain behaviour—experimenters typically standardize their instructions or even use a computer to present them.

Researchers often walk a tightrope in designing experiments that will be involving yet ethical. To believe that you are hurting someone or to be subjected to strong social pressure to see if it will change your opinion or behaviour may be temporarily uncomfortable. Such experiments raise the age-old question of whether ends justify means. Do the insights gained justify deceiving and sometimes distressing people?

University ethics committees now review social–psychological research to ensure that it will treat people humanely. Ethical principles developed by major psychological organizations and government organizations (such as

What influences occasionally trigger post-game violence among sports fans? Social psychologists have proposed hypotheses that have been tested with groups behaving under controlled conditions.
Source: The Canadian Press/Ryan Remiorz.

informed consent An ethical principle requiring that research participants be told enough to enable them to choose whether they wish to participate.

Canada's Tri-Council, which funds natural science, social science, humanities, and health research) urge investigators to follow these practices:

- Tell potential participants enough about the experiment to enable their **informed consent**.
- Be truthful. Use deception only if essential and justified by a significant purpose and if there is no alternative.
- Protect people from harm and significant discomfort.
- Treat information about the individual participants confidentially.
- Debrief participants. Fully explain the experiment afterward, including any deception. The only exception to this rule is when the feedback would be distressing, such as by making participants realize they have been stupid or cruel.

The experimenter should be sufficiently informative and considerate to leave subjects feeling at least as good about themselves as when they came in. Better yet, the participants should be repaid by having learned something (Sharpe & Faye, 2009). When treated respectfully, few participants mind being deceived (Epley & Huff, 1998; Kimmel, 1998). Indeed, say social psychology's defenders, professors provoke far greater anxiety and distress by giving and returning course exams than researchers now do in their experiments.

Increasingly, social psychologists have recognized that research ethics go beyond how participants in their studies are treated. Part of this realization occurred when three established social psychologists were exposed for making up all or part of their data in several experiments (Funder et al., 2014).

The shock from these cases of fraud caused most social psychologists to do a lot of soul searching about how this could happen in the field. How could someone work in the field for 20 years, make up the data in all or most of their papers, and by all appearances be successful? Why didn't colleagues, editors, reviewers, and students notice? The answers to these questions have not been simple and have caused social psychologists to rethink the standards for conducting, reporting, and reviewing research (John, Loewenstein, & Prelec, 2012).

Researchers now have become more vigilant, not only in trying to detect and eliminate fraud but also in conducting and reviewing research to eliminate subtle biases, such as the tendency to confirm hypotheses, as much as possible. Among the practices that are gaining wider adoption are making the data from one's experiments publicly available, providing fuller reports of the methods used in experiments, and carefully describing the statistical tests used to test hypotheses. It remains to be seen whether these practices will make fraud more difficult, but they do reflect a trend among researchers to hold one another to a higher standard and to reduce bias in conducting research.

Generalizing From Laboratory to Life

As the research on children, television, and violence illustrates, social psychology mixes everyday experience and laboratory analysis. Throughout this book, we will do the same by drawing our data mostly from the laboratory and our illustrations mostly from life. Social psychology displays a healthy interplay between laboratory research and everyday life. Hunches gained from everyday experience often inspire laboratory research, which deepens our understanding of our experience.

This interplay appears in the children's television experiment. What people saw in everyday life suggested experimental research. Network and government policymakers, those with the power to make changes, are now aware of the results. This consistency of findings on television's effects—in the lab and in the field—is true of research in many other areas, including studies of helping, of leadership style, of depression, and of achievement. The effects found in the lab have been mirrored by effects in the field.

"The psychology laboratory has generally produced psychological truths rather than trivialities," noted Craig Anderson and his colleagues (1999).

We need to be cautious, however, in generalizing from the laboratory to life. Although the laboratory uncovers basic dynamics of human existence, it is still a simplified, controlled reality. It tells us what effect to expect of variable *X*, all other things being equal—which, in real life, they never are. Moreover, as you will see, the participants in many experiments are university students. Although this may help you identify with them, university students are hardly a random sample of all humanity. Would we get similar results with people of different ages, educational levels, and cultures? This is always an open question.

SUMMING UP

What Is Social Psychology?

- *Social psychology* is the scientific study of how people think about, influence, and relate to one another. Its central themes are listed below.

What Are the Major Themes of Social Psychology?

- We construct our social reality.
- Our social intuitions are often powerful but sometimes perilous.
- Social influences shape our behaviour.
- Personal attitudes and dispositions also shape behaviour.
- Social behaviour is biologically rooted.
- Relating to others is a basic need.
- Social psychology's principles are applicable in everyday life.

How Do Values Affect Social Psychology?

- Social psychologists' values penetrate their work in obvious ways, such as their choice of research topics and the types of people who are attracted to various fields of study.
- They also do this in subtler ways, such as their hidden assumptions when forming concepts, choosing labels, and giving advice.
- This penetration of values into science is not a reason to fault social psychology or any other science. That human thinking is seldom dispassionate is precisely why we need systematic observation and experimentation if we are to check our cherished ideas against reality.

Is Social Psychology Merely Common Sense?

- Social psychology is criticized for being trivial because it documents things that seem obvious.
- Experiments, however, reveal that outcomes are more "obvious" *after* the facts are known.
- This *hindsight bias* (the *I-knew-it-all-along phenomenon*) often makes people overconfident about the validity of their judgments and predictions.

Research Methods: How Do We Do Social Psychology?

- Social psychologists organize their ideas and findings into *theories.* A good theory will distill an array of facts into a much shorter list of predictive principles. We can use those predictions to confirm or modify the theory, to generate new research, and to suggest practical application.
- Most social–psychological research is either *correlational* or *experimental.* Correlational studies, sometimes conducted with systematic survey methods, discern the relationship between variables, such as between amount of education and amount of income. Knowing that two things are naturally related is valuable information, but it is not a reliable indicator of what is causing what—or whether a third variable is involved.
- When possible, social psychologists prefer to conduct experiments that explore cause and effect. By constructing a miniature reality that is under their control, experimenters can vary one thing and then another and discover how those things, separately or in combination, affect behaviour. We *randomly assign* (Figure 1–6) participants to an experimental condition, which receives the experimental treatment, or to a control condition, which does not. We can then attribute any resulting difference between the two conditions to the *independent variable.*
- In creating experiments, social psychologists sometimes stage situations that engage people's emotions. In doing so, they are obliged to follow professional ethical guidelines, such as obtaining people's *informed consent,* protecting them from harm, and, afterward, fully disclosing any temporary deceptions. Laboratory experiments enable social psychologists to test ideas gleaned from life experience and then apply the principles and findings to the real world.

Key Terms

correlational research
culture
demand characteristics
dependent variable
experimental realism
experimental research
field research
hindsight bias
hypotheses
independent variables
informed consent
mundane realism
naturalistic fallacy
observational research methods
random assignment
random sample
social neuroscience
social psychology
social representations
theory

Answers to Common Sense Questions

Answers to Activity:

1. F **2.** F **3.** F **4.** F **5.** T **6.** F **7.** F **8.** F **9.** F **10.** F

Part One

Social Thinking

This book unfolds around its definition of social psychology: the scientific study of how we *think about* (Part One), *influence* (Part Two), and *relate to* (Part Three) one another.

Part One examines the scientific study of how we think about one another (also called social cognition). Each chapter confronts some overriding questions: How reasonable are our social attitudes, explanations, and beliefs? Are our impressions of ourselves and others generally accurate? How does our social thinking form? How is it prone to bias and error, and how might we bring it closer to reality?

Chapter 2 explores the interplay between our sense of self and our social worlds. How do our social surroundings shape our self-identities? How does self-interest colour our social judgments and motivate our social behaviour?

Chapter 3 looks at the amazing and sometimes amusing ways we form beliefs about our social worlds. It also alerts us to some pitfalls of social thinking and suggests how to avoid them and think smarter.

Chapter 4 explores the links between our thinking and our actions, between our attitudes and behaviours: Do our attitudes determine our behaviours, or vice versa? Or does it work both ways?

CHAPTER 2

The Self in a Social World

Source: ©Adam Lubroth/Getty Images.

CHAPTER OUTLINE

Spotlights and Illusions: What Do They Teach Us About Ourselves?

Self-Concept: Who Am I?

What Is the Nature and Motivating Power of Self-Esteem?

What Is Self-Serving Bias?

How Do People Manage Their Self-Presentation?

What Does It Mean to Have Perceived Self-Control?

At the centre of our worlds, more pivotal for us than anything else, is ourselves. As we navigate our daily lives, our sense of self continually engages the world.

Consider this example: One morning, you wake up to find your hair sticking up at strange angles on your head. You can't find a hat, so you smooth down the random spikes of your hair and dash out the door to class. All morning, you are acutely self-conscious about your very bad hair day. To your surprise, your friends in class don't say anything. Are they secretly laughing to themselves about how ridiculous you look, or are they too preoccupied with themselves to notice your spiky hair?

Spotlights and Illusions: What Do They Teach Us About Ourselves?

What is the spotlight effect? And how does it relate to the illusion of transparency?

Why do we often feel that others are paying more attention to us than they really are? The **spotlight effect** means seeing ourselves at centre stage, thus intuitively overestimating the extent to which others' attention is aimed at us.

Timothy Lawson (2010) explored the spotlight effect by having university students change into a sweatshirt emblazoned with "American Eagle" before meeting a group of peers. Nearly 40 percent were sure the other students would remember what the shirt said, but only 10 percent actually did. Most observers did not even notice when the students changed sweatshirts after leaving the room for a few minutes. In another experiment, even noticeably embarrassing clothes, such as a T-shirt with singer Barry Manilow on it, provoked only 23 percent of observers to notice—much less than the 50 percent estimated by the unfortunate students sporting the 1970s soft-rock warbler on their chests (Gilovich et al., 2000).

spotlight effect The belief that others are paying more attention to our appearance than they really are.

illusion of transparency The illusion that our concealed emotions leak out and can be easily read by others.

What's true of our dorky clothes and bad hair is also true of our emotions: our anxiety, irritation, disgust, deceit, or attraction to someone else (Gilovich et al., 1998). Keenly aware of our own emotions, we often suffer an **illusion of transparency**. We feel especially transparent when we feel self-conscious and worry about being evaluated negatively by others (Vorauer & Ross, 1999). If we're happy and we know it, then our face will surely show it—and others, we presume, will notice. Actually, we can be more opaque than we realize.

Savitsky and Gilovich (2003) wondered whether an "illusion of transparency" might surface among inexperienced public speakers—and whether it might disrupt their performance. To find out, they invited 40 university students to their laboratory in pairs. One person stood at the podium and spoke for three minutes (on a topic such as "The Best and Worst Things About Life Today") as the other sat and listened. Then the two switched positions and the other person gave a different three-minute impromptu talk. Afterward, each rated how nervous they thought they appeared while speaking (from 0, *not at all,* to 10, *very*) and how nervous the other person seemed.

> ***"There are three things extremely hard: steel, a diamond, and to know one's self."***
>
> Benjamin Franklin

The results? People rated themselves as appearing relatively nervous (6.65, on average). But to their partner they appeared not so nervous (5.25), a difference great enough to be statistically significant (meaning that a difference this great, for this sample of people, is very unlikely to have been due to chance variation). Twenty-seven of the 40 participants (68%) believed that they appeared more nervous than their partner did.

Savitsky and Gilovich (2003) next wondered whether informing speakers that their nervousness isn't so obvious might help them relax and perform better. They invited 77 more university students to come to the lab and, after five minutes' preparation, give a three-minute videotaped speech on race relations at their university. Those in one group—the *control condition*—were given no further instructions. Those in the *reassured condition*

TABLE 2-1 Average Ratings of Speeches by Speakers and Observers on a 1 to 7 Scale.

Type of Rating	Control Condition	Reassured Condition	Informed Condition
Speakers' self-ratings			
Speech quality	3.04	2.83	3.50*
Relaxed appearance	3.35	2.69	4.20*
Observers' ratings			
Speech quality	3.50	3.62	4.23*
Composed appearance	3.90	3.94	4.65*

*Each of these results differs by a statistically significant margin from those of the control and reassured condition.

were told that it was natural to feel anxious but that "You shouldn't worry much about what other people think. . . . With this in mind you should just relax and try to do your best. Know that if you become nervous, you probably shouldn't worry about it." To those in the informed condition he explained the illusion of transparency. After telling them it was natural to feel anxious, the experimenter added, "Research has found that audiences can't pick up on your anxiety as well as you might expect. . . . Those speaking feel that their nervousness is transparent, but in reality their feelings are not so apparent. . . . With this in mind, you should just relax and try to do your best. Know that if you become nervous, you'll probably be the only one to know."

After the speeches, the speakers rated their speech quality and their perceived nervousness (this time using a seven-point scale) and were also rated by the observers. As Table 2–1 shows, those informed about the illusion-of-transparency phenomenon felt better about their speech and their appearance than did those in the control and reassurance conditions. What's more, the observers confirmed the speakers' self-assessments.

So, the next time you feel nervous about looking nervous, pause to remember the lesson of these experiments: Other people are noticing less than you might suppose.

In addition to thinking our emotions are transparent, we also overestimate the visibility of our social blunders and public mental slips. When we trigger the library alarm or accidentally insult someone, we may be mortified ("Everyone thinks I'm a jerk"). But research shows that what we agonize over, others may hardly notice and soon forget (Savitsky et al., 2001).

The spotlight effect and the related illusion of transparency are but two of many examples of the interplay between our sense of self and our social worlds. Here are a few more:

- *Social surroundings affect our self-awareness.* When we are the only members of our race, gender, or nationality in a group, we notice how we differ and how others are reacting to our difference. For example, the only woman in an executive meeting is likely to be acutely aware of her gender. When travelling abroad, you may be keenly aware of being Canadian; while at home, however, you might not think about your nationality very much.
- *Self-interest colours our social judgment.* When problems arise in a close relationship, we usually attribute more responsibility to our partners than to ourselves. When things go well at home or work or play, we see ourselves as more responsible. After Canadians Frederick Banting and John Macleod received a 1923 Nobel Prize for discovering insulin, they both thought the discovery was primarily their own. Banting claimed that Macleod, who headed the laboratory, had been more a hindrance than a help. Macleod omitted Banting's name in speeches about the discovery (Ross, 1981).

- *Self-concern motivates our social behaviour.* In hopes of making a positive impression, we agonize about our appearance. Like savvy politicians, we also monitor others' behaviour and expectations and adjust our behaviour accordingly.
- *Social relationships help define the self.* In our varied relationships, we have varying selves (Andersen & Chen, 2002). We may be one self with Mom, another with friends, another with teachers. How we think of ourselves is linked to the person we're with at the moment. And when relationships change, our self-concepts can change as well. University students who recently broke up with a romantic partner shifted their self-perceptions and felt less certain about who they were—one reason breakups can be so emotionally distressing (Slotter, Gardner, & Finkel, 2010).

As these examples suggest, the traffic between self and society runs both ways. Our ideas and feelings about ourselves affect how we respond to others. And others help shape our sense of self.

No topic in psychology is more researched today than the self. In 2018, the word *self* appeared in 29 445 book and article summaries in *PsycINFO* (the online archive of psychological research)—more than 25 times the number that had appeared in 1970. Our sense of self organizes our thoughts, feelings, and actions (Figure 2–1). Our sense of self enables us to remember our past, assess our present, and project our future—and, thus, enables us to behave adaptively.

In later chapters, we will see that much of our behaviour is not consciously controlled but, rather, automatic and unselfconscious. However, the self does enable long-term planning, goal setting, and restraint. It imagines alternatives, compares itself with others, and manages its reputation and relationships. Moreover, as Mark Leary (2004a) noted in his aptly titled *The Curse of the Self,* the self can sometimes be an impediment to a satisfying life. That's why religious or spiritual meditation practices seek to prune the self's egocentric preoccupations, by quieting the ego, reducing its attachments to material pleasures, and redirecting it. "Mysticism," adds psychologist Jonathan Haidt (2006), "everywhere and always, is about losing the self, transcending the self, and merging with something larger than the self."

In the remainder of this chapter, we examine our self-concept (how we come to know ourselves) and the self in action (how our sense of self drives our attitudes and actions).

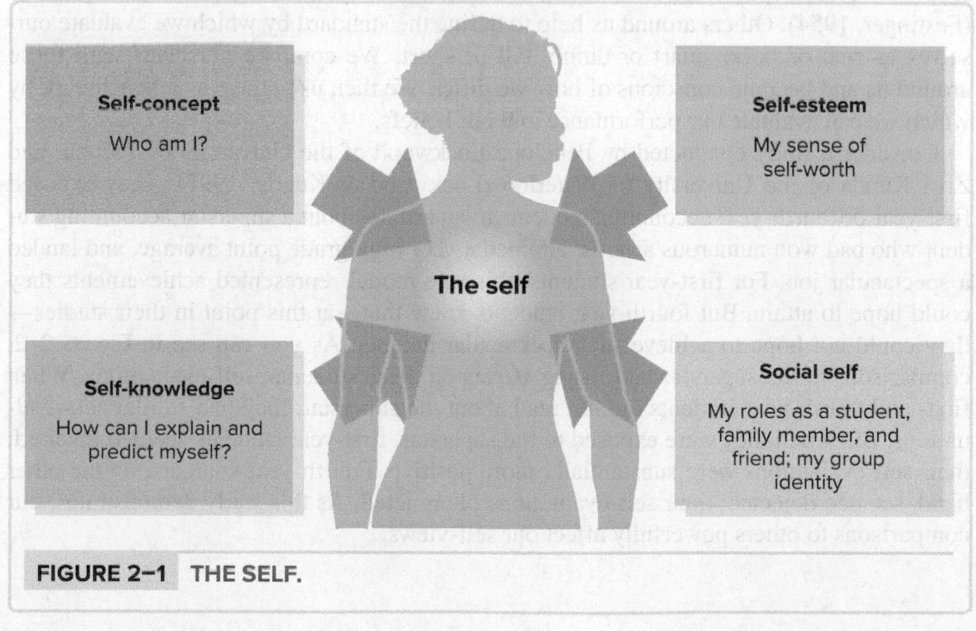
Self-concept
Who am I?
Self-esteem
My sense of self-worth
The self
Self-knowledge
How can I explain and predict myself?
Social self
My roles as a student, family member, and friend; my group identity

FIGURE 2–1 THE SELF.

Self-Concept: Who Am I?

How and how accurately do we know ourselves? What determines our **self-concept**?

At the Centre of Our Worlds: Our Sense of Self

The most important aspect of yourself is your self. To discover where this sense of self arises, neuroscientists are exploring the brain activity that underlies our constant sense of being oneself. Most studies suggest an important role for the right hemisphere (van Veluw & Chance, 2014). Put yours to sleep (with an anaesthetic to your right carotid artery) and you likely will have trouble recognizing your own face. One patient with right-hemisphere damage failed to recognize that he owned and was controlling his left hand (Decety & Sommerville, 2003). The "medial prefrontal cortex," a neuron path located in the cleft between your brain hemispheres just behind your eyes, seemingly helps stitch together your sense of self. It becomes more active when you think about yourself (Farb et al., 2007; Zimmer, 2005).

The elements of your self-concept, the specific beliefs by which you define yourself, are your **self-schemas** (Markus & Wurf, 1987). *Schemas* are mental templates by which we organize our worlds. Our *self*-schemas—our perceiving ourselves as athletic, overweight, smart, or whatever—powerfully affect how we perceive, remember, and evaluate other people and ourselves. If, for example, athletics is central to your self-concept (if being an athlete is one of your self-schemas), then you will tend to notice others' bodies and skills. You will quickly recall sports-related experiences. And you will welcome information that is consistent with your self-schema (Kihlstrom & Cantor, 1984). Because birthdays are often central pieces of information within self-schemas, if your friend's birthday is close to yours, you're more likely to remember it (Kesebir & Oishi, 2010). The self-schemas that make up our self-concepts help us organize and retrieve our experiences.

self-concept How a person answers the question "Who am I?" provides a glimpse of their self-concept.

self-schemas Beliefs about self that organize and guide the processing of self-relevant information.

social comparison Evaluating your abilities and opinions by comparing yourself to others.

Social Comparisons

How do we decide if we are rich, smart, or short? One way is through **social comparison** (Festinger, 1954). Others around us help to define the standard by which we evaluate ourselves as rich or poor, smart or dumb, tall or short: We compare ourselves with those around us and become conscious of how we differ. We then use others as a benchmark by which we can evaluate our performance and our beliefs.

Consider a study conducted by Penelope Lockwood of the University of Toronto and Ziva Kunda of the University of Waterloo (Lockwood & Kunda, 1997). They exposed first-year or fourth-year accounting students to an article about a superstar accounting student who had won numerous awards, attained a very high grade point average, and landed a spectacular job. For first-year students, this role model represented achievements they could hope to attain. But fourth-year students knew that—at this point in their studies—they could not hope to achieve such spectacular heights. As you can see in Figure 2–2, comparisons to the superstar had strong effects on these students' self-evaluations. When first- and fourth-year students did not read about the superstar, they had similar self-evaluations. But when they were exposed to the superstar, first-year students seemed inspired; their self-evaluations were substantially more positive. Fourth-year students, on the other hand, seemed dejected; their self-evaluations plummeted. As this study demonstrates, our comparisons to others powerfully affect our self-views.

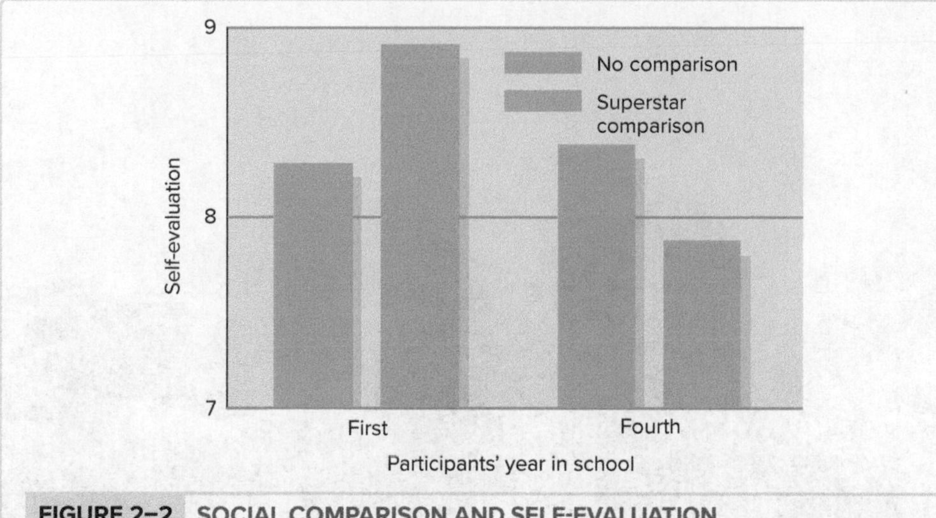

FIGURE 2–2 SOCIAL COMPARISON AND SELF-EVALUATION.

People are inspired by a role model if they can attain similar success, but they are demoralized if they cannot.

Source: Adapted from P. Lockwood and Z. Kunda, "Superstars and me: Predicting the impact of role models on the self," *Journal of Personality and Social Psychology, 73*(1), 91–103. Copyright © 1997 by the American Psychological Association. Adapted with permission.

Social comparison explains why students tend to have a higher academic self-evaluation if they attend a school with mostly average students (Marsh et al., 2000; Wang, 2015) and how self-concept can be threatened after graduation when a student who excelled in an average high school goes on to an academically selective university. The "big fish" is no longer in a small pond.

Much of life revolves around social comparisons. We feel handsome when others seem homely, smart when others seem dull, caring when others seem callous. When we witness a peer's performance, we cannot resist implicitly comparing ourselves (Gilbert, Giesler, & Morris, 1995). We may, therefore, privately take some pleasure in a peer's failure, especially when it happens to someone we envy and when we don't feel vulnerable to such misfortune ourselves (Lockwood, 2002, Smith et al., 1996). You might have heard the German word for this: *schadenfreude*.

> ***"Make no comparisons!"***
>
> King Charles I, 1600–1649

Sometimes social comparison is based on incomplete information. Have you ever been on Facebook or Instagram and thought, "All of my friends are having a lot more fun than I am"? If so, you're not alone. Among students in one study, those who spent more time on Facebook were more likely to believe that other people were happier and had better lives than they did (Chou & Edge, 2012). Of course, it can't be true that everybody is having more fun then everyone else—it's just that Facebook users feature the more exciting and positive aspects of their lives. Sure enough, Facebook users who socially compared themselves to others on the site were more likely to be depressed—a phenomenon the researchers called "seeing everyone else's highlight reels" (Steers et al., 2014). This biased social comparison might be one reason young adults who used Facebook more often were more anxious, more lonely, and less satisfied with their lives (Huang, 2017; Kross et al., 2013). An experiment found the same result: People who were randomly assigned to give up Facebook for a week ended the week happier than those who kept using Facebook (Tromholt, 2016).

Social comparison: Because people tend to highlight only the best and most exciting parts of their lives on social media, social comparison online is often based on incomplete information.
Source: ©Hero Images Inc./Alamy Stock Photo.

Social comparisons can also diminish our satisfaction in other ways. When we experience an increase in affluence, status, or achievement, we "compare upward"—we raise the standards by which we evaluate our attainments. When climbing the ladder of success, we tend to look up, not down (Gruder, 1977; Suls & Tesch, 1978; Wheeler, Koestner, & Driver, 1982). People living in communities where a few residents are very wealthy tend to feel less satisfied as they compare upward (Fiske, 2011).

When facing competition, we often protect our shaky self-concept by perceiving the competitor as advantaged. For example, college swimmers believed that their competitors had better coaching and more practice time (Shepperd & Taylor, 1999). Even sexual activity is subject to social comparison. Adults who have sex more often are happier—you might have guessed that! But then social comparison kicks in: Even people who have a lot of sex are less happy if their peers are having more sex than they are (Wadsworth, 2014). Apparently, we judge not just how much fun we're having—but how it measures up to the fun everyone else is having.

Other people's judgments

When people think well of us, it helps us think well of ourselves. Children whom others label as gifted, hard-working, or helpful tend to incorporate such ideas into their self-concepts and behaviour (see Chapter 3). Children who are praised for "being a helper" (rather than "helping") later help more—it has become part of their identity (Bryan et al., 2014). If minority students feel threatened by negative stereotypes of their academic ability, or if women feel threatened by low expectations for their math and science performance, they may "disidentify" with those realms. Rather than fight such prejudgments, they may identify their interests elsewhere (Steele, 2010) (and see Chapter 11).

The *looking-glass self* was how sociologist Charles H. Cooley (1902) described our use of how we think others perceive us as a mirror for perceiving ourselves. Fellow sociologist George Herbert Mead (1934) refined this concept, noting that what matters for our self-concept is not how others actually see us but the way we imagine they see us. People generally feel freer to praise than to criticize; they voice their compliments and restrain their insults. We may, therefore, overestimate others' appraisal, inflating our self-images. For example, people tend to see themselves as more physically attractive than they actually are (Epley & Whitchurch, 2008). Our self-esteem, moreover, corresponds with how we see ourselves on traits that we believe are valued by others (Anthony, Holmes, & Wood, 2007).

Self and Culture

How would you complete this statement: "I am ______"? Would you give information about your personal traits, such as "I am honest," "I am tall," or "I am outgoing"? Or would you also describe your social identity, such as "I am a Pisces," "I am a MacDonald," or "I am a Muslim"?

For some people, especially those in industrialized Western cultures, **individualism** prevails. Identity is self-contained. Becoming an adult means separating from parents, becoming self-reliant, and defining one's personal, **independent self**. One's identity—as a unique individual with particular abilities, traits, values, and dreams—remains fairly constant.

Western culture assumes that your life will be enriched by believing in your power of personal control. Western literature, from *The Iliad* to *Anne of Green Gables,* celebrates the self-reliant individual. Movie plots feature rugged heroes who buck the establishment. Songs proclaim "I've Gotta Be Me" and extol the virtues of loving yourself (Schoeneman, 1994). Individualism flourishes when people experience affluence, mobility, urbanism, and mass media, and when economies shift away from manufacturing and toward information and service industries (Bianchi, 2016; Grossmann & Varnum, 2015; Triandis, 2000). Such changes are occurring worldwide and, as we might therefore expect, individualism is increasing globally (Santos et al., 2017).

Most cultures native to Asia, Africa, and Central and South America place a greater value on **collectivism** by respecting and identifying with the group. They nurture what Shinobu Kitayama and Hazel Markus (1995) call the **interdependent self**. In these cultures, people are more self-critical and focus less on positive self-views (Heine et al., 1999). Malaysians, Indians, Japanese, and traditional Kenyans, such as the Maasai, for example, are much more likely than Australians, Canadians, Americans, and the British to complete the "I am" statement with their group identities (Kanagawa, Cross, & Markus, 2001; Ma & Schoeneman, 1997). When speaking, people using the languages of collectivist countries say "I" less often (Kashima & Kashima, 1998, 2003). Compared with U.S. church websites, Korean church websites place more emphasis on social connections and participation and less on personal spiritual growth and self-betterment (Sasaki & Kim, 2011).

individualism The concept of giving priority to one's own goals over group goals and defining one's identity in terms of personal attributes rather than group identifications.

independent self Construing one's identity as an autonomous self.

collectivism Giving priority to the goals of one's groups (often, one's extended family or work group) and defining one's identity accordingly.

interdependent self Construing one's identity in relation to others.

Collectivist cultures focus less on individual identity and more on group identity.

Source: ©xavierarnau/Getty Images.

Of course, pigeonholing cultures as solely individualist or collectivist oversimplifies because within any culture individualism varies from person to person (Oyserman, Coon, & Kemmelmeier, 2002; Oyserman, Kemmelmeier, & Coon, 2002). There are individualist Chinese and collectivist Americans, and most of us behave communally at some times and individualistically at others (Bandura, 2004). Individualism–collectivism also varies across a country's regions and political views. Conservatives tend to be economic individualists ("Don't tax or regulate me") and moral collectivists ("Legislate against immorality"). Liberals tend to be economic collectivists (supporting universal health care) and moral individualists ("Let people choose for themselves"). In China, people living in areas that grow rice (which requires more collective cooperation) are more collectivistic than those in areas that grow wheat (Talhelm et al., 2014). Despite individual and subcultural variations, however, researchers continue to regard individualism and collectivism as genuine cultural variables (Schimmack, Oishi, & Diener, 2005).

Growing individualism within cultures

Cultures can also change over time, and many seem to be growing more individualistic. One way to see this is using the Google Books Ngram Viewer, which shows the usage of words and phrases in the full text of 5 million books since the 1800s. (Try it yourself; it's online and free.) In the 2000s, compared to previous decades, books published in the United States used the word *get* more and *give* less (Greenfield, 2013), and used *I*, *me*, and *you* more and *we* and *us* a little less (Twenge et al., 2013) (see Figure 2–3). This pattern of increasing individualism also appears in books in eight other languages worldwide (Yu et al., 2016).

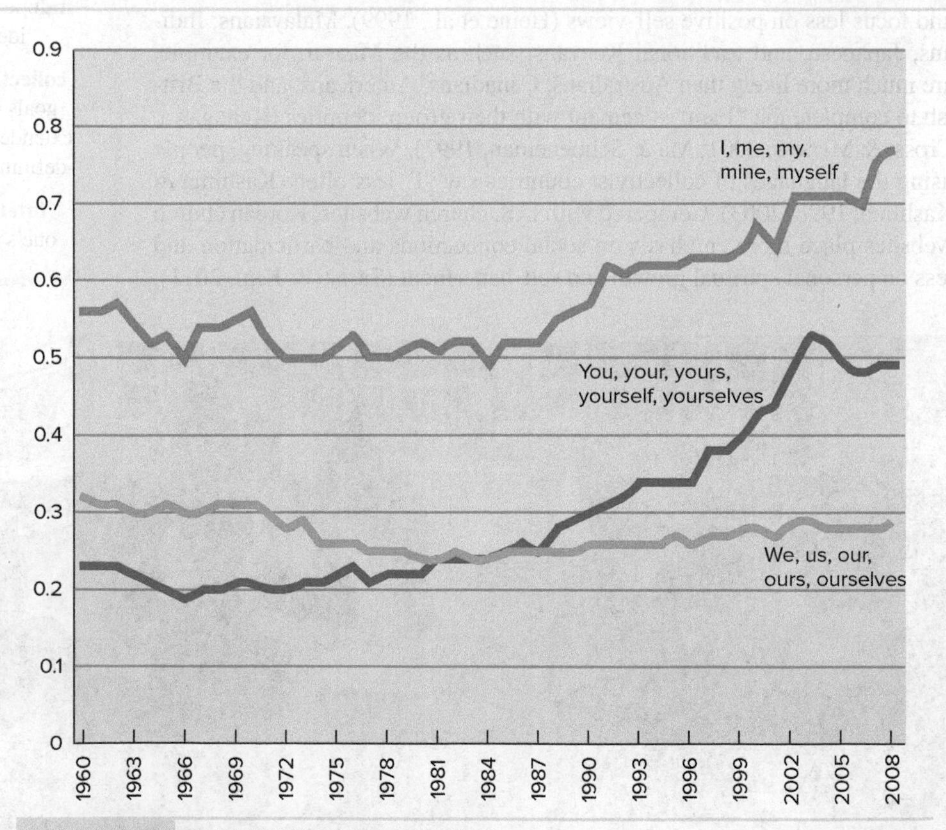

FIGURE 2–3 CHANGING PRONOUN USE.

In the Google Books database, American books in the 2000s (versus those from the 1960s–1970s) used *I*, *me*, *my*, *mine*, and *myself* and *you*, *your*, *yours*, *yourself*, and *yourselves* more often.

Popular song lyrics also became more likely to use *I* and *me* and less likely to use *we* and *us* between 1980 and 2007 (DeWall et al., 2011), with the norm shifting from the sappy love songs of the 1980s ("Endless Love," 1981) to the self-celebration of the 2000s (Justin Timberlake singlehandedly bringing "SexyBack," 2006).

Even your name might show the shift toward individualism: Parents are now less likely to give their children common names and more likely to help them stand out with an unusual name. Although nearly 20 percent of boys born in 1990 received one of the 10 most common names, only 8 percent received such a common name by 2010, with the numbers similar for girls (Twenge et al., 2016). Today, you don't have to be the child of a celebrity to have a name as unique as North, Suri, or Apple.

Americans and Australians, most of whom are descended from those who struck out on their own to emigrate, are more likely than Europeans to give their children uncommon names. Parents in the western United States and Canada, descended from independent pioneers, are also more likely than those in the more established east to give their children uncommon names (Varnum & Kitayama, 2011). The more individualistic the time or the place, the more children receive unique names.

These changes demonstrate a principle that goes deeper than a name: the interaction between individuals and society. Did the culture focus on uniqueness first and cause the parents' name choices, or did individual parents decide they wanted their children to be unique, thus creating the culture? A similar chicken-and-egg question applies to song lyrics: Did a more self-focused population listen to more self-focused songs, or did listening to more self-focused songs make people more self-focused? The answer, although not yet fully understood, is probably "both" (Markus & Kitayama, 2010).

Culture and cognition

In his book *The Geography of Thought* (2003), social psychologist Richard Nisbett contends that collectivism also results in different ways of thinking. When shown an animated underwater scene (Figure 2–4), Japanese respondents spontaneously recalled 60 percent more background features than did Americans, and they spoke of more relationships (the frog beside the plant). Americans look more at the focal object, such as a single big fish, and less at the surroundings (Chua, Boland, & Nisbett, 2005; Nisbett, 2003), a result duplicated when studies examine activation in different areas of the brain (Goh et al., 2007; Lewis, Goto, & Kong, 2008). When shown drawings of groups of children, Japanese students took the facial expressions of all of the children into account when rating the happiness or anger of an individual child, whereas Americans focused on only the child they were asked to rate (Masuda et al., 2008). Facebook profile pictures show a similar cultural effect: U.S. students' selfies were more likely to be close-ups of their faces, whereas Taiwanese students were more likely to choose a picture with more background (Huang & Park, 2012). Nisbett and Takahido Masuda (2003) concluded from such studies that East Asians think more holistically—perceiving and thinking about objects and people in relationship to one another and to their environment.

FIGURE 2–4 ASIAN AND WESTERN THINKING. When shown an underwater scene such as this one, Asians often describe the environment and the relationships among the fish. Americans attend more to a single big fish (Nisbett, 2003).

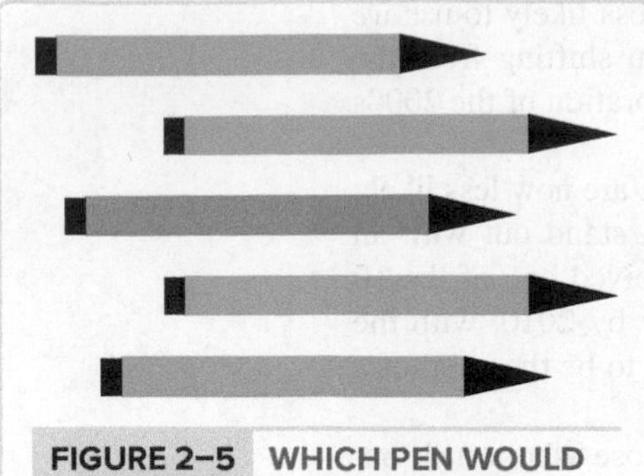

FIGURE 2–5 WHICH PEN WOULD YOU CHOOSE?

When Heejun Kim and Hazel Markus (1999) invited people to choose one of these pens, 77 percent of Americans but only 31 percent of Asians chose the uncommon colour (regardless of whether it was orange, as here, or green). This result illustrates differing cultural preferences for uniqueness and conformity, noted Kim and Markus.

If you grew up in a Western culture, you were probably told to "express yourself"—through writing, through the choices you make, through the products you buy, and perhaps through your tattoos or piercings. When asked about the purpose of language, American students were more likely to explain that it allows self-expression, whereas Korean students focused on how language allows communication with others. American students were also more likely to see their choices as expressions of themselves and to evaluate their choices more favourably (Kim & Sherman, 2007). The individualized latté—"decaf, single shot, skinny, extra hot"—that seems just right at a North American espresso shop would seem strange in Seoul, noted Heejun Kim and Hazel Markus (1999). In Korea, people place less value on expressing their uniqueness and more on tradition and shared practices (Choi & Choi, 2002) (Figure 2–5). Korean advertisements tend to feature people together; they seldom highlight personal choice or freedom (Markus, 2001; Morling & Lamoreaux, 2008).

Collectivist cultures also promote a greater sense of belonging and more integration between the self and others. When Chinese participants were asked to think about their mothers, a brain region associated with the self became activated—an area that became more active for Western participants only when they thought about themselves (Zhu et al., 2007). Interdependent selves have not one self but many selves: self-with-parents, self-at-work, self-with-friends (Cross, Liao, & Josephs, 1992). As Figure 2–6 and Table 2–2 suggest, the interdependent self is embedded in social memberships. Conversation is less direct and more polite (Holtgraves, 1997), and people focus more on gaining social approval (Lalwani, Shavitt, & Johnson, 2006). Among Chinese students, half said they would stop dating someone if their parents disapproved, compared with less than one-third of American students (Zhang & Kline, 2009). In a collectivist culture, the goal of social life is to harmonize with and support one's communities, not—as it is in more individualistic societies—to enhance one's individual self and make independent choices.

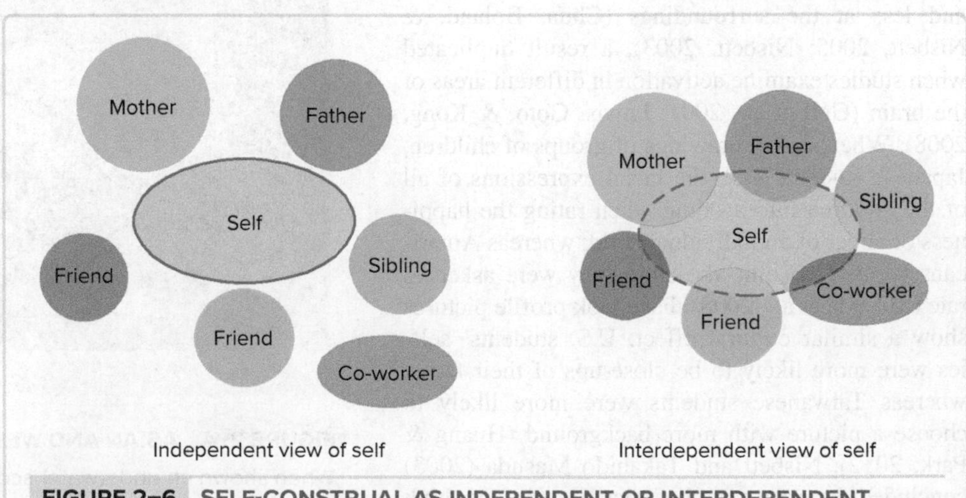

FIGURE 2–6 SELF-CONSTRUAL AS INDEPENDENT OR INTERDEPENDENT.

The independent self acknowledges relationships with others; the interdependent self is more deeply embedded in others (Markus & Kitayama, 1991).

TABLE 2-2	Self-Concept: Independent or Interdependent.	
	Independent	**Interdependent**
Identity is	Personal, defined by individual traits and goals	Social, defined by connections with others
What matters	Me—personal achievement and fulfillment; my rights and liberties	We—group goals and solidarity; our social responsibilities and relationships
Disapproves of	Conformity	Egotism
Illustrative motto	"To thine own self be true"	"No one is an island"
Cultures that support	Individualistic Western	Collectivistic Asian and developing world

Culture and self-esteem

In collectivist cultures, self-esteem is malleable (context-specific) rather than stable (enduring across situations). In one study, four in five Canadian students agreed that they remain essentially the same person in different situations, compared with one in three Chinese and Japanese students (Tafarodi et al., 2004).

For those in individualistic cultures, self-esteem is more personal and less relational. If a Westerner's *personal* identity is threatened, she'll feel angrier and sadder than when her collective identity is threatened (Gaertner, Sedikides, & Graetz, 1999). Unlike Japanese subjects, who persist more on tasks when they are failing, people in individualistic countries persist more when succeeding because, for them, success elevates self-esteem (Heine et al., 2001). Western individualists like to make comparisons with others that boost their self-esteem. Asian collectivists make comparisons (often upward, with those doing better) in ways that facilitate self-improvement (White & Lehman, 2005).

So when, do you suppose, are university students in collectivist Japan and individualist United States most likely to report positive emotions, such as happiness and elation? For Japanese students, happiness comes with positive social engagement—with feeling close, friendly, and respectful. For American students, happiness more often comes with disengaged emotions—with feeling effective, superior, and proud (Kitayama & Markus, 2000). Conflict in collectivist cultures often takes place between groups; individualist cultures breed more conflict (and crime and divorce) between individuals (Triandis, 2000).

When Shinobu Kitayama (1999), after 10 years of teaching and researching in America, visited his Japanese alma mater, Kyoto University, graduate students were "astounded" when he explained the Western idea of the independent self. "I persisted in explaining this Western notion of self-concept—one that my American students understood intuitively—and finally began to persuade them that, indeed, many Americans do have such a disconnected notion of self. Still, one of them, sighing deeply, said at the end, 'Could this *really* be true?'"

When East meets West, does the self-concept become more individualized? What happens when Japanese are exposed to Western advice to "believe in one's own possibilities" and to movies in which the heroic individual police officer catches the crook *despite*

In collectivist cultures, harmony comes from sameness and agreement.
Source: Visage/Getty Images.

THE INSIDE STORY

We began our collaboration by wondering out loud. Shinobu wondered why American life was so weird. Hazel countered with anecdotes about the strangeness of Japan. Cultural psychology is about making the strange familiar and the familiar strange. Our shared cultural encounters astonished us and convinced us that, when it comes to psychological functioning, culture matters.

After weeks of lecturing in Japan to students with a good command of English, Hazel wondered why the students did not say anything—no questions, no comments. She assured students she was interested in ideas that were different from hers, so why was there no response? Where were the arguments, debates, and signs of critical thinking? Even if she asked a straightforward question—for example, "Where is the best noodle shop?"—the answer was invariably an audible intake of air followed by "It depends." Didn't Japanese students have preferences, ideas, opinions, and attitudes? How could you know someone if she didn't tell you what she was thinking?

On the other hand, Shinobu was curious about why students shouldn't just listen to a lecture and why American students felt the need to be constantly interrupting each other and talking over each other and the professor. Why did the comments and questions reveal strong emotions and have a competitive edge? What was the point of this arguing? Why did intelligence seem to be associated with getting the best of another person, even within a class where people knew each other well?

Shinobu expressed his amazement at American hosts who bombard their guests with choices. Do you want wine or beer, or soft drinks or juice, or coffee or tea? Why burden the guest with trivial decisions? Surely the host knew what would be good refreshment on this occasion and could simply provide something appropriate.

Choice as a burden? Hazel wondered if this could be the key to one particularly humiliating experience in Japan. A group of eight was in a French restaurant, and everyone was following the universal restaurant script and was studying the menu. The waiter approached and stood nearby. Hazel announced her choice of appetizer and entree. Next was a tense conversation among the Japanese host and the Japanese guests. When the meal was served, it was not what Hazel had ordered. Everyone at the table was served the same meal. This was deeply disturbing. If you can't choose your own dinner, how could it be enjoyable? What was the point of the menu if everybody is served the same meal? Could a sense of sameness be a good or a desirable feeling in Japan?

Offering a guest a choice of beverage may be greeted with surprise by people from some cultures.
Source: ©Pixtal/SuperStock.

When Hazel walked around the grounds of a temple in Kyoto, there was a fork in the path and a sign that read, "Ordinary path." Who would want to take the ordinary path? Where was the special, less travelled path? Choosing the nonordinary path may be an obvious course for Americans, but in this case, it led to the temple dump outside the temple grounds. The ordinary path did not denote the dull and unchallenging way; it meant the good and appropriate way.

These exchanges inspired our experimental studies and reminded us that there are ways of life beyond the ones that each of us knows best. So far, most of psychology has been produced by psychologists in middle-class White American settings studying middle-class White American respondents. In other sociocultural contexts, there can be different ideas and practices about how to be a person and how to live a meaningful life, and these differences have an influence on psychological functioning. It is this realization that fuels our continuing interest in collaboration and in cultural psychology.

Hazel Rose Markus *Stanford University*

Shinobu Kitayama *University of Michigan*

others' interference? As Steven Heine and his co-researchers (1999) report, they become more individualistic. Being an exchange student has a similar effect: Personal self-esteem increased among Japanese exchange students after spending seven months at the University of British Columbia. Individual self-esteem is also higher among long-term Asian immigrants to Canada than among more recent immigrants (and higher than among those living in Asia).

Self-Knowledge

"Know thyself," admonished an ancient Greek oracle. We certainly try. We readily form beliefs about ourselves, and we in Western cultures don't hesitate to explain why we feel and act as we do. But how well do we actually know ourselves?

"There is one thing, and only one in the whole universe which we know more about than we could learn from external observation," noted C. S. Lewis (1952, pp. 18–19). "That one thing is [ourselves]. We have, so to speak, inside information; we are in the know." Indeed. Yet sometimes we think we know, but our inside information is wrong. That is the unavoidable conclusion of some fascinating research.

> ***"You don't know your own mind."***
>
> Jonathan Swift, *Polite Conversation,* 1738

Predicting our behaviour

Consider two examples of how people's self-predictions can err:

- *Movie watching*. Netflix at one time invited users to predict what films they later wanted to watch. What they actually later watched, however, were lower-brow films. "Faced with this disparity," reported Seth Stephens-Davidowitz (2017), "Netflix stopped asking people to tell them what they wanted to see in the future" and instead offered them suggestions "based on millions of clicks and views from similar customers. . . . The result: customers . . . watched more movies."
- *Dating and romance future.* Inevitably, dating couples are optimistic about how long their relationships will last. Their friends and family often know better, reported Tara MacDonald and Michael Ross (1997). Among University of Waterloo students, their roommates were better predictors of whether their romances would survive than they were. Medical residents weren't very good at predicting whether they would do well on a surgical skills exam, but their peers in the program predicted each other's performance with startling accuracy (Lutsky, Risucci, & Tortolani, 1993). Observers predicted psychology students' exam grades better than the students themselves—mostly because observers relied on past performance rather than on the students' hopes for acing the test (Helzer & Dunning, 2012). So, if you're in love and want to know whether it will last, don't listen to your heart—ask your roommate.

> **planning fallacy** The tendency to underestimate how long it will take to complete a task.

One of the most common errors in behaviour prediction is underestimating how long it will take to complete a task (called the **planning fallacy**). The Sydney Opera House, for example, was supposed to be completed in six years; it took 16. In 1969, Montreal mayor Jean Drapeau proudly announced that a stadium with a retractable roof would be built for the 1976 Olympics; the roof was completed in 1989. Less than a third of couples engaged to be married completed their wedding planning in the amount of time they had anticipated, and only four out of 10 sweethearts bought a planned Valentine's Day gift by their self-imposed deadline (Min & Arkes, 2012). Coursework doesn't fare any better. Wilfrid Laurier University students writing an honours thesis were asked to predict when they would complete the project. On average, students finished three weeks later than their "most realistic" estimate—and a week later than their "worst-case scenario" estimate (Buehler, Griffin, & Ross, 2002). However,

When will you finish your term paper? Your friends might have a more accurate answer than you do. Estimating each step separately might help you estimate more accurately.
Source: ©Dean Drobot/Shutterstock.

friends and teachers were able to predict just how late these papers would be. Just as you should ask your friends how long your relationship is likely to survive, if you want to know when you will finish your term paper, ask your roommate or your mom. You could also do what Microsoft does: Managers automatically add 30 percent onto a software developer's estimate of completion—and 50 percent if the project involves a new operating system (Dunning, 2006).

So, how can you improve your self-predictions? The best way is to be more realistic about how long tasks took in the past. Apparently, people underestimate how long something will take because they misremember previous tasks as taking less time than they actually did (Roy et al., 2005). Another useful strategy: Estimate how long each step in the project will take. Engaged couples who described their wedding-planning steps in more detail more accurately predicted how long the process would take (Min & Arkes, 2012).

Are people equally bad at predicting how much money they will spend? Johanna Peetz of Carleton University and Roger Buehler of Wilfrid Laurier University (2009) found that the answer was "yes." Undergraduates predicted that they would spend $94 over the next week but actually spent $122. Considering they had spent $126 in the week before the study, their guess should have been more accurate. When they came back a week later, they still predicted they would spend only $85 in the coming week. Students who said they wanted to save money were more likely to predict they would spend less—but ended up spending the same amount as everyone else. So, just as we think we will complete tasks quickly, we think we will save our money. The difficulty lies in actually doing so.

> *"When a feeling was there, they felt as if it would never go; when it was gone, they felt as if it had never been; when it returned, they felt as if it had never gone."*
>
> George MacDonald, *What's Mine's Mine,* 1886

Predicting feelings

Many of life's big decisions involve predicting our future feelings. Would marrying this person lead to lifelong contentment? Would entering this profession make for satisfying work? Would going on this vacation produce a happy experience? Or would the likelier results be divorce, job burnout, and holiday disappointment?

Sometimes we know how we will feel—if we fail that exam, win that big game, or soothe our tensions with a half-hour jog. We know what exhilarates us and what makes us anxious or bored. Other times we may mispredict our responses. Asked how they would feel if asked sexually harassing questions on a job interview, most women studied by Julie Woodzicka and Marianne LaFrance (2001) said they would feel angry. When actually asked such questions, however, women more often experienced fear.

Studies of "affective forecasting" reveal that people have the greatest difficulty predicting the intensity and the duration of their future emotions (Wilson & Gilbert, 2003). People mispredict how they would feel some time after experiencing a romantic breakup, receiving a gift, losing an election, winning a game, and being insulted (Gilbert & Ebert, 2002; Loewenstein & Schkade, 1999). Some examples follow:

- When young men are sexually aroused by erotic photographs and then exposed to a passionate date scenario in which their date asks them to "stop," they admit that they might not stop. If not shown sexually arousing pictures first, they are less likely to say that they might be sexually aggressive. When not aroused, they easily mispredict how they will feel and act when aroused—which can lead to unexpected professions of love during lust, to unintended pregnancies, and to repeat offences among sex abusers who have sincerely vowed "never again."

- Hungry shoppers are more likely to impulse buy ("Those doughnuts would be delicious!") than shoppers who have just enjoyed a mega-sized blueberry muffin (Gilbert & Wilson, 2000). When hungry, we mispredict how gross those deep-fried doughnuts will seem when we are sated. When stuffed, we underestimate how yummy those doughnuts might be—a purchase whose appeal quickly fades when you've eaten one or two.
- When natural disasters, such as hurricanes, occur, people predict that their sadness will be greater if more people are killed. But after Hurricane Katrina struck in 2005, students' sadness was similar when they believed 50 people had been killed or 1000 had been killed (Dunn & Ashton-James, 2008). What did influence how sad people felt? Seeing pictures of victims. No wonder poignant images of disasters on TV have so much influence on us.
- People overestimate how much their well-being would be affected by both bad events (a romantic breakup, failure to reach an athletic goal [Eastwick, Finkel, Krishnamurti, et al., 2007; van Dijk, Finkenauer, & Pollmann, 2008]) and good events (warmer winters, losing weight, more television channels, or more free time). Even extreme events, such as winning a provincial lottery or suffering a paralyzing accident, impact long-term happiness less than most people suppose.

Our intuitive theory seems to be this: We want; we get; we are happy. If that were true, this chapter would have fewer words. In reality, noted Daniel Gilbert and Timothy Wilson (2000), we often "miswant." People who imagine an idyllic desert island holiday with sun, surf, and sand may be disappointed when they discover "how much they require daily structure, intellectual stimulation, or regular infusions of Pop Tarts" (p. 182). We think that if our candidate or team wins we will be delighted for a long while. But study after study reveals our vulnerability to **impact bias**—overestimating the enduring impact of emotion-causing events. Faster than we expect, the emotional traces of such good tidings evaporate.

Impact bias Overestimating the enduring impact of emotion-causing events.

We are especially prone to impact bias after negative events. Let's make this personal. Gilbert and Wilson invite you to imagine how you might feel a year after losing your nondominant hand. Compared with today, how happy would you be?

You may have focused on what the calamity would mean: no clapping, no shoe tying, no competitive basketball, no speedy keyboarding. Although you likely would forever regret the loss, your general happiness some time after the event would be influenced by "two things: (a) the event, and (b) everything else" (Gilbert & Wilson, 2000). In focusing on the negative event, we discount the importance of everything else that contributes to happiness, and so we overpredict our enduring misery. "Nothing that you focus on will make as much difference as you think," concurred researchers David Schkade and Daniel Kahneman (1998).

Moreover, said Wilson and Gilbert (2003), people neglect the speed and power of their *coping mechanisms,* which include rationalizing, discounting, forgiving, and limiting emotional trauma. Because we are unaware of the speed and strength of our coping, we adapt to disabilities, romantic breakups, exam failures, layoffs, and personal and team defeats more readily than we would expect. Ironically, Gilbert and his colleagues report (2004) that major negative events (which activate our psychological defences) can be less enduringly distressing than minor irritations (which don't activate our defences). We are, under most circumstances, remarkably resilient.

The wisdom and illusions of self-analysis

To a striking extent, then, our intuitions are often dead wrong about what has influenced us and what we will feel and do. But let's not overstate the case. When the causes of our behaviour are conspicuous and the correct explanation fits our intuition, our self-perceptions will be accurate (Gavanski & Hoffman, 1987). When the causes of behaviour are obvious to an observer, they are usually obvious to us as well. Overall, the correlation between predicted feelings and actual feelings is 0.28—a modest, although far from perfect, correlation (Mathieu & Gosling, 2012).

We are unaware of much that goes on in our minds. Perception and memory studies show that we are more aware of the results of our thinking than of the process. Creative scientists and artists often cannot report the thought processes that produced their insights, although they have superb knowledge of the results.

Timothy Wilson (1985, 2002) offers a bold idea: Analyzing why we feel the way we do can actually make our judgments less accurate. In nine experiments, Wilson and his colleagues (1989) found that the attitudes people consciously expressed toward things or people usually predicted their subsequent behaviour reasonably well. Their attitude reports became useless, however, if the participants were first asked to analyze their feelings. For example, dating couples' current happiness with their relationship accurately predicted whether they would still be dating several months later. But participants who first listed all the reasons they could think of why their relationship was good or bad before rating their happiness were misled—their happiness ratings were useless in predicting the future of the relationship! Apparently, the process of dissecting the relationship drew attention to easily verbalized factors that were not as important as harder-to-verbalize happiness. We are often "strangers to ourselves," Wilson concluded (2002).

dual attitudes Differing implicit (automatic) and explicit (consciously controlled) attitudes toward the same object. Verbalized explicit attitudes may change with education and persuasion; implicit attitudes change slowly, with practice that forms new habits.

self-esteem A person's overall self-evaluation or sense of self-worth.

Such findings illustrate that we have **dual attitudes**, say Wilson and colleagues (Wilson, Lindsey, & Schooler, 2000). Our automatic, *implicit* attitudes regarding someone or something often differ from our consciously controlled, *explicit* attitudes (Gawronski & Bodenhausen, 2006; Nosek, 2007). When someone purports to make decisions by "trusting my gut," they're referring to their implicit attitudes (Kendrick & Olson, 2012). Although explicit attitudes may change with relative ease, notes Wilson, "implicit attitudes, like old habits, change more slowly" (p. 104). With repeated practice, however, new habitual attitudes can replace old ones.

This research on the limits of our self-knowledge has two practical implications. The first is for psychological inquiry. *Self-reports are often untrustworthy*. Errors in self-understanding limit the scientific usefulness of subjective personal reports.

The second implication is for our everyday lives. Even if people report and interpret their experiences with complete honesty, that does not mean their reports are true. Personal testimonies are powerfully persuasive. But they may also be wrong. Keeping this potential for error in mind can help us feel less intimidated by others and become less gullible.

What Is the Nature and Motivating Power of Self-Esteem?

What is self-esteem and how does it affect behaviour and cognition?

Everyone desires and seeks to bolster self-esteem. But can self-esteem be problematic?

First, we must decide how much self-esteem we have. Is **self-esteem** the sum of all our self-views across various domains? If we see ourselves as attractive, athletic, smart, and destined to be rich and loved, will we have high self-esteem? Yes, say Jennifer Crocker and Connie Wolfe (2001). When we feel good about the domains (looks, smarts, or whatever) important to our self-esteem, we will have high self-esteem. One person may have self-esteem that is highly contingent on doing well in school and being physically attractive, whereas another may have self-esteem that is contingent on being loved by God and adhering to moral standards. Thus, the first person will feel high self-esteem when made to feel smart and good-looking; the second person, when made to feel moral.

But Jonathon Brown and Keith Dutton (1994) argue that this "bottom-up" view of self-esteem is not the whole story. The causal arrow, they believe, also goes the other way. People who value themselves in a general way—those with high self-esteem—are more likely to value their looks, abilities, and so forth. They are like new parents, who, loving their infant, delight in the baby's fingers, toes, and hair: The parents do not first evaluate their infant's fingers or toes and then decide how much to value the whole baby.

Specific self-perceptions do have some influence, however. If you think you're good at math, you will be more likely to do well at math. Although general self-esteem does not predict academic performance very well, academic self-concept—whether you think you are good in school—does predict performance (Marsh & O'Mara, 2008). Of course, each causes the other: Doing well at math makes you think you are good at math, which then motivates you to do even better. So if you want to encourage someone (or yourself!), it's better if your praise is specific ("You're good at math") instead of general ("You're great"), and better if your kind words reflect true ability and performance ("You really improved on your last test") rather than unrealistic optimism ("You can do anything"). Feedback is best when it is true and specific (Swann, Chang-Schneider, & Angulo, 2007).

One intriguing study examined the effects of very general feedback on self-esteem. Imagine you're getting your grade back for the first test in a psychology class. When you see your grade, you groan—it's a D–. But then you get an encouraging email with some review questions for the class and this message: "Students who have high self-esteem not only get better grades, but they remain self-confident and assured. . . . Bottom line: Hold your head—and your self-esteem—high." Another group of students instead get a message about taking personal control of their performance or receive review questions only. So which group does better on the final exam? To the surprise of the researchers, the students whose self-esteem was boosted did by far the worst on the final; in fact, they flunked it (Forsyth et al., 2007). Struggling students told to feel good about themselves, the researchers suggested, may have thought, "I'm already great—why study?"

Self-Esteem Motivation

Most people are extremely motivated to maintain their self-esteem. In fact, a study found that university students preferred getting a boost to their self-esteem to eating their favourite food, engaging in their favourite sexual activity, seeing a best friend, drinking alcohol, or receiving a paycheque (Bushman, Moeller, & Crocker, 2011). So, somewhat incredibly, self-esteem was more important than sex, pizza, and beer!

What happens when your self-esteem is threatened—for example, by a failure or an unflattering comparison with someone else? When brothers have markedly different ability levels—for example, one is a great athlete and the other is not—they report not getting along well (Tesser, 1988). Dutch university students who experienced a "double whammy" of low self-evaluation and negative feedback felt more *schadenfreude* (joy at another's misfortune) when they watched a young woman sing horribly out of tune in an audition for the Dutch version of *American Idol* (van Dijk et al., 2012). Misery loves to laugh at others' misery.

Self-esteem threats occur among friends, whose success can be more threatening than that of strangers (Zuckerman & Jost, 2001). In contrast, researchers at the University of Toronto found that people often react more positively to upward comparisons, rather than

Activity: How Good Are You?

Compared to other students of the same class level as you, how would you rate yourself on the characteristics below? Use the following scale in making your response:

1 = well below average, 2 = below average, 3 = slightly below average, 4 = average, 5 = slightly above average, 6 = above average, 7 = well above average

_____ leadership ability

_____ athletic ability

_____ ability to get along with others

_____ tolerance

_____ energy level

_____ helpfulness

_____ responsibility

_____ creativity

_____ patience

_____ trustworthiness

_____ sincerity

_____ thoughtfulness

_____ cooperativeness

_____ reasonableness

_____ intelligence

Now that you have rated yourself on all of these characteristics, take a look at your responses again. Do you see yourself in a positive light? A negative one? How do you compare to others? Most people rate themselves above average on most of the characteristics.

downward comparisons, to romantic partners (Pinkus et al., 2008). When a partner outperforms us in a domain important to both our identities, we may reduce the threat by affirming our relationship, saying, "My capable partner, with whom I'm very close, is part of who I am" (Lockwood et al., 2004). Self-esteem level also makes a difference: High-self-esteem people usually react to a self-esteem threat by compensating for it (blaming someone else or trying harder next time). These reactions help them preserve their positive feelings about themselves. Low-self-esteem people, however, are more likely to blame themselves or to give up (VanDellen et al., 2011).

What underlies the motive to maintain or enhance self-esteem? Mark Leary (1998, 2004b, 2007) believes that our self-esteem feelings are similar to a fuel gauge. Relationships enable surviving and thriving, so the self-esteem gauge alerts us to threatened social rejection, motivating us to act with greater sensitivity to others' expectations. Studies confirmed that social rejection lowers our self-esteem and makes us more eager for approval. Spurned or jilted, we feel unattractive or inadequate. Like a blinking dashboard light, this pain can motivate action: self-improvement and a search for acceptance and inclusion elsewhere. Self-esteem can also serve as a gauge of status with others, growing higher when we are respected as well as liked (Gebauer et al., 2015).

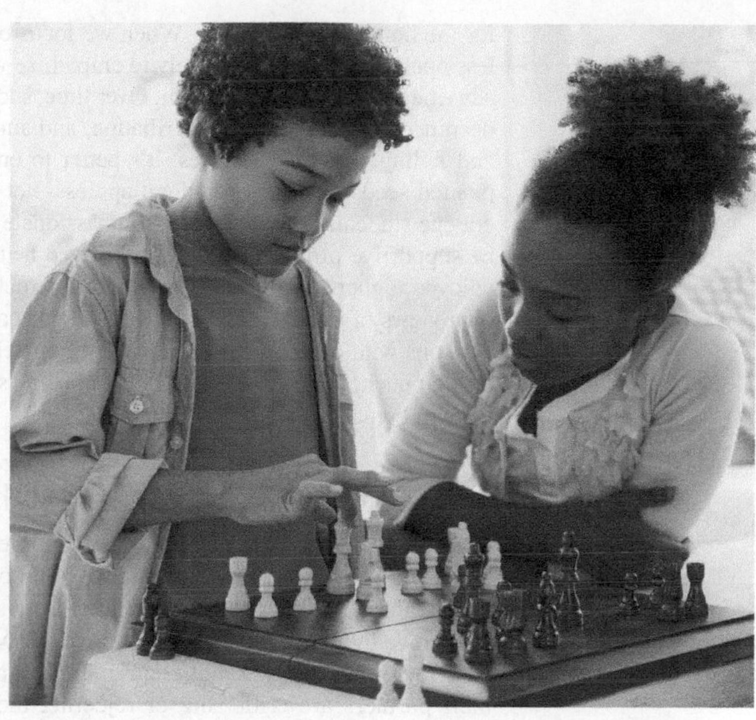

Among sibling relationships, the threat to self-esteem is greatest for an older child with a highly capable younger brother or sister.

Source: ©Hero/Corbis/Glow Images.

Consistent with this view, our self-esteem tracks how we view ourselves on traits we believe are valued by others. People believe that social acceptance often depends on easily observable traits, such as physical appearance and social skills. Although people say they value communal traits—traits that denote a concern for and connection to other people, such as kindness and understanding—they recognize that appearance is often what attracts others. And self-esteem generally corresponds more closely to such superficial traits than to communal qualities (Anthony, Holmes, & Wood, 2007). But self-esteem is related to communal qualities for people whose roles make these qualities attractive to others. Society values kindness and caring in women (more so than in men) and in people in romantic relationships. For these individuals, self-esteem tracks communal qualities. Self-esteem thus depends on whether we believe we have traits that make us attractive to others, and not necessarily on the traits that we say we value most.

Jeff Greenberg (2008) offers another perspective, called "terror management theory," which argues that humans must find ways to manage their overwhelming fear of death. If self-esteem is only about acceptance, he counters, why do "people strive to be great rather than to just be accepted" (p. 51)? The reality of our own death, he argues, motivates us to gain recognition from our work and values. There's a worm in the apple, however: Not everyone can achieve such recognition, which is exactly why it is valuable and why self-esteem can never be wholly unconditional (or not based on anything, such as when parents say, "You're special just for being you"). To feel our lives are not in vain, Greenberg maintains, we must continually pursue self-esteem by meeting the standards of our societies.

However, actively pursuing self-esteem can backfire. Jennifer Crocker and colleagues found that students whose self-worth was contingent on external sources (such as grades or others' opinions) experienced more stress, anger, relationship problems, drug and alcohol use, and eating disorders than did those whose sense of self-worth was rooted more in internal sources, such as personal virtues (Crocker, 2002; Crocker & Knight, 2005; Crocker & Luhtanen, 2003; Crocker & Park, 2004).

Ironically, note Crocker and Lora Park (2004), those who pursue self-esteem, perhaps by seeking to become beautiful, rich, or popular, may lose sight of what really makes them feel good about themselves. University students who tried to impress their roommates by emphasizing their good qualities and hiding their bad ones found that their roommates actually liked them *less*, which then undermined their self-esteem (Canevello & Crocker, 2011). Pursuing self-esteem, Crocker explains, is like reaching into a small hole in a barrel to grasp a delicious apple—and then getting stuck because your hand's tight grip has made it too big for the hole (Crocker, 2011). When we focus on boosting our self-esteem, we may become less open to criticism, less likely to empathize with others, and more pressured to succeed at activities rather than enjoy them. Over time, such pursuit of self-esteem can fail to satisfy our deep needs for competence, affiliation, and autonomy. So, instead of reaching for the apple and failing, Crocker observes, it's better to emulate Johnny Appleseed, who altruistically planted seeds so others could eat apples—not so he could eat them himself. For example, college students who embraced compassionate goals regarding their roommates ("I want to be supportive of my roommate") achieved better relationships with them and subsequently enjoyed higher self-esteem (Canevello & Crocker, 2011). A similar approach works for our own views of ourselves. Kristin Neff (2011) calls it self-compassion—leaving behind comparisons with others and instead treating ourselves with kindness. As an adage of uncertain origin puts it, "There is nothing noble in being superior to some other person. The true nobility is in being superior to your previous self."

The Trade-Off of Low vs. High Self-Esteem

People low in self-esteem are more vulnerable to anxiety, loneliness, and eating disorders. When feeling bad or threatened, those with low self-esteem often take a negative view of everything. They notice and remember others' worst behaviours and think their partners don't love them (Murray, Rose, et al., 2002; Vorauer & Quesnel, 2013). Although people with low self-esteem do not choose less desirable partners, they are quick to believe that their partners are criticizing or rejecting them. Perhaps as a result, those low in self-esteem are less satisfied with their relationships (Fincham & Bradbury, 1993). They may also be more likely to leave those relationships. Low-self-esteem undergraduates decided not to stay with roommates who saw them in a positive light (Swann & Pelham, 2002). Unfortunately, trying to boost low self-esteem by repeating positive phrases (such as "I'm a lovable person") backfires: It actually makes low-self-esteem people feel worse (Wood et al., 2009). Those low in self-esteem also don't want to hear positive things about negative experiences (such as "At least you learned something"). Instead, they prefer to hear understanding responses, even if they are negative (such as "That really sucks") (Marigold et al., 2014).

People with low self-esteem also experience more problems in life: They make less money, abuse drugs, and are more likely to be depressed and engage in acts of self-harm such as cutting (Forrester et al., 2017; Orth & Robins, 2013; Salmela-Aro & Nurmi, 2007). Several studies that took the crucial step of following people as they grew older (called a longitudinal study), found that those who had low self-esteem as teens were more likely to later be depressed, suggesting that low self-esteem causes depression rather than the other way around (Sowislo & Orth, 2013). As you learned in Chapter 1, a correlation between two variables is sometimes caused by a third factor. Perhaps people low in self-esteem also faced poverty as children, experienced sexual abuse, or had parents who used drugs—all possible causes of later struggling. Sure enough, a study that controlled for these factors found that the link between self-esteem and negative outcomes disappeared (Boden, Fergusson, & Horwood, 2008). Self-esteem was seemingly a symptom of an underlying disease—in this case, a tough childhood.

When good things happen, people with high self-esteem are more likely to savour and sustain the good feelings (Wood et al., 2003). As research on depression and anxiety suggests, self-serving perceptions can be useful. It may be strategic to believe we are smarter, stronger, and more socially successful than we are. Belief in our superiority can also motivate us to achieve—creating a self-fulfilling prophecy—and can sustain our hope through difficult times (Willard & Gramzow, 2009).

High self-esteem has other benefits: It fosters initiative, resilience, and pleasant feelings (Baumeister et al., 2003). Yet teen gang leaders, extreme ethnocentrists, terrorists, and men in prison for committing violent crimes also tend to have higher than average self-esteem (Bushman & Baumeister, 1998; Dawes, 1994, 1998). "Hitler had very high self-esteem," note Baumeister and his co-authors (2003). Nor is self-esteem the key to success: Self-esteem does not cause better academic achievement or superior work performance (Baumeister et al., 2003). "The enthusiastic claims of the self-esteem movement mostly range from fantasy to hogwash," says Baumeister (1996), who suspects he has "probably published more studies on self-esteem than anybody else. … The effects of self-esteem are small, limited, and not all good." Folks with high self-esteem, he reports, are more likely to be obnoxious, to interrupt, and to talk *at* people rather than *with* them (in contrast to the more shy, modest folks with low self-esteem). "My conclusion is that self-control is worth 10 times as much as self-esteem."

Narcissism: Self-esteem's conceited sister

High self-esteem becomes especially problematic if it crosses over into narcissism or having an inflated sense of self. Most people with high self-esteem value both individual achievement and relationships with others. Narcissists usually have high self-esteem, but they are missing the piece about caring for others (Campbell, Rudich, & Sedikides, 2002; Jones & Brunell, 2014). Narcissism goes beyond just very high self-esteem—people high in self-esteem think they're worthy and good, but narcissists think they are better than others (Brummelman et al., 2016). Although narcissists are often outgoing and charming early on, their self-centredness often leads to relationship problems in the long run (Campbell, 2005). The link between narcissism and problematic social relations led Delroy Paulhus and Kevin Williams (2002) of the University of British Columbia to include narcissism in the "Dark Triad" of negative traits, along with Machiavellianism (manipulativeness) and antisocial psychopathy.

In a series of experiments conducted by Brad Bushman and Roy Baumeister (1998), undergraduate volunteers wrote essays and received rigged feedback that said, "This is one of the worst essays I've read!" Those who scored high on narcissism were much more likely to retaliate, blasting painful noise into the headphones of the student they believed had criticized them. Narcissists weren't aggressive toward someone who praised them ("Great essay!"); it was the insult that set them off. But what about self-esteem? Maybe only the "insecure" narcissists—those low in self-esteem—would lash out. But that's not how it turned out; instead, the students high in both self-esteem and narcissism were the most aggressive. The same was true in a classroom setting: Those who were high in narcissism were most likely to retaliate against a classmate's criticism by giving the person a bad grade (Bushman et al., 2009; Figure 2–7). Narcissists are especially likely to lash out when the insult is delivered publicly—and thus punctures their carefully constructed bubble of superiority. For that, someone must pay (Ferriday et al., 2011). It's true that narcissists can be charming and entertaining. But, as one wit has said, "God help you if you cross them."

Narcissistic people are more active and more popular on social media sites, increasing their influence in these online communities.
Source: ©gpointstudio/Shutterstock.

Narcissists' deep-seated feeling of superiority may originate in childhood. In a longitudinal study, when parents believed their children deserved special treatment, the children scored higher on narcissism six months later. In contrast, parents' feelings of love and kindness to their children were not linked to narcissism (Brummelman et al., 2015). This study suggests a straightforward piece of advice for parents: Instead of telling your children that they are special, tell them you love them.

Due to their self-confidence, narcissists are often initially popular with others. In one experiment, those higher in narcissism were more likely to emerge as the leader of a

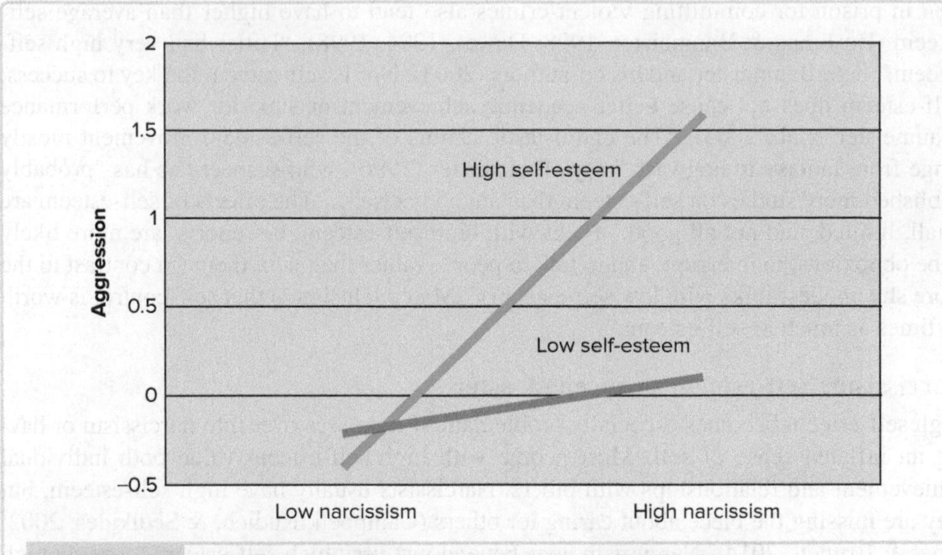

FIGURE 2–7 NARCISSISM, SELF-ESTEEM, AND AGGRESSION.
Narcissism and self-esteem interact to influence aggression. In an experiment by Brad Bushman and colleagues (2009), the recipe for retaliation against a critical classmate required both narcissism and high self-esteem.

group of students they hadn't met before (Brunell et al., 2008). However, once groups meet more than a few times, the popularity of narcissistic leaders declines as the group realizes the leader doesn't have their best interests at heart (Rosenthal & Pittinsky, 2006). As time passes, narcissists' antagonism and aggression toward others makes them less and less popular with their peers (Leckelt et al., 2015). That can become particularly problematic on social media, where narcissists are both more active (posting more status updates and tweets) and more popular (having more friends and followers) (Gnambs & Appel, 2017; Liu & Baumeister, 2016; McCain & Campbell, 2017).

Narcissists seem to be aware of their own narcissism, too. Simply asking people if they agree with the statement "I am a narcissist" predicts narcissistic behaviour nearly as well as the standard 40-item measure (Konrath et al., 2014). Narcissists realize that they see themselves more positively than others see them and admit that they are arrogant and exaggerate their abilities (Carlson et al., 2011). They also recognize that they make good first impressions but are often actively disliked in the long run (Paulhus, 1998; Paulhus et al., 2013). "Early in life I had to choose between honest arrogance and hypocritical humility," observed Frank Lloyd Wright. "I chose honest arrogance and have seen no occasion to change."

Self-Efficacy

self-efficacy A sense that one is competent and effective, distinguished from self-esteem, which is one's sense of self-worth. A sharpshooter in the military might feel high self-efficacy and low self-esteem.

Stanford psychologist Albert Bandura (1997, 2000, 2008) captured the power of positive thinking in his research and theorizing about **self-efficacy** (how competent we feel on a task). Believing in our own competence and effectiveness pays dividends (Bandura et al., 1999; Maddux & Gosselin, 2003). Children and adults with strong feelings of self-efficacy are more persistent, less anxious, and less depressed. They also live healthier lives and are more academically successful.

Someone who thinks, "If I work hard, I can swim fast," has high self-efficacy. Someone who thinks, "I am a great swimmer," has high self-esteem.
Source: ©Dean Drobot/ Shutterstock.

In everyday life, self-efficacy leads us to set challenging goals and to persist. More than 100 studies show that self-efficacy predicts worker productivity (Stajkovic & Luthans, 1998). The results of 241 studies show that performance self-efficacy is one of the strongest predictors of students' GPAs in college (Richardson et al., 2012). When problems arise, a strong sense of self-efficacy leads people to stay calm and seek solutions rather than ruminate on their inadequacy. Competence plus persistence equals accomplishment. And with accomplishment, self-confidence grows. Self-efficacy, then, like self-esteem, grows with hard-won achievements.

Self-efficacy and self-esteem sound similar but are different concepts. If you believe you can do something, that's self-efficacy. If you like yourself overall, that's self-esteem. When you were a child, your parents may have encouraged you by saying things such as, "You're special!" (intended to build self-esteem) or "I know you can do it!" (intended to build self-efficacy). One study showed that self-efficacy feedback ("You tried really hard") led to better performance than self-esteem feedback ("You're really smart"). Children told they were smart were afraid to try again—maybe they wouldn't look so smart next time. Those praised for working hard, however, knew they could exert more effort again (Mueller & Dweck, 1998). If you want to encourage someone, focus on their self-efficacy, not their self-esteem.

What Is Self-Serving Bias?

What is self-serving bias? What are its adaptive and maladaptive aspects?

Most of us have a good reputation with ourselves. In studies of self-esteem, even low-scoring people respond in the mid-range of possible scores. (Someone with low self-esteem responds to such statements as "I have good ideas" with a qualifying adjective, such as "somewhat" or "sometimes.") In a study of self-esteem across 53 nations, including Canada, the average self-esteem score was above the midpoint in every single country (Schmitt & Allik, 2005). One of social psychology's most provocative yet firmly established conclusions concerns the potency of **self-serving bias**.

self-serving bias The tendency to perceive yourself favourably.

Explaining Positive and Negative Events

Many dozens of experiments have found that people accept credit when told they have succeeded. They attribute the success to their ability and effort, but they attribute failure to such external factors as bad luck or the problem's inherent "impossibility" (Campbell & Sedikides, 1999). Similarly, in explaining their victories, athletes commonly credit themselves, but they attribute losses to something else: bad breaks, bad referee calls, or the other team's super effort or dirty play (Grove, Hanrahan, & McInman, 1991; Lalonde, 1992; Mullen & Riordan, 1988). And how much responsibility do you suppose car drivers tend to accept for their accidents? On insurance forms, drivers have described their accidents in words such as these: "An invisible car came out of nowhere, struck my car and vanished," "As I reached an intersection, a hedge sprang up, obscuring my vision, and I did not see the other car," and "A pedestrian hit me and went under my car" (*Toronto News*, 1977).

self-serving attributions A form of self-serving bias; the tendency to attribute positive outcomes to yourself and negative outcomes to other factors.

Situations that combine skill and chance (games, exams, job applications) are especially prone to the phenomenon: Winners can easily attribute their successes to their skill, while losers can attribute their losses to chance. When you win at Scrabble, it's because of your verbal dexterity; when you lose, it's "Who could get anywhere with a *Q* but no *U*?" Politicians similarly tend to attribute their wins to themselves (hard work, constituent service, reputation, and strategy) and their losses to factors beyond their control (their district's party makeup, their opponent's name, and political trends) (Kingdon, 1967). This phenomenon of **self-serving attributions** (attributing positive outcomes to oneself and negative outcomes to something else) is one of the most potent of human biases. That might be for a good reason: Making self-serving attributions activates brain areas associated with reward and pleasure (Seidel et al., 2010).

"I never blame myself when I'm not hitting. I just blame the bat and if it keeps up, I change bats."

Yogi Berra

Self-serving attributions contribute to marital discord, worker dissatisfaction, and bargaining impasses (Kruger & Gilovich, 1999). Small wonder that divorced people usually blame their partner for the breakup (Gray & Silver, 1990) or that managers usually blame poor performance on workers' lack of ability or effort while workers blame external factors, such as excessive workload or difficult co-workers (Imai, 1994; Rice, 1985). Small wonder, too, that people evaluate reward distributions, such as pay raises, as fair when they receive a bigger raise than most of their co-workers (Diekmann et al., 1997).

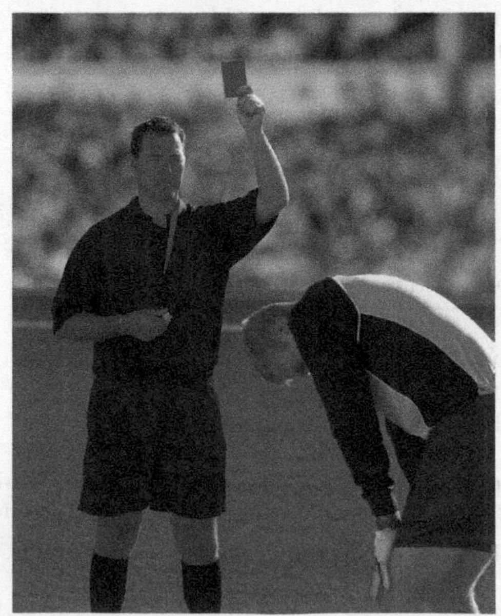

Self-serving bias at work: If his team loses the game, the player getting the penalty might blame the referee's call instead of his own lacklustre play.

Source: ©Corbis/VCG/Getty Images.

Ironically, we are even biased against seeing our own bias. People claim they avoid self-serving bias themselves but readily acknowledge that others show this bias (Pronin, Lin, & Ross, 2002). This "bias blind spot" can have serious consequences during conflicts. If you're negotiating with your roommate over who does household chores and you believe your roommate has a biased view of the situation, you're much more likely to become angry (Pronin & Ross, 2006). Apparently we see ourselves as objective and everyone else as biased. No wonder we fight: We're each convinced we're "right" and free from bias. As the T-shirt slogan says, "Everyone is entitled to my opinion."

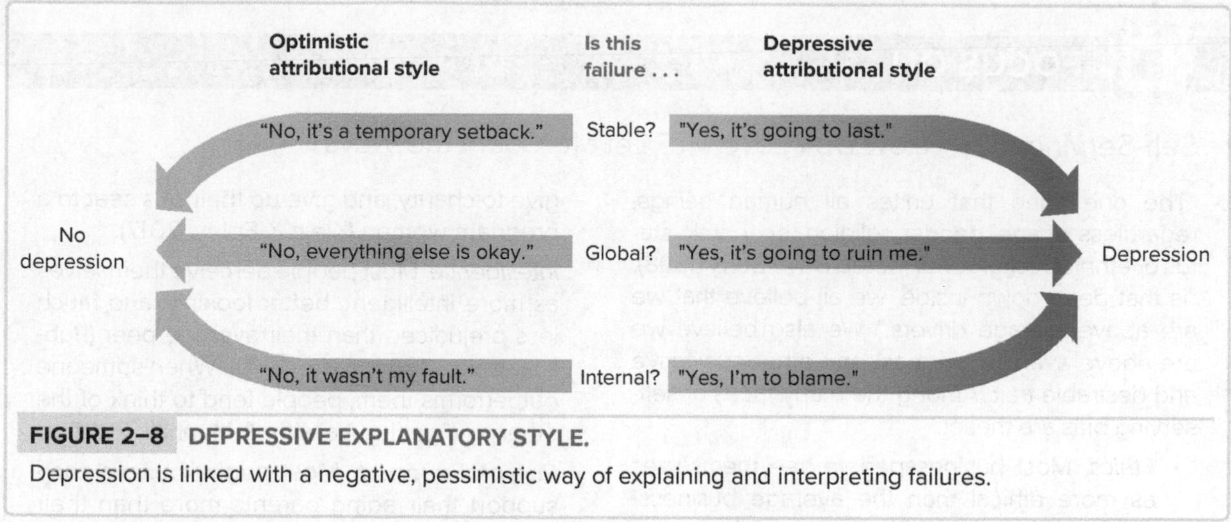
Optimistic attributional style
Is this failure . . .
Depressive attributional style
"No, it's a temporary setback."
Stable?
"Yes, it's going to last."
No depression
"No, everything else is okay."
Global?
"Yes, it's going to ruin me."
Depression
"No, it wasn't my fault."
Internal?
"Yes, I'm to blame."

FIGURE 2–8 DEPRESSIVE EXPLANATORY STYLE.

Depression is linked with a negative, pessimistic way of explaining and interpreting failures.

Is the self-serving bias universal, or are people in collectivistic cultures immune? People in collectivistic cultures associate themselves with positive words and valued traits (Gaertner, Sedikides, & Chang, 2008; Yamaguchi et al., 2007). However, in some studies, collectivists are less likely to self-enhance by believing they are better than others (Church et al., 2014; Heine & Hamamura, 2007), particularly in individualistic domains such as leadership or individual achievement (Sedikides, Gaertner, & Toguchi, 2003).

One group of people, however, do not display self-serving bias: those who suffer depression. Depressed people are more likely to believe they are to blame for negative events. For example, if you fail an exam and blame yourself, you may conclude that you are stupid or lazy; consequently, you may feel depressed. If you attribute the failure to an unfair exam or to other circumstances beyond your control, you may instead feel angry. In more than 100 studies of 15 000 participants, depressed people have been more likely than nondepressed people to exhibit a negative **explanatory style** (Haeffel et al., 2008; Peterson & Steen, 2002; Sweeney et al., 1986). As shown in Figure 2–8, this explanatory style attributes failure and setbacks to causes that are *stable* ("It's going to last forever"), *global* ("It's going to affect everything I do"), and *internal* ("It's all my fault"). The result of this pessimistic, overgeneralized, self-blaming thinking is a depressing sense of hopelessness (Abramson et al., 1989).

explanatory style A person's habitual way of explaining life events. A negative, pessimistic, and depressive explanatory style attributes failures to stable, global, and internal causes.

Can We All Be Better Than Average?

Self-serving bias also appears when people compare themselves with others. If Chinese philosopher Lao-tzu was right that "at no time in the world will a man who is sane over-reach himself, overspend himself, overrate himself," then most of us are a little insane. On *subjective, socially desirable,* and *common* dimensions, most people see themselves as better than the average person. Compared with people in general, most people see themselves as more ethical, more competent at their job, friendlier, more intelligent, better looking, less prejudiced, healthier, and even more insightful and less biased in their self-assessments. Even men convicted of violent crimes rated themselves as more moral, kind, and trustworthy than most people (Sedikides et al., 2014). (See Focus On: Self-Serving Bias—How Do I Love Me? Let Me Count the Ways.)

FOCUS ON

Self-Serving Bias—How Do I Love Me? Let Me Count the Ways

"The one thing that unites all human beings, regardless of age, gender, religion, economic status or ethnic background," noted Dave Barry (1998), "is that deep down inside, we all believe that we are above-average drivers." We also believe we are above average on most any other subjective and desirable trait. Among the many faces of self-serving bias are these:

- *Ethics.* Most businesspeople see themselves as more ethical than the average businessperson (Baumhart, 1968; Brenner & Molander, 1977). One national survey asked, "How would you rate your own morals and values on a scale from 1 to 100 (100 being perfect)?" Fifty percent of people rated themselves 90 or above; only 11 percent said 74 or less (Lovett, 1997).
- *Professional competence.* In one survey, 90 percent of business managers rated their performance as superior to their average peer (French, 1968). In Australia, 86 percent of people rated their job performance as above average, while only 1 percent rated it as below average (Headey & Wearing, 1987). Most surgeons believed their patients' mortality rate to be lower than average (Gawande, 2002).
- *Virtues.* In the Netherlands, most high school students rated themselves as more honest, persistent, original, friendly, and reliable than the average high school student (Hoorens, 1993, 1995). Most people see themselves as more likely than others to donate blood, give to charity, and give up their bus seat to a pregnant woman (Klein & Epley, 2017).
- *Intelligence.* Most people perceive themselves as more intelligent, better looking, and much less prejudiced than their average peer (Public Opinion, 1984; Wylie, 1979). When someone outperforms them, people tend to think of the other as a genius (Lassiter & Munhall, 2001).
- *Parental support.* Most adults believe they support their aging parents more than their siblings do (Lerner et al., 1991).
- *Health.* Los Angeles residents view themselves as healthier than most of their neighbours, and most university students believe they will outlive their actuarially predicted age of death by about 10 years (Larwood, 1978; Snyder, 1978).
- *Attractiveness.* Is it your experience, as it is ours, that most photos of you seem not to do you justice? One experiment showed people a lineup of faces—one their own, the others being their face morphed into those of less and more attractive faces (Epley & Whitchurch, 2008). When asked which was their actual face, people tended to identify an attractively enhanced version of their face.
- *Driving.* Most drivers—even most drivers who have been hospitalized for accidents—believe themselves to be safer and more skilled than the average driver (Guerin, 1994; McKenna & Myers, 1997; Svenson, 1981). Dave Barry was right!

Every community, it seems, is like Garrison Keillor's fictional Lake Wobegon, where "all the women are strong, all the men are good-looking, and all the children are above average." Many people believe that they will become even more above average in the future—"If I'm good now, I will be even better soon," they seem to think (Kanten & Teigen, 2008). The phenomenon lurks in Freud's joke about the husband who told his wife, "If one of us dies, I shall move to Paris."

Michael Ross and Fiore Sicoly (1979) observed that the self-serving bias is also common in marriages. They found that young, married Canadians usually felt that they did more of the work of cleaning the house and caring for the children than their spouses believed they did. In a 2008 survey, 49 percent of married men said they did half to most of the child care. But only 31 percent of wives said their husbands did this much. In the same survey, 70 percent of women said they did most of the cooking, but 56 percent of the men

THE INSIDE STORY

Suppose that you have collaborated on a project with another student and that the two of you evaluated each other's contributions to the final product. You may be disappointed to discover that your partner is less impressed with the quality and extent of your contribution than you are. In the history of science, there are many examples of such disagreements; erstwhile friends and colleagues become bitter enemies as they contest each other's contributions to important discoveries.

[Fiore] Sicoly and I suggested that individuals generally tend to accept more responsibility for a joint product than other contributors attribute to them. In many everyday activities, participants are unaware of their divergent views because they don't share their opinions with each other. After cleaning the kitchen, for example, spouses don't usually discuss how much each contributed to the cleanup.

When such opinions are voiced, people are likely to be upset because they believe that the other person is not giving them sufficient credit. If the consequences are high (e.g., academic grades, job promotions, or Nobel Prizes at stake), they may well assume that their partner is deliberately downgrading their contributions to enhance his or her own achievements.

Source: Mast3r/Dreamstime.com/GetStock.com.

In our research, Sicoly and I showed that differences in assessments of responsibility are common in many everyday contests and that contrasting judgments may reflect normal cognitive processes rather than deliberate deceit. Differences in judgment can result from honest evaluation of information that is differentially available to the two participants.

Michael Ross *University of Waterloo*

said *they* did most of the cooking (Galinsky, Aumann, & Bond, 2009). The general rule: Group members' estimates of how much they contribute to a joint task typically sum to more than 100 percent (Savitsky et al., 2005).

Self-serving bias is stronger for traits that are more subjective or difficult to measure. Seventy-six percent of university students in 2016 believed they were above average in "drive to achieve" (a more subjective attribute), but only 48 percent thought they were above average in the more quantifiable realm of math ability (Twenge, 2017). Subjective qualities give us leeway in constructing our own definitions of success (Dunning, Meyerowitz, & Holzberg, 1989; Dunning, Perie, & Story, 1991). When I consider my "athletic ability," I ponder my proficiency at cycling, not the evenings I spent in Little League cowering in right field hoping no one would hit the ball my way. Assessing my "leadership ability," I conjure up an image of a great leader whose style is similar to mine. By defining ambiguous criteria in our own terms, each of us can see ourselves as relatively successful. In one University Entrance Examination Board survey of 829 000 high school seniors, *none* rated themselves as below average in "ability to get along with others" (a subjective, desirable trait), 60 percent rated themselves in the top 10 percent, and 25 percent saw themselves among the top 1 percent! In one survey in Britain, 98 percent of 17- to 25-year-olds believed they were good drivers—even though 20 percent got into an accident within six months of passing their driving test (AFP, 2013).

Researchers have wondered: Do people really believe their above-average self-estimates? Is their self-serving bias partly a function of how the questions are phrased (Krizan & Suls, 2008)? When Elanor Williams and Thomas Gilovich (2008) had people bet real money when estimating their relative performance on tests, they found that, yes, "people truly believe their self-enhancing self-assessments."

Unrealistic Optimism

Studies of more than 90 000 people across 22 cultures reveal that most humans are more disposed to optimism than pessimism (Fischer & Chalmers, 2008; Shepperd et al., 2013, 2015). Indeed, many of us have what researcher Neil Weinstein (1980, 1982) termed "an unrealistic optimism about future life events." Partly because of their relative pessimism about others' fates (Hoorens, Smits, & Shepperd, 2008; Shepperd, 2003), students perceive themselves as far more likely than their classmates to get a good job, draw a good salary, and own a home. They also see themselves as far less likely to experience negative events, such as developing a drinking problem, having a heart attack before age 40, or being fired. Indeed, adult women are much more likely to be unduly optimistic than pessimistic about their relative risk of breast cancer (Waters et al., 2011). Football fans, moreover, believe that their favourite team has a 70 percent chance of winning its next game (Massey, Simmons, & Armor, 2011).

"God, give us grace to accept with serenity the things that cannot be changed, courage to change the things which should be changed, and the wisdom to distinguish the one from the other."

Reinhold Niebuhr, "The Serenity Prayer," 1943

Illusory optimism increases our vulnerability. Believing ourselves immune to misfortune, we do not take sensible precautions. Sexually active undergraduate women who don't consistently use contraceptives perceive themselves, compared to other women at their university, as much *less* vulnerable to unwanted pregnancy (Burger & Burns, 1988). People trying to quit smoking who believe they are above average in willpower are more likely to keep cigarettes around and stand near others who are smoking—behaviours likely to lead to a relapse (Nordgren et al., 2009). Elderly drivers who rated themselves as "above average" were four times more likely than more modest drivers to flunk a driving test and be rated "unsafe" (Freund et al., 2005). Students who enter university with inflated assessments of their academic ability often suffer deflating self-esteem and well-being and are more likely to drop out (Robins & Beer, 2001). In perhaps the most wide-ranging example, many home buyers, mortgage lenders, and investors in the mid-2000s displayed unrealistic optimism in their belief that "housing never goes down," accumulating large amounts of debt. The eventual result was a wave of home foreclosures that spawned the 2007–2009 recession, the most severe economic downturn since the Great Depression. Even the seventeenth-century economist Adam Smith, a defender of human economic rationality, foresaw that people would overestimate their chances of gain. This "absurd presumption in their own good fortune," he said, arises from "the overweening conceit which the greater part of men have of their own abilities" (Spiegel, 1971, p. 243).

On the other hand, optimism definitely beats pessimism in promoting self-efficacy, health, and well-being (Armor & Taylor, 1996). As natural optimists, most people believe they will be happier with their lives in the future—a belief that surely helps create happiness in the present (Robinson & Ryff, 1999). Pessimists even die sooner—apparently because they are more likely to suffer unfortunate accidents (Peterson et al., 2001). If our optimistic prehistoric ancestors were more likely than their pessimistic neighbours to surmount challenges and survive, then small wonder that we are disposed to optimism (Haselton & Nettle, 2006).

Yet a dash of realism—or what Julie Norem calls **defensive pessimism**—can sometimes save us from the perils of unrealistic optimism. Defensive pessimism anticipates problems and motivates effective coping. As a Chinese proverb says, "Be prepared for danger while staying in peace." Students who exhibit excess optimism (as many students destined for low grades do) can benefit from having some self-doubt, which motivates study (Prohaska, 1994; Sparrell & Shrauger, 1984). Students who are overconfident tend to underprepare, whereas their equally able but less confident peers study harder and get higher grades (Goodhart, 1986; Norem & Cantor, 1986; Showers & Ruben, 1987). Viewing things in a more immediate, realistic way often helps. Students in one

defensive pessimism The adaptive value of anticipating problems and harnessing one's anxiety to motivate effective action.

experiment were wildly optimistic in predicting their test performance when the test was hypothetical, but they were surprisingly accurate when the test was imminent (Armor & Sackett, 2006). Believing you're great when nothing can prove you wrong is one thing, but with an evaluation fast approaching, it's best not to look like a bragging fool.

It's also important to listen to criticism. "One gentle rule I often tell my students," writes David Dunning (2006), "is that if two people independently give them the same piece of negative feedback, they should at least consider the possibility that it might be true" (p. 603). So, there is a power to negative as well as positive thinking. The moral: Success in school and beyond requires enough optimism to sustain hope and enough pessimism to motivate concern.

False Consensus and Uniqueness

We have a curious tendency to further enhance our self-images by overestimating or underestimating the extent to which others think and act as we do. On matters of *opinion,* we find support for our positions by overestimating the extent to which others agree—a phenomenon called the **false consensus effect** (Krueger & Clement, 1994; Marks & Miller, 1987; Mullen & Goethals, 1990). Facebook users were 90 percent accurate in guessing when they agreed with their friends on political and other issues, but they were only 41 percent accurate in guessing disagreement (Goel et al., 2010). In other words, they thought their friends agreed with them more than they actually did. This goes beyond politics: When university students thought about their favourite celebrity, they significantly underestimated how much others would express dislike for their idolized star (Bui, 2012). White Australians prejudiced against Aborigines were more likely to believe that other Whites were also prejudiced (Watt & Larkin, 2010). The sense we make of the world seems like common sense.

false consensus effect The tendency to overestimate the commonality of one's opinions and one's undesirable or unsuccessful behaviours.

false uniqueness effect The tendency to underestimate the commonality of one's abilities and one's desirable or successful behaviours.

When we behave badly or fail in a task, we reassure ourselves by thinking that such lapses also are common. After one person lies to another, the liar begins to perceive the *other* person as dishonest (Sagarin, Rhoads, & Cialdini, 1998). People guess that others think and act as they do: "I lie, but doesn't everyone?" If we smoke or cheat on our income taxes, we are likely to overestimate the number of other people who do likewise. If we feel sexual desire toward someone, we may overestimate that person's reciprocal desire. "We don't see things as they are," says a proverb. "We see things as we are."

> ***"I think few people have conventional family relationships."***
>
> Madonna, 2000

Dawes (1990) proposes that false consensus may occur because we generalize from a limited sample, which prominently includes ourselves. Lacking other information, why not "project" ourselves; why not impute our own knowledge to others and use our responses as a clue to their likely responses? Also, we're more likely to spend time with people who share our attitudes and behaviours and consequently judge the world from the people we know. Small wonder that Germans tend to think that the typical European looks rather German, whereas the Portuguese see Europeans as looking more Portuguese (Imhoff et al., 2011).

On matters of ability or when we behave well or successfully, however, a **false uniqueness effect** more often occurs (Goethals, Messick, & Allison, 1991). We serve our self-image by seeing our talents and moral behaviours as relatively unusual. Dutch college students preferred being part of a larger group in matters of opinion, such as politics (false consensus), but wanted to be part of a smaller group in matters of taste, such as musical preferences (false uniqueness) (Spears, Ellemers, & Doosje, 2009). After all, a band isn't cool anymore if too many people like it. Female university students who protect themselves while drinking (by, for example, designating a driver or drinking only with a meal) underestimate how many other women take the same precaution (Benton et al., 2008). Thus we may see our failings as relatively normal and our virtues as relatively exceptional.

Temporal Comparison

Comparisons with others can enhance self-esteem and so can comparisons to the person we used to be. **Temporal comparisons** with our own past selves are typically flattering to our current selves.

temporal comparisons Comparisons between how the self is viewed now and how the self was viewed in the past or how the self is expected to be viewed in the future.

Anne Wilson of Wilfrid Laurier University and Mike Ross of the University of Waterloo (Wilson & Ross, 2001; Ross & Wilson, 2002) observe that people maintain positive self-views in the present by disparaging distant past selves while complimenting recent past selves, creating a sense of improvement. When university students and their parents rated the students now and when they were 16, they both believed the students had improved, on a variety of traits (see Figure 2–9). These evaluations, however, could simply indicate a developmental trend—maybe people just get better with time. But Wilson and Ross (2001) also had students, at the end of term, recall what they were like at the beginning of term. The catch was that they had actually surveyed the students at the beginning of term and could compare their two sets of ratings. The students remembered being much worse off at the start of term than they actually rated themselves as being at the time—their sense of improvement, it seems, was more wishful thinking than reality.

"Always remember that you are absolutely unique. Just like everyone else."

Anonymous, sometimes attributed to Jim Wright

Ross and Wilson (2002) also observe that we perceive positive past selves as psychologically closer in time and negative past selves as more distant. Students who recall being popular in high school report that high school feels more recent ("It seems like yesterday!") than those who recall high school as a more socially awkward time ("It's ancient history"). This tendency extends to our social groups: German but not Canadian students felt as though the Holocaust had occurred in the more distant past when they read about German atrocities committed at that time (Peetz, Gunn, & Wilson, 2010).

"The past is to be respected and acknowledged, but not to be worshipped. It is our future in which we will find our greatness."

Pierre Elliott Trudeau, *Canadian Museum of History Library*

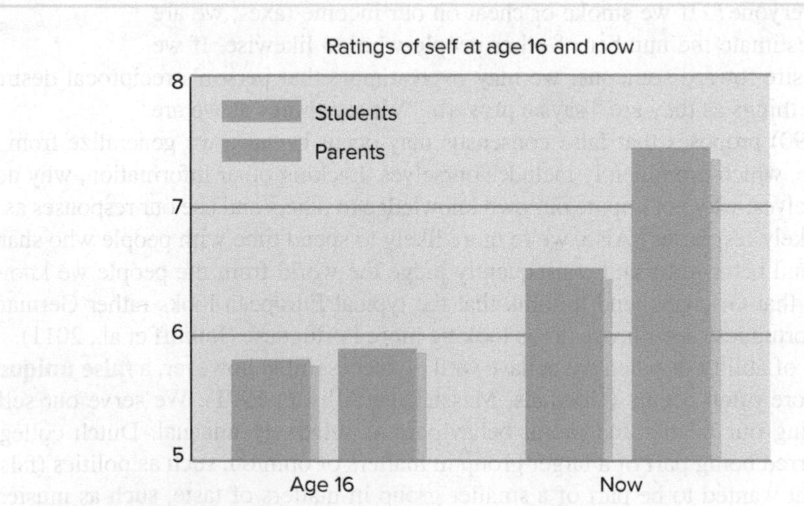

FIGURE 2–9 BETTER WITH TIME?

Both university students and their parents believe they have improved with time.

Source: Adapted from A. Wilson and M. Ross, "From chump to champ: People's appraisals of their earlier and present selves," *Journal of Personality and Social Psychology, 80*(4), 572–584. Copyright © 2001 by the American Psychological Association. Adapted with permission.

Illusory optimism: Most couples marry feeling confident of long-term love. Actually, in individualistic cultures, new marriages often fail.
Source: ©Studio Zanello/Streetstock Images/Blend Images/Getty Images.

To sum up, these tendencies toward self-serving attributions, self-congratulatory comparisons, illusory optimism, false consensus for our failings, and an illusory sense of improvement are major sources of self-serving bias (Figure 2–10).

Explaining Self-Serving Bias

Why do people perceive themselves in self-enhancing ways? Perhaps the self-serving bias exists because of errors in how we process and remember information about ourselves. Comparing ourselves with others requires us to notice, assess, and recall their behaviour and ours. This creates multiple opportunities for flaws in our information processing (Chambers & Windschitl, 2004). Recall that married people gave themselves credit for doing more housework than their spouses did. That might occur because we remember what we've done but not what our partner

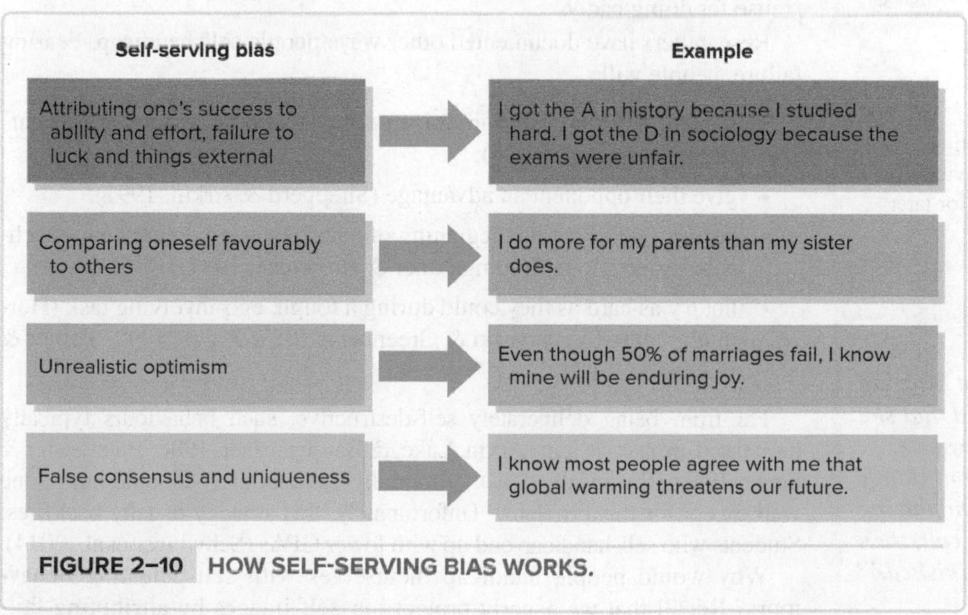

Self-serving bias
Example
Attributing one's success to ability and effort, failure to luck and things external
I got the A in history because I studied hard. I got the D in sociology because the exams were unfair.
Comparing oneself favourably to others
I do more for my parents than my sister does.
Unrealistic optimism
Even though 50% of marriages fail, I know mine will be enduring joy.
False consensus and uniqueness
I know most people agree with me that global warming threatens our future.

FIGURE 2–10 HOW SELF-SERVING BIAS WORKS.

did (Kahneman & Deaton, 2010). We can easily picture ourselves picking up the laundry from the bedroom floor, but we are less aware of the times we absentmindedly overlook it.

Are the biased perceptions, then, simply a perceptual error, an emotion-free glitch in how we process information? Or are self-serving *motives* also involved? It's now clear from research that we have multiple motives. Questing for self-knowledge, we're motivated to *assess our competence* (Dunning, 1995). Questing for self-confirmation, we're motivated to *verify our self-conceptions* (Sanitioso, Kunda, & Fong, 1990; Swann, 1996, 1997). Questing for self-affirmation, we're especially motivated to *enhance our self-image* (Sedikides, 1993). Trying to increase self-esteem, then, helps power self-serving bias. As social psychologist Daniel Batson (2006) surmised, "The head is an extension of the heart."

How Do People Manage Their Self-Presentation?

What is self-presentation? How can impression management explain behaviour?

So far we have seen that the self is at the centre of our social worlds, that self-esteem and self-efficacy pay some dividends, and that self-serving bias influences self-evaluations. But are self-enhancing expressions always sincere? Do people have the same feelings privately as those they express publicly? Or are they just putting on a positive face even while living with self-doubt?

Self-Handicapping

Sometimes people sabotage their chances for success by creating impediments that make success less likely—known as **self-handicapping**.

Imagine yourself in the position of the participants of a study conducted by Steven Berglas and Edward Jones (1978). You guess answers to some difficult aptitude questions and are told, "Yours was one of the best scores seen to date!" Feeling incredibly lucky, you are then offered a choice between two drugs before answering more of these items. One drug will aid intellectual performance and the other will inhibit it. Which drug do you want? Most students wanted the drug that would supposedly disrupt their thinking, thus providing a handy excuse for doing badly.

> ***"With no attempt there can be no failure; with no failure no humiliation."***
>
> William James, *Principles of Psychology*, 1890

Researchers have documented other ways people self-handicap. Fearing failure, people will

> **self-handicapping** Protecting one's self-image with behaviours that create a handy excuse for later failure.

- reduce their preparation for important individual athletic events (Rhodewalt et al., 1984).
- give their opponent an advantage (Shepperd & Arkin, 1991).
- perform poorly at the beginning of a task so as not to create unreachable expectations (Baumgardner & Brownlee, 1987).
- not try as hard as they could during a tough, ego-involving task (Hormuth, 1986; Pyszczynski & Greenberg, 1987; Riggs, 1992; Turner & Pratkanis, 1993).

> ***"After losing to some younger rivals, tennis great Martina Navratilova confessed that she was 'afraid to play my best. … I was scared to find out if they could beat me when I'm playing my best because if they can, then I am finished.'"***
>
> Frankel & Snyder (1987)

Far from being deliberately self-destructive, such behaviours typically have a self-protective aim (Arkin, Lake, & Baumgardner, 1986; Baumeister & Scher, 1988; Rhodewalt, 1987): "I'm really not a failure—I would have done well except for this problem." Unfortunately, this strategy usually backfires: Students who self-handicap end up with lower GPAs (Schwinger et al., 2014).

Why would people handicap themselves with self-defeating behaviours? Recall that we eagerly protect our self-images by attributing failures to external factors. Thus, *fearing failure,* people might handicap themselves by partying half the night before a job interview or playing video games instead of studying before a big exam. When self-image is tied up with performance, it can be more self-deflating to try hard and fail than to procrastinate and have a ready excuse. If we fail while handicapped in some way, we can cling to a sense of competence; if we succeed under such conditions, it can only boost our self-image. Handicaps protect both self-esteem and public image by allowing us to attribute failures to something temporary or external ("I was feeling sick" or "I was out too late the night before") rather than to lack of talent or ability.

Impression Management

Self-serving bias, false modesty, and self-handicapping reveal the depth of our concern for self-image. To varying degrees, we are continually managing the impressions we create. Whether we wish to impress, to intimidate, or to seem helpless, we are social animals, playing to an audience. So great is the human desire for social acceptance that it can lead people to risk harming themselves through smoking, binge eating, premature sex, or drug and alcohol abuse (Rawn & Vohs, 2011).

Self-presentation refers to our wanting to present a desired image both to an external audience (other people) and to an internal audience (ourselves). We work at managing the impressions we create. We excuse, justify, or apologize as necessary to shore up our self-esteem and verify our self-image (Schlenker & Weigold, 1992). Just as we preserve our self-esteem, we also must make sure not to brag too much and risk the disapproval of others (Anderson et al., 2006). In one study, students who were told to "put your best face forward" actually made a more negative impression on people they had just met than those who were not under self-presentational demands (Human et al., 2012). One self-presentation strategy is the "humblebrag," an attempt to disguise bragging behind complaints or false humility ("I still can't believe I was the one who got the job out of 300 applicants!" "I go out wearing grubby clothes and I still get hit on!"). One study found that humblebragging usually backfires, failing to either convey humility or impress others (Sezer et al., 2018).

self-presentation The act of expressing yourself and behaving in ways designed to create a favourable impression or an impression that corresponds to your ideals.

Social interaction is a careful balance of looking good while not looking *too* good. That seems to be particularly true in collectivistic cultures, where modesty is a "default strategy" to avoid offending others. When there was no risk of offence, Japanese participants self-enhanced as much as Americans (Yamagishi et al., 2012).

In familiar situations, self-presentation happens without conscious effort. In unfamiliar situations, perhaps at a party with people we would like to impress or in conversation with someone we have a romantic interest in, we are acutely self-conscious of the impressions we are creating, and we are, therefore, less modest than when among friends who know us well (Leary et al., 1994; Tice et al., 1995). Preparing to present ourselves in a photograph, we may even try out different faces in a mirror. We do so even though active self-presentation depletes energy, which often leads to diminished effectiveness—for example, to less persistence on a tedious experimental task or to more difficulty stifling emotional expressions (Vohs, Baumeister, & Ciarocco, 2005). The upside is that self-presentation can unexpectedly improve mood. People felt significantly better than they thought they would after doing their best to "put their best face forward" and concentrate on making a positive impression on their boyfriend or girlfriend. Elizabeth Dunn of the University of British Columbia and her colleagues (2008) concluded that "date nights" for long-term couples work because they encourage active self-presentation, which improves mood.

"Public opinion is always more tyrannical towards those who obviously fear it than towards those who feel indifferent to it."

Bertrand Russell, *The Conquest of Happiness,* 1930

Social networking sites provide a new and sometimes intense venue for self-presentation. They are, according to communications professor Joseph Walther, "like impression management on steroids" (Rosenbloom, 2008). Users make careful decisions about which

In the age of the selfie, self-presentation can be a nearly constant concern.
Source: ©mindof/123RF.

pictures, activities, and interests to highlight in their profiles. Tinkering with self-presentation online apparently has benefits: People who edit their own Facebook profile subsequently report higher self-esteem (Gentile et al., 2012; Gonzales & Hancock, 2011). Given the concern with status and attractiveness on social networking sites, it is not surprising that people high in narcissistic traits thrive on Facebook, tallying up more friends and choosing more attractive pictures of themselves to display (Buffardi & Campbell, 2008).

Given our concern for self-presentation, it's no wonder, say self-presentation researchers, that people will self-handicap when failure might make them look bad. It's no wonder that people take health risks: tanning their skin with wrinkle- and cancer-causing radiation; having piercings or tattoos done without proper hygiene; becoming anorexic; or yielding to peer pressure to smoke, get drunk, and do drugs (Leary et al., 1994). It's no wonder that people express more modesty when their self-flattery is vulnerable to being debunked, perhaps by experts who will be scrutinizing their self-descriptions (Arkin, Appleman, & Burger, 1980; Riess et al., 1981; Weary et al., 1982). Professor Smith will express less confidence in the significance of her work, for example, when presenting it to professional colleagues, who are better able to scrutinize the claims, than when presenting it to students.

For some people, conscious self-presentation is a way of life. They continually monitor their own behaviour and note how others react, then adjust their social performance to gain a desired effect. Those who score high on a scale of **self-monitoring** (who, for example, agree that "I tend to be what people expect me to be") act like social chameleons—they adjust their behaviour in response to external situations (Gangestad & Snyder, 2000; Snyder, 1987). Having attuned their behaviour to the situation, they are more likely to express attitudes they don't really hold and less likely to express or act on their own attitudes (Zanna & Olson, 1982). As Mark Leary (2004b) observed, the self they know often differs from the self they show. As social chameleons, those who score high in self-monitoring are also less committed to their relationships and more likely to be dissatisfied in their marriages (Leone & Hawkins, 2006). On the other hand, high self-monitors may rack up more connections online. For example, they post more on Facebook and receive more "likes" from friends (Hall & Pennington, 2013).

self-monitoring Being attuned to the way you present yourself in social situations and adjusting your performance to create the desired impression.

Those low in self-monitoring care less about what others think. They are more internally guided and thus more likely to talk and act as they feel and believe (McCann & Hancock, 1983). For example, if asked to list their thoughts about gay couples, they simply express what they think, regardless of the attitudes of their anticipated audience (Klein, Snyder, & Livingston, 2004). As you might imagine, someone who is extremely low in self-monitoring could come across as an insensitive boor, whereas extremely high self-monitoring could result in dishonest behaviour worthy of a con artist. Most of us fall somewhere between those two extremes.

Presenting oneself in ways that create a desired impression is a delicate balancing act. People want to be seen as able but also as modest and honest (Carlston & Shovar, 1983). In most situations, modesty creates a good impression while unsolicited boasting creates a bad one (Forsyth, Berger, & Mitchell, 1981; Holtgraves & Srull, 1989; Schlenker & Leary, 1982)—hence, the false modesty phenomenon: We often display lower self-esteem than we privately feel (Miller & Schlenker, 1985). But when we have obviously done extremely

Group identity: In Asian countries, self-presentation is restrained. Children learn to identify themselves with their groups.

Source: ©imtmphoto/Shutterstock.

well, the insincerity of a disclaimer ("I did well, but it's no big deal") may be evident. To make good impressions—as modest yet competent—requires social skill.

Self-presented modesty is greatest in cultures that value self-restraint, such as those of China and Japan (Heine & Lehman, 1995, 1997a, 1997b; Lee & Seligman, 1997; Markus & Kitayama, 1991). In China and Japan, people exhibit less self-serving bias. Unlike Westerners, who (as we have seen in this chapter) tend to take credit for successes and attribute failures to the situation, Japanese children learn to share credit for success and to accept responsibility for failures. "When I fail, it's my fault, not my group's" is a typical Japanese attitude (Anderson, 1999).

Doubting Our Ability in Social Situations

What causes us to feel anxious in social situations? Why are some people shackled in the prison of their own social anxiety? Barry Schlenker and Mark Leary (1982, 1985; Leary & Kowalski, 1995) answer those questions by applying **self-presentation theory**. Self-presentation theory assumes that we are eager to present ourselves in ways that make a good impression. Thus, *we feel social anxiety when we are motivated to impress others but have self-doubts.* This simple principle helps explain a variety of research findings, each of which may ring true in your experience. We feel most anxious when we are

self-presentation theory A theory positing that we are eager to present ourselves in ways that make a good impression.

- with powerful, high-status people—people whose impressions of us matter.
- in an evaluative context, such as when making a first interview.
- self-conscious (as shy people often are), with our attention focused on ourselves and how we are coming across.
- focused on something central to our self-image, as when a university professor presents research before peers at a professional conference.
- in novel or unstructured situations, such as a first school dance or first formal dinner, where we are unsure of the social rules.

For most people, the tendency in all such situations is to be cautiously self-protective: to talk less; to avoid topics that reveal one's ignorance; to be guarded about oneself; to be unassertive, agreeable, and smiling. Ironically, such anxious concern with making a good impression often makes a bad impression (Broome & Wegner, 1994; Meleshko & Alden, 1993). With time, however, shy people often become well-liked. Their lack of egotism and their modesty, sensitivity, and discretion wear well (Gough & Thorne, 1986; Paulhus & Morgan, 1997; Shepperd et al., 1995).

Overpersonalizing Situations

Compared with outgoing people, shy, self-conscious people (whose numbers include many adolescents) see incidental events as somehow relevant to themselves (Fenigstein, 1984; Fenigstein & Vanable, 1992). Shy, anxious people overpersonalize situations, a tendency that breeds anxious concern and, in extreme cases, paranoia. They are especially prone to *the spotlight effect*—they overestimate the extent to which other people are watching and evaluating them. If their hair won't comb right or they have a facial blemish, they assume everyone else notices and judges them accordingly. Shy people may even be conscious of their self-consciousness. They wish they could stop worrying about blushing, about what others are thinking, or about what to say next.

To reduce social anxiety, some people turn to alcohol. Alcohol lowers anxiety and reduces self-consciousness (Hull & Young, 1983). Thus, chronically self-conscious people are especially likely to drink following a failure. If recovering from alcoholism, they are more likely than those low in self-consciousness to relapse when they again experience stress or failure.

Alcohol can also reduce social anxiety by restricting people's ability to think about their internal states. Claude Steele and Robert Josephs (1990) call this effect "alcohol myopia." Steele and Josephs showed that when people are intoxicated they can focus on only the most salient cues in their environment. If drinking at a rowdy party, anxious people are likely to focus on the party, not their anxiety. On the other hand, if they drink alone in a quiet room, they will more likely focus on their anxiety (as there is little else to focus on) and become more anxious. This may be one reason people drink mainly in social situations.

Alcohol myopia can have serious consequences, as Queen's University professor Tara MacDonald and University of Waterloo professors Mark Zanna and Geoff Fong (1995) have shown. They had students at a campus bar answer a survey about drinking and driving either when they arrived at the bar (i.e., when they were sober) or at the end of the night after they'd been drinking. They asked them their attitudes about "drinking and driving" or "drinking and driving only a short distance." How they asked the question made no difference to sober students, but intoxicated students were more accepting of drinking and driving "only a short distance" (see Figure 2–11). It seems that alcohol myopia made these students focus on the encouraging cue that it was only a short distance, and not on their more general belief that drinking and driving is dangerous. This same effect of alcohol—a narrowing of attention—can also contribute to potentially costly decisions to have unprotected casual sex (MacDonald et al., 2000).

Symptoms as diverse as anxiety and alcohol abuse can serve a self-handicapping function. Labelling oneself as anxious, shy, depressed, or under the influence of alcohol can provide an excuse for failure (Snyder & Smith, 1986). Behind a barricade of symptoms, the person's ego stands secure. "Why don't I date? Because I'm shy, so people don't easily get to know the real me." The symptom is an unconscious strategic ploy to explain away negative outcomes.

What if we were to remove the need for such a ploy by providing people with a handy alternative explanation for their anxiety and therefore for possible failure? Would a shy

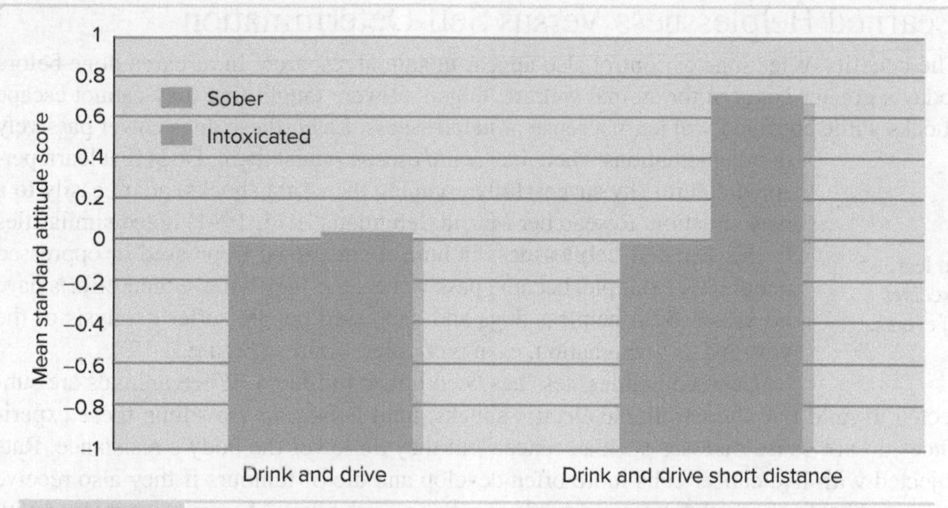

FIGURE 2–11 ALCOHOL MYOPIA AND ATTITUDES TOWARD DRINKING AND DRIVING.

When people are intoxicated, they can only focus on a very limited amount of information, an effect called alcohol myopia. If people focus on cues that lower their inhibition, such as the short distance home, then they may be more likely to drink and drive.

Source: Adapted from T. K. MacDonald, M. P. Zanna, and G. T. Fong, "Decision making in altered states: Effects of alcohol on attitudes toward drinking and driving," *Journal of Personality and Social Psychology, 68*(6), 973–985. Copyright © 1995 by the American Psychological Association. Adapted with permission.

person no longer need to be shy? That is precisely what Susan Brodt and Philip Zimbardo (1981) found when they brought shy and not-shy college women to the laboratory and had them converse with a handsome man who posed as another participant. Before the conversation, the women were cooped up in a small chamber and blasted with loud noise. Some of the shy women (but not others) were told that the noise would leave them with a pounding heart, a common symptom of social anxiety. Thus, when these women later talked with the man, they could attribute their pounding hearts and any conversational difficulties to the noise, not to their shyness or social inadequacy. Compared with the shy women who were not given this handy explanation for their pounding hearts, these women were no longer so shy. They talked fluently once the conversation got going and asked questions of the man. In fact, unlike the other shy women (whom the man could easily spot as shy), these women were to him indistinguishable from the not-shy women.

What Does It Mean to Have Perceived Self-Control?

How can we understand "self-control" through examination of the self in action?

We have considered what our self-concept is, how it develops, and how well (or poorly) we know ourselves. Now let's see why our self-concept matters, by viewing the self in action. Our self-concepts influence our behaviour (Graziano, Jensen-Campbell, & Finch, 1997). Given challenging tasks, people who imagine themselves as hard-working and successful outperform those who imagine themselves as failures (Ruvolo & Markus, 1992). Envision your positive possibilities and you become more likely to plan and enact a successful strategy.

Learned Helplessness Versus Self-Determination

The benefits of feelings of control also appear in animal research. In research done before today's greater concern for animal welfare, dogs that were taught that they cannot escape shocks while confined will learn a sense of helplessness. Later, these dogs cower passively in other situations when they *could* escape punishment. Dogs that learn personal control (by successfully escaping their first shocks) adapt easily to a new situation. Researcher Martin Seligman (1975, 1991) noted similarities to this **learned helplessness** in human situations. Depressed or oppressed people, for example, become passive because they believe their efforts have no effect. Both helpless dogs and depressed people suffer paralysis of the will, passive resignation, even motionless apathy (Figure 2–12).

learned helplessness The hopelessness and resignation learned when a human or animal perceives no control over repeated bad events.

Learned helplessness has been linked to illness. When animals are subjected to mild but uncontrollable electric shocks, loud noises, or crowding, these experiences do not cause diseases such as cancer, but they do lower the body's resistance. Rats injected with live cancer cells more often develop and die of tumours if they also receive inescapable shocks (rather than escapable shocks or no shocks). Moreover, compared with juvenile rats given controllable shocks, those given uncontrollable shocks are twice as likely in adulthood to develop tumours if given cancer cells and another round of shocks (Visintainer & Seligman, 1985). Animals that have learned helplessness react more passively, and blood tests reveal a weakened immune response.

It's a big leap from rats to humans. But a growing body of evidence reveals that people who undergo highly stressful experiences become more vulnerable to disease (Segerstrom & Miller, 2004). Stress doesn't make us sick, but it does divert energy from our disease-fighting immune system, leaving us more vulnerable to infections and malignancy (Cohen, 2002, 2004). The death of a spouse, the stress of a space flight landing, and even the strain of an exam week have all been associated with depressed immune defences (Jemmott & Locke, 1984).

Consider the following:

- Stress magnifies the severity of respiratory infections and of symptoms experienced by volunteers who are knowingly infected with a cold virus (Cohen et al., 2003, 2006, 2012; Pedersen et al., 2010).
- Newlywed couples who became angry while discussing problems suffered more immune system suppression the next day (Kiecolt-Glaser et al., 1993). When people are stressed by marital conflict, puncture wounds inflicted in the laboratory take a day or two longer to heal (Kiecolt-Glaser et al., 2005). Studies in 11 countries following 6.5 million lives through time reveal that, among men and younger adults, divorce increases the later risk of early death (Sbarra et al., 2011).

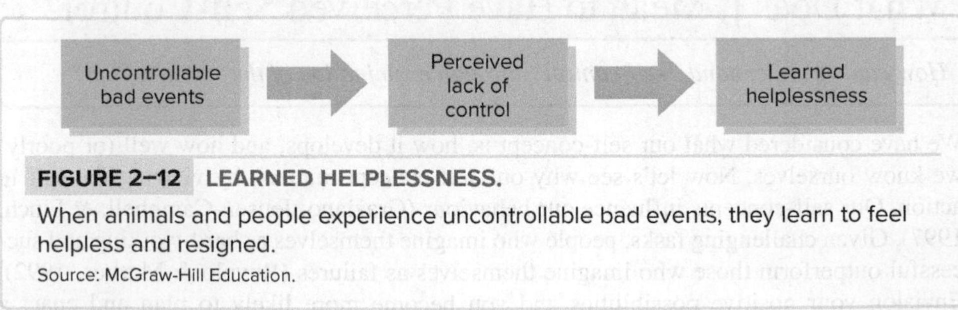

FIGURE 2–12 LEARNED HELPLESSNESS.
When animals and people experience uncontrollable bad events, they learn to feel helpless and resigned.
Source: McGraw-Hill Education.

- Work stress can literally be disheartening. In one study that followed 17 415 middle-aged women, researchers found that significant work stress predicted an 88 percent increased risk of heart attacks (Slopen et al., 2010). In Denmark, a study of 12 116 female nurses found that those reporting "much too high" work pressures had a 40 percent increased risk of heart disease (Allesøe et al., 2010).
- Stress increases the production of inflammation-producing proteins. Those who experience social stress, including children reared in abusive families, are therefore more prone to inflammation responses (Dickerson et al., 2009; Miller et al., 2011). Inflammation fights infections, but persistent inflammation contributes to asthma, clogged arteries, and depression. Researchers have even discovered molecular, *epigenetic* mechanisms by which stress, in some people, activates genes that control inflammation (Cole et al., 2010).

On the other hand, people benefit by training their self-control "muscles." University students who practised self-control by sticking with an exercise program or reducing their impulse buying also ate less junk food, cut down on alcohol, and studied more (Oaten & Cheng, 2006a, 2006b). So if you'd like to increase your willpower, don't make a long list of New Year's resolutions and tackle them all at once in January. A better strategy, the research suggests, is to start with one area and then let your increased self-control spread throughout your newly improved life. Another life hack is to stop doing things you shouldn't by reducing the possibility you'll be tempted—don't leave the cookies on the counter, and keep your phone out of reach (Milyavskaya et al., 2015). As Roy Baumeister and John Tierney write in their book, *Willpower,* "The best way to reduce stress in your life is to stop screwing up" (2011, p. 238). A little self-control now means you need less self-control later.

Ellen Langer and Judith Rodin (1976) tested the importance of personal control by treating elderly patients in a highly rated nursing home in one of two ways. With one group, the benevolent caregivers stressed "our responsibility to make this a home you can be proud of and happy in." They gave the passive patients their normal well-intentioned, sympathetic care, and they allowed them to assume a passive care-receiving role. Three weeks later, most were rated by themselves, by interviewers, and by nurses as being further debilitated. Langer and Rodin's other treatment promoted personal control. It emphasized opportunities for choice, the possibilities for influencing nursing-home policy, and the person's responsibility "to make of your life whatever you want." These patients were given small decisions to make and responsibilities to fulfill. Over the ensuing three weeks, 93 percent of this group showed improved alertness, activity, and happiness.

Studies have confirmed that systems of governing or managing people that promote self-efficacy—a belief in your own competence—will, indeed, promote health and happiness (Deci & Ryan, 1987). Here are some additional examples:

- University students who develop a sense of control over school gain a greater sense of control over their lives (Guay, Mageau, & Vallerand, 2003).
- Prisoners given some control over their environments—by being able to move chairs, control TV sets, and switch the lights—experience less stress, exhibit fewer health problems, and commit less vandalism (Ruback, Carr, & Hoper, 1986; Wener, Frazier, & Farbstein, 1987).
- Workers given leeway in carrying out tasks and making decisions experience improved morale (Miller & Monge, 1986), as do telecommuting workers who have more flexibility in balancing their work and personal life (Valcour, 2007).
- In all countries studied, including Canada, people who perceive themselves as having free choice experience greater satisfaction with their lives. And countries where people experience more freedom have more satisfied citizens (Inglehart & Welzel, 2005).

> *"Argue for your limitations, and sure enough they're yours."*
>
> Richard Bach, *Illusions: Adventures of a Reluctant Messiah,* 1977

Research on self-control gives us greater confidence in traditional virtues, such as perseverance and hope. Bandura (2004) acknowledges that self-efficacy is fed by social persuasion ("You have what it takes to succeed") and by self-persuasion ("I think I can, I think I can"). Modelling—seeing similar others succeed with effort—helps, too. But the biggest source of self-efficacy, he says, is *mastery experiences:* "Successes build a robust belief in one's efficacy." If your initial efforts to lose weight, stop smoking, or improve your grades succeed, your self-efficacy increases.

A team of researchers led by Roy Baumeister (Baumeister et al., 2003) concurs with Bandura's conclusion about mastery experiences. "Praising all the children just for being themselves," they contend, "simply devalues praise." Better to praise and bolster self-esteem "in recognition of good performance. … As the person performs or behaves better, self-esteem is encouraged to rise, and the net effect will be to reinforce both good behavior and improvement. Those outcomes are conducive to both the happiness of the individual and the betterment of society" (p. 39).

SUMMING UP

Spotlights and Illusions: What Do They Teach Us About Ourselves?

- Concerned with the impression we make on others, we tend to believe that others are paying more attention to us than they are (the *spotlight effect*).
- We also tend to believe that our emotions are more obvious than they are (the *illusion of transparency*).

Self-Concept: Who Am I?

- Our sense of self helps organize our thoughts and actions. Self-concept consists of two elements: the self-schemas that guide our processing of self-relevant information, and the possible selves that we dream of or dread.
- Cultures shape the self, too. Many people in individualistic Western cultures assume an *independent self.* Others, often in collectivistic cultures, assume a more *interdependent self.* These contrasting ideas contribute to cultural differences in social behaviour.
- Our self-knowledge is curiously flawed. We often do not know why we behave the way we do. When influences upon our behaviour are not conspicuous enough for any observer to see, we, too, can miss them. The unconscious, implicit processes that control our behaviour may differ from our conscious, explicit explanations of it.
- We also tend to mispredict our emotions. We underestimate the power of our psychological immune systems and thus tend to overestimate the durability of our emotional reactions to significant events.

What Is the Nature and Motivating Power of Self-Esteem?

- Self-esteem is the overall sense of self-worth we use to appraise our traits and abilities. Our self-concepts are determined by multiple influences, including the roles we play, the comparisons we make, our social identities, how we perceive others appraising us, and our experiences of success and failure.
- Self-esteem motivation influences our cognitive processes: Facing failure, high-self-esteem people sustain their self-worth by perceiving other people as failing, too, and by exaggerating their superiority over others.
- Although high self-esteem is generally more beneficial than low, researchers have found that people high in both self-esteem and narcissism are the most aggressive. Someone with a big ego who is threatened or deflated by social rejection is potentially aggressive.
- Self-efficacy is the belief that one is effective and competent and can do something. Unlike high self-esteem, high self-efficacy is consistently linked to success.

What Is Self-Serving Bias?

- Contrary to the presumption that most people suffer from low self-esteem or feelings of inferiority, researchers consistently find that most people exhibit a *self-serving bias*. In experiments and everyday life, we often take credit for successes while blaming failures on the situation.
- Most people rate themselves as better than average on subjective, desirable traits and abilities. We exhibit unrealistic optimism about our futures.
- We overestimate the commonality of our opinions and foibles (*false consensus*) while underestimating the commonality of our abilities and virtues (*false uniqueness*).
- We also remember ourselves in the past in ways that flatter the current self.
- Such perceptions arise partly from a motive to maintain and enhance—a motive that protects people from depression but contributes to misjudgment and group conflict.
- Self-serving bias can be adaptive in that it allows us to savour the good things that happen in our lives. When bad things happen, however, self-serving bias can have the maladaptive effect of causing us to blame others or feel cheated out of something we "deserved."

How Do People Manage Their Self-Presentation?

- As social animals, we adjust our words and actions to suit our audiences. To varying degrees, we self-monitor; we note our performance and adjust it to create the impressions we desire.
- Sometimes, people will even *self-handicap* with self-defeating behaviours that protect self-esteem by providing excuses for failure.
- *Self-presentation* refers to our wanting to present a favourable image both to an external audience (other people) and to an internal audience (ourselves). With regard to an external audience, those who score high on a scale of self-monitoring adjust their behaviour to each situation, whereas those low in self-monitoring may do so little social adjusting that they seem insensitive.

What Does It Mean to Have Perceived Self-Control?

- Our sense of self helps organize our thoughts and actions.
- Learned helplessness often occurs when attempts to improve a situation have proven fruitless; self-determination, in contrast, is bolstered by experiences of successfully exercising control and improving one's situation.
- People who believe in their own competence and effectiveness cope better and achieve more than those who have learned a helpless, pessimistic outlook.

Key Terms

collectivism
defensive pessimism
dual attitudes
explanatory style
false consensus effect
false uniqueness effect
illusion of transparency
impact bias
independent self
individualism
interdependent self
learned helplessness
planning fallacy
self-concept
self-efficacy
self-esteem
self-handicapping
self-monitoring
self-presentation
self-schemas
self-serving attributions
self-serving bias
social comparison
spotlight effect
temporal comparisons

CHAPTER 3

Social Beliefs and Judgments

Source: ©CREATISTA/Shutterstock.

CHAPTER OUTLINE

How Do We Judge Our Social Worlds, Consciously and Unconsciously?

How Do We Perceive Our Social Worlds?

How Do We Explain Our Social Worlds?

How Do Our Social Beliefs Matter?

What Can We Conclude About Social Beliefs and Judgments?

In June 2010, Canada hosted the 2010 G20 Toronto summit of world financial leaders. To prepare for the summit, to be held at the Metro Toronto Convention Centre, an integrated security unit was formed of police officers and Canadian military personnel.

Large segments of downtown Toronto were cordoned off to secure the summit and protect delegates from harm. Then, just prior to the summit, a bank in Ottawa was firebombed by a group of anarchists who threatened to be in Toronto to violently oppose the meeting.

As the summit began, many activist groups gathered in downtown Toronto to protest issues such as poverty, Indigenous rights, and capitalism and globalization. A few downtown streets were closed off to accommodate the growing number of protesters. Most of the protests were peaceful. Some individuals, however, began using "black bloc" tactics: They dressed entirely in black, concealed their faces, and vandalized local businesses, broke windows, and set police cruisers on fire.

In response, over the course of the weekend, the Toronto police (as part of the integrated security unit) arrested over 900 people. Many were detained for hours without any charges, including hundreds of citizens who, without warning, were corralled and held in the pouring rain at the corner of Spadina Avenue and Queen Street. Cold, wet, hungry, and without access to bathrooms, most were ultimately released without questioning.

To what should we attribute the police's actions? Should protesters and onlookers have expected such treatment after getting so close to the summit with tensions running high? Were the police simply reacting as best they could to control a complex and perilous situation? Or did they unjustifiably abuse their power, ignoring citizens' rights and treating everyone like "black bloc" hooligans?

These differing reactions illustrate the extent to which we construct social perceptions and beliefs as we

- *judge* events, informed by implicit rules that guide our snap judgments, and by our moods;
- *perceive* and recall events through the filters of our own assumptions;
- *explain* events by sometimes attributing them to the situation, sometimes to the person; and
- *expect* certain events, sometimes helping to actually bring them about as a result.

This chapter explores how we judge, perceive, and explain our social worlds, and why our expectations matter.

How Do We Judge Our Social Worlds, Consciously and Unconsciously?

How are judgments influenced by both unconscious and conscious systems?

System 1 The intuitive, automatic, unconscious, and fast way of thinking.

System 2 The deliberate, controlled, and slower way of thinking.

We have two brain systems, notes Nobel Prize-winner Daniel Kahneman in *Thinking, Fast and Slow* (2011). **System 1** functions automatically and out of our awareness (often called "intuition" or a "gut feeling"), whereas **System 2** requires our conscious attention and effort. The big lesson of recent research: System 1 influences more of our actions than we realize.

Priming

Things we don't even consciously notice can subtly influence how we interpret and recall events. Imagine wearing earphones and concentrating on ambiguous spoken sentences, such as "We stood by the bank." When a pertinent word (*river* or *money*) is simultaneously sent to your other ear, you don't consciously hear it. Yet the unheard word "primes" your interpretation of the sentence (Baars & McGovern, 1994).

Our memory system is a web of associations, and **priming** is the awakening or activating of certain associations. Experiments show that priming one thought, even without awareness, can influence another thought or even an action (Herring et al., 2013). John Bargh has likened primes to bells that only mental butlers (who manage the small unconscious stuff) can hear. In a host of studies, priming effects surface even when the stimuli are presented subliminally—too briefly to be perceived consciously. What's out of sight may not be completely out of mind, however. An electric shock too slight to be felt may increase the perceived intensity of a later shock. If the word *bread* is flashed so briefly that it's just below your conscious awareness, you'll detect a related word, such as *butter*, more quickly than an unrelated word, like *bubble* (Epley et al., 1999; Merikle et al., 2001). Religious people subliminally exposed to words associated with religion are more likely to help others (Shariff et al., 2016). In each case, an imperceptible image or word primes a response to a later task. In another experiment, students were more likely to wobble on a balance beam in a room with posters of beer and vodka as opposed to apple or orange juice (Cox et al., 2014).

Unnoticed events can also subtly prime our thinking and behaviour. Rob Holland and colleagues (2005) observed that Dutch students exposed to the scent of an all-purpose cleaner were quicker to identify cleaning-related words, recalled more cleaning-related activities when describing their day, and even kept their desk cleaner while eating a crumbly cookie. Another team of Dutch psychologists found that people exposed to the scent of a cleaning product were less likely to litter (de Lange et al., 2012). And, in a laboratory experiment, exposure to a fishy smell caused people to be suspicious of each other and to cooperate less—priming notions of a shady deal as "fishy" (Lee & Schwarz, 2012). All of these effects occurred without the participants' conscious awareness of the scent and its influence.

priming Activating particular associations in memory.

embodied cognition The mutual influence of bodily sensations on cognitive preferences and social judgments.

Priming experiments have their counterparts in everyday life, reports John Bargh (2006):

- Watching a scary movie alone at home can activate emotions that, without our realizing it, cause us to interpret furnace noises as a possible intruder.
- Depressed moods, as this chapter explains later, prime negative associations. But put people in a good mood and suddenly their past seems more wonderful; and their future, brighter.
- For many psychology students, reading about psychological disorders primes how they interpret their own anxieties and gloomy moods. Reading about disease symptoms similarly primes medical students to worry about their congestion, fever, or headache.

Studies of how implanted ideas and images can prime our interpretations and recall illustrate one of this book's take-home lessons: *Much of our social information processing is automatic*. It is unintentional, is out of sight, and happens without our conscious awareness—relying on System 1. As John Bargh and Tanya Chartrand (1999) explain, "Most of a person's everyday life is determined not by their conscious intentions and deliberate choices but by mental processes that are put into motion by features of the environment and that operate outside of conscious awareness and guidance" (p. 462).

Even physical sensations, thanks to our **embodied cognition**, prime our social judgments and vice versa:

- After assessing a cold person, people judge the room as colder than do those who instead assessed a warm person (Szymkow et al., 2013; Zhong & Leonardelli, 2008). People who ate alone judged room temperature as colder than those who ate with others (Lee et al., 2014). Social exclusion literally feels cold.
- When holding a *hard* rather than *soft* ball, people judge the same face as more likely to be Republican than Democrat and more likely to be a physicist than a historian (Slepian et al., 2012).

- People who feel hopeless perceive rooms to be darker—they don't have a "ray of hope" (Dong et al., 2015).
- When sitting in a wobbly chair, people rate other couples' relationships as more unstable (Kille et al., 2013).
- Embodied cognition can also be social. When two people synchronize their bodies, as when dancing, singing, or walking together, they may also synchronize their spirits. As two walkers together attend to their environment and coordinate their steps, mutual rapport and empathy increases and conflicts sometimes resolve (Webb et al., 2017).

The bottom line: Our social cognition is embodied. The brain systems that process our bodily sensations communicate with the brain systems responsible for our social thinking.

Intuitive Judgments

What are our powers of intuition—of immediately knowing something without reasoning or analysis? Advocates of "intuitive management" believe we should tune into our hunches—use System 1. When judging others, they say, we should plug into the nonlogical smarts of our "right brain." When hiring, firing, and investing, we should listen to our premonitions. In making judgments, we should trust the force within.

Are the intuitionists correct that important information is immediately available apart from our conscious analysis? Or are the skeptics right in saying that intuition is "our knowing we are right, whether we are or not" and finding that self-described "intuitive" people are actually no better than others at tasks that assess intuition (Leach & Weick, 2018).

The powers of intuition

"The heart has its reasons of which reason knows nothing," observed seventeenth-century philosopher–mathematician Blaise Pascal. Three centuries later, scientists have proven Pascal correct. We know more than we know we know. Studies of our unconscious information processing confirm our limited access to what's going on in our minds (Bargh, 1997; Greenwald & Banaji, 1995; Strack & Deutsch, 2004). Our thinking combines both **automatic processing** (impulsive, effortless, and without our awareness—System 1) and **controlled processing** (reflective, deliberate, and conscious—System 2). Automatic, intuitive thinking occurs not "onscreen" but offscreen, out of sight, where reason does not go. Consider these examples of automatic thinking:

automatic processing "Implicit" thinking that is effortless, habitual, and without awareness; roughly corresponds to "intuition." Also known as System 1.

controlled processing "Explicit" thinking that is deliberate, reflective, and conscious. Also known as System 2.

- *Schemas* are mental concepts or templates that intuitively guide our perceptions and interpretations of our experience. Whether we hear someone speaking of religious *sects* or *sex* depends on how we automatically interpret the sound.
- *Emotional reactions* are often nearly instantaneous, before there is time for deliberate thinking. One neural shortcut takes information from the eye or ear to the brain's sensory switchboard (the thalamus) and out to its emotional control centre (the amygdala) before the thinking cortex has had any chance to intervene (LeDoux, 1994, 1996). Our ancestors who intuitively feared a sound in the bushes were usually fearing nothing. But when they were right and the sound was made by a dangerous predator, they became more likely to survive to pass on their genes to us.
- Given sufficient *expertise,* people may intuitively know the answer to a problem. Many skills, from playing the piano to swinging a golf club, begin as a controlled, deliberate process and gradually become automatic and intuitive (Kruglanski & Gigerenzer, 2011). Master chess players intuitively recognize meaningful patterns

that novices miss and often make their next move with only a glance at the board, as the situation cues information stored in their memory.

- Given very little information about someone—even just a fraction of a second's glance at their photo—people's snap judgments can beat chance at guessing whether someone is outgoing or shy, straight or gay (Rule, 2014).

Some things—facts, names, and past experiences—we remember explicitly (consciously) using System 2. But other things—skills and conditioned dispositions—we remember *implicitly* with System 1, without consciously knowing or declaring that we know. It's true of us all but most strikingly evident in people with brain damage who cannot form new explicit memories. One such person never could learn to recognize her physician, who would need to reintroduce himself with a handshake each day. One day, the physician affixed a tack to his hand, causing the patient to jump with pain when they shook hands. When the physician next returned, the patient still didn't recognize him. But, due to her implicit memory, she wouldn't shake his hand.

Equally dramatic are the cases of *blindsight.* Having lost a portion of the visual cortex to surgery or stroke, people may be functionally blind in part of their field of vision. Shown a series of sticks in the blind field, they reported seeing nothing. When asked to guess whether the sticks were vertical or horizontal, the patients, remarkably, got them all right. Like the patient who "remembered" the painful handshake, these people know more than they know they know.

Subliminal stimuli, as we have already noted, can have intriguing effects. Consider the following study: Mark Baldwin of McGill University and his colleagues (1990) had Catholic women read a sexually explicit passage and then Baldwin and colleagues subliminally flashed either a picture of the Pope frowning, a picture of a stranger frowning, or a blank screen. As you can see in Figure 3–1, the women subsequently reported lower self-esteem if they were exposed to the frowning Pope. This effect was particularly pronounced for women who reported being more devout Catholics. Even outside awareness, the image of a disapproving Pope made these women feel worse after reading a steamy passage.

So, many routine cognitive functions occur automatically, unintentionally, without awareness. We might remember how automatic processing helps us get through life by

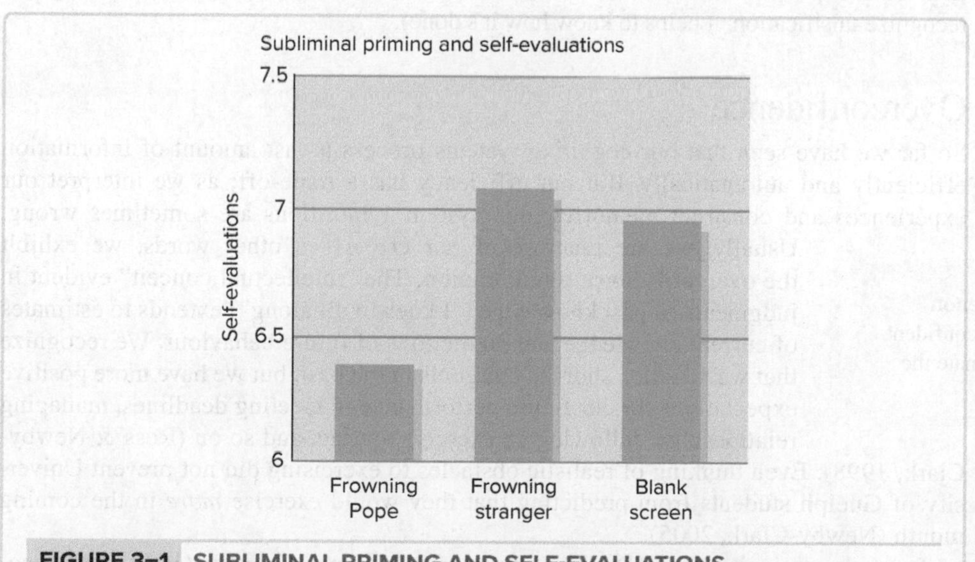

FIGURE 3–1 **SUBLIMINAL PRIMING AND SELF-EVALUATIONS.**

Catholic students primed with a subliminal picture of the Pope frowning rated themselves lower on a number of traits.

picturing our minds as functioning much as big corporations. Our CEO—our controlled consciousness—attends to many of the most important, complex, and novel issues while subordinates deal with routine affairs and matters requiring instant action. Like a CEO, consciousness sets goals and priorities, often with little knowledge of operational activities in the underlying departments. This delegation of resources enables us to react to many situations quickly and efficiently. The bottom line: Our brain knows much more than it tells us.

The limits of intuition

We have seen how automatic, intuitive thinking can "make us smart" (Gigerenzer, 2010). Elizabeth Loftus and Mark Klinger (1992), nevertheless, spoke for other cognitive scientists in having doubts about the brilliance of intuition. They reported "a general consensus that the unconscious may not be as smart as previously believed." Although subliminal stimuli can trigger a weak, fleeting response—enough to evoke a feeling if not conscious awareness—there is no evidence that (for example) commercial subliminal audio recordings can "reprogram your unconscious mind" for success. In fact, a significant body of evidence indicates that they can't (Greenwald, 1992).

Social psychologists have explored not only our error-prone hindsight judgments but also our capacity for illusion—for perceptual misinterpretations, fantasies, and constructed beliefs. Michael Gazzaniga (1992, 1998, 2008) reported that patients whose brain hemispheres have been surgically separated will instantly fabricate—and believe—explanations of their own puzzling behaviours. If the patient gets up and takes a few steps after the experimenter flashes the instruction "walk" to the patient's nonverbal right hemisphere, the verbal left hemisphere will instantly provide the patient with a plausible explanation ("I felt like getting a drink").

Illusory intuition also appears in how we take in, store, and retrieve social information. As perception researchers study visual illusions for what they reveal about our normal perceptual mechanisms, social psychologists study illusory thinking for what it reveals about normal information processing. These researchers want to give us a map of everyday social thinking, with the hazards clearly marked.

As we examine some of these efficient thinking patterns, remember this: Demonstrations of how people create false beliefs do not prove that all beliefs are false (although, to recognize falsification, it helps to know how it's done).

Overconfidence

So far we have seen that our cognitive systems process a vast amount of information efficiently and automatically. But our efficiency has a trade-off; as we interpret our experiences and construct memories, our System 1 intuitions are sometimes wrong. Usually, we are unaware of our errors—in other words, we exhibit the **overconfidence phenomenon**. The "intellectual conceit" evident in judgments of past knowledge ("I knew it all along") extends to estimates of current knowledge and predictions of future behaviour. We recognize that we've fallen short of our goals in the past, but we have more positive expectations for our future performance in meeting deadlines, managing relationships, following an exercise routine, and so on (Ross & Newby-Clark, 1998). Even thinking of realistic obstacles to exercising did not prevent University of Guelph students from predicting that they would exercise *more* in the coming month (Newby-Clark, 2005).

overconfidence phenomenon
The tendency to be more confident than correct—to overestimate the accuracy of one's beliefs.

To study overconfidence, Daniel Kahneman and Amos Tversky (1979) gave people factual questions and asked them to fill in the blanks, as in the following: "I feel 98 percent certain that the air distance between New Delhi and Beijing is more than

_____ miles but less than ______ miles." Most individuals were overconfident: About 30 percent of the time, the correct answer lay outside the range they felt 98 percent confident about. Even when participants were offered lottery tickets for a correct answer, they were still too overconfident, identifying too narrow a range (also known as overprecision). "The consequences of overprecision are profound," note Albert Mannes and Don Moore (2013, p. 1196). "People frequently cut things too close—arriving late, missing planes, [or] bouncing checks." In thinking we know exactly how something will go, we too often miss the window.

Ironically, *incompetence feeds overconfidence.* It takes competence to recognize competence, note Justin Kruger and David Dunning (1999). Students who score the lowest on tests of grammar, humour, and logic are the most prone to overestimating their abilities. Those who don't know what good logic or grammar is are often unaware that they lack it. If you make a list of all the words you can form out of the letters in *psychology*, you may feel brilliant—but then stupid when a friend starts naming the ones you missed. Deanna Caputo and David Dunning (2005) recreated this phenomenon in experiments, confirming that our ignorance of our ignorance sustains our self-confidence. Follow-up studies indicate that this "ignorance of one's incompetence" occurs mostly on relatively easy-seeming tasks, such as forming words out of *psychology*. On difficult tasks, poor performers more often appreciate their lack of skill (Burson et al., 2006).

Robert Vallone and his colleagues (1990) had university students predict in September whether they would drop a course, declare a major, elect to live off campus next year, and so forth. Although the students felt, on average, 84 percent sure of these self-predictions, they were wrong nearly twice as often as they expected to be. Even when feeling 100 percent sure of their predictions, they were right only 85 percent of the time. Ignorance of one's incompetence helps explain David Dunning's (2005) startling

The perils of overconfidence. Before its exploded drilling platform spewed oil into the Gulf of Mexico, BP downplayed safety concerns, and then was overconfident that the spill would be modest (Mohr et al., 2010; Urbina, 2010).

Source: ©U.S. Coast Guard/Getty Images.

THE INSIDE STORY

As a graduate student, I noticed something peculiar about my work-related predictions. Most evenings, I would stuff my briefcase with work to complete at home and then return the following day with much of it untouched. Yet each time I packed that briefcase, I was sure my plans were realistic. In my PhD dissertation and subsequent research (conducted with Dale Griffin and Michael Ross), I have addressed two related questions: Why do people often underestimate how long it will take to finish tasks? Why don't people learn from past experience and adjust their estimates accordingly? The findings suggest that people's unwarranted optimism stems in part from a desire to finish projects promptly and in part from the thought processes that they naturally engage in to generate predictions. People tend to focus narrowly on their plans for completing the task at hand and consequently dismiss other valuable sources of information, such as how long similar tasks have taken in the past. These research insights have, unfortunately, had little impact on my own predictions, and I'm still lugging around an overweight briefcase.

Roger Buehler *Wilfrid Laurier University*

conclusion from employee assessment studies that "what others see in us . . . tends to be more highly correlated with objective outcomes than what we see in ourselves." If ignorance can beget false confidence, then—yikes!—where, we may ask, are you and I unknowingly deficient?

Part of the problem may be that people often give too much weight to their intentions when predicting their future behaviour (Koehler & Poon, 2006; Koehler, White, & John, 2011). When University of Waterloo students predicted whether they would donate blood, they relied heavily on their intentions to do so. But their intentions were a poor predictor of whether they actually donated. The students failed to appreciate how much their busy schedules, looming deadlines, or simple forgetfulness got in the way of donating.

In estimating their chances for success on a task, such as a major exam, people's confidence runs highest when the moment of truth is off in the future. By exam day, the possibility of failure looms larger and confidence typically drops (Gilovich, Kerr, & Medvec, 1993). Roger Buehler and his colleagues (1994, 2010) report that most students confidently underestimate how long it will take them to complete major assignments and overestimate how much money they will save in coming weeks (Peetz & Buehler, 2009). These students are not alone:

- *Stockbroker overconfidence*. Mutual fund portfolios selected by investment analysts perform about as well as randomly selected stocks (Malkiel, 2016). The analysts might think they can pick the best stocks, but everyone else does, too—stocks are a confidence game. Worse, people who are overconfident invest more and more even when things aren't going well, digging in their heels after publicly declaring their choices (Ronay et al., 2017).
- *Student overconfidence*. In one study, students memorizing psychology terms for a test typed in each term's definition and then predicted how much credit they expected to receive. The overconfident students—those who thought they were more accurate than they actually were—did worse on the test, mostly because they stopped studying (Dunlosky & Rawson, 2012).

Why does overconfidence persist? Perhaps because we like those who are confident: Group members rewarded highly confident individuals with higher status—even when their confidence was not justified by actual ability. Overconfident individuals spoke first, talked longer, and used a more factual tone, making them appear more competent than they actually were (Anderson et al., 2012). Even when groups worked together repeatedly and learned that the overconfident individuals were not as accurate as presented, group members continued to accord them status (Kennedy et al., 2013). Overconfident people are seen as more desirable romantic partners than the less confident (Murphy et al., 2015). If confidence, but not ability, helps people become leaders, pervasive overconfidence seems less surprising—but perhaps more distressing.

"When you know a thing, to hold that you know it; and when you do not know a thing, to allow that you do not know it; this is knowledge."

Confucius, *Analects*

Confirmation bias

People also tend not to seek information that might disprove what they believe. We are eager to verify our beliefs but less inclined to seek evidence that might disprove them. We call this phenomenon the **confirmation bias**. For example, opponents of same-sex marriage gave up the chance to win money to avoid hearing from those on the other side—and so did supporters of same-sex marriage. Across a variety of political and social issues, both liberals and conservatives preferred not to learn more about the other side's arguments (Frimer et al., 2017). Thus, people often choose their news sources and Facebook friends to align with their beliefs, a phenomenon known as "ideological echo chambers" (Del Vicario et al., 2017).

confirmation bias A tendency to search for information that confirms one's preconceptions.

Confirmation bias appears to be a System 1 snap judgment, where our default reaction is to look for information consistent with our presupposition. Stopping and thinking a little—calling up System 2—makes us less likely to commit this error. For example, Ivan Hernandez and Jesse Lee Preston (2013) had college students read an article arguing for the death penalty. Those who read the article in a dark, standard font did not change their opinions. But when the words were in light grey and italics, more shifted their beliefs—probably because straining to read the words slowed down participants' thinking enough for them to consider both sides. Contemplation curtails confirmation.

Confirmation helps explain why our self-images are so remarkably stable. In several experiments, William Swann and Stephen Read (1981; Swann, Stein-Seroussi, & Giesler, 1992; Swann, Stein-Seroussi, & McNulty, 1992; Swann, Chang-Schneider, & Angulo, 2007) discovered that students seek, elicit, and recall feedback that confirms their beliefs about themselves. People seek as friends and spouses those who verify their own self-views—even if they think poorly of themselves (Swann et al., 1991, 2003).

Swann and Read (1981) compared this *self-verification* to how someone with a domineering self-image might behave at a party. When she arrives, she seeks out those guests who she knows acknowledge her dominance. In conversation, she then presents her views in ways that elicit the respect she expects. After the party, she has trouble recalling conversations in which her influence was minimal and more easily recalls her persuasiveness in the conversations she dominated. Thus her experience at the party confirms her self-image.

Although we may normally gravitate to people who see us as we see ourselves, we may sometimes interact with someone who has different expectations of us. Can confirmation bias cause them to confirm their beliefs, even if they are inaccurate? To get a feel for how this possibility might be tested experimentally, imagine yourself on a blind date with someone who has been told that you are an uninhibited, outgoing person. To see whether this is true, your date slips questions into the conversation, such as "Have you ever done anything crazy in front of other people?" As you answer such questions, will you reveal a different "you" than if your date had been told you were shy and reserved?

In a clever series of experiments, Mark Snyder (1984), in collaboration with William Swann and others, gave interviewers some hypotheses to test concerning individuals' traits. Snyder and Swann found that people often test for a trait by looking for information that confirms it. As in the above blind-date example, if people are trying to find out if someone is an extrovert, they often solicit instances of extroversion ("What would you do if you wanted to liven things up at a party?"). Testing for introversion, they are more likely to ask,

"What factors make it hard for you to really open up to people?" In response, those probed for extroversion seem more sociable, and those probed for introversion seem more shy. Our assumptions and expectations about another help elicit the behaviour we expect.

Russell Fazio and his colleagues (1981) reproduced this finding and also discovered that those asked the "extroverted questions" later perceived themselves as actually more outgoing than those asked the introverted questions. Moreover, they really became noticeably more outgoing. An accomplice of the experimenter later met each participant in a waiting room and 70 percent of the time correctly guessed from the person's behaviour which condition the person had come from. These findings reveal that confirmation bias can sometimes cause our self-concepts to shift, even while it generally upholds the stability of our self-concepts through self-verification.

Confirmation bias can affect how people evaluate themselves. Consider for a moment: Are you happy with your social life? Ziva Kunda and colleagues (Kunda et al., 1993) put this question to students at the University of Waterloo and elsewhere. The students searched their memories for confirming instances and thus ended up feeling happier than students asked, "Are you unhappy with your social life?" Seek and you shall find.

Confidence in intuition versus statistical prediction

Not surprisingly, given tendencies toward overconfidence and confirmation bias, decision-makers often trust their intuitive judgments more than statistical data (such as using past grades and aptitude scores to predict success in graduate or professional school). Yet when researchers pit statistical prediction against intuitive prediction, the statistics usually win. Statistical predictions are indeed unreliable. But human intuition—even expert intuition—is even more unreliable (Faust & Ziskin, 1988; Meehl, 1954; Swets et al., 2000).

Three decades after demonstrating the superiority of statistical over intuitive prediction, Paul Meehl (1986) found the evidence stronger than ever:

> There is no controversy in social science which shows [so many] studies coming out so uniformly in the same direction as this one . . . When you are pushing 90 investigations, predicting everything from the outcome of football games to the diagnosis of liver disease and when you can hardly come up with a half dozen studies showing even a weak tendency in favour of the clinician, it is time to draw a practical conclusion.

One research team conducted an all-encompassing digest ("meta-analysis") of 134 studies predicting human behaviour or making psychological or medical diagnoses and prognoses (Grove et al., 2000). In only eight of the studies did clinical prediction surpass "mechanical" (statistical) prediction. In eight times as many (63 studies), statistical prediction fared better. Daniel Kahneman (2011, p. 223) notes that we now have some 200 studies comparing clinical and statistical prediction, most of which favour the latter, with the rest a draw. These include efforts to predict the following:

- *Medical outcomes:* cancer patients' longevity, hospital stays, cardiac diagnoses, babies' susceptibility to sudden infant death syndrome
- *Economic outcomes:* new business success, credit risks, career satisfaction
- *Government agency outcomes:* foster parent assessments, juvenile offender re-offence, violent behaviour
- *Miscellaneous other outcomes:* football winners, Bordeaux wine prices

What if we combined statistical prediction with expert intuition? What if we gave professional clinicians the statistical prediction of someone's future academic performance or risk of parole violation or suicide and asked them to refine or improve on the prediction? Alas, in the few studies where that has been done, prediction was better if the "improvements" were ignored (Dawes, 1994).

These findings have important implications for the assessment of human potential by graduate admissions interviewers. Dawes (1976) explained why statistical prediction is so often superior to an interviewer's intuition when predicting certain outcomes, such as graduate school success:

> What makes us think that we can do a better job of selection by interviewing (students) for a half hour, than we can by adding together relevant (standardized) variables, such as undergraduate GPA, GRE score, and perhaps ratings of letters of recommendation? The most reasonable explanation to me lies in our overevaluation of our cognitive capacity. And it is really cognitive conceit. Consider, for example, what goes into a GPA. Because for most graduate applicants it is based on at least 3½ years of undergraduate study, it is a composite measure arising from a minimum of 28 courses and possibly, with the popularity of the quarter system, as many as 50 . . . Yet you and I, looking at a folder or interviewing someone for a half hour, are supposed to be able to form a better impression than one based on 3½ years of the cumulative evaluations of 20–40 different professors. . . . Finally, if we do wish to ignore GPA, it appears that the only reason for doing so is believing that the candidate is particularly brilliant even though his or her record may not show it. What better evidence for such brilliance can we have than a score on a carefully devised aptitude test? Do we really think we are better equipped to assess such aptitude than is the Educational Testing Service, whatever its faults?

The bottom line, contended Dawes (2005) after three decades pressing his point, is that, lacking evidence, using intuition rather than statistical prediction "is simply unethical."

Remedies for overconfidence

What lessons can we draw from research on overconfidence? One lesson is to be wary of other people's dogmatic statements. Even when people seem sure they are right, they may be wrong. Confidence and competence need not coincide.

Two techniques have successfully reduced the overconfidence bias. One is *prompt feedback* (Lichtenstein & Fischhoff, 1980). In everyday life, weather forecasters and those who set the odds in horse racing both receive clear, daily feedback. Experts in both groups, therefore, do quite well at estimating their probable accuracy (Fischhoff, 1982).

When people think about why an idea might be true, it begins to seem true (Koehler, 1991). Thus, a second way to reduce overconfidence is to get people to think of one good reason *why* their judgments *might be wrong*: Force them to consider disconfirming information (Koriat, Lichtenstein, & Fischhoff, 1980). Managers might foster more realistic judgments by insisting that all proposals and recommendations include reasons why they might *not* work.

Still, we should be careful not to undermine people's reasonable self-confidence or to destroy their decisiveness. In times when their wisdom is needed, those lacking self-confidence may shrink from speaking up or making tough decisions. Overconfidence can cost us, but realistic self-confidence is adaptive.

Heuristics: Mental Shortcuts

With precious little time to process so much information, our cognitive system is fast and frugal. It specializes in mental shortcuts. With remarkable ease, we form impressions, make judgments, and invent explanations. We do so by using **heuristics**—simple, efficient thinking strategies. In most situations, our System 1 snap generalizations—"That's dangerous!"—are adaptive. The speed of these intuitive guides promotes our survival. The biological purpose of thinking is less to make us right than to keep us alive. In some situations, however, haste makes error.

heuristics A thinking strategy that enables quick, efficient judgments.

Representativeness heuristic

Suppose a panel of psychologists interviewed a sample of 30 engineers and 70 lawyers and summarized their impressions in thumbnail descriptions. Suppose further that the following description was drawn at random from the sample of 30 engineers and 70 lawyers:

> Twice divorced, Frank spends most of his free time hanging around the country club. His clubhouse bar conversations often centre on his regrets at having tried to follow his esteemed father's footsteps. The long hours he had spent at academic drudgery would have been better invested in learning how to be less quarrelsome in his relations with other people.
>
> *Question:* What is the probability that Frank is a lawyer rather than an engineer?

Asked to guess Frank's occupation, more than 80 percent of students in one study surmised he was one of the lawyers (Fischhoff & Bar-Hillel, 1984). Fair enough. But how do you suppose their estimates changed when the sample description was changed to say that 70 percent were engineers? Not in the slightest. The students took no account of the base rate of engineers (70 percent) and lawyers (30 percent); in their minds, Frank was more *representative* of lawyers, and that was all that seemed to matter. Or consider John, a 23-year-old White man who is an atheist and abuses drugs. What kind of music does he like? Most people guessed heavy metal, even though heavy metal fans are a very small minority of the population (Lonsdale & North, 2011).

To judge something by intuitively comparing it to our mental representation of a category is to use the **representativeness heuristic**. Representativeness (typicalness) usually reflects reality. But, as we saw with "Frank" above, it doesn't always. Consider Linda, who is 31, single, outspoken, and very bright. She majored in philosophy in university. As a student, she was deeply concerned with discrimination and other social issues, and she participated in anti-nuclear demonstrations. Based on this description, which of the following statements would you say is more likely?

a. Linda is a bank teller.

b. Linda is a bank teller and active in the feminist movement.

Most people think *b* is more likely, partly because Linda better *represents* their image of feminists. Consider: Is there a better chance that Linda is *both* a bank teller *and* a feminist than that she's a bank teller (whether feminist or not)? As Amos Tversky and Daniel Kahneman (1983) remind us, the conjunction of two events can't be more likely than either one of the events alone.

representativeness heuristic The tendency to presume, sometimes despite contrary odds, that someone or something belongs to a particular group if resembling (representing) a typical member.

availability heuristic A cognitive rule that judges the likelihood of things in terms of their availability in memory. If instances of something come readily to mind, we presume it to be commonplace.

Availability heuristic

Consider: Do more people live in Iraq or in Tanzania?

You probably answered in terms of how readily Iraqis and Tanzanians come to mind. If examples are readily *available* in our memory—as Iraqis tend to be—then we presume that the event is commonplace. Usually it is, so we are often well served by this cognitive rule, called the **availability heuristic**. Said simply, the more easily we can recall something, the more likely it seems. (*Answer: Tanzania's 57 million people greatly outnumber Iraq's 38 million. Most people, having more vivid images of Iraqis, guess wrong.*)

If people hear a list of famous people of one sex (Oprah Winfrey, Lady Gaga, Margaret Atwood) intermixed with an equal size list of unfamous people of the other sex (Donald Scarr, William Wood, Mel Jasper), the famous names will later be more cognitively available and people will believe they heard more women's names (McKelvie, 1995, 1997; Tversky & Kahneman, 1973). Likewise, media attention to gay–lesbian issues makes gay people cognitively available. Thus, the average person in one survey estimated that 25 percent of people are gay or lesbian (Morales, 2011)—more than five times the number who self-identify as gay, lesbian, or bisexual in surveys (4.1 percent [Gates, 2017]).

Even fictional happenings in novels, television, and movies leave images that later penetrate our judgments (Gerrig & Prentice, 1991; Green, Strange, & Brock, 2002). The more absorbed and "transported" the reader ("I could easily picture the events"), the more the story affects the reader's later beliefs (Diekman, McDonald, & Gardner, 2000). Readers who are captivated by romance novels, for example, may gain readily available sexual scripts that influence their own sexual attitudes and behaviours.

Our use of the availability heuristic highlights a basic principle of social thinking: People are slow to deduce particular instances from a general truth, but they are remarkably quick to infer general truth from a vivid instance. No wonder that after hearing and reading stories of rapes, robberies, and beatings, nine out of ten Canadians overestimated—usually by a considerable margin—the percentage of crimes that involve violence (Doob & Roberts, 1988).

The availability heuristic explains why vivid, easy-to-imagine events, such as shark attacks or diseases with easy-to-picture symptoms, may seem more likely to occur than harder-to-picture events (MacLeod & Campbell, 1992; Sherman et al., 1985). Likewise, powerful anecdotes can be more compelling than statistical information. We fret over extremely rare child abduction, even if we don't buckle children into their car seats every time. We dread terrorism but are indifferent to global climate change—"Armageddon in slow motion." Especially after the 2011 Japanese tsunami and nuclear power catastrophe, we have feared nuclear power, with little concern for the many more deaths related to coal mining and burning (von Hippel, 2011). In short, we worry about remote possibilities while ignoring higher probabilities, a phenomenon that social scientists call our "probability neglect."

Because news footage of airplane crashes is a readily available memory for most of us, we often suppose we are more at risk travelling in commercial airplanes than in cars. Actually, from 2010 to 2014, U.S. travellers were nearly 2000 times more likely to die in a car crash than on a commercial flight covering the same distance (National Safety Council, 2017). For most air travellers, the most dangerous part of the journey is the drive to the airport.

The availability heuristic may also make us more sensitive to unfairness, as our struggles are more memorable than our advantages. Students think that their parents were harder on them than on their siblings. And academics believe that they have had a more difficult time with journal-article reviewers than average (Davidai & Gilovich, 2016).

By now it is clear that our naive statistical intuitions, and our resulting fears, are driven not by calculation and reason but by emotions attuned to the availability heuristic. After this book is published, there likely will be another dramatic natural or terrorist event, which will again propel our fears, vigilance, and resources in a new direction. Terrorists, aided by the media, may again achieve their objective of capturing our attention, draining our resources, and distracting us from the mundane, undramatic, insidious risks that, over time, devastate lives, such as the rotavirus (an intestinal infection) that each day claims the equivalent of four 747s filled with children (Parashar et al., 2006). But, then again, dramatic events can also serve to awaken us to real risks. That, say some scientists, is what happens when extreme weather events remind us that global climate change, by raising sea levels and spawning extreme weather, is destined to become nature's own weapon of mass destruction. A hot day can prime people to believe more in global warming (Li et al., 2011). Even feeling hot in an *indoor* room increases people's belief in global warming (Risen & Critcher, 2011).

Vivid, memorable—and therefore cognitively available—events influence our perception of the social world. The resulting "probability neglect" often leads people to fear the wrong things, such as fearing flying or terrorism more than smoking, driving, or climate change. If four jumbo jets filled with children crashed every day—approximating the number of childhood diarrhea deaths resulting from the rotavirus—something would have been done about it.

Counterfactual Thinking

Easily imagined, cognitively available events also influence our experiences of guilt, regret, frustration, and relief. If our team loses (or wins) a big game by one point, we can easily imagine how the game might have gone the other way, and thus we feel greater regret (or relief). Imagining worse alternatives helps us feel better. When skier Lindsey Vonn lost a World Cup slalom event by just 0.03 seconds, she was happy for her competitor but noted that "I'd rather she beat me by a second" (Associated Press, 2012). Imagining better alternatives, and pondering what we might do differently next time, helps us prepare to do better in the future (Epstude & Roese, 2008; Scholl & Sassenberg, 2014).

counterfactual thinking Imagining alternative scenarios and outcomes that might have happened, but didn't.

In Olympic competition, athletes' emotions after an event reflect mostly how they did relative to expectations; but they also reflect the athletes' **counterfactual thinking**—their *mentally simulating what might have been* (McGraw, Mellers, & Tetlock, 2005; Medvec, Madey, & Gilovich, 1995). Bronze medallists (who could easily imagine finishing without a medal) exhibited more joy than silver medallists (who could more easily imagine having won the gold). On the medal stand, happiness is as simple as 1-3-2. Similarly, the higher a student's score within a grade category (such as B+), the *worse* they feel (Medvec & Savitsky, 1997). The B+ student who misses an A− by a point feels worse than the B+ student who actually did worse and just made a B+ by a point. In sports games or TV game shows, near misses are especially distressing when they occur near the end of the competition when there is little chance for future success (Zhang & Covey, 2014).

Such counterfactual thinking—imagining what could have been—occurs when we can easily picture an alternative outcome (Kahneman & Miller, 1986; Markman & McMullen, 2003; Petrocelli et al., 2011):

- If we barely miss a plane or bus, we imagine making it *if only* we had left at our usual time, taken our usual route, or not paused to talk. If we miss our connection by a half-hour or after taking our usual route, it's harder to simulate a different outcome, so we feel less frustration.

- If we change an exam answer, then get it wrong, we inevitably think, "If only . . ." and will vow next time to trust our immediate intuition—although, contrary to student lore, answer changes are more often from incorrect to correct (Kruger et al., 2005).
- Students who chose a university major but then thought about the benefits of a major they didn't choose were less satisfied with their choice and predicted they would not perform as well (Leach & Patall, 2013).

Counterfactual thinking underlies our feelings of luck. When we have barely escaped a bad event—avoiding defeat with a last-minute goal or standing near a falling icicle—we easily imagine a negative counterfactual (losing, being hit) and, therefore, feel "good luck" (Teigen et al., 1999). "Bad luck," on the other hand, refers to bad events that did happen but easily might not have.

The more significant and unlikely the event, the more intense the counterfactual thinking. Bereaved people who have lost a spouse or child in a vehicle accident, or a child to sudden infant death syndrome, commonly report replaying and undoing the event (Davis et al., 1995, 1996). One man survived a head-on collision with a drunk driver that killed his wife, daughter, and mother. "For months," he recalled, "I turned the events of that day over and over in my mind. I kept reliving the day, changing the order of events so that the accident wouldn't occur" (Sittser, 1994).

Most people, however, live with more regret over things they *didn't* do than what they did, such as, "I should have told my father I loved him before he died" or "I wish I had been more serious in university" (Gilovich & Medvec, 1994; Rajagopal et al., 2006). In one survey of adults, the most common regret was not taking their education more seriously (Kinnier & Metha, 1989). Would we live with less regret if we dared more often to reach beyond our comfort zone—to venture out, risking failure, but at least having tried?

Illusory Thinking

Another influence on everyday thinking is our search for order in random events, a tendency that can lead us down all sorts of wrong paths.

Illusory correlation

It's easy to see a correlation where none exists. When we expect significant relationships, we easily associate random events, perceiving an **illusory correlation**. William Ward and Herbert Jenkins (1965) showed people the results of a hypothetical 50-day cloud-seeding experiment. They told their subjects which of the 50 days the clouds had been seeded and which days it had rained. This information was nothing more than a random mix of results: Sometimes it rained after seeding; sometimes it didn't. People nevertheless became convinced—in conformity with their ideas about the effects of cloud seeding—that they really had observed a relationship between cloud seeding and rain.

illusory correlation A perception of a relationship where none exists or a perception of a stronger relationship than actually exists.

Other experiments confirmed this: ***People easily misperceive random events as confirming their beliefs*** (Crocker, 1981; Jennings, Amabile, & Ross, 1982; Trolier & Hamilton, 1986). If we believe a correlation exists, we are more likely to notice and recall confirming instances. If we believe that premonitions correlate with events, we notice and remember the joint occurrence of the premonition and the event's later occurrence. We seldom notice or remember all the times unusual events do not coincide. If, after we think about a friend, the friend calls us, we notice and remember this coincidence. We don't notice all the times we think of a friend without any ensuing call or receive a call from a friend about whom we've not been thinking.

Illusory correlation can help explain why clinicians continue to express confidence in uninformative or ambiguous tests. Pioneering experiments by Loren Chapman and Jean Chapman (1969) help us see why. They invited both university students and professional clinicians to study some test performances and diagnoses. If the students or clinicians *expected* a particular association, they generally *perceived* it. For example, clinicians who believed that suspicious people draw peculiar eyes on the Draw-a-Person test did, in fact, perceive such a relationship—even when shown cases in which suspicious people drew peculiar eyes *less* often than nonsuspicious people. If they believed in a connection, they were more likely to notice confirming instances.

In fairness to clinicians, illusory thinking also occurs among political analysts, historians, sportscasters, personnel directors, stockbrokers, and many other professionals, including research psychologists. As researchers, we have often been unaware of the shortcomings of our theoretical analyses. We so eagerly presume that our idea of truth is *the* truth that, no matter how hard we try, we cannot see our own errors. This is evident in the editorial review process that precedes any research publication. Over the years, we have read dozens of reviews of our own manuscripts and have been reviewers for dozens of others. Our experience is that it is far easier to spot someone else's sloppy thinking than to perceive our own.

Gambling

Compared to those given an assigned lottery number, people who chose their own number demanded four times as much money when asked if they would sell their ticket. When playing a game of chance against an awkward and nervous person, they bet significantly more than when playing against a dapper, confident opponent (Langer, 1977). Michael Wohl of Carleton University and Michael Enzle of the University of Alberta have found that being the person who throws the dice or spins the wheel increases people's confidence (Wohl & Enzle, 2002). In these and other ways, more than 50 experiments have consistently found people acting as though they could predict or control chance events (Stefan & David, 2013).

Observations of real-life gamblers confirm these experimental findings (Orgaz et al., 2013). Dice players may throw gently for low numbers and forcefully for high numbers (Henslin, 1967). The gambling industry thrives on gamblers' illusions. Gamblers attribute wins to their skill and foresight. Losses become "near misses" or "flukes"—perhaps (for the sports gambler) a bad call by the referee or a freakish bounce of the ball (Gilovich & Douglas, 1986).

Stock traders also like the "feeling of empowerment" that comes from being able to choose and control their own stock trades, as if their being in control can enable them to outperform the market average. One ad declared that online investing "is about control." Alas, the illusion of control breeds overconfidence and frequent losses after stock market trading costs are subtracted (Barber & Odean, 2001a, 2001b).

People like feeling in control and so, when experiencing a lack of control, will act to create a sense of predictability. In experiments, loss of control has led people to form illusory correlations in stock market information, to perceive nonexistent conspiracies, and to develop superstitions (Whitson & Galinsky, 2008).

regression toward the average
The statistical tendency for extreme scores or extreme behaviour to return toward the person's average.

Regression toward the average

Tversky and Kahneman (1974) noted another way by which an illusion of control may arise: when we fail to recognize the statistical phenomenon of **regression toward the average**. Because exam scores fluctuate partly by chance, most students who get extremely high scores on an exam will get lower scores on the next exam. If their first score is at the ceiling, their second score is more likely to fall back ("regress") toward their own average than to push the ceiling even higher. That is why a student who does consistently good work, even if never the best, will sometimes end a course at the top of the class. Conversely, the lowest-scoring students on the first exam are likely to improve. If those who scored lowest go for tutoring after the first exam, the tutors are likely to feel effective when the student improves, even if the tutoring had no effect.

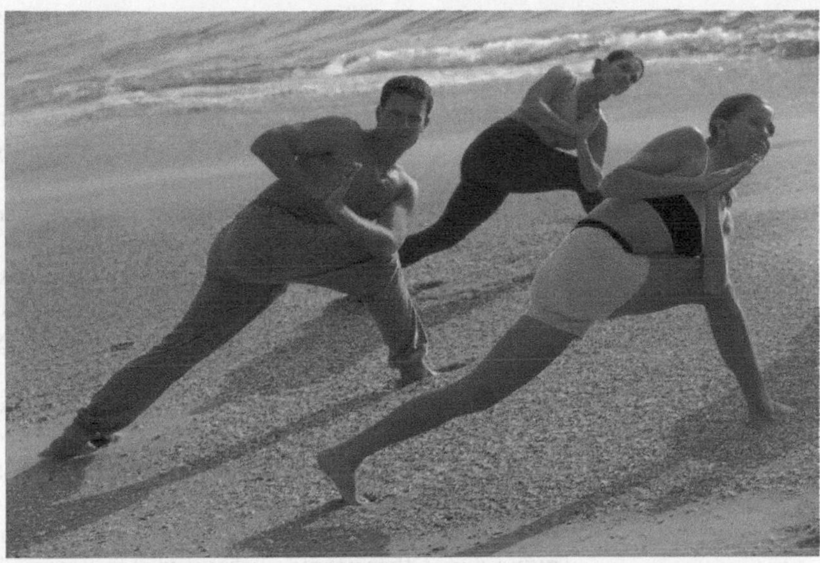

Regression toward the average: When we are at an extremely low point, anything we try, such as meditation or yoga, will usually seem effective as we return to our more usual state.

Source: ©Purestock/SuperStock.

Indeed, when things reach a low point, we will try anything, and whatever we try—going to a psychotherapist, starting a new diet-exercise plan, reading a self-help book—is more likely to be followed by improvement than by further deterioration. Sometimes we recognize that events are not likely to continue at an unusually good or bad extreme. Experience has taught us that when everything is going great, something will go wrong, and that when life is dealing us terrible blows, we can usually look forward to things getting better. Often, though, we fail to recognize this regression effect. We puzzle at why baseball's rookie-of-the-year often has a more ordinary second year: Did they become overconfident? Self-conscious? We forget that exceptional performance tends to regress toward normality.

By simulating the consequences of using praise and punishment, Paul Schaffner (1985) showed how the illusion of control might infiltrate human relations. He invited students to train an imaginary Grade 4 boy, "Harold," to come to school by 8:30 each morning. For each school day of a three-week period, a computer displayed Harold's arrival time, which was always between 8:20 and 8:40. The students would then select a response to Harold, ranging from strong praise to strong reprimand. As you might expect, they usually praised Harold when he arrived before 8:30 and reprimanded him when he arrived after 8:30. Because Schaffner had programmed the computer to display a random sequence of arrival times, Harold's arrival time tended to improve (to regress toward 8:30) after being reprimanded. For example, if Harold arrived at 8:39, he was almost sure to be reprimanded, and his randomly selected next-day arrival time was likely to be earlier than 8:39. Thus, *even though their reprimands were having no effect*, most subjects ended the experiment believing that their reprimands had been effective.

This experiment demonstrates Tversky and Kahneman's provocative conclusion: *Nature operates in such a way that we often feel punished for rewarding others and rewarded for punishing them.* In actuality, as every student of psychology knows, positive reinforcement for doing things right is usually more effective and has fewer negative side effects.

Mood and Judgment

Social judgment involves efficient information processing. It also involves our feelings: Our moods infuse our judgments. Unhappy people—especially those bereaved or depressed—tend to be more self-focused and brooding (Myers, 1993, 2000). But there is also a bright side to sadness (Forgas, 2013). A depressed mood motivates intense thinking—a search for information that makes one's environment more memorable, understandable, and controllable.

Happy people, by contrast, are more trusting, more loving, more responsive. If people are made temporarily happy by receiving a small gift while shopping, they will report, a few moments later on an unrelated survey, that their cars and TV sets are working beautifully—better, if you took their word for it, than those belonging to folks who replied after not receiving gifts.

Moods pervade our thinking. From Germans enjoying their team's World Cup soccer victory (Schwarz et al., 1987) to Australians emerging from a heartwarming movie (Forgas & Moylan, 1987), people seem good-hearted; life seems wonderful. When we are in a happy mood, the world seems friendlier, decisions are easier, and good news more readily comes to mind (DeSteno et al., 2000; Isen & Means, 1983; Stone & Glass, 1986).

Let a mood turn gloomy, however, and thoughts switch onto a different track. Now the bad mood primes our recollections of negative events (Bower, 1987; Johnson & Magaro, 1987). Our relationships seem to sour. Our self-image takes a dive. Our hopes for the future dim. Other people's behaviour seems more sinister (Brown & Taylor, 1986; Esses, 1989; Mayer & Salovey, 1987).

Joseph Forgas (2007, 2008, 2010, 2011) had often been struck by how people's "memories and judgments change with the colour of their mood." Let's say that you're put in a good or a bad mood and then watch a recording (made the day before) of you talking with someone. If made to feel happy, you feel pleased with what you see, and you are able to detect many instances of your poise, interest, and social skill. If you've been put in a bad mood, viewing the same video seems to reveal a quite different you—one who is stiff, nervous, and inarticulate (Figure 3–2). Given how your mood colours your judgments, you feel relieved at how things brighten when the experimenter switches you to a happy mood before leaving the experiment. Curiously, note Michael Ross and Garth Fletcher (1985), we don't attribute our changing perceptions to our mood shifts. Rather, the world really seems different.

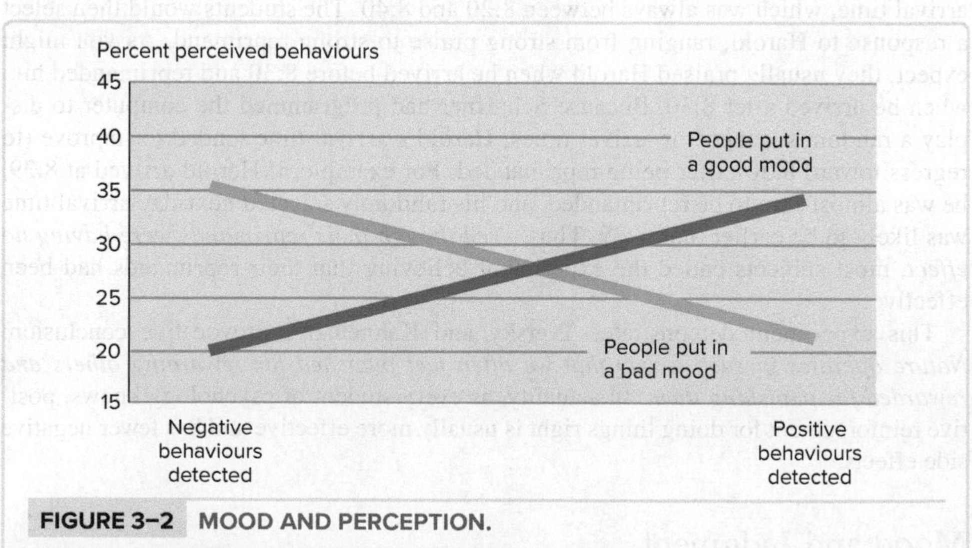

FIGURE 3–2 MOOD AND PERCEPTION.

A temporary good or bad mood strongly influenced people's ratings of their videotaped behaviour. Those in a bad mood detected far fewer positive behaviours.

THE INSIDE STORY

We all know moody people, and I have often been struck by how their feelings seem to invade their thinking. It almost appears that their memories and judgments change with the colour of their mood. For some years now, I have been trying to understand how and why this mood infusion occurs.

One day while sitting in a restaurant, I noticed an odd couple at the next table—a beautiful young woman with an unattractive elderly man. As I found myself repeatedly wondering about this relationship, it occurred to me that the more I thought about them, the more opportunity there might be for my mood to infuse my thoughts. Testing this idea in the laboratory, we found that, indeed, mood had a greater effect on complex judgments of odd couples than on snap judgments of well-matched couples. Such findings have helped us to develop a theory that predicts when moodiness will infuse judgments.

Joseph Forgas *University of New South Wales, Sydney, Australia*

Our moods colour how we see our worlds partly by bringing to mind past experiences associated with the mood. When we are in a bad mood, we have more depressing thoughts. Mood-related thoughts may distract us from complex thinking about something else. Thus, when emotionally aroused—when angry or even in a very good mood—we become more likely to make snap judgments and evaluate others based on stereotypes (Bodenhausen, Sheppard, & Kramer, 1994; Paulhus & Lim, 1994). But if our attention is explicitly drawn to our moods, we may "correct" our judgments. People in a bad mood have less flattering views of another person than do people in a happy mood, unless they first think about their moods. In that case, mood has little impact on their impressions of the other person (McFarland, White, & Newth, 2003). It seems that if we acknowledge our moods, we can keep them from biasing our judgments.

How Do We Perceive Our Social Worlds?

How do our assumptions and prejudgments guide our perceptions, interpretations, and recall?

Our preconceptions guide how we perceive and interpret information. We construe the world through belief-tinted glasses. "Sure, preconceptions matter," people agree; yet they fail to fully appreciate the impact of their own predispositions.

Let's consider some provocative experiments. The first group examines how *pre*dispositions and *pre*judgments affect how we perceive and interpret information. The second group plants a judgment in people's minds *after* they have been given information to study how after-the-fact ideas bias recall. The overarching point: *We respond not to reality as it is but to reality as we construe it.*

Perceiving and Interpreting Events

Despite some startling biases and logical flaws in how we perceive and understand one another, we're mostly accurate (Jussim, 2005). Our first impressions of one another are more often right than wrong. Moreover, the better we know people, the more accurately we can read their minds and feelings.

But, on occasion, our prejudgments *err*. The effects of prejudgments and expectations are standard fare for psychology's introductory course. Consider this phrase:

A
BIRD
IN THE
THE HAND

Did you notice anything wrong with it? There is more to perception than meets the eye.

Political perceptions

The same is true of political perceptions. Because social perceptions are very much in the eye of the beholder, even a simple stimulus may strike two people quite differently. An experiment by Robert Vallone, Lee Ross, and Mark Lepper (1985) reveals just how powerful preconceptions can be. The researchers showed pro-Israeli and pro-Arab students six network news segments describing the 1982 killing of civilian refugees at two camps in Beirut, Lebanon. As Figure 3–3 illustrates, each group perceived the networks as hostile to its side.

> ***"Once you have a belief, it influences how you perceive all other relevant information. Once you see a country as hostile, you are likely to interpret ambiguous actions on their part as signifying their hostility."***
>
> Political scientist Robert Jervis (1985)

The phenomenon is commonplace: Sports fans perceive referees as partial to the other side. Presidential candidates and their supporters nearly always view the media as unsympathetic to their cause. Saying that Justin Trudeau is "an okay prime minister" may seem like a put-down to those who admire him but praise to those who despise him.

It's not just fans and politicians. People everywhere perceive media and mediators as biased against their position. "There is no subject about which people are less objective than objectivity," noted one media commentator (Poniewozik, 2003). Indeed, people's perceptions of bias can be used to assess their attitudes (Saucier & Miller, 2003). Tell someone where you see bias, and you will signal your attitudes.

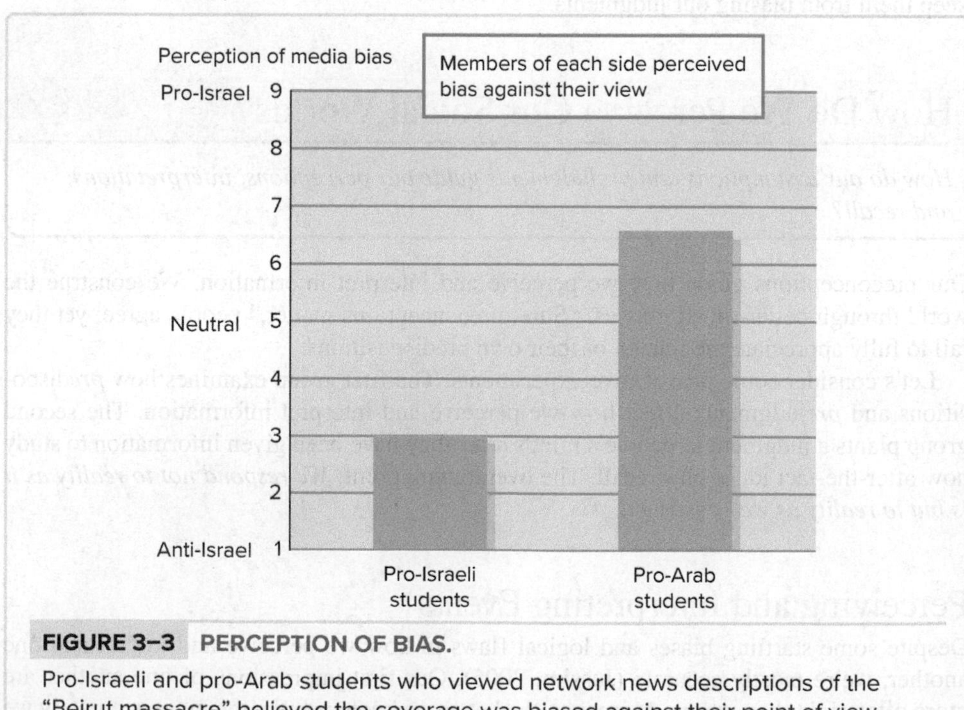

FIGURE 3–3 PERCEPTION OF BIAS.

Pro-Israeli and pro-Arab students who viewed network news descriptions of the "Beirut massacre" believed the coverage was biased against their point of view.

Is that why, in politics, religion, and science, ambiguous information often fuels conflict? When political debates have no clear-cut winner, they mostly reinforce pre-debate opinions. By nearly a 10-to-1 margin, those who already favoured one candidate over the others perceived their candidate as having won (Kinder & Sears, 1985). Not only do people think their candidate won, but they report becoming even more supportive of them after viewing a debate (Munro et al., 1997).

The bottom line: We view our social worlds through the spectacles of our beliefs, attitudes, and values. That is one reason our beliefs and schemas are so important; they shape our interpretation of everything else.

Supporters of a particular cause or candidate tend to see the media as favouring the other side.

Source: The Canadian Press/Ian Barrett.

Belief Perseverance

Imagine a babysitter who decides, during an evening with a crying infant, that bottle-feeding produces colicky babies: "Formula is obviously no substitute for breast milk." If the infant turns out to be suffering a high fever, will the sitter nevertheless persist in believing that bottle-feeding causes colic (Ross & Anderson, 1982)? To find out, Craig Anderson, Mark Lepper, and Lee Ross (1980) planted a falsehood in people's minds and then tried to discredit it.

Their research reveals that it is surprisingly difficult to demolish a falsehood, once the person conjures up a rationale for it. Each experiment first *implanted a belief*, either by proclaiming it to be true or by showing the participants some anecdotal evidence. Then the participants were asked to *explain why* it is true. Finally, the researchers totally *discredited* the initial information by telling the participants the truth: The information was manufactured for the experiment, and half the people in the experiment had received opposite information. Nevertheless, the new belief survived approximately 75 percent intact, presumably because the participants still retained their invented explanations for the belief. This phenomenon, named **belief perseverance**, shows that beliefs can take on a life of their own and survive the discrediting of the evidence that inspired them. In a time when "fake news" (false stories often designed to attract clicks and thus advertising profits or to sway opinions of politicians or politicized issues) spreads on social media (Fulgoni & Lipsman, 2017), it's especially important to understand why people continue to believe false information.

> ***"We hear and apprehend only what we already half know."***
>
> Henry David Thoreau, 1817–1862

Another example of belief perseverance: Anderson, Lepper, and Ross (1980) asked people to decide whether people who take risks make good or bad firefighters. One group considered a risk-prone person who was a successful firefighter and a cautious person who was an unsuccessful one. The other group considered cases suggesting the opposite conclusion. After forming their theory that risk-prone people make better (or worse) firefighters, the individuals wrote explanations for it—for example, that risk-prone people are brave or that cautious people have fewer accidents. After each explanation was formed, it could exist independently of the information that initially created the belief. When that information was discredited, the people still held their self-generated

belief perseverance Persistence of your initial conceptions, as when the basis for your belief is discredited but an explanation of why the belief might be true survives.

Do people who take risks make the best firefighters? Or the worst?
Source: ©Mike Kemp/age fotostock.

explanations and, therefore, continued to believe that risk-prone people really *do* make better (or worse) firefighters.

These experiments also show that the more we examine our theories and explain how they *might* be true, the more closed we become to information that challenges our belief. Once we consider why an accused person might be guilty, why someone of whom we have a negative first impression acts that way, or why a favoured stock might rise in value, our explanations may survive challenges (Davies, 1997; Jelalian & Miller, 1984).

The evidence is compelling: Our beliefs and expectations powerfully affect how we mentally construct events. Usually, we benefit from our preconceptions, just as scientists benefit from creating theories that guide them in noticing and interpreting events. But the benefits sometimes entail a cost: We become prisoners of our own thought patterns. Thus, the "canals" that were so often seen on Mars *did* turn out to be the product of intelligent life—but an intelligence on Earth's side of the telescope.

Constructing Memories of Ourselves and Our Worlds

Do you agree or disagree with this statement?

> Memory can be likened to a storage chest in the brain into which we deposit material and from which we can withdraw it later if needed. Occasionally, something is lost from the "chest," and then we say we have forgotten.

In one survey, 85 percent of university students surveyed agreed (Lamal, 1979). As one magazine ad put it, "Science has proven the accumulated experience of a lifetime is preserved perfectly in your mind."

Actually, psychological research has proven the opposite. Our memories are not exact copies of experiences that remain on deposit in a memory bank. Rather, we construct memories at the time of withdrawal. Like a paleontologist inferring the appearance of a dinosaur from bone fragments, we reconstruct our distant past by using our current feelings and expectations to combine fragments of information (Hirt, 1990; Ross & Buehler, 1994). Thus, we can easily (though unconsciously) revise our memories to suit our current knowledge. When one of the authors' sons complained, "The June issue of *Cricket* never came" and was then shown where it was, he delightedly responded, "Oh good, I knew I'd gotten it."

When an experimenter or a therapist manipulates people's presumptions about their past, a sizable fraction will construct false memories. Asked to vividly imagine a childhood time when they ran, tripped, fell, and stuck their hand through a window, or a time when they knocked over a punch bowl at a wedding, about one-fourth will later recall the fictitious event as something that actually happened (Loftus & Bernstein, 2005). In its search for truth, the mind sometimes constructs a falsehood.

> ***"Memory isn't like reading a book: it's more like writing a book from fragmentary notes."***
>
> John F. Kihlstrom, 1994

In experiments involving more than 20 000 people, Elizabeth Loftus (2003, 2007, 2011a) and her collaborators explored our mind's tendency to construct memories. In the typical experiment, people witness an event, receive misleading information about it (or not), and then take a memory test. The results find a **misinformation effect** in which people incorporate the misinformation into their memories: They recall a yield sign as a stop sign, hammers as screwdrivers, *Vogue* magazine as *Mademoiselle,* Dr. Henderson as "Dr. Davidson," breakfast cereal as eggs, and a clean-shaven man as having a moustache. Suggested misinformation may even produce false memories of supposed child sexual abuse, argued Loftus.

misinformation effect Incorporating "misinformation" into one's memory of an event, after witnessing an event and then receiving misleading information about it.

This process affects our recall of social as well as physical events. Jack Croxton and colleagues (1984) had students spend 15 minutes talking with someone. The students who were later informed that this person reported liking them recalled the person's behaviour as relaxed, comfortable, and happy. Those informed that the person disliked them recalled the person as nervous, uncomfortable, and not so happy.

It is troubling to realize that false memories feel and look like real memories. Thus, they can be as persuasive as real memories—convincingly sincere, yet sincerely wrong. This is true of young children (who are especially susceptible to misinformation) as well as adults. Stephen Ceci and Maggie Bruck (1993a, 1993b) demonstrated children's suggestibility by asking children, once a week for 10 weeks, to "Think real hard, and tell me if this ever happened to you." For example, "Can you remember going to the hospital with the mousetrap on your finger?" Remarkably, when then interviewed by a new adult who asked the same question, 58 percent of preschoolers produced false and often detailed stories about the fictitious event. One boy explained that his brother had pushed him into a basement woodpile, where his finger got stuck in the trap: "And then we went to the hospital, and my mommy, daddy, and Colin drove me there, to the hospital in our van, because it was far away. And the doctor put a bandage on this finger."

Given such vivid stories, professional psychologists were often fooled. They could not reliably separate real from false memories; neither could the children. Told the incident never actually happened, some protested: "But it really did happen. I remember it!" For Bruck and Ceci (1999, 2004), such findings raise the possibility of false accusations, as in alleged child sex abuse cases where children's memories may have been contaminated by repeated suggestive questioning and where there is no corroborating evidence. Given suggestive interview questions, Bruck and Ceci reported, most preschoolers and many older children will produce false reports, such as of having seen a thief steal food in their daycare centre.

Even among university students, imagining childhood events, such as breaking a window with their hand or having a nurse remove a skin sample, led one-fourth to recall that the imagined event had actually happened (Garry et al., 1996; Mazzoni & Memon, 2003). This "imagination inflation" happens partly because visualizing something activates similar areas in the brain as does actually experiencing it (Gonsalves et al., 2004).

Misinformation-induced false memories provide one explanation for a worrying phenomenon: *false confessions* (Kassin et al., 2010; Lassiter, 2010; Loftus, 1974, 1979a, 1979b, 2003). Among 250 closely studied cases in which DNA evidence cleared wrongfully convicted people, 40 involved false confessions (Garrett, 2011). Many of these were *compliant confessions*—people who confessed when worn down and often sleep-deprived ("If you will just tell us you accidentally rather than deliberately set the fire, you can go home"). Others were *internalized confessions*—ones apparently believed after people were fed misinformation.

Reconstructing past attitudes

Five years ago, how did you feel about nuclear power? About Canada's prime minister? About your parents? If your attitudes have changed, how much have they changed?

Experimenters have explored such questions, and the results have been unnerving. People whose attitudes have changed often insist that they have always felt much as they now feel (Wolfe & Williams, 2018). University students in one study answered a long survey that included a question about student control over the university curriculum. A week later, they agreed to write an essay opposing student control. After doing so, their attitudes shifted toward greater opposition to student control. When asked to recall how they had answered the question before writing the essay, they "remembered" holding the opinion that they *now* held and denied that the experiment had affected them (Bem & McConnell, 1970).

"Travel is glamorous only in retrospect."

Paul Theroux, in *The Observer*

After observing students similarly denying their former attitudes, researchers D. R. Wixon and James Laird (1976) commented, "The speed, magnitude, and certainty" with which the students revised their own histories "was striking." As George Vaillant (1977, p. 197) noted after following adults through time, "It is all too common for caterpillars to become butterflies and then to maintain that in their youth they had been little butterflies. Maturation makes liars of us all."

The construction of positive memories brightens our recollections. Terence Mitchell, Leigh Thompson, and colleagues (1994, 1997) report that people often exhibit *rosy retrospection*—they recall mildly pleasant events more favourably than they experienced them. University students on a three-week bike trip, older adults on a guided tour of Austria, and undergraduates on vacation all reported enjoying their experiences as they were having them. But they later recalled such experiences even more fondly, minimizing the unpleasant or boring aspects and remembering the high points. With any positive experience, some of the pleasure resides in the anticipation, some in the actual experience, and some in the rosy retrospection.

Cathy McFarland and Michael Ross (1985) found that as our relationships change, we also revise our recollections of other people. They had university students rate their steady dating partners. Two months later, they rated them again. Students who were more in love than ever had a tendency to recall love at first sight. Those who had broken up were more likely to recall having recognized the partner as somewhat selfish and bad-tempered.

Diane Holmberg and John Holmes (1994) discovered the same phenomenon among 373 newlywed couples, most of whom reported being very happy. When resurveyed two years later, those whose marriages had soured recalled that things had always been bad. The results are "frightening," said Holmberg and Holmes: "Such biases can lead to a dangerous downward spiral. The worse your current view of your partner is, the worse your memories are, which only further confirms your negative attitudes."

Fight now, and you might falsely recall that your relationship was never that happy.
Source: ©Tetra Images/Getty Images.

It's not that we are totally unaware of how we used to feel, just that when memories are hazy, current feelings guide our recall. When widowed people try to recall the grief they felt upon their spouse's death five years earlier, their current emotional state colours their memories (Safer et al., 2001). When patients recall their previous day's headache pain, their current feelings sway their recollections (Eich et al., 1985). Depressed people who get Botox—which prevents them from frowning—recover from depression more quickly, perhaps because they find it more difficult to remember why they were sad (Lewis & Bowler, 2009).

> ***"A man should never be ashamed to own that he has been in the wrong, which is but saying, in other words, that he is wiser today than he was yesterday."***
>
> Jonathan Swift, *Thoughts on Various Subjects,* 1711

Reconstructing past behaviour

Memory construction enables us to revise our own histories. In one study, University of Waterloo students read a message about the benefits of toothbrushing. Later, in a supposedly different experiment, these students recalled brushing their teeth more often during the preceding two weeks than did students who had not heard the message (Ross et al., 1981). Likewise, projecting from surveys, people report smoking many fewer cigarettes than are actually sold (Hall, 1985). And they recall casting more votes than are actually recorded (Census Bureau, 1993).

Social psychologist Anthony Greenwald (1980) noted the similarity of such findings to happenings in George Orwell's novel *1984,* in which it was "necessary to remember that events happened in the desired manner." Indeed, argued Greenwald, we all have "totalitarian egos" that revise the past to suit our present views. Thus, we underreport bad behaviour and overreport good behaviour.

> ***"Vanity plays lurid tricks with our memory."***
>
> Novelist Joseph Conrad, 1857–1924

Sometimes, our present view is that we've improved—in which case we may misrecall our past as more unlike the present than it actually was. This tendency resolves a puzzling pair of consistent findings: Those who participate in psychotherapy and self-improvement programs for weight control, anti-smoking, and exercise show only modest improvement on average. Yet they often claim considerable benefit. Michael Conway and Michael Ross (1986) explain why: Having expended so much time, effort, and money on self-improvement, people may think, "I may not be perfect now, but I was worse before; this did me a lot of good."

Unlike photos, memories get reconstructed when withdrawn from the memory bank.
Source: ©PeopleImages/DigitalVision/Getty Images.

How Do We Explain Our Social Worlds?

How–and how accurately–do we explain others' behaviour?

People make it their business to explain other people, and social psychologists make it their business to explain people's explanations.

Our judgments of people depend on how we explain their behaviour. Depending on our explanation, we may judge killing as murder, manslaughter, self-defence, or heroism. Depending on our explanation, we may view a homeless person as lacking initiative or as victimized by job and social assistance cutbacks. Depending on our explanation, we may attribute someone's friendly behaviour as genuine warmth or as ingratiation. Attribution theory helps us make sense of how this explanation works.

Attributing Causality: To the Person or the Situation?

We endlessly analyze and discuss why things happen as they do, especially when we experience something negative or unexpected (Weiner, 1985, 2008, 2010). If worker productivity declines, do we assume the workers are getting lazier? Or has their workplace become less efficient? Does a young boy who hits his classmates have a hostile personality? Or is he responding to relentless teasing?

Researchers found that married people often analyze their partners' behaviours, especially their negative behaviours. Cold hostility is more likely than a warm hug to leave the partner wondering, "Why?" (Holtzworth-Munroe & Jacobson, 1985; Holtzworth & Jacobson, 1988). Spouses' answers correlate with their marriage satisfaction. Unhappy couples usually offer internal explanations for negative acts ("She was late because she doesn't care about me"). Happy couples more often externalize ("She was late because of heavy traffic"). Explanations for positive acts similarly work either to maintain distress ("He brought me flowers because he wants sex") or to enhance the relationship ("He brought me flowers to show he loves me") (Hewstone & Fincham, 1996; McNulty, O'Mara, & Karney, 2008; Weiner, 1995).

Antonia Abbey (1987, 1991, 2011) and her colleagues repeatedly found that men are more likely than women to attribute a woman's friendliness to mild sexual interest. Men's misreading of women's warmth as a sexual come-on—an example of **misattribution**—can lead to behaviour that women regard as sexual harassment or even to rape (Farris et al., 2008; Kolivas & Gross, 2007; Pryor et al., 1997). Many men believe women are flattered by repeated requests for dates, which women more often view as harassment (Rotundo, Nguyen, & Sackett, 2001).

misattribution Mistakenly attributing a behaviour to the wrong cause.

Misattribution is especially likely when men are in positions of power. A male manager may misinterpret a subordinate woman's submissive or friendly behaviour and, full of himself, may see the woman only in sexual terms (Bargh & Raymond, 1995). Men think about sex more often than women do. Men also are more likely than women to assume that others share their feelings. Thus, a man with sex on his mind may greatly overestimate the sexual significance of a woman's courteous smile (Levesque, Nave, & Lowe, 2006; Nelson & LeBoeuf, 2002). Misattributions help explain why, in one national survey, 23 percent of American women said they had been forced into unwanted sexual behaviour, but only 3 percent of American men said they had ever forced a woman into a sexual act (Laumann et al., 1994).

Notably, men's tendency to overestimate women's sexual interest wanes in long-term relationships. Amy Muise, of York University, and colleagues (2016) find that men in ongoing, intimate relationships err in the opposite direction: They *underestimate* their

To what should we attribute this student's sleepiness? Lack of sleep? Boredom? Whether we make internal or external attributions depends on whether we notice her consistently sleeping in this and other classes, and whether other students react as she does to this particular class.

Source: ©Wavebreakmedia/Shutterstock.

partners' sexual interest. Such underestimation, moreover, benefits their relationships because it prevents them from becoming complacent about attracting their partners' interest. Partners of men who underestimate their sexual interest are more satisfied and committed to their relationships.

Attribution theory analyzes how we explain people's behaviour and what we infer from it (Gilbert & Malone, 1995). We sometimes attribute people's behaviour to *internal* causes (for example, the person's disposition) or *external* causes (for example, something about the person's situation). A teacher may wonder whether a child's underachievement is due to lack of motivation and ability (a **dispositional attribution**) or to physical and social circumstances (a **situational attribution**). Some people are more inclined to attribute behaviour to stable personality; others tend to attribute behaviour to situations (Bastian & Haslam, 2006; Robins et al., 2004).

attribution theory The theory of how people explain the behaviour of others—for example, by attributing it either to internal dispositions (enduring traits, motives, and attitudes) or to external situations.

dispositional attribution Attributing behaviour to the person's disposition and traits.

situational attribution Attributing behaviour to the environment.

spontaneous trait inference An effortless, automatic inference of a trait after exposure to someone's behaviour.

Inferring traits

We often infer that other people's actions are indicative of their intentions and dispositions (Jones & Davis, 1965). If I observe Mason making a sarcastic comment to Ashley, I infer that Mason is a hostile person. When are people more likely to infer that others' behaviour is caused by traits? For one thing, normal or expected behaviour tells us less about the person than does behaviour that is unusual for that situation. If Samantha is sarcastic in a job interview, where a person would normally be pleasant, this tells us more about Samantha than if she is sarcastic with her siblings.

The ease with which we infer traits—a phenomenon called **spontaneous trait inference**—is remarkable. In experiments at New York University, James Uleman (1989) gave students statements to remember, such as "The librarian carries the old woman's groceries across the street." The students would instantly, unintentionally, and unconsciously infer a trait. When later they were helped to recall the sentence, the most valuable clue word was not "books" (to cue "librarian") or "bags" (to cue "groceries") but "helpful"—the inferred trait that we suspect you, too, spontaneously attributed to the librarian. Exposure for just one-tenth of a second to someone's face leads people to spontaneously infer some personality traits (Willis & Todorov, 2006).

The Fundamental Attribution Error

Social psychology's most important lesson concerns the influence of our social environment. At any moment, our internal state and, therefore, what we say and do depends on the situation, as well as on what we bring to the situation. In experiments, a slight difference between two situations sometimes greatly affects how people respond. As professors, we have seen this when teaching classes at both 8:30 a.m. and 7:00 p.m. Silent stares greet us at 8:30 a.m.; at 7:00 p.m., one of the authors had to break up a party. In each situation, some individuals are more talkative than others, but the difference between the two situations exceeds the individual differences.

Attribution researchers have found that we often fail to appreciate this important lesson. When explaining someone's behaviour, we underestimate the impact of the situation and overestimate the extent to which it reflects the individual's traits and attitudes. Thus, even knowing the effect of the time of day on classroom conversation, we have found it terribly tempting to assume that the people in the 7:00 p.m. class are more extroverted than the "silent types" who attend class at 8:30 a.m. Likewise, we may infer that people fall because they're clumsy rather than because they were tripped, that people smile because they're happy rather than because they're faking friendliness, and that people speed past us on the highway because they're aggressive rather than late for an important meeting.

fundamental attribution error The tendency for observers to underestimate situational influences and overestimate dispositional influences on others' behaviour; also called correspondence bias because we so often see behaviour as corresponding to a disposition.

This discounting of the situation, called the **fundamental attribution error** (Ross, 1977), appears in many experiments. In the first such study, Edward Jones and Victor Harris (1967) had students read debaters' speeches supporting or attacking Cuba's leader, Fidel Castro. When the position taken was said to have been chosen by the debater, the students logically enough assumed it reflected the person's own attitude. But what happened when the students were told that the debate coach had assigned the position? Students still inferred that the debater had the assigned leanings (Figure 3–4).

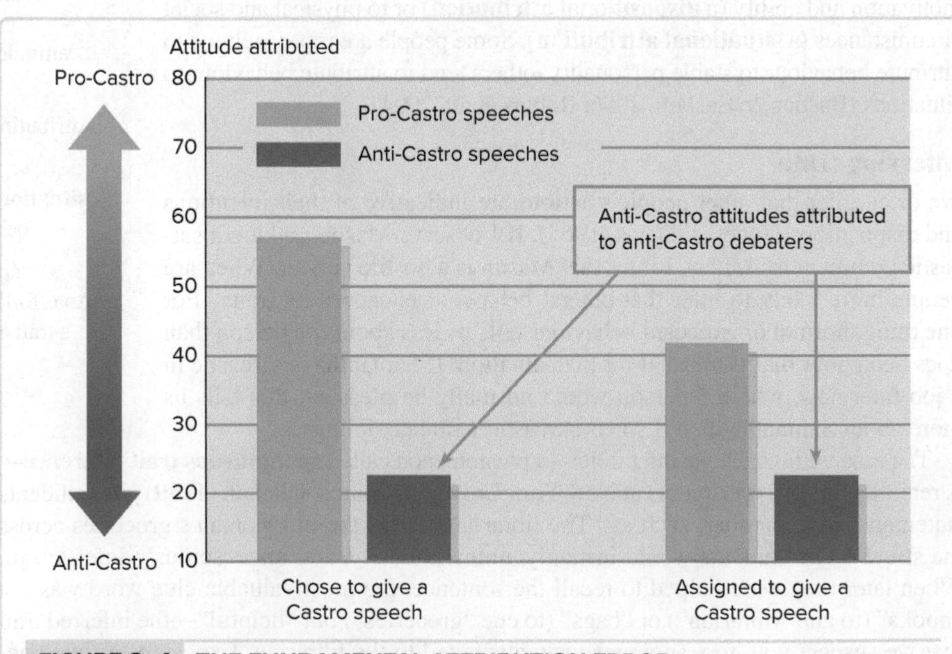

FIGURE 3–4 THE FUNDAMENTAL ATTRIBUTION ERROR.
When people read a debate speech supporting or attacking Fidel Castro, they attributed corresponding attitudes to the speech writer, even when the debate coach assigned the writer's position.

People seemed to think, "Yeah, I know he was assigned that position, but, you know, I think he really believes it."

Even when people know they are *causing* someone else's behaviour, they still underestimate external influences. If individuals dictate an opinion that someone else must then express, they still tend to see the person as actually holding that opinion (Gilbert & Jones, 1986). If people are asked to be either self-enhancing or self-deprecating during an interview, they are very aware of why they are acting so. But they are *unaware* of their effect on another person. If Juan acts modestly, his conversation partner Ethan is likely to exhibit modesty as well. Juan will easily understand his own behaviour, but he will think that poor Ethan suffers from low self-esteem (Baumeister et al., 1988). In short, we tend to presume that others *are* the way they act—even when we don't make the same presumption about ourselves. Observing Cinderella cowering in her oppressive home, people (ignoring the situation) infer that she is meek; dancing with her at the ball, the prince sees a suave and glamorous person. Cinderella knows that she is the same person in both situations.

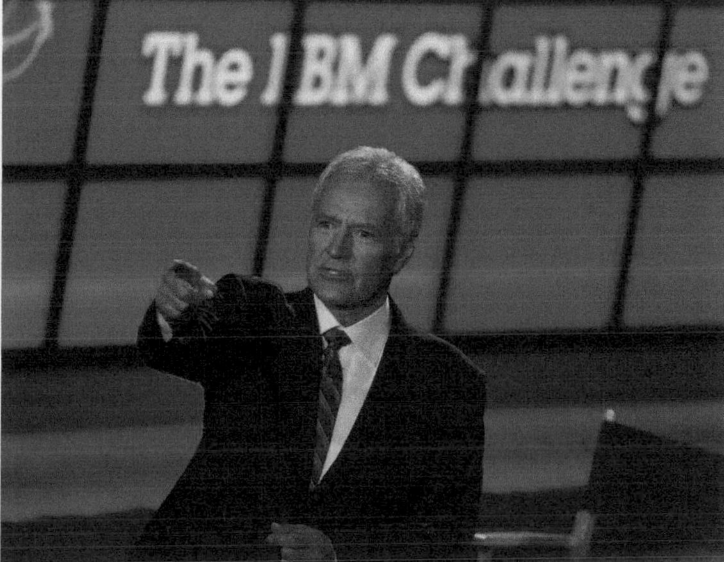

People often attribute keen intelligence to those, such as teachers and quiz show hosts, who test others' knowledge.

Source: ©Ben Hider/Stringer/Getty Images.

One experiment recreated Lee Ross's first-hand experience of moving from graduate student to professor. His doctoral oral exam had proven to be a humbling experience as his apparently brilliant professors quizzed him on topics they specialized in. Six months later, *Dr.* Ross was himself an examiner, now able to ask penetrating questions on *his* favourite topics. Ross's hapless student later confessed to feeling exactly as Ross had a half-year before—dissatisfied with his ignorance and impressed with the apparent brilliance of the examiners.

In an experiment mimicking his student-to-professor experience, Ross set up a simulated quiz game. He randomly assigned some students to play the role of questioner, some to play the role of contestant, and others to observe. The researchers invited the questioners to make up difficult questions that would demonstrate their wealth of knowledge. Any one of us can imagine such questions, using our own domain of competence: "Where are the clearest waters for scuba diving in Canada?" "What is the seventh book in the Old Testament?" "Which has the longer coastline, Europe or Africa?" If even these few questions have you feeling a little uninformed, then you will appreciate the results of this experiment (Ross et al., 1977).*

Everyone had to know that the questioner would have the advantage. Yet both contestants and observers (but not the questioners) came to the erroneous conclusion that the questioners really were more knowledgeable than the contestants (Figure 3–5). Follow-up research shows that these misimpressions are hardly a reflection of low social intelligence. If anything, university students and other intelligent and socially competent people are *more* likely to make the attribution error (Bauman & Skitka, 2010; Block & Funder, 1986).

In real life, those with social power usually initiate and control conversations, and this often leads underlings to overestimate their knowledge and intelligence (Jouffre & Croizet, 2016). Medical doctors, for example, are often presumed to be experts on all sorts of questions unrelated to medicine. Similarly, students often overestimate the brilliance of their teachers. (As in the experiment, teachers are questioners on subjects of their special expertise.) When some of these students later become teachers, they are usually amazed to discover that teachers are not so brilliant after all.

*Tobermory, Ontario, has the clearest waters in Canada. The seventh Old Testament book is Judges. Although the African continent is more than double the area of Europe, Europe's coastline is longer. (It is more convoluted, with lots of harbours and inlets, a geographical fact that contributed to its role in the history of maritime trade.)

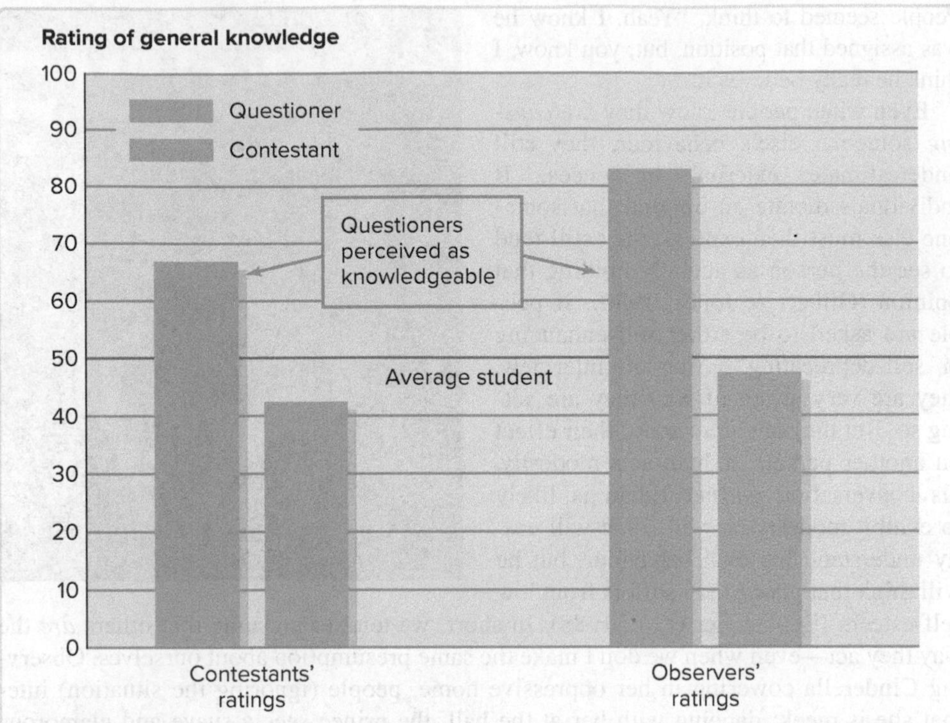

FIGURE 3–5 MISPERCEPTIONS AND THE FUNDAMENTAL ATTRIBUTION ERROR. Both contestants and observers of a simulated quiz game assumed that a person who had been randomly assigned the role of questioner was far more knowledgeable than the contestant. Actually, the assigned roles of questioner and contestant simply made the questioner seem more knowledgeable. The failure to appreciate this illustrates the fundamental attribution error.

To illustrate the fundamental attribution error, most of us need look no further than our own experiences. Determined to make some new friends, Nicole plasters a smile on her face and anxiously plunges into a party. Everyone else seems quite relaxed and happy as they laugh and talk with one another. Nicole wonders to herself, "Why is everyone always so at ease in groups like this while I'm feeling shy and tense?" Actually, everyone else is feeling nervous, too, and making the same attribution error in assuming that Nicole and the others are as they *appear*—that is, confidently convivial.

Why Do We Make the Attribution Error?

So far, we have seen a bias in the way we explain other people's behaviour: We often ignore powerful situational determinants. Why do we tend to underestimate the situational determinants of others' behaviour but not of our own?

Perspective and situational awareness

An actor–observer difference

Attribution theorists point out that we observe others from a different perspective than we observe ourselves (Jones & Nisbett, 1971; Jones, 1976). When we act, the *environment* commands our attention. When we watch another person act, that *person* occupies the centre of our attention and the situation becomes relatively invisible. If I'm mad, it's the situation that's making me angry. But someone else getting mad may seem like an ill-tempered person.

From his analysis of 173 studies, Bertram Malle (2006) concluded that the actor–observer difference is often minimal. When our action feels intentional and admirable, we attribute it to our own good reasons, not to the situation. It's only when we behave badly that we're more likely to attribute our behaviour to the situation. Meanwhile, someone observing us may spontaneously infer a trait.

When people viewed a video of a suspect confessing during a police interview, with the camera focused on the suspect, they perceived the confession as genuine. If the camera was instead focused on the detective, they perceived it as more coerced (Lassiter & Irvine, 1986; Lassiter et al., 2005, 2007). The camera perspective influenced people's guilt judgments even when the judge instructed them not to allow it to happen (Lassiter et al., 2002).

In courtrooms, most confession videos focus on the confessor. As we might expect, noted Daniel Lassiter and Kimberly Dudley (1991), such videos yield a nearly 100 percent conviction rate when played by prosecutors. Aware of Lassiter's research on the *camera perspective bias*, New Zealand has made it a national policy that police interrogations be filmed with equal focus on the officer and the suspect.

The passage of time decreases the tendency toward the fundamental attribution error. A week after hearing someone argue a position that they did not choose, people were more likely to credit the situation (Burger & Palmer, 1991). The day after a major election, Jerry Burger and Julie Pavelich (1994) asked voters why the election turned out the way it did. Most attributed the outcome to the candidates' personal traits and positions. When they asked other voters the same question a year later, only one-third attributed the verdict to the candidates. More people now credited the circumstances, such as the country's good mood and robust economy.

Consider this: Are you generally quiet or talkative, or does it depend on the situation? "Depends on the situation" is a common answer. Likewise, when asked to predict their feelings two weeks after receiving grades or learning the outcome of their country's national election, people expect the situation to rule their emotions; they underestimate the importance of their own sunny or dour dispositions (Quoidbach & Dunn, 2010). But when asked to describe a friend—or to describe what they themselves were like five years ago—people more often ascribed trait descriptions. *When recalling our past, we become like observers of someone else* (Pronin & Ross, 2006). For most of us, the "old you" is someone other than today's "real you." We regard our distant past selves (and our distant future selves) almost as if they were other people occupying our body.

All these experiments point to a reason for the attribution error: *We find causes where we look for them.* To see this in your own experience, consider this: Would you say your social psychology instructor is a quiet or a talkative person?

You may have guessed that they are fairly outgoing. But consider: Your attention focuses on your instructor while they behave in a public context that demands speaking. The instructor, on the other hand, observes their own behaviour in many different situations—in the classroom, in meetings, at home. "Me, talkative?" your instructor might say. "Well, it all depends on the situation. When I'm in class or with good friends, I'm rather outgoing. But at conferences and in unfamiliar situations, I'm rather shy." Because we are acutely aware of how our behaviour varies with the situation, we see ourselves as more variable than other people (Baxter & Goldberg, 1987; Kammer, 1982; Sande, Goethals, & Radloff, 1988). "Nigel is uptight; Fiona is relaxed. With me, it varies."

Cultural differences

Cultures also influence attribution errors (Ickes, 1980; Watson, 1982). A Western worldview predisposes people to assume that people, not situations, cause events. Internal explanations are more socially approved (Jellison & Green, 1981). "You can do it!" we are assured by the pop psychology of positive-thinking Western culture. You get what you deserve and deserve what you get.

Activity: How Do We Assess People's Traits?

This demonstration was adapted from work by Richard Nisbett. For each of the following 10 pairs of traits, circle the one trait in each pair that is most characteristic of Jon Stewart, formerly of *The Daily Show*. (Actually, you can use any celebrity you wish if you object to Jon Stewart.) If neither of the traits in a trait pair is the most characteristic, indicate that by circling "depends on the situation."

serious	fun-loving	depends on the situation
subjective	analytic	depends on the situation
future oriented	present oriented	depends on the situation
energetic	relaxed	depends on the situation
unassuming	self-asserting	depends on the situation
lenient	firm	depends on the situation
reserved	emotionally expressive	depends on the situation
dignified	casual	depends on the situation
realistic	idealistic	depends on the situation
intense	calm	depends on the situation

Go back and complete the same responses for you. Now, go back and count the number of times you circled "depends on the situation" for Jon Stewart, and how many times you circled it for you. Are you more willing to ascribe traits to Jon Stewart than to yourself? Were you more likely to circle "depends on the situation"? If so, why? If so, it is probably because, as the actor, you are better able to see the external factors that influence your behaviour than you are able to see them for a celebrity.

Source: Myers/Smith, *Exploring Social Psychology, Fourth Canadian Edition*, p. 78.

The fundamental attribution error: People are biased to assume that people's behaviour corresponds to their inner dispositions. Such assumptions are sometimes, but not always, correct. Some weekend bikers are weekday professionals.

Source: The Globe and Mail-John Lehmann/The Canadian Press.

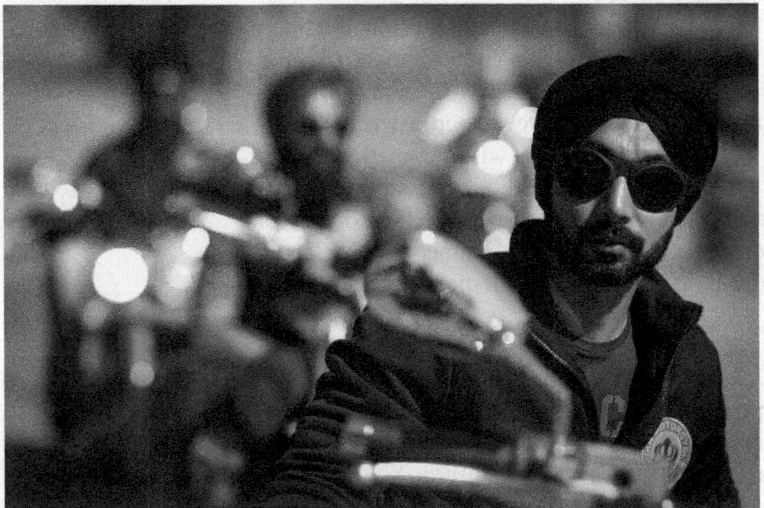

As Western children grow up, they learn to explain behaviour in terms of others' personal characteristics (Rholes, Newman, & Ruble, 1990). As a Grade 1 student, one of the authors' sons brought home an example. He unscrambled the words "gate the sleeve caught Tom on his" into "The gate caught Tom on his sleeve." His teacher, applying the Western cultural assumptions of the curriculum materials, marked that wrong. The "right" answer located the cause within Tom: "Tom caught his sleeve on the gate."

The fundamental attribution error occurs across varied cultures (Krull et al., 1999). Yet people in Eastern Asian cultures are somewhat more sensitive to the importance of situations. Thus, when aware of the social context, they are less inclined to assume that others' behaviour corresponds to their traits (Choi, Nisbett, & Norenzayan, 1999; Farwell & Weiner, 2000; Masuda & Kitayama, 2004).

Some languages promote external attributions. Instead of "I was late," Spanish idiom allows one to say, "The clock caused me to be late." In collectivist cultures, people less often perceive others in terms of personal dispositions (Lee, Hallahan, & Herzog, 1996; Zebrowitz-McArthur, 1988). They are also less likely to spontaneously interpret a behaviour as reflecting an inner trait (Newman, 1993). When told of someone's actions, Hindus in India are less likely than Americans to offer dispositional explanations ("She is kind") and more likely to offer situational explanations ("Her friends were with her") (Miller, 1984).

The fundamental attribution error is *fundamental* because it colours our explanations in basic and important ways. Researchers in Britain, India, Australia, and the United States have found, for example, that people's attributions predict their attitudes toward the poor and unemployed (Feather, 1983; Furnham, 1982; Pandey et al., 1982; Wagstaff, 1983; Weiner, Osborne, & Rudolph, 2011). Those who attribute poverty and unemployment to personal dispositions ("They're just lazy and undeserving") tend to adopt political positions unsympathetic to such people (Figure 3–6). This *dispositional attribution* ascribes behaviour to the person's dispositions and traits. Those who make *situational attributions* ("If you or I were to live with the same overcrowding, poor education, and discrimination, would we be any better off?") tend to adopt political positions that offer more direct support to the poor. Tell me your attributions for poverty and I will guess your politics.

> ***"Most poor people are not lazy. . . . They catch the early bus. . . . They raise other people's children. . . . They clean the streets. No, no, they're not lazy."***
>
> The Reverend Jesse Jackson, address to the Democratic National Convention, July 1988

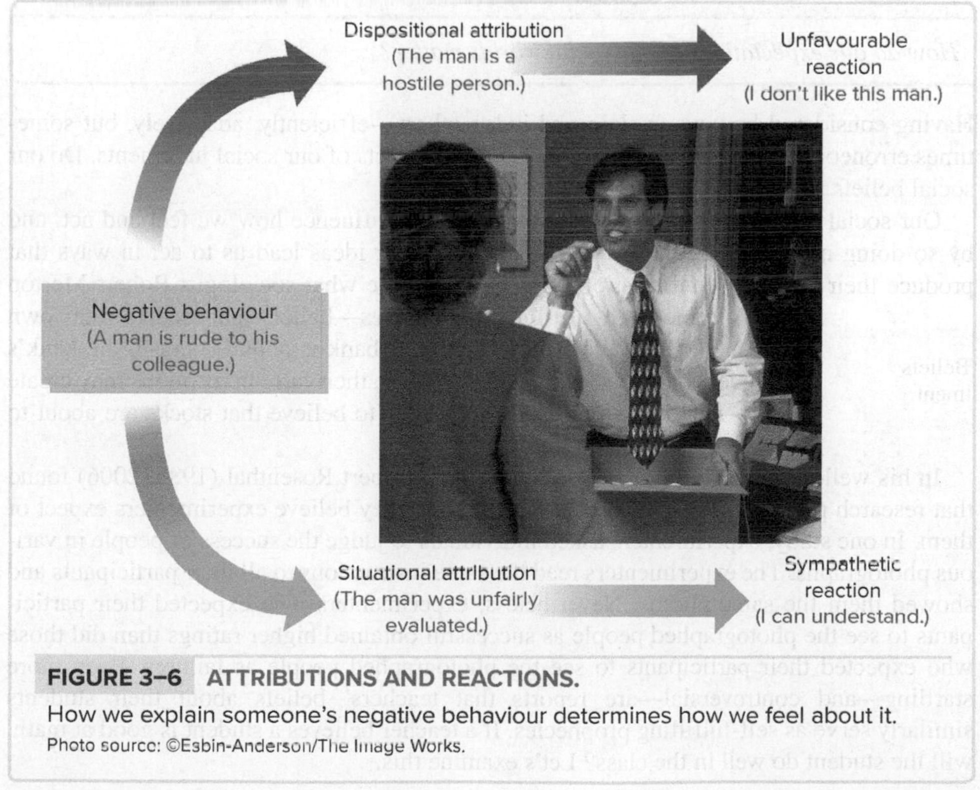

FIGURE 3–6 ATTRIBUTIONS AND REACTIONS.

How we explain someone's negative behaviour determines how we feel about it.

Photo source: ©Esbin-Anderson/The Image Works.

Why Do We Study Attribution Errors?

This chapter, like the one before, explains some foibles and fallacies in our social thinking. Reading these may make it seem, as one of our students put it, that "social psychologists get their kicks out of playing tricks on people." Actually, the experiments, though sometimes amusing, are not designed to demonstrate "what fools these mortals be." Their serious purpose is to reveal how we think about ourselves and others.

If our capacity for illusion and self-deception is shocking, remember that our modes of thought are generally adaptive. Illusory thinking is often a by-product of our mind's strategies for simplifying complex information. It parallels our perceptual mechanisms, which generally give us a useful image of the world but sometimes lead us astray.

A second reason for focusing on biases such as the fundamental attribution error is humanitarian. One of social psychology's "great humanizing messages," noted Thomas Gilovich and Richard Eibach (2001), is that people should not always be blamed for their problems: "More often than people are willing to acknowledge, failure, disability, and misfortune are . . . the product of real environmental causes" (p. 26).

A third reason for focusing on the biases is that we are mostly unaware of them and can benefit from greater awareness. As with other biases, such as the self-serving bias (Chapter 2), people see themselves as less susceptible than others to attribution errors (Pronin, Gilovich, & Ross, 2004). Our hunch is that you will find more surprises, more challenges, and more benefit in an analysis of errors and biases than you would in a string of testimonies to the human capacity for logic and intellectual achievement. That is also why world literature so often portrays pride and other human failings. Social psychology aims to expose us to fallacies in our thinking in the hope that we will become more rational, more in touch with reality. and more receptive to critical thinking.

How Do Our Social Beliefs Matter?

How do our expectations of our social worlds matter?

Having considered how we explain and judge others—efficiently, adaptively, but sometimes erroneously—we conclude by pondering the effects of our social judgments. Do our social beliefs matter? Can they change reality?

Our social beliefs and judgments do matter. They influence how we feel and act, and by so doing may generate their own reality. When our ideas lead us to act in ways that produce their apparent confirmation, they have become what sociologist Robert Merton (1948) termed **self-fulfilling prophecies**—beliefs that lead to their own fulfillment. If, led to believe that their bank is about to crash, the bank's customers race to withdraw their money, their false perceptions may create reality, noted Merton. If people are led to believe that stocks are about to soar, they will indeed soar.

self-fulfilling prophecies Beliefs that lead to their own fulfillment.

In his well-known studies of *experimenter bias*, Robert Rosenthal (1985, 2006) found that research participants sometimes live up to what they believe experimenters expect of them. In one study, experimenters asked individuals to judge the success of people in various photographs. The experimenters read the same instructions to all their participants and showed them the same photos. Nevertheless, experimenters who expected their participants to see the photographed people as successful obtained higher ratings than did those who expected their participants to see the photographed people as failures. Even more startling—and controversial—are reports that teachers' beliefs about their students similarly serve as self-fulfilling prophecies. If a teacher believes a student is good at math, will the student do well in the class? Let's examine this.

Teacher Expectations and Student Performance

Teachers do have higher expectations for some students than for others. Perhaps you have detected this yourself after having a brother or sister precede you in school, after receiving a label such as "gifted" or "learning disabled," or after taking "honours" classes. Or perhaps your new teacher scrutinized your school file or discovered your family's social status. It's clear that teachers' evaluations *correlate* with student achievement: Teachers think well of students who do well. That's mostly because teachers accurately perceive their students' abilities and achievements. "About 75 percent of the correlation between teacher expectations and student future achievement reflects accuracy," report Lee Jussim, Stacy Robustelli, and Thomas Cain (2009).

But are teachers' evaluations ever a *cause* as well as a consequence of student performance? One correlational study of 4300 British schoolchildren suggested yes: Students whose teachers expected them to perform well indeed performed well (Crano & Mellon, 1978). Not only is high performance followed by higher teacher evaluations, but the reverse is true as well—teachers' judgments predicted students' later performance even beyond their actual ability (Sorhagen, 2013).

Could we test this "teacher-expectations effect" experimentally? Imagine we gave a teacher the impression that Dana, Marisa, Todd, and Jamal—four randomly selected students—are unusually capable. Will the teacher give special treatment to these four and elicit superior performance from them? In a now-famous experiment, Rosenthal and Lenore Jacobson (1968) reported precisely that. Randomly selected children in an elementary school who were said (on the basis of a fictitious test) to be on the verge of a dramatic intellectual spurt did then spurt ahead in IQ score.

> ***"To judge a teacher or professor's overall warmth and enthusiasm also takes but a thin slice of behaviour—mere seconds."***
>
> Ambady & Rosenthal, 1992, 1993

That dramatic result seemed to suggest that the school problems of "disadvantaged" children might reflect their teachers' low expectations. The findings were soon publicized in the media as well as in many university textbooks in psychology and education. However, further analysis—which was not as highly publicized—revealed the teacher-expectations effect to be not so powerful and reliable as this initial study had led many people to believe (Jussim et al., 2009; Spitz, 1999). By Rosenthal's own count, in only about 40 percent of the nearly 500 published experiments did expectations significantly affect performance (Rosenthal, 1991, 2002). Low expectations do not doom a capable child, nor do high expectations magically transform a slow learner into a valedictorian. Human nature is not so pliable.

High expectations do, however, seem to boost low achievers, for whom a teacher's positive attitude may be a hope-giving breath of fresh air (Madon, Jussim, & Eccles, 1997). How are such expectations transmitted? Rosenthal and other investigators reported that teachers look, smile, and nod more at "high-potential students." Teachers also may teach more to their "gifted" students, set higher goals for them, call on them more, and give them more time to answer (Cooper, 1983; Harris & Rosenthal, 1985, 1986; Jussim, 1986).

In one study, teachers were videotaped talking to, or about, unseen students for whom they held high or low expectations. A random 10-second clip of either the teacher's voice or the teacher's face was enough to tell viewers—both children and adults—whether this was a good or poor student and how much the teacher liked the student. (You read that right: 10 seconds.) Although teachers may think they can conceal their feelings, students are acutely sensitive to teachers' facial expressions and body movements (Figure 3–7).

What about the effect of *students'* expectations on their teachers? You, no doubt, begin many of your courses having heard "Professor Smith is interesting" and "Professor Jones is a bore." Robert Feldman and Thomas Prohaska (1979; Feldman & Theiss, 1982) found that such expectations can affect both student and teacher. Students in a learning

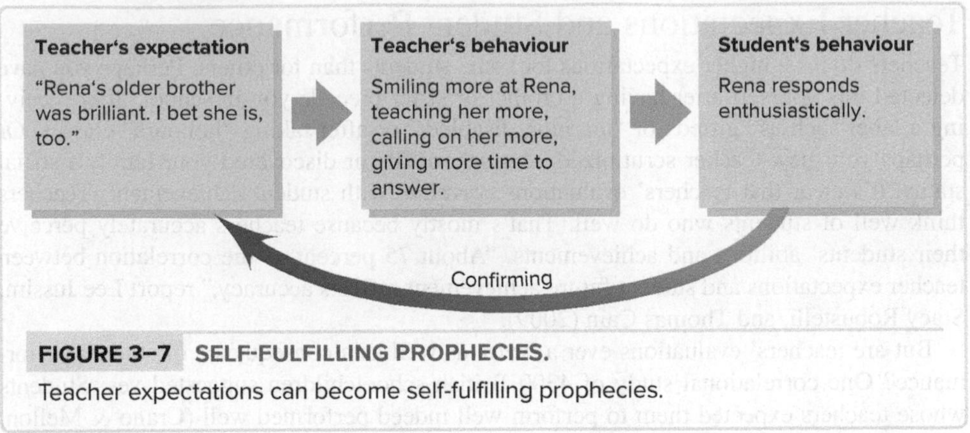
Teacher's expectation
"Rena's older brother was brilliant. I bet she is, too."
Teacher's behaviour
Smiling more at Rena, teaching her more, calling on her more, giving more time to answer.
Student's behaviour
Rena responds enthusiastically.
Confirming

FIGURE 3–7 SELF-FULFILLING PROPHECIES.
Teacher expectations can become self-fulfilling prophecies.

experiment who expected to be taught by a competent teacher perceived their teacher (who was unaware of their expectations) as more competent and interesting than did students with low expectations. Furthermore, the students actually learned more. In a later experiment, women who were led to expect their male instructor to be sexist had a less positive experience with him, performed worse, and rated him as less competent than did women not given the expectation of sexism (Adams et al., 2006).

Were these results due entirely to the students' perceptions or also to a self-fulfilling prophecy that affected the teacher? In a follow-up experiment, Feldman and Prohaska videotaped teachers and had observers rate their performances. Teachers were judged most capable when assigned a student who nonverbally conveyed positive expectations.

To see whether such effects might also occur in actual classrooms, a research team led by David Jamieson (Jamieson et al., 1987) experimented with four Ontario high school classes taught by a newly transferred teacher. During individual interviews, researchers told students in two of the classes that both other students and the research team rated the teacher very highly. Compared to the control classes, whose expectations they did not raise, the students given positive expectations paid better attention during class. At the end of the teaching unit, they also got better grades and rated the teacher as clearer in her teaching. The attitudes that a class has toward its teacher are as important, it seems, as the teacher's attitude toward the students.

Getting From Others What We Expect

So, the expectations of experimenters and teachers, though usually reasonably accurate assessments, occasionally act as self-fulfilling prophecies. Overall, our perceptions of others are more accurate than biased (Jussim, 2012). Self-fulfilling prophecies have "less than extraordinary power." Yet, sometimes, self-fulfilling prophecies do operate in work settings (with managers who have high or low expectations), in courtrooms (as judges instruct juries), and in simulated police contexts (as interrogators with expectations of guilt or innocence interrogate and pressure suspects) (Kassin, Goldstein, & Savitsky, 2003; Rosenthal, 2003). Teens whose parents thought they had tried marijuana—even though they hadn't—were more likely to subsequently try it (Lamb & Crano, 2014).

Do self-fulfilling prophecies colour our personal relationships? There are times when negative expectations of someone lead us to be extra nice to that person, which induces them to be nice in return—thus *disconfirming* our expectations. But a more common finding in studies of social interaction is that, yes, we do to some extent get what we expect (Olson, Roese, & Zanna, 1996).

In laboratory games, hostility nearly always begets hostility: People who perceive their opponents as noncooperative will readily induce them to be noncooperative (Kelley &

What we believe about someone can lead us to treat the person in ways that create a self-fulfilling prophecy. Consider this in the context of Internet dating and email exchanges with strangers.
Source: ©Wavebreak Media LTD/123RF.

Stahelski, 1970). Each party's perception of the other as aggressive, resentful, and vindictive induces the other to display these behaviours in self-defence, thus creating a vicious self-perpetuating circle. In another experiment, people anticipated interacting with another person of a different race. When led to expect that the person disliked interacting with someone of their race, they felt more anger and displayed more hostility toward the person (Butz & Plant, 2006). Likewise, whether someone expects her partner to be in a bad mood or in a warm, loving mood may affect how she relates to her partner, thereby inducing the partner to confirm her belief.

So do intimate relationships prosper when partners idealize each other? Are positive illusions of the other's virtues self-fulfilling? Or are they more often self-defeating, by creating expectations that can't be met? Among University of Waterloo dating couples followed by Sandra Murray and associates (1996a, 2000), positive ideals of one's partner were good omens. Idealization helped buffer conflict, bolster satisfaction, and turn self-perceived frogs into princes or princesses. When someone loves and admires us, it helps us become more the person our admirer imagines us to be.

When dating couples deal with conflicts, hopeful optimists and their partners tend to perceive each other as engaging constructively. Compared to those with more pessimistic expectations, they then feel more supported and more satisfied with the outcome (Srivastava et al., 2006). Among married couples, too, those who worry that their partner doesn't love and accept them interpret slight hurts as rejections, which motivate them to devalue the partner and distance themselves. Those who presume their partner's love and acceptance respond less defensively, read less into stressful events, and treat the partner better (Murray et al., 2003). Love helps create its presumed reality.

Several experiments conducted by Mark Snyder (1984) show how, once formed, erroneous beliefs about the social world can induce others to confirm those beliefs, a phenomenon called **behavioural confirmation**. In a classic study, Snyder, Elizabeth Tanke, and Ellen Berscheid (1977) had male students talk on the telephone with women they thought (from having been shown a picture) were either attractive or unattractive. Analysis of just the women's comments during the conversations revealed that the supposedly attractive women spoke more warmly than the supposedly unattractive women. The men's erroneous beliefs had become a self-fulfilling prophecy by leading

behavioural confirmation A type of self-fulfilling prophecy whereby people's social expectations lead them to act in ways that cause others to confirm their expectations.

them to act in a way that influenced the women to fulfill their stereotype that beautiful people are desirable people.

Behavioural confirmation also occurs as people interact with partners holding mistaken beliefs. People who are believed to be lonely behave less sociably (Rotenberg, Gruman, & Ariganello, 2002). People who believe they are accepted and liked (rather than disliked) then behave warmly—and do get accepted and liked (Stinson et al., 2009). Men who are believed to be sexist behave less favourably toward women (Pinel, 2002). Job interviewees who are believed to be warm behave more warmly.

Imagine yourself as one of the 60 young men or 60 young women in an experiment by Robert Ridge and Jeffrey Reber (2002). Each man is to interview one of the women to assess her suitability for a teaching assistant position. Before doing so, he is told either that she feels attracted to him (based on his answers to a biographical questionnaire) or not attracted to him. (Imagine being told that someone you were about to meet reported considerable interest in getting to know you and in dating you, or had no interest whatsoever.) The result was behavioural confirmation: Applicants believed to feel an attraction exhibited more flirtatiousness (and without being aware of doing so). Ridge and Reber believe this process, like the misattribution phenomenon discussed previously, may be one of the roots of sexual harassment. If a man thinks a woman's behaviour seems to confirm the man's beliefs, he may then escalate his overtures until they become sufficiently overt for the woman to recognize and interpret them as inappropriate or harassing.

Expectations influence children's behaviour, too. After observing the amount of litter in three classrooms, Richard Miller and his colleagues (1975) had the teacher and others repeatedly tell one class that they should be neat and tidy. This persuasion increased the amount of litter placed in wastebaskets from 15 percent to 45 percent, but only temporarily. Another class, which also had been placing only 15 percent of its litter in wastebaskets, was repeatedly congratulated for being so neat and tidy. After eight days of hearing this, and still two weeks later, these children were fulfilling the expectation by putting more than 80 percent of their litter in wastebaskets. Tell children they are hard-working and kind (rather than lazy and mean), and they may live up to their labels.

Overall, these experiments help us understand how social beliefs, such as stereotypes about people with disabilities or about people of a particular race or sex, may be self-confirming. How others treat us reflects how we and others have treated them.

What Can We Conclude About Social Beliefs and Judgments?

How can we view human nature through cognitive social psychology?

Social cognition studies reveal that our information-processing powers are impressive for their efficiency and adaptiveness ("in apprehension how like a god!" exclaimed Shakespeare's Hamlet). Yet we are also vulnerable to predictable errors and misjudgments ("headpiece filled with straw," said T. S. Eliot). What practical lessons, and what insights into human nature, can we take home from all of this research?

We have reviewed reasons why people sometimes form false beliefs. We cannot easily dismiss these experiments: Most of the participants were intelligent people, mostly students at leading universities. Moreover, people's intelligence scores are uncorrelated with their vulnerability to many different thinking biases (Stanovich & West, 2008). One can be very smart and exhibit seriously bad judgment.

Trying hard also doesn't eliminate biased thinking. These predictable distortions and biases occur even when payment for right answers motivates people to think optimally.

Research in cognitive social psychology thus mirrors the mixed review given humanity in literature, philosophy, and religion. Many research psychologists have spent lifetimes exploring the awesome capacities of the human mind. We are smart enough to have cracked our own genetic code, to have invented talking computers, and to have sent people to the moon. Three cheers for human reason.

Well, two cheers—because the mind's premium on efficient judgment makes our intuition more vulnerable to misjudgment than we suspect. With remarkable ease, we form and sustain false beliefs. Led by our preconceptions, overconfident, persuaded by vivid anecdotes, perceiving correlations and control even where none may exist, we construct our social beliefs and then influence others to confirm them.

But have these experiments just been intellectual tricks played on hapless participants, thus making them look worse than they are? Richard Nisbett and Lee Ross (1980) contended that, if anything, laboratory procedures overestimate our intuitive powers. The experiments usually present people with clear evidence and warn them that their reasoning ability is being tested. Seldom does life say to us, "Here is some evidence. Now put on your intellectual Sunday best and answer these questions."

> ***"In creating these problems we didn't set out to fool people. All our problems fooled us, too."***
>
> Amos Tversky (1985)

Often, our everyday failings are inconsequential, but not always. False impressions, interpretations, and beliefs can produce serious consequences. Even small biases can have profound social effects when we are making important social judgments: Why are so many people homeless? Unhappy? Homicidal? Does my friend love me or my money? Cognitive biases even creep into sophisticated scientific thinking. Apparently, human nature has not changed in the 3000 years since the Old Testament psalmist noted that "no one can see his own errors."

Is this too cynical? Leonard Martin and Ralph Erber (2005) invited us to imagine that an intelligent being swooped down just for a moment and begged for information that would help it understand the human species. When you hand it this social psychology text, the alien says, "Thank you," and zooms back off into space. After (we'd like to presume) resolving your remorse over giving up this book, how would you feel about having offered social psychology's analysis? Joachim Krueger and David Funder (2003a, 2003b) wouldn't feel too good. Social psychology's preoccupation with human foibles needs balancing with "a more positive view of human nature," they argue.

Fellow social psychologist Lee Jussim (2005) agreed, adding, "Despite the oft-demonstrated existence of a slew of logical flaws and systematic biases in lay judgment and social perception, such as the fundamental attribution error, false consensus, over-reliance on imperfect heuristics, self-serving biases, etc., people's perceptions of one another are surprisingly (though rarely perfectly) accurate." The elegant analyses of the imperfections of our thinking are themselves a tribute to human wisdom. Were one to argue that all human thought is illusory, the assertion would be self-refuting, for it, too, would be but an illusion. It would be logically equivalent to contending, "All generalizations are false, including this one."

Just as medicine assumes that any given body organ serves a function, so behavioural scientists find it useful to assume that our modes of thought and behaviour are adaptive (Funder, 1987; Kruglanski & Ajzen, 1983; Swann, 1984). The rules of thought that produce false beliefs and striking deficiencies in our statistical intuition usually serve us well. Frequently, the errors are a by-product of our mental shortcuts that simplify the complex information we receive.

Nobel laureate psychologist Herbert Simon (1957) was among the modern researchers who first described the bounds of human reason. Simon contended that to cope with reality, we simplify it. Consider the complexity of a chess game: The number of possible games is greater than the number of particles in the universe. How do we cope? We adopt some simplifying rules of thumb: heuristics. These heuristics sometimes lead us to defeat. But they do enable us to make efficient snap judgments.

Illusory thinking can likewise spring from useful heuristics that aid our survival. In many ways, as mentioned earlier in the chapter, heuristics make us smart (Gigerenzer & Gaissmaier, 2011). The belief in our power to control events helps maintain hope and effort. If things are sometimes subject to control and sometimes not, we maximize our outcomes by positive thinking. Optimism pays dividends. We might even say that our beliefs are like scientific theories—sometimes in error yet useful as generalizations. As Susan Fiske (1992) said, "Thinking is for doing."

Might we reduce errors in our social thinking? In school, math teachers teach, teach, teach until the mind is finally trained to process numerical information accurately and automatically. We assume that such ability does not come naturally; otherwise, why bother with the years of training? Research psychologist Robyn Dawes (1980b)—who was dismayed that "study after study has shown [that] people have very limited abilities to process information on a conscious level, particularly social information"—suggested that we should also teach, teach, teach how to process social information.

Richard Nisbett and Lee Ross (1980) believed that education could, indeed, reduce our vulnerability to certain types of error. They offered the following recommendations:

- Train people to recognize likely sources of error in their own social intuition.
- Set up statistics courses geared to everyday problems of logic and social judgment. Given such training, people do, in fact, reason better about everyday events (Lehman, Lempert, & Nisbett, 1988; Nisbett et al., 1987).
- Make such teaching more effective by richly illustrating it with concrete, vivid anecdotes and examples from everyday life.
- Teach memorable and useful slogans, such as, "It's an empirical question. Where did the sample come from?" or "You can lie with statistics, but a well-chosen example does the job better."

SUMMING UP

How Do We Judge Our Social Worlds, Consciously and Unconsciously?

- We have an enormous capacity for automatic, efficient, intuitive thinking (*System 1*). Our cognitive efficiency, though generally adaptive, comes at the price of occasional error. Since we are generally unaware of those errors entering our thinking, it is useful to identify ways in which we form and sustain false beliefs.
- Our preconceptions strongly influence how we interpret and remember events. In a phenomenon called *priming,* people's prejudgments have striking effects on how they perceive and interpret information.
- We often overestimate our judgments. This *overconfidence phenomenon* stems partly from the much greater ease with which we can imagine why we might be right than why we might be wrong. Moreover, people are much more likely to search for information that can confirm their beliefs than information that can disconfirm them.
- When given compelling anecdotes or even useless information, we often ignore useful base-rate information. This is partly due to the later ease of recall of vivid information (the *availability heuristic*).
- We are often swayed by illusions of correlation and personal control. It is tempting to perceive correlations where none exist (*illusory correlation*) and to think we can predict or control chance events.

- Moods infuse judgments. Good and bad moods trigger memories of experiences associated with those moods. Moods colour our interpretation of current experiences. And, by distracting us, moods can also influence how deeply or superficially we think when making judgments.

How Do We Perceive Our Social Worlds?

- Experiments have planted judgments or false ideas in people's minds *after* they have been given information. These experiments reveal that as *before-the-fact judgments* bias our perceptions and interpretations, so, too, *after-the-fact judgments* bias our recall.
- *Belief perseverance* is the phenomenon in which people cling to their initial beliefs and the reasons why a belief might be true, even when the basis for the belief is discredited.
- Far from being a repository for facts about the past, our memories are actually formed when we retrieve them; they are subject to strong influence by the attitudes and feelings we hold at the time of retrieval.

How Do We Explain Our Social Worlds?

- *Attribution theory* involves how we explain people's behaviour. Misattribution—attributing a behaviour to the wrong source—is a major factor in sexual harassment, as a person in power (typically male) interprets friendliness as a sexual come-on.
- Although we usually make reasonable attributions, we often commit the *fundamental attribution error* when explaining other people's behaviour. We attribute their behaviour so much to their inner traits and attitudes that we discount situational constraints, even when those are obvious. We make this attribution error partly because when we watch someone act, that *person* is the focus of our attention and the situation is relatively invisible. When *we* act, our attention is usually on what we are reacting to—the situation is more visible.

How Do Our Social Beliefs Matter?

- Our beliefs sometimes take on a life of their own. Usually, our beliefs about others have a basis in reality. But studies of experimenter bias and teacher expectations show that an erroneous belief that certain people are unusually capable (or incapable) can lead teachers and researchers to give those people special treatment. This may elicit superior (or inferior) performance and, therefore, seem to confirm an assumption that is actually false.
- Similarly, in everyday life, we often get *behavioural confirmation* of what we expect. Told that someone we are about to meet is intelligent and attractive, we may come away impressed with just how intelligent and attractive that person is.

What Can We Conclude About Social Beliefs and Judgments?

- Research on social beliefs and judgments reveals how we form and sustain beliefs that usually serve us well but sometimes lead us astray. A balanced social psychology will appreciate both the powers and perils of social thinking.

Key Terms

attribution theory
automatic processing
availability heuristic
behavioural confirmation
belief perseverance
confirmation bias
controlled processing
counterfactual thinking
dispositional attribution
embodied cognition
fundamental attribution error
heuristics
illusory correlation
misattribution
misinformation effect
overconfidence phenomenon
priming
regression toward the average
representativeness heuristic
self-fulfilling prophecies
situational attribution
spontaneous trait inference
System 1
System 2

CHAPTER 4

Behaviour and Attitudes

Source: The Canadian Press/Jonathan Hayward.

CHAPTER OUTLINE

How Well Do Our Attitudes Predict Our Behaviours?

When Does Our Behaviour Affect Our Attitudes?

Why Does Our Behaviour Affect Our Attitudes?

Latisha is active and health conscious. She enjoys rock climbing, cycling, and Ultimate Frisbee, and she recently ran a half-marathon. She eats well and takes good care of her body with one exception: She smokes. Latisha started smoking when she was 14 and has tried to quit several times. She quit once for almost two years but returned to smoking when hanging out with a group of friends who smoked.

How are we to understand Latisha's behaviour (i.e., smoking) and her attitudes (i.e., being health conscious)? What is the relationship between what we *are* (on the inside) and what we *do* (on the outside)? Philosophers, theologians, and educators have long speculated about the connections between attitude and action, character and conduct, private word and public deed. Underlying most teaching, counselling, and child-rearing is an assumption: Our private beliefs and feelings determine our public behaviour, so if we wish to change behaviour we must first change hearts and minds.

In the beginning, social psychologists agreed: To know people's attitudes is to predict their actions. As demonstrated by genocidal killers and suicide bombers, extreme attitudes can produce extreme behaviour. Countries whose people detest another country's leaders are more likely to produce terrorist acts against them (Krueger & Malečková, 2009). Hateful attitudes spawn violent behaviour.

But Leon Festinger (1957) concluded that the evidence showed that *changing* people's attitudes hardly affects their behaviour. Festinger believed the attitude–behaviour relation works the other way around. As Robert Abelson (1972) put it, we are "very well trained and very good at finding reasons for what we do, but not very good at doing what we find reasons for." This chapter explores the interplay between attitudes and behaviour.

attitude A favourable or unfavourable evaluative reaction toward something or someone, exhibited in one's beliefs, feelings, or intended behaviour.

When social psychologists talk about someone's attitude, they refer to beliefs and feelings related to a person or an event and the resulting behaviour tendency. Taken together, favourable or unfavourable evaluative reactions toward something—often rooted in beliefs and exhibited in feelings and inclinations to act—define a person's **attitude** (Olson & Zanna, 1993). Thus, a person may have a negative attitude toward coffee, a neutral attitude toward cats, and a positive attitude toward the next-door neighbour. Attitudes efficiently size up the world. When we have to respond quickly to something, how we feel about it can guide how we react (Bassili & Roy, 1998; Breckler & Wiggins, 1989; Sanbonmatsu & Fazio, 1990). For example, a person who believes that a particular ethnic group is lazy and aggressive may feel dislike for such people and, therefore, tend to act in a discriminatory manner. You can remember these three dimensions as the ABCs of attitudes: *a*ffect (feelings), *b*ehaviour tendency, and *c*ognition (thoughts).

How Well Do Our Attitudes Predict Our Behaviours?

To what extent, and under what conditions, do attitudes drive our outward actions? Why were social psychologists at first surprised by a seemingly small connection between attitudes and actions?

Are We All Hypocrites?

A blow to the supposed power of attitudes came when social psychologist Allan Wicker (1969) reviewed several dozen research studies covering a wide variety of people, attitudes, and behaviours, and offered a shocking conclusion: People's expressed attitudes hardly predicted their varying behaviours.

"The ancestor of every action is a thought."

Ralph Waldo Emerson, *Essays, First Series,* 1841

- Student attitudes toward cheating bore little relation to the likelihood of them actually cheating.
- Attitudes toward the Church were only modestly linked with church attendance on any given Sunday.
- Self-described racial attitudes provided little clue to behaviours in actual situations. Many people *say* they would be upset with someone making racist remarks; yet, when they hear racism (such as someone using the *N*-word), they respond indifferently (Kawakami et al., 2009).

An example of the disjuncture between attitudes and actions is what Daniel Batson and his colleagues (1997, 2001, 2002; Valdesolo & DeSteno, 2007, 2008) called "moral hypocrisy" (appearing moral without being so). Their studies presented people with an appealing task (where the participant could earn raffle tickets toward a $30 prize) and a dull task with no rewards. The participants had to assign themselves to one of the tasks and a supposed second participant to the other. Only one in 20 believed that assigning the positive task to themselves was the most moral thing to do, yet 80 percent did so. In follow-up experiments on moral hypocrisy, participants could toss a coin to assign roles—privately, if they wished. Even if they chose to use a coin toss, 90 percent assigned themselves to the positive task! Was this because they could specify the consequences of heads and tails after the coin toss? In yet another experiment, Batson put a sticker on each side of the coin, indicating what the flip outcome would signify. Still, 24 of 28 people who made the toss assigned themselves to the positive task. When morality and greed were put on a collision course, greed won. People are particularly likely to behave in an unethical manner if their identity is publicly threatened (see Zhou et al., 2019).

If people don't do what they say they would do, it's little wonder that attempts to change behaviour by changing attitudes often fail. Warnings about the dangers of smoking only minimally affect those who already smoke. Increasing public awareness of the desensitizing and brutalizing effects of a prolonged diet of television violence has stimulated many people to voice a desire for less violent programming—yet they still watch such programming as much as ever. Sex education programs have often influenced attitudes toward abstinence and condom use without affecting long-term abstinence and condom-use behaviours. It seems, at base, that we are all hypocrites.

> ***"It may be desirable to abandon the attitude concept."***
>
> Allan Wicker, 1971

All in all, the developing picture of what controls behaviour emphasized external social influences, such as others' behaviour and expectations, and played down internal factors, such as attitudes and personality. The surprising finding that what people say often differs from what they do sent social psychologists scurrying to find out why.

When Attitudes Predict Behaviour

The reason—now obvious—why our behaviour and our expressed attitudes differ is that both are subject to other influences. One social psychologist counted 40 separate factors that complicate their relationship (Triandis, 1982; see also Kraus, 1995). Our attitudes do predict our behaviour when social and other influences on what we say and do are minimal, when the attitude is specific to the behaviour, and when the attitude is potent (that is, strong and on our mind).

When social influences on what we say are minimal

Unlike a physician measuring heart rate, social psychologists never get a direct reading on attitudes. Rather, we typically measure expressed attitudes. Like other behaviours, expressions are subject to outside influences. This was vividly demonstrated when politicians once overwhelmingly passed a salary increase for themselves in an off-the-record vote, then moments later overwhelmingly defeated the same bill on a roll-call vote. Fear of criticism had distorted the true sentiment on the roll-call vote. We sometimes say what we think others want to hear.

Today's social psychologists have some clever means at their disposal for minimizing social influences on people's attitude reports. Some of these complement traditional self-report measures of *explicit* (conscious) attitudes with measures of *implicit* (unconscious) attitudes. One such test measures facial muscle responses to various statements (Cacioppo & Petty, 1981). Such measurements, the researchers hope, can reveal enough of a microsmile or a microfrown to indicate the participant's attitude about a given statement.

Implicit Association Test (IAT) A computer-driven assessment of implicit attitudes that uses reaction times to measure people's automatic associations between attitude objects and evaluative words, where easier pairings (and faster responses) are taken to indicate stronger unconscious associations.

A widely used attitude measure, the **Implicit Association Test (IAT)**, uses reaction times to measure how quickly people associate concepts (Greenwald et al., 2002; Greenwald, Nosek, & Banaji, 2003). One can, for example, measure implicit racial attitudes by assessing whether White people take longer to associate positive words with Black faces as compared with White faces. Implicit attitude researchers have offered various IAT assessments online (projectimplicit.net), and report that approximately 5 million completed tests since 1998 have shown the following:

- *Implicit biases are pervasive.* For example, 80 percent of people show more implicit negativity toward the elderly compared with the young.
- *People differ in implicit bias.* Depending on their group memberships, their conscious attitudes, and the bias in their immediate environment, some people exhibit more implicit bias than others.
- *People are often unaware of their implicit biases.* Despite thinking themselves unprejudiced, even the researchers exhibit some implicit biases (negative associations with various social groups).
- *Implicit biases can harm.* Implicit biases toward Indigenous people in Canada can lead to their not receiving necessary life-saving health care (Wylie & McConkey, 2019).

Do implicit biases predict behaviour? A review of the available research reveals that both explicit (self-report) and implicit attitudes do help predict people's behaviours and judgments (Greenwald et al., 2008; Nosek, Hawkins, & Frazier, 2011). Implicit attitudes can predict a wide range of behaviours, including people's exercise behaviour (Forrest et al., 2016), voting choices (e.g., Friese et al., 2016), and the age at which adolescents begin to drink alcohol (Payne, Brown-Iannuzzi, et al., 2016; Payne, Lee, et al., 2016).

In one study, managers received job applications that were matched on credential strength, but on one of those applications, the applicant's photos were digitally altered to make the person appear obese. Several months later, when 153 of the managers completed an IAT, their automatic anti-obesity bias score predicted which applicants they had invited for interviews (Agerström & Rooth, 2011).

Further, evidence has been found that explicit and implicit attitudes may *together* predict behaviour better than either would alone (Spence & Townsend, 2007). The behaviour predictions range from dental flossing to the fate of romantic relationships to suicide attempts to helmet use (Lee, Rogge, & Reis, 2010; Millar, 2011; Nock et al., 2010; Ledesma et al., 2015).

For attitudes formed early in life—such as racial and gender attitudes—implicit and explicit attitudes frequently diverge, with implicit attitudes often being the better predictor of behaviour. For example, implicit racial attitudes have successfully predicted interracial roommate relationships (Towles-Schwen & Fazio, 2006). For other attitudes, such as those related to consumer behaviour and support for political candidates, explicit self-reports are the better predictor.

Recent neuroscience studies have identified brain centres that produce our automatic, implicit reactions (Stanley, Phelps, & Banaji, 2008). One area deep in the brain (the amygdala, a centre for threat perception) is active as we automatically evaluate social stimuli. For example, White people who show strong unconscious racial bias on the IAT also exhibit high amygdala activation when viewing unfamiliar Black faces. Other frontal lobe areas are involved in detecting and regulating implicit attitudes.

A word of caution: Despite much excitement over these studies of implicit attitudes hiding in the mind's basement, the Implicit Association Test has detractors (Arkes & Tetlock, 2004; Blanton et al., 2007, 2009). They note that, unlike an aptitude test, the IAT is not reliable enough for use in assessing and comparing individuals. Moreover, a score that suggests some relative bias doesn't distinguish a positive bias for one group (or greater familiarity with one group) from a negative bias against another. The critics also wonder whether compassion and guilt rather than latent hostility might slow one's speed in associating Black people with positive words. Regardless, the existence of distinct explicit and implicit attitudes confirms one of twenty-first-century psychology's biggest lessons: our "dual processing" capacity for both *controlled* (deliberate, conscious, explicit) and *automatic* (effortless, habitual, implicit) thinking.

When other influences on behaviour are minimal

On any occasion, it's not only our inner attitudes that guide us but also the situation we face. As Chapter 5, Chapter 6, and Chapter 7 will illustrate again and again, social influences can be huge—enormous enough to induce people to violate their deepest convictions. Government aides may go along with actions they know are wrong. Prisoners of war may lie to placate their captors.

So, would averaging our behaviour on many occasions enable us to detect more clearly the impact of our attitudes? Predicting people's behaviour is like predicting a baseball or cricket player's hitting. The outcome of any particular time at bat is nearly impossible to predict because it is affected not only by the batter but also by what the pitcher throws and by chance factors. When we aggregate many times at bat, we neutralize these complicating factors. Knowing the players, we can predict their approximate batting averages.

> ***"Do I contradict myself? Very well then I contradict myself. (I am large, I contain multitudes.)"***
>
> Walt Whitman, *Song of Myself,* 1855

To use a research example, people's general attitude toward religion poorly predicts whether they will go to worship next weekend (because the weather, the preacher, how they are feeling, and so forth also influence attendance). But religious attitudes predict quite well the total quantity of religious behaviours over time (Fishbein & Ajzen, 1974; Kahle & Berman, 1979). The findings define a *principle of aggregation:* The effects of an attitude on behaviour become more apparent when we look at a person's aggregate or average behaviour rather than at isolated acts.

When attitudes specific to behaviour are examined

Other conditions further improve the predictive accuracy of attitudes. As Icek Ajzen and Martin Fishbein (1977; Ajzen, 1982) point out, when the measured attitude is a general one—say, an attitude toward Asians—and the behaviour is very specific—say, a decision whether to help a particular Asian couple—we should not expect a close correspondence between words and actions. Indeed, reported Fishbein and Ajzen, in 26 out of 27 such research studies, attitudes did not predict behaviour. But attitudes *did* predict behaviour in all 26 studies they could find in which the measured attitude was directly pertinent to the situation. Thus, attitudes toward the general concept of "health fitness" poorly predict specific exercise and dietary practices, but an individual's attitudes about the costs and benefits of jogging are a fairly strong predictor of whether that person jogs regularly.

Better yet for predicting behaviour, said Ajzen in his and Fishbein's *Theory of Reasoned Action,* is knowing people's *intended* behaviours and *subjective norms* (in other words, what we think other people think about our behaviour). Later Ajzen added the concept of perceived self-efficacy and control (Figure 4–1) which further validated the theory (and changed the name to the *Theory of Planned Behaviour*). Moreover, four dozen experimental tests confirm that inducing new intentions induces new behaviour (Webb & Sheeran, 2006). Even simply asking people about their intentions to engage in a behaviour increases its likelihood (Levav & Fitzsimons, 2006). Ask people if they intend to floss their teeth in the next two weeks or to vote in an upcoming election, and they will become more likely to do so.

Further studies—more than 700 studies with 276 000 participants—confirmed that specific, relevant attitudes do predict intended and actual behaviour (Armitage & Conner, 2001; Bassili, 1995; Six & Eckes, 1996; Wallace et al., 2005). For example, attitudes toward condoms strongly predict condom use (Albarracin et al., 2001). And attitudes toward recycling (but not general attitudes toward environmental issues) predict participation in recycling (Oskamp, 1991). To change habits through persuasion, we had best alter people's attitudes toward *specific* practices.

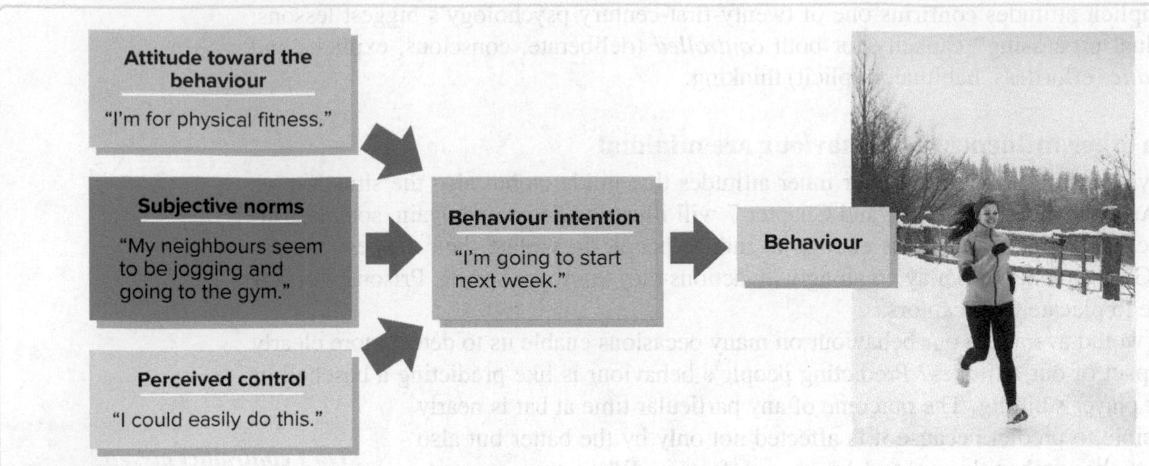

FIGURE 4–1 THE THEORY OF PLANNED BEHAVIOUR.

Icek Ajzen, working with Martin Fishbein, has shown that one's (a) attitudes, (b) perceived social norms, and (c) feelings of control together determine one's intentions, which guide behaviour.

Photo source: ©Jozef Polc/123RF.

So far we have seen two conditions under which attitudes will predict behaviour: (1) when we minimize other influences on our attitude statements and our behaviour, and (2) when the attitude is specifically relevant to the observed behaviour. There is a third condition: An attitude predicts behaviour better when it is potent (strong and on one's mind).

When attitudes are potent

Much of our behaviour is automatic. We act out familiar scripts, without reflecting on what we're doing. We respond to people we meet in the hall with an automatic "Hi." We answer the restaurant cashier's question, "How was your meal?" by saying, "Fine," even if we found the food tasteless.

Such mindless reaction is adaptive. It frees our minds to work on other things. For habitual behaviours—seat belt use, coffee consumption, class attendance—conscious intentions are hardly activated (Ouellette & Wood, 1998). As the philosopher Alfred North Whitehead argued, "Civilization advances by extending the number of operations which we can perform without thinking about them."

> ***"Thinking is easy, acting difficult, and to put one's thoughts into action, the most difficult thing in the world."***
>
> Johann Wolfgang Von Goethe, 1749–1832

Bringing attitudes to mind

If we were prompted to think about our attitudes before acting, would we be truer to ourselves? Mark Snyder and William Swann (1976) wanted to find out. So, two weeks after 120 of their students indicated their attitudes toward affirmative-action employment policies, Snyder and Swann invited them to act as jurors in a sex-discrimination court case. Only if they first induced the students to remember their attitudes—by giving them "a few minutes to organize your thoughts and views on the affirmative-action issue"—did attitudes predict verdicts. Similarly, people who take a few moments to review their past behaviour express attitudes that better predict their future behaviour (Zanna, Olson, & Fazio, 1981). Our attitudes become potent *if* we think about them.

Self-conscious people usually are in touch with their attitudes (Miller & Grush, 1986). This suggests another way to induce people to focus on their inner convictions: Make them self-conscious, perhaps by having them act in front of a mirror (Carver & Scheier, 1981). Maybe you can recall suddenly being acutely aware of yourself upon entering a room with a large mirror. Making people self-aware in this way promotes consistency between words and deeds (Froming, Walker, & Lopyan, 1982; Gibbons, 1978).

"Without doubt it is a delightful harmony when doing and saying go together."

Montaigne, *Essays,* 1588

Edward Diener and Mark Wallbom (1976) noted that nearly all university students say that cheating is morally wrong. But will they follow the advice of Shakespeare's Polonius, "To thine own self be true"? Diener and Wallbom set students to work on an anagram-solving task (said to predict IQ) and told them to stop when a bell in the room sounded. Left alone, 71 percent cheated by working past the bell. Among students made self-aware—by working in front of a mirror while hearing their tape-recorded voices—only 7 percent cheated.

Remember Batson's studies of moral hypocrisy? In a later experiment, Batson and his colleagues (1999) found that mirrors did bring behaviour into line with espoused moral attitudes. When people flipped a coin while facing a mirror, the coin flip became scrupulously fair. Exactly half of the self-conscious participants assigned the other person to the positive task.

Forging strong attitudes through experience

When attitudes are forged by experience, not just by hearsay, they are more accessible, more enduring, and more likely to guide actions (Fazio & Zanna, 1981; Glasman & Albarracin, 2006). In one study, university students all expressed negative attitudes about their school's response to a housing shortage. But, given opportunities to act (to sign a petition, solicit signatures, join a committee, or write a letter), only those whose attitudes grew from direct experience acted (Regan & Fazio, 1977).

"It is easier to preach virtue than to practise it."

La Rochefoucauld, *Maxims,* 1665

When Does Our Behaviour Affect Our Attitudes?

If social psychology has taught us anything, it is that we are likely not only to think ourselves into a way of acting but also to act ourselves into a way of thinking. What lines of evidence support this assertion?

Now we turn to a more startling idea: behaviour determines attitudes. It's true that we sometimes stand up for what we believe. But it's also true that we come to believe in what we stand up for. Social–psychological theories inspired much of the research that underlies this conclusion. Instead of beginning with these theories, however, let's first see what there is to explain. As we engage evidence that behaviour affects attitudes, speculate *why* this is and then compare your ideas with social psychologists' explanations.

"Thought is the child of Action."

Benjamin Disraeli, *Vivian Grey,* 1826

Consider the following incidents, each based on actual happenings:

- Azat is hypnotized and told to take off her shoes when a book drops on the floor. Fifteen minutes later, a book drops, and Azat quietly slips out of her loafers. "Azat," asks the hypnotist, "why did you take off your shoes?" "Well… my feet are hot and tired," Azat replies. "It has been a long day." The act produces the idea.
- Brad has electrodes temporarily implanted in the brain region that controls his head movements. When neurosurgeon José Delgado (1973) stimulates the electrodes by remote control, Brad always turns his head. Unaware of the remote stimulation, he offers a reasonable explanation for it: "I heard a noise." "I'm restless." "I was looking under the bed."

- Yemi's severe seizures were relieved by surgically separating her two brain hemispheres. Now, in an experiment, psychologist Michael Gazzaniga (1985) flashes a picture of a nude woman to the left half of Yemi's field of vision and thus to her nonverbal right hemisphere. A sheepish smile spreads over her face, and she begins chuckling. Asked why, she invents—and apparently believes—a plausible explanation: "Oh—that funny machine."

The mental after-effects of our behaviour also appear in many social–psychological examples of self-persuasion. As we will see over and over, attitudes follow behaviour.

Role-Playing

role A set of norms that define how people in a given social position ought to behave.

norms Rules for accepted and expected behaviour that prescribe "proper" behaviour.

The word **role** is borrowed from the theatre and, as in the theatre, refers to actions expected of those who occupy a particular social position. Each social position is defined by a set of prescribed **norms** for behaviour. When stepping into a new social role, we must perform its actions, even if we feel phony. But our unease seldom lasts.

Think of a time when you stepped into some new role—perhaps your first days on a job, at university, or on a sports team. That first week on campus, for example, you may have been super-sensitive to your new social situation and tried valiantly to act appropriately and root out your high school behaviour. At such times, we feel self-conscious. We observe our new speech and actions because they aren't natural to us. Then, one day, an amazing thing happens: We notice that our team cohesion or our intellectual discussion no longer feels forced. The role has begun to fit as comfortably as our favourite clothes.

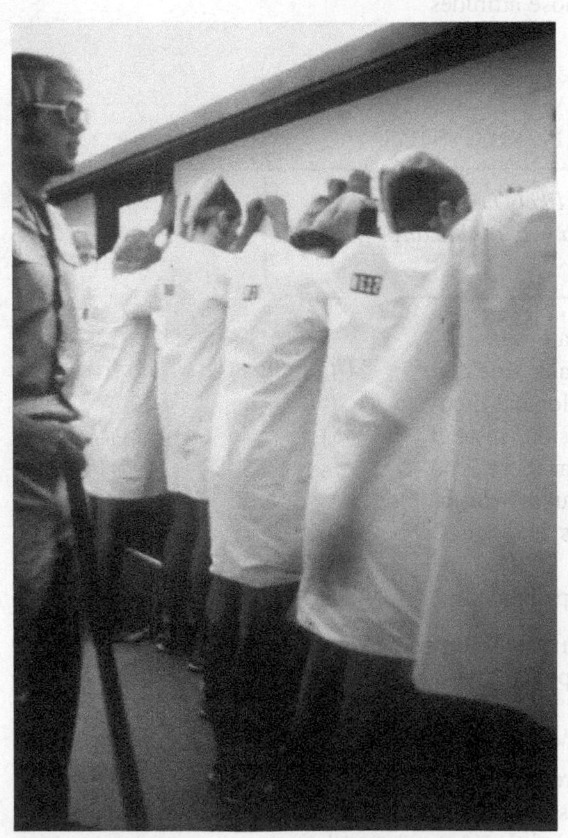

Guards and prisoners in a prison simulation quickly absorbed the roles they played.

Source: ©Philip Zimbardo.

In one study, university men volunteered to spend time in a simulated prison constructed in a psychology department by Philip Zimbardo (1972). Zimbardo, like so many others, wondered whether prison brutality is a product of evil prisoners and malicious guards or whether the institutional roles of guard and prisoner would embitter and harden even compassionate people. Do the people make the place violent, or does the place make the people violent?

By a flip of a coin, he designated half of the students as guards. He gave them uniforms, billy clubs, and whistles, and instructed them to enforce the rules. The other half were designated as prisoners and were locked in cells and made to wear humiliating outfits. After a jovial first day of "playing" their roles, the guards and prisoners, and even the experimenters, got caught up in the situation. The guards began to disparage the prisoners, and some devised cruel and degrading routines. The prisoners broke down, rebelled, or became apathetic. There developed, reported Zimbardo (1972), a "growing confusion between reality and illusion, between role-playing and self-identity . . . This prison which we had created . . . was absorbing us as creatures of its own reality." Observing the emerging social pathology, Zimbardo was forced to call off the planned two-week simulation after only six days. Although widely criticized on ethical and methodological grounds (e.g., Toppo, 2018; Haslam et al., 2019), it has had a lasting impact on how we view the role of behaviours on attitudes.

U.S. soldiers acting as prison guards engaged in brutal and demeaning treatment of their Iraqi prisoners. Most soldiers

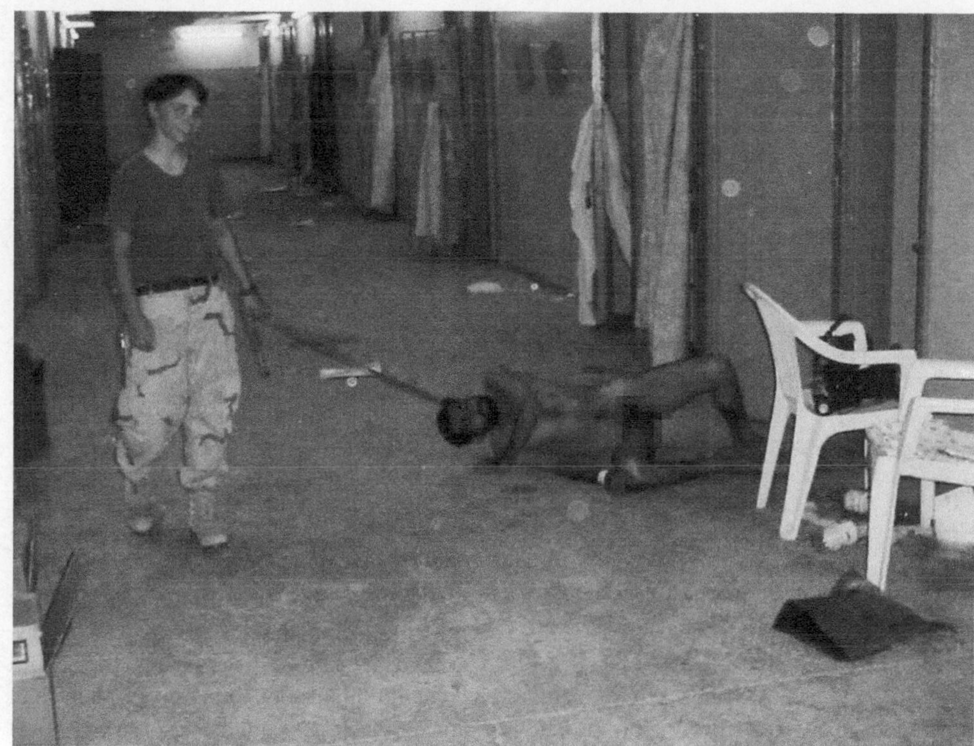

After the degradation of Iraqi prisoners by some U.S. military personnel, Philip Zimbardo (2004) noted "direct and sad parallels between similar behaviour of the 'guards' in the Stanford Prison Experiment." Such behaviour, he contended, is attributable to a toxic situation that can make good people into perpetrators of evil. "It's not that we put bad apples in a good barrel. We put good apples in a bad barrel. The barrel corrupts anything that it touches."
Source: ©AP Photo.

sat by and watched the atrocities occur without raising a warning or trying to stop them. This reaction, too, resembled the Stanford Prison Experiment. The role of prison guard brought out hostility in some, but an even more common result of the role seems to be that it prevents intervening even to help those who are clearly in need.

The deeper lesson of role-playing studies concerns how what is unreal (an artificial role) can evolve into what is real. In a new career, as teacher, soldier, or businessperson, we act a role that shapes our attitudes.

Take the case of Stephen Reid. In the 1970s, Reid was part of the notorious group of bank robbers called the "Stop Watch Gang." They robbed over 100 banks, stealing more than $15 million. Reid was eventually arrested. While in prison, he wrote the highly regarded novel, *Jackrabbit Parole.* Award-winning Canadian poet Susan Musgrave edited the book and then asked Reid to marry her. They were married; when he was released, they raised two children. By all accounts, Reid was a happy and devoted husband and father. He was fond of saying, "My criminal career ended the day I began writing."

Sadly, his criminal career had not ended. In 1998, Reid began using drugs and became addicted. On June 9, 1999, he robbed a Victoria bank, shot at a police officer, and held an elderly couple hostage.

If Reid had been a bank robber all along and only pretended to be a good family man, people could have more easily understood his actions. What they could not understand was that he could really be a bank robber, then really be a devoted husband and father, and then really be a bank robber again.

> ***"No man, for any considerable period, can wear one face to himself and another to the multitude without finally getting bewildered as to which may be true."***
>
> Nathaniel Hawthorne, 1850

Could such a thing happen to you or me? Yes and no. Our actions depend not only on the social situation but also on our dispositions. Reid may have had a predisposition to drug abuse, which probably played a role in his criminal activities. You might well have responded differently.

Stephen Reid, serving his sentence for bank robbery (left), and with his wife, poet and author Susan Musgrave (right).
(left): Source: The Canadian Press/Don Denton; (right): Source: Victoria Times Colonist/ The Canadian Press.

Nevertheless, some social situations can move most "normal" people to behave in "abnormal" ways. This is clear from experiments that put well-intentioned people in a bad situation to see whether good or evil prevails. To a dismaying extent, evil wins. Nice guys often don't finish nice.

Gender roles

One prominent role given to us by our society is our gender. Early on, we are socialized into gender roles. Gender socialization, it has been said, gives girls "roots" and boys "wings," in that girls are told of the limited roles that are expected of them, whereas boys are told they can accomplish anything. For example, in children's books over the second half of the 20th century, girls were shown using household objects (such as a broom, a sewing needle, or pots and pans) four times more often than boys, and boys were shown using production objects (such as a pitchfork, a plough, or a gun) five times more often than girls (Crabb & Bielawski, 1994). Women are more likely to be judged on their appearance than men (e.g., Xie et al., 2019). The adult result: "Everywhere," reported the United Nations (1991), women do most household work. And "everywhere, cooking and dishwashing are the least shared household chores." Even though since 1965 men have doubled the amount of housework they do, women still do on average one hour more per day (New York Times, 2020). Such behaviour expectations for males and females define **gender roles.**

gender roles Behaviour expectations (norms) for males and females.

Do you ever present one self to members of your own sex and a different self to members of the other sex?

In an experiment with undergraduate women, Mark Zanna and Susan Pack (1975) showed the impact of gender role expectations. The women answered a questionnaire on which they described themselves to a man they expected to meet—a man they were told was tall, unattached, and a fourth-year student. Those led to believe that the man's ideal woman was home-oriented and deferential to her husband presented themselves as more traditionally feminine than did women expecting to meet a man who liked strong, ambitious women. Moreover, given a problem-solving test, those expecting to meet the nonsexist man behaved more intelligently: They solved 18 percent more problems than those expecting to meet the man with the traditional views. This adapting of themselves to fit the man's image was much less pronounced if the man was less desirable—a short, already attached first-year student. In a companion experiment by Dean Morier and Cara Seroy (1994), men similarly adapted their self-presentations to meet desirable women's gender role expectations. Clearly, our gender roles can shape our actions.

When Saying Becomes Believing

People often adapt what they say to please their listeners. They are quicker to tell people good news than bad, and they adjust their message toward the listener's position (Manis, Cornell, & Moore, 1974; Tesser, Rosen, & Conlee, 1972; Tetlock, 1983). When induced to give spoken or written support to something they doubt, people will often feel bad about the deceit. Nevertheless, they begin to believe what they are saying—provided they weren't bribed or coerced into doing so. When there is no compelling external explanation for one's words, saying becomes believing (Klaas, 1978).

Tory Higgins and his colleagues (Higgins & McCann, 1984; Higgins & Rholes, 1978) illustrated how saying becomes believing. They had university students read a personality description of someone and then summarize it for someone else who was believed either to like or to dislike this person. The students wrote a more positive description when the recipient liked the person, and, having said positive things, then liked the person more themselves. Asked to recall what they had read, they remembered the description as being more positive than it was. In short, it seems that we are prone to adjust our messages to our listeners and, having done so, to believe the altered message.

"Good God! He's giving the white-collar voters' speech to the blue collars."

Saying becomes believing: In expressing our thoughts to others, we sometimes tailor our words to what we think the others will want to hear, and then come to believe our own words.

Source: ©Joseph Farris. All rights reserved. Used with permission.

The Foot-in-the-Door Phenomenon

Social psychologist Robert Cialdini is a self-described "patsy": "For as long as I can recall, I've been an easy mark for the pitches of peddlers, fundraisers, and operators of one sort or another." To better understand why one person says yes to another, he spent three years as a trainee in various sales, fundraising, and advertising organizations, discovering how they exploit "the weapons of influence."

Most of us can recall times when, after agreeing to help out with a project or an organization, we ended up more involved than we ever intended, vowing that in the future we would say no to such requests. How does this happen?

In keeping with the "attitude follows behaviour" principle, experiments suggest that if you want people to do a big favour for you, one technique is to get them to do a small favour first. In the best-known demonstration of this **foot-in-the-door phenomenon**, researchers posing as safety-drive volunteers asked people to permit the installation of a huge, poorly lettered "Drive carefully" sign in their front yards. Only 17 percent consented. Others were first approached with a small request: Would they display a 7.5 cm "Be a safe driver" window sign? Nearly all readily agreed. When approached two weeks later to allow the large, ugly sign in their front yards, 76 percent consented (Freedman & Fraser, 1966). One project helper who went from house to house later recalled that, not knowing who had been previously visited, "I was simply stunned at how easy it was to convince some people and how impossible to convince others" (Ornstein, 1991).

foot-in-the-door phenomenon The tendency for people who have first agreed to a small request to comply later with a larger request.

Other researchers have confirmed the foot-in-the-door phenomenon with a variety of behaviours:

- Patricia Pliner and her collaborators (1974) found that 46 percent of Toronto suburbanites were willing to give to the Cancer Society when approached directly. Others who had been asked a day ahead to wear a lapel pin publicizing the drive (which all agreed to do) were nearly twice as likely to donate.
- Angela Lipsitz and others (1989) reported that ending blood-drive reminder calls with "We'll count on seeing you then, OK?" increased the show-up rate from 62 to 81 percent.

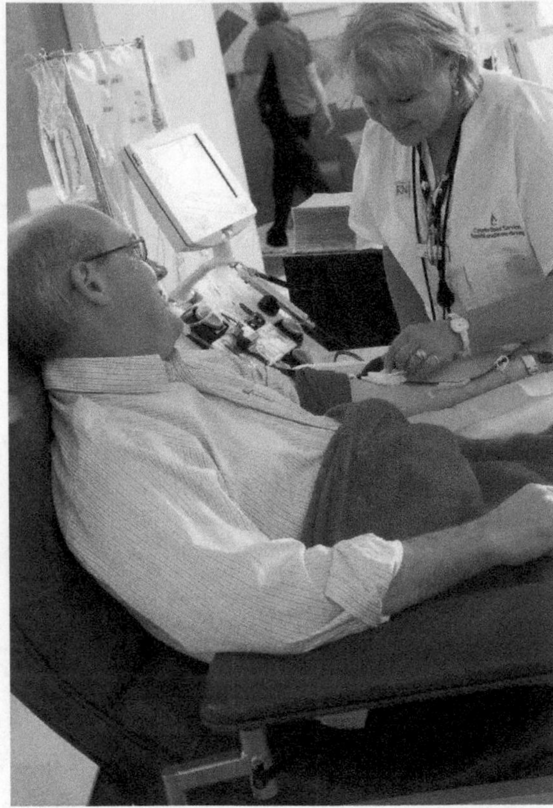

A foot in the door. To get people to donate blood or money, it often helps to first elicit a smaller commitment to the same cause.

Source: © Canadian Blood Services.

- Nicolas Guéguen and Celine Jacob (2001) tripled the rate of French Internet users contributing to a child land-mine victims organization (from 1.6 to 4.9 percent) by first inviting them to sign a petition against land mines.
- Guéguen and his colleagues (2016) also used the foot-in-the-door technique to reduce driver aggressiveness by first asking drivers to help a lost pedestrian.

Note that in these experiments, as in many of the over 1000 other foot-in-the-door experiments, the initial compliance—signing a petition, helping a stranger, stating one's intention—was voluntary (Burger & Guadagno, 2003). We will see again and again that when people commit themselves to public behaviours and perceive these acts to be their own doing, they come to believe more strongly in what they have done. But this research is not without criticism. Because stronger initial attitudes increase the likelihood of the effect occurring, some of the foot-in-the-door results found might be "pseudo"-effects (e.g., a result of the underlying attitude rather than the technique itself) (Arnold & Kaiser, 2018).

Low-Ball Technique

Cialdini and his collaborators (1978) explored a variation of the foot-in-the-door phenomenon by experimenting with the **low-ball technique**. After the customer agrees to buy a new car because of its bargain price and begins completing the sales forms, the salesperson removes the price advantage by charging for options the customer thought were included or by checking with a boss who disallows the deal because "we'd be losing money." Folklore has it that more customers stick with the higher-priced purchase than would have agreed to it at the outset.

Cialdini and his collaborators found that this technique indeed works. When they invited introductory psychology students to participate in an experiment at 7:00 a.m., only 24 percent showed up. But if the students first agreed to participate without knowing the time and only then were asked to participate at 7:00 a.m., 53 percent came.

> ***"You can use small commitments to manipulate a person's self-image; you can use them to turn citizens into 'public servants,' prospects into 'customers,' prisoners into 'collaborators.'"***
>
> Robert Cialdini, *Influence,* 1988

Marketing researchers and salespeople have found that the principle works even when we are aware of a profit motive (Cialdini, 1988). A harmless initial commitment—returning a card for more information and a gift, agreeing to listen to an investment possibility—often moves us toward a larger commitment. Salespeople may exploit the power of small commitments when trying to bind people to purchase agreements. Many places now have laws that allow customers of door-to-door salespeople a few days to think over their purchases and cancel. (For example, the Ontario Consumer Protection Act of 2002 allows a 10-day *cooling-off period* during which you may cancel a contract.) To combat the effect of these laws, many companies use what the sales-training program of one encyclopedia company calls "a very important psychological aid in preventing customers from backing out of their contracts" (Cialdini, 1988, p. 78). They simply have the customer, rather than the salesperson, fill out the agreement. Having written it themselves, people usually live up to their commitment.

low-ball technique A tactic for getting people to agree to something. People who agree to an initial request will often still comply when the requester ups the ante. People who receive only the costly request are less likely to comply with it.

The foot-in-the-door phenomenon is well worth learning about. Someone trying to seduce us—financially, politically, or sexually—usually will try to create a momentum of compliance. Before agreeing to a small request, think about what may follow.

Door-in-the-Face Technique

Cialdini and his colleagues (e.g., Cialdini et al., 1975; Cialdini & Goldstein, 2004) have also identified the **door-in-the-face-technique**—the tendency for people who have first declined a large request to comply with a subsequent, but smaller, request. The door-in-the-face technique works through the principle of reciprocity.

door-in-the-face technique A strategy for gaining a concession. After someone first turns down a large request (the door in the face), the same requester counteroffers with a more reasonable request.

The basic idea is that an initial large request is presented—one that is so large that people will almost all say no (e.g., "Can you donate $100 for cancer research?"). The requester acquiesces and then makes a smaller request ("Well, if you can't donate $100, how about $10?"). We feel bad about saying no at first so we say yes to the second request to "be nice." Cialdini and his colleagues (1975) have shown that this "request then moderation" procedure is very effective at gaining compliance.

In their initial study, Cialdini had students recruit volunteers to chaperone a group of children from the "County Juvenile Detention Center" on a trip to the zoo. For half of the participants, this request was preceded by a larger request—to act as a volunteer, unpaid counsellor at the detention centre. When people received the small request only (to chaperone) they agreed 16.7 percent of the time. But when they received the large request first (which no one agreed to), 50 percent of those asked agreed to chaperone the children to the zoo. The technique has also been used to get six- to eight-year-olds to do more schoolwork (Chan & Au, 2011). Clearly, this is a very effective technique.

Activity: Do Compliance Tactics Work on You?

Now that you know some of the tactics used in compliance, can you think about how to counter them? Let's take a concrete example. Have you ever received a free sample at a grocery store? Often there is a booth set up for tasting a new product. Conveniently, the product is on display with the samples. People try the sample and then take the product. It has been demonstrated that people are much more likely to take the product after having a free sample than they are if no sample is provided. This may be an example of the reciprocity principle—we get something (the sample) and we reciprocate by taking the product (although there are likely other elements at play as well, such as the taste of the product, hunger, etc.).

What about other principles? Companies use scarcity with "limited time offers" and "limited quantities." Authority and attraction are being used when sports and movie stars advertise products.

Now, here is your task: Pull out a magazine (or find one online). How many of the ads in that magazine use one or more of these principles? Look at the ads on these pages. What principles are they getting at? Marketing researchers and salespeople have found that these principles work even when we are aware of a profit motive (Cialdini, 1988). As noted above, a harmless initial commitment can move us toward a larger one. Remember, just because you have initially agreed to something (and even signed something) does not necessarily mean you have to follow through if the deal changes.

Interestingly, the door-in-the-face technique can work even better when we are motivated to reciprocate (i.e., the norm activated when using the technique; Cantarero et al., 2017) and when the requests are associated with strong arguments (Howard, 2019).

Immoral and Moral Acts

The attitudes-follow-behaviour principle works with more immoral acts as well. Such acts sometimes result from gradually escalating commitments. An early (seemingly innocuous) negative behaviour can make it easier for us to perform a worse act later. But these acts gnaw at the actor's moral sensitivity. To paraphrase La Rochefoucauld's *Maxims* (1665), it is not as difficult to find a person who has never succumbed to a given temptation as to find a person who has succumbed only once. After telling a "white lie" and thinking, "Well, that wasn't so bad," the person may go on to tell a bigger lie.

Another way in which immoral acts influence attitudes lies in the paradoxical fact that we tend not only to hurt those we dislike but also to dislike those we hurt. Several studies (Berscheid, Boye, & Walster, 1968; Davis & Jones, 1960; Glass, 1964) found that harming an innocent victim—by uttering hurtful comments or delivering electric shocks—typically leads aggressors to disparage their victims, thus helping them justify their cruel behaviour. This is especially so when we are coaxed into something, not coerced. When we voluntarily agree to do a deed, we take more responsibility for it.

The phenomenon appears in wartime. Soldiers ordered to kill may initially react with revulsion to the point of sickness over their act but not for long (Waller, 2002). Often, they will denigrate their enemies with dehumanizing nicknames.

> ***"Our self-definitions are not constructed in our heads; they are forged by our deeds."***
>
> Robert McAfee Brown, *Creative Dislocation—The Movement of Grace,* 1980

Attitudes also follow behaviour in peacetime. A group that holds another in slavery will likely come to perceive the enslaved people as having traits that justify their oppression. For example, prison staff who participate in executions experience "moral disengagement" by coming to believe (more strongly than do other prison staff) that their victims deserve their fate (Osofsky, Bandura, & Zimbardo, 2005).

The Canadian Residential School system (founded in the 1800s) and the "'60s scoop" program were Canadian government initiatives intended to assimilate Indigenous children into Euro-Canadian culture (Miller et al., 2019). Over 170 000 Indigenous children from across Canada were removed from their homes and forced to suppress their own language and traditions. As a consequence, generations of Indigenous families were left with deep psychological, emotional, and physical scars, as well as a lack of models to demonstrate effective parenting skills. Importantly, as noted in the *Final Report of the Truth and Reconciliation Commission of Canada* (2015), the government's actions created the social conditions that allowed prejudice against Indigenous peoples to flourish. The government's behaviour, in part, *caused* racist beliefs about Canada's Indigenous people to develop—beliefs that persist to this day. Remarkably, the final residential school did not close until 1996.

Actions and attitudes feed each other, sometimes to the point of moral numbness. The more one harms another and adjusts one's attitudes, the easier harm-doing becomes. To simulate the "killing begets killing" process, Andy Martens and his collaborators (2007) asked University of Arizona students to kill some bugs. They wondered: Would killing initial bugs in a "practice" trial increase students' willingness to kill more bugs later? To find out, they asked some students to look at one small bug in a container, then to dump it into a coffee grinder and press the "on" button for three seconds. (No bugs were actually killed. An unseen stopper at the base of the insert tube prevented the bug from actually entering the opaque killing machine, which had torn bits of paper to simulate the sound of a killing.) Others, who initially killed five bugs (or so they thought), went on to "kill" significantly more bugs during an ensuing 20-second period.

Harmful acts shape the self, but, thankfully, so do moral acts. Character is reflected in what we do when we think no one is looking. Researchers have tested character by giving children temptations when it seems no one is watching. Consider what happens when children resist the temptation. They internalize the conscientious act if the deterrent is strong enough to elicit the desired behaviour yet mild enough to leave them with a sense of choice. In a dramatic experiment, Jonathan Freedman (1965) introduced elementary-school children to an enticing battery-controlled robot, instructing them not to play with it while he was out of the room. Freedman used a severe threat with half the children and a mild threat with the others. Both were sufficient to deter the children.

Several weeks later, a different researcher, with no apparent relation to the earlier events, left each child to play in the same room with the same toys. Of the 18 children who had been given the severe threat, 14 now freely played with the robot, but two-thirds of those who had been given the mild deterrent still resisted playing with it. Having earlier made a conscious choice not to play with the toy, the mildly deterred children apparently had internalized their decision. This new attitude controlled their subsequent action. Thus, moral action, especially when chosen rather than coerced, affects moral thinking.

If moral action feeds moral attitudes, can laws and rules that require moral conduct lead to genuine moral beliefs? Elliot Aronson (1992) argued that such change is possible. His argument went like this: If we wait for the heart to change—through preaching and teaching—we will wait a long time. But if we legislate moral action, we can, under the right conditions, indirectly affect heartfelt attitudes.

The idea runs counter to the presumption that "you can't legislate morality." Yet attitude change has, in fact, followed changes in the laws. Consider some of the following:

- In the 1980s and 1990s, many governments began requiring the use of seat belts by all people riding in automobiles. Initially, these laws were seen as burdensome and were opposed by many. But, over time, seat belt use has risen dramatically. Now, most people in these jurisdictions favour mandatory seat belt laws.

Mourners leave flowers and messages at the site of a deadly shooting at a Quebec mosque.

Source: ©ALICE CHICHE/ AFP via Getty Images.

- In 1954, the Supreme Court of the United States ruled that schools segregated by race were inherently unfair and that such schools were required to desegregate. Since that decision, the percentage of Whites in the U.S. favouring integrated schools has more than doubled and now includes nearly everyone.
- In the 1970s, many National Hockey League players did not wear helmets. Older players saw this as a measure of toughness. But in the 1980s, almost all bantam and junior hockey leagues required players to wear helmets. Now, all players in the NHL wear helmets and see them as an important safety measure. Having grown up with helmets, they now believe they are useful.

> ***"We do not love people so much for the good they have done us, as for the good we have done them."***
>
> Leo Tolstoy, *War and Peace,* 1867–1869

Do laws always lead to the adoption of consistent attitudes? Almost certainly not. There are times when it is true that "you can't legislate morality." But research in social psychology confirms that, under the right conditions, people's attitudes follow their behaviours even when these behaviours are required.

Experiments demonstrate that positive behaviour toward someone fosters liking for that person. Doing a favour for an experimenter or another subject or tutoring a student usually increases liking of the person helped (Blanchard & Cook, 1976). It is a lesson worth remembering: If you wish to love someone more, act as if you do.

Social Movements

We have now seen that a society's laws, and therefore its behaviour, can have a strong influence on people's behaviour. But a danger lies in the possibility of employing the same idea for political socialization on a mass scale. For many Germans during the 1930s, participating in Nazi rallies, wearing uniforms, demonstrating, and especially using the public greeting "Heil Hitler" established a profound inconsistency between behaviour and belief. Historian Richard Grunberger (1971) reported that for those who had their doubts about Hitler, "The 'German greeting' was a powerful conditioning device. Having once decided to intone it as an outward token of conformity, many experienced schizophrenic discomfort at the contradiction between their words and their feelings. Prevented from saying what they believed, they tried to establish their psychic equilibrium by consciously making themselves believe what they said" (p. 27).

The practice is not limited to totalitarian regimes. Political rituals, such as singing the national anthem, use public conformity to build a private belief in patriotism. One of the authors was amazed at the strong sense of being a Canadian that his son developed in junior kindergarten. Before school, his son had virtually no identity as a Canadian, but after three weeks of singing *O Canada* on Mondays, he was Canadian through and through. Interestingly, one of your other co-authors grew up in Quebec, where singing the Canadian national anthem was not done in schools. The focus in Quebec at that time (the 1970s) was to build Quebec Nationalist affiliations. In another example, observers noted how the civil rights marches of the 1960s strengthened the demonstrators' commitments. Their actions expressed an idea whose time had come and drove that idea more deeply into their hearts. In the 1980s, the move toward gender-inclusive language similarly strengthened inclusive attitudes.

Many people assume that most social indoctrination comes through *brainwashing,* a term coined to describe what happened to prisoners of war (POWs) during the Korean War in the 1950s. Actually, this Chinese "thought-control" program, developed to re-educate the Chinese populace into communism, was not nearly as irresistible as this term suggests. But the results still were disconcerting. Hundreds of prisoners cooperated with their captors. Twenty-one chose to remain after being granted permission to return to their home countries. And many of those who returned to the United States arrived believing that "although communism won't work in America, I think it's a good thing for Asia" (Segal, 1954).

Edgar Schein (1956) interviewed many of the POWs during their journey home and reported that the captors' methods included a gradual escalation of demands. The Chinese always started with trivial requests and gradually worked up to more significant ones: "Thus after a prisoner had once been 'trained' to speak or write out trivia, statements on more important issues were demanded." Moreover, they always expected active participation, be it just copying something or participating in group discussions, writing self-criticism, or uttering public confessions. Once a prisoner had spoken or written a statement, he felt an inner need to make his beliefs consistent with his acts. This often drove prisoners to persuade themselves of the good of what they had done. The "start-small-and-build" tactic was an effective application of the foot-in-the-door technique, as it continues to be today in the socialization of terrorists and torturers (Chapter 7).

Now, before reading further, let us ask you to play theorist. Ask yourself this: Why, in these studies and in real-life examples, did attitudes follow behaviour? Why might playing a role or making a speech influence your attitude?

Celebrating Canada Day: Patriotic actions strengthen patriotic attitudes.

Source: Ginaellen/Dreamstime.com/GetStock.com.

Why Does Our Behaviour Affect Our Attitudes?

What theories help explain the attitudes-follow-behaviour phenomenon? How do the tests between these competing ideas illustrate the process of scientific explanation?

We have seen that several streams of evidence merge to form a river: the effect of actions on attitudes. Do these observations contain any clues to why action affects attitude? Social psychology's detectives suspect three possible sources: (1) Self-presentation theory assumes that, for strategic reasons, we express attitudes that make us appear consistent; (2) cognitive dissonance theory assumes that to reduce discomfort, we justify our actions to ourselves; and (3) self-perception theory assumes that our actions are self-revealing (when uncertain about our feelings or beliefs, we look to our behaviour, much as anyone else would). Let's examine each explanation.

Self-Presentation: Impression Management

The first explanation began as a simple idea, which you may recall from Chapter 2. Who among us does not care what people think? We spend countless dollars on clothes, diets, cosmetics, even plastic surgery—all because we worry about what others think of us. We see making a good impression as a way to gain social and material rewards, to feel better about ourselves, even to become more secure in our social identities (Leary, 1994, 2001, 2004b, 2007, 2010).

No one wants to look foolishly inconsistent. To avoid seeming so, we express attitudes that match our actions. To appear consistent, we may pretend. Even if it means displaying a little insincerity or hypocrisy, it can pay off in managing the impression we are making. Or so self-presentation theory suggests.

Does our feigning consistency explain why expressed attitudes shift toward consistency with behaviour? To some extent, yes. People exhibit a much smaller attitude change when a bogus pipeline—a technique in which researchers lead participants to believe that any false statements will be detected—inhibits trying to make a good impression (Paulhus, 1982; Tedeschi, Nesler, & Taylor, 1987).

But there is more to the attitude changes we have reviewed than self-presentation, for people express their changed attitudes even to someone who doesn't know how they have behaved. Two other theories explain why people sometimes internalize their self-presentations as genuine attitude changes.

Self-Justification: Cognitive Dissonance

One theory is that our attitudes change because we are motivated to maintain consistency among our cognitions. This is the implication of Leon Festinger's (1957) **cognitive dissonance theory**. The theory is simple, but its range of applications is enormous. It assumes we feel tension ("dissonance") when two simultaneously accessible thoughts or beliefs ("cognitions") are psychologically inconsistent—as when we decide to say or do something we have mixed feelings about. Festinger argued that to reduce this unpleasant arousal, we often adjust our thinking. This simple idea and some surprising predictions derived from it have spawned more than 2000 studies (Cooper, 1999).

cognitive dissonance theory Tension that arises when we are simultaneously aware of two inconsistent cognitions. For example, dissonance may occur when we realize that we have, with little justification, acted contrary to our attitudes or made a decision favouring one alternative despite reasons favouring another.

One way that people minimize dissonance, Festinger believed, is through selective exposure to agreeable information (more about this in Chapter 5). Studies have asked people about their views on various topics and then invited them to choose whether they want to view information supporting or opposing their viewpoint. By about a two-to-one ratio, people (less secure and open-minded people, especially) preferred supporting rather than challenging information (Fischer & Greitemeyer, 2010; Hart et al., 2009; Sweeny et al., 2010; see Smith et al., 2008, for a review). People are especially keen on reading information that supports their political, religious, and ethical views—a phenomenon that most of us can illustrate from our own favourite news and blog sources. On more practical and less values-relevant topics, "accuracy motives" are more likely to drive us. Thus, we welcome a home inspection before buying or a second opinion before surgery.

Dissonance theory pertains mostly to discrepancies between behaviour and attitudes. We are aware of both. Thus, if we sense some inconsistency, perhaps some hypocrisy, we feel pressure for change, either in our attitudes or in our behaviours. That helps explain why, in a British survey, half of cigarette smokers disagreed with the near-consensus among nonsmokers that smoking is "really as dangerous as people say" (Eiser, Sutton, & Wober, 1979; Saad, 2002) and why the perception of risk among those who have quit declines after relapsing (Gibbons, Eggleston, & Benthin, 1997). However, it is not all bad news—dissonance has been effectively used to get people to pay more attention to their health and has effectively been used to prevent the development of eating disorders (e.g., Stice et al., 2015). For example, in one study (Nabi et al., 2019), people who posted a melanoma (skin cancer) awareness video to their Facebook page reported more sun safety behaviour the following week than those who did not post the video.

Insufficient justification

Imagine you are a participant in a famous experiment staged by the creative Festinger and his student, J. Merrill Carlsmith (1959). For an hour, you are required to perform dull tasks, such as turning wooden knobs again and again. After you finish, the experimenter (Carlsmith) explains that the study concerns how expectations affect performance. The next subject, waiting outside, must be led to expect an interesting experiment. The seemingly distraught experimenter, whom Festinger had spent hours coaching until he became extremely convincing, explains that the assistant who usually creates this expectation couldn't make this session. Wringing his hands, he pleads, "Could you fill in and do this?"

It's for science and you are being paid, so you agree to tell the next subject (who is actually the experimenter's real assistant) what a delightful experience you have just had. "Really?" responds the supposed subject. "A friend of mine was in this experiment a week ago, and she said it was boring." "Oh, no," you respond, "it's really very interesting. You get good exercise while turning some knobs. I'm sure you'll enjoy it." Finally, someone else who is studying how people react to experiments has you complete a questionnaire that asks how much you actually enjoyed your knob-turning experience.

"A foolish consistency is the hobgoblin of little minds."

Ralph Waldo Emerson, "Self-Reliance," 1841

Now for the prediction: Under which condition are you most likely to believe your little lie and say the experiment was, indeed, interesting? When you are paid $1 for doing so, as some of the subjects were? Or when you are paid a then-generous $20, as others were? Contrary to the common notion that big rewards produce big effects, Festinger and Carlsmith made an outrageous prediction: Those paid just $1 (hardly sufficient justification for a lie) would be most likely to adjust their attitudes to their actions. Having **insufficient justification** for their action, they would experience more discomfort (dissonance) and thus be more motivated to believe in what they had done. Those paid $20 had sufficient justification for what they did and hence should have experienced less dissonance. As Figure 4–2 shows, the results fit this intriguing prediction.*

insufficient justification Reduction of dissonance by internally justifying one's behaviour when external justification is "insufficient."

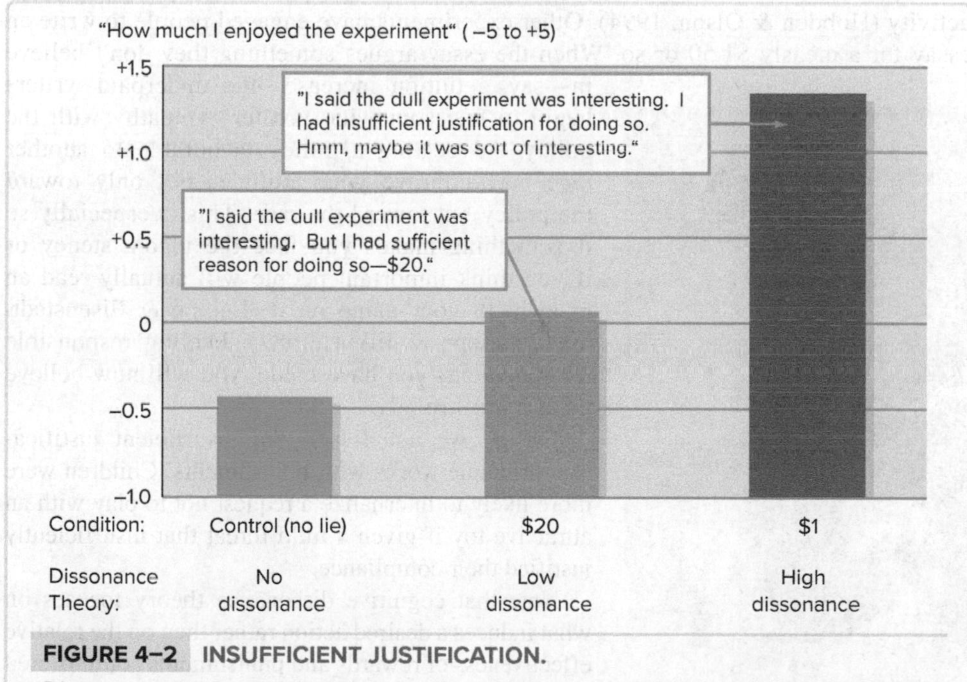

FIGURE 4–2 INSUFFICIENT JUSTIFICATION.

Dissonance theory predicts that when our actions are not fully explained by external rewards or coercion, we will experience dissonance, which we can reduce by believing in what we have done.

---

*There is a seldom-reported final aspect of this 1950s experiment. Imagine that you are back with the experimenter, who is truthfully explaining the whole study. Not only do you learn that you've been duped, but the experimenter asks for the $20 back. Do you comply? Festinger and Carlsmith noted that all their student subjects willingly reached into their pockets and gave back the money. This is a foretaste of some quite amazing observations on compliance and conformity, discussed in Chapter 6. As we will see, when the social situation makes clear demands, people usually respond accordingly.

THE INSIDE STORY

Following a 1934 earthquake in India, there were rumours outside the disaster zone of worse disasters to follow. It occurred to me that these rumours might be "anxiety-justifying"—cognitions that would justify their lingering fears. From that germ of an idea, I developed my theory of dissonance reduction—making your view of the world fit with how you feel or what you've done.

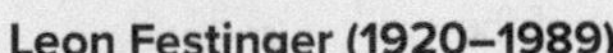

Leon Festinger (1920–1989)

Source: ©Mark Benham/Alamy Stock Photo.

Dissonance theory suggests that parents should aim to elicit desired behaviour non-coercively, thus motivating children to internalize the appropriate attitudes.

Source: ©Monkey Business Images/Shutterstock.

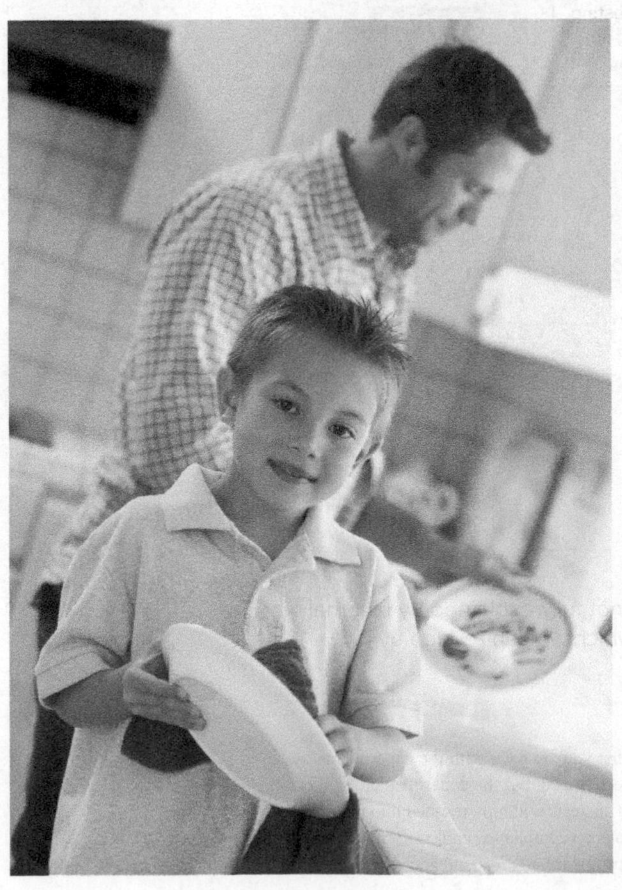

In dozens of later experiments, the attitudes-follow-behaviour effect was strongest when people felt some choice and when their actions had foreseeable consequences. One experiment had people read disparaging lawyer jokes into a recorder (for example, "How can you tell when lawyers are lying? Their lips are moving"). The reading produced more negative attitudes toward lawyers when it was a chosen rather than coerced activity (Hobden & Olson, 1994). Other experiments have engaged people to write an essay for a measly $1.50 or so. When the essay argues something they don't believe in—say, a tuition increase—the underpaid writers begin to feel somewhat greater sympathy with the policy. Advocating a policy favourable to another race may improve your attitudes not only toward the policy but toward the race. This is especially so if something makes you face the inconsistency or if you think important people will actually read an essay with your name on it (Leippe & Eisenstadt, 1994; Leippe & Elkin, 1987). Feeling responsible for statements you have made, you will now believe them more strongly.

Earlier, we noted how the insufficient justification principle works with punishments. Children were more likely to internalize a request not to play with an attractive toy if given a mild threat that insufficiently justified their compliance.

Note that cognitive dissonance theory focuses on what induces a desired action rather than on the relative effectiveness of rewards and punishments administered after the act. It aims to have Jesse say "I am cleaning up my room because I want a clean room" rather than "I am cleaning up my room because I'll lose my phone if I don't." Students who perceive their required community service as something they would have chosen to do are more likely to anticipate future volunteering than those who feel coerced (Stukas, Snyder, & Clary, 1999). The principle: Attitudes follow behaviours for which we feel some responsibility.

Dissonance after decisions

The emphasis on perceived choice and responsibility implies that decisions produce dissonance. When faced with an important decision—what university to attend, whom to date, which job to accept—we are sometimes torn between two equally attractive alternatives. Perhaps you can recall a time when, having committed yourself, you became painfully aware of dissonant cognitions—the desirable features of what you rejected and the undesirable features of what you chose. If you decided to live on campus, you may have realized you were forgoing the spaciousness and freedom of an apartment in favour of cramped, noisy dorm quarters. If you elected to live off campus, you may have realized that your decision meant physical separation from campus and friends and having to cook for yourself.

After making important decisions, we usually reduce dissonance by upgrading the chosen alternative and downgrading the unchosen option. In the first published dissonance experiment (1956), Jack Brehm had women rate eight products, such as a toaster, a radio, and a hair dryer. Brehm then showed the women two objects they had rated closely and told them they could have whichever they chose. Later, when re-rating the eight objects, the women increased their evaluations of the item they had chosen and decreased their evaluations of the rejected item. It seems that after we have made our choice, the grass does *not* then grow greener on the other side of the fence. (Afterwards, Brehm confessed he couldn't afford to let them keep what they had chosen.)

With simple decisions, this deciding-becomes-believing effect can breed overconfidence (Blanton et al., 2001): "What I have decided must be right." The effect can occur very quickly. Robert Knox and James Inkster (1968) found that bettors at a Vancouver racetrack who had just put down their money on a horse felt more optimistic about their bet than did those who were about to bet. In the few moments that intervened between standing in line and walking away from the betting window, nothing had changed—except the decisive action and the person's feelings about it. Contestants in carnival games of chance feel more confident of winning right after agreeing to play than right before. Similarly, voters indicate more esteem and confidence in a candidate just after voting than just before (Younger, Walker, & Arrowood, 1977). Making such a decision is one way we express ourselves, and once we make such a decision we are motivated to bolster our attitudes (Kokkoris & Kühnen, 2015).

Our preferences influence our decisions, which then sharpen our preferences. This choices-influence-preferences effect occurs even after people press a button to choose what they think is a subliminally presented vacation alternative (nothing was actually shown to them). They later tended to prefer the holiday that they believed they had chosen (Sharot, Velasquez, & Dolan, 2010). However, if the choice disappoints, our attitudes toward a product can change significantly in the negative direction as well. Wilkins, Beckenuyte, and Butt (2016) found that when people selected products (bags of chips) that had misleading labels or that were overfilled with air, they were less likely to buy that product in the future.

Children (Egan, Santos, & Bloom, 2007) and older adults (Cooper & Feldman, 2019a, 2019b) also display dissonance reactions. Louisa Egan and her colleagues (2007) invited four-year-olds to rate different stickers on a scale of smiley faces. With each child, the researchers then picked three stickers that the child had rated equally, and randomly identified two (let's call them Sticker A and Sticker B), from which the children could choose to take one home. Next the researchers let the child choose one more—either the unchosen sticker or the third one, Sticker C. The result: The children apparently reduced dissonance by downplaying the appeal of the unchosen first sticker, thus moving them to favour Sticker C 63 percent of the time (rather than half the time, as we might have expected). They repeated the experiment with capuchin monkeys using alternative sweets instead of stickers. As with the children, so with the monkeys: They, too, revised their attitudes after making an initial decision.

Cognitive dissonance can also be used to increase intention to exercise in the elderly (Cooper & Feldman, 2019b). Maintaining physical activity levels is especially important for older adults. The Princeton researchers found that asking older adults to generate arguments for why people should exercise led their attitudes to change such that they became more positive toward exercise. In addition, they were also more likely to say they would exercise in the future.

Culture and cognitive dissonance

Do cultural differences lead to differences in the experience of cognitive dissonance? Recall from Chapter 2 that people from Eastern cultures tend to have a more collectivist self-concept, whereas people from Western cultures tend to have a more individualistic self-concept. Note that all the early studies on dissonance after making a decision took place in Western cultures. Does the tendency in these studies for people to justify their decisions arise out of a Western cultural desire to individualistically claim that they made good choices?

Steve Heine and Darrin Lehman (1997a) from the University of British Columbia (UBC) thought so. They had Canadian students from UBC and Japanese exchange students complete a typical dissonance experiment. All the students were asked to rate a number of music CDs and then were given a choice between two of the CDs as a reward for being in the experiment. Previous studies conducted in individualistic cultures have shown that when people are given such a choice and then rate the CDs again, their ratings of the CD they chose become more positive and their ratings of the CD they did not choose become more negative. Heine and Lehman found this exact pattern among their Canadian participants. Apparently, Canadians protected their individualistic self-concepts by seeing their choices as good choices.

But what about the Japanese participants? Did they protect themselves by justifying their choices? No. Showing no evidence of the typical Western pattern, they rated the CDs the same regardless of what choice they had made.

Does this mean that people who have a collectivistic self-concept do not experience cognitive dissonance? Etsuko Hoshino-Browne and her colleagues (Hoshino-Browne et al., 2005) thought that they would experience dissonance if their collectivist self-concepts were threatened. They tested this idea by modifying the typical dissonance experiment. They had University of Waterloo students born in Canada or Kyoto University students from Japan make a choice for themselves or for a close friend. They reasoned that when Canadian students made a choice for themselves, their individualistic self-concept would be threatened, but when Japanese students made a choice for a friend, their collectivistic self-concept would be threatened. Consistent with this reasoning, they found that Canadian students justified the choices they made for themselves but not the choices they made for their friends; Japanese students, on the other hand, justified the choices they made for their friends but not the choices they made for themselves.

These studies suggest that culture can shape the experience of cognitive dissonance. Having an individualistic versus a collectivistic self-concept will affect when and how people experience cognitive dissonance. The studies also suggest, however, that the experience of feeling cognitive dissonance may be shared across many cultures.

Self-Perception

Although dissonance theory has inspired much research, an even simpler theory explains its phenomena. Consider how we make inferences about other people's attitudes. We see how a person acts in a particular situation, and then we attribute the behaviour either to the person's traits and attitudes or to environmental forces. If we see parents coercing their little Myuki into saying "I'm sorry," we attribute Myuki's reluctant behaviour to the situation, not to her personal regret. If we see Myuki apologizing with no apparent inducement, we attribute the apology to Myuki herself.

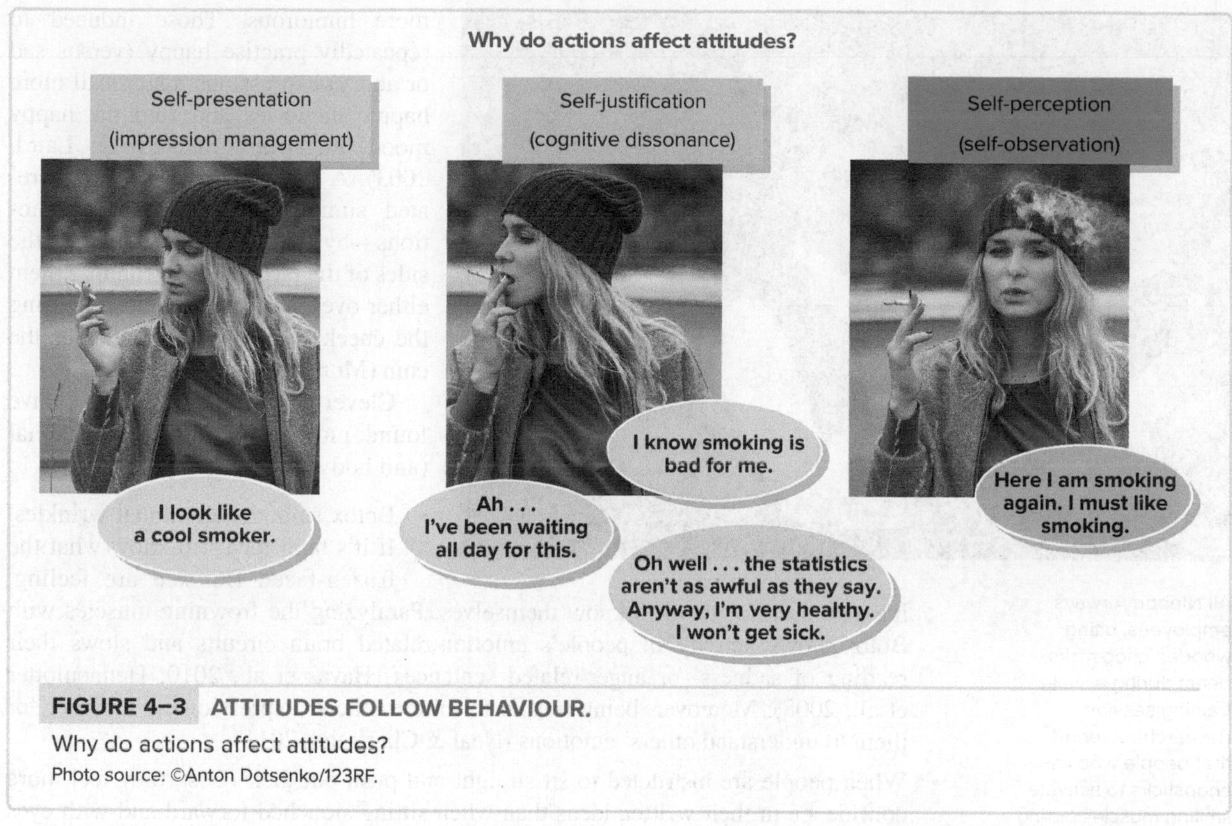

FIGURE 4–3 ATTITUDES FOLLOW BEHAVIOUR.

Why do actions affect attitudes?

Photo source: ©Anton Dotsenko/123RF.

Self-perception theory (proposed by Daryl Bem, 1972) assumes that we make similar inferences when we observe our own behaviour. When our attitudes are weak or ambiguous, we are in the position of someone who observes us from the outside. Hearing ourselves talk informs us of our attitudes; seeing our actions provides clues to how strong our beliefs are. This is especially so when we can't easily attribute our behaviour to external constraints. The acts we freely commit are self-revealing (Figure 4–3).

self-perception theory The theory that, when unsure of our attitudes, we infer them much as would someone observing us—by looking at our behaviour and the circumstances under which it occurs.

The pioneering psychologist William James proposed a similar explanation for emotion a century ago. We infer our emotions, he suggested, by observing our bodies and our behaviours. A stimulus, such as a growling bear, confronts a woman in the forest. She tenses, her heartbeat increases, adrenalin flows, and she runs away. Observing all this, she then experiences fear. Before big lectures, one of the authors often wakes before dawn and is unable to get back to sleep. Noting his wakefulness, he concludes that he must be anxious.

Do people who observe themselves agreeing to a small request come to perceive themselves as the helpful sort of person who responds positively to requests for help? Is that why, in the foot-in-the-door experiments, people will then later agree to larger requests? Indeed, yes, reported Jerry Burger and David Caldwell (2003). Behaviour can modify self-concept.

Expressions and attitude

You may be skeptical of the self-perception effect. We were when we first heard it. Experiments on the effects of facial expressions, however, suggest a way for you to experience it. When James Laird (1974, 1984; Duclos et al., 1989) induced university students to frown with electrodes attached to their faces—"Contract these muscles," "Pull your brows together"—the students reported feeling angry. It's more fun to try out Laird's other finding: Those induced to make a smiling face felt happier and found cartoons

"Self-knowledge is best learned, not by contemplation, but action."

Goethe, 1749–1832

All Nippon Airways employees, biting wooden chopsticks, beam during a smile training session. Researchers report that people who use chopsticks to activate smiling muscles during laboratory stress experiences also recover more quickly (Kraft & Pressman, 2012).
Source: ©Kyodo News International, Inc.

more humorous. Those induced to repeatedly practise happy (versus sad or angry) expressions may recall more happy memories and find the happy mood lingering (Schnall & Laird, 2003). A Japanese research team created similar expressions—and emotions—by taping rubber bands to the sides of the face and then running them either over the top of the head (raising the cheeks into a smile) or under the chin (Mori & Mori, 2009).

Clever follow-up studies have found more examples of this facial (and body) feedback effect:

- Botox smooths emotional wrinkles. If it's hard for us to know what the frozen-faced Botoxed are feeling, it's also hard for them to know themselves. Paralyzing the frowning muscles with Botox slows activity in people's emotion-related brain circuits and slows their reading of sadness- or anger-related sentences (Havas et al., 2010; Hennenlotter et al., 2008). Moreover, being unable to mimic others' expressions, it's harder for them to understand others' emotions (Neal & Chartrand, 2011).
- When people are instructed to sit straight and push out their chest, they feel more confidence in their written ideas than when sitting slouched forward and with eyes downcast (Briñol, Petty, & Wagner, 2009).
- People who assume high-power rather than low-power poses (think hands on hips rather than a contracted posture) experience increased testosterone, feelings of power, and risk tolerance (Carney, Cuddy, & Yap, 2010).

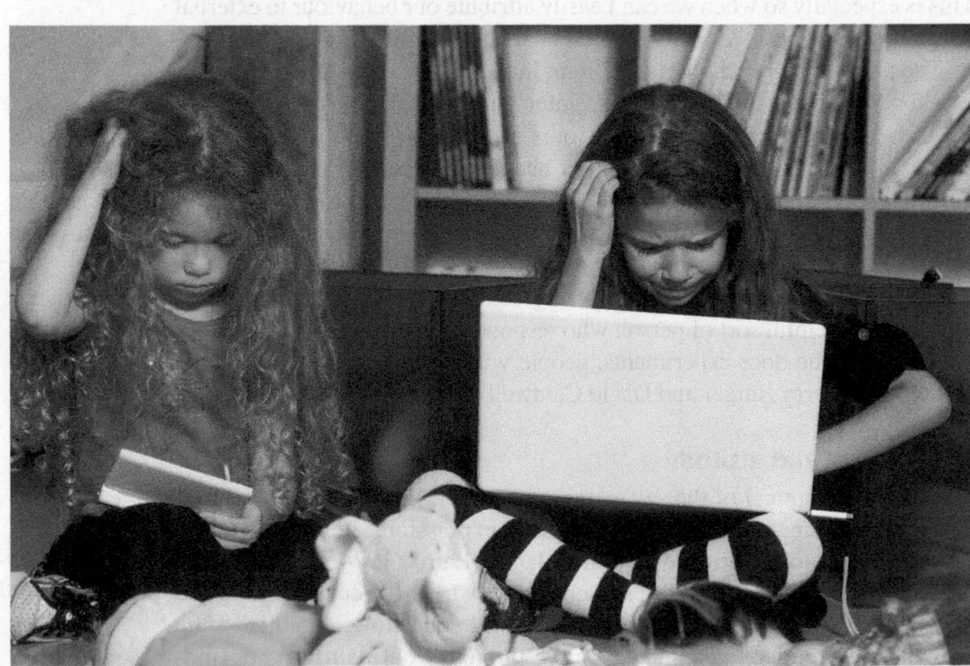

Natural mimicry and emotional contagion. People in sync, like these children working out math problems, feel more rapport with each other.
Source: ©PEOPLE AND TECHNOLOGY by VISION/ Alamy Stock Photo.

We have all experienced this phenomenon. We're feeling crabby, but then the phone rings or someone comes to the door and elicits from us warm, polite behaviour. "How's everything?" "Just fine, thanks. How are things with you?" This warm behaviour may change our whole attitude. It's tough to smile and feel grouchy. Going through the motions can trigger the emotions. It is also true, however, that extending the middle finger makes others' ambiguous expressions seem more hostile (Chandler & Schwarz, 2009).

> ***"I can watch myself and my actions, just like an outsider."***
>
> Anne Frank, *The Diary of a Young Girl,* 1947

> ***"The free expression by outward signs of emotion intensifies it. On the other hand, the repression as far as possible, of all outward signs softens our emotions."***
>
> Charles Darwin, *The Expression of the Emotions in Man and Animals,* 1897

Even your gait can affect how you feel. When you get up from reading this chapter, walk for a minute, taking short, shuffling steps, with eyes downcast. It's a great way to feel depressed. "Sit all day in a moping posture, sigh, and reply to everything with a dismal voice, and your melancholy lingers," noted William James (1890, p. 463). Want to feel better? Walk for a minute taking long strides with your arms swinging and your eyes straight ahead.

If our expressions influence our feelings, then would imitating others' expressions help us know what they are feeling? An experiment by Katherine Burns Vaughan and John Lanzetta (1981) suggested it would. They asked students to observe someone who was receiving electric shock. They told some of the observers to make a pained expression whenever the shock occurred. If, as Freud and others supposed, expressing an emotion allows us to discharge it, then the pained expression should be inwardly calming (Cacioppo et al., 1991). Actually, compared to other students who did not act out the expressions, these grimacing students perspired more and had a faster heart rate whenever they saw the person being shocked. Acting out the person's emotion apparently enabled the observers to feel more empathy. The implication: To sense how other people are feeling, let your own face mirror their expressions.

Actually, you hardly need try. Observing others' faces, postures, and voices, we naturally and unconsciously mimic their moment-to-moment reactions (Hatfield, Cacioppo, & Rapson, 1992; Ireland & Pennebaker, 2010). We synchronize our movements, postures, and tones of voice with theirs. Doing so helps us tune in to what they're feeling. It also makes for "emotional contagion," helping to explain why it's fun to be around happy people and depressing to be around depressed people.

Our movements can also influence our attitudes. In a clever experiment, Gary Wells and Richard Petty (1980) had University of Alberta students "test headphone sets" by making either vertical or horizontal head movements while listening to a radio editorial. Who most agreed with the editorial? Those who had been nodding their heads up and down. Why? Wells and Petty surmised that positive thoughts are compatible with vertical nodding and incompatible with horizontal motion. Try it yourself when listening to someone: Do you feel more agreeable when nodding rather than shaking your head?

At the University of Cologne, Thomas Mussweiler (2006) likewise discovered that stereotyped actions feed stereotyped thinking. In one experiment, he induced some people to move about in the manner of an obese person—by having them wear a life vest and putting weights on their wrists and ankles—and then give their impression of someone described on paper. Those whose movements simulated obesity, more than those in a control condition, perceived the person (described on paper) as exhibiting traits (friendliness, sluggishness, unhealthiness) that people often perceive in obese people. In follow-up experiments, people induced to move slowly, as an elderly person might, ascribed more elderly stereotypic traits to a target person. Doing influenced thinking.

Postures also affect performance. After noting that people associate an arms-folded posture with determination and persistence, Ron Friedman and Andrew Elliot (2008) had students attempt to solve impossible anagrams. Those instructed to work with their arms folded persevered for an average 55 seconds, nearly double the 30 seconds of those with their hands on their thighs.

Overjustification and intrinsic motivations

Recall the insufficient justification effect—the smallest incentive that will get people to do something is usually the most effective in getting them to like the activity and keep on doing it. Cognitive dissonance theory offers one explanation for this: When external inducements are insufficient to justify our behaviour, we reduce dissonance by internally justifying the behaviour.

Self-perception theory offers another explanation: People explain their behaviour by noting the conditions under which it occurs. Imagine hearing someone proclaim the wisdom of a tuition increase after they are paid $20 to do so. Surely the statement would seem less sincere than if you thought the person was expressing those opinions for no pay. Perhaps we make similar inferences when observing ourselves. We observe our uncoerced action and infer our attitude.

Self-perception theory goes even a step further. Contrary to the notion that rewards always increase motivation, it suggests that unnecessary rewards sometimes have a hidden cost. Rewarding people for doing what they already enjoy may lead them to attribute their doing it to the reward, thus undermining their self-perception that they do it because they like it. Experiments by Edward Deci and Richard Ryan (1991, 1997), by Mark Lepper and David Greene (1979), and by Ann Boggiano and her colleagues (1985, 1987; Boggiano & Ruble, 1985) confirmed this **overjustification effect**. Pay people for playing with puzzles, and they will later play with the puzzles less than those who play without being paid; promise children a reward for doing what they intrinsically enjoy (for example, playing with magic markers) and you will turn their play into work (Figure 4–4).

overjustification effect The result of bribing people to do what they already like doing; they may then see their action as externally controlled rather than intrinsically appealing.

A folk tale illustrates the overjustification effect. An old man lived alone on a street where boys played noisily every afternoon. The din annoyed him, so one day he called the boys to his door. He told them he loved the cheerful sound of children's voices and promised them each 50 cents if they would return the next day. Next afternoon, the youngsters raced back and played more lustily than ever. The old man paid them and promised another reward the next day. Again they returned, whooping it up, and

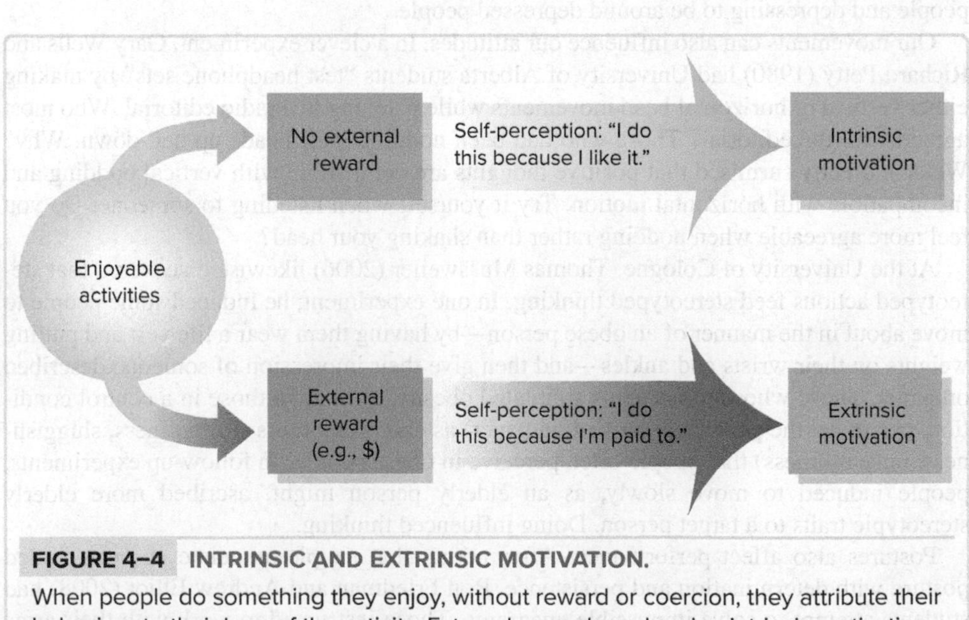

FIGURE 4–4 INTRINSIC AND EXTRINSIC MOTIVATION.

When people do something they enjoy, without reward or coercion, they attribute their behaviour to their love of the activity. External rewards undermine intrinsic motivation by leading people to attribute their behaviour to the incentive.

the man again paid them; this time, 25 cents. The following day they got only 15 cents, and the man explained that his meagre resources were being exhausted. "Please, though, would you come to play for 10 cents tomorrow?" The disappointed boys told the man they would not be back. It wasn't worth the effort, they said, to play all afternoon at his house for only 10 cents.

As self-perception theory implies, an unanticipated reward does not diminish intrinsic interest because people can still attribute their action to their own motivation (Bradley & Mannell, 1984; Tang & Hall, 1995). And if compliments for a good job make us feel more competent and successful, this can actually increase our intrinsic motivation. When rightly administered, rewards may also boost creativity (Eisenberger & Armeli, 2001; Eisenberger & Cameron, 1999; Eisenberger & Rhoades, 2001; Eisenberger, Rhoades, & Cameron, 1999; Eisenberger & Shanock, 2003).

The overjustification effect occurs when someone offers an unnecessary reward beforehand in an obvious effort to control behaviour. What matters is what a reward implies: Rewards and praise that inform people of their achievements (that make them feel, "I'm very good at this") boost intrinsic motivation. Rewards that seek to control people and lead them to believe it was the reward that caused their effort ("I did it for the money") diminish the intrinsic appeal of an enjoyable task (Freedman, Cunningham, & Krismer, 1992; Rosenfeld, Folger, & Adelman, 1980; Sansone, 1986).

How then can we cultivate people's enjoyment of tasks that are not intrinsically appealing? Courtney may find her first piano lessons frustrating. Sydney may not have an intrinsic love of Grade 5 science. Katelynn may not look forward to making those first sales calls. In such cases, the parent, teacher, or manager should probably use some incentives to coax the desired behaviour (Boggiano & Ruble, 1985; Cooke et al., 2011; Workman & Williams, 1980). After the person complies, suggest an intrinsic reason for doing so: "I'm not surprised that sales call went well because you are so good at making a first impression."

If we provide students with just enough justification to perform a learning task and use rewards and labels to help them feel competent, we may enhance their enjoyment and their eagerness to pursue the subject on their own. When there is too much justification—as happens in classrooms where teachers dictate behaviour and use rewards to control the children—child-driven learning may diminish (Deci & Ryan, 1985, 1991, 2008). One of the authors' sons eagerly consumed six or eight library books a week—until his library started a reading club that promised a party to those who read 10 books in three months. Three weeks later, he began checking out only one or two books during his weekly visit. Why? "Because you only need to read 10 books, you know."

Comparing the Theories

We have seen one explanation of why our actions seem to affect our attitudes (self-presentation theory). And we have seen two explanations of why our actions genuinely affect our attitudes: (1) the dissonance-theory assumption that we justify our behaviour to reduce our internal discomfort, and (2) the self-perception theory assumption that we observe our behaviour and make reasonable inferences about our attitudes, as we observe other people and infer their attitudes.

The last two explanations seem to contradict one another. Which is right? It's difficult to find a definitive test. In most instances, they make the same predictions, and we can bend each theory to accommodate most of the findings we have considered (Greenwald, 1975). Daryl Bem (1972), the self-perception theorist, even suggested that it boils down to a matter of loyalties and aesthetics. This illustrates the subjectivity of scientific theorizing (see Chapter 1). Neither dissonance theory nor self-perception theory has been handed to us by nature. Both are products of human imagination—creative attempts to simplify and explain what we've observed.

It is not unusual in science to find that a principle, such as "attitudes follow behaviour," is predictable from more than one theory. Physicist Richard Feynman (1967) marvelled that "one of the amazing characteristics of nature" is the "wide range of beautiful ways" in which we can describe it: "I do not understand the reason why it is that the correct laws of physics seem to be expressible in such a tremendous variety of ways" (pp. 53–55). Like different roads leading to the same place, different sets of assumptions can lead to the same principle. If anything, this *strengthens* our confidence in the principle. It becomes credible not only because of the data supporting it but also because it rests on more than one theoretical pillar.

Dissonance as arousal

Can we say that one of our theories is better? On one key point, strong support has emerged for dissonance theory. Recall that dissonance is, by definition, an aroused state of uncomfortable tension. To reduce this tension, we supposedly change our attitudes. Self-perception theory says nothing about tension being aroused when our actions and attitudes are not in harmony. It assumes merely that when our attitudes are weak to begin with, we will use our behaviour and its circumstances as a clue to those attitudes (like the person who said, "How do I know how I feel until I hear what I say?" [Forster, 1976]).

Are conditions that supposedly produce dissonance (for example, making decisions or acting contrary to one's attitudes) actually uncomfortably arousing? Clearly, yes, considering the classic study by the University of Waterloo's Mark Zanna and Princeton University's Joel Cooper (1974). They had students write an essay banning all speakers on campus, a view with which all the students disagreed. Half the students were told that they had no choice but to write the essay, while the other half were given the illusion that they chose to write the essay. Thus far, the study is just a replication of many previous dissonance studies, but Zanna and Cooper added a simple manipulation that helped establish arousal as central to the experience of dissonance. They had all the students take a pill (actually filled with powdered milk) at the beginning of the experiment. One-third of the students were told that the pill would make them feel aroused, one-third were told that it would make them feel relaxed, and one-third were given no information about the effects of the pill. Zanna and Cooper reasoned that if students thought the pill would make them feel aroused, when they experienced the arousal from the cognitive dissonance they were feeling, they would blame the arousal on the pill and would not change their attitude.

As you can see in Figure 4–5, the results of the experiment supported this reasoning. When students thought the pill would be arousing, students who had high and low choice to write the essay did not differ in their attitudes. When they were given no information about the pill, students showed the typical dissonance pattern of attitude change—those who were given the illusion of choice to write the essay changed their attitudes more than those who were given no choice to write it. Finally, the students who were told the pill would be relaxing showed an especially large amount of attitude change. These results demonstrate that feeling aroused is a central part of the experience of cognitive dissonance and that people must attribute this arousal to their own actions before they engage in self-justifying attitude change.

self-affirmation theory A theory that people often experience self-image threat after engaging in an undesirable behaviour, and they compensate for this threat by affirming another aspect of the self. Threaten people's self-concept in one domain, and they will compensate either by refocusing or by doing good deeds in some other domain.

Why is "volunteering" to say or do undesirable things so arousing? Because, suggests Claude Steele's (1988) **self-affirmation theory**, such acts are embarrassing. They make us feel foolish. They threaten our sense of personal competence and goodness. Justifying our actions and decisions is, therefore, self-affirming; it maintains our sense of integrity and self-worth. And when people engage in dissonance-generating actions—uncoerced counterattitudinal actions—their left frontal lobes (where thinking occurs) buzz with extra arousal (Harmon-Jones, Gerdjikov, & Harmon-Jones, 2008). This is the grinding gears of belief change at work.

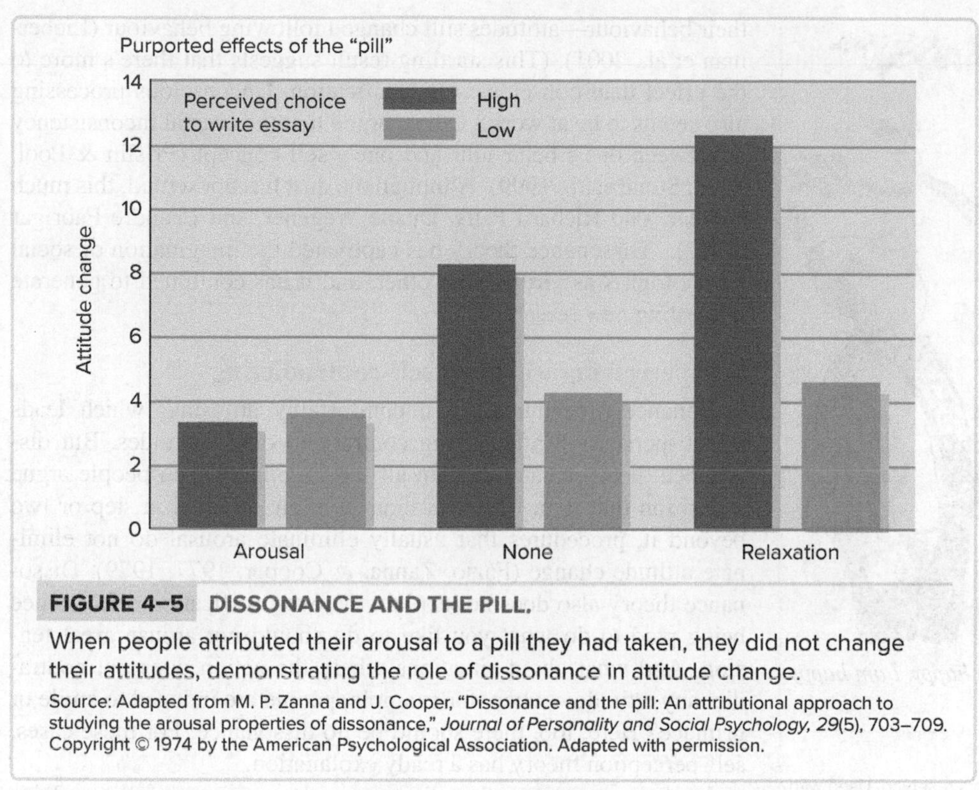

FIGURE 4–5 DISSONANCE AND THE PILL.

When people attributed their arousal to a pill they had taken, they did not change their attitudes, demonstrating the role of dissonance in attitude change.

Source: Adapted from M. P. Zanna and J. Cooper, "Dissonance and the pill: An attributional approach to studying the arousal properties of dissonance," *Journal of Personality and Social Psychology, 29*(5), 703–709. Copyright © 1974 by the American Psychological Association. Adapted with permission.

What do you suppose happens if, after committing a self-contradictory act, we offer people some other way to reaffirm their sense of self-worth, such as by doing a good deed? In several experiments, Steele found that, with their self-concepts secure, people (especially those who came to the experiments with strong self-concepts) feel much less need to justify their acts (Steele, Spencer, & Lynch, 1993). People with secure and stable high self-esteem also engage in less self-justification (Holland, Meertens, & Van Vugt, 2002; Jordan et al., 2003).

Self-affirming also seems to help people let down their guard and pay attention to health messages—researchers have found that providing opportunities to self affirm allows people to be more receptive to messages about quitting smoking (DiBello et al., 2015) and about responsible drinking (Armitage & Arden, 2016).

So dissonance conditions do, indeed, arouse tension, especially when they threaten positive feelings of self-worth. (In the study of relapsed smokers, it was those with high self-esteem who especially downplayed the risks.) But is this arousal necessary for the attitudes-follow-behaviour effect? Steele and his colleagues (1981) believed the answer to be yes. When drinking alcohol reduces dissonance-produced arousal, the attitudes-follow-behaviour effect disappears. In one of their experiments, they induced students to write an essay favouring a big tuition increase. The students reduced their resulting dissonance by softening their anti-tuition attitudes—unless after writing the unpleasant essay they drank alcohol.

Nearly seven decades after Festinger first proposed his theory, social psychologists continue to study and debate alternative views of what causes dissonance. Some say Festinger was right to think that merely behaving inconsistently with one's attitudes—say, writing privately that you liked a foul-tasting drink and being simultaneously aware of the inconsistency—is enough to provoke some attitude change (Harmon-Jones et al., 1996; Johnson, Kelly, & LeBlanc, 1995; McGregor, Newby-Clark, & Zanna, 1998). In fact, in studies with people suffering from amnesia—and thus with an inability to explicitly remember

I don't sing because I am happy. I am happy because I sing.

Self-perception at work.

Source: ©Ed Frascino.

their behaviour—attitudes still changed following behaviour (Lieberman et al., 2001). (This startling result suggests that there's more to the effect than conscious self-justification. Unconscious processing also seems to be at work.) Others argue that the crucial inconsistency is between one's behaviour and one's self-concept (Prislin & Pool, 1996; Stone et al., 1999). Although the dust has not settled, this much is clear, said Richard Petty, Duane Wegener, and Leandre Fabrigar (1997): "Dissonance theory has captivated the imagination of social psychologists as virtually no other, and it has continued to generate interesting new research."

Self-perceiving when not self-contradicting

Dissonance procedures are uncomfortably arousing, which leads to self-persuasion after acting contrary to one's attitudes. But dissonance theory cannot explain all the findings. When people argue a position that is in line with their opinion, although a step or two beyond it, procedures that usually eliminate arousal do not eliminate attitude change (Fazio, Zanna, & Cooper, 1977, 1979). Dissonance theory also does not explain the overjustification effect, since being paid to do what you like to do should not arouse great tension. And what about situations where the action does not contradict any attitude—when, for example, people are induced to smile or grimace? Here, too, there should be no dissonance. For these cases, self-perception theory has a ready explanation.

In short, it appears that dissonance theory successfully explains what happens when we act contrary to clearly defined attitudes: We feel tension, so we adjust our attitudes to reduce it. Dissonance theory, then, explains attitude change. In situations where our attitudes are not well formed, self-perception theory explains attitude formation. As we act and reflect, we develop a more readily accessible attitude to guide our future behaviour (Fazio, 1987; Roese & Olson, 1994).

SUMMING UP

How Well Do Our Attitudes Predict Our Behaviours?

- Attitudes do not predict behaviour as well as most people believe.
- Attitudes are better predictors of behaviour, however, when social influences are minimal, attitudes are specific to behaviours, and attitudes are potent (strong and on one's mind).

When Does Our Behaviour Affect Our Attitudes?

- When taking on a role, our actions in that role often shape our attitudes.
- When we state a belief (even if we do not initially believe it), our words often shape our attitudes.
- When we engage in small actions inconsistent with our attitudes, these small actions can lead to larger actions that can dramatically shape our attitudes and behaviour.

- When we engage in moral or evil acts, these actions can powerfully shape our attitudes.
- When we participate in social movements, our actions can profoundly shape our attitudes.

Why Does Our Behaviour Affect Our Attitudes?

- One reason our behaviours affect our attitudes is that we want to present ourselves to others and ourselves as consistently rational people.
- Our behaviours also affect our attitudes because holding beliefs that are inconsistent with our actions is arousing and uncomfortable. Because it is often easier to change our beliefs than our actions, we change our beliefs to match our actions and reduce the discomfort.
- Cultures vary in what beliefs and actions arouse feelings of discomfort, but when discrepancies between beliefs and action cause discomfort, similar processes of reducing this discomfort seem to occur across cultures.
- We also change our beliefs to match our actions because in observing our actions we have powerful clues about our beliefs.
- Several theories have been proposed to explain how our behaviour shapes our attitudes (i.e., self-presentation theory, cognitive dissonance theory, and self-perception theory). All three theories account for important phenomena, but cognitive dissonance theory is best at explaining what happens when the discrepancy between attitudes and behaviour is large, while self-perception theory is best at explaining what happens when the discrepancy between attitudes and behaviour is small.

Key Terms

attitude
cognitive dissonance theory
door-in-the-face-technique
foot-in-the-door phenomenon
gender roles
Implicit Association Test (IAT)
insufficient justification
low-ball technique
norms
overjustification effect
role
self-affirmation theory
self-perception theory

Part Two
Social Influence

So far in this book we have considered mostly intrapersonal phenomena—how we think about one another. Now we consider interpersonal happenings—how we influence and relate to one another. Therefore, in Chapter 5, Chapter 6, and Chapter 7, we probe social psychology's central concern: the powers of social influence.

What are these unseen social forces that push and pull us? How powerful are they? Research on social influence helps illuminate the invisible strings by which our social worlds move us about. This part reveals these subtle powers, especially the principles of persuasion (Chapter 5), the forces of social conformity (Chapter 6), the consequences of participation in groups (Chapter 7), and how all these influences operate together in everyday situations.

Seeing these influences, we may better understand why people feel and act as they do. And we may ourselves become less vulnerable to unwanted manipulation and more adept at pulling our own strings.

CHAPTER 5

Persuasion

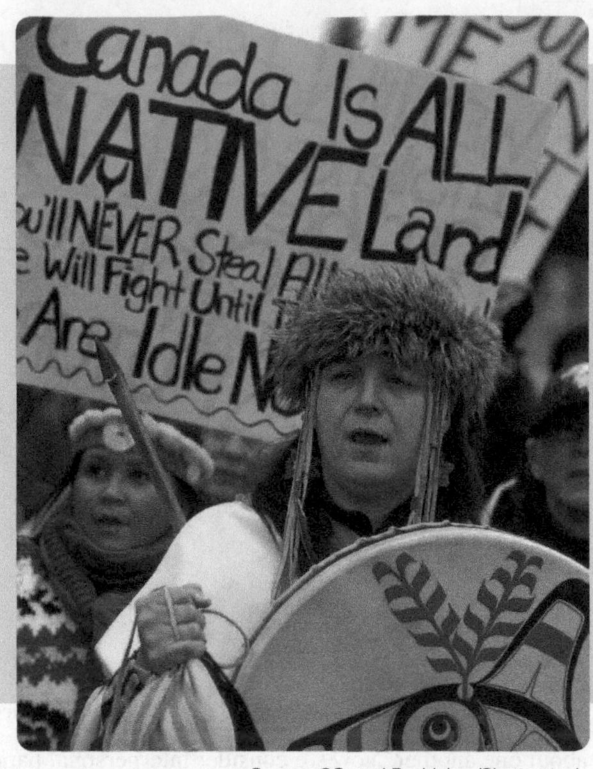

Source: ©Sergei Bachlakov/Shutterstock.

CHAPTER OUTLINE

What Paths Lead to Persuasion?

What Are the Elements of Persuasion?

Extreme Persuasion: How Do Cults Indoctrinate?

Persuasion and Climate Change: How Do We Address Global Warming?

How Can Persuasion Be Resisted?

Think of the best advertisement you have ever seen. What made it good? Was it artistic? Was it funny? Was it sad? What was the ad for? Did you buy the product? Most people think about a very poignant ad or a very funny one. Interestingly, most people cannot remember what the ad was for, and most never bought the product. Regardless, the advertisement was trying to persuade you to buy whatever product it was selling.

persuasion The process by which a message induces change in beliefs, attitudes, or behaviours.

Similarly, the power of **persuasion** enables us to promote health or to sell addiction, to advance peace or to stir up hate, to enlighten or to deceive. Persuasion is everywhere: at the heart of politics, marketing, courtship, parenting, social media, negotiation, conflict resolution, and courtroom decision making. Social psychologists therefore seek to understand what leads to effective, long-lasting attitude change.

Consider the following:

- *The spread of weird beliefs and conspiracy theories:* About one American in four and one European in three thinks the sun revolves around the earth (Grossman, 2014). Others deny that the moon landing and the Holocaust happened. A relatively new trend is the increase in "flat-earthers," people who believe the world is flat. In the United States, QAnon (an online source) claims that Democrats are Satan-worshipping child molesters (who drink children's blood) and that Donald Trump is secretly battling against them. Interestingly, Trump has not denied this, and there are elected officials within the Republican Party that support these theories.
- *Climate change skepticism:* The scientific community, represented by various national academies of science and the Intergovernmental Panel on Climate Change, is in a virtual consensus about three facts of life: (1) Atmospheric greenhouse gases are accumulating; (2) diminishing sea ice and rising land, sea, and atmospheric temperatures all confirm the world is warming; and (3) this climate change will almost certainly produce rising sea levels and more extreme weather, including record floods, tornadoes, droughts, and high temperatures (National Geographic, 2020). Nevertheless, over the past two decades, popular climate *skepticism* has grown. The number of people who believe that global warming has been happening declined from 84 to 74 percent between 2007 and 2010 in the United States, as concern diminished (Krosnick, 2010). That number now stands at 69 percent (Leiserowitz et al., 2019). As a comparison, 83 percent of Canadians believe climate change is happening, with the greatest number of believers in Halifax (93 percent) and the lowest in rural Saskatchewan (60 percent). Researchers wondered: Why is the scientific consensus failing to persuade and to motivate action? And what might be done?
- *The promotion of healthier living:* Due partly to health-promotion campaigns, the Canadian Tobacco Use Monitoring Survey reveals that the Canadian smoking rate has plunged to 15.8 percent, less than half the rate of 30 years ago (Statistics Canada, 2019). And the rate of lifetime abstainers from alcohol use among Canadian university students had increased to 12.2 percent in 2016, and 35.5 percent of Canadians over 15 had not had a drink in a year (WHO, 2018).

Persuasion is everywhere. When we approve of it, we may call it "education."

Source: Ad developed by ChangeMakers for the Winnipeg Regional Health Authority.

Persuasion is neither inherently good nor inherently bad. It is usually the content of the message that elicits judgments of good or bad. The bad, we call "propaganda"; the good, we call "education." *Education* is more believable than *propaganda* (Lumsden, Zanna, & Darley, 1980).

Persuasion is everywhere—and it is inevitable. What factors affect persuasion? And how, as persuaders, can we most effectively "educate" others? Imagine that you are a marketing or advertising executive. Or imagine that you want to promote energy conservation, to encourage breast-feeding, or to campaign for a political candidate. What could you do to make yourself and your message persuasive? And if you are wary of being influenced, what tactics should you be alert to?

To answer such questions, social psychologists usually study persuasion the way some geologists study erosion—by observing the effects of various factors in brief, controlled experiments that enable us to understand how, given enough time, such factors could produce big effects.

What Paths Lead to Persuasion?

What two paths lead to persuasion? What type of cognitive processing does each involve—and with what effects?

When people try to persuade others, they can try to use good arguments; they can convince people that if they really think through the issues, they will become persuaded to change their minds. At the opposite extreme, they can try to change people's minds without having them think about the issue at all.

In the 1940s and 1950s, Carl Hovland and his colleagues (Hovland, Lumsdaine, & Sheffield, 1949) at Yale University studied the barriers that can prevent a message from being persuasive. They approached their task carefully, manipulating factors related to the communicator, the content of the message, the channel of communication, and the audience.

Researchers at Ohio State University then focused on people's thoughts in response to persuasive messages. If a message is clear but unconvincing, then you will easily counterargue the message and won't be persuaded. If the message offers convincing arguments, however, then your thoughts will be more favourable toward the message and you will most likely be persuaded. People's "cognitive responses" matter. As shown in Figure 5–1, persuasion entails clearing several hurdles. Any factors that help people clear the hurdles increase persuasion. For example, if an attractive source increases your attention to a message, then the message should have a better chance of persuading you.

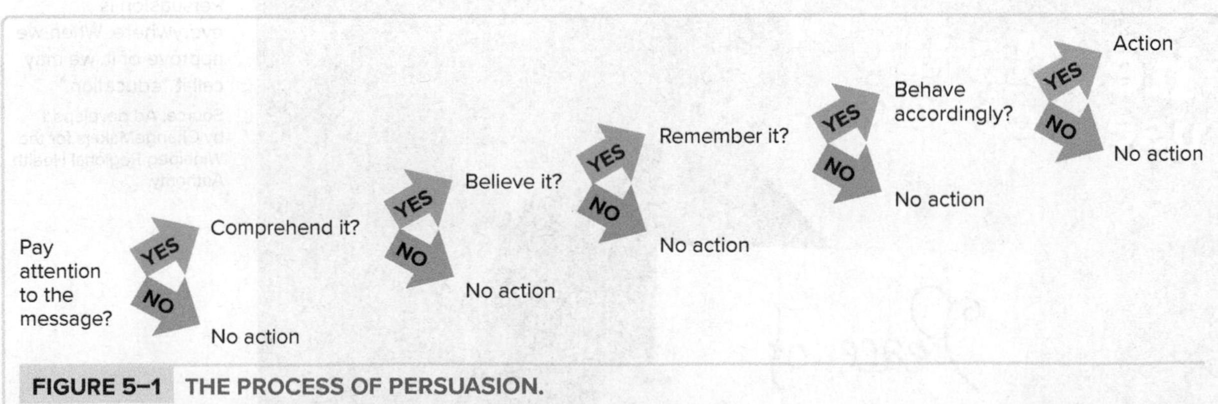

FIGURE 5–1 THE PROCESS OF PERSUASION.

To elicit action, a persuasive message must clear several hurdles. What is crucial is not so much remembering the message itself as remembering one's own thoughts in response.

The Central Route and the Peripheral Route

Richard Petty and John Cacioppo (1986; Petty & Wegener, 1999; see also Eagly & Chaiken, 1998) took this one step further. They theorized that persuasion is likely to occur via one of two routes (Figure 5–2).

When people are motivated and able to think systematically about an issue, they are likely to take the **central route to persuasion**—focusing on the arguments. If those arguments are strong and compelling, persuasion is likely. If the message contains only weak arguments, thoughtful people will notice that the arguments aren't very compelling and will counter-argue.

But sometimes the strength of the arguments doesn't matter. Sometimes we're not motivated enough or able to think carefully. If we're distracted, uninvolved, or just plain busy, we may not take the time to reflect on the message's content. Rather than noticing whether the arguments are particularly compelling, we might follow the **peripheral route to persuasion**—focusing on cues that trigger acceptance without much thinking.

Smart advertisers adapt ads to their consumers' thinking and the context in which they will see their ads. They do so for good reason. Much of consumers' behaviour is done unthinkingly (Dijksterhuis et al., 2005). Our opinions regarding products such as food, drink, and clothing are often

central route to persuasion Occurs when interested people focus on the arguments and respond with favourable thoughts.

peripheral route to persuasion Occurs when people are influenced by incidental cues, such as a speaker's attractiveness.

"Attitude changes are stronger the more they are based on issue-relevant thinking."

Richard Petty and Duane Wegener (1998)

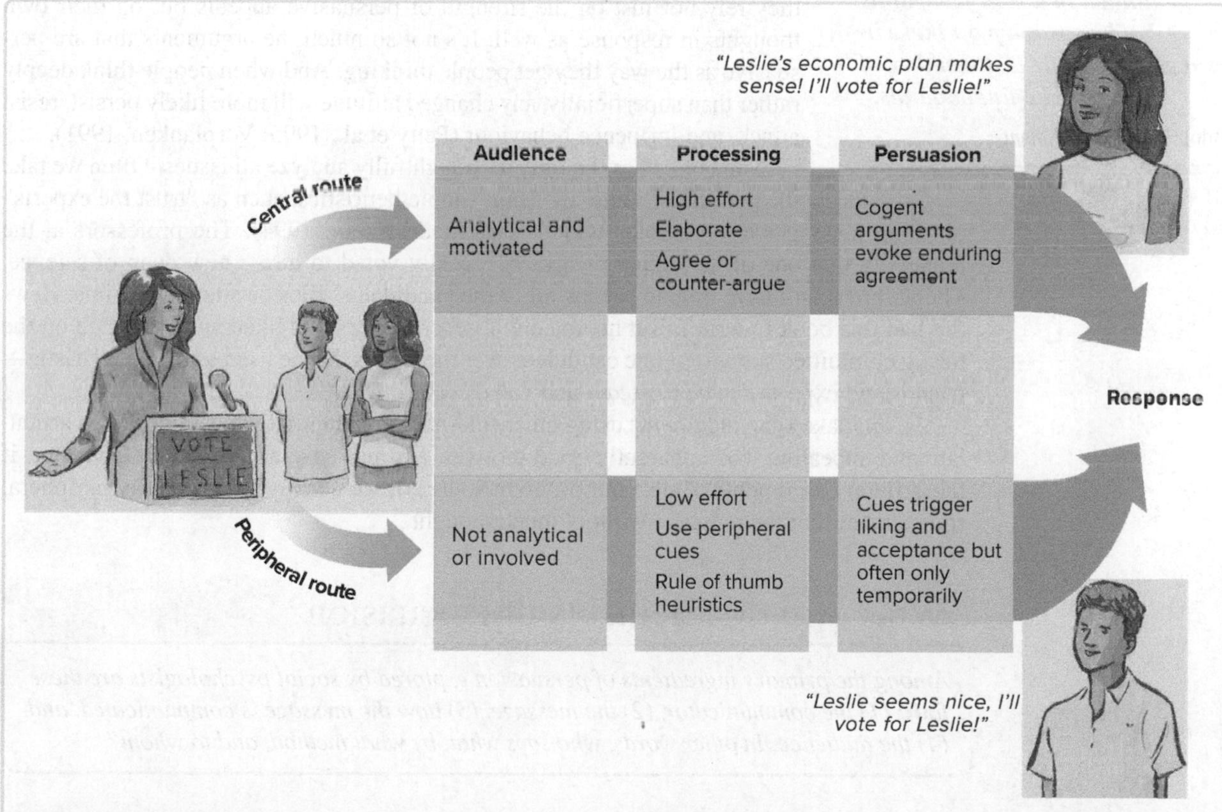

FIGURE 5–2 THE CENTRAL AND PERIPHERAL ROUTES TO PERSUASION.

Computer ads typically take the central route, by assuming that their audience wants to systematically compare features and prices. Soft-drink ads usually take the peripheral route, by merely associating their product with glamour, pleasure, and good moods. Central route processing more often produces enduring attitude change.

based more on feelings than on logic. Billboards and television commercials—media that consumers are able to take in only for brief amounts of time—typically use visual images as peripheral cues. Instead of providing arguments in favour of consuming alcohol, beer ads associate the product with images of beauty and pleasure. Tim Hortons and Molson ads promote their products as being quintessentially Canadian. On the other hand, computer ads and car ads—which interested, logical consumers may pore over for some time—are less likely to feature Hollywood stars or great athletes; instead, they offer customers information on competitive features and prices.

These two routes to persuasion—one explicit and reflective, the other more implicit and automatic—were forerunners to today's "dual processing" models of the human mind. Central route processing often swiftly changes explicit attitudes. Peripheral route processing more slowly builds implicit attitudes, through repeated associations between an attitude object and an emotion (Jones, Fazio, & Olson, 2009; Petty & Brinõl, 2008; Walther, Weil, & Düsing, 2011).

Different Routes for Different Purposes

The ultimate goal of the persuader is not just to have people pay attention to the message and move on. Typically, the goal is behaviour change (buying a product, quitting smoking, or studying more effectively). Are both routes to persuasion equally likely to fulfill that goal? Petty and his colleagues (Petty, Haugtvedt, & Smith, 1995) noted how central route processing can lead to more enduring change than does the peripheral route.

> ***"All effective propaganda must be limited to a very few points and must harp on these in slogans until the last member of the public understands."***
>
> Adolf Hitler, *Mein Kampf*

When people are thinking carefully and mentally elaborating on issues, they rely not just on the strength of persuasive appeals but on their own thoughts in response as well. It's not so much the arguments that are persuasive as the way they get people thinking. And when people think deeply rather than superficially, any changed attitude will more likely persist, resist attack, and influence behaviour (Petty et al., 1995; Verplanken, 1991).

None of us has the time to thoughtfully analyze all issues. Often we take the peripheral route, by using simple heuristics, such as "trust the experts" or "long messages are credible" (Chaiken & Maheswaran, 1994). The professors at the university that one of the authors works at recently voted to hire a new dean of science. The author didn't have time to review all of the candidates' files or attend their interviews (he had this book to write). But he noted that several people he liked and respected on the hiring committee supported one candidate over the others. So he used a simple heuristic—friends and experts can be trusted—and voted accordingly.

We all make snap judgments using other rule-of-thumb heuristics: If a speaker is articulate and appealing, has apparently good motives, and has several arguments (or better, if the different arguments come from different sources), we usually take the easy peripheral route and accept the message without much thought.

What Are the Elements of Persuasion?

Among the primary ingredients of persuasion explored by social psychologists are these four: (1) the communicator, (2) the message, (3) how the message is communicated, and (4) the audience. In other words, who says what, by what method, and to whom?

Who Says? The Communicator

Imagine you are talking to a car salesperson who tells you that the car you are interested in is the most fuel-efficient in its class, has the best handling, and is cheaper than the competition. The salesperson also tells you that all of her customers have loved the car—no one has complained. Would you believe her? Would you buy the car? Now, what if you read the same information in *Consumer Reports* magazine or in online reviews? Most people would be more likely to believe the magazine and online sources over the salesperson. The salesperson clearly has something to gain, whereas the magazine and online reviewers do not.

Social psychologists have found that who is saying something affects how an audience receives it. In one experiment, when the Socialist and Liberal leaders in the Dutch parliament argued identical positions using the same words, each was most effective with members of his own party (Wiegman, 1985). Your belief about who wins a political debate depends on who you supported initially.

Credibility

What, then, makes one communicator more persuasive than another? It's not just the central message that matters but also who says it. Interestingly, advertisers know this and have tried to adapt. One strategy is to mask the source: Advertisers prepare "video news releases" and give them to news shows, which play them without indicating their source. Viewers think that they are seeing a news story when in fact they are viewing a carefully crafted ad. Research has shown (e.g., Nelson & Park, 2015) that these approaches are more effective than regular advertising because people's natural distrust of the advertiser is circumvented. You might also have noticed short "Brand Power" news segments that come on during TV commercials or before YouTube videos. They are written to appear to be consumer information but they are really just ads for the products they talk about.

Any of us would find a statement about the benefits of exercise more believable if it came from a scientific journal rather than from a tabloid newspaper. But the effects of source **credibility** (perceived expertise and trustworthiness) diminish after a month or so. If a credible person's message is persuasive, its impact may fade as its source is forgotten or dissociated from the message. And the impact of a non-credible person may correspondingly increase over time if people remember the message better than the reason for discounting it (Cook & Flay, 1978; Gruder et al., 1978; Pratkanis et al., 1988; Foos, Keeling, & Keeling, 2016). This delayed persuasion, after people forget the source or its connection with the message, is called the **sleeper effect**. Interestingly, the sleeper effect is particularly effective when attitudes are based on beliefs rather than on emotional information (Isaac & Poor, 2016).

credibility Believability. A credible communicator is perceived as both expert and trustworthy.

sleeper effect A delayed impact of a message; occurs when we remember the message but forget a reason for discounting it.

CBarsotti
"If I seem excited, Mr. Bolling, it's only because I know that I can make you a very rich man."

Skilled persuaders know how to convey a message effectively.
Source: ©Charles Barsotti. All rights reserved. Used with permission.

Perceived expertise

How does someone become an authoritative "expert"? One way is to begin by saying things the audience agrees with, which makes the speaker seem smart. Indeed, one reason the scientific consensus about climate change fails to persuade is that people count as "expert" someone whose conclusions support their own pre-existing values and views. Researchers have observed this "congenial views seem more expert" phenomenon on topics ranging from climate change to nuclear waste to gun laws (Kahan, Jenkins-Smith, & Braman, 2010).

Another way to be perceived as credible is to be seen as *knowledgeable* on the topic. A message about tooth brushing from "Dr. James Rundle of the Canadian Dental Association" is much more convincing than the same message from "Jim Rundle, a local high school student who did a project with some of his classmates on dental hygiene" (Olson & Cal, 1984). After more than a decade studying high school marijuana use, researchers concluded that scare messages from unreliable sources did not affect marijuana use during the 1960s and 1970s. However, from a credible source, scientific reports of the biological and psychological results of long-term marijuana use "can play an important role in reducing . . . drug use" (Bachman et al., 1988).

"Believe an expert."

Virgil, *Aeneid*

Another way to appear credible is to speak confidently (e.g., Pulford et al., 2018). Whether pitching a business plan or giving advice, a charismatic, energetic, confident-seeming person often is convincing (Moore & Swift, 2011; Pentland, 2010). Bonnie Erickson and her collaborators (1978) had students evaluate courtroom testimony given in a straightforward manner or in a more hesitant manner. Here is an example:

QUESTION: Approximately how long did you stay there before the ambulance arrived?

ANSWER A: [*Straightforward*] Twenty minutes. Long enough to help get Mrs. David straightened out.

ANSWER B: [*Hesitating*] Oh, it seems like it was about, uh, 20 minutes. Just long enough to help my friend Mrs. David, you know, get straightened out.

The students found the straightforward witnesses much more competent and credible.

Perceived trustworthiness

Speech style also affects a speaker's apparent trustworthiness. Gordon Hemsley and Anthony Doob (1978) found that if, while testifying, videotaped witnesses looked their questioner straight in the eye instead of gazing downward, they impressed people as more believable.

Trustworthiness is also higher if the audience believes the communicator is not trying to persuade them. In an experimental version of what later became the "hidden-camera" method of television advertising, Elaine Hatfield and Leon Festinger (Walster & Festinger, 1962) had some undergraduates eavesdrop on graduate students' conversations. (What they actually heard was a tape recording.) When the conversational topic was relevant to the eavesdroppers (having to do with campus regulations), the speakers had more influence if the listeners presumed the speakers were unaware of the eavesdropping. After all, if people don't know someone's listening, why would they be less than fully honest?

We also perceive as sincere those who argue against their own self-interest. Alice Eagly, Wendy Wood, and Shelly Chaiken (1978) presented students with a speech attacking a company's pollution of a river. When they said the speech was given by a political candidate with a business background or to an audience of company supporters, it seemed unbiased and was persuasive. When a supposedly pro-environment politician gave the same anti-business speech to environmentalists, listeners could attribute the politician's arguments to personal bias or to the audience. Being willing to suffer for one's beliefs—which Mahatma Gandhi, Nelson Mandela, Martin Luther King, Jr., and other great leaders have done—also helps convince people of one's sincerity (Knight & Weiss, 1980).

As well, Norman Miller and his colleagues (1976) found that trustworthiness and credibility increase when people talk fast. People who listened to tape-recorded messages rated fast speakers (about 190 words per minute) as more objective, intelligent, and knowledgeable than slow speakers (about 110 words per minute). They also found the more rapid speakers more persuasive.

Some television ads are obviously constructed to make the communicator appear both expert and trustworthy. A drug company may promote its pain relievers using a speaker in a white lab coat, who declares confidently that most doctors recommend their ingredient (which is merely aspirin). Given such peripheral cues, people who don't care enough to analyze the evidence may reflexively infer that the product is special. Other ads seem not to use the credibility principle. It's not primarily for his expertise about sports apparel that Nike signed a deal with Lebron James that might be worth up to $1 billion (*Sports Illustrated*, 2016).

Thus, communicators gain credibility if they seem expert and trustworthy (Pornpitakpan, 2004). When we know in advance that a source is credible, we think more favourable thoughts in response to the message. If we learn the source after a message generates favourable thoughts, high credibility strengthens our confidence in our thinking, which strengthens the persuasive impact of the message (Briñol, Petty, & Tormala, 2004; Briñol, Tormala, & Petty, 2002; Tormala, Briñol, & Petty, 2006).

An interesting finding is that sources who are clearly biased (e.g., who are in a conflict of interest) but who openly declare that bias, are actually seen as more credible (see Sah et al., 2018). Participants who read a blog post from a blogger who openly declared their conflict of interest perceived the blogger, the blogger's recommendation, and the blogger's sponsor as more credible than those with no disclosure. Given the new ubiquity of social media "influencers" and the fact that with the number of sources online people struggle to separate credible from non-credible sources (e.g., Zha et al., 2018), this is a very important finding.

Attractiveness and liking

Most of us deny that endorsements by star athletes and entertainers affect us. We know that stars are seldom knowledgeable about the products they endorse. Besides, we know the intent is to persuade us: We don't just casually get to observe Ryan Reynolds's morning routine, getting dressed and spraying himself with a specific brand of cologne. Such ads are based on another characteristic of an effective communicator: **attractiveness**.

We may think we are not influenced by attractiveness or likeability, but researchers have found otherwise. We're more likely to respond to those we like, a phenomenon well known to those organizing charitable solicitations and candy sales. Even a fleeting conversation with someone is enough to increase our liking for that person and our responsiveness to their influence (Burger et al., 2001). Our liking may open us up to the communicator's arguments (central route persuasion), or it may trigger positive associations when we see the product later (peripheral route persuasion). As with credibility, the liking-begets-persuasion principle suggests applications (see Table 5–1).

attractiveness Having qualities that appeal to an audience. An appealing communicator (often someone similar to the audience) is most persuasive on matters of subjective preference.

Attractiveness exists in several forms. Physical attractiveness is one. Arguments, especially emotional ones, are often more influential when they come from people we consider beautiful (Chaiken, 1979; Dion & Stein, 1978; Pallak, Murroni, & Koch, 1983). Most people understand that attractiveness matters most when people are making superficial judgments. In experiments, people exploit opportunities to use attractive communicators with less analytical recipients (Vogel et al., 2010).

Similarity is another form of attractiveness. As Chapter 10 will emphasize, we tend to like people who are like us. We also are influenced by them, a fact that has been harnessed by a successful anti-smoking campaign that features youth appealing to other youth through ads that challenge the tobacco industry about its destructiveness and its marketing

TABLE 5-1 Six Persuasion Principles.

In his book *Influence: Science and Practice*, persuasion researcher Robert Cialdini (2000) illustrates six principles that underlie human relationships and human influence.

Principle	Application
Authority: People defer to credible experts.	Establish your expertise; identify problems you have solved and people you have served.
Liking: People respond more affirmatively to those they like.	Win friends and influence people. Create bonds based on similar interests; praise freely.
Social proof: People allow the example of others to validate how to think, feel, and act.	Use "peer power"—have respected others lead the way.
Reciprocity: People feel obliged to repay in kind what they've received.	Be generous with your time and resources. What goes around, comes around.
Consistency: People tend to honour their public commitments.	Have others write or voice their intentions. Don't say "Please do this by . . ." Instead, elicit a "yes" by asking.
Scarcity: People prize what's scarce.	Highlight genuinely exclusive information or opportunities.

practices (Krisberg, 2004). People who act as we do, subtly mimicking our postures, are likewise more influential (Bailenson & Yee, 2005). Thus, salespeople are sometimes taught to "mimic and mirror": If the customer's arms or legs are crossed, cross yours; if they smile, smile back.

Another example: Theodore Dembroski, Thomas Lasater, and Albert Ramirez (1978) gave Black junior high school students a taped appeal for proper dental care. When a dentist assessed the cleanliness of their teeth the next day, those who heard the appeal from a Black dentist had cleaner teeth. As a general rule, people respond better to a message that comes from someone in their group (Van Knippenberg & Wilke, 1992; Wilder, 1990).

Is similarity more important than credibility? Sometimes yes, sometimes no. Timothy Brock (1965) found that paint-store customers were more influenced by the testimony of an ordinary person who had recently bought the same amount of paint they planned to buy than by an expert who had recently purchased 20 times as much. But recall that when discussing dental hygiene, a leading dentist (a dissimilar but expert source) was more persuasive than a student (a similar but inexpert source).

Such seemingly contradictory findings bring out the detective in us. They suggest that an undiscovered factor is at work—that similarity is more important given the presence of factor X, and credibility is more important given the absence of factor X. Factor X, as George Goethals and Erick Nelson (1973) discovered, is whether the topic is one of subjective preference or objective reality. When the choice concerns matters of personal value, taste, or way of life, similar communicators have the most influence. But on judgments of fact—e.g., Does Sydney have less rainfall than London?—confirmation of belief by a dissimilar person does more to boost confidence. A dissimilar person provides a more independent judgment.

Importantly, if we believe that communicators truly like, use, or desire the product they are endorsing, then we are more likely to have positive views on the product as well and are presumably more likely to buy the product (Kapitan & Silvera, 2016).

What Is Said? The Message Content

It matters not only who says something but also what that person says. If you were to help organize an appeal to get people to vote for an increase in school taxes, or to stop smoking, or to give money to world hunger relief, you might wonder how to concoct a recipe for central route persuasion. Common sense could lead you to either side of these questions:

- Is a logical message one that is more persuasive—or one that arouses emotion?
- Will you get more opinion change by advocating a position that is only slightly different from the listeners' existing opinions or by advocating an extreme point of view?
- Should the message express your side only, or should it acknowledge and refute the opposing views?
- If people are to present both sides—say, in successive talks at a community meeting or in a political debate—is there an advantage to going first or last?

Let's examine these questions one at a time.

Attractive communicators—such as David and Victoria Beckham—often trigger peripheral route persuasion. We associate their message or product with our good feelings toward the communicator, and we approve and believe.
Source: ©Everett Collection/Shutterstock.

Reason versus emotion

Suppose you were campaigning in support of world hunger relief. Would it be best to itemize your arguments and cite an array of impressive statistics? Or would you be more effective presenting an emotional approach—say, the compelling story of one starving child? Of course, an argument can be both reasonable and emotional. You can marry passion and logic. Still, which is more influential—reason or emotion? Was Shakespeare's Lysander right: "The will of man is by his reason sway'd"? Or was Lord Chesterfield's advice wiser: "Address yourself generally to the senses, to the heart, and to the weaknesses of mankind, but rarely to their reason"?

The answer: It depends on the audience. Well-educated or analytical people are responsive to rational appeals (Cacioppo et al., 1996; Cacioppo, Petty, & Morris, 1983; Hovland et al., 1949). Thoughtful, involved audiences travel the central route; they are most responsive to reasoned arguments. Disinterested audiences travel the peripheral route; they are more affected by how much they like the communicator (Chaiken, 1980; Petty, Cacioppo, & Goldman, 1981).

It also depends on how people's attitudes were formed. When people's initial attitudes are formed primarily through emotion, they are more persuaded by later emotional appeals; when their initial attitudes are formed primarily through reason, they are more persuaded by later intellectual arguments (Edwards, 1990; Fabrigar & Petty, 1999). New emotions may sway an emotion-based attitude. But to change an information-based attitude, more information may be needed.

The effect of good feelings

> ***"The truth is always the strongest argument."***
>
> Sophocles, *Phaedra*

Messages can also become more persuasive through association with good feelings (e.g., Petty & Brinol, 2015). Irving Janis and his colleagues (Janis, Kaye, & Kirschner, 1965; Dabbs & Janis, 1965) found that students were more convinced by persuasive messages if they were allowed to enjoy peanuts and Pepsi while reading them (Figure 5–3). Similarly, Mark Galizio and Clyde Hendrick (1972) found that students were more persuaded by folk-song lyrics accompanied by pleasant guitar music than by unaccompanied lyrics. There is, it seems, something to be gained from conducting business over sumptuous lunches with pleasant background music.

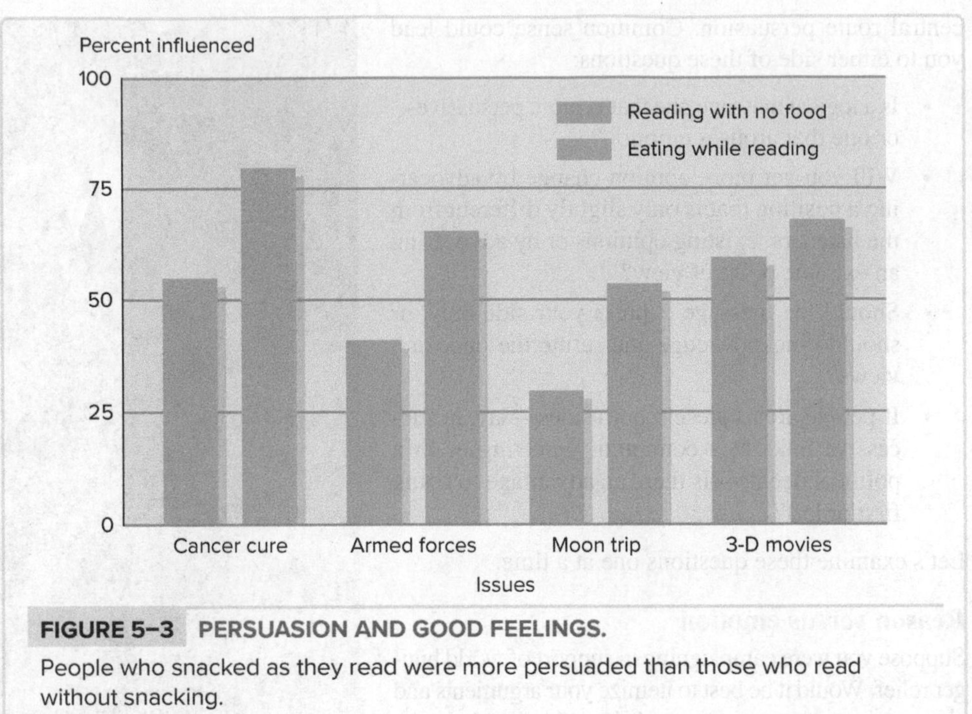

FIGURE 5–3 PERSUASION AND GOOD FEELINGS.

People who snacked as they read were more persuaded than those who read without snacking.

Good feelings often enhance persuasion, partly by enhancing positive thinking and partly by linking good feelings with the message (Petty et al., 1993; Petty & Brinol, 2015). As noted in Chapter 3, people in a good mood view the world through rose-coloured glasses. But they also make faster, more impulsive decisions; they rely more on peripheral cues (Bodenhausen, 1993; Moons & Mackie, 2007). Unhappy people, on the other hand, ruminate more before reacting so they are less easily swayed by weak arguments. (They also produce more cogent persuasive messages [Forgas, 2007].) Thus, if you can't make a strong case, it's a smart idea to put your audience members in a good mood and hope they'll feel good about your message without thinking too much about it.

> ***"Opinion is ultimately determined by the feelings and not by the intellect."***
>
> Herbert Spencer, *Social Statics*, 1851

Knowing that humour can put people in a good mood, a Dutch research team led by Madelijn Strick (Strick et al., 2009) invited people to view ads of either funny cartoons (Figure 5–4) or the same cartoons altered to be unfunny. Their finding: Products associated with humour were better liked, as measured by an implicit attitude test, and were more often chosen.

The effect of arousing fear

Messages also can be effective by evoking negative emotions. When trying to convince people to cut down on smoking, to brush their teeth more often, to get a tetanus shot, or to drive carefully, a fear-arousing message can be potent (de Hoog, Stroebe, & de Wit, 2007; Muller & Johnson, 1990). By requiring cigarette makers to include graphic warning labels on each pack of cigarettes depicting the hazards of smoking, the Canadian government assumed—correctly, it turns out—that showing cigarette smokers the horrible things that can happen to smokers adds to persuasiveness (O'Hegarty et al., 2007; Peters et al., 2007; Stark et al., 2008).

But how much fear should you arouse? Should you evoke just a little fear, lest people become so frightened that they tune out your painful message? Or should you try to scare the daylights out of them? Experiments by Howard Leventhal (1970) and his collaborators,

FIGURE 5–4 HUMOUR IN ADVERTISING.

In experiments at Radboud University in Nijmegen, Netherlands, humour enhanced people's liking of products such as these.

Source: (left): ©Sun Media Corporation. Reprinted by permission; (right): ©Chones/Shutterstock.

by Ronald Rogers and his collaborators (Robberson & Rogers, 1988), and by Natascha de Hoog and her colleagues (2007) show that, often, the more frightened people are, the more they respond.

The effectiveness of fear-arousing communications is being applied in ads discouraging not only smoking but also drinking and driving and risky sexual behaviours. When Claude Levy-Leboyer (1988) found that attitudes toward alcohol and drinking habits among French youth were effectively changed by fear-arousing pictures, the French government incorporated this kind of information in its TV spots.

One effective anti-smoking ad campaign offered graphic "truth" ads. In one, vans pull up outside an unnamed corporate tobacco office. Teens pile out and unload 1200 body bags covering two city blocks. As a curious corporate suit peers out a window above, a teen shouts into a loudspeaker that smoking kills 1200 people per day and the body bags were being left there to show what that meant (Nicholson, 2007). While teens who viewed a cerebral Philip Morris ad (that lectured, "Think. Don't Smoke") were not less likely to smoke, those viewing the more dramatic and edgy ad became significantly less inclined to smoke (Farrelly et al., 2002, 2008).

"If the jury had been sequestered in a nicer hotel, this would probably never have happened."

Good feelings help create positive attitudes.

Source: ©Frank Cotham. All rights reserved. Used with permission.

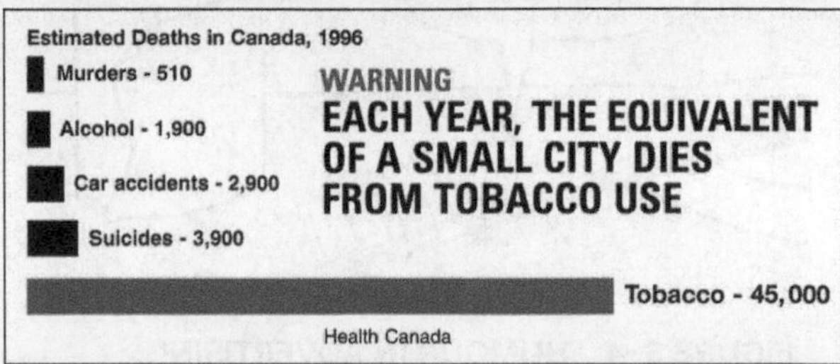

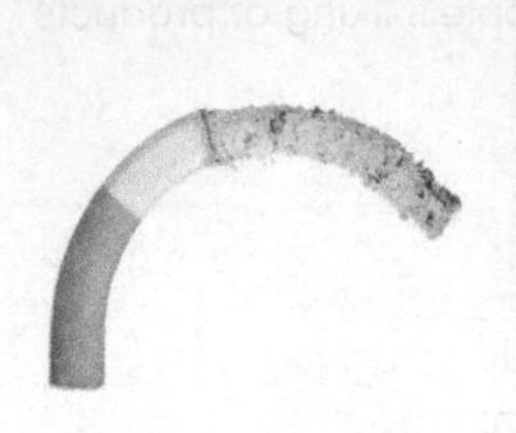

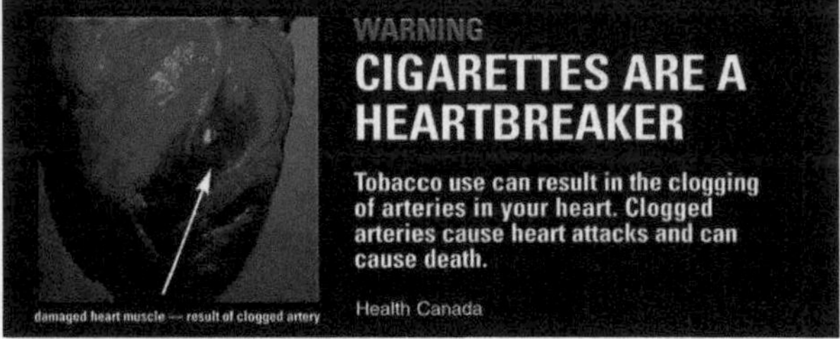

Canadian cigarette warnings, sampled here, use fear arousal.

Source: (top left, middle left, middle right, and bottom left): Health Canada, 2011 Reproduced with the permission of the Minister of Health, 2011; (top right): Health Canada, 2011 Reproduced with the permission of the Minister of Health, 2011. Copyright (c) Province of British Columbia. All rights reserved. Reproduced with permission of the Province of British Columbia; (bottom right): Health Canada, 2011 Reproduced with the permission of the Minister of Health, 2011. Copyright Health Sciences Centre Winnipeg, an operating division of Winnipeg Regional Health Authority.

Fear-arousing communications are increasing people's detection behaviours, such as getting mammograms, doing breast or testicular self-exams, and checking for signs of skin cancer. Sara Banks, Peter Salovey, and their colleagues (1995) had women aged 40 to 66 who had not obtained mammograms view an educational video on mammography. Of those who had received a positively framed message (emphasizing that getting a mammogram can save your life through early detection), only half got a mammogram within 12 months. Of those who had received a fear-framed message (emphasizing that not getting a mammogram can cost you your life), two-thirds got a mammogram within 12 months.

Playing on fear works best if a message leads people not only to fear the severity and likelihood of a threatened event but also to perceive a solution and feel capable of implementing it (Devos-Comby & Salovey, 2002; Maddux & Rogers, 1983). Many ads aimed at reducing sexual risks aim both to arouse fear—"AIDS kills"—and to offer a protective strategy: Abstain, or wear a condom, or save sex for a committed relationship. Also, "gain-framed" messages are often equally effective as "loss-framed" messages (O'Keefe & Jensen, 2011). Gain-framed messages focus on the advantages of healthy behaviour (for example, "If you wear sunscreen, you'll have attractive skin" rather than "If you don't wear sunscreen, you'll have unattractive skin"). Thus, a global climate change article that ends by describing future catastrophic consequences is less persuasive to many skeptics than one that concludes by discussing possible solutions (Feinberg & Willer, 2010).

Vivid propaganda often exploits fears. The Nazi newspaper *Der Stürmer* aroused fear with hundreds upon hundreds of unsubstantiated anecdotes about Jews who were said to have ground rats to make food, seduced non-Jewish women, and cheated families out of their life savings. These appeals, like most Nazi propaganda, were emotional, not logical. The appeals also gave clear, specific instructions on how to combat "the danger": They listed Jewish businesses so readers would avoid them, encouraged readers to submit for publication the names of Germans who patronized Jewish shops and professionals, and directed readers to compile lists of Jews in their area (Bytwerk & Brooks, 1980).

Vivid stories can also be used for good, however, especially when what's most memorable conveys the central message rather than distracting from it (Guadagno, Rhoads, & Sagarin, 2011). After the genocidal conflict between Rwanda's Hutus and Tutsis, a year-long field experiment explored the impact of a radio soap opera that featured stories of prejudice, conflict, communication, reconciliation, and even love across group lines in two fictional communities. Compared with a control group exposed to a health-related radio soap opera, listeners became more accepting of empathy, cooperation, trauma healing, and even intermarriage (Paluck, 2009).

Another approach is to enhance people's perceptions of susceptibility to a particular illness to make them more likely to expose themselves to messages about the topic. They were also more likely to be motivated to engage in adaptive behaviours to address the potential health threat (Hastall & Wagner, 2018).

Discrepancy

Picture the following scene: Ritu arrives home on spring vacation and hopes to convert her portly, middle-aged father to her new "health-fitness lifestyle." She runs eight kilometres a day. Her father says his idea of exercise is "channel surfing." Ritu thinks, "Would I be more likely to get Dad off his chair by urging him to try a modest exercise program—say, a daily walk—or by trying to get him involved in something strenuous, like a program of calisthenics and running? Maybe if I asked him to take up a rigorous exercise program, he would compromise and at least do something worthwhile. But then again, maybe he'd write me off and do nothing."

Like Ritu, social psychologists can reason either way. Disagreement produces discomfort, and discomfort prompts people to change their opinions. (Recall from Chapter 4 the effects of dissonance.) So, perhaps, greater disagreement will produce more change. Then again, a communicator who proclaims an uncomfortable message may be discredited. People who disagree with conclusions drawn by a newscaster rate the newscaster as biased, inaccurate, and untrustworthy. People are more open to conclusions within their range of acceptability (Liberman & Chaiken, 1992; Zanna, 1993). So, perhaps, greater disagreement will produce less change.

Elliot Aronson, Judith Turner, and Merrill Carlsmith (1963) reasoned that a credible source—one hard to discount—would elicit considerable opinion change when advocating a position greatly discrepant from the recipient's. Sure enough, when credible poet T. S. Eliot was said to have highly praised a disliked poem, people changed their opinion more than when he gave it faint praise. But when the less credible "Agnes Stearns," a teacher's college student, evaluated a disliked poem, high praise was no more persuasive than faint praise. Thus, as Figure 5–5 shows, discrepancy and credibility interact: The effect of a large versus small discrepancy depends on whether the communicator is credible.

So the answer to Ritu's question "Should I argue an extreme position?" is "It depends." Is Ritu, in her adoring father's eyes, a highly prestigious, authoritative source? If so, she should push for a complete fitness program. If not, she would be wise to make a more modest appeal.

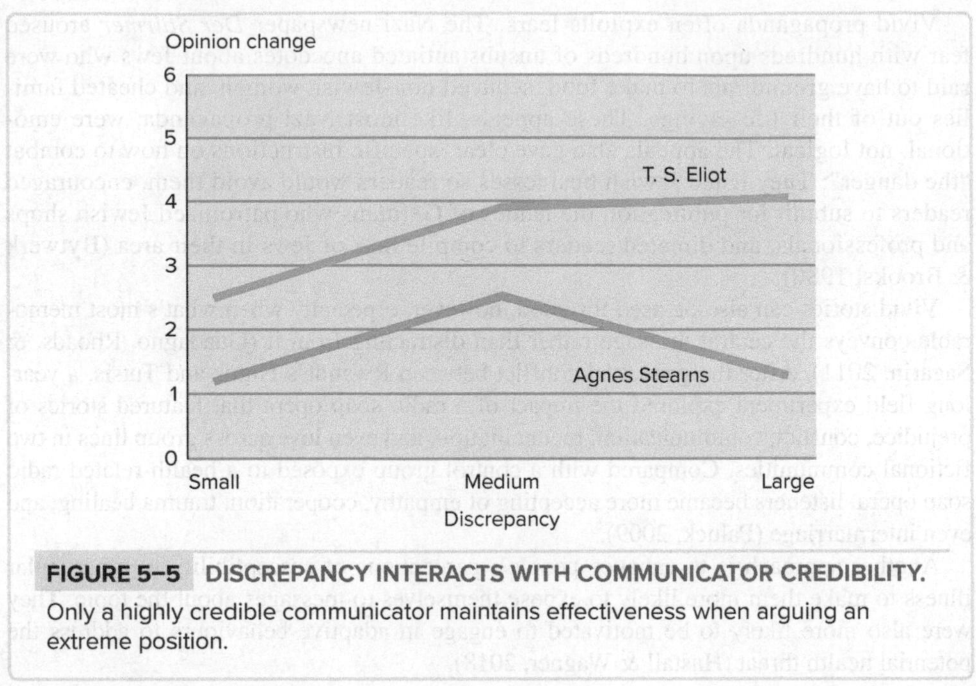

FIGURE 5–5 DISCREPANCY INTERACTS WITH COMMUNICATOR CREDIBILITY. Only a highly credible communicator maintains effectiveness when arguing an extreme position.

The answer also depends on how involved her father is in the issue. Deeply involved people tend to accept only a narrow range of views. To them, a moderately discrepant message may seem foolishly radical, especially if the message argues an opposing view rather than being a more extreme version of their own view (Maio, Bell, & Esses, 1996; Pallak et al., 1972; Petty & Cacioppo, 1979; Rhine & Severance, 1970). Thus, social psychologists Arie Kruglanski, Michele Gelfand, and Rohan Gunaratna (2010) advise how to construct messages that may help deradicalize committed terrorists: Build such messages upon elements of their pre-existing beliefs.

On the other hand, if Ritu's father has not yet thought or cared much about exercise, she can probably take a more extreme position. So, if you are a credible authority and your audience isn't much concerned with your issue, go for it: Advocate a discrepant view.

One-sided versus two-sided appeals

Persuaders face another practical issue: how to deal with opposing arguments. Once again, common sense offers no clear answer. Acknowledging the opposing arguments might confuse the audience and weaken the case. On the other hand, a message might seem fairer and be more disarming if it recognizes the opposition's arguments.

Carol Werner and her colleagues (2002) showed the disarming power of a simple two-sided message in experimental messages that promoted aluminum can recycling. Signs added to wastebaskets in a university classroom said, for example, "No Aluminum Cans Please!!!!! Use the Recycler Located on the First Floor, Near the Entrance." When a final persuasive message acknowledged and responded to the main counter-argument—"It May Be Inconvenient. But It Is Important!!!!!!!!!!"—recycling reached 80 percent (double the rate before any message and more than in other message conditions).

After Germany's defeat in the Second World War, the Allies did not want soldiers to relax and think that the still ongoing war with Japan would become easy. So Carl Hovland and his colleagues (1949) designed two radio broadcasts arguing that the war in the Pacific would last at least two more years. One broadcast was one-sided; it did not acknowledge the existence of contradictory arguments, such as the advantage of fighting only one enemy instead of two. The other broadcast was two-sided; it mentioned and responded to the

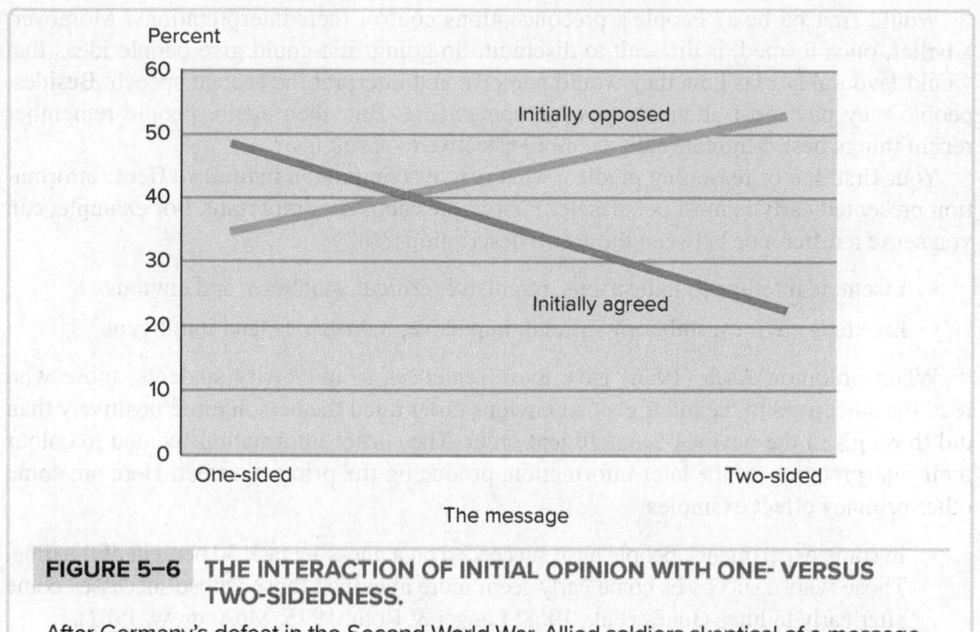

FIGURE 5–6 THE INTERACTION OF INITIAL OPINION WITH ONE- VERSUS TWO-SIDEDNESS.

After Germany's defeat in the Second World War, Allied soldiers skeptical of a message suggesting Japan's strength were more persuaded by a two-sided communication. Soldiers initially agreeing with the message were strengthened more by a one-sided message.

opposing arguments. As Figure 5–6 illustrates, the effectiveness of the message depended on the listener. A one-sided appeal was most effective with those who already agreed. An appeal that acknowledged opposing arguments worked better with those who disagreed.

Experiments also revealed that a two-sided presentation is more persuasive and enduring if people are (or will be) aware of opposing arguments (Jones & Brehm, 1970; Lumsdaine & Janis, 1953). In simulated trials, a defence case becomes more credible when the defence brings up damaging evidence before the prosecution does (Williams, Bourgeois, & Croyle, 1993). Thus, a political candidate speaking to a politically informed group would, indeed, be wise to respond to the opposition. So, if your audience will be exposed to opposing views, offer a two-sided appeal.

> ***"Opponents fancy they refute us when they repeat their own opinion and pay no attention to ours."***
>
> Goethe (1749–1832), *Maxims and Reflections*

This interaction effect typifies persuasion research. For optimists, positive persuasion works best ("The new plan reduces tuition in exchange for part-time university service"). For pessimists, negative persuasion is more effective ("All students will have to work part-time for the university, lest they pay exorbitant tuition fees") (Geers, Handley, & McLarney, 2003). We might wish that persuasion variables had simple effects. (It would make this an easier chapter to study.) Alas, most variables, noted Richard Petty and Duane Wegener (1998), "have complex effects—increasing persuasion in some situations and decreasing it in others."

As students and scientists, we cherish "Occam's razor"—seeking the simplest possible principles. But if human reality is complex, our principles will need to have some complexity—to acknowledge interaction effects—as well.

Primacy versus recency

Imagine that you are a consultant to a cabinet minister who must soon debate her opposition critic regarding a proposed carbon tax. Three weeks before the vote, each politician is to appear on CBC and present a prepared statement. By the flip of a coin, your side receives the choice of whether to speak first or last. Knowing that you are a former social psychology student, everyone looks to you for advice.

Would first be best? People's preconceptions control their interpretations. Moreover, a belief, once formed, is difficult to discredit. So going first could give people ideas that would favourably bias how they would perceive and interpret the second speech. Besides, people may pay most attention to what comes first. But, then again, people remember recent things best. Might it really be more effective to speak last?

Your first line of reasoning predicts what is most common, a **primacy effect**: Information presented early is most persuasive. First impressions *are* important. For example, can you sense a difference between these two descriptions?

- Lisette is intelligent, industrious, impulsive, critical, stubborn, and envious.
- Lisette is envious, stubborn, critical, impulsive, industrious, and intelligent.

When Solomon Asch (1946) gave these sentences to university students, those who read the adjectives in the intelligent-to-envious order rated the person more positively than did those given the envious-to-intelligent order. The earlier information seemed to colour their interpretation of the later information, producing the primacy effect. Here are some other primacy effect examples:

- In some experiments, people have succeeded on a guessing task 50 percent of the time. Those whose successes come early seem more able than those whose successes come after early failures (Jones et al., 1968; Langer & Roth, 1975; McAndrew, 1981).
- In political polls and in election voting, candidates benefit from being listed first on the ballot (Moore, 2004).
- Norman Miller and Donald Campbell (1959) gave university students a condensed transcript from an actual civil trial. They placed the plaintiff's testimony and arguments in one block, and those for the defence in another. The students read both blocks. When they returned a week later to declare their opinions, most sided with the information they had read first.

What about the opposite possibility? Would our better memory for the most recent information we've received ever create a **recency effect**? We know from our experience (as well as from memory experiments) that today's events can temporarily outweigh significant past events. As we noted in Chapter 3, today's blizzard makes long-term global warming seem less a threat, just as today's sweltering heat makes it seem more a threat.

primacy effect Other things being equal, information presented first usually has the most influence.

recency effect Information presented last sometimes has the most influence. Recency effects are less common than primacy effects.

channel of communication The way the message is delivered—whether face to face, in writing, on film, or in some other way.

To test for a possible recency effect, Miller and Campbell (1959) gave another group of students one block of testimony to read. A week later, the researchers had them read the second block and then immediately state their opinions. Now the results were just the reverse—a recency effect. Apparently, the first block of arguments, being a week old, had largely faded from memory.

Forgetting creates the recency effect (1) when enough time separates the two messages, and (2) when the audience commits itself soon after the second message. When the two messages are back to back, followed by a time gap, a primacy effect usually occurs (Figure 5–7). This is especially so when the first message stimulates thinking (Haugtvedt & Wegener, 1994). So, what advice would you now give to the political debater?

How Is It Said? The Channel of Communication

For persuasion to occur, there must be communication. And for communication to occur, there must be a **channel of communication**: a face-to-face appeal, a written sign or document, a media advertisement, or some other method.

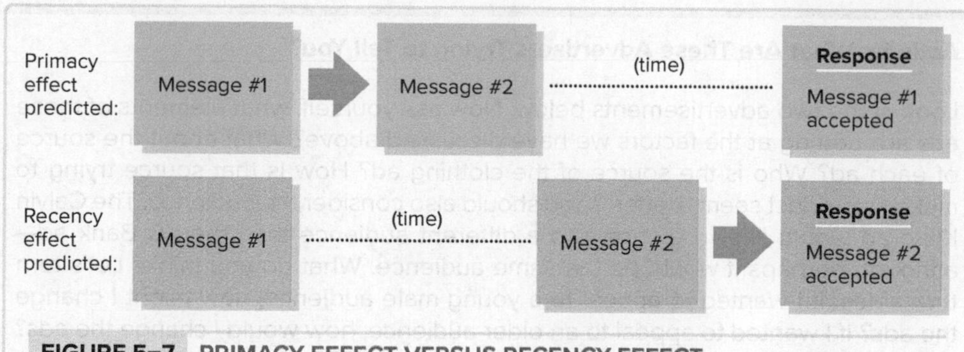

FIGURE 5–7 PRIMACY EFFECT VERSUS RECENCY EFFECT.
When two persuasive messages are back to back and the audience then responds at some later time, the first message has the advantage (primacy effect). When the two messages are separated in time and the audience responds soon after the second message, the second message has the advantage (recency effect).

Common-sense psychology places faith in the power of written words. How do we try to get people out to a campus event? We post notices. How do we get drivers to slow down and keep their eyes on the road? We put "Drive carefully" messages on billboards. How do we discourage students from dropping garbage on campus? We post anti-litter messages on campus bulletin boards.

Active experience or passive reception?

Are spoken appeals more persuasive? Not necessarily. Those of us who do public speaking can become so easily enamoured with our spoken words that we are tempted to overestimate their power. Ask university students what aspect of their school experience has been most valuable or what they remember from their first year, and few, we are sad to say, recall the brilliant lectures that we faculty remember giving.

When you stop to think about it, an effective speaker has many hurdles to surmount. As Figure 5–1 showed, a persuasive speaker must deliver a message that not only gets attention but also is understandable, convincing, memorable, and compelling. A carefully thought-out appeal must consider each of those steps in the persuasion process.

> ***"The medium is the message."***
>
> Marshall McLuhan, 1964

Consider another well-intentioned effort. At one university, a week-long anti-litter campaign urged students with slogans such as "Let's clean up our garbage." Such slogans were placed in students' mailboxes each morning and displayed on prominent posters. The day before the campaign began, social psychologist Raymond Paloutzian (1979) placed litter near a garbage can along a well-travelled sidewalk. Then he stepped back to record the behaviour of 180 passersby. No one picked up anything. On the last day of the campaign, he repeated the test with 180 more passersby. Did the pedestrians now race one another in their zeal to comply with the appeals? Hardly. Only 2 of the 180 picked up the trash.

Passively received appeals are not always futile, however. A drugstore that one of the authors shops at sells two brands of aspirin, one heavily advertised and one unadvertised. Apart from slight differences in how fast each tablet crumbles in your mouth, the two brands are identical, as any pharmacist will tell you. Aspirin is aspirin. Our bodies cannot tell the difference. But our wallets can. The advertised brand sells for three times the price of the unadvertised brand.

> ***"In study after study, most people agree that mass media influence attitudes— other people's attitudes, but not their own."***
>
> Duck, Hogg, & Terry, 1995

With such power, can the media help a wealthy political candidate buy an election? In politics, those who spend the most usually get the most

Activity: What Are These Advertisers Trying to Tell You?

Look at the two advertisements below. Now ask yourself, what elements of these ads are getting at the factors we have discussed above? What about the source of each ad? Who is the source of the clothing ad? How is that source trying to make its product seem "better"? You should also consider the audience. The Calvin Klein ad would likely be shown to a different audience than the TD Bank ad—although perhaps it would be the same audience. What do you think? Let's turn the tables. If I wanted to appeal to a young male audience, how might I change the ads? If I wanted to appeal to an older audience, how would I change the ads? Can you see how the audience matters?

Source: ©Caroline Cortizo/Alamy Stock Photo.

Source: ©Torontonian/Alamy Stock Photo.

votes (Grush, 1980; Open Secrets, 2005). Advertising exposure helps make an unfamiliar candidate into a familiar one. As we will see in Chapter 10, mere exposure to unfamiliar stimuli breeds liking. Moreover, mere repetition can make things believable (Dechêne et al., 2010; Moons, Mackie, & Garcia-Marques, 2009). Researcher Hal Arkes (1990) calls such findings "scary." As political manipulators know, believable lies can displace hard truths. Repeated clichés can cover complex realities. Even repeatedly saying that a consumer claim ("Shark cartilage is good for arthritis") is false can, when the discounting is presented amid other true and false claims, lead older adults to later misremember it as true (Skurnik et al., 2005). As they forget the discounting, their lingering familiarity with the claim can make it seem believable.

Mere repetition of a statement also serves to increase its fluency—the ease with which it spills off our tongue—which, in turn, increases believability (McGlone & Tofighbakhsh, 2000). Other factors, such as rhyming, also increase fluency—and believability. "Haste makes waste" may say essentially the same thing as "Rushing causes mistakes," but it seems more true. Whatever makes for fluency (familiarity, rhyming) also makes for credibility.

Because passively received appeals are sometimes effective and sometimes not, can we specify in advance the topics on which a persuasive appeal will be successful? There is a simple rule: Persuasion decreases as the significance of the issue increases. On minor issues, such as which brand of aspirin to buy, it's easy to demonstrate the media's power. On more important issues, such as whether the federal government is doing enough to reduce greenhouse gas emissions, persuading people is like trying to push a piano uphill. It is not impossible, but one shove won't do it.

As we saw in Chapter 4, active experience also strengthens attitudes. When we act, we amplify the idea behind what we've done, especially when we feel responsible. What is more, attitudes more often endure and influence our behaviour when rooted in our own experience. Compared with attitudes formed passively, experience-based attitudes are more confident, more stable, and less vulnerable to attack. These principles are evident in many studies that show that the most effective HIV-prevention interventions not only give people information but also give them behavioural training, such as practising assertiveness in refusing sex and using protection (Albarracin et al., 2005).

Personal versus media influence

Persuasion studies demonstrate that the major influence on us is not the media but our contact with people. Modern selling strategies seek to harness the power of word-of-mouth personal influence through "viral marketing," "creating a buzz," and "seeding" sales (Walker, 2004). As noted above, we have seen an incredible increase in online marketing through "social influencers." The *Harry Potter* series was not expected to be a bestseller (*Harry Potter and the Philosopher's Stone* had a first printing of 500 copies), but young people talking to other young people made it so.

> ***"You do realize, you will never make a fortune out of writing children's books?"***
>
> J. K. Rowling's literary agent before the release of *Harry Potter and the Philosopher's Stone*

Two classic field experiments illustrate the strength of personal influence. Some years ago, Samuel Eldersveld and Richard Dodge (1954) studied political persuasion in a local election. They divided citizens intending not to vote for a revision of the city charter into three groups. Among those exposed only to what they saw and heard in the mass media, 19 percent changed their minds and voted in favour of the revision on election day. Of a second group, who received four mailings in support of the revision, 45 percent voted for it. Among people in a third group, who were visited personally and given the appeal face to face, 75 percent cast their votes for the revision.

In another field experiment, a research team led by John Farquhar and Nathan Maccoby (Farquhar et al., 1977; Maccoby, 1980; Maccoby & Alexander, 1980) tried to reduce the frequency of heart disease among middle-aged adults in three small California cities. To check the relative effectiveness of personal and media influence, they interviewed and medically examined some 1200 people before the project began and at the end of each of the following three years. Residents of Tracy, California, received no persuasive appeals other than those occurring in their regular media. In Gilroy, California, a two-year multimedia campaign used TV, radio, newspapers, and direct mail to teach people about coronary risk and what they could do to reduce it. In Watsonville, California, this media campaign was supplemented by personal contacts with two-thirds of those whose blood pressure, weight, and age put them in a high-risk group. Using behaviour-modification principles, the researchers helped people set specific goals and reinforced their successes.

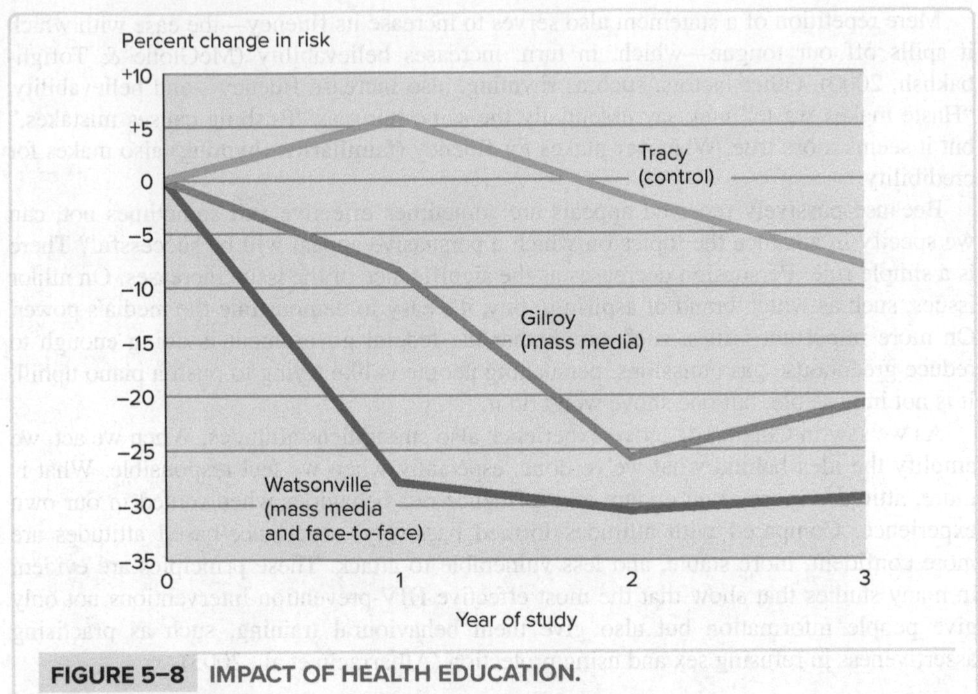

FIGURE 5–8 IMPACT OF HEALTH EDUCATION.

Percentage change from baseline (0) in coronary risk after one, two, or three years of health education.

As Figure 5–8 shows, after one, two, and three years, the high-risk people in Tracy (the control town) were about as much at risk as before. High-risk people in Gilroy, which was deluged with media appeals, improved their health habits and were now somewhat less at risk. Those in Watsonville, who also received the personal contacts, changed most.

Media influence: The two-step flow

Although face-to-face influence is usually greater than media influence, we should not underestimate the media's power. Those who personally influence our opinions must get their ideas from somewhere, and often their sources are the media. Elihu Katz (1957) observed that much of the media's effects operate in a **two-step flow of communication**: from media to opinion leaders to the rank and file. In any large group, it is these opinion leaders and trendsetters—"the influentials"—that marketers and politicians seek to woo (Keller & Berry, 2003). Opinion leaders are individuals perceived as experts. Traditionally they may have included talk show hosts and editorial columnists; doctors, teachers, and scientists; and people in all walks of life who have made it their business to absorb information and to inform their friends and family. More recently, and certainly with younger consumers, social media influencers are very persuasive.

two-step flow of communication
The process by which media influence often occurs through opinion leaders, who in turn influence others.

The two-step flow of information may influence the drugs your physician prescribes (Nair, Manchanda, & Bhatia, 2008). Physicians look to opinion leaders within their social network—often, a university hospital–based specialist—when deciding which drugs to favour. For more than nine in ten physicians, this influence comes through personal contact. The largest drug companies know that opinion leaders drive sales, and, therefore, they target about one-third of their marketing dollars on these influential people.

The two-step flow model reminds us that media influences penetrate the culture in subtle ways. Even if the media had little direct effect on people's attitudes, they could still have a big indirect effect. Those rare children who grow up without watching television do not grow up beyond television's influence. Unless they live as hermits, they will join in TV-imitative play on the school playground. They will watch YouTube videos of kids playing with toys or games they will then want. They will ask their parents for the toys their friends have. They will beg or demand to watch their friends' favourite programs. Parents can say no, but they cannot switch off television's influence.

Comparing media

Lumping together all media, from mass mailings to television to social networking, oversimplifies. Studies comparing different media find that the more lifelike the medium, the more persuasive its message. Thus, the order of persuasiveness seems to be this: live (face to face), video, audio, and written.

To add to the complexity, messages are best comprehended and recalled when written. Comprehension is one of the first steps in the persuasion process. So Shelly Chaiken and Alice Eagly (1976) reasoned that if a message is difficult to comprehend, persuasion should be greatest when the message is written because readers will be able to work through the message at their own pace. The researchers gave students easy or difficult messages in writing, on audio, or on video. Figure 5–9 displays their results: Difficult messages were, indeed, most persuasive when written; easy messages, when videotaped. The video medium takes control of the pacing of the message away from the recipients. By drawing attention to the communicator and away from the message itself, the video is also able to focus on peripheral cues, such as the communicator's attractiveness (Chaiken & Eagly, 1983).

To Whom Is It Said? The Audience

Persuasion varies with who says what, by what medium, to whom. Let's also consider two other characteristics of those who receive a message: (1) their age and (2) their thoughtfulness.

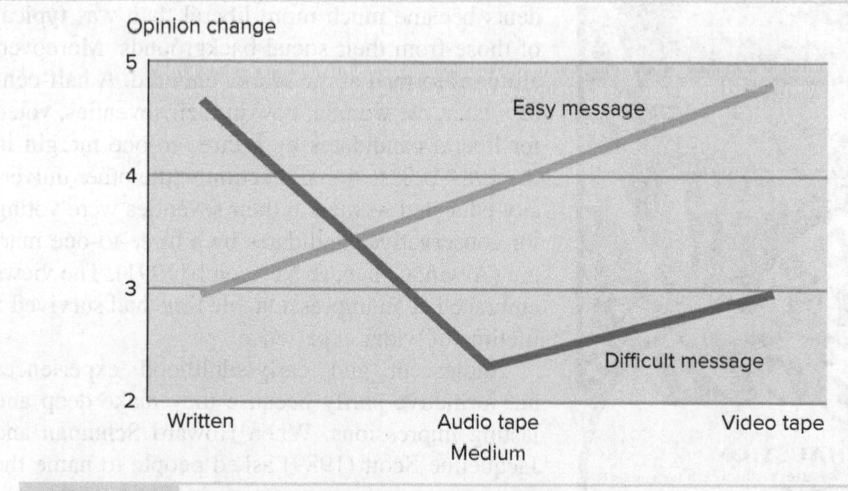

FIGURE 5–9 WRITTEN VS. TAPED MESSAGES.

Easy-to-understand messages are most persuasive when videotaped. Difficult messages are most persuasive when written. Thus, the difficulty of the message interacts with the medium to determine persuasiveness.

How old are they?

As evident in polls leading up to the 2015 Canadian federal election—with the Conservative Party favoured by older voters and the New Democratic Party by younger voters—people's social and political attitudes correlate with their age (Angus Reid, 2015). Social psychologists offer two explanations for age differences:

- *A life cycle explanation:* Attitudes change (for example, become more conservative) as people grow older.
- *A generational explanation:* Attitudes do not change; older people largely hold onto the attitudes they adopted when they were young. Because these attitudes are different from those now being adopted by young people today, a generation gap develops.

The evidence mostly supports the generational explanation. In surveying and resurveying groups of younger and older people over several years, the attitudes of older people usually change less than those of younger people. As David Sears (1979, 1986) put it, researchers have "almost invariably found generational rather than life cycle effects."

The teens and early twenties are important formative years (Koenig, McGue, & Iacono, 2008; Krosnick & Alwin, 1989). Attitudes are changeable during that time, and the attitudes formed then tend to stabilize through middle adulthood. Gallup interviews of more than 120 000 people suggest that political attitudes formed at age 18 tend to last (Silver, 2009). Young people might, therefore, be advised to choose their social influences—the groups they join, the media they consume, the roles they adopt—carefully.

Although illegal, companies used to make a wide variety of (untested) medical claims about their products, like in this Coke ad.

Source: ©Bettmann/Getty Images.

A striking example: During the late 1930s and early 1940s, students at one small prestigious school—women from privileged, conservative families—encountered a free-spirited environment led by a left-leaning, young faculty. One member of the faculty, social psychologist Theodore Newcomb, later denied that the faculty members were trying to make "good little liberals" out of students. Nevertheless, they succeeded. The students became much more liberal than was typical of those from their social backgrounds. Moreover, attitudes formed at the school endured. A half-century later, the women, now in their seventies, voted for liberal candidates by a three-to-one margin in the 1984 U.S. national election while other university-educated women in their seventies were voting for conservative candidates by a three-to-one margin (Alwin, Cohen, & Newcomb, 1991). The views embraced at an impressionable time had survived a lifetime of wider experience.

Adolescent and early-adulthood experiences are formative partly because they make deep and lasting impressions. When Howard Schuman and Jacqueline Scott (1989) asked people to name the one or two most important world events of the previous half-century, most recalled events from their teens or early twenties. For those who had experienced the Great Depression or the Second World War as 16- to 24-year-olds, those events overshadowed more recent events that were imprinted on the minds of those who had experienced them as 16- to 24-year-olds. We may, therefore, expect that today's young adults will include events such as COVID-19 and the ensuing economic recession as key factors in their lives.

That is not to say that older adults are inflexible. Studies conducted by Norval Glenn (1980) found that most people in their fifties and sixties had more liberal sexual and racial attitudes than they had had in their thirties and forties. Given the "sexual revolution" that began in the 1960s and became mainstream in the 1970s, these middle-aged people had apparently changed with the times. Few of us are utterly uninfluenced by changing cultural norms. Moreover, near the end of their lives, older adults may again become more susceptible to attitude change, perhaps because of the decline in the strength of their attitudes (Visser & Krosnick, 1998).

What are they thinking?

The crucial aspect of central route persuasion is not the message but the responses it evokes in a person's mind. Our minds are not sponges that soak up whatever pours over them. If the message summons favourable thoughts, it persuades us. If it provokes us to think of contrary arguments, we remain unpersuaded.

Forewarned is forearmed—if you care enough to counter-argue

What circumstances breed counter-arguing? One is a warning that someone is going to try to persuade you. If you had to tell your family that you wanted to drop out of school, you would likely anticipate their pleading with you to stay. So you might develop a list of arguments to counter every conceivable argument they might make.

Jonathan Freedman and David Sears (1965) demonstrated the difficulty of trying to persuade people under such circumstances. They warned one group of high school students that they were going to hear a talk entitled "Why Teenagers Should Not Be Allowed to Drive." Those forewarned did not budge in their opinions. Others, not forewarned, did budge. In courtrooms, too, defence attorneys sometimes forewarn juries about prosecution evidence to come. With mock juries, such "stealing thunder" neutralizes its impact (Dolnik, Case, & Williams, 2003).

Distraction disarms counter-arguing

Persuasion is also enhanced by a distraction that inhibits counter-arguing (Festinger & Maccoby, 1964; Keating & Brock, 1974; Osterhouse & Brock, 1970). Political ads often use this technique. The words promote the candidate, and the visual images keep us occupied so that we don't analyze the words. Distraction is especially effective when the message is simple (Harkins & Petty, 1981; Regan & Cheng, 1973). Sometimes, though, distraction precludes our processing an ad. That helps explain why ads viewed during violent or sexual TV programs are so often unremembered and ineffective (Bushman, 2005, 2007).

need for cognition The motivation to think and analyze; assessed by agreement with items such as "the notion of thinking abstractly is appealing to me" and disagreement with items such as "I only think as hard as I have to."

Uninvolved audiences use peripheral cues

Recall the two routes to persuasion—the central route of systematic thinking and the peripheral route of heuristic cues. Like the road through town, the central route has starts and stops as the mind analyzes arguments and formulates responses. Like the highway around town, the peripheral route zips people to their destination. Analytical people—those with a high **need for cognition**—enjoy thinking carefully and prefer central routes (Cacioppo et al., 1996). People who like to conserve their mental resources—those with a low need for cognition—are quicker to respond to such peripheral cues as the communicator's attractiveness and the pleasantness of the surroundings.

"To be forewarned and therefore forearmed . . . is eminently rational if our belief is true; but if our belief is a delusion, this same forewarning and forearming would obviously be the method whereby the delusion rendered itself incurable."

C. S. Lewis, *Screwtape Proposes a Toast,* 1965

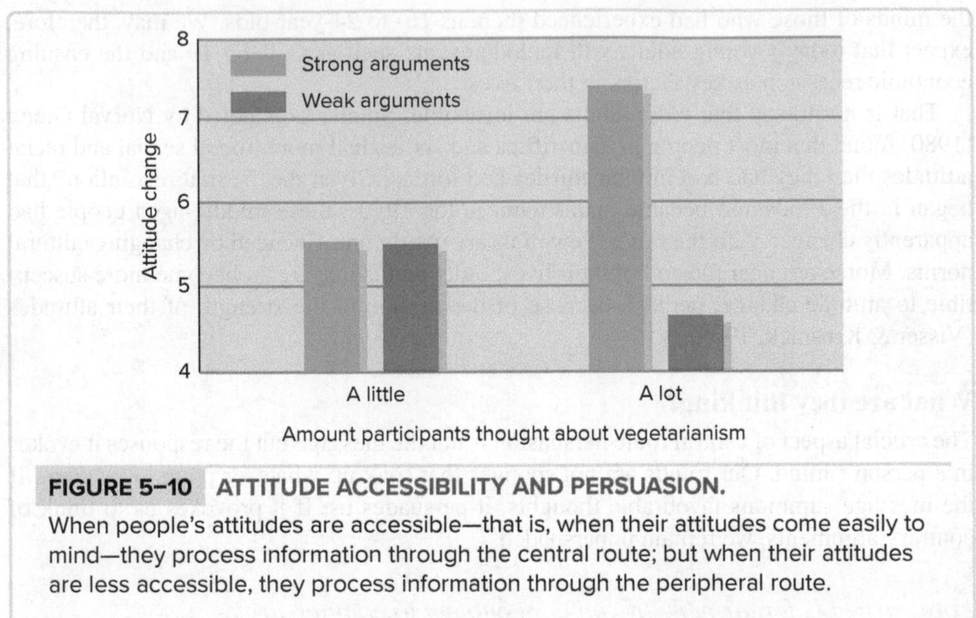

FIGURE 5–10 ATTITUDE ACCESSIBILITY AND PERSUASION.
When people's attitudes are accessible—that is, when their attitudes come easily to mind—they process information through the central route; but when their attitudes are less accessible, they process information through the peripheral route.

But the issue matters, too. All of us struggle actively with issues that involve us while making snap judgments about things that matter little (Johnson & Eagly, 1990; Maio & Olson, 1990). The more we think about an issue, the more we take the central route. Consider the following study conducted by Queen's University's Leandre Fabrigar and his colleagues (1998). They made some students think about their attitudes toward vegetarianism by asking them a lot of questions about it; others were asked about their views only once. As you can see in Figure 5–10, those who had thought a lot about their views were persuaded by strong arguments about vegetarianism but were uninfluenced by weak arguments. But for people who had not thought much about the topic, the strength of the arguments did not matter.

This simple theory—that what we think in response to a message is crucial, especially if we are motivated and able to think about it—has generated many predictions, most of which have been confirmed by Petty, Cacioppo, and others (Axsom, Yates, & Chaiken, 1987; Haddock et al., 2008; Harkins & Petty, 1987). Many experiments have explored different ways to stimulate people's thinking:

- By using rhetorical questions
- By presenting multiple speakers (for example, having three speakers each give one argument instead of one speaker giving three)
- By making people feel responsible for evaluating or passing along the message
- By repeating the message
- By getting people's undistracted attention

The consistent finding with each of these techniques: Stimulating thinking makes strong messages more persuasive and (because of counter-arguing) weak messages less persuasive.

The theory also has practical implications. Effective communicators care not only about their images and their messages but also about how their audience is likely to react. The best instructors tend to get students to think actively. They ask rhetorical questions, provide intriguing examples, and challenge students with difficult problems. Such techniques foster the central route to persuasion. In classes where the instruction is less engaging, you can provide your own central processing. If you think about the material and elaborate on the arguments, you are likely to do better in the course.

Extreme Persuasion: How Do Cults Indoctrinate?

What persuasion and group influence principles are harnessed by new religious movements ("cults")?

We are inundated with up to 15 000 persuasive communications every day (O'Reilly & Tennant, 2009). Most of the time, these communications are mundane, with little meaning or consequence. Perhaps we buy a chocolate bar or maybe even a car we had not intended to, but our decisions are typically harmless (except to our bank accounts). However, sometimes we are persuaded to do things that are very harmful, even deadly. People who kill innocent civilians in the name of some cause are good examples. But how does it come to this? No one grows up thinking, "I want to blow up innocent civilians for a cause one day."

At the very least you should understand by now that social influence is pervasive and often affects us without our knowing. But we do resist. Now we will discuss some of the ways in which groups use social influence tactics to change individual behaviour and how we might resist their attempts more effectively.

> ***"To swallow and follow, whether old doctrine or new propaganda, is a weakness still dominating the human mind."***
>
> Charlotte Perkins Gilman, *Human Work*, 1904

Depending on their perspective, people discuss and believe (and are presented with) somewhat differing information. On the positive side of the equation, however, persuasive forces have also been harnessed for good—to promote healthier living, safer driving, and better education and child care. For example, the rate of new U.S. university students reporting abstinence from beer has increased—from 25 percent in 1981 to 57 percent in 2005 (Pryor et al., 2005). In the fall of 2011, when the University of Alberta offered 80 spots in an alcohol-free residence, over 200 new students applied. Alcohol-free (and "quiet") floors and buildings are becoming the norm on Canadian campuses. More than at any time in recent decades, health- and safety-conscious educated adults are shunning cigarettes and beer. Nonetheless, because persuasion tactics can be used among a wide variety of groups, we need to be aware of how they work and how to counteract them.

Group Indoctrination Tactics

On March 22, 1997, Marshall Applewhite, leader of Heaven's Gate, and 37 of his disciples decided the time had come to shed their bodies—mere "containers"—and be whisked up to a UFO trailing Comet Hale-Bopp, en route to heaven's gate. So they put themselves to sleep by mixing phenobarbital into pudding or applesauce, washing it down with vodka, and then fixing plastic bags over their heads so they would suffocate in their sleep. On that same day, a cottage in the French-Canadian village of St. Casimir exploded in an inferno, consuming five people—the latest of 74 members of the Order of the Solar Temple to have died by suicide in Canada, Switzerland, and France. All were hoping to be transported to the star Sirius, nine light-years away.

The question on many minds is this: What persuades people to leave behind their former beliefs and join these groups? Shall we attribute their strange behaviours to strange personalities? Or do their experiences illustrate the common dynamics of social influence and persuasion?

Keep three things in mind: First, this is hindsight analysis. It uses persuasion principles as categories for explaining, after the fact, fascinating and sometimes disturbing social phenomena. Second, explaining why people believe something says nothing about the truth of their beliefs. That is a logically separate issue. A psychology of religion might tell us why a believer believes in God and an atheist doesn't, but it cannot tell us who is right. Third, we must bear in mind that indoctrination tactics are used by a wide variety of groups, from mainstream religious groups, to biker and other gangs, to corporations, sports teams, and governments trying to win over the hearts and minds of their citizens.

Cults provide useful case studies to explore persuasion because these groups are often intently analyzed. Therefore, we will focus here on some of the tactics they use.

Several **cults**, also known as new religious movements, have gained much publicity: Sun Myung Moon's Unification Church, Jim Jones's Peoples Temple, and David Koresh's Branch Davidians.

Sun Myung Moon's mixture of Christianity, anti-communism, and glorification of Moon himself as a new messiah attracted a worldwide following. Many committed themselves and their incomes to his Unification Church.

cults Groups typically characterized by (1) the distinctive ritual of their devotion to a god or a person, (2) isolation from the surrounding "evil" culture, and (3) a charismatic leader; also called *new religious movements*. (A sect, by contrast, is a spinoff from a major religion.)

In 1978 in Guyana, 914 followers of the Reverend Jim Jones, who had followed him there from San Francisco, shocked the world when they died by following his order to down a strawberry drink laced with tranquilizers, painkillers, and a lethal dose of cyanide.

In 1993, high-school dropout David Koresh used his talent for memorizing scripture and mesmerizing people to seize control of a faction of a sect called the Branch Davidians. Over time, members were gradually relieved of their bank accounts and possessions. Koresh also persuaded the men to be celibate while he slept with their wives and daughters, and he convinced his 19 "wives" that they should bear his children. Under siege after a shootout that killed six members and four U.S. federal agents, Koresh told his followers they would soon die and go with him straight to heaven. Federal agents rammed the compound with tanks, hoping to inject tear gas. By the end of the assault, 86 people had been consumed in a fire.

How could these things happen? What persuaded these people to give such total allegiance to these leaders? Let's explore.

Attitudes Follow Behaviour

As Chapter 4 showed over and over again, people usually internalize commitments made voluntarily, publicly, and repeatedly. Cult leaders seem to know this.

Compliance breeds acceptance

New converts soon learn that membership is no trivial matter. They are quickly made active members of the team. Behavioural rituals, public recruitment, and fundraising strengthen the initiates' identities as members. Just as those in social–psychological experiments come to believe in what they bear witness to (Aronson & Mills, 1959; Gerard & Mathewson, 1966), cult initiates become committed advocates. The greater the personal commitment, the more the need to justify it.

The foot-in-the-door phenomenon

One does not suddenly decide, "I'm gonna find a cult." Nor do cult recruiters approach people on the street with, "Hi. I'm a cult member. Care to join us?" Rather, the recruitment strategy exploits the foot-in-the-door principle. Let's consider one man's encounter with a group in Montreal. Craig Silverman (2004) described his first meeting with members of the Raelians, who believe that their leader, Rael, was visited by aliens and is the "brother of Jesus" sent to save us by telling us our true origins and preparing us for a visit from our creators. In the Raelian philosophy, life on Earth was created by extraterrestrials and they will come back once an extraterrestrial embassy is built on Earth.

At the meeting, everyone was very polite and friendly. They watched a video that asked all of the questions to which we want answers: Why are we here? What is the meaning of life? Where do we come from? The video answered some (but not all) of these questions, and the newcomers were encouraged to buy the movement's books and DVDs to learn more and to obtain additional answers to their questions. At the end of the session they were invited to sign up for additional lectures. Do you see the foot-in-the-door technique at work? Presumably, once you have bought the book or agreed to a new meeting, you have committed (albeit in a small way) to find out more.

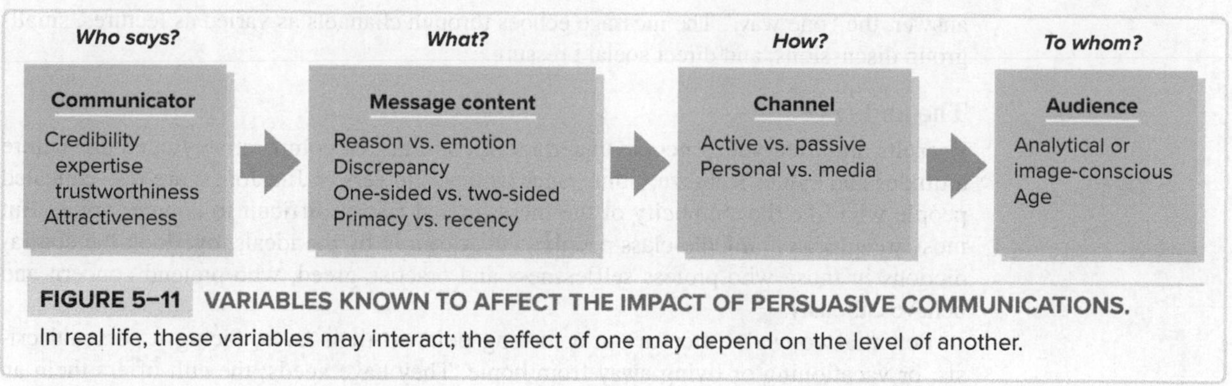

FIGURE 5–11 VARIABLES KNOWN TO AFFECT THE IMPACT OF PERSUASIVE COMMUNICATIONS.
In real life, these variables may interact; the effect of one may depend on the level of another.

Consistent with their approach at individual meetings, the Raelians operate a visitors' centre in the Eastern Townships of Quebec that is designed to work in a similar way. As it turns out, the brother of one of your authors (interestingly, also a psychologist) was once visiting the Eastern Townships with his wife and saw a sign for a "UFO museum." On a whim, they decided to visit. Upon paying the fee, they gained entry to a building (intriguingly, billed as the largest building made of hay bales in the world) and started to wander through. They found themselves being shadowed by one of the group members, who offered information about the group and asked if they had questions. They were given several opportunities to purchase information and soon found that the path they were on was deliberately complex with no obvious exits—so that they had to go through all of the exhibits and "sales pitches" before they could leave.

Persuasive Elements

We can also analyze cult persuasion using the factors discussed in this chapter (and summarized in Figure 5–11): *Who* (the communicator) said *what* (the message), *how* (the channel), and to *whom* (the audience)?

The communicator

Successful cults typically have a charismatic leader—someone who attracts and directs the members. As in experiments on persuasion, a credible communicator is someone the audience perceives as expert and trustworthy—for example, as "Father" Moon.

Jim Jones used "psychic readings" to establish his credibility. Newcomers were asked to identify themselves as they entered the church before services. Then one of his aides would call the person's home and say, "Hi. We're doing a survey, and we'd like to ask you some questions." During the service, one ex-member recalled, Jones would call out the person's name and say things like this:

> Have you ever seen me before? Well, you live in such and such a place, your phone number is such and such, and in your living room you've got this, that, and the other, and on your sofa you've got such and such a pillow. . . . Now do you remember me ever being in your house? (Conway & Siegelman, 1979, p. 234)

Trust is another aspect of credibility. Many cult members have been recruited by friends or relatives—people they trust (Stark & Bainbridge, 1980). Hundreds of thousands of people in recent years have been recruited by members of some 2500 religious cults but seldom through an abrupt decision.

The message

The vivid, emotional messages and the warmth and acceptance that the group showers newcomers with can be strikingly appealing: Trust the master, join the family; we have the answer, the "one way." The message echoes through channels as varied as lectures, small-group discussions, and direct social pressure.

The audience

Recruits are often young people under age 25, still at that comparatively open age before attitudes and values stabilize. Some, such as the followers of Jim Jones, are less-educated people who like the simplicity of the message and find it difficult to counter-argue. But most are educated, middle-class people, who, taken in by the ideals, overlook the contradictions in those who profess selflessness and practise greed, who pretend concern and behave callously.

Potential converts often are at a turning point in their lives, facing a personal crisis, or vacationing or living away from home. They have needs; the cult offers them an answer (Lofland & Stark, 1965; Singer, 1979). Gail Maeder joined Heaven's Gate after her T-shirt shop failed. David Moore joined when he was 19, just out of high school and searching for direction. Times of social and economic upheaval are especially conducive to someone who can make apparent simple sense out of the confusion (O'Dea, 1968; Sales, 1973).

Most of those who have carried out suicide bombings around the world are young men at the transition between adolescence and maturity. Like cult recruits, they come under the influence of authoritative, religiously oriented communicators who indoctrinate them into seeing themselves as "living martyrs" whose fleeting moment of self-destruction will be their portal into bliss and heroism. To overcome the will to survive, each candidate makes public commitments—creating a will, writing goodbye letters, making a farewell video—that create a psychological point of no return (Kruglanski & Golec de Zavala, 2005). All of this typically transpires in the relative isolation of small cells, with group influences that fan hatred for the enemy.

Group Effects

Cults also illustrate the theme of Chapter 7: the power of a group to shape members' views and behaviour. The cult typically separates members from their previous social support systems and isolates them with other cult members. There may then occur what Rodney Stark and William Bainbridge (1980) called a "social implosion": External ties weaken until the group collapses inward socially, each person engaging only with other group members. Cut off from families and former friends, they lose access to counter-arguments. The group now offers identity and defines reality. Because the cult frowns on or punishes disagreements, the apparent consensus helps eliminate any lingering doubts. Moreover, stress and emotional arousal narrow attention, making people "more susceptible to poorly supported arguments, social pressure, and the temptation to derogate non-group members" (Baron, 2000). Importantly, these connections do not need to be physical—for example, some research has shown that online groups can be equally effective. High-risk gamblers who connect with other high-risk gamblers in online forums tend to engage in even riskier behaviour (Russell, Langham, & Hing, 2018).

Marshall Applewhite and Bonnie Nettles at first formed their own group of two, reinforcing each other's aberrant thinking—a phenomenon that psychiatrists call *folie à deux* (French for "insanity of two"). As others joined them, the group's social isolation facilitated more peculiar thinking. Internet conspiracy groups can likewise foster paranoia. Heaven's Gate was skilled in Internet recruiting, as is ISIS.

These techniques—increasing behavioural commitments, persuasion, and group isolation—do not have unlimited power, however. Toward the end, the leaders of the Solar Temple became increasingly eccentric. One of the leaders' own sons exposed the frauds of the "religious experiences." Many of the members left, and some demanded that their "contributions" of money be returned.

It is important to recognize that cult influence techniques are in some ways similar to techniques used by groups more familiar to us. We might also ask why people join gangs. Wendy Craig at Queen's University and her colleagues (e.g., Craig et al., 2002) have demonstrated that the decision can start in childhood. Youth join gangs as young as age 10 or 11, and by 13 their gang membership has become stable. Researchers at the University of Alberta (Grekul & LaBoucane-Benson, 2008) have found that Indigenous youth join gangs due to their perceptions of discrimination, marginalization, and lack of opportunity and because joining the gang provides them with a sense of identity. Police in Toronto have blamed a number of structural problems—such as poverty, unemployment, nonintegrated neighbourhoods, and a weak legal system—for the increase in gun violence in that city (Ezeonu, 2010). These factors not only encourage participation in gangs but provide a basis for increasing gang cohesion and influence on its members.

The same techniques used in cults are used in sports teams and in the military during "hazing," such as the well-publicized 2012 events that resulted in the women's hockey team at Dalhousie University being suspended for a full year and the 2013 hazing of Grade 9 and 10 students by senior students at the Lanigan Central High School near Saskatoon. The latter incident resulted in 39 charges being laid against 11 students. One study found that martial arts rituals also enhance social identification among group members and help develop a shared identity (Kavanagh et al., 2019). Any group that wants cohesion among its members will likely use some form of these tactics.

Military training creates cohesion and commitment through some of the same tactics used by leaders of cults, fraternities, and therapeutic communities.

Source: ©dario photography/Alamy Stock Photo.

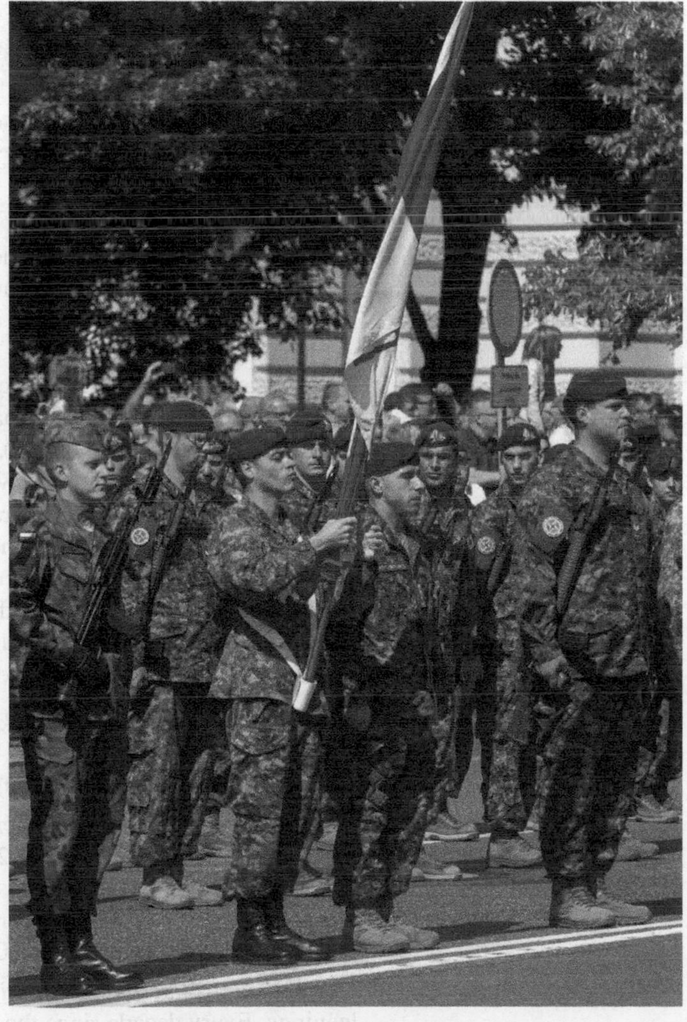

Much the same is true of some therapeutic communities for recovering drug and alcohol abusers and for people who claim to have recalled repressed memories of sexual abuse. Some self-help groups form a cohesive "social cocoon," have intense beliefs, and exert a profound influence on members' behaviour (Galanter, 1989, 1990). Keep in mind that many groups use these indoctrination techniques. For example, terrorist organizations isolate individuals and promise benefits in the afterlife as a potential reward (Aslan, 2010). Some movements can be broad-ranging and generally seem socially acceptable (Scientology and the rise of the more extreme right-wing politicians in the United States are examples), but these groups can use similar tactics—even if they are not considered "cults." However, aside from terrorist groups, cults are perhaps the most documented and analyzed of these types of groups in terms of their social–psychological approaches to persuasion and indoctrination.

But the power may be fleeting: The Unification Church has successfully recruited fewer than one in ten people who attend its workshops (Ennis & Verrilli, 1989). Most who joined Heaven's Gate had left before that fateful day. David Koresh ruled with a mix of persuasion, intimidation, and violence. As Jim Jones made his demands more extreme, he, too, increasingly had to control people with intimidation. He used threats of harm to those who fled the community, beatings for noncompliance, and drugs to neutralize disagreeable members.

Another constructive use of persuasion is in counselling and psychotherapy. Jerome Frank (1974, 1982) recognized years ago that it takes persuasion to change self-defeating attitudes and behaviours. Frank noted that the psychotherapy setting, like cults and zealous self-help groups, provides (1) a supportive, confiding social relationship; (2) an offer of expertise and hope; (3) a special rationale that explains one's difficulties and offers a new perspective; and (4) a set of rituals and learning experiences that promise a new sense of peace and happiness.

We chose the examples of the military, self-help groups, and psychotherapy not to disparage them but to illustrate two concluding observations. First, if we attribute the existence of a movement to the leader's mystical force or to the followers' peculiar weaknesses, we may delude ourselves into thinking we are immune to social control techniques. In truth, our own groups—and countless political leaders, educators, and other persuaders—successfully use many of these tactics on us. Between education and indoctrination, enlightenment and propaganda, conversion and coercion, therapy and mind control, there is but a blurry line.

Second, the fact that Jim Jones and other cult leaders abused the power of persuasion does not mean persuasion is intrinsically bad. Knowing that persuasive power, much like nuclear power, can be harnessed for evil purposes should alert us, as scientists and citizens, to guard against its immoral use. But the power itself is neither inherently evil nor inherently good; it is how we use it that determines whether its effect is destructive or constructive. Condemning persuasion because of deceit is like condemning eating because of gluttony.

Persuasion and Climate Change: How Do We Address Global Warming?

How can we change attitudes and behaviours regarding climate change?

Psychology and Climate Change

In 1960, Earth carried 3 billion people and 127 million motor vehicles. Today, it has more than 7 billion people and nearly 1.2 billion motor vehicles, and we are on track to have 2 billion by 2035. The greenhouse gases we emit (through vehicles, heating, etc.) are changing Earth's climate (Figure 5–12). To ascertain how much and how fast climate change is occurring, several thousand scientists worldwide have collaborated to create and review the evidence via the Intergovernmental Panel on Climate Change (IPCC). The past chair of its scientific assessment committee, John Houghton (2011), reports that the panel's conclusions—supported by the national academies of science of the world's 11 most developed countries—are undergirded by the most "thoroughly researched and reviewed" scientific effort in human history.

In scientific gatherings hosted by the United Nations, Britain's Royal Society, and the U.S. National Academy of Sciences, a consensus has emerged: Increasing population and increasing consumption have combined to overshoot Earth's ecological carrying capacity; in other words we are using more resources than our planet can support.

As the IPCC reports illustrate, converging evidence verifies climate change:

- *A warming greenhouse gas blanket is growing.* About half the carbon dioxide emitted by human activity since the Industrial Revolution (since 1750) remains in the atmosphere (Royal Society, 2010).
- *Reported emissions levels are increasing.* There is now over 140 percent more atmospheric carbon dioxide and over 250 percent more atmospheric methane than before industrial times—and the increase has recently accelerated (World Meteorological Organization, 2019). As the permafrost thaws, methane gas release threatens to compound the problem (Gillis, 2011; National Geographic, 2020).
- *Sea and air temperatures are rising.* The numbers—the facts—have no political leanings. Every decade since the 1970s has been warmer than the one preceding it,

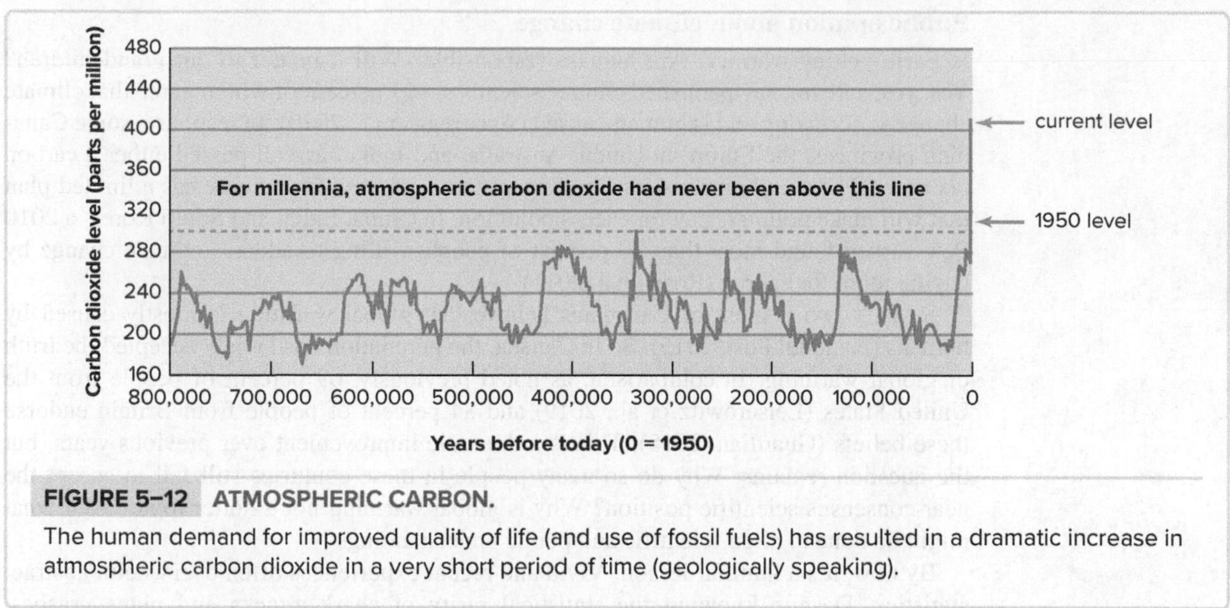

FIGURE 5–12 ATMOSPHERIC CARBON.
The human demand for improved quality of life (and use of fossil fuels) has resulted in a dramatic increase in atmospheric carbon dioxide in a very short period of time (geologically speaking).

with eight of the ten warmest years on record occurring since 2007 (NASA, 2017). If the world were not warming, random weather variations should produce equal numbers of record-breaking high and low temperatures. In reality, record highs have been greatly outnumbering record lows—by about two to one in the United States, for example (Meehl et al., 2009). After amassing 1.6 billion temperature reports from more than 39 000 weather stations, one-time climate change skeptic Richard Muller (2011) became convinced: "Global warming is real."

- *Various plant and animal species are migrating.* In response to the warming world, they are creeping northward and upward, with anticipated loss of biodiversity (Houghton, 2011).
- *The Arctic sea ice is melting.* The late-summer ice cover has shrunk from nearly 7.8 million sq. km (3 million sq. mi.) in the late 1970s to 4.33 million sq. km (1.67 million sq. mi.) in 2011. The West Antarctica and Greenland glacial ice sheets are also melting—faster than ever (Kerr, 2011; National Geographic, 2020).
- *The seas are rising.* Ocean water expands as it warms. Moreover, what happens in the Arctic doesn't stay in the Arctic. Projections of rising sea levels portend large problems for coastal and low-lying areas, including Pakistan, southern China, and Indian and Pacific Ocean islands (Houghton, 2011).
- *Extreme weather is increasing.* Any single weather event cannot be attributed to climate change. Weird weather happens. Nevertheless, climate scientists predict that global warming will make extreme weather events—hurricanes, heat waves, droughts, and floods—more intense (Kerr, 2011). As precipitation in a warming and wetter world falls more as rain and less as snow, the likely result will be rainy-season floods and less dry-season snow and ice melt to sustain rivers.

Throughout its history, social psychology has responded to human events: to the civil rights era with studies of stereotyping and prejudice, to years of civil unrest and increasing crime with studies of aggression, to the women's movement with studies of gender development and gender-related attitudes. If global climate change is now "the greatest problem the world faces" (Houghton, 2011), surely we will see more and more studies of the likely effects of climate change on human behaviour, of public opinion about climate change, and of ways to modify the human sources of climate change. Already, such inquiry is underway.

Public opinion about climate change

Is Earth getting warmer? Are humans responsible? Will it matter to our grandchildren? Yes, yes, and yes, say published climate scientists—97 percent of whom agree that climate change is occurring and is human-caused (Anderegg et al., 2010). In response, some Canadian provinces, the European Union, Australia, and India have all passed either a carbon tax on coal or a carbon emissions trading system, and even China now has a limited plan that will make polluters pay for excess pollution. In China, India, and South Korea, a 2010 Pew survey found more than 70 percent of people willing to address climate change by paying more for energy (Rosenthal, 2011).

Seventy-two percent of Canadians believe that global warming is mostly caused by humans (National Post, 2015). So in Canada, the population has largely accepted the truth of global warming. In comparison, as noted previously, 69 percent of people from the United States (Leiserowitz et al., 2019) and 84 percent of people from Britain endorse these beliefs (Guardian, 2015). This is a dramatic improvement over previous years, but the question remains: Why do so many people in these countries still fail to accept the near-consensus scientific position? Why is global warming not a hotter topic? And what might be done to align scientific and public understandings?

By now, it's a familiar lesson: Vivid and recent experiences often overwhelm abstract statistics. Despite knowing the statistical rarity of shark attacks and plane crashes, vivid images of such—being readily available in memory—often hijack our emotions and distort our judgments. We make our intuitive judgments under the influence of the availability heuristic—and thus we often fear the wrong things. If an airline misplaces our bag, we likely will overweight our immediate experience; ignoring data on the airline's overall lost-bag rate, we belittle the airline. Our ancient brains come designed to attend to the immediate situation, not out-of-sight data and beyond-the-horizon dangers (Gifford, 2011). Likewise, people will often scorn global warming in the face of a winter freeze. One climate skeptic declared a record blizzard "a coup de grâce" for global warming (Breckler, 2010).

As you may recall, persuasive messages must first be understood. Thanks in part to the media's mixed messages—its framing of two opposing sides, those concerned about and those dismissive of climate change—and perceiving uncertainty, and reassured by the natural human optimism bias, people discount the threat (Gifford, 2011). U.S. president Donald Trump, himself a climate change denier, appointed in January 2017 a fellow skeptic to run the U.S. Environmental Protection Agency, the impact of which may be felt for decades.

People also exhibit a "system justification" tendency—a tendency to believe in and justify the way things are in their culture and, thus, especially when comfortable, to not want to change the familiar status quo (Feygina, Jost, & Goldsmith, 2010). We tend to like our habitual ways of living—of travelling, of eating, and of heating and cooling our spaces. More encouraging news comes from an experiment that showed global temperature trends to people. Regardless of their prior assumptions about global climate change, people were able to understand the trend and project it into the near future—and to adjust their beliefs. Education matters.

We also benefit from framing energy savings in attention-getting ways. An information sheet or store sign might read, "If you do not install CFL light bulbs, you will lose $_____." Another effective strategy is to use long time periods. For example, instead of saying "This Energy Star refrigerator will save you $120 a year on your electric bills," say it "will save you $2400 in wasted energy bills over the next 20 years" (Hofmeister, 2010).

What shall we do? Eat, drink, and be merry, for tomorrow is doom? Behave as so many participants have in Prisoner's Dilemma games, by pursuing self-interest to our collective detriment? ("Heck, on a global scale, my consumption is infinitesimal; it makes my life comfortable and costs the world practically nothing.")

Those more optimistic about the future see two routes to sustainable lifestyles: (1) increasing technological efficiency and agricultural productivity, and (2) moderating consumption and population.

New Technologies

One component in a sustainable future is improved eco-technologies. Newer refrigerators consume half the energy of those sold 10 years earlier (Heap & Comim, 2005). We have replaced many incandescent bulbs with energy-saving fluorescent bulbs, replaced printed and delivered letters and catalogues with email and ecommerce, and replaced many commuter kilometres driven with telecommuting.

There is also good news about cars. To begin with, today's middle-aged adults drive cars that get twice the mileage and produce a twentieth of the pollution of the ones they drove as teenagers. For the near future, we have hybrid cars—which conserve gasoline by using an electric power cell—and flex-fuel cars, which can run on ethanol produced from a variety of vegetable sources, such as soybeans, or on a mixture of ethanol and gasoline.

Plausible future technologies include diodes that emit light for 20 years without bulbs; ultrasound washing machines that consume no water, heat, or soap; reusable and compostable plastics; cars running on fuel cells that combine hydrogen and oxygen and produce water exhaust; lightweight materials that are stronger than steel; and roofs and roads that double as solar energy collectors (N. Myers, 2000; Zhang et al., 2007).

Some energy solutions are low-tech. One Philippine nonprofit is working with the government and volunteers to install zero-energy solar light bulbs in 1 million low-income homes. The "bulbs" are nothing more than discarded clear plastic soda bottles that, when filled with water and wedged in a hole in the roof—with half the bottle exposed to the sun and half jutting into the room—transmit 55 watts of light. The result? Daytime light is provided without electricity bills (Orendain, 2011).

Given the speed of innovation (who could have imagined today's world a century ago?), the future will surely bring solutions that we aren't yet imagining. Surely, say the optimists, the future will bring increased material well-being for more people requiring many fewer raw materials and much less polluting waste.

Reducing Consumption

The second component of a sustainable future is the control of consumption. Instead of more people consuming and polluting more all the time, a stable population will need to consume and pollute less.

Thanks to family planning efforts, the world's population growth rate has decelerated, especially in developed nations. Even in less-developed countries, when food security has improved and women have become educated and empowered, birth rates have fallen. But even if birth rates everywhere instantly fell to a replacement level of 2.1 children per woman, the lingering momentum of population growth, fed by the bulge of younger humans, would continue for years to come.

Given that humans have already overshot Earth's carrying capacity, individual consumption must moderate. With our material appetites continually swelling—as more people seek more—what can be done to moderate consumption by those who can afford to overconsume?

One way is through public policies that harness the motivating power of incentives. As a general rule, we get less of what we tax and more of what we reward. Many cities are using tax monies to build bike lanes and subsidize improved mass transportation, thus encouraging alternatives to cars. On jammed highways, many regions have created high-occupancy-vehicle lanes that reward carpooling and penalize driving solo. Gregg Esterbrook (2004) noted that if the United States had raised its gasoline tax by 50 cents a decade ago, as was proposed, the country would now have smaller, more fuel-efficient cars (as do Europeans, with their higher petrol taxes) and would, therefore, import less oil. This, in turn, would have led to lower oil consumption, less global warming, lower gas prices, and a smaller trade deficit weighing down the economy. A higher gas tax would have similar effects in Canada.

Europe leads the way in incentivizing mass transit and bicycle use over personal vehicle use. Cities such as Vienna, Munich, Zurich, and Copenhagen have closed many city centre streets to car traffic. London and Stockholm drivers pay congestion fees when entering the heart of the city. Amsterdam is a bicycle haven. Dozens of German cities have "environmental zones" where only low CO_2 cars may enter (Rosenthal, 2011). The Netherlands has even experimented with a car meter that would tax drivers a fee for distance driven, rather like paying a phone fee for minutes talked (Rosenthal, 2011).

Some free-market proponents object to carbon taxes because they are taxes. Others respond that carbon taxes are simply payment for external damage to today's health and tomorrow's environment. If not today's CO_2 emitters, who should pay for the cost of tomorrow's more threatening floods, tornadoes, hurricanes, droughts, and sea rise? "Markets are truly free only when everyone pays the full price for his or her actions," contends Environmental Defense Fund economist Gernot Wagner (2011).

Another way to encourage greener homes and businesses is to harness the power of immediate feedback to the consumer by installing "smart meters" that provide a continuous readout of electricity use and its cost. Turn off a computer monitor or the lights in an empty room, and the meter displays the decreased wattage. Turn on the air conditioning, and you immediately know the usage and cost. In Britain, smart meters are being installed in businesses, and some politicians have supported a plan to have them installed in all homes (Rosenthal, 2008).

In one survey, the top reason people gave for buying a Prius hybrid car was that it "makes a statement about me" (Clayton & Myers, 2009, p. 9). Indeed, argue Tom Crompton and Tim Kasser (2010), our sense of who we are—our identity—has profound implications for our climate-related behaviours. Does our social identity, the in-group that defines our circle of concern, include only those around us now? Or does it encompass vulnerable people in places unseen, our descendants and others in the future, and even the creatures in the planet's natural environment?

Support for new energy policies will require a shift in public consciousness not unlike that which occurred during the 1960s civil rights movement and the 1970s women's movement. James Gustave Speth (2008) is calling for an enlarged identity—a "new consciousness"—in which people do the following:

- See humanity as part of nature.
- See nature as having intrinsic value that we must steward.
- Value the future and its inhabitants as well as the present.
- Appreciate our human interdependence, by thinking "we" and not just "me."
- Define quality of life in relational and spiritual rather than materialistic terms.
- Value equity, justice, and the human community.

Is there any hope that human priorities might shift from accumulating money to finding meaning, and from aggressive consumption to nurturing connections? The British government's plan for achieving sustainable development includes an emphasis on promoting personal well-being and social health. Perhaps social psychology can help point the way to greater well-being, by suggesting *ways to reduce consumption*—and also by documenting *materialism,* by informing people that *economic growth does not automatically improve human morale,* and by helping people understand *why materialism and money fail to satisfy* and encouraging *alternative, intrinsic values.*

How Can Persuasion Be Resisted?

What are some tactics for resisting influence? How might we prepare people to resist unwanted persuasion?

Martial arts trainers devote as much time to teaching defensive blocks, deflections, and parries as they do to teaching attack. "On the social influence battlefield," noted Brad Sagarin and his colleagues (2002), researchers have focused more on persuasive attack than on defence. Being persuaded comes naturally, Daniel Gilbert and his colleagues (Gilbert, Krull, & Malone, 1990; Gilbert, Tafarodi, & Malone, 1993) reported. It is easier to accept persuasive messages than to doubt them. To understand an assertion (say, that lead pencils are a health hazard) is to believe it—at least temporarily, until one actively undoes the initial, automatic acceptance. If a distracting event prevents the undoing, the acceptance lingers.

Still, blessed with logic, information, and motivation, we do resist falsehoods. If the credible-seeming repair person's uniform and the doctor's title have intimidated us into unquestioning agreement, we can rethink our habitual responses to authority. We can seek more information before committing time or money. We can question what we don't understand.

Attitude Strength

Strong attitudes are more likely to lead to behaviour, whereas weak attitudes are not. Similarly, strong attitudes are consequential in that they bias how we perceive incoming information, whereas weak attitudes do so to a lesser degree (Krosnick & Petty, 1995).

There has been research exploring people's subjective beliefs about the strength of their attitudes. Indeed, subjective beliefs are probably the most common approach to assessing attitude strength. Think back to any opinion survey you have ever done. You were probably asked how "certain" you were or how "important the topic was to you." **Certainty** refers to the level of subjective confidence or validity that people attach to their attitudes. Certainty is high when people have a clear notion of what their attitudes are and believe that their attitudes are accurate (Petrocelli, Tormala, & Rucker, 2007). Studies conducted by multiple researchers have found that higher certainty is associated with attitude stability over time (Bassili, 1996), resistance to persuasion (Bassili, 1996; Tormala & Petty, 2002), and impact on social judgments (Marks & Miller, 1985). Thus, the more certain you are, the harder it will be for someone to change your mind.

certainty Refers to the level of subjective confidence or validity that people attach to their attitudes.

"A fanatic is one who can't change his mind and won't change the subject."

Winston Churchill, 1954

Information-Processing Biases

Perhaps not surprisingly, given the extensive work on attitude strength and its relation to information processing, strong attitudes have been demonstrated to result in biases in how we process information. Leon Festinger (1957), who developed cognitive dissonance theory, provided one of the earliest discussions and conducted the first systematic research into the impact of attitudes on information processing. Festinger argued that, because individuals are motivated to maintain cognitive consistency, people should be motivated to incorporate information that is consistent with their attitudes and to avoid information that is inconsistent. And there is some evidence that we are better at incorporating new information if it is consistent with our existing knowledge. For example, Teena Willoughby at Brock University (Willoughby et al., 2009) has demonstrated that, when doing Internet searches for assigned essays, we are much better at getting information if we already know something about the topic. Having that basic knowledge helps both subjectively (how we feel about it) and objectively (how well we write the essay).

Typically, these biases have been broken down by the stages at which they have an influence on information processing: selective exposure and attention to information, selective processing and judgment, and selective memory. Although more sophisticated approaches to the concept of information processing have been developed, and the "stage" model is not as supported as it once was, it is still a useful way to think about information processing biases (Eagly & Chaiken, 1998; Smith et al., 2007).

Selective exposure and attention

Early work on exposure found that people were biased in how they exposed themselves to information. **Selective exposure** is the extent to which people's attitudes affect the information they expose themselves to. **Selective attention** is the extent to which people's attitudes affect how much of this information they pay attention to, once they've been exposed to it. For example, Ehrlich and colleagues (1957) found that car owners who had recently made a car purchase read more ads about the cars they purchased than they did ads for cars they had considered but decided not to buy. More recently, Steven Smith (one of your authors) and his colleagues (2007) found that motivation and the ability to process information are important. In order to be a complete information processor, a person must both be able (e.g., have the appropriate cognitive resources, not be distracted) and be motivated (e.g., want or be predisposed) to first process all of the available information, and then be unbiased when processing that information. However, as you can imagine, there are many times when motivation to be unbiased may be low and times when being biased in an attitude-congruent way would be common. Thus, under many conditions, people are indeed biased in how they expose themselves to information. However, there are occasions (e.g., when we are uniquely responsible for decisions or our decisions have important consequences) where we will strive to be unbiased (see Jonas et al., 2005; Smith et al., 2007, 2008).

selective exposure The extent to which people's attitudes bias the attitude-relevant information they expose themselves to.

selective attention The extent to which people's attitudes bias the attitude-relevant information they attend to, once exposed.

selective memory The extent to which people's attitudes bias recall and recognition of attitude-relevant information.

Selective perception and judgment

In a classic study, Lord, Ross, and Lepper (1979) demonstrated biased perception and judgment regarding the death penalty. The researchers first assessed people with existing attitudes toward the death penalty. Next, participants were presented with the results of two purportedly real studies. One study supported the effectiveness of capital punishment as a deterrent; the other did not. As predicted, participants rated the study that agreed with their own point of view as more convincing and more scientifically rigorous than the study they disagreed with. In general, these selectivity effects have been found to be particularly likely to occur when attitudes are strong. For example, Houston and Fazio (1989) found that people whose attitudes toward capital punishment were more accessible engaged in biased processing to a greater degree than people whose attitudes were not as accessible.

Selective memory

Of the various attitude-based information processing biases, perhaps the most controversial has been the relationship between attitudes and recall. Within this literature, the dominant perspective has been that attitudes should produce congeniality biases in recall. This perspective postulates that people use **selective memory** when they process social information: they remember information that is congruent with their attitudes better than information that is incongruent with their attitudes (e.g., see Eagly et al., 1999). Meghan Norris at Queen's University and her colleagues (Smith et al., 2008; Norris, 2007; Norris et al., 2014) have shown that, similar to selective exposure effects, people's motivation and ability to be biased are important factors in biased memory.

Overall, however, we can consider that attitude strength and biases in information processing work as somewhat "passive" factors in protecting our attitudes from inconsistent information. Most people are not aware of the natural biases they may be exhibiting (Wegener & Petty, 1996). Yet the effects are quite consistent. If we cannot ignore the inconsistent information, we can judge it as irrelevant or inconsequential, or we can simply forget it. This does not necessarily require any conscious decision making. However, there are certainly more "active" approaches we can take to defend our attitudes. We will discuss some of these below.

Reactance

Knowing that someone is trying to coerce us may even prompt us to react in the opposite direction. For example, think back to some of your early romantic relationships. Did you ever have a relationship with someone your guardian did not like? Most of us have had this experience. You bring home the new love of your life, only to discover that your parent absolutely despises them. If your parents were social psychologists, they probably said nothing. However, if they were like most parents, they probably told you how they felt about your new amour. How did you react to this information? If you are like many of the students in the authors' classes, you probably liked your new love interest even more after you discovered your parents' true feelings about them. This is called **reactance**, which we will discuss more in Chapter 6.

Strengthening Personal Commitment

Before encountering others' judgments, you can resist persuasion by making a public commitment to your position. Having stood up for your convictions, you will become less susceptible (or should we say less "open") to what others have to say. In mock civil trials, straw polls of jurors can foster a hardening of expressed positions, leading to more dead locks (Davis et al., 1993).

Challenging beliefs

How might we stimulate people to commit themselves? Charles Kiesler (1971) offered one possible way: by mildly attacking their position. Kiesler found that when committed people were attacked strongly enough to cause them to react, but not so strongly as to overwhelm them, they became even more committed. Kiesler explained: "When you attack committed people and your attack is of inadequate strength, you drive them to even more extreme behaviours in defense of their previous commitment" (p. 88). Perhaps you can recall a time when this happened in an argument, as those involved escalated their rhetoric, committing themselves to increasingly extreme positions.

reactance A motive to protect or restore our sense of freedom. Reactance arises when someone threatens our freedom of action.

attitude inoculation Exposing people to weak attacks on their attitudes so that when stronger attacks come, they will have refutations available.

Developing counter-arguments

There is a second reason a mild attack might build resistance. Like inoculations against disease, even weak arguments will prompt counter-arguments, which are then available for a stronger attack. William McGuire (1964) documented this in a series of experiments. McGuire wondered if we could inoculate people against persuasion much as we inoculate them against a virus. Is there such a thing as **attitude inoculation**? Could we take people raised in a "germ-free ideological environment"—people who hold some unquestioned belief—and stimulate their mental defences? And would subjecting them to a small dose of belief-threatening material inoculate them against later persuasion?

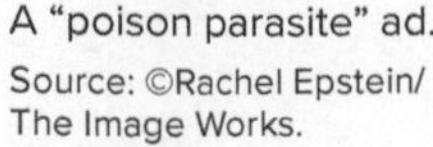

A "poison parasite" ad.
Source: ©Rachel Epstein/The Image Works.

That is what McGuire did. First, he found some cultural truisms, such as, "It's a good idea to brush your teeth after every meal if at all possible." He then showed that people were vulnerable to a massive, credible assault on these truisms (for example, prestigious authorities were said to have discovered that too much tooth brushing can damage your gums). If, however, before having their belief attacked, they were "immunized" by first receiving a small challenge to their belief, and if they read or wrote an essay in refutation of this mild attack, then they were better able to resist the powerful attack.

Robert Cialdini and his colleagues (2003) agree that appropriate counter-arguments are a great way to resist persuasion, but they wondered how to bring them to mind in response to an opponent's ads. The answer, they suggest, is a "poison parasite" defence—one that combines a poison (strong counter-arguments) with a parasite (retrieval cues that bring those arguments to mind when seeing the opponent's ads). In their studies, participants who viewed a familiar political ad were least persuaded by it when they had earlier seen counter-arguments overlaid on a replica of the ad. Seeing the ad again thus also brought to mind the puncturing counter-arguments. Anti-smoking ads have effectively done this, for example, by recreating a "Marlboro Man" commercial set in the rugged outdoors but now showing a coughing, decrepit cowboy.

Inoculation Programs

Could attitude inoculation indeed prepare people to resist unwanted persuasion? Applied research on smoking prevention and consumer education offers encouraging answers.

Inoculating children against peer pressure to smoke

Consider how laboratory research findings can lead to practical applications. One research team had high school students "inoculate" students in Grade 7 against peer pressures to smoke (McAlister et al., 1980). The Grade 7 students were taught to respond to advertisements implying that liberated women smoke by saying, "She's not really liberated if she is hooked on tobacco." They also acted in role-plays; after being called "chicken" for not taking a cigarette, they answered with statements like "I'd be a real chicken if I smoked just to impress you." After several of these sessions during Grades 7 and 8, the inoculated students were half as likely to begin smoking as uninoculated students at another junior high school that had an identical parental smoking rate (Figure 5–13).

Other research teams have confirmed that such inoculation procedures, sometimes supplemented by other life-skills training, reduce teen smoking (Botvin, Epstein, &

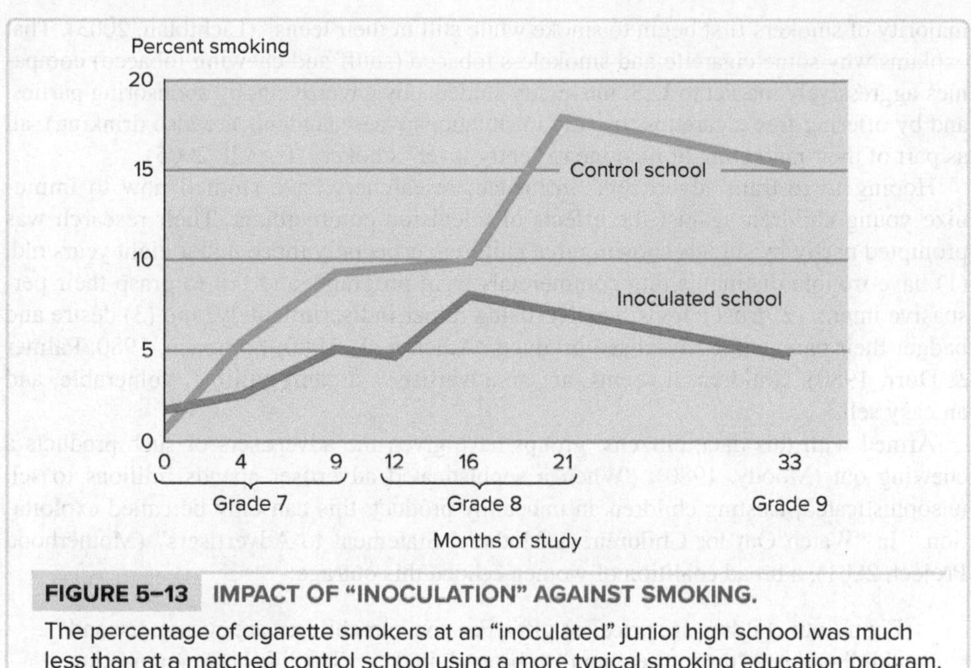

FIGURE 5–13 IMPACT OF "INOCULATION" AGAINST SMOKING.

The percentage of cigarette smokers at an "inoculated" junior high school was much less than at a matched control school using a more typical smoking education program.

Griffin, 2008; Botvin, Schinke, & Orlandi, 1995; Evans, Smith, & Raines, 1984; Flay et al., 1985). Most newer efforts emphasize strategies for resisting social pressure. One study exposed students in Grades 6 to 8 to anti-smoking films or to information about smoking, together with role-plays of student-generated ways of refusing a cigarette (Hirschman & Leventhal, 1989). A year-and-a-half later, 31 percent of those who had watched the anti-smoking films had taken up smoking. Among those who had role-played refusing a cigarette, only 19 percent had begun smoking.

Anti-smoking and drug education programs apply other persuasion principles, too. They use attractive peers to communicate information. They trigger the students' own cognitive processing ("Here's something you might want to think about"). They get the students to make a public commitment (by making a rational decision about smoking and then announcing it, along with their reasoning, to their classmates). Some of these smoking-prevention programs require only two to six hours of class time, using prepared printed materials or videotapes. Today, any school district or teacher wishing to use the social–psychological approach to smoking prevention can do so easily, inexpensively, and with the hope of significant reductions in future smoking rates and associated health costs.

Inoculating children against the influence of advertising

Belgium, Denmark, Greece, Ireland, Italy, and Sweden all restrict advertising that targets children (McGuire, 2002). Advertising to children is prohibited by law in Quebec and regulated in other provinces. Nevertheless, in North America, noted Robert Levine in *The Power of Persuasion: How We're Bought and Sold,* the average child sees over 10 000 commercials a year. "Two decades ago," he noted, "children drank twice as much milk as soda. Thanks to advertising the ratio is now reversed" (2003, p. 16).

> ***"In general, my children refuse to eat anything that hasn't danced on television."***
>
> Erma Bombeck

Smokers often develop an "initial brand choice" in their teens, said a 1981 report from researchers at Philip Morris (FTC, 2003). Indeed, "today's teenager is tomorrow's potential regular customer, and the overwhelming majority of smokers first begin to smoke while still in their teens" (Lichtblau, 2003). That explains why some cigarette and smokeless tobacco (snuff and chewing tobacco) companies aggressively market to U.S. university students by advertising, by sponsoring parties, and by offering free cigarettes (usually in situations where students are also drinking), all as part of their marketing of nicotine to "entry level" smokers (Farrell, 2005).

Hoping to restrain advertisers' influence, researchers have studied how to immunize young children against the effects of television commercials. Their research was prompted partly by studies showing that children, especially those under eight years old, (1) have trouble distinguishing commercials from programs and fail to grasp their persuasive intent, (2) trust television advertising rather indiscriminately, and (3) desire and badger their parents for advertised products (Adler et al., 1980; Feshbach, 1980; Palmer & Dorr, 1980). Children, it seems, are an advertiser's dream: gullible, vulnerable, and an easy sell.

Armed with this data, citizens' groups have given the advertisers of such products a chewing out (Moody, 1980): "When a sophisticated advertiser spends millions to sell unsophisticated, trusting children an unhealthy product, this can only be called exploitation." In "Watch Out for Children: A Mothers' Statement to Advertisers" (Motherhood Project, 2001), a broad coalition of women echoed this outrage:

> For us, our children are priceless gifts. For you, our children are customers, and childhood is a "market segment" to be exploited. . . . The line between meeting and creating consumer needs and desire is increasingly being crossed, as your battery of highly trained and creative experts study, analyze, persuade, and manipulate our children. . . . The driving messages are "You deserve a break today," "Have it your way," "Follow your instincts. Obey your thirst," "Just Do It," "No Boundaries," "Got the Urge?" These [exemplify] the dominant message of advertising and marketing: that life is about selfishness, instant gratification, and materialism.

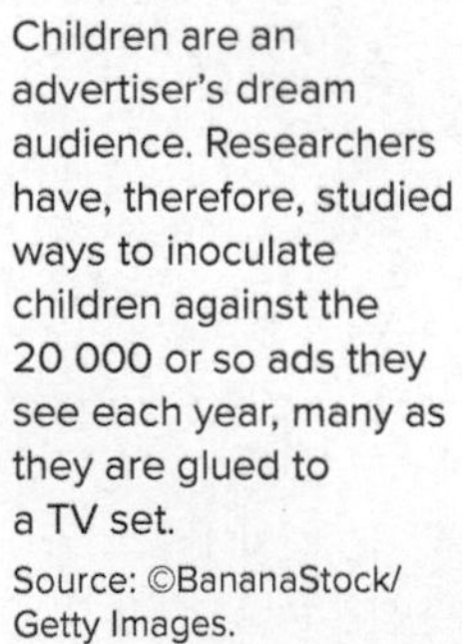

Children are an advertiser's dream audience. Researchers have, therefore, studied ways to inoculate children against the 20 000 or so ads they see each year, many as they are glued to a TV set.

Source: ©BananaStock/Getty Images.

On the other side are the commercial interests. They claim that ads allow parents to teach their children consumer skills and, more important, finance children's television programs. Government agencies that oversee the media are often stuck in the middle, pushed by research findings and political pressures while trying to decide whether to place new constraints on TV ads aimed at underage youth.

Meanwhile, researchers have found that urban Grade 7 students who are able to think critically about ads—who have "media resistance skills"—also better resist peer pressure when they are in Grade 8 and are less likely to drink alcohol in Grade 9 (Epstein & Botvin, 2008). Researchers have also wondered whether children can be taught to resist deceptive ads. In one such effort, a team of investigators led by Norma Feshbach (1980; Cohen, 1980) gave small groups of elementary schoolchildren three half-hour lessons in analyzing commercials. The children were inoculated by viewing ads and discussing them. For example, after viewing a toy ad, they were immediately given the toy and challenged to make it do what they had just seen in the commercial. Such experiences helped breed a more realistic understanding of commercials.

Consumer advocates worry that inoculation may be insufficient. Better to clean the air than to wear a gas mask. It is no surprise, then, that parents resent it when advertisers market products to children and then place them on lower store shelves where children will see them, pick them up, and nag and whine until they sometimes wear the parent down. For that reason, urges the "Mothers' Code for Advertisers," there should be no advertising in schools, no targeting of children under eight years of age, no product placement in movies and programs targeting children and adolescents, and no ads directed at children and adolescents "that promote an ethic of selfishness and a focus on instant gratification" (Motherhood Project, 2001).

Implications of Attitude Inoculation

The best way to build resistance to brainwashing probably is not just stronger indoctrination into one's current beliefs. If parents are worried that their children could become members of a cult, they might better teach their children about the various cults and prepare them to counter persuasive appeals.

For the same reason, religious educators should be wary of creating a "germ-free ideological environment" in their churches and schools. People who live amid diverse views become more discerning and more likely to modify their views only in response to credible arguments (Levitan & Visser, 2008). Also, a challenge to one's views, if refuted, is more likely to solidify one's position than to undermine it, particularly if the threatening material can be examined with like-minded others (Visser & Mirabile, 2004). Cults apply this principle by forewarning members of how families and friends will attack the cult's beliefs. When the expected challenge comes, the member is armed with counter-arguments.

Another implication is that, for the persuader, an ineffective appeal can be worse than none. Can you see why? Those who reject an appeal are inoculated against further appeals. Consider an experiment in which Susan Darley and Joel Cooper (1972) invited students to write essays advocating a strict dress code. Because that was against the students' own positions and the essays were to be published, all chose not to write the essay—even those offered money to do so. After turning down the money, they became even more extreme and confident in their anti–dress-code opinions. Those who have rejected initial appeals to quit smoking may likewise become immune to further appeals. Ineffective persuasion, by stimulating the listener's defences, may be counterproductive. It may "harden the heart" against later appeals.

SUMMING UP

What Paths Lead to Persuasion?

- Sometimes persuasion occurs as people focus on arguments and respond with favourable thoughts. Such systematic, or "central route," persuasion occurs when people are naturally analytical or involved in the issue.
- When issues don't engage systematic thinking, persuasion may occur through a faster "peripheral route" as people use heuristics or incidental cues to make snap judgments.
- Central route persuasion, being more thoughtful and less superficial, is more durable and more likely to influence behaviour.

What Are the Elements of Persuasion?

- What makes persuasion effective? Researchers have explored four factors: the communicator (who says it), the message (what is said), the channel (how it is said), and the audience (to whom it is said).
- Credible communicators have the best success in persuading. People who speak unhesitatingly, who talk fast, and who look listeners straight in the eye seem more credible. So do people who argue against their own self-interest. An attractive communicator is effective on matters of taste and personal values.
- The message itself persuades; associating it with good feelings makes it more convincing. People often make quicker, less reflective judgments while in good moods. Fear-arousing messages can also be effective, especially if recipients can take protective action.
- How discrepant a message should be from an audience's existing opinions depends on the communicator's credibility. And whether a one- or a two-sided message is most persuasive depends on whether the audience already agrees with the message, is unaware of opposing arguments, and is unlikely later to consider the opposition.
- When two sides of an issue are included, the primacy effect often makes the first message more persuasive. If a time gap separates the presentations, the more likely result will be a recency effect in which the second message prevails.
- Another important consideration is how the message is communicated. Usually face-to-face appeals work best. Print media can be effective for complex messages; the mass media can be effective when the issue is minor or unfamiliar and when the media reach opinion leaders.
- The age of the audience makes a difference; young people's attitudes are more subject to change. What does the audience think while receiving a message? Do they think favourable thoughts? Do they counter-argue? Were they forewarned?

Extreme Persuasion: How Do Cults Indoctrinate?

- The successes of religious cults provide an opportunity to see powerful persuasion processes at work.
- It appears that the success of cults has resulted from three general techniques: eliciting behavioural commitments (as described in Chapter 4); applying principles of effective persuasion (this chapter); and isolating members in like-minded groups (to be discussed in Chapter 7).

Persuasion and Climate Change: How Do We Address Global Warming?

- There is overwhelming scientific evidence and consensus that global warming is a fact and caused by human activity. Global warming has psychological costs in that people must cope with the natural disasters, wars, and aggression that are promoted by global warming. Many people in Canada, the United States and Britain accept that climate change is caused by human activity.
- Humanity can prepare for a sustainable future by increasing technological efficiency. We can also create incentives and change actions and attitudes to control population and moderate consumption.
- Attending to concepts in social psychology that address our attitudes and our behaviours may help accomplish those objectives. Rapid cultural change has happened in the last 40 years, and there is hope that in response to the global crisis it can happen again.

How Can Persuasion Be Resisted?

- Attitude strength is important: the stronger our attitudes, the more likely we are to avoid, dismiss, forget, or counter-argue information that is inconsistent with our existing attitudes.
- If we feel that our freedoms to think and behave in a certain way are being unreasonably challenged, we will "react" (i.e., reactance) and often end up strengthening our pre-existing attitudes and beliefs.
- How do people resist persuasion? A prior public commitment to one's own position, stimulated perhaps by a mild attack on the position, breeds resistance to later persuasion.
- A mild attack can also serve as an inoculation, stimulating one to develop counter-arguments that will then be available if and when a strong attack comes.
- This implies, paradoxically, that one way to strengthen existing attitudes is to challenge them, though the challenge must not be so strong as to overwhelm them.

Key Terms

attitude inoculation
attractiveness
central route to persuasion
certainty
channel of communication
credibility
cults
need for cognition
peripheral route to persuasion
persuasion
primacy effect
reactance
recency effect
selective attention
selective exposure
selective memory
sleeper effect
two-step flow of communication

CHAPTER 6

Conformity

Source: ©Daniel Megias/iStock/Getty Images Plus.

CHAPTER OUTLINE

What Is Conformity?

What Are the Classic Conformity and Obedience Studies?

What Predicts Conformity?

Why Conform?

Who Conforms?

Do We Ever Want to Be Different?

You have surely experienced this phenomenon: You are at a local play, or a school concert, and the admiring fans (parents) near the front leap to their feet, applauding.

The folks just behind them follow their example and join the standing ovation. Now the wave of people standing reaches people who, unprompted, would merely be giving polite applause from their seats. Seated among them, you partly want to stay seated ("This was fine, but . . ."). But as the wave of standing people sweeps by, will you alone stay seated? It's not easy, being a minority of one.

Unless you heartily dislike what you've experienced, you will probably rise to your feet, at least briefly. Such scenes of conformity raise this chapter's questions:

- Why, given our diversity, do we so often behave as social clones?
- Under what circumstances are we most likely to conform?
- Are certain people more likely than others to conform?
- Who resists the pressure to conform?
- Is conformity as bad as our image of a docile "herd" implies? Should we instead be describing "group solidarity" and "social sensitivity"?

What Is Conformity?

Is conformity good or bad? Assuming the values most of us share, conformity is at times bad (when it leads someone to drink and drive or to join in racist behaviour), at times good (when people collectively social distance to minimize disease transmission), and at times inconsequential (when it disposes tennis players to wear white).

In Western individualistic cultures, where submitting to peer pressure is not admired, the word *conformity* tends to carry a negative connotation. Most North Americans and Europeans would not like to be called a "real conformist." North American and European social psychologists, reflecting their individualistic cultures, give conformity negative labels (submission, compliance) rather than positive ones (communal sensitivity, responsiveness, cooperative team play). However, there are times in individualistic cultures where conformity is naturally encouraged, such as times of national (or local) crises where people are exhorted to "stand together." This was a common refrain early in the COVID-19 pandemic outbreak.

"The social pressures community brings to bear are a mainstay of our moral values."

Amitai Etzioni, *The Spirit of Community,* 1993

In Japan, going along with others is a sign not of weakness but of tolerance, self-control, and maturity (Markus & Kitayama, 1994). "Everywhere in Japan," observed Lance Morrow (1983), "one senses an intricate serenity that comes to a people who know exactly what to expect from each other." Such is also true of self-organized U2 fans whom Marie Helweg-Larsen and Barbara LoMonaco (2008) observed queuing overnight for unreserved concert places at or near the front rail. A U2 fan code of honour mandates first come, first served.

"The race of men, while sheep in credulity, are wolves for conformity."

Carl Van Doren, "Why I Am an Unbeliever," 1926

The moral: We choose labels to suit our values and judgments. Labels both describe and evaluate, and they are inescapable. We cannot discuss the topics of this chapter without labels. So let us be clear on the meanings of the following labels: *conformity*, *obedience*, *compliance*, and *acceptance*.

Conformity is not just acting as other people act; it is also being affected by how they act. It is acting or thinking differently from the way you would act and think if you were alone. Thus, **conformity** is a change in behaviour or belief to accord with others. When, as part of a crowd, you rise to cheer a game-winning goal, are you conforming? When, along with millions of others, you drink milk or coffee, are you conforming? Maybe, maybe not. The key is whether your behaviour and beliefs would be the same apart from the group. Would you rise to cheer the goal if you were the only fan in the stands?

conformity A change in behaviour or belief to accord with others.

"Whatever crushes individuality is despotism, by whatever name it may be called."

John Stuart Mill, *On Liberty*, 1859

compliance Conformity that involves publicly acting in accord with social pressure while privately disagreeing.

obedience Acting in accord with a direct order.

acceptance Conformity that involves both acting and believing, in accord with social pressure.

There are several varieties of conformity (Nail, MacDonald, & Levy, 2000). Sometimes we conform to an expectation or request without really believing in what we are doing. We put on the necktie or dress, although we dislike doing so. This insincere, outward conformity is **compliance**. We comply primarily to reap a reward or avoid a punishment. If our compliance is to an explicit command, we call it **obedience**.

Sometimes we genuinely believe in what the group has persuaded us to do. The general population's reaction to the COVID-19 pandemic is a good example of this. Around the world, countries and regions spent significant time in self-isolation despite the real personal, social, and economic impact this had on millions of people. Although there was enforcement in most countries, the majority of people complied because they believed that social distancing would keep them and their families safer. This sincere, inward conformity is called **acceptance**. There is even a neuroscience of compliance and acceptance: The shorter-lived memories that underlie public compliance have a different neural basis than the memories that underlie longer-term private acceptance (Edelson et al., 2011; Zaki, Schirmer, & Mitchell, 2011).

Acceptance sometimes follows compliance; we may come to inwardly believe something we initially questioned. As Chapter 4 emphasized, attitudes follow behaviour. Unless we feel no responsibility for our behaviour, we usually become sympathetic to what we have stood up for.

What Are the Classic Conformity and Obedience Studies?

How have social psychologists studied conformity in the laboratory? What do their results reveal about the potency of social forces and the nature of evil?

Researchers who study conformity construct miniature social worlds—laboratory microcultures that simplify and simulate important features of everyday social influence. Some of these studies revealed such startling findings that they have been widely replicated and widely reported by other researchers, earning them the name "classic" experiments. We will consider three, each of which provides a method for studying conformity—and plenty of food for thought.

Sherif's Studies of Norm Formation

The first of the three classics bridges between culture's power to create and perpetuate arbitrary norms and processes of conformity. Muzafer Sherif (1935, 1937) wondered whether it was possible to observe the emergence of a social norm in the laboratory. Like biologists seeking to isolate a virus so that they can then experiment with it, Sherif wanted to isolate and then experiment with the social phenomenon of norm formation.

Imagine yourself a participant in one of Sherif's experiments. You find yourself seated in a dark room. Five metres in front of you a pinpoint of light appears. At first, nothing happens. Then for a few seconds it moves erratically and finally disappears. Now you must guess how far it moved. The dark room gives you no way to judge distance, so you offer an uncertain "15 centimetres." The experimenter repeats the procedure. This time you say "25 centimetres." With further repetitions, your estimates continue to average about 20 centimetres.

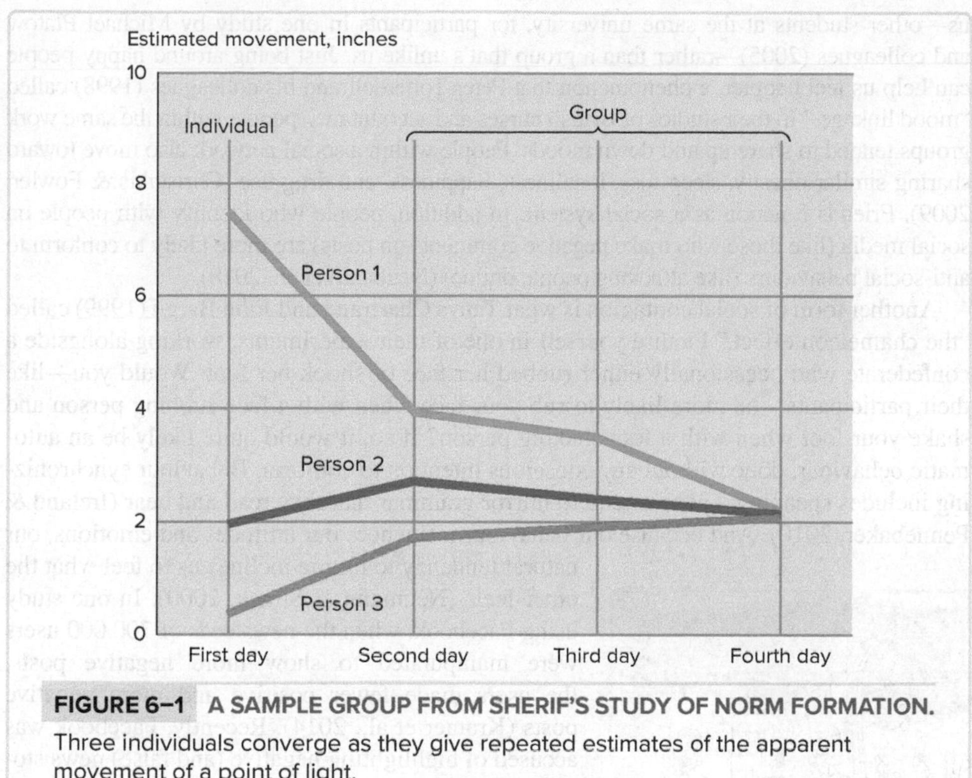

FIGURE 6–1 A SAMPLE GROUP FROM SHERIF'S STUDY OF NORM FORMATION.
Three individuals converge as they give repeated estimates of the apparent movement of a point of light.

The next day you return, joined by two other participants who had the same experience the day before. When the light goes off for the first time, the other two people offer their best guesses from the day before. "Five centimetres," says one. "Two centimetres," says the other. A bit taken aback, you nevertheless say "15 centimetres." With successive repetitions of this group experience, both on this day and for the next two days, will your responses change? The participants whom Sherif tested changed their estimates markedly. As Figure 6–1 illustrates, a group norm typically emerged. (The norm was false. Why? The light never moved! Sherif had taken advantage of an optical illusion called the **autokinetic phenomenon**.)

autokinetic phenomenon Self (*auto*) motion (*kinetic*). The apparent movement of a stationary point of light in the dark. Perhaps you have experienced this when thinking you have spotted a moving satellite in the sky, only to realize later that it was merely an isolated star.

confederate An accomplice of the experimenter.

Sherif and others have used this technique to answer questions about people's suggestibility. When people were retested alone a year later, would their estimates again diverge or would they continue to follow the group norm? Remarkably, they continued to support the group norm (Rohrer et al., 1954). (Does this suggest compliance or acceptance?)

Struck by culture's seeming power to perpetuate false beliefs, Robert Jacobs and Donald Campbell (1961) studied the transmission of false beliefs. Using the autokinetic phenomenon, they had a **confederate** give an inflated estimate of how far the light moved. The confederate then left the experiment and was replaced by another real subject, who was in turn replaced by a still newer member. The inflated illusion persisted (although diminishing) for five generations of participants. These people had become "unwitting conspirators in perpetuating a cultural fraud." The lesson of these experiments: Our views of reality are not ours alone.

In everyday life, the results of suggestibility are sometimes amusing. One person coughs, laughs, or yawns, and others are soon doing the same (Joly-Mascheroni et al., 2008; Silva & Teixeira, 2012; Provine, 2005). Comedy-show laugh tracks capitalize on our suggestibility. Laugh tracks work especially well when we presume that the laughing audience is like us—other students at the same university, for participants in one study by Michael Platow and colleagues (2005)—rather than a group that's unlike us. Just being around happy people can help us feel happier, a phenomenon that Peter Totterdell and his colleagues (1998) called "mood linkage." In their studies of British nurses and accountants, people within the same work groups tended to share up and down moods. People within a social network also move toward sharing similar obesity, sleep loss, loneliness, happiness, and drug use (Christakis & Fowler, 2009). Friends function as a social system. In addition, people who identify with people on social media (like those who make negative comments on posts) are more likely to conform to anti-social behaviours (like attacking people online) (Neubaum et al., 2018).

Another form of social contagion is what Tanya Chartrand and John Bargh (1999) called "the chameleon effect." Picture yourself in one of their experiments, working alongside a confederate who occasionally either rubbed her face or shook her foot. Would you—like their participants—be more likely to rub your face when with a face-rubbing person and shake your foot when with a foot-shaking person? If so, it would quite likely be an automatic behaviour, done without any conscious intention to conform. Behaviour synchronizing includes speaking—people tend to mirror grammar that they read and hear (Ireland & Pennebaker, 2010). And because our behaviour influences our attitudes and emotions, our natural tendency to mimic inclines us to feel what the other feels (Neumann & Strack, 2000). In one study using Facebook, when the newsfeeds of 700 000 users were manipulated to show more negative posts, the users made fewer positive and more negative posts (Kramer et al., 2014). Recently, Facebook was accused of highlighting negative (and false) news stories during the 2016 U.S. presidential election and, potentially, of biasing users toward Donald Trump (CBC, 2016b). In the fall of 2017, Facebook was forced by the U.S. Congress to turn over ads created in Russia and distributed on Facebook which were purported to have influenced the outcome of the election. More recently, Facebook, Google, and Twitter have been pressured to take down false posts related to the COVID-19 pandemic, leading to further calls for social media regulation (CBC, 2020c).

"I don't know why. I just suddenly felt like calling."

Source: ©Mick Stevens. All rights reserved. Used with permission.

Suggestibility can also occur on a large scale. In late March 1954, one city's newspapers reported damage to car windshields in an area 125 kilometres to the north. On the morning of April 14, similar windshield damage was reported 105 kilometres away; and later that day, only 70 kilometres away. By nightfall, whatever was causing the windshield-pitting had reached the city itself. Before the end of April 15, the police department had received complaints of damage to more than 3000 windshields (Medalia & Larsen, 1958). That evening, the mayor called on the federal government for help.

David Myers was an 11-year-old at the time. He recalls searching the family car's windshield, frightened by the explanation that an H-bomb test was raining fallout on his city. On April 16, however, the newspapers hinted that the real culprit might be mass suggestibility. After April 17, there were no more complaints. Later analysis of the pitted windshields concluded that the cause was ordinary road damage. Why did people notice this only after April 14? Given the suggestion, they had looked carefully at their windshields instead of through them.

> *"Why doth one man's yawning make another yawn?"*
>
> Robert Burton, *Anatomy of Melancholy,* 1621

Suggestibility is not always so amusing. Hijackings, UFO sightings, illnesses, and even suicides tend to come in waves. Shortly after the 1774 publication of *The Sorrows of Young Werther,* Johann Wolfgang von Goethe's first novel, young European men started dressing in yellow trousers and blue jackets, as had Goethe's protagonist, a young man named Werther.

Although the fashion epidemic triggered by the book was amusing, another apparent effect was less amusing and led to the book's banning in several areas. In the novel, Werther commits suicide with a pistol after being rejected by the woman whose heart he failed to win; after the book's publication, reports began accumulating of young men imitating Werther's desperate act.

Two centuries later, sociologist David Phillips confirmed such imitative suicidal behaviour and described it as "the Werther effect." Phillips and his colleagues (1985, 1989) discovered that suicides, as well as fatal auto accidents and private airplane crashes (which sometimes disguise suicides), increase after well-publicized suicides. For example, following Marilyn Monroe's August 6, 1962, suicide, there were 200 more August suicides than normal. Moreover, the increase happened only in areas where the suicide story had been publicized. The more publicity, the greater the increase in later fatalities.

Although not all studies have found the copycat suicide phenomenon, it has surfaced in Germany and in a London psychiatric unit, and is considered a major problem in Canada's Indigenous communities, such as Attawapiskat First Nation (Joiner, 1999; Jonas, 1992; CBC, 2016a, 2020b). In both Germany and the United States, suicide rates rise slightly following fictional suicides on soap operas and, ironically, even after serious dramas that focus on the suicide problem (Gould & Shaffer, 1986). Phillips reports that teenagers are most susceptible, a finding that would help explain the occasional clusters of teen copycat suicides.

Asch's Studies of Group Pressure

Participants in Sherif's darkened-room autokinetic experiments faced an ambiguous reality. Solomon Asch (1907–1996) had been fascinated with conformity since his childhood. Imagine yourself as one of Asch's volunteer subjects. You are seated sixth in a row of seven people. After explaining that you will be taking part in a study of perceptual judgments, the experimenter asks you to say which of the three lines in Figure 6–2 matches the standard line. You can easily see that it's line 2. So it's no surprise when the five people responding before you all say, "Line 2."

The next comparison proves as easy, and you settle in for what seems to be a simple test. But the third trial startles you. Although the correct answer seems just as clear-cut, the first person gives a wrong answer. When the second person gives the same wrong answer, you sit up in your chair and stare at the cards. The third person agrees with the first two. Your jaw drops; you start to perspire. "What is this?" you ask yourself. "Are they blind? Or am I?"

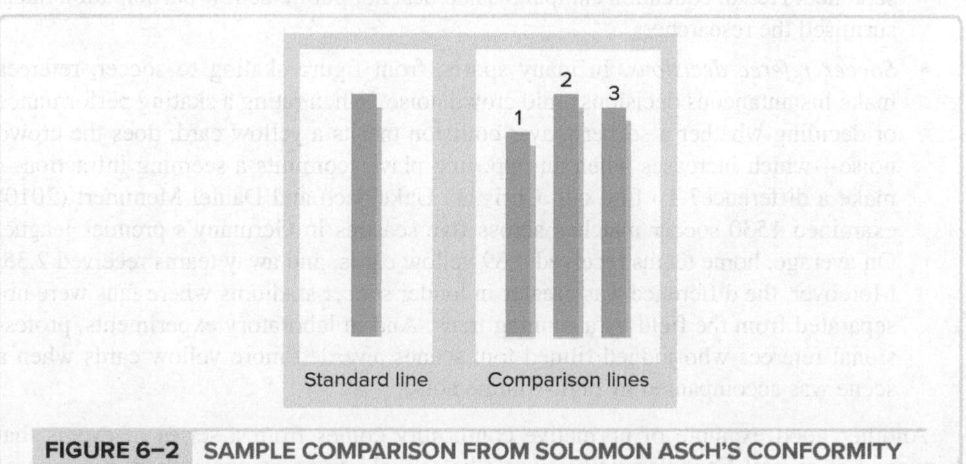

FIGURE 6–2 SAMPLE COMPARISON FROM SOLOMON ASCH'S CONFORMITY PROCEDURE.

The participants judged which of three comparison lines matched the standard.

The fourth and fifth people agree with the others. Then the experimenter looks at you. Now you are experiencing a real dilemma: "How am I to know what is true? Is it what my peers tell me or what my eyes tell me?"

Dozens of university students experienced this conflict during Asch's experiments. Those in a control condition who answered alone were correct more than 99 percent of the time. Asch wondered: If several others (confederates coached by the experimenter) gave identical wrong answers, would people declare what they would otherwise have denied? Although some people never conformed, three-quarters did so at least once. All told, 37 percent of the responses were conforming.

> ***"He who sees the truth, let him proclaim it, without asking who is for it or who is against it."***
>
> Henry George, *The Irish Land Question*, 1881

Of course, that means 63 percent of the time people did not conform. The experiments show that most people "tell the truth even when others do not," noted Bert Hodges and Ann Geyer (2006). Despite the independence shown by many of his subjects, Asch's (1955) feelings about the conformity were as clear as the correct answers to his questions: "That reasonably intelligent and well-meaning young people are willing to call white black is a matter of concern. It raises questions about our ways of education and about the values that guide our conduct."

Asch's procedure became the standard for hundreds of later experiments. These experiments lack what Chapter 1 called the "mundane realism" of everyday conformity, but they do have "experimental realism." People became emotionally involved in the experience. The Sherif and Asch results are startling because they involve no obvious pressure to conform—there are no rewards for "team play," no punishments for individuality. Other experiments have explored conformity in everyday situations, such as these:

- *Dental flossing.* Sarah Schmiege and her colleagues (2010) told students either that "Our studies show that [fellow students] your age floss approximately [X] times per week," where X was either the participant's own flossing rate, as reported in prior questioning, or five greater than that number. Those given the inflated estimate not only expressed increased intent to floss but also flossed more over the ensuing three months.
- *Cancer screening.* Monika Sieverding and her colleagues (2010) approached middle-aged German men on the street and invited them to sign up to receive information about cancer screening. If led to believe few other men ("only 18 percent!") in Germany had undergone the screening, a similar 18 percent signed up. But 39 percent signed up after being told that most other men ("indeed 65 percent!") had been screened. Health education campaigns had best not publicize low participation rates, surmised the researchers.
- *Soccer referee decisions.* In many sports, from figure skating to soccer, referees make instantaneous decisions amid crowd noise. When rating a skating performance or deciding whether a soccer player collision merits a yellow card, does the crowd noise—which increases when an opposing player commits a seeming infraction—make a difference? To find out, Christian Unkelbach and Daniel Memmert (2010) examined 1530 soccer matches across five seasons in Germany's premier league. On average, home teams received 1.89 yellow cards, and away teams received 2.35. Moreover, the difference was greater in louder soccer stadiums where fans were not separated from the field by a running track. And in laboratory experiments, professional referees who judged filmed foul scenes awarded more yellow cards when a scene was accompanied by high-volume noise.

Another good example of normative conformity comes from a series of events that happened at several Canadian universities (the school of one of our authors was one of them) in the fall of 2013. Canadian university orientations received a great deal of attention and international scrutiny when a YouTube video of students singing a sexist chant promoting non-consensual underage sex went viral (CBC, 2013b). What struck many people was that there were equal numbers of men and women singing the chant and that it had apparently been going on for several years. Why would young women on university campuses, the most likely target of unwanted sexual advances, sing these chants? What most commentators did not address was the issue of normative influence. Undoubtedly, most women singing this chant (and indeed most men) probably recognized that the chant was offensive (and promoted illegal activity), but "Everyone was doing it, right?" It is hard to stand up to a group of people you have just met, especially when you are trying to fit in with a new crowd.

If people are this compliant in response to such minimal pressure, how much more compliant would they be if they were directly coerced? Could someone force average North Americans to perform cruel acts? We would have guessed not: Their humane, democratic, individualistic values would make them resist such pressure. Besides, the easy verbal pronouncements of these experiments are a giant step away from actually harming someone; we would never yield to coercion to hurt another. Or would we? Social psychologist Stanley Milgram wondered.

Milgram's Obedience Studies

Milgram's (1965, 1974) controversial studies—"the most famous, or infamous, stud[ies] in the annals of scientific psychology" (Benjamin & Simpson, 2009, p. 12)—tested what happens when the demands of authority clash with the demands of conscience. Lee Ross (1988) noted that these are some of the most influential studies in social psychology, despite the serious ethical (e.g., Griggs et al., 2020) and methodological flaws (e.g., Perry, 2013). Although you may recall a mention of this research in a prior course, let's go backstage and examine the studies in depth.

Here is the scene staged by Milgram, a creative artist who wrote stories and stage plays: Two men come to the psychology laboratory to participate in a study of learning and memory. A stern experimenter in a grey technician's coat explains that this is a pioneering study of the effect of punishment on learning. The experiment requires one of them to teach a list of word pairs to the other and to punish errors by delivering shocks of increasing intensity. To assign the roles, they draw slips of paper out of a hat. One of the men (a mild-mannered, 47-year-old accountant who is the experimenter's confederate) says that his slip says "learner," and he is ushered into an adjacent room. The other man (a volunteer who has come in response to a newspaper ad) is assigned the role of "teacher." He takes a mild sample shock and then looks on as the experimenter straps the learner into a chair and attaches an electrode to his wrist.

> ***"It is too easy to go over to the majority."***
>
> Seneca, *Epistulae Ad Lucilium*

Teacher and experimenter then return to the main room, where the teacher takes his place before a "shock generator" with switches ranging from 15 to 450 volts in 15-volt increments. The switches are labelled "Slight Shock," "Very Strong Shock," "Danger: Severe Shock," and so forth. Under the 435- and 450-volt switches appears "XXX." The experimenter tells the teacher to "move one level higher on the shock generator" each time the learner gives a wrong answer. With each flick of a switch, lights flash, relay switches click, and an electric buzzer sounds.

If the participant complies with the experimenter's requests, he hears the learner grunt at 75, 90, and 105 volts. At 120 volts, the learner shouts that the shocks are painful; at 150 volts, he cries out, "Experimenter, get me out of here! I won't be in the experiment anymore! I refuse to go on!" By 270 volts, his protests have become screams of agony, and his pleas to be let out continue. At 300 and 315 volts, he screams his refusal to answer. After 330 volts, he falls silent. In answer to the teacher's inquiries and pleas to end the experiment, the experimenter states that the non-responses should be treated as wrong answers. To keep the participant going, he uses four verbal prods:

Prod 1: Please continue (*or* Please go on).

Prod 2: The experiment requires that you continue.

Prod 3: It is absolutely essential that you continue.

Prod 4: You have no other choice; you *must* go on.

How far would you go? Milgram described the study to 110 psychiatrists, university students, and middle-class adults. People in all three groups guessed that they would disobey by about 135 volts, which perhaps isn't surprising. But they also said that they thought other people would disobey by 200 volts; virtually no one expected anyone to proceed to XXX on the shock panel. (The psychiatrists guessed about one in a thousand.)

But when Milgram conducted the study with 40 men—a vocational mix of 20- to 50-year-olds—26 of them (65 percent) went all the way to 450 volts. Those who stopped often did so at the 150-volt point, when the learner's protestations became more compelling (Packer, 2008).

Wondering if people today would similarly obey, Jerry Burger (2009; 2014) replicated Milgram's study—though only to the 150-volt point. At that point, 70 percent of participants were still obeying, a slight reduction from Milgram's results. (In Milgram's study, most who were obedient to this point continued to the end. In fact, all who reached 450 volts complied with a command to continue the procedure until, after two further trials, the experimenter called a halt.)

Having expected a low rate of obedience, and with plans to replicate the study in Germany and assess the culture difference, Milgram was disturbed (A. Milgram, 2000). So instead of going to Germany, Milgram next made the learner's protests even more compelling. As the learner was strapped into the chair, the teacher heard him mention his "slight heart condition" and heard the experimenter's reassurance that "although the shocks may be painful, they cause no permanent tissue damage." The learner's anguished protests were to little avail; of 40 new men in this study, 25 (63 percent) fully complied with the experimenter's demands (Figure 6–3). Ten later studies that included women found that women's compliance rates were similar to men's (Blass, 1999).

It is worth noting that there are significant methodological issues with the experiments. Later researchers (e.g., Packer, 2012; Griggs et al., 2020) who reviewed the audiotapes of the sessions noted that although the "experimenter" was given four prods to use to encourage participation, they often departed significantly from the script, becoming more insistent and demanding of the participants. This was particularly true for female participants, which raises questions about the validity of lack of gender differences in behaviour.

Others have argued that what Milgram did in his research wasn't obedience at all, because the experimenter did not have any actual power over the participants (e.g., Gibson, 2013, 2019; Gibson et al., 2018). Indeed, perhaps only the fourth prod suggests any actual obedience. However, how often do we "obey" when no direct order is given, or no specific authority is present? This is why we must consider all social behaviour in the context of how we are influenced by our social situation.

The ethics of Milgram's studies

The obedience of his subjects disturbed Milgram. The procedures he used disturbed many social psychologists (Miller, 1986; Stam, Lubeck, & Radtke, 1998, Griggs et al., 2020). The "learner" in these studies actually received no shock (he disengaged himself from the electric chair and turned on a tape player that delivered the protests). Nevertheless, some critics said that Milgram did to his participants what they did to their victims: He stressed them against their will. Indeed, many of the "teachers" did experience agony.

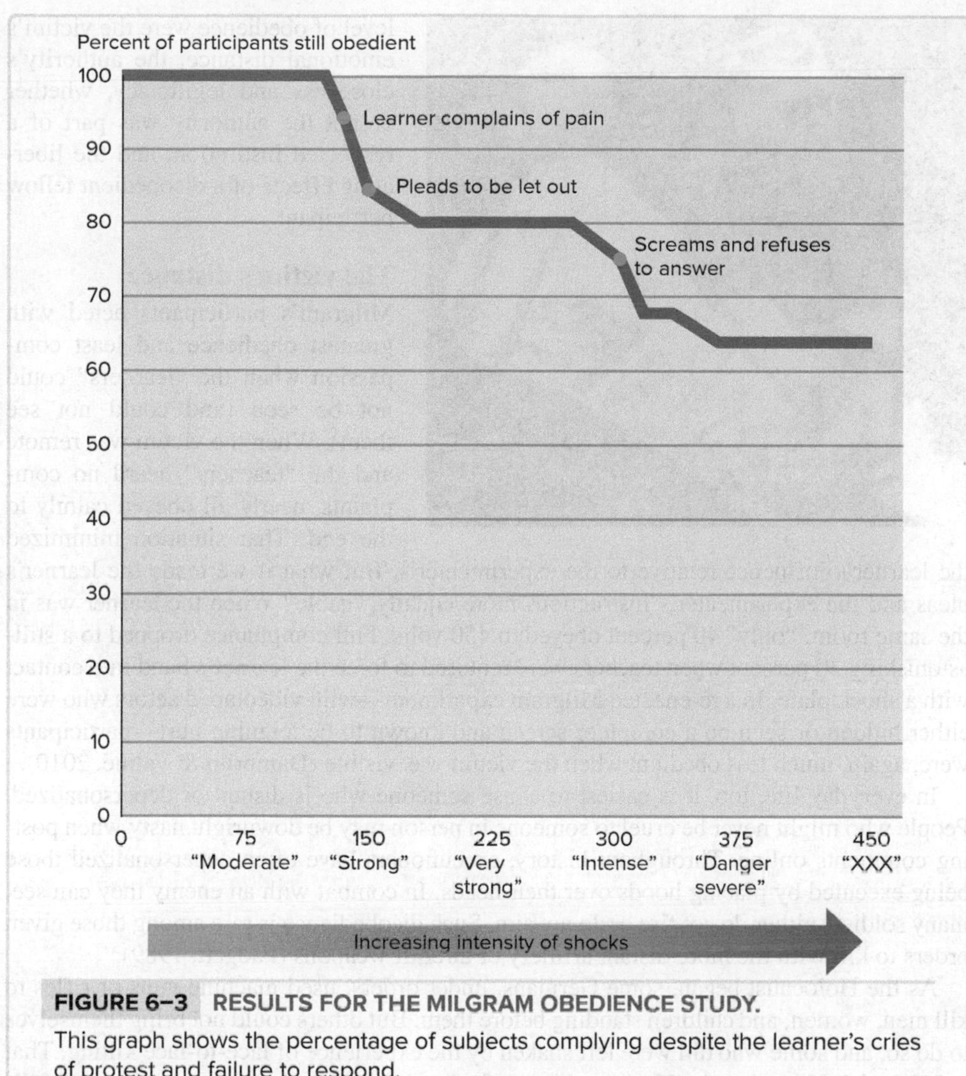

FIGURE 6–3 RESULTS FOR THE MILGRAM OBEDIENCE STUDY.
This graph shows the percentage of subjects complying despite the learner's cries of protest and failure to respond.

They sweated, trembled, stuttered, bit their lips, groaned, or even broke into uncontrollable nervous laughter. A *New York Times* reviewer complained that the cruelty inflicted by the studies "upon their unwitting subjects is surpassed only by the cruelty that they elicit from them" (Marcus, 1974).

In his own defence, Milgram pointed to the lessons taught by his nearly two dozen studies with a diverse sample of more than 1000 participants. He also reminded critics of the support he received from the participants after the deception was revealed and the study explained. When surveyed afterwards, 84 percent said they were glad to have participated; only 1 percent regretted volunteering. A year later, a psychiatrist interviewed 40 of those who had suffered most and concluded that, despite the temporary stress, none were harmed. However, only about a quarter of the participants were fully debriefed so the impact cannot truly be known (Griggs et al., 2020).

What Breeds Obedience?

Milgram did more than reveal the extent to which people will obey an authority; he also examined the conditions that breed obedience. When he varied the social conditions, compliance ranged from 0 to 93 percent fully obedient. Four factors that determined the

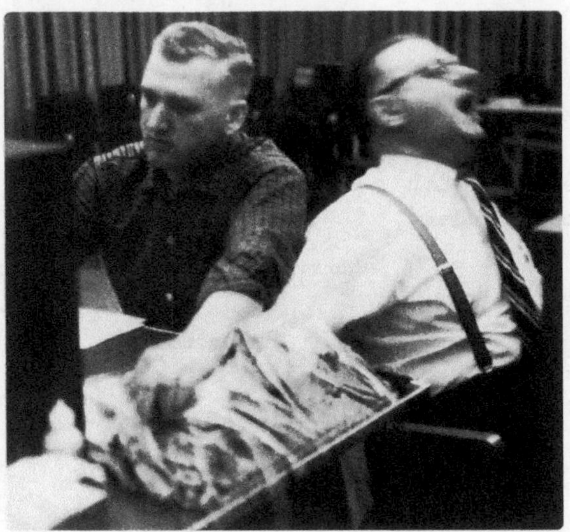

An obedient subject in Milgram's "touch" condition forces the victim's hand onto the shock plate. Usually, however, those in the teacher role were more merciful to victims who were this close to them.

Source: ©Stanley Milgram, 1965, from the film *Obedience*, distributed by Alexandra Street Press.

level of obedience were the victim's emotional distance, the authority's closeness and legitimacy, whether or not the authority was part of a respected institution, and the liberating effects of a disobedient fellow participant.

The victim's distance

Milgram's participants acted with greatest obedience and least compassion when the "learners" could not be seen (and could not see them). When the victim was remote and the "teachers" heard no complaints, nearly all obeyed calmly to the end. That situation minimized the learner's influence relative to the experimenter's. But what if we made the learner's pleas and the experimenter's instructions more equally visible? When the learner was in the same room, "only" 40 percent obeyed to 450 volts. Full compliance dropped to a still-astonishing 30 percent when teachers were required to force the learner's hand into contact with a shock plate. In a re-enacted Milgram experiment—with videotaped actors who were either hidden or seen on a computer screen and known to be feigning hurt—participants were, again, much less obedient when the victim was visible (Dambrun & Vatiné, 2010).

In everyday life, too, it is easiest to abuse someone who is distant or depersonalized. People who might never be cruel to someone in person may be downright nasty when posting comments online. Throughout history, executioners have often depersonalized those being executed by placing hoods over their heads. In combat with an enemy they can see, many soldiers either do not fire or do not aim. Such disobedience is rare among those given orders to kill with the more distant artillery or aircraft weapons (Padgett, 1989).

As the Holocaust began, some Germans, under orders, used machine guns or rifles to kill men, women, and children standing before them. But others could not bring themselves to do so, and some who did were left shaken by the experience of face-to-face killing. That led Heinrich Himmler, the Nazi "architect of genocide," to devise a "more humane" killing, one that would visually separate the killers and their victims. The solution was the construction of concrete gas chambers, where the killers would not see or hear the human consequences of their horror (Russell & Gregory, 2005).

Closeness and legitimacy of the authority

The physical presence of the experimenter also affected obedience. When Milgram gave the commands by telephone, full obedience dropped to 21 percent (although many lied and said they were obeying). Other studies confirmed that when the one making the request is physically close, compliance increases. Given a light touch on the arm, people were more likely to comply by lending a dime, signing a petition, or sampling a new pizza (Kleinke, 1977; Smith, Gier, & Willis, 1982; Willis & Hamm, 1980).

The authority, however, must normally be perceived as legitimate (but see Hays & Goldstein, 2015). In another twist on the basic study, the experimenter received a rigged telephone call that required him to leave the laboratory. He said that since the equipment recorded data automatically, the "teacher" should just go ahead. After the experimenter left, another person who had been assigned a clerical role (actually a second confederate) assumed command. The clerk "decided" that the shock should be increased one level for each wrong answer and instructed the teacher accordingly. Now 80 percent of the teachers refused to comply fully. The confederate, feigning disgust at this defiance, sat down in front of the shock generator and tried to take over the teacher's role. At this point, most of the defiant participants protested. Some tried to unplug the generator. One large man lifted the zealous confederate from his chair and threw him across the room. This rebellion against an illegitimate authority contrasted sharply with the deferential politeness usually shown the experimenter.

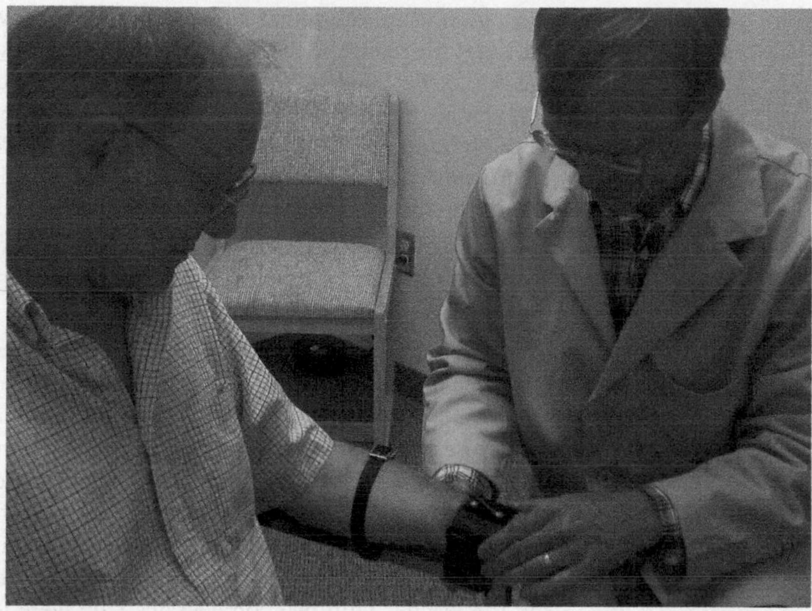

Recent replications of Milgram's obedience study have shown levels of obedience somewhat lower than in the 1960s, but two-thirds of men still administer high levels of shock.

Source: ©Jerry Burger.

It also contrasts with the behaviour of hospital nurses who in one study were called by an unknown physician and ordered to administer an obvious overdose of a drug (Hofling et al., 1966). The researchers told one group of nurses and nursing students about the experiment and asked how they would react. Nearly all said they would not have given the medication as ordered. Nevertheless, when 22 other nurses were actually given the phoned-in overdose order, all but one obeyed without delay (until being intercepted on their way to the patient). Although not all nurses are so compliant (Krackow & Blass, 1995; Rank & Jacobson, 1977), these nurses were following a familiar script: Doctor (a legitimate authority) orders; nurse obeys. However, in recognition (in part) of this issues, the ensuing decades have resulted in a multitude of checks that have been put in place to minimize the possibility of medication and other errors.

Another example of obedience to a perceived authority comes from cases of at least 70 fast-food restaurant managers who, between 1995 and 2006, complied with orders from a self-described authority, usually posing as a police officer over the phone (ABC News, 2004; Snopes, 2008). This supposed officer described a generic employee or customer. Once the manager had identified someone fitting the description, the authoritative-sounding caller gave an order to strip-search the person to see if he or she had stolen property. One male Taco Bell manager pulled aside a 17-year-old female customer who fit the description and, with the caller giving orders, carried out a search that included body cavities. After forcing a 19-year-old female employee to strip against her will, a restaurant manager explained that he was just doing as he was told, and feared that disobedience might mean losing his job or going to jail.

In another incident, a McDonald's manager received a call from an "Officer Scott," who described an employee he said was suspected of stealing. The female manager brought an 18-year-old woman who fit the description into the office and followed a series of orders to have her empty her pockets and successive pieces of clothing. Over three-and-a-half hours of humiliating detention, the requests became progressively more bizarre, including sexual contact with a male. The traumatized teen sued McDonald's, claiming it had not adequately forewarned staff of the scam, and was awarded $6.1 million (CNN, 2007).

Institutional authority

If the prestige of the authority is important, then perhaps the institutional prestige of Yale University, where the Milgram studies were conducted, legitimized the commands. In post-study interviews, many participants volunteered that, had it not been for Yale's reputation, they would not have obeyed. To see whether this was true, Milgram moved the study to Bridgeport, Connecticut. He set himself up in a modest commercial building as the "Research Associates of Bridgeport." When the "learner-has-a-heart-condition" study was run with the same personnel, what percentage of the men do you suppose fully obeyed? Although the obedience rate (48 percent) was still remarkably high, it was significantly lower than the 65 percent rate at Yale. In a recent replication in France, a TV game show host did a similar demonstration, and 81 percent obeyed until the end (Beauvois et al., 2012).

The liberating effects of group influence

These classic experiments give us a negative view of conformity. But conformity can also be constructive. The heroic figures who rushed into the flaming World Trade Center towers were "incredibly brave," noted Susan Fiske and her colleagues (2004), but they were also "partly obeying their superiors, partly conforming to extraordinary group loyalty." Consider, too, the occasional liberating effect of conformity. Perhaps you can recall a time you felt justifiably angry at an unfair teacher or with someone's offensive behaviour, but you hesitated to object. Then one or two others objected, and you followed their example. Milgram captured this liberating effect of conformity by placing the teacher with two confederates who were to help conduct the procedure. During the study, both defied the experimenter, who then ordered the real subject to continue alone. Did he? No. Ninety percent liberated themselves by conforming to the defiant confederates.

Given orders, some soldiers will torch people's homes or kill people—behaviours that in other contexts they would consider immoral.
Source: ©STR/AP Images.

Reflections on the Classic Studies

The common response to Milgram's results is to note their counterparts in recent history: the "I was only following orders" defences of Adolf Eichmann in Nazi Germany, and the "ethnic cleansing" occurring more recently in Iraq, Rwanda, Bosnia, Syria, and Kosovo. Soldiers are trained to obey superiors. The "safe" scientific contexts of the obedience studies differ from the wartime contexts. Moreover, much of the mockery and brutality of war and genocide goes beyond obedience (Miller, 2004). Some of those who implemented the Holocaust were "willing executioners" who hardly needed to be commanded to kill (Goldhagen, 1996).

The obedience studies also differ from the other conformity studies in the strength of the social pressure: Obedience is explicitly commanded. Without the coercion, people did not act cruelly. Yet both the Asch and Milgram studies share certain commonalities. They show how compliance can take precedence over moral sense. They succeeded in pressuring people to go against their own conscience. They did more than teach us an academic lesson; they sensitized us to moral conflicts in our own lives. And they illustrated and affirmed some familiar social psychological principles: the link between behaviour and attitudes and the power of the situation.

"Maybe I was too patriotic." So said ex-torturer Jeffrey Benzien, shown here demonstrating the "wet bag" technique to South Africa's Truth and Reconciliation Commission. He would place a cloth over victims' heads, bringing them to the terrifying brink of asphyxiation over and over again. Such terror by the former security police, who routinely denied such acts, was used to get an accused person to disclose, for example, where guns were hidden. "I did terrible things," Benzien admitted with apologies to his victims, though he claimed only to be following orders.

Source: ©Benny Gool/Capetown Independent Newspaper.

Behaviour and attitudes

Chapter 4 noted a situation in which attitudes fail to determine behaviour: when external influences override inner convictions. These experiments vividly illustrated that principle. When responding alone, Asch's subjects nearly always gave the correct answer. It was another matter when they stood alone against a group.

In the obedience studies, a powerful social pressure (the experimenter's commands) overcame a weaker one (the remote victim's pleas). Torn between the pleas of the victim and the orders of the experimenter, between the desire to avoid doing harm and the desire to be a good participant, a surprising number chose to obey.

Why were the participants unable to disengage themselves? How had they become trapped? Imagine yourself as the teacher in yet another version of Milgram's study, one he never conducted. Assume that when the learner gives the first wrong answer, the experimenter asks you to zap him with 330 volts. After flicking the switch, you hear the learner scream, complain of a heart disturbance, and plead for mercy. Do you continue?

We doubt it. Recall the step-by-step entrapment of the foot-in-the-door phenomenon (Chapter 4) as we compare this hypothetical experiment to what Milgram's participants experienced. Their first commitment was mild—15 volts—and it elicited no protest. You, too, would agree to do that much. By the time they delivered 75 volts and heard the learner's first groan, they had already complied five times, and the next request was to deliver only slightly more. By the time they delivered 330 volts, the participants had complied 22 times and reduced some of their dissonance. They were, therefore, in a different psychological state from that of someone beginning the experiment at that point. The same thing occurred with the fast-food restaurant managers in the strip-search scam, after they had complied with initially reasonable-seeming orders from a supposed authority. This progressive effect has also been demonstrated in studies of cheating (Welch et al., 2005). As we saw in Chapter 4, external behaviour and internal disposition can feed one another, sometimes in an escalating spiral. Thus, reported Milgram (1974, p. 10),

> Many subjects harshly devalue the victim as a consequence of acting against him. Such comments as "He was so stupid and stubborn he deserved to get shocked" were common. Once having acted against the victim, these subjects found it necessary to view him as an unworthy individual, whose punishment was made inevitable by his own deficiencies of intellect and character.

THE INSIDE STORY

While working for Solomon E. Asch, I wondered whether his conformity experiments could be made more humanly significant. First, I imagined an experiment similar to Asch's except that the group induced the person to deliver shocks to a protesting victim. But a control was needed to see how much shock a person would give in the absence of group pressure. Someone, presumably the experimenter, would have to instruct the subject to give the shocks. But now a new question arose: Just how far would a person go when ordered to administer such shocks? In my mind, the issue had shifted to the willingness of people to comply with destructive orders. It was an exciting moment for me. I realized that this simple question was both humanly important and capable of being precisely answered.

The laboratory procedure gave scientific expression to a more general concern about authority, a concern forced upon members of my generation, in particular upon Jews such as myself, by the atrocities of the Second World War. The impact of the Holocaust on my own psyche energized my interest in obedience and shaped the particular form in which it was examined.

Source: Courtesy of Alexandra Milgram.

Stanley Milgram (1933–1984)

Abridged from the original for this book and from Milgram, 1977, with permission of Alexandra Milgram.

During the early 1970s, Greece's military junta used this "blame-the-victim" process to train torturers (Haritos-Fatouros, 1988; Staub, 1989, 2003). There, as in the training of SS officers in Nazi Germany, the military selected candidates based on their respect for and submission to authority. But such tendencies alone do not a torturer make. Thus Greece's military junta would first assign the trainee to guard prisoners, then to participate in arrest squads, then to hit prisoners, then to observe torture, and only then to practise it. Step by step, an obedient but otherwise decent person evolved into an agent of cruelty. Compliance bred acceptance. If we focus on the end point—450 volts of torture administered—we are aghast at the evil conduct. If we consider how one gets there—in tiny steps—we understand.

But humans also have a capacity for heroism. During the Holocaust, the French village of Le Chambon sheltered 5000 Jews and other refugees destined for deportation to Germany. These people were mostly Protestants, whose own authorities, their pastors, had taught them to "resist whenever our adversaries will demand of us obedience contrary to the orders of the Gospel" (Rochat, 1993; Rochat & Modigliani, 1995). Ordered to expose the sheltered Jews, the head pastor modelled disobedience: "I don't know of Jews, I only know of human beings." Without knowing how terrible the war would be or how much they would suffer, the resisters made an initial commitment and then—supported by their beliefs, by their own authorities, and by one another—remained defiant to the war's end. Here and elsewhere, the ultimate response to Nazi occupation came early. Initial helping heightened commitment, leading to more helping.

> ***"Human beings have the capacity to come to experience killing other people as nothing extraordinary."***
>
> Erwin Staub, Holocaust survivor, 1989, p. 13

The power of the situation

This chapter's most important lesson—that immediate situational forces are powerful—reveals the strength of the social context. To feel this for yourself, imagine violating some minor norms: standing up in the middle of a class, singing out loud in a restaurant, greeting some distinguished senior professors by their first names, playing a sport in a suit. In trying to break with social constraints, we suddenly realize how strong they are.

The students in one experiment found it surprisingly difficult to violate the norm of being "nice" rather than confrontational. Participants imagined themselves discussing with three others whom to select for survival on a desert island. They were asked to imagine one of the others, a man, injecting three sexist comments, such as "I think we need more women on the island to keep the men satisfied." How would they react to such sexist remarks? Only 5 percent predicted they would ignore each of the comments or wait to see how others reacted. But when Janet Swim and Lauri Hyers (1998) engaged other students in discussions where such comments were actually made by a male confederate, 55 percent (not 5 percent) said nothing. Likewise, although people predicted they would be upset by witnessing a person making a racial slur—and would avoid picking the racist person as a partner in an experiment—Kerry Kawakami of York University and her colleagues (2009) found that people actually experiencing such an event typically exhibited indifference. These experiments demonstrated the power of normative pressures and showed how hard it is to predict behaviour, even our own.

This lesson is further illustrated by a painful episode in Canadian history. In 1994, two soldiers in the Canadian Airborne Regiment tortured and killed Shidane Arone, a Somali teenager who had been caught stealing from their camp in Somalia. An inquiry into Arone's death suggested that 16 people passed through the area where he was tortured and that his screams could be heard throughout the camp, yet no one intervened. The Canadian public was outraged: They had prided their military as peacekeepers and did not believe that such atrocity could happen on Canada's watch. They likely believed that they would have stepped in to stop torture. But the lessons of history, of bystander response (see Chapter 8), and of these experiments remind us that *saying* what we would do in a hypothetical situation is often easier than *doing* it in a real situation.

Milgram's studies also offer a lesson about evil. According to what we see in horror movies and suspense novels, evil results from a few bad apples, a few depraved killers. In real life, we similarly think of Hitler's extermination of Jews or of Osama bin Laden's terrorist plots. But evil also results from social forces—from the heat, humidity, and disease that help make a whole barrel of apples go bad. The U.S. military police, whose abuse of Iraqi prisoners at Abu Ghraib prison horrified the world, were under stress, taunted by many of those they had come to save, angered by comrades' deaths, overdue to return home, and under lax supervision—an evil situation that produced evil behaviour (Fiske et al., 2004). Similar conditions prevailed in Somalia when Canadian soldiers turned a blind eye to Shidane Arone's murder. Situations can induce ordinary people to capitulate to cruelty.

Procrastination involves a similar unintended drift, toward self-harm (Sabini & Silver, 1982). A student knows the deadline for a term paper weeks ahead. Each diversion from work on the paper—a video game here, a TV program there—seems harmless enough. Yet gradually, the student veers toward not doing the paper without ever consciously deciding not to do it.

It is tempting to assume that Eichmann and the Auschwitz death camp commanders were uncivilized monsters. Indeed, their evil was fueled by virulent anti-Semitism. And the social situation alone does not explain why, in the same death camp, some personalities displayed vicious cruelty and others heroic kindness. Still, the commanders would not have stood out to us as monsters. After a hard day's work, they would relax by listening to Beethoven and Schubert. Like most other Nazis, Eichmann himself was outwardly indistinguishable from common people with ordinary jobs (Arendt, 1963). Or consider the German police battalion responsible for shooting nearly 40 000 Jews in Poland, many of them women, children, and elderly people who were gruesomely shot in the back of the head. Christopher Browning (1992) portrayed the "normality" of these men. Like the many, many others who ravaged Europe's Jewish ghettos, operated the deportation trains, and administered the death camps (Goldhagen, 1996), they were not Nazis, SS members, or racial fanatics. They were labourers, salesmen, clerks, and artisans—family men who were too old for military service but who, when directly ordered to kill, were unable to refuse.

Under the sway of evil forces, even nice people are sometimes corrupted as they construct moral rationalizations for immoral behaviour (Tsang, 2002). So it is that ordinary soldiers will follow orders to shoot defenceless civilians, ordinary employees will follow instructions to produce and distribute degrading products, and ordinary group members will heed commands to brutally haze initiates.

So, does a situational analysis of harm-doing exonerate harm-doers? Does it absolve them of responsibility? In laypeople's minds, the answer is, to some extent, yes, noted Arthur Miller (2006). But the psychologists who study the roots of evil insist otherwise. To explain is not to excuse. To understand is not to forgive. You can forgive someone whose behaviour you don't understand, and you can understand someone whom you do not forgive. Moreover, added James Waller (2002), "When we understand the ordinariness of extraordinary evil, we will be less surprised by evil, less likely to be unwitting contributors to evil, and perhaps better equipped to forestall evil."

> ***"Eichmann did not hate Jews, and that made it worse, to have no feelings. To make Eichmann appear a monster renders him less dangerous than he was. If you kill a monster you can go to bed and sleep, for there aren't many of them. But if Eichmann was normality, then this is a far more dangerous situation."***
>
> Hannah Arendt, *Eichmann in Jerusalem: A Report on the Banality of Evil,* 1963

Finally, a comment on the experimental method used in conformity research (see synopsis, Table 6–1): Conformity situations in the laboratory differ from those in everyday life. How often are we asked to judge line lengths or administer shock? But as combustion is similar for a burning match and a forest fire, so we assume that psychological processes in the laboratory and in everyday life are similar (Milgram, 1974). We must be careful in generalizing from the simplicity of a burning match to the complexity of a forest fire. Yet controlled experiments on burning matches can give us insights into combustion that we cannot gain by observing forest fires. So, too, the social–psychological experiment offers insights into behaviour not readily revealed in everyday life. The experimental situation is unique, but so is every social situation. By testing with a variety of unique tasks, and by repeating experiments in different times and places, researchers probe for the common principles that lie beneath the surface diversity.

Sometimes people conform; sometimes they do not. The classic conformity studies answered some questions but raised others: (1) What predicts conformity? When do we conform? (2) Why do people conform? Why don't they ignore the group and "to their own selves be true"? (3) Is there a type of person who is likely to conform? The next sections will address these questions one at a time.

TABLE 6-1 Summary of Classic Obedience Studies.

Topic	Researcher	Method	Real-Life Example
Norm formation	Sherif	Assessing suggestibility regarding seeming movement of light	Interpreting events differently after hearing from others; appreciating a tasty food that others love
Conformity	Asch	Agreement with others' obviously wrong perceptual judgments	Doing as others do; fads such as tattoos
Obedience	Milgram	Complying with commands to shock another	Soldiers or employees following questionable orders

What Predicts Conformity?

Some situations trigger much conformity; others, little. If you want to produce maximum conformity, what conditions would you choose?

Social psychologists wondered: If even Asch's noncoercive, unambiguous situation could elicit a 37 percent conformity rate, would other settings produce a greater rate? Researchers soon discovered that conformity did grow if the judgments were difficult or if the subjects felt incompetent. The more insecure we are about our judgments, the more influenced we are by others.

Group attributes also matter. Conformity is highest when the group has three or more people and is cohesive, unanimous, and high in status. Conformity is also highest when the response is public and made without prior commitment. Let's look at each of these conditions.

Group Size

In laboratory experiments, a group need not be large to have a large effect. Asch and other researchers found that three to five people will elicit much more conformity than just one or two. Increasing the number of people beyond five yields diminishing returns (Gerard, Wilhelmy, & Conolley, 1968; Rosenberg, 1961). In a field experiment, Milgram and his colleagues (1969) had 1, 2, 3, 5, 10, or 15 people pause on a busy sidewalk and look up. As Figure 6–4 shows, the percentage of people passing by who also looked up increased as the number looking up increased from one to five persons.

The way the group is "packaged" also makes a difference. Researcher David Wilder (1977) gave students a jury case. Before giving their own judgments, the students watched videotapes of four confederates giving their judgments. When the confederates were presented as two independent groups of two people, the participants conformed more than when the four confederates presented their judgments as a single group. Similarly, two groups of three people elicited more conformity than one group of six, and three groups of two people elicited even more. The agreement of several small groups makes a position more credible.

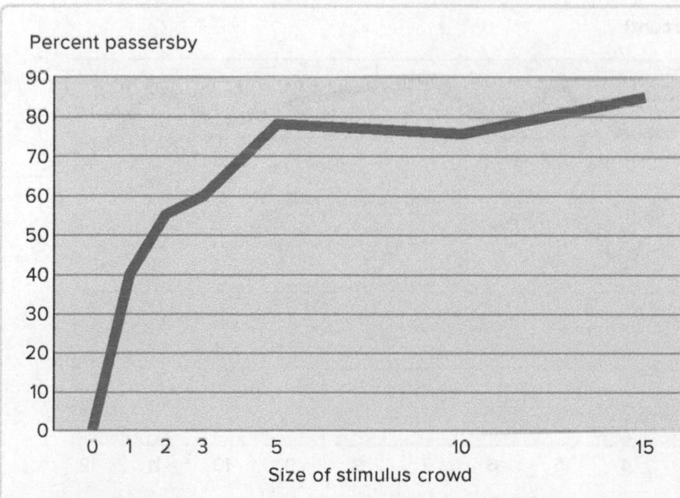

FIGURE 6–4 GROUP SIZE AND CONFORMITY.

The percentage of passersby who imitated a group looking upward increased as group size increased to five persons.

Photo source: ©dolgachov/123RF.

Unanimity

Imagine yourself in a conformity experiment in which all but one of the people responding before you give the same wrong answer. Would the example of this one nonconforming confederate be as liberating as it was for the subjects in Milgram's obedience experiment? Several experiments reveal that someone who punctures a group's unanimity deflates its social power (Allen & Levine, 1969; Asch, 1955; Morris & Miller, 1975). As Figure 6–5 illustrates, people will nearly always voice their convictions if just one other person has also differed from the majority. The participants in such experiments often later say they felt warm toward and close to their nonconforming ally. Yet they deny that the ally influenced them: "I would have answered just the same if they weren't there."

It's difficult to be a minority of one; few juries are hung because of one dissenting juror. Conformity experiments teach the practical lesson that it is easier to stand up for something if you can find someone else to stand up with you. Many religious groups recognize this. Following the example of Jesus, who sent his disciples out in pairs, Jehovah's Witnesses send two missionaries into a neighbourhood together. The support of the one comrade greatly increases a person's social courage.

> *"My opinion, my conviction, gains infinitely in strength and success, the moment a second mind has adopted it."*
>
> Novalis, *Fragment*

Observing someone else's dissent—even when it is wrong—can increase our own independence. Charlan Nemeth and Cynthia Chiles (1988) discovered this after having people observe a lone individual in a group of four misjudge blue stimuli as green. Although the dissenter was wrong, observing him enabled the observers to exhibit their own form of independence: 76 percent of the time they correctly labelled red slides "red" even when everyone else was calling them "orange." Participants who had no opportunity to observe the "green" dissenter conformed 70 percent of the time.

Cohesion

A minority opinion from someone outside the groups we identify with—from someone at another university or of a different religion, for example—sways us less than

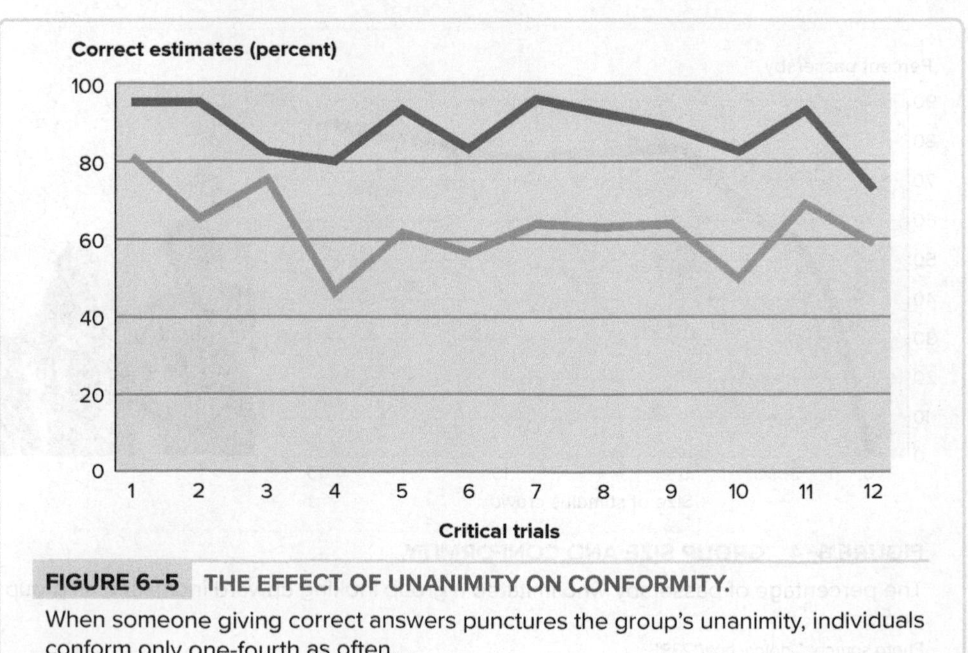

FIGURE 6–5 THE EFFECT OF UNANIMITY ON CONFORMITY.

When someone giving correct answers punctures the group's unanimity, individuals conform only one-fourth as often.

the same minority opinion from someone within our group (Clark & Maass, 1988). A heterosexual arguing for LGBTQ+ rights would sway heterosexuals more effectively than would a homosexual. People even comply more readily with requests from those said to share their birthday, their first name, or features of their fingerprint (Burger et al., 2004; Silvia, 2005). The more **cohesiveness** a group exhibits, the more power it gains over its members. In university sororities, for example, friends tend to share binge-eating tendencies, especially as they grow closer (Crandall, 1988). In experiments, too, group members who feel attracted to the group are more responsive to its influence (Berkowitz, 1954; Boldt, 1976; Lott & Lott, 1961; Sakurai, 1975). Fearing rejection by group members whom they like, they allow them a certain power.

cohesiveness A "we feeling"—the extent to which members of a group are bonded together, such as by attraction for one another.

Our inclination to go with our group—to think what it thinks and do what it does—surfaced in one experiment as people reported greater liking for a piece of music that was said to be liked by people akin to themselves, but disliked the music more when it was liked by someone unlike themselves (Hilmert, Kulik, & Christenfeld, 2006). Likewise, when university students compare themselves with drinkers who are dissimilar to themselves, they become *less* likely to drink (Lane et al., 2011). And after observing cheating by someone wearing a T-shirt from their own university, participants in another experiment became more likely to cheat. But if the cheater wore a T-shirt from a competing university, it had the opposite effect: the participants became more honest (Gino, Ayal, & Ariely, 2009). Cohesion-fed conformity also appears in university dorms, where students' attitudes over time become more similar to those living near them (Cullum & Harton, 2007).

Status

As you might suspect, higher-status people tend to have more impact (Driskell & Mullen, 1990). Junior group members—even junior social psychologists—acknowledge more conformity to their group than do senior group members (Jetten, Hornsey, & Adarves-Yorno, 2006). Or consider this: U.S. studies of jaywalking behaviour, conducted with the unwitting aid of nearly 24 000 pedestrians, revealed that the baseline jaywalking rate of 25 percent decreases to 17 percent in the presence of a non-jaywalking confederate and increases to 44 percent in the presence of another jaywalker (Mullen, Copper, & Driskell, 1990). The non-jaywalker best discourages jaywalking when well dressed. Children aged three and five imitate as well, by watching the behaviour of high-status others (e.g., adults; Flynn et al., 2018). Even chimps are more likely to imitate the behaviours of high-ranking group members (Horner et al., 2010). Among both humans and other primates, prestige begets influence. Milgram (1974) reported that in his obedience studies, people of lower status accepted the experimenter's commands more readily than people of higher status. After delivering 450 volts, one participant, a 37-year-old welder, turned to the experimenter and deferentially asked, "Where do we go from here, Professor?" (p. 46). Another participant, a divinity school professor who disobeyed at 150 volts, said, "I don't understand why the experiment is placed above this person's life" and plied the experimenter with questions about "the ethics of this thing" (p. 48).

Public Response

One of conformity researchers' first questions was this: Would people conform more in their public responses than in their private opinions? Or would they wobble more in their private opinions but be unwilling to conform publicly lest they appear wishy-washy?

The answer is now clear: As shown in experiments, people conform more when they must respond in front of others rather than when they write their answer privately. Asch's participants, after hearing others respond, were less influenced by group pressure if they could write an answer that only the experimenter would see. Likewise, when university instructors ask controversial questions, students express more diverse opinions when answering anonymously, with clickers, than when raising hands (Stowell, Oldham, & Bennett, 2010). It is much easier to stand up for what we believe in the privacy of the voting booth than before a group.

No Prior Commitment

In 1980, Genuine Risk became the second filly ever to win the Kentucky Derby. In her next race, the Preakness, she came off the last turn gaining on the leader, Codex, a colt. As they came out of the turn neck and neck, Codex moved sideways toward Genuine Risk, causing her to hesitate and giving him a narrow victory. Had Codex brushed Genuine Risk? Had his jockey even whipped Genuine Risk in the face? The race referees huddled. After a brief deliberation, they judged that no foul had occurred and confirmed Codex as the winner. The decision caused an uproar. Televised instant replays showed that Codex had, indeed, brushed Genuine Risk, the sentimental favourite. A protest was filed. The officials reconsidered their decision, but they did not change it.

> *"If you worry about missing the boat—remember the* Titanic.*"*
>
> Anonymous

Did their declared judgment immediately after the race affect officials' openness toward reaching a different decision later? We will never know for sure. We can, however, put people through a laboratory version of this event—with and without the immediate commitment—and observe whether the commitment makes a difference. Again, imagine yourself in an Asch-type experiment. The experimenter displays the lines and asks you to respond first. After you have given your judgment and then heard everyone else disagree, the experimenter offers you an opportunity to reconsider. In the face of group pressure, do you now back down?

People almost never do (Deutsch & Gerard, 1955). Having made a public commitment, they stick to it. At most, they will change their judgments in later situations (Saltzstein & Sandberg, 1979). We may, therefore, expect that judges of diving or gymnastics competitions, for example, will seldom change their ratings after seeing the other judges' ratings, although they might adjust their later performance ratings.

Did Codex brush against Genuine Risk? Once race referees publicly announced their decision, no amount of evidence could budge them.
Source: ©IRA SCHWARZ/AP Images.

Prior commitments restrain persuasion, too. When simulated juries make decisions, hung verdicts are more likely in cases when jurors are polled by a show of hands rather than by secret ballot (Kerr & MacCoun, 1985). Making a public commitment makes people hesitant to back down.

Smart persuaders know this. Salespeople ask questions that prompt us to make statements for, rather than against, what they are marketing. Environmentalists ask people to commit themselves to recycling, energy conservation, or bus riding. That's because behaviour then changes more than when environmental appeals are heard without inviting a commitment (Katzev & Wang, 1994).

Why Conform?

What two forms of social influence explain why people will conform to others?

One of your authors was attending his first lecture during an extended visit at a German university. As the lecturer finished, the author lifted his hands to join in the clapping. But rather than clap, the other people began rapping the tables with their knuckles. What did this mean? Did they disapprove of the speech? Surely, not everyone would be so openly rude. Nor did their faces express displeasure. No, the author decided, this must be a German ovation. Whereupon, he added his knuckles to the chorus.

What causes such conformity? There are two possibilities: A person may bow to the group (a) to be accepted and avoid rejection or (b) to obtain important information. Morton Deutsch and Harold Gerard (1955) named these two possibilities **normative influence** and **informational influence**. The first springs from our desire to be liked; the second, from our desire to be right.

normative influence Conformity based on a person's desire to fulfill others' expectations, often to gain acceptance.

informational influence Conformity that results from accepting evidence about reality provided by other people.

Normative influence is "going along with the crowd" to avoid rejection, to stay in people's good graces, or to gain their approval. In the laboratory and in everyday life, groups often reject those who consistently deviate from the norm (Miller & Anderson, 1979; Schachter, 1951). That's a lesson learned by a media studies professor who became an outcast while playing the online game "City of Heroes" (Vargas, 2009). The professor, with whom we empathize, played by the rules but did not conform to the customs. Much as drivers who go 70 in a 100 km/hour zone are disliked for violating norms but not rules, the professor was derided with instant messages: "I hope your mother gets cancer." "EVERYONE HATES YOU." "If you kill me one more time I will come and kill you for real and I am not kidding."

As most of us know, social rejection is painful; when we deviate from group norms, we often pay an emotional price. Brain scans show that group judgments differing from one's own activate a brain area that also is active when one feels the pain of bad betting decisions (Klucharev et al., 2009; see also Toelch & Dolan, 2015). Sometimes, the high price of deviation compels people to support what they do not believe in or at least to suppress their disagreement.

Informational influence, on the other hand, leads people to privately accept others' influence. When reality is ambiguous, as it was for subjects in the autokinetic situation, other people can be a valuable source of information. The participant may reason, "I can't tell how far the light is moving. But this person seems to know."

Our friends have extra influence on us for informational as well as normative reasons (Denrell, 2008; Denrell & Le Mens, 2007). If our friend buys a particular car and takes us to a particular restaurant, we will gain information that may lead us to like what our friend likes—even if we don't care what our friend likes. Our friends influence the experiences that inform our attitudes.

To discover what the brain is doing when people experience an Asch-type conformity experiment, a neuroscience team put participants in a functional magnetic resonance imaging (fMRI) brain scanner while having them answer perceptual questions after hearing others' responses (Berns et al., 2005). (The task involved mentally rotating a figure to find its match among several possibilities.) When the participants conformed to a wrong answer, the brain regions dedicated to perception became active. And when they went *against* the group, brain regions associated with emotion became active. These results suggest that when people conform, their perceptions may be genuinely influenced. Follow-up fMRI studies have identified neural activity associated with normative influence (in a brain area that is active when people are anxious about social rejection) and with informational

Activity: How Have You Experienced Conformity?

We have all experienced conformity. We have seen it in others and we too have conformed. The interesting thing about conformity is that we may not recognize it until we think back. Let's consider a time when we are most likely to conform: in high school. When you were in high school, were there norms that dictated how you were supposed to look?

Write down your answers to the following questions:

- What was the norm for clothing in your group?
- What about hairstyles? Were there common themes based on popular people in the media?
- What were the consequences of failing to meet those norms?
  - Do you remember people who weren't groomed or dressed that way?
  - How were they regarded and treated?
  - Did they form their own group and their own "cultural" norms?

For each of the examples above, identify if this illustrated normative or informational influence or both.

influence (in areas involved with one's judgments of a stimulus) (Zaki et al., 2011; Toelch & Dolan, 2015). When we deviate from the norm and perceive the risk of being socially rejected, the same part of our brain is activated as when we make errors that need to be corrected (Shestakova et al., 2013).

So, concern for social image produces normative influence, and the desire to be correct produces informational influence. In day-to-day life, normative and informational influence often occur together. Dale Griffin of the University of British Columbia and Roger Buehler of Wilfrid Laurier University found that normative influence can even cause informational influence as people construct reasons to justify their conformity (Griffin & Buehler, 1993). They found that participants who conformed to a group standard subsequently interpreted information in ways that upheld their decision to conform. Participants read about "Robert," who needed to decide whether to take a chance and pursue his dream of studying music or play it safe and accept an offer to attend medical school. Some participants were told that "most people" thought that Robert should make the risky choice and pursue his dream. Others were told that "most people" thought that he should play it safe. As Figure 6–6 demonstrates, participants who conformed changed their perceptions of acceptable risk for Robert. Those who conformed to the recommendation that Robert attend medical school subsequently believed that he should consider studying music only if he was quite certain of success; those who

Normative influence: Newly elected politicians often dream of changing the system. Then, seeking to climb within the system, normative influences compel them to comply with its social rules.
Source: The Canadian Press/Ryan Remiorz.

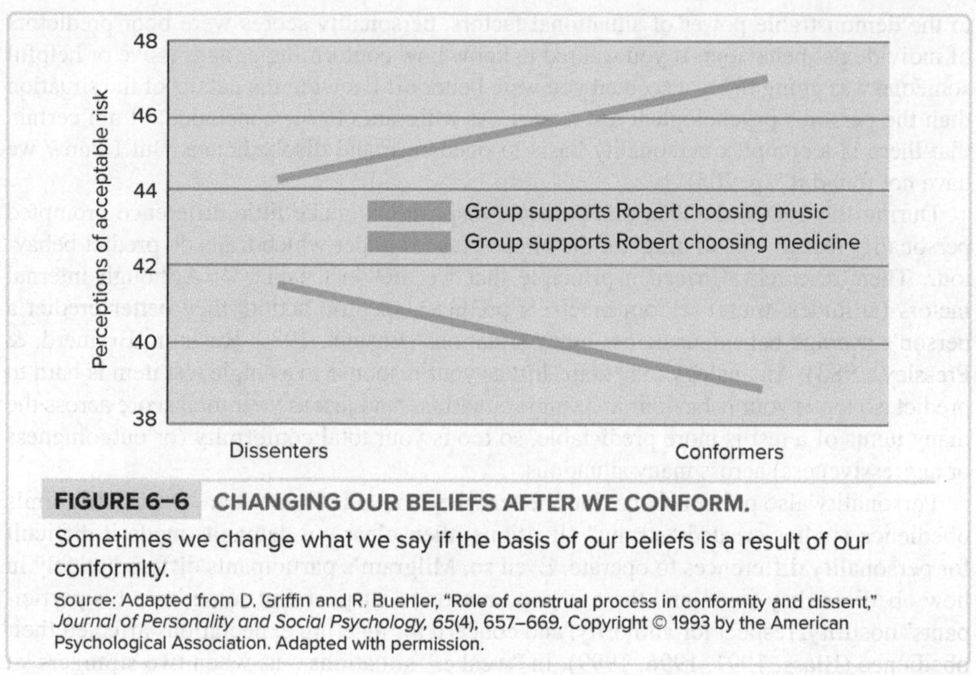

FIGURE 6–6 CHANGING OUR BELIEFS AFTER WE CONFORM.

Sometimes we change what we say if the basis of our beliefs is a result of our conformity.

Source: Adapted from D. Griffin and R. Buehler, "Role of construal process in conformity and dissent," *Journal of Personality and Social Psychology, 65*(4), 657–669. Copyright © 1993 by the American Psychological Association. Adapted with permission.

conformed to the recommendation that Robert study music thought that he should do so even if success was only a remote possibility. Participants also changed their interpretation of the situation in ways that justified their decision to conform or dissent. Those who conformed to the recommendation that Robert go to the music conservatory, for example, thought that "success" meant "international fame" rather than a career with a "local symphony orchestra." Thus, the act of dissenting or conforming driven by normative influence—led participants to interpret the situation differently.

Conformity experiments have sometimes isolated either normative or informational influence. Conformity is greater when people respond before a group; this surely reflects normative influence (because subjects receive the same information whether they respond publicly or privately). On the other hand, conformity is greater when participants feel incompetent, when the task is difficult, and when the subjects care about being right—all signs of informational influence.

> ***"Do as most do and men will speak well of thee."***
>
> Thomas Fuller, *Gnomologia*, 1732

Who Conforms?

Conformity varies not only with situations but also with personality differences. How much so? And in what social contexts do personality traits shine through?

Are some people generally more susceptible (or, should we say, more open) to social influence? Among your friends, can you identify some who are "conformists" and others who are "independent"? In their search for the conformer, researchers have focused on personality, culture, gender, and social roles.

Personality

During the late 1960s and 1970s, researchers observed only weak connections between personality traits and social behaviours, such as conformity (Mischel, 1968). In contrast to the demonstrable power of situational factors, personality scores were poor predictors of individuals' behaviour. If you wanted to know how conforming or aggressive or helpful someone was going to be, it seemed you were better off knowing the details of the situation than the person's psychological test scores. As Milgram (1974) concluded, "I am certain that there is a complex personality basis to obedience and disobedience. But I know we have not found it" (p. 205).

During the 1980s, the idea that personal dispositions make little difference prompted personality researchers to pinpoint the circumstances under which traits do predict behaviour. Their research affirmed a principle that we met in Chapter 4: Although internal factors (attitudes, traits) seldom precisely predict a specific action, they better predict a person's average behaviour across many situations (Epstein, 1980; Rushton, Brainerd, & Pressley, 1983). An analogy may help: Just as your response to a single test item is hard to predict, so too is your behaviour in a single situation. And just as your total score across the many items of a test is more predictable, so too is your total conformity (or outgoingness or aggressiveness) across many situations.

Personality also predicts behaviour better when social influences are weak. Milgram's obedience studies created "strong" situations; their clear-cut demands made it difficult for personality differences to operate. Even so, Milgram's participants differed widely in how obedient they were, and there is good reason to suspect that sometimes his participants' hostility, respect for authority, and concern for meeting expectations affected their obedience (Blass, 1991, 1996, 1999). In "weaker" situations—as when two strangers sit in a waiting room with no cues to guide their behaviour—individual personalities are even freer to shine (Ickes et al., 1982; Monson, Hesley, & Chernick, 1982).

The pendulum of professional opinion swings. Without discounting the undeniable power of social forces, the pendulum is now swinging back toward an appreciation of individual personality and its genetic predispositions. Like the attitude researchers we considered earlier, personality researchers are clarifying and reaffirming the connection between who we are and what we do. Thanks to their efforts, today's social psychologists now agree with pioneering theorist Kurt Lewin's (1936) dictum: "Every psychological event depends

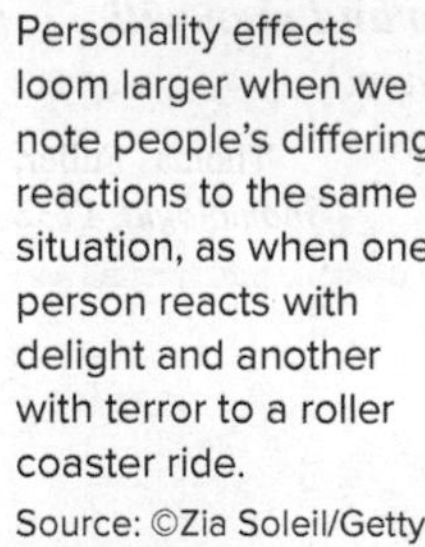

Personality effects loom larger when we note people's differing reactions to the same situation, as when one person reacts with delight and another with terror to a roller coaster ride.

Source: ©Zia Soleil/Getty Images.

upon the state of the person and at the same time on the environment, although their relative importance is different in different cases" (p. 12).

Culture

Does cultural background help predict how conforming people will be? Indeed it does. James Whittaker and Robert Meade (1967) repeated Asch's conformity experiment in several countries and found similar conformity rates in most—31 percent in Lebanon, 32 percent in Hong Kong, 34 percent in Brazil—but 51 percent among the Bantu of Zimbabwe, a tribe with strong sanctions for nonconformity. When Milgram (1961) used a different conformity procedure to compare Norwegian and French students, he consistently found the French students to be less conforming. An analysis by Roy Bond and Peter Smith (1996) of 133 studies in 17 countries showed how cultural values influence conformity. Compared with people in individualistic countries, those in collectivist countries (where social harmony is prized) are more responsive to others' influence. In collectivist Japan, Western observers were struck by the absence of looting and lawlessness following the 2011 earthquake and tsunami; respect for social norms prevailed (Cafferty, 2011). In individualist countries, university students see themselves as more nonconforming than others in their consumer purchases and political views—as individuals amid the sheep (Pronin, Berger, & Molouki, 2007).

Why do people in some countries conform more than others? Conformity may reflect an evolutionary response to survival threats, such as disease-bearing pathogens. Norms for food preparation and personal hygiene protect people from pathogens, and conformity to these norms reduces the spread of disease. Damian Murray and his collaborators (2011) at the University of British Columbia found that cultures that display greater conformity in experiments had historically greater prevalence of pathogens, such as those that cause malaria, dengue, and tuberculosis. Cultural norms promoting greater conformity may have emerged in these areas to protect people from these dangerous diseases. Cultural differences also exist within any country. For example, in five studies, Nicole Stephens and her co-researchers (2007) found that working-class people tend to prefer similarity to others, while middle-class people more strongly preferred to see themselves as unique individuals. In one experiment, people chose a pen from among five green and orange pens (with three or four of one colour). Of university students from working-class backgrounds, 72 percent picked one from the majority colour, as did only 44 percent of those from middle-class backgrounds (with a university-graduate parent). Those from working-class backgrounds also came to like their chosen pen more after seeing someone else make the same choice. They responded more positively to a friend's knowingly buying the same car they had just bought. And they were also more likely to prefer visual images that they knew others had chosen.

In addition, cultures may change over time. Replication of Asch's experiment with university students in Canada, Britain, and the United States sometimes triggers less conformity than Asch observed two or three decades earlier (Lalancette & Standing, 1990; Larsen, 1974, 1990; Nicholson, Cole, & Rocklin, 1985; Perrin & Spencer, 1981). So conformity and obedience are universal phenomena, yet they vary across cultures and eras.

Gender

Does gender matter? In early work, there was an assumption that women were more susceptible to influence than men (see Crutchfield, 1955), showing that women conformed more than men in many situations. However, when Milgram specifically explored this in the paradigm above, he found no difference between men and women (Milgram, 1974), and this has been replicated (Burger, 2009; though again, there were differences in how some women were treated in the Milgram experiments; Perry, 2013).

Alice Eagly and her colleagues (e.g., Eagly & Carli, 1981; Eagly, 1987), in a meta-analysis of 145 studies spanning over 21 000 people, found that men were slightly less influenceable than women. However, this effect was fairly weak and varied considerably across studies. Interestingly, women were more likely to conform when they were in situations where people could observe the participant's behaviours, such as the group pressure situations in the Asch study. When behaviours were less observable, the difference went away. One of Eagly's findings was particularly notable. Researchers found that studies with male researchers were more likely to find increased conformity effects for women than studies run by women. Why? Eagly argues this is because men tend to choose more male-oriented topics, where women are less knowledgeable, thus leading to increased "informational" conformity. In essence, then, the gender difference may be in part a confound effect.

There is some research to back this up. In a study of University of Saskatchewan students, males were found to conform more to female-oriented topics, where women displayed superior skills and/or knowledge. Similarly, Sistrunk and McDavid (1971) found that, in general, men conformed more to topics where women would typically know more (e.g., fashion) whereas women conformed more when the topics were more male-oriented (e.g., mechanics).

Social Roles

> All the world's a stage,
> And all the men and women merely players:
> They have their exits and their entrances;
> And one man in his time plays many parts.
>
> —William Shakespeare

Role theorists assume, as did William Shakespeare's character Jaques in *As You Like It,* that social life is like acting on a theatrical stage, with all its scenes, masks, and scripts. And those roles have much to do with conformity. Social roles allow some freedom of interpretation to those who act them out, but some aspects of any role *must* be performed. A student must at least show up for exams, turn in papers, and maintain some minimum grade point average.

When only a few norms are associated with a social category (for example, riders on an escalator should stand to the right and walk to the left), we do not regard the position as a social role. It takes a whole cluster of norms to define a role (such as the expectations on health care workers during a pandemic). Roles have powerful effects. In Chapter 4, we noted that we tend to absorb our roles. On a first date or in a new job, we may act the role self-consciously. As we internalize the role, self-consciousness subsides. What felt awkward now feels genuine.

That is the experience of many immigrants, international students, and expatriate executives. After arriving in a new country, it takes time to learn how to talk and act appropriately in the new context—to conform, as your author did with the Germans who rapped their knuckles on their desks. And the almost universal experience of those who repatriate to their home country is re-entry distress (Sussman, 2000). In ways they may not have been aware of, their behaviour, values, and identity will have shifted to accommodate a different place. They must "re-conform" to their former roles before being back in sync.

So far in this chapter, we have discussed classic studies of conformity and obedience, identified the factors that predict conformity, and considered who conforms and why.

Remember that our primary quest in social psychology is not to catalogue differences but to identify universal principles of behaviour. Social roles will always vary with culture, but the processes by which those roles influence behaviour vary much less. People in Nigeria and Japan define teen roles differently from people in Europe and North America, for example; but in all cultures, role expectations guide the conformity found in social relations.

Do We Ever Want to Be Different?

Will people ever actively resist social pressure? What would motivate such anti-conformity?

This chapter emphasizes the power of social forces. It is, therefore, fitting that we conclude by again reminding ourselves of the power of the person. We are not just billiard balls moving where pushed. We may and can act according to our own values, independently of the forces that push on us. Knowing that someone is trying to coerce us may even prompt us to react in the opposite direction.

"To do just the opposite is also a form of imitation."

Lichtenberg, *Aphorisms,* 1764–1799

Reactance

Individuals value their sense of freedom and self-efficacy. When blatant social pressure threatens their sense of freedom, they often rebel. Think of Romeo and Juliet, whose love was intensified by their families' opposition. Or think of children asserting their freedom and independence by doing the opposite of what their parents ask. Savvy parents, therefore, offer their children choices instead of commands: "It's time to clean up: Do you want a bath or a shower?"

The theory of psychological **reactance**—that people act to protect their sense of freedom—was supported by experiments showing that attempts to restrict a person's freedom often produce an anti-conformity "boomerang effect" (Brehm & Brehm, 1981; Nail et al., 2000; Rains, 2013). In one field experiment, many non-"nerdy" students stopped wearing a "Livestrong" wristband when nearby "nerdy" academic students started wearing the band (Berger & Heath, 2008). Likewise, rich Brits dissociated themselves from a dissimilar group when they stopped wearing Burberry caps after the headwear caught on among soccer hooligans (Clevstrom & Passariello, 2006).

reactance A motive to protect or restore our sense of freedom. Reactance arises when someone threatens our freedom of action.

Reactance may contribute to underage drinking. A survey of 18- to 24-year-olds by the Canadian Centre on Substance Use and Addiction (1997) revealed that 69 percent of those over the legal drinking age had been drunk in the previous year, as had 77 percent of those who were underage. In the United States, a survey of students on 56 campuses revealed a 25 percent rate of abstinence among students of legal drinking age (21) but only a 19 percent abstinence rate among students under 21. The researchers, Ruth Engs and David Hanson (1989), also found that 15 percent of the legal-age students and 24 percent of the underage students were heavy drinkers.

Likewise, 21.5 percent of underage drinkers, but only 17 percent of legal drinkers, reported that their drinking had caused personal problems in their life. Even warning teens against binge drinking can increase their drinking intentions (e.g., Shorey-Fennell & Magnan, 2019). They suspect this reflects a reactance against the restriction. It probably also reflects peer influence. With alcohol use, as with drugs, peers influence attitudes, provide the substance, and offer a context for its use. This helps explain why post-secondary

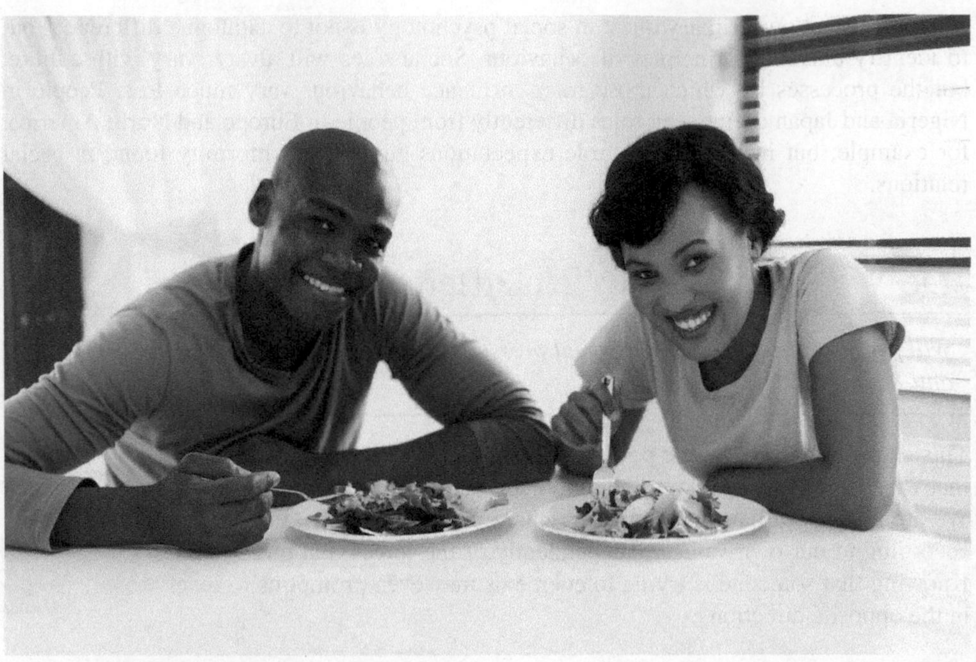

We're more likely to eat healthy when others do (normative influence)—but not when we're lectured about how healthy it is (reactance).
Source: ©michaeljung/123RF.

students, living in a peer culture that often supports alcohol use, drink more alcohol than their nonstudent peers (Atwell, 1986).

Reactance may also play a role in more antisocial behaviours. Baumeister and colleagues (2002) have suggested that reactance processes may have an impact on sexual assault. They argue that when a woman refuses to comply with a man's desire for sex, he may react with frustration over this restriction, resulting in increased desire for the forbidden activity (in this case, sex). Mix this reactance with narcissism—a self-serving sense of entitlement and low empathy for others—and the result can be rape.

Reactance can occur in some rather unexpected situations as well. It may surprise you that in the 2001 census, 20 000 Canadians indicated their religion as "Jedi." The Jedi, as you may know, are the guardians of peace and justice who manipulate the Force to maintain order in the blockbuster *Star Wars* movies. Is this actually a religion that 20 000 Canadians follow? Not likely. The move to choose Jedi as a religion was begun by Denis Dion, a man living outside Vancouver, as a protest (that is, reactance) against what he believed to be an intrusive Statistics Canada question concerning religion. Dion felt that this question was none of the government's business and began an email campaign to encourage others to defy the government by giving a bogus response: Jedi. Obviously, many others had a similar reaction and indicated Jedi as their religion. Interestingly, this reaction has been seen in other countries as well—apparently there were 400 000 Jedi in the United Kingdom in 2001 (compared with 260 000 self-identified Jews), and 70 000 Australians listed themselves as Jedi in 2002.

People have also begun to identify themselves as vampires (and even zombies). Due to the popularity of shows like *The Walking Dead*, there are regular "zombie runs" in many major cities. Some vampire groups, says Adam Possami at the University of West Sydney in Australia, are a form of "hyper real" religion, groups that use elements of existing religions, unique philosophy, and pop culture elements (such as the *True Blood* and *Twilight* novels) to create their own reality (Metcalfe, 2010). These groups are typically harmless and short-lived but at times can develop into dangerous obsessions. In 2003, for example, a 12-year-old Toronto boy was reportedly stabbed to death by his brother and two friends, who all claimed to be members of a vampire group (CTV, 2005a).

Asserting Uniqueness

Imagine a world of complete conformity, where there were no differences among people. Would such a world be a happy place? If nonconformity can create discomfort, can sameness create comfort?

People feel uncomfortable when they appear too different from others. But, at least in Western cultures, they also feel uncomfortable when they appear exactly like everyone else. As experiments by C. R. Snyder and Howard Fromkin (1980) have shown, people feel better when they see themselves as moderately unique. Moreover, they act in ways that will assert their individuality. In one experiment, Snyder (1980) led university students to believe that their "10 most important attitudes" were either distinct from or nearly identical to the attitudes of 10 000 other students. When they then participated in a conformity experiment, those deprived of their feeling of uniqueness were most likely to assert their individuality through nonconformity. Moreover, individuals who have the highest "need for uniqueness" tend to be the least responsive to majority influence (Imhoff & Erb, 2009).

"When I'm in America, I have no doubt I'm a Jew, but I have strong doubts about whether I'm really an American. And when I get to Israel, I know I'm an American, but I have strong doubts about whether I'm a Jew."

Leslie Fiedler,
Fiedler on the Roof: Essays on Literature and Jewish Identity, 1991

Seeing oneself as unique also appears in people's "spontaneous self-concepts." William McGuire and his colleagues (McGuire & Padawer-Singer, 1978; McGuire, McGuire, & Winton, 1979) reported that when children are invited to "tell us about yourself," they are most likely to mention their distinctive attributes. Foreign-born children are more likely than others to mention their birthplace. Redheads are more likely than black- and brown-haired children to volunteer their hair colour. Light and heavy children are the most likely to refer to their body weight. Minority children are the most likely to mention their race.

Likewise, we become more keenly aware of our gender when we are with people of the other gender (Cota & Dion, 1986). When one of the authors attended a Psychological Association meeting with 10 others—all women, as it happened—he immediately became aware of his gender. As the group took a break at the end of the second day, he joked that the line would be short in front of his bathroom, triggering the woman sitting next to him to notice what hadn't crossed her mind until then—the group's gender makeup.

The principle, says McGuire, is that "one is conscious of oneself insofar as, and in the ways that, one is different." Thus, "If I am a Black woman in a group of White women, I tend to think of myself as a Black; if I move to a group of Black men, my blackness loses salience and I become more conscious of being a woman" (McGuire et al., 1978). This insight helps us understand why White people who grow up amid non-White people tend to have a strong White identity, and why any minority group tends to be conscious of its distinctiveness and how the surrounding culture relates to it (Knowles & Peng, 2005). The majority group, being less conscious of race, may see the minority group as hypersensitive.

When the people of two cultures are nearly identical, they still will notice their differences, however small. Even trivial distinctions may provoke scorn and conflict. Jonathan Swift satirized the phenomenon in *Gulliver's Travels* with the Little-Endians' war against the Big-Endians. Their difference: The Little-Endians preferred to break their eggs on the small end; the Big-Endians, on the large end. On a world scale, the differences may not seem great between Scots and English people, Hutus and Tutsis, Serbs and Croatians, Sunnis and Shias, or Catholic and Protestant Northern Irish. But small differences can mean big conflicts (Rothbart & Taylor, 1992). Rivalry is often most intense when the other group closely resembles your own.

"There are no exceptions to the rule that everybody likes to be an exception to the rule."

Malcolm Forbes,
Forbes Magazine

So, although we do not like being greatly deviant, we are, ironically, all alike in wanting to feel distinctive and in noticing how we are distinctive. But as research on self-serving bias (Chapter 2) has made clear, it is not just any kind of distinctiveness we seek but distinctiveness in the right direction. Our quest is not merely to be different from the average but to be better than average.

SUMMING UP

What Is Conformity?

- *Conformity*—changing one's behaviour or belief as a result of group pressure—comes in two forms. *Compliance* is outwardly going along with the group while inwardly disagreeing; a subset of compliance is *obedience*, compliance with a direct command. *Acceptance* is believing as well as acting in accord with social pressure.

What Are the Classic Conformity and Obedience Studies?

Three classic sets of experiments illustrate how researchers have studied conformity:

- Muzafer Sherif observed that others' judgments influenced people's estimates of the movement of a point of light that actually did not move. Norms for "proper" answers emerged and survived both over long periods of time and through succeeding generations of research participants.
- Solomon Asch had people listen to others' judgments of which of three comparison lines was equal to a standard line and then make the same judgment themselves. When the others unanimously gave a wrong answer, the subjects conformed 37 percent of the time.
- Stanley Milgram's obedience studies elicited an extreme form of compliance. Under optimum conditions—a legitimate, close-at-hand commander, a remote victim, and no one else to exemplify disobedience—65 percent of his adult male subjects fully obeyed instructions to deliver what were supposedly traumatizing electric shocks to a screaming, innocent victim in an adjacent room.
- These classic studies expose the potency of several phenomena. Behaviour and attitudes are mutually reinforcing, enabling a small act of evil to foster the attitude that leads to a larger evil act. The power of the situation is seen when good people, faced with dire circumstances, commit reprehensible acts (although dire situations may produce heroism in others).

What Predicts Conformity?

- Using conformity testing procedures, experimenters have explored the circumstances that produce conformity. Certain situations appear to be especially powerful. For example, conformity is affected by the characteristics of the group: People conform most when faced with the unanimous reports of three or more people, or groups, who model the behaviour or belief.
- Conformity is reduced if the model behaviour or belief is not unanimous.
- Conformity is enhanced by group cohesion.
- The higher the status of those modelling the behaviour or belief, the greater the likelihood of conformity.
- People also conform most when their responses are public (in the presence of the group).
- A prior commitment to a certain behaviour or belief increases the likelihood that a person will stick with that commitment rather than conform.

Why Conform?

Experiments reveal two reasons people conform:

- Normative influence results from a person's desire for acceptance: We want to be liked. The tendency to conform more when responding publicly reflects normative influence.
- Informational influence results from others' providing evidence about reality. The tendency to conform more on difficult decision-making tasks reflects informational influence: We want to be right.

Who Conforms?

- The question "Who conforms?" has produced few definitive answers. Personality scores are poor predictors of specific acts of conformity but better predictors of average conformity. Trait effects sometimes seem strongest in "weak" situations where social forces do not overwhelm individual differences.
- Although conformity and obedience are universal, culture and gender socialize people to be more or less socially responsive.
- Social roles involve a certain degree of conformity, and conforming to expectations is an important task when stepping into a new social role.

Do We Ever Want to Be Different?

- Social psychology's emphasis on the power of social pressure must be joined by a complementary emphasis on the power of the person. We are not puppets. When social coercion becomes blatant, people often experience reactance—a motivation to defy the coercion in order to maintain a sense of freedom.
- We are not comfortable being too different from a group, but neither do we want to appear the same as everyone else. Thus, we act in ways that preserve our sense of uniqueness and individuality. In a group, we are most conscious of how we differ from the others.

Key Terms

acceptance
autokinetic phenomenon
cohesiveness
compliance
confederate
conformity
informational influence
normative influence
obedience
reactance

CHAPTER 7

Group Influence

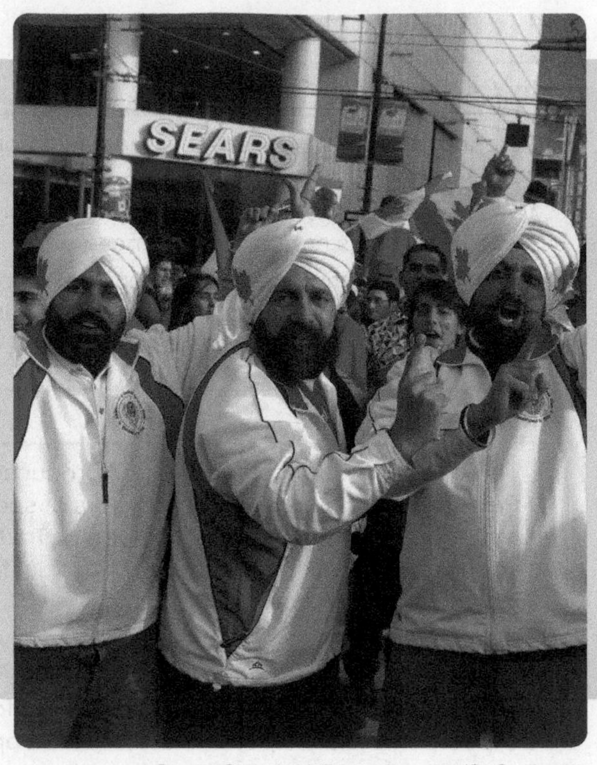

Source: Sergeibach/Dreamstime.com/GetStock.com.

CHAPTER OUTLINE

What Is a Group?

Social Facilitation: How Are We Affected by the Presence of Others?

Social Loafing: Do Individuals Exert Less Effort in a Group?

Deindividuation: When Do People Lose Their Sense of Self in Groups?

Group Polarization: Do Groups Intensify Our Opinions?

Groupthink: Do Groups Hinder or Assist Good Decisions?

Leadership: How Do Leaders Shape the Group's Actions?

The Influence of the Minority: How Do Individuals Influence the Group?

One of your authors (Steven) is a runner. He had always wanted to run a "10k" (10 km distance) in less than an hour, but he had never been able to. Five years ago he signed up for a 10k charity race. He trained for three months but never got close to beating his one-hour goal. The day of the race, he completed the 10k in 55 minutes and 56 seconds. How did he manage it? Is it important that during the race he was competing against 100 others while when training he was always alone?

Imagine yourself in front of a crowd. You are preparing to give a speech to a class of 150 students. How do you feel? Is your heart beating fast? Are your palms sweating? Do you feel ill? You might well be suffering from some performance anxiety—you might be afraid of performing badly. Do you think you would feel differently if you were speaking in front of only three friends instead of 150 strangers? Would your performance anxiety go away? When do you think you would perform your best? Do you perform best on your own or when there are other people around you?

At almost every turn, we are involved in groups. Our world contains not only more than 7 billion individuals but almost 200 nation–states, 4 million local communities, 20 million economic organizations, and hundreds of millions of other formal and informal groups—couples having dinner, housemates hanging out, clubs planning activities. How do these groups influence us?

Group interactions often have more dramatic effects. Intellectual university students hang out with other intellectuals, accentuating one another's interests. Deviant youth hang out with other deviant youth, amplifying one another's antisocial tendencies. But how do groups affect attitudes? And what influences lead groups to smart or to foolish decisions?

Individuals influence their groups. As the movie *Twelve Angry Men* opens, 12 wary murder trial jurors file into a jury room. It is a hot day. The tired jurors are close to agreement and eager for a quick verdict convicting a teenage boy of knifing his father. But one maverick refuses to vote for a guilty verdict. As the heated deliberation proceeds, the jurors one by one change their verdict until consensus is reached: "Not guilty." In real trials, a lone individual seldom sways the entire group. Yet, minorities that sway majorities make history. What helps make a minority—or an effective leader—persuasive?

We will examine these intriguing phenomena of group influence one at a time. But, first things first: What is a group and why do groups exist?

What Is a Group?

We all belong to groups: friends, clubs, teams, etc. But what defines a group? Do we have to know we are in a group to be part of one? These are the types of questions social psychologists ask.

The answer to this question seems self-evident—until several people compare their definitions. Are jogging partners a group? Are airplane passengers a group? Is a group a set of people who identify with one another, who sense they belong together? Is a group those who share common goals and rely on one another? Does a group form when individuals become organized? When their relationships with one another continue over time? These are among the social psychological definitions of a group (McGrath, 1984).

Group dynamics expert Marvin Shaw (1981) argued that all groups have one thing in common: Their members interact. He, therefore, defined a **group** as two or more people who interact with and influence one another. Moreover, suggested Australian National University social psychologist John Turner (1987), groups perceive themselves as "us" in contrast to "them." A pair of joggers, then, would indeed constitute a group, if they were jogging together. Different groups help us meet different human needs: to affiliate (to belong to and connect with others), to achieve, and to gain a social identity (Johnson et al., 2006).

By Shaw's definition, students working individually in a computer lab would not be a group. Although physically together, they are more a collection of individuals than an interacting group (though each may be part of a group with dispersed others in an online forum). The distinction between collections of unrelated individuals in a computer lab and the more influential group behaviour among interacting individuals sometimes blurs. People who are merely in one another's presence do sometimes influence one another. At a hockey game, they may perceive themselves as "us" fans in contrast with "them" (people who root for the other team).

In this chapter, we consider three examples of such collective influence: social facilitation, social loafing, and deindividuation. These three phenomena can occur with minimal interaction (in what we call "minimal group situations"), but they also influence people's behaviour while interacting. Then we will consider four examples of social influence in interacting groups: group polarization, groupthink, leadership, and minority influence.

Social Facilitation: How Are We Affected by the Presence of Others?

Are we affected by the mere presence of another person? Would the mere presence of others affect a person's jogging, eating, ice skating, or exam performance?

The Mere Presence of Others

"Mere presence" means that the people are not competing, do not reward or punish, and in fact do nothing except be present as a passive audience or as **co-actors**. More than a century ago, Norman Triplett (1898), a psychologist interested in bicycle racing, noticed that cyclists' times were faster when racing together than when racing alone against the clock (maybe that's why Steve performed best in his 10k race?). Triplett conducted one of social psychology's early laboratory experiments. Children told to wind string on a fishing reel as rapidly as possible wound faster when they worked with co-actors than when they worked alone.

A modern reanalysis of Triplett's data revealed that the difference did not reach statistical significance (Stroebe, 2012; Strube, 2005). But ensuing experiments found that the presence of others improves the speed with which people do simple multiplication problems and cross out designated letters. It also improves the accuracy with which people perform simple motor tasks, such as keeping a metal stick in contact with a dime-sized disc on a moving turntable (F. H. Allport, 1920; Dashiell, 1930; Travis, 1925). This **social facilitation** effect also occurs with animals. In the presence of others of their species, ants excavate more sand, chickens eat more grain, and sexually active rat pairs mate more often (Bayer, 1929; Chen, 1937; Larsson, 1956). More recently, researchers have found the presence of others even makes us better at recognizing faces (e.g., Garcia-Marques et al., 2015). And people do not even need to be physically

group Two or more people who, for longer than a few moments, interact with and influence one another and perceive one another as "us."

co-actors A group of people working simultaneously and individually on a noncompetitive task.

social facilitation (1) *Original meaning:* the tendency of people to perform simple or well-learned tasks better when others are present. (2) *Current meaning:* the strengthening of dominant (prevalent, likely) responses owing to the presence of others.

Activity: How Does the Presence of Others Affect You?

On a scale of 1 to 10, **where 1 is poor and 10 is excellent**, how good are you at:

Playing an instrument _____ Driving a car _____

Skateboarding _____ Snowboarding _____

Public speaking _____ Running _____

Now, *imagine you have an audience* (e.g., speaking in front of a group of strangers, driving with your mother, running in a race). On the same rating scale, **where 1 is poor and 10 is excellent**, how good are you at:

Playing an instrument _____ Driving a car _____

Skateboarding _____ Snowboarding _____

Public speaking _____ Running _____

Did your ratings change? If you are like most people, the presence of an audience should improve your performance on tasks you are good at (e.g., driving, running) but hinder your performance when the task is difficult (e.g., public speaking, playing a musical instrument). How does this match with your own experience?

present for the facilitation to occur; simply knowing you are in an online "group" enhances performance on simple tasks (e.g., Liu & Yu, 2018).

But wait: Other studies revealed that on some tasks the presence of others hinders performance. In the presence of others, cockroaches, parakeets, and green finches learn mazes more slowly (Allee & Masure, 1936; Gates & Allee, 1933; Klopfer, 1958). This disruptive effect also occurs with people. The presence of others diminishes efficiency at learning nonsense syllables, completing a maze, and performing complex multiplication problems (Dashiell, 1930; Pessin, 1933; Pessin & Husband, 1933). We can even be worse at learning new faces (Hills et al., 2019).

Saying that the presence of others sometimes facilitates performance and sometimes hinders it is about as satisfying as a Nova Scotia weather forecast—

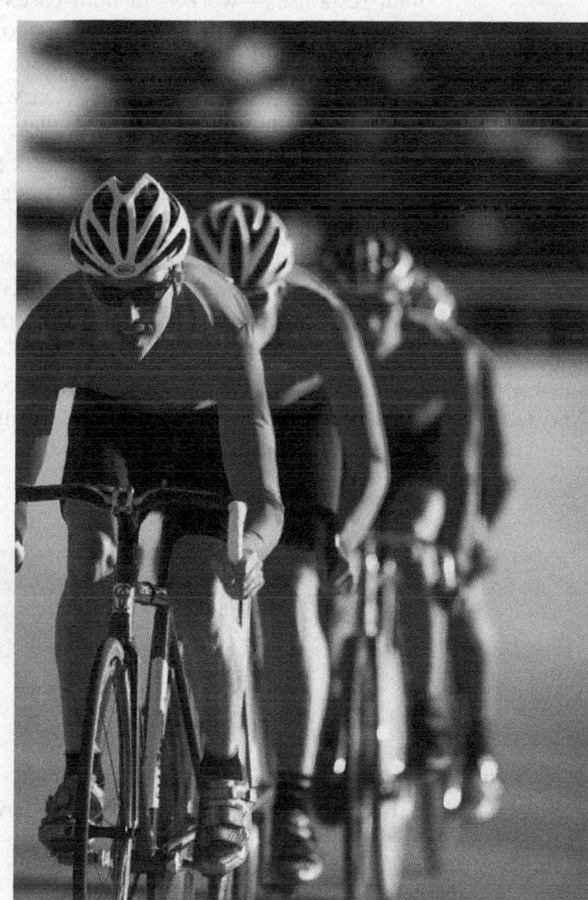

Social facilitation: The motivating presence of a co-actor or audience strengthens well-learned responses.

Source: ©Ryan McVay/Getty Images.

"It might be sunny but then again it might rain." By 1940, research activity in this area had ground to a halt. It lay dormant for 25 years until awakened by the touch of a new idea.

Social psychologist Robert Zajonc (pronounced *Zyence;* rhymes with *science*) wondered whether these seemingly contradictory findings could be reconciled. As often happens at creative moments in science, Zajonc (1965) used one field of research to illuminate another. The illumination came from a well-established principle in experimental psychology: Arousal enhances whatever response tendency is dominant. Increased arousal enhances performance on easy tasks for which the most likely—"dominant"—response is correct. People solve easy anagrams, such as *akec,* fastest when they are anxious. On complex tasks, for which the correct answer is not dominant, increased arousal promotes incorrect responding. On harder anagrams, such as *theloacco,* people do worse when anxious.

Could this principle solve the mystery of social facilitation? It seemed reasonable to assume that others' presence will arouse or energize people (Mullen, Bryant, & Driskell, 1997); most of us can recall feeling more tense or excited before an audience. If social arousal facilitates dominant responses, it should boost performance on easy tasks and hurt performance on difficult tasks.

With that explanation, confusing results made sense. Winding fishing reels, doing simple multiplication problems, and eating were all easy tasks for which the responses were well-learned or naturally dominant. Sure enough, having others around boosted performance. Learning new material, doing a maze, and solving complex math problems were more difficult tasks for which the correct responses were initially less probable. In these cases, the presence of others increased the number of incorrect responses on these tasks. The same general rule—arousal facilitates dominant responses—worked in both cases (see Figure 7–1). Suddenly, what had looked like contradictory results no longer seemed contradictory.

> ***"Mere social contact begets . . . a stimulation of the animal spirits that heightens the efficiency of each individual workman."***
>
> Karl Marx, *Das Kapital,* 1867

Zajonc's solution, so simple and elegant, left other social psychologists thinking what Thomas H. Huxley thought after first reading Darwin's *Origin of the Species:* "How extremely stupid not to have thought of that!" (Huxley, 1900, p. 189). It seemed obvious—once Zajonc had pointed it out. Perhaps, however, the pieces appeared to merge so neatly only because we viewed them through the spectacles of hindsight. Would the solution survive direct experimental tests?

After almost 300 studies, conducted with the help of more than 25 000 volunteers, the solution has indeed survived (Bond & Titus, 1983; Guerin, 1993, 1999). Social arousal facilitates dominant responses, whether right or wrong. For example, Peter Hunt and Joseph Hillery (1973) found that in the presence of others, students took less time to learn a simple maze and more time to learn a complex one (just as the cockroaches do!). And James Michaels and his collaborators (1982) found that good pool players (who had

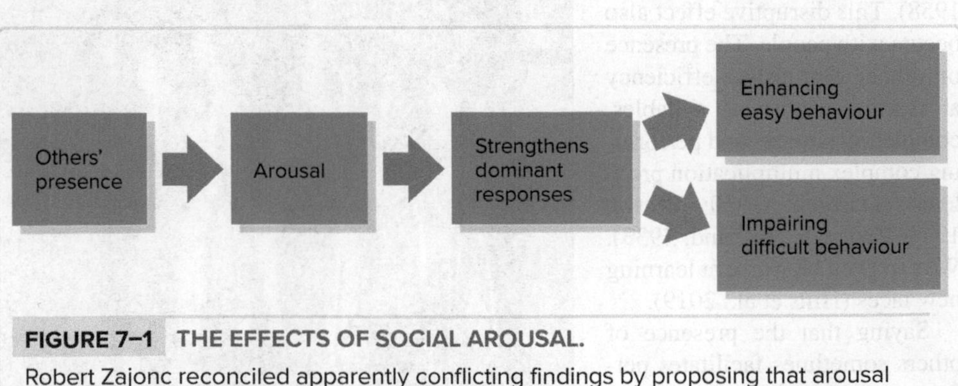

FIGURE 7–1 THE EFFECTS OF SOCIAL AROUSAL.

Robert Zajonc reconciled apparently conflicting findings by proposing that arousal from others' presence strengthens dominant responses (the correct responses only on easy or well-learned tasks).

TABLE 7–1 Home Advantage in Major Team Sports.		
Sport	**Games Studied**	**Winning Percentage**
Baseball	135 665	54.3%
Football	2 592	57.3
Hockey	4 322	61.1
Basketball	13 596	64.4
Soccer	37 202	69.0

made 71 percent of their shots while being unobtrusively observed) did even better (80 percent) when four observers came up to watch them play. Poor shooters (who had previously averaged 36 percent) did even worse (25 percent) when closely observed. Likewise, novice drivers more often fail driving tests when tested with another to-be-tested person in the car rather than alone (Rosenbloom et al., 2007).

> ***"Discovery consists of seeing what everybody has seen and thinking what nobody has thought."***
>
> Albert von Szent-Györgyi, *The Scientist Speculates*, 1962

Athletes, actors, and musicians perform well-practised skills, which helps explain why they often perform best when energized by the responses of a supportive audience. Studies of more than 80 000 university and professional athletic events in Canada, the United States, and Great Britain revealed that home teams win about six in 10 games (somewhat fewer for baseball and football, somewhat more for basketball and soccer) (see Table 7–1).

In the last several Olympic games, home teams did much better than they typically have in previous games. The Chinese dominance at Beijing's 2008 Summer Olympics was a frequent topic of discussion; Canada won more gold medals at the 2010 Winter Olympics in Vancouver than any Canadian team has ever won. In 2012, the British in London did the best they had in an Olympics since 1920. The Russians won the most medals during the Sochi 2014 Winter Olympics. In 2016, host country Brazil won the most medals (and gold medals) it had ever won at an Olympics; and South Korea did the same in Seoul in 2018. At the time of this writing, the 2020 Summer Olympics in Tokyo have been postponed to 2021 due to COVID-19. It is unclear what impact this will have on the games, or on individual country performance.

Yet some research by Stephen Bray and his colleagues at the University of Lethbridge (see Bray et al., 2003) suggests that home-field advantage is not always an advantage. In this research the authors found that home field was more of an advantage for good teams than for poorly performing teams. More specifically, they found that British professional soccer teams were more likely to tie their home games if they were poorly performing teams. Higher-quality teams were less likely to tie home games. The home advantage may, however, also stem from the players' familiarity with their home environment, less travel fatigue, feelings of dominance derived from territorial control, or increased team identity when cheered by fans (Zillmann & Paulus, 1993; Allen & Jones, 2014; van de Ven, 2011; Unkelbach & Memmert, 2010).

Crowding: The Presence of Many Others

So people do respond to the mere presence of others. But does the presence of observers always arouse people? In times of stress, a comrade can be comforting. Nevertheless, with others present, people perspire more, breathe faster, tense their muscles more, and have higher blood pressure and a faster heart rate (Geen & Gange, 1983; Moore & Baron, 1983). Even a supportive audience may elicit poorer performance on challenging tasks (Butler & Baumeister, 1998). Having your family at your first piano recital likely won't boost your performance.

A good house is a full house, as James Maas's Cornell University introductory psychology students experienced in this 2000-seat auditorium. If the class had 100 students meeting in this large space, it would feel much less energized.

Source: ©Mike Okoniewski.

The effect of others' presence increases with their number (Jackson & Latané, 1981; Knowles, 1983). Sometimes, the arousal and self-conscious attention created by a large audience interferes even with well-learned, automatic behaviours, such as speaking. Given extreme pressure, we're vulnerable to "choking." Stutterers tend to stutter more in front of larger audiences than when speaking to just one or two people (Mullen, 1986b). Even professional golfers feel the effects—scores on the final day of four-day tournaments tend to be worse than those on the previous day (Wells & Skowronski, 2012).

Being in a crowd also intensifies positive or negative reactions. When they sit close together, friendly people are liked even more, and unfriendly people are disliked even more (Schiffenbauer & Schiavo, 1976; Storms & Thomas, 1977). In experiments with Columbia University students and with Ontario Science Centre visitors, Jonathan Freedman and his co-workers (1979, 1980) had an accomplice listen to a humorous tape or watch a movie with other participants. When they all sat close together, the accomplice could more readily induce them to laugh and clap. As theatre directors and sports fans know, and as researchers have confirmed, a "good house" is a full house (Agnew & Carron, 1994; Aiello, Thompson, & Brodzinsky, 1983; Worchel & Brown, 1984).

Perhaps you've noticed that a class of 35 students feels warmer and livelier in a room that seats just 35 than when spread around a room that seats 100. When others are close by, we are more likely to notice and join in their laughter or clapping. But crowding also enhances arousal, as Gary Evans (1979) found. He tested 10-person groups in two rooms: with dimensions of 7 metres by 10 metres or 3 metres by 4 metres. Compared to those in the large room, those who were densely packed had higher pulse rates and blood pressure (indicating arousal). On difficult tasks, they made more errors, an effect of crowding replicated by Dinesh Nagar and Janak Pandey (1987) with university students in India. Crowding, then, has a similar effect to being observed by a crowd: It enhances arousal, which facilitates dominant responses.

> *"Heightened arousal in crowded homes also tends to increase stress. Crowding produces less distress in homes divided into many spaces, however, enabling people to withdraw in privacy."*
>
> Evans, Lepore, & Schroeder (1996)

Why Are We Aroused in the Presence of Others?

What you do well, you will be energized to do best in front of others (unless you become hyper-aroused and self-conscious). What you find difficult may seem impossible in the same circumstances. What is it about other people that creates arousal? There is evidence to support three possible factors (Aiello & Douthitt, 2001; Feinberg & Aiello, 2006): evaluation apprehension, distraction, and mere presence.

Evaluation apprehension

Nickolas Cottrell surmised that observers make us apprehensive because we wonder how they are evaluating us. To test whether **evaluation apprehension** exists, Cottrell and his associates (1968) examined social facilitation for the pronunciation of nonsense syllables and well-learned, easy-to-pronounce syllables. In this "mere presence" condition, they blindfolded observers, supposedly in preparation for a perception experiment. In contrast to the effect of the watching audience, the mere presence of these blindfolded people did not boost well-practised responses.

evaluation apprehension Concern for how others are evaluating us.

Other experiments confirmed Cottrell's conclusion: The enhancement of dominant responses is strongest when people think they are being evaluated. In one experiment, joggers on a jogging path sped up as they came upon a woman seated on the grass—if she was facing them rather than sitting with her back turned (Worringham & Messick, 1983).

The self-consciousness we feel when being evaluated can also interfere with behaviours that we perform best automatically (Mullen & Baumeister, 1987). If self-conscious basketball players analyze their body movements while shooting critical free throws, they are more likely to miss.

Driven by distraction

Glenn Sanders, Robert Baron, and Danny Moore (1978; Baron, 1986) carried evaluation apprehension a step further. They theorized that when people wonder how co-actors are doing or how an audience is reacting, they get distracted. This *conflict* between paying attention to others and paying attention to the task overloads our cognitive system, causing arousal. We are "driven by distraction." This arousal comes not just from the presence of another person but even from a non-human distraction, such as bursts of light (Sanders, 1981a, 1981b).

Mere presence

Zajonc, however, believed that the mere presence of others produces some arousal even without evaluation apprehension or arousing distraction. Recall that facilitation effects also occur with non-human creatures, such as cockroaches. This finding hints at an innate social arousal mechanism common to much of the zoological world. (Animals probably are not consciously worrying about how other animals are evaluating them.) At the human level, most runners are energized when running with someone else, even one who neither competes nor evaluates. And university rowing team members, perhaps aided by an endorphin boost from the communal activity, tolerate twice as much pain after rowing together rather than solo (E. Cohen et al., 2009).

This is a good time to remind ourselves that a good theory is scientific shorthand: It simplifies and summarizes a variety of observations. Social facilitation theory does this well. It is a simple summary of many research findings. A good theory also offers clear predictions that (1) help confirm or modify the theory, (2) guide new exploration, and (3) suggest practical application. Social facilitation theory has definitely generated the first two types of prediction: (1) The basics of the theory (that the presence of others is arousing and that this social arousal enhances dominant responses) have been confirmed, and (2) the theory has brought new life to a long-dormant field of research. Are there (3) some practical applications? We can make some educated guesses. Many new office buildings have replaced private offices with large, open areas divided by low partitions. Might the resulting awareness of others' presence help boost the performance of well-learned tasks but disrupt creative thinking on complex tasks? Can you think of other possible applications?

Social Loafing: Do Individuals Exert Less Effort in a Group?

In a team tug of war, will eight people on a side exert as much force as the sum of their best efforts in individual tugs of war? If not, why not? What level of individual effort can we expect from members of work groups?

Think about the last time you worked on a group project. (Many of you may be doing one right now!) Have you ever been in a group where one person was not pulling their weight? Have you ever been that person, slacking off a bit because you know you can get away with it? We all do it, under certain conditions. This can be particularly frustrating when a person who has done little or no work will get the same credit as those who did more work. What can you do in these situations to make that person work harder? Does the culture you come from make a difference?

Social facilitation usually occurs when people work toward individual goals and when their efforts, whether winding fishing reels or solving math problems, can be individually evaluated. These situations parallel some everyday work situations—not those where people cooperatively pool their efforts toward a common goal but those where individuals are not accountable for their efforts. A team tug of war provides one such example. Organizational fundraising—pooling candy-sale proceeds to pay for the class trip—provides another. So does a class project where all get the same grade. On such "additive tasks"—tasks where the group's achievement depends on the sum of the individual efforts—will team spirit boost productivity? Will bricklayers lay bricks faster when working as a team than when working alone? One way to attack such questions is with laboratory simulations.

Many Hands Make Light Work

Nearly a century ago, French engineer Max Ringelmann (reported by Kravitz & Martin, 1986) found that the collective effort of tug-of-war teams was but half the sum of the individual efforts. Contrary to the common notion that "in unity there is strength," this suggested that group members may actually be less motivated when performing additive tasks. Maybe, though, poor performance stemmed from poor coordination—people pulling a rope in slightly different directions at slightly different times. A group of researchers led by Alan Ingham (1974) cleverly eliminated this problem by making individuals think others were pulling with them, when in fact they were pulling alone. Blindfolded participants who were assigned the first position in the apparatus shown in Figure 7–2 and told to "pull as hard as you can" pulled 18 percent harder when they knew they were pulling alone than when they believed that behind them two to five people were also pulling. While completing his PhD at Carleton University, Frederick Lichacz replicated the original Ringelmann study and added a couple of other twists (see Lichacz & Partington, 1996).

FIGURE 7–2 THE ROPE-PULLING APPARATUS.

People in the first position pulled less hard when they thought people behind them were also pulling.

Source: Alan G. Ingham.

He found that giving feedback to the participants on their performance was effective at increasing their individual efforts. In addition, he found that if people had experience with the task, they exerted a greater effort than if the task was a novel one for them.

Researchers Bibb Latané, Kipling Williams, and Stephen Harkins (1979; Harkins, Latané, & Williams, 1980) kept their ears open for other ways to investigate this phenomenon, which they labelled **social loafing**. They observed that the noise produced by six people shouting or clapping "as loud as you can" was less than three times that produced by one person alone. Like the tug-of-war task, however, noisemaking is vulnerable to group inefficiency. So Latané and his associates followed Ingham's example by leading their participants to believe that others were shouting or clapping with them, when in fact they were doing so alone.

Their method was to blindfold six people, seat them in a semicircle, and have them put on headphones, over which they were blasted with the sound of people shouting or clapping. People could not hear their own shouting or clapping, much less that of others. On various trials, they were instructed to shout or clap either alone or along with the group. People who were told about this experiment guessed that the participants would shout louder when with others because they would be less inhibited (Harkins, 1981). The actual result? Social loafing. When the participants believed five others were also either shouting or clapping, they produced one-third less noise than when they thought they were alone. Social loafing occurred even when the participants were high school cheerleaders who believed themselves to be cheering together rather than alone (Hardy & Latané, 1986).

social loafing The tendency for people to exert less effort when they pool their efforts toward a common goal than when they are individually accountable.

free-ride Benefiting from the group, but giving little in return.

Curiously, those who clapped both alone and in groups did not view themselves as loafing; they perceived themselves as clapping the same in both situations. This parallels what happens when students work on group projects for a shared grade. Williams reports that all agree that loafing occurs—but no one admits to doing the loafing.

John Sweeney (1973), a political scientist interested in the policy implications of social loafing, obtained similar results. Students pumped exercise bicycles more energetically (as measured by electrical output) when they knew they were being individually monitored than when they thought their output was being pooled with that of other riders. In the group condition, people were tempted to **free-ride** on the group effort.

In this and some 160 other studies (Karau & Williams, 1993, 1997; Figure 7–3), we see a twist on one psychological force that makes for social facilitation: evaluation apprehension. In the social loafing experiments, individuals believe they are evaluated only when they act alone. The group situation (rope pulling, shouting, and so forth) decreases evaluation apprehension. When people are not accountable and cannot evaluate their own efforts, responsibility is diffused across all group members (Harkins & Jackson, 1985; Kerr & Bruun, 1981). By contrast, the social facilitation experiments increased exposure to evaluation. When made the centre of attention, people self-consciously monitor their behaviour (Mullen & Baumeister, 1987). So, when being observed increases evaluation concerns, social facilitation occurs; when being lost in a crowd decreases evaluation concerns, social loafing occurs (Figure 7–4).

To motivate group members, one strategy is to make individual performance identifiable. Some football coaches do this by filming and evaluating each player individually. Whether in a group or not, people exert more effort when their outputs are individually identifiable: University swim team members swim faster in intrasquad relay races when someone monitors and announces their individual times (Williams et al., 1989).

Social Loafing in Everyday Life

How widespread is social loafing? In the laboratory, the phenomenon occurs not only among people who are pulling ropes, cycling, shouting, and clapping but also among those

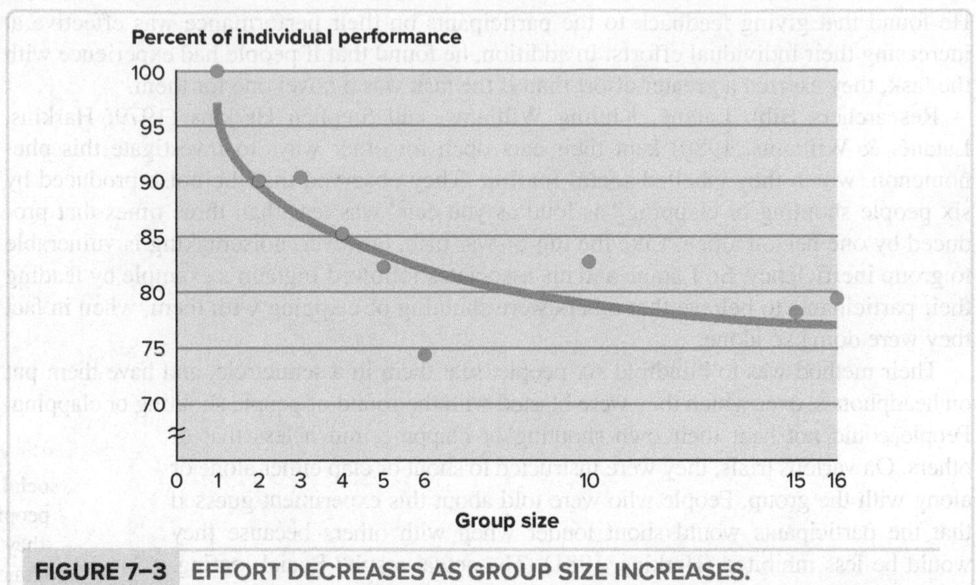

FIGURE 7–3 EFFORT DECREASES AS GROUP SIZE INCREASES.

A statistical digest of 49 studies, involving more than 4000 participants, revealed that effort decreases (loafing increases) as the size of the group increases. Each dot represents the aggregate data from one of these studies.

who are pumping water or air, evaluating poems or editorials, producing ideas, typing, and detecting signals. Do these results generalize to everyday worker productivity?

In one small experiment, assembly-line workers produced 16 percent more product when their individual output was identified, even though they knew their pay would not be affected (Faulkner & Williams, 1996). And consider: A key job in a pickle factory is picking the right-size dill-pickle halves off the conveyor belt and stuffing them in jars.

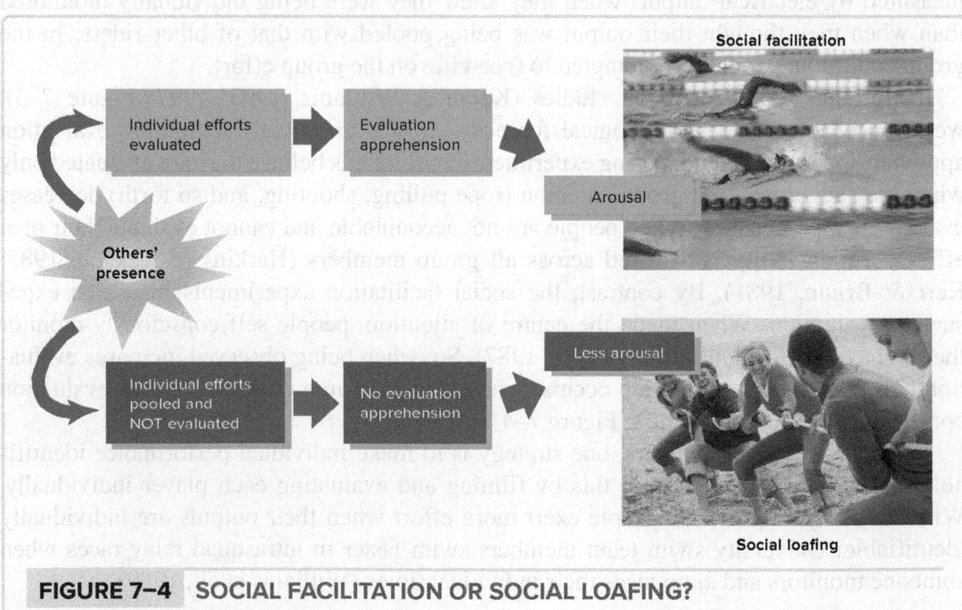

FIGURE 7–4 SOCIAL FACILITATION OR SOCIAL LOAFING?

When individuals cannot be evaluated or held accountable, loafing becomes more likely. An individual swimmer is evaluated on ability to win the race. In tug of war, no single person on the team is held accountable, so any one member might relax or loaf.

Photo source: (top): ©imagenavi/Getty Images; (bottom): ©Thinkstock Images/Getty Images.

Unfortunately, workers are tempted to stuff any size pickle in because their output is not identifiable. (The jars go into a common hopper before reaching the quality-control section.) Williams, Harkins, and Latané (1981, p. 311) noted that research on social loafing suggests "making individual production identifiable, and raises the question: 'How many pickles could a pickle packer pack if pickle packers were only paid for properly packed pickles?'"

Researchers have also found evidence of social loafing in varied cultures, particularly by assessing agricultural output in formerly communist countries. On their collective farms under communism, Russian peasants worked one field one day, another field the next, with little direct responsibility for any given plot. For their own use, they were given small private plots. One analysis found that the private plots occupied 1 percent of the agricultural land yet produced 27 percent of the Soviet farm output (H. Smith, 1976). In communist Hungary, private plots accounted for 13 percent of the farmland but produced one-third of the output (Spivak, 1979). When China began allowing farmers to sell food grown in excess of that owed to the state, food production jumped 8 percent per year—2.5 times the annual increase in the preceding 26 years (Church, 1986). In an effort to tie rewards to productive effort, today's Russia has "decollectivized" many of its farms (Kramer, 2008).

What about collectivist cultures under non-communist regimes? Latané and his co-researchers (Gabrenya et al., 1985) repeated their sound-production experiments in Japan, Thailand, Taiwan, India, and Malaysia. Their findings? Social loafing was evident in all of those countries, too. Seventeen later studies in Asia revealed that people in collectivist cultures do, however, exhibit less social loafing than do people in individualist cultures (Karau & Williams, 1993; Kugihara, 1999). As we noted in Chapter 2, loyalty to family and work groups is strong in collectivist cultures. Likewise, women tend to be less individualistic than men—and to exhibit less social loafing.

In North America, workers who do not pay dues or volunteer time to their unions or professional associations nevertheless are usually happy to accept the benefits those organizations provide. So, too, are public television viewers who don't respond to their station's fund drives. This hints at another possible explanation of social loafing: When rewards are divided equally, regardless of how much one contributes to the group, any individual gets more reward per unit of effort by free-riding on the group. So people may be motivated to slack off when their efforts are not individually monitored and rewarded. Situations that welcome free-riders can, therefore, be, in the words of one commune member, a "paradise for parasites."

But surely collective effort does not always lead to slacking off. Sometimes, the goal is so compelling and maximum output from everyone is so essential that team spirit maintains or intensifies effort. In an Olympic crew race, will the individual rowers in a four-person crew pull their oars with less effort than those in a one- or two-person crew?

The evidence assures us they will not. People in groups loaf less when the task is challenging, appealing, or involving (Karau & Williams, 1993). On challenging tasks, people may perceive their efforts as indispensable (Harkins & Petty, 1982; Kerr, 1983; Kerr & Bruun, 1983). When people see others in their group as unreliable or as unable to contribute much, they work harder (Plaks & Higgins, 2000; Williams & Karau, 1991). But in many situations, so do less capable individuals as they strive to keep up with others' greater productivity (Weber & Hertel, 2007). Adding incentives or challenging a group to strive for

People usually give reduced effort when working in a group; but when group members are highly committed to one another and to the success of the group—like these rowers for the Canadian national team—such social loafing may not occur.
Source: The Canadian Press/Dave Chidley.

certain standards also promotes collective effort (Harkins & Szymanski, 1989; Shepperd & Wright, 1989). Group members will work hard when convinced that high effort will bring rewards (Shepperd & Taylor, 1999), particularly for those who are high in achievement motivation (Hilkenmeier, 2018). Swimmers perform their best when swimming the final legs of relay races (Hüffmeier et al., 2012). Mihelič and Culiberg (2019) found that business students who engaged in mindfulness were less likely to social loaf.

Groups also loaf less when their members are friends or are identified with or indispensable to their group (Davis & Greenlees, 1992; Gockel et al., 2008; Karau & Williams, 1997; Worchel, Jenner, & Hebl, 1998). Even just expecting to interact with someone again serves to increase efforts on team projects (Groenenboom, Wilke, & Wit, 2001). Students who are more similar are also less likely to social loaf when working on a project together (Harding, 2018). Collaborate on a class project with others whom you will be seeing often, and you will probably feel more motivated than you would if you never expected to see them again. Cohesiveness intensifies effort.

These findings parallel those from studies of everyday work groups. When groups are given challenging objectives, when they are rewarded for group success, and when there is a spirit of commitment to the "team," group members work hard (Hackman, 1986). Keeping work groups small can also help members believe that their contributions are indispensable (Comer, 1995). Social loafing is common when group members work without individual accountability; so it would seem that many hands need not always make light work.

Deindividuation: When Do People Lose Their Sense of Self in Groups?

Group situations may cause people to lose self-awareness, with resulting loss of individuality and self-restraint. What circumstances trigger such "deindividuation"?

The suicide attempt and subsequent death of Cole Harbour District High School student Rehtaeh Parsons led national and international news in the spring of 2013. In November of 2011, Rehtaeh, then 15, was drinking at a party and while intoxicated was gang-raped by four other teenagers. The assault was photographed, and photos of the event were widely distributed on Facebook. Rehtaeh was bullied and teased and was repeatedly sent messages online asking for sex. Though the rape was reported to police, no charges were laid until after her death 17 months later. Ultimately, two of the teenagers who posted photos of the rape were charged with creating and distributing child pornography. Sadly, this is only one of many stories like this that have unfolded across Canada and the world over the last 20 years. A question that people asked themselves was this: "How could these kids have done this?" Would they have committed the same crime if they had been on their own, or did being in the group influence their behaviour? In this case, was distributing the photos easier because it could be done essentially anonymously, online?

Doing Together What We Would Not Do Alone

Social facilitation experiments show that groups can arouse people, and social loafing experiments show that groups can diffuse responsibility. When arousal and diffused responsibility combine and normal inhibitions diminish, the results may be startling. Acts may range from a mild lessening of restraint (throwing food in the dining hall, snarling at a referee, screaming during a rock concert) to impulsive self-gratification (group vandalism, orgies, thefts) to destructive social explosions (police brutality, riots, mass suicide).

These unrestrained behaviours have something in common: They are somehow provoked by the power of a group. Groups can generate a sense of excitement, of being caught up in something bigger than one's self. It is hard to imagine a single rock fan screaming deliriously at a private rock concert or a single sports fan setting multiple cars on fire after a championship win. In certain kinds of group situations, people are more likely to abandon normal restraints, to lose their sense of individual responsibility—a state that Leon Festinger, Albert Pepitone, and Theodore Newcomb (1952) labelled **deindividuation**. What circumstances elicit this psychological state?

Prompted by group influence, an anarchist vandalized a police cruiser on Bay Street in Toronto before setting it on fire, Saturday, June 26, 2010.
Source: The Globe and Mail-Kevin Van Paassen/The Canadian Press.

Group size

A group has the power not only to arouse its members but also to render them unidentifiable. The snarling crowd hides the snarling hockey fan. A mob enables its members to believe they will not be prosecuted; they perceive the action as the group's. Rioters, made faceless by the mob, are freed to loot. Why does this happen? Perfectly normal and respectable people can find themselves involved in and participating in rioting. Indeed, one of the authors' friends—now a tenured full professor at a Canadian university—actually participated in a Toronto riot that occurred after the Blue Jays won the World Series.

deindividuation Loss of self-awareness and evaluation apprehension; occurs in group situations that foster anonymity and draw attention away from the individual.

Interestingly, this seems to occur even when people are identifiable and will be prosecuted. In the riots that ensued after the Vancouver Canucks lost the Stanley Cup in 2011, people acted as though they would not be identified and prosecuted even though several people were. In an analysis of 21 instances in which crowds were present as someone threatened to jump from a building or bridge, Leon Mann (1981) found that when the crowd was small and exposed by daylight, people usually did not try to bait the person. But when a large crowd or the cover of night gave people anonymity, the crowd usually baited and jeered.

From sports crowds to rioters, evaluation apprehension plummets. And because "everyone is doing it," all can attribute their behaviour to the situation rather than to their own choices.

Physical anonymity

How can we be sure that the effect of crowds means greater anonymity? We can't. But we can experiment with anonymity to see if it actually lessens inhibitions. Philip Zimbardo (1970, 2002) got the idea for such an experiment from his undergraduate students, who questioned how good boys in William Golding's *Lord of the Flies* could so suddenly become monsters after painting their faces. To experiment with such anonymity, he dressed women in identical white coats and hoods, rather like Ku Klux Klan members (Figure 7–5). Asked to deliver electric shocks to a woman, anonymous hooded women pressed the shock button twice as long as did women who were visible and wearing large name tags.

"A mob is a society of bodies voluntarily bereaving themselves of reason."

Ralph Waldo Emerson, "Compensation," *Essays: First Series,* 1841

The Internet offers similar anonymity. Indeed, the anonymity offered by social media has been observed to foster higher levels of hostile, uninhibited "flaming" behaviour than observed in face-to-face conversations (Douglas & McGarty, 2001; Bae, 2016). Internet

FIGURE 7–5 EFFECT OF PHYSICAL ANONYMITY.

Anonymous women delivered longer electric shocks to helpless victims than did identifiable women.

Source: ©Philip Zimbardo.

bullies who would never to someone's face say "Why don't you just go die" will hide behind their anonymity, particularly if they have high self-esteem (Christie & Dill, 2016). Facebook, to its credit, requires people to use their real names, which may constrain the bullying, hate-filled, and inflammatory comments. When people are deindividuated online, they are no longer influenced by the same norms as when they can be identified individually (Perfumi et al., 2019).

On several occasions, anonymous online bystanders have egged on people who are threatening suicide, sometimes with live video feeding the scene to scores of people. Online communities "are like the crowd outside the building with the guy on the ledge," noted one analyst of technology's social effects (quoted by Stelter, 2008). Sometimes, a caring person has tried to talk the person down, while others, in effect, have chanted, "Jump, jump": "The anonymous nature of these communities only emboldens the meanness or callousness of the people on these sites."

> ***"The use of self-control is like the use of brakes on a train. It is useful when you find yourself going in the wrong direction, but merely harmful when the direction is right."***
>
> Bertrand Russell, *Marriage and Morals,* 1929

Testing deindividuation on the streets, Patricia Ellison, John Govern, and their colleagues (1995) had a confederate driver stop at a red light and wait for 12 seconds whenever she was followed by a convertible or a Jeep. While enduring the wait, she recorded any horn-honking (a mildly aggressive act) by the car behind. Compared to drivers of convertibles and Jeeps with the top down, those with the top up, who were relatively anonymous, honked one-third sooner, twice as often, and for nearly twice as long.

A research team led by Ed Diener (1976) cleverly demonstrated both the effect of being in a group and the effect of being physically anonymous. At Halloween, they observed 1352 children trick-or-treating. As the children, either alone or in groups, approached one of 27 homes scattered throughout the city, an experimenter greeted them warmly, invited them to "take *one* of the candies," and then left the room. Hidden observers noted that, compared to solo children, those in groups were more than twice as likely to take extra candy. Also, compared to children who had been asked their names and where they lived, those left anonymous were also more than twice as likely to transgress. As Figure 7–6 shows, the transgression rate thus varied dramatically with the situation. When deindividuated by group immersion combined with anonymity, most children stole extra candy.

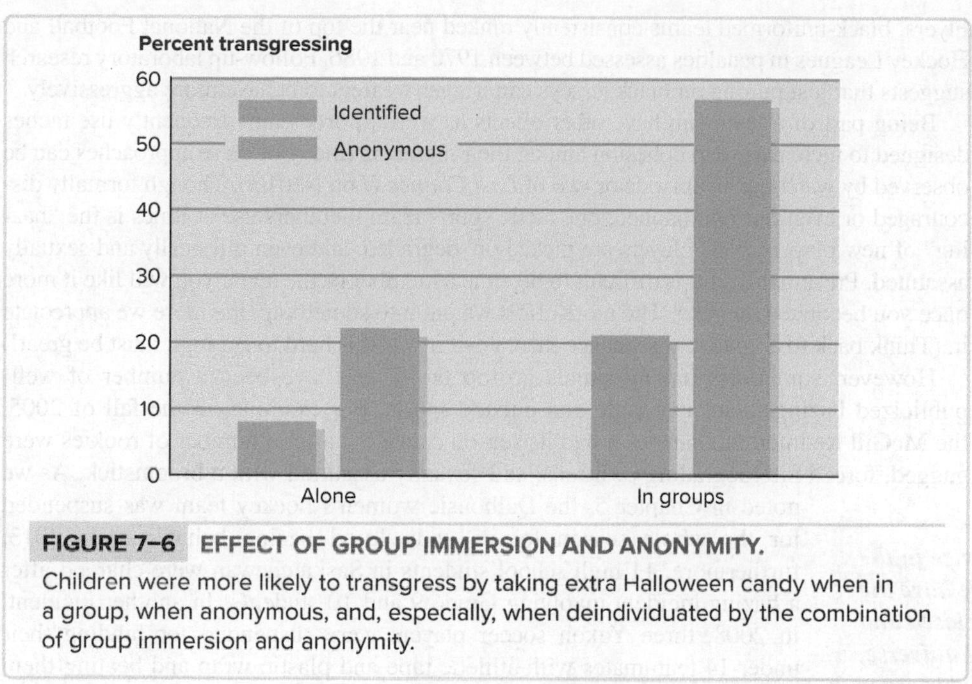

FIGURE 7–6 EFFECT OF GROUP IMMERSION AND ANONYMITY.
Children were more likely to transgress by taking extra Halloween candy when in a group, when anonymous, and, especially, when deindividuated by the combination of group immersion and anonymity.

These experiments make us wonder about the effect of wearing uniforms. Preparing for battle, warriors in some tribal cultures (much like rabid fans of some sports teams) depersonalize themselves with body and face paints or special masks. After the battle, some cultures kill, torture, or mutilate any remaining enemies; other cultures take prisoners alive. Robert Watson (1973) scrutinized anthropological files and discovered that the cultures with depersonalized warriors were also the cultures that brutalized the enemy. The uniformed Canadian soldiers who tortured and killed Shidane Arone in Somalia in 1993 were reportedly angered and aroused by their frustrating mission and the brutal desert heat; enjoying one another's camaraderie, they were unaware that outsiders would view their actions. Thus, forgetting their normal standards, they were swept away by the situation. During the 2010 G20 summit in Toronto, many of the police officers violated explicit regulations and did not wear their name tags or other identification.

Similarly, during the 2020 Black Lives Matter protests in the United States many law enforcement officials also did not wear nametags or insignia, and refused to identify themselves when asked (CNN, 2020). This may be one of the factors that led to the excessive violence used by these officers, who regularly fired on peaceful protesters, and seemed to target journalists covering the protests (CBC, 2020d).

Does becoming physically anonymous always unleash our worst impulses? Fortunately, no. For one thing, the situations in which some of these experiments took place had clear antisocial cues. Robert Johnson and Leslie Downing (1979) pointed out that the Klan-like outfits worn by Zimbardo's subjects may have encouraged hostility. In an experiment, they had women put on nurses' uniforms before deciding how much shock someone should receive. When those wearing the nurses' uniforms were made anonymous, they became *less* aggressive in administering shocks than when their names and personal identities were stressed. From their analysis of 60 deindividuation studies, Tom Postmes and Russell Spears (1998; Reicher, Spears, & Postmes, 1995) concluded that being anonymous makes one less self-conscious and more responsive to cues present in the situation, whether negative (Klan uniforms) or positive (nurses' uniforms).

This helps explain why wearing black uniforms—which are traditionally associated with evil and death—has an effect opposite to that of wearing nurses' uniforms. Mark Frank and Thomas Gilovich (1988) report that, led by the Los Angeles Raiders and the Philadelphia

Flyers, black-uniformed teams consistently ranked near the top of the National Football and Hockey Leagues in penalties assessed between 1970 and 1986. Follow-up laboratory research suggests that just putting on black jerseys can trigger wearers to behave more aggressively.

Being part of a team can have other effects as well. Sports teams frequently use tactics designed to increase group cohesion among their members (many of these approaches can be observed by watching an episode or two of *Last Chance U* on Netflix). Though formally discouraged or even outright banned, one tactic sports team members use at times is the "hazing" of new players. New players are picked on, degraded, and even physically and sexually assaulted. Presumably, if it is difficult to become a member of the team, you will like it more once you become a member. The more effort we put into something, the more we appreciate it. (Think back to cognitive dissonance theory—if it was this hard to get in, it must be great!)

However, sometimes hazing rituals go too far. There have been a number of well-publicized hazing incidents inside and outside sports. For example, in the fall of 2005, the McGill Redmen football team had its season cancelled after a number of rookies were gagged, forced into degrading positions, and sexually assaulted with a broomstick. As we noted in Chapter 5, the Dalhousie women's hockey team was suspended for the whole season for its undisclosed hazing behaviour. In 2013, furthermore, 11 high school students in Saskatchewan were charged after a hazing incident involving Grade 9 and 10 students. In another incident, in 2008, three Yukon soccer players were suspended for binding their under-14 teammates with athletic tape and plastic wrap and beating them with wet towels. And in June of 2010, two Mississauga transportation and works department supervisors were suspended for hazing other employees, including videotaping them while they were bound and having water balloons thrown at them. Although these behaviours are widely condemned, they are still disturbingly frequent.

> ***"Attending a service in the Gothic cathedral, we have the sensation of being enclosed and steeped in an integral universe, and of losing a prickly sense of self in the community of worshippers."***
>
> Yi-Fu Tuan, *Escapism*, 1982

Arousing and distracting activities

Aggressive outbursts by large crowds are often preceded by minor actions that arouse and divert people's attention. Group shouting, chanting, clapping, or dancing serve to both hype people up and reduce self-consciousness.

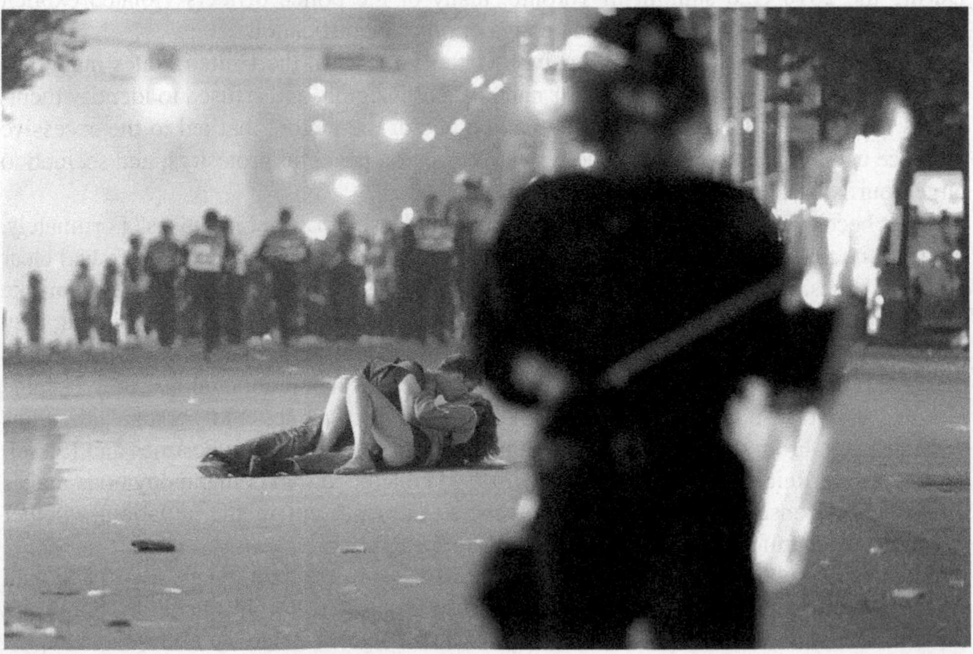

Deindividuation, such as is seen in a riot, can lead to expressions of affection as well as violence.

Source: ©Rich Lam/Stringer/Getty Images.

Ed Diener's experiments (1976, 1979) showed that such activities as throwing rocks and group singing can set the stage for more uninhibited behaviour. There is a self-reinforcing pleasure in doing an impulsive act while observing others doing it also. When we see others act as we are acting, we think they feel as we do, which reinforces our own feelings (Orive, 1984). Moreover, impulsive group action absorbs our attention. When we yell at the referee, we are not thinking about our values; we are reacting to the immediate situation. Later, when we stop to think about what we have done or said, we sometimes feel chagrined—sometimes. At other times, we seek deindividuating group experiences—dances, worship experiences, group encounters—where we can enjoy intense positive feelings and feel close to others.

Diminished Self-Awareness

Group experiences that diminish self-consciousness tend to disconnect behaviour from attitudes. Experiments by Ed Diener (1980) and Steven Prentice-Dunn and Ronald Rogers (1980, 1989) revealed that unselfconscious, deindividuated people are less restrained, less self-regulated, more likely to act without thinking about their own values, and more responsive to the situation. These findings complement and reinforce the experiments on self-awareness considered in Chapter 3.

Self-awareness is the opposite of deindividuation. Those made self-aware—say, by acting in front of a mirror or TV camera—exhibit increased self-control; their actions more clearly reflect their attitudes. In front of a mirror, people taste-testing cream cheese varieties eat less of the high-fat alternative (Sentyrz & Bushman, 1997).

People made self-aware are also less likely to cheat (Beaman et al., 1979; Diener & Wallbom, 1976). So are those who generally have a strong sense of themselves as distinct and independent (Nadler, Goldberg, & Jaffe, 1982). In Japan, where (mirror or no mirror) people more often imagine how they might look to others, people are no more likely to cheat when not in front of a mirror (Heine et al., 2008). The principle: People who are self-aware, or who are temporarily made so, exhibit greater consistency between their words outside a situation and their deeds in it.

We can apply those findings to many situations in everyday life. Circumstances that decrease self-awareness, as alcohol consumption does, increase deindividuation (Hull & Young, 1983). And deindividuation decreases in circumstances that increase self-awareness: in front of mirrors and cameras, in small towns, under bright lights, wearing large name tags, in undistracted quiet, wearing individual clothes, and living in houses (Ickes, Layden, & Barnes, 1978). When a teenager leaves for a party, a parent's parting advice should perhaps be this: "Have fun, and remember who you are." In other words, enjoy being with the group, but be self-aware; maintain your personal identity; and be wary of being deindividuated.

Group Polarization: Do Groups Intensify Our Opinions?

Many conflicts grow as people on both sides talk mostly with like-minded others. Does such interaction amplify pre-existing attitudes? If so, why?

Have you ever sat on a committee that had to make a decision? Have you ever been part of a student group or a group of friends trying to plan an event? Have you ever seen this turn into an absolute disaster? Typically, when groups get together to make decisions, this is a good thing. Group members can share the effort, as well as provide multiple cognitive resources and different ways of thinking about the problem and solutions. However, group decision-making must be done carefully. Because of the social influences working within them, groups can make poor decisions—decisions that sometimes have devastating consequences.

For example, in 2013, a scandal erupted in the Canadian Senate. Senator Mike Duffy had been forced to pay back travel expense reimbursements that were, allegedly, fraudulent. Later, it was revealed that Prime Minister Stephen Harper's chief of staff had personally reimbursed Duffy $90 000 after he paid back the money. This was apparently a deal made involving members of the Prime Minister's Office. Debate raged about "who knew what when" and whether or not the prime minister had been involved. Clearly, some very poor decisions had been made. Ultimately, Duffy was found not guilty on 31 criminal charges and (at the time of this writing) he is suing the government for $7.8 million over how he was treated (CTV, 2020; Globe and Mail, 2017).

Which effects—good or bad—does group interaction more often have? Police brutality and mob violence demonstrate its destructive potential. Yet support-group leaders, management consultants, and educational theorists proclaim its benefits, and social and religious movements urge their members to strengthen their identities by fellowship with like-minded others.

Studies of people in small groups have produced a principle that helps explain both bad and good outcomes: Group discussion often strengthens members' initial inclinations. The unfolding of this research on group polarization illustrates the process of inquiry—how an interesting discovery often leads researchers to hasty and erroneous conclusions, which ultimately are replaced with more accurate conclusions. This is a scientific mystery we can discuss first-hand, one of your authors (David) having been one of the detectives.

The Case of the "Risky Shift"

Among the more than 300 studies of risk-taking behaviour was a study by James Stoner (1961), a study that led to a surprising result. For his master's thesis in industrial management, Stoner compared risk-taking by individuals and groups. To test the commonly held belief that groups are more cautious than individuals, Stoner posed decision dilemmas faced by fictional characters. The participant's task was to advise the imagined character how much risk to take. How do you think the group decisions compared to the average decision before the discussions? Would the groups be likely to take greater risks? To be more cautious? Or would the decisions stay the same?

To everyone's amazement, the group decisions were usually riskier. Dubbed the "risky shift phenomenon," this finding set off a wave of investigation into group risk taking. The studies revealed that this effect occurs not only when a group decides by consensus; after a brief discussion, individuals, too, will alter their decisions. What is more, researchers successfully repeated Stoner's finding with people of varying ages and occupations in a dozen different nations.

During discussion, opinions converged. Curiously, however, the point toward which they converged was usually a lower (riskier) number than their initial average. Here was a delightful puzzle: The small risky shift effect was reliable, unexpected, and without any immediately obvious explanation. What group influences produce such an effect? And how widespread is it? Do discussions in juries, business committees, and military organizations also promote risk taking? Does this explain why teenage reckless driving, as measured by death rates, nearly doubles when a 16- or 17-year-old driver has two teenage passengers rather than none (Chen et al., 2000)? Does it explain stock bubbles, as people discuss why stocks are rising, thus creating an informational cascade that drives stocks even higher (Sunstein, 2009)?

Impact of Group Discussion on Individuals' Opinions

Later research showed that this group phenomenon was not a consistent shift to risk but, rather, a tendency for group discussion to enhance the individuals' initial leanings. This idea led investigators to propose what Serge Moscovici and Marisa Zavalloni (1969) called a **group polarization** phenomenon: Discussion typically strengthens the average inclination of group members.

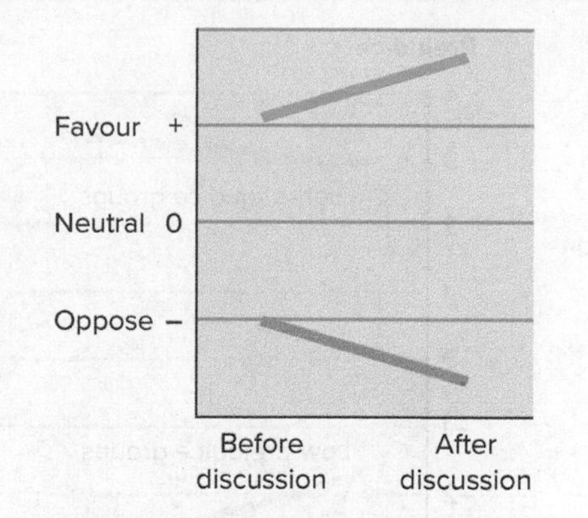

FIGURE 7–7 GROUP POLARIZATION.

The group-polarization hypothesis predicts that discussion will strengthen an attitude shared by group members. If people initially tend to favour something (say, taking a risk), they tend to favour it even more after discussion, and vice versa.

Group polarization experiments

This new view of the changes induced by group discussion prompted experimenters to have people discuss statements that most of them favoured or most of them opposed. Would talking in groups enhance their initial inclinations as it did with the decision dilemmas? That's what the group polarization hypothesis predicts (Figure 7–7).

Dozens of studies confirm group polarization. Moscovici and Zavalloni (1969) observed that discussion enhanced French students' initially positive attitude toward their president and negative attitude toward Americans. Mititoshi Isozaki (1984) found that Japanese university students gave more pronounced "guilty" judgments after discussing a traffic case. Markus Brauer and his co-workers (2001) found that French students' dislike for certain other people was exacerbated after discussing their shared negative impressions. And Glen Whyte (1993) reported that groups exacerbate the "too much invested to quit" phenomenon (also called the "sunk cost fallacy" or "gamblers' fallacy") that has cost many businesses (and gamblers) huge sums of money. Canadian business students imagined themselves having to decide whether to invest more money in the hope of preventing losses in various failing projects (for example, whether to make a high-risk loan to protect an earlier investment). They exhibited the typical effect: 72 percent reinvested money they would seldom have invested if they were considering it as a new investment on its own merits. When making the same decision in groups, 94 percent opted for reinvestment. Importantly, as noted in Chapter 5, in our discussion of cults, these connections do not need to be physical—high-risk gamblers who connect with other high-risk gamblers online tend to engage in riskier behaviour (Russell, Langham, & Hing, 2018).

group polarization Group-produced enhancement of members' pre-existing tendencies; a strengthening of the members' *average* tendency, not a split within the group.

Another research strategy has been to pick issues on which opinions are divided and then isolate people who hold the same view. Does discussion with like-minded people strengthen shared views? Does it magnify the attitude gap that separates the two sides? George Bishop and David Myers wondered. So they set up groups of relatively prejudiced and unprejudiced high school students and asked them to respond—before and after discussion—to issues involving racial attitudes, such as property rights versus open housing (Myers & Bishop, 1970). They found that the discussions among like-minded students did, indeed, increase the initial gap between the two groups (Figure 7–8). This has been replicated many times—for example, Trump supporters get more extreme after talking with other Trump supporters (Bekafigo et al., 2019).

Group polarization in everyday life

In everyday life, people associate mostly with others whose attitudes are similar to their own (see Chapter 10—or just look at your own circle of friends). Does everyday group interaction with like-minded friends intensify shared attitudes?

Group polarization in schools

One real-life parallel to the laboratory phenomenon is what education researchers have called the "accentuation phenomenon": Over time, initial differences among groups of university

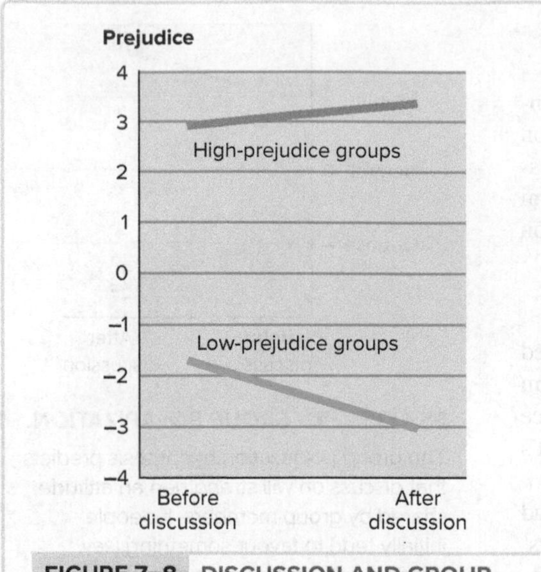

FIGURE 7–8 DISCUSSION AND GROUP POLARIZATION.

Discussion increased polarization between homogeneous groups of high- and low-prejudice high school students. Talking over racial issues increased prejudice in a high-prejudice group and decreased it in a low-prejudice group.

students become accentuated. If the students at university X are initially more intellectual than the students at university Y, that gap is likely to grow during university. Likewise, compared to fraternity and sorority members, independents tend to have more liberal political attitudes, a difference that grows with time in university (Pascarella & Terenzini, 1991). Researchers believe that this results partly from group members reinforcing shared inclinations.

Group polarization in communities

Polarization also occurs in communities. During community conflicts, like-minded people associate increasingly with one another, amplifying their shared tendencies. Gang hostility emerges from a process of mutual reinforcement within neighbourhood gangs, whose members share attributes and hostilities (Cartwright, 1975). If, on your block, "a second out-of-control 15-year-old moves in," surmised David Lykken (1997, p. 263), "the mischief they get into as a team is likely to be more than merely double what the first would do on his own. … A gang is more dangerous than the sum of its individual parts." Indeed, unsupervised peer groups are the strongest predictor of a neighbourhood's crime victimization rate, reported Bonita Veysey and Steven Messner (1999). Moreover, experimental interventions that group young offenders with other young offenders actually—no surprise to any group polarization researcher—increase the rate of problem behaviour (Dishion, McCord, & Poulin, 1999).

Group polarization on the Internet

Email, social media, blogs, and forums offer an easy medium for group interaction. By 2019, 94 percent of Canadians had Internet access, and 91 percent of people over 15 used the Internet. The largest growth in use comes from seniors (Statistics Canada, 2020; 71 percent versus 48 percent in 2012). Almost half of Canadians use the Internet more than 10 hours per week. Almost 70 percent use video streaming services, and 49 percent use music streaming services. Facebook hit 2.7 billion monthly users in 2020 (Statista, 2020). On average, Canadians are online more than 41 hours per month (Canadian Press, 2013; and this has probably increased significantly since COVID-19 hit and many people are working remotely and online).

The Internet's countless virtual groups enable peacemakers and neo-Nazis, geeks and goths, vegans and vampires, conspiracy theorists and cancer survivors to isolate themselves with one another and find support for their shared concerns, interests, and suspicions (Gerstenfeld, Grant, & Chiang, 2003; McKenna & Bargh, 1998, 2000; Sunstein, 2001, 2007, 2009). Even terrorist groups, such as Al Qaeda and ISIS, are using the Internet to recruit new members (CBS, 2009). Indeed, a study in the early 2000s noted that terrorist websites grew from about a dozen in 1997 to 4700 in 2005, a rate of increase that is four times faster than the total number of websites (Ariza, 2006).

Will such discussions produce group polarization? Will socially networked birds of a feather find support for their shared beliefs, values, and suspicions? Evidence suggests yes. Email, Google, and social media "make it much easier for small groups to rally like-minded people, crystallize diffuse hatreds, and mobilize lethal force," observes Robert Wright (2003). Like-minded people share like-minded views, leading to increased extremity and avoidance of counter-attitudinal information (Iyengar & Westwood, 2015; Chen, 2012). We also tend to frame arguments within our groups as related to ourselves and our emotions: we are caring and trustworthy; they are deceptive and irrational (Stevens, Aarts, & Dewulf, 2020).

Group polarization in terrorist organizations
From their analysis of terrorist organizations throughout the world, Clark McCauley and Mary Segal (1987; McCauley, 2002) note that terrorism does not erupt suddenly. Rather, it arises among people whose shared grievances bring them together and fan their fire. As they interact in isolation from moderating influences, they become progressively more extreme. The social amplifier brings the signal in more strongly. The result is violent acts that the individuals, apart from the group, would never have committed.

According to one analysis of terrorists who were members of the Salafi-Jihad, 70 percent had joined while living as expatriates. After moving to foreign places in search of jobs or education, they became keenly mindful of their Muslim identity and often gravitated to mosques and moved in with other expatriate Muslims, who sometimes recruited them into cell groups that provided "mutual emotional and social support" and "development of a common identity" (Sageman, 2004).

But there are many "home grown" terrorists as well. Timothy McVeigh bombed a United States federal building in Oklahoma City in 1994 as revenge against what he viewed as a tyrannical federal government (CNN, 2001). He killed 168 people and injured over 600 more. Reportedly inspired by McVeigh, Dylan Klebold and Eric Harris killed 13 people at Columbine High School. Closer to home, James Gamble, Randall Shepherd, and Lindsay Souvannarath plotted a mass shooting at the Halifax Shopping Centre in February 2015 after meeting and plotting the attack online. A tip to Crime Stoppers foiled the attack (CBC, 2015b).

Massacres, similarly, have been found to be group phenomena. The violence is enabled and escalated by the killers egging one another on, noted Robert Zajonc (2000), who knew violence as a survivor of a Second World War Warsaw air raid that killed both his parents (Burnstein, 2009). It is difficult to influence someone once "in the pressure cooker of the terrorist group," notes Jerrold Post (2005, p. 634) after interviewing many accused terrorists. "In the long run, the most effective anti-terrorist policy is one that inhibits potential recruits from joining in the first place."

Explaining Polarization

Why do groups adopt stances that are more exaggerated than the average opinions of their individual members? Researchers hoped that solving the mystery of group polarization might provide some insights. Solving small puzzles sometimes provides clues for solving larger ones.

Among several proposed theories of group polarization, two have survived scientific scrutiny. One deals with the arguments presented during a discussion, the other with how members of a group view themselves in relation to the other members. The first idea is an example of what Chapter 6 called informational influence (influence that results from accepting evidence about reality). The second is an example of normative influence (influence based on a person's desire to be accepted or admired by others).

In two trials, South African courts reduced sentences after learning how social–psychological phenomena, including deindividuation and group polarization, led crowd members to commit murderous acts (Colman, 1991). Would you agree that courts should consider social–psychological phenomena as possible extenuating circumstances?

Informational influence and group polarization

According to the best-supported explanation, group discussion elicits a pooling of ideas, most of which favour the dominant viewpoint. Ideas that were common knowledge to group members will often be brought up in discussion or, even if unmentioned, will jointly influence their discussion (Gigone & Hastie, 1993; Larson, Foster-Fishman, & Keys, 1994; Stasser, 1991). Other ideas mentioned in discussion may include persuasive arguments that some group members had not previously considered. But when people hear relevant arguments without learning the specific stands that other people assume, they still shift their positions (Burnstein & Vinokur, 1977; Hinsz, Tindale, & Vollrath, 1997). Arguments, in and of themselves, matter.

But there's more to attitude change than merely hearing someone else's arguments. Active participation in discussion produces more attitude change than does passive listening.

Participants and observers hear the same ideas, but when participants put them into their own words, the verbal commitment magnifies the impact. The more group members repeat one another's ideas, the more they rehearse and validate them (Brauer, Judd, & Gliner, 1995).

This illustrates a point made in Chapter 5: People's minds are not just blank tablets for persuaders to write on. In the central route to persuasion, what people think in response to a message is crucial; in fact, just thinking about an issue for a couple of minutes can strengthen opinions (Tesser, Martin, & Mendolia, 1995). (Perhaps you can recall your feelings becoming polarized as you merely ruminated about someone you disliked or liked.) Even expecting to discuss an issue with an equally expert person holding an opposing view can motivate people to marshal their arguments and thus adopt a more extreme position (Fitzpatrick & Eagly, 1981). But, fascinatingly, we can change our attitudes without hearing an argument at all (e.g., Levitan & Verhulst, 2016). Simply knowing that people in a group have an opinion influences ours.

But, as we learned in Chapter 5, the source of the information we get is important as well. People also make assumptions about the quality of the information based on where it comes from. For example, one study (Hanel et al., 2018) found that we are more likely to believe information that comes from a group we are affiliated with than one we are not. They found that Christians are more likely to accept an aphorism (a short observation assumed to be truthful, such as, "If it ain't broke, don't fix it") than atheists are, if both are told that the aphorism comes from a Bible verse. They found the same pattern for Democrats and Republicans in the United States. Interestingly, we assume our chosen groups are more similar to us and out groups are more dissimilar than they typically are. For example, evangelicals in the United States believe that the Republican party has more evangelicals than it does, and that the Democratic party has more atheists than is in fact the case (Claassen et al., 2019).

Normative influence and group polarization

As Leon Festinger (1954) argued in his influential theory of social comparison, and as already discussed in Chapter 2, it is human nature to want to evaluate our abilities and opinions, something we can do by comparing our views with those of others. We are most persuaded by people in our "reference groups"—that is, groups we identify with (Abrams et al., 1990; Hogg, Turner, & Davidson, 1990). Moreover, because we want people to like us, we may express stronger opinions after discovering that others share our views.

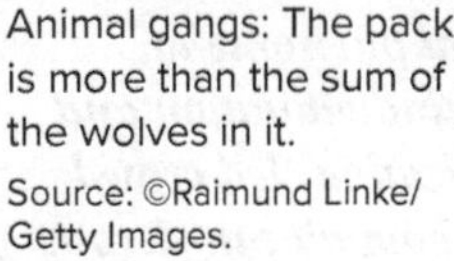
Animal gangs: The pack is more than the sum of the wolves in it.
Source: ©Raimund Linke/Getty Images.

pluralistic ignorance A false impression of how other people are thinking, feeling, or responding.

When we ask people (as we asked you earlier in the Rehtaeh Parsons case) to predict how others would respond to social dilemmas, they typically exhibit **pluralistic ignorance**: They don't realize how strongly others support the socially preferred tendency. Typically, people will say that they would never act the way those teenagers did. (This finding is reminiscent of the self-serving bias: People tend to view themselves as a better-than-average embodiment of socially desirable traits and attitudes.)

Perhaps you have been in the situation where you have wanted to go out with someone, but you were afraid to make the first move. You wait and watch, but the other person doesn't seem to be expressing any interest in you, so you think that they would probably reject you. Have you ever stopped to think that the other person might be doing the same thing you are? University of Manitoba researchers Jacquie Vorauer and Rebecca Ratner (1996) have shown that such reactions make it difficult for people to start up relationships.

Dale Miller and Cathy McFarland (1987) created a similar phenomenon in a laboratory experiment. They asked people to read an article and to seek help if they ran into "any really serious problems in understanding the paper." Although the article was incomprehensible, none of the subjects sought help, but they presumed other subjects would not be similarly restrained by fear of embarrassment. They wrongly inferred that people who didn't seek help didn't need any. To overcome such pluralistic ignorance, someone must break the ice and enable others to reveal and reinforce their shared reactions.

Social comparison theory prompted experiments that exposed people to others' positions but not to their arguments. This is roughly the experience we have when reading the results of an opinion poll. When people learn others' positions—without discussion—will they adjust their responses to maintain a socially favourable position? When people have made no prior commitment to a particular response, seeing others' responses does stimulate a small polarization (Goethals & Zanna, 1979; Sanders & Baron, 1977). (See Figure 7–9 for an example.) This polarization from mere social comparison is usually

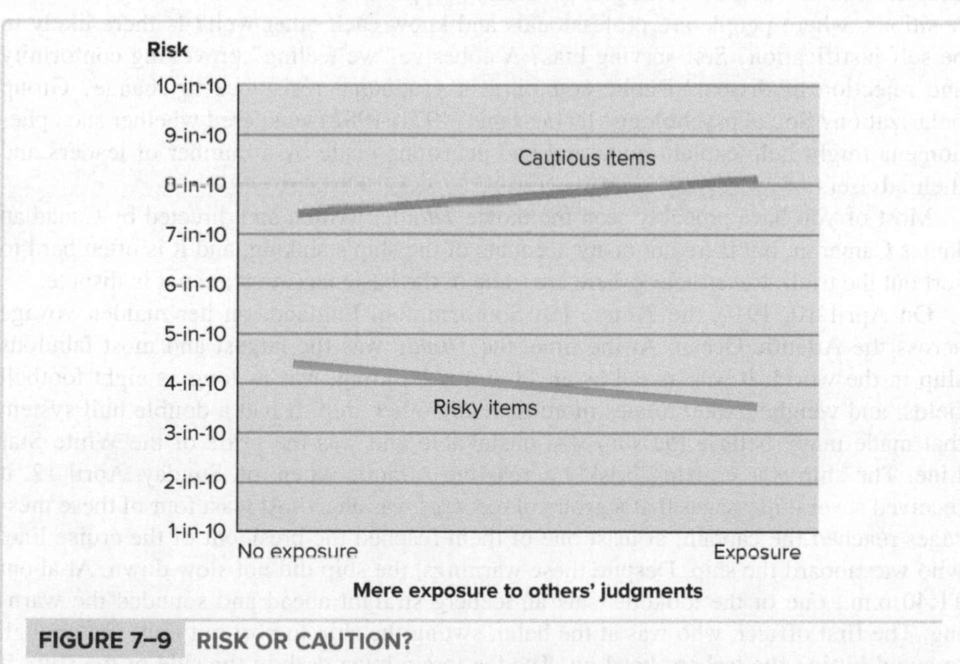

FIGURE 7–9 RISK OR CAUTION?

On "risky" dilemma items, mere exposure to others' judgments enhanced individuals' risk-prone tendencies. On "cautious" dilemma items, exposure to others' judgments enhanced their cautiousness.

less than that produced by a lively discussion. Still, it's surprising that, instead of simply conforming to the group average, people often go it one better.

Merely learning others' choices also contributes to the bandwagon effect that creates blockbuster songs, books, and movies. Sociologist Matthew Salganik and colleagues (2006) experimented with the phenomenon by engaging 14 341 Internet participants in listening to and, if they wished, downloading previously unknown songs. The researchers randomly assigned some participants to a condition that disclosed previous participants' download choices. Among those given that information, popular songs became more popular and unpopular songs became less popular.

Group polarization research illustrates the complexity of social–psychological inquiry. As much as we like our explanations of a phenomenon to be simple, one explanation seldom accounts for all the data. Because people are complex, more than one factor frequently influences an outcome. In group discussions, persuasive arguments predominate on issues that have a factual element ("Is she guilty of the crime?"). Social comparison sways responses on value-laden judgments ("How long a sentence should she serve?") (Kaplan, 1989). On the many issues that have both factual and value-laden aspects, the two factors work together. Discovering that others share one's feelings (social comparison) unleashes arguments (informational influence) supporting what everyone secretly favours.

Groupthink: Do Groups Hinder or Assist Good Decisions?

When do group influences hinder smart decisions? When do groups promote good decisions, and how can we lead groups to make optimal decisions?

Do the social–psychological phenomena we have been considering in these first seven chapters occur in sophisticated groups, such as corporate boards, or in senior government positions, where people are professionals and know each other well? Is there likely to be self-justification? Self-serving bias? A cohesive "we feeling" provoking conformity and rejection of dissent? Public commitment producing resistance to change? Group polarization? Social psychologist Irving Janis (1971, 1982) wondered whether such phenomena might help explain good and bad decisions made by a number of leaders and their advisers.

Most of you have probably seen the movie *Titanic,* written and directed by Canadian James Cameron, but there are many accounts of the ship's sinking, and it is often hard to sort out the truth. Nevertheless, here are some of the basic facts that are not in dispute.

On April 10, 1912, the *Titanic* left Southampton, England, on her maiden voyage across the Atlantic Ocean. At the time, the *Titanic* was the largest and most fabulous ship in the world. It was as tall as an 11-storey building, was as long as eight football fields, and weighed 1000 tonnes more than any other ship. It had a double hull system that made many believe the ship was unsinkable and was the pride of the White Star Line. The ship was cruising briskly across the Atlantic when, on Sunday, April 12, it received several messages that a group of icebergs was ahead. At least four of these messages reached the captain; at least one of them reached the president of the cruise line, who was aboard the ship. Despite these warnings, the ship did not slow down. At about 11:40 p.m., one of the lookouts saw an iceberg straight ahead and sounded the warning. The first officer, who was at the helm, swung the ship to port but only fast enough to avoid hitting the iceberg head-on. The ice tore a huge gash in the side of the ship. It didn't take crew members a great deal of time to know the extent of the damage—by 12:15 a.m., they knew the ship was going to sink. The *Titanic* had only 20 lifeboats, which was not even enough for half of the passengers. These lifeboats were lowered and

Groupthink on a titanic scale. Despite four messages of possible icebergs ahead, Captain Edward Smith—a directive and respected leader—kept his ship sailing at full speed into the night. There was an illusion of invulnerability (many believed the ship to be unsinkable). There was conformity pressure (crew mates chided the lookout for not being able to use his naked eye and dismissed his misgivings). And there was mindguarding (a *Titanic* telegraph operator failed to pass the last and most complete iceberg warning to Captain Smith).

Source: ©Everett Historical/Shutterstock.

filled—or only partially filled—with passengers, and distress calls were sent out to other ships. The ship finally went under at 2:20 a.m. Only 705 people survived the shipwreck; at least twice that many died. The exact number is one of the facts that is in dispute: Estimates range from 1490 to 1635.

Janis believed that such tragedies could be traced to the tendency of decision-making groups to suppress dissent in the interests of group harmony, a phenomenon he called **groupthink**. In work groups, camaraderie boosts productivity (Mullen & Copper, 1994; Mellers et al., 2014). Moreover, team spirit is good for morale, and a shared group identity motivates people to persist (Haslam et al., 2014). But when making decisions, close-knit groups may pay a price. Janis believed that the soil from which groupthink sprouts includes an amiable, cohesive group; relative isolation of the group from dissenting viewpoints; and a directive leader who signals what decision is favoured. When deciding what to do with the threat of the icebergs ahead, there is little doubt that Captain Edward J. Smith, the senior captain of the cruise line, who had served for 38 years, was a respected and directive leader. He and his crew enjoyed a strong *esprit de corps*. As one source (Lord, 1955) put it, Smith was "worshiped by crew and passenger alike. … They loved everything about him." It is also clear that in the middle of the Atlantic, they were isolated from other points of view. It is quite possible that groupthink may have influenced their decision making. Let's see if they displayed the symptoms of groupthink.

groupthink The tendency for groups, in the process of decision making, to suppress dissenting cognitions in the interest of ensuring harmony within the group.

Symptoms of Groupthink

From historical records and the memoirs of participants and observers, Janis identified eight groupthink symptoms. These symptoms are a collective form of dissonance reduction that surfaces as group members try to maintain the positive group feeling when facing a threat (Turner et al., 1992; Turner & Pratkanis, 1994, 1997).

The first two groupthink symptoms lead group members to overestimate their group's might and right:

- *An illusion of invulnerability:* There is little question that Captain Smith and his crew had developed an illusion that nothing bad could happen to them or their ship. Five years before the crash, it was clear that Smith believed a disaster with loss of life could not happen to one of his ships. He was quoted as saying, "I cannot conceive of any vital disaster happening … Modern shipbuilding has gone beyond that" (Marshall, 1912). As the ship departed from Southampton, one of the crew members expressed a view that seemed to be widespread. When asked if the *Titanic* was really unsinkable, he replied, "God Himself could not sink this ship" (Lord, 1955).
- *Unquestioned belief in the group's morality:* Group members assume the inherent morality of their group and ignore ethical and moral issues. Looking back on the tragedy of the *Titanic,* it is clear that there should have been more lifeboats aboard the vessel, and, sadly, this would not have been difficult. But the builders of the ship and especially the president of the cruise line decided they were not needed.

Group members also become closed-minded:

- *Rationalization:* The group discounts challenges by collectively justifying its decisions. The officers on the *Titanic* knew they were in the vicinity of icebergs, but they continued on at full speed. In one critical conversation at 9:00 p.m., the second officer and Captain Smith discussed how they should handle the ship. Both knew that they were in the vicinity of icebergs, but Smith remarked that it was an exceptionally clear night and, therefore, they did not need to slow down (Davie, 1986).
- *Stereotyped view of opponent:* One of the most controversial stories surrounding the *Titanic* is whether the ship was trying to break a speed record in crossing the Atlantic. You may recall that the movie *Titanic* portrayed the president of the cruise line as pressuring the captain to do so. This story has been suggested several times and many believe it—even though the president of the cruise line, who survived, vehemently denied it. One reason the story is believable to some is that the shipping business was intensely competitive in the early 1900s; cruise lines had very derogatory views of other cruise lines. These stereotyped views of their opponents might well have led Smith and his crew to ignore the warnings from other ships.

Self-censorship contributes to an illusion of unanimity.
Source: ©Henry Martin.

Finally, the group suffers from pressures toward uniformity:

- *Conformity pressure:* Group members rebuff those who raise doubts about the group's assumptions and plans, at times not by argument but by ridicule. When Frederick Fleet—the lookout who eventually saw the iceberg—complained that the crew did not have binoculars, he was chided by his colleagues for not being able to use his naked eye.
- *Self-censorship:* Since disagreements are often uncomfortable and the group seems to be in consensus, members often withhold or discount their misgivings (Hampton et al., 2014). Despite Fleet's belief that he needed a pair of binoculars for his task as a lookout, he did not suggest that they pick up a new pair at the next port. He was at a loss to describe his failure to do so. He maintained until his dying day that if he had had a pair of binoculars, he would have seen the iceberg soon enough to avoid hitting it.

- *Illusion of unanimity:* Self-censorship and pressure not to puncture the consensus create an illusion of unanimity. What is more, the apparent consensus confirms the group's decision. Did none of the experienced crew on the *Titanic* think they should slow down? It seems likely that the apparent unanimity about the decision to go full speed ahead was merely an illusion. This sort of illusion has been seen in other groups as well. Albert Speer (1971), an adviser to Hitler, described the atmosphere around Hitler as one where pressure to conform suppressed all deviance. The absence of dissent created the illusion of unanimity.
- *Mindguards:* Some members protect the group from information that would call into question the effectiveness or the morality of its decisions. The telegraph operator on the *Titanic* provided a compelling example of this symptom. After receiving several warning messages about icebergs, he failed to take down the final and most complete message about the iceberg that was struck and he failed to pass this message to the captain. Thus the operator deprived Captain Smith of the latest information that would have challenged Smith's decision to go full steam ahead.

People "are never so likely to settle a question rightly as when they discuss it freely."

John Stuart Mill, *On Liberty,* 1859

Groupthink symptoms can produce a failure to seek and discuss contrary information and alternative possibilities. When a leader promotes an idea and when a group insulates itself from dissenting views, groupthink may produce defective decisions (McCauley, 1989).

The management of the Walkerton, Ontario, water crisis in May 2000 by Stan Koebel, who ran the water treatment plant, shows many of the symptoms of groupthink. Koebel and his employees certainly showed an illusion of invulnerability. They believed that the water in Walkerton had always been safe and that little needed to be done to ensure its safety. They viewed the new chlorinator that they had never installed as unnecessary. Koebel even continued to drink tap water long after people began getting sick and he knew that the water had tested positive for *E. coli.* The men at the water plant also engaged in massive rationalization. Even though they, too, knew that the water had tested positive for contaminants, they continued to believe for days that the water was not what was making people sick. Self-censorship was also an important part of the group's response. Frank Koebel (Stan's brother) testified in the inquiry into the crisis that he knew the failure to chlorinate the water and to take proper samples could lead to problems, but he never raised his objections to his brother. Finally, the group clearly employed mindguards by failing to report the results of the tainted water to the Ministry of the Environment and the chief medical officer of health.

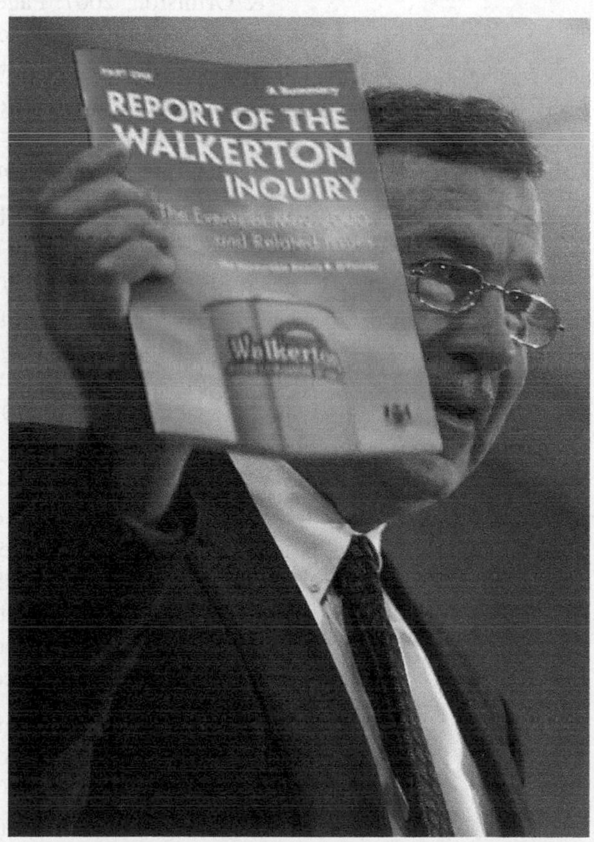

The contaminated water tragedy in Walkerton, Ontario, demonstrated the negative aspects of groupthink in action. Source: The Canadian Press/Frank Gunn.

How the COVID-19 pandemic is handled worldwide will undoubtedly induce significant discussion around the role of groupthink in decision making across the globe. While some countries and regions (e.g., New Zealand, South Korea, Taiwan, Alberta, the Maritime provinces) are being lauded for their rapid and effective response, others (e.g., Iran, the United Kingdom, the United States and Florida in particular) are being sharply criticized for their perceived lack of action in the face of "clear" warnings. For example, public health officials in Alberta saw the risks far enough ahead of the pandemic to order more supplies than they needed (and in fact shared with the rest of Canada; CBC, 2020b), whereas the U.S. federal government has been lambasted for failing to prepare and downplaying the severity of the crisis until it was too late.

Critiquing Groupthink

Although Janis's ideas and observations have received enormous attention, some researchers are skeptical (Fuller & Aldag, 1998; Hart, 1998). The evidence being retrospective, Janis could pick supporting cases.

Some follow-up experiments have supported aspects of Janis's theory:

- Directive leadership is indeed associated with poorer decisions because subordinates sometimes feel too weak or insecure to speak up (Granstrom & Stiwne, 1998; McCauley, 1998).
- Groups that make smart decisions have widely distributed conversation, with socially attuned members who take turns speaking (Woolley et al., 2010).
- Groups do prefer supporting over challenging information (Schulz-Hardt et al., 2000).
- When members look to a group for acceptance, approval, and social identity, they may suppress disagreeable thoughts (Hogg & Hains, 1998; Turner & Pratkanis, 1997).
- Groups that have broad discussions, and take turns speaking, make better decisions (Woolley et al., 2010). Group success depends on what the group members know and how effective they are at sharing that information (Bonner & Baumann, 2012).
- Groups with diverse perspectives outperform groups of like-minded experts (Nemeth & Ormiston, 2007; Page, 2007). Engaging people who think differently from you can make you feel uncomfortable; but compared with comfortably homogeneous groups, diverse groups tend to produce more ideas and greater creativity.
- In discussion, information that is shared by group members does tend to dominate and crowd out unshared information, meaning that groups often do not benefit from all that their members know (Sunstein & Hastie, 2008).

Yet, friendships need not breed groupthink (Esser, 1998; Mullen et al., 1994). In a secure, highly cohesive group (say, a family), committed members will often care enough to voice disagreement (Packer, 2009). The norms of a cohesive group can favour either consensus, which can lead to groupthink, or critical analysis, which prevents it (Postmes, Spears, & Cihangir, 2001). When Philip Tetlock and his colleagues (1992) looked at a broader sample of historical episodes, it became clear that even good group procedures sometimes yield ill-fated decisions.

Preventing Groupthink

Flawed group dynamics help explain many failed decisions; sometimes too many cooks spoil the broth. But, given open leadership, a cohesive team spirit can improve decisions. Sometimes two (or more) heads are better than one.

In search of conditions that breed good decisions, Janis also analyzed successful ventures. Janis's (1982) recommendations for preventing groupthink incorporate many of the following effective group procedures:

- Be impartial; do not endorse any position. Don't start group discussions by having people state their positions; doing so suppresses information sharing and degrades the quality of decisions (Mojzisch & Schulz-Hardt, 2010).
- Encourage critical evaluation; assign a "devil's advocate." Better yet, welcome the input of a genuine critic, which does even more to stimulate original thinking and to open a group to opposing views, report Charlan Nemeth and her colleagues (Nemeth, Brown, & Rogers, 2001; Nemeth, Connell, et al., 2001).

- Occasionally subdivide the group, and then reunite to air differences.
- Welcome critiques from outside experts and associates.
- Before implementing a decision, call a "second-chance" meeting to air any lingering doubts.

Some of these practical principles for improved group dynamics are now being taught to airline flight crews. Training programs called crew resource management developed from the realization that flight crew mistakes contribute to more than two-thirds of plane accidents. Having two or three people in the cockpit should increase the odds that someone will notice a problem or see its solution—if the information is shared. Sometimes, however, groupthink pressures lead to conformity or self-censorship.

On the night of September 2, 1998, Swissair Flight 111 crashed just off of Peggy's Cove, Nova Scotia, killing all 229 people on board. The crash appears to have occurred because faulty wiring led to a fire in the cockpit. Several stories in the media reported that the two pilots were at odds over how to respond to the fire. These reports suggested that the co-pilot wanted to forget about procedure and land the plane immediately. The pilot, on the other hand, was allegedly firm in his insistence that they follow the standard procedure and was so busy with a checklist that he was not able to discuss a plan of action with the co-pilot. Could these faulty group dynamics have played a role in the crash? We do not even know if the media reports are accurate, but faulty group dynamics have been linked to other crashes (Helmrich, 1997).

But not always. In 1989, a three-person crew facing a similar problem responded as a model team to imminent disaster. The crew, which had been trained in crew resource management, faced the disintegration of the centre engine, severing lines to the rudder and ailerons needed to manoeuvre the plane. In the 34 minutes before crash-landing just short of the airport runway, the crew had to devise a strategy for bringing the plane under control, assessing damage, choosing a landing site, and preparing the crew and passengers for the crash. Minute-by-minute analysis of the cockpit conversation revealed intense interaction—31 communications per minute (one per second at the incident's peak). In those minutes, the crew members recruited a fourth pilot, who was flying as a passenger, prioritized their work, and kept one another aware of unfolding events and decisions. Junior crew members freely suggested alternatives, and the captain responded with appropriate commands. Bursts of social conversation provided emotional support, enabling the crew to cope with the extreme stress and to save the lives of 185 of the 296 people on board.

Effective group dynamics enabled the crew of a disabled Denver-to-Chicago United Airlines flight to devise a technique for steering by adjusting relative power from its two remaining engines, enabling the survival of most passengers. Recognizing the importance of cockpit group dynamics, airlines now provide crew management training and seek pilots who are capable of functioning as team members.
Source: ©Bettmann/Getty Images.

Group Problem Solving

Not every group decision is flawed by groupthink. Under some conditions, two or more heads *are* better than one. Patrick Laughlin and his colleagues (Laughlin, 1996; Laughlin & Adamopoulos, 1980; Laughlin et al., 2003) have shown this with various intellectual tasks. Consider one of their analogy problems:

Assertion is to *disproved* as *action* is to

1. *hindered*
2. *opposed*
3. *illegal*
4. *precipitate*
5. *thwarted*

Most university students miss this question when answering alone but choose the correct answer (*thwarted*) after discussion. Moreover, Laughlin finds that if two members of a six-person group are initially correct, two-thirds of the time they convince all the others. (If only one person is correct, on the other hand, this "minority of one" almost three-fourths of the time fails to convince the group.) And when given tricky logic problems, three, four, or five heads are better than two (Laughlin et al., 2006).

Several heads critiquing each other can also allow the group to avoid some forms of cognitive bias and produce some higher-quality ideas (McGlynn, Tubbs, & Holzhausen, 1995; Wright, Lüüs, & Christie, 1990). In science, the benefits of diverse minds collaborating have led to more and more "team science"—to an increasing proportion of scientific publication, especially highly cited publication, by multi-author teams (Cacioppo, 2007). However, this diversity can backfire if there is interpersonal relationship conflict between the members. Culturally diverse groups make better decisions, as long as the members of the group can get along (Manata, 2019; Maznevski, 1994). We will discuss more on this topic in Chapter 12.

But, contrary to the popular idea that face-to-face brainstorming generates more creative ideas than do the same people working alone, researchers agree it isn't so (Paulus, Dzindolet, & Kohn, 2011; Paulus, Larey, & Ortega, 1995; Paulus & Yang, 2000; Stroebe & Diehl, 1994). People feel more productive when generating ideas in groups, but, time and again, researchers have found that people working alone generate more good ideas (Nijstad, Stroebe, & Lodewijkx, 2006; Rietzschel, Nijstad, & Stroebe, 2006).

Large brainstorming groups are especially inefficient. In accordance with social loafing theory, large groups cause some individuals to free-ride on others' efforts. In accordance with normative influence theory, they cause others to feel apprehensive about voicing oddball ideas. Large groups can cause "production blocking"—losing one's ideas while awaiting a turn to speak (Nijstad & Stroebe, 2006). And contrary to the popular idea that brainstorming is most productive when the brainstormers are admonished "not to criticize," encouraging people to debate ideas appears to stimulate ideas and to extend creative thinking beyond the brainstorming session (Nemeth et al., 2004).

Creative work teams tend to be small and to alternate working alone, working in pairs, and meeting as a circle (Paulus & Coskun, 2012). Moreover, when leaders urge people to generate lots of ideas (rather than just good ideas), they generate both more ideas *and* more good ideas (Paulus et al., 2011). Finally, writing down ideas, and sharing ideas via electronic means, may enhance the positive effects of brainstorming (Brown & Paulus, 2002; Heslin, 2009; Kohn, Paulus, & Choi, 2011).

As James Watson and Francis Crick demonstrated in discovering DNA, challenging two-person conversations can more effectively engage creative thinking. Watson later recalled that he and Crick benefited from *not* being the most brilliant people seeking to crack the genetic code. The most brilliant researcher, Rosalind Franklin, "was so intelligent that she rarely sought advice" (quoted by Cialdini, 2005). If you are (and regard yourself as) the most gifted person, why seek others' input? Like Watson and Crick, psychologists Daniel Kahneman and the late Amos Tversky similarly collaborated in their exploration of intuition and its influence on economic decision making. (See "The Inside Story" shown next.)

THE INSIDE STORY

In the spring of 1969, Amos Tversky, my younger colleague at the Hebrew University of Jerusalem, and I met over lunch and shared our own recurrent errors of judgment. From there were born our studies of human intuition.

I had enjoyed collaboration before, but this was magical. Amos was very smart, and also very funny. We could spend hours of solid work in continuous mirth. His work was always characterized by confidence and by a crisp elegance, and it was a joy to find those characteristics now attached to my ideas as well. As we were writing our first paper, I was conscious of how much better it was than the more hesitant piece I would have written by myself.

All our ideas were jointly owned. We did almost all the work on our joint projects while physically together, including the drafting of questionnaires and papers. Our principle was to discuss every disagreement until it had been resolved to our mutual satisfaction.

Source: Skypixel/Dreamstime.com/GetStock.com.

Some of the greatest joys of our collaboration—and probably much of its success—came from our ability to elaborate on each other's nascent thoughts: If I expressed a half-formed idea, I knew that Amos would be there to understand it, probably more clearly than I did, and that if it had merit, he would see it.

Amos and I shared the wonder of together owning a goose that could lay golden eggs—a joint mind that was better than our separate minds. We were a team, and we remained in that mode for well over a decade. The Nobel Prize was awarded for work that we produced during that period of intense collaboration.

Daniel Kahneman *Princeton University, Nobel Laureate, 2002*

The wisdom of groups is evident in everyday life as well as in the laboratory:

- *Weather forecasting.* "Two forecasters will come up with a forecast that is more accurate than either would have come up with working alone," reported Joel Myers (1997), president of the largest private forecasting service.
- *Google.* Google has become the dominant search engine by harnessing what James Surowiecki (2004) called "the wisdom of crowds." Google interprets a link to Page X as a vote for Page X, and weights most heavily links from pages that are themselves highly ranked. Harnessing the democratic character of the web, Google often takes less than one-tenth of a second to lead you right to what you want. Unfortunately, the data that tech companies collect can be used in more nefarious ways as well, using our data to target us with ads and political messages.
- *Game shows.* For a befuddled contestant on *Who Wants to Be a Millionaire?*, a valuable lifeline was to "ask the audience," which usually offered wisdom superior to the contestant's intuition. This is because the average judgment from a crowd of people typically errs less than does the average judgment by an individual.
- *The "crowd within."* Likewise, the average of different guesses from the same person tends to surpass the person's individual guesses (Herzog & Hertwig, 2009). Edward Vul and Harold Pashler (2008) discovered this when asking people to guess the correct answers to factual questions, such as "What percentage of the world's airports are in the United States?" Then the researchers asked their participants to make a second guess, either immediately or three weeks later. The result? "You can gain about one-tenth as much from asking yourself the same question twice as you can from getting a second opinion from someone else, but if you wait three weeks, the benefit of re-asking yourself the same question rises to one-third the value of a second opinion."

- *Prediction markets.* In U.S. presidential elections since 1988, the final public opinion polls have provided a good gauge to the election result (with the exception of the 2016 race, which heavily favoured Hillary Clinton but which Donald Trump won in a landslide). An even better predictor, however, has been the Iowa Election Market. Taking everything (including polls) into account, people buy and sell shares in candidates. Other prediction markets have harnessed collective wisdom in gauging the likelihood of other events, such as an avian flu epidemic (Arrow et al., 2008; Stix, 2008).

Thus, we can conclude that when information from many diverse people is combined, all of us together can become smarter than almost any of us alone. We're in some ways like a flock of geese, no one of which has a perfect navigational sense. Nevertheless, by staying close to one another, a group of geese can navigate accurately. The flock is smarter than the bird.

Leadership: How Do Leaders Shape the Group's Actions?

What is leadership, and what roles do effective leaders perform in groups?

In 1910, the Norwegians and the English engaged in an epic race to the South Pole. The Norwegians, effectively led by Roald Amundsen, made it. The English, ineptly led by Robert Falcon Scott, did not; Scott and three team members died. Some coaches of sports teams move from team to team, transforming losers into winners each time; for example, Scotty Bowman led three different teams to Stanley Cup championships. What makes one leader effective and another a failure? This is something social psychologists have been investigating for some time.

Task Leadership and Social Leadership

Some leaders are formally appointed or elected; others emerge informally as the group interacts. What makes for good **leadership** often depends on the situation; the best person to lead an engineering team may not make the best leader of a sales force. Some people excel at *task leadership:* organizing work, setting standards, and focusing on goal attainment. Others excel at *social leadership:* building teamwork, mediating conflicts, and being supportive.

leadership The process by which certain group members motivate and guide the group.

Task leaders often have a directive style—one that can work well if the leader is bright enough to give good orders (Fiedler, 1987). Being goal oriented, such leaders also keep the group's attention and effort focused on its mission. Experiments show that the combination of specific, challenging goals and periodic progress reports helps motivate high achievement (Locke & Latham, 1990, 2002, 2009). Men that exhibit "masculine" traits—e.g., height, fitness, wide faces—tend to be perceived as dominant leaders and to be successful CEOs (Blaker et al., 2013; Wong et al., 2011).

Social leaders often have a democratic style: one that delegates authority, welcomes input from team members, and, as we have seen, helps prevent groupthink. Women, in general, are more egalitarian than men and are more likely to oppose hierarchies (Lee et al., 2011). Many experiments reveal that such leadership is good for morale. Group members usually feel more satisfied when they participate in making decisions (Spector, 1986; Vanderslice, Rice, & Julian, 1987). Given control over their tasks, workers also become more motivated to achieve (Burger, 1987). People who value good group feeling and take pride in achievement, therefore, thrive under democratic leadership (Lortie-Lussier, Lemieux, & Godbout, 1989).

Women more often than men have a democratic leadership style.

Eagly & Johnson, 1990

Participative management, illustrated in this "quality circle," requires democratic rather than autocratic leaders.

Source: ©Stockbroker/MBI /Alamy Stock Photo.

Democratic leadership can be seen in the move by many businesses toward participative management, a management style common in Sweden and Japan (Naylor, 1990; Sundstrom, De Meuse, & Futrell, 1990). Ironically, a major influence on this "Japanese-style" management was social psychologist Kurt Lewin. In laboratory and factory experiments, Lewin and his students demonstrated the benefits of inviting workers to participate in decision making. Shortly before the Second World War, Lewin visited Japan and explained his findings to industrial and academic leaders (Nisbett & Ross, 1991). Japan's collectivist culture provided a receptive audience for Lewin's ideas about teamwork. Eventually, his influence circled back to North America.

Transactional Leadership

The once-popular "great person" theory of leadership—that all great leaders share certain traits—has fallen into disrepute. Effective leadership styles, we now know, vary with the situation. People who know what they are doing may resent task leadership, while those who don't may welcome it. Recently, however, social psychologists have again wondered if there might be qualities that mark a good leader in many situations (Hogan, Curphy, & Hogan, 1994). British social psychologists Peter Smith and Monir Tayeb (1989) reported that studies done in India, Taiwan, and Iran found that the most effective supervisors in coal mines, banks, and government offices score high on tests of both task and social leadership. They are actively concerned with how work is progressing and sensitive to the needs of their subordinates.

These transactional leaders (Hollander, 1958) focus on getting to know their subordinates and listening carefully. They seek to fulfill the subordinates' needs but maintain high expectations for how subordinates will perform. Such leaders, who allow people to express their opinions, both learn from others and receive strong support from their followers (Tyler, Rasinski, & Spodick, 1985).

Transformational Leadership

Studies also reveal that many effective leaders of laboratory groups, work teams, and large corporations exhibit behaviours that help make a minority view persuasive. Such leaders engender trust by consistently sticking to their goals. And they often exude a self-confident charisma that kindles the allegiance of their followers (Bennis, 1984; House & Singh, 1987; Tintoré, 2019). Charismatic leaders typically have a compelling vision of some desired state of affairs, an ability to communicate this to others in clear and simple language, and enough optimism and faith in their group to inspire others to follow.

In one analysis of 50 Dutch companies, the highest morale was at firms with chief executives who most inspired their colleagues "to transcend their own self-interests for the sake of the collective" (de Hoogh et al., 2004). Leadership of this kind—transformational leadership—motivates others to identify with and commit themselves to the group's mission. Transformational leaders—many of whom are charismatic, energetic, self-confident extroverts—articulate high standards, inspire people to share their vision, and offer personal attention (Bono & Judge, 2004). The frequent result of such leadership in organizations is a more engaged, trusting, and effective workforce (Turner et al., 2002).

To be sure, groups also influence their leaders. Sometimes, those at the front of the herd have simply sensed where it is already heading. Political candidates know how to read the opinion polls. A leader who deviates too radically from the group's standards may be rejected. Smart leaders usually remain with the majority and spend their influence prudently. Nevertheless, effective individual leaders can sometimes exhibit a type of minority influence by mobilizing and guiding their group's energy.

When an apt combination of intelligence, skill, determination, self-confidence, and social charisma meets a rare opportunity, the result is sometimes a new government, a Nobel Prize, or a social revolution.

The Influence of the Minority: How Do Individuals Influence the Group?

Groups influence individuals, but when—and how—do individuals influence their groups?

Each chapter in this social influence unit concludes with a reminder of our power as individuals. We have seen these phenomena:

- Persuasive forces are powerful, but we can resist persuasion by making public commitments and by anticipating persuasive appeals.
- Pressures to conform sometimes overwhelm our better judgment, but blatant pressure can motivate us to assert our individuality and freedom.
- The groups we create and belong to influence our behaviour; but if we act consistently, we can sometimes influence the group.

This chapter has emphasized group influences on the individual, so we conclude by seeing how individuals and minorities can influence their groups. (Note that in this context, "minority influence" refers to minority opinions, not to ethnic minorities.)

At the beginning of most social movements, a small minority will sometimes sway, and then even become, the majority. "All history," wrote Ralph Waldo Emerson, "is a record of the power of minorities, and of minorities of one." For good or bad, minorities of one often have a huge impact. Innovative minorities also make technological history—think Steve Jobs, Elon Musk, and Mark Zuckerberg.

What makes a minority persuasive? What might the crew of the *Titanic* have done to convince Captain Smith that the ship needed to slow down? Experiments initiated by Serge Moscovici in Paris have identified several determinants of minority influence: consistency, self-confidence, and defection.

Consistency

More influential than a minority that wavers is a minority that sticks to its position. Moscovici and his associates (Moscovici, 1985; Moscovici, Lage, & Naffrechoux, 1969) found that if a minority consistently judges blue slides as green, members of the majority will occasionally agree. But if the minority wavers, saying "blue" to one-third of the blue slides and "green" to the rest, virtually no one in the majority will ever agree with "green."

> ***"If the single man plant himself indomitably on his instincts, and there abide, the huge world will come round to him."***
>
> Ralph Waldo Emerson, *Nature, Address, and Lectures: The American Scholar,* 1849

Experiments show—and experience confirms—that nonconformity, especially persistent nonconformity, is often painful (Levine, 1989; Lücken & Simon, 2005). That helps explain a *minority slowness effect*—a tendency for people with minority views to express them less quickly than people in the majority (Bassili, 2003). If you set out to be Emerson's minority of one, prepare yourself for ridicule—especially when you argue an issue that's personally relevant to the majority and when the group wants to settle an issue by reaching consensus (Kameda & Sugimori, 1993; Kruglanski & Webster, 1991; Trost, Maass, & Kenrick, 1992). Even when people in the majority know that the disagreeing person is factually or morally right, they may still, unless they change their position, dislike the person (Chan, Louis, & Jetten, 2010).

People may attribute your dissent to psychological peculiarities (Papastamou & Mugny, 1990). When Charlan Nemeth (1979, 2011) planted a minority of two within a simulated jury and had them oppose the majority's opinions, the two were inevitably disliked. Nevertheless, the majority acknowledged that the persistence of the two did more than anything else to make them rethink their positions. Compared to majority influence that often triggers unthinking agreement, minority influence stimulates a deeper processing of arguments, often with increased creativity (Kenworthy et al., 2008; Martin, Hewstone, & Martin, 2007; Martin et al., 2008).

On the other hand, a minority may stimulate creative thinking (Martin, 1996; Mucchi-Faina, Maass, & Volpato, 1991; Peterson & Nemeth, 1996). With dissent from within one's own group, people take in more information, think about the issue in new ways, and often make better decisions (Page, 2007). Believing that one need not win friends to influence people, Nemeth quotes Oscar Wilde: "We dislike arguments of any kind; they are always vulgar, and often convincing."

A persistent minority is influential, even if not popular, partly because it soon becomes the focus of debate (Schachter, 1951). Being the centre of conversation allows one to contribute a disproportionate number of arguments. And Nemeth reported that in experiments on minority influence, as in the studies dealing with group polarization, the position supported by the most arguments usually wins. Talkative group members are usually influential (Mullen, Salas, & Driskell, 1989).

Self-Confidence

Consistency and persistence convey self-confidence. Furthermore, Nemeth and Joel Wachtler (1974) reported that any behaviour by a minority that conveys self-confidence—for example, taking the head seat at the table—tends to raise self-doubts among the majority. By being firm and forceful, the minority's apparent self-assurance may prompt the majority to reconsider its position. This is especially so on matters of opinion rather than fact. In research at Italy's University of Padova, Anne Maass and her colleagues (1996) reported that minorities are less persuasive regarding fact ("From which country does Italy import most of its raw oil?") than regarding attitude ("From which country should Italy import most of its raw oil?").

Defections From the Majority

A persistent minority punctures any illusion of unanimity. When a minority consistently doubts the majority wisdom, majority members become freer to express their own doubts and may even switch to the minority position. John Levine (1989) found that a minority person who had defected from the majority was more persuasive than a consistent minority voice. In her jury-simulation experiments, Nemeth found that once defections begin, others often soon follow, initiating a snowball effect.

Are these factors that strengthen minority influence unique to minorities? Sharon Wolf and Bibb Latané (1985; Wolf, 1987) and Russell Clark (1995) believed not. They argued that the same social forces work for both majorities and minorities. Informational and normative influence fuels both group polarization and minority influence. And if consistency, self-confidence, and defections from the other side strengthen the minority, such variables also strengthen a majority. The social impact of any position depends on the strength, immediacy, and number of those who support it. Minorities have less influence than majorities simply because they are smaller.

Anne Maass and Russell Clark (1984, 1986) agreed with Moscovici, however, that minorities are more likely to convert people to accepting their views. And from their analyses of how groups evolve over time, John Levine and Richard Moreland (1985) concluded that new recruits to a group exert a different type of minority influence than do longtime members. Newcomers exert influence through the attention they receive and the group awareness they trigger in the old-timers. Established members feel freer to dissent and to exert leadership.

There is a delightful irony in this emphasis on how individuals can influence the group. Until this research was done, the idea that the minority could sway the majority was itself a minority view in social psychology. Nevertheless, by arguing consistently and forcefully, Moscovici, Nemeth, Maass, Clark, and others have convinced the majority of group influence researchers that minority influence is a phenomenon worthy of study.

And the way that several of these minority influence researchers came by their interests should, perhaps, not surprise us. Anne Maass (1998) became interested in how minorities could effect social change after growing up in post-war Germany and hearing her grandmother's personal accounts of fascism. Charlan Nemeth (1999) developed her interest while she was a visiting professor in Europe "working with Henri Tajfel and Serge Moscovici. The three of us were 'outsiders'—I am an American Roman Catholic female in Europe, they having survived World War II as Eastern European Jews. Sensitivity to the value and the struggles of the minority perspective came to dominate our work."

Group Influences in Juries

Imagine a jury that, having finished a trial, has entered the jury room to begin its deliberations. Researchers Harry Kalven and Hans Zeisel (1966) reported that chances are about two in three that the jurors will initially *not* agree on a verdict. Yet, after discussion, 95 percent emerge with a consensus. Obviously, group influence has occurred.

Thousands of times a year, small groups sampled from the people called for jury duty convene to seek a group decision (Kagehiro, 1990). Are they subject to the social influences that mould other decision groups—to patterns of majority and minority influence, to group polarization, to groupthink? Let's start with a simple question: If we knew the jurors' initial leanings, could we predict their verdict?

The law prohibits observation of actual juries. So researchers simulate the jury process by presenting a case to mock juries and having them deliberate as a real jury would. In a series of such studies, James Davis, Robert Holt, Norbert Kerr, and Garold Stasser tested various mathematical schemes for predicting group decisions, including decisions by mock juries (Davis et al., 1975, 1977, 1989; Kerr et al., 1976). Will some mathematical combination of initial decisions predict the final group decision? Davis and his colleagues found that the scheme that predicts best varies according to the nature of the case. But in several experiments, a "two-thirds-majority" scheme fared best: The group verdict was usually the alternative favoured by at least two-thirds of the jurors at the outset. Without such a majority, a hung jury was likely.

Likewise, in Kalven and Zeisel's survey of juries, nine in 10 reached the verdict favoured by the majority on the first ballot. Although you might fantasize about someday being the courageous lone juror who sways the majority, as Henry Fonda's character did in the famous play and movie *Twelve Angry Men,* the fact is that it seldom happens.

Minority influence

Sometimes, however, what was initially a minority prevails. A typical 12-person jury is like a typical small university class: The three quietest people rarely talk and the three most vocal people contribute more than half of the talking (Hastie, Penrod, & Pennington, 1983). If jurors who favour a particular verdict are vocal and persist in their views, they are more likely to eventually prevail. From the research on minority influence, we know that jurors in the minority will be most persuasive when they are consistent, persistent, and self-confident. This is especially so if they can begin to trigger some defections from the majority (Gordijn, De Vries, & De Dreu, 2002).

Group polarization

Confirmation that group polarization can occur in juries comes from an ambitious study in which Reid Hastie, Steven Penrod, and Nancy Pennington (1983) put together 69 twelve-person juries, made up of Massachusetts citizens, on jury duty. Each jury was shown a re-enactment of an actual murder case, with roles played by an experienced judge and actual attorneys. Then they were given unlimited time to deliberate the case in a jury room. As Figure 7–10 shows, the evidence was incriminating: Four out of five jurors voted guilty before deliberation but felt unsure enough that a weak verdict of manslaughter was their most popular preference. After deliberation, nearly all agreed that the accused was guilty, and most now preferred a stronger verdict—second-degree murder. Through deliberation, their initial leanings had grown stronger.

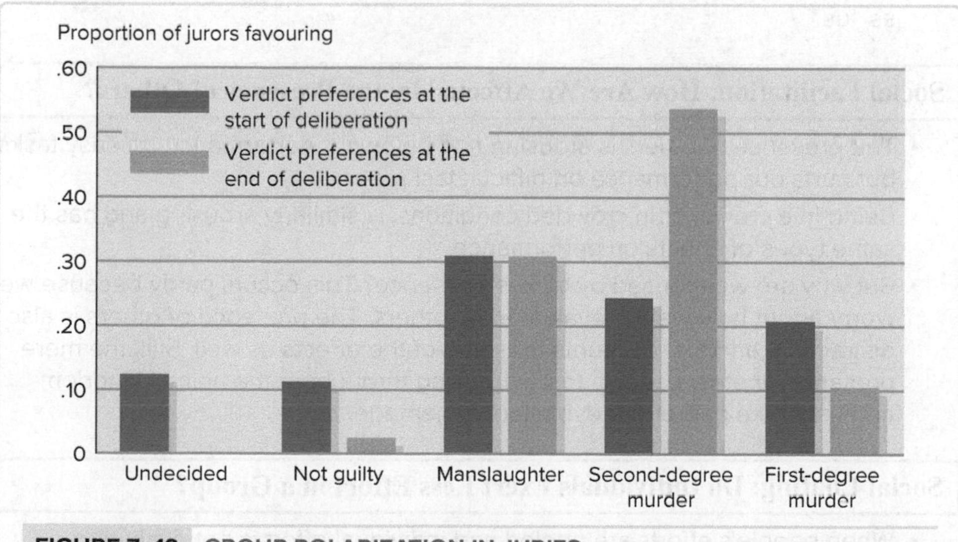

FIGURE 7–10 GROUP POLARIZATION IN JURIES.

In highly realistic simulations of a murder trial, 828 Massachusetts jurors stated their initial verdict preferences, and then deliberated the case for periods ranging from three hours to five days. Deliberation strengthened initial tendencies, which favoured the prosecution.

Leniency

In many experiments, one other curious effect of deliberation has surfaced: Especially when the evidence is not highly incriminating, as in the experiment just described, deliberating jurors often become more lenient (MacCoun & Kerr, 1988). This qualifies the "two-thirds-majority-rules" finding, for if even a bare majority initially favours acquittal, it usually will prevail (Stasser, Kerr, & Bray, 1981). Moreover, a minority that favours acquittal stands a better chance of prevailing than one that favours conviction (Tindale et al., 1990).

> *"It is better that ten guilty persons escape than one innocent suffer."*
>
> William Blackstone, 1769

Once again, a survey of actual juries confirms the laboratory results. Kalven and Zeisel (1966) reported that in those cases where the majority does not prevail, it usually shifts to acquittal. When a judge disagrees with the jury's decision, it is usually because the jury acquits someone the judge would have convicted.

Might "informational influence" (stemming from others' persuasive arguments) account for the increased leniency? The "innocent-unless-proven-guilty" and "proof-beyond-a-reasonable-doubt" rules put the burden of proof on those who favour conviction. Perhaps this makes evidence of the defendant's innocence more persuasive. Or perhaps "normative influence" creates the leniency effect, as jurors who view themselves as fair-minded confront other jurors who are even more concerned with protecting a possibly innocent defendant.

SUMMING UP

What Is a Group?

- A group exists when two or more people interact for more than a few moments, affect one another in some way, and think of themselves as "us."

Social Facilitation: How Are We Affected by the Presence of Others?

- The presence of others is arousing and helps our performance on easy tasks but hurts our performance on difficult tasks.
- Being in a crowd, or in crowded conditions, is similarly arousing and has the same types of effects on performance.
- But why are we aroused by others' presence? This occurs partly because we worry about how we are evaluated by others. The presence of others is also distracting, and that accounts for some of the effects as well. Still, the mere presence of others seems to be arousing throughout the animal kingdom and may be a part of our evolutionary heritage.

Social Loafing: Do Individuals Exert Less Effort in a Group?

- When people's efforts are pooled and individual effort is not evaluated, people generally exert less effort in groups than individually.
- Such social loafing is common in everyday life, but when the task is challenging, the group is cohesive, and people are committed to the group, social loafing is less evident.

Deindividuation: When Do People Lose Their Sense of Self in Groups?

- Deindividuation occurs when people are in a large group, are physically anonymous, and are aroused and distracted.
- The resulting diminished self-awareness and self-restraint tend to increase people's responsiveness to the immediate situation, be it negative or positive.

Group Polarization: Do Groups Intensify Our Opinions?

- When researchers originally studied the ways that groups make decisions differently from individuals, they found that groups make riskier decisions; but as they examined more types of decisions, they found that groups make more polarized decisions. If individuals would tend to be risky, then groups would make riskier decisions, but if individuals would tend to play it safe, then groups would make less risky decisions.
- Groups intensify decisions through group discussions.
- Group discussions intensify decisions by exposing us to new arguments and through our comparisons with others in the group.

Groupthink: Do Groups Hinder or Assist Good Decisions?

- Analysis of several international fiascos indicates that group cohesion can override realistic appraisal of a situation, leading to bad decisions. This is especially true when group members strongly desire unity, when they are isolated from opposing ideas, and when the leader signals what he or she wants from the group.
- Symptomatic of this overriding concern for harmony, labelled groupthink, are (1) an illusion of invulnerability, (2) rationalization, (3) unquestioned belief in the group's morality, (4) stereotyped views of the opposition, (5) pressure to conform, (6) self-censorship of misgivings, (7) an illusion of unanimity, and (8) "mindguards" who protect the group from unpleasant information.
- Critics have noted that some aspects of Janis's groupthink model (such as directive leadership) seem more implicated in flawed decisions than others (such as cohesiveness).
- Both in experiments and in actual history, groups sometimes decide wisely. These cases suggest ways to prevent groupthink: upholding impartiality, encouraging "devil's advocate" positions, subdividing and then reuniting to discuss a decision, seeking outside input, and having a "second-chance" meeting before implementing a decision.
- Research on group problem solving suggests that groups can be more accurate than individuals; groups also generate more and better ideas if the group is small or if, in a large group, individual brainstorming follows the group session.

Leadership: How Do Leaders Shape the Group's Actions?

- Some leaders focus more on tasks and other leaders focus more on the social functioning of the group. Leaders who focus on tasks are often most effective for very high- and very low-functioning groups.

- Some leaders, however, combine social and task leadership by listening to followers and seeking to meet their needs but, at the same time, holding them to high standards for performance. These transactional leaders are often very effective.
- Other leaders gain a following through their charisma and by offering personal attention. These transformational leaders inspire people to make self-sacrifices for the sake of the group and can lead others to be committed and engaged in the task at hand.

The Influence of the Minority: How Do Individuals Influence the Group?

- When minority group members are consistent, they are more likely to influence the group.
- When minority group members have self-confidence, they are more likely to influence the group.
- When minority group members are consistent and self-confident, they create an atmosphere in which defection from the majority viewpoint can occur.

Key Terms

co-actors
deindividuation
evaluation apprehension
free-ride
group
group polarization
groupthink
leadership
pluralistic ignorance
social facilitation
social loafing

Part Three
Social Relations

Social psychology is the scientific study of how people think about, influence, and relate to one another. Having explored how we think about (Part One) and influence (Part Two) one another, we now consider social psychology's third facet: how we relate to one another. Our feelings and actions toward people are sometimes negative, sometimes positive. Chapter 8, "Altruism: Helping Others," and Chapter 9, "Aggression: Hurting Others," examine why and when we help and hurt one another. Then in Chapter 10, "Attraction and Intimacy: Liking and Loving Others," Chapter 11, "Prejudice," and Chapter 12, "Conflict and Peacemaking," we explore why and when we love and hate one another.

CHAPTER 8

Altruism: Helping Others

Source: ©SanchaiRat/Shutterstock.

CHAPTER OUTLINE

Why Do We Help?

When Will We Help?

Who Helps?

How Can We Increase Helping?

Helping comes in many forms, most strikingly in heroic, caring acts.

In January 2020, the world learned a new term: "coronavirus." As COVID-19 spread across the globe, and country after country went into lockdown, the apocalyptic predictions of movies like *Contagion*, *World War Z*, and *Outbreak* did not occur. There was no panic in the streets (though there were toilet paper shortages), and overall people settled into a new life of social distancing and extreme hygiene. Although national borders did close, and many groups (domestic abuse sufferers, Indigenous people, people experiencing homelessness, and those in precarious work conditions) did suffer significant hardships (CBC, 2020b; Global News, 2020), what was perhaps most telling was the outpouring of support by people and in particular by health care workers who risked their lives daily to take care of the sick and those suffering from COVID-19. But this is not an isolated event—this type of heroism has been seen over and over in our history.

In May 2020, George Floyd was detained by police for allegedly passing a fake $20 bill in Minneapolis, Minnesota. What was caught on video next was horrifying—a police officer knelt on Floyd's neck for 8 minutes and 46 seconds, callously mocking his pleas to be released, until Floyd died. The outrage that followed, from another Black man being killed by a White police officer, spread across the city, the state, the entire United States, and internationally, until protests were being held in solidarity in over 1600 cities and towns worldwide (ABC News, 2020). What was it about a singular case in a small U.S. city that caused so many people around the world to stand up to defend those who have traditionally been disadvantaged, targeted, and even killed?

On November 12, 1999, Rohan Wilson saw smoke and flames spewing out of an Edmonton, Alberta, apartment building. He quickly called 911 and then climbed up the outside of the building to a balcony where three children were stranded. He brought them down to safety and then climbed to another balcony and saved a pregnant woman. When asked if he was a hero, he said, "Someone needed help, I hope someone would do the same for me if I was in that position" (CBC 4 Kids, 1999).

Less dramatic acts of comforting, caring, and helping abound: Without asking anything in return, people offer directions, donate money, give blood, and volunteer time.

- Why, and when, will people help?
- Who will help?
- What can be done to lessen indifference and increase helping?

Those are this chapter's primary questions.

Black Lives Matter protesters take to the streets in Montreal.
Source: ©Amru Salahuddien/Anadolu Agency/Getty Images.

Activity: What Is Altruism?

Before you read on, let's try a little activity: For each question that follows, indicate whether or not you think the item is an example of helping behaviour.

Yes	Maybe	No	
_____	_____	_____	**1.** Mohammed, a college student, spends three hours per week as a "Big Brother" to an eight-year-old boy.
_____	_____	_____	**2.** Marie, a lawyer, stops to aid the victim of an automobile accident.
_____	_____	_____	**3.** Jim notifies the bookstore manager when he sees a college student attempt to shoplift some notebook paper.
_____	_____	_____	**4.** Ngocwa, a firefighter, rescues an elderly woman from an apartment building fire.
_____	_____	_____	**5.** Nasrin anonymously donates $500 to a local charity.
_____	_____	_____	**6.** Samin attempts to save her three-year-old from drowning.
_____	_____	_____	**7.** Sally buys a 50-50 ticket at a minor league hockey game.
_____	_____	_____	**8.** Ashraf agrees to donate his organs for transplant after he dies.
_____	_____	_____	**9.** Boazhai, a university student, gives a unit of blood.
_____	_____	_____	**10.** Wanda, a police officer, arrests a bank robber who is fleeing the scene of the crime.
_____	_____	_____	**11.** Believing that those who give will receive great blessings in return, Rick and Sophie contribute 10 percent of their family's monthly income to their church.

Now that you have completed this activity, read the following section on altruism carefully. Afterward, come back and answer the questions again, this time assessing whether or not these are true examples of altruism. Did your answers change? Why or why not?

Altruism is selfishness in reverse. An altruistic person is concerned and helpful even when no benefits are offered or expected in return.

altruism A motive to increase another's welfare without conscious regard for one's own self-interests.

Consider another situation: You are trolling through your favourite social media streams over an early breakfast when you come across a thread entitled "This is it." Curious, you open up the thread, see a picture, and read, "Today at 11:30 GMT, I will attack my school with arson and other forms of violence—the bastards will pay!" You can see from the picture on the post that the school is in a specific country, but you do not know which school. What do you do? Ignore it as a ridiculous and meaningless threat? Or do you report it?

This was the dilemma faced by J. P. Neufeld in Montreal. What should he do? He could tell by the photo and a link that this person was in Norfolk, England. He decided to act: He googled the Norfolk police department, found a number, and called it. Feeling ridiculous when the police department answered, he said "Hi. I'm a guy from Canada … there is someone about to set fire to a school" (Fitterman & Bouquet, 2009, p. 63). Much to his surprise, they took his information and put detectives on the case. With the help of another tip, within the hour the Norfolk police arrested the young student outside his school—he was carrying a flammable liquid, some matches, and a knife. The Internet is powerful: It can provide anonymity, but it can also empower people to help—even from the other side of the world.

Why Do We Help?

To study altruistic acts, social psychologists identify circumstances in which people perform such deeds. Before looking at what the experiments reveal, let's consider what motivates helping.

Social Exchange

Several theories of helping agree that, in the long run, helping benefits the giver as well as the receiver. One explanation assumes that human interactions are guided by "social economics." We exchange not only material goods and money but also social goods: love, services, information, status (Foa & Foa, 1975). In doing so, we use a "minimax" strategy—minimize costs, maximize rewards. **Social-exchange theory** does not contend that we consciously monitor costs and rewards, only that such considerations predict our behaviour.

Suppose your campus is having a blood drive and someone asks you to participate. Might you not implicitly weigh the costs of donating (needle prick, time, fatigue) against those of not donating (guilt, disapproval)? Might you not also weigh the benefits of donating (feeling good about helping someone, receiving free refreshments) against those of not donating (saving the time, discomfort, and anxiety)? According to social-exchange theory—supported by studies of Wisconsin blood donors by Jane Allyn Piliavin and her research team (Piliavin, 2003)—such subtle calculations precede decisions to help or not.

social-exchange theory The theory that human interactions are transactions that aim to maximize one's rewards and minimize one's costs.

Rewards

Rewards that motivate helping may be external or internal. When businesses donate money to improve their corporate image or when someone offers someone else a ride hoping to receive appreciation or friendship, the reward is external. We give to get. Thus we are most eager to help someone attractive to us, someone whose approval we desire (Krebs, 1970; Unger, 1979). In experiments, and in everyday life, public generosity boosts one's status, while selfish behaviour can lead to punishment (Hardy & Van Vugt, 2006; Henrich et al., 2006).

Rewards may also be internal. Nearly all blood donors in Jane Piliavin's research agreed that giving blood "makes you feel good about yourself" and "gives you a feeling of self-satisfaction" (Piliavin, 2003; Piliavin et al., 1982). This helps explain why people far from home will leave tips for waiters and do kindnesses for strangers whom they will never see again.

"Men do not value a good deed unless it brings a reward."

Ovid, *Epistulae Ex Ponto*, AD 10

Helping's boost to self-worth explains why so many people feel good after doing good. One month-long study of 85 couples found that giving emotional support to one's partner was positive for the giver, boosting the giver's mood (Gleason et al., 2003). Jane Piliavin (2003) and Susan Andersen (1998) reviewed studies showing that youth who engage in community service projects, school-based "service learning," or tutoring children develop social skills and positive social values. Such youth are at markedly less risk for delinquency, pregnancy, and school dropout and are more likely to become engaged citizens. Volunteering likewise benefits morale and health, especially when self-initiated rather than imposed (Weinstein & Ryan, 2010). Bereaved spouses recover from their depressed feelings faster when they are engaged in helping others (S. L. Brown et al., 2008, 2009). Those who do good tend to do well.

The same goes for giving money. Making donations activates brain areas linked with reward (Harbaugh, Mayr, & Burghart, 2007). Generous people are happier than those whose spending is self-focused. In one experiment, people received an envelope with cash: Some were instructed to spend it on themselves while others were directed to spend it on other people. At the day's end, the happiest people were those assigned to the spend-it-on-others condition (Dunn et al., 2008). Other research confirms that giving increases happiness (Anik et al., 2010).

This cost–benefit analysis can seem demeaning. In defence of the theory, however, is it not a credit to humanity that much of our behaviour is not antisocial but "prosocial" and that we can find fulfillment in the giving of love? How much worse if we gained pleasure only by serving ourselves.

"True," some readers may reply. "Still, doesn't social-exchange theory imply that a helpful act is never truly altruistic—that we merely call it 'altruistic' when its rewards are inconspicuous? If we help the screaming person so we can gain social approval, relieve our distress, or boost our self-image, is it really altruistic?" This is reminiscent of B. F. Skinner's (1971) analysis of altruism. We credit people for their good deeds, said Skinner, only when we can't explain them. We attribute their behaviour to their inner dispositions only when we lack external explanations. When the external causes are obvious, we credit the causes, not the person.

There is, however, a weakness in social-exchange theory: It easily degenerates into explaining-by-naming. If someone volunteers for the Big Brothers Big Sisters tutor program, it is tempting to "explain" that compassionate action by the satisfaction it brings. But such after-the-fact naming of rewards creates a circular explanation: "Why did the person volunteer?" "Because of the inner rewards." "How do you know there are inner rewards?" "Why else would the person have volunteered?" Because of this circular reasoning, **egoism**—the idea that self-interest motivates all behaviour—has fallen into disrepute.

egoism A motive (supposedly underlying all behaviour) to increase your own welfare; the opposite of *altruism*, which aims to increase someone else's welfare.

To escape the circularity, we must define the rewards and costs independently of the helping behaviour. If social approval motivates helping, then in experiments we should find that when approval follows helping, helping increases. And it does (Staub, 1978).

Internal rewards

The benefits of helping include internal self-rewards. When we are near someone in distress, we may feel distress. A scream outside your window arouses and distresses you. If you cannot reduce your arousal by interpreting the scream as a playful shriek, then you may investigate or give aid, thereby reducing your distress (Piliavin & Piliavin, 1973). Altruism researcher Dennis Krebs (1975) found that university men whose physiological responses and self-reports revealed the most arousal in response to another's distress also gave the most help to the person.

Guilt

Throughout recorded history, guilt has been a painful emotion that people avoid and seek to relieve. To examine the consequences of guilt, social psychologists have induced people to transgress: to lie, to deliver shock, to knock over a table loaded with alphabetized cards, to break a machine, to cheat. Afterwards, the guilt-laden participants may be offered a way to relieve their guilt: by confessing, by disparaging the one harmed, or by doing a good deed to offset the bad one. The results are remarkably consistent: People will do whatever can be done to expunge the guilt and restore their self-image.

Picture yourself as a participant in one such experiment conducted with university students by David McMillen and James Austin (1971). You and another student, each seeking to earn credit toward a course requirement, arrive for the experiment. Soon after, a confederate enters, portraying himself as a previous subject looking for a lost book. He strikes up a conversation in which he mentions that the experiment involves taking a multiple-choice test, for which most of the correct answers are "B." After the accomplice departs, the experimenter arrives, explains the experiment, and then asks, "Have either of you been in this experiment before or heard anything about it?"

Would you lie? The behaviour of those who have gone before you in this experiment—100 percent of whom told the little lie—suggests that you would. After you have taken the test (without receiving any feedback on it), the experimenter says: "You are free to leave. However, if you have some spare time, I could use your help in scoring some questionnaires." Assuming you have told the lie, do you think you would now be more willing to volunteer some time? Judging from the results, the answer again is yes. On average, those who had not been induced to lie volunteered only two minutes of time. Those who had lied were apparently eager to redeem their self-image; on average, they offered a whopping 63 minutes. One moral of this experiment was well expressed by a seven-year-old girl, who, in one of our own experiments, wrote this: "Don't Lie or youl Live with gilt" (and you will feel a need to relieve it).

Our eagerness to do good after doing bad reflects both our need to reduce private guilt and restore our shaken self-image and our desire to reclaim a positive public image. We are more likely to redeem ourselves with helpful behaviour when other people know about our misdeeds (Carlsmith & Gross, 1969).

All in all, guilt leads to much good. By motivating people to confess, apologize, help, and avoid repeated harm, it boosts sensitivity and sustains close relationships.

Among adults, the inner rewards of prosocial behaviour—feeling good about oneself after donating blood or helping pick up someone's dropped materials—can offset other negative moods as well (Cialdini, Kenrick, & Baumann, 1981; Williamson & Clark, 1989). Thus, when an adult is in a guilty, sad, or otherwise negative mood, a helpful deed (or any other mood-improving experience) helps neutralize the bad feelings.

Exceptions to the feel bad–do good scenario

Among well-socialized adults, should we always expect to find the "feel bad–do good" phenomenon? No. One negative mood, anger, produces anything but compassion (as we will see in Chapter 9). Another exception is depression, which is characterized by brooding self-concern (Carlson & Miller, 1987; Wood, Saltzberg, & Goldsamt, 1990). Yet another exception is profound grief. People who suffer the loss of a spouse or a child, whether through death or separation, often undergo a period of intense self-preoccupation, a state that makes it difficult to be giving (Aderman & Berkowitz, 1983; Gibbons & Wicklund, 1982).

In a powerfully involving laboratory simulation of self-focused grief, William Thompson, Claudia Cowan, and David Rosenhan (1980) had Stanford University students privately listen to a taped description of a person (whom they were to imagine as their best friend of the other sex) dying of cancer. The experiment focused some subjects' attention on their own worry and grief, and others' attention on the friend. When immediately thereafter the subjects were given a chance to anonymously help a graduate student with her research, 25 percent of those whose attention had been self-focused helped. Of those whose attention was other-focused, 83 percent helped. The two groups were equally touched. But only the other-focused participants found helping someone especially rewarding. In short, the feel bad–do good effect occurs with people whose attention is on others, people for whom prosocial behaviour is, therefore, rewarding (Barnett et al., 1980; McMillen, Sanders, & Solomon, 1977). If not self-preoccupied by depression or grief, sad people are sensitive, helpful people.

Feel good–do good

Are happy people unhelpful? Quite the contrary. There are few more consistent findings in the entire literature of psychology: Happy people are helpful people. This effect occurs with both children and adults, regardless of whether the good mood comes from a success, from thinking happy thoughts, or from any of several other positive experiences (Salovey, Mayer, & Rosenhan, 1991).

In experiments on happiness and helpfulness, the person who is helped may be someone seeking a donation, an experimenter seeking help with paperwork, or a woman who drops papers. Here are three other examples:

- Joseph Forgas and his colleagues (2008) had a confederate offer a Target department store salesperson either a mood-boosting compliment or a neutral or mood-deflating comment. Moments later, a second confederate, who was "blind" to the mood-induction condition, sought the employee's help in locating a nonexistent item. Among less-experienced staff (who lacked a practised routine for answering such requests), those receiving the mood boost made the greatest effort to help.
- Dariusz Dolinski and Richard Nawrat (1998) found that a positive mood of relief can dramatically boost helping. Imagine yourself as one of their unwitting subjects. After illegally parking your car for a few moments, you return to discover what looks like a ticket under your windshield wiper (where parking tickets are placed). Groaning inwardly, you pick up the apparent ticket and then are much relieved to discover it is only an ad (or a blood drive appeal). Moments later, a university student approaches you and asks you to spend 15 minutes answering questions—to "help me complete my MA thesis." Would your positive, relieved mood make you more likely to help? Indeed, 62 percent of people whose fear had just turned to relief agreed willingly. That was nearly double the number who did so when no ticket-like paper was left or when it was left on the car door (not a place for a ticket).
- Alice Isen, Margaret Clark, and Mark Schwartz (1976) had a confederate call people who had, 0 to 20 minutes earlier, received a free sample of stationery. The confederate said she had used her last dime to dial this (supposedly wrong) number and asked each person to relay a message by phone. As Figure 8–1 shows, the individuals' willingness to relay the phone message rose during the five minutes afterward. Then, as the good mood wore off, helpfulness dropped.

If sad people are sometimes extra helpful, how can it be that happy people are also helpful? Experiments reveal that several factors are at work (Carlson, Charlin, & Miller, 1988; Schaller & Cialdini, 1988). Helping softens a bad mood and sustains a good mood. (Perhaps you can recall feeling good after giving someone directions.) A positive mood is, in turn, conducive to positive thoughts and positive self-esteem, which predispose us to positive behaviour (Berkowitz, 1987; Cunningham et al., 1990; Isen et al., 1978). In a good mood—after being given a gift or while feeling the warm glow of success—people are more likely to have positive

> ***"It's curious how, when you're in love, you yearn to go about doing acts of kindness to everybody."***
>
> P. G. Wodehouse, *The Mating Season*, 1949

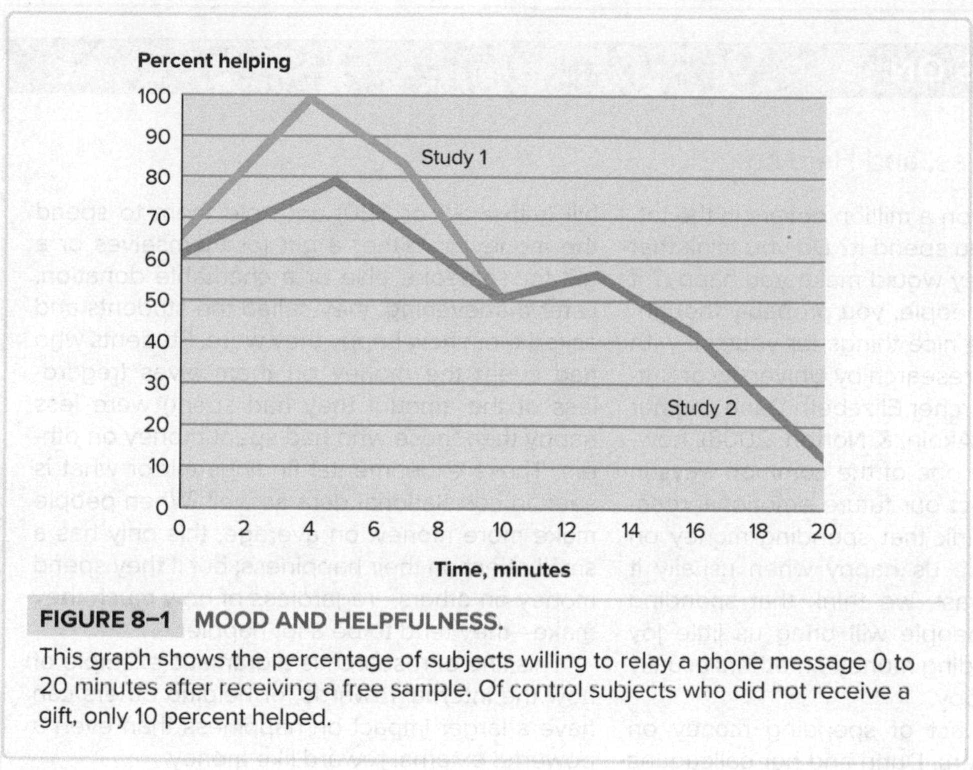

FIGURE 8–1 MOOD AND HELPFULNESS.

This graph shows the percentage of subjects willing to relay a phone message 0 to 20 minutes after receiving a free sample. Of control subjects who did not receive a gift, only 10 percent helped.

thoughts and to have positive associations with being helpful. Positive thinkers are likely to be positive actors.

Social Norms

Often, we help others not because we have consciously calculated that such behaviour is in our self-interest but simply because something tells us we ought to. We ought to help a new neighbour move in. We ought to return the wallet we found. We ought to protect our teammates in video games from (virtual) harm. Norms, the "oughts" of our lives, are social expectations. They prescribe proper behaviour. Researchers studying helping behaviour have identified two social norms that motivate prosocial behaviour: (1) the reciprocity norm and (2) the social-responsibility norm.

> ***"There is no duty more indispensable than that of returning a kindness."***
>
> Cicero, quoted in Gouldner, 1960

The reciprocity norm

One universal moral code is a **reciprocity norm**: *To those who help us, we should return help, not harm* (Gouldner, 1960). This norm is as universal as the incest taboo. We "invest" in others and expect dividends. Politicians know that the one who gives a favour can later expect a favour. Mail surveys and solicitations sometimes include a little gift of money or personalized address labels, assuming that some people will reciprocate the favour. Even 21-month-old infants display reciprocity, by being more willing to help those who have tried to give them a toy (Dunfield & Kuhlmeier, 2010). The reciprocity norm even applies in marriage. At times, one may give more than one receives, but, in the long run, the exchange should balance out. In all such interactions, to receive without giving in return violates the reciprocity norm.

> **reciprocity norm** An expectation that people will help, not hurt, those who have helped them.

Money, Happiness, and Helping

Imagine that you won a million dollars in the lottery. How would you spend it? Do you think that spending the money would make you happy? If you are like most people, you probably thought about buying some nice things for yourself with the money. Recent research by University of British Columbia researcher Elizabeth Dunn and her colleagues (Dunn, Aknin, & Norton, 2008), however, suggests that one of the common ways in which we mispredict our future emotional reactions is that we think that spending money on ourselves will make us happy when usually it does not. In contrast, we think that spending money on other people will bring us little joy when, in fact, spending money on others usually makes us quite happy.

To test the impact of spending money on oneself versus others, Dunn and her colleagues gave students an envelope with a fresh new bill (either $5 or $20) and told them to spend the money on either a gift for themselves or a gift for someone else or a charitable donation. Later that evening, they called the students and asked them how happy they were. Students who had spent the money on themselves (regardless of the amount they had spent) were less happy than those who had spent money on others. These experimental findings mirror what is seen in correlational data as well. When people make more money, on average, this only has a small effect on their happiness; but if they spend money on others—regardless of how much they make—they tend to be a lot happier.

This line of research is a dramatic example of how the internal rewards for helping others can have a larger impact on happiness than even a powerful external reward like money.

Reciprocity within social networks helps define the "social capital"—the supportive connections, information flow, trust, and cooperative actions—that keeps a community healthy. Neighbours keeping an eye on each other's homes is social capital in action.

The norm operates most effectively as people respond publicly to deeds earlier done to them. In laboratory games, as in everyday life, fleeting one-shot encounters produce greater selfishness than sustained relationships. But even when people respond anonymously, they sometimes do the right thing and repay the good done to them. In one experiment, Mark Whatley and his colleagues (1999) found that more university students willingly made a pledge to the charity of someone who had previously bought them some candy (Figure 8–2).

When people cannot reciprocate, they may feel threatened and demeaned by accepting aid. Thus, proud, high-self-esteem people are often reluctant to seek help (Nadler & Fisher, 1986). Receiving unsolicited help can take one's self-esteem down a notch (Schneider et al., 1996; Shell & Eisenberg, 1992). Studies show that this can happen to beneficiaries of affirmative action, especially when affirmative action fails to affirm the person's competence and chances for future success (Pratkanis & Turner, 1996). Asians, for whom social ties and the reciprocity norm are stronger than for North Americans, are therefore more likely to refuse a gift from a casual acquaintance to avoid the felt need to reciprocate (Shen, Wan, & Wyer, 2011). And the reciprocity norm starts young—one study showed that children as young as four years old respond to prosocial behaviour by behaving prosocially themselves (Beeler-Duden & Vaish, 2020).

The social-responsibility norm

The reciprocity norm reminds us to balance giving and receiving in social relations. With people who clearly are dependent and unable to reciprocate, such as children, the severely impoverished, and those with disabilities, another social norm motivates our helping. The **social-responsibility norm** is the belief that people should help those who need help, without regard to future exchanges (Berkowitz, 1975; Schwartz, 1975). If a person on crutches drops a book, you honour the social-responsibility norm as you pick it up. In India, a relatively collectivist culture, people support the social-responsibility norm more strongly than in the individualist West (Baron & Miller, 2000). They voice an obligation to help even when the need is not life-threatening or when the needy person—perhaps a stranger needing a bone marrow transplant—is outside their family circle.

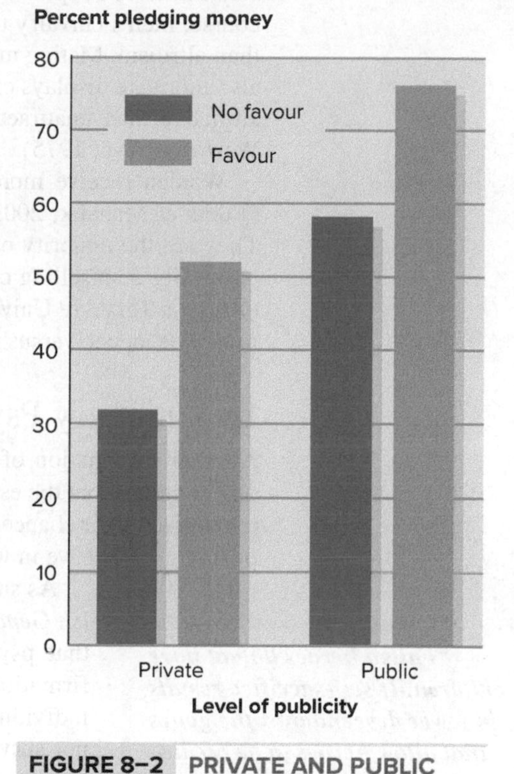

FIGURE 8–2 **PRIVATE AND PUBLIC RECIPROCATION OF A FAVOUR.**

People were more willing to pledge to an experimental confederate's charity if the confederate had done a small favour for them earlier, especially when their reciprocation was made known to the confederate.

Even when helpers in Western countries remain anonymous and have no expectation of any reward, they often help needy people (Harrel, 1994; Shotland & Stebbins, 1983). However, they usually apply the social-responsibility norm selectively to those whose need appears not to be due to their own negligence. Especially among political conservatives (Skitka & Tetlock, 1993), the norm seems to be this: Give people what they deserve. If they are victims of circumstance, such as a natural disaster, then by all means be compassionate (Goetz, Keltner, & Simon-Thomas, 2010; Zagefka et al., 2011). If they seem to have created their own problems (through laziness, immorality, or lack of foresight, for example), then the norm suggests they don't deserve help.

Responses are thus closely tied to attributions. If we attribute the need to an uncontrollable predicament, we help. If we attribute the need to the person's choices, fairness does not require us to help; we say it's the person's own fault (Weiner, 1980). The key, suggested Udo Rudolph and his colleagues (2004) from their review of more than three dozen pertinent studies, is whether your attributions evoke sympathy, which in turn motivates helping.

social-responsibility norm An expectation that people will help those dependent upon them.

Gender and receiving help

If, indeed, perception of someone else's need strongly determines your willingness to help, will women, if perceived as less competent and more dependent, receive more help than men? That is indeed the case. Alice Eagly and Maureen Crowley (1986) located 35 studies that compared help received by male or female victims. (Virtually all the studies involved short-term encounters with strangers in need—the very situations in which people expect males to be chivalrous, noted Eagly and Crowley.)

Women offered help equally to males and females, whereas men offered more help when the strangers in need were females. Several experiments in the 1970s found that women with disabled cars (for example, with a flat tire) got many more offers of help than men did (Penner, Dertke, & Achenbach, 1973; Pomazal & Clore, 1973; West, Whitney, & Schnedler, 1975). Similarly, solo female hitchhikers received far more offers of help than solo males or couples did (Pomazal & Clore, 1973; Snyder, Grether, & Keller, 1974). Of course, men's chivalry toward lone women may have been motivated by something other than altruism. Mating motives increase men's spending on conspicuous luxuries, and they also motivate displays of heroism (Griskevicius et al., 2007). Men more frequently helped attractive than unattractive women (Mims, Hartnett, & Nay, 1975; Stroufe et al., 1977; West & Brown, 1975).

Women receive more offers of help in certain situations; they also seek more help (Addis & Mahalik, 2003). They are twice as likely to seek medical and psychiatric help. They are the majority of callers to radio counselling programs and clients of college and university counselling centres. They more often welcome help from friends. Arie Nadler (1991), a Tel Aviv University expert on help-seeking, attributed this to gender differences in independence versus interdependence.

Evolutionary Psychology

Another explanation of helping comes from evolutionary theory. Evolutionary psychology contends that the essence of life is gene survival. Our genes drive us in ways that have maximized their chance of survival. When our ancestors died, their genes lived on, predisposing us to behave in ways that will spread them into the future.

As suggested by the title of Richard Dawkins's (1976) book, *The Selfish Gene,* evolutionary psychology offers a humbling human image—one that psychologist Donald Campbell (1975b) called a biological reaffirmation of a deep, self-serving "original sin." Genes that predispose individuals to self-sacrifice in the interests of strangers' welfare would not survive in the evolutionary competition. Evolutionary success does, however, come from cooperation. And humans, say Martin Nowak and Roger Highfield (2011), are the animal kingdom's super-cooperators because we exhibit multiple mechanisms for overcoming selfishness, including the following:

> ***"Fallen heroes do not have children. If self-sacrifice results in fewer descendants, the genes that allow heroes to be created can be expected to disappear gradually from the population."***
>
> E. O. Wilson, *On Human Nature*, 1978

- *Kin selection:* If you carry my genes, I'll favour you.
- *Direct reciprocity:* You scratch my back, and I'll scratch yours.
- *Indirect reciprocity:* I'll scratch your back, you scratch someone's, and someone will scratch mine.
- *Group selection:* Back-scratching groups survive.

Kin selection

Our genes dispose us to care for relatives. Thus, one form of self-sacrifice that would increase gene survival is devotion to one's children. Compared with neglectful parents, parents who put their children's welfare ahead of their own are more likely to pass on their genes. As evolutionary psychologist David Barash (1979, p. 153) wrote, "Genes help themselves by being nice to themselves, even if they are enclosed in different bodies." Genetic egoism (at the biological level) fosters parental altruism (at the psychological level). Although evolution favours self-sacrifice for one's children, children have less at stake in the survival of their parents' genes. Thus, according to the theory, parents will generally be more devoted to their children than their children are to them.

> **kin selection** The idea that evolution has selected altruism toward one's close relatives to enhance the survival of mutually shared genes.

Other relatives share genes in proportion to their biological closeness. You share one-half of your genes with your brothers and sisters, one-eighth with your cousins. **Kin selection**—favouritism toward those who share our genes—led the evolutionary biologist J. B. S. Haldane to joke that while he would not give up his life for his brother, he would sacrifice himself for three brothers—or for nine cousins. Haldane would not have been surprised that, compared to fraternal twins, genetically identical twins are noticeably more mutually supportive (Segal, 1984; Stewart-Williams, 2007). In one laboratory game experiment, identical twins were half again as likely to cooperate with their twin for a shared gain when playing for money (Segal & Hershberger, 1999).

The point is not that we calculate genetic relatedness before helping but that nature (as well as culture) programs us to care about close relatives. The Carnegie medal for heroism is seldom awarded for saving an immediate family member. When Carlos Rogers, formerly of the Toronto Raptors NBA basketball team, volunteered to end his career and donate a kidney to his sister (who sadly died before she received it), people applauded his self-sacrificial love. But such acts for close kin are not totally unexpected. What we do not expect (and, therefore, honour) is the altruism of those who, like our apartment fire hero Rohan Wilson, risk themselves to save a stranger.

> ***"Morality governs our actions toward others in much the same way that gravity governs the motions of the planets: its strength is in inverse proportion to the square of the distance between them."***
>
> James Q. Wilson, "The Universal Aspiration," 1993

We share common genes with many besides our relatives. Are we, therefore, biologically biased to be more helpful to those who look similar to us and to those who live near us? In the aftermath of natural disasters and other life-and-death situations, the order of who gets helped would not surprise an evolutionary psychologist: the children before the old, family members before friends, neighbours before strangers (Burnstein, Crandall, & Kitayama, 1994; Form & Nosow, 1958). We feel more empathy for a distressed or tortured person in our in-group and even s*chadenfreude* (secret pleasure at their misfortune) for rivals or out-group members (Batson, Chao, & Givens, 2009; Cikara, Bruneau, & Saxe, 2011; Tarrant, Dazeley, & Cottom, 2009). Helping starts close to home.

Reciprocity

Genetic self-interest also predicts reciprocity. One organism helps another, biologist Robert Trivers argued, because it expects help in return (Binham, 1980). The giver expects to be the receiver later on.

Reciprocity works best in small, isolated groups, groups in which one will often see the people for whom one does favours. Sociable female baboons—those who groom and stay in close contact with their peers—gain a reproductive advantage: Their infants more often live to see a first birthday (Silk, Alberts, & Altmann, 2003). If a vampire bat has gone a day or two without food—it can't go much more than 60 hours without starving to death—it prompts a well-fed nestmate to regurgitate food for a meal (Wilkinson, 1990). The donor bat does so willingly, losing fewer hours till starvation than the recipient gains. But such favours occur only among familiar nestmates who share in the give-and-take. Those who always take and never give, and those who have no relationship with the donor bat, go hungry.

For similar reasons, reciprocity is stronger in the remote Cook Islands of the South Pacific than in New York City (Barash, 1979). Small schools, towns, churches, work teams, and dorms are all conducive to a community spirit in which people care for each other. Compared to people in small-town or rural environments, those in big cities are less willing to relay a phone message, less likely to mail "lost" letters, less cooperative with survey interviewers, less helpful to a lost child, and less willing to do small favours (Hedge & Yousif, 1992; Steblay, 1987).

Group selection

If individual self-interest inevitably wins in genetic competition, then why will we help strangers? Why will we help those whose limited resources or abilities preclude their reciprocating? What caused Mother Teresa to act as she did? What causes soldiers to throw themselves on grenades? One answer is group selection: When groups are in competition, groups of mutually supportive altruists outlast groups of non-altruists (Krebs, 1998; Sober & Wilson, 1998; Wilson & Wilson, 2008). This is most dramatically evident with the social insects, which function like cells in a body. Bees and ants will labour sacrificially for their colony's survival.

To a much lesser extent, humans exhibit in-group loyalty by sometimes sacrificing to support "us" against "them." Natural selection is, therefore, "multi-level," according to some researchers (Mirsky, 2009): It operates at both individual and group levels.

But these effects can be mitigated. As you will see in Chapter 11, contact between different racial groups reduces expressions of racism, and researchers have also found that it may increase helping. For example, when White women were asked if they would intervene in a situation where Black women were at risk of sexual assault, the positivity and frequency of intergroup contact positively correlated with their intentions to help (Merrilees et al., 2018).

Comparing and Evaluating Theories of Altruism

By now, you have perhaps noticed similarities among the social exchange, social norm, and evolutionary views of altruism. As Table 8–1 shows, each proposes two types of prosocial behaviour: a tit-for-tat reciprocal exchange and a more unconditional helpfulness. They do so at three complementary levels of explanation. If the evolutionary view is correct, then our genetic predispositions should manifest themselves in psychological and sociological phenomena.

Each theory appeals to logic. Yet each is vulnerable to charges of being speculative and after the fact. When we start with a known effect (the give-and-take of everyday life) and explain it by conjecturing a social-exchange process, a "reciprocity norm," or an evolutionary origin, we might be merely explaining-by-naming. The argument that a behaviour occurs because of its survival function is hard to disprove. With hindsight, it's easy to think it had to be that way. If we can explain any conceivable behaviour after the fact as the result of a social exchange, a norm, or natural selection, then we cannot disprove the theories. Each theory's task is, therefore, to generate predictions that enable us to test it.

An effective theory also provides a coherent scheme for summarizing a variety of observations. On this criterion, the three altruism theories get high marks. Each offers us a broad perspective from which we can understand both enduring commitments and spontaneous help.

Genuine altruism

Are life-saving heroes, everyday blood donors, and relief workers *ever* motivated by an ultimate goal of selfless concern for others? Or is their ultimate goal always some form of self-benefit, such as relief from distress or avoidance of guilt?

TABLE 8-1 Comparing Theories of Altruism.

		How Is Altruism Explained?	
Theory	**Level of Explanation**	**Mutual Altruism**	**Intrinsic Altruism**
Social norms	Sociological	Reciprocity norm	Social-responsibility norm
Social exchange	Psychological	External rewards for helping	Distress → inner rewards for helping
Evolutionary	Biological	Reciprocity	Kin selection

THE INSIDE STORY

The reasons why people do things aren't always what they seem. For instance, the things I'll tell you shortly may imply that my motive for going to graduate school was to study interesting questions about helping behaviour. It's more likely, though, that I went to graduate school because I didn't fancy having to find a job in the real world. Before going to graduate school, I heard about research suggesting that the emotional experience of empathy leads to a truly altruistic motive to help others. I didn't buy it. Neither did Bob Cialdini, and so I chose to go work with him.

We conducted several studies supporting the hypothesis that the alleged altruistic motive to help is actually a mood-management motive in disguise. So even when people feel empathic toward someone else, they may help that person for selfish, not selfless, motives. Of course, these motives may not account fully for the effects of empathy on helping behaviour. Recently, I've been thinking that some of the effects on helping may be so automated that they may not be driven by motives and goals at all, even though they appear to be. After all, the reasons why people do things aren't always what they seem.

Source: Ken Karp/ McGraw-Hill Education.

Mark Schaller, *University of British Columbia*

Philosophers have debated this question for centuries. Consider Rohan Wilson, whom we discussed at the beginning of this chapter. Was this truly a selfless act of concern? Perhaps he only helped because he would not have been able to live with himself if he had not. Or maybe he helped because he expected the praise and accolades he received. The skeptic can always see a hidden motive of self-interest in even the most heroic acts.

We can all be skeptical of some acts of helping. Take as an example corporate donations to charity. John Cleghorn (2000), the chairman and CEO of Royal Bank of Canada (RBC), noted that in 1999 his bank gave over $25 million to charity but it was as much to enhance the business as to support the community. So, do people help just so they won't feel bad, and do companies give to charities only to increase their bottom lines? Until recently, psychologists have generally argued that self-interest is behind most instances of helping.

Helpfulness so reliably makes helpers feel better that Daniel Batson (2011) has devoted much of his career to discerning whether helpfulness also contains a streak of genuine altruism. Batson theorizes that our willingness to help is influenced by both self-serving and selfless considerations (Figure 8–3). Distress over someone's suffering motivates us to relieve our upset feelings, either by escaping the distressing situation or by helping. But especially when we feel attached to someone, reported Batson and a team of attachment researchers led by Mario Mikulincer (2005), we also feel **empathy**. Loving parents suffer when their children suffer and rejoice over their children's joys—an empathy lacking in child abusers and other perpetrators of cruelty (Miller & Eisenberg, 1988).

empathy The vicarious experience of someone else's feeling; putting yourself in someone else's shoes.

We also feel empathy for those we identify with. In September 1997, millions of people who never came anywhere close to Princess Diana (but who felt as though they knew her after hundreds of tabloid stories and 44 *People* magazine cover articles) wept for her and her motherless sons—but shed no tears for the nearly 1 million faceless Rwandans murdered or dying in squalid refugee camps since 1994. We feel more empathy for a real person than a suffering aggregate, more sadness over the death of a Diana than over a mass "statistic." This "collapse of compassion"—decreasing concern

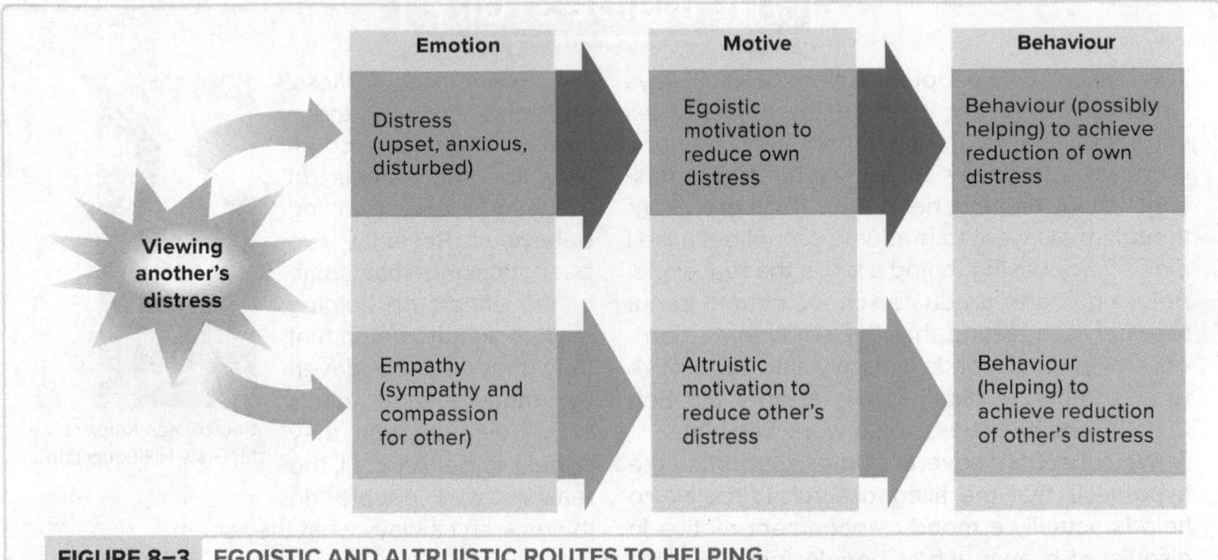

FIGURE 8–3 EGOISTIC AND ALTRUISTIC ROUTES TO HELPING.
Viewing someone else's distress can evoke a mixture of self-focused distress and other-focused empathy. Researchers agree that distress triggers egoistic motives. But they debate whether empathy can trigger a purely altruistic motive.

as the number of suffering people increases—also occurs as people regulate their painful emotional responses to large tragedies (Cameron & Payne, 2011).

When we feel empathy, we focus not so much on our own distress as on the sufferer. Genuine sympathy and compassion motivate us to help others for their own sake. When we value another's welfare, perceive the person as in need, and take the person's perspective, we feel empathic concern (Batson et al., 2007).

To increase empathy, it helps to get a small dose of what another feels. A specific torture technique becomes less acceptable when people experience even a small dose of it. For example, when people are moderately sleep-deprived, they become more likely to say that, yes, extreme sleep deprivation is torture (Nordgren, Banas, & MacDonald, 2011).

In humans, empathy comes naturally. Even day-old infants cry more when they hear another infant cry (Hoffman, 1981). In hospital nurseries, one baby's crying sometimes evokes a chorus of crying. Most 18-month-old infants, after observing an unfamiliar adult accidentally drop a marker or clothespin and have trouble reaching it, will readily help (Tomasello, 2009). To some, this suggests that humans are hard-wired for empathy. Primates and even mice also display empathy, indicating that the building blocks of prosocial behaviour predate humanity (de Waal, 2005; de Waal, Leimgruber, & Greenberg, 2008; Langford et al., 2006; Wynne & de Waal, 2006). In one classic experiment, most rhesus monkeys refused to operate a device that gained them food if it would cause another monkey to receive an electric shock (Masserman, Wechkin, & Terris, 1964). Chimpanzees will choose a token that gives both themselves and another chimp a food treat over a token that gratifies only themselves (Horner et al., 2010).

Often, distress and empathy together motivate responses to a crisis (Russell & Mentzel, 1990). In 1983, people watched on television as an Australian bushfire wiped out hundreds of homes near Melbourne. Afterwards, Paul Amato (1986) studied donations of money and goods. He found that those who felt angry or indifferent gave less than those who felt either distressed (shocked and sickened) or empathic (sympathetic and worried for the victims).

To separate egoistic distress reduction from altruistic empathy, Batson's research group conducted studies that aroused feelings of empathy. Then the researchers noted whether the aroused people would reduce their own distress by escaping the situation or whether they would go out of their way to aid the person. The results were consistent: Their empathy aroused, they usually helped.

In one of these experiments, Batson and his associates (1981) had women observe a young woman suffering while she supposedly received electric shocks. During a pause in the experiment, the obviously upset victim explained to the experimenter that a childhood fall against an electric fence had left her acutely sensitive to shocks. In sympathy, the experimenter suggested that perhaps the observer (the actual subject in this experiment) might trade places and take the remaining shocks for her. Previously, half of these actual subjects had been led to believe that the suffering person was a kindred spirit on matters of values and interests (thus arousing their empathy). Some also had been led to believe that their part in the experiment was completed so that in any case they were done observing the woman's suffering. Nevertheless, their empathy aroused, virtually all of these student observers willingly offered to substitute for the victim.

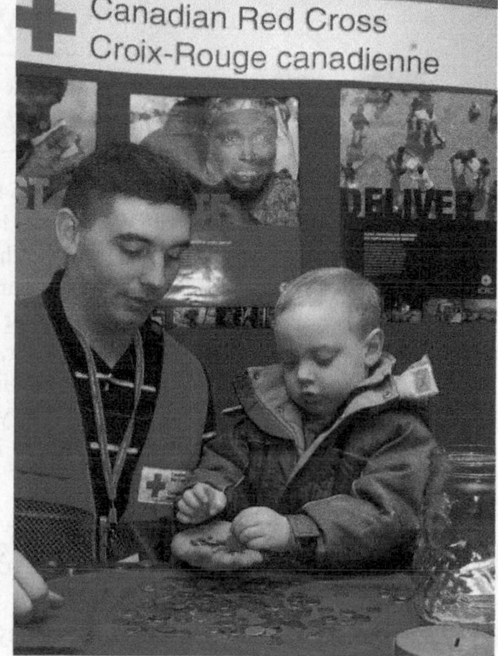

Might genuine empathy motivate humanitarian aid workers to travel across the world? This Red Cross worker believes that, yes, it does.

Source: St. John's Telegram-Joe Gibbons/The Canadian Press.

Is this genuine altruism? Mark Schaller and Robert Cialdini (1988) doubted it. Feeling empathy for a sufferer makes one sad, they noted. In one of their experiments, they led people to believe that their sadness was going to be relieved by a different sort of mood-boosting experience—listening to a comedy tape. Under such conditions, people who felt empathy were not especially helpful. Schaller and Cialdini concluded that if we feel empathy but know that something else will make us feel better, we aren't so likely to help.

> ***"How selfish soever man may be supposed, there are evidently some principles in his nature, which interest him in the fortune of others, and render their happiness necessary to him, though he derives nothing from it except the pleasure of seeing it."***
>
> Adam Smith, *The Theory of Moral Sentiments*, 1759

Everyone agrees that some helpful acts are either obviously egoistic (done to gain rewards or avoid punishment) or subtly egoistic (done to relieve inner distress). Is there a third type of helpfulness—an altruism that aims simply to increase another's welfare (producing happiness for oneself merely as a by-product)? Is empathy-based helping a source of such altruism? Cialdini (1991) and his colleagues Mark Schaller and Jim Fultz thought not. They noted that no experiment rules out all possible egoistic explanations for helpfulness.

However, after some 25 experiments testing egoism versus empathy, Batson (2001) and others (Dovidio, 1991; Staub, 1991) believed that sometimes people do focus on the welfare of others, not themselves. Genuine "empathy-induced altruism is part of human nature" (Batson 1999b). And that, said Batson, raises the hope—confirmed by research—that inducing empathy might improve attitudes toward stigmatized people: people with AIDS, the homeless, the imprisoned, and other minorities.

Alright—now that you have completed this section, go back and answer the questions from the activity at the beginning of the chapter again, but this time assessing whether or not these are true examples of altruism. Did your answers change? Why or why not?

When Will We Help?

What circumstances prompt people to help or not to help? How is helping influenced by the number and behaviour of other bystanders, and why?

On March 13, 1964, bar manager Kitty Genovese was attacked by a knife-wielding rapist as she returned to her apartment house at 3:00 a.m. Her screams of terror and pleas for help—"Oh my God, he stabbed me! Please help me! Please help me!"—aroused 38 of her neighbours. Many came to their windows and saw her plight while she struggled for 35 minutes to escape her attacker. Not until her attacker departed did anyone so much as call the police. Soon after, she died.

A later analysis disputed the initial report that there were actually 38 witnesses who observed the murder yet remained inactive (Manning, Levine, & Collins, 2007). Nevertheless, the story helped inspire research on bystander inaction, which was illustrated in other incidents:

- Seventeen-year-old Andrew Mormille was stabbed in the stomach as he rode the subway home. After his attackers left the car, 11 other riders watched the young man bleed to death.
- Eleanor Bradley tripped and broke her leg while shopping. Dazed and in pain, she pleaded for help. For 40 minutes, the stream of pedestrians simply parted and flowed around her. Finally, a cab driver helped her to a doctor (Darley & Latané, 1968).
- As more than a million locals and tourists mingled in the warm sun during and after a June 2000 parade alongside New York's Central Park, a pack of alcohol-fuelled young men became sexually aggressive—groping, and in some cases stripping, 60 women. In the days that followed, media attention focused on the mob psychology behind this sexual aggression and on police inaction. (At least two victims had approached nearby police, who failed to respond.) But what about the thousands of people milling around? Why did they tolerate this? Among the many bystanders with cellphones, why did not one person call 911 (*Dateline,* 2000)?

What is shocking in these cases is not that *some* people failed to help, but that in each of these groups, *almost 100 percent* of those present failed to respond. Why? In the same or similar situations, would you or I react as they did?

Social psychologists were curious and concerned about bystanders' lack of involvement. So they undertook experiments to identify when people will help in an emergency and when they will not.

Number of Bystanders

Bystander passivity during emergencies has prompted social commentators to lament people's "alienation," "apathy," "indifference," and "unconscious sadistic impulses." By attributing the nonintervention to the bystanders' dispositions, we can reassure ourselves that, as caring people, *we* would have helped. But were the bystanders such inhumane characters?

Social psychologists Bibb Latané and John Darley (1970) were unconvinced. So they staged ingenious emergencies and found that a single situational factor—the presence of other bystanders—greatly decreased intervention. By 1980, some four dozen experiments had compared help given by bystanders who perceived themselves to be either alone or with others. Given unrestricted communication among the bystanders, a person was at least as likely to be helped by a lone bystander as when observed by several bystanders (Latané & Nida, 1981; Stalder, 2008). In Internet communication, people are more likely to respond helpfully to a request for help (such as from someone seeking the link to the campus library) if they believe they alone (and not several others as well) have received the request (Blair, Thompson, & Wuensch, 2005).

When Latané and James Dabbs (1975) and 145 collaborators "accidentally" dropped coins or pencils during 1497 elevator rides, they were helped 40 percent of the time when one other person was on the elevator and less than 20 percent of the time when there were six passengers.

Why does the presence of other bystanders sometimes inhibit helping? Latané and Darley surmised that as the number of bystanders increases, any given bystander is less likely to notice the incident, less likely to interpret the incident as a problem or emergency, and less likely to assume responsibility for taking action (Figure 8–4).

Noticing

Imagine that 20 minutes after Eleanor Bradley has fallen and broken her leg on a crowded city sidewalk, you come along. Your eyes are on the backs of the pedestrians in front of you (it is bad manners to stare at those you pass), and your private thoughts are on the day's events. Would you, therefore, be less likely to notice the injured woman than if the sidewalk were virtually deserted?

To find out, Latané and Darley (1968) had men fill out a questionnaire in a room, either by themselves or with two strangers. While they were working (and being observed through a one-way mirror), there was a staged emergency: Smoke poured into the room through a wall vent. Solitary students, who often glanced idly about the room while working, noticed the smoke almost immediately—usually in less than five seconds. Those in groups kept their eyes on their work. It typically took them about 20 seconds to notice the smoke.

Interpreting

Once we notice an ambiguous event, we must interpret it. Put yourself in the room filling with smoke. Though worried, you don't want to embarrass yourself by getting flustered. You glance at the others. They look calm, indifferent. Assuming everything must be okay, you shrug it off and go back to work. Then one of the others notices the smoke and, noting your apparent unconcern, reacts similarly. This is an example of informational influence. Each person uses others' behaviour as clues to reality. Such misinterpretations can contribute to a delayed response to actual fires in offices, restaurants, and other multiple-occupancy settings (Canter, Breaux, & Sime, 1980).

The misinterpretations are fed by what Thomas Gilovich, Victoria Husted Medvec, and Kenneth Savitsky (2000) called an *illusion of transparency*—a tendency to overestimate

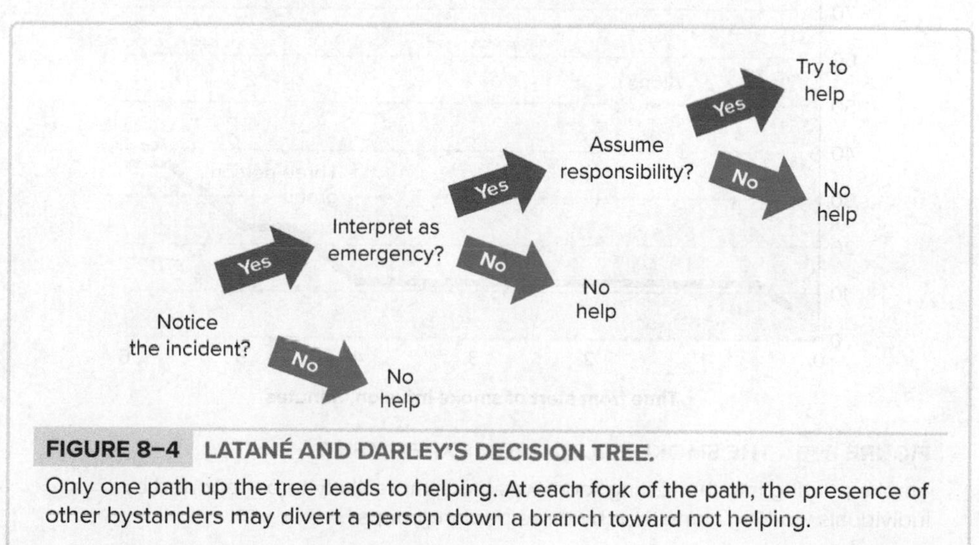

FIGURE 8–4 LATANÉ AND DARLEY'S DECISION TREE.

Only one path up the tree leads to helping. At each fork of the path, the presence of other bystanders may divert a person down a branch toward not helping.

others' ability to "read" our internal states. More than we usually suppose, our disgust, our deceit, and our alarm are opaque. Keenly aware of our emotions, we presume that others see right through us. Sometimes others do. But often we appear quite effectively to keep our cool. The result is what Chapter 7 called *pluralistic ignorance*—the assumption that others are thinking and feeling what we are. Thus, in emergencies, each person may think, "I'm very concerned," but perceive others as not looking alarmed—"so maybe it's not an emergency."

So it happened in the actual experiment. When those working alone noticed the smoke, they usually hesitated a moment, then got up, walked over to the vent, felt, sniffed, and waved at the smoke, hesitated again, and then went to report it. In dramatic contrast, those in groups of three did not move. Among the 24 men in eight groups, only one person reported the smoke within the first four minutes (Figure 8–5). By the end of the six-minute experiment, the smoke was so thick it was obscuring the men's vision and they were rubbing their eyes and coughing. Still, in only three of the eight groups did even a single person leave to report the problem.

Equally interesting, the group's passivity affected its members' interpretations. When asked what they thought had caused the smoke, these were the replies: "a leak in the air conditioning," "chemistry labs in the building," "steam pipes," and "truth gas." They offered many explanations. Not one person, however, said, "fire." The group members, by serving as nonresponsive models, influenced each other's interpretation of the situation.

That experimental dilemma parallels dilemmas each of us faces. Is the boys' scuffling a friendly tussle or a vicious fight? Is the person slumped in the doorway sleeping, high on drugs, or seriously ill, perhaps in a diabetic coma? That surely was the question confronting those who in 2003 watched Brandon Vedas overdose and die online. As his life ebbed, his audience, which was left to wonder whether he was putting on an act, failed to decipher available clues to his whereabouts and to contact police (Nichols, 2003). A recent meta-analysis of bystander effect research has shown that the seemingly counterintuitive result is that the bystander effect is reduced in dangerous situations. When the situation is obviously dangerous, people are more likely to provide help (Fischer et al., 2011). Why?

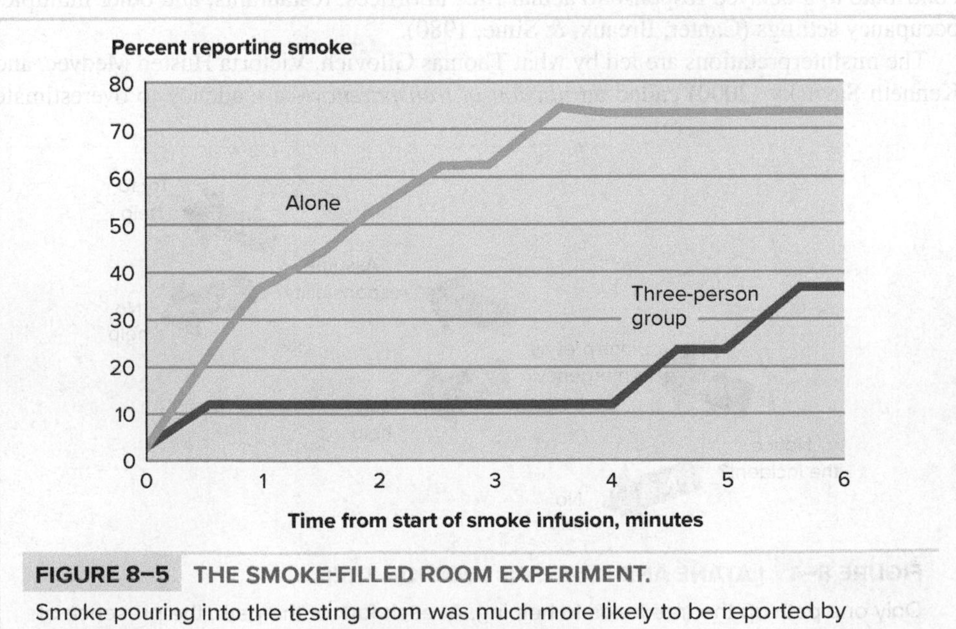

FIGURE 8–5 THE SMOKE-FILLED ROOM EXPERIMENT.

Smoke pouring into the testing room was much more likely to be reported by individuals working alone than by three-person groups.

Because a dangerous situation is easy to interpret. We know that a person needs help so that overrides people's difficulty with interpreting the situation.

Amanda Todd, a 15-year-old from British Columbia, took her own life after being severely bullied online. Experts argued that passive bystanders were partly to blame (CBC, 2012). In Nova Scotia, this has been addressed head-on in the legal definition of bullying (which also applies to bullying online) (CBC, 2013a). Now, people who passively watch someone being bullied and do not act are also considered responsible and are subject to sanctions.

Assuming responsibility

Unlike the smoke-filled-room experiment, however, each of these everyday situations involves someone in desperate need. To see if the same **bystander effect** occurs in such situations, Latané and Judith Rodin (1969) staged an experiment around a woman in distress. A female researcher set men to work on a questionnaire and then left through a curtained doorway to work in an adjacent office. Four minutes later, she could be heard (from a tape recorder) climbing on a chair to reach some papers. This was followed by a scream and a loud crash as the chair collapsed and she fell to the floor. "Oh, my God, my foot . . . I . . . I . . . can't move it," she sobbed. "Oh . . . my ankle . . . I . . . can't get this . . . thing . . . off me." Only after two minutes of moaning did she manage to make it out of her office door.

bystander effect The finding that a person is less likely to provide help when there are other bystanders.

Seventy percent of those alone when they overheard the "accident" came into the room or called out to offer help. Among pairs of strangers confronting the emergency, only 40 percent of the time did either person offer help. Those who did nothing apparently interpreted the situation as a nonemergency. "A mild sprain," said some. "I didn't want to embarrass her," explained others. This again demonstrates the bystander effect: As the number of people known to be aware of an emergency increases, any given person becomes less likely to help. For the victim, there is, therefore, no safety in numbers.

People's interpretations also affect their reactions to street crimes. In staging physical fights between a man and a woman, Lance Shotland and Margaret Straw (1976) found that bystanders intervened 65 percent of the time when the woman shouted, "Get away from me; I don't know you" but only 19 percent of the time when she shouted, "Get away from me; I don't know why I ever married you." People seemed to think it wasn't their business when the woman was married to the attacker. Spousal abuse, it seems, just doesn't trigger as much concern as stranger abuse. In such dangerous situations where a perpetrator is present and intervention requires physical risk, the bystander effect is less evident (Fischer et al., 2011).

Interpretations matter: Is this man locked out of his car or is he a burglar? Our answer affects how we respond.

Source: ©Peter Dazeley/Photographer's Choice/Getty Images.

Failure to notice and misinterpretation are not the only causes of the bystander effect. Would you intervene if you saw someone breaking into a car? Even when a 14-year-old was the "burglar," when someone simultaneously broke into two adjacent cars, or when onlookers saw a different person breaking into the car than had just gotten out of it, Takooshian and Bodinger (1982) reported that there was virtually no intervention.

To explore bystander inaction in clear emergencies, Darley and Latané (1968) simulated the Genovese case. They placed people in separate rooms from which the participants would hear a victim crying for help. To create this situation, Darley and Latané asked some students to discuss, over a laboratory intercom, their problems with university life. The students were told that, to guarantee their anonymity, no one would be visible and the experimenter would not eavesdrop. During the ensuing discussion, the

Responsibility diffusion. The nine paparazzi photographers on the scene immediately after Princess Diana's fatal car accident all had cell phones. Only one called for help. Nearly all said they assumed "someone else" had already called (Sancton, 1997).
Source: ©Pierre Boussel/Getty Images.

participants heard one person, when the experimenter turned his microphone on, lapse into an epileptic seizure. With increasing intensity and speech difficulty, he pleaded for someone to help.

Of those led to believe they were the only listener, 85 percent left their room to seek help. Of those who believed that four others also overheard the victim, only 31 percent went for help. Were those who didn't respond apathetic and indifferent? When the experimenter came in to end the experiment, she did not find this response. Most immediately expressed concern. Many had trembling hands and sweating palms. They believed an emergency had occurred but were undecided whether to act.

After the smoke-filled room, the woman-in-distress, and the seizure experiments, Latané and Darley asked the participants whether the presence of others had influenced them. We know that presence of others had a dramatic effect. Yet the participants almost invariably denied the influence. The typical reply? "I was aware of the others, but I would have reacted just the same if they weren't there." This response reinforces a familiar point: We often do not know why we do what we do. That is why experiments such as these are revealing. A survey of uninvolved bystanders following a real emergency would have left the bystander effect hidden.

Further experiments revealed situations in which the presence of others sometimes did not inhibit people from offering help. Irving Piliavin and his colleagues (1969) staged an emergency in a laboratory on wheels—the unwitting subjects being 4450 riders of the subway. On each of 103 occasions, a confederate entered a subway car and stood in the centre next to a pole. After the train pulled out of the station, he staggered, then collapsed. When the victim carried a cane, one or more bystanders almost always promptly offered help. Even when the victim carried a bottle and smelled of liquor, he was often promptly offered aid—aid that was especially prompt when several male bystanders were close by. Why? Did the presence of other passengers provide a sense of security to those who helped? Or did they help because the situation was unambiguous? (The passengers couldn't help noticing and realizing what was happening.)

To test this latter possibility, Linda Solomon, Henry Solomon, and Ronald Stone (1978) conducted experiments in which people either saw and heard someone's distress, as in the subway experiment, or only heard it, as in the woman-in-distress

The guilt many people feel after passing by someone experiencing homelessness might motivate them to help someone in the next situation they encounter.
Source: ©Ruben Sanchez @lostintv/Getty Images.

experiment (leaving the situation more open to interpretation). When the emergencies were very clear, those in groups were only slightly less likely to help than were those who were alone. When the emergencies were somewhat ambiguous, however, the subjects in groups were far less likely to help than were solitary bystanders.

Most people who live in large cities are seldom alone in public places, which helps account for why city people often are less helpful than country people. *Compassion fatigue* and *sensory overload* from encountering so many people in need further restrain helping in large cities across the world (Yousif & Korte, 1995). This explains what happened when Robert Levine and colleagues (1994) approached several thousand people in 36 cities, dropping an unnoticed pen, asking for change, simulating a blind person needing help at a corner, and so forth. The bigger and more densely populated the city, the less likely people were to help. In large cities, bystanders are also more often strangers—whose increasing numbers depress helping. When bystanders are friends or people who share a group identity, increased numbers may, instead, increase helping (M. Levine & Crowther, 2008).

A significant amount of work has been done around how to impact helping behaviour at school and in the workplace, particularly to reduce bullying behaviours and avoid what happened to youth such as Rehteah Parsons and Amanda Todd (see Sanderson, 2020; Staub, 2019, for reviews). Some findings are that how connected students are to the school increases helping behaviour (Jouriles et al., 2020), and that people who are mindful help more (Hafenbrack et al., 2019). Importantly, we are more likely to help people we know and like (Coyne et al., 2019) and our friends reinforce our social norms—if we are expected to help, we will (Moisuc & Brauer, 2019; Patrick et al., 2019). A very important outcome of this is that we know training people (e.g., not to use the word "retard" in school, and to stop people who do) can be very effective (Siperstein et al., 2018) and anti-bullying programs reduce that behaviour (see Sanderson, 2020, for a review).

Levine and his collaborators (R. V. Levine, 2001, 2003; Levine, Norenzayan, & Philbrick, 2001) have also found that willingness to help strangers also varies around the world (Figure 8–6). People in economically advanced countries tended to offer less help to strangers, and those in cultures marked by amiable and agreeable *simpatia* (in Spanish) or *simpatico* (in Portuguese) were more helpful.

Nations, too, have often been bystanders to catastrophes, even to genocide. As 750 000 people were murdered in Rwanda, we all stood by. "With many potential actors, each feels less responsible," noted Ervin Staub (1997a). "It's not our responsibility," say the leaders of unaffected nations. This was particularly noticeable when COVID-19 began to hit in early 2020. Many countries focused on their own concerns, rather than helping other countries control their outbreaks. However, as we saw, our global interconnectivity means that what happens in one country will inevitably affect many others.

Revisiting research ethics

These experiments raise an ethical issue: Is it right to force unwitting people to overhear someone's apparent collapse? Were the researchers in the seizure experiment ethical when they forced people to decide whether to interrupt their discussion to report the problem? Would you object to being in such a study? Note that it would have been impossible to get your "informed consent"; doing so would have destroyed the experiment's cover.

The researchers were always careful to debrief the laboratory participants. Other researchers have confirmed that the overwhelming majority of participants in such experiments say that their participation was both instructive and ethically justified (Schwartz & Gottlieb, 1981). In field experiments, an accomplice assisted the victim if no one else did, thus reassuring bystanders that the problem was being dealt with.

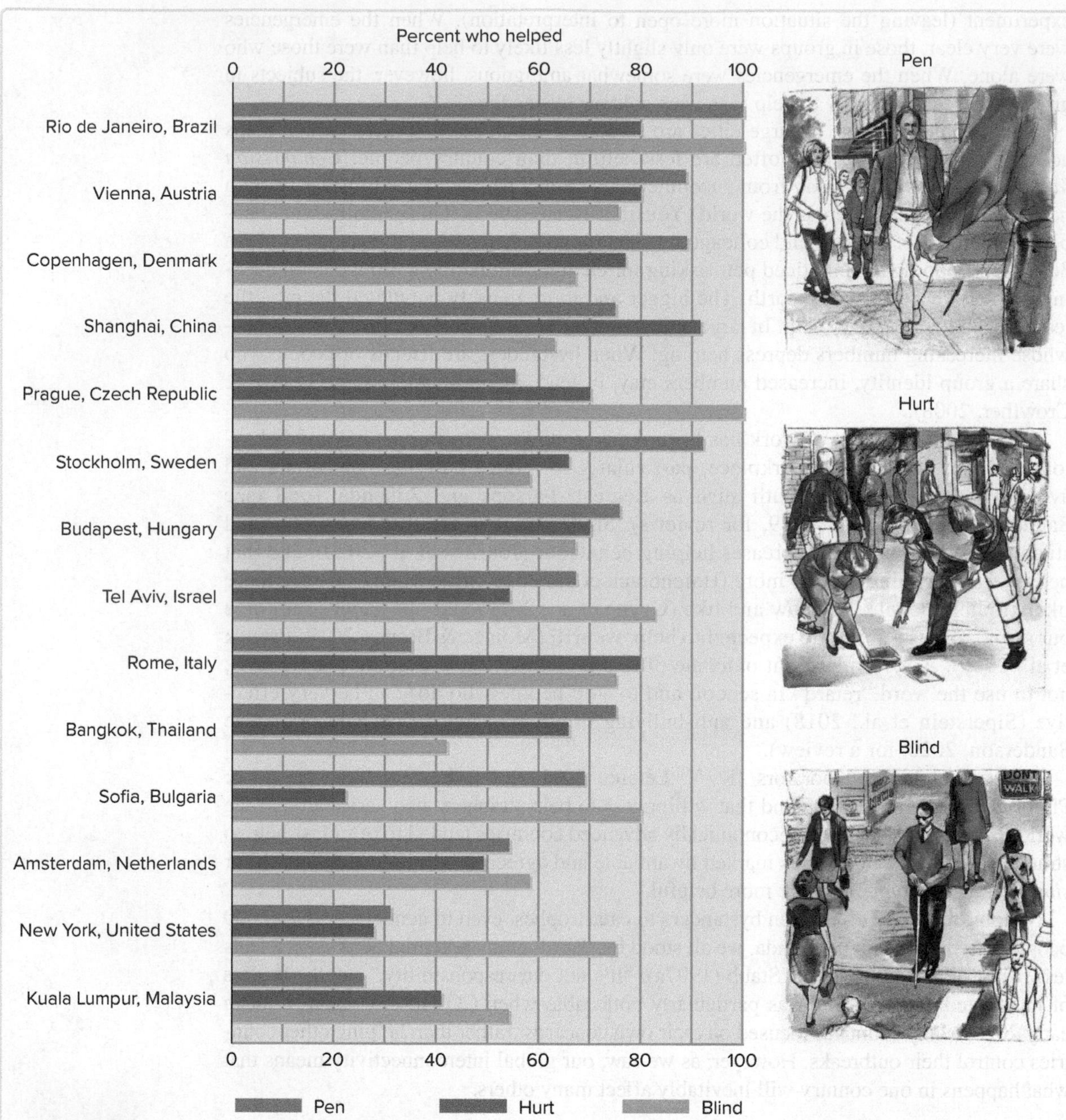

FIGURE 8–6 A WORLD OF DIFFERENCE IN HELPING STRANGERS.

To compare helping in different cities and cultures, Robert Levine and his collaborators would "accidentally" drop a pen, drop magazines while limping with an apparently injured leg, or feign blindness when approaching an intersection as the light turned green. Those dropping a pen in Rio were, for example, four times more likely to be helped than those doing so in New York City or Kuala Lumpur. (This is a sample of data from 14 countries.)

Source: Adapted from R. V. Levine. (2003). The kindness of strangers. *American Scientist, 91,* 226–233.

Remember that the social psychologist has a twofold ethical obligation: to protect the participants and to enhance human welfare by discovering influences upon human behaviour. Such discoveries can alert us to unwanted influences and show us how we might exert positive influences. The ethical principle seems to be this: After protecting participants' welfare, social psychologists fulfill their responsibility to society by giving us insight into our behaviour.

Helping When Someone Else Does

Imagine hearing a crash followed by sobs and moans. If another bystander said, "Uh-oh. This is an emergency! We've got to do something," would this stimulate others to help?

The evidence is clear: Prosocial models do promote prosocial behaviour. Here are some examples:

- In one field study, James Bryan and Mary Ann Test (1967) found that drivers were more likely to offer help to a female driver with a flat tire if a quarter-mile (0.4 km) earlier they had witnessed someone helping another woman change a tire.
- In another experiment, Bryan and Test observed that Christmas shoppers were more likely to drop money in a Salvation Army kettle if they had just seen someone else do the same.
- Philippe Rushton and Anne Campbell (1977) found that British adults were more willing to donate blood if they were approached after observing a confederate consent to donating.
- A glimpse of extraordinary human kindness and charity often triggers what Jonathan Haidt (2003) called *elevation,* "a distinctive feeling in the chest of warmth and expansion" that may provoke chills, tears, and throat-clenching and that often inspires people to become more self-giving.

> ***"We are, in truth, more than half what we are by imitation. The great point is, to choose good models and to study them with care."***
>
> Lord Chesterfield, quoted in *The Best Letters ofLord Chesterfield,* 1890

One of these findings is especially meaningful for parents: Models sometimes contradict in practice what they preach. Parents may tell their children, "Do as I say, not as I do." Experiments show that children learn moral judgments from both what they hear preached and what they see practised (Rice & Grusec, 1975; Rushton, 1975). When exposed to these discrepancies, they imitate: They say what the model says and do what the model does.

Time Pressures

Darley and Batson (1973) discerned another determinant of helping. In their experiment, after collecting their thoughts prior to recording a brief extemporaneous talk (which, for half the participants, was on the Good Samaritan parable), theological seminary students were directed to a recording studio in an adjacent building. En route, they passed a man sitting slumped in a doorway, head down, coughing and groaning. Some of the students had been sent off nonchalantly: "It will be a few minutes before they're ready for you, but you might as well head on over." Of these, almost two-thirds stopped to offer help. Others were told, "Oh, you're late. They were expecting you a few minutes ago … so you'd better hurry." Of these, only 10 percent offered help.

Darley and Batson (1973), reflecting on these findings, wrote:

> A person not in a hurry may stop and offer help to a person in distress. A person in a hurry is likely to keep going. Ironically, he is likely to keep going even if he is hurrying to speak on the parable of the Good Samaritan, thus inadvertently confirming the point of the parable. (Indeed, on several occasions, a seminary student going to give his talk on the parable of the Good Samaritan literally stepped over the victim as he hurried on his way!) (p. 107)

Are we being unfair to the seminary students, who were, after all, hurrying to help the experimenter? Perhaps they keenly felt the social-responsibility norm but found it pulling them two ways—toward the experimenter and toward the victim. In another enactment of the Good Samaritan situation, Batson and his associates (1978) directed 40 university students to an experiment in another building. Half were told they were late; half knew they had plenty of time. Half thought their participation was vitally important to the experimenter; half thought it was not essential. The results: Those on their way to an unimportant appointment usually stopped to help. But people seldom stopped to help if they were late.

Can we conclude that those who were rushed were callous? Did the seminarians notice the victim's distress and then consciously choose to ignore it? No. In their hurry, they never fully grasped the situation. Harried, preoccupied, rushing to meet a deadline, they simply did not take time to tune in to the person in need. As social psychologists have so often observed, their behaviour was influenced more by context than by conviction.

Similarity to the Victim

Because similarity is conducive to liking, and liking is conducive to helping, we are more empathic and helpful toward those similar to us (Miller, Kozu, & Davis, 2001). This similarity bias applies to both dress and beliefs. Tim Emswiller and his fellow researchers (1971) had confederates, dressed either conservatively or in counterculture garb, approach "conservative" or "hip" students seeking money for a phone call. Fewer than half the students did the favour for those dressed differently than themselves. Two-thirds did so for those dressed similarly. Likewise, Scottish shoppers in a more anti-gay era were less willing to make change for someone if the person wore a T-shirt with a pro-gay slogan (Gray, Russell, & Blockley, 1991).

No face is more familiar than one's own. That explains why, when Lisa DeBruine (2002) had McMaster University students play an interactive game with a supposed other player, they were more trusting and generous when the other person's pictured face had some features of their own morphed into it (Figure 8–7): In me I trust. Even just sharing a birthday, a first name, or a fingerprint pattern leads people to respond more to a request for help (Burger et al., 2004).

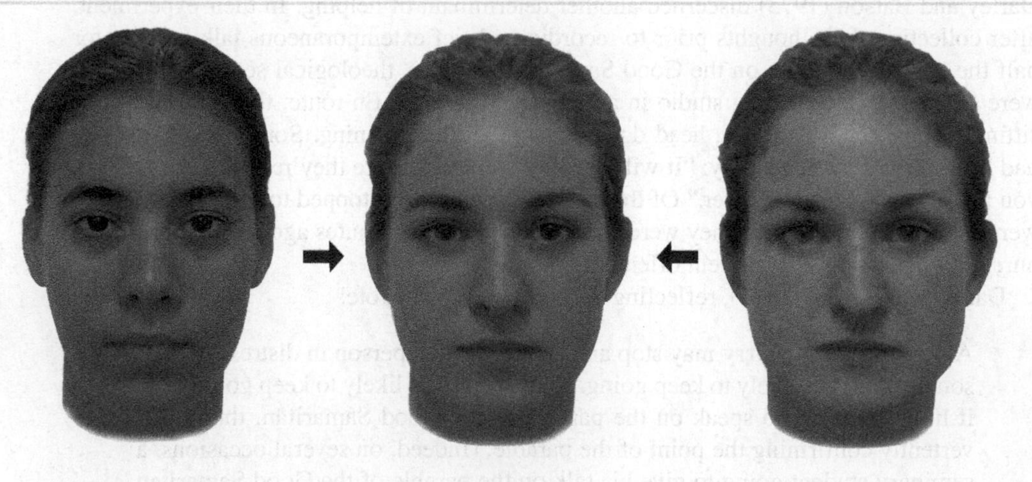

FIGURE 8–7 SIMILARITY BREEDS COOPERATION.

Lisa DeBruine (2002) morphed participants' faces (left) with strangers' faces (right) to make the composite faces (centre)—toward whom the participants were more generous than toward the stranger.

Source: Courtesy of Lisa DeBruine.

Who Helps?

We have considered internal influences on the decision to help (such as guilt and mood) and external influences as well (such as social norms, number of bystanders, time pressure, and similarity to the victim). We also need to consider the helper's personality and gender.

Personality Traits

Faced with identical situations, some people will respond helpfully while others won't bother. Some people will run to the disaster while others run away. Many (such as first responders and health care workers) face the risks of pandemics like COVID-19 on a daily basis. But what distinguishes these people from those who don't (or won't) help?

For many years, social psychologists were unable to discover a single personality trait that predicted altruistic behaviour with anything close to the predictive power of the situation, guilt, and mood factors. Modest relationships were found between helping and certain personality variables, such as need for social approval. But, by and large, the personality tests were unable to identify the helpers. Studies of rescuers of Jews in Nazi Europe reveal a similar conclusion: Although the social context clearly influenced willingness to help, there was no definable set of altruistic personality traits (Darley, 1995).

"There are … reasons why personality should be rather unimportant in determining people's reactions to the emergency. For one thing, the situational forces affecting a person's decision are so strong."

Bibb Latané and John Darley, 1970, p. 115

If that has a familiar ring, it could be from a similar conclusion by conformity researchers (Chapter 6): Conformity, too, seemed more influenced by the situation than by measurable personality traits. Perhaps, though, you recall from Chapter 2 that who we are does affect what we do. Attitude and trait measures seldom predict a specific act, which is what most experiments on prosocial behaviour measure, in contrast to the lifelong altruism of someone like Mother Teresa. But such measures more accurately predict average behaviour across many situations.

Personality researchers have responded to the challenge. First, they have found individual differences in helpfulness, and they have shown that these differences persist over time and are noticed by a person's peers (Hampson, 1984; Rushton, Chrisjohn, & Fekken, 1981). Some people are reliably more helpful.

Second, researchers are gathering clues to the network of traits that predispose a person to helpfulness. Those high in emotionality, empathy, and self-efficacy are most likely to be concerned and helpful (Eisenberg et al., 1991; Krueger, Hicks, & McGue, 2001; Walker & Frimer, 2007).

Third, personality influences how particular people react to particular situations (Carlo et al., 1991; Romer, Gruder, & Lizzadro, 1986; Wilson & Petruska, 1984). Those high in self-monitoring are attuned to the expectations of others and are especially helpful if they think helpfulness will be socially rewarded (White & Gerstein, 1987). Others' opinions matter less to internally guided, low-self-monitoring people.

Gender

This interaction of person and situation also appears in the 172 studies that have compared the helpfulness of nearly 50 000 male and female subjects. After analyzing these results, Alice Eagly and Maureen Crowley (1986) reported that, when faced with potentially dangerous situations in which strangers need help (such as with a flat tire or a fall in a subway), men more often help. Eagly (2009) also reported that among 6767 individuals who have received the Carnegie medal for heroism in saving human life, 90 percent have been men.

Would gender norms—"women and children first"—more likely come into play in situations when people have time to reflect on social norms (as opposed to acting instinctively, on impulse)? To explore this possibility, some fiendish experimenter might wish to assign passengers to fast- or slow-sinking ships and observe behaviour. Actually, note Zurich researcher Bruno Frey and his colleagues (2010), the course of human events has conducted this experiment. In 1915, a German U-boat sank the passenger liner *Lusitania* in a panicked 18 minutes, with women on board being 1 percent less likely to survive than men. In 1912, the *Titanic,* carrying a similar mix of passengers, hit an iceberg and took nearly three hours to sink—and women were 53 percent more likely to survive than men. In this natural experiment, time enabled prosocial behaviour and the activation of gender norms.

In safer situations, such as volunteering to help with an experiment or spending time with children with developmental disabilities, women are slightly more likely to help. In one survey of 272 036 university students, 63 percent of men and 75 percent of women rated "helping others in difficulty" as "very important" or "essential" (Pryor et al., 2007). Women also have been as likely as, or more likely than, men to risk death as Holocaust rescuers, to donate a kidney, and to volunteer with the Peace Corps and Doctors of the World (Becker & Eagly, 2004). Faced with a friend's problems, women respond with greater empathy and spend more time helping (George et al., 1998). Thus, the gender difference interacts with (depends on) the situation.

How Can We Increase Helping?

To increase helping, we can reverse the factors that inhibit helping, or we can teach altruistic norms and socialize people to see themselves as helpful.

As social scientists, our goal is to understand human behaviour and, thus, to also suggest ways to improve it. So, how might we apply research-based understanding to increase helping? One way to promote prosocial behaviour is to reverse those factors that inhibit it. Given that hurried, preoccupied people are less likely to help, can we think of ways to encourage them to slow down and turn their attention outward? If the presence of others diminishes each bystander's sense of responsibility, how can we enhance responsibility?

Reduce Ambiguity, Increase Responsibility

If Latané and Darley's decision tree (Figure 8–4) describes the dilemmas that bystanders face, then assisting people to interpret an incident correctly and to assume responsibility should increase their involvement. Leonard Bickman and his colleagues (1975, 1979; Bickman & Green, 1977) tested this presumption in a series of experiments on crime reporting. In each, supermarket or bookstore shoppers witnessed a shoplifting. Some witnesses had seen signs that attempted to sensitize them to shoplifting and to inform them how to report it. But the signs had little effect. Other witnesses heard a bystander interpret the incident: "Say, look at her. She's shoplifting. She put that into her purse." (The bystander then left to look for a lost child.) Still others heard this person add, "We saw it. We should report it. It's our responsibility." Both face-to-face comments substantially boosted reporting of the crime.

The potency of personal influence is no longer in doubt. Robert Foss (1978) surveyed several hundred blood donors and found that new donors, unlike regular donors, were usually there at someone's personal invitation. Leonard Jason and his collaborators (1984) confirmed that personal appeals for blood donation are much more effective than posters and media announcements—if the personal appeals come from friends.

Personal appeal

Personalized nonverbal appeals can also be effective. Mark Snyder and his co-workers (1974; Omoto & Snyder, 2002) found that hitchhikers doubled the number of ride offers by looking drivers straight in the eye and that most AIDS volunteers got involved through someone's personal influence. A personal approach makes people feel less anonymous, more responsible.

Henry Solomon and Linda Solomon (1978; Solomon et al., 1981) explored ways to reduce anonymity. They found that bystanders who had identified themselves to one another—by name, age, and so forth—were more likely to offer aid to a sick person than were anonymous bystanders. Similarly, when a female experimenter caught the eye of another shopper and gave her a warm smile prior to stepping on an elevator, that shopper was far more likely than other shoppers to offer help when the experimenter later said, "Damn. I've left my glasses. Can anyone tell me what floor the umbrellas are on?" Even a trivial momentary conversation with someone ("Excuse me, aren't you Suzie Spear's sister?" "No, I'm not") dramatically increased the person's later helpfulness.

Helpfulness also increases when one expects to meet the victim and other witnesses again. Using a laboratory intercom system, Jody Gottlieb and Charles Carver (1980) led students to believe that they were discussing problems of university living with other students. (Actually, the other discussants were tape-recorded.) When one of the supposed fellow discussants had a choking fit and cried out for help, she was helped most quickly by subjects who believed they would soon be meeting the discussants face-to-face. In short, anything that personalizes bystanders—a personal request, eye contact, stating one's name, anticipation of interaction—increases willingness to help. In experiments, restaurant patrons tipped more when their servers introduced themselves by name, touched guests on the arm or shoulder, sat or squatted at the table during the service encounter, and wrote friendly messages on checks before they gave them to customers (Leodoro & Lynn, 2007; Schirmer et al., 2011).

Personal treatment makes bystanders more self-aware and, therefore, more attuned to their own altruistic ideals. Recall from earlier chapters that people made self-aware by acting in front of a mirror or TV camera exhibited increased consistency between attitudes and actions. By contrast, *deindividuated* people were less responsible. Thus, circumstances that promote self-awareness—name tags, being watched and evaluated, undistracted quiet—should also increase helping.

Shelley Duval, Virginia Duval, and Robert Neely (1979) confirmed this. They showed some women their own image on a TV screen or had them complete a biographical questionnaire just before giving them a chance to contribute time and money to people in need. Those made self-aware contributed more. Similarly, pedestrians who have just had their picture taken by someone became more likely to help another pedestrian pick up dropped envelopes (Hoover, Wood, & Knowles, 1983). And among those who had just seen themselves in a mirror, 70 percent of Italian pedestrians helped a stranger by mailing a postcard, as did 13 percent of others approached (Abbate et al., 2006). Self-aware people more often put their ideals into practice.

Guilt and Concern for Self-Image

Previously, we noted that people who feel guilty will act to reduce guilt and restore their self-worth. Can awakening people's guilt therefore increase their desire to help? Have university students think about their past transgressions and they become more likely to agree to volunteer to help with a school project.

A research team led by Richard Katzev (1978) experimented with guilt-induced helping in everyday contexts. When visitors to an art museum disobeyed a "Please do not touch" sign, experimenters reprimanded some of them: "Please don't touch the objects. If everyone touches them, they will deteriorate." Likewise, when visitors to a zoo fed unauthorized food to the bears, some of them were admonished with, "Hey, don't feed unauthorized food to the animals. Don't you know it could hurt them?" In both cases, 58 percent of the now guilt-laden subjects shortly thereafter offered help to another experimenter who had "accidentally" dropped something. Of those not reprimanded, only one-third helped. Guilt-laden people are helpful people.

Socializing Prosocial Behaviour

If we can learn prosocial behaviour, then how might we teach it? Here are five ways.

Teaching moral inclusion

Rescuers of Jews in Nazi Europe, relief workers in foreign countries, and volunteers at homeless shelters share at least one thing in common: **moral inclusion**. They include people who differ from themselves within the human circle to which their moral values and rules of justice apply. These people are morally inclusive, as illustrated by one rescuer who faked a pregnancy on behalf of a pregnant hidden Jew—thus including the soon-to-be-born child within the circle of her own children's identities (Fogelman, 1994).

moral inclusion Regarding others as within your circle of moral concern.

moral exclusion The perception of certain individuals or groups as outside the boundary within which you apply moral values and rules of fairness.

Moral exclusion—omitting certain people from one's circle of moral concern—has the opposite effect. It justifies all sorts of harm, from discrimination to genocide (Opotow, 1990; Staub, 1990; Tyler & Lind, 1990). Exploitation or cruelty becomes acceptable, even appropriate, toward those we regard as undeserving or as nonpersons. The Nazis excluded Jews from their moral community. Anyone who participates in enslavement, death squads, or torture demonstrates moral exclusion. To a lesser extent, moral exclusion describes any of us who concentrate our concerns, favours, and financial inheritance on "our people" (for example, our children) to the exclusion of others.

We easily become numbed by impersonal big numbers of out-group fatalities, note Paul Slovic (2007) and Elizabeth Dunn and Claire Ashton-James (2008). People presume that they would be more upset about a hurricane that killed 5000 rather than 50 people. But whether Dunn and Ashton-James told people that Hurricane Katrina claimed 50, 500, 1000, or 5000 lives, their sadness was unaffected by the number. Ditto for the scale of other tragedies, including a forest fire in Spain and the war in Iraq. "If I look at the mass I will never act," said Mother Teresa. "If I look at the one, I will." Shown a single victim, a seven-year-old girl named Rokia, people responded with more money for a hunger charity than when told the organization was working to save millions (Slovic & Västfjäll, 2010).

> ***"We consider humankind our family."***
>
> Parliament of the World's Religions, *Towards a Global Ethic*, 1993

A first step toward socializing prosocial behaviour is, therefore, to counter the natural in-group bias favouring kin and tribe by broadening the range of people whose well-being concerns us. If everyone is part of our family, then everyone has a moral claim on us. The boundaries between "us" and "them" fade. Inviting advantaged people to put themselves in others' shoes, to imagine how less advantaged people feel, also helps (Batson et al., 2003). To "do unto others as you would have them do unto you," one must take the other's perspective (see Figure 8–8).

Modelling prosocial behaviour

Previously, we noted that seeing unresponsive bystanders makes us less likely to help. People reared by extremely punitive parents, as were many delinquents and chronic criminals, also show much less of the empathy and principled caring that typify altruists.

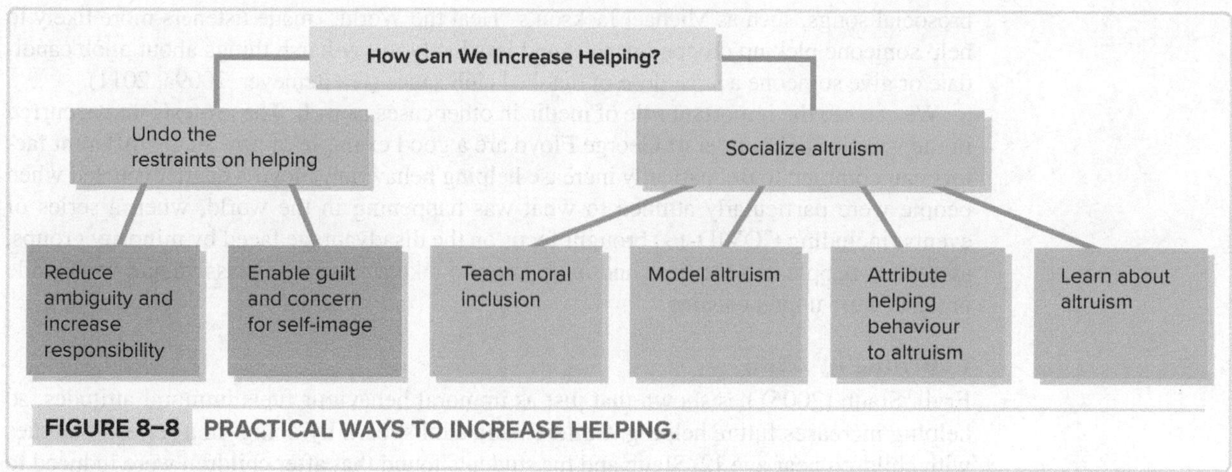

FIGURE 8–8 **PRACTICAL WAYS TO INCREASE HELPING.**

If we see or read about someone helping, we are more likely to offer assistance. It's better, found Robert Cialdini (2003), not to publicize rampant tax cheating, littering, and teen drinking, and instead to emphasize—to define a norm of—people's widespread honesty, cleanliness, and abstinence. In one experiment, researchers asked visitors not to remove petrified wood from along the paths of the U.S. Petrified Forest National Park. Some subjects were also told that "past visitors have removed the petrified wood." Those subjects who were told that "past visitors have left the petrified wood" in order to preserve the park were much less likely to pick up samples placed along a path.

Modelling effects were also apparent in the families of European Christians who risked their lives to rescue Jews in the 1930s and 1940s and in the civil rights activists of the late 1950s. In both cases, these exceptional altruists had warm and close relationships with at least one parent who was, similarly, a strong "moralist" or committed to humanitarian causes (London, 1970, Oliner & Oliner, 1988, Rosenhan, 1970). This *prosocial value orientation* led them to include people from other groups in their circle of moral concern and to feel responsible for others' welfare (Staub, 1989, 1991, 1992).

Can positive models in the media promote helping? Prosocial TV models have actually had even greater effects than antisocial models. Susan Hearold (1986) statistically combined 108 comparisons of prosocial programs with neutral programs or no program. She found that, on average, "If the viewer watched prosocial programs instead of neutral programs, he would [at least temporarily] be elevated from the 50th to the 74th percentile in prosocial behaviour—typically altruism."

Other media also effectively model prosocial behaviour. Recent studies show positive effects on attitudes or behaviour from playing prosocial video games and listening to prosocial music lyrics (Gentile et al., 2009; Greitemeyer, 2009a; Greitemeyer, Osswald, & Brauer, 2010). For example, playing *Lemmings,* where the goal is to help others, increases later real-life empathy and helping in response to another's misfortune (Greitemeyer & Osswald, 2010; Greitemeyer et al., 2010). Listening to

Warren Buffett, co-creator of the Giving Pledge, earned admiration for pledging to give away 99 percent of his fortune to philanthropic causes.

Source: ©dpa picture alliance archive/Alamy Stock Photo.

prosocial songs, such as Michael Jackson's "Heal the World," made listeners more likely to help someone pick up dropped pencils and less likely to say harsh things about a job candidate or give someone a large dose of disliked chili sauce (Greitemeyer, 2009a, 2011).

We can see the important role of media in other cases as well. The protests that occurred in the wake of the murder of George Floyd are a good example of how many different factors can combine to dramatically increase helping behaviour. Floyd's death occurred when people were particularly attuned to what was happening in the world, when a series of events (including COVID-19) brought focus on the disadvantage faced by minority groups, and when people had the time and inclination to take action. The massive and worldwide protests were unprecedented.

Learning by doing

Ervin Staub (2005) has shown that just as immoral behaviour fuels immoral attitudes, so helping increases future helping. Children and adults learn by doing. In a series of studies with children near age 12, Staub and his students found that after children were induced to make toys for hospitalized children or for an art teacher, they became more helpful. So did children who first taught younger children to make puzzles or use first aid.

When children act helpfully, they develop helping-related values, beliefs, and skills, noted Staub. Helping also contributes to satisfying their needs for a positive self-concept. On a larger scale, community service and volunteer programs woven into a school curriculum have been shown to increase later citizen involvement, social responsibility, cooperation, and leadership (Andersen, 1998; Putnam, 2000). Attitudes follow behaviour. Helpful actions, therefore, promote the self-perception that one is caring and helpful, which in turn promotes further helping.

Attributing helpful behaviour to altruistic motives

Another clue to socializing prosocial behaviour comes from research on the overjustification effect (see also Chapter 4): When the justification for an act is more than sufficient, the person may attribute the act to the extrinsic justification rather than to an inner motive. Rewarding people for doing what they would do anyway undermines intrinsic motivation. We can state the principle positively: By providing people with just enough justification to prompt a good deed (weaning them from bribes and threats when possible), we may increase their pleasure in doing such deeds on their own.

Daniel Batson and his associates (1978, 1979) put the overjustification phenomenon to work. In several experiments, they found that University of Kansas students felt most altruistic after they agreed to help someone without payment or implied social pressure. When pay had been offered or social pressures were present, people felt less altruistic after helping.

In another experiment, the researchers led students to attribute a helpful act to compliance ("I guess we really don't have a choice") or to compassion ("The guy really needs help"). Later, when the students were asked to volunteer their time to a local service agency, 25 percent of those who had been led to perceive their previous helpfulness as mere compliance now volunteered; of those led to see themselves as compassionate, 60 percent volunteered. The moral? When people wonder, "Why am I helping?" it's best if the circumstances enable them to answer, "Because help was needed, and I am a caring, giving, helpful person."

As you may recall from Chapter 4, rewards undermine intrinsic motivation when they function as controlling bribes. An unanticipated compliment, however, can make people feel competent and worthy. When Joe is coerced with "If you quit being chicken and give blood, we'll win the fraternity prize for most donations," he isn't likely to attribute his donation to altruism. When Jocelyn is rewarded with "That's terrific that you'd choose to take an hour out of such a busy week to give blood," she's more likely to walk away with an altruistic self-image—and thus to contribute again (Piliavin et al., 1982; Thomas & Batson, 1981; Thomas, Batson, & Coke, 1981).

To predispose more people to help in situations where most don't, it can also pay to induce a tentative positive commitment, from which people may infer their own helpfulness. Delia Cioffi and Randy Garner (1998) observed that only about 5 percent of students responded to a campus blood drive after receiving an email announcement a week ahead. They asked other students to reply to the announcement with a yes, "if you think you probably will donate." Of these, 29 percent replied and the actual donation rate was 8 percent. They asked a third group to reply with a no if they did not anticipate donating. Now 71 percent implied they might give (by not replying). Imagine yourself in this third group. Might you have decided not to say no because, after all, you are a caring person so there's a chance you might give? And might that thought have opened you to persuasion as you encountered campus posters and flyers during the ensuing week? That, apparently, is what happened because 12 percent of these students—more than twice the normal rate—showed up to offer their blood.

Inferring that one is a helpful person seems also to have happened when Dariusz Dolinski (2000) stopped pedestrians on the streets of Wroclaw, Poland, and asked them for directions to a nonexistent "Zubrzyckiego Street" or to an illegible address. Everyone tried unsuccessfully to help. After doing so, about two-thirds (twice the number of those not given the opportunity to try to help) agreed when asked by someone 100 metres farther down the road to watch their heavy bag or bicycle for five minutes.

Learning about prosocial behaviour

Researchers have found another way to boost prosocial behaviour, one that provides a happy conclusion to this chapter. Some social psychologists worry that as people become more aware of social psychology's findings, their behaviour may change, thus invalidating the findings (Gergen, 1982). Will learning about the factors that inhibit helping reduce their influence? Sometimes, such "enlightenment" is not our problem but one of our goals.

Experiments by Arthur Beaman and his colleagues (1978) revealed that once people understand why the presence of bystanders inhibits helping, they become more likely to help in group situations. The researchers used a lecture to inform some students how bystander inaction can affect the interpretation of an emergency and feelings of responsibility. Other students heard either a different lecture or no lecture at all. Two weeks later, as part of a different experiment in a different location, the participants found themselves walking (with an unresponsive confederate) past someone slumped over or past a person sprawled beneath a bicycle. Of those who had not heard the helping lecture, one-quarter paused to offer help; twice as many of those who had been "enlightened" did so.

Postscript: The Kitty Genovese Case Revisited

As we mentioned at the beginning of the chapter, the rape and murder of Kitty Genovese was the catalyst for an entire line of research on helping. Because of this research, we now have a much better understanding of the factors that influence whether or not people will engage in prosocial behaviour and when they will intervene in an emergency. We also now know the things we can do as the victims to encourage people to help us. Perhaps it is ironic, then, that the case that started it all turns out to have been misreported and misinterpreted from the time it happened (see Manning et al., 2007).

As it turns out, there were not 38 witnesses. There may have been as few as 8. Several witnesses saw a man and a woman talking on the street and some saw them on the ground, but only a couple seem to have seen the actual attack (i.e., there was some difficulty interpreting the events). After the initial attack on the street, Kitty Genovese cried out. One witness who saw the actual struggle yelled at the attacker (Winston Mosley) to leave (i.e., the person recognized the danger and intervened).

Mosley then ran away. Apparently, more than one person called the police immediately (i.e., identified the emergency situation and acted), but the police did not show up (apparently the attack occurred near a neighbourhood bar that was known for frequent fights and disturbances; this resulted in the police not recognizing the calls as an emergency). It was only after Kitty Genovese got up and stumbled away (perhaps sending a further message to the witnesses that the emergency had passed) and into her apartment building that the attacker returned, raped her, and inflicted the wound that would ultimately kill her. In the entryway to her apartment building, she was no longer in sight of any of the witnesses, and her building neighbours were unlikely to have heard the struggle or her screams (i.e., no one could notice the crisis). Finally, the police did arrive at the scene, but Genovese was already mortally wounded. She died a short time later.

Thus, perhaps the iconic story of apathy in a big city, which led to 40 years of research on helping, was not as bleak a story as originally told. Indeed, some of the people who saw the problem and identified it as an emergency acted, just as we would predict based on the research literature.

What to Do When You Need Help

If you are in an emergency situation, what should you do to increase the chances someone will help you? As highlighted above, the natural tendency of bystanders, especially when there are a lot of them, will be to ignore your emergency. They may not notice, they may interpret it incorrectly, they may not know how to help, or they may feel someone else has already helped. You, as the person in the middle of the situation, need to take action. Get the attention of a specific person. Point that person out and make eye contact. Make it clear, through your words, that you need help. This personal approach has been shown to be effective to get help in different situations: for blood donations (Foss, 1978), rides for hitchhikers (Snyder et al., 1974), and volunteers for AIDS workers (Omoto & Snyder, 2002). A personal approach reduces people's perceptions of anonymity and increases personal responsibility. Doing this, and identifying an individual, will reduce any ambiguity in the situation and reduce any diffusion of responsibility.

Conclusions

We have heard of a number of cases where people ignored situations or even refused to help when people were in need. But could something as simple as a psychology class change people's behaviours in such situations? What if you saw a man about to jump off a bridge? What would you do? That very scenario unfolded in Ithaca, New York, in 1993. Pablo Salanova, Rob Lee, and Gretchen Goldfarb were walking through town when they saw a naked man leap onto the railing of a bridge. Initially they thought it was all a joke, but Gretchen, whose introductory psychology class had recently covered helping and prosocial behaviour, realized that the situation might be an emergency. At Gretchen's prompting, her two friends grabbed the man and kept him from jumping (likely to his death) from the bridge.

Coincidentally, a similar thing has happened to one of your authors. A former student, now living in Washington, D.C., stopped by his office one day. The student mentioned that she had recently found herself as part of a stream of pedestrians striding past a man lying unconscious on the sidewalk. "It took my mind back to our social psych class and the accounts of why people fail to help in such situations. Then I thought, 'Well, if I just walk by, too, who's going to help him?'" So she made a call to an emergency help number and waited with the victim—and other bystanders who then joined her—until help arrived.

So, how will learning about social influences upon helping affect you? Will the knowledge you've gained affect your actions? We hope so.

SUMMING UP

Why Do We Help?

We help for the following reasons:

- Because of social exchange: We help those who have helped us
- Because social norms dictate helping in some situations
- To aid our survival—helping kin and those who may help us makes it more likely for us to pass on our genes

When Will We Help?

We will help under the following circumstances:

- When there are few bystanders
- When we observe someone else helping
- When we are not in a hurry
- When the person needing help is similar to us

Who Helps?

The following determines who will help:

- People high in emotionality, empathy, and self-efficacy
- Men in risky situations but women in less risky situations; overall, men and women do not differ in helpfulness

How Can We Increase Helping?

We can increase helping by doing the following:

- Reducing ambiguity and increasing responsibility
- Evoking feelings of guilt
- Socializing prosocial behaviour

Key Terms

altruism
bystander effect
egoism
empathy
kin selection
moral exclusion
moral inclusion
reciprocity norm
social-exchange theory
social-responsibility norm

CHAPTER 9

Aggression: Hurting Others

Source: ©Mike Kemp/InPictures/Getty Images.

CHAPTER OUTLINE

What Is Aggression?

What Are Some Theories of Aggression?

What Are Some Influences on Aggression?

How Can Aggression Be Reduced?

During the past century, some 250 wars killed 110 million people, enough to populate a "nation of the dead" with more than the combined populations of France, Belgium, the Netherlands, Denmark, Finland, Norway, and Sweden.

The tolls resulted not only from the two world wars but also from genocides, including the 1915–1923 genocide of 1 million Armenians by the Ottoman Empire, the slaughter of some 250 000 Chinese in Nanking after it had surrendered to Japanese troops, the 1.5 million Cambodians murdered between 1975 and 1979, the murder of 1 million in Rwanda in 1994 (Sternberg, 2003), and the more than one-half million killed in Syria since 2011 (SOHR, 2018). As Hitler's genocide of millions of Jews, Stalin's genocide of millions of Russians, Mao's genocide of millions of Chinese, and the genocide of millions of Indigenous people from the time of Columbus through the nineteenth century make plain, the human potential for extraordinary cruelty crosses cultures.

> ***"Our behaviour toward each other is the strangest, most unpredictable, and most unaccountable of all the phenomena with which we are obliged to live. In all of nature, there is nothing so threatening to humanity as humanity itself."***
>
> Lewis Thomas, *Notes of a Biology Watcher,* 1981

Less severe aggression is even more common. One study found that 90 percent of young couples are verbally aggressive toward each other, including yelling, screaming, and insults (Munoz-Rivas et al., 2007). In a survey of children across 35 countries, more than one out of ten reported being bullied at school (Craig & Harel, 2004). Half of Canadian middle school and high school students said they had been bullied online in the previous three months. Their experiences included being called names, having rumours spread about them, or having their private pictures distributed without their consent (Mishna et al., 2010). Seventy-five percent of children and adolescents have experienced **cyberbullying**, defined as intentional and repeated aggression via email, texts, social networking sites, and other electronic media (Katzer et al., 2009). Cyberbullying often results in negative outcomes, such as depression, fear, drug abuse, dropping out of school, poor physical health, and suicide—even years after the bullying occurred (Kowalski et al., 2014; Ortega et al., 2012; Sigurdson et al., 2014).

> **cyberbullying** Bullying, harrassing, or threatening someone using electronic communication, such as texts, online social networks, or email.

> ***"Is there any way of delivering mankind from the menace of war?"***
>
> Albert Einstein, letter to Sigmund Freud, 1932

Are we like the mythical Minotaur, half human, half beast? What explains that midsummer day in 1941 when the non-Jewish half of the Polish town of Jedwabne murdered the other half in a macabre frenzy of violence, leaving only a dozen or so survivors among the 1600 Jews (Gross, 2001)? Why would a university student broadcast his gay roommate's sexual encounter, driving him to suicide, as happened at Rutgers University in 2010? Why would middle school students bully 13-year-old Hailee Lamberth so cruelly and relentlessly ("Why don't you die?") that she died by suicide in December 2013 (Wagner, 2014)? Why, in 2011, would a gunman in peaceful Norway bomb government buildings and then shoot and kill 69 people, mostly teenagers? Why would a gunman shoot 15 pedestrians and restaurant-goers on Danforth Avenue in Toronto on a July night in 2018? What explains such monstrous behaviour? In this chapter, we ask these questions:

- Is aggression biologically predisposed, or do we learn it?
- What circumstances prompt hostile outbursts?
- Do the media influence aggression?
- How might we reduce aggression?

First, however, we need to clarify the term *aggression.*

What Is Aggression?

What is aggression and what are its different forms?

The original Thugs, members of a sect in northern India, were aggressing when, between 1550 and 1850, they strangled more than 2 million people, which they claimed to do in the service of the goddess Kali. But people also use "aggressive" to describe a dynamic salesperson. Social psychologists distinguish such self-assured, energetic, go-getting behaviour as the salesperson's from behaviour that hurts, harms, or destroys. The former is assertiveness; the latter, aggression.

To a social psychologist, **aggression** is physical or verbal behaviour intended to cause harm. This definition excludes unintentional harm, such as auto accidents or sidewalk collisions; it also excludes actions that may involve pain as an unavoidable side effect of helping someone, such as dental treatments or—in the extreme—assisted suicide.

The definition of aggression includes kicks and slaps, threats and insults, gossip or snide "digs," and "trolling" behaviour such as online name-calling and harassment (Cheng et al., 2017). It includes ugly confrontational rudeness, such as giving the finger to another driver or yelling at someone who is walking too slow (Park et al., 2014). It includes decisions during experiments about how much to hurt someone, such as how much electric shock to impose. It also includes destroying property, lying, and other behaviour that aims to hurt. As these examples illustrate, aggression includes both **physical aggression** (hurting someone's body) and **social aggression** (such as bullying and cyberbullying, insults, harmful gossip, or social exclusion that hurts feelings) (Dehue et al., 2008). Social aggression can have serious consequences, with victims suffering from depression and sometimes—as happened in several well-publicized cases—dying by suicide. Dan Olweus and Kyrre Breivik (2013), who research bullying, describe the consequences of bullying as "the opposite of well-being."

aggression Physical or verbal behaviour intended to hurt someone.

physical aggression Hurting someone else's body.

social aggression Hurting someone else's feelings or threatening their relationships. Sometimes called relational aggression, it includes cyberbullying and some forms of in-person bullying.

hostile aggression Aggression driven by anger and performed as an end in itself.

instrumental aggression Aggression that is a means to some other end.

However, the social psychology definition of aggression does not include microaggressions, usually defined as words or actions that unintentionally convey prejudice toward marginalized groups; to fit the definition, aggression must be intentional. For that reason and others, some have recommended abandoning the term "microaggressions" and replacing it with another term that better captures their unintentional nature, such as "inadvertent racial slights" (Lilienfeld, 2017).

Psychologists also make a distinction between **hostile aggression** (which springs from anger and aims to injure) and **instrumental aggression** (which aims to injure, too—but is committed in the pursuit of another goal). Both physical and social aggression can be either hostile or instrumental. For example, bullying can be hostile (one teen is angry at another for stealing her boyfriend) or instrumental (a high school student believes she can become popular by rejecting an unpopular girl [Juvonen & Graham, 2014; Prinstein & Cillessen, 2003]).

Most terrorism is instrumental aggression. "What nearly all suicide terrorist campaigns have in common is a specific secular and strategic goal," concludes Robert Pape (2003) after studying all suicide bombings from 1980 to 2001. That goal is "to compel liberal democracies to withdraw military forces from territory that the terrorists consider to be their homeland." Terrorism is rarely committed by someone with a mental illness, noted Arie Kruglanski and his colleagues (2009); instead, terrorists seek personal significance through, for example, attaining hero or martyr status. Terrorism is also a strategic tool used during conflict.

Because it is intended to hurt, online bullying is aggression even though its harm is emotional rather than physical.

Source: ©oliveromg/ Shutterstock.

Most wars are instrumental aggression. In 2003, U.S. and British leaders justified attacking Iraq not as a hostile effort to kill Iraqis but as an instrumental act of liberation and of self-defence against presumed weapons of

Activity: Defining Aggression?

How do you define aggression? Below are a number of examples of behaviours that some might see as aggressive. Read each one and indicate whether or not the acts described are aggression.

Yes	No		
____	____	1.	A criminal is executed under China's capital punishment law.
____	____	2.	A father spanks his six-year-old daughter.
____	____	3.	A woman uses pepper spray on her would-be-rapist.
____	____	4.	A batter's line drive hits the pitcher in the knee.
____	____	5.	A frustrated wife yells at her "messy slob of a husband."
____	____	6.	A soldier in Afghanistan shoots at a car that refuses to stop at a checkpoint.
____	____	7.	A professor lowers a student's grade on a late paper.
____	____	8.	A man passes along rumours about his business rival's ethical transgressions.
____	____	9.	A boy tells his little sister that her art project is "dumb and ugly."
____	____	10.	Two girls create a website to spread rumours about another girl at school.

mass destruction. Adolescents who bully others—either verbally or physically—are also often engaged in instrumental aggression because they frequently seek to demonstrate their dominance and high status. In the strange hierarchy of adolescence, being mean and disliked can sometimes make you popular and revered (Salmivalli, 2009).

Most murders, on the other hand, are hostile aggression. Approximately half erupt from arguments, and others result from romantic triangles or from brawls that involve the influence of alcohol or drugs (Ash, 1999). Such murders are impulsive, emotional outbursts—which helps explain why data from 110 nations show that enforcing the death penalty has not resulted in fewer homicides (Costanzo, 1998; Wilkes, 1987). Some murders and many other violent acts of retribution and sexual coercion, however, are instrumental (Felson, 2000). Most of Chicago's more than 1000 murders carried out by organized crime during the Prohibition era and the years following were cool and calculated.

What Are Some Theories of Aggression?

What are the important theories of aggression?

In analyzing causes of hostile and instrumental aggression, social psychologists have focused on three big ideas: biological influences, frustration, and learned behaviour.

Aggression as a Biological Phenomenon

Philosophers have debated whether our human nature is fundamentally that of a benign, contented "noble savage" or that of a brute. The first view, argued by the eighteenth-century French philosopher Jean-Jacques Rousseau (1712–1778), blames society, not human nature, for social evils. The second, associated with the English philosopher Thomas Hobbes (1588–1679), credits society for restraining the human brute. In the twentieth century, the "brutish" view—that aggressive drive is inborn and thus inevitable—was argued in Vienna by Sigmund Freud and in Germany by Konrad Lorenz, an animal behaviour expert.

Instinct theory and evolutionary psychology

Freud speculated that human aggression springs from a self-destructive impulse. It redirects toward others the energy of a primitive death urge (the *death instinct*). Lorenz saw aggression as adaptive rather than self-destructive. The two agreed that aggressive energy involves **instinctive behaviour** (it is innate, unlearned, and universal). If not discharged, it supposedly builds up until it explodes or until an appropriate stimulus "releases" it, like a mouse releasing a mousetrap.

instinctive behaviour An innate, unlearned behaviour pattern exhibited by all members of a species.

The idea that aggression is an instinct collapsed as the list of supposed human instincts grew to include nearly every conceivable human behaviour. Nearly 6000 supposed instincts were enumerated in one 1924 survey of social science books (Barash, 1979). The social scientists had tried to *explain* social behaviour by *naming* it. It's tempting to play this explaining-by-naming game: "Why do sheep stay together?" "Because of their herd instinct." "How do you know they have a herd instinct?" "Just look at them: They're always together!"

The idea that aggression is instinctive also fails to account for the variations in aggressiveness from person to person and culture to culture. How would a shared human instinct for aggression explain the difference between the peaceful Iroquois before White invaders came and the hostile Iroquois after the invasion (Hornstein, 1976)? Although aggression is biologically influenced, the human propensity to aggress does not qualify as instinctive behaviour.

However, aggression is sometimes rooted in basic evolutionary impulses. Throughout much of human history, men especially have found aggression adaptive, note evolutionary psychologists such as John Archer (2006) and Francis McAndrew (2009). Purposeful aggression improved the odds of survival and reproduction. The losers, notes McAndrew, "ran the risk of genetic annihilation."

Mating-related aggression often occurs when males are competing with other males. In one study, men primed to think about mating delivered louder and longer bursts of painful noise against another man who provoked them (Ainsworth & Maner, 2012). Evolutionary psychologists also posit a "selfish gene" theory of the relationship between genetic relatedness and aggression, including the unfortunate statistic that men are much more likely to harm stepchildren than their genetic children (Archer, 2013).

Male aggression can be heightened in the context of dating and mating.

Source: ©Valua Vitaly/Shutterstock.

Men may also become more aggressive when their social status is challenged. "Violence committed against the right people at the right time was a ticket to social success," McAndrew observes. Consider professional basketball player Charles Barkley, who was drinking in a bar in 1997 when a man threw a glass of water at him. Barkley promptly hurled the man through a plate-glass window—even though Barkley was not hurt by the water, even though the man might have retaliated, and even though Barkley was arrested within minutes of the assault. Nevertheless, witnesses praised Barkley in news reports, seemingly impressed by his aggression. When Barkley was asked if he regretted throwing the man through the window, he replied, "I regret we weren't on a higher floor" (Griskevicius et al., 2009).

Apparently, Barkley was not an isolated example. Across three experiments, college men motivated to increase their status were more aggressive toward others in face-to-face confrontations (Griskevicius et al., 2009). Status-based aggression also helps explain why aggression is highest during adolescence and early adulthood, when the competition for status and mates is the most intense. Although violence is less rewarded than it once was, young men scuffling for status and mates are still very much in evidence at many bars and campuses around the world. Sometimes that struggle for status is taken to extremes; as Jill Filipovic (2017) writes, "Another mass shooting in America, another round of questions: Did he have a political agenda? Was he mentally ill? . . . A question we never ask: Was the shooter a man? The answer is always the same." Ninety-six percent of mass shooters have been male, a 24 to 1 ratio (Stone, 2015).

Neural influences

Because aggression is a complex behaviour, no single spot in the brain controls it. But researchers have found neural systems in both animals and humans that facilitate aggression. When the scientists activate these brain areas, such as the hypothalamus (Falkner et al., 2016; Falkner & Lin, 2014), hostility increases; when they deactivate them, hostility decreases. Docile animals can thus be provoked into rage; and raging animals, into submission.

In one experiment, researchers placed an electrode in an aggression-inhibiting area of a domineering monkey's brain. A smaller monkey, given a button that activated the electrode, learned to push it every time the tyrant monkey became intimidating. Brain activation works with humans, too. After receiving painless electrical stimulation in her amygdala (a brain core area involved with emotion), one woman became enraged and smashed her guitar against the wall, barely missing her psychiatrist's head (Moyer, 1976, 1983).

Does this mean that violent people's brains are in some way abnormal? To find out, Adrian Raine and his colleagues (1998, 2000, 2005, 2008) used brain scans to measure brain activity in murderers and to measure the amount of grey matter in men with antisocial conduct disorder. They found that the prefrontal cortex, which acts like an emergency brake on deeper brain areas involved in aggressive behaviour, was 14 percent less active than normal in murderers (excluding those who had been abused by their parents) and 15 percent smaller in the antisocial men. Another study found that more aggressive and violent men had smaller amygdalas (Pardini et al., 2014). As other studies of murderers and death-row inmates confirm, abnormal brains can contribute to abnormally aggressive behaviour (Davidson, Putnam, & Larson, 2000; Lewis, 1998; Pincus, 2001). Situational factors can also play a role: Sleep deprivation reduces activity in the prefrontal cortex, an area of the brain responsible for self-control. In aggression-prone individuals, poor sleep can lead to violent and aggressive behaviour (Kamphuis

Another reason to get enough sleep: Aggressive people are often tired people.

Source: ©Lorena Fernandez/Shutterstock.

et al., 2012). Even in a sample of 425 normal German college students, those who slept for fewer hours were more physically and verbally aggressive (Randler & Vollmer, 2013).

What about mental illness? When news of a mass shooting breaks, politicians often blame mental illness. In fact, being young, male, or drunk is a better predictor of being violent than is being mentally ill (Corrigan et al., 2005; Metzl & MacLeish, 2014), and 78 percent of mass shooters are not mentally ill (Stone, 2015). If someone magically cured schizophrenia, bipolar disorder, and depression overnight, violent crime in the United States would fall by only 4 percent, according to Duke University professor Jeffrey Swanson (2016). People with mental illnesses are more likely to be the victims of violence than be the perpetrators (Brekke et al., 2001).

Genetic influences

Heredity influences the neural system's sensitivity to aggressive cues. It has long been known that animals of many species can be bred for aggressiveness. Sometimes, this is done for practical purposes (the breeding of fighting cocks). Sometimes, breeding is done for research. Finnish psychologist Kirsti Lagerspetz (1979) took normal albino mice and bred the most aggressive ones together and the least aggressive ones together. After repeating the procedure for 26 generations, she had one set of fierce mice and one set of placid mice.

Aggressiveness also varies among individuals (Asher, 1987; Bettencourt et al., 2006; Denson, Pedersen, & Miller, 2006; Olweus, 1979). Our temperaments—how intense and reactive we are—are partly brought with us into the world, influenced by our sympathetic nervous system's reactivity (Kagan, 1989; Wilkowski & Robinson, 2008). A person's temperament, observed in infancy, usually endures (Larsen & Diener, 1987; Wilson & Matheny, 1986). A three-year-old who exhibits little conscientiousness and self-control is more vulnerable to substance abuse and arrest by age 32 (Moffitt et al., 2011). A child who is nonaggressive at age eight will very likely still be nonaggressive at age 48 (Huesmann et al., 2003). Identical twins, when asked separately, are more likely than fraternal twins to agree on whether they have "a violent temper" or have gotten into fights (Rowe, Almeida, & Jacobson, 1999; Rushton et al., 1986). Of convicted criminals who are twins, fully half of their identical twins (but only one in five fraternal twins) also have criminal records (Raine, 1993, 2008).

In a study examining 12.5 million residents of Sweden, those with a genetic sibling convicted of a violent crime were four times as likely to be convicted themselves. Rates were much lower for adopted siblings, suggesting a strong genetic component and a more modest environmental influence (Frisell, Lichtenstein, & Långström, 2011). Recent research has identified a specific gene (MAOA-L) linked to aggression; some even call it the "warrior gene" or the "violence gene." Among 900 criminals in Finland, those with the gene were 13 times more likely to have repeatedly committed violent crimes, explaining up to 10 percent of severe violent crime in the country (Tiihonen et al., 2015). In several lab studies, people with the gene were more likely to act aggressively when provoked (Ficks & Waldman, 2014; McDermott et al., 2009). Long-term studies following several hundred New Zealand children reveal that the recipe for aggressive behaviour combines the MAOA-L gene with childhood maltreatment (Caspi et al., 2002; Moffitt et al., 2003). Neither "bad" genes nor a "bad" environment alone predispose later aggressiveness and antisocial behaviour; rather, genes predispose some children to be more sensitive and responsive to maltreatment. Nature and nurture interact.

Biochemical influences

Blood chemistry also influences neural sensitivity to aggressive stimulation.

Alcohol

Both laboratory experiments and police data indicate that alcohol unleashes aggression when people are provoked (Bushman, 1993; Bushman & Cooper, 1990; Taylor & Chermack, 1993). A huge analysis of studies confirmed that alcohol consumption is associated with higher levels of aggression, especially among men (Duke et al., 2018). Consider the following:

- When asked to think back on relationship conflicts, intoxicated people administer stronger shocks and feel angrier than do sober people in lab experiments (MacDonald, Zanna, & Holmes, 2000).
- University students primed to think about alcohol responded more aggressively to ambiguous insults (Pederson et al., 2014). Apparently, alcohol led to interpreting neutral statements as hostile.
- Fifty percent of murders worldwide involve alcohol (Kuhns et al., 2014). Thirty-seven percent of U.S. rapes and sexual assaults involved alcohol (NCADD, 2014). Four in ten prisoners convicted of a violent crime were drinking when they committed murder, assault, robbery, or sexual assault (Karberg & James, 2005).
- University students followed for two months using electronic diaries showed a clear pattern: Those who drank alcohol were more likely to act aggressively toward their dating partners. With each drink, rates of abuse went up (Moore et al., 2011).
- Heavy men who drank alcohol were significantly more aggressive after drinking alcohol, but alcohol had little effect on women's or smaller men's aggression. Alcohol, note the researchers, seemed to encourage "heavy men to 'throw their weight around' and intimidate others by behaving aggressively" (DeWall et al., 2010a). Apparently, people really are wise to avoid the "big, drunk guy" in the bar.

Alcohol enhances aggressiveness by reducing people's self-awareness, by focusing their attention on a provocation, and by people's mentally associating alcohol with aggression (Bartholow & Heinz, 2006; Giancola & Corman, 2007; Ito, Miller, & Pollock, 1996). Alcohol also predisposes people to interpret ambiguous acts (such as a bump in a crowd) as provocations (Bègue et al., 2010). Alcohol deindividuates, and it disinhibits.

Testosterone

Hormonal influences appear much stronger in lower animals than in humans. But human aggressiveness does correlate with testosterone, the male sex hormone. Consider the following:

- Drugs that diminish testosterone levels in violent human males will subdue their aggressive tendencies.
- After people reach age 25, their testosterone and rates of violent crime decrease together.
- Testosterone levels tend to be higher among prisoners convicted of planned and unprovoked violent crimes compared with those convicted of nonviolent crimes (Dabbs, 1992; Dabbs et al., 1995, 2001).
- Among the normal range of teen boys and adult men, those with high testosterone levels are more prone to delinquency, hard drug use, and aggressive responses to provocation (Archer, 1991; Dabbs & Morris, 1990; Olweus et al., 1988).
- Men high in dominance or low in self-control who received an administration of testosterone became more aggressive after being provoked (Carré et al., 2017).
- University students reporting higher levels of anger after being ostracized had higher levels of testosterone in their saliva (Peterson & Harmon-Jones, 2012).
- After handling a gun, people's testosterone levels rise; and the more their testosterone rises, the more aggressive they are toward others (Kleinsmith, Kasser, & McAndrew, 2006).
- People with brain structures indicative of greater testosterone exposure were more aggressive from childhood to adulthood (Nguyen et al., 2016).

Young, male, and restless. In the 2011 riots that swept English cities, those arrested overwhelmingly shared one genetic characteristic—a Y chromosome—and were testosterone-fuelled teens or people in their early twenties (Somaiya, 2011).

Source: ©Matt Dunham/AP Images.

Some violent sex offenders, wishing to free themselves of persistent, damaging impulses and to reduce their prison terms, have requested castration. Should their requests be granted? If so, and if they are deemed no longer at risk of sexual violence, should their prison terms be reduced or eliminated?

Poor diet

When British researcher Bernard Gesch first tried to study the effect of diet on aggression, he stood in front of hundreds of inmates at an English prison—but no matter how loudly he talked, none of them would listen. Finally, he talked privately to the "daddy"—the inmates' "tough guy" leader—and 231 inmates signed on to receive nutritional supplements or a placebo. Prisoners who got the extra nutrition were involved in 35 percent fewer violent incidents (Gesch et al., 2002). Such programs may eventually help people outside prison as well because many people have diets deficient in important nutrients, such as omega-3 fatty acids (found in fish and important for brain function) and calcium (which guards against impulsivity).

In another study, researchers surveyed Boston public high school students about their diets and their aggressive or violent actions. Those who drank more than five cans of non–diet soda a week were more likely to have been violent toward peers, siblings, or dating partners and more likely to have carried a weapon, such as a gun or knife. This was true even after the researchers accounted for eight other possible factors (Solnick & Hemenway, 2012). Another correlational study found that men and women who consumed more trans fat—also known as hydrogenated oils—were more aggressive, even after adjusting for third factors (Golomb et al., 2012). Thus, perhaps surprisingly, there may have been at least some truth to the classic "Twinkie Defense," in which an accused murderer's attorneys argued he had been eating a junk food diet of Twinkies and Coca-Cola. The upshot: To lower aggression, eat a diet high in omega-3 fatty acids, low in trans fat, and without sweetened drinks.

Biology and behaviour interact

The traffic between biology and behaviour flows both ways. For example, higher levels of testosterone may cause dominant and aggressive behaviour, but dominant and aggressive behaviour also leads to higher testosterone levels (Mazur & Booth, 1998). After a World Cup soccer match or a big basketball game between arch-rivals, testosterone levels rise in the winning fans and fall in the losing fans (Bernhardt et al., 1998). The phenomenon also occurs in the laboratory, where socially anxious men exhibit a pronounced drop in their testosterone level after losing a rigged face-to-face competition (Maner et al., 2008). Testosterone surges, plus celebration-related drinking, probably explain the finding of Cardiff University researchers that fans of *winning* rather than losing soccer and rugby teams commit more post-game assaults (Sivarajasingam, Moore, & Shepherd, 2005).

So neural, genetic, and biochemical influences predispose some people to react aggressively to conflict and provocation. But is aggression so much a part of human nature that it makes peace unattainable? The International Council of Psychologists has joined other organizations in unanimously endorsing a statement on violence developed by scientists from a dozen nations (Adams, 1991): "It is scientifically incorrect [to say that] war or any other violent behaviour is genetically programmed into our human nature [or that] war is caused by 'instinct' or any single motivation." Thus, there are, as we will see, ways to reduce human aggression.

frustration–aggression theory The theory that frustration triggers a readiness to aggress.

frustration The blocking of goal-directed behaviour.

displacement The redirection of aggression to a target other than the source of the frustration. Generally, the new target is a safer or more socially acceptable target.

Aggression as a Response to Frustration

It is a warm evening. Tired and thirsty after two hours of studying, you borrow some change from a friend and head for the nearest soft-drink machine. As the machine devours the change, you can almost taste the cold, refreshing cola. But when you push the button, nothing happens. You push it again. Then you flip the coin return button. Still nothing. Again, you hit the buttons. You slam the machine. Alas, no money and no drink. You stomp back to your studies, empty-handed and short-changed. Should your roommate beware? Are you now more likely to say or do something hurtful?

One of the first psychological theories of aggression, the popular **frustration–aggression theory**, answers "yes" (Dollard, 1939). **Frustration** is anything (such as the malfunctioning vending machine) that blocks us from attaining a goal. Frustration grows when our motivation to achieve a goal is very strong, when we expected gratification, and when the blocking is complete. When Rupert Brown and his colleagues (2001) surveyed British ferry passengers heading to France, they found much higher aggressive attitudes on a day when French fishing boats blockaded the port, preventing their travel. Blocked from obtaining their goal, the passengers became more likely (in responding to various vignettes) to agree with an insult toward a French person who had spilled coffee. University students who were frustrated by losing a multiplayer video soccer game blasted their opponents with longer and louder bursts of painful noise (Breuer et al., 2014). Cyberbullying is often rooted in frustration, such as after a breakup. Some cyberbullies direct their aggression against the person now dating their ex-partner. One woman described her experience this way: "A girl was upset that I was dating her ex-boyfriend. She would harass me with text messages telling me I was a bad friend and a slut. Then, she turned to Facebook and started posting between her and her friend bad things about me and said my boyfriend was cheating. This went on for a good six months" (Rafferty & Vander Ven, 2014).

Frustration-triggered aggression sometimes appears as road rage. Road rage is fed by perceptions of hostile intentions from other drivers, as when someone is cut off in traffic (Britt & Garrity, 2006).

Source: ©O. Burriel/ Science Source.

The aggressive energy need not explode directly against its source. Most people learn to inhibit direct retaliation, especially when others might disapprove or punish; instead, we *displace* our hostilities to safer targets. **Displacement** occurs in the old anecdote about a man who, humiliated by his boss, berates his wife, who yells at their son, who kicks the dog, which bites the mail carrier (who goes home and berates his wife . . .). In experiments and in real life, displaced aggression is most likely when the target shares some similarity to the instigator and does some minor irritating act that unleashes the displaced aggression (Marcus-Newhall et al., 2000; Pedersen, Gonzales, & Miller, 2000). When someone is harbouring anger from a prior provocation, even a trivial offence may elicit an explosive overreaction (as you may realize if you have ever yelled at your roommate after losing money in a malfunctioning vending machine).

In one experiment, Eduardo Vasquez and his co-researchers (2005) provoked some university students (but not others) by having an experimenter insult their performance on an anagram-solving test. Shortly afterward, the students had to decide how long another supposed student should be required to immerse their hand in painful cold water while completing a task. When the supposed student committed a trivial offence—by giving a mild insult—the previously provoked participants responded punitively, by recommending a longer cold-water treatment than did the unprovoked participants. This phenomenon of displaced aggression helps us understand, noted Vasquez, why a previously provoked and still-angry person might respond to mild highway offences with road rage or react to spousal criticism with spouse abuse. It also helps explain why frustrated Major League Baseball pitchers, in one analysis of nearly 5 million at-bats from 74 197 games since 1960, were most likely to hit batters after the batter hit a home run the last time at bat or after the previous batter did so (Timmerman, 2007).

Even irrational frustration can cause devastating violence. On December 6, 1989, Marc Lépine took a semi-automatic rifle into the École Polytechnique de Montréal, the engineering school he applied to twice but failed to get into. He shot and killed 14 women and wounded 10 more before turning the gun on himself. He blamed women for his failures and for taking positions in traditionally male careers and educational programs, and claimed to be fighting feminism. His frustrations exploded in deadly violence. More recently, on April 23, 2018, Alek Minassian drove a rented van down Yonge Street in the bustling business district of Toronto, deliberately hitting pedestrians. He killed 10 people and seriously injured 14 more, most of them women. He had earlier self-identified on social media as an incel ("involuntary celibate"), one of an online group who define themselves as being unable to find romantic and sexual partners despite wanting them. The online incel community is defined by frustration and misogyny, and actively advocates violence against sexually active people. Marc Lépine and Alek Minassian both believed that women blocked their personal goals. A misplaced sense of entitlement and irrational frustration played a key role in both of these terrible tragedies.

Frustration–aggression theory revised

Laboratory tests of the frustration–aggression theory have produced mixed results: Sometimes frustration increases aggressiveness, sometimes not. For example, if the frustration was understandable—if, as in one experiment, a confederate disrupted a group's problem-solving because his hearing aid malfunctioned (rather than just because he wasn't paying attention)—then frustration led to irritation but not aggression (Burnstein & Worchel, 1962). Similarly, we are less likely to react aggressively toward someone who frustrates us if that person apologizes, accepts responsibility, or otherwise tries to make amends (Eaton & Struthers, 2006).

Leonard Berkowitz (1978, 1989) realized that the original theory overstated the frustration–aggression connection, so he revised it. Berkowitz theorized that frustration produces aggression only when people become upset—for instance, when someone who frustrates us could have chosen to act otherwise, leading to feelings of anger (Averill, 1983; Weiner, 1981). For example, many people are frustrated in their goals while playing sports, but they usually aren't aggressive unless they are angered by a deliberate, unfair act by an opposing player.

FIGURE 9–1 SIMPLIFIED FRUSTRATION–AGGRESSION THEORY.
A simplified synopsis of Leonard Berkowitz's revised frustration–aggression theory.

A frustrated person is especially likely to lash out when aggressive cues pull the cork, releasing bottled-up anger (Figure 9–1). Sometimes the cork will blow without such cues. But, as we will see, cues associated with aggression amplify aggression (Carlson, Marcus-Newhall, & Miller, 1990).

Relative deprivation

Frustration is not only caused by complete deprivation; more often, *frustration arises from the gap between expectations and attainments.* The most economically frustrated people are probably not the impoverished residents of third-world shantytowns, who might know no other way of life, but middle-class North Americans who aspire to be rich—or, at least, upper middle class. When your expectations are fulfilled by your attainments, and when your desires are reachable at your income, you feel satisfied rather than frustrated (Solberg et al., 2002). But when being rich feels out of reach, aggression might be the result.

> ***"A house may be large or small; as long as the surrounding houses are equally small, it satisfies all social demands for a dwelling. But let a palace arise beside the little house, and it shrinks from a little house into a hut."***
>
> Karl Marx

Such feelings, called **relative deprivation**, explain why happiness tends to be lower and crime rates higher in communities and nations with large income inequality (a larger gap between the rich and poor) (Coccia, 2017). The greater the income gap, the higher the sense that others are getting something you're not (Cheung & Lucas, 2016). British low-income boys with rich neighbours—who were aware of what they were missing—were more aggressive than boys surrounded by concentrated poverty (Odgers et al., 2015). Among university students, those who reported experiencing stress during an economic recession were more aggressive, and those randomly assigned to watch a news story about the poor economy reported feeling more hostile (Barlett & Anderson, 2014). People who saw themselves as lower in socioeconomic status—whether they actually were or not—were more aggressive, as were those assigned to feel they were relatively deprived compared to others (Greitemeyer & Sagioglou, 2016).

relative deprivation The perception that one is less well off than others to whom one compares oneself.

Feelings of relative deprivation predict reactions to perceived inequities by minority groups (K. L. Dion, 1985; Kawakami & Dion, 1993, 1995). They also explain why women who make less than men working in the same occupations feel underpaid only if they compare themselves with male rather than female colleagues (Bylsma & Major, 1994).

The term *relative deprivation* was coined by researchers studying the satisfaction felt by soldiers in the Second World War (Merton & Kitt, 1950; Stouffer et al., 1949). Ironically, those in the air corps felt *more* frustrated about their own rate of promotion than those in the military police, for whom promotions were actually slower. The air corps' promotion rate was rapid, and most air corps personnel probably perceived themselves as better than the average air corps member (the self-serving bias). Thus, their aspirations soared higher than their achievements. The result? Frustration.

THE INSIDE STORY

For the last 25+ years, I have been exploring the psychology of perceived prejudice and discrimination from the "victim" or target's perspective. When I began this work in the early 1970s, little systematic or definitive research on the topic existed. Most research on prejudice concerned the bigot and ignored the target of the bigot's negative attitudes and behaviour. I felt, then as now, that there was an equally important story to be told about how people who experience prejudice and discrimination from others respond to these experiences.

Source: ©SolStock/Getty Images.

I began with the assumption that perceived discrimination was vital for understanding the psychology of oppressed groups. My research has indicated that perceived discrimination is a social stressor and produces negative effects, but it also prompts perceivers to identify more closely with the positive aspects of their membership groups (as a likely response to stress). Perceived discrimination also has complex effects on self-esteem.

My more recent studies document the stressfulness of perceived discrimination by oppressed group members in the real social world rather than the artificial laboratory, and explore conditions under which they will take corrective action in response. This research shows that collective deprivation consistently predicts militancy better than "egoistic" or personal deprivation.

Ken Dion *University of Toronto*

One possible source of such frustration today is the affluence depicted in television programs and commercials. In cultures where television is a universal appliance, it helps turn absolute deprivation (lacking what others have) into relative deprivation (feeling deprived). Karen Hennigan and her co-workers (1982) analyzed crime rates in several cities around the time television was introduced. In 34 cities where television ownership became widespread in 1951, the 1951 larceny theft rate (for crimes such as shoplifting and bicycle stealing) took an observable jump. In 34 other cities, where a government freeze had delayed the introduction of television until 1955, a similar jump in the theft rate occurred—in 1955.

Aggression as Learned Social Behaviour

Theories of aggression based on instinct and frustration assume that hostile urges erupt from inner emotions, which naturally "push" aggression from within. Social psychologists contend that learning also "pulls" aggression out of us.

The rewards of aggression

Aggression as revenge can feel satisfying: most people report feeling good after they stick pins in a voodoo doll representing a hated person (Chester et al., 2017). There are other rewards as well; by experience and observing others, we learn that aggression often pays. A child whose aggressive acts successfully intimidate other children will likely become increasingly aggressive (Patterson, Littman, & Bricker, 1967). Aggressive hockey players—the ones sent most often to the penalty box for rough play—score more goals than nonaggressive players (McCarthy & Kelly, 1978a, 1978b). Canadian teenage hockey players whose fathers applaud physically aggressive play show the most aggressive attitudes and style of play (Ennis & Zanna, 1991). In the waters off Somalia, paying ransom to hijackers of ships—a reported $150 million in 2008 (BBC, 2008)—rewarded the pirates, thus fuelling further hijackings. In such cases, aggression is instrumental in achieving certain rewards.

The same is true of terrorist acts, which enable powerless people to garner widespread attention. "The primary targets of suicide-bombing attacks are not those who are injured but those who are made to witness it through media coverage," noted Paul Marsden and Sharon Attia (2005). Terrorism's purpose is, with the help of media amplification, to terrorize. "Kill one, frighten ten thousand," asserts an ancient Chinese proverb. Deprived of what Margaret Thatcher called "the oxygen of publicity," terrorism would surely diminish, concluded Jeffrey Rubin (1986). It's like the 1970s incidents of naked spectators "streaking" onto football fields for a few seconds of television exposure. Once the networks decided to ignore the incidents, the phenomenon ended.

Observational learning

Albert Bandura (1997) proposed a **social learning theory** of aggression. He believed that we learn aggression not only by experiencing its payoffs but also by observing others. As with most social behaviours, we acquire aggression by watching others act and noting the consequences.

social learning theory The theory that we learn social behaviour by observing and imitating and by being rewarded and punished.

Picture this scene from one of Bandura's experiments (Bandura, Ross, & Ross, 1961). A preschool child is put to work on an interesting art activity. An adult is in another part of the room, where there are Tinkertoys, a mallet, and a big, inflated "Bobo doll." After a minute of working with the Tinkertoys, the adult gets up and for almost 10 minutes attacks the inflated doll. She pounds it with the mallet, kicks it, and throws it, all the while yelling, "Sock him in the nose. . . . Knock him down. . . . Kick him."

After observing this outburst, the child goes to a different room with many very attractive toys. But after two minutes, the experimenter interrupts, saying these are her best toys and she must "save them for the other children." The frustrated child now goes into another room with various toys for aggressive and nonaggressive play, two of which are a Bobo doll and a mallet.

Children who were not exposed to the aggressive adult model rarely displayed any aggressive play or talk. Although frustrated, they nevertheless played calmly. Those who had observed the aggressive adult were many times more likely to pick up the mallet and lash out at the doll. Watching the adult's aggressive behaviour lowered their inhibitions. Moreover, the children often reproduced the model's acts and said her words. Observing aggressive behaviour had both lowered their inhibitions and taught them ways to aggress.

Bandura (1997) believed that everyday life exposes us to aggressive models in the family, in the subculture, and, as we will see, in the mass media.

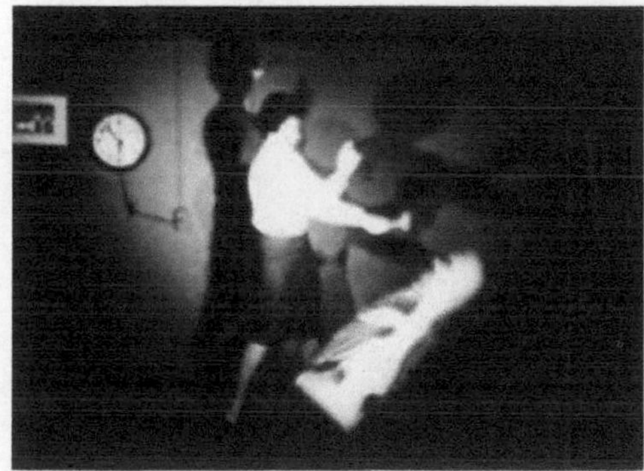

Monkey see, monkey do: In Bandura's famous experiment, children exposed to an adult's aggression against a Bobo doll were likely to reproduce the observed aggression.
Source: Courtesy of Albert Bandura.

The family

Physically aggressive children tend to have physically punitive parents, who disciplined them by modelling aggression with screaming, slapping, and beating (Patterson, Chamberlain, & Reid, 1982). These parents often had parents who were themselves physically punitive (Bandura & Walters, 1959; Straus & Gelles, 1980). A study of 975 Canadian children six years of age or younger found that those with more hostile parents were more aggressive (Benzies, Keown, & Magill-Evans, 2009). Such punitive behaviour may escalate into abuse, and although most abused children do not become criminals or abusive parents, 30 percent do later abuse their own children—four times the rate of the general population (Kaufman & Zigler, 1987; Widom, 1989). Even more mild physical punishment, such as spanking, is linked to later aggression (Gershoff, 2002). Violence often begets violence.

The culture

The social environment outside the home also provides models. In communities where "macho" images are admired, aggression is readily transmitted to new generations (Cartwright, 1975; Short, 1969). The violent subculture of teenage gangs, for instance, provides its junior members with aggressive models. Among adolescents who are otherwise equally at risk for violence, those who have observed gun violence are twice as likely to be violent (Bingenheimer, Brennan, & Earls, 2005).

The broader culture also matters. Men from cultures that are nondemocratic, high in income inequality, and focused on teaching men to be warriors and that have gone to war are more likely to behave aggressively than those from cultures with the opposite characteristics (Bond, 2004).

Richard Nisbett and Dov Cohen (Cohen, 1998; Cohen et al., 1996) explored the effects of culture on attitudes toward violence. They report that the U.S. South, settled by Scots–Irish herders ever wary of threats to their flocks, has a "culture of honour," which maintains that insults deserve retaliation. After squeezing past another man in a hallway and hearing him mutter an insult, White Southern men expressed more aggressive thoughts and experienced a surge in testosterone. White Northern men were more likely to find the encounter funny (Cohen et al., 1996). To the present day, U.S. cities populated by Southerners have higher-than-average White homicide rates (Vandello, Cohen, & Ransom, 2008). More students in "culture of honour" states bring weapons to school, and these states have had three times as many school shootings as others (R. P. Brown, Osterman, & Barnes, 2009).

People learn aggressive responses both by experience and by observing aggressive models. But when will aggressive responses actually occur? Bandura (1997) contended that aggressive acts are motivated by a variety of aversive experiences, such as frustration, pain, or insults (Figure 9–2). Such experiences arouse us emotionally. But whether we act

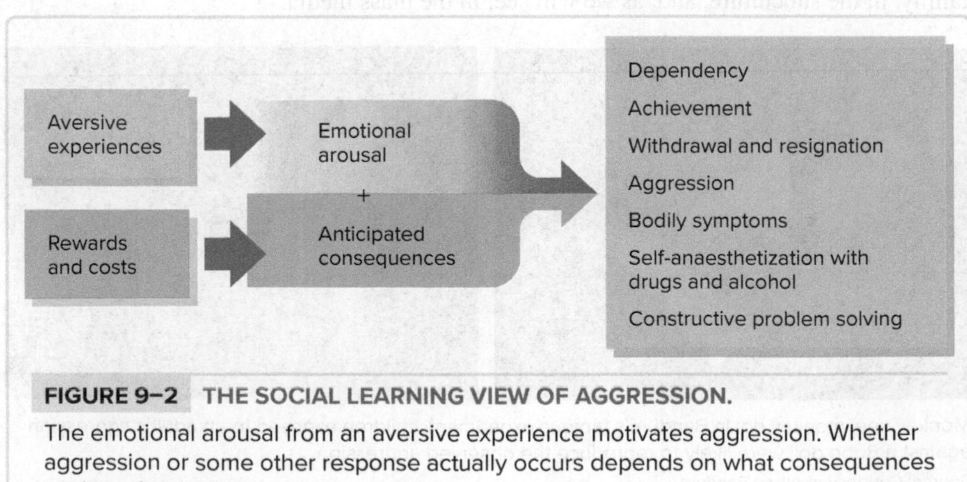

FIGURE 9–2 THE SOCIAL LEARNING VIEW OF AGGRESSION.

The emotional arousal from an aversive experience motivates aggression. Whether aggression or some other response actually occurs depends on what consequences we have learned to expect.

aggressively depends on the consequences we anticipate. Aggression occurs most likely when we are aroused *and* when it seems safe and rewarding to aggress.

What Are Some Influences on Aggression?

What are the influences on aggression and how do they work?

Consider some specific influences on aggression: aversive incidents, arousal, aggression cues, the media, and the group context.

Aversive Incidents

Recipes for aggression often include some type of aversive experience. These include pain, uncomfortable heat, or an attack.

Pain

Today's ethical guidelines restrict researchers' use of painful stimuli.

Researcher Nathan Azrin (1967) was doing experiments with laboratory rats in a cage wired to deliver shocks to the animals' feet. Azrin wanted to know if switching off the foot shocks would reinforce two rats' positive interactions with each other. Azrin planned to turn on the shock and then, once the rats approached each other, cut off the pain. To his great surprise, the experiment proved impossible. As soon as the rats felt pain, they attacked each other before the experimenter could switch off the shock. The greater the shock (and pain), the more violent the attack. The same effect occurred across a long list of species, including cats, turtles, and snakes. The animals were not selective about their targets. They would attack animals of their own species and those of a different species, or stuffed dolls, or even tennis balls.

The researchers also varied the source of pain. They found that shocks weren't the only stimuli that induced attack; intense heat and "psychological pain"—for example, suddenly not rewarding hungry pigeons that had been trained to expect a grain reward after pecking at a disk—brought the same reaction as shocks. This "psychological pain" is, of course, frustration.

Pain heightens aggressiveness in humans, too. Many of us can recall such a reaction after stubbing a toe or suffering a headache. Leonard Berkowitz and his associates demonstrated this by having university students hold one hand in lukewarm water or painfully cold water. Those whose hands were submerged in the cold water reported feeling more irritable and more annoyed, and they were more willing to blast another person with unpleasant noise. In view of such results, Berkowitz (1983, 1989) proposed that aversive stimulation rather than frustration is the basic trigger of hostile aggression. Frustration is certainly one important type of unpleasantness. But any aversive event, whether a dashed expectation, a personal insult, or physical pain, can incite an emotional outburst. Even the torment of a depressed state increases the likelihood of hostile aggressive behaviour.

Heat

Temporary climate variations can affect behaviour. Offensive odours, cigarette smoke, and air pollution have all been linked with aggressive behaviour (Rotton & Frey, 1985). But the most-studied environmental irritant is heat. William Griffitt (1970; Griffitt & Veitch, 1971) found that, compared to students who answered questionnaires in a room with a normal temperature, those who did so in an uncomfortably hot room (over 32°C/90°F) reported feeling more tired and aggressive and expressed more hostility toward a stranger. Follow-up experiments revealed that heat also triggers retaliation in response to an attack or injury (Bell, 1980; Rule, Taylor, & Dobbs, 1987).

Does uncomfortable heat increase aggression in the real world as well as in the laboratory? Consider the following:

- In uncomfortably hot weather, drivers without air conditioning are more likely to honk at a stalled car (Kenrick & MacFarlane, 1986).
- In an analysis of 57 293 Major League Baseball games since 1952, batters were more likely to be hit by a pitch during hot weather—nearly 50 percent more likely when the temperature was 32°C or above (versus 27°C or below) and when three of the pitcher's teammates had previously been hit (Larrick et al., 2011). This wasn't due to reduced accuracy: Pitchers had no more walks or wild pitches. They just clobbered more batters.
- Studies in six cities have found that when the weather is hot, violent crimes are more likely (Anderson & Anderson, 1984; Cohn, 1993; Cotton, 1981, 1986; Harries & Stadler, 1988; Rotton & Frey, 1985).
- Across the northern hemisphere, it is not only hotter days that have more violent crimes but also hotter seasons of the year, hotter summers, hotter years, hotter cities, and hotter regions (Anderson & Anderson, 1998; Anderson et al., 2000). Anderson and his colleagues projected that if global warming increases temperatures by four degrees Fahrenheit (about 2°C), the United States alone will see at least 50 000 more serious assaults annually.

> ***"I pray thee, good Mercutio, let's retire; The day is hot, the Capulets abroad, And, if we meet, we shall not 'scape a brawl, For now, these hot days, is the mad blood stirring."***
>
> William Shakespeare, *Romeo and Juliet*

Can climate change affect large-scale violence and war? Jeffrey Sachs (2006) argues this is often the case. The recent deadly carnage in Darfur, Sudan, for example, had its roots in drought and the competition for water. And so it has happened across history. Many human maladies—from economic downturns to wars—have been traced to climate fluctuations (Zhang et al., 2007). When the climate changes, agriculture often suffers, leading to increased famine, epidemics, economic crises, and overall misery. Poorer countries, with fewer resources, are especially vulnerable to climate-produced misery (Fischer & Van de Vliert, 2011). And, when miserable, people become more prone to anger with their governments and with one another, leading to war. For social stability, climate matters.

Do these real-world findings show that heat discomfort directly fuels aggressiveness? Although the conclusion appears plausible, these *correlations* between temperature and aggression don't prove a connection. People certainly could be more irritable in hot, sticky weather. And in the laboratory, hot temperatures do increase arousal and hostile thoughts and feelings (Anderson et al., 1999). Other factors may contribute, though. Perhaps hot summer evenings drive people into the streets, where other influences may well take over. Then again (researchers have debated this), there may come a point where stifling heat suppresses violence—when it's too hot to do anything, much less hurt someone (Bell, 2005; Bushman, Wang, & Anderson, 2005a, 2005b; Cohn & Rotton, 2005).

Attacks

Being attacked or insulted by someone is especially conducive to aggression. Several experiments confirmed that intentional attacks breed retaliatory attacks. In most of these experiments, one person competed with another in a reaction-time contest. After each test trial, the winner chose how much shock to give the loser. Actually, each subject was playing a programmed opponent, who steadily escalated the amount of shock. Do the real participants respond more charitably? Hardly. Extracting "an eye for an eye" is the more likely response (Ohbuchi & Kambara, 1985).

Arousal

So far we have seen that various aversive stimuli can arouse anger. Do other types of arousal, such as those that occur during exercise or sexual excitement, have a similar effect? Imagine that Tawna, having just finished a stimulating short run, comes home to discover that her date for the evening has called and left word that they have made other plans. Will Tawna be more likely to explode in fury after her run than if she discovered the same message after awakening from a nap? Or, because she just exercised, will her aggressive tendencies be exorcised? To discover an answer, consider how we interpret and label our bodily states.

In a famous experiment, Stanley Schachter and Jerome Singer (1962) found that we can experience an aroused bodily state in different ways. They aroused men by injecting them with adrenaline. The drug produced body flushing, heart palpitations, and more rapid breathing. When forewarned that the drug would produce these effects, the men felt little emotion, even when waiting with either a hostile or a euphoric person. Of course, they could readily attribute their bodily sensations to the drug. Schachter and Singer led another group of men to believe the drug produced no such side effects. Then they, too, were placed in the company of a hostile or euphoric person. How did they feel and act? They were angry when with the hostile person, and amused when with the euphoric person. The principle seemed to be this: *A state of arousal can be interpreted in different ways depending on the context.*

Other experiments indicate that arousal is not as emotionally undifferentiated as Schachter believed. Yet being physically stirred up does intensify just about any emotion (Reisenzein, 1983). For example, people find radio static unpleasant, *especially* when they are aroused by bright lighting (Biner, 1991). People who have just pedalled an exercise bike or watched a film of a rock concert find it easy to misattribute their arousal to a provocation and then retaliate with heightened aggression (Zillman et al., 1988). Although common sense might lead us to assume that Tawna's run would have drained her aggressive tensions, it's more likely that she would react with more anger and aggression. As these studies show, *arousal fuels emotions*.

Sexual arousal and other forms of arousal (such as anger) can, therefore, amplify one another (Zillmann, 1989a). Love is never so passionate as after a fight or a fright—one reason it's so popular to take a date to a horror movie. In the laboratory, erotic stimuli are more arousing to people who have just been frightened. Similarly, the arousal of a roller-coaster ride may spill over into romantic feelings for one's partner.

A frustrating or insulting situation heightens arousal. When it does, the arousal, combined with hostile thoughts and feelings, may form a recipe for aggressive behaviour (Figure 9–3).

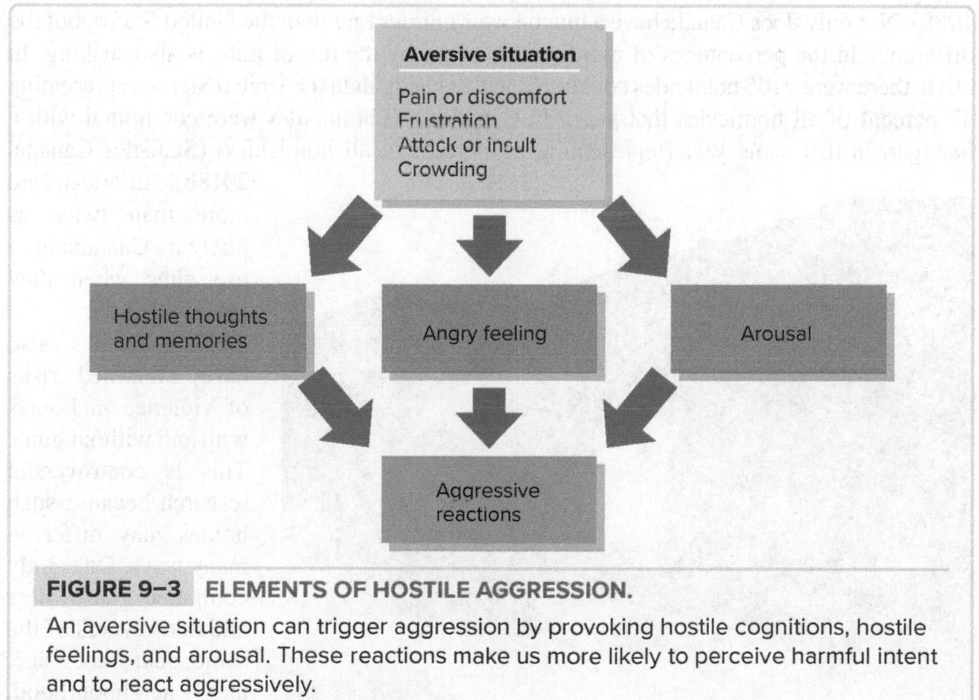

FIGURE 9–3 ELEMENTS OF HOSTILE AGGRESSION.

An aversive situation can trigger aggression by provoking hostile cognitions, hostile feelings, and arousal. These reactions make us more likely to perceive harmful intent and to react aggressively.

Aggression Cues

As we noted when considering the frustration–aggression hypothesis, violence is more likely when aggressive cues release pent-up anger. Leonard Berkowitz (1968, 1981, 1995) and others have found that the sight of a weapon is such a cue. In one experiment, children who had just played with toy guns became more willing to knock down another child's blocks. In another, angered University of Wisconsin men gave more electric shocks to their tormentor when a rifle and a revolver (supposedly left over from a previous experiment) were nearby than when badminton racquets had been left behind (Berkowitz & LePage, 1967). In a more recent experiment, people who used a driving simulator while a gun (vs. a tennis racquet) was on the passenger seat drove more aggressively (Bushman et al., 2017). In a meta-analysis of 78 independent studies, the mere presence of weapons increased aggressive thoughts and behaviours, known as the "weapons effect" (Benjamin et al., 2018). What's in sight is in mind.

The weapons effect might be why in the United States, home to about 300 million privately owned guns, half of all murders are committed with handguns, or that handguns in homes are far more likely to kill household members than intruders. "Guns not only permit violence," Berkowitz reported, "they can stimulate it as well. The finger pulls the trigger, but the trigger may also be pulling the finger."

Berkowitz was further unsurprised that countries that ban handguns have lower murder rates. Compared to the United States, Britain has one-fourth as many people and one-sixteenth as many murders. The United States has the most firearms per capita in the world, and the rate of gun murders in the United States is 25 times higher than that of other high-income countries (Grinshteyn & Hemenway, 2016). In 130 studies across 10 countries, laws restricting firearms sales were followed by reductions in gun crimes (Santaella-Tenorio et al., 2016). When Australia instituted stricter gun laws and bought back 700 000 guns after a 1996 mass shooting, gun-related murders fell 59 percent, and no mass shootings have occurred since (Howard, 2013). Vancouver, British Columbia, and Seattle, Washington, have similar populations, climates, economies, and rates of criminal activity and assault—except that Vancouver, which carefully restricts handgun ownership, had one-fifth as many handgun murders as Seattle and thus a 40 percent lower overall murder rate (Sloan et al., 1988). Not only does Canada have a much lower murder rate than the United States, but the difference in the percentages of murders that occur by the use of guns is also striking. In 2016, there were 7105 homicides committed with a handgun in the United States (representing 47 percent of all homicides that year). In Canada, 130 homicides were committed with a handgun in that same year (representing 21 percent of all homicides) (Statistics Canada, 2018b). Americans are more than twice as likely as Canadians to use guns when they commit murder.

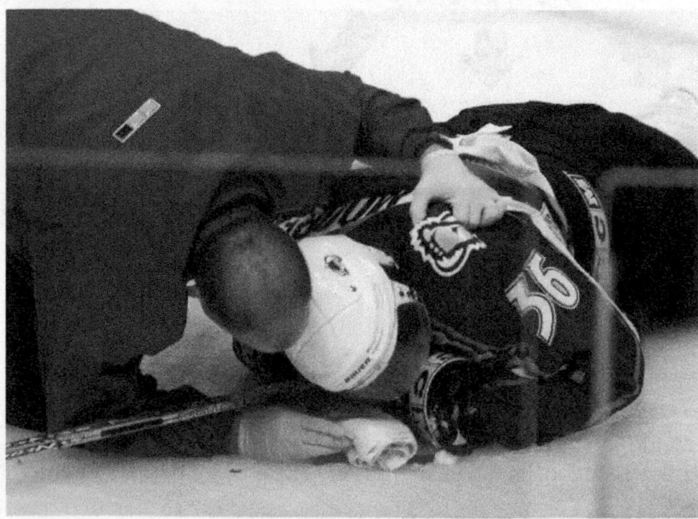

The NHL's Steve Moore collapsed on the ice with three broken vertebrae and a concussion after being viciously sucker-punched by Todd Bertuzzi in March 2004. Bertuzzi's captain had taken a hard hit earlier in the season, and it appears the attack on Moore was retaliatory.
Source: The Canadian Press/Chuck Stoody.

Researchers also have examined risks of violence in homes with and without guns. This is controversial research because such homes may differ in many ways. One study compared gun owners and non-owners of the same sex, race, age, and neighbourhood.

Is violent crime rising? Perceptions of increased crime can trigger gun purchases, but this gun is more likely to be used against a household member than as originally intended—against an intruder or attacker. Countries with fewer guns have lower murder rates.

Source: ©tommaso altamura/Alamy Stock Photo.

The ironic and tragic result was that those who kept a gun in the home (often for protection) were 2.7 times more likely to be murdered—nearly always by a family member or close acquaintance (Kellermann, 1997; Kellermann et al., 1993). A meta-analysis found that those with guns in their homes were three times more likely to be murdered and twice as likely to die by suicide (Anglemyer et al., 2014). Even after controlling for gender, age, and race, people with guns at home were 41 percent more likely to be murdered and three times as likely to die by suicide (Wiebe, 2003). A gun in the home is 12 times more likely to kill a household member than an intruder (Narang et al., 2010). A gun in the home has often meant the difference between a fight and a funeral or between suffering and suicide.

Guns serve as aggression cues, and they also put psychological distance between aggressor and victim. As Milgram's obedience studies taught us, remoteness from the victim facilitates cruelty. A knife can kill someone, but a knife attack is more difficult than pulling a trigger from a distance.

Media Influences: Pornography and Sexual Violence

Pornography is now a bigger business in North America than professional football, basketball, and baseball combined, thanks to some $13 billion a year spent on the industry's cable and satellite networks, theatres, and pay-per-view movies, and in-room hotel movies, phone sex, sex magazines, and Internet sites (D'Orlando, 2011). The easy availability of pornography on the Internet has accelerated its popularity. In a recent survey of 18- to 26-year-old men, 87 percent said they viewed pornography at least once a month, and nearly half used it at least once a week. However, only 31 percent of women reported viewing pornography at all (Carroll et al., 2008). Pornography use is more common among men who are younger, are less religious, and have had more sexual partners than average (Wright, 2013). Social–psychological research on pornography has focused mostly on depictions of sexual violence, which is commonplace in pornography videos (Sun et al., 2008). A typical sexually violent episode finds a man forcing himself on a woman. She at first resists and tries to fight off her attacker. Gradually, as she resists and he persists, she becomes sexually aroused, and her resistance melts. By the end, she is in ecstasy, pleading for more. The problem, of course, is that women do not actually respond this way to rape or sexual harassment—this scenario is pure fantasy.

"Repeated exposure to erotic films featuring quick, uncommitted sex also tends to

- *decrease attraction for one's partner*
- *increase acceptance of extramarital sex and of women's sexual submission to men*
- *increase men's perceiving women in sexual terms"*

N. Myers (2000)

Social psychologists report that viewing such fictional scenes of a man overpowering and arousing a woman can (a) distort men's (and possibly women's) perceptions of how women actually respond to sexual coercion and (b) increase men's aggression against women.

Distorted perceptions of sexual reality

Does viewing sexual violence reinforce the "rape myth"—that some women would welcome sexual assault and that "no doesn't really mean no"? Researchers have observed a correlation between the amount of TV viewing and rape myth acceptance (Kahlor & Morrison, 2007). To explore the relationship experimentally, Neil Malamuth and James Check (1981) showed University of Manitoba men either two nonsexual movies or two movies depicting a man sexually overcoming a woman. A week later, when surveyed by a different experimenter, those who saw the films with mild sexual violence were more accepting of violence against women. This was especially true if they had been aroused by the films (Hald & Malamuth, 2015).

"Pornography that portrays sexual aggression as pleasurable for the victim increases the acceptance of the use of coercion in sexual relations."

Social Science Consensus at Surgeon General's Workshop on Pornography and Public Health (Koop, 1987)

Other studies confirm that exposure to pornography increases acceptance of the rape myth (Oddone-Paolucci, Genuis, & Violato, 2000). For example, while spending three evenings watching sexually violent movies, men became progressively less bothered by the raping and slashing (Mullin & Linz, 1995). Compared with men not exposed to the films, the men expressed less sympathy for domestic violence victims and rated the victims' injuries as less severe—even three days later. In fact, noted the researchers, what better way for an evil character to get people to react calmly to the torture and mutilation of women than to show a gradually escalating series of such films (Donnerstein, 1980)?

Aggression against women

Evidence also suggests that pornography contributes to men's actual aggression toward women (Kingston et al., 2009). Boys and girls aged 10–15 who had seen movies, magazines, or websites with violent sexual content were six times more likely to be sexually aggressive toward others (defined as having "kissed, touched, or done anything sexual with another person when that person did not want you to do so"), even after

Did Paul Bernardo's use of pornography (police found pornographic tapes in his house) contribute to his derangement? Did it incite his sexual violence against young women?

Source: ©Jim Rankin/Toronto Star/Getty Images.

adjusting for factors such as gender, aggressive traits, and family background (Ybarra et al., 2011). Across 43 studies, teens and young adults who consumed more sexually explicit and sexually violent media were more likely to have been involved in dating violence and sexual violence (Rodenhizer & Edwards, 2017). A meta-analysis of 22 studies found that people who watch pornography often were more likely to be sexually aggressive, including both physical force and verbal coercion and harassment (Wright et al., 2016).

Canadian and American sexual offenders commonly acknowledge pornography use. Among 155 men arrested for Internet-based child pornography, 85 percent admitted they had molested a child at least once, and the average offender had 13 victims (Bourke & Hernandez, 2009). The reverse is also true: Rapists, serial killers, and child molesters report using pornography at unusually high rates (Bennett, 1991; Ressler, Burgess, & Douglas, 1988).

But perhaps pornography doesn't actually cause violence; instead, violent men like violent pornography. To rule out this explanation, it is necessary to perform an experiment—for example, to randomly assign some people to watch pornography. In one such study, 120 men watched a neutral, an erotic, or an aggressive erotic (rape) film. Then the men, supposedly as part of another experiment, "taught" a male or female confederate some nonsense syllables by choosing how much shock to administer for incorrect answers. The men who had watched the rape film administered markedly stronger shocks (Figure 9–4), particularly to women, and particularly when angered. A consensus statement by 21 leading social scientists summed up the results of experiments in this area: "Exposure to violent pornography increases punitive behavior toward women" (Koop, 1987).

If the ethics of conducting such experiments trouble you, rest assured that these researchers appreciate the controversial and powerful experience they are giving participants. Only after giving their knowing consent do people participate. Moreover, after the experiment, researchers effectively debunk any myths the film communicated (Check & Malamuth, 1984).

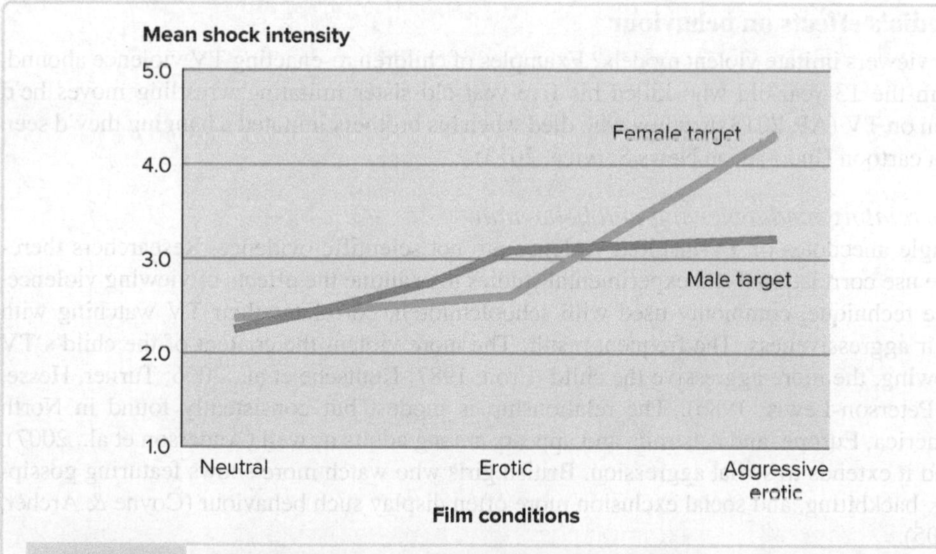

FIGURE 9–4 PORNOGRAPHY AND PUNITIVE BEHAVIOUR.

After viewing an aggressive erotic film, university and college men delivered stronger shocks than before, especially to a woman.

Media Influences: Television, Movies, and the Internet

We have seen that watching an aggressive model attack a Bobo doll can unleash children's aggressive urges and teach them new ways to aggress. And we have seen that after viewing movies depicting sexual violence, many angry men will act more violently toward women. Does everyday television viewing have any similar effects?

Today, in much of the industrialized world, nearly all households (99.2 percent in Australia, for example) have a TV set. Most homes have more than one set, which helps explain why parents and children often give differing reports of what the children are watching (Nielsen, 2010). In some households these days, each member of the family has their own computer, tablet, or smartphone, making it even more difficult for parents to monitor children's media use.

In the average home, the TV is on seven hours a day, with individual teens averaging about three hours and adults six hours (Nielsen, 2011). Teens make up some of the difference by watching video on their phones more often.

> ***"One of television's great contributions is that it brought murder back into the home where it belongs. Seeing a murder on television can be good therapy. It can help work off one's antagonisms."***
>
> Alfred Hitchcock

All told, television beams its electromagnetic waves into children's eyeballs for more growing-up hours than they spend in school—more hours, in fact, than they spend in any other waking activity. In one content analysis of TV dramas airing in 2012–13, a gun, knife, or sword appeared on screen every three minutes. Children watching four episodes of the show *Criminal Minds* in fall 2012 were exposed to nearly 53 acts of violence per episode—one every minute and eight seconds (PTC, 2013). Social aggression (such as bullying and social exclusion) is just as frequent; in the 50 most popular TV shows among 2- to 11-year-olds, 92 percent featured at least some social aggression. This bullying often came from an attractive perpetrator, was portrayed as funny, and was neither rewarded nor punished (Martins & Wilson, 2012).

Studies of television viewing and aggression aim to identify effects more subtle and pervasive than the occasional "copycat" murders that capture public attention. They ask this: How does television affect viewers' *behaviour* and viewers' *thinking*?

Media's effects on behaviour

Do viewers imitate violent models? Examples of children re-enacting TV violence abound, from the 13-year-old who killed his five-year-old sister imitating wrestling moves he'd seen on TV (AP, 2013) to a boy who died when his brothers imitated a hanging they'd seen in a cartoon (Indo-Asian News Service, 2013).

Correlating media viewing and behaviour

Single anecdotes of TV-inspired violence are not scientific evidence. Researchers therefore use correlational and experimental studies to examine the effects of viewing violence. One technique, commonly used with schoolchildren, correlates their TV watching with their aggressiveness. The frequent result: The more violent the content of the child's TV viewing, the more aggressive the child (Eron, 1987; Kuntsche et al., 2006; Turner, Hesse, & Peterson-Lewis, 1986). The relationship is modest but consistently found in North America, Europe, and Australia and appears among adults as well (Anderson et al., 2007). And it extends to social aggression. British girls who watch more shows featuring gossiping, backbiting, and social exclusion more often display such behaviour (Coyne & Archer, 2005).

Can we conclude, then, that a diet of violent TV fuels aggression? Perhaps you are already thinking that, because this is a correlational study, the cause–effect relation could also work in the opposite direction. Maybe aggressive children prefer aggressive programs. Or maybe some underlying third factor, such as lower intelligence, predisposes some children both to prefer aggressive programs and to exhibit aggressive behaviour.

Researchers have developed ways to test these alternative explanations, reducing hidden third factors by statistically pulling out their influence. For example, British researcher William Belson (1978; Muson, 1978) studied 1565 London boys. Compared to those who watched little violence, those who watched a great deal (especially realistic rather than cartoon violence) admitted to 50 percent more violent acts during the preceding six months. Belson also examined 22 likely third factors, such as family size. The "heavy violence" and "light violence" viewers still differed after these third factors were included. Belson surmised that the heavy viewers were, indeed, more violent *because* of their TV exposure.

Similarly, Leonard Eron and Rowell Huesmann (1980, 1985) found that violence viewing among 875 eight-year-olds correlated with aggressiveness even after statistically pulling out several obvious possible third factors. Moreover, when they restudied these individuals as 19-year-olds, they discovered that viewing violence at age eight modestly predicted aggressiveness at age 19 but that aggressiveness at age eight did *not* predict viewing violence at age 19. Aggression followed viewing, not the reverse. Moreover, by age 30, those who had watched the most violence in childhood were more likely to have been convicted of a crime. Another longitudinal study followed 1037 New Zealand children from age five to age 26. Children and teens who spent more time watching TV were more likely to become young adults convicted of crimes, diagnosed with antisocial personality disorder, and high in aggressive personality traits. This was true even when the researchers controlled for possible third variables, such as sex, IQ, socioeconomic status, previous antisocial behaviour, and parenting style (Robertson et al., 2013) (see Figure 9–5). Researchers are *not* saying that everyone who watches violent media becomes aggressive in real life—instead, they find it is one of several risk factors for aggressive behaviour, combined with family troubles, gender, and being the victim of someone else's aggression. Even taking these factors into account, though, exposure to violent media is a significant predictor (Gentile & Bushman, 2012).

Many people now spend more screen time in front of their computers than in front of the television. In many ways, the Internet allows an even greater variety of options for

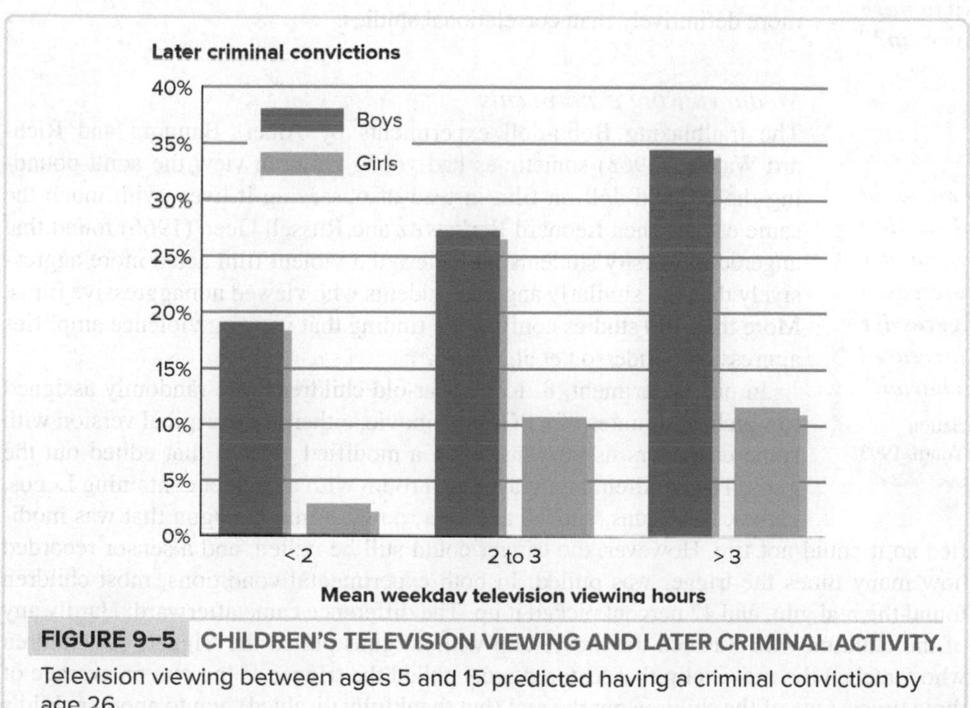

FIGURE 9–5 CHILDREN'S TELEVISION VIEWING AND LATER CRIMINAL ACTIVITY.
Television viewing between ages 5 and 15 predicted having a criminal conviction by age 26.

Watching violent media leads to social and physical aggression in real life.
Source: ©AJPhoto/Science Source.

viewing violence than television does, including violent videos, violent pictures, and hate-group websites (Donnerstein, 2011). It also allows people to create and distribute violent media themselves and to bully others through email, via instant messaging, or on social networking websites (Donnerstein, 2011). In a survey of European adolescents, one-third reported seeing violent or hateful content online (Livingstone & Haddon, 2009). Among U.S. youth, those who frequently visited violent websites were five times more likely to report engaging in violent behaviour (Ybarra et al., 2008). Even books influence people: Middle-school students who read more books featuring aggression and violence were more likely to behave aggressively (Stockdale et al., 2013).

Other studies have confirmed these results in various ways, including the following:

- Eight-year-olds' violence viewing predicted spouse abuse as an adult (Huesmann et al., 1984, 2003).
- Adolescents' violence viewing predicted engaging in assault, robbery, and threats of injury (Johnson et al., 2002).
- Elementary schoolchildren's violent media exposure predicted how often they got into fights two to six months later (Gentile et al., 2004).

In all these studies, the investigators were careful to adjust for likely third factors, such as intelligence or hostility. Nevertheless, an infinite number of possible third factors could be creating a merely coincidental relation between viewing violence and aggression. Fortunately, the experimental method can control these extraneous factors. If we randomly assign some children to watch a violent film and others a nonviolent film, any later aggression difference between the two groups will be due to the only factor that distinguishes them: what they watched. In the next section, we discuss studies using the experimental method that can prove causation more definitively than correlational studies.

> ***"Then shall we simply allow our children to listen to any story anyone happens to make up, and so receive into their minds ideas often the very opposite of those we shall think they ought to have when they are grown up?"***
>
> Plato, *Republic*

> ***"There is absolutely no doubt that higher levels of viewing violence on television are correlated with increased acceptance of aggressive attitudes and increased aggressive behavior."***
>
> American Psychological Association Commission on Violence and Youth, 1993

Media viewing experiments

The trailblazing Bobo-doll experiments by Albert Bandura and Richard Walters (1963) sometimes had young children view the adult pounding the inflated doll on film instead of observing it live—with much the same effect. Then Leonard Berkowitz and Russell Geen (1966) found that angered university students who viewed a violent film acted more aggressively than did similarly angered students who viewed nonaggressive films. More than 100 studies confirm the finding that viewing violence amplifies aggression (Anderson et al., 2003).

In one experiment, 8- to 12-year-old children were randomly assigned to watch 20 minutes of a PG-rated movie, either in its original version with some characters using guns, or in a modified version that edited out the guns. The children then played in a room with a cabinet containing Legos, games, Nerf guns, and, in a drawer, a real 9-mm handgun that was modified so it could not fire. However, the trigger could still be pulled, and a sensor recorded how many times the trigger was pulled. In both experimental conditions, most children found the real gun, and 42 percent picked it up. The difference came afterward: Hardly any of the children who watched the movie clip without guns pulled the trigger, but children who watched the movie clip that featured guns pulled the trigger of the gun an average of three times. One of the children put the real (but thankfully disabled) gun to another child's temple and pulled the trigger (Dillon & Bushman, 2017).

The effects appear among adults as well. In another experiment, female university students were randomly assigned to watch portions of a physically aggressive film (*Kill Bill*), a relationally aggressive film (*Mean Girls*), or a nonaggressive control film (*What Lies Beneath*). Compared to the control group, those who watched the aggressive films were more aggressive toward an innocent person, blasting her headphones with loud, uncomfortable noise. They were also more subtly aggressive, giving negative evaluations to another participant (actually a confederate) who annoyed them (Coyne et al., 2008). Even reading about physical or relational aggression produced the same results (Coyne et al., 2012). Dolf Zillmann and James Weaver (1999) similarly exposed men and women, on four consecutive days, to violent or nonviolent films. When participating in a different project on the fifth day, those exposed to the violent films were more hostile to the research assistant. Children in Grade 5 who watched a tween sitcom featuring social aggression (compared with those watching a control show) were more likely to agree that a student from a different group should be excluded from joining their team for a school competition (Mares & Braun, 2013).

"The irrefutable conclusion," said one commission of psychologists on youth violence, is "that viewing violence increases violence." This is especially so among people with aggressive tendencies and when an attractive person commits justified, realistic violence that goes unpunished and that shows no pain or harm (Comstock, 2008; Gentile, Saleem, & Anderson, 2007; Zillmann & Weaver, 2007). That description is, of course, consistent with much of the violence shown on TV and in the movies.

If increased exposure to media violence causes aggression, would less exposure lead to less aggression? One group of researchers found that the answer was "yes." German middle school students were randomly assigned to either a control group or an intervention group and encouraged to reduce their media use and critically question it. Among those already high in aggressive behaviour, the intervention group later reported less aggressive behaviour than the control group (Krahé & Busching, 2015; Moller et al., 2012).

All in all, concluded researchers Brad Bushman and Craig Anderson (2001), the evidence for media effects on aggression is now "overwhelming." The research base is large, the methods diverse, and the overall findings consistent, agreed a task force of leading media violence researchers (C. A. Anderson et al., 2003): "Our in-depth review . . . reveals unequivocal evidence that exposure to media violence can increase the likelihood of aggressive and violent behaviour in both immediate and long-term contexts." This conclusion has been questioned by some critics (Elson & Ferguson, 2014) but is endorsed by the researchers with the most expertise in the field. Although viewing violent media is of course only one among many causes of aggression (and thus not *the* cause of aggression), experiments do show that it is *a* cause (Bushman & Anderson, 2015).

Why does media viewing affect behaviour?

Given the convergence of correlational and experimental evidence, researchers have explored *why* viewing violence has this effect. Consider three possibilities (Geen & Thomas, 1986). First, viewing violence produces *arousal* (Mueller, Donnerstein, & Hallam, 1983; Zillmann, 1989a). As we noted earlier, arousal tends to spill over: One type of arousal energizes other behaviours.

Second, viewing violence *disinhibits*. In Bandura's experiment, the adult's punching of the Bobo doll seemed to make such outbursts legitimate and to lower the children's inhibitions. Viewing violence primes the viewer for aggressive behaviour by activating violence-related thoughts (Berkowitz, 1984; Bushman & Geen, 1990; Josephson, 1987). Listening to music with sexually violent lyrics seems to have a similar effect (Barongan & Hall, 1995; Johnson, Jackson, & Gatto, 1995; Pritchard, 1998).

Third, media portrayals also evoke *imitation*. The children in Bandura's experiments re-enacted the specific behaviours they had witnessed. The commercial television industry is hard-pressed to dispute that television leads viewers to imitate what they have seen:

Its advertisers model consumption. Are media executives right, however, to argue that TV merely holds a mirror to a violent society, that art imitates life, and that the "reel" world therefore shows us the real world? Actually, on TV programs, acts of assault outnumber affectionate acts four to one. In other ways as well, television models an unreal world.

But there is good news here, too. If the ways of relating and problem solving modelled on television do trigger imitation, especially among young viewers, then modelling of **prosocial behaviour** should be socially beneficial. Chapter 8 explored how television's subtle influence can, indeed, teach children positive lessons in behaviour. A character who helps others (like Dora or Doc McStuffins) can teach children prosocial behaviour.

Media's effects on thinking

We have focused on television's effect on behaviour, but researchers have also examined the cognitive effects of viewing violence: Does prolonged viewing *desensitize* us to cruelty? Does it give us mental *scripts* for how to act? Does it distort our *perceptions* of reality? Does it *prime* aggressive thoughts?

Children who watch more violent media can become desensitized to cruelty and feel less empathy for others.
Source: ©MachineHeadz/iStockphoto/Getty Images.

Desensitization

Repeat an emotion-arousing stimulus, such as an obscene word, over and over. What happens? From introductory psychology, you may recall that the emotional response will "extinguish." After witnessing thousands of acts of cruelty, there is good reason to expect a similar emotional numbing. The most common response might well become, "Doesn't bother me at all." Such a response is precisely what Barbara Krahé and her colleagues (2010) observed when they measured the physiological arousal of 303 university students who watched a clip from a violent movie. Regular viewers of violence on TV and in movies showed a lessened response, compared to infrequent viewers, reacting to violence with a shrug rather than concern. A longitudinal study of German adolescents found the same thing: media violence exposure decreased feelings of empathy for others (Krahé & Moller, 2010).

prosocial behaviour Positive, constructive, helpful social behaviour; the opposite of antisocial behaviour.

social scripts Culturally provided mental instructions for how to act in various situations.

In a clever experiment, Brad Bushman and Craig Anderson (2009) had a young woman with a taped-up ankle drop her crutches while outside a movie theatre and then struggle to retrieve them. Moviegoers who had just seen a violent film (*The Ruins*) took longer to help than those who had just seen a nonviolent film (*Nim's Island*). When the woman dropped her crutches *before* the movie, however, there was no difference in helping—suggesting it was the violent film itself, and not the type of people who watch violent films, that desensitized moviegoers to her dilemma.

Social scripts

When we find ourselves in new situations, uncertain how to act, we often rely on **social scripts**—culturally provided mental instructions for how to act. After so many action films, youngsters may acquire a script that is played when they face real-life conflicts. Challenged, they may "act like a man" by intimidating or eliminating the threat. Likewise, after viewing multiple sexual innuendoes and acts on TV and in music lyrics—mostly involving impulsive or short-term relationships—youths may acquire sexual scripts they later enact in real-life relationships (Escobar-Chaves & Anderson, 2008; Fischer & Greitemeyer, 2006; Kunkel, 2001). Thus, the more sexual content that adolescents view (even when controlling for other predictors of early sexual activity), the more likely they are to perceive their peers as sexually active, to develop sexually permissive attitudes, and to experience early intercourse (Escobar-Chaves et al., 2005; Martino et al., 2005). Media portrayals implant social scripts.

Altered perceptions

Does television's fictional world also mould our conceptions of the real world? George Gerbner and his associates (1979, 1994) suspect that this is television's most potent effect. Their surveys of both adolescents and adults showed that heavy viewers (four hours a day or more) are more likely than light viewers (two hours or fewer) to exaggerate the frequency of violence in the world around them and to fear being personally assaulted. Similar feelings of vulnerability have been expressed by South African women after viewing violence against women (Reid & Finchilescu, 1995). One survey of 7- to 11-year-old children found that heavy viewers were more likely than light viewers to admit fears "that somebody bad might get into your house" or that "when you go outside, somebody might hurt you" (Peterson & Zill, 1981). For those who watch a lot of television, the world becomes a scary place. Media portrayals shape perceptions of reality.

> ***"The more fully that any given generation was exposed to television in its formative years, the lower its civic engagement [its rate of voting, joining, meeting, giving, and volunteering]."***
>
> Robert Putnam, *Bowling Alone* (2000)

Cognitive priming

Research also reveals that watching violent videos primes aggression-related ideas (Bushman, 1998). After viewing violence, people offer more hostile explanations for others' behaviour (Was the shove intentional?). They interpret spoken homonyms with the more aggressive meaning (interpreting *punch* as a hit rather than a drink). And they recognize aggressive words more quickly. Media portrayals prime thinking.

Another Media Influence: Video Games

The scientific debate over the effects of media violence "is basically over," contended Douglas Gentile and Craig Anderson (2003). Researchers are now shifting their attention to video games, which are extremely popular and can be extremely violent. Educational research shows that "video games are excellent teaching tools," noted Gentile and Anderson. "If health video games can successfully teach health behaviours, and flight simulator video games can teach people how to fly, then what should we expect violent murder-simulating games to teach?"

Since the first video game in 1972, we have moved from electronic ping-pong to splatter games (Anderson, Gentile, & Buckley, 2007). In a 2015 poll, two out of three 18- to 29-year-olds said they play video games: 77 percent of men, and 57 percent of women (Duggan, 2015). Half said they had played a video game the day before. In an earlier poll of teens, 97 percent said they played video games. Half said they played first-person shooter games, such as *Halo* or *Counter-Strike*, and two out of three played action games that often involve violence, such as *Grand Theft Auto* (Pew Research Center, 2008). Younger children are also playing violent games: In one survey of Grade 4 students, 59 percent of girls and 73 percent of boys reported that their favourite games were violent ones (Anderson, 2003, 2004).

In the popular video game *Grand Theft Auto: San Andreas*, youth are invited to play psychopath, noted Gentile (2004): "You can run down pedestrians with the car, you can do carjackings, you can do drive-by shootings, you can run down to the red-light district, pick up a prostitute, have sex with her in your car, and then kill her to get your money back." In effective 3D graphics, you can knock people over, stomp on them until they cough up blood, and watch them die.

Effects of video games

Concerns about violent video games heightened after teen murderers in several mass shootings enacted the horrific violence they had so often played onscreen. Adam Lanza, who shot 20 Grade 1 students and six teachers at Sandy Hook Elementary School in Connecticut in 2012, spent many hours playing the warfare game *Call of Duty* (Kleinfield et al., 2013). In 2013, an eight-year-old boy shot and killed a 90-year-old woman after playing *Grand Theft Auto IV* (Stegall, 2013). People wondered: What do youth learn from endless hours of role-playing attacking and dismembering people? And was anything accomplished when some Norwegian stores responded to the 2011 killing of teens by a game-addicted shooter by pulling violent games from their shelves (Anderson, 2011)?

Most smokers don't die of lung cancer. Most abused children don't become abusive. And most people who spend hundreds of hours rehearsing human slaughter live gentle lives. "I play violent video games," some may protest, "but I'm not aggressive." This enables video game defenders, like tobacco and TV interests, to say that their products are harmless. The problem with this common argument is that one isolated example proves nothing—it's not a scientific study. Just as a mass shooter playing video games doesn't show that video games cause aggression, a nonviolent person playing video games doesn't show that video games don't cause aggression. A better approach is to examine large samples of people to find out if, on average, violent video games increase aggression.

Gentile and Anderson (2003) offer some reasons why violent game playing *might* have a more toxic effect than watching violent television. With game playing, players:

- Identify with, and play the role of, a violent character.
- Actively rehearse violence, instead of passively watching it.
- Engage in the whole sequence of enacting violence—selecting victims, acquiring weapons and ammunition, stalking the victim, aiming the weapon, pulling the trigger.
- Engage with continual violence and threats of attack.
- Repeat violent behaviours over and over.
- Are rewarded for violent acts.

For such reasons, military organizations often prepare soldiers to fire in combat by engaging them with attack-simulation games.

Research that examines large samples of people shows that playing violent video games does, on average, increase aggressive behaviour, thoughts, and feelings outside of the game. Combining data from 381 studies with 130 296 participants, Craig Anderson and his colleagues (2010) found a clear effect: Violent video game playing increased aggression—for children, adolescents, and young adults; in North America, Japan, and Western Europe; and across three research designs (correlational, experimental, and longitudinal). That means that violent video games caused aggression even when participants were randomly assigned to play them (versus a nonviolent game), which rules out the possibility that, for example, aggressive people like to play aggressive games. Violent games lead to aggressive actions—though the size of the effect is a matter of debate (Hilgard et al., 2017; Kepes et al., 2017).

First-person shooter games teach and reward aggression, leading to increased aggression after the game is over.
Source: ©Andrey_Popov/Shutterstock.

In one experiment, for example, French university students

were randomly assigned to play either a violent video game (*Condemned 2, Call of Duty 4, The Club*) or a nonviolent video game (*S3K Superbike, Dirt 2, or Pure*) for 20 minutes each day for three days. Those randomly assigned to play a violent game blasted longer and louder unpleasant noise into the headphones of an innocent person than those who played the nonviolent game, with their aggression increasing each day they played the violent game (Hasan et al., 2013).

Studies examining real-world aggression find similar results. Among 3372 Finnish adolescents, those who spent more time playing violent video games were more likely to commit real-world aggressive acts such as attacking someone with the intention of seriously hurting them or threatening someone with a weapon (Exelmans et al., 2015). Longitudinal studies, which follow people over time, produce similar results: Among German adolescents, today's violent game playing predicted later aggression, but today's aggression did not predict future violent game playing (Moller & Krahé, 2008). The same was true for Canadian adolescents followed for four years (Willoughby et al., 2012). In 2015, an American Psychological Association task force reviewing 300 studies between 2005 and 2013 concluded that the evidence linking violent video games and aggression was strong enough to warrant recommending that the video game industry include violence in its game rating system (American Psychological Association, 2015).

Playing violent video games has an array of effects, including the following:

- *Increases in aggressive behaviours.* After violent game play, children and youth play more aggressively with their peers, get into more arguments with their teachers, and participate in more fights. The effect occurs inside and outside the laboratory; across self-reports, teacher reports, and parent reports; and for reasons illustrated in Figure 9–6. Even among young adolescents who scored low in hostility, 10 times more of the high-violence gamers got into fights compared with their nongaming counterparts. And after they started playing the violent games, previously nonhostile kids became more likely to have fights (Gentile et al., 2004). In Japan, too, playing violent games early in a school year predicted physical aggressiveness later in the year, even after controlling for gender and prior aggressiveness (Anderson et al., 2008).
- *Increases in aggressive thoughts.* After playing a violent game, students became more likely to guess that a man whose car was just rear-ended would respond aggressively, by using abusive language, kicking out a window, or starting a fight

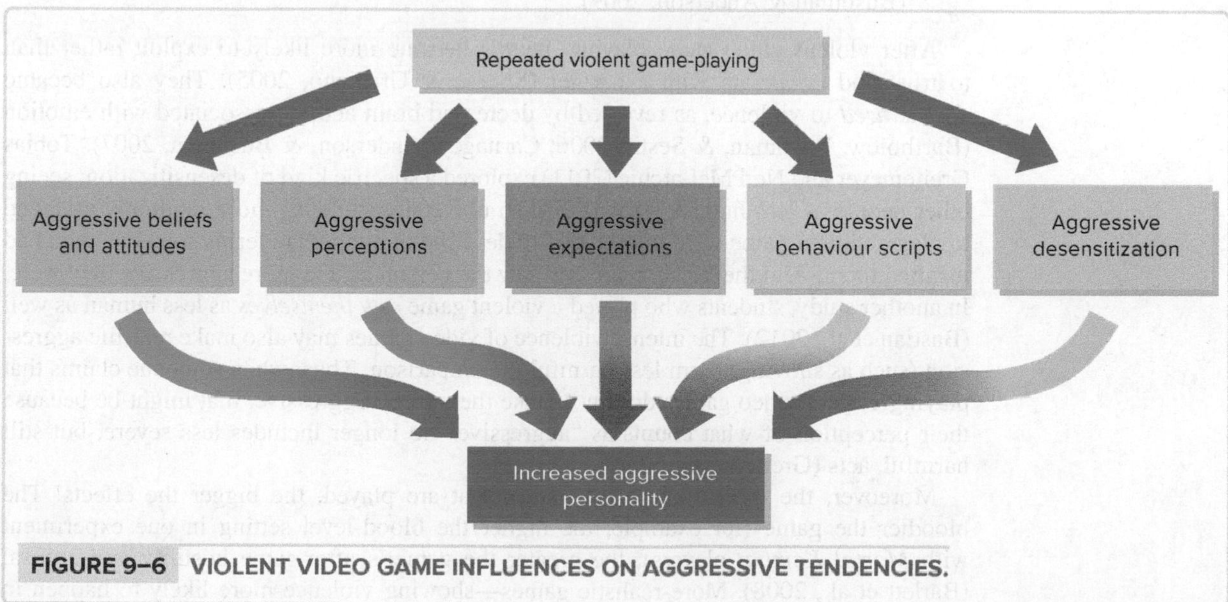

FIGURE 9–6 **VIOLENT VIDEO GAME INFLUENCES ON AGGRESSIVE TENDENCIES.**

(Bushman & Anderson, 2002; Gentile et al., 2017). Those who played violent games were also more likely to have a hostile attribution bias—they expected other people to act aggressively when provoked, and the greater this bias, the more aggressively they behaved themselves. Those who play violent games, conclude the researchers, see the world through "blood-red tinted glasses" (Hasan et al., 2012).

- *Increases in aggressive feelings,* including hostility, anger, or revenge. Students who played a violent video game had more aggressive thoughts and feelings than those who watched a recording of someone else playing the same game or who watched a violent film, suggesting that violent video games heighten aggression even more than other violent media—most likely because people actually act aggressively when they play video games instead of being passive observers (Lin, 2013). Those randomly assigned to play a violent video game also reported feeling less happy than those who played prosocial or neutral games (Saleem et al., 2012).
- *Habituation in the brain.* Compared with those who did not play violent games, frequent gamers' brains reacted less strongly to negative images. Apparently, their brains have become habituated to violence, numbing their reactions (Montag et al., 2012).
- *Greater likelihood of carrying a weapon.* Among 9- to 18-year-olds in one longitudinal study, those who had played violent video games in the past year were five times more likely to carry a weapon to school, even when adjusted for third factors (Ybarra et al., 2014).
- *Decreases in self-control and increases in antisocial behaviour.* High school students who played a violent video game (compared with a control group who played a nonviolent game) ate four times more M&Ms out of a bowl next to the computer, suggesting lowered self-control. They were also more likely to steal, taking more raffle tickets for attractive prizes than they actually earned (Gabbiadini et al., 2014). A correlational study found that youth who played violent video games were more likely to have stolen, vandalized property, or sold drugs (DeLisi et al., 2013).
- *Decreases in helping others and in empathy for others.* Students randomly assigned to play a violent or nonviolent video game later overheard a loud fight that ended with one person writhing on the floor in pain from a sprained ankle. Students who had just played a violent game took more than one minute on average to come to the person's aid, almost four times as long as those who had played a nonviolent game (Bushman & Anderson, 2009).

After violent video game playing, people became more likely to exploit rather than to trust and cooperate with a partner (Sheese & Graziano, 2005). They also became *desensitized* to violence, as revealed by decreased brain activity associated with emotion (Bartholow, Bushman, & Sestir, 2006; Carnagey, Anderson, & Bushman, 2007). Tobias Greitemeyer and Neil McLatchie (2011) explored a specific kind of desensitization: seeing other people as less human. Among British university students, those randomly assigned to play a violent game were more likely to describe in nonhuman terms someone who had insulted them. And the less human they saw the person as, the more aggressive they were. In another study, students who played a violent game saw *themselves* as less human as well (Bastian et al., 2012). The intense violence of video games may also make real-life aggression (such as shoving) seem less harmful in comparison. Thus, when someone claims that playing violent video games does not make them more aggressive, that might be because their perception of what counts as "aggressive" no longer includes less severe, but still harmful, acts (Greitemeyer, 2014).

Moreover, the more violent the games that are played, the bigger the effects. The bloodier the game (for example, the higher the blood-level setting in one experiment with *Mortal Kombat* players), the greater the gamer's after-game hostility and arousal (Barlett et al., 2008). More-realistic games—showing violence more likely to happen in

THE INSIDE STORY

Understanding the clearly harmful effects being documented by TV/film researchers, I was disturbed as I noticed the increasing violence in video games. With one of my graduate students, Karen Dill, I therefore began correlational and experimental investigations that intersected with growing public concern and led to my testifying before the U.S. Senate subcommittee and consulting for a wide array of government and public policy groups, including parent and child advocacy organizations.

Although it is gratifying to see one's research have a positive impact, the video game industry has gone to great lengths to dismiss the research, much as 30 years ago cigarette manufacturers ridiculed basic medical research by asking how many Marlboros a lab rat had to smoke before contracting cancer. I also got some pretty nasty mail from gamers, and the volume of requests for information led me to offer resources and answers at **psychology.iastate.edu/faculty/caa.**

Many people believe that the best way to enhance understanding of a complicated topic is to find people who will give opposite views and give each "side" equal time. Media violence news stories typically give equal time to industry representatives and their preferred "experts" along with reassuring words from a carefree four-year-old, which can leave the impression that we know less than we do. If all the experts in a given area agree, does this idea of "fairness" and "balance" make sense? Or should we expect that legitimate experts will have published peer-reviewed original research articles on the issue at hand?

Is violent video game playing cathartic? Toxic? Or neutral? Experiments offer some answers.

Source: ©James Woodson/Getty Images.

Craig A. Anderson *Iowa State University*

real life—also produced more aggressive feelings than less-realistic games (Barlett & Rodeheffer, 2009). Although much remains to be learned, these studies challenge the **catharsis** hypothesis—the idea that violent games allow people to safely express their aggressive tendencies and "get their anger out" (Kutner & Olson, 2008). Practising violence breeds rather than releases violence, say catharsis critics. Yet the idea that games might relieve angry feelings is one of the main draws of violent games for angry people (Bushman & Whitaker, 2010). Unfortunately, say critics, this strategy is likely to backfire, leading to more anger and aggression.

catharsis Emotional release. The catharsis view of aggression is that aggressive drive is reduced when one "releases" aggressive energy, either by acting aggressively or by fantasizing aggression.

In 2005, California state senator Leland Yee proposed a law banning the sale of violent video games to those under 18. The bill was signed into law, but video game manufacturers immediately sued, and it never went into effect. The U.S. Supreme Court heard the case in 2010, and more than 100 social scientists signed a statement in support of the law, writing that "Overall, the research data conclude that exposure to violent video games causes an increase in the likelihood of aggressive behavior."

But Christopher Ferguson and John Kilburn (2010) signed a statement to the U.S. Supreme Court criticizing the California law. They point out that from 1996 to 2006, when violent video game sales were increasing, real-life youth violence was decreasing (Markey et al., 2015). Ferguson and Kilburn also argue that the effects of violent video games on aggression are small—only some people who play violent video games will act aggressively in real life. In return, Craig Anderson and his colleagues (2010) argue that the violent gaming effect is larger than the toxic effects of asbestos or the effect of second-hand smoke on lung cancer. Not everyone exposed to asbestos or second-hand smoke will develop cancer, they point out, but they are still considered public health dangers. Other critics point out that most experiments on violent video games have not used control games similar in competitiveness or pace of action, creating the possibility that *these* factors increase aggression, rather than the violence in the games per se (Adachi & Willoughby, 2011).

In 2011, the U.S. Supreme Court struck down the law, primarily citing the First Amendment's guarantee of free speech but also expressing doubts that the research showed "a direct causal link between playing violent video games and actual harm to minors" (Scalia, 2011).

Video games are not all bad—not all of them are violent, and even the violent games improve hand–eye coordination, reaction time, spatial ability, and selective attention (Dye, Green, & Bavelier, 2009; Wu et al., 2012), though these effects are limited to those who play frequently and for many hours (Unsworth et al., 2015). Moreover, game playing is focused fun that helps satisfy basic needs for a sense of competence, control, and social connection (Przybylski, Rigby, & Ryan, 2010). No wonder an experiment that randomly assigned six- to nine-year-old boys to receive a game system found them spending an average of 40 minutes a day on it over the next few months. The downside: They spent less time on schoolwork, resulting in lower reading and writing scores than the control group that did not get a game system (Weis & Cerankosky, 2010).

What about playing prosocial games in which people help each other—the conceptual opposite of violent games? In three studies with children and adults in Singapore, Japan, and the United States, those who played prosocial video games helped others, shared, and cooperated more in real-life situations (Gentile et al., 2009). German students randomly assigned to play a prosocial (vs. neutral) game were less physically and socially aggressive toward someone who had insulted them (Greitemeyer et al., 2010). A meta-analysis of 98 studies found the same: Violent video games are linked to more antisocial acts and fewer prosocial acts, and prosocial games are linked to fewer antisocial acts and more prosocial acts (Greitemeyer & Mugge, 2014). As Douglas Gentile and Craig Anderson (2011) conclude, "Video games are excellent teachers." Educational games teach children reading and math, prosocial games teach prosocial behaviour, and violent games teach violence, they note. We do what we're taught to do, whether that's to help or to hurt.

As a concerned scientist, Craig Anderson (2003, 2004; see "The Inside Story," p. 331) therefore encourages parents to discover what their kids are ingesting and to ensure that their media diet, at least in their own home, is healthy. Parents may not be able to control what their child watches, plays, and eats in someone else's home. Nor can they control the media's effect on their children's peer culture. (That is why advising parents to "just say no" is naive.) But parents can oversee consumption in their own home and provide increased time for alternative activities. Networking with other parents can build a kid-friendly neighbourhood. And schools can help by providing media awareness education.

Group Influences

We have considered what provokes *individuals* to aggress. If frustrations, insults, and aggressive models heighten the aggressive tendencies of isolated people, then such factors are likely to prompt the same reaction in groups. As a riot begins, aggressive acts often spread rapidly after the "trigger" example of one antagonistic person. Seeing looters freely helping themselves to TV sets, normally law-abiding bystanders may drop their moral inhibitions and imitate.

Groups can amplify aggressive reactions partly by diffusing responsibility. Decisions to attack in war typically are made by strategists remote from the front lines. They give orders, but others carry them out. Does such distancing make it easier to recommend aggression?

In one experiment, students either *shocked* someone or simply *advised* someone else how much shock to administer. When the recipient had not done anything to provoke the aggressor, characteristic of most victims of mass aggression, the advisers recommended more shock than given by the front-line participants, who felt more directly responsible for any hurt (Gaebelein & Mander, 1978).

Social contagion: When 17 juvenile, orphaned bull elephants were relocated during the mid-1990s to a South African park, they became an out-of-control adolescent gang and killed 40 white rhinoceroses. When, in 1998, concerned park officials relocated six older, stronger bull elephants into their midst, the rampaging soon quieted down (Slotow et al., 2000). One of these dominant bulls, at left, faces down several of the juveniles.

Source: ©Gus van Dyk.

Diffusion of responsibility increases not only with distance but with numbers. (Recall from Chapter 7 the phenomenon of deindividuation.) Brian Mullen (1986a) analyzed information from 60 lynchings between 1899 and 1946 and made an interesting discovery: The greater the number of people in a lynch mob, the more vicious the murder and mutilation.

Through social "contagion," groups magnify aggressive tendencies, much as they polarize other tendencies. Examples include youth gangs, soccer fans, rapacious soldiers, urban rioters, and what Scandinavians call "mobbing"—schoolchildren in groups repeatedly harassing or attacking an insecure, weak schoolmate (Lagerspetz et al., 1982). Mobbing is a group activity.

Youths sharing antisocial tendencies and lacking close family bonds and expectations of academic success may find social identity in a gang. As group identity develops, conformity pressures and deindividuation increase (Staub, 1996). Self-identity diminishes as members give themselves over to the group, often feeling a satisfying oneness with the others. The frequent result is social contagion—group-fed arousal, disinhibition, and polarization. As gang expert Arnold Goldstein (1994) observed, until gang members marry out, age out, get a job, go to prison, or die, they hang out. They define their turf, display their colours, challenge rivals, and sometimes commit delinquent acts and fight over drugs, territory, honour, women, or insults.

The twentieth-century massacres that claimed more than 150 million lives were "not the sums of individual actions," noted Robert Zajonc (2000). "*Genocide is not the plural of homicide.*" Massacres are *social* phenomena fed by "moral imperatives"—a collective mentality (including images, rhetoric, and ideology) that mobilizes a group or a culture for extraordinary actions. The massacres of Rwanda's Tutsis, of Europe's Jews, and of North America's Indigenous population were collective phenomena requiring widespread support, organization, and participation. Before launching the genocidal initiative, Rwanda's Hutu government and business leaders bought and distributed 2 million Chinese machetes. Over three months, the Hutu attackers reportedly would get up, eat a hearty breakfast, gather together, and then go hunt their former neighbours, who had fled. They would hack to death anyone they found, then return home, wash, and socialize over a few beers (Dalrymple, 2007; Hatzfeld, 2007).

> ***"Genocide is not the plural of homicide."***
>
> Robert Zajonc, "Massacres: Mass Murders in the Name of Moral Imperatives," 2000

Experiments in Israel (Jaffe & Yinon, 1983) confirmed that groups can amplify aggressive tendencies. In one such experiment, university men angered by a supposed fellow participant retaliated with decisions to give much stronger shocks when in groups than when alone. In another experiment (Jaffe, Shapir, & Yinon, 1981), people decided, either alone or in groups, how much punishing shock to give someone for incorrect answers on a task. As Figure 9–7 shows, individuals gave progressively more of the assumed shock as

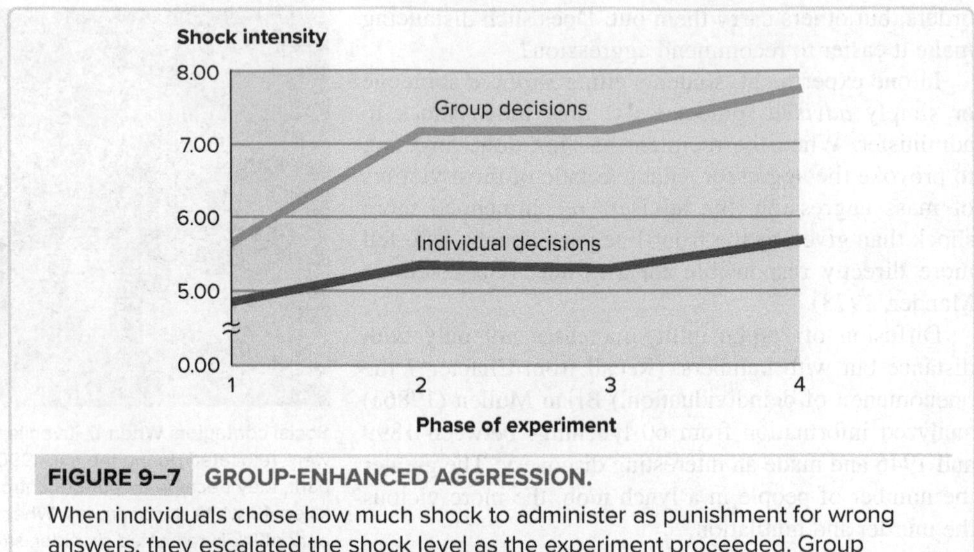

FIGURE 9–7 GROUP-ENHANCED AGGRESSION.
When individuals chose how much shock to administer as punishment for wrong answers, they escalated the shock level as the experiment proceeded. Group decision making further polarized this tendency.

the experiment proceeded, and group decision making magnified this individual tendency. When circumstances provoke an individual's aggressive reaction, the addition of group interaction will often amplify it.

Perhaps you can remember a time in school when you were bullied or someone you knew was—either verbally or physically. Much of the time, other students watch bullying as it happens, or even join in. These bystanders can play an active role in the aggressive act of bullying—for example, by contributing to the humiliation by laughing or cheering (Salmivalli et al., 1999). Or they may defend the victim. An effective anti-bullying program in Finland found that when bystanders stopped rewarding bullies with positive feedback and status, bullying declined (Karna et al., 2011).

Aggression studies provide an apt opportunity to ask how well social psychology's laboratory findings generalize to everyday life. Do the circumstances that trigger someone to deliver electric shock or other aversive stimuli really tell us anything about the circumstances that trigger verbal abuse or a punch in the face? Craig Anderson and Brad Bushman (1997; Bushman & Anderson, 1998) noted that social psychologists have studied aggression in both the laboratory and the everyday world, and the findings are strikingly consistent. In both contexts, increased aggression is predicted by the following:

- Being male
- Aggressive or anger-prone personalities
- Alcohol use
- Violence viewing
- Anonymity
- Provocation
- The presence of weapons
- Group interaction

The laboratory allows us to test and revise theories under controlled conditions. Real-world events inspire ideas and provide the venue for applying our theories.

Aggression research illustrates that an interplay between studies in the controlled lab and the complex real world advances psychology's contribution to human welfare. Hunches gained from everyday experience inspire theories, which stimulate laboratory research, which then deepens our understanding and our ability to apply psychology to real problems.

How Can Aggression Be Reduced?

Can we reduce aggression? Do theory and research suggest ways to control it?

Catharsis?

Ann Landers (1969) advised that youth express their annoyance rather than bottle it up. If a person "bottles up his rage, we have to find an outlet. We have to give him an opportunity of letting off steam," asserted psychiatrist Fritz Perls (1973). Both statements assume the "hydraulic model," which implies accumulated aggressive energy, like dammed-up water, needs a release.

The concept of catharsis is usually credited to Aristotle. Although Aristotle actually said nothing about aggression, he did argue that we can purge emotions by experiencing them and that viewing the classic tragedies, therefore, enabled a catharsis (purging) of pity and fear. To have an emotion excited, he believed, is to have that emotion released (Butcher, 1951). The catharsis hypothesis has been extended to include the emotional release supposedly obtained not only by observing drama but also through recalling and reliving past events, through expressing emotions, and through our actions.

Assuming that aggressive action or fantasy drains pent-up aggression, some therapists and group leaders encourage people to ventilate suppressed aggression by acting it out—by whopping one another with foam bats or beating a bed with a tennis racquet while screaming. If led to believe that catharsis effectively vents emotions, people will react more aggressively to an insult as a way to improve their mood (Bushman, Baumeister, & Phillips, 2001). Some psychologists, believing that catharsis is therapeutic, advise parents to encourage children's release of emotional tension through aggressive play. As you saw earlier, it is also a common argument to defend violent video games. But does catharsis work? Do those who vent their anger become less—or more—aggressive?

Many laypeople have also bought the catharsis idea, as reflected in their nearly two-to-one agreement with the statement, "Sexual materials provide an outlet for bottled-up impulses" (Niemi, Mueller, & Smith, 1989). But other surveys reveal that most people also agree that "Sexual materials lead people to commit rape." So is the catharsis approach valid or not?

In laboratory tests of the catharsis hypothesis, angered participants hit a punching bag while either ruminating about someone who angered them or thinking about becoming physically fit. A third group did not hit the punching bag. When given a chance to administer loud blasts of noise to the person who angered them, people in the "punching bag plus rumination" condition felt angrier and were most aggressive. Moreover, doing nothing at all more effectively reduced aggression than did "blowing off steam" by hitting the bag (Bushman, 2002). Venting anger caused more aggression, not less.

> ***"The worst barbarity of war is that it forces men collectively to commit acts against which individually they would revolt with their whole being."***
>
> Ellen Key, *War, Peace, and the Future*, 1916

Real-life experiments have produced similar results. One study examined Internet users who frequently visit "rant" sites where people are encouraged to express their anger. Did the opportunity to express their hostility reduce it? No. Their hostility and anger increased and their happiness decreased (Martin et al., 2013). Expressing hostility bred more hostility. Several studies have found that Canadian and American spectators of football, wrestling, and hockey games exhibit more hostility after viewing the event than before (Arms et al., 1979; Goldstein & Arms, 1971; Russell, 1983). Instead of reducing their anger, viewing these aggressive sports increased their anger. As Brad Bushman (2002) notes, "Venting to reduce anger is like using gasoline to put out a fire."

> *"He who gives way to violent gestures will increase his rage."*
>
> Charles Darwin,
> *The Expression of the Emotion in Man and Animals,* 1872

Cruel acts beget cruel attitudes. Furthermore, little aggressive acts can breed their own justification. People derogate their victims, rationalizing further aggression.

Retaliation may, in the short run, reduce tension and even provide pleasure (Ramirez, Bonniot-Cabanac, & Cabanac, 2005). But in the long run, it fuels more negative feelings. When people who have been provoked hit a punching bag, even when they believe it will be cathartic, the effect is the opposite—leading them to exhibit *more* cruelty, reported Bushman and his colleagues (Bushman, Baumeister, & Stack, 1999; Bushman, Baumeister, & Phillips, 2001). "It's like the old joke," reflected Bushman (1998). "How do you get to Carnegie Hall? Practice, practice, practice. How do you become a very angry person? The answer is the same. Practice, practice, practice."

Should we, therefore, bottle up anger and aggressive urges? Silent sulking is hardly more effective because it allows us to continue reciting our grievances as we conduct conversations in our head. Brad Bushman and his colleagues (2005) experimented with the toxic effect of such rumination. First, an obnoxious experimenter provoked subjects with insults such as, "Can't you follow directions? Speak louder!" Then half were given a distraction (by being asked to write an essay about their campus landscape), and half were induced to ruminate (by writing an essay about their experiences as a research participant). Next they were mildly insulted by a supposed fellow participant (actually a confederate), to whom they responded by prescribing a hot sauce dose this person would have to consume. The distracted participants, their anger now abated, prescribed only a mild dose; the still-seething ruminators displaced their aggressive urge and prescribed twice as much.

Fortunately, there are nonaggressive ways to express our feelings and to tell others how their behaviour affects us. Across cultures, those who reframe accusatory "you" messages as "I" messages—"I feel angry about what you said" or "I get irritated when you leave dirty dishes"—communicate their feelings in a way that better enables the other person to make a positive response (Kubany et al., 1995). We can be assertive without being aggressive.

A Social Learning Approach

If aggressive behaviour is learned, then there is hope for its control. Let us briefly review factors that influence aggression and speculate how to counteract them.

Aversive experiences, such as frustrated expectations and personal attacks, predispose hostile aggression. So it is wise to refrain from planting false, unreachable expectations in people's minds. Anticipated rewards and costs influence instrumental aggression. This suggests that we should reward cooperative, nonaggressive behaviour.

In experiments, children become less aggressive when caregivers ignore their aggressive behaviour and reinforce their nonaggressive behaviour (Hamblin et al., 1969). Punishing the aggressor is less consistently effective. Threatened punishment deters aggression only under ideal conditions: when the punishment is strong, prompt, and sure; when it is combined with reward for the desired behaviour; and when the recipient is not angry (Baron, 1977).

Moreover, there are limits to punishment's effectiveness. Most homicide is impulsive, hot aggression—the result of an argument, an insult, or an attack. If mortal aggression were cool and instrumental, we could hope that waiting until it happens and severely punishing the criminal afterwards would deter such acts. In that world, countries that impose the death penalty might have a lower murder rate than countries without the death penalty. But in our world of hot homicide, that is not so (Costanzo, 1998). As John Darley and Adam Alter (2009) noted, "A remarkable amount of crime is committed by impulsive individuals, frequently young males, who are frequently drunk or high on drugs, and who often are in packs of similar and similarly mindless young men." No wonder, they say, that trying to reduce crime by increasing sentences has proven so fruitless, while on-the-street policing that produces more arrests has produced encouraging results, such as a 50 percent drop in gun-related crimes in some cities.

Thus, we must *prevent* aggression before it happens. We must teach nonaggressive conflict-resolution strategies. When psychologists Sandra Jo Wilson and Mark Lipsey (2005) assembled data from 249 studies of school violence-prevention programs, they found encouraging results, especially for programs focused on selected "problem" students. After being taught problem-solving skills, emotion-control strategies, and conflict-resolution techniques, the typical 20 percent of students engaging in some violent or disruptive behaviour in a typical school year was reduced to 13 percent. Children whose parents were more permissive (and thus rarely set limits on behaviour and did not enforce rules) grew into more aggressive adolescents (Ehrenreich et al., 2014), suggesting that more authoritative parenting can prevent aggression (but not overly harsh parenting—spanking and other forms of physical punishment can also cause aggression) (Gershoff, 2002). Bullying (including cyberbullying) is reduced when parents or teachers monitor children closely (M. A. Campbell, 2005; Wingate et al., 2013) and when children are educated about what behaviours are considered bullying (Mishna, 2004). Other programs focus on teaching empathy and encourage children not to ignore bullying (Noble, 2003).

To foster a gentler world, we could model and reward sensitivity and cooperation from an early age, perhaps by training parents how to discipline without violence. Training programs encourage parents to reinforce desirable behaviours and to frame statements positively ("When you finish cleaning your room, you can play," rather than "If you don't clean your room, you're grounded."). One "aggression-replacement program" has reduced re-arrest rates of juvenile offenders and gang members by teaching the youths and their parents communication skills, training them to control anger, and raising their level of moral reasoning (Goldstein & Glick, 1994).

If observing aggressive models lowers inhibitions and elicits imitation, then we might also reduce brutal, dehumanizing portrayals in films and on television—steps comparable to those already taken to reduce racist and sexist portrayals. We can also inoculate children against the effects of media violence. Wondering if the TV networks would ever "face the facts and change their programming," Eron and Huesmann (1984) taught 170 children that television portrays the world unrealistically, that aggression is less common and effective than TV suggests, and that aggressive behaviour is undesirable. (Drawing upon attitude research, Eron and Huesmann encouraged children to draw these inferences themselves and to attribute their expressed criticisms of television to their own convictions.) When restudied two years later, these children were less influenced by TV violence than were untrained children. In a more recent study, Stanford University used 18 classroom lessons to persuade children to simply reduce their TV watching and video game playing (Robinson et al., 2001). They reduced their TV viewing by a third—and their aggressive behaviour at school dropped 25 percent compared to children in a control school. Even music can help reduce aggression when it models the right attitude:

German students who were randomly assigned to hear prosocial music like "We Are the World" and "Help" behaved less aggressively than those who heard neutral music (Greitemeyer, 2011). Other ideas for how to prevent aggression come from studies of differences among people. For example, people who are sensitive to disgust are less aggressive (Pond et al., 2012), suggesting that emphasizing the disgusting aspects of violence might help prevent aggression. People who see moral rules as negotiable (agreeing, for example, that "Cheating is appropriate behaviour because no one gets hurt") are more aggressive (Gini et al., 2014), suggesting that teaching some non-negotiable rules and moral reasoning ("It's never okay to hit," "Cheating hurts everyone") might reduce aggressive behaviour.

Suggestions such as these can help us minimize aggression. But given the complexity of aggression's causes and the difficulty of controlling them, it is difficult to feel the optimism expressed by Andrew Carnegie's forecast that in the twentieth century, "To kill a man will be considered as disgusting as we in this day consider it disgusting to eat one." Since Carnegie uttered those words in 1900, some 200 million human beings have been killed. It is a sad irony that, although today we understand human aggression better than ever before, humanity's inhumanity endures.

Culture Change and World Violence

Nevertheless, cultures can change. "The Vikings slaughtered and plundered," noted science writer Natalie Angier. "Their descendants in Sweden haven't fought a war in nearly 200 years." Indeed, as psychologist Steven Pinker (2014) documents, across centuries, humans have become more civilized, and all forms of violence—including wars, genocide, and murders—are less common in recent years than in past eras. We've graduated from plundering neighbouring tribes to economic interdependence, from a world in which Western European countries initiated two new wars per year over 600 years to, for the past seven decades, zero wars. Surprisingly, to those of us who love modern British murder mysteries, "a contemporary Englishman has about a 50-fold less chance of being murdered than his compatriot in the Middle Ages," notes Pinker. In all but one Western democracy, the death penalty has been abolished. And the sole exception—the United States—no longer practises it for witchcraft, counterfeiting, and horse theft. Many aggressive and violent acts have become less common, including lynchings, hate crimes, rapes, corporal punishment, and anti-gay attitudes and intimidation. We can, Pinker concludes, be grateful "for the institutions of civilization and enlightenment [economic trade, education, government policing, and justice] that have made it possible."

SUMMING UP

What Is Aggression?

- *Aggression* (defined as behaviour intended to cause harm) can be *physical* (hurting someone's body) or *social* (hurting someone's feelings or status). *Social aggression* includes bullying and *cyberbullying* (bullying carried out online or through texting).
- *Aggression* (either physical or social) can be *hostile aggression*, which springs from emotions such as anger, or *instrumental aggression*, which aims to injure as a means to some other end.

What Are Some Theories of Aggression?

There are three broad theories of aggression:

- The *instinct* view, most commonly associated with Sigmund Freud and Konrad Lorenz, contended that aggressive energy will accumulate from within, like water accumulating behind a dam. Although the available evidence offers little support for this view, aggression is biologically influenced by heredity, blood chemistry, and the brain.
- According to the second view, *frustration* causes anger and hostility. Given aggressive cues, anger may provoke aggression. Frustration stems not from deprivation itself but from the gap between expectations and achievements.
- The *social learning* view presents aggression as learned behaviour. By experience and by observing others' success, we sometimes learn that aggression pays. Social learning enables family and subculture influences on aggression, as well as media influences.

What Are Some Influences on Aggression?

- Many factors exert influence on aggression. One factor is aversive experiences, which include not only frustrations but also discomfort, heat, pain, and personal attacks, both physical and verbal.
- Arousal from almost any source, even physical exercise or sexual stimulation, can be transformed into other emotions, such as anger.
- Aggressive cues, such as the presence of a gun, increase the likelihood of aggressive behaviour.
- Viewing violence (1) breeds a modest increase in aggressive behaviour, especially in people who are provoked; (2) desensitizes viewers to aggression; and (3) alters viewers' perceptions of reality. These findings parallel the results of research on the effects of viewing violent pornography, which can increase men's aggression against women and distort their perceptions of women's responses to sexual coercion.
- Television permeates the daily life of millions of people and portrays considerable violence. Correlational and experimental studies converge on the conclusion that heavy exposure to televised violence correlates with aggressive behaviour.
- Playing violent video games may increase aggressive thinking, feelings, and behaviour even more than television or movies do because the experience involves much more active participation than those other media.
- Much aggression is committed by groups. Circumstances that provoke individuals may also provoke groups. By diffusing responsibility and polarizing actions, group situations amplify aggressive reactions.

How Can Aggression Be Reduced?

- How can we minimize aggression? Contrary to the *catharsis* hypothesis, expressing aggression by catharsis tends to breed further aggression, not reduce it.
- The social learning approach suggests controlling aggression by counteracting the factors that provoke it: by reducing aversive stimulation, by rewarding and modelling nonaggression, and by eliciting reactions incompatible with aggression.

Key Terms

aggression
catharsis
cyberbullying
displacement
frustration
frustration–aggression theory
hostile aggresssion
instrumental aggression
instinctive behaviour
physical aggression
prosocial behaviour
relative deprivation
social aggression
social learning theory
social scripts

CHAPTER 10

Attraction and Intimacy: Liking and Loving Others

Source: ©Jack Hollingsworth/Blend Images LLC.

CHAPTER OUTLINE

What Leads to Friendship and Attraction?

What Is Love?

What Enables Close Relationships?

How Do Relationships End?

Our lifelong dependence on one another puts relationships at the core of our existence. In your beginning, there very likely was an attraction—an attraction between two specific people. Aristotle called humans "the social animal."

Indeed, we have what today's social psychologists call a **need to belong**—to connect with others in enduring, close relationships. This need forms the basis for what we explore in this chapter: How and why we like and love others, both romantically and as friends.

Social psychologists Roy Baumeister and Mark Leary (1995) illustrated the power of social attachments:

- For our ancestors, mutual attachments enabled group survival. When hunting game or erecting shelter, 10 hands were better than two.
- The bonds of love can lead to children, whose survival chances are boosted by the nurturing of two bonded parents who support each other (Fletcher et al., 2015).
- Relationships consume much of life. How much of your waking life is spent talking with people? One sampling of 10 000 tape recordings of half-minute slices of students' waking hours (using belt-worn recorders) found them talking to someone 28 percent of the time—and that doesn't count the time they spent listening to someone (Mehl & Pennebaker, 2003).

need to belong A motivation to bond with others in relationships that provide ongoing, positive interactions.

- When not face to face, the world's nearly 8 billion people connect by voice and texting or through social networks such as Instagram. The average 18-year-old spends about two hours a day sending texts and just under two hours on social media (Twenge, 2017). Our need to belong motivates our investment in being continuously connected.
- For people everywhere, actual and hoped-for close relationships can dominate thinking and emotions. Finding a supportive person in whom we can confide, we feel accepted and prized. Falling in love, we feel irrepressible joy. When relationships with partners, family, and friends are healthy, self-esteem—a barometer of our relationships—rides high (Denissen et al., 2008). Longing for acceptance and love, we spend billions on cosmetics, clothes, and diets. Even people who seem unconcerned with pleasing others relish being accepted (Carvallo & Gabriel, 2006).
- Exiled, imprisoned, or in solitary confinement, people ache for their own people and places. Rejected, we are at risk for depression (Nolan, Flynn, & Garber, 2003). Time passes more slowly and life seems less meaningful (Twenge, Catanese, & Baumeister, 2003). When queried three months after arriving on a large university campus, many international students, like some homesick domestic students, reported declining feelings of well-being (Cemalcilar & Falbo, 2008).
- For the jilted, the widowed, and the sojourner in a strange place, the loss of social bonds triggers pain, loneliness, or withdrawal. Losing a close relationship, adults feel jealous, lonely, distraught, or bereaved, as well as mindful of death and the fragility of life (Strachman & Schimel, 2006). After relocating, people—especially those with the strongest need to belong—typically feel homesick (Watt & Badger, 2009).
- Reminders of death in turn heighten our need to belong, to be with others, and to hold close those we love (Mikulincer, Florian, & Hirschberger, 2003; Wisman & Koole, 2003). The shocking death of a classmate, co-worker, or family member brings people together, their differences no longer mattering.

We are indeed social animals. We need to belong. As with other motivations, we pursue belonging when we don't have it and seek less when our needs are fulfilled (DeWall et al., 2009). And when we do belong—when we feel supported by close, intimate relationships—we tend to be healthier and happier. Satisfy the need to belong in balance with two other human needs—to feel *autonomy* and *competence*—and the typical result is a deep sense of well-being (Deci & Ryan, 2002; Milyavskaya et al., 2009; Sheldon & Niemiec, 2006). Happiness is feeling connected, free, and capable.

Social psychologist Kipling Williams (2002, 2007, 2011) has explored what happens when our need to belong is thwarted by ostracism (acts of excluding or ignoring). Humans in all cultures, whether in schools, workplaces, or homes, use ostracism to regulate social behaviour. Some of us know what it is like to be shunned—to be avoided, met with averted eyes, or given the silent treatment. The silent treatment is "emotional abuse" and "a terrible, terrible weapon to use," say those who have experienced it from a family member or co-worker. In experiments, people who are left out of a simple game of ball tossing feel deflated and stressed. Ostracism hurts, and the social pain is keenly felt—more than those who are not ostracized ever know (Nordgren, Banas, & MacDonald, 2011). Ostracism may be even worse than bullying: Bullying, though extremely negative, at least acknowledges someone's existence and importance, whereas ostracism treats a person as though they don't exist at all (Williams & Nida, 2009). In one study, children who were ostracized but not bullied felt worse than those who were bullied but not ostracized (Carpenter, 2012). If only we better empathized with those rejected, there might be less tolerance of ostracism.

Sometimes deflation turns nasty, as when people lash out at the very people whose acceptance they desire (Reijntjes et al., 2011) or engage in self-defeating behaviour. In several experiments, students randomly assigned to be rejected by their peers (versus those who were accepted) became more likely to engage in self-defeating behaviours (such as procrastinating by reading magazines) and less able to regulate their behaviour (such as eating cookies [Baumeister et al., 2005; Twenge et al., 2002]). Apparently the stereotype of someone eating lots of ice cream after a breakup isn't far off. Nor is the trope of the rejected person drowning their sorrows in alcohol: People who were socially rejected by those close to them subsequently drank more alcohol (Laws et al., 2017).

Such overeating and alcohol use might result from a self-control breakdown: Ostracized people show deficits in brain mechanisms that inhibit unwanted behaviour (Otten & Jonas, 2013). Outside the laboratory, rejected children were, two years later, more likely to have self-regulation issues, such as not finishing tasks and not listening to directions (Stenseng et al., 2014). In lab experiments, socially rejected people also became more likely to disparage or blast unpleasant noise at someone who had insulted them, were less likely to help others, and were more likely to cheat and steal (Kouchaki & Wareham, 2015; Poon et al., 2013; Twenge et al., 2001, 2007). If a small laboratory experience of rejection could produce such aggression, noted the researchers, one wonders what aggressive and antisocial tendencies "might arise from a series of important rejections or chronic exclusion."

Williams and Steve Nida (2011) were surprised to discover that even "cyberostracism," by faceless people whom one will never meet, takes a toll. Their experimental procedure was inspired by Williams's experience at a park picnic. When a Frisbee landed near his feet, and Williams threw it back to two others, they then included him in the tossing for a while. When suddenly they stopped tossing the Frisbee his way, Williams was "amazed" at how hurt he felt by the ostracism (Storr, 2018).

Taking this experience into the laboratory, the researchers have had more than 5000 participants from dozens of countries play a Web-based game of throwing a ball with two others (actually, computer-generated fellow players). Those ostracized by the other players experienced poorer moods and became more likely to conform to others' wrong judgments on a subsequent perceptual task. Exclusion, whether it's cyberostracism or in the real world, hurts longest for anxious people (Zadro et al., 2006). It hurts more for younger than older adults (Hawkley et al., 2011). And it hurts no less when it comes from a group that the rest of society spurns—Australian Ku Klux Klan members, in one experiment

(Gonsalkorale & Williams, 2006). Exclusion even hurts when the rejection comes from a robot instead of a person (Nash et al., 2018).

Cyberostracism can also occur when you feel ignored on social media. Wouter Wolf and his colleagues (2015) created an experimental paradigm to test this type of ostracism online, having participants create a personal profile ("write a paragraph [to] introduce yourself to the group") and then, in the ostracism condition, receiving a very low number of "likes." Participants ostracized in this way reported just as much negative mood and lack of meaning as those excluded during the online ball-toss game. So the next time you feel hurt because you didn't get many likes, realize you're not the only one who sometimes feels that way.

Williams and his colleagues (Williams, Cheung, & Choi, 2000) found ostracism stressful even when each of them was ignored for an agreed-upon day by the unresponsive four others. Contrary to their expectations that this would be a laughter-filled role-playing game, the simulated ostracism disrupted work, interfered with pleasant social functioning, and "caused temporary concern, anxiety, paranoia, and general fragility of spirit." To thwart our deep need to belong is to unsettle our life.

Evidence collected by Geoff MacDonald of the University of Toronto and his colleagues suggests a convergence between social and physical pain (MacDonald & Leary, 2005). Ostracized people exhibit heightened activity in a brain cortex area that also activates in response to physical pain. Ostracism's social pain, much like physical pain, increases aggression (Riva, Wirth, & Williams, 2011). Hurt feelings are also embodied in a depressed heart rate (Moor, Crone, & van der Molen, 2010). Heartbreak makes one's heart brake.

Indeed, the pain of social rejection is so real that a pain-relieving Tylenol can reduce hurt feelings (DeWall et al., 2010b), as can sending a light electrical current to the brain region in which rejection is felt (Riva et al., 2012). Ostracism's opposite—feeling love—activates brain reward systems. When looking at their beloved's picture, deeply in love university students feel markedly less pain when immersing their hands in cold water (Younger et al., 2010). Ostracism is a real pain. And love is a natural painkiller.

Asked to recall a time when they were socially excluded—perhaps left alone in the dorm when others went out—University of Toronto students in one experiment even perceived the room temperature as five degrees colder than did those asked to recall a social acceptance experience (Zhong & Leonardelli, 2008). Such recollections come easily: People remember and relive past social pain more easily than past physical pain (Chen et al., 2008). The effect moves the other way as well: Students who were ordered to ostracize others were just as distressed as those who were ostracized (Legate et al., 2013) and felt less human (Bastian et al., 2012).

Roy Baumeister (2005) finds a silver lining in the rejection research. When recently excluded people experience a safe opportunity to make a new friend, they "seem willing and even eager to take it." They become more attentive to smiling, accepting faces (DeWall, Maner, & Rouby, 2009). An exclusion experience also triggers increased mimicry of others' behaviour as a nonconscious effort to build rapport (Lakin, Chartrand, & Arkin, 2008). And, at a societal level, notes Baumeister (2005), meeting the need to belong should pay dividends:

> My colleagues in sociology have pointed out that minority groups who feel excluded show many of the same patterns that our laboratory manipulations elicit: high rates of aggression and antisocial behaviour, decreased willingness to cooperate and obey rules, poorer intellectual performance, more self-destructive acts, short-term focus, and the like. If we could promote a more inclusive society in which more people feel themselves accepted as valued members, some of these tragic patterns might be reduced.

What Leads to Friendship and Attraction?

What factors nurture liking and loving? How do proximity, physical attractiveness, similarity, and feeling liked nurture liking and loving?

What predisposes one person to like, or to love, another? Few questions about human nature arouse greater interest. The ways affections flourish and fade form the stuff and fluff of soap operas, popular music, novels, and much of our everyday conversation.

So much has been written about liking and loving that almost every conceivable explanation—and its opposite—has already been proposed. For most people—and for you—what factors nurture liking and loving?

- Does absence make the heart grow fonder, or is someone who is out of sight also out of mind?
- Do likes attract? Or opposites?
- How much do good looks matter?
- What has fostered your close relationships?

Let's start with those factors that lead to friendship and then consider those that sustain and deepen a relationship.

"I cannot tell how my ankles bend, nor whence the cause of my faintest wish, nor the cause of the friendship I emit, nor the cause of the friendship I take again."

Walt Whitman, *Song of Myself,* 1855

Proximity

One powerful predictor of whether any two people are friends is sheer **proximity**. Proximity can also breed hostility; most assaults and murders involve people living close to each other. But, far more often, proximity prompts liking. Mitja Back and his colleagues (2008) confirmed this by randomly assigning students to seats at their first class meeting and then having each make a brief self-introduction to the whole class. One year after this one-time seating assignment, students reported greater friendship with those who just happened, during that first class, to be seated next to or near them. In baseball, umpires are less likely to call a strike on batters they have stood closer to throughout the game (Mills, 2014).

proximity Geographical nearness. Proximity (more precisely, "functional distance") powerfully predicts liking.

"I do not believe that friends are necessarily the people you like best, they are merely the people who got there first."

Sir Peter Ustinov, *Dear Me,* 1979

Though it may seem trivial to those pondering the mysterious origins of romantic love, sociologists long ago found that most people marry someone who lives in the same neighbourhood, or works at the same company or job, or sits in the same class (Bossard, 1932; Burr, 1973; Clarke, 1952; Katz & Hill, 1958). In a survey of people married or in long-term relationships, 38 percent met at work or at school; some of the rest met when their paths crossed in their neighbourhood, church, or gym, or while growing up (Pew Research Center, 2007). Look around. If you marry, it will likely be to someone who has lived or worked or studied within walking distance.

Interaction

Even more significant than geographical distance is "functional distance"—how often people's paths cross. We frequently become friends with those who use the same entrances, parking lots, and recreation areas. Randomly assigned university roommates, who can hardly avoid frequent interaction, are far more likely to become good friends than enemies (Newcomb, 1961). At the university where one of us teaches, the men and women once lived on opposite sides of the campus. They understandably bemoaned the lack of cross-sex friendships. Now that they occupy different areas of the same dormitories and share common sidewalks, lounges, and laundry facilities, friendships between men and women are far more frequent. Interaction enables people to explore their similarities, to sense one another's liking, and to perceive themselves as a social unit (Arkin & Burger, 1980). In one study, strangers liked each other more the longer they talked (Reis et al., 2010).

So if you're new in town and want to make friends, try to get an apartment near the mailboxes, an office desk near the coffee pot, a parking spot near the main buildings, or a room in a dormitory with shared bathroom facilities (Easterbrook & Vignoles, 2015). Such is the architecture of friendship.

The chance nature of such contacts helps explain a surprising finding. Consider this: If you had an identical twin who became engaged to someone, wouldn't you (being in so many ways similar to your twin) expect to share your twin's attraction to that person? But no, reported researchers David Lykken and Auke Tellegen (1993); only half of identical twins recalled really liking their twin's selection, and only 5 percent said, "I could have fallen for my twin's fiancé(e)." Romantic love is often rather like ducklings' imprinting, in which ducklings bond to whomever is near, surmised Lykken and Tellegen. With repeated exposure to someone, our infatuation may fix on almost anyone who has roughly similar characteristics and who reciprocates our affection.

Why does proximity breed liking? One factor is availability; obviously there are fewer opportunities to get to know someone who attends a different school or lives in another town. But there is more to it than that. Most people like their roommates, or those one door away, better than those two doors away. Those just a few doors away, or even a floor below, hardly live at an inconvenient distance. Moreover, those close by are potential enemies as well as friends. So why does proximity encourage affection more often than animosity?

Anticipation of interaction

Proximity enables people to discover commonalities and exchange rewards. But merely anticipating interaction also boosts liking. John Darley and Ellen Berscheid (1967) discovered this when they gave women ambiguous information about two other women, one of whom they expected to talk with intimately. Asked how much they liked each one, the women preferred the person they expected to meet. Expecting to date someone similarly boosts liking (Berscheid et al., 1976). Even voters on the losing side of an election will find their opinions of the winning candidate—whom they are now stuck with—rising (Gilbert et al., 1995).

The phenomenon is adaptive. Anticipatory liking—expecting that someone will be pleasant and compatible—increases the chance of a rewarding relationship (Klein & Kunda, 1992; Knight & Vallacher, 1981; Miller & Marks, 1982). It's a good thing that we are biased to like those we often see, for our lives are filled with relationships with people whom we may not have chosen but with whom we need to have continuing interactions—roommates, siblings, grandparents, teachers, classmates, co-workers. Liking such people is surely conducive to better relationships with them, which in turn makes for happier, more productive living.

Mere exposure

Proximity leads to liking not only because it enables interaction and anticipatory liking but also for another reason: More than 200 experiments revealed that, contrary to an old proverb, familiarity does not breed contempt. Rather, it fosters fondness (Bornstein, 1989, 1999). Simply being repeatedly exposed to all sorts of novel stimuli—nonsense syllables, Chinese calligraphy characters, musical selections, faces—boosts people's ratings of them; this phenomenon is called the **mere-exposure effect**. Do the "words" *nansoma, saricik,* and *afworbu* mean something better or something worse than the words *iktitaf, biwojni,* and *kadirga*? Told these words were Turkish (they are not), students tested by Robert Zajonc (1968, 1970) preferred whichever of these words they had seen most frequently. The more times they had seen a meaningless word or a Chinese ideograph,

mere-exposure effect The tendency for novel stimuli to be liked more or rated more positively after the rater has been repeatedly exposed to them.

the more likely they were to say it meant something good. This can make for a good class demonstration. Periodically flash certain nonsense words on a screen. By the end of the semester, students will rate those "words" more positively than other nonsense words they have never before seen. When hurricanes do significant damage—and thus the hurricane name is mentioned frequently—babies are more likely to receive names starting with that letter, presumably due to mere exposure (Berger et al., 2012). Attitudes toward social groups can also be changed by mere exposure: When people read stories about transgender individuals accompanied by pictures, they become more comfortable and less afraid of transgender people (Flores et al., 2018).

Or consider this: What are your favourite letters of the alphabet? People of differing nationalities, languages, and ages prefer the letters appearing in their own names and those that frequently appear in their own languages (Hoorens, 1990, 1993; Kitayama & Karasawa, 1997; Nuttin, 1987). French students rate capital *W*, the least frequent letter in French, as their least favourite letter. In a stock market simulation study, business students preferred to buy stocks that shared the same first letter as their name (Knewtson & Sias, 2010). Japanese students prefer not only letters from their names but also numbers corresponding to their birth dates. Consumers prefer products whose prices remind them of their birthdates ($49.15 for a birthday on the fifteenth) and their names (55 dollars for a name starting with *F*). The preference persists even when the price is higher (Coulter & Grewal, 2014).

The mere-exposure effect violates the common-sense prediction of boredom—*decreased* interest—regarding repeatedly heard music or tasted foods (Kahneman & Snell, 1992). When completed in 1889, the Eiffel Tower in Paris was mocked as grotesque (Harrison, 1977). Today, it is the beloved symbol of Paris. Familiarity usually doesn't breed contempt; it increases liking.

However, there is such a thing as too much exposure—if repetitions are incessant, liking eventually drops (Montoya et al., 2017). Music provides a vivid example: You may grow to like a popular song as you hear it more often, but there eventually comes a point—*ugh*—when you've heard it too much. "Even the best song becomes tiresome if heard too often," says a Korean proverb.

So, do visitors to the Louvre in Paris really adore the *Mona Lisa* for the artistry it displays, or are they simply delighted to find a familiar face? It might be both: To know her is to like her. Eddie Harmon-Jones and John Allen (2001) explored this phenomenon

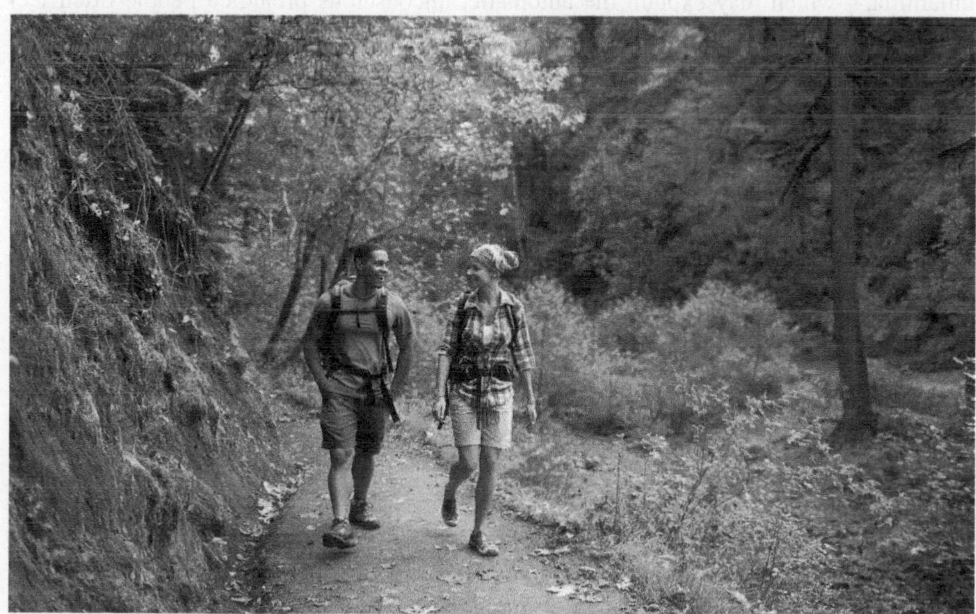

Feeling close to those close by: People often become attached to, and sometimes fall in love with, those with whom they share activities.

Source: ©Isaac Koval/Getty Images.

experimentally. When they showed people a woman's face, their cheek (smiling) muscle typically became more active with repeated viewings. Mere exposure breeds pleasant feelings.

Mere-exposure effects are even stronger when people receive stimuli without awareness (Hansen & Wänke, 2009; Kunst-Wilson & Zajonc, 1980; Moreland & Zajonc, 1977; Wilson, 1978; Willems et al., 2010). In one experiment, women heard music in one headphone and words in the other; they were asked to repeat the words out loud, focusing attention toward the words and away from the tunes. Later, when the women heard the tunes interspersed among similar ones not previously played, they did not recognize them. Nevertheless, they liked best the tunes they had previously heard. Even patients with amnesia—who can consciously recall very little of what they have experienced—prefer faces they saw recently (Marin-Garcia et al., 2013).

Note that conscious judgments about the stimuli in these experiments provided fewer clues to what people had heard or seen than did their instant feelings. You can probably recall immediately liking or disliking something or someone without consciously knowing why. Zajonc (1980) argued that *emotions are often more instantaneous than thinking*. Zajonc's rather astonishing idea—that emotions are semi-independent of thinking ("affect may precede cognition")—has found support in recent brain research. Emotion and cognition are enabled by distinct brain regions. Lesion a monkey's amygdala (the emotion-related brain structure) and its emotional responses will be impaired, but its cognitive functions will be intact. Lesion its hippocampus (a memory-related structure) and its cognition will be impaired, but its emotional responses remain intact (Zola-Morgan et al., 1991).

The mere-exposure effect has "enormous adaptive significance," noted Zajonc (1998). It is a "hard-wired" phenomenon that predisposes our attractions and attachments and that helped our ancestors categorize things and people as either familiar and safe or unfamiliar and possibly dangerous. The more two strangers interact, the more attractive they tend to find each other (Reis et al., 2010). The mere-exposure effect colours our evaluations of others: We like familiar people (Swap, 1977), and perceive them as happy (Carr et al., 2017) and more trustworthy (Sofer et al., 2015). "If it's familiar, it has not eaten you yet," Zajonc used to say (Bennett, 2010). It works the other way around, too: People we like (for example, smiling rather than unsmiling strangers) seem more familiar (Garcia-Marques et al., 2015).

Mere exposure's negative side, as we will note in Chapter 11, is our wariness of the unfamiliar—which may explain the automatic, unconscious prejudice people often feel when confronting those who are different. Infants as young as three months old exhibit an own-race preference: If they are typically surrounded by others of the same race in their environments, then they prefer to gaze at faces of their own familiar race (Bar-Haim et al., 2006; Kelly et al., 2005, 2007).

We even like ourselves better when we are the way we're used to seeing ourselves. In a delightful experiment, researchers showed women pictures of themselves and their mirror images. Asked which picture they liked better, most preferred the mirror image—the image they were used to seeing in the mirror. (No wonder our photographs never look quite right.) When close friends of the subjects were shown the same two pictures, they preferred the true picture—the image *they* were used to seeing (Mita et al., 1977). Now that we see our own selfies so frequently, do you think the results would be different?

Advertisers and politicians exploit this phenomenon. When people have no strong feelings about a product or a candidate, repetition alone can increase sales or votes (McCullough & Ostrom, 1974; Winter, 1973). After endless repetition of a commercial, shoppers often have an unthinking, automatic, favourable response to the product. Students who saw pop-up ads for brand-name products on web pages had a more positive attitude toward the brand, even when they didn't remember seeing the ads (Courbet et al., 2014). If candidates are relatively unknown, those with the most media exposure usually win (Patterson, 1980; Schaffner, Wandersman, & Stang, 1981). Political strategists who understand the mere-exposure effect have replaced reasoned argument with brief ads that hammer home a candidate's name and a sound-bite message.

Physical Attractiveness

What do (or did) you look for in a potential date? Sincerity? Character? Humour? Good looks? Sophisticated, intelligent people are unconcerned with such superficial qualities as good looks; they know that "beauty is only skin deep" and that "you can't judge a book by its cover." At least they know that's how they *ought* to feel. As Cicero counselled, "Resist appearance."

> ***"We should look to the mind, and not to the outward appearances."***
>
> Aesop, *Fables*

The belief that looks are unimportant may be another instance of how we deny real influences on us, for there is now a filing cabinet full of research studies showing that appearance does matter. The consistency and pervasiveness of this effect is astonishing. Good looks are a great asset.

Attractiveness and dating

Like it or not, a young woman's physical attractiveness is a moderately good predictor of how frequently she dates, and a young man's attractiveness is a modestly good predictor of how frequently he dates (Berscheid et al., 1971; Krebs & Adinolfi, 1975; Reis et al., 1982; Reis, Nezlek, & Wheeler, 1980; Walster et al., 1966). However, women more than men say they would prefer a mate who's homely and warm over one who's attractive and cold (Fletcher et al., 2004). In a worldwide BBC Internet survey of nearly 220 000 people, men more than women ranked attractiveness as important in a mate, while women more than men assigned importance to honesty, humour, kindness, and dependability (Lippa, 2007). In a longitudinal study following heterosexual married couples over four years, the wife's physical attractiveness predicted the husband's marital satisfaction better than the husband's physical attractiveness predicted the wife's satisfaction. In other words, attractive wives led to happier husbands, but attractive husbands had less effect on wives' happiness (Meltzer et al., 2014). Gay men and lesbian women display these sex differences as well, with gay and straight men both valuing appearance more than lesbian or straight women do (Ha et al., 2012).

Do such self-reports imply, as many have surmised, that women are better at following Cicero's advice? Or that nothing has changed since 1930, when the English philosopher

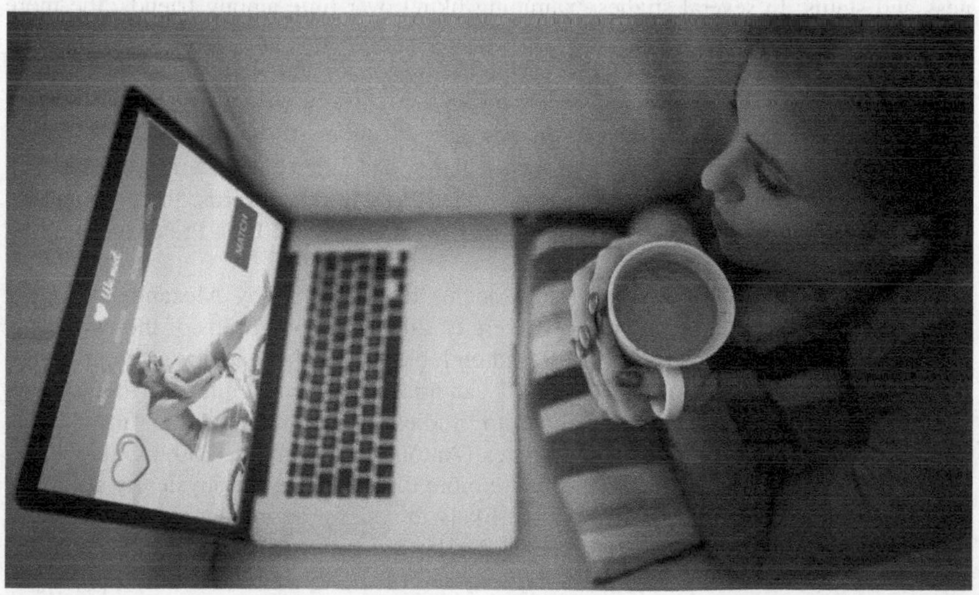

Attractiveness and dating: For online daters, looks are part of what is offered and sought.

Source: ©Wavebreak Media Ltd/123RF.

> *"Personal beauty is a greater recommendation than any letter of introduction."*
>
> Aristotle, *Diogenes Laertius*

Bertrand Russell (1930, p. 139) wrote, "On the whole women tend to love men for their character while men tend to love women for their appearance." Or does it merely reflect the fact that men more often do the inviting? If women were to indicate their preferences among various men, would looks be as important to them as looks are to men?

In one classic study, Elaine Hatfield and her co-workers (1966) matched 752 first-year students for a "Welcome Week" matching dance. The researchers gave each student personality and aptitude tests but then matched the heterosexual couples randomly. On the night of the dance, the couples danced and talked for two-and-a-half hours and then evaluated their dates. How well did the personality and aptitude tests predict attraction? Did people like someone better who was high in self-esteem, or low in anxiety, or different from themselves in outgoingness? The researchers examined a long list of possibilities. But as far as they could determine, only one thing mattered: how physically attractive the person was (as previously rated by the researchers). The more attractive a woman was, the more he liked her and wanted to date her again. And the more attractive the man was, the more she liked him and wanted to date him again. Pretty pleases.

More recent studies have gathered data from speed-dating evenings, during which people interact with a succession of potential dates for only a few minutes each and later indicate which ones they would like to see again (mutual "yeses" are given contact information). The procedure is rooted in research showing that we can form durable impressions of others based on seconds-long "thin slices" of their social behaviour (Ambady, Bernieri, & Richeson, 2000). In speed-dating research, men (vs. women) thought they would care more about a potential date's physical attractiveness; but when it came time to decide whom to date, a prospect's attractiveness was similarly important to both men and women (Eastwick & Finkel, 2008).

A recent meta-analysis (statistical digest) of 97 studies found that men and women placed about the same, fairly high, importance on physical attractiveness and about the same, lower, importance on earning prospects (Eastwick et al., 2014). As you saw earlier, other studies have found otherwise. Thus, whether men value physical attractiveness more than women is debated, but the overall importance of physical attractiveness in dating is fairly large—especially when dates stem from first impressions. However, once people have gotten to know each other over months or years through jobs or friendships, they focus more on each person's unique qualities rather than their physical attractiveness and status. In several studies examining liking over time among friends, the more time that went by, the more the friends diverged over who was most attractive as a mate. Among 167 couples, those who knew each other for longer and were friends before they dated were less similar in physical attractiveness than those who had known each other a shorter time and were not friends before they dated (Hunt et al., 2015). In a 2012 survey, 43 percent of women and 33 percent of men said they had fallen in love with someone they were not initially attracted to (Fisher & Garcia, 2013). In other words, there's someone for everyone—once you get to know them (Eastwick & Hunt, 2014). Pretty pleases, but perhaps only for a time.

Looks even influence voting, or so it seems from a study by Alexander Todorov and colleagues (2005). They showed university students photographs of the two major candidates in 695 political elections. Based on looks alone, the students (who preferred competent-looking over more baby-faced candidates) correctly guessed the winners of 67 percent of the elections. Follow-up studies have confirmed the finding that voters prefer competent-looking candidates (Antonakis & Dalgas, 2009; Chiao et al., 2008). But gender also mattered: Men were more likely to vote for physically attractive female candidates, and women were more likely to vote for approachable-looking male candidates. Likewise, heterosexual people display a positive bias toward attractive job candidates and university applicants—*if* they are of the other sex (Agthe, Spörrle, & Maner, 2011).

Physical appearance matters less among couples who were friends before they started dating.
Source: ©Cathy Yeulet/123RF.

The matching phenomenon

Not everyone can end up paired with someone stunningly attractive. So how do people pair off? Judging from research by Bernard Murstein (1986) and others, they get real. They pair off with people who are about as attractive as they are. Several studies have found a strong correspondence between the attractiveness of husbands and wives, of dating partners, and even of those within particular fraternities (Feingold, 1988; Montoya, 2008). People tend to select as friends and especially to marry those who are a "good match" not only to their level of intelligence, popularity, and self-worth but also to their level of attractiveness (McClintock, 2014; Taylor et al., 2011).

> ***"If you would marry wisely, marry your equal."***
>
> Ovid, 43 BC–17 AD

Experiments confirm this **matching phenomenon**. When choosing whom to approach, knowing that the other is free to say yes or no, people usually approach and invest more in pursuing someone whose attractiveness roughly matches their own (Berscheid et al., 1971; van Straaten et al., 2009). They seek out someone who seems desirable, but they are mindful of the limits of their own desirability. Good physical matches may also be conducive to good relationships, reported Gregory White (1980) from a study of dating couples. Those who were most similar in physical attractiveness were most likely, nine months later, to have fallen more deeply in love. When couples are instead dissimilar in attractiveness, they are more likely to consider leaving the relationship for someone else (Davies & Shackelford, 2017).

matching phenomenon The tendency for men and women to choose as partners those who are a "good match" in attractiveness and other traits.

Perhaps this research prompts you to think of happy couples who differ in perceived "hotness." In such cases, the less attractive person often has compensating qualities. Each partner brings assets to the social marketplace, and the value of the respective assets creates an equitable match. Personal advertisements and self-presentations to online dating services exhibit this exchange of assets (Cicerello & Sheehan, 1995; Hitsch, Hortacsu, & Ariely, 2006; Koestner & Wheeler, 1988). Men typically offer wealth or status and seek youth and attractiveness; women more often do the reverse: "Attractive, bright woman, 26, slender, seeks warm, professional male." Men who advertise their income and education, and women who advertise their youth and looks, receive more responses to their ads (Baize & Schroeder, 1995). The asset-matching process helps explain why beautiful young women often marry older men of higher social status (Elder, 1969). The richer the man, the younger and more beautiful the woman.

Asset matching: High-status Rolling Stones guitarist Keith Richards has been married to supermodel Patti Hansen, 19 years his junior, since 1983.
Source: ©s_bukley/Shutterstock.

The physical-attractiveness stereotype

Does the attractiveness effect spring entirely from sexual attractiveness? Clearly not, as researchers discovered when they used a makeup artist to give an accomplice a scarred, bruised, or birthmarked face. Glasgow train commuters of both sexes avoided sitting next to an apparently facially disfigured accomplice (Houston & Bull, 1994). In one experiment, two groups of observers were asked to surmise people's traits based on their photographs. Those seeing photos of facially disfigured people judged them as less intelligent, emotionally stable, and trustworthy than did those seeing photos of those same people after plastic surgery (Jamrozik et al., 2019). Moreover, much as adults are biased toward attractive adults, young children are biased toward attractive children (Dion, 1973; Dion & Berscheid, 1974; Langlois et al., 2000). Judging from how long they gaze at someone, even three-month-old infants prefer attractive faces (Langlois et al., 1987).

Adults show a similar bias when judging children. Grade 5 teachers were given identical information about a boy or girl but with the photograph of an attractive or unattractive child attached. The teachers perceived the attractive child as more intelligent and successful in school (Clifford & Walster, 1973). Imagine being a playground supervisor having to discipline an unruly child. Might you, like the women studied by Karen Dion (1972), show less warmth and tact to an unattractive child? The sad truth is that most of us assume that homely children are less able and socially competent than their beautiful peers.

What is more, we assume that beautiful people possess certain desirable traits. Other things being equal, we guess that beautiful people are happier; sexually warmer; and more outgoing, intelligent, and successful—although not more honest (Eagly et al., 1991; Feingold, 1992; Jackson, Hunter, & Hodge, 1995). In one study, students judged attractive women as more agreeable, open, outgoing, ambitious, and emotionally stable (Segal-Caspi et al., 2012). We are more eager to bond with attractive people, which motivates our projecting desirable attributes, such as kindness and reciprocal interest, onto them (Lemay, Clark, & Greenberg, 2010). When attractive CEOs of companies appear on television, the stock prices of their companies rise—but being quoted in the newspaper, without a photo, has no effect (Halford & Hsu, 2014).

> *"Love is often nothing but a favourable exchange between two people who get the most of what they can expect, considering their value on the personality market."*
> Erich Fromm, *The Sane Society*, 1955

physical-attractiveness stereotype The presumption that physically attractive people possess other socially desirable traits as well: What is beautiful is good.

Added together, the findings define a **physical-attractiveness stereotype**: What is beautiful is good. Children learn the stereotype quite early—and one of the ways they learn it is through stories told to them by adults. "Disney movies promote the stereotype that what is beautiful is good," report Doris Bazzini and colleagues (2010) from an analysis of human characters in 21 animated films. Snow White and Cinderella are beautiful—and kind. The witch and the stepsisters are ugly—and wicked. "If you want to be loved by somebody who isn't already in your family, it doesn't hurt to be beautiful," surmised one eight-year-old girl. Or as one kindergarten girl put it when asked what it means to be pretty, "It's like to be a princess. Everybody loves you" (Dion, 1979).

If physical attractiveness is that important, then permanently changing people's attractiveness should change the way others react to them. But is it ethical to alter someone's looks? Such manipulations are performed millions of times a year by plastic surgeons and orthodontists. With teeth and nose straightened, hair dyed, face lifted, fat liposuctioned, and breasts enlarged, lifted, or reduced, most self-dissatisfied people do express satisfaction with the results of their procedures, though some unhappy patients seek out repeat procedures (Honigman, Phillips, & Castle, 2004).

To examine the effect of such alterations, Michael Kalick (1977) had students rate their impressions of eight women based on profile photographs taken before or after cosmetic surgery. Not only did they judge the women as more physically attractive after the surgery but also as kinder, more sensitive, more sexually warm and responsive, more likeable, and so on.

> ***"Even virtue is fairer in a fair body."***
>
> Virgil, *Aeneid*, BC 1st Century

First impressions

To say that attractiveness is important, other things being equal, is not to say that physical appearance always outranks other qualities. Some people more than others judge people by their looks (Livingston, 2001). Moreover, attractiveness most affects first impressions. But first impressions are important—and are becoming more so as societies become increasingly mobile and urbanized and as contacts with people become more fleeting (Berscheid, 1981). Your Facebook self-presentation starts with your face. In speed-dating experiments, the attractiveness effect is strongest when people's choices are superficially made—when meeting lots of people quickly (Lenton & Francesconi, 2010). That helps explain why attractiveness better predicts happiness and social connections for those in urban rather than rural settings (Plaut, Adams, & Anderson, 2009).

Though interviewers may deny it, attractiveness and grooming affect first impressions in job interviews—especially when the evaluator is of another sex (Agthe et al., 2011; Cash & Janda, 1984; Mack & Rainey, 1990; Marvelle & Green, 1980). People rate new products more favourably when they are associated with attractive inventors (Baron, Markman, & Bollinger, 2006). Such impressions help explain why attractive people and tall people have more prestigious jobs and make more money (Engemann & Owyang, 2003; Persico, Postelwaite, & Silverman, 2004).

Patricia Roszell and her colleagues (1990) looked at the incomes of a national sample of Canadians whom interviewers had rated on a 1 (homely) to 5 (strikingly attractive) scale. They found that for each additional scale unit of rated attractiveness, people earned, on average, an additional $1988 annually. Irene Hanson Frieze and her associates (1991) did the same analysis with 737 MBA graduates after rating them on a similar 1-to-5 scale using student yearbook photos. For each additional scale unit of rated attractiveness, men earned an added $2600 and women earned an additional $2150. In *Beauty Pays,* economist Daniel Hamermesh (2011) argues that, for a man, good looks have the earnings effect of another year-and-a-half of schooling.

The speed with which first impressions form, and their influence on thinking, helps explain why good-looking people prosper. Even an exposure as brief as 0.013 seconds—too brief to actually discern a face—is enough to enable people to guess a face's attractiveness (Olson & Marchuetz, 2005). Moreover, when categorizing subsequent words as either good or bad, an attractive face predisposes people to categorize good words faster. Attractiveness is perceived promptly and primes positive processing.

Is the "beautiful is good" stereotype accurate?

Do beautiful people, indeed, have desirable traits? For centuries, those who considered themselves serious scientists thought so when they sought to identify physical traits (shifty eyes, a weak chin) that would predict criminal behaviour. Despite others' perceptions, physically attractive people do not differ from others in basic personality traits, such as agreeableness, openness, extroversion, ambition, or emotional stability (Segal-Caspi et al., 2012). However, there is some truth to the stereotype. Attractive children and young adults are somewhat more relaxed, outgoing, and socially polished (Feingold, 1992; Langlois et al., 2000).

THE INSIDE STORY

I vividly remember the afternoon I began to appreciate the far-reaching implications of physical attractiveness. Graduate student Karen Dion (now a professor at the University of Toronto) learned that some researchers at our Institute of Child Development had collected popularity ratings from nursery school children and taken a photo of each child. Although teachers and caregivers of children had persuaded us that "all children are beautiful" and no physical-attractiveness discriminations could be made, Dion suggested we instruct some people to rate each child's looks and correlate these with popularity. After doing so, we realized our long shot had hit home: Attractive children were popular children. Indeed, the effect was far more potent than we and others had assumed, with a host of implications that investigators are still tracing.

Source: ©andresr/E+/Getty Images.

Ellen Berscheid, *University of Minnesota*

In one study, 60 men called and talked for five minutes with each of three women students. Afterwards, the men and women rated the most attractive of their unseen telephone partners as somewhat more socially skillful and likeable. The same is true online: Even when they hadn't seen the men's photos, women rated the text of attractive men's dating website profiles as more desirable and confident. What is beautiful is good, even online (Brand et al., 2012). Physically attractive individuals also tend to be more popular, more outgoing, and more gender-typed—more traditionally masculine, if male; more traditionally feminine, if female (Langlois et al., 1996).

These small average differences between attractive and unattractive people probably result from self-fulfilling prophecies. Attractive people are valued and favoured and so may develop more social self-confidence. (Recall from Chapter 3 an experiment in which men evoked a warm response from unseen women they *thought* were attractive.) By that analysis, what's crucial to your social skill is not how you look but how people treat you and how you feel about yourself—whether you accept yourself, like yourself, feel comfortable with yourself.

Who is attractive?

We have described attractiveness as if it were an objective quality, such as height, that some people have more of, and some less. Strictly speaking, attractiveness is whatever the people of any given place and time find attractive. This, of course, varies. The beauty standards by which Miss Universe is judged hardly apply to the whole planet. People in various places and times have pierced noses, lengthened necks, dyed hair, whitened teeth, painted skin, gorged themselves to become voluptuous, starved themselves to become thin, and bound themselves with leather garments to make their breasts seem small—or used silicone and padded bras to make them seem big. For cultures with scarce resources and for poor or hungry people, plumpness is considered attractive; for cultures and individuals with abundant resources, beauty more often equals slimness (Nelson & Morrison, 2005). Moreover, attractiveness influences life outcomes less in cultures where relationships are based more on kinship or social arrangement than on personal choice (Anderson et al., 2008). Despite such variations, there remains "strong agreement both

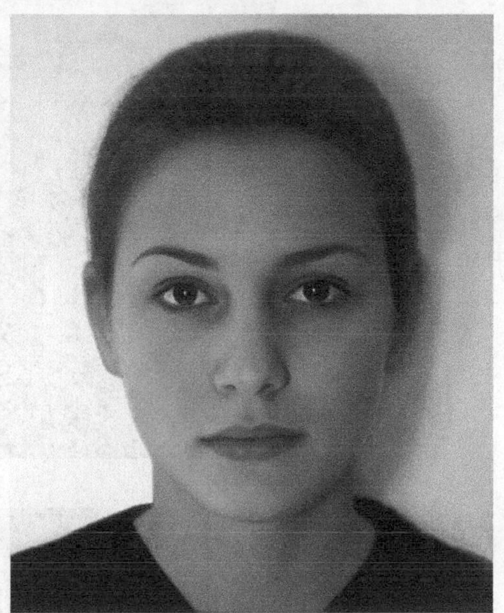

FIGURE 10–1 WHO'S THE FAIREST OF THEM ALL?

Each year's selection of Miss Germany provides one country's answer. A University of Regensburg student research team, working with a German television channel, offered an alternative. Christof Braun and his compatriots (Gruendl, 2005) photographed the 2002 "Queen of Beauty" finalists, without makeup and with hair tied back, and then created a "Virtual Miss Germany" that was the blended composite of all 22 of them (right). When adults in a local shopping mall were shown the finalists and the Virtual Miss Germany, they easily rated Virtual Miss Germany as the most attractive of them all. Although the winning real Miss Germany (left) may have been disappointed by the news that everyone preferred her virtual competitor to herself, she can reassure herself that she will never meet her virtual competitor.

Source: (left): ©Oliver Bodmer/Action Press/ZUMAPRESS.com; (right): ©Dr. Martin Gruendl.

within and across cultures about who is and who is not attractive," note Judith Langlois and colleagues (2000).

To be really attractive is, ironically, to be *perfectly average* (Rhodes, 2006). Researchers have digitized multiple faces and averaged them using a computer. Inevitably, people find the composite faces more appealing than almost all of the actual faces (Langlois & Roggman, 1990; Langlois et al., 1994; Perrett, 2010) (Figure 10–1). Across 27 nations, even an average leg-length-to-body ratio looks more attractive than very short or long legs (Sorokowski et al., 2011). With both humans and animals, averaged looks best embody prototypes (for your typical man, woman, dog, or whatever) and, thus, are easy for the brain to process and categorize, noted Jamin Halberstadt (2006). Let's face it: Perfectly average is easy on the eyes (and brain).

Computer-averaged faces also tend to be perfectly *symmetrical*—another characteristic of strikingly attractive (and reproductively successful) people (W. M. Brown et al., 2008; Gangestad & Thornhill, 1997). If you could merge either half of your face with its mirror image—thus forming a perfectly symmetrical new face—you would boost your looks (Penton-Voak et al., 2001; Rhodes et al., 1999). With a few facial features excepted (Said & Todorov, 2011), averaging a number of such attractive, symmetrical faces produces an even better-looking face.

Standards of beauty differ from culture to culture. Yet some people are considered attractive throughout most of the world.

Source: (top left): ©2009 Jupiterimages Corporation; (top right): ©John Lund/Getty Images; (bottom left): Courtesy of Catherine Karnow; (bottom right): ©Marc Romanelli/ Getty Images.

Evolution and attraction

Psychologists working from the evolutionary perspective explain the human preference for attractive partners in terms of reproductive strategy. They assume that beauty signals biologically important information: health, youth, and fertility. And so it does. Men with attractive faces have higher-quality sperm. Women with hourglass figures have more regular menstrual cycles and are more fertile (Gallup et al., 2008). Over time, men who preferred fertile-looking women out-reproduced those who were as happy to mate with post-menopausal females. That, David Buss (1989) believed, explains why the males he studied in 37 cultures—from Australia to Zambia—did, indeed, prefer youthful female characteristics that signify reproductive capacity.

Evolutionary psychologists also assume that evolution predisposes women to favour male traits that signify an ability to provide and protect resources. In screening potential mates, reported Norman Li and his follow researchers (2002), men require a modicum of physical attractiveness, women require status and resources, and both welcome kindness and intelligence. Women's emphasis on men's physical attractiveness may also depend on their goals: Those focused on short-term relationships prefer symmetrical and thus attractive men, whereas those focused on the long term find this less important, perhaps because physical attractiveness may come with more negative qualities, such as infidelity (Quist et al., 2012).

Evolutionary psychologists have also explored men's and women's responses to other cues to reproductive success. Men everywhere are most attracted to women whose waists are 30 percent narrower than their hips—a shape associated with peak sexual fertility (Singh, 1993, 1995; Singh & Randall, 2007; Streeter & McBurney, 2003; Zotto & Pegna, 2017). Circumstances that reduce a woman's fertility—malnutrition, pregnancy, menopause—also change her shape.

When judging males as potential marriage partners, women, too, prefer a male waist-to-hip ratio suggesting health and vigour. They rate muscular men as sexier, and muscular men do feel sexier and report more lifetime sex partners (Frederick & Haselton, 2007). This makes evolutionary sense, noted Jared Diamond (1996): A muscular hunk was more likely than a scrawny fellow to gather food, build houses, and defeat rivals. But today, women prefer men with high incomes even more (Muggleton & Fincher, 2017; Singh, 1995).

During ovulation, women show increased accuracy in judging male sexual orientation, finds Nicholas Rule of the University of Toronto and his colleagues (2011). And they show increased wariness of out-group men (McDonald et al., 2011). One study found that, when ovulating, young women tend to wear and prefer more revealing outfits than when infertile (Durante et al., 2008). In another study, ovulating lap dancers averaged $70 in tips per hour—double the $35 of those who were menstruating (Miller et al., 2007).

We are, evolutionary psychologists suggest, driven by primal attractions. Like eating and breathing, attraction and mating are too important to leave to the whims of culture.

Evolutionary psychology theorizes that strong men would have been more likely to survive and reproduce over the course of human history, explaining women's preference for muscular men.
Source: ©dash/123RF

Social comparison

Although our mating psychology has wisdom, attraction is not all hard-wired. What's attractive to you also depends on your comparison standards.

To men who have recently been gazing at centrefolds, average women and even their own wives seem less attractive (Kenrick, Gutierres, & Goldberg, 1989). Viewing pornographic films simulating passionate sex similarly decreases satisfaction with the viewer's own partner (Zillmann, 1989b). Being sexually aroused may *temporarily* make a person of the other sex seem more attractive. But the lingering effect of exposure to "perfect 10s," or of unrealistic sexual depictions, is to make a person's own partner seem less appealing.

It works the same way with our self-perceptions. After viewing a very attractive person of the same gender, people rate themselves as being *less* attractive than after viewing a homely person (J. D. Brown et al., 1992; Thornton & Maurice, 1997). Men's self-rated desirability is also deflated by exposure to more dominant, successful men. Thanks to modern media, we may see in an hour "dozens of individuals who are more attractive and more successful than any of our ancestors would have seen in a year, or even a lifetime," noted Sara Gutierres and her co-researchers (1999). Moreover, we often see slim, wrinkle-free, photoshopped people who don't exist. Such extraordinary comparison standards trick us into devaluing our potential mates and ourselves and spending billions and billions of dollars on cosmetics, diet aids, and plastic surgery. But even after another 17 million annual cosmetic procedures, there may be no net gain in human satisfaction. If others get their teeth straightened, capped, and whitened, and you don't, the social comparison may leave you more dissatisfied with your normal, natural teeth than you would have been if you were surrounded by peers whose teeth were also natural.

> ***"Love is only a dirty trick played on us to achieve a continuation of the species."***
>
> Novelist W. Somerset Maugham (1874–1965)

> ***"Do I love you because you are beautiful, or are you beautiful because I love you?"***
>
> Prince Charming, in Rodgers and Hammerstein's *Cinderella*

The attractiveness of those we love

Let's conclude our discussion of attractiveness on an upbeat note. First, a 17-year-old girl's facial attractiveness is a surprisingly weak predictor of her attractiveness at ages 30 and 50. Sometimes, an average-looking adolescent becomes a quite attractive middle-aged adult (Zebrowitz, Collins, & Dutta, 1998; Zebrowitz, Olson, & Hoffman, 1993).

Second, not only do we perceive attractive people as likeable, but we also perceive likeable people as attractive. Perhaps you can recall individuals who, as you grew to like them, became more attractive. Their physical imperfections were no longer so noticeable. Alan Gross and Christine Crofton (1977) had students view someone's photograph after reading a favourable or unfavourable description of the person's personality. Those portrayed as warm, helpful, and considerate also *looked* more attractive. It may be true, then, that "handsome is as handsome does" and that "what is good is beautiful." Discovering someone's similarities to us also makes the person seem more attractive (Beaman & Klentz, 1983; Klentz et al., 1987).

> ***"Can two walk together except they be agreed?"***
>
> Amos 3:3

Moreover, love sees loveliness: The more in love a woman is with a man, the more physically attractive she finds him (Price et al., 1974). And the more in love people are, the less attractive they find all others of the opposite sex (Johnson & Rusbult, 1989; Simpson, Gangestad, & Lerma, 1990). Research by John Lydon of McGill University and his colleagues (1999) finds that this is especially true for people in more committed relationships. They had people in relationships rate an attractive, "single and not currently involved" member of the opposite sex who was apparently also a participant in the study. This attractive person was supposedly matched with them randomly (a moderate threat to their relationship) or because he or she thought the participant was attractive (a more serious threat). As you can see in Figure 10–2, when people

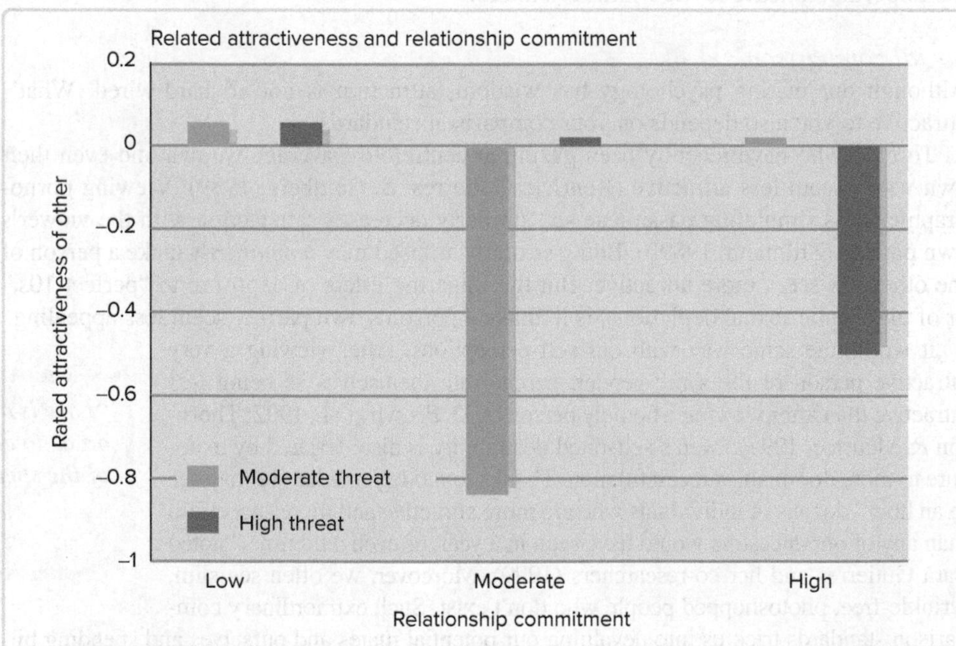

FIGURE 10–2 RELATED ATTRACTIVENESS AND RELATIONSHIP COMMITMENT.
When an attractive member of the opposite sex threatens people's relationships, they rate this person as less attractive if the threat posed by the person matches their level of commitment.

were threatened at the same level as they were committed, they saw the competition as less attractive. It seems that people modulate how attractive they find others in a way that maintains their close relationships. Beauty really is, to some extent, in the eye of the beholder.

Similarity Versus Complementarity

From our discussion so far, one might surmise that Leo Tolstoy was entirely correct: "Love depends . . . on frequent meetings, and on the style in which the hair is done up, and on the colour and cut of the dress." As people get to know one another, however, other factors influence whether acquaintance develops into friendship.

Do birds of a feather flock together?

Of this much we may be sure: Birds that flock together are of a feather. Friends, engaged couples, and spouses are far more likely than people randomly paired to share common attitudes, beliefs, and values. Furthermore, the greater the similarity between husband and wife, the happier they are and the less likely they are to divorce (Byrne, 1971; Caspi & Herbener, 1990). Dating couples with more similar political and religious attitudes were more likely to still be together after 11 months (Bleske-Recheck et al., 2009). Such correlational findings are intriguing. But cause and effect remain an enigma. Does similarity lead to liking? Or does liking lead to similarity?

Likeness begets liking

To discern cause and effect, we experiment. Imagine that at a campus party Lakesha gets involved in a long discussion of politics, religion, and personal likes and dislikes with Les and Lon. She and Les discover they agree on almost everything; she and Lon, on few things. Afterwards, she reflects, "Les is really intelligent . . . and so likeable. I hope we meet again." In experiments, Donn Byrne (1971) and his colleagues captured the essence of Lakesha's experience. Over and over again, they found that the more similar someone's attitudes are to your own, the more you will like the person.

Recent studies have replicated these effects, finding that students like others with similar attitudes (Montoya & Horton, 2012; Reid et al., 2013). Facebook friends and fraternity co-members tend to share facial similarities (Hehman, Flake, & Freeman, 2018). Likeness produces liking not only for college students but also for children and the elderly, for people of various occupations, and for those in various cultures

The likeness-leads-to-liking effect has been tested in real-life situations:

- *Roommates and speed daters*. At two of Hong Kong's universities, Royce Lee and Michael Bond (1996) found that roommate friendships flourished over a six-month period when roommates shared values and personality traits but more so when they *perceived* their roommates as similar. Perceived similarity also mattered more than actual similarity during speed dating (Tidwell et al., 2013). As so often happens, reality matters, but perception matters more.
- *Strangers*. In various settings, researchers at Wilfrid Laurier University found that people entering a room of strangers sit closer to those like themselves (Mackinnon, Jordan, & Wilson, 2011). People with glasses sit closer to others with glasses. Long-haired people sit closer to people with long hair. Dark-haired people sit closer to people with dark hair (even after controlling for race and sex).
- *Babies*. Eleven-month-old infants were more likely to choose a stuffed animal that pretended to eat the same food or wore the same colour mittens that they did. This suggests that the preference for similar others develops very early, even before babies can talk (Mahajan & Wynn, 2012).

- *Mimicry as behavioural similarity*. People like not only those who think as they do but also those who act as they do. Subtle mimicry fosters fondness. Have you noticed that when people nod their head as you do and echo your thoughts, you feel a certain rapport and liking? That's a common experience, reported Rick van Baaren and his colleagues (van Baaren, Holland, Karremans, et al., 2003; van Baaren, Holland, Steenaert, et al., 2003), and one result is higher tips for Dutch restaurant servers who mimic their customers by merely repeating their order. Natural mimicry increases rapport, noted Jessica Lakin and Tanya Chartrand (2003), and desire for rapport increases mimicry.
- *Throughout different cultures*. In cultures as diverse as those in China, Israel, and California, similar attitudes, traits, and values help bring couples together and predict their satisfaction (Chen et al., 2009; Gaunt, 2006; Gonzaga, Campos, & Bradbury, 2007).

"And they are friends who have come to regard the same things as good and the same things as evil, they who are friends of the same people, and they who are the enemies of the same people. . . . We like those who resemble us, and are engaged in the same pursuits."

Aristotle, *Rhetoric*, BC 4th Century

So similarity breeds content. Birds of a feather *do* flock together. Surely you have noticed this upon discovering a person who shares your ideas, values, and desires—a special someone who likes the same foods, the same activities, the same music you do. (When liking the same music as another, people infer similar values as well [Boer et al., 2011].)

The principle that similarity attracts is a key selling point for online dating sites such as Chemistry.com and eHarmony.com that match users with similar others via secret formulas. With that in mind, Samantha Joel of Western University and her co-authors (2017) gave college students an exhaustive battery of 100 personality and attitude questionnaires and fed the results into a sophisticated computer program. However, the program couldn't predict who would like each other after they actually met during a series of four-minute speed dates. So why do so many people not only use online dating sites but find long-term partners on them? Probably because the sites expand your pool of potential dates (Finkel et al., 2012). What happens afterward is much more unpredictable.

Dissimilarity breeds dislike

We have a bias—the false consensus bias—toward assuming that others share our attitudes. We also tend to see those we like as being like us (Castelli et al., 2009). Getting to know someone—and discovering that the person is actually dissimilar—tends to decrease liking (Norton, Frost, & Ariely, 2007). If those dissimilar attitudes pertain to our strong moral convictions, we dislike and distance ourselves from them all the more (Skitka, Bauman, & Mullen, 2004). People in one political party often are not so much fond of fellow party members as they are disdainful of the opposition (Hoyle, 1993; Rosenbaum, 1986).

In general, dissimilar attitudes depress liking more than similar attitudes enhance it (Singh & Ho, 2000; Singh & Teoh, 1999). Within their own groups, where they expect similarity, people find it especially hard to like someone with dissimilar views (Chen & Kenrick, 2002). That perhaps explains why dating partners and roommates become more similar over time in their emotional responses to events and in their attitudes (C. Anderson, Keltner, & John, 2003; Davis & Rusbult, 2001). "Attitude alignment" helps promote and sustain close relationships, a phenomenon that can lead partners to overestimate their attitude similarities (Kenny & Acitelli, 2001; Murray, Holmes, et al., 2002).

Whether people perceive those of another race as similar or dissimilar influences their racial attitudes. Wherever one group of people regards another as "other"—as creatures who speak differently, live differently, and think differently—the potential for conflict is high. In fact, except for intimate relationships, such as dating, the perception of like minds seems more important for attraction than like skins. In one study, liberals expressed dislike of conservatives and conservatives of liberals, but race did not affect liking (Chambers et al., 2012). Likewise, the more that Montreal residents perceived a Canadian ethnic group as similar to themselves, the more willing they were to associate with its members (Osbeck, Moghaddam, & Perreault, 1996).

"Cultural racism" persists, argued social psychologist James Jones (1988, 2003, 2004), because cultural differences are a fact of life. Black culture tends to be present-oriented, spontaneously expressive, spiritual, and emotionally driven. White culture tends to be more future-oriented, materialistic, and achievement-driven. Rather than trying to eliminate such differences, suggested Jones, we might better appreciate what they "contribute to the cultural fabric of a multicultural society." There are situations in which expressiveness is advantageous and situations in which future orientation is advantageous. Each culture has much to learn from the other. In places such as Canada, Great Britain, and the United States, where migration and different birthrates make for growing diversity, educating people to respect and enjoy those who differ is a major challenge. Given increasing cultural diversity and given our natural wariness of differences, this may, in fact, be the major social challenge of our time.

Do opposites attract?

Are we not also attracted to people who in some ways *differ* from ourselves? We are physically attracted to people whose scent suggests dissimilar enough genes to prevent inbreeding (Garver-Apgar et al., 2006). But what about attitudes and behavioural traits? Researchers have explored this question by comparing not only friends' and spouses' attitudes and beliefs but also their age, religion, race, smoking behaviour, economic level, education, height, intelligence, and appearance. In all these ways and more, similarity still prevails (Buss, 1985; Kandel, 1978). Among 410 Grade 7 students, those who were similar in popularity, aggressiveness, and academic performance were more likely to still be friends a year later (Hartl et al., 2015). Smart birds flock together. So do rich birds, Protestant birds, tall birds, and pretty birds.

Still we resist: Are we not attracted to people whose needs and personalities complement our own? Would a sadist and a masochist find true love? Even the *Reader's Digest* has told us that "opposites attract. . . . Socializers pair with loners, novelty-lovers with those who dislike change, free spenders with scrimpers, risk-takers with the very cautious" (Jacoby, 1986). Sociologist Robert Winch (1958) reasoned that the needs of someone who is outgoing and domineering would naturally complement those of someone who is shy and submissive. The logic seems compelling, and most of us can think of couples who view their differences as complementary: "My husband and I are perfect for each other. I'm Aquarius—a decisive person. He's Libra—can't make decisions. But he's always happy to go along with arrangements I make."

Given the idea's persuasiveness, the inability of researchers to confirm it is astonishing. For example, most people feel attracted to expressive, outgoing people (Friedman, Riggio, & Casella, 1988). Would this be especially so when one is down in the dumps? Do depressed people seek those whose gaiety will cheer them up? To the contrary, it is nondepressed people who most prefer the company of happy people (Locke & Horowitz, 1990; Rosenblatt & Greenberg, 1988, 1991; Wenzlaff & Prohaska, 1989). When you're feeling blue, someone else's bubbly personality can be aggravating. The contrast effect that makes average people feel homely in the company of beautiful people also makes sad people more conscious of their misery in the company of cheerful people.

Some **complementarity** may evolve as a relationship progresses (even a relationship between identical twins). Yet people seem slightly more prone to like and to marry those whose needs and personalities are *similar* (Botwin, Buss, & Shackelford, 1997; Buss, 1984; Fishbein & Thelen, 1981a, 1981b; Nias, 1979). Perhaps we shall yet discover some ways in which differences commonly breed liking. Dominance/submissiveness may be one such way (Dryer & Horowitz, 1997). But, as a general rule, opposites do not attract.

complementarity The popularly supposed tendency, in a relationship between two people, for each to complete what is missing in the other.

Liking Those Who Like Us

Liking is usually mutual. Proximity and attractiveness influence our initial attraction to someone, and similarity influences longer-term attraction as well. If we have a deep need to belong and to feel liked and accepted, would we not also take a liking to those who like us? Are the best friendships mutual admiration societies? Indeed, one person's liking for another does predict the other's liking in return (Kenny & Nasby, 1980; Montoya & Insko, 2008). One common way to show interest in someone—asking them questions—is especially effective in increasing liking (Huang et al., 2017).

But does one person's liking another *cause* the other to return the appreciation? People's reports of how they fell in love suggest this is true (Aron et al., 1989). Discovering that an appealing someone really likes you seems to awaken romantic feelings. Experiments confirm it: Those told that certain others like or admire them usually feel a reciprocal affection (Berscheid & Walster, 1978). And all the better, one speed-dating experiment suggested, when someone likes *you* especially (Eastwick, Finkel, et al., 2007). A dash of uncertainty can also fuel desire. Thinking that someone probably likes you—but you aren't sure—tends to increase your thinking about, and feeling attracted to, another (Whitechurch, Wilson, & Gilbert, 2011).

"The average man is more interested in a woman who is interested in him than he is in a woman with beautiful legs."

Actress Marlene Dietrich, *The Quotable Woman, 1800–1975*, 1978

And consider this finding: Students like another student who said eight positive things about them more than one who said seven positive things and one negative thing (Berscheid & Walster, 1978). We are sensitive to the slightest hint of criticism. Writer Larry L. King spoke for many in noting, "I have discovered over the years that good reviews strangely fail to make the author feel as good as bad reviews make him feel bad."

Whether we are judging ourselves or others, negative information carries more weight because, being less usual, it grabs more attention (Yzerbyt & Leyens, 1991). People's votes are more influenced by their impressions of candidates' weaknesses than by their impressions of strengths (Klein, 1991), a phenomenon that has not been lost on those who design negative campaigns. It's a general rule of life: Bad is stronger than good (Baumeister et al., 2001).

Our liking for those we perceive as liking us was recognized long ago. Observers from the ancient philosopher Hecato ("If you wish to be loved, love") to Ralph Waldo Emerson ("The only way to have a friend is to be one") to Dale Carnegie ("Dole out praise lavishly") anticipated the findings. What they did not anticipate was the precise conditions under which the principle works.

"Well—and I'm not just saying this because you're my husband—it stinks."

Source: ©Robert Mankoff.

Attribution

As we've seen, flattery will get you somewhere—but not everywhere. If praise clearly violates what we know is true—if someone says, "Your hair looks great," when we haven't washed it in days—we may lose respect for the flatterer and wonder whether the compliment springs from ulterior motives (Shrauger, 1975). Thus we often perceive criticism to be more sincere than praise (Coleman, Jussim, & Abraham, 1987).

Laboratory experiments reveal something we've noted in previous chapters: Our reactions depend on our attributions. Do we attribute the flattery to **ingratiation**—to a self-serving strategy? Is the person trying to get us to buy something, to acquiesce sexually, to do a favour? If so, both the flatterer and the praise lose appeal (Gordon, 1996; Jones, 1964). But if there is no apparent ulterior motive, then we warmly receive both flattery and flatterer.

ingratiation The use of strategies, such as flattery, by which people seek to gain another's favour.

Some people embrace compliments more readily than others do, however. Denise Marigold of Renison University College and her colleagues found that people with low self-esteem focus narrowly on the literal meaning of compliments—to them, "You have a nice smile" means just that (Marigold, Holmes, & Ross, 2007). People with high self-esteem, in contrast, attribute more abstract significance to compliments—that their partner is attentive, and values and cares for them—and this makes them feel more secure in their relationships. It's not that low-self-esteem people can't derive the same benefit from compliments; they do if they are specifically directed to think about what compliments mean for their relationship. Everyone feels more secure and valued if they attribute compliments to caring and affection, but people with low self-esteem need more encouragement to do so.

Self-esteem and attraction

Elaine Hatfield (Walster, 1965) wondered if another's approval is especially rewarding after we have been deprived of approval, much as eating is most powerfully rewarding after fasting. To test this idea, she gave some women either very favourable or very unfavourable analyses of their personalities, affirming some and wounding others. Then she asked them to evaluate several people, including an attractive male confederate who just before the experiment had struck up a warm conversation with each woman and had asked each for a date. (Not one turned him down.) Which women do you suppose most liked the man? It was those whose self-esteem had been temporarily shattered and who were presumably hungry for social approval.

This helps explain why people sometimes fall passionately in love on the rebound, after an ego-bruising rejection. Indeed, after a breakup, the prospect of someone new helps people get over their ex-partners (Spielmann, MacDonald, & Wilson, 2009). Unfortunately, people with low self-esteem tend to underestimate how much potential partners will like and accept them. Jessica Cameron of the University of Manitoba, Danu Stinson of the University of Victoria, and their collaborators (2010) found that, even when partners behave in an equally friendly way, low-self-esteem individuals believe they will be less accepted than high-self-esteem individuals. These lower expectations of acceptance lead low-self-esteem individuals to behave in a less warm and friendly manner, which ultimately leads them to actually be less accepted by others (Stinson et al., 2009).

Even in established relationships, low-self-esteem people underestimate how much their romantic partners value them. They also have less generous views of their partner and are, therefore, less happy with the relationship (Murray et al., 2000). If you feel down about yourself, you will likely feel pessimistic about your relationships. Feel good about yourself and you're more likely to feel confident of your dating partner's or spouse's regard. Accordingly, when low-self-esteem people are focused on their own strengths, they feel more secure in their relationships (Murray et al., 2005).

Gaining another's esteem

If approval that comes after disapproval is powerfully rewarding, then would we most like someone who liked us after initially disliking us? Or would we most like someone who liked us from the start (and, therefore, gave us more total approval)? Ray is in a small discussion class with his roommate's cousin, Sophia. After the first week of classes, Ray learns via his "pipeline" that Sophia thinks him rather shallow. As the semester progresses, however, he learns that Sophia's opinion of him is steadily rising; gradually, she comes to view him as bright, thoughtful, and charming. Would Ray like Sophia more if she had thought well of him from the beginning? If Ray is simply counting the number of approving comments he receives, then the answer will be "yes": He would like Sophia better had she consistently praised him. But if, after her initial disapproval, Sophia's rewards become more potent, Ray then might like her better than if she had been consistently affirming.

To see which is more often true, Elliot Aronson and Darwyn Linder (1965) captured the essence of Ray's experience in a clever experiment. They "allowed" 80 women to overhear a sequence of evaluations of themselves by another woman. Some women heard consistently positive things about themselves; some, consistently negative. Others heard evaluations that changed either from negative to positive (like Sophia's evaluations of Ray) or from positive to negative. In this and other experiments, the target person was well liked when the subject experienced a gain in the other's esteem, especially when the gain occurred gradually and reversed the earlier criticism (Aronson & Mettee, 1974; Clore, Wiggins, & Itkin, 1975). Perhaps Sophia's nice words have more credibility coming after her not-so-nice words. Or, perhaps after being withheld, they are especially gratifying.

Aronson (1988) speculated that constant approval can lose value. When a husband says for the five-hundredth time, "Gee, honey, you look great," the words carry far less impact than were he now to say, "Gee, honey, you look awful in that dress." A loved one you've doted upon is hard to reward but easy to hurt. This suggests that an open, honest relationship—one where people enjoy one another's esteem and acceptance yet are honest—is more likely to offer continuing rewards than one dulled by the suppression of unpleasant emotions, one in which people try only, as Dale Carnegie advised, to "lavish praise." Aronson (1988) put it this way:

> As a relationship ripens toward greater intimacy, what becomes increasingly important is authenticity—our ability to give up trying to make a good impression and begin to reveal things about ourselves that are honest even if unsavory. . . . If two people are genuinely fond of each other, they will have a more satisfying and exciting relationship over a longer period of time if they are able to express both positive and negative feelings than if they are completely "nice" to each other at all times. (p. 323)

In most social interactions, we self-censor our negative feelings. Thus, noted William Swann and his colleagues (1991), some people receive no corrective feedback. Living in a world of pleasant illusion, they continue to act in ways that alienate their would-be friends. A true friend is one who can let us in on bad news—nicely.

Someone who really loves us will be honest with us but will also tend to see us through rose-coloured glasses. The happiest dating and married couples (and those who became happier) are those who see their partners more positively than their partners see themselves (Murray & Holmes, 1997; Murray et al., 1996a, 1996b). When we're in love, we're biased to find those we love not only physically attractive but socially attractive as well (Boyes & Fletcher, 2007). Moreover, the most satisfied married couples tend to have idealized one another as newlyweds and to approach problems without immediately criticizing their partners and finding fault (P. J. E. Miller, Niehuis, & Huston, 2006). Honesty has its place in a good relationship, but so does a presumption of the other person's basic goodness.

"It takes your enemy and your friend, working together, to hurt you to the heart; the enemy to slander you and the friend to get the news to you."

Mark Twain, *Pudd'nhead Wilson's New Calendar,* 1897

Relationship Rewards

Asked why they are friends with someone or why they were attracted to their partner, most people can readily answer: "I like Carol because she's warm, witty, and well-read." What such explanations leave out—and what social psychologists believe is most important—is ourselves. Attraction involves the one who is attracted as well as the attractor. Thus a more psychologically accurate answer might be, "I like Carol because of how I feel when I'm with her." We are attracted to those we find it satisfying and gratifying to be with. Attraction is in the eye (and brain) of the beholder.

"No one is perfect until you fall in love with them."

Andy Rooney

The point can be expressed as a simple **reward theory of attraction**: Those who reward us, or whom we associate with rewards, we like. If a relationship gives us more rewards than costs, we will like it and will want it to continue. Canadian children randomly assigned to perform three acts of kindness (versus to visit three places) became more socially accepted and were less likely to be bullied—they gained friends as they helped others (Layous et al., 2012). In his 1665 book, *Maxims*, La Rochefoucauld conjectured, "Friendship is a scheme for the mutual exchange of personal advantages and favors whereby self-esteem may profit."

reward theory of attraction
The theory that we like those whose behaviour is rewarding to us or whom we associate with rewarding events.

Not only do we like people who are rewarding to be with, but, also, according to the second version of the reward principle, we like those we *associate* with good feelings. Conditioning creates positive feelings toward things and people linked with rewarding events (Byrne & Clore, 1970; De Houwer, Thomas, & Baeyens, 2001; Lott & Lott, 1974). When, after a strenuous week, we relax in front of a fire, enjoying good food, drink, and music, we will likely feel a special warmth toward those around us. We are less likely to take a liking to someone we meet while suffering a splitting headache.

Experiments confirm this phenomenon of liking—and disliking—by association (Hofmann et al., 2010). When an experimenter was friendly, participants chose to interact with someone who looked similar to her, but if she was unfriendly, they avoided the similar-looking woman (Lewicki, 1985). Elaine Hatfield and William Walster (1978) found a practical tip in these research studies: "Romantic dinners, trips to the theatre, evenings at home together, and vacations never stop being important. . . . If your relationship is to survive, it's important that you *both* continue to associate your relationship with good things."

This simple theory of attraction—we like those who reward us and those whom we associate with rewards—helps us understand why people everywhere feel attracted to those who are warm, trustworthy, and responsive (Fletcher et al., 1999; Regan, 1998; Wojciszke, Bazinska, & Jaworski, 1998). The reward theory also helps explain some of the influences on attraction:

- *Proximity* is rewarding. It costs less time and effort to receive friendship's benefits with someone who lives or works close by.
- We like *attractive* people because we perceive that they offer other desirable traits and because we benefit by associating with them.
- If others have *similar* opinions, we feel rewarded because we presume that they like us in return. Moreover, those who share our views help validate those views. We especially like people if we have successfully converted them to our way of thinking (Lombardo, Weiss, & Buchanan, 1972; Riordan, 1980; Sigall, 1970).
- We like to be liked and love to be loved. Thus, liking is usually *mutual*. We like those who like us.

What Is Love?

What are the varieties and components of love?

Loving is more complex than liking and thus more difficult to measure, more perplexing to study. People yearn for it, live for it, die for it.

Researchers report that sustained eye contact, nodding, and smiling are indicators of passionate love.
Source: ©rawpixel/123RF.

Most attraction researchers have studied what is most easily studied—responses during brief encounters between strangers. The influences on our initial liking of another—proximity, attractiveness, similarity, being liked, and other rewarding traits—also influence our long-term, close relationships. The impressions that dating couples quickly form of each other provide a clue to their long-term future (Berg, 1984; Berg & McQuinn, 1986). Indeed, if North American romances flourished *randomly*, without regard to proximity and similarity, then most Catholics (being a minority) would marry Protestants, most Blacks would marry Whites, and college graduates would be as apt to marry high school dropouts as fellow graduates.

So first impressions are important. Nevertheless, long-term loving is not merely an intensification of initial liking. Social psychologists therefore study enduring, close relationships.

Passionate Love

The first step in scientifically studying romantic love, as in studying any variable, is to decide how to define and measure it. We have ways to measure aggression, altruism, prejudice, and liking—but how do we measure love?

"How do I love thee? Let me count the ways," wrote Elizabeth Barrett Browning. Social scientists have counted various ways. Psychologist Robert Sternberg (1988, 1998) viewed love as a triangle consisting of three components: passion, intimacy, and commitment (Figure 10–3). Some elements are common to all loving relationships: mutual understanding, giving and receiving support, enjoying the loved one's company. Some are distinctive. If we experience passionate love, we express it physically, we expect the relationship to be exclusive, and we are intensely fascinated with our partner. You can see it in our eyes.

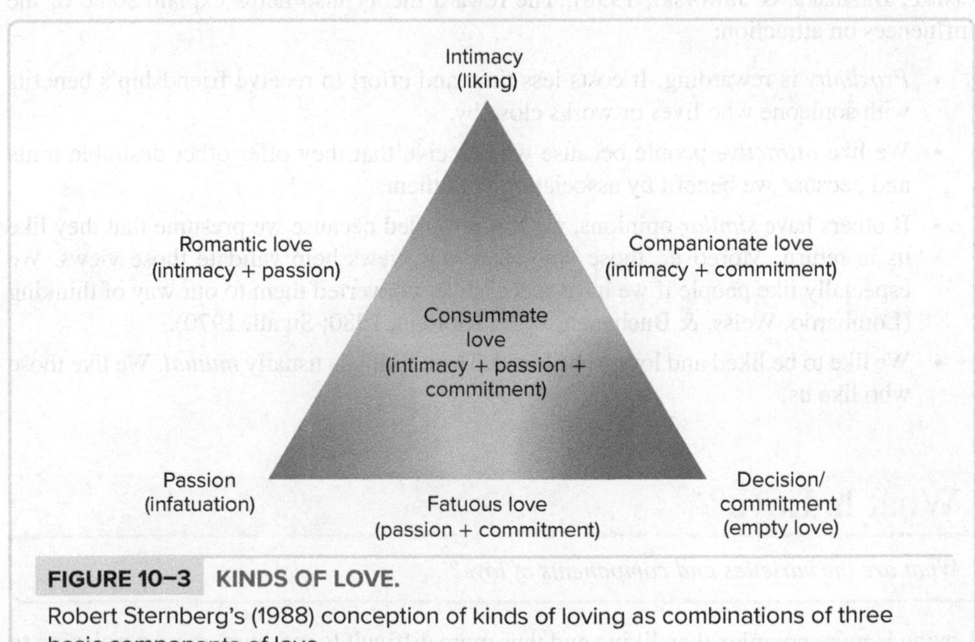

FIGURE 10–3 KINDS OF LOVE.
Robert Sternberg's (1988) conception of kinds of loving as combinations of three basic components of love.

Zick Rubin confirmed this (1973). He administered a love scale to hundreds of dating couples. Later, from behind a one-way mirror in a laboratory waiting room, he clocked eye contact among "weak-love" and "strong-love" couples (mutual gaze conveys liking and averted eye gaze conveys ostracism [Wirth et al., 2010]). So Rubin's result will not surprise you: The strong-love couples gave themselves away by gazing for a long time into one another's eyes. When talking, they also nod their head, smile naturally, and lean forward (Gonzaga et al., 2001). When observing speed daters, it takes but a few seconds to make a reasonably accurate guess as to whether one person is interested in another (Place et al., 2009).

Passionate love is emotional, exciting, and intense. Elaine Hatfield (1988) defined it as "a state of intense longing for union with another" (p. 193). If reciprocated, a person feels fulfilled and joyous; if not, they feel empty or despairing. Like other forms of emotional excitement, passionate love involves a mix of elation and gloom, tingling exhilaration and dejected misery. Passionate love preoccupies the lover with thoughts of the other, involving the same reward pathways in the brain as addiction to substances (Fisher et al., 2016; Takahashi et al., 2015).

passionate love A state of intense longing for union with another. Passionate lovers are absorbed in one another; they feel ecstatic at attaining their partner's love, and they are disconsolate on losing it.

two-factor theory of emotion Arousal × its label = emotion.

Passionate love is what you feel not only when you love someone but also when you are "in love" with them. As Sarah Meyers and Ellen Berscheid (1997) note, we understand that someone who says "I love you, but I'm not in love with you" means to say "I like you. I care about you. I think you're marvellous. But I don't feel sexually attracted to you." That person feels friendship but not passion.

A theory of passionate love

To explain passionate love, Hatfield noted that a given state of arousal can be steered into any of several emotions, depending on how we attribute the arousal. An emotion involves both body and mind—both arousal and how we interpret and label that arousal. Imagine yourself with pounding heart and trembling hands. Are you experiencing fear, anxiety, or joy? Physiologically, one emotion is quite similar to another. You may, therefore, experience the arousal as joy if you are in a euphoric situation, as anger if your environment is hostile, or as passionate love if the situation is romantic. In this view, passionate love is the psychological experience of being biologically aroused by someone we find attractive.

If, indeed, passion is a revved-up state that's labelled "love," then whatever revs one up should intensify feelings of love. In several experiments, university men aroused sexually by reading or viewing erotic materials had a heightened response to a woman—for example, by scoring much higher on a love scale when describing their girlfriend (Carducci, Cosby, & Ward, 1978; Dermer & Pyszczynski, 1978; Stephan, Berscheid, & Walster, 1971). Proponents of the **two-factor theory of emotion**, developed by Stanley Schachter and Jerome Singer (1962), argue that when the revved-up men responded to a woman, they easily misattributed some of their arousal to her.

According to this theory, being aroused by *any* source should intensify passionate feelings—providing the mind is free to attribute some of the arousal to a romantic stimulus. In a dramatic illustration of this phenomenon, Donald Dutton and Arthur Aron (1974, 1989) had an attractive young woman approach individual young men as they crossed a narrow, wobbly, 150-metre-long suspension walkway hanging 75 metres above British Columbia's rocky Capilano River. The woman asked each man to help her fill out a class questionnaire. When he had finished, she scribbled her name and phone number and invited him to call if he wanted to hear more about the project. Most accepted the phone number, and half who did so called. By contrast, men approached by the woman on a low, solid bridge and men approached on the high bridge by a male interviewer rarely called. Once again, physical arousal accentuated romantic responses.

> *"The 'adrenaline' associated with a wide variety of highs can spill over and make passion more passionate. (Sort of a 'Better loving through chemistry' phenomenon.)"*
>
> Elaine Hatfield and Richard Rapson (1987)

Scary movies, roller-coaster rides, and physical exercise have the same effect, especially to those we find attractive (Cohen, Waugh, & Place, 1989; White & Kight, 1984). The effect holds true with married couples, too. Those who do exciting activities together report the best relationships. And after doing an arousing rather than a mundane laboratory task (roughly the equivalent of a three-legged race on their hands and knees), couples also reported higher satisfaction with their overall relationship (Aron et al., 2000). Adrenalin makes the heart grow fonder.

As this suggests, passionate love is a biological as well as a psychological phenomenon. Research by Aron and his colleagues (2005) indicated that passionate love engages dopamine-rich brain areas associated with reward (see Figure 10-4).

Love is also a social phenomenon. Love is more than lust, notes Ellen Berscheid (2010). Supplement sexual desire with a deepening friendship and the result is romantic love. Passionate love = lust + attachment.

Variations in love: Culture and gender

There is always a temptation to assume that most others share our feelings and ideas. We assume, for example, that love is a precondition for marriage. Most cultures—89 percent in one analysis of 166 cultures—do have a concept of romantic love, as reflected in flirtation or couples running off together (Jankowiak & Fischer, 1992). But in some cultures, notably those practising arranged marriages, love tends to follow rather than to precede marriage.

Do males and females differ in how they experience passionate love? Studies of men and women falling in and out of love reveal some surprises. Although most people suppose

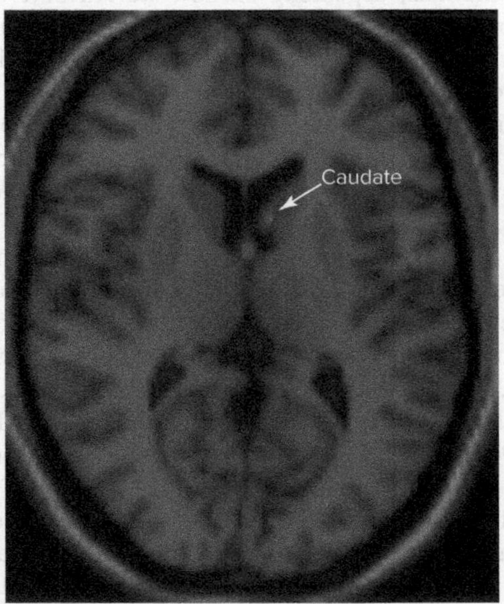

FIGURE 10–4 LOVE IS IN THE BRAIN.

MRI scans from young adults intensely in love revealed areas, such as the caudate nucleus, that became more active when gazing at the loved one's photo (but not when gazing at the photo of another acquaintance).

Source: ©From Aron, A., Fisher, H., Mashek, D. J., Strong, G., Li, H., & Brown, L. L. (2005). Reward, Motivation, and emotion systems associated with early-stage intense romance love. *Journal of Neurophysiology, 94,* 327-337. Image courtesy of Lucy L. Brown.

THE INSIDE STORY

For a number of years, I have been studying the social/developmental psychology of physical attractiveness. There is now considerable evidence that attractiveness affects judgments and evaluations of others. More recently, I've been interested in whether cultural values are related to the occurrence and/or strength of stereotyping based on attractiveness. Are there culture-related differences in the impact of physical attractiveness on evaluations of others?

This question reflects my more general research interest in the cultural context of attraction and interpersonal relationships. Increasingly, the importance of cultural perspectives is being acknowledged by social psychologists, as well as researchers in other areas of psychology—a promising trend within the field.

Karen Dion, *University of Toronto, Scarborough*

Source: ©Tetra Images/Alamy.

that women fall in love more readily, the repeated finding is that men tend to fall in love more readily (Ackerman, Griskevicius, & Li, 2011; Dion & Dion, 1985; Peplau & Gordon, 1985). Men also seem to fall out of love more slowly and are less likely than women to break up a premarital romance. Surprisingly to most people, in heterosexual relationships it's men, not women, who most often are first to say "I love you" (Ackerman et al., 2011).

Once in love, however, women are typically as emotionally involved as their partners, or more so. They are more likely to report feeling euphoric and "giddy and carefree," as if they were "floating on a cloud." Women are also somewhat more likely than men to focus on the intimacy of the friendship and on their concern for their partner. Men are more likely than women to think about the playful and physical aspects of the relationship (Hendrick & Hendrick, 1995).

Companionate Love

Although passionate love burns hot, it inevitably simmers down. The high of romance may be sustained for a few months, even a couple of years. But no high lasts forever. "When you're in love, it's the most glorious two-and-a-half days of your life," jested comedian Richard Lewis. The novelty, the intense absorption in the other, the thrill of the romance, the giddy "floating on a cloud" feeling—they all fade. After two years of marriage, spouses express affection about half as often as when they were newlyweds (Huston & Chorost, 1994). About four years after marriage, the divorce rate peaks in cultures worldwide (H. Fisher, 1994). If a close relationship is to endure, it will settle to a steadier but still warm afterglow called **companionate love**. The passion-facilitating hormones (testosterone, dopamine, adrenalin) subside, while the hormone oxytocin supports feelings of attachment and trust (Taylor, Saphire-Bernstein, & Seeman, 2010).

companionate love The affection we feel for those with whom our lives are deeply intertwined.

Unlike the wild emotions of passionate love, companionate love is lower key; it's a deep, affectionate attachment. It activates different parts of the brain (Aron et al., 2005). And it is just as real. Nisa, a !Kung San woman of the African Kalahari desert,

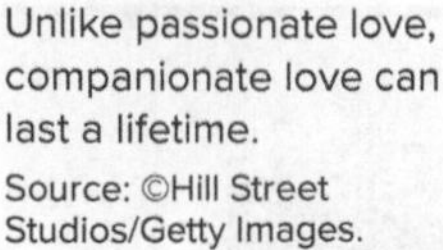

Unlike passionate love, companionate love can last a lifetime.

Source: ©Hill Street Studios/Getty Images.

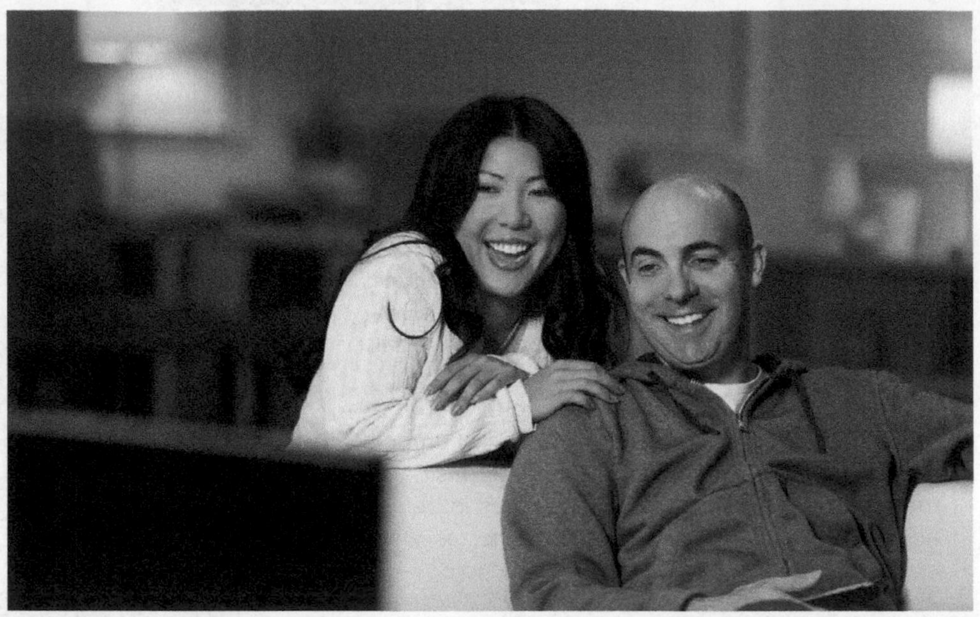

explained it this way: "When two people are first together, their hearts are on fire and their passion is very great. After a while, the fire cools and that's how it stays. They continue to love each other, but it's in a different way—warm and dependable" (Shostak, 1981).

The flow and ebb of romantic love follows the pattern of addictions to coffee, alcohol, and other drugs. At first, a drug gives a big kick, perhaps a high. With repetition, opponent emotions gain strength and tolerance develops. An amount that once was highly stimulating no longer gives a thrill. Stopping the substance, however, does not return you to where you started. Rather, it triggers withdrawal symptoms—malaise, depression, the blahs. The same often happens in love. The passionate high is fated to become lukewarm. The no-longer-romantic relationship becomes taken for granted—until it ends. Then the jilted lover or the widowed or divorced person is surprised at how empty life now seems without the person they long ago stopped feeling passionately attached to. Having focused on what was not working, they stopped noticing what was (Carlson & Hatfield, 1992).

The cooling of passionate love over time and the growing importance of other factors, such as shared values, can be seen in the feelings of those who enter arranged versus love-based marriages in India. Those who married for love reported diminishing feelings of love after a five-year newlywed period. By contrast, those in arranged marriages reported *more* love after five years (Gupta & Singh, 1982) (Figure 10–5).

The cooling of intense romantic love often triggers a period of disillusionment, especially among those who believe that passionate love is essential both for a marriage and for its continuation. Compared to North Americans, Asians tend to focus less on personal feelings and more on the practical aspects of social attachments (Dion & Dion, 1993; Sprecher et al., 1994). Thus, they are less vulnerable to disillusionment. Asians are also less prone to the self-focused individualism that in the long run can undermine a relationship and lead to divorce (Dion & Dion, 1991, 1996; Triandis et al., 1988).

> ***"Grow old along with me! The best is yet to be."***
>
> Robert Browning, "Rabbi ben Ezra," in *Dramatis Personae*, 1864

The decline in intense mutual fascination may be natural and adaptive for species survival. The result of passionate love frequently is children, whose survival is aided by the parents' waning obsession with one another (Kenrick & Trost, 1987). Nevertheless, for those married more than 20 years, some of the lost romantic feeling is often renewed as the family nest empties and the parents are once again free to focus their attention on each other (Hatfield & Sprecher, 1986). "No man or woman really knows

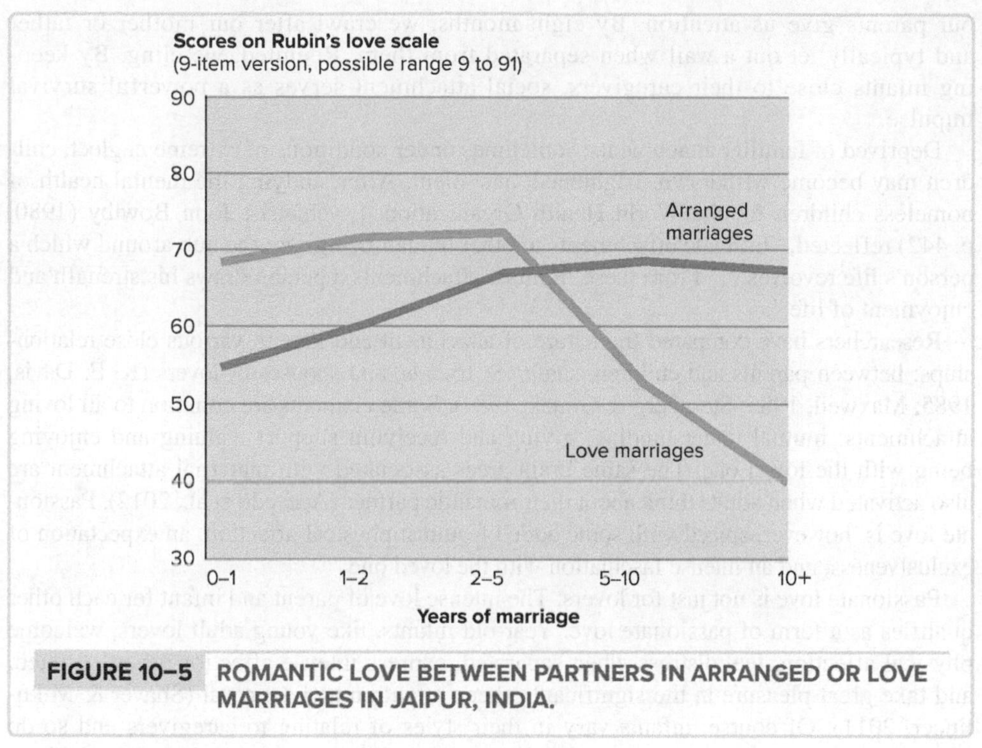

FIGURE 10–5 ROMANTIC LOVE BETWEEN PARTNERS IN ARRANGED OR LOVE MARRIAGES IN JAIPUR, INDIA.

what love is until they have been married a quarter of a century," said Mark Twain. If the relationship has been intimate, mutually rewarding, and rooted in a shared life history, companionate love deepens.

What Enables Close Relationships?

What factors influence the ups and downs of our close relationships? Let's consider three factors: attachment styles, equity, and self-disclosure.

Attachment

Love is a biological imperative. We are social creatures, destined to bond with others. Our need to belong is adaptive. Cooperation promotes survival. In solo combat, our ancestors were not the toughest predators; but as hunter–gatherers, and in fending off predators, they gained strength from numbers. Because group dwellers survived and reproduced, we today carry genes that predispose us to form such bonds.

Researchers have found that different forms of a particular gene predict mammalian pair bonding. In the mouse-like prairie vole, and in humans, injections of hormones such as oxytocin (which is released in females during nursing and during mating) and vasopressin produce good feelings that trigger male–female bonding (Donaldson & Young, 2008; Young, 2009). In humans, genes associated with vasopressin activity predict marital stability (Walum et al., 2008). Such is the biology of enduring love.

Our dependence as infants strengthens our human bonds. Soon after birth, we exhibit various social responses—love, fear, anger. But the first and greatest of these is love. As babies, we almost immediately prefer familiar faces and voices. We coo and smile when our parents give us attention. By eight months, we crawl after our mother or father and typically let out a wail when separated from them. Reunited, we cling. By keeping infants close to their caregivers, social attachment serves as a powerful survival impulse.

Deprived of familiar attachments, sometimes under conditions of extreme neglect, children may become withdrawn, frightened, and silent. After studying the mental health of homeless children for the World Health Organization, psychiatrist John Bowlby (1980, p. 442) reflected, "Intimate attachments to other human beings are the hub around which a person's life revolves . . . From these intimate attachments a person draws his strength and enjoyment of life."

Researchers have compared the nature of attachment and love in various close relationships: between parents and children, same-sex friends, and spouses or lovers (K. E. Davis, 1985; Maxwell, 1985; Sternberg & Grajek, 1984). Some elements are common to all loving attachments: mutual understanding, giving and receiving support, valuing and enjoying being with the loved one. The same brain areas associated with maternal attachment are also activated when adults think about their romantic partner (Acevedo et al., 2012). Passionate love is, however, spiced with some added features: physical affection, an expectation of exclusiveness, and an intense fascination with the loved one.

Passionate love is not just for lovers. The intense love of parent and infant for each other qualifies as a form of passionate love. Year-old infants, like young adult lovers, welcome physical affection, feel distress when separated, express intense affection when reunited, and take great pleasure in the significant other's attention and approval (Shaver & Mikulincer, 2011). Of course, infants vary in their styles of relating to caregivers and so do adults in how they relate to their romantic partners. This made Phillip Shaver and Cindy Hazan (1993, 1994) wonder whether infant attachment styles might carry over to adult relationships.

Attachment styles

About seven in 10 infants, and nearly that many adults, exhibit **secure attachment** (Baldwin et al., 1996; Jones & Cunningham, 1996; Mickelson, Kessler, & Shaver, 1997). When placed as infants in a strange situation (usually a laboratory playroom), they play comfortably in their mother's presence, happily exploring this strange environment. If she leaves, they get distressed; when she returns, they run to her, hold her, then relax and return to exploring and playing (Ainsworth, 1973, 1979). This trusting attachment style, many researchers believe, forms a working model of intimacy—a blueprint for one's adult intimate relationships, in which underlying trust sustains relationships through times of conflict (Miller & Rempel, 2004). Secure adults find it easy to get close to others and don't fret about getting too dependent or being abandoned. As lovers, they enjoy sexuality within the context of a continuing relationship. And their relationships tend to be satisfying and enduring (Feeney, 1996; Feeney & Noller, 1990; Keelan, Dion, & Dion, 1998; Simpson, Rholes, & Nelligan, 1992).

Approximately two in 10 infants and adults exhibit **avoidant attachment**, one of the two types of insecure attachment. Although internally aroused, avoidant infants reveal little distress during separation and little clinging upon reunion. Avoiding closeness, avoidant adults tend to be less invested in relationships and more likely to leave them. They also are more likely to engage in uncommitted hookups (Garneau et al., 2013) and are more likely to be sexually unfaithful to their partners in both straight (DeWall et al., 2011) and gay (Starks & Parsons, 2014) relationships. Kim Bartholomew of Simon Fraser University and Leonard Horowitz of Stanford University (1991) note that avoidant individuals may be either *fearful* ("I am uncomfortable getting close to others") or *dismissing* ("It is very important to me to feel independent and self-sufficient"). More North

secure attachment Attachment rooted in trust and marked by intimacy.

avoidant attachment Attachments are marked by discomfort over, or resistance to, being close to others. An insecure attachment style.

THE INSIDE STORY

My interest in adult attachment stems from an obvious, but perplexing, observation. On the one hand, people are highly motivated to form satisfying intimate relationships. And yet, despite this motivation, the goal of finding and maintaining the perfect (or at least good enough) intimate relationship all too often proves elusive. I have looked to attachment theory as a theoretical framework for understanding the range of difficulties people experience in their intimate relationships. My research has focused on how adult attachment orientations, as assessed through semi-structured interviews, may affect functioning in close relationships. During the course of a longitudinal study of attachment processes in young established couples, I became acutely aware of the high levels of abuse in some relationships and the surprisingly high stability of most of these relationships. Through this work and through an association with Donald Dutton, a family-violence researcher at UBC, my students and I became interested in violent relationships. Working with both clinical and community samples, we have applied an attachment perspective to understanding the dynamics of abusive relationships and the difficulty many individuals experience leaving abusive relationships. We have observed that individuals who lack confidence in the acceptance and responsiveness of their partners are prone to experiencing high levels of attachment anxiety, leading them (in some cases) to act in aggressive, seemingly counterproductive, ways in an attempt to gain proximity to their partners. In our most recent line of research, we are investigating attachment, childhood socialization, and partner abuse in gay men.

Source: Ximagination/Dreamstime.com/GetStock.com.

Kim Bartholomew, *Simon Fraser University*

American university students had a dismissing attachment style in the 2010s (vs. the 1980s), and fewer had a secure attachment style. The researchers speculate that this shift may be rooted in changing family structures and an increasing emphasis on individualism (Konrath et al., 2014).

Approximately one in 10 infants and adults exhibit the anxiousness and ambivalence that mark **anxious attachment**, the second type of insecure attachment. In the strange situation, infants are more likely to cling tightly to their mother. If she leaves, they cry; when she returns, they may be indifferent or hostile. As adults, anxious–ambivalent individuals are less trusting and more possessive and jealous. They may break up repeatedly with the same person. When discussing conflicts, they get emotional and often angry (Cassidy, 2000; Simpson, Rholes, & Phillips, 1996), and their self-esteem fluctuates more based on feedback from others, especially romantic partners (Hepper & Carnelly, 2012). Their eagerness to form relationships can hamper their efforts because others perceive their anxiety and the interaction becomes awkward (McClure & Lydon, 2014). Anxiously attached people can even transfer their anxious attachment style to their smartphones, causing them to rely on their phones more and check their phones more often—even while driving (Bodford et al., 2017).

anxious attachment Attachment marked by anxiety or ambivalence. An insecure attachment style.

Some researchers attribute these varying attachment styles, which have been observed across 62 cultures (Schmitt et al., 2004), to parental responsiveness. Cindy Hazan (2004) sums up the idea: "Early attachment experiences form the basis for *internal working models* or characteristic ways of thinking about relationships." Thus, sensitive, responsive mothers—mothers who engender a sense of basic trust in the world's reliability—typically have securely attached infants, observed Mary Ainsworth (1979) and Erik Erikson (1963). In fact, one study of 100 Israeli grandmother–daughter–granddaughter threesomes found intergenerational consistency of attachment styles (Besser & Priel, 2005). Youths who have experienced nurturing and involved parenting teams tend later to have warm and supportive relationships with their romantic partners (Conger et al., 2000). However, young adults whose parents were divorced did not differ in attachment style from those whose parents were still married (Washington & Hans, 2013). Attachment styles may be partially based in inherited temperament (Gillath et al., 2008; Harris, 1998). A gene that predisposes prairie voles to cuddle and mate for life (and has the same effect on laboratory mice genetically engineered to have the gene) has varying human forms. This gene is more commonly found in faithful, married men (Caldwell et al., 2008; Walum et al., 2008).

The effects of attachment can last a lifetime: In a 22-year longitudinal study, infants who were insecurely attached to their mothers became adults who struggled to feel more positive emotions (Moutsiana et al., 2014). Attachment styles also have obvious impacts on adult relationships: In an analysis of 188 studies, avoidantly attached people were less satisfied and supported in their relationships, and anxiously attached people experienced more relationship conflict (Li & Chan, 2012).

Which attachment style combinations are the best—and the worst? Two securely attached partners would seem to be ideal, and pairings in which at least one partner is insecurely attached may have more issues. The most difficult pairing appears to be an anxious woman and an avoidant man; these couples showed the highest levels of stress hormones when they anticipated talking over a conflict, and they found it more difficult to give and seek care from their partner (Beck et al., 2013). This makes sense: The anxious woman, uncertain of her partner's love, seeks closeness, while the avoidant man, uncomfortable with closeness, distances himself. For better or for worse, early attachment styles do seem to lay foundations for future relationships.

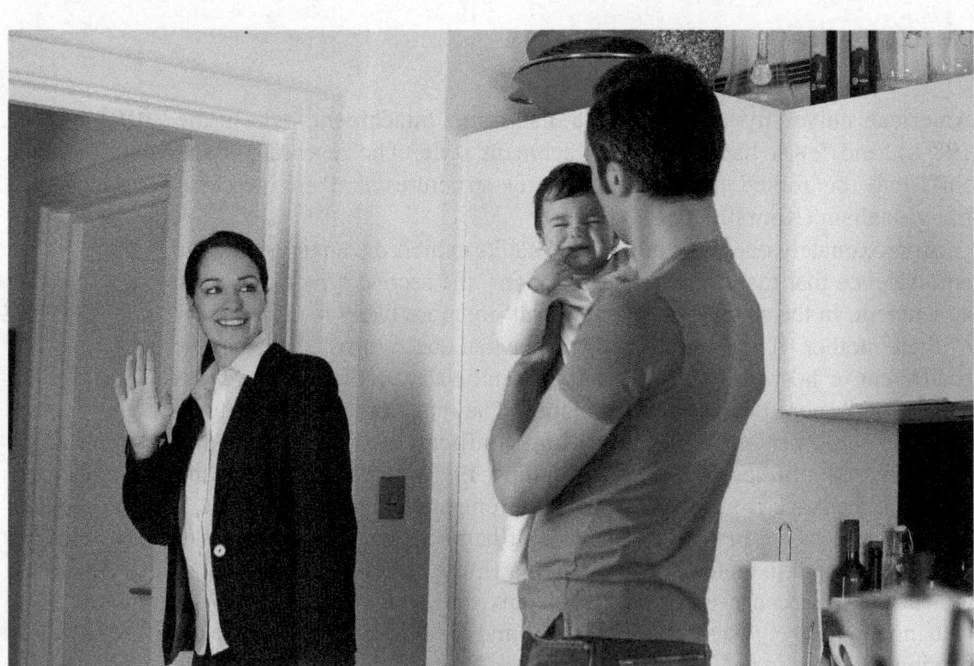

Attachment, especially to caretakers, is a powerful survival impulse.

Source: ©Juice Images/Alamy Stock Photo.

Equity

If each partner in a relationship pursues their personal desires willy-nilly, the relationship will die. Therefore, our society teaches us to exchange rewards by the **equity** principle of attraction: What you and your partner get out of a relationship should be proportional to what you each put into it (Hatfield et al., 1985). If two people receive equal outcomes, they should contribute equally; otherwise, one or the other will feel the relationship is unfair. If both feel their outcomes correspond to the assets and efforts each contributes, then both perceive equity.

equity A condition in which the outcomes people receive from a relationship are proportional to what they contribute to it. Note: Equitable outcomes needn't always be equal outcomes.

Strangers and casual acquaintances maintain equity by exchanging benefits: You lend me your class notes; later, I'll lend you mine. I invite you to my party; you invite me to yours. Those in an enduring relationship, including roommates and those in love, do not feel bound to trade similar benefits—notes for notes, parties for parties (Berg, 1984). They feel freer to maintain equity by exchanging a variety of benefits ("When you drop by to lend me your notes, why don't you stay for dinner?") and eventually to stop keeping track of who owes whom. A sense of equity underlies nearly all of the qualities that a group of university students identified as "deal breakers" in considering long-term partners. Most said they would not consider being with someone who was inattentive or uncaring, was dismissive of their interests, or was already in a relationship or married (Jonason et al., 2015).

Long-term equity

Is it crass to suppose that friendship and love are rooted in an equitable exchange of rewards? Don't we sometimes give in response to a loved one's need without expecting anything in return? Indeed, those involved in an equitable, long-term relationship are unconcerned with short-term equity. Margaret Clark and Judson Mills (1979, 1993; Clark, 1984, 1986) argued that people even take pains to *avoid* calculating any exchange benefits. When we help a good friend, we do not want instant repayment. If someone invites us for dinner, we wait before reciprocating, lest the person attribute the motive for our return invitation to be merely paying off a social debt. True friends tune in to one another's needs even when reciprocation is impossible (Clark, Mills, & Corcoran, 1989; Clark, Mills, & Powell, 1986). Similarly, happily married people tend not to keep track of how much they are giving and getting (Buunk & Van Yperen, 1991). As people observe their partners being self-giving, their sense of trust grows (Wieselquist et al., 1999).

In a series of experiments, Clark and Mills confirmed that *not* being calculating is a mark of friendship. Tit-for-tat exchanges boosted people's liking when the relationship was relatively formal but diminished liking when the two sought friendship. Clark and Mills surmised that marriage contracts in which each partner specifies what is expected from the other are more likely to undermine than enhance love. Only when the other's positive behaviour is voluntary can we attribute it to love.

> ***"Love is the most subtle kind of self-interest."***
>
> Holbrook Johnson

Previously, we noted an equity principle at work in the matching phenomenon: People usually bring equal assets to romantic relationships. Often, they are matched for attractiveness, status, and so forth. If they are mismatched in one area, such as attractiveness, they tend to be mismatched in some other area, such as status. But in total assets, they are an equitable match. No one says, and few even think, "I'll trade you my good looks for your big income." But, especially in relationships that last, equity is the rule.

Perceived equity and satisfaction

In one survey, "sharing household chores" ranked third (after "faithfulness" and a "happy sexual relationship") among nine things that people saw as marks of successful marriages (Pew Research Center, 2007). Indeed, those in an equitable relationship are typically

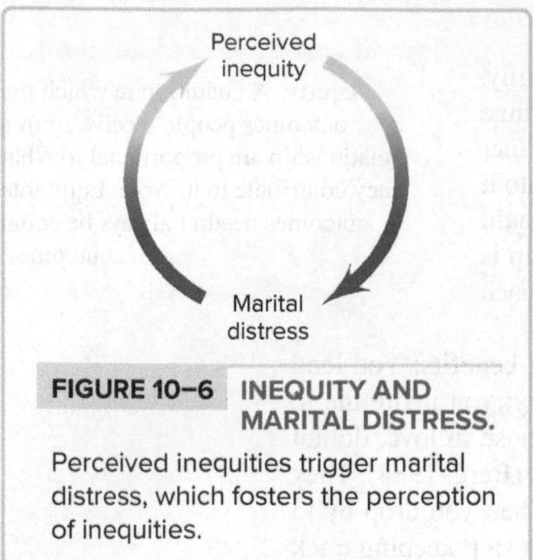

FIGURE 10–6 INEQUITY AND MARITAL DISTRESS.

Perceived inequities trigger marital distress, which fosters the perception of inequities.

content (Fletcher et al., 1987; Hatfield et al., 1985; Van Yperen & Buunk, 1990). Those who perceive their relationship as inequitable feel discomfort: The one who has the better deal may feel guilty, and the one who senses a raw deal may feel strong irritation. (Given the self-serving bias—most husbands perceive themselves as contributing more housework than their wives credit them for—the person who is "overbenefited" is less sensitive to the inequity.)

Robert Schafer and Patricia Keith (1980) surveyed several hundred married couples of all ages, noting those who felt their marriages were somewhat unfair because one spouse contributed too little to the cooking, housekeeping, parenting, or providing. Inequity took its toll: Those who perceived inequity also felt more distressed and depressed. During the child-rearing years, when wives often feel underbenefited and husbands feel overbenefited, marital satisfaction tends to dip. During the honeymoon and empty-nest stages, spouses are more likely to perceive equity and to feel satisfaction with their marriages (Feeney, Peterson, & Noller, 1994). When both partners freely give and receive, and make decisions together, the odds of sustained, satisfying love are good.

Perceived inequity triggers marital distress, agreed Nancy Grote and Margaret Clark (2001) from their tracking of married couples over time. But they also reported that the traffic between inequity and distress runs both ways: Marital distress exacerbates the perception of unfairness (Figure 10–6).

Self-Disclosure

Deep, companionate relationships are intimate. They enable us to be known as we truly are and feel accepted. We discover this exquisite experience in a good marriage or a close friendship—a relationship where trust displaces anxiety and where we are free to open ourselves without fear of losing the other's affection (Holmes & Rempel, 1989). Such relationships are characterized by **self-disclosure** (Derlega et al., 1993). As a relationship grows, self-disclosing partners reveal more and more of themselves to one another; their knowledge of one another penetrates to deeper levels. In relationships that flourish, much of this self-disclosure shares successes, triumphs, and mutual delight over good happenings (Gable, Gonzaga, & Strachman, 2006). When a friend rejoices with us over good news, it not only increases our joy about the happy event but also helps us feel better about the friendship (Reis et al., 2010).

self-disclosure Revealing intimate aspects of oneself to others.

Most of us enjoy such intimacy. It's gratifying to be singled out for another's disclosure. We feel pleased when a normally reserved person says that something about us "made me feel like opening up," when that person shares confidential information (Archer & Cook, 1986; D. Taylor, Gould, & Brounstein, 1981).

Not only do we like those who disclose, but we also disclose to those whom we like. And, after disclosing to them, we like them more (Collins & Miller, 1994). One way to feed intimacy and love is by talking about your emotions and views. Couples who discussed questions such as "Given the choice of anyone in the world, whom would you want as a dinner guest?" and "What is the greatest accomplishment of your life?" later felt more passionate love for each other (Welker et al., 2014). Lacking opportunities for intimacy, on the other hand, we experience the pain of loneliness (Berg & Peplau, 1982; Solano, Batten, & Parish, 1982).

Experiments have probed both the *causes* and the *effects* of self-disclosure. When are people most willing to disclose intimate information concerning "what you like and don't like about yourself" or "what you're most ashamed and most proud of"? And what effects do such revelations have on those who reveal and receive them?

disclosure reciprocity
The tendency for one person's intimacy of self-disclosure to match that of a conversational partner.

The most reliable finding is the **disclosure reciprocity** effect: Disclosure begets disclosure (Berg, 1987; L. C. Miller, 1990; Reis & Shaver, 1988). We reveal more to those who have been open with us. But intimacy is seldom instant. (If it is, the person may seem indiscreet and unstable.) Appropriate intimacy progresses like a dance: I reveal a little, you reveal a little—but not too much. You then reveal more, and I reciprocate.

For those in love, deepening intimacy is exciting. "Rising intimacy will create a strong sense of passion," noted Roy Baumeister and Ellen Bratslavsky (1999). This helps explain why those who remarry after the loss of a spouse tend to begin the new marriage with an increased frequency of sex and why passion often rides highest when intimacy is restored following severe conflict.

Some people—most of them women—are especially skilled "openers"; they easily elicit intimate disclosures from others, even from those who normally don't reveal very much of themselves (L. C. Miller, Berg, & Archer, 1983; Pegalis et al., 1994; Shaffer, Pegalis, & Bazzini, 1996). Such people tend to be good listeners. During conversation, they maintain attentive facial expressions and appear to be comfortably enjoying themselves (Purvis, Dabbs, & Hopper, 1984). They may also express interest by uttering supportive phrases while their conversational partner is speaking. They are what psychologist Carl Rogers (1980) called "growth-promoting" listeners—people who are genuine in revealing their own feelings, who are accepting of others' feelings, and who are empathetic, sensitive, reflective listeners.

What are the effects of such self-disclosure? Humanistic psychologist Sidney Jourard (1964) argued that dropping our masks, letting ourselves be known as we are, nurtures love. He presumed that it is gratifying to open up to another and then to receive the trust another implies by being open with us. People feel better on days when they have disclosed something significant about themselves (such as their being lesbian or gay), and feel worse when concealing their identity (Beals, Peplau, & Gable, 2009). Those whose days include more deep or substantive discussions, rather than just small talk, tend to be happier. That's what Mathias Mehl and coresearchers (2010) found after equipping 70 undergraduates with recording devices that snatched 30-second conversational snippets five times each hour over four days.

"What is a friend? I will tell you. It is a person with whom you dare to be yourself."

Frank Crane, "A Definition of Friendship," *Four Minute Essays,* 1919

Having an intimate friend with whom we can discuss threats to our self-image seems to help us survive such stress (Swann & Predmore, 1985). A true friendship is a special relationship that helps us cope with our other relationships. "When I am with my friend," reflected the Roman playwright Seneca, "methinks I am alone, and as much at liberty to speak anything as to think it." At its best, marriage is such a friendship, sealed by commitment.

Intimate self-disclosure is also one of companionate love's delights. The most self-revealing dating and married couples tend to enjoy the most satisfying and enduring relationships (Berg & McQuinn, 1986; Hendrick, Hendrick, & Adler, 1988; Sprecher, 1987). For example, in a study of newlywed couples who were all equally in love, those who most deeply and accurately knew each other were most likely to enjoy enduring love (Neff & Karney, 2005). Married partners who most strongly agree that "I try to share my most intimate thoughts and feelings with my partner" tend to have the most satisfying marriages (Sanderson & Cantor, 2001). For very reticent people, marriage may not be as satisfying as it is for those more willing to share their feelings (Baker & McNulty, 2010). When the inevitable disagreements occur, couples who believe that their partner understands their perspective—even if they don't agree with it—report more relationship satisfaction (Gordon & Chen, 2016).

Researchers have also found that women are often more willing to disclose their fears and weaknesses than men are (Cunningham, 1981). As feminist writer Kate Millett (1975) put it, "Women express, men repress." Small wonder that both men and women report friendships with women to be more intimate, enjoyable, and nurturing, and that on social networks, both males and females seem to prefer female friends (Thelwall, 2008).

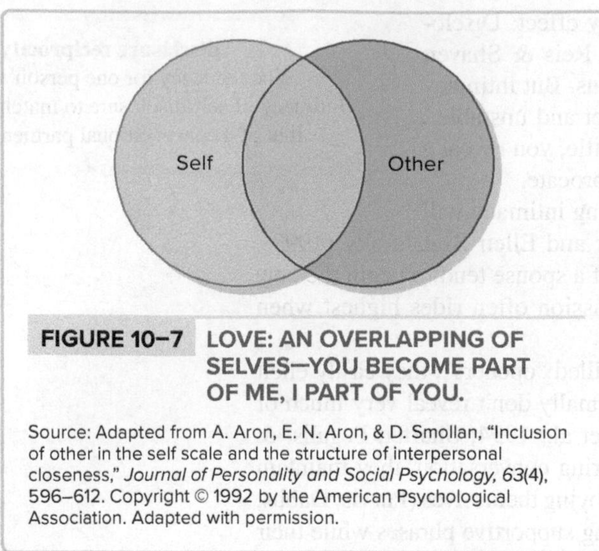

FIGURE 10–7 **LOVE: AN OVERLAPPING OF SELVES—YOU BECOME PART OF ME, I PART OF YOU.**

Source: Adapted from A. Aron, E. N. Aron, & D. Smollan, "Inclusion of other in the self scale and the structure of interpersonal closeness," *Journal of Personality and Social Psychology, 63*(4), 596–612. Copyright © 1992 by the American Psychological Association. Adapted with permission.

Nevertheless, men today, particularly men with egalitarian gender-role attitudes, seem increasingly willing to reveal intimate feelings and to enjoy the satisfactions that accompany a relationship of mutual trust and self-disclosure. And that, say Arthur Aron and Elaine Aron (1994), is the essence of love—two selves connecting, disclosing, and identifying with one another; two selves, each retaining their individuality, yet sharing activities, delighting in similarities, and being mutually supporting. The result for many romantic partners is "self–other integration": intertwined self-concepts (Slotter & Gardner, 2009) (Figure 10–7).

That being so, might we cultivate closeness by experiences that mirror the escalating closeness of budding friendships? The Arons and their collaborators (1997) wondered. They paired volunteer students who were strangers to each other. The students talked for 45 minutes. For the first 15 minutes, they shared thoughts on a list of personal but low-intimacy topics, such as "When did you last sing to yourself?" The next 15 minutes were spent on more intimate topics, such as "What is your most treasured memory?" The last 15 minutes invited even more self-disclosure, with questions such as this: "Complete this sentence: 'I wish I had someone with whom I could share . . .'" and "When did you last cry in front of another person? By yourself?"

Compared to control participants who spent the 45 minutes in small talk ("What was your high school like?" "What is your favourite holiday?"), those who experienced the escalating self-disclosure ended the hour feeling remarkably close to their conversation partners—in fact, "closer than the closest relationship in the lives of 30 percent of similar students," reported the researchers. These relationships surely were not yet marked by the loyalty and commitment of true friendship. Nevertheless, the experiment provided a striking demonstration of how readily a sense of closeness to others can grow, given open self-disclosure.

To promote self-disclosure in ongoing dating relationships, Richard Slatcher and James Pennebaker (2006) invited one member of 86 couples to spend 20 minutes on each of three days writing their deepest thoughts and feelings about the relationship (or, in a control condition, writing merely about their daily activities). Those who pondered and wrote about their feelings expressed more emotion to their partners in the days following. Three months later, 77 percent were still dating (compared with 52 percent in the control group).

How Do Relationships End?

What factors predict marital dissolution? How do couples typically detach or renew their relationships?

In 1971, a man wrote a love poem to his bride, slipped it into a bottle, and dropped it into the Pacific Ocean. A decade later, a jogger found it on a Guam beach:

> If, by the time this letter reaches you, I am old and grey, I know that our love will be as fresh as it is today. It may take a week or it may take years for this note to find you. . . . If this should never reach you, it will still be written in my heart that I will go to extreme means to prove my love for you. Your husband, Bob.

The woman to whom the love note was addressed was reached by phone. When the note was read to her, she burst out laughing. And the more she heard, the harder she laughed. "We're divorced," she finally said, and hung up the phone.

So it often goes. Comparing their unsatisfying relationship with the support and affection they imagine is available elsewhere, many relationships end. Each year, Canada and the United States record one divorce for every two marriages. As economic and social barriers to divorce weakened during the 1960s and 1970s, divorce rates rose. "We are living longer, but loving more briefly," quipped Os Guiness (1993, p. 309).

Divorce

To predict a culture's divorce rates, it helps to know its values (Triandis, 2000). Individualistic cultures (where love is a feeling and people ask, "What does my heart say?") have more divorce than do communal cultures (where love entails obligation and people ask, "What will other people say?"). Individualists marry "for as long as we both shall love"; collectivists, more often for life. Individualists expect more passion and personal fulfillment in a marriage, which puts greater pressure on the relationship (Dion & Dion, 1993). In one pair of surveys, "keeping romance alive" was rated as important to a good marriage by 78 percent of American women surveyed and 29 percent of Japanese women (*American Enterprise,* 1992). Eli Finkel and his colleagues (2014) argue that marriage has become more challenging in individualistic recent times as couples expect more fulfillment from marriage but invest fewer resources in it—a potentially impossible equation.

Even in Western society, however, those who enter relationships with a long-term orientation and an intention to persist do experience healthier, less turbulent, and more durable partnerships (Arriaga, 2001; Arriaga & Agnew, 2001). Enduring relationships are rooted in enduring love and satisfaction but also in fear of the termination cost, a sense of moral obligation, and inattention to possible alternative partners (Adams & Jones, 1997; Maner et al., 2009; R. S. Miller, 1997). Those who fear being single, who dread the thought of growing old alone, are likely to persist in relationships, even if they are not satisfying (Spielmann et al., 2013). For those determined that their marriage should last, it usually does.

> ***"Passionate love is in many ways an altered state of consciousness. . . . In many states today, there are laws that a person must not be in an intoxicated condition when marrying. But passionate love is a kind of intoxication."***
>
> Roy Baumeister, *Meanings of Life,* 1991

Those whose commitment to a union outlasts the desires that gave birth to it will endure times of conflict and unhappiness. One national survey found that 86 percent of those who were unhappily married but who stayed with the marriage were, when reinterviewed five years later, now mostly "very" or "quite" happy with their marriages (Popenoe, 2002). By contrast, narcissistic people enter relationships with less likelihood of long-term relational success (Campbell & Foster, 2002).

Risk of divorce also depends on who marries whom (Fergusson et al., 1984; D. G. Myers, 2000; Tzeng, 1992). People usually stay married if they:

- Married after age 20
- Both grew up in stable, two-parent homes
- Dated for a long while before marriage
- Are well and similarly educated
- Enjoy a stable income from a good job
- Live in a small town or on a farm
- Did not cohabit or conceive a pregnancy before marriage
- Are religiously committed
- Are of similar age, faith, and education

None of these predictors, by itself, is essential to a stable marriage. But if none of these things is true for someone, marital breakdown is an almost sure bet. If all are true, they are very likely to stay together until death. The English perhaps had it right, several centuries ago, when presuming that the temporary intoxication of passionate love was a foolish basis for permanent marital decisions. It was better, they felt, to choose a mate based on stable friendship and compatible backgrounds, interests, habits, and values (Stone, 1977).

The Detachment Process

Our close relationships help define the social identity that shapes our self-concept (Slotter, Gardner, & Finkel, 2010). Thus, much as we experience life's best moments when relationships begin—e.g., having a baby, making a friend, falling in love—so we experience life's worst moments when relationships end, with death or a broken bond (Jaremka, Gabriel, & Carvallo, 2011). Severing bonds produces a predictable sequence of agitated preoccupation with the lost partner, followed by deep sadness and, eventually, the beginnings of emotional detachment, a letting go of the old while focusing on someone new, and a renewed sense of self (Hazan & Shaver, 1994; Lewandowski & Bizzoco, 2007; Spielmann, MacDonald, & Wilson, 2009). Because humans often mate with more than one partner, we must have evolved psychological processes for cutting ties, a mechanism evolutionary psychologists dubbed the "mate rejection module" (Boutwell et al., 2015). Deep and long-standing attachments seldom break quickly; detaching is a process, not an event.

Among dating couples, the closer and longer the relationship and the fewer the available alternatives, the more painful the breakup (Simpson, 1987). Surprisingly, Roy Baumeister and Sara Wotman (1992) report that, months or years later, people recall more pain over spurning someone's love than over having been spurned. Their distress arises from guilt over hurting someone, from sadness over the heartbroken lover's persistence, or from uncertainty over how to respond. Among married couples, breakup has additional costs: shocked parents and friends, guilt over broken vows, anguish over reduced household income, and possibly less time with the children. Still, each year millions of couples are willing to pay those costs to extricate themselves from what they perceive as the greater price of continuing a painful, unrewarding relationship. Such costs include, in one study of 328 married couples, a tenfold increase in depression symptoms when a marriage is marked by discord rather than satisfaction (O'Leary, Christian, & Mendell, 1994).

When relationships suffer, those without better options or those who feel invested in a relationship (through time, energy, mutual friendships, possessions, and perhaps children) will seek alternatives to exiting the relationship. Caryl Rusbult and her colleagues (1986, 1987) have explored three ways of coping with a failing relationship. Some people exhibit *loyalty*—by waiting for conditions to improve. The problems are too painful to confront and the risks of separation are too great, so the loyal partner perseveres, hoping the good old days will return. Others (especially men) exhibit *neglect*; they ignore the partner and allow the relationship to deteriorate. With painful dissatisfactions ignored, an insidious emotional uncoupling ensues as the partners talk less and begin redefining their lives without each other. Still others will *voice* their concerns and take active steps to improve the relationship by discussing problems, seeking advice, and attempting to change.

Study after study—in fact, 115 studies of 45 000 couples—reveal that unhappy couples disagree, command, criticize, and put down. Happy couples more often agree, approve, assent, and laugh (Karney & Bradbury, 1995; Noller & Fitzpatrick, 1990). After observing 2000 couples, John Gottman (1994) noted that healthy marriages were not necessarily devoid of conflict. Rather, they were marked by an ability to reconcile differences and to overbalance criticism with affection. In successful marriages, positive interactions (smiling, touching, complimenting, laughing) outnumbered negative interactions (sarcasm, disapproval, insults) by at least a five-to-one ratio. Gay and lesbian couples may have an advantage here. Same-sex couples, compared to straight couples, are more positive when raising disagreements; they are more sensitive, are less defensive, and use more humour (Gottman et al., 2003). As a result, they remain more positive after discussing disagreements.

TABLE 10-1 Responses to Relationship Distress.

	Passive	Active
Constructive	*Loyalty*: Await improvement	*Voice*: Seek to improve relationship
Destructive	*Neglect*: Ignore the partner	*Exit*: End the relationship

Successful couples have learned, sometimes aided by communication training, to restrain the poisonous putdowns and gut-level reactions and to think and behave more positively (McNulty, 2010). They fight fairly (by stating feelings without insulting). They depersonalize conflict with comments like "I know it's not your fault" (Markman et al., 1988; Notarius & Markman, 1993; Yovetich & Rusbult, 1994). Couples randomly assigned to think less emotionally and more like an observer during fights were later more satisfied with their marriages (Finkel et al., 2013). Would unhappy relationships get better if the partners agreed to *act* more as happy couples do—by complaining and criticizing less? By affirming and agreeing more? By setting time aside to voice their concerns and doing so calmly? By having fun together daily? As attitudes trail behaviours, do affections trail actions?

Joan Kellerman, James Lewis, and James Laird (1989) wondered. They knew that among couples passionately in love, eye gazing is typically prolonged and mutual (Rubin, 1973). Would intimate eye gazing similarly stir feelings between those not in love (much as 45 minutes of escalating self-disclosure evoked feelings of closeness among those unacquainted students)? To find out, they asked unacquainted male–female pairs to gaze intently for two minutes either at one another's hands or into one another's eyes. When they separated, the eye gazers reported a tingle of attraction and affection toward each other. Simulating love had begun to stir it.

Enacting and expressing love, believed researcher Robert Sternberg (1988), can cause the passion of initial romance to evolve into enduring love:

> "Living happily ever after" need not be a myth, but if it is to be a reality, the happiness must be based upon different configurations of mutual feelings at various times in a relationship. Couples who expect their passion to last forever, or their intimacy to remain unchallenged, are in for disappointment. . . . We must constantly work at understanding, building, and rebuilding our loving relationships. Relationships are constructions, and they decay over time if they are not maintained and improved. We cannot expect a relationship simply to take care of itself, any more than we can expect that of a building. Rather, we must take responsibility for making our relationships the best they can be.

SUMMING UP

What Leads to Friendship and Attraction?

- The best predictor of whether any two people are friends is their sheer *proximity* to one another. Proximity is conducive to repeated *exposure* and interaction, which enables us to discover similarities and to feel each other's liking.
- A second determinant of initial attraction is physical attractiveness. Both in laboratory studies and in field experiments involving blind dates, university students tend to prefer attractive people. In everyday life, however, people tend to choose and marry someone whose attractiveness roughly matches their own (or someone who, if less attractive, has other compensating qualities). Positive attributions about attractive people define a *physical-attractiveness stereotype*—an assumption that what is beautiful is good.
- Liking is greatly aided by similarity of attitudes, beliefs, and values. Likeness leads to liking; opposites rarely attract.
- We are also likely to develop friendships with people who like us.
- According to the *reward theory of attraction*, we like people whose behaviour we find rewarding or whom we have associated with rewarding events.

What Is Love?

- Researchers have characterized love as having components of intimacy, passion, and commitment. *Passionate love* is experienced as a bewildering confusion of ecstasy and anxiety, elation and pain. The *two-factor theory of emotion* suggests that in a romantic context, arousal from any source, even painful experiences, can be steered into passion.
- In the best of relationships, the initial romantic high settles to a steadier, more affectionate relationship called *companionate love*.

What Enables Close Relationships?

- From infancy to old age, attachments are central to human life. *Secure attachments*, as in an enduring marriage, mark happy lives.
- Companionate love is most likely to endure when both partners feel the partnership is *equitable*, with both perceiving themselves receiving from the relationship in proportion to what they contribute to it.
- One reward of companionate love is the opportunity for intimate *self-disclosure*, a state achieved gradually as each partner reciprocates the other's increasing openness (*disclosure reciprocity*).

How Do Relationships End?

- Often love does not endure. As divorce rates rose in the twentieth century, researchers discerned predictors of marital dissolution. One predictor is an individualistic culture that values feelings over commitment; other factors include the couple's age, education, values, and similarity.
- Researchers are also identifying the process through which couples either detach or rebuild their relationships, and they are identifying the positive and nondefensive communication styles that mark healthy, stable marriages.

Key Terms

anxious attachment
avoidant attachment
companionate love
complementarity
disclosure reciprocity
equity
ingratiation
matching phenomenon
mere-exposure effect
need to belong
passionate love
physical-attractiveness stereotype
proximity
reward theory of attraction
secure attachment
self-disclosure
two-factor theory of emotion

CHAPTER 11

Prejudice

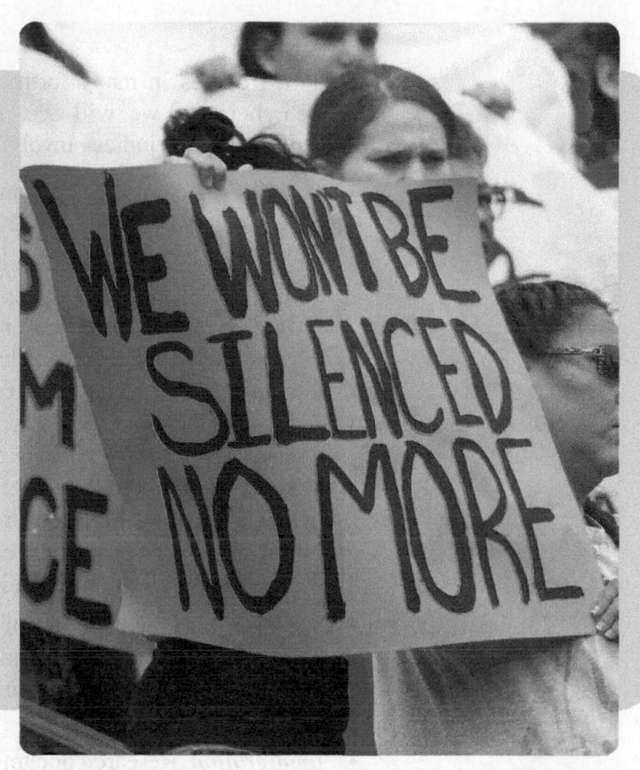

Source: The Canadian Press/Adrian Wyld.

CHAPTER OUTLINE

What Is the Nature and Power of Prejudice?

What Are the Social Sources of Prejudice?

What Are the Motivational Sources of Prejudice?

What Are the Cognitive Sources of Prejudice?

What Are the Consequences of Prejudice?

Racism, sexism, homophobia, transphobia: These are a few of the prominent forms of prejudice that are prevalent in our society. We are all members of social groups—we may be gay, Canadian, a student, a hockey player—and may derive a sense of pride or identity from these groups. Belonging to particular social groups may also inadvertently position us against other social groups, however, and contribute to more negative tendencies, like prejudice, stereotyping, and discrimination.

Prejudice comes in many forms—for our own group and against some other group. Researchers, as we will see, have explored race, gender, and sexual orientation prejudice but also prejudices involving the following:

- *Religion*. If told a job applicant is Muslim, many managers have not been inclined to hire or pay well (Park et al., 2009).
- *Obesity*. One analysis of 2.2 million social media posts containing *obese* or *fat* revealed a stream of shaming and flaming—insults, criticisms, and derogatory jokes (Chou et al., 2014). When seeking love and employment, overweight people—especially White women—face significant challenges. Overweight people marry less often, gain entry to less-desirable jobs, and make less money (Swami et al., 2008). For example, they seldom (relative to their numbers in the general population) become the CEOs of large corporations or get elected to office (Roehling, Roehling, & Odland, 2008; Roehling, Roehling, Vandlen, et al., 2009; Roehling, Roehling, Johnston, et al., 2010). Weight discrimination, in fact, exceeds racial or gender discrimination and occurs at every employment stage—hiring, placement, promotion, compensation, discipline, and discharge (Roehling, 2000). It is also at the root of much child bullying (Brody, 2017; Reece, 2017).
- *Age*. People's perceptions of the elderly—as generally kind but frail, incompetent, and unproductive—predispose patronizing behaviour. Baby-talk speech, for example, leads elderly people to feel less competent and act less capably (Bugental & Hehman, 2007).
- *Immigration*. Research documents anti-immigrant prejudice among Germans toward Turks, French toward North Africans, British toward West Indians and Pakistanis, and Americans toward Latin American immigrants, especially unauthorized immigrants (Murray & Marx, 2013; Pettigrew, 2006). In the aftermath of the refugee surge into Europe, Europeans are less likely than North Americans to say that growing ethnic diversity makes their country "a better place to live" (Drake & Poushter, 2016).
- *Politics*. Liberals and conservatives dislike—and sometimes despise—one another, and to roughly equal degrees (Crawford et al., 2017). They also display "virtually identical" amounts of bias toward their side (Ditto et al., 2019). When processing political information, each side is more accepting of information that supports its view.

What Is the Nature and Power of Prejudice?

What is the nature of prejudice? What are the differences between prejudice, stereotypes, and discrimination?

Prejudice, stereotyping, discrimination, racism, sexism—the terms overlap. Let's clarify them.

Defining *Prejudice*

prejudice A negative prejudgment of a group and its individual members.

Each of the situations described in the introduction to this chapter involved a negative evaluation of some group. And that is the essence of **prejudice**: a preconceived negative judgment of a group and its individual members. (Some "prejudice" definitions include *positive* judgments, but nearly all uses of "prejudice" refer to *negative* ones.)

Prejudice is an attitude. As we noted in Chapter 4, an attitude is a combination of feelings, inclinations to act, and beliefs. It can be easily remembered as the ABCs of attitudes: *a*ffect (feelings), *b*ehaviour tendency (inclination to act), and *c*ognition (beliefs). Prejudiced

What stereotypes might each of these people hold about the others? Even if stereotypes are somewhat accurate of a group as a whole, they are often not accurate for a particular individual.

Source: ©Adam Hester/Blend Images.

people might *dislike* those who are different from themselves and *behave* toward them in a discriminatory manner, *believing* them to be ignorant and dangerous.

The negative evaluations that mark prejudice often are supported by negative beliefs, called **stereotypes**. To stereotype is to generalize. To simplify the world, we generalize: "The British are reserved. Italians are outgoing. Professors are absent-minded. The elderly are frail."

Such generalizations can be more or less true (and are not always negative). The elderly *are* generally more frail. People may stereotype Asians as good at math, and those of African heritage as superior athletes (Kay et al., 2013). Such stereotypes often arise from the occupational roles we observe people playing (Koenig & Eagly, 2014). Black men are about 40 times more likely than White men to play basketball in the NBA (Stephens-Davidowitz, 2017).

So stereotypes may be accurate (they may reflect sensitivity to diversity). People perceive Australians as having a wilder culture than Britons—and they do use more profanity in their millions of Facebook posts (Kramer & Chung, 2011). To stereotype the British as more concerned about punctuality than Mexicans are is to understand what to expect and how to get along in each culture. "Accuracy dominates bias," notes Lee Jussim (2005, 2012). "The social perception glass (of people judging others) is about 90 percent full."

Familiar stereotypes: "Heaven is a place with an American house, Chinese food, British police, a German car, and French art. Hell is a place with a Japanese house, Chinese police, British food, German art, and a French car."

Anonymous, as reported by Yueh-Ting Lee (1996)

The "10 percent problem" with stereotypes arises when they are *overgeneralized* or just plain wrong, as when liberals and conservatives overestimate the extremity of each other's views (Graham et al., 2012; Wilson et al., 2017). To presume that most Indigenous peoples suffer from alcoholism is to overgeneralize because it just isn't so. To presume that people with disabilities are incompetent and asexual, as did participants in one study, misrepresents reality (Nario-Redmond, 2010). To stigmatize the obese as slow, lazy, and undisciplined is inaccurate (Puhl & Heuer, 2009, 2010). To presume that priests are pedophiles or evangelicals hate gay people overgeneralizes from the worst examples of each. And it's especially when we have strong views about group difference—say, that women have superior empathic skill at reading others' minds—that our beliefs exaggerate reality (Eyal & Epley, 2017).

Prejudice is a negative *attitude*; **discrimination** is negative *behaviour*. Discriminatory behaviour often, but not always, has its source in prejudicial attitudes (Dovidio et al., 1996; Wagner, Christ, & Pettigrew, 2008). As Chapter 4 emphasized, however, attitudes and behaviour are often loosely linked. Prejudiced attitudes need not breed hostile acts, nor does all oppression

stereotypes Beliefs about the personal attributes of a group of people. Stereotypes can be overgeneralized, inaccurate, and resistant to new information.

discrimination Unjustifiable negative behaviour toward a group or its members.

racism (1) An individual's prejudicial attitudes and discriminatory behaviour toward people of a given race, or (2) institutional practices (even if not motivated by prejudice) that subordinate people of a given race.

sexism (1) An individual's prejudicial attitudes and discriminatory behaviour toward people of a given sex, or (2) institutional practices (even if not motivated by prejudice) that subordinate people of a given sex.

spring from prejudice. **Racism** and **sexism** are institutional practices that discriminate, even when there is no prejudicial intent. If word-of-mouth hiring practices in an all-White business have the effect of excluding potential non-White employees, the practice could be called racism—even if an employer intended no discrimination. Much discrimination reflects no intended harm; it's simply favouritism toward people like oneself (Greenwald & Pettigrew, 2014). And that perhaps explains why 1000 recent popular fictional films (the top 100 each from 2007 through 2016) have had one female director for every 24 male directors (Smith et al., 2017).

Consider this: When job ads for male-dominated vocations feature words associated with male stereotypes ("We are a dominant engineering firm seeking individuals who can perform in a competitive environment"), and job ads for female-dominated vocations feature the opposite ("We seek people who will be sensitive to clients' needs and can develop warm client relationships"), the result may be institutional sexism. Without intending any prejudice, the gendered wording helps sustain gender inequality (Gaucher, Friesen, & Kay, 2011).

Prejudice: Implicit and Explicit

Prejudice illustrates our *dual attitude* system. As hundreds of studies using the Implicit Association Test (IAT) have shown, we can have different explicit (conscious) and implicit (automatic) attitudes toward the same target (Banaji & Greenwald, 2013). The test, which has been taken more than 20 million times, assesses "implicit cognition"—what you know without knowing that you know. It does so by measuring people's speed of associations. Much as we more quickly associate a hammer with a nail than with a pail, so the test can measure how speedily we associate "White" with "good" versus "Black" with "good." Thus, people may retain from childhood a habitual, automatic fear or dislike of people for whom they now express respect and admiration. Although explicit attitudes may change dramatically with education, implicit attitudes may linger, changing only as we form new habits through practice (Kawakami et al., 2000).

"Although our [conscious] minds are in the right places, and we may truly believe we are not prejudiced, our hearts aren't quite there yet."

Prejudice researcher John Dovidio, *Time*, 2009

Critics contend that the Implicit Association Test does not predict behaviour well enough to assess or label individuals (Blanton et al., 2007, 2009, 2015; Oswald et al., 2013, 2015). Perhaps the test's modest predictive power reflects its merely revealing common cultural associations, much as your associating bread with butter faster than bread with carrot need not reveal a vegetable prejudice.

The test is more appropriate for research, which has shown, for example, that implicit biases help predict behaviours ranging from acts of friendliness to work evaluations. In the 2008 U.S. election, both implicit and explicit prejudice predicted voters' support for Barack Obama, and his election in turn led to some reduction in both explicit and implicit prejudice (Bernstein et al., 2010; Goldman, 2012; Payne et al., 2010; Stephens-Davidowitz, 2014). And, as in elections, even a small effect of implicit prejudice may, over time and across people, accumulate to a large societal effect (Greenwald et al., 2015). Thus, while the IAT, like most psychological measures, only modestly predicts individual acts, it better predicts average outcomes. For example, metropolitan areas with higher implicit bias scores have also had larger racial differences in police shootings (Hehman et al., 2018).

A raft of other experiments converge in pointing to one of social psychology's big lessons: *prejudiced and stereotypic evaluations can occur outside people's awareness*. Some of these studies briefly flash words or faces that "prime" (automatically activate) stereotypes for some racial, gender, or age group. Without their awareness, the participants' activated stereotypes may then bias their behaviour. Having been primed with images associated with Black persons, for example, they may then react with more hostility to an experimenter's (intentionally) annoying request.

Keeping in mind the distinction between conscious, explicit prejudice and unconscious, implicit prejudice, let's examine three common forms of prejudice: racial prejudice, gender prejudice, and LGBT (lesbian, gay, bisexual, and transgender) prejudice. In each case, we will look first at explicit prejudice, which is the greater (though not the only) predictor of discriminatory actions.

Racial Prejudice

In the context of the world, every race is a minority. Non-Hispanic Whites, for example, are one-fifth of the world's people and will be one-eighth within another half-century. Thanks to mobility and migration over the past two centuries, the world's races now intermingle, in relations that are sometimes hostile, sometimes amiable.

To a molecular biologist, skin colour is a trivial human characteristic, one controlled by a minuscule genetic difference. Moreover, nature doesn't cluster races in neatly defined categories. It is people, not nature, who label Barack Obama (the son of a White woman and Black man) and Meghan Markle (the daughter of a Black woman and White man) as "Black." (To people whose exposure has been mostly to Black faces, mixed-race people are somewhat more likely to be categorized as White [Lewis, 2016].)

Is racial prejudice disappearing?

Explicit prejudicial attitudes can change very quickly.

- In 1942, most Americans agreed that "There should be separate sections for Negroes on streetcars and buses" (Hyman & Sheatsley, 1956). Today, the question would seem bizarre because such blatant prejudice has nearly disappeared.
- In 1942, less than 33 percent of all American Whites (only 2 percent in the South) supported school integration; by 1980, 90 percent supported it.

Considering what a thin slice of history is covered by the years since 1942 or even since slavery was practised, the changes are dramatic. In Britain, overt racial prejudice, as expressed in opposition to interracial marriage or having an ethnic minority boss, has similarly plummeted, especially among younger adults (Ford, 2008).

Psychologists usually capitalize "Black" and "White" to emphasize that these are socially applied race labels, not literal colour labels for persons of African and European ancestry.

In Canada, Africville was a small community in the north end of Halifax, founded in the early 1800s by free formerly enslaved people from the United States and by free Canadians of African descent. In the 1950s and 1960s, Halifax "reclaimed" this land from Africville residents and relocated them to slum housing, transporting their belongings in garbage trucks. Little to no compensation was offered to them. In the twenty-first century, such blatant discrimination is a major embarrassment, and the Halifax Regional Municipality apologized for its actions (CBC, 2002).

Shall we conclude, then, that racial prejudice is extinct in places such as the United States, Great Britain, and Canada? Not if we consider the recent increase in hate crime incidents—6121 during 2016 in the United States or 1798 in Canada in 2018 (Federal Bureau of Investigation [FBI], 2017; Statistics Canada, 2018). And not if we consider that people tend to underreport their negative stereotypes and feelings (Bergsieker et al., 2012). In the United States, Canada, and countries throughout the world, many large protests against police brutality were sparked in 2020 by the murder of George

Africville: A symbol of African identity in Nova Scotia and of the fight against racism.

Source: ©AA Images/Alamy Stock Photo.

Floyd, a Black man, by a White police officer in Minneapolis—just one of many cases of race-based police brutality in recent years.

So, how great is the progress toward racial equality? Majority group members tend to contrast the present with the oppressive past and to perceive swift and radical progress. Minority group members tend to compare the present with their ideal world, which has not yet been realized, and to perceive somewhat less progress (Eibach & Ehrlinger, 2006).

Subtle racial prejudice

Despite lingering animosities, the bigger problem in today's world is not overt, conscious prejudice. Most people support racial equality and deplore discrimination. Yet three in four people who take the Implicit Association Test (IAT) display an automatic tendency to associate White, more than Black, with favourable words (Banaji & Greenwald, 2013). Modern prejudice also appears subtly, in our preferences for what is familiar, similar, and comfortable (Dovidio et al., 1992; Esses et al., 1993a; Gaertner & Dovidio, 2005).

> ***"I cannot totally grasp all that I am. . . . For that darkness is lamentable in which the possibilities in me are hidden from myself."***
>
> St. Augustine, *Confessions,* 398 AD

Prejudiced attitudes and discriminatory behaviour surface when they can hide behind the screen of some other motive. In Australia, Great Britain, France, Germany, and the Netherlands, blatant prejudice has been replaced by subtle prejudice (exaggerating ethnic differences; feeling less admiration and affection for immigrant minorities, rejecting them for supposedly nonracial reasons) (Pedersen & Walker, 1997; Tropp & Pettigrew, 2005a). Some researchers call such subtle prejudice "modern racism" or "cultural racism."

We can also detect bias in *behaviours*:

- *Employment discrimination*. To test for possible labour market discrimination, Massachusetts Institute of Technology (MIT) researchers sent out 5000 resumés in response to 1300 varied employment ads (Bertrand & Mullainathan, 2003). Applicants with randomly assigned White names (Emily, Greg) received one callback for every 10 resumés sent. Those given Black names (Lakisha, Jamal) received one callback for every 15 resumés sent.
- *Favouritism galore*. Similar experiments have found
  - Airbnb hosts less likely to accept applications from would-be guests with Black names (Edelman et al., 2017),
  - longer Uber and Lyft wait times and more cancellations for passengers with Black names (Ge et al., 2016), and
  - half as much willingness of Australian bus drivers to admit dark-skinned people with an empty fare card (Mujcic & Frijters, 2014).
- *Traffic stops*. In one analysis of traffic stops, Blacks and Latinos were four times more likely than Whites to be searched, twice as likely to be arrested, and three times more likely to be handcuffed and to have excessive force used against them (Lichtblau, 2005). Another analysis found that Blacks were more likely than Whites to be stopped and physically grabbed or pushed to the ground during encounters with the police (Fryer, 2016). And one analysis of traffic stops in Kingston, Ontario, found that police were 3.7 times as likely to stop Black drivers and 1.4 times as likely to stop Indigenous drivers as White drivers (CBC, 2005).
- *Patronization*. Modern prejudice even appears as race sensitivity that leads to exaggerated reactions to isolated minority persons—for example, overpraising their accomplishments, overcriticizing.their mistakes, and failing to warn Black students, as they would White students, about potential academic difficulty (Crosby & Monin, 2007; Fiske, 1989; Hart & Morry, 1997; Hass et al., 1991). At Stanford University, Kent Harber (1998) gave White students a poorly written essay to evaluate. When the students thought the writer was Black, they rated it *higher* than when they were led

to think the author was White, and they rarely offered harsh criticisms. The evaluators, perhaps wanting to avoid the appearance of bias, patronized the Black essayists with lower standards. Such "inflated praise and insufficient criticism" may hinder minority student achievement, Harber noted. In follow-up research, Harber and his colleagues (2010) found that Whites concerned about appearing biased not only rate and comment more favourably on weak essays attributed to Black students, but also recommend less time for skill development. To protect their own self-image as unprejudiced, they bend over backward to give positive and unchallenging feedback.

Automatic racial prejudice

Does automatic (implicit) prejudice, like explicit prejudice, matter? Critics note that unconscious *associations* may only indicate cultural assumptions, perhaps without *prejudice* (which involves negative feelings and action tendencies). Or perhaps people's knee-jerk responses relate to familiarity or to actual race differences (Tetlock, 2007). But some studies find that implicit bias can leak into behaviour. Those who display implicit prejudice on the IAT—by taking longer to identify positive words such as *peace* and *paradise* as "good" when associated with Black rather than White faces—also have been observed to judge White job applicants more favourably, to recommend better treatment for White than Black emergency room patients, and to perceive anger in Black faces more quickly than in White ones (Green et al., 2007; Hugenberg & Bodenhausen, 2003; Rooth, 2007).

In some situations, automatic, implicit prejudice can have life or death consequences. In separate experiments, Joshua Correll and his co-workers (2002, 2007; 2015; Sadler et al., 2012) and Anthony Greenwald and his co-workers (Greenwald, Oakes, & Hoffman, 2003) invited people to press buttons quickly to "shoot" or "not shoot" men who suddenly appeared onscreen holding either a gun or a harmless object, such as a flashlight or a bottle. The participants (both Blacks and Whites, in one of the studies) more often misperceived the object and mistakenly shot harmless targets who were Black. (Follow-up computerized simulations revealed that it's Black *males*—not females, whether Black or White—who are more likely to be associated with a threat and to be shot [Plant, Goplen, & Kunstman, 2011].)

Other studies have found that, when primed with a Black rather than a White face, people think of guns: They more quickly recognize a gun and they more often mistake a tool, such as a wrench, for a gun (Judd et al., 2004; Payne, 2001, 2006). Even when race does not bias *perception*, it may bias reaction—as people require less evidence before firing (Klauer & Voss, 2008).

When people are fatigued or feeling threatened by a dangerous world, they become even more likely to mistakenly shoot a minority person (Ma et al., 2013; Miller et al., 2012). Brain activity in the amygdala, a region that underlies fear and aggression, facilitates such automatic responding (Eberhardt et al., 2004; Harris & Fiske, 2006). These studies help explain why, in 1999, Amadou Diallo (a Black immigrant in New York City) was shot 41 times by police officers for removing his wallet from his pocket. The good news is that implicit-bias training is now part of modern police education and that, when trained to overcome the influence of stereotypes, police are less racially influenced than most people in the decision to shoot (Correll et al., 2014).

Automatic prejudice: When Joshua Correll and his colleagues invited people to react quickly to individuals holding either a gun or a harmless object, race influenced perceptions and reactions.
Source: ©Pawel Radomski/Shutterstock.

Even the social scientists who study prejudice seem vulnerable to automatic prejudice, noted Anthony Greenwald and Eric Schuh (1994). They analyzed biases in authors' citations of social science articles by people with selected non-Jewish names (Erickson, McBride, etc.) and Jewish names (Goldstein, Siegel, etc.). Their analysis of nearly 30 000 citations, including 17 000 citations of prejudice research, found something remarkable: Compared with Jewish authors, non-Jewish authors had 40 percent higher odds of citing non-Jewish names. (Greenwald and Schuh could not determine whether Jewish authors were overciting their Jewish colleagues or whether non-Jewish authors were overciting their non-Jewish colleagues, or both.)

Gender-Based Prejudice

How pervasive is prejudice against women? In Chapter 4, we examined gender norms—people's ideas about how women and men *ought* to behave. Here we consider gender *stereotypes*—people's beliefs about how women and men *do* behave. Norms are *pre*scriptive; stereotypes are *de*scriptive.

Gender stereotypes

From research on stereotypes, two conclusions are indisputable: Strong gender stereotypes exist; and, as often happens, members of the stereotyped group accept them. Men and women agree that you *can* judge a book by its gendered cover. In one survey, 87 percent of respondents agreed that men and women are "basically different" in "how they experience their feelings" (Parker et al., 2017).

Google's diversity training workshops aim to inform people about and restrain the implicit biases uncovered by social psychologists (Manjoo, 2014).

Remember that stereotypes are generalizations about a group of people and may be true, false, or overgeneralized from a kernel of truth. The average man and woman do differ somewhat in social connectedness, empathy, social power, aggressiveness, and sexual initiative (although not in intelligence). Do we then conclude that gender stereotypes are accurate? Sometimes, stereotypes exaggerate differences—but not always, observed Janet Swim (1994). She found that university students' stereotypes of men's and women's restlessness, nonverbal sensitivity, aggressiveness, and so forth were reasonable approximations of actual gender differences.

"All the pursuits of men are the pursuits of women also, and in all of them a woman is only a lesser man."

Plato, *Republic,* 360 BC

Gender stereotypes have persisted across time and culture. Averaging data from 27 countries, John Williams and his colleagues (Williams, Satterwhite, & Best, 1999, 2000) found that folks everywhere perceive women as more agreeable; men, as more outgoing. The persistence and omnipresence of gender stereotypes leads some evolutionary psychologists to believe that they reflect innate, stable reality (Lueptow, Garovich, & Lueptow, 1995).

Stereotypes (beliefs) are not prejudices (attitudes). Stereotypes may support prejudice. Yet one might believe, without prejudice, that men and women are "different yet equal." Let us, therefore, see how researchers probe for gender prejudice.

Sexism: Benevolent and hostile

Judging from what people tell survey researchers, attitudes toward women have changed as rapidly as racial attitudes. Alice Eagly and her associates (1991) and Geoffrey Haddock and Mark Zanna (1994) also report that people don't respond to women with gut-level negative emotions as they do to certain other groups; in fact, most people *like* women more than men. They perceive women as more understanding, kind, and helpful. Eagly dubbed this *favourable* stereotype the *women-are-wonderful effect.*

But gender attitudes often are ambivalent, report Peter Glick and Susan Fiske (1996, 2007, 2011) from their surveys of 15 000 people in 19 nations. Gender attitudes frequently mix a *benevolent sexism* ("Women have a superior moral sensibility") with a *hostile sexism* ("Once a man commits, she puts him on a tight leash"). Moreover, in one 57-nation study, hostile sexist beliefs ("On the whole, men make better political leaders than women do") predicted increased future gender inequality (Brandt, 2011). Hostile sexism is overtly negative. Benevolent sexism, though sounding positive ("Women deserve protection"), may still impede gender equity by discouraging the hiring of women in traditionally male-dominated occupations (Hideg & Ferris, 2016).

Gender discrimination

Being male isn't all roses. Compared to women, men are three times more likely to die by suicide and be murdered. They comprise nearly all of the battlefield and death row casualties. They die five years sooner than women. And males represent the majority of those with intellectual disability or autism and the majority of students in special education programs (Baumeister, 2007; Pinker, 2008).

One publicized finding of seeming pro-male bias came from a 1968 study in which women students were given several short articles and asked to judge the value of each (Goldberg, 1968). Sometimes, a given article was attributed to a male author (for example, John T. McKay); sometimes, to a female author (for example, Joan T. McKay). In general, the articles received lower ratings when attributed to a female. That's right: Women discriminated against women.

> **Question:** *Misogyny is the hatred of women. What is the corresponding word for the hatred of men?*
> **Answer:** *In most dictionaries, no such word exists.*

Eager to demonstrate the subtle reality of gender discrimination, in 1980 David Myers obtained the materials from the 1968 study and repeated the experiment with his own students. They (women and men) showed no such tendency to deprecate women's work. So Janet Swim, Eugene Borgida, Geoffrey Maruyama, and David Myers (1989) searched the literature and corresponded with investigators to learn all they could about studies of gender bias in the evaluation of men's and women's work. To their surprise, the biases that occasionally surfaced were as often against men as women. But the most common result across 104 studies involving almost 20 000 people was *no difference.* On most comparisons, judgments of someone's work were unaffected by whether the work was attributed to a female or a male. Summarizing other studies of people's evaluations of women and men as leaders, professors, and so forth, Alice Eagly (2009) concluded, "Experiments have *not* demonstrated any *overall* tendency to devalue women's work." Moreover, as Stephen Ceci and Wendy Williams (2015) report, in the academic sciences, five national studies reveal that "faculty prefer female job candidates over identically qualified male ones."

Is gender bias fast becoming extinct in Western countries? Has the women's movement nearly completed its work? (See Figure 11–1.)

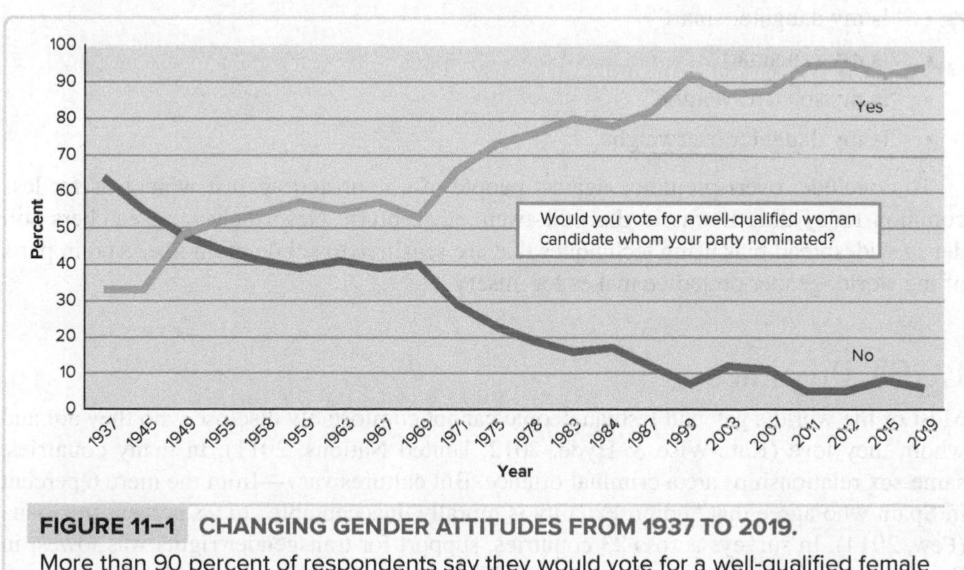

FIGURE 11–1 CHANGING GENDER ATTITUDES FROM 1937 TO 2019.
More than 90 percent of respondents say they would vote for a well-qualified female candidate for president. As with racial prejudice, blatant gender prejudice is dying, but subtle bias lives on.

Violate gender stereotypes and others may react. People take notice of a cigar-smoking woman and a tearful man and denigrate them (Phelan & Rudman, 2010). A woman whom people see as power hungry suffers more voter backlash than does a similarly power-hungry man (Okimoto & Brescoll, 2010).

In the non-Western world, gender discrimination is less subtle. Although 86 percent of Europeans say it "is very important that women have the same rights as men," only 48 percent of Middle Easterners agree (Zainulbhai, 2016). Women are two-thirds of the world's illiterate (UN, 2015). And worldwide, some 30 percent of women have experienced intimate partner violence (Devries et al., 2013). Such tendencies are especially likely among men who objectify women by implicitly associating them with animals or objects (Rudman & Mescher, 2012). Labels some use for women—like "honey," "sweetie," and "chick"—are both infantilizing and focused on food and animals.

But the biggest violence against women may occur prenatally. Around the world, people tend to prefer having baby boys. In the United States in 1941, for example, 38 percent of expectant parents said they preferred a boy if they could have only one child, 24 percent preferred a girl, and 23 percent said they had no preference. In 2011, the answers were virtually unchanged, with 40 percent still preferring a boy (Newport, 2011).

With the widespread use of ultrasound to determine the sex of a fetus and the growing availability of abortion, these preferences are, in some countries, affecting the number of boys and girls. With 108 males for every 100 females, India has 63 million "missing women" (Subramanian, 2018; United Nations, 2017). In China, where 95 percent of children in orphanages are girls (Webley, 2009), there are 106 males for every 100 females. The 32 million missing women in China correspond to an excess of 32 million under-20 men; these are tomorrow's "bare branches"—bachelors who will have trouble finding mates (Hvistendahl, 2009, 2010, 2011; Zhu et al., 2009). This female shortage also contributes to increased violence, crime, prostitution, and trafficking of women (Brooks, 2012). In response, China has made sex-selective abortions a criminal offence. And in South Korea, which also for many years had experienced a deficit of female births, the sex ratio for children has returned to normal (Gupta, 2017).

Aggregated data from Google searches reveal that parents' hopes for their children are also not gender neutral (Stephens-Davidowitz, 2014). Many parents seem eager to have smart sons and slender, beautiful daughters. You can see this for yourself. Google the following (using quotation marks as indicated), and note the number of results:

- "Is my daughter smart"
- "Is my son smart"
- "Is my son overweight"
- "Is my daughter overweight"

To conclude, overt prejudice against people of colour and against women is far less common today than it was in the mid–twentieth century. Nevertheless, researchers still detect widespread bias using techniques that are sensitive to subtle prejudice. And in parts of the world, gender prejudice makes for misery.

LGBT Prejudice

Most of the world's gay and lesbian people cannot comfortably disclose who they are and whom they love (Katz-Wise & Hyde, 2012; United Nations, 2011). In many countries, same-sex relationships are a criminal offence. But cultures vary—from the mere 6 percent in Spain who agree that "homosexuality is morally unacceptable" to 98 percent in Ghana (Pew, 2014). In surveys across 23 countries, support for transgender rights was lowest in Russia and highest in Spain (Flores et al., 2016). Anti-gay attitudes worldwide are strongest among those who are older, less educated, and male (Jäckle & Wenzelburger, 2015). Similarly, heterosexual men who value masculinity express the most prejudice against transgender individuals (Anderson, 2017).

In Western countries, anti-gay prejudice, though rapidly diminishing, endures:

- *Job discrimination.* Experiments have submitted many hundreds of fictitious pairs of women's and men's resumés to Austrian, Greek, and American job openings (Drydakis, 2009; Tilcsik, 2011; Weichselbaumer, 2003). By random assignment, one applicant in each pair acknowledged, among other activities, volunteering in a gay–lesbian organization. In response, callbacks were much less likely to the gay-associated applicants. In the American experiment, for example, 7.2 percent of applicants whose activities included being "Treasurer, Gay and Lesbian Alliance," received replies, as did 11.5 percent of those associated with a different left-seeming group ("Treasurer, Progressive and Socialist Alliance"). Job discrimination is even more pronounced for transgender people, 90 percent of whom report being harassed or mistreated at work (Grant et al., 2011), with many saying they have been fired for their gender preference (Mizock et al., 2018).
- *Gay marriage support is mixed but increasing.* In Western countries, support for same-sex marriage has soared over the past two decades—in Canada, for example, from 41 percent in 1997 to 74 percent in 2017 (CROP, 2017).
- *Harassment hurts.* In a national survey, 14.2 percent of lesbian and gay Canadians and 26.7 percent of bisexual Canadians reported experiencing sexual assault, physical assault, or robbery (compared to 6.9 percent of straight Canadians) (Statistics Canada, 2018b). Gay and lesbian Canadians are frequently victimized in hate crimes (Statistics Canada, 2018c). Forty-nine patrons of a gay nightclub in Orlando, Florida, were murdered by a gunman in 2016 (Sherman, 2016). Two-thirds of British gay youth report experiencing homophobic bullying (Hunt & Jensen, 2007).
- *Rejection happens.* In national surveys, 40 percent of gay and lesbian Americans have said it would be difficult for someone in their community "to live openly as gay or lesbian" (Jones, 2012). Thirty nine percent report having "a friend or family member" reject them because of their sexual orientation or gender identity (Pew, 2013). A majority (54 percent) of transgender people report being harassed at school, and 8 percent were kicked out of the house for being transgender (James et al., 2016).

As the public's support for same-sex marriage has increased, more countries have legalized marriages between two men or two women.

Source: ©Lisa F. Young/ Shutterstock.

Do disparaging attitudes and discriminatory practices against gay and lesbian people increase LGBT people's risk of ill health and psychological disorder? Consider (from research summarized by Hatzenbuehler, 2014):

- *Community attitudes predict LGBT health.* Communities where anti-gay prejudice is commonplace are communities with high rates of gay–lesbian suicide and cardiovascular death. Moreover, gay and lesbian individuals who experience discrimination are at increased risk of depression and anxiety (Schmitt et al., 2014). Overall, the suicide rate among gay and lesbian teens—who often experience bullying—is three times higher than the general rate for teens (Raifman et al., 2017). In one survey, more than 40 percent of transgender people reported having attempted suicide (Haas et al., 2014), but were less likely to do so if their families supported them (Klein & Golub, 2016).
- *Two quasi-experiments confirm the toxicity of gay stigma and the benefits of its removal.* Between 2001 and 2005, 16 U.S. states banned same-sex marriage. In those states, gays and lesbians (but not heterosexuals) experienced a 37 percent increase in mood disorders, a 42 percent increase in alcohol use disorders, and a 248 percent increase in general anxiety disorders (Hatzenbuehler, 2014). In other U.S. states, gays and lesbians experienced no such increases in psychiatric disorder. And when the tide turned and some states legalized same-sex marriage between 2004 and 2015, fewer teens in those states attempted suicide in the years afterward (Raifman et al., 2017).

What Are the Social Sources of Prejudice?

What influences give rise to and maintain prejudice?

Prejudice springs from several sources. It may arise from people's differing social status and their desires to justify and maintain those differences. It may also be learned from our parents as they socialize us about what differences they believe matter between people. Our social institutions, too, may maintain and support prejudice. Consider first how prejudice can function to defend one's social position.

Social Inequalities: Unequal Status and Prejudice

A principle to remember: *Unequal status breeds prejudice*. Enslavers viewed enslaved people as lazy, irresponsible, and lacking ambition—as having traits that justified the slavery. Historians debate the forces that create unequal status. But once these inequalities exist, prejudice helps justify the economic and social superiority of those who have wealth and power. Tell us the economic relationship between two groups, and we'll predict the intergroup attitudes. Upper-class individuals are more likely than those in poverty to see people's fortunes as the outcomes they have earned, thanks to skill and effort, and not as the result of having connections, money, and luck (Costa-Lopes et al., 2013; Kraus & Keltner, 2013).

> ***"Prejudice is never easy unless it can pass itself off for reason."***
>
> William Hazlitt, 1778–1830, "On Prejudice"

Historical examples abound. Where slavery was practised, prejudice ran strong. Nineteenth-century politicians justified imperial expansion by describing exploited colonized people as "inferior," "requiring protection," and a "burden" to be borne (G. W. Allport, 1958, pp. 204–205). Sociologist Helen Mayer Hacker (1951) noted how stereotypes of Blacks and women helped rationalize the inferior status of each: Many people thought that both groups were mentally slow, emotional, primitive, and "contented" with their subordinate role. Blacks were "inferior"; women were "weak." Blacks were alright in their place; women's place was in the home.

Theresa Vescio and her colleagues (2005) tested that reasoning. They found that powerful men who stereotype their female subordinates give them plenty of praise but fewer resources, thus undermining their performance and allowing the men to maintain their power. In the laboratory, too, patronizing benevolent sexism (statements implying that women, as the weaker sex, need support) has undermined women's cognitive performance by planting intrusive thoughts—self-doubts, preoccupations, and decreased self-esteem (Dardenne, Dumont, & Bollier, 2007).

Racial prejudice often begins during times of conflict, as during the Second World War when Japanese Canadians were sent to internment camps.
Source: National Archives of Canada-Tak Toyota/The Canadian Press.

Peter Glick and Susan Fiske's distinction between "hostile" and "benevolent" sexism extends to other prejudices (2001). We see other groups as *competent* or as *likeable* but not usually as both. These two culturally universal dimensions of social perception—likeability (warmth) and competence—were illustrated by one European's comment that "Germans love Italians, but don't admire them. Italians admire Germans, but don't love them" (Cuddy et al., 2009). We typically *respect* the competence of those high in status and *like* those who agreeably accept a lower status. Depending on the situation, we may seek to impress people with either our competence or warmth. When wanting to appear competent, people will often downplay their warmth. And when wanting to appear warm and likeable, people will downplay their competence (Holoien & Fiske, 2013).

In the United States, report Fiske and her colleagues (1999), Asians, Jews, Germans, nontraditional women, assertive Blacks, and gay men tend to be respected but are not so well liked. Traditionally subordinate Blacks and Hispanics, traditional women, feminine gay men, and people with disabilities tend to be seen as less competent but liked for their emotional, spiritual, artistic, or athletic qualities.

Some people, more than others, notice and justify status differences. Those high in **social dominance orientation** tend to view people in terms of hierarchies. They like their social groups to be high status; that is, they like to be on the top. Being in a dominant, high-status position also tends to promote this orientation (Guimond et al., 2003). Jim Sidanius, Felicia Pratto, and their colleagues (Levin et al., 2011; Pratto et al., 1994; Sidanius et al., 2004) suggested that this desire to be on top leads people high in social dominance to embrace prejudice and to support political positions that justify prejudice.

social dominance orientation
A motivation to have your own group be dominant over other social groups.

Indeed, people high in social dominance orientation often support policies that maintain hierarchies, such as tax cuts for the well-off. They tend to prefer professions, such as politics and business, that increase their status and maintain hierarchies. They typically avoid jobs, such as social work, that, by virtue of their aid to disadvantaged groups, undermine hierarchies. And they frequently express more negative attitudes toward minority persons who exhibit strong racial identities (Kaiser & Pratt-Hyatt, 2009). Status breeds prejudice, especially for people high in social dominance orientation.

Socialization

Prejudice springs from unequal status and from other social sources, including our acquired values and attitudes. The influence of family socialization appears in children's prejudices, which often mirror those perceived in their mothers (Castelli et al., 2007). For example,

Swedish teens display increasing anti-immigrant prejudice over time if their parents voice such prejudice (Miklikowska, 2017). Even children's implicit racial attitudes reflect their parents' explicit prejudice (Sinclair, Dunn, & Lowery, 2005). Our families and cultures pass on all kinds of information—how to find mates, drive cars, and divide the household labours, and whom to distrust and dislike. Indeed, parental attitudes assessed shortly after their babies are born predict their children's attitudes 17 years later (Fraley et al., 2012).

The authoritarian personality

In the 1940s, University of California at Berkeley researchers—two of whom had fled Nazi Germany—set out on an urgent research mission: to uncover the psychological roots of the poisonous anti-Semitism that caused Nazis to slaughter millions of Jews. In studies of American adults, Theodor Adorno and his colleagues (1950) discovered that hostility toward Jews often coexisted with hostility toward other minorities. In those who were strongly prejudiced, prejudice appeared to be less an attitude specific to one group than a way of thinking about those who are "different" or marginalized. These **ethnocentric** people shared certain tendencies: an intolerance for weakness, a punitive attitude, and a submissive respect for their group's authorities, as reflected in their agreement with statements such as: "Obedience and respect for authority are the most important virtues children should learn." Adorno and his colleagues (1950) surmised that these tendencies define a prejudice-prone **authoritarian personality**.

ethnocentric Believing in the superiority of your own ethnic and cultural group and having a corresponding disdain for all other groups.

authoritarian personality A personality that is disposed to favour obedience to authority and intolerance of outgroups and those lower in status.

Studies of authoritarian people's early lives have revealed that, as children, they often face harsh discipline. Extremism, on both the political left and right, shares some common themes, such as catastrophizing, desiring vengeance, dehumanizing the enemy, and seeking a sense of control (Kay & Eibach, 2013;

Activity: How Authoritarian Are You?

For each of these statements, indicate whether or not you agree:

1. Gays and lesbians are just as healthy and moral as anybody else.
2. Women should have to promise to obey their husbands when they get married.
3. There is no "one right way" to live life; everybody has to create their own way.
4. Our country needs free thinkers who have the courage to defy traditional ways, even if this upsets many people.
5. The only way our country can get through the crisis ahead is to get back to our traditional values, put some tough leaders in power, and silence the troublemakers spreading bad ideas.
6. The "old fashioned ways" and "old-fashioned values" still show the best way to live.

These items are from a recent version of the Right-Wing Authoritarianism Scale (Altemeyer, 2006). If you agreed with items 1, 3, and 4, and disagreed with 2, 5, and 6, this suggests you are low in authoritarianism. However, if the opposite is true, you may have some authoritarian tendencies. So, how authoritarian are you really?

Saucier et al., 2009). Moreover, people on both the left and right express similar intolerance of groups with values and beliefs unlike their own (Brandt & van Tongeren, 2017; Kossowska et al., 2017; Toner et al., 2013; van Prooijen et al., 2015). Ironically, people who strongly support ethnic tolerance can display considerable intolerance and discrimination toward those who disagree (Bizumic et al., 2017).

Research into authoritarianism also suggests that the insecurity of authoritarian individuals predisposes them toward an excessive concern with power and status and an inflexible right–wrong way of thinking that makes ambiguity difficult to tolerate. Authoritarian people therefore tend to be submissive to those with power over them and aggressive or punitive toward those whom they consider lower in status than themselves (Altemeyer, 1988). "It's my way or the highway." Authoritarians' feelings of moral superiority may go hand in hand with brutality toward perceived inferiors (McAdams, 2017; Taub, 2016). Becky Choma of Ryerson University and Yaniv Hanoch of Plymouth University (2017) find that authoritarianism also predicts support for politicians who channel dominance and promise to restore hierarchies.

Particularly striking are people high in social dominance orientation and authoritarian personality. University of Manitoba psychologist Bob Altemeyer (2004) reported that these "Double Highs" are, not surprisingly, "among the most prejudiced persons in our society." What is perhaps most surprising and more troubling is that they seem to display the worst qualities of each type of personality, striving for status often in manipulative ways while being dogmatic and ethnocentric. Altemeyer argued that although these people are relatively rare, they are predisposed to be leaders of hate groups.

Although authoritarianism and social dominance can coexist, they appear to be rooted in different beliefs and to serve different functions. Authoritarianism is more related to concern with security and control, whereas social dominance orientation is more related to a person's group status (Cohrs et al., 2005). They can function together to form a toxic environment in groups. Leanne Son Hing from the University of Guelph and her colleagues (2007) examined combinations of authoritarian and high social dominance leaders and followers. They found that high social dominance orientation leaders who had high authoritarian followers were more likely than others to throw ethics out the window in the blind pursuit of profit.

Religion and prejudice

Consider those who benefit from social inequalities while avowing that "all are created equal." They need to justify keeping things the way they are. And what could be a more powerful justification than to believe that God has ordained the existing social order? For all sorts of cruel deeds, noted William James, "piety is the mask" (1902, p. 264).

In almost every country, leaders invoke religion to sanctify the present order. The use of religion to support injustice helps explain a consistent pair of findings concerning North American Christianity: (1) White church members express more racial prejudice than non-members, and (2) those professing traditional or fundamentalist Christian beliefs express more prejudice than those professing more progressive beliefs (Hall, Matz, & Wood, 2010; Johnson et al., 2011).

> ***"We have just enough religion to make us hate, but not enough to make us love one another."***
>
> Jonathan Swift, "Thoughts on Various Subjects," 1706

Knowing the correlation between two variables—religion and prejudice—tells us nothing about their causal connection. Consider three possibilities:

- There might be *no causal connection*. Perhaps people with less education are both more fundamentalist and more prejudiced. (In one study of 7070 Brits, those scoring high on IQ tests at age 10 expressed more nontraditional and anti-racist views at age 30 [Deary et al., 2008].)
- Perhaps *prejudice causes religion*, such as by leading people to create religious ideas to support their prejudices. People who feel hatred may use religion, even God, to justify their contempt for the other.

- Perhaps *religion causes prejudice*, such as by leading people to believe that, because all individuals possess free will, impoverished minorities have themselves to blame for their status, and gays and lesbians choose their orientation.

If, indeed, religion causes prejudice, then more religious church members should also be more prejudiced. But three other findings consistently indicate otherwise:

- *Faithful attenders are less prejudiced.* Among church members, faithful church attenders were, in 24 out of 26 mid-20th-century comparisons, less prejudiced than occasional attenders (Batson & Ventis, 1982).
- *Intrinsically religious are less prejudiced.* Gordon Allport and Michael Ross (1967) compared "intrinsic" and "extrinsic" religiosity. They found that those for whom religion is an intrinsic end in itself (those who agree, for example, with the statement, "My religious beliefs are what really lie behind my whole approach to life") express *less* prejudice than those for whom religion is more a means to other ends (who agree that "A primary reason for my interest in religion is that my church is a congenial social activity"). Faced with reminders of their mortality, such as what people experience during terrorist threats, intrinsic religiosity also has predicted decreased out-group hostility among American Christians and Jews, Iranian Muslims, and Polish Christians (Golec de Zavala et al., 2012). And those who score highest on Gallup's "spiritual commitment" index are more welcoming of a person of another race moving in next door (Gallup & Jones, 1992).
- *Clergy are less prejudiced.* Protestant ministers and Roman Catholic priests have historically given more support to human rights than laypeople do (Fichter, 1968; Hadden, 1969). In Germany, 45 percent of clergy in 1934 had aligned themselves with the Confessing Church, which was organized to oppose Nazi influence on the German Protestant Church (Reed, 1989).

What, then, is the relationship between religion and prejudice? The answer we get depends on *how* we ask the question. If we define *religiousness* as church membership or willingness to agree at least superficially with traditional beliefs, then the more religious people have been the more racially prejudiced. Bigots often rationalize bigotry with religion. But if we assess depth of religious commitment in any of several other ways, then the very devout are less prejudiced—hence the religious roots of the modern civil rights and anti-apartheid movements among whose leaders were many ministers and priests. It was Thomas Clarkson and William Wilberforce's faith-inspired values ("Love your neighbour as yourself") that, two centuries ago, motivated their successful campaign to end the British Empire's slave trade and the practice of slavery. As Gordon Allport concluded, "The role of religion is paradoxical. It makes prejudice and it unmakes prejudice" (1958, p. 413).

Conformity

Once established, prejudice is maintained largely by inertia. If prejudice is socially accepted, many people will follow the path of least resistance and conform to the fashion. They will act not so much out of a need to hate as out of a need to be liked and accepted. Thus, people become more likely to favour (or oppose) discrimination after hearing someone else do so, and they are less supportive of women after hearing sexist humour (Ford et al., 2008; Zitek & Hebl, 2007).

During the 1950s, Thomas Pettigrew (1958) studied Whites in South Africa and the American South. His discovery: Those who conformed most to other social norms were also most prejudiced; those who were less conforming mirrored less of the surrounding prejudice.

So, if a country's head of government expressed contempt for immigrants, Muslims, and ethnic minorities, would that matter? Following the 2016 election of U.S. president Donald Trump, and his declaration in August 2017 that White supremacist marchers included "very fine people," the U.S. Southern Poverty Law Center (2017) reported, based on anecdotes of bullying and harassment, that hate-mongering had been "emboldened" and "energized."

Still, we might wonder: Does prejudicial political speech simply give voice to existing attitudes? Or does it normalize prejudice?

Two large surveys plus an experiment confirm that hate speech can be socially toxic. University of Warsaw psychologist Wiktor Soral and his colleagues (2018) report that "frequent and repetitive exposure to hate speech leads to desensitization" to such speech and to "increasing out-group prejudice." Moreover, the U.S. FBI's (2017) annual hate crimes report confirms that, yes, 2016 saw a 5 percent increase in hate crime incidents. Despite increased overall American acceptance of LGBT people, they—as well as ethnic and religious minorities—experienced an uptick in hate crime incidents. Likewise, the United Kingdom experienced a jump in reported hate crimes following passage of the Brexit vote, fuelled partly by anti-immigrant sentiments (Kenyon, 2016).

Should we be surprised? As social psychologists Chris Crandall and Mark White (2016) remind us: Political leaders have the power to influence norms, and norms matter. "People express the prejudices that are socially acceptable and they hide the ones that are not."

Conformity also maintains gender prejudice. "If we have come to think that the nursery and the kitchen are the natural sphere of a woman," wrote George Bernard Shaw in an 1891 essay, "we have done so exactly as English children come to think that a cage is the natural sphere of a parrot—because they have never seen one anywhere else." Children who *have* seen women elsewhere—children of employed women—have less stereotyped views of men and women (Hoffman, 1977). Women students exposed to female science, technology, engineering, and mathematics (STEM) experts likewise express more positive implicit attitudes toward STEM studies and display more effort on STEM tests (Stout et al., 2011).

In all these findings, there is a message of hope. If prejudice is not deeply ingrained in personality, then as fashions change and new norms evolve, prejudice can diminish. And so it has.

Institutional Supports

Social institutions (schools, government, the media) may bolster prejudice through overt policies, such as segregation, or by passively reinforcing the status quo. Until the 1970s many banks routinely denied mortgages to unmarried women and to minority applicants, with the result that most homeowners were White married couples.

Media may also strengthen harmful stereotypes. In several studies, exposure to portrayals of Muslims as terrorists was associated with increased perceptions of Muslims as aggressive, and increased support for military action in Muslim territories and for Muslim-harming policies (Saleem et al., 2017).

Institutional supports for prejudice are often unintended and unnoticed. Here is one that most of us failed to notice, although it was right before our eyes: By examining 1750 photographs of people in magazines and newspapers, Dane Archer and his associates (1983) discovered that about two-thirds of the average male photo, but less than half of the average female photo, was devoted to the face. As Archer widened his search, he discovered that such "face-ism" is common: He found it in the periodicals of 11 other countries, in 920 portraits gathered from the artwork of six centuries, and in the amateur drawings of university students. Follow-up studies have confirmed the face-ism phenomenon in more magazines (including the feminist *Ms.* magazine) and in website photos of male and female politicians—even in countries with gender equality (Konrath et al., 2012; Nigro et al., 1988). The researchers suspect that the visual prominence given men's faces and women's bodies both reflects and perpetuates gender bias.

What Are the Motivational Sources of Prejudice?

What human motivations fuel prejudice?

Various motivations underlie prejudice. But motivations can also lead people to avoid prejudice.

Frustration and Aggression: The Scapegoat Theory

Frustration (from the blocking of a goal) feeds hostility (as discussed in Chapter 9). When the cause of our frustration is intimidating or unknown, we often redirect our hostility. This phenomenon of "displaced aggression" (scapegoating) contributed to the lynchings of Blacks in the southern United States after the Civil War. Between 1882 and 1930, there were more lynchings in years when cotton prices were low and economic frustration was, therefore, presumably high (Hepworth & West, 1988; Hovland & Sears, 1940). When living standards are rising, societies tend to be more open to diversity and to the passage and enforcement of antidiscrimination laws (Frank, 1999). Ethnic peace is easier to maintain during prosperous times.

Targets for this displaced aggression vary. Following their defeat in the First World War and their country's subsequent economic chaos, many Germans saw Jews as villains. Long before Hitler came to power, one German leader explained it this way: "The Jew is just convenient. . . . If there were no Jews, the anti-Semites would have to invent them" (quoted by Allport, 1958, p. 325).

More recently, Americans who reacted to 9/11 with more anger than fear expressed greater intolerance toward immigrants and Middle Easterners (Skitka et al., 2004). As twenty-first century Greece sank into economic misery, rage against foreign immigrants increased (Becatoros, 2012). Even threats from distant groups, such as terrorist acts, can heighten local prejudices (Bouman et al., 2014; Greenaway et al., 2014). Passions provoke prejudice.

By contrast, individuals who experience no negative emotional response to social threats—namely, children with the genetic disorder Williams syndrome—display a notable lack of racial stereotypes and prejudice (Santos et al., 2010): No passion, no prejudice.

Competition is an important source of frustration that can fuel prejudice. When two groups compete for jobs, housing, or social prestige, one group's goal fulfillment can become the other group's frustration. Thus, the **realistic group conflict theory** suggests that prejudice arises when groups compete for scarce resources (Esses, Jackson, & Armstrong, 1998; Maddux, Mullen, & Galinsky, 2008; Pereira, Vala, & Costa-Lopes, 2010; Sassenberg et al., 2007). In evolutionary biology, Gause's law states that maximum competition will exist between species with identical needs.

realistic group conflict theory
The theory that prejudice arises from competition between groups for scarce resources.

Consider how this has played out across the world:

- In Western Europe, economically frustrated people express relatively high levels of blatant prejudice toward ethnic minorities (Pettigrew et al., 2008, 2010).
- In Canada, opposition to immigration since 1975 has gone up and down with the unemployment rate (Palmer, 1996).
- In the United States, concerns about immigrants taking jobs are greatest among those with the lowest income (AP/Ipsos, 2006).
- In South Africa, dozens of African immigrants were killed by mobs, and 35 000 people were hounded from squatter camps by poor South Africans who resented the economic competition. "These foreigners have no IDs, no papers, and yet they get the jobs," said one unemployed South African, noting that "They are willing to work for 15 rand [about $2] a day" (Bearak, 2010). When interests clash, prejudice may be the result.

"Whoever is dissatisfied with himself is continually ready for revenge."

Nietzsche, *The Gay Science*, 1882

Social Identity Theory: Feeling Superior to Others

Humans are a group-bound species. Our ancestral history prepares us to feed and protect ourselves—to live—in groups. Humans cheer for their groups, kill for their groups, die for their groups. Evolution prepares us, when encountering strangers, to make a quick judgment: friend or foe? Those from our group, those who look like us, even those who *sound* like us—with accents like our own—we instantly tend to like (Gluszek & Dovidio, 2010; Kinzler et al., 2009).

Not surprisingly, as noted by social psychologists John Turner (1981, 2000), Michael Hogg (1992, 2010, 2014), and their colleagues, we also define ourselves by our groups. Self-concept—our sense of who we are—contains not just a *personal identity* (our sense of our personal attributes and attitudes) but also a **social identity** (Chapter 2) (Chen et al., 2006; Haslam et al., 2014). Fiona identifies herself as a woman, an Aussie, a supporter of the Labour Party, a University of New South Wales student, and a MacDonald family member.

social identity The "we" aspect of our self-concept; the part of our answer to "Who am I?" that comes from our group memberships.

in-groups "Us": groups of people who share a sense of belonging, a feeling of common identity.

out-groups "Them": groups that people perceive as distinctively different from or apart from their in-group.

Working with the late British social psychologist Henri Tajfel, a Polish native who had lost family and friends in the Holocaust and then devoted much of his career to studying ethnic hatred, Turner (1947–2011) proposed *social identity theory*. Turner and Tajfel observed the following:

- *We categorize*: We find it useful to put people, ourselves included, into categories. To label someone as a Hindu, a Scot, or a bus driver is a shorthand way of saying some other things about the person.
- *We identify*: We associate ourselves with certain groups (our **in-groups**) and gain self-esteem by doing so.
- *We compare:* We contrast our groups with other groups (**out-groups**), with a favourable bias toward our own groups.

Beginning in our preschool years, we humans naturally divide others into those inside and those outside our group (Buttlemann & Bohm, 2014; Dunham et al., 2013). We also evaluate ourselves partly by our group memberships. Having a sense of "we-ness" strengthens our self-concept. It *feels* good. We seek not only *respect* for ourselves but also *pride* in our groups (Greenaway et al., 2016; Sani et al., 2012). Moreover, seeing our groups as superior helps us to feel even better. It's as though we all think, "I am an X [name your group]. X is good. Therefore, I am good."

Lacking a positive personal identity, people often seek self-esteem by identifying with a group. Thus, many youths find pride, power, and identity in gang affiliations. Much as dissonance motivates its reduction and insecurity feeds authoritarianism, so too uncertainty motivates people to seek social identity. Their uncertainty subsides as they perceive who "we" and "they" are. Especially in a chaotic or an uncertain world, being part of a zealous, tightly knit group feels good; it validates who one is (Hogg et al., 2017). And that explains part of the appeal of extreme radical groups in today's world.

When people's personal and social identities become *fused*—when the boundary between self and group blurs—they become more willing to fight or die for their group (Gómez et al., 2011; Swann et al., 2009). Many patriotic individuals, for example, define themselves by their national identities (Staub, 1997b, 2005). And many people at loose ends find identity in their associations with new religious movements, self-help groups, or fraternal clubs (Figure 11–2).

Because of our social identifications, we conform to our group norms. We sacrifice ourselves for team, family, and nation. The more important our social identity and the more strongly attached we feel to a group, the more we react prejudicially to threats from another group (Crocker & Luhtanen, 1990).

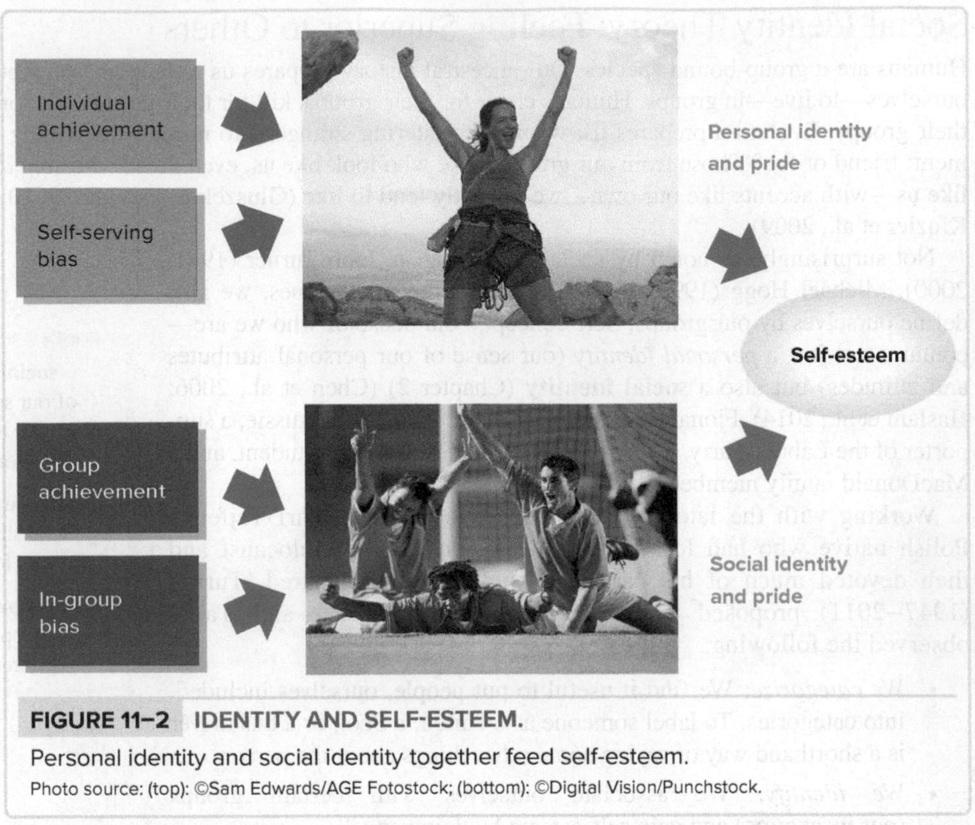

FIGURE 11–2 IDENTITY AND SELF-ESTEEM.

Personal identity and social identity together feed self-esteem.

Photo source: (top): ©Sam Edwards/AGE Fotostock; (bottom): ©Digital Vision/Punchstock.

In-group bias

The group definition of who you are—your race, religion, gender, academic major—implies a definition of who you are not. The circle that includes "us" (the in-group) excludes "them" (the out-group). The more that ethnic Turks in the Netherlands see themselves as Turks or as Muslims, the less they see themselves as Dutch (Verkuyten & Yildiz, 2007).

in-group bias The tendency to favour your own group.

The mere experience of being formed into groups may promote **in-group bias**. Ask children, "Which are better, the children in your school or the children at [another school nearby]?" Virtually all will say their own school has the better children.

In-group bias expresses and supports a positive self-concept

In-group bias is one more example of the human quest for a positive self-concept (Chapter 2). When our group has been successful, we can make ourselves feel better by identifying more strongly with it. College and university students whose team has just been victorious frequently report, "*We* won." After their team's defeat, students are more likely to say, "*They* lost." Basking in the reflected glory of a successful in-group is strongest among those who have just experienced an ego blow, such as learning they did poorly on a "creativity test" (Cialdini et al., 1976). We can also bask in the reflected glory of a friend's achievement—except when the friend outperforms us on something pertinent to our identity (Tesser, Millar, & Moore, 1988). If you think of yourself as an outstanding psychology student, you will likely take more pleasure in a friend's excellence in mathematics.

In-group bias feeds favouritism

We are so group conscious that, given any excuse to think of ourselves as a group, we will do so—and will then exhibit in-group bias. Even forming conspicuous groups on no logical basis—for instance, merely by composing groups X and Y with the flip of a coin—will produce some in-group bias (Billig & Tajfel, 1973; Brewer & Silver, 1978; Locksley et al., 1980). In Kurt Vonnegut's novel *Slapstick,* computers gave everyone a new middle name; all "Daffodil-11s" then felt unity with one another and distance from "Raspberry-13s." The self-serving bias (Chapter 2) rides again, enabling people to achieve a more positive social identity: "We" are better than "they," even when "we" and "they" are defined randomly!

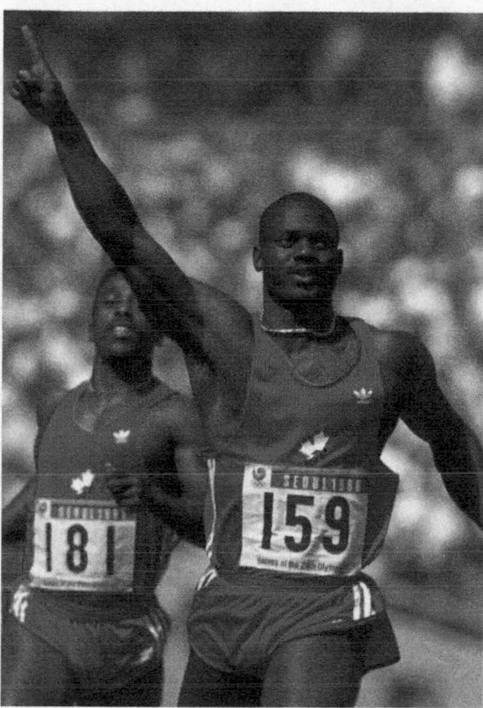

Basking in reflected glory: After Jamaican-Canadian sprinter Ben Johnson won the Olympic 100-metre race in 1988, Canadian media described this victory by a "Canadian." After Johnson's gold medal was taken away due to steroid use, Canadian media then emphasized his "Jamaican" identity (Stelzl, Janes, & Seligman, 2008).
Source: ©DIETER ENDLICHER/AP Images.

In a series of experiments, Tajfel and Michael Billig (1974; Tajfel, 1970, 1981, 1982) further explored how little it takes to provoke favouritism toward "us" and unfairness toward "them." In one study, Tajfel and Billig had British teenagers evaluate modern abstract paintings and then told them that they and some others had favoured the art of Paul Klee over that of Wassily Kandinsky, while others favoured Kandinsky. Finally, without ever meeting the other members of their Klee-favouring group, each teen divided some money among members of the Klee- and Kandinsky-favouring groups. In this and other experiments, defining groups even in this trivial way produced in-group favouritism. David Wilder (1981) summarized the typical result: "When given the opportunity to divide 15 points [worth money], subjects generally award 9 or 10 points to their own group and 5 or 6 points to the other group."

> ***"There is a tendency to define one's own group positively in order to evaluate oneself positively."***
>
> John C. Turner, "Social Identity," (1984)

We are more prone to in-group bias when our group is small and differs in status relative to the out-group (Ellemers et al., 1997; Mullen, Brown, & Smith, 1992). When we're part of a small group surrounded by a larger group, we are conscious of our group membership; when our in-group is the majority, we think less about it. To be a foreign student, to be gay or lesbian, or to be of a minority race or gender at some social gathering is to feel your own social identity more keenly and to react accordingly.

Must in-group liking foster out-group disliking?
Does in-group bias reflect liking for the in-group, dislike for the out-group, or both? Does ethnic pride cause prejudice? Does a strong feminist identity lead feminists to dislike non-feminists? Does loyalty to a particular university lead its students to deprecate students of other universities and those who don't go to university at all? Or do people merely favour their own group without any animosity toward others?

Experiments reveal both in-group liking and out-group disliking. Sometimes love and hate are opposite sides of the same coin. If you love the Toronto Blue Jays, you may hate the Detroit Tigers. Patriots' love of tribe or country motivates their fighting to defend it against enemies. To the extent that we see virtue in *us*, we likely see evil in *them*. Moreover, out-group stereotypes prosper when people feel their in-group identity most keenly, such as when they are with other in-group members (Wilder & Shapiro, 1991).

We also ascribe uniquely human emotions (love, hope, contempt, resentment) to in-group members and are more reluctant to see such human emotions in out-group members (Demoulin, Saroglou, & Van Pachterbeke, 2008; Leyens et al., 2003, 2007). There is a long history of denying human attributes to out-groups—a process called "infrahumanization."

European explorers pictured many of the peoples they encountered as savages ruled by animal instinct. "Africans have been likened to apes, Jews to vermin, and immigrants to parasites," noted Australian social psychologists Stephen Loughman and Nick Haslam (2007). We humanize pets and dehumanize out-groups.

Yet in-group bias and discrimination result less from hostility than from in-group favouritism (Balliet et al., 2014; Greenwald & Pettigrew, 2014). Bias is less a matter of dislike toward those who are different than of networking and mutual support among those in one's group. Even when there is no "them" (imagine yourself bonding with a handful of fellow survivors on a deserted island), one can come to love "us" (Gaertner et al., 2006). Thus, positive feelings for our own groups need not be mirrored by equally strong negative feelings for out-groups.

Need for status, self-regard, and belonging

Status is relative: To perceive ourselves as having status, we need people below us. Thus one psychological benefit of prejudice, or of any status system, is a feeling of superiority. Most of us can recall a time when we took secret satisfaction in someone else's failure—perhaps seeing a sibling punished or a classmate failing a test. In Europe and North America, prejudice is often greater among those low or slipping on the socioeconomic ladder and among those whose positive self-image is threatened (Lemyre & Smith, 1985; Pettigrew et al., 2008; Thompson & Crocker, 1985). In one study, members of lower-status sororities were more disparaging of other sororities than were members of higher-status sororities (Crocker et al., 1987). If our status is secure, we have less need to feel superior, and we express less prejudice (Ashton-James & Tracey, 2012).

> ***"Father, mother, and me, sister and auntie say all the people like us are We, and every one else is they. And they live over the sea, while we live over the way. But would you believe it? They look upon we as only a sort of they!"***
>
> Rudyard Kipling, "We and They," in *Debits and Credits,* 1926

In study after study, thinking about our own mortality—by writing a short essay on dying and the emotions aroused by thinking about death—also provokes enough insecurity to intensify in-group favouritism and out-group prejudice (Greenberg et al., 1990, 2013; Schimel et al., 2000, 2001). One study found that among Whites, thinking about death can even promote liking for racists who argue for their group's superiority (Greenberg et al., 2008). With death on their minds, people exhibit **terror management**. They shield themselves from the threat of their own death by derogating those whose challenges to their worldviews further arouse their anxiety. When people are already feeling vulnerable about their mortality, prejudice helps bolster a threatened belief system. But thinking about death can also heighten communal feelings, such as in-group identification, togetherness, and altruism (McGregor et al., 2001; Sani et al., 2009).

> **terror management** According to "terror management theory," people's self-protective emotional and cognitive responses (including adhering more strongly to their cultural worldviews and prejudices) when confronted with reminders of their mortality.

All this suggests that a man who doubts his own strength and independence might, by proclaiming women to be weak and dependent, boost his masculine image. Indeed, when university men in one study viewed young women's videotaped job interviews, men with low self-acceptance disliked strong, nontraditional women. Men with high self-acceptance preferred them (Grube et al., 1982). Similarly, a humiliating experience—accidentally knocking over a stack of someone's important computer cards—provoked English-speaking Canadian students to express increased hostility toward French-speaking Canadians (Meindl & Lerner, 1984). Experiments confirm the connection between self-image and prejudice: Affirm people and they will evaluate an out-group more positively; threaten their self-esteem and they will restore it by denigrating an out-group (Fein & Spencer, 1997; Spencer et al., 1998).

> ***"By exciting emulation and comparisons of superiority, you lay the foundation of lasting mischief; you make brothers and sisters hate each other."***
>
> Samuel Johnson, quoted in James Boswell's *Life of Samuel Johnson,* 1791

Despising out-groups strengthens the in-group. School spirit is seldom so strong as when the game is with the archrival. The sense of comradeship among workers is often highest when they all feel a

THE INSIDE STORY

I grew up in Toronto and watched it evolve from a very homogeneous city to one of the most ethnically diverse cities in the world. This planted the seed for my later interest in studying intergroup attitudes. I began to study intergroup attitudes as a postdoctoral fellow at the University of Waterloo in the late 1980s, conducting research on the effects of mood on the expression of ethnic stereotypes, and the role of values, stereotypes, and emotions in determining intergroup attitudes. Since then, my interest in this topic has moved in several different directions. One important direction is the investigation of attitudes toward immigrants and immigration, which again came out of my experiences in Toronto. It struck me that immigrants seemed to be the target of considerable prejudice and discrimination, even among people who were themselves immigrants only a generation or two ago. In addition, it seemed that people justified their negative attitudes and behaviour toward immigrants on the basis of competition for resources, such as jobs. This led to my research on the role of group competition in determining prejudice and discrimination toward immigrants. I feel fortunate to be able to work in an area in which I can apply theory and research in social psychology to important social issues.

Source: ©Victor Korchenko/Alamy Stock Photo.

Victoria Esses *University of Western Ontario*

common antagonism toward management. To solidify the Nazi hold over Germany, Hitler threatened Germans with the "Jewish menace."

When the need to belong is met, people become more accepting of out-groups, report Mario Mikulincer and Phillip Shaver (2001). They subliminally primed some Israeli students with words that fostered a sense of belonging (*love, support, hug*) and primed others with neutral words. The students then read an essay that was supposedly written by a fellow Jewish student and another by an Arab student. When primed with neutral words, the Israeli students evaluated the supposed Israeli student's essay as superior to the supposed Arab student's essay. When the participants were primed with a sense of belonging, that bias disappeared.

Motivation to Avoid Prejudice

Motivations lead people not only to be prejudiced but also to avoid prejudice. But try as we might to suppress unwanted thoughts—thoughts about food, thoughts about romance with a friend's partner, judgmental thoughts about another group—they sometimes refuse to go away (Macrae, Bodenhausen, et al., 1994; Macrae, Stangor, et al., 1994; Wegner & Erber, 1992). This is especially so for older adults, who lose some of their ability to inhibit unwanted thoughts and, therefore, to suppress old stereotypes (von Hippel, Silver, & Lynch, 2000). Patricia Devine and her colleagues (1989; Forscher & Devine, 2014) report that people low and high in prejudice sometimes have similar automatic (unintentional) prejudicial responses. The result: Unwanted (dissonant) thoughts and feelings often persist. Breaking the prejudice habit is not easy.

In real life, a majority person's encountering a minority person may trigger a knee-jerk stereotype. Those with accepting attitudes and those with disapproving attitudes toward gay people may both feel uncomfortable sitting with a gay male on a bus seat (Monteith, 1993).

Encountering an unfamiliar Black male, White people—even those who pride themselves on not being prejudiced—may respond warily. Seeking not to appear prejudiced, they may divert their attention away from the person (Richeson & Trawalter, 2008).

Researchers who study stereotyping contend, however, that prejudicial reactions are not inevitable (Crandall, Eshleman, & O'Brien, 2002; Kunda & Spencer, 2003). The motivation to avoid prejudice can lead people to modify their thoughts and actions. Aware of the gap between how they *should* feel and how they *do* feel, self-conscious people will feel guilt and try to inhibit their prejudicial response (Bodenhausen & Macrae, 1998; Dasgupta & Rivera, 2006; Zuwerink et al., 1996). Even automatic prejudices subside, noted Devine and her colleagues (2005), when people's motivation to avoid prejudice is internal (because they believe prejudice is wrong) rather than external (because they don't want others to think badly of them).

The moral: Overcoming what Devine called "the prejudice habit" isn't easy. But it can be done. One team of 24 researchers held a "research contest" that compared 17 interventions for reducing implicit prejudice among more than 17 000 individuals (Lai et al., 2014). Eight of the interventions proved effective, especially those giving people experiences with vivid, positive examples of Black people who countered stereotypes. A similar technique, with people going door to door and having 10-minute nonjudgmental conversations, also worked to reduce prejudice against transgender individuals (Broockman & Kalla, 2016). In another study, Devine and her colleagues (2005) raised the awareness and concern of willing volunteers and trained them to replace biased with unbiased knee-jerk responses. Throughout the two-year study follow-up period, participants in the experimental intervention condition displayed reduced implicit prejudice. If you find yourself reacting with knee-jerk presumptions or feelings, don't despair; that's not unusual. It's what you do with that awareness that matters. Do you let those feelings hijack your behaviour? Or do you compensate by monitoring and correcting your behaviour in future situations?

What Are the Cognitive Sources of Prejudice?

What are the different cognitive sources of prejudice?

How does the way we think about the world influence our stereotypes? And how do our stereotypes affect our everyday judgments? Stereotypes, beliefs, and prejudiced attitudes exist not only because of socialization and because they displace hostilities but also as by-products of normal thinking processes. Stereotypes spring less from malice of the heart than from the machinery of the mind. Like perceptual illusions, which are by-products of our knack for interpreting the world, stereotypes can be by-products of how we simplify our complex worlds.

Categorization: Classifying People Into Groups

One way we simplify our environment is to *categorize*—to organize the world by clustering objects into groups (Macrae & Bodenhausen, 2000, 2001). A biologist classifies plants and animals. A human classifies people. Having done so, we think about them more easily. If persons in a group share some similarities—if most MENSA members are smart, and most basketball players are tall—knowing their group memberships can provide useful information with minimal effort (Macrae, Stangor, & Milne, 1994). Stereotypes sometimes offer "a beneficial ratio of information gained to effort expended" (Sherman et al., 1998). Stereotypes represent cognitive efficiency: They are energy-saving schemes for making speedy judgments and predicting how others will think and act. We judge people in out-groups more quickly;

when assessing in-group individuals, we take longer to form impressions (Vala et al., 2012). Thus, stereotypes and out-group bias may have served ultimate, evolutionary functions by enabling our ancestors to cope and survive (Navarrete et al., 2010).

Spontaneous categorization

We find it especially easy and efficient to rely on stereotypes when we are

- pressed for time (Kaplan, Wanshula, & Zanna, 1993),
- preoccupied (Gilbert & Hixon, 1991),
- tired (Bodenhausen, 1990), and
- emotionally aroused (Esses, Haddock, & Zanna, 1993b; Stroessner & Mackie, 1993).

Ethnicity and sex are, in our current world, powerful ways of categorizing people. Imagine Julius, a 45-year-old Black real estate agent in New Brunswick. We suspect that your image of "Black male" predominates over the categories "middle-aged," "business-person," and "Maritimer."

Experiments expose our spontaneous categorization of people by race. Much as we organize what is actually a colour continuum into what we perceive as distinct colours, such as red, blue, and green, so our "discontinuous minds" (Dawkins, 1993) cannot resist categorizing people into groups. We label people of widely varying ancestry as simply "Black" or "White," as if such categories were black and white. By itself, such categorization is not prejudice, but it does provide a foundation for prejudice.

Perceived similarities and differences

Picture the following objects: apples, chairs, pencils.

There is a strong tendency to see objects within a group as being more uniform than they really are. Were your apples all red? Your chairs, all straight-backed? Your pencils, all yellow? Once we classify two days as in the same month, they seem more alike, temperature-wise, than the same interval across months. People guess the eight-day average temperature difference between, say, November 15 and 23 to be less than the eight-day difference between November 30 and December 8 (Krueger & Clement, 1994).

It's the same with people. When we assign people to groups—athletes, drama majors, math professors—we are likely to exaggerate the similarities within the groups and the differences between them (S. E. Taylor, 1981; Wilder, 1978). We assume that other groups are more homogeneous than our own. Mere division into groups can create an **out-group homogeneity effect**—a sense that *they* are "all alike" and different from "us" and "our" group (Ostrom & Sedikides, 1992). Consider:

out-group homogeneity effect
Perception of out-group members as more similar to one another than are in-group members. Thus, "they are alike; we are diverse."

- Many non-Europeans see the Swiss as a fairly homogeneous people. But to the people of Switzerland, the Swiss are diverse, encompassing groups who speak French, German, Italian, and Romansh.
- Many non-Latino Americans lump "Latinos" together. Mexican Americans, Cuban Americans, and Puerto Ricans—among others—see important differences (Huddy & Virtanen, 1995).
- Sorority sisters perceive the members of any other sorority as less diverse than the members of their own (Park & Rothbart, 1982).

"Women are more like each other than men [are]."
Lord (not Lady) Chesterfield

In general, the greater our familiarity with a social group, the more we see its diversity (Brown & Wootton-Millward, 1993; Linville, Gischer, & Salovey, 1989). The less our familiarity, the more we stereotype.

Perhaps you have noticed: *They*—the members of any racial group other than your own—even *look* alike. Many people can recall embarrassing ourselves by confusing two people of

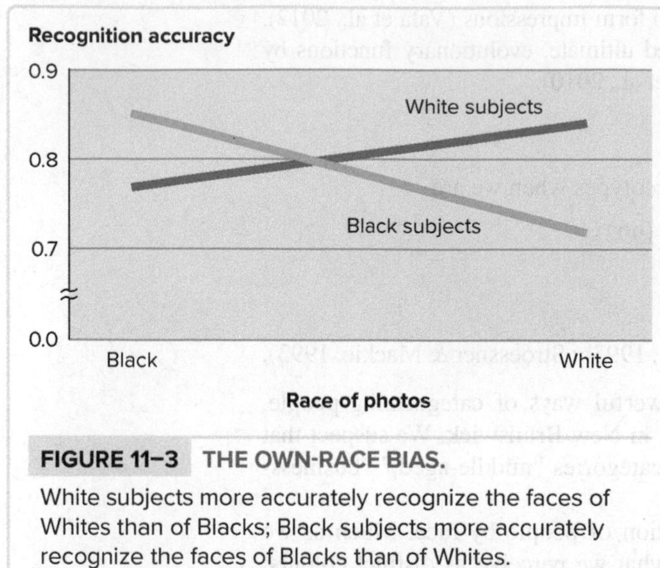

FIGURE 11–3 THE OWN-RACE BIAS.

White subjects more accurately recognize the faces of Whites than of Blacks; Black subjects more accurately recognize the faces of Blacks than of Whites.

another racial group, prompting the person we've misnamed to say, "You think we all look alike." Experiments in the United States, Scotland, and Germany reveal that people of other races do, in fact, *seem* to look more alike than do people of your own race (Chance & Goldstein, 1981; Ellis, 1981; Meissner & Brigham, 2001; Sporer & Horry, 2011). When White students are shown faces of a few White and a few Black individuals and then asked to pick these individuals out of a photographic lineup, they show an **own-race bias**: They more accurately recognize the White faces than the Black, and they often falsely recognize Black faces never before seen. (See Figure 11–3.) (Individuals do differ, however, with some showing no own-race bias while others have an extreme inability to recognize other-race faces [Wan et al., 2017].)

own-race bias The tendency for people to more accurately recognize faces of their own race.

As Figure 11–3 illustrates, Blacks more easily recognize another Black than they do a White, and vice versa (Bothwell et al., 1989). Hispanics, Blacks, and Asians all recognize faces from their own races better than from one another's (Gross, 2009). Likewise, British South Asians are quicker than White Brits to recognize South Asian faces (Walker & Hewstone, 2008). And 10- to 15-year-old Turkish children are quicker than Austrian children to recognize Turkish faces (Sporer et al., 2007). Even infants as young as nine months display better own-race recognition of faces (Kelly et al., 2005, 2007; Sugden & Marquie, 2017).

The term "own-race bias" is a misnomer in the case of Anglo and Hispanic identifications. Most Hispanic people are classified as Caucasians.

It's not that we cannot perceive differences among faces of another group. Rather, when looking at a face from another racial group, we often pay attention, first, to race ("that man is Black") rather than to individual features. When viewing someone of our own race, we are less attentive to the race category and more attentive to individual details, such as the eyes (Kawakami et al., 2014; Shriver et al., 2008; Young, Bernstein, & Hugenberg, 2010).

Our attending to someone's being in a different social category may also be contributing to a parallel *own-age bias*—the tendency for both children and older adults to more accurately identify faces from their own age groups (Anastasi & Rhodes, 2005, 2006; He, Ebner, & Johnson, 2011; Wright & Stroud, 2002). (Perhaps you have noticed that senior citizens look more alike than your fellow students do?)

Distinctiveness: Perceiving People Who Stand Out

Other ways we perceive our worlds also breed stereotypes. Distinctive people and vivid or extreme occurrences often capture attention and distort judgments.

Distinctive people

Have you ever found yourself in a situation where you were the only person of your gender, race, or nationality? If so, your difference from the others probably made you more noticeable and the object of more attention. A Black person in an otherwise White group, a male in an otherwise female group, and a female in an otherwise male group seem more prominent and influential; they appear to have exaggerated good and bad qualities (Crocker & McGraw, 1984; S. E. Taylor et al., 1979). When someone in a group is made conspicuous, we tend to see that person as causing whatever happens (S. E. Taylor & Fiske, 1978). If we are positioned to look at Joe, even if Joe is merely an average group member, Joe will seem to have a greater-than-average influence on the group.

Have you noticed that people also define you by your most distinctive traits and behaviours? Tell people about someone who is a skydiver and a tennis player, reported Lori Nelson and Dale Miller (1995), and they will think of the person as a skydiver. Asked to choose a gift book for the person, they will pick a skydiving book over a tennis book. A person who has both a pet snake and a pet dog is seen more as a snake owner than as a dog owner.

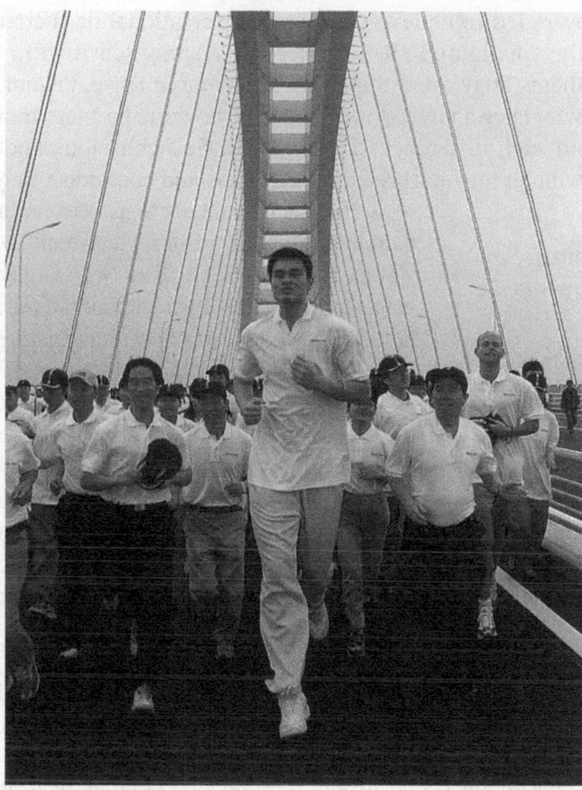

Distinctive people, such as the Houston Rockets' 7'6" player Yao Ming, now retired, draw attention.

Source: ©Eugene Hoshiko/AP Images.

Ellen Langer and Lois Imber (1980) cleverly demonstrated the attention that is paid to distinctive people. They asked Harvard students to watch a video of a man reading. The students paid closer attention when they were led to think he was out of the ordinary—a cancer patient, gay, or a millionaire. They detected characteristics that other viewers ignored, and their evaluation of him was more extreme. Those who thought the man was a cancer patient noticed distinctive facial characteristics and bodily movements and thus perceived him as much more "different from most people" than did the other viewers. The extra attention we pay to distinctive people creates an illusion that they differ more from others than they really do. If people thought you had a genius-level IQ, they would probably notice things about you that otherwise would pass unnoticed.

Distinctiveness feeds self-consciousness

When surrounded by Whites, Blacks sometimes detect people reacting to their distinctiveness. Many report being stared or glared at, being subject to insensitive comments, and receiving bad service (Swim, Cohen, & Hyers, 1998). Whites, when alone amid those of another race, may be similarly sensitive to others' reactions. Sometimes, however, we misperceive others as reacting to our distinctiveness. Researchers Robert Kleck and Angelo Strenta (1980) discovered this when they led Dartmouth College women to feel disfigured. The women thought the purpose of the experiment was to assess how someone would react to a facial scar created with theatrical makeup; the scar was on the right cheek, running from the ear to the mouth. Actually, the purpose was to see how the women themselves, when made to feel deviant, would perceive others' behaviour toward them. After applying the makeup, the experimenter gave each woman a small hand mirror so that she could see the authentic-looking scar. When the woman put the mirror down, the experimenter then applied some "moisturizer" to "keep the makeup from cracking." What the "moisturizer" really did was remove the scar.

The scene that followed was poignant. A young woman, feeling terribly self-conscious about her supposedly disfigured face, talked with another woman who saw no such disfigurement and knew nothing of what had gone on before. If you have ever felt similarly self-conscious—perhaps about a physical handicap, acne, or even just a bad hair day—then perhaps you can empathize with the self-conscious woman. Compared with women who were led to believe that their conversational partners merely thought they had an allergy, the "disfigured" women became acutely sensitive to how their partners were looking at them. They rated their partners as more tense, distant, and patronizing. In fact, observers who later analyzed videotapes of how the partners treated "disfigured" persons could find no such differences in treatment. Self-conscious about being different, the "disfigured" women misinterpreted mannerisms and comments they would otherwise not have noticed.

Self-conscious interactions between a majority and a minority person can, therefore, feel tense even when both are well-intentioned (Devine, Evett, & Vasquez-Suson, 1996). Tom, who is gay, meets Bill, who is straight and who wants to respond to Tom without prejudice. But, feeling unsure of himself, Bill holds back a bit. Tom, expecting negative attitudes from most people, misreads Bill's hesitancy as hostility and responds with a seeming chip on his shoulder.

"If we foresee evil in our fellow man, we tend to provoke it; if good, we elicit it."

Gordon Allport, *The Nature of Prejudice*, 1958

Anyone can experience this phenomenon. Majority group members (in one study, White residents of Manitoba) often have beliefs—"meta-stereotypes"—about how minorities stereotype them (Vorauer, Main, & O'Connell, 1998). Even relatively unprejudiced Canadian Whites, Israeli Jews, or American Christians may sense that out-group minorities stereotype them as prejudiced, arrogant, or patronizing. If George worries that Gamal perceives him as "your typical educated racist," he may be self-consciously on guard when talking with Gamal.

Vivid cases

Our minds also use distinctive cases as a shortcut to judging groups. Are the Japanese good baseball players? "Well, there's Ichiro Suzuki and Hideki Matsui and Yu Darvish. Yeah, I'd say so." Note the thought processes at work here: If one has limited experience with a particular social group, they recall examples of it and generalize from those (Sherman, 1996). Moreover, encountering exemplars of negative stereotypes can prime the stereotype, leading people to minimize contact with the group (Hendersen-King & Nisbett, 1996).

Such generalizing from single cases can cause problems. Vivid instances, though more available in memory, are seldom representative of the larger group. Exceptional athletes, though distinctive and memorable, are not the best basis for judging the distribution of athletic talent in an entire group.

Those in a numerical minority, being more distinctive, also may be numerically overestimated by the majority. What proportion of your country's population would you say is Muslim? People in non-Muslim countries often overestimate this proportion. (In Canada, for example, 3.2 percent declared themselves as Muslim in the 2011 census.) Consider a U.S. poll that found that the average American thought that 25 percent of people are exclusively gay (Morales, 2011). The best evidence suggests that 4 percent or fewer have a same-sex orientation (Chandra et al., 2011; Gates, 2017; Herbenick et al., 2010).

Myron Rothbart and his colleagues (1978) showed how distinctive cases also fuel stereotypes. They had University of Oregon students view 50 slides, each of which stated a man's height. For one group of students, 10 of the men were identified as being slightly over 6 feet (up to 6 feet, 4 inches). For other students, these 10 men were identified as being well over 6 feet (up to 6 feet, 11 inches). When asked later how many of the men were over 6 feet, those given the moderately tall examples recalled 5 percent too many. Those given the extremely tall examples recalled 50 percent too many. In a follow-up experiment, students read descriptions of the actions of 50 men, 10 of whom had committed either nonviolent crimes, such as forgery, or violent crimes, such as rape. Of those shown the list with the violent crimes, most overestimated the number of criminal acts. Vivid cases distort judgments and create stereotypes.

Distinctive events foster illusory correlations

Stereotypes assume a correlation between group membership and individuals' characteristics ("Italians are emotional," "Jews are shrewd," "Accountants are perfectionists"). Often, people's stereotypes are accurate (Jussim, 2012). But sometimes our attentiveness to unusual occurrences creates illusory correlations (see Chapter 3). Because we are sensitive to distinctive events, the co-occurrence of two such events is especially noticeable—more noticeable than each of the times the unusual events do *not* occur together.

In a classic experiment, David Hamilton and Robert Gifford (1976) demonstrated illusory correlation in a clever experiment. They showed students slides on which various people, members of "Group A" or "Group B," were said to have done something desirable or undesirable; for example, "John, a member of Group A, visited a sick friend in the hospital." Twice as many statements described members of Group A as Group B, but both groups did nine desirable acts for every four undesirable behaviours. Since both Group B and the undesirable acts were less frequent, their co-occurrence—for example, "Allen, a member of Group B, dented the fender of a parked car and didn't leave his name"—was an unusual combination that caught people's attention. The students then overestimated the frequency with which the "minority" group (B) acted undesirably and judged Group B more harshly.

Remember, Group B members actually committed undesirable acts in the same *proportion* as Group A members (thus they committed only half as many). Moreover, the students had no pre-existing biases for or against Group B, and they received the information more systematically than daily experience ever offers it. Although researchers debate why it happens, they agree that illusory correlation occurs and provides yet another source for the formation of racial stereotypes (Berndsen et al., 2002). Thus, the features that most distinguish a minority from a majority are those that become associated with it (Sherman et al., 2009). Your ethnic or social group may be like other groups in most ways, but people will notice how it differs.

In experiments, even single co-occurrences of an unusual act by someone in an atypical group—"Ben, a Jehovah's Witness, owns a pet sloth"—can embed illusory correlations in people's minds (Risen, Gilovich, & Dunning, 2007). This enables the mass media to feed illusory correlations. When a self-described gay person murders someone, their sexual orientation is often mentioned. When a straight person does the same, the person's sexual orientation is seldom mentioned. Such reporting adds to the illusion of a large correlation between (1) violent tendencies and (2) gay people or mental hospitalization.

Unlike the students who judged Groups A and B, we often have pre-existing biases. David Hamilton's further research with Terrence Rose (1980) revealed that our pre-existing stereotypes can lead us to "see" correlations that aren't there. The researchers had University of California Santa Barbara students read sentences in which various adjectives described the members of different occupational groups ("Juan, an accountant, is timid and thoughtful"). In actuality, each occupation was described equally often by each adjective; accountants, doctors, and salespeople were equally often timid, wealthy, and talkative. The students, however, *thought* they had more often read descriptions of timid accountants, wealthy doctors, and talkative salespeople. Their stereotyping led them to perceive correlations that weren't there, thus helping to perpetuate the stereotypes.

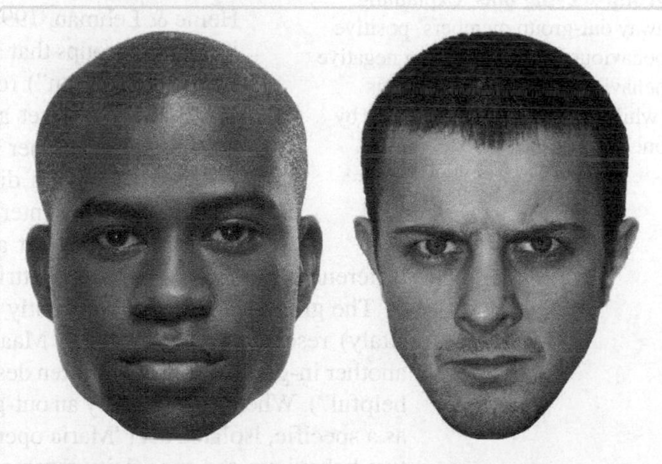

FIGURE 11–4 IN-GROUP BIASES INFLUENCE PERCEPTIONS.

When briefly shown two faces, one neutral, one angry, people more often misrecalled the Black rather than the White face as angry (Becker et al., 2010).

Photo source: (left): ©Paul Burns/Getty Images; (right): ©Cordelia Molloy/Science Source.

Likewise, guess what happened when Vaughn Becker and his colleagues (2010) invited university students to view a White and a Black face—one angry, one not—for one-tenth of a second (see Figure 11–4). The participants' subsequent recollections of what they had viewed revealed racial bias: "White anger flowed to neutral Black faces (34 percent likelihood) more readily than Black anger flowed to neutral White faces (19 percent likelihood)."

Attributions: Is It a Just World?

In explaining others' actions, we frequently commit the fundamental attribution error (Chapter 3): We attribute others' behaviour so much to their inner dispositions that we discount important situational forces. The error occurs partly because our attention focuses on the person, not on the situation. A person's race or sex is vivid and gets attention; the situational forces working on that person are usually less visible. Slavery was often overlooked as an explanation for the behaviour of people who were enslaved; the behaviour was instead attributed to the enslaved people's own nature.

Until recently, the same was true of how we explained the perceived differences between women and men. Because gender-role constraints were hard to see, we attributed men's and women's behaviour solely to their innate dispositions. The more people assume that human traits are fixed dispositions, the stronger are their stereotypes and the greater their acceptance of racial inequalities (Levy, Stroessner, & Dweck, 1998; Williams & Eberhardt, 2008).

Group-serving bias

Thomas Pettigrew (1979, 1980) showed how attribution errors can bias people's explanations of group members' behaviours. We grant members of our own group the benefit of the doubt: "She donated because she has a good heart; he refused because he's using every penny to help support his mother." When explaining acts by members of other groups, we more often assume the worst: "She donated to gain favour; he refused because he's selfish." In one classic study, the light shove that Whites perceive as mere "horsing around" when done by another White person became a "violent gesture" when done by a Black person (Duncan, 1976).

Positive behaviour by out-group members is more often dismissed. It may be seen as a "special case" ("He is certainly bright and hard-working—not at all like other …"), as owing to luck or some special advantage ("She probably got admitted just because her med school had to fill its quota for women applicants"), as demanded by the situation ("Under the circumstances, what could the cheap Scot do but pay the whole cheque?"), or as attributable to extra effort ("Asian students get better grades because they're so compulsive").

group-serving bias Explaining away out-group members' positive behaviours; also attributing negative behaviours to their dispositions (while excusing such behaviour by one's own group).

Disadvantaged groups and groups that stress modesty (such as the Chinese) exhibit less of this **group-serving bias** (Fletcher & Ward, 1989; Heine & Lehman, 1997b; Jackson, Sullivan, & Hodge, 1993). By contrast, immodest groups that are invested in their own greatness (that display "collective narcissism") react to threats with group-serving bias and hostility (Golec de Zavala et al., 2013). University of Manitoba social psychologists Jacquie Vorauer and Stacey Sasaki (2010, 2011) note that multiculturalism's focus on differences, which can be positive in the absence of conflict (making intergroup exchanges seem interesting and stimulating), sometimes comes at a cost. When there is conflict or threat, a focus on differences can foster group-level attributions and increased hostility.

The group-serving bias can subtly colour our language. A team of University of Padua (Italy) researchers led by Anne Maass (1995, 1999) found that positive behaviours by another in-group member are often described as general dispositions (for example, "Lucy is helpful"). When performed by an out-group member, the same behaviour is often described as a specific, isolated act ("Maria opened the door for the man with the cane"). With negative behaviour, the specificity reverses: "Eric shoved her" (an isolated act by an in-group member) but "Enrique was aggressive" (an out-group member's general disposition).

Earlier we noted that blaming the victim can justify the blamer's own superior status (see Table 11–1). Blaming occurs as people attribute an out-group's failures to its members' flawed dispositions, noted Miles Hewstone (1990): "They fail because they're stupid; we fail because we didn't try." If women, Blacks, or Jews have been abused, they must somehow have brought it on themselves. When the British made a group of German

TABLE 11-1 How Self-Enhancing Social Identities Support Stereotypes.		
	In-Group	**Out-Group**
Attitude	Favouritism	Denigration
Perceptions	Heterogeneity (we differ)	Homogeneity (they're all alike)
Attributions for negative behaviour	To situations	To dispositions

civilians walk through the Bergen–Belsen concentration camp at the close of the Second World War, one German responded, "What terrible criminals these prisoners must have been to receive such treatment." (Such group-serving bias illustrates the motivations that underlie prejudice, as well as the cognition. Motivation and cognition, emotion and thinking, are inseparable.)

Motivation to See the World as Just

In a series of experiments conducted at the University of Waterloo and the University of Kentucky, Melvin Lerner and his colleagues (Lerner & Miller, 1978; Lerner, 1980) discovered that merely *observing* an innocent person being victimized is enough to make the victim seem less worthy.

Lerner (1980) noted that the unfortunate and problematic tendency to disparage hapless victims results from the human need to believe that "I am a just person living in a just world, a world where people get what they deserve." From early childhood, we are taught that good is rewarded and evil punished. We are told that hard work and virtue pay dividends; laziness and immorality do not. From this, it is but a short leap to assume that those who flourish must be good and those who suffer must deserve their fate.

Numerous studies have confirmed this **just-world phenomenon** (Hafer & Bègue, 2005). Imagine that you, along with some others, are participating in one of Lerner's studies—supposedly on the perception of emotional cues (Lerner & Simmons, 1966). One of the participants, a confederate, is selected by lottery to perform a memory task. This person receives painful shocks whenever they give a wrong answer. You and the others note their emotional responses.

just-world phenomenon People's tendency to believe that the world is just and that, therefore, people get what they deserve and deserve what they get.

After watching the victim receive these apparently painful shocks, the experimenter asks you to evaluate the victim. How would you respond? With compassionate sympathy? We might expect so. As Ralph Waldo Emerson wrote, "The martyr cannot be dishonoured." On the contrary, in these experiments, the martyrs *were* dishonoured. When observers were powerless to alter the victim's fate, they often rejected and devalued the victim. Juvenal, the Roman satirist, anticipated these results: "The Roman mob follows after Fortune … and hates those who have been condemned." And the more ongoing the suffering, as with Jews even after the Holocaust, the greater the dislike of the victims (Imhoff & Banse, 2009).

Linda Carli and her colleagues (Carli, 1999; Carli & Leonard, 1989) reported that this just-world phenomenon colours our impressions of rape victims. Carli had people read detailed descriptions of interactions between a man and a woman. In one scenario, a woman and her boss meet for dinner, go to his home, and each have a glass of wine. Some read a scenario that has a happy ending: "Then he led me to the couch. He held my hand and asked me to marry him." In hindsight, people find the ending unsurprising and admire the man's and woman's character traits. Others read the same scenario with a different ending: "But then he became very rough and pushed me onto the couch. He held me down on the couch and raped me." Given this ending, people see it as inevitable and blame the woman for provocative behaviour that seems faultless in the first scenario.

Carolyn Hafer of Brock University and her colleagues (Hafer, 2000; Hafer & Bègue, 2005; Hafer & Olson, 2003) find that blameless victims threaten people's sense of justice. Participants who observed a boy describing being beaten and robbed while travelling in South America (compared to those who did not) took longer to recognize words related to justice, much like spider phobics take longer to recognize words related to spiders. They also distanced themselves from the victim by reporting that they were not like him. The more they distanced themselves from him, the more they derogated him. Confronted with an innocent victim of a serious crime, people avoid thinking about justice, blame the victim, and see themselves as different from the victim.

Research on belief in a just world suggests that people are indifferent to social injustice, not because they have no concern for justice but because they see no injustice. Those who assume the world is just believe that:

- rape victims must have behaved seductively (Borgida & Brekke, 1985)
- battered spouses must have provoked their beatings (Summers & Feldman, 1984)
- poor people don't deserve better (Furnham & Gunter, 1984)
- sick people are responsible for their illnesses (Gruman & Sloan, 1983), and
- teens who are bullied online deserve it (Chapin & Coleman, 2017).

Such beliefs enable successful people to reassure themselves that they, too, deserve what they have. The wealthy and healthy can see their own good fortune, and others' misfortune, as justly deserved. Linking good fortune with virtue and misfortune with moral failure enables the fortunate to feel pride and to avoid responsibility for the unfortunate. But on the positive side, believing the world is just also motivates us to invest our energies in long-term goals (Hafer & Sutton, 2016).

People loathe a loser even when the loser's misfortune obviously stems from mere bad luck. Children, for example, tend to view lucky others—such as someone who has found money on a sidewalk—as more likely than unlucky children to do good things and be a nice person (Olson et al., 2008). Adults *know* that gambling outcomes are just good or bad luck and should not affect their evaluations of the gambler. Still, they can't resist playing Monday-morning quarterback—judging people by their results. Ignoring the fact that reasonable decisions can bring bad results, they judge losers as less competent (Baron & Hershey, 1988). Lawyers and stock market speculators may similarly judge themselves by their outcomes, becoming smug after successes and self-reproachful after failures. Talent and initiative matter. But the just-world assumption discounts the uncontrollable factors that can derail good efforts even by talented people.

When people violate our stereotypes, we salvage the stereotype by splitting off a new subgroup stereotype, such as "senior athletes."

Source: ©Shih-Hao Liao/123RF.

Just-world thinking also leads people to justify their culture's familiar social systems (Jost et al., 2009; Kay et al., 2009; Osborne & Sibley, 2013). The way things are, we're inclined to think, is the way things essentially are and ought to be (Brescoll et al., 2013; Hussak & Cimpian, 2015). Such natural conservatism makes it difficult to pass new social policies, such as voting rights laws or tax or health-care reform. But after a new policy is in place, our "system justification" works to sustain it. Thus, Canadians mostly approve of our government policies, such as national health care, strict gun control, and no capital punishment, whereas Americans likewise mostly support differing policies to which they are accustomed.

What Are the Consequences of Prejudice?

How can stereotypes create their own reality? How can prejudice impede performance? Prejudice has consequences as well as causes.

Self-Perpetuating Prejudgments

Prejudice involves preconceived judgments. Prejudgments are inevitable: None of us is a dispassionate bookkeeper of social happenings, tallying evidence for and against our biases. Our prejudgments matter.

"It is understandable that the suppressed people should develop an intense hostility towards a culture whose existence they make possible by their work, but in whose wealth they have too small a share."

Sigmund Freud, *The Future of an Illusion*, 1927

Prejudgments guide our attention and our memories. People who accept gender stereotypes often misrecall their own school grades in stereotype-consistent ways. For example, women often recall receiving worse math grades and better arts grades than were actually the case (Chatard, Guimond, & Selimbegovic, 2007).

Moreover, after we judge an item as belonging to a category, such as a particular race or gender, our memory for it shifts toward the features we associate with that category. In one experiment, Belgian university students viewed a face that was a blend of 70 percent of the features of the typical male and 30 percent of the typical female (or vice versa). Later, those shown the 70 percent of the features of a typical male recalled seeing a male (as you might expect) but also misrecalled the face as being even more prototypically male (Huart et al., 2005).

Prejudgments are self-perpetuating. Whenever a group member behaves as expected, we duly note the fact; our prior belief is confirmed. When a member of a group behaves inconsistently with our expectation, we may explain away the behaviour as due to special circumstances (Crocker, Hannah, & Weber, 1983).

Perhaps you can recall a time when, try as you might, you could not overcome someone's opinion of you, a time when no matter what you did you were misinterpreted. Misinterpretations are likely when someone *expects* an unpleasant encounter with you (Wilder & Shapiro, 1989). William Ickes and his colleagues (1982) demonstrated this in an experiment with pairs of university-age men. As the men arrived, the experimenters falsely forewarned one member of each pair that the other subject was "one of the *unfriendliest* people I've talked to lately." The two were then introduced and left alone together for five minutes. Students in another condition were led to think that the other subject was exceptionally *friendly*.

Those who expected him to be *un*friendly went out of their way to be friendly, and their friendly behaviour elicited a warm response. But unlike the positively biased students, their expecting an unfriendly person led them to attribute this reciprocal friendliness to their own "kid-gloves" treatment of him. Afterwards, they expressed more mistrust and dislike for the person and rated his behaviour as less friendly. Despite their partner's actual friendliness, the negative bias induced these students to "see" hostilities lurking beneath his "forced smiles." They would never have seen it if they hadn't believed it.

We do notice information that is strikingly inconsistent with a stereotype, but even this information has less impact than we might expect. When we focus on an atypical

subtyping Accommodating groups of individuals who deviate from one's stereotype by thinking of them as a special category of people with different properties.

subgrouping Accommodating groups of individuals who deviate from one's stereotype by forming a new stereotype about this subset of the group.

example, we can salvage the stereotype by splitting off a new category (Brewer, 1988; Hewstone, 1994; Kunda & Oleson, 1995, 1997). The positive image that British schoolchildren formed of their friendly school police officers (whom they perceived as a special category) didn't improve their image of police officers in general (Hewstone, Hopkins, & Routh, 1992). This **subtyping**—putting people who deviate into a different class of people—helps maintain the stereotype that police officers are unfriendly and dangerous. High-prejudice people tend to subtype *positive* out-group members (seeing them as atypical exceptions); low-prejudice people more often subtype *negative* out-group members (Riek et al., 2013).

A different way to accommodate the inconsistent information is to form a new stereotype for those who don't fit the original stereotype. Recognizing that the stereotype does not apply to everyone in the category, homeowners who have "desirable" Black neighbours can form a new and different stereotype of "professional, middle-class Blacks." This **subgrouping**—forming a subgroup stereotype—tends to lead to modest change in the stereotype as the stereotype becomes more differentiated (Richards & Hewstone, 2001). Subtypes are *exceptions* to the group; subgroups are acknowledged as a *part* of the overall diverse group.

Discrimination's Impact: The Self-Fulfilling Prophecy

Attitudes may coincide with the social hierarchy not only as a rationalization for it but also because discrimination affects its victims. "One's reputation," wrote Gordon Allport, "cannot be hammered, hammered, hammered into one's head without doing something to one's character" (1958, p. 139). If we could snap our fingers and end all discrimination today, the tough times would not instantly end for people who have been systematically targeted by discrimination. When the oppression ends, its effects linger, like a societal hangover.

In *The Nature of Prejudice,* Allport (1954) catalogued 15 possible effects of victimization. Allport believed these reactions were reducible to two basic types: (1) those that involve *blaming oneself* (withdrawal, self-hate, aggression against your own group) and (2) those that involve *blaming external causes* (fighting back, suspiciousness, increased group pride). If victimization takes a toll—for instance, resulting in higher crime rates—people can use the result to justify the discrimination: "If we let those people into our nice neighbourhood, property values will plummet."

"If we foresee evil in our fellow man, we tend to provoke it; if good, we elicit it."

Gordon Allport, *The Nature of Prejudice,* 1958

Discrimination *does* significantly affect its victims. Social beliefs can be self-confirming, as demonstrated in a clever pair of experiments by Carl Word, Mark Zanna, and Joel Cooper (1974). In the first experiment, Princeton University White male volunteers interviewed White and Black research assistants posing as job applicants. When the applicant was Black, the interviewers sat farther away, ended the interview 25 percent sooner, and made 50 percent more speech errors than when the applicant was White. Imagine being interviewed by someone who sat at a distance, stammered, and ended the interview rather quickly. Would it affect your performance or your feelings about the interviewer?

To find out, the researchers conducted a second experiment in which trained interviewers treated students in the same way as the interviewers in the first experiment had treated either the White or Black applicants. When videotapes of the interviews were later rated, those who were treated like the Blacks in the first experiment seemed more nervous and less effective. Moreover, the interviewees could themselves sense a difference; those treated like the Black applicants judged their interviewers to be less adequate and less friendly. The experimenters concluded that part of "the 'problem' of Black performance resides … within the interaction setting itself." As with other self-fulfilling prophecies (recall Chapter 3), prejudice affects its targets.

Stereotype Threat

Just being sensitive to prejudice is enough to make us self-conscious when living as a numerical minority—perhaps as a Black person in a White community or as a White person in a Black community. As with other circumstances that siphon off our mental energy and attention, the result can be diminished mental and physical stamina (Inzlicht et al., 2006, 2012). Placed in a situation where others expect you to perform poorly, your anxiety may also cause you to confirm the belief. One of the authors is a short, older man. When he joins a pick-up basketball game with bigger, younger players, he often suspects that they expect him to be a detriment to their team, and that tends to undermine his confidence and performance. Claude Steele and his colleagues called this phenomenon **stereotype threat**—a self-confirming apprehension that one will be evaluated based on a negative stereotype (Steele, 2010; Steele, Spencer, & Aronson, 2002; see also ReducingStereotypeThreat.org).

stereotype threat A disruptive concern, when facing a negative stereotype, that one will be evaluated based on a negative stereotype.

In several experiments, Steven Spencer, Claude Steele, and Diane Quinn (1999) gave a very difficult math test to men and women students who had similar math backgrounds. When told that there were *no* gender differences on the test and no evaluation of any group stereotype, the women's performance consistently equalled the men's. Told that there *was* a gender difference, the women dramatically confirmed the stereotype (Figure 11–5). Frustrated by the extremely difficult items, they apparently felt added apprehension, which undermined their performances. For female engineering students, interacting with a sexist man likewise undermines test performance (Logel, Walton, et al., 2009). Even before exams, stereotype threat can also hamper women's learning of math rules and operations (Rydell, Rydell, & Boucher, 2010). The same is true for older people, for whom age-related stereotype threats (and resulting underperformance) have appeared across nearly three dozen studies (Lamont et al., 2015). Ditto in 19 more experiments which reveal stereotype threat's influence on immigrants' performance (Appel et al., 2015).

"Math class is tough!"

"Teen Talk" Barbie (later removed from the market)

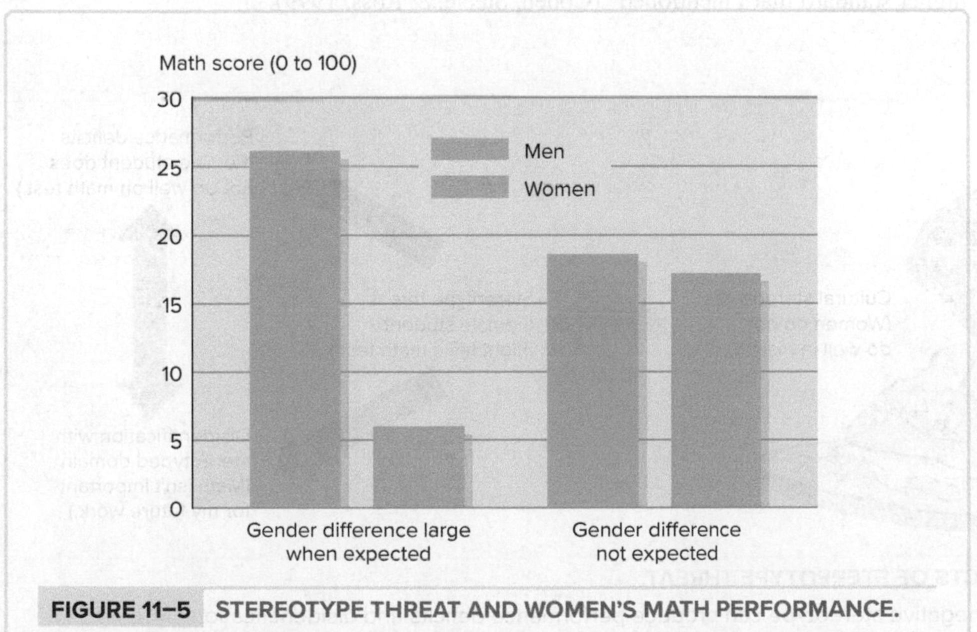

FIGURE 11–5 STEREOTYPE THREAT AND WOMEN'S MATH PERFORMANCE.
Experiments confirmed the effects of stereotype threat on women's math scores.

The media can provoke stereotype threat. Paul Davies and his colleagues (2002) had women and men watch a series of commercials, expecting that they would be tested for their memory of details. For half the participants, the commercials contained only neutral stimuli; for the other half, some of the commercials contained images of "air-headed" women. After seeing the stereotypic images, women not only performed worse than men on a math test, but also reported less interest in obtaining a math or science major or entering a math or science career.

Might racial stereotypes be similarly self-fulfilling? Claude Steele and Joshua Aronson (1995) confirmed that they are, by giving difficult verbal abilities tests to Whites and Blacks. Blacks underperformed Whites only when taking the tests under conditions high in stereotype threat. A similar stereotype threat effect has occurred with Hispanic Americans (Nadler & Clark, 2011).

Jeff Stone and his colleagues (1999) reported that stereotype threat affects athletic performance, too. Blacks did worse than usual when a golf task was framed as a test of "sports intelligence," and Whites did worse when it was a test of "natural athletic ability." "When people are reminded of a negative stereotype about themselves—'White men can't jump' or 'Black men can't think'—it can adversely affect performance," Stone (2000) surmised. The same is true for people with disabilities, for whom concern about others' negative stereotypes can hinder achievement (Silverman & Cohen, 2014).

If you tell students that they are at risk of failure (as is often suggested by minority support programs), the stereotype may erode their performance, says Steele (1997). It may cause them to "disidentify" with school and seek self-esteem elsewhere (Figure 11–6). Indeed, studies have shown that as Black students move from Grade 8 to Grade 10, their school performance becomes more weakly linked to their self-esteem (Osborne, 1995). Moreover, students led to think they have benefited from gender- or race-based preferences in gaining admission to a college or an academic group tend to underperform those who are led to feel competent (Brown et al., 2000).

Better, therefore, to challenge students to believe in their potential, observes Steele. In another of his research team's experiments, Black students responded well to criticism of their writing when also told, "I wouldn't go to the trouble of giving you this feedback if I didn't think, based on what I've read in your letter, that you are capable of meeting the higher standard that I mentioned" (Cohen, Steele, & Ross, 1999).

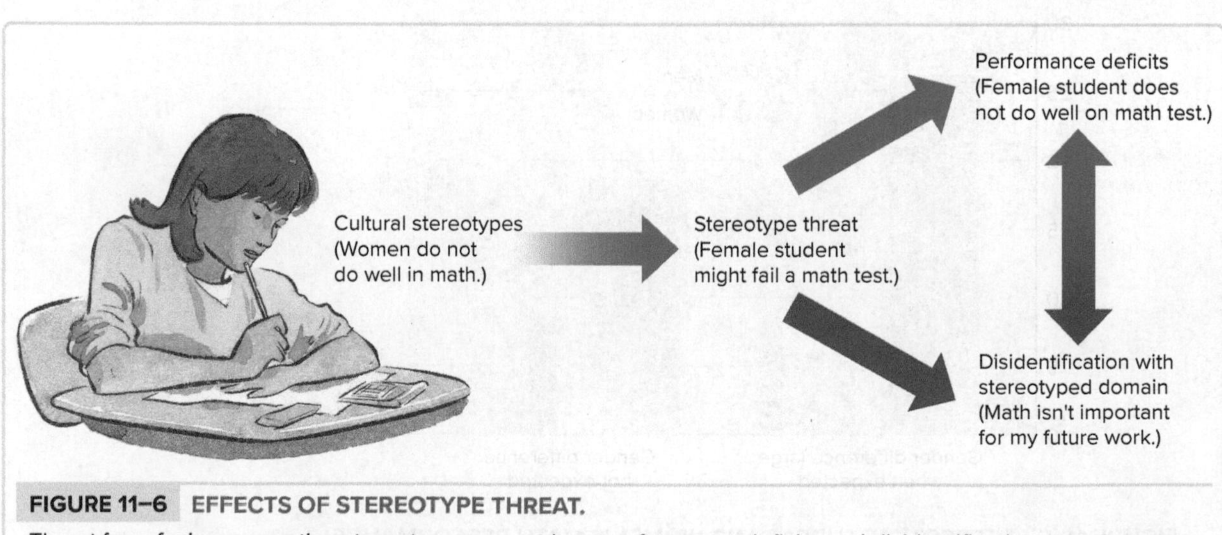

FIGURE 11–6 EFFECTS OF STEREOTYPE THREAT.
Threat from facing a negative stereotype can produce performance deficits and disidentification.

"Values affirmation"—getting people to affirm who they are—also helps (Walton, 2014). A Stanford research team invited Black Grade 7 students to write about their most important values several times. Compared to their peers, they earned higher grades over the next two years (G. L. Cohen et al., 2006, 2009). Ensuing studies have extended the values affirmation effect (such as by getting people to recall times they felt successful or proud) to populations ranging from female college physics students to soup kitchen clients (Bowen et al., 2013; Hall et al., 2014; Miyake et al., 2010; Sherman et al., 2013).

How does stereotype threat undermine performance? It does so in three ways, contend Toni Schmader, Michael Johns, and Chad Forbes (2008):

1. *Stress.* fMRI brain scans suggest that the stress of stereotype threat impairs brain activity associated with mathematical processing and increases activity in areas associated with emotion processing (Derks, Inzlicht, & Kang, 2008; Krendl et al., 2008; Wraga et al., 2007).
2. *Self-monitoring.* Worrying about making mistakes disrupts focused attention (Keller & Dauenheimer, 2003; Seibt & Forster, 2004). In interracial interactions, Blacks and Latinos (concerned with stereotypes of their intelligence) seek respect and to be seen as competent, whereas Whites (concerned with their image as racist) seek to be liked and seen as moral (Bergsieker, Shelton, & Richeson, 2010).
3. *Suppressing unwanted thoughts and emotions.* The effort required to regulate one's thinking takes energy and disrupts working memory (Bonnot & Croizet, 2007; Logel, Iserman, et al., 2009).

If stereotype threats can disrupt performance, could positive stereotypes enhance it? Margaret Shih, Todd Pittinsky, and Nalini Ambady (1999) confirmed this possibility. When Asian-American females were asked biographical questions that reminded them of their gender identity before taking a math test, their performance plunged (compared to a control group). When similarly reminded of their Asian identity, their performance rose. Negative stereotypes disrupt performance, and positive stereotypes, it seems, facilitate performance (Rydell, McConnell, & Beilock, 2009).

Do Stereotypes Bias Judgments of Individuals?

Yes, stereotypes bias judgments, but here is some good news: First, *our stereotypes mostly reflect* (though sometimes distort) *reality.* As multiculturalism recognizes, people differ—and can perceive and appreciate those differences. "Stereotype accuracy is one of the largest effects in all of social psychology," argues Lee Jussim (2012).

Second, *people often evaluate individuals more positively than the individuals' groups* (Miller & Felicio, 1990). Anne Locksley, Eugene Borgida, and Nancy Brekke have found that once someone knows a person, "stereotypes may have minimal, if any, impact on judgments about that person" (Borgida, Locksley, & Brekke, 1981; Locksley et al., 1980; Locksley, Hepburn, & Ortiz, 1982). They discovered this by giving university students anecdotal information about recent incidents in the life of "Nancy." In a supposed transcript of a telephone conversation, Nancy told a friend how she responded to three different situations (for example, being harassed by a seedy character while shopping). Some of the students read transcripts that portrayed Nancy as responding assertively (telling the seedy character to leave); others read a report of passive responses (simply ignoring the character until he finally drifts away). Still other students received the same information, except that the person was named "Paul" instead of Nancy. A day later, the students predicted how Nancy (or Paul) would respond to other situations.

Did knowing the person's gender have any effect on these predictions? None at all. Expectations of the person's assertiveness were influenced solely by what the students had learned about that individual the day before. Even their judgments of masculinity and femininity were unaffected by knowing the person's gender. Gender stereotypes had been left on the shelf; the students evaluated Nancy and Paul as individuals.

An important principle discussed in Chapter 3 explains that finding. Given general (base-rate) information about a group and trivial but vivid information about a particular group member, the vivid information usually overwhelms the effect of the general information. This is especially so when the person doesn't fit our image of the typical group member (Fein & Hilton, 1992; Lord et al., 1979). For example, imagine yourself being told how most people in an experiment actually behaved and then viewing a brief interview with one of the supposed participants. Would you, like the typical viewer, guess the person's behaviour solely from the interview? Would you ignore the base-rate information on how most people actually behaved?

People often believe such stereotypes, yet ignore them when given personal, anecdotal information. Thus, many people believe that "politicians are crooks" but "our MP Mr. Jones has integrity." No wonder people have such a low opinion of politicians yet usually re-elect their own representatives. These findings resolve a puzzling set of findings considered early in this chapter. We know that gender stereotypes are strong, yet they have little effect on people's judgments of work attributed to a man or a woman. Now we see why. People may have strong gender stereotypes yet ignore them when judging an individual they meet or learn about.

THE INSIDE STORY

During a committee meeting on campus diversity at the University of Michigan in the late 1980s, I noticed an interesting fact: At every level of entering SAT score, minority students were getting lower college grades than their non-minority counterparts. Soon, Steven Spencer, Joshua Aronson, and I found that this was a national phenomenon; it happened at most colleges and it happened to other groups whose abilities were negatively stereotyped, such as women in advanced math classes. This underperformance wasn't caused by group differences in preparation. It happened at all levels of preparation (as measured by SATs).

Eventually, we produced this underperformance in the laboratory by simply having motivated people perform a difficult task in a domain where their group was negatively stereotyped. We also found that we could eliminate this underperformance by making the same task irrelevant to the stereotype, by removing the "stereotype threat," as we had come to call it. This latter finding spawned more research: figuring out how to reduce stereotype threat and its ill effects. Through this work, we have gained an appreciation for two big things: first, the importance of life context in shaping psychological functioning, and second, the importance of social identities like age, race, and gender in shaping that context.

Source: ©Simon Jarratt/Corbis.

Claude Steele *Stanford University*

Strong stereotypes matter

However, stereotypes, when *strong,* do colour our judgments of individuals (Krueger & Rothbart, 1988). When researchers had students estimate the heights of individually pictured men and women, they judged the individual men as taller—even when their heights were equal, even when they were told that gender didn't predict height in this sample, and even when they were offered cash rewards for accuracy (Nelson et al., 1990).

In a follow-up study, university students viewed photos of other students from the university's engineering and nursing schools, along with descriptions of each student's interests (Nelson et al., 1996). Even when informed that the sample contained an equal number of males and females from each school, a description attached to a female face was judged more likely to come from a nursing student. Thus, even when a strong gender stereotype is known to be irrelevant, it has an irresistible force.

Outside the laboratory, strong stereotypes affect everyday experience. For example, men who endorse "hostile sexism" behave more negatively toward their female partners and experience less relationship satisfaction (Hammond & Overall, 2013).

Stereotypes bias interpretations

Stereotypes also colour how we interpret events, noted David Dunning and David Sherman (1997). If told that "some felt the politician's statements were untrue," people will infer that the politician was lying. If told that "some felt the physicist's statements were untrue," they infer only that the physicist was mistaken. When told two people had an altercation, people perceive it as a fist fight if told it involved two lumberjacks but as a verbal spat if told it involved two marriage counsellors. A person concerned about their physical condition seems vain if they are a model, but health-conscious if they are a triathlete. Like a prison guiding and constraining its inmates, conclude Dunning and Sherman, the "cognitive prison" of our stereotypes guides and constrains our impressions.

Sometimes we make judgments, or begin interacting with someone, with little to go on but our stereotypes. In such cases, stereotypes can strongly bias our interpretations and memories of people. For example, Charles Bond and his colleagues (1988) found that, after getting to know their patients, White psychiatric nurses put Black and White patients in physical restraints equally often. But they restrained *incoming* Black patients more often than their White counterparts. With little else to go on, stereotypes mattered.

Stereotypes can also operate subtly. In an experiment by John Darley and Paget Gross (1983), students viewed a videotape of a Grade 4 girl, Hannah. The tape depicted her either in a depressed urban neighbourhood, supposedly the child of lower-class parents, or in an affluent suburban setting, the child of professional parents. Asked to guess Hannah's ability level in various subjects, both groups of viewers refused to use Hannah's class background to prejudge her ability level; each group rated her ability level at her grade level.

Two additional groups of students also viewed a second videotape, showing Hannah taking an oral achievement test in which she got some questions right and some wrong. Those who had previously been introduced to professional-class Hannah judged her answers as showing high ability and later recalled her getting most questions right; those who had met lower-class Hannah judged her ability as below grade level and recalled her missing almost half the questions. But remember: The second videotape was *identical* for both groups. So we see that when stereotypes are strong and the information about someone is ambiguous (unlike the cases of Nancy and Paul), stereotypes can subtly bias our judgments of individuals.

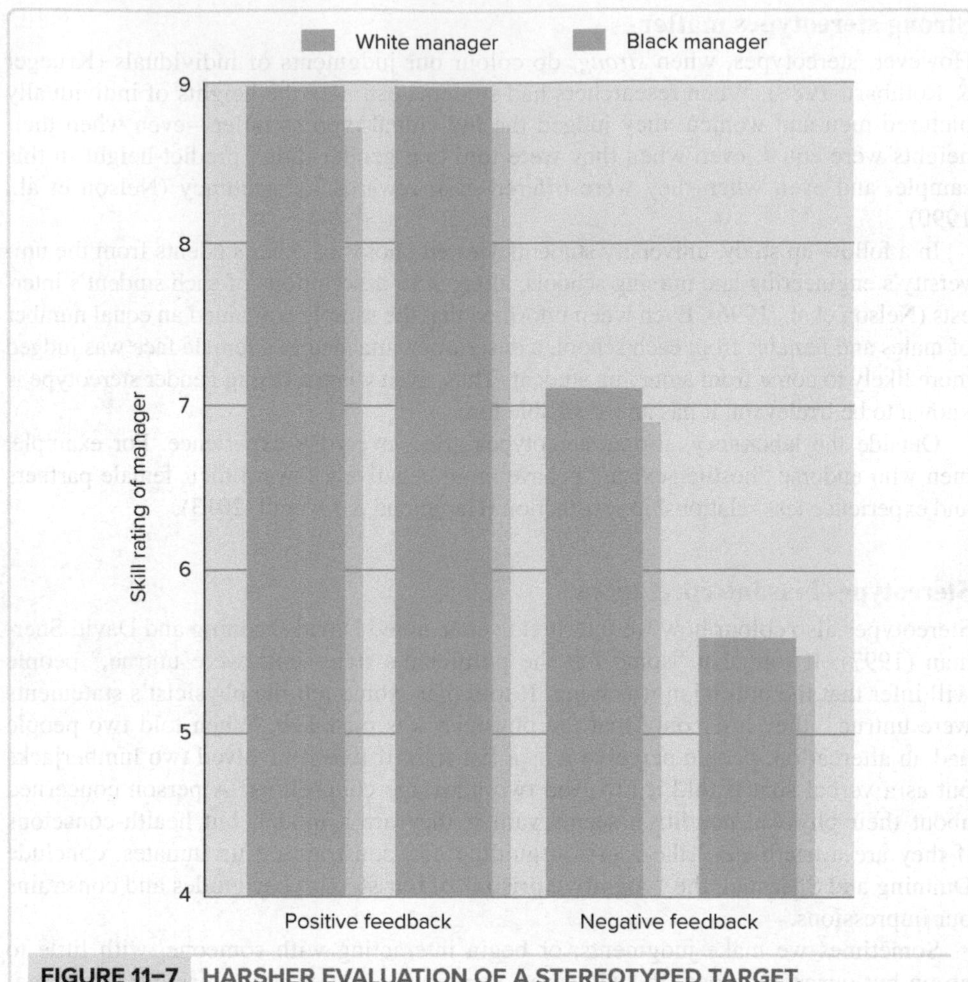

FIGURE 11–7 HARSHER EVALUATION OF A STEREOTYPED TARGET.
When University of Waterloo students received positive feedback from a "manager," his race did not matter; but when they received negative feedback, they saw a Black manager as less competent than a White manager.

Finally, we evaluate people more extremely when their behaviour violates our stereotypes (Bettencourt et al., 1997). A woman who rebukes someone cutting in front of her in a movie line ("Shouldn't you go to the end of the line?") may seem more assertive than a man who reacts similarly (Manis, Nelson, & Shedler, 1988). Do stereotypes similarly affect how students evaluate professors? Studies conducted by University of Winnipeg professor Lisa Sinclair and University of Waterloo professor Ziva Kunda suggests they do. They analyzed students' evaluations of their professors and found that when students get good grades they rate their professors highly, whether they are women or men. But when students get bad grades, they rate female professors especially low (Kunda & Sinclair, 1999; Sinclair & Kunda, 1999, 2000).

Kunda and Sinclair found similar findings in a series of laboratory studies. After completing a test of leadership ability while being observed by a "manager" in an adjacent room, participants were praised or criticized on their performance by the manager. When praised, participants liked the male and female manager equally; but when criticized, they evaluated the female manager much more negatively. They found similar results for White and Black male managers (see Figure 11–7).

THE INSIDE STORY

Ziva Kunda had long been interested in how people's motives and desires coloured their judgment. Her earlier work suggested that people attempted to be rational and drew their desired conclusions only if they could justify them. However, they often did not realize that their justifications could be biased by their motives—when constructing justifications, people search selectively for those beliefs that lend support to their desired conclusion. If they could successfully recruit such beliefs, they could draw their desired conclusion, not realizing that they may also possess other beliefs that argue against it. It occurred to Kunda and Lisa Sinclair that a negative group stereotype may sometimes provide a handy justification for disparaging a group member whom one is otherwise motivated to discredit. People may be motivated to discredit anyone who has criticized them, but may be better able to justify disparaging a woman or a member of a visible minority than disparaging a White man. As a result, people may view a woman or a Black man who criticizes them more negatively than they view a White man who delivers the same criticism.

Ziva Kunda *University of Waterloo*

SUMMING UP

What Is the Nature and Power of Prejudice?

- *Prejudice* is a preconceived negative attitude. *Stereotypes* are beliefs about another group—beliefs that may be accurate, inaccurate, or overgeneralized but based on a kernel of truth. *Discrimination* is unjustified negative behaviour. *Racism* and *sexism* may refer to individuals' prejudicial attitudes or discriminatory behaviour or to oppressive institutional practices (even if not intentionally prejudicial).
- Prejudice exists in subtle and unconscious (implicit) guises as well as overt, conscious (explicit) forms. Researchers have devised subtle survey questions and indirect methods for assessing people's attitudes and behaviour to detect unconscious prejudice.
- Racial prejudice was widely accepted until the 1960s; since that time it has become far less prevalent, but it still exists.
- Similarly, prejudice against women and gays and lesbians has lessened in recent decades. Nevertheless, strong gender stereotypes and a significant amount of gender and sexual orientation bias are still found around the world.

What Are the Social Sources of Prejudice?

- The social situation breeds and maintains prejudice in several ways. A group that enjoys social and economic superiority will often use prejudicial beliefs to justify its privileged position.

- Children are also brought up in ways that foster or reduce prejudice. Those with *authoritarian personalities* are said to be socialized into obedience and intolerance. The family, religious communities, and the broader society can sustain or reduce prejudices.
- Social institutions (government, schools, the media) also support prejudice, sometimes through overt policies and sometimes through unintentional inertia.

What Are the Motivational Sources of Prejudice?

- People's motivations affect prejudice. Frustration breeds hostility, which people sometimes vent on scapegoats and sometimes express more directly against competing groups.
- People also are motivated to view themselves and their groups as superior to other groups. Even trivial group memberships lead people to favour their own group over others. A threat to self-image heightens such *in-group favouritism*, as does the need to belong.
- On a more positive note, if people are motivated to avoid prejudice, they can break the prejudice habit.

What Are the Cognitive Sources of Prejudice?

- The stereotyping that underlies prejudice is a by-product of our thinking—our ways of simplifying the world. Clustering people into categories exaggerates the uniformity within a group and the differences between groups.
- A distinctive individual, such as a lone minority person, has a compelling quality that makes us aware of differences that would otherwise go unnoticed. The occurrence of two distinctive events (for example, a minority person committing an unusual crime) helps create an illusory correlation between people and behaviour.
- Attributing others' behaviour to their dispositions can lead to the *group-serving bias*: assigning out-group members' negative behaviour to their natural character while explaining away their positive behaviours.
- Blaming the victim results from the common presumption that because this is a *just world*, people get what they deserve.

What Are the Consequences of Prejudice?

- Prejudice and stereotyping have important consequences, especially when strongly held, when judging unknown individuals, and when deciding policies regarding whole groups.
- Once formed, stereotypes tend to perpetuate themselves and resist change. They also create their own realities through self-fulfilling prophecies.
- Prejudice can undermine people's performance through *stereotype threat*, by making people apprehensive that others will view them stereotypically.
- Stereotypes, especially when strong, can predispose how we perceive people and interpret events.

Key Terms

authoritarian personality
discrimination
ethnocentric
group-serving bias
in-group bias
in-groups
just-world phenomenon
out-group homogeneity effect
out-groups
own-race bias
prejudice
racism
realistic group conflict theory
sexism
social dominance orientation
social identity
stereotype threat
stereotypes
subgrouping
subtyping
terror management

CHAPTER 12

Conflict and Peacemaking

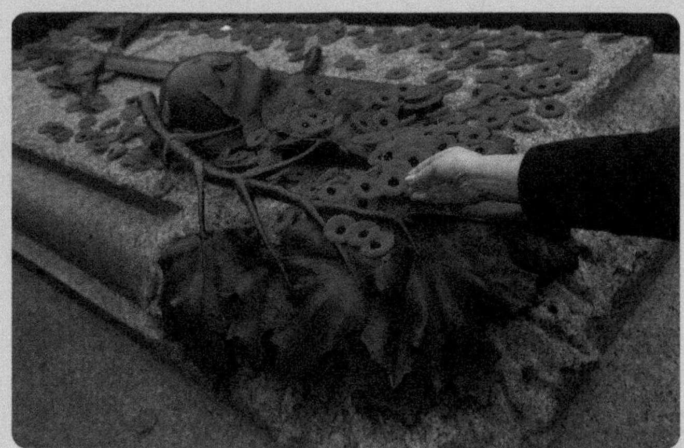

Source: The Canadian Press/Sean Kilpatrick.

CHAPTER OUTLINE

What Creates Conflict?

How Can Peace Be Achieved?

There is a speech that has been spoken in many languages by the leaders of many countries. It goes like this: "The intentions of our country are entirely peaceful. Yet, we are also aware that other nations, with their new weapons, threaten us. Thus we must defend ourselves against attack. By so doing, we shall protect our way of life and preserve the peace" (Richardson, 1960).

Almost every nation claims concern only for peace but, mistrusting other nations, arms itself in self-defence. The result is a world that has been spending $5 billion per day on arms and armies while hundreds of millions of people die of malnutrition and untreated disease (SIPRI, 2014).

The elements of **conflict** (a perceived incompatibility of actions or goals) are similar at many levels, whether we examine conflict between nations in an arms race, religious factions disputing points of doctrine, corporate executives and workers disputing salaries, or a married couple bickering. Whether their perceptions are accurate or inaccurate, people in conflict sense that one side's gain is the other's loss.

"We want peace and security." "So do we, but you threaten us."

"We want more pay." "We can't afford to give it to you."

"I'd like the music off." "I'd like it on."

Sometimes, the result is that everybody loses, as when a salary cap impasse between owners and players caused the 2004–05 National Hockey League season to be cancelled.

An organization or a relationship without conflict is probably apathetic. Conflict signifies involvement, commitment, and caring. If conflict is understood and recognized, it can end oppression and stimulate renewed relationships. Without conflict, people seldom face and resolve their problems.

Genuine **peace** is more than the suppression of open conflict, more than a fragile, superficial calm. Peace is the outcome of a creatively managed conflict. Peace is reconciling perceived differences to reach genuine accord: "We got our increased pay. You got your increased profit. Now each of us is helping the other achieve the organization's goals."

conflict A perceived incompatibility of actions or goals.

peace A condition marked by low levels of hostility and aggression and by mutually beneficial relationships.

What Creates Conflict?

What factors create conflict?

Social–psychological studies have identified several ingredients that create conflict. What is striking (and what simplifies our task) is that these ingredients are common to all levels of social conflict, whether intergroup (us versus them), or interpersonal (me versus us).

Social Dilemmas

Many of the problems that most threaten our future—nuclear arms, climate change, overpopulation, low stocks of ocean fish—arise as various parties pursue their self-interest—but, ironically, to their collective detriment. One individual may think, "It would cost me a lot to buy expensive greenhouse emission controls. Besides, the greenhouse gases I personally generate are trivial." Many others reason similarly, and the result is a warming climate, melting ice cover, rising seas, and more extreme weather.

When individually rewarding choices become collectively punishing, we have a dilemma: How can we reconcile individual self-interest with communal well-being?

To isolate and illustrate this dilemma, social psychologists have used laboratory games that expose

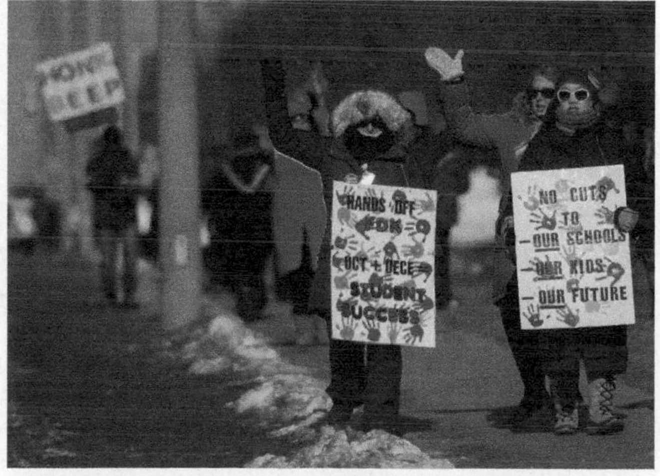

Although workers and management often cooperate, they also can experience conflict, which is most evident during a strike.
Source: The Canadian Press/Nathan Denette.

the heart of many real social conflicts. "Social psychologists who study conflict are in much the same position as the astronomers," noted conflict researcher Morton Deutsch (1999). "We cannot conduct true experiments with large-scale social events. But we can identify the conceptual similarities between the large scale and the small, as the astronomers have between the planets and Newton's apple. That is why the games people play as subjects in our laboratory may advance our understanding of war, peace, and social justice."

social trap A situation in which the conflicting parties, by rationally pursuing their own self-interest, become caught in mutually destructive behaviour.

Let's consider two laboratory games that are each an example of a **social trap** (a situation when conflicting parties are caught in mutually destructive behaviour): the Prisoner's Dilemma and the Tragedy of the Commons.

The Prisoner's Dilemma

The Prisoner's Dilemma originated from a story about two suspects questioned separately by the Crown attorney, the lawyer who can bring charges against suspects (Rapoport, 1960). The Crown knows that both suspects are jointly guilty but has only enough evidence to convict them of a lesser offence. So the Crown creates an incentive for each to confess privately:

> If Prisoner A confesses and Prisoner B doesn't, the Crown will grant immunity to A and will use A's confession to convict B of a maximum offence (and vice versa if B confesses and A doesn't).
>
> If both confess, each will receive a moderate sentence.
>
> If neither confesses, each will be convicted of a lesser crime and receive a light sentence.

The matrix of Figure 12–1 summarizes the choices. If you were a prisoner faced with such a dilemma, with no chance to talk to the other prisoner, would you confess?

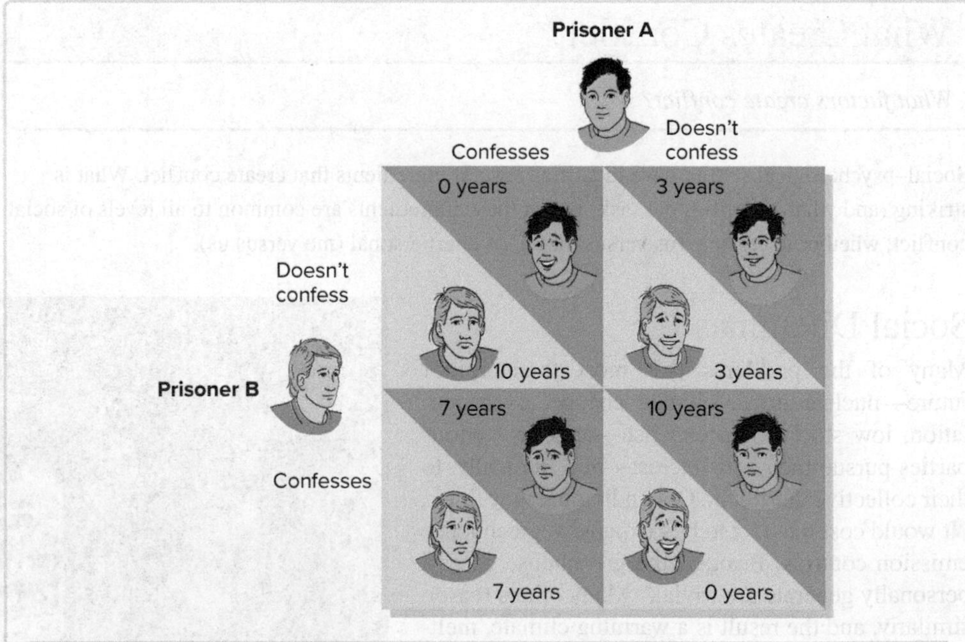

FIGURE 12–1 THE CLASSIC PRISONER'S DILEMMA.

In each box, the number above the diagonal is Prisoner A's outcome. Thus, if both prisoners confess, both get seven years. If neither confesses, each gets three years. If one confesses, that prisoner is set free in exchange for evidence used to convict the other of a crime bringing a ten-year sentence. If you were one of the prisoners, would you confess?

Many people say they would confess to be granted immunity, even though mutual *non*confession elicits lighter sentences than mutual confession. Perhaps this is because (as shown in the matrix of Figure 12–1) no matter what the other prisoner decides, each is better off confessing than being convicted individually. If the other also confesses, the sentence is moderate rather than severe.

> *"When multiplied by 2, a national policy of Peace Through Strength leads inevitably to an arms race."*
>
> George Levinger (1987)

University students have faced variations of the Prisoner's Dilemma with the choices being to defect or cooperate, and the outcome not being prison terms but chips, money, or course points. As Figure 12–2 illustrates, on any given decision, a person is better off defecting (because such behaviour exploits the other's cooperation or protects against the other's exploitation). However—and here's the rub—by not cooperating, both parties end up far worse off than if they had trusted each other and thus had gained a joint profit. This dilemma often traps each one in a maddening predicament in which both realize they *could* mutually profit. But, unable to communicate and mistrusting each other, they often become "locked in" to not cooperating. Outside the university, examples abound: seemingly intractable and costly conflicts between Israelis and Palestinians over borders, Canadian political parties over taxation and deficits, and employers and striking employees over pay.

Punishing another's lack of cooperation might seem like a smart strategy, but in the laboratory it can be counterproductive (Dreber et al., 2008). Punishment typically triggers retaliation, which means that those who punish tend to escalate conflict, worsening their outcomes, while nice guys finish first. What punishers see as a defensive reaction, recipients see as an aggressive escalation (Anderson, Buckley, & Carnagey, 2008). When hitting back, they may hit harder while seeing themselves as merely returning tit for tat. In one experiment, volunteers used a mechanical device to press back on someone else's finger after receiving pressure on their own. Although they tried to reciprocate with the same degree of pressure, they typically responded with 40 percent more force. Thus, touches soon escalated to hard presses, much like a child saying "I just *touched* him, and then he *hit* me!" (Shergill et al., 2003).

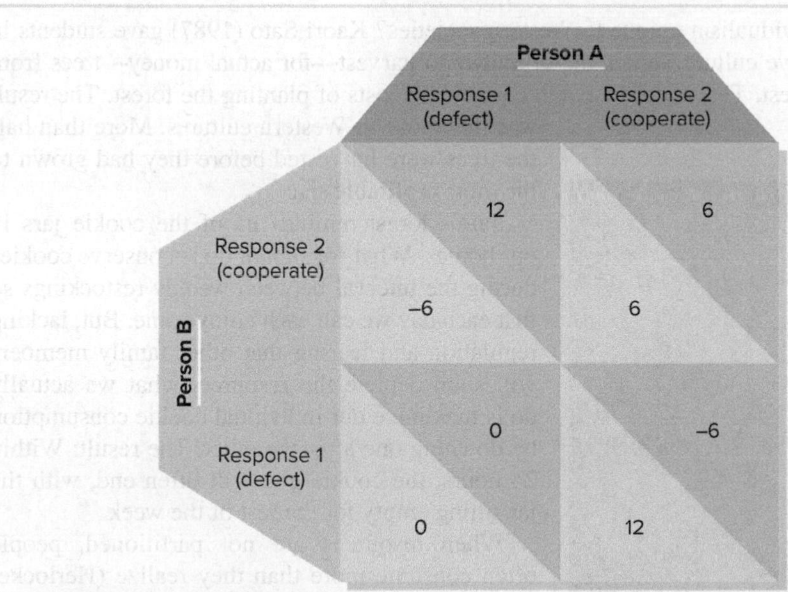

FIGURE 12–2 LABORATORY VERSION OF THE PRISONER'S DILEMMA.

The numbers represent some reward, such as money. In each box, the number above the diagonal lines is the outcome for Person A. Unlike the classic Prisoner's Dilemma (a one-shot decision), most laboratory versions involve repeated plays.

The Tragedy of the Commons

Many social dilemmas involve more than two parties. Climate change, for example, stems from deforestation and from the carbon dioxide emitted by vehicles, furnaces, and coal-fired power plants. Each car contributes infinitesimally to the problem, and the harm each does is diffused over many people. To model such social predicaments, researchers have developed laboratory dilemmas that involve multiple people.

A metaphor for the insidious nature of social dilemmas is what ecologist Garrett Hardin (1968) called the **Tragedy of the Commons**. He derived the name from the centrally located pasture area in old English towns. Imagine 100 farmers surrounding a commons capable of sustaining 100 cows. When each grazes one cow, the common feeding ground is optimally used. But then a farmer reasons, "If I put a second cow in the pasture, I'll double my output, minus the mere 1 percent overgrazing" and adds a second cow. So does each of the other farmers. The inevitable result? The Tragedy of the Commons—a mud field and famished cows.

Tragedy of the Commons
The "commons" is any shared resource, including air, water, energy sources, and food supplies. The tragedy occurs when individuals consume more than their share, with the cost of their doing so dispersed among all, causing the ultimate collapse—the tragedy—of the commons.

In today's world, the "commons" can be air, water, fish, cookies, or any shared and limited resource. If all use the resource in moderation, it may replenish itself as rapidly as it is harvested. The grass will grow, the fish will reproduce, and the cookie jar will get restocked. If not, there occurs a tragedy of the commons.

Likewise, environmental pollution is the sum of many minor pollutions, each of which benefits the individual polluters much more than they could benefit themselves (and the environment) if they stopped polluting. We litter public places—parks, zoos, residence lounges—while keeping our personal spaces clean. And we deplete our natural resources because the immediate personal benefits of, say, taking a long, hot shower outweigh the seemingly inconsequential costs. Whalers knew that others would exploit the whales if they didn't and that taking a few whales would hardly diminish the species. Therein lay the tragedy: *Everybody's business (conservation) becomes nobody's business.*

Is such individualism unique to Western societies? Kaori Sato (1987) gave students in a more collective culture, Japan, opportunities to harvest—for actual money—trees from a simulated forest. The students shared equally the costs of planting the forest. The result was like those in Western cultures. More than half the trees were harvested before they had grown to the most profitable size.

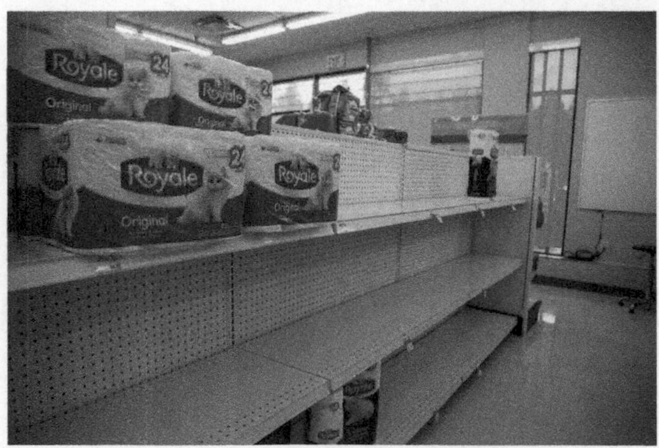

It's tempting to hoard a resource that other people also want. But if everyone hoards, the resource is soon depleted. For many weeks during the COVID-19 epidemic, toilet paper was hard to find as people bought extra rolls for themselves and their families, leaving little for everyone else.
Source: ©Adam Melnyk/Alamy Stock Photo.

Sato's forest reminds us of the cookie jars in our homes. What we *should* do is conserve cookies during the interval between weekly restockings so that each day we can each enjoy some. But, lacking regulation and fearing that other family members will soon deplete the resource, what we actually do is maximize our individual cookie consumption by downing one after the other. The result: Within 24 hours, the cookie glut will often end, with the jar sitting empty for the rest of the week.

When resources are not partitioned, people often consume more than they realize (Herlocker et al., 1997). As a bowl of mashed potatoes is passed around a table of 10, it is likely that more people will scoop out a disproportionate share than when a platter of 10 chicken drumsticks is passed.

The Prisoner's Dilemma and the Tragedy of the Commons games have several similar features.

The fundamental attribution error

First, both games tempt people to explain *their own behaviour situationally* ("I had to protect myself against exploitation by my opponent") and to explain their partners' behaviour dispositionally ("She was greedy," "He was untrustworthy"). Most never realize that their counterparts are viewing them with the same fundamental attribution error (Hine & Gifford, 1996).

When Muslims have killed Westerners, Western media have attributed the killings to evil dispositions—to fanatical, hateful terrorists. When an American soldier killed 16 Afghans, including 9 children, he was said to be experiencing financial stress, suffering marital problems, and experiencing frustration from being passed over for a promotion (Greenwald, 2012). Violence explanations vary depending on whether the act is by or toward one's side.

Evolving motives

Second, *motives often change*. At first, people are eager to make some easy money, then to minimize their losses, and finally to save face and avoid defeat (Brockner et al., 1982; Teger, 1980). These shifting motives can make it harder to negotiate a solution. Early on, mediators can focus on proposing resolutions that maximize the benefits to both sides. As time progresses, however, solutions must increasingly address the substantive issues, and they must also let all parties enter an agreement with the sense that they have prevented important losses and avoided defeat.

Outcomes need not sum to zero

Third, most real-life conflicts, like the Prisoner's Dilemma and the Tragedy of the Commons, are **non-zero-sum games**. The two sides' profits and losses need not add up to zero. Both can win; both can lose. Each game pits the immediate interests of individuals against the well-being of the group. Each is a diabolical social trap that shows how, even when each individual behaves rationally, harm can result. No malicious person planned for the earth's atmosphere to be warmed by a blanket of carbon dioxide.

non-zero-sum games Games in which outcomes need not sum to zero. With cooperation, both can win; with competition, both can lose. (Also called *mixed-motive situations*.)

Not all self-serving behaviour leads to collective doom. In a plentiful commons—as in the world of the eighteenth-century capitalist economist Adam Smith (1976, p. 18)—individuals who seek to maximize their own profit may also give the community what it needs: "It is not from the benevolence of the butcher, the brewer, or the baker, that we expect our dinner," he observed, "but from their regard to their own interest."

Resolving social dilemmas

In real-life situations, many people approach commons dilemmas with a cooperative outlook and expect similar cooperation from others, thus enabling their collective betterment (Krueger et al., 2012; Ostrom, 2014). Research with the laboratory dilemmas has identified several ways to further encourage such mutual betterment (Gifford & Hine, 1997; Nowak, 2012).

Regulation

If taxes were entirely voluntary, how many would pay their full share? Modern societies do not depend on charity to pay for schools, parks, and social and military security. We also develop rules to safeguard our common good. Fishing and hunting have long been regulated by local seasons and limits; at the global level, an International Whaling Commission sets an agreed-upon "harvest" that enables whales to regenerate. Likewise, where fishing industries, such as the Alaskan halibut fishery, have implemented "catch shares"—guaranteeing each fisher a percentage of each year's allowable catch—competition and overfishing have been greatly reduced (Costello, Gaines, & Lynham, 2008).

In everyday life, however, regulation has costs—costs of administering and enforcing the regulations, costs of diminished personal freedom. A volatile political question thus arises: At what point does a regulation's cost exceed its benefits?

Small is beautiful

There is another way to resolve social dilemmas: Make the group small. In small commons, each person feels more responsible and effective (Kerr, 1989). As a group grows larger, people become more likely to think "I couldn't have made a difference anyway"—a common excuse for non-cooperation (Kerr & Kaufman-Gilliland, 1997).

In small groups, people also identify more with a group's success. Residential stability also strengthens communal identity and pro-community behaviour (Oishi, Rothman, et al., 2007). In small rather than large groups, individuals are less likely to take more than their equal share of available resources (Allison, McQueen, & Schaerf, 1992). On the Puget Sound island where one of the authors grew up, for example, the small neighbourhood shared a communal water supply. On hot summer days when the reservoir ran low, a light came on, signalling the community's 15 families to conserve. Recognizing their responsibility to one another, and feeling as if conservation really mattered, each family conserved. Never did the reservoir run dry.

In a much larger commons—say, a city—voluntary conservation is less successful. In 2018 as Cape Town was facing becoming the world's first major city to run out of water, its nearly 4 million people were admonished to take extreme measures to conserve. Yet it was easy for any individual to think, "My flushing the toilet or taking a shower won't make a noticeable difference in the city's reservoir." Thus, residents and businesses did not conserve as much as anticipated, hastening the reservoir depletion (Maxmen, 2018).

> ***"For that which is common to the greatest number has the least care bestowed upon it."***
>
> Aristotle (BC 384–322)

Evolutionary psychologist Robin Dunbar (1992, 2010) notes that tribal villages and clans often have averaged about 150 people—enough to afford mutual support and protection but not more people than one can monitor. This seemingly natural group

Small is cooperative. On Scotland's Isle of Muck, Constable Lawrence MacEwan has had an easy time policing the island's 33 residents. Over his 40 years on the job, there was never a crime (Scottish Life, 2001). In 2010, a row between two friends who had been drinking at a wedding became the first recorded crime in 50 years, but the next morning, they shook hands and all was well (Cameron, 2010). In 2015, the nearby island of Canna experienced its "crime of the century" (its first crime since the 1960s) when thieves stole crafts, food, and money from its shop. The shop was left unlocked so that fishing people resting at the pier overnight could buy what they needed, paying via an "honesty box."
Source: ©Catherine Karnow.

size is also, he believes, the optimum size for business organizations, religious congregations, and military fighting units.

Communication

To resolve a social dilemma, people must communicate. In the laboratory as in real life, group communication sometimes degenerates into threats and name-calling (Deutsch & Krauss, 1960). More often, communication enables cooperation (Bornstein & Rapoport, 1988; Bornstein et al., 1989). Discussing the dilemma forges a group identity, which enhances concern for everyone's welfare. It devises group norms and expectations and pressures members to follow them. It enables them to commit themselves to cooperation (Bouas & Komorita, 1996; Drolet & Morris, 2000; Kerr & Kaufman-Gilliland, 1994, 1997; Pruitt, 1998). Humans, thanks to full-blown language, are the most cooperative, reciprocally helpful species (Nowak, 2012).

A clever experiment by researcher Robyn Dawes (1980a, 1994) illustrates the importance of communication. Imagine that an experimenter offered you and six strangers a choice: You can each have $6, or you can donate your $6 to the other six. If you give away your money, the experimenter will double your gift. No one will be told whether you chose to give or keep your $6. Thus, if all seven give, everyone pockets $12. If you alone keep your $6 and all the others give theirs, you pocket $18. If you give and all the others don't, you pocket nothing. In this experiment, cooperation is mutually advantageous, but it requires risk. Dawes found that, without discussion, about 30 percent of people gave. With discussion, in which they could establish trust and cooperation, about 80 percent gave.

Open, clear, forthright communication between two parties reduces mistrust. Without communication, those who expect others not to cooperate will usually refuse to cooperate themselves (Messé & Sivacek, 1989; Pruitt & Kimmel, 1977). One who mistrusts is almost sure to be uncooperative (to protect against exploitation). Noncooperation, in turn, feeds further mistrust ("What else could I do? It's a dog-eat-dog world"). In experiments, communication reduces mistrust, enabling people to reach agreements that lead to their common betterment.

Changing the payoffs

Laboratory cooperation rises when experimenters change the payoff matrix to reward cooperation and punish exploitation (Balliet & Van Lange, 2013). Changing payoffs also helps resolve actual dilemmas. In some cities, freeways clog and skies fill with smog because people prefer the convenience of driving to work by themselves. Each knows that one more car does not add noticeably to the congestion and pollution. To alter the personal cost–benefit calculations, many cities now give carpoolers and electric cars incentives, such as designated freeway lanes or reduced tolls.

To change behaviour, many cities have changed the payoff matrix. Fast carpool-only lanes increase the benefits of carpooling and increase the costs of driving alone.

Source: ©Lester Balajadia/Shutterstock.

Appeals to altruistic norms

In Chapter 8, we described how increasing bystanders' feelings of responsibility for others boosts altruism. Will appeals to altruistic motives similarly prompt people to act for the common good?

The evidence is mixed. On the one hand, just *knowing* the dire consequences of noncooperation has little effect. In laboratory games, people realize that their self-serving choices are mutually destructive, yet they continue to make them. People know that climate change is underway, yet they continue to buy gas-guzzling SUVs. Outside the laboratory, warnings of doom and appeals to conserve have brought little response. As we have seen many times in this book, attitudes sometimes fail to influence behaviour. *Knowing* what is good does not necessarily lead to *doing* what is good.

Still, most people do adhere to norms of social responsibility, reciprocity, equity, and keeping one's commitments (Kerr, 1992). The problem is how to tap into such feelings. One way is through the influence of a charismatic leader who inspires others to cooperate (De Cremer, 2002). In China, those who were educated during Mao's "planned economy" era—an era that emphasized equal wealth distribution—make more cooperative social dilemma game choices than those who were not (Zhu et al., 2013).

Another way to tap into feelings of social responsibility, reciprocity, and equity is by defining situations in ways that invoke cooperative norms. In one experiment, only a third of participants cooperated in a simulation labelled the "Wall Street Game." Two-thirds did so when the same social dilemma was labelled the "Community Game" (Liberman et al., 2004).

> *"Never in the field of human conflict was so much owed by so many to so few."*
>
> Sir Winston Churchill, House of Commons, August 20, 1940

Communication can also activate altruistic norms. When permitted to communicate, participants in laboratory games frequently appeal to the social-responsibility norm: "If you defect on the rest of us, you're going to have to live with it for the rest of your life" (Dawes, McTavish, & Shaklee, 1977). So Robyn Dawes (1980a) and his associates gave people a short sermon about group benefits, exploitation, and ethics. Then the participants played a dilemma game. The sermon worked: People were convinced to forgo immediate personal gain for the common good.

Could such appeals work in large-scale dilemmas? In the 1960s struggle for civil rights, many marchers willingly agreed, for the sake of the larger group, to suffer harassment, beatings, and jail. In wartime, people make great personal sacrifices for the good of their group. As Winston Churchill said of the Battle of Britain, the actions of the Royal Air Force pilots were genuinely altruistic: A great many people owed a great deal to those who flew into battle knowing there was a high probability—70 percent for those on a standard tour of duty—that they would not return (Levinson, 1950).

To summarize, we can minimize destructive entrapment in social dilemmas by establishing rules that regulate self-serving behaviour, by keeping groups small, by enabling people to communicate, by changing payoffs to make cooperation more rewarding, and by invoking compelling altruistic norms.

Competition

Hostilities often arise when groups compete for scarce jobs, housing, or resources. When interests clash, conflict erupts. Feeling threatened, such as by economic or terrorist threats, predicts Dutch citizens' increased right-wing authoritarianism (Onraet et al., 2014). Even perceived distant threats—from another ethnic group's population growth or a pandemic disease—can increase people's intolerance (Beall et al., 2016; Bouman et al., 2015). Moreover, not only do perceived threats feed prejudice and conflict, prejudice—in a vicious cycle—also amplifies the perception of a threat (Bahns, 2017).

To experiment on competition's effect, we could randomly divide people into two groups, have the groups compete for a scarce resource, and note what happens. That is precisely what Muzafer Sherif (1966) and his colleagues did in a famous series of experiments with typical 11- and 12-year-old boys. The inspiration for those experiments dated back to Sherif's witnessing, as a teenager, Greek troops invading his Turkish province in 1919.

> They started killing people right and left. [That] made a great impression on me. There and then I became interested in understanding why these things were happening among human beings. … I wanted to learn whatever science or specialization was needed to understand this intergroup savagery. (Quoted by Aron & Aron, 1989, p. 131.)

After studying the social roots of savagery, Sherif introduced the seeming essentials into several three-week summer camping experiences. In one study, he divided 22 unacquainted boys into two groups, took them to a Boy Scout camp in separate buses, and settled them in bunkhouses about a half-mile apart at Robber's Cave State Park. For most of the first week, each group was unaware of the other's existence. By cooperating in various activities—preparing meals, camping out, fixing up a swimming hole, building a rope bridge—each group soon became close-knit. They gave themselves names: "Rattlers" and "Eagles." Typifying the good feeling, a sign appeared in one cabin: "Home Sweet Home."

Group identity thus established, the stage was set for the conflict. Near the first week's end, the Rattlers discovered the Eagles "on 'our' baseball field." When the camp staff then proposed a tournament of competitive activities between the two groups (baseball games, tugs-of-war, cabin inspections, treasure hunts, and so forth), both groups responded enthusiastically. This was win–lose competition. The spoils (medals, knives) would all go to the tournament victor.

The result? The camp degenerated into open warfare. It was like a scene from William Golding's novel, *Lord of the Flies,* which depicts the social disintegration of boys marooned on an island. In Sherif's study, the conflict began with each side calling the other names during the competitive activities. Soon it escalated to dining hall "garbage wars," flag burnings, cabin ransackings, even fistfights. Asked to describe the other group, the boys said they were "sneaky," "smart alecks," and "stinkers," but referred to their own group as "brave," "tough," and "friendly." It was a tough experience, driving some of the boys to bedwetting, running away, being homesick, and later recalling an unhappy experience (Perry, 2014).

The win–lose competition had produced intense conflict, negative images of the outgroup, and strong in-group cohesiveness and pride. Group polarization no doubt exacerbated the conflict. In competition-fostering situations, groups behave more competitively than do individuals (Wildschut et al., 2003, 2007). Even after hearing tolerance-advocating messages, in-group discussion often exacerbates dislike of the conflicting group (Paluck, 2010).

All this occurred without any cultural, physical, or economic differences between the two groups, and with boys who were their communities' "cream of the crop." Sherif noted that, had we visited the camp at that point, we would have concluded these "were wicked, disturbed, and vicious bunches of youngsters" (1966, p. 85). Actually, their evil behaviour was triggered by an evil situation. Fortunately, as we will see, Sherif not only made strangers into enemies, but also made the enemies into friends.

Competition kindles conflict. In competition-fostering situations, groups act more competitively, as in this raid, than do individuals.
Source: Muzafer Sherif.

Perceived Injustice

"That's unfair!" "What a rip-off!" "We deserve better!" Such comments typify conflicts bred by perceived injustice.

But what is "justice"? According to some social–psychological theorists, people perceive justice as equity—the distribution of rewards in proportion to individuals' contributions (Starmans et al., 2017; Walster (Hatfield), Walster, & Berscheid, 1978). If you and "Jamie" have a relationship (employer–employee, teacher–student, spouse–spouse, colleague–colleague), it is equitable if

$$\frac{\text{Your outcomes}}{\text{Your inputs}} = \frac{\text{Jamie's outcomes}}{\text{Jamie's inputs}}$$

"Do unto others 20 percent better than you would expect them to do unto you, to correct for subjective error."

Linus Pauling, response to audience question at Monterey Peninsula College, 1961

If you contribute more and benefit less than Jamie does, you will feel exploited and irritated; Jamie may feel exploitative and guilty. Chances are, though, that you will be more sensitive to the inequity than I am (Greenberg, 1986; Messick & Sentis, 1979).

We may agree with the equity principle's definition of justice yet disagree on whether our relationship is equitable. If two people are colleagues, what will each consider a relevant input? The older person may favour basing pay on seniority; the younger, on current productivity. Given such a disagreement, whose definition is likely to prevail? Those with social power usually convince themselves and others that they deserve what they're getting (Guinote, 2017; Mikula, 1984). This has been called a "golden" rule: Whoever has the gold makes the rules.

"From each according to his abilities, to each according to his needs."

Karl Marx

Critics argue that equity is not the only conceivable definition of justice. (Pause a moment: Can you imagine any other?) Edward Sampson (1975) pointed out that equity theorists wrongly assume that the economic principles that guide Western, capitalist nations are universal. Some noncapitalist cultures define justice not as equity but as either **equality** or even fulfillment of need (or **need-based distribution**): From each according to his abilities, to each according to his needs (to paraphrase Karl Marx). Compared with people from individualistic

equality The equal distribution of rewards to all individuals.

need-based distribution The distribution of rewards based on need for those rewards.

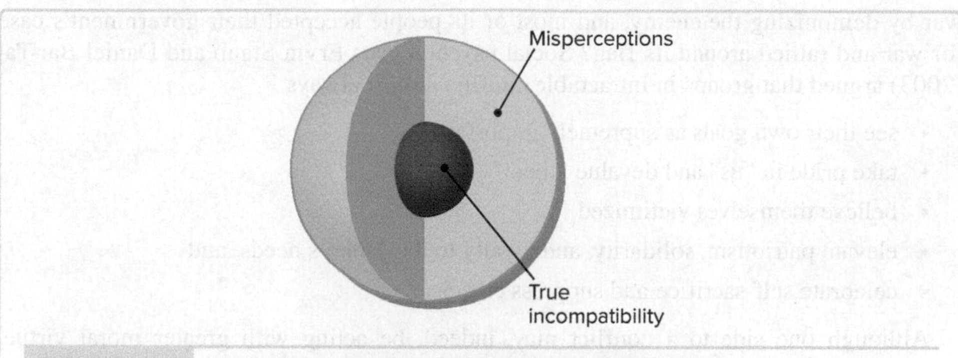

FIGURE 12–3 INCOMPATIBLE GOALS VS. MISPERCEPTIONS.

Many conflicts contain a core of truly incompatible goals surrounded by a larger exterior of misperceptions.

cultures, such as Canada and the United States, children and adults socialized under the influence of collectivist cultures, such as China and India, have defined justice more as equality or need fulfillment (Hui, Triandis, & Yee, 1991; Leung & Bond, 1984; Schäfer et al., 2015).

On what basis *should* rewards be distributed? Need? Equality? Merit? Some combination of those? Political philosopher John Rawls (1971) invited us to consider a future in which our own place on the economic ladder was unknown. Which standard of justice would we prefer?

Misperception

Recall that conflict is a *perceived* incompatibility of actions or goals. Many conflicts contain but a small core of truly incompatible goals; the bigger problem is the misperceptions of the others' motives and goals (Figure 12–3). The Eagles and the Rattlers did indeed have some genuinely incompatible aims. But their perceptions subjectively magnified their differences.

In earlier chapters, we considered the seeds of such misperception:

- The *self-serving bias* leads individuals and groups to accept credit for their good deeds and shirk responsibility for bad deeds.
- A tendency to *self-justify* inclines people to deny the wrong of the evil acts ("You call that hitting? I hardly touched him!").
- Thanks to the *fundamental attribution error*, each side sees the other's hostility as reflecting an evil disposition.
- One filters the information and interprets it to fit one's *preconceptions*.
- Groups frequently *polarize* these self-serving, self-justifying, biasing tendencies.
- One symptom of *groupthink* is the tendency to perceive one's own group as moral and strong and the opposition as evil and weak. Acts of terrorism that in most people's eyes are despicable brutality are seen by others as "holy war."
- Indeed, the mere fact of being in a group triggers an *in-group bias*.
- Negative *stereotypes*, once formed, are often resistant to contradictory evidence.

So it should not surprise us, although it should sober us, to discover that people in conflict form distorted images of one another. Wherever in the world you live, is it not true that, when your country was last at war, it clothed itself in moral virtue and prepared for war by demonizing the enemy, and most of its people accepted their government's case for war and rallied around its flag? Social psychologists Ervin Staub and Daniel Bar-Tal (2003) argued that groups in intractable conflict almost always

- see their own goals as supremely important
- take pride in "us" and devalue "them"
- believe themselves victimized
- elevate patriotism, solidarity, and loyalty to the group's needs, and
- celebrate self-sacrifice and suppress criticism.

Although one side to a conflict may, indeed, be acting with greater moral virtue, the point is that enemy images are predictable. Even the types of misperception are intriguingly predictable.

Mirror-image perceptions

To a striking degree, the misperceptions of those in conflict are mutual. People in conflict attribute similar virtues to themselves and vices to the other. When the American psychologist Urie Bronfenbrenner (1961) visited the Soviet Union in 1960 and conversed with many ordinary citizens in Russian, he was astonished to hear them saying the same things about America that Americans were saying about Russia. The Russians said that the U.S. government was militarily aggressive; that it exploited and deluded the American people; that in diplomacy, it was not to be trusted. "Slowly and painfully, it forced itself upon one that the Russians' distorted picture of us was curiously similar to our view of them—a mirror image."

When two sides have clashing perceptions, at least one is misperceiving the other. And when such misperceptions exist, noted Bronfenbrenner, "It is a psychological phenomenon without parallel in the gravity of its consequences … for *it is characteristic of such images that they are self-confirming.*" If A expects B to be hostile, A may treat B in such a way that B fulfills A's expectations, thus beginning a vicious circle (Kennedy & Pronin, 2008). Morton Deutsch (1986) explained:

> You hear the false rumor that a friend is saying nasty things about you; you snub him; he then badmouths you, confirming your expectation. Similarly, if the policymakers of East and West believe that war is likely and either attempts to increase its military security vis-à-vis the other, the other's response will justify the initial move.

Negative mirror-image perceptions have been an obstacle to peace in many places:

- *Middle East perceptions.* Both sides of the Arab–Israeli conflict insist that "we" are motivated by our need to protect our security and our territory, whereas "they" want to obliterate us and gobble up our land. "We" are the indigenous people here; "they" are the invaders. "We" are the victims; "they" are the aggressors (Bar-Tal, 2004, 2013; Heradstveit, 1979; Kelman, 2007). Given such intense mistrust, negotiation is difficult.
- *What defines terrorism?* Terrorism is in the eye of the beholder. In the Middle East, in a public opinion survey of Palestinians, 98 percent agreed that the killing of 29 Palestinians by an assault-rifle-bearing Israeli at a mosque constituted terrorism, and 82 percent *dis*agreed that the killing of 21 Israeli youths in a Palestinian suicide bombing constituted terrorism (Kruglanski & Fishman, 2006). Israelis likewise have responded to violence with intensified perceptions of Palestinian evil intent (Bar-Tal, 2004, 2013).

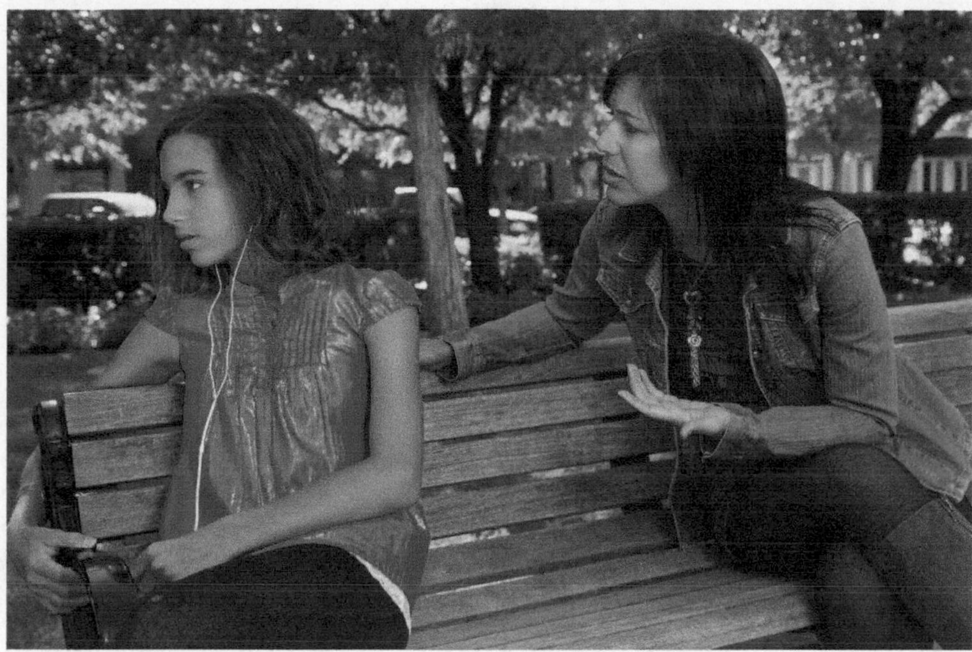

Self-confirming, mirror-image perceptions are a hallmark of intense conflict.
Source: ©asiseeit/E+/Getty Images.

- *Myside bias.* People, regardless of their intelligence, also display a *myside bias*. In one experiment, American students were much more likely to favour banning an accident-prone German car from American roads than a comparably accident-prone American car from German roads (Stanovich et al., 2013). Even torture seems more morally justified when "we" rather than "they" do it (Tarrant et al., 2009).
- *Political polarization.* In polarized North America, both liberals and conservatives see love and benevolence on their side, and hatred and evil on the other (Waytz et al., 2014).

Such conflicts, noted Philip Zimbardo (2004), engage "a two-category world—of good people, like US, and of bad people, like THEM." "In fact," noted Daniel Kahneman and Jonathan Renshon (2007), all the biases uncovered in 40 years of psychological research are conducive to war. They "incline national leaders to exaggerate the evil intentions of adversaries, to misjudge how adversaries perceive them, to be overly sanguine when hostilities start, and overly reluctant to make necessary concessions in negotiations."

Opposing sides in a conflict tend to exaggerate their differences. On issues related to abortion and politics, partisans perceive exaggerated differences from their adversaries—who actually agree with them more often than they guess (Chambers et al., 2006). On immigration and affirmative action, proponents aren't as liberal and opponents aren't as conservative as their adversaries suppose (Sherman et al., 2003). Opposing sides also tend to have a "bias blind spot," notes Cynthia McPherson Frantz (2006). They see their own understandings as not biased by their liking or disliking others, but those who disagree with them seem unfair and biased.

Group conflicts are often fuelled by an illusion that the enemy's top leaders are evil but their people, though controlled and manipulated, are on our side. This *evil leader–good people* perception characterized Americans' and Russians' views of each other during the

Cold War. The United States entered the Vietnam War believing that, in areas dominated by the Communist Vietcong "terrorists," many of the people were allies in waiting. As suppressed information later revealed, those beliefs were mere wishful thinking. In 2003, the United States began the Iraq War presuming the existence of "a vast underground network that would rise in support of coalition forces to assist security and law enforcement" (Phillips, 2003). Alas, the network didn't materialize, and the resulting postwar security vacuum enabled looting, sabotage, and persistent attacks on American forces and their allies, including those deployed by Canada.

Simplistic thinking

When tension rises—as happens during an international crisis—rational thinking becomes more difficult (Janis, 1989). Views of the enemy become more simplistic and stereotyped, and hasty, uninformed judgments become more likely. Even the mere expectation of conflict can serve to freeze thinking and impede creative problem solving (Carnevale & Probst, 1998). Social psychologist Philip Tetlock (1988) observed inflexible thinking when he analyzed the complexity of Russian and American rhetoric since 1945. During the Berlin blockade, the Korean War, and the Russian invasion of Afghanistan, political statements became simplified into stark, good-versus-bad terms.

Researchers have also analyzed political rhetoric preceding the outset of major wars, surprise military attacks, regional conflicts, and revolutions (Conway et al., 2001). In nearly every case, attacking leaders displayed increasingly simplistic we-are-good/they-are-bad thinking immediately prior to their aggressive actions. But shifts *away* from simplistic rhetoric typically preceded major peace agreements.

Shifting perceptions

If misperceptions accompany conflict, then they should appear and disappear as conflicts wax and wane. And they do, with startling regularity. The same processes that create the enemy's image can reverse that image when the enemy becomes an ally. Thus, the "bloodthirsty, cruel, treacherous little Japs" of the Second World War (who were deemed so dangerous that innocent Canadian citizens of Japanese descent were sent to internment camps) soon became—in North American minds and in the media—our "intelligent, hard-working, self-disciplined, resourceful allies" (Gallup, 1972)

The Germans—who after two world wars had been hated, then admired, and then hated again—were once again admired, apparently no longer plagued by what earlier was presumed to be cruelty in their national character. So long as Iraq was attacking unpopular Iran, even while using chemical weapons and massacring its own Kurds, many nations supported it. Our enemy's enemy is our friend. When Iraq ended its war with Iran and invaded oil-rich Kuwait, Iraq's behaviour suddenly became "barbaric." Images of our enemies change with amazing ease.

The extent of misperceptions during conflict provides a chilling reminder that people need not be insane or abnormally malicious to form distorted images of their antagonists. When we experience conflict with another nation, another group, or simply a roommate or a parent, we readily misperceive our own motives as good and the other's as evil. And just as readily, our antagonists form a mirror-image perception of us.

So, with antagonists trapped in a social dilemma, competing for scarce resources, or perceiving injustice, the conflict continues until something enables both parties to peel away their misperceptions and work at reconciling their actual differences. Good advice, then, is this: When in conflict, do not assume that the other fails to share your values and morality. Rather, share and compare perceptions, assuming that the other likely perceives the situation differently.

How Can Peace Be Achieved?

What processes enable the achievement of peace?

We have seen how conflicts are ignited by social traps, competition, perceived injustices, and misperceptions. Although the picture is grim, it is not hopeless. Sometimes closed fists give way to open arms as hostilities evolve into harmony. To explore the transition from conflict to community, social psychologists have focused on four peacemaking strategies. We can remember these as the four Cs of peacemaking: contact, cooperation, communication, and conciliation.

Contact

Might putting two conflicting individuals or groups into close contact enable them to know and like each other? Perhaps not: We have seen how negative expectations can bias judgments and create self-fulfilling prophecies. When tensions run high, contact may fuel a fight.

But we have also seen that proximity—and the accompanying interaction, anticipation of interaction, and mere exposure—boosts liking. And we have noted how blatant racial prejudice has declined following desegregation, showing that *attitudes follow behaviour*. If this social–psychological principle now seems obvious, remember: That's how things usually seem after you know them.

Does contact predict attitudes?

In general, contact predicts tolerance. In a painstaking analysis, researchers assembled data from 516 studies of 250 055 people in 38 nations (Tropp & Pettigrew, 2005a, 2005b; Pettigrew & Tropp, 2008, 2011). In 94 percent of studies, *increased contact predicted decreased prejudice*. This is especially so for majority group attitudes toward minorities (Durrheim et al., 2011; Gibson & Claassen, 2010).

Newer studies—in Bosnia, Israel/Palestine, Turkey, Northern Ireland, Lebanon, Liberia, South Africa, and Britain (Wright et al., 2017)—extend other studies of the correlation between contact and positive attitudes:

- *South Africa*. The more interracial contact that South African Blacks and Whites have, the less prejudice they feel and the more sympathetic their policy attitudes are to those of the other group (Dixon et al., 2003, 2007; Tredoux & Finchilescu, 2010).
- *Sexual orientation and transgender identity*. The more contact that straight people have with gays and lesbians, the more accepting they become (Collier et al., 2012; Smith et al., 2009). The more contact cisgender people have with transgender individuals, the less trans-prejudice they express (Norton & Herek, 2013). What matters is not *what* you know about gay or transgender people, but *who* you know.
- *Muslims*. The more contact Dutch adolescents have with Muslims, the more accepting of Muslims they are (González et al., 2008).
- *Roommates and family*. For White students, having a Black roommate improves racial attitudes and leads to greater comfort with those of another race (Gaither & Sommers, 2013). Other potent connections with a single out-group member, such as through adopting an interracial child or having a gay child, similarly link people with the out-group and reduce implicit prejudice (Gulker & Monteith, 2013).
- *Intergenerational*. The more contact younger people have with older adults, the more favourable their attitudes toward older people are (Drury et al., 2016).
- *Indirect contact*. Even vicarious indirect contact, via story reading or imagination or through friends who have an out-group friend, tends to reduce prejudice (Bilewicz &

Kogan, 2014; Crisp et al., 2011; Turner, Hewstone, & Voci, 2007; Turner, Hewstone, Voci, Paolini, et al., 2007; Turner, Hewstone, Voci, & Vanofakou, 2008; Turner & Crisp 2010). Those who read the *Harry Potter* books—with their themes of supportive contact with stigmatized groups—have better attitudes toward immigrants, gay people, and refugees (Vezzali et al., 2014). This indirect contact effect, also called the *extended-contact effect*, can spread more positive attitudes through a peer group (Christ et al., 2010; Wright et al., 2008).

As interracial contact has increased, expressed prejudice has diminished. But was interracial contact the *cause* of these improved attitudes?

Does contact improve racial attitudes?

Sometimes desegregation improves racial attitudes, but sometimes—especially when there is anxiety or perceived threat (Pettigrew, 2004)—it doesn't. Such disagreements excite the scientist's detective spirit. What explains the difference? So far, we've been lumping all kinds of contact together. Actual interracial contact occurs in many ways and under vastly different conditions.

Morton Deutsch and Mary Collins (1951) took advantage of a made-to-order natural experiment to test whether desegregation improves racial attitudes. In accordance with state law, New York City desegregated its public housing units; it assigned families to apartments without regard to race. In a similar development across the river in Newark, New Jersey, Blacks and Whites were assigned to separate buildings. When surveyed, White women in the desegregated development were far more likely to favour interracial housing and to say their attitudes toward Blacks had improved. Exaggerated stereotypes had wilted in the face of reality. As one woman put it, "I've really come to like it. I see they're just as human as we are."

Given that "mere exposure" can produce liking, might exposure to other-race faces produce increased liking for other-race strangers? Indeed, yes, Leslie Zebrowitz and her colleagues (2008) discovered, when exposing White participants to Asian and Black faces.

When it might not: Self-segregation

Providing the opportunity for contact does not mean that people will take the opportunity. Researchers have gone into dozens of schools and observed with whom children of a given race eat, talk, and loiter. Race influences contact. Whites have disproportionately associated with Whites; Blacks, with Blacks (Schofield, 1982, 1986). The same self-imposed segregation was evident on a South African beach, as John Dixon and Kevin Durrheim (2003) discovered when they recorded the locations of Black, White, and Indian beachgoers one midsummer afternoon (see Figure 12–4).

In school cafeterias, people may wonder, "Why are all the Black kids sitting together?" (a question that could as easily be asked of the White kids). One naturalistic study observed 119 class sessions of 26 University of Cape Town tutorial groups, which averaged six Black and 10 White students per group (Alexander & Tredoux, 2010). On average, the researchers calculated that 71 percent of Black students would have needed to change seats to achieve a fully integrated seating pattern.

Even within the same race, likes tend to self-segregate. That's what University of Ulster (Northern Ireland) researchers discerned when noting the lecture hall seating patterns of Catholic and Protestant students (Orr et al., 2012).

In one study that tracked the attitudes of more than 1600 European students, contact reduced prejudice. But prejudice also minimized contact (Binder et al., 2009). Prejudice, however, is not the only obstacle to contact. Anxiety also helps explain why those placed in interracial relationships (when students are paired as roommates or as partners in an experiment) may engage in less intimate self-disclosure than those in same-race relationships (Johnson et al., 2009; Trail et al., 2009).

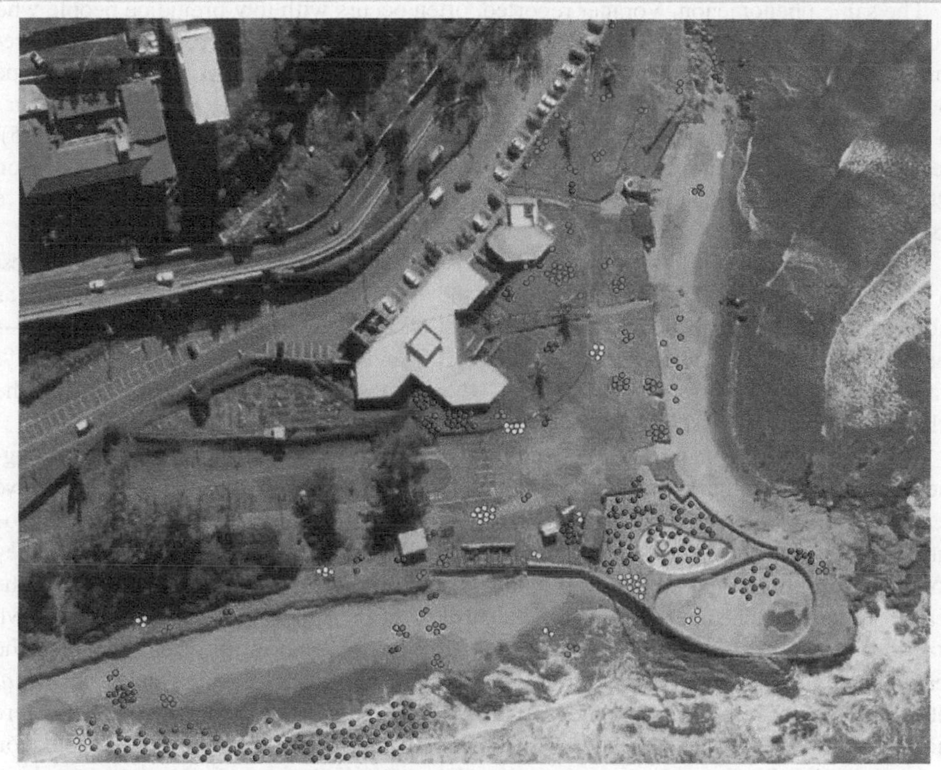

FIGURE 12–4 DESEGREGATION NEED NOT MEAN CONTACT.

After this Scottburgh, South Africa, beach became "open" and desegregated in the new South Africa, Blacks (represented by red dots), Whites (blue dots), and Indians (yellow dots) tended to cluster with their own race.

Source: From Dixon & Durrheim, 2003.

Efforts to facilitate contact sometimes help but sometimes fall flat. "We had one day when some of the Protestant schools came over," explained one Catholic youngster after a Northern Ireland school exchange (Cairns & Hewstone, 2002). "It was supposed to be like … mixing, but there was very little mixing. It wasn't because we didn't want to; it was just really awkward." The lack of mixing stems partly from "pluralistic ignorance." Many Whites and Blacks say they would like more contact but misperceive that the other does not reciprocate their feelings.

Perhaps you can recall a time when you really would have liked to reach out to someone. Maybe it was someone to whom you felt attracted. But, doubting that your feelings were reciprocated, you didn't risk rebuff. Or maybe it was someone of another race whom you wanted to welcome to the open seat at your dining hall or library table, but you worried that the person might be wary of sitting with you. On some such occasions, the other person shared your wish to connect but assumed that your distance signified indifference or even prejudice. Alas, thanks to pluralistic ignorance—shared false impressions of another's feelings—you passed like ships in the night.

Studies by University of Manitoba psychologist Jacquie Vorauer (2001, 2005; Vorauer & Sakamoto, 2006) illuminate this phenomenon. In new relationships, people often overestimate the transparency of their feelings, Vorauer reported. Presuming that their feelings are leaking out, they experience the *illusion of transparency*. Thus, they may assume that their body language conveys their romantic interest, when actually the intended recipient never gets the message. If the other person shares the positive feelings, and is similarly overestimating their own transparency, then the possible relationship is quenched.

The same phenomenon, Vorauer reported, often occurs with low-prejudice people who would love more friendships with those outside their racial or social group. If Whites presume that Blacks think them prejudiced, and if Blacks presume that Whites stereotype them, both will feel anxious about making the first move. Such anxiety is "a central factor" in South Africa's "continuing informal segregation," reported Gillian Finchilescu (2005). Seeking to replicate and extend Vorauer's work, Nicole Shelton and Jennifer Richeson (2006; Richeson & Shelton, 2012; Shelton, Richeson, & Vorauer, 2006) undertook a coordinated series of surveys and behavioural tests.

In their studies, White students viewed themselves as having more-than-average interest in cross-racial contacts and friendships, and they perceived White students in general as more eager for such than were Black students. Black students had mirror-image views—seeing themselves as more eager for cross-racial friendships than were White students. "I want to have friendships across racial lines," thought the typical student. "But those in the other racial group don't share my desire."

This pluralistic ignorance generalized to a specific setting. White students who imagined entering their dining hall and noticing several Black (or White) "students who live near you sitting together," believed that they, more than those of the other race, would be interested in contact. Other students contemplated a dining hall situation in which they noticed a table with familiar-looking students of the other race, but neither they nor the seated students reached out to the other. Regardless of their race, they attributed their own inaction in such a situation primarily to fear of rejection, and more often attributed the seated students' inaction to lack of interest. These social misperceptions constrain *actual* interracial contact. In one of Richeson and Shelton's studies, White students who were most prone to pluralistic ignorance—to presuming that they feared interracial rejection more than did Black students—were also the most likely to experience diminishing cross-racial contacts in the ensuing weeks.

Misperceptions alone do not impede romances and cross-racial friendships. But misperceptions do restrain people from risking an overture. Understanding this phenomenon—recognizing that others' coolness may actually reflect motives and feelings similar to our own—may help us reach out to others, and sometimes to transform potential friendships into real ones.

Friendship

The encouraging older studies involved more than enough contact to reduce the anxiety that marks interracial interaction. Other studies show similar benefits when they involve prolonged, personal contact—between Black and White prison inmates, between Black and White girls in an interracial summer camp, between Black and White university roommates, and between Black, Coloured, and White South Africans (Al Ramiah & Hewstone, 2013; Beelmann & Heinemann, 2014). The same has been true of intergroup contact programs in Northern Ireland, Cyprus, and Bosnia (Hewstone et al., 2014). One program that brought Israeli and Palestinian youth to a three-week camp produced significant and sustained improvement in intergroup attitudes (Schroeder & Risen, 2014).

So how does intergroup contact reduce prejudice and increase support for racial equality? It does so, report contact researchers Ananthi Al Ramiah and Miles Hewstone (2013), by

- *reducing anxiety* (more contact brings greater comfort),
- *increasing empathy* (contact helps people put themselves in others' shoes),
- *humanizing others* (enabling people to discover their similarities), and
- *decreasing perceived threats* (alleviating overblown fears and increasing trust).

Among American students who have studied in Germany or in Britain, the more contact they have with the host country's people, the more positive their attitudes are (Stangor et al., 1996). Exchange students' hosts also are transformed by the experience, becoming

THE INSIDE STORY

We noticed that both White and ethnic minority students in our classes often indicated that they genuinely wanted to interact with people outside of their ethnic group but were afraid that they would not be accepted. However, they assumed that members of other groups simply did not want to connect. This sounded very much like Dale Miller's work on pluralistic ignorance. Over the course of a few weeks, we designed a series of studies to explore pluralistic ignorance during interracial interactions.

Since the publication of our article, we have had researchers tell us that we should use our work in new student orientation sessions in order to reduce students' fears about reaching across racial lines. We are delighted that when we present this work in our courses, students of all racial backgrounds tell us that it indeed has opened their eyes about making the first move to develop interracial friendships.

Source: ©Justin Pumfrey/The Image Bank/Getty Images.

Nicole Shelton *Princeton University*
Jennifer Richeson *Yale University*

Cross-racial friendships can reduce prejudice if people see their friends both as individuals and as members of their groups. Saying "I don't see colour" is both inaccurate and often counterproductive.

Source: ©Felix Sanchez/Blend Images LLC.

more open to new experiences and more likely to see things from the visitor's cultural perspective (Sparkman et al., 2016; Vollhardt, 2010).

Group salience (visibility) also helps bridge divides between people. If you forever think of that friend solely as an individual, your affective ties may not generalize to other members of the friend's group (Miller, 2002). Ideally, then, we should form trusting friendships across group lines but also recognize that the friend represents those in another group (Brown et al., 2007).

We are especially likely to befriend dissimilar people when their out-group identity is initially minimized. If our liking for our new friends is then to generalize to others, their group identity must at some point become salient. So, to reduce prejudice and conflict, we had best initially minimize group diversity, then acknowledge it, and then transcend it.

Surveys of nearly 4000 Europeans reveal that friendship is key to successful contact: If you have a minority group friend, you become much more likely to express sympathy and support for the friend's group and even somewhat more support for immigration by that group. It's true of West Germans' attitudes toward Turks, French people's attitudes toward Asians and North Africans, Netherlanders' attitudes toward Surinamers and Turks, British people's attitudes toward West Indians and Asians, and Northern Ireland Protestants' and Catholics' attitudes toward each other (Brown et al., 1999; Hamberger & Hewstone, 1997; Paolini et al., 2004; Pettigrew, 1997).

equal-status contact Contact on an equal basis. Just as a relationship between people of unequal status breeds attitudes consistent with their relationship, so do relationships between those of equal status. Thus, to reduce prejudice, interracial contact should ideally be between persons equal in status.

Equal-status contact

Social psychologists never claimed that all contact would improve attitudes. Much as positive contact boosts liking, negative contact increases *disliking* (Guffler & Wagner, 2017; Hayward et al., 2017, 2018; McKeown & Psaltis, 2017). Positive contact is more commonplace, but negative experiences have greater effect (Graf et al., 2014; Paolini et al., 2014).

Social psychologists had expected poor results when contacts were competitive, unsupported by authorities, and unequal (Pettigrew, 1988; Stephan, 1987). Before 1954, many prejudiced Whites had frequent contact with Blacks—as shoeshine men and domestic workers. As we have seen, such unequal contact breeds attitudes that merely justify the continuation of inequality. So it's important that the contact be **equal-status contact**.

Cooperation

Although equal-status contact can help, it is sometimes not enough. It didn't help when Muzafer Sherif stopped the competition between the Eagles and Rattlers and brought the groups together for noncompetitive activities, such as watching movies, shooting off fireworks, and eating. By that time, their hostility was so strong that mere contact only provided opportunities for taunts and attacks. When an Eagle was bumped by a Rattler, for example, his fellow Eagles urged him to "brush off the dirt." Desegregating the two groups hardly promoted their social integration.

Given entrenched hostility, what can a peacemaker do? Desegregation was most successful at reducing prejudice when it brought people together into equal-status contact and made them interdependent, fighting a common enemy, or striving toward a shared goal.

Does that suggest a second factor that predicts whether the effect of desegregation will be favourable? Does competitive contact divide and *cooperative* contact unite? Consider what happens to people who together face a common predicament. In conflicts at all levels, from couples to teams to nations, *shared threats* and *common goals* breed unity.

Common external threats build cohesiveness

Together with others, have you ever been caught in a blizzard, punished by a teacher, or persecuted and ridiculed because of your social, racial, or religious identity? If so, you may recall feeling close to those with whom you shared the predicament. Perhaps previous social barriers fell as you helped one another dig out of the snow or struggled to cope with your common enemy. Survivors of shared pain or more extreme crises, such as a bombing, also often report a spirit of cooperation and solidarity rather than all-for-themselves panic (Bastian et al., 2014; Drury et al., 2009).

Such friendliness is common among those who experience a shared threat. John Lanzetta (1955) observed this when he put four-man groups of naval cadets to work on problem-solving tasks and then began informing them over a loudspeaker that their answers were wrong; their productivity, inexcusably low; their thinking, stupid. Other groups did not receive this harassment. Lanzetta observed that the group members under duress became friendlier to one another, more cooperative, less argumentative, and less competitive. They were in it together. And the result was a cohesive spirit. Recent experiments confirm a silver lining of mistreatment by a boss: those mistreated become more cohesive (Stoverink et al., 2014). Misery loves company.

Having a common enemy unified the groups of competing boys in Sherif's camping experiments—and in many subsequent experiments (Dion, 1979). Just being reminded of an out-group (say, a rival school) heightens people's responsiveness to their own group (Wilder & Shapiro, 1984). To perceive discrimination against one's racial or religious group is to feel more bonded and identified with that group (Craig & Richeson, 2012;

Martinovic & Verkuyten, 2012; Ramos et al., 2012). When keenly conscious of who "they" are, we also know who "we" are.

Shared predicaments trigger cooperation, as these Walmart workers on strike in Germany demonstrate.
Source: ©FRANK AUGSTEIN/AP Images.

When facing a well-defined external threat during wartime, the we-feeling soars. Membership in civic organizations mushrooms (Putnam, 2000). Shared threats also produce a political "rally around the flag" effect (Lambert et al., 2011). Children and youth who survive war exposure later display a more cooperative spirit toward their in-group (Bauer et al., 2014).

Even just imagining or fearing the extinction of one's group often serves to strengthen in-group solidarity (Wohl et al., 2010). Likewise, merely imagining the shared climate-change threat reduces international antagonism (Pyszczynski et al., 2012). Leaders may therefore *create* a threatening external enemy as a technique for building group cohesiveness. George Orwell's novel *1984* illustrates this tactic: The leader of the protagonist nation uses border conflicts with the other two major powers to lessen internal strife. From time to time the enemy shifts, but there is always an enemy. Indeed, the nation seems to *need* an enemy. For the world, for a nation, for a group, then, having a common enemy is powerfully unifying. Sunni and Shia Islamic differences that seem significant in Iraq will not seem so significant to Muslims in countries where both must cope with anti-Muslim attitudes.

The roots of rivalry run deep. Our ancestors, living in a world where neighbouring tribes occasionally raided and pillaged one another's camps, knew that there was safety in solidarity. (Those who didn't band together left fewer descendants.) Whether hunting, defending, or attacking, many hands were better than just two. Dividing the world into "us" and "them" entails significant costs, such as racism and war, but also provides the benefits of communal solidarity. To identify us and them, our ancestors—not so far removed from today's rabid sports fans—dressed or painted themselves in group-specific costumes and colours. Sports and warfare, notes evolutionary psychologist Benjamin Winegard (2010), are mostly done by males associated with geographical areas and wearing group-identifying uniforms. Both use war-relevant skills (running, tackling, throwing). And both offer rewards to the victors.

As social animals, we live in groups, cheer for our groups, kill for our groups, die for our groups. We also define ourselves by our groups. Our self-concept—our sense of who we are—consists not only of our personal attributes and attitudes but also of our social identity. Our social identities—our knowing who "we" are—strengthens self-concept and pride, especially when perceiving that "we" are superior. Lacking a positive individual identity, many youths find pride, power, and identity in gangs. Many patriots define themselves by their national identities.

The group definition of who we *are* also implies who we are *not*. Social–psychological experiments reveal that being formed into groups—even arbitrary groups—promotes in-group bias. Cluster people into groups defined by nothing more than their birth date or even the last digit of their driver's licence and they'll feel a certain kinship with their number mates and will show them favouritism. So strong is our group consciousness that "we" seem better than "they" even when "we" and "they" are defined randomly.

Group solidarity soars when people face a common enemy. As Muzafer Sherif's Robber's Cave boys' camp experiment vividly demonstrated, competition creates enemies. Fuelled by competition and unleashed by the anonymity of a crowd, passions can culminate in sport's worst moments—fans taunting opponents, screaming at umpires, even pelting referees with beer bottles.

Group identification soars further with success. Fans find self-respect, in at least small measure, by their association with the victorious athletes when their team wins. Queried after a big football victory, university students commonly report that "*we* won" (Cialdini et al., 1976). They bask in reflected glory. Asked the outcome after a defeat, students more often distance themselves from the team by saying, "*They* lost."

Ironically, we often reserve our most intense passions for rivals most similar to us. Freud long ago recognized that animosities formed around small differences: "Of two neighbouring towns, each is the other's most jealous rival; every little canton looks down upon the others with contempt. Closely related races keep one another at arm's length; the South German cannot endure the North German, the Englishman casts every kind of aspersion upon the Scot, the Spaniard despises the Portuguese."

To today's non-Muslims, antagonist Sunni and Shia Muslims might seem pretty similar (both revere the Qur'an, follow Muhammad, and pray to Allah). Likewise, to non-Christians, Northern Ireland's formerly combative Protestants and Catholics (both followers of the same Prince of Peace) seemed religiously and ethnically so similar. But with those near us, our attention focuses not on our considerable similarities but on our differences.

As rabid Toronto Blue Jays fans are happy if either the Jays win or the Yankees lose, so ardent New Zealand rugby fans root for New Zealand and whoever is playing against Australia (Halberstadt et al., 2006). Fervent fans of Scottish soccer likewise rejoice in either a Scotland victory or an England defeat. "Phew! They Lost," rejoiced one Scottish tabloid front-page headline after England's 1996 Euro Cup defeat—by Germany. To a sports fan, few things are so sweet as an archrival's misfortune. Both a rival's failure and a favoured team's success activate pleasure-associated brain areas (Cikara et al., 2011).

Numerical minorities, such as the Scots in Britain, are especially conscious of their social identities. The 5 million Scots and their descendants are more conscious of their national identity vis-à-vis the neighbouring 53 million English than vice versa. (The United States and Canada have but nine English social organizations and 111 Scottish ones [Watson, 2015].) Likewise, the 5 million New Zealanders are more conscious of their identity vis-à-vis the 24 million Australians, and they are more likely to root for Australia's sports opponents (Halberstadt et al., 2006).

Superordinate goals foster cooperation

superordinate goals Shared goals that necessitate cooperative effort: goals that override people's differences from one another.

Closely related to the unifying power of an external threat is the unifying power of **superordinate goals,** goals that unite all in a group and require cooperative effort. To promote harmony among his warring campers, Sherif introduced such goals. He created a problem with the camp water supply, necessitating both groups' cooperation to restore the water. As well, given an opportunity to rent a movie, one expensive enough to require the joint resources of the two groups, they again cooperated. When a truck "broke down" on a camp excursion, a staff member casually left the tug-of-war rope nearby, prompting one boy to suggest that they all pull the truck to get it started. When it started, a backslapping celebration ensued over their victorious "tug-of-war against the truck."

After working together to achieve such superordinate goals, the boys ate together and enjoyed themselves around a campfire. Friendships sprouted across group lines. Hostilities plummeted (Figure 12–5). On the last day, the boys decided to travel home together on one bus. During the trip, they no longer segregated by groups. As the bus approached home, they, as one, spontaneously sang "Oklahoma" and then bade their friends farewell. With isolation and competition, Sherif made strangers into bitter enemies. With superordinate goals, he made enemies into friends.

Are Sherif's experiments mere child's play? Or can pulling together to achieve superordinate goals be similarly beneficial with conflicting adults? Robert Blake and Jane

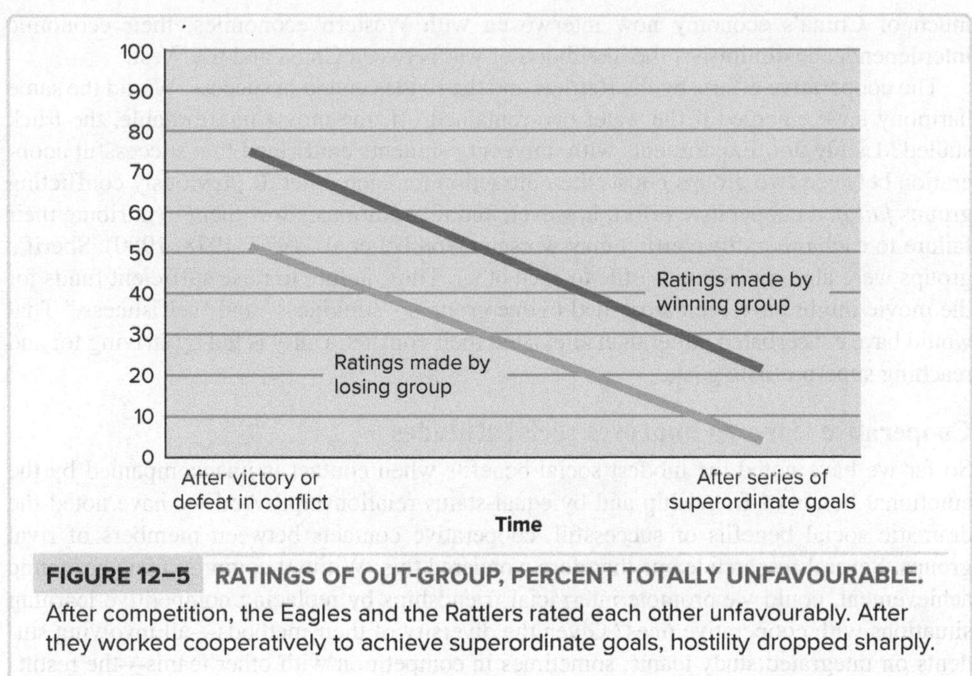

FIGURE 12–5 RATINGS OF OUT-GROUP, PERCENT TOTALLY UNFAVOURABLE.
After competition, the Eagles and the Rattlers rated each other unfavourably. After they worked cooperatively to achieve superordinate goals, hostility dropped sharply.

Mouton (1962, 1979) wondered. So, in a series of two-week experiments involving more than 1000 executives in 150 different groups, they recreated the essential features of the situation experienced by the Rattlers and the Eagles. Each group first engaged in activities by itself, then competed with another group, and then cooperated with the other group in working toward jointly chosen superordinate goals. Their results provided "unequivocal evidence that adult reactions parallel those of Sherif's younger subjects."

Extending those findings, John Dovidio, Samuel Gaertner, and their collaborators (2005, 2009) report that working cooperatively has especially favourable effects under conditions that lead people to define a new, inclusive group that dissolves their former subgroups. Old feelings of bias against another group diminish when members of the two groups sit alternately around a table (rather than on opposite sides), give their new group a single name, and then work together under conditions that foster a good mood. "Us" and "them" become "we."

Promoting "common in-group identity." The banning of gang colours and the common European practice of school uniforms aim to change "us" and "them" into "we."
Source: ©Ian Shaw/Getty Images.

To combat Germany, Italy, and Japan during the Second World War, Canada, the United States, and the former USSR, along with other nations, formed one united group named the Allies. So long as the superordinate goal of defeating a common enemy lasted, so did supportive Canadian and U.S. attitudes toward the Russians. From Amazon tribes to European countries, peace arises when groups become interconnected and interdependent and develop an overarching social identity (Fry, 2012). To reduce Muslim–Christian tension in the Central African Republic, Catholic Relief Services has paid people to dig drainage ditches, with one condition: Muslims and Christians work together (Kristof, 2018).

Economic interdependence through international trade also motivates peace. "Where goods cross frontiers, armies won't," noted Michael Shermer (2006). With so much of China's economy now interwoven with Western economies, their economic interdependence diminishes the likelihood of war between China and the West.

The cooperative efforts by the Rattlers and the Eagles ended in success. Would the same harmony have emerged if the water had remained off, the movie unaffordable, the truck stalled? Likely not. Experiments with university students confirmed that successful cooperation between two groups boosts their attraction for each other. If previously conflicting groups *fail* in a cooperative effort, however, and if conditions allow them to attribute their failure to each other, the conflict may worsen (Worchel et al., 1977, 1978, 1980). Sherif's groups were already feeling hostile to each other. Thus, failure to raise sufficient funds for the movie might have been attributed to one group's "stinginess" and "selfishness." That would have exacerbated rather than alleviated their conflict. Unity is fed by striving for and reaching superordinate goals.

Cooperative learning improves racial attitudes

So far we have noted the modest social benefits when contact is unaccompanied by the emotional bonds of friendship and by equal-status relationships. And we have noted the dramatic social benefits of successful, cooperative contacts between members of rival groups. Several research teams therefore wondered this: Without compromising academic achievement, could we promote interracial friendships by replacing competitive learning situations with cooperative ones? Given the diversity of their methods—all involving students on integrated study teams, sometimes in competition with other teams—the results are striking and heartening.

Are students who participate in existing cooperative activities, such as interracial athletic teams and class projects, less prejudiced? In one experiment, White youth on two- to three-week Outward Bound expeditions (involving intimate contact and cooperation) expressed improved attitudes toward Blacks a month after the expedition *if* they had been randomly assigned to an interracial expedition group (Green & Wong, 2008).

Robert Slavin and Nancy Madden (1979) analyzed survey data from 2400 students in 71 high schools and found similarly encouraging results. Those of different races who play and work together are more likely to report having friends of another race and to express positive racial attitudes. Charles Green and his colleagues (1988) confirmed this in a study of 3200 middle-school students. Compared with students at traditional, competitive schools, those at schools with interracial "learning teams" had more positive racial attitudes.

From such correlational findings, can we conclude that cooperative interracial activity improves racial attitudes? To find out, we experiment, by randomly designating some students, but not others, to work together in racially mixed groups. Slavin (1985; Slavin et al., 2003, 2009) and his colleagues divided classes into interracial teams, each composed of four or five students from all achievement levels. Team members sat together, studied a variety of subjects together, and at the end of each week competed with the other teams in a class tournament. All members contributed to their team's score by doing well, sometimes by competing with other students whose recent achievements were similar to their own, sometimes by competing with their own previous scores. Everyone had a chance to succeed. Moreover, team members were motivated to help one another prepare for the weekly tournament—by drilling each other on fractions, spelling, or historical events—whatever the next event was. Rather than isolating students from one another, team competition brought them into closer contact and drew out mutual support.

Another research team, led by Elliot Aronson (2004; Aronson & Gonzalez, 1988), elicited similar group cooperation with a "jigsaw" technique. In experiments in Texas and California elementary schools, the researchers assigned children to racially and academically diverse six-member groups. The subject matter was then divided into six parts, with each student becoming the expert on one part. In a unit on Chile, one student might be the expert on Chile's history, another on its geography, another on its culture. First, the various "historians," "geographers," and so forth got together to master their material. Then they returned to the home groups to teach it to their classmates. Each group member held, so to speak, a piece of the jigsaw.

Self-confident students therefore had to listen to and learn from reticent students who, in turn, soon realized they had something important to offer their peers. Other research teams have devised additional methods for cooperative learning. Studies (148 of them across 11 countries) show that adolescents, too, have more positive peer relationships and may even achieve more when working cooperatively rather than competitively (Lemmer & Wagner, 2015; Roseth et al., 2008).

What can we conclude from all this research? With cooperative learning, students learn not only the material but other lessons. Cooperative learning, said Slavin and Cooper (1999), promotes "the academic achievement of all students while simultaneously improving intergroup relations." Aronson reported that "children in the interdependent, jigsaw classrooms grow to like each other better, develop a greater liking for school, and develop greater self-esteem than children in traditional classrooms" (1980, p. 232).

Cross-racial friendships also begin to blossom. The exam scores of minority students improve (perhaps because academic achievement is now peer supported). After the experiments are over, many teachers continue using cooperative learning (D. W. Johnson et al., 1981; Slavin, 1990). "It is clear," wrote race-relations expert John McConahay (1981), that cooperative learning "is the most effective practice for improving race relations in desegregated schools that we know of to date."

Should we have "known it all along"? At the time of the 1954 Supreme Court decision, Gordon Allport spoke for many social psychologists in predicting that "Prejudice … may be reduced by equal status contact between majority and minority groups in the pursuit of common goals" (1954, p. 281). Cooperative learning experiments confirmed Allport's insight, making Robert Slavin and his colleagues (1985, 2003) optimistic: "Thirty years after Allport laid out the basic principles operationalized in cooperative learning methods, we finally have practical, proven methods for implementing contact theory in the desegregated classroom. … Research on cooperative learning is one of the greatest success stories in the history of educational research."

Interracial cooperation—on athletic teams, in class projects, and in extracurricular activities—melts differences and improves racial attitudes. White teen athletes who play cooperative team sports (such as basketball) with Black teammates express more liking and support for Blacks than do their counterparts involved in individual sports (such as wrestling) (Brown et al., 2003).

Source: ©sirtravelalot/Shutterstock.

To sum up, cooperative, equal-status contacts exert a positive influence on boy campers, industrial executives, college students, and schoolchildren. Does the principle extend to all levels of human relations? Are families unified by pulling together to farm the land, restore an old house, or sail a sloop? Are communal identities forged by raising a barn, singing as a group, or cheering for the football team? Is international understanding bred by international collaboration in science and space? By joint efforts to feed the world and conserve resources? By friendly personal contacts between people of different nations? Indications are that the answer to all of those questions is "yes" (Brewer & Miller, 1988; Desforges et al., 1991, 1997; Deutsch, 1985, 1994). Thus, an important challenge facing our divided world is to identify and agree on our superordinate goals and to structure cooperative efforts to achieve them.

Group and superordinate identities

In everyday life, we often reconcile multiple identities (Gaertner et al., 2000, 2001). We acknowledge our subgroup identity (as parent or child) and then transcend it (sensing our superordinate identity as a family). Pride in our ethnic heritage can complement our larger communal or national identity. Being mindful of our multiple social identities enables social cohesion (Brewer & Pierce, 2005; Crisp & Hewstone, 1999, 2000): "I am many things, some of which you are, too."

But in ethnically diverse cultures, how do people balance their ethnic identities with their national identities? They may have a "bicultural" or "omnicultural" identity, one that identifies with both the larger culture and their own ethnic and religious culture (Moghaddam, 2009, 2010; Phinney, 1990): "In many ways, I am like everyone around me, but I also affirm my own cultural heritage." Thus, ethnically conscious Asians living in England may also feel strongly British (Hutnik, 1985). French Canadians who identify with their ethnic roots may or may not also feel strongly Canadian (Driedger, 1975).

> ***"Most of us have overlapping identities which unite us with very different groups. We can love what we are, without hating what—and who—we are not. We can thrive in our own tradition, even as we learn from others, and come to respect their teachings."***
>
> Kofi Annan, Nobel Peace Prize lecture, 2001

Over time, identification with a new culture often grows. Former East and West Germans come to see themselves as "German" (Kessler & Mummendey, 2001). The children of Chinese immigrants to Australia and the United States feel their Chinese identity somewhat less keenly, and their new national identity more strongly, than do immigrants who were born in China (Rosenthal & Feldman, 1992). Often, however, the grandchildren of immigrants feel more comfortable identifying with their ethnicity (Triandis, 1994).

Researchers have wondered whether pride in one's group competes with identification with the larger culture. We evaluate ourselves partly in terms of our social identities. Seeing our own group (our school, our employer, our family, our race, our nation) as good helps us feel good about ourselves. A positive ethnic identity can therefore contribute to positive self-esteem—and so can a positive mainstream cultural identity. "Marginal" people, who have neither a strong ethnic nor a strong mainstream cultural identity (Table 12–1), often have low self-esteem. Bicultural people, who affirm both identities, typically have a strongly positive self-concept (Phinney, 1990; Sam & Berry, 2010). Often, they alternate between their two cultures, adapting their language and behaviour to whichever group they are with (LaFromboise et al., 1993).

TABLE 12-1 Ethnic and Cultural Identity.

	Ethnic Group Identification	
Majority Group Identification	**Strong**	**Weak**
Strong	Bicultural	Assimilated
Weak	Separated	Marginal

Is it better to recognize and affirm group differences or to look beyond them (Hahn et al., 2015)? Debate continues over the ideals of multiculturalism (celebrating differences) versus assimilation (meshing one's values and habits with the prevailing culture). Compared with university minority students, those in the majority racial group have been more likely to favour assimilation. They more often agree, for example, that "there should be a single center on campus for all students, rather than separate cultural centers for students of different racial groups" (Hehman et al., 2012).

On one side of the multiculturalism vs. assimilation debate are those who believe, as the Department of Canadian Heritage (2006) has declared, that "multiculturalism ensures that all citizens can keep their identities, can take pride in their ancestry and have a sense of belonging. Acceptance gives Canadians a feeling of security and self-confidence, making them open to and accepting of diverse cultures."

On the other side are those who concur with Britain's Commission for Racial Equality chair, Trevor Phillips (2004), in worrying that multiculturalism separates people. Experiments by Jacquie Vorauer and Stacey Sasaki (2011) showed that, in threatening situations, highlighting multicultural differences enhanced hostility. Focusing on differences prompted people to attend and attach meaning to out-group members' threatening behaviours. Likewise, highlighting genetic differences between ethnic groups contributes to violence risk, while learning about genetic similarities helps foster peace (Kimel et al., 2016). Thus, an alternative common values view inspired the Rwandan government to declare that "there is no ethnicity here. We are all Rwandan." In the aftermath of Rwanda's ethnic bloodbath, government documents and government-controlled radio and newspapers have ceased mentioning Hutu and Tutsi (Lacey, 2004).

In the space between multiculturalism and assimilation lies "diversity within unity," an omnicultural perspective advocated by cultural psychologist Fathali Moghaddam (2009, 2010) and by sociologist Amitai Etzioni (2005): "It presumes that all members of a given society will fully respect and adhere to those basic values and institutions that are considered part of the basic shared framework of the society. At the same time, every group in society is free to maintain its distinct subculture—those policies, habits, and institutions that do not conflict with the shared core."

By forging unifying ideals, immigrant countries (such as the United States, Canada, and Australia) have avoided ethnic wars. In these countries, Irish and Italians, Swedes and Scots, Asians and Africans seldom kill in defence of their ethnic identities. Nevertheless, even the immigrant nations struggle between separation and wholeness, between people's pride in their distinct heritage and unity as one nation, between acknowledging the reality of diversity and questing for shared values and identity.

Communication

Conflicting parties have ways to resolve their differences. When spouses, or labour and management, or Nation X and Nation Y disagree, they can try **bargaining** with one another directly. They can ask for **mediation** by a third party who will make suggestions and facilitate their negotiations. Or they can try **arbitration**, submitting their disagreement to someone who will study the issues and impose a settlement.

bargaining Seeking an agreement through direct negotiation between parties.

mediation An attempt by a neutral third party to resolve a conflict by facilitating communication and offering suggestions.

arbitration Resolution of a conflict by a neutral third party who studies both sides and imposes a settlement.

Bargaining

If you want to buy or sell a new car, are you better off adopting a tough bargaining stance—opening with an extreme offer so that splitting the difference will yield a favourable result? Or are you better off beginning with a sincere "good-faith" offer?

Experiments suggest no simple answer. On the one hand, those who demand more will often get more. Robert Cialdini, Leonard Bickman, and

John Cacioppo (1979) provide a typical result: In a control condition, they approached various Chevrolet dealers and asked the price of a new Monte Carlo sports coupe. In an experimental condition, they approached other dealers and first struck a tougher bargaining stance, asking for and rejecting a price on a *different* car ("I need a lower price than that. That's a lot"). When they then asked the price of the Monte Carlo, exactly as in the control condition, they received offers that averaged some $200 lower.

Tough bargaining may lower the other party's expectations, making the other side willing to settle for less (Yukl, 1974). But toughness can sometimes backfire. Many a conflict is not over a pie of fixed size but over a pie that shrinks if the conflict continues. A time delay is often a lose–lose scenario. When a strike is prolonged, labour loses wages and management loses income. Being tough is therefore a potential lose–lose scenario. If the other party responds with an equally tough stance, both may be locked into positions from which neither can back down without losing face.

The nurses' strike in Quebec in the summer of 1999 had some of these features. Premier Lucien Bouchard had announced before the strike that he would not give a raise greater than 5 percent over three years, and the nurses announced they would not accept such a deal. After such statements, it is difficult for either side to compromise and reach an agreement.

Mediation

A third-party mediator may offer suggestions that enable conflicting parties to make concessions and still save face (Pruitt, 1998). If my concession can be attributed to a mediator, who is gaining an equal concession from my antagonist, then neither of us will be viewed as weakly caving in.

Turning win–lose into win–win

Mediators also help resolve conflicts by facilitating constructive communication. Their first task is to help the parties rethink the conflict and gain information about the other's interests (Thompson, 1998). Typically, people on both sides have a competitive win–lose orientation: They think that they are successful if their opponent is unhappy with the result and unsuccessful if their opponent is pleased (Thompson, Valley, & Kramer, 1995). The mediator aims to replace this win–lose orientation with a cooperative win–win orientation, by prodding them to set aside their conflicting demands and instead think about each other's underlying needs, interests, and goals.

A classic win–win story concerns two sisters who quarrelled over an orange (Follett, 1940). Finally they compromised and split the orange in half, whereupon one sister squeezed her half for juice while the other used the peel to make a cake. If the sisters had each explained *why* they wanted the orange, they very likely would have agreed to share it, giving one sister all the juice and the other all the peel. This is an example of an integrative agreement (Pruitt & Lewis, 1975, 1977). Compared with compromises, in which each party sacrifices something important, **integrative agreements** are more enduring. Because they are mutually rewarding, they also lead to better ongoing relationships (Pruitt, 1986).

integrative agreements Win–win agreements that reconcile both parties' interests to their mutual benefit.

Unravelling misperceptions with controlled communications

Communication often helps reduce self-fulfilling misperceptions. Perhaps you can recall experiences similar to that of this university student:

> Often, after a prolonged period of little communication, I perceive Martha's silence as a sign of her dislike for me. She, in turn, thinks that my quietness is a result of my being mad at her. My silence induces her silence, which makes me even more silent … until this snowballing effect is broken by some occurrence that makes it necessary for us to interact. And the communication then unravels all the misinterpretations we had made about one another.

TABLE 12–2 How People Can Argue Constructively.

Do Not	Do
• evade the argument, give the silent treatment, or walk out.	• clearly define the issue and repeat the other's arguments in your own words.
• use your intimate knowledge of the other person to hit below the belt and humiliate.	• divulge your positive and negative feelings.
• bring in unrelated issues.	• welcome feedback about your behaviour.
• feign agreement while harbouring resentment.	• clarify where you agree and disagree and what matters most to each of you.
• tell the other party how they are feeling.	• ask questions that help the other find words to express the concern.
• attack indirectly by criticizing someone or something that the other person values.	• wait for spontaneous explosions to subside, without retaliating.
• undermine the other by intensifying their insecurity or threatening disaster.	• offer positive suggestions for mutual improvement.

The outcome of such conflicts often depends on *how* people communicate their feelings. Psychologists Ian Gotlib and Catherine Colby (1988) offered advice on how to avoid destructive quarrels and how to have good quarrels (see Table 12–2). Children, for example, learn that conflict is normal, that people can learn to get along with those who are different, that most disputes can be resolved with two winners, and that nonviolent communication strategies are an alternative to a world of bullies and victims. This "violence prevention curriculum … is not about passivity," noted Deborah Prothrow-Stith (1991, p. 183). "It is about using anger not to hurt oneself or one's peers, but to change the world."

"[There is] a psychological barrier between us, a barrier of suspicion, a barrier of rejection; a barrier of fear, of deception, a barrier of hallucination."

Egyptian president Anwar al-Sadat, to the Israeli Knesset, 1977

David Johnson and Roger Johnson (1995, 2003) put children from Grades 1 to 9 through about a dozen hours of conflict resolution training in six schools, with very heartening results. Before the training, most students were involved in daily conflicts—put-downs and teasing, playground turn-taking conflicts, conflicts over possessions—conflicts that nearly always resulted in a winner and a loser. After training, the children more often found win–win solutions, better mediated friends' conflicts, and retained and applied their new skills in and out of school throughout the school year. When implemented with a whole student body, the result is a more peaceful student community and increased academic achievement.

Communication facilitators work to break down barriers, as in this diversity training exercise. In work organizations, too, diversity training can improve attitudes (Kalinoski et al., 2013).
Source: ©Rawpixel.com/Shutterstock.

Conflict researchers report that a key factor is *trust* (Balliet & Van Lange, 2013). If you believe the other person is well-intentioned, you are more likely to divulge your needs and concerns. Lacking trust, you may fear that being open will give the other party information that might be used against you. Even simple behaviours can enhance trust. In experiments, negotiators who were instructed to mimic the others' mannerisms, as naturally empathic people often do, elicited more trust and greater discovery of compatible interests and mutually

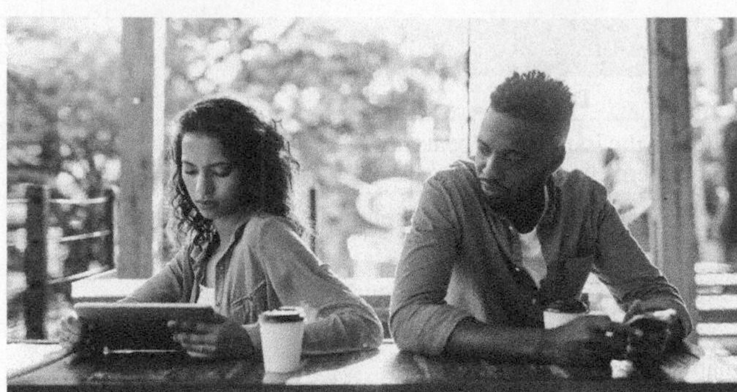

Trust, like other social behaviours, is also a biological phenomenon. Social neuroscientists have found that individuals with lowered levels of serotonin, the brain neurotransmitter, become more likely to see a low offer in a laboratory game as unfair, and to reject it (Bilderbeck et al., 2014; Colzato et al., 2013; Crockett et al., 2008). Infusions of the hormone oxytocin have something of an opposite effect, increasing people's trust of strangers in a laboratory game (Zak, 2008).

Source: ©PeopleImages/E+/Getty Images.

satisfying deals (Maddux, Mullen, & Galinsky, 2008). Meeting people face to face, and hearing their views in their own voice (rather than in writing) also helps to humanize them (Schroeder et al., 2018).

When the two parties mistrust each other and communicate unproductively, a third-party mediator—a marriage counsellor, a labour mediator, a diplomat—sometimes helps. Often, the mediator is someone trusted by both sides. In the 1980s, it took an Algerian Muslim to mediate the conflict between Iran and Iraq, and the Pope to resolve a geographical dispute between Argentina and Chile (Carnevale & Choi, 2000).

After coaxing the conflicting parties to rethink their perceived win–lose conflict, the mediator often has each party identify and rank its goals. When goals are compatible, the ranking procedure makes it easier for each to concede on less important goals so that both achieve their chief goals (Erickson et al., 1974; Schulz & Pruitt, 1978). South Africa achieved internal peace when White and Black South Africans granted each other's top priorities—replacing apartheid with majority rule and safeguarding the security, welfare, and rights of Whites (Kelman, 1998).

When labour and management both believe that management's goal of higher productivity and profit is compatible with labour's goal of better wages and working conditions, they can begin to work for an integrative win–win solution. If workers will forgo benefits that are moderately beneficial to them but very costly to management (perhaps company-provided dental care), and if management will forgo moderately valuable arrangements that workers very much resent (perhaps inflexibility of working hours), both sides may gain (Ross & Ward, 1995). Rather than seeing itself as making a concession, each side can see the negotiation as an effort to exchange bargaining chips for things more valued.

When the parties convene to communicate directly, they are usually not set loose in the hope that, eyeball-to-eyeball, the conflict will resolve itself. In the midst of a threatening, stressful conflict, emotions often disrupt the ability to understand the other party's point of view. Although happiness and gratitude can increase trust, anger decreases it (Dunn & Schweitzer, 2005). Communication may become most difficult just when it is most needed (Tetlock, 1985).

The mediator will, therefore, often structure the encounter to help each party understand and feel understood by the other. The mediator may ask the conflicting parties to restrict their arguments to statements of fact, including statements of how they feel and how they respond when the other acts in a given way: "I enjoy music. But when you play it loud, I find it hard to concentrate. That makes me crabby." To increase empathy, the mediator may ask people to reverse roles and argue the other's position or to imagine and explain what the other person is experiencing (Yaniv, 2012). The mediator may have them restate one another's positions before replying with their own: "It annoys you when I play my music and you're trying to study."

Experiments show that taking the other's perspective and inducing empathy decreases stereotyping and increases cooperation (Batson & Moran, 1999; Galinsky & Moskowitz, 2000; Todd et al., 2011). Hearing an out-group person criticizing their own group—as when Israeli Jews heard a Palestinian criticizing Palestinians—opens people to the out-group's perspective (Saguy & Halperin, 2014). It helps to humanize rather than demonize the other. Igor Grossman of the University of Waterloo and his colleagues (2010) observe that older people often find that easier to do, by having the wisdom to appreciate multiple

"Adversarial collaboration"—turning rivals into teammates. Groups with conflicting ideas may want to lay out where they agree, identify points of disagreement, and jointly propose solutions to those points.

Source: ©Photononstop/Alamy Stock Photo.

perspectives and the limits of knowledge. Sometimes our elders are older, wiser, and better able to navigate social conflicts.

When parties—perhaps two colleagues or two partners—are at an impasse and need to move on from their standstill, one simple strategy is literally to take steps forward together … *to go for a walk*. Walking together, like other forms of movement synchrony, engages people in jointly attending to their environment and coordinating their steps. Doing so increases their empathy and rapport, softens the boundary between them, and engenders cooperation (Good et al., 2017; Webb et al., 2017).

Neutral third parties may also suggest mutually agreeable proposals that would be dismissed—"reactively devalued"—if offered by either side. The very same proposal that is seen as a cheap trick when presented by the opposition is often seen as an interesting suggestion when presented by the mediator. Likewise, people will often reactively devalue a concession offered by an adversary ("They must not value it"); the same concession may seem more than a token gesture when suggested by a third party.

These peacemaking principles—based partly on laboratory experiments, partly on practical experience—have helped mediate both international and industrial conflicts (Blake & Mouton, 1962, 1979; R. J. Fisher, 1994; Wehr, 1979). Social psychologists have conducted workshops bringing together influential Arabs and Israelis (Kelman, 1998, 2007, 2010). Kelman and colleagues counter misperceptions and have participants seek creative solutions for their common good. Isolated, the participants are free to speak directly to their adversaries without fearing that their constituents are second-guessing what they were saying. The result? Those from both sides typically come to understand the other's perspective and how the other side responds to their own group's actions.

Arbitration

Some conflicts are so intractable, with underlying interests so divergent, that a mutually satisfactory resolution is unattainable. Conflicting claims to Jerusalem as the capital of an independent Palestine versus a secure Israel have, so far, proven insurmountable. In a divorce dispute over custody of a child, both parents cannot enjoy full custody. In these and many other cases (disputes over tenants' repair bills, athletes' wages, and national territories), a third-party mediator may—or may not—help resolve the conflict.

If not, the parties may turn to *arbitration* by having the mediator or another third party *impose* a settlement. Disputants usually prefer to settle their differences without arbitration so that they retain control over the outcome. Neil McGillicuddy and others (1987) observed this preference in an experiment involving disputants coming to a dispute settlement centre. When people knew they would face an arbitrated settlement if mediation failed, they tried harder to resolve the problem, exhibited less hostility, and thus were more likely to reach agreement.

In cases where differences seem large and irreconcilable, however, the prospect of arbitration may cause disputants to freeze their positions, hoping to gain an advantage when the arbitrator chooses a compromise. To combat that tendency, some disputes, such as those involving salaries of individual baseball players, are settled with "final-offer arbitration" in which the third party chooses one of the two final offers. Final-offer arbitration motivates each party to make a reasonable proposal.

Typically, however, the final offer is not as reasonable as it would be if each party, free of self-serving bias, saw its own proposal through others' eyes. Negotiation researchers report that most disputants are made stubborn by "optimistic overconfidence" (Kahneman & Tversky, 1995). Successful mediation is hindered when, as often happens, both parties believe they have a two-thirds chance of winning a final-offer arbitration (Bazerman, 1986, 1990).

Conciliation

Sometimes, tension and suspicion run so high that communication, let alone resolution, becomes all but impossible. Each party may threaten, coerce, or retaliate against the other. Unfortunately, such acts tend to be reciprocated, thus escalating the conflict. So, would a strategy of appeasing the other party by being unconditionally cooperative produce a satisfying result? Often not. In laboratory games, those who are 100 percent cooperative often are exploited. Politically, a one-sided pacifism is out of the question.

GRIT

GRIT An acronym for "graduated and reciprocated initiatives in tension reduction"—a strategy designed to de-escalate international tensions.

Social psychologist Charles Osgood (1962, 1980) advocated a third alternative—one that is conciliatory, yet strong enough to discourage exploitation. Osgood called it "graduated and reciprocated initiatives in tension reduction." He nicknamed it **GRIT**, a label that suggests the determination it requires. GRIT aims to reverse the "conflict spiral" by triggering reciprocal de-escalation. To do so, it draws upon social–psychological concepts, such as the norm of reciprocity and the attribution of motives.

GRIT requires one side to initiate a few small de-escalatory actions, after *announcing a conciliatory intent*. The initiator states a desire to reduce tension, declares each conciliatory act prior to making it, and invites the adversary to reciprocate. Such announcements create a framework that helps the adversary correctly interpret what otherwise might be seen as weak or tricky actions. They also bring public pressure on the adversary to follow the reciprocity norm.

Next, the initiator establishes credibility and genuineness by carrying out, exactly as announced, several verifiable *conciliatory acts*. This intensifies the pressure to reciprocate. Making conciliatory acts diverse—perhaps offering medical information, closing a military base, and lifting a trade ban—keeps the initiator from making a significant sacrifice in any one area and leaves the adversary freer to choose its own means of reciprocation. If the adversary reciprocates voluntarily, this conciliatory behaviour may soften its attitudes.

GRIT *is* conciliatory. But it is not "surrender on the installment plan." The remaining aspects of the plan protect each side's self-interest by *maintaining retaliatory capability*.

The initial conciliatory steps entail some small risk but do not jeopardize either one's security; rather, they are calculated to begin edging both sides down the tension ladder. If one side takes an aggressive action, the other side reciprocates in kind, making it clear it will not tolerate exploitation. Yet the reciprocal act is not an over-response that would re-escalate the conflict. If the adversary offers its own conciliatory acts, these, too, are matched or even slightly exceeded. Morton Deutsch (1993) captured the spirit of GRIT in advising negotiators to be "'firm, fair, and friendly': *firm* in resisting intimidation, exploitation, and dirty tricks; *fair* in holding to one's moral principles, not reciprocating the other's immoral behaviour despite his or her provocations; and *friendly* in the sense that one is willing to initiate and reciprocate cooperation."

"I am not suggesting that principles of individual behavior can be applied to the behavior of nations in any direct, simpleminded fashion. What I am trying to suggest is that such principles may provide us with hunches about inter-nation behavior that can be tested against experience in the larger arena."

Charles E. Osgood, *Our Crisis in Perspective*, 1966

Does GRIT really work? In a lengthy series of experiments, Svenn Lindskold and his associates (Lindskold, Bennett, & Wayner, 1976; Lindskold, Betz, & Walters, 1986; Lindskold, Han, & Betz, 1986a, 1986b; Lindskold & Han, 1988) found "strong support for the various steps in the GRIT proposal." In laboratory games, announcing cooperative intent *does* boost cooperation. Repeated conciliatory acts *do* breed greater trust (Klapwijk & Van Lange, 2009). Maintaining an equality of power *does* protect against exploitation.

Lindskold was not contending that the world of laboratory experiment mirrors the more complex world of everyday life. Rather, experiments enable us to formulate and verify powerful theoretical principles, such as the reciprocity norm and the self-serving bias. As Lindskold (1981) noted, "It is the theories, not the individual experiments, that are used to interpret the world."

Real-world applications

GRIT-like strategies have occasionally been tried outside the laboratory, with promising results. One of the best examples of such a strategy was Lester B. Pearson's handling of the Suez Canal crisis. In the summer of 1956, Egyptian president Gamal Abdel Nasser declared that the Egyptian government was taking control of the Suez Canal. He hoped to raise money from tolls charged to ships traversing the canal to finance the Aswan High Dam on the Nile River. A company controlled by British and French interests had previously controlled the canal. Britain and France were taken aback by the announcement and were worried that Egyptian control of the canal might restrict the flow of goods (particularly oil) to Western Europe. In October 1956, these worries led Great Britain, France, and their ally Israel to invade the canal zone. They gained control of the area but were criticized in international circles, precipitating a major international crisis. International outrage forced Great Britain, France, and Israel to withdraw from the canal zone, and Anthony Eden, the British foreign minister, to resign.

In response to this pressure-cooker situation, Lester B. Pearson, then Canada's foreign minister, formulated a plan in which concessions were made to both Egypt and Britain, as well as France and Israel. In exchange, United Nations peacekeeping troops were sent to the canal zone to ensure the plan was implemented. Egypt was allowed to collect tolls on ships going through the canal. Britain and France were assured that the canal would remain open and that trade would not be restricted. Israel was given shipping rights it had not previously enjoyed.

Lester B. Pearson received international acclaim (and the Nobel Peace Prize in 1957) for his role in handling the crisis; and, of course, he went on to become prime minister of Canada.

Might conciliatory efforts also help reduce tension between individuals? There is every reason to expect so. When a relationship is strained and communication nonexistent, it sometimes takes only a conciliatory gesture—a soft answer, a warm smile, a gentle touch—for both parties to begin easing down the tension ladder, to a rung where contact, cooperation, and communication again become possible.

SUMMING UP

What Creates Conflict?

- Whenever two people, two groups, or two nations interact, their perceived needs and goals may conflict.
- Many social dilemmas arise as people pursue individual self-interest, to their collective detriment. Two *non-zero-sum* laboratory games, the Prisoner's Dilemma and the Tragedy of the Commons, exemplify such dilemmas.
- In real life, we can avoid such traps by establishing rules that regulate self-serving behaviour; by keeping social groups small so people feel responsibility for one another; by enabling communication, thus reducing mistrust; by changing payoffs to make cooperation more rewarding; and by invoking altruistic norms.
- When people compete for scarce resources, human relations often sink into prejudice and hostility. In his famous experiment, Muzafer Sherif found that win–lose competition quickly made strangers into enemies, triggering outright warfare even among normally upstanding boys.
- *Conflicts* also arise when people perceive injustice. According to equity theory, people define justice as the distribution of rewards in proportion to one's contributions. Conflicts occur when people disagree on the extent of their contributions and thus on the equity of their outcomes.
- Conflicts frequently contain a small core of truly incompatible goals, surrounded by a thick layer of misperceptions of the adversary's motives and goals. Often, conflicting parties have *mirror-image perceptions*. When both sides believe, "We are peace-loving; they are hostile," each may treat the other in ways that provoke confirmation of its expectations. International conflicts are sometimes also fed by an evil leader–good people illusion.

How Can Peace Be Achieved?

- Although conflicts are readily kindled and fuelled by social dilemmas, competition, perceived injustices, and misperceptions, some equally powerful forces (contact, cooperation, communication, and conciliation) can transform hostility into harmony. Despite some encouraging early studies, other studies show that mere contact has little effect upon racial attitudes. But when contact encourages emotional ties with individuals identified with an out-group, and when it is structured to convey *equal status*, hostilities often lessen.
- Contacts are especially beneficial when people work together to overcome a common threat or to achieve a *superordinate goal*. Taking their cue from experiments on cooperative contact, several research teams have replaced competitive classroom learning situations with opportunities for cooperative learning, with heartening results.
- Conflicting parties often have difficulty communicating. The communication techniques of bargaining, mediation, and arbitration can bring conciliation and transform hostility into harmony.
- A third-party mediator can promote communication by prodding the antagonists to replace their competitive win–lose view of the conflict with a more cooperative win–win orientation, leading to an *integrative agreement*.

Mediators can also structure communications that will peel away misperceptions and increase mutual understanding and trust. When a negotiated settlement is not reached, the conflicting parties may defer the outcome to an *arbitrator*, who either dictates a settlement or selects one of the two final offers.

- Sometimes tensions run so high that genuine communication is impossible. In such cases, small conciliatory gestures by one party may elicit reciprocal conciliatory acts by the other party. One such conciliatory strategy, graduated and reciprocated initiatives in tension reduction (GRIT), aims to alleviate tense international situations. Those who mediate tense labour–management and international conflicts sometimes use another peacemaking strategy. They instruct the participants in the dynamics of conflict and peacemaking in the hope that understanding can help them establish and enjoy peaceful, rewarding relationships.

Key Terms

- arbitration
- bargaining
- conflict
- equal-status contact
- equality
- GRIT
- integrative agreements
- mediation
- need-based distribution
- non-zero-sum-games
- peace
- social trap
- superordinate goals
- Tragedy of the Commons

References

Abbate, C. S., Isgro, A., Wicklund, R. A., & Boca, S. (2006). A field experiment on perspective-taking, helping, and self-awareness. *Basic and Applied Social Psychology, 28,* 283–287.

Abbey, A. (1987). Misperceptions of friendly behavior as sexual interest: A survey of naturally occurring incidents. *Psychology of Women Quarterly, 11,* 173–194.

Abbey, A. (1991). Misperception as an antecedent of acquaintance rape: A consequence of ambiguity in communication between women and men. In A. Parrot (Ed.), *Acquaintance rape.* New York: Wiley.

Abbey, A. (2011). Alcohol and dating risk factors for sexual assault: Double standards are still alive and well entrenched. *Psychology of Women Quarterly, 35,* 362–368.

Abbey, A., & Andrews, F. M. (1985). Modeling the psychological determinants of life quality. *Social Indicators Research, 16,* 1–34.

ABC News. (2004, March 31). Bizarre hoax leads to strip searches. Retrieved from http://abcnews.go.com

ABC News. (2020). George Floyd protests aren't just happening in big cities. Retrieved from https://abcnews.go.com/US/article/george-floyd-protests-happening-big-cities/story?id=71327256

Abelson, R. (1972). Are attitudes necessary? In B. T. King & E. McGinnies (Eds.), *Attitudes, conflict and social change.* New York: Academic Press.

Abrams, D., Wetherell, M., Cochrane, S., Hogg, M. A., & Turner, J. C. (1990). Knowing what to think by knowing who you are: Self-categorization and the nature of norm formation, conformity and group polarization. *British Journal of Social Psychology, 29,* 97–119.

Abramson, L. Y., Metalsky, G. I., & Alloy, L. B. (1989). Hopelessness depression: A theory-based subtype. *Psychological Review, 96,* 358–372.

Acevedo, B. P., Aron, A., Fisher, H. E., & Brown, L. L. (2012). Neural correlates of long-term intense romantic love. *Scan, 7,* 145–159.

Ackerman, J. M., Griskevicius, V., & Li, N. P. (2011). Let's get serious: Communicating commitment in romantic relationships. *Journal of Personality and Social Psychology, 100,* 1079–1094.

Adachi, P. J. C., & Willoughby, T. (2011). The effect of violent video games on aggression: Is it more than just the violence? *Aggression and Violent Behavior, 16,* 55–62.

Adair, J. G., Dushenko, T. W., & Lindsay, R. C. L. (1985). Ethical regulations and their impact on research practice. *American Psychologist, 40,* 59–72.

Adams, D. (Ed.) (1991). The Seville statement on violence: Preparing the ground for the constructing of peace. UNESCO.

Adams, G., Garcia, D. M., Purdie-Vaughns, V., & Steele, C. M. (2006). The detrimental effects of a suggestion of sexism in an instruction situation. *Journal of Experimental Social Psychology, 42,* 602–615.

Adams, J. M., & Jones, W. H. (1997). The conceptualization of marital commitment: An integrative analysis. *Journal of Personality and Social Psychology, 72,* 1177–1196.

Addis, M. E., & Mahalik, J. R. (2003). Men, masculinity, and the contexts of help seeking. *American Psychologist, 58,* 5–14.

Aderman, D., & Berkowitz, L. (1983). Self-concern and the unwillingness to be helpful. *Social Psychology Quarterly, 46,* 293–301.

Adler, N. E., Boyce, T., Chesney, M. A., Cohen, S., Folkman, S., Kahn, R. L., & Syme, S. L. (1993). Socioeconomic inequalities in health: No easy solution. *Journal of the American Medical Association, 269,* 3140–3145.

Adler, N. E., Boyce, T., Chesney, M. A., Cohen, S., Folkman, S., Kahn, R. L., & Syme, S. L. (1994). Socioeconomic status and health: The challenge of the gradient. *American Psychologist, 49,* 15–24.

Adler, R. P., Lesser, G. S., Meringoff, L. K., Robertson, T. S., & Ward, S. (1980). The *effects of television advertising on children.* Lexington, MA: Lexington Books.

Adorno, T., Frenkel-Brunswik, E., Levinson, D., & Sanford, R. N. (1950). *The authoritarian personality.* New York: Harper.

AFP relaxnews. (2013, March 13). Young UK drivers overconfident of their abilities: Survey (https://sg.news.yahoo.com/young-uk-drivers-overconfident-abilitiessurvey-165114562.html).

Agerström, J., & Rooth, D-O. (2011). The role of automatic obesity stereotypes in real hiring discrimination. *Journal of Applied Psychology, 96,* 790–805.

Agnew, G. A., & Carron, A. V. (1994). Crowd effects and the home advantage. *International Journal of Sport Psychology, 25,* 53–62.

Agthe, M., Spörrle, M., & Maner, J. K. (2011). Does being attractive always help? Positive and negative effects of attractiveness on social decision making. *Personality and Social Psychology Bulletin, 37,* 1042–1054.

Aiello, J. R., & Douthitt, E. Z. (2001). Social facilitation from Triplett to electronic performance monitoring. *Group Dynamics: Theory, Research, and Practice, 5,* 163–180.

Aiello, J. R., Thompson, D. E., & Brodzinsky, D. M. (1983). How funny is crowding anyway? Effects of room size, group size, and the introduction of humor. *Basic and Applied Social Psychology, 4,* 193–207.

Ainsworth, M. D. S. (1973). The development of infant-mother attachment. In B. Caldwell & H. Ricciuti (Eds.), *Review of child development research* (Vol. 3). Chicago: University of Chicago Press.

Ainsworth, M. D. S. (1979). Infant-mother attachment. *American Psychologist, 34,* 932–937.

Ainsworth, S. E., & Maner, J. K. (2012). Sex begets violence: Mating motives, social dominance, and physical aggression in men. *Journal of Personality and Social Psychology, 103,* 819–829.

Ajzen, I. (1982). On behaving in accordance with one's attitudes. In M. P. Zanna, E. T. Higgins, & C. P. Herman (Eds.). *Consistency in social behavior: The Ontario Symposium* (Vol. 2). Hillside, NJ: Erlbaum.

Ajzen, I., & Fishbein, M. (1977). Attitude-behavior relations: A theoretical analysis and review of empirical research. *Psychological Bulletin, 84,* 888–918.

Al Ramiah, A., & Hewstone, M. (2013). Intergroup contact as a tool for reducing, resolving, and preventing intergroup conflict: Evidence, limitations, and potential. *American Psychologist, 68,* 527–542.

Albarracin, D., Gillette, J. C., Earl, A. N., Glasman, L. R., Durantini, M. R., & Ho, M. (2005). A test of major assumptions about behavior change: A comprehensive look at the effects of passive and active HIV-prevention interventions since the beginning of the epidemic. *Psychological Bulletin, 131,* 856.

Albarracin, D., Johnson, B. T., Fishbein, M., & Muellerleile, P. A. (2001). Theories of reasoned action and planned behavior as models of condom use: A meta-analysis. *Psychological Bulletin, 127,* 142–161.

Alexander, L., & Tredoux, C. (2010). The spaces between us: A spatial analysis of informal segregation at a South African university. *Journal of Social Issues, 66,* 367–386.

Allee, W. C., & Masure, R. M. (1936). A comparison of maze behavior in paired and isolated shell-parakeets (Melopsittacus undulatus Shaw) in a two-alley problem box. *Journal of Comparative Psychology, 22,* 131–155.

Allen, M. S., & Jones, M. V. (2014). The "home advantage" in athletic competitions. *Current Directions in Psychological Science, 23*(1), 48–53.

Allen, V. L., & Levine, J. M. (1969). Consensus and conformity. *Journal of Experimental Social Psychology, 5,* 389–399.

Allesøe, K., Hundrup, V. A., Thomsen, J. F., & Osler, M. (2010). Psychosocial work environment and risk of ischaemic heart disease in women: The Danish Nurse Cohort Study. *Occupational and Environmental Medicine, 67,* 318–322.

Allison, S. T., Mackie, D. M., Muller, M. M., & Worth, L. T. (1993). Sequential correspondence biases and perceptions of change: The Castro studies revisited. *Personality and Social Psychology Bulletin, 19,* 151–157.

Allison, S. T., McQueen, L. R., & Schaerf, L. M. (1992). Social decision making processes and the equal partitioning of shared resources. *Journal of Experimental Social Psychology, 28,* 23–42.

Allport, F. H. (1920). The influence of the group upon association and thought. *Journal of Experimental Psychology, 3,* 159–182.

Allport, G. (1954). *The nature of prejudice.* Cambridge, MA: Addison-Wesley.

Allport, G. W. (1958). *The nature of prejudice* (abridged). Garden City, NY: Anchor Books.

Allport, G. W., & Ross, J. M. (1967). Personal religious orientation and prejudice. *Journal of Personality and Social Psychology, 5,* 432–443.

Altemeyer, B. (2004). Highly dominating, highly authoritarian personalities. *Journal of Social Psychology, 144,* 421.

Altemeyer, R. (1988). *Enemies of freedom: Understanding right-wing authoritarianism.* San Francisco: Jossey-Bass.

Altemeyer, R. (2006). *The authoritarians.* Unpublished manuscript, University of Manitoba, Winnipeg, Canada.

Alwin, D. F., Cohen, R. L., & Newcomb, T. M. (1991). *Political attitudes over the life span: The Bennington women after fifty years.* Madison, WI: University of Wisconsin Press.

Amato, P. R. (1986). Emotional arousal and helping behavior in a real-life emergency. *Journal of Applied Social Psychology, 16,* 633–641.

Ambady, N., Bernieri, F. J., & Richeson, J. A. (2000). Toward a histology of social behavior: Judgmental accuracy from thin slices of the behavioral stream. In M. P. Zanna (Ed.), *Advances in Experimental Social Psychology, 32,* 201–271.

Ambady, N., & Rosenthal, R. (1992). Thin slices of expressive behavior as predictors of interpersonal consequences: A meta-analysis. *Psychological Bulletin, 111,* 256–274.

Ambady, N., & Rosenthal, R. (1993). Half a minute: Predicting teacher evaluations from thin slices of nonverbal behavior and physical attractiveness. *Journal of Personality and Social Psychology, 64,* 431–441.

American Enterprise. (1992, January/February). Women, men, marriages & ministers, 106.

American Psychological Association (1993). *Violence and youth: Psychology's response.* Vol I: Summary report of the American Psychological Association Commission on Violence and Youth. Washington DC: Public Interest Directorate, American Psychological Association.

American Psychological Association. (2015). Resolution on violent video games (http://www.apa.org/about/policy /violent-video-games.aspx).

Amodio, D. H., & Devine, P. G. (2010). Control in the regulation of intergroup bias. In R. R. Hassin, K. H. Ochsner, & Y. Trope (Eds.), *Self-control in society, mind, and brain.* New York: Oxford University Press.

Anastasi, J. S., & Rhodes, M. G. (2005). An own-age bias in face recognition for children and older adults. *Psychonomic Bulletin & Review, 12,* 1043–1047.

Anastasi, J. S., & Rhodes, M. G. (2006). Evidence for an own-age bias in face recognition. *North American Journal of Psychology, 8,* 237–252.

Anderegg, W. R. L., Prall, J. W., Harold, J., & Schneider, S. H. (2010). Expert credibility in climate change. *PNAS, 107,* 12107–12109.

Andersen, S. M. (1998). *Service learning: A national strategy for youth development. A position paper issued by the Task Force on Education Policy.* Washington, DC: Institute for Communitarian Policy Studies, George Washington University.

Andersen, S. M., & Chen, S. (2002). The relational self: An interpersonal social-cognitive theory. *Psychological Review, 109,* 619–645.

Anderson, C. (2011, August 2). Norway: War games and toys pulled from shelves. *New York Times.* Retrieved from http://www.nytimes.com

Anderson, C., Brion, S., Moore, D. A., & Kennedy, J. A. (2012). A status-enhancement account of overconfidence. *Journal of Personality and Social Psychology, 103,* 718–735.

Anderson, C., Keltner, D., & John, O. P. (2003). Emotional convergence between people over time. *Journal of Personality and Social Psychology, 84,* 1054–1068.

Anderson, C., Srivastava, S., Beer, J. S., Spataro, S. E., & Chatman, J. A. (2006). Knowing your place: Self-perceptions of status in face-to-face groups. *Journal of Personality and Social Psychology, 91,* 1094–1110.

Anderson, C. A. (1982). Inoculation and counter-explanation: Debiasing techniques in the perseverance of social theories. *Social Cognition, 1,* 126–139.

Anderson, C. A. (1999). Attributional style, depression, and loneliness: A cross-cultural comparison of American and Chinese students. *Personality and Social Psychology Bulletin, 25,* 482–499.

Anderson, C. A. (2003). Video games and aggressive behavior. In D. Ravitch and J. P. Viteritti (Eds.), *Kids stuff: Marking violence and vulgarity in the popular culture.* Baltimore, MD: Johns Hopkins University Press.

Anderson, C. A. (2004). An update on the effects of violent video games. *Journal of Adolescence, 27,* 113–122.

Anderson, C. A., & Anderson, D. C. (1984). Ambient temperature and violent crime: Tests of the linear and curvilinear hypotheses. *Journal of Personality and Social Psychology, 46,* 91–97.

Anderson, C. A., & Anderson, K. B. (1998). Temperature and aggression: Paradox, controversy, and a (fairly) clear picture. In R. G. Geen & E. Donnerstein (Eds.), *Human aggression: Theories, research, and implications for social policy.* San Diego: Academic Press.

Anderson, C. A., Anderson, K. B., Dorr, N., DeNeve, K. M., & Flanagan, M. (2000). Temperature and aggression. In M. P.

Zanna (Ed.), *Advances in experimental social psychology.* San Diego: Academic Press.
Anderson, C. A., Andrighetto, L., Bartholow, B. D., Bègue, L., Boxer, P., Brockmyer, J. F., Burgess, M. C. R., Calvete, E., Cantor, J., Coyne, S. M., Dill-Shackleford, K., Donnerstein, E., Gabbiadini, A., Gibson, B., Youssef, H., Lueke, A. K., Orue, I., Riva, P., Strasburger, V. C., Volpato, C., & Warburton, W. (2015). Consensus on media violence effects: Comment on Bushman, Gollwitzer, and Cruz (2015). *Psychology of Popular Media Culture, 4,* 215–221.
Anderson, C. A., Benjamin, A. J., Jr., & Bartholow, B. D. (1998). Does the gun pull the trigger? Automatic priming effects of weapon pictures and weapon names. *Psychological Science, 9,* 308–314.
Anderson, C. A., Berkowitz, L., Donnerstein, E., Huesmann, L. R., Johnson, J. D., Linz, D., Malamuth, N. M., & Wartella, E. (2003). The influence of media violence on youth. *Psychological Science in the Public Interest, 4*(3), 81–110.
Anderson, C. A., Buckley, K. E., & Carnagey, N. L. (2008). Creating your own hostile environment: A laboratory examination of trait aggressiveness and the violence escalation cycle. *Personality and Social Psychology Bulletin, 34,* 462–473
Anderson, C. A., & Bushman, B. J. (1997). External validity of "trivial" experiments: The case of laboratory aggression. *Review of General Psychology, 1,* 19–41.
Anderson, C. A., & Bushman, B. J. (2001). Effects of violent video games on aggressive behavior, aggressive cognition, aggressive affect, physiological arousal, and prosocial behavior: A meta-analytic review of the scientific literature. *Psychological Science, 12,* 353–359.
Anderson, C. A., Deuser, W. E., & DeNeve, K. M. (1995). Hot temperatures, hostile affect, hostile cognition, and arousal: Tests of a general model of affective aggression. *Personality and Social Psychology Bulletin, 21,* 434–448.
Anderson, C. A., Gentile, D. A., & Buckley, K. E. (2007). *Violent video game effects on children and adolescents: Theory, research, and public policy.* New York: Oxford University Press.
Anderson, C. A., Horowitz, L. M., & French, R. D. (1983). Attributional style of lonely and depressed people. *Journal of Personality and Social Psychology, 45,* 127–136.
Anderson, C. A., Lepper, M. R., & Ross, L. (1980). Perseverance of social theories: The role of explanation in the persistence of discredited information. *Journal of Personality and Social Psychology, 39,* 1037–1049.
Anderson, C. A., Lindsay, J. J., & Bushman, B. J. (1999). Research in the psychological laboratory: Truth or triviality? *Current Directions in Psychological Science, 8,* 3–9.
Anderson, C. A., Sakamoto, A., Gentile, D. A., Ihori, N., Shibuya, A., Yukawa, S., Naito, M., & Kobayashi, K. (2008). Longitudinal effects of violent video games on aggression in Japan and the United States. *Pediatrics, 122,* e1067–e1072.
Anderson, C. A., & Sechler, E. S. (1986). Effects of explanation and counterexplanation on the development and use of social theories. *Journal of Personality and Social Psychology, 50,* 24–34.
Anderson, C. A., Shibuya, A., Ihori, N., Swing, E. L., Bushman, B. J., Sakamoto, A., Rothstein, C. R., & Saleen, M. (2010). Violent video game effects on aggression, empathy, and prosocial behavior in Eastern and Western countries: A meta-analytic review. *Psychological Bulletin, 136,* 151–173.
Anderson, R. (2004). A definition of peace. *Peace and Conflict: Journal of Peace Psychology. Special Issue: Assessing Cultures of Peace, 10,* 101–116.
Anderson, S. L., Adams, G., & Plaut, V. C. (2008). The cultural grounding of personal relationship: The importance of attractiveness in everyday life. *Journal of Personality and Social Psychology, 95,* 352–368.
Anderson, V. N. (2017). Cisgender men and trans prejudice: Relationships with sexual orientation and gender self-esteem. *Psychology of Men & Masculinity.*
Anglemyer, A., Horvath, T., & Rutherford, G. (2014). The accessibility of firearms and risk for suicide and homicide victimization among household members: A systematic review and meta-analysis. *Annals of Internal Medicine, 160,* 101–110.
Angus Reid. (2012, June). Global warming skepticism higher in U.S. and Britain than Canada.
Angus Reid. (2015). Election 2015: Race narrows to Conservative-Liberal contest with NDP in third place; soft voters still cause for volatility. Retrieved from: http://angusreid.org/election-2015-race-narrows-to-conservative-liberal-contest/
Angus Reid Public Opinion. (2011). Tories lead in Canada, NDP firmly in second place due to Quebec strength.
Anik, L., Aknin, L. B., Norton, M. I., & Dunn, E. W. (2010). Feeling good about giving: The benefits (and costs) of self-interested charitable behavior. In D. M. Oppenheimer & C. Y. Olivola (Eds.), *The science of giving: Experimental approaches to the study of charity.* New York: Psychology Press.
Anthony, D. B., Holmes, J. G., & Wood, J. V. (2007). Social acceptance and self-esteem: Tuning the sociometer to interpersonal value. *Journal of Personality and Social Psychology, 92,* 1024.
Antonakis, J., & Dalgas, O. (2009). Predicting elections: Child's play! *Science, 323,* 1183.
AP. (2013, November 25). Man breaks woman's jump from Oakland stadium deck. Associated Press release.
AP/Ipsos. (2006, May 4). Associated Press/Ipsos Poll data reported by personal correspondence with Michael Gross.
Appel, M., Weber, S., & Kronberger, N. (2015). The influence of stereotype threat on immigrants: Review and meta-analysis. *Frontiers in Psychology, 6,* 900.
Archer, D., Iritani, B., Kimes, D. B., & Barrios, M. (1983). Face-ism: Five studies of sex differences in facial prominence. *Journal of Personality and Social Psychology, 45,* 725–735.
Archer, J. (1991). The influence of testosterone on human aggression. *British Journal of Psychology, 82,* 1–28.
Archer, J. (2006). Testosterone and human aggression: An evaluation of the challenge hypothesis. *Neuroscience and Biobehavioral Reviews, 30,* 319–345.
Archer, J. (2013). Can evolutionary principles explain patterns of family violence? *Psychological Bulletin, 139,* 403–440.
Archer, R. L., & Cook, C. E. (1986). Personalistic self-disclosure and attraction: Basis for relationship or scarce resource. *Social Psychology Quarterly, 49,* 268–272.
Arendt, H. (1963). *Eichmann in Jerusalem: A report on the banality of evil.* New York: Viking Press.
Ariza, L. M. (2006, January). Virtual Jihad: The Internet as the ideal terrorism recruiting tool. *Scientific American,* pp. 18–21.
Arkes, H. R. (1990). *Some practical judgment/decision making research.* Paper presented at the American Psychological Association convention.
Arkes, H. R., & Tetlock, P. E. (2004). Attributions of implicit prejudice, or "would Jesse Jackson 'fail' the implicit association test?" *Psychological Inquiry, 15,* 257–278.
Arkin, R. M., Appleman, A., & Burger, J. M. (1980). Social anxiety, self-presentation, and the self-serving bias in causal attribution. *Journal of Personality and Social Psychology, 38,* 23–35.
Arkin, R. M., & Burger, J. M. (1980). Effects of unit relation tendencies on

interpersonal attraction. *Social Psychology Quarterly, 43,* 380–391.

Arkin, R. M., Lake, E. A., & Baumgardner, A. H. (1986). Shyness and self-presentation. In W. H. Jones, J. M. Cheek, & S. R. Briggs (Eds.), *Shyness: Perspectives on research and treatment.* New York: Plenum.

Armitage, C. J., & Arden, M. A. (2016). Enhancing the effectiveness of alcohol warning labels with a self-affirming implementation intention. *Health Psychology, 35*(10), 1159–1163.

Armitage, C. J., & Conner, M. (2001). Efficacy of the theory of planned behaviour: A meta-analytic review. *British Journal of Social Psychology, 40,* 471–499.

Armor, D. A., & Sackett, A. M. (2006). Accuracy, error, and bias in predictions for real versus hypothetical events. *Journal of Personality and Social Psychology, 91,* 583–600.

Armor, D. A., & Taylor, S. E. (1996). Situated optimism: Specific outcome expectancies and self-regulation. In M. P. Zanna (Ed.), *Advances in experimental social psychology* (Vol. 30). San Diego, CA: Academic Press.

Arms, R. L., Russell, G. W., & Sandilands, M. L. (1979). Effects on the hostility of spectators of viewing aggressive sports. *Social Psychology Quarterly, 42,* 275–279.

Arnold, O., & Kaiser, F. G. (2018). Understanding the foot-in-the-door effect as a pseudo-effect from the perspective of the Campbell paradigm. *International Journal of Psychology, 53*(2), 157–165. https://doi-org.library.smu.ca/10.1002/ijop.12289

Aron, A., & Aron, E. (1989). *The heart of social psychology* (2nd ed.). Lexington, MA: Lexington Books.

Aron, A., & Aron, E. N. (1994). Love. In A. L. Weber & J. H. Harvey (Eds.), *Perspective on close relationships.* Boston: Allyn & Bacon.

Aron, A., Dutton, D. G., Aron, E. N., & Iverson, A. (1989). Experiences of falling in love. *Journal of Social and Personal Relationships, 6,* 243–257.

Aron, A., Fisher, H., Mashek, D. J., Strong, G., Li, H., & Brown, L. L. (2005). Reward, motivation, and emotion systems associated with early-stage intense romantic love. *Journal of Neurophysiology, 94*(1), 327.

Aron, A., Melinat, E., Aron, E. N., Vallone, R. D., & Bator, R. J. (1997). The experimental generation of interpersonal closeness: A procedure and some preliminary findings. *Personality and Social Psychology Bulletin, 23,* 363–377.

Aron, A., Norman, C. C., Aron, E. N., McKenna, C., & Heyman, R. E. (2000). Couples' shared participation in novel and arousing activities and experienced relationship quality. *Journal of Personality and Social Psychology, 78,* 273–284.

Aronson, E. (1980). The *social animal* (3rd ed.). New York: Freeman.

Aronson, E. (1988). *The social animal.* New York: Freeman.

Aronson, E. (1992). Stateways can change folkways. In R. M. Baird & S. E. Rosenbaum (Eds.), *Bigotry, prejudice, and hatred: Definitions, causes and solutions* (pp. 185–201). Buffalo, NY: Prometheus.

Aronson, E. (2004). Reducing hostility and building compassion: Lessons from the jigsaw classroom. In A. G. Miller (Ed.), *The social psychology of good and evil.* New York: Guilford.

Aronson, E., Brewer, M., & Carlsmith, J. M. (1985). Experimentation in social psychology. In G. Lindzey & E. Aronson (Eds.), *Handbook of social psychology* (Vol. 1). Hillsdale, NJ: Erlbaum.

Aronson, E., & Gonzalez, A. (1988). Desegregation, jigsaw, and the Mexican-American experience. In P. A. Katz & D. Taylor (Eds.), *Towards the elimination of racism: Profiles in controversy.* New York: Plenum.

Aronson, E., & Linder, D. (1965). Gain and loss of esteem as determinants of interpersonal attractiveness. *Journal of Experimental Social Psychology, 1,* 156–171.

Aronson, E., & Mettee, D. R. (1974). *Affective reactions to appraisal from others. Foundations of interpersonal attraction.* New York: Academic Press.

Aronson, E., & Mills, J. (1959). The effect of severity of initiation on liking for a group. *Journal of Abnormal and Social Psychology, 59,* 177–181.

Aronson, E., Turner, J. A., & Carlsmith, J. M. (1963). Communicator credibility and communicator discrepancy as determinants of opinion change. *Journal of Abnormal and Social Psychology, 67,* 31–36.

Arora, R. (2005). China's "Gen Y" bucks tradition. Gallup Poll. Retrieved from http://www.gallup.com/poll/15934/Chinas-Gen-Bucks-Tradition.aspx

Arriaga, X. B. (2001). The ups and downs of dating: Fluctuations in satisfaction in newly formed romantic relationships. *Journal of Personality and Social Psychology, 80,* 754.

Arriaga, X. B., & Agnew, C. R. (2001). Being committed: Affective, cognitive, and conative components of relationship commitment. *Personality and Social Psychology Bulletin, 27,* 1190.

Arrow, K. J., Forsythe, R., Gorham, M., Hahn, R., Hanson, R., Ledyard, J., Levmore, S., Litan, R., Milgrom, P., Nelson, F. D., Neumann, G. R., Ottaviani, M., Schelling, T. C., Shiller, R. J., Smith, V. L., Snowberg, E., Sunstein, C., Tetlock, P. E., … Zitzewitz, E. (2008). Economics: The promise of prediction markets. *Science, 320,* 877–878.

Asch, S. E. (1946). Forming impressions of personality. *Journal of Abnormal and Social Psychology, 41,* 258–290.

Asch, S. E. (1955, November). Opinions and social pressure. *Scientific American,* 31–35.

Ash, R. (1999). *The top 10 of everything 2000.* New York: DK Publishing.

Asher, J. (1987, April). Born to be shy? *Psychology Today,* 56–64.

Ashton-James, C., & Tracey, J. L. (2012). Pride and prejudice: How feelings about the self influence judgments of others. *Personality and Social Psychology Bulletin, 38, 466–476.*

Aslan, R. (2010). *Beyond Fundamentalism: Confronting Religious Extremism in the Age of Globalization.* Random House, NY:NY

Associated Press (AP). (2007, January 15). Kids copying execution accidentally hang selves. *Grand Rapids Press,* p. A3.

Associated Press. (2012, January 29). Maria Hoefl-Riesch edges Lindsey Vonn. Retrieved from http://espn.go.com/olympics/skiing/story/_/id/7516020/lindsey-vonn-denied-weekend-sweep-003-seconds

Associated Press. (2013, November 25). Man breaks women's jump from Oakland stadium deck. *Associated Press.*

Atwell, R. H. (1986, July 28). Drugs on campus: A perspective. *Higher Education and National Affairs,* 5.

Augoustinos, M., & Innes, J. M. (1990). Towards an integration of social representations and social schema theory. *British Journal of Social Psychology, 29,* 213–231.

Averill, J. R. (1983). Studies on anger and aggression: Implications for theories of emotion. *American Psychologist, 38,* 1145–1160.

Axelrod, R., & Dion, D. (1988). The further evolution of cooperation. *Science, 242,* 1385–1390.

Axsom, D., Yates, S., & Chaiken, S. (1987). Audience response as a heuristic cue in persuasion. *Journal of Personality and Social Psychology, 53,* 30–40.

Ayres, I. (1991). Fair driving: Gender and race discrimination in retail car negotiations. *Harvard Law Review, 104,* 817–872.

Azrin, N. H. (1967, May). Pain and aggression. *Psychology Today,* 27–33.

Baars, B. J., & McGovern, K. (1994). *How not to start a scientific revolution.* US: American Psychological Association.

Baars, B. J., & McGovern, K. A. (1994). Consciousness. In V. Ramachandran (Ed.), *Encyclopedia of human behavior.* Orlando, FL: Academic Press.

Babad, E., Bernieri, F., & Rosenthal, R. (1991). Students as judges of teachers' verbal and nonverbal behavior. *American Educational Research Journal, 28,* 211–234.

Bachman, J. G., Johnston, L. D., O'Malley, P. M., & Humphrey, R. N. (1988). Explaining the recent decline in marijuana use: Differentiating the effects of perceived risks, disapproval, and general lifestyle factors. *Journal of Health and Social Behavior, 29,* 92–112.

Bachman, J. G., & O'Malley, P. M. (1977). Self-esteem in young men: A longitudinal analysis of the impact of educational and occupational attainment. *Journal of Personality and Social Psychology, 35,* 365–380.

Back, M. D., Schmukle, S. C., & Egloff, B. (2008). Becoming friends by chance. *Psychological Science, 19,* 439–440.

Bae, M. (2016). The effects of anonymity on computer-mediated communication: The case of independent versus interdependent self-construal influence. *Computers in Human Behavior*, *55*, 300–309.

Bahns, A. (2017). Threat as justification of prejudice. *Group Processes & Intergroup Relations, 20,* 52–74.

Bailenson, J. N., & Yee, N. (2005). Digital chameleons: Automatic assimilation of nonverbal gestures in immersive virtual environments. *Psychological Science, 16,* 814.

Baize, H. R., Jr., & Schroeder, J. E. (1995). Personality and mate selection in personal ads: Evolutionary preferences in a public mate selection process. *Journal of Social Behavior and Personality, 10,* 517–536.

Baker, L., & McNulty, J. K. (2010). Shyness and marriage: Does shyness shape even established relationships? *Personality and Social Psychology Bulletin, 36,* 665–676.

Baldwin, M. W., & Carrell, S. E., & Lopez, D. F. (1990). Priming relationship schemas: My advisor and the Pope are watching me from the back of my mind. *Journal of Experimental Social Psychology, 26,* 435–454.

Baldwin, M. W., Keelan, J. P. R., Fehr, B., Enns, V., & Koh-Rangarajoo, E. (1996). Social-cognitive conceptualization of attachment working models: Availability and accessibility effects. *Journal of Personality and Social Psychology, 71,* 94–109.

Balliet, D., & Van Lange, P. A. M. (2013). Trust, conflict. and cooperation: A meta-analysis. *Psychological Bulletin, 139,* 1090–1112.

Balliet, D., Wu, J., & De Dreu, Carsten, K. W. (2014). Ingroup favoritism in cooperation: A meta-analysis. *Psychological Bulletin, 140,* 1556–1581.

Banaji, M. R. (2004). The opposite of a great truth is also true: Homage of Koan #7. In J. T. Jost, M. R. Banaji, & D. A. Prentice (Eds.), *Perspectivism in social psychology: The yin and yang of scientific progress.* Washington, DC: American Psychological Association.

Banaji, M. R., & Greenwald, A. G. (2013). *Blindspot: Hidden biases of good people.* New York: Delacorte Press.

Bandura, A. (1997). *Self-efficacy: The exercise of control.* New York: Freeman.

Bandura, A. (2000). Social cognitive theory: An agentic perspective. *Annual Review of Psychology, 52,* 1–26.

Bandura, A. (2004). Swimming against the mainstream: The early years from chilly tributary to transformative mainstream. *Behaviour Research and Therapy, 42,* 613–630.

Bandura, A. (2008). Reconstrual of "free will" from the agentic perspective of social cognitive theory. In J. Baer, J. C. Kaufman, & R. F. Baumeister (Eds.), *Are we free? Psychology and free will.* New York: Oxford University Press.

Bandura, A., Pastorelli, C., Barbaranelli, C., & Caprara, G. V. (1999). Self-efficacy pathways to childhood depression. *Journal of Personality and Social Psychology, 76,* 258–269.

Bandura, A., Ross, D., & Ross, S. A. (1961). Transmission of aggression through imitation of aggressive models. *Journal of Abnormal and Social Psychology, 63,* 575–582.

Bandura, A., & Walters, R. H. (1959). *Adolescent aggression.* New York: Ronald Press.

Bandura, A., & Walters, R. H. (1963). *Social learning and personality development.* New York: Holt, Rinehart and Winston.

Banks, S. M., Salovey, P., Greener, S., Rothman, A. J., Moyer, A., Beauvais, J., & Epel, E. (1995). The effects of message framing on mammography utilization. *Health Psychology, 14,* 178–184.

Bar-Haim, Y., Ziv, T., Lamy, D., & Hodes, R. M. (2006). Nature and nurture in own-race face processing. *Psychological Science, 17,* 159–163.

Bar-Tal, D. (2004). The necessity of observing real life situations: Palestinian-Israeli violence as a laboratory for learning about social behaviour. *European Journal of Social Psychology, 34,* 677–701.

Bar-Tal, D. (2013). *Intractable conflicts: Socio-psychological foundations and dynamics.* New York: Cambridge University Press.

Barash, D. (1979). *The whisperings within.* New York: Harper & Row.

Barber, B. M., & Odean, T. (2001a). Boys will be boys: Gender, overconfidence and common stock investment. *Quarterly Journal of Economics, 116,* 261–292.

Barber, B. M., & Odean, T. (2001b). The Internet and the investor. *Journal of Economic Perspectives, 15,* 41–54.

Bargh, J. A. (1997). The automaticity of everyday life. In R. S. Wyer (Ed.), *The automaticity of everyday life: Advances in social cognition* (Vol. 10) (pp. 1–61). Mahwah, NJ: Lawrence Erlbaum Associates.

Bargh, J. A. (2006). What have we been priming all these years? On the development, mechanisms, and ecology of nonconscious social behavior. *European Journal of Social Psychology, 36,* 147–168.

Bargh, J. A., & Chartrand, T. L. (1999). The unbearable automaticity of being. *American Psychologist*, 54, 462–479.

Bargh, J. A., & McKenna, K. Y. A. (2004). The Internet and social life. *Annual Review of Psychology, 55,* 573–590.

Bargh, J. A., McKenna, K. Y. A., & Fitzsimons, G. M. (2002). Can you see the real me? Activation and expression of the "true self" on the Internet. *Journal of Social Issues, 58,* 33–48.

Bargh, J. A., & Raymond, P. (1995). The naive misuse of power: Nonconscious sources of sexual harassment. *Journal of Social Issues. Special Issue: Gender Stereotyping, Sexual Harassment, and the Law, 51*(1), 85–96.

Barlett, C. P., & Anderson, C. A. (2014). Bad news, bad times, and violence: The link between economic distress and aggression. *Psychology of Violence, 4,* 309–321.

Barlett, C. P., Harris, R. J., & Bruey, C. (2008). The effect of the amount of blood in a violence video game on aggression, hostility, and arousal. *Journal of Experimental Social Psychology, 44,* 539–546.

Barlett, C. P., & Rodeheffer, C. (2009). Effects of realism on extended violent and nonviolent video game play on aggressive thoughts, feelings, and physiological arousal. *Aggressive Behavior, 35,* 213–224.

Barnes, R. D., Ickes, W., & Kidd, R. F. (1979). Effects of the perceived intentionality and stability of another's dependency on helping behavior. *Personality and Social Psychology Bulletin, 5,* 367–372.

Barnett, M. A., King, L. M., Howard, J. A., & Melton, E. M. (1980). *Experiencing negative affect about self or other: Effects on helping behavior in children and adults.* Paper presented at the Midwestern Psychological Association convention.

Barnett, T. A., O'Loughlin, J., Lambert, M., Gauvin, L., Kestens, Y., & Daniel, M. (2008). *Many teens spend 30 hours a week on "screen time" during high school.* American Heart Association 48th Annual Conference.

Baron J., & Hershey, J. C. (1988). Outcome bias in decision evaluation. *Journal of Personality and Social Psychology, 54,* 569–579.

Baron, J., & Miller, J. G. (2000). Limiting the scope of moral obligations to help: A cross-cultural investigation. *Journal of Cross-Cultural Psychology, 31,* 703–725.

Baron, R. A. (1977). *Human aggression.* New York: Plenum Press.

Baron, R. A., Markman, G. D., & Bollinger, M. (2006). Exporting social psychology: Effects of attractiveness on perceptions of entrepreneurs, their ideas for new products, and their financial success. *Journal of Applied Social Psychology, 36,* 467–492.

Baron, R. S. (1986). Distraction-conflict theory: Progress and problems. In L. Berkowitz (Ed.), *Advances in experimental social psychology.* Orlando, FL: Academic Press.

Baron, R. S. (2000). Arousal, capacity, and intense indoctrination. *Personality and Social Psychology Review, 4,* 238–254.

Baron, R. S., Kerr, N. L., & Miller, N. (1992). *Group process, group decision, group action.* Pacific Grove, CA: Brooks/Cole.

Barongan, C., & Hall, G. C. N. (1995). The influence of misogynous rap music on sexual aggression against women. *Psychology of Women Quarterly, 19,* 195–207.

Barry, D. (1998). *Dave Barry turns 50.* New York: Crown.

Bartholomew, K., & Horowitz, L. (1991). Attachment styles among young adults: A test of a four-category model. *Journal of Personality and Social Psychology, 61,* 226–244.

Bartholow, B. C., Anderson, C. A., Carnagey, N. L., & Benjamin, A. J., Jr. (2004). Interactive effects of life experience and situational cues on aggression: The weapons priming effect in hunters and nonhunters. *Journal of Experimental Social Psychology, 41,* 48–60.

Bartholow, B. D., Bushman, B. J., & Sestir, M. A. (2006). Chronic violent video game exposure and desensitization to violence: Behavioral and event-related brain potential data. *Journal of Experimental Social Psychology, 42,* 532.

Bartholow, B. D., & Heinz, A. (2006). Alcohol and aggression without consumption: Alcohol cues, aggressive thoughts, and hostile perception bias. *Psychological Science, 17,* 30.

Basile, K. C., Chen, J., Lynberg, M. C., & Saltzman, L. E. (2007). Prevalence and characteristics of sexual violence victimization. *Violence and Victims, 22,* 437–448.

Bassili, J. N. (1995). Response latency and the accessibility of voting intentions: What contributes to accessibility and how it affects vote choice. *Personality and Social Psychology Bulletin, 21,* 686–695.

Bassili, J. N. (1996). Meta-judgmental versus operative indexes of psychological attributes: The case of measures of attitude strength. *Journal of personality and social psychology, 71*(4), 637.

Bassili, J. N. (2003). The minority slowness effect: Subtle inhibitions in the expression of views not shared by others. *Journal of Personality and Social Psychology, 84,* 261–276.

Bassili, J. N., & Roy, J. P. (1998). On the representation of strong and weak attitudes about policy in memory. *Political Psychology, 19,* 669–681.

Bastardi, A., Uhlmann, E. L., & Ross, L. (2011). Wishful thinking: Belief, desire, and the motivated evaluation of scientific evidence. *Psychological Science, 22,* 731–732.

Bastian, B., & Haslam, N. (2006). Psychological essentialism and stereotype endorsement. *Journal of Experimental Social Psychology, 42,* 228–235.

Bastian, B., Jetten, J., Chen, H., Radke, H. R. M., Harding, J. F., & Fasoli, F. (2012). Losing our humanity: The self-dehumanizing consequences of social ostracism. *Personality and Social Psychology Bulletin, 39,* 156–169.

Bastian, B., Jetten, J., & Ferris, L. J. (2014). Pain as social glue: Shared pain increased cooperation. *Psychological Science, 25,* 2079–2085.

Batson, C. D. (1983). Sociobiology and the role of religion in promoting prosocial behavior: An alternative view. *Journal of Personality and Social Psychology, 45,* 1380–1385.

Batson, C. D. (1999a). Behind the scenes. In D. G. Myers, *Social psychology* (6th ed.). New York: McGraw-Hill.

Batson, C. D. (1999b). *Addressing the altruism question experimentally.* Paper presented at a Templeton Foundation/Fetzer Institute Symposium on Empathy, Altruism, and Agape, Cambridge, MA.

Batson, C. D. (2001). Addressing the altruism question experimentally. In S. G. Post, L. B. Underwood, J. P. Schloss, & W. B. Hurlbut (Eds.), *Altruism and altruistic love: Science, philosophy, and religion in dialogue.* New York: Oxford University Press.

Batson, C. D. (2006). "Not all self-interest after all": Economics of empathy-induced altruism. In D. De Cremer, M. Zeelenberg, & J. K. Murnighan (Eds.), *Social psychology and economics* (pp. 281–299). Mahwah, NJ: Lawrence Erlbaum Associates Publishers.

Batson, C. D. (2011). *Altruism in humans.* New York: Oxford University Press.

Batson, C. D., Chang, J., Orr, R., & Rowland, J. (2002). Empathy, attitudes, and action: Can feeling for a member of a stigmatized group motivate one to help the group? *Personality and Social Psychology Bulletin, 28*(12), 1656–1666.

Batson, C. D., Chao, M. C., & Givens, J. M. (2009). Pursuing moral outrage: Anger at torture. *Journal of Experimental Social Psychology, 45,* 155–160.

Batson, C. D., Coke, J. S., Jasnoski, M. L., & Hanson, M. (1978). Buying kindness: Effect of an extrinsic incentive for helping on perceived altruism. *Personality and Social Psychology Bulletin, 4,* 86–91.

Batson, C. D., Duncan, B. D., Ackerman, P., Buckley, T., & Birch, K. (1981). Is empathic emotion a source of altruistic motivation? *Journal of Personality and Social Psychology, 40,* 290–302.

Batson, C. D., Early, S., & Salvarani, G. (1997). Perspective taking: Imagining how another feels versus imaging how you would feel. *Personality and social psychology bulletin, 23*(7), 751–758.

Batson, C. D., Eklund, J. H., Chermok, V. L., Hoyt, J. L., & Ortiz, B. G. (2007). An additional antecedent of empathic concern: Valuing the welfare of the person in need. *Journal of Personality and Social Psychology, 93,* 65–74.

Batson, C. D., Fultz, J., & Schoenrade, P. A. (1987). Distress and empathy: Two qualitatively distinct vicarious emotions with different motivational consequences. *Journal of Personality, 55,* 19–40.

Batson, C. D., Harris, A. C., McCaul, K. D., Davis, M., & Schmidt, T. (1979). Compassion or compliance: Alternative dispositional attributions for one's helping behavior. *Social Psychology Quarterly, 42,* 405–409.

Batson, C. D., Kobrynowicz, D., Dinnerstein, J. L., Kampf, H. C., & Wilson, A. D. (1997). In a very different voice: Unmasking moral hypocrisy. *Journal of Personality and Social Psychology, 72,* 1335–1348.

Batson, C. D., Lishner, D. A., Carpenter, A., Dulin, L., Harjusola-Webb, S., Stocks, E. L., Gale, S., Hassam, O., & Sampat, B. (2003). "… As you would have them do unto you": Does imagining yourself in the other's place stimulate moral action? *Personality and Social Psychology Bulletin, 29,* 1190–1201.

Batson, C. D., & Moran, T. (1999). Empathy-induced altruism in a prisoner's dilemma. *European Journal of Social Psychology, 29,* 909–924.

Batson, C. D., & Thompson, E. R. (2001). Why don't moral people act morally? Motivational considerations. *Current Directions in Psychological Science, 10,* 54–57.

Batson, C. D., Thompson, E. R., & Chen, H. (2002). Moral hypocrisy: Addressing some alternatives. *Journal of Personality and Social Psychology, 83*(2), 330–339.

Batson, C. D., Thompson, E. R., Seuferling, G., Whitney, H., & Strongman, J. A. (1999). Moral hypocrisy: Appearing moral to oneself without being so. *Journal of Personality and Social Psychology, 77,* 525–537.

Batson, C. D., & Ventis, W. L. (1982). *The religious experience: A social psychological perspective.* New York: Oxford University Press.

Bauer, M., Cassar, A., Chytilová, J., & Henrich, J. (2014). War's enduring effects on the development of egalitarian motivations and in-group biases. *Psychological Science, 25,* 47–57.

Bauman, C. W., & Skitka, L. J. (2010). Making attributions for behaviors: The prevalence of correspondence bias in the general population. *Basic and Applied Social Psychology, 32,* 269–277.

Baumeister, R. (2005). Rejected and alone. *The Psychologist, 18,* 732.

Baumeister, R. (2007). Is there anything good about men? Address to the American Psychological Association convention.

Baumeister, R. F. (1996). Self-regulation and ego threat: Motivated cognition, self deception, and destructive goal setting. In P. M. Gollwitzer, & J. A. Bargh (Eds.), *The psychology of action: Linking cognition and motivation to behavior* (pp. 27–47). New York: Guilford Press.

Baumeister, R. F., & Bratslavsky, E. (1999). Passion, intimacy, and time: Passionate love as a function of change in intimacy. *Personality and Social Psychology Review, 3,* 49–67.

Baumeister, R. F., Bratslavsky, E., Finkenauer, C., & Vohs, D. K. (2001). Bad is stronger than good. *Review of General Psychology, 5,* 323–370.

Baumeister, R. F., Bratslavsky, E., Muraven, M., & Tice, D. M. (1998). Ego depletion: Is the active self a limited resource? *Journal of Personality and Social Psychology,* 74, 1252–1265.

Baumeister, R. F., Campbell, J. D., Krueger, J. I., & Vohs, K. D. (2003). Does high self-esteem cause better performance, interpersonal success, happiness, or healthier lifestyles? *Psychological Science in the Public Interest, 4*(1), 1–44.

Baumeister, R. F., Chesner, S. P., Senders, P. S., & Tice, D. M. (1988). Who's in charge here? Group leaders do lend help in emergencies. *Personality and Social Psychology Bulletin, 14,* 17–22.

Baumeister, R. F., DeWall, C. N., Ciarocco, N. J., & Twenge, J. M. (2005). Social exclusion impairs self-regulation. *Journal of Personality and Social Psychology, 88,* 589–604.

Baumeister, R. F., DeWall, C. N., & Vohs, K. D. (2009). Social rejection, control, numbness, and emotion: How not to be fooled by Gerber and Wheeler (2009). *Perspectives on Psychological Science, 4,* 489–493.

Baumeister, R. F., & Exline, J. J. (2000). Self-control, morality, and human strength. *Journal of Social and Clinical Psychology, 19,* 29–42.

Baumeister, R. F., & Leary, M. R. (1995). The need to belong: Desire for interpersonal attachment as a fundamental human motivation. *Psychological Bulletin, 117,* 495–527.

Baumeister, R. F., Muraven, M., & Tice, D. M. (2000). Ego depletion: A resource model of volition, self-regulation, and controlled processing. *Social Cognition, 18,* 130–150.

Baumeister, R. F., & Scher, S. J. (1988). Self-defeating behavior patterns among normal individuals: Review and analysis of common self-destructive tendencies. *Psychological Bulletin, 104,* 3–22.

Baumeister, R. F., & Tierney, J. (2011). *Willpower: The rediscovery of humans' greatest strength.* New York: Penguin.

Baumeister, R. F., Twenge, J. M., & Nuss, C. K. (2002). Effects of social exclusion on cognitive processes: Anticipated aloneness reduces intelligent thought. *Journal of Personality and Social Psychology, 83*(4), 817–827.

Baumeister, R. F., & Wotman, S. R. (1992). *Breaking hearts: The two sides of unrequited love.* New York: Guilford.

Baumgardner, A. H., & Brownlee, E. A. (1987). Strategic failure in social interaction: Evidence for expectancy disconfirmation process. *Journal of Personality and Social Psychology, 52,* 525–535.

Baumhart, R. (1968). *An honest profit.* New York: Holt, Rinehart & Winston.

Baxter, T. L., & Goldberg, L. R. (1987). Perceived behavioral consistency underlying trait attributions to oneself and another: An extension of the actor-observer effect. *Personality and Social Psychology Bulletin, 13,* 437–447.

Bayer, E. (1929). Beitrage zur zeikomponenten theorie des hungers. *Zeitschrift fur Psychologie, 112,* 1–54.

Bazerman, M. H. (1986, June). Why negotiations go wrong. *Psychology Today,* 54–58.

Bazerman, M. H. (1990). *Judgment in managerial decision making* (2nd ed.). New York: Wiley.

Bazzini, D., Curtin, L., Joslin, S., Regan, S., & Martz, D. (2010). Do animated Disney characters portray and promote the beauty-goodness stereotype? *Journal of Applied Social Psychology, 40,* 2687–2709.

BBC (2008, November 21). Pirates "gained $150m this year." Retrieved from http://www.bbc.com/news

Beall, A. T., Hofer, M. K., & Schaller, M. (2016). Infections and elections: Did an ebola outbreak influence the 2014 U.S. federal elections (and if so, how)? *Psychological Science, 27,* 595–605.

Beals, K. P., Peplau, L. A., & Gable, S. L. (2009). Stigma management and well-being: The role of perceived social support, emotional processing, and suppression. *Personality and Social Psychology Bulletin, 35,* 867–879.

Beaman, A. L., Barnes, P. J., Klentz, B., & McQuirk, B. (1978). Increasing helping rates through information dissemination: Teaching pays. *Personality and Social Psychology Bulletin, 4,* 406–411.

Beaman, A. L., & Klentz, B. (1983). The supposed physical attractiveness bias against supporters of the women's movement: A meta-analysis. *Personality and Social Psychology Bulletin, 9,* 544–550.

Beaman, A. L., Klentz, B., Diener, E., & Svanum, S. (1979). Self-awareness and transgression in children: Two field studies. *Journal of Personality and Social Psychology, 37,* 1835–1846.

Bearak, B. (2010, July 9). South Africa braces for new attacks on immigrants. *New York Times.* Retrieved from http://www.nytimes.com

Beauvois, J. L., Courbet, D., & Oberlé, D. (2012). The prescriptive power of the television host. A transposition of Milgram's obedience paradigm to the context of TV game show. *European Review of Applied Psychology, 62*(3), 111–119.

Becatoros, E. (2012, November 13). On streets of Athens, racist attacks increase.

Associated Press. Retrieved from http://www.yahoo.com/news

Beck, L. A., Pietrimonoco, P. R., DeBuse, C. J., Powers, S. I., & Sayer, A. G. (2013). Spouses' attachment pairings predict neuroendocrine, behavioral, and psychological responses to marital conflict. *Journal of Personality and Social Psychology, 105,* 388–424.

Becker, D. V., Neel, R., & Anderson, U. S. (2010). Illusory conjunctions of angry facial expressions follow intergroup biases. *Psychological Science, 21,* 938–940.

Becker, S. W., & Eagly, A. H. (2004). The heroism of women and men. *American Psychologist, 59,* 163–178.

Beeler-Duden, S., & Vaish, A. (2020). Paying it forward: The development and underlying mechanisms of upstream reciprocity. *Journal of Experimental Child Psychology, 192*. https://doi-org.library.smu.ca/10.1016/j.jecp.2019.104785

Beelmann, A., & Heinemann, K. S. (2014). Preventing prejudice and improving intergroup attitudes: A meta-analysis of child and adolescent training programs. *Journal of Applied Developmental Psychology, 35,* 10–24.

Bègue, L., Bushman, B., Giancola, P., Subra, B., & Rosset, E. (2010). "There is no such thing as an accident," especially when people are drunk. *Personality and Social Psychology Bulletin, 36,* 1301–1304.

Bekafigo, M. A., Stepanova, E. V., Eiler, B. A., Noguchi, K., & Ramsey, K. L. (2019). The effect of group polarization on opposition to Donald Trump. *Political Psychology*. https://doi-org.library.smu.ca/10.1111/pops.12584

Bell, P. A. (1980). Effects of heat, noise, and provocation on retaliatory evaluative behavior. *Journal of Social Psychology, 110,* 97–100.

Bell, P. A. (2005). Reanalysis and perspective in the heat-aggression debate. *Journal of Personality and Social Psychology, 89,* 71–73.

Belson, W. A. (1978). *Television violence and the adolescent boy.* Westmead, UK: Saxon House, Teakfield Ltd.

Beltrani, A., Reed, A., Zapf, P. & Otto, R. (2018). Is Hindsight Really 20/20?: The Impact of Outcome Information on the Decision-Making Process, *International Journal of Forensic Mental Health, 17:3*, 285-296, DOI: 10.1080/14999013.2018.1505790

Bem, D. J. (1972). Self-perception theory. In L. Berkowitz (Ed.), *Advances in experimental social psychology* (Vol. 6). New York: Academic Press.

Bem, D. J., & McConnell, H. K. (1970). Testing the self-perception explanation of dissonance phenomena: On the salience of premanipulation attitudes. *Journal of Personality and Social Psychology, 14,* 23–31.

Benjamin, A. J., Kepes, S., & Bushman, B. J. (2018). Effects of weapons on aggressive thoughts, angry feelings, hostile appraisals, and aggressive behavior: A meta-analytic review of the weapons effect. *Personality and Social Psychology Bulletin*.

Benjamin, L. T., Jr., & Simpson, J. A. (2009). The power of the situation: The impact of Milgram's obedience studies on personality and social psychology. *American Psychologist, 64,* 12–19.

Bennett, D. (2010, January 31). *How "cognitive fluency" shapes what we believe, how we invest, and who will become a supermodel.* Retrieved from http://www.boston.com

Bennett, R. (1991, February). *Pornography and extrafamilial child sexual abuse: Examining the relationship.* Unpublished manuscript, Los Angeles Police Department Sexually Exploited Child Unit.

Bennis, W. (1984). Transformative power and leadership. In T. J. Sergiovani & J. E. Corbally (Eds.), *Leadership and organizational culture.* Urbana: University of Illinois Press.

Benton, S. L., Downey, R. G., Gilder, P. J., & Benton, S. A. (2008). College students' norm perception predicts reported use of protective behavioral strategies for alcohol consumption. *Journal of Studies on Alcohol and Drugs, 69,* 859–866.

Benzies, K., Keown, L., & Magill-Evans, J. (2009). Immediate and sustained effects of parenting on physical aggression in Canadian children aged 6 years and younger. *The Canadian Journal of Psychiatry, 54,* 55–64.

Berg, J. H. (1984). Development of friendship between roommates. *Journal of Personality and Social Psychology, 46,* 346–356.

Berg, J. H. (1987). Responsiveness and self-disclosure. In V. J. Derlega & J. H. Berg (Eds.), *Self-disclosure: Theory, research, and therapy.* New York: Plenum.

Berg, J. H., & McQuinn, R. D. (1986). Attraction and exchange in continuing and noncontinuing dating relationships. *Journal of Personality and Social Psychology, 50,* 942–952.

Berg, J. H., & Peplau, L. A. (1982). Loneliness: The relationship of self-disclosure and androgyny. *Personality and Social Psychology Bulletin, 8,* 624–630.

Berger, J., Bradlow, E. T., Braumstein, A., & Zhang, Y. (2012). From Karen to Katie: Using baby names to understand cultural evolution. *Psychological Science, 23,* 1067–1073.

Berger, J., & Heath, C. (2008). Who drives divergence? Identity signaling, outgroup dissimilarity, and the abandonment of cultural tastes. *Journal of Personality and Social Psychology, 95,* 593–607.

Berglas, S., & Jones, E. E. (1978). Drug choice as a self-handicapping strategy in response to noncontingent success. *Journal of Personality and Social Psychology, 36,* 405–417.

Bergsieker, H. B., Leslie, L. M., Constantine, V. S., & Fiske, S. T. (2012). Stereotyping by omission: Eliminate the negative, accentuate the positive. *Journal of Personality and Social Psychology, 102,* 1214–1238.

Bergsieker, H. B., Shelton, J. N., & Richeson, J. A. (2010). To be liked versus respected: Divergent goals in interracial interactions. *Journal of Personality and Social Psychology, 99,* 248–264.

Berkowitz, L. (1954). Group standards, cohesiveness, and productivity. *Human Relations, 7,* 509–519.

Berkowitz, L. (1968, September). Impulse, aggression and the gun. *Psychology Today,* 18–22.

Berkowitz, L. (1969, July). The case for bottling up rage. *Psychology Today*, 24–30.

Berkowitz, L. (1973, September). The case for bottling up rage. *Psychology Today*, 24–31.

Berkowitz, L. (1975). Social norms, feelings, and other factors affecting helping and altruism. In L. Berkowitz (Ed.), *Advances in experimental social psychology* (Vol. 6). New York: Academic Press.

Berkowitz, L. (1978). Whatever happened to the frustration-aggression hypothesis? *American Behavioral Scientists, 21,* 691–708.

Berkowitz, L. (1981, June). How guns control us. *Psychology Today,* 11–12.

Berkowitz, L. (1983). Aversively stimulated aggression: Some parallels and differences in research with animals and humans. *American Psychologist, 38,* 1135–1144.

Berkowitz, L. (1984). Some effects of thoughts on anti- and prosocial influences of media events: A cognitive-neoassociation analysis. *Psychological Bulletin, 95,* 410–427.

Berkowitz, L. (1987). Mood, self-awareness, and willingness to help. *Journal of Personality and Social Psychology, 52,* 721–729.

Berkowitz, L. (1989). Frustration-aggression hypothesis: Examination and reformulation. *Psychological Bulletin, 106,* 59–73.

Berkowitz, L. (1995). A career on aggression. In G. G. Brannigan & M. R. Merrens (Eds.), *The social psychologists: Research adventures.* New York: McGraw-Hill.

Berkowitz, L., & Geen, R. G. (1966). Film violence and the cue properties of available targets. *Journal of Personality and Social Psychology, 3,* 525–530.

Berkowitz, L., & LePage, A. (1967). Weapons as aggression-eliciting stimuli. *Journal of Personality and Social Psychology, 7,* 202–207.

Berndsen, M., Spears, R., Pligt, J. V. D., & McGarty, C. (2002). Illusory correlation and stereotype formation: Making sense of group differences and cognitive biases. In C. McGarty, V. Y. Yzerbyt, & R. Spears (Eds.), *Stereotypes as explanations: The formation of meaningful beliefs about social groups* (pp. 90–110). New York: Cambridge University Press.

Bernhardt, P. C., Dabbs, J. M., Jr., Fielden, J. A., & Lutter, C. D. (1998). Testosterone changes during vicarious experiences of winning and losing among fans at sporting events. *Physiology & Behavior, 65,* 59.

Berns, G. S., Chappelow, J., Zink, C. F., Pagnoni, G., Martin-Skurski, M. E., & Richards, J. (2005). Neurobiological correlates of social conformity and independence during mental rotation. *Biological Psychiatry, 58,* 245.

Bernstein, M. J., Young, S. G., & Claypool, H. M. (2010). Is Obama's win a gain for Blacks? Changes in implicit racial prejudice following the 2008 election. *Social Psychology, 41,* 147–151.

Bernstein, M. J., Young, S. G., & Hugenberg, K. (2007). The cross-category effect. Mere social categorization is sufficient to elicit an own-group bias in face recognition. *Psychological Science, 18,* 706–712.

Berscheid, E. (1981). An overview of the psychological effects of physical attractiveness and some comments upon the psychological effects of knowledge of the effects of physical attractiveness. In W. Lucker, K. Ribbens, & J. A. McNamera (Eds.), *Logical aspects of facial form (craniofacial growth series).* Ann Arbor: University of Michigan Press.

Berscheid, E. (1985). Interpersonal attraction. In G. Lindzey & E. Aronson (Eds.), *The handbook of social psychology.* New York: Random House.

Berscheid, E. (2010). Love in the fourth dimension. *Annual Review of Psychology, 61,* 1–25.

Berscheid, E., Boye, D., & Walster (Hatfield), E. (1968). Retaliation as a means of restoring equity. *Journal of Personality and Social Psychology, 10,* 370–376.

Berscheid, E., Dion, K., Walster (Hatfield), E., & Walster, G. W. (1971). Physical attractiveness and dating choice: A test of the matching hypothesis. *Journal of Experimental Social Psychology, 7,* 173–189.

Berscheid, E., Graziano, W., Monson, T., & Dermer, M. (1976). Outcome dependency: Attention, attribution, and attraction. *Journal of Personality and Social Psychology, 34,* 978–989.

Berscheid, E., & Peplau, L. A. (1983). The emerging science of relationships. In Kelley, H. H., Berscheid, E., Christensen, A., Harvey, J. H., Huston, T. L., Levinger, G., McClintock, E., Peplau, L. A., & Peterson, D. R. (Eds.), *Close relationships.* New York: Freeman.

Berscheid, E., Snyder, M., & Omoto, A. M. (1989). Issues in studying close relationships: Conceptualizing and measuring closeness. In C. Hendrick (Ed.), *Review of personality and social psychology* (Vol. 10). Newbury Park, CA: Sage.

Berscheid, E., & Walster (Hatfield), E. (1978). *Interpersonal attraction.* Reading, MA: Addison-Wesley.

Berscheid, E., Walster, G. W., & Hatfield (was Walster), E. (1969). *Effects of accuracy and positivity of evaluation on liking for the evaluator.* Unpublished manuscript. Summarized by E. Berscheid and E. Walster (Hatfield) (1978), *Interpersonal attraction.* Reading, MA: Addison-Wesley.

Bertrand, M., & Mullainathan, S. (2003). Are Emily and Greg more employable than Lakisha and Jamal? A field experiment on labor market discrimination. Massachusetts Institute of Technology, Department of Economics, Working Paper 03–22.

Besser, A., & Priel, B. (2005). The apple does not fall far from the tree: Attachment styles and personality vulnerabilities to depression in three generations of women. *Personality and Social Psychology Bulletin, 31,* 1052–1073.

Bettencourt, B. A., Dill, K. E., Greathouse, S. A., Charlton, K., & Mulholland, A. (1997). Evaluations of ingroup and outgroup members: The role of category-based expectancy violation. *Journal of Experimental Social Psychology, 33,* 244–275.

Bettencourt, B. A., Talley, A., Benjamin, A. J., & Valentine, J. (2006). Personality and aggressive behavior under provoking and neutral conditions: A meta-analytic review. *Psychological Bulletin, 132,* 751–777.

Beyer, L. (1990, Fall issue on women). Life behind the veil. *Time,* p. 37.

Bianchi, E. (2016). American individualism rises and falls with the economy: Cross-temporal evidence that individualism declines when the economy falters. *Journal of Personality and Social Psychology, 111,* 567–584.

Bianchi, S. M., Milkie, M. A., Sayer, L. C., & Robinson, J. P. (2000). Is anyone doing the housework? Trends in the gender division of household labor. *Social Forces, 79,* 191–228.

Bickman, L. (1975). Bystander intervention in a crime: The effect of a mass-media campaign. *Journal of Applied Social Psychology, 5,* 296–302.

Bickman, L. (1979). Interpersonal influence and the reporting of a crime. *Personality and Social Psychology Bulletin, 5,* 32–35.

Bickman, L., & Green, S. K. (1977). Situational cues and crime reporting: Do signs make a difference? *Journal of Applied Social Psychology, 7,* 1–18.

Biernat, M., Vescio, T. K., & Green, M. L. (1996). Selective self-stereotyping. *Journal of Personality and Social Psychology, 71,* 1194–1209.

Biernat, M., Vescio, T. K., & Theno, S. A. (1996). Violating American values: A "Value congruence" approach to understanding outgroup attitudes. *Journal of Experimental Social Psychology, 32,* 387–410.

Biernat, M., & Wortman, C. B. (1991). Sharing of home responsibilities between professionally employed women and their husbands. *Journal of Personality and Social Psychology, 60,* 844–860.

Bilderbeck, A. C., Brown, G. D. A., Read, J., Woolrich, M., Cowen, P. J., Behrens, T. E. J., & Rogers, R. D. (2014). Serotonin and social norms: Tryptophan depletion impairs social comparison and leads to resource depletion in a multiplayer harvesting game. *Psychological Science, 25,* 1303–1313.

Bilewicz, M., & Kogan, A. (2014). Embodying imagined contact: Facial feedback moderates the intergroup consequences of mental simulation. *British Journal of Social Psychology, 53,* 387–395

Billig, M., & Tajfel, H. (1973). Social categorization and similarity in intergroup behaviour. *European Journal of Social Psychology, 3,* 27–52.

Binder, J., Zagefka, H., Brown, R., Funke, F., Kessler, T., Mummendey, A., Maquil, A., Demoulin, S., & Leyens, J-P. (2009). Does contact reduce prejudice or does prejudice reduce contact? A longitudinal test of the contact hypothesis among majority and minority groups in three European countries. *Journal of Personality and Social Psychology, 96,* 843–856.

Biner, P. M. (1991). Effects of lighting-induced arousal on the magnitude of goal valence. *Personality and Social Psychology Bulletin, 17,* 219–226.

Bingenheimer, J. B., Brennan, R. T., & Earls, F. J. (2005). Firearm violence exposure and serious violent behavior. *Science, 308,* 1323.

Binham, R. (1980, March–April). Trivers in Jamaica. *Science, 80,* 57–67.

Bizumic, B., Kenny, A., Iyer, R., Tanuwira, J., & Huxley, E. (2017). Are the ethnically tolerant free of discrimination, prejudice and political intolerance? *European Journal of Social Psychology, 47,* 457–471.

Blackburn, R. T., Pellino, G. R., Boberg, A., & O'Connell, C. (1980). Are instructional improvement programs off target? *Current Issues in Higher Education, 1,* 31–48.

Blackhart, G. C., Nelson, B. C., Knowles, M. L., & Baumeister, R. F. (2009). Rejection elicits emotional reactions but neither causes immediate distress nor lowers self-esteem: A meta-analytic review of 192 studies on social exclusion. *Personality and Social Psychology Review, 13,* 269–309.

Blair, C. A., Thompson, L. F., & Wuensch, K. L. (2005). Electronic helping behavior: The virtual presence of others makes a difference. *Basic and Applied Social Psychology, 27,* 171–178.

Blake, R. R., & Mouton, J. S. (1962). The intergroup dynamics of win-lose conflict and problem-solving collaboration in union management relations. In M. Sherif (Ed.), *Intergroup relations and leadership.* New York: Wiley.

Blake, R. R., & Mouton, J. S. (1979). Intergroup problem solving in organizations: From theory to practice. In W. G. Austin and S. Worchel (Eds.), *The social psychology of intergroup relations.* Monterey, CA: Brooks/Cole.

Blaker, N. M., Rompa, I., Dessing, I. H., Vriend, A. F., Herschberg, C., & Van Vugt, M. (2013). The height leadership advantage in men and women: Testing evolutionary psychology predictions about the perceptions of tall leaders. *Group Processes & Intergroup Relations, 16*(1), 1–27.

Blanchard, F. A., & Cook, S. W. (1976). Effects of helping a less competent member of a cooperating interracial group on the development of interpersonal attraction. *Journal of Personality and Social Psychology, 34,* 1245–1255.

Blanton, H., Jaccard, J., Christie, C., & Gonzales, P. M. (2007). Plausible assumptions, questionable assumptions and post hoc rationalizations: Will the real IAT please stand up? *Journal of Experimental Social Psychology, 43,* 399–409.

Blanton, H., Jaccard, J., Klick, J., Mellers, B., Mitchell, G., & Tetlock P. E. (2009). Strong claims and weak evidence: Reassessing the predictive validity of the IAT. *Journal of Applied Psychology, 94,* 583–603.

Blanton, H., Jaccard, J., Strauts, E., Mitchell, G., & Tetlock, P. E. (2015). Toward a meaningful metric of implicit prejudice. *Journal of Applied Psychology, 100,* 1468–1481.

Blanton, H., Pelham, B. W., DeHart, T., & Carvallo, M. (2001). Overconfidence as dissonance reduction. *Journal of Experimental Social Psychology, 37,* 373–385.

Blass, T. (1991). Understanding behavior in the Milgram obedience experiment: The role of personality, situations, and their interactions. *Journal of Personality and Social Psychology, 60,* 398–413.

Blass, T. (1996). Stanley Milgram: A life of inventiveness and controversy. In G. A. Kimble, C. A. Boneau, & M. Wertheimer (Eds.). *Portraits of pioneers in psychology* (Vol. II). Washington, DC: American Psychological Association.

Blass, T. (1999). The Milgram paradigm after 35 years: Some things we now know about obedience to authority. *Journal of Applied Social Psychology, 29,* 955–978.

Bleske-Rechek, A., Remiker, M. W., & Baker, J. P. (2009). Similar from the start: Assortment in young adult dating couples and its link to relationship stability over time. *Individual Differences Research, 7,* 142–158.

Block J., & Funder, D. C. (1986). Social roles and social perception: Individual differences in attribution and error. *Journal of Personality and Social Psychology, 51,* 1200–1207.

Boden, J. M., Fergusson, D. M., & Horwood, L. J. (2007). Self-esteem and violence: Testing links between adolescent self-esteem and later hostility and violent behavior. *Social Psychiatry and Psychiatric Epidemiology, 42,* 881–891.

Boden, J. M., Fergusson, D. M., & Horwood, L. J. (2008). Does adolescent self-esteem predict later life outcomes? A test of the causal role of self-esteem. *Development and Psychopathology, 20,* 319–339.

Bodenhausen, G. V. (1990). Stereotypes as judgmental heuristics: Evidence of circadian variations in discrimination. *Psychological Science, 1,* 319–322.

Bodenhausen, G. V. (1993). Emotions, arousal, and stereotypic judgments: A heuristic model of affect and stereotyping. In D. M. Mackie & D. L. Hamilton (Eds.), *Affect, cognition, and stereotyping: Interactive processes in group perception.* San Diego, CA: Academic Press.

Bodenhausen, G. V., & Macrae, C. N. (1998). Stereotype activation and inhibition. In R. S. Wyer, Jr., *Stereotype activation and inhibition: Advances in social cognition* (Vol. 11). Mahwah, NJ: Erlbaum.

Bodenhausen, G. V., Sheppard, L. A., & Kramer, G. F. (1994). Negative affect and social judgment: The differential impact of anger and sadness. *European Journal of Social Psychology, 24,* 45–62.

Bodford, J. E., Kwan, V. Y., & Sobota, D. S. (2017). Fatal attractions: Attachment to smartphones predicts anthropomorphic beliefs and dangerous behaviors. *Cyberpsychology, Behavior, and Social Networking, 20,* 320–326.

Boer, D., Fischer, R., Strack, M., Bond, M. H., Lo, E., & Lam, J. (2011). How shared preferences in music create bonds between people: Values as the missing link. *Personality and Social Psychology Bulletin, 37,* 1159–1171.

Boggiano, A. K., Barrett, M., Weiher, A. W., McClelland, G. H., & Lusk, C. M. (1987). Use of the maximal-operant principle to motivate children's intrinsic interest. *Journal of Personality and Social Psychology, 53,* 866–879.

Boggiano, A. K., Harackiewicz, J. M., Bessette, J. M., & Main, D. S. (1985). Increasing children's interest through performance-contingent reward. *Social Cognition, 3,* 400–411.

Boggiano, A. K., & Ruble, D. N. (1985). Children's responses to evaluative feedback. In R. Schwarzer (Ed.), *Self-related cognitions in anxiety and motivation.* Hillsdale, NJ: Erlbaum.

Boldt, E. D. (1976). Acquiescence and conventionality in a communal society. *Journal of Cross Cultural Psychology, 7,* 21–36.

Bonanno, G. A., Rennicke, C., & Dekel, S. (2005). Self-enhancement among high-exposure survivors of the September 11th terrorist attack: Resilience or social maladjustment? *Journal of Personality and Social Psychology, 88,* 984–998.

Bond, C. F., Jr., DiCandia, C. G., & MacKinnon, J. R. (1988). Responses to violence in a psychiatric setting: The role of patient's race. *Personality and Social Psychology Bulletin, 14,* 448–458.

Bond, C. F., Jr., & Titus, L. J. (1983). Social facilitation: A meta-analysis of 241 studies. *Psychologial Bulletin, 94,* 265–292.

Bond, M. H. (2004). Culture and aggression: From context to coercion. *Personality and Social Psychology Review, 8,* 62–78.

Bond, R., & Smith, P. B. (1996). Culture and conformity: A meta-analysis of studies using Asch's (1952b, 1956) line judgment task. *Psychological Bulletin, 119,* 111–137.

Bonner, B. L., & Baumann, M. R. (2012). Leveraging member expertise to improve knowledge transfer and demonstrability in groups. *Journal of Personality and Social Psychology, 102*(2), 337

Bonnot, V., & Croizet, J-C. (2007). Stereotype internalization and women's math performance: The role of interference in working memory. *Journal of Experimental Social Psychology, 43,* 857–866.

Bono, J. E., & Judge, T. A. (2004). Personality and transformational and transactional leadership: A meta-analysis. *Journal of Applied Psychology, 89,* 901.

Booth, D. (2019). Motor Mouth: As it turns out, money can buy you happiness after all. *Driving.ca*. Retrieved from: https://driving.ca/features/feature-story/motor-mouth-as-it-turns-out-money-can-buy-you-happiness-after-all

Borgida, E., & Brekke, N. (1985). Psycholegal research on rape trials. In A. W. Burgess (Ed.), *Rape and sexual assault: A research handbook.* New York: Garland.

Borgida, E., Locksley, A., & Brekke, N. (1981). Social stereotypes and social judgment. In N. Cantor & J. Kihlstrom (Eds.), *Cognition, social interaction, and personality.* Hillsdale, NJ: Erlbaum.

Borkenau, P., & Liebler, A. (1993). Consensus and self-other agreement for trait inferences from minimal information. *Journal of Personality. Special Issue: Viewpoints on Personality: Consensus, Self-Other Agreement, and Accuracy in Personality Judgment, 61*(4), 477.

Bornstein, G., & Rapoport, A. (1988). Intergroup competition for the provision of step-level public goods: Effects of preplay communication. *European Journal of Social Psychology, 18,* 125–142.

Bornstein, G., Rapoport, A., Kerpel, L., & Katz, T. (1989). Within- and between-group communication in intergroup competition for public goods. *Journal of Experimental Social Psychology, 25,* 422–436.

Bornstein, R. F. (1989). Exposure and affect: Overview and meta-analysis of research, 1968–1987. *Psychological Bulletin, 106,* 265–289.

Bornstein, R. F. (1999). Source amnesia, misattribution and the power of unconscious perceptions and memories. *Psychoanalytic Psychology, 16,* 155–178.

Bossard, J. H. S. (1932). Residential propinquity as a factor in marriage selection. *American Journal of Sociology, 38,* 219–224.

Bothwell, R. K., Brigham, J. C., & Malpass, R. S. (1989). Cross-racial identification. *Personality and Social Psychology Bulletin, 15,* 19–25.

Botvin, G. J., Epstein, J. A., & Griffin, K. W. (2008). A social influence model of alcohol use for inner-city adolescents: Family drinking, perceived drinking norms, and perceived social benefits of drinking. *Journal of Studies on Alcohol and Drugs, 69,* 397–405.

Botvin, G. J., Schinke, S., & Orlandi, M. A. (1995). School-based health promotion: Substance abuse and sexual behavior. *Applied & Preventive Psychology, 4,* 167–184.

Botwin, M. D., Buss, D. M., & Shackelford, T. K. (1997). Personality and mate preferences: Five factors in mate selection and marital satisfaction. *Journal of Personality, 65,* 107–136.

Bouas, K. S., & Komorita, S. S. (1996). Group discussion and cooperation in social dilemmas. *Personality and Social Psychology Bulletin, 22,* 1144–1150.

Bouman, T., van Zomeren, M., & Otten, S. (2014). Threat by association: Do distant intergroup threats carry-over into local intolerance? *British Journal of Social Psychology*, 53, 405–421.

Bouman, T., van Zomeren, M., & Otten, S. (2015). When threats foreign turn domestic: Two ways for distant realistic intergroup threats to carry over into local intolerance. *British Journal of Social Psychology, 54,* 581–600.

Bourke, M. L., & Hernandez, A. E. (2009). The "Butner Study" Redux: A report of the incidence of hands-on child victimization by child pornography offenders. *Journal of Family Violence, 24,* 183–191.

Boutwell, B. B., Barnes, J. C., & Beaver, K. M. (2015). When love dies: Further elucidating the existence of a mate ejection module. *Review of General Psychology, 19,* 30–38.

Bowen, E. (1988, April 4). Whatever became of Honest Abe? *Time.*

Bowen, N. K., Wegmann, K. M., & Webber, K. C. (2013). Enhancing a brief writing intervention to combat stereotype threat among middle-school students. *Journal of Educational Psychology, 105,* 427–435.

Bower, G. H. (1987). Commentary on mood and memory. *Behavioral Research and Therapy, 25,* 443–455.

Bowlby, J. (1980). Loss, sadness and depression. In *Attachment and loss* (Vol. 2). London: Basic Books.

Boyatzis, C. J., Matillo, G. M., & Nesbitt, K. M. (1995). Effects of the "Mighty Morphin Power Rangers" on children's aggression with peers. *Child Study Journal, 25,* 45–55.

Boyes, A. D., & Fletcher, G. J. O. (2007). Metaperceptions of bias in intimate relationships. *Journal of Personality and Social Psychology, 92,* 286–306.

Bradley, W., & Mannell, R. C. (1984). Sensitivity of intrinsic motivation to reward procedure instructions. *Personality and Social Psychology Bulletin, 10,* 426–431.

Brand, R. J., Bonatsos, A., D'Orazio, R., & DeShong, H. (2012). What is beautiful is good, even online: Correlations between photo attractiveness and text attractiveness in men's online dating profiles. *Computers in Human Behavior. 28,* 166–170.

Brandt, M. J. (2011). Sexism and gender inequality across 57 societies. *Psychological Science, 22,* 1413–1418.

Brandt, M. J., & Van Tongeren, D. R. (2017). People both high and low on religious fundamentalism are prejudiced toward dissimilar groups. *Journal of Personality and Social Psychology, 112,* 76–97.

Branscombe, N. R., Schmitt, M. T., & Harvey, R. D. (1999). Perceiving pervasive discrimination among African Americans: Implications for group identification and well-being. *Journal of Personality and Social Psychology, 77,* 135–149.

Brauer, M., Judd, C. M., & Gliner, M. D. (1995). The effects of repeated expressions on attitude polarization during group discussions. *Journal of Personality and Social Psychology, 68,* 1014–1029.

Brauer, M., Judd, C. M., & Jacquelin, V. (2001). The communication of social stereotypes: The effects of group discussion and information distribution on stereotypic appraisals. *Journal of Personality and Social Psychology, 81,* 463.

Bray, R. M., & Noble, A. M. (1978). Authoritarianism and decisions of mock juries: Evidence of jury bias and group polarization. *Journal of Personality and Social Psychology, 36,* 1424–1430.

Bray, S. R., Law, J., & Foyle, J. (2003). Team quality and game location effects in English professional soccer. *Journal of Sport Behavior, 26,* 319–334.

Breckler, S. J. (2010, April). In the heat of the moment. *Monitor on Psychology,* 39.

Breckler, S. J., & Wiggins, E. C. (1989). Affect versus evaluation in the structure of attitudes. *Journal of Experimental Social Psychology, 25,* 253–271.

Brehm, J. W. (1956). Post-decision changes in desirability of alternatives. *Journal of Abnormal Social Psychology, 52,* 384–389.

Brehm, S., & Brehm, J. W. (1981). *Psychological reactance: A theory of freedom and control.* New York: Academic Press.

Brekke, J. S., Prindle, C., Bae, S. W., & Long, J. D. (2001). Risks for individuals with schizophrenia who are living in the community. *Psychiatric Services, 52,* 1358–1366.

Brenner, S. N., & Molander, E. A. (1977, January-February). Is the ethics of business changing? *Harvard Business Review,* 57–71.

Brescoll, V. L., Uhlmann, E. L., & Newman, G. E. (2013). The effects of system-justifying motives on endorsement of essentialist explanations of gender differences. *Journal of Personality and Social Psychology, 105,* 891–908.

Breuer, J., Scharkow, M., & Quandt, T. (2014). Sore losers? A reexamination of the frustration-aggression hypothesis for collocated video game play. *Psychology of Popular Media Culture, 4,* 126–137.

Brewer, M. B. (1979). In-group bias in the minimal intergroup situation: A cognitive-motivational analysis. *Psychological Bulletin, 86,* 307–324.

Brewer, M. B. (1987). Collective decisions. *Social Science, 72,* 140–143.

Brewer, M. B. (1988). A dual process model of impression formation. In T. Srull & R. Wyer (Eds.), *Advances in social cognition* (Vol. 1). Hillsdale, NJ: Erlbaum.

Brewer, M. B., & Miller, N. (1988). Contact and cooperation: When do they work? In P. A. Katz & D. Taylor (Eds.), *Towards the elimination of racism: Profiles in controversy.* New York: Plenum.

Brewer, M. B., & Pierce, K. P. (2005). Social identity complexity and outgroup tolerance. *Personality and Social Psychology Bulletin, 31,* 428–437.

Brewer, M. B., & Silver, M. (1978). In-group bias as a function of task characteristics. *European Journal of Social Psychology, 8,* 393–400.

Brewer, N., & Wells, G. L. (2011). Eyewitness identification. *Current Directions in Psychological Science,* 20, 24–27.

Brickman, P. (1978). Is it real? In J. Harvey, W. Ickes, & R. Kidd (Eds.), *New directions in attribution research* (Vol. 2). Hillsdale, NJ: Erlbaum.

Brickman, P., Coates, D., & Janoff-Bulman, R. J. (1978). Lottery winners and accident victims: Is happiness relative? *Journal of Personality and Social Psychology, 36,* 917–927.

Briñol, P., Petty, R. E., & Tormala, Z. L. (2004). Self-validation of cognitive responses to advertisements. *Journal of Consumer Research, 30,* 559–573.

Briñol, P., Petty, R. E., & Wagner, B. (2009). Body posture effects on self-evaluation: A self-validation approach. *European Journal of Social Psychology, 39*(6), 1053-1064.

Briñol, P., Tormala, Z. L., & Petty, R. E. (2002). *Source credibility as a determinant of self-validation effects in persuasion.* Poster presented at the European Association of Experimental Social Psychology, San Sebastian, Spain.

Britt, T. W., & Garrity, M. J. (2006). Attributions and personality as predictors of the road rage response. *British Journal of Social Psychology, 45,* 127–147.

Brock, T. C. (1965). Communicator-recipient similarity and decision change. *Journal of Personality and Social Psychology, 1,* 650–654.

Brockner, J., Rubin, J. Z., Fine, J., Hamilton, T. P., Thomas, B., & Turetsky, B. (1982). Factors affecting entrapment in escalating conflicts: The importance of timing. *Journal of Research in Personality, 16,* 247–266.

Brodt, S. E., & Zimbardo, P. G. (1981). Modifying shyness-related social behavior through symptom misattribution. *Journal of Personality and Social Psychology, 41,* 437–449.

Brody, J. (2017, August 21). Fat bias starts early and takes a serious toll. *New York Times* (www.nytimes.com).

Bronfenbrenner, U. (1961). The mirror image in Soviet-American relations. *Journal of Social Issues, 17*(3), 45–56.

Broockman, D., & Kalla, J. (2016). Durably reducing transphobia: A field experiment on door-to-door canvassing. *Science, 352,* 220–224.

Brooks, R. (2012). "Asia's missing women" as a problem in applied evolutionary psychology? *Evolutionary Psychology, 12,* 910–925.

Broome, A., & Wegner, D. M. (1994). *Some positive effects of releasing socially anxious people from the need to please.* Paper presented to the American Psychological Society convention.

Brown, H. J., Jr. (1990). *P.S. I love you.* Nashville, TN: Rutledge Hill.

Brown, J. D., & Dutton, K. A. (1994). *From the top down: Self-esteem and self-evaluation.* Unpublished manuscript, University of Washington, Seattle.

Brown, J. D., Novick, N. J., Lord, K. A., & Richards, J. M. (1992). When Gulliver travels: Social context, psychological closeness, and self-appraisals. *Journal of Personality and Social Psychology, 62,* 717–727.

Brown, J. D., & Taylor, S. E. (1986). Affect and the processing of personal information: Evidence for mood-activated self-schemata. *Journal of Experimental Social Psychology, 22,* 436–452.

Brown, R., Eller, A., Leeds, S., & Stace, K. (2007). Intergroup contact and intergroup attitudes: A longitudinal study. *European Journal of Social Psychology, 37,* 692–703.

Brown, R., Maras, P., Masser, B., Vivian, J., & Hewstone, M. (2001). Life on the ocean wave: Testing some intergroup hypotheses in a naturalistic setting. *Group Processes and Intergroup Relations, 4,* 81–97.

Brown, R., Vivian, J., & Hewstone, M. (1999). Changing attitudes through intergroup contact: The effects of group membership salience. *European Journal of Social Psychology, 29,* 741–764.

Brown, R., & Wootton-Millward, L. (1993). Perceptions of group homogeneity during group formation and change. *Social Cognition, 11,* 126–149.

Brown, R. P., Charnsangavej, T., Keough, K. A., Newman, M. L., & Rentfrom, P. J. (2000). Putting the "affirm" into affirmative action: Preferential selection and academic performance. *Journal of Personality and Social Psychology, 79,* 736–747.

Brown, R. P., Osterman, L. L., & Barnes, C. D. (2009). School violence and the culture of honor. *Psychological Science, 20,* 1400–1405.

Brown, S. L., Brown, R. M., House, J. S., & Smith, D. M. (2008). Coping with spousal loss: Potential buffering effects of self-reported helping behavior. *Personality and Social Psychology Bulletin, 34,* 849–861.

Brown, S. L., Nesse, R. M., Vinokur, A. D., & Smith, D. M. (2003). Providing social support may be more beneficial than receiving it. *Psychological Science, 14,* 320–327.

Brown, S. L., Smith, D. M., Schulz, R., Kabeto, M. U., Ubel, P. A., Poulin, M., Yi, J. Kim, C., & Langa, K. M. (2009). Caregiving behavior is associated with decreased mortality risk. *Psychological Science, 20,* 488–494.

Brown, V. R., & Paulus, P. B. (2002). Making group brainstorming more effective: Recommendations from an associative memory perspective. *Current Directions in Psychological Science, 11,* 208–212.

Brown, W. M., Price, M. E., Kang, J., Pound, N., Zhao, Y., & Yu, H. (2008). Fluctuating asymmetry and preferences for sex-typical bodily characteristics. *Proceedings of the National Academy of Sciences, 105,* 12938–12943. Retrieved from http://www.pnas.org

Browning, C. (1992). *Ordinary men: Reserve police battalion 101 and the final solution in Poland.* New York: HarperCollins.

Bruck, M., & Ceci, S. (2004). Forensic developmental psychology: Unveiling four common misconceptions. *Current*

Directions in Psychological Science, 15, 229–232.

Bruck, M., & Ceci, S. J. (1999). The suggestibility of children's memory. *Annual Review of Psychology, 50,* 419–439.

Brummelman, E., Thomaes, S., Nelemans, S. A., de Castro, B. O., Overbeek, G., & Bushman, B. J. (2015). Origins of narcissism in children. *Proceedings of the Natural Academy of Sciences, 112,* 3659–3662.

Brummelman, E., Thomaes, S., & Sedikides, C. (2016). Separating narcissism from self-esteem. *Current Directions in Psychological Science, 25,* 8–13.

Brunell, A. B., Gentry, W. A., Campbell, W. K., Hoffman, B. J., Kuhnert, K. W., & DeMarree, K. G. (2008). Leader emergence: The case of the narcissistic leader. *Personality and Social Psychology Bulletin, 34,* 1663–1676.

Bryan, C. J., Master, A., & Walton, G. M. (2014). "Helping" versus "being a helper": Invoking the self to increase helping in young children. *Child Development, 85,* 1836–1842.

Bryan, J. H., & Test, M. A. (1967). Models and helping: Naturalistic studies in aiding behavior. *Journal of Personality and Social Psychology, 6,* 400–407.

Buckhout, R. (1974, December). Eyewitness testimony. *Scientific American,* 23–31.

Buehler, R., Griffin, D., & Ross, M. (1994). Exploring the "planning fallacy": When people underestimate their task completion times. *Journal of Personality and Social Psychology, 67,* 366–381.

Buehler, R., Griffin, D., & Ross, M. (2002). Inside the planning fallacy: The causes and consequences of optimistic time predictions. In T. Gilovich, D. Griffin, & D. Kahneman (Eds.), *Heuristics and biases: The psychology of intuitive judgment* (pp. 250–270). New York: Cambridge University Press.

Buehler, R., Peetz, J., & Griffin, D. (2010). Finishing on time: When do predictions influence completion times? *Organizational Behavior and Human Decision Processes, 111,* 23–32.

Buffardi, L. E., & Campbell, W. K. (2008). Narcissism and social networking websites. *Personality and Social Psychology Bulletin, 34,* 1303–1314.

Bugental, D. B., & Hehman, J. A. (2007). Ageism: A review of research and policy implications. *Social Issues and Policy Review, 1,* 173–216.

Bui, N. H. (2012). False consensus in attitudes toward celebrities. *Psychology of Popular Media Culture, 1,* 236–243.

Burger, J. M. (1987). Increased performance with increased personal control: A self-presentation interpretation. *Journal of Experimental Social Psychology, 23,* 350–360.

Burger, J. M. (1991). Changes in attributions over time: The ephemeral fundamental attribution error. *Social Cognition, 9,* 182–193.

Burger, J. M. (2009, January). Replicating Milgram: Would people still obey today? *American Psychologist, 64,* 1–11.

Burger, J. M. (2014). Situational features in Milgram's experiment that kept his participants shocking. *Journal of Social Issues, 70*(3), 489-500.

Burger, J. M., & Burns, L. (1988). The illusion of unique invulnerability and the use of effective contraception. *Personality and Social Psychology Bulletin, 14,* 264–270.

Burger, J. M., & Caldwell, D. F. (2003). The effects of monetary incentives and labeling on the foot-in-the-door effect: Evidence for a self-perception process. *Basic and Applied Social Psychology, 25,* 235–241.

Burger, J. M., & Guadagno, R. E. (2003). Self-concept clarity and the foot-in-the-door procedure. *Basic and Applied Social Psychology, 25,* 79–86.

Burger, J. M., Messian, N., Patel, S., del Prade, A., & Anderson, C. (2004). What a coincidence! The effects of incidental similarity on compliance. *Personality and Social Psychology Bulletin, 30,* 35–43.

Burger, J. M., & Palmer, M. L. (1991). Changes in and generalization of unrealistic optimism following experiences with stressful events: Reactions to the 1989 California earthquake. *Personality and Social Psychology Bulletin, 18,* 39–43.

Burger, J. M., & Pavelich, J. L. (1994). Attributions for presidential elections: The situational shift over time. *Basic and Applied Social Psychology, 15,* 359–371.

Burger, J. M., Soroka, S., Gonzago, K., Murphy, E., & Somervell, E. (2001). The effect of fleeting attraction on compliance to requests. *Personality and Social Psychology Bulletin, 27,* 1578–1586.

Burnstein, E. (2009). Robert B. Zajonc (1923–2008). *American Psychologist, 64,* 558–559.

Burnstein, E., Crandall, R., & Kitayama, S. (1994). Some neo-Darwinian decision rules for altruism: Weighing cues for inclusive fitness as a function of the biological importance of the decision. *Journal of Personality and Social Psychology, 67,* 773–789.

Burnstein, E., & Vinokur, A. (1977). Persuasive argumentation and social comparison as determinants of attitude polarization. *Journal of Experimental Social Psychology, 13,* 315–332.

Burnstein, E., & Worchel, P. (1962). Arbitrariness of frustration and its consequences for aggression in a social situation. *Journal of Personality, 30,* 528–540.

Burr, W. R. (1973). *Theory construction and the sociology of the family.* New York: Wiley.

Burson, K. A., Larrick, R. P., & Klayman, J. (2006). Skilled or unskilled, but still unaware of it: How perceptions of difficulty drive miscalibration in relative comparisons. *Journal of Personality and Social Psychology, 90*(1), 60.

Bushman, B. J. (1993). Human aggression while under the influence of alcohol and other drugs: An integrative research review. *Current Directions in Psychological Science, 2,* 148–152.

Bushman, B. J. (1998). Priming effects of media violence on the accessibility of aggressive constructs in memory. *Personality and Social Psychology Bulletin, 24,* 537–545.

Bushman, B. J. (2002). Does venting anger feed or extinguish the flame? Catharsis, rumination, distraction, anger, and aggressive responding. *Personality and Social Psychology Bulletin, 28,* 724–731.

Bushman, B. J. (2005). Violence and sex in television programs do not sell products in advertisements. *Psychological Science, 16,* 702–708.

Bushman, B. J. (2007). That was a great commercial, but what were they selling? Effects of violence and sex on memory for products in television commercials. *Journal of Applied Social Psychology, 37,* 1784–1796.

Bushman, B. J., & Anderson, C. A. (1998). Methodology in the study of aggression: Integrating experimental and nonexperimental findings. In R. Geen & E. Donnerstein (Eds.), *Human aggression: Theories, research and implications for policy.* San Diego: Academic Press.

Bushman, B. J., & Anderson, C. A. (2001). Media violence and the American public: Scientific facts versus media misinformation. *American Psychologist, 56,* 477–489.

Bushman, B. J., & Anderson, C. A. (2002). Violent video games and hostile expectations: A test of the general aggression model. *Personality and Social Psychology Bulletin, 28,* 1679–1686.

Bushman, B. J., & Anderson, C. A. (2009). Comfortably numb: Desensitizing effects of violent media on helping others. *Psychological Science, 20,* 273–277.

Bushman, B. J., & Anderson, C. A. (2015). Understanding causality in the effects of media violence. *American Behavioral Scientist, 59,* 1807–1821.

Bushman, B. J., & Baumeister, R. (1998). Threatened egotism, narcissism, self-esteem, and direct and displaced aggression: Does self-love or self-hate lead to violence? *Journal of Personality and Social Psychology, 75,* 219–229.

Bushman, B. J., Baumeister, R. F., & Phillips, C. M. (2001). Do people aggress to improve their mood? Catharsis beliefs, affect regulation opportunity, and aggressive responding. *Journal of Personality and Social Psychology, 81,* 17–32.

Bushman, B. J., Baumeister, R. F., & Stack, A. D. (1999). Catharsis, aggression, and persuasive influence: Self-fulfilling or self-defeating prophecies? *Journal of Personality and Social Psychology, 76,* 367–376.

Bushman, B. J., Baumeister, R. F., Thomaes, S., Ryu, E., Begeer, S., & West, S. G. (2009). Looking again, and harder, for a link between low self-esteem and aggression. *Journal of Personality,* published online February 2, 2009.

Bushman, B. J., Bonacci, A. M., Pedersen, W. C., Vasquez, E. A., & Miller, N. (2005). Chewing on it can chew you up: Effects of rumination on triggered displaced aggression. *Journal of Personality and Social Psychology, 88,* 969.

Bushman, B. J., & Cooper, H. M. (1990). Effects of alcohol on human aggression: An integrative research review. *Psychological Bulletin, 107,* 341–354.

Bushman, B. J., & Geen, R. G. (1990). Role of cognitive-emotional mediators and individual differences in the effects of media violence on aggression. *Journal of Personality and Social Psychology, 58,* 156–163.

Bushman, B. J., Kerwin, T., Whitlock, T., & Weisenberger, J. M. (2017). The weapons effect on wheels: Motorists drive more aggressively when there is a gun in the vehicle. *Journal of Experimental Social Psychology, 73,* 82–85.

Bushman, B. J., Moeller, S. J., & Crocker, J. (2011). Sweets, sex, or self-esteem? Comparing the value of self-esteem boosts with other pleasant rewards. *Journal of Personality, 79,* 993–1012.

Bushman, B. J., Wang, M. C., & Anderson, C. A. (2005a). Is the curve relating temperature to aggression linear or curvilinear? Assaults and temperature in Minneapolis reexamined. *Journal of Personality and Social Psychology, 89,* 62–66.

Bushman, B. J., Wang, M. C., & Anderson, C. A. (2005b). Is the curve relating temperature to aggression linear or curvilinear? A response to Bell (2005) and to Cohn and Rotton (2005). *Journal of Personality and Social Psychology, 89,* 74–77.

Bushman, B. J., & Whitaker, J. L. (2010). Like a magnet: Catharsis beliefs attract angry people to violent video games. *Psychological Science, 21,* 790–792.

Buss, D. M. (1984). Toward a psychology of person-environment (PE) correlation: The role of spouse selection. *Journal of Personality and Social Psychology, 47,* 361–377.

Buss, D. M. (1985). Human mate selection. *American Scientist, 73,* 47–51.

Buss, D. M. (1989). Sex differences in human mate preferences: Evolutionary hypotheses tested in 37 cultures. *Behavioral and Brain Sciences, 12,* 1–49.

Butcher, S. H. (1951). *Aristotle's theory of poetry and fine art.* New York: Dover Publications.

Butler, J. L., & Baumeister, R. F. (1998). The trouble with friendly faces: Skilled performance with a supportive audience. *Journal of Personality and Social Psychology, 75,* 1213–1230.

Buttlemann, D., & Bohm, R. (2014). The ontogeny of the motivation that underlies in-group bias. *Psychological Science, 25,* 921–927.

Butz, D. A., & Plant, E. A. (2006). Perceiving outgroup members as unresponsive: Implications for approach-related emotions, intentions, and behavior. *Journal of Personality and Social Psychology, 91,* 1066–1079.

Buunk, B. P., & van der Eijnden, R. J. J. M. (1997). Perceived prevalence, perceived superiority, and relationship satisfaction: Most relationships are good, but ours is the best. *Personality and Social Psychology Bulletin, 23,* 219–228.

Buunk, B. P., & Van Yperen, N. W. (1991). Referential comparisons, relational comparisons, and exchange orientation: Their relation to marital satisfaction. *Personality and Social Psychology Bulletin, 17,* 709–717.

Byers, S., & Wang, A. (2004). Understanding sexuality in close relationships from the social exchange perspective. In J. H. Harvey, A. Wenzel, & S. Sprecher (Eds.), *The handbook of sexuality in close relationships.* Mahwah, NJ: Erlbaum.

Bylsma, W. H., & Major, B. (1994). Social comparisons and contentment. *Psychology of Women Quarterly, 18,* 241–249.

Byrne, D. (1971). *The attraction paradigm.* New York: Academic Press.

Byrne, D., & Clore, G. L. (1970). A reinforcement model of evaluative responses. *Personality: An International Journal, 1,* 103–128.

Bytwerk, R. L., & Brooks, R. D. (1980). *Julius Streicher and the rhetorical foundations of the holocaust.* Paper presented to the Central States Speech Association convention.

Cacioppo, J. T. (2007, October). The rise in collaborative science. *Association for Psychological Science Observer,* 52–53.

Cacioppo, J. T., Berntson, G. G., & Decety, J. (2010). Social neuroscience and its relationship to social psychology. *Social Cognition,* 28, 675–685.

Cacioppo, J. T., Cacioppo, S., Gonzaga, G. C., Ogburn, E. L., & VanderWeele, T. J. (2013). Marital satisfaction and break-ups differ across on-line and off-line meeting venues. *Proceedings of the National Academy of Sciences, 110,* 10135–10140.

Cacioppo, J. T., & Petty, R. E. (1981). Electromyograms as measures of extent and affectivity of information processing. *American Psychologist, 36,* 441–456.

Cacioppo, J. T., Petty, R. E., Feinstein, J. A., & Jarvis, W. B. G. (1996). Dispositional differences in cognitive motivation: The life and times of individuals varying in need for cognition. *Psychological Bulletin, 119,* 197–253.

Cacioppo, J. T., Petty, R. E., & Morris, K. J. (1983). Effects of need for cognition on message evaluation, recall, and persuasion. *Journal of Personality and Social Psychology, 45,* 805–818.

Cacioppo, J. T., Uchino, B. N., Crites, S. L., Snydersmith, M. A., Smith, G., Berntson, G. G., & Lang, P. J. (1991). Relationship between facial expressiveness and sympathetic activation in emotion: A critical review, with emphasis on modeling underlying mechanisms and individual differences. *Journal of Personality and Social Psychology, 62,* 110–128.

Cafferty, J. (2011, March 15). Why is there no looting in Japan? [Web log comment].

Cairns, E., & Hewstone, M. (2002). The impact of peacemaking in Northern Ireland on intergroup behavior. In S. Gabi & B. Nevo (Eds.), *Peace education: The concept, principles, and practices around the world.* Mahwah, NJ: Erlbaum.

Caldwell, H. K., Lee, H-J., MacBeth, A. H., & Young, W. S. (2008). Vasopressin: Behavioral roles of an "original" neuropeptide. *Progress in Neurobiology, 84,* 1–24.

Cameron, C. D., & Payne, B. K. (2011). Escaping affect: How motivated emotion regulation creates insensitivity to mass suffering. *Journal of Personality and Social Psychology, 100,* 1–15.

Cameron, G. (2010, May 7). The Muck files. *The Scottish Sun* (www.thesun.co.uk/scotsol).

Cameron, J. J., Stinson, D. A., Gaetz, R., & Balchen, S. (2010). Acceptance is in the eye of the beholder: Self-esteem and motivated perceptions of acceptance from the opposite sex. *Journal of Personality and Social Psychology, 99,* 513–529.

Campbell, D. T. (1975a). On the conflicts between biological and social evolution and between psychology and oral tradition. *American Psychologist, 30,* 1103–1126.

Campbell, D. T. (1975b). The conflict between social and biological evolution and the concept of original sin. *Zygon, 10,* 234–249.

Campbell, M. A. (2005). Cyberbullying: An old problem in a new guise? *Australian Journal of Guidance and Counselling, 15,* 68–76.

Campbell, W. K. (2005). *When you love a man who loves himself.* Chicago: Sourcebooks.

Campbell, W. K., Bosson, J. K., Goheen, T. W., Lakey, C. E., & Kernis, M. H. (2007). Do narcissists dislike themselves "deep down inside"? *Psychological Science, 18,* 227–229.

Campbell, W. K., Bush, C. P., Brunell, A. B., & Shelton, J. (2005). Understanding the social costs of narcissism: The case of the Tragedy of the Commons. *Personality and Social Psychology Bulletin, 31,* 1358.

Campbell, W. K., & Foster, C. A. (2002). Narcissism and commitment in romantic relationships: An investment model analysis. *Personality and Social Psychology Bulletin, 28,* 484.

Campbell, W. K., Rudich, E., & Sedikides, C. (2002). Narcissism, self-esteem, and the positivity of self-views: Two portraits of self-love. *Personality and Social Psychology Bulletin, 28,* 358–368.

Campbell, W. K., & Sedikides, C. (1999). Self-threat magnifies the self-serving bias: A meta-analytic integration. *Review of General Psychology, 3,* 23–43.

Canadian Centre on Substance Use and Addiction. (1997). *Canadian profile: Alcohol, tobacco, & other drugs.* Ottawa: Canadian Centre on Substance Use and Addiction.

Canadian Museum of History. (n.d.). Pierre Elliott Trudeau. Retrieved from https://www.historymuseum.ca/cmc/exhibitions/hist/biography/biographi270e.html

Canadian Press. (2013*). Front-row seat to history: National news agency the Canadian Press marks 100 years.* Retrieved from http://www.news1130.com/2017/09/01/front-row-seat-to-history-national-news-agency-the-canadian-press-marks-100-years/

Canevello, A., & Crocker, J. (2011). Interpersonal goals, others' regard for the self, and self-esteem: The paradoxical consequences of self-image and compassionate goals. *European Journal of Social Psychology, 41,* 422–434.

Cantarero, K., Gamian-Wilk, M., & Dolinski, D. (2017). Being inconsistent and compliant: The moderating role of the preference for consistency in the door-in-the-face technique. *Personality and Individual Differences, 115,* 54–57.

Canter, D., Breaux, J., & Sime, J. (1980). Domestic, multiple occupancy, and hospital fires. In D. Canter (Ed.), *Fires and human behavior.* Hoboken, NJ: Wiley.

Cantril, H., & Bumstead, C. H. (1960). *Reflections on the human venture.* New York: New York University Press.

Caputo, D., & Dunning, D. (2005). What you don't know: The role played by errors of omission in imperfect self-assessments. *Journal of Experimental Social Psychology, 41*(5), 488.

Carducci, B. J., Cosby, P. C., & Ward, D. D. (1978). Sexual arousal and interpersonal evaluations. *Journal of Experimental Social Psychology, 14,* 449–457.

Carli, L. L. (1999). Cognitive reconstruction, hindsight, and reactions to victims and perpetrators. *Personality and Social Psychology Bulletin, 25,* 966–979.

Carli, L. L., & Leonard, J. B. (1989). The effect of hindsight on victim derogation. *Journal of Social and Clinical Psychology, 8,* 331–343.

Carlo, G., Eisenberg, N., Troyer, D., Switzer, G., & Speer, A. L. (1991). The altruistic personality: In what contexts is it apparent? *Journal of Personality and Social Psychology, 61,* 450–458.

Carlsmith, J. M., & Gross, A. E. (1969). Some effects of guilt on compliance. *Journal of Personality and Social Psychology, 11,* 232–239.

Carlson, E. N., Vazire, S., & Oltmanns, T. F. (2011). You probably think this paper's about you: Narcissists' perceptions of their personality and reputation. *Journal of Personality and Social Psychology, 101,* 185–201.

Carlson, J., & Hatfield, E. (1992). *The psychology of emotion.* Fort Worth, TX: Holt, Rinehart & Winston.

Carlson, J., & Miller, N. (1987). Explanation of the relation between negative mood and helping. *Psychological Bulletin, 102,* 91–108.

Carlson, M., Charlin, V., & Miller, N. (1988). Positive mood and helping behavior: A test of six hypotheses. *Journal of Personality and Social Psychology, 55,* 211–229.

Carlson, M., Marcus-Newhall, A., & Miller, N. (1990). Effects of situational aggression cues: A quantitative review. *Journal of Personality and Social Psychology, 58,* 622–633.

Carlston, D. E., & Shovar, N. (1983). Effects of performance attributions on others' perceptions of the attributor. *Journal of Personality and Social Psychology, 44,* 515–525.

Carlston, D. E., & Skowronski, J. J. (2005). Linking versus thinking: Evidence for the different associative and attributional bases of spontaneous trait transference and spontaneous trait inference. *Journal of Personality and Social Psychology, 89*(6), 884.

Carnagey, N. L., Anderson, C. A., & Bushman, B. J. (2007). The effect of video game violence on physiological desensitization to real-life violence. *Journal of Experimental Social Psychology, 43,* 489–496.

Carnevale, P. J., & Choi, D-W. (2000). Culture in the mediation of international disputes. *International Journal of Psychology, 35,* 105–110.

Carnevale, P. J., & Probst, T. M. (1998). Social values and social conflict in creative problem solving and categorization. *Journal of Personality and Social Psychology, 74,* 1300–1309.

Carney, D. R., Cuddy, A. J. C., & Yap, A. J. (2010). Power posing: Brief nonverbal displays affect neuroendocrine levels and risk tolerance. *Psychological Science, 21,* 1363–1368.

Carpenter, C. J. (2012). A meta-analysis and an experiment investigating the effects of speaker disfluency on persuasion. *Western Journal of Communication, 76,* 552–569.

Carpenter, S. (2008, April/May). Buried prejudice. *Scientific American,* 32–39.

Carr, E. W., Brady, T. F., & Winkielman, P. (2017). Are you smiling, or have I seen you before? Familiarity makes faces look happier. *Psychological Science, 28,* 1087–1102.

Carré, J. M., Geniole, S. N., Ortiz, T. L., Bird, B. M., Videto, A., & Bonin, P. L. (2017). Exogenous testosterone rapidly increases aggressive behavior in dominant and impulsive men. *Biological Psychiatry, 82,* 249–256.

Carré, J. M., & McCormick, C. M. (2008). In your face: Facial metrics predict aggressiveness behaviour in the laboratory and in varsity and professional hockey players. *Proceedings of the Royal Society B, 275,* 2651–2656.

Carré, J. M., McCormick, C. M., & Mondloch, C. J. (2009). Facial structure is a reliable cue of aggressive behavior. *Psychological Science, 20,* 1194–1198.

Carroll, D., Davey Smith, G., & Bennett, P. (1994, March). Health and socio-economic status. *The Psychologist,* 122–125.

Carroll, J. S., Padilla-Walker, L. M., Nelson, L. J., Olson, C. D., Barry, C. M., & Madsen, S. D. (2008). Generation XXX: Pornography acceptance and use among emerging adults. *Journal of Adolescent Research, 23,* 6–30.

Carter, S., & Snow, C. (2004, May). Helping singles enter better marriages using predictive models of marital success. Paper presented at the annual meeting of the American Psychological Society. Chicago, IL.

Carter, S. L. (1993). *Reflections of an affirmative action baby.* New York: Basic Books.

Cartwright, D. S. (1975). The nature of gangs. In D. S. Cartwright, B. Tomson, & H. Schwartz (Eds.), *Gang delinquency.* Monterey, CA: Brooks/Cole.

Carvallo, M., & Gabriel, S. (2006). No man is an island: The need to belong and dismissing avoidant attachment style. *Personality and Social Psychology Bulletin, 32,* 697–709.

Carver, C. S., & Scheier, M. F. (1981). *Attention and self-regulation.* New York: Springer-Verlag.

Cash, T. F., & Janda, L. H. (1984, December). The eye of the beholder. *Psychology Today,* 46–52.

Caspi, A., & Herbener, E. S. (1990). Continuity and change: Assortative marriage and the consistency of personality in adulthood. *Journal of Personality and Social Psychology, 58,* 250–258.

Caspi, A., McClay, J., Moffitt, T., Mill, J., Martin, J., Craig, I. W., Taylor, A., & Poulton, R. (2002). Role of genotype in the cycle of violence in maltreated children. *Science, 297,* 851–854.

Cassidy, J. (2000). Adult romantic attachments: A developmental perspective on individual differences. *Review of General Psychology, 4,* 111–131.

Castelli, L., Arcuri, L., & Carraro, L. (2009). Projection processes in the perception of political leaders. *Basic and Applied Social Psychology, 31,* 189–196.

Castelli, L., Carraro, L., Tomelleri, S., & Amari, A. (2007). White children's alignment to the perceived racial attitudes of the parents: Closer to the mother than father. *British Journal of Developmental Psychology, 25,* 353–357.

CBC. (2002). Africville: Expropriating black Nova Scotians. *CBC News.* Retrieved from http://archives.cbc.ca/society/racism/topics/96/

CBC. (2005). Racial profiling: Frequently asked questions *CBC News.*

CBC. (2012). Amanda Todd tribute honours life of bullied teen. Retrieved from http://www.cbc.ca/news/canada/british-columbia/amanda-todd-tribute-honours-life-of-bullied-teen-1.1138838

CBC. (2013a). N.S. cyberbullying legislation allows victims to sue. *CBC News.* Retrieved from http://www.cbc.ca/news/canada/nova-scotia/n-s-cyberbullying-legislation-allows-victims-to-sue-1.1307338

CBC. (2013b). Saint Mary's sex chant highlights risk of student-led frosh events. *CBC News.* Retrieved from http://www.cbc.ca/news/canada/saint-mary-s-sex-chant-highlights-risk-of-student-led-frosh-events-1.1321822

CBC. (2015a). Poll Tracker: Liberals poised for win barring Conservative surprise. Retrieved from https://www.cbc.ca/news/politics/canada-election-2015-grenier-polls-oct18-1.3276755

CBC. (2015b). Randall Steven Shepherd, Lindsay Kanittha Souvannarath charged in Halifax shooting plot https://www.cbc.ca/news/canada/nova-scotia/randall-steven-shepherd-lindsay-kanittha-souvannarath-charged-in-halifax-shooting-plot-1.2957685

CBC. (2016a). Attawapiskat declares state of emergency over spate of suicide attempts. *CBC News.* Retrieved from http://www.cbc.ca/news/canada/sudbury/attawapiskat-suicide-first-nations-emergency-1.3528747

CBC. (2016b). Only Facebook knows how it spreads fake election news. *CBC News.* Retrieved from http://www.cbc.ca/news/technology/facebook-fake-news-us-election-algorithm-transparency-1.3846073

CBC. (2019). Close elections like this one are rare—and hard to predict. Retrieved from: https://www.cbc.ca/news/politics/grenier-history-close-elections-1.5304892

CBC. (2020a, Jan. 3). Recent suicides in northern communities during holiday season "shocking," MPP says. Retrieved from https://www.cbc.ca/news/canada/thunder-bay/suicide-deaths-northern-communities-1.5413478

CBC. (2020b, Mar. 31). Overcrowding, vulnerable population make COVID-19 big worry for First Nations. Retrieved from https://www.cbc.ca/news/canada/new-brunswick/first-nations-coronavirus-overcrowding-1.5516174

CBC. (2020c, April 20). Social media firms catching more misinformation, but critics say "they could be doing more." Retrieved from https://www.cbc.ca/news/technology/social-media-platforms-pandemic-moderation-1.5536594

CBC. (2020d, May 31). Unrest overshadows peaceful U.S. protests against police killings of black people. Retrieved from https://www.cbc.ca/news/world/minneapolis-george-floyd-protest-may31-1.5592200

CBC 4 Kids. (1999, Nov. 15). A hero saves three children. CBC LICENSING.

CBS. (2009). Terrorists take recruitment effort online. *60 Minutes.* Retrieved from http://www.cbsnews.com/stories/2007/03/02/60minutes/main2531546.shtml

Ceci, S. J., & Bruck, M. (1993a). Child witnesses: Translating research into policy. *Social Policy Report (Society for Research in Child Development), 7*(3), 1–30.

Ceci, S. J., & Bruck, M. (1993b). Suggestibility of the child witness: A historical review and synthesis. *Psychological Bulletin, 113,* 403–439.

Ceci, S. J., & Williams, W. M. (2015, September 10). Passions supplant reason in dialogue on women in science. *The Chronicle of Higher Education* (www.chronicle.com).

Cemalcilar, Z., & Falbo, T. (2008). A longitudinal study of the adaptation of international students in the United States. *Journal of Cross-Cultural Psychology, 39,* 799–804.

Census Bureau. (1993, May 4). Voting survey, reported by Associated Press.

Centers for Disease Control (CDC). (2008, Spring). Sexual violence: Facts at a glance. Centers for Disease Control and Prevention. Retrieved from http://www.cdc.gov/injury

Centerwall, B. S. (1989). Exposure to television as a risk factor for violence. *American Journal of Epidemiology, 129,* 643–652.

Chaiken, S. (1979). Communicator physical attractiveness and persuasion. *Journal of Personality and Social Psychology, 37,* 1387–1397.

Chaiken, S. (1980). Heuristic versus systematic information processing and the use of source versus message cues in persuasion. *Journal of Personality and Social Psychology, 39,* 752–766.

Chaiken, S., & Eagly, A. H. (1976). Communication modality as a determinant of message persuasiveness and message comprehensibility. *Journal of Personality and Social Psychology, 34,* 605–614.

Chaiken, S., & Eagly, A. H. (1983). Communication modality as a determinant of persuasion: The role of communicator salience. *Journal of Personality and Social Psychology, 45,* 241–256.

Chaiken, S., & Maheswaran, D. (1994). Heuristic processing can bias systematic processing: Effects of source credibility, argument ambiguity, and task importance on attitude judgment. *Journal of Personality and Social Psychology, 66,* 460–473.

Chambers, J. R., Baron, R. S., & Inman, M. L. (2006). Misperceptions in intergroup conflict: Disagreeing about what we disagree about. *Psychological Science, 17,* 38–45.

Chambers, J. R., Schlenker, B. R., & Collisson, B. (2012). Ideology and prejudice: The role of value conflicts. *Psychological Science, 24,* 140–149.

Chambers, J. R., & Windschitl, P. D. (2004). Biases in social comparative judgments: The role of nonmotivated factors in above-average and comparative-optimism effects. *Psychological Bulletin, 130,* 813.

Chan, A. C., & Au, T. K. (2011). Getting children to do more academic work: Foot-in-the-Door versus Door-in-the-Face. *Teaching and Teacher Education, 27*(6), 982–985.

Chan, M. K. H., Louis, W. R., & Jetten, J. (2010). When groups are wrong and deviants are right. *European Journal of Social Psychology, 40,* 1103–1109.

Chance, J. E., & Goldstein, A. G. (1981). Depth of processing in response to own and other-race faces. *Personality and Social Psychology Bulletin, 7,* 475–480.

Chandler, J., & Schwarz, N. (2009). How extending your middle finger affects your perception of others: Learned movements influence concept accessibility. *Journal of Experimental Social Psychology, 45,* 123–128.

Chandra, A., Mosher, W. D., & Copen, C. (2011, March). Sexual behavior, sexual attraction, and sexual identity in the United States: Data from the 2006–2008 National Survey of Family Growth. *National Health Statistics Reports*, Number 36 (Centers for Disease Control and Prevention).

Chapin, J., & Coleman, G. (2017). The cycle of cyberbullying: Some experience required. *The Social Science Journal, 54,* 314–318.

Chapman, L. J., & Chapman, J. P. (1969). Genesis of popular but erroneous psychodiagnostic observations. *Journal of Abnormal Psychology, 74,* 272–280.

Chartrand, T. L., & Bargh, J. A. (1999). The chameleon effect: The perception-behavior link and social interaction. *Journal of Personality and Social Psychology, 76,* 893–910.

Chatard, A., Guimond, S., & Selimbegovic, L. (2007). "How good are you in math?" The effect of gender stereotypes on students' recollection of their school marks. *Journal of Experimental Social Psychology, 43,* 1017–1024.

Check, J., & Malamuth, N. (1984). Can there be positive effects of participation in pornography experiments? *Journal of Sex Research, 20,* 14–31.

Chen, F. F., & Kenrick, D. T. (2002). Repulsion or attraction? Group membership and assumed attitude similarity. *Journal of Personality and Social Psychology, 83,* 111–125.

Chen, H., Luo, S., Yue, G., Xu, D., & Zhaoyang, R. (2009). Do birds of a feather flock together in China? *Personal Relationships, 16,* 167–186.

Chen, H. T. (2012). Multiple issue publics in the high-choice media environment: Media use, online activity, and political knowledge. *Asian Journal of Communication, 22*(6), 621–641.

Chen, L.-H., Baker, S. P., Braver, E. R., & Li, G. (2000). Carrying passengers as a risk factor for crashes fatal to 16- and 17-year-old drivers. *Journal of the American Medical Association, 283,* 1578–1582.

Chen, S., Boucher, H. C., & Tapias, M. P. (2006). The relational self revealed: Integrative conceptualization and implications for interpersonal life. *Psychological Bulletin, 132,* 151–179.

Chen, S. C. (1937). Social modification of the activity of ants in nest-building. *Physiological Zoology, 10,* 420–436.

Chen, Y., Yao, M., & Yan, W. (2014). Materialism and well-being among Chinese college students: The mediating role of basic psychological need satisfaction. *Journal of Health Psychology, 19*(10), 1232–1240.

Chen, Z., Williams, K. D., Fitness, J., & Newton, N. C. (2008). When hurt will not heal: Exploring the capacity to relive social and physical pain. *Psychological Science, 19,* 789–795.

Cheng, J., Bernstein, M., Danescu-Niculescu-Mizil, C., & Leskovec, J. (2017, February). *Anyone can become a troll: Causes of trolling behavior in online discussions.* Paper presented at the Proceedings of the 2017 ACM Conference on Computer Supported Cooperative Work and Social Computing.

Chester, D. S., Dewall, C. N., & Enjaian, B. (2017). *Sadism and aggression: Inflicting pain to feel pleasure.* Unpublished manuscript.

Cheung, F., & Lucas, R. E. (2016). Income inequality is associated with stronger social comparison effects: The effect of relative income on life satisfaction. *Journal of Personality and Social Psychology, 110*(2), 332–341.

Chiao, J. Y., Bowman, N. E., & Gill, H. (2008). The political gender gap: Gender bias in facial inferences that predict voting behavior. *PLoS One 3*(10): e3666. doi:10.1371/journal.pone.0003666

Choi, I., & Choi, Y. (2002). Culture and self-concept flexibility. *Personality & Social Psychology Bulletin, 28,* 1508–1517.

Choi, I., Nisbett, R. E., & Norenzayan, A. (1999). Causal attribution across cultures: Variation and universality. *Psychological Bulletin, 125,* 47–63.

Choma, B. L., & Hanoch, Y. (2017). Cognitive ability and authoritarianism: Understanding support for Trump and Clinton. *Personality and Individual Differences, 106,* 287–291.

Chou, H. G., & Edge, N. (2012). "They are happier and having better lives than I am": The impact of using Facebook on perceptions of others' lives. *Cyberpsychology, Behavior, and Social Networking, 15,* 117–121.

Chou, W. S., Prestin, A., & Kunath, S. (2014). Obesity in social media: A mixed methods analysis. *Translational Behavioral Medicine, 4,* 314–323.

Christ, O., Hewstone, M., Tausch, N., Wagner, U., Voci, A., Hughes, J., & Cairns, E. (2010). Direct contact as a moderator of extended contact effects: Cross-sectional and longitudinal impact on outgroup attitudes, behavioral intentions, and attitude certainty. *Personality and Social Psychology Bulletin, 36,* 1662–1674.

Christakis, N. A., & Fowler, J. H. (2009). *Connected: The surprising power of social networks and how they shape our lives.* New York: Little, Brown.

Christie, C., & Dill, E. (2016). Evaluating peers in cyberspace: The impact of anonymity. *Computers in Human Behavior, 55,* 292–299.

Chua, H. F., Boland, J. E., & Nisbett, R. E. (2005). Cultural variation in eye movements during scene perception. *Proceedings of the National Academy of Sciences, 102,* 12629–12633.

Chua-Eoan, H. (1997, April 7). Imprisoned by his own passions. *Time,* 40–42.

Church, A. T., Aria, R. M., Rincon, B. C., Vargas-Flores, J. J., Ibanez-Eyes, J., Wang, L., Alvarez, J. M., Wang, C., & Ortiz, F. A. (2014). A four-culture study of self-enhancement and adjustment using the social relations model: Do alternative conceptualizations and indices make a difference? *Journal of Personality and Social Psychology, 106,* 997–1014.

Church, G. J. (1986, January 6). China. *Time,* 6–19.

CIA: Central Intelligence Agency. (2014). The World Factbook. Retrieved from https://www.cia.gov/library/publications/the-world-factbook/geos/ja.html

Cialdini, R. B. (1988). *Influence: Science and practice.* Glenview, IL: Scott, Foresman/Little, Brown.

Cialdini, R. B. (1989). *Agents of influence: Bunglers, smugglers, and sleuths.* Paper presented at the American Psychological Association convention.

Cialdini, R. B. (1991). Altruism or egoism? That is (still) the question. *Psychological Inquiry, 2,* 124–126.

Cialdini, R. B. (1995). A full-cycle approach to social psychology. In G. G. Brannigan & M. R. Merrens (Eds.), *The social psychologists: Research adventures.* New York: McGraw-Hill.

Cialdini, R. B. (2000). *Influence: Science and practice* (4th ed.). Boston: Allyn & Bacon.

Cialdini, R. B. (2003). Crafting normative messages to protect the environment. *Current Directions in Psychological Science, 12*(4), 105–109.

Cialdini, R. B. (2005). Basic social influence is underestimated. *Psychological Inquiry, 16,* 158–161.

Cialdini, R. B., Bickman, L., & Cacioppo, J. T. (1979). An example of consumeristic social psychology: Bargaining tough in the new car showroom. *Journal of Applied Social Psychology, 9,* 115–126.

Cialdini, R. B., Borden, R. J., Thorne, A., Walker, M. R., Freeman, S., & Sloan, L. R. (1976). Basking in reflected glory: Three (football) field studies. *Journal of Personality and Social Psychology, 39,* 406–415.

Cialdini, R. B., Cacioppo, J. T., Bassett, R., & Miller, J. A. (1978). Lowball procedure for producing compliance: Commitment then cost. *Journal of Personality and Social Psychology, 36,* 463–476.

Cialdini, R. B., Demaine, L. J., Barrett, D. W., Sagarin, B. J., & Rhoads, K. L. V. (2003). *The poison parasite defense: A strategy for sapping a stronger opponent's persuasive strength.* Unpublished manuscript, Arizona State University. Tempe, Arizona.

Cialdini, R. B., & Goldstein, N. J. (2004). Social influence: Compliance and conformity. *Annual Review of Psychology, 55,* 591–621.

Cialdini, R. B., Kenrick, D. T., & Baumann, D. J. (1981). Effects of mood on prosocial behavior in children and adults. In N. Eisenberg-Berg (Ed.), *The development of prosocial behavior.* New York: Academic Press.

Cialdini, R. B., & Schroeder, D. A. (1976). Increasing compliance by legitimizing paltry contributions: When even a penny helps. *Journal of Personality and Social Psychology, 34,* 599–604.

Cialdini, R. B., Vincent, J. E., Lewis, S. K., Catalan, J., Wheeler, D., & Danby, B. L. (1975). Reciprocal concessions procedure for inducing compliance: The door-in-the-face technique. *Journal of Personality and Social Psychology, 31,* 206–215.

Cialdini, R. B., Wosinska, W., Dabul, A. J., Whetstone-Dion, R., & Heszen, I. (1998). When social role salience leads to social role rejection: Modest self-presentation among women and men in two cultures. *Personality and Social Psychology Bulletin, 24,* 473–481.

Cicerello, A., & Sheehan, E. P. (1995). Personal advertisements: A content analysis. *Journal of Social Behavior and Personality, 10,* 751–756.

Cikara, M., Bruneau, E. G., & Saxe, R. R. (2011). Us and them: Intergroup failures of empathy. *Current Directions in Psychological Science, 20,* 149–153.

Cioffi, D., & Garner, R. (1998). The effect of response options on decisions and subsequent behavior: Sometimes inaction is better. *Personality and Social Psychology Bulletin, 24,* 463–472.

Claassen, R. L., Djupe, P. A., Lewis, A. R., & Neiheisel, J. R. (2019). Which party represents my group? The group foundations of partisan choice and polarization. *Political Behavior.* https://doi-org.library.smu.ca/10.1007/s11109-019-09565-6

Clark, M. S. (1984). Record keeping in two types of relationships. *Journal of Personality and Social Psychology, 47,* 549–557.

Clark, M. S. (1986). Evidence for the effectiveness of manipulations of desire for communal versus exchange relationships. *Personality and Social Psychology Bulletin, 12,* 414–425.

Clark, M. S., & Mills, J. (1979). Interpersonal attraction in exchange and communal relationships. *Journal of Personality and Social Psychology, 37,* 12–24.

Clark, M. S., & Mills, J. (1993). The difference between communal and exchange relationships: What it is and is not. *Personality and Social Psychology Bulletin, 19,* 684–691.

Clark, M. S., Mills, J., & Corcoran, D. (1989). Keeping track of needs and inputs of friends and strangers. *Personality and Social Psychology Bulletin, 15,* 533–542.

Clark, M. S., Mills, J., & Powell, M. C. (1986). Keeping track of needs in communal and exchange relationships. *Journal of Personality and Social Psychology, 51,* 333–338.

Clark, R. D., III (1995). A few parallels between group polarization and minority influence. In S. Moscovici, H. Mucchi-Faina, & A. Maass (Eds.), *Minority influence.* Chicago: Nelson-Hall.

Clark, R. D., III, & Maass, S. A. (1988). The role of social categorization and perceived source credibility in minority influence. *European Journal of Social Psychology, 18,* 381–394.

Clarke, A. C. (1952). An examination of the operation of residual propinquity as a factor in mate selection. *American Sociological Review, 27,* 17–22.

Clayton, S., & Myers, G. (2009). *Conservation psychology: Understanding and promoting human care for nature.* Hoboken, NJ: Wiley-Blackwell.

Cleghorn, J. (2000). *Beyond the bottom line: Redefining philanthropy in the 21st century.* Ketchum Leaders in Philanthropy Series. Toronto: Canadian Centre for Philanthropy.

Cleghorn, R. (1980, October 31). ABC News, meet the Literary Digest. *Detroit Free Press,* p. 22.

Clement, J. (2019, November 15). Global number of Facebook users 2015-2020. Retrieved from: https://www.statista.com/statistics/490424/number-of-worldwide-facebook-users/

Clevstrom, J., & Passariello, C. (2006, August 18). No kicks from "champagne." *Wall Street Journal,* p. A11.

Clifford, M. M., & Walster, E. H. (1973). The effect of physical attractiveness on teacher expectation. *Sociology of Education, 46,* 248–258.

Clore, G. L., Wiggins, N. H., & Itkin, G. (1975). Gain and loss in attraction: Attributions from nonverbal behavior. *Journal of Personality and Social Psychology, 31,* 706–712.

CNN. (2001). Timothy McVeigh: Convicted Oklahoma City Bomber. https://web.archive.org/web/20100301192549/; http://archives.cnn.com/2001/US/03/29/profile.mcveigh/

CNN. (2007, October 6). Jury awards $6.1 million in McDonald's strip search case. Retrieved from http://www.cnn.com

CNN. (2020). Columbine: Fast Facts. https://www.cnn.com/2013/09/18/us/columbine-high-school-shootings-fast-facts/index.html

Coates, B., Pusser, H. E., & Goodman, I. (1976). The influence of "Sesame Street" and "Mister Rogers' Neighborhood" on children's social behavior in the preschool. *Child Development, 47,* 138–144.

Coccia, M. (2017). A theory of the general causes of violent crime: Homicides, income inequality and the deficiencies of the heat hypothesis and the model of CLASH. *Aggression and Violent Behavior, 37,* 190-200.

Codol, J. P. (1976). On the so-called superior conformity of the self behavior: Twenty experimental investigations. *European Journal of Social Psychology, 5,* 457–501.

Cohen, B., Waugh, G., & Place, K. (1989). At the movies: An unobtrusive study of arousal attraction. *Journal of Social Psychology, 129,* 691–693.

Cohen, D. (1998). Culture, social organization, and patterns of violence. *Journal of Personality and Social Psychology, 75,* 408–419.

Cohen, D., Nisbett, R. E., Bowdle, B. F., & Schwarz, N. (1996). Insult, aggression, and the southern culture of honor: An "Experimental Ethnography." *Journal of*

Personality and Social Psychology, 70, 945–960.

Cohen, E. E. A., Ejsmond-Frey, R., Knight, N., & Dunbar, R. I. M. (2009, September 15). Rowers' high: Behavioural synchrony is correlated with elevated pain thresholds. *Biology Letters.* doi:10.1098/rsbl.2009.0670

Cohen, G. L., Garcia, J., Apfel, N., & Master, A. (2006). Reducing the racial achievement gap: A social-psychological intervention. *Science, 313,* 1307–1310.

Cohen, G. L., Garcia, J., Purdie-Vaugns, V., Apfel, N., & Brzustoski, P. (2009). Recursive processes in self-affirmation: Intervening to close the minority achievement gap. *Science, 324,* 400–403.

Cohen, G. L., Steele, C. M., & Ross, L. D. (1999). The mentor's dilemma: Providing critical feedback across the racial divide. *Personality and Social Psychology Bulletin, 25,* 1302–1318.

Cohen, M., & Davis, N. (1981). *Medication errors: Causes and prevention.* Philadelphia: G. F. Stickley Co.

Cohen, S. (1980). *Training to understand TV advertising: Effects and some policy implications.* Paper presented at the American Psychological Association convention.

Cohen, S. (2002). Psychosocial stress, social networks, and susceptibility to infection. In H. G. Koenig, & H. J. Cohen (Eds.), *The link between religion and health: Psychoneuroimmunology and the faith factor* (pp. 101–123). New York: Oxford University Press.

Cohen, S. (2004). Social relationships and health. *American Psychologist. Special Issue: Awards Issue 2004, 59,* 676.

Cohen, S., Alper, C. M., Doyle, W. J., Treanor, J. J., & Turner, R. B. (2006). Positive emotional style predicts resistance to illness after experimental exposure to rhinovirus or influenza A virus. *Psychosomatic Medicine, 68,* 809–815.

Cohen, S., Doyle, W. J., Turner, R., Alper, C. M., & Skoner, D. P. (2003). Sociability and susceptibility to the common cold. *Psychological Science, 14,* 389–395.

Cohen, S., Janicki-Deverts, D., Doyle, W. J., Miller, G. E., Frank, E., Rabin, B. S., & Turner, R. B. (2012). Chronic stress, glucocorticoid receptor resistance, inflammation, and disease risk. *PNAS Proceedings of the National Academy of Sciences of the United States of America, 109,* 5995–5999.

Cohen, S., & Rodriguez, M. S. (1995). Pathways linking affective disturbances and physical disorders. *Health Psychology, 14,* 374–380.

Cohn, E. G. (1993). The prediction of police calls for service: The influence of weather and temporal variables on rape and domestic violence. *Environmental Psychology, 13,* 71–83.

Cohn, E. G., & Rotton, J. (2005). The curve is still out there: A reply to Bushman, Wang, and Anderson (2005), Is the curve relating temperature to aggression linear or curvilinear? *Journal of Personality and Social Psychology, 89,* 67–70.

Cohrs, J. C., Moschner, B., Maes, J., & Kielmann, S. (2005). The motivational bases of right-wing authoritarianism and social dominance orientation: Relations to values and attitudes in the aftermath of September 11, 2001. *Personality and Social Psychology Bulletin, 31,* 1425.

Cole, S. W., Arevalo, J. M. G., Takahashi, R., Sloan, E. K., Lutgendorf, S. K., Sood, A. K., Sheridan, J. F., & Seeman, T. E. (2010). Computational identification of gene-social environment interaction at the human IL6 locus. *PNAS, 107,* 5681–5686.

Coleman, L. M., Jussim, L., & Abraham, J. (1987). Students' reactions to teachers' evaluations: The unique impact of negative feedback. *Journal of Applied Social Psychology, 17,* 1051–1070.

Collier, K. L., Bos, H. M. W., & Sandfort, T. G. M. (2012). Intergroup contact, attitudes toward homosexuality, and the role of acceptance of gender non-conformity in young adolescents. *Journal of Adolescence, 35,* 899–907.

Collins, N. L., & Miller, L. C. (1994). Self-disclosure and liking: A meta-analytic review. *Psychological Bulletin, 116,* 457–475.

Colman, A. M. (1991). Crowd psychology in South African murder trials. *American Psychologist, 46,* 1071–1079. See also, A. M. Colman (1991), Psychological evidence in South African murder trials. *The Psychologist, 14,* 482–486.

Colzato, L. S., Steenbergen, L., de Kwaadsteniet, E. W., Sellaro, R., Liepelt, R., & Hommel, B. (2013). Tryptophan promotes interpersonal trust. *Psychological Science, 24,* 2575–2577.

Comer, D. R. (1995). A model of social loafing in real work group. *Human Relations, 48,* 647–667.

Comstock, G. (2008). A sociological perspective on television violence and aggression. *American Behavioral Scientist, 51,* 1184–1211.

Conger, R. D., Cui, M., Bryant, C. M., & Elder, G. H. (2000). Competence in early adult romantic relationships: A developmental perspective on family influences. *Journal of Personality and Social Psychology, 79,* 224–237.

Conway, F., & Siegelman, J. (1979). *Snapping: America's epidemic of sudden personality change.* New York: Delta Books.

Conway, L. G., III, Suedfeld, P., & Tetlock, P. E. (2001). Integrative complexity and political decisions that lead to war or peace. In D. J. Christie, R. V. Wagner, & D. Winter (Eds.), *Peace, conflict, and violence: Peace psychology for the 21st century.* Englewood Cliffs, NJ: Prentice-Hall.

Conway, M., & Ross, M. (1986). Remembering one's own past: The construction of personal histories. In R. Sorrentino & E. T. Higgins (Eds.), *Handbook of motivation and cognition.* New York: Guilford.

Cook, T. D., & Flay, B. R. (1978). The persistence of experimentally induced attitude change. In L. Berkowitz (Ed.), *Advances in experimental social psychology* (Vol. 11). New York: Academic Press.

Cooke, L., Chambers, L., Anez, E., Croker, H., Boniface, D., Yeomans, M., & Wardle, J. (2011). Eating for pleasure or profit: The effect of incentives on children's enjoyment of vegetables. *Psychological Science, 22,* 190–196.

Cooley, C. H. (1902). *Human nature and the social order.* New York: Schocken Books.

Cooper, H. (1983). Teacher expectation effects. In L. Bickman (Ed.), *Applied social psychology annual* (Vol. 4). Beverly Hills, CA: Sage.

Cooper, J. (1999). Unwanted consequences and the self: In search of the motivation for dissonance reduction. In E. Harmon-Jones & J. Mills (Eds.), *Cognitive dissonance: Progress on a pivotal theory in social psychology.* Science conference series (pp. 149–173). Washington, DC: American Psychological Association.

Cooper, J., & Feldman, L. A. (2019a). Does cognitive dissonance occur in older age? A study of induced compliance in a healthy elderly population. *Psychology and Aging, 34*(5), 709–713. https://doi - org.library.smu.ca/10.1037/pag0000338

Cooper, J., & Feldman, L. A. (2019b). Helping the "couch potato": A cognitive dissonance approach to increasing exercise in the elderly. *Journal of Applied Social Psychology.*https://doi- org.library.smu .ca/10.1111/jasp.12639

Cooper, M. (1999, Feb. 5). Officers in Bronx fire 41 shots, and an unarmed man is killed. *New York Times.* Retrieved from http://www.nytimes.com

Correll, J., Hudson, S. M., Guillermo, S., & Ma, D. S. (2014). The police officer's dilemma: A decade of research on racial bias in the decision to shoot. *Social and Personality Psychology Compass, 8,* 201–213.

Correll, J., Park, B., Judd, C. M., & Wittenbrink, B. (2002). The police officer's dilemma: Using ethnicity to disambiguate potentially threatening individuals. *Journal of Personality and Social Psychology, 83,* 1314–1329.

Correll, J., Park, B., Judd, C. M., & Wittenbrink, B. (2007). The influence of stereotypes on decisions to shoot. *European Journal of Social Psychology, 37,* 1102–1117.

Correll, J., Urland, G. R., & Ito, T. A. (2006). Event-related potentials and the decision to shoot: The role of threat perception and cognitive control. *Journal of Experimental Social Psychology, 42,* 120–128.

Correll, J., Wittenbrink, B., Crawford, M. T., & Sadler, M. S. (2015). Stereotypic vision: How stereotypes disambiguate visual stimuli. *Journal of Personality and Social Psychology, 108,* 219–233.

Corrigan, P. W., Watson, A. C., Byrne, P., & Davis, K. E. (2005). Mental illness stigma: Problem of public health or social justice? *Social Work, 50,* 363–368.

Costa-Lopes, R., Dovidio, J. F., Pereira, C., & Jost, J. T. (2013). Social psychological perspectives on the legitimation of social inequality: Past, present and future. *European Journal of Social Psychology, 43,* 229–237.

Costanzo, M. (1998). *Just revenge.* New York: St. Martins.

Costello, C., Gaines, S. D., & Lynham, J. (2008). Can catch shares prevent fisheries' collapse? *Science, 321,* 1678–1682.

Cota, A. A., & Dion, K. L. (1986). Salience of gender and sex composition of ad hoc groups: An experimental test of distinctiveness theory. *Journal of Personality and Social Psychology, 50,* 770–776.

Cotton, J. L. (1981). *Ambient temperature and violent crime.* Paper presented at the Midwestern Psychological Association convention, Washington, D.C.

Cotton, J. L. (1986). Ambient temperature and violent crime. *Journal of Applied Social Psychology, 16,* 786–801.

Cottrell, N. B., Wack, D. L., Sekerak, G. J., & Rittle, R. M. (1968). Social facilitation of dominant responses by the presence of an audience and the mere presence of others. *Journal of Personality and Social Psychology, 9,* 245–250.

Coulter, K. S., & Grewal, D. (2014). Name-letters and birthday-numbers: Implicit egotism effects in pricing. *Journal of Marketing, 78,* 102–120.

Council of Ontario Universities (2013). *Aboriginal Self-Identification Project Final Report.* Council of Ontario Universities, Toronto, ON.

Courbet, D., Fourquet-Courbet, M. P., Kazan, R., & Intartaglia, J. (2014). The long-term effects of e-advertising: The influence of Internet pop-ups viewed at a low level of attention in implicit memory. *Journal of Computer-Mediated Communication, 19,* 274–293.

Courneya, K. S., & Carron, A. V. (1992). The home advantage in sport competitions: A literature review. *Journal of Sport and Exercise Psychology, 14,* 13–27.

Cox, C. R., Van Enkevort, E. A., Hicks, J. A., Kahn-Weintraub, M., & Morin, A. (2014). The relationship between alcohol cues, alcohol expectancies, and physical balance. *Experimental and Clinical Psychopharmacology, 22,* 307–315.

Coyne, I., Gopaul, A.-M., Campbell, M., Pankász, A., Garland, R., & Cousans, F. (2019). Bystander responses to bullying at work: The role of mode, type and relationship to target. *Journal of Business Ethics, 157*(3), 813–827. https://doi-org.library.smu.ca/10.1007/s10551-017-3692-2

Coyne, S. M., & Archer, J. (2005). The relationship between indirect and physical aggression on television and in real life. *Social Development, 14,* 324–338.

Coyne, S. M., Nelson, D. A., Lawton, F., Haslam, S., Rooney, L., Titterington, L., Trainor, H., Remnant, J., & Ogunlaja, L. (2008). The effects of viewing physical and relational aggression in the media: Evidence for a cross-over effect. *Journal of Experimental Social Psychology, 44,* 1551–1554.

Coyne, S. M., Ridge, R., Stevens, M., Callister, M., & Stockdale, L. (2012). Backbiting and bloodshed in books: Short-term effects of reading physical and relational aggression in literature. *British Journal of Social Psychology, 51,* 188–196.

Cozzolino, P. J. (2011). Trust, cooperation, and equality: A psychological analysis of the formation of social capital. *British Journal of Social Psychology, 50,* 302–320.

Crabb, P. B., & Bielawski, D. (1994). The social representation of material culture and gender in children's books. *Sex Roles, 30,* 69–79.

Craig, M. A., & Richeson, J. A. (2012). Coalition or derogation? How perceived discrimination influences intraminority intergroup relations. *Journal of Personality and Social Psychology, 102,* 759–777.

Craig, M. A., & Richeson, J. A. (2014). On the precipice of a "majority-minority" America: Perceived status threat from the racial demographic shift affects White Americans' political ideology. *Psychological Science, 25,* 1189–1197.

Craig, W., & Harel, Y. (2004). Bullying, physical fighting, and victimization. In C. Currie (Ed.), *Young people's health in context: International report from the HSBC 2001/2 survey.* WHO Policy Series: Health policy for children and adolescents, issue 4. Copenhagen: WHO Regional Office for Europe.

Craig, W. M., Vitaro, F., Gagnon, C., & Tremblay, R. E. (2002). The road to gang membership: Characteristics of male gang and nongang members from ages 10 to 14. *Social Development, 11*(1), 53–68.

Crandall, C. S. (1988). Social contagion of binge eating. *Journal of Personality and Social Psychology, 55,* 588–598.

Crandall, C. S., Eshleman, A., & O'Brien, L. (2002). Social norms and the expression and suppression of prejudice: The struggle for internalization. *Journal of Personality and Social Psychology, 82*(3), 359–378.

Crandall, C. S., & White, M. H. (2016, November 17). Trump and the social psychology of prejudice (https://undark.org/article/trump-social-psychology-prejudice-unleashed/).

Crano, W. D., & Mellon, P. M. (1978). Causal influence of teachers' expectations on children's academic performance: A cross-legged panel analysis. *Journal of Educational Psychology, 70,* 39–49.

Crawford, J. T., Brandt, M. J., Inbar, Y., Chambers, J. R., & Motyl, M. (2017). Social and economic ideologies differentially predict prejudice across the political spectrum, but social issues are most divisive. *Journal of Personality and Social Psychology, 112,* 383–412.

Crawford, M., Stark, A. C., & Renner, C. H. (1998). The meaning of Ms.: Social assimilation of a gender concept. *Psychology of Women Quarterly, 22,* 197–208.

Crawford, T. J. (1974). Sermons on racial tolerance and the parish neighborhood context. *Journal of Applied Social Psychology, 4,* 1.

Crisp, R. J., Birtel, M. D., & Meleady, R. (2011). Mental simulations of social thought and action: Trivial tasks or tools for transforming social policy? *Current Directions in Psychological Science, 20,* 261–264.

Crisp, R. J., & Hewstone, M. (1999). Differential evaluation of crossed category groups: Patterns, processes, and reducing intergroup bias. *Group Processes & Intergroup Relations, 2,* 307–333.

Crisp, R. J., & Hewstone, M. (2000). Multiple categorization and social identity. In D. Capozza & R. Brown (Eds.), *Social identity theory: Trends in theory and research.* Beverly Hills, CA: Sage.

Crocker, J. (1981). Judgment of covariation by social perceivers. *Psychological Bulletin, 90,* 272–292.

Crocker, J. (2002). The costs of seeking self-esteem. *Journal of Social Issues, 58,* 597–615.

Crocker, J. (2011). Presidential address: Self-image and compassionate goals and construction of the social self: Implications for social and personality psychology. *Personality and Social Psychology Review, 15,* 394–407.

Crocker, J., Hannah, D. B., & Weber, R. (1983). Personal memory and causal attributions. *Journal of Personality and Social Psychology, 44,* 55–56.

Crocker, J., & Knight, K. M. (2005). Contingencies of self-worth. *Current Directions in Psychological Science, 14,* 200–203.

Crocker, J., & Luhtanen, R. (1990). Collective self-esteem and ingroup bias. *Journal of Personality and Social Psychology, 58,* 60–67.

Crocker, J., & Luhtanen, R. (2003). Level of self-esteem and contingencies of self-worth: Unique effects on academic, social, and financial problems in college students. *Personality and Social Psychology Bulletin, 29,* 701–712.

Crocker, J., Luhtanen, R. K., Cooper, M. L., & Bouvrette, S. (2003). Contingencies of self-worth in college students: Theory and measurement. *Journal of Personality and Social Psychology, 85,* 894–908.

Crocker, J., & Major, B. (1989). Social stigma and self-esteem: The self-protective properties of stigma. *Psychological Review, 96,* 608–630.

Crocker, J., & McGraw, K. M. (1984). What's good for the goose is not good for the gander: Solo status as an obstacle to occupational achievement for males and females. *American Behavioral Scientist, 27,* 357–370.

Crocker, J., & Park, L. E. (2004). The costly pursuit of self-esteem. *Psychological Bulletin, 130,* 392–414.

Crocker, J., Sommers, S., & Luhtanen, R. (2002). Hopes dashed and dreams fulfilled: Contingencies of self-worth in the graduate school admissions process. *Personality and Social Psychology Bulletin, 28,* 1275–1286.

Crocker, J., Thompson, L. L., McGraw, K. M., & Ingerman, C. (1987). Downward comparison, prejudice, and evaluations of others: Effects of self-esteem and threat. *Journal of Personality and Social Psychology, 52,* 907–916.

Crocker, J., Voelkl, K., Testa, M., & Major, B. (1991). Social stigma: The affective consequences of attributional ambiguity. *Journal of Personality and Social Psychology, 60,* 218–228.

Crocker, J., & Wolfe, C. (2001). Contingencies of self-worth. *Psychological Review, 108,* 593–623.

Crockett, M. J., Clark, L., Tabibnia, G., Lieberman, M. D., & Robbins, T. W. (2008). Serotonin modulates behavioral reactions to unfairness. *Science, 320,* 1739.

Crompton, T., & Kasser, T. (2010, July/August). Human identity: A missing link in environmental campaigning. *Environment Magazine,* 23–33. Retrieved from http://www.environmentmagazine.org

CROP (2017, November). Are you in favour of same-sex marriage? 74% of Canadians and 80% of Quebecers support it (and Death in Venice by Benjamin Britten). Retrieved from https://www.crop.ca/en/blog/2017/207/

Crosby, J. R., & Monin, B. (2007). Failure to warn: How student race affects warnings of potential academic difficulty. *Journal of Experimental Social Psychology, 43,* 663–670.

Cross, P. (1977, Spring). Not can but will college teaching be improved? *New Directions for Higher Education, 17,* 1–15.

Cross, S. E., Liao, M-H., & Josephs, R. (1992). *A cross-cultural test of the self-evaluation maintenance model.* Paper presented at the American Psychological Association convention.

Cross-National Collaborative Group. (1992). The changing rate of major depression. *Journal of the American Medical Association, 268,* 3098–3105.

Crowley, G. (1996, June 3). The biology of beauty. *Newsweek,* 61–69.

Croxton, J. S., Eddy, T., & Morrow, N. (1984). Memory biases in the reconstruction of interpersonal encounters. *Journal of Social & Clinical Psychology, 2*(4), 348.

Crutchfield, R. S. (1955). Conformity and character. *American Psychologist, 1,* 191–198.

Csikszentmihalyi, M. (1990). *Flow: The psychology of optimal experience.* New York: Harper & Row.

Csikszentmihalyi, M. (1999). If we are so rich, why aren't we happy? *American Psychologist, 54,* 821–827.

CTV. (2005a). Mistrial declared in Toronto murder trial. Retrieved from http://www.cp24.com/servlet/an/local/CTVNews/20050216/johnathan_murder_050215?hubWinnipegHome.

CTV. (2005b). Rosie O'Donnell praises Canada, condemns Bush. Retrieved from http://www.ctv.ca/CTVNews/2/20050712/rosie_halifax_050712/.

CTV. (2020, January). Sen. Mike Duffy begins appeal of ruling blocking him from suing Senate. https://www.ctvnews.ca/politics/sen-mike-duffy-begins-appeal-of-ruling-blocking-him-from-suing-senate-1.4770187

Cuddy, A. J. C., Fiske, S. T., Kwan, V. S. Y., Glick, P., Demoulin, S., Leyens, J. P., Harris Bond, M., Croizet, J. C., Ellemers, N., Sleebos, E., Htun, T. T., Kim, H. J., Maio, G. Perry, J., Petkova, K., Todorov, V., Rodríguez-Bailón, R., Morales, E., Moya, M., & Ziegler, Z. (2009). Stereotype content model across cultures: Towards universal similarities and some differences. *British Journal of Social Psychology, 48,* 1–33.

Cullum, J., & Harton, H. C. (2007). Cultural evolution: Interpersonal influence, issue importance, and the development of shared attitudes in college residence halls. *Personality and Social Psychology Bulletin, 33,* 1327–1339.

Cunningham, J. D. (1981). Self-disclosure intimacy: Sex, sex-of-target, cross-national, and generational differences. *Personality and Social Psychology Bulletin, 7,* 314–319.

Cunningham, M. R., Shaffer, D. R., Barbee, A. P., Wolff, P. L., & Kelley, D. J. (1990). Separate processes in the relation of elation and depression to helping: Social versus personal concerns. *Journal of Experimental Social Psychology, 26,* 13–33.

Cunningham, W. A., Raye, C. L., & Johnson, M. K. (2004). Implicit and explicit evaluation: FMRI correlates of valence, emotional intensity, and control in the processing of attitudes. *Journal of Cognitive Neuroscience. Special Issue: Social Cognitive Neuroscience, 16,* 1717.

Dabbs, J. M., & Janis, I. L. (1965). Why does eating while reading facilitate opinion change? An experimental inquiry. *Journal of Experimental Social Psychology, 1,* 133–144.

Dabbs, J. M., Jr. (1992). Testosterone measurements in social and clinical psychology. *Journal of Social and Clinical Psychology, 11,* 302–321.

Dabbs, J. M., Jr. (2000). *Heroes, rogues, and lovers: Testosterone and behavior.* New York: McGraw-Hill.

Dabbs, J. M., Jr., Carr, T. S., Frady, R. L., & Riad, J. K. (1995). Testosterone, crime, and misbehavior among 692 male prison inmates. *Personality and Individual Differences, 18,* 627–633.

Dabbs, J. M., Jr., & Morris, R. (1990). Testosterone, social class, and antisocial behavior in a sample of 4462 men. *Psychological Science, 1,* 209–211.

Dabbs, J. M., Jr., Riad, J. K., & Chance, S. E. (2001). Testosterone and ruthless homicide. *Personality and Individual Differences, 31,* 599.

Dalrymple, T. (2007). On evil. *New English Review.* Retrieved from http://www.newenglishreview.org

Dambrun, M., & Vatiné, E. (2010). Reopening the study of extreme social behaviors: Obedience to authority within an immersive video environment. *European Journal of Social Psychology, 40,* 760–773.

Damon, W. (1995). *Greater expectations: Overcoming the culture of indulgence in America's homes and schools.* New York: Free Press.

Dardenne, B., Dumont, M., & Bollier, T. (2007). Insidious dangers of benevolent sexism: Consequences for women's performance. *Journal of Personality and Social Psychology, 93,* 764–779.

Darley, J. M. (1995). Book review essay. *Political Psychology,* in press.

Darley, J. M., & Batson, C. D. (1973). From Jerusalem to Jericho: A study of situational and dispositional variables in helping behavior. *Journal of Personality and Social Psychology, 27,* 100–108.

Darley, J. M., & Berscheid, E. (1967). Increased liking as a result of the anticipation of personal contact. *Human Relations, 20,* 29–40.

Dabbs, J. M., Jr., Strong, R., & Milun, R. (1997). Exploring the mind of testosterone: A beeper study. *Journal of Research in Personality, 31,* 577–588.

Darley, J., & Alter, A. (2009). Behavioral issues of punishment and deterrence. In E. Shafir (Ed.), *The behavioral foundations of policy.* Princeton, NJ: Princeton University Press.

Darley, J. M., & Gross, P. H. (1983). A hypothesis-confirming bias in labelling effects. *Journal of Personality and Social Psychology, 44,* 20–33.

Darley, J. M., & Latané, B. (1968). Bystander intervention in emergencies: Diffusion of responsibility. *Journal of Personality and Social Psychology, 8,* 377–383.

Darley, S., & Cooper, J. (1972). Cognitive consequences of forced noncompliance. *Journal of Personality and Social Psychology, 24,* 321–326.

Dasgupta, N., & Rivera, L. M. (2006). From automatic antigay prejudice to behavior: The moderating role of conscious beliefs about gender and behavioral control. *Journal of Personality and Social Psychology, 91,* 268–280.

Dashiell, J. F. (1930). An experimental analysis of some group effects. *Journal of Abnormal and Social Psychology, 25,* 190–199.

Dateline. (2000, June 20). *Dateline NBC* [Television broadcast]. New York: NBC.

Davidai, S., & Gilovich, T. (2016). The headwinds/tailwinds asymmetry: An availability bias in assessments of barriers and blessings. *Journal of Personality and Social Psychology, 111,* 835–851.

Davidson, R. J., Putnam, K. M., & Larson, C. L. (2000). Dysfunction in the neural circuitry of emotion regulation—A possible prelude to violence. *Science, 289,* 591–594.

Davie, M. (1986). *The Titanic: The full story of a tragedy.* London: Collins.

Davies, A. C., & Shackelford, T. K. (2017). Don't you wish your partner was hot like me? The effectiveness of mate poaching across relationship types considering the relative mate-values of the poacher and the partner of the poached. *Personality and Individual Differences, 106,* 32–35.

Davies, M. F. (1997). Belief persistence after evidential discrediting: The impact of generated versus provided explanations on the likelihood of discredited outcomes. *Journal of Experimental Social Psychology, 33,* 561–578.

Davies, P. G., Spencer, S. J., Quinn, D. M., & Gerhardstein, R. (2002). Consuming images: How television commercials that elicit stereotype threat can restrain women academically and professionally. *Personality and Social Psychology Bulletin, 28,* 1615–1628.

Davis, C. G., Lehman, D. R., Silver, R. C., Wortman, C. B., & Ellard, J. H. (1996). Self-blame following a traumatic event: The role of perceived avoidability. *Personality and Social Psychology Bulletin, 22,* 557–567.

Davis, C. G., Lehman, D. R., Wortman, C. B., Silver, R. C., & Thompson, S. C. (1995). The undoing of traumatic life events. *Personality and Social Psychology Bulletin, 21,* 109–124.

Davis, J. H., Kameda, T., Parks, C., Stasson, M., & Zimmerman, S. (1989). Some social mechanics of group decision making: The distribution of opinion, polling sequence, and implications for consensus. *Journal of Personality and Social Psychology, 57,* 1000–1012.

Davis, J. H., Kerr, N. L., Atkin, R. S., Holt, R., & Meek, D. (1975). The decision processes of 6- and 12-person mock juries assigned unanimous and two-thirds majority rules. *Journal of Personality and Social Psychology, 32,* 1–14.

Davis, J. H., Kerr, N. L., Strasser, G., Meek, D., & Holt, R. (1977). Victim consequences, sentence severity, and decision process in mock juries. *Organizational Behavior and Human Performance, 18,* 346–365.

Davis, J. H., Stasson, M. F., Parks, C. D., Hulbert, L., Kameda, T., Zimmerman, S. K., & Ono, K. (1993). Quantitative decisions by groups and individuals: Voting procedures and monetary awards by mock civil juries. *Journal of Experimental Social Psychology, 29,* 326–346.

Davis, J. L., & Rusbult, C. E. (2001). Attitude alignment in close relationships. *Journal of Personality and Social Psychology, 81,* 65–84.

Davis, K. E. (1985, February). Near and dear: Friendship and love compared. *Psychology Today,* 22–30.

Davis, K. E., & Jones, E. E. (1960). Changes in interpersonal perception as a means of reducing cognitive dissonance. *Journal of Abnormal and Social Psychology, 61,* 402–410.

Davis, L., & Greenlees, C. (1992). *Social loafing revisited: Factors that mitigate—and reverse—performance loss.* Paper presented at the Southwestern Psychological Association convention.

Davis, S. C., Diegel, S. W., & Boundy, R. G. (2011, June). *Transportation Energy Data Book: Edition 30* (Tables 3.1 and 3.2). Office of Energy Efficiency and Renewable Energy, U.S. Department of Energy.

Dawes, R. M. (1976). Shallow psychology. In J. S. Carroll & J. W. Payne (Eds.), *Cognition and social behavior.* Hillsdale, NJ: Erlbaum.

Dawes, R. M. (1980a). Social dilemmas. *Annual Review of Psychology, 31,* 169–193.

Dawes, R. M. (1980b). You can't systematize human judgment: Dyslexia. In R. A. Shweder (Ed.), *New directions for methodology of social and behavioral science: Fallible judgment in behavioral research.* San Francisco: Jossey-Bass.

Dawes, R. M. (1990). The potential nonfalsity of the false consensus effect. In R. M. Hogarth (Ed.), *Insights in decision making: A tribute to Hillel J. Einhorn.* Chicago: University of Chicago Press.

Dawes, R. M. (1991). Social dilemmas, economic self-interest, and evolutionary theory. In D. R. Brown & J. E. Keith Smith (Eds.), *Frontiers of mathematical psychology: Essays in honor of Clyde Coombs.* New York: Springer-Verlag.

Dawes, R. M. (1994). *House of cards: Psychology and psychotherapy built on myth.* New York: Free Press.

Dawes, R. M. (1998). Behavioral decision making and judgment. In D. T. Gilbert, S. T. Fiske, & G. Lindzey (Eds.), *The handbook of social psychology* (Vol. 1 and 2) (4th ed.) (pp. 497–548). New York: McGraw-Hill.

Dawes, R. M. (2005). The ethical implications of Paul Meehl's work on comparing clinical versus actuarial prediction methods. *Journal of Clinical Psychology, 61,* 1245–1255.

Dawes, R. M., McTavish, J., & Shaklee, H. (1977). Behavior, communication, and assumptions about other people's behavior in a commons dilemma situation. *Journal of Personality and Social Psychology, 35,* 1–11.

Dawkins, R. (1976). *The selfish gene.* New York: Oxford University Press.

Dawkins, R. (1993). Gaps in the mind. In P. Cavalieri & P. Singer (Eds.), *The great ape project: Equality beyond humanity* (pp. 80–87). London: Fourth Estate.

Dawson, N. V., Arkes, H. R., Siciliano, C., Blinkhorn, R., Lakshmanan, M., & Petrelli, M. (1988). Hindsight bias: An impediment to accurate probability estimation in clinicopathologic conferences. *Medical Decision Making, 8*(4), 259–264.

De Cremer, D. (2002). Charismatic leadership and cooperation in social dilemmas: A matter of transforming motives? *Journal of Applied Social Psychology, 32,* 997–1016.

de Hoog, N., Stroebe, W., & de Wit, J. B. F. (2007). The impact of vulnerability to and severity of a health risk on processing and acceptance of fear-arousing communications: A meta-analysis. *Review of General Psychology, 11,* 258–285.

de Hoogh, A. H. B., den Hartog, D. N., Koopman, P. L., Thierry, H., van den Berg, P. T., van der Weide, J. G., & Wilderom, C. P. M. (2004). Charismatic leadership, environmental dynamism, and performance. *European Journal of Work and Organizational Psychology, 13,* 447.

De Houwer, J., Thomas, S., & Baeyens, F. (2001). Associative learning of likes and dislikes: A review of 25 years of research on human evaluative conditioning. *Psychological Bulletin, 127,* 853–869.

de Lange, M. A., Debets, L. W., Ruitenburg, K., & Holland, R. W. (2012). Making less of a mess: Scent exposure as a tool for behavioral change. *Social Influence, 7,* 90–97.

de Waal, F. B. M. (2005–2006, Fall–Winter). The evolution of empathy. *Greater Good,* 6–9.

de Waal, F. B. M., Leimgruber, K., & Greenberg, A. R. (2008). Giving is self-rewarding for monkeys. *Proceedings of the National Academy of Sciences, 105,* 13685–13689.

de Zavala, A. G., Cichocka, A., & Iskra-Golec, I. (2013). Collective narcissism moderates the effect of in-group image threat on intergroup hostility. *Journal of Personality and Social Psychology, 104,* 1019–1039.

Dean, C. (2005, August 30). Scientific savvy? In U.S., not much. *New York Times.* Retrieved from http://www.nytimes.com

Deary, I. J., Batty, G. D., & Gale, C. R. (2008). Bright children become enlightened adults. *Psychological Science, 19,* 1–6.

DeBruine, L. M. (2002). Facial resemblance enhances trust. *Proceedings of the Royal Society of London, 269,* 1307–1312.

Decety, J., & Sommerville, J. A. (2003). Shared representations between self and other: A social cognitive neuroscience view. *Trends in Cognitive Sciences, 7,* 527–533.

Dechêne, A., Stahl, C., Hansen, J., & Wänke, M. (2010). The truth about the truth: A meta-analysis review of the truth effect. *Personality and Social Psychology Review, 14,* 238–257.

Deci, E. L., & Ryan, R. M. (1985). *Intrinsic motivation and self-determination in human behavior.* New York: Plenum.

Deci, E. L., & Ryan, R. M. (1987). The support of autonomy and the control of behavior. *Journal of Personality and Social Psychology, 53,* 1024–1037.

Deci, E. L., & Ryan, R. M. (1991). A motivational approach to self: Integration in personality. In R. Dienstbier (Ed.), *Perspectives on motivation* (Vol. 38) (pp. 237–288). Lincoln, NE: University of Nebraska Press. Nebraska Symposium on Motivation.

Deci, E. L., & Ryan, R. M. (1997). *Behaviorists in search of the null: Revisiting the undermining of intrinsic motivation by extrinsic rewards.* Unpublished manuscript, University of Rochester.

Deci, E. L., & Ryan, R. M. (2008). Facilitating optimal motivation and psychological well-being across life's domains. *Canadian Psychology, 49,* 14–23.

Deci, E. L., & Ryan, R. M. (Eds.). (2002). *Handbook of self-determination research.* Rochester, NY: University of Rochester Press.

Dehue, F., Bolman, C., & Vollink, T. (2008). Cyberbullying: Youngsters' experiences and parental perception. *Cyberpsychology & Behavior, 11,* 217–223.

Del Vicario, M., Zollo, F., Caldarelli, G., Scala, A., & Quattrociocchi, W. (2017). Mapping social dynamics on Facebook: The Brexit debate. *Social Networks, 50,* 6–16.

Delgado, J. (1973). In M. Pines, *The brain changers.* New York: Harcourt Brace Jovanovich.

DeLisi, M., Vaughn, M. G., Gentile, D. A., Anderson, C. A., & Shook, J. J. (2013). Violent video games, delinquency, and youth violence: New evidence. *Youth Violence and Juvenile Justice, 11,* 132–142.

Dembroski, T. M., Lasater, T. M., & Ramirez, A. (1978). Communicator similarity, fear arousing communications, and compliance with health care recommendations. *Journal of Applied Social Psychology, 8,* 254–269.

Demoulin, S., Saroglou, V., & Van Pachterbeke, M. (2008). Infra-humanizing others, supra-humanizing gods: The emotional hierarchy. *Social Cognition, 26,* 235–247.

Denissen, J. J. A., Penke, L., Schmitt, D. P., & van Aken, M. A. G. (2008). Self-esteem reactions to social interactions: Evidence for sociometer mechanisms across days, people, and nations. *Journal of Personality and Social Psychology, 95,* 181–196.

Denrell, J. (2008). Indirect social influence. *Science, 321,* 47–48.

Denrell, J., & Le Mens, G. (2007). Interdependent sampling and social influence. *Psychological Review, 114,* 398–422.

Denson, T. F., Pedersen, W. C., & Miller, N. (2006). The displaced aggression questionnaire. *Journal of Personality and Social Psychology, 90,* 1032–1051.

Department of Canadian Heritage. (2006). *What is multiculturalism?* Retrieved from http://www.pch.gc.ca

DePaulo, B. M., Charlton, K., Cooper, H., Lindsay, J. J., & Muhlenbruck, L. (1997). The accuracy-confidence correlation in the detection of deception. *Personality and Social Psychology Review, 1,* 346–357.

Derks, B., Inzlicht, M., & Kang, S. (2008). The neuroscience of stigma and stereotype threat. *Group Processes and Intergroup Relations, 11,* 163–181.

Derlega, V., Metts, S., Petronio, S., & Margulis, S. T. (1993). *Self-disclosure.* Newbury Park, CA: Sage.

Dermer, M., Cohen, S. J., Jacobsen, E., & Anderson, E. A. (1979). Evaluative judgments of aspects of life as a function of vicarious exposure to hedonic extremes. *Journal of Personality and Social Psychology, 37,* 247–260.

Dermer, M., & Pyszczynski, T. A. (1978). Effects of erotica upon men's loving and liking responses for women they love. *Journal of Personality and Social Psychology, 36,* 1302–1309.

Desforges, D. M., Lord, C. G., Pugh, M. A., Sia, T. L., Scarberry, N. C., & Ratcliff, C. D. (1997). Role of group representativeness in generalization part of the contact hypothesis. *Basic Applied Social Psychology, 19,* 183–204.

Desforges, D. M., Lord, C. G., Ramsey, S. L., Mason, J. A., Van Leeuwen, M. D., West, S. C., & Lepper, M. R., (1991). Effects of structured cooperative contact on changing negative attitudes toward stigmatized social groups. *Journal of Personality and Social Psychology, 60,* 531–544.

DeSteno, D., Petty, R. E., Wegener, D. T., & Rucker, D. D. (2000). Beyond valence in the perception of likelihood: The role of emotion specificity. *Journal of Personality and Social Psychology, 78,* 397–416.

Deutsch, M. (1985). *Distributive justice: A social psychological perspective.* New Haven: Yale University Press.

Deutsch, M. (1986). Folie à deux: A psychological perspective on Soviet-American relations. In M. P. Kearns (Ed.), *Persistent patterns and emergent structures in a waning century.* New York, NY: Praeger.

Deutsch, M. (1993). Educating for a peaceful world. *American Psychologist, 48,* 510–517.

Deutsch, M. (1994). Constructive conflict resolution: Principles, training, and research. *Journal of Social Issues, 50,* 13–32.

Deutsch, M. (1999). Behind the scenes. In D. G. Myers, *Social psychology* (6th ed.). New York: McGraw-Hill.

Deutsch, M., & Collins, M. E. (1951). *Interracial housing: A psychological evaluation of a social experiment.* Minneapolis: University of Minnesota Press.

Deutsch, M., & Gerard, H. B. (1955). A study of normative and informational social influence upon individual judgment. *Journal of Abnormal and Social Psychology, 51,* 629–636.

Deutsch, M., & Krauss, R. M. (1960). The effect of threat upon interpersonal bargaining. *Journal of Abnormal and Social Psychology, 61,* 181–189.

Devine, P. A., Brodish, A. B., & Vance, S. L. (2005). Self-regulatory processes in interracial interactions: The role of internal and external motivation to respond without prejudice. In J. P. Forgas, K. D. Williams, & S. M. Laham (Eds.), *Social motivation: Conscious and unconscious processes.* New York: Cambridge University Press.

Devine, P. G. (1989). Stereotypes and prejudice: Their automatic and controlled components. *Journal of Personality and Social Psychology, 56,* 5–18.

Devine, P. G., Evett, S. R., & Vasquez-Suson, K. A. (1996). Exploring the interpersonal dynamics of intergroup contact. In R. Sorrentino & E. T. Higgins (Eds.), *Handbook of motivation and cognition: The interpersonal content* (Vol. 3). New York: Guilford.

Devine, P. G., & Malpass, R. S. (1985). Orienting strategies in differential face recognition. *Personality and Social Psychology Bulletin, 11*(1), 33–40.

Devine, P. G., & Sharp, L. B. (2008). Automatic and controlled processes in stereotyping and prejudice. In T. Nelson (Ed.), *Handbook of prejudice, stereotyping, and discrimination.* New York: Psychology Press.

DeVoe, S. E., House, J., & Zhong, C.-B. (2013). Fast food and financial impatience: A socio-ecological approach. *Journal of Personality and Social Psychology, 105,* 476–494.

Devos-Comby, L., & Salovey, P. (2002). Applying persuasion strategies to alter HIV-relevant thoughts and behavior. *Review of General Psychology, 6,* 287–304.

Devries, K. M., Mak, J. Y. T., García-Moreno, C., Petzold, M., Child, J. C., Falder, G., Lim, S., Bacchus, L. J., Engell, R. E., Rosenfeld, L., Pallitto, C., Vos, T., Abrahams, N., & Watts, C. H. (2013). The global prevalence of intimate partner violence against women. *Science, 340,* 1527.

DeWall, C. N., Baumeister, R. F., Stillman, T. F., & Gailliot, M. T. (2007). Violence restrained: Effects of self-regulation and its depletion on aggression. *Journal of Experimental Social Psychology, 43,* 62–76.

DeWall, C. N., Bushman, B. J., Giancola, P. R., & Webster, G. D. (2010). The big, the bad, and the boozed-up: Weight moderates the effect of alcohol on aggression. *Journal of Experimental Social Psychology, 46,* 619–623.

DeWall, C. N., MacDonald, G., Webster, G. D., Masten, C. L., Baumeister, R. F., Powell, C., Combs, D., Schurtz, D. R., Stillman, T. F. Tice, D. M., & Eisenberger, N. I. (2010). Acetaminophen reduces social pain: Behavioural and neural evidence. *Psychological Science, 21,* 931–937.

DeWall, C. N., Maner, J. K., & Rouby, D. A. (2009). Social exclusion and early-stage interpersonal perception: Selective attention to signs of acceptance. *Journal of Personality and Social Psychology, 96,* 729–741.

DeWall, C. N., Pond, R. S., Jr., Campbell, W. K., & Twenge, J. M. (2011). Tuning in to psychological change: Linguistic markers of psychological traits and emotions over time in popular U.S. song lyrics. *Psychology of Aesthetics, Creativity, and the Arts, 5,* 200–207.

DeWall, C. N., Twenge, J. M., Gitter, S. A., & Baumeister, R. F. (2009). It's the thought that counts: The role of hostile cognition in shaping aggressive responses to social exclusion. *Journal of Personality and Social Psychology, 96,* 45–59.

Diamond, J. (1996, December). The best ways to sell sex. *Discover,* 78–86.

DiBello, A. M., Neighbors, C., & Ammar, J. (2015). Self-affirmation theory and cigarette smoking warning images. *Addictive behaviors, 41,* 87–96.

Dickerson, S. S., Gable, S. L., Irwin, M. R., Aziz, N., & Kemeny, M. E. (2009). Social-evaluative threat and proinflammatory cytokine regulation: An experimental laboratory investigation. *Psychological Science, 20,* 1237–1243.

Dicum, J. (2003, November 11). Letter to the editor. *New York Times,* p. A20.

DiDonato, T. E., Ullrich, J., & Krueger, J. I. (2011). Social perception as induction and inference: An integrative model of intergroup differentiation, ingroup favoritism, and differential accuracy. *Journal of Personality and Social Psychology, 100,* 66–83.

Diekman, A. B., McDonald, M., & Gardner, W. L. (2000). Love means never having to be careful: The relationship between reading romance novels and safe sex behavior. *Psychology of Women Quarterly, 24,* 179–188.

Diekmann, K. A., Samuels, S. M., Ross, L., & Bazerman, M. H. (1997). Self-interest and fairness in problems of resource allocation: Allocators versus recipients. *Journal of Personality and Social Psychology, 72,* 1061–1074.

Diener, E. (1976). Effects of prior destructive behavior, anonymity, and group presence on deindividuation and aggression. *Journal of Personality and Social Psychology, 33,* 497–507.

Diener, E. (1979). Deindividuation, self-awareness, and disinhibition. *Journal of Personality and Social Psychology, 37,* 1160–1171.

Diener, E. (1980). Deindividuation: The absence of self-awareness and self-regulation in group members. In P. Paulus (Ed.), *The psychology of group influence.* Hillsdale, NJ: Erlbaum.

Diener, E., Horwitz, J., & Emmons, R. A. (1985). Happiness of the very wealthy. *Social Indicators, 16,* 263–274.

Diener, E., & Wallbom, M. (1976). Effects of self-awareness on antinormative behavior. *Journal of Research in Personality, 10,* 107–111.

Dijksterhuis, A., Bos, M. W., Nordgren, L. F., & van Baaren, R. B. (2006). Complex choices better made unconsciously? *Science, 313,* 760–761.

Dijksterhuis, A., & Nordgren, L. F. (2006). A theory of unconscious thought. *Perspectives on Psychological Science, 1,* 95–109.

Dijksterhuis, A., Smith, P. K., van Baaren, R. B., & Wigboldus, D. H. J. (2005). The unconscious consumer: Effects of environment on consumer behavior. *Journal of Consumer Psychology, 15,* 193–202.

Dillon, K. P., & Bushman, B. J. (2017). Effects of exposure to gun violence in movies on children's interest in real guns. *JAMA Pediatrics, 171,* 1057–1062.

Dion, K. K. (1972). Physical attractiveness and evaluations of children's transgressions. *Journal of Personality and Social Psychology, 24,* 207–213.

Dion, K. K. (1973). Young children's stereotyping of facial attractiveness. *Developmental Psychology, 9,* 183–188.

Dion, K. K. (1979). Physical attractiveness and interpersonal attraction. In M. Cook & G. Wilson (Eds.), *Love and attraction.* New York: Pergamon Press.

Dion, K. K., & Berscheid, E. (1974). Physical attractiveness and peer perception among children. *Sociometry, 37,* 1–12.

Dion, K. K., & Dion, K. L. (1985). Personality, gender, and the phenomenology of romantic love. In P. R. Shaver (Ed.), *Review of personality and social psychology* (Vol. 6). Beverly Hills, CA: Sage.

Dion, K. K., & Dion, K. L. (1991). Psychological individualism and romantic love. *Journal of Social Behavior and Personality, 6,* 17–33.

Dion, K. K., & Dion, K. L. (1993). Individualistic and collectivistic perspectives on gender and the cultural context of love and intimacy. *Journal of Social Issues, 49,* 53–69.

Dion, K. K., & Dion, K. L. (1996). Cultural perspectives on romantic love. *Personal Relationships, 3,* 5–17.

Dion, K. K., & Stein, S. (1978). Physical attractiveness and interpersonal influence. *Journal of Experimental Social Psychology, 14,* 97–109.

Dion, K. L. (1975). Women's reactions to discrimination from members of the same or opposite sex. *Journal of Research in Personality, 9,* 294–306.

Dion, K. L. (1985). Responses to perceived discrimination and relative deprivation. In J. M. Olson, C. P. Herman, & M. P. Zanna (Eds.), *Relative deprivation and social comparison: The Ontario symposium* (Vol. 4). Hillsdale, NJ: Erlbaum.

Dion, K. L. (1987). What's in a title? The Ms. stereotype and images of women's titles of address. *Psychology of Women Quarterly, 11,* 21–36.

Dion, K. L. (1998). *The social psychology of perceived prejudice and discrimination.* Colloquium presentation, Carleton University, Ottawa, ON.

Dion, K. L., & Cota, A. A. (1991). The Ms. stereotype: Its domain and the role of explicitness in title preference. *Psychology of Women Quarterly, 15,* 403–410.

Dion, K. L., & Dion, K. K. (1979). Personality and behavioral correlates of romantic love. In M. Cook & G. Wilson (Eds.), *Love and attraction.* Oxford: Pergamon.

Dion, K. L., & Dion, K. K. (1988). Romantic love: Individual and cultural perspectives. In R. J. Sternberg & M. L. Barnes (Eds.), *The psychology of love.* New Haven, CT: Yale University Press.

Dion, K. L., Dion, K. K., & Keelan, J. P. (1990). Appearance anxiety as a dimension of social-evaluative anxiety: Exploring the ugly duckling syndrome. *Contemporary Social Psychology, 14*(4), 220–224.

Dion, K. L., & Earn, B. M. (1975). The phenomenology of being a target of prejudice. *Journal of Personality and Social Psychology, 32,* 944–950.

Dion, K. L., & Kawakami, K. (1996). Ethnicity and perceived discrimination in Toronto: Another look at the personal/group discrimination discrepancy. *Canadian Journal of Behavioural Science, 28,* 203–213.

Dion, K. L., & Schuller, R. A. (1991). The Ms. stereotype: Its generality and its relation to managerial and marital status stereotypes. *Canadian Journal of Behavioural Science, 23,* 25–40.

DiPietro, L. (2000). Tackling race and sports: A review of *Taboo,* by Jon Entine. *Scientific American,* May, 112–118.

Dishion, T. J., McCord, J., & Poulin, F. (1999). When interventions harm: Peer groups and problem behavior. *American Psychologist, 54,* 755–764.

Ditto, P. H., Liu, B. S., Clark, C. J., Wojcik, S. P., Chen, E. E., Grady, R. H., & Celniker, J. B., & Zinger, J. F. (2019). At least bias is bipartisan: A meta-analytic comparison of partisan bias in liberals and conservatives. *Perspectives on Psychological Science,* 273-291.

Dixon, J., & Durrheim, K. (2003). Contact and the ecology of racial division: Some varieties of informal segregation. *British Journal of Social Psychology, 42,* 1–23.

Dixon, J., Durrheim, K., & Tredoux, C. (2007). Intergroup contact and attitudes toward the principle and practice of racial equality. *Psychological Science, 18,* 867–872.

Dolinski, D. (2000). On inferring one's beliefs from one's attempt and consequences for subsequent compliance. *Journal of Personality and Social Psychology, 78,* 260–272.

Dolinski, D., & Nawrat, R. (1998). "Fear-then-relief" procedure for producing compliance: Beware when the danger is over. *Journal of Experimental Social Psychology, 34,* 27–50.

Dollard, J., Doob, L., Miller, N., Mowrer, O. H., & Sears, R. R. (1939). *Frustration and aggression.* New Haven, CT: Yale University Press.

Dolnik, L., Case, T. I., & Williams, K. D. (2003). Stealing thunder as a courtroom tactic revisited: Processes and boundaries. *Law and Human Behavior, 27,* 267.

Donaldson, Z. R., & Young, L. J. (2008). Oxytocin, vasopressin, and the neurogenetics of sociality. *Science, 322,* 900–904.

Donders, N. C., Correll, J., & Wittenbrink, B. (2008). Danger stereotypes predict racially biased attentional allocation. *Journal of Experimental Social Psychology, 44,* 1328–1333.

Dong, P., Huang, X., & Zhong, C. (2015). Ray of hope: Hopelessness increases preferences for brighter lighting. *Social Psychological and Personality Science, 6,* 84–91.

Donnellan, M. B., Larsen-Rife, D., & Conger, R. D. (2005). Personality, family history, and competence in early adult romantic relationships. *Journal of Personality and Social Psychology, 88,* 562–576.

Donnerstein, E. (1980). Aggressive erotica and violence against women. *Journal of Personality and Social Psychology, 39,* 269–277.

Donnerstein, E. (1998). Why do we have those new ratings on television? Invited address to the National Institute on the Teaching of Psychology.

Donnerstein, E. (2011). The media and aggression: From TV to the Internet. In J. Forgas, A. Kruglanski, & K. Williams (Eds), *The psychology of social conflict and aggression.* New York: Psychology Press.

Doob, A. N., & Roberts, J. (1988). Public attitudes toward sentencing in Canada. In N. Walker & M. Hough (Eds.), *Sentencing and the public.* London: Gower.

Doolittle, R. (2007). Bizarre assaults hit quiet town. *Toronto Star.* Retrieved from http://www.thestar.com/News/GTA/article/260646

D'Orlando, F. (2011). The demand for pornography. *Journal of Happiness Studies, 12,* 51–75.

Dotan-Eliaz, O., Sommer, K. L., & Rubin, S. (2009). Multilingual groups: Effects of linguistic ostracism on felt rejection and anger, coworker attraction, perceived team potency, and creative performance. *Basic and Applied Social Psychology, 31,* 363–375.

Dotsch, R., & Wigboldus, D. H. J. (2008). Virtual prejudice. *Journal of Experimental Social Psychology, 44,* 1194–1198.

Douglas, K. M., & McGarty, C. (2001). Identifiability and self-presentation: Computer-mediated communication and intergroup interaction. *British Journal of Social Psychology, 40,* 399–416.

Dovidio, J. F. (1991). The empathy-altruism hypothesis: Paradigm and promise. *Psychological Inquiry, 2,* 126–128.

Dovidio, J. F., Brigham, J. C., Johnson, B. T., & Gaertner, S. L. (1996). Stereotyping, prejudice, and discrimination: Another look. In N. Macrae, M. Hewstone, & C. Stangor (Eds.), *Stereotypes and stereotyping.* New York: Guilford.

Dovidio, J. F., Gaertner, S. L., Anastasio, P. A., & Sanitioso, R. (1992). Cognitive and motivational bases of bias: Implications of aversive racism for attitudes toward Hispanics. In S. Knouse, P. Rosenfeld, & A. Culbertson (Eds.), *Hispanics in the workplace.* Newbury Park, CA: Sage.

Dovidio, J. F., Gaertner, S. L., Hodson, G., Houlette, M., & Johnson, K. M. (2005). Social inclusion and exclusion: Recategorization and the perception of intergroup boundaries. In D. Abrams, M. A. Hogg, & J. M. Marques (Eds.), *The social psychology of inclusion and exclusion.* New York: Psychology Press.

Dovidio, J. F., Gaertner, S. L., & Saguy, T. (2009). Commonality and the complexity of "we": Social attitudes and social change. *Personality and Social Psychology Bulletin, 13,* 3–20.

Drake, B., & Poushter, J. (2016, July 13). In views of diversity, many Europeans are less positive than Americans. Pew Research Center (www.pewresearch.org).

Dreber, A., Rand, D. G., Fudenberg, D., & Nowak, M. A. (2008). Winners don't punish. *Nature, 452,* 348–351.

Driedger, L. (1975). In search of cultural identity factors: A comparison of ethnic students. *Canadian Review of Sociology and Anthropology, 12,* 150–161.

Driskell, J. E., & Mullen, B. (1990). Status, expectations, and behavior: A meta-analytic review and test of the theory. *Personality and Social Psychology Bulletin, 16,* 541–553.

Drolet, A. L., & Morris, M. W. (2000). Rapport in conflict resolution: Accounting for how face-to-face contact fosters mutual cooperation in mixed-motive conflicts. *Journal of Experimental Social Psychology, 36,* 26–50.

Drury, J., Cocking, C., & Reicher, S. (2009). Everyone for themselves? A comparative study of crowd solidarity among emergency survivors. *British Journal of Social Psychology, 48,* 487–506.

Drury, L., Hutchison, P., & Abrams, D. (2016). Direct and extended intergenerational contact and young people's attitudes towards older adults. *British Journal of Social Psychology, 55,* 522–543.

Drydakis, N. (2009). Sexual orientation discrimination in the labour market. *Labour Economics, 16,* 364–372.

Dryer, D. C., & Horowitz, L. M. (1997). When do opposites attract? Interpersonal complementarity versus similarity. *Journal of Personality and Social Psychology, 72,* 592–603.

Duck, J. M., Hogg, M. A., & Terry, D. J. (1995). Me, us and them: Political identification and the third-person effect in the 1993 Australian federal election. *European Journal of Social Psychology, 25*(2), 195–215.

Duclos, S. E., Laird, J. D., Schneider, E., Sexter, M., Stern, L., & Van Lighten, O. (1989). Emotion-specific effects of facial expressions and postures on emotional experience. *Journal of Personality and Social Psychology, 57,* 100–108.

Duggan, M. (2015, December 15). Gaming and gamers. Pew Research Center (www.PewInternet.org).

Dugger, C. W. (2001, April 22). Abortions in India spurred by sex test skew the ratio against girls. *New York Times* (late edition), p. 12. Retrieved from https://www.nytimes.com/2001/04/22/world/abortions-in-india-spurred-by-sex-test-skew-the-ratio-against-girls.html

Duke, A. A., Smith, K. Z., Oberleitner, L. S., Westphal, A., & McKee, S. A. (2018). Alcohol, drugs, and violence: A meta-meta-analysis. *Psychology of Violence, 8,* 238–249.

Dunbar, R. (1992). Neocortex size as a constraint on group size in primates. *Journal of Human Evolution, 22,* 469–493

Dunbar, R. (2010, December 25). You've got to have (150) friends. *New York Times.* Retrieved from http://www.nytimes.com

Duncan, B. L. (1976). Differential social perception and attribution of intergroup violence: Testing the lower limits of stereotyping of blacks. *Journal of Personality and Social Psychology, 34,* 590–598.

Dunfield, K. A., & Kuhlmeier, V. A. (2010). Intention-mediated selective helping in infancy. *Psychological Science, 21,* 523–527.

Dunham, Y., Chen, E. E., & Banaji, M. R. (2013). Two signatures of implicit intergroup attitudes: Developmental invariance and early enculturation. *Psychological Science,*24, 860–868.

Dunlosky, J., & Rawson, K. A. (2012). Overconfidence produces underachievement: Inaccurate self evaluations undermine students' learning and retention. *Learning and Instruction, 22,* 271–280.

Dunn, E., & Ashton-James, C. (2008). On emotional innumeracy: Predicted and actual affective response to grand-scale tragedies. *Journal of Experimental Social Psychology, 44,* 692–698.

Dunn, E. W., Aknin, L. B., & Norton, M. I. (2008). Spending money on others promotes happiness. *Science, 319,* 1687–1688.

Dunn, J. R., & Schweitzer, M. E. (2005). Feeling and believing: The influence of emotion on trust. *Journal of Personality and Social Psychology, 88,* 736–748.

Dunning, D. (1995). Trait importance and modifiability as factors influencing self-assessment and self-enhancement motives. *Personality and Social Psychology Bulletin, 21,* 1297–1306.

Dunning, D. (2005). *Self-insight: Roadblocks and detours on the path to knowing thyself.* London: Psychology Press.

Dunning, D. (2006). Strangers to ourselves? *The Psychologist, 19,* 600–603.

Dunning, D., Griffin, D. W., Milojkovic, J. D., & Ross, L. (1990). The overconfidence effect in social prediction. *Journal of Personality and Social Psychology, 58,* 568–581.

Dunning, D., Meyerowitz, J. A., & Holzberg, A. D. (1989). Ambiguity and self-evaluation. *Journal of Personality and Social Psychology, 57,* 1082–1090.

Dunning, D., Perie, M., & Story, A. L. (1991). Self-serving prototypes of social categories. *Journal of Personality and Social Psychology, 61,* 957–968.

Dunning, D., & Sherman, D. A. (1997). Stereotypes and tacit inference. *Journal of Personality and Social Psychology, 73,* 459–471.

Durante, K. M., Li, N. P., & Haselton, M. G. (2008). Changes in women's dress across the ovulatory cycle: Naturalistic and laboratory task-based evidence. *Personality and Social Psychology Bulletin, 34,* 1451–1460.

Durrheim, K., Tredoux, C., Foster, D., & Dixon, J. (2011). Historical trends in South African race attitudes. *South African Journal of Psychology, 41,* 263–278.

Dutton, D. G., & Aron, A. (1989). Romantic attraction and generalized liking for others who are sources of conflict-based arousal. *Canadian Journal of Behavioural Science, 21,* 246–257.

Dutton, D. G., & Aron, A. P. (1974). Some evidence for heightened sexual attraction under conditions of high anxiety. *Journal of Personality and Social Psychology, 30,* 510–517.

Dutton, D. G., Boyanowsky, E. O., & Bond, M. H. (2005). Extreme mass homicide: From military massacre to genocide.

Aggression and Violent Behavior, 10, 437–473.

Duval, S., Duval, V. H., & Neely, R. (1979). Self-focus, felt responsibility, and helping behavior. *Journal of Personality and Social Psychology, 37,* 1769–1778.

Dye, M. W. G., Green, C. S., & Bavelier, D. (2009). Increasing speed of processing with action video games. *Current Directions in Psychological Science, 18,* 321–326.

Eagly, A. H. (1987). *Sex differences in social behavior: A social-role interpretation.* Lawrence Erlbaum Associates, Inc.

Eagly, A. H. (2009). The his and hers of prosocial behavior: An examination of the social psychology of gender. *American Psychologist, 64,* 644–658.

Eagly, A. H., Ashmore, R. D., Makhijani, M. G., & Longo, L. C. (1991). What is beautiful is good, but … : A meta-analytic review of research on the physical attractiveness stereotype. *Psychological Bulletin, 110,* 109–128.

Eagly, A. H., & Carli, L. L. (1981) Sex of researchers and sex-typed communications as determinants of sex differences in influenceability: A meta-analysis of social influence studies. *Psychological Bulletin, 90*(1), 1–20.

Eagly, A. H., & Chaiken, S. (1993). *The psychology of attitudes.* San Diego: Harcourt Brace Jovanovich.

Eagly, A. H., & Chaiken, S. (1998). Attitude structure and function. In D. Gilbert, S. Fiske, and G. Lindzey (Eds.), *The handbook of social psychology* (4th ed.). New York: McGraw-Hill.

Eagly, A. H., Chen, S., Chaiken, S., & Shaw-Barnes, K . (1999). The impact of attitudes on memory: An affair to remember. *Psychological Bulletin, 125,* 64-89.

Eagly, A. H., & Crowley, M. (1986). Gender and helping behavior: A meta-analytic review of the social psychological literature. *Psychological Bulletin, 100,* 283–308.

Eagly, A. H., & Johnson, B. T. (1990). Gender and leadership style: A meta-analysis. *Psychological Bulletin, 108,* 233–256.

Eagly, A. H., & Wood, W. (1999). The origins of sex differences in human behavior: Evolved dispositions versus social roles. *American Psychologist, 54*(6), 408–423.

Eagly, A. H., Wood, W., & Chaiken, S. (1978). Causal inferences about communicators and their effect on opinion change. *Journal of Personality and Social Psychology, 36,* 424–435.

Easterbrook, G. (2004, May 25). The 50-cent-a-gallon solution. *New York Times*. Retrieved from http://www.nytimes.com/2004/05/25/opinion/the-50-cent-a-gallon-solution.html October 17, 2020.

Easterbrook, M., & Vignoles, V. (2015). When friendship formation goes down the toilet: Design features of share accommodation influence interpersonal bonds and well-being. *British Journal of Social Psychology, 54,* 125–139.

Easterlin, R. (1995). Will raising the incomes of all increase the happiness of all? *Journal of Economic Behavior and Organization, 27,* 35–47.

Eastwick, P. W., & Finkel, E. J. (2008). Sex differences in mate preferences revisited: Do people know what they initially desire in a romantic partner? *Journal of Personality and Social Psychology, 94,* 245.

Eastwick, P. W., Finkel, E. J., Krishnamurti, T., & Loewenstein, G. (2007). Mispredicting distress following romantic breakup: Revealing the time course of the affective forecasting error. *Journal of Experimental Social Psychology, 44,* 800–807.

Eastwick, P. W., Finkel, E. J., Mochon, D., & Ariely, D. (2007). Selective versus unselective romantic desire. *Psychological Science, 18,* 317–319.

Eastwick, P. W., & Hunt, L. L. (2014). Relational mate value: Consensus and uniqueness in romantic evaluations. *Journal of Personality and Social Psychology, 106,* 728–751.

Eastwick, P. W., Luchies, L. B., Finkel, E. J., & Hunt, L. L. (2014). The predictive validity of ideal partner preferences: A review and meta-analysis. *Psychological Bulletin, 140,* 623–665.

Eaton, J., & Struthers, C. W. (2006). The reduction of psychological aggression across varied interpersonal contexts through repentance and forgiveness. *Aggressive Behavior, 32,* 195.

Ebbesen, E. B., Duncan, B., & Konecni, V. J. (1975). Effects of content of verbal aggression on future verbal aggression: A field experiment. *Journal of Experimental Social Psychology, 11,* 192–204.

Eberhardt, J. L., Goff, P. A., Purdie, V. J., & Davies, P. G. (2004). Seeing black: Race, crime, and visual processing. *Journal of Personality and Social Psychology, 87,* 876.

Eckersley, R. (2005, November 22). Is modern Western culture a health hazard? *International Journal of Epidemiology.* Online.

Edelman, B., Luca, M., & Svirsky, D. (2017). Racial discrimination in the sharing economy: Evidence from a field experiment. *American Economic Journal: Applied Economics, 9,* 1–22.

Edelson, M., Sharot, T., Dolan, R. J., & Dudai, Y. (2011). Following the crowd: Brain substrates of long-term memory conformity. *Science, 333,* 108–111.

Editors of TIME. (2017, February). TIME Innocent: The fight against wrongful convictions. *Time Magazine,* pp. 1–96.

Edney, J. J. (1980). The commons problem: Alternative perspectives. *American Psychologist, 35,* 131–150.

Edwards, K. (1990). The interplay of affect and cognition in attitude formation and change. *Journal of Personality and Social Psychology, 59,* 202–216.

Egan, L. C., Santos, L. R., & Bloom, P. (2007). The origins of cognitive dissonance: Evidence from children and monkeys. *Psychological Science, 18,* 978–983.

Ehrenreich, S. E., Beron, K. J., Brinkley, D. Y., & Underwood, M. K. (2014). Family predictors of continuity and change in social and physical aggression from ages 9 to 18. *Aggressive Behavior, 40,* 421–439.

Ehrlich, D., Guttman, I., Schönbach, P., & Mills, J. (1957). Postdecision exposure to relevant information. *The Journal of Abnormal and Social Psychology, 54*(1), 98–102.

Eibach, R. P., & Ehrlinger, J. (2006). "Keep your eyes on the prize": Reference points and racial differences in assessing progress toward equality. *Personality and Social Psychology Bulletin, 32,* 66–77.

Eich, E., Reeves, J. L., Jaeger, B., & Graff-Radford, S. B. (1985). Memory for pain: Relation between past and present pain intensity. *Pain, 23,* 375–380.

Eisenberg, N., Miller, P. A., Shell, R., McNalley, S., & Shea, C. (1991). Prosocial development in adolescence: A longitudinal study. *Developmental psychology, 27*(5), 849.

Eisenberger, N. I., Lieberman, M. D., & Williams, K. D. (2003). Does rejection hurt? An fMRI study of social exclusion. *Science, 302,* 290–292.

Eisenberger, R., & Armeli, S. (2001). Can salient reward increase creative performance without reducing intrinsic creative interest? *Journal of Personality and Social Psychology, 72,* 652–660.

Eisenberger, R., & Cameron, J. (1999). Detrimental effects of reward: Reality or myth? *American Psychologist, 51,* 1153–1166.

Eisenberger, R., & Rhoades, L. (2001). Incremental effects of reward on creativity. *Journal of Personality and Social Psychology, 81,* 728–741.

Eisenberger, R., Rhoades, L., & Cameron, J. (1999). Does pay for performance increase or decrease perceived self-determination and intrinsic motivation? *Journal of Personality and Social Psychology, 77,* 1026–1040.

Eisenberger, R. & Shanock, L. (2003). Rewards, intrinsic motivation, and creativity: A case study of conceptual and methodological isolation. *Creativity Research Journal, 15,* 121–130.

Eiser, J. R., Sutton, S. R., & Wober, M. (1979). Smoking, seat-belts, and beliefs about health. *Addictive Behaviors, 4,* 331–338.

Elder, G. H., Jr. (1969). Appearance and education in marriage mobility. *American Sociological Review, 34,* 519–533.

Eldersveld, S. J., & Dodge, R. W. (1954). Personal contact or mail propaganda? An experiment in voting turnout and attitude change. In D. Katz, D. Cartwright, S. Eldersveld, & A. M. Lee (Eds.), *Public opinion and propaganda.* New York: Dryden Press.

Ellemers, N., Van Rijswijk, W., Roefs, M., & Simons, C. (1997). Bias in intergroup perceptions: Balancing group identity with social reality. *Personality and Social Psychology Bulletin, 23,* 186–198.

Ellis, H. D. (1981). Theoretical aspects of face recognition. In G. H. Davies, H. D. Ellis, & J. Shepherd (Eds.), *Perceiving and remembering faces.* London: Academic Press.

Ellison, P. A., Govern, J. M., Petri, H. L., & Figler, M. H. (1995). Anonymity and aggressive driving behavior: A field study. *Journal of Social Behavior and Personality, 10,* 265–272.

Elms, A. C. (1995). Obedience in retrospect. *Journal of Social Issues, 51,* 21–31.

Elson, M., & Ferguson, C. J. (2014). Twenty-five years of research on violence in digital games and aggression: Empirical evidence, perspectives, and a debate gone astray. *European Psychologist, 19,* 33–46.

Emerson, R. W. (1993). Self-reliance and other essays. CreateSpace Independent Publishing.

Emmons, R. A., Larsen, R. J., Levine, S., & Diener, E. (1983). *Factors predicting satisfaction judgments: A comparative examination.* Paper presented at the Midwestern Psychological Association.

Emswiller, T., Deaux, K., & Willits, J. E. (1971). Similarity, sex, and requests for small favors. *Journal of Applied Social Psychology, 1,* 284–291.

Engemann, K. M., & Owyang, M. T. (2003, April). So much for that merit raise: The link between wages and appearance. *The Regional Economist.* Retrieved from http://www.stlouisfed.org

Engs, R., & Hanson, D. J. (1989). Reactance theory: A test with collegiate drinking. *Psychological Reports, 64,* 1083–1086.

Ennis, B. J., & Verrilli, D. B., Jr. (1989). Motion for leave to file brief amicus curiae and brief of Society for the Scientific Study of Religion, American Sociological Association, and others. U.S. Supreme Court Case No. 88–1600, *Holy Spirit Association for the Unification of World Christianity, et al., v. David Molko and Tracy Leal.* On petition for write of certiorari to the Supreme Court of California. Washington, DC: Jenner & Block, 21 Dupont Circle NW.

Ennis, R., & Zanna, M. P. (1991). *Hockey assault: Constitutive versus normative violations.* Paper presented at the Canadian Psychological Association convention.

Epley, N., & Huff, C. (1998). Suspicion, affective response, and educational benefit as a result of deception in psychology research. *Personality and Social Psychology Bulletin, 24,* 759–768.

Epley, N., & Huff, C. (1998). Suspicion, affective response, and educational benefit of deception in psychological research. *Personality and Social Psychology Bulletin, 67,* 371–378.

Epley, N., & Whitchurch, E. (2008). Mirror, mirror on the wall: Enhancement in self-recognition. *Personality and Social Psychology Bulletin, 34,* 1159–1170.

Epstein, J. A., & Botvin, G. J. (2008). Media refusal skills and drug skill refusal techniques: What is their relationship with alcohol use among inner-city adolescents? *Addictive Behavior, 33,* 528–537.

Epstein, S. (1980). The stability of behavior: II. Implications for psychological research. *American Psychologist, 35,* 790–806.

Epstude, K., & Roese, N. J. (2008). The functional theory of counterfactual thinking. *Personality and Social Psychology Review, 12,* 168–192.

Erickson, B., Holmes, J. G., Frey, R., Walker, L., & Thibaut, J. (1974). Functions of a third party in the resolution of conflict: The role of a judge in pretrial conferences. *Journal of Personality and Social Psychology, 30,* 296–306.

Erickson, B., Lind, E. A. Johnson, B. C., & O'Barr, W. M. (1978). Speech style and impression formation in a court setting: The effects of powerful and powerless speech. *Journal of Experimental Social Psychology, 14,* 266–279.

Erikson, E. H. (1963). *Childhood and society.* New York: Norton.

Eron, L. D. (1987). The development of aggressive behavior from the perspective of a developing behaviorism. *American Psychologist, 42,* 425–442.

Eron, L. D., & Huesmann, L. R. (1980). Adolescent aggression and television. *Annals of the New York Academy of Sciences, 347,* 319–331.

Eron, L. D., & Huesmann, L. R. (1984). The control of aggressive behavior by changes in attitudes, values, and the conditions of learning. In R. J. Blanchard & C. Blanchard (Eds.), *Advances in the study of aggression* (Vol. 1). Orlando, FL: Academic Press.

Eron, L. D., & Huesmann, L. R. (1985). The role of television in the development of prosocial and antisocial behavior. In D. Olweus, M. Radke-Yarrow, and J. Block (Eds.), *Development of antisocial and prosocial behavior.* Orlando, FL: Academic Press.

Escobar-Chaves, S. L., & Anderson, C. A. (2008). Media and risky behaviors. *The Future of Children, 18,* 147–180.

Escobar-Chaves, S. L., Tortolero, S. R., Markham, C. M., Low, B. J., Eitel, P., & Thickstun, P. (2005). Impact of the media on adolescent sexual attitudes and behaviors. *Pediatrics, 116,* 303–326.

Esser, J. K. (1998). Alive and well after 25 years: A review of groupthink research. *Organizational behavior and human decision processes, 73*(2–3), 116–141.

Esses, V. M. (1989). Mood as a moderator of acceptance of interpersonal feedback. *Journal of Personality and Social Psychology, 57,* 769–781.

Esses, V. M., Haddock, G., & Zanna, M. P. (1993a). Values, stereotypes, and emotions as determinants of intergroup attitudes. In D. Mackie & D. Hamilton (Eds.), *Affect, cognition and stereotyping: Interactive processes in intergroup perception.* San Diego, CA: Academic Press.

Esses, V. M., Haddock, G., & Zanna, M. P. (1993b). The role of mood in the expression of intergroup stereotypes. In M. P. Zanna & J. M. Olson (Eds.), *The psychology of prejudice: The Ontario symposium* (Vol. 7). Hillsdale, NJ: Erlbaum.

Esses, V. M., Jackson, L. M., & Armstrong, T. L. (1998). Intergroup competition and attitudes toward immigrants and immigration: An instrumental model of group conflict. *Journal of Social Issues, 54,* 699–724.

Esterbrook, G. (2004, May 25). The 50-cent a gallon solution. *New York Times.* Retrieved December 14, 2017, from http://www.nytimes.com/2004/05/25/opinion/the-50-cent-a-gallon-solution.html.

Etaugh, C. E., Bridges, J. S., Cummings-Hill, M., & Cohen, J. (1999). "Names can never hurt me": The effects of surname use on perceptions of married women.

Psychology of Women Quarterly, 23, 819–823.

Etzioni, A. (2005). *The diversity within unity platform.* Washington, DC: The Communitarian Network.

Evans, G. W. (1979). Behavioral and physiological consequences of crowding in humans. *Journal of Applied Social Psychology, 9,* 27–46.

Evans, G. W., Lepore, S. J., & Schroeder, A. (1996). The role of interior design elements in human responses to crowding. *Journal of Personality and Social Psychology, 70,* 41–46.

Evans, R. I., Smith, C. K., & Raines, B. E. (1984). Deterring cigarette smoking in adolescents: A psycho-social-behavioral analysis of an intervention strategy. In A. Baum, J. Singer, & S. Taylor (Eds.), *Handbook of psychology and health: Social psychological aspects of health* (Vol. 4). Hillsdale, NJ: Erlbaum.

Evelo, A. J., & Greene, E. (2013). Judgments about felony-murder in hindsight. *Applied Cognitive Psychology, 27*(3), 277–285.

Exelmans, L., Custers, K., & van den Bulck, J. (2015). Violent video game and delinquent behavior in adolescents. *Aggressive Behavior, 41*, 267–279.

Eyal, T., & Epley, N. (2017). Exaggerating accessible differences: When gender stereotypes overestimate actual group differences. *Personality and Social Psychology Bulletin, 43*, 1323–1336.

Ezeonu, I. (2010). Gun violence in Toronto: Perspectives from the police. *The Howard Journal of Crime and Justice*, *49*(2), 147–165.

Fabrigar, L. R., & Petty, R. E. (1999). The role of the affective and cognitive bases of attitudes in susceptibility to affectively and cognitively based persuasion. *Personality and Social Psychology Bulletin, 25,* 363–381.

Fabrigar, L. R., Priester, J. R., Petty, R. E., & Wegener, D. T. (1998). The impact of attitude accessibility on elaboration of persuasive messages. *Personality and Social Psychology Bulletin, 24,* 339–352.

Fachner, G., & Carter, S. (2015). *Collaborative reform initiative: An assessment of deadly force in the Philadelphia Police Department*. Washington, DC: Office of Community Oriented Policing Services, U.S. Department of Justice.

Falkner, A., & Lin, D. (2014). Recent advances in understanding the role of the hypothalmic circuit during aggression. *Frontiers in Systems Neuroscience, 25,* 168.

Falkner, A. L., Grosenick, L., Davidson, T., Deisseroth, K., & Lin, D. (2016). Hypothalamic control of male aggression-seeking behavior. *Nature Neuroscience, 19,* 596–604.

Farb, N. A. S., Segal, Z. V., Mayberg, H., Bean, J., & McKeon, D. (2007). Attending to the present: Mindfulness meditation reveals distinct neural modes of self-reference. Social Cognitive and Affective Neuroscience, 2, 313–322.

Farquhar, J. W., Maccoby, N., Wood, P. D., Alexander, J. K., Breitrose, H., Brown, B. W., Haskell, W. L., McAlister, A. L., Meyer, A. J., Nash, J. D., & Stern, M. P. (1977, June 4). Community education for cardiovascular health. *Lancet,* 1192–1195.

Farrell, M. A. (2005). The effect of a market-oriented organisational culture on salesforce behaviour and attitudes. *Journal of Strategic Marketing, 13,* 261.

Farrelly, M. C., Davis, K. C., Duke, J., & Messeri, P. (2008, January 17). Sustaining "truth": Changes in youth tobacco attitudes and smoking intentions after three years of a national antismoking campaign. *Health Education Research.* doi:10.1093/her/cym087

Farrelly, M. C., Healton, C. G., Davis, K. C., Messeri, P., Hersey, J. C., & Haviland, M. L. (2002). Getting to the truth: Evaluating national tobacco countermarketing campaigns. *American Journal of Public Health, 92,* 901–907.

Farris, C., Treat, T. A., Viken, R. J., & McFall, R. M. (2008). Perceptual mechanisms that characterize gender differences in decoding women's sexual intent. *Psychological Science, 19,* 348–354.

Farwell, L., & Weiner, B. (2000). Bleeding hearts and the heartless: Popular perceptions of liberal and conservative ideologies. *Personality and Social Psychology Bulletin, 26,* 845–852.

Faulkner, S. L., & Williams, K. D. (1996). *A study of social loafing in industry.* Paper presented to the Midwestern Psychological Association convention.

Faust, D., & Ziskin, J. (1988). The expert witness in psychology and psychiatry. *Science, 241,* 31–35.

Fazio, R. (1987). Self-perception theory: A current perspective. In M. P. Zanna, J. M. Olson, & C. P. Herman (Eds.), *Social influence: The Ontario symposium* (Vol. 5). Hillsdale, NJ: Erlbaum.

Fazio, R. H. (2007). Attitudes as object-evaluation associations of varying strength. *Social Cognition, 25,* 603–637.

Fazio, R. H., Effrein, E. A., & Falender, V. J. (1981). Self-perceptions following social interaction. *Journal of Personality and Social Psychology, 41,* 232–242.

Fazio, R. H., Jackson, J. R., Dunton, B. C., & Williams, C. J. (1995). Variability in automatic activation as an unobtrusive measure of racial attitudes: A bona fide pipeline? *Journal of Personality and Social Psychology, 69,* 1013–1027.

Fazio, R. H., & Zanna, M. P. (1981). Direct experience and attitude-behavior consistency. In L. Berkowitz (Ed.), *Advances in experimental social psychology* (Vol. 14). New York: Academic Press.

Fazio, R. H., Zanna, M. P., & Cooper, J. (1977). Dissonance versus self-perception: An integrative view of each theory's proper domain of application. *Journal of Experimental Social Psychology, 13,* 464–479.

Fazio, R. H., Zanna, M. P., & Cooper, J. (1979). On the relationship of data to theory: A reply to Ronis and Greenwald. *Journal of Experimental Social Psychology, 15,* 70–76.

FBI. (2017). Uniform crime reports: Crime in the United States. Table 1: Violent crime.

Feather, N. T. (1983). Causal attributions for good and bad outcomes in achievement and affiliation situations. *Australian Journal of Psychology, 35,* 37–48.

Feather, N. T. (2005). Social psychology in Australia: Past and present. *International Journal of Psychology, 40,* 263–276.

Federal Bureau of Investigation. (2008). Uniform crime report: Hate crimes 2008. Retrieved from http://www.fbi.gov/about-us/cjis/ucr/hate-crime/2008

Federal Bureau of Investigation. (2013, November 25). Latest hate crime statistics. Washington, DC: Federal Bureau of Investigation. Retrieved from http://www.fbi.gov.

Federal Trade Commission (FTC). (2003, June 12). Federal Trade Commission cigarette report for 2001. Retrieved from http://www.ftc.gov/opa/2003/06/2001cigrpt.htm

Feeney, J., Peterson, C., & Noller, P. (1994). Equity and marital satisfaction over the family life cycle. *Personality Relationships, 1,* 83–99.

Feeney, J. A. (1996). Attachment, caregiving, and marital satisfaction. *Personal Relationships, 3,* 401–416.

Feeney, J. A., & Noller, P. (1990). Attachment style as a predictor of adult romantic relationships. *Journal of Personality and Social Psychology, 58,* 281–291.

Fein, S., & Hilton, J. L. (1992). Attitudes toward groups and behavioral intentions toward individual group members: The impact of nondiagnostic information. *Journal of Experimental Social Psychology, 28,* 101–124.

Fein, S., & Spencer, S. J. (1997). Prejudice as self-image maintenance: Affirming the self through derogating others. *Journal of Personality and Social Psychology, 73,* 31–44.

Feinberg, J. M., & Aiello, J. R. (2006). Social facilitation: A test of competing theories. *Journal of Applied Social Psychology, 36,* 1–23.

Feinberg, M., & Willer, R. (2010). Apocalypse soon? Dire messages reduce belief in global warming by contradicting just-world beliefs. *Psychological Science, 22,* 34–38.

Feingold, A. (1988). Matching for attractiveness in romantic partners and same-sex friends: A meta-analysis and theoretical critique. *Psychological Bulletin, 104,* 226–235.

Feingold, A. (1990). Gender differences in effects of physical attractiveness on romantic attraction: A comparison across five research paradigms. *Journal of Personality and Social Psychology, 59,* 981–993.

Feingold, A. (1991). Sex differences in the effects of similarity and physical attractiveness on opposite-sex attraction. *Basic and Applied Social Psychology, 12,* 357–367.

Feingold, A. (1992). Gender differences in mate selection preferences: A test of the parental investment model. *Psychological Bulletin, 112,* 125–139.

Feldman, R. S., & Prohaska, T. (1979). The student as Pygmalion: Effect of student expectation on the teacher. *Journal of Educational Psychology, 71,* 485–493.

Feldman, R. S., & Theiss, A. J. (1982). The teacher and student as Pygmalions: Joint effects of teacher and student expectations. *Journal of Educational Psychology, 74,* 217–223.

Felson, R. B. (1984). The effect of self-appraisals of ability on academic performance. *Journal of Personality and Social Psychology, 47,* 944–952.

Felson, R. B. (2000). A social psychological approach to interpersonal aggression. In V. B. Van Hasselt, & M. Hersen (Eds.), *Aggression and violence: An introductory text* (pp. 9–22). Needham Heights, MA: Allyn & Bacon.

Fenigstein, A. (1984). Self-consciousness and the overperception of self as a target. *Journal of Personality and Social Psychology, 47,* 860–870.

Fenigstein, A., & Vanable, P. A. (1992). Paranoia and self-consciousness. *Journal of Personality and Social Psychology, 62,* 129–138.

Ferguson, C. J., & Kilburn, J. (2010). Much ado about nothing: The misestimation and overinterpretation of violent video game effects in Eastern and Western nations: Comment on Anderson et al. (2010). *Psychological Bulletin, 136,* 174–178.

Fergusson, D. M., Horwood, L. J., & Shannon, F. T. (1984). A proportional hazards model of family breakdown. *Journal of Marriage and the Family, 46,* 539–549.

Ferriday, C., Vartanian, O., & Mandel, D. R. (2011). Public but not private ego threat triggers aggression in narcissists. *European Journal of Social Psychology, 41,* 564–568.

Feshbach, N. D. (1980). *The child as "psychologist" and "economist": Two curricula.* Paper presented at the American Psychological Association convention.

Festinger, L. (1954). A theory of social comparison processes. *Human Relations, 7,* 117–140.

Festinger, L. (1957). *A theory of cognitive dissonance.* Stanford: Stanford University Press.

Festinger, L. (1987). *Reflections on cognitive dissonance theory: 30 years later.* Paper presented at the American Psychological Association convention.

Festinger, L., & Carlsmith, J. M. (1959). Cognitive consequences of forced compliance. *Journal of Abnormal and Social Psychology, 58,* 203–210.

Festinger, L., & Maccoby, N. (1964). On resistance to persuasive communications. *Journal of Abnormal and Social Psychology, 68,* 359–366.

Festinger, L., Pepitone, A., & Newcomb, T. (1952). Some consequences of deindividuation in a group. *Journal of Abnormal and Social Psychology, 47,* 382–389.

Feygina, I., Jost, J. T., & Goldsmith, R. E. (2010). System justification, the denial of global warming, and the possibility of "system-sanctioned change." *Personality and Social Psychology Bulletin, 36,* 326–338.

Feynman, R. (1967). *The character of physical law.* Cambridge, MA: MIT Press.

Fichter, J. (1968). *America's forgotten priests: What are they saying?* New York: Harper.

Ficks, C. A., & Waldman, I. D. (2014). Candidate genes for aggression and antisocial behavior: A meta-analysis of association studies of the 5HTTLPR and MAOA-uVNTR. *Behavior Genetics, 44,* 427–444.

Fiedler, F. E. (1987, September). When to lead, when to stand back. *Psychology Today, 26–27.*

Filipovic, J. (2017, October 4). One undeniable factor in gun violence: men. *Time.com.*

Fincham, F. D., & Bradbury, T. N. (1993). Marital satisfaction, depression, and attributions: A longitudinal analysis. *Journal of Personality and Social Psychology, 64,* 442–452.

Finchilescu, G. (2005). Meta-stereotypes may hinder interracial contact. *South African Journal of Psychology, 35,* 460–472.

Finkel, E. J., & Campbell, W. K. (2001). Self-control and accommodation in close relationships: An interdependence analysis. *Journal of Personality and Social Psychology, 81,* 263–277.

Finkel, E. J., Eastwick, P. W., Karney, B. R., Reis, H. T., & Sprecher, S. (2012). Online dating: A critical analysis from the perspective of psychological science. *Psychological Science in the Public Interest, 13,* 3–66.

Finkel, E. J., Hui, C. M., Carswell, K. L., & Larson, G. M. (2014). The suffocation of marriage: Climbing Mount Maslow without enough oxygen. *Psychological Inquiry, 25,* 1–41.

Finkel, E. J., Slotter, E. B., Luchies, L. B., Walton, G. M., & Gross, J. J. (2013). A brief intervention to promote conflict reappraisal preserves marital quality over time. *Psychological Science, 24,* 1595–1601.

Fischer, P., & Greitemeyer, T. (2006). Music and aggression: The impact of sexual-aggressive song lyrics on aggression-related thoughts, emotions, and behavior toward the same and the opposite sex. *Personality and Social Psychology Bulletin, 32,* 1165–1176.

Fischer, P., & Greitemeyer, T. (2010). A new look at selective-exposure effects: An integrative model. *Current Directions in Psychological Science, 19,* 384–389.

Fischer, P., Krueger, J., Greitemeyer, T., Vogrincic, C., Kastenmüller, A., Frey, D., Heene, M., Wicher, M., & Kainbacher, M. (2011). The bystander-effect: A meta-analytic review on bystander intervention in dangerous and non-dangerous emergencies. *Psychological Bulletin, 137,* 517–537.

Fischer, R., & Chalmers, A. (2008). Is optimism universal? A meta-analytical investigation of optimism levels across 22 nations. *Personality and Individual Differences, 45,* 378–382.

Fischer, R., & Van de Vliert, E. (2011). Does climate undermine subjective well-being? A 58-nation study. *Personality and Social Psychology Bulletin, 37,* 1031–1041.

Fischhoff, B. (1982). Debiasing. In D. Kahneman, P. Slovic, & A. Tversky (Eds.), *Judgment under uncertainty: Heuristics and biases.* New York: Cambridge University Press.

Fischhoff, B., & Bar-Hillel, M. (1984). Diagnosticity and the base rate effect. *Memory and Cognition, 12,* 402–410.

Fishbein, D., & Thelen, M. H. (1981a). *Husband-wife similarity and marital satisfaction: A different approach.* Paper presented at the Midwestern Psychological Association convention.

Fishbein, D., & Thelen, M. H. (1981b). Psychological factors in mate selection and marital satisfaction: A review (Ms. 2374). *Catalog of Selected Documents in Psychology, 11,* 84.

Fishbein, M., & Ajzen, I. (1974). Attitudes toward objects as predictive of single and multiple behavioral criteria. *Psychological Review, 81,* 59–74.

Fisher, H. (1994, April). The nature of romantic love. *Journal of NIH Research,* 59–64.

Fisher, H., & Garcia, J. R. (2013, February 5). Singles in America. Match.com survey of single population.

Fisher, H. E., Xu, X., Aron, A., & Brown, L. L. (2016). Intense, passionate, romantic love: A natural addiction? How the fields that investigate romance and substance abuse can inform each other. *Frontiers In Psychology, 7.*

Fisher, R. J. (1994). Generic principles for resolving intergroup conflict. *Journal of Social Issues, 50,* 47–66.

Fiske, S. T. (1989). *Interdependence and stereotyping: From the laboratory to the Supreme Court (and back).* Invited address, American Psychological Association convention.

Fiske, S. T. (1992). Thinking is for doing: Portraits of social cognition from Daguerrotype to Laserphoto. *Journal of Personality and Social Psychology, 63,* 877–889.

Fiske, S. T. (1993). Controlling other people: The impact of power on stereotyping. *American Psychologist, 48,* 621–628.

Fiske, S. T. (2004). Mind the gap: In praise of informal sources of formal theory. *Personality and Social Psychology Review, 8,* 132–137.

Fiske, S. T. (2011). *Envy up, scorn down: How status divides us.* New York: Sage Foundation.

Fiske, S. T., Harris, L. T., & Cuddy, A. J. C. (2004). Why ordinary people torture enemy prisoners. *Science, 306,* 1482.

Fiske, S. T., Xu, J., Cuddy, A. C., & Glick, P. (1999). (Dis)respecting versus (Dis)liking: Status and interdependence predict ambivalent stereotypes of competence and warmth. *Journal of Social Issues, 55,* 473–489.

Fitterman, L., & Bouquet, T. (2009, September). Web of conscience. *Reader's Digest,* 60–64.

Fitzpatrick, A. R., & Eagly, A. H. (1981). Anticipatory belief polarization as a function of the expertise of a discussion partner. *Personality and Social Psychology Bulletin, 1,* 636–642.

Flay, B. R., Ryan, K. B., Best, J. A., Brown, K. S., Kersell, M. W., d'Avernas, J. R., & Zanna, M. P. (1985). Are social-psychological smoking prevention programs effective? The Waterloo study. *Journal of Behavioral Medicine, 8,* 37–59.

Fletcher, G. J. O., Fincham, F. D., Cramer, L., & Heron, N. (1987). The role of attributions in the development of dating relationships. *Journal of Personality and Social Psychology, 53,* 481–489.

Fletcher, G. J. O., Simpson, J. A., Campbell, L., & Overall, N. C. (2015). Pair-bonding, romantic love, and evolution: The curious case of Homo sapiens. *Perspectives on Psychological Science, 10,* 20–36.

Fletcher, G. J. O., Simpson, J. A., Thomas, G., & Giles, L. (1999). Ideals in intimate relationships. *Journal of Personality and Social Psychology, 76,* 72–89.

Fletcher, G. J. O., Tither, J. M., O'Loughlin, C., Friesen, M., & Overall, N. (2004). Warm and homely or cold and beautiful? Sex differences in trading off traits in mate selection. *Personality and Social Psychology Bulletin, 30,* 659.

Fletcher, G. J. O., & Ward, C. (1989). Attribution theory and processes: A cross-cultural perspective. In M. H. Bond (Ed.), *The cross-cultural challenge to social psychology.* Newbury Park, CA: Sage.

Flores, A. R., Brown, T. N. T., & Park, A. S. (2016). Public support for transgender rights: A twenty-three country survey. The Williams Institute, UCLA School of Law. https://williamsinstitute.law.ucla.edu/wp-content/uploads/23-Country-Survey.pdf

Flores, A. R., Haider-Markel, D. P., Lewis, D. C., Miller, P. R., Tadlock, B. L., & Taylor, J. K. (2018). Challenged expectations: Mere exposure effects on attitudes about transgender people and rights. *Political Psychology.*

Flynn, E., Turner, C., & Giraldeau, L.-A. (2018). Follow (or don't follow) the crowd: Young children's conformity is influenced by norm domain and age. *Journal of Experimental Child Psychology, 167,* 222–233. https://doi-org.library.smu.ca/10.1016/j.jecp.2017.10.014

Flynn, F. J., & Wiltermuth, S. S. (2010). Who's with me? False consensus, brokerage, and ethical decision-making in organizations. *Academic of Management Journal, 53,* 1074–1089.

Foa, U. G., & Foa, E. B. (1975). *Resource theory of social exchange.* Morristown, NJ: General Learning Press.

Fogelman, E. (1994). *Conscience and courage: Rescuers of Jews during the Holocaust.* New York: Doubleday Anchor.

Follett, M. P. (1940). Constructive conflict. In H. C. Metcalf & L. Urwick (Eds.), *Dynamic administration: The collected papers of Mary Parker Follett.* New York: Harper.

Foos, A. E., Keeling, K., & Keeling, D. (2016). Redressing the sleeper effect: Evidence for the favorable persuasive impact of discounting information over time in a contemporary advertising context. *Journal of Advertising, 45*(1), 19–25.

Ford, R. (2008). Is racial prejudice declining in Britain? *British Journal of Sociology, 59,* 609–636.

Ford, T. E., Boxer, C. F., Armstrong, J., & Edel, J. R. (2008). More than "just a joke": The prejudice-releasing function of sexist humor. *Personality and Social Psychology Bulletin, 34,* 159–170.

Forgas, J. P. (2007). When sad is better than happy: Negative affect can improve the quality and effectiveness of persuasive messages and social influence strategies. *Journal of Experimental Social Psychology, 43,* 513–528.

Forgas, J. P. (2008). Affect and cognition. *Perspectives on Psychological Science, 3,* 94–101.

Forgas, J. P. (2010). Affective influences on the formation, expression, and change of attitudes. In J. P. Forgas, J. Cooper, & W. D. Crano (Eds.), *The psychology of attitudes and attitude change.* New York: Psychology Press.

Forgas, J. P. (2011). Affect and global versus local processing: The processing benefits of negative affect for memory, judgments, and behavior. *Psychological Inquiry, 21,* 216–224.

Forgas, J. P. (2013). Don't worry, be sad! On the cognitive, motivational, and interpersonal benefits of negative mood. *Current Directions in Psychological Science, 22,* 225–232.

Forgas, J. P., Bower, G. H., & Krantz, S. E. (1984). The influence of mood on perceptions of social interactions. *Journal of Experimental Social Psychology, 20,* 497–513.

Forgas, J. P., Dunn, E., & Granland, S. (2008). Are you being served ... ? An unobtrusive experiment of affective influences on helping in a department store. *European Journal of Social Psychology, 38,* 333–342.

Forgas, J. P., & Moylan, S. (1987). After the movies: Transient mood and social judgments. *Personality and Social Psychology Bulletin, 13,* 467–477.

Form, W. H., & Nosow, S. (1958). *Community in disaster.* New York: Harper.

Forrest, L. N., Smith, A. R., Fussner, L. M., Dodd, D. R., & Clerkin, E. M. (2016).

Using implicit attitudes of exercise importance to predict explicit exercise dependence symptoms and exercise behaviors. *Psychology of sport and exercise, 22*, 91–97.

Forrester, R. L., Slater, H., Jomar, K., Mitzman, S., & Taylor, P. J. (2017). Self-esteem and non-suicidal self-injury in adulthood: A systematic review. *Journal of Affective Disorders,* 221, 172–183.

Forscher, P. S., & Devine, P. G. (2014). Breaking the prejudice habit: Automaticity and control in the context of long-term goal. In J. W. Sherman, B. Gawronski, & Y. Trope (Eds.), *Dual-process theories of the social mind* (pp. 468–482). New York: Guilford Press.

Forster, E. M. (1976). *Aspects of the novel.* O. Stallybrass (Ed.). Harmondsworth: Penguin. (Original work published 1927.)

Forsyth, D. R., Berger, R. E., & Mitchell, T. (1981). The effects of self-serving vs. other-serving claims of responsibility on attraction and attribution in groups. *Social Psychology Quarterly, 44,* 59–64.

Forsyth, D. R., Kerr, N. A., Burnette, J. L., & Baumeister, R. F. (2007). Attempting to improve the academic performance of struggling college students by bolstering their self-esteem: An intervention that backfired. *Journal of Social and Clinical Psychology, 26,* 447–459.

Foss, R. D. (1983). Community Norms and Blood Donation 1. *Journal of Applied Social Psychology, 13*(4), 281–290.

Foster, E. M., & McCombs-Thornton, K. (2013). Child welfare and the challenge of causal inference. *Children and Youth Services Review, 35*(7), 1130–1142.

Fowler, S. P., Williams, K., Hunt, K. J., Resendez, G. R., Hazuda, H. P., & Stern, M. P.(2005, June 10–14). Diet soft drink consumption is associated with increased incidence of overweight and obesity in the San Antonio Heart Study. Slideshow presented at the 65th Annual Scientific Sessions, American Diabetes Association.

Fraley, R. C., Griffin, B. N., Belsky, J., & Roisman, G. I. (2012). Developmental antecedents of political ideology: A longitudinal investigation from birth to age 18 years. *Psychological Science, 23,* 1425–1431.

Frank, J. (1974). *Persuasion and healing: A comparative study of psychotherapy.* New York: Schocken.

Frank, J. D. (1982). Therapeutic components shared by all psychotherapies. In J. H. Harvey, & M. M. Parks (Eds.), *Psychotherapy research and behavior change* (Vol. 1) (pp. 9–37). Washington, DC: American Psychological Association.

Frank, M. G., & Gilovich, T. (1988). The dark side of self and social perception: Black uniforms and aggression in professional sports. *Journal of Personality and Social Psychology*, 54, 74–85.

Frank, R. (1999). *Luxury fever: Why money fails to satisfy in an era of excess.* New York: The Free Press.

Frankel, A., & Snyder, M. L. (1987). *Egotism among the depressed: When self-protection becomes self-handicapping.* Paper presented at the American Psychological Association convention. New York, NY.

Frantz, C. M. (2006). I AM being fair: The bias blind spot as a stumbling block to seeing both sides. *Basic and Applied Social Psychology,* 28, 157–167.

Frederick, D. A., & Haselton, M. G. (2007). Why is muscularity sexy? Tests of the fitness indicator hypothesis. *Personality and Social Psychology Bulletin, 8,* 1167–1183.

Freedman, J. L., Birsky, J., & Cavoukian, A. (1980). Environmental determinants of behavioral contagion: Density and number. *Basic and Applied Social Psychology, 1,* 155–161.

Freedman, J. L., Cunningham, J. A., & Krismer, K. (1992). Inferred values and the reverse-incentive effect in induced compliance. *Journal of Personality and Social Psychology, 62,* 357–368.

Freedman, J. L., & Fraser, S. C. (1966). Compliance without pressure: The foot-in-the-door technique. *Journal of Personality and Social Psychology, 4,* 195–202.

Freedman, J. L., & Perlick, D. (1979). Crowding, contagion, and laughter. *Journal of Experimental Social Psychology, 15,* 295–303.

Freedman, J. L., & Sears, D. O. (1965). Warning, distraction, and resistance to influence. *Journal of Personality and Social Psychology, 1,* 262–266.

Freedman, J. S. (1965). Long-term behavioral effects of cognitive dissonance. *Journal of Experimental Social Psychology, 1,* 145–155.

French, J. R. P. (1968). The conceptualization and the measurement of mental health in terms of self-identity theory. In S. B. Sells (Ed.), *The definition and measurement of mental health.* Washington, DC: Department of Health, Education, and Welfare.

Freund, B., Colgrove, L. A., Burke, B. L., & McLeod, R. (2005). Self-rated driving performance among elderly drivers referred for driving evaluation. *Accident Analysis and Prevention, 37,* 613–618.

Frey, B. S., Savage, D. A., & Torgler, B. (2010). Interaction of natural survival instincts and internalized social norms exploring the Titanic and Lusitania disasters. *Proceedings of the National Academy of Sciences USA, 107,* 4862–4865.

Friedman, H. S., Riggio, R. E., & Casella, D. F. (1988). Nonverbal skill, personal charisma, and initial attraction. *Personality and Social Psychology Bulletin, 14,* 203–211.

Friedman, R., & Elliot, A. J. (2008). The effect of arm crossing on persistence and performance. *European Journal of Social Psychology, 38,* 449–461.

Friedrich, J. (1996). On seeing oneself as less self-serving than others: The ultimate self-serving bias? *Teaching of Psychology, 23,* 107–109.

Friedrich, L. K., & Stein, A. H. (1973). Aggressive and prosocial television programs and the natural behavior of preschool children. *Monographs of the Society of Research in Child Development, 38* (4, Serial No. 151).

Friedrich, L. K., & Stein, A. H. (1975). Prosocial television and young children: The effects of verbal labeling and role playing on learning and behavior. *Child Development, 46,* 27–38.

Friese, M., Smith, C. T., Koever, M., & Bluemke, M. (2016). Implicit measures of attitudes and political voting behavior. *Social and Personality Psychology Compass, 10*(4), 188–201.

Frieze, I. H., Olson, J. E., & Russell, J. (1991). Attractiveness and income for men and women in management. *Journal of Applied Social Psychology, 21,* 1039–1057.

Frimer, J. A., Skitka, L. J., & Motyl, M. (2017). Liberals and conservatives are similarly motivated to avoid exposure to one another's opinions. *Journal of Experimental Social Psychology, 7,* 21–12.

Frisell, T., Lichtenstein, P., & Långström, N. (2011). Violent crime runs in families: A total population study of 12.5 million individuals. *Journal of Research in Psychiatry and the Allied Sciences, 41,* 97–105.

Froming, W. J., Walker, G. R., & Lopyan, K. J. (1982). Public and private self-awareness: When personal attitudes conflict with societal expectations. *Journal of Experimental Social Psychology, 18,* 476–487.

Fry, D. P. (2012). Life without war. *Science, 336,* 879–884.

Fryer, R. G. (2016). *An empirical analysis of racial differences in police use of force.* NBER Working Paper no. 22399 (http://www.nber.org/papers/w22399).

Fulgoni, G. M., & Lipsman, A. (2017). The downside of digital word of mouth and the pursuit of media quality: How social sharing is disrupting digital advertising models and metrics. *Journal of Advertising Research, 57,* 127–131.

Fuller, S. R., & Aldag, R. J. (1998). Organizational Tonypandy: Lessons from a quarter century of the groupthink phenomenon. *Organizational Behavior and Human Decision Processes,* in press.

Funder, D. C. (1987). Errors and mistakes: Evaluating the accuracy of social judgment. *Psychological Bulletin, 101,* 75–90.

Funder, D. C., Levine, J. M., Mackie, D. M., Morf, C. C., Vazire, S. & West, S. G. (2014). Notice: PSPB articles by authors with retracted articles at PSPB or other journals: Stapel, Smeesters, and Sanna. *Personality and Social Psychology Bulletin, 40,* 132–135.

Furnham, A. (1982). Explanations for unemployment in Britain. *European Journal of Social Psychology, 12,* 335–352.

Furnham, A., & Gunter, B. (1984). Just world beliefs and attitudes towards the poor. *British Journal of Social Psychology, 23,* 265–269.

Gabbiadini, A., Riva, P., Andrighetto, L., Volpato, C., & Bushman, B. J. (2014). Interactive effect of moral disengagement and violent video games on self-control, cheating, and aggression. *Social Psychological and Personality Science, 5,* 451–458.

Gable, S. L., Gonzaga, G. C., & Strachman, A. (2006). Will you be there for me when things go right? Supportive responses to positive event disclosures. *Journal of Personality and Social Psychology, 91,* 904–917.

Gabrenya, W. K., Jr., Wang, Y.-E., & Latané, B. (1985). Social loafing on an optimizing task: Cross-cultural differences among Chinese and Americans. *Journal of Cross-Cultural Psychology, 16,* 223–242.

Gaebelein, J. W., & Mander, A. (1978). Consequences for targets of aggression as a function of aggressor and instigator roles: Three experiments. *Personality and Social Psychology Bulletin, 4,* 465–468.

Gaertner, L., Iuzzini, J., Witt, M. G., & Oriña, M. M. (2006). Us without them: Evidence for an intragroup origin of positive in-group regard. *Journal of Personality and Social Psychology, 90,* 426–439.

Gaertner, L., Sedikides, C., & Chang, K. (2008). On pancultural self-enhancement: Well-adjusted Taiwanese self-enhance on personally valued traits. *Journal of Cross-Cultural Psychology, 39,* 463–477.

Gaertner, L., Sedikides, C., & Graetz, K. (1999). In search of self-definition: Motivational primacy of the individual self, motivational primacy of the collective self, or contextual primacy? *Journal of Personality and Social Psychology, 76,* 5–18.

Gaertner, S. L., & Dovidio, J. F. (2005). Understanding and addressing contemporary racism: From aversive racism to the Common Ingroup Identity Model. *Journal of Social Issues, 61,* 615–639.

Gaertner, S. L., Dovidio, J. F., Nier, J. A., Banker, B. S., Ward, C. M., Houlette, M., & Loux, S. (2000). The common ingroup identity model for reducing intergroup bias: Progress and challenges. In D. Capozza & R. Brown (Eds.), *Social identity processes: Trends in theory and research.* London: Sage.

Gaertner, S. L., Mann, J., Murrell, A., & Dovidio, J. F. (2001). Reducing intergroup bias: The benefits of recategorization. In M. A. Hogg & D. Abrams (Eds.), *Intergroup relations: Essential readings.* Philadelphia: Psychology Press.

Gailliot, M. T. (2008). Unlocking the energy dynamics of executive function: Linking executive functioning to brain glycogen. *Perspectives on Psychological Science, 3,* 245–263.

Gailliot, M. T., & Baumeister, R. F. (2007). Self-regulation and sexual restraint. Dispositionally and temporarily poor self-regulatory abilities contribute to failures at restraining sexual behavior. *Personality and Social Psychology Bulletin, 33,* 173–186.

Gaither, S. E., & Sommers, S. R. (2013). Living with an other-race roommate shapes Whites' behavior in subsequent diverse settings. *Journal of Experimental Social Psychology, 49,* 272–276.

Galanter, M. (1989). *Cults: Faith, healing, and coercion.* New York: Oxford University Press.

Galanter, M. (1990). Cults and zealous self-help movements: A psychiatric perspective. *American Journal of Psychiatry, 147,* 543–551.

Galinsky, A. D., & Moskowitz, G. B. (2000). Perspective-taking: Decreasing stereotype expression, stereotype accessibility, and in-group favoritism. *Journal of Personality and Social Psychology, 78,* 708–724.

Galinsky, E., Aumann, K., & Bond, J. T. (2009). *Times are changing: Gender and generation at work and at home.* New York: Families and Work Institute.

Galizio, M., & Hendrick, C. (1972). Effect of musical accompaniment on attitude: The guitar as a prop for persuasion. *Journal of Applied Social Psychology, 2,* 350–359.

Gall, G., Millette, D., & Lambert, M. (2015). Quebec Referendum (1995). The Canadian Encyclopedia. Retrieved from: https://thecanadianencyclopedia.ca/en/article/quebec-referendum-1995

Gallup, G. G., Jr., & Frederick, D. A. (2010). The science of sex appeal: An evolutionary perspective. *Journal of General Psychology, 14,* 240–250.

Gallup, G. G., Jr., Frederick, M. J., & Pipitone, R. N. (2008). Morphology and behavior: Phrenology revisited. *Review of General Psychology, 12,* 297–304.

Gallup, G. H. (1972). *The Gallup poll: Public opinion 1935–1971* (Vol. 3) (pp. 551, 1716). New York: Random House.

Gallup, G. H., Jr., & Jones, T. (1992). *The saints among us.* Harrisburg, PA: Morehouse.

Gangestad, S. W., & Snyder, M. (2000). Self-monitoring: Appraisal and reappraisal. *Psychological Bulletin, 126,* 530–555.

Gangestad, S. W., & Thornhill, R. (1997). Human sexual selection and developmental stability. In J. A. Simpson & D. T. Kenrick (Eds.), *Evolutionary social psychology.* Mahway, NJ: Erlbaum.

Gangestad, S. W., Simpson, J. A., Cousins, A. J., Garver-Apgar, C. E., & Christensen, P. N. (2004). Women's preferences for male behavioral displays change across the menstrual cycle. *Psychological Science, 15,* 203.

Garcia-Marques, T., Fernandes, A., Fonseca, R., & Prada, M. (2015). Social presence and the composite face effect. *Acta Psychologica, 158,* 61–66.

Gardner, M. (1997, July/August). Heaven's Gate: The UFO cult of Bo and Peep. *Skeptical Inquirer,* 15–17.

Garneau, C., Olmstead, S. B., Pasley, K., & Fincham, F. D. (2013). The role of family structure and attachment in college student hookups. *Archives of Sexual Behavior, 42,* 1473–1486.

Garrett, B. L. (2011, April 12). Getting it wrong: Convicting the innocent. *Slate.* Retrieved from http://www.slate.com

Garry, M., Manning, C. G., Loftus, E. F., & Sherman, S. J. (1996). Imagination inflation: Imagining a childhood event inflates confidence that it occurred. *Psychonomic Bulletin & Review, 3,* 208–214.

Garver-Apgar, C. E., Gangestad, S. W., Thornhill, R., Miller, R. D., & Olp, J. J. (2006). Major histocompatibility complex alleles, sexual responsivity, and unfaithfulness in romantic couples. *Psychological Science, 17,* 830–834.

Gates, G. J. (2017, January 11). In US, more adults identifying as LGBT (www.gallup.com).

Gates, M. F., & Allee, W. C. (1933). Conditioned behavior of isolated and grouped cockroaches on a simple maze. *Journal of Comparative Psychology, 15,* 331–358.

Gaucher, D., Friesen, J., & Kay, A. C. (2011). Evidence that gendered wording in job advertisements exists and sustains gender inequality. *Journal of Personality and Social Psychology, 101,* 109–128.

Gaunt, R. (2006). Couple similarity and marital satisfaction: Are similar spouses happier? *Journal of Personality, 74,* 1401–1420.

Gavanski, I., & Hoffman, C. (1987). Awareness of influences on one's own judgments: The roles of covariation detection and attention to the judgment process. *Journal of Personality and Social Psychology, 52,* 453–463.

Gawande, A. (2002). *Complications: A surgeon's notes on an imperfect science.* New York: Metropolitan Books, Holt and Company.

Gawronski, B., & Bodenhausen, G. V. (2006). Associative and propositional processes in evaluation: An integrative review of implicit and explicit attitude change. *Psychological Bulletin, 132,* 692–731.

Gazzaniga, M. (1985). *The social brain: Discovering the networks of the mind.* New York: Basic Books.

Gazzaniga, M. (1998). *The mind's past.* Berkeley, CA: University of California Press.

Gazzaniga, M. (2008). *Human: The science behind what makes us unique.* New York: Ecco.

Gazzaniga, M. S. (1992). *Nature's mind: The biological roots of thinking, emotions, sexuality, language, and intelligence.* New York: Basic Books.

Ge, Y., Knittel, C. R., MacKenzie, D., & Zoepf, S. (2016). *Racial and gender discrimination in transportation network companies.* National Bureau of Economic Research, Inc., NBER Working Papers: 22776.

Gebauer, J. E., Sedikides, C., Wagner, J., Bleidorn, W., Rentfrow, P. J., Potter, J., & Gosling, S. D. (2015). Cultural norm fulfillment, interpersonal belonging, or getting ahead? A large-scale, cross-cultural test of three perspectives on the function of self-esteem. Journal of Personality and Social Psychology, 109, 526–548.

Geen, R. G. (1998). Aggression and antisocial behavior. In D. Gilbert, S. Fiske, & G. Lindzey (Eds.), *Handbook of social psychology* (4th ed). New York: McGraw-Hill.

Geen, R. G., & Gange, J. J. (1983). Social facilitation: Drive theory and beyond. In H. H. Blumberg, A. P. Hare, V. Kent, & M. Davies (Eds.), *Small groups and social interaction* (Vol. 1). London: Wiley.

Geen, R. G., & Thomas, S. L. (1986). The immediate effects of media violence on behavior. *Journal of Social Issues, 42*(3), 7–28.

Geers, A. L., Handley, I. M., & McLarney, A. R. (2003). Discerning the role of optimism in persuasion: The valence-enhancement hypothesis. *Journal of Personality and Social Psychology, 85,* 554–565.

Gentile, B., Twenge, J. M., Freeman, E. C., & Campbell, W. K. (2012). The effect of social networking websites on positive self-views: An experimental investigation. *Computers in Human Behavior, 28,* 1929–1933.

Gentile, D. A. (2004, May 14). Quoted by K. Laurie in *Violent games.* Retrieved from http://ScienCentral.com

Gentile, D. A., & Anderson, C. A. (2003). Violent video games: The newest media violence hazard. In D. A. Gentile (Ed.), *Media violence and children.* Westport, CT: Ablex.

Gentile, D. A., & Anderson, C. A. (2011, June 30). Don't read more into the Supreme Court's ruling on the California video game law. News release, Iowa State University. *Newswise.* Retrieved from http://www.newswise.com

Gentile, D. A., Anderson, C. A., Yukawa, S., Ihori, N., Saleem, M., Ming, L. K., Shibuya, A., Liau, A. K., Khoo, A., Bushman, B. J., Huesmann, L. R., & Sakamoto, A. (2009). The effects of prosocial video games on prosocial behaviors: International evidence from correlational, longitudinal, and experimental studies. *Personality and Social Psychology Bulletin, 35,* 752–763.

Gentile, D. A., Bender, P. K., & Anderson, C. A. (2017). Violent video game effects on salivary cortisol, arousal, and aggressive thoughts in children. *Computers in Human Behavior, 70,* 39–43.

Gentile, D. A., & Bushman, B. J. (2012). Reassessing media violence effects using a risk and resilience approach to understanding aggression. *Psychology of Popular Media Culture, 1,* 138–151.

Gentile, D. A., Lynch, P. J., Linder, J. R., & Walsh, D. A. (2004). The effects of violent video game habits on adolescent hostility, aggressive behaviors, and school performance. *Journal of Adolescence, 27,* 5.

Gentile, D. A., Saleem, M., & Anderson, C. A. (2007). Public policy and the effects of media violence on children. *Social Issues and Policy Review, 1,* 15–61.

George, D., Carroll, P., Kersnick, R., & Calderon, K. (1998). Gender-related patterns of helping among friends. *Psychology of Women Quarterly, 22,* 685–704.

Gerard, H. B. (1999). A social psychologist examines his past and looks to the future. In A. Rodrigues, & R. V. Levine (Eds.), *Reflections on 100 years of experimental social psychology* (pp. 47–81). New York: Basic Books.

Gerard, H. B., & Mathewson, G. C. (1966). The effects of severity of initiation on liking for a group: A replication. *Journal of Experimental Social Psychology, 2,* 278–287.

Gerard, H. B., Wilhelmy, R. A., & Conolley, E. S. (1968). Conformity and group size. *Journal of Personality and Social Psychology, 8,* 79–82.

Gerber, J., & Wheeler, L. (2009a). On being rejected: A meta-analysis of experimental research on rejection. *Perspectives on Psychological Science, 4,* 468–488.

Gerber, J., & Wheeler, L. (2009b). Rejoinder to Baumeister, DeWall, and Vohs (2009). *Perspectives on Psychological Science, 4,* 494–495.

Gerbner, G. (1994). The politics of media violence: Some reflections. In C. Hamelink & O. Linne (Eds.), *Mass communication research: On problems and policies.* Norwood, NJ: Ablex.

Gerbner, G., Gross, L., Signorielli, N., Morgan, M., & Jackson-Beeck, M. (1979). The demonstration of power: Violence profile No. 10. *Journal of Communication, 29,* 177–196.

Gergen, K. E. (1982). *Toward transformation in social knowledge.* New York: Springer-Verlag.

Gergen, K. J., Gergen, M. M., & Barton, W. H. (1973, October). Deviance in the dark. *Psychology Today,* 129–130.

Gerrig, R. J., & Prentice, D. A. (1991, September). The representation of fictional information. *Psychological Science, 2,* 336–340.

Gershoff, E. T. (2002). Corporal punishment by parents and associated child behaviors and experiences: A meta-analytic and theoretical review. *Psychological Bulletin, 128,* 539–579.

Gerstenfeld, P. B., Grant, D. R., & Chiang, C. (2003). Hate online: A content analysis of extremist Internet sites. *Analyses of Social Issues and Public Policy (ASAP), 3,* 29.

Gesch, C. B., Hammond, S. M., Hampson, S. E., Eves, A., & Crowder, M. J. (2002). Influence of supplementary vitamins, minerals and essential fatty acids on the antisocial behavior of young adult prisoners. Randomised, placebo-controlled trial. *British Journal of Psychiatry, 181,* 22–28.

Giancola, P. R., & Corman, M. D. (2007). Alcohol and aggression: A test of the attention-allocation model. *Psychological Science, 18,* 649–655.

Gibbons, F. X. (1978). Sexual standards and reactions to pornography: Enhancing behavioral consistency through self-focused attention. *Journal of Personality and Social Psychology, 36,* 976–987.

Gibbons, F. X., Eggleston, T. J., & Benthin, A. C. (1997). Cognitive reactions to smoking relapse: The reciprocal relation between dissonance and self-esteem. *Journal of Personality and Social Psychology, 72,* 184–195.

Gibbons, F. X., & Wicklund, R. A. (1982). Self-focused attention and helping behavior. *Journal of Personality and Social Psychology, 43,* 462–474.

Gibson, B., & Sanbonmatsu, D. M. (2004). Optimism, pessimism, and gambling: The downside of optimism. *Personality and Social Psychology Bulletin, 30,* 149–160.

Gibson, J. I., & Claassen, C. (2010). Racial reconciliation in South Africa: Interracial contact. *Journal of Social Issues, 66,* 255–272.

Gibson, S. (2013). Milgram's obedience experiments: A rhetorical analysis. *British Journal of Social Psychology, 52(2)*, 290–309. https://doi.org/10.1111/j.2044-8309.2011.02070.x

Gibson, S. (2019). Obedience without orders: Expanding social psychology's conception of 'obedience.' *British Journal of Social Psychology, 58*(1), 241–259. https://doi-org.library.smu.ca/10.1111/bjso.12272

Gibson, S., Blenkinsopp, G., Johnstone, E., & Marshall, A. (2018). Just following orders? The rhetorical invocation of 'obedience' in Stanley Milgram's post-experiment interviews. *European Journal of Social Psychology, 48*(5), 585–599. https://doi-org.library.smu.ca/10.1002/ejsp.2351

Gifford, R. (2011). The dragons of inaction: Psychological barriers that limit climate change mitigation and adaptation. *American Psychologist, 66,* 290–302.

Gifford, R., & Hine, D. W. (1997). Toward cooperation in commons dilemmas. *Canadian Journal of Behavioural Science, 29,* 167–179.

Gigerenzer, G. (2010). *Rationality for mortals: How people cope with uncertainty.* New York: Oxford University Press.

Gigerenzer, G., & Gaissmaier, W. (2011). Heuristic decision making. *Annual Review of Psychology, 62,* 451–482.

Gigone, D., & Hastie, R. (1993). The common knowledge effect: Information sharing and group judgment. *Journal of Personality and Social Psychology, 65,* 959–974.

Gilbert, D. (2007). *Stumbling on happiness.* New York: Knopf.

Gilbert, D. (2011, June 7). Introduction (to conversation with Timothy Wilson). *The Edge.* Retrieved from http://www.edge.org

Gilbert, D. T., & Ebert, J. E. J. (2002). *Decisions and revisions: The affective forecasting of escapable outcomes.* Unpublished manuscript, Harvard University, Cambridge, MA.

Gilbert, D. T., Giesler, R. B., & Morris, K. A. (1995). When comparisons arise. *Journal of Personality and Social Psychology, 69,* 227–236.

Gilbert, D. T., & Hixon, J. G. (1991). The trouble of thinking: Activation and application of stereotypic beliefs. *Journal of Personality and Social Psychology, 60,* 509–517.

Gilbert, D. T., & Jones, E. E. (1986). Perceiver-induced constraint: Interpretations of self-generated reality. *Journal of Personality and Social Psychology, 50,* 269–280.

Gilbert, D. T., Killingsworth, M. A., Eyre, R. N., & Wilson, T. D. (2009). The surprising power of neighborly advice. *Science, 323,* 1617–1619.

Gilbert, D. T., Krull, D. S., & Malone, P. S. (1990). Unbelieving the unbelievable: Some problems in the rejection of false information. *Journal of personality and social psychology, 59*(4), 601.

Gilbert, D. T., Lieberman, M. D., Morewedge, C. K., & Wilson, T. D. (2004). The peculiar longevity of things not so bad. *Psychological Science, 15,* 14–19.

Gilbert, D. T., & Malone, P. S. (1995). The correspondence bias. *Psychological Bulletin, 117,* 21–38.

Gilbert, D. T., Tafarodi, R. W., & Malone, P. S. (1993). You can't not believe everything you read. *Journal of Personality and Social Psychology, 65,* 221–233.

Gilbert, D. T., & Wilson, T. D. (2000). Miswanting: Some problems in the forecasting of future affective states. In J. Forgas (Ed.), *Feeling and thinking: The role of affect in social cognition.* Cambridge, UK: Cambridge University Press.

Gillath, O. M., Shaver, P. R., Baek, J-M., & Chun, D. S. (2008). Genetic correlates of adult attachment. *Personality and Social Psychology Bulletin, 34,* 1396–1405.

Gillis, J. (2011, December 16). As permafrost thaws, scientists study the risks. *New York Times.* Retrieved from http://www.nytimes.com

Gilovich, T., & Douglas, C. (1986). Biased evaluations of randomly determined gambling outcomes. *Journal of Experimental Social Psychology, 22,* 228–241.

Gilovich, T., & Eibach, R. (2001). The fundamental attribution error where it really counts. *Psychological Inquiry, 12*(1), 23.

Gilovich, T., Kerr, M., & Medvec, V. H. (1993). Effect of temporal perspective on subjective confidence. *Journal of Personality and Social Psychology, 64,* 552–560.

Gilovich, T., & Medvec, V. H. (1994). The temporal pattern to the experience of regret. *Journal of Personality and Social Psychology, 67,* 357–365.

Gilovich, T., Medvec, V. H., & Savitsky, K. (2000). The spotlight effect in social judgment: An egocentric bias in estimates of the salience of one's own actions and appearance. *Journal of Personality and Social Psychology, 78,* 211–222.

Gilovich, T., Savitsky, K., & Medvec, V. H. (1998). The illusion of transparency: Biased assessments of others' ability to read one's emotional states. *Journal of Personality and Social Psychology, 75,* 332–346.

Gilovich, T., Wang, R. F., Regan, D., & Nishina, S. (2003). Regrets of action and inaction across cultures. *Journal of Cross-Cultural Psychology, 34,* 61–71.

Gini, G., Pozzoli, T., & Hymel, S. (2014). Moral disengagement among children and youth: A meta-analytic review of links to aggressive behavior. *Aggressive Behavior, 40,* 56–68.

Gino, F., Ayal, S., & Ariely, D. (2009). Contagion and differentiation in unethical behavior: The effect of one bad apple on the barrel. *Psychological Science, 20,* 393–398.

Ginsburg, B., & Allee, W. C. (1942). Some effects of conditioning on social dominance and subordination in inbred strains of mice. *Physiological Zoology, 15,* 485–506.

Glasman, L. R., & Albarracin, D. (2006). Forming attitudes that predict future behavior: A meta-analysis of the attitude-behavior relation. *Psychological Bulletin, 132,* 778–822.

Glass, D. C. (1964). Changes in liking as a means of reducing cognitive discrepancies between self-esteem and aggression. *Journal of Personality, 32,* 531–549.

Gleason, M. E. J., Masumi, I., Bolger, N., & Shrout, P. E. (2003). Daily supportive equity in close relationships. *Personality and Social Psychology Bulletin, 29,* 1036–1045.

Glenn, N. D. (1980). Aging and attitudinal stability. In O. G. Brim, Jr., & J. Kagan (Eds.), *Constancy and change in human development.* Cambridge, MA: Harvard University Press.

Glick, P., & Fiske, S. T. (1996). The ambivalent sexism inventory: Differentiating hostile and benevolent sexism. *Journal of Personality and Social Psychology, 70,* 491–512.

Glick, P., & Fiske, S. T. (2001). An ambivalent alliance: Hostile and benevolent sexism as complementary justifications for gender inequality. *American Psychologist, 56,* 109–118.

Glick, P., & Fiske, S. T. (2007). Sex discrimination: The psychological approach. In F. J. Crosby, M. S. Stockdale, & S. Ropp (Eds.), *Sex discrimination in the workplace: Multidisciplinary perspectives.* Malden, MA: Blackwell.

Glick, P., & Fiske, S. T. (2011). Ambivalent sexism revisited. *Psychology of Women Quarterly, 35,* 530–535.

Glick, P., Lameiras, M., Fiske, S. T., Eckes, T., Masser, B., Volpato, C., et al. (2004). Bad but bold: Ambivalent attitudes toward men predict gender inequality in 16 nations. *Journal of Personality and Social Psychology, 86,* 713.

Global News. (2020, April 10). Coronavirus: Toronto's homeless COVID-19 patients sent to hospital due to lack of recovery sites. Retrieved from https://globalnews.ca/news/6806485/coronavirus-toronto-homeless-hospitals-covid-19-recovery-site/

Globe and Mail. (2017). Mike Duffy sues Ottawa for unfair treatment in Senate scandal. Retrieved from https://www.theglobeandmail.com/news/politics/mike-duffy-sues-government-senate/article36078625/

Gluszek, A., & Dovidio, J. F. (2010). The way *they* speak: A social psychological perspective on the stigma of nonnative accents in communication. *Personality and Social Psychology Review, 14,* 214–237.

Gnambs, T., & Appel, M. (2017). Narcissism and social networking behavior: A meta-analysis. Journal of Personality, 86, 200-212.

Gockel, C., Kerr, N. L., Seok, D-H., & Harris, D. W. (2008). Indispensability and group identification as sources of task motivation. *Journal of Experimental Social Psychology, 44,* 1316–1321.

Goel, S., Mason, W., & Watts, D. J. (2010). Real and perceived attitude agreement in social networks. *Journal of Personality and Social Psychology, 99,* 611–621.

Goethals, G. R., Messick, D. M., & Allison, S. T. (1991). The uniqueness bias: Studies of constructive social comparison. In J. Suls & T. A. Wills (Eds.), *Social comparison: Contemporary theory and research.* Hillsdale, NJ: Erlbaum.

Goethals, G. R., & Nelson, E. R. (1973). Similarity in the influence process: The belief-value distinction. *Journal of Personality and Social Psychology, 25,* 117–122.

Goethals, G. R., & Zanna, M. P. (1979). The role of social comparison in choice shifts. *Journal of Personality and Social Psychology, 37,* 1469–1476.

Goetz, J. L., Keltner, D., & Simon-Thomas, E. (2010). Compassion: An evolutionary analysis and empirical review. *Psychological Bulletin, 136,* 351–374.

Goetz, S. M. M., Tang, L., Thomason, M. E., Diamond, M. P., Hariri, A. R., & Carre, J. M. (2014). Testosterone rapidly increases neural reactivity to threat in healthy men: A novel two-step pharmacological challenge paradigm. *Biological Psychiatry, 76,* 324–331.

Goggin, W. C., & Range, L. M. (1985). The disadvantages of hindsight in the perception of suicide. *Journal of Social and Clinical Psychology, 3,* 232–237.

Goh, J. O., Chee, M. W., Tan, J. C., Venkatraman, V., Hebrank, A., Leshikar, E. D., Jenkins, L., Sutton, B. P., Gutchess, A. H., & Park, D. C. (2007). Age and culture modulate object processing and object-science binding in the ventral visual area. *Cognitive, Affective & Behavioral Neuroscience, 7,* 44–52.

Goldberg, P. (1968). Are women prejudiced against women? *Transaction, 5,* 28–30.

Goldhagen, D. J. (1996). *Hitler's willing executioners.* New York: Knopf.

Goldman, S. K. (2012). Effects of the 2008 Obama presidential campaign on White racial prejudice. *Public Opinion Quarterly, 76,* 663–687.

Goldman, W., & Lewis, P. (1977). Beautiful is good: Evidence that the physically attractive are more socially skillful. *Journal of Experimental Social Psychology, 13,* 125–130.

Goldstein, A. P. (1994). Delinquent gangs. In A. P. Goldstein, B. Harootunian, and J. C. Conoley (Eds.), *Student aggression: Prevention, control, and replacement.* New York: Guilford.

Goldstein, A. P., & Glick, B. (1994). Aggression replacement training: Curriculum and evaluation. *Simulation and Gaming, 25,* 9–26.

Goldstein, J. H., & Arms, R. L. (1971). Effects of observing athletic contests on hostility. *Sociometry, 34,* 83–90.

Golec de Zavala, A., Cichocka, A., Eidelson, R., & Jayawickreme, N. (2009). Collective narcissism and its social consequences. *Journal of Personality and Social Psychology, 97,* 1074–1096.

Golec de Zavala, A., Cichocka, A., & Iskra-Golec, I. (2013). Collective narcissism moderates the effect of in-group image threat on intergroup hostility. *Journal of Personality and Social Psychology, 104,* 1019–1039.

Golec de Zavala, A., Cichocka, A., Orehek, E., & Abdollahi, A. (2012). Intrinsic religiosity reduces intergroup hostility under mortality salience. *European Journal of Social Psychology, 42,* 451–461.

Goleman, D. (1993, June 22). Scientist at work: Ervin Staub; studying the pivotal role of bystanders. *New York Times.*

Golomb, B. A., Evans, M. A., White, H. L., & Dimsdale, J. E. (2012). Trans fat consumption and aggression. *Plos ONE,* 7. doi:10.1371/journal.pone.0032175

Gómez, A., Brooks, M. L., Buhrmester, M. D., Vázquez, A., Jetten, J., & Swann, Jr., W. B. (2011). On the nature of identity fusion: Insights into the construct and a new measure. *Journal of Personality and Social Psychology, 100,* 918–933.

Gonsalkorale, K., & Williams, K. D. (2006). The KKK would not let me play: Ostracism even by a despised outgroup hurts. *European Journal of Social Psychology, 36,* 1–11.

Gonsalves, B., Reber, P. J., Gitelman, D. R., Parrish, T. B., Mesulam, M., & Paller, K. A. (2004). Neural evidence that vivid imagining can lead to false remembering. *Psychological Science, 15,* 655.

Gonzaga, G. C., Campos, B., & Bradbury, T. (2007). Similarity, convergence, and relationship satisfaction in dating and married couples. *Journal of Personality and Social Psychology, 93,* 34–48.

Gonzaga, G. C., Keltner, D., Londahl, E. A., & Smith, M. D. (2001). Love and the commitment problem in romantic relations and friendship. *Journal of Personality and Social Psychology, 81,* 247–262.

Gonzales, A. L., & Hancock, J. T. (2011). Mirror, mirror on my Facebook wall: Effects of exposure to Facebook on self-esteem. *Cyberpsychology, Behavior, and Social Networking, 14,* 79–83.

González, K. V., Verkuyten, M., Weesie, J., & Poppe, E. (2008). Prejudice towards Muslims in the Netherlands: Testing integrated threat theory. *British Journal of Social Psychology, 47,* 667–685.

González-Vallejo, C., Lassiter, G. D., Bellezza, F. S., & Lindberg, M. J. (2008). "Save angels perhaps": A critical examination of unconscious thought theory and the deliberation-without-attention effect. *Review of General Psychology, 12,* 282–296.

Good, A., Choma, B., & Russo, F. A. (2017). Movement synchrony influences intergroup relations in a minimal groups paradigm. *Basic and Applied Social Psychology, 39,* 231–238.

Goodhart, D. E. (1986). The effects of positive and negative thinking on performance in an achievement situation. *Journal of Personality and Social Psychology, 51,* 117–124.

Gordijn, E. H., De Vries, N. K., & De Dreu, C. K. W. (2002). Minority influence on focal and related attitudes: Change in size, attributions and information processing. *Personality and Social Psychology Bulletin, 28,* 1315.

Gordon, A. M., & Chen, S. (2016). Do you get where I'm coming from? Perceived understanding buffers against the negative impact of conflict on relationship satisfaction. *Journal of Personality and Social Psychology, 110,* 239–260.

Gordon, R. A. (1996). Impact of ingratiation on judgments and evaluations: A meta-analytic investigation. *Journal of Personality and Social Psychology, 71,* 54–70.

Gortmaker, S. L., Must, A., Perrin, J. M., Sobol, A. M., & Dietz, W. H. (1993). Social and economic consequences of overweight in adolescence and young adulthood. *New England Journal of Medicine, 329,* 1008–1012.

Gotlib, I. H., & Colby, C. A. (1988). How to have a good quarrel. In P. Marsh (Ed.), *Eye to eye: How people interact.* Topsfield, MA: Salem House.

Gottlieb, J., & Carver, C. S. (1980). Anticipation of future interaction and the bystander effect. *Journal of Experimental Social Psychology, 16,* 253–260.

Gottman, J. (with N. Silver). (1994). *Why marriages succeed or fail.* New York: Simon & Schuster.

Gottman, J. M., Levenson, R. W., Swanson, C., Swanson, K., Tyson, R., & Yoshimoto, D. (2003). Observing gay, lesbian and heterosexual couples' relationships: Mathematical modeling of conflict interaction. *Journal of homosexuality, 45,* 65-91.

Gough, H. G., & Thorne, A. (1986). Positive, negative, and balanced shyness. In W. H. Jones, J. M. Cheek, & S. R. Briggs (Eds.), *Shyness: Perspectives on research and treatment.* New York: Plenum.

Gould, M. S., & Shaffer, D. (1986). The impact of suicide in television movies: Evidence of imitation. *New England Journal of Medicine, 315,* 690–694.

Gould, S. J. (1988, July). Kropotkin was no crackpot. *Natural History,* 12–21.

Gouldner, A. W. (1960). The norm of reciprocity: A preliminary statement. *American Sociological Review, 25,* 161–178.

Graf, S., Paolini, S., & Rubin, M. (2014). Negative intergroup contact is more influential, but positive intergroup contact is more common: Assessing contact prominence and contact prevalence in five Central European countries. *European Journal of Social Psychology, 44,* 536–547.

Graham, J., Nosek, B. A., & Haidt, J. (2012, December 12). The moral stereotypes of liberals and conservatives: Exaggeration of differences across the political spectrum. *PLoS ONE 7*: e50092.

Granstrom, K., & Stiwne, D. (1998). A bipolar model of groupthink: An expansion of Janis's concept. *Small Group Research, 29,* 32–56.

Grant, J. M., Mottet, L. A., Tanis, J., Herman, J. L., Harrison, J., & Keisling, M. (2011). *National transgender discrimination survey report on health and health care.* National Center for Transgender Equality and National Gay and Lesbian Task Force.

Gray, C., Russell, P., & Blockley, S. (1991). The effects upon helping behaviour of wearing pro-gay identification. *British Journal of Social Psychology, 30*(2), 171-178.

Gray, J. D., & Silver, R. C. (1990). Opposite sides of the same coin: Former spouses' divergent perspectives in coping with their divorce. *Journal of Personality and Social Psychology, 59,* 1180–1191.

Graziano, W. G., Jensen-Campbell, L. A., & Finch, J. F. (1997). The self as a mediator between personality and adjustment. *Journal of Personality and Social Psychology, 73,* 392–404.

Green, A. R., Carney, D. R., Pallin, D. J., Ngo, L. H., Raymond, K. L., Iezzoni, L. I., & Banaji, M. R. (2007). Implicit bias among physicians and its prediction of thrombolysis decisions for Black and White patients. *Journal of General Internal Medicine, 22,* 1231–1238.

Green, C. W., Adams, A. M., & Turner, C. W. (1988). Development and validation of the school interracial climate scale. *American Journal of Community Psychology, 16,* 241–259.

Green, D. P, Strolovitch, D. Z., & Wong, S. J. (1998). Defended neighborhoods, integration, and racially motivated crime. *American Journal of Sociology,* 104, 372–403.

Green, D. P., & Wong, J. S. (2008). Tolerance and the contact hypothesis: A field experiment. In E. Borgida (Ed.), *The political psychology of democratic citizenship.* London: Oxford University Press.

Green, M. C., Strange, J. J., & Brock, T. C. (Eds.) (2002). *Narrative impact: Social and cognitive foundations.* Mahwah, NJ: Erlbaum.

Greenaway, K. H., Cruwys, T., Haslam, S. A., & Jetten, J. (2016). Social identities promote well-being because they satisfy global psychological needs. *European Journal of Social Psychology, 46,* 294–307.

Greenaway, K. H., Louis, W. R., Hornsey, M. J., & Jones, J. M. (2014). Perceived control qualifies the effects of threat on prejudice. *British Journal of Social Psychology, 75,* 82–92.

Greenberg, J. (1986). Differential intolerance for inequity from organizational and individual agents. *Journal of Applied Social Psychology, 16,* 191–196.

Greenberg, J. (2008). Understanding the vital human quest for self-esteem. *Perspectives on Psychological Science, 3,* 48–55.

Greenberg, J., Landau, M. J., & Arndt, J. (2013). Mortal cognition: Viewing self and the world from the precipice. In Carlston, D. E. (Ed.). *The Oxford handbook of social cognition* (pp.680–701). New York: Oxford University Press.

Greenberg, J., Landau, M. J., Kosloff, S., & Solomon, S. (2008). How our dreams of death transcendence breed prejudice, stereotyping, and conflict. In T. Nelson (Ed.), *Handbook of prejudice, stereotyping, and discrimination.* New York: Psychology Press.

Greenberg, J., Pyszczynski, T., Solomon, S., Rosenblatt, A., Veeder, M., Kirkland, S., & Lyon, D. (1990). Evidence for terror management theory II: The effects of mortality salience on reactions to those who threaten or bolster the cultural worldview. *Journal of Personality and Social Psychology, 58,* 308–318.

Greenberg, J., Pyszczynski, T., Solomon, S., Simon, L., & Breus, M. (1994). Role of consciousness and accessibility of death-related thoughts in mortality salience effects. *Journal of Personality and Social Psychology, 67,* 627–637.

Greenberg, J., Solomon, S., & Pyszczynski, T. (1997). Terror management theory of self-esteem and cultural worldviews: Empirical assessments and conceptual refinements. *Advances in Experimental Social Psychology, 29,* in press.

Greenfield, P. M. (2013). The changing psychology of culture from 1800 through 2000. *Psychological Science, 24,* 1722–1731.

Greenwald, A. G. (1975). On the inconclusiveness of crucial cognitive tests of dissonance versus self-perception theories. *Journal of Experimental Social Psychology, 11,* 490–499.

Greenwald, A. G. (1980). The totalitarian ego: Fabrication and revision of personal history. *American Psychologist, 35,* 603–618.

Greenwald, A. G. (1992). New look 3: Unconscious cognition reclaimed. *American Psychologist, 47,* 766–779.

Greenwald, A. G., & Banaji, M. R. (1995). Implicit social cognition: Attitudes, self-esteem, and stereotypes. *Psychological Review, 102,* 4–27.

Greenwald, A. G., Banaji, M. R., & Nosek, B. A. (2015). Statistically small effects of the implicit association test can have societally large effects. *Journal of Personality and Social Psychology, 108,* 553–561.

Greenwald, A. G., Banaji, M. R., Rudman, L. A., Farnham, S. D., Nosek, B. A., & Mellott, D. S. (2002). A unified theory of implicit attitudes, stereotypes, self-esteem, and self-concept. *Psychological Bulletin, 109,* 3–25.

Greenwald, A. G., Banaji, M. R., Rudman, L. A., Farnham, S. D., Nosek, B. A., & Rosier, M. (2000). Prologue to a unified theory of attitudes, stereotypes, and self-concept. In J. P. Forgas (Ed.), *Feeling and thinking: The role of affect in social cognition and behavior.* New York: Cambridge University Press.

Greenwald, A. G., McGhee, D. E., & Schwartz, J. L. K. (1998). Measuring individual differences in implicit cognition: The implicit association test. *Journal of Personality and Social Psychology, 74,* 1464–1480.

Greenwald, A. G., Nosek, B. A., & Banaji, M. R. (2003). Understanding and using the Implicit Association Test: I. An improved scoring algorithm. *Journal of Personality and Social Psychology, 85,* 197–216.

Greenwald, A. G., Oakes, M. A., & Hoffman, H. G. (2003). Targets of discrimination: Effects of race on responses to weapons holders. *Journal of Experimental Social Psychology, 39,* 399–405.

Greenwald, A. G., & Pettigrew, T. F. (2014). With malice toward none and charity for some: Ingroup favoritism enables discrimination. *American Psychologist, 69,* 669–684.

Greenwald, A. G., Poehlman, T. A., Uhlmann, E. L., & Banaji, M. R. (2008). Understanding and using the Implicit Association Test: III. Meta-analysis of predictive validity. *Journal of Personality and Social Psychology, 97*(1), 17–41.

Greenwald, A. G., & Schuh, E. S. (1994). An ethnic bias in scientific citations. *European Journal of Social Psychology, 24,* 623–639.

Greenwald, G. (2012, March 19). Discussing the motives of the Afghan shooter: The contrast is glaring in how we talk about violence by Americans versus violence toward Americans. *Salon.* Retrieved from http://www.salon.com

Greitemeyer, T. (2009a). Effects of songs with prosocial lyrics on prosocial thoughts, affect, and behavior. *Journal of Experimental Social Psychology, 45,* 186–190.

Greitemeyer, T. (2009b). Stereotypes of singles: Are singles what we think? *European Journal of Social Psychology, 39,* 368–383.

Greitemeyer, T. (2011). Exposure to music with prosocial lyrics reduces aggression: First evidence and test of the underlying mechanism. *Journal of Experimental Social Psychology, 47,* 28–36.

Greitemeyer, T. (2014). Intense acts of violence during video game play make daily life aggression appear innocuous: A new mechanism why violent video games increase aggression. *Journal of Experimental Social Psychology, 50,* 52–56.

Greitemeyer, T., & McLatchie, N. (2011). Denying humanness to others: A newly discovered mechanism by which violent video games increase aggressive behavior. *Psychological Science, 22,* 659–665.

Greitemeyer, T., & Mugge, D. O. (2014). Video games do affect social outcomes: A meta-analytic review of the effects of violent and prosocial video game play. *Personality and Social Psychology Bulletin, 40,* 578–589.

Greitemeyer, T., & Osswald, S. (2010). Effects of prosocial video games on prosocial behavior. *Journal of Personality and Social Psychology, 98,* 211–221.

Greitemeyer, T., Osswald, S., & Brauer, M. (2010). Playing prosocial video games increases empathy and decreases Schadenfreude. *Emotion, 10,* 796–802.

Greitemeyer, T., & Sagioglou, C. (2016). Subjective socioeconomic status causes aggression: A test of the theory of social deprivation. *Journal of Personality and Social Psychology, 111,* 178–194.

Grekul, J., & LaBoucane-Benson, P. (2008). Aboriginal gangs and their (dis)placement: Contextualizing recruitment, membership, and status. *Canadian Journal of Criminology and Criminal Justice, 50*(1), 59–82.

Griffin, D., & Buehler, R. (1993). Role of construal processes in conformity and dissent. *Journal of Personality and Social Psychology, 65,* 657.

Griffitt, W. (1970). Environmental effects on interpersonal affective behavior. Ambient effective temperature and attraction. *Journal of Personality and Social Psychology, 15,* 240–244.

Griffitt, W., & Veitch, R. (1971). Hot and crowded: Influences of population density and temperature on interpersonal affective behavior. *Journal of Personality and Social Psychology, 17,* 92–98.

Griggs, R. A., Blyler, J., & Jackson, S. L. (2020). Using research ethics as a springboard for teaching Milgram's obedience study as a contentious classic. *Scholarship of Teaching and Learning in Psychology.* https://doi-org.library.smu.ca/10.1037/stl0000182

Grinshteyn, E., & Hemenway, D. (2016). Violent death rates: The US compared with other high-income OECD countries, 2010. *American Journal of Medicine, 129,* 266–273.

Grise, E., Boer, C., Turim, A., Manaugh, K., & El-Geneidy, A. (2019). The impacts of varying survey design on reported trip satisfaction, *Transportation Research, 60,* 761-768. https://doi.org/10.1016/j.trf.2018.12.003

Griskevicius, V., Tybur, J. M., Gangestad, S. W., Perea, E. F., Shapiro, J. R., & Kenrick, D. T. (2009). Aggress to impress: Hostility as an evolved context-dependent strategy. *Journal of Personality and Social Psychology, 96,* 980–994.

Griskevicius, V., Tybur, J. M., Sundie, J. M., Cialdini, R. B., Miller, G. F., & Kenrick, D. T. (2007). Blatant benevolence and conspicuous consumption: When romantic motives elicit strategic costly signals. *Journal of Personality and Social Psychology, 93,* 85–102.

Groenenboom, A., Wilke, H. A. M., & Wit, A. P. (2001). Will we be working together again? The impact of future interdependence on group members' task motivation. *European Journal of Social Psychology, 31,* 369.

Gross, A. E., & Crofton, C. (1977). What is good is beautiful. *Sociometry, 40,* 85–90.

Gross, J. T. (2001). *Neighbors: The destruction of the Jewish community in Jedwabne, Poland.* Princeton: Princeton University Press.

Gross, T. F. (2009). Own-ethnicity bias in the recognition of Black, East Asian, Hispanic, and White faces. *Basic and Applied Social Psychology, 31,* 128–135.

Grossman, S. (2014, February 16). 1 in 4 Americans apparently unaware the Earth orbits the Sun. Time.com. Retrieved from http://time.com/7809/1-in-4-americans-thinks-sun-orbits-earth/

Grossmann, I., Na, J., Varnum, M. E. W., Park, D. C., Kitayama, S., & Nisbett, R. E. (2010). Reasoning about social conflicts improves into old age. *PNAS, 107,* 7246–7250.

Grossmann, I., & Varnum, M. E. W. (2015). Social structure, infectious diseases, disasters, secularism, and cultural change in America. *Psychological Science, 26,* 311–324.

Grote, N. K., & Clark, M. S. (2001). Perceiving unfairness in the family: Cause or consequence of marital distress? *Journal of Personality and Social Psychology, 80,* 281.

Grove, J. R., Hanrahan, S. J., & McInman, A. (1991). Success/failure bias in attributions across involvement categories in sport. *Personality and Social Psychology Bulletin, 17,* 93–97.

Grove, W. M., Zald, D. H., Lebow, B. S., Snitz, B. E., & Nelson, C. (2000). Clinical versus mechanical prediction: A meta-analysis. *Psychological Assessment, 12,* 19–30.

Grube, J. W., Kleinhesselink, R. R., & Kearney, K. A. (1982). Male self-acceptance and attraction toward women. *Personality and Social Psychology Bulletin, 8,* 107–112.

Gruder, C. L. (1977). Choice of comparison persons in evaluating oneself. In J. M. Suls & R. L. Miller (Eds.), *Social comparison processes.* Washington, DC: Hemisphere.

Gruder, C. L., Cook, T. D., Hennigan, K. M., Flay, B., Alessis, C., & Kalamaj, J. (1978). Empirical tests of the absolute sleeper effect predicted from the discounting cue hypothesis. *Journal of Personality and Social Psychology, 36,* 1061–1074.

Gruendl, M. (2005, December 14). Beautycheck. Retrieved from http://www.beautycheck.de

Gruman, J. C., & Sloan, R. P. (1983). Disease as justice: Perceptions of the victims of physical illness. *Basic and Applied Social Psychology, 4,* 39–46.

Grunberger, R. (1971). *The 12-year reich: A social history of Nazi Germany 1933–1945.* New York: Holt, Rinehart & Winston.

Grush, J. E. (1980). Impact of candidate expenditures, regionality, and prior outcomes on the 1976 Democratic presidential primaries. *Journal of Personality and Social Psychology, 38,* 337–347.

Grush, J. E., & Glidden, M. V. (1987). *Power and satisfaction among distressed and nondistressed couples.* Paper presented at the Midwestern Psychological Association convention.

Grzyb, T., Doliński, D., Trojanowski, J., & Bar-Tal, Y. (2018). Cognitive structuring and obedience toward authority.*Personality and Individual Differences, 133,* 115–120. https://doi-org.library.smu.ca/10.1016/j.paid.2017.08.032

Guadagno, R. E., Rhoads, K. V. L., & Sagarin, B. J. (2011). Figural vividness and persuasion: Capturing the "elusive" vividness effect. *Personality and Social Psychology Bulletin, 37,* 626–638.

Guardian (2015). British belief in climate change on the rise, research finds. Retrieved from: https://www.theguardian.com/environment/2015/jan/29/british-belief-in-climate-change-at-highest-level-in-past-decade-survey

Guay, F., Mageau, G. A., & Vallerand, R. J. (2003). On the hierarchical structure of self-determined motivation: A test of top-down, bottom-up, reciprocal, and horizontal effects. *Personality & Social Psychology Bulletin, 29*(8), 992–1004.

Guéguen, N. & Jacob, C. (2001). Fund-raising on the Web: The effect of an electronic foot-in-the-door on donation. *CyberPsychology and Behavior, 4,* 705–709.

Guéguen, N., Martin, A., Silone, F., & David, M. (2016). Foot-in-the-door technique and reduction of driver's aggressiveness: A field study. *Transportation Research Part F: Traffic Psychology and Behaviour, 36,* 1–5.

Guerin, B. (1993). *Social facilitation.* Paris: Cambridge University Press.

Guerin, B. (1994). What do people think about the risks of driving? Implications for traffic safety interventions. *Journal of Applied Social Psychology, 24,* 994–1021.

Guerin, B. (1999). Social behaviors as determined by different arrangements of social consequences: Social loafing, social facilitation, deindividuation, and a modified social loafing. *The Psychological Record, 49,* 565–578.

Guffler, K., & Wagner, U. (2017). Backfire of good intentions: Unexpected long-term contact intervention effects in an intractable conflict area. *Peace and Conflict: Journal of Peace Psychology, 23,* 383–391.

Guimond, S., Dambrun, N., Michinov, N., & Duarte, S. (2003). Does social dominance generate prejudice? Integrating individual and contextual determinants of intergroup cognitions. *Journal of Personality and Social Psychology, 84,* 697–721.

Guiness, O. (1993). *The American hour: A time of reckoning and the once and future role of faith.* New York: Free Press.

Guinote, A. (2017). How power affects people: Activating, wanting, and goal seeking. *Annual Review of Psychology, 68,* 353–381.

Gulker, J. E., & Monteith, M. J. (2013). Intergroup boundaries and attitudes: The power of a single potent link. *Personality and Social Psychology Bulletin, 39,* 943–955.

Gupta, M. D. (2017, September). Return of the missing daughters. *Scientific American,* pp. 78–85.

Gupta, U., & Singh, P. (1982). Exploratory study of love and liking and type of marriages. *Indian Journal of Applied Psychology, 19,* 92–97.

Gutierres, S. E., Kenrick, D. T., & Partch, J. J. (1999). Beauty, dominance, and the mating game: Contrast effects in self-assessment reflect gender differences in mate selection. *Journal of Personality and Social Psychology, 25,* 1126–1134.

Ha, T., van denBerg, J. E. M., Engels, R. C., & Lichtwarck-Aschoff, A. (2012). Effects of attractiveness and status in dating desire in homosexual and heterosexual men and women. *Archives of Sexual Behavior, 41,* 673–682.

Haas, A. P., Rodgers, P. L., & Herman, J. L. (2014). *Suicide attempts among transgender and gender non-conforming adults.* American Foundation for Suicide Prevention and the Williams Institute, UCLA (https://williamsinstitute.law.ucla.edu/wp-content/uploads/AFSP-Williams-Suicide-Report-Final.pdf).

Hacker, H. M. (1951). Women as a minority group. *Social Forces, 30,* 60–69.

Hackman, J. R. (1986). The design of work teams. In J. Lorsch (Ed.), *Handbook of organizational behavior.* Englewood Cliffs, NJ: Prentice-Hall.

Hadden, J. K. (1969). *The gathering storm in the churches.* Garden City, NY: Doubleday.

Haddock, G., Maio, G. R., Arnold, K., & Huskinson, T. (2008). Should persuasion be affective or cognitive? The moderating effects of need for affect and need for cognition. *Personality and Social Psychology Bulletin, 34,* 769–778.

Haddock, G., & Zanna, M. P. (1994). Preferring "housewives" to "feminists." *Psychology of Women Quarterly, 18,* 25–52.

Haeffel, G. J., Gibb, B. E., Metalsky, G. I., Alloy, L. B., Abramson, L. Y., Hankin, B. L., Joiner, T. E., Jr., & Swendsen, J. D. (2008). Measuring cognitive vulnerability to depression: Development and validation of the cognitive style questionnaire. *Clinical Psychology Review, 28,* 824–836.

Hafenbrack, A. C., Cameron, L. D., Spreitzer, G. M., Zhang, C., Noval, L. J., & Shaffakat, S. (2019). Helping people by being in the present: Mindfulness increases prosocial behavior. Organizational Behavior and Human Decision Processes. https://doi-org.library.smu.ca/10.1016/j.obhdp.2019.08.005

Hafer, C. L. (2000). Do innocent victims threaten the belief in a just world? Evidence from a modified Stroop task. *Journal of Personality and Social Psychology, 79*(2), 165–173.

Hafer, C. L., & Bègue, L. (2005). Experimental research on just-world theory: Problems, developments, and future challenges. *Psychological Bulletin, 131,* 128.

Hafer, C. L., & Olson, J. M. (2003). An analysis of empirical research on the scope of justice. *Personality and Social Psychology Review, 7*(4), 311–323.

Hafer, C. L., & Sutton, R. (2016). Belief in a just world. In C. Sabbagh & M. Schmitt (Eds.), *Handbook of social justice theory and research.* New York: Springer.

Haidt, J. (2003). The moral emotions. In R. J. Davidson (Ed.), *Handbook of affective sciences.* Oxford: Oxford University Press.

Haidt, J. (2006). *The happiness hypothesis: Finding modern truth in ancient wisdom.* New York: Basic Books.

Hahn, A., Banchefsky, S., Park, B., & Judd, C. M. (2015). Measuring intergroup ideologies: Positive and negative aspects of emphasizing versus looking beyond group differences. *Personality and Social Psychology Bulletin, 41,* 1646–1664.

Halberstadt, J. (2006). The generality and ultimate origins of the attractiveness of prototypes. *Personality and Social Psychology Review, 10,* 166–183.

Halberstadt, J., O'Shea, R. P., & Forgas, J. (2006). Outgroup fanship in Australia and New Zealand. *Australian Journal of Psychology, 58,* 159–165.

Hald, G. M., & Malamuth, N. N. (2015). Experimental effects of exposure to pornography: The moderating effect of personality and mediating effect of sexual arousal. *Archives of Sexual Behavior, 44,* 99–109.

Halford, J. T., & Hsu, H-C. (2014). Beauty is wealth: CEO appearance and shareholder value. Retrieved from https://papers.ssrn.com/sol3/papers.cfm?abstract_id=2357756

Hall, C. C., Zhao, J., & Shafir, E. (2014). Self-affirmation among the poor: Cognitive and behavioral implications. *Psychological Science, 25,* 619–625.

Hall, D. L., Matz, D. C., & Wood, W. (2010). Why don't we practice what we preach? A meta-analytic review of religious racism. *Personality and Social Psychology Review, 14,* 126–139.

Hall, J. A., & Pennington, N. (2013). Self-monitoring, honesty, and cue use on Facebook: The relationship with user extraversion and conscientiousness. *Computers in Human Behavior, 29,* 1556–1564.

Hall, T. (1985, June 25). The unconverted: Smoking of cigarettes seems to be becoming a lower-class habit. *Wall Street Journal, 1,* 25.

Hamberger, J., & Hewstone, M. (1997). Inter-ethnic contact as a predictor of blatant and subtle prejudice: Tests of a model in four West European nations. *British Journal of Social Psychology, 36,* 173–190.

Hamblin, R. L., Buckholdt, D., Bushell, D., Ellis, D., & Feritor, D. (1969, January). Changing the game from get the teacher to learn. *Transaction,* 20–25, 28–31.

Hamermesh, D. S. (2011). *Beauty pays: Why attractive people are more successful.* Princeton, NJ: Princeton University Press.

Hamilton, D. L., & Gifford, R. K. (1976). Illusory correlation in interpersonal perception: A cognitive basis of stereotypic judgments. *Journal of Experimental Social Psychology, 12,* 392–407.

Hamilton, D. L., & Rose, T. L. (1980). Illusory correlation and the maintenance of stereotypic beliefs. *Journal of Personality and Social Psychology, 39,* 832–845.

Hammond, M. D., & Overall, N. C. (2013). Men's hostile sexism and biased perceptions of intimate partners: Fostering dissatisfaction and negative behavior in close relationships. *Personality and Social Psychology Bulletin, 39,* 1585–1599.

Hampson, R. B. (1984). Adolescent prosocial behavior: Peer-group and situational factors associated with helping. *Journal of Personality and Social Psychology, 46,* 153–162.

Hampton, K. N., Rainie, H., Lu, W., Dwyer, M., Shin, I., & Purcell, K. (2014). *Social media and the "spiral of silence."* PewResearchCenter.

Hancock, K. J., & Rhodes, G. (2008). Contact, configural coding and the other-race effect in face recognition. *British Journal of Psychology, 99,* 45–56.

Hanel, P. H. P., Wolfradt, U., Maio, G. R., & Manstead, A. S. R. (2018). The source attribution effect: Demonstrating pernicious disagreement between ideological groups on non-divisive aphorisms. *Journal of Experimental Social Psychology, 79,* 51–63. https://doi-org.library.smu.ca/10.1016/j.jesp.2018.07.002

Hansen, J., & Wänke, M. (2009). Liking what's familiar: The importance of unconscious familiarity in the mere-exposure effect. *Social Cognition, 27,* 161–182.

Harbaugh, W. T., Mayr, U., & Burghart, D. R. (2007). Neural responses to taxation and voluntary giving reveal motives for charitable donations. *Science, 316,* 1622–1625.

Harber, K. D. (1998). Feedback to minorities: Evidence of a positive bias. *Journal of Personality and Social Psychology, 74,* 622–628.

Harber, K. D., Stafford, R., & Kennedy, K. A. (2010). The positive feedback bias as a response to a self-image threat. *Journal of Social Psychology, 49,* 207–218.

Hardes, J. (2006). Retention of Aboriginal students in postsecondary education. *Alberta Counsellor, 29*(1), 28–33.

Hardin, G. (1968). The tragedy of the commons. *Science, 162,* 1243–1248.

Harding, L. M. (2018). Students of a feather "flocked" together: A group assignment method for reducing free-riding and improving group and individual learning outcomes. *Journal of Marketing Education, 40*(2), 117–127. https://doi-org.library.smu.ca/10.1177/0273475317708588

Hardy, C., & Latané, B. (1986). Social loafing on a cheering task. *Social Science, 71,* 165–172.

Hardy, C. L., & Van Vugt, M. (2006). Nice guys finish first: The competitive altruism hypothesis. *Personality and Social Psychology Bulletin, 32,* 1402–1413.

Haritos-Fatouros, M. (1988). The official torturer: A learning model for obedience to the authority of violence. *Journal of Applied Social Psychology, 18,* 1107–1120.

Harkins, S. G. (1981). *Effects of task difficulty and task responsibility on social loafing.* Presentation to the First International Conference on Social Processes in Small Groups, Kill Devil Hills, NC.

Harkins, S. G., & Jackson, J. M. (1985). The role of evaluation in eliminating social loafing. *Personality and Social Psychology Bulletin, 11,* 457–465.

Harkins, S. G., Latané, B., & Williams, K. (1980). Social loafing: Allocating effort or taking it easy? *Journal of Experimental Social Psychology, 16,* 457–465.

Harkins, S. G., & Petty, R. E. (1981). Effects of source magnification of cognitive effort on attitudes: An information-processing view. *Journal of Personality and Social Psychology, 40,* 401–413.

Harkins, S. G., & Petty, R. E. (1982). Effects of task difficulty and task uniqueness on social loafing. *Journal of Personality and Social Psychology, 43,* 1214–1229.

Harkins, S. G., & Petty, R. E. (1987). Information utility and the multiple source effect. *Journal of Personality and Social Psychology, 52,* 260–268.

Harkins, S. G., & Szymanski, K. (1989). Social loafing and group evaluation. *Journal of Personality and Social Psychology, 56,* 934–941.

Harmon-Jones, E., & Allen, J. J. B. (2001). The role of affect in the mere exposure effect: Evidence from psychophysiological and individual differences approaches.

Personality and Social Psychology Bulletin, 27, 889–898.

Harmon-Jones, E., Brehm, J. W., Greenberg, J., Simon, L., & Nelson, D. E. (1996). Evidence that the production of aversive consequences is not necessary to create cognitive dissonance. *Journal of Personality and Social Psychology, 70,* 5–16.

Harmon-Jones, E., Gerdjikov, T., & Harmon-Jones, C. (2008). The effect of induced compliance on relative left frontal cortical activity: A test of the action-based model of dissonance. *European Journal of Social Psychology, 38,* 35–45.

Harrel, W. A. (1994). Effects of blind pedestrians on motorists. *Journal of Social Psychology, 134,* 529–539.

Harries, K. D., & Stadler, S. J. (1988). Heat and violence: New findings from Dallas field data, 1980–1981. *Journal of Applied Social Psychology, 18,* 129–138.

Harris, J. R. (1998). *The nurture assumption.* New York: Free Press.

Harris, L. T., & Fiske, S. T. (2006). Dehumanizing the lowest of the low: Neuroimaging responses to extreme out-groups. *Psychological Science, 17,* 847–853.

Harris, M. J., & Rosenthal, R. (1985). Mediation of interpersonal expectancy effects: 31 meta-analyses. *Psychological Bulletin, 97,* 363–386.

Harris, M. J., & Rosenthal, R. (1986). Four factors in the mediation of teacher expectancy effects. In R. S. Feldman (Ed.), *The social psychology of education.* New York: Cambridge University Press.

Harrison, A. A. (1977). Mere exposure. In L. Berkowitz (Ed.), *Advances in experimental social psychology* (Vol. 10). New York: Academic Press, 39–83.

Hart, A. J., & Morry, M. M. (1997). Trait inferences based on racial and behavioral cues. *Basic and Applied Social Psychology, 19,* 33–48.

Hart, C. (1998). *Doing a literature review: Releasing the social science research imagination.* London: Sage.

Hart, W., Albarracin, D., Eagly, A. H., Brechan, I., Lindberg, M. J., & Merrill, L. (2009). Feeling validated versus being correct: A meta-analysis of selective exposure to information. *Psychological Bulletin, 135,* 555–588.

Hartl, A. C., Laursen, B., & Cillessen, A. H. (2015). A survival analysis of adolescent friendships: The downside of dissimilarity. *Psychological Science, 26,* 1304–1315.

Hasan, Y., Begue, L., & Bushman, B. J. (2012). Viewing the world through "blood-red tinted glasses": The hostile expectation bias mediates the link between violent video game exposure and aggression. *Journal of Experimental Social Psychology, 48,* 953–956.

Hasan, Y., Begue, L., Scharkow, M., & Bushman, B. J. (2013). The more you play, the more aggressive you become: A long-term experimental study of cumulative violent video game effects on hostile expectations and aggressive behavior. *Journal of Experimental Social Psychology, 49,* 224–227.

Haselton, M. G., & Nettle, D. (2006). The paranoid optimist: An integrative evolutionary model of cognitive biases. *Personality and Social Psychology Review, 10,* 47.

Haslam, C., Cruwys, T., & Haslam, S. A. (2014). "The we's have it": Evidence for the distinctive benefits of group engagement in enhancing cognitive health in aging. *Social Science & Medicine, 120,* 57–66.

Haslam, S. A., Reicher, S. D., & Van Bavel, J. J. (2019). Rethinking the nature of cruelty: The role of identity leadership in the Stanford Prison Experiment. *American Psychologist, 74*(7), 809–822. https://doi-org.library.smu.ca/10.1037/amp0000443.supp (Supplemental)

Hass, R. G., Katz, I., Rizzo, N., Bailey, J., & Eisenstadt, D. (1991). Cross-racial appraisal as related to attitude ambivalence and cognitive complexity. *Personality and Social Psychology Bulletin, 17,* 83–92.

Hastall, M. R., & Wagner, A. J. M. (2018). Enhancing selective exposure to health messages and health intentions: Effects of susceptibility cues and gain–loss framing. *Journal of Media Psychology: Theories, Methods, and Applications, 30*(4), 217–231. https://doi- org.library.smu.ca/10.1027/1864-1105/a000197

Hastie, R., Penrod, S. D., & Pennington, N. (1983). *Inside the jury.* Cambridge, MA: Harvard University Press.

Hatfield, E. (1988). Passionate and compassionate love. In R. J. Sternberg & M. L. Barnes (Eds.), *The psychology of love.* New Haven, CT: Yale University Press.

Hatfield (Walster), E., Aronson, V., Abrahams, D., & Rottman, L. (1966). Importance of physical attractiveness in dating behavior. *Journal of Personality and Social Psychology, 4,* 508–516.

Hatfield, E., Cacioppo, J. T., & Rapson, R. (1992). The logic of emotion: Emotional contagion. In M. S. Clark (Ed.), *Review of personality and social psychology.* Newbury Park, CA: Sage.

Hatfield, E., & Rapson, R. L. (1987). Passionate love/sexual desire: Can the same paradigm explain both? *Archives of Sexual Behavior, 16,* 259–278.

Hatfield, E., & Sprecher, S. (1986). *Mirror, mirror: The importance of looks in everyday life.* Albany, NY: SUNY Press.

Hatfield, E., Traupmann, J., Sprecher, S., Utne, M., & Hay, J. (1985). Equity and intimate relations: Recent research. In W. Ickes (Ed.), *Compatible and incompatible relationships.* New York: Springer-Verlag.

Hatfield, E., & Walster, G. W. (1978). *A new look at love.* Reading, MA: Addison-Wesley. (Note: originally published as Walster, E., & Walster, G. W.)

Hatzenbuehler, M. L. (2014). Structural stigma and the health of lesbian, gay, and bisexual populations. *Current Directions in Psychological Science, 23,* 127–132.

Hatzfeld, J. (2007). *Machete season: The killers in Rwanda speak.* New York: Farrar, Straus and Giroux.

Haugtvedt, C. P., & Wegener, D. T. (1994). Message order effects in persuasion: An attitude strength perspective. *Journal of Consumer Research, 21,* 205–218.

Havas, D. A., Glenberg, A. M., Gutowski, K. A., Lucarelli, M. J., & Davidson, R. J. (2010). Cosmetic use of Botulinum Toxin-A affects processing of emotional language. *Psychological Science, 21,* 895–900.

Hawkley, L. C., Williams, K. D., & Cacioppo, J. T. (2011). Responses to ostracism across adulthood. *Social, Cognitive, and Affective Neuroscience, 6,* 234–243.

Hays, N. A., & Goldstein, N. J. (2015). Power and legitimacy influence conformity. *Journal of Experimental Social Psychology, 60,* 17–26.

Hayward, L. E., Tropp, L. R., Hornsey, M. J., & Barlow, F. K. (2017). Toward a comprehensive understanding of intergroup contact: Descriptions and mediators of positive and negative contact among majority and minority groups. *Personality and Social Psychology Bulletin, 43,* 347–364.

Hayward, L. E., Tropp, L. R., Hornsey, M. J., & Barlow, F. K. (2018). How negative contact and positive contact with whites predict collective action among racial and ethnic minorities. *British Journal of Social Psychology, 57,* 1–20.

Hazan, C. (2004). Intimate attachment/capacity to love and be loved. In C. Peterson & M. E. P. Seligman (Eds.), *The values in action classification of strengths and virtues.* Washington, DC: American Psychological Association.

Hazan, C., & Shaver, P. R. (1994). Attachment as an organizational framework for research on close relationships. *Psychological Inquiry, 5,* 1–22.

He, Y., Ebner, N. C., & Johnson, M. K. (2011). What predicts the own-age bias in face recognition memory? *Social Cognition, 29,* 97–109.

Headey, B., & Wearing, A. (1987). The sense of relative superiority—central to well-being. *Social Indicators Research, 20,* 497–516.

Health Canada. (2012). Canadian tobacco use monitoring survey (CTUMS). Retrieved from http://www.hc-sc.gc.ca/hc-ps/tobac-tabac/research-recherche/stat/ctums-esutc_2012-eng.php

Heap, B., & Comim, F. (2005). Consumption and happiness: Christian values and an approach towards sustainability. Capability and Sustainability Centre, St. Edmund's College, University of Cambridge. Address to Christians in Science annual meeting.

Hearold, S. (1986). A synthesis of 1043 effects of television on social behavior. In G. Comstock (Ed.), *Public communication and behavior* (Vol. 1). Orlando, FL: Academic Press.

Hedge, A., & Yousif, Y. H. (1992). Effects of urban size, urgency, and cost on helpfulness: A cross-cultural comparison between the United Kingdom and the Sudan. *Journal of Cross-Cultural Psychology, 23,* 107–115.

Hehman, E., Flake, J. K., & Calanchini, J. (2018). Disproportionate use of lethal force in policing is associated with regional racial biases of residents. *Social Psychological and Personality Science,* in press.

Hehman, E., Flake, J. K., & Freeman, J. B. (2018). The faces of group members share physical resemblance. *Personality and Social Psychology Bulletin, 44,* 3–15.

Hehman, E., Gaertner, S. L., Dovidio, J. F., Mania, E. W., Guerra, R., Wilson, D. C., & Friel, B. M. (2012). Group status drives majority and minority integration preferences. *Psychological Science, 23,* 46–52.

Heider, F. (1958). *The psychology of interpersonal relations.* New York: Wiley.

Heine, S. J., & Hamamura, T. (2007). In search of East Asian self-enhancement. *Personality and Social Psychology Review, 11,* 4–27.

Heine, S. J., Kitayama, S., Lehman, D. R., Takata, T., Ide, E., Leung, C., & Matsumoto, H. (2001). Divergent consequences of success and failure in Japan and North America: An investigation of self- improving motivations and malleable selves. *Journal of Personality and Social Psychology, 81,* 599–615.

Heine, S. J., & Lehman, D. R. (1995). Cultural variation in unrealistic optimism: Does the West feel more invulnerable than the East? *Journal of Personality and Social Psychology, 68,* 595–607.

Heine, S. J., & Lehman, D. R. (1997a). Culture, dissonance, and self-affirmation. *Personality and Social Psychology Bulletin, 23,* 389–400.

Heine, S. J., & Lehman, D. R. (1997b). The cultural construction of self-enhancement: An examination of group-serving biases. *Journal of Personality and Social Psychology, 72,* 1268–1283.

Heine, S. J., Lehman, D. R., Markus, H. R., & Kitayama, S. (1999). Is there a universal need for positive self-regard? *Psychological Review, 106,* 766–794.

Heine, S. J., Takemoto, T., Moskalenko, S., Lasaleta, J., & Heinrich, J. (2008). Mirrors in the head: Cultural variation in objective self-awareness. *Personality and Social Psychology Bulletin, 34,* 879–887.

Heintzman, C. (2011). Stephen Reid and the Stopwatch Gang. *Zero1Magazine.com.* Retrieved from: http://zero1magazine.com/2011/01/stephen-reidstopwatch-gang-video/

Hellman, P. (1980). *Avenue of the righteous of nations.* New York: Atheneum.

Helmrich, R. L. (1997, May). Managing human error in aviation. *Scientific American,* 62–67.

Helweg-Larsen, M., & LoMonaco, B. L. (2008). Queuing among U2 fans: Reactions to social norm violations. *Journal of Applied Social Psychology, 38,* 2378–2393.

Helzer, E. G., & Dunning, D. (2012). Why and when peer prediction is superior to self-prediction: The weight given to future aspiration versus past achievement. *Journal of Personality and Social Psychology Bulletin, 103,* 38–53.

Hemsley, G. D., & Doob, A. N. (1978). The effect of looking behavior on perceptions of a communicator's credibility. *Journal of Applied Social Psychology, 8,* 136–144.

Hendersen-King, E. I., & Nisbett, R. E. (1996). Anti-black prejudice as a function of exposure to the negative behavior of a single black person. *Journal of Personality and Social Psychology, 71,* 654–664.

Hendrick, S. S., & Hendrick, C. (1995). Gender differences and similarities in sex and love. *Personal Relationships, 2,* 55–65.

Hendrick, S. S., Hendrick, C., & Adler, N. L. (1988). Romantic relationships: Love, satisfaction, and staying together. *Journal of Personality and Social Psychology, 54,* 980–988.

Hennenlotter, A., Dresel, C., Castrop, F., Ceballos Baumann, A., Wohschlager, A., & Haslinger, B. (2008). The link between facial feedback and neural activity within central circuitries of emotion: New insights from Botulinum Toxin-induced denervation of frown muscles. *Cerebral Cortex, 19,* 537–542.

Hennigan, K. M., Del Rosario, M. L., Health, L., Cook, T. D., Wharton, J. D., & Calder, B. J. (1982) Impact of the introduction of television on crime in the United States: Empirical findings and theoretical implications. *Journal of Personality and Social Psychology, 42,* 461–477.

Henrich, J., McElreath, R., Barr, A., Ensminger, J., Barrett, C., Bolyanatz, A., Cardenas, J. C., Gurven, M., Gwako, E., Henrich, N., Lesorogol, C., Marlowe, F., Tracer, D., & Ziker, J. (2006). Costly punishment across human societies. *Science, 312,* 1767–1770.

Henslin, M. (1967). Craps and magic. *American Journal of Sociology, 73,* 316–330.

Hepper, E. G., & Carnelley, K. B. (2012). The self-esteem roller coaster: Adult attachment moderates the impact of daily feedback. *Personal Relationships, 19,* 504–520.

Hepworth, J. T., & West, S. G. (1988). Lynchings and the economy: A time-series reanalysis of Hovland and Sears (1940). *Journal of Personality and Social Psychology, 55,* 239–247.

Heradstveit, D. (1979). *The Arab-Israeli conflict: Psychological obstacles to peace* (Vol. 28). Oslo, Norway: Universitetsforlaget. Distributed by Columbia University Press. Reviewed by R. K. White (1980), *Contemporary Psychology, 25,* 11–12.

Herbenick, D., Reece, M., Schick, V., S. A., Dodge, B., & Fortenberry, J. D. (2010). Sexual behaviors, relationships, and perceived health among adult women in the United States: Results from a national probability sample. *Journal of Sexual Medicine, 7* (suppl 5), 277–290.

Herlocker, C. E., Allison, S. T., Foubert, J. D., & Beggan, J. K. (1997). Intended and unintended overconsumption of physical, spatial, and temporal resources. *Journal of Personality and Social Psychology, 73,* 992–1004.

Hernandez, I., & Preston, J. L. (2013). Disfluency disrupts the confirmation bias. *Journal of Experimental Social Psychology, 49,* 178–182.

Herring, D. R., White, K. R., Jabeen, L. N., Hinojos, M., Terrazas, G., Reyes, S. M., Taylor, J. H., & Crites, S. J. (2013). On the automatic activation of attitudes: A quarter century of evaluative priming research. *Psychological Bulletin, 139,* 1062–1089.

Herzog, S. M., & Hertwig, R. (2009). The wisdom of many in one mind: Improving individual judgments with dialectical bootstrapping. *Psychological Science, 20,* 231–237.

Heslin, P. A. (2009). Better than brainstorming? Potential contextual boundary conditions to brainwriting for idea generation in organizations. *Journal of Occupational and Organizational Psychology, 82,* 129–145.

Hewstone, M. (1990). The "ultimate attribution error"? A review of the literature on intergroup causal attribution. *European Journal of Social Psychology, 20,* 311–335.

Hewstone, M. (1994). Revision and change of stereotypic beliefs: In search of the elusive subtyping model. In S. Stroebe & M. Hewstone (Eds.), *European review of social psychology* (Vol. 5). Chichester, England: Wiley.

Hewstone, M., & Fincham, F. (1996). Attribution theory and research: Basic issues and applications. In M. Hewstone, W. Stroebe, and G. M. Stephenson (Eds.), *Introduction to social psychology: A European perspective.* Oxford, UK: Blackwell..

Hewstone, M., Hopkins, N., & Routh, D. A. (1992). Cognitive models of stereotype change: Generalization and subtyping in young people's views of the police. *European Journal of Social Psychology, 22,* 219–234.

Hewstone, M., Lolliot, S., Swart, H., Myers, E., Voci, A., Al Ramiah, A., & Cairns, E. (2014). Intergroup contact and intergroup conflict. *Peace and Conflict: Journal of Peace Psychology, 20,* 39–53.

Hideg, I., & Ferris, D. L. (2016). The compassionate sexist? How benevolent sexism promotes and undermines gender equality in the workplace. *Journal of Personality and Social Psychology, 111,* 706–727.

Higbee, K. L., Millard, R. J., & Folkman, J. R. (1982). Social psychology research during the 1970s: Predominance of experimentation and college students. *Personality and Social Psychology Bulletin, 8,* 180–183.

Higgins, E. T., & McCann, C. D. (1984). Social encoding and subsequent attitudes, impressions and memory: "Context-driven" and motivational aspects of processing. *Journal of Personality and Social Psychology, 47,* 26–39.

Higgins, E. T., & Rholes, W. S. (1978). Saying is believing: Effects of message modification on memory and liking for the person described. *Journal of Experimental Social Psychology, 14,* 363–378.

Hilgard, J., Engelhardt, C. R., & Rouder, J. N. (2017). Overstated evidence for short-term effects of violent games on affect and behavior: A reanalysis of Anderson et al. (2010). *Psychological Bulletin, 143,* 757–774.

Hilkenmeier, F. (2018). The impact of motive disposition on group performance. *Cogent Psychology, 5*(1). https://doi-org.library.smu.ca/10.1080/23311908.2018.1507123

Hills, P. J., Dickinson, D., Daniels, L. M., Boobyer, C. A., & Burton, R. (2019). Being observed caused physiological stress leading to poorer face recognition. *Acta Psychologica, 196,* 118–128. https://doi-org.library.smu.ca/10.1016/j.actpsy.2019.04.012

Hilmert, C. J., Kulik, J. A., & Christenfeld, N. J. S. (2006). Positive and negative opinion modeling: The influence of another's similarity and dissimilarity. *Journal of Personality and Social Psychology, 90,* 440.

Hilton, J. L., & von Hippel, W. (1990). The role of consistency in the judgment of stereotype-relevant behaviors. *Personality and Social Psychology Bulletin, 16,* 430–448.

Hine, D. W., & Gifford, R. (1996). Attributions about self and others in commons dilemmas. *European Journal of Social Psychology, 26,* 429–445.

Hinsz, V. B. (1990). Cognitive and consensus processes in group recognition memory performance. *Journal of Personality and Social Psychology, 59,* 705–718.

Hinsz, V. B., Tindale, R. S., & Vollrath, D. A. (1997). The emerging conceptualization of groups as information processors. *Psychological Bulletin, 121,* 43–64.

Hirschman, R. S., & Leventhal, H. (1989). Preventing smoking behavior in school children: An initial test of a cognitive-development program. *Journal of Applied Social Psychology, 19,* 559–583.

Hirt, E. R. (1990). Do I see only what I expect? Evidence for an expectancy-guided retrieval model. *Journal of Personality and Social Psychology, 58,* 937–951.

Hitsch, G. J., Hortacsu, A., & Ariely, D. (2006, February). What makes you click? Mate preferences and matching outcomes in online dating. MIT Sloan Research Paper No. 4603–06. Retrieved from http://ssrn.com/abstract=895442

Hobden, K. L., & Olson, J. M. (1994). From jest to antipathy: Disparagement humor as a source of dissonance-motivated attitude change. *Basic and Applied Social Psychology, 15,* 239–249.

Hodges, B. H., & Geyer, A. L. (2006). A nonconformist account of the Asch experiments: Values, pragmatics, and moral dilemmas. *Personality and Social Psychology Review, 10,* 2.

Hoffman, L. W. (1977). Changes in family roles, socialization, and sex differences. *American Psychologist, 32,* 644–657.

Hoffman, M. L. (1981). Is altruism part of human nature? *Journal of Personality and Social Psychology, 40,* 121–137.

Hofling, C. K., Brotzman, E., Dalrymple, S., Graves, N., & Pierce, C. M. (1966). An experimental study in nurse-physician relationships. *The Journal of Nervous and Mental Disease, 143*(2), 171–180.

Hofmann, W., De Houwer, J., Perugini, M., Baeyens, F., & Crombez, G. (2010). Evaluative conditioning in humans: A meta-analysis. *Psychological Review, 136,* 390–421.

Hofmeister, B. (2010). Bridging the gap: Using social psychology to design market interventions to overcome the energy efficiency gap in residential energy markets. *Southeastern Environmental Law Journal, 19,* pp. 1ff.

Hogan, R., Curphy, G. J., & Hogan, J. (1994). What we know about leadership: Effectiveness and personality. *American Psychologist, 49,* 493–504.

Hogg, M. (2014). From uncertainty to extremism: Social categorization and identity formation. *Current Directions in Psychological Science, 23,* 338–342.

Hogg, M. A. (1992). *The social psychology of group cohesiveness: From attraction to social identity.* London: Harvester Wheatsheaf.

Hogg, M. A. (2010). Human groups, social categories, and collective self: Social identity and the management of self-uncertainty. In R. M. Arkin, K. C. Oleson, & P. J. Carroll (Eds.), *Handbook of the uncertain self.* New York: Psychology Press, 2010.

Hogg, M. A., Abrams, D., & Brewer, M. B. (2017). Social identity: The role of self in group processes and intergroup relations. *Group Processes & Intergroup Relations, 20,* 570–581.

Hogg, M. A., & Hains, S. C. (1998). Friendship and group identification: A new look at the role of cohesiveness in groupthink. *European Journal of Social Psychology, 28,* 323.

Hogg, M. A., Turner, J. C., & Davidson, B. (1990). Polarized norms and social frames of reference: A test of the self-categorization theory of group polarization. *Basic and Applied Social Psychology, 11,* 77–100.

Hohnen, J. (2000, March). My friend Madonna. *Jane,* 116-121.

Holland, R. W., Hendriks, M., & Aarts, H. (2005). Smells like clean spirit: Nonconscious effect of scent on cognition and behavior. *Psychological Science, 16,* 689–693.

Holland, R. W., Meertens, R. M., & Van Vugt, M. (2002). Dissonance on the road: Self-esteem as a moderator of internal and external self-justification strategies. *Personality and Social Psychology Bulletin, 28,* 1712–1724.

Hollander, E. P. (1958). Conformity, status, and idiosyncrasy credit. *Psychological Review, 65,* 117–127.

Holmberg, D., & Holmes, J. G. (1994). Reconstruction of relationship memories: A mental models approach. In N. Schwarz & S. Sudman (Eds.), *Autobiographical memory and the validity of retrospective reports.* New York: Springer-Verlag.

Holmes, J. G., & Rempel, J. K. (1989). Trust in close relationships. In C. Hendrick (Ed.), *Review of personality and social psychology* (Vol. 10). Newbury Park, CA: Sage.

Holoien, D. S., & Fiske, S. T. (2013). Downplaying positive impressions: Compensation between warmth and competence in impression management. *Journal of Experimental Social Psychology, 49,* 33–41.

Holtgraves, T. (1997). Styles of language use: Individual and cultural variability in conversational indirectness. *Journal of Personality and Social Psychology, 73,* 624–637.

Holtgraves, T., & Srull, T. K. (1989). The effects of positive self-descriptions on impressions: General principles and individual differences. *Personality and Social Psychology Bulletin, 15,* 452–462.

Holtzworth, A., & Jacobson, N. S. (1988). An attributional approach to marital dysfunction and therapy. In J. E. Maddux, C. D. Stoltenberg, & R. Rosenwein (Eds.), *Social processes in clinical and counseling psychology.* New York: Springer-Verlag.

Holtzworth-Munroe, A., & Jacobson, N. S. (1985). Causal attributions of married couples: When do they search for causes? What do they conclude when they do? *Journal of Personality and Social Psychology, 48*(6), 1398–1412.

Hom, H., & Van Nuland, A. (2019). Evaluating scientific research: Belief, hindsight bias, ethics, and research evaluation. *Applied Cognitive Psychology, 33,* 675-681. https://doi.org/10.1002/acp.3519

Honigman, R. J., Phillips, K. A., & Castle, D. J. (2004). A review of psychosocial outcomes for patients seeking cosmetic surgery. *Plastic and Reconstructive Surgery, 113,* 1229–1237.

Hoorens, V. (1993). Self-enhancement and superiority biases in social comparison. In W. Stroebe & M. Hewstone (Eds.), *European Review of Social Psychology* (Vol. 4). Chichester, UK: Wiley.

Hoorens, V. (1995). Self-favoring biases, self-presentation and the self-other asymmetry in social comparison. *Journal of Personality, 63,* 793–819.

Hoorens, V., Smits, T., & Shepperd, J. A. (2008). Comparative optimism in the spontaneous generation of future life-events. *British Journal of Social Psychology, 47,* 441–451.

Hoover, C. W., Wood, E. E., & Knowles, E. S. (1983). Forms of social awareness and helping. *Journal of Experimental Social Psychology, 19,* 577–590.

Hormuth, S. E. (1986). Lack of effort as a result of self-focused attention: An attributional ambiguity analysis. *European Journal of Social Psychology, 16,* 181–192.

Horner, V., Proctor, D., Bonnie, K. E., Whiten, A., & de Waal, F. B. M. (2010). Prestige affects cultural learning in chimpanzees. *PLoS One, 5,* e10625. Retrieved from http://www.plosone.org

Hornstein, H. (1976). *Cruelty and kindness.* Englewood Cliffs, NJ: Prentice-Hall.

Horowitz, S. V., & Boardman, S. K. (1994). Managing conflict: Policy and research implications. *Journal of Social Issues, 50,* 197–211.

Hoshino-Browne, E., Zanna, A. S., Spencer, S. J., Zanna, M. P., Kitayama, S., & Lackenbauer, S. (2005). On the cultural guises of cognitive dissonance: The easterners and westerners. *Journal of Personality and Social Psychology, 89,* 294–310.

Houghton, J. (2011). Global warming, climate change and sustainability: A challenge to scientists, policymakers and religious believers. Cambridge, England: The International Society for Science and Religion. Retrieved from http://www.issr.org.uk/latest-news/global warming

House, R. J., & Singh, J. V. (1987). Organizational behavior: Some new directions for I/O psychology. *Annual Review of Psychology, 38,* 669–718.

Houston, D. A., & Fazio, R. H. (1989). Biased processing as a function of attitude accessibility: Making objective judgments subjectively. *Social Cognition, 7*(1), 51–66.

Houston, V., & Bull, R. (1994). Do people avoid sitting next to someone who is facially disfigured? *European Journal of Social Psychology, 24,* 279–284.

Hovland, C. I., Lumsdaine, A. A., & Sheffield, F. D. (1949). *Experiments on mass communication. Studies in social psychology in World War II* (Vol. III). Princeton, NJ: Princeton University Press.

Hovland, C. I., & Sears, R. (1940). Minor studies of aggression: Correlation of lynchings with economic indices. *Journal of Psychology, 9,* 301–310.

Howard, D. J. (1997). Familiar phrases as peripheral persuasion cues. *Journal of Experimental Social Psychology, 33,* 231–243.

Howard, D. J. (2019). A dual process theory explanation for door-in-the-face effectiveness. *Basic and Applied Social Psychology, 41*(5), 273–286. https://doi-org.library.smu.ca/10.1080/01973533.2019.1648265

Howard, J. (2013, January 16). I went after guns. Obama can, too. *New York Times,* p. A27.

Howell, R. T., & Howell, C. J. (2008). The relation of economic status to subjective well-being in developing countries: A meta-analysis. *Psychological Bulletin, 134,* 536–560.

Hoyle, R. H. (1993). Interpersonal attraction in the absence of explicit attitudinal information. *Social Cognition, 11,* 309–320.

Hsee, C. K., & Hastie, R. (2006). Decision and experience: Why don't we choose what makes us happy? *Trends in Cognitive Sciences, 10,* 31–37.

Huang, C. (2017). Time spent on social network sites and psychological well-being: A meta-analysis. *Cyberpsychology, Behavior, and Social Networking, 20,* 346–354.

Huang, C., & Park, D. (2012). Cultural influences on Facebook photographs. *International Journal of Psychology,* 1–10.

Huang, K., Yeomans, M., Brooks, A. W., Minson, K., & Gino, F. (2017). It doesn't hurt to ask: Question-asking increases liking. *Journal of Personality and Social Psychology, 113,* 430–452.

Huart, J., Corneille, O., & Becquart, E. (2005). Face-based categorization, context-based categorization, and distortions in the recollection of gender ambiguous faces. *Journal of Experimental Social Psychology, 41,* 598–608.

Huberman, B., & Lukose, R. (1997). Social dilemmas and internet congestion. *Science, 277,* 535–537.

Huddy, L., & Virtanen, S. (1995). Subgroup differentiation and subgroup bias among Latinos as a function of familiarity and positive distinctiveness. *Journal of Personality and Social Psychology, 68,* 97–108.

Huesmann, L. R., Lagerspetz, K., & Eron, L. D. (1984). Intervening variables in the TV violence-aggression relation: Evidence from two countries. *Developmental Psychology, 20,* 746–775.

Huesmann, L. R., Moise-Titus, J., Podolski, C-L., & Eron, L. D. (2003). Longitudinal relations between children's exposure to TV violence and their aggressive and violent behavior in young adulthood:

1977–1992. *Developmental Psychology, 39,* 201–222.

Hüffmeier, J., Krumm, S., Kanthak, J., & Hertel, G. (2012). "Don't let the group down": Facets of instrumentality moderate the motivating effects of groups in a field experiment. *European Journal of Social Psychology, 42*(5), 533–538.

Hugenberg, K., & Bodenhausen, G. V. (2003). Facing prejudice: Implicit prejudice and the perception of facial threat. *Psychological Science, 14,* 640–643.

Hui, C. H., Triandis, H. C., & Yee, C. (1991). Cultural differences in reward allocation: Is collectivism the explanation? *British Journal of Social Psychology, 30,* 145–157.

Hull, J. G., & Young, R. D. (1983). The self-awareness-reducing effects of alcohol consumption: Evidence and implications. In J. Suls & A. G. Greenwald (Eds.), *Psychological perspectives on the self* (Vol. 2). Hillsdale, NJ: Erlbaum.

Human, L. J., Biesanz, J. C., Prisotto, K. L., & Dunn, E. W. (2012). Your best self helps reveal your true self: Positive self-presentation leads to more accurate personality impressions. *Social Psychological and Personality Science, 3,* 23–30.

Hunt, L. L., Eastwick, P. W., & Finkel, E. J. (2015). Leveling the playing field: Longer acquaintance predicts reduced assortative mating on attractiveness. *Psychological Science, 26,* 1046–1053.

Hunt, P. J., & Hillery, J. M. (1973). Social facilitation in a location setting: An examination of the effects over learning trials. *Journal of Experimental Social Psychology, 9,* 563–571.

Hunt, R., & Jensen, J. (2007). The experiences of young gay people in Britain's schools. *Stonewall* (www.stonewall.org.uk).

Hussak, L. J., & Cimpian, A. (2015). An early-emerging explanatory heuristic promotes support for the status quo. *Journal of Personality and Social Psychology, 109,* 739–752.

Huston, A. C., Donnerstein, E., Fairchild, H., Feshbach, N. D., Katz, P. A., & Murray, J. P. (1992). *Big world, small screen: The role of television in American society.* Lincoln, NE: University of Nebraska Press.

Huston, T. L., & Chorost, A. F. (1994). Behavioral buffers on the effect of negativity on marital satisfaction: A longitudinal study. *Personal Relationships, 1,* 223–239.

Hutnik, N. (1985). Aspects of identity in a multi-ethnic society. *New Community, 12,* 298–309.

Huxley, L. (1900). *The life and letters of Thomas Henry Huxley. 2 vols 8vo,* London: Macmillan.

Hvistendahl, M. (2009). Making every baby girl count. *Science, 323,* 1164–1166.

Hvistendahl, M. (2010). Has China outgrown the one-child policy? *Science, 329,* 1458–1461.

Hvistendahl, M. (2011). *Unnatural selection: Choosing boys over girls, and the consequences of a world full of men.* New York: PublicAffairs.

Hyde, J. S., Mezulis, A. H., & Abramson, L. Y. (2008). The ABCs of depression: Integrating affective, biological, and cognitive models to explain the emergence of the gender difference in depression. *Psychological Review, 115,* 291–313.

Hyman, H. H., & Sheatsley, P. B. (1956 & 1964). Attitudes toward desegregation. *Scientific American, 195*(6), 35–39, and *211*(1), 16–23.

Ickes, B. (1980). *On disconfirming our perceptions of others.* Paper presented at the American Psychological Association convention.

Ickes, W., Layden, M. A., & Barnes, R. D. (1978). Objective self-awareness and individuation: An empirical link. *Journal of Personality, 46,* 146–161.

Ickes, W., Patterson, M. L., Rajecki, D. W., & Tanford, S. (1982). Behavioral and cognitive consequences of reciprocal versus compensatory responses to preinteraction expectancies. *Social Cognition, 1,* 160–190.

Ijzerman, H., & Semin, G. R. (2009). The thermometer of social relations: Mapping social proximity on temperature. *Psychological Science, 20,* 1214–1220.

Imai, Y. (1994). Effects of influencing attempts on the perceptions of powerholders and the powerless. *Journal of Social Behavior and Personality, 9,* 455–468.

Imhoff, R., & Banse, R. (2009). Ongoing victim suffering increases prejudice: The case of secondary anti-Semitism. *Psychological Science, 20,* 1443–1447.

Imhoff, R., Dotsch, R., Bianchi, M., Banse, R., & Wigboldus, D. (2011). Facing Europe: Visualizing spontaneous ingroup projection. *Psychological Science, 22,* 1583–1590.

Imhoff, R., & Erb, H-P. (2009). What motivates nonconformity? Uniqueness seeking blocks majority influence. *Personality and Social Psychology Bulletin, 35,* 309–320.

Indo-Asian News Service. (2013, March 13). Child killed after imitating TV hanging scene. Retrieved from http://www.ndtv.com/article/cities/child-killed-after-imitating-tv-hanging-scene-346554

Ingham, A. G., Levinger, G., Graves, J., & Peckham, V. (1974). The Ringelmann effect: Studies of group size and group performance. *Journal of Experimental Social Psychology, 10,* 371–384.

Inglehart, M. R., Markus, H., & Brown, D. R. (1989). The effects of possible selves on academic achievement—a panel study. In J. P. Forgas & J. M. Innes (Eds.), *Recent advances in social psychology: An international perspective.* Amsterdam: North-Holland–Elsevier Science Publishers.

Inglehart, R. (1990). *Culture shift in advanced industrial society.* Princeton, NJ: Princeton University Press.

Inglehart, R. F., & Welzel, C. (2005). Liberalism, postmaterialism and the growth of freedom. *International Review of Sociology, 15,* 81–108.

Insko, C. A., Nacoste, R. W., & Moe, J. L. (1983). Belief congruence and racial discrimination: Review of the evidence and critical evaluation. *European Journal of Social Psychology, 13,* 153–174.

International Telecommunication Union (ITU). (2010). *The world in 2010: ICT facts and figures.* ITU. Retrieved from http://www.itu.int/ict

Inzlicht, M., McKay, L., & Aronson, J. (2006). Stigma as ego depletion: How being the target of prejudice affects self-control. *Psychological Science, 17,* 262–269.

Inzlicht, M., & Schmeichel, B. J. (2012). What is ego depletion? Toward a mechanistic revision of the resource model of self-control. *Perspectives on Psychological Science, 7,* 450–463.

Ireland, M. E., & Pennebaker, J. W. (2010). Language style matching in writing: Synchrony in essays, correspondence, and poetry. *Journal of Personality and Social Psychology, 99,* 549–571.

Ireland, M. E., Slatcher, R. B., Eastwick, P. W., Scissors, L. E., Finkel, E. J., & Pennebaker, J. W. (2011). Language style matching predicts relationship initiation and stability. *Psychological Science, 22,* 39–44.

Isaac, M. S., & Poor, M. (2016). The sleeper framing effect: The influence of frame valence on immediate and retrospective judgments. *Journal of Consumer Psychology, 26*(1), 53–65.

Isen, A. M., Clark, M., & Schwartz, M. F. (1976). Duration of the effect of good mood on helping: Footprints on the sands of time. *Journal of Personality and Social Psychology, 34,* 385–393.

Isen, A. M., & Means, B. (1983). The influence of positive affect on decision-making strategy. *Social Cognition, 2,* 28–31.

Isen, A. M., Shalker, T. E., Clark, M., & Karp, L. (1978). Affect, accessibility of material in memory, and behavior: A cognitive loop. *Journal of Personality and Social Psychology, 36,* 1–12.

Isozaki, M. (1984). The effect of discussion on polarization of judgments. *Japanese Psychological Research, 26,* 187–193.

Ito, T. A., Miller, N., & Pollock, V. E. (1996). Alcohol and aggression: A meta-analysis on the moderating effects of inhibitory cues, triggering events, and self-focused attention. *Psychological Bulletin, 120,* 60–82.

Iyengar, S., & Westwood, S. J. (2015). Fear and loathing across party lines: New evidence on group polarization. *American Journal of Political Science, 59*(3), 690–707.

Iyengar, S. S., & Lepper, M. R. (2000). When choice is demotivating: Can one desire too much of a good thing? *Journal of Personality and Social Psychology, 79,* 995–1006.

Jäckle, S., & Wenzelburger, G. (2015). Religion, religiosity, and the attitudes toward homosexuality—A multilevel analysis of 79 countries. *Journal of Homosexuality, 62,* 207-241.

Jackman, M. R., & Senter, M. S. (1981). Beliefs about race, gender, and social class different, therefore unequal: Beliefs about trait differences between groups of unequal status. In D. J. Treiman & R. V. Robinson (Eds.), *Research in stratification and mobility* (Vol. 2). Greenwich, CT: JAI Press.

Jackson, J. M., & Latané, B. (1981). All alone in front of all those people: Stage fright as a function of number and type of co-performers and audience. *Journal of Personality and Social Psychology, 40,* 73–85.

Jackson, L. A., Hunter, J. E., & Hodge, C. N. (1995). Physical attractiveness and intellectual competence: A meta-analytic review. *Social Psychology Quarterly, 58,* 108–122.

Jackson, L. A., Sullivan, L. A., & Hodge, C. N. (1993). Stereotype effects on attributions, predictions, and evaluations: No two social judgments are quite alike. *Journal of Personality and Social Psychology, 65,* 69–84.

Jacobs, R. C., & Campbell, D. T. (1961). The perpetuation of an arbitrary tradition through several generations of a laboratory microculture. *Journal of Abnormal and Social Psychology, 62,* 649–658.

Jacoby, S. (1986, December). When opposites attract. *Reader's Digest,* 95–98.

Jacques-Tiura, A. J., Abbey, A., Parkhill, M. R., & Zawacki, T. (1997). Why do some men misperceive women's sexual intentions more frequently than others do? An application of the confluence model. *Personality and Social Psychology Bulletin, 33,* 1467–1480.

Jaffe, Y., Shapir, N., & Yinon, Y. (1981). Aggression and its escalation. *Journal of Cross-Cultural Psychology, 12,* 21–36.

Jaffe, Y., & Yinon, Y. (1983). Collective aggression: The group-individual paradigm in the study of collective antisocial behavior. In H. H. Blumberg, A. P. Hare, V. Kent, & M. Davies (Eds.), *Small groups and social interaction* (Vol. 1). Cambridge: Wiley.

James, S. E., Herman, J. L., Rankin, S., Keisling, M., Mottet, L., & Anafi, M. (2016). *Executive summary of the report of the 2015 U.S. Transgender Survey.* Washington, DC: National Center for Transgender Equality.

James, W. (1890, reprinted 1950). *The principles of psychology* (Vol. 2). New York: Dover Publications.

James, W. (1902, reprinted 1958). *The varieties of religious experience.* New York: Mentor Books.

Jamieson, D. W., Lydon, J. E., Stewart, G., & Zanna, M. P. (1987). Pygmalion revisited: New evidence for student expectancy effects in the classroom. *Journal of Educational Psychology, 79,* 461–466.

Jamrozik, A., Oraa Ali, M., Sarwer, D. B., & Chatterjee, A. (2019). More than skin deep: Judgments of individuals with facial disfigurement. *Psychology of Aesthetics, Creativity, and the Arts, 13, 117-129.*

Janis, I. (1989). *Crucial decisions: Leadership in policymaking and crisis management.* New York: Free Press.

Janis, I. L. (1971, November). Groupthink. *Psychology Today,* 43–46.

Janis, I. L. (1982). Counteracting the adverse effects of concurrence-seeking in policy-planning groups: Theory and research perspectives. In H. Brandstatter, J. H. Davis, & G. Stocker-Kreichgauer (Eds.), *Group decision making.* New York: Academic Press.

Janis, I. L., Kaye, D., & Kirschner, P. (1965). Facilitating effects of eating while reading on responsiveness to persuasive communications. *Journal of Personality and Social Psychology, 1,* 181–186.

Jankowiak, W. R., & Fischer, E. F. (1992). A cross-cultural perspective on romantic love. *Ethnology, 31,* 149–155.

Jaremka, L. M., Gabriel, S., & Carvallo, M. (2011). What makes us feel the best also makes us feel the worst: The emotional impact of independent and interdependent experiences. *Self and Identity, 10,* 44–63.

Jason, L. A., Rose, T., Ferrari, J. R., & Barone, R. (1984). Personal versus impersonal methods for recruiting blood donations. *Journal of Social Psychology, 123,* 139–140.

Jelalian, E., & Miller, A. G. (1984). The perseverance of beliefs: Conceptual perspectives and research developments. *Journal of Social and Clinical Psychology, 2,* 25–56.

Jellison, J. M., & Green, J. (1981). A self-presentation approach to the fundamental attribution error: The norm of internality. *Journal of Personality and Social Psychology, 40,* 643–649.

Jemmott, J. B., III., & Locke, S. E. (1984). Psychosocial factors, immunologic mediation, and human susceptibility to infectious diseases: How much do we know? *Psychological Bulletin, 95,* 78–108.

Jenkins, A. C., Macrae, C. N., & Mitchell, J. P. (2008). Repetition suppression of ventromedial prefrontal activity during judgments of self and others. *Proceedings of the National Academy of Sciences, 105,* 4507–4512. Retrieved from http://www.pnas.org

Jennings, D. L., Amabile, T. M., & Ross, L. (1982). Informal covariation assessment: Data-based vs theory-based judgments. In D. Kahneman, P. Slovic, & A. Tversky (Eds.), *Judgment under uncertainty: Heuristics and biases.* New York: Cambridge University Press.

Jetten, J., Hornsey, M. J., & Adarves-Yorno, I. (2006). When group members admit to being conformist: The role of relative intragroup status in conformity self-reports. *Personality and Social Psychology Bulletin, 32,* 162.

Ji, L., Guo, T., Zhang, Z., & Messervey, D. (2009). Looking into the past: Cultural differences in perception and representation of past information. *Journal of Personality and Social Psychology, 96,* 761–769.

Jiang, L. C., Bazarova, N. N., & Hancock, J. T. (2013). From perception to behavior: Disclosure reciprocity and the intensification of intimacy in computer-mediated communication. *Communication Research, 40,* 125–143.

Job, V., Dweck, C., & Walton, G. (2010). Ego depletion: Is it all in your head? Implicit theories about willpower affect self-regulation. *Psychological Science, 21,* 1686–1693.

Joel, S., Eastwick, P. W., & Finkel, E. J. (2017). Is romantic desire predictable? Machine learning applied to initial romantic attraction. *Psychological Science, 28,* 1478–1489.

John, L. K., Loewenstein, G., & Prelec, D. (2012). Measuring the prevalence of questionable research practices with incentives for truth telling. *Psychological Science, 23,* 524–532.

Johnson, A. L., Crawford, M. T., Sherman, S. J., Rutchick, A. M., Hamilton, D. L., Ferreira, M. B., & Petrocelli, J. V. (2006). A functional perspective on group memberships: Differential need fulfillment in group typology. *Journal of Experimental Social Psychology, 42,* 707–719.

Johnson, B. T., & Eagly, A. H. (1990). Involvement and persuasion: Types, traditions, and the evidence. *Psychological Bulletin, 107,* 375–384.

Johnson, C. S., Olson, M. A., & Fazio, R. H. (2009). Getting acquainted in interracial interactions: Avoiding intimacy but approaching race. *Personality and Social Psychology Bulletin, 35,* 557–571.

Johnson, D. J., & Rusbult, C. E. (1989). Resisting temptation: Devaluation of alternative partners as a means of maintaining commitment in close relationships. *Journal of Personality and Social Psychology, 57,* 967–980.

Johnson, D. W., & Johnson, R. T. (1995). Teaching students to be peacemakers: Results of five years of research. *Peace and Conflict: Journal of Peace Psychology, 1,* 417–438.

Johnson, D. W., & Johnson, R. T. (2003). Field testing integrative negotiations. *Peace and Conflict, 9,* 39–68.

Johnson, D. W., Maruyama, G., Johnson, R., Nelson, D., & Skon, L. (1981). Effects of cooperative, competitive, and individualistic goal structures on achievement: A meta-analysis. *Psychological Bulletin, 89,* 47–62.

Johnson, J. D., Jackson, L. A., & Gatto, L. (1995). Violent attitudes and deferred academic aspirations: Deleterious effects of exposure to rap music. *Basic and Applied Social Psychology, 16,* 27–41.

Johnson, J. G., Cohen, P., Smailes, E. M., Kasen, S. & Brook, J. S. (2002). Television viewing and aggressive behavior during adolescence and adulthood. *Science, 295,* 2468–2471.

Johnson, M. H., & Magaro, P. A. (1987). Effects of mood and severity on memory processes in depression and mania. *Psychological Bulletin, 101,* 28–40.

Johnson, M. K., Rowatt, W. C., Barnard-Brak, L. M., Patock-Peckham, J. A., LaBouff, J. P., & Carlisle, R. D. (2011). A mediational analysis of the role of right-wing authoritarianism and religious fundamentalism in the religiosity-prejudice link. *Personality and Individual Differences, 50,* 851–856.

Johnson, R. D., & Downing, L. J. (1979). Deindividuation and valence of cues: Effects of prosocial and antisocial behavior. *Journal of Personality and Social Psychology, 37,* 1532–1538.

Johnson, R. W., Kelly, R. J., & LeBlanc, B. A. (1995). Motivational basis of dissonance: Aversive consequences or inconsistency. *Personality and Social Psychology Bulletin, 21,* 850–855.

Johnson, W., & Krueger, R. F. (2006). How money buys happiness: Genetic and environmental processes linking finances and life satisfaction. *Journal of Personality and Social Psychology, 90,* 680.

Joiner, T. E., Jr. (1999). The clustering and contagion of suicide. *Current Directions in Psychological Science, 8,* 89–92.

Joinson, A. N. (2001). Self-disclosure in computer-mediated communication: The role of self-awareness and visual anonymity. *European Journal of Social Psychology, 31,* 177–192.

Joly-Mascheroni, R. M., Senju, A., & Shepherd, A. J. (2008). Dogs catch human yawns. *Biology Letters, 4*(5), 446-448.

Jonas, E., Schulz-Hardt, S., & Frey, D. (2005). Giving advice or making decisions in someone else's place: The influence of impression, defense, and accuracy motivation on the search for new information. *Personality and Social Psychology Bulletin, 31*, 977–990.

Jonas, K. (1992). Modelling and suicide: A test of the Werther effect. *British Journal of Social Psychology, 31,* 295–306.

Jonason, P. K., Garcia, J. R., Webster, G. D., Li, N. P., & Fisher, H. E. (2015). Relationship dealbreakers: Traits people avoid in potential mates. *Personality and Social Psychology Bulletin, 41*, 1697–1711.

Jones, C. R., Fazio, R. H., & Olson, M. A. (2009). Implicit misattribution as a mechanism underlying evaluative conditioning. *Journal of Personality and Social Psychology, 96,* 933–948.

Jones, E. E. (1964). *Ingratiation.* New York: Appleton-Century-Crofts.

Jones, E. E. (1976). How do people perceive the causes of behavior? *American Scientist, 64,* 300–305.

Jones, E. E., & Davis, K. E. (1965). From acts to dispositions: The attribution process in person perception. In L. Berkowitz (Ed.), *Advances in experimental social psychology* (Vol. 2). New York: Academic Press.

Jones, E. E., & Harris, V. A. (1967). The attribution of attitudes. *Journal of Experimental Social Psychology, 3,* 2–24.

Jones, E. E., & Nisbett, R. E. (1971). *The actor and the observer: Divergent perceptions of the cases of behavior.* Morristown, NJ: General Learning Press.

Jones, E. E., Rock, L., Shaver, K. G., Goethals, G. R., & Ward, L. M. (1968). Pattern of performance and ability attribution: An unexpected primacy effect. *Journal of Personality and Social Psychology, 10,* 317–340.

Jones, J. M. (1988). *Piercing the veil: Bicultural strategies for coping with prejudice and racism.* Invited address at the national conference, "Opening Doors: An Appraisal of Race Relations in America," University of Alabama, June 11.

Jones, J. M. (2003). TRIOS: A psychological theory of the African legacy in American culture. *Journal of Social Issues, 59,* 217–242.

Jones, J. M. (2004). TRIOS: A model for coping with the universal context of racism? In G. Philogène (Ed.), *Racial identity in context: The legacy of Kenneth B. Clark.* Washington, DC: American Psychological Association.

Jones, J. M. (2012, December 6). Most in U.S. say gay/lesbian bias is a serious problem. Gallup Poll (www.gallup.com).

Jones, J. T., & Cunningham, J. D. (1996). Attachment styles and other predictors of relationship satisfaction in dating couples. *Personal Relationships, 3,* 387–399.

Jones, L. L., & Brunell, A. B. (2014). Clever and crude but not kind: Narcissism, self-esteem, and the self-reference effect. *Memory, 22,* 307–322.

Jones, R. A., & Brehm, J. W. (1970). Persuasiveness of one- and two-sided communications as a function of awareness there are two sides. *Journal of Experimental Social Psychology, 6,* 47–56.

Jordan, C. H., Spencer, S. J., Zanna, M. P., Hoshino-Browne, E., & Correll, J. (2003). Secure and defensive high self-esteem. *Journal of personality and social psychology, 85*(5), 969.

Josephson, W. L. (1987). Television violence and children's aggression: Testing the priming, social script, and disinhibition predictions. *Journal of Personality and Social Psychology, 53,* 882–890.

Jost, J. T., & Kay, A. C. (2005). Exposure to benevolent sexism and complementary gender stereotypes: Consequences for specific and diffuse forms of system justification. *Journal of Personality and Social Psychology, 88,* 498.

Jost, J. T., Kay, A. C., & Thorisdottir, H. (Eds.) (2009). *Social and psychological bases of ideology and system justifications.* New York: Oxford University Press.

Jouffre, S., & Croizet, J. (2016). Empowering and legitimizing the fundamental attribution error: Power and legitimization exacerbate the translation of role-constrained behaviors into ability differences. *European Journal of Social Psychology, 46*, 621–631.

Jourard, S. M. (1964). *The transparent self.* Princeton, NJ: Van Nostrand.

Jourden, F. J., & Heath, C. (1996). The evaluation gap in performance perceptions: Illusory perceptions of groups and individuals. *Journal of Applied Psychology, 81,* 369–379.

Jouriles, E. N., Krauss, A., Sargent, K. S., Grych, J. H., Cascardi, M., O'Leary, K. D., Murphy, C., Nguyen, J., McDonald, R., & Rosenfield, D. (2020). College students' feelings of campus connectedness, party safety behavior and intervening to prevent sexual assault and intimate partner violence. *Psychology of Violence.* https://doi-org.library.smu.ca/10.1037/vio0000284

Judd, C. M., Blair, I. V., & Chapleau, K. M. (2004). Automatic stereotypes vs. automatic prejudice: Sorting out the possibilities in the Payne (2001) weapon paradigm. *Journal of Experimental Social Psychology, 40,* 75–81 .

Jussim, L. (1986). Self-fulfilling prophecies: A theoretical and integrative review. *Psychological Review, 93,* 429–445.

Jussim, L. (2005). Accuracy in social perception: Criticisms, controversies, criteria, components, and cognitive processes. In M. P. Zanna (Ed.), *Advances in experimental social psychology* (Vol. 37) (pp. 1–93). San Diego, CA: Elsevier Academic Press.

Jussim, L. (2012). *Social perception and social reality: Why accuracy dominates bias and self-fulfilling prophecy.* New York: Oxford University Press.

Jussim, L., McCauley, C. R., & Lee, Y-T. (1995). Introduction: Why study stereotype accuracy and inaccuracy? In Y. T. Lee, L. Jussim, & C. R. McCauley (Eds.), *Stereotype accuracy: Toward appreciating group differences.* Washington, DC: American Psychological Association.

Jussim, L., Robustelli, S. L., & Cain, T. R. (2009). Teacher expectations and self-fulfilling prophecies. In K. R. Wenzel & A. Wigfield (Eds.), *Handbook of motivation at school.* New York: Routledge/Taylor & Francis.

Juvonen, J., & Graham, S. (2014). Bullying in schools: The power of bullies and the plight of victims. *Annual Review of Psychology, 65,* 159–185.

Kagan, J. (1989). Temperamental contributions to social behavior. *American Psychologist, 44,* 668–674.

Kagan, J. (2009). Historical selection. *Review of General Psychology, 13,* 77–88.

Kagehiro, D. K. (1990). Defining the standard of proof in jury instructions. *Psychological Science, 1,* 194–200.

Kahan, D. M., Jenkins-Smith, H., & Braman, D. (2010). Cultural cognition of scientific consensus. *Journal of Risk Research, 14,* 147–174.

Kahle, L. R., & Berman, J. (1979). Attitudes cause behaviors: A cross-lagged panel analysis. *Journal of Personality and Social Psychology, 37,* 315–321.

Kahlor, L., & Morrison, D. (2007). Television viewing and rape myth acceptance among college women. *Sex Roles, 56,* 729–739.

Kahn, M. W. (1951). The effect of severe defeat at various age levels on the aggressive behavior of mice. *Journal of Genetic Psychology, 79,* 117–130.

Kahneman, D. (2011). *Thinking, fast and slow.* New York: Farrar, Straus, and Giroux.

Kahneman, D., & Deaton, A. (2010). High income improves evaluation of life but not emotional well-being. *PNAS, 107,* 16489–16493.

Kahneman, D., & Miller, D. T. (1986). Norm theory: Comparing reality to its alternatives. *Psychological Review, 93,* 75–88.

Kahneman, D., & Renshon, J. (2007, January/February). Why hawks win. *Foreign Policy.* Retrieved from www.foreignpolicy.com

Kahneman, D., & Snell, J. (1992). Predicting a changing taste: Do people know what they will like? *Journal of Behavioral Decision Making, 5,* 187–200.

Kahneman, D., & Tversky, A. (1979). Intuitive prediction: Biases and corrective procedures. *Management Science, 12,* 313–327.

Kahneman, D., & Tversky, A. (1995). Conflict resolution: A cognitive perspective. In K. Arrow, R. Mnookin, L. Ross, A. Tversky, & R. Wilson (Eds.), *Barriers to the negotiated resolution of conflict.* New York: Norton.

Kaiser, C. R., & Pratt-Hyatt, J. S. (2009). Distributing prejudice unequally: Do Whites direct their prejudice toward strongly identified minorities? *Journal of Personality and Social Psychology, 96,* 432–445.

Kaiser Family Foundation. (2005, November 9). Sex on TV 4. Retrieved from http://www.kff.org

Kalick, S. M. (1977). Plastic surgery, physical appearance, and person perception. Unpublished doctoral dissertation, Harvard University.

Kalin, R., & Berry, J. W. (1995). Ethnic and civic self-identity in Canada: Analyses of 1974 and 1991 national surveys. *Canadian Ethnic Studies, 27,* 1–15.

Kalinoski, Z. T., Steele-Johnson, D., Peyton, E. J., Leas, K. A., Steinke, J., & Bowling, N. A. (2013). A meta-analytic evaluation of diversity training outcomes. *Journal of Organizational Behavior, 34,* 1076–1104.

Kalven, H., Jr., & Zeisel, H. (1966). *The American jury.* Chicago: University of Chicago Press.

Kameda, T., & Sugimori, S. (1993). Psychological entrapment in group decision making: An assigned decision rule and a groupthink phenomenon. *Journal of Personality and Social Psychology, 65,* 282–292.

Kammer, D. (1982). Differences in trait ascriptions to self and friend: Unconfounding intensity from variability. *Psychological Reports, 51,* 99–102.

Kamphuis, J., Meerlo, P., Koolhaas, J. M., & Lancel, M. (2012). Poor sleep as a potential causal factor in aggression and violence. *Sleep Medicine, 13,* 327–334.

Kanagawa, C., Cross, S. E., & Markus, H. R. (2001). "Who am I?" The cultural psychology of the conceptual self. *Personality and Social Psychology Bulletin, 27,* 90–103.

Kandel, D. B. (1978). Similarity in real-life adolescent friendship pairs. *Journal of Personality and Social Psychology, 36,* 306–312.

Kanekar, S., & Nazareth, A. (1988). Attributed rape victim's fault as a function of her attractiveness, physical hurt, and emotional disturbance. *Social Behaviour, 3,* 37–40.

Kanten, A. B., & Teigen, K. H. (2008). Better than average and better with time. Relative evaluations of self and others in the past, present, and future. *European Journal of Social Psychology, 38,* 343–353.

Kapitan, S., & Silvera, D. H. (2016). From digital media influencers to celebrity endorsers: Attributions drive endorser effectiveness. *Marketing Letters, 27*(3), 553–567.

Kaplan, M. F. (1989). Task, situational, and personal determinants of influence processes in group decision making. In E. J. Lawler (Ed.), *Advances in group processes* (Vol. 6). Greenwich, CT: JAI Press.

Kaplan, M. F., Wanshula, L. T., & Zanna, M. P. (1993). Time pressure and information integration in social judgment: The effect of need for structure. In O. Svenson & J. Maule (Eds.), *Time pressure and stress in human judgment and decision making.* Cambridge: Cambridge University Press.

Karau, S. J., & Williams, K. D. (1993). Social loafing: A meta-analytic review and theoretical integration. *Journal of Personality and Social Psychology, 65,* 681–706.

Karau, S. J., & Williams, K. D. (1997). The effects of group cohesiveness on social loafing and social compensation. *Group Dynamics: Theory, Research, and Practice, 1,* 156–168.

Karberg, J. C., & James, D. J. (2005). Substance dependence, abuse, and treatment of jail inmates, 2002. Bureau of Justice Statistics Special Report. Washington, DC: U.S. Department of Justice.

Karna, A., Voeten, M., Little, T. D., Poskiparta, E., Kalijonen, A., & Salmivalli, C. (2011). A large-scale evaluation of the KiVa antibullying program. *Child Development, 82,* 311–330.

Karney, B. R., & Bradbury, T. N. (1995). The longitudinal course of marital quality and stability: A review of theory, method, and research. *Psychological Bulletin, 118,* 3–34.

Kashima, E. S., & Kashima, Y. (1998). Culture and language: the case of cultural dimensions and personal pronoun use. *Journal of Cross-Cultural Psychology, 29,* 461–486.

Kashima, Y., & Kashima, E. S. (2003). Individualism, GNP, climate, and pronoun drop: Is individualism determined by affluence and climate, or does language use play a role? *Journal of Cross-Cultural Psychology, 34,* 125–134.

Kasser, T. (2000). Two versions of the American dream: Which goals and values make for a high quality of life? In E. Diener and D. Rahtz (Eds.), *Advances in quality of life: Theory and research.* Dordrecth, Netherlands: Kluwer.

Kasser, T., & Ahuvia, A. (2002). Materialistic values and well-being in business students. *European Journal of Social Psychology, 32,* 137.

Kassin, S. M., Drizin, S. A., Grisso, T., Gudjonsson, G. H., Leo, R. A., & Redlich, A. D. (2010). Police-induced confessions: Risk factors and recommendations. *Law and Human Behavior, 34,* 3–38.

Kassin, S. M., Goldstein, C. C., & Savitsky, K. (2003). Behavioral confirmation in the interrogation room: On the dangers of presuming guilt. *Law and Human Behavior, 27*(2), 187.

Katz, A. M., & Hill, R. (1958). Residential propinquity and marital selection: A review of theory, method, and fact. *Marriage and Family Living, 20,* 237–335.

Katz, E. (1957). The two-step flow of communication: An up-to-date report on a hypothesis. *Public Opinion Quarterly, 21,* 61–78.

Katz-Wise, S. L., & Hyde, J. S. (2012). Victimization experiences of lesbian, gay, and bisexual individuals: A meta-analysis. *Journal of Sex Research, 49,* 142–167.

Katzer, C., Fetchenhauer, D., & Belschak, F. (2009). Cyberbullying: Who are the victims? A comparison of victimization in Internet chatrooms and victimization in school. *Journal of Media Psychology, 21,* 25–36.

Katzev, R., Edelsack, L., Steinmetz, G., & Walker, T. (1978). The effect of reprimanding transgressions on subsequent helping behavior: Two field experiments. *Personality and Social Psychology Bulletin, 4,* 126–129.

Katzev, R., & Wang, T. (1994). Can commitment change behavior? A case study of environmental actions. *Journal of Social Behavior and Personality, 9,* 13–26.

Kaufman, J., & Zigler, E. (1987). Do abused children become abusive parents? *American Journal of Orthopsychiatry, 57,* 186–192.

Kavanagh, C. M., Jong, J., McKay, R., & Whitehouse, H. (2019). Positive experiences of high arousal martial arts rituals are linked to identity fusion and costly pro-group actions. *European Journal of Social Psychology, 49*(3), 461–481. https://doi-org.library.smu.ca/10.1002/ejsp.2514

Kawakami, K., & Dion, K. L. (1993). The impact of salient self-identities on relative deprivation and action intentions. *European Journal of Social Psychology, 23,* 525–540.

Kawakami, K., & Dion, K. L. (1995). Social identity and affect as determinants of collective action: Toward an integration of relative deprivation and social identity theories. *Theory & Psychology, 5,* 551–577.

Kawakami, K., Dovidio, J. F., Moll, J., Hermsen, S., & Russin, A. (2000). Just say no (to stereotyping): Effects of training in the negation of stereotypic associations on stereotype activation. *Journal of Personality and Social Psychology, 78,* 871–888.

Kawakami, K., Dunn, E., Kiarmali, F., & Dovidio, J. F. (2009). Mispredicting affective and behavioral responses to racism. *Science, 323,* 276–278.

Kawakami, K., Williams, A., Sidhu, D., Choma, B. L., Rodriguez-Bailón, R., Cañadas, E., Chung, B. L., & Hugenberg, K. (2014). An eye for the I: Preferential attention to the eyes of ingroup members. *Journal of Personality and Social Psychology, 107,* 1–20.

Kay, A. C., Baucher, D., Peach, J. M., Laurin, K., Friesen, J., Zanna, M. P., & Spencer, S. J. (2009). Inequality, discrimination, and the power of the status quo: Direct evidence for a motivation to see the ways things are as they way they should be. *Journal of Personality and Social Psychology, 97,* 421–434.

Kay, A. C., Day, M. V., Zanna, M. P., & Nussbaum, A. D. (2013). The insidious (and ironic) effects of positive stereotypes. *Journal of Experimental Social Psychology, 49,* 287–291.

Kay, A. C., & Eibach, R. P. (2013). Compensatory control and its implications for ideological extremism. *Journal of Social Issues, 69,* 564–585.

Kay, A. C., Jost, J. T., Mandisodza, A. N., Sherman, S. J., Petrocelli, J. V., & Johnson, A. L. (2007). Panglossian ideology in the service of system justification: How complementary stereotypes help us to rationalize inequality. In M. P. Zanna (Ed.), *2005 Society of Experimental Social Psychology Conference, 2005,* San Diego, CA (pp. 305–358). San Diego: Elsevier Academic Press.

Kay, A. C., Jost, J. T., & Young, S. (2005). Victim derogation and victim enhancement as alternate routes to system justification. *Psychological Science, 16,* 240.

Keating, J. P., & Brock, T. C. (1974). Acceptance of persuasion and the inhibition of counterargumentation under various distraction tasks. *Journal of Experimental Social Psychology, 10,* 301–309.

Keelan, J. P., Dion, K. K., & Dion, K. L. (1998). Attachment style and relationship satisfaction: Test of a self-disclosure explanation. *Canadian Journal of Behavioural Science, 30,* 24–35.

Keller, E., & Berry, J. L. (2003). *The influentials.* New York: Simon & Schuster.

Keller, J., & Dauenheimer, D. (2003). Stereotype threat in the classroom: Dejection mediates the disrupting threat effect on women's math performance. *Personality and Social Psychology Bulletin, 29,* 371–381.

Kellerman, J., Lewis, J., & Laird, J. D. (1989). Looking and loving: The effects of mutual gaze on feelings of romantic love. *Journal of Research in Personality, 23,* 145–161.

Kellermann, A. L. (1997). Comment: Gunsmoke-changing public attitudes toward smoking and firearms. *American Journal of Public Health, 87,* 910–912.

Kellermann, A. L., Rivara, F. P., Rushforth, N. B., Banton, J. G., Reay, D. T., Francisco, J. T., Locci, A. B., Prodzinski, J., Hackman, B. B., & Somes, G. (1993). Gun ownership as a risk factor for homicide in the home. *New England Journal of Medicine, 329,* 1084-1091.

Kelley, H. H. (1973). The process of causal attribution. *American Psychologist, 28,* 107–128.

Kelley, H. H., & Stahelski, A. J. (1970). The social interaction basis of cooperators' and competitors' beliefs about others. *Journal of Personality and Social Psychology, 16,* 66–91.

Kelley, K., Dawson, L., & Musialowski, D. M. (1989). Three faces of sexual explicitness: The good, the bad, and the useful. In D. Zillmann & J. Bryant (Eds.),

Pornography: Research advances and policy considerations. Hillsdale, NJ: Erlbaum.

Kelly, D. J., Liu, S., Ge, L., Quinn, P. C., Slater, A. M., Lee, K., Liu, Q., & Pascalis, O. (2007). Cross-race preferences for same-race faces extended beyond the African versus Caucasian contrast in 3-month-old infants. *Infancy, 11,* 87–95.

Kelly, D. J., Quinn, P. C., Slater, A. M., Lee, K., Gibson, A., Smith, M., Ge, L., & Y Pascalis, O. (2005). Three-month-olds, but not newborns prefer own-race faces. *Developmental Science, 8,* F31–F36.

Kelman, H. C. (1998). *Building a sustainable peace: The limits of pragmatism in the Israeli-Palestinian negotiations.* Address to the American Psychological Association convention.

Kelman, H. C. (2007). The Israeli-Palestinian peace process and its vicissitudes: Insights from attitude theory. *American Psychologist, 62,* 287–303.

Kelman, H. C. (2010). Looking back at my work on conflict resolution in the Middle East. *Peace and Conflict: Journal of Peace Psychology, 16,* 361–387.

Kendrick, R. V., & Olson, M. A. (2012). When feeling right leads to being right in the reporting of implicitly-formed attitudes, or how I learned to stop worrying and trust my gut. *Journal of Experimental Social Psychology, 48,* 1316–1321.

Kennedy, J. A., Anderson, C., & Moore, D. A. (2013). When overconfidence is revealed to others: Testing the status-enhancement theory of overconfidence. *Organizational Behavior and Human Decision Processes, 122,* 266–279.

Kennedy, K. A., & Pronin, E. (2008). When disagreement gets ugly: Perceptions of bias and the escalation of conflict. *Personality and Social Psychology Bulletin, 34,* 833–848.

Kenny, D. A., & Acitelli, L. K. (2001). Accuracy and bias in the perception of the partner in a close relationship. *Journal of Personality and Social Psychology, 80,* 439–448.

Kenny, D. A., & Nasby, W. (1980). Splitting the reciprocity correlation. *Journal of Personality and Social Psychology, 38,* 249–256.

Kenrick, D. T., & Gutierres, S. E. (1980). Contrast effects and judgments of physical attractiveness: When beauty becomes a social problem. *Journal of Personality and Social Psychology, 38,* 131–140.

Kenrick, D. T., Gutierres, S. E., & Goldberg, L. L. (1989). Influence of popular erotica on judgments of strangers and mates. *Journal of Experimental Social Psychology, 25,* 159–167.

Kenrick, D. T., & MacFarlane, S. W. (1986). Ambient temperature and horn-honking: A field study of the heat/aggression relationship. *Environment and Behavior, 18,* 179–191.

Kenrick, D. T., & Trost, M. R. (1987). A biosocial theory of heterosexual relationships. In K. Kelly (Ed.), *Females, males, and sexuality.* Albany: State University of New York Press.

Kenworthy, J. B., Hewstone, M., Levine, J. M., Martin, R., & Willis, H. (2008). The phenomenology of minority–majority status: Effects of innovation in argument generation. *European Journal of Social Psychology, 38,* 624–636.

Kenyon, P. (2016, June 29). After Brexit vote, U.K. sees a wave of hate crimes and racist abuse. NPR. Retrieved from www.npr.org/sections/parallels/2016/06/29/484038396/after-brexit-vote-u-k-sees-a-wave-of-hate-crimes-and-racist-abuse

Kepes, S., Bushman, B. J., & Anderson, C. A. (2017). Violent video game effects remain a societal concern: Reply to Hilgard, Engelhardt, and Rouder (2017). *Psychological Bulletin, 143,* 775–782.

Kernis, M. H. (2003). High self-esteem: A differentiated perspective. In E. C. Chang & L. J. Sanna (Eds.), *Virtue, vice, and personality: The complexity of behavior.* Washington, DC: APA Books.

Kerr, N. L. (1983). Motivation losses in small groups: A social dilemma analysis. *Journal of Personality and Social Psychology, 45,* 819–828.

Kerr, N. L. (1989). Illusions of efficacy: The effects of group size on perceived efficacy in social dilemmas. *Journal of Experimental Social Psychology, 25,* 287–313.

Kerr, N. L. (1992). Norms in social dilemmas. In D. Schroeder (Ed.), *Social dilemmas: Psychological perspectives.* New York: Praeger.

Kerr, N. L., Atkin, R. S., Stasser, G., Meek, D., Holt, R. W., & Davis, J. H. (1976). Guilt beyond a reasonable doubt: Effects of concept definition and assigned decision rule on the judgments of mock jurors. *Journal of Personality and Social Psychology, 34,* 282–294.

Kerr, N. L., & Bruun, S. E. (1981). Ringelmann revisted: Alternative explanations for the social loafing effect. *Personality and Social Psychology Bulletin, 7,* 224–231.

Kerr, N. L., & Bruun, S. E. (1983). Dispensibility of member effort and group motivation losses: Free-rider effects. *Journal of Personality and Social Psychology, 44,* 78–94.

Kerr, N. L., & Kaufman-Gilliland, C. M. (1994). Communication, commitment, and cooperation in social dilemmas. *Journal of Personality and Social Psychology, 66,* 513–529.

Kerr, N. L., & Kaufman-Gilliland, C. M. (1997). "… and besides, I probably couldn't have made a difference anyway": Justification of social dilemma defection via perceived self-inefficacy. *Journal of Experimental Social Psychology, 33,* 211–230.

Kerr, N. L., & MacCoun, R. J. (1985). The effects of jury size and polling method on the process and product of jury deliberation. *Journal of Personality and Social Psychology, 48,* 349–363.

Kerr, R. A. (2009). Amid worrisome signs of warming, "climate fatigue" sets in. *Science, 326,* 926–928.

Kerr, R. A. (2011). Humans are driving extreme weather; time to prepare. *Science, 334,* 1040.

Kesebir, S., & Oishi, S. (2010). A spontaneous self-reference effect in memory: Why some birthdays are harder to remember than others. Psychological Science, 21, 1525–1531.

Kessler, T., & Mummendey, A. (2001). Is there any scapegoat around? Determinants of intergroup conflicts at different categorization levels. *Journal of Personality and Social Psychology, 81,* 1090–1102.

Kidd, J. B., & Morgan, J. R. (1969). A predictive information system for management. *Operational Research Quarterly, 20,* 149–170.

Kiecolt-Glaser, J. K., Loving, T. J., Stowell, J. R., Malarkey, W. B., Lemeshow, S., Dickinson, S. L., & Glaser, R. (2005). Hostile marital interactions, proinflammatory cytokine production, and wound healing. *Archives of General Psychiatry, 62,* 1377–1384.

Kiecolt-Glaser, J. K., Malarkey, W. B., Chee, M., Newton, T., Cacioppo, J. T., Mao, H-Y., & Glaser, R. (1993). Negative behavior during marital conflict is associated with immunological downregulation. *Psychosomatic Medicine, 55,* 395–409.

Kiesler, C. A. (1971). *The psychology of commitment: Experiments linking behavior to belief.* New York: Academic Press.

Kihlstrom, J. F., & Cantor, N. (1984). Mental representations of the self. In L. Berkowitz (Ed.), *Advances in experimental social psychology* (Vol. 17). New York: Academic Press.

Kille, D. R., Forest, A. L., & Wood, J. V. (2013). Tall, dark, and stable: Embodiment motivates mate selection preferences. *Psychological Science, 24,* 112–114.

Kim, H., & Markus, H. R. (1999). Deviance of uniqueness, harmony or conformity? A cultural analysis. *Journal of Personality and Social Psychology, 77,* 785–800.

Kim, H. S., & Sherman, D. K. (2007). "Express yourself": Culture and the effect of self-expression on choice. *Journal of Personality and Social Psychology, 92,* 1–11.

Kimel, S. Y., Huesmann, R., Kunst, J. R., & Halperin, E. (2016). Living in a genetic world: How learning about interethnic genetic similarities and differences affects peace and conflict. *Personality and Social Psychology Bulletin, 42*, 688–700.

Kimmel, A. J. (1998). In defense of deception. *American Psychologist, 53,* 803–804.

Kimmel, M. J., Pruitt, D. G., Magenau, J. M., Konar-Goldband, E., & Carnevale, P. J. D. (1980). Effects of trust, aspiration, and gender on negotiation tactics. *Journal of Personality and Social Psychology, 38,* 9–22.

Kinder, D. R., & Sears, D. O. (1985). Public opinion and political action. In G. Lindzey & E. Aronson (Eds.), *The handbook of social psychology* (3rd ed.). New York: Random House.

Kingdon, J. W. (1967). Politicans' beliefs about voters. *The American Political Science Review, 61,* 137–145.

Kingston, D. A., Malamuth, N. M., Federoff, P., & Marshall, W. L. (2009). The importance of individual differences in pornography use: Theoretical perspectives and implications for treating sexual offenders. *Journal of Sex Research, 46,* 216–232.

Kinnier, R. T., & Metha, A. T. (1989). Regrets and priorities at three stages of life. *Counseling and Values, 33,* 182–193.

Kinzler, K. D., Shutts, K., Dejesus, J., & Spelke, E. S. (2009). Accent trumps race in guiding children's social preferences. *Social Cognition, 27,* 623–634.

Kirsh, S. J. (2006). Cartoon violence and aggression in youth. *Aggression and Violent Behavior, 11,* 547–557.

Kitaigorodskii, A. I. (1975, August). Lecture. ICU, Amsterdam.

Kitayama, S. (1996). *The mutual constitution of culture and the self: Implications for emotion.* Paper presented to the American Psychological Society convention.

Kitayama, S. (1999). Behind the scenes. In D. G. Myers, *Social psychology* (6th ed.). New York: McGraw-Hill.

Kitayama, S., & Karasawa, M. (1997). Implicit self-esteem in Japan: Name letters and birthday numbers. *Personality and Social Psychology Bulletin, 23,* 736–742.

Kitayama, S., & Markus, H. R. (1995). Culture and self: Implications for internationalizing psychology. In N. R. Godlberger & J. B. Veroff (Eds.), *The culture and psychology reader.* New York: New York University Press.

Kitayama, S., & Markus, H. R. (2000). The pursuit of happiness and the realization of sympathy: Cultural patterns of self, social relations, and well-being. In E. Diener & E. M. Suh (Eds.), *Subjective well-being across cultures.* Cambridge, MA: MIT Press.

Kite, M. E. (2001). Changing times, changing gender roles: Who do we want women and men to be? In R. K. Unger (Ed.), *Handbook of the psychology of women and gender.* New York: Wiley.

Klaas, E. T. (1978). Psychological effects of immoral actions: The experimental evidence. *Psychological Bulletin, 85,* 756–771.

Klapwijk, A., & Van Lange, P. A. M. (2009). Promoting cooperation and trust in "noisy" situations: The power of generosity. *Journal of Personality and Social Psychology, 96,* 83–103.

Klauer, K. C., & Voss, A. (2008). Effects of race on responses and response latencies in the weapon identification task: A test of six models. *Personality and Social Psychology Bulletin, 34,* 1124–1140.

Kleck, R. E., & Strenta, A. (1980). Perceptions of the impact of negatively valued physical characteristics on social interaction. *Journal of Personality and Social Psychology, 39,* 861–873.

Kleiman, T., & Hassin, R. R. (2013). When conflicts are good: Nonconscious goal conflicts reduce confirmatory thinking. *Journal of Personality and Social Psychology, 105,* 374–387.

Klein, A., & Golub, S. A. (2016). Family rejection as a predictor of suicide attempts and substance misuse among transgender and gender nonconforming adults. *LGBT Health, 3,* 193–199.

Klein, J. G. (1991). Negative effects in impression formation: A test in the political arena. *Personality and Social Psychology Bulletin, 17,* 412–418.

Klein, N., & Epley, N. (2017). Less evil than you: Bounded self-righteousness in character inferences, emotional reactions, and behavioral extremes. *Personality and Social Psychology Bulletin, 43,* 1202–1212.

Klein, O., Snyder, M., & Livingston, R. W. (2004). Prejudice on the stage: Self-monitoring and the public expression of group attitudes. *British Journal of Social Psychology, 43,* 299–314.

Klein, S. B., Lax, M. L., & Gangi, C. E. (2010). A call for an inclusive approach to the social cognitive neurosciences. *Social Cognition, 28,* 748–756.

Klein, W. M., & Kunda, Z. (1992). Motivated person perception: Constructing justifications for desired beliefs. *Journal of Experimental Social Psychology, 28,* 145–168.

Kleinfield, N. R., Rivera, R., & Kovaleski, S. F. (2013, March 28). Newtown killer's obsessions, in chilling detail. *New York Times,* p. A1.

Kleinke, C. L. (1977). Compliance to requests made by gazing and touching experimenters in field settings. *Journal of Experimental Social Psychology, 13,* 218–223.

Kleinsmith, J., Kasser, T., & McAndrew, F. T. (2006). Guns, testosterone, and aggression: An experimental test of a mediational hypothesis. *Psychological Science, 17,* 568.

Klentz, B., Beaman, A. L., Mapelli, S. D., & Ullrich, J. R. (1987). Perceived physical attractiveness of supporters and nonsupporters of the women's movement: An attitude-similarity-mediated error (AS-ME). *Personality and Social Psychology Bulletin, 13,* 513–523.

Klopfer, P. H. (1958). Influence of social interaction on learning rates in birds. *Science, 128,* 903.

Klucharev, V., Hytönen, K., Rijpkema, M., Smidts, A., & Fernández, G. (2009). Reinforcement learning signal predicts conformity. *Neuron, 61,* 140–151.

Knewtson, H. S., & Sias, R. W. (2010). Why Susie owns Starbucks: The name letter effect in security selection. *Journal of Business Research, 63,* 1324–1327.

Knight, J. A., & Vallacher, R. R. (1981). Interpersonal engagement in social perception: The consequences of getting into the action. *Journal of Personality and Social Psychology, 40,* 990–999.

Knight, P. A., & Weiss, H. M. (1980). *Benefits of suffering: Communicator suffering, benefiting, and influence.* Paper presented at the American Psychological Association convention.

Knowles, E. D., & Peng, K. (2005). White selves: Conceptualizing and measuring a dominant-group identity. *Journal of Personality and Social Psychology, 89,* 223–241.

Knowles, E. S. (1983). Social physics and the effects of others: Tests of the effects of audience size and distance on social judgment and behavior. *Journal of Personality and Social Psychology, 45,* 1263–1279.

Knox, R. E., & Inkster, J. A. (1968). Postdecision dissonance at post-time. *Journal of Personality and Social Psychology, 8,* 319–323.

Knudson, R. M., Sommers, A. A., & Golding, S. L. (1980). Interpersonal perception and mode of resolution in marital conflict. *Journal of Personality and Social Psychology, 38,* 751–763.

Koehler, D. J. (1991). Explanation, imagination, and confidence in judgment. *Psychological Bulletin, 110,* 499–519.

Koehler, D. J., & Poon, C. S. K. (2006). Self-predictions overweight strength of current intentions. *Journal of Experimental Social Psychology, 42*(4), 517.

Koehler, D. J., White, R. J., & John, L. K. (2011). Good intentions, optimistic self-predictions, and missed opportunities. *Social Psychological and Personality Science, 2,* 90–96.

Koenig, A. M., & Eagly, A. H. (2014). Evidence for the social role theory of stereotype content: Observations of groups' roles shape stereotypes. *Journal of Personality and Social Psychology, 107,* 371–392.

Koenig, L. B., McGue, M., & Iacono, W. G. (2008). Stability and change in religiousness during emerging adulthood. *Developmental Psychology, 44,* 531–543.

Koestner, R., & Wheeler, L. (1988). Self-presentation in personal advertisements: The influence of implicit notions of attraction and role expectations. *Journal of Social and Personal Relationships, 5,* 149–160.

Kohn, N. W., Paulus, P. B., & Choi, Y. (2011). Building on the ideas of others. An examination of the idea combination process. *Journal of Experimental Social Psychology, 47,* 554–561.

Kokkoris, M. D., & Kühnen, U. (2015). You are (not only) what you choose: A self-expression account of post-choice dissonance. *Motivation and Emotion, 39*(1), 34–48.

Kolivas, E. D., & Gross, A. M. (2007). Assessing sexual aggression: Addressing the gap between rape victimization and perpetration prevalence rates. *Aggression and Violent Behavior, 12,* 315–328.

Konrath, S., Au, J., & Ramsey, L. R. (2012). Cultural differences in face-ism: Male politicians have bigger heads in more gender-equal cultures. *Psychology of Women Quarterly, 36,* 476–487.

Konrath, S. H., Chopik, W. J., Hsing, C. K., & O'Brien, E. (2014). Changes in adult attachment styles in American college students over time: A meta-analysis. *Personality and Social Psychology Review, 18,* 326–348.

Koomen, W., & Bahler, M. (1996). National stereotypes: Common representations and ingroup favouritism. *European Journal of Social Psychology, 26,* 325–331.

Koop, C. E. (1987). Report of the Surgeon General's workshop on pornography and public health. *American Psychologist, 42,* 944–945.

Koriat, A., Lichtenstein, S., & Fischhoff, B. (1980). Reasons for confidence. *Journal of Experimental Social Psychology: Human Learning and Memory, 6,* 107–118.

Korn, J. H., & Nicks, S. D. (1993). *The rise and decline of deception in social psychology.* Poster presented at the American Psychological Society convention.

Koss, M. P., Heise, L., & Russo, N. F. (1994). The global health burden of rape. *Psychology of Women Quarterly, 18,* 509–537.

Kossowska, M., Czernatowicz-Kukuczka, A., & Sekerdej, M. (2017). Many faces of dogmatism: Prejudice as a way of protecting certainty against value violations among dogmatic believers and atheists. *British Journal of Psychology, 108,* 127–147.

Kouchaki, M., & Wareham, J. (2015). Excluded and behaving unethically: Social exclusion, physiological responses, and unethical behavior. *Journal of Applied Psychology, 100,* 547–556.

Kowalski, R. M., Guimetti, G. W., Schroeder, A. N., & Lattanner, M. R. (2014). Bullying in the digital age: A critical review and meta-analysis of cyberbulling research among youth. *Psychological Bulletin, 140,* 1073–1137.

Krackow, A., & Blass, T. (1995). When nurses obey or defy inappropriate physician orders: Attributional differences. *Journal of Social Behavior and Personality, 10,* 585–594.

Kraft, T. L., & Pressman, S. D. (2012). Grin and bear it: The influence of manipulated facial expression on the stress response. *Psychological science, 23*(11), 1372-1378.

Krahé, B. (1998). Sexual aggression among adolescents: Prevalence and predictors in a German sample. *Psychology of Women Quarterly, 22,* 537–554.

Krahé, B., & Busching, R. (2015). Breaking the vicious cycle of media violence use and aggression: A test of intervention effects over 30 months. *Psychology of Violence, 5,* 217–226.

Krahé, B., & Möller, I. (2010). Longitudinal effects of media violence on aggression and empathy among German adolescents. *Journal of Applied Developmental Psychology, 31,* 401–409.

Krahé, B., Moller, I., Huesmann, L. R., Kirwil, L., Felber, J., & Berger, A. (2010). Desensitization to media violence: Links with habitual media violence exposure, aggressive cognitions, and aggressive behavior. *Journal of Personality and Social Psychology, 100,* 630–646.

Kramer, A. D., Guillory, J. E., & Hancock, J. T. (2014). Experimental evidence of massive-scale emotional contagion through social networks. *Proceedings of the National Academy of Sciences, 111*(24), 8788–8790.

Kramer, A. D. I., & Chung, C. K. (2011). Dimensions of self-expression in Facebook status updates. Proceedings of the Fifth International AAAI Conference on Weblogs and Social Media. Retrieved from http://www.aaai.org

Kramer, A. E. (2008, August 31). Russia's collective farms: Hot capitalist property. *New York Times.* Retrieved from http://www.nytimes.com

Kraus, M. W., & Keltner, D. (2013). Social class rank, essentialism, and punitive judgment. *Journal of Personality and Social Psychology, 105,* 247–261.

Kraus, M. W., Piff, P. K., & Keltner, D. (2011). Social class as culture: the convergence of resources and rank in the social realm. *Current Directions in Psychological Science, 20,* 246–250.

Kraus, S. J. (1995). Attitudes and the prediction of behavior: A meta-analysis of the empirical literature. *Personality and Social Psychology Bulletin, 21,* 58–75.

Kraut, R. E. (1973). Effects of social labeling on giving to charity. *Journal of Experimental Social Psychology, 9,* 551–562.

Kravitz, D. A., & Martin, B. (1986). Ringelmann rediscovered: The original article. *Journal of Personality and Social Psychology, 50,* 936–941.

Krebs, D. (1970). Altruism—An examination of the concept and a review of the literature. *Psychological Bulletin, 73,* 258–302.

Krebs, D. (1975). Empathy and altruism. *Journal of Personality and Social Psychology, 32,* 1134–1146.

Krebs, D., & Adinolfi, A. A. (1975). Physical attractiveness, social relations, and personality style. *Journal of Personality and Social Psychology, 31,* 245–253.

Krebs, D. L. (1998). The evolution of moral behaviors. In C. Crawford & D. L. Krebs (Eds.), *Handbook of evolutionary psychology: Ideas, issues, and applications.* Mahwah, NJ: Erlbaum.

Krendl, A. C., Richeson, J. A., Kelley, W. M., & Heatherton, T. F. (2008). The negative consequences of threat: A functional magnetic resonance imaging investigation of the neural mechanisms underlying women's underperformance in math. *Psychological Science, 19,* 168–175.

Krisberg, K. (2004). Successful "truth" anti-smoking campaign in funding jeopardy: New commission works to save campaign. *Nation's Health, 34*(4).

Kristof, N. (2018, March 23). Conflict is more profitable than peace. *New York Times*. Retrieved from www.nytimes.com

Krizan, Z., & Suls, J. (2008). Losing sight of oneself in the above-average effect: When egocentrism, focalism, and group diffuseness collide. *Journal of Experimental Social Psychology, 44,* 929–942.

Krosnick, J. A. (2010, June 8). The climate majority. *New York Times*. Retrieved from http://www.nytimes.com

Krosnick, J. A., & Alwin, D. F. (1989). Aging and susceptibility to attitude change. *Journal of Personality and Social Psychology, 57,* 416–425.

Krosnick, J. A., & Petty, R. E. (1995). *Attitude strength: Antecedents and consequences*. Ohio State University Series on Attitudes and Persuasion, 4, 1–24.

Krosnick, J. A., & Schuman, H. (1988). Attitude intensity, importance, and certainty and susceptibility to response effects. *Journal of Personality and Social Psychology, 54,* 940–952.

Kross, E., Verduyn, P., Demiralp, E., Park, J., Lee, D. S., Lin, N., Shablack, H., Jonides, J., & Ybarra, O. (2013). Facebook use predicts declines in subjective well-being in young adults. *Plos One, 8,* e69841.

Krueger, A. B., & Malečková, J. (2009). Attitudes and action: Public opinion and the occurrence of international terrorism. *Science, 325,* 1534–1536.

Krueger, J., & Clement, R. W. (1994). Memory-based judgments about multiple categories: A revision and extension of Tajfel's accentuation theory. *Journal of Personality and Social Psychology, 67,* 35–47.

Krueger, J., & Rothbart, M. (1988). Use of categorical and individuating information in making inferences about personality. *Journal of Personality and Social Psychology, 55,* 187–195.

Krueger, J. I., DiDonato, T. E., & Freestone, D. (2012). Social projection can solve social dilemmas. *Psychological Inquiry, 23,* 1–27.

Krueger, J. I., & Funder, D. C. (2003a). Towards a balanced social psychology: Causes, consequences and cures for the problem-seeking approach to social behavior and cognition. *Behavior and Brain Sciences, 27,* 313–349.

Krueger, J. I., & Funder, D. C. (2003b). Social psychology: A field in search of a center—Response. *Behavior and Brain Sciences, 27,* 361–376.

Krueger, R. F., Hicks, B. M., & McGue, M. (2001). Altruism and antisocial behavior: Independent tendencies, unique personality correlates, distinct etiologies. *Psychological Science, 12,* 397–402.

Kruger, J., & Dunning, D. (1999). Unskilled and unaware of it: How difficulties in recognizing one's own incompetence lead to inflated self-assessments. *Journal of Personality and Social Psychology, 77,* 1121–1134.

Kruger, J., Epley, N., Parker, J., & Ng, Z. (2005). Egocentrism over e-mail: Can we communicate as well as we think? *Journal of Personality and Social Psychology, 89*(6), 925.

Kruger, J., & Gilovich, T. (1999). "Naive cynicism" in everyday theories of responsibility assessment: On biased assumptions of bias. *Journal of Personality and Social Psychology, 76,* 743–753.

Kruger, J., Gordon, C. L., & Kuban, J. (2006). Intentions in teasing: When "just kidding" just isn't good enough. *Journal of Personality and Social Psychology,* 90, 412–425.

Kruglanski, A. W., & Ajzen, I. (1983). Bias and error in human judgment. *European Journal of Social Psychology, 13,* 1–44.

Kruglanski, A. W., Chen, X., Dechesne, M., Fishman, S., & Orehek E. (2009). Fully committed: Suicide bombers' motivation and the quest for personal significance. *Political Psychology, 30,* 331–357.

Kruglanski, A. W., & Fishman, S. (2006). The psychology of terrorism: "Syndrome" versus "tool" perspective. *Journal of Terrorism and Political Violence, 18(2),* 193–215.

Kruglanski, A. W., Gelfand, M., & Gunaratna, R. (2010, January). Detainee deradicalization: A challenge for psychological science. *APS Observer, 23,* 20–22.

Kruglanski, A. W., & Gigerenzer, G. (2011). Intuitive and deliberate judgments are based on common principles. *Psychological Review, 118,* 97–109.

Kruglanski, A. W., & Golec de Zavala, A. (2005). Individual motivations, the group process and organizational strategies in suicide terrorism. *Psychology and Sociology (Psycologie et sociologie).*

Kruglanski, A. W., & Webster, D. M. (1991). Group members' reactions to opinion deviates and conformists at varying degrees of proximity to decision deadline and of environmental noise. *Journal of Personality and Social Psychology, 61,* 212–225.

Krull, D. S., Loy, M. H-M., Lin, J., Wang, C-F., Chen, S., & Zhao, X. (1999). The fundamental fundamental attribution error: Correspondence bias in individualist and collectivist cultures. *Personality and Social Psychology Bulletin, 25,* 1208–1219.

Kubany, E. S., Bauer, G. B., Pangilinan, M. E., Muroka, M. Y., & Enriquez, V. G. (1995). Impact of labeled anger and blame in intimate relationships. *Journal of Cross-Cultural Psychology, 26,* 65–83.

Kubey, R., & Csikszentmihalyi, M. (2002, February). Television addiction is no mere metaphor. *Scientific American, 286,* 74–82.

Kugihara, N. (1999). Gender and social loafing in Japan. *Journal of Social Psychology, 139,* 516–526.

Kuhns, J. B., Exum, M. L., Clodfelter, T. A., & Bottia, M. C. (2014). The prevalence of alcohol-involved homicide offending: A meta-analytic review. *Homicide Studies,* 18, 251–270.

Kunda, Z., Fong, G. T., Sanitioso, R., & Reber, E. (1993). Directional questions direct self-conceptions. *Journal of Experimental Social Psychology, 29,* 63–86.

Kunda, Z., & Oleson, K. C. (1995). Maintaining stereotypes in the face of disconfirmation: Constructing grounds for subtyping deviants. *Journal of Personality and Social Psychology, 68,* 565–579.

Kunda, Z., & Oleson, K. C. (1997). When exceptions prove the rule: How extremity of deviance determines the impact of deviant examples on stereotypes. *Journal of Personality and Social Psychology, 72,* 965–979.

Kunda, Z., & Sinclair, L. (1999). Motivated reasoning with stereotypes: Activation, application, and inhibition. *Psychological Inquiry, 10,* 12–22.

Kunda, Z., & Spencer, S. J. (2003). When do stereotypes come to mind and when do they color judgment? A goal-based theoretical framework for stereotype activation and application. *Psychological Bulletin, 129,* 522–544.

Kunkel, D. (2001, February 4). Sex on TV. Menlo Park, CA: Henry J. Kaiser Family Foundation. Retrieved from http://www.kff.org

Kunst-Wilson, W. R., & Zajonc, R. B. (1980). Affective discrimination of stimuli that cannot be recognized. *Science, 207,* 557–558.

Kuntsche, E. K., Picket, W., Overpeck, M. Craig, W., Boyce, W., & de Matos, M. G. (2006). Television viewing and forms of bullying among adolescents from eight countries. *Journal of Adolescent Health, 39,* 908–915.

Kutner, L., & Olson, C. K. (2008). *Grand theft childhood: The surprising truth about violent video games and what parents can do* (pp. 111–137). New York: Simon & Schuster.

Lacey, M. (2004, April 9). A decade after massacres, Rwanda outlaws ethnicity. *New York Times.* Retrieved from http://www.nytimes.com

LaFromboise, T., Coleman, H. L. K., & Gerton, J. (1993). Psychological impact of biculturalism: Evidence and theory. *Psychological Bulletin, 114,* 395–412.

Lagerspetz, K. (1979). Modification of aggressiveness in mice. In S. Feshbach & A. Fraczek (Eds.), *Aggression and behavior change.* New York: Praeger.

Lagerspetz, K. M. J., Bjorkqvist, K., Berts, M., & King, E. (1982). Group aggression among school children in three schools. *Scandinavian Journal of Psychology, 23,* 45–52.

Lai, C. K., Marini, M., Lehr, S. A., Cerruti, C., Shin, J. E., Joy-Gaba, J. A., Ho, A. K., Teachman, B. A., Wojcik, S. P., Koleva, S. P., Frazier, R. S., Heiphetz, L., Chen, E. E., Turner, R. N., Haidt, J., Kesebir, S., Hawkins, C. B., Schaefer, H. S., Rubichi, S., … Nosek, B. A. (2014). Reducing implicit racial preferences: I. A comparative investigation of 17 interventions. *Journal of Experimental Psychology: General, 143,* 1765–1785.

Laird, J. D. (1974). Self-attribution of emotion: The effects of expressive behavior on the quality of emotional experience. *Journal of Personality and Social Psychology, 29,* 475–486.

Laird, J. D. (1984). The real role of facial response in the experience of emotion: A reply to Tourangeau and Ellsworth, and others. *Journal of Personality and Social Psychology, 47,* 909–917.

Lakin, J. L., & Chartrand, T. L. (2003). Using nonconscious behavioral mimicry to create affiliation and rapport. *Psychological Science, 14,* 334–339.

Lakin, J. L., Chartrand, T. L., & Arkin, R. M. (2008). I am too just like you: Nonconscious mimicry as an automatic behavioral response to social exclusion. *Psychological Science, 19,* 816–821.

Lalancette, M-F., & Standing, L. (1990). Asch fails again. *Social Behavior and Personality, 18,* 7–12.

Lalonde, R. N. (1992). The dynamics of group differentiation in the face of defeat. *Personality and Social Psychology Bulletin, 18,* 336–342.

Lalwani, A. K., Shavitt, S., & Johnson, T. (2006). What is the relation between cultural orientation and socially desirable responding? *Journal of Personality and Social Psychology, 90,* 165–178.

Lamal, P. A. (1979). College student common beliefs about psychology. *Teaching of Psychology, 6,* 155–158.

Lamb, C. S., & Crano, W. D. (2014). Parents' beliefs and children's marijuana use: Evidence for a self-fulfilling prophecy effect. *Addictive Behaviors, 39,* 127–132.

Lambert, N. M., DeWall, C. N., Bushman, B. J., Stillman, T. F., Fincham, F. D., & Pond, R. S. (2011). Lashing out in lust: Effect of pornography on nonsexual, physical aggression against relationship partners. Unpublished manuscript, Florida State University.

Lambert, N. M., Negash, S., Stillman, T. F., Olmstead, S. B., & Fincham, F. D. (2012). A love that doesn't last: Pornography consumption and weakened commitment to a romantic partner. *Journal of Social and Clinical Psychology, 31,* 410–438.

Lamont, R. A., Swift, H. J., & Abrams, D. (2015). A review and meta-analysis of age-based stereotype threat: Negative stereotypes, not facts, do the damage. *Psychology and Aging, 30,* 180–193.

Landers, A. (1969, April 8). Syndicated newspaper column.

Landers, A. (1985, August). Is affection more important than sex? *Reader's Digest,* 44–46.

Lane, D. J., Gibbons, F. X., O'Hara, R. E., & Gerrard, M. (2011). Standing out from the crowd: How comparison to prototypes can decrease health-risk behavior in young adults. *Basic and Applied Social Psychology, 33,* 228–238.

Langer, E. J. (1977). The psychology of chance. *Journal for the Theory of Social Behavior, 7,* 185–208.

Langer, E. J., & Imber, L. (1980). The role of mindlessness in the perception of deviance. *Journal of Personality and Social Psychology, 39,* 360–367.

Langer, E. J., & Rodin, J. (1976). The effects of choice and enhanced personal responsibility for the aged: A field experiment in an institutional setting. *Journal of Personality and Social Psychology, 334,* 191–198.

Langer, E. J., & Roth, J. (1975). Heads I win, tails it's chance: The illusion of control as a function of the sequence of outcomes in a purely chance task. *Journal of Personality and Social Psychology, 32,* 951–955.

Langford, D. J., Crager, S. E., Shehzad, Z., Smith, S. B., Sotocinal, S. G., Levenstadt, J. S., Chanda, M. L., Levitin, D. J., & Mogil, J. S. (2006). Social modulation of pain as evidence for empathy in mice. *Science, 312,* 1967–1970.

Langlois, J., Kalakanis, L., Rubenstein, A., Larson, A., Hallam, M., & Smoot, M. (1996). *Maxims and myths of beauty: A meta-analytic and theoretical review.* Paper presented to the American Psychological Society convention.

Langlois, J. H., Kalakanis, L., Rubenstein, A. J., Larson, A., Hallam, M., & Smoot, M. (2000). Maxims or myths of beauty? A meta-analytic and theoretical review. *Psychological Bulletin, 126,* 390–423.

Langlois, J. H., & Roggman, L. A. (1990). Attractive faces are only average. *Psychological Science, 1,* 115–121.

Langlois, J. H., Roggman, L. A., Casey, R. J., Ritter, J. M., Rieser-Danner, L. A., & Jenkins, V. Y. (1987). Infant preferences for attractive faces: Rudiments of a stereotype? *Developmental Psychology, 23,* 363–369.

Langlois, J. H., Roggman, L. A., & Musselman, L. (1994). What is average and what is not average about attractive faces? *Psychological Science, 5,* 214–220.

Lanzetta, J. T. (1955). Group behavior under stress. *Human Relations, 8,* 29–53.

Larrick, R. P., Timmerman, T. A., Carton, A. M., and Abrevaya, J. (2011). Temper, temperature, and temptation: Heat-related retaliation in baseball. *Psychological Science, 23*(6), 1–6.

Larsen, K. (1974). Conformity in the Asch experiment. *Journal of Social Psychology, 94,* 303–304.

Larsen, K. S. (1990). The Asch conformity experiment: Replication and transhistorical comparisons. *Journal of Social Behavior and Personality, 5*(4), 163–168.

Larson, J. R., Jr., Foster-Fishman, P. G., & Keys, C. B. (1994). Discussion of shared and unshared information in decision-making groups. *Journal of Personality and Social Psychology, 67,* 446–461.

Larsen, R. J., & Diener, E. (1987). Affect intensity as an individual difference characteristic: A review. *Journal of Research in Personality, 21,* 1–39.

Larsson, K. (1956). *Conditioning and sexual behavior in the male albino rat.* Stockholm: Almqvist & Wiksell.

Larwood, L. (1978). Swine flu: A field study of self-serving biases. *Journal of Applied Social Psychology, 18,* 283–289.

Larwood, L., & Whittaker, W. (1977). Managerial myopia: Self-serving biases in organizational planning. *Journal of Applied Psychology, 62,* 194–198.

Lassiter, G. D. (2010). Psychological science and sound public policy: Video recording of custodial interrogations. *American Psychologist, 65,* 768–779.

Lassiter, G. D., Diamond, S. S., Schmidt, H. C., & Elek, J. K. (2007). Evaluating videotaped confessions. *Psychological Science, 18,* 224–226.

Lassiter, G. D., & Dudley, K. A. (1991). The a priori value of basic research: The case of videotaped confessions. *Journal of Social Behavior and Personality, 6,* 7–16.

Lassiter, G. D., Geers, A. L., Handley, I. M., Weiland, P. E., & Munhall, P. J. (2002). Videotaped interrogations and confessions: A simple change in camera perspective alters verdicts in simulated trials. *Journal of Applied Psychology, 87,* 867–874.

Lassiter, G. D., & Irvine, A. A. (1986). Videotaped confessions: The impact of camera point of view on judgments of coercion. *Journal of Applied Social Psychology, 16,* 268–276.

Lassiter, G. D., & Munhall, P. J. (2001). The genius effect: Evidence for a nonmotivational interpretation. *Journal of Experimental Social Psychology, 37,* 349–355.

Lassiter, G. D., Munhall, P. J., Berger, I. P., Weiland, P. E., Handley, I. M., & Geers, A. L. (2005). Attributional complexity and the camera perspective bias in videotaped confessions. *Basic and Applied Social Psychology, 27,* 27–35.

Latané, B., & Dabbs, J. M., Jr. (1975). Sex, group size and helping in three cities. *Sociometry, 38,* 180–194.

Latané, B., & Darley, J. M. (1968). Group inhibition of bystander intervention in emergencies. *Journal of Personality and Social Psychology, 10,* 215–221.

Latané, B., & Darley, J. M. (1970). *The unresponsive bystander: Why doesn't he help?* New York: Appleton-Century-Crofts.

Latané, B., & Nida, S. (1981). Ten years of research on group size and helping. *Psychological Bulletin, 89,* 308–324.

Latané, B., & Rodin, J. (1969). A lady in distress: Inhibiting effects of friends and strangers on bystander intervention. *Journal of Experimental Social Psychology, 5,* 189–202.

Latané, B., Williams, K., & Harkins. S. (1979). Many hands make light the work: The causes and consequences of social loafing. *Journal of Personality and Social Psychology, 37,* 822–832.

Lau, G. P., Kay, A. C., & Spencer, S. J. (2008). Loving those who justify inequality: The effects of system threat on attraction to women who embody benevolent sexist ideals. *Psychological Science, 19,* 20.

Laughlin, P. R. (1996). Group decision making and collective induction. In E. H. Witte & J. H. Davis (Eds.), *Understanding group behavior: Consensual action by small groups.* Mahwah, NJ: Erlbaum.

Laughlin, P. R., & Adamopoulos, J. (1980). Social combination processes and individual learning for six-person cooperative groups on an intellective task. *Journal of Personality and Social Psychology, 38,* 941–947.

Laughlin, P. R., Hatch, E. C., Silver, J. S., & Boh, L. (2006). Groups perform better than the best individuals on letters-to-numbers problems: Effects of group size. *Journal of Personality and Social Psychology, 90,* 644–651.

Laughlin, P. R., Zander, M. L., Knievel, E. M., & Tan, T. K. (2003). Groups perform better than the best individuals on letters-to-numbers problems: Informative equations and effective strategies. *Journal of Personality and Social Psychology, 85,* 684–694.

Laumann, E. O., Gagnon, J. H., Michael, R. T., & Michaels, S. (1994). *The social organization of sexuality: Sexual practices in the United States.* Chicago: University of Chicago Press.

Laws, H. B., Ellerbeck, N. E., Rodrigues, A. S., Simmons, J. A., & Ansell, E. B. (2017). Social rejection and alcohol use in daily life. *Alcoholism: Clinical and Experimental Research, 41,* 820–827.

Lawson, T. J. (2010). The social spotlight increases blindness to change blindness. *Basic and Applied Social Psychology, 32,* 360–368.

Layous, K., Nelson, S. K., Oberle, E., Schonert-Reichl, K. A., & Lyubomirsky, S. (2012). Kindness counts: Prompting prosocial behavior in preadolescents boosts peer acceptance and well-being. *Plos One, 7,* e51380.

Lazarsfeld, P. F. (1949). The American soldier—an expository review. *Public Opinion Quarterly, 13,* 377–404.

Lazer, D., Pentland, A., Adamic, L., Aral, S., Barabási, A-L., Brewer, D., Christakis, N., Contractor, N., Fowler, J., Gutmann, M., Jebara, T., King, G., Macy, M., Roy, D., & Van Alstyne, M. (2009). Computational social science. *Science, 323,* 721–723.

Leach, J. K., & Patall, E. A. (2013). Maximizing and counterfactual thinking in academic major decision making. *Journal of Career Assessment, 21,* 414–429.

Leach, S., & Weick, M. (2018). Can people judge the veracity of their intuitions? *Social Psychological and Personality Science, 9,* 40–49.

Leary, M. (1994). *Self-presentation: Impression management and interpersonal behavior.* Pacific Grove, CA: Brooks/Cole.

Leary, M. R. (1998). The social and psychological importance of self-esteem. In R. M. Kowalski & M. R. Leary (Eds.), *The social psychology of emotional and behavioral problems.* Washington, DC: American Psychological Association.

Leary, M. R. (2001). Social anxiety as an early warning system: A refinement and extension of the self-presentation theory of social anxiety. In S. G. Hofmann & P. M. DiBartolo (Eds.), *From social anxiety to social phobia: Multiple perspectives.* Needham Heights, MA: Allyn & Bacon.

Leary, M. R. (2004a). *The curse of the self: Self-awareness, egotism, and the quality of human life.* New York: Oxford University Press.

Leary, M. R. (2004b). The self we know and the self we show: Self-esteem, self-presentation, and the maintenance of interpersonal relationships. In M. Brewer & M. Hewstone (Eds.), *Emotion and motivation.* Malden, MA: Usishers.

Leary, M. R. (2007). Motivational and emotional aspects of the self. *Annual Review of Psychology, 58,* 317–344.

Leary, M. R. (2010). Affiliation, acceptance, and belonging: The pursuit of interpersonal connection. In S. T. Fiske, D. T. Gilbert, & G. Lindzey (Eds.), *Handbook of social psychology* (5th ed.). Hoboken, NJ: Wiley.

Leary, M. R. (2016). *Introduction to behavioral research methods*. Pacific Grove: Brooks/Cole Publishing Company.

Leary, M. R., & Baumeister, R. F. (2000). The nature and function of self-esteem: Sociometer theory. In M. P. Zanna (Ed.) *Advances in experimental social psychology* (Vol. 32) (pp. 1–62). San Diego, CA: Academic Press.

Leary, M. R., & Kowalski, R. M. (1995). *Social anxiety.* New York: Guilford.

Leary, M. R., Kowalski, R. M., Smith, L., & Phillips, S. (2003). Teasing, rejection, and violence: Case studies of the school shootings. *Aggressive Behavior, 29,* 202–214.

Leary, M. R., Nezlek, J. B., Radford-Davenport, D., Martin, J., & McMullen, A. (1994). Self-presentation in everyday interactions: Effects of target familiarity and gender composition. *Journal of Personality and Social Psychology, 67,* 664–673.

Leary, M. R., Twenge, J. M., & Quinlivan, E. (2006). Interpersonal rejection as a determinant of anger and aggression. *Personality and Social Psychology Review, 10,* 111–132.

Leckelt, M., Kufner, A. C. P., Nestler, S., & Back, M. D. (2015). Behavioral processes underlying the decline of narcissists' popularity over time. *Journal of Personality and Social Psychology, 109,* 856–871.

Ledesma, R. D., Tosi, J., Poó, F. M., Montes, S. A., & López, S. S. (2015). Implicit attitudes and road safety behaviors. The helmet-use case. *Accident Analysis & Prevention, 79,* 190–197.

LeDoux, J. (1994, June). Emotion, memory and the brain. *Scientific American,* 50–57.

LeDoux, J. (1996). *The emotional brain: The mysterious underpinnings of emotional life.* New York: Simon & Schuster.

Lee, F., Hallahan, M., & Herzog, T. (1996). Explaining real-life events: How culture and domain shape attributions.

Personality and Social Psychology Bulletin, 22, 732–741.

Lee, I. C., Pratto, F., & Johnson, B. T. (2011). Intergroup consensus/disagreement in support of group-based hierarchy: An examination of socio-structural and psycho-cultural factors. *Psychological Bulletin, 137*(6), 1029–1064.

Lee, S., Rogge, R. D., & Reis, H. T. (2010). Assessing the seeds of relationship decay: Using implicit evaluations to detect the early stages of disillusionment. *Psychological Science, 21,* 857–864.

Lee, S. H., Rotman, J. D., & Perkins, A. W. (2014). Embodied cognition and social consumption: Self-regulating temperature through social products and behaviors. *Journal of Consumer Psychology, 24,* 234–240.

Lee, S. W. S., & Schwarz, N. (2012). Bidirectionality, mediation, and moderation of metaphorical effects: The embodiment of social suspicion and fishy smells. *Journal of Personality and Social Psychology, 103,* 737–749.

Lee, Y-P., & Bond, M. H. (1996). *How friendship develops out of personality and values: A study of interpersonal attraction in Chinese culture.* Unpublished manuscript, Chinese University of Hong Kong.

Lee, Y-T. (1996). Difference, not prejudice, engenders intergroup tension. *American Psychologist, 51,* 267–268.

Lee, Y-T., & Seligman, M. E. P. (1997). Are Americans more optimistic than the Chinese? *Personality and Social Psychology Bulletin, 23,* 32–40.

Legate, N., DeHaan, C. R., Weinstein, N., & Ryan, R. M. (2013). Hurting you hurts me too: The psychological costs of complying with ostracism. *Psychological Science, 24,* 583–588.

Lehavot, K., & Lambert, A. J. (2007). Toward a greater understanding of antigay prejudice: On the role of sexual orientation and gender role violation. *Basic and Applied Social Psychology, 29,* 279–292.

Lehman, D. R., Krosnick, J. A., West, R. L., & Fan, L. (1992). The focus of judgment effect: A question wording effect due to hypothesis confirmation bias. *Personality and Social Psychology Bulletin, 18,* 690–699.

Lehman, D. R., Lempert, R. O., & Nisbett, R. E. (1988). The effects of graduate training on reasoning: Formal discipline and thinking about everyday-life events. *American Psychologist, 43,* 431–442.

Leippe, M. R., & Eisenstadt, D. (1994). Generalization of dissonance reduction: Decreasing prejudice through induced compliance. *Journal of Personality and Social Psychology, 67,* 395–413.

Leippe, M. R., & Elkin, R. A. (1987). *Dissonance reduction strategies and accountability to self and others: Ruminations and some initial research.* Presentation to the Fifth International Conference on Affect, Motivation, and Cognition, Nags Head Conference Center, Nags Head, NC.

Leiserowitz, A., Maibach, E., Rosenthal, S., Kotcher, J., Bergquist, P., Ballew, M., Goldberg, M., & Gustafson, A., (2019). Climate Change in the American Mind. Retrieved from https://climatecommunication.yale.edu/publications/climate-change-in-the-american-mind-april-2019/2/ on December 23, 2019.

Leiserowitz, A., Maibach, E., Roser-Renouf, C., & Smith, N. (2011). *Climate change in the American mind: Americans' global warming beliefs and attitudes in May 2011.* Yale University and George Mason University. New Haven, CT: Yale Project on Climate Change Communication.

Lemay, E. P., Jr., Clark, M. S., & Greenberg, A. (2010). What is beautiful is good because what is beautiful is desired: Physical attractiveness stereotyping as projection of interpersonal goals. *Personality and Social Psychology Bulletin, 36,* 339–353.

Lemmer, G., & Wagner, U. (2015). Can we really reduce ethnic prejudice outside the lab? A meta-analysis of direct and indirect contact interventions. *European Journal of Social Psychology, 45,* 152–168.

Lemyre, L., & Smith, P. M. (1985). Intergroup discrimination and self-esteem in the minimal group paradigm. *Journal of Personality and Social Psychology, 49,* 660–670.

Lench, H. C., Quas, J. A., & Edelstein, R. S. (2006). My child is better than average: The extension and restriction of unrealistic optimism. *Journal of Applied Social Psychology, 36,* 2963–2979.

Lenton, A. P., & Francesconi, M. (2010). How humans cognitively manage an abundance of mate options. *Psychological Science, 21,* 528–533.

Leodoro, G., & Lynn, M. (2007). The effect of server posture on the tips of Whites and Blacks. *Journal of Applied Social Psychology, 37,* 201–209.

Leone, C., & Hawkins, L. B. (2006). Self-monitoring and close relationships. *Journal of Personality, 74,* 739–778.

Lepore, S. J., Ragan, J. D., & Jones, S. (2000). Talking facilitates cognitive-emotional processes of adaptation to an acute stressor. *Journal of Personality and Social Psychology, 78,* 499–508.

Lepper, M. R., & Greene, D. (Eds.) (1979). *The hidden costs of reward.* Hillsdale, NJ: Erlbaum.

Lerner, M. J. (1980). *The belief in a just world: A fundamental delusion.* New York: Plenum.

Lerner, M. J., & Miller, D. T. (1978). Just world research and the attribution process: Looking back and ahead. *Psychological Bulletin, 85,* 1030–1051.

Lerner, M. J., & Simmons, C. H. (1966). Observer's reaction to the "innocent victim": Compassion or rejection? *Journal of Personality and Social Psychology, 4,* 203–210.

Lerner, M. J., Somers, D. G., Reid, D., Chiriboga, D., & Tierney, M. (1991). Adult children as caregivers: Egocentric biases in judgments of sibling contributions. *The Gerontologist, 31,* 746–755.

Leshner, A. I. (2005, October). Science and religion should not be adversaries. *APS Observer.* Retrieved from http://www.psychologicalscience.org

Leung, K., & Bond, M. H. (1984). The impact of cultural collectivism on reward allocation. *Journal of Personality and Social Psychology, 47,* 793–804.

Levav, J., & Fitzsimons, G. J. (2006). When questions change behavior: The role of ease of representation. *Psychological Science, 17,* 207–213.

Leventhal, H. (1970). Findings and theory in the study of fear communications. In L. Berkowitz (Ed.), *Advances in experimental social psychology* (Vol. 5). New York: Academic Press.

Levesque, M. J., Nave, C. S., & Lowe, C. A. (2006). Toward an understanding of gender differences in inferring sexual interest. *Psychology of Women Quarterly, 30,* 150–158.

Levin, S., Matthews, M., Guimond, S., Sidanius, J., Pratto, F., Kteily, N., Pitpitan, E. V., & Dover, T. (2011). Assimilation, multiculturalism, and colorblindness: Mediated and moderated relationships between social dominance orientation and prejudice. *Journal of Experimental Social Psychology, 47,* 208–214.

Levine, J. M. (1989). Reaction to opinion deviance in small groups. In P. Paulus (Ed.), *Psychology of group influence: New perspectives.* Hillsdale, NJ: Erlbaum.

Levine, J. M., & Moreland, R. L. (1985). Innovation and socialization in small groups. In S. Moscovici, G. Mugny, & E. Van Avermaet (Eds.), *Perspectives on minority influence.* Cambridge: Cambridge University Press.

Levine, M., & Crowther, S. (2008). The responsive bystander: How social group membership and group size can encourage as well as inhibit bystander intervention. *Journal of Personality and Social Psychology, 95,* 1429–1439.

Levine, R. (2003). *The power of persuasion: How we're bought and sold.* New York: Wiley.

Levine, R. V. (2001). Cross-cultural differences in helping strangers. *Journal of Cross-Cultural Psychology, 32,* 543–560.

Levine, R. V. (2003). The kindness of strangers. *American Scientist, 91,* 226–233.

Levine, R. V., Martinez, T. S., Brase, G., & Sorenson, K. (1994). Helping in 36 U.S. cities. *Journal of Personality and Social Psychology, 67,* 69–82.

Levine, R. V., Norenzayan, A., & Philbrick, K. (2001). Cross-cultural differences in helping strangers. *Journal of Cross-Cultural Psychology, 32*(5), 543–560.

Levinger, G. (1987). The limits of deterrence: An introduction. *Journal of Social Issues, 43,* 1–4.

Levinson, H. (1950). *The science of chance: From probability to statistics.* New York: Rinehart.

Levitan, L. C., & Verhulst, B. (2016). Conformity in groups: The effects of others' views on expressed attitudes and attitude change. *Political Behavior, 38*(2), 277–315.

Levitan, L. C., & Visser, P. S. (2008). The impact of the social context on resistance to persuasion: Effortful versus effortless responses to counter-attitudinal information. *Journal of Experimental Social Psychology, 44,* 640–649.

Levy, S. R., Stroessner, S. J., & Dweck, C. S. (1998). Stereotype formation and endorsement: The role of implicit theories. *Journal of Personality and Social Psychology, 74,* 1421–1436.

Levy-Leboyer, C. (1988). Success and failure in applying psychology. *American Psychologist, 43,* 779–785.

Lewandowski, G. W., & Bizzoco, N. M. (2007). Addition through subtraction: Growth following the dissolution of a low-quality relationship. *Journal of Positive Psychology, 2,* 40–54.

Lewicki, P. (1985). Nonconscious biasing effects of single instances on subsequent judgments. *Journal of Personality and Social Psychology, 48,* 563–574.

Lewin, K. (1936). *A dynamic theory of personality.* New York: McGraw-Hill.

Lewin, K. (1952). *Field theory in social science: Selected theoretical papers by Kurt Lewin.* London: Tavistock.

Lewis, C. S. (1952). *Mere Christianity.* New York: Macmillan.

Lewis, C. S. (1974). *The horse and his boy.* New York: Collier Books.

Lewis, D. O. (1998). *Guilty by reason of insanity.* London: Arrow.

Lewis, M. B., & Bowler, P. J. (2009). Botulinum toxin cosmetic therapy correlates with a more positive mood. *Journal of Cosmetic Dermatology, 8,* 24–26.

Lewis, M. B. (2016). Arguing that Black is White: Racial categorization of mixed-race faces. *Perception, 45,* 505–514.

Lewis, R. S., Goto, S. G., & Kong, L. L. (2008). Culture and context: East Asian American and European American differences in P3 event-related potentials and self-construal. *Personality and Social Psychology Bulletin, 34,* 623–634.

Leyens, J-P., Camino, L., Parke, R. D., & Berkowitz, L. (1975). Effects of movie violence on aggression in a field setting as a function of group dominance and cohesion. *Journal of Personality and Social Psychology, 32,* 346–360.

Leyens, J-P., Cortes, B., Demoulin, S., Dovidio, J. F., Fiske, S. T., Gaunt, R., Paladino, M-P., Rodriguez-Perez, A., Rodriguez-Torres, R, & Vaes, J. (2003). Emotional prejudice, essentialism, and nationalism. *European Journal of Social Psychology, 33,* 703–717.

Leyens, J-P., Demoulin, S., Vaes, J., Gaunt, R., & Paladino, M. P. (2007). Infrahumanization: The wall of group differences. *Social Issues and Policy Review, 1,* 139–172.

Li, N. P., Bailey, J. M., Kenrick, D. T., & Linsenmeier, J. A. W. (2002). The necessities and luxuries of mate preferences: Testing the tradeoffs. *Journal of Personality and Social Psychology, 82,* 947–955.

Li, T., & Chan, D. K-S. (2012). How anxious and avoidant attachment affect romantic relationship quality differently: A meta-analytic review. *European Journal of Social Psychology, 42,* 406–419.

Li, Y., Johnson, E. J., & Zaval, L. (2011). Local warming: Daily temperature influences belief in global warming. *Psychological Science, 22,* 454–459.

Liberman, A., & Chaiken, S. (1992). Defensive processing of personally relevant health messages. *Personality and Social Psychology Bulletin, 18,* 669–679.

Liberman, V., Samuels, S. M., & Ross, L. (2004). The name of the game: Predictive power of reputations vs. situational labels in determining Prisoner's Dilemma game moves. *Personality and Social Psychology Bulletin, 30,* 1175–1185.

Lichacz, F. M., & Partington, J. T. (1996). Collective efficacy and true group performance. *International Journal of Sport Psychology, 27,* 146.

Lichtblau, E. (2003, March 18). U.S. seeks $289 billion in cigarette makers' profits. *New York Times.* Retrieved from http://www.nytimes.com

Lichtblau, E. (2005, August 24). Profiling report leads to a demotion. *New York Times.* Retrieved from http://www.nytimes.com

Lichtenstein, S., & Fischhoff, B. (1980). Training for calibration. *Organizational Behavior and Human Performance, 26,* 149–171.

Lieberman, M. D., Ochsner, K. N., Gilbert, D. T., & Schacter, D. L. (2001). Do amnesics exhibit cognitive dissonance reduction? The role of explicit memory and attention in attitude change. *Psychological Science, 12,* 135–140.

Lilienfeld, S. O. (2017). Microaggressions: Strong claims, inadequate evidence. *Perspectives on Psychological Science, 12,* 138–169.

Lin, J-H. (2013). Do video games exert stronger effects on aggression than film? The role of media interactivity and identification on the association of violent content and aggressive outcomes. *Computers in Human Behavior, 29,* 535–543.

Lindskold, S. (1978). Trust development, the GRIT proposal, and the effects of conciliatory acts on conflict and cooperation. *Psychological Bulletin, 85,* 772–793.

Lindskold, S. (1981). The laboratory evaluation of GRIT: Trust, cooperation, aversion to using conciliation. Paper presented at the American Association for the Advancement of Science convention.

Lindskold, S., Bennett, R., & Wayner, M. (1976). Retaliation level as a foundation for subsequent conciliation. *Behavioral Science, 21,* 13–18.

Lindskold, S., Betz, B., & Walters, P. S. (1986). Transforming competitive or cooperative climate. *Journal of Conflict Resolution, 30,* 99–114.

Lindskold, S., & Collins, M. G. (1978). Inducing cooperation by groups and individuals. *Journal of Conflict Resolution, 22,* 679–690.

Lindskold, S., & Finch, M. L. (1981). Styles of announcing conciliation. *Journal of Conflict Resolution, 25,* 145–155.

Lindskold, S., & Han, G. (1988). GRIT as a foundation for integrative bargaining. *Personality and Social Psychology Bulletin, 14,* 335–345.

Lindskold, S., Han, G., & Betz, B. (1986a). Repeated persuasion in interpersonal conflict. *Journal of Personality and Social Psychology, 51,* 1183–1188.

Lindskold, S., Han, G., & Betz, B. (1986b). The essential elements of communication in the GRIT strategy. *Personality and Social Psychology Bulletin, 12,* 179–186.

Lindskold, S., Walters, P. S., Koutsourais, H., & Shayo, R. (1981). *Cooperators, competitors, and response to GRIT.*

Unpublished manuscript, Ohio University, Athens, OH.

Linssen, H., & Hagendoorn, L. (1994). Social and geographical factors in the explanation of the content of European nationality stereotypes. *British Journal of Social Psychology, 33,* 165–182.

Linville, P. W., Gischer, W. G., & Salovey, P. (1989). Perceived distributions of the characteristics of in-group and out-group members: Empirical evidence and a computer simulation. *Journal of Personality and Social Psychology, 57,* 165–188.

Lippa, R. A. (2007). The preferred traits of mates in a cross-national study of heterosexual and homosexual men and women: An examination of biological and cultural influences. *Archives of Sexual Behavior, 36,* 193–208.

Lipsitz, A., Kallmeyer, K., Ferguson, M., & Abas, A. (1989). Counting on blood donors: Increasing the impact of reminder calls. *Journal of Applied Social Psychology, 19,* 1057–1067.

LISPOP. (2011). Post-morten, 2011. Laurier Institute for the Study of Public Opinion and Policy. Retrieved from: https://www.lispop.ca/seat-projection/federal/2011-10-07/post-mortem-2011

Little, A., & Perrett, D. (2002). Putting beauty back in the eye of the beholder. *The Psychologist, 15,* 28–32.

Liu, D., & Baumeister, R. F. (2016). Social networking online and personality of self-worth: A meta-analysis. *Journal of Research In Personality, 64,* 79–89.

Liu, N., & Yu, R. (2018). Determining effects of virtually and physically present co-actor in evoking social facilitation. *Human Factors and Ergonomics in Manufacturing & Service Industries, 28*(5), 260–267. https://doi-org.library.smu.ca/10.1002/hfm.20743

Livingston, R. W. (2001). What you see is what you get: Systematic variability in perceptual-based social judgment. *Personality and Social Psychology Bulletin, 27,* 1086.

Livingstone, S., & Haddon, L. (2009). *EU Kids Online: Final report.* LSE, London: EU Kids Online.

Locke, E. A., & Latham, G. P. (1990). Work motivation and satisfaction: Light at the end of the tunnel. *Psychological Science, 1,* 240–246.

Locke, E. A., & Latham, G. P. (2002). Building a practically useful theory of goal setting and task motivation: A 35-year odyssey. *American Psychologist, 57*(9), 705.

Locke, E. A., & Latham, G. P. (2009). Has goal setting gone wild, or have its attackers abandoned good scholarship? *Academy of Management Perspectives, 23*(1).

Locke, K. D., & Horowitz, L. M. (1990). Satisfaction in interpersonal interactions as a function of similarity in level of dysphoria. *Journal of Personality and Social Psychology, 58,* 823–831.

Locksley, A., Borgida, E., Brekke, N., & Hepburn, C. (1980). Sex stereotypes and social judgment. *Journal of Personality and Social Psychology, 39,* 821–831.

Locksley, A., Hepburn, C., & Ortiz, V. (1982). Social stereotypes and judgments of individuals: An instance of the base-rate fallacy. *Journal of Experimental Social Psychology, 18,* 23–42.

Lockwood, P. (2002). Could it happen to you? Predicting the impact of downward comparisons on the self. *Journal of Personality and Social Psychology, 87,* 343–358.

Lockwood, P., Dolderman, D., Sadler, P., & Gerchak, E. (2004). Feeling better about doing worse: Social comparisons within romantic relationships. *Journal of Personality and Social Psychology, 87,* 80.

Lockwood, P., & Kunda, Z. (1997). Superstars and me: Predicting the impact of role models on the self. *Journal of Personality and Social Psychology, 73,* 91–103.

Loewenstein, G., & Schkade, D. (1999). Wouldn't it be nice? Predicting future feelings. In D. Kahneman, E. Diener, & N. Schwarz (Eds.), *Understanding well-being: Scientific perspectives on enjoyment and suffering.* New York: Russell Sage Foundation, 85–105.

Lofland, J., & Stark, R. (1965). Becoming a worldsaver: A theory of conversion to a deviant perspective. *American Sociological Review, 30,* 862–864.

Loftin, C., McDowall, D., Wiersema, B., & Cottey, T. J. (1991). Effects of restrictive licensing of handguns on homicide and suicide in the District of Columbia. *New England Journal of Medicine, 325,* 1615–1620.

Loftus, E. F. (1974, December). Reconstructing memory: The incredible eyewitness. *Psychology Today,* 117–119.

Loftus, E. F. (1979a). *Eyewitness testimony.* Cambridge, MA: Harvard University Press.

Loftus, E. F. (1979b). The malleability of human memory. *American Scientist, 67,* 312–320.

Loftus, E. F. (2003). Make-believe memories. *American Psychologist, 58*(11), 867.

Loftus, E. F. (2007). Memory distortions: Problems solved and unresolved. In M. Garry & H. Hayne (Eds.), *Do justice and let the sky fall: Elizabeth Loftus and her contributions to science, law, and academic freedom.* Mahway, NJ: Erlbaum.

Loftus, E. F. (2011a, August 31). The risk of ill-informed juries. *New York Times.* Retrieved from http://www.nytimes.com

Loftus, E. F. (2011b, September). Intelligence gathering post-9/11. *American Psychologist, 66,* 532–541.

Loftus, E. F., & Bernstein, D. M. (2005). Rich false memories: The royal road to success. In A. F. Healy (Ed.), *Experimental cognitive psychology and its applications.* Washington, DC: American Psychological Association.

Loftus, E. F., & Klinger, M. R. (1992). Is the unconscious smart or dumb? *American Psychologist, 47,* 761–765.

Logel, C., Walton, G. M., Spencer, S. J., Iserman, E. C., von Hippel, W., & Bell, A. E. (2009). Interacting with sexist men triggers social identity threat among female engineers. *Journal of Personality and Social Psychology, 96,* 1089–1103.

Logel, C. E. R., Iserman, E. C., Spencer, S. J., Davies, P. G., & Quinn, D. M. (2009). The perils of avoiding negative thoughts: Thought suppression as a mediator of stereotype threat. *Journal of Experimental Social Psychology, 45,* 299–312.

Lombardo, J. P., Weiss, R. F., & Buchanan, W. (1972). Reinforcing and attracting functions of yielding. *Journal of Personality and Social Psychology, 21,* 359–368.

London, P. (1970). The rescuers: Motivational hypotheses about Christians who saved Jews from the Nazis. In J. Macaulay & L. Berkowitz (Eds.), *Altruism and helping behavior.* New York: Academic Press.

Lonsdale, A. J., & North, A. C. (2011). Musical taste and the representativeness heuristic. *Psychology of Music, 40,* 131–142.

Lord, C. G., Lepper, M. R., & Preston, E. (1984). Considering the opposite: A corrective strategy for social judgment. *Journal of Personality and Social Psychology, 47,* 1231–1243.

Lord, C. G., Ross, L., & Lepper, M. (1979). Biased assimilation and attitude polarization: The effects of prior theories on subsequently considered evidence. *Journal of Personality and Social Psychology, 37,* 2098–2109.

Lord, W. (1955). *A night to remember.* New York: Holt.

Lortie-Lussier, M., Lemieux, S., & Godbout, L. (1989). Reports of a public manifestation: Their impact according to minority influence theory. *Journal of Social Psychology, 129,* 285–295.

Lott, A. J., & Lott, B. E. (1961). Group cohesiveness, communication level, and conformity. *Journal of Abnormal and Social Psychology, 62,* 408–412.

Lott, A. J., & Lott, B. E. (1974). The role of reward in the formation of positive interpersonal attitudes. In T. Huston (Ed.), *Foundations of interpersonal attraction.* New York: Academic Press.

Loughman, S., & Haslam, N. (2007). Animals and androids: Implicit associations between social categories and nonhumans. *Psychological Science, 18,* 116–121.

Lovett, F. (1997). Thinking about values (report of December 13, 1996, *Wall Street Journal* national survey). *The Responsive Community, 7*(2), 87.

Lowenstein, D. (2000, May 20). Interview. *The World.* Retrieved from http://www.cnn.com/TRANSCRIPTS/0005/20/stc.00.html

Lücken, M., & Simon, B. (2005). Cognitive and affective experiences of minority and majority members: The role of group size, status, and power. *Journal of Experimental Social Psychology, 41,* 396–413.

Lueptow, L. B., Garovich, L., & Lueptow, M. B. (1995). The persistence of gender stereotypes in the face of changing sex roles: Evidence contrary to the sociocultural model. *Ethology and Sociobiology, 16,* 509–530.

Lumsdaine, A. A., & Janis, I. L. (1953). Resistance to "counter-propaganda" produced by one-sided and two-sided "propaganda" presentations. *Public Opinion Quarterly, 17,* 311–318.

Lumsden, A., Zanna, M. P., & Darley, J. M. (1980). *When a newscaster presents counter-additional information: Education or propaganda?* Paper presented to the Canadian Psychological Association annual convention.

Lutsky, L. A., Risucci, D. A., & Tortolani, A. J. (1993). Reliability and accuracy of surgical resident peer ratings. *Evaluation Review, 17,* 444–456.

Lydon, J., & Dunkel-Schetter, C. (1994). Seeing is committing: A longitudinal study of bolstering commitment in amniocenesis patients. *Personality and Social Psychology Bulletin, 20,* 218–227.

Lydon, J. E., Meana, M., Sepinwall, D., Richards, N., & Mayman, S. (1999). The commitment calibration hypothesis: When do people devalue attractive alternatives? *Personality and Social Psychology Bulletin, 25,* 152–161.

Lykken, D. T. (1997). The American crime factory. *Psychological Inquiry, 8,* 261–270.

Lykken, D. T., & Tellegen, A. (1993). Is human mating adventitious or the result of lawful choice? A twin study of mate selection. *Journal of Personality and Social Psychology, 65,* 56–68.

Lynn, M., & Oldenquist, A. (1986). Egoistic and nonegoistic motives in social dilemmas. *American Psychologist, 41,* 529–534.

Lyons, L. (2003, September 23). Oh, boy: Americans still prefer sons. *Gallup Poll Tuesday Briefing.* Retrieved from http://www.gallup.com

Lyons, P. A., Kenworthy, J. B., & Popan, J. R. (2010). Ingroup identification and group-level narcissism as predictors of U.S. citizens' attitudes and behavior toward Arab immigrants. *Personality and Social Psychology Bulletin, 36,* 1267–1280.

Ma, D. S., Correll, J., Wittenbrink, B., Bar-Anan, Y., Sriram, N., & Nosek, B. A. (2013). When fatigue turns deadly: The association between fatigue and racial bias in the decision to shoot. *Basic and Applied Social Psychology, 35,* 515–524.

Ma, V., & Schoeneman, T. J. (1997). Individualism versus collectivism: A comparison of Kenyan and American self-concepts. *Basic and Applied Social Psychology, 19,* 261–273.

Maass, A. (1998). Personal communication from Universita degli Studi di Padova.

Maass, A. (1999). Linguistic intergroup bias: Stereotype perpetuation through language. In M. P. Zanna (Ed.), *Advances in experimental social psychology* (Vol. 31) (pp. 79–121). San Diego, CA: Academic Press.

Maass, A., & Clark, R. D., III (1984). Hidden impact of minorities: Fifteen years of minority influence research. *Psychological Bulletin, 95,* 428–450.

Maass, A., & Clark, R. D., III (1986). Conversion theory and simultaneous majority/minority influence: Can reactance offer an alternative explanation? *European Journal of Social Psychology, 16,* 305–309.

Maass, A., Milesi, A., Zabbini, S., & Stahlberg, D. (1995). Linguistic intergroup bias: Differential expectancies or in-group protection? *Journal of Personality and Social Psychology, 68,* 116–126.

Maass, A., Volparo, C., & Mucchi-Faina, A. (1996). Social influence and the verifiability of the issue under discussion: Attitudinal versus objective items. *British Journal of Social Psychology, 35,* 15–26.

Maccoby, N. (1980). Promoting positive health behaviors in adults. In L. A. Bond & J. C. Rosen (Eds.), *Competence and coping during adulthood.* Hanover, NH: University Press of New England.

Maccoby, N., & Alexander, J. (1980). Use of media in lifestyle programs. In P. O. Davidson & S. M. Davidson (Eds.). *Behavioral medicine: Changing health lifestyles.* New York: Brunner/Mazel.

MacCoun, R. J., & Kerr, N. L. (1988). Asymmetric influence in mock jury deliberation: Jurors' bias for leniency. *Journal of Personality and Social Psychology, 54,* 21–33.

MacDonald, G., & Leary, M. R. (2005). Why does social exclusion hurt? The relationship between social and physical pain. *Psychological Bulletin, 131,* 202.

MacDonald, G., Zanna, M. P., & Holmes, J. G. (2000). An experimental test of the role of alcohol in relationship conflict. *Journal of Experimental Social Psychology, 36,* 182–193.

MacDonald, T. K., & Ross, M. (1997). *Assessing the accuracy of predictions about dating relationships: How and why do lovers' predictions differ from those made by observers?* Unpublished manuscript, University of Lethbridge, Lethbridge, AB.

MacDonald, T. K., Zanna, M. P., & Fong, G. T. (1995). Decision making in altered states: Effects of alcohol on attitudes toward drinking and driving. *Journal of Personality and Social Psychology, 68,* 973–985.

Mack, D., & Rainey, D. (1990). Female applicants' grooming and personnel selection. *Journal of Social Behavior and Personality, 5,* 399–407.

Mackinnon, S. P., Jordan, C. H., & Wilson, A. E. (2011). Birds of a feather sit together: Physical similarity predicts seating choice. *Personality and Social Psychology Bulletin, 37,* 879–892.

MacLeod, C., & Campbell, L. (1992). Memory accessibility and probability judgments: An experimental evaluation of the availability heuristic. *Journal of Personality and Social Psychology, 63,* 890–902.

Macrae, C. N., Alnwick, M. A., Milne, A. B., & Schloerscheidt, A. M. (2002). Person perception across the menstrual cycle: Hormonal influences on social-cognitive functioning. *Psychological Science,* 13, 532–536.

Macrae, C. N., & Bodenhausen, G. V. (2000). Social cognition: Thinking categorically about others. *Annual Review of Psychology, 51,* 93–120.

Macrae, C. N., & Bodenhausen, G. V. (2001). Social cognition: Categorical person perception. *British Journal of Psychology, 92,* 239–255.

Macrae, C. N., Bodenhausen, G. V., Milne, A. B., & Jetten, J. (1994). Out of mind but back in sight: Stereotypes on the rebound. *Journal of Personality and Social Psychology, 67,* 808–817.

Macrae, C. N., Stangor, C., & Milne, A. B. (1994). Activating social stereotypes: A functional analysis. *Journal of Experimental Social Psychology, 30,* 370–389.

Maddux, J. E., & Gosselin, J. T. (2003). Self-efficacy. In M. R. Leary & J. P. Tangney (Eds.), *Handbook of self and identity.* New York: Guilford.

Maddux, J. E., & Rogers, R. W. (1983). Protection motivation and self-efficacy: A revised theory of fear appeals and attitude change. *Journal of Experimental Social Psychology, 19,* 469–479.

Maddux, W. W., Galinsky, A. D., Cuddy, A. J. C., & Polifroni, M. (2008). When being a model minority is good … and bad: Realistic threat explains negativity towards Asian Americans. *Personality and Social Psychology Bulletin, 34,* 74–89.

Maddux, W. W., Mullen, E., & Galinsky, A. D. (2008). Chameleons bake bigger pies and take bigger pieces: Strategic behavioral mimicry facilitates negotiation outcomes. *Journal of Experimental Social Psychology, 44,* 461–468.

Madon, S., Jussim, L., & Eccles, J. (1997). In search of the powerful self-fulfilling prophecy. *Journal of Personality and Social Psychology, 72,* 791–809.

Mae, L., Carlston, D. E., & Skowronski, J. (1999). Spontaneous trait transference to familiar communicators: Is a little knowledge a dangerous thing? *Journal of Personality and Social Psychology, 77,* 233–246.

Mahajan, N., & Wynn, K. (2012). Origins of "us" versus "Them": Prelinguistic infants prefer similar others. *Cognition, 124,* 227–233.

Maio, G. R., Bell, D., & Esses, V. M. (1996). Ambivalence in persuasion: The processing of messages about immigrant groups. *Journal of Experimental Social Psychology, 32,* 513–536.

Maio, G. R., & Olson, J. M. (1990). Involvement and persuasion: Evidence for different types of involvement. *Canadian Journal of Behavioural Science, 27,* 64–78.

Major, B., Quinton, W. J., & McCoy, S. K. (2002). Antecedents and consequences of attributions to discrimination: Theoretical and empirical advances. In M. P. Zanna (Ed.), *Advances in experimental social psychology* (Vol. 34) (pp. 251–330). San Diego: Academic Press.

Malahy, L. W., Rubinlicht, M. A., & Kaiser, C. R. (2009). Justifying inequality: A cross-temporal investigation of U.S. income disparities and just-world beliefs from 1973 to 2006. *Social Justice Research, 22,* 369–383.

Malamuth, N. M. (1996). The confluence model of sexual aggression. In D. M. Buss & N. M. Malamuth (Eds.), *Sex, power, conflict: Evolutionary and feminist perspectives.* New York: Oxford University Press.

Malamuth, N. M. (2003). Criminal and noncriminal sexual aggressors: Integrating psychopathy in a hierarchical-mediational confluence model. In R. A. Prentky, E. Janus, & M. Seto (Eds.), *Sexually coercive behavior: Understanding and management.* New York: Annals of the New York Academy of Sciences.

Malamuth, N. M., & Check, J. V. P. (1981). The effects of media exposure on acceptance of violence against women: A field experiment. *Journal of Research in Personality, 15,* 436–446.

Malamuth, N. M., Haber, S., & Feshbach, S. (1980, March). Testing hypotheses regarding rape: Exposure to sexual violence, sex difference, and the "normality" of rapists. *Journal of Research in Personality, 14,* 121–137.

Malkiel, B. G. (1985). *A random walk down Wall Street* (4th ed.). New York: W. W. Norton.

Malkiel, B. G. (1995, June). Returns from investing in equity mutual funds 1971 to 1991. *Journal of Finance,* 549–572.

Malkiel, B. G. (2016). *A random walk down Wall Street.* New York: W. W. Norton.

Malle, B. F. (2006). The actor-observer asymmetry in attribution: A (surprising) meta-analysis. *Psychological Bulletin, 132,* 895–919.

Mallet, R. K., & Swim, J. K. (2003). Collective guilt in the United States: Predicting support for social policies that alleviate social injustice. In N. Branscombe & B. Doosje (Eds.), *Collective guilt: International perspectives.* New York: Cambridge University Press.

Manata, B. (2019). Investigating the impact of racial diversity in decision-making groups: The moderating role of relationship conflict. *Negotiation and Conflict Management Research.* https://doi-org.library.smu.ca/10.1111/ncmr.12173

Maner, J. K., Gailliot, M. T., & Miller, S. L. (2009). The implicit cognition of relationship maintenance: Inattention to attractive alternatives. *Journal of Experimental Social Psychology, 45,* 174–179.

Maner, J. K., Miller, S. L., Schmidt, N. B., & Eckel, L. A. (2008). Submitting to defeat: Social anxiety, dominance threat, and decrements in testosterone. *Psychological Science, 19,* 764–768.

Manis, M., Cornell, S. D., & Moore, J. C. (1974). Transmission of attitude-relevant information through a communication chain. *Journal of Personality and Social Psychology, 30,* 81–94.

Manis, M., Nelson, T. E., & Shedler, J. (1988). Stereotypes and social judgment: Extremity, assimilation, and contrast. *Journal of Personality and Social Psychology, 55,* 28–36.

Manjoo, F. (2014, September 24). Exposing hidden bias at Google. *New York Times.* Retrieved from www.nytimes.com

Mann, L. (1981). The baiting crowd in episodes of threatened suicide. *Journal of Personality and Social Psychology, 41,* 703–709.

Mannes, A. E., & Moore, D. A. (2013). A behavioral demonstration of overconfidence in judgment. *Psychological Science, 24,* 1190–1197.

Manning, R., Levine, M., & Collins, A. (2007). The Kitty Genovese murder and the social psychology of helping: The parable of the 38 witnesses. *American Psychologist, 62,* 555–562.

Marcus, S. (1974, January 13). Review of *Obedience to authority. New York Times* Book Review, 1–2.

Marcus-Newhall, A., Pedersen, W. C., Carlson, M., & Miller, N. (2000). Displaced aggression is alive and well: A meta-analytic review. *Journal of Personality and Social Psychology, 78,* 670–689.

Mares, M-L., & Braun, M. T. (2013). Effects of conflict in tween sitcoms on U.S. students' moral reasoning about social exclusion. *Journal of Children and Media, 7,* 428–445.

Marigold, D. C., Holmes, J. G., & Ross, M. (2007). More than words: Reframing compliments from romantic partners fosters security in low self-esteem individuals. *Journal of Personality and Social Psychology, 92,* 232.

Marigold, D. C., Holmes, J. G., Wood, J. V., & Cavallo, J. V. (2014). You can't always give what you want: The challenge of providing social support to low self-esteem individuals. *Journal of Personality and Social Psychology, 107,* 56–80.

Marin-Garcia, E., Ruiz-Vargas, J. M., & Kapur, N. (2013). Mere exposure effect can be elicited in transient global amnesia. *Journal of Clinical and Experimental Neuropsychology, 35,* 1007–1014.

Markey, P. M., Markey, C. N., & French, J. E. (2015). Violent video games and real-world violence: Rhetoric versus data. *Psychology of Popular Media Culture, 4,* 277–295.

Markey, P. M., Wells, S. M., & Markey, C. N. (2002). In S. P. Shohov (Ed.), *Advances in psychology research* (Vol. 9) (pp. 94–113). Huntington, NY: Nova Science.

Markman, H. J., Floyd, F. J., Stanley, S. M., & Storaasli, R. D. (1988). Prevention of marital distress: A longitudinal investigation. *Journal of Consulting and Clinical Psychology, 56,* 210–217.

Markman, K. D., & McMullen, M. N. (2003). A reflection and evaluation model of comparative thinking. *Personality and Social Psychology Review, 7,* 244–267.

Marks, G., & Miller, N. (1985). The effect of certainty on consensus judgments. *Personality and Social Psychology Bulletin, 11(*2), 165–177.

Marks, G., & Miller, N. (1987). Ten years of research on the false-consensus effect: An empirical and theoretical review. *Psychological Bulletin, 102,* 72–90.

Markus, H. (2001, October 7). Culture and the good life. Address to the Positive Psychology Summit conference, Washington, DC.

Markus, H., & Kitayama, S. (1991). Culture and the self: Implications for cognition, emotion, and motivation. *Psychological Review, 98,* 224–253.

Markus, H., & Nurius, P. (1986). Possible selves. *American Psychologist, 41,* 954–969.

Markus, H., & Wurf, E. (1987). The dynamic self-concept: A social psychological perspective. *Annual Review of Psychology, 38,* 299–337.

Markus, H. R. (2005). On telling less than we can know: The too tacit wisdom of social psychology. *Psychological Inquiry, 16,* 180–184.

Markus, H. R., & Kitayama, S. (1994). A collective fear of the collective: Implications for selves and theories of selves. *Personality and Social Psychology Bulletin, 20,* 568–579.

Markus, H. R., & Kitayama, S. (2010). Cultures and selves: A cycle of mutual constitution. *Perspectives on Psychological Science, 5,* 420–430.

Marquis, D. G. (1962). Individual responsibility and group decisions involving risk. *Industrial Management Review, 3,* 8–23.

Marsden, P., & Attia, S. (2005). A deadly contagion? *The Psychologist, 18,* 152–155.

Marsh, H. W., Kong, C-K., & Hau, K-T. (2000). Longitudinal multilevel models of the big-fish-little-pond effect on academic self-concept: Counterbalancing contrast and reflected-glory effects in Hong Kong schools. *Journal of Personality and Social Psychology, 78,* 337–349.

Marsh, H. W., & O'Mara, A. (2008). Reciprocal effects between academic self-concept, self-esteem, achievement, and attainment over seven adolescent years: Unidimensional and multidimensional perspectives of self-concept. *Personality and Social Psychology Bulletin, 34,* 542–552.

Marsh, H. W., & Young, A. S. (1997). Causal effects of academic self-concept on academic achievement: Structural equation models of longitudinal data. *Journal of Educational Psychology, 89,* 41–54.

Marshall, L. (Ed.) (1912). *Sinking of the* Titanic *and great sea disasters.* Philadelphia, PA: Universal Book and Bible House.

Martens, A., Kosloff, S., Greenberg, J., Landau, M. J., & Schmader, R. (2007). Killing begets killing: Evidence from a bug-killing paradigm that initial killing fuels subsequent killing. *Personality and Social Psychology Bulletin, 33,* 1251–1264.

Martin, L. L., & Erber, R. (2005). Can social psychology impart any wisdom to the world? *Psychological Inquiry, 16*(4), 151.

Martin, R. (1996). Minority influence and argument generation. *British Journal of Social Psychology, 35,* 91–103.

Martin, R., Hewstone, M., & Martin, P. Y. (2007). Majority versus minority influence: The role of message processing in determining resistance to counter-persuasion. *European Journal of Social Psychology, 38,* 16–34.

Martin, R., Martin, P. Y., Smith, J. R., & Hewstone, M. (2008). Majority versus minority influence and prediction of behavioural intentions and behaviour. *Journal of Experimental Social Psychology, 43,* 763–771.

Martin, R. C., Coyier, K. R., VanSistine, L. M., & Schroeder, K. L. (2013). Anger on the Internet: The perceived value of rant-sites. *Cyberpsychology, Behavior, and Social Networking, 16,* 119–122.

Martino, S. C., Collins, R. L., Kanouse, D. E., Elliott, M., & Berry, S. H. (2005). Social cognitive processes mediating the relationship between exposure to television's sexual content and adolescents' sexual behavior. *Journal of Personality and Social Psychology, 89,* 914–924.

Martinovic, B., & Verkuyten, M. (2012). Host national and religious identification among Turkish Muslims in Western Europe: The role of ingroup norms, perceived discrimination and value incompatibility. *European Journal of Social Psychology, 42,* 893–903.

Martins, N., & Wilson, B. J. (2012). Mean on the screen: Social aggression in programs popular with children, *Journal of Communications, 62,* 991–1009.

Maruyama, G., Rubin, R. A., & Kingbury, G. (1981). Self-esteem and educational achievement: Independent constructs with a common cause? *Journal of Personality and Social Psychology, 40,* 962–975.

Marvelle, K., & Green, S. (1980). Physical attractiveness and sex bias in hiring decisions for two types of jobs. *Journal of the National Association of Women Deans, Administrators, and Counselors, 44*(1), 3–6.

Masserman, J. H., Wechkin, S., & Terris, W. (1964). "Altruistic" behavior in rhesus monkeys. *American Journal of Psychiatry, 121,* 584–585.

Massey, C., Simmons, J. P., & Armor, D. A. (2011). Hope over experience: Desirability and the persistence of optimism. *Psychological Science, 22,* 274–281.

Mast, M. S., & Hall, J. A. (2006). Women's advantage at remembering others' appearance: A systematic look at the why and when of a gender difference. *Personality and Social Psychology Bulletin, 32,* 353–364.

Masuda, T., Gonzalez, R., Kwan, L., & Nisbett, R. E. (2008). Culture and aesthetic preference: Comparing the attention to context of East Asians and Americans. *Personality and Social Psychology Bulletin, 34,* 1260–1275.

Masuda, T., & Kitayama, S. (2004). Perceiver-induced constraint and attitude attribution in Japan and the US: A case for the cultural dependence of the correspondence bias. *Journal of Experimental Social Psychology, 40,* 409.

Mathieu, M. T., & Gosling, S. D. (2012). The accuracy or inaccuracy of affective forecasts depends on how accuracy is indexed: A meta-analysis of past studies. *Psychological Science, 23,* 161–162.

Matthews, K. A. (2005). Psychological perspectives on the development of coronary heart disease. *American Psychologist, 60,* 783–796.

Maxmen, A. (2018, January 24). As Cape Town water crisis deepens, scientists prepare for "Day Zero." *Nature.* Retrieved from ww.nature.com/articles/d41586-018-01134-x

Maxwell, G. M. (1985). Behaviour of lovers: Measuring the closeness of relationships. *Journal of Personality and Social Psychology, 2,* 215–238.

Mayer, J. D., & Salovey, P. (1987). Personality moderates the interaction of mood and cognition. In K. Fiedler & J. Forgas (Eds.), *Affect, cognition, and social behavior.* Toronto: Hogrefe.

Maznevski, M. L. (1994). Understanding our differences: Performance in decision-making groups with diverse members. *Human Relations*, *47*(5), 531–552. https://doi-org.library.smu.ca/10.1177/001872679404700504

Mazur, A., & Booth, A. (1998). Testosterone and dominance in men. *Behavioral and Brain Sciences, 21,* 353–363.

Mazzoni, G., & Memon, A. (2003). Imagination can create false autobiographical memories. *Psychological Science, 14,* 186.

Mazzuca, J. (2002, August 20). Teens shrug off movie sex and violence. Gallup Tuesday Briefing. Retrieved from http://www.gallup.com

McAdams, D. P. (2017). The appeal of the primal leader: Human evolution and Donald J. Trump. *Evolutionary Studies in Imaginative Culture, 1*(2), DOI: 10.26613/esic/1.2.45/

McAlister, A., Perry, C., Killen, J., Slinkard, L. A., & Maccoby, N. (1980). Pilot study of smoking, alcohol and drug abuse prevention. *American Journal of Public Health, 70,* 719–721.

McAndrew, F. T. (1981). Pattern of performance and attributions of ability and gender. *Journal of Personality and Social Psychology, 7,* 583–587.

McAndrew, F. T. (2009). The interacting roles of testosterone and challenges to status in human male aggression. *Aggression and Violent Behavior, 14,* 330–335.

McCain, J. L., & Campbell, W. K. (2017). Narcissism and social media use: A meta-analytic review. *Psychology of Popular Media Culture, 7,* 308-327.

McCann, C. D., & Hancock, R. D. (1983). Self-monitoring in communicative interactions: Social cognitive consequences of goal-directed message modification. *Journal of Experimental Social Psychology, 19,* 109–121.

McCarthy, J. F., & Kelly, B. R. (1978a). Aggression, performance variables, and anger self-report in ice hockey players. *Journal of Psychology, 99,* 97–101.

McCarthy, J. F., & Kelly, B. R. (1978b). Aggressive behavior and its effect on performance over time in ice hockey athletes: An archival study. *International Journal of Sport Psychology, 9,* 90–96.

McCauley, C. (1989). The nature of social influence in groupthink: Compliance and internalization. *Journal of Personality and Social Psychology, 57,* 250–260.

McCauley, C. (1998). Group dynamics in Janis's theory of groupthink: Backward and forward. *Organizational Behavior and Human Decision Processes, 73,* 142–163.

McCauley, C. R. (2002). Psychological issues in understanding terrorism and the response to terrorism. In C. E. Stout (Ed.), *The psychology of terrorism* (Vol. 3). Westport, CT: Praeger/Greenwood.

McCauley, C. R., & Segal, M. E. (1987). Social psychology of terrorist groups. In C. Hendrick (Ed.), *Group processes and intergroup relations: Review of personality and social psychology* (Vol. 9). Newbury Park, CA: Sage.

McClintock, E. A. (2014). Beauty and status: The illusion of exchange in partner selection? *American Sociological Review, 79,* 575–604.

McClure, J. (1998). Discounting causes of behavior: Are two reasons better than one? *Journal of Personality and Social Psychology, 74,* 7–20.

McClure, M. J., & Lydon, J. E. (2014). Anxiety doesn't become you: How attachment anxiety compromises relational opportunities. *Journal of Personality and Social Psychology, 106,* 89–111.

McConahay, J. B. (1981). Reducing racial prejudice in desegregated schools. In W. D. Hawley (Ed.), *Effective school desegregation.* Beverly Hills, CA: Sage.

McConahay, J. B. (1986). Modern racism, ambivalence, and the Modern Racism Scale. In J. F. Dovidio & S. L. Gaertner (Eds.), *Prejudice, discrimination, and racism* (pp. 91–125). San Diego, CA: Academic Press.

McCullough, J. L., & Ostrom, T. M. (1974). Repetition of highly similar messages and attitude change. *Journal of Applied Psychology, 59,* 395–397.

McDermott, R., Tingley, D. Cowden, J., Frazzetto, G., & Johnson, D. D. P. (2009). Monoamine oxidase A gene (MAOA) predicts behavioral aggression following provocation. *Proceedings of the National Academy of Sciences of the United States of America, 106,* 2118–2123.

McDonald, M. M., Asher, B. D., Kerr, N. L., & Navarrete, C. D. (2011). Fertility and intergroup bias in racial and minimal-group contexts: Evidence for shared architecture. *Psychological Science, 22,* 860–865.

McFarland, C., & Ross, M. (1985). *The relation between current impressions and memories of self and dating partners.* Unpublished manuscript, University of Waterloo, Waterloo, ON.

McFarland, C., White, K., & Newth, S. (2003). Mood acknowledgement and correction for the mood-congruency bias in social judgment. *Journal of Experimental Social Psychology, 39,* 483–491.

McGillicuddy, N. B., Welton, G. L., & Pruitt, D. G. (1987). Third-party intervention: A field experiment comparing three different models. *Journal of Personality and Social Psychology, 53,* 104–112.

McGlone, M. S., & Tofighbakhsh, J. (2000). Birds of a feather flock conjointly (?): Rhyme as reason in aphorisms. *Psychological Science, 11,* 424–428.

McGlynn, R. P., Tubbs, D. D., & Holzhausen, K. G. (1995). Hypothesis generation in groups constrained by evidence. *Journal of Experimental Social Psychology, 31,* 64–81.

McGrath, J. E. (1984). *Groups: Interaction and performance.* Englewood Cliffs, NJ: Prentice-Hall.

McGraw, A. P., Mellers, B. A., & Tetlock, P. E. (2005). Expectations and emotions of Olympic athletes. *Journal of Experimental Social Psychology, 41,* 438–446.

McGregor, I., & Marigold, D. C. (2003). Defensive zeal and the uncertain self: What makes you so sure? *Journal of Personality & Social Psychology, 85*(5), 838–852.

McGregor, I., Nail, P. R., Marigold, D. C., & Kang, S. (2005). Defensive pride and consensus: Strength in imaginary numbers. *Journal of Personality and Social Psychology, 89,* 978.

McGregor, I., Newby-Clark, I. R., & Zanna, M. P. (1998). Epistemic discomfort is moderated by simultaneous accessibility of inconsistent elements. In E. Harmon-Jones and J. Mills (Eds.), *Cognitive dissonance theory 40 years later: A revival with revisions and controversies.* Washington, DC: American Psychological Association.

McGregor, I., Zanna, M. P., Holmes, J. G., & Spencer, S. J. (2001). Conviction in the face of uncertainty: Going to extremes and being oneself. *Journal of Personality and Social Psychology, 80,* 472–478.

McGuire, A. (2002, August 19). Charity calls for debate on adverts aimed at children. *The Herald* (Scotland), p. 4.

McGuire, W. J. (1964). Inducing resistance to persuasion: Some contemporary approaches. In L. Berkowitz (Ed.), *Advances in experimental social psychology* (Vol. 1). New York: Academic Press.

McGuire, W. J. (1978). An information-processing model of advertising effectiveness. In H. L. Davis & A. J. Silk (Eds.), *Behavioral and management sciences in marketing.* New York: John Wiley & Sons, Inc.

McGuire, W. J., McGuire, C. V., Child, P., & Fujioka, T. (1978). Salience of ethnicity in the spontaneous self-concept as a function of one's ethnic distinctiveness in the social environment. *Journal of Personality and Social Psychology, 36,* 511–520.

McGuire, W. J., McGuire, C. V., & Winton, W. (1979). Effects of household sex composition on the salience of one's gender in the spontaneous self-concept. *Journal of Experimental Social Psychology, 15,* 77–90.

McGuire, W. J., & Padawer-Singer, A. (1978). Trait salience in the spontaneous self-concept. *Journal of Personality and Social Psychology, 33,* 743–754.

McKelvie, S. J. (1995). Bias in the estimated frequency of names. *Perceptual and Motor Skills, 81,* 1331–1338.

McKelvie, S. J. (1997). The availability heuristic: Effects of fame and gender on the estimated frequency of male and female names. *Journal of Social Psychology, 137,* 63–78.

McKenna, F. P., & Myers, L. B. (1997). Illusory self-assessments—Can they be reduced? *British Journal of Psychology, 88,* 39–51.

McKenna, K. Y. A., & Bargh, J. A. (1998). Coming out in the age of the Internet: Identity demarginalization through virtual group participation. *Journal of Personality and Social Psychology, 75,* 681–694.

McKenna, K. Y. A., & Bargh, J. A. (2000). Plan 9 from cyberspace: The implications of the Internet for personality and social psychology. *Personality and Social Psychology Review, 4,* 57–75.

McKenna, K. Y. A., Green, A. S., & Gleason, M. E. J. (2002). What's the big attraction? Relationship formation on the Internet. *Journal of Social Issues, 58,* 9–31.

McKenzie-Mohr, D., & Zanna, M. P. (1990). Treating women as sexual objects: Look to the (gender schematic) male who has viewed pornography. *Personality and Social Psychology Bulletin, 16,* 296–308.

McKeown, S., & Psaltis, C. (2017). Intergroup contact and the mediating role of intergroup trust on outgroup evaluation and future contact intentions in Cyprus and Northern Ireland. *Peace and Conflict: Journal of Peace Psychology, 23,* 392–404.

McLuhan, M. (1964). *Understanding Media: The Extensions of Man.* New York: Mentor.

McMillen, D. L., & Austin, J. B. (1971). Effect of positive feedback on compliance following transgression. *Psychonomic Science, 24,* 59–61.

McMillen, D. L., Sanders, D. Y., & Solomon, G. S. (1977). Self-esteem, attentiveness, and helping behavior. *Journal of Personality and Social Psychology, 3,* 257–261.

McNulty, J. K. (2010). When positive processes hurt relationships. *Current Directions in Psychological Science, 19,* 167–171.

McNulty, J. K., O'Mara, E. M., & Karney, B. R. (2008). Benevolent cognitions as a strategy of relationship maintenance: "Don't sweat the small stuff" … But it is not all small stuff. *Journal of Personality and Social Psychology, 94,* 631–646.

Mead, G. H. (1934). *Mind, self, and society.* Chicago: University of Chicago Press.

Medalia, N. Z., & Larsen, O. N. (1958). Diffusion and belief in collective delusion: The Seattle windshield pitting epidemic. *American Sociological Review, 23,* 180–186.

Medvec, V. H., Madey, S. F., & Gilovich, T. (1995). When less is more: Counterfactual thinking and satisfaction among Olympic medalists. *Journal of Personality and Social Psychology, 69,* 603–610.

Medvec, V. H., & Savitsky, K. (1997). When doing better means feeling worse: The effects of categorical cutoff points on counterfactual thinking and satisfaction. *Journal of Personality and Social Psychology, 72,* 1284–1296.

Meehl, G. A., Tebaldi, C., Walton, G., Easterling, D., & McDaniel, L. (2009). Relative increase of record high maximum temperatures compared to record low minimum temperatures in the U.S. *Geophysical Research Letters, 36,* L23701.

Meehl, P. E. (1954). *Clinical vs. statistical prediction: A theoretical analysis and a review of evidence.* Minneapolis: University of Minnesota Press.

Meehl, P. E. (1986). Causes and effects of my disturbing little book. *Journal of Personality Assessment, 50,* 370–375.

Mehl, M. R., & Pennebaker, J. W. (2003). The sounds of social life: A psychometric analysis of students' daily social environments and natural conversations. *Journal of Personality and Social Psychology, 84,* 857–870.

Mehl, M. R., Vazire, S., Holleran, S. E., & Clark, C. S. (2010). Eavesdropping on happiness: Well-being is related to having less small talk and more substantive conversations. *Psychological Science, 21,* 539–541.

Meindl, J. R., & Lerner, M. J. (1984). Exacerbation of extreme responses to an outgroup. *Journal of Personality and Social Psychology, 47,* 71–84.

Meissner, C. A., & Brigham, J. C. (2001). Thirty years of investigating the own-race bias in memory for faces: A meta-analytic review. *Psychology, Public Policy, & Law, 7,* 3–35.

Meleshko, K. G. A., & Alden, L. E. (1993). Anxiety and self-disclosure: Toward a motivational model. *Journal of Personality and Social Psychology, 64,* 1000–1009.

Mellers, B., Ungar, L., Baron, J., Ramos, J., Gurcay, B., Fincher, K., Scott, S. E., Moore, D., Atanasov, P., Swift, S. A., Murray, T., Stone, E., & Tetlock, P. E. (2014). Psychological strategies for winning a geopolitical forecasting tournament. *Psychological science*, *25*(5), 1106–1115.

Meltzer, A. L., McNulty, J. K., Jackson, G. L., & Karney, B. R. (2014). Sex differences in the implications of partner physical attractiveness for the trajectory of marital satisfaction. *Journal of Personality and Social Psychology, 106,* 418–428.

Merikle, P. M., Smilek, D., & Eastwood, J. D. (2001). Perception without awareness: Perspectives from cognitive psychology. *Cognition, 79,* 115–134.

Merrilees, C. E., Katz, J., DuBois, N., & Grant, C. (2018). White female bystanders' responses to a Black woman at risk for sexual assault: Positive effects of intergroup contact. *Violence and Victims, 33*(4), 739–754. https://doi-org.library.smu.ca/10.1891/0886-6708.VV-D-17-00062

Merton, R. K. (1948). The self-fulfilling prophecy. *Antioch Review, 8,* 193–210.

Merton, R. K., & Kitt, A. S. (1950). Contributions to the theory of reference group behavior. In R. K. Merton & P. F. Lazarsfeld (Eds.), *Continuities in social research: Studies in the scope and method of the American soldier.* Glencoe, IL: Free Press.

Messé, L. A., & Sivacek, J. M. (1979). Predictions of others' responses in a mixed-motive game: Self-justification or false consensus? *Journal of Personality and Social Psychology, 37,* 602–607.

Messick, D. M., & Sentis, K. P. (1979). Fairness and preference. *Journal of Experimental Social Psychology, 15,* 418–434.

Metcalfe, C. (2010, July 8). Vampires reach cult religion status. *Penwirth Press.*

Metzl, J. M., & MacLeish, K. T. (2014). Mental illness, mass shootings, and the politics of American firearms. *American Journal of Public Health, 105*, 240–249.

Meyers, S. A., & Berscheid, E. (1997). The language of love: The difference a preposition makes. *Personality and Social Psychology Bulletin, 23,* 347–362.

Michaels, J. W., Blommel, J. M., Brocato, R. M., Linkous, R. A., & Rowe, J. S. (1982). Social facilitation and inhibition in a natural setting. *Replications in Social Psychology, 2,* 21–24.

Mickelson, K. D., Kessler, R. C., & Shaver, P. R. (1997). Adult attachment in a nationally representative sample. *Journal of Personality and Social Psychology, 73,* 1092–1106.

Mihelič, K. K., & Culiberg, B. (2019). Reaping the fruits of another's labor: The role of moral meaningfulness, mindfulness, and motivation in social loafing. *Journal of Business Ethics, 160*(3), 713–727. https://doi-org.library.smu.ca/10.1007/s10551-018-3933-z

Miklikowska, M. (2017). Development of anti-immigrant attitudes in adolescence: The role of parents, peers, intergroup friendships, and empathy. *British Journal of Psychology, 108,* 626–648.

Mikula, G. (1984). Justice and fairness in interpersonal relations: Thoughts and suggestions. In H. Taijfel (Ed.), *The social dimension: European developments in social psychology* (Vol. 1). Cambridge: Cambridge University Press.

Mikulincer, M., Florian, V., & Hirschberger, G. (2003). The existential function of close relationships: Introducing death into the science of love. *Personality and Social Psychology Review, 7,* 20–40.

Mikulincer, M., & Shaver, P. R. (2001). Attachment theory and intergroup bias: Evidence that priming the secure base schema attenuates negative reactions to out-groups. *Journal of Personality and Social Psychology, 81,* 97–115.

Mikulincer, M., Shaver, P. R., Gillath, O., & Nitzberg, R. A. (2005). Attachment, caregiving, and altruism: Boosting attachment security increases compassion and helping. *Journal of Personality and Social Psychology, 89,* 817–839.

Mildenberger, M., Howe, P.D., Lachapelle, E., Stokes, L.C., Marlon, J., and Gravelle, T. The distribution of climate change public opinion in Canada. *PLoS ONE* 11(8) eo159774. Retrieved from https://journals.plos.org/plosone/article?id=10.1371/journal.pone.0159774

Milgram, A. (2000). My personal view of Stanley Milgram. In T. Blass (Ed.), *Obedience to authority: Current perspectives on the Milgram paradigm.* Mahwah, NJ: Erlbaum.

Milgram, S. (1961, December). Nationality and conformity. *Scientific American,* 45–51.

Milgram, S. (1965). Liberating effects of group pressure. *Journal of Personality and Social Psychology, 1*(2), 127.

Milgram, S. (1974). *Obedience to authority.* New York: Harper and Row.

Milgram, S., Bickman, L., & Berkowitz, L. (1969). Note on the drawing power of crowds of different size. *Journal of Personality and Social Psychology, 13,* 79–82.

Millar, M. G. (2011). Predicting dental flossing behavior: The role of implicit and explicit responses and beliefs. *Basic and Applied Social Psychology, 33,* 7–15.

Miller, A. G. (1986). *The obedience experiments: A case study of controversy in social science.* New York: Praeger.

Miller, A. G. (2006). *Exonerating harmdoers: Some problematic implications of social-psychological explanations.* Paper presented to the Society of Personality and Social Psychology convention.

Miller, A. G., Ashton, W., & Mishal, M. (1990). Beliefs concerning the features of constrained behavior: A basis for the fundamental attribution error. *Journal of Personality and Social Psychology, 59,* 635–650.

Miller, C. E., & Anderson, P. D. (1979). Group decision rules and the rejection of deviates. *Social Psychology Quarterly, 42,* 354–363.

Miller, C. T., & Felicio, D. M. (1990). Person-positivity bias: Are individuals liked better than groups? *Journal of Experimental Social Psychology, 26,* 408–420.

Miller, D. T., Downs, J. S., & Prentice, D. A. (1998). Minimal conditions for the creation of a unit relationship: The social bond between birthdaymates. *European Journal of Social Psychology, 28,* 475–481.

Miller, D. T., & McFarland, C. (1987). Pluralistic ignorance: When similarity is interpreted as dissimilarity. *Journal of Personality and Social Psychology, 53,* 298–305.

Miller, G., Tybur, J. M., & Jordan, B. D. (2007). Ovulatory cycle effects on tip earnings by lap dancers: Economic evidence for human estrus? *Evolution and Human Behavior, 28,* 375–381.

Miller, G. E., & Blackwell, E. (2006). Turning up the heat: Inflammation as a mechanism linking chronic stress, depression, and heart disease. *Current Directions in Psychological Science, 15,* 269–272.

Miller, G. E., Chen, E., & Parker, K. J. (2011). Psychological stress in childhood and susceptibility to the chronic diseases of aging: Moving toward a model of behavioral and biological mechanisms. *Psychological Bulletin, 137,* 959–997.

Miller, J. G. (1984). Culture and the development of everyday social explanation. *Journal of Personality and Social Psychology, 46,* 961–978.

Miller, J. R., Marshall, T., & Gallant, D. (2019). Residential schools in Canada. *The Canadian Encyclopedia.* Retrieved from https://www.thecanadianencyclopedia.ca/en/article/residential-schools

Miller, K. I., & Monge, P. R. (1986). Participation, satisfaction, and productivity: A meta-analytic review. *Academy of Management Journal, 29,* 727–753.

Miller, L. (2004). Psychotherapeutic interventions for survivors of terrorism. *American Journal of Psychotherapy, 58,* 1.

Miller, L. C. (1990). Intimacy and liking: Mutual influence and the role of unique relationships. *Journal of Personality and Social Psychology, 59,* 50–60.

Miller, L. C., Berg, J. H., & Archer, R. L. (1983). Openers: Individuals who elicit intimate self-disclosure. *Journal of Personality and Social Psychology, 44,* 1234–1244.

Miller, L. E., & Grush, J. E. (1986). Individual differences in attitudinal versus normative determination of behavior. *Journal of Experimental Social Psychology, 22,* 190–202.

Miller, N. (2002). Personalization and the promise of contact theory. *Journal of Social Issues, 58,* 387–410.

Miller, N., & Campbell, D. T. (1959). Recency and primacy in persuasion as a function of the timing of speeches and measurements. *Journal of Abnormal and Social Psychology, 59,* 1–9.

Miller, N., & Marks, G. (1982). Assumed similarity between self and other: Effect of expectation of future interaction with that other. *Social Psychology Quarterly, 45,* 100–105.

Miller, N., Maruyama, G., Beaber, R. J., & Valone, K. (1976). Speed of speech and persuasion. *Journal of Personality and Social Psychology, 34,* 615–624.

Miller, P. A., & Eisenberg, N. (1988). The relation of empathy to aggressive and externalizing/antisocial behavior. *Psychological Bulletin, 103,* 324–344.

Miller, P. A., Kozu, J., & Davis, A. C. (2001). Social influence, empathy, and prosocial behavior in cross-cultural perspective. In W. Wosinska, R. B. Cialdini, D. W. Barrett, & J. Reykowski (Eds.), *The practice of social influence in multiple cultures.* Mahwah, NJ: Erlbaum.

Miller, P. J. E., Niehuis, S., & Huston, T. L. (2006). Positive illusions in marital relationships: A 13-year longitudinal study. *Personality and Social Psychology Bulletin, 32,* 1579–1594.

Miller, P. J. E., & Rempel, J. K. (2004). Trust and partner-enhancing attributions in close relationships. *Personality and Social Psychology Bulletin, 30,* 695.

Miller, R. L., Brickman, P., & Bolen, D. (1975). Attribution versus persuasion as a means for modifying behavior. *Journal of Personality and Social Psychology, 31,* 430–441.

Miller, R. S. (1997). Inattentive and contented: Relationship commitment and attention to alternatives. *Journal of Personality and Social Psychology, 73,* 758–766.

Miller, R. S., & Schlenker, B. R. (1985). Egotism in group members: Public and private attributions of responsibility for group performance. *Social Psychology Quarterly, 48,* 85–89.

Miller, S. L., Zielaskowski, K., & Plant, E. A. (2012). The basis of shooter biases: Beyond cultural stereotypes. *Personality and Social Psychology Bulletin, 38,* 1358–1366.

Millett, K. (1975, January). The shame is over. *Ms.,* 26–29.

Millette, D., Lambert, M., & Gall, G. (2015). Quebéc referendum (1995). The Canadian Encyclopedia. Retrieved from https://thecanadianencyclopedia.ca/en/article/quebec-referendum-1995

Mills, B. M. (2014). Social pressure at the plate: Inequality aversion, status, and mere exposure. *Managerial and Decision Economics, 35,* 387–403.

Milyavskaya, M., Gingras, I., Mageau, G. A., Koestner, R., Gagnon, H., Fang, J., & Boiché, J. (2009). Balance across contexts: Importance of balanced need satisfaction across various life domains. *Personality and Social Psychology Bulletin, 35,* 1031–1045.

Milyavskaya, M., Inzlicht, M., Hope, N., & Koestner, R. (2015). Saying "no" to temptation: Want-to motivation improves self-regulation by reducing temptation rather than by increasing self-control. *Journal of Personality and Social Psychology, 109,* 677–693.

Mims, P. R., Hartnett, J. J., & Nay, W. R. (1975). Interpersonal attraction and help volunteering as a function of physical attractiveness. *Journal of Psychology, 89,* 125–131.

Min, K. S., & Arkes, H. R. (2012). When is difficult planning good planning? The effects of scenario-based planning on optimistic prediction bias. *Journal of Applied Social Psychology, 42,* 2701–2729.

Mio, J. S., Thompson, S. C., & Givens, G. H. (1993). The commons dilemma as a metaphor: Memory, influence, and implications for environmental conservation. *Metaphor and Symbolic Activity, 8,* 23–42.

Mirsky, S. (2009, January). What's good for the group. *Scientific American,* 51.

Mischel, W. (1968). *Personality and assessment.* New York: Wiley.

Mishna, F. (2004). A qualitative study of bullying from multiple perspectives. *Children & Schools, 26,* 234–247.

Mishna, F., Cook, C., Gadallo, T., Daciuk, J., & Solomon, S. (2010). Cyberbullying behaviors among middle and high school students. *American Journal of Orthopsychiatry, 80,* 362–374.

Mita, T. H., Dermer, M., & Knight, J. (1977). Reversed facial images and the mere-exposure hypothesis. *Journal of Personality and Social Psychology, 35,* 597–601.

Mitchell, G., Tetlock, P. E., Mellers, B. A., & Ordonez, L. D. (1993). Judgments of social justice: Compromises between equality and efficiency. *Journal of Personality and Social Psychology, 65,* 629–639.

Mitchell, J., McCrae, C. N, & Banaji, M. R. (2006). Dissociable medial prefrontal contributions to judgments of similar and dissimilar others. *Neuron, 18,* 655–663.

Mitchell, T. R., & Thompson, L. (1994). A theory of temporal adjustments of the evaluation of events: Rosy prospection and rosy retrospection. In C. Stubbart, J. Porac, & J. Meindl (Eds.), *Advances in managerial cognition and organizational information processing.* Greenwich, CT: JAI Press.

Mitchell, T. R., Thompson, L., Peterson, E., & Cronk, R. (1997). Temporal adjustments in the evaluation of events: The "rosy view." *Journal of Experimental Social Psychology, 33,* 421–448.

Miyake, A., Kost-Smith, L., Finkelstein, N. D., Pollock, S. J., Cohen, G. L., & Ito, T. A. (2010). Reducing the gender achievement gap in college science: A classroom study of values affirmation. *Science, 330,* 1234–1237.

Mizock, L., Riley, J., Yuen, N., Woodrum, T. D., Sotilleo, E. A., & Ormerod, A. J. (2018). Transphobia in the workplace: A qualitative study of employment stigma. *Stigma and Health, 3,* 275-282.

Moffitt, T., Caspi, A., Sugden, K., Taylor, A., Craig, I. W., Harrington, H., McClay, J., Mill, J., Martin, J., Braithwaite, A., & Poulton, R. (2003). Influence of life stress on depression: Moderation by a polymorphism in the 5-HTT gene. *Science, 301,* 386–389.

Moffitt, T. E., Arseneault, L., Belsky, D., Dickson, N., Hancox, R. J., Harrington, H. L., Houts, R., Poulton, R., Roberts, B. W., Ross, S., Sears, M. R., Thomson, W. M., & Caspi, A. (2011). A gradient of childhood self-control predicts health, wealth, and public safety. *PNAS, 108*(7): 2693–2698.

Moghaddam, F. M. (2009). Omniculturalism: Policy solutions to fundamentalism in the era of fractured globalization. *Culture and Psychology, 15,* 337–347.

Moghaddam, F. M. (2010). *The new global insecurity.* New York: Praeger.

Moghaddam, F. M., & Studer, C. (1997). The sky is falling, but not on me: A cautionary tale of illusions of control, in four acts. *Cross-Cultural Research: The Journal of Comparative Social Science, 31,* 155–167.

Mohr, H., Pritchard, J., & Lush, T. (2010, May 29). BP has been good at downplaying disaster. *Associated Press.*

Moisuc, A., & Brauer, M. (2019). Social norms are enforced by friends: The effect of relationship closeness on bystanders' tendency to confront perpetrators of uncivil, immoral, and discriminatory behaviors. *European Journal of Social Psychology, 49*(4), 824–830. https://doi-org.library.smu.ca/10.1002/ejsp.2525

Mojzisch, A., & Schulz-Hardt, S. (2010). Knowing others' preferences degrades the quality of group decisions. *Journal of Personality and Social Psychology, 98,* 784–808.

Moller, I., & Krahé, B. (2008). Exposure to violent video games and aggression in German adolescents: A longitudinal analysis. *Aggressive Behavior, 34,* 1–14.

Moller, I., Krahé, B., Busching, R., & Krause, C. (2012). Efficacy of an intervention to reduce the use of media violence and aggression: An experimental evaluation with adolescents in Germany. *Journal of Youth and Adolescence, 41,* 105–120.

Monson, T. C., Hesley, J. W., & Chernick, L. (1982). Specifying when personality traits can and cannot predict behavior: An alternative to abandoning the attempt to predict single-act criteria. *Journal of Personality and Social Psychology, 43,* 385–399.

Montag, C., Weber, B., Trautner, P., Newport, B., Markett, S., Walter, N. T., Felten, A., & Reuter, M. (2012). Does excessive play of violent first-person-shooter-video-games dampen brain activity in response to emotional stimuli? *Biological Psychology, 89,* 107–111.

Monteith, M. J. (1993). Self-regulation of prejudiced responses: Implications for progress in prejudice-reduction efforts. *Journal of Personality and Social Psychology, 65,* 469–485.

Montoya, R. M. (2008). I'm hot, so I'd say you're not: The influence of objective physical attractiveness on mate selection. *Personality and Social Psychology Bulletin, 34,* 1315–1331.

Montoya, R. M., & Horton, R. S. (2012). A meta-analytic investigation of the processes underlying the similarity-attraction effect. *Journal of Social and Personal Relationships, 30,* 64–94.

Montoya, R. M., Horton, R. S., Vevea, J. L., Citkowicz, M., & Lauber, E. A. (2017). A re-examination of the mere exposure effect: The influence of repeated exposure on recognition, familiarity, and liking. *Psychological Bulletin, 143,* 459–498.

Montoya, R. M., & Insko, C. A. (2008). Toward a more complete understanding of the reciprocity of liking effect. *European Journal of Social Psychology, 38,* 477–498.

Moody, K. (1980). *Growing up on television: The TV effect.* New York: Times Books.

Moons, W. G., & Mackie, D. M. (2007). Thinking straight while seeing red: The influence of anger on information processing. *Personality and Social Psychology Bulletin, 33,* 706–720.

Moons, W. G., Mackie, D. M., & Garcia-Marques, T. (2009). The impact of repetition-induced familiarity on agreement with weak and strong arguments. *Journal of Personality and Social Psychology, 96,* 32–44.

Moor, B. G., Crone, E. A., & van der Molen, M. W. (2010). The heartbrake of social rejection: Heart rate deceleration in response to unexpected peer rejection. *Psychological Science, 21,* 1326–1333.

Moore, D. A., & Swift, S. A. (2011). The three faces of overconfidence in organizations. In D. De Cremer, R. van Dick, & J. K. Murnighan (Eds.), *Social psychology and organizations.* New York: Routledge /Taylor & Francis.

Moore, D. A., Swift, S. A., Sharek, Z. S., & Gino, F. (2010). Correspondence bias in performance evaluation: Why grade inflation works. *Personality and Social Psychology Bulletin, 36,* 843–852.

Moore, D. L., & Baron, R. S. (1983). Social facilitation: A physiological analysis. In J. T. Cacioppo & R. Petty (Eds.), *Social psychophysiology.* New York: Guilford Press.

Moore, D. W. (2004, April 20). Ballot order: Who benefits? *Gallup Poll Tuesday Briefing.* Retrieved from http://www.gallup.com

Moore, T. M., Elkins, S. R., McNulty, J. K., Kivisto, A. J., & Handsel, V. A. (2011). Alcohol use and intimate partner violence perpetration among college students: Assessing the temporal association using electronic diary technology. *Psychology of Violence, 1*(4), 315–328.

Morales, L. (2011, May 27). U.S. adults estimate that 25% of Americans are gay or lesbian [news release]. Retrieved from http://www.gallup.com/poll/147824/adults-estimate-americans-gay-lesbian.aspx

Moreland, R. L., & Zajonc, R. B. (1977). Is stimulus recognition a necessary condition for the occurrence of exposure effects? *Journal of Personality and Social Psychology, 35,* 191–199.

Mori, K., & Mori, H. (2009). Another test of the passive facial feedback hypothesis: When your face smiles, you feel happy. *Perceptual and Motor Skills, 109,* 1–3.

Morier, D., & Seroy, C. (1994). The effect of interpersonal expectancies on men's self-presentation of gender role attitudes to women. *Sex Roles, 31,* 493–504.

Morling, B., & Lamoreaux, M. (2008). Measuring culture outside the head: A meta-analysis of individualism-collectivism in cultural products. *Personality and Social Psychology Bulletin, 12,* 199–221.

Morris, W. N., & Miller, R. S. (1975). The effects of consensus-breaking and consensus-preempting partners on reduction of conformity. *Journal of Experimental Social Psychology, 11,* 215–223.

Morrow, L. (1983, August 1). All the hazards and threats of success. *Time,* 20–25.

Moscovici, S. (1985). Social influence and conformity. In G. Lindzey & E. Aronson (Eds.), *The handbook of social psychology* (3rd ed.). Hillsdale, NJ: Erlbaum.

Moscovici, S. (1988). Notes towards a description of social representations. *European Journal of Social Psychology, 18,* 211–250.

Moscovici, S. (2001). Why a theory of social representation? In K. Deaux & G. Philogène (Eds.), *Representations of the social: Bridging theoretical traditions.* Malden, MA: Blackwell.

Moscovici, S., Lage, S., & Naffrechoux, M. (1969). Influence of a consistent minority on the responses of a majority in a color perception task. *Sociometry, 32,* 365–380.

Moscovici, S., & Zavalloni, M. (1969). The group as a polarizer of attitudes. *Journal of Personality and Social Psychology, 12,* 124–135.

Motherhood Project. (2001, May 2). Watch out for children: A mothers' statement to advertisers. Institute for American Values.

Moutsiana, C., Fearon, P., Murray, L., Cooper, P., Goodyer, I., Johnstone, T., & Halligan, S. (2014). Making an effort to feel positive: Insecure attachment in infancy predicts the neural underpinnings of emotion regulation in adulthood. *Journal of Child Psychology and Psychiatry, 55,* 999–1008.

Moyer, K. E. (1976). *The psychobiology of aggression.* New York: Harper & Row.

Moyer, K. E. (1983). The physiology of motivation: Aggression as a model. In C. J. Scheier & A. M. Rogers (Eds.), *G. Stanley Hall Lecture Series* (Vol. 3). Washington, DC: American Psychological Association.

Moynihan, D. P. (1979). Social science and the courts. *Public Interest, 54,* 12–31.

Mucchi-Faina, A., Maass, A., & Volpato, C. (1991). Social influence: The role of originality. *European Journal of Social Psychology, 21,* 183–197.

Muehlenhard, C. L. (1988). Misinterpreted dating behaviors and the risk of date rape. *Journal of Social and Clinical Psychology, 6,* 20–37.

Mueller, C. M., & Dweck, C. S. (1998). Praise for intelligence can undermine children's motivation and performance. *Journal of Personality and Social Psychology, 75,* 33–52.

Mueller, C. W., Donnerstein, E., & Hallam, J. (1983). Violent films and prosocial behavior. *Personality and Social Psychology Bulletin, 9,* 83–89.

Muggleton, N. K., & Fincher, C. L. (2017). Unrestricted sexuality promotes distinctive short- and long-term mate preferences in women. *Personality and Individual Differences, 111,* 169–173.

Muise, A., Stanton, S. C. E., Kim, J. J., & Impett, E. A. (2016). Not in the mood? Men under- (not over-) perceive their partner's sexual desire in established intimate relationships. *Journal of Personality and Social Psychology, 110,* 725–742.

Mujcic, R., & Frijters, P. (2014, December). Still not allowed on the bus: It matters if you're Black or White. Working paper, University of Queensland.

Mullen, B. (1986a). Atrocity as a function of lynch mob composition: A self-attention perspective. *Personality and Social Psychology Bulletin, 12,* 187–197.

Mullen, B. (1986b). Stuttering, audience size, and the other-total ratio: A self-attention perspective. *Journal of Applied Social Psychology, 16,* 139–149.

Mullen, B., Anthony, T., Salas, E., & Driskell, J. E. (1994). Group cohesiveness and quality of decision making: An integration of tests of the groupthink hypothesis. *Small Group Research, 25,* 189–204.

Mullen, B., & Baumeister, R. F. (1987). Group effects on self-attention and performance: Social loafing, social facilitation, and social impairment. In C. Hendrick (Ed.), *Group processes and intergroup relations: Review of personality and social psychology* (Vol. 9). Newbury Park, CA: Sage.

Mullen, B., Brown, R., & Smith, C. (1992). Ingroup bias as a function of salience, relevance, and status: An integration. *European Journal of Social Psychology, 22,* 103–122.

Mullen, B., Bryant, B., & Driskell, J. E. (1997). Presence of others and arousal: An integration. *Group Dynamics: Theory, Research, and Practice, 1,* 52–64.

Mullen, B., & Copper, C. (1994). The relation between group cohesiveness and performance: An integration. *Psychological Bulletin, 115,* 210–227.

Mullen, B., Copper, C., & Driskell, J. E. (1990). Jaywalking as a function of model behavior. *Personality and Social Psychology Bulletin, 16,* 320–330.

Mullen, B., & Goethals, G. R. (1990). Social projection, actual consensus and valence. *British Journal of Social Psychology, 29,* 279–282.

Mullen, B., & Hu, L. (1989). Perceptions of ingroup and outgroup variability: A meta-analytic integration. *Basic and Applied Social Psychology, 10,* 233–252.

Mullen, B., & Riordan, C. A. (1988). Self-serving attributions for performance in naturalistic settings: A meta-analytic review. *Journal of Applied Social Psychology, 18,* 3–22.

Mullen, B., Salas, E., & Driskell, J. E. (1989). Salience, motivation, and artifact as contributions to the relation between participation rate and leadership. *Journal of Experimental Social Psychology, 25,* 545–559.

Muller, R. A. (2011, October 21). The case against global-warming skepticism. *Wall Street Journal.* Retrieved from https://www.wsj.com/

Muller, S., & Johnson, B. T. (1990). *Fear and persuasion: A linear relationship?* Paper presented to the Eastern Psychological Association convention.

Mullin, C. R., & Linz, D. (1995). Desensitization and resensitization to violence against women: Effects of exposure to sexually violent films on judgments of domestic violence victims. *Journal of Personality and Social Psychology, 69,* 449–459.

Munoz-Rivas, M. J., Grana, J. L., O'Leary, K. D., & Gonzalez, M. P. (2007). Aggression in adolescent dating relationships: Prevalence, justification, and health consequences. *Journal of Adolescent Health, 40,* 298–304.

Munro, G. D., Ditto, P. H., Lockhart, L. K., Fagerlin, A., Gready, M., & Peterson, E. (1997). *Biased assimilation of sociopolitical arguments: Evaluating the 1996 U.S. Presidential debate.* Unpublished manuscript, Hope College, Holland, MI.

Muraven, M., & Slessareva, E. (2003). Mechanism of self-control failure: Motivation and limited resources. *Personality and Social Psychology Bulletin, 29,* 894–906.

Muraven, M., Tice, D. M., & Baumeister, R. F. (1998). Self-control as a limited resource: Regulatory depletion patterns. *Journal of Personality and Social Psychology, 74,* 774–790.

Murphy, C. (1990, June). New findings: Hold on to your hat. *The Atlantic,* 22–23.

Murphy, S. C., von Hippel, W., Dubbs, S. L., Angilletta, M. J., Wilson, R. S., Trivers, R., & Barlow, F. K. (2015). The role of overconfidence in romantic desirability and competition. *Personality and Social Psychology Bulletin, 41,* 1036–1052.

Murray, D. R., Trudeau, R., & Schaller, M. (2011). On the origins of cultural differences in conformity: Four tests of the pathogen prevalence hypothesis. *Personality and Social Psychology Bulletin, 37,* 318–329.

Murray, K. E., & Marx, D. M. (2013). Attitudes toward unauthorized immigrants, authorized immigrants, and refugees. *Cultural Diversity and Ethnic Minority Psychology, 19,* 332–341.

Murray, S. L., Gellavia, G. M., Rose, P., & Griffin, D. W. (2003). Once hurt, twice hurtful: How perceived regard regulates daily marital interactions. *Journal of Personality and Social Psychology, 84,* 126–147.

Murray, S. L., & Holmes, J. G. (1997). A leap of faith? Positive illusions in romantic relationships. *Personality and Social Psychology Bulletin, 23,* 586–604.

Murray, S. L., Holmes, J. G., Gellavia, G., Griffin, D. W., & Dolderman, D. (2002). Kindred spirits? The benefits of egocentrism in close relationships. *Journal of Personality and Social Psychology, 82,* 563–581.

Murray, S. L., Holmes, J. G., & Griffin, D. W. (1996a). The self-fulfilling nature of positive illusions in romantic relationships: Love is not blind, but prescient. *Journal of Personality and Social Psychology, 71,* 1155–1180.

Murray, S. L., Holmes, J. G., & Griffin, D. W. (1996b). The benefits of positive illusions: Idealization and the construction of satisfaction in close relationships. *Journal of Personality and Social Psychology, 70,* 79–98.

Murray, S. L., Holmes, J. G., & Griffin, D. W. (2000). Self-esteem and the quest for felt security: How perceived regard regulates attachment processes. *Journal of Personality and Social Psychology, 78,* 478–498.

Murray, S. L., Holmes, J. G., MacDonald, G., & Ellsworth, P. C. (1998). Through the looking glass darkly? When self-doubts turn into relationship insecurities. *Journal of Personality and Social Psychology, 75,* 1459–1480.

Murray, S. L., Rose, P., Bellavia, G. M., Holmes, J. G., & Kusche, A. G. (2002). When rejection stings: How self-esteem constrains relationship-enhancement processes. *Journal of Personality and Social Psychology, 83,* 556–573.

Murray, S. L., Rose, P., Holmes, J. G., Derrick, J., Podchaski, E. J., Bellavia, G., & Griffin, D. W. (2005). Putting the partner within reach: A dyadic perspective on felt security in close relationships. *Journal of Personality and Social Psychology, 88,* 327.

Murstein, B. L. (1986). *Paths to marriage.* Newbury Park, CA: Sage.

Muson, G. (1978, March). Teenage violence and the telly. *Psychology Today,* 50–54.

Mussweiler, T. (2006). Doing is for thinking! Stereotype activation by stereotypic movements. *Psychological Science, 17,* 17–21.

Myers, D. G. (1978). Polarizing effects of social comparison. *Journal of Experimental Social Psychology, 14,* 554–563.

Myers, D. G. (1993). *The pursuit of happiness.* New York: Avon.

Myers, D. G. (2000). *The American paradox: Spiritual hunger in an age of plenty.* New Haven, CT: Yale University Press.

Myers, D. G., & Bishop, G. D. (1970). Discussion effects on racial attitudes. *Science, 169,* 778–789.

Myers, J. N. (1997, December). Quoted by S. A. Boot, Where the weather reigns. *World Traveler,* 86, 88, 91, 124.

Myers, N. (2000). Sustainable consumption: The meta-problem. In B. Heap & J. Kent (Eds.), *Towards sustainable consumption: A European perspective.* London: The Royal Society.

Nabi, R. L., Huskey, R., Nicholls, S. B., Keblusek, L., & Reed, M. (2019). When audiences become advocates: Self-induced behavior change through health message posting in social media. *Computers in Human Behavior, 99,* 260–267. https://doi- org.library.smu.ca/10.1016/j.chb.2019.05.030

Nadler, A. (1991). Help-seeking behavior: Psychological costs and instrumental benefits. In M. S. Clark (Ed.), *Prosocial behavior.* Newbury Park, CA: Sage.

Nadler, A., & Fisher, J. D. (1986). The role of threat to self-esteem and perceived control in recipient reaction to help: Theory development and empirical validation. In L. Berkowitz (Ed.), *Advances in experimental social psychology* (Vol. 19). Orlando, FL: Academic Press.

Nadler, A., Goldberg, M., & Jaffe, Y. (1982). Effect of self-differentiation and anonymity in group on deindividuation. *Journal of Personality and Social Psychology, 42,* 1127–1136.

Nadler, J. T., & Clark, M. H. (2011). Stereotype threat: A meta-analysis comparing African Americans to Hispanic Americans. *Journal of Applied Social Psychology, 41,* 872–890.

Nagar, D., & Pandey, J. (1987). Affect and performance on cognitive task as a function of crowding and noise. *Journal of Applied Social Psychology, 17,* 147–157.

Nail, P. R., MacDonald, G., & Levy, D. A. (2000). Proposal of a four-dimensional model of social response. *Psychological Bulletin, 126,* 454–470.

Nair, H., Manchanda, P., & Bhatia, T. (2008, May). Asymmetric social interactions in physician prescription behavior: The role of opinion leaders. Stanford University Graduate School of Business Research Paper No. 1970. Retrieved from http://ssrn.com/abstract=937021

Narang, P., Paladugu, A., Manda, S. R., Smock, W., Cosnay, C., & Lippmann, S. (2010). Do guns provide safety? At what cost? *Southern Medical Journal*, *103,* 151–153.

Nario-Redmond, M. R. (2010). Cultural stereotypes of disabled and non-disabled men and women: Consensus for global category representations and diagnostic domains. *British Journal of Social Psychology, 49,* 471–488.

NASA. (2017). NASA, NOAA data show 2016 warmest year on record globally. Retrieved from https://www.nasa.gov/press-release/nasa-noaa-data-show-2016-warmest-year-on-record-globally

Nash, K., Lea, J. M., Davies, T., & Yogeeswaran, K. (2018). The bionic blues: Robot rejection lowers self-esteem. *Computers in Human Behavior, 78,* 59–63.

National Geographic. (2020). See how your city's climate may change by 2070. Retrieved from https://www.nationalgeographic.com/magazine/2020/04/see-how-your-citys-climate-might-change-by-2070-feature/

National Post. (2015). Just over half of Canadians believe humans causing climate change, while 15 per cent don't believe in it all. Retrieved from https://nationalpost.com/news/politics/just-over-half-of-canadians-believe-humans-causing-climate-change-while-15-per-cent-dont-believe-in-it-all

National Safety Council. (2017). Transportation mode comparisons: Passenger death and death rates, United States 2007–2014. *Injury Facts 2017 Edition,* p. 156. Itasca, IL: National Safety Council.

National Television Violence Study. (1997). Thousand Oaks, CA: Sage.

Navarrete, C. D., McDonald, M. M., Molina, L. E., & Sidanius, J. (2010). Prejudice at the nexus of race and gender: An outgroup male target hypothesis. *Journal of Personality and Social Psychology, 98,* 933–945.

Naylor, T. H. (1990). Redefining corporate motivation, Swedish style. *Christian Century, 107,* 566–570.

NCADD–National Council of Alcoholism and Drug Dependence. (2014). Alcohol and crime. Retrieved from https://ncadd.org/learn-about-alcohol/alcohol-and-crime

Neal, D. T., & Chartrand, T. L. (2011). Embodied emotion perception: Amplifying and dampening facial feedback modulates emotion perception accuracy. *Social Psychological and Personality Science, 2,* 673–678.

Neff, K. D. (2011). Self-compassion, self-esteem, and well-being. *Social and Personality Psychology Compass, 5,* 1–12.

Neff, L. A., & Karney, B. R. (2005). To know you is to love you: The implications of global adoration and specific accuracy for marital relationships. *Journal of Personality and Social Psychology, 88,* 480.

Nelson, L., & LeBoeuf, R. (2002). Why do men overperceive women's sexual intent? False consensus vs. evolutionary explanations. Paper presented to the annual meeting of the Society for Personality and Social Psychology.

Nelson, L. D., & Morrison, E. L. (2005). The symptoms of resource scarcity: Judgments of food and finances influence preferences for potential partners. *Psychological Science, 16,* 167.

Nelson, L. J., & Miller, D. T. (1995). The distinctiveness effect in social categorization: You are what makes you unusual. *Psychological Science, 6,* 246.

Nelson, M. R., & Park, J. (2015). Publicity as covert marketing? The role of persuasion knowledge and ethical perceptions on beliefs and credibility in a video news release story. *Journal of Business Ethics, 130*(2), 327–341.

Nelson, T. E., Acker, M., & Manis, M. (1996). Irrepressible stereotypes. *Journal of Experimental Social Psychology, 32,* 13–38.

Nelson, T. E., Biernat, M. R., & Manis, M. (1990). Everyday base rates (sex stereotypes): Potent and resilient. *Journal of Personality and Social Psychology, 59,* 664–675.

Nemeth, C. (1979). The role of an active minority in intergroup relations. In W. G. Austin and S. Worchel (Eds.), *The social psychology of intergroup relations.* Monterey, CA: Brooks/Cole.

Nemeth, C., & Chiles, C. (1988). Modelling courage: The role of dissent in fostering independence. *European Journal of Social Psychology, 18,* 275–280.

Nemeth, C., & Wachtler, J. (1974). Creating the perceptions of consistency and confidence: A necessary condition for minority influence. *Sociometry, 37,* 529–540.

Nemeth, C. J. (1999). Behind the scenes. In D. G. Myers, *Social psychology* (6th ed.). New York: McGraw-Hill.

Nemeth, C. J. (2011). Minority influence theory. In P. Van Lange, A. Kruglanski, & E. T. Higgins (Eds.), *Handbook of theories in social psychology.* New York: Sage.

Nemeth, C. J., Brown, K., & Rogers, J. (2001). Devil's advocate versus authentic dissent: Stimulating quantity and quality. *European Journal of Social Psychology, 31,* 1–13.

Nemeth, C. J., Connell, J. B., Rogers, J. D., & Brown, K. S. (2001). Improving decision making by means of dissent. *Journal of Applied Social Psychology, 31,* 48.

Nemeth, C. J., & Ormiston, M. (2007). Creative idea generation: Harmony versus stimulation. *European Journal of Social Psychology, 37,* 524–535.

Nemeth, C. J., Personnaz, B., Personnaz, M., & Goncalo, J. A. (2004). The liberating role of conflict in group creativity: A study in two countries. *European Journal of Social Psychology, 34,* 365–374.

Neubaum, G., Rösner, L., Ganster, T., Hambach, K., & Krämer, N. C. (2018). United in the name of justice: How conformity processes in social media may influence online vigilantism. *Psychology of Popular Media Culture, 7*(2), 185–199. https://doi-org.library.smu.ca/10.1037/ppm0000112

Neumann, R., & Strack, F. (2000). Approach and avoidance: The influence of proprioceptive and exteroceptive cues on encoding of affective information. *Journal of Personality and Social Psychology, 79,* 39–48.

New York Times. (2020, February 12). The household work men and women do, and why. Retrieved from https://www.nytimes.com/2020/02/12/us/the-household-work-men-and-women-do-and-why.html

Newby-Clark, I. R. (2005). Plans and predictions for exercise frequency change. *Basic and Applied Social Psychology, 27,* 97–106.

Newcomb, T. M. (1961). *The acquaintance process.* New York: Holt, Rinehart and Winston.

Newell, B. R., Wong, K. Y., Cheung, J. C. H., & Rakow, T. (2008, August 23). Think, blink, or sleep on it? The impact of modes of thought on complex decision making. *Quarterly Journal of Experimental Psychology.* doi:10.1080/17470210802215202

Newman, H. M., & Langer, E. J. (1981). Post-divorce adaptation and the attribution of responsibility. *Sex Roles, 7,* 223–231.

Newman, L. S. (1993). How individualists interpret behavior: Idiocentrism and spontaneous trait inference. *Social Cognition, 11,* 243–269.

Newport, F. (2011). Americans prefer boys to girls, just as they did in 1941. Retrieved from http://www.gallup.com

Nguyen, T., McCracken, J. T., Albaugh, M. D., Botteron, K. N., Hudziak, J. J., & Ducharme, S. (2016). A testosterone-related structural brain phenotype predicts aggressive behavior from childhood to adulthood. *Psychoneuroendocrinology, 63,* 109–118.

Nias, D. K. B. (1979). Marital choice: Matching or complementation? In M. Cook and G. Wilson (Eds.), *Love and attraction.* Oxford: Pergamon.

Nichols, J. (2003, February 9). Man overdoses online as chatters watch him die. *Grand Rapids Press,* p. A20.

Nicholson, C. (2007, January). Framing science: Advances in theory and technology are fueling a new era in the science of persuasion. *APS Observer.* Retrieved from http://www.psychologicalscience.org

Nicholson, N., Cole, S. G., & Rocklin, T. (1985). Conformity in the Asch situation: A comparison between contemporary British and U.S. university students. *British Journal of Social Psychology, 24,* 59–63.

Nicholson, S. P. (2012). Polarizing cues. *American Journal of Political Science, 56*(1), 52–66.

Nie, N. H., & Erbring, L. (2000, February 17). *Internet and society: A preliminary report.* Stanford, CA: Stanford Institute for the Quantitative Study of Society.

Nielsen. (2008a, May). *Nielsen's three screen report.* The Nielsen Company. Retrieved from http://www.nielsen.com

Nielsen. (2008b, February 14). Nielsen reports DVR playback is adding to TV viewing levels. The Nielsen Company. Retrieved from http://www.nielsen.com

Nielsen Company. (2011, April). State of the media: Trends in TV viewing–2011 TV upfront. Retrieved from http://www.nielsen.com/content/dam/corporate/us/en/newswire/uploads/2011/04/State-of-the-Media-2011-TV-Upfronts.pdf.

Nielsen Company. (2010, April 28). U.S. homes add even more TV sets in 2010. Television Audience Report, 2009.

Niemi, R. G., Mueller, J., & Smith, T. W. (1989). *Trends in public opinion: A compendium of survey data.* New York: Greenwood Press.

Nigro, G. N., Hill, D. E., Gelbein, M. E., & Clark, C. L. (1988). Changes in the facial prominence of women and men over the last decade. *Psychology of Women Quarterly, 12,* 225–235.

Nijstad, B. A., & Stroebe, W. (2006). How the group affects the mind: A cognitive model of idea generation in groups. *Personality and Social Psychology Review, 10,* 186–213.

Nijstad, B. A., Stroebe, W., & Lodewijkx, H. F. M. (2006). The illusion of group productivity. A reduction of failures explanation. *European Journal of Social Psychology, 36,* 31–48.

Nisbett, R. (2003). *The geography of thought: How Asians and Westerners think differently ... and why.* New York: Free Press.

Nisbett, R. E., Fong, G. T., Lehman, D. R., & Cheng, P. W. (1987). Teaching reasoning. *Science, 238,* 625–631.

Nisbett, R. E., & Masuda, T. (2003). Culture and point of view. *Proceedings of the National Academy of Sciences, 100,* 11163–11170.

Nisbett, R. E., & Ross, L. (1980). *Human inference: Strategies and shortcomings of social judgment.* Englewood Cliffs, NJ: Prentice-Hall.

Nisbett, R. E., & Ross, L. (1991). *The person and the situation.* New York: McGraw-Hill.

Noble, T. (2003). Nobody left to hate. *EQ Australia, 4,* 8–9.

Nock, M. K., Park, J. M., Finn, C. T., Deliberto, T. L., Dour, H. J., & Banaji, M. R. (2010). Measuring the suicidal mind: Implicit cognition predicts suicidal behavior. *Psychological Science, 21,* 511–517.

Nolan, S. A., Flynn, C., & Garber, J. (2003). Prospective relations between rejection and depression in young adolescents. *Journal of Personality and Social Psychology, 85,* 745–755.

Noller, P., & Fitzpatrick, M. A. (1990). Marital communication in the eighties. *Journal of Marriage and the Family, 52,* 832–843.

Noor, M., Brown, R., Gonzalez, R., Manzi, J., & Lewis, C. A. (2008). On positive psychological outcomes: What helps groups with a history of conflict to forgive and reconcile with each other? *Personality and Social Psychology Bulletin, 34,* 819–832.

Nordgren, L. F., Banas, K., & MacDonald, G. (2011). Empathy gaps for social pain: Why people underestimate the pain of social suffering. *Journal of Personality and Social Psychology, 100,* 120–128.

Nordgren, L. F., van Harreveld, F., & van der Pligt, J. (2009). The restraint bias: How the illusion of self-restraint promotes impulsive behavior. *Psychological Science, 20,* 1523–1528.

Norem, J. K., & Cantor, N. (1986). Defensive pessimism: Harnessing anxiety as motivation. *Journal of Personality and Social Psychology, 51,* 1208–1217.

Norris, M. (2007). The impact of information processing goals and capacity restrictions on attitude-memory. Unpublished Master's Thesis. Queen's University, Kingston, ON.

Norris, M. E., Smith, S. M., Fabrigar, L. R., & Wegener, D. T. (2014). Attitude-memory biases from auditory information: Exploring the moderating roles of information processing goals and capacity restrictions. Poster presented at the 15th annual meeting of the Society for Personality and Social Psychology, Austin, TX.

Norton, A. T., & Herek, G. M. (2013). Heterosexuals' attitudes toward transgender people: Findings from a national probability sample of U.S. adults. *Sex Roles, 68,* 738–753.

Norton, M. I., Frost, J. H., & Ariely, D. (2007). Less is more: The lure of ambiguity, or why familiarity breeds contempt. *Journal of Personality and Social Psychology, 92,* 97–105.

Nosek, B. A. (2007). Implicit-explicit relations. *Current Directions in Psychological Science, 16,* 65–69.

Nosek, B. A., Hawkins, C. B., & Frazier, R. S. (2011). Implicit social cognition: From measures to mechanisms. *Trends in Cognitive Sciences, 15,* 152–159.

Nosek, B. A., Smyth, F. L., Hansen, J. J., Devos, T., Lindner, N. M., Ranganath, K. A., Tucker Smith, C., Olson, K. R., Chugh, D., Greenwald, A. G., & Banaji, M. R. (2007). Pervasiveness and correlates of implicit attitudes and stereotypes. *European Review of Social Psychology, 18,* 36–88.

Notarius, C., & Markman, H. J. (1993). *We can work it out.* New York: Putnam.

Nowak, M. A. (2012, July). Why we help. *Scientific American,* 34–39.

Nowak, M. A., & Highfield, R. (2011). *SuperCooperators: Altruism, evolution, and why we need each other to succeed.* New York: Free Press.

Nuttin, J. M., Jr. (1987). Affective consequences of mere ownership: The name letter effect in twelve European languages. *European Journal of Social Psychology, 17,* 318–402.

O'Brien, E., Konrath, S. H., Grühn, D., & Hagen, A. (2013). Empathic concern and perspective taking: Linear and quadratic effects of age across the adult life span. *The Journals of Gerontology: Series B: Psychological Sciences and Social Sciences, 68B,* 168–175.

O'Dea, T. F. (1968). Sects and cults. In D. L. Sills (Ed.), *International encyclopedia of the social sciences* (Vol. 14). New York: Macmillan.

O'Hegarty, M., Pederson, L. L., Yenokyan, G., Nelson, D., & Wortley, P. (2007). Young adults' perceptions of cigarette warning labels in the United States and

Canada. *Preventing Chronic Disease: Public Health Research, Practice, and Policy, 30,* 467–473.

O'Keefe, D. J., & Jensen, J. D. (2011). The relative effectiveness of gain-framed and loss-framed persuasive appeals concerning obesity-related behaviors: Meta-analytic evidence and implications. In R. Batra, P. A. Keller, & V. J. Strecher (Eds.), *Leveraging consumer psychology for effective health communications: The obesity challenge* (pp. 171–185). Armonk, NY: Sharpe.

O'Leary, K. D., Christian, J. L., & Mendell, N. R. (1994). A closer look at the link between marital discord and depressive symptomatology. *Journal of Social and Clinical Psychology, 13,* 33–41.

O'Reilly, T., & Tennant, M. (2009). *The age of persuasion: How marketing ate our culture.* Toronto: Knopf Canada.

Oaten, M., & Cheng, K. (2006a). Improved self-control: The benefits of a regular program of academic study. *Basic and Applied Social Psychology, 28,* 1.

Oaten, M., & Cheng, K. (2006b). Longitudinal gains in self-regulation from regular physical exercise. *British Journal of Health Psychology, 11,* 717–733.

Oddone-Paolucci, E., Genuis, M., & Violato, C. (2000). A meta-analysis of the published research on the effects of pornography. In C. Violata (Ed.), *The changing family and child development.* Aldershot, UK: Ashgate Publishing.

Odgers, C. L., Donley, S., Caspi, A., Bates, C. J., & Moffitt, T. E. (2015). Living alongside more affluent neighbors predicts greater involvement in antisocial behavior among low-income boys. *Journal of Child Psychology and Psychiatry, 56,* 1055–1064.

Ohbuchi, K., & Kambara, T. (1985). Attacker's intent and awareness of outcome, impression management, and retaliation. *Journal of Experimental Social Psychology, 21,* 321–330.

Oishi, S., Lun, J., & Sherman, G. D. (2007). Residential mobility, self-concept, and positive affect in social interactions. *Journal of Personality and Social Psychology, 93,* 131–141.

Oishi, S., Rothman, A. J., Snyder, M., Su, J., Zehm, K., Hertel, A. W., Gonzales, M. H., & Sherman, G. D. (2007). The socioecological model of procommunity action: The benefits of residential stability. *Journal of Personality and Social Psychology, 93,* 831–844.

Okimoto, T. G., & Brescoll, V. L. (2010). The price of power: Power seeking and backlash against female politicians. *Personality and Social Psychology Bulletin, 36,* 923–936.

Oliner, S. P., & Oliner, P. M. (1988). *The altruistic personality: Rescuers of Jews in Nazi Europe.* New York: The Free Press.

Olson, I. R., & Marchuetz, C. (2005). Facial attractiveness is appraised in a glance. *Emotion, 5,* 498.

Olson, J. M., & Cal, A. V. (1984). Source credibility, attitudes, and the recall of past behaviours. *European Journal of Social Psychology, 14,* 203–210.

Olson, J. M., Roese, N. J., & Zanna, M. P. (1996). Expectancies. In E. T. Higgins & A. W. Kruglanski (Eds.), *Social psychology: Handbook of basic principles.* New York: Guilford Press.

Olson, J. M., & Zanna, M. P. (1993). Attitudes and attitude change. *Annual Review of Psychology, 44,* 117–154.

Olson, K. R., Dunham, Y., Dweck, C. S., Spelke, E. S., & Banaji, M. R. (2008). Judgments of the lucky across development and culture. *Journal of Personality and Social Psychology, 94,* 757–776.

Olweus, D. (1979). Stability of aggressive reaction patterns in males: A review. *Psychological Bulletin, 86,* 852–875.

Olweus, D., & Breivik, K. (2013). The plight of victims of school bullying: The opposite of well-being. In B. A. Asher, F. Casas, I. Frones, & J. E. Korbin, (Eds.), *International handbook of child well-being.* Heidelberg, Germany: Springer.

Olweus, D., Mattsson, A., Schalling, D., & Low, H. (1988). Circulating testosterone levels and aggression in adolescent males: A causal analysis. *Psychosomatic Medicine, 50,* 261–272.

Omoto, A. M., & Snyder, M (2002). Considerations of community: The context and process of volunteerism. *American Behavioral Scientist, 45,* 846–867.

Onraet, E., Dhont, K., & Van Hiel, A. (2014). The relationships between internal and external threats and right-wing attitudes: A three-wave longitudinal study. *Personality and Social Psychology Bulletin, 40,* 712–725.

Open Secrets. (2005). 2004 election overview: Winning vs. spending. Retrieved from http://www.opensecrets.org

Opotow, S. (1990). Moral exclusion and injustice: An introduction. *Journal of Social Issues, 46,* 1–20.

Orbell, J. M., van de Kragt, A. J. C., & Dawes, R. M. (1988). Explaining discussion-induced cooperation. *Journal of Personality and Social Psychology, 54,* 811–819.

Orendain, S. (2011, December 29). In Philippine slums, capturing light in a bottle. National Public Radio. Retrieved from http://www.npr.org

Orgaz, C., Estévez, A., & Matute, H. (2013). Pathological gamblers are more vulnerable to the illusion of control in a standard associative learning task. *Frontiers in Psychology, 4.* doi:10.3389/fpsyg.2013.00306

Orive, R. (1984). Group similarity, public self-awareness, and opinion extremity: A social projection explanation of deindividuation effects. *Journal of Personality and Social Psychology, 47,* 727–737.

Ornstein, R. (1991). *The evolution of consciousness: Of Darwin, Freud, and cranial fire: The origins of the way we think.* New York: Prentice-Hall.

Orr, R., McKeown, S., Cairns, E., & Stringer, M. (2012). Examining non-racial segregation: A micro-ecological approach. *British Journal of Social Psychology, 51,* 717–723.

Ortega, R., Elipe, P., Mora-Merchan, J. A., Genta, M. L., Brighi, A., Guarini, A., Smith, P. K., Thompson, F., & Tippett, N. (2012). The emotional impact of bullying and cyberbullying on victims: A European cross-national study. *Aggressive Behavior, 38,* 342–356.

Orth, U., & Robins, R. W. (2013). Understanding the link between low self-esteem and depression. *Current Directions in Psychological Science, 22,* 455–460.

Osbeck, L. M., Moghaddam, F. M., & Perreault, S. (1996). Similarity and attraction among majority and minority groups in a multicultural context. *International Journal of Intercultural Relations, 20,* 1–10.

Osborne, D., & Sibley, C. G. (2013). Through rose-colored glasses: System-justifying beliefs dampen the effects of relative deprivation on well-being and political mobilization. *Personality and Social Psychology Bulletin, 39,* 991–1004.

Osborne, J. W. (1995). Academics, self-esteem, and race: A look at the underlying assumptions of the disidentification hypothesis. *Personality and Social Psychology Bulletin, 21,* 449–455.

Osgood, C. E. (1962). *An alternative to war or surrender.* Urbana, IL: University of Illinois Press.

Osgood, C. E. (1980). *GRIT: A strategy for survival in mankind's nuclear age?* Paper presented at the Pugwash Conference on New Directions in Disarmament, Racine, WI.

Oskamp, S. (1991). *Curbside recycling: Knowledge, attitudes, and behavior.* Paper presented at the Society for Experimental Social Psychology meeting, Columbus, Ohio.

Osofsky, M. J., Bandura, A., & Zimbardo, P. G. (2005). The role of moral disengagement in the execution process. *Law and Human Behavior, 29,* 371–393.

Osterhouse, R. A., & Brock, T. C. (1970). Distraction increases yielding to propaganda by inhibiting counterarguing. *Journal of Personality and Social Psychology, 15,* 344–358.

Ostrom, E. (2014). Do institutions for collective action evolve? *Journal of Bioeconomics, 16,* 3–30.

Ostrom, T. M., & Sedikides, C. (1992). Outgroup homogeneity effects in natural and minimal groups. *Psychological Bulletin, 112,* 536–552.

Oswald, F. L., Mitchell, G., Blanton, H., Jaccard, J., & Tetlock, P. E. (2013). Predicting ethnic and racial discrimination: A meta-analysis of IAT criterion studies. *Journal of Personality and Social Psychology, 105,* 171–192.

Oswald, F. L., Mitchell, G., Blanton, H., Jaccard, J., & Tetlock, P. E. (2015). Using the IAT to predict ethnic and racial discrimination: Small effect sizes of unknown societal significance. *Journal of Personality and Social Psychology, 108,* 562–571.

Otten, M., & Jonas, K. J. (2013). Out of the group, out of control? The brain responds to social exclusion with changes in cognitive control. *Scan, 8,* 789–794.

Ouellette, J. A., & Wood, W. (1998). Habit and intention in everyday life: The multiple processes by which past behavior predicts future behavior. *Psychological Bulletin, 124,* 54–74.

Oyserman, D., Coon, H. M., & Kemmelmeier, M. (2002). Rethinking individualism and collectivism: Evaluation of theoretical assumptions and meta-analyses. *Psychological Bulletin, 128,* 3–72.

Oyserman, D., Kemmelmeier, M., & Coon, H. M. (2002). Cultural psychology, a new look: Reply to Bond (2002), Fiske (2002), Kitayama (2002), and Miller (2002). *Psychological Bulletin, 128,* 110–117.

Packer, D. J. (2008). Identifying systematic disobedience in Milgram's obedience experiments: A meta-analytic review. *Perspectives on Psychological Science, 3*(4), 301–304.

Packer, D. J. (2009). Avoiding groupthink: Whereas weakly identified members remain silent, strongly identified members dissent about collective problems. *Psychological Science, 20,* 546–548.

Packer, D. J. (2012). *Conformity and Obedience.* Encyclopedia of Human Behavior (2nd Ed). Elsevier.

Padgett, V. R. (1989). *Predicting organizational violence: An application of 11 powerful principles of obedience.* Paper presented at the American Psychological Association convention.

Page, S. E. (2007). *The difference: How the power of diversity creates better groups, firms, schools, and societies.* Princeton, NJ: Princeton University Press.

Pallak, M. S., Mueller, M., Dollar, K., & Pallak, J. (1972). Effect of commitment on responsiveness to an extreme consonant communication. *Journal of Personality and Social Psychology, 23,* 429–436.

Pallak, S. R., Murroni, E., & Koch, J. (1983). Communicator attractiveness and expertise, emotional versus rational appeals, and persuasion: A heuristic versus systematic processing interpretation. *Social Cognition, 2,* 122–141.

Palmer, D. L. (1996). Determinants of Canadian attitudes toward immigration: More than just racism? *Canadian Journal of Behavioural Science, 28,* 180–192.

Palmer, E. L., & Dorr, A. (Eds.) (1980). *Children and the faces of television: Teaching, violence, selling.* New York: Academic Press.

Paloutzian, R. (1979). *Pro-ecology behavior: Three field experiments on litter pickup.* Paper presented at the Western Psychological Association convention.

Paluck, E. L. (2009). Reducing intergroup prejudice and conflict using the media: A field experiment in Rwanda. *Journal of Personality and Social Psychology, 96,* 574–587.

Paluck, E. L. (2010). Is it better not to talk? Group polarization, extended contact, and perspective taking in Eastern Democratic Republic of Congo. *Personality and Social Psychology Bulletin, 36,* 1170–1185.

Pandey, J., Sinha, Y., Prakash, A., & Tripathi, R. C. (1982). Right-left political ideologies and attribution of the causes of poverty. *European Journal of Social Psychology, 12,* 327–331.

Paolini, S., Harwood, J., Rubin, M., Husnu, S., Joyce, N., & Hewstone, M. (2014). Positive and extensive intergroup contact in the past buffers against the disproportionate impact of negative contact in the present. *European Journal of Social Psychology, 44,* 548–562.

Paolini, S., Hewstone, M., Cairns, E., & Voci, A. (2004). Effects of direct and indirect cross-group friendships on judgments of Catholics and Protestants in Northern Ireland: The mediating role of an anxiety-reduction mechanism. *Personality and Social Psychology Bulletin, 30,* 770–786.

Papastamou, S., & Mugny, G. (1990). Synchronic consistency and psychologization in minority influence. *European Journal of Social Psychology, 20,* 85–98.

Pape, R. A. (2003, September 22). Dying to kill us. *New York Times.* Retrieved from http://www.nytimes.com

Parashar, U. D., Gibson, C. J., Bresse, J. S., & Glass, R. I. (2006). Rotavirus and severe childhood diarrhea. *Emerging Infectious Diseases, 12,* 304–306.

Pardini, D. A., Raine, A., Erickson, K., & Loeber, R. (2014). Low amygdala volume in men is associated with childhood aggression, early psychopathic traits, and future violence. *Biological Psychiatry, 75,* 73–80.

Parents Television Council (PTC). (2007, January 10). Dying to entertain: Violence on prime time broadcast TV, 1998 to 2006. Retrieved from http://www.parentstv.org

Park, A., Ickes, W., & Robinson, R. L. (2014). More f#!%ing rudeness: Reliable personality predictors of verbal rudeness and other ugly confrontational behaviors. *Journal of Aggression, Conflict, and Peace Research, 6,* 26–43.

Park, B., & Rothbart, M. (1982). Perception of out-group homogeneity and levels of social categorization: Memory for the subordinate attributes of in-group and out-group members. *Journal of Personality and Social Psychology, 42,* 1051–1068.

Park, J., Malachi, E., Sternin, O., & Tevet, R. (2009). Subtle bias against Muslim job applicants in personnel decisions. *Journal of Applied Social Psychology, 39,* 2174–2190.

Parke, R. D., Berkowitz, L., Leyens, J. P., West, S. G., & Sebastian, J. (1977). Some effects of violent and nonviolent movies on the behavior of juvenile delinquents. In L. Berkowitz (Ed.), *Advances in experimental social psychology* (Vol. 10). New York: Academic Press.

Parker, K., Horowitz, J. M., Igielnik, R., Oliphant, B., & Brown, A. (2017, June 22). Protection tops the list of reasons for owning a gun. Pew Research Center.

Parker, K. D., Ortega, S. T., & VanLaningham, J. (1995). Life satisfaction, self-esteem, and personal happiness among Mexican and African Americans. *Sociological Spectrum, 15,* 131–145.

Parks, C. D., & Rumble, A. C. (2001). Elements of reciprocity and social value orientation. *Personality and Social Psychology Bulletin, 27,* 1301–1309.

Pascarella, E. T., & Terenzini, P. T. (1991). *How college affects students: Findings and insights from twenty years of research.* San Francisco: Jossey-Bass.

Patrick, R. B., Rote, W. M., Gibbs, J. C., & Basinger, K. S. (2019). Defend, stand by, or join in?: The relative influence of moral identity, moral judgment, and social self-efficacy on adolescents' bystander behaviors in bullying situations. *Journal of Youth and Adolescence, 48*(10),

2051–2064. https://doi-org.library.smu.ca/10.1007/s10964-019-01089-w

Patterson, G. R., Chamberlain, P., & Reid, J. B. (1982). A comparative evaluation of parent training procedures. *Behavior Therapy, 13,* 638–650.

Patterson, G. R., Littman, R. A., & Bricker, W. (1967). Assertive behavior in children: A step toward a theory of aggression. *Monographs of the Society of Research in Child Development* (Serial No. 113), *32,* 5.

Patterson, T. E. (1980). The role of the mass media in presidential campaigns: The lessons of the 1976 election. *Items, 34,* 25–30. Social Science Research Council, 605 Third Avenue, New York, NY 10016.

Paulhus, D. (1982). Individual differences, self-presentation, and cognitive dissonance: Their concurrent operation in forced compliance. *Journal of Personality and Social Psychology, 43,* 838–852.

Paulhus, D. L. (1998). Interpersonal and intrapsychic adaptiveness of trait self-enhancment: A mixed blessing? *Journal of Personality and Social Psychology, 75,* 1197–1208.

Paulhus, D. L., & Lim, D. T. K. (1994). Arousal and evaluative extremity in social judgments: A dynamic complexity model. *European Journal of Social Psychology, 24,* 89–99.

Paulhus, D. L., & Morgan, K. L. (1997). Perceptions of intelligence in leaderless groups: The dynamic effects of shyness and acquaintance. *Journal of Personality and Social Psychology, 72,* 581–591.

Paulhus, D. L., Westlake, B. G., Calvez, S. S., & Harms, P. D. (2013). Self-presentation style in job interviews: The role of personality and culture. *Journal of Applied Social Psychology, 43,* 2042–2059.

Paulhus, D. L., & Williams, K. M. (2002). The Dark Triad of personality: Narcissism, Machiavellianism and psychopathy. *Journal of Research in Personality, 36,* 556–563.

Paulus, P. B. (1998). Developing consensus about groupthink after all these years. *Organizational behavior and human decision processes,* in press.

Paulus, P. B., & Coskun, H. (2012). Group creativity: Understanding collaborative creativity processes. In J. M. Levine (Ed.), *Group processes.* Boca Raton, FL: Psychology Press.

Paulus, P. B., Dzindolet, M., & Kohn, N. W. (2011). Collaborative creativity—Group creativity and team innovation. In M. D. Mumford (Ed.), *Handbook of organizational creativity.* New York: Elsevier.

Paulus, P. B., Larey, T. S., & Ortega, A. H. (1995). Performance and perceptions of brainstormers in an organizational setting. *Basic and Applied Social Psychology, 17,* 249–265.

Paulus, P. B., & Yang, H. (2000). Idea generation in groups: A basis for creativity in organizations. *Organizational Behavior and Human Decision Processes, 82,* 76–87.

Payne, B. K. (2001). Prejudice and perception: The role of automatic and controlled processes in misperceiving a weapon. *Journal of Personality and Social Psychology, 81,* 181–192.

Payne, B. K. (2006). Weapon bias: Split-second decisions and unintended stereotyping. *Current Directions in Psychological Science, 15,* 287–291.

Payne, B. K., Brown-Iannuzzi, J. L., & Loersch, C. (2016). Replicable effects of primes on human behavior. *Journal of Experimental Psychology: General, 145*(10), 1269.

Payne, B. K., Krosnick, J. A., Pasek, J., Lelkes, Y., Akhtar, O., & Tompson, T. (2010). Implicit and explicit prejudice in the 2008 American presidential election. *Journal of Experimental Social Psychology, 46,* 367–374.

Payne, B. K., Lee, K. M., Giletta, M., & Prinstein, M. J. (2016). Implicit attitudes predict drinking onset in adolescents: Shaping by social norms. *Health psychology, 35*(8), 829.

Pedersen, A., & Walker, I. (1997). Prejudice against Australian Aborigines: Old-fashioned and modern forms. *European Journal of Social Psychology, 27,* 561–587.

Pedersen, A., Zachariae, R., & Bovbjerg, D. H. (2010). Influence of psychological stress on upper respiratory infection—A meta-analysis of prospective studies. *Psychosomatic Medicine, 72,* 823–832.

Pedersen, W. C., Gonzales, C., & Miller, N. (2000). The moderating effect of trivial triggering provocation on displaced aggression. *Journal of Personality and Social Psychology, 78,* 913–927.

Pedersen, W. C., Vasquez, E. A., Bartholow, B. D., Grosvenor, M., & Truong, A. (2014). Are you insulting me? Exposure to alcohol primes increases aggression following ambiguous provocation. *Personality and Social Psychology Bulletin, 40,* 1037–1049.

Peetz, J., & Buehler, R. (2009). Is there a budget fallacy? The role of savings goals in the prediction of personal spending. *Personality and Social Psychology Bulletin, 35,* 1579–1591.

Peetz, J., Gunn, G. R., & Wilson, A. E. (2010). Crimes of the past: Defensive temporal distancing in the face of past in-group wrongdoing. *Personality and Social Psychology Bulletin, 36,* 598–611.

Pegalis, L. J., Shaffer, D. R., Bazzini, D. G., & Greenier, K. (1994). On the ability to elicit self-disclosure: Are there gender-based and contextual limitations on the opener effect? *Personality and Social Psychology Bulletin, 20,* 412–420.

Pennebaker, J. W., Rime, B., & Sproul, G. (1996). Stereotypes of emotional expressiveness of northerners and southerners: A cross-cultural test of Montesquieu's hypotheses. *Journal of Personality and Social Psychology, 70,* 372–380.

Penner, L. A., Dertke, M. C., & Achenbach, C. J. (1973). The "flash" system: A field study of altruism. *Journal of Applied Social Psychology, 3,* 362–370.

Pentland, A. (2010). To signal is human. *American Scientist, 98,* 204–211.

Penton-Voak, I. S., Perrett, D. I., & Peirce, J. W. (2001). *Computer graphic studies of the role of facial similarity in judgements of attractiveness.* New Brunswick, NJ: Transaction Publishers.

Peplau, L. A., & Gordon, S. L. (1985). Women and men in love: Gender differences in close heterosexual relationships. In V. E. O'Leary, R. K. Unger, & B. S. Wallston (Eds.), *Women, gender, and social psychology.* Hillsdale, NJ: Erlbaum.

Pereira, C., Vala, J., & Costa-Lopes, R. (2010). From prejudice to discrimination: The legitimizing role of perceived threat in discrimination against immigrants. *European Journal of Social Psychology, 40,* 1231–1250.

Pereira, J. (2003, January 10). Just how far does First Amendment protection go? *Wall Street Journal,* pp. B1, B3.

Perfumi, S. C., Bagnoli, F., Caudek, C., & Guazzini, A. (2019). Deindividuation effects on normative and informational social influence within computer-mediated-communication. *Computers in Human Behavior, 92,* 230–237. https://doi-org.library.smu.ca/10.1016/j.chb.2018.11.017

Perkins, H. W. (1991). Religious commitment, Yuppie values, and well-being in post-collegiate life. *Review of Religious Research, 32,* 244–251.

Perlman, D., & Rook, K. S. (1987). Social support, social deficits, and the family: Toward the enhancement of well-being. In S. Oskamp (Ed.), *Family processes and problems: Social psychological aspects.* Newbury Park, CA: Sage.

Perls, F. S. (1973). *Ego, hunger and aggression: The beginning of Gestalt therapy.* New York: Random House.

Perrett, D. (2010). *In your face: The new science of human attraction.* New York: Palgrave Macmillan.

Perrin, S., & Spencer, C. (1981). Independence or conformity in the Asch experiment as a reflection of cultural or situational factors. *British Journal of Social Psychology, 20,* 205–209.

Perry, G. (2013). *Behind the shock machine: The untold story of the notorious Milgram psychology experiments*. New York, NY: The New Press.

Perry, G. (2014). The view from the boys. *Psychologist, 27,* 834–836.

Persico, N., Postelwaite, A., & Silverman, D. (2004). The effect of adolescent experience on labor market outcomes: The case of height. *Journal of Political Economy, 112,* 1019–1053.

Pessin, J. (1933). The comparative effects of social and mechanical stimulation on memorizing. *American Journal of Psychology, 45,* 263–270.

Pessin, J., & Husband, R. W. (1933). Effects of social stimulation on human maze learning. *Journal of Abnormal and Social Psychology, 28,* 148–154.

Peters, E., Romer, D., Slovic, P., Jamieson, K. H., Whasfield, L., Mertz, C. K., & Carpenter, S. M. (2007). The impact and acceptability of Canadian-style cigarette warning labels among U.S. smokers and nonsmokers. *Nicotine and Tobacco Research, 9,* 473–481.

Peterson, C., Bishop, M. P., Fletcher, C. W., Kaplan, M. R., Yesko, E. S., Moon, C. H., Smith, J. S., Michaels, C. E., & Michaels, A. J. (2001). Explanatory style as a risk factor for traumatic mishaps. *Cognitive Therapy and Research, 25,* 633–649.

Peterson, C., & Bossio, L. M. (2000). Optimism and physical well-being. In E. C. Chang (Ed.), *Optimism and pessimism.* Washington, DC: APA Books.

Peterson, C., Schwartz, S. M., & Seligman, M. E. P. (1981). Self-blame and depression symptoms. *Journal of Personality and Social Psychology, 41,* 253–259.

Peterson, C., & Steen, T. A. (2002). Optimistic explanatory style. In C. R. Snyder & S. J. Lopez (Ed.), *Handbook of positive psychology.* London: Oxford University Press.

Peterson, C. K., & Harmon-Jones, E. (2012). Anger and testosterone: Evidence that situationally-induced anger relates to situationally-induced testosterone. *Emotion, 12,* 899–902.

Peterson, J. L., & Zill, N. (1981). Television viewing in the United States and children's intellectual, social, and emotional development. *Television and Children,* 2(2), 21–28.

Peterson, R. S., & Nemeth, C. J. (1996). Focus versus flexibility: Majority and minority influence can both improve performance. *Personality and Social Psychology Bulletin, 22,* 14–23.

Petrocelli, J. V., Percy, E. J., Sherman, S. J., & Tormala, Z. L. (2011). Counterfactual potency. *Journal of Personality and Social Psychology, 100,* 30–46.

Petrocelli, J. V., Seta, C. E., & Seta, J. J. (2013). Dysfunctional counterfactual thinking: When simulating alternatives to reality impedes experiential learning. *Thinking & Reasoning, 19*(2), 205-230.

Petrocelli, J. V., Tormala, Z. L., & Rucker, D. D. (2007). Unpacking attitude certainty: Attitude clarity and attitude correctness. *Journal of Personality and Social Psychology, 92*(1), 30–41.

Pettigrew, T. F. (1958). Personality and socio-cultural factors in intergroup attitudes: A cross-national comparison. *Journal of Conflict Resolution, 2,* 29–42.

Pettigrew, T. F. (1979). The ultimate attribution error: Extending Allport's cognitive analysis of prejudice. *Personality and Social Psychology Bulletin, 55,* 461–476.

Pettigrew, T. F. (1980). Prejudice. In S. Thernstrom et al. (Eds.), *Harvard encyclopedia of American ethnic groups.* Cambridge, MA: Harvard University Press.

Pettigrew, T. F. (1988). Advancing racial justice: Past lessons for future use. Paper for the University of Alabama conference "Opening Doors: An appraisal of Race Relations in America."

Pettigrew, T. F. (1997). Generalized intergroup contact effects on prejudice. *Personality and Social Psychology Bulletin, 23,* 173–185.

Pettigrew, T. F. (1997, May 12). *New York Times,* p. 20.

Pettigrew, T. F. (1998). Intergroup contact theory. *Annual Review of Psychology,* in press.

Pettigrew, T. F. (2004). Intergroup contact: Theory, research, and new perspectives. In J. A. Banks & C. A. McGee Banks (Eds.), *Handbook of research on multicultural education.* San Francisco: Jossey-Bass.

Pettigrew, T. F. (2006). A two-level approach to anti-immigrant prejudice and discrimination. In R. Mahalingam (Ed.), *Cultural psychology of immigrants.* Mahwah, NJ: Erlbaum.

Pettigrew, T. F., Jackson, J. S., Brika, J. B., Lemaine, G., Meertens, R. W., Wagner, U., & Zick, A. (1998). Outgroup prejudice in western Europe. *European Review of Social Psychology, 8,* 241–273.

Pettigrew, T. F., & Meertens, R. W. (1995). Subtle and blatant prejudice in western Europe. *European Journal of Social Psychology, 25,* 57–76.

Pettigrew, T. F., & Tropp, L. R. (2008). How does intergroup contact reduce prejudice? Meta-analytic tests of three mediators. *European Journal of Social Psychology, 38,* 922–934.

Pettigrew, T. F., & Tropp, L. R. (2011). *When groups meet: The dynamics of intergroup contact.* New York: Psychology Press.

Pettigrew, T. F., Wagner, U., & Christ, O. (2010). Population ratios and prejudice: Modeling both contact and threat effects. *Journal of Ethnic and Migration Studies, 36,* 635–650.

Petty, R. E., & Briñol, P. (2008). Persuasion: From single to multiple to metacognitive processes. *Perspectives on Psychological Science, 3,* 137–147.

Petty, R. E., & Briñol, P. (2015). Emotion and persuasion: Cognitive and meta-cognitive processes impact attitudes. *Cognition and Emotion, 29*(1), 1–26.

Petty, R. E., & Cacioppo, J. T. (1979). Effects of forewarning of persuasive intent and involvement on cognitive response and persuasion. *Personality and Social Psychology Bulletin, 5,* 173–176.

Petty, R. E., & Cacioppo, J. T. (1986). *Communication and persuasion: Central and peripheral routes to attitude change.* New York: Springer-Verlag.

Petty, R. E., Cacioppo, J. T., & Goldman, R. (1981). Personal involvement as a determinant of argument-based persuasion. *Journal of Personality and Social Psychology, 41,* 847–855.

Petty, R. E., Haugtvedt, C. P., & Smith, S. M. (1995). Elaboration as a determinant of attitude strength: Creating attitudes that are persistent, resistant, and predictive of behavior. In R. E. Petty & J. A. Krosnick (Eds.), *Attitude strength: Antecedents and consequences.* Hillsdale, NJ: Erlbaum.

Petty, R. E., Schumann, D. W., Richman, S. A., & Strathman, A. J. (1993). Positive mood and persuasion: Different roles for affect under high and low elaboration conditions. *Journal of Personality and Social Psychology, 64,* 5–20.

Petty, R. E., & Wegener, D. T. (1998). Attitude change: Multiple roles for persuasion variables. In D. Gilbert, S. Fiske, & G. Lindzey (Eds), *Handbook of social psychology* (4th ed.). New York: McGraw-Hill.

Petty, R. E., & Wegener, D. T. (1999). The elaboration likelihood model: Current status and controversies. In S. & Y. Trope (Eds.), *Dual-process theories in social psychology* (pp. 41–72). New York: Guilford.

Petty, R. E., Wegener, D. T., & Fabrigar, L. R. (1997). Attitudes and attitude change. *Annual Review of Psychology, 48,* 609–647.

Pew. (2006, March 30). America's immigration quandary. Pew Research Center. Retrieved from www. pewglobal.org.

Pew Research Center. (2000, May 10). Tracking online life: How women use the Internet to cultivate relationships with family and friends. Washington, DC: Pew Internet and American Life Project.

Pew Research Center. (2007, July 18). Modern marriage: "I like hugs. I like kisses. But what I really love is help with the dishes." Pew Research Center. Retrieved from pewresearch.org

Pew Research Center. (2008). Video gamers galore.

Pew Research Center. (2011, January 27). The future of the global Muslim population: Projections for 2010–2030. Retrieved from http://www.pewforum.org

Pew Research Center. (2013). Big racial divide over Zimmerman verdict. July 22, 2013.

Pew Research Center. (2014). Global views on morality. Pew Research Global Attitudes Project (www.pewglobal.org).

Pew Research Center. (2014). The Web at 25 in the U.S. Retrieved from http://www.pewinternet.org/2014/02/27/the-web-at-25-in-the-u-s/

Phelan, J. E., & Rudman, L. A. (2010). Reactions to ethnic deviance: The role of backlash in racial stereotype maintenance. *Journal of Personality and Social Psychology, 99,* 265–281.

Phillips, D. L. (2003, September 20). Listening to the wrong Iraqi. *New York Times* (www.nytimes.com)

Phillips, D. P. (1985). Natural experiments on the effects of mass media violence on fatal aggression: Strengths and weaknesses of a new approach. In L. Berkowitz (Ed.), *Advances in experimental social psychology* (Vol. 19). Orlando, FL: Academic Press.

Phillips, D. P., Carstensen, L. L., & Paight, D. J. (1989). Effects of mass media news stories on suicide, with new evidence on the role of story content. In D. R. Pfeffer (Ed.), *Suicide among youth: Perspectives on risk and prevention.* Washington, DC: American Psychiatric Press.

Phillips, T. (2004, April 3). Quoted by T. Baldwin & D. Rozenberg, "Britain 'must scrap multiculturalism.'" *The Times,* p. A1.

Phinney, J. S. (1990). Ethnic identity in adolescents and adults: Review of research. *Psychological Bulletin, 108,* 499–514.

Piliavin, I. M., Rodin, J., & Piliavin, J. A. (1969). Good Samaritanism: An underground phenomenon. *Journal of Personality and Social Psychology, 13,* 289–299.

Piliavin, J. A. (2003). Doing well by doing good: Benefits for the benefactor. In C. L. M. Keyes, & J. Haidt (Eds.), *Flourishing: Positive psychology and the life well-lived* (pp. 227–247). Washington, DC: APA Press.

Piliavin, J. A., Evans, D. E., & Callero, P. (1982). Learning to "Give to unnamed strangers": The process of commitment to regular blood donation. In E. Staub, D. Bar-Tal, J. Karylowski, & J. Reykawski (Eds.), *The development and maintenance of prosocial behavior: International perspectives.* New York: Plenum.

Piliavin, J. A., & Piliavin, I. M. (1973). *The Good Samaritan: Why does he help?* Unpublished manuscript, University of Wisconsin, Madison, WI.

Pincus, J. H. (2001). *Base instincts: What makes killers kill?* New York: W. W. Norton & Co., Inc.

Pinel, E. C. (1999). Stigma consciousness: The psychological legacy of social stereotypes. *Journal of Personality and Social Psychology, 76,* 114–128.

Pinel, E. C. (2002). Stigma consciousness in intergroup contexts: The power of conviction. *Journal of Experimental Social Psychology, 38,* 178–185.

Pinker, S. (2008). *The sexual paradox: Men, women, and the real gender gap.* New York: Scribner.

Pinker, S. (2014). *The village effect: How face-to-face contact can make us healthier, happier, and smarter.* New York: Spiegel & Grau.

Pinkus, R. T., Lockwood, P., Schimmack, U., & Fournier, M. A. (2008). For better and for worse: Everyday social comparisons between romantic partners. *Journal of Personality and Social Psychology, 95,* 1180–1201.

Place, S. S., Todd, P. M., Penke, L., & Asendorpf, J. B. (2009). The ability to judge the romantic interest of others. *Psychological Science, 20,* 22–26.

Plaks, J. E., & Higgins, E. T. (2000). Pragmatic use of stereotyping in teamwork: Social loafing and compensation as a function of inferred partner-situation fit. *Journal of Personality and Social Psychology, 79,* 962–974.

Plant, E. A., Devine, P. G., & Peruche, B. M. (2010). Regulatory concerns for interracial interactions: Approaching egalitarianism versus avoiding prejudice. *Personality and Social Psychology Bulletin, 36,* 1135–1147.

Plant, E. A., Goplen, J., & Kunstman, J. W. (2011). Selective responses to threat: The roles of race and gender in decisions to shoot. *Personality and Social Psychology, 37,* 1274–1281.

Platow, M. J., Haslam, S. A., Both, A., Chew, I., Cuddon, M., Goharpey, N., Maurer, J., Rosini, S., Tsekouras, A., & Grace, D. M. (2005). "It's not funny if they're laughing": Self-categorization, social influence, and responses to canned laughter. *Journal of Experimental Social Psychology, 41,* 542–550.

Plaut, V. C., Adams, G., & Anderson, S. L. (2009). Does attractiveness buy happiness? "It depends on where you're from." *Personal Relationships, 16,* 619–630.

Pliner, P., Hart, H., Kohl, J., & Saari, D. (1974). Compliance without pressure: Some further data on the foot-in-the-door technique. *Journal of Experimental Social Psychology, 10,* 17–22.

Poincaré, J. H. (1905). *Science and hypothesis* (W. J. Greenstreet, Trans.). London: Walter Scott Publishing Co. (Original work published 1901).

Pomazal, R. J., & Clore, G. L. (1973). Helping on the highway: The effects of dependency and sex. *Journal of Applied Social Psychology, 3,* 150–164.

Pond, R. S., DeWall, C. N., Lambert, N. M., Deckman, T., Bonser, I. M., & Fincham, F. D. (2012). Repulsed by violence: Disgust sensitivity buffers trait, behavioral, and daily aggression. *Journal of Personality and Social Psychology, 102,* 175–188.

Poniewozik, J. (2003, November 24). All the news that fits your reality. *Time,* 90.

Poon, K-T., Chen, Z., & DeWall, C. N. (2013). Feeling entitled to more: Ostracism increases dishonest behavior. *Personality and Social Psychology Bulleting, 39,* 1227–1239.

Popenoe, D. (2002). *Seven secrets to a happy marriage.* New York: Ladies Home Journal.

Pornpitakpan, C. (2004). The persuasiveness of source credibility: A critical review of five decades' evidence. *Journal of Applied Social Psychology, 34,* 243–281.

Post, J. M. (2005). The new face of terrorism: Socio-cultural foundations of contemporary terrorism. *Behavioral Sciences and the Law, 23,* 451–465.

Postmes, T., & Spears, R. (1998). Deindividuation and antinormative behavior: A meta-analysis. *Psychological Bulletin, 123,* 238–259.

Postmes, T., Spears, R., & Cihangir, S. (2001). Quality of decision making and group norms. *Journal of Personality and Social Psychology, 80,* 918–930.

Pratkanis, A. R., Greenwald, A. G., Leippe, M. R., & Baumgardner, M. H. (1988). In search of reliable persuasion effects: III.

The sleeper effect is dead. Long live the sleeper effect. *Journal of Personality and Social Psychology, 54,* 203–218.

Pratkanis, A. R., & Turner, M. E. (1996). The proactive removal of discriminatory barriers: Affirmative action as effective help. *Journal of Social Issues, 52,* 111–132.

Pratto, F., Sidanius, J., Stallworth, L. M., & Malle, B. F. (1994). Social dominance orientation: A personality variable predicting social and political attitudes. *Journal of Personality and Social Psychology, 67,* 741–763.

Prentice-Dunn, S., & Rogers, R. W. (1980). Effects of deindividuating situational cues and aggressive models on subjective deindividuation and aggression. *Journal of Personality and Social Psychology, 39,* 104–113.

Prentice-Dunn, S., & Rogers, R. W. (1989). Deindividuation and the self-regulation of behavior. In P. B. Paulus (Ed.), *Psychology of group influence* (2nd ed.). Hillsdale, NJ: Erlbaum.

Price, G. H., Dabbs, J. M., Jr., Clower, B. J., & Resin, R. P. (1974). *At first glance Or, is physical attractiveness more than skin deep?* Paper presented at the Eastern Psychological Association convention.

Prinstein, M. J., & Cillessen, A. N. (2003). Forms and functions of adolescent peer aggression associated with high levels of peer status. *Merrill-Palmer Quarterly, 49,* 310–342.

Prislin, R., & Pool, G. J. (1996). Behavior, consequences, and the self: Is all well that ends well? *Personality and Social Psychology Bulletin, 22,* 933–948.

Pritchard, I. L. (1998). *The effects of rap music: On aggressive attitudes toward women.* Master's thesis, Humboldt State University, Arcata, CA.

Prohaska, V. (1994). "I know I'll get an A": Confident overestimation of final course grades. *Teaching of Psychology, 21,* 141–143.

Pronin, E., Berger, J., & Molouki, S. (2007). Alone in a crowd of sheep: Asymmetric perceptions of conformity and their roots in an introspection illusion. *Journal of Personality and Social Psychology, 92,* 585–595.

Pronin, E., Gilovich, T., & Ross, L. (2004). Objectivity in the eye of the beholder: Divergent perceptions of bias in self versus others. *Psychological Review, 111*(3), 781.

Pronin, E., Kruger, J., Savitsky, K., & Ross, L. (2001). You don't know me, but I know you: The illusion of asymmetric insight. *Journal of Personality and Social Psychology, 81,* 639–656.

Pronin, E., Lin, D. Y., & Ross, L. (2002). The bias blind spot: Perceptions of bias in self versus others. *Personality and Social Psychology Bulletin, 28,* 369–381.

Pronin, E., & Ross, L. (2006). Temporal differences in trait self-ascription: When the self is seen as an other. *Journal of Personality and Social Psychology, 90*(2), 197.

Prothrow-Stith, D. (with M. Wiessman) (1991). *Deadly consequences.* New York: HarperCollins.

Provine, R. R. (2005). Yawning: the yawn is primal, unstoppable and contagious, revealing the evolutionary and neural basis of empathy and unconscious behavior. *American Scientist, 93*(6), 532–539.

Pruitt, D. G. (1986, July). Trends in the scientific study of negotiation. *Negotiation Journal,* 237–244.

Pruitt, D. G. (1998). Social conflict. In D. Gilbert, S. T. Fiske, & G. Lindzey (Eds.), *Handbook of social psychology* (4th ed.). New York: McGraw-Hill.

Pruitt, D. G., & Kimmel, M. J. (1977). Twenty years of experimental gaming: Critique, synthesis, and suggestions for the future. *Annual Review of Psychology, 28,* 363–392.

Pruitt, D. G., & Lewis, S. A. (1975). Development of integrative solutions in bilateral negotiation. *Journal of Personality and Social Psychology, 31,* 621–633.

Pruitt, D. G., & Lewis, S. A. (1977). The psychology of integrative bargaining. In D. Druckman (Ed.), *Negotiations: A social-psychological analysis.* New York: Halsted.

Pryor, J. B., DeSouza, E. R., Fitness, J., Hutz, C., Kumpf, M., Lubbert, K., Pesonen, O., & Erber, M. W. (1997). Gender differences in the interpretation of social-sexual behavior: A cross-cultural perspective on sexual harassment. *Journal of Cross-Cultural Psychology, 28*(5), 509.

Pryor, J. H., Hurtado, S., DeAngelo, L., Blake, L. P., & Tran, S. (2010). *The American freshman: National norms fall 2010.* Los Angeles: Higher Education Research Institute, UCLA.

Pryor, J. H., Hurtado, S., Saenz, V. B., Lindholm, J. A., Korn, W. S., & Mahoney, K. M. (2005). *The American freshman: National norms for fall 2005.* Los Angeles: Higher Education Institute, UCLA.

Pryor, J. H., Hurtado, S., Sharkness, J., & Korn, W. S. (2007). *The American freshman: National norms for Fall 2007.* Los Angeles: Higher Education Research Institute, UCLA.

Przybylski, A. K., Rigby, C. S., & Ryan, R. M. (2010). A motivational model of video game engagement. *Review of General Psychology, 14,* 154–166.

PTC: Parents Television Council. (2013). Media violence: An examination of violence, graphic violence, and gun violence in the media (2012–2013). Retrieved from http://w2.parentstv.org/MediaFiles/PDF/Studies/VStudy_dec2013.pdf

Public Opinion (1984, August/September). *Vanity Fair,* 22.

Puhl, R. M., & Heuer, C. A. (2009). The stigma of obesity: A review and update. *Obesity, 17,* 941–964.

Puhl, R. M., & Heuer, C. A. (2010). Obesity stigma: Important considerations for public health. *American Journal of Public Health, 100,* 1019–1028.

Pulford, B. D., Colman, A. M., Buabang, E. K., & Krockow, E. M. (2018). The persuasive power of knowledge: Testing the confidence heuristic. *Journal of Experimental Psychology: General, 147*(10), 1431–1444. https://doi-org.library.smu.ca/10.1037/xge0000471.supp

Purvis, J. A., Dabbs, J. M., Jr., & Hopper, C. H. (1984). The "opener": Skilled user of facial expression and speech pattern. *Personality and Social Psychology Bulletin, 10,* 61–66.

Putnam, R. D. (2000). Bowling alone: America's declining social capital. In *Culture and politics* (pp. 223-234). Palgrave Macmillan, New York.

Pyszczynski, T., & Greenberg, J. (1987). Self-regulatory perseveration and the depressive self-focusing style: A self-awareness theory of reactive depression. *Psychological Bulletin, 102,* 122–138.

Pyszczynski, T., Motyl, M., Vail, Kenneth E., III, Hirschberger, G., Arndt, J., & Kesebir, P. (2012). Drawing attention to global climate change decreases support for war. *Peace and Conflict: Journal of Peace Psychology, 18,* 354–368.

Quist, M. C., Watkins, C. D., Smith, F. G., Little, A. C., Debruine, L. M., & Jones, B. C. (2012). Sociosexuality predicts women's preferences for symmetry in men's faces. *Archives of Sexual Behavior, 41,* 1415–1421.

Quoidbach, J., & Dunn, E. W. (2010). Personality neglect: The unforeseen impact of personal dispositions on emotional life. *Psychological Science, 21,* 1783–1786.

Rafferty, R., & Vander Ven, T. (2014). "I hate everything about you": A qualitative examination of cyberbullying and on-line aggression in a college sample. *Deviant Behavior, 35,* 364–377.

Raifman, J., Moscoe, E., & Austin, S. B. (2017). Difference-in-differences analysis of the association between state same-sex marriage policies and adolescent suicide attempts. *Journal of the American Medical Association, 171,* 350–356.

Raine, A. (1993). *The psychopathology of crime: Criminal behavior as a clinical disorder.* San Diego, CA: Academic Press.

Raine, A. (2005). The interaction of biological and social measures in the explanation of antisocial and violent behavior. In D. M. Stoff & E. J. Susman (Eds.), *Developmental psychobiology of aggression.* New York: Cambridge University Press.

Raine, A. (2008). From genes to brain to antisocial behavior. *Current Directions in Psychological Science, 17,* 323–328.

Raine, A., Lencz, T., Bihrle, S., LaCasse, L., & Colletti, P. (2000). Reduced prefrontal gray matter volume and reduced autonomic activity in antisocial personality disorder. *Archives of General Psychiatry, 57,* 119–127.

Raine, A., Stoddard, J., Bihrle, S., & Buchsbaum, M. (1998). Prefrontal glucose deficits in murderers lacking psychosocial deprivation. *neuropsychiatry, NeuroPsychology, & Behavioral Neurology, 11,* 1–7.

Rains, S. A. (2013). The nature of psychological reactance revisited: A meta-analytic review. *Human Communication Research, 39*(1), 47–73.

Rajagopal, P., Raju, S., & Unnava, H. R. (2006). Differences in the cognitive accessibility of action and inaction regrets. *Journal of Experimental Social Psychology, 42,* 302–313.

Ramirez, J. M., Bonniot-Cabanac, M-C., & Cabanac, M. (2005). Can aggression provide pleasure? *European Psychologist, 10,* 136–145.

Ramos, M. R., Cassidy, C., Reicher, S., & Haslam, S. A. (2012). A longitudinal investigation of the rejection–identification hypothesis. *British Journal of Social Psychology, 51,* 642–660.

Randler, C., & Kretz, S. (2011). Assortative mating in morningness-eveningness. *International Journal of Psychology, 46,* 91–96.

Randler, C., & Vollmer, C. (2013). Aggression in young adults—A matter of short sleep and social jetlag? *Psychological Reports: Disability and Trauma, 113,* 754–765.

Rank, S. G., & Jacobson, C. K. (1977). Hospital nurses' compliance with medication overdose orders: A failure to replicate. *Journal of Health and Social Behavior, 18,* 188–193.

Rapoport, A. (1960). *Fights, games, and debates.* Ann Arbor: University of Michigan Press.

Rawls, J. (1971). *A theory of justice.* Cambridge, MA: Belknap Press of Harvard University Press.

Rawn, C. D., & Vohs, K. D. (2011). People use self-control to risk personal harm: An intra-interpersonal dilemma. *Personality and Social Psychology Review, 15,* 267–289.

Reece, R. L. (2017, Fall). Fighting fat stigma with science. *Teaching Tolerance,* pp. 35–37 (www.tolerance.org/magazine/fall-2017/fighting-fat-stigma-with-science).

Reed, D. (1989, November 25). Video collection documents Christian resistance to Hitler. Associated Press release in *Grand Rapids Press,* pp. B4, B5.

Regan, D. T., & Cheng, J. B. (1973). Distraction and attitude change: A resolution. *Journal of Experimental Social Psychology, 9,* 138–147.

Regan, D. T., & Fazio, R. (1977). On the consistency between attitudes and behavior: Look to the method of attitude formation. *Journal of Experimental Social Psychology, 13,* 28–45.

Regan, P. C. (1998). What if you can't get what you want? Willingness to compromise ideal mate selection standards as a function of sex, mate value, and relationship context. *Personality and Social Psychology Bulletin, 24,* 1294–1303.

Reicher, S., Spears, R., & Postmes, T. (1995). A social identity model of deindividuation phenomena. In W. Storebe & M. Hewstone (Eds.), *European review of social psychology* (Vol. 6). Chichester, England: Wiley.

Reid, C. A., Davis, J. L., & Green, J. D. (2013). The power of change: Interpersonal attraction as a function of attitude similarity and attitude alignment. *Journal of Social Psychology, 153,* 700–719.

Reid, P., & Finchilescu, G. (1995). The disempowering effects of media violence against women on college women. *Psychology of Women Quarterly, 19,* 397–411.

Reijntjes, A., Thomaes, S., Kamphuis, J. H., Bushman, B. J., de Castro, B. O., & Telch, M. J. (2011). Explaining the paradoxical rejection–aggression link: The mediating effects of hostile intent attributions, anger, and decreases in state self-esteem on peer rejection-induced aggression on youth. *Personality and Social Psychology Bulletin, 37,* 955–963.

Reis, H. T., & Shaver, P. (1988). Intimacy as an interpersonal process. In S. Duck (Ed.), *Handbook of personal relationships: Theory, relationships and interventions.* Chichester, UK: Wiley.

Reis, H. T., Nezlek, J., & Wheeler, L. (1980). Physical attractiveness in social interaction. *Journal of Personality and Social Psychology, 38,* 604–617.

Reis, H. T., Smith, S. M., Carmichael, C. L., Caprariello, P. A., Tsa, F.-F., Rodrigues, A., & Maniaci, M. R. (2010). Are you happy for me? How sharing positive events with others provides personal and interpersonal benefits. *Journal of Personality and Social Psychology, 99,* 311–329.

Reis, H. T., Wheeler, L., Spiegel, N., Kernis, M. H., Nezlek, J., & Perri, M. (1982). Physical attractiveness in social interaction: II. Why does appearance affect social experience? *Journal of Personality and Social Psychology, 43,* 979–996.

Reisenzein, R. (1983). The Schachter theory of emotion: Two decades later. *Psychological Bulletin, 94,* 239–264.

Ressler, R. K., Burgess, A. W., & Douglas, J. E. (1988). *Sexual homicide patterns.* Boston: Lexington Books.

Rhine, R. J., & Severance, L. J. (1970). Ego-involvement, discrepancy, source credibility, and attitude change. *Journal of Personality and Social Psychology, 16,* 175–190.

Rhodes, G., Sumich, A., & Byatt, G. (1999). Are average facial configurations attractive only because of their symmetry. *Psychological Science, 10,* 52–58.

Rhodewalt, F. (1987). *Is self-handicapping an effective self-protective attributional strategy?* Paper presented at the American Psychological Association convention.

Rhodewalt, F., Saltzman, A. T., & Wittmer J. (1984). Self-handicapping among competitive athletes: The role of practice in self-esteem protection. *Basic and Applied Social Psychology, 5,* 197–209.

Rholes, W. S., Newman, L. S., & Ruble, D. N. (1990). Understanding self and other: Developmental and motivational aspects of perceiving persons in terms of invariant dispositions. In E. T. Higgins & R. M. Sorrentino (Eds.), *Handbook of motivation and cognition: Foundations of social behavior* (Vol. 2). New York: Guilford.

Rice, B. (1985, September). Performance review: The job nobody likes. *Psychology Today,* 30–36.

Rice, M. E., & Grusec, J. E. (1975). Saying and doing: Effects on observer performance. *Journal of Personality and Social Psychology, 32,* 584–593.

Richards, Z., & Hewstone, M. (2001). Subtyping and subgrouping: Processes for the prevention and promotion of stereotype change. *Personality and Social Psychology Review, 5,* 52–73.

Richardson, L. F. (1960). Generalized foreign policy. *British Journal of Psychology Monographs Supplements,* 23.

Richardson, M., Abraham, C., & Bond, R. (2012). Psychological correlates of university students' academic performance:

A systematic review and meta-analysis. *Psychological Bulletin, 138,* 353–387.

Richeson, J. A., & Shelton, J. N. (2012). Stereotype threat in interracial interactions. In M. Inzlicht & T. Schmader (eds.), *Stereotype threat: Theory, process, and application,* pp. 231–245. New York: Oxford University Press

Richeson, J. A., & Trawalter, S. (2008). The threat of appearing prejudiced, and race-based attentional biases. *Psychological Science, 19,* 98–102.

Ridge, R. D., & Reber, J. S. (2002). "I think she's attracted to me": The effect of men's beliefs on women's behavior in a job interview scenario. *Basic and Applied Social Psychology, 24,* 1–14.

Riek, B. M., Mania, E. W., & Gaertner, S. L. (2013). Reverse subtyping: The effects of prejudice level on the subtyping of counterstereotypic outgroup members. *Basic and Applied Social Psychology, 35,* 409–417.

Riess, M., Rosenfeld, P., Melburg, V., & Tedeschi, J. T. (1981). Self-serving attributions: Biased private perceptions and distorted public descriptions. *Journal of Personality and Social Psychology, 41,* 224–231.

Rietzschel, E. F., Nijstad, B. A., & Stroebe, W. (2006). Productivity is not enough: A comparison of interactive and nominal brainstorming groups on idea generation and selection. *Journal of Experimental Social Psychology, 42,* 244–251.

Riggs, J. M. (1992). Self-handicapping and achievement. In A. K. Boggiano & T. S. Pittman (Eds.), *Achievement and motivation: A social-developmental perspective.* New York: Cambridge University Press.

Riordan, C. A. (1980). *Effects of admission of influence on attributions and attraction.* Paper presented at the American Psychological Association convention.

Risen, J. L., & Critcher, C. R. (2011). Visceral fit: While in a visceral state, associated states of the world seem more likely. *Journal of Personality and Social Psychology, 100,* 777–793.

Risen, J. L., Gilovich, T., & Dunning, D. (2007). One-shot illusory correlations and stereotype formation. *Personality and Social Psychology Bulletin, 33,* 1492–1502.

Riva, P., Romero Lauro, L. J., DeWall, C. N., & Bushman, B. J. (2012). Buffer the pain away: Stimulating the right ventrolateral prefrontal cortex reduces pain following social exclusion. *Psychological Science, 23,* 1473–1475.

Riva, P., Wirth, J. H., & Williams, K. D. (2011). The consequences of pain: The social and physical overlap on psychological responses. *European Journal of Social Psychology, 41,* 681–687.

Robberson, M. R., & Rogers, R. W. (1988). Beyond fear appeals: Negative and positive persuasive appeals to health and self-esteem. *Journal of Applied Social Psychology, 18,* 277–287.

Robertson, L. A., McAnally, H. M., & Hancox, R. J. (2013). Childhood and adolescent television viewing and antisocial behavior in early adulthood. *Pediatrics, 131,* 439–446.

Robins, R. W., & Beer, J. S. (2001). Positive illusions about the self: Short-term benefits and long-term costs. *Journal of Personality and Social Psychology, 80,* 340–352.

Robins, R. W., Mendelsohn, G. A., Connell, J. B., & Kwan, V. S. Y. (2004). Do people agree about the causes of behavior? A social relations analysis of behavior ratings and causal attributions. *Journal of Personality and Social Psychology, 86,* 334–344.

Robinson, J. (2002, October 8). What percentage of the population is gay? *Gallup Tuesday Briefing.* Retrieved from http://www.gallup.com

Robinson, M. D., & Ryff, C. D. (1999). The role of self-deception in perceptions of past, present, and future happiness. *Personality and Social Psychology Bulletin, 25,* 595–606.

Robinson, T. N., Wilde, M. L., Navracruz, L. C., Haydel, F., & Varady, A. (2001). Effects of reducing children's television and video game use on aggressive behavior. *Archives of Pediatric and Adolescent Medicine, 155,* 17–23.

Rochat, F. (1993). How did they resist authority? Protecting refugees in Le Chambon during World War II. Paper presented at the American Psychological Association convention.

Rochat, F., & Modigliani, A. (1995). The ordinary quality of resistance: From Milgram's laboratory to the village of Le Chambon. *Journal of Social Issues, 51,* 195–210.

Rodenhizer, K. A. E., & Edwards, K. M. (2019). The impacts of sexual media exposure on adolescent and emerging adults' dating and sexual violence attitudes and behaviors: A critical review of the literature. *Trauma, Violence, and Abuse, 20,* 439-452.

Roehling, M. V. (2000). Weight-based discrimination in employment: Psychological and legal aspects. *Personnel Psychology, 52,* 969–1016.

Roehling, M. V., Roehling, P. V., & Odland, I. M. (2008). Investigating the validity of stereotypes about overweight employees. *Group and Organization Management, 23,* 392–424.

Roehling, P. V., Roehling, M. V., Johnston, A., Brennan, A., & Drew, A. (2010). Weighty decisions: The effect of weight bias on the selection and election of U.S. political candidates. Unpublished manuscript, Hope College, Holland, MI.

Roehling, P. V., Roehling, M. V., Vandlen, J. D., Blazek, J., & Guy, W. C. (2009). Weight discrimination and the glass ceiling effect among top U.S. male and female CEOs. *Equal Opportunities International, 28,* 179–196.

Roese, N. J., & Jamieson, D. W. (1993). Twenty years of bogus pipeline research: A critical review and meta-analysis. *Psychological Bulletin, 114,* 363–375.

Roese, N. L., & Olson, J. M. (1994). Attitude importance as a function of repeated attitude expression. *Journal of Experimental Social Psychology, 66,* 805–818.

Rogers, C. R. (1980). *A way of being.* Boston: Houghton Mifflin.

Rohrer, J. H., Baron, S. H., Hoffman, E. L., & Swander, D. V. (1954). The stability of autokinetic judgments. *Journal of Abnormal and Social Psychology, 49,* 595–597.

Rokeach, M. (1968). *Beliefs, attitudes, and values.* San Francisco: Jossey-Bass.

Romer, D., Gruder, D. L., & Lizzadro, T. (1986). A person-situation approach to altruistic behavior. *Journal of Personality and Social Psychology, 51,* 1001–1012.

Ronay, R., Oostrom, J. K., Lehmann-Willenbrock, N., & Van Vugt, M. (2017). Pride before the fall: (Over)confidence predicts escalation of public commitment. *Journal of Experimental Social Psychology, 69,* 13–22.

Rooth, D-O. (2007). Implicit discrimination in hiring: Real-world evidence. IZA Discussion Paper No. 2764, University of Kalmar, Institute for the Study of Labor (IZA), Kalmar, Sweden.

Rosenbaum, M. E. (1986). The repulsion hypothesis: On the nondevelopment of relationships. *Journal of Personality and Social Psychology, 51,* 1156–1166.

Rosenbaum, M. E., & Holtz, R. (1985). *The minimal intergroup discrimination effect: Out-group derogation, not in-group favorability.* Paper presented at the American Psychological Association convention.

Rosenberg, L. A. (1961). Group size, prior experience and conformity. *Journal of Abnormal and Social Psychology, 63,* 436–437.

Rosenberg, M. (1979). *Conceiving the self.* New York: Basic Books.

Rosenblatt, A., & Greenberg, J. (1988). Depression and interpersonal attraction: The role of perceived similarity. *Journal of Personality and Social Psychology, 55,* 112–119.

Rosenblatt, A., & Greenberg, J. (1991). Examining the world of the depressed: Do depressed people prefer others who are depressed? *Journal of Personality and Social Psychology, 60,* 620–629.

Rosenbloom, S. (2008, January 3). Putting your best cyberface forward. *New York Times,* Style section.

Rosenbloom, T., Shahar, A., Perlman, A., Estreich, D., & Kirzner, E. (2007). Success on a practical driver's license test with and without the presence of another testee. *Accident Analysis and Prevention, 39,* 1296–1301.

Rosenfeld, D., Folger, R., & Adelman, H. F. (1980). When rewards reflect competence: A qualification of the overjustification effect. *Journal of Personality and Social Psychology, 39,* 368–376.

Rosenhan, D. L. (1970). The natural socialization of altruistic autonomy. In J. Macaulay & L. Berkowitz (Eds.), *Altruism and helping behavior.* New York: Academic Press.

Rosenthal, D. A., & Feldman, S. S. (1992). The nature and stability of ethnic identity in Chinese youth: Effects of length of residence in two cultural contexts. *Journal of Cross-Cultural Psychology, 23,* 214–227.

Rosenthal, E. (2008, July 15). Britons shine a light on energy use at home. *New York Times.* Retrieved from http://www.nytimes.com

Rosenthal, E. (2010, May 24). Climate fears turn to doubts among Britons. *New York Times.* Retrieved from http://www.nytimes.com

Rosenthal, E. (2011, October 15). Where did global warming go? *New York Times.* Retrieved from http://www.nytimes.com

Rosenthal, R. (1985). From unconscious experimenter bias to teacher expectancy effects. In J. B. Dusek, V. C. Hall, & W. J. Meyer (Eds.), *Teacher expectancies.* Hillsdale, NJ: Erlbaum.

Rosenthal, R. (1991). Teacher expectancy effects: A brief update 25 years after the Pygmalion experiment. *Journal of Research in Education, 1,* 3–12.

Rosenthal, R. (2002). Covert communication in classrooms, clinics, courtrooms, and cubicles. *American Psychologist, 57*(11), 839.

Rosenthal, R. (2003). Covert communication in laboratories, classrooms, and the truly real world. *Current Directions in Psychological Science, 12*(5), 151.

Rosenthal, R. (2006). Applying psychological research on interpersonal expectations and covert communication in classrooms, clinics, corporations, and courtrooms. In S. I. Donaldson, D. E. Berger, & K. Pezdek (Eds.), *Applied psychology: New frontiers and rewarding careers.* Mahwah, NJ: Erlbaum.

Rosenthal, R., & Jacobson, L. (1968). *Pygmalion in the classroom: Teacher expectation and pupils' intellectual development.* New York: Holt, Rinehart & Winston.

Rosenthal, S. A., & Pittinsky, T. L. (2006). Narcissistic leadership. *Leadership Quarterly,* 17, 617–633.

Roseth, C. J., Johnson, D. W., & Johnson, R. T. (2008). Promoting early adolescents' achievement and peer relationships: The effects of cooperative, competitive, and individualistic goal structures. *Psychological Bulletin, 134,* 223–246.

Ross, L. (1977). The intuitive psychologist and his shortcomings: Distortions in the attribution process. In L. Berkowitz (Ed.), *Advances in experimental social psychology* (Vol. 10). New York: Academic Press.

Ross, L. (1981). The "intuitive scientist" formulation and its developmental implications. In J. H. Havell & L. Ross (Eds.), *Social cognitive development: Frontiers and possible futures.* Cambridge, UK: Cambridge University Press.

Ross, L. (1988). Situationist perspectives on the obedience experiments. Review of A. G. Miller's *The obedience experiments. Contemporary Psychology, 33,* 101–104.

Ross, L., Amabile, T. M., & Steinmetz, J. L. (1977). Social roles, social control, and biases in social-perception processes. *Journal of Personality and Social Psychology, 35,* 485–494.

Ross, L., & Anderson, C. A. (1982). Shortcomings in the attribution process: On the origins and maintenance of erroneous social assessments. In D. Kahneman, P. Slovic, & A. Tversky (Eds.), *Judgment under uncertainty: Heuristics and biases.* New York: Cambridge University Press.

Ross, L., & Lepper, M. R. (1980). The perseverance of beliefs: Empirical and normative considerations. In R. A. Shweder (Ed.), *New directions for methodology of behavioral science: Fallible judgment in behavioral research.* San Francisco: Jossey-Bass.

Ross, L., & Ward, A. (1995). Psychological barriers to dispute resolution. In M. P. Zanna (Ed.), *Advances in experimental social psychology* (Vol. 27). San Diego: Academic Press.

Ross, L., & Ward, A. (1996). Naive realism in everyday life: Implications for social conflict and misunderstanding. In T. Brown, E. Reed, & E. Turiel (Eds.), *Values and knowledge.* Hillsdale, NJ: Erlbaum.

Ross, M., & Buehler, R. (1994). Creative remembering. In U. Neisser & R. Fivush (Eds.), *The remembering self.* New York: Cambridge University Press.

Ross, M., & Fletcher, G. J. O. (1985). Attribution and social perception. In G. Lindzey & E. Aronson (Eds.), *The handbook of social psychology* (3rd ed.). New York: Random House.

Ross, M., McFarland, C., & Fletcher, G. J. O. (1981). The effect of attitude on the recall of personal histories. *Journal of Personality and Social Psychology, 40,* 627–634.

Ross, M., & Newby-Clark, I. R. (1998). Construing the past and future. *Social Cognition, 16,* 133–150.

Ross, M., & Sicoly, F. (1979). Egocentric biases in availability and attribution. *Journal of Personality and Social Psychology, 37,* 322–336.

Ross, M. & Wilson, A. E. (2002). It feels like yesterday: Self-esteem, valence of personal past experiences, and judgments of subjective distance. *Journal of Personality and Social Psychology, 82,* 792–803.

Roszell, P., Kennedy, D., & Grabb, E. (1990). Physical attractiveness and income attainment among Canadians. *Journal of Psychology, 123,* 547–559.

Rotenberg, K. J., Gruman, J. A., & Ariganello, M. (2002). Behavioral confirmation of the loneliness stereotype. *Basic and Applied Social Psychology, 24,* 81–89.

Rothbart, M., & Birrell, P. (1977). Attitude and perception of faces. *Journal of Research Personality, 11,* 209–215.

Rothbart, M., Fulero, S., Jensen, C., Howard, J., & Birrell, P. (1978). From individual to group impressions: Availability heuristics in stereotype formation. *Journal of Experimental Social Psychology, 14,* 237–255.

Rothbart, M., & Taylor, M. (1992). Social categories and social reality. In G. R. Semin & K. Fielder (Eds.), *Language, interaction and social cognition.* London: Sage.

Rotton, J., & Frey, J. (1985). Air pollution, weather, and violent crimes: Concomitant time-series analysis of archival data. *Journal of Personality and Social psychology, 49,* 1207–1220.

Rotundo, M., Nguyen, D-H., & Sackett, P. R. (2001). A meta-analytic review of gender differences in perceptions of sexual harassment. *Journal of Applied Psychology, 86,* 914–922.

Rowe, D. C., Almeida, D. M., & Jacobson, K. C. (1999). School context and genetic influences on aggression in adolescence. *Psychological Science, 10,* 277–280.

Roy, M. M., Christenfeld, N. J. S., & McKenzie, C. R. M. (2005). Underestimating the duration of future events: Memory incorrectly used or memory bias? *Psychological Bulletin, 131,* 738–756.

Royal Society. (2010, September). *Climate change: A summary of the science.* London: The Royal Society.

Ruback, R. B., Carr, T. S., & Hoper, C. H. (1986). Perceived control in prison: Its relation to reported crowding, stress, and symptoms. *Journal of Applied Social Psychology, 16,* 375–386.

Rubin, J. Z. (1986). *Can we negotiate with terrorists: Some answers from psychology.* Paper presented at the American Psychological Association convention.

Rubin, Z. (1973). *Liking and loving: An invitation to social psychology.* New York: Holt, Rinehart and Winston.

Rudman, L. A., & Mescher, K. (2012). Of animals and objects: Men's implicit dehumanization of women and likelihood of sexual aggression. *Personality and Social Psychology Bulletin, 38,* 734–746.

Rudolph, U., Roesch, S. C., Greitemeyer, T., & Weiner, B. (2004). A meta-analytic review of help giving and aggression from an attributional perspective: Contributions to a general theory of motivation. *Cognition & Emotion, 18,* 815.

Rule, B. G., Taylor, B. R., & Dobbs, A. R. (1987). Priming effects of heat on aggressive thoughts. *Social Cognition, 5,* 131–143.

Rule, N. (2014, May-June). Snap-judgment science. *APS Observer.* Retrieved from http://www.psychologicalscience.org/index.php/publications/observer/2014/may-june-14/snap-judgment-science.html

Rule, N. O., Rosen, K. S., Slepian, M. L., & Ambady, N. (2011). Mating interest improves women's accuracy in judging male sexual orientation. *Psychological Science, 22,* 881–886.

Rusbult, C. E. (1980). Commitment and satisfaction in romantic associations: A test of the investment model. *Journal of Experimental Social Psychology, 16,* 172–186.

Rusbult, C. E., Johnson, D. J., & Morrow, G. D. (1986). Impact of couple patterns of problem solving on distress and nondistress in dating relationships. *Journal of Personality and Social Psychology, 50,* 744–753.

Rusbult, C. E., Morrow, G. D., & Johnson, D. J. (1987). Self-esteem and problem-solving behaviour in close relationships. *British Journal of Social Psychology, 26,* 293–303.

Rushton, J. P. (1975). Generosity in children: Immediate and long-term effects of modeling, preaching, and moral judgment. *Journal of Personality and Social Psychology, 31,* 459–466.

Rushton, J. P. (1991). Is altruism innate? *Psychological Inquiry, 2,* 141–143.

Rushton, J. P., Brainerd, C. J., & Pressley, M. (1983). Behavioral development and construct validity: The principle of aggregation. *Psychological Bulletin, 94,* 18–38.

Rushton, J. P., & Campbell, A. C. (1977). Modeling, vicarious reinforcement and extraversion on blood donating in adults: Immediate and long-term effects. *European Journal of Social Psychology, 7,* 297–306.

Rushton, J. P., Chrisjohn, R. D., & Fekken, G. C. (1981). The altruistic personality and the self-report altruism scale. *Personality and Individual Differences, 2,* 293–302.

Rushton, J. P., Fulker, D. W., Neale, M. C., Nias, D. K. B., & Eysenck, H. J. (1986). Altruism and aggression: The heritability of individual differences. *Journal of Personality and Social Psychology, 50,* 1192–1198.

Russell, A. M. T., Langham, E., & Hing, N. (2018). Social influences normalize gambling-related harm among higher risk gamblers. *Journal of Behavioral Addictions, 7*(4), 1100–1111. https://doi-org.library.smu.ca/10.1556/2006.7.2018.139

Russell, B. (1930/1980). *The conquest of happiness.* London: Unwin Paperbacks, p. 139.

Russell, G. W. (1983). Psychological issues in sports aggression. In J. H. Goldstein (Ed.), *Sports violence.* New York: Springer-Verlag.

Russell, G. W., & Mentzel, R. K. (1990). Sympathy and altruism in response to disasters. *Journal of Social Psychology, 130,* 309–316.

Russell, N. J. C., & Gregory, R. J. (2005). Making the undoable doable: Milgram, the Holocaust, and modern government. *American Review of Public Administration, 35,* 327–349.

Ruvolo, A., & Markus, H. (1992). Possible selves and performance: The power of self-relevant imagery. *Social Cognition, 9,* 95–124.

Ryan, R. (1999, February 2). Quoted by A. Kohn, In pursuit of affluence, at a high price. *New York Times.* Retrieved from http://www.nytimes.com

Ryckman, R. M., Robbins, M. A., Kaczor, L. M., & Gold, J. A. (1989). Male and female raters' stereotyping of male and female physiques. *Personality and Social Psychology Bulletin, 15,* 244–251.

Rydell, R. J., McConnell, A. R., & Beilock, S. L. (2009). Multiple social identities and stereotype threat: Imbalance, accessibility, and working memory. *Journal of Personality and Social Psychology, 96,* 949–966.

Rydell, R. J., Rydell, M. T., & Boucher, K. L. (2010). The effect of negative performance stereotypes on learning. *Journal of Personality and Social Psychology, 99,* 883–896.

Saad, L. (2002, November 21). Most smokers wish they could quit. Gallup News Service.

Sabini, J., & Silver, M. (1982). *Moralities of everyday life.* New York: Oxford University Press.

Sachs, J. D. (2006, July). Ecology and political upheaval. *Scientific American, 291,* 37.

Sack, K., & Elder, J. (2000, July 11). Poll finds optimistic outlook but enduring racial division. *New York Times.* Retrieved from http://www.nytimes.com

Sadler, M. S., Correll, J., Park, B., & Judd, C. M. (2012). The world is not Black and White: Racial bias in the decision to shoot in a multiethnic context. *Journal of Social Issues, 68,* 286–313.

Safer, M. A., Bonanno, G. A., & Field, N. P. (2001). It was never that bad: Biased recall of grief and long-term adjustment to the death of a spouse. *Memory, 9,* 195–204.

Sagarin, B. J., Cialdini, R. B., Rice, W. E., & Serna, S. B. (2002). Dispelling the illusion of invulnerability: The motivations and mechanisms of resistance to persuasion. *Journal of Personality and Social Psychology, 83,* 526–541.

Sagarin, B. J., Rhoads, K. V. L., & Cialdini, R. B. (1998). Deceiver's distrust: Denigration as a consequence of undiscovered deception. *Personality and Social Psychology Bulletin, 24,* 1167–1176.

Sageman, M. (2004). *Understanding terror networks.* Philadelphia: University of Pennsylvania Press.

Saguy, T., & Halperin, E. (2014). Exposure to outgroup members criticizing their own group facilitates intergroup openness. *Personality and Social Psychology Bulletin, 40,* 791–802.

Sah, S., Malaviya, P., & Thompson, D. (2018). Conflict of interest disclosure as an expertise cue: Differential effects due to automatic versus deliberative processing. *Organizational Behavior and Human Decision Processes, 147,* 127–146. https://doi- org.library.smu.ca/10.1016/j.obhdp.2018.05.008

Said, C. P., & Todorov, A. (2011). A statistical model of facial attractiveness. *Psychological Science, 22,* 1183–1190.

Sakurai, M. M. (1975). Small group cohesiveness and detrimental conformity. *Sociometry, 38,* 340–357.

Saleem, M., Anderson, C. A., & Gentile, D. A. (2012). Effects of prosocial, neutral, and violent video games on college students' affect. *Aggressive Behavior, 38,* 263–271.

Saleem, M., Prot, S., Anderson, C. A., & Lemieux, A. F. (2017). Exposure to Muslims in media and support for public policies harming Muslims. *Communication Research, 44,* 841–869.

Sales, S. M. (1973). Threat as a factor in authoritarianism: An analysis of archival data. *Journal of Personality & Social Psychology, 28,* 44–57.

Salganik, M. J., Dodds, P. S., & Watts, D. J. (2006). Experimental study of inequality and unpredictability in an artificial cultural market. *Science, 311,* 854–856.

Salmela-Aro, K., & Nurmi, J-E. (2007). Self-esteem during university studies predicts career characteristics 10 years later. *Journal of Vocational Behavior, 70,* 463–477.

Salmivalli, C. (2009). Bullying and the peer group: A review. *Aggression and Violent Behavior, 15,* 112–120.

Salmivalli, C., Kaukiainen, A., Kaistaniemi, L., & Lagerspetz, K. M. J. (1999). Self-evaluated self-esteem, peer-evaluated self-esteem, and defensive egotism as predictors of adolescents' participation in bullying situations. *Personality and Social Psychology Bulletin, 25,* 1268–1278.

Salovey, P., Mayer, J. D., & Rosenhan, D. L. (1991). Mood and healing: Mood as a motivator of helping and helping as a regulator of mood. In M. S. Clark (Ed.), *Prosocial behavior.* Newbury Park, CA: Sage.

Saltzstein, H. D., & Sandberg, L. (1979). Indirect social influence: Change in judgmental processor anticipatory conformity. *Journal of Experimental Social Psychology, 15,* 209–216.

Sam, D. L., & Berry, J. W. (2010). Acculturation: When individuals and groups of different cultural backgrounds meet. *Perspectives on Psychological Science, 5,* 472–481.

Sampson, E. E. (1975). On justice as equality. *Journal of Social Issues, 31*(3), 45–64.

Sanbonmatsu, D. M., & Fazio, R. H. (1990). The role of attitudes in memory-based decision making. *Journal of Personality and Social Psychology, 59,* 614–622.

Sancton, T. (1998). Death of a princess—The investigation. Retrieved from http://www.larouchepub.com/eiw/public/1998/eirv25n11-19980313/eirv25n11-19980313_044-the_murder_of_a_princess.pdf

Sande, G. N., Goethals, G. R., & Radloff, C. E. (1988). Perceiving one's own traits and others': The multifaceted self. *Journal of Personality and Social Psychology, 54,* 13–20.

Sanders, G. S. (1981a). Driven by distraction: An integrative review of social facilitation and theory and research. *Journal of Experimental Social Psychology, 17,* 227–251.

Sanders, G. S. (1981b). Toward a comprehensive account of social facilitation: Distraction/conflict does not mean theoretical conflict. *Journal of Experimental Social Psychology, 17,* 262–265.

Sanders, G. S., & Baron, R. S. (1977). Is social comparison irrelevant for producing choice shifts? *Journal of Experimental Social Psychology, 13*(4), 303-314.

Sanders, G. S., Baron, R. S., & Moore, D. L. (1978). Distraction and social comparison as mediators of social facilitation effects. *Journal of Experimental Social Psychology, 14,* 291–303.

Sanderson, C. A., (2020). *Why we act: Turning bystanders into moral rebels.* Belknap Press, Cambridge MA, USA.

Sanderson, C. A., & Cantor, N. (2001). The association of intimacy goals and marital satisfaction: A test of four mediational hypotheses. *Personality and Social Psychology Bulletin, 27,* 1567.

Sani, F., Herrera, M., & Bowe, M. (2009). Perceived collective continuity and ingroup identification as defence against death awareness. *Journal of Experimental Social Psychology, 45,* 242–245.

Sani, F., Herrera, M., Wakefield, J. R. H., Boroch, O., & Gulyas, C. (2012). Comparing social contact and group identification as predictors of mental health. *British Journal of Social Psychology, 51,* 781 790.

Sanitioso, R., Kunda, Z., & Fong, G. T. (1990). Motivated recruitment of autobiographical memories. *Journal of Personality and Social Psychology, 59,* 229–241.

Sansone, C. (1986). A question of competence: The effects of competence and task feedback on intrinsic interest. *Journal of Personality and Social Psychology, 51,* 918–931.

Santaella-Tenorio, J., Cerda, M., Villaveces, A., & Galea, S. (2016). What do we know about the association between firearm legislation and firearm-related injuries? *Epidemiologic Reviews, 38,* 140–157.

Santos, A., Meyer-Lindenberg, A., & Deruelle, C. (2010). Absence of racial, but not gender, stereotyping in Williams syndrome children. *Current Biology, 20,* 307–308.

Santos, H. C., Varnum, M. E. W., & Grossman, I. (2017). Global increases in individualism. *Psychological Science, 28*(9), 1228–1239.

Sartre, J-P. (1946/1948). *Anti-Semite and Jew.* New York: Shocken Books.

Sasaki, J. Y., & Kim, H. S. (2011). At the intersection of culture and religion: A cultural analysis of religion's implications for secondary control and social affiliation. *Journal of Personality and Social Psychology, 101,* 401–414.

Saslow, L. R., Muise, A., Impett, E. A., & Dubin, M. (2013). Can you see how happy we are? Facebook images and relationship satisfaction. *Social Psychological and Personality Science, 4,* 411–418.

Sassenberg, K., Moskowitz, G. B., Jacoby, J., & Hansen, N. (2007). The carry-over effect of competition: The impact of competition on prejudice towards uninvolved outgroups. *Journal of Experimental Social Psychology, 43,* 529–538.

Sato, K. (1987). Distribution of the cost of maintaining common resources. *Journal of Experimental Social Psychology, 23,* 19–31.

Saucier, D. A., & Miller, C. T. (2003). The persuasiveness of racial arguments as a subtle measure of racism. *Personality and Social Psychology Bulletin, 29,* 1303–1315.

Saucier, G., Akers, L. G., Shen-Miller, S., Knežević, G., & Stankov, L. (2009). Patterns of thinking in militant extremism. *Perspectives on Psychological Science, 4,* 256–271.

Savitsky, K., Epley, N., & Gilovich, T. (2001). Do others judge us as harshly as we think? Overestimating the impact of our failures, shortcomings, and mishaps. *Journal of Personality and Social Psychology, 81,* 44–56.

Savitsky, K., & Gilovich, T. (2003). The illusion of transparency and the alleviation of speech anxiety. *Journal of Experimental Social Psychology, 39,* 618–625.

Savitsky, K., Medvec, V. H., & Gilovich, T. (1997). Remembering and regretting: The Zeigarnik effect and the cognitive availability of regrettable actions and inactions. *Personality and Social Psychology Bulletin, 23,* 248–257.

Savitsky, K., Van Voven, L., Epley, N., & Wright, W. M. (2005). The unpacking effect in allocations of responsibility for group tasks. *Journal of Experimental Social Psychology, 41,* 447–457.

Sbarra, D. A., Law, R. W., & Portley, R. M. (2011). Divorce and death: A meta-analysis and research agenda for clinical, social, and health psychology. *Perspectives on Psychological Science, 6,* 454–474.

Scalia, A. (2011, June 27). Opinion of the Supreme Court of the United States,

Brown v. Entertainment Merchants Association.

Schachter, S. (1951). Deviation, rejection and communication. *Journal of Abnormal and Social Psychology, 46,* 190–207.

Schachter, S., & Singer, J. E. (1962). Cognitive, social and physiological determinants of emotional state. *Psychological Review, 69,* 379–399.

Schäfer, M., Haun, D. B. M., & Tomasello, M. (2015). Fair is not fair everywhere. *Psychological Science, 26,* 1252–1260.

Schafer, R. B., & Keith, P. M. (1980). Equity and depression among married couples. *Social Psychology Quarterly, 43,* 430–435.

Schaffner, P. E. (1985). Specious learning about reward and punishment. *Journal of Personality and Social Psychology, 48,* 1377–1386.

Schaffner, P. E., Wandersman, A., & Stang, D. (1981). Candidate name exposure and voting: Two field studies. *Basic and Applied Social Psychology, 2,* 195–203.

Schaller, M., & Cialdini, R. B. (1988). The economics of empathic helping: Support for a mood management motive. *Journal of Experimental Social Psychology, 24,* 163–181.

Schein, E. H. (1956). The Chinese indoctrination program for prisoners of war: A study of attempted brainwashing. *Psychiatry, 19,* 149–172.

Schiffenbauer, A., & Schiavo, R. S. (1976). Physical distance and attraction: An intensification effect. *Journal of Experimental Social Psychology, 12,* 274–282.

Schimel, J., Arndt, J., Pyszczynski, T., & Greenberg, J. (2001). Being accepted for who we are: Evidence that social validation of the intrinsic self reduces general defensiveness. *Journal of Personality and Social Psychology, 80,* 35–52.

Schimel, J., Pyszczynski, T., Greenberg, J., O'Mahen, H., & Arndt, J. (2000). Running from the shadow: Psychological distancing from others to deny characteristics people fear in themselves. *Journal of Personality and Social Psychology, 78,* 446.

Schimmack, U., Oishi, S., & Diener, E. (2005). Individualism: A valid and important dimension of cultural differences between nations. *Personality and Social Psychology Review, 9,* 17.

Schirmer, A., Teh, K., Wang, S., Vijayakumar, R., Ching, A., Nithianantham, D., Escoffier, N., & Cheok, A. (2011). Squeeze me, but don't tease me: Human and mechanical touch enhance visual attention and emotion discrimination. *Social Neuroscience, 6*(3), 219–230.

Schkade, D. A., & Kahneman, D. (1998). Does living in California make people happy? A focusing illusion in judgments of life satisfaction. *Psychological Science, 9,* 340–346.

Schlenker, B. R. (1976). *Egocentric perceptions in cooperative groups: A conceptualization and research review.* Final Report, Office of Naval Research Grant NR 170–797.

Schlenker, B. R., & Leary, M. R. (1982). Social anxiety and self-presentation: A conceptualization and model. *Psychological Bulletin, 92,* 641–669.

Schlenker, B. R., & Leary, M. R. (1985). Social anxiety and communication about the self. *Journal of Language and Social Psychology, 4,* 171–192.

Schlenker, B. R., & Miller, R. S. (1977a). Egocentrism in groups: Self-serving biases or logical information processing? *Journal of Personality and Social Psychology, 35,* 755–764.

Schlenker, B. R., & Miller, R. S. (1977b). Group cohesiveness as a determinant of egocentric perceptions in cooperative groups. *Human Relations, 30,* 1039–1055.

Schlenker, B. R., Phillips, S. T., Boniecki, K. A., & Schlenker, D. R. (1995). Championship pressures: Choking or triumphing in one's own territory? *Journal of Personality and Social Psychology, 68(4),* 632–643.

Schlenker, B. R., & Weigold, M. F. (1992). Interpersonal processes involving impression regulation and management. *Annual Review of Psychology, 43,* 133–168.

Schlesinger, A., Jr. (1949). The statistical soldier. *Partisan Review, 16,* 852–856.

Schmader, T., Johns, M., & Forbes, C. (2008). An integrated process model of stereotype threat effects on performance. *Psychological Review, 115,* 336.

Schmiege, S. J., Klein, W. M. P., & Bryan, A. D. (2010). The effect of peer comparison information in the context of expert recommendations on risk perceptions and subsequent behavior. *European Journal of Social Psychology, 40,* 746–759.

Schmitt, D. P., Alcalay, L., Allensworth, M., Allik, J., Ault, L., Austers, I., Bennett, K. L., Bianchi, G., Boholst, F., Borg Cunen, M. A., Braeckman, J., Brainerd, E. G., Caral, L. G. A., Caron, G., Casullo, M. M., Cunningham, M., Daibo, I., De Backer, C., De Souza, E., … Zupan, A. (2004). Patterns and universals of adult romantic attachment across 62 cultural regions: Are models of self and of other pancultural constructs? *Journal of Cross-Cultural Psychology, 35,* 367.

Schmitt, D. P., & Allik, J. (2005). Simultaneous administration of the Rosenberg Self-Esteem Scale in 53 nations: Exploring the universal and culture-specific features of global self-esteem. *Journal of Personality and Social Psychology, 89,* 623–642.

Schmitt, M. T., Branscombe, N. R., Postmes, T., & Garcia, A. (2014). The consequences of perceived discrimination for psychological well-being: A meta-analytic review. *Psychological Bulletin, 140,* 921–948.

Schnall, S., & Laird, J. D. (2003). Keep smiling: Enduring effects of facial expressions and postures on emotional experience and memory. *Cognition and Emotion, 17,* 787–797.

Schneider, M. E., Major, B., Luhtanen, R., & Crocker, J. (1996). Social stigma and the potential costs of assumptive help. *Personality and Social Psychology Bulletin, 22,* 201–209.

Schoeneman, T. J. (1994). Individualism. In V. S. Ramachandran (Ed.), *Encyclopedia of human behavior.* San Diego, CA: Academic Press.

Schofield, J. (1982). *Black and white in school: Trust, tension, or tolerance?* New York: Praeger.

Schofield, J. W. (1986). Causes and consequences of the colorblind perspective. In J. F. Dovidio & S. L. Gaertner (Eds.), *Prejudice, discrimination, and racism.* Orlando, FL: Academic Press.

Scholl, A., & Sassenberg, K. (2014). Where could we stand if I had …? How social power impacts counterfactual thinking after failure. *Journal of Experimental Social Psychology, 53,* 51–61.

Schor, J. B. (1998). *The overworked American.* New York: Basic Books.

Schroeder, J., Kardas, M., & Epley, N. (2018). The humanizing voice: Speech reveals, and text conceals, a more thoughtful mind in the midst of disagreement. *Psychological Science,* in press.

Schroeder, J., & Risen, J. L. (2014). Befriending the enemy: Outgroup friendship longitudinally predicts intergroup attitudes in a coexistence program for Israelis and Palestinians. *Group processes and intergroup relations,* in press.

Schulz, J. W., & Pruitt, D. G. (1978). The effects of mutual concern on joint welfare. *Journal of Experimental Social Psychology, 14,* 480–492.

Schulz-Hardt, S., Frey, D., Luthgens, C., & Moscovici, S. (2000). Biased information search in group decision making. *Journal of Personality and Social Psychology, 78,* 655–669.

Schuman, H., & Kalton, G. (1985). Survey methods. In G. Lindzey & E. Aronson (Eds.), *Handbook of social psychology* (Vol. 1). Hillsdale, NJ: Erlbaum.

Schuman, H., & Ludwig, J. (1983). The norm of even-handedness in surveys as in life. *American Sociological Review, 48,* 112–120.

Schuman, H., & Scott, J. (1989). Generations and collective memories. *American Sociological Review, 54,* 359–381.

Schutte, J. W., & Hosch, H. M. (1997). Gender differences in sexual assault verdicts. *Journal of Social Behavior and Personality, 12,* 759–772.

Schwartz, B. (2000). Self-determination: The tyranny of freedom. *American Psychologist, 55,* 79–88.

Schwartz, B. (2004). *The tyranny of choice.* New York: Ecco/HarperCollins.

Schwartz, S. H. (1975). The justice of need and the activation of humanitarian norms. *Journal of Social Issues, 31*(3), 111–136.

Schwartz, S. H., & Gottlieb, A. (1981). Participants' post-experimental reactions and the ethics of bystander research. *Journal of Experimental Social Psychology, 17,* 396–407.

Schwarz, N., Bless, H., Strack, F., Klumpp, G., Rittenauer-Schatka, H., & Simons, A. (1991). Ease of retrieval of information: Another look at the availability heuristic. *Journal of Personality and Social Psychology, 61,* 195–202.

Schwarz, N., & Clore, G. L. (1983). Mood, misattribution, and judgments of well-being: Informative and directive functions of affective states. *Journal of Personality and Social Psychology, 45,* 513–523.

Schwarz, N., Strack, F., Kommer, D., & Wagner, D. (1987). Soccer, rooms, and the quality of your life: Mood effects on judgments of satisfaction with life in general and with specific domains. *Journal of Applied Social Psychology, 17,* 69–79.

Schweitzer, K., Zillmann, D., Weaver, J. B., & Luttrell, E. S. (1992, Spring). Perception of threatening events in the emotional aftermath of a televised college football game. *Journal of Broadcasting and Electronic Media,* 75–82.

Schweitzer, L., & Lyons, S. (2019). *The truth about Gen Z: What we really know about their education experience and career aspirations*. Presentation at Strategic Enrolment Management and Marketing 2019 conference. Toronto, ON.

Schwinger, M., Wirthwein, L., Lemmer, G., & Steinmayr, R. (2014). Academic self-handicapping and achievement: A meta-analysis. *Journal of Educational Psychology, 106,* 744–761.

Scott, J. P., & Marston, M. V. (1953). Non-adaptive behavior resulting from a series of defeats in fighting mice. *Journal of Abnormal and Social Psychology, 48,* 417–428.

Scottish Life. (2001, Winter). Isle of Muck without a crime for decades. *Scottish Life,* p. 11.

Sears, D. O. (1979, May 3–5). *Life stage effects upon attitude change, especially among the elderly.* Manuscript prepared for Workshop on the Elderly of the Future, Committee on Aging, National Research Council, Annapolis, MD.

Sears, D. O. (1986). College sophomores in the laboratory: Influences of a narrow data base on social psychology's view of human nature. *Journal of Personality and Social Psychology, 51,* 515–530.

Sedikides, C. (1993). Assessment, enhancement, and verification determinants of the self-evaluation process. *Journal of Personality and Social Psychology, 65,* 317–338.

Sedikides, C., Gaertner, L., & Toguchi, Y. (2003). Pancultural self-enhancement. *Journal of Personality and Social Psychology, 84,* 60–79.

Sedikides, C., Meek, R., Alicke, M. D., & Taylor, S. (2014). Behind bars but above the bar: Prisoners consider themselves more prosocial than non-prisoners. *British Journal of Social Psychology, 53,* 396–403.

Segal, H. A. (1954). Initial psychiatric findings of recently repatriated prisoners of war. *American Journal of Psychiatry, 61,* 358–363.

Segal, N. L. (1984). Cooperation, competition, and altruism within twin sets: A reappraisal. *Ethology and Sociobiology, 5,* 163–177.

Segal, N. L., & Hershberger, S. L. (1999). Cooperation and competition between twins: Findings from a Prisoner's Dilemma game. *Evolution and Human Behavior, 20,* 29–51.

Segal-Caspi, L., Roccas, S., & Sagiv, L. (2012). Don't judge a book by its cover, revisited: Perceived and reported traits and values of attractive women. *Psychological Science, 23,* 1112–1116.

Segerstrom, S. C., & Miller, G. E. (2004). Psychological stress and the human immune system: A meta-analytic study of 30 years of inquiry. *Psychological Bulletin, 130,* 601.

Seibt, B., & Forster, J. (2004). Stereotype threat and performance: How self-stereotypes influence processing by inducing regulatory foci. *Journal of Personality and Social Psychology, 87*(1), 38–56.

Seidel, E., Eickhoff, S. B., Kellermann, T., Schneider, F., Gur, R. C., Habel, U., & Birgit, D. (2010). Who is to blame? Neural correlates of causal attribution in social situations. *Social Neuroscience, 5,* 335–350.

Seligman, M. (1994). *What you can change and what you can't.* New York: Knopf.

Seligman, M. E. P. (1975). *Helplessness: On depression, development and death.* San Francisco: W. H. Freeman.

Seligman, M. E. P. (1991). *Learned optimism.* New York: Knopf.

Sentyrz, S. M., & Bushman, B. J. (1997). *Mirror, mirror on the wall, who's the thinnest one of all? Effects of self-awareness on consumption of fatty, reduced-fat, and fat-free products.* Unpublished manuscript, Iowa State University, Ames, Iowa.

Sezer, O., Gino, F., & Norton, M. I. (2018). Humblebragging: A distinct—and ineffective—self-presentation strategy. *Journal of Personality and Social Psychology, 114,* 52–74.

Shaffer, D. R., Pegalis, L. J., & Bazzini, D. G. (1996). When boy meets girls (revisited): Gender, gender-role orientation, and prospect of future interaction as determinants of self-disclosure among same- and opposite-sex acquaintances. *Personality and Social Psychology Bulletin, 22,* 495–506.

Shah, J. Y. (2005). The automatic pursuit and management of goals. *Current Directions in Psychological Science, 14,* 10.

Shariff, A. F., Willard, A. K., Andersen, T., & Norenzayan, A. (2016). Religious priming: A meta-analysis with a focus on prosociality. *Personality and Social Psychology Review, 20,* 27–48.

Sharot, T., Velasquez, C. M., & Dolan, R. J. (2010). Do decisions shape preference? Evidence from blind chance. *Psychological Science, 21,* 1231–1235.

Sharpe, D., & Faye, C. (2009). A second look at debriefing practices: Madness in our methods? *Ethics and Behavior, 19,* 432–447.

Shaver, P. R., & Hazan, C. (1993). Adult romantic attachment: Theory and evidence. In D. Perlman & W. Jones (Eds.), *Advances in personal relationships* (Vol. 4). Greenwich, CT: JAI.

Shaver, P. R., & Hazan, C. (1994). Attachment. In A. L. Weber & J. H. Harvey (Eds.), *Perspectives on close relationships*. Boston: Allyn & Bacon.

Shaver, P. R., & Mikulincer, M. (2011). An attachment-theory framework for conceptualizing interpersonal behavior. In L. M. Horowitz & S. Strack (Eds.), *Handbook of interpersonal psychology: Theory, research, assessment, and therapeutic interventions.* Hoboken, NJ: Wiley.

Shaw, M. E. (1981). *Group dynamics: The psychology of small group behavior.* New York: McGraw-Hill.

Sheese, B. E., & Graziano, W. G. (2005). Deciding to defect: The effects of video-game violence on cooperative behavior. *Psychological Science, 16,* 354.

Sheldon, K. M., & Niemiec, C. P. (2006). It's not just the amount that counts: Balanced need satisfaction also affects well-being. *Journal of Personality and Social Psychology, 91,* 331–341.

Sheldon, K. M., Ryan, R. M., Deci, E. L., & Kasser, T. (2004). The independent effects of goal contents and motives on well-being: It's both what you pursue and why you pursue it. *Personality and Social Psychology Bulletin, 30,* 475.

Shell, R. M., & Eisenberg, N. (1992). A developmental model of recipients' reactions to aid. *Psychological Bulletin, 111,* 413–433.

Shelton, J. N., & Richeson, J. A. (2006). Ethnic minorities' racial attitudes and contact experiences with white people. *Cultural Diversity and Ethnic Minority Psychology, 12,* 149–164.

Shelton, J. N., Richeson, J. A., & Vorauer, J. D. (2006). Threatened identities and interethnic interactions. *European Review of Social Psychology, 17,* 321–358.

Shen, H., Wan, F., & Wyer, R. S., Jr. (2011). Cross-cultural differences in the refusal to accept a small gift: The differential influence of reciprocity norms on Asians and North Americans. *Journal of Personality and Social Psychology, 100,* 271–281.

Shepperd, J. A. (2003). *Interpreting comparative risk judgments: Are people personally optimistic or interpersonally pessimistic?* Unpublished manuscript, University of Florida, Gainesville, FL.

Shepperd, J. A., & Arkin, R. M. (1991). Behavioral other-enhancement: Strategically obscuring the link between performance and evaluation. *Journal of Personality and Social Psychology, 60,* 79–88.

Shepperd, J. A., Arkin, R. M., & Slaughter, J. (1995). Constraints on excuse making: The deterring effects of shyness and anticipated retest. *Personality and Social Psychology Bulletin, 21,* 1061–1072.

Shepperd, J. A., Klein, W. M. P., Waters, E. A., & Weinstein, N. D. (2013). Taking stock of unrealistic optimism. *Perspectives on Psychological Science, 8,* 395–411.

Shepperd, J. A., & Taylor, K. M. (1999). Ascribing advantages to social comparison targets. *Basic and Applied Social Psychology, 21,* 103–117.

Shepperd, J. A., Waters, E., Weinstein, N. D., & Klein, W. M. P. (2015). A primer on unrealistic optimism. *Current Directions in Psychological Science,* in press.

Shepperd, J. A., & Wright, R. A. (1989). Individual contributions to a collective effort: An incentive analysis. *Personality and Social Psychology Bulletin, 15,* 141–149.

Shergill, S. S., Bays, P. M., Frith, C. D., & Wolpert, D. M. (2003). Two eyes for an eye: The neuroscience of force escalation. *Science, 301,* 187.

Sherif, M. (1935). A study of some social factors in perception. *Archives of Psychology,* No. 187.

Sherif, M. (1937). An experimental approach to the study of attitudes. *Sociometry, 1,* 90–98.

Sherif, M. (1966). *In common predicament: Social psychology of intergroup conflict and cooperation.* Boston: Houghton Mifflin.

Sherif, M., & Sherif, C. (1969). *Social psychology.* New York: Harper & Row.

Sherman, A. (2016, June 23). Loretta Lynch says gays and lesbians are most frequently targeted for hate crimes. Politifact (www.politfact.com)

Sherman, D. K., Hartson, K. A., Binning, K. R., Purdie-Vaughns, V., Garcia, J., Taborsky-Barba, S., Tomassetti, S., Nussbaum, A. D., & Cohen, G. L. (2013). Deflecting the trajectory and changing the narrative: How self-affirmation affects academic performance and motivation under identity threat. *Journal of Personality and Social Psychology, 104,* 591–618.

Sherman, D. K., Nelson, L. D., & Ross, L. D. (2003). Naive realism and affirmative action: Adversaries are more similar than they think. *Basic and Applied Social Psychology, 25,* 275–289.

Sherman, L. E., Payton, A. A., Hernandez, L. M., Greenfield, P. M., & Dapretto, M. (2016). The power of the Like in adolescence: Effects of peer influence on neural and behavioral responses to social media. *Psychological Science, 27*(7), 1027–1035. https://doi-org.library.smu.ca/10.1177/0956797616645673

Sherman, J. W. (1996). Development and mental representation of stereotypes. *Journal of Personality and Social Psychology, 70,* 1126–1141.

Sherman, J. W., Kruschke, J. K., Sherman, S. J., Percy, E. J., Petrocelli, J. V., & Conrey, F. R. (2009). Attentional processes in stereotype formation: A common model for category accentuation and illusory correlation. *Journal of Personality and Social Psychology, 96,* 305–323.

Sherman, J. W., Lee, A. Y., Bessenoff, G. R., & Frost, L. A. (1998). Stereotype efficiency reconsidered: Encoding flexibility under cognitive load. *Journal of Personality and Social Psychology, 75,* 589–606.

Sherman, S. J., Cialdini, R. B., Schwartzman, D. F., & Reynolds, K. D. (1985). Imagining can heighten or lower the perceived likelihood of contracting a disease: The mediating effect of ease of imagery. *Personality and Social Psychology Bulletin, 11,* 118–127.

Shermer, M. (2006). Answer on World Question Center 2006. *The Edge.* Retrieved from http://www.edge.org

Shestakova, A., Rieskamp, J., Tugin, S., Ossadtchi, A., Krutitskaya, J., & Klucharev, V. (2013). Electrophysiological precursors of social conformity. *Social Cognitive and Affective Neuroscience, 8*(7), 756–763. https://doi-org.library.smu.ca/10.1093/scan/nss064

Shih, M., Pittinsky, T. L., & Ambady, N. (1999). Stereotype susceptibility: Identity salience and shifts in quantitative performance. *Psychological Science, 10,* 80–83.

Shorey-Fennell, B. R., & Magnan, R. E. (2019). Reactance to anti-binge drinking messages: Testing cognitive and affective mechanisms among noncollege emerging adults. *Journal of Behavioral Medicine, 42*(5), 984–990. https://doi-org.library.smu.ca/10.1007/s10865-019-00018-3

Short, J. F., Jr. (Ed.) (1969). *Gang delinquency and delinquent subcultures.* New York: Harper & Row.

Shostak, M. (1981). *Nisa: The life and words of a !Kung woman.* Cambridge, MA: Harvard University Press.

Shotland, R. L. (1989). A model of the causes of date rape in developing and close relationships. In C. Hendrick (Ed.), *Review of personality and social psychology* (Vol. 10). Beverly Hills, CA: Sage.

Shotland, R. L., & Stebbins, C. A. (1983). Emergency and cost as determinants of helping behavior and the slow accumulation of social psychological knowledge. *Social Psychology Quarterly, 46,* 36–46.

Shotland, R. L., & Straw, M. K. (1976). Bystander response to an assault: When a man attacks a woman. *Journal of Personality and Social Psychology, 34,* 990–999.

Showers, C., & Ruben, C. (1987). *Distinguishing pessimism from depression: Negative expectations and positive coping mechanisms.* Paper presented at the American Psychological Association convention.

Shrauger, J. S. (1975). Responses to evaluation as a function of initial self-perceptions. *Psychological Bulletin, 82,* 581–596.

Shriver, E. R., Young, S. G., Hugenberg, K., Bernstein, M. J., & Lanter, J. R. (2008, February). Class, race, and the face: Social context modulates the cross-race effect in face recognition. *Personality and Social Psychology Bulletin, 34,* 260–274.

Sidanius, J., Van Laar, C., Levin, S., & Sinclair, S. (2004). Ethnic enclaves and the dynamics of social identity on the college campus: The good, the bad, and the ugly. *Journal of Personality and Social Psychology, 87,* 96–110.

Sieverding, M., Decker, S., & Zimmerman, F. (2010). Information about low participation in cancer screening demotivates other people. *Psychological Science, 21,* 941–943.

Sigall, H. (1970). Effects of competence and consensual validation on a communicator's liking for the audience. *Journal of Personality and Social Psychology, 16,* 252–258.

Sigurdson, J. F., Wallander, J., & Sund, A. M. (2014). Is involvement in school bullying associated with general health and psychosocial adjustment outcomes in adulthood? *Child Abuse & Neglect, 38,* 1607–1617.

Silk, J. B., Alberts, S. C., & Altmann, J. (2003). Social bonds of female baboons enhance infant survival. *Science, 302,* 1231–1234.

Silva, M. N., & Teixeira, P. J. (2012). Promotion of and adherence to physical activity. In *Encyclopedia of Exercise Medicine in Health and Disease* (pp. 727–731). Springer Berlin Heidelberg.

Silver, M., & Geller, D. (1978). On the irrelevance of evil: The organization and individual action. *Journal of Social Issues, 34,* 125–136.

Silver, N. (2009, May 9). Bush may haunt Republicans for generations. Retrieved from http://www.fivethirtyeight.com

Silverman, A. M. & Cohen, G. L. (2014). Stereotypes as stumbling-blocks: How coping with stereotypes threat affects life outcomes for people with physical disabilities. *Personality and Social Psychology Bulletin, 40,* 1330–1340.

Silverman, C. (2004, March/April). Canadian cults: Blind faith or new religion? *The New Canadian Magazine,* 1–4. Retrieved June 1, 2006, from http://ordinary.blogs.com/clips/Cults.pdf

Silvia, P. J. (2005). Deflecting reactance: The role of similarity in increasing compliance and reducing resistance. *Basic and Applied Social Psychology, 27,* 277–284.

Simmons, W. W. (2000, December). When it comes to having children, Americans still prefer boys. *The Gallup Poll Monthly,* 63–64.

Simon, H. A. (1957). *Models of man: Social and rational.* New York: Wiley.

Simon, P. (1996, April 17). American provincials. *Christian Century,* 421–422.

Simon, R. (2011). SCOTUS: Violence OK. Sex? Maybe. Retrieved from https://politico.com

Simonton, D. K. (1994). *Greatness: Who makes history and why.* New York: Guilford.

Simpson, J. A. (1987). The dissolution of romantic relationships: Factors involved in relationship stability and emotional distress. *Journal of Personality and Social Psychology, 53,* 683–692.

Simpson, J. A., Gangestad, S. W., & Lerma, M. (1990). Perception of physical attractiveness: Mechanisms involved in the maintenance of romantic relationships. *Journal of Personality and Social Psychology, 59,* 1192–1201.

Simpson, J. A., Rholes, W. S., & Nelligan, J. S. (1992). Support seeking and support giving within couples in an anxiety-provoking situation: The role of attachment styles. *Journal of Personality and Social Psychology, 62,* 434–446.

Simpson, J. A., Rholes, W. S., & Phillips, D. (1996). Conflict in close relationships: An attachment perspective. *Journal of Personality and Social Psychology, 71,* 899–914.

Sinclair, L., & Kunda, Z. (1999). Reactions to a Black professional: Motivated inhibition and activation of conflicting stereotypes. *Journal of Personality and Social Psychology, 77,* 885–904.

Sinclair, L., & Kunda, Z. (2000). Motivated stereotyping of women: She's fine if she praised me but incompetent if she criticized me. *Personality and Social Psychology Bulletin, 26,* 1329–1342.

Sinclair, S., Dunn, E., & Lowery, B. S. (2005). The relationship between parental racial attitudes and children's implicit prejudice. *Journal of Experimental Social Psychology, 41,* 283–289.

Singer, M. (1979) *Cults and cult members.* Address to the American Psychological Association convention.

Singh, D. (1993). Adaptive significance of female physical attractiveness: Role of waist-to-hip ratio. *Journal of Personality and Social Psychology, 65,* 293–307.

Singh, D. (1995). Female judgment of male attractiveness and desirability for relationships: Role of waist-to-hip ratio and financial status. *Journal of Personality and Social Psychology, 69,* 1089–1101.

Singh, D., & Randall, P. K. (2007). Beauty is in the eye of the plastic surgeon: Waist-hip ratio (WHR) and women's attractiveness. *Personality and Individual Differences, 43,* 329–340.

Singh, R., & Ho, S. J. (2000). Attitudes and attraction: A new test of the attraction, repulsion and similarity-dissimilarity asymmetry hypotheses. *British Journal of Social Psychology, 39,* 197–211.

Singh, R., & Teoh, J. B. P. (1999). Attitudes and attraction: A test of two hypotheses for the similarity-dissimilarity asymmetry. *British Journal of Social Psychology, 38,* 427–443.

Siperstein, G. N., Albert, A. B., Jacobs, H. E., Osborne, K. J., & Stokes, J. E. (2018). A schoolwide approach to promoting student bystander behavior in response to the use of the word "retard." *Research in Developmental Disabilities, 80,* 142–152. https://doi-org.library.smu.ca/10.1016/j.ridd.2018.06.016

SIPRI. (2011). Appendix 4A. Military expenditure data, 2001–10. Stockholm International Peace Research Institute.

SIPRI. (2014). Recent trends. Stockholm International Peace Research Institute. Retrieved from http://www.sipri.org/research/armaments/milex.

Sistrunk, F., & McDavid, J. W. (1971). Sex variable in conforming behaviour. *Journal of Personality and Social Psychology, 17*(2), 200–207.

Sittser, G. L. (1994, April). Long night's journey into light. *Second Opinion,* 10–15.

Sivarajasingam, V., Moore, S., & Shepherd, J. P. (2005). Winning, losing, and violence. *Injury Prevention, 11,* 69–70.

Six, B., & Eckes, T. (1996). Metaanalysen in der Einstellungs-Verhaltens-Forschung. *Zeitschrift fur Sozialpsychologie,* 7–17.

Skaalvik, E. M., & Hagtvet, K. A. (1990). Academic achievement and self-concept: An analysis of causal predominance in a developmental perspective. *Journal of Personality and Social Psychology, 58,* 292–307.

Skinner, B. F. (1971). *Beyond freedom and dignity.* New York: Knopf.

Skitka, L. J., & Tetlock, P. E. (1993). Providing public assistance: Cognitive and motivational processes underlying liberal and conservative policy preferences. *Journal of Personality and Social Psychology, 65,* 1205–1223.

Skitka, L. R., Bauman, C. E., & Mullen, E. (2004). Political tolerance and coming to psychological closure following the September 11, 2001 terrorist attacks: An integrative approach. *Personality and Social Psychology Bulletin, 30,* 743–756.

Skurnik, I., Yoon, C., Park, D. C., & Schwarz, N. (2005). How warnings about false claims become recommendations. *Journal of Consumer Research, 31,* 713.

Slatcher, R. B., & Pennebaker, J. W. (2006). How do I love thee? Let me count the words: The social effects of expressive writing. *Psychological Science, 17,* 660–664.

Slavin, R. E. (1985). Cooperative learning: Applying contact theory in desegregated schools. *Journal of Social Issues, 41*(3), 45–62.

Slavin, R. E. (1990, December/January). Research on cooperative learning: Consensus and controversy. *Educational Leadership,* 52–54.

Slavin, R. E., & Cooper, R. (1999). Improving intergroup relations: Lessons learned from cooperative learning programs. *Journal of Social Issues, 55,* 647–663.

Slavin, R. E., Hurley, E. A., & Chamberlain, A. (2003). Cooperative learning and achievement: Theory and research. In W. M. Reynolds & G. E. Miller (Eds.), *Handbook of psychology: Educational psychology* (Vol. 7). New York: Wiley.

Slavin, R. E., Lake, C., & Groff, C. (2009). Effective programs in middle and high school mathematics: A best-evidence synthesis. *Review of Educational Research, 79,* 839–911.

Slavin, R. E., & Madden, N. A. (1979). School practices that improve race relations. *Journal of Social Issues, 16,* 169–180.

Slepian, M. L., Rule, N. O., & Ambady, N. (2012). Proprioception and person perception: Politicians and professors. *Personality and Social Psychology Bulletin, 38,* 1621–1628.

Sloan, J. H., Kellerman, A. L., Reay, D. T., Ferris, J. A., Koepsell, T., Rivara, F. P., Rice, C., Gray, L., & LoGerfo, J. (1988). Handgun regulations, crime, assaults, and homicide: A tale of two cities. *New England Journal of Medicine, 319,* 1256–1262.

Slopen, N., Glynn, R. J., Buring, J., & Albert, M. A. (2010, November 23). Job strain, job insecurity, and incident cardiovascular disease in the Women's Health Study (Abstract 18520). *Circulation, A18520.* Retrieved from circ.ahajournals.org

Slotow, R., Van Dyke, G., Poole, J., Page, B., & Klocke, A. (2000). Older bull elephants control young males. *Nature, 408,* 425–426.

Slotter, E. B., & Gardner, W. L. (2009). Where do you end and I begin? Evidence for anticipatory, motivated self-other integration between relationship partners. *Journal of Personality and Social Psychology, 96,* 1137–1151.

Slotter, E. B., Gardner, W. L., & Finkel, E. (2010). Who am I without you? The influence of romantic breakup on the self-concept. *Personality and Social Psychology Bulletin, 36,* 147–160.

Slovic, P. (1972). From Shakespeare to Simon: Speculations—and some evidence—about man's ability to process information. *Oregon Research Institute Research Bulletin, 12*(2).

Slovic, P. (2007). "If I look at the mass I will never act": Psychic numbing and genocide. *Judgment and Decision Making, 2,* 79–95.

Slovic, P., & Fischhoff, B. (1977). On the psychology of experimental surprises. *Journal of Experimental Psychology: Human Perception and Performance, 3,* 455–551.

Slovic, P., & Västfjäll, D. (2010). Affect, moral intuition, and risk. *Psychological Inquiry, 21,* 387–398.

Smith, A. (1976). *The wealth of nations.* Book 1. Chicago: University of Chicago Press. (Originally published, 1776.)

Smith, D. E., Gier, J. A., & Willis, F. N. (1982). Interpersonal touch and compliance with a marketing request. *Basic and Applied Social Psychology, 3,* 35–38.

Smith, H. (1976). *The Russians.* New York: Balantine Books.

Smith, P. B. (2005). Is there an indigenous European social psychology? *International Journal of Psychology, 40,* 254–262.

Smith, P. B., & Tayeb, M. (1989). Organizational structure and processes. In M. Bond (Ed.), *The cross-cultural challenge to social psychology.* Newbury Park, CA: Sage.

Smith, R. H., Turner, T. J., Garonzik, R., Leach, C. W., Urch-Druskat, V., & Weston, C. M. (1996). Envy and Schadenfreude. *Personality and Social Psychology Bulletin, 22,* 158–168.

Smith, S. J., Axelton, A. M., & Saucier, D. A. (2009). The effects of contact on sexual prejudice: A meta-analysis. *Sex Roles, 61,* 178–191.

Smith, S. L., Pieper, K., & Choueiti, M. (2017, February). Inclusion in the director's chair? Gender, race, & age of film directors across 1,000 films from 2007–2016. Media, Diversity, & Social Change Initiative, University of Southern California Annenberg School for Communications and Journalism.

Smith, S. M., Fabrigar, L. R., MacDougall, B. L., & Wiesenthal, N. L. (2008). The role of amount, cognitive elaboration, and structural consistency of attitude-relevant knowledge in the formation of attitude certainty. *European Journal of Social Psychology, 38,* 280–295.

Smith, S. M., Fabrigar, L. R., & Norris, M. E. (2008). Reflecting on six decades of selective exposure research: Progress, challenges, and opportunities. *Social and Personality Compass, 2,* 464-493.

Smith, S. M., Fabrigar, L. R., Powell, D. M., & Estrada, M. (2007). The role of information-processing capacity and goals in attitude-congruent selective exposure effects. *Personality and Social Psychology Bulletin, 33*(7), 948–960.

Smith, T. W. (1998, December). *American sexual behavior: Trends, socio-demographic differences, and risk behavior.* National Opinion Research Center GSS Topical Report No. 25.

Snopes. (2008). The naked truth. Retrieved from http://www.snopes.com/humor/iftrue/pollster.asp

Snyder, C. R. (1978). The "illusion" of uniqueness. *Journal of Humanistic Psychology, 18,* 33–41.

Snyder, C. R. (1980, March). The uniqueness mystique. *Psychology Today,* 86–90.

Snyder, C. R., & Fromkin, H. L. (1980). *Uniqueness: The human pursuit of difference.* New York, NY: Plenum.

Snyder, C. R., & Higgins, R. L. (1988). Excuses: Their effective role in the negotiation of reality. *Psychological Bulletin, 104,* 23–35.

Snyder, C. R., & Smith, T. W. (1986). On being "shy like a fox": A self-handicapping analysis. In W. H. Jones et al. (Eds.), *Shyness: Perspectives on research and treatment.* New York: Plenum.

Snyder, M. (1981). Seek, and ye shall find: Testing hypotheses about other people. In E. T. Higgins, C. P. Herman, & M. P. Zanna (Eds.), *Social cognition: The Ontario symposium on personality and social psychology.* Hillsdale, NJ: Erlbaum.

Snyder, M. (1984). When belief creates reality. In L. Berkowitz (Ed.), *Advances in experimental social psychology* (Vol. 18). New York: Academic Press.

Snyder, M. (1987). *Public appearances/private realities: The psychology of self-monitoring.* New York: Freeman.

Snyder, M., Campbell, B., & Preston, E. (1982). Testing hypotheses about human nature: Assessing the accuracy of social stereotypes. *Social Cognition, 1,* 256–272.

Snyder, M., Grether, J., & Keller, K. (1974). Staring and compliance: A field experiment on hitch-hiking. *Journal of Applied Social Psychology, 4,* 165–170.

Snyder, M., & Haugen, J. A. (1994). Why does behavioral confirmation occur? A functional perspective on the role of the perceiver. *Journal of Experimental Social Psychology, 30,* 218–246.

Snyder, M., & Haugen, J. A. (1995). Why does behavioral confirmation occur? A functional perspective on the role of the target. *Personality and Social Psychology Bulletin, 21,* 963–974.

Snyder, M., & Swann, W. B., Jr. (1976). When actions reflect attitudes: The politics of impression management. *Journal of Personality and Social Psychology, 34,* 1034–1042.

Snyder, M., Tanke, E. D., & Berscheid, E. (1977). Social perception and interpersonal behavior: On the self-fulfilling nature of social stereotypes. *Journal of Personality and Social Psychology, 35,* 656–666.

Sober, E., & Wilson, D. S. (1998). *Unto others: The evolution and psychology of unselfish behavior.* Cambridge, MA: Harvard University Press.

Sofer, C., Dotsch, R., Wigboldus, D. H. J., & Todorov, A. (2015). What is typical is good: The influence of face typicality on perceived trustworthiness. *Psychological Science, 26,* 39–47.

Solano, C. H., Batten, P. G., & Parish, E. A. (1982). Loneliness and patterns of self-disclosure. *Journal of Personality and Social Psychology, 43,* 524–531.

Solberg, E. C., Diener, E., Wirtz, D., Lucas, R. E., & Oishi, S. (2002). Wanting, having, and satisfaction: Examining the role of desire discrepancies in satisfaction with income. *Journal of Personality and Social Psychology, 83,* 725.

Solnick, S. J., & Hemenway, D. (2012). The "Twinkie Defense": The relationship between carbonated non-diet soft drinks and violence perpetration among Boston high school students. *Injury Prevention, 18,* 259–263.

Solomon, H., & Solomon, L. Z. (1978). *Effects of anonymity on helping in emergency situations.* Paper presented at the Eastern Psychological Association convention.

Solomon, H., Solomon, L. Z., Arnone, M. M., Maur, B. J., Reda, R. M., & Rother, E. O. (1981). Anonymity and helping. *Journal of Social Psychology, 113,* 37–43.

Solomon, L. Z., Solomon, H., & Stone, R. (1978). Helping as a function of number of bystanders and ambiguity of emergency. *Personality and Social Psychology Bulletin, 4,* 318–321.

Solomon, S., Greenberg, J., & Pyszczynski, T. (2000). Pride and prejudice: Fear of death and social behavior. *Current Directions in Psychological Science, 9,* 200–203.

Somaiya, R. (2011, August 13). After British riots, conflicting answers as to "why." New York Times (www.nytimes.com).

Sommer, F., Leuschner, V., & Scheithauer, H. (2014). Bullying, romantic rejection, and conflicts with teachers: The crucial role of social dynamics in the development of school shootings—A systematic review. *International Journal of Developmental Science, 8,* 3–24.

Son Hing, L. S., Bobocel, D. R., Zanna, M. P., & McBride, M. V. (2007). Authoritarian dynamics and unethical decision making: High social dominance orientation leaders and high right-wing authoritarianism followers. *Journal of Personality and Social Psychology, 92,* 67.

Soral, W., Bilewicz, M., & Winiewski, M. (2018). Exposure to hate speech increases prejudice through desensitization. *Aggressive Behavior, 44,* 136-146.

Sorhagen, N. S. (2013). Early teacher expectations disproportionately affect poor children's high school performance. *Journal of Educational Psychology, 105,* 465–477.

Sorokowski, P., et al. (2011). Attractiveness of leg length: Report from 27 nations. *Journal of Cross-Cultural Psychology, 42,* 131–139.

Southern Poverty Law Center (2017). *Hate and extremism in 2017.* Montgomery, AL: Southern Poverty Law Center.

Sowislo, J. F., & Orth, U. (2013). Does low self-esteem predict depression and anxiety? A meta-analysis of longitudinal studies. *Psychological Bulletin, 139,* 213–240.

Sparkman, D. J., Eidelman, S., & Blanchar, J. C. (2016). Multicultural experiences reduce prejudice through personality shifts in openness to experience. *European Journal of Social Psychology, 46,* 840–853.

Sparrell, J. A., & Shrauger, J. S. (1984). *Self-confidence and optimism in self-prediction.* Paper presented at the American Psychological Association convention.

Spears, R., Ellemers, N., & Doosje, B. (2009). Strength in numbers or less is more? A matter of opinion and a question of taste. *Personality and Social Psychology Bulletin, 35,* 1099–1111.

Spector, P. E. (1986). Perceived control by employees: A meta-analysis of studies concerning autonomy and participation at work. *Human Relations, 39,* 1005–1016.

Speer, A. (1971). *Inside the Third Reich: Memoirs* (R. Winston & C. Winston, Trans.). New York: Avon Books.

Spence, A., & Townsend, E. (2007). Predicting behaviour towards genetically modified food using implicit and explicit attitudes. *British Journal of Social Psychology, 46,* 437–457.

Spencer, S. J., Fein, S., Wolfe, C. T., Fong, C., & Dunn, M. A. (1998). Automatic activation of stereotypes: The role of self-image threat. *Personality and Social Psychology Bulletin, 24,* 1139–1152.

Spencer, S. J., Steele, C. M., & Quinn, D. M. (1999). Stereotype threat and women's math performance. *Journal of Experimental Social Psychology, 35,* 4–28.

Speth, J. G. (2008). Foreword. In A. A. Leiserowitz & L. O. Fernandez, *Toward a new consciousness: Values to sustain human and natural communities.* New Haven: Yale School of Forestry & Environmental Studies.

Spiegel, H. W. (1971). *The growth of economic thought.* Durham, NC: Duke University Press.

Spielmann, S. S., Joel, S., MacDonald. G., & Kogan, A. (2013). Ex appeal: Current relationship quality and emotional attachment to ex-partners. *Social Psychological and Personality Science, 4,* 175–180.

Spielmann, S. S., MacDonald, G., & Wilson, A. E. (2009). On the rebound: Focusing on someone new helps anxiously attached individuals let go of ex-partners. *Personality and Social Psychology Bulletin, 35,* 1382–1394.

Spitz, H. H. (1999). Beleaguered Pygmalion: A history of the controversy over claims that teacher expectancy raises intelligence. *Intelligence, 27,* 199–234.

Spivak, J. (1979, June 6). *Wall Street Journal.*

Sporer, S. L., & Horry, R. (2011). Recognizing faces from ethnic in-groups and outgroups: Importance of outer face features and effects of retention interval. *Applied Cognitive Psychology, 25,* 424–431.

Sporer, S. L., Trinkl, B., & Guberova, E. (2007). Matching faces. Differences in processing speed of out-group faces by different ethnic groups. *Journal of Cross-Cultural Psychology, 38,* 398–412.

Sports Illustrated. (2016, May 17). LeBron James's Nike deal may be worth more than $1 billion. Retrieved from https://www.si.com/nba/2016/05/17/lebron-james-nike-deal-contract-one-billion

Sprecher, S. (1987). The effects of self-disclosure given and received on affection for an intimate partner and stability of the relationship. *Journal of Personality and Social Psychology, 4,* 115–127.

Sprecher, S., Aron, A., Hatfield, E., Cortese, A., Potapova, E., & Levitskaya, A. (1994). Love: American style, Russian style, and Japanese style. *Personal Relationships, 1,* 349–369.

Srivastava, S., McGonigal, K. M., Richards, J. M., Butler, E. A., & Gross, J. J. (2006). Optimism in close relationships: How seeing things in a positive light makes them so. *Journal of Personality and Social Psychology, 91,* 143–153.

Stajkovic, A., & Luthans, F. (1998). Self-efficacy and work-related performance: A meta-analysis. *Psychological Bulletin, 124,* 240–261.

Stalder, D. R. (2008). Revisiting the issue of safety in numbers: The likelihood of receiving help from a group. *Social Influence, 3,* 24–33.

Stam, H., Lubeck, I., & Radtke, H. L. (1998). Repopulating social psychology texts: Disembodied "subjects" and embodied subjectivity. In B. M. Bayer & J. Shotter (Eds.), *Reconstructing the psychological subject: Bodies, practices and technologies. Inquiries in social construction* (pp. 153–186). London: Sage Publications, Inc.

Stangor, C., Jonas, K., Stroebe, W., & Hewstone, M. (1996). Influence of student exchange on national stereotypes, attitudes, and perceived group variability. *European Journal of Social Psychology, 26,* 663–675.

Stanley, D., Phelps, E., & Banaji, M. (2008). The neural basis of implicit attitudes. *Current Directions in Psychological Science, 17,* 164–170.

Stanovich, K. E., & West, R. F. (2008). On the relative independence of thinking biases and cognitive ability. *Journal of Personality and Social Psychology, 94,* 672–695.

Stanovich, K. E., West, R. F., & Toplak, M. E. (2013). Myside bias, rational thinking, and intelligence. *Current Directions in Psychological Science, 22,* 259–264.

Staples, B. (2000, June 26). Playing "catch and grope" in the schoolyard. *New York Times.* Retrieved from http://www.nytimes.com

Stark, E., Kim, A., Miller, C., & Borgida, E. (2008). Effects of including a graphic warning label in advertisements for reduced-exposure products: Implications for persuasion and policy. *Journal of Applied Social Psychology, 38,* 281–293.

Stark, R., & Bainbridge, W. S. (1980). Networks of faith: Interpersonal bonds and recruitment of cults and sects. *American Journal of Sociology, 85,* 1376–1395.

Starks, T. J., & Parsons, J. T. (2014). Adult attachment among partnered gay men: Patterns and associations with sexual relationship quality. *Archives of Sexual Behavior, 43,* 107–117.

Starmans, C., Sheskin, M., & Bloom, P. (2017). Why people prefer unequal societies. *Nature Human Behavior, 1,* 0082.

Stasser, G. (1991). Pooling of unshared information during group discussion. In S. Worchel, W. Wood, & J. Simpson (Eds.), *Group process and productivity.* Beverly Hills, CA: Sage.

Stasser, G., Kerr, N. L., & Bray, R. M. (1981). The social psychology of jury deliberations: Structure, process, and product. In N. L. Kerr & R. M. Bray (Eds.), *The psychology of the courtroom.* New York: Academic Press.

Statista. (2020). Facebook: Number of monthly active users worldwide 2008–2020. Retrieved from https://www.statista.com/statistics/264810/number-of-monthly-active-facebook-users-worldwide/

Statistics Canada. (1998). General social survey: Overview of the time use of Canadians in 1998. Ottawa: Statistics Canada.

Statistics Canada. (2009). Police reported hate crime in Canada, 2009. Retrieved from http://www.statcan.gc.ca/pub/85-002-x/2011001/article/11469-eng.htm

Statistics Canada. (2018a). Smoking, 2018. Retrieved from https://www150.statcan.gc.ca/n1/pub/82-625-x/2019001/article/00006-eng.htm

Statistics Canada. (2018b). Firearm-related violent crime, 2009–2017. Retrieved from https://www150.statcan.gc.ca/n1/pub/89-28-0001/2018001/article/00004-eng.htm

Statistics Canada. (2018c). Violent victimization of lesbians, gays and bisexuals in Canada, 2014. Retrieved from https://www150.statcan.gc.ca/n1/pub/85-002-x/2018001/article/54923-eng.htm

Statistics Canada. (2018d). Police-reported hate crime, number of incidents and rate per 100,000 population, Census Metropolitan Areas. Retrieved from https://www150.statcan.gc.ca/t1/tbl1/en/tv.action?pid=3510019101

Statistics Canada. (2018e). Police-reported hate crime, by type of motivation, Canada (selected police services). Retrieved from https://www150.statcan.gc.ca/t1/tbl1/en/tv.action?pid=3510006601

Statistics Canada. (2019). Smoking, 2018. Retrieved from https://www150.statcan.gc.ca/n1/pub/82-625-x/2019001/article/00006-eng.htm

Statistics Canada. (2020). Canadian internet usage survey. Retrieved from https://www150.statcan.gc.ca/n1/daily-quotidien/191029/dq191029a-eng.htm

Staub, E. (1978). *Positive social behavior and morality: Social and personal influences* (Vol. 1). Hillsdale, NJ: Erlbaum.

Staub, E. (1989). *The roots of evil: The origins of genocide and other group violence.* Cambridge: Cambridge University Press.

Staub, E. (1990). Moral exclusion: Personal goal theory, and extreme destructiveness. *Journal of Social Issues, 46,* 47–64.

Staub, E. (1991). Altruistic and moral motivations for helping and their translation into action. *Psychological Inquiry, 2,* 150–153.

Staub, E. (1992). The origins of caring, helping, and nonaggression: Parental socialization, the family system, schools, and cultural influence. In P. M. Oliner, S. P. Oliner, L. Baron, L. A. Blum, D. L. Krebs, & M. Z. Smolenska (Eds.), *The origins of caring, helping, and nonaggression: Parental socialization, the family system, schools, and cultural influence.* New York: New York University Press.

Staub, E. (1996). Altruism and aggression in children and youth: Origins and cures. In R. Feldman (Ed.), *The psychology of adversity.* Amherst, MA: University of Massachusetts Press.

Staub, E. (1997a). Halting and preventing collective violence: The role of bystanders. Background paper for symposium organized by the Friends of Raoul Wallenberg, Stockholm, June 13–16.

Staub, E. (1997b). Blind versus constructive patriotism: Moving from embeddedness in the group to critical loyalty and action. In D. Bar-Tal and E. Staub (Eds.), *Patriotism in the lives of individuals and nations.* Chicago: Nelson-Hall.

Staub, E. (2003). *The psychology of good and evil: Why children, adults, and groups help and harm others.* New York: Cambridge University Press.

Staub, E. (2005). The roots of goodness: The fulfillment of basic human needs and the development of caring, helping and nonaggression, inclusive caring, moral courage, active bystandership, and altruism born of suffering. In G. Carlo & C. P. Edwards (Eds.), *Moral motivation through the life span: Theory, research, applications. Nebraska Symposium on Motivation* (Vol. 51). Lincoln, NE: University of Nebraska Press.

Staub, E. (2019). Witnesses/bystanders: The tragic fruits of passivity, the power of bystanders, and promoting active bystandership in children, adults, and groups. *Journal of Social Issues, 75*(4), 1262–1293. https://doi-org.library.smu.ca/10.1111/josi.12351

Staub, E., & Bar-Tal, D. (2003). Genocide, mass killings, and intractable conflict. In D. Sears, L. Huddy, & R. Jervis (Eds.), *Handbook of political psychology.* New York: Oxford University Press.

Staub, E., & Pearlman, L. A. (2005a). Advancing healing and reconciliation. In L. Barbanel & R. Sternberg (Eds.), *Psychological interventions in times of crisis* (pp. 213–243). New York: Springer.

Staub, E., & Pearlman, L. A. (2005b). Psychological recovery and reconciliation after the genocide in Rwanda and in other post-conflict settings. In R. Sternberg & L. Barbanel (Eds.), *Psychological interventions in times of crisis.* New York: Springer.

Steblay, N. M. (1987). Helping behavior in rural and urban environments: A meta-analysis. *Psychological Bulletin, 102,* 346–356.

Steele, C. M. (1988). The psychology of self-affirmation: Sustaining the integrity of the self. In L. Berkowitz (Ed.), *Advances in experimental social psychology* (Vol. 21). Orlando, FL: Academic Press.

Steele, C. M. (1997). A threat in the air: How stereotypes shape intellectual identity and performance. *American Psychologist, 52,* 613–629.

Steele, C. M. (2010). *Whistling Vivaldi: And other clues to how stereotypes affect us.* New York: Norton.

Steele, C. M., & Aronson, J. (1995). Stereotype threat and the intellectual test performance of African Americans. *Journal of Personality and Social Psychology, 69,* 797–811.

Steele, C. M., & Josephs, R. A. (1990). Alcohol myopia: Its prized and dangerous effects. *American Psychologist, 45,* 921–933.

Steele, C. M., Southwick, L. L., & Critchlow, B. (1981). Dissonance and alcohol: Drinking your troubles away. *Journal of Personality and Social Psychology, 41,* 831–846.

Steele, C. M., Spencer, S. J., & Aronson, J. (2002). Contending with group image: The psychology of stereotype and social identity threat. In M. P. Zanna (Ed.), *Advances in experimental social psychology,* 34, 379–440. San Diego, CA: Academic Press, Inc.

Steele, C. M., Spencer, S. J., & Lynch, M. (1993). Self-image resilience and dissonance: The role of affirmational resources. *Journal of Personality and Social Psychology, 64,* 885–896.

Steers, M. N., Wickham, R. E., & Acitelli, L. K. (2014). Seeing everyone else's highlight reels: How Facebook usage is linked to depressive symptoms. *Journal of Social and Clinical Psychology, 33,* 701–731.

Stefan, S., & David, D. (2013). Recent developments in the experimental investigation of the illusion of control. A meta-analytic review. *Journal of Applied Social Psychology, 43,* 377–386.

Stegall, A. (2013, August 26). Investigators believe 8-year-old intentionally killed 90-year-old woman. WAFB News. Retrieved from http://www.wafb.com/story/23242078/investigators-believe-8-year-old-intentionally-killed-90-year-old-woman

Stein, A. H., & Friedrich, L. K. (1972). Television content and young children's behavior. In J. P. Murray, E. A. Rubinstein, & G. A. Comstock (Eds.), *Television and social learning.* Washington, DC: Government Printing Office.

Stelter, B. (2008, November 25). Web suicide viewed live and reaction spur a debate. *New York Times.* Retrieved from http://www.nytimes.com

Stelzl, M., Janes, L., & Seligman, C. (2008). Champ or chump: Strategic utilization of dual social identities of others. *European Journal of Social Psychology, 38,* 128–138.

Stenseng, F., Belsky, J., Skalicka, V., & Wichstrøm, L. (2014). Preschool social exclusion, aggression, and cooperation: A longitudinal evaluation of the need-to-belong and the social-reconnection hypotheses. *Personality and Social Psychology Bulletin, 40,* 1637–1647.

Stephan, W. G. (1987). The contact hypothesis in intergroup relations. In C. Hendrick (Ed.), *Group processes and intergroup relations.* Newbury Park, CA: Sage.

Stephan, W. G., Berscheid, E., & Walster, E. (1971). Sexual arousal and heterosexual perception. *Journal of Personality and Social Psychology, 20,* 93–101.

Stephens, N. M., Markus, H. R., & Townsend, S. S. M. (2007). Choice as an act of meaning: The case of social class. *Journal of Personality and Social Psychology, 93,* 814–830.

Stephens-Davidowitz, S. (2014, January 18). Google, tell me. Is my son a genius? *New York Times.* Retrieved from http://www.nytimes.com

Stephens-Davidowitz, S. (2017). *Everybody lies: Big data, new data, and what the internet call tell us about who we really are.* New York: Dey Street.

Sternberg, R. J. (1988). Triangulating love. In R. J. Sternberg & M. L. Barnes (Eds.), *The psychology of love.* New Haven, CT: Yale University Press.

Sternberg, R. J. (1998). *Cupid's arrow: The course of love through time.* New York: Cambridge University Press.

Sternberg, R. J. (2003). A duplex theory of hate and its development and its application to terrorism, massacres, and genocide. *Review of General Psychology, 7,* 299–328.

Sternberg, R. J., & Grajek, S. (1984). The nature of love. *Journal of Personality and Social Psychology, 47,* 312–329.

Stevens, T. M., Aarts, N., & Dewulf, A. (2020). Using emotions to frame issues and identities in conflict: Farmer movements on social media. *Negotiation and Conflict Management Research.* https://doi-org.library.smu.ca/10.1111/ncmr.12177

Stewart-Williams, S. (2007). Altruism among kin vs. nonkin: Effects of cost of help and reciprocal exchange. *Evolution and Human Behavior, 28,* 193–198.

Stice, E., Rohde, P., Butryn, M. L., Shaw, H., & Marti, C. N. (2015). Effectiveness trial of a selective dissonance-based eating disorder prevention program with female college students: Effects at 2- and 3-year follow-up. *Behaviour Research and Therapy, 71,* 20–26.

Stinson, D. A., Cameron, J. J., Wood, J. V., Gaucher, D. G., & Holmes, J. G. (2009). Deconstructing the "reign of error": Interpersonal warmth explains the self-fulfilling prophecy of anticipated acceptance. *Personality and Social Psychology Bulletin, 35,* 1165–1178.

Stix, G. (2008, March). When markets beat the polls. *Scientific American Mind,* 38–45.

Stockdale, L. A., Coyne, S. M., Nelson, D. A., & Padilla-Walker, L. M. (2013). Read anything mean lately? Associations between reading aggression in books and aggressive behavior in adolescents. *Aggressive Behavior, 39,* 493–502.

Stone, A. A., Hedges, S. M., Neale, J. M., & Satin, M. S. (1985). Prospective and cross sectional mood reports offer no evidence of a "blue Monday" phenomenon. *Journal of Personality and Social Psychology, 49,* 129–134.

Stone, A. L., & Glass, C. R. (1986). Cognitive distortion of social feedback in depression. *Journal of Social and Clinical Psychology, 4,* 179–188.

Stone, J. (2000, November 6). Quoted by Sharon Begley, The stereotype trap. *Newsweek.*

Stone, J., Lynch, C. I., Sjomeling, M., & Darley, J. M. (1999). Stereotype threat effects on Black and White athletic performance. *Journal of Personality and Social Psychology, 77,* 1213–1227.

Stone, L. (1977). *The family, sex and marriage in England, 1500–1800.* New York: Harper & Row.

Stone, M. H. (2015). Mass murder, mental illness, and men. *Violence and Gender, 2,* 51–86.

Stoner, J. A. F. (1961). *A comparison of individual and group decisions involving risk.* Unpublished master's thesis, Massachusetts Institute of Technology, Cambridge, MA.

Storms, M. D., & Thomas, G. C. (1977). Reactions to physical closeness. *Journal of Personality and Social Psychology, 35,* 412–418.

Storr, W. (2018, April 25). How scientists invented a test to measure hurt feelings. *The Cut (*https://amp.thecut.com/2018/04/book-excerpt-selfie-by-will-storr.html?__twitter_impression=true).

Stouffer, S. A., Suchman, E. A., DeVinney, L. C., Star, S. A., & Williams, R. M., Jr. (1949). *The American soldier: Adjustment during army life* (Vol. 1.). Princeton, NJ: Princeton University Press.

Stout, J. G., Dasgupta, N., Hunsinger, M., & McManus, M. A. (2011). STEMing the tide: Using ingroup experts to inoculate women's self-concept in science, technology, engineering, and mathematics (STEM). *Journal of Personality and Social Psychology, 100,* 255–270.

Stoverink, A., Umphress, E., Gardner, R., & Miner, K. (2014). Misery loves company: Team dissonance and the influence of supervisor-focused interpersonal justice climate on team cohesiveness. *Journal of Applied Psychology, 99,* 1059–1073.

Stowell, J. R., Oldham, T., & Bennett, D. (2010). Using student response systems ("clickers") to combat conformity and shyness. *Teaching of Psychology, 37,* 135–140.

Strachman, A., & Schimel, J. (2006). Terror management and close relationships: Evidence that mortality salience reduces commitment among partners with different worldviews. *Journal of Social and Personal Relationships, 23*, 965–978.

Strack, F., & Deutsch, R. (2004). Reflective and impulsive determinants of social behavior. *Personality and Social Psychology Review, 8*(3), 220–247.

Strack, F., Martin, L. & Stepper, S. (1988). Inhibiting and facilitating conditions of the human smile: A nonobtrusive test of the facial feedback hypothesis. *Journal of Personality and Social Psychology, 54,* 768–777.

Straus, M. A., & Gelles, R. J. (1980). *Behind closed doors: Violence in the American family.* New York: Anchor/Doubleday.

Streeter, S. A., & McBurney, D. H. (2003). Waist–hip ratio and attractiveness: New evidence and a critique of "a critical test." *Evolution and Human Behavior, 24,* 88–98.

Strick, M., van Baaren, R. B., Holland, R. W., & van Knippenberg, A. (2009). Humor in advertisements enhances product liking by mere association. *Journal of Experimental Psychology: Applied, 15,* 35–45.

Stroebe, W. (2012). The truth about Triplett (1898), but nobody seems to care. *Perspectives on Psychological Science, 7,* 54–57.

Stroebe, W., & Diehl, M. (1994). Productivity loss in idea-generating groups. In W. Stroebe & M. Hewstone (Eds.), *European review of social psychology* (Vol. 5). Chichester: Wiley.

Stroessner, S. J., & Mackie, D. M. (1993). Affect and perceived group variability: Implications for stereotyping and prejudice. In D. M. Mackie & D. L. Hamilton (Eds.), *Affect, cognition, and stereotyping: Interactive processes in group perception.* San Diego, CA: Academic Press.

Strong, S. R. (1978). Social psychological approach to psychotherapy research. In S. L. Garfield & A. E. Bergin (Eds.), *Handbook of psychotherapy and behavior change* (2nd ed.). New York: Wiley.

Stroufe, B., Chaikin, A., Cook, R., & Freeman, V. (1977). The effects of physical attractiveness on honesty: A socially desirable response. *Personality and Social Psychology, 3,* 59–62.

Strube, M. J. (2005). What did Triplett really find? A contemporary analysis of the first experiment in social psychology. *American Journal of Psychology, 118,* 271–286.

Stukas, A. A., Snyder, M., & Clary, E. G. (1999). The effects of "mandatory volunteerism" on intentions to volunteer. *Psychological Science, 10,* 59–64.

Subramanian, A. (2018). Gender and son meta-preference: Is development itself an antidote? Ministry of Finance, Government of India (http://mofapp.nic.in:8080/economicsurvey/pdf/102-118_Chapter_07_ENGLISH_Vol_01_2017-18.pdf).

Suedfeld, P. (2000). Reverberations of the Holocaust fifty years later: Psychology's contributions to understanding persecution and genocide. *Canadian Psychology, 41,* 1–9.

Sugden, N. A., & Marquis, A. R. (2017). Meta-analytic review of the development of face discrimination in infancy: Face race, face gender, infant age, and methodology moderate face discrimination. *Psychological Review, 143,* 1201–1244.

Suls, J., & Tesch, F. (1978). Students' preferences for information about their test performance: A social comparison study. *Journal of Applied Social Psychology, 8,* 189–197.

Summers, G., & Feldman, N. S. (1984). Blaming the victim versus blaming the perpetrator: An attributional analysis of spouse abuse. *Journal of Social and Clinical Psychology, 2,* 339–347.

Sun, C., Bridges, A., Wosnitzer, R., Scharrer, E., & Liberman, R. (2008). A comparison of male and female directors in popular pornography: What happens when women are at the helm? *Psychology of Women Quarterly, 32,* 312–325.

Sundstrom, E., De Meuse, K. P., & Futrell, D. (1990). Work teams: Applications and effectiveness. *American Psychologist, 45,* 120–133.

Sunstein, C. R. (2001). *Republic.com.* Princeton, NJ: Princeton University Press.

Sunstein, C. R. (2007). On the divergent American reactions to terrorism and climate change. *Columbia Law Review, 107,* 503–557.

Sunstein, C. R. (2009). *Going to extremes: How like minds unite and divide.* New York: Oxford University Press.

Sunstein, C. R., & Hastie, R. (2008). *Four failures of deliberating groups.* Economics Working Paper Series, University of Chicago Law School. Retrieved from http://www.law.uchicago.edu

Surowiecki, J. (2004). *The wisdom of crowds.* New York: Doubleday.

Sussman, N. M. (2000). The dynamic nature of cultural identity throughout cultural transitions: Why home is not so sweet. *Personality and Social Psychology Review, 4,* 355–373.

Svenson, O. (1981). Are we all less risky and more skillful than our fellow drivers? *Acta Psychologica, 47,* 143–148.

Swami, V., Chan, F., Wong, V., Furnham, A., & Tovée, M. J. (2008). Weight-based discrimination in occupational hiring and helping behavior. *Journal of Applied Social Psychology, 38,* 968–981.

Swann, W. B., Jr. (1984). Quest for accuracy in person perception: A matter of pragmatics. *Psychological Review, 91,* 457–475.

Swann, W. B., Jr. (1996). *Self-traps: The elusive quest for higher self-esteem.* New York: Freeman.

Swann, W. B., Jr. (1997). The trouble with change: Self-verification and allegiance to the self. *Psychological Science, 8,* 177–180.

Swann, W. B., Jr., Chang-Schneider, C., & Angulo, S. (2007). Self-verification in relationships as an adaptive process. In J. Wood, A. Tesser, & J. Holmes (Eds.), *Self and relationships.* New York: Psychology Press.

Swann, W. B., Jr., & Gill, M. J. (1997). Confidence and accuracy in person perception: Do we know what we think we know about our relationship partners? *Journal of Personality and Social Psychology, 73,* 747–757.

Swann, W. B., Jr., Gómez, Á., Seyle, D. C., Morales, J. F., & Huici, C. (2009). Identity fusion: The interplay of personal and social identities in extreme group behavior. *Journal of Personality and Social Psychology, 96,* 995–1011.

Swann, W. B., Jr., & Pelham, B. (2002, July–September). Who wants out when the going gets good? Psychological investment and preference for self-verifying college roommates. *Self and Identity, 1,* 219–233.

Swann, W. B., Jr., & Predmore, S. C. (1985). Intimates as agents of social support: Sources of consolation or despair? *Journal of Personality and Social Psychology, 49,* 1609–1617.

Swann, W. B., Jr., & Read, S. J. (1981). Acquiring self-knowledge: The search for feedback that fits. *Journal of Personality and Social Psychology, 41,* 1119–1128.

Swann, W. B., Jr., Rentfrow, P. J., & Gosling, S. D. (2003). The precarious couple effect: Verbally inhibited men + critical, disinhibited women = bad chemistry. *Journal of Personality and Social Psychology, 85,* 1095–1106.

Swann, W. B., Jr., Stein-Seroussi, A., & Giesler, R. B. (1992). Why people self-verify. *Journal of Personality and Social Psychology, 62,* 392–401.

Swann, W. B., Jr., Stein-Seroussi, A., & McNulty, S. E. (1992). Outcasts in a white lie society. The enigmatic worlds of people with negative self-conceptions. *Journal of Personality and Social Psychology, 62,* 618–624.

Swann, W. B., Jr., Wenzlaff, R. M., Krull, D. S., & Pelham, B. W. (1991). Seeking truth, reaping despair: Depression, self-verification and selection of relationship partners. *Journal of Abnormal Psychology, 101,* 293–306.

Swanson, J. W. (2016). On thoughts, threats, and throwing the spear. *Schizophrenia Bulletin, 42,* 883–884.

Swap, W. C. (1977). Interpersonal attraction and repeated exposure to rewarders and punishers. *Personality and Social Psychology Bulletin, 3,* 248–251.

Sweeney, J. (1973). An experimental investigation of the free rider problem. *Social Science Research, 2,* 277–292.

Sweeney, P. D., Anderson, K., & Bailey, S. (1986). Attributional style in depression: A meta-analytic review. *Journal of Personality and Social Psychology, 50,* 947–991.

Sweeny, K., Melnyk, D., Miller, W., & Shepperd, J. A. (2010). Information avoidance: Who, what, when, and why. *Review of General Psychology, 14,* 340–353.

Swets, J. A., Dawes, R. M., & Monahan, J. (2000). Psychological science can improve diagnostic decisions. *Psychological Science in the Public Interest, 1,* 1–26.

Swim, J., Borgida, E., Maruyama, G., & Myers, D. G. (1989). Joan McKay vs. John McKay: Do gender stereotypes bias evaluations? *Psychological Bulletin, 105,* 409–429.

Swim, J. K. (1994). Perceived versus meta-analytic effect sizes: An assessment of the accuracy of gender stereotypes. *Journal of Personality and Social Psychology, 66,* 21–36.

Swim, J. K., Aikin, J. K., Hall, W. S., & Hunter, B. A. (1995). Sexism and racism: Old-fashioned and modern prejudices. *Journal of Personality and Social Psychology, 68,* 199–214.

Swim, J. K., & Cohen, L. L. (1997). Overt, covert, and subtle sexism. *Psychology of Women Quarterly, 21,* 103–118.

Swim, J. K., Cohen, L. L., & Hyers, L. L. (1998). Experiencing everyday prejudice and discrimination. In J. K. Swim & C. Stangor (Eds.), *Prejudice: The target's perspective.* San Diego: Academic Press.

Swim, J. K., & Hyers, L. L. (1998). Excuse me—What did you just say?!: Women's public and private reactions to sexist remarks. *Journal of Experimental Social Psychology,* in press.

Swindle, R., Jr., Heller, K., Bescosolido, B., & Kikuzawa, S. (2000). Responses to nervous breakdowns in America over a 40-year period: Mental health policy implications. *American Psychologist, 55,* 740–749.

Syrian Observatory for Human Rights (SOHR). (2018, August). Death toll from Syrian conflict passes half a million. www.syriahr.com/en/?p=94610

Szymkow, A., Chandler, J., IJzerman, H., Parzuchowski, M., & Wojciszke, B. (2013). Warmer hearts, warmer rooms: How positive communal traits increase estimates of ambient temperature. *Social Psychology, 44,* 167–176.

Taborsky-Barba, S., Tomassetti, S., Nussbaum, A. D., & Cohen, G. L. (2013). Deflecting the trajectory and changing the narrative: How self-affirmation affects academic performance and motivation under identity threat. *Journal of Personality and Social Psychology, 104,* 591–618.

Tafarodi, R. W., Lo, C., Yamaguchi, S., Lee, W. W-S., & Katsura, H. (2004). The inner self in three countries. *Journal of Cross-Cultural Psychology, 35,* 97–117.

Tajfel, H. (1970, November). Experiments in intergroup discrimination. *Scientific American,* 96–102.

Tajfel, H. (1981). *Human groups and social categories: Studies in social psychology.* London: Cambridge University Press.

Tajfel, H. (1982). Social psychology of intergroup relations. *Annual Review of Psychology, 33,* 1–39.

Tajfel, H., & Billig, M. (1974). Familiarity and categorization in intergroup behavior. *Journal of Experimental Social Psychology, 10,* 159–170.

Takahashi, K., Mizuno, K., Sasaki, A. T., Wada, Y., Tanaka, M., Ishii, A., Tajima, K., Tsuyuguchi, N., Watanabe, K., Zeki, S., & Watanabe, Y. (2015). Imaging the passionate stage of romantic love by dopamine dynamics. *Frontiers In Human Neuroscience, 9.*

Takooshian, H., & Bodinger, H. (1982). Bystander indifference to street crime. In L. Savitz & N. Johnston (Eds.), *Contemporary criminology.* New York: Wiley.

Talhelm, T., Zhang, X., Oishi, S., Shimin, C., Duan, D., Lan, X., & Kitayama, S. (2014). Large-scale psychological differences within China explained by rice versus wheat agriculture. *Science, 344,* 603–608.

Tandoc, E., Ferruci, P., & Duffy, M. (2015). Facebook use, envy, and depression among college students: Is facebooking depressing*?Computers in Human Behavior, 43,* 139-146. https://doi.org/10.1016/j.chb.2014.10.053

Tang, S-H., & Hall, V. C. (1995). The overjustification effect: A meta-analysis. *Applied Cognitive Psychology, 9,* 365–404.

Tanner, R. J., Ferraro, R., Chartrand, T. L., Bettman, J. R., & van Baaren, R. (2008). Of chameleons and consumption: The impact of mimicry on choice and preferences. *Journal of Consumer Research, 34,* 754–766.

Tarmann, A. (2002, May/June). Out of the closet and onto the Census long form. *Population Today, 30,* 1, 6.

Tarrant, M., Dazeley, S., & Cottom, T. (2009). Social categorization and empathy for outgroup members. *British Journal of Social Psychology, 48,* 427–446.

Taub, A. (2016, March 1). The rise of American authoritarianism. *Vox.* (www.vox.com/2016/3/1/11127424/trump-authoritarianism).

Taubes, G. (1992). Violence epidemiologists tests of hazards of gun ownership. *Science, 258,* 213–215.

Tavris, C., & Offir, C. (1977). *The longest war: Sex differences in perspective.* New York: Harcourt Brace Jovanovich.

Taylor, D. A., Gould, R. J., & Brounstein, P. J. (1981). Effects of personalistic self-disclosure. *Personality and Social Psychology Bulletin, 7,* 487–492.

Taylor, D. G., Sheatsley, P. B., & Greeley, A. M. (1978). Attitudes toward racial integration. *Scientific American, 238*(6), 42–49.

Taylor, D. M., & Doria, J. R. (1981). Self-serving and group-serving bias in attribution. *Journal of Social Psychology, 113,* 201–211.

Taylor, D. M., Wright, S. C., Moghaddam, F. M., & Lalonde, R. N. (1990). The personal/group discrimination discrepancy: Perceiving my group, but not myself, to be a target for discrimination. *Personality and Social Psychology Bulletin, 16,* 254–262.

Taylor, L. S., Fiore, A. T., Mendelsohn, G. A., & Cheshire, C. (2011). "Out of my league": A real-world test of the matching hypothesis. *Personality and Social Psychology Bulletin, 37,* 942–954.

Taylor, S. E. (1981). A categorization approach to stereotyping. In D. L. Hamilton (Ed.), *Cognitive processes in stereotyping and intergroup behavior.* Hillsdale, NJ: Erlbaum.

Taylor, S. E., Crocker, J., Fiske, S. T., Sprinzen, M., & Winkler, J. D. (1979). The generalizability of salience effects. *Journal of Personality and Social Psychology, 37,* 357–368.

Taylor, S. E., & Fiske, S. T. (1978). Salience, attention, and attribution: Top of the head phenomena. In L. Berkowitz (Ed.), *Advances in experimental social psychology* (Vol. 11). New York: Academic Press.

Taylor, S. E., Lerner, J. S., Sherman, D. K., Sage, R. M., & McDowell, N. K. (2003). Are self-enhancing cognitions associated with healthy or unhealthy biological profiles? *Journal of Personality and Social Psychology, 85,* 605.

Taylor, S. E., Saphire-Bernstein, S., & Seeman, T. E. (2010). Are plasma oxytocin in women and plasma vasopressin in men biomarkers of distressed pair-bond relationships? *Psychological Science, 21,* 3–7.

Taylor, S. P., & Chermack, S. T. (1993). Alcohol, drugs and human physical aggression. *Journal of Studies on Alcohol,* Supplement No. 11, 78–88.

Tedeschi, J. T., Nesler, M., & Taylor, E. (1987). *Misattribution and the bogus pipeline: A test of dissonance and impression management theories.* Paper presented at the American Psychological Association convention.

Teger, A. I. (1980). *Too much invested to quit.* New York: Pergamon Press.

Teigen, K. H. (1986). Old truths or fresh insights? A study of students' evaluations of proverbs. *British Journal of Social Psychology, 25,* 43–50.

Teigen, K. H., Evensen, P. C., Samoilow, D. K., & Vatne, K. B. (1999). Good luck and bad luck: How to tell the difference. *European Journal of Social Psychology, 29,* 981–1010.

Telch, M. J., Killen, J. D., McAlister, A. L., Perry, C. L., & Maccoby, N. (1981). *Long-term follow-up of a pilot project on smoking prevention with adolescents.* Paper presented at the American Psychological Association convention.

Tennen, H., & Affleck, G. (1987). The costs and benefits of optimistic explanations and dispositional optimism. *Journal of Personality, 55,* 377–393.

Tennov, D. (1979). *Love and limerence: The experience of being in love.* New York: Stein and Day, 22.

Tesser, A. (1988). Toward a self-evaluation maintenance model of social behavior. In L. Berkowitz (Ed.), *Advances in experimental social psychology* (Vol. 21). San Diego, CA: Academic Press.

Tesser, A., Martin, L., & Mendolia, M. (1995). The impact of thought on attitude extremity and attitude-behavior consistency. In R. E. Petty and J. A Krosnick (Eds.), *Attitude strength: Antecedents and consequences.* Hillsdale, NJ: Erlbaum.

Tesser, A., Millar, M., & Moore, J. (1988). Some affective consequences of social comparison and reflection processes: The pain and pleasure of being close. *Journal of Personality and Social Psychology, 54,* 49–61.

Tesser, A., Rosen, S., & Conlee, M. C. (1972). News valence and available recipient as determinants of news transmission. *Sociometry, 35,* 619–628.

Tetlock, P. E. (1983). Accountability and complexity of thought. *Journal of Personality and Social Psychology, 45,* 74–83.

Tetlock, P. E. (1985). Integrative complexity of American and Soviet foreign policy rhetoric: A time-series analysis. *Journal of Personality and Social Psychology, 49,* 1565–1585.

Tetlock, P. E. (1988). Monitoring the integrative complexity of American and Soviet policy rhetoric: What can be learned? *Journal of Social Issues, 44,* 101–131.

Tetlock, P. E. (1998). Close-call counterfactuals and belief-system defenses: I was not almost wrong but I was almost right. *Journal of Personality and Social Psychology, 75,* 639–652.

Tetlock, P. E. (1999). Theory-driven reasoning about plausible pasts and probable futures in world politics: Are we prisoners of our preconceptions? *American Journal of Political Science, 43,* 335–366.

Tetlock, P. E. (2005). *Expert political judgment: How good is it? How can we know?* Princeton, NJ: Princeton University Press.

Tetlock, P. E. (2007). Psychology and politics: The challenges of integrating levels of analysis in social science. In E. T. Higgins & A. Kruglanski (Eds.), *Social psychology: Handbook of basic principles.* New York: Guilford.

Tetlock, P. E., Peterson, R. S., McGuire, C., Chang, S., & Feld, P. (1992). Assessing political group dynamics: A test of the groupthink model. *Journal of Personality and Social Psychology, 63,* 403–425.

t'Hart, P. (1998). Preventing groupthink revisited: Evaluating and reforming groups in government. *Organizational Behavior and Human Decision Processes, 73,* 306–326.

Thelwall, M. (2008). Social networks, gender and friending: An analysis of MySpace member profiles. *Journal of the American Society for Information Science and Technology, 59,* 1321–1330.

Thomas, G. C., & Batson, C. D. (1981). Effect of helping under normative pressure on self-perceived altruism. *Social Psychology Quarterly, 44,* 127–131.

Thomas, G. C., Batson, C. D., & Coke, J. S. (1981). Do Good Samaritans discourage helpfulness? Self-perceived altruism after exposure to highly helpful others. *Journal of Personality and Social Psychology, 40,* 194–200.

Thompson, L. (1990). An examination of naive and experienced negotiators. *Journal of Personality and Social Psychology, 59,* 82–90.

Thompson, L. (1998). *The mind and heart of the negotiator.* Upper Saddle River, NJ: Prentice-Hall.

Thompson, L., Valley, K. L., & Kramer, R. M. (1995). The bittersweet feeling of success: An examination of social perception in negotiation. *Journal of Experimental Social Psychology, 31,* 467–492.

Thompson, L. L., & Crocker, J. (1985). *Prejudice following threat to the self-concept. Effects of performance expectations and attributions.* Unpublished manuscript, Northwestern University, Evanston, IL.

Thompson, W. C., Cowan, C. L., & Rosenhan, D. L. (1980). Focus of attention mediates the impact of negative affect on altruism. *Journal of Personality and Social Psychology, 38,* 291–300.

Thornton, B., & Maurice, J. (1997). Physique contrast effect: Adverse impact of idealized body images for women. *Sex Roles, 37,* 433–439.

Tice, D. M., Butler, J. L., Muraven, M. B., & Stillwell, A. M. (1995). When modesty prevails: Differential favorability of self-presentation to friends and strangers. *Journal of Personality and Social Psychology, 69,* 1120–1138.

Tidwell, N. D., Eastwick, P. W., & Finkel, E. J. (2013). Perceived, not actual, similarity predicts initial attraction in a live romantic context: Evidence from the speed-dating paradigm. *Personal Relationships, 20,* 199–215.

Tiihonen, J., Rautiainen, M., Ollila, H. M., Repo-Tiihonen, E., Virkkunen, M., Palotie, A., Pietiläinen, O., Kristiansson,

K., Joukamaa, M., Lauerma, H., Saarela, J., Tyni, S., Vartiainen, H., Paananen, J., Goldman, D., & Paunio, T. (2015). Genetic background of extreme violent behavior. *Molecular Psychiatry, 20,* 786–792.

Tilcsik, A. (2011). Pride and prejudice: Employment discrimination against openly gay men in the United States. *American Journal of Sociology, 117,* 586–626.

Timmerman, T. A. (2007). "It was a thought pitch": Personal, situational, and target influences on hit-by-pitch events across time. *Journal of Applied Psychology, 92,* 876–884.

Tindale, R. S., Davis, J. H., Vollrath, D. A., Nagao, D. H., & Hinsz, V. B. (1990). Asymmetrical social influence in freely interacting groups: A test of three models. *Journal of Personality and Social Psychology, 58,* 438–449.

Tintoré, M. (2019). Introducing a model of transformational prosocial leadership. *Journal of Leadership Studies.* https://doi-org.library.smu.ca/10.1002/jls.21664

Todd, A. R., Bodenhausen, G. V., Richeson, J. A., & Galinsky, A. D. (2011). Perspective taking combats automatic expressions of racial bias. *Journal of Personality and Social Psychology, 100,* 1027–1042.

Todorov, A., Mandisodza, A. N., Goren, A., & Hall, C. C. (2005). Inferences of competence from faces predict election outcomes. *Science, 308,* 1623–1626.

Toelch, U., & Dolan, R. J. (2015). Informational and normative influences in conformity from a neurocomputational perspective. *Trends in cognitive sciences, 19*(10), 579–589.

Tomasello, M. (2009). *Why we cooperate.* Boston: MIT Press.

Toner, K., Leary, M. R., Asher, M. W., & Jongman-Sereno, K. (2013). Feeling superior is a bipartisan issue: Extremity (not direction) of political views predicts perceived belief superiority. *Psychological Science, 24,* 2454–2462.

Toppo, G. (2018). Time to dismiss the Stanford Prison Experiment? *Inside Higher Ed.* Retrieved from https://www.insidehighered.com/news/2018/06/20/new-stanford-prison-experiment-revelations-question-findings on December 23, 2019.

Tormala, Z. L., Briñol, P., & Petty, R. E. (2006). When credibility attacks: The reverse impact of source credibility on persuasion. *Journal of Experimental Social Psychology, 42,* 684–691.

Tormala, Z. L., & Petty, R. E. (2002). What doesn't kill me makes me stronger: The effects of resisting persuasion on attitude change. *Journal of Personality and Social Psychology, 83,* 1298–1313.

Toronto News. (1977, July 26).

Totterdell, P., Kellett, S., Briner, R. B., & Teuchmann, K. (1998). Evidence of mood linkage in work groups. *Journal of Personality and Social Psychology, 74,* 1504–1515.

Towles-Schwen, T., & Fazio, R. H. (2006). Automatically activated racial attitudes as predictors of the success of interracial roommate relationships. *Journal of Experimental Social Psychology, 42,* 698–705.

Trail, T. E., Shelton, J. N., & West, T. V. (2009). Interracial roommate relationships: Negotiating daily interactions. *Personality and Social Psychology Bulletin, 35,* 671–684.

Trautwein, U., & Lüdtke, O. (2006). Self-esteem, academic self-concept, and achievement: How the learning environment moderates the dynamics of self-concept. *Journal of Personality and Social Psychology, 90,* 334–349.

Travis, L. E. (1925). The effect of a small audience upon eye-hand coordination. *Journal of Abnormal and Social Psychology, 20,* 142–146.

Trawalter, S., Todd, A. R., Baird, A. A., & Richeson, J. A. (2008). Attending to threat: Race-based patterns of selective attention. *Journal of Experimental Social Psychology, 44,* 1322–1327.

Tredoux, C., & Finchilescu, G. (2010). Mediators of the contact-prejudice relation amongst South African students on four university campuses. *Journal of Social Issues, 66,* 289–308.

Trewin, D. (2001). *Australian social trends 2001.* Canberra: Australian Bureau of Statistics.

Triandis, H. C. (1982). Incongruence between intentions and behavior: A review. Paper presented at the American Psychological Association convention.

Triandis, H. C. (1994). *Culture and social behavior.* New York: McGraw-Hill.

Triandis, H. C. (2000). Culture and conflict. *International Journal of Psychology, 55,* 145–152.

Triandis, H. C., Bontempo, R., Villareal, M. J., Asai, M., & Lucca, N. (1988). Individualism and collectivism: Cross-cultural perspectives on self-ingroup relationships. *Journal of Personality and Social Psychology, 54,* 323–338.

Triplett, N. (1898). The dynamogenic factors in pacemaking and competition. *American Journal of Psychology, 9,* 507–533.

Trolier, T. K., & Hamilton, D. L. (1986). Variables influencing judgments of correlational relations. *Journal of Personality and Social Psychology, 50,* 879–888.

Tromholt, M. (2016). The Facebook experiment: Quitting Facebook leads to higher levels of well-being. *Cyberpsychology, Behavior, and Social Networking, 19,* 661–666.

Tropp, L. R., & Pettigrew, T. F. (2005a). Differential relationships between intergroup contact and affective and cognitive dimensions of prejudice. *Personality and Social Psychology Bulletin, 31,* 1145–1158.

Tropp, L. R., & Pettigrew, T. F. (2005b). Relationships between intergroup contact and prejudice among minority and majority status groups. *Psychological Science, 16,* 951–957.

Trost, M. R., Maass, A., & Kenrick, D. T. (1992). Minority influence: Personal relevance biases cognitive processes and reverses private acceptance. *Journal of Experimental Social Psychology, 28,* 234–254.

Truth and Reconciliation Commission of Canada (2015). *Honouring the Truth, Reconciling for the Future Summary of the Final Report of the Truth and Reconciliation Commission of Canada.*

Trzesniewski, K. H., & Donnellan, M. B. (2010). Rethinking "Generation Me": A study of cohort effects from 1976–2006. *Perspectives in Psychological Science, 5,* 58–75.

Trzesniewski, K. H., Donnellan, M. B., Moffitt, T. E., Robins, R. W., Poulton, R., & Caspi, A. (2006). Low self-esteem during adolescence predicts poor health, criminal behavior, and limited economic prospects during adulthood. *Developmental Psychology, 42,* 381–390.

Tsang, J-A. (2002). Moral rationalization and the integration of situational factors and psychological processes in immoral behavior. *Review of General Psychology, 6,* 25–50.

Turner, C. W., Hesse, B. W., & Peterson-Lewis, S. (1986). Naturalistic studies of the long-term effects of television violence. *Journal of Social Issues, 42*(3), 51–74.

Turner, J. C. (1981). The experimental social psychology of intergroup behaviour. In J. Turner & H. Giles (Eds.), *Intergroup behaviour.* Oxford, England: Blackwell.

Turner, J. C. (1987). *Rediscovering the social group: A self-categorization theory.* New York: Basil Blackwell.

Turner, J. C. (2000). Social identity. In A. E. Kazdin (Ed.), *Encyclopedia of Psychology* (Vol. 7). Washington, DC: American Psychological Association.

Turner, M. E., & Pratkanis, A. R. (1993). Effects of preferential and meritorious selection on performance: An examination of intuitive and self-handicapping perspectives. *Personality and Social Psychology Bulletin, 19,* 47–58.

Turner, M. E., & Pratkanis, A. R. (1994). Social identity maintenance prescriptions for preventing groupthink: Reducing identity protection and enhancing intellectual conflict. *International Journal of Conflict Management, 5,* 254–270.

Turner, M. E., & Pratkanis, A. R. (1997). Mitigating groupthink by stimulating constructive conflict. In C. K. W. De Dreu & E. Van de Vliert (Eds.), *Using conflict in organizations.* London: Sage.

Turner, M. E., Pratkanis, A. R., Probasco, P., & Leve, C. (1992). Threat cohesion, and group effectiveness: Testing a social identity maintenance perspective on groupthink. *Journal of Personality and Social Psychology, 63,* 781–796.

Turner, N., Barling, J., Epitropaki, O., Butcher, V., & Milner, C. (2002). Transformational leadership and moral reasoning. *Journal of Applied Psychology, 87,* 304.

Turner, R. N., & Crisp, R. J. (2010). Imagining intergroup contact reduces implicit prejudice. *British Journal of Social Psychology, 49,* 129–142.

Turner, R. N., Hewstone, M., & Voci, A. (2007). Reducing explicit and implicit outgroup prejudice via direct and extended contact: The mediating role of self-disclosure and intergroup anxiety. *Journal of Personality and Social Psychology, 93,* 369–388.

Turner, R. N., Hewstone, M., Voci, A., Paolini, S., & Christ, O. (2007). Reducing prejudice via direct and extended cross-group friendship. *European Review of Social Psychology, 18,* 212–255.

Turner, R. N., Hewstone, M., Voci, A., & Vonofakou, C. (2008). A test of the extended intergroup contact hypothesis: The mediating role of intergroup anxiety, perceived ingroup and outgroup norms, and inclusion of the outgroup in the self. *Journal of Personality and Social Psychology, 95,* 843–860.

TV Guide. (1977, January 26), 5–10.

Tversky, A., & Kahneman, D. (1973). Availability: A heuristic for judging frequency and probability. *Cognitive Psychology, 5,* 207–302.

Tversky, A., & Kahneman, D. (1974). Judgment under uncertainty: Heuristics and biases. *Science, 185,* 1123–1131.

Tversky, A., & Kahneman, D. (1983). Extensional versus intuitive reasoning: The conjunction fallacy in probability judgment. *Psychological Review, 90,* 293–315.

Twenge, J. M. (2006). *Generation Me.* New York: Free Press.

Twenge, J. M. (2017). *iGen: Why today's super-connected kids are growing up less rebellious, more tolerant, less happy—and completely unprepared for adulthood.* New York: Atria Books.

Twenge, J. M., Baumeister, R. F., Tice, D. M., & Stucke, T. S. (2001). If you can't join them, beat them: Effects of social exclusion on aggressive behavior. *Journal of Personality and Social Psychology, 81,* 1058–1069.

Twenge, J. M., & Campbell, W. K. (2008). Increases in positive self-views among high school students: Birth cohort changes in anticipated performance, self-satisfaction, self-liking, and self-competence. *Psychological Science, 19,* 1082–1086.

Twenge, J. M., Campbell, W. K., & Gentile, B. (2012). Generational increases in agentic self-evaluations among American college students, 1966–2009. *Self and Identity, 11,* 409–427.

Twenge, J. M., Campbell, W. K., & Gentile, B. (2013). Changes in pronoun use in American books and the rise of individualism, 1960–2008. *Journal of Cross-Cultural Psychology, 44,* 406–415.

Twenge, J. M., Catanese, K. R., & Baumeister, R. F. (2002). Social exclusion causes self-defeating behavior. *Journal of Personality and Social Psychology, 83,* 606–615.

Twenge, J. M., Catanese, K. R., & Baumeister, R. F. (2003). Social exclusion and the deconstructed state: Time perception, meaninglessness, lethargy, lack of emotion, and self-awareness. *Journal of Personality and Social Psychology, 85,* 409–423.

Twenge, J. M., & Foster, J. D. (2008). Mapping the scale of the narcissism epidemic: Increases in narcissism 2002–2007 within ethnic groups. *Journal of Research in Personality, 42,* 1619–1622.

Twenge, J. M., Honeycutt, N., Prislin, R., & Sherman, R. A. (2016). More polarized but more Independent: Political party identification and ideological self-categorization among U.S. adults, college students, and late adolescents, 1970–2015. *Personality and Social Psychology Bulletin, 42,* 1364–1383.

Twenge, J. M., Konrath, S., Foster, J. D., Campbell, W. K., & Bushman, B. J. (2008). Egos inflating over time: A cross-temporal meta-analysis of the Narcissistic Personality Inventory. *Journal of Personality, 76,* 875–902.

Twenge, J. M., Zhang, L., Catanese, K. R., Dolan-Pascoe, B., Lyche, L. F., & Baumeister, R. F. (2007). Replenishing connectedness: Reminders of social activity reduce aggression after social exclusion. *British Journal of Social Psychology, 46,* 205–224.

Tyler, T. R., & Lind, E. A. (1990). Intrinsic versus community-based justice models: When does group membership matter? *Journal of Social Issues, 46,* 83–94.

Tyler, T. R., Rasinski, K. A., & Spodick, N. (1985). Influence of voice on satisfaction with leaders: Exploring the meaning of process control. *Journal of Personality and Social Psychology, 48,* 72–81.

Tzeng, M. (1992). The effects of socioeconomic heterogamy and changes on marital dissolution for first marriages. *Journal of Marriage and the Family, 54,* 609–619.

Uleman, J. S. (1989). A framework for thinking intentionally about unintended thoughts. In J. S. Uleman & J. A. Bargh (Eds.), *Unintended thought: The limits of awareness, intention, and control.* New York: Guilford.

Unger, R. K. (1979, April). *Whom does helping help?* Paper presented at the Eastern Psychological Association convention.

Unger, R. K. (1985). Epistemological consistency and its scientific implications. *American Psychologist, 40,* 1413–1414.

United Nations (UN). (1991). *The world's women 1970–1990: Trends and statistics.* New York: United Nations.

United Nations (UN). (2006). *Ending violence against women: From words to action.* Study of the Secretary-General. New York: United Nations. Retrieved from http://www.un.org

United Nations (UN). (2011, November 17). *Discriminatory laws and practices and acts of violence against individuals based on their sexual orientation and gender identity.* Report of the United Nations High Commissioner for Human Rights.

United Nations (UN). (2015, November 23). *The human cost of weather related disasters, 1995–2015.* Geneva: The United Nations Office for Disaster Risk Reduction (www.unisdr.org).

United Nations (UN). (2017, June 21). *World population prospects: The 2017 revision.* Bureau of Economic and Social Affairs (https://esa.un.org/unpd/wpp/DataQuery).

Unkelbach, C., Forgas, J. P., & Denson, T. F. (2008). The turban effect: The influence of Muslim headgear and induced affect on aggressive responses in the shooter bias paradigm. *Journal of Experimental Social Psychology, 44,* 1409–1413.

Unkelbach, C., & Memmert, D. (2010). Crowd noise as a cue in referee decisions contributes to the home advantage. *Journal of Sport & Exercise Psychology, 32,* 483–498.

Unsworth, N., Redick, T. S., McMillan, B. D., Hambrick, D. Z., Kane, M. J., & Engle, R. W. (2015). Is playing video games related to cognitive abilities? *Psychological Science, 26,* 759–774.

Urbina, I. (2010, May 29). Documents show early worries about safety of rig. *New York Times* (www.nytimes.com).

Vaillant, G. E. (1977). *Adaptation to life.* Boston: Little, Brown.

Vaillant, G. E. (1997). *Report on distress and longevity.* Paper presented to the American Psychiatric Association convention.

Vala, J., Pereira, C., Oliveira Lima, M. E., & Leyens, J. (2012). Intergroup time bias and racialized social relations. *Personality and Social Psychology Bulletin, 38,* 491–504.

Valcour, M. (2007). Work-based resources as moderators of the relationship between work hours and satisfaction with work-family balance. *Journal of Applied Psychology, 92,* 1512–1523.

Valdesolo, P., & DeSteno, D. (2007). Moral hypocrisy: Social groups and the flexibility of virtue. *Psychological Science, 18,* 689–690.

Valdesolo, P., & DeSteno, D. (2008). The duality of virtue: Deconstructing the moral hypocrite. *Journal of Experimental Social Psychology, 44,* 1334–1338.

Vallone, R. P., Griffin, D. W., Lin, S., & Ross, L. (1990). Overconfident prediction of future actions and outcomes by self and others. *Journal of Personality and Social Psychology, 58,* 582–592.

Vallone, R. P., Ross, L., & Lepper, M. R. (1985). The hostile media phenomenon: Biased perception and perceptions of media bias in coverage of the "Beirut Massacre." *Journal of Personality and Social Psychology, 49,* 577–585.

van Baaren, R. B., Holland, R. W., Karremans, R. W., & van Knippenberg, A. (2003). *Mimicry and interpersonal closeness.* Unpublished manuscript, University of Nijmegen, Nijmegen, Netherlands.

van Baaren, R. B., Holland, R. W., Kawakami, K., & van Knippenberg, A. (2004). Mimicry and prosocial behavior. *Psychological Science, 15,* 71.

van Baaren, R. B., Holland, R. W., Steenaert, B., & van Knippenberg, A. (2003). Mimicry for money: Behavioral consequences of imitation. *Journal of Experimental Social Psychology, 39,* 393–398.

van de Ven, N. (2011). Supporters are not necessary for the home advantage: Evidence from same-stadium derbies and games without an audience. *Journal of Applied Social Psychology, 41*(12), 2785–2792.

Van de Vyver, J., Houston, D. M., Abrams, D., & Vasiljevic, M. (2016). Boosting belligerence: How the July 7, 2005, London bombings affected liberals' moral foundations and prejudice. *Psychological Science, 27,* 169–177.

Van Den Bergh, B., Schmitt, J., & Warlop, L. (2011). Embodied myopia. *Journal of Marketing Research, 48,* 1033–44.

van der Plight, J., Eise, J. R., & Spears, R. (1987). Comparative judgments and preferences: The influence of the number of response alternatives. *British Journal of Social Psychology, 26,* 269–280.

van der Velde, S. W., Stapel, D. A., & Gordijn, E. H. (2010). Imitation of emotion: When meaning leads to aversion. *European Journal of Social Psychology, 40*(3), 536–542.

van Dijk, W. W., Finkenauer, C., & Pollmann, M. (2008). The misprediction of emotions in track athletics: Is experience the teacher of all things? *Basic and Applied Social Psychology, 30,* 369–376.

van Dijk, W. W., Ouwerkerk, J. W., van Koningsbruggen, G. M., & Wesseling, Y. M. (2012). "So you wanna be a pop star?": Schadenfreude following another's misfortune on TV. *Basic & Applied Social Psychology, 34,* 168–174.

Van Knippenberg, D., & Wilke, H. (1992). Prototypicality of arguments and conformity to ingroup norms. *European Journal of Social Psychology, 22,* 141–155.

Van Lange, P. A. M., & Visser, K. (1999). Locomotion in social dilemmas: How people adapt to cooperative, tit-for-tat, and noncooperative partners. *Journal of Personality and Social Psychology, 77,* 762–773.

van Prooijen, J., Krouwel, A. P. M., Boiten, M., & Eendebak, L. (2015). Fear among the extremes: How political ideology predicts negative emotions and outgroup derogation. *Personality and Social Psychology Bulletin, 41,* 485–497.

van Straaten, I., Engels, R. C. M. E., Finkenauer, C., & Holland, R. W. (2009). Meeting your match: How attractiveness similarity affects approach behavior in mixed-sex dyads. *Personality and Social Psychology Bulletin, 35,* 685–697.

van Veluw, S. J., & Chance, S. A. (2014). Differentiating between self and others: An ALE meta-analysis of fMRI studies of self-recognition and theory of mind. *Brain Imaging and Behavior, 8,* 24–38.

Van Vugt, M., Van Lange, P. A. M., & Meertens, R. M. (1996). Commuting by car or public transportation? A social dilemma analysis of travel mode judgements. *European Journal of Social Psychology, 26,* 373–395.

Van Yperen, N. W., & Buunk, B. P. (1990). A longitudinal study of equity and satisfaction in intimate relationships. *European Journal of Social Psychology, 20,* 287–309.

VanDellen, M. R., Campbell, W. K., Hoyle, R. H., & Bradfield, E. K. (2011). Compensating, resisting, and breaking: A meta-analytic examination of reactions to self-esteem threat. *Personality and Social Psychology Review, 15,* 51–74.

Vandello, J. A., Cohen, D., & Ransom, S. (2008). U.S. southern and northern differences in perceptions of norms about aggression: Mechanisms for the perpetuation of a culture of honor. *Journal of Cross-Cultural Psychology, 39,* 162–177.

Vanderslice, V. J., Rice, R. W., & Julian, J. W. (1987). The effects of participation in decision-making on worker satisfaction and productivity: An organizational simulation. *Journal of Applied Social Psychology, 17,* 158–170.

Vargas, R. A. (2009, July 6). "City of Heroes" character "Twixt" becomes game's most hated outcast courtesy of Loyola professor. *The Times-Picayune.* Retrieved from http://www.nola.com

Varnum, M. E. W., & Kitayama, S. (2011). What's in a name? Popular names are less common on frontiers. *Psychological Science, 22,* 176–183.

Vasquez, E. A., Denson, T. F., Pedersen, W. C., Stenstrom, D. M., & Miller, N. (2005). The moderating effect of trigger intensity on triggered displaced aggression. *Journal of Experimental Social Psychology, 41,* 61.

Vaughan, K. B., & Lanzetta, J. T. (1981). The effect of modification of expressive displays on vicarious emotional arousal. *Journal of Experimental Social Psychology, 17,* 16–30.

Vazire, S., & Mehl, M. R. (2008). Knowing me, knowing you: The accuracy and unique predictive validity of self-ratings and other-ratings of daily behavior. *Journal of Personality and Social Psychology, 95,* 1202–1216.

Verkuyten, M., & Yildiz, A. A. (2007). National (dis)identification and ethnic and religious identity: A study among Turkish-Dutch Muslims. *Personality and Social Psychology, 33,* 1448–1462.

Verplanken, B. (1991). Persuasive communication of risk information: A test of cue versus message processing effects in a field experiment. *Personality and Social Psychology Bulletin, 17,* 188–193.

Vescio, T. K., Gervais, S. J., Snyder, M., & Hoover, A. (2005). Power and the creation of patronizing environments: The stereotype-based behaviors of the powerful and their effects on female performance in masculine domains. *Journal of Personality and Social Psychology, 88,* 658–672.

Veysey, B. M., & Messner, S. F. (1999). Further testing of social disorganization theory: An elaboration of Sampson and Groves's "Community structure and crime." *Journal of Research in Crime and Delinquency, 36,* 156–174.

Vezzali, L., Stathi, S., Giovannini, D., Capozza, D., & Trifiletti, E. (2014). The greatest magic of Harry Potter: Reducing prejudice. *Journal of Applied Social Psychology,* in press.

Visher, C. A. (1987). Juror decision making: The importance of evidence. *Law and Human Behavior, 11,* 1–17.

Visintainer, M. A., & Seligman, M. E. P. (1985). *Tumor rejection and early experience of uncontrollable shock in the rat.* Unpublished manuscript, University of Pennsylvania, Philadelphia, PA. See also, M. A. Visintainer et al. (1982). Tumor rejection in rats after inescapable versus escapable shock. *Science, 216,* 437–439.

Visser, P. S., & Krosnick, J. A. (1998). Development of attitude strength over the life cycle: Surge and decline. *Journal of Personality and Social Psychology, 75,* 1389.

Visser, P. S., & Mirabile, R. R. (2004). Attitudes in the social context: The impact of social network composition on individual-level attitude strength. *Journal of Personality and Social Psychology, 87,* 779–795.

Vitelli, R. (1988). The crisis issue assessed: An empirical analysis. *Basic and Applied Social Psychology, 9,* 301–309.

Vogel, T., Kutzner, F., Fiedler, K., & Freytag, P. (2010). Exploiting attractiveness in persuasion: Senders' implicit theories about receivers' processing motivation. *Personality and Social Psychology Bulletin, 36,* 830–842.

Vohs, K. D., Baumeister, R. F., & Ciarocco, N. J. (2005). Self-regulation and self-presentation: Regulatory resource depletion impairs impression management and effortful self-presentation depletes regulatory resources. *Journal of Personality and Social Psychology, 88,* 632.

Vohs, K. D., Baumeister, R. F., Schmeichel, B. J., Twenge, J. M., Nelson, N. M., & Tice, D. M. (2008). Making choices impairs subsequent self-control: A limited-resource account of decision making, self-regulation, and active initiative. *Journal of Personality and Social Psychology, 94,* 883–898.

Vollhardt, J. R. (2010). Enhanced external and culturally sensitive attributions after extended intercultural contact. *British Journal of Social Psychology, 49,* 363–383.

von Hippel, F. N. (2011, March 22). It could happen here. *New York Times.* Retrieved from http://www.nytimes.com

von Hippel, W., Brener, L., & von Hippel, C. (2008). Implicit prejudice toward injecting drug users predicts intentions to change jobs among drug and alcohol nurses. *Psychological Science, 19,* 7–12.

von Hippel, W., Silver, L. A., & Lynch, M. E. (2000). Stereotyping against your will: The role of inhibitory ability in stereotyping and prejudice among the elderly. *Personality and Social Psychology Bulletin, 26,* 523–532.

Vorauer, J. D. (2001). The other side of the story: Transparency estimation in social interaction. In G. Moskowitz (Ed.), *Cognitive social psychology: The Princeton symposium on the legacy and future of social cognition.* Mahwah, NJ: Erlbaum.

Vorauer, J. D. (2005). Miscommunications surrounding efforts to reach out across group boundaries. *Personality and Social Psychology Bulletin, 31,* 1653–1664.

Vorauer, J. D., Hunter, A. J., Main, K. J., & Roy, S. A. (2000). Meta-stereotype activation: Evidence from indirect measures for specific evaluative concerns experienced by members of dominant groups in intergroup interaction. *Journal of Personality and Social Psychology, 78,* 690–707.

Vorauer, J. D., Main, K. J., & O'Connell, G. B. (1998). How do individuals expect to be viewed by members of lower status groups? Content and implications of meta-stereotypes. *Journal of Personality and Social Psychology, 75,* 917–937.

Vorauer, J. D., & Miller, D. T. (1997). Failure to recognize the effect of implicit social influence on the presentation of self. *Journal of Personality and Social Psychology, 73,* 281–295.

Vorauer, J. D., & Quesnel, M. (2013). You don't really love me, do you? Negative effects of imagine-other perspective-taking on lower self-esteem individuals' relationship well-being. *Personality and Social Psychology Bulletin, 39,* 1428–1440.

Vorauer, J. D., & Ratner, R. K. (1996). Who's going to make the first move? Pluralistic ignorance as an impediment to relationship formation. *Journal of Social and Personal Relationships, 13,* 483–506.

Vorauer, J. D., & Ross, M. (1999). Self-awareness and feeling transparent: Failing to suppress one's self. *Journal of Experimental Social Psychology, 35,* 415–440.

Vorauer, J. D., & Sakamoto, Y. (2006). I thought we could be friends, but … Systematic miscommunication and defensive distancing as obstacles to cross-group friendship formation. *Psychological Science 17,* 326–331.

Vorauer, J. D., & Sasaki, S. J. (2010). In need of liberation or constraint? How intergroup attitudes moderate the behavioral implications of intergroup ideologies. *Journal of Experimental Social Psychology, 46,* 133–138.

Vorauer, J. D., & Sasaki, S. J. (2011). In the worst rather than the best of times; Effect of salient intergroup ideology in threatening intergroup interactions. *Journal of Personality and Social Psychology, 101,* 307–320.

Vul, E., & Pashler, H. (2008). Measuring the crowd within: Probabilistic representations within individuals. *Psychological Science, 19,* 646–647.

Wadsworth, T. (2014). Sex and the pursuit of happiness: How other people's sex lives are related to our sense of well-being. *Social Indicators Research, 116,* 115–135.

Wagner, G. (2011, September 7). Going green but getting nowhere. *New York Times.* Retrieved from http://www.nytimes.com

Wagner, M. (2014, October 23). Nevada school knew 13-year-old was being bullied before suicide, didn't tell girl's parents: Lawsuit. *New York Daily News* (http://www.nydailynews.com/news/national/nev-school-didn-girl-parents-bullying-suicide-lawsuit-article-1.1984436).

Wagner, U., Christ, O., & Pettigrew, T. F. (2008). Prejudice and group-related behavior in Germany. *Journal of Social Issues, 64,* 403–416.

Wagstaff, G. F. (1983). Attitudes to poverty, the Protestant ethic, and political affiliation: A preliminary investigation. *Social Behavior and Personality, 11,* 45–47.

Walfish, D. (2001). China's census: National count reveals major societal changes. *Science, 292* (5523), 1823.

Walker, L. J., & Frimer, J. A. (2007). Moral personality of brave and caring exemplars. *Journal of Personality and Social Psychology, 93,* 845–860.

Walker, P. M., & Hewstone, M. (2008). The influence of social factors and implicit racial bias on a generalized own-race effect. *Applied Cognitive Psychology, 22,* 441–453.

Walker, R. (2004, December 5). The hidden (in plain sight) persuaders. *New York Times Magazine.*

Wallace, D. S., Paulson, R. M., Lord, C. G., & Bond, C. F., Jr. (2005). Which behaviors do attitudes predict? Meta-analyzing the effects of social pressure and perceived difficulty. *Review of General Psychology, 9,* 214–227.

Wallace, M. (1969, November 25). *New York Times.*

Waller, J. (2002). *Becoming evil: How ordinary people commit genocide and mass killing.* Oxford: Oxford University Press.

Walster (Hatfield), E. (1965). The effect of self-esteem on romantic liking. *Journal of Experimental Social Psychology, 1,* 184–197.

Walster (Hatfield), E., Aronson, V., Abrahams, D., & Rottman, L. (1966). Importance of physical attractiveness in dating behavior. *Journal of Personality and Social Psychology, 4,* 508–516.

Walster (Hatfield), E., & Festinger, L. (1962). The effectiveness of "overheard" persuasive communications. *Journal of Abnormal and Social Psychology, 65,* 395–402.

Walster (Hatfield), E., Walster, G. W., & Berscheid, E. (1978). *Equity: Theory and research.* Boston: Allyn and Bacon.

Walther, E., Weil, R., & Düsing, J. (2011). The role of evaluative conditioning in attitude formation. *Current Directions in Psychological Science, 20,* 190–196.

Walther, J. B., Van Der Heide, B., Kim, S-Y., Westerman, D., & Tong, S. T. (2008). The role of friends' appearance and behavior on evaluations of individuals on Facebook: Are we known by the company we keep? *Human Communication Research, 34,* 28–49.

Walton, G. M. (2014). The new science of wise psychological interventions. *Current Directions in Psychological Science, 23,* 73–82.

Walum, H., Westberg, L., Henningsson, S., Neiderhiser, J. M., Reiss, D., Igl, W., Ganiban, J. M., Spotts, E. L., Pedersen, N. L., Eriksson, E., & Lichtenstein, P. (2008). Genetic variation in the vasopressin receptor 1a gene (*AVPR1A*) associates with pair-bonding behavior in humans. *Proceedings of the National Academy of Sciences, 105,* 14153–14156.

Wan, L., Crookes, K., Dawel, A., Pidcock, M., Hall, A., & McKone, E. (2017). Face-blind for other-race faces: Individual differences in other-race recognition impairments. *Journal of Experimental Psychology: General, 146,* 102–122.

Wang, Z. (2015). Examining big-fish-little-pond effects across 49 countries: A multilevel latent variable modeling approach. *Educational Psychology, 35,* 228–251.

Ward, W. C., & Jenkins, H. M. (1965). The display of information and the judgment of contingency. *Canadian Journal of Psychology, 19,* 231–241.

Warnick, D. H., & Sanders, G. S. (1980). The effects of group discussion on eyewitness accuracy. *Journal of Applied Social Psychology, 10,* 249–259.

Warren, N. C. (2005, March 4). Personal correspondence from founder of eHarmony.com.

Washington, K. N., & Hans, J. D. (2013). Romantic attachment among young adults: The effects of parental divorce and residential instability. *Journal of Divorce & Remarriage, 54,* 95–111.

Waters, E. A., Klein, W. M. P., Moser, R. P., Yu, M., Waldron, W. R., McNeel, T. S., & Freedman, A. N. (2011). Correlates of unrealistic risk beliefs in a nationally representative sample. *Journal of Behavioral Medicine, 34,* 225–235.

Watson, D. (1982, November). The actor and the observer: How are their perceptions of causality divergent? *Psychological Bulletin, 92,* 682–700.

Watson, M. (2015, August). Ethnic anchors—differences between the Scots and the English. *The Scottish Banner (North American Edition),* p. 10.

Watson, R. I., Jr. (1973). Investigation into deindividuation using a cross-cultural survey technique. *Journal of Personality and Social Psychology, 25,* 342–345.

Watt, S. E., & Badger, A. J. (2009). Effects of social belonging on homesickness: An application of the belongingness hypothesis. *Personality and Social Psychology Bulletin, 35,* 516–530.

Watt, S. E., & Larkin, C. (2010). Prejudiced people perceive more community support for their views: The role of own, media, and peer attitudes in perceived consensus. *Journal of Applied Social Psychology, 40,* 710–731.

Waytz, A., Young, L. L., & Ginges, J. (2014). Motive attribution asymmetry for love vs. hate drives intractable conflict. *PNAS Proceedings of the National Academy of Sciences of the United States of America, 111,* 15687–15692.

Weary, G., & Edwards, J. A. (1994). Social cognition and clinical psychology: Anxiety, depression, and the processing of social information. In R. Wyer & T. Srull (Eds.), *Handbook of social cognition* (Vol. 2). Hillsdale, NJ: Erlbaum.

Weary, G., Harvey, J. H., Schwieger, P., Olson, C. T., Perloff, R., & Pritchard, S. (1982). Self-presentation and the moderation of self-serving biases. *Social Cognition, 1,* 140–159.

Webb, C. E., Rossignac-Milon, M., & Higgins, E. T. (2017). Stepping forward together: Could walking facilitate interpersonal conflict resolution? *American Psychologist, 72,* 374–385

Webb, T. L., & Sheeran, P. (2006). Does changing behavioral intentions engender behavior change? A meta-analysis of the experimental evidence. *Psychological*

Weber, A. L., & Harvey, J. H. (1994). *Perspective on close relationships.* Boston, MA: Allyn & Bacon, Pearson Education.

Weber, B., & Hertel, G. (2007). Motivation gains of inferior group members: A meta-analytical review. *Journal of Personality and Social Psychology, 93,* 973–993.

Webley, K. (2009, June 15). Behind the drop in Chinese adoptions. *Time,* 55.

Wegener, D. T., & Petty, R. E. (1996). Effects of mood on persuasion processes: Enhancing, reducing, and biasing scrutiny of attitude-relevant information. In L. L. Martin & A. Tesser, (Eds.), *Striving and feeling: Interactions among goals, affect, and self-regulation* (pp. 329–362). Hillsdale, NJ: Erlbaum

Wegner, D. M., & Erber, R. (1992). The hyperaccessibility of suppressed thoughts. *Journal of Personality and Social Psychology, 63,* 903–912.

Wehr, P. (1979). *Conflict regulation.* Boulder, CO: Westview Press.

Weichselbaumer, D. (2003). Sexual orientation discrimination in hiring. *Labour Economics, 10,* 629–642.

Weiner, B. (1980). A cognitive (attribution)-emotion-action model of motivated behavior: An analysis of judgments of help-giving. *Journal of Personality and Social Psychology, 39,* 186–200.

Weiner, B. (1981). *The emotional consequences of causal ascriptions.* Unpublished manuscript, UCLA.

Weiner, B. (1985). "Spontaneous" causal thinking. *Psychological Bulletin, 97,* 74–84.

Weiner, B. (1995). *Judgments of responsibility: A foundation for a theory of social conduct.* New York: Guilford.

Weiner, B. (2008). Reflections on the history of attribution theory and research: People, personalities, publications, problems. *Social Psychology, 39,* 151–156.

Weiner, B. (2010). The development of an attribution-based theory of motivation: A history of ideas. *Educational Psychologist, 45,* 28–36.

Weiner, B., Osborne, D., & Rudolph, U. (2011). An attributional analysis of reactions to poverty: The political ideology of the giver and the perceived morality of the receiver. *Personality and Social Psychology Review, 15,* 199–213.

Weinstein, N., & Ryan, R. M. (2010). When helping helps: Autonomous motivation for prosocial behavior and its influence on well-being for the helper and recipient. *Journal of Personality and Social Psychology, 98,* 222–244.

Weinstein, N. D. (1980). Unrealistic optimism about future life events. *Journal of*

Personality and Social Psychology, 39, 806–820.
Weinstein, N. D. (1982). Unrealistic optimism about susceptibility to health problems. *Journal of Behavioral Medicine, 5,* 441–460.
Weis, R., & Cerankosky, B. C. (2010). Effects of video-game ownership on young boys' academic and behavioral functioning: A randomized, controlled study. *Psychological Science, 21,* 463–470.
Weiss, J., & Brown, P. (1976). *Self-insight error in the explanation of mood.* Unpublished manuscript, Harvard University, Cambridge, MA.
Welch, M. R., Xu, Y., Bjarnason, T., Petee, T., O'Donnell, P., & Magro, P. (2005). "But Everybody Does It …": The Effects of Perceptions, Moral Pressures, and Informal Sanctions on Tax Cheating. *Sociological Spectrum, 25*(1), 21–52.
Welker, K. M., Baker, L., Padilla, A., Holmes, H., Aron, A., & Slatcher, R. B. (2014). Effects of self-disclosure and responsiveness between couples on passionate love within couples. *Personal Relationships, 21,* 692–708.
Wells, B. M., & Skowronski, J. J. (2012). Evidence of choking under pressure on the PGA tour. *Basic and Applied Social Psychology, 34*(2), 175–182.
Wells, G. L., & Petty, R. E. (1980). The effects of overt head movements on persuasion: Compatibility and incompatibility of responses. *Basic and Applied Social Psychology, 1,* 219–230.
Wener, R., Frazier, W., & Farbstein, J. (1987, June). Building better jails. *Psychology Today,* 40–49.
Wenzlaff, R. M., & Prohaska, M. L. (1989). When misery prefers company: Depression, attributions, and responses to others' moods. *Journal of Experimental Social Psychology, 25,* 220–233.
Werner, C. M., Stoll, R., Birch, P., & White, P. H. (2002). Clinical validation and cognitive elaboration: Signs that encourage sustained recycling. *Basic and Applied Social Psychology, 24,* 185–203.
West, S. G., & Brown, T. J. (1975). Physical attractiveness, the severity of the emergency and helping: A field experiment and interpersonal simulation. *Journal of Experimental Social Psychology, 11,* 531–538.
West, S. G., Whitney, G., & Schnedler, R. (1975). Helping a motorist in distress: The effects of sex, race, and neighborhood. *Journal of Personality and Social Psychology, 31,* 691–698.
Weyant, J. M. (1984). Applying social psychology to induce charitable donations. *Journal of Applied Social Psychology, 14,* 441–447.
Weyant, J. M., & Smith, S. L. (1987). Getting more by asking for less: The effects of request size on donations of charity. *Journal of Applied Social Psychology, 17,* 392–400.
Whatley, M. A., Webster, J. M., Smith, R. H., & Rhodes, A. (1999). The effect of a favor on public and private compliance: How internalized is the norm of reciprocity? *Basic and Applied Social Psychology, 21,* 251–261.
Wheeler, L., Koestner, R., & Driver, R. E. (1982). Related attributes in the choice of comparison others: It's there, but it isn't all there is. *Journal of Experimental Social Psychology, 18,* 489–500.
White, G. L. (1980). Physical attractiveness and courtship progress. *Journal of Personality and Social Psychology, 39,* 660–668.
White, G. L., & Kight, T. D. (1984). Misattribution of arousal and attraction: Effects of salience of explanations for arousal. *Journal of Experimental Social Psychology, 20,* 55–64.
White, K., & Lehman, D. R. (2005). Culture and social comparison seeking: The role of self-motives. *Personality and Social Psychology Bulletin, 31,* 232.
White, M. J., & Gerstein, L. H. (1987). Helping: The influence of anticipated social sanctions and self-monitoring. *Journal of Personality, 55,* 41–54.
Whitechurch, E. R., Wilson, T. D., & Gilbert, D. T. (2011). "He loves me, he loves me not …"; Uncertainty can increase romantic attraction. *Psychological Science, 22,* 172–175.
Whitson, J. A., & Galinsky, A. D. (2008). Lacking control increases illusory pattern perception. *Science, 322,* 115–117.
Whittaker, J. O., & Meade, R. D. (1967). Social pressure in the modification and distortion of judgment: A cross-cultural study. *International Journal of Psychology, 2,* 109–113.
WHO. (2018). *Canada: Alcohol Consumption: Levels and Patterns.* World Health Organisation. Retrieved from https://www.who.int/substance_abuse/publications/global_alcohol_report/profiles/can.pdf?ua=1
Whooley, M. A., de Jonge, P., Vittinghoff, E., Otte, C., Moos, R., Carney, R., Ali, S., Dowray, S., Na, B., Feldman, M. D., Schiller, N. B., & Browner, W. S. (2008). Depressive symptoms, health behaviors, and risk of cardiovascular events in patients with coronary heart disease. *Journal of the American Medical Association, 300,* 2379–2388.
Whyte, G. (1993). Escalating commitment in individual and group decision making: A prospect theory approach. *Organizational Behavior and Human Decision Processes, 54,* 430–455.
Wicker, A. W. (1969). Attitudes versus actions: The relationship of verbal and overt behavioral responses to attitude objects. *Journal of Social Issues, 25*(4), 41–78.
Wicker, A. W. (1971). An examination of the "other variables" explanation of attitude behavior inconsistency. *Journal of Personality and Social Psychology, 19,* 18–30.
Widom, C. S. (1989). Does violence beget violence? A critical examination of the literature. *Psychological Bulletin, 106,* 3–28.
Wiebe, D. J. (2003). Homicide and suicide risks associated with firearms in the home: A national case-control study. *Annals of Emergency Medicine, 41,* 771–782.
Wiegman, O. (1985). Two politicians in a realistic experiment: Attraction, discrepancy, intensity of delivery, and attitude change. *Journal of Applied Social Psychology, 15,* 673–686.
Wiesel, E. (1985, April 6). The brave Christians who saved Jews from the Nazis. *TV Guide,* 4–6.
Wieselquist, J., Rusbult, C. E., Foster, C. A., & Agnew, C. R. (1999). Commitment, pro-relationship behavior, and trust in close relationships. *Journal of Personality and Social Psychology, 77,* 942–966.
Wikipedia. (2008). Strip search prank call scam. Retrieved from https://en.wikipedia.org
Wilder, D. A. (1977). Perception of groups, size of opposition, and social influence. *Journal of Experimental Social Psychology, 13,* 253–268.
Wilder, D. A. (1978). Perceiving persons as a group: Effect on attributions of causality and beliefs. *Social Psychology, 41,* 13–23.
Wilder, D. A. (1981). Perceiving persons as a group: Categorization and intergroup relations. In. D. L. Hamilton (Ed.), *Cognitive processes in stereotyping and intergroup behavior.* Hillsdale, NJ: Lawrence Erlbaum.
Wilder, D. A. (1990). Some determinants of the persuasive power of in-groups and out-groups: Organization of information and attribution of independence. *Journal of Personality and Social Psychology, 59,* 1202–1213.
Wilder, D. A. (1996). Challenging stereotypes about stereotypes. *PsycCRITIQUES, 41,* 429–430.
Wilder, D. A., & Shapiro, P. (1991). Facilitation of outgroup stereotypes by enhanced ingroup identity. *Journal of Experimental Social Psychology, 27,* 431–452.
Wilder, D. A., & Shapiro, P. N. (1984). Role of out-group cues in determining social

identity. *Journal of Personality and Social Psychology, 47,* 342–348.

Wilder, D. A., & Shapiro, P. N. (1989). Role of competition-induced anxiety in limiting the beneficial impact of positive behavior by out-group members. *Journal of Personality and Social Psychology, 56,* 60–69.

Wildschut, T., Insko, C. A., & Pinter, B. (2007). Interindividual-intergroup discontinuity as a joint function of acting as a group and interacting with a group. *European Journal of Social Psychology, 37,* 390–399.

Wildschut, T., Pinter, B., Vevea, J. L., Insko, C. A., & Schopler, J. (2003). Beyond the group mind: A quantitative review of the interindividual-intergroup discontinuity effect. *Psychological Bulletin, 129,* 698–722.

Wilke, R., Stokes, B., & Simmons, K. (2016, July 11). Europeans fear waves of refugees will mean more terrorism, fewer jobs. Pew Research Center (www.pewglobal.org).

Wilkes, J. (1987, June). Murder in mind. *Psychology Today,* 27–32.

Wilkins, S., Beckenuyte, C., & Butt, M. M. (2016). Consumers' behavioural intentions after experiencing deception or cognitive dissonance caused by deceptive packaging, package downsizing or slack filling. *European Journal of Marketing, 50*(1/2), 213–235.

Wilkinson, G. S. (1990, February). Food sharing in vampire bats. *Scientific American, 262,* 76–82.

Wilkinson, R., & Pickett K. (2009). *The spirit level: Why greater equality makes societies stronger.* New York: Penguin.

Wilkowski, B. M., & Robinson, M. D. (2008). The cognitive basis of trait anger and reactive aggression: An integrative analysis. *Personality and Social Psychology Bulletin, 12,* 3–21.

Willard, G., & Gramzow, R. H. (2009). Beyond oversights, lies, and pies in the sky: Exaggeration as goal projection. *Personality and Social Psychology Bulletin, 35,* 477–492.

Willems, S., Dedonder, J., & Van der Linden, M. (2010). The mere exposure effect and recognition depend on the way you look! *Experimental Psychology, 57,* 185–192.

Williams, D. K., Bourgeois, M. J., & Croyle, R. T. (1993). The effects of stealing thunder in criminal and civil trials. *Law and Human Behavior, 17,* 597–609.

Williams, E. F., & Gilovich, T. (2008). Do people really believe they are above average? *Journal of Experimental Social Psychology, 44,* 1121–1128.

Williams, J. E., Satterwhite, R. C., & Best, D. L. (1999). Pancultural gender stereotypes revisited: The Five Factor model. *Sex Roles, 40,* 513–525.

Williams, J. E., Satterwhite, R. C., & Best, D. L. (2000). *Five-factor gender stereotypes in 27 countries.* Paper presented at the XV Congress of the International Association for Cross-Cultural Psychology, Pultusk, Poland.

Williams, K. D. (2002). *Ostracism: The power of silence.* New York: Guilford.

Williams, K. D. (2007). Ostracism. *Annual Review of Psychology, 58,* 425–452.

Williams, K. D. (2011, January/February). The pain of exclusion. *Scientific American Mind,* 30–37.

Williams, K. D., Cheung, C. K. T., & Choi, W. (2000). Cyberostracism: Effects of being ignored over the Internet. *Journal of Personality and Social Psychology, 79,* 748–762.

Williams, K. D., Harkins, S., & Latané, B. (1981). Identifiability as a deterrent to social loafing: Two cheering experiments. *Journal of Personality and Social Psychology, 40,* 303–311.

Williams, K. D., Jackson, J. M., & Karau, S.J. (1992). Collective hedonism: A social loafing analysis of social dilemmas. In D. A. Schroeder (Ed.), *Social dilemmas: Social psychological perspectives.* New York: Praeger.

Williams, K. D., & Karau, S. J. (1991). Social loafing and social compensation: The effects of expectations of coworker performance. *Journal of Personality and Social Psychology, 61,* 570–581.

Williams, K. D., & Nida, S. A. (2009). Is ostracism worse than bullying? In M. J. Harris (Ed.), *Bullying, rejection, and peer victimization: A social cognitive neuroscience perspective* (pp. 279–296). New York: Springer.

Williams, K. D., & Nida, S. A. (2011). Ostracism: Consequences and coping. *Current Directions in Psychological Science, 20,* 71–75.

Williams, K. D., Nida, S. A., Baca, L. D., & Latané, B. (1989). Social loafing and swimming: Effects of identifiability on individual and relay performance of intercollegiate swimmers. *Basic and Applied Social Psychology, 10,* 73–81.

Williams, K. D., & Zadro, L. (2001). Ostracism: On being ignored, excluded and rejected. In M. Leary (Ed.), *Interpersonal rejection.* New York: Oxford.

Williams, L. E., & Bargh, J. A. (2008). Experiencing physical warmth promotes interpersonal warmth. *Science, 322,* 606–607.

Williams, M. J., & Eberhardt, J. L. (2008). Biological conceptions of race and the motivation to cross racial boundaries. *Journal of Personality and Social Psychology, 94,* 1033–1047.

Williams, T. M. (Ed.) (1986). *The impact of television: A natural experiment in three communities.* Orlando, FL: Academic Press.

Williamson, G. M., & Clark, M. S. (1989). Providing help and desired relationship type as determinants of changes in moods and self-evaluations. *Journal of Personality and Social Psychology, 56,* 722–734.

Willis, F. N., & Hamm, H. K. (1980). The use of interpersonal touch in securing compliance. *Journal of Nonverbal Behavior, 5,* 49–55.

Willis, J., & Todorov, A. (2006). First impressions: Making up your mind after a 100-ms exposure to a face. *Psychological Science, 17,* 592–598.

Willoughby, T., Adachi, P. J. C., & Good, M. (2012). A longitudinal study of the association between violent video game play and aggression among adolescents. *Developmental Psychology, 48,* 1044–1057.

Willoughby, T., Anderson, S. A., Wood, E., Mueller, J., & Ross, C. (2009). Fast searching for information on the Internet to use in a learning context: The impact of domain knowledge. *Computers & Education, 52,* 640–648.

Wilson, A. E., & Ross, M. (2001). From chump to champ: People's appraisals of their earlier and present selves. *Journal of Personality and Social Psychology, 80,* 572–584.

Wilson, D. S., & Wilson, E. O. (2008). Evolution for "the good of the group." *American Scientist, 96,* 380–389.

Wilson, E. O. (1978). *On human nature.* Cambridge, MA: Harvard University Press.

Wilson, J. P., & Petruska, R. (1984). Motivation, model attributes, and prosocial behavior. *Journal of Personality and Social Psychology, 46,* 458–468.

Wilson, J. P., Hugenberg, K., & Rule, N. O. (2017). Racial bias in judgments of physical size and formidability: From size to threat. *Journal of Personality and Social Psychology, 113,* 59–80.

Wilson, L. C., & Scarpa, A. (2011). The link between sensation seeking and aggression: A meta-analytic review. *Aggressive Behavior, 37,* 81–90.

Wilson, R. S., & Matheny, A. P., Jr. (1986). Behavior-genetics research in infant temperament: The Louisville twin study. In R. Plomin & J. Dunn (Eds.), *The study of temperament: Changes, continuities, and challenges.* Hillsdale, NJ: Erlbaum.

Wilson, S. J., & Lipsey, M. W. (2005). The effectiveness of school-based violence prevention programs for reducing disruptive and aggressive behavior. Revised Report for the National Institute of Justice School Violence Prevention Research Planning Meeting, May 2005.

Wilson, T. D. (1985). Strangers to ourselves: The origins and accuracy of beliefs about one's own mental states. In J. H. Harvey & G. Weary (Eds.), *Attribution in contemporary psychology.* New York: Academic Press.

Wilson, T. D. (2002). *Strangers to ourselves: Discovering the adaptive unconscious.* Cambridge, MA: Harvard University Press.

Wilson, T. D., Dunn, D. S., Kraft, D., & Lisle, D. J. (1989). Introspection, attitude change, and attitude-behavior consistency: The disruptive effects of explaining why we feel the way we do. In L. Berkowitz (Eds.), *Advances in experimental social psychology* (Vol. 22). San Diego, CA: Academic Press.

Wilson, T. D., & Gilbert, D. T. (2003). Affective forecasting. *Advances in Experimental Social Psychology, 35,* 346–413.

Wilson, T. D., & Gilbert, D. T. (2005). Affective forecasting: Knowing what to want. *Current Directions in Psychological Science, 14,* 131–134.

Wilson, T. D., Laser, P. S., & Stone, J. I. (1982). Judging the predictors of one's mood: Accuracy and the use of shared theories. *Journal of Experimental Social Psychology, 18,* 537–556.

Wilson, T. D., Lindsey, S., & Schooler, T. Y. (2000). A model of dual attitudes. *Psychological Review, 107,* 101–126.

Wilson, W. R. (1979). Feeling more than we can know: Exposure effects without learning. *Journal of Personality and Social Psychology, 37,* 811–821.

Winch, R. F. (1958). *Mate selection: A study of complementary needs.* New York: Harper & Row.

Winegard, B. (2010). The evolutionary significance of Red Sox Nation: Sports fandom as a by-product of coalitional psychology. *Evolutionary Psychology, 8,* 432–446.

Wingate, V. S., Minney, J. A., & Guadagno, R. E. (2013). Sticks and stones may break your bones, but words will always hurt you: A review of cyberbulling. *Social Influence, 8,* 87–106.

Winter, F. W. (1973). A laboratory experiment of individual attitude response to advertising exposure. *Journal of Marketing Research, 10,* 130–140.

Wirth, J. H., Sacco, D. F., Hugenberg, K., & Williams, K. D. (2010). Eye gaze as relational evaluation: Averted eye gaze leads to feelings of ostracism and relational devaluation. *Personality and Social Psychology Bulletin, 36,* 869–882.

Wisman, A., & Koole, S. L. (2003). Hiding in the crowd: Can mortality salience promote affiliation with others who oppose one's worldviews? *Journal of Personality and Social Psychology, 84,* 511–526.

Wittenbrink, B. (2007). Measuring attitudes through priming. In B. Wittenbrink & N. Schwarz (Eds.), *Implicit measures of attitudes.* New York: Guilford.

Wittenbrink, B., Judd, C. M., & Park, B. (1997). Evidence for racial prejudice at the implicit level and its relationship with questionnaire measures. *Journal of Personality and Social Psychology, 72,* 262–274.

Wixon, D. R., & Laird, J. D. (1976). Awareness and attitude change in the forced-compliance paradigm: The importance of when. *Journal of Personality and Social Psychology, 34,* 376–384.

Wohl, M. J. A., Branscombe, N. R., & Reysen, S. (2010). Perceiving your group's future to be in jeopardy: Extinction threat induces collective angst and the desire to strengthen the ingroup. *Personality and Social Psychology Bulletin, 36,* 898–910.

Wohl, M. J. A., & Enzle, M. E. (2002). The deployment of personal luck: Sympathetic magic and illusory control in games of pure chance. *Personality and Social Psychology Bulletin, 28,* 1388–1397.

Wojciszke, B., Bazinska, R., & Jaworski, M. (1998). On the dominance of moral categories in impression formation. *Personality and Social Psychology Bulletin, 24,* 1251–1263.

Wolf, S. (1987). Majority and minority influence: A social impact analysis. In M. P. Zanna, J. M. Olson, & C. P. Herman (Eds.), *Social influence: The Ontario symposium on personality and social psychology* (Vol. 5). Hillsdale, NJ: Erlbaum.

Wolf, S., & Latané, B. (1985). Conformity, innovation and the psycho-social law. In S. Moscovici, G. Mugny, & E. Van Avermaet (Eds.), *Perspectives on minority influence.* Cambridge: Cambridge University Press.

Wolf, W., Levordashka, A., Ruff, J. R., Kraaijeveld, S., Lueckmann, J-M., & Williams, K. D. (2015). Ostracism online: A social media ostracism paradigm. *Behavior Research, 47,* 361–373.

Wolfe, M. B., & Williams, T. J. (2018). Poor metacognitive awareness of belief change. *Quarterly Journal of Experimental Psychology, 71,* 1898-1910.

Women on Words and Images. (1972). *Dick and Jane as victims: Sex stereotyping in children's readers.* Princeton: Women on Words and Images.

Wong, E. M., Ormiston, M. E., and Haselhuhn, M. P. (2011). A face only an investor could love: CEOs' facial structure predicts their firms' financial performance. *Psychological Science, 22,* 1478–1483

Wood, J. V., Heimpel, S. A., & Michela, J. L. (2003). Savoring versus dampening: Self-esteem differences in regulating positive affect. *Journal of Personality and Social Psychology, 85,* 566–580.

Wood, J. V., Perunovic, W. Q. E., & Lee, J. W. (2009). Positive self-statements: Power for some, peril for others. *Psychological Science, 20,* 860–866.

Wood, J. V., Saltzberg, J. A., & Goldsamt, L. A. (1990). Does affect induce self-focused attention? *Journal of Personality and Social Psychology, 58,* 899–908.

Wood, W., Rhodes, N., & Whelan, M. (1989). Sex differences in positive well-being: A consideration of emotional style and marital status. *Psychological Bulletin, 106,* 249–264.

Woodzicka, J. A., & LaFrance, M. (2001). Real versus imagined gender harassment. *Journal of Social Issues, 57*(1), 15–30.

Woolley, A. W., Chabris, C. F., Pentland, A., Hasmi, N., & Malone, T. W. (2010). Evidence for a collective intelligence factor in the performance of human groups. *Science, 330,* 686–688.

Worchel, S., Andreoli, V. A., & Folger, R. (1977). Intergroup cooperation and intergroup attraction: The effect of previous interaction and outcome of combined effort. *Journal of Experimental Social Psychology, 13,* 131–140.

Worchel, S., Axsom, D., Ferris, F., Samah, G., & Schweitzer, S. (1978). Deterrents of the effect of intergroup cooperation on intergroup attraction. *Journal of Conflict Resolution, 22,* 429–439.

Worchel, S., & Brown, E. H. (1984). The role of plausibility in influencing environmental attributions. *Journal of Experimental Social Psychology, 20,* 86–96.

Worchel, S., Jenner, S. M., & Hebl, M. R. (1998). Changing the guard: How origin of new leader and disposition of ex-leader affect group performance and perceptions. *Small Group Research, 29,* 436.

Worchel, S., & Norvell, N. (1980). Effect of perceived environmental conditions during cooperation on intergroup attraction. *Journal of Personality and Social Psychology, 38,* 764–772.

Word, C. O., Zanna, M. P., & Cooper, J. (1974). The nonverbal mediation of self-fulfilling prophecies in interracial interaction. *Journal of Experimental Social Psychology, 10,* 109–120.

Workman, E. A., & Williams, R. L. (1980). Effects of extrinsic rewards on intrinsic motivation in the classroom. *Journal of School Psychology, 18,* 141–147.

World Meteorological Association (2019). Greenhouse gas concentrations in atmosphere reach yet another high. Retrieved from https://public.wmo.int/en/media/press-release/greenhouse-gas-concentrations-atmosphere-reach-yet-another-high#:~:text=The%20WMO%20Greenhouse%20Gas%20Bulletin,million%20(ppm)%20in%202017.

Worringham, C. J., & Messick, D. M. (1983). Social facilitation of running: An unobtrusive study. *Journal of Social Psychology, 121,* 23–29.

Wraga, M., Helt, M., Jacobs, E., & Sullivan, K. (2007). Neural basis of stereotype-induced shifts in women's mental rotation performance. *Social Cognitive and Affective Neuroscience, 2,* 12–19.

Wright, D. B., & Stroud, J. N. (2002). Age differences in lineup identification accuracy: People are better with their own age. *Law and Human Behavior, 26,* 641–654.

Wright, E. F., Lüüs, C. A., & Christie, S. D. (1990). Does group discussion facilitate the use of consensus information in making causal attributions? *Journal of Personality and Social Psychology, 59,* 261–269.

Wright, P. J. (2013). U.S. males and pornography, 1973–2010: Consumption, predictors, correlates. *Journal of Sex Research, 50,* 60–71.

Wright, P. J., Tokunaga, R. S., & Kraus, A. (2016). A meta-analysis of pornography consumption and actual acts of sexual aggression in general population studies. *Journal of Communication, 66,* 183–205.

Wright, R. (2003, June 29). Quoted by Thomas L. Friedman, "Is Google God?" *New York Times.* Retrieved from http://www.nytimes.com

Wright, S. C., Aron, A., & Brody, S. M. (2008). Extended contact and including others in the self: Building on the Allport/Pettigrew legacy. In U. Wagner, L. R. Tropp, G. Finchilescu, & C. Tredoux (Eds.), *Social issues and interventions. Improving intergroup relations: Building on the legacy of Thomas F. Pettigrew* (p. 143–159). Blackwell Publishing.

Wright, S. C., Tropp, L. R., & Mazziotta, A. (2017). Contact between groups, peace, and conflict. *Peace and Conflict: Journal of Peace Psychology, 23,* 207–209.

Wu, A. (2017). Gender stereotyping in academia: Evidence from economics job market rumors forum. Paper presented at Harvard Business School (https://growthecon.com/assets/Wu_EJMR_paper.pdf).

Wylie, L., & McConkey, S. Insiders' insight: Discrimination against Indigenous peoples through the eyes of health care professionals. *J. Racial and Ethnic Health Disparities, 6,* 37–45 (2019) doi:10.1007/s40615-018-0495-9

Wylie, R. C. (1979). *The self-concept (Vol. 2): Theory and research on selected topics.* Lincoln, NE: University of Nebraska Press.

Wynne, C. D. L., & de Waal, F. B. M. (2006). Chimps are from Mars, bonobos from Venus. *Ethology, 112*(3), 310–311.

Xie, S. Y., Flake, J. K., & Hehman, E. (2019). Perceiver and target characteristics contribute to impression formation differently across race and gender. *Journal of Personality and Social Psychology, 117*(2), 364–385. https://doi-org.library.smu.ca/10.1037/pspi0000160.supp

Yamagishi, T., Hashimoto, H., Cook, K. S., Kiyonari, T., Shinada, M., Mifune, N., Inukai, K., Takagishi, H., Horita, Y., & Li, Y. (2012). Modesty in self-presentation: A comparison between the USA and Japan. *Asian Journal of Social Psychology, 15,* 60–68.

Yamaguchi, S., Greenwald, A. G., Banaji, M. R., Murakami, F., Chen, D., Shiomura, K., Kobayashi, C., Cai, H., & Krendl, A. (2007). Apparent universality of positive implicit self-esteem. *Psychological Science, 18,* 498–500.

Yaniv, D. (2012). Dynamics of creativity and empathy in role reversal: Contributions from neuroscience. *Review of General Psychology, 16,* 70–77.

Ybarra, M. L., Huesmann, L. R., Korchmaros, J. D., & Reisner, S. L. (2014). Cross-sectional associations between violent video and computer game playing and weapon carrying in a national cohort of children. *Aggressive Behavior, 40,* 345–358.

Ybarra, M. L., Mitchell, K. J., Hamburger, M., Diener-West, M., & Leaf, P. J. (2011). X-rated material and perpetration of sexually aggressive behavior among children and adolescents: Is there a link? *Aggressive Behavior, 37,* 1–18.

Ybarra, M. L., West, M. D., Markow, D., Leaf, P. J., Hamburger, M. & Boxer, P. (2008). Linkages between Internet and other media violence with seriously violent behavior by youth. *Pediatrics, 122,* 929–937.

Ybarra, O. (1999). Misanthropic person memory when the need to self-enhance is absent. *Personality and Social Psychology Bulletin, 25,* 261–269.

Young, L. (2009). Love: Neuroscience reveals all . *Nature, 457,* 148.

Young, S. G., Bernstein, M. J., & Hugenberg, K. (2010). When do own-group biases in face recognition occur? Encoding versus post-encoding. *Social Cognition, 28,* 240–250.

Younger, J. C., Walker, L., & Arrowood, A. J. (1977). Postdecision dissonance at the fair. *Personality and Social Psychology Bulletin, 3*(2), 284-287.

Younger, J., Aron, A., Parke, S., Chatterjee, N., & Mackey, S. (2010). Viewing pictures of a romantic partner reduces experimental pain: Involvement of neural reward systems. *PLoS One, 5*(10), e13309.

Yousif, Y., & Korte, C. (1995). Urbanization, culture, and helpfulness. *Journal of Cross-Cultural Psychology, 26,* 474–489.

Yovetich, N. A., & Rusbult, C. E. (1994). Accommodative behavior in close relationships: Exploring transformation of motivation. *Journal of Experimental Social Psychology, 30,* 138–164.

Yu, F., Peng, T., Peng, K., Tang, S., Chen, C. S., Qian, X., Sun, P., Han, T., & Chai, F. (2016). Cultural value shifting in pronoun use. *Journal of Cross-Cultural Psychology, 47,* 310–316.

Yuchtman (Yaar), E. (1976). Effects of social-psychological factors on subjective economic welfare. In B. Strumpel (Ed.), *Economic means for human needs.* Ann Arbor: Institute for Social Research, University of Michigan.

Yukl, G. (1974). Effects of the opponent's initial offer, concession magnitude, and concession frequency on bargaining behavior. *Journal of Personality and Social Psychology, 30,* 323–335.

Yzerbyt, V. Y., & Leyens, J-P. (1991). Requesting information to form an impression: The influence of valence and confirmatory status. *Journal of Experimental Social Psychology, 27,* 337–356.

Zadro, L., Boland, C., & Richardson, R. (2006). How long does it last? The persistence of the effects of ostracism in the socially anxious. *Journal of Experimental Social Psychology, 42,* 692–697.

Zagefka, H., Noor, M., Brown, R., De Moura, G. R., & Hopthrow, T. (2011). Donating to disaster victims: Responses to natural and humanly caused events. *European Journal of Social Psychology, 41,* 353–363.

Zainulbhai, H. (2016, March 8). Strong global support for gender equality, especially among women. Pew Research Center (www.pewresearch.org).

Zajonc, R. B. (1965). Social facilitation. *Science, 149,* 269–274.

Zajonc, R. B. (1968). Attitudinal effects of mere exposure. *Journal of Personality and Social Psychology, 9,* Monograph Suppl. No. 2, part 2.

Zajonc, R. B. (1970, February). Brainwash: Familiarity breeds comfort. *Psychology Today,* 32–35, 60–62.

Zajonc, R. B. (1980). Feeling and thinking: Preferences need no inferences. *American Psychologist, 35,* 151–175.

Zajonc, R. B. (1998). Emotions. In D. Gilbert, S. T. Fiske, & G. Lindzey (Eds.), *Handbook of social psychology* (4th ed.). New York: McGraw-Hill.

Zajonc, R. B. (2000). *Massacres: Mass murders in the name of moral imperatives.* Unpublished manuscript, Stanford University, Stanford, CA.

Zak, P. J. (2008, June). The neurobiology of trust. *Scientific American,* 88–95.

Zaki, J., Schirmer, J., & Mitchell, J. P. (2011). Social influence modulates the neural computation of value. *Psychological Science, 22,* 894–900.

Zanna, M. P. (1993). Message receptivity: A new look at the old problem of open- vs. closed-mindedness. In A. Mitchell (Ed.), *Advertising: Exposure, memory and choice.* Hillsdale, NJ: Erlbaum.

Zanna, M. P., & Cooper, J. (1974). Dissonance and the pill: An attributional approach to studying the arousal properties of dissonance. *Journal of Personality and Social Psychology, 29,* 703–709.

Zanna, M. P., & Olson, J. M. (1982). Individual differences in attitudinal relations. In M. P. Zanna, E. T. Higgins, & C. P. Herman, (Eds.) *Consistency in social behavior: The Ontario symposium* (Vol. 2). Hillsdale, NJ: Erlbaum.

Zanna, M. P., Olson, J. M., & Fazio, R. H. (1981). Self-perception and attitude-behavior consistency. *Personality and Social Psychology Bulletin, 7,* 252–256.

Zanna, M. P., & Pack, S. J. (1975). On the self-fulfilling nature of apparent sex differences in behavior. *Journal of Experimental Social Psychology, 11,* 583–591.

Zebrowitz, L. A., Collins, M. A., & Dutta, R. (1998). The relationship between appearance and personality across the life span. *Personality and Social Psychology Bulletin, 24,* 736–749.

Zebrowitz, L. A., Olson, K., & Hoffman, K. (1993). Stability of babyfaceness and attractiveness across the life span. *Journal of Personality and Social Psychology, 64,* 453–466.

Zebrowitz, L. A., White, B., & Wieneke, K. (2008). Mere exposure and racial prejudice: Exposure to other-race faces increases liking for strangers of that race. *Social Cognition, 26,* 259–275.

Zebrowitz-McArthur, L. (1988). Person perception in cross-cultural perspective. In M. H. Bond (Ed.), *The cross-cultural challenge to social psychology.* Newbury Park, CA: Sage.

Zha, X., Yang, H., Yan, Y., Liu, K., & Huang, C. (2018). Exploring the effect of social media information quality, source credibility and reputation on informational fit-to-task: Moderating role of focused immersion. *Computers in Human Behavior, 79,* 227–237. https://doi- org .library.smu.ca/10.1016/j.chb.2017.10.038

Zhang, Q., & Covey, J. (2014). Past and future implications of near-misses and their emotional consequences. *Experimental Psychology, 61,* 118–126.

Zhang, S., & Kline, S. L. (2009). Can I make my own decision? A cross-cultural study of perceived social network influence in mate selection. *Journal of Cross-Cultural Psychology, 40,* 3–23.

Zhang, Y. F., Wyon, D. P., Fang, L., & Melikov, A. K. (2007). The influence of heated or cooled seats on the acceptable ambient temperature range. *Ergonomics, 50,* 586–600.

Zhong, C.-B., & Leonardelli, G. F. (2008). Cold and lonely: Does social exclusion literally feel cold? *Psychological Science, 19,* 838–842.

Zhou, J., Dou, J., & Wang, X. (May). (2019). A double-edged sword: When does identity threat affect unethical behavior? *Journal of Management & Organization.* https://doi- org.library.smu.ca/10 .1017/jmo.2019.80

Zhu, L., Gigerenzer, G., & Huangfu, G. (2013). Psychological traces of China's socio-economic reforms in the ultimatum and dictator games. *PLOS ONE, 8,* e70769.

Zhu, W. X., Lu, L., & Hesketh, T. (2009). China's excess males, sex selective abortion, and one child policy: Analysis of data from 2005 national intercensus survey. *British Medical Journal (BMJ), 338,* b1211.

Zhu, Y., Zhang, L., Fan, L., & Han, S. (2007). Neural basis of cultural influence on self-representation. *NeuroImage, 34,* 1310–1316.

Zillmann, D. (1988). Cognition-excitation interdependencies in aggressive behavior. *Aggressive Behavior, 14,* 51–64.

Zillmann, D. (1989a). Aggression and sex: Independent and joint operations. In H. L. Wagner & A. S. R. Manstead (Eds.), *Handbook of psychophysiology: Emotion and social behavior.* Chichester, UK: Wiley.

Zillmann, D. (1989b). Effects of prolonged consumption of pornography. In D. Zillmann & J. Bryant (Eds.), *Pornography: Research advances and policy considerations.* Hillsdale, NJ: Erlbaum.

Zillmann, D., & Paulus, P. B. (1993). Spectators: Reactions to sports events and effects on athletic performance. In R. N. Singer, N. Murphey, & L. K. Tennant (Eds.), *Handbook of research on sport psychology.* New York: Macmillan.

Zillmann, D., & Weaver, J. B. (2007). Aggressive personality traits in the effects of violence imagery on unprovoked impulsive aggression. *Journal of Research in Personality, 41,* 753–771.

Zillmann, D., & Weaver, J. B., III. (1999). Effects of prolonged exposure to gratuitous media violence on provoked and unprovoked hostile behavior. *Journal of Applied Social Psychology, 29,* 145–165.

Zimbardo, P. G. (1970). The human choice: Individuation, reason, and order versus deindividuation, impulse, and chaos. In W. J. Arnold & D. Levine (Eds.), *Nebraska symposium on motivation, 1969.* Lincoln: University of Nebraska Press.

Zimbardo, P. G. (1972). *The Stanford prison experiment.* A slide/tape presentation produced by Philip G. Zimbardo, Inc., P. O. Box 4395, Stanford, CA 94305.

Zimbardo, P. G. (2002, April). Nurturing psychological synergies. *APA Monitor, 5,* 38.

Zimbardo, P. G. (2004). A situationist perspective on the psychology of evil: Understanding how good people are transformed into perpetrators. In A. G. Miller (Ed.), *The social psychology of good and evil.* New York: Guilford.

Zimmer, C. (2005, November). The neurobiology of the self. *Scientific American,* 93–101.

Zitek, E. M., & Hebl, M. R. (2007). The role of social norm clarity in the influenced expression of prejudice over time. *Journal of Experimental Social Psychology, 43,* 867–876.

Zola-Morgan, S., Squire, L. R., Alvarez-Royo, P., & Clower, R. P. (1991). Independence of memory functions and emotional behavior. *Hippocampus, 1,* 207–220.

Zotto, M., & Pegna, A. J. (2017). Electrophysiological evidence of perceived sexual attractiveness for human female bodies varying in waist-to-hip ratio. *Cognitive, Affective & Behavioral Neuroscience, 17,* 577–591.

Zuckerman, E. W., & Jost, J. T. (2001). What makes you think you're so popular? Self-evaluation maintenance and the subjective side of the "friendship paradox." *Social Psychology Quarterly, 64,* 207–223.

Zuwerink, J. R., Monteith, M. J., Devine, P. G., & Cook, D. A. (1996). Prejudice toward blacks: With and without compunction? *Basic and Applied Social Psychology, 18,* 131–150.

Chapter Sources

Chapter Two

Figure 2.3: Twenge et al., 2012.

Chapter Three

Figure 3.1: Data from Baldwin, Carrell, & Lopez, 1990.
Figure 3.2: Forgas, Bower, & Krantz, 1984.
Figure 3.3: Data from Vallone, Ross, & Lepper, 1985.
Figure 3.4: Data from Forgas, Bower, & Krantz, 1984.
Figure 3.5: Data from Vallone, Ross, & Lepper, 1985.
Figure 3.7: Jussim & Harber, 2005.

Chapter Four

Figure 4.2: Data from Festinger & Carlsmith, 1959.

Chapter Five

Figure 5.1: Adapted from McGuire, 1978.
Figure 5.3: Data from Janis, Kaye, & Kirschner, 1965.
Figure 5.5: Data from Aronson, Turner, & Carlsmith, 1963.
Figure 5.6: Data from Hovland, Lumsdaine, & Sheffield, 1949.
Figure 5.8: Data from Maccoby, 1980.
Figure 5.9: Data from Chaiken & Eagly, 1976.
Figure 5.10: Based on Fabrigar et al., 1998.
Figure 5.12: Data: Luthi, D., et al., 2008; Etheridge, D.M., et al., 2010; Vostok ice core data/J.R. Petit et al.; NOAA Mauna Loa CO_2 record. Some description adapted from the Scripps CO_2 Program website, "Keeling Curve Lessons."
Figure 5.13: Data from McAlister et al., 1980; Telch et al., 1981.

Chapter Six

Figure 6.1: Data from Sherif & Sherif, 1969.
Figure 6.3: From Milgram, 1965.
Figure 6.4: Data from Milgram, Bickman, & Berkowitz, 1969.
Figure 6.5: Data from Asch, 1955.

Chapter Seven

Table 7.1: Data from Courneya & Carron, 1992, except for Major League Baseball, 1900 to 1992, from Schlenker et al., 1995.
Figure 7.3: Williams et al., 1992.
Figure 7.6: Data from Diener et al., 1976.
Figure 7.8: Data from Myers & Bishop, 1970.
Figure 7.9: Data from Myers, 1978.
Figure 7.10: From Hastie et al., 1983.

Chapter Eight

Figure 8.1: Data from Isen et al., 1976.
Figure 8.2: Whatley et al., 1999.
Figure 8.3: Adapted from Batson et al., 1987.
Figure 8.4: Adapted from Darley & Latané, 1968.
Figure 8.5: Data from Darley & Latané, 1968.

Chapter Nine

Figure 9.2: Based on Bandura, 1979, 1997.
Figure 9.3: Simplified from Anderson, Deuser, & DeNeve, 1995. For an updated but more complex version, see Anderson & Bushman, 2018.
Figure 9.4: Data from Donnerstein, 1980.
Figure 9.6: Adapted from Anderson & Bushman, 2001.
Figure 9.7: Data from Jaffe et al., 1981.

Chapter Ten

Figure 10.2: Based on Lydon et al. 1999.
Figure 10.5: Data from Gupta & Singh, 1982.
Figure 10.6: Adapted from Grote & Clark, 2001.
Table 10.1: Rusbult et al., 1986, 1987, 1998, 2001.

Chapter Eleven

Figure 11.1: Data from Gallup Polls (https://news.gallup.com/poll/4729/presidency.aspx).
Figure 11.3: Devine & Malpass, 1985.
Figure 11.5: Spencer, Steele, & Quinn, 1999.
Figure 11.7: Data from Kunda & Sinclair, 1999.

Chapter Twelve

Figure 12.5: Data from Sherif, M. (1966). *In common predicament: Social psychology of intergroup conflict and cooperation.* Boston, MA: Houghton Mifflin, p. 84.
Table 12.1: Adapted from Phinney, J. S. (1990). Ethnic identity in adolescents and adults: Review of research. *Psychological Bulletin,* 108, 499–514.

Glossary

A

acceptance Conformity that involves both acting and believing, in accord with social pressure.

aggression Physical or verbal behaviour intended to hurt someone.

altruism A motive to increase another's welfare without conscious regard for one's own self-interests.

anxious attachment Attachment marked by anxiety or ambivalence. An insecure attachment style.

arbitration Resolution of a conflict by a neutral third party who studies both sides and imposes a settlement.

attitude A favourable or unfavourable evaluative reaction toward something or someone, exhibited in one's beliefs, feelings, or intended behaviour.

attitude inoculation Exposing people to weak attacks on their attitudes so that when stronger attacks come, they will have refutations available.

attractiveness Having qualities that appeal to an audience. An appealing communicator (often someone similar to the audience) is most persuasive on matters of subjective preference.

attribution theory The theory of how people explain the behaviour of others—for example, by attributing it either to internal dispositions (enduring traits, motives, and attitudes) or to external situations.

authoritarian personality A personality that is disposed to favour obedience to authority and intolerance of outgroups and those lower in status.

autokinetic phenomenon Self (*auto*) motion (*kinetic*). The apparent movement of a stationary point of light in the dark. Perhaps you have experienced this when thinking you have spotted a moving satellite in the sky, only to realize later that it was merely an isolated star.

automatic processing "Implicit" thinking that is effortless, habitual, and without awareness; roughly corresponds to "intuition." Also known as System 1.

availability heuristic A cognitive rule that judges the likelihood of things in terms of their availability in memory. If instances of something come readily to mind, we presume it to be commonplace.

avoidant attachment Attachments are marked by discomfort over, or resistance to, being close to others. An insecure attachment style.

B

bargaining Seeking an agreement through direct negotiation between parties.

behavioural confirmation A type of self-fulfilling prophecy whereby people's social expectations lead them to act in ways that cause others to confirm their expectations.

belief perseverance Persistence of your initial conceptions, as when the basis for your belief is discredited but an explanation of why the belief might be true survives.

bystander effect The finding that a person is less likely to provide help when there are other bystanders.

C

catharsis Emotional release. The catharsis view of aggression is that aggressive drive is reduced when one "releases" aggressive energy, either by acting aggressively or by fantasizing aggression.

central route to persuasion Occurs when interested people focus on the arguments and respond with favourable thoughts.

certainty Refers to the level of subjective confidence or validity that people attach to their attitudes.

channel of communication The way the message is delivered—whether face to face, in writing, on film, or in some other way.

co-actors A group of people working simultaneously and individually on a noncompetitive task.

cognitive dissonance theory Tension that arises when we are simultaneously aware of two inconsistent cognitions. For example, dissonance may occur when we realize that we have, with little justification, acted contrary to our attitudes or made a decision favouring one alternative despite reasons favouring another.

cohesiveness A "we feeling"—the extent to which members of a group are bonded together, such as by attraction for one another.

collectivism Giving priority to the goals of one's groups (often, one's extended family or work group) and defining one's identity accordingly.

companionate love The affection we feel for those with whom our lives are deeply intertwined.

complementarity The popularly supposed tendency, in a relationship between two people, for each to complete what is missing in the other.

compliance Conformity that involves publicly acting in accord with social pressure while privately disagreeing.

confederate An accomplice of the experimenter.

confirmation bias A tendency to search for information that confirms one's preconceptions.

conflict A perceived incompatibility of actions or goals.

conformity A change in behaviour or belief to accord with others.

controlled processing "Explicit" thinking that is deliberate, reflective, and conscious. Also known as System 2.

correlational research The study of the naturally occurring relationships among variables.

counterfactual thinking Imagining alternative scenarios and outcomes that might have happened, but didn't.

credibility Believability. A credible communicator is perceived as both expert and trustworthy.

cults Groups typically characterized by (1) the distinctive ritual of their devotion to a god or a person, (2) isolation from the surrounding "evil" culture, and (3) a charismatic leader; also called *new religious movements.* (A sect, by contrast, is a spinoff from a major religion.)

culture The enduring behaviours, ideas, attitudes, traditions, products, and institutions shared by a large group of people and transmitted from one generation to the next.

cyberbullying Bullying, harrassing, or threatening someone using electronic communication, such as texts, online social networks, or email.

D

defensive pessimism The adaptive value of anticipating problems and harnessing one's anxiety to motivate effective action.

deindividuation Loss of self-awareness and evaluation apprehension; occurs in group situations that foster anonymity and draw attention away from the individual.

demand characteristics Cues in an experiment that tell the participant what behaviour is expected.

dependent variable The variable being measured, so called because it may *depend* on manipulations of the independent variable.

disclosure reciprocity The tendency for one person's intimacy of self-disclosure to match that of a conversational partner.

discrimination Unjustifiable negative behaviour toward a group or its members.

displacement The redirection of aggression to a target other than the source of the frustration. Generally, the new target is a safer or more socially acceptable target.

dispositional attribution Attributing behaviour to the person's disposition and traits.

door-in-the-face technique A strategy for gaining a concession. After someone first turns down a large request (the door in the face), the same requester counteroffers with a more reasonable request.

dual attitudes Differing implicit (automatic) and explicit (consciously controlled) attitudes toward the same object. Verbalized explicit attitudes may change with education and persuasion; implicit attitudes change slowly, with practice that forms new habits.

E

egoism A motive (supposedly underlying all behaviour) to increase your own welfare; the opposite of *altruism,* which aims to increase someone else's welfare.

embodied cognition The mutual influence of bodily sensations on cognitive preferences and social judgments.

empathy The vicarious experience of someone else's feeling; putting yourself in someone else's shoes.

equal-status contact Contact on an equal basis. Just as a relationship between people of unequal status breeds attitudes consistent with their relationship, so do relationships between those of equal status. Thus, to reduce prejudice, interracial contact should ideally be between persons equal in status.

equality The equal distribution of rewards to all individuals.

equity A condition in which the outcomes people receive from a relationship are proportional to what they contribute to it. *Note:* Equitable outcomes needn't always be equal outcomes.

ethnocentric Believing in the superiority of your own ethnic and cultural group and having a corresponding disdain for all other groups.

evaluation apprehension Concern for how others are evaluating us.

experimental realism Degree to which an experiment absorbs and involves its participants.

experimental research Studies that seek clues to cause–effect relationships by manipulating one or more factors (independent variables) while controlling others (holding them constant).

explanatory style A person's habitual way of explaining life events. A negative, pessimistic, and depressive explanatory style attributes failures to stable, global, and internal causes.

F

false consensus effect The tendency to overestimate the commonality of one's opinions and one's undesirable or unsuccessful behaviours.

false uniqueness effect The tendency to underestimate the commonality of one's abilities and one's desirable or successful behaviours.

field research Research done in natural, real-life settings outside the laboratory.

foot-in-the-door phenomenon The tendency for people who have first agreed to a small request to comply later with a larger request.

free-ride Benefiting from the group, but giving little in return.

frustration The blocking of goal-directed behaviour.

frustration–aggression theory The theory that frustration triggers a readiness to aggress.

fundamental attribution error The tendency for observers to underestimate situational influences and overestimate dispositional influences on others' behaviour; also called *correspondence bias* because we so often see behaviour as corresponding to a disposition.

G

gender roles Behaviour expectations (norms) for males and females.

GRIT An acronym for "graduated and reciprocated initiatives in tension reduction"—a strategy designed to de-escalate international tensions.

group Two or more people who, for longer than a few moments, interact with and influence one another and perceive one another as "us."

group polarization Group-produced enhancement of members' pre-existing tendencies; a strengthening of the members' *average* tendency, not a split within the group.

group-serving bias Explaining away out-group members' positive behaviours; also attributing negative behaviours to their dispositions (while excusing such behaviour by one's own group).

groupthink The tendency for groups, in the process of decision making, to suppress dissenting cognitions in the interest of ensuring harmony within the group.

H

heuristics A thinking strategy that enables quick, efficient judgments.

hindsight bias The tendency to exaggerate, after learning an outcome, one's ability to have foreseen how something turned out; also known as the *I-knew-it-all-along phenomenon.*

hostile aggression Aggression driven by anger and performed as an end in itself.

hypotheses Testable propositions that describe relationships that may exist between events.

I

illusion of transparency The illusion that our concealed emotions leak out and can be easily read by others.

illusory correlation A perception of a relationship where none exists or a perception of a stronger relationship than actually exists.

impact bias Overestimating the enduring impact of emotion-causing events.

Implicit Association Test (IAT) A computer-driven assessment of implicit attitudes that uses reaction times to measure people's automatic associations between attitude objects and evaluative words, where easier pairings (and faster responses) are taken to indicate stronger unconscious associations.

independent self Construing one's identity as an autonomous self.

independent variables Experimental factors that a researcher manipulates.

individualism The concept of giving priority to one's own goals over group goals and defining one's identity in terms of personal attributes rather than group identifications.

informational influence Conformity that results from accepting evidence about reality provided by other people.

informed consent An ethical principle requiring that research participants be told enough to enable them to choose whether they wish to participate.

ingratiation The use of strategies, such as flattery, by which people seek to gain another's favour.

in-group bias The tendency to favour your own group.

in-groups "Us": groups of people who share a sense of belonging, a feeling of common identity.

instinctive behaviour An innate, unlearned behaviour pattern exhibited by all members of a species.

instrumental aggression Aggression that is a means to some other end.

insufficient justification Reduction of dissonance by internally justifying one's behaviour when external justification is "insufficient."

integrative agreements Win–win agreements that reconcile both parties' interests to their mutual benefit.

interdependent self Construing one's identity in relation to others.

J

just-world phenomenon People's tendency to believe that the world is just and that, therefore, people get what they deserve and deserve what they get.

K

kin selection The idea that evolution has selected altruism toward one's close relatives to enhance the survival of mutually shared genes.

L

leadership The process by which certain group members motivate and guide the group.

learned helplessness The hopelessness and resignation learned when a human or animal perceives no control over repeated bad events.

low-ball technique A tactic for getting people to agree to something. People who agree to an initial request will often still comply when the requester ups the ante. People who receive only the costly request are less likely to comply with it.

M

matching phenomenon The tendency for men and women to choose as partners those who are a "good match" in attractiveness and other traits.

mediation An attempt by a neutral third party to resolve a conflict by facilitating communication and offering suggestions.

mere-exposure effect The tendency for novel stimuli to be liked more or rated more positively after the rater has been repeatedly exposed to them.

misattribution Mistakenly attributing a behaviour to the wrong cause.

misinformation effect Incorporating "misinformation" into one's memory of an event, after witnessing an event and then receiving misleading information about it.

moral exclusion The perception of certain individuals or groups as outside the boundary within which you apply moral values and rules of fairness.

moral inclusion Regarding others as within your circle of moral concern.

mundane realism Degree to which an experiment is superficially similar to everyday situations.

N

naturalistic fallacy The error of defining what is good in terms of what is observable: For example, what's typical is normal; what's normal is good.

need-based distribution The distribution of rewards based on need for those rewards.

need for cognition The motivation to think and analyze; assessed by agreement with items such as "the notion of thinking abstractly is appealing to me" and disagreement with items such as "I only think as hard as I have to."

need to belong A motivation to bond with others in relationships that provide ongoing, positive interactions.

non-zero-sum games Games in which outcomes need not sum to zero. With cooperation, both can win; with competition, both can lose. (Also called *mixed-motive situations.*)

normative influence Conformity based on a person's desire to fulfill others' expectations, often to gain acceptance.

norms Rules for accepted and expected behaviour that prescribe "proper" behaviour.

O

obedience Acting in accord with a direct order.

observational research methods Where individuals are observed in natural settings, often without awareness, in order to provide the opportunity for objective analysis of behaviour.

out-group homogeneity effect Perception of out-group members as more similar to one another than are in-group members. Thus, "they are alike; we are diverse."

out-groups "Them": groups that people perceive as distinctively different from or apart from their in-group.

overconfidence phenomenon The tendency to be more confident than correct—to overestimate the accuracy of one's beliefs.

overjustification effect The result of bribing people to do what they already like doing; they may then see their action as externally controlled rather than intrinsically appealing.

own-race bias The tendency for people to more accurately recognize faces of their own race.

P

passionate love A state of intense longing for union with another. Passionate lovers are absorbed in one another; they feel ecstatic at attaining their partner's love, and they are disconsolate on losing it.

peace A condition marked by low levels of hostility and aggression and by mutually beneficial relationships.

peripheral route to persuasion Occurs when people are influenced by incidental cues, such as a speaker's attractiveness.

persuasion The process by which a message induces change in beliefs, attitudes, or behaviours.

physical aggression Hurting someone else's body.

physical-attractiveness stereotype The presumption that physically attractive people possess other socially desirable traits as well: What is beautiful is good.

planning fallacy The tendency to underestimate how long it will take to complete a task.

pluralistic ignorance A false impression of how other people are thinking, feeling, or responding.

prejudice A negative prejudgment of a group and its individual members.

primacy effect Other things being equal, information presented first usually has the most influence.

priming Activating particular associations in memory.

prosocial behaviour Positive, constructive, helpful social behaviour; the opposite of antisocial behaviour.

proximity Geographical nearness. Proximity (more precisely, "functional distance") powerfully predicts liking.

R

racism (1) An individual's prejudicial attitudes and discriminatory behaviour toward people of a given race, or (2) institutional practices (even if not motivated by prejudice) that subordinate people of a given race.

random assignment The process of assigning participants to the conditions of an experiment such that all persons have the same chance of being in a given condition.

random sample Survey procedure in which every person in the population being studied has an equal chance of inclusion.

reactance A motive to protect or restore our sense of freedom. Reactance arises when someone threatens our freedom of action.

realistic group conflict theory The theory that prejudice arises from competition between groups for scarce resources.

recency effect Information presented last sometimes has the most influence. Recency effects are less common than primacy effects.

reciprocity norm An expectation that people will help, not hurt, those who have helped them.

regression toward the average The statistical tendency for extreme scores or extreme behaviour to return toward the person's average.

relative deprivation The perception that one is less well off than others to whom one compares oneself.

representativeness heuristic The tendency to presume, sometimes despite contrary odds, that someone or something belongs to a particular group if resembling (representing) a typical member.

reward theory of attraction The theory that we like those whose behaviour is rewarding to us or whom we associate with rewarding events.

role A set of norms that define how people in a given social position ought to behave.

S

secure attachment Attachment rooted in trust and marked by intimacy.

selective attention The extent to which people's attitudes bias the attitude-relevant information they attend to, once exposed.

selective exposure The extent to which people's attitudes bias the attitude-relevant information they expose themselves to.

selective memory The extent to which people's attitudes bias recall and recognition of attitude-relevant information.

self-affirmation theory A theory that people often experience self-image threat after engaging in an undesirable behaviour, and they compensate for this threat by affirming another aspect of the self. Threaten people's self-concept in one domain, and they will compensate either by refocusing or by doing good deeds in some other domain.

self-concept How a person answers the question "Who am I?" provides a glimpse of their self-concept.

self-disclosure Revealing intimate aspects of oneself to others.

self-efficacy A sense that one is competent and effective, distinguished from self-esteem, which is one's sense of self-worth. A sharpshooter in the military might feel high self-efficacy and low self-esteem.

self-esteem A person's overall self-evaluation or sense of self-worth.

self-fulfilling prophecies Beliefs that lead to their own fulfillment.

self-handicapping Protecting one's self-image with behaviours that create a handy excuse for later failure.

self-monitoring Being attuned to the way you present yourself in social situations and adjusting your performance to create the desired impression.

self-perception theory The theory that, when unsure of our attitudes, we infer them much as would someone observing us—by looking at our behaviour and the circumstances under which it occurs.

self-presentation The act of expressing yourself and behaving in ways designed to create a favourable impression or an impression that corresponds to your ideals.

self-presentation theory A theory positing that we are eager to present ourselves in ways that make a good impression.

self-schemas Beliefs about self that organize and guide the processing of self-relevant information.

self-serving attributions A form of self-serving bias; the tendency to attribute positive outcomes to yourself and negative outcomes to other factors.

self-serving bias The tendency to perceive yourself favourably.

sexism (1) An individual's prejudicial attitudes and discriminatory behaviour toward people of a given sex, or (2) institutional practices (even if not motivated by prejudice) that subordinate people of a given sex.

situational attribution Attributing behaviour to the environment.

sleeper effect A delayed impact of a message; occurs when we remember the message but forget a reason for discounting it.

social aggression Hurting someone else's feelings or threatening their relationships. Sometimes called relational aggression, it includes cyberbullying and some forms of in-person bullying.

social comparison Evaluating your abilities and opinions by comparing yourself to others.

social dominance orientation A motivation to have your own group be dominant over other social groups.

social-exchange theory The theory that human interactions are transactions that aim to maximize one's rewards and minimize one's costs.

social facilitation (1) *Original meaning*: the tendency of people to perform simple or well-learned tasks better when others are present. (2) *Current meaning*: the strengthening of dominant (prevalent, likely) responses owing to the presence of others.

social identity The "we" aspect of our self-concept; the part of our answer to "Who am I?" that comes from our group memberships.

social learning theory The theory that we learn social behaviour by observing and imitating and by being rewarded and punished.

social loafing The tendency for people to exert less effort when they pool their efforts toward a common goal than when they are individually accountable.

social neuroscience An integration of biological and social perspectives that explores the neural and psychological bases of social and emotional behaviours.

social psychology The scientific study of how people think about, influence, and relate to one another.

social representations Socially shared beliefs; widely held ideas and values, including our assumptions and cultural ideologies. Our social representations help us make sense of our world.

social-responsibility norm An expectation that people will help those dependent upon them.

social scripts Culturally provided mental instructions for how to act in various situations.

social trap A situation in which the conflicting parties, by rationally pursuing their own self-interest, become caught in mutually destructive behaviour.

spontaneous trait inference An effortless, automatic inference of a trait after exposure to someone's behaviour.

spotlight effect The belief that others are paying more attention to our appearance than they really are.

stereotype threat A disruptive concern, when facing a negative stereotype, that one will be evaluated based on a negative stereotype.

stereotypes Beliefs about the personal attributes of a group of people. Stereotypes can be overgeneralized, inaccurate, and resistant to new information.

subgrouping Accommodating groups of individuals who deviate from one's stereotype by forming a new stereotype about this subset of the group.

subtyping Accommodating groups of individuals who deviate from one's stereotype by thinking of them as a special category of people with different properties.

superordinate goals Shared goals that necessitate cooperative effort: goals that override people's differences from one another.

System 1 The intuitive, automatic, unconscious, and fast way of thinking.

System 2 The deliberate, controlled, and slower way of thinking.

T

temporal comparisons Comparisons between how the self is viewed now and how the self was viewed in the past or how the self is expected to be viewed in the future.

terror management According to "terror management theory," people's self-protective emotional and cognitive responses (including adhering more strongly to their cultural worldviews and prejudices) when confronted with reminders of their mortality.

theory An integrated set of principles that explain and predict observed events.

Tragedy of the Commons The "commons" is any shared resource, including air, water, energy sources, and food supplies. The tragedy occurs when individuals consume more than their share, with the cost of their doing so dispersed among all, causing the ultimate collapse—the tragedy—of the commons.

two-factor theory of emotion Arousal × its label = emotion.

two-step flow of communication The process by which media influence often occurs through opinion leaders, who in turn influence others.

Name Index

A

Aarts, N., 244
Abbate, C. S., 293
Abbey, A., 98
ABC News, 203, 267
Abelson, R., 116
Abrams, D., 246
Abramson, L., 55
Acevedo, B. P., 372
Achenbach, C. J., 275
Acitelli, L. K., 360
Ackerman, J. M., 369
Adair, J. G., 22
Adamopoulos, J., 253
Adams, D., 309
Adams, G., 108, 353
Adams, J. M., 379
Adarves-Yorno, I., 211
Addis, M. E., 276
Adelman, H. F., 141
Aderman, D., 271
Adinolfi, A. A., 349
Adler, N. L., 377
Adler, R. P., 188
Adorno, T., 396
Aesop, 349
AFP, 57
Agerström, J., 118
Agnew, C. R., 379
Agnew, G. A., 230
Agthe, M., 350, 353
Ahuvia, A., 13
Aiello, J. R., 230
Ainsworth, M., 304, 372, 374
Ajzen, I., 116, 119, 120f
Aknin, L. B., 274
Al Ramiah, A., 444
Al-Sadat, A., 455
Albarracin, D., 119, 121, 167
Alberts, S. C., 277
Aldag, R. J., 252
Alden, L. E., 66
Alexander, J., 167
Alexander, L., 442
Allee, W. C., 227
Allen, J., 346
Allen, M. S., 229
Allen, V. L., 210
Allesøe, K., 69
Allik, J., 54
Allison, S. T., 59, 432
Almeida, D. M., 306
Allport, F. W., 226
Allport, G. W., 394, 398, 400, 410, 416, 451
Altemeyer, B., 396, 397
Alter, A., 337
Altmann, J., 277
Alwin, D. E., 170
Amabile, T. M., 87
Amato, P., 280
Ambady, N., 107, 350, 419
American Enterprise, 379
American Psychological Association, 324, 329
Amos, 358
Amundsen, R., 256
Anastasi, J. S., 408
Anderegg, W. R. L., 180
Andersen, S., 270
Andersen, S. M., 33
Anderson, C., 81
Anderson, C. A., 27, 63, 65, 93, 311, 316, 322, 324–332, 334, 360, 429
Anderson, D. C., 316, 325
Anderson, P. D., 213
Anderson, S. L., 353, 354
Anderson, V. N., 392
Anglemyer, A., 319
Angulo, S., 47, 81
Angus Reid, 170
Anik, L., 270
Annan, K., 452
Anthony, D. B., 36, 49
Antonakis, J., 350
AP/Ipsos, 322, 400
Appel, M., 52, 417
Appleman, A. J., 64
Appleseed, J., 50
Applewhite, M. H., 173, 176
Archer, D., 399
Archer, J., 304, 307, 322
Archer, R. L., 376, 377
Arden, M. A., 143
Arendt, H., 207, 208
Ariely, D., 211, 351, 360
Ariganello, M., 110
Aristotle, 335, 350, 360, 432
Ariza, L. M., 244
Arkes, H. R., 43, 44, 118, 166
Arkin, R. M., 62, 64, 344, 346
Armeli, S., 141
Armitage, C. J., 119, 143
Armor, D. A., 58, 59
Arms, R. L., 336
Armstrong, T. L., 400
Arnold, O., 126
Aron, A., 362, 367, 368, 368f, 369, 378, 378f, 435
Aron, E., 378, 378f, 435
Arone, S., 207, 239
Aronson, E., 25, 129, 161, 174, 364, 450, 451
Aronson, J., 417, 418
Arriaga, X. B., 379
Arrow, J., 256
Arrowood, A. J., 135
Asch, S. E., 164, 197, 198, 205, 208t, 209, 210, 212, 213, 217, 218
Ash, E., 303
Asher, S. R., 306
Ashton-James, C. E., 45, 294, 404
Aslan, R., 177
Associated Press, 86
Attia, S., 313
Atwell, R. H., 220
Au, T.K., 127
Augoustinos, M., 9
Aumann, K., 57
Aurelius, M., 15
Austin, J. B., 271
Averill, J., 310
Axsom, D., 172
Ayal, S., 211
Azrin, N. H., 315

B

Baars, B. J., 74
Bachman, J. G., 19, 154
Back, M., 345
Badger, A. J., 342
Bae, M., 237
Baeyens, F., 365
Bailenson, J. N., 156
Bainbridge, W. S., 175, 176
Baize, H. R., 351
Baker, L. R., 377
Baldwin, M. W., 77, 372
Balliet, D., 404, 433, 455
Banaji, M. R., 76, 118, 386, 388
Banas, K., 280, 343
Bandura, A., 38, 53, 70, 128, 313, 314, 324, 325
Banks, S. M., 160
Banse, R., 413
Banting, F., 32
Bar-Haim, Y., 348
Bar-Hillel, M., 84
Bar-Tal, D., 438

Barash, D. P., 276, 177, 304
Barber, B. M., 88
Bargh, J. A., 75, 76, 98, 196, 244
Barkley, C., 305
Barlett, C. P., 311, 330, 331
Barnes, R. D., 241
Barnett, M. A., 272
Baron, J., 275, 414
Baron, R. A., 336, 353
Baron, R. S., 176, 229, 231, 247
Barongan, C., 325
Barry, D., 56
Bartholomew, K., 372, 373
Bartholow, B. D., 307, 330
Bassili, J. N., 116, 119, 183, 259
Bastian, B., 99, 330, 344, 446
Batson, C. D., 62, 117, 121, 277, 279, 280, 281, 289, 294, 296, 398, 456
Batten, P. G., 376
Bauer, M., 447
Bauman, C. W., 101, 360
Baumann, L. J., 271
Baumann, M. R., 252
Baumgardner, A. H., 62
Baumeister, R. F., 8, 51, 52, 62, 63, 69, 70, 101, 220, 229, 231, 233, 335, 336, 342, 343, 344, 362, 377, 379, 380, 391
Baumhart, R., 56
Bavelier, D., 332
Baxter, T. L., 103
Bayer, E., 226
Bazerman, M. H., 458
Bazinska, R., 365
Bazzini, D., 352, 377
Beall, A. T., 434
Beals, K. P., 377
Beaman, A. L., 241, 358
Bearak, B., 400
Beauvois, J. L., 204
Becatoros, E., 400
Beck, L. A., 374
Beckenuyte, C., 135
Becker, S., 292
Becker, V., 411, 411f
Beckham, D., 157
Beckham, V., 157
Beeler-Duden, S., 274
Beelmann, A., 444
Beer, J. S., 58
Bègue, L., 307, 413, 414
Beilock, S. L., 419
Bekafigo, M. A., 243
Bell, D. W., 162
Bell, P. A., 315, 316
Belson, W. A., 323
Beltrani, A., 14
Bem, D., 96, 137, 141
Benjamin, A. J. Jr., 318
Benjamin, L. T. Jr., 199
Bennett, D., 212, 348
Bennett, R., 459
Bennett, T., 321
Bennis, W. G., 258
Benthin, A. C., 132
Benton, S. L., 59
Benzien, J., 205
Benzies, K., 314
Berg, J. H., 366, 375, 376, 377
Berger, J., 217, 219, 346
Berger, R., 64
Berglas, S., 62
Bergsieker, H., 387, 419
Berkowitz, L., 211, 271, 272, 275, 310, 311f, 315, 318, 324, 325
Berman, J. J., 119
Bernardo, P., 320
Berndsen, M., 411
Bernhardt, P. C., 309
Bernieri, F., 350
Berns, G. S., 213
Bernstein, D. M., 94
Bernstein, M. J., 386, 408
Berra, Y., 54
Berry, J. L., 168
Berry, J. W., 452
Berscheid, E., 109, 128, 346, 349, 351, 352, 353, 354, 362, 367, 368, 436
Bertrand, M., 388
Besser, A., 374
Best, D. L., 390
Bettencourt, B. A., 306, 422
Betz, B., 459
Bhatia, T., 168
Bianchi, E., 37
Bickman, L., 292, 453
Biden, J., 20
Bielawski, D. M., 124
Bilderdeck, A. C., 456
Bilewicz, M., 441
Billig, M. G., 403
bin Laden, O., 207
Binder, J., 442
Biner, P., 317
Bingenheimer, J. B., 314
Binham, R., 277
Bishop, G. D., 243
Bizumic, B., 397
Bizzoco, N., 380
Blair, J., 283
Blake, R. R., 448, 457
Blaker, N. M., 256
Blanchard, F. A., 130
Blanton, H., 118, 386
Blass, T., 200, 203, 216
Block, J., 101
Blockley, S., 290
Bloom, P., 135
Boden, J. M., 50
Bodenhausen, G. V., 46, 91, 158, 389, 405, 406, 407
Bodford, J. E., 373
Bodinger, H., 285
Boer, D., 360
Boggiano, A. K., 140, 141
Bohm, R., 401
Boland, J. E., 39
Boldt, E. D., 395
Bollinger, M., 353
Bombeck, E., 187
Bond, A. J., 314
Bond, C. F. Jr., 228, 421
Bond, J. T., 57
Bond, M. H., 359, 437
Bond, R., 217
Bonner, B. L., 252
Bonniot-Cabanac, M-C., 336
Bonnot, V., 419
Bono, J. E., 258
Booth, A., 208
Booth, D., 12
Borgida, E., 391, 414, 419
Bornstein, B. H., 433
Bornstein, R. F., 346
Bossard, J. H. S., 345
Bothwell, R. K., 408
Botvin, G. J., 186, 187, 189
Botwin, M. D., 361
Bouas, K. S., 433
Boucher, K. L., 417
Bouman, T., 434
Bourgeois, M. J., 163
Bourke, M. L., 321
Boutwell, B. B., 380
Bowen, E., 3
Bowen, N. K., 419
Bower, G. H., 90
Bowlby, J., 372
Bowler, P. J., 97
Bowman, S., 256
Boyatzis, C. J., 23
Boye, D., 128
Boyes, A. D., 364
Bradbury, T., 360
Bradbury, T. N., 50, 380
Bradley, E., 282, 283
Bradley, W., 141
Brainerd, C. J., 216
Braman, D., 154
Brand, R. J., 354
Brandt, M. J., 390, 397
Bratslavsky, E., 377
Brauer, M., 243, 246, 287, 295
Braun, C., 355f
Braun, M. T., 325
Bray, R. M., 262
Bray, S., 229
Breaux, J., 283
Breckler, S. J., 116, 180
Brehm, J. W., 135, 163, 219
Brehm, S. S., 219
Breivik, K., 302
Brekke, N., 306, 414, 419
Brennan, R. T., 314
Brenner, S. N., 56
Brescoli, V. L., 392
Brescoll, V. L., 414
Breuer, J., 309
Brewer, M. B., 25, 403, 416, 451, 452
Bricker, W., 312

Brickman, P., 13
Brigham, J. C., 408
Briñol, P., 138, 152, 155, 157, 158
Britt, T. W., 309
Brock, T. C., 85, 156, 171
Brockner, J., 431
Brodt, S., 67
Brody, J., 384
Brodzinsky, D. M., 230
Bronfenbrenner, U., 438
Broockman, D., 406
Brooks, R., 392
Brooks, R. D., 161
Broome, A., 66
Brounstein, P., 376
Brown, E. H., 230
Brown, J., 47
Brown, J. D., 90, 35
Brown, K., 252
Brown, L. L., 368f
Brown, R., 309, 314, 403, 407, 418, 445
Brown, S. L., 270, 451
Brown, T. J., 276
Brown, V. R., 254
Brown, W. M., 355
Brown-Iannuzzi, J. L., 118
Browning, C., 208
Browning, E. B., 366
Browning, R., 370
Brownlee, E. A., 62
Bruck, M., 95
Brummelman, E., 51, 52
Bruneau, E., 277
Brunell, A. B., 51, 52
Bruun, S. E., 233, 235
Bryan, C. J., 36
Bryan, J., 289
Bryant, B., 228
Buchanan, W., 365
Buckley, K. E., 327, 429
Buehler, R., 43, 44, 80, 94, 214, 215f
Buffardi, L. E., 64
Buffett, W., 295
Bui, N. H., 59
Bull, R., 352
Burger, J. M., 58, 64, 103, 126, 137, 155, 200, 211, 218, 256, 290, 346
Burgess, A. W., 321
Burghart, D., 270
Burns, L., 58
Burnstein, E., 245, 277, 310
Burr, W. R., 345
Burson, A. K., 79
Burton, R., 196
Busching, R., 325
Bushman, B. J., 47, 51, 52f, 171, 306, 316, 318, 323–327, 330, 331, 334, 335, 336
Buss, D. M., 356, 361
Butcher, S. H., 335
Buttlemann, D., 401
Butz, D. A., 109
Buunk, A. P., 375, 376
Bylsma, W. H., 311
Byrne, D., 359, 365
Bytwerk, R. L., 161

C

Cabanac, M., 336
Cacioppo, J. T., 7, 117, 139, 151, 157, 162, 171, 172, 254, 454
Cafferty, J., 217
Cain, T. R., 107
Cairns, E., 443
Cal, A. V., 154
Caldwell, D., 137
Caldwell, H. K., 374
Cameron, C. D., 280
Cameron, G., 432
Cameron, J., 141, 248, 363
Campbell, A. C., 289
Campbell, D. T., 9, 164, 195, 276
Campbell, L., 85, 379
Campbell, M. A., 337
Campbell, W. K., 51, 52, 54, 64
Campos, B., 360
Canadian Centre on Substance Abuse and Addiction, 219
Canadian Press, 244
Canevello, A., 50
Cantarero, K., 128
Canter, D., 283
Cantor, N., 34, 58, 37
Caputo, D., 79
Carducci, B. J., 367
Carli, L. L., 218, 413
Carlo, G., 291
Carlsmith, J. M., 25, 132, 161, 271
Carlson, E. N., 52
Carlson, J. G., 370
Carlson, M., 271, 272, 311
Carlston, D. E., 64
Carnagey, N. L., 330, 429
Carnegie, A., 338
Carnegie, D., 362, 364
Carnelly, K. B., 373
Carnevale, P. J., 440, 456
Carney, D. R., 138
Carpenter, C. J., 343
Carr, E. W., 348
Carr, R. B., 69
Carré, J. M., 307
Carroll, J. S., 319
Carron, A. V., 230
Cartwright, D. S., 244, 314
Carvallo, M., 342, 380
Carver, C. S., 121, 293
Case, T. I., 171
Casella, D., 361
Cash, T. F., 353
Caspi, A., 306, 359
Cassidy, J., 373
Castelli, L., 360, 395
Castle, D. J., 353
Castro, F., 100, 100f
Catanese, K. R., 342
CBC, 20, 196, 197, 199, 239, 245, 252, 267, 285, 387, 388
CBS, 244
Ceci, S. J., 95, 391
Cemalcilar, Z., 342
Census Bureau, 97
Cerankosky, B. C., 332
Chaiken, S., 151, 152, 154, 155, 157, 161, 169, 172, 184
Chalmers, A., 58
Chamberlain, P., 314
Chambers, J. R., 61, 360, 439
Chan, A. C., 127
Chan, D. K-S., 374
Chan, M. K. H., 259
Chance, J. E., 408
Chance, S. A., 34
Chandler, J., 139
Chandra, A., 410
Chang, K., 55
Chang-Schneider, C., 47, 81
Chao, M., 277
Chapin, J., 414
Chapman, J. P., 87
Chapman, L. J., 87
Charlin, V., 272
Chartrand, T. L., 75, 138, 196, 344, 360
Chatard, A., 415
Check, J., 320, 321
Chen, F. F., 360
Chen, L., 242
Chen, S., 33, 377, 401
Chen, S. C., 226
Chen, Y., 13
Chen, Z., 344
Cheng, J., 302
Cheng, J. B., 171
Cheng, K., 69
Chermack, S. M., 306
Chernick, L., 216
Chester, D. S., 312
Chesterfield, Lord, 157, 289, 407
Cheung, C. K. T., 7, 344
Cheung, F., 311
Chiang, C. P., 244
Chiao, J., 350
Chiles, C., 210
Choi, D-W., 456
Choi, I., 40, 15
Choi, J., 40
Choi, W., 7, 344
Choi, Y., 254
Choma, B., 397
Chorost, A. F., 369
Chou, H. G., 35
Chou, W. S., 383
Christ, O., 385, 442
Christakis, N. A., 196
Chrisjohn, R. D., 291
Christenfeld, N., 211
Christian, J. L., 380
Christie, C., 238
Christie, S. D., 254

Chua, H. F., 39
Chung, C. K., 385
Church, A. H., 235
Church, A. T., 55
Churchill, W., 183, 434
Cialdini, R. B., 59, 125, 126, 127, 156t, 186, 254, 271, 281, 295, 402, 448, 453
Ciarocco, N. J., 63
Ciccone, M., 59
Cicerello, A., 351
Cicero, 273
Cihangir, S., 252
Cikara, M., 277, 448
Cillessen, A. N., 302
Cimpian, A., 414
Cioffi, D., 297
Claassen, C., 441
Claassen, R. L., 246
Clark, M. H., 418
Clark, M. S., 271, 272, 352, 375, 376
Clark, R. D. III, 211, 260
Clarke, A. C., 345
Clarkson, T., 398
Clary, E. G., 134
Clayton, S., 182
Cleghorn, J., 279
Clement, R. W., 59, 407
Clevstrom, J., 219
Clifford, M. M., 352
Clinton, H., 20, 256
Clore, G. L., 275, 276, 364, 365
CNN, 203, 239, 245
Coates, D., 13
Coccia, M., 311
Cohen, B., 368
Cohen, D., 314
Cohen, E. E. A., 231
Cohen, G. L., 418, 419
Cohen, L. L., 409
Cohen, R. L., 170
Cohen, S., 68, 181
Cohn, E., 316
Cohrs, J. C., 397
Coke, J. S., 296
Colby, C. A., 455
Cole, S. W., 69
Coleman, G., 414
Collier, K. L., 441
Collins, A., 282
Collins, M. A., 358
Collins, M. E., 442
Collins, N. L., 376
Colman, A. M., 245
Colzato, L. S., 456
Comer, D. R., 236
Comim, F., 181
Comstock, G., 325
Confucius, 81
Conger, R. D., 374
Conlee, M. C., 124
Connell, J. B., 252
Conner, M., 119
Conolley, E. S., 209
Conrad, J., 97
Conway, F., 175
Conway, L. G. III, 440
Conway, M., 98
Cook, S. W., 130
Cooke, L. J., 141
Cooley, C. H., 36
Coon, H. M., 38
Cooper, H., 306
Cooper, H. M., 107
Cooper, J., 132, 135, 136, 142, 143f, 144, 189, 416
Cooper, R., 451
Copper, C., 211, 249
Corcoran, D. M., 375
Corman, M. D., 307
Cornell, S. D., 124
Cornwallis, E., 10
Correl, J., 389
Corrigan, P. W., 306
Cosby, P. C., 367
Coskun, H., 254
Costa-Lopes, R., 394, 400
Costanzo, M., 303, 337
Costello, C., 431
Cota, A. A., 221
Cottom, T., 277
Cotton, J. L., 316
Cottrell, N. B., 230, 231
Coulter, K. S., 346
Council of Ontario Universities, 8
Courbet, D., 348
Covey, J., 86
Cowan, C. L., 271
Cox, C. R., 75
Coyne, I., 287
Coyne, S. M., 322, 325
Crabb, P. B., 124
Craig, W. M., 177, 301
Crandall, C. S., 211, 277, 399, 406
Crane, F., 377
Crano, W., 107, 108
Crawford, J. T., 384
Crick, F., 254
Crisp, R. J., 442, 452
Critcher, C. R., 85
Crocker, J., 46, 47, 49, 50, 87, 401, 404, 408, 415
Crockett, M. J., 456
Crofton, C., 358
Croizet, J., 101
Croizet, J.-C., 419
Crompton, T., 182
Crone, E. A., 344
CROP, 393
Crosby, J. R., 388
Cross, S. E., 37, 40
Crowley, M., 275, 291
Crowther, S., 287
Croxton, J., 95
Croyle, R. T., 163
Crutchfield, R. S., 217
CTV, 220, 242
Cuddy, A. J. C., 138, 395
Culiberg, B., 236
Cullum, J. G., 211
Cunningham, J. A., 141
Cunningham, J. D., 372, 377
Cunningham, M. R., 272
Curphy, G. J., 257

D

Dabbs, J., 377
Dabbs, J. M., 157, 283, 307
Dalgas, O., 350
Dalrymple, T., 333
Dambrun, M., 202
Damon, W., 19
Dardenne, B., 395
Darley, J. M., 150, 282, 283, 283f, 285, 286, 289, 291, 292, 337, 346, 421
Darley, S., 189
Darvish, Y., 410
Darwin, C., 15, 139, 228
Dasgupta, N., 406
Dashiell, J. F., 226, 227
Dateline, 282
Dauenheimer, D., 419
David, D., 88
Davidai, S., 85
Davidson, B., 246
Davidson, R., 305
Davie, M., 250
Davies, A. C., 351
Davies, P. G., 418
Davies, W. H., 94
Davila, J., 493
Davis, A. C., 290
Davis, C. G., 87
Davis, J. H., 185, 260
Davis, J. L., 360
Davis, K. E., 99, 128, 372
Davis, L., 236
Dawes, R., 19, 51, 59, 112
Dawes, R. M., 82, 83, 433, 434
Dawkins, R., 276, 407
Dawson, L., 14
Dazeley, S., 277
De Cremer, D., 434
De Dreu, C. K. W., 261
de Hoog, N., 158, 159
de Hoogh, A. H. B., 258
De Houwer, J., 365
de Lange, M. A., 75
de Meuse, K. P., 257
de Vries, N. K., 261
de Waal, F. B. M., 280
de Wit, J. B. F., 158
Del Vicario, M., 81
Deary, I. J., 397
Deaton, A., 62
DeBruine, L. M., 290, 290f
Decety, J., 34
Dechêne, A., 166
Deci, E. L., 69, 140, 141, 343

Dehue, F., 302
Delgado, J., 121
DeLisi, M., 330
Dembroski, T. M., 156
Demoulin, S., 403
Denissen, J. J. A., 342
Denrell, J., 213
Denson, T. F., 306
Department of Canadian Heritage, 453
Derks, B., 419
Derlega, V. J., 376
Dermer, M., 367
Dertke, M. C., 275
Desforges, D. M., 452
DeSteno, D., 90, 117
Deutsch, M., 212, 213, 428, 433, 438, 442, 452, 459
Deutsch, R., 76
Devine, P. G., 405, 406, 410
DeVos-Comby, L., 160
Devries, K. M., 392
DeWall, C. N., 39, 307, 342, 344, 372
Dewulf, A., 244
Diallo, A., 389
DiBello, A. M., 143
Dickerson, S. S., 69
Diehl, M., 254
Dickman, A. B., 85
Diekmann, K. A., 54
Diener, E., 13, 38, 121, 238, 241, 306
Dietrich, M., 362
Dijksterhuis, A., 151
Dill, E., 238
Dill, K., 331
Dillon, K. P., 324
Dion, K. K., 155, 352, 354, 369, 370, 372, 379, 446
Dion, K. L., 221, 311, 312, 369, 370, 372, 379
Dishion, T. J., 244
Disraeli, B., 121
Ditto, P. H., 384
Dixon, J., 441, 442, 443f
Dobbs, A. R., 315
Dodge, R. W., 167
Dolan, R. J., 135, 213, 214
Dolinski, D., 272, 297
Dollard, J., 309
Dolnik, L., 171
Donaldson, Z. R., 371
Dong, P., 76
Donnerstein, E., 320, 324, 325
Doob, A. N., 85, 154
Doosje, B., 59
D'Orlando, F., 319
Dorr, A., 188
Douglas, C., 88
Douglas, J. E., 321
Douglas, K. M., 237
Douthitt, E. A., 230
Dovidio, J. F., 281, 385, 386, 388, 401, 449
Downing, L., 239
Drake, B., 384
Drapeau, J., 43
Dreber, A., 429
Driedger, L., 452
Driskell, J. E., 211, 228, 259
Driver, R., 36
Drolet, A. L., 433
Drury, L., 441, 446
Drydakis, N., 393
Dryer, D. C., 361
Duck, J. M., 165
Duclos, S. E., 137
Dudley, K. A., 103
Duffy, M., 242
Duggan, M., 327
Duke, A. A., 307
Dumont, M., 395
Dunbar, R., 432
Duncan, B. L., 412
Dunfield, K. A., 273
Dunham, Y., 401
Dunlosky, J., 80
Dunn, E. W., 45, 63, 103, 270, 274, 294
Dunn, J. R., 456
Dunn, L., 396
Dunning, D., 43, 44, 57, 59, 62, 79, 411, 421
Durante, K. M., 357
Durrheim, K., 441, 442, 443f
Dushenko, T. W., 22
Düsing, J., 152
Dutta, R., 358
Dutton, D., 367, 373
Dutton, K. A., 47
Duval, S., 293
Duval, V. H., 293
Dweck, C. S., 53, 412
Dye, M. W. G., 331
Dzindolet, M. T., 254

E

Eagly, A. H., 151, 154, 169, 172, 184, 218, 246, 256, 275, 291, 292, 352, 384, 390, 391
Earls, F. J., 314
Easterbrook, M., 346
Eastwick, P. W., 45, 350, 362
Eaton, J., 310
Eberhardt, J. L., 412
Ebert, J. E. J., 44
Ebner, N. C., 408
Eccles, J., 107
Eckersley, R., 13
Eckes, T., 119
Edelman, B., 388
Edelson, M. G., 194
Edge, N., 35
Edwards, J. A., 157
Edwards, K. M., 321
Egan, L., 135
Eggleston, T. J., 132
Ehrenreich, S. E., 337
Ehrlich, D., 184
Ehrlinger, J., 106, 388
Eibach, R. P., 388, 396
Eich, E., 97
Eichmann, A., 204, 207, 208
Einstein, A., 301
Eisenberg, N., 274, 278, 291
Eisenberger, R., 141
Eisenstadt, D., 134
Eiser, J. R., 132
Elder, G. H. Jr., 351
Eldersveld, S., 167
Eliot, T. S., 110, 161
Elkin, R. A., 134
Ellemers, N., 59, 403
Elliot, A., 139
Ellis, H., 408
Ellison, P., 238
Elson, M., 325
Emerson, R. W., 133, 237, 258, 259, 362, 413
Emmons, R. A., 13
Engemann, K. M., 353
Ennis, B. J., 177, 313
Enzle, M., 88
Epley, N., 26, 36, 56, 75, 385
Epstein, J. A., 186, 189
Epstein, S., 216
Epstude, K., 86
Erb, H.-P., 221
Erber, R., 111, 405
Erickson, B., 154
Erickson, S. K., 56
Erikson, E. H., 374
Eron, L. D., 322, 323, 337
Escobar-Chaves, L. S., 326, 327
Eshleman, A., 406
Esser, J. K., 252
Esses, V. M., 90, 162, 388, 400, 405, 407
Esterbrook, G., 181
Etzioni, A., 193, 453
Evans, G. W., 230
Evans, R. I., 187
Evelo, A.J., 14410
Eyal, T., 385
Ezeonu, I., 177

F

Fabrigar, L. R., 144, 157, 172
Falbo, T., 342
Falkener, A., 305
Falkener, A. L., 305
Farb, N. A. S., 34
Farbstein, F., 69
Farquhar, J. W., 167
Farrell, C., 188
Farrelly, M. C., 159
Farris, K. B., 98
Farwell, L., 105
Faulkner, S. L., 234
Faust, D., 82
Faye, C., 26
Fazio, R. H., 82, 116, 118, 120, 121, 144, 152, 184

Feather, N. T., 9, 105
Federal Bureau of Investigation, 387, 399
Federal Trade Commission, 187
Feeney, J., 376
Feeney, J. A., 372
Fein, S., 404, 420
Feinberg, J. M., 230
Feinberg, M., 160
Feingold, A., 351, 352, 353
Fekken, G. C., 291
Feldman, L. A., 135, 136
Feldman, N. S., 414
Feldman, R. S., 107, 108
Feldman, S. S., 452
Felicio, D. M., 419
Felson, R. B., 303
Fenigstein, A., 66
Ferguson, C. J., 325, 331
Fergusson, D. M., 51, 379
Ferriday, C., 51
Ferris, D. L., 390
Feshbach, N. D., 188, 189
Festinger, L., 34, 116, 132, 133, 134, 154, 171, 183, 237, 246
Feygina, J. T., 180
Feynman, R., 142
Fichter, J. H., 398
Ficks, C. A., 306
Fiedler, F. E., 256
Fielder, L., 221
Filipovic, J., 305
Final Report of the Truth and Reconciliation Commission of Canada, 128
Finch, J. F., 57
Fincham, F. D., 50, 98
Fincher, C. L., 357
Finchilescu, G., 327, 441, 444
Finkel, E., 350
Finkel, E. J., 33, 45, 360, 362, 379, 380
Finkenauer, C., 45
Fischer, E. F., 368
Fischer, P., 132, 284, 285, 316, 32
Fischer, R., 58
Fischhoff, B., 13, 83, 84
Fishbein, D., 361
Fishbein, M., 119, 120f
Fisher, H., 350, 369
Fisher, H. E., 367, 368f
Fisher, J. D., 274
Fisher, R. J., 457
Fishman, S., 438
Fiske, S. T., 9, 36, 112, 204, 207, 388, 389, 390, 395, 408
Fitterman, L., 269
Fitzpatrick, A. R., 246
Fitzpatrick, M. A., 380
Fitzsimons, G. J., 119
Flake, J. K., 359
Flay, B. R., 153, 187
Fleet, F., 250
Fletcher, G. J. O., 90, 342, 364, 365, 376, 412
Flores, A. R., 392
Florian, V., 342
Floyd, G., 267, 296
Flynn, C., 342
Flynn, E., 211
Foa, E. B., 269
Foa, U. G., 269
Fogelman, E., 294
Folger, R., 141
Folkman, J. R., 22
Follett, M. P., 454
Fonda, H., 261
Fong, G. T., 62, 66, 67f
Foos, A. E., 153
Forbes, C., 419
Forbes, M., 221
Ford, J. D., 398
Ford, R., 387
Forgas, J. P., 90, 91, 158, 272
Form, W. H., 277
Forrest, L. N., 118
Forrester, R. L., 50
Forscher, P. S., 405
Forster, E. M., 142
Förster, J., 419
Forsyth, D. R., 47, 64
Foss, R. D., 292, 298
Foster, C. A., 379
Foster, E. M., 24
Foster-Fishman, P. G., 245
Fowler, J. H., 196
Fowler, S., 17
Fraley, R. C., 396
Francesconi, M., 353
Frank, A., 139
Frank, B., 400
Frank, J. D., 178
Frank, M., 239
Frankel, A., 62
Franklin, B., 31
Franklin, R., 254
Frantz, C. M., 439
Fraser, S. C., 125
Frazier, R. S., 118
Frazier, W., 69
Frederick, D. A., 357
Freedman, J. L., 125, 129, 141, 171, 230
Freeman, J. B., 359
French, S., 56
Freud, S., 304, 415
Freund, B., 58
Frey, B., 292
Frey, J., 315, 316
Friedman, H. S., 361
Friedman, R., 139
Friesen, J., 386
Frijters, P., 388
Frieze, I. H., 353
Frimer, J. A., 81, 291
Frisell, T., 306
Froming, W. J., 121
Fromkin, H., 221
Fromm, E., 352
Frost, J. H., 360
Fry, D. P., 449
Fryer, R. G., 388
Fulgoni, G. M., 93
Fuller, S. R., 252
Fuller, T., 215
Fultz, J., 281
Funder, D. C., 26, 101, 111
Furnham, A., 105, 414
Futrell, D., 257

G

Gabbiadini, A., 330
Gable, S. L., 376, 377
Gabrenya, W. K. Jr., 235
Gabriel, S., 342, 380
Gaebelein, J. W., 333
Gaertner, S. L., 41, 55, 388, 404, 449, 452
Gaines, S. D., 431
Gaissmaier, W., 112
Gaither, S. E., 441
Galanter, M., 177
Galinsky, A. D., 88, 400, 456
Galinsky, E., 57
Galizio, M., 157
Gall, G. L., 21
Gallup, G. H. Jr., 356, 398, 440
Gamble, J., 245
Gandhi, M., 154
Gange, J. J., 229
Gangestad, S. W., 64, 355, 358
Garber, J., 342
Garcia-Marques, T., 166, 226, 348
Gardner, W. L., 33, 85, 378, 380
Garner, R., 297
Garovich, L., 390
Garrett, B. L., 95
Garrity, M. J., 309
Garry, M., 95
Garver-Apgar, C. E., 361
Gates, G. J., 85, 410
Gates, M. F., 227
Gatto, K., 325
Gaucher, D., 386
Gaunt, R., 360
Gavanski, I., 46
Gawande, A., 56
Gawronski, B., 46
Gazzaniga, M., 78, 122
Ge, Y., 388
Gebauer, J. E., 48
Geen, R. G., 229, 324, 325
Geers, A. L., 163
Gelfand, M., 162
Geller, D., 213
Gelles, R., 314
Genovese, K., 282, 285, 297, 298
Gentile, B., 64
Gentile, D. A., 295, 323, 324, 325, 327, 328, 330, 332
Genuis, M., 320
George, D., 292
Gerard, H. B., 174, 209, 212, 213

Gerbner, G., 327
Gerdjikov, T., 142
Gergen, K. J., 297
Gerrig, R. J., 85
Gershoff, E., 314
Gershoff, E. T., 337
Gerstein, L. H., 291
Gerstenfeld, P. B., 244
Gesch, B., 308
Giancola, P. R., 307
Gibbons, F. X., 121, 132, 271
Gibson, J. I., 441
Gier, J., 202
Giesler, R. B., 35, 81
Gifford, R., 180, 410, 431
Gigerenzer, G., 76, 78, 112
Gigone, D., 245
Gilbert, D. T., 35, 44, 45, 99, 101, 183, 346, 362, 407
Gillath, O., 374
Gillis, J., 17
Gilman, C. P., 173
Gilovich, T., 31, 54, 57, 80, 85, 86, 87, 88, 106, 239, 283, 411
Gini, G., 338
Gino, F., 211
Gischer, W. G., 407
Givens, J., 277
Glasman, L. R., 121
Glass, C., 90, 128
Gleason, M. E. J., 270
Glenn, N. D., 171
Glick, B., 337
Glick, P., 390, 395
Gliner, M. D., 246
Globe and Mail, 242
Gluszek, A., 401
Gnambs, T., 52
Gockel, C., 236
Godbout, L., 256
Goel, S., 59
Goethals, G. R., 59, 103, 156, 247
Goethe, J. W., 137, 163
Goetz, J. L., 275
Goh, J., 39
Goldberg, L. L., 357
Goldberg, L. R., 103
Goldberg, M., 241
Goldberg, P., 391
Goldhagen, D. J., 204, 208
Golding, W., 237, 435
Goldman, R., 157
Goldman, S. K., 386
Goldsamt, L. A., 271
Goldsmith, R. E., 180
Goldstein, A. G., 408
Goldstein, A. P., 333, 337
Goldstein, C. C., 108
Goldstein, J. H., 336
Goldstein, N. J., 127, 202
Golec de Davala, A., 176, 398, 412
Golomb, B. A., 308
Golub, S. A., 394
Gómez, A., 401
Gonsalkorale, K., 344
Gonsalves, B., 95
Gonzaga, G. C., 360, 376
Gonzales, A. L., 64
Gonzales, C., 310
Gonzalez, A., 450
Gonzalez, K. V., 441
Gonzalez-Vallejo, 58
Good, A., 457
Goplen, J., 389
Gordjin, E., 261
Gordon, A. M., 377
Gordon, S. L., 363, 369
Gortmaker, S. L., 22
Gosling, S. D., 46
Gosselin, J. T., 53
Gotlib, I. H., 455
Goto, S. G., 39
Gottlieb, J., 293
Gottlieb, M. C., 287
Gottman, J., 380
Gough, H. G., 66
Gould, M. S., 197
Gould, R., 376
Gouldner, A. W., 273
Govern, J., 238
Graetz, K., 41
Graf, S., 446
Graham, J., 385
Graham, S., 302
Grajek, S., 372
Gramzow, R. H., 51
Granstrom, K., 252
Grant, D. R., 244
Grant, J. M., 393
Gray, C., 290
Gray, J. D., 54
Graziano, W. G., 67, 330
Green, A. R., 389
Green, C., 450
Green, C. S., 332
Green, D. P., 450
Green, J., 103
Green, M. C., 85
Green, S., 353
Green, S. K., 292
Greenaway, K. H., 400, 401
Greenberg, A., 352
Greenberg, A. R., 280
Greenberg, J., 49, 62, 361, 404, 436
Greene, D., 140
Greene, E., 14
Greenlees, C., 236
Greenwald, A. G., 76, 78, 97, 118, 141, 386, 388, 389, 390, 404, 431
Gregory, R., 202
Greitemeyer, T., 132, 295, 296, 311, 326, 330, 332, 338
Grekul, J., 177
Grether, J., 276
Grewal, D., 346
Griffin, D., 43
Griffin, D. W., 80, 214, 215f
Griffin, K. W., 187
Griffitt, W., 315
Griggs, R. A., 199, 200, 201
Grinshteyn, E., 318
Grise, E., 20
Griskevicius, V., 276, 305, 369
Groenenboom, A., 236
Gross, A. E., 271, 358
Gross, A. M., 98
Gross, J. T., 301
Gross, P. H., 421
Gross, T. F., 408
Grossman, I., 456
Grossman, S., 149
Grossmann, I., 37
Grote, M., 376
Grove, J. R., 54
Grove, W. M., 82
Grube, J. W., 404
Gruder, C. L., 36, 153, 291
Gruendl, M., 355f
Gruman, J. A., 110
Gruman, J. C., 414
Grunberger, R., 130
Grusec, J. E., 289
Grush, J. E., 120, 166
Guadagno, R. E., 126, 161
Guardian, 180
Guay, F., 69
Gueguen, N., 126
Guerin, B., 56, 228
Guffler, K., 446
Guimond, S., 395, 415
Guiness, O., 379
Guinote, A., 436
Gulker, J. E., 441
Gunaratna, R., 162
Gunn, G., 60
Gunter, B., 414
Gupta, U., 370, 392
Gutierres, S. E., 357

H

Ha, T., 349
Haas, A. P., 394
Hacker, H. M., 394
Hackman, J. R., 236
Hadden, J. K., 398
Haddock, G., 172, 390, 407
Haddon, L., 324
Haeffel, G. J., 55
Hafenbrack, A. C., 287
Hafer, C. L., 413, 414Hagtvet, K. A., 19
Haidt, J., 33, 289
Hains, S. C., 252
Hahn, A., 453
Halberstadt, J., 355, 448
Hald, G. M., 320
Haldane, J. B. S., 276
Halford, J. T., 352
Hall, C. C., 419

Hall, D. L., 397
Hall, G. C. N., 325
Hall, J. A., 64
Hall, T., 97
Hall, V. C., 141
Hallahan, M., 105
Hallam, J., 325
Halperin, E., 456
Hamamura, T., 55
Hamberger, J., 445
Hamblin, R. L., 336
Hamermesh, D., 353
Hamilton, D. L., 87, 411
Hamm, H. K., 202
Hammond, M. D., 421
Hampson, R. B., 291
Hampton, K. N., 250
Han, G., 459
Hancock, J. T., 64
Handley, I. M., 163
Hanel, P. H. P., 246
Hannah, D. B., 415
Hanoch, Y., 397
Hanrahan, S. J., 54
Hans, J. D., 374
Hansen, P., 348, 352
Harbaugh, W. T., 270
Harber, K., 388, 389
Hardes, 7
Hardin, G., 430
Harding, L. M., 236
Hardy, C. H., 33
Hardy, C. L., 269
Harel, Y., 301
Haritos-Fatouros, M., 206
Harkins, S. G., 171, 172, 233, 235, 236
Harmon-Jones, C., 142
Harmon-Jones, E., 142, 143, 307, 346
Harper, S., 242
Harrel, W. A., 275
Harries, K. D., 316
Harris, E., 245
Harris, L. T., 389
Harris, M. J., 107
Harris, V. A., 100
Harrison, A. A., 346
Hart, P. T., 252
Hart, W., 132
Hartl, A. C., 361
Hartnett, J. J., 276
Harton, H. C., 211
Hasan, Y., 329, 330
Haselton, M. G., 58, 357
Haslam, C., 249, 401
Haslam, N., 99, 404
Haslam, S. A., 122
Hass, R. G., 388
Hastall, M. R., 161
Hastie, R., 245, 252, 261
Hatfield, E. C., 139, 154, 350, 367, 368, 370, 375, 376
Hatzenbuehler, M. L., 394
Hatzfeld, J., 333
Haugen, J., 22
Haugtvedt, C. P., 152, 164
Havas, D. A., 138
Hawkins, C. B., 118
Hawkins, L. B., 64
Hawkley, L. C., 343
Hawthorne, N., 123
Hays, N. A., 202
Hayward, L. E., 446
Hazan, C., 372, 374, 380
Hazlitt, W., 394
He, Y., 408
Headey, B., 56
Heap, B., 181
Hearold, S., 295
Heath, C., 219
Hebl, M. R., 236, 398
Hecato, 362
Hedge, A., 277
Hehman, E., 359, 384, 386, 453
Heine, S. J., 37, 41, 43, 55, 65, 136, 241, 412
Heinemann, K. S., 444
Heinz, A., 307
Heisenberg, W., 9
Helmreich, R. L., 253
Helwig-Larsen, M., 193
Helzer, E. G., 43
Hemenway, D., 308, 318
Hemsley, G., 154
Henderson-King, E. I., 410
Hendrick, C., 157, 369, 377
Hendrick, S. S., 369, 377
Hennenlotter, A., 138
Hennigan, K., 312
Henrich, J., 269
Henslin, M., 88
Hepburn, C., 419
Hepper, E. G., 373
Hepworth, J. T., 400
Heradstveit, D., 438
Herbenick, D., 410
Herek, G. M., 441
Herlocker, C. E., 430
Hernandez, A., 321
Hernandez, I., 81
Herring, D. R., 75
Hershberger, S. L., 277
Hershey, J. C., 414
Hertel, G., 235
Hertwig, R., 255
Herzog, S. M., 255
Herzog, T., 105
Hesley, J. W., 216
Heslin, P. A., 254
Hesse, B., 322
Heuer, C. A., 385
Hewstone, M., 98, 408, 412, 416, 442, 443, 444, 445, 452
Hicks, B. M., 291
Hideg, I., 390
Higbee, K. L., 22
Higgins, E. T., 125, 235
Highfield, R., 276
Hilgard, J., 328
Hilkenmeier, K., 236
Hill, R., 345
Hillery, J. M., 228
Hills, P. J., 227
Hilmert, C. J., 211
Hilton, J. L., 420
Hine, D. W., 431
Hing, N., 176, 243
Hinsz, V. B., 245
Hirschberger, G., 342
Hirschman, R. S., 187
Hirt, E. R., 94
Hitchcock, A., 322
Hitler, A., 152, 207, 251, 301, 405
Hitsch, G. J., 351
Hixon, J. G., 407
Ho, S. Y., 360
Hobbes, T., 304
Hobden, K. L., 134
Hodge, C. N., 352, 412
Hoffman, C., 46, 389
Hoffman, K., 358
Hoffman, L. W., 399
Hoffman, M. L., 280
Hofling, C. K., 203
Hofmann, W., 365
Hofmeister, J., 180
Hogan, J., 257
Hogan, R., 257
Hogg, M. A., 165, 246, 252, 401
Holland, R. W., 75, 143, 360
Hollander, E. P., 257
Holmberg, D., 96, 97
Holmes, J. G., 36, 49, 96, 97, 307, 360, 363, 364, 376
Holoien, D. S., 395
Holt, R., 260
Holtgraves, T. M., 40, 64
Holtzworth, A., 98
Holtzworth-Munroe, A., 98
Holzberg, A. D., 57
Holzhausen, K. G., 254
Hom, H.L., 13
Honigman, R., 353
Hoorens, V., 56, 58, 346
Hoover, C. W., 293
Hopkins, N., 416
Hopper, C., 377
Hopper, T. S., 69
Hormuth, S. E., 62
Horner, V., 211, 280
Hornsey, M. J., 211
Hornstein, H. A., 304
Horowitz, L. M., 361, 372
Horry, R., 408
Hortacsu, A., 351
Horton, R. S., 359
Horwitz, A. V., 13
Horwood, L. J., 51
Hoshino-Browne, E., 136
Houghton, J., 178, 179

Houghton, R. A., 179
House, R. J., 258
Houston, D. A., 184
Houston, V., 352
Howard, D. J., 128
Howard, J., 318
Howell, C. J., 13
Howell, R. T., 13
Hovland, C. I., 150, 157, 162, 400
Hoyle, R. H., 360
Hsu, H-C., 352
Huang, C., 35, 39, 362
Huart, J., 415
Huddy, L., 407
Huesmann, L. R., 306, 323, 324, 337
Huff, C., 26
Hüffmeier, J., 236
Hugenberg, K., 389, 408
Hui, C. H., 437
Hull, J. G., 66, 241
Human, L. J., 63
Hume, D., 10
Hunt, L. L., 350
Hunt, P., 228
Hunt, R., 393
Hunter, J. E., 352
Husband, R. W., 227
Hussak, L. J., 414
Huston, T. L., 364, 369
Hutnik, N., 452
Huxley, T. H., 228
Hvistendahl, M., 392
Hyde, J. S., 392
Hyers, L., 207
Hyers, L. L., 409
Hyman, H. H., 387

I

Iacono, W. G., 170
Ickes, W., 103, 216, 241, 415
Imai, Y., 54
Imber, L., 409
Imhoff, R., 59, 21, 413
Indo-Asian News Service, 322
Ingham, A. G., 232, 232f
Inglehart, M. R., 13, 69
Inkster, J. A., 135
Innes, J. M., 9
Insko, C. A., 362
Inzlicht, M., 417, 419
Ireland, M. E., 139, 196
Irvine, A. A., 103
Isaac, M. S., 153
Isen, A. M., 90, 272
Iserman, E. C., 419
Isozaki, M., 243
Itkin, S., 364
Ito, T., 307
Iyengar, S., 244

J

Jäckle, S., 392
Jackson, E. F., 412
Jackson, J. M., 105, 230, 233
Jackson, L. A., 325, 352, 400
Jackson, M., 296
Jacob, C., 126
Jacobs, R. C., 195
Jacobson, C. K., 203
Jacobson, K. C., 306
Jacobson, L., 107
Jacobson, N. S., 98
Jacoby, S., 361
Jaffe, Y., 241, 333
James, J., 307
James, S. E., 393
James, W., 62, 137, 139, 397
Jamieson, D. W., 108
Jamrozik, A., 352
Janda, L. H., 353
Janes, L. M., 403
Janis, I. L., 157, 163, 248, 252, 252, 440
Jankowiak, W. R., 368
Janoff-Bullman, R., 13
Jaremka, L. M., 380
Jason, L., 292
Jaworski, M., 365
Jelalian, E., 94
Jellison, J. M., 103
Jemmott, J. B. III, 68
Jenkins, H. M., 87
Jenkins-Smith, H., 154
Jenner, S., 236
Jennings, D., 87
Jensen, J., 393
Jensen, J. D., 160
Jensen-Campbell, L. A., 67
Jervis, R., 92
Jetten, J., 211, 259
Jobs, S., 258
Joel, S., 360
John, L. J., 26
John, L. K., 80
John, O. P., 360
Johns, M., 419
Johnson, A. L., 226
Johnson, B., 403
Johnson, B. T., 158, 172, 256
Johnson, C. S., 442
Johnson, D. J., 358
Johnson, D. W., 451, 455
Johnson, H., 375
Johnson, J. D., 143, 325
Johnson, J. G., 324
Johnson, M. H., 90
Johnson, M. K., 397, 408
Johnson, R. D., 239
Johnson, R. T., 455
Johnson, S., 404
Johnson, T. P., 40
Johnson, W., 13
Joiner, T. E., 197
Joly-Mascheroni, R. M., 195
Jonas, E., 184
Jonas, K., 197
Jonas, K. J., 343
Jonason, P. K., 375
Jones, C. R., 152
Jones, E. E., 62, 99, 100, 101, 102, 128, 363
Jones, J. M., 174, 177, 393
Jones, J. T., 361f, 372
Jones, L. L., 51
Jones, M. V., 229
Jones, R. A., 163, 164
Jones, T. K., 398
Jones, W. H., 379
Jordan, C. H., 143, 359
Josephs, R., 40, 66
Josephson, W. L., 325
Jost, J. T., 47, 180, 414
Jouffre, S., 101
Jourard, S., 377
Judd, C. M., 246, 389
Judge, T. A., 258
Julian, J. W., 256
Jussim, L., 9, 91, 107, 108, 111, 385, 410, 419
Juvonen, J., 302

K

Kagan, J., 8, 9
Kagehiro, D. K., 260
Kahan, D. M., 154
Kahle, L. R., 119
Kahlor, L. A., 320
Kahneman, D., 45, 62, 74, 78, 82, 84, 85, 86, 88, 89, 254, 255, 346, 458
Kaiser, C. R., 395
Kaiser, F. G., 126
Kalick, M., 353
Kalinoski, Z. T., 455
Kalla, J., 406
Kalton, G., 21
Kalven, H. Jr., 260, 261, 262
Kambara, T., 316
Kameda, T., 259
Kammer, D., 103
Kamphuis, J., 305
Kanagawa, C., 37
Kandel, D. B., 361
Kandinsky, W., 403
Kang, S., 419
Kanten, A. B., 56
Kapitan, S., 156
Kaplan, M. F., 248, 407
Karasawa, M., 346
Karau, S. J., 233, 235, 236
Karberg, J., 307
Karna, A., 334
Karney, B. R., 98, 377, 380
Karremans, R. W., 360
Kashima, E. S., 37
Kashima, Y., 37
Kasser, T., 13, 182, 307

Kassin, S. M., 95, 108
Katz, A. M., 345
Katz, E., 168
Katz-Wise, S. L., 392
Katzer, C., 301
Katzev, R., 293
Katzev, T., 212
Kaufman, J., 314
Kaufman-Gilliland, C. M., 432, 433
Kavanagh, C. M., 177
Kawakami, K., 116, 207, 311, 386, 408
Kay, A. C., 384, 386, 396, 414
Kaye, D., 157
Keating, J. P., 171
Keelan, J. P. R., 372
Keeling, D., 153
Keeling, K., 153
Keillor, G., 56
Keith, P., 376
Keller, E. B., 168
Keller, J., 419
Keller, K., 276
Kellerman, A., 319
Kellerman, J., 381
Kelley, H. H., 108
Kelly, B. R., 312
Kelly, D. J., 348, 408
Kelly, R. J., 143
Kelman, H. C., 438, 456, 457
Keltner, D., 275, 360, 394
Kemmelmeir, M., 38
Kendrick, R. V., 46
Kennedy, J. A., 81
Kennedy, K. A., 438
Kenny, D. A., 360, 362
Kenrick, D. T., 259, 271, 316, 357, 360, 370
Kenworthy, L., 259
Kenyon, P., 399
Keown, L. A., 314
Kepes, S., 328
Kerr, M., 80
Kerr, N. L., 179, 212, 233, 235, 260, 262, 432, 433, 434
Kesebir, S., 34
Kessler, R. C., 372
Kessler, T., 452
Key, E., 335
Keys, C. B., 245
Kiecolt-Glaser, J. K., 68
Kierkegaard, S., 13
Kiesler, C. A., 185
Kight, T. D., 368
Kihlstrom, J. F., 34, 94
Kilburn, J., 331
Kille, D. R., 76
Kim, H. S., 37, 40, 40f
Kimel, S. Y., 453
Kimmel, A. J., 26
Kimmel, M. J., 433
Kinder, D. R., 93
King, L. L., 362
King, M. L. Jr., 154
Kingdon, J. W., 54
Kingsbury, G. G., 19
Kingston, D. A., 320
Kinnier, R. T., 87
Kinzler, K. D., 401
Kipling, R., 404
Kirschner, P., 157
Kitaigorodskii, A. I., 11
Kitayama, S., 37, 39, 40f, 41, 42, 65, 105, 193, 277, 346
Kitt, A. S., 311
Klaas, E. T., 125
Klapwijk, A., 459
Klauer, K. C., 389
Klebold, D., 245
Kleck, R. E., 409
Klee, P., 403
Klein, A., 394
Klein, D. J., 7
Klein, N., 56
Klein, R., 362
Klein, S. B., 64
Klein, W. M., 346
Kleinfield, N. R., 328
Kleinke, C. L., 202
Kleinsmith, J., 307
Klentz, B., 358
Kline, S. L., 40
Klinger, M., 78
Klopfer, P. H., 227
Klucharev, V., 213
Knewtson, H. S., 346
Knight, J. A., 346
Knight, K. M., 50
Knight, P. A., 154
Knowles, E., 221, 230
Knowles, E. S., 293
Knox, R., 135
Koch, J., 155
Koebel, F., 251
Koebel, S., 251
Koehler, D. J., 80, 83
Koenig, A. M., 170, 384
Koestner, R., 36
Koestner, R. F., 351
Kogan, A., 442
Kohn, N. W., 254
Kokkoris, M. D., 135
Kolivas, E. D., 98
Komorita, S. S., 433
Kong, L. L., 42
Konrath, S. H., 52, 373, 399
Koole, S. L., 342
Koop, C. E., 320, 321
Koresh, D., 174, 177
Koriat, A., 83
Korn, J. H., 25
Korte, C., 287
Kossowska, M., 397
Kouchaki, M., 343
Kowalski, R. M., 65, 301
Kozu, J., 290
Krackow, A., 203
Krahe, B., 325, 326, 329
Kramer, A. D., 196, 385
Kramer, A. E., 91, 235
Kramer, R. M., 454
Kraus, M. W., 394
Kraus, S. J., 117
Krauss, R. M., 433
Kravitz, D. A., 232
Krebs, D., 269, 270, 278, 349
Krendl, A. C., 419
Krisberg, K., 156
Krishnamurti, T., 45
Krismer, K., 141
Kristof, N., 449
Krizan, Z., 57
Kross, E., 35
Krosnick, J. A., 21, 149, 170, 171, 183
Krueger, A., 116
Krueger, J., 59, 111, 407
Krueger, R. F., 13, 421, 431
Krueger, W. K., 291
Kruger, J., 54, 79, 87
Kruglanski, A. W., 76, 111, 162, 176, 259, 302, 438
Krull, D. S., 104, 183
Kubany, E. S., 336
Kugihara, N., 235
Kuhlmeier, V. A., 273
Kühnen, U., 135
Kuhns, J. B., 307
Kulik, J. A., 211
Kunda, Z., 34, 35f, 62, 82, 346, 406, 416, 422, 423
Kunkel, S., 326
Kunst-Wilson, W., 348
Kuntsche, E. N., 322
Kuntsman, J. W., 389
Kutner, L. A., 331

L

La Rochefoucauld, 121, 128, 365
LaBoucane-Benson, P., 177
Lacey, M., 453
LaFramboise, T., 452
LaFrance, M., 44
Lage, S., 259
Lagerspetz, K., 306, 333
Lai, C. K., 406
Laird, J. D., 96, 137, 138, 381
Lake, E. A., 62
Lakin, J. L., 344, 360
Lalancette, M-F., 217
Lalonde, R. N., 54
Lalwani, A. K., 40
Lamal, P. A., 94
Lamb, C. S., 108
Lambert, M.-E., 21
Lambert, N. M., 447
Lamberth, H., 301
Lamont, R. A., 417
Lamoreaux, M., 40
Landers, A., 20, 335
Lane, T., 211

Langer, E. J., 69, 88, 164, 409
Langford, D. J., 280
Langham, E., 176, 243
Langlois, J. H., 352, 353, 354, 355
Långström, N., 306
Lanzetta, J. T., 139, 446
Lao-tzu, 55
Larey, T. S., 254
Larkin, C., 59
Larrick, R. P., 316
Larsen, K. S., 217
Larsen, O. N., 196
Larsen, R. J., 306
Larson, C. L., 305
Larson, J. R. Jr., 245
Larsson, K., 226
Larwood, L., 56
Lasater, T. M., 156
Lassiter, G. D., 56, 95, 103
Latané, B., 230, 233, 235, 260, 282, 283, 283f, 285, 286, 291, 292
Latham, G. P., 256
Laughlin, P. R., 253, 254
Laumann, E. O., 98
Laurier Institute for the Study of Public Opinion and Policy (LISPOP), 20
Lawson, T., 31
Layden, M. A., 241
Layous, K., 365
Le Mens, G., 213
Leach, S., 76
Leary, M. R., 5, 8, 19, 33, 48, 63, 64, 65, 131, 342, 344
LeBlanc, B. A., 98, 149
Leckelt, M., 52
Ledesma, R. D., 118
LeDoux, J. E., 76
Lee, I. C., 256
Lee, K. M., 118
Lee, R., 298
Lee, R. Y. P., 359
Lee, S., 118
Lee. S. H., 75
Lee, S. W. S., 75
Lee, Y. T., 65, 105, 385
Lehman, D. R., 21, 41, 65, 112, 136, 412
Leimgruber, K., 280
Leippe, M. R., 134
Leiserowitz, A., 149, 180
Lemay, E. P. Jr., 352
Lemmer, G., 451
Lempert, R. O., 112
Lemyre, L., 404
Lenton, A. P., 353
Leodoro, G., 293
Leonard, J. B., 413 .
Leonardelli, G. J., 75, 344
Leone, C., 64
LePage, A., 318
Lepine, M., 310
Lepore, S. J., 230
Lepper, M., 92, 93, 140, 184
Lerma, M., 358
Lerner, M. J., 56, 404, 413
Leshner, A., 15
Leung, K., 437
Levav, J., 119
Leventhal, H., 158, 187
Levesque, M. J., 98
Levin, S., 395
Levine, J. M., 210, 259, 260
Levine, M., 282, 287
Levine, R., 187
Levine, R. V., 287, 288f
Levinger, G., 429
Levinson, M., 434
Levitan, L. C., 189, 246
Levy, D. A., 194
Levy, S. R., 412
Levy-Leboyer, C., 159
Lewandowski, G., 380
Lewicki, P., 365
Lewin, K., 4, 216, 257
Lewis, C. S., 43, 171
Lewis, D. O., 305
Lewis, E. D., 39
Lewis, J., 381
Lewis, M. B., 97, 387
Lewis, R., 369
Lewis, S. A., 454
Leyens, J. P., 362, 403
Li, H., 368f
Li, N., 356
Li, T., 374
Li, Y., 85
Liao, M., 40
Liberman, A., 161
Liberman, V., 434
Lichacz, F. M., 232
Lichtblau, E., 188, 388
Lichtenberg, 219
Lichtenstein, P., 306
Lichtenstein, S., 83
Lieberman, M. D., 144
Lilienfeld, S. O., 302
Lim, D. T. K., 91
Lin, D., 305
Lin, D. Y., 54
Lin, J-H., 330
Lin, N., 227
Lind, E. A., 294
Linder, D., 364
Lindsay, R. C. L., 22
Lindsey, S., 46
Lindskold, S., 459
Linville, P., 407
Linz, D., 320
Lippa, R. A., 349
Lipsey, M., 337
Lipsitz, A., 125
Lipsman, A., 93
Littman, R. A., 312
Liu, D., 52
Livingston, R. W., 64, 353
Livingstone, S., 324
Lizzadro, T., 291
Locke, E. A., 256
Locke, K. D., 361
Locke, S. B., 468
Locksley, A., 419
Lockwood, P., 34, 35, 35f, 47
Lodewijkx, H. F. M., 254
Loewenstein, G., 26, 44
Lofland, J., 176
Loftus, E. F., 78, 94, 95
Logel, C. E. R., 417, 419
Lombardo, J. P., 365
LoMonaco, B., 193
London, P., 295
Lonsdale, A. J., 84
Lopyan, K. J., 121
Lord, C. G., 184, 420
Lord, W., 249
Lorenz, K., 304
Lortie-Lussier, M., 256
Lott, A. J., 211, 365
Lott, B. E., 211, 365
Loughman, S., 404
Louis, W. R., 259
Lovett, F., 56
Lowe, C. A., 98
Lowery, B. S., 396
Lubek, H. J., 200
Lucas, R. E., 311
Lücken, M., 259
Lüdtke, O., 19
Lueptow, L. B., 390
Lueptow, M. B., 390
Luhtanen, R., 50, 401
Lumsdaine, A. A., 150, 163
Lumsden, A., 150
Luthans, F., 53
Lutsky, N., 43
Lüüs, C. A. E., 254
Lydon, J., 358
Lydon, J. E., 373
Lykken, D. T., 244, 346
Lynch, M., 143
Lynch, M. E., 405
Lynham, J., 431
Lynn, M., 293
Lyons, 12
Lyons, P. A., 383

M

Maas, J., 230
Maass, A., 211, 259, 260, 412
Macchiavelli, N., 5
Maccoby, N., 167, 171
MacCoun, R. J., 212, 262
MacDonald, G., 194, 280, 307, 343, 344, 363, 380
MacDonald, S., 307
MacDonald, T. K., 43, 66, 67f
MacEwan, L., 432
MacFarlane, S. W., 316
Mack, D., 353
Mackie, D. M., 158, 166, 407

Mackinnon, S. P., 359
MacLeish, K. T., 306
MacLeod, C., 85
Macleod, J., 32
Macrae, C. N., 405, 406
Madden, N., 450
Maddux, J. E., 53, 160
Maddux, W. M., 400
Madey, S. F., 86
Madison, J., 107
Maeder, G., 176
Magaro, P. A., 90
Mageau, G. A., 69
Magill-Evans, J., 314
Magnan, R. E., 219
Mahajan, N., 359
Mahalik, J. R., 276
Maheswaran, D., 152
Main, K. J., 410
Maio, G. R., 162, 172
Major, B., 311
Malamuth, N., 320, 321
Maleckovà, J., 116
Malkiel, B., 80
Malle, B., 103
Malone, D. T., 183
Malone, P. S., 99
Manata, B., 254
Manchanda, P., 168
Mandela, N., 7, 154
Mander, A., 333
Maner, J. K., 304, 309, 344, 350, 379
Manis, M., 124, 422
Manjoo, F., 390
Mann, L., 237
Mannell, R. C., 141
Mannes, A., 79
Manning, R., 282, 297
Marchuetz, C., 353
Marcus, S., 201
Marcus-Newhall, A., 310, 311
Mares, M-L., 325
Marigold, D. C., 50, 363
Marin-Garcia, E., 348
Markman, G. D., 353
Markman, H. J., 381
Markman, K. D.,86
Marks, G., 59, 183, 346
Markus, H. R., 6, 34, 37, 39, 40, 40f, 41, 42, 65, 67, 193
Marquis, A. R., 408
Marsden, P., 313
Marsh, H. W., 35, 47
Marshall, R., 250
Martens, A., 128
Martin, B., 232
Martin, L., 246
Martin, L. L., 111
Martin, P. Y., 259
Martin, R. C., 336
Martino, S. C., 327
Martinovic, B., 447
Maruyama, G. M., 19, 391
Marvelle, K., 353
Marx, D. M., 384
Marx, K., 228, 311, 436
Mashek, D. J., 368f
Masserman, J. H., 280
Massey, C., 58
Masuda, T., 39, 105
Masure, R. H., 227
Matheny, A., 306
Mathieu, M. T., 46
Matsui, H., 410
Mathewson, G. C., 174
Matz, D. C., 397
Maugham, W. S., 357
Maurice, J. K., 357
Maxmen, A., 432
Maxwell, G. M., 372
Mayer, J. D., 90, 272
Mayr, U., 270
Maznevski, M. L., 254
Mazur, A., 308
Mazzoni, G., 95
McAdams, D. P., 397
McAlister, A., 186
McAndrew, F. T., 164, 307
McBurney, D. H., 357
McCain, J. L., 52
McCann, C. D., 64, 125
McCarthy, J. F., 312
McCauley, C., 245, 251, 252
McClintock, E. A., 351
McClure, M. J., 373
McCombs-Thornton, K., 24
McConahay, J. B., 451
McConkey, S., 118
McConnell, A. R., 419
McConnell, H. K., 96
McCord, J., 244
McCullough, J. L., 348
McDavid, J. W., 218
McDermott, R., 306
McDonald, M., 85
McDonald, M. M., 357
McFarland, C., 91, 96, 247
McGarty, C., 237
McGillicuddy, N., 458
McGlone, M. S., 167
McGlynn, F. D., 254
McGovern, K., 74
McGrath, J. E., 225
McGraw, A. P., 86
McGraw, K. M., 408
McGregor, I., 143, 404
McGue, M., 170, 291
McGuire, C. V., 221
McGuire, W. J., 185, 186, 187, 221
McInman, A. D., 54
McKelvie, S. J., 85
McKenna, F. P., 56
McKenna, K. Y. A., 244
McKeown, S., 446
McLarney, A., 163
McLatchie, N., 330
McLuhan, M., 165
McMillen, D., 271, 272
McMullen, M. N., 86
McNulty, J. K., 377, 381
McNulty, S. E., 81, 98
McQueen, L. R., 432
McQuinn, R. D., 366, 377
McTavish, J., 434
McVeigh, T., 245
Mead, G. H., 36
Meade, R. D., 217
Means, B., 90
Medalia, N., 196
Medvec, V. H., 80, 86, 87, 283
Meehl, G. A., 82, 179
Meertens, R. W., 143
Mehl, M. R., 6, 342, 377
Meindl, J. R., 404
Meissner, A., 408
Meleshko, K. A., 66
Mellers, B., 249
Mellers, B. A., 86
Mellon, P., 107
Meltzer, A. L., 349
Memmert, D., 198, 229
Memon, A., 95
Mendell, N. R., 380
Mendolia, M., 246
Mentzel, R. K., 280
Merikle, P., 75
Merrilees, C. E., 278
Merton, R., 106
Merton, R. K., 311
Mescher, K., 392
Messé, L., 433
Messick, D. M., 59, 231, 436
Messner, S. F., 244
Metcalfe, C., 220
Metha, A. T., 87
Mettee, D. R., 364
Metzl, J. M., 306
Meyerowitz, J. A., 57
Meyers, S., 367
Michaels, J., 228
Mickelson, K. D., 372
Mihelic, K. K., 236
Miklikowska, M., 396
Mikula, G., 436
Mikulincer, M., 278, 342, 372, 405
Milgram, A., 200, 206
Milgram, S., 3, 199–211, 201f, 208t, 216–218
Mill, J. S., 194, 251
Millar, M., 402
Millar, M. G., 118
Millard, R. J., 22
Miller, A. G., 200, 208
Miller, C. E., 213
Miller, C. T., 92, 105, 419
Miller, D. L., 94
Miller, D. T., 86, 247, 409, 413
Miller, F. A., 69
Miller, G., 357

Miller, G. E., 59, 68, 69
Miller, J. G., 275, 290
Miller, J. R., 128
Miller, L., 204
Miller, L. C., 376, 377
Miller, L. E., 120, 164
Miller, N., 155, 183, 271, 272, 306, 307, 310, 311, 346, 445, 452
Miller, P. A., 278
Miller, P. J. E., 364, 372
Miller, R. L., 110
Miller, R. S., 64, 210, 379
Miller, S. L., 389
Millett, K., 377
Millette, D., 21
Mills, B. M., 345
Mills, J., 174, 375
Milne, A. B., 406
Milyavskaya, M., 69, 343
Mims, P. R., 276
Min, K. S., 43, 44
Minassian, A., 310
Ming, Y., 409
Mirabile, R. R., 189
Mirsky, S., 278
Mischel, W., 215
Mishna, F., 301, 337
Mita, T., 348
Mitchell, J. P., 194
Mitchell, T., 64
Mitchell, T. R., 96
Miyake, A., 419
Mizock, L., 393
Modigliani, A., 206
Moeller, S. J., 47
Moffitt, T. E., 306
Moghaddam, F. M., 361, 452
Moisuc, A., 287
Mojzisch, A., 252
Molander, E. A., 56
Moller, I., 325, 326, 329
Molouki, S., 217
Monge, P. R., 69
Monin, B., 388
Monroe, M., 197
Monson, T. C., 216
Montag, C., 330
Montaigne, 121
Monteith, M. J., 405, 441
Montoya, R. M., 346, 351, 359, 362
Moody, K., 188
Moon, S. M., 174
Moons, W. G., 158, 166
Moor, B. G., 344
Moore, D., 176
Moore, D. A., 79, 154
Moore, D. L., 229, 231
Moore, D. W., 164
Moore, J., 402
Moore, J. C., 124
Moore, S., 307, 309, 318
Morales, L., 85, 410
Moran, T., 456
Moreland, R. L., 260, 348
Morgan, K. L., 66
Mori, H., 138
Mori, K., 138
Morier, D., 124
Morling, B., 40
Mormille, A., 282
Morris, K., 157
Morris, K. A., 35
Morris, M. W., 433
Morris, R., 307
Morris, W. N., 210
Morrison, D., 320
Morrison, E. L., 354
Morrow, L., 193
Moscovici, S., 9, 243, 258, 259, 260
Moskowitz, G. B., 456
Mosley, W., 297
Motherhood Project, 188, 189
Mouton, J. S., 448, 449, 457
Moutsiana, C., 374
Moyer, K. E., 305
Moylan, S., 90
Moynihan, D. P., 9
Mucchi-Faina, A., 259
Mueller, C. M., 53
Mueller, J., 335
Mueller, U., 325
Mugge, D. O., 332
Muggleton, N. K., 357
Mugny, G., 259
Muise, A., 98
Mujcic, R., 388
Mullainathan, S., 388
Mullen, B., 54, 59, 211, 228, 230, 231, 233, 249, 252, 259, 333, 403
Mullen, E., 360, 400, 456
Muller, R., 179
Muller, S., 158
Mullin, C. R., 320
Mummendey, A., 452
Munhall, P. J., 56
Munoz-Rivas, M. J., 301
Munro, G. D., 93
Murphy, C. M., 11
Murphy, S. C., 81
Murray, D., 50, 217
Murray, K. E., 384
Murray, S. L., 109, 360, 363, 364
Murroni, E., 155
Murstein, B., 351
Musgrave, S., 123
Musk, E., 258
Muson, G., 323
Mussweiler, T., 139
Myers, D., 196, 243, 391
Myers, D. G., 379
Myers, J., 255
Myers, K. M., 90
Myers, L. B., 56
Myers, N., 181, 182, 319

N

Nabi, R. L., 132
Nadler, A., 241, 274, 276, 418
Naffrechoux, M., 259
Nagar, D., 230
Nail, P. R., 194, 219
Nair, H., 168
Narang, P., 319
Nario-Redmond, M. R., 385
NASA, 179
Nasby, W., 362
Nash, K., 344
Nasser, G. A., 459
National Geographic, 149, 178
National Post, 180
National Safety Council, 85
Navarette, C. D., 407
Nave, C. S., 98
Nawrat, R., 272
Nay, W. R., 276
Naylor, J. C., 257
NCADD, 307
Neal, T. L., 138
Neely, R., 293
Neff, K., 50
Neff, L. A., 377
Nelligan, J. S., 372
Nelson, E., 156
Nelson, L., 98, 409
Nelson, L. D., 354
Nelson, M. R., 153
Nelson, T. E., 421
Nemeth, C. J., 210, 252, 254, 259, 260
Nesler, M. S., 132
Nettle, D., 58
Nettles, B. L., 176
Neubaum, G., 196
Neufeld, J. P., 269
Neumann, R., 196
New York Times, 124
Newby-Clark, I. R., 78, 143
Newcomb, T. M., 170, 237, 345
Newman, L. S., 104, 105
Newport, F., 392
Newth, S., 91
Nezlek, J. B., 349
Nguyen, D-H., 98
Nguyen, T., 307
Nias, D. K. B., 361
Nichols, J., 284
Nicholson, C., 159
Nicholson, N., 217
Nicks, S. D., 25
Nida, S., 282, 343
Niebuhr, R., 58
Niehuis, S., 364
Nielsen, 322
Niemi, G. J., 335
Niemiec, C. P., 343
Nietzsche, F., 400
Nigro, G. N., 399
Nijstad, B. A., 254

Nisbett, R. E., 39, 39f, 102, 104, 111, 112, 257, 314, 410
Nock, S. L., 118
Noble, T., 337
Nolan, S. A., 342
Noller, P., 372, 376, 380
Nordgren, L. F., 58, 280, 343
Norem, J. K., 58
Norenzayan, A., 105, 287
Norris, M., 184
North, A. C., 84
North, O., 209
Norton, A. T., 441
Norton, M. I., 274, 360
Nosek, B. A., 46, 118
Nosow, S., 277
Notarius, C. I., 381
Nowak, M. A., 431, 433
Nurmi, J.-E., 50
Nuttin, J. M. Jr., 346

O

Oakes, P. J., 389
Oaten, M., 69
Obama, B., 386, 387
O'Brien, L. T., 406
O'Connell, G. B., 410
Odean, T., 88
Oddone-Paolucci, E., 320
O'Dea, T. F., 176
Odgers, C. L., 311
Odland, I. M., 384
Ohbuchi, K., 316
O'Hegarty, M., 158
Oishi, S., 34, 38, 432
O'Keefe, D. J., 160
Okimoto, T. G., 392
Oldham, T., 212
O'Leary, K. D., 380
Oleson, K. C., 416
Oliner, P. M., 295
Oliner, S. P., 295
Olson, C. K., 331
Olson, I. R., 353
Olson, J. M., 64, 108, 116, 120, 134, 144, 154, 172, 414
Olson, K., 358
Olson, M. A., 46, 152
Olweus, D., 302, 306, 307
O'Malley, P. M., 19
O'Mara, A., 47
O'Mara, E. M., 98
Omoto, A. M., 293, 298
Onraet, E., 434
Open Secrets, 166
O'Reilly, T., 173
Orendain, S., 181
Orgaz, C., 88
Orive, R., 241
Orlandi, M. A., 187
Ormiston, M., 252
Ornstein, R., 125
Orr, R., 442
Ortega, A. H., 254
Ortega, R., 301
Orth, U., 50
Ortiz, V., 419
Orwell, G., 97, 447
Osbeck, L. M., 361
Osborne, D., 105, 414
Osgood, C. E., 458, 459
Oskamp, S., 119
Osofsky, M. J., 128
Osswald, S., 295
Osterhouse, R. A., 171
Osterman, L. L., 314
Ostrom, T. M., 348, 407, 431
Oswald, F. L., 386
Otten, M., 343
Ouellette, J. A., 120
Overall, N. C., 421
Ovid, 269, 351
Owyang, M. T., 353
Oyserman, D., 38

P

Pack, S. J., 124
Packer, D. J., 200, 252
Padawer-Singer, A., 221
Padgett, V. R., 202
Page, S. E., 252, 259
Pallak, M. S., 155, 162
Palmer, D. L., 400
Palmer, E. L., 188
Palmer, M. L., 103
Paloutzian, R., 165
Paluck, E. L., 161, 435
Pandey, J., 105, 230
Paolini, S., 442, 445, 446
Papastamou, S., 259
Pape, R., 302
Parashar, U. D., 85
Pardini, D. A., 305
Parish, E. A., 376
Park, A., 302
Park, B. M., 407
Park, D., 39
Park, J., 153
Park, L. E., 50
Parker, K., 390
Parsons, J. T., 372
Parsons, R., 236, 247, 287
Partington, J. T., 232
Pascal, B., 76
Pascarella, E. T., 244
Pashler, H., 255
Passariello, C., 219
Patall, E. A., 87
Patrick, R. B., 287
Patterson, G. R., 312, 314, 348
Paulhus, D. L., 51, 52, 66, 91, 132
Pauling, L., 436
Paulus, P. B., 229, 254
Pavelich, J. L., 103
Payne, B. K., 118, 386, 389
Pearson, L. B., 459
Pedersen, A., 388
Pedersen, A. F., 68
Pedersen, W. C., 306, 310
Pederson, 307
Peetz, J., 44, 60, 80
Pegalis, L. J., 377
Pegna, A. J., 357
Pelham, B. W., 50
Peng, K., 221
Pennebaker, J. W., 6, 139, 196, 342, 378
Penner, L., 275
Pennington, N., 64, 261
Penrod, S. D., 261
Pentland, S., 154
Penton-Voak, I. S., 355
Pepitone, A., 237
Peplau, L. A., 369, 376, 377
Pereira, C., 400
Perfumi, S. C., 238
Perie, M., 62
Perls, F. S., 335
Perrault, S., 361
Perrin, S., 217
Perry, G., 199, 218, 435
Persico, N., 353
Pessin, J., 227
Peters, E., 158
Peterson, C., 55, 58, 376
Peterson, C. K., 307
Peterson, J. L., 327
Peterson, R. S., 259
Peterson-Lewis, S., 322
Peto, R., 121
Petrocelli, J. V., 14, 86, 183
Pettigrew, T. F., 384, 385, 386, 388, 398, 400, 404, 412, 441, 442, 445, 446
Petty, R. E., 117, 138, 139, 144, 151, 152, 155, 157, 158, 162, 163, 171, 172, 183, 185, 235
Pew Research Center, 327, 345, 375, 383, 392, 393
Phelan, J. E., 392
Phelps, E., 118
Philbrick, K., 287
Phillips, C. M., 335, 336
Phillips, D., 373
Phillips, D. L., 440
Phillips, D. P., 197
Phillips, K. A., 353
Phillips, T., 453
Phinney, J. S., 452
Pierce, K. P., 452
Piliavin, I. M., 270, 286
Piliavin, J. A., 269, 270, 296
Pincus, J. H, 305
Pinel, E. C., 110
Pinker, S., 338, 391
Pinkus, R. T., 47
Pittinsky, T., 419
Pittinsky, T. L., 52
Place, K., 368

Place, S. S., 367
Plaks, J. E., 235
Plant, E. A., 109, 389
Plato, 324, 390
Platow, M., 196
Plaut, V. C., 353
Pliner, P., 125
Poincaré, J. H., 15
Pollmann, M. M. H., 45
Pollock, V. E., 307
Pomazal, J. R., 275, 276
Pond, R. S., 338
Poniewozik, J., 92
Pool, G. J., 144
Poon, C. S. K., 80
Poon, K. T., 343
Poor, M., 153
Popenoe, D., 379
Pornpitakpan, C., 155
Possami, A., 220
Post, J., 245
Postelwaite, A., 353
Postmes, T., 239, 252
Poulin, F., 244
Poushter, J., 384
Powell, M. C., 375
Pratkanis, A. R., 62, 153, 249, 252, 274
Pratt-Hyatt, J. S., 395
Pratto, F., 395
Predmore, S. C., 377
Prelec, D., 26
Prentice, D. A., 85
Prentice-Dunn, S., 241
Pressley, M., 216
Preston, J. L., 81
Price, G. H., 358
Priel, B., 374
Prinstein, M. J., 302
Prislin, R., 144
Pritchard, C., 325
Probst, T., 440
Prohaska, M. L., 361
Prohaska, T., 58, 107, 108
Pronin, E., 54, 103, 106, 217, 438
Prothrow-Stith, D., 455
Provine, R. R., 195
Pruitt, D. G., 433, 454, 456
Pryor, J. B., 98
Pryor, J. H., 292
Przybylski, A. K., 332
Psaltis, C., 446
PTC, 322
Public Opinion, 56
Puhl, R. M., 385
Pulford, B. D., 154
Purvis, J. A., 377
Putnam, K. M., 305
Putnam, R., 296, 327
Putnam, R. D., 447
Pyszczynski, T., 62, 367, 447

Q

Quesnel, M., 50
Quist, M. C., 356
Quoidbach, J., 103

R

Radloff, C., 103
Radtke, H. L., 200
Rafferty, R., 309
Raifman, J., 394
Raine, A., 305, 306
Raines, B. E., 187
Rainey, D., 353
Rains, S. A., 219
Rajagopal, P., 87
Ramirez, A., 156
Ramirez, J. M., 336
Ramos, M. R., 447
Randall, P. K., 357
Randler, C., 306
Rank, S. G., 203
Ransom, S., 314
Rapoport, A., 428, 433
Rapson, R., 139, 368
Rasinski, K. A., 257
Ratner, R. K., 247
Rawls, J., 437
Rawn, C. D., 63
Rawson, K. A., 80
Raymond, P., 98
Read, S. J., 81
Reber, J., 110
ReducingStereotypeThreat.org, 417
Reece, R. L., 384
Reed, D., 398
Regan, D. T., 121, 171, 365
Reicher, S., 239
Reid, C. A., 359
Reid, J. B., 314
Reid, P., 327
Reid, S., 123, 124
Reijntjes, A., 343
Reis, H. T., 118, 346, 348, 349, 376, 377
Reisenzein, R., 317
Rempel, J. K., 372, 376
Renshon, J., 439
Ressler, R. K., 321
Reynolds, R., 155
Rhine, R. J., 162
Rhoades, L., 141
Rhoads, K., 59
Rhoads, K. V. L., 161
Rhodes, G., 355
Rhodes, M. G., 408
Rhodewalt, F., 62
Rholes, W. S., 104, 125, 372, 373
Rice, B., 54
Rice, M. E., 289
Rice, R. W., 256
Richards, K., 352
Richards, Z., 416
Richardson, L. F., 426
Richardson, M., 53
Richeson, J. A., 350, 406, 419, 444, 445, 446
Ridge, R. D., 110
Riek, B. M., 416
Riess, M., 64
Rietzschel, E. F., 254
Rigby, C. S., 332
Riggio, R. E., 361
Riggs, J. M., 62
Ringelmann, M., 232
Riordan, C. A., 54, 365
Risen, J. L., 85, 411, 444
Risucci, D. A., 43
Riva, P., 344
Rivera, L. M., 406
Robberson, M. R., 159
Roberts, J. V., 85
Robertson, L. A., 323
Robins, G., 99
Robins, R. W., 50, 58
Robinson, M. D., 58, 306
Robinson, T. N., 337
Robustelli, S. L., 107
Rochat, F., 206
Rocklin, T., 217
Rodeheffer, C., 331
Rodenhizer, K., 321
Roehling, M. V., 384
Roehling, P. V., 384
Rodin, J., 69, 285
Roese, N. L., 86, 144
Roese, N. J., 108
Rogers, C., 277
Rogers, C. R., 377
Rogers, J. D., 252
Rogers, R. W., 159, 160, 241
Rogge, R. D., 118
Roggman, L., 355
Rohrer, J. H., 195
Romer, D., 291
Ronay, R., 80
Rooney, A., 365
Rooth, D. O., 118, 389
Rose, P., 50
Rose, T. L., 411
Rosen, S., 124
Rosenbaum, M. E., 360
Rosenberg, L. A., 209
Rosenblatt, A., 361
Rosenbloom, S., 63
Rosenbloom, T., 228
Rosenfeld, D., 141
Rosenhan, D. L., 271, 272, 295
Rosenthal, D. A., 452
Rosenthal, E., 180, 182
Rosenthal, R., 106, 107, 108
Rosenthal, S. A., 52
Roseth, C. J., 451
Ross, D., 313

Ross, L., 31, 32, 54, 55, 87, 92, 93, 94, 100, 101, 103, 106, 111, 112, 184, 199, 257, 456
Ross, L. D., 418
Ross, M., 43, 56, 57, 60, 60f, 78, 80, 90, 96, 97, 98, 363
Ross, M. J., 398
Ross, S. A., 313
Roszell, P., 353
Rotenberg, K. J., 110
Roth, J., 164
Rothbart, M., 221, 407, 421
Rothman, A. J., 432
Rotton, J., 315, 316
Rotundo, M., 98
Rouby, D. A., 344
Rousseau, J-J., 304
Routh, D. A., 416
Rowe, D. C., 306
Roy, J-P., 116
Roy, M.-M., 44
Royal Society, 178
Ruback, R. B., 69
Ruben, C., 58
Rubin, J. Z., 313
Rubin, R. A., 19
Rubin, Z., 367, 381
Ruble, D. N., 104, 140, 141
Rucker, D. D., 183
Rudich, E. A., 51
Rudman, L. A., 392
Rudolph, U., 105, 275
Ruge, J., 316
Rule, B. G., 315
Rule, N., 77, 357
Rusbult, C. E., 358, 360, 380, 381
Rushton, J. P., 216, 291, 306
Rushton, P., 289
Russell, A. M. T., 176, 243
Russell, B., 63, 238, 350
Russell, G. W., 280, 336
Russell, N., 202
Russell, P., 290
Ruvolo, A., 67
Ryan, R. M., 13, 69, 140, 141, 270, 332, 343
Ryckman, R. M., 22
Rydell, M. T., 417
Rydell, R. J., 417, 419
Ryff, C. D., 58

S

Saad, L., 132
Sabini, J., 207
Sachs, J., 316
Sacket, A. M., 59
Sackett, P. R., 98
Sadler, M. S., 389
Safer, M. A., 97
Sagarin, B. J., 59, 161, 183
Sageman, M., 245
Sagioglou, C., 311
Saguy, T., 456
Sah, S., 155
Said, C. P., 355
Sakamoto, Y., 443
Sakurai, M. M., 211
Salanova, P., 298
Salas, E., 259
Saleem, M., 325, 330, 399
Sales, S. M., 176
Salganik, M., 248
Salmela-Aro, K., 50
Salmivalli, C., 303, 334
Salovey, P., 90, 160, 272, 40
Saltzberg, J. A., 271
Saltzstein, H. D., 212
Sam, D. L., 452
Sampson, E. E., 436
Sanbonmatsu, D. M., 116
Sancton, T., 286
Sandberg, L., 212
Sande, G. N., 103
Sanders, D. Y., 272
Sanders, G. S., 231, 247
Sanderson, C. A., 287, 377
Sani, F., 401, 404
Sansone, C., 141
Santaella-Tenorio, J., 318
Santos, A., 400
Santos, H. C., 37
Santos, L. R., 135
Saphire-Bernstein, S., 369
Saroglou, V., 403
Sartre, J. P., 2
Sasaki, J. Y., 37
Sasaki, S., 412, 453
Sassenberg, K., 86, 400
Sato, K., 430
Satterwhite, R. C., 390
Saucier, D. A., 92, 397
Savitsky, K., 31, 32, 57, 86, 108, 283
Saxe, R., 277
Sbarra, D. A., 68
Scalia, A., 331
Schachter, S., 259, 317, 367
Schaerf, L., 432
Schäfer, M., 437
Schafer, R., 376
Schaffner, P. E., 89, 348
Schaller, M., 272, 279, 281
Scheier, M. F., 121
Schein, E., 131
Scher, S. J., 62
Schiavo, R. S., 230
Schiffenbauer, A., 30
Schimel, J., 342, 404
Schimmack, U., 38
Schinke, S., 187
Schirmer, J., 194, 293
Schkade, D., 44, 45
Schlenker, B. R., 63, 64, 65
Schmader, T., 419
Schmiege, S., 198
Schmitt, D. P., 54, 374
Schmitt, M. T., 394
Schnall, S., 138
Schnedler, R., 275
Schneider, C., 274
Schoeneman, T. J., 37
Schofield, J., 442
Scholl, A., 86
Schooler, S., 46
Schor, J. B., 11
Schroeder, A., 230
Schroeder, J., 444, 456
Schroeder, J. E., 351
Schuh, E., 389, 390
Schulz, R. W., 456
Schulz-Hardt, S., 252
Schuman, H., 21, 170
Schwartz, D. A., 287
Schwartz, M., 272, 275
Schwarz, N., 75, 90, 139
Schweitzer, L., 12
Schwinger, M., 62
Schweitzer, M. E., 456
Scott, J., 170
Scott, R. F., 256
Scottish Life, 432
Sears, D. O., 93, 170, 171
Sears, R., 400
Sedikides, C., 41, 51, 54, 55, 62, 407
Seeman, T. E., 369
Segal, H. A., 131
Segal, M., 245
Segal, N. L., 277
Segal-Caspi, L., 352, 353
Segerstrom, S. C., 68
Seibt, B., 419
Seidel, E. M., 54
Seligman, C., 403
Seligman, M. E. P., 19, 65, 68
Selimbegovic, L., 415
Seneca, 199, 377
Sentis, K. P., 436
Sestir, M. A., 330
Seroy, C., 124
Seta, C.E., 14
Seta, J.J., 14
Severance, L. J., 162
Sezer, O., 63
Shackelford, T. K., 351, 361
Shaffer, D., 197
Shaffer, D. R., 377
Shah, A., 11
Shakespeare, W., 110, 121, 157, 218, 316
Shaklee, H., 434
Shanock, L., 141
Shapir, N., 333
Shapiro, P. N., 403, 415, 446
Shariff, A. F., 75
Sharot, T., 135
Sharpe, D., 26
Shaver, P., 372, 377, 380, 405
Shavitt, S., 40
Shaw, G. B., 399
Shaw, M., 226

Sheatsley, P. B., 387
Shedler, J., 422
Sheehan, E. P., 351
Sheeran, P., 119
Sheese, B. E., 330
Sheffield, F. D., 150
Sheldon, K. M., 13, 343
Shell, R. M., 274
Shelton, J. N., 419
Shelton, N., 444, 445
Shen, H., 274
Shepherd, J., 309
Shepherd, R., 245
Sheppard, L., 91
Shepperd, J. A., 36, 58, 62, 66, 236
Shergill, S. S., 429
Sherif, M., 194, 195, 197, 198, 208t, 435, 436, 447, 448
Sherman, A., 393
Sherman, D. K., 40, 419, 421
Sherman, J. W., 406, 410, 411
Sherman, S. J., 85
Shermer, M., 449
Shestakova, A., 214
Shih, M., 419
Shorey-Fennell, B. R., 219
Short, J. F. Jr., 314
Shostak, M., 370
Shotland, R. L., 275, 285
Shovar, N., 64
Showers, C., 58
Shrauger, J. S., 58, 362
Shriver, E. R., 408
Sias, R. W., 346
Sibley, C. G., 414
Sicoly, F., 56, 57
Sidanius, J., 395
Siegelman, J., 175
Sieverding, M., 198
Sigall, H., 365
Sigurdson, J. F., 301
Silk, J. B., 277
Silva, M. N., 195
Silver, L. A., 405
Silver, M., 170, 207, 403
Silver, R. C., 54
Silvera, D. H., 156
Silverman, A. M., 418
Silverman, C., 174
Silverman, D., 353
Silvia, P. J., 211
Sime, J., 283
Simmons, C. H., 413
Simmons, J., 58
Simon, B., 259
Simon, H., 111
Simon, P., 21
Simon-Thomas, E., 275
Simpson, J. A., 199, 358, 372, 373, 380
Sinclair, L., 422
Sinclair, S., 396
Singer, J. E., 317, 367
Singer, M., 176
Singh, D., 357
Singh, J. V., 258
Singh, P., 370
Singh, R., 360
Siperstein, G. N., 287
SIPRI, 427
Sistrunk, F., 218
Sittser, G. L., 87
Sivacek, J. M., 433
Sivarajasingham, V., 309
Six, B., 119
Skaalvik, E. M., 19
Skinner, B. F., 270
Skitka, L. J., 101, 275, 360, 400
Skowronski, J. J., 230
Skurnik, I., 166
Slatcher, R., 378
Slavin, R., 450, 451
Slepian, M. L., 75
Sloan, J. H., 318
Sloan, R. P., 414
Slopen, N., 69
Slotter, E. B., 33, 378, 380
Slotow, R., 333
Slovic, P., 13, 294
Smith, A., 58, 281, 431
Smith, C., 403
Smith, C. K., 187
Smith, D. E., 202
Smith, E. J., 249–251, 258
Smith, H., 235
Smith, P. B., 3, 217, 257
Smith, P. M., 404
Smith, R. H., 35
Smith, S. J., 441
Smith, S. L., 386
Smith, S. M., 132, 152, 184
Smith, T. W., 66, 335
Smits, T., 58
Smollan, D., 378f
Snell, J., 346
Snopes, 203
Snyder, C. R., 56, 66, 221
Snyder, M., 22, 64, 81, 109, 120, 134, 276, 293, 298
Snyder, M. L., 62
Sober, E., 278
Sofer, C., 348
SOHR, 301
Solano, C. H., 376
Solberg, N. L., 311
Solnick, S. J., 308
Solomon, G. S., 272
Solomon, H., 286, 293
Solomon, L. Z., 286, 293
Somaiya, R., 308
Sommers, S. R., 441
Sommerville, J. A., 34
Son Hing, L. S., 397
Sophocles, 157
Soral, W., 399
Sorhagen, N. S., 107
Souvanarath, L., 245
Sowislo, J. F., 50
Sparkman, D. J., 445
Sparrell, J. A., 58
Spears, R., 59, 239, 252
Spector, P. E., 256
Speer, A., 251
Spence, A., 118
Spencer, C. P., 217
Spencer, H., 158
Spencer, S. J., 143, 404, 406, 417
Speth, J. G., 182
Spiegel, H. W., 58
Spielman, S., 363
Spielmann, S. S., 379, 380
Spitz, H. H., 107
Spivak, G., 235
Spodick, N., 257
Sporer, S. L., 408
Spörrle, M., 350
Sprecher, S., 370, 377
Srivastava, S., 109
Srull, T. K., 64
St. Augustine, 388
Stadler, S. J., 316
Stalder, D. R., 282
Stahelski, A. J., 109
Stajkovic, A., 53
Stalin, J., 301
Stam, H. J., 200
Standing, L. G., 217
Stang, D. J., 348
Stangor, C., 405, 406, 444
Stanley, D., 118
Stanovich, K. E., 110, 439
Stark, R., 158, 175, 176
Starks, T. J., 372
Starmans, C., 436
Stasser, G., 245, 260, 262
Statista, 244
Statistics Canada, 149, 244, 318, 387, 393
Staub, E., 206, 270, 281, 287, 294, 295, 296, 333, 401, 438
Stebbins, C. A., 275
Steblay, N. M., 277
Steele, C. M., 36, 66, 142, 143, 417, 418, 420
Steen, T. A., 55
Steers, M. N., 35
Stefan, S., 88
Stegall, A., 328
Stein, S., 155
Stein-Seroussi, A., 81
Stelter, B., 238
Stelzl, M., 403
Stenseng, F., 343
Stephan, W. G., 367, 446
Stephens, N., 217
Stephens-Davidowitz, S., 43, 384, 386, 392
Sternberg, R. J., 301, 366, 366f, 372, 381
Stevens, T. M., 244
Stewart, J., 104
Stewart-Williams, S., 277
Stinson, D., 363

Stinson, D. A., 110
Stiwne, D., 252
Stix, G., 256
Stockdale, L. A., 324
Stone, J., 418
Stone, J. I., 90, 144
Stone, L., 379
Stone, M. H., 305, 306
Stone, R., 286
Stoner, J. A. F., 242
Storms, M. D., 230
Storr, W., 343
Story, A. L., 57
Stouffer, S. A., 311
Stout, J. G., 399
Stoverink, A., 446
Stowell, J. R., 212
Strachman, A., 342, 376
Strack, F., 76, 196
Strange, J. J., 85
Strauss, M., 314
Straw, M. K., 285
Streeter, S. A., 357
Strenta, A., 409
Strick, M., 158
Stroebe, W., 158, 226, 254
Stroessner, S. J., 407, 412
Strong, G., 368f
Stroud, J. N., 408
Stroufe, R., 276
Strube, M. J., 226
Struthers, C. W., 310
Stukas, A. A., 134
Subramanian, A., 392
Sugden, N. A., 408
Sugimori, S., 259
Sullivan, L. A., 412
Suls, J. M., 36, 57
Summers, G., 414
Sun, C., 319
Sundstrom, E., 257
Sunstein, C., 242, 244, 252
Surowiecki, J., 255
Sussman, N. M., 218
Sutton, R., 414
Sutton, S. R., 132
Suzuki, I., 410
Svenson, O., 56
Swami, V., 383
Swann, W. B. Jr., 47, 62, 81, 111, 120, 364, 377, 401
Swanson, J., 306
Swap, W. C., 348
Sweeney, J., 233
Sweeny, K., 132
Swets, J. A., 82
Swift, J., 43, 97, 221, 397
Swift, S. A., 154
Swim, J., 207, 390, 391, 409
Szymanski, K., 236

T

Tafarodi, R. W., 41, 183
Tajfel, H., 9, 260, 401, 403
Takooshian, H., 285
Talhelm, T., 38
Tandoc, E., 6
Tang, S. H., 141
Tanke, E. D., 109
Tarrant, M., 277, 439
Taub, A., 397
Tayeb, M., 257
Taylor, B. R., 315
Taylor, D. G., 376
Taylor, K., 36
Taylor, K. M., 236
Taylor, L. S., 351
Taylor, M., 221
Taylor, R. D., 132
Taylor, S. E., 58, 90, 369, 407, 408
Taylor, S. P., 306
Tedeschi, J. T., 132
Teger, A. I., 431
Teigen, K. H., 56, 87
Teixeira, P. J., 195
Tellegen, A., 346
Tennant, M., 173
Teoh, J. B. P., 360
Terenzini, P. T., 244
Terris, W., 280
Terry, D. J., 165
Tesch, F. E., 36
Tesser, A., 47, 124, 246, 402
Test, M. A., 289
Tetlock, P. E., 86, 118, 124, 252, 275, 389, 440, 456
Thelen, M. H., 361
Thelwall, M., 377
Thomas, G. C., 230, 296
Thomas, L., 301
Thomas, S., 365
Thomas, S. L., 325
Thompson, D. E., 230
Thompson, L., 96, 454
Thompson, L. F., 283
Thompson, L. L., 404
Thompson, W., 271
Thoreau, H. D., 93
Thorne, A., 66
Thornhill, R., 355
Thornton, B., 357
Tice, D. M., 63
Tidwell, N. D., 359
Tierney, J., 69
Tiihonen, J., 306
Tilcsik, A., 393
Timberlake, J., 39
Timmerman, T. A., 310
Tindale, R. S., 245, 262
Tintoré, M., 258
Titus, L. J., 228
Todd, A., 285, 287
Todd, A. R., 456
Todorov, A., 99, 350, 355
Toelch, U., 213, 214
Tofighbakhsh, J., 167
Toguchi, Y., 55
Tolstoy, L., 130
Tomasello, M., 280
Toner, K., 397
Toppo, G., 122
Tormala, Z. L., 155, 183
Toronto News, 54
Tortolani, A. J., 43
Totterdell, P., 196
Towles-Schwen, T., 118
Townsend, E., 118
Tracey, J. L., 404
Trail, T. E., 442
Trautwein, U., 19
Travis, L. E., 226
Trawalter, S., 406
Tredoux, C., 441, 442
Trewin, D., 331
Triandis, H. C., 37, 41, 117, 370, 379, 437, 452
Triplett, N., 226
Trolier, T. K., 87
Tromholt, M., 35
Tropp, L. R., 388, 441
Trost, M. R., 259, 370
Trudeau, P. E., 60
Trump, D., 5, 10, 20, 149, 180, 196, 256, 398
Tsang, J-A., 208
Tuan, Y-F., 240
Tubbs, D. D., 254
Turner, C., 322
Turner, J. A., 161
Turner, J. C., 9, 226, 246, 401, 403
Turner, M. E., 62, 249, 252, 274
Turner, N., 258
Turner, R. N., 442
Tversky, A., 78, 84, 85, 88, 89, 111, 254, 255, 458
Twain, M., 364, 371
Twenge, J. M., 38, 39, 57, 342, 343
Tyler, T. R., 257, 294
Tzeng, O., 379

U

Uleman, J., 99
Unger, R. K., 9, 269
United Nations, 124, 392
Unkelbach, C., 198, 229
Unsworth, N., 332
U.S. Southern Poverty Law Center, 399
Ustinov, P., 345

V

Vaillant, G. E., 96
Vaish, A., 274
Vala, J., 400, 407
Valcour, P. M., 69

Valdesolo, P., 117f
Vallacher, R. R., 346
Vallerand, R. J., 69
Valley, K. L., 454
Vallone, R. P., 79, 92
van Baaren, R., 360
van de Ven, N., 229
Van de Vliert, E., 316
Van de Vyver, J., 434
van der Molen, M. W., 344
van der Plight, J., 20
Van Dijk, J., 45, 47
Van Doren, C., 193
van Knippenberg, A., 156
Van Lange, P. A. M., 433, 455, 459
Van Nuland, A.L., 13
Van Pachterbeke, M., 403
van Prooijen, J., 397
Van Straaten, I., 351
Van Tongeren, D. R., 397
van Velow, S. J., 34
Van Vugt, M., 143, 269
Van Yperen, N. W., 375, 376
Vanable, P., 66
VanDellen, M. R., 48
Vandello, J. A., 314
Vanderslice, R. R., 256
Vandlen, J. D., 384
Vanofakou, C., 442
Vargas, R. A., 213
Varnum, M. E. W., 37, 39
Vasquez, E., 310
Vasquez-Suson, K. A., 410
Västfjäll, D., 294
Vatiné, E., 202
Vaughan, K. B., 139
Vedas, B., 284
Veitch, R., 315
Velasquez, C. M., 135
Ventis, W. L., 398
Verkuyten, M., 447
Verkuyten, M. J. A. M., 402
Verplanken, B., 152
Verrilli, D. B. Jr., 177
Vescio, T., 395
Veysey, B., 244
Vezzali, L., 442
Vignoles, V., 346
Vinokur, A., 245
Violato, C., 320
Virgil, 353
Virtanen, S. V., 407
Visintainer, M. A., 68
Visser, P. S., 171, 189
Vitelli, S., 25
Voci, A., 442
Vogel, T., 155
Vohs, K. D., 63
Vollhardt, J. R., 445
Vollmer, C., 306
Vollrath, D. A., 245
Volpato, C., 259
von Goethe, J. W., 196
von Hippel, W., 85, 405
von Szent-Györgyi, A., 229
Vonn, L., 86
Vonnegut, K., 403
Vorauer, J. D., 31, 50, 247, 410, 412, 443, 444, 453
Voss, A., 389
Vul, E., 255

W

Wachtler, J., 259
Wadsworth, T., 36
Wagner, A. J. M., 161
Wagner, B., 138
Wagner, G., 182, 301
Wagner, U., 385, 446, 451
Wagstaff, J. F., 105
Waldman, I. D., 306
Walker, G. R., 121
Walker, I., 388
Walker, L., 135
Walker, L. J., 291
Walker, P. M., 408
Walker, R., 167
Wallace, D. S., 119
Wallbom, M., 121, 241
Waller, J., 128, 208
Walster (Hatfield), E., 128, 154, 349, 352, 362, 363, 365, 367, 436
Walster, G. W., 436
Walster, W., 365
Walters, R. H., 314, 324
Walther, E., 152
Walther, J., 63
Walton, G. M., 417, 419
Walum, H., 371, 374
Wan, F., 274
Wan, L., 408
Wandersman, A., 348
Wang, M. C., 316
Wang, T., 212
Wang, Z., 35
Wänke, M., 348
Wanshula, L. T., 407
Ward, A., 456
Ward, C., 412
Ward, C. D., 367
Wareham, J., 343
Waters, E. A., 58
Watson, D., 103
Watson, J., 254
Watson, M., 448
Watson, R. I. Jr., 239
Watt, S. E., 59, 342
Waugh, G., 368
Wayner, M., 459
Waytz, A., 439
Wearing, A., 56
Weaver, J. B. III, 325
Weary, G., 64
Webb, C. E., 76, 457
Webb, T. L., 119
Weber, B., 235
Weber, R., 415
Webley, K., 392
Webster, D. M., 259
Wechkin, S., 280
Wegener, D. T., 144, 151, 163, 164, 185
Wegner, D. M., 66, 405
Wehr, P., 457
Weichselbaumer, D., 393
Weick, M., 76
Weigold, M. F., 63
Weil, R., 152
Weiner, B., 98, 105, 275, 310
Weinstein, N., 58, 270
Weis, R., 332
Weiss, H. M., 154
Weiss, R. F., 365
Welch, M. R., 205
Welker, K. M., 376
Wells, B. M., 230
Wells, G. L., 139
Welzel, C., 69
Wener, R., 69
Wenzelburger, G., 392
Wenzlaff, R. M., 361
Werner, C. M., 162
West, R. F., 110
West, S. G., 275, 276, 400
Westwood, S. J., 244
Whatley, M., 274
Wheeler, L., 36, 349, 351
Whitaker, J. L., 331
Whitchurch, E., 36, 56
White, G., 351
White, G. L., 368
White, K., 41, 91
White, M. H., 399
White, M. J., 291
White, R. J., 80
Whitechurch, E. R., 362
Whitehead, A. N., 120
Whitman, W., 119, 345
Whitney, G., 275
Whitson, J. A., 88
Whittaker, J. O., 217
Whyte, G., 243
Wicker, A., 116, 117
Wicklund, R. A., 271
Widom, C., 314
Wiebe, D. J., 319
Wiegman, O., 153
Wieselquist, J., 375
Wiggins, E. C., 116
Wiggins, N. H., 364
Wilberforce, W., 398
Wilde, O., 259
Wilder, D. A., 156, 209, 403, 415, 446
Wildschut, T., 435
Wilhelmy, R. A., 209
Wilke, H., 156
Wilke, H. A. M., 236
Wilkes, D. E. Jr., 303
Wilkes, R., 383

Wilkins, S., 135
Wilkinson, G. S., 277
Wilkowski, B. M., 330613
Willard, G., 51
Willems, S., 348
Willer, R., 160
Williams, D. K., 163
Williams, E., 57
Williams, J. E., 390
Williams, K., 233
Williams, K. D., 7, 171, 233, 234, 235, 236, 343, 344
Williams, K. M., 51
Williams, M. J., 412
Williams, R. L., 141
Williams, T. J., 96
Williams, W., 391
Williamson, G. M., 271
Willis, F. N., 202
Willoughby, T., 183, 329, 331
Wilson, A. E., 60, 60f, 359, 363, 380
Wilson, B. J., 322
Wilson, D. S., 278
Wilson, E. O., 276, 284
Wilson, J. P., 291, 385
Wilson, J. Q., 277
Wilson, R., 267, 277, 279, 306
Wilson, S. J., 337
Wilson, T. D., 44, 45, 46, 362
Wilson, W. R., 348
Winch, R., 361
Windschitl, P. D., 61
Winegard, B., 447
Wingate, V. S., 337
Winter, F. W., 348
Winton, W., 221
Wirth, J. H., 344, 367
Wisman, A., 342
Wit, A. P., 236
Wixon, D. R., 96
Wober, M., 132
Wodehouse, P. G., 272
Wohl, M., 88. 447
Wojciszke, B., 365
Wolf, S., 60
Wolf, W., 344
Wolfe, C., 46
Wolfe, M. B., 96
Wong, E. M., 256
Wong, J. S., 450
Wood, E. E., 293
Wood, J. V., 36, 49, 50, 51
Wood, V. R., 271
Wood, W., 120, 154, 397
Woodzicka, J., 44
Woolley, J., 252
Wootton-Millward, L., 407
Worchel, S., 230, 236, 310, 450
Word, C., 416
Workman, E. A., 141
World Health Organization, 149
World Meteorological Organization, 178
Worringham, C., 231
Wotman, S., 380
Wraga, M., 419
Wright, D. B., 408
Wright, F. L., 52
Wright, J., 60
Wright, K. D., 254
Wright, P. J., 319, 321
Wright, R. A., 236, 244
Wright, S. C., 441, 442
Wu, A., 332
Wuensch, K. L., 283
Wurf, E., 34
Wyer, R. S., 274
Wylie, L., 118
Wylie, R. C., 56
Wynn, K., 359
Wynne, C. D. L., 280

X

Xie, S. Y., 124

Y

Yamagishi, T., 63
Yamaguchi, S., 55
Yang, H-C., 254
Yaniv, D., 456
Yap, A. J., 138
Yates, S., 172
Ybarra, O., 321, 324, 330
Yee, C., 437
Yee, L., 331
Yee, N., 56
Yildiz, A. A., 402
Yinon, Y., 333
Young, L. J., 371
Young, R. D., 66, 241
Young, S. G., 408
Younger, J. C., 135, 344
Yousif, Y., 277, 287
Yovetich, N. A., 381
Yu, F., 38
Yu, R., 227
Yukl, G., 454
Yzerbyt, V. Y., 362

Z

Zadro, L., 7, 343
Zagefka, H., 275
Zainulbhai, H., 392
Zajonc, R. B., 228, 228f, 231, 245, 333, 346, 348
Zak, P. J., 456
Zaki, J., 194, 214
Zanna, M. P., 64, 66, 67f, 108, 116, 120, 121, 124, 142, 143, 143f, 150, 161, 247, 307, 313, 390, 407, 416
Zavalloni, M., 243
Zebrowitz, L. A., 358, 442
Zebrowitz-McArthur, L., 105
Zeisel, H., 260, 261, 262
Zha, X., 155
Zhang, D. D., 181
Zhang, Q., 86
Zhang, S., 40
Zhang, Y. F., 316
Zhong, C. B., 75, 344
Zhou, J., 117
Zhu, L., 434
Zhu, Y., 40
Zigler, E., 314
Zill, N., 327
Zillman, D., 229, 317, 325, 357
Zimbardo, P. G., 67, 122, 123, 128, 237, 238f, 439
Zimmer, C., 34
Ziskin, J., 82
Zitek, E. M., 398
Zola-Morgan, S., 348
Zotto, M., 357
Zuckerberg, M., 258
Zuckerman, E. W., 47
Zuwerink, J. R., 406

Subject Index

A

Abu Ghraib, 207
academic achievement, and self-esteem, 18–19, 51
accentuation phenomenon, 243–244
acceptance
  see also conformity
  and compliance, 174
  defined, 194
achievement, and self-concept, 19
active experience, 165–167
active participation, 245–246
actor-observer difference, 102–103
additive tasks, 232
advertising
  and children, 187–189
  humour in, 159f
advice, 10
affective forecasting, 44
Africville, 387
age
  and attitudes, 170–171
  of audience, 170–171
  generational explanation, 170
  prejudice, 384
  life cycle explanation, 170
aggression
  adaptive nature of, 304
  aggression cues, 318–319
  alcohol and, 306–307
  altered perceptions, 327
  arousal, 316–317
  attacks, 316
  aversive incidents, 315–316
  biochemical influences, 306–309
  as biological phenomenon, 304–309
  biology and behaviour, 308–309
  catharsis, 331, 335–336
  cognitive priming, 327
  correlational studies, 322–323
  and culture, 239, 314–315
  culture change and world violence, 338
  defined, 302
  described, 301–303
  desensitization, 326
  displaced aggression, 309–310, 400
  distorted perceptions of sexual reality, 320
  evolutionary psychology, 304–305
  experimental studies, 320–321, 324–325
  and the family, 314
  frustration-aggression theory, 309–312, 311f, 400
  genetic influences, 306
  group influences, 332–335, 334f
  guns, 318–319, 337
  heat, 315–316
  hostile aggression, 302, 315, 317f
  influences on, 315–335
  instinct theory, 304–305
  instinctive behaviour, 304
  instrumental aggression, 302
  as learned social behaviour, 312–315
  media awareness education, 332
  media influences, 319–332
  murders, 303
  and narcissism, 52f
  neural influences, 305–306
  observational learning, 313–315
  pain, 315
  poor diet, 308
  and pornography, 319–321, 321f
  primates *vs.* humans, 305–306
  reducing aggression, 335–338
  relative deprivation, 311–312
  retaliation, 309, 336
  rewards of, 312–313
  scapegoat theory, 400
  and self-esteem, 52f
  sexual violence, 319–321
  social aggression, 302
  social learning theory, 313–315, 314f, 336–338
  social scripts, 326–327
  television, influences of, 23, 322–327
  terrorism, 302, 313
  and testosterone, 307
  theories of aggression, 303–315
  types of aggression, 302
  video games, 327–332, 329f
  wars, 302–303
  against women, 320–321
aggression cues, 318–319
aggressive behaviours, 23, 329
aggressive feelings, 330
alcohol
  and aggression, 306–307
  myopia, 66, 67f
Algo Centre Mall, 13
altered perceptions, 327
altruism
  altruistic norms, 434
  ambiguity, reducing, 292–293
  anonymity, 285–286, 293
  attributing helpful behaviour to, 296–297
  comparison and evaluation of theories, 278–281, 278t
  and culture, 288f
  defined, 268
  egoistic distress reduction, 280–281, 280f
  empathy and distress, 280–281
  encouraging altruistic behaviour, 292–298, 295f
  evolutionary psychology, 276–278
  examples of, 268
  and foot-in-the-door phenomenon, 125–126
  and gender, 275–276, 291–292
  genuine altruism, 278–281, 280f
  Good Samaritan parable, 289
  group selection, 277–278
  guilt, 271, 293–294
  how to increase helping, 292–298, 295f
  kin selection, 276–277
  learning about, 297
  modelling altruism, 294–296
  money and happiness, 274
  moral inclusion, 294
  and number of bystanders, 282–288
  overjustification effect, 296–297
  personality traits, 291
  and prejudice, 404
  and prosocial models, 289
  reciprocity norm, 273–274, 278
  responsibility, increase in, 292 293
  rewards, 269–273
  self-image, concern for, 293–294
  similarity to victim, 290
  social-exchange theory, 269–273
  and social norms, 273–276
  social-responsibility norm, 275–276
  socialization and, 294–297
  teaching altruism, 294
  theories of altruism, 278–281, 278t
  time pressures, 289–290
  what to do when you need help, 298
  when we help, 282–290
  who helps, 291–292
  why we help, 269–281
altruistic norms, 434
ambiguity, and altruism, 292–293
ambiguous events, 283–285
ambiguous information, 93
ambiguous reality, 197
amygdala, 118
anecdotes, power of, 85
anonymity, 237–240, 238f, 239f, 293
anticipation of interaction, 346
anticipatory liking, 346
anticonformity
  motivation for, 219–221
  reactance, 185, 219–220
  uniqueness, assertion of, 221

anti-gay prejudice, 393
anti-smoking programs, 158–159
antisocial behaviour
and self-esteem, 51
and video games, 330
antisocial tendencies, 332
anxious-ambivalent attachment, 373
approval, 363–364
arbitration, 453, 457–458
arguments, 245
arousal
and aggression, 316–317
and deindividuation, 241
dissonance as arousal, 142–144
dominant responses, facilitation of, 228
effects of, 228f
mere presence of others, 226–229, 228f, 230–231
and passionate love, 366–369
and romantic responses, 367
and self-affirmation theory, 142
sexual arousal, 316–317
television, 325
video games, 330–331
arousing and distracting activities, 240–241
Asch's studies of group pressure, 197–199, 197f, 208t
assumption of responsibility, 285–287
assumptions, power of, 82
athletic performance, and stereotypes, 418
atmospheric carbon, 179f
attachment
anxious-ambivalent attachment, 373
avoidant attachment, 372
and close relationships, 371–374
dismissive attachment, 372–373
fearful attachment, 372–373
insecure attachment, 373
internal working models, 374
secure attachment, 372
styles, 372–374
attacks, 316
attitude alignment, 360
attitude inoculation, 185, 186–189
attitude strength, 183
attitudes
accessibility of, and persuasion, 172f
and active participation, 245–246
and age, 170–171
behaviour, effect on, 6–7, 46, 137f
and conformity and obedience, 205–206
contact, and prediction of, 441–442
defined, 116
dissimilar attitudes, 360–361
dual attitude system, 46, 386
experience and, 121
explicit attitudes, 46, 117
and expressions, 137–139
facial expressions, 137–139
and hypocrisy, 116–117
implicit attitudes, 46, 117
minimal social influences, 117–119
in novel, 123
and persuasive messages, 150
power of, 120–121
and prediction of behaviour, 117–121
predictive accuracy of, 119–120
prejudice, and contact, 442–445
reconstruction of past attitudes, 95–97
and self-conscious people, 120–121
self-perception theory, and attitude formation, 141
strong, 183
attitudes-follow-behaviour principle
cognitive dissonance theory, 132–136
comparison of theories, 141–144
culture, 136
cults, 174
evil acts, 128–130
explanations of, 121–122
foot-in-the-door phenomenon, 125–126, 174–175
gender roles, 124
impression management, 131–132
moral acts, 128–130
role playing, 122–124
self-justification, 132–136
self-perception theory, 131–132, 136–141, 144
self-presentation theory, 131–132
social movements, 130–131
when saying becomes believing, 124–125
attraction
attribution, 362–363
beautiful is good stereotype, 353–354
complementarity, 361
and dating, 349–350
dissimilarity breeds dislike, 360–361
and evolution, 356–357
first impressions, 353
gaining another's esteem, 363–364
ingratiation, 363
interaction and, 345–346
likeness-leads-to-liking effect, 359–360
liking by association, 365
liking those who like us, 362–364
love and, 358–359
matching phenomenon, 351
mere-exposure effect, 346–349
mutual liking, 362–364
open, honest relationship, 364
opposites, 361
physical attractiveness, 155, 349–359
proximity and, 345–349
reward theory of attraction, 365
and self-esteem, 363
similarity, 155–156, 359–361
social comparison, 357
attractiveness, 56, 155–156, 349–350. *See* physical attractiveness
attribution theory, 99
attributions
attraction, 362–363
causality, 98–99
cognitive source of prejudice, 412–413
and culture, 103–105
dispositional attribution, 99
fundamental attribution error, 100–102, 100f, 102–105, 102f, 106
group-serving bias, 412–413
helpful behaviour to altruistic motives, 296–297
inferring traits, 99
language, and external attributions, 105
misattribution, 98
prejudice, 412–413
and reactions, 105f
self-serving attributions, 54
situational attribution, 99, 105
and social-responsibility norm, 275–276
audience
age of audience, 170–171
counterarguing, 171
cults, 176
distraction, 171
peripheral cues, 171–172
and persuasion, 169–172
thoughts of, 170–172
uninvolved audiences, 171–172
authoritarian personality, 396–397
authority
closeness and legitimacy, and obedience, 202–203
institutional authority, 203–204
persuasion, 156t
autokinetic phenomenon, 195
automatic prejudice, 386, 389–390, 406
automatic processing, 46, 76
autonomy, 342
availability heuristics, 84–85
aversive incidents
and aggression, 315–316
attacks, 316
heat, 315–316
pain, 315
avoidance, 372
avoidant attachment, 372

B

bad luck, 87
bargaining, 453–454
beautiful is good stereotype, 353–354
behaviour
affect on attitudes, 121–131
aggressive behaviours, 329
attitudes, and prediction of behaviour, 116–121
attitudes, effect of, 6–7, 46, 137f
biological roots of, 7
and biology, interaction between, 308–309
and conformity and obedience, 205–206
and culture, 98–106
discrimination, 385
and evolution, 276–278
examining attitudes specific to, 119–120
and expectations, 108–110
expected behaviour. *See* norms
helping behaviour. *See* altruism

instinctive behaviour, 304
looking good, as motivator, 63–65
mental after-effects of, 122
minimal social influences, 117–119
past behaviour, reconstruction of, 97–98
personality, effect of, 6
planned behaviour, 120f
predicting our behaviour, 43–44, 82
prosocial behaviour, 294–297, 326, 330, 332
social influences, effect of, 6
television, effects of, 322–325
behaviour tendency, 384
behavioural confirmation, 108–110
belief perseverance, 93–94
beliefs
challenging, 185
changing after conforming, 215f
belonging, and social identity, 404–405
benevolent sexism, 390
bias
blind spot, 54
camera perspective bias, 103
confirmation bias, 81–82
correspondence bias, 100–102
detection of, in behaviour, 409
experimenter bias, 106
false consensus bias, 360
fundamental attribution error, 100–102, 100f, 102–105, 102f, 106
gender bias, 391–392
group-serving bias, 412–413
hindsight bias, 13
impact bias, 45
implicit bias, 117
information-processing biases, 183–185
in-group bias, 294, 402–404, 411f
in interpretations, 421–422
knowledge of issues, 21
linguistic intergroup bias, 412
media bias, 92, 92f
in memories, 421–422
myside bias, 439
own-age bias, 408
own-race bias, 408, 408f
perception of, 92f
response bias, 20–21
self-serving bias. *See* self-serving bias
study of, 106
subtle biases in social psychology, 9
survey, 19–21
bio-psycho-social organisms, 7
biochemical influences on aggression, 306–309
biology
and aggression, 304–309
and behaviour, interaction between, 7, 308–309
and culture, 304
natural selection, 278
passionate love and, 367
black bloc tactics, 74
Black Lives Matter, 239
blame-the-victim process, 206
blindsight, 77
blood chemistry, 306
Bobo doll, 313, 322, 324, 325
boomerang effect, 219
boredom, 347
the brain
and aggression, 305–306
and conformity, 213–214
habituation, 330
and love, 368f
and stereotyping, 419
brainstorming, 254
brainwashing, 10, 130
bullying, 287, 334
bystander effect, 285
bystander passivity
assumption of responsibility, 285–287
decision tree, 283f
interpretation, 283–285
nations as bystanders, 287
noticing, 283
number of bystanders, effect of, 282–288
research ethics, 287–288
similarity to victim, 290
smoke-filled room experiment, 284f
time pressures, 289–290

C

camera perspective bias, 103
Canada
alcohol and tobacco use, 149
aggression in, 318
immigration, 400
murders in, 318
prejudice and discrimination in, 387, 393, 400, 410
Residential School system, 128
Senate scandal, 242
self-concept, 136
social identity, 39
cancer screening, 198
carbon taxes, 182,
cases, distinctive, 410
castration, 308
categorization, 406–408
catharsis, 331, 335–336
causality, attributing, 98–99
causation, 18–19, 18f, 23
central route to persuasion, 151–152, 151f
certainty, 183
chameleon effect, 196
channel of communication
active experience *vs.* passive reception, 165–167
defined, 164
personal *vs.* media influence, 167–169
charismatic leaders, 175
charitable donations, 279
cheating, 241
children
advertising, influence of, 187–189
and aggression, 313, 314
altruism, teaching, 294
attitude inoculation, 185
and dissonance, 136
expectations, and behaviour, 110
games they play, 328–332
and Halloween anonymity, 238–239, 239f
peer pressure to smoke, 186–187, 187f
and physical-attractiveness stereotype, 352–354
sexual scripts, 326–327
television viewing, 322–324, 323f
video games, 327–332
choices-influence-preferences effect, 135
classification, 406–408
climate change
evidence of, 178–179
and persuasion, 178–182
new technologies, 181
psychology and, 178–181
public opinion about, 180–181
reducing consumption, 181–182
skepticism, 149
close relationships
see also love
arranged marriages *vs.* love marriages, 371f
attachment, 371–374
collectivism and, 235
and culture, 235
detachment process, 380–381
divorce, 379
ending relationships, 378–381
equity, 375–376
and expectations, 108–112
happily *vs.* unhappily married, 3
individualism and, 41
long-term equity, 375
love, 358–359, 365–371
open, honest relationship, 364
perceived equity and satisfaction, 375–376
physical attractiveness of loved ones, 358–359, 359f
positive illusions, 364
predictions of, 43–44
self-disclosure, 376–378
successful couples, 381
co-actors, 226
cognition, 39–40, 171, 384, 386
cognitive dissonance theory
application of, 132
and culture, 136
defined, 132
dissonance after decisions, 135–136
dissonance as arousal, 142–144
insufficient justification effect, 132–134, 133f
cognitive priming, 327
cognitive processes, and prejudice, 406–414
cognitive response approach, 150
cohesiveness, 210–211, 446–448
collapse of compassion, 279–280

collective narcissism, 51–52
collectivism
cognitive dissonance, 136
defined, 37
intimate relationships, formation of, 379
language, 40
and the self, 37–43
and self-esteem, 41–43
and social loafing, 235
variations in, 38
commitment
effect of, on social loafing, 236
prior commitments, 212
relationship commitment, and related attractiveness, 358f
common external threats, and cohesiveness, 446–448
common-sense attributions, 11–15
communal qualities, 49
communication
arbitration, 453, 457–458
bargaining, 453–454
channel of communication, 164–169
fear-rousing communications, 158–161
mediation, 453, 454–457
peace, achievemtn of, 453–458
persuasion. *See* persuasion
social dilemmas, 433
two-step flow of communication, 168–169
the communicator
attractiveness and liking, 155–156
credibility, 153–155, 162f
cults, 175
communities, and group polarization, 244
community spirit, 277
companionate love, 369–371
comparison
downward, 47
media comparison, 169
self-serving bias, and, 55–57
social comparison. *See* social comparison
temporal comparison, 60–61
upward, 36
compassion fatigue, 287
competence, 342
competition, 434–435
complementarity, 361
compliance
see also conformity
and acceptance, 174
defined, 194
with legitimate authority, 202–203
compliant confessions, 95
compliments, 362–363
companionate love, 369–371
competition, and prejudice, 400
concepts, formation of, 10
conciliation, 458–459
conciliatory acts, 458–459
confederate, 7, 195–196
confident speaking, 154
confirmation bias, 81–82
confirming evidence, 79
conflict
creation of conflict, 427–440
defined, 427
misperception, 437–440
non-zero-sum games, 431
perceived injustice, 436–437
Prisoner's Dilemma, 428–429, 428f, 429f, 431
resolution of, 453–458
social dilemmas, 427–434
Tragedy of the Commons, 430
conformity
acceptance, 194
anti-conformity, motivation for, 219–221
behaviour and attitudes, 205–206
and the brain, 213–214
changing beliefs after conforming, 215f
classic conformity and obedience studies, 194–208, 208t
cohesiveness, 210–211
compliance, 194
conformists, 215–219
and culture, 217
defined, 193–194
gender prejudice, 398–399
group influence, liberating effects of, 204
group size, 209, 209f
groupthink, and conformity pressure, 250
informational influence, 213, 214–215
negative value judgment, 193
no prior commitment, 212
normative influence, 213, 214–215
obedience, 194, 201–204
and personality, 215–217
predicting conformity, 209–212
prejudice, 398–399
public response, 211–212
reactance, 185, 219–220
reasons for conformity, 213–215
situation, power of, 207–208
and social movements, 100–102
social roles, 218–219
status, 211
suggestibility, 195–196
unanimity, 210, 210f
and uniqueness, 221
varieties of, 194
conformity and obedience studies
Asch's studies of group pressure, 197–199, 197f, 208t
Milgram's obedience studies, 199–201, 201f, 208t
reflections on, 204–208
Sherif's studies of norm formation, 194–197, 195f, 208t
summary, 208t
confounded variables, 19
conscious self-presentation, 64
Conservative Party, 170
consistency, 156t, 259
conspiracy theories, 149
construction of memories, 94–98
constructive fighting, 455t
consumption, reduction of, 181–182
contact
affect on prejudice, 442–445
equal-status contact, 446
friendship, 444–445
peace, achievement of, 441–446
personal vs, media influence, 167–168
prediction of attitudes, 441–442
reciprocity, 277
self-segregation, 442–444, 443f
contrast effect, 361
control
in experimental research, 22–23
illusion of control, 88–89
personal control, 69
self-control, 67–70, 241
social control, 178
control condition, 31–32, 32t
controlled processing, 76
conventional wisdom, 15
cooling-off period, 126
cooperation
altruistic norms, appeals to, 434
attachment, 371
changing payoffs, 433
common external threats, 446–448
communication, 433
cooperative learning and prejudice, 450–452
ethnic and cultural identity, 452t
group and superordinate identities, 452–453
out-group ratings, 449f
peace, achievement of, 446–453
regulation, 431–432
similarity breeds cooperation, 290f
small groups, 432–433
and social dilemmas, 431–434
and social loafing, 232
superordinate goals, 448–450
coping mechanisms, 45
coronavirus. *See* COVID-19 pandemic
correlation
vs. causation, 18–19, 18f
illusory correlation, 87–89, 410–411
obesity, marital status and income, 22
quantifying, 19
recognition of, 24t
television viewing and behaviour, 322–324
temperature and aggression, 315–316
time-lagged correlation, 19
violence on television, 23
correlational research
aggression against women, 320–321
and causation, 18–19, 18f
cause-effect relations, 19
defined, 17
detecting natural associations, 17–21
and experiments, 22–23, 22f, 24t
longitudinal research, 19
prejudice against obese, 22–23

recognizing, 24t
survey research, 19–21
television violence viewing, 23
time-lagged correlation, 19
correspondence bias, 100–102
cosmetic surgery, 353, 357
counterarguing, 185–186
counterarguments, 171, 185–186
counterfactual thinking, 86–87
COVID-19 pandemic, 251–252, 267
credibility, 153–155, 156, 162f
credible source, 161–162
crowd within, 255
crowding, 229–230
cruelty, 6
cults
attitudes-follow-behaviour principle, 174–175
audience, 176
the communicator, 175
compliance, effect of, 174
defined, 174
extreme persuasion, 173–178
foot-in-the-door phenomenon, 174–175
group effects, 176–178
the message, 175–176
persuasive elements of, 175–176
cultural psychology, 42
cultural racism, 360–361
culture
and aggression, 314–315
and altruism, 288f
and attributions, 103–105
and behaviour, 98 106
and biology, 304
cognition and, 39–40
and cognitive dissonance, 136
and conformity, 217
conformity, and negative value judgment, 193
cultural racism, 360–361
defined, 9
Eastern cultural assumptions, 104, 136
and emotional expression, 137–139
facial expressions, 137–139
false beliefs, perpetuation of, 195
and friendships, 277
and fundamental attribution error, 103–105
and gender stereotypes, 390
and group behaviour, 235
individualism. *See* individualism
language, influence of, 105
likeness begets liking, 360
love, variations in, 368–369
and norms, 277
perceptions, 38f
and persuasion, 150
and physical attractiveness, 354–355
pigeonholing, 38
self and, 37–43
and self-esteem, 41, 43
social influence, impact on, 6, 231–236
and social loafing, 235
and social relations, 314–315
social roles, 218–219
thinking, effect on, 37–43
and uniqueness, 221
values, differences in, 9
Western cultural assumptions, 37–38
world violence, and change, 338
cyberbullying, 301
cyberostracism, 343–344

D

dating, and attractiveness, 349–350
death instinct, 304
deciding-becomes-believing effect, 135
decision tree, 283f
decisions, and dissonance, 135–136
defections from the majority, 260
defensive pessimism, 58
deflation, 343
deindividuation
arousing and distracting activities, 240–241
defined, 237
diminished self-awareness, 241
group size, 237
physical anonymity, 237–240, 238f
unrestrained behaviours, 236–237
demand characteristics, 25
democratic leadership, 256–257
dental flossing, 198
dependent variable, 23
depersonalization, 202
depressive explanatory style, 55f
deprivation, 311–312
desegregation, 443f
desensitization, 327
detachment process, 380–381
devil's advocate, 252
diet, and aggression, 308
differences, perceived, 408–411
diffusion of responsibility, 332–333
diminished self-awareness, 241
disagreement, 161
disclosure reciprocity, 377
discomfort, 161
discrepancy, 161–162, 162f
discrimination
see also prejudice
defined, 385
effect of, 416
gender discrimination, 391–392
influence of prejudice on, 414–422
obesity and, 23
perceived discrimination, 419
discrepancy, 161–162, 162f
vs. prejudice, 385
self-fulfilling prophecy, 416
disinhibition, 325, 333
dismissive attachment, 372–373
displaced aggression, 309–310, 400
displacement, 309
disposition and behaviour, 6–7
dispositional attribution, 99, 105
dissimilarity, 360–361
dissonance
as arousal, 142–144
and decisions, 135–136
minimizing, 132
and the Pill, 143f
distinctiveness
cases, 410
events, 410–411
illusory correlation, 87–89, 410–411
people, 408–409
and prejudice, 408–411
and self-consciousness, 409–410
shortcut to judging groups, 410
stereotypes, 410
distracting activities, 240–241
distraction, 171, 231
distress, 280–281
divorce, 379
door-in-the-face technique, 127–128
driven by distraction, 231
drivers, and self-serving bias, 56
drunk driving attitudes, 67f
drug education programs, 187
dual attitude system, 46, 386
dual processing, 5, 119

E

eco-technologies, 181
education
health, 168f
media awareness education, 332
persuasion as, 150
egoism, 270
egoistic distress reduction, 280–281, 280f
electronic brainstorming, 254
elevation, 289
embodied cognition, 75
emergency situations, 298
emotional expression, 137–139
emotional reactions, 76
emotions
expressions, influence of, 137–139
fear-arousing communications, 158–161
good feelings, effect of, 157–158, 158f
perception of, 157–161
predicting our future feelings, 44–45
vs. reason, 157–161
and self-perception theory, 137
stereotype threat and, 419
two-factor theory of emotion, 367
video games, and aggressive feelings, 329–330
empathy, 279–280, 330
employment discrimination, 388
ending relationships, 378–381
environmental influences, 315–16
environmental zones, 182
equal-status contact, 446
equality, 436

equity, 375–376, 436
erotic photographs, 44
ethics
  of experimentation, 25–26
  explanation of experiment, 198
  informed consent, 26, 287
  Milgram's studies, 200–201
  and self-serving bias, 56
  twofold obligation, 288
  university ethics committees, 25–26
ethnic and cultural identity, 452t
ethnicity, 407
ethnocentric, 396
evaluation apprehension, 230–231, 233, 237
events
  distinctive, 410–411
  perceiving and interpreting, 91–93
everyday life
  group brainstorming, 255–256
  group polarization, 243–245
  social loafing, 233–236
  social psychology in, 8
evil acts, 128–130, 205–206
evil leader-good people perception, 439–440
evolution
  and aggression, 304–305
  and altruism, 276–277
  and attraction, 356–357
  and behaviour, 276–278
  genetic self-interest, 277
  instinct theory, 304–305
  kin selection, 276–277
  physical attractiveness, 356–357
  reciprocity, 277
evolutionary psychology, 7, 276–278, 304–305, 356–357
exchanging benefits, and equity, 375–376
expectations
  and children's behaviour, 110
  influence of, 108–110
  of our social world, 106–110
  self-fulfilling prophecy, 106, 108f
  teacher expectations and student performance, 107–108, 108f
experimental realism, 25, 198
experimental research
  see also specific research topics
  aggression against women, 320–321
  confederate, 7, 195–196
  control, 22–23
  and correlations, 22–23, 22f, 24t
  defined, 17
  demand characteristics, 25
  dependent variables, 23
  described, 22
  ethics of experimentation, 25–26
  experimental realism, 25
  generalizations from laboratory to life, 26–27
  independent variables, 22
  informed consent, 26
  manipulating variables, 22–23
  and mundane realism, 25
  observational research methods, 24
  prejudice against obese, 22–23
  random assignment, 23–25, 24f
  recognizing, 24t
  television violence viewing, 23, 324–325
experimenter bias, 106
expertise, perceived, 76, 154
explanatory style, 55, 55f
explicit attitudes, 46, 117
explicit memory, 77
explicit prejudice, 386, 387, 389, 396
express yourself, 40
expressions
  and attitudes, 137–139
  emotional expression, and culture, 137–139
  of prejudice, 386
extended-contact effect, 442
external causes, 99
external rewards, 269
extreme persuasion, 173–178
extrinsic motivation, 140f

F

faces
  see also physical attractiveness
  computer averaged faces, and attractiveness, 355
  facial expressions, 39, 107, 137–139, 377
facial expressions, 29, 107, 137–139, 377
facts, 15
failure, 35, 62
fallacies
  naturalistic fallacy, 10
  planning fallacy, 43
false confessions, 95
false consensus bias, 360
false consensus effect, 59
false modesty, 63
false uniqueness effect, 59
family
  and aggression, 314
  and contact, 441
favour, reciprocation of, 275f
favourable stereotype, 390
favouritism, 388, 402–403
fear of failure, 62
fear-rousing communications, 158–161
fearful attachment, 372–373
federalists, 21
feel bad-do good scenario, 271–272
feel good-do good scenario, 272–273
feelings
  see also emotions
  expressions, influence of, 137–139
  good feelings, effect of, 157–158, 158f
  predicting our future feelings, 44–45
  video games, and aggressive feelings, 329–330
feminist critics, 9
field research, 17
first impressions, 353
fitting in, and social comparison, 34–36
Floyd, George, 267, 296
folie à deux, 176
folk tale, 2
foot-in-the-door phenomenon, 125–126, 174–175, 205
fraud, 26
free-ride, 233
friendship
  complementarity, 361
  and contact, 444–445
  and culture, 277
  and groupthink, 252
  long-term equity, 375
  mere-exposure effect, 346–349
  mutual liking, 362–364
  norms, 273
  physical attractiveness, 349–359
  proximity and, 345–349
  relationship rewards, 364–365
  similarity, 359–361
frustration
  aggression as response to, 309–312, 400
  defined, 309
  vs. deprivation, 311
  scapegoat theory, 400
frustration-aggression theory
  classic theory, 311f
  defined, 309
  displacement, 309–310
  relative deprivation, 311–312
  revision of theory, 310–311
full house, 230
functional distance, 345
fundamental attribution error
  actor-observer difference, 102–103
  attributions, 412–413
  camera perspective bias, 103
  changes in perspective, 102–103
  and culture, 103–105
  defined, 100
  described, 100–102
  illustration of, 100f
  misperception and, 102f, 437
  perspective and situational awareness, 102–103
  prejudice, 412–413
  reasons for, 102–105
  social dilemmas, 431
  study of, 106
future technologies, 181

G

G-20 summit, 73–74, 239
gain-framed messages, 160
gambling, 88
game shows, 255
gangs, 333
gender
  and altruism, 291–292
  awareness of, 217–218
  bias, 391–392
  changing attitudes, 391f

discrimination, 391–392
gender roles, 124, 412
love, variations in, 368–369
passionate love, 368–369
prejudice, and conformity, 398–399
prejudice based on, 390–392
and receiving help, 275–276
and self-disclosure, 377–378
stereotypes, 385, 390
gender-based prejudice, 390–392
gender-inclusive language, 130
generalization of positive attitudes, 384
generational explanation, 170
genes and genetics
and aggression, 306
altruism, 276–278
attachment, 374
genetic selfishness, and altruistic behaviour, 279
kin selection, 276–277
genetic self-interest, 277
genocide, 301, 333
Genovese, Kitty, 282, 285, 297–298
genuine altruism, 278–281, 280f
The Geography of Thought (Nisbett), 39
global warming, 178–182
"going along with the crowd," 213
good feelings, 157–158, 158f
good life, 12
good luck, 87
Good Samaritan parable, 289
good subjects, 25
Google, 255
gravity, 15
"great person" theory of leadership, 257
GRIT, 458–459
group identities, 287, 452–453
group immersion, and anonymity, 239f
group indoctrination tactics, 173–174
group polarization
in communities, 244
defined, 243
discussion, 244f
in everyday life, 243–245
experiments, 243
explanations for, 245–248
illustration of, 243f
informational influence, 245–246
intensification of opinions, 241–248
on the Internet, 244
jury as a group, 261, 261f
misperception and, 437
normative influence, 246–248
pluralistic ignorance, 247
research on, 248
risky shift phenomenon, 242
schools, 243–244
social comparison, 247–248
terrorist organizations, 245
group salience, 445
group selection, 277–278
group-serving bias, 412–413
group size
and conformity, 209, 209f
and deindividuation, 236–237
and social dilemmas, 432–433
and social loafing, 234f
group solidarity, 447–448
groups
aggression, influences on, 332–335, 334f
Asch's studies of group pressure, 197–199, 197f, 208t
and brainstorming, 254
categorization, 406–408
co-actors, 226
cohesiveness, 210–211
cults, and group effects, 176–178
and culture, 235
defined, 225–226
deindividuation, 236–241
group polarization, 241–248
groupthink, 248–256
and humans, 401
in-group, 401
in-group bias, 402–404
leadership, 256–258
liberating effects of group influence, 204
minority influence, 258–262
out-group, 401, 403–405
problem solving, 253–256
reference groups, 246–247
social facilitation, 226–231
social loafing, 231–236
unanimity, 210, 210f
unquestioned belief in morality of, 250
groupthink
and brainstorming, 254
closed-mindedness, 250
conformity pressure, 250
COVID-19 pandemic, 251–252
critique of, 252
defined, 249
everyday examples, 255–256
group problem solving, 253–256
illusion of invulnerability, 250
illusion of unanimity, 251
mindguards, 251
misperception and, 437
overestimate of might and right, 250
prevention of, 252–253
rationalization, 250
self-censorship, 250
stereotyped view of opponent, 250
symptoms of, 249–252
the *Titanic*, 248–249
uniformity, 240–251
unquestioned belief in group's morality, 250
Walkerton water crisis, 251
growth-promoting listeners, 377
guilt, 271, 293–294
guns, 318–319, 330, 337

H

handguns, 318–319, 330, 337
happiness, 274
hazing, 177
health
and persuasion, 150
and self-efficacy, 53
and self-serving bias, 56
health education, 168f
healthier living, 149
healthy self-concept, 19
heat, 315–316
helping, 295f
heroism, 206
heuristics
availability heuristics, 84–85
defined, 83
representativeness heuristics, 84
hidden-camera method, 154
hidden third factor, 323
hidden values, 10–11
high self-esteem, 46–47, 50–52, 52f, 64
hindsight bias, 13
the Holocaust, 6, 149, 202, 204, 206
see also Nazi Germany
home advantage in team sports, 229, 229t
hormones
aggression, 307
stress hormones, 7
testosterone, 307
hostile aggression, 302, 315, 317f
hostile sexism, 390
hostility, 108–109
humility, 63
humour in advertising, 159f
Hurricane Katrina, 45
hypocrisy, 116–117
hypotheses
defined, 15
forming and testing, 15–17
purposes of, 15–16

I

I know it all along phenomenon, 13
illusion, capacity for, 78
illusion of control, 88–89
illusion of invulnerability, 250
illusion of transparency, 31, 283–284, 443
illusion of unanimity, 251, 260
illusory correlation, 87–89, 410–411
illusory optimism, 58
illusory thinking
illusion of control, 88–89
illusory correlation, 87–89, 410–411
limits of intuition, 78
regression toward the average, 88
imitation, 325–326
immigration, and prejudice, 384, 400
immoral acts, 128–130
impact bias, 45
Implicit Association Test (IAT), 118, 386
implicit attitudes, 46, 117
implicit bias, 118
implicit cognition, 386
implicit measures, 21

implicit memory, 77
implicit prejudice, 386, 389–390
impression management, 63–65, 131-132
impulse buying, 45
incest taboo, 273
income and marital status, and obesity
correlation, 22–23
incompatibility *vs.* misconceptions, 437f
incompetence, and overconfidence, 79
independent self, 37, 40f, 41t
independent variables, 22
indirect contact, 441–442
individualism
cognitive dissonance, 136
defined, 37
growing within cultures, 38–39
and the self, 37–38
and self-esteem, 41, 43
and Tragedy of the Commons, 430
variations in, 38
ineffective appeals, 189
inequity
marital distress, and, 376f
perceived, 375–376
information-processing biases, 183–185
informational influence, 213, 214–215,
245–246, 262
informed consent, 26, 287
infrahumanization, 403–404
ingratiation, 363
in-group, 401
in-group bias, 294, 402–404, 411f, 437
injustice, perceived, 436–437
inoculation programs, 186–189
insecure attachment, 373
insight, 46
instinct theory, 304–305
instinctive behaviour, 304
institutional authority, 203–204
institutional supports, 399
instrumental aggression, 302
insufficient justification, 132–134, 133f
definition, 133
intellectual conceit, 78
intelligence
and self-serving bias, 56
and social status, 19
interaction, 269, 291–292, 293, 345–346
interdependent self, 37, 40f, 41t
intergenerational contact, 441
integrative agreements, 454
intergroup relations
generalization of positive attitudes, 385
group identities, 287
internal causes, 99
internal rewards, 269, 270–273
internal working models, 374
internalized confessions, 95
Internet
and anonymity, 237–238
cyberostracism, 343–344
and group polarization, 244
and violence, 323
interpretation, bias in, 421–422
interpretation of events, 91–93, 283–285
intrinsic motivation, 140–141, 140f
intuition
about the self, 43–46
limits of, 78
power of, 5
powers of, 76–78
predicting our feelings, 44–45
predicting our own behaviour, 43–44
social intuitions, 5
and self-concept, 34–46
statistical prediction versus, 82–83
intuitive judgments, 76–78

J

Japan, 6, 41
Japanese-style management, 257
judgments. *See* social judgment
jurors and juries
group polarization, 261, 261f
influences, 260–262
leniency, effect of, 262
minority influence, 261
just-world phenomenon, 413–414

K

kin selection, 276–277
knowledge of issues, and bias, 21

L

labelling, 10
language
collectivist language, 38–39
culture, influence of, 103
external attributions, 99
gender-inclusive language, 130
group-serving bias, 412–413
preferences, 346–347
purpose of, 40
value judgments within, 10
law and social science. *See* courtroom;
jurors and juries
leadership
defined, 256
democratic leadership, 256–257
"great person" theory of leadership, 257
social leadership, 256–257
task leadership, 256–257
transactional leadership, 257
transformational leadership, 257–258
learned helplessness, 68, 68f
learning
about altruism, 297
aggression, 312–315, 314f
by doing, 296
observational learning, 313–315
social learning theory, 313–315, 314f,
336–338
Lemmings, 295
leniency, 262
LGBT prejudice, 392–394
Liberal Party, 20
life cycle explanation, 170
likeness-leads-to-liking effect, 359–360
liking, 155–156, 156t, 341–382
see also attraction
liking by association, 346, 365
liking those who like us, 362–364
linguistic intergroup bias, 412
long-term equity, 375
longitudinal research, 19
looking-glass self, 36
love
see also close relationships
arranged marriages *vs.* love marriages,
371f
and attractiveness, 358–359, 366–369
brain and, 368f
companionate love, 369–371
and culture, 368–369
described, 366–367, 368
and gender, 368–369
overlapping of selves, 378f
passionate love, 366–369
two-factor theory of emotion, 367
types, 366f
low-ball techniques, 126–127
low self-esteem, 19, 48, 50–52, 52f, 53, 64,
363
luck, 87

M

major themes in social psychology, 4–8, 4f
mammalian pair bonding, 371
mammograms, and fear-arousing
communications, 160
marital distress, and inequity, 376f
marital status and income, and obesity
correlation, 22–23
marriage. *See* close relationships
massacres, 245
mastery experiences, 70
matching phenomenon, 351
media
aggression, influences on, 319–332
comparison of, 169
influence, 168–169
media awareness education, 332
pornography, 319–321
sexual violence, 319–321
stereotype threat, 417–419, 417f, 418f
television, movies, and the Internet,
322–327
two-step flow of communication,
168–169
video games, 327–332, 329f
media bias, 92–93, 92f
medial prefrontal cortex, 34
mediation
constructive arguing, 455t

defined, 453
integrative agreements, 454
turning win-lose into win-win, 454
unravelling misperceptions, 454–457
memory
bias in, 421–422
construction of memories, 94–98
explicit memory, 77
implicit memory, 77
misinformation effect, 95
past attitudes, reconstruction of, 95–97
past behaviour, reconstruction of, 97–98
positive memories, 96
priming, 75
rosy retrospection, 96
selective memory, 184–185
stereotypes, influence of, 417–419
men
see also gender
falling in love, 351
looks, and attraction, 350
stereotypes about, 390
mere-exposure effect, 346–349
mere presence of others, 226–229, 230–231
mere repetition, 166–167
message
audience, 169–172
content of, and persuasion, 156–164
cults, 175–176
discrepancy, 161–162, 162f
fear-rousing communications, 158–161
good feelings, effect of, 157–158, 158f
one-sided appeals, 162–163, 163f
personal *vs.* media influence, 167–169
primacy *vs.* recency, 163–164, 165f
reason *vs.* emotion, 157–161
two-sided appeals, 162–163, 163f
written message, 169, 169f
meta-stereotypes, 410
Middle East perceptions, 438
Milgram's obedience studies, 199–204, 201f, 208t
mimic and mirror, 156
mimicry, 196, 360
mindguards, 251
minimal group situations, 226
minority influence
consistency, 259
defections from the majority, 260
jury as a group, 261
minority slowness effect, 259
self-confidence, 259
minority slowness effect, 259
mirror image, 348
mirror-image perceptions, 438–440
misattribution, 98
misconceptions *vs.* incompatibility, 437f
misinformation effect, 95
misperception, 102f, 437–440, 437f, 454–457
miswant, 45
modelling altruism, 294–296
moment of truth, 80
money, and happiness, 270, 274
mood
and helpfulness, 273f
and judgment, 90–91
and perception, 90f
and self-presentation, 63
and social judgment, 90–91
and thinking, 90–91
mood infusion, 90–91
mood linkage, 196
moral acts, 128–130
moral disengagement, 128–130
moral exclusion, 294
moral hypocrisy, 116–117, 121
moral imperative, 333
moral inclusion, 294
morality
legislation of, 129–130
unquestioned belief in, 250
motivation
for anti-conformity, 219–221
avoidance of prejudice, 405–406
extrinsic motivation, 140f
frustration and aggression, 400
internal rewards, 269, 270–273
intrinsic motivation, 140–141, 140f
just-world phenomenon, 413–414
need for cognition, 171
need to belong, 342
and prejudice, 400–406
rewards, 269–273
self-esteem, 47–50
social identity theory, 401–405
motives, and social dilemmas, 431
motives *vs.* perceptions, 62
multiculturalism, 412, 419, 452–453
mundane realism, 25, 198
murders, 303, 318–319
Muslims, 441
myside bias, 439

N

name letter effect, 347
narcissism, 51–52, 52f
nation of the dead, 300–301
natural associations, 17–27, 17f, 24t, 24f
natural disasters, 45
natural mimicry, 360
natural selection, 278
naturalistic fallacy, 10
Nazi Germany, 3, 6, 130, 161, 202, 204, 206, 207–208
see also the Holocaust
need-based distribution, 436
need for cognition, 171
need to belong, 342
negative events
explanations for, 54–55
and impact bias, 45
negative persuasion, 163
negative stereotypes, 437
neurobiology, 7
neuroscience
and aggression, 305–306
social neuroscience, 7
neutral third parties, 457
new consciousness, 182
New Democratic Party (NDP), 21, 170
new technologies, 181
no prior commitment, 212
Nobel Prize, 32, 255
non-zero-sum games, 431
normative influence, 213, 214–215, 246–248
norms
and altruism, 273–276
altruistic norms, 434
and culture, 275
defined, 122
reciprocity norm, 273–274, 278
Sherif's studies of norm formation, 194–197, 195f, 208t
social-responsibility norm, 275–276
universal norms, 273
noticing, 283

O

obedience
see also conformity
Asch's studies of group pressure, 197–199, 197f, 208t
behaviour and attitudes, 205–206
classic conformity and obedience studies, 194–208, 208t
closeness and legitimacy of the authority, 202–203
conditions that breed obedience, 202–204
defined, 194
factors, 202–204
group influence, liberating effects of, 204
institutional authority, 203–204
Milgram's obedience studies, 199–204, 201f, 208t
Sherif's studies of norm formation, 194–197, 195f, 208t
situation, power of, 207–208
soldiers, 202, 204
victims' distance, 202
obesity
prejudice against, 22–23, 383–384
soft drink consumption, and, 17f
objective reality, 156
observable traits, 49
observational learning, 313–315
observational research methods, 24
Occam's razor, 163
one-sided appeals, 162–163, 163f
open, honest relationship, 364
openers, 377
operationalization, 16
opposites, 361
optimism, 58–59, 163
ostracism, 343–344
out-group, 401, 403–405, 449f
out-group homogeneity effect, 407

overconfidence
confirmation bias, 81–82
and incompetence, 79
intuition versus statistical prediction, 82–83
overconfidence phenomenon, 78–81
remedies for, 83
stockbroker overconfidence, 80
student overconfidence, 80
overconfidence phenomenon, 78–81
overjustification effect, 140–141, 296–297
overpersonalization, 66–67
own-age bias, 408
own-race bias, 408, 408f
oxygen of publicity, 313

P

pain, 315
parental support, 56
Parti Quebecois, 21
passionate love, 366–369
passive reception, 165–167, 245–246
patronization, 388–389
peace
achievement of, 441–459
applications in the real world, 459
arbitration, 453, 457–458
bargaining, 453–454
communication, 453–458
conciliation, 458–459
contact, 441–446
cooperation, 446–453
defined, 427
GRIT, 458–459
mediation, 453, 454–457
people, distinctive, 408–409
people-watching, 15
perception
altered perceptions, 327
of bias, 92f
culture, 40f
of differences, 407–408
distinctiveness, 408–411
discrimination, 419
of emotion, 157–161
of equity, and satisfaction, 375–376
of events, 91–93
of expertise, 76, 154
of facial expressions, 138
of inequity and marital distress, 375–376, 376f
in-group biases, 411f
of injustice, 436–437
and mood, 90f
vs. motives, 62
misperception, 437–440, 437f
political, 92–93
of prejudice, 406–414
of sexual reality, 320
shifting perceptions, and conflict, 440
of similarities, 407–408
of social worlds, 91–98
trustworthiness, 154–155
peripheral cues, 151–152, 171–172
peripheral route to persuasion, 151–152, 151f
persistence, 259, 260
person, power of the, 219–221
personal appeal, 293
personal commitment, 185–186
personal control, 69
personal identity, 41, 401, 402f
personal influence, 167–169, 293
personal judgment, and stereotypes, 419–422
personality
and altruism, 291
authoritarian personality, 396–397
behaviour, effect on, 6–7
and conformity, 215–217
social dominance orientation, 395, 397
personality disposition, 6–7
personality psychology, 3
perspective
actor-observer difference, 102–103
camera perspective bias, 103
change in, over time, 103
and situational awareness, 102–103
persuasion
active experience *vs.* passive reception, 165–167
age, 170–171
attitude accessibility, 172f
attitude inoculation, 185, 186–189
attitudes follow behaviour, 174–175
and attractiveness, 155–156
audience, 169–172, 176
central route to persuasion, 151–152, 151f
challenging beliefs, 185
channel of communication, 164–169
and climate change, 178–182
the communicator, 152–156, 175
comprehension, 169
constructive uses of, 177–178
counterarguments, 171, 185–186
credibility, 153–155
cults, 173–178
defined, 149
different routes and purposes, 152
discrepancy, 161–162, 162f
as education, 150
extreme persuasion, 173–178
fear-rousing communications, 158–161
good feelings, effect of, 157–158, 158f
group effects, 176–178
and health, 149
ineffective appeals, 189
influencing variables, 175f
inoculation programs, 186–189
and liking, 155–156
message content, 156–164, 175–176
negative persuasion, 163
one-sided appeals, 162–163, 163f
paths to persuasion, 150–152, 151f
perceived expertise, 154
perceived trustworthiness, 154–155
peripheral cues, 171–172
peripheral route to persuasion, 151–152, 151f
personal commitment, strengthening, 185–186
personal *vs.* media influence, 167–169
persuasive elements, 175–176
positive persuasion, 163
power of, 149–150
primacy *vs.* recency, 163–164, 165f
and prior commitments, 212
process, 150f
propaganda, 150, 161
reason *vs.* emotion, 157–161
resistance to, 183–189
six persuasion principles, 156t
thought, 171–172
two-sided appeals, 162–163, 163f
pessimism, 58–59, 163
physical anonymity, 237–240, 238f
physical appeal, 155
physical attractiveness
across cultures, 354–355
and attraction, 349–359
beautiful is good stereotype, 353–354
of the communicator, 155–156
computer averaged faces, 355
and dating, 349–350
and evolution, 356–357
first impressions, 353
and liking, 155–156
of loved ones, 358–359
matching phenomenon, 351
physical-attractiveness stereotype, 352–354
and relationship commitment, 358f
social comparison, 357
subjective nature of, 354–359
physical-attractiveness stereotype, 352–354
physical punishment, 337
planned behaviour, 120f
planning fallacy, 43
pluralistic ignorance, 247, 284, 443, 444
poison parasite defence, 186
political correctness, 9
political debate, 92–93
political perceptions, 92–93
political polarization, 439
politics, and prejudice, 384
polls, 20
pop psychology, 103
pornography, and aggression, 319–321, 321f
positive events, explanations for, 54–55
positive illusions, 364
positive memories, 96
positive persuasion, 163
post-decision dissonance, 135–136
posture and performance, 139
power of the person, 219–221
The Power of Persuasion: How We're Bought and Sold (Levine), 187
Power Rangers, 23
preconceptions, 81, 91, 92, 94, 111, 437
prediction markets, 256

predictions
  about our behaviour, 43–44
  about our future feelings, 44–45
  affective forecasting, 44
  attitudes, and behaviour, 119–120
  of conformity, 209–212
  money and, 44
  relationship, fate of, 58
  in research, 18, 19, 20
  theoretical predictions, 16
prejudgments, 384, 415–416
prejudice
  age, 384
  attitude of, 384, 386
  attributions, 412–413
  authoritarian personality, 396–397
  automatic prejudice, 386, 389–390, 405, 406
  avoidance of prejudice, and motivation, 405–406
  categorization, 406–408
  cognitive sources of, 406–414
  conformity, 398–399
  consequences of, 414–422
  contact, improvement through, 442–445
  cooperative learning, and improvement, 450–452
  defined, 384
  vs. discrimination, 385
  distinctiveness, 408–411
  ethnocentric, 396
  explicit prejudice, 386, 387, 389, 396
  facing, 418f
  and friendship, 444–445
  frustration and aggression, 400
  fundamental attribution error, 412
  gender-based prejudice, 390–392
  gender roles, 412
  group-serving bias, 412–413
  immigration, 384
  implicit prejudice, 386, 389–390
  in-group bias, 402–404
  institutional supports, 399
  just-world phenomenon, 413–414
  LGBT prejudice, 392–394
  measuring, 386
  motivational sources of, 400–406
  nature and power of, 384–394
  need for status, self-regard and belonging, 404–405
  against obesity, 23, 383–384
  out-group homogeneity effect, 407
  own-race bias, 408, 408f
  perceived similarities and differences, 407–408
  personal judgment, 419–422
  politics, 384
  prejudgments, 384, 415–416
  racial prejudice, 387–390
  vs. racism, 385–386
  realistic group conflict theory, 400
  and religion, 383, 397–398
  scapegoat theory, 400
  self-consciousness, 417
  self-fulfilling prophecy, 416
  self-perpetuating stereotypes, 415–416
  self-segregation, 442–444, 443f
  vs. sexism, 385–386
  social desirability and, 20–21
  social dominance orientation, 395, 397
  social identity theory, 401–405
  social inequalities, 394–395
  social sources of, 394–399
  socialization, 395–399
  vs. stereotype, 384–385, 394–395
  stereotype threat, 417–419, 417f, 418f
  subtle forms of, 388–389
  values and, 10–11
primacy effect, 163–164, 165f
primal attractions, 357
priming, 74–76, 77f
principle of aggregation, 119
prior commitments, 212
Prisoner's Dilemma, 428–429, 428f, 429f, 431
probability neglect, 86
problem-solving, group, 253–256
production blocking, 254
professional advice, 10
professional competence, 56
professional opinion, 216–217
prompt feedback, 83
pronoun use, 38f
propaganda, 150, 161
prosocial behaviour, 289, 294–297, 326, 332
prosocial models, 289, 294–296
prosocial value orientation, 295
proverbs, 14
proximity
  anticipation of interaction, 346
  defined, 345
  interaction, 345–346
  mere-exposure effect, 346–349
psychological concepts, hidden values in, 10–11
psychological immune system, 68
psychological pain, 315
psychology and climate change, 178–181
psychotherapy, 178
PsycINFO, 33
public commitment, 212
public opinion, 20, 180–181
public response, 211–212
punishment, 336–337
punitive behaviour, 321f

Q

quantifying correlations, 19
Quebec sovereignty, 21
questions
  order of, 20
  timing of, 20
  wording of, 21

R

r, coefficient of, 19
race, categorization by, 407–408, 408f
racial attitudes. *See* prejudice
racial prejudice, 387–390
racism
  see also prejudice
  cultural, 360–361
  defined, 385
  vs. prejudice, 385–386
random assignment, 23–25, 24f
random events, 87
random sample, 19, 24
rape myth, 320
rationalization, 250
reactance, 185, 219–220
reactions, and attributions, 105f
realism, 58
realistic group conflict theory, 400
reason *vs.* emotion, 157–161
reassured condition, 31–32, 32t
recency effect, 163–164, 165f
reciprocity, 156t, 277
reciprocity norm, 273–274, 278
recollections, 96–97
reference groups, 246–247
regression toward the average, 88–89
regulation of social dilemmas, 431–432
relating to others, 7–8
relationships
  close relationships. *See* close relationships
  ending relationships, 378–381
  love, 358–359, 365–371
  related attractiveness, and commitment, 358f
  responses to distress, 380t
  and self-esteem, 8
  social relationships, 33
relative deprivation, 311–312
religion, and prejudice, 383, 397–398
repetition, 166–167
representativeness, 20
representativeness heuristics, 84
research methods
  correlational research, 17–21, 18f, 22f, 24t
  experimental research, 17, 21–26, 22f, 24t
  experimenter bias, 106
  field research, 17
  generalizations from laboratory to life, 26–27
  hypotheses, forming and testing, 15–17
  longitudinal research, 19
  manipulating variables, 22–23
  random assignment, 23–25, 24f
  survey research, 19–21
  theory, 15
  time-lagged correlations, 19
resisting persuasion, 183–189
response bias, 20–21
responsibility
  and altruism, 292–293
  assumption of, 285–287

responsibility diffusion, 332–333
retaliation, 309, 314, 336
reward theory of attraction, 365
rewards, 269–273, 312–313, 365
rioters, 237
risky shift phenomenon, 242
risk *vs.* caution, 247f
rivalry, 447
role
  defined, 122
  effects of, 218
  gender roles, 124, 217–218
  social roles, 218–219
role playing, 122–124
romantic love. *See* love
roommates, 441
rope-pulling, 232f
rosy retrospection, 96

S

satisfaction
  and perceived equity, 375–376
  and social comparison, 36
saying, and believing, 124–125
scapegoat theory, 400
scarcity, 156t
schadenfreude, 35, 47
schemas, 34, 76
school
  group polarization in, 243–244
  success in, 59
science, subjective aspects of, 9
secure attachment, 372
secure self-esteem, 51
selective attention, 184
selective exposure, 184
selective memory, 184–185
selective perception, 184
the self
  in action, 67–70
  and culture, 37–43
  defining, 33, 33f
  evaluation of, 53–62
  independent self, 37, 40f, 41t
  interdependent self, 37, 40, 40f, 41t
  intuitions about, 43–46
  looking-glass self, 36
  sense of self, 34
  social comparison, 34–36, 35f
self-affirmation theory, 142
self-analysis, 46
self-awareness, 32, 241, 293
self-censorship, 250, 364
self-concept
  defined, 34
  healthy self-concept, and achievement, 19
  importance of, 34
  independent *vs.* interdependent, 40f, 41t
  intuition, 34–46
  malleability of, 41
  self and culture, 37–43
  self-determination, 68–70
  self-knowledge, 43–46
  sense of self, 34
  social identity, 401, 403
  spontaneous self-concepts, 221
self-concern, 33
self-confidence, 259
self-consciousness, 89, 120–121, 409–410
self-construal, 40f
self-contradictory acts, 144
self-control, 67–70, 241, 330
self-defeating behaviour, 62
self-determination, 68–70
self-disclosure, 376–378
self-doubt, 58
self-efficacy
  defined, 53
  and health and happiness, 53
  and optimism, 58–59
self-esteem
  and achievement, 18, 51
  and aggression, 52f
  and attraction, 363
  and communal qualities, 49
  and culture, 41, 43
  defined, 46
  gaining another's esteem, 363–364
  high self-esteem, 46–47, 50–52, 52f, 64
  low self-esteem, 19, 48, 50–52, 52f, 53, 64, 363
  motivation, 47–50
  narcissism and, 51–52, 52f
  observable traits, 49
  and personal identity, 402f
  and relationships, 8
  secure self-esteem, 51
  and self-serving bias, 53–55
  and social identity, 401, 402f
  success and, 41
  threats, 47
  and violence, 51
self-evaluation, 34–35, 35f, 77f
self-fulfilling prophecy
  defined, 106
  and discrimination, 416
  influence of, 108–110
  teacher expectations and student performance, 107–108, 108f
self-handicapping, 62–63
self-image, 293–294
self-interest, and judgment, 32
self-justification, 132–136, 437
self-knowledge
  dual attitude system, 46, 386
  impact bias, 45
  planning fallacy, 43
  predicting behaviour, 43–44
  predicting feelings, 44–45
  self-analysis, 46
self-monitoring, 64, 419
self-perception theory
  defined, 137
  described, 136–137
  expressions and attitude, 137–139
  intrinsic motivations, 140–141
  overjustification effect, 140–141
  physical attractivness, 357
  when not self-contradicting, 144
self-perpetuating stereotypes, 415–416
self-persuasion, 122, 144
self-presentation
  conscious self-presentation, 63–64
  defined, 63
  false modesty, 64–65
  impression management, 63–65, 131-132
  overpersonalizing situations, 66–67
  self-handicapping, 62–63
  self-monitoring, 64
  social influence on, 33
  and social networking, 63–64
self-presentation theory, 65–66, 131–132
self-presented modesty, 65
self-regard, and social identity, 404–405
self-reports, 46
self-sacrifice, 276
self-schema, 34
self-segregation, 442–444, 443f
self-serving attributions, 54
self-serving bias
  as adaptive, 53–55
  attractiveness, 56
  comparisons with others, 55–57
  defensive pessimism, 58
  defined, 54
  and driving, 56
  and ethics, 56
  evaluating self, 53–62
  explanations for, 61–62, 61f
  false consensus effect, 59
  false uniqueness effect, 59
  group self-serving bias, 55
  and health, 56
  and humility, 63
  and insight, 55
  and intelligence, 56
  as maladaptive, 53–55
  and marriage, 56
  misperception and, 437
  negative events, explanations for, 54–55
  parental support, 56
  perceptions *vs.* motives, 62
  positive events, explanations for, 54–55
  and professional competence, 56
  and self-esteem, 53–55
  and stress, 68–70
  temporal comparison, 60–61, 60f
  types of, 56
  unrealistic optimism, 58–59
  and virtues, 56
self-verification, 81
self-worth, 270
sensitivity to diversity, 385
sensory overload, 287
sexism, 385, 386, 390
sexual arousal, 44, 317
sexual assault, 320
sexual orientation, and contact, 441

sexual scripts, 326–327
sexual violence
  aggression against women, 320–321
  correlational studies, 320
  depictions of, in pornography, 319–320
  distorted perceptions of sexual reality, 320
  experimental studies, 320–321
  increase in incidents of, 320–321
  media awareness education, 332
  rape myth, acceptance of, 320
  violent pornography, exposure to, 321
Sherif's studies of norm formation, 194–197, 195f, 208t
shifting perceptions, 440
silent sulking, 336
silent treatment, 343
similarity
  and attraction, 155–156, 359–361
  bystander passivity, 282–283
  and cooperation, 290f
  cultural similarity, 217
  and liking, 359–360
  perceived similarities, 362–364, 407–408
  to victim, 290
simplistic thinking, 440
situational attribution, 99, 105
situational awareness, and perspective, 102–103
situational influences
  conformity, predicting, 209–212
  the person, influence of, 163–164, 293
  power of, 6, 207–208
"'60s scoop" program, 128
sleeper effect, 153
smart meters, 182
smoke-filled room experiment, 284f
smoking, and children, 186–187, 187f
snap judgments, 5, 74
soccer referee decisions, 198
social acceptance, 49
social aggression, 302
social animal, 341, 342
social arousal, 228f
social attachment, 342
social behaviour, 3, 7, 33, 312–315
social beliefs
  behavioural confirmation, 108–110
  belief perseverance, 93–94
  challenging beliefs, 185
  changing, after conforming, 215f
  conclusions on, 110–112
  constructing, 91
  and mental construction of events, 93–94
  saying, and believing, 124–125
  self fulfilling, 51
social capital, 274
social cocoon, 177
social comparison
  defined, 34
  and group polarization, 243–245
  physical attractiveness, 357
  and self-evaluation, 34–35, 35f
social competence, 342
social contagion
  and aggressive tendencies, 333
  chameleon effect, 196
  suggestibility, 195–196
social control, 178
Social Credit Party, 21
social desirability, 20–21
social dilemmas
  altruistic norms, appeal to, 434
  changing payoffs, 433
  communication, 433
  described, 427–428
  Prisoner's Dilemma, 428–429, 428f, 429f, 431
  regulation, 431–432
  resolution of, 431–434
  small groups, 432–433
  social trap, 428
  Tragedy of the Commons, 430
social dominance orientation, 395, 397
social-exchange theory
  defined, 269
  described, 269
  egoism, 270
  feel bad-do good scenario, exceptions to, 271–272
  feel good-do good scenario, 272–273
  guilt, 271
  internal rewards, 270–273
  rewards, 269–270
  weakness in, 270
social facilitation
  crowding, 229–230
  defined, 226
  driven by distraction, 231
  evaluation apprehension, 230–231
  mere presence of others, 226–229, 230–231
  reasons for arousal, 228f, 230–231
  vs. social loafing, 234f
social history, 8
social identity
  and belonging, 404–405
  categorization and, 407
  defined, 37
  Europe and, 9
  in-group, 401
  in-group bias, 402–404
  motivational source of prejudice, 401–405
  other people's judgments, 36
  out-group, 401, 403–405
  perceived prejudice and discrimination, 395–399
  self-enhancing, 413t
  self-esteem, 401, 402f
  self-regard, need for, 404–405
  social comparisons, 34–36
  status, need for, 404–405
  success and failure, 35
social image, 214
social implosion, 176
social indoctrination, 130
social inequalities, and prejudice, 394–395
social influence
  and behaviour, 6, 117–119
  culture, impact of, 6, 217
  jurors and juries, 508–510
  and personality, 215–217
  social psychology, 2f
social intuitions, 5
social judgment
  confirmation bias, 81–82
  counterfactual thinking, 86–87
  heuristics, 83–85
  illusory thinking, 87–89
  intuitive judgment, 76–78
  mood and, 90–91
  overconfidence phenomenon, 78–83
  other people's judgments, 36
  and selective perception, 184
  self-interest and, 32
social leadership, 256–257
social learning theory, 313–315, 314f, 336–338
social loafing
  challenging tasks, effect of, 236
  collective effort of teams, 232–233
  commitment, effect of, 236
  and culture, 235
  defined, 233
  in everyday life, 233–236
  free riders, 233
  group size, effect of, 234f
  vs. social facilitation, 234f
social movements, 130–131, 258
social networking, 63, 64
social neuroscience, 7
social norms. *See* norms
social perception, 74
social proof, 156t
social psychology
  behaviour, and effect of social influences, 6
  behaviour, and effect of personal attitudes and dispositions, 6–7
  biological roots of social behaviour, 7
  and climate change, 179
  and common sense, 11–15
  defined, 2, 2f
  everyday life and, 8
  hidden values and, 9–11
  and human values, 8–11
  major themes in, 4–8, 4f
  new technologies, 181
  obvious values and, 8–9
  parameters of, 2–4
  vs. personality psychology, 3
  purposes of, 2–4
  questions, 3–4
  reducing consumption, 181–182
  relating to others, 7–8
  research methods, 15–27
  social intuitions, power of, 5
  social reality, construction of, 4–5
  vs. sociology, 3
  unexamined assumptions, 9

social reality, construction of, 4–5
social rejection, 213, 344
social relations
  see also aggression; altruism; attraction; relationships
  culture and, 314–315
  reward theory of attraction, 365
  social psychology, 2f
social relationships, and self, 33
social representations, 9
social-responsibility norm, 275–276
social roles, 218–219
social scripts, 326–327
social self, 33f
social status, and intelligence, 20
social surroundings, 32
social thinking, 2f
social trap, 428
social world
  behavioural confirmation, 108–110
  expectations of, 106–112
  explaining, 98–106
  judging, 74–98
  perception of, 91–98
socialization
  altruism, 294–297
  and prejudice, 395–399
sociology, 3
soldiers, 204
Somalia, 207, 239
source credibility, 153–155
South Africa, 441
sovereignty, 21
speech ratings, 32t
speed dating, 350, 353, 359
spoken appeals, 165–166
spontaneous categorization, 407
spontaneous self-concepts, 221
spontaneous trait inference, 99
spotlight effect, 31, 66
Stanley Cup riots, 237
start-small-and-build technique, 131
statistical prediction versus intuition, confidence in, 82–83
status
  and conformity, 211
  marital, 22
  need for, and social identity, 404–405
  unequal status, 394–395
stereotype threat, 417–419, 417f, 418f
stereotypes
  actions and thinking, 139
  and athletic performance, 418
  beautiful is good stereotype, 353–354
  defined, 384
  and distinctiveness, 410
  favourable stereotypes, 390
  gender stereotypes, 384, 390
  harsher evaluation of target, 422
  influence on judgment, 419–422
  interpretations, influence on, 421–422
  memories, influence on, 421–422
  negative stereotypes, 437
  overgeneralization, 385
  and personal judgment, 419–422
  physical-attractiveness stereotype, 352–354
  vs. prejudice, 384–385, 394–395
  self-enhancing social identities, supporting, 413t
  self-perpetuating stereotypes, 415–416
  stereotyped view of opponent, 250
  strong stereotypes, 421
  subgrouping, 416
  subtyping, 416
  and unequal status, 394–395
Stop Watch Gang, 123
strangers
  helping, 288f
  liking, 359
stress
  and self-serving bias, 68–70
  and stereotype threat, 419
student expectations, and teacher performance, 107–108, 108f
subgrouping, 416
subjective aspects of science, 9
subjective preference, 156
subliminal priming, 77f
subliminal stimuli, 77, 78
subtle prejudice, 388–389
subtyping, 416
success
  and failure, 35
  in school, 59
  and self-control, 68
  and self-esteem, 41
  and subjective qualities, 55–57
suggestibility, 195–196
suicide, 197
superordinate goals, 448–450
superordinate identities, 452–453
suppressing thoughts and emotions, 419
survey research
  biases, sensitivity to, 21
  described, 19–20
  order of questions, 20
  random sample, 19
  response bias, 20–21
  social desirability, 20–21
  timing of questions, 20
  unrepresentative sample, 20
  wording of question, 21
sustainability
  consumption, reduction of, 181–182,
  eco-technologies, 181
  psychology and climate change, 178–181
  sustainable future, 178–182
Swissair flight 111, 253
System 1 functions, 74
System 2 functions, 74

T

task leadership, 256–257
teacher expectations, and student performance, 107–108, 108f
team science, 254
television
  and aggression, 322–327
  altered perceptions, 327
  arousal, 325
  behaviour, effects on, 322–326
  catharsis, 331
  children, and latent criminal activity, 323f
  cognitive priming, 327
  correlating viewing and behaviour, 23, 322–324
  desensitization, 326
  disinhibition, 325
  hidden third factor, 323
  imitation, 325–326
  prosocial behaviour, 326
  prosocial models, 294–296
  social scripts, 326–327
  thinking, effects on, 326–327
  viewing, and violence, 23, 325
  viewing experiments, 324–325
temperament, 306, 374
temporal comparison, 60–61
temporary climate, 315
terror management theory, 49, 404
terrorism, 302, 313, 438
terrorist organizations, group polarization in, 245
testosterone, and aggression, 307
theoretical explanation, 15
theoretical predictions, 16
theory, 15
thinking
  Asian and Western thinking, 39–40, 39f
  automatic processing, 46, 76
  controlled processing, 76
  counterfactual thinking, 86–87
  culture, effect of, 37–43
  heuristics, 83–85
  illusory thinking, 87–89, 410–411
  intuition and, 5
  and mood, 90–91
  persuasion and, 171–172
  simplistic thinking, 440
  stereotype threat and, 419
  television, effects of, 326–327
  unconscious thinking, 78
  video games, and aggressive thinking, 329–330
third variable, 18
threatened punishment, 336
time-lagged correlations, 19
time pressures, 289–290
Titanic, 248–249
Todd, Amanda, 285
totalitarian egos, 86, 97
traffic stops, 388
Tragedy of the Commons, 428, 430
traits, inference of, 99
transactional leadership, 257
transformational leadership, 257–258
transgender identity, and contact, 441
Tri-Council, 26

truisms, 186
trust, 455–456
trustworthiness, 154–155
two-factor theory of emotion, 367
two-sided appeals, 162–163, 163f
two-step flow of communication, 168–169

U

unanimity, 210, 210f , 251
unanticipated reward, 141
unconscious mind, 5
unconscious thinking, 78
unequal status, 394–395
unhappy people, 90
uniforms, 239–240
uninvolved audiences, 171–172
uniqueness, 59, 221
universal norms, 273
university ethics committees, 25–26
unrealistic optimism, 58–59
unrepresentative samples, 20
unrestrained behaviours, 236–237

V

value judgments, 10
values
  concept formation, 10
  differences across time and culture, 9
  hidden values, 9–11
  labelling, 10
  naturalistic fallacy, 10
  obvious values, 8–9
  psychological concepts, 10–11
  and social psychology, 8–11
  and subjective aspects of science, 9
values affirmation, 419
variables
  dependent variable, 23
  independent variables, 22
victimization, 416
victims
  blame-the-victim process, 206
  discrimination and, 416
  distance of, 202
  similarity to, 290
video games, 327–332, 329f
violence
  operationalizing, 16
  sexual violence, 319–321
  and television viewing, 22, 324–325
  world, and culture change, 338
virtues, 56
vivid cases, 410
vivid stories, 161
voting, and looks, 350

W

Walkerton, Ontario water crisis, 251
wars, 302–303
weather forecasting, 255
weird beliefs, 149
well-being, and good or bad events, 45
Werther effect, 197
women
  see also gender
  aggression against, 320–321
  looks, and attraction, 350
  math performance, and stereotype threat, 417f
  as "openers," 377
  prejudice against, 390–392
  self-disclosure, 377
  stereotypes of, 390
women-are-wonderful effect, 390
world violence, 338
written *vs.* taped messages, 169, 169f

Z

Zimbardo's prison study, 122–123

INFORMATION TECHNOLOGY PROJECT MANAGEMENT

INFORMATION TECHNOLOGY PROJECT MANAGEMENT

Sixth Edition

Kathy Schwalbe, Ph.D., PMP
Augsburg College

Australia • Brazil • Japan • Korea • Mexico • Singapore • Spain • United Kingdom • United States

Information Technology Project Management, Sixth Edition

Kathy Schwalbe

Vice President, Publisher: Jack Calhoun

Senior Acquisitions Editor: Charles McCormick, Jr.

Product Manager: Kate Hennessy Mason

Development Editor: Deb Kaufmann

Editorial Assistant: Bryn Lathrop

Marketing Director: Brian Joyner

Marketing Manager: Bryant Chrzan

Marketing Communications Manager: Libby Shipp

Marketing Coordinator: Suellen Ruttkay

Content Project Manager: Matthew Hutchinson

Media Editor: Chris Valentine

Senior Art Director: Stacy Jenkins Shirley

Cover Designer: Craig Ramsdell

Cover Image: ©Getty Images/Digital Vision

Manufacturing Coordinator: Julio Esperas

Compositor: Pre-Press PMG

ISBN-13: 978-0-324-78692-7
ISBN-10: 0-324-78692-1

Course Technology
20 Channel Center Street
Boston, MA 02210
USA

Cengage Learning is a leading provider of customized learning solutions with office locations around the globe, including Singapore, the United Kingdom, Australia, Mexico, Brazil, and Japan. Locate your local office at: **international. cengage.com/region**

Cengage Learning products are represented in Canada by Nelson Education, Ltd.

For your course and learning solutions, visit **www.cengage.com**

Purchase any of our products at your local college store or at our preferred online store **www.ichapters.com**

Printed in the United States of America
3 4 5 6 7 14 13 12 11 10

For Dan, Anne, Bobby, and Scott

BRIEF CONTENTS

Chapter 1	*Introduction to Project Management*	1
Chapter 2	*The Project Management and Information Technology Context*	43
Chapter 3	*The Project Management Process Groups: A Case Study*	77
Chapter 4	*Project Integration Management*	129
Chapter 5	*Project Scope Management*	177
Chapter 6	*Project Time Management*	211
Chapter 7	*Project Cost Management*	253
Chapter 8	*Project Quality Management*	291
Chapter 9	*Project Human Resource Management*	337
Chapter 10	*Project Communications Management*	381
Chapter 11	*Project Risk Management*	421
Chapter 12	*Project Procurement Management*	461
Appendix A	*Guide to Using Microsoft Project 2007*	A.1
Appendix B	*Advice for the Project Management Professional (PMP) Exam and Related Certifications*	B.1
Appendix C	*Additional Running Cases and Simulation Software*	C.1
Glossary		G.1
Index		I.1

TABLE OF CONTENTS

Preface xvii

Chapter 1 *Introduction to Project Management* 1

Introduction 2
What Is a Project? 4
Examples of Information Technology Projects 4
Project Attributes 6
The Triple Constraint 8
What Is Project Management? 10
Project Stakeholders 10
Project Management Knowledge Areas 12
Project Management Tools and Techniques 12
Project Success 14
Program and Project Portfolio Management 17
Programs 17
Project Portfolio Management 18
The Role of the Project Manager 21
Project Manager Job Description 21
Suggested Skills for Project Managers 22
Importance of People and Leadership Skills 24
Careers for Information Technology Project Managers 25
The Project Management Profession 27
History of Project Management 27
The Project Management Institute 29
Project Management Certification 30
Ethics in Project Management 31
Project Management Software 32
Chapter Summary 35
Quick Quiz 35
Discussion Questions 37
Exercises 38
Companion Web Site 39
Key Terms 39
End Notes 40

Chapter 2 *The Project Management and Information Technology Context* 43

A Systems View of Project Management 44
What Is a Systems Approach? 45
The Three-Sphere Model for Systems Management 45

Understanding Organizations 47
The Four Frames of Organizations 47
Organizational Structures 48
Organizational Culture 51
Stakeholder Management 52
The Importance of Top Management Commitment 54
The Need for Organizational Commitment to Information Technology 55
The Need for Organizational Standards 56
Project Phases and the Project Life Cycle 57
Product Life Cycles 59
The Importance of Project Phases and Management Reviews 61
The Context of Information Technology Projects 63
The Nature of Information Technology Projects 63
Characteristics of Information Technology Project Team Members 64
Diverse Technologies 64
Recent Trends Affecting Information Technology Project Management 65
Globalization 65
Outsourcing 66
Virtual Teams 67
Chapter Summary 70
Quick Quiz 71
Discussion Questions 72
Exercises 73
Companion Web Site 74
Key Terms 74
End Notes 75

Chapter 3 *The Project Management Process Groups: A Case Study* 77
Project Management Process Groups 78
Mapping the Process Groups to the Knowledge Areas 83
Developing an Information Technology Project Management Methodology 85
Case Study: JWD Consulting's Project Management Intranet Site Project 86
Project Pre-Initiation and Initiation 87
Project Planning 96
Project Execution 106
Project Monitoring and Controlling 111
Project Closing 114
Chapter Summary 123
Quick Quiz 123
Discussion Questions 125
Exercises 125
Companion Web Site 126
Key Terms 127
End Notes 127

Chapter 4 *Project Integration Management* 129
What Is Project Integration Management? 130
Strategic Planning and Project Selection 133
Strategic Planning 133
Identifying Potential Projects 135
Aligning Information Technology with Business Strategy 136
Methods for Selecting Projects 138
Developing a Project Charter 147
Developing a Project Management Plan 151
Project Management Plan Contents 151
Using Guidelines to Create Project Management Plans 154
Directing and Managing Project Execution 155
Coordinating Planning and Execution 156
Providing Strong Leadership and a Supportive Culture 157
Capitalizing on Product, Business, and Application Area Knowledge 157
Project Execution Tools and Techniques 158
Monitoring and Controlling Project Work 159
Performing Integrated Change Control 161
Change Control on Information Technology Projects 162
Change Control System 162
Closing Projects or Phases 164
Using Software to Assist in Project Integration Management 165
Chapter Summary 167
Quick Quiz 168
Discussion Questions 169
Exercises 170
Running Case 171
Tasks 172
Companion Web Site 173
Key Terms 173
End Notes 174

Chapter 5 *Project Scope Management* 177
What Is Project Scope Management? 178
Collecting Requirements 179
What Are Requirements? 179
How Do You Collect Requirements? 181
How Do You Document Requirements? 182
Defining Scope 183
Creating the Work Breakdown Structure 186
Approaches to Developing Work Breakdown Structures 191
The WBS Dictionary and Scope Baseline 194
Advice for Creating a WBS and WBS Dictionary 196
Verifying Scope 196
Controlling Scope 198

Suggestions for Improving User Input 200
Suggestions for Reducing Incomplete and Changing Requirements 200
Using Software to Assist in Project Scope Management 202
Chapter Summary 204
Quick Quiz 204
Discussion Questions 206
Exercises 206
Running Case 207
Tasks 208
Companion Web Site 208
Key Terms 209
End Notes 210

Chapter 6 *Project Time Management* 211
The Importance of Project Schedules 212
Defining Activities 214
Sequencing Activities 217
Dependencies 217
Network Diagrams 218
Estimating Activity Resources 221
Estimating Activity Durations 222
Developing the Schedule 223
Gantt Charts 224
Critical Path Method 228
Critical Chain Scheduling 233
Program Evaluation and Review Technique (PERT) 236
Controlling the Schedule 237
Reality Checks on Scheduling and the Need for Discipline 238
Using Software to Assist in Project Time Management 239
Words of Caution on Using Project Management Software 240
Chapter Summary 243
Quick Quiz 244
Discussion Questions 245
Exercises 246
Running Case 249
Tasks 249
Key Terms 250
End Notes 252

Chapter 7 *Project Cost Management* 253
The Importance of Project Cost Management 254
What Is Cost? 255
What Is Project Cost Management? 256
Basic Principles of Cost Management 257
Estimating Costs 261
Types of Cost Estimates 261

Cost Estimation Tools and Techniques 263
Typical Problems with Information Technology Cost Estimates 264
Sample Cost Estimate 265
Determining the Budget 270
Controlling Costs 272
Earned Value Management 273
Project Portfolio Management 278
Using Project Management Software to Assist in Project Cost Management 279
Chapter Summary 282
Quick Quiz 282
Discussion Questions 284
Exercises 285
Running Case 286
Tasks 286
Companion Web Site 287
Key Terms 288
End Notes 289

Chapter 8 *Project Quality Management* 291
The Importance of Project Quality Management 292
What Is Project Quality Management? 294
Planning Quality 296
Performing Quality Assurance 298
Performing Quality Control 299
Tools and Techniques for Quality Control 300
Statistical Sampling 306
Six Sigma 307
Testing 313
Modern Quality Management 315
Deming and his 14 Points for Management 315
Juran and the Importance of Top Management Commitment to Quality 316
Crosby and Striving for Zero Defects 316
Ishikawa's Guide to Quality Control 317
Taguchi and Robust Design Methods 317
Feigenbaum and Workers' Responsibility for Quality 318
Malcolm Baldrige National Quality Award 318
ISO Standards 318
Improving Information Technology Project Quality 319
Leadership 319
The Cost of Quality 320
Organizational Influences, Workplace Factors, and Quality 321
Expectations and Cultural Differences in Quality 322
Maturity Models 323
Using Software to Assist in Project Quality Management 326
Chapter Summary 327
Quick Quiz 328

Discussion Questions 329
Exercises 330
Running Case 331
Tasks 331
Companion Web Site 332
Key Terms 332
End Notes 334

Chapter 9 *Project Human Resource Management* 337
The Importance of Human Resource Management 338
The Global IT Workforce 338
Implications for the Future of IT Human Resource Management 340
What Is Project Human Resource Management? 342
Keys to Managing People 344
Motivation Theories 344
Thamhain and Wilemon's Influence and Power 348
Covey and Improving Effectiveness 350
Developing the Human Resource Plan 352
Project Organizational Charts 352
Responsibility Assignment Matrices 354
Staffing Management Plans and Resource Histograms 356
Acquiring the Project Team 357
Resource Assignment 358
Resource Loading 359
Resource Leveling 361
Developing the Project Team 362
Training 363
Team-Building Activities 364
Reward and Recognition Systems 368
Managing the Project Team 368
Tools and Techniques for Managing Project Teams 368
General Advice on Managing Teams 369
Using Software to Assist in Human Resource Management 370
Chapter Summary 372
Quick Quiz 373
Discussion Questions 375
Exercises 375
Running Case 376
Companion Web Site 377
Key Terms 377
End Notes 378

Chapter 10 *Project Communications Management* 381
The Importance of Project Communications Management 382
Identifying Stakeholders 385
Planning Communications 386

Distributing Information 388
Using Technology to Enhance Information Distribution 389
Formal and Informal Methods for Distributing Information 390
Distributing Important Information in an Effective and Timely Manner 391
Selecting the Appropriate Communications Medium 392
Understanding Group and Individual Communication Needs 394
Setting the Stage for Communicating Bad News 394
Determining the Number of Communications Channels 395
Managing Stakeholders 396
Reporting Performance 398
Suggestions for Improving Project Communications 399
Using Communication Skills to Manage Conflict 399
Developing Better Communication Skills 400
Running Effective Meetings 402
Using e-Mail, Instant Messaging, and Collaborative Tools Effectively 403
Using Templates for Project Communications 406
Using Software to Assist in Project Communications 410
Chapter Summary 414
Quick Quiz 414
Discussion Questions 416
Exercises 417
Running Case 418
Companion Web Site 418
Key Terms 418
End Notes 419

Chapter 11 *Project Risk Management* 421
The Importance of Project Risk Management 422
Planning Risk Management 428
Common Sources of Risk on Information Technology Projects 430
Identifying Risks 434
Suggestions for Identifying Risks 434
The Risk Register 436
Performing Qualitative Risk Analysis 438
Using Probability/Impact Matrixes to Calculate Risk Factors 438
Top Ten Risk Item Tracking 441
Performing Quantitative Risk Analysis 442
Decision Trees and Expected Monetary Value 442
Simulation 444
Sensitivity Analysis 446
Planning Risk Responses 447
Monitoring and Controlling Risks 450
Using Software to Assist in Project Risk Management 450
Chapter Summary 452
Quick Quiz 453
Discussion Questions 455

Exercises 455
Running Case 456
Companion Web Site 457
Key Terms 457
End Notes 459

Chapter 12 *Project Procurement Management* 461
The Importance of Project Procurement Management 462
Planning Procurements 466
Tools and Techniques for Planning Procurements 468
Procurement Management Plan 473
Statement of Work 474
Procurement Documents 475
Source Selection Criteria 476
Conducting Procurements 477
Administering Procurements 479
Closing Procurements 481
Using Software to Assist in Project Procurement Management 481
Chapter Summary 484
Quick Quiz 485
Discussion Questions 486
Exercises 487
Running Case 488
Companion Web Site 488
Key Terms 489
End Notes 490

Appendix A *Guide to Using Microsoft Project 2007* A.1
Introduction A.2
New Features of Project 2007 A.3
Backward Compatibility A.4
Before You Begin A.4
Overview of Project 2007 A.5
Starting Project 2007 and Using the Getting Started and Project Guide Features A.5
Main Screen Elements A.8
Project 2007 Views A.14
Project 2007 Filters A.18
Project Scope Management A.19
Creating a New Project File A.20
Developing a Work Breakdown Structure A.22
Saving Project Files with or without a Baseline A.25
Project Time Management A.26
Entering Task Durations A.27
Establishing Task Dependencies A.32
Changing Task Dependency Types and Adding Lead or Lag Time A.35

Gantt Charts A.38
Network Diagrams A.40
Critical Path Analysis A.42
Project Cost Management A.44
Fixed and Variable Cost Estimates A.44
Assigning Resources to Tasks A.48
Baseline Plan, Actual Costs, and Actual Times A.54
Earned Value Management A.59
Project Human Resource Management A.62
Resource Calendars A.62
Resource Histograms A.64
Resource Leveling A.67
Project Communications Management A.70
Common Reports and Views A.70
Using Templates and Inserting Hyperlinks and Comments A.71
Using the Copy Picture Feature A.75
Discussion Questions A.77
Exercises A.77
Exercise A-1: Homework Assignments A.77
HW1: Project 2007, Part 1 (100 points, 25 points for each item) A.77
HW2: Project 2007, Part 2 (100 points, 25 points for each item) A.78
Exercise A-2: Web Site Development A.78
Exercise A-3: Software Training Program A.80
Exercise A-4: Project Tracking Database A.81
Exercise A-5: Real Project Application A.84

Appendix B *Advice for the Project Management Professional (PMP) Exam and Related Certifications* B.1
Introduction to Project Management Certification Programs B.1
What Is PMP Certification? B.1
What Are the Requirements for Earning and Maintaining PMP Certification? B.3
What Is the Structure and Content of the PMP Exam? B.5
How Should You Prepare for the PMP Exam? B.6
Ten Tips for Taking the PMP Exam B.7
Sample PMP Exam Questions B.8
What Is Project+ Certification? B.13
What Are the Requirements for Earning and Maintaining Project+ Certification? B.14
Additional Information on the Project+ Exam B.15
Sample Project+ Exam Questions B.16
What Other Exams or Certifications Related to Project Management Are Available? B.17
Discussion Questions B.19
Exercises B.19
Answers to Sample PMP Exam Questions B.20
Answers to Sample Project+ Exam Questions B.20
End Notes B.20

Appendix C *Additional Running Cases and Simulation Software* C.1
Introduction C.1
Additional Case 1: Green Computing Research Project C.1
Part 1: Project Integration Management C.1
Part 2: Project Scope Management C.3
Part 3: Project Time Management C.4
Part 4: Project Cost Management C.6
Part 5: Project Quality Management C.7
Part 6: Project Human Resource Management C.7
Part 7: Project Communications Management C.8
Part 8: Project Risk Management C.9
Part 9: Project Procurement Management C.9
Additional Case 2: Project Management Videos Project C.10
Part 1: Initiating C.10
Part 2: Planning C.11
Part 3: Executing C.12
Part 4: Monitoring and Controlling C.12
Part 5: Closing C.13
Fissure Simulation Software C.13
Introduction C.13
Instructions C.13

Glossary G.1
Index I.1

PREFACE

The future of many organizations depends on their ability to harness the power of information technology, and good project managers continue to be in high demand. Colleges have responded to this need by establishing courses in project management and making them part of the information technology, management, engineering, and other curriculum. Corporations are investing in continuing education to help develop effective project managers and project teams. This text provides a much-needed framework for teaching courses in project management, especially those that emphasize managing information technology projects. The first five editions of this text were extremely well received by people in academia and the workplace. The Sixth Edition builds on the strengths of the previous editions and adds new, important information and features.

It's impossible to read a newspaper, magazine, or Web page without hearing about the impact of information technology on our society. Information is traveling faster and being shared by more individuals than ever before. You can buy just about anything online, surf the Web on a mobile phone, or use a wireless Internet connection at your local coffee shop. Companies have linked their many systems together to help them fill orders on time and better serve their customers. Software companies are continually developing new products to help streamline our work and get better results. When technology works well, it is almost invisible. But did it ever occur to you to ask, "Who makes these complex technologies and systems happen?"

Because you're reading this text, you must have an interest in the "behind-the-scenes" aspects of technology. If I've done my job well, as you read you'll begin to see the many innovations society is currently experiencing as the result of thousands of successful information technology projects. In this text, you'll read about IT projects around the world that went well, including Mittal Steel Poland's Implementation of SAP project that unified IT systems to improve business and financial processes; Dell Earth and other green computing projects that save energy and millions of dollars; and Six Sigma projects such as the project to improve case load management at Baptist St. Anthony's Hospital in Amarillo, Texas; the systems infrastructure project at the Boots Company in the United Kingdom that is taking advantage of supplier competition to cut costs and improve services; Kuala Lumpur's state-of-the-art Integrated Transport Information System (ITIS) project; and many more. Of course, not all projects are successful. Factors such as time, money, and unrealistic expectations, among many others can sabotage a promising effort if it is not properly managed. In this text, you'll also learn from the mistakes made on many projects that were not successful. I have written this book in an effort to educate you, tomorrow's project managers, about what will help make a project succeed—and what can make it fail. You'll also see how projects are used in everyday media, such as television and film, and how companies use best practices in project management. Many readers tell me how much they enjoy reading these real-world examples in the What Went Right?, What Went Wrong?, Media Snapshot, and Best Practice features. As practitioners know, there is no "one size fits all" solution to managing projects. By seeing how different organizations successfully implement project management, you can help your organization do the same.

Although project management has been an established field for many years, managing information technology projects requires ideas and information that go beyond standard project management. For example, many information technology projects fail because of a lack of user input, incomplete and changing requirements, and a lack of executive support. This book includes suggestions on dealing with these issues. New technologies can also aid in managing information technology projects, and examples of using software to assist in project management are included throughout the book.

Information Technology Project Management, Sixth Edition, is still the only textbook to apply all nine project management knowledge areas—project integration, scope, time, cost, quality, human resource, communications, risk, and procurement management—and all five process groups—initiating, planning, executing, monitoring and controlling, and closing—to information technology projects. This text builds on the *PMBOK® Guide, Fourth Edition,* an American National Standard, to provide a solid framework and context for managing information technology projects. It also includes an appendix, *Guide to Using Microsoft Project 2007,* which many readers find invaluable. A second appendix provides advice on earning and maintaining Project Management Professional (PMP) certification from the Project Management Institute (PMI) as well as information on other certification programs, such as CompTIA's Project+ certification. A third appendix provides new case studies and information on using simulation software to help readers apply their project management skills.

Information Technology Project Management, Sixth Edition, provides practical lessons in project management for students and practitioners alike. By weaving together theory and practice, this text presents an understandable, integrated view of the many concepts, skills, tools, and techniques involved in information technology project management. The comprehensive design of the text provides a strong foundation for students and practitioners in project management.

New to the Sixth Edition

Building on the success of the previous editions, *Information Technology Project Management, Sixth Edition,* introduces a uniquely effective combination of features. The main changes made to the Sixth Edition include the following:

- Several changes were made to synchronize this edition with the *PMBOK® Guide, Fourth Edition,* which PMI published in December 2008. Several processes have changed, a few have been deleted, and a few have been added. For example, project scope management now includes a process for collecting requirements, which produces requirements documentation, a requirements management plan, and a requirements traceability matrix as outputs. This text describes this and other new processes and provides more details and examples of their outputs.
- Appendix C, Additional Running Cases, provides two new cases and information about using Fissure's simulation software. One of the new cases focuses on green computing projects, and the other involves finding or creating video clips related to project management. There is also a running case at the end of each knowledge area chapter, and the old cases from the Fifth Edition text

are available on the new companion (premium) Web site. Several additional exercises are also provided at the end of chapters.

- A new Jeopardy-like game is provided on the companion (premium) Web site to help students study important concepts from each chapter in a fun and engaging way.
- A new companion (premium) Web site for the Sixth Edition (*www.cengage.com/mis/schwalbe*) provides you with access to informative links from the end notes, lecture notes, interactive quizzes, templates, additional running cases, suggested readings, podcasts, the new Jeopardy-like game, and many other items to enhance your learning.

ACCESSING THE COMPANION (PREMIUM) WEB SITE

To access the companion (premium) Web site, open a Web browser and go to *www.cengage.com/login.* Locate your companion (premium) access card in the front of each new book purchase, and click "Create My Account" to begin the registration process. If you've purchased a used book, please search for ***Information Technology Project Management, Sixth Edition*** at *www.ichapters.com* where you can purchase instant access.

- Updated examples are provided throughout the text. You'll notice several new examples in the Sixth Edition that explain recent events in managing real information technology projects. Several of the What Went Right?, What Went Wrong?, Media Snapshot, and Best Practice examples have been updated to keep you up-to-date. Additional examples and results of new studies are also included throughout the text, with appropriate citations.
- User feedback is incorporated. Based on feedback from reviewers, students, instructors, practitioners, and translators (this book has been translated into Chinese, Japanese, Russian, and Czech), you'll see several additional changes to help clarify information.

Approach

Many people have been practicing some form of project management with little or no formal study in this area. New books and articles are being written each year as we discover more about the field of project management, and project management software continues to advance. Because the project management field and the technology industry change rapidly, you cannot assume that what worked even a few years ago is still the best approach today. This text provides up-to-date information on how good project management and effective use of software can help you manage projects, especially information technology projects. Five distinct features of this text include its relationship to the Project Management Body of Knowledge, its detailed guide for using Microsoft Project 2007, its value in preparing for Project Management Professional and other certification exams, its inclusion of running case studies and online templates, and its companion (premium) Web site. You can also purchase a special bundling of this text that includes simulation software by Fissure, or you can order the Fissure simulation separately.

Based on the *PMBOK® Guide, Fourth Edition*

The Project Management Institute (PMI) created the Guide to the Project Management Body of Knowledge (the *PMBOK® Guide*) as a framework and starting point for understanding project management. It includes an introduction to project management, brief descriptions of all nine project management knowledge areas, and a glossary of terms. The *PMBOK® Guide* is, however, just that—a guide. This text uses the *PMBOK® Guide, Fourth Edition-like* (December 2008) *as a foundation, but goes beyond it by providing more details, highlighting additional topics, and providing a real-world context for project management.* Information Technology Project Management, Sixth Edition, *explains project management specifically as it applies to managing information technology projects in the twenty-first century. It includes several unique features to bring you the excitement of this dynamic field (for more information on features, see the section entitled "Pedagogical Features").*

Contains a Detailed Guide on How to Use Microsoft Project 2007

Software has advanced tremendously in recent years, and it is important for project managers and their teams to use software to help manage information technology projects. Each copy of *Information Technology Project Management, Sixth Edition,* includes a detailed guide in Appendix A on using the leading project management software on the market—Microsoft Project 2007. Examples using Project 2007 and other software tools are integrated throughout the text, not as an afterthought. Appendix A, Guide to Using Microsoft Project 2007, teaches you in a systematic way to use this powerful software to help in project scope, time, cost, human resource, and communications management.

Resource for PMP and Other Certification Exams

Professional certification is an important factor in recognizing and ensuring quality in a profession. PMI provides certification as a Project Management Professional (PMP), and this text is an excellent resource for studying for the certification exam. This text will also help you pass other certification exams, such as CompTIA's Project+ exam. Having experience working on projects does not mean you can easily pass the PMP or other certification exams.

I like to tell my students a story about taking a driver's license test after moving to Minnesota. I had been driving very safely and without accidents for over 16 years, so I thought I could just walk in and take the test. I was impressed by the sophisticated computer system used to administer the test. The questions were displayed on a large touch-screen monitor, often along with an image or video to illustrate different traffic signs or driving situations. I became concerned when I found I had no idea how to answer several questions, and I was perplexed when the test seemed to stop and a message displayed saying, "Please see the person at the service counter." This was a polite way of saying I had failed the test! After controlling my embarrassment, I picked up one of the Minnesota driving test brochures, studied it for an hour or two that night, and successfully passed the test the next day.

The point of this story is that it is important to study information from the organization that creates the test and not be overconfident that your experience is enough. Because this text is based on PMI's *PMBOK® Guide, Fourth Edition,* it provides a valuable reference for studying for PMP certification. It is also an excellent reference for CompTIA's Project+ exam. I have earned both of those certifications and kept them in mind when writing this text.

Provides Exercises, Running Cases, Templates, Sample Documents, and Optional Simulation Software

Based on feedback from readers, the Sixth Edition continues to provide challenging exercises and running cases to help students apply concepts in each chapter. There are over 50 templates, examples of real project documents, and optional simulation software developed by Fissure, a PMI Registered Education Provider, that you can use to actively practice your skills in managing a project. All of these features help the subject matter come alive and have more meaning.

Includes a Companion (Premium) Web site

A companion (premium) Web site provides you with a one-stop location to access informative links and tools to enhance your learning. Similar to other companion (premium) Web sites provided by Course Technology, this site will be a valuable resource as you view lecture notes, templates, interactive quizzes, podcasts, student files for Project 2007, important articles, references, and more. You can also link to the author's site to see real class syllabi, samples of student projects, and other helpful links.

Organization and Content

Information Technology Project Management, Sixth Edition, is organized into three main sections to provide a framework for project management, a detailed description of each project management knowledge area, and three appendices to provide practical information for applying project management. The first three chapters form the first section, which introduces the project management framework and sets the stage for the remaining chapters.

Chapters 4 through 12 form the second section of the text, which describes each of the project management knowledge areas—project integration, scope, time, cost, quality, human resource, communications, risk, and procurement management—in the context of information technology projects. An entire chapter is dedicated to each knowledge area. Each knowledge area chapter includes sections that map to their major processes as described in the *PMBOK® Guide, Fourth Edition.* For example, the chapter on project quality management includes sections on planning quality, performing quality assurance, and performing quality control. Additional sections highlight other important concepts related to each knowledge area, such as Six Sigma, testing, maturity models, and using software to assist in project quality management. Each chapter also includes detailed examples of key project management tools and techniques as applied to information technology projects. For example, the chapter on project integration management includes samples of various project-selection documents, such as net present value analyses, ROI calculations, payback analyses, and weighted scoring models. The project scope management chapter includes a sample project charter, a project scope statement, and several work breakdown structures for information technology projects.

Appendices A through C form the third section of the text, which provides practical information to help you apply project management skills on real or practice projects. By following the detailed, step-by-step guide in Appendix A, which includes more than 60 screen shots, you will learn how to use Project 2007. Appendix B summarizes what you need to know to earn PMP or other certifications related to project management. Appendix C provides additional running cases and information on using simulation software to help you practice your new skills.

Pedagogical Features

Several pedagogical features are included in this text to enhance presentation of the materials so that you can more easily understand the concepts and apply them. Throughout the text, emphasis is placed on applying concepts to current, real-world information technology project management.

Learning Objectives, Chapter Summaries, Discussion Questions, Exercises, Quick Quizzes, Running Cases, and Companion (Premium) Web site

Learning Objectives, Chapter Summaries, Quick Quizzes, Discussion Questions, Exercises, Running Cases, and the companion (premium) Web site are designed to function as integrated study tools. Learning Objectives reflect what you should be able to accomplish after completing each chapter. Chapter Summaries highlight key concepts you should master. The Discussion Questions help guide critical thinking about those key concepts. Quick Quizzes test knowledge of essential chapter concepts and include an answer key. Exercises provide opportunities to practice important techniques, as do the Running Cases. The companion (premium) Web site provides several study aids, such as podcasts, the new Jeopardy-like game, and interactive quizzes for each chapter, which are different from the Quick Quizzes in the text.

Opening Case and Case Wrap-Up

To set the stage, each chapter begins with an opening case related to the material presented in that chapter. These "real-life" case scenarios (most based on the author's experiences) spark student interest and introduce important concepts in a real-world context. As project management concepts and techniques are discussed, they are applied to the opening case and other similar scenarios. Each chapter then closes with a case wrap-up—with some ending successfully and some, realistically, failing—to further illustrate the real world of project management.

What Went Right? and What Went Wrong?

Failures, as much as successes, can be valuable learning experiences. Each chapter of the text includes one or more examples of real information technology projects that went right as well as examples of projects that went wrong. These examples further illustrate the importance of mastering key concepts in each chapter.

Media Snapshot

The world is full of projects. Several televisions shows, movies, newspapers, Web sites, and other media highlight project results, good and bad. Relating project management concepts to all types of projects highlighted in the media will help you understand and see the importance of this growing field. Why not get people excited about studying project management by showing them how to recognize project management concepts in popular television shows, movies, or other media?

Best Practice

Every chapter includes an example of a best practice related to topics in that chapter. For example, Chapter 1 describes best practices written by Robert Butrick, author of *The Project Workout,* from the *Ultimate Business Library's Best Practice* book. He suggests that organizations ensure their projects are driven by their strategy and engage project stakeholders.

Key Terms

The fields of information technology and project management both include many unique terms that are vital to creating a workable language when the two fields are combined. Key terms are displayed in bold face and are defined the first time they appear. Definitions of key terms are provided in alphabetical order at the end of each chapter and in a glossary at the end of the text.

Application Software

Learning becomes much more dynamic with hands-on practice using the top project management software tool in the industry, Microsoft Project 2007, as well as other tools, such as spreadsheet software and the Internet. Each chapter offers you many opportunities to get hands-on experience and build new software skills. This text is written from the point of view that reading about something only gets you so far—to really understand project management, you have to do it for yourself. In addition to the exercises and running cases found at the end of each chapter and in Appendix C, several challenging exercises are provided at the end of Appendix A, Guide to Using Microsoft Project 2007.

SUPPLEMENTS

The following supplemental materials are available when this text is used in a classroom setting. All of the teaching tools available with this text are provided to the instructor on a single CD-ROM.

- **Electronic Instructor's Manual** The Instructor's Manual that accompanies this textbook includes additional instructional material to assist in class preparation, including suggestions for lecture topics and additional discussion questions.
- **ExamView®** This textbook is accompanied by ExamView, a powerful testing software package that allows instructors to create and administer printed, computer (LAN-based), and Internet exams. ExamView includes hundreds of questions that correspond to the topics covered in this text, enabling students to

generate detailed study guides that include page references for further review. The computer-based and Internet testing components allow students to take exams at their computers, and also save the instructor time by grading each exam automatically.

- **PowerPoint Presentations** This text comes with Microsoft PowerPoint slides for each chapter. These are included as a teaching aid for classroom presentation, to make available to students on the network for chapter review, or to be printed for classroom distribution. Instructors can add their own slides for additional topics they introduce to the class.
- **Solution Files** Solutions to end-of-chapter questions can be found on the Instructor Resource CD-ROM and may also be found on the Course Technology Web site at *www.cengage.com/mis/schwalbe.* The solutions are password-protected.
- **Distance Learning** Course Technology is proud to present online courses in WebCT and Blackboard, to provide the most complete and dynamic learning experience possible. When you add online content to one of your courses, you're adding a lot: self tests, links, glossaries, and, most of all, a gateway to the twenty-first century's most important information resource. We hope you will make the most of your course, both online and offline. For more information on how to bring distance learning to your course, contact your Course Technology sales representative.

ACKNOWLEDGMENTS

I never would have taken on this project—writing this book, the first, second, third, fourth, fifth, and sixth edition—without the help of many people. I thank the staff at Course Technology for their dedication and hard work in helping me produce this book and in doing such an excellent job of marketing it. Kate Mason (formerly Hennessy), Deb Kaufmann, Matthew Hutchinson, Patrick Franzen, and many more people did a great job in planning and executing all of the work involved in producing this book.

I thank my many colleagues and experts in the field who contributed information to this book. David Jones, Rachel Hollstadt, Cliff Sprague, Michael Branch, Barb Most, Jodi Curtis, Rita Mulcahy, Karen Boucher, Bill Munroe, Tess Galati, Joan Knutson, Neal Whitten, Brenda Taylor, Quentin Fleming, Jesse Freese, Nick Matteucci, Nick Erndt, Dragan Milosevic, Bob Borlink, Arvid Lee, Kathy Christenson, Peeter Kivestu, and many other people who provided excellent materials included in the Sixth Edition of this book. I really enjoy the network of project managers, authors, and consultants in this field who are very passionate about improving the theory and practice of project management.

I also thank my students and colleagues at Augsburg College and the University of Minnesota for providing feedback on the earlier editions of this book. I received many valuable comments from them on ways to improve the text and structure of my courses. I learn something new about project management and teaching all the time by interacting with students, faculty, and staff.

I also thank faculty reviewers for providing excellent feedback for me in writing this edition: Brian Ameling, Limestone College; Michel Avital, University of Amsterdam; Al Fundaburk, Bloomsburg University; Suleyman Guleyupoglu, University of Phoenix; Aurore

Kamssu, Tennessee State University; Angela Lemons, North Carolina A&T State University; Alan L. Matthews, Travecca Nazarene University; Thyra Nelson, Macon State College; Samir Shah, Pennsylvania State University—York; and Andrew Urbaczewski, University of Michigan-Dearborn. I also wish to thank the many reviewers of the earlier editions of this text. I also thank the many other instructors and readers who have contacted me directly with praise as well as suggestions for improving this text. I really appreciate the feedback and do my best to incorporate as much as I can.

Most of all, I am grateful to my family. Without their support, I never could have written this book. My wonderful husband, Dan, has always supported me in my career, and he helps me keep up-to-date with software development since he is a lead architect for ComSquared Systems, Inc. Our three children, Anne, Bobby, and Scott, actually think it's cool that their mom writes books and speaks at conferences. They also see me managing projects all the time. Anne, now 25, teases me for being the only quilter she knows who treats each quilt as a project. (Maybe that's why I get so many done!) Our children all understand the main reason why I write—I have a passion for educating future leaders of the world, including them.

As always, I am eager to receive your feedback on this book. Please send comments to me at schwalbe@augsburg.edu.

Kathy Schwalbe, Ph.D., PMP
Professor, Department of Business Administration

Augsburg College

ABOUT THE AUTHOR

Kathy Schwalbe is a Professor in the Department of Business Administration at Augsburg College in Minneapolis, where she teaches courses in project management, problem solving for business, systems analysis and design, information systems projects, and electronic commerce. Kathy was also an adjunct faculty member at the University of Minnesota, where she taught a graduate-level course in project management in the engineering department. She also provides training and consulting services to several organizations and speaks at several conferences. Kathy worked for ten years in industry before entering academia in 1991. She was an Air Force officer, systems analyst, project manager, senior engineer, and information technology consultant. Kathy is an active member of PMI, having served as the Student Chapter Liaison for the Minnesota chapter of PMI, VP of Education for the Minnesota chapter, Director of Communications and Editor of the Information Systems Specific Interest Group (ISSIG) Review, and member of PMI's test-writing team. Kathy earned her Ph.D. in Higher Education at the University of Minnesota, her MBA at Northeastern University's High Technology MBA program, and her B.S. in mathematics at the University of Notre Dame.

CHAPTER 1

INTRODUCTION TO PROJECT MANAGEMENT

LEARNING OBJECTIVES

After reading this chapter, you will be able to:

- Understand the growing need for better project management, especially for information technology projects
- Explain what a project is, provide examples of information technology projects, list various attributes of projects, and describe the triple constraint of project management
- Describe project management and discuss key elements of the project management framework, including project stakeholders, the project management knowledge areas, common tools and techniques, and project success
- Discuss the relationship between project, program, and portfolio management and the contributions they each make to enterprise success
- Understand the role of the project manager by describing what project managers do, what skills they need, and what the career field is like for information technology project managers
- Describe the project management profession, including its history, the role of professional organizations like the Project Management Institute (PMI), the importance of certification and ethics, and the advancement of project management software

OPENING CASE

Anne Roberts, the Director of the Project Management Office for a large retail chain, stood in front of 500 people in the large corporate auditorium to explain the company's new strategies. She was also broadcasting to thousands of other employees, suppliers, and stockholders throughout the world using live video via the Internet. The company had come a long way in implementing new information systems to improve inventory control, sell products using the Web, streamline the sales and distribution processes, and improve customer service. However, the stock price was down, the nation's economy was weak, and people were anxious to hear about the company's new strategies.

Anne began to address the audience, "Good morning. As many of you know, our CEO promoted me to this position as Director of the Project Management Office two years ago. Since then, we have completed many projects, including the advanced data networks project. That project enabled us to provide persistent broadband between headquarters and our retail stores throughout the world, allowing us to make timely decisions and continue our growth strategy. Our customers love that they can return items to any store, and any sales clerk can look up past sales information. Local store managers can make timely decisions using up-to-date information. Of course, we've had some project failures, too, and we need to continually assess our portfolio of projects to meet business needs. Two big IT initiatives this coming year include meeting new green IT regulations and providing enhanced online collaboration tools for our employees, suppliers, and customers. Our challenge is to work even smarter to decide what projects will most benefit the company, how we can continue to leverage the power of information technology to support our business, and how we can exploit our human capital to successfully plan and execute those projects. If we succeed, we'll continue to be a world-class corporation."

"And if we fail?" someone asked from the audience.

"Let's just say that failure is not an option," Anne replied.

INTRODUCTION

Many people and organizations today have a new—or renewed—interest in project management. Until the 1980s, project management primarily focused on providing schedule and resource data to top management in the military, computer, and construction industries. Today's project management involves much more, and people in every industry and every country manage projects. New technologies have become a significant factor in many businesses. Computer hardware, software, networks, and the use of interdisciplinary and global work teams have radically changed the work environment. The following statistics demonstrate the significance of project management in today's society, especially for projects involving information technology (IT). Note that IT projects involve using hardware, software, and/or networks to create a product, service, or result.

- Total global spending on technology goods, services, and staff was projected to reach $2.4 trillion in 2008, an 8 percent increase from 2007. IT purchases in the U.S. grew less than 3 percent, while the rest of the Americas expanded in local currencies at 6-percent rates. Asia Pacific and the oil-exporting areas of Eastern Europe, the Middle East, and Africa were the main engines of growth.[1]

- In the U.S. the size of the IT workforce topped 4 million workers for the first time in 2008. Unemployment rates in many information technology occupations were among the lowest in the labor force at only 2.3 percent. Demand for talent is high, and several organizations throughout the world cannot grow as desired due to difficulties in hiring and recruiting the people they need.[2]
- In 2007 the total compensation for the average senior project manager in U.S. dollars was $104,776 per year in the United States, $111,412 in Australia, and $120,364 in the United Kingdom. The average total compensation of a program manager was $122,825 in the United States, $133,718 in Australia, and $165,489 in the United Kingdom. The average total compensation for a Project Management Office (PMO) Director was $134,422 in the United States, $125,197 in Australia, and $210,392 in the United Kingdom. This survey was based on self-reported data from more than 5,500 practitioners in 19 countries.[3]
- The number of people earning their Project Management Professional (PMP) certification continues to increase each year.
- A research report showed that the U.S. spends $2.3 trillion on projects every year, an amount equal to 25 percent of the nation's gross domestic product. The world as a whole spends nearly $10 trillion of its $40.7 trillion gross product on projects of all kinds. More than 16 million people regard project management as their profession.[4]

Today's companies, governments, and nonprofit organizations are recognizing that to be successful, they need to be conversant with and use modern project management techniques. Individuals are realizing that to remain competitive in the workplace, they must develop skills to become good project team members and project managers. They also realize that many of the concepts of project management will help them in their everyday lives as they work with people and technology on a day-to-day basis.

WHAT WENT WRONG?

In 1995, the Standish Group published an often-quoted study entitled "The CHAOS Report." This consulting firm surveyed 365 information technology executive managers in the United States who managed more than 8,380 information technology application projects. As the title of the study suggests, the projects were in a state of chaos. U.S. companies spent more than $250 billion each year in the early 1990s on approximately 175,000 information technology application development projects. Examples of these projects included creating a new database for a state department of motor vehicles, developing a new system for car rental and hotel reservations, and implementing a client-server architecture for the banking industry. The study reported that the overall success rate of information technology projects was *only* 16.2 percent. The surveyors defined success as meeting project goals on time and on budget. The study also found that more than 31 percent of information technology projects were canceled before completion, costing U.S. companies and

continued

government agencies more than $81 billion. The study authors were adamant about the need for better project management in the information technology industry. They explained, "Software development projects are in chaos, and we can no longer imitate the three monkeys—hear no failures, see no failures, speak no failures."[5]

In a more recent study, PricewaterhouseCoopers surveyed 200 companies from 30 different countries about their project management maturity and found that *over half of all projects fail.* They also found that only 2.5 percent of corporations consistently meet their targets for scope, time, and cost goals for all types of project.[6]

Although several researchers question the methodology of such studies, their popularity has prompted managers throughout the world to examine their practices in managing projects. Many organizations assert that using project management provides advantages, such as:

- Better control of financial, physical, and human resources
- Improved customer relations
- Shorter development times
- Lower costs and improved productivity
- Higher quality and increased reliability
- Higher profit margins
- Better internal coordination
- Positive impact on meeting strategic goals
- Higher worker morale

This chapter introduces projects and project management, explains how projects fit into programs and portfolio management, discusses the role of the project manager, and provides important background information on this growing profession. Although project management applies to many different industries and types of projects, this text focuses on applying project management to information technology projects.

WHAT IS A PROJECT?

To discuss project management, it is important to understand the concept of a project. A **project** is "a temporary endeavor undertaken to create a unique product, service, or result."[7] Operations, on the other hand, is work done in organizations to sustain the business. Projects are different from operations in that they end when their objectives have been reached or the project has been terminated.

Examples of Information Technology Projects

Projects can be large or small and involve one person or thousands of people. They can be done in one day or take years to complete. As described earlier, information technology projects involve using hardware, software, and/or networks to create a product, service, or result. Examples of information technology projects include the following:

- A technician replaces ten laptops for a small department
- A small software development team adds a new feature to an internal software application for the finance department

- A college campus upgrades its technology infrastructure to provide wireless Internet access across the whole campus
- A cross-functional taskforce in a company decides what Voice-over-Internet-Protocol (VoIP) system to purchase and how it will be implemented
- A company develops a new system to increase sales force productivity and customer relationship management
- A television network implements a system to allow viewers to vote for contestants and provide other feedback on programs
- The automobile industry develops a Web site to streamline procurement
- A government group develops a system to track child immunizations
- A large group of volunteers from organizations throughout the world develops standards for environmentally friendly or green IT

Gartner, Inc., a prestigious consulting firm, identified the top ten strategic technologies for 2008. A few of these technologies include the following:

- *Green IT:* Simply defined, **green IT** or **green computing** involves developing and using computer resources in an efficient way to improve economic viability, social responsibility, and environmental impact. For example, government regulations now encourage organizations and IT departments to use low-emission building materials, recycle computing equipment, and use alternative energy and other green technologies.
- *Unified communications:* The majority of organizations are expected to migrate from PBX (private branch exchange) to IP (Internet protocol) telephony in the next three years.
- *Business process modeling:* Enterprise and process architects, senior developers, and business process analysts must work together to help organizations effectively use IT to improve processes. Business process modeling (BPM) suites are expected to fill a critical role as a compliment to service-oriented architecture (SOA).
- *Virtualization 2.0:* **Virtualization** hides the physical characteristics of computing resources from their users, such as making a single server, operating system, application, or storage device appear to function as multiple virtual resources. Virtualization technologies can improve IT resource management and increase flexibility for adapting to changing requirements and workloads. Virtualization 2.0 adds automation technologies so that resource efficiency can improve dramatically.
- *Social software:* Most students and professionals today use online social networking sites such as MySpace, Facebook, LinkedIn, and YouTube to collaborate with others. Organizations will increasingly use social software technologies to augment traditional collaboration.[8]

As you can see, a wide variety of projects use information technologies, and organizations rely on them for their success.

MEDIA SNAPSHOT

Nicholas Carr published his exposé "IT Doesn't Matter" in the May 2003 issue of *Harvard Business Review,* a topic he expanded on in the following year with his book *Does IT Matter? Information Technology and the Corrosion of Competitive Advantage.*[9] Both sparked heated debates on the value of information technology in today's society. Carr suggested that information technology has followed a pattern similar to earlier infrastructure technologies like railroads and electric power. As availability increased and costs decreased, information technology has become a commodity; therefore, Carr argued, it can no longer provide companies with a competitive advantage. In 2006, *Baseline* magazine published the article, "Where I.T. Matters: How 10 Technologies Transformed 10 Industries" as a retort to Carr's ideas. Below are a few of the technologies and industries that have made IT an important part of their business strategy. (Visit *www.nicholasgcarr.com* to see more recent work by Carr, including a free 2008 eBook, *IT in 2018: From Turing's Machine to the Computing Cloud.*)

- *VoIP:* VoIP has totally transformed the telecommunications industry and broadband Internet access. Phone companies do not have a lock on dial tones anymore; you can make a phone call through a cable TV provider or over any Internet channel for less than the cost of ordinary phone service. These technologies, along with regulatory changes, have forced major phone companies to be more competitive to keep and attract customers. VoIP is more efficient and less expensive than traditional phone networks. The ramp-up to VoIP is expected to happen quickly. Research firm IDC estimates that U.S. subscribers to residential VoIP services will grow from 3 million in 2005 to 27 million by the end of 2009.
- *Global Positioning Systems (GPS) and Business Intelligence:* "Farming is the oldest known human activity," says Michael Swanson, an agricultural economist at Wells Fargo bank, the largest lender to U.S. farmers. "You'd think that after 10,000 years there'd be nothing left to improve. Not true." How have GPS and Business Intelligence changed the farming industry? In 1950, American farmers planted 83 million acres of corn, which produced 38 bushels per acre. In 2004, farmers planted 81 million acres of corn, which produced 160 bushels. That means that 2.5 percent fewer acres produced more than four times as much corn. Swanson estimates that if farmers did not use the technology they do today, they would have had to plant 320 million acres of corn last year to meet demand: "We'd be planting parking lots and backyards," Swanson joked.
- *Digital Supply Chain:* The entertainment industry's distribution system has changed dramatically due to new information technologies. "The great promise of digital technology is that consumers will be able to choose how they want to consume content," says Kevin Tsujihara, president of Warner Home Entertainment Group, a new department formed to handle the digital delivery of entertainment to consumers. Before Warner underwent a major digital transformation, they were only able to process one or two pictures at a time. "Today, we have the capability of taking upward of 10 simultaneous motion picture projects and working on them in this environment. The creation of these digital masters obviously is important in that we can make a transformation to whatever channel we need to get to the consumer."[10]

Project Attributes

As you can see, projects come in all shapes and sizes. The following attributes help to define a project further:

- *A project has a unique purpose.* Every project should have a well-defined objective. For example, Anne Roberts, the Director of the Project Management Office in the opening case, might sponsor an information technology collaboration project to develop a list and initial analysis of potential information technology projects that might improve operations for the company. The unique purpose of this project would be to create a collaborative report with ideas from people throughout the company. The results would provide the basis for further discussions and projects. As in this example, projects result in a unique product, service, or result.
- *A project is temporary.* A project has a definite beginning and a definite end. In the information technology collaboration project, Anne might form a team of people to work immediately on the project, and then expect a report and an executive presentation of the results in one month.
- *A project is developed using progressive elaboration.* Projects are often defined broadly when they begin, and as time passes, the specific details of the project become clearer. Therefore, projects should be developed in increments. A project team should develop initial plans and then update them with more detail based on new information. For example, suppose a few people submitted ideas for the information technology collaboration project, but they did not clearly address how the ideas would support the business strategy of improving operations. The project team might decide to prepare a questionnaire for people to fill in as they submit their ideas to improve the quality of the inputs.
- *A project requires resources, often from various areas.* Resources include people, hardware, software, and other assets. Many projects cross departmental or other boundaries to achieve their unique purposes. For the information technology collaboration project, people from information technology, marketing, sales, distribution, and other areas of the company would need to work together to develop ideas. The company might also hire outside consultants to provide input. Once the project team has selected key projects for implementation, they will probably require additional resources. And to meet new project objectives, people from other companies—product suppliers and consulting companies—may be added. Resources, however, are limited and must be used effectively to meet project and other corporate goals.
- *A project should have a primary customer or sponsor.* Most projects have many interested parties or stakeholders, but someone must take the primary role of sponsorship. The **project sponsor** usually provides the direction and funding for the project. In this case, Anne Roberts would be the sponsor for the information technology collaboration project. Once further information technology projects are selected, however, the sponsors for those projects would be senior managers in charge of the main parts of the company affected by the projects. For example, if the vice president of sales initiates a project to

improve direct product sales using the Internet, he or she might be the project sponsor.

- *A project involves uncertainty.* Because every project is unique, it is sometimes difficult to define its objectives clearly, estimate how long it will take to complete, or determine how much it will cost. External factors also cause uncertainty, such as a supplier going out of business or a project team member needing unplanned time off. This uncertainty is one of the main reasons project management is so challenging, especially on projects involving new technologies.

An effective **project manager** is crucial to a project's success. Project managers work with the project sponsors, the project team, and the other people involved in a project to meet project goals.

The Triple Constraint

Every project is constrained in different ways by its scope, time, and cost goals. These limitations are sometimes referred to in project management as the **triple constraint**. To create a successful project, a project manager must consider scope, time, and cost and balance these three often-competing goals. He or she must consider the following:

- *Scope:* What work will be done as part of the project? What unique product, service, or result does the customer or sponsor expect from the project? How will the scope be verified?
- *Time:* How long should it take to complete the project? What is the project's schedule? How will the team track actual schedule performance? Who can approve changes to the schedule?
- *Cost:* What should it cost to complete the project? What is the project's budget? How will costs be tracked? Who can authorize changes to the budget?

Figure 1-1 illustrates the three dimensions of the triple constraint. Each area—scope, time, and cost—has a target at the beginning of the project. For example, the information technology collaboration project might have an initial scope of producing a 40- to 50-page report and a one-hour presentation on about 30 potential information technology projects. The project manager might further define project scope to include providing a description of each potential project, an investigation of what other companies have implemented for similar projects, a rough time and cost estimate, and assessments of the risk and potential payoff as high, medium, or low. The initial time estimate for this project might be one month, and the cost estimate might be $45,000–$50,000. These expectations provide the targets for the scope, time, and cost dimensions of the project. Note that the scope and cost goals in this example include ranges—the report can be between 40- to 50-pages long and the project can cost between $45,000 and $50,000. Because projects involve uncertainty and limited resources, projects rarely finish according to discrete scope, time, and cost goals originally planned. Instead of discrete target goals, it is often more realistic to set a range of goals such as spending between $45,000 and $50,000 and having the length of the report between 40 and 50 pages. These goals might mean hitting the target, but not the bull's eye.

Managing the triple constraint involves making trade-offs between scope, time, and cost goals for a project. For example, you might need to increase the budget for a project to meet

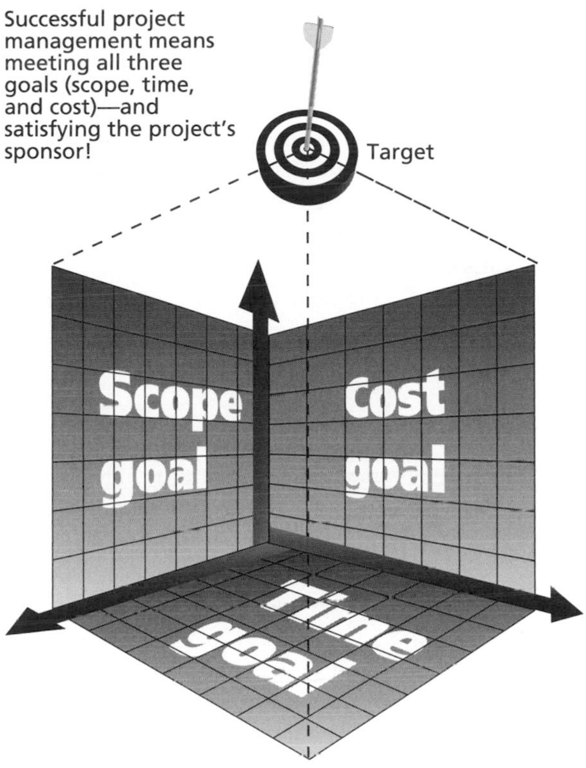
Successful project management means meeting all three goals (scope, time, and cost)—and satisfying the project's sponsor!
Target
Scope goal
Cost goal
Time goal

FIGURE 1-1 The triple constraint of project management

scope and time goals. Alternatively, you might have to reduce the scope of a project to meet time and cost goals. Experienced project managers know that you must decide which aspect of the triple constraint is most important. If time is most important, you must often change the initial scope and/or cost goals to meet the schedule. If scope goals are most important, you may need to adjust time and/or cost goals.

For example, to generate project ideas, suppose the project manager for the information technology collaboration project sent an e-mail survey to all employees, as planned. The initial time and cost estimate may have been one week and $5,000 to collect ideas based on this e-mail survey. Now, suppose the e-mail survey generated only a few good project ideas, and the scope goal was to collect at least 30 good ideas. Should the project team use a different method like focus groups or interviews to collect ideas? Even though it was not in the initial scope, time, or cost estimates, it would really help the project. Since good ideas are crucial to project success, it would make sense to inform the project sponsor that you want to make adjustments.

Although the triple constraint describes how the basic elements of a project—scope, time, and cost—interrelate, other elements can also play significant roles. Quality is often a key factor in projects, as is customer or sponsor satisfaction. Some people, in fact, refer to the *quadruple constraint* of project management, which includes quality as well as scope, time, and cost. Others believe that quality considerations, including customer satisfaction, must be inherent in setting the scope, time, and cost goals of a project. A project team may meet scope, time, and cost goals but fail to meet quality standards or satisfy their sponsor, if they have not adequately addressed these concerns. For example, Anne Roberts may receive a 50-page report describing 30 potential information technology projects and hear a presentation on the findings of the report. The project team may have completed the work on time and within the cost constraint, but the quality may have been unacceptable. Anne's view of an executive presentation may be very different from the project team's view. The project manager should be communicating with the sponsor throughout the project to make sure the project meets his or her expectations.

How can you avoid the problems that occur when you meet scope, time, and cost goals, but lose sight of quality or customer satisfaction? The answer is *good project management, which includes more than meeting the triple constraint.*

WHAT IS PROJECT MANAGEMENT?

Project management is "the application of knowledge, skills, tools and techniques to project activities to meet project requirements."[11] Project managers must not only strive to meet specific scope, time, cost, and quality goals of projects, they must also facilitate the entire process to meet the needs and expectations of the people involved in or affected by project activities.

Figure 1-2 illustrates a framework to help you understand project management. Key elements of this framework include the project stakeholders, project management knowledge areas, project management tools and techniques, and the contribution of successful projects to the enterprise.

Project Stakeholders

Stakeholders are the people involved in or affected by project activities and include the project sponsor, project team, support staff, customers, users, suppliers, and even

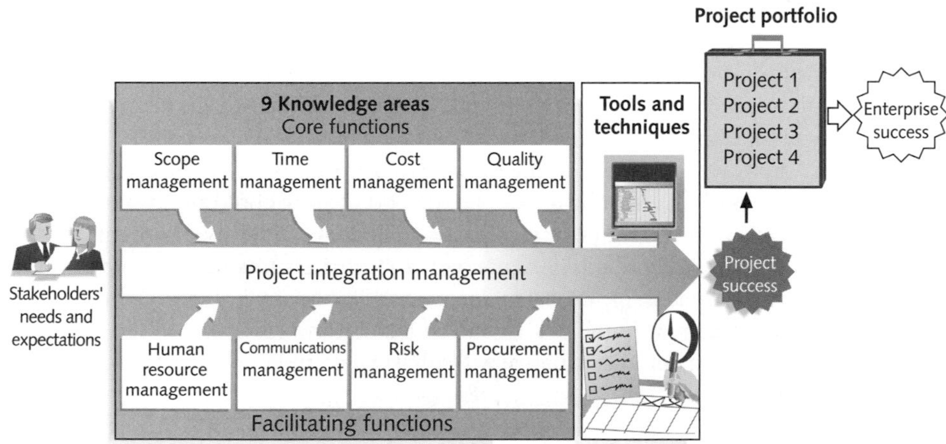

FIGURE 1-2 Project management framework

opponents of the project. These stakeholders often have very different needs and expectations. For example, building a new house is a well-known example of a project. There are several stakeholders involved in a home construction project.

- The project sponsors would be the potential new homeowners. They would be the people paying for the house and could be on a very tight budget, so they would expect the contractor to provide accurate estimates of the costs involved in building the house. They would also need a realistic idea of when they could move in and what type of home they could afford given their budget constraints. The new homeowners would have to make important decisions to keep the costs of the house within their budget. Can they afford to finish the basement right away? If they can afford to finish the basement, will it affect the projected move-in date? In this example, the project sponsors are also the customers and users for the product, which is the house.
- The project manager in this example would normally be the general contractor responsible for building the house. He or she needs to work with all the project stakeholders to meet their needs and expectations.
- The project team for building the house would include several construction workers, electricians, carpenters, and so on. These stakeholders would need to know exactly what work they must do and when they need to do it. They would need to know if the required materials and equipment will be at the construction site or if they are expected to provide the materials and equipment. Their work would need to be coordinated since there are many interrelated factors involved. For example, the carpenter cannot put in kitchen cabinets until the walls are completed.
- Support staff might include the buyers' employers, the general contractor's administrative assistant, and other people who support other stakeholders. The buyers' employers might expect their employees to still complete their work but allow some flexibility so they can visit the building site or take phone calls related to building the house. The contractor's administrative assistant would support the project by coordinating meetings between the buyers, the contractor, suppliers, and so on.
- Building a house requires many suppliers. The suppliers would provide the wood, windows, flooring materials, appliances, and so on. Suppliers would expect exact details on what items they need to provide, where and when to deliver those items, and so on.
- There may or may not be opponents of a project. In this example, there might be a neighbor who opposes the project because the workers are making so much noise that she cannot concentrate on her work at home, or the noise might wake her sleeping children. She might interrupt the workers to voice her complaints or even file a formal complaint. Or, the neighborhood might have association rules concerning new home design and construction. If the homeowners did not follow these rules, they might have to halt construction due to legal issues.

As you can see from this example, there are many different stakeholders on projects, and they often have different interests. Stakeholders' needs and expectations are important in the beginning and throughout the life of a project. Successful project managers develop good relationships with project stakeholders to understand and meet their needs and expectations.

Project Management Knowledge Areas

Project management knowledge areas describe the key competencies that project managers must develop. The center of Figure 1-2 shows the nine knowledge areas of project management. The four core knowledge areas of project management include project scope, time, cost, and quality management. These are core knowledge areas because they lead to specific project objectives.

- Project scope management involves defining and managing all the work required to complete the project successfully.
- Project time management includes estimating how long it will take to complete the work, developing an acceptable project schedule, and ensuring timely completion of the project.
- Project cost management consists of preparing and managing the budget for the project.
- Project quality management ensures that the project will satisfy the stated or implied needs for which it was undertaken.

The four facilitating knowledge areas of project management are human resource, communications, risk, and procurement management. These are called facilitating knowledge areas because they are the processes through which the project objectives are achieved.

- Project human resource management is concerned with making effective use of the people involved with the project.
- Project communications management involves generating, collecting, disseminating, and storing project information.
- Project risk management includes identifying, analyzing, and responding to risks related to the project.
- Project procurement management involves acquiring or procuring goods and services for a project from outside the performing organization.

Project integration management, the ninth knowledge area, is an overarching function that affects and is affected by all of the other knowledge areas. Project managers must have knowledge and skills in all nine of these areas. This text includes an entire chapter on each of these knowledge areas because all of them are crucial to project success.

Project Management Tools and Techniques

Thomas Carlyle, a famous historian and author, stated, "Man is a tool-using animal. Without tools he is nothing, with tools he is all." As the world continues to become more complex, it is even more important for people to develop and use tools, especially for managing important projects. **Project management tools and techniques** assist project managers and their teams in carrying out work in all nine knowledge areas. For example, some popular time-management tools and techniques include Gantt charts, project network diagrams, and critical path analysis. Table 1-1 lists some commonly used tools and techniques by knowledge area. You will learn more about these and other tools and techniques throughout this text.

TABLE 1-1 Common project management tools and techniques by knowledge area

Knowledge area/category	Tools and techniques
Integration management	Project selection methods, project management methodologies, stakeholder analyses, project charters, project management plans, **project management software, change requests,** change control boards, project review meetings, **lessons-learned reports**
Scope management	**Scope statements, work breakdown structures,** statements of work, **requirements analyses,** scope management plans, scope verification techniques, and scope change controls
Time management	**Gantt charts,** project network diagrams, critical path analysis, crashing, fast tracking, schedule performance measurements
Cost management	Net present value, return on investment, payback analysis, earned value management, project portfolio management, cost estimates, cost management plans, cost baselines
Quality management	Quality metrics, checklists, quality control charts, Pareto diagrams, fishbone diagrams, maturity models, statistical methods
Human resource management	Motivation techniques, empathic listening, responsibility assignment matrices, project organizational charts, resource histograms, team building exercises
Communications management	Communications management plans, **kick-off meetings,** conflict management, communications media selection, status and **progress reports,** virtual communications, templates, project Web sites
Risk management	Risk management plans, risk registers, probability/impact matrices, risk rankings
Procurement management	Make-or-buy analyses, contracts, requests for proposals or quotes, source selections, supplier evaluation matrices

A 2006 survey of 753 project and program managers was conducted to rate several project management tools. Respondents were asked to rate tools on a scale of 1–5 (low to high) based on the extent of their use and the potential of the tools to help improve project success. "Super tools" were defined as those that had high use and high potential for improving project success. These super tools included software for task scheduling (such as project management software), scope statements, requirement analyses, and lessons-learned reports. Tools that are already extensively used and have been found to improve project importance include progress reports, kick-off meetings, Gantt charts, and change requests. These super tools are bolded in Table 1-1.[12] Of course, different tools can be more effective in different situations. It is crucial for project managers and their team members to determine which tools will be most useful for their particular projects.

WHAT WENT RIGHT?

Follow-up studies by the Standish Group (see the previously quoted CHAOS study in the What Went Wrong? passage) showed some improvement in the statistics for information technology projects in the past decade:

- The number of successful IT projects has more than doubled, from 16 percent in 1994 to 35 percent in 2006.
- The number of failed projects decreased from 31 percent in 1994 to 19 percent in 2006.
- The United States spent more money on IT projects in 2006 than 1994 ($346 billion and $250 billion, respectively), but the amount of money wasted on challenged projects (those that did not meet scope, time, or cost goals, but were completed) and failed projects was down to $53 billion in 2006 compared to $140 billion in 1994.[13]

The good news is that project managers are learning how to succeed more often; the bad news is that it is still very difficult to lead successful IT projects. "The reasons for the increase in successful projects vary. First, the average cost of a project has been more than cut in half. Better tools have been created to monitor and control progress and better skilled project managers with better management processes are being used. The fact that there are processes is significant in itself."[14]

Despite its advantages, project management is not a silver bullet that guarantees success on all projects. Project management is a very broad, often complex discipline. What works on one project may not work on another, so it is essential for project managers to continue to develop their knowledge and skills in managing projects. It is also important to learn from the mistakes and successes of others.

Project Success

How do you define the success or failure of a project? There are several ways to define project success. The list that follows outlines a few common criteria for measuring the success of a project using the example of upgrading 500 desktop computers within three months for $300,000:

1. *The project met scope, time, and cost goals.* If all 500 computers were upgraded and met other scope requirements, the work was completed in three months or less, and the cost was $300,000 or less, you could consider it a

successful project based on this criterion. The Standish Group studies used this definition of success. Several people question this simple definition of project success and the methods used for collecting the data. (See the references by Glass on the companion Web site for this text to read more about this debate.)

2. *The project satisfied the customer/sponsor.* Even if the project met initial scope, time, and cost goals, the users of the computers or their managers (the main customers or sponsors in this example) might not be satisfied. Perhaps the project manager or team members never returned calls or were rude. Perhaps users had their daily work disrupted during the upgrades or had to work extra hours due to the upgrades. If the customers were not happy with important aspects of the project, it would be deemed a failure. Conversely, a project might not meet initial scope, time, and cost goals, but the customer could still be very satisfied. Perhaps the project team took longer and spent more money than planned, but they were very polite and helped the users and managers solve several work-related problems. Many organizations implement a customer satisfaction rating system for projects to measure project success instead of only tracking scope, time, and cost performance.
3. *The results of the project met its main objective, such as making or saving a certain amount of money, providing a good return on investment, or simply making the sponsors happy.* Even if the project cost more than estimated, took longer to complete, and the project team was hard to work with, if the users were happy with the upgraded computers it would be a successful project, based on this criterion. As another example, suppose the sponsor really approved the upgrade project to provide a good return on investment by speeding up work and therefore generating more profits. If those goals were met, the sponsor would deem the project a success, regardless of other factors involved.

Why do some IT projects succeed and others fail? Table 1-2 summarizes the results of the 2001 CHAOS study, describing, in order of importance, what factors contribute most to the success of information technology projects. The study lists executive support as the most important factor, overtaking user involvement, which was ranked first in earlier studies. Also note that several other success factors can be strongly influenced by executives such as encouraging user involvement, providing clear business objectives, assigning an experienced project manager, using a standard software infrastructure, and following a formal methodology. Other success factors are related to good project scope and time management such as having a minimized scope, firm basic requirements, and reliable estimates. In fact, experienced project managers, who can often help influence all of these factors to improve the probability of project success, led 97 percent of successful projects.

It is interesting to compare success factors for information technology projects in the U.S. with those in other countries. A 2004 study summarizes the results of a survey of 247 information systems project practitioners in mainland China. One of the study's key findings is that relationship management is viewed as a top success factor for information systems in China, while it is not mentioned in U.S. studies. The study also suggested that having competent team members is less important in China than in the U.S. The Chinese, like the Americans, included top management support, user involvement, and a competent project manager as vital to project success.[15]

TABLE 1-2 What helps projects succeed?

1. Executive support
2. User involvement
3. Experienced project manager
4. Clear business objectives
5. Minimized scope
6. Standard software infrastructure
7. Firm basic requirements
8. Formal methodology
9. Reliable estimates
10. Other criteria, such as small milestones, proper planning, competent staff, and ownership

The Standish Group, "Extreme CHAOS," (2001).

It is also important to look beyond individual project success rates and focus on how organizations as a whole can improve project performance. Research comparing companies that excel in project delivery—the "winners"—from those that do not found four significant best practices. The winners:

1. *Use an integrated toolbox.* Companies that consistently succeed in managing projects clearly define what needs to be done in a project, by whom, when, and how. They use an integrated toolbox, including project management tools, methods, and techniques. They carefully select tools, align them with project and business goals, link them to metrics, and provide them to project managers to deliver positive results.
2. *Grow project leaders.* The winners know that strong project managers—referred to as project leaders—are crucial to project success. They also know that a good project leader needs to be a business leader as well, with strong interpersonal and intrapersonal skills. Companies that excel in project management often grow their project leaders internally, providing them with career opportunities, training, and mentoring.
3. *Develop a streamlined project delivery process.* Winning companies have examined every step in the project delivery process, analyzed fluctuations in workloads, searched for ways to reduce variation, and eliminated bottlenecks to create a repeatable delivery process. All projects go through clear stages and clearly define key milestones. All project leaders use a shared road map, focusing on key business aspects of their projects while integrating goals across all parts of the organization.

4. *Measure project health using metrics.* Companies that excel in project delivery use performance metrics to quantify progress. They focus on a handful of important measurements and apply them to all projects. Metrics often include customer satisfaction, return on investment, and percentage of schedule buffer consumed.[16]

Project managers play an important role in making projects, and therefore organizations, successful. Project managers work with the project sponsors, the project team, and the other stakeholders involved in a project to meet project goals. They also work with the sponsor to define success for that particular project. Good project managers do not assume that their definition of success is the same as the sponsors'. They take the time to understand their sponsors' expectations and then track project performance based on important success criteria.

PROGRAM AND PROJECT PORTFOLIO MANAGEMENT

As mentioned earlier, about one-quarter of the world's gross domestic product is spent on projects. Projects make up a significant portion of work in most business organizations or enterprises, and successfully managing those projects is crucial to enterprise success. Two important concepts that help projects meet enterprise goals are the use of programs and project portfolio management.

Programs

A **program** is "a group of related projects managed in a coordinated way to obtain benefits and control not available from managing them individually."[17] As you can imagine, it is often more economical to group projects together to help streamline management, staffing, purchasing, and other work. The following are examples of common programs in the IT field.

- *Infrastructure:* An IT department often has a program for IT infrastructure projects. Under this program, there could be several projects, such as providing more wireless Internet access, upgrading hardware and software, and developing and maintaining corporate standards for IT.
- *Applications development:* Under this program, there could be several projects, such as updating an enterprise resource planning (ERP) system, purchasing a new off-the-shelf billing system, or developing a new capability for a customer relationship management system.
- *User support:* In addition to the many operational tasks related to user support, many IT departments have several projects to support users. For example, there could be a project to provide a better e-mail system or one to develop technical training for users.

A **program manager** provides leadership and direction for the project managers heading the projects within a program. Program managers also coordinate the efforts of project teams, functional groups, suppliers, and operations staff supporting the projects to ensure that project products and processes are implemented to maximize benefits. Program managers are responsible for more than the delivery of project results; they are change agents responsible for the success of products and processes produced by those projects. For example, the popular video game *Rock Band*™ lists the program manager and team first under the credits section for the game.

Program managers often have review meetings with all their project managers to share important information and coordinate important aspects of each project. Many program managers worked as project managers earlier in their careers, and they enjoy sharing their wisdom and expertise with their project managers. Effective program managers recognize that managing a program is much more complex than managing a single project. They recognize that technical and project management skills are not enough—program managers must also possess strong business knowledge, leadership capabilities, and communication skills.

Project Portfolio Management

In many organizations, project managers also support an emerging business strategy of **project portfolio management** (also called just **portfolio management** in this text), in which organizations group and manage projects and programs as a portfolio of investments that contribute to the entire enterprise's success. Portfolio managers help their organizations make wise investment decisions by helping to select and analyze projects from a strategic perspective. Portfolio managers may or may not have previous experience as project or program managers. It is most important that they have strong financial and analytical skills and understand how projects and programs can contribute to meeting strategic goals.

Figure 1-3 illustrates the differences between project management and project portfolio management. Notice that the main distinction is a focus on meeting tactical or strategic goals. Tactical goals are generally more specific and short-term than strategic goals, which emphasize long-term goals for an organization. Individual projects often address tactical goals, whereas portfolio management addresses strategic goals. Project management addresses questions like "Are we carrying out projects well?", "Are projects on time and budget?", and "Do project stakeholders know what they should be doing?"

Portfolio management addresses questions like "Are we working on the right projects?", "Are we investing in the right areas?", and "Do we have the right resources to be competitive?" Pacific Edge Software's product manager, Eric Burke, defines project portfolio management as "the continuous process of selecting and managing the optimum set of project initiatives that deliver maximum business value."[18]

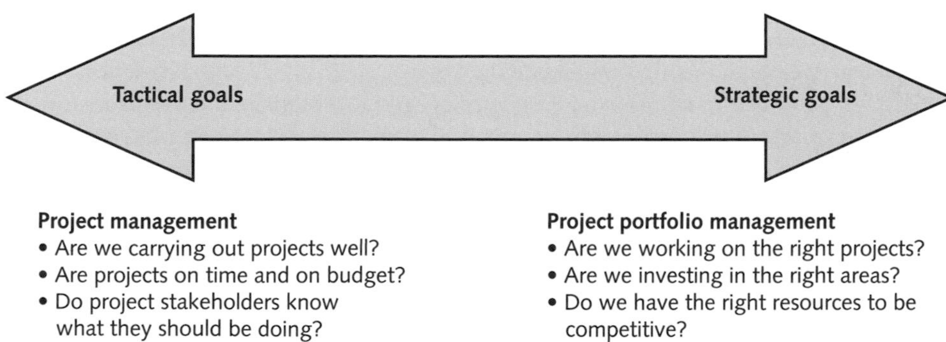
Tactical goals
Strategic goals
Project management
• Are we carrying out projects well?
• Are projects on time and on budget?
• Do project stakeholders know what they should be doing?
Project portfolio management
• Are we working on the right projects?
• Are we investing in the right areas?
• Do we have the right resources to be competitive?

FIGURE 1-3 Project management compared to project portfolio management

Many organizations use a more disciplined approach to portfolio management by developing guidelines and software tools to assist in project portfolio management. The Project Management Institute (described later in this chapter) first published the *Organizational Project Management Maturity Model (OPM3) Knowledge Foundation* in 2003,[19] which describes the importance not only of managing individual projects or programs well, but the importance of following organizational project management to align projects, programs, and portfolios with strategic goals. OPM3 is a standard that organizations can use to measure their organizational project management maturity against a comprehensive set of best practices.

BEST PRACTICE

A **best practice** is "an optimal way recognized by industry to achieve a stated goal or objective."[20] Rosabeth Moss Kanter, a Professor at Harvard Business School and well-known author and consultant, says that visionary leaders know "the best practice secret: Stretching to learn from the best of the best in any sector can make a big vision more likely to succeed."[21] Kanter also emphasizes the need to have measurable standards for best practices. An organization can measure performance against its own past, against peers, and even better, against potential. Kanter suggests that organizations need to continue to reach for higher standards. She suggests the following exercise regime for business leaders who want to adapt best practices in an intelligent way to help their own organizations:

- Reach high. Stretch. Raise standards and aspirations. Find the best of the best and then use it as inspiration for reaching full potential.
- Help everyone in your organization become a professional. Empower people to manage themselves through benchmarks and standards based on best practice exchange.
- Look everywhere. Go far afield. Think of the whole world as your laboratory for learning.

Robert Butrick, author of *The Project Workout,* wrote an article on best practices in project management for the *Ultimate Business Library's Best Practice* book. He suggests that organizations need to follow basic principles of project management, including these two mentioned earlier in this chapter.

- Make sure your projects are driven by your strategy. Be able to demonstrate how each project you undertake fits your business strategy, and screen out unwanted projects as soon as possible.
- Engage your stakeholders. Ignoring stakeholders often leads to project failure. Be sure to engage stakeholders at all stages of a project, and encourage teamwork and commitment at all times.[22]

As you can imagine, project portfolio management is not an easy task. Figure 1-4 illustrates one approach for project portfolio management where one large portfolio exists for the entire organization. This allows top management to view and manage all projects at an enterprise level. Sections of that portfolio are then broken down to improve the management of projects in each sector. For example, a company might have the main

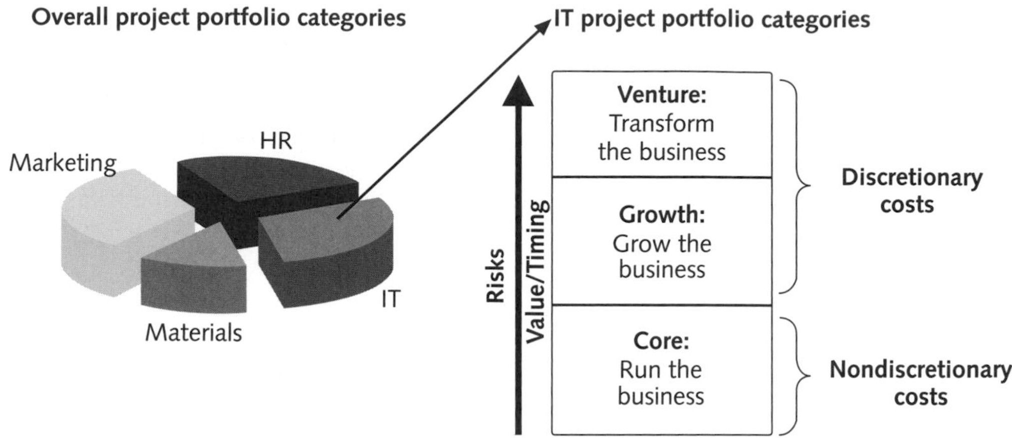

FIGURE 1-4 Sample project portfolio approach

portfolio categories as shown in the left part of Figure 1-4—marketing, materials, IT, and human resources (HR)—and divide each of those categories further to address their unique concerns. The right part of this figure shows how the IT projects could be categorized in more detail to assist in their management. In this example, there are three basic IT project portfolio categories:

- *Venture:* Projects in this category help transform the business. For example, the large retail chain described in the opening case might have an IT project to provide kiosks in stores and similar functionality on the Internet where customers and suppliers could quickly provide feedback on products or services. This project could help transform the business by developing closer partnerships with customers and suppliers.
- *Growth:* Projects in this category would help the company grow in terms of revenues. For example, a company might have an IT project to provide information on their corporate Web site in a new language, such as Chinese or Japanese. This capability could help them grow their business in those countries.
- *Core:* Projects in this category must be accomplished to run the business. For example, an IT project to provide computers for new employees would fall under this category.

Note on the right part of Figure 1-4 that the Core category of IT projects is labeled as nondiscretionary costs. This means that the company has no choice in whether to fund these projects; they must fund them to stay in business. Projects that fall under the Venture or Growth category are discretionary costs because the company can use its own discretion or judgment in deciding whether or not to fund them. Notice the arrow in the center of Figure 1-4 labeled Risks, Value/Timing. This arrow indicates that the risks, value, and timing of projects normally increase as you move from Core to Growth to Venture projects. However, some core projects can also be high risk, have high value, and require good timing. As you can see, many factors are involved in portfolio management.

Many organizations use specialized software to organize and analyze all types of project data into project portfolios. **Enterprise** or **portfolio project management software** integrates information from multiple projects to show the status of active, approved, and future projects across an entire organization. For example, Figure 1-5 provides a sample screen from portfolio management software provided by Planview. The charts and text in the upper half of the screen show the number and percentage of projects in this project portfolio that are on target and in trouble in terms of schedule and cost variance. The bottom half of the screen lists the names of individual projects, percent complete, schedule variance, cost variance, budget variance, and risk percentage. The last section in this chapter provides more information on project management software.

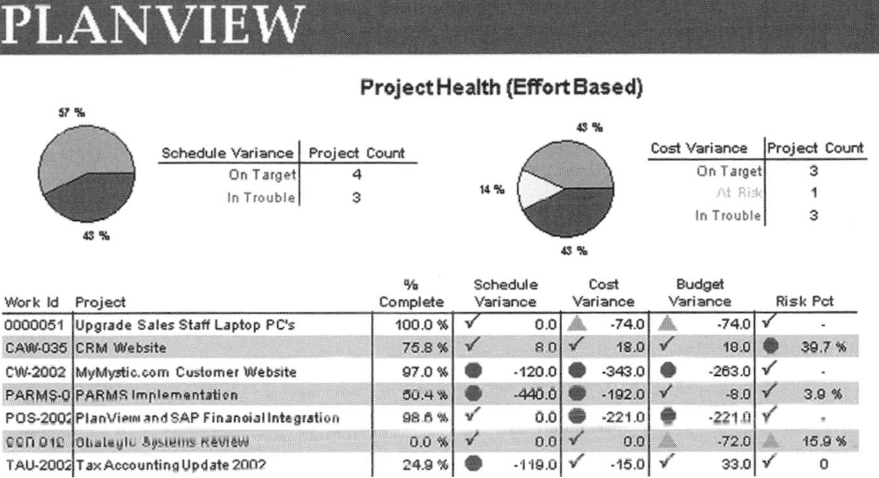

FIGURE 1-5 Sample project portfolio management screen showing project health

THE ROLE OF THE PROJECT MANAGER

You have already read that project managers must work closely with the other stakeholders on a project, especially the sponsor and project team. They are also more effective if they are familiar with the nine project management knowledge areas and the various tools and techniques related to project management. Experienced project managers help projects succeed. But what do project managers do exactly? What skills do they really need to do a good job? The next section provides brief answers to these questions, and the rest of this book gives more insight into the role of the project manager. Even if you never become a project manager, you will probably be part of a project team, and it is important for team members to help their project managers.

Project Manager Job Description

A project manager can have many different job descriptions, which can vary tremendously based on the organization and the project. For example, Monster.com includes thousands of job listings for project managers. They even have a job category for project/program managers. Here are a few edited postings:

- *Project manager for a consulting firm:* Plans, schedules, and controls activities to fulfill identified objectives applying technical, theoretical, and managerial skills to satisfy project requirements. Coordinates and integrates team and individual efforts and builds positive professional relationships with clients and associates.
- *IT project manager for a financial services firm:* Manages, prioritizes, develops, and implements information technology solutions to meet business needs. Prepares and executes project plans using project management software following a standard methodology. Establishes cross-functional end-user teams defining and implementing projects on time and within budget. Acts as a liaison between third-party service providers and end-users to develop and implement technology solutions. Participates in vendor contract development and budget management. Provides post implementation support.
- *IT project manager for a nonprofit consulting firm:* Responsibilities include business analysis, requirements gathering, project planning, budget estimating, development, testing, and implementation. Responsible for working with various resource providers to ensure development is completed in a timely, high-quality, and cost-effective manner.

The job description for a project manager can vary by industry and by organization, but there are similar tasks that most project managers perform regardless of these differences. In fact, project management is a skill needed in every major information technology field, from database administrator to network specialist to technical writer.

Suggested Skills for Project Managers

In an interview with two chief information officers (CIOs), John Oliver of True North Communications, Inc. and George Nassef of *Hotjobs.com*, both men agreed that the most important project management skills seem to depend on the uniqueness of the project and the people involved.[23] Project managers need to have a wide variety of skills and be able to decide which particular skills are more important in different situations. As you can imagine, good project managers should have many skills. *A Guide to the Project Management Body of Knowledge*—the *PMBOK® Guide*—recommends that the project management team understand and use expertise in the following areas:

- The Project Management Body of Knowledge
- Application area knowledge, standards, and regulations
- Project environment knowledge
- General management knowledge and skills
- Soft skills or human relations skills

This chapter introduced the nine project management knowledge areas, as well as some general tools and techniques project managers use. The following section focuses on the IT application area, including skills required in the project environment, general management, and soft skills. Note that the *PMBOK® Guide, Fourth Edition* describes three dimensions of project management competency: project management knowledge and performance competency (knowing about project management and being able to apply that knowledge) as well as personal competency (attitudes and personality characteristics). Consult PMI's Web site at *www.pmi.org* for further information on skills for project managers and PMI's Career Framework for Practitioners.

The project environment differs from organization to organization and project to project, but some skills will help in almost all project environments. These skills include understanding change, and understanding how organizations work within their social, political, and physical environments. Project managers must be comfortable leading and handling change, since most projects introduce changes in organizations and involve changes within the projects themselves. Project managers need to understand the organization in which they work and how that organization develops products and provides services. The skills and behavior needed to manage a project for a Fortune 100 company in the United States may differ greatly from those needed to manage a government project in Poland. Chapter 2, The Project Management and Information Technology Context, provides detailed information on these topics.

Project managers should also possess general management knowledge and skills. They should understand important topics related to financial management, accounting, procurement, sales, marketing, contracts, manufacturing, distribution, logistics, the supply chain, strategic planning, tactical planning, operations management, organizational structures and behavior, personnel administration, compensation, benefits, career paths, and health and safety practices. On some projects, it will be critical for the project manager to have a lot of experience in one or several of these general management areas. On other projects, the project manager can delegate detailed responsibility for some of these areas to a team member, support staff, or even a supplier. Even so, the project manager must be intelligent and experienced enough to know which of these areas are most important and who is qualified to do the work. He or she must also make and/or take responsibility for all key project decisions.

Achieving high performance on projects requires soft skills, otherwise called human relations skills. Some of these soft skills include effective communication, influencing the organization to get things done, leadership, motivation, negotiation, conflict management, and problem solving. Why do project managers need good soft skills? One reason is that to understand, navigate, and meet stakeholders' needs and expectations, project managers need to lead, communicate, negotiate, solve problems, and influence the organization at large. They need to be able to listen actively to what others are saying, help develop new approaches for solving problems, and then persuade others to work toward achieving project goals. Project managers must lead their project teams by providing vision, delegating work, creating an energetic and positive environment, and setting an example of appropriate and effective behavior. Project managers must focus on teamwork skills to employ people effectively. They need to be able to motivate different types of people and develop *esprit de corps* within the project team and with other project stakeholders. Since most projects involve changes and trade-offs between competing goals, it is important for project managers to have strong coping skills as well. It helps project managers maintain their sanity and reduce their stress levels if they cope with criticism and constant change. Project managers must be flexible, creative, and sometimes patient in working toward project goals; they must also be persistent in making project needs known.

Lastly, project managers, especially those managing IT projects, must be able to make effective use of technology as it relates to the specific project. Making effective use of technology often includes special product knowledge or experience with a particular industry.

Project managers must make many decisions and deal with people in a wide variety of disciplines, so it helps tremendously to have a project manager who is confident in using the special tools or technologies that are the most effective in particular settings. Project managers do not normally have to be experts on any specific technology, but they have to know enough to build a strong team and ask the right questions to keep things on track. For example, project managers for large information technology projects do not have to be experts in the field of information technology, but they must have working knowledge of various technologies and understand how the project would enhance the business. Many companies have found that a good business manager can be a very good information technology project manager because they focus on meeting business needs and rely on key project members to handle the technical details.

All project managers should continue to develop their knowledge and experience in project management, general management, soft skills, and the industries they support. Non-IT business people are now very savvy with information technology, but few information technology professionals have spent the time developing their business savvy.[24] IT project managers must be willing to develop more than their technical skills to be productive team members and successful project managers. Everyone, no matter how technical they are, should develop business and soft skills.

Importance of People and Leadership Skills

In a recent study, project management experts from various industries were asked to identify the ten most important skills and competencies for effective project managers. Table 1-3 shows the results.

Respondents were also asked what skills and competencies were most important in various project situations:

- *Large projects:* Leadership, relevant prior experience, planning, people skills, verbal communication, and team-building skills were most important.
- *High uncertainty projects:* Risk management, expectation management, leadership, people skills, and planning skills were most important.
- *Very novel projects:* Leadership, people skills, having vision and goals, self confidence, expectations management, and listening skills were most important.[25]

Notice that a few additional skills and competencies not cited in the top 10 list were mentioned when people thought about the context of a project. To be the most effective, project managers require a changing mix of skills and competencies depending on the project being delivered.

Also notice the general emphasis on people and leadership skills. As mentioned earlier, all project managers, especially those working on technical projects, need to demonstrate leadership and management skills. *Leadership* and *management* are terms often used interchangeably, although there are differences. Generally, a **leader** focuses on long-term goals and big-picture objectives, while inspiring people to reach those goals. A **manager** often deals with the day-to-day details of meeting specific goals. Some people say that, “Managers do things right, and leaders do the right things.” “Leaders determine the vision, and managers achieve the vision.” “You lead people and manage things.”

TABLE 1-3 Ten most important skills and competencies for project managers

1. People skills
2. Leadership
3. Listening
4. Integrity, ethical behavior, consistent
5. Strong at building trust
6. Verbal communication
7. Strong at building teams
8. Conflict resolution, conflict management
9. Critical thinking, problem solving
10. Understands, balances priorities

Jennifer Krahn, "Effective Project Leadership: A Combination of Project Manager Skills and Competencies in Context," *PMI Research Conference Proceedings* (July 2006).

However, project managers often take on the role of both leader and manager. Good project managers know that people make or break projects, so they must set a good example to lead their team to success. They are aware of the greater needs of their stakeholders and organizations, so they are visionary in guiding their current projects and in suggesting future ones. As mentioned earlier, companies that excel in project management grow project "leaders," emphasizing development of business and communication skills. Yet good project managers must also focus on getting the job done by paying attention to the details and daily operations of each task. Instead of thinking of leaders and managers as specific people, it is better to think of people as having leadership skills, such as being visionary and inspiring, and management skills, such as being organized and effective. Therefore, the best project managers have leadership and management characteristics; they are visionary yet focused on the bottom line. Above all else, good project managers focus on achieving positive results!

Careers for Information Technology Project Managers

A recent article suggests that, "The most sought-after corporate IT workers in 2010 may be those with no deep-seated technical skills at all. The nuts-and-bolts programming and easy-to-document support jobs will have all gone to third-party providers in the U.S. or abroad. Instead, IT departments will be populated with 'versatilists'—those with a technology background who also know the business sector inside and out, can architect and carry out IT plans that will add business value, and can cultivate relationships both inside and outside the company."[26]

A recent survey by CIO.com supports this career projection. IT executives listed the skills they predicted would be the most in demand in the next two to five years. Project/

program management came in first place, followed by business process management, business analysis, and application development. Table 1-4 shows these results, as well as the percentage of respondents who listed the skill as most in demand. Even if you choose to stay in a technical role, you still need project management knowledge and skills to help your team and your organization succeed.

TABLE 1-4 Top information technology skills

Skill	Percentage of Respondents
Project/program management	60%
Business process management	55%
Business analysis	53%
Application development	52%
Database management	49%
Security	42%
Enterprise architect	41%
Strategist/internal consultant	40%
Systems analyst	39%
Relationship management	39%
Web services	33%
Help desk/user support	32%
Networking	32%
Web site development	30%
QA/testing	28%
IT finance	28%
Vendor management/ procurement	27%
IT HR	21%
Other	3%

Carolyn Johnson, "2006 Midyear Staffing Updates," *CIO Research Reports*, October 2, 2006.

THE PROJECT MANAGEMENT PROFESSION

The profession of project management is growing at a very rapid pace. To understand this line of work, it is helpful to briefly review the history of project management, introduce you to the Project Management Institute (PMI) and some of its services (such as certification), and discuss the growth in project management software.

History of Project Management

Although people have worked on projects for centuries, most agree that the modern concept of project management began with the Manhattan Project, which the U.S. military led to develop the atomic bomb in World War II. The Manhattan Project involved many people with different skills at several different locations. It also clearly separated the overall management of the project's mission, schedule, and budget under General Leslie R. Groves and the technical management of the project under the lead scientist, Dr. Robert Oppenheimer. The Manhattan Project lasted about three years and cost almost $2 billion in 1946.

In developing the project, the military realized that scientists and other technical specialists often did not have the desire or the necessary skills to manage large projects. For example, after being asked several times for each team member's responsibilities at the new Los Alamos laboratory in 1943, Dr. Oppenheimer tossed a piece of paper with an organization chart on it at his director and said, "Here's your damn organization chart."[27] Project management was recognized as a distinct discipline requiring people with special skills and, more importantly, the desire to lead project teams.

In 1917, Henry Gantt developed the famous Gantt chart for scheduling work in factories. A **Gantt chart** is a standard format for displaying project schedule information by listing project activities and their corresponding start and finish dates in a calendar format. Initially, managers drew Gantt charts by hand to show project tasks and schedule information, and this tool provided a standard format for planning and reviewing all the work on early military projects.

Today's project managers still use the Gantt chart as the primary tool to communicate project schedule information, but with the aid of computers, it is no longer necessary to draw the charts by hand and they can be more easily shared and disseminated to project stakeholders. Figure 1-6 displays a Gantt chart created with Microsoft Project, the most widely used project management software today. You will learn more about using Project 2007 in Appendix A.

During the Cold War years of the 1950s and '60s, the military continued to be key in refining several project management techniques. Members of the U.S. Navy Polaris missile/submarine project first used network diagrams in 1958. These diagrams helped managers model the relationships among project tasks, which allowed them to create schedules that were more realistic. Figure 1-7 displays a network diagram created using Microsoft Project. Note that the diagram includes arrows that show which tasks are related and the sequence in which team members must perform the tasks. The concept of determining relationships among tasks is essential in helping to improve project scheduling. This concept allows you to find and monitor the **critical path**—the longest path through a network diagram that determines the earliest completion of a project. You will learn more about Gantt charts, network diagrams, critical path analysis, and other time management concepts in Chapter 6, Project Time Management.

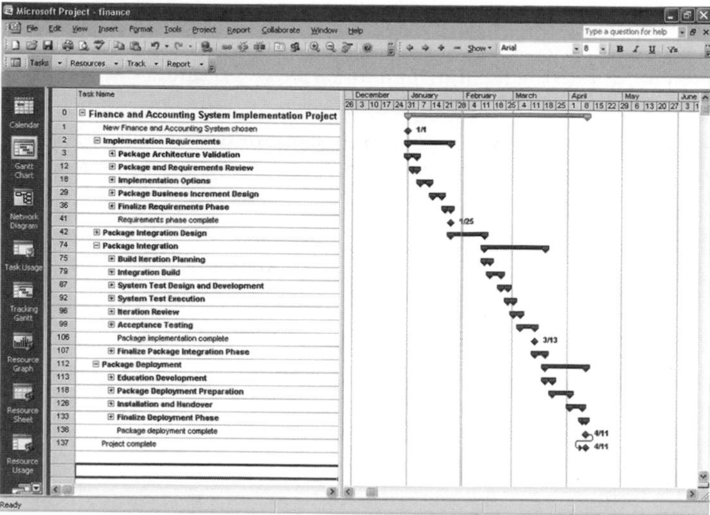

FIGURE 1-6 Sample Gantt chart created with Project 2007

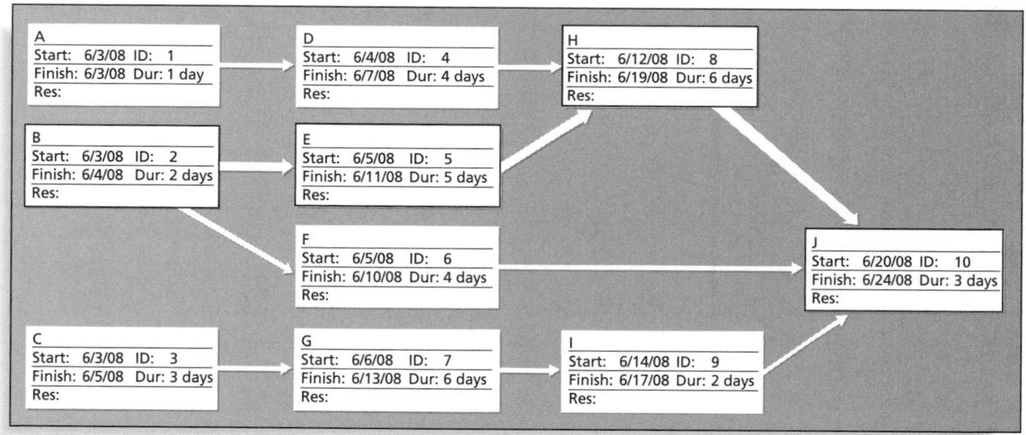

FIGURE 1-7 Sample network diagram in Microsoft Project

By the 1970s, the U.S. military and its civilian suppliers developed software to assist in managing large projects. Early project management software was very expensive to purchase and it ran exclusively on mainframe computers. For example, Artemis was an early project management software product that helped managers analyze complex schedules for designing aircraft. A full-time employee was often required to run the complicated software, and expensive pen plotters were used to draw network diagrams and Gantt charts.

As computer hardware became smaller and more affordable and software included graphical, easy-to-use interfaces, project management software became less expensive and more widely used. This made it possible—and affordable—for many industries worldwide to use project management software on all types and sizes of projects. New software makes basic tools, such as Gantt charts and network diagrams, inexpensive, easy to create, and available for anyone to update. See the section in this chapter on project management software for more information.

In the 1990s, many companies began creating project management offices to help them handle the increasing number and complexity of projects. A **Project Management Office (PMO)** is an organizational group responsible for coordinating the project management function throughout an organization. There are different ways to structure a PMO, and they can have various roles and responsibilities. Below are possible goals of a PMO:

- Collect, organize, and integrate project data for the entire organization.
- Develop and maintain templates for project documents.
- Develop or coordinate training in various project management topics.
- Develop and provide a formal career path for project managers.
- Provide project management consulting services.
- Provide a structure to house project managers while they are acting in those roles or are between projects.

By the end of the twentieth century, people in virtually every industry around the globe began to investigate and apply different aspects of project management to their projects. The sophistication and effectiveness with which project management tools are being applied and used today is influencing the way companies do business, use resources, and respond to market requirements with speed and accuracy. As mentioned earlier in this chapter, many organizations are now using enterprise or project portfolio management software to help manage portfolios of projects.

Many colleges, universities, and companies around the world now offer courses related to various aspects of project management. You can even earn bachelor's, master's, and doctoral degrees in project management. PMI reported in 2008 that of the 280 institutions it has identified that offer degrees in project management, 103 are in mainland China. "When Western companies come into China they are more likely to hire individuals who have PMP certification as an additional verification of their skills. In our salary survey, the salary difference in IT, for example, was dramatic. A person with certification could make five to six times as much salary, so there is terrific incentive to get certified and work for these Western companies."[28]

The problems in managing projects, the publicity about project management, and the belief that it really can make a difference continue to contribute to the growth of this field.

The Project Management Institute

Although many professional societies suffer from declining membership, the **Project Management Institute (PMI)**, an international professional society for project managers founded in 1969, has continued to attract and retain members, reporting 277,221 members worldwide by August 31, 2008. A large percentage of PMI members work in the information technology field and more than 13,000 pay additional dues to join the Information Systems Specific Interest Group. Because there are so many people working on projects in various industries, PMI has created specific interest groups (SIGs) that enable members to share ideas about project management in their particular application areas, such as information systems. PMI also has SIGs for aerospace/defense, financial services, healthcare, hospitality management, manufacturing, new product development, retail, and urban development, to name a few. Note that there are also other project management professional societies. See the companion Web site for more information.

PMI STUDENT MEMBERSHIP

As a student, you can join PMI for a reduced fee. Consult PMI's Web site (*www.pmi.org*) for more information. You can also network with other students studying project management by joining the Students of Project Management Specific Interest Group (SIG) at *www.studentsofpm.org*. Note that PMI is changing the SIGs into Virtual Communities, so you may see that term used.

Project Management Certification

Professional certification is an important factor in recognizing and ensuring quality in a profession. PMI provides certification as a **Project Management Professional (PMP)**—someone who has documented sufficient project experience and education, agreed to follow the PMI code of professional conduct, and demonstrated knowledge of the field of project management by passing a comprehensive examination. Appendix B provides more information on PMP certification as well as other certification programs, such as CompTIA's Project+ certification.

The number of people earning PMP certification continues to increase. In 1993, there were about 1,000 certified project management professionals. By December 31, 2008, there were 318,289 active PMPs.[29] Figure 1-8 shows the rapid growth in the number of people earning project management professional certification from 1993 to 2008.

Several studies show that organizations supporting technical certification programs tend to operate in more complex information technology environments and are more

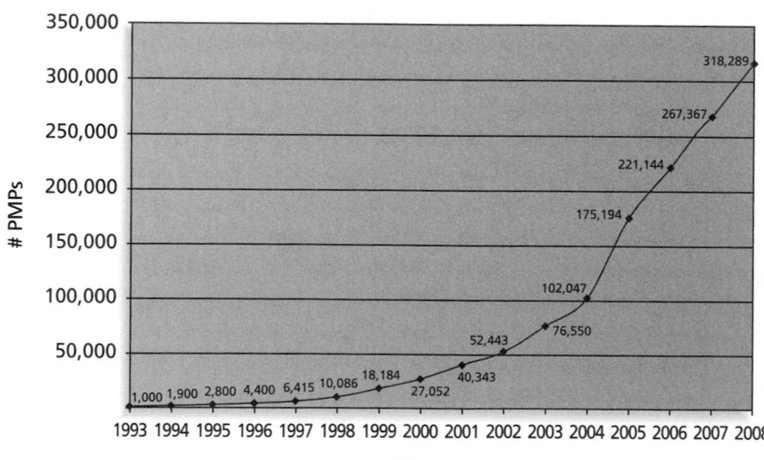

FIGURE 1-8 Growth in PMP Certification, 1993–2008

efficient than companies that do not support certification. Likewise, organizations that support PMP certification see the value of investing in programs to improve their employees' knowledge in project management. Many employers today require specific certifications to ensure their workers have current skills, and job seekers find that they often have an advantage when they earn and maintain marketable certifications. A 2006 *Certification Magazine* survey of over 35,000 IT workers from 197 countries found that average salaries for workers in project management were among the highest for all IT specialties. IT workers with a PMP certification earned among the highest salaries for all IT workers who hold professional certifications.[30]

As information technology projects become more complex and global in nature, the need for people with demonstrated knowledge and skills in project management will continue. Just as passing the CPA exam is a standard for accountants, passing the PMP exam is becoming a standard for project managers. Some companies require that all project managers be PMP certified. Project management certification is also enabling professionals in the field to share a common base of knowledge. For example, any person with PMP certification can list, describe, and use the nine project management knowledge areas. Sharing a common base of knowledge is important because it helps advance the theory and practice of project management. PMI also offers additional certifications, including new ones in scheduling, risk, and program management. See Appendix B of this text for detailed information on certification.

Ethics in Project Management

Ethics, loosely defined, is a set of principles that guide our decision making based on personal values of what is "right" and "wrong." Making ethical decisions is an important part of our personal and professional lives because it generates trust and respect with other people. Project managers often face ethical dilemmas. For example, several projects involve different payment methods. If a project manager can make more money by doing a job poorly, should he or she do the job poorly? No! If a project manager is personally opposed to the development of nuclear weapons, should he or she refuse to manage a project that helps produce them? Yes! Ethics guide us in making these types of decisions.

PMI approved a new Code of Ethics and Professional Conduct effective January 1, 2007. This new code applies not only to PMPs, but to all PMI members and individuals who hold a PMI certification, apply for a PMI certification, or serve PMI in a volunteer capacity. It is vital for project management practitioners to conduct their work in an ethical manner. Even if you are not affiliated with PMI, these guidelines can help you conduct your work in an ethical manner, which helps the profession earn the confidence of the public, employers, employees, and all project stakeholders. The PMI Code of Ethics and Professional Conduct includes short chapters addressing vision and applicability, responsibility, respect, fairness, and honestly. A few excerpts from this document include the following:

"As practitioners in the global project management community:

2.2.1 We make decisions and take actions based on the best interests of society, public safety, and the environment.

2.2.2 We accept only those assignment that are consistent with our background, experience, skills, and qualifications.

2.2.3 We fulfill the commitments that we undertake—we do what we say we will do.

3.2.1 We inform ourselves about the norms and customs of others and avoid engaging in behaviors they might consider disrespectful.

3.2.2 We listen to others' points of view, seeking to understand them.

3.2.3 We approach directly those persons with whom we have a conflict or disagreement.

4.2.1 We demonstrate transparency in our decision-making process.

4.2.2 We constantly reexamine our impartiality and objectivity, taking corrective action as appropriate.

4.3.1 We proactively and fully disclose any real or potential conflicts of interest to appropriate stakeholders.

5.2.1 We earnestly seek to understand the truth.

5.2.2 We are truthful in our communications and in our conduct."[31]

In addition, PMI added a new series of questions to the PMP certification exam in March 2002 to emphasize the importance of ethics and professional responsibility. See Appendix B for information on the PMP exam.

Project Management Software

Unlike the cobbler neglecting to make shoes for his own children, the project management and software development communities have definitely responded to the need to provide more software to assist in managing projects. The Project Management Center, a Web site for people involved in project management, provides an alphabetical directory of more than 300 project management software solutions (*www.infogoal.com/pmc*). This site and others demonstrate the growth in available project management software products, especially Web-based tools. Deciding which project management software to use has become a project in itself. This section provides a summary of the basic types of project management software available and references for finding more information. In Appendix A, you will learn how to use Microsoft Project 2007, the most widely used project management software tool today.

MICROSOFT PROJECT 2007

Appendix A includes a *Guide to Using Microsoft Project 2007,* which will help you develop hands-on skills using this most popular project management software tool. You can also access a trial version of VPMi Express—a Web-based product from VCS (*www.vcsonline.com*)—by following the information provided on the resources page in the front of this text or by going directly to the VCS Web site.

Many people still use basic productivity software such as Microsoft Word and Excel to perform many project management functions, including determining project scope, time, and cost, assigning resources, preparing project documentation, and so on. People often use productivity software instead of specialized project management software because they already have it and know how to use it. However, there are hundreds of project management software tools that provide specific functionality for managing projects. These project management software tools can be divided into three general categories based on functionality and price:

- *Low-end tools:* These tools provide basic project management features and generally cost less than $200 per user. They are often recommended for small projects and single users. Most of these tools allow users to create Gantt charts, which cannot be done easily using current productivity software. Top Ten Reviews listed MinuteMan ($49.95) and Project Kickstart ($199.95) in their list of top 10 project management software tools for 2008.[32] Basecamp (*www.basecamphq.com*) is another popular tool with low-end through high-end versions ranging in price from $24 to $149 per month. Several companies provide add-in features to Excel (see *www.business-spreadsheets.com*) to provide basic project management functions using a familiar software product.
- *Midrange tools:* A step up from low-end tools, midrange tools are designed to handle larger projects, multiple users, and multiple projects. All of these tools can produce Gantt charts and network diagrams, and can assist in critical path analysis, resource allocation, project tracking, status reporting, and so on. Prices range from about $200 to $600 per user, and several tools require additional server software for using workgroup features. Microsoft Project is still the most widely used project management software today in this category, and there is also an enterprise version, as described briefly below and in Appendix A. In the summer of 2008, Top Ten Reviews listed Microsoft Project as the number one choice ($599), along with Milestones ($249). A product called Copper also made the top ten list, with a price of $999 for up to 50 users. As noted earlier, this text includes a trial version of Project 2007 as well as one of VPMi Express, a totally Web-based tool. Note that students and educators can purchase software like Microsoft Project 2007 at reduced prices from sites like *www.journeyed.com* ($59.98 for Project 2007 Standard in October 2008), and anyone can download a trial version from Microsoft's Web site. Many other suppliers also provide trial versions of their products.
- *High-end tools:* Another category of project management software is high-end tools, sometimes referred to as enterprise project management software. These tools provide robust capabilities to handle very large projects, dispersed workgroups, and enterprise and portfolio management functions that summarize and combine individual project information to provide an enterprise view of all projects. These products are generally licensed on a per-user basis, integrate with enterprise database management software, and are accessible via the Internet. In mid-2002, Microsoft introduced the first version of their Enterprise Project Management software, and in 2003, they introduced the Microsoft Enterprise Project Management solution, which was updated in 2007 to include Microsoft Office Project Server 2007 and Microsoft Office Project Portfolio Server 2007A. Several inexpensive, Web-based products that provide enterprise and portfolio management capabilities are also on the market. For example, VPMi Enterprise Online (*www.vcsonline.com*) is available for a low monthly fee per user (see the front cover of this text for free trial information). See the Project Management Center Web site (*www.infogoal.com/pmc*) or Top Ten Reviews

(*http://project-management-software-review.toptenreviews.com*) for links to many companies that provide project management software.

There are also several free or open-source tools available. For example, Open Workbench (*www.openworkbench.org*), dotProject (*www.dotproject.net*), and TaskJuggler (*www.taskjuggler.org*) are all free online project management tools. Remember, however, that these tools are developed, managed, and maintained by volunteers. They also often run on limited platforms and may not be well supported.

As mentioned earlier, there are many reasons to study project management, particularly as it relates to information technology projects. The number of information technology projects continues to grow, the complexity of these projects continues to increase, and the profession of project management continues to expand and mature. As more people study and work in this important field, the success rate of information technology projects should improve.

CASE WRAP-UP

Anne Roberts worked with the VPs and the CEO to form teams to help identify potential IT projects that would support their business strategies. They formed a project team to implement a project portfolio management software tool across the organization. They formed another team to develop project-based reward systems for all employees. They also authorized funds for a project to educate all employees in project management, to help people earn PMP and related certifications, and to develop a mentoring program. Anne had successfully convinced everyone that effectively managing projects was crucial to their company's future.

Chapter Summary

There is a new or renewed interest in project management today as the number of projects continues to grow and their complexity continues to increase. The success rate of information technology projects has more than doubled since 1995, but still only about a third are successful in meeting scope, time, and cost goals. Using a more disciplined approach to managing projects can help projects and organizations succeed.

A project is a temporary endeavor undertaken to create a unique product, service, or result. An information technology project involves the use of hardware, software, and/or networks. Projects are unique, temporary, and developed incrementally; they require resources, have a sponsor, and involve uncertainty. The triple constraint of project management refers to managing the scope, time, and cost dimensions of a project.

Project management is the application of knowledge, skills, tools, and techniques to project activities to meet project requirements. Stakeholders are the people involved in or affected by project activities. A framework for project management includes the project stakeholders, project management knowledge areas, and project management tools and techniques. The nine knowledge areas are project integration management, scope, time, cost, quality, human resource, communications, risk, and procurement management. There are many tools and techniques in each knowledge area. There are different ways to define project success, and project managers must understand the success criteria for their unique projects.

A program is a group of related projects managed in a coordinated way to obtain benefits and control not available from managing them individually. Project portfolio management involves organizing and managing projects and programs as a portfolio of investments that contribute to theentire enterprise's success. Portfolio management emphasizes meeting strategic goals while project management focuses on tactical goals. Studies show that executive support is crucial to project success, as are other factors like user involvement, an experienced project manager, and clear business objectives.

Project managers play a key role in helping projects and organizations succeed. They must perform various job duties, possess many skills, and continue to develop skills in project management, general management, and their application area, such as information technology. Soft skills, especially leadership, are particularly important for project managers.

The profession of project management continues to grow and mature. In the U.S., the military took the lead in project management and developed many tools such as Gantt charts and network diagrams, but today people use project management in virtually every industry around the globe. The Project Management Institute (PMI) is an international professional society that provides certification as a Project Management Professional (PMP) and upholds a code of ethics. Today, hundreds of project management software products are available to assist people in managing projects.

Quick Quiz

1. Approximately what percentage of the world's gross domestic product is spent on projects?
    a. 10 percent
    b. 25 percent
    c. 50 percent
    d. 75 percent

2. Which of the following is a not a potential advantage of using good project management?
   a. Shorter development times
   b. Higher worker morale
   c. Lower cost of capital
   d. Higher profit margins
3. A ______ is a temporary endeavor undertaken to create a unique product, service, or result.
   a. program
   b. process
   c. project
   d. portfolio
4. Which of the following is not an attribute of a project?
   a. projects are unique
   b. projects are developed using progressive elaboration
   c. projects have a primary customer or sponsor
   d. projects involve little uncertainty
5. Which of the following is not part of the triple constraint of project management?
   a. meeting scope goals
   b. meeting time goals
   c. meeting communications goals
   d. meeting cost goals

6. ______ is the application of knowledge, skills, tools and techniques to project activities to meet project requirements.
   a. Project management
   b. Program management
   c. Project portfolio management
   d. Requirements management
7. Project portfolio management addresses ______ goals of an organization, while project management addresses ______ goals.
   a. strategic, tactical
   b. tactical, strategic
   c. internal, external
   d. external, internal

8. Several application development projects done for the same functional group might best be managed as part of a ______.
   a. portfolio
   b. program
   c. investment
   d. collaborative
9. Which of the following is not one of the top ten skills or competencies of an effective project manager?
   a. people skills
   b. leadership
   c. integrity
   d. technical skills
10. What is the certification program called that the Project Management Institute provides?
   a. Certified Project Manager (CPM)
   b. Project Management Professional (PMP)
   c. Project Management Expert (PME)
   d. Project Management Mentor (PMM)

Quick Quiz Answers

1. b; 2. c; 3. c; 4. d; 5. c; 6. a; 7. a; 8. b; 9. d; 10. b

Discussion Questions

1. Why is there a new or renewed interest in the field of project management?
2. What is a project, and what are its main attributes? How is a project different from what most people do in their day-to-day jobs? What is the triple constraint?
3. What is project management? Briefly describe the project management framework, providing examples of stakeholders, knowledge areas, tools and techniques, and project success factors.
4. What is a program? What is a project portfolio? Discuss the relationship between projects, programs, and portfolio management and the contributions they each make to enterprise success.
5. What is the role of the project manager? What are suggested skills for all project managers and for information technology project managers? Why is leadership so important for project managers? How is the job market for information technology project managers?
6. Briefly describe some key events in the history of project management. What role does the Project Management Institute and other professional societies play in helping the profession?
7. What functions can you perform with project management software? What are some popular names of low-end, midrange, and high-end project management tools?

Exercises

1. Visit the Standish Group's Web site at *www.standishgroup.com*. Read one of the CHAOS articles, and also read at least one report or article that questions the findings of the CHAOS studies. See the Suggested Readings by Robert L. Glass on the companion Web site for references. Write a two-page summary of the reports, key conclusions, and your opinion of them.
2. Find someone who works as a project manager or someone who works on projects, such as a worker in your school's IT department or the president of a social club. Prepare several interview questions to learn more about projects and project management, and then ask them your questions in person, through e-mail, or over the phone. Write a two-page summary of your findings. Guidelines for your interview and sample questions are available on the companion Web site.
3. Search the Internet for the terms *project management, project management careers, project portfolio management,* and *information technology project management.* Write down the number of hits that you received for each of these phrases. Find at least three Web sites that provide interesting information on one of the topics. Write a two-page paper summarizing key information about these three Web sites as well as the Project Management Institute's Web site (*www.pmi.org*).
4. Find any example of a real project with a real project manager. Feel free to use projects in the media (the Olympics, television shows, movies, etc.) or a project from your work, if applicable. Write a two-page paper describing the project in terms of its scope, time, and cost goals. Discuss what went right and wrong on the project and the role of the project manager and sponsor. Also describe if the project was a success or not and why. Include at least one reference and cite it on the last page.
5. Skim through Appendix A on Microsoft Project 2007. Review information about Project 2007 from Microsoft's Web site (*www.microsoft.com/project*) and information about VPMi Express from *www.vcsonline.com*. Also, visit The Project Management Center (*www.infogoal.com/pmc*) and Top Ten Reviews (*http://project-management-software-review.toptenreviews.com*). Research two project management software tools besides Project 2007. Write a two-page paper answering the following questions:
    a. What functions does project management software provide that you cannot do easily using other tools such as a spreadsheet or database?
    b. How do the different tools you reviewed compare, based on cost of the tool, key features, and other relevant criteria?
    c. How can organizations justify investing in enterprise or portfolio project management software?
6. Research information about PMP and related certifications. Skim through Appendix B for information and find at least two articles on this topic. What are benefits of certification in general? Do you think it is worthwhile for most project managers to get certified? Is it something you would consider? Write a two-page paper summarizing your findings and opinions.

Companion Web Site

Visit the companion Web site for this text at *www.cengage.com/mis/schwalbe* to access:

- References cited in the text and additional suggested readings for each chapter
- Template files
- Lecture notes
- Interactive quizzes
- Podcasts
- Links to general project management Web sites
- And more

See the Preface of this text for additional information on accessing the companion Web site.

Key Terms

best practice — An optimal way recognized by industry to achieve a stated goal or objective

critical path — The longest path through a network diagram that determines the earliest completion of a project

enterprise project management software — Software that integrates information from multiple projects to show the status of active, approved, and future projects across an entire organization; also called portfolio project management software

ethics — A set of principles that guide our decision making based on personal values of what is "right" and "wrong"

Gantt chart — A standard format for displaying project schedule information by listing project activities and their corresponding start and finish dates in a calendar format

green IT or **green computing** — Developing and using computer resources in an efficient way to improve economic viability, social responsibility, and environmental impact

leader — A person who focuses on long-term goals and big-picture objectives, while inspiring people to reach those goals

manager — A person who deals with the day-to-day details of meeting specific goals

portfolio project management software — Software that integrates information from multiple projects to show the status of active, approved, and future projects across an entire organization; also called enterprise project management software

program — A group of projects managed in a coordinated way to obtain benefits and control not available from managing them individually

program manager — A person who provides leadership and direction for the project managers heading the projects within a program

project — A temporary endeavor undertaken to create a unique product, service, or result

project management — The application of knowledge, skills, tools, and techniques to project activities to meet project requirements

Project Management Institute (PMI) — An international professional society for project managers

project management knowledge areas — Project integration management, scope, time, cost, quality, human resource, communications, risk, and procurement management

Project Management Office (PMO) — An organizational group responsible for coordinating the project management functions throughout an organization

Project Management Professional (PMP) — Certification provided by PMI that requires documenting project experience and education, agreeing to follow the PMI code of ethics, and passing a comprehensive exam

project management tools and techniques — Methods available to assist project managers and their teams; some popular tools in the time management knowledge area include Gantt charts, network diagrams, and critical path analysis

project manager — The person responsible for working with the project sponsor, the project team, and the other people involved in a project to meet project goals

project portfolio management or **portfolio management —** When organizations group and manage projects as a portfolio of investments that contribute to the entire enterprise's success

project sponsor — The person who provides the direction and funding for a project

stakeholders — People involved in or affected by project activities

triple constraint — Balancing scope, time, and cost goals

virtualization — Hiding the physical characteristics of computing resources from their users, such as making a single server, operating system, application, or storage device appear to function as multiple virtual resources

End Notes

1 Andrew H. Bartels, "Teleconference: Global IT 2008 Market Forecast," *Forrester Research* (February 11, 2008).

2 Eric Chabrow, "Computer Jobs Hit Record High," *CIO Insight* (July 7, 2008).

3 Project Management Institute, *Project Management Salary Survey*, Fifth Edition, 2007.

4 Project Management Institute, *PMI Today*, October 2006 and June 2008.

5 Standish Group, "The CHAOS Report" (*www.standishgroup.com*) (1995). Another reference is Jim Johnson, "CHAOS: The Dollar Drain of IT Project Failures," *Application Development Trends* (January 1995).

6 PricewaterhouseCoopers, "Boosting Business Performance through Programme and Project Management" (June 2004).

7 Project Management Institute, *A Guide to the Project Management Body of Knowledge (PMBOK® Guide)*, Fourth Edition (2008).

8 Gartner, Inc. "Gartner Identifies the Top 10 Strategic Technologies for 2008," *Gartner Symposium/ITxpo* (October 9, 2007).

9 Nicholas G. Carr, *Does IT Matter?* (Harvard Business School Press, 2004).

10 "Where I.T. Matters: How 10 Technologies Transformed 10 Industries," *Baseline* (October 2, 2006).

11 Project Management Institute, Inc., *A Guide to the Project Management Body of Knowledge* (*PMBOK® Guide*), Fourth Edition (2008).

[12] Claude Besner and Brian Hobbs, "The Perceived Value and Potential Contribution of Project Management Practices to Project Success," *PMI Research Conference Proceedings* (July 2006).

[13] Jim Johnson, "CHAOS 2006 Research Project," *CHAOS Activity News*, 2:no. 1 (2007).

[14] Standish Group, "CHAOS 2001: A Recipe for Success" (2001).

[15] Chang Dong, K.B. Chuah, and Li Zhai, "A Study of Critical Success Factor of Information System Projects in China," *Proceedings of PMI Research Conference* (2004).

[16] Dragan Milosevic and And Ozbay, "Delivering Projects: What the Winners Do," *Proceedings of the Project Management Institute Annual Seminars & Symposium* (November 2001).

[17] Project Management Institute, *A Guide to the Project Management Body of Knowledge* (*PMBOK® Guide*), Fourth Edition (2008).

[18] Eric Burke, "Project Portfolio Management," *PMI Houston Chapter Meeting* (July 10, 2002).

[19] Project Management Institute, *Organizational Project Management Maturity Model (OPM3) Knowledge Foundation* (2003).

[20] Ibid., p. 13.

[21] Ultimate Business Library, *Best Practice: Ideas and Insights from the World's Foremost Business Thinkers* (New York: Perseus 2003), p. 1.

[22] Ibid., p. 8.

[23] Mary Brandel, "The Perfect Project Manager," *ComputerWorld* (August 6, 2001).

[24] Lauren Thomsen-Moore, "No 'soft skills' for us, we're techies," *ComputerWorld* (December 16, 2002)

[25] Jennifer Krahn, "Effective Project Leadership: A Combination of Project Manager Skills and Competencies in Context," *PMI Research Conference Proceedings* (July 2006).

[26] Stacy Collett, "Hot Skills: Cold Skills," *ComputerWorld* (July 17, 2006).

[27] Regents of the University of California, Manhattan Project History, "Here's Your Damned Organization Chart," (1998–2001).

[28] Venessa Wong, "PMI On Specialization and Globalization," *Projects@Work* (June 23, 2008)

[29] Project Management Institute, "PMI Today," (February 2009).

[30] Project Management Institute, "PMI Community Post," (February 9, 2007).

[31] Project Management Institute, "PMI Today," (December 2006), p. 12–13.

[32] Top Ten Reviews, "2006 Project Management Report," *http://project-management-software-review.toptenreviews.com*, (accessed September 10, 2008).

CHAPTER 2

THE PROJECT MANAGEMENT AND INFORMATION TECHNOLOGY CONTEXT

LEARNING OBJECTIVES

After reading this chapter, you will be able to:

- Describe the systems view of project management and how it applies to information technology projects
- Understand organizations, including the four frames, organizational structures, and organizational culture
- Explain why stakeholder management and top management commitment are critical for a project's success
- Understand the concept of a project phase and the project life cycle and distinguish between project development and product development
- Discuss the unique attributes and diverse nature of information technology projects
- Describe recent trends affecting IT project management, including globalization, outsourcing, and virtual teams

OPENING CASE

Tom Walters recently accepted a new position at his college as the Director of Information Technology. Tom had been a respected faculty member at the college for the past 15 years. The college—a small, private institution in the Southwest—offered a variety of programs in the liberal arts and professional areas. Enrollment included 1,500 full-time traditional students and about 1,000 working-adult students attending evening programs. Many instructors supplemented their courses with information on the Internet and course Web sites, but they did not offer any distance-learning programs. The college's niche was serving students in that region who liked the setting of a small liberal arts college.

Like other institutions of higher learning, the use of information technology at the college had grown tremendously in the past 10 years. There were a few classrooms on campus with computers for the instructors and students, and a few more with just instructor stations and projection systems. Tom knew that several colleges throughout the country required that all students lease laptops and that these colleges incorporated technology components into most courses. This idea fascinated him. He and two other members of the Information Technology department visited a local college that had required all students to lease laptops for the past three years, and they were very impressed with what they saw and heard. Tom and his staff developed plans to start requiring students to lease laptops at their college the next year.

Tom sent an e-mail to all faculty and staff in September, which briefly described this and other plans. He did not get much response, however, until the February faculty meeting when, as he described some of the details of his plan, the chairs of the History, English, Philosophy, and Economics departments all voiced their opposition to the idea. They eloquently stated that the college was not a technical training school, and they thought the idea was ludicrous. Members of the Computer Science department voiced their concern that almost all of their students already had state-of-the art laptops and would not want to pay a mandatory fee to lease less-powerful ones. The director of the adult education program expressed her concern that many adult-education students would balk at an increase in fees. Tom was in shock to hear his colleagues' responses, especially after he and his staff had spent a lot of time planning details of how to implement laptops at their campus. Now what should he do?

Many of the theories and concepts of project management are not difficult to understand. What *is* difficult is implementing them in various environments. Project managers must consider many different issues when managing projects. Just as each project is unique, so is its environment. This chapter discusses some of the components involved in understanding the project environment, such as using a systems approach, understanding organizations, managing stakeholders, matching product life cycles to the project environment, understanding the context of information technology projects, and reviewing recent trends affecting IT project management.

A SYSTEMS VIEW OF PROJECT MANAGEMENT

Even though projects are temporary and intended to provide a unique product or service, you cannot run projects in isolation. If project managers lead projects in isolation, it is unlikely that those projects will ever truly serve the needs of the organization. Therefore, projects must operate in a broad organizational environment, and project managers need to consider projects within the greater organizational context. To handle complex situations effectively, project managers need to take a holistic view of a project and understand how it relates to the larger organization. **Systems thinking** describes this holistic view of carrying out projects within the context of the organization.

What Is a Systems Approach?

The term **systems approach** emerged in the 1950s to describe a holistic and analytical approach to solving complex problems that includes using a systems philosophy, systems analysis, and systems management. A **systems philosophy** is an overall model for thinking about things as systems. **Systems** are sets of interacting components working within an environment to fulfill some purpose. For example, the human body is a system composed of many subsystems—the nervous system, the skeletal system, the circulatory system, the digestive system, and so on. **Systems analysis** is a problem-solving approach that requires defining the scope of the system, dividing it into its components, and then identifying and evaluating its problems, opportunities, constraints, and needs. Once this is completed, the systems analyst then examines alternative solutions for improving the current situation, identifies an optimum, or at least satisfactory, solution or action plan, and examines that plan against the entire system. **Systems management** addresses the business, technological, and organizational issues associated with creating, maintaining, and making changes to a system.

Using a systems approach is critical to successful project management. Top management and project managers must follow a systems philosophy to understand how projects relate to the whole organization. They must use systems analysis to address needs with a problem-solving approach. They must use systems management to identify key business, technological, and organizational issues related to each project in order to identify and satisfy key stakeholders and do what is best for the entire organization.

In the opening case, when Tom Walters planned the laptop project, he did not use a systems approach. Members of his IT department did all of the planning. Even though Tom sent an e-mail describing the laptop project to all faculty and staff, he did not address many of the organizational issues involved in such a complex project. Most faculty and staff are very busy at the beginning of fall term and many may not have read the entire message. Others may have been too busy to communicate their concerns to the Information Technology department. Tom was unaware of the effects the laptop project would have on other parts of the college. He did not clearly define the business, technological, and organizational issues associated with the project. Tom and the Information Technology department began work on the laptop project in isolation. If they had taken a systems approach, considering other dimensions of the project, and involving key stakeholders, they could have identified and addressed many of the issues raised at the February faculty meeting *before* the meeting.

The Three-Sphere Model for Systems Management

Many business and information technology students understand the concepts of systems and performing a systems analysis. However, they often gloss over the topic of systems management. The simple idea of addressing the three spheres of systems management—business, organization, and technology—can have a huge impact on selecting and managing projects successfully.

Figure 2-1 provides a sample of some of the business, organizational, and technological issues that could be factors in the laptop project. In this case, technological issues, though

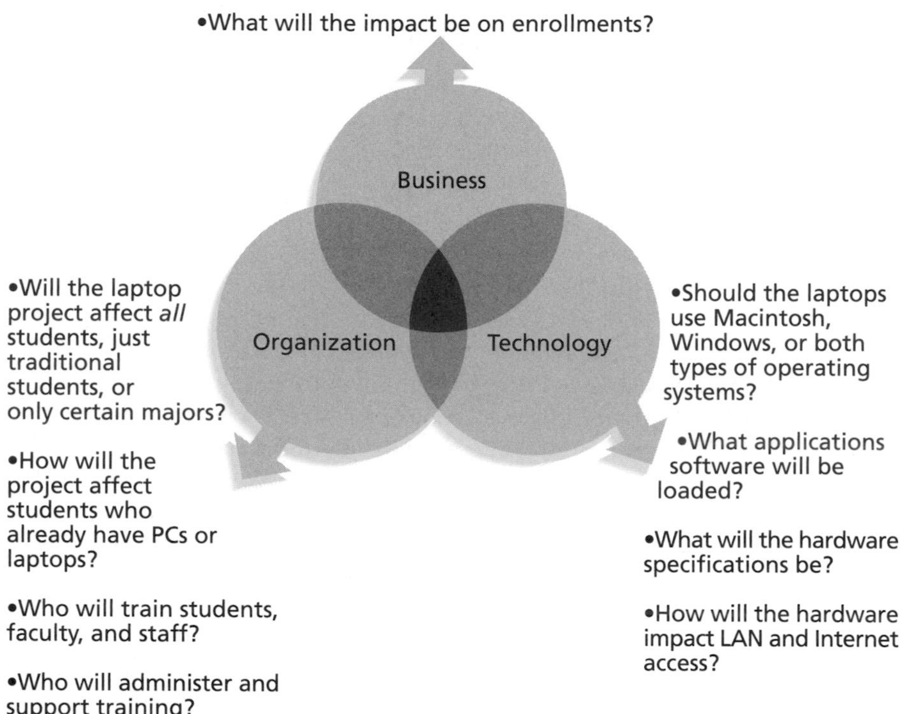
•What will the laptop project cost the college?
•What will it cost students?
•What will support costs be?
•What will the impact be on enrollments?
Business
Organization
Technology
•Will the laptop project affect *all* students, just traditional students, or only certain majors?
•How will the project affect students who already have PCs or laptops?
•Who will train students, faculty, and staff?
•Who will administer and support training?
•Should the laptops use Macintosh, Windows, or both types of operating systems?
•What applications software will be loaded?
•What will the hardware specifications be?
•How will the hardware impact LAN and Internet access?

FIGURE 2-1 Three-sphere model for systems management

not simple by any means, are probably the least difficult to identify and resolve. However, projects must address issues in all three spheres of the systems management model. Although it is easier to focus on the immediate and sometimes narrow concerns of a particular project, project managers and other staff must keep in mind the effects of any project on the interests and needs of the entire system or organization.

Many information technology professionals become captivated with the technology and day-to-day problem solving involved in working with information systems. They tend to become frustrated with many of the "people problems" or politics involved in most organizations. In addition, many information technology professionals ignore important business issues—such as, "Does it make financial sense to pursue this new technology?" or, "Should the company develop this software in-house or purchase it off-the-shelf?" Using a more holistic approach helps project managers integrate business and organizational issues into their planning. It also helps them look at projects as a series of interrelated phases. When you integrate business and organizational issues into project management planning and look at projects as a series of interrelated phases, you do a better job of ensuring project success.

UNDERSTANDING ORGANIZATIONS

The systems approach requires that project managers always view their projects in the context of the larger organization. Organizational issues are often the most difficult part of working on and managing projects. For example, many people believe that most projects fail because of company politics. Project managers often do not spend enough time identifying all the stakeholders involved in projects, especially the people opposed to the projects. In fact, the latest edition of the *PMBOK® Guide* added a new initiating process under project communications management called "identify stakeholders." (See Chapter 10 for more information.) Project managers also often do not spend enough time considering the political context of a project or the culture of the organization. To improve the success rate of information technology projects, it is important for project managers to develop a better understanding of people as well as organizations.

The Four Frames of Organizations

Organizations can be viewed as having four different frames: structural, human resources, political, and symbolic:[1]

- The **structural frame** deals with how the organization is structured (usually depicted in an organizational chart) and focuses on different groups' roles and responsibilities in order to meet the goals and policies set by top management. This frame is very rational and focuses on coordination and control. For example, within the structural frame, a key information technology issue is whether a company should centralize the information technology personnel in one department or decentralize across several departments. You will learn more about organizational structures in the next section.
- The **human resources (HR) frame** focuses on producing harmony between the needs of the organization and the needs of the people. It recognizes that there are often mismatches between the needs of the organization and the needs of individuals and groups and works to resolve any potential problems. For example, many projects might be more efficient for the organization if personnel worked 80 or more hours a week for several months. This work schedule would probably conflict with the personal lives of those people. Important issues in information technology related to the human resources frame are the shortage of skilled information technology workers within the organization and unrealistic schedules imposed on many projects.
- The **political frame** addresses organizational and personal politics. **Politics** in organizations take the form of competition among groups or individuals for power and leadership. The political frame assumes that organizations are coalitions composed of varied individuals and interest groups. Often, important decisions need to be made based on the allocation of scarce resources. Competition for scarce resources makes conflict a central issue in organizations, and power improves the ability to obtain scarce resources. Project managers must pay attention to politics and power if they are to be effective. It is important to know who opposes your projects as well as who supports them. Important issues in information technology related to the political frame are the power shifts from central functions to operating units or from functional managers to project managers.

- The **symbolic frame** focuses on symbols and meanings. What is most important about any event in an organization is not what actually happened, but what it means. Was it a good sign that the CEO came to a kickoff meeting for a project, or was it a threat? The symbolic frame also relates to the company's culture. How do people dress? How many hours do they work? How do they run meetings? Many information technology projects are international and include stakeholders from various cultures. Understanding those cultures is also a crucial part of the symbolic frame.

WHAT WENT WRONG?

Several large organizations have installed or tried to install enterprise resource planning (ERP) systems to integrate business functions such as ordering, inventory, delivery, accounting, and human resource management. They understand the potential benefits of an ERP system and can analyze its various technical issues, but many companies do not realize how important the organizational issues are to ERP implementations.

For example, in early 2001, Sobey's, Canada's second largest grocery store chain with 1,400 stores, abandoned its two-year, $90 million investment in an ERP system. The system was developed by SAP, the largest enterprise software company and the third-largest software supplier. Unfortunately, the system did not work properly due to several organizational challenges. People in different parts of the company had different terms for various items, and it was difficult to make the necessary decisions for the ERP system. Also, no one wanted to take the time required to get the new system to work because they had their daily work to do. Every department has to work together to implement an ERP system, and it is often difficult to get departments to communicate their needs. As Dalhousie University Associate Professor Sunny Marche states, "The problem of building an integrated system that can accommodate different people is a very serious challenge. You can't divorce technology from the sociocultural issues. They have an equal role." Sobey's ERP system shut down for five days and employees were scrambling to stock potentially empty shelves in several stores for weeks. The system failure cost Sobey's more than $90 million and caused shareholders to take an 82-cent after-tax hit per share.[2]

Project managers must learn to work within all four organizational frames to function well in organizations. Chapter 9, Project Human Resource Management, and Chapter 10, Project Communications Management, further develop some of the organizational issues. The following sections on organizational structures, organizational culture, stakeholder management, and the need for top management commitment provide additional information related to the structural and political frames.

Organizational Structures

Many discussions of organizations focus on organizational structure. Three general classifications of organizational structures are functional, project, and matrix. Most companies today involve all three structures somewhere in the organization, but one is usually most common. Figure 2-2 portrays these three organizational structures. A **functional organizational structure** is the hierarchy most people think of when picturing an organizational

Functional

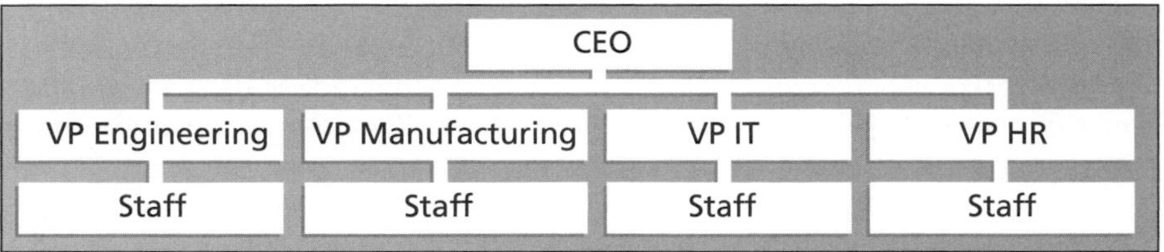

Project

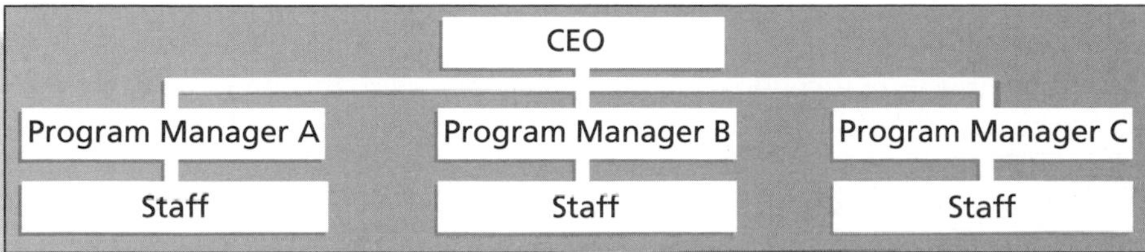

Matrix

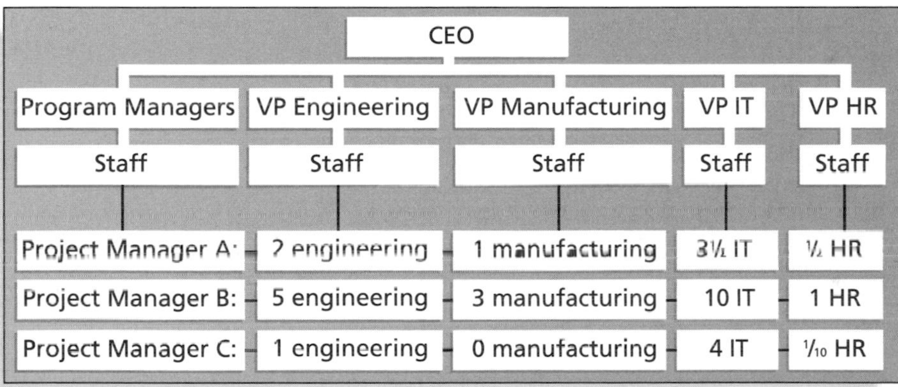

FIGURE 2-2 Functional, project, and matrix organizational structures

chart. Functional managers or vice presidents in specialties such as engineering, manufacturing, information technology, and human resources report to the chief executive officer (CEO). Their staffs have specialized skills in their respective disciplines. For example, most colleges and universities have very strong functional organizations. Only faculty in the business department teach business courses; faculty in the history department teach history; faculty in the art department teach art, and so on.

A **project organizational structure** also has a hierarchical structure, but instead of functional managers or vice presidents reporting to the CEO, program managers report to the CEO. Their staffs have a variety of skills needed to complete the projects within their programs. An organization that uses this structure earns their revenue primarily from performing projects for other groups under contract. For example, many defense, architectural, engineering, and consulting companies use a project organizational structure. These companies often hire people specifically to work on particular projects.

A **matrix organizational structure** represents the middle ground between functional and project structures. Personnel often report to both a functional manager and one or more project managers. For example, information technology personnel at many companies often split their time between two or more projects, but they report to their manager in the information technology department. Project managers in matrix organizations have staff from various functional areas working on their projects, as shown in Figure 2-2. Matrix organizational structures can be strong, weak, or balanced, based on the amount of control exerted by the project managers.

Table 2-1 summarizes how organizational structures influence projects and project managers, based on information from several versions of the *PMBOK® Guide*. Project managers have the most authority in a pure project organizational structure and the least amount of authority in a pure functional organizational structure. It is important that project managers understand the current organizational structure under which they are working. For example, if someone in a functional organization is asked to lead a project that requires strong support from several different functional areas, he or she should ask for top management sponsorship. This sponsor should solicit support from all relevant functional managers to ensure that they cooperate on the project and that qualified people are

TABLE 2-1 Organizational structure influences on projects

Project Characteristics	Organizational Structure Type				
	Functional	Matrix			Project
		Weak Matrix	**Balanced Matrix**	**Strong Matrix**	
Project manager's authority	Little or none	Limited	Low to Moderate	Moderate to High	High to almost total
Percent of organization's personnel assigned full-time to project work	Virtually none	0–25%	15–60%	50–95%	85–100%
Who controls the project budget	Functional manager	Functional manager	Mixed	Project manager	Project manager
Project manager's role	Part-time	Part-time	Full-time	Full-time	Full-time
Common title for project manager's role	Project Coordinator/ Project Leader	Project Coordinator/ Project Leader	Project Manager/ Project Officer	Project Manager / Program Manager	Project Manager/ Program Manager
Project management administrative staff	Part-time	Part-time	Part-time	Full-time	Full-time

available to work as needed. The project manager might also ask for a separate budget to pay for project-related trips, meetings, and training or to provide financial incentives to the people supporting the project.

Even though project managers have the most authority in the project organizational structure, this type of organization is often inefficient for the company as a whole. Assigning staff full-time to the project often creates underutilization and/or misallocation of staff resources. For example, if a technical writer is assigned full-time to a project, but there is no work for him or her on a particular day, the organization is wasting money by paying that person a full-time wage. Project organizations may also miss economies of scale available through the pooling of requests for materials with other projects.

Disadvantages such as these illustrate the benefit of using a systems approach to managing projects. For example, the project manager might suggest hiring an independent contractor to do the technical writing work instead of using a full-time employee. This approach would save the organization money while still meeting the needs of the project. When project managers use a systems approach, they are better able to make decisions that address the needs of the entire organization.

Organizational Culture

Just as an organization's structure affects its ability to manage projects, so does an organization's culture. **Organizational culture** is a set of shared assumptions, values, and behaviors that characterize the functioning of an organization. It often includes elements of all four frames described previously. Organizational culture is very powerful, and many people believe the underlying causes of many companies' problems are not in the organizational structure or staff; they are in the culture. It is also important to note that the same organization can have different subcultures. The information technology department may have a different organizational culture than the finance department, for example. Some organizational cultures make it easier to manage projects.

According to Stephen P. Robbins and Timothy Judge, authors of a popular textbook on organizational behavior, there are ten characteristics of organizational culture:

1. *Member identity*: The degree to which employees identify with the organization as a whole rather than with their type of job or profession. For example, a project manager or team member might feel more dedicated to his or her company or project team than to their job or profession, or they might not have any loyalty to a particular company or team. As you can guess, an organizational culture where employees identify more with the whole organization are more conducive to a good project culture.
2. *Group emphasis*: The degree to which work activities are organized around groups or teams, rather than individuals. An organizational culture that emphasizes group work is best for managing projects.
3. *People focus*: The degree to which management's decisions take into account the effect of outcomes on people within the organization. A project manager might assign tasks to certain people without considering their individual needs, or the project manager might know each person very well and focus on individual needs when assigning work or making other decisions. Good project managers often balance the needs of individuals and the organization.

4. *Unit integration*: The degree to which units or departments within an organization are encouraged to coordinate with each other. Most project managers strive for strong unit integration to deliver a successful product, service, or result. An organizational culture with strong unit integration makes the project manager's job easier.
5. *Control*: The degree to which rules, policies, and direct supervision are used to oversee and control employee behavior. Experienced project managers know it is often best to balance the degree of control to get good project results.
6. *Risk tolerance*: The degree to which employees are encouraged to be aggressive, innovative, and risk seeking. An organizational culture with a higher risk tolerance is often best for project management since projects often involve new technologies, ideas, and processes.
7. *Reward criteria*: The degree to which rewards, such as promotions and salary increases, are allocated according to employee performance rather than seniority, favoritism, or other nonperformance factors. Project managers and their teams often perform best when rewards are based mostly on performance.
8. *Conflict tolerance*: The degree to which employees are encouraged to air conflicts and criticism openly. It is very important for all project stakeholders to have good communications, so it is best to work in an organization where people feel comfortable discussing conflict openly.
9. *Means-ends orientation*: The degree to which management focuses on outcomes rather than on techniques and processes used to achieve results. An organization with a balanced approach in this area is often best for project work.
10. *Open-systems focus*: The degree to which the organization monitors and responds to changes in the external environment. As discussed earlier in this chapter, projects are part of a larger organizational environment, so it is best to have a strong open-systems focus.[3]

As you can see, there is a definite relationship between organizational culture and successful project management. Project work is most successful in an organizational culture where employees identify more with the organization, where work activities emphasize groups, and where there is strong unit integration, high risk tolerance, performance-based rewards, high conflict tolerance, an open-systems focus, and a balanced focus on people, control, and means orientation.

STAKEHOLDER MANAGEMENT

Recall from Chapter 1 that project stakeholders are the people involved in or affected by project activities. Stakeholders can be internal to the organization, external to the organization, directly involved in the project, or simply affected by the project. Internal project stakeholders generally include the project sponsor, project team, support staff, and internal customers for the project. Other internal stakeholders include top management, other functional managers, and other project managers. Since organizations have limited resources, projects affect top management, other functional managers, and other project managers by using some of the organization's limited resources. Thus, while additional internal stakeholders may not be directly involved in the project, they are still stakeholders because the project affects them in some way. External project stakeholders include the project's customers (if they are external to the organization), competitors, suppliers, and other external groups potentially involved in or affected by the project, such as government officials or concerned citizens. Since the purpose of project management is to meet project requirements and satisfy stakeholders, it is critical that project managers take adequate time to identify, understand, and manage relationships with all project stakeholders. Using the four frames of organizations to think about project stakeholders can help you meet their expectations.

Consider again the laptop project from the opening case. Tom Walters seemed to focus on just a few internal project stakeholders. He viewed only part of the structural frame of the college. Since his department would do most of the work in administering the laptop project, he concentrated on those stakeholders. Tom did not even involve the main customers for this project—the students at the college. Even though Tom sent an e-mail to faculty and staff, he did not hold meetings with senior administration or faculty at the college. Tom's view of who the stakeholders were for the laptop project was very limited.

During the faculty meeting, it became evident that the laptop project had many stakeholders in addition to the Information Technology department and students. If Tom had expanded his view of the structural frame of his organization by reviewing an organizational chart for the entire college, he could have identified other key stakeholders. He would have been able to see that the laptop project would affect academic department heads and members of different administrative areas. If Tom had focused on the human resources frame, he would have been able to tap his knowledge of the college and identify individuals who would most support or oppose requiring laptops. By using the political frame, Tom could have considered the main interest groups that would be most affected by this project's outcome. Had he used the symbolic frame, Tom could have tried to address what moving to a laptop environment would really mean for the college. He then could have anticipated some of the opposition from people who were not in favor of increasing the use of technology on campus. He also could have solicited a strong endorsement from the college president or dean before talking at the faculty meeting.

Tom Walters, like many new project managers, learned the hard way that his technical and analytical skills were not enough to guarantee success in project management. To be more effective, he had to identify and address the needs of different stakeholders and understand how his project related to the entire organization.

MEDIA SNAPSHOT

The *New York Times* reported that the project to rebuild Ground Zero in New York City is having severe problems. Imagine all of the stakeholders involved in this huge, highly emotional project. A 34-page report (see the article reference for further information) describes the many challenges faced in the reconstruction of the former World Trade Center site nearly seven years after the terrorist attack of September 11, 2001. The report listed at least 15 fundamental unresolved issues, including the lack of final designs for the proposed World Trade Center Transportation Hub; the unfinished decontamination and

continued

dismantling of the former Deutsche Bank tower; and the resolution of a land-rights issue with the St. Nicholas Greek Orthodox Church.

"Perhaps most pressingly, the report identified a need for 'a more efficient, centralized decision-making structure—a steering committee—with authority to make final decisions on matters which fundamentally drive schedule and cost.'"[4] The "What Went Right?" example later in this chapter describes the benefits of having an executive steering committee to help projects succeed, especially when there are many stakeholders and challenges involved.

The Importance of Top Management Commitment

People in top management positions, of course, are key stakeholders in projects. A very important factor in helping project managers successfully lead projects is the level of commitment and support they receive from top management. Without top management commitment, many projects will fail. Some projects have a senior manager called a **champion** who acts as a key proponent for a project. The sponsor can serve as the champion, but often another manager can more successfully take on this role. As described earlier, projects are part of the larger organizational environment, and many factors that might affect a project are out of the project manager's control. Several studies cite executive support as one of the key factors associated with virtually all project success.

Top management commitment is crucial to project managers for the following reasons:

- Project managers need adequate resources. The best way to kill a project is to withhold the required money, human resources, and visibility for the project. If project managers have top management commitment, they will also have adequate resources and not be distracted by events that do not affect their specific projects.
- Project managers often require approval for unique project needs in a timely manner. For example, on large information technology projects, top management must understand that unexpected problems may result from the nature of the products being produced and the specific skills of the people on the project team. For example, the team might need additional hardware and software halfway through the project for proper testing, or the project manager might need to offer special pay and benefits to attract and retain key project personnel. With top management commitment, project managers can meet these specific needs in a timely manner.
- Project managers must have cooperation from people in other parts of the organization. Since most information technology projects cut across functional areas, top management must help project managers deal with the political issues that often arise in these types of situations. If certain functional managers are not responding to project managers' requests for necessary information, top management must step in to encourage functional managers to cooperate.
- Project managers often need someone to mentor and coach them on leadership issues. Many information technology project managers come from technical positions and are inexperienced as managers. Senior managers should take the time to pass on advice on how to be good leaders. They should encourage new

project managers to take classes to develop leadership skills and allocate the time and funds for them to do so.

Information technology project managers work best in an environment in which top management values information technology. Working in an organization that values good project management and sets standards for its use also helps project managers succeed.

BEST PRACTICE

A major element of good practice concerns **IT governance**, which addresses the authority and control for key IT activities in organizations, including IT infrastructure, IT use, and project management. (The term *project governance* can also used to describe a uniform method of controlling all types of projects.) The IT Governance Institute (ITGI) was established in 1998 to advance international thinking and standards in directing and controlling an organization's use of technology. Effective IT governance helps ensure that IT supports business goals, maximizes investment in IT, and addresses IT-related risks and opportunities. A 2004 book by Peter Weill and Jeanne Ross called *IT Governance: How Top Performers Manage IT Decision Rights for Superior Results*[5] includes research stating that firms with superior IT governance systems have 20 percent higher profits than firms with poor governance. (See the ITGI's Web site *www.itgi.org* for more information, including many case studies and best practices in this area.)

A lack of IT governance can be dangerous, as evidenced by three well-publicized IT project failures in Australia—Sydney Water's customer relationship management system, the Royal Melbourne Institute of Technology's academic management system, and One.Tel's billing system. Researchers explained how these projects were catastrophic for their organizations, primarily due to a severe lack of IT governance, which the authors dubbed *managerial IT unconsciousness*, the title of their article.

> "All three projects suffered from poor IT governance. Senior management in all three organizations had not ensured that prudent checks and balances were in place to enable them to monitor either the progress of the projects or the alignment and impact of the new systems on their business. Proper governance, particularly with respect to financial matters, auditing, and contract management, was not evident. Also, project-level planning and control were notably absent or inadequate—with the result that project status reports to management were unrealistic, inaccurate, and misleading."[6]

The Need for Organizational Commitment to Information Technology

Another factor affecting the success of information technology projects is the organization's commitment to information technology in general. It is very difficult for a large information technology project (or a small one, for that matter) to be successful if the organization itself does not value information technology. Many companies have realized that information technology is integral to their business and have created a vice president or equivalent-level position for the head of information technology, often called the Chief Information Officer (CIO). Some companies assign people from non-information technology areas to work on large projects full-time to increase involvement from end users of the systems. Some CEOs even take a strong leadership role in promoting the use of information technology in their organizations.

Gartner, Inc., a well-respected information technology consulting firm, provides awards to organizations for excellence in applying various technologies. For example, in 2006, Gartner announced the winners of its eighth annual Customer Relationship Management (CRM) Excellence Awards. BNSF Railway received the award in the "Excellence in Enterprise CRM" category, and UnitedHealth Group received the award in the "Excellence in Sales, Marketing or Customer Service" category. (Electronic Arts, an independent producer of electronic games, won the award in 2007.) The 2006 award winners had the following to say:

- *Elizabeth Obermiller, director of ERM systems for BNSF Railway*: "Our success was driven by the ongoing executive commitment and passionate and talented teams, who were able to implement a planned and phased approach with advanced application of analytics to monitor, measure and drive success."
- *John Reinke, a senior vice president of Uniprise, a UnitedHealth Group*: "We are excited to receive this award for our partnership with eLoyalty to implement a new, cutting-edge call center technology application called Behavioral Analytics™. This technology allows us to engage in deeper, more personally relevant phone conversations with each consumer who speaks with a customer care professional. Health care consumers often face complex and emotional issues, and this is a great example of how technology can help improve their experience."[7]

The Need for Organizational Standards

Another problem in most organizations is not having standards or guidelines to follow that could help in performing project management. These standards or guidelines might be as simple as providing standard forms or templates for common project documents, examples of good project management plans, or guidelines on how the project manager should provide status information to top management. The content of a project management plan and how to provide status information might seem like common sense to senior managers, but many new information technology project managers have never created plans or given a non-technical status report. Top management must support the development of these standards and guidelines and encourage or even enforce their use. For example, an organization might require all potential project information in a standard format to make project portfolio management decisions. If a project manager does not submit a potential project in the proper format, it could be rejected.

As described in Chapter 1, some organizations invest heavily in project management by creating a project management office or center of excellence, an organizational entity created to assist project managers in achieving project goals and maintaining project governance. Rachel Hollstadt, founder and CEO of a project management consulting firm, suggests that organizations consider adding a new position, a Chief Project Officer (CPO). Some organizations develop career paths for project managers. Some require that all project managers have Project Management Professional (PMP) certification and that all employees have some type of project management training. The implementation of all of these standards demonstrates an organization's commitment to project management.

PROJECT PHASES AND THE PROJECT LIFE CYCLE

Since projects operate as part of a system and involve uncertainty, it is good practice to divide projects into several phases. A **project life cycle** is a collection of project phases. Some organizations specify a set of life cycles for use on all of their projects, while others follow common industry practices based on the types of projects involved. In general, project life cycles define what work will be performed in each phase, what deliverables will be produced and when, who is involved in each phase, and how management will control and approve work produced in each phase. A **deliverable** is a product or service, such as a technical report, a training session, a piece of hardware, or a segment of software code, produced or provided as part of a project. (See Chapter 5, Project Scope Management, for detailed information on deliverables.)

In early phases of a project life cycle, resource needs are usually lowest and the level of uncertainty is highest. Project stakeholders have the greatest opportunity to influence the final characteristics of the project's products, services, or results during the early phases of a project life cycle. It is much more expensive to make major changes to a project during latter phases. During the middle phases of a project life cycle, the certainty of completing a project improves as a project continues, more information is known about the project requirements and objectives, and more resources are usually needed than during the initial or final phase. The final phase of a project focuses on ensuring that project requirements were met and that the project sponsor approves completion of the project.

Project phases vary by project or industry, but some general phases in traditional project management are often called the concept, development, implementation, and close-out phases. The *PMBOK Guide®, Fourth Edition* calls these phases starting the project, organizing and preparing, carrying out the project work, and finishing the project. These phases should not be confused with the project management process groups of initiating, planning, executing, monitoring and controlling, and closing, as described in Chapter 3. The first two traditional project phases (concept and development) focus on planning and are often referred to as **project feasibility**. The last two phases (implementation and close-out) focus on delivering the actual work and are often referred to as **project acquisition**. A project should successfully complete each phase before moving on to the next. This project life cycle approach provides better management control and appropriate links to the ongoing operations of the organization.

Figure 2-3 provides a summary framework for the general phases of the traditional project life cycle. In the concept phase of a project, managers usually develop some type of business case, which describes the need for the project and basic underlying concepts. A preliminary or rough cost estimate is developed in this first phase, and an overview of the work involved is created. A work breakdown structure (WBS) outlines project work by decomposing the work activities into different levels of tasks. The WBS is a deliverable-oriented document that defines the total scope of the project. (You will learn more about the work breakdown structure in Chapter 5, Project Scope Management.) For example, if Tom

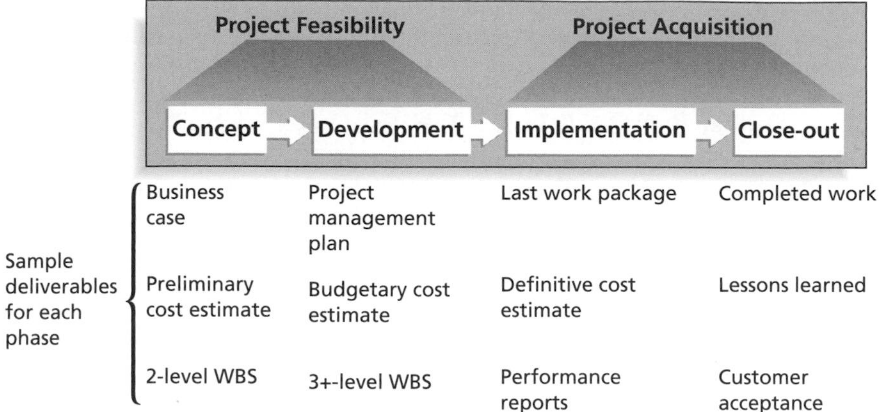

FIGURE 2-3 Phases of the traditional project life cycle

Walters (from the opening case) had followed the project life cycle instead of moving full-steam ahead with the laptop project, he could have created a committee of faculty and staff to study the concept of increasing the use of technology on campus. This committee might have developed a business case and plan that included an initial, smaller project to investigate alternative ways of increasing the use of technology. They might have estimated that it would take six months and $20,000 to conduct a detailed technology study. The WBS at this phase of the study might have three levels and partition the work to include a competitive analysis of what five similar campuses were doing, a survey of local students, staff, and faculty, and a rough assessment of how using more technology would affect costs and enrollments. At the end of the concept phase, the committee would be able to deliver a report and presentation on its findings. The report and presentation would be an example of a deliverable.

After the concept phase is completed, the next project phase—development—begins. In the development phase, the project team creates more detailed project management plans, a more accurate cost estimate, and a more thorough WBS. In the example under discussion, suppose the concept phase report suggested that requiring students to have laptops was one means of increasing the use of technology on campus. The project team could then further expand this idea in the development phase. They would have to decide if students would purchase or lease the laptops, what type of hardware and software the laptops would require, how much to charge students, how to handle training and maintenance, how to integrate the use of the new technology with current courses, and so on. If, however, the concept phase report showed that the laptop idea was not a good idea for the college, then the project team would no longer consider increasing the use of technology by requiring laptops in the development phase and would cancel the project before development. This phased approach minimizes the time and money spent developing inappropriate projects. A project idea must pass the concept phase before evolving into the development phase.

The third phase of the traditional project life cycle is implementation. In this phase, the project team creates a definitive or very accurate cost estimate, delivers the required work, and provides performance reports to stakeholders. Suppose Tom Walters' college took the idea of requiring students to have laptops through the development phase. During the implementation phase, the project team would need to obtain the required hardware and software, install the necessary network equipment, deliver the laptops to the students, create a process for collecting fees, provide training to students, faculty, and staff, and so on. Other people on campus would also be involved in the implementation phase. Faculty would need to consider how best to take advantage of the new technology. The recruiting staff would have to update their materials to reflect this new feature of the college. Security would need to address new problems that might result from having students carry around expensive equipment. The project team usually spends the bulk of their efforts and money during the implementation phase of projects.

The last phase of the traditional project life cycle is close-out. In the close-out phase, all of the work is completed, and there should be some sort of customer acceptance of the entire project. The project team should document its experiences on the project in a lessons-learned report. If the laptop idea made it all the way through the implementation phase and all students received laptops, the project team would then complete the project by closing out any related activities. Team members might administer a survey to students, faculty, and staff in order to gather opinions on how the project fared. They would ensure that any contracts with suppliers were completed and appropriate payments made. They would transition future work related to the laptop project to other parts of the organization. The project team could also share its lessons-learned report with other college campuses that are considering implementing a similar program.

Many projects, however, do not follow this traditional project life cycle. They still have general phases with some similar characteristics as the traditional project life cycle, but they are much more flexible. For example, there may be just three phases, the initial, intermediate, and final phase. Or there may be multiple intermediate phases. There might be a separate project just to complete a feasibility study. Regardless of the project life cycle's specific phases, it is good practice to think of projects as having phases that connect the beginning and the end of the project, so that people can measure progress toward achieving project goals during each phase.

Just as a *project* has a life cycle, so does a *product*. Information technology projects help produce products and services such as new software, hardware, networks, research reports, and training on new systems. Understanding the product life cycle is just as important to good project management as understanding the phases of the traditional project life cycle.

Product Life Cycles

Recall from Chapter 1 that a project is defined as "a temporary endeavor undertaken to create a unique product, service, or result," and a program is defined as "a group of projects managed in a coordinated way." A program often refers to the creation of a product, like an automobile or a new operating system. Therefore, developing a product often involves many projects.

All products follow some type of life cycle—cars, buildings, even amusement parks. The Walt Disney Company, for example, follows a rigorous process to design, build, and test new products. They assign project managers to oversee the development of all new products, such as rides, parks, and cruise lines. Likewise, major automotive companies follow product life cycles to produce new cars, trucks, and other products. Most information technology professionals are familiar with the concept of a product life cycle, especially for developing software.

Software development projects are one subset of information technology projects. Many information technology projects involve researching, analyzing, and then purchasing and installing new hardware and software with little or no actual software development required. However, some projects involve minor software modifications to enhance existing software or to integrate one application with another. Other projects involve a major amount of software development. Many argue that developing software requires project managers to modify traditional project management methods, depending on a particular product's life cycle.

A **systems development life cycle (SDLC)** is a framework for describing the phases involved in developing information systems. Some popular models of an SDLC include the waterfall model, the spiral model, the incremental build model, the prototyping model, and the Rapid Application Development (RAD) model. These life cycle models are examples of a **predictive life cycle**, meaning that the scope of the project can be clearly articulated and the schedule and cost can be accurately predicted. The project team spends a large portion of the project effort attempting to clarify the requirements of the entire system and then producing a design. Users are often unable to see any tangible results in terms of working software for an extended period. Below are brief descriptions of several predictive SDLC models.[8]

- The waterfall life cycle model has well-defined, linear stages of systems analysis, design, construction, testing, and support. This life cycle model assumes that requirements will remain stable after they are defined.
- The spiral life cycle model was developed based on experience with various refinements of the waterfall model as applied to large government software projects. It recognizes the fact that most software is developed using an iterative or spiral approach rather than a linear approach.
- The incremental build life cycle model provides for progressive development of operational software, with each release providing added capabilities.
- The prototyping life cycle model is used for developing software prototypes to clarify user requirements for operational software. It requires heavy user involvement, and developers use a model to generate functional requirements and physical design specifications simultaneously. Developers can throw away or keep prototypes, depending on the project.
- The RAD life cycle model uses an approach in which developers work with an evolving prototype. This life cycle model also requires heavy user involvement and helps produce systems quickly without sacrificing quality. Developers use RAD tools such as CASE (computer-aided software engineering), JRP (joint requirements planning), and JAD (joint application design) to facilitate rapid prototyping and code generation.

In contrast to the predictive life cycle models, the **Adaptive Software Development (ASD)** life cycle model assumes that software development follows an adaptive approach because the requirements cannot be clearly expressed early in the life cycle. An adaptive approach is also used to provide more freedom than the prescriptive approaches. It allows the development to proceed by creating components that provide the functionality specified by the business group as these needs are discovered in a more free-form approach.

Important attributes of this approach are that the projects are mission driven and component based, using time-based cycles to meet target dates. Requirements are developed using an iterative approach, and development is risk driven and change tolerant to address and incorporate rather than mitigate risks. More recently, the term **agile software development** has become popular to describe new approaches that focus on close collaboration between programming teams and business experts. (See the companion Web site for the Suggested Readings related to agile and other software development methodologies.)

These life cycle models are all examples of SDLCs. Many Web sites and introductory management information systems texts describe each of them in detail. The type of software and complexity of the information system in development determines which life cycle model to use. It is important to understand the product life cycle to meet the needs of the project environment.

Most large information technology products are developed as a series of projects. For example, the systems planning phase for a new information system can include a project to hire an outside consulting firm to help identify and evaluate potential strategies for developing a particular business application, such as a new order processing system or general ledger system. It can also include a project to develop, administer, and evaluate a survey of users to get their opinions on the current information systems used for performing that business function in the organization. The systems analysis phase might include a project to create process models for certain business functions in the organization. It can also include a project to create data models of existing databases in the company related to the business function and application. The implementation phase might include a project to hire contract programmers to code a part of the system. The close-out phase might include a project to develop and run several training sessions for users of the new application. All of these examples show that large information technology projects are usually composed of several smaller projects. It is often good practice to view large projects as a series of smaller, more manageable ones, especially when there is a lot of uncertainty involved. Successfully completing one small project at a time will help the project team succeed in completing the larger project.

Because some aspects of project management need to occur during each phase of the product life cycle, it is critical for information technology professionals to understand and practice good project management throughout the product life cycle.

The Importance of Project Phases and Management Reviews

Due to the complexity and importance of many information technology projects and their resulting products, it is important to take time to review the status of a project at each phase. A project should successfully pass through each of the main project or product phases before continuing to the next. Since the organization usually commits more money as a project continues, a management review should occur after each phase to evaluate progress, potential success, and continued compatibility with organizational goals. These management reviews, called **phase exits** or **kill points**, are very important for keeping projects on track and determining if they should be continued, redirected, or terminated. Recall that projects are just one part of the entire system of an organization. Changes in other parts of the organization might affect a project's status, and a project's status might likewise affect what is happening in other parts of the organization. By breaking projects into phases, top management can make sure that the projects are still compatible with the needs of the rest of the organization.

Let's take another look at the opening case. Suppose Tom Walters' college did a study on increasing the use of technology that was sponsored by the college president. At the end of the concept phase, the project team could have presented information to the faculty, president, and other staff members that described different options for increasing the use of technology, an analysis of what competing colleges were doing, and results of a survey of local stakeholders' opinions on the subject. This presentation at the end of the concept phase represents one form of a management review. Suppose the study reported that 90 percent of students, faculty, and staff surveyed strongly opposed the idea of requiring all students to have laptops and that many adult students said they would attend other colleges if they were required to pay for the additional technology. The college would probably decide not to pursue this idea any further. Had Tom taken a phased approach, he and his staff would not have wasted the time and money it took to develop detailed plans.

In addition to formal management reviews, it is important to have top management involvement throughout the life cycle of most projects. It is unwise to wait for the end of project or product phases to have management inputs. Many projects are reviewed by management on a regular basis, such as weekly or even daily, to make sure they are progressing well. Everyone wants to be successful in accomplishing goals at work, and having management involvement ensures that they are on track in accomplishing both project and organizational goals.

WHAT WENT RIGHT?

Having specific deliverables and kill points at the end of project or product phases helps managers make better decisions about whether to proceed, redefine, or kill a project. Improvement in information technology project success rates reported by the Standish Group has been due, in part, to an increased ability to know when to cancel failing projects. Standish Group Chairman Jim Johnson made the following observation: "The real improvement that I saw was in our ability to—in the words of Thomas Edison—know when to stop beating a dead horse . . .. Edison's key to success was that he failed fairly often; but as he said, he could recognize a dead horse before it started to smell . . .. In information technology we ride dead horses—failing projects—a long time before we give up. But what we are seeing now is that we are able to get off them; able to reduce cost overrun and time overrun. That's where the major impact came on the success rate."[9]

Another example of the power of management oversight comes from Huntington Bancshares, Inc. This company, like many others, had an **executive steering committee**, a group of senior executives from various parts of the organization who regularly reviewed important corporate projects and issues. This Ohio-based, $26 billion bank holding company completed a year-long Web site redesign effort using XML technology to give its online customers access to real-time account information as well as other banking services. The CIO, Joe Gottron, said there were "four or five very intense moments" when the whole project was almost stopped due to its complexity. An executive steering committee met

continued

weekly to review the project's progress and discuss work planned for the following week. Gottron said the meetings ensured that "if we were missing a beat on the project, no matter which company [was responsible], we were on top of it and adding additional resources to make up for it."[10]

Managers in the motorcycle industry now understand the importance of overseeing their IT projects. Harley-Davidson Motor Company used to focus only on producing and selling high-quality motorcycles. In 2003, however, management realized that it had to improve its IT operations and control to stay in business and adhere to new government laws such as the accounting reporting regulations of Sarbanes-Oxley. Harley-Davidson had no standardized processes for user access, change management, or backup and recovery at that time. "Although complying with Sarbanes-Oxley was going to be a challenge, the company took strong action, utilized COBIT (Control Objectives for Information and related Technology) and passed Sarbanes-Oxley year one compliance.... One of the major benefits of using COBIT as its overall internal control and compliance model was getting everyone—especially non-technical motorcycle experts—revved up about control activities and why controls are important.[11]

THE CONTEXT OF INFORMATION TECHNOLOGY PROJECTS

As described earlier, software development projects can follow several different product life cycles based on the project context. There are several other issues related to managing information technology projects. This section highlights some of the issues unique to the information technology industry that affect project management, including the nature of projects, the characteristics of project team members, and the diverse nature of technologies involved.

The Nature of Information Technology Projects

Unlike projects in many other industries, projects labeled as information technology projects can be very diverse. Some involve a small number of people installing off-the-shelf hardware and associated software. Others involve hundreds of people analyzing several organizations' business processes and then developing new software in a collaborative effort with users to meet business needs. Even for small hardware-oriented projects, there is a wide diversity in the types of hardware that could be involved—personal computers, mainframe computers, network equipment, kiosks, or small mobile devices, to name a few. The network equipment might be wireless, phone-based, cable-based, or require a satellite connection. The nature of software development projects is even more diverse than hardware-oriented projects. A software development project might include developing a simple, standalone Microsoft Excel or Access application or a sophisticated, global e-commerce system using state-of-the-art programming languages.

Information technology projects also support every possible industry and business function. Managing an information technology project for a film company's animation department would require different knowledge and skills of the project manager and team members than a project to improve a federal tax collection system or install a communication infrastructure in a third-world country. Because of the diversity of information technology projects and the newness of the field, it is important to develop and follow best practices in managing these varied projects. That way, information technology project managers will have a common starting point and method to follow with every project.

Characteristics of Information Technology Project Team Members

Because of the nature of information technology projects, the people involved come from very diverse backgrounds and possess different skill sets. Most trade schools, colleges, and universities did not start offering degrees in computer technology, computer science, management information systems, or other information technology areas until the 1970s. Therefore, many people in the field do not have a common educational background. Many companies purposely hire graduates with degrees in other fields such as business, mathematics, or the liberal arts to provide different perspectives on information technology projects. Even with these different educational backgrounds, there are some common job titles for people working on most information technology projects such as business analyst, programmer, network specialist, database analyst, quality assurance expert, technical writer, security specialist, hardware engineer, software engineer, and system architect. Within the category of programmer, there are several other job titles used to describe the specific technologies the programmer uses, such as Java programmer, XML programmer, C/C++ programmer, and so on.

Some information technology projects require the skills of people in just a few of these job functions, but many require inputs from many or all of them. Occasionally, information technology professionals move around between these job functions, but more often people become technical experts in one area or they decide to move into a management position. It is also rare for technical specialists or project managers to remain with the same company for a long time, and in fact, many information technology projects include a large number of contract workers. Working with this "army of free agents," as Rob Thomsett, author and consultant for the Cutter Consortium, calls them, creates special challenges. (See the companion Web site for an article on this topic by Thomsett and other suggested readings.)

Diverse Technologies

Many of the job titles for IT professionals reflect the different technologies required to hold that position. Unfortunately, hardware specialists might not understand the language of database analysts, and vice versa. Security specialists may have a hard time communicating with business analysts. It is also unfortunate that people within the same information technology job function often do not understand each other because each uses different technology. For example, someone with the title of programmer can often use several different programming languages. A COBOL programmer, however, cannot be of much help on a Java project. These highly specialized positions also make it difficult for project managers to form and lead project teams.

Another problem with diverse technologies is that many of them change rapidly. A project team might be close to finishing a project when it discovers a new technology that can greatly enhance the project and better meet long-term business needs. New technologies have also shortened the time frame many businesses have to develop, produce, and distribute new products and services. This fast-paced environment requires equally fast-paced processes to manage and produce information technology projects and products.

RECENT TRENDS AFFECTING INFORMATION TECHNOLOGY PROJECT MANAGEMENT

Additional challenges and opportunities face IT project managers and their teams in the form of the recent trends of increased globalization, outsourcing, and virtual teams. Each of these trends and suggestions for addressing them are provided in this section.

Globalization

In his popular book, *The World Is Flat*, Thomas L. Friedman describes the effects of globalization, which has created a "flat" world where everyone is connected and the "playing field" is level for many more participants.[12] Lower trade and political barriers and the digital revolution have made it possible to interact almost instantaneously with billions of other people across the planet, and for individuals and small companies to compete with large corporations. Friedman also discusses the increase in "uploading," where people share information through blogging, podcasts, and open-source software.

Information technology is a key enabler of globalization, and globalization has significantly affected the field of IT. Even though major IT companies such as Microsoft and IBM started in the United States, much of their business is global—indeed, companies and individuals throughout the world contribute to the growth of information technologies and work and collaborate on various IT projects. As mentioned in Chapter 1, the total global spending on technology goods, services, and staff was projected to reach $2.4 trillion in 2008, and the main engines of growth were Asia Pacific and the oil-exporting areas of Eastern Europe, the Middle East, and Africa.

It is important for project managers to address several issues when working on global projects. Several key issues include the following:

- *Communications*: Since people will be working in different time zones, speak different languages, have different cultural backgrounds, celebrate different holidays, etc., it is important to address how people will communicate in an efficient and timely manner. A communications management plan (like the one described in Chapter 10, Project Communications Management) is vital.
- *Trust*: Trust is an important issue for all teams, especially when they are global teams. It is important to start building trust immediately by recognizing and respecting others' differences and the value they add to the project.
- *Common work practices*: It is important to align work processes to come up with an agreed-upon modus operandi with which everyone is comfortable. Project managers must allow time for the team to develop these common work practices. Using special tools, as described in the next section, can facilitate this process.
- *Tools*: Information technology plays a vital role in globalization, especially in enhancing communications and work practices. For example, Timothy Porter, a project manager for Hundsun Technologies, a Chinese domestic software company building a global services business, describes several tools they use as follows:
    - XPlanner is used for project planning and project monitoring. This tool is suitable for agile software development and is Web-based for ease of distributed geographic access.

- TRAC is an enhanced issue-tracking system for software development projects. TRAC includes features such as defect management, source code control, project roadmap management, and an integrated wiki—a collaborative, Web-based feedback system—for project documentation that is very easy for stakeholders to review.
- CruiseControl is a framework for a continuous build process. It includes plug-ins for e-mail notification, source control tools, and so on. A Web interface is provided to view the details of the current and previous builds.
- WebEx, a Web-based conferencing tool, is used to record each development cycle's demo, which is stored on our wikis. These demos provide stakeholders visibility into our progress and can also be used as training materials for new staff members or the test team.
- E-mail, telephone, SKYPE (software that allows users to make telephone calls over the Internet), and instant messaging (IM) are used for routine daily communication among team members.[13]

After researching over 600 global organizations, KPMG International summarized several suggestions for managing global project teams:

- Employ greater project discipline for global projects, otherwise weaknesses within the traditional project disciplines may be amplified by the geographical differences.
- Think global, but act local to align and integrate stakeholders at all project levels.
- Consider collaboration over standardization to help balance the goals and project approach.
- Keep project momentum going for projects, which will typically have a long duration.
- Consider the use of newer, perhaps more innovative, tools and technology.[14]

Outsourcing

As described in detail in Chapter 12, Project Procurement Management, **outsourcing** is when an organization acquires goods and/or sources from an outside source. The term **offshoring** is sometimes used to describe outsourcing from another country. Offshoring is a natural outgrowth of globalization. IT projects continue to rely more and more on outsourcing, both within and outside of their country boundaries.

Organizations remain competitive by using outsourcing to their advantage. For example, many organizations have found ways to reduce costs by outsourcing. Their next challenge is to make strategic IT investments with outsourcing by improving their enterprise architecture to ensure that IT infrastructure and business processes are integrated and standardized. (See the Suggested Readings on the companion Web site for this chapter by Ross and Beath and KPMG International. Chapter 12, Project Procurement Management, also features more information.)

Because of the increased use of outsourcing for IT projects, project managers should become more familiar with negotiating contracts and many other issues, including working on and managing virtual teams.

Virtual Teams

Increased globalization and outsourcing have increased the need for virtual teams. A **virtual team** is a group of individuals who work across time and space using communication technologies. Team members might all work for the same company in the same country, or they might include employees as well as independent consultants, suppliers, or even volunteers providing their expertise from around the globe.

The main advantages of virtual teams include:

- Increasing competiveness and responsiveness by having a team of workers available 24/7.
- Lowering costs because many virtual workers do not require office space or support beyond their home offices.
- Providing more expertise and flexibility by having team members from across the globe working any time of day or night.
- Increasing the work/life balance for team members by eliminating fixed office hours and the need to travel to work.

Disadvantages of virtual teams include:

- Isolating team members who may not adjust well to working in a virtual environment.
- Increasing the potential for communications problems since team members cannot use body language or other communications to understand each other and build relationships and trust.
- Reducing the ability for team members to network and transfer information informally.
- Increasing the dependence on technology to accomplish work.

Like any team, a virtual team should focus on achieving a common goal.

Research on virtual teams reveals a growing list of factors that influence their success including:

- *Team processes*: It is important to define how the virtual team will operate. For examples, teams must agree on how and when work will be done, what technologies will be used, how decisions will be made, and other important process issues.
- *Leadership style*: The project manager's leadership style affects all teams, especially virtual ones.
- *Trust and relationships*: Many virtual teams fail because of a lack of trust. It is difficult to build relationships and trust from a distance. Some project managers like to have a face-to-face meeting so team members can get to know each other and build trust. If that is not possible, phone or video conferences can help.
- *Team member selection and role preferences*: Dr. Meredith Belbin defined a team role as "a tendency to behave, contribute and interrelate with others in a particular way."[15] It is important to select team members carefully and to form a team where all roles are covered. Each virtual team member must also understand his or her role(s) on the team. (Visit *www.belbin.com* for more information on this topic.)

- *Task-technology fit*: IT is more likely to have a positive impact on individual performance if the capabilities of the technologies match the tasks that the user must perform.
- *Cultural differences*: It is important to address cultural differences, including the dimensions of directness, hierarchy, consensus, and individualism. These dimensions will affect many aspects of the team such as communications and decision making.
- *Computer-mediated communication*: It is crucial to provide reliable and appropriate computer-mediated communication to virtual team members, including e-mail, instant messaging, text messaging, chat rooms, and so on.
- *Team life cycles*: Just as projects and products have life cycles, so do teams. Project managers must address the team life cycle especially in assigning team members and determining deliverable schedules.
- *Incentives*: Virtual teams may require different types of incentives in order to accomplish quality work on time. They do not have the benefit of physical contact with their project managers or other team members, so it important to provide frequent positive incentives like a thank you via e-mail or phone, or even a bonus on occasion. Negative incentives, such as payment withholding or fines, can also be effective if virtual team members are not being productive.
- *Conflict management*: Even though they may never physically meet, virtual teams will still have conflict. It is important to address conflict management, as described in more detail in Chapter 10, Project Communications Management.

Several studies have been done to try to determine factors that are positively correlated to the effectiveness of virtual teams. Research suggests that team processes, trust/relationships, leadership style, and team member selection provide the strongest relationships to team performance and team member satisfaction.[16] See the companion Web site for suggested readings on virtual teams and other topics discussed in this chapter.

As you can see, working as an information technology project manager or team member is an exciting and challenging job. It's important to focus on successfully completing projects that will have a positive impact on the organization as a whole.

CASE WRAP-UP

After several people voiced concerns about the laptop idea at the faculty meeting, the president of the college directed that a committee be formed to formally review the concept of requiring students to have laptops in the near future. Because the college was dealing with several other important enrollment-related issues, the president named the vice president of enrollment to head the committee. Other people soon volunteered or were assigned to the committee, including Tom Walters as head of Information Technology, the director of the adult education program, the chair of the Computer Science department, and the chair of the History department. The president also insisted that the committee include at least two members of the student body. The president knew everyone was busy, and he questioned whether the laptop idea was a high-priority issue for the college. He directed the committee to present a proposal at the next month's faculty meeting, either to recommend the creation of a formal project team (of which these committee members would commit to be a part) to fully investigate requiring laptops, or to recommend terminating the concept. At the next faculty meeting, few people were surprised to hear the recommendation to terminate the concept. Tom Walters learned that he had to pay much more attention to the needs of the entire college before proceeding with detailed information technology plans.

Chapter Summary

Projects operate in an environment broader than the project itself. Project managers need to take a systems approach when working on projects; they need to consider projects within the greater organizational context.

Organizations have four different frames: structural, human resources, political, and symbolic. Project managers need to understand all of these aspects of organizations to be successful. The structural frame focuses on different groups' roles and responsibilities to meet the goals and policies set by top management. The human resources frame focuses on producing harmony between the needs of the organization and the needs of people. The political frame addresses organizational and personal politics. The symbolic frame focuses on symbols and meanings.

The structure of an organization has strong implications for project managers, especially in terms of the amount of authority the project manager has. The three basic organizational structures include functional, matrix, and project. Project managers have the most authority in a pure project organization, an intermediate amount of authority in a matrix organization, and the least amount of authority in a pure functional organization.

Organizational culture also affects project management. A culture where employees have a strong identity with the organization, where work activities emphasize groups, where there is strong unit integration, high risk tolerance, performance-based rewards, high conflict tolerance, an open-systems focus, and a balance on the dimensions of people focus, control, and means-orientation is more conducive to project work.

Project stakeholders are individuals and organizations who are actively involved in the project or whose interests may be positively or negatively affected because of project execution or successful project completion. Project managers must identify and understand the different needs of all stakeholders on their projects.

Top management commitment is crucial for project success. Since projects often affect many areas in an organization, top management must assist project managers if they are to do a good job of project integration. Organizational commitment to information technology is also important to the success of information technology projects. Development standards and guidelines assist most organizations in managing projects.

A project life cycle is a collection of project phases. Traditional project phases include concept, development, implementation, and close-out phases. Projects often produce products, which follow product life cycles. Examples of product life cycles for software development include the waterfall, spiral, incremental build, prototyping, RAD, and the adaptive software development models. Project managers must understand the specific life cycle of the products they are producing as well as the general project life cycle model.

A project should successfully pass through each of the project phases in order to continue to the next phase. A management review should occur at the end of each project phase, and more frequent management inputs are often needed. These management reviews and inputs are important for keeping projects on track and determining if projects should be continued, redirected, or terminated.

Project managers need to consider several factors due to the unique context of information technology projects. The diverse nature of these projects and the wide range of business areas and technologies involved make information technology projects especially challenging to manage. Leading project team members with a wide variety of specialized skills and understanding rapidly changing technologies are also important considerations.

Several recent trends have affected information technology project management. Increased globalization, outsourcing, and virtual teams have changed the way many IT projects are staffed and managed. Project managers must stay abreast of these and other trends and discover ways to use them to their advantage.

Quick Quiz

1. Which of the following is not part of the three-sphere model for systems management?
   a. business
   b. information
   c. technology
   d. organization
2. Which of the four frames of organizations addresses how meetings are run, employee dress codes, and expected work hours?
   a. structural
   b. human resources
   c. political
   d. symbolic
3. Personnel in a ______ organizational structure often report to two or more bosses.
   a. functional
   b. project
   c. matrix
   d. hybrid
4. Project work is most successful in an organizational culture where all of the following characteristics are high except ______.
   a. member identity
   b. group emphasis
   c. risk tolerance
   d. control
5. A ______ is a product or service, such as a technical report, a training session, or hardware, produced or provided as part of a project.
   a. deliverable
   b. product
   c. work package
   d. tangible goal

6. Which of the following is not a phase of the traditional project life cycle?
   a. systems analysis
   b. concept
   c. development
   d. implementation
7. What is the term used to describe a framework of the phases involved in developing information systems?
   a. systems development life cycle
   b. rapid application development
   c. predictive life cycle
   d. extreme programming
8. Another name for a phase exit is a _____ point.
   a. review
   b. stage
   c. meeting
   d. kill
9. The nature of information technology projects is different from projects in many other industries because they are very ______.
   a. expensive
   b. technical
   c. diverse
   d. challenging
10. What term is used to describe when an organization acquires goods and/or sources from an outside source in another country?
    a. globalization
    b. offshoring
    c. exporting
    d. global sourcing

Quick Quiz Answers

1. b; 2. d; 3. c; 4. d; 5. a; 6. a; 7. a; 8. d; 9. c; 10. b

Discussion Questions

1. What does it mean to take a systems view of a project? How does taking a systems view of a project apply to project management?
2. Explain the four frames of organizations. How can they help project managers understand the organizational context for their projects?

3. Briefly explain the differences between functional, matrix, and project organizations. Describe how each structure affects the management of the project.
4. Describe how organizational culture is related to project management. What type of culture promotes a strong project environment?
5. Discuss the importance of top management commitment and the development of standards for successful project management. Provide examples to illustrate the importance of these items based on your experience on any type of project.
6. What are the phases in a traditional project life cycle? How does a project life cycle differ from a product life cycle? Why does a project manager need to understand both?
7. What makes information technology projects different from other types of projects? How should project managers adjust to these differences?
8. Define globalization, outsourcing, and virtual teams and describe how these trends are changing IT project management.

Exercises

1. Summarize the three-sphere model of systems management in your own words. Then use your own experience or interview someone who recently completed an information technology project and list several business, technology, and organizational issues addressed during the project. Which issues were most important to the project and why? Summarize your answers in a two-page paper.
2. Apply the four frames of organizations to an information technology project with which you are familiar. If you cannot think of a good information technology project, use your personal experience in deciding where to attend college to apply this framework. Write a two-page paper describing key issues related to the structural, human resources, political, and symbolic frames. Which frame seemed to be the most important and why? For example, did you decide where to attend college primarily because of the curriculum and structure of the program? Did you follow your friends? Did your parents have a lot of influence in your decision? Did you like the culture of the campus?
3. Search the Internet for two interesting articles about software development life cycles, including agile software development. Also review the Web site *www.agilealliance.org*. What do these sources say about project management? Write a two-page summary of your findings, citing your references.

   Note: For this exercise and others, remember that you can find references cited in this text, suggested readings, and links to general project management Web sites on the companion Web site.
4. Search the Internet and scan information technology industry magazines or Web sites to find an example of an information technology project that had problems due to organizational issues. Write a two-page paper summarizing who the key stakeholders were for the project and how they influenced the outcome.
5. Write a two-page summary of an article about the importance of top management support for successful information technology projects and your opinion on this topic.

6. Research the trend of using virtual teams. Review the information on team role theory from *www.belbin.com* and other related sources. Write a two-page summary of your findings, citing at least three references. Also include your personal experience and/or opinion on the topic. For example, what role(s) would you prefer to play on a team? Do you like working on virtual teams? If you have not yet worked on one, how do you think it would be different from working on a face-to-face team?

Companion Web Site

Visit the companion Web site for this text at *www.cengage.com/mis/schwalbe* to access:

- References cited in the text and additional suggested readings for each chapter
- Template files
- Lecture notes
- Interactive quizzes
- Podcasts
- Links to general project management Web sites
- And more

See the Preface of this text for additional information on accessing the companion Web site.

Key Terms

adaptive software development (ASD) — A software development approach used when requirements cannot be clearly expressed early in the life cycle

agile software development — A method for software development that uses new approaches, focusing on close collaboration between programming teams and business experts

champion — A senior manager who acts as a key proponent for a project

deliverable — A product or service, such as a technical report, a training session, a piece of hardware, or a segment of software code, produced or provided as part of a project

executive steering committee — A group of senior executives from various parts of the organization who regularly review important corporate projects and issues

functional organizational structure — An organizational structure that groups people by functional areas such as information technology, manufacturing, engineering, and human resources

human resources frame — Focuses on producing harmony between the needs of the organization and the needs of people

IT governance — Addresses the authority and control for key IT activities in organizations, including IT infrastructure, IT use, and project management

kill point — Management review that should occur after each project phase to determine if projects should be continued, redirected, or terminated; also called a phase exit

matrix organizational structure — An organizational structure in which employees are assigned to both functional and project managers

offshoring — Outsourcing from another country

organizational culture — A set of shared assumptions, values, and behaviors that characterize the functioning of an organization

outsourcing — When an organization acquires goods and/or sources from an outside source

phase exit — Management review that should occur after each project phase to determine if projects should be continued, redirected, or terminated; also called a kill point

political frame — Addresses organizational and personal politics

politics — Competition between groups or individuals for power and leadership

predictive life cycle — A software development approach used when the scope of the project can be clearly articulated and the schedule and cost can be accurately predicted

project acquisition — The last two phases in a project (implementation and close-out) that focus on delivering the actual work

project feasibility — The first two phases in a project (concept and development) that focus on planning

project life cycle — A collection of project phases, such as concept, development, implementation, and close-out

project organizational structure — An organizational structure that groups people by major projects, such as specific aircraft programs

structural frame — Deals with how the organization is structured (usually depicted in an organizational chart) and focuses on different groups' roles and responsibilities to meet the goals and policies set by top management

symbolic frame — Focuses on the symbols, meanings, and culture of an organization

systems — Sets of interacting components working within an environment to fulfill some purpose

systems analysis — A problem-solving approach that requires defining the scope of the system to be studied, and then dividing it into its component parts for identifying and evaluating its problems, opportunities, constraints, and needs

systems approach — A holistic and analytical approach to solving complex problems that includes using a systems philosophy, systems analysis, and systems management

systems development life cycle (SDLC) — A framework for describing the phases involved in developing and maintaining information systems

systems management — Addressing the business, technological, and organizational issues associated with creating, maintaining, and making changes to a system

systems philosophy — An overall model for thinking about things as systems

systems thinking — Taking a holistic view of an organization to effectively handle complex situations

virtual team — A group of individuals who work across time and space using communication technologies

End Notes

[1] Lee G. Bolman and Terrence E. Deal, *Reframing Organizations* (San Francisco: Jossey-Bass, 1991).

[2] Eva Hoare, "Software hardships," *Herald* (Halifax: Nova Scotia) (February 4, 2001).

[3] Stephen P. Robbins and Timothy A. Judge, *Organizational Behavior, 13th Edition* (Prentice Hall, 2008).

[4] Charles V. Bagli, "Higher Costs and Delays Expected at Ground Zero," *New York Times* (June 30, 2008).

5 Peter Weill and Jeanne Ross, *IT Governance: How Top Performers Manage IT Decision Rights for Superior Results* (Harvard Business School Press, 2004).

6 David Avison, Shirely Gregor, and David Wilson, "Managerial IT Unconsciousness," *Communications of the ACM* 49, no. 7 (July 2006), p. 92.

7 Gartner Inc., "BNSF and UnitedHealth Group Win 2006 Gartner CRM Excellence Awards," press release (September 25, 2006).

8 Douglas H. Desaulniers and Robert J. Anderson, "Matching Software Development Life Cycles to the Project Environment," Proceedings of the Project Management Institute Annual Seminars & Symposium, (November 1–10, 2001).

9 Jeannette Cabanis, "A Major Import: The Standish Group's Jim Johnson on Project Management and IT Project Success," *PM Network* (PMI), (September 1998), p. 7.

10 Lucas Mearian, "Bank Hones Project Management Skills with Redesign," *ComputerWorld* (April 29, 2002).

11 IT Governance Institute, "COBIT and IT Governance Case Study: Harley-Davidson," *www.itgi.org* (September 2006).

12 Thomas L. Friedman, *The World Is Flat: A Brief History of the Twenty-First Century* (Farrar, Straus, and Giroux, 2005).

13 Timothy Porter, "Tools for Facilitating Project Communication in an Onshore-Offshore Engagement Model," *PMI-ISSIG.org* (June 30, 2008).

14 KPMG International, "Managing Global Projects: Observations from the front-line," *www.kpmg.com* (2007).

15 Belbin® Team Role Theory, *Belbin.com* (accessed July 1, 2008).

16 Jeremy S. Lurey and Mahesh S. Raisinghani, "An Empirical Study of Best Practices in Virtual Teams," *Information & Management* 38, no. 8 (2001).

CHAPTER 3

THE PROJECT MANAGEMENT PROCESS GROUPS: A CASE STUDY

LEARNING OBJECTIVES

After reading this chapter, you will be able to:

- Describe the five project management process groups, the typical level of activity for each, and the interactions among them
- Understand how the project management process groups relate to the project management knowledge areas
- Discuss how organizations develop information technology project management methodologies to meet their needs
- Review a case study of an organization applying the project management process groups to manage an information technology project, describe outputs of each process group, and understand the contribution that effective initiating, planning, executing, monitoring and controlling, and closing make to project success

OPENING CASE

Erica Bell was in charge of the Project Management Office (PMO) for her consulting firm. The firm, JWD—for Job Well Done—Consulting, had grown to include more than 200 full-time consultants and even more part-time consultants. JWD Consulting provides a variety of consulting services to assist organizations in selecting and managing information technology projects. The firm focuses on finding and managing high-payoff projects and developing strong metrics to measure project performance and benefits to the organization after the project is implemented. The firm's emphasis on metrics and working collaboratively with its customers gives it an edge over many competitors.

Joe Fleming, the CEO, wanted his company to continue to grow and become a world-class consulting organization. Since the core of the business was helping other organizations with project management, he felt it was crucial for JWD Consulting to have an exemplary process for managing its own projects. He asked Erica to work with her team and other consultants in the firm to develop several intranet site applications that would allow them to share their project management knowledge. He also thought it would make sense to make some of the information available to the firm's clients. For example, the firm could provide project management templates, tools, articles, links to other sites, and an "Ask the Expert" feature to help build relationships with current and future clients. Since JWD Consulting emphasizes the importance of high-payoff projects, Joe also wanted to see a business case for this project before proceeding.

Recall from Chapter 1 that project management consists of nine knowledge areas: integration, scope, time, cost, quality, human resources, communications, risk, and procurement. Another important concept to understand is that projects involve five project management process groups: initiating, planning, executing, monitoring and controlling, and closing. Tailoring these process groups to meet individual project needs increases the chance of success in managing projects. This chapter describes each project management process group in detail through a simulated case study based on JWD Consulting. It also includes samples of typical project documents applied to this case. You can download templates for these and other project documents from the companion Web site for this text. Although you will learn more about each knowledge area in Chapters 4 though 12, it is important first to learn how they fit into the big picture of managing a project. Understanding how the knowledge areas and project management process groups function together will lend context to the remaining chapters.

PROJECT MANAGEMENT PROCESS GROUPS

Project management is an integrative endeavor; decisions and actions taken in one knowledge area at a certain time usually affect other knowledge areas. Managing these interactions often requires making trade-offs among the project's scope, time, and cost—the triple constraint of project management described in Chapter 1. A project manager may also need to make trade-offs between other knowledge areas, such as between risk and human resources. Consequently, you can view project management as a number of related processes.

- A **process** is a series of actions directed toward a particular result. **Project management process groups** progress from initiating activities to planning activities, executing activities, monitoring and controlling activities, and closing activities. **Initiating processes** include defining and authorizing a project or project phase. Initiating processes take place during *each* phase of a project. Therefore, you cannot equate process groups with project phases. Recall that there can be different project phases, but all projects will include all five process groups. For example, project managers and teams should reexamine the business need for the project during every phase of the project life cycle to determine if the project is worth continuing. Initiating processes are also required to end a project. Someone must initiate activities to ensure that the project team completes all the work, documents lessons learned, assigns project resources, and that the customer accepts the work.
- **Planning processes** include devising and maintaining a workable scheme to ensure that the project addresses the organization's needs. There are several plans for projects, such as the scope management plan, schedule management plan, cost management plan, procurement management plan, and so on, defining each knowledge area as it relates to the project at that point in time. For example, a project team must develop a plan to define the work that needs to be done for the project, to schedule activities related to that work, to estimate costs for performing the work, to decide what resources to procure to accomplish the work, and so on. To account for changing conditions on the project and in the organization, project teams often revise plans during each phase of the project life cycle. The project management plan, described in Chapter 4, coordinates and encompasses information from all other plans.
- **Executing processes** include coordinating people and other resources to carry out the various plans and produce the products, services, or results of the project or phase. Examples of executing processes include acquiring and developing the project team, performing quality assurance, distributing information, managing stakeholder expectations, and conducting procurements.
- **Monitoring and controlling processes** include regularly measuring and monitoring progress to ensure that the project team meets the project objectives. The project manager and staff monitor and measure progress against the plans and take corrective action when necessary. A common monitoring and controlling process is reporting performance, where project stakeholders can identify any necessary changes that may be required to keep the project on track.
- **Closing processes** include formalizing acceptance of the project or project phase and ending it efficiently. Administrative activities are often involved in this process group, such as archiving project files, closing out contracts, documenting lessons learned, and receiving formal acceptance of the delivered work as part of the phase or project.

The process groups are not mutually exclusive. For example, project managers must perform monitoring and controlling processes throughout the project's life span. The level of activity and length of each process group varies for every project. Normally, executing tasks requires the most resources and time, followed by planning tasks. Initiating and closing tasks are usually the shortest (at the beginning and end of a project or phase, respectively), and they require the least amount of resources and time. However, every project is unique, so there can be exceptions. You can apply the process groups for each major phase of a project, or you can apply the process groups to an entire project, as the JWD Consulting case study does in this chapter.

Many people ask for guidelines on how much time to spend in each process group. In his book, *Alpha Project Managers: What the Top 2% Know That Everyone Else Does Not*, Andy Crowe collected data from 860 project managers in various companies and industries in the United States. He found that the best—the "alpha"—project managers spent more time on every process group than their counterparts except for executing, as shown in Figure 3-1. This breakdown suggests that the most time should be spent on executing, followed by planning. Spending a fair amount of time on planning should lead to less time spent on execution. Notice that the alpha project managers spent almost twice as much time on planning (21 percent versus 11 percent) as other project managers.[1]

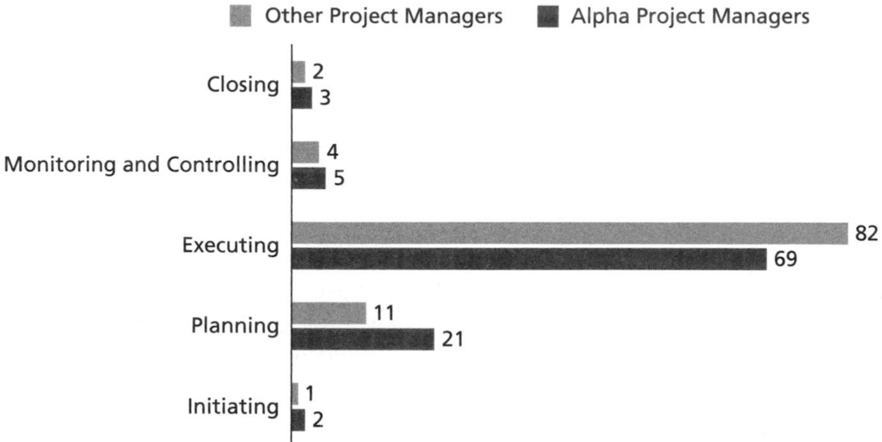

FIGURE 3-1 Percentage of time spent on each process group

WHAT WENT WRONG?

Many readers of *CIO Magazine* commented on its cover story about problems with information systems at the U.S. Internal Revenue Service (IRS). The article described serious problems the IRS has had in managing information technology projects. Philip A. Pell, PMP,

continued

believes that having a good project manager and following a good project management process would help the IRS and many organizations tremendously. Mr. Pell provided the following feedback:

> Pure and simple, good, methodology-centric, predictable, and repeatable project management is the SINGLE greatest factor in the success (or in this case failure) of any project. When a key stakeholder says, 'I didn't know how bad things were,' it is a direct indictment of the project manager's communications management plan. When a critical deliverable like the middleware infrastructure that makes the whole thing work is left without assigned resources and progress tracking, the project manager has failed in his duty to the stakeholders. When key stakeholders (people and organizations that will be affected by the project, not just people who are directly working on the project) are not informed and their feedback incorporated into the project plan, disaster is sure to ensue. The project manager is ultimately responsible for the success or failure of the project.[2]

The IRS continues to have problems managing IT projects. A 2008 U.S. Government Accountability Office (GAO) report stated that IRS had fixed just 29 of 98 information security weaknesses identified the previous year. The report stated that the IRS has "persistent information security weaknesses that place [it] at risk of disruption, fraud or inappropriate disclosure of sensitive information."[3]

Each of the five project management process groups is characterized by the completion of certain tasks. During initiating processes for a new project, the organization recognizes that a new project exists, and completes a project charter as part of this recognition (see Chapter 4 for more information on project charters). Tables are provided later in this chapter with detailed lists of possible outputs for each process group by knowledge area. For example, Tables 3-3 through 3-7 list potential outputs for the initiating and planning process groups. Samples of some outputs are provided for each process group in a case study of JWD Consulting's Project Management Intranet Site project. Project managers and their teams must decide which outputs are required for their particular projects.

Outputs of the planning process group include completing the project scope statement, the work breakdown structure, the project schedule, and many other items. Planning processes are especially important for information technology projects. Everyone who has ever worked on a large information technology project that involves new technology knows the saying, "A dollar spent up front in planning is worth one hundred dollars spent after the system is implemented." Planning is crucial in information technology projects because once a project team implements a new system, it takes a considerable amount of effort to change the system. Research suggests that companies working to implement best practices should spend at least 20 percent of project time in initiating and planning.[4] This percentage is backed up by evidence from Alpha Project Managers, as described earlier.

The executing process group takes the actions necessary to complete the work described in the planning activities. The main outcome of this process group is delivering the actual work of the project. For example, if an information technology project involves providing new hardware, software, and training, the executing processes would include leading the project team and other stakeholders to purchase the hardware, develop and test the software, and deliver and participate in the training. The executing process group should overlap the other process groups and generally requires the most resources.

Monitoring and controlling processes measure progress toward the project objectives, monitor deviation from the plan, and take corrective action to match progress with the plan. Performance reports are common outputs of monitoring and controlling. The project manager should be monitoring progress closely to ensure that deliverables are being completed and objectives are being met. The project manager must work closely with the project team and other stakeholders and take appropriate actions to keep the project running smoothly. The ideal outcome of the monitoring and controlling process group is to complete a project successfully by delivering the agreed-upon project scope within time, cost, and quality constraints. If changes to project objectives or plans are required, monitoring and controlling processes ensure that these changes are made efficiently and effectively to meet stakeholder needs and expectations. Monitoring and controlling processes overlap all of the other project management process groups because changes can occur at any time.

During the closing processes, the project team works to gain acceptance of the end products, services, or results and bring the phase or project to an orderly end. Key outcomes of this process group are formal acceptance of the work and creation of closing documents, such as a final project report and lessons-learned report.

MEDIA SNAPSHOT

Just as information technology projects need to follow the project management process groups, so do other projects, such as the production of a movie. Processes involved in making movies might include screenwriting (initiating), producing (planning), acting and directing (executing), editing (monitoring and controlling), and releasing the movie to theaters (closing). Many people enjoy watching the extra features on a DVD that describe how these processes lead to the creation of a movie. For example, the DVD for *Lord of the Rings: The Two Towers Extended Edition* includes detailed descriptions of how the script was created, how huge structures were built, how special effects were made, and how talented professionals overcame numerous obstacles to complete the project. This acted "not as promotional filler but as a serious and meticulously detailed examination of the entire filmmaking process."[5] New Line Cinema made history by shooting all three Lord of the Rings films consecutively during one massive production. It took three years of preparation to build the sets, find the locations, write the scripts, and cast the actors. Director Peter Jackson said that the amount of early planning they did made it easier than he imagined to produce the films. Project managers in any field know how important it is to have good plans and to follow a good process.

MAPPING THE PROCESS GROUPS TO THE KNOWLEDGE AREAS

You can map the main activities of each project management process group into the nine project management knowledge areas. Table 3-1 provides a big-picture view of the relationships among the 42 project management activities, the process groups in which they are typically completed, and the knowledge areas into which they fit. The activities listed in the table are the main processes for each knowledge area listed in the *PMBOK® Guide, Fourth Edition*. This text also includes additional activities not listed in the *PMBOK® Guide*, such as creating a business case and team contract, which can also assist in managing projects.

Several organizations use PMI's *PMBOK® Guide* information as a foundation for developing their own project management methodologies, as described in the next section. Notice in Table 3-1 that many of the project management processes occur as part of the planning process group. Since each project is unique, project teams are always trying to do something that has not been done before. To succeed at unique and new activities, project teams must do a fair amount of planning. Recall, however, that the most time and money is normally spent on executing. It is good practice for organizations to determine how project management will work best in their own organizations.

TABLE 3-1 Project management process groups and knowledge area mapping

Knowledge Area	Project Management Process Groups				
	Initiating	Planning	Executing	Monitoring and Controlling	Closing
Project Integration Management	Develop project charter	Develop project management plan	Direct and manage project execution	Monitor and control project work, Perform integrated change control	Close project or phase
Project Scope Management		Collect requirements, Define scope, Create WBS		Verify scope, Control scope	
Project Time Management		Define activities, Sequence activities,		Control schedule	

(continued)

TABLE 3-1 Project management process groups and knowledge area mapping (*continued*)

Knowledge Area	Project Management Process Groups				
	Initiating	Planning	Executing	Monitoring and Controlling	Closing
Project Time Management (continued)		Estimate activity resources, Estimate activity durations, Develop schedule			
Project Cost Management		Estimate costs, Determine budget		Control costs	
Project Quality Management		Plan quality	Perform quality assurance	Perform quality control	
Project Human Resource Management		Develop human resource plan	Acquire project team, Develop project team, Manage project team		
Project Communi-cations Management	Identify stake-holders	Plan communi-cations	Distribute information, Manage stakeholders expectations	Report performance	
Project Risk Management		Plan risk man-agement, Identi-fy risks, Perform qualitative risk analysis, Perform quantitative risk analysis, Plan risk responses		Monitor and control risks	
Project Procurement Management		Plan procurements	Conduct procurements	Administer procurements	Close procurements

Source: PMBOK® Guide, Fourth Edition, 2008.

DEVELOPING AN INFORMATION TECHNOLOGY PROJECT MANAGEMENT METHODOLOGY

Some organizations spend a great deal of time and money on training efforts for general project management skills, but after the training, project managers may still not know how to tailor their project management skills to the organization's particular needs. Because of this problem, some organizations develop their own internal information technology project management methodologies. The *PMBOK® Guide* is a **standard** that describes best practices for *what* should be done to manage a project. A **methodology** describes *how* things should be done, and different organizations often have different ways of doing things.

In addition to using the *PMBOK® Guide* as a basis for project management methodology, many organizations use others, such as the following:

- **PRojects IN Controlled Environments (PRINCE2):** Originally developed for information technology projects, PRINCE2 was released in 1996 as a generic project management methodology by the U.K. Office of Government Commerce (OCG). It is the de facto standard in the United Kingdom and is used in over 50 countries. (See *www.prince2.com* for more information.) PRINCE2 defines 45 separate subprocesses and organizes these into eight process groups as follows:

  1. Starting Up a Project
  2. Planning
  3. Initiating a Project
  4. Directing a Project
  5. Controlling a Stage
  6. Managing Product Delivery
  7. Managing Stage Boundaries
  8. Closing a Project

- **Agile methodologies:** As described in Chapter 2, agile software development is a form of adaptive software development. All agile methodologies include an iterative workflow and incremental delivery of software in short iterations. Several popular agile methodologies include extreme programming, scrum, feature driven development, lean software development, Agile Unified Process (AUP), Crystal, and Dynamic Systems Development Method (DSDM). (See Web sites like *www.agilealliance.org* and the Suggested Readings on the companion Web site for this text for more information.)
- **Rational Unified Process (RUP) framework:** RUP is an iterative software development process that focuses on team productivity and delivers software best practices to all team members. According to RUP expert Bill Cottrell, "RUP embodies industry-standard management and technical methods and techniques to provide a software engineering process particularly suited to creating and maintaining component-based software system solutions."[6] Cottrell explains that you can tailor RUP to include the PMBOK process groups, since several customers asked for that capability. There are several other project management methodologies specifically for software development projects such as Joint Application Development (JAD) and Rapid Application Development

(RAD). (See Web sites such as *www.ibm.com/software/awdtools/rup* for more information.)

- **Six Sigma methodologies:** Many organizations have projects underway that use Six Sigma methodologies. The work of many project quality experts contributed to the development of today's Six Sigma principles. Two main methodologies are used on Six Sigma projects: DMAIC (Define, Measure, Analyze, Improve, and Control) is used to improve an existing business process, and DMADV (Define, Measure, Analyze, Design, and Verify) is used to create new product or process designs to achieve predictable, defect-free performance. (See Chapter 8, Project Quality Management, for more information on Six Sigma.)

Many organizations tailor a standard or methodology to meet their unique needs. For example, if organizations use the *PMBOK® Guide* as the basis for their project management methodology, they still have to do a fair amount of work to adapt it to their work environment. See the suggested reading on the companion Web site by William Munroe for an example of how Blue Cross Blue Shield of Michigan developed its IT project management methodology.

WHAT WENT RIGHT?

AgênciaClick, an interactive advertising and online communications company based in São Paulo, Brazil, made PMI's list of outstanding organizations in project management in 2007. Since 2002, the company saw revenues jump 132 percent, primarily due to their five-year emphasis on practicing good project management across the entire company. AgênciaClick launched a PMO in 2002 and used the *PMBOK® Guide* as the basis for developing their methodology and project management training program. The company also developed a custom project tracking system to help calculate physical work progress each day and alert managers of any schedule or cost issues. PMO Director Fabiano D'Agostinho said, "We realized the only way to manage multiple dynamic projects and deliver great products is to focus on project management ... By monitoring and controlling projects and programs more efficiently, senior managers can focus on issues within the portfolio that need more attention."[7]

The following section describes an example of applying the project management process groups to a project at JWD Consulting. It uses some of the ideas from the *PMBOK® Guide, Fourth Edition*, some ideas from other methodologies, and some new ideas to meet unique project needs.

CASE STUDY: JWD CONSULTING'S PROJECT MANAGEMENT INTRANET SITE PROJECT

The following fictitious case provides an example of the elements involved in managing a project from start to finish. This example also uses Microsoft Project to demonstrate how project management software can assist in several aspects of managing a project. Several templates illustrate how project teams prepare various project management documents. Files for these and other templates are available on the companion Web site for this text. Details on creating many of the documents shown are provided in later chapters, so do not worry if you do not understand everything right now. You might want to read this section again to enhance your learning.

Project Pre-Initiation and Initiation

In project management, initiating includes recognizing and starting a new project. An organization should put considerable thought into project selection to ensure that it initiates the right kinds of projects for the right reasons. *It is better to have a moderate or even small amount of success on an important project than huge success on one that is unimportant*. The selection of projects for initiation, therefore, is crucial, as is the selection of project managers. Ideally, the project manager would be involved in initiating a project, but often the project manager is selected after many initiation decisions have already been made. You will learn more about project selection in Chapter 4, Project Integration Management. Organizations must also understand and plan for the ongoing support that is often required after implementing a new system or other product or service resulting from a project.

It is important to remember that strategic planning should serve as the foundation for deciding which projects to pursue. The organization's strategic plan expresses the vision, mission, goals, objectives, and strategies of the organization. It also provides the basis for information technology project planning. Information technology is usually a support function in an organization, so it is critical that the people initiating information technology projects understand how those projects relate to current and future needs of the organization. For example, JWD Consulting's main business is providing consulting services to other organizations, not developing its own intranet site applications. Information systems, therefore, must support the firm's business goals, such as providing consulting services more effectively and efficiently.

An organization may initiate information technology projects for several reasons, but the most important reason is to support business objectives. Providing a good return on investment at a reasonable level of risk is also important, especially in tough economic times. As mentioned in the opening case, JWD Consulting wants to follow an exemplary process for managing its projects since its core business is helping other organizations manage projects. Developing an intranet to share its project management knowledge could help JWD Consulting reduce internal costs by working more effectively, and by allowing existing and potential customers to access some of the firm's information. JWD Consulting could also increase revenues by bringing in more business. Therefore, they will use these metrics—reducing internal costs and increasing revenues—to measure their own performance on this project.

Pre-Initiation Tasks

It is good practice to lay the groundwork for a project *before* it officially starts. Senior managers often perform several tasks, sometimes called pre-initiation tasks, including the following:

- Determine the scope, time, and cost constraints for the project
- Identify the project sponsor

- Select the project manager
- Develop a business case for a project
- Meet with the project manager to review the process and expectations for managing the project
- Determine if the project should be divided into two or more smaller projects

As described in the opening case, the CEO of JWD Consulting, Joe Fleming, defined the high-level scope of the project, and he wanted to sponsor it himself since it was his idea and it was of strategic importance to the business. He wanted Erica Bell, the PMO Director, to manage the project after proving there was a strong business case for it. If there was a strong business case for pursuing the project, then Joe and Erica would meet to review the process and expectations for managing the project. If there was not a strong business case, the project would not continue. As for the necessity of the last pre-initiation task, many people know from experience that it is easier to successfully complete a small project than a large one, especially for IT projects. It often makes sense to break large projects down into two or more smaller ones to help increase the odds of success. In this case, however, Joe and Erica decided that the work could be done in one project that would last about six months. To justify investing in this project, Erica drafted a business case for the project, getting input and feedback from Joe, from one of her senior staff members in the PMO, and from a member of the Finance department. She also used a corporate template and sample business cases from past projects as a guide. Table 3-2 provides the business case. (Note that this example and others are abbreviated examples. See the companion Web site for additional examples of project documents and to download a business case template and other templates.) Notice that the following information is included in this business case:

- Introduction/background
- Business objective
- Current situation and problem/opportunity statement
- Critical assumptions and constraints
- Analysis of options and recommendation
- Preliminary project requirements
- Budget estimate and financial analysis
- Schedule estimate
- Potential risks
- Exhibits

Since this project is relatively small and is for an internal sponsor, the business case is not as long as many other business cases. Erica reviewed the business case with Joe, and he agreed that the project was definitely worth pursuing. He was quite pleased to see that payback was estimated within a year, and the return on investment was projected to be 112 percent. He told Erica to proceed with the formal initiation tasks for this project, as described in the next section.

TABLE 3-2 JWD Consulting's business case

1.0 Introduction/Background

JWD Consulting's core business goal is to provide world-class project management consulting services to various organizations. The CEO, Joe Fleming, believes the firm can streamline operations and increase business by providing information related to project management on its intranet site, making some information and services accessible to current and potential clients.

2.0 Business Objective

JWD Consulting's strategic goals include continuing growth and profitability. The Project Management Intranet Site Project will support these goals by increasing visibility of the firm's expertise to current and potential clients by allowing client and public access to some sections of the intranet. It will also improve profitability by reducing internal costs by providing standard tools, techniques, templates, and project management knowledge to all internal consultants. Since JWD Consulting focuses on identifying profitable projects and measuring their value after completion, this project must meet those criteria.

3.0 Current Situation and Problem/Opportunity Statement

JWD Consulting has a corporate Web site as well as an intranet. The firm currently uses the Web site for marketing information. The primary use of the intranet is for human resource information, such as where consultants enter their hours on various projects, change and view their benefits information, access an online directory and Web-based e-mail system, and so on. The firm also uses an enterprise-wide project management system to track all project information, focusing on the status of deliverables and meeting scope, time, and cost goals. There is an opportunity to provide a new section on the intranet dedicated to sharing consultants' project management knowledge across the organization. JWD Consulting only hires experienced consultants and gives them freedom to manage projects as they see fit. However, as the business grows and projects become more complex, even experienced project managers are looking for suggestions on how to work more effectively.

4.0 Critical Assumption and Constraints

The proposed intranet site must be a valuable asset for JWD Consulting. Current consultants and clients must actively support the project, and it must pay for itself within one year by reducing internal operating costs and generating new business. The Project Management Office manager must lead the effort, and the project team must include participants from several parts of the company, as well as current client organizations. The new system must run on existing hardware and software, and it should require minimal technical support. It must be easily accessible by consultants and clients and be secure from unauthorized users.

5.0 Analysis of Options and Recommendation

There are three options for addressing this opportunity:

1. Do nothing. The business is doing well, and we can continue to operate without this new project.
2. Purchase access to specialized software to support this new capability with little in-house development.

(continued)

3. Design and implement the new intranet capabilities in-house using mostly existing hardware and software.

Based on discussions with stakeholders, we believe that option 3 is the best option.

6.0 Preliminary Project Requirements

The main features of the project management intranet site include the following:

1. Access to several project management templates and tools. Users must be able to search for templates and tools, read instructions on using these templates and tools, and see examples of how to apply them to real projects. Users must also be able to submit new templates and tools, which should be first screened or edited by the Project Management Office.
2. Access to relevant project management articles. Many consultants and clients feel as though there is an information overload when they research project management information. They often waste time they should be spending with their clients. The new intranet should include access to several important articles on various project management topics, which are searchable by topic, and allow users to request the Project Management Office staff to find additional articles to meet their needs.
3. Links to other, up-to-date Web sites, with brief descriptions of the main features of the external site.
4. An "Ask the Expert" feature to help build relationships with current and future clients and share knowledge with internal consultants.
5. Appropriate security to make the entire intranet site accessible to internal consultants and certain sections accessible to others.
6. The ability to charge money for access to some information. Some of the information and features of the intranet site should prompt external users to pay for the information or service. Payment options should include a credit card option or similar online payment transactions. After the system verifies payment, the user should be able to access or download the desired information.
7. Other features suggested by users, if they add value to the business.

7.0 Budget Estimate and Financial Analysis

A preliminary estimate of costs for the entire project is $140,000. This estimate is based on the project manager working about 20 hours per week for six months and other internal staff working a total of about 60 hours per week for six months. The customer representatives would not be paid for their assistance. A staff project manager would earn $50 per hour. The hourly rate for the other project team members would be $70 per hour, since some hours normally billed to clients may be needed for this project. The initial cost estimate also includes $10,000 for purchasing software and services from suppliers. After the project is completed, maintenance costs of $40,000 are included for each year, primarily to update the information and coordinate the "Ask the Expert" feature and online articles.

Projected benefits are based on a reduction in hours consultants spend researching project management information, appropriate tools and templates, and so on. Projected benefits are also based on a small increase in profits due to new business generated by this project. If each of more than 400 consultants saved just 40 hours each year (less than one hour per week) and could bill that time to other projects that generate a conservative estimate of $10 per hour in *profits*, then the projected benefit would be $160,000 per year. If the new intranet increased business by just 1 percent, using past profit information, increased profits due to new business would be at least $40,000 each year. Total projected benefits, therefore, are about $200,000 per year.

Exhibit A summarizes the projected costs and benefits and shows the estimated net present value (NPV), return on investment (ROI), and year in which payback occurs. It also lists assumptions made in performing this preliminary financial analysis. All of the financial estimates are very encouraging. The estimated payback is within one year, as requested by the sponsor. The NPV is $272,800, and the discounted ROI based on a three-year system life is excellent at 112 percent.

8.0 Schedule Estimate

The sponsor would like to see the project completed within six months, but there is some flexibility in the schedule. We also assume that the new system will have a useful life of at least three years.

9.0 Potential Risks

There are several risks involved with this project. The foremost risk is a lack of interest in the new system by our internal consultants and external clients. User inputs are crucial for populating information into this system and realizing the potential benefits from using the system. There are some technical risks in choosing the type of software used to search the system, check security, process payments, and so on, but the features of this system all use proven technologies. The main business risk is investing the time and money into this project and not realizing the projected benefits.

10.0 Exhibits

Exhibit A: Financial Analysis for Project Management Intranet Site Project

Discount rate	8%				
Assume the project is done in about 6 months		Year			
	0	1	2	3	Total
Costs	140,000	40,000	40,000	40,000	
Discount factor	1	0.93	0.86	0.79	
Discounted costs	140,000	37,037	34,294	31,753	243,084
Benefits	0	200,000	200,000	200,000	
Discount factor	1	0.93	0.86	0.79	
Discounted benefits	0	186,185	171,468	158,766	515,419
Discounted benefits - costs	(140,000)	148,148	137,174	127,013	
Cumulative benefits - costs	(140,000)	8,148	145,322	272,336	← NPV
	Payback in Year 1				
Discounted life cycle ROI----------->	**112%**				
Assumptions					
Costs	# hours				
PM (500 hours, $50/hour)	25,000				
Staff (1500 hours, $70/hour)	105,000				
Outsourced software and services	10,000				
Total project costs (all applied in year 0)	140,000				
Benefits					
# consultants	400				
Hours saved	40				
$/hour profit	10				
Benefits from saving time	160,000				
Benefits from 1% increase in profits	40,000				
Total annual projected benefits	200,000				

Initiating

To officially initiate the Project Management Intranet Site project, Erica knew that main tasks were to identify all of the project stakeholders and to develop the project charter. Table 3-3 shows these processes and their outputs, based on the *PMBOK® Guide Fourth Edition*. The main outputs are a project charter, stakeholder register, and stakeholder management strategy. Another output that Erica found very useful for initiating projects was a formal project kick-off meeting. Descriptions of how these outputs were created and sample documents related to each of them are provided for this particular project. Recall that every project and every organization is unique, so not all project charters, stakeholder registers, etc. will look the same. You will see examples of several of these documents in later chapters.

TABLE 3-3 Project initiation knowledge areas, processes, and outputs

Knowledge Area	Initiating Process	Outputs
Project Integration Management	Develop project charter	Project charter
Project Communications Management	Identify stakeholders	Stakeholder register Stakeholder management strategy

Identifying Project Stakeholders

Erica met with Joe Fleming, the project's sponsor, to help identify key stakeholders for this project. Recall from Chapter 1 that stakeholders are people involved in or affected by project activities and include the project sponsor, project team, support staff, customers, users, suppliers, and even opponents to the project. Joe, the project sponsor, knew it would be important to assemble a strong project team, and he was very confident in Erica's ability to lead that team. They decided that key team members should include one of their full-time consultants with an outstanding record, Michael Chen, one part-time consultant, Jessie Faue, who was new to the company and supported the Project Management Office, and two members of the Information Technology (IT) department who supported the current intranet, Kevin Dodge and Cindy Dawson. They also knew that client inputs would be important for this project, so Joe agreed to call the CEOs of two of the firm's largest clients to see if they would be willing to provide representatives to work on this project at their own expense. All of the internal staff Joe and Erica recommended agreed to work on the project, and the two client representatives would be Kim Phuong and Page Miller. Since many other people would be affected by this project as future users of the new intranet, they also identified other key stakeholders including their directors of IT, Human Resources (HR), and Public Relations (PR), as well as Erica's administrative assistant.

After Joe and Erica made the preliminary contacts, Erica documented the stakeholders' roles, names, organizations, and contact information in a **stakeholder register**, a document that includes details related to the identified project stakeholders. Table 3-4 provides an example of part of the initial stakeholder register. Since this document would be public, Erica was careful not to include information that might be sensitive, such as how strongly the stakeholder supported the project, potential influence on the project, requirements and

TABLE 3-4 Stakeholder register

Name	Position	Internal/ External	Project Role	Contact Information
Joe Fleming	CEO	Internal	Sponsor	joe_fleming@jwdconsulting.com
Erica Bell	PMO Director	Internal	Project manager	erica_bell@jwdconsulting.com
Michael Chen	Team member	Internal	Team member	michael_chen@jwdconsulting.com
Kim Phuong	Business analyst	External	Advisor	kim_phuong@client1.com
Louise Mills	PR Director	Internal	Advisor	louise_mills@jwdconsulting.com

expectations, etc. She would keep these issues in mind discretely and use them in developing the stakeholder management strategy.

A stakeholder management strategy is an approach to help increase the support of stakeholders throughout the project. It includes basic information such as stakeholder names, level of interest in the project, level of influence on the project, and potential management strategies for gaining support or reducing obstacles from that particular stakeholder. Since much of this information can be sensitive, it should be considered confidential. Some project managers do not even write down this information, but they do consider it since stakeholder management is a crucial part of their jobs. Table 3-5 provides an example of part of Erica's stakeholder management strategy for the Project Management Intranet Site project. You will see other examples of documenting stakeholder information in later chapters.

TABLE 3-5 Stakeholder management strategy

Name	Level of Interest	Level of Influence	Potential Management Strategies
Joe Fleming	High	High	Joe likes to stay on top of key projects and make money. Have a lot of short, face-to-face meetings and focus on achieving the financial benefits of the project.
Louise Mills	Low	High	Louise has a lot of things on her plate, and she does not seem excited about this project. She may be looking at other job opportunities. Show her how this project will help the company and her resume.

Drafting the Project Charter

Erica drafted a project charter and had the project team members review it before showing it to Joe. Joe made a few minor changes, which Erica incorporated. Table 3-6 shows the final project charter (see Chapter 4 for more information on project charters). Note the items included on the project charter and its short length. JWD Consulting believes that project charters should preferably be one or two pages long, and they may refer to other documents, such as a business case, as needed. Erica felt the most important parts of the project charter were the signatures of key stakeholders (not included for brevity) and their individual comments. It is hard to get stakeholders to agree on even a one-page project charter, so everyone has a chance to make their concerns known in the comments section. Note that Michael Chen, the senior consultant asked to work on the project, was concerned about working on this project when he felt that his other assignments with external clients might have a higher priority. He offered to have an assistant help as needed. The information technology staff members mentioned their concerns about testing and security issues. Erica knew that she would have to consider these concerns when managing the project.

TABLE 3-6 Project charter

Project Title: Project Management Intranet Site Project
Project Start Date: May 2 **Projected Finish Date:** November 4

Budget Information: The firm has allocated $140,000 for this project. The majority of costs for this project will be internal labor. An initial estimate provides a total of 80 hours per week.

Project Manager: Erica Bell, (310) 555-5896, erica_bell@jwdconsulting.com

Project Objectives: Develop a new capability accessible on JWD Consulting's intranet site to help internal consultants and external customers manage projects more effectively. The intranet site will include several templates and tools that users can download, examples of completed templates and related project management documents used on real projects, important articles related to recent project management topics, an article retrieval service, links to other sites with useful information, and an "Ask the Expert" feature, where users can post questions they have about their projects and receive advice from experts in the field. Some parts of the intranet site will be accessible free to the public, other parts will only be accessible to current customers and/or internal consultants, and other parts of the intranet site will be accessible for a fee.

Main Project Success Criteria: The project should pay for itself within one year of completion.

Approach:

- Develop a survey to determine critical features of the new intranet site and solicit input from consultants and customers.
- Review internal and external templates and examples of project management documents.
- Research software to provide security, manage user inputs, and facilitate the article retrieval and "Ask the Expert" features.
- Develop the intranet site using an iterative approach, soliciting a great deal of user feedback.

TABLE 3-6 Project charter (*continued*)

- Determine a way to measure the value of the intranet site in terms of reduced costs and new revenues, both during the project and one year after project completion.

ROLES AND RESPONSIBILITIES

Name	Role	Position	Contact Information
Joe Fleming	Sponsor	JWD Consulting, CEO	joe_fleming@jwdconsulting.com
Erica Bell	Project Manager	JWD Consulting, manager	erica_bell@jwdconsulting.com
Michael Chen	Team Member	JWD Consulting, senior consultant	michael_chen@jwdconsulting.com
Jessie Faue	Team Member	JWD Consulting, consultant	jessie_faue@jwdconsulting.com
Kevin Dodge	Team Member	JWD Consulting, IT department	kevin_dodge@jwdconsulting.com
Cindy Dawson	Team Member	JWD Consulting, IT department	cindy_dawson@jwdconsulting.com
Kim Phuong	Advisor	Client representative	kim_phuong@client1.com
Page Miller	Advisor	Client representative	page_miller@client2.com

Sign-Off: (Signatures of all the above stakeholders)
Comments: (Handwritten or typed comments from above stakeholders, if applicable)
"I will support this project as time allows, but I believe my client projects take priority. I will have one of my assistants support the project as needed." —Michael Chen
"We need to be extremely careful testing this new system, especially the security in giving access to parts of the intranet site to the public and clients." —Kevin Dodge and Cindy Dawson

Holding a Project Kick-off Meeting

Experienced project managers like Erica know that it is crucial to get projects off to a great start. Holding a good kick-off meeting is an excellent way to do this. A **kick-off meeting** is a meeting held at the beginning of a project so that stakeholders can meet each other, review the goals of the project, and discuss future plans. The kick-off meeting is often held after the business case and project charter are completed, but it could be held sooner, as needed. Even if some or even all project stakeholders must meet virtually, it is still important to have a kick-off meeting.

Erica also knows that all project meetings with major stakeholders should include an agenda. Figure 3-2 shows the agenda that Erica provided for the Project Management Intranet Site project kick-off meeting. Notice the main topics in an agenda:

- Meeting objective
- Agenda (lists in order the topics to be discussed)

- A section for documenting action items, who they are assigned to, and when each person will complete the action
- A section to document the date and time of the next meeting

Kick-Off Meeting
[Date of Meeting]

Project Name: Project Management Intranet Site Project

Meeting Objective: Get the project off to an effective start by introducing key stakeholders, reviewing project goals, and discussing future plans

Agenda:

- Introductions of attendees
- Review of the project background
- Review of project-related documents (i.e., business case, project charter)
- Discussion of project organizational structure
- Discussion of project scope, time, and cost goals
- Discussion of other important topics
- List of action items from meeting

Action Item	Assigned To	Due Date

Date and time of next meeting:

FIGURE 3-2 Kick-off meeting agenda

It is good practice to focus on results of meetings, and having sections for documenting action items and deciding on the next meeting date and time on the agenda helps to do so. It is also good practice to document meeting minutes, focusing on key decisions and action items. Erica planned to send the meeting minutes to all meeting participants and other appropriate stakeholders within a day or two of the meeting.

Project Planning

Planning is often the most difficult and unappreciated process in project management. Because planning is not always used to facilitate action, many people view planning negatively. The main purpose of project plans, however, is *to guide project execution*. To guide execution, plans must be realistic and useful, so a fair amount of time and effort must go into the planning process; people knowledgeable with the work need to plan the work.

Chapter 4, Project Integration Management, provides detailed information on preparing a project management plan, and Chapters 5 through 12 describe planning processes for each of the other knowledge areas.

Table 3-7 lists the project management knowledge areas, processes, and outputs of project planning according to the *PMBOK® Guide, Fourth Edition*. There are many potential outputs from the planning process group, and every knowledge area is included. Just a few planning documents from JWD Consulting's Project Management Intranet Site Project are provided in this chapter as examples, and later chapters include many more examples. Recall that the *PMBOK® Guide* is only a guide, so many organizations may have different planning outputs based on their particular needs, as is the case in this example. There are many templates related to planning as well, with several listed in the last section of this chapter.

TABLE 3-7 Planning processes and outputs

Knowledge Area	Planning Process	Outputs
Project Integration Management	Develop project management plan	Project management plan
Project Scope Management	Collect requirements	Requirements documents Requirements management plan Requirements traceability matrix
	Define scope	Project scope statement Project document updates
	Create WBS	WBS WBS dictionary Scope baseline Project document updates
Project Time Management	Define activities	Activity list Activity attributes Milestone list
	Sequence activities	Project schedule network diagrams Project document updates
	Estimate activity resources	Activity resource requirements Resource breakdown structure Project document updates
	Estimate activity durations	Activity duration estimates Project document updates
	Develop schedule	Project schedule Schedule baseline

(continued)

TABLE 3-7 Planning processes and outputs (*continued*)

Knowledge Area	Planning Process	Outputs
		Schedule data Project document updates
Project Cost Management	Estimate costs	Activity cost estimates Basis of estimates Project document updates
	Determine budget	Cost performance baseline Project funding requirements Project document updates
Project Quality Management	Plan quality	Quality management plan Quality metrics Quality checklists Process improvement plan Project document updates
Project Human Resource Management	Develop human resource plan	Human resource plan
Project Communications Management	Plan communications	Communications management plan Project document updates
Project Risk Management	Plan risk management	Risk management plan
	Identify risks	Risk register
	Perform qualitative risk analysis	Risk register updates
	Perform quantitative risk analysis	Risk register updates
	Plan risk responses	Risk register updates Project management plan updates Risk related contract decisions Project document updates
Project Procurement Management	Plan procurements	Procurement management plan Procurement statement of work Make-or-buy decisions Procurement documents Source selection criteria Change requests

Since the Project Management Intranet Site project is relatively small, Erica believes some of the most important planning documents to focus on are the following:

- A team contract (not listed in Table 3-7, which is based only on the *PMBOK® Guide*)
- A project scope statement
- A work breakdown structure (WBS)
- A project schedule, in the form of a Gantt chart with all dependencies and resources entered
- A list of prioritized risks (part of a risk register)

All of these documents, as well as other project-related information, will be available to all team members on a project Web site. JWD Consulting has used project Web sites for several years, and has found that they really help facilitate communications and document project information. For larger projects, JWD Consulting also creates many of the other outputs listed in Table 3-7. (You will learn more about these documents by knowledge area in the following chapters.)

Soon after the project team signed the project charter, Erica organized a team-building meeting for the Project Management Intranet Site Project. An important part of the meeting was helping the project team get to know each other. Erica had met and talked to each member separately, but this was the first time the project team would spend much time together. Jessie Faue worked in the Project Management Office with Erica, so they knew each other well, but Jessie was new to the company and did not know any of the other team members. Michael Chen was a senior consultant and often worked on the highest priority projects for external clients. He attended the meeting with his assistant, Jill Anderson, who would also support the project when Michael was too busy. Everyone valued Michael's expertise, and he was extremely straightforward in dealing with people. He also knew both of the client representatives from past projects. Kevin Dodge was JWD Consulting's intranet guru who tended to focus on technical details. Cindy Dawson was also from the Information Technology department and had experience working as a business consultant and negotiating with outside suppliers. Kim Phuong and Page Miller, the two client representatives, were excited about the project, but they were wary of sharing sensitive information about their company.

Erica had everyone introduce him or herself, and then she facilitated an icebreaker activity so everyone would be more relaxed. She asked everyone to describe his or her dream vacation, assuming cost was no issue. This activity helped everyone get to know each other and show different aspects of their personalities. Erica knew that it was important to build a strong team and have everyone work well together.

Erica then explained the importance of the project, again reviewing the signed project charter. She explained that an important tool to help a project team work together was to have members develop a team contract that everyone felt comfortable signing. JWD Consulting believed in using team contracts for all projects to help promote teamwork and clarify team communications. She explained the main topics covered in a team contract and showed them a team contract template. She then had the team members form two smaller groups, with one consultant, one Information Technology department member, and one client representative in each group. These smaller groups made it easier for everyone to contribute ideas. Each group shared their ideas for what should go into the contract, and then they worked together to form one project team contract. Table 3-8 shows the resulting team contract, which took about 90 minutes to create. Erica could see that

TABLE 3-8 Team contract

Code of Conduct: As a project team, we will:

- Work proactively, anticipating potential problems and working to prevent them.
- Keep other team members informed of information related to the project.
- Focus on what is best for the entire project team.

Participation: We will:

- Be honest and open during all project activities.
- Encourage diversity in team work.
- Provide the opportunity for equal participation.
- Be open to new approaches and consider new ideas.
- Have one discussion at a time.
- Let the project manager know well in advance if a team member has to miss a meeting or may have trouble meeting a deadline for a given task.

Communication: We will:

- Decide as a team on the best way to communicate. Since a few team members cannot meet often for face-to-face meetings, we will use e-mail, a project Web site, and other technology to assist in communicating.
- Have the project manager facilitate all meetings and arrange for phone and video conferences, as needed.
- Work together to create the project schedule and enter actuals into our enterprise-wide project management system by 4 p.m. every Friday.
- Present ideas clearly and concisely.
- Keep discussions on track.

Problem Solving: We will:

- Encourage everyone to participate in solving problems.
- Only use constructive criticism and focus on solving problems, not blaming people.
- Strive to build on each other's ideas.

Meeting Guidelines: We will:

- Plan to have a face-to-face meeting the first and third Tuesday morning of every month.
- Meet more frequently the first month.
- Arrange for telephone or videoconferencing for participants as needed.
- Hold other meetings as needed.
- Record meeting minutes and send them out via e-mail within 24 hours of all project meetings, focusing on decisions made and action items from each meeting.

there were different personalities on this team, but she felt they all could work together well.

Erica wanted to keep their meeting to its two-hour time limit. Their next task would be to clarify the scope of the project by developing a project scope statement and WBS. She knew it took time to develop these documents, but she wanted to get a feel for what everyone thought were the main deliverables for this project, their roles in producing those deliverables, and what areas of the project scope needed clarification. She reminded everyone what their budget and schedule goals were so they would keep that in mind as they discussed the scope of the project. She also asked each person to provide the number of hours he or she would be available to work on this project each month for the next six months. She then had each person write down his or her answers to the following questions:

1. List one item that is most unclear to you about the scope of this project.
2. What other questions do you have or issues do you foresee about the scope of the project?
3. List what you believe to be the main deliverables for this project.
4. Which deliverables do you think you will help create or review?

Erica collected everyone's inputs. She explained that she would take this information and work with Jessie to develop the first draft of the scope statement that she would e-mail to everyone by the end of the week. She also suggested that they all meet again in one week to develop the scope statement further and to start creating the WBS for the project.

Erica and Jessie reviewed all the information and created the first draft of the scope statement. At their next team meeting, they discussed the scope statement and got a good start on the WBS. Table 3-9 shows a portion of the scope statement that Erica created after a few more e-mails and another team meeting. Note that the scope statement lists the product characteristics and requirements, summarizes the deliverables, and describes project success criteria in detail.

TABLE 3-9 Scope statement (draft version)

Project Title: Project Management Intranet Site Project
Date: May 18 **Prepared by:** Erica Bell, Project Manager, erica_bell@jwdconsulting.com

Project Summary and Justification: Joe Fleming, CEO of JWD Consulting, requested this project to assist the company in meeting its strategic goals. The new intranet site will increase visibility of the company's expertise to current and potential clients. It will also help reduce internal costs and improve profitability by providing standard tools, techniques, templates, and project management knowledge to all internal consultants. The budget for the project is $140,000. An additional $40,000 per year will be required for operational expenses after the project is completed. Estimated benefits are $200,000 each year. It is important to focus on the system paying for itself within one year of its completion.

Product Characteristics and Requirements:

1. Templates and tools: The intranet site will allow authorized users to download files they can use to create project management documents and to help them use project

(continued)

management tools. These files will be in Microsoft Word, Excel, Access, Project, or in HTML or PDF format, as appropriate.

2. User submissions: Users will be encouraged to e-mail files with sample templates and tools to the Webmaster. The Webmaster will forward the files to the appropriate person for review and then post the files to the intranet site, if desired.
3. Articles: Articles posted on the intranet site will have appropriate copyright permission. The preferred format for articles will be PDF. The project manager may approve other formats.
4. Requests for articles: The intranet site will include a section for users to request someone from the Project Management Office (PMO) at JWD Consulting to research appropriate articles for them. The PMO manager must first approve the request and negotiate payments, if appropriate.
5. Links: All links to external sites will be tested on a weekly basis. Broken links will be fixed or removed within five working days of discovery.
6. The "Ask the Expert" feature must be user-friendly and capable of soliciting questions and immediately acknowledging that the question has been received in the proper format. The feature must also be capable of forwarding the question to the appropriate expert (as maintained in the system's expert database) and capable of providing the status of questions that are answered. The system must also allow for payment for advice, if appropriate.
7. Security: The intranet site must provide several levels of security. All internal employees will have access to the entire intranet site when they enter their security information to access the main, corporate intranet. Part of the intranet will be available to the public from the corporate Web site. Other portions of the intranet will be available to current clients based on verification with the current client database. Other portions of the intranet will be available after negotiating a fee or entering a fixed payment using pre-authorized payment methods.
8. Search feature: The intranet site must include a search feature for users to search by topic, key words, etc.
9. The intranet site must be accessible using a standard Internet browser. Users must have appropriate application software to open several of the templates and tools.
10. The intranet site must be available 24 hours a day, 7 days a week, with one hour per week for system maintenance and other periodic maintenance, as appropriate.

Summary of Project Deliverables

Project management-related deliverables: Business case, charter, team contract, scope statement, WBS, schedule, cost baseline, progress reports, final project presentation, final project report, lessons-learned report, and any other documents required to manage the project.

Product-related deliverables:

1. Survey: Survey current consultants and clients to help determine desired content and features for the intranet site.
2. Files for templates: The intranet site will include templates for at least 20 documents when the system is first implemented, and it will have the capacity to store up to 100 documents. The project team will decide on the initial 20 templates based on survey results.
3. Examples of completed templates: The intranet site will include examples of projects that have used the templates available on the intranet site. For example, if there is a

template for a business case, there will also be an example of a real business case that uses the template.

4. Instructions for using project management tools: The intranet site will include information on how to use several project management tools, including the following as a minimum: work breakdown structures, Gantt charts, network diagrams, cost estimates, and earned value management. Where appropriate, sample files will be provided in the application software appropriate for the tool. For example, Microsoft Project files will be available to show sample work breakdown structures, Gantt charts, network diagrams, cost estimates, and applications of earned value management. Excel files will be available for sample cost estimates and earned value management charts.
5. Example applications of tools: The intranet site will include examples of real projects that have applied the tools listed in number 4 above.
6. Articles: The intranet site will include at least 10 useful articles about relevant topics in project management. The intranet site will have the capacity to store at least 1,000 articles in PDF format with an average length of 10 pages each.
7. Links: The intranet site will include links with brief descriptions for at least 20 useful sites. The links will be categorized into meaningful groups.
8. Expert database: In order to deliver an "Ask the Expert" feature, the system must include and access a database of approved experts and their contact information. Users will be able to search for experts by pre-defined topics.
9. User Requests feature: The intranet site will include an application to solicit and process requests from users.
10. Intranet site design: An initial design of the new intranet site will include a site map, suggested formats, appropriate graphics, etc. The final design will incorporate comments from users on the initial design.
11. Intranet site content: The intranet site will include content for the templates and tools section, articles section, article retrieval section, links section, "Ask the Expert" section, User Requests feature, security, and payment features.
12. Test plan: The test plan will document how the intranet site will be tested, who will do the testing, and how bugs will be reported.
13. Promotion: A plan for promoting the intranet site will describe various approaches for soliciting inputs during design. The promotion plan will also announce the availability of the new intranet site.
14. Project benefit measurement plan: A project benefit plan will measure the financial value of the intranet site.

Project Success Criteria: Our goal is to complete this project within six months for no more than $140,000. The project sponsor, Joe Fleming, has emphasized the importance of the project paying for itself within one year after the intranet site is complete. To meet this financial goal, the intranet site must have strong user inputs. We must also develop a method for capturing the benefits while the intranet site is being developed and tested, and after it is rolled out. If the project takes a little longer to complete or costs a little more than planned, the firm will still view it as a success if it has a good payback and helps promote the firm's image as an excellent consulting organization.

As the project team worked on the scope statement, they also developed the work breakdown structure (WBS) for the project. The WBS is a very important tool in project management because it provides the basis for deciding how to do the work. The WBS also provides a basis for creating the project schedule and performing earned value management for measuring and forecasting project performance. Erica and her team decided to use the project management process groups as the main categories for the WBS, as shown in Figure 3-3. They included completed work from the initiating process to provide a complete picture of the project's scope. The group also wanted to list several milestones on their schedule, such as the completion of key deliverables, so they prepared a separate list of milestones that they would include on the Gantt chart. You will learn more about creating a WBS in Chapter 5, Project Scope Management.

After preparing the WBS, the project team held another face-to-face meeting to develop the project schedule, following the steps outlined in section 2.5 of the WBS. Several of the project schedule tasks are dependent on one another. For example, the intranet site testing was dependent on the construction and completion of the content tasks. Everyone participated in the development of the schedule, especially the tasks on which each would be working. Some of the tasks were broken down further so the team members had a better understanding of what they had to do and when. They also kept their workloads and cost constraints in mind when developing the duration estimates. For example, Erica was scheduled to work 20 hours per week on this project, and the other project team members combined should not spend more than 60 hours per week on average for the project. As team members provided duration estimates, they also estimated how many work hours they would spend on each task.

After the meeting, Erica worked with Jessie to enter all of the information into Microsoft Project. Erica was using the intranet site project to train Jessie in applying several project management tools and templates. They entered all of the tasks, duration estimates, and dependencies to develop the Gantt chart. Erica decided to enter the resource and cost information after reviewing the schedule. Their initial inputs resulted in a completion date a few weeks later than planned. Erica and Jessie reviewed the critical path for the project, and Erica had to shorten the duration estimates for a few critical tasks in order to meet their schedule goal of completing the project within six months. She talked to the team members working on those tasks, and they agreed that they could plan to work more hours each week on those tasks, if required, in order to complete them on time. Figure 3-4 shows the resulting Gantt chart created in Microsoft Project. Only the executing tasks are expanded to show the subtasks under that category. (You will learn how to use Project 2007 in Appendix A. Chapter 6, Project Time Management, explains Gantt charts and other time management tools.) The baseline schedule projects a completion date of November 1. The project charter had a planned completion date of November 4. Erica wanted to complete the project on time, and although three extra days was not much of a buffer, she felt the baseline schedule was very realistic. She would do her best to help everyone meet their deadlines.

The majority of the costs for this project were internal labor, and the team kept their labor hour constraints in mind when developing task duration estimates. Erica and Jessie entered each project team member's name and labor rate in the resource sheet for their Microsoft Project file. The client representatives were not being paid for their time, so she left their labor rates at the default value of zero. Erica had also included $10,000 for procurement in the financial analysis she prepared for the business case, and she showed Jessie how to enter that amount as a fixed cost split equally between the "Ask the Expert" and User Requests features,

- 1.0 Initiating
  - 1.1 Identify key stakeholders
  - 1.2 Prepare project charter
  - 1.3 Hold project kick-off meeting
- 2.0 Planning
  - 2.1 Hold team planning meeting
  - 2.2 Prepare team contract
  - 2.3 Prepare scope statement
  - 2.4 Prepare WBS
  - 2.5 Prepare schedule and cost baseline
    - 2.5.1 Determine task resources
    - 2.5.2 Determine task durations
    - 2.5.3 Determine task dependencies
    - 2.5.4 Create draft Gantt chart
    - 2.5.5 Review and finalize Gantt chart
  - 2.6 Identify, discuss, and prioritize risks
- 3.0 Executing
  - 3.1 Survey
  - 3.2 User inputs
  - 3.3 Intranet site content
    - 3.3.1 Templates and tools
    - 3.3.2 Articles
    - 3.3.3 Links
    - 3.3.4 Ask the Expert
    - 3.3.5 User requests feature
  - 3.4 Intranet site design
  - 3.5 Intranet site construction
  - 3.6 Intranet site testing
  - 3.7 Intranet site promotion
  - 3.8 Intranet site roll-out
  - 3.9 Project benefits measurement
- 4.0 Monitoring and Controlling
  - 4.1 Progress reports
- 5.0 Closing
  - 5.1 Prepare final project report
  - 5.2 Prepare final project presentation
  - 5.3 Lessons learned

FIGURE 3-3 JWD Consulting intranet project work breakdown structure (WBS)

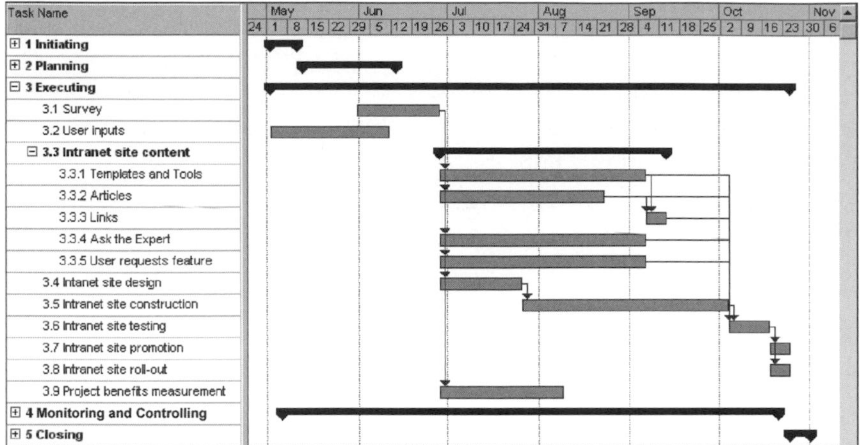

FIGURE 3-4 JWD Consulting intranet site project baseline Gantt chart

where she thought they would have to purchase some external software and/or services. Erica then helped Jessie assign resources to tasks, entering the projected number of hours everyone planned to work each week on each task. They then ran several cost reports and made a few minor adjustments to resource assignments to make their planned total cost meet their budget constraints. Their cost baseline was very close to their planned budget of $140,000.

The last deliverable her team needed to create within the planning process group was a list of prioritized risks. This information will be updated and expanded as the project progresses in a risk register, which also includes information on root causes of the risks, warning signs that potential risks might occur, and response strategies for the risks. (See Chapter 12, Project Risk Management, for more information on risk registers.) Erica reviewed the risks she had mentioned in the business case as well as the comments team members made on the project charter and in their team meetings. She held a special meeting for everyone to brainstorm and discuss potential risks. They posted all of the risks they identified on a probability/impact matrix, and then they grouped some of the ideas. There was only one risk in the high probability and high impact category, and several with medium impact in one or both categories. They chose not to list the low probability and low impact risks. After some discussion, the team developed the list of prioritized risks shown in Table 3-10.

Project Execution

Executing the project involves taking the actions necessary to ensure that activities in the project plan are completed. It also includes work required to introduce any new hardware, software, and procedures into normal operations. The products of the project are produced during project execution, and it usually takes the most resources to accomplish this process. Table 3-11 lists the knowledge areas, executing processes, and outputs of project execution listed in the *PMBOK® Guide, Fourth Edition*. Many project sponsors and customers focus on deliverables related to providing the products, services, or results desired from the project. It is also important to document change requests and prepare updates to planning documents as part of execution. Templates related to this process group are also listed later in this chapter.

TABLE 3-10 List of prioritized risks

Ranking	Potential Risk
1	Lack of inputs from internal consultants
2	Lack of inputs from client representatives
3	Security of new system
4	Outsourcing/purchasing for the article retrieval and "Ask the Expert" features
5	Outsourcing/purchasing for processing online payment transactions
6	Organizing the templates and examples in a useful fashion
7	Providing an efficient search feature
8	Getting good feedback from Michael Chen and other senior consultants
9	Effectively promoting the new system
10	Realizing the benefits of the new system within one year

For this relatively small project, Erica would work closely with all the team members to make sure they were producing the desired work results. She also used her networking skills to get input from other people in the firm and from external sources at no additional cost to the project. She made sure that everyone who would use the resulting intranet application also understood what they were producing as part of the project and how it would help them in the future. She knew that providing strong leadership and using good communication skills were crucial to good project execution. The firm did have a formal change request form, but primarily used it for external projects. The firm also had contract specialists and templates for several procurement documents that the project team would use for the portions of the project they planned to outsource.

As mentioned earlier, Erica knew that Joe, the CEO and project sponsor, liked to see progress on projects through milestone reports. He also wanted Erica to alert him to any potential issues or problems. Table 3-12 shows a sample of a milestone report for the Project Management Intranet Site Project that Erica reviewed with Joe in mid-June. Erica met with most of her project team members often, and she talked to Joe about once a week to review progress on completing milestones and to discuss any other project issues. Although Erica could have used project management software to create milestone reports, she used word processing software instead because this project was small and she could more easily manipulate the report format.

Human resource issues often occur during project execution, especially conflicts. At several of the team meetings, Erica could see that Michael seemed to be bored and often left the room to make phone calls to clients. She talked to Michael about the situation, and she discovered that Michael was supportive of the project, but he knew he could only spend a minimal amount of time on it. He was much more productive outside of meetings, so Erica agreed to have Michael attend a minimal amount of project team meetings. She could see

TABLE 3-11 Executing processes and outputs

Knowledge Area	Executing Process	Outputs
Project Integration Management	Direct and manage project execution	Deliverables Work performance information Change requests Project management plan updates Project document updates
Project Quality Management	Perform quality assurance	Organizational process asset updates Change requests Project management plan updates Project document updates
Project Human Resource Management	Acquire project team Develop project team Manage project team	Project staff assignments Resource calendars Project management plan updates Team performance assessment Enterprise environmental factor updates Enterprise environmental factors updates Organizational process assets updates Project management plan updates Change requests
Project Communications Management	Distribute information Manage stake-holders expectations	Organizational process assets updates Organizational process assets updates Change requests Project management plan updates Project document updates
Project Procurement Management	Conduct procurements	Selected sellers Procurement contract award Resource calendars Change requests Project management plan updates Project documents updates

that Michael was contributing to the team by the feedback he provided and his leadership on the "Ask the Expert" feature for the intranet site. Erica adjusted her communication style to meet his specific needs.

Another problem occurred when Cindy was contacting potential suppliers for software to help with the "Ask the Expert" and User Requests features. Kevin wanted to write all of the software for the project himself, but Cindy knew it made better business sense to

TABLE 3-12 Milestone Report as of June 17

Milestone	Date	Status	Responsible	Issues/ Comments
Initiating Stakeholders identified	May 2	Completed	Erica and Joe	
Project charter signed	May 10	Completed	Erica	
Project kick-off meeting held	May 13	Completed	Erica	Went very well
Planning Team contract signed	May 13	Completed	Erica	
Scope statement completed	May 27	Completed	Erica	
WBS completed	May 31	Completed	Erica	
List of prioritized risks completed	June 3	Completed	Erica	Reviewed with sponsor and team
Schedule and cost baseline completed	June 13	Completed	Erica	
Executing Survey completed	June 28		Erica	Poor response so far!
Intranet site design completed	July 26		Kevin	
Project benefits measurement completed	August 9		Erica	
User inputs collected	August 9		Jessie	
Articles completed	August 23		Jessie	
Templates and tools completed	September 6		Erica	
Ask the Expert completed	September 6		Michael	
User Requests feature completed	September 6		Cindy	
Links completed	September 13		Kevin	

(continued)

TABLE 3-12 Milestone Report as of June 17 (*continued*)

Milestone	Date	Status	Responsible	Issues/ Comments
Intranet site construction completed	October 4		Kevin	
Intranet site testing completed	October 18		Cindy	
Intranet site promotion completed	October 25		Erica	
Intranet site roll-out completed	October 25		Kevin	
Monitoring and Controlling Progress reports	Every Friday		All	
Closing Final project presentation completed	October 27		Erica	
Sponsor sign-off on project completed	October 27		Joe	
Final project report completed	October 28		Erica	
Lessons-learned reports submitted	November 1		All	

purchase these new software capabilities from a reliable source. Cindy had to convince Kevin that it was worth buying some software from other sources.

Cindy also discovered that their estimate of $10,000 was only about half the amount they needed. She discussed the problem with Erica, explaining the need for some custom development no matter which supplier they chose. Erica agreed that they should go with an outside source, and she asked their sponsor to approve the additional funds. Joe agreed, but he stressed the importance of still having the system pay for itself within a year.

Erica also had to ask Joe for help when the project team received a low response rate to their survey and requests for user inputs. Joe sent out an e-mail to all of JWD Consulting's consultants describing the importance of the project. He also offered five extra vacation days to the person who provided the best examples of how they used tools and templates to manage their projects. Erica then received informative input from the consultants. Having effective communication skills and strong top management support are essential to good project execution.

BEST PRACTICE

One way to learn about best practices in project management is by studying recipients of PMI's Project of the Year award. The Quartier International de Montréal (QIM), Montreal's international district, was a 66-acre urban revitalization project in the heart of downtown Montreal. This $90 million, five-year project turned a once unpopular area into a thriving section of the city with a booming real estate market and has generated $770 million in related construction. Clement Demers, PMP, was the director general for the QIM project. He said the team "took a unique project execution approach by dividing work into packages that allowed for smaller-scale testing of management techniques and contract awards. Benefiting from experience gained in each stage, managers could then adjust future work segments and management styles accordingly."[8]

Other strategies that helped the team succeed included the following:

- The team identified champions in each stakeholder group to help inspire others to achieve project goals.
- The team's communications plan included a Web site dedicated to public concerns.
- There were two-day reviews at the beginning of each project phase to discuss problems and develop solutions to prevent conflict.
- Financial investors were asked for input to increase their stake in the project.
- The team recognized the cost value of hiring high-quality experts, such as architects, engineers, lawyers, and urban planners. They paid all professionals a fixed price for their services and paid their fees quickly.

Project Monitoring and Controlling

Monitoring and controlling is the process of measuring progress toward project objectives, monitoring deviation from the plan, and taking corrective action to match progress with the plan. Monitoring and controlling is done throughout the life of a project. It also involves eight of the nine project management knowledge areas. Table 3-13 lists the knowledge areas, monitoring and controlling processes, and outputs, according to the *PMBOK® Guide, Fourth Edition*. Templates related to this process group are listed later in this chapter.

TABLE 3-13 Monitoring and controlling processes and outputs

Knowledge Area	Monitoring and Controlling Process	Outputs
Project Integration Management	Monitor and control project work	Change requests Project management plan updates Project document updates
	Perform integrated change control	Change request status updates Project management plan updates Project document updates
Project Scope Management	Verify scope	Accepted deliverables Change requests Project document updates

TABLE 3-13 Monitoring and controlling processes and outputs (*continued*)

Knowledge Area	Monitoring and Controlling Process	Outputs
	Control scope	Work performance measurements Organizational process assets updates Change requests Project management plan updates Project document updates
Project Time Management	Control schedule	Work performance measurements Organizational process assets updates Change requests Project management plan updates Project document updates
Project Cost Management	Control cost	Work performance measurements Budget forecasts Organizational process assets updates Change requests Project management plan updates Project document updates
Project Quality Management	Perform quality control	Quality control measurements Validated deliverables Organizational process assets updates Change requests Project management plan updates Project document updates
Project Communications Management	Report performance	Performance reports Organizational process assets updates Change requests
Project Risk Management	Monitor and control risks	Risk register updates Organizational process assets updates Change requests Project management plan updates Project document updates
Project Procurement Management	Administer procurements	Procurement documentation Organizational process assets updates Change requests Project management plan updates

On the Project Management Intranet Site Project, there were several updates to the project management plan to reflect changes made to the project scope, schedule, and budget. Erica and other project team members took corrective action when necessary. For example, when they were not getting many responses to their survey, Erica asked Joe for help. When Cindy had trouble negotiating with a supplier, she got help from another senior consultant who had worked with that supplier in the past. Erica also had to request more funds for that part of the project.

Project team members submitted a brief progress report every Friday. They were originally using a company template for progress reports, but Erica found that by modifying the old template, she received better information to help her team work more effectively. She wanted team members not only to report what they did but also to focus on what was going well or not going well and why. This extra information helped team members reflect on the project's progress and identify areas in need of improvement. Table 3-14 is an example of one of Cindy's progress reports.

TABLE 3-14 Sample weekly progress report

Project Name: Project Management Intranet Project
Team Member Name: Cindy Dawson, cindy_dawson@jwdconsulting.com
Date: August 5

Work completed this week:
–Worked with Kevin to start the intranet site construction
–Organized all the content files
–Started developing a file naming scheme for content files
–Continued work on "Ask the Expert" and User Requests features
–Met with preferred supplier
–Verified that their software would meet our needs
–Discovered the need for some customization

Work to complete next week:
–Continue work on intranet site construction
–Prepare draft contract for preferred supplier
–Develop new cost estimate for outsourced work

What's going well and why:
The intranet site construction started well. The design was very clear and easy to follow. Kevin really knows what he's doing.

What's not going well and why:
It is difficult to decide how to organize the templates and examples. Need more input from senior consultants and clients.

Suggestions/Issues:
–Hold a special meeting to decide how to organize the templates and examples on the intranet site.
–Get some sample contracts and help in negotiating with the preferred supplier.

(continued)

TABLE 3-14 Sample weekly progress report (*continued*)

Project changes:
I think we can stay on schedule, but it looks like we'll need about $10,000 more for outsourcing. That's doubling our budget in that area.

In addition to progress reports, an important tool for monitoring and controlling the project was using project management software. Each team member submitted his or her actual hours worked on tasks each Friday afternoon by 4 p.m. via the firm's enterprise-wide project management software. They were using the enterprise version of Microsoft Project 2007, so they could easily update their task information via the Web. Erica worked with Jessie to analyze the information, paying special attention to the critical path and earned value data. (See Chapter 6 on Project Time Management for more information on critical path analysis; Chapter 7 on Project Cost Management for a description of earned value management; and Appendix A for more information on using Project 2007 to help control projects.) Erica wanted to finish the project on time, even if it meant spending more money. Joe agreed with that approach, and approved the additional funding Erica projected they would need based on the earned value projections and the need to make up a little time on critical tasks.

Joe again emphasized the importance of the new system paying for itself within a year. Erica was confident that they could exceed the projected financial benefits, and she decided to begin capturing benefits as soon as the project team began testing the system. When she was not working on this project, Erica was managing JWD Consulting's Project Management Office (PMO), and she could already see how the intranet site would help her staff save time and make their consultants more productive. One of her staff members wanted to move into the consulting group, and she believed the PMO could continue to provide its current services with one less person due to this new system—a benefit she had not considered before. Several of the firm's client contracts were based on performance and not hours billed, so she was excited to start measuring the value of the new intranet site to their consultants as well.

Project Closing

The closing process involves gaining stakeholder and customer acceptance of the final products and services and bringing the project, or project phase, to an orderly end. It includes verifying that all of the deliverables are complete, and it often includes a final project report and presentation. Even though many information technology projects are canceled before completion, it is still important to formally close any project and reflect on what can be learned to improve future projects. As philosopher George Santayana said, "Those who cannot remember the past are condemned to repeat it."

It is also important to plan for and execute a smooth transition of the project into the normal operations of the company. Most projects produce results that are integrated into the existing organizational structure. For example, JWD Consulting's Project Management Intranet Site Project will require staff to support the intranet site after it is operational. Erica included support costs of $40,000 per year for the projected three-year life of the new system. She also created a transition plan as part of the final report to provide for a smooth transition of the system into the firm's operations. The plan included a list of issues that had to be resolved before the firm could put the new intranet site into production. For example,

Michael Chen would not be available to work on the intranet site after the six-month project was complete, so they had to know who would support the "Ask the Expert" feature and plan some time for Michael to work with him or her.

Table 3-15 lists the knowledge areas, processes, and outputs of project closing based on the *PMBOK® Guide, Fourth Edition*. During the closing processes of any project, project team members must deliver the final product, service, or result of the project, and update organizational process assets, such as project files and a lessons-learned report. If the project team procured items during the project, they must formally complete or close out all contracts. Templates related to project closing are listed later in this chapter.

TABLE 3-15 Closing processes and output

Knowledge Area	Closing Process	Outputs
Project Integration Management	Close project or phase	Final product, service, or result transition Organizational process assets updates
Project Procurement Management	Close procurements	Closed procurements Organizational process assets updates

Erica and her team prepared a final report, final presentation, contract files, and lessons-learned report in closing the project. Erica reviewed the confidential, individual lessons-learned report from each team member and wrote one summary lessons-learned report to include in the final documentation, part of which is provided in Table 3-16. Notice the bulleted items in the fourth question, such as the importance of having a good kick-off meeting, working together to develop a team contract, using project management software, and communicating well with the project team and sponsor.

TABLE 3-16 Lessons-learned report (abbreviated)

Project Name:	JWD Consulting Project Management Intranet Site Project
Project Sponsor:	Joe Fleming
Project Manager:	Erica Bell
Project Dates:	May 2 – November 4
Final Budget:	$150,000
1.	Did the project meet scope, time, and cost goals? *We did meet scope and time goals, but we had to request an additional $10,000, which the sponsor did approve.*

(continued)

TABLE 3-16 Lessons-learned report (abbreviated) (*continued*)

2.	What were the success criteria listed in the project scope statement? *Below is what we put in our project scope statement under project success criteria*: *"Our goal is to complete this project within six months for no more than $140,000. The project sponsor, Joe Fleming, has emphasized the importance of the project paying for itself within one year after the intranet site is complete. To meet this financial goal, the intranet site must have strong user input. We must also develop a method for capturing the benefits while the intranet site is being developed and tested, and after it is rolled out. If the project takes a little longer to complete or costs a little more than planned, the firm will still view it as a success if it has a good payback and helps promote the firm's image as an excellent consulting organization."*
3.	Reflect on whether or not you met the project success criteria. *As stated above, the sponsor was not too concerned about going over budget as long as the system would have a good payback period and help promote our firm's image. We have already documented some financial and image benefits of the new intranet site. For example, we have decided that we can staff the PMO with one less person, resulting in substantial cost savings. We have also received excellent feedback from several of our clients about the new intranet site.*
4.	In terms of managing the project, what were the main lessons your team learned from this project? *The main lessons we learned include the following*: • *Having a good project sponsor was instrumental to project success. We ran into a couple of difficult situations, and Joe was very creative in helping us solve problems.* • *Teamwork was essential. It really helped to take time for everyone to get to know each other at the kick-off meeting. It was also helpful to develop and follow a team contract.* • *Good planning paid off in execution. We spent a fair amount of time developing a good project charter, scope statement, WBS, schedules, and so on. Everyone worked together to develop these planning documents, and there was strong buy-in.* • *Project management software was very helpful throughout the project.*
5.	Describe one example of what went right on this project.
6.	Describe one example of what went wrong on this project.
7.	What will you do differently on the next project based on your experience working on this project?

Erica also had Joe sign a client acceptance form, one of the sample templates on the new intranet site that the project team suggested all consultants use when closing their projects. (You can find this and other templates on the companion Web site for this text.)

Table 3-17 provides the table of contents for the final project report. The cover page included the project title, date, and team member names. Notice the inclusion of a

TABLE 3-17 Final project report table of contents

1. Project Objectives
2. Summary of Project Results
3. Original and Actual Start and End Dates
4. Original and Actual Budget
5. Project Assessment (Why did you do this project? What did you produce? Was the project a success? What went right and wrong on the project?)
6. Transition Plan
7. Annual Project Benefits Measurement Approach

Attachments:

A. Project Management Documentation

- Business case
- Project charter
- Team contract
- Scope statement
- WBS and WBS dictionary
- Baseline and actual Gantt chart
- List of prioritized risks
- Milestone reports
- Progress reports
- Contract files
- Lessons-learned reports
- Final presentation
- Client acceptance form

B. Product-Related Documentation

- Survey and results
- Summary of user inputs
- Intranet site content
- Intranet site design documents
- Test plans and reports
- Intranet site promotion information
- Intranet site roll-out information
- Project benefits measurement information

transition plan and a plan to analyze the benefits of the system each year in the final report. Also, notice that the final report includes attachments for all the project management and product-related documents. Erica knew how important it was to provide good final documentation on projects. The project team produced a hard copy of the final documentation and an electronic copy to store on the new intranet site for other consultants to use as desired.

Erica also organized a project closure luncheon for the project team right after their final project presentation. She used the luncheon to share lessons learned and celebrate a job well done!

As you can see, there are many documents that project teams prepare throughout the life of a project. Many people use templates as a standard format for preparing those documents. Table 3-18 lists templates used in this text for preparing the documents

TABLE 3-18 Templates by process group

Template Name	Process Group	Chapter(s) Where Used	Application Software	File Name
Business Case	Pre-initiating	3	Word	business_case.doc
Business Case Financial Analysis	Pre-initiating	3, 4	Excel	business_case_ financials.xls
Stakeholder Register	Initiating	3, 10	Word	stakeholder_register.doc
Stakeholder Management Strategy	Initiating	3, 10	Word	stakeholder_strategy.doc
Kick-off Meeting	Initiating	3	Word	kick-off_meeting.doc
Payback Chart	Initiating	4	Excel	payback.xls
Weighted Decision Matrix	Initiating	4, 12	Excel	wtd_decision_matrix.xls
Project Charter	Initiating	3, 4, 5	Word	charter.doc
Team Contract	Planning	3	Word	team_contract.doc
Requirements Traceability Matrix	Planning	5	Word	reqs_matrix.xls
Scope Statement	Planning	3, 4, 5	Word	scope_ statement.doc
Statement of Work	Planning	12	Word	statement_of_work.doc

TABLE 3-18 Templates by process group (*continued*)

Template Name	Process Group	Chapter(s) Where Used	Application Software	File Name
Request for Proposal	Planning	12	Word	rfp_outline.doc
Software Project Management Plan	Planning	4	Word	sw_project_mgt_plan.doc
Work Breakdown Structure	Planning	3, 5, 6	Word	wbs.doc
Gantt Chart	Planning, Executing	3, 5, 6	Project	Gantt_chart.mpp
Network Diagram	Planning, Executing	3, 6	Project	network_ diagram.mpp
Project Cost Estimate	Planning	7	Excel	cost_estimate.xls
Earned Value Data and Chart	Monitoring and Controlling	7	Excel	earned_value.xls
Quality Assurance Plan	Executing	8	Word	quality_assurance_ plan.doc
Pareto Chart	Monitoring and Controlling	8	Excel	pareto_chart.xls
Project Organizational Chart	Planning, Executing	9	PowerPoint	project_org_chart.ppt
Responsibility Assignment Matrix	Planning, Executing	9	Excel	ram.xls
Resource Histogram	Planning, Executing	9	Excel	resource_histogram.xls
Communications Management Plan	Planning	10	Word	comm_plan.doc

(*continued*)

TABLE 3-18 Templates by process group (*continued*)

Template Name	Process Group	Chapter(s) Where Used	Application Software	File Name
Project Description (text)	Planning	10	Word	project_desc_text.doc
Project Description (Gantt chart)	Planning	10	Project	project_desc_Gantt.mpp
Milestone Report	Executing	3, 6	Word	milestone_report.doc
Change Request Form	Planning, Monitoring and Controlling	4	Word	change_request.doc
Progress Report	Monitoring and Controlling	3, 10	Word	progress_report.doc
Expectations Management Matrix	Monitoring and Controlling	10	Word	expectations.doc
Issue Log	Monitoring and Controlling	10	Word	issue_log.doc
Probability/ Impact Matrix	Planning, Executing, Monitoring and Controlling	11	PowerPoint	prob_impact_matrix.ppt
List of Prioritized Risks	Planning, Executing, Monitoring and Controlling	3, 11	Word	list_of_risks.doc
Risk Register	Planning, Monitoring and Controlling	11	Excel	risk_register.xls

TABLE 3-18 Templates by process group (*continued*)

Template Name	Process Group	Chapter(s) Where Used	Application Software	File Name
Top 10 Risk Item Tracking	Planning, Monitoring and Controlling	11	Excel	top_10.xls
Breakeven/ Sensitivity Analysis	Planning	11	Excel	breakeven.xls
Client Acceptance Form	Closing	3, 10	Word	client_acceptance.doc
Lessons-Learned Report	Closing	3, 10	Word	lessons_learned_ report.doc
Final Project Documentation	Closing	3, 10	Word	final_documentation.doc

shown in this chapter and in later chapters. It lists the template name, chapter number, process group(s) where you normally use the template, application software used to create it, and the file name for the template. You can download all of these files in one compressed file from the companion Web site for this text or from the author's Web site at *www.kathyschwalbe.com*. Note that the templates were saved in Office 2003 and 2007 format to allow for easier compatibility. Feel free to modify the templates to meet your needs.

The project management process groups—initiating, planning, executing, monitoring and controlling, and closing—provide a useful framework for understanding project management. They apply to most projects (information technology and non-information technology) and, along with the project management knowledge areas, help project managers see the big picture of managing a project in their particular organization.

CASE WRAP-UP

Erica Bell and her team finished the Project Management Intranet Site Project on November 4, as planned in their project charter. They did go over budget, however, but Joe had approved Erica's request for additional funds, primarily for purchasing external software and customization. Like any project, they had a few challenges, but they worked together as a team and used good project management to meet their sponsor's and users' needs. They received positive initial feedback from internal consultants and some of their clients on the new intranet site. People were asking for templates, examples, and expert advice even before the system was ready. About a year after the project was completed, Erica worked with a member of the Finance department to review the benefits of the new system. The Project Management Office did lose one of its staff members, but it did not request a replacement since the new system helped reduce the PMO's workload. This saved the firm about $70,000 a year for the salary and benefits of that staff position. They also had data to show that the firm saved more than $180,000 on contracts with clients due to the new system, while they had projected just $160,000. The firm was breaking even with the "Ask the Expert" feature the first year, and Erica estimated that the system provided $30,000 in additional profits the first year by generating new business, not the $40,000 they had projected. However, savings from the PMO staff position salary and the extra savings on contracts more than made up for the $10,000 difference. Joe was proud of the project team and the system they produced to help make JWD Consulting a world-class organization.

Chapter Summary

Project management involves a number of interlinked processes. The five project management process groups are initiating, planning, executing, monitoring and controlling, and closing. These processes occur at varying levels of intensity throughout each phase of a project, and specific outcomes are produced as a result of each process. Normally the executing processes require the most resources and time, followed by the planning processes.

Mapping the main activities of each project management process group into the nine project management knowledge areas provides a big picture of what activities are involved in project management.

Some organizations develop their own information technology project management methodologies, often using the standards found in the *PMBOK® Guide* as a foundation. It is important to tailor project management methodologies to meet the organization's particular needs. Popular methodologies like PRINCE2, agile methodologies, RUP, and Six Sigma include project management processes.

The JWD Consulting case study demonstrates how one organization managed an information technology project from its initiation through its closure. The case study provides several samples of outputs produced for initiating (including pre-initiating), planning, executing, monitoring and controlling, and closing as follows:

- Business case
- Stakeholder register
- Stakeholder management strategy
- Project charter
- Kick-off meeting agenda
- Team contract
- Work breakdown structure
- Gantt chart
- List of prioritized risks
- Milestone report
- Progress report
- Lessons-learned report
- Final project report

Later chapters in this text provide detailed information on creating these and other project management documents and using several of the tools and techniques described in this case study.

Quick Quiz

1. A ______ is a series of actions directed toward a particular result.
   a. goal
   b. process
   c. plan
   d. project

2. ______ processes include coordinating people and other resources to carry out the project plans and produce the products, services, or results of the project or phase.
   a. Initiating
   b. Planning
   c. Executing
   d. Monitoring and controlling
   e. Closing
3. Which process group normally requires the most resources and time?
   a. Initiating
   b. Planning
   c. Executing
   d. Monitoring and controlling
   e. Closing
4. What methodology was developed in the U.K., defines 45 separate subprocesses, and organizes these into eight process groups?
   a. Six Sigma
   b. RUP
   c. *PMBOK® Guide*
   d. PRINCE2
5. Which of the following outputs is often completed before initiating a project?
   a. stakeholder register
   b. business case
   c. project charter
   d. kick-off meeting
6. A work breakdown structure, project schedule, and cost estimates are outputs of the ______ process.
   a. initiating
   b. planning
   c. executing
   d. monitoring and controlling
   e. closing
7. Initiating involves developing a project charter, which is part of the project ______ management knowledge area.
   a. integration
   b. scope
   c. communications
   d. risk

8. ______ involves measuring progress toward project objectives and taking corrective actions.
    a. Initiating
    b. Planning
    c. Executing
    d. Monitoring and controlling
    e. Closing
9. What type of report do project teams create to reflect on what went right and what went wrong with the project?
    a. lessons-learned report
    b. progress report
    c. final project report
    d. business case
10. Many people use ______ to have a standard format for preparing various project management documents.
    a. methodologies
    b. templates
    c. project management software
    d. standards

Quick Quiz Answers

1. b; 2. c; 3. c; 4. d; 5. b; 6. b; 7. a; 8. d; 9. a; 10. b

Discussion Questions

1. Briefly describe what happens in each of the five project management process groups (initiating, planning, executing, monitoring and controlling, and closing). What types of activities are done before initiating a project?
2. Approximately how much time do good project managers spend on each process group and why?
3. Why do organizations need to tailor project management concepts, such as those found in the *PMBOK® Guide*, to create their own methodologies?
4. What are some of the key outputs of each process group?
5. What are some of the typical challenges project teams face during each of the five process groups?

Exercises

1. Study the WBS and Gantt charts provided in Figures 3-3 and 3-4. Enter the WBS into Project 2007, indenting tasks as shown to create the WBS hierarchy. Do not enter durations or dependencies. Print the resulting Gantt chart. See the scope management section of Appendix A for help using Project 2007.

2. Read the article by William Munroe regarding BlueCross BlueShield of Michigan's information technology project management methodology (available on the companion Web site for this text under Chapter 3). Or, research another methodology, such as PRINCE2, an agile methodology, RUP, or Six Sigma, and how organizations use it, citing at least two references. Why do you think organizations spend time and money tailoring a methodology to their environment? Write a two-page summary of your findings and your opinion on the topic.
3. Read the "ResNet Case Study" (available from the companion Web site for this text under Chapter 3). This real case study about Northwest Airlines' reservation system illustrates another application of the project management process groups. Write a three-page paper summarizing the main outputs produced during each project process group in this case. Also, include your opinion of whether or not Peeter Kivestu was an effective project manager. If you prefer, find another well-documented project and summarize it instead.
4. JWD Consulting wrote a business case before officially initiating the Project Management Intranet Site project. Review the contents of this document (Table 3-2) and find two articles describing the need to justify investing in IT projects. In addition, describe whether you think most projects should include a business case before the project sponsors officially approve the project. Write a two-page paper summarizing your findings and opinions.
5. Read an article about a recipient of PMI's Project of the Year award. Past winners include Fluor Corporation's Fernald Closure Project, Kaiser-Hill's Rocky Flats Nuclear Plant Closing, the Quartier International de Montréal district revitalization project, Saudi Aramco Haradh Gas Plant, and the Winter Olympics Salt Lake Organizing Committee. Write a one-page paper summarizing the project, focusing on how the project manager and team used good project management practices.
6. Download the template files used in this text from the companion Web site or from *www.kathyschwalbe.com*. Review several of them, and look at examples of how they are used in this text. Also search the Internet for other template files. Summarize what you think about using templates and how you think they can help project managers and their teams in a two-page paper. Also discuss potential problems with using templates.

Companion Web Site

Visit the companion Web site for this text at *www.cengage.com/mis/schwalbe* to access:

- References cited in the text and additional suggested readings for each chapter
- Template files
- Lecture notes
- Interactive quizzes
- Podcasts
- Links to general project management Web sites
- And more

See the Preface of this text for more information on accessing the companion Web site.

Key Terms

closing processes — formalizing acceptance of the project or project phase and ending it efficiently

executing processes — coordinating people and other resources to carry out the project plans and produce the products, services, or results of the project or project phase

initiating processes — defining and authorizing a project or project phase

kick-off meeting — a meeting held at the beginning of a project so that stakeholders can meet each other, review the goals of the project, and discuss future plans

methodology — describes *how* things should be done

monitoring and controlling processes — regularly measuring and monitoring progress to ensure that the project team meets the project objectives

planning processes — devising and maintaining a workable scheme to ensure that the project addresses the organization's needs

process — a series of actions directed toward a particular result

project management process groups — the progression of project activities from initiation to planning, executing, monitoring and controlling, and closing

PRojects IN Controlled Environments (PRINCE2) — a project management methodology developed in the U.K. that defines 45 separate sub-processes and organizes these into eight process groups

Rational Unified Process (RUP) — an iterative software development process that focuses on team productivity and delivers software best practices to all team members

Six Sigma methodologies — DMAIC (Define, Measure, Analyze, Improve, and Control) is used to improve an existing business process and DMADV (Define, Measure, Analyze, Design, and Verify) is used to create new product or process designs

stakeholder register — a document that includes details related to the identified project stakeholders

standard — describes best practices for *what* should be done

End Notes

[1] Andy Crowe, Alpha Project Managers: What the Top 2% Know That Everyone Else Does Not, Velociteach Press, Atlanta, GA, (2006).

[2] Phillip A. Pell, Comments posted at Elaine Varron, "No Easy IT Fix for IRS [formerly "For the IRS, There's No EZ Fix"], *CIO.com* (April 1, 2004).

[3] Grant Gross, "Report: IRS information security still poor," *InfoWorld* (January 8, 2008).

[4] PCI Group, "PM Best Practices Report," (October 2001).

[5] Brian Jacks, "Lord of the Rings: The Two Towers Extended Edition (New Line)," *Underground Online (UGO.com)* (accessed August 4, 2004).

[6] Bill Cottrell, "Standards, compliance, and Rational Unified Process, Part I: Integrating RUP and the PMBOK," IBM Developerworks (May 10, 2004).

[7] Sarah Fister Gale, "Outstanding Organizations 2007," *PM Network*, (October 2007), p. 5.

[8] Libby Elis, "Urban Inspiration," *PM Network,* (January 2006), p. 30.

CHAPTER 4

PROJECT INTEGRATION MANAGEMENT

LEARNING OBJECTIVES

After reading this chapter, you will be able to:

- Describe an overall framework for project integration management as it relates to the other project management knowledge areas and the project life cycle
- Explain the strategic planning process and apply different project selection methods
- Explain the importance of creating a project charter to formally initiate projects
- Describe project management plan development, understand the content of these plans, and review approaches for creating them
- Explain project execution, its relationship to project planning, the factors related to successful results, and tools and techniques to assist in managing project execution
- Describe the process of monitoring and controlling a project
- Understand the integrated change control process, planning for and managing changes on information technology projects, and developing and using a change control system
- Explain the importance of developing and following good procedures for closing projects
- Describe how software can assist in project integration management

OPENING CASE

Nick Carson recently became project manager of a critical biotech enterprise at his Silicon Valley company. This project involved creating the hardware and software for a DNA-sequencing instrument used in assembling and analyzing the human genome. The biotech project was the company's largest endeavor, and it had tremendous potential for future growth and revenues. Unfortunately, there were problems managing this large project. It had been underway for three years and had already gone through three different project managers. Nick had been the lead software developer on the project before top management made him the project manager. The CEO told him to do whatever it took to deliver the first version of the software for the DNA-sequencing instrument in four months and a production version in nine months. Negotiations for a potential corporate buyout with a larger company influenced top management's sense of urgency to complete the project.

Highly energetic and intelligent, Nick had the technical background to make the project a success. He delved into the technical problems and found some critical flaws that kept the DNA-sequencing instrument from working. Nevertheless, he was having difficulty in his new role as project manager. Although Nick and his team got the product out on time, top management was upset because Nick did not focus on managing all aspects of the project. He never provided them with accurate schedules or detailed plans of what was happening on the project. Instead of performing the work of project manager, Nick had taken on the role of software integrator and troubleshooter. Nick, however, did not understand top management's problem—he delivered the product, didn't he? Didn't they realize how valuable he was?

WHAT IS PROJECT INTEGRATION MANAGEMENT?

Project integration management involves coordinating all of the other project management knowledge areas throughout a project's life cycle. This integration ensures that all the elements of a project come together at the right times to complete a project successfully. According to the *PMBOK® Guide, Fourth Edition* there are six main processes involved in project integration management:

1. *Developing the project charter* involves working with stakeholders to create the document that formally authorizes a project—the charter.
2. *Developing the project management plan* involves coordinating all planning efforts to create a consistent, coherent document—the project management plan.
3. *Directing and managing project execution* involves carrying out the project management plan by performing the activities included in it. The outputs of this process are deliverables, work performance information, change requests, project management plan updates, and project document updates.
4. *Monitoring and controlling project work* involves overseeing activities to meet the performance objectives of the project. The outputs of this process are

change requests, project management plan updates, and project document updates.

5. *Performing integrated change control* involves identifying, evaluating, and managing changes throughout the project life cycle. The outputs of this process include change request status updates, project management plan updates, and project document updates.
6. *Closing the project or phase* involves finalizing all activities to formally close the project or phrase. Outputs of this process include final product, service, or result transition and organizational process assets updates. Figure 4-1 summarizes these processes and outputs, showing when they occur in a typical project.

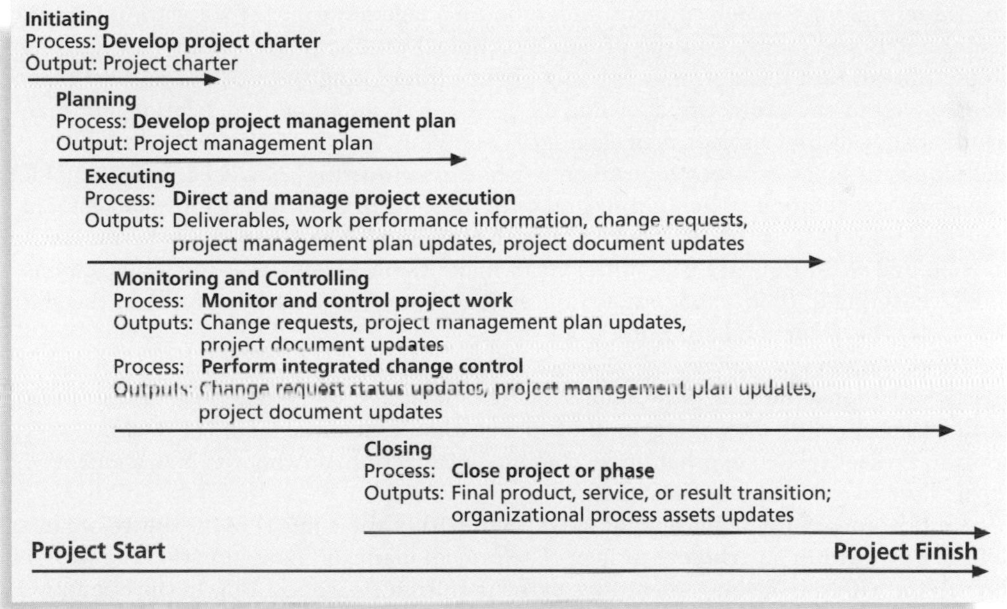

FIGURE 4-1 Project integration management summary

Many people consider project integration management the key to overall project success. Someone must take responsibility for coordinating all of the people, plans, and work required to complete a project. Someone must focus on the big picture of the project and steer the project team toward successful completion. Someone must make the final decisions when there are conflicts among project goals or people. Someone must communicate key project information to top management. This someone is the project manager, and the project manager's chief means for accomplishing all these tasks is project integration management.

Good project integration management is critical to providing stakeholder satisfaction. Project integration management includes interface management. **Interface management** involves identifying and managing the points of interaction between various elements of the project. The number of interfaces can increase exponentially as the number of people involved in a project increases. Thus, one of the most important jobs of a project manager is to establish and maintain good communication and relationships across organizational interfaces. The project manager must communicate well with all project stakeholders, including customers, the project team, top management, other project managers, and opponents of the project.

What happens when a project manager does not communicate well with all stakeholders? In the opening case, Nick Carson seemed to ignore a key stakeholder for the DNA-sequencing instrument project—his top management. Nick was comfortable working with other members of the project team, but he was not familiar with his new job as project manager or the needs of the company's top management. Nick continued to do his old job of software developer and took on the added role of software integrator. He mistakenly thought project integration management meant software integration management and focused on the project's technical problems. He totally ignored what project integration management is really about—integrating the work of all of the people involved in the project by focusing on good communication and relationship management. Recall that project management is applying knowledge, skills, tools, and techniques to meet project requirements, while also meeting or exceeding stakeholder needs and expectations. Nick did not take the time to find out what top management expected from him as the project manager; he assumed that completing the project on time and within budget was sufficient to make them happy. Yes, top management should have made their expectations more clear, but Nick should have taken the initiative to get the guidance he needed from them.

In addition to not understanding project integration management, Nick did not use holistic or systems thinking (see Chapter 2). He burrowed into the technical details of his particular project. He did not stop to think about what it meant to be the project manager, how this project related to other projects in the organization, or what top management's expectations were of him and his team.

Project integration management must occur within the context of the entire organization, not just within a particular project. The project manager must integrate the work of the project with the ongoing operations of the performing organization. In the opening case, Nick's company was negotiating a potential buyout with a larger company. Consequently, top management needed to know when the DNA-sequencing instrument would be ready, how big the market was for the product, and if they had enough in-house staff to continue to manage projects like this one in the future. They wanted to see a project management plan and a schedule to help them monitor the project's progress and show their potential buyer what was happening. When top managers tried to talk to Nick about these issues, Nick soon returned to discussing the technical details of the project. Even though Nick was very bright, he had no experience or real interest in many of the business aspects of how the company operated. Project managers must always view their projects in the context of the changing needs of their organizations and respond to requests from top management. Likewise, top management must keep project managers informed of major issues that could affect their projects and strive to make processes consistent throughout their organization.

The Airbus A380 megajet project was two years behind schedule in October 2006, causing Airbus' parent company to face an expected loss of $6.1 billion over the next four years. Why? The project suffered from severe integration management problems, or "*integration disintegration*. ... [W]hen pre-assembled bundles containing hundreds of miles of cabin wiring were delivered from a German factory to the assembly line in France, workers discovered that the bundles, called harnesses, didn't fit properly into the plane. Assembly slowed to a near-standstill, as workers tried to pull the bundles apart and re-thread them through the fuselage. Now Airbus will have to go back to the drawing board and redesign the wiring system."[1]

How did this lack of integration occur? At the end of 2000, just as Airbus was giving the go-ahead to the A380 project, the company announced that it was completing the process of transforming itself into an integrated corporation. Since its founding in 1970, Airbus had operated as a loose consortium of aerospace companies in several countries, including France, Germany, Britain, and Spain. The company wanted to integrate all of its operations into one cohesive business. Unfortunately, that integration was much easier said than done and caused major problems on the A380 project. For example, the Toulouse assembly plant used the latest version of a sophisticated design software tool called CATIA, but the design center at the Hamburg factory used an earlier version—a completely different system dating from the 1980s. As a result, design specs could not flow easily back and forth between the two systems. Airbus's top managers should have made it a priority to have all sites use the latest software, but they didn't, resulting in this project disaster.

Following a standard process for managing projects can help prevent some of the typical problems new and experienced project managers face, including communicating with and managing stakeholders. Before organizations begin projects, however, they should go through a formal process to decide what projects to pursue.

STRATEGIC PLANNING AND PROJECT SELECTION

Successful leaders look at the big picture or strategic plan of the organization to determine what types of projects will provide the most value. Some may argue that project managers should not be involved in strategic planning and project selection because top management is usually responsible for these types of business decisions. But successful organizations know that project managers can provide valuable insight into the project selection process.

Strategic Planning

Strategic planning involves determining long-term objectives by analyzing the strengths and weaknesses of an organization, studying opportunities and threats in the business environment, predicting future trends, and projecting the need for new products and services. Strategic planning provides important information to help organizations identify and then select potential projects.

Many people are familiar with **SWOT analysis**—analyzing **S**trengths, **W**eaknesses, **O**pportunities, and **T**hreats—which is used to aid in strategic planning. For example, a group of four people who want to start a new business in the film industry could perform a SWOT analysis to help identify potential projects. They might determine the following based on a SWOT analysis:

Strengths:

- As experienced professionals, we have numerous contacts in the film industry.
- Two of us have strong sales and interpersonal skills.
- Two of us have strong technical skills and are familiar with several filmmaking software tools.
- We all have impressive samples of completed projects.

Weaknesses:

- None of us have accounting/financial experience.
- We have no clear marketing strategy for products and services.
- We have little money to invest in new projects.
- We have no company Web site and limited use of technology to run the business.

Opportunities:

- A current client has mentioned a large project she would like us to bid on.
- The film industry continues to grow.
- There are two major conferences this year where we could promote our company.

Threats:

- Other individuals or companies can provide the services we can.
- Customers might prefer working with more established individuals/organizations.
- There is high risk in the film business.

Based on their SWOT analysis, the four entrepreneurs outline potential projects as follows:

- Find an external accountant or firm to help run the business.
- Hire someone to develop a company Web site, focusing on our experience and past projects.
- Develop a marketing plan.
- Develop a strong proposal to get the large project the current client mentioned.
- Plan to promote the company at two major conferences this year.

Some people like to perform a SWOT analysis by using **mind mapping**, which is a technique that uses branches radiating out from a core idea to structure thoughts and ideas. The human brain does not work in a linear fashion. People come up with many unrelated ideas. By putting those ideas down in a visual mind map format, you can often generate more ideas than by just creating lists. You can create mind maps by hand, using sticky notes, using presentation software such as Microsoft PowerPoint, or by using mind mapping software.

Figure 4-2 shows a sample mind map for the SWOT analysis presented earlier. This diagram was created using MindManager software by Mindjet. (You can download a free trial of this software from *www.mindjet.com* or use a similar free tool called FreeMind available at *www.freemind.sourceforge.net*.) Notice that this map has four main branches representing strengths, weaknesses, opportunities, and threats. Icons are added to each of those main branches to more visually identify them, such as the thumbs up for strengths and thumbs down for weaknesses. Ideas in each category are added to the appropriate branch. You could also add sub-branches to show ideas under those categories. For example, under the first branch for strengths, you could start adding sub-branches to list the most important contacts you have. This mind map includes branches for project ideas related to different categories, with text markers used to identify the project names. From this visual example, you can see that there are no project ideas identified to address strengths or threats, so these areas should be discussed further.

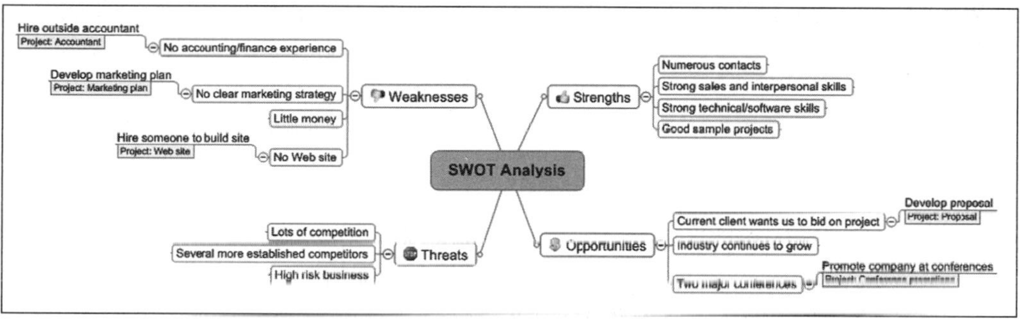

FIGURE 4-2 Mind map of a SWOT analysis to help identify potential projects

Identifying Potential Projects

The first step in project management is deciding what projects to do in the first place. Therefore, project initiation starts with identifying potential projects, using realistic methods to select which projects to work on, and then formalizing their initiation by issuing some sort of project charter.

In addition to using a SWOT analysis, organizations often follow a detailed process for project selection. Figure 4-3 shows a four-stage planning process for selecting information technology projects. Note the hierarchical structure of this model and the results produced from each stage. The first step in this process, starting at the top of the hierarchy, is to tie the information technology strategic plan to the organization's overall strategic plan. It is very important to have managers from outside the information technology department assist in the information technology planning process, as they can help information technology personnel understand organizational strategies and identify the business areas that support them.

After identifying strategic goals, the next step in the planning process for selecting information technology projects is to perform a business area analysis. This analysis outlines

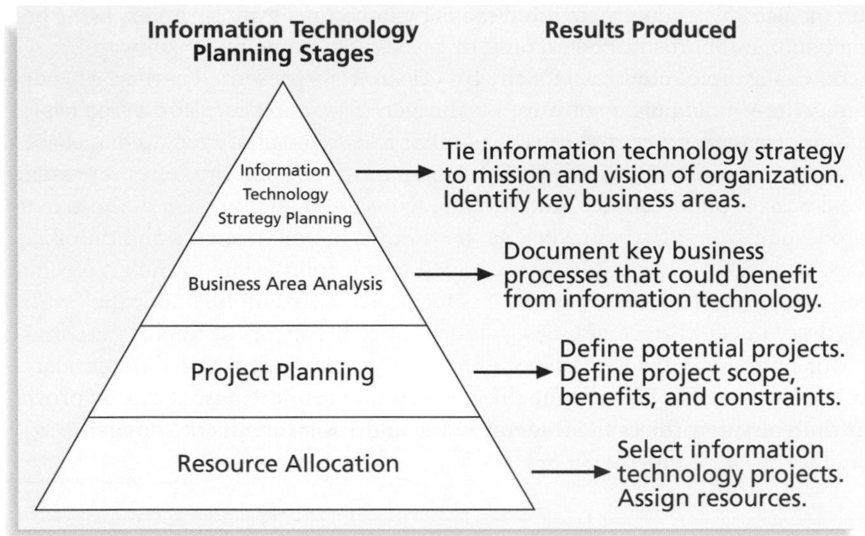

FIGURE 4-3 Planning process for selecting information technology projects

business processes that are central to achieving strategic goals and helps determine which ones could most benefit from information technology. The next step is to start defining potential information technology projects, their scope, benefits, and constraints. The last step in the planning process for selecting information technology projects is choosing which projects to do and assigning resources for working on them.

Aligning Information Technology with Business Strategy

Aligning IT projects with business strategy is consistently the top concern for CIOs. It is often difficult to educate line managers on technology's possibilities and limitations and keep IT professionals in tune with changing business needs. Most organizations face thousands of problems and opportunities for improvement. Therefore, an organization's strategic plan should guide the information technology project selection process. Recall from Chapter 2's Best Practice feature that IT governance is also important in ensuring that IT supports business goals. IT governance helps organizations maximize their investments in IT and address IT-related risks and opportunities.

An organization must develop a strategy for using information technology to define how it will support the organization's objectives. This information technology strategy must align with the organization's strategic plans and strategy. In fact, research shows that supporting explicit business objectives is the number one reason cited for why organizations invest in information technology projects. Other top criteria for investing in information technology projects include supporting implicit business objectives and providing financial incentives, such as a good internal rate of return (IRR) or net present value (NPV).[2] You will learn more about these financial criteria later in this section.

Information systems can be and often are central to business strategy. Author Michael Porter, who developed the concept of the strategic value of competitive advantage, has written several books and articles on strategic planning and competition. He and many other experts have emphasized the importance of using information technology to support strategic plans and provide a competitive advantage. Many information systems are classified as "strategic" because they directly support key business strategies. For example, information systems can help an organization support a strategy of being a low-cost producer. As one of the largest retailers in the United States, Wal-Mart's inventory control system is a classic example of such a system. Information systems can support a strategy of providing specialized products or services that set a company apart from others in the industry. Consider the classic example of Federal Express's introduction of online package tracking systems. They were the first company to provide this type of service, which gave them a competitive advantage until others developed similar systems. Information systems can also support a strategy of selling to a particular market or occupying a specific product niche. Owens-Corning developed a strategic information system that boosted the sales of its home-insulation products by providing its customers with a system for evaluating the energy efficiency of building designs.

BEST PRACTICE

Many organizations rely on effective new product development (NPD) to increase growth and profitability, yet according to Robert Cooper, of McMaster University and New Product Development Institute in Ontario, Canada, only one in seven product concepts comes to fruition. Why is it that some companies such as Procter & Gamble, Johnson & Johnson, Hewlett-Packard, and Sony are consistently successful in NPD? Because they use a disciplined, systematic approach to NPD projects based on best practices. Four important forces behind NPD success include the following:

1. A product innovation and technology strategy for the business
2. Resource commitment and focusing on the right projects, or solid portfolio management
3. An effective, flexible and streamlined idea-to-launch process
4. The right climate and culture for innovation, true cross-functional teams, and senior management commitment to NPD

Cooper's study compared companies that were the best at performing NPD with those that were the worst. For example, 65.5 percent of companies performing the best at NPD align projects with business strategy. However, within the group of companies performing the worst at NPD, only 46 percent align projects with business strategy. Even more telling is that 65.5 percent of best performing NPD companies have their resource breakdown aligned to business strategy while only 8 percent of worst performing companies do. It's easy for a company to say that its projects are aligned with business strategy, but assigning its resources based on that strategy is a measurable action that produces results. Best performing NPD companies are also more customer-focused in identifying new product ideas. Sixty-nine percent of them identify customer needs and problems based on customer input, while only 15 percent of worst performing companies do. Also, 80 percent of best performing companies have an identifiable NPD project manager compared to only 50 percent of worst performing companies.[3] These best practices apply to all projects: align projects *and* resources with business strategy, focus on customer needs when identifying potential projects, and assign project managers to lead the projects.

Methods for Selecting Projects

Organizations identify many potential projects as part of their strategic planning processes, and they often rely on experienced project managers to help them make project selection decisions. However, organizations need to narrow down the list of potential projects to those projects that will be of most benefit. Selecting projects is not an exact science, but it is a necessary part of project management. Many methods exist for selecting from among possible projects. Five common techniques are:

- Focusing on broad organizational needs
- Categorizing information technology projects
- Performing net present value or other financial analyses
- Using a weighted scoring model
- Implementing a balanced scorecard

In practice, organizations usually use a combination of these approaches to select projects. Each approach has advantages and disadvantages, and it is up to management to decide the best approach for selecting projects based on their particular organization.

Focusing on Broad Organizational Needs

Top managers must focus on meeting their organization's many needs when deciding what projects to undertake, when to undertake them, and to what level. Projects that address broad organizational needs are much more likely to be successful because they will be important to the organization. For example, a broad organizational need might be to improve safety, increase morale, provide better communications, or improve customer service. However, it is often difficult to provide a strong justification for many information technology projects related to these broad organizational needs. For example, it is often impossible to estimate the financial value of such projects, but everyone agrees that they do have a high value. As the old proverb says, "It is better to measure gold roughly than to count pennies precisely."

One method for selecting projects based on broad organizational needs is to determine whether they first meet three important criteria: *need*, *funding*, and *will*. Do people in the organization agree that the project needs to be done? Does the organization have the desire and the capacity to provide adequate funds to perform the project? Is there a strong will to make the project succeed? For example, many visionary CEOs can describe a broad need to improve certain aspects of their organizations, such as communications. Although they cannot specifically describe how to improve communications, they might allocate funds to projects that address this need. As projects progress, the organization must reevaluate the need, funding, and will for each project to determine if the project should be continued, redefined, or terminated.

Categorizing Information Technology Projects

Another method for selecting projects is based on various categorizations, such as the impetus for the project, the time window for the project, and the general priority for the project. The impetus for a project is often to respond to a problem, an opportunity, or a directive.

- **Problems** are undesirable situations that prevent an organization from achieving its goals. These problems can be current or anticipated. For example, users of an information system may be having trouble logging onto the system or getting information in a timely manner because the system has reached its capacity. In response, the company could initiate a project to enhance the current system by adding more access lines or upgrading the hardware with a faster processor, more memory, or more storage space.

- **Opportunities** are chances to improve the organization. For example, the project described in the opening case involves creating a new product that can make or break the entire company.
- **Directives** are new requirements imposed by management, government, or some external influence. For example, many projects involving medical technologies must meet rigorous government requirements.

Organizations select projects for any of these reasons. It is often easier to get approval and funding for projects that address problems or directives because the organization must respond to these categories of projects to avoid hurting their business. Many problems and directives must be resolved quickly, but managers must also apply systems thinking and seek opportunities for improving the organization through information technology projects.

Another categorization for information technology projects is based on the time it will take to complete a project or the date by which it must be done. For example, some potential projects must be finished within a specific time window. If they cannot be finished by this set date, they are no longer valid projects. Some projects can be completed very quickly—within a few weeks, days, or even minutes. Many organizations have an end user support function to handle very small projects that can be completed quickly. Even though many information technology projects can be completed quickly, it is still important to prioritize them.

Organizations can also prioritize information technology projects as being high-, medium-, or low-priority based on the current business environment. For example, if it is crucial to cut operating costs quickly, projects that have the most potential to do so would be given a high priority. The organization should always complete high-priority projects first, even if a low- or medium-priority project could be finished in less time. Usually there are many more potential information technology projects than an organization can undertake at any one time, so it is very important to work on the most important ones first.

Performing Net Present Value Analysis, Return on Investment, and Payback Analysis

Financial considerations are often an important aspect of the project selection process, especially during tough economic times. As authors Dennis Cohen and Robert Graham put it, "Projects are never ends in themselves. Financially they are always a means to an end, cash."[4] Many organizations require an approved business case before pursuing projects, and financial projections are a critical component of the business case. (See Chapter 3 for a sample business case.) Three primary methods for determining the projected financial value of projects include net present value analysis, return on investment, and payback analysis. Because project managers often deal with business executives, they must understand how to speak their language, which often boils down to these important financial concepts.

Net Present Value Analysis

Everyone knows that a dollar earned today is worth more than a dollar earned five years from now. **Net present value (NPV) analysis** is a method of calculating the expected net monetary gain or loss from a project by discounting all expected future cash inflows and outflows to the present point in time. An organization should consider only projects with a positive NPV if financial value is a key criterion for project selection. This is because a positive NPV means the return from a project exceeds the **cost of capital**—the return available by investing the capital elsewhere. Projects with higher NPVs are preferred to projects with lower NPVs, if all other factors are equal.

Figure 4-4 illustrates this concept for two different projects. Note that this example starts discounting right away in Year 1 and uses a 10 percent discount rate. You can use the NPV function in Microsoft Excel to calculate the NPV quickly. Detailed steps on performing this calculation manually are provided later in this section. Note that Figure 4-4 lists the projected benefits first, followed by the costs, and then the calculated cash flow amount. Note that the sum of the **cash flow**—benefits minus costs or income minus expenses—is the same for both projects at $5,000. The net present values are different, however, because they account for the time value of money. Project 1 has a negative cash flow of $5,000 in the first year, while Project 2 has a negative cash flow of only $1,000 in the first year. Although both projects have the same total cash flows without discounting, these cash flows are not of comparable financial value. Project 2's NPV of $3,201 is better than Project 1's NPV of $2,316. NPV analysis, therefore, is a method for making equal comparisons between cash flows for multi-year projects.

There are some items to consider when calculating NPV. Some organizations refer to the investment years for project costs as Year 0 instead of Year 1 and do not discount costs in Year 0. Other organizations start discounting immediately based on their financial procedures; it's simply a matter of preference for the organization. The discount rate can also vary, often based on the prime rate and other economic considerations. Financial experts in your organization can tell you what discount rate to use. Some people consider it to be the rate at which you could borrow money for the project. You can enter costs as negative numbers

	A	B	C	D	E	F	G
1	Discount rate	10%					
2							
3	PROJECT 1	YEAR 1	YEAR 2	YEAR 3	YEAR 4	YEAR 5	TOTAL
4	Benefits	$0	$2,000	$3,000	$4,000	$5,000	$14,000
5	Costs	$5,000	$1,000	$1,000	$1,000	$1,000	$9,000
6	Cash flow	($5,000)	$1,000	$2,000	$3,000	$4,000	$5,000
7	NPV ——→	$2,316					
8		Formula =npv(b1,b6:f6)					
9							
10	PROJECT 2	YEAR 1	YEAR 2	YEAR 3	YEAR 4	YEAR 5	TOTAL
11	Benefits	$1,000	$2,000	$4,000	$4,000	$4,000	$15,000
12	Costs	$2,000	$2,000	$2,000	$2,000	$2,000	$10,000
13	Cash flow	($1,000)	$0	$2,000	$2,000	$2,000	$5,000
14	NPV ——→	$3,201					
15		Formula =npv(b1,b13:f13)					
16							
17							

Note that totals are equal, but NPVs are not because of the time value of money

FIGURE 4-4 Net present value example

instead of positive numbers, and you can list costs first and then benefits. For example, Figure 4-5 shows the financial calculations JWD Consulting provided in the business case for the Project Management Intranet Site Project described in Chapter 3. Note that the discount rate is 8 percent, costs are not discounted right away (note the Year 0), the discount factors are rounded to two decimal places, costs are listed first, and costs are entered as positive numbers. The NPV and other calculations are the same; only the format is different. A project manager must be sure to check with his or her organization to find out its guidelines for when discounting starts, what discount rate to use, and what format the organization prefers.

To determine NPV, follow these steps:

1. Determine the estimated costs and benefits for the life of the project and the products it produces. For example, JWD Consulting assumed the project would produce a system in about six months that would be used for three years, so costs are included in Year 0, when the system is developed, and ongoing system costs and projected benefits are included for Years 1, 2, and 3.
2. Determine the discount rate. A **discount rate** is the rate used in discounting future cash flow. It is also called the **capitalization rate** or **opportunity cost of capital**. In Figure 4-4, the discount rate is 10 percent per year, and in Figure 4-5, the discount rate is 8 percent per year.
3. Calculate the net present value. There are several ways to calculate NPV. Most spreadsheet software has a built-in function to calculate NPV. For example, Figure 4-4 shows the formula that Microsoft Excel uses: =npv(discount rate, range of cash flows), where the discount rate is in cell B1 and the range of cash flows for Project 1 are in cells B6 through F6. (See Chapter 7, Project Cost Management, for more information on cash flow and other cost-related terms.) To use the NPV function, there must be a row in the spreadsheet (or column,

Discount rate	8%					
Assume the project is completed in Year 0			**Year**			
	0	1	2	3	**Total**	
Costs	140,000	40,000	40,000	40,000		
Discount factor	1	0.93	0.86	0.79		
Discounted costs	**140,000**	**37,200**	**34,400**	**31,600**	**243,200**	
Benefits	0	200,000	200,000	200,000		
Discount factor	1	0.93	0.86	0.79		
Discounted benefits	**0**	**186,000**	**172,000**	**158,000**	**516,000**	
Discounted benefits - costs	(140,000)	148,800	137,600	126,400	**272,800**	←**NPV**
Cumulative benefits - costs	(140,000)	8,800	146,400	272,800		
		↑				
ROI ⟶	**112%**					
	Payback In Year 1					

FIGURE 4-5 JWD Consulting net present value example

depending how it is organized) for the cash flow each year, which is the benefit amount for that year minus the cost amount. The result of the formula yields an NPV of $2316 for Project 1 and $3201 for Project 2. Since both projects have positive NPVs, they are both good candidates for selection. However, since Project 2 has a higher NPV than Project 1 (38 percent higher), it would be the better choice. If the two numbers are close, then other methods should be used to help decide which project to select.

The mathematical formula for calculating NPV is:

$$\text{NPV} = \sum_{t=0...n} A_t/(1+r)^t$$

where t equals the year of the cash flow, n is the last year of the cash flow, A is the amount of cash flow each year, and r is the discount rate. If you cannot enter the data into spreadsheet software, you can perform the calculations by hand or with a simple calculator. First, determine the annual **discount factor**—a multiplier for each year based on the discount rate and year—and then apply it to the costs and benefits for each year. The formula for the discount factor is $1/(1 + r)t$ where r is the discount rate, such as 8 percent, and t is the year. For example, the discount factors used in Figure 4-5 are calculated as follows:

$$\text{Year } 0: \text{discount factor} = 1/(1+0.08)^0 = 1$$

$$\text{Year } 1: \text{discount factor} = 1/(1+0.08)^1 = .93$$

$$\text{Year } 2: \text{discount factor} = 1/(1+0.08)^2 = .86$$

$$\text{Year } 3: \text{discount factor} = 1/(1+0.08)^3 = .79$$

After determining the discount factor each year, multiply the costs and benefits each year by the appropriate discount factor. For example, in Figure 4-5, the discounted cost for Year 1 is $40,000 * .93 = $37,200. Next, sum all of the discounted costs and benefits each year to get a total. For example, the total discounted costs in Figure 4-5 are $243,200. To calculate the NPV, take the total discounted benefits and subtract the total discounted costs. In this example, the NPV is $516,000 – $243,200 = $272,800.

Return on Investment

Another important financial consideration is return on investment. **Return on investment (ROI)** is the result of subtracting the project costs from the benefits and then dividing by the costs. For example, if you invest $100 today and next year it is worth $110, your ROI is ($110 – 100)/100 or 0.10 (10 percent). Note that the ROI is always a percentage. It can be positive or negative. It is best to consider discounted costs and benefits for multi-year projects when calculating ROI. Figure 4-5 shows an ROI of 112 percent. You calculate this number as follows:

$$\text{ROI} = (\text{total discounted benefits} - \text{total discounted costs})/\text{discounted costs}$$

$$\text{ROI} = (516,000 - 243,200)/243,200 = 112\%$$

The higher the ROI, the better. An ROI of 112 percent is outstanding. Many organizations have a required rate of return for projects. The **required rate of return** is the minimum acceptable rate of return on an investment. For example, an organization might have a required rate of return of at least 10 percent for projects. The organization bases the required rate of return on what it could expect to receive elsewhere for an investment of comparable risk. You can also determine a project's **internal rate of return (IRR)** by finding what discount rate results in an NPV of zero for the project. You can use the Goal Seek function in Excel (use Excel's Help function for more information on Goal Seek) to determine the IRR quickly. Simply set the cell containing the NPV calculation to zero while changing the cell containing the discount rate. For example, in Figure 4-4, you could set cell b7 to zero while changing cell b1 to find that the IRR for Project 1 is 27 percent.

Many organizations use ROI in the project selection process. In a recent *Information Week* study, more than 82 percent of IT decisions required an ROI analysis.[5]

Payback Analysis

Payback analysis is another important financial tool to use when selecting projects. **Payback period** is the amount of time it will take to recoup, in the form of net cash inflows, the total dollars invested in a project. In other words, payback analysis determines how much time will lapse before accrued benefits overtake accrued and continuing costs. Payback occurs when the net cumulative benefits equals the net cumulative costs, or when the net cumulative benefits minus costs equals zero. Figure 4-6 shows how to find the payback period. The cumulative benefits minus costs for Year 0 are ($140,000). Adding that number

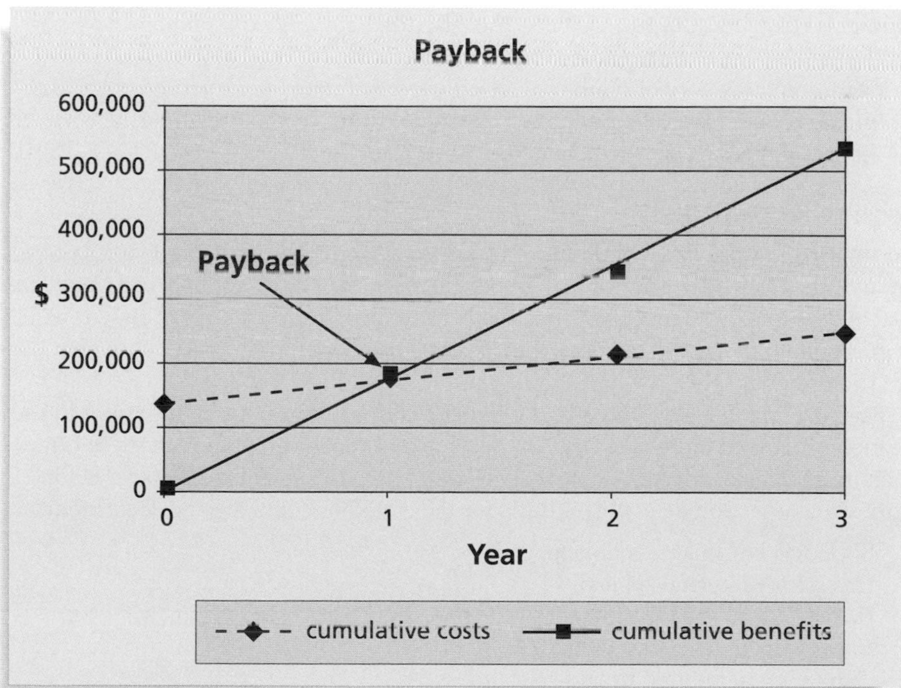

FIGURE 4-6 Charting the payback period

to the discounted benefits minus costs for Year 1 results in $8,800. Since that number is positive, the payback occurs in Year 1.

Creating a chart helps illustrate more precisely when the payback period occurs. Figure 4-6 charts the cumulative discounted costs and cumulative discounted benefits each year using the numbers from Figure 4-5. Note that the lines cross right around Year 1. This is the point where the cumulative discounted benefits equal the cumulative discounted costs, so that the cumulative discounted benefits minus costs are zero. Beyond this point, discounted benefits exceed discounted costs and the project is showing a profit. Since this project started in Year 0, a payback in Year 1 actually means the project reached payback in its second year. The cumulative discounted benefits and costs are equal to zero where the lines cross. An early payback period, such as in the first or second year, is normally considered very good.

Many organizations have certain recommendations for the length of the payback period of an investment. They might require all information technology projects to have a payback period of less than two years or even one year, regardless of the estimated NPV or ROI. Dan Hoover, vice president and area director at Ciber Inc., an international systems integration consultancy, suggests that organizations, especially small firms, should focus on payback period when making IT investment decisions. "If your costs are recovered in the first year," Hoover says, "the project is worthy of serious consideration, especially if the benefits are high. If the payback period is more than a year, it may be best to look elsewhere."[6] However, organizations must also consider long-range goals when making technology investments. Many crucial projects cannot achieve a payback so quickly or be completed in such a short time period.

To aid in project selection, it is important for project managers to understand the organization's financial expectations for projects. It is also important for top management to understand the limitations of financial estimates, particularly for information technology projects. For example, it is very difficult to develop good estimates of projected costs and benefits for information technology projects. You will learn more about estimating costs and benefits in Chapter 7, Project Cost Management.

Using a Weighted Scoring Model

A **weighted scoring model** is a tool that provides a systematic process for selecting projects based on many criteria. These criteria can include factors such as meeting broad organizational needs; addressing problems, opportunities, or directives; the amount of time it will take to complete the project; the overall priority of the project; and projected financial performance of the project.

The first step in creating a weighted scoring model is to identify criteria important to the project selection process. It often takes time to develop and reach agreement on these criteria. Holding facilitated brainstorming sessions or using groupware to exchange ideas can aid in developing these criteria. Some possible criteria for information technology projects include:

- Supports key business objectives
- Has strong internal sponsor
- Has strong customer support
- Uses realistic level of technology
- Can be implemented in one year or less
- Provides positive NPV
- Has low risk in meeting scope, time, and cost goals

Next, you assign a weight to each criterion. Once again, determining weights requires consultation and final agreement. These weights indicate how much you value each criterion or how important each criterion is. You can assign weights based on percentages, and the sum of all of the criteria's weights must total 100 percent. You then assign numerical scores to each criterion (e.g. 0 to 100) for each project. The scores indicate how much each project meets each criterion. At this point, you can use a spreadsheet application to create a matrix of projects, criteria, weights, and scores. Figure 4-7 provides an example of a weighted scoring model to evaluate four different projects. After assigning weights for the criteria and scores for each project, you calculate a weighted score for each project by multiplying the weight for each criterion by its score and adding the resulting values.

For example, you calculate the weighted score for Project 1 in Figure 4-7 as:

$$25\% * 90 + 15\% * 70 + 15\% * 50 + 10\% * 25 + 5\% * 20 + 20\% * 50 + 10\% * 20 = 56$$

Note that in this example, Project 2 would be the obvious choice for selection because it has the highest weighted score. Creating a bar chart to graph the weighted

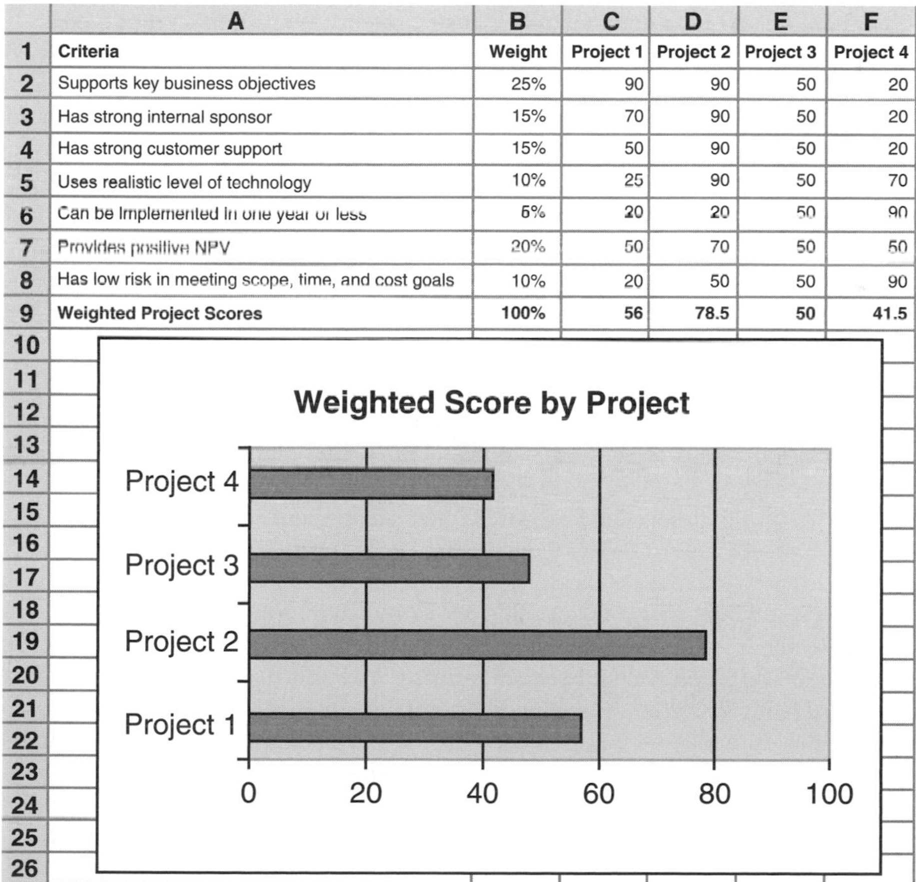

	A	B	C	D	E	F
1	**Criteria**	**Weight**	**Project 1**	**Project 2**	**Project 3**	**Project 4**
2	Supports key business objectives	25%	90	90	50	20
3	Has strong internal sponsor	15%	70	90	50	20
4	Has strong customer support	15%	50	90	50	20
5	Uses realistic level of technology	10%	25	90	50	70
6	Can be implemented in one year or less	5%	20	20	50	90
7	Provides positive NPV	20%	50	70	50	50
8	Has low risk in meeting scope, time, and cost goals	10%	20	50	50	90
9	**Weighted Project Scores**	**100%**	**56**	**78.5**	**50**	**41.5**

FIGURE 4-7 Sample weighted scoring model for project selection

scores for each project allows you to see the results at a glance. If you create the weighted scoring model in a spreadsheet, you can enter the data, create and copy formulas, and perform a "what-if" analysis. For example, suppose you change the weights for the criteria. By having the weighted scoring model in a spreadsheet, you can easily change the weights to update the weighted scores and charts automatically. This capability allows you to investigate various options for different stakeholders quickly. Ideally, the result should be reflective of the group's consensus, and any major disagreements should be documented.

Teachers often use a weighted scoring model to determine grades. Suppose grades for a class are based on two homework assignments and two exams. To calculate final grades, the teacher would assign a weight to each of these items. Suppose Homework One is worth 10 percent of the grade, Homework Two is worth 20 percent of the grade, Test One is worth 20 percent of the grade, and Test Two is worth 50 percent of the grade. Students would want to do well on each of these items, but they should focus on performing well on Test Two since it is 50 percent of the grade.

You can also establish weights by assigning points. For example, a project might receive 10 points if it definitely supports key business objectives, 5 points if it somewhat supports them, and 0 points if it is totally unrelated to key business objectives. With a point model, you can simply add all the points to determine the best projects for selection, without having to multiply weights and scores and sum the results.

You can also determine minimum scores or thresholds for specific criteria in a weighted scoring model. For example, suppose an organization really should not consider a project if it does not score at least 50 out of 100 on every criterion. You can build this type of threshold into the weighted scoring model to reject projects that do not meet these minimum standards. As you can see, weighted scoring models can aid in project selection decisions.

Implementing a Balanced Scorecard

Drs. Robert Kaplan and David Norton developed another approach to help select and manage projects that align with business strategy. A **balanced scorecard** is a methodology that converts an organization's value drivers, such as customer service, innovation, operational efficiency, and financial performance, to a series of defined metrics. Organizations record and analyze these metrics to determine how well projects help them achieve strategic goals. Using a balanced scorecard involves several detailed steps. You can learn more about how balanced scorecards work from the Balanced Scorecard Institute (*www.balancedscorecard.org*) or other sources. Although this concept can work within an information technology department specifically. It is best to implement a balanced scorecard throughout an organization because it helps foster alignment between business and information technology.[7] The Balanced Scorecard Institute's Web site includes several examples of how organizations use this methodology, For example, the U.S. Defense Finance and Accounting Services (DFAS) organization uses a balanced scorecard to measure performance and track progress in achieving its strategic goals. Its strategy focuses on four perspectives: customer, financial, internal, and growth and learning. Figure 4-8 shows how the balanced scorecard approach ties together the organization's mission, vision, and goals based on these four perspectives. The DFAS continuously monitors this corporate scorecard and revises it based on identified priorities.

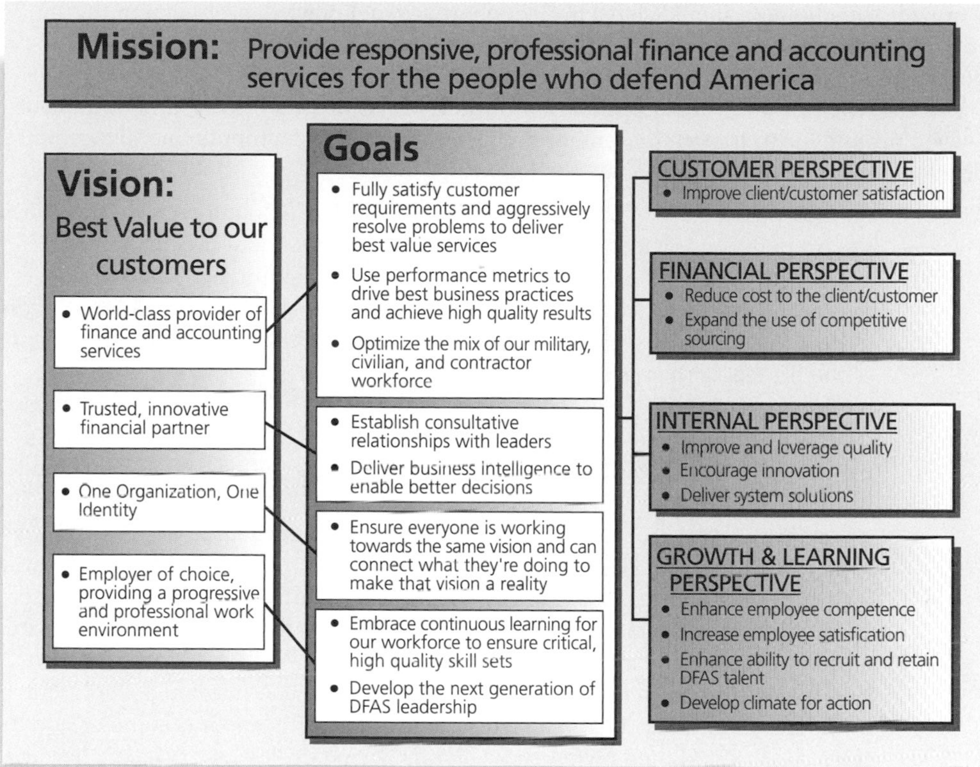

Mission: Provide responsive, professional finance and accounting services for the people who defend America
Vision: Best Value to our customers
• World-class provider of finance and accounting services
• Trusted, innovative financial partner
• One Organization, One Identity
• Employer of choice, providing a progressive and professional work environment
Goals
• Fully satisfy customer requirements and aggressively resolve problems to deliver best value services
• Use performance metrics to drive best business practices and achieve high quality results
• Optimize the mix of our military, civilian, and contractor workforce
• Establish consultative relationships with leaders
• Deliver business intelligence to enable better decisions
• Ensure everyone is working towards the same vision and can connect what they're doing to make that vision a reality
• Embrace continuous learning for our workforce to ensure critical, high quality skill sets
• Develop the next generation of DFAS leadership
CUSTOMER PERSPECTIVE
• Improve client/customer satisfaction
FINANCIAL PERSPECTIVE
• Reduce cost to the client/customer
• Expand the use of competitive sourcing
INTERNAL PERSPECTIVE
• Improve and leverage quality
• Encourage innovation
• Deliver system solutions
GROWTH & LEARNING PERSPECTIVE
• Enhance employee competence
• Increase employee satisfaction
• Enhance ability to recruit and retain DFAS talent
• Develop climate for action

FIGURE 4-8 Balanced scorecard example

Defense Finance and Accounting Service, "DFAS Strategic Plan," Nov 2001 *(http:/balancedscorecard.org/Portals/0/PDF/DFAS-strategic-plan.pdf)*, p. 13.

As you can see, organizations can use many approaches to select projects. Many project managers have some say in which projects their organization select for implementation. Even if they do not, they need to understand the motives and overall business strategies for the projects they are managing. Project managers and team members are often called upon to explain the importance of their projects, and understanding many of these project selection methods can help them represent the project effectively.

Developing a Project Charter

After top management decides on which projects to pursue, it is important to let the rest of the organization know about these projects. Management needs to create and distribute documentation to authorize project initiation. This documentation can take many different forms, but one common form is a project charter. A **project charter** is a document that formally recognizes the existence of a project and provides direction on the project's objectives and management. It authorizes the project manager to use organizational resources to complete the project. Ideally, the project manager will provide a major role in developing the project charter. Instead of project charters, some organizations initiate projects using a simple letter of agreement, while others use much longer documents or formal contracts.

Key project stakeholders should sign a project charter to acknowledge agreement on the need for and intent of the project. A project charter is a key output of the initiation process, as described in Chapter 3.

The *PMBOK® Guide, Fourth Edition* lists inputs, tools and techniques, and outputs of the seven project integration management processes. For example, inputs that are helpful in developing a project charter include the following:

- *A project statement of work*: A statement of work is a document that describes the products or services to be created by the project team. It usually includes a description of the business need for the project, a summary of the requirements and characteristics of the products or services, and organizational information, such as appropriate parts of the strategic plan, showing the alignment of the project with strategic goals.
- *A business case*: As explained in Chapter 3, many projects require a business case to justify their investment. Information in the business case, such as the project objective, high-level requirements, and time and cost goals are included in the project charter.
- *A contract*: If you are working on a project under contract for an external customer, the contract should include much of the information needed for creating a good project charter. Some people might use a contract in place of a charter; however, many contracts are difficult to read and can often change, so it is still a good idea to create a project charter.
- *Enterprise environmental factors*: These factors include relevant government or industry standards, the organization's infrastructure, and marketplace conditions. Managers should review these factors when developing a project charter.
- *Organizational process assets*: **Organizational process assets** include formal and informal plans, policies, procedures, guidelines, information systems, financial systems, management systems, lessons learned, and historical information that can be used to influence a project's success.

The main tool and technique for developing a project charter is expert judgment. Experts from within as well as outside the organization should be consulted when creating a project charter to make sure it is useful and realistic.

The only output of the process to develop a project charter is a project charter. Although the format of project charters can vary tremendously, they should include at least the following basic information:

- The project's title and date of authorization
- The project manager's name and contact information
- A summary schedule, including the planned start and finish dates; if a summary milestone schedule is available, it should also be included or referenced
- A summary of the project's budget or reference to budgetary documents
- A brief description of the project objectives, including the business need or other justification for authorizing the project
- Project success criteria, including project approval requirements and who signs off on the project
- A summary of the planned approach for managing the project, which should describe stakeholder needs and expectations, important assumptions, and

constraints, and refer to related documents, such as a communications management plan, as available
- A roles and responsibilities matrix
- A sign-off section for signatures of key project stakeholders
- A comments section in which stakeholders can provide important comments related to the project

Unfortunately, many internal projects, like the one in the opening case of this chapter, do not have project charters. They often have a budget and general guidelines, but no formal, signed documentation. If Nick had a project charter to refer to—especially if it included information on the approach for managing the project—top management would have received the business information they needed, and managing the project might have been easier. Project charters are usually not difficult to write. What is difficult is getting people with the proper knowledge and authority to write and sign the project charters. Top management should have reviewed the charter with Nick, since he was the project manager. In their initial meeting, they should have discussed roles and responsibilities, as well as their expectations of how Nick should work with them. If there is no project charter, the project manager should work with key stakeholders, including top management, to create one. Table 4-1 shows a possible charter that Nick could have created for completing the DNA-sequencing instrument project.

Many projects fail because of unclear requirements and expectations, so starting with a project charter makes a lot of sense. If project managers are having difficulty obtaining support from project stakeholders, for example, they can refer to what everyone agreed to in the project charter. Note that the sample project charter in Table 4-1 includes several items under the Approach section to help Nick in managing the project and the sponsor in overseeing it. To help Nick transition to the role of project manager, the charter said that they would hire a technical replacement and part-time assistant for Nick as soon as possible. To help Ahmed, the project sponsor, feel more comfortable with how the project was being managed, there were items included to ensure proper planning and communications. Recall from Chapter 2 that executive support contributes the most to successful information technology projects. Since Nick was the fourth project manager on this project, top management at his company obviously had some problems choosing and working with project managers.

TABLE 4-1 Project charter for the DNA-sequencing instrument completion project

Project Title: DNA-Sequencing Instrument Completion Project
Date of Authorization: February 1
Project Start Date: February 1 **Projected Finish Date:** November 1

Key Schedule Milestones:

- Complete first version of the software by June 1
- Complete production version of the software by November 1

Budget Information: The firm has allocated $1.5 million for this project, and more funds are available if needed. The majority of costs for this project will be internal labor. All hardware will be outsourced.

TABLE 4-1 Project charter for the DNA-sequencing instrument completion project (cont)

Project Manager: Nick Carson, (650) 949-0707, ncarson@dnaconsulting.com

Project Objectives: The DNA-sequencing instrument project has been underway for three years. It is a crucial project for our company. This is the first charter for the project, and the objective is to complete the first version of the software for the instrument in four months and a production version in nine months.

Main Project Success Criteria: The software must meet all written specifications, be thoroughly tested, and be completed on time. The CEO will formally approve the project with advice from other key stakeholders.

Approach:

- Hire a technical replacement for Nick Carson and a part-time assistant as soon as possible.
- Within one month, develop a clear work breakdown structure, scope statement, and Gantt chart detailing the work required to complete the DNA sequencing instrument.
- Purchase all required hardware upgrades within two months.
- Hold weekly progress review meetings with the core project team and the sponsor.
- Conduct thorough software testing per the approved test plans.

ROLES AND RESPONSIBILITIES

Name	Role	Position	Contact Information
Ahmed Abrams	Sponsor	CEO	aabrams@dnaconsulting.com
Nick Carson	Project Manager	Manager	ncarson@dnaconsulting.com
Susan Johnson	Team Member	DNA expert	sjohnson@dnaconsulting.com
Renyong Chi	Team Member	Testing expert	rchi@dnaconsulting.com
Erik Haus	Team Member	Programmer	ehaus@dnaconsulting.com
Bill Strom	Team Member	Programmer	bstrom@dnaconsulting.com
Maggie Elliot	Team Member	Programmer	melliot@dnaconsulting.com

Sign-off: (Signatures of all the above stakeholders)

Ahmed Abrams *Nick Carson*
Susan Johnson *Renyong Chi*
Erik Haus *Bill Strom*
Maggie Elliot

Comments: (Handwritten or typed comments from above stakeholders, if applicable)

"I want to be heavily involved in this project. It is crucial to our company's success, and I expect everyone to help make it succeed." —Ahmed Abrams

"The software test plans are complete and well documented. If anyone has questions, do not hesitate to contact me." —Renyong Chi

Taking the time to discuss, develop, and sign off on a simple project charter could have prevented several problems in this case.

After creating a project charter, the next step in project integration management is preparing a project management plan.

DEVELOPING A PROJECT MANAGEMENT PLAN

To coordinate and integrate information across project management knowledge areas and across the organization, there must be a good project management plan. A **project management plan** is a document used to coordinate all project planning documents and help guide a project's execution and control. Plans created in the other knowledge areas are considered subsidiary parts of the overall project management plan. Project management plans also document project planning assumptions and decisions regarding choices, facilitate communication among stakeholders, define the content, extent, and timing of key management reviews, and provide a baseline for progress measurement and project control. Project management plans should be dynamic, flexible, and subject to change when the environment or project changes. These plans should greatly assist the project manager in leading the project team and assessing project status.

To create and assemble a good project management plan, the project manager must practice the art of project integration management, since information is required from all of the project management knowledge areas. Working with the project team and other stakeholders to create a project management plan will help the project manager guide the project's execution and understand the overall project. The main inputs for developing a project management plan include the project charter, outputs from planning processes, enterprise environment factors, and organizational process assets. The main tool and technique is expert judgment, and the output is a project management plan.

Project Management Plan Contents

Just as projects are unique, so are project management plans. A small project involving a few people over a couple of months might have a project management plan consisting of only a project charter, scope statement, and Gantt chart. A large project involving a hundred people over three years would have a much more detailed project management plan. It is important to tailor project management plans to fit the needs of specific projects. The project management plans should guide the work, so they should be only as detailed as needed for each project.

There are, however, common elements to most project management plans. Parts of a project management plan include an introduction or overview of the project, a description of how the project is organized, the management and technical processes used on the project, and sections describing the work to be performed, the schedule, and the budget.

The introduction or overview of the project should include, as a minimum, the following information:

- *The project name*: Every project should have a unique name. Unique names help distinguish each project and avoid confusion among related projects.

- *A brief description of the project and the need it addresses*: This description should clearly outline the goals of the project and reason for the project. It should be written in layperson's terms, avoid technical jargon, and include a rough time and cost estimate.
- *The sponsor's name*: Every project needs a sponsor. Include the name, title, and contact information of the sponsor in the introduction.
- *The names of the project manager and key team members*: The project manager should always be the contact for project information. Depending on the size and nature of the project, names of key team members may also be included.
- *Deliverables of the project*: This section should briefly list and describe the products that will be produced as part of the project. Software packages, pieces of hardware, technical reports, and training materials are examples of deliverables.
- *A list of important reference materials*: Many projects have a history preceding them. Listing important documents or meetings related to a project helps project stakeholders understand that history. This section should reference the plans produced for other knowledge areas. (Recall from Chapter 3 that every single knowledge area includes some planning processes.) Therefore, the project management plan should reference and summarize important parts of the scope management, schedule management, cost management, quality management, human resource management, communications management, risk management, and procurement management plans.
- *A list of definitions and acronyms, if appropriate*: Many projects, especially information technology projects, involve terminology unique to a particular industry or technology. Providing a list of definitions and acronyms will help avoid confusion.

The description of how the project is organized should include the following information:

- *Organizational charts*: In addition to an organizational chart for the company sponsoring the project and for the customer's company (if it is an external customer), there should be a project organizational chart to show the lines of authority, responsibilities, and communication for the project. For example, the Manhattan Project introduced in Chapter 1 had a very detailed organizational chart to show all the people working on the project.
- *Project responsibilities*: This section of the project plan should describe the major project functions and activities and identify those individuals who are responsible for them. A responsibility assignment matrix (described in Chapter 9) is a tool often used for displaying this information.
- *Other organizational or process-related information*: Depending on the nature of the project, there may be a need to document major processes followed on the project. For example, if the project involves releasing a major software upgrade, it might help everyone involved in the project to see a diagram or timeline of the major steps involved in this process.

The section of the project management plan describing management and technical approaches should include the following information:

- *Management objectives*: It is important to understand top management's view of the project, what the priorities are for the project, and any major assumptions or constraints.
- *Project controls*: This section describes how to monitor project progress and handle changes. Will there be monthly status reviews and quarterly progress reviews? Will there be specific forms or charts to monitor progress? Will the project use earned value management (described in Chapter 7) to assess and track performance? What is the process for change control? What level of management is required to approve different types of changes? (You will learn more about change control later in this chapter.)
- *Risk management*: This section briefly addresses how the project team will identify, manage, and control risks. It should refer to the risk management plan, if one is required for the project.
- *Project staffing*: This section describes the number and types of people required for the project. It should refer to the human resource plan, if one is required for the project.
- *Technical processes*: This section describes specific methodologies a project might use and explains how to document information. For example, many information technology projects follow specific software development methodologies or use particular Computer Aided Software Engineering (CASE) tools. Many companies or customers also have specific formats for technical documentation. It is important to clarify these technical processes in the project management plan.

The next section of the project management plan should describe the work to perform and reference the scope management plan. It should summarize the following:

- *Major work packages*: A project manager usually organizes the project work into several work packages using a work breakdown structure (WBS), and produces a scope statement to describe the work in more detail. This section should briefly summarize the main work packages for the project and refer to appropriate sections of the scope management plan.
- *Key deliverables*: This section lists and describes the key products produced as part of the project. It should also describe the quality expectations for the product deliverables.
- *Other work-related information*: This section highlights key information related to the work performed on the project. For example, it might list specific hardware or software to use on the project or certain specifications to follow. It should document major assumptions made in defining the project work.

The project schedule information section should include the following:

- *Summary schedule*: It is helpful to see a one-page summary of the overall project schedule. Depending on the size and complexity of the project, the summary schedule might list only key deliverables and their planned completion dates. For smaller projects, it might include all of the work and associated dates for the entire project in a Gantt chart. For example, the Gantt chart and milestone schedule provided in Chapter 3 for JWD Consulting were fairly short and simple.

- *Detailed schedule*: This section provides information on the project schedule that is more detailed. It should reference the schedule management plan and discuss dependencies among project activities that could affect the project schedule. For example, it might explain that a major part of the work cannot start until an external agency provides funding. A network diagram can show these dependencies (see Chapter 6, Project Time Management).
- *Other schedule-related information*: Many assumptions are often made in preparing project schedules. This section should document major assumptions and highlight other important information related to the project schedule.

The budget section of the project management plan should include the following:

- *Summary budget*: The summary budget includes the total estimate of the overall project's budget. It could also include the budget estimate for each month or year by certain budget categories. It is important to provide some explanation of what these numbers mean. For example, is the total budget estimate a firm number that cannot change, or is it a rough estimate based on projected costs over the next three years?
- *Detailed budget*: This section summarizes what is in the cost management plan and includes more detailed budget information. For example, what are the fixed and recurring cost estimates for the project each year? What are the projected financial benefits of the project? What types of people are needed to do the work, and how are the labor costs calculated? (See Chapter 7, Project Cost Management, for more information on creating cost estimates and budgets.)
- *Other budget-related information*: This section documents major assumptions and highlights other important information related to financial aspects of the project.

Using Guidelines to Create Project Management Plans

Many organizations use guidelines to create project management plans. Microsoft Project 2007 and other project management software packages come with several template files to use as guidelines. However, do not confuse a project management plan with a Gantt chart. The project management plan is much more than a Gantt chart, as described earlier.

Many government agencies also provide guidelines for creating project management plans. For example, the U.S. Department of Defense (DOD) Standard 2167, Software Development Plan, describes the format for contractors to use in creating a plan for software development for DOD projects. The Institute of Electrical and Electronics Engineers (IEEE) Standard 1058–1998 describes the contents of a Software Project Management Plan (SPMP). Table 4-2 provides some of the categories for the IEEE SPMP. Companies working on software development projects for the Department of Defense must follow this or a similar standard.

In many private organizations, specific documentation standards are not as rigorous; however, there are usually guidelines for developing project management plans. It is good

TABLE 4-2 Sample contents for a software project management plan (SPMP)

Major section headings	Section topics
Overview	Purpose, scope, and objectives; assumptions and constraints; project deliverables; schedule and budget summary; evolution of the plan
Project Organization	External interfaces; internal structure; roles and responsibilities
Managerial Process Plan	Start-up plans (estimation, staffing, resource acquisition, and project staff training plans); work plan (work activities, schedule, resource, and budget allocation); control plan; risk management plan; closeout plan
Technical Process Plans	Process model; methods, tools, and techniques; infrastructure plan; product acceptance plan
Supporting Process Plans	Configuration management plan; verification and validation plan; documentation plan; quality assurance plan; reviews and audits; problem resolution plan; subcontractor management plan; process improvement plan

Source: IEEE Standard 1058–1998.

practice to follow standards or guidelines for developing project management plans in an organization to facilitate the development and execution of those plans. The organization can work more efficiently if all project management plans follow a similar format. Recall from Chapter 1 that companies that excel in project management develop and deploy standardized project delivery systems.

> The winners clearly spell out what needs to be done in a project, by whom, when, and how. For this they use an integrated toolbox, including PM tools, methods, and techniques … If a scheduling template is developed and used over and over, it becomes a repeatable action that leads to higher productivity and lower uncertainty. Sure, using scheduling templates is neither a breakthrough nor a feat. But laggards exhibited almost no use of the templates. Rather, in constructing schedules their project managers started with a clean sheet, a clear waste of time.[8]

For example, in the opening case, Nick Carson's top managers were disappointed because he did not provide them with the project planning information they needed to make important business decisions. They wanted to see detailed project management plans, including schedules and a means for tracking progress. Nick had never created a project management plan or even a simple progress report before, and the organization did not provide templates or examples to follow. If it had, Nick might have been able to deliver the information top management was expecting.

DIRECTING AND MANAGING PROJECT EXECUTION

Directing and managing project execution involves managing and performing the work described in the project management plan, one of the main inputs for this process. Other inputs include approved change requests, enterprise environmental factors, and organizational process assets. The majority of time on a project is usually spent on execution, as is most of the project's budget. The application area of the project directly affects project execution because the products of the project are produced during project execution. For example, the DNA-sequencing instrument project from the opening case and all associated software and documentation would be produced during project execution. The project team would need to use their expertise in biology, hardware and software development, and testing to produce the product successfully.

The project manager would also need to focus on leading the project team and managing stakeholder relationships to execute the project management plan successfully. Project human resource management and project communications management are crucial to a project's success. See Chapters 9 and 10 respectively for more information on those knowledge areas. If the project involves a significant amount of risk or outside resources, the project manager also needs to be well versed in project risk management and project procurement management. See Chapters 11 and 12 for details on those knowledge areas. Many unique situations occur during project execution, so project managers must be flexible and creative in dealing with them. Review the situation Erica Bell faced during project execution in Chapter 3. Also review the ResNet case study (available on the companion Web site for this text) to understand the execution challenges project manager Peeter Kivestu and his project team faced.

Coordinating Planning and Execution

In project integration management, project planning and execution are intertwined and inseparable activities. The main function of creating a project management plan is to guide project execution. A good plan should help produce good products or work results. Plans should document what good work results consist of. Updates to plans should reflect knowledge gained from completing work earlier in the project. Anyone who has tried to write a computer program from poor specifications appreciates the importance of a good plan. Anyone who has had to document a poorly programmed system appreciates the importance of good execution.

A commonsense approach to improving the coordination between project plan development and execution is to follow this simple rule: Those who will do the work should plan the work. All project personnel need to develop both planning and executing skills and need experience in these areas. In information technology projects, programmers who have had to write detailed specifications and then create the code from their own specifications become better at writing specifications. Likewise, most systems analysts begin their careers as programmers, so they understand what type of analysis and documentation they need to write good code. Although project managers are responsible for developing the overall project management plan, they must solicit input from the project team members who are developing plans in each knowledge area.

Providing Strong Leadership and a Supportive Culture

Strong leadership and a supportive organizational culture are crucial during project execution. Project managers must lead by example to demonstrate the importance of creating good project plans and then following them in project execution. Project managers often create plans for things they need to do themselves. If project managers follow through on their own plans, their team members are more likely to do the same.

Good project execution also requires a supportive organizational culture. For example, organizational procedures can help or hinder project execution. If an organization has useful guidelines and templates for project management that everyone in the organization follows, it will be easier for project managers and their teams to plan and do their work. If the organization uses the project plans as the basis for performing and monitoring progress during execution, the culture will promote the relationship between good planning and execution. On the other hand, if organizations have confusing or bureaucratic project management guidelines that hinder getting work done or measuring progress against plans, project managers and their teams will be frustrated.

Even with a supportive organizational culture, project managers may sometimes find it necessary to break the rules to produce project results in a timely manner. When project managers break the rules, politics will play a role in the results. For example, if a particular project requires use of nonstandard software, the project manager must use his or her political skills to convince concerned stakeholders of the need to break the rules on using only standard software. Breaking organizational rules—and getting away with it—requires excellent leadership, communication, and political skills.

Capitalizing on Product, Business, and Application Area Knowledge

In addition to possessing strong leadership, communication, and political skills, project managers also need to possess product, business, and application area knowledge to execute projects successfully. It is often helpful for information technology project managers to have prior technical experience or at least a working knowledge of information technology products. For example, if the project manager were leading a Joint Application Design (JAD) team to help define user requirements, it would be helpful for him or her to understand the language of the business and technical experts on the team. See Chapter 5, Project Scope Management, for more information on JAD and other methods for collecting requirements.

Many information technology projects are small, so project managers may be required to perform some technical work or mentor team members to complete the project. For example, a three-month project to develop a Web-based application with only three team members would benefit most from a project manager who can complete some of the technical work. On larger projects, however, the project manager's primary responsibility is to lead the team and communicate with key project stakeholders. He or she would not have time to do any of the technical work. In this case, it is usually best that the project manager understand the business and application area of the project more than the technology involved.

However, it is very important on large projects for the project manager to understand the business and application area of his or her project. For example, Northwest Airlines completed a series of projects in the last several years to develop and upgrade its reservation systems. The company spent millions of dollars and had more than 70 full-time people working on the projects at peak periods. The project manager, Peeter Kivestu, had never worked in an information technology department, but he had extensive knowledge of the airline industry and the reservations process. He carefully picked his team leaders, making sure they had the required technical and product knowledge. ResNet was the first large information technology project at Northwest Airlines led by a business manager instead of a technical expert, and it was a roaring success. Many organizations have found that large information technology projects require experienced general managers who understand the business and application area of the technology, not the technology itself. (You can find the entire ResNet case study on the companion Web site for this text.)

Project Execution Tools and Techniques

Directing and managing project execution requires specialized tools and techniques, some of which are unique to project management. Project managers can use specific tools and techniques to perform activities that are part of execution processes. These include:

- *Expert judgment*: Anyone who has worked on a large, complex project appreciates the importance of expert judgment in making good decisions. Project managers should not hesitate to consult experts on different topics, such as what methodology to follow, what programming language to use, what training approach to follow, and so on.
- *Project management information systems*: As described in Chapter 1, there are hundreds of project management software products on the market today. Many large organizations use powerful enterprise project management systems that are accessible via the Internet and tie into other systems, such as financial systems. Even in smaller organizations, project managers or other team members can create Gantt charts that include links to other planning documents on an internal network. For example, Nick or his assistant could have created a detailed Gantt chart for their project in Project 2007 and created a link to other key planning documents created in Word, Excel, or PowerPoint. Nick could have shown the summary tasks during the progress review meetings, and if top management had questions, Nick could have shown them supporting details. Nick's team could also have set baselines for completing the project and tracked their progress toward achieving those goals. See Appendix A for details on using Project 2007 to perform these functions.

Although project management information systems can aid in project execution, project managers must remember that positive leadership and strong teamwork are critical to successful project management. Project managers should delegate the detailed work involved in using these tools to other team members and focus on providing leadership for the whole project to ensure project success. Stakeholders often focus on what to them is the most important output of execution: the deliverables. For example, a production version of the DNA-sequencing instrument was the main deliverable for the project in the opening case. Of course there were many other deliverables created along the way, such as software modules, tests, reports, and so on. Other outputs of project execution include work performance information, change requests, and updates to the project management plan and project documents.

WHAT WENT RIGHT?

Malaysia's capital, Kuala Lumpur, has become one of Asia's busiest, most exciting cities. With growth, however, came traffic. To help alleviate this problem, the city hired a local firm in mid-2003 to manage a MYR $400 million (U.S. $105 million) project to develop a state-of-the-art Integrated Transport Information System (ITIS). The Deputy Project Director, Lawrence Liew, explained that they broke the project into four key phases and focused on several key milestones. They deliberately kept the work loosely structured to allow the team to be more flexible and creative in handling uncertainties. They based the entire project team within a single project office to streamline communications and facilitate quick problem solving through ad hoc working groups. They also used a dedicated project intranet to exchange information between the project team and sub-contractors. The project was completed in 2005, and ITIS continues to improve traffic flow into Kuala Lumpur.[9]

Project managers and their teams are most often remembered for how well they executed a project and handled difficult situations. Likewise, sports teams around the world know that, the key to winning is good execution. Team coaches can be viewed as project managers, with each game a separate project. Coaches are often judged primarily based on their win-loss record, not on how well they planned for each game. On a humorous note, when one *losing* coach was asked what he thought about his team's execution, he responded, "I'm all for it!"

MONITORING AND CONTROLLING PROJECT WORK

On large projects, many project managers say that 90 percent of the job is communicating and managing changes. Changes are inevitable on most projects, so it's important to develop and follow a process to monitor and control changes.

Monitoring project work includes collecting, measuring, and disseminating performance information. It also involves assessing measurements and analyzing trends to determine what process improvements can be made. The project team should continuously monitor project performance to assess the overall health of the project and identify areas that require special attention.

The project management plan, performance reports, enterprise environmental factors, and organizational process assets are all important inputs for monitoring and controlling project work.

The project management plan provides the baseline for identifying and controlling project changes. A **baseline** is the approved project management plan plus approved changes. For example, the project management plan includes a section describing the work to perform on a project. This section of the plan describes the key deliverables for the project, the products of the project, and quality requirements. The schedule section of the project management plan lists the planned dates for completing key deliverables, and the budget section of the project management plan provides the planned cost for these deliverables. The project team must focus on delivering the work as planned. If the project team or someone else causes changes during project execution, they must revise the project management plan and have it approved by the project sponsor. Many people refer to different types of baselines, such as a cost baseline or schedule baseline, to describe different project goals more clearly and performance toward meeting them.

Performance reports use this data to provide information on how project execution is going. The main purpose of these reports is to alert the project manager and project team of issues that are causing problems or might cause problems in the future. The project manager and project team must continuously monitor and control project work to decide if corrective or preventive actions are needed, what the best course of action is, and when to act.

MEDIA SNAPSHOT

Few events get more media attention than the Olympic Games. Imagine all the work involved in planning and executing an event that involves thousands of athletes from around the world with millions of spectators. The 2002 Olympic Winter Games and Paralympics took five years to plan and cost more than $1.9 billion. PMI awarded the Salt Lake Organizing Committee (SLOC) the Project of the Year award for delivering world-class games that, according to the International Olympic Committee, "made a profound impact upon the people of the world."[10]

Four years before the Games began, the SLOC used a Primavera software-based system with a cascading color-coded WBS to integrate planning. A year before the Games, they added a Venue Integrated Planning Schedule to help the team integrate resource needs, budgets, and plans. For example, this software helped the team coordinate different areas involved in controlling access into and around a venue, such as roads, pedestrian pathways, seating and safety provisions, and hospitality areas, saving nearly $10 million.

When the team experienced a budget deficit three years before the games, they separated "must-have" from "nice-to-have" items and implemented a rigorous expense approval process. According to Matthew Lehman, SLOC managing director, using classic project management tools turned a $400 million deficit into a $100 million surplus.

The SLOC also used an Executive Roadmap, a one-page list of the top 100 Games-wide activities, to keep executives apprised of progress. Activities were tied to detailed project information within each department's schedule. A 90-day highlighter showed which managers were accountable for each integrated activity. Fraser Bullock, SLOC Chief Operating Officer and Chief, said, "We knew when we were on and off schedule and where we had to apply additional resources. The interrelation of the functions meant they could not run in isolation—it was a smoothly running machine."[11]

An important output of monitoring and controlling project work is a change request, which includes recommended corrective and preventive actions and defect repairs. Corrective actions should result in improvements in project performance. Preventive actions reduce the probability of negative consequences associated with project risks. Defect repairs involve bringing defective deliverables into conformance with requirements. For example, if project team members have not been reporting hours that they worked, a corrective action would be to show them how to enter the information and let them know that they need to do it. A preventive action might be modifying a time-tracking system screen to avoid common errors people made in the past. A defect repair might be having someone redo an entry that was incorrect. Many organizations use a formal change request process and forms to keep track of project changes, as described in the next section.

PERFORMING INTEGRATED CHANGE CONTROL

Integrated change control involves identifying, evaluating, and managing changes throughout the project life cycle. The three main objectives of integrated change control are:

- *Influencing the factors that create changes to ensure that changes are beneficial*: To ensure that changes are beneficial and that a project is successful, project managers and their teams must make trade-offs among key project dimensions, such as scope, time, cost, and quality.
- *Determining that a change has occurred*: To determine that a change has occurred, the project manager must know the status of key project areas at all times. In addition, the project manager must communicate significant changes to top management and key stakeholders. Top management and other key stakeholders do not like surprises, especially ones that mean the project might produce less, take longer to complete, cost more than planned, or be of lower quality than desired.
- *Managing actual changes as they occur*: Managing change is a key role of project managers and their teams. It is important that project managers exercise discipline in managing the project to help minimize the number of changes that occur.

Important inputs to the integrated change control process include the project management plan, work performance information, change requests, enterprise environmental factors, and organizational process assets. Important outputs include updates to change request status, the project management plan, and project documents.

Change requests are common on projects and occur in many different forms. They can be oral or written, formal or informal. For example, a project team member responsible for installing a server needed to support the project might ask the project manager at a progress review meeting if it is all right to order a server with a faster processor than planned, from the same manufacturer for the same approximate cost. Since this change is positive and should have no negative effects on the project, the project manager might give a verbal approval at the progress review meeting. Nevertheless, it is still important that the project manager document this change to avoid any potential problems. The appropriate team member should update the section of the scope statement with the new specifications for the server. Still, keep in mind that many change requests can have a major impact on a project. For example, customers changing their minds about the number of pieces of hardware they want as part of a project will have a definite impact on the scope and cost of the project. Such a change might also affect the project's schedule. The project team must present such significant changes in written form, and there should be a formal review process for analyzing and deciding whether to approve these changes.

Change is unavoidable and often expected on most information technology projects. Technologies change, personnel change, organizational priorities change, and so on. Careful change control on information technology projects is a critical success factor. A good change control system is also important for project success.

Change Control on Information Technology Projects

From the 1950s to the 1980s, a widely held view of information technology (then often referred to as data automation or data processing) project management was that the project team should strive to do exactly what they planned on time and within budget. The problem with this view was that project teams could rarely meet original project goals, especially on projects involving new technologies. Stakeholders rarely agreed up front on what the scope of the project really was or what the finished product should really look like. Time and cost estimates created early in a project were rarely accurate.

Beginning in the 1990s, most project managers and top management realized that project management is a process of constant communication and negotiation about project objectives and stakeholder expectations. This view assumes that changes happen throughout the project life cycle and recognizes that changes are often beneficial to some projects. For example, if a project team member discovers a new hardware or software technology that could satisfy the customers' needs for less time and money, the project team and key stakeholders should be open to making major changes in the project.

All projects will have some changes, and managing them is a key issue in project management, especially for information technology projects. Many information technology projects involve the use of hardware and software that is updated frequently. For example, the initial plan for the specifications of the server described earlier may have been cutting-edge technology at that time. If the actual ordering of the server occurred six months later, it is quite possible that a more powerful server could be ordered at the same cost. This example illustrates a positive change. On the other hand, the manufacturer of the server specified in the project plan could go out of business, which would result in a negative change. Information technology project managers should be accustomed to changes such as these and build some flexibility into their project plans and execution. Customers for information technology projects should also be open to meeting project objectives in different ways.

Even if project managers, project teams, and customers are flexible, it is important that projects have a formal change control system. This formal change control system is necessary to plan for managing change.

Change Control System

A **change control system** is a formal, documented process that describes when and how official project documents may be changed. It also describes the people authorized to make changes, the paperwork required for this change, and any automated or manual tracking systems the project will use. A change control system often includes a change control board, configuration management, and a process for communicating changes.

A **change control board (CCB)** is a formal group of people responsible for approving or rejecting changes to a project. The primary functions of a change control board are to provide guidelines for preparing change requests, evaluating change requests, and managing the implementation of approved changes. An organization could have key stakeholders for the entire organization on this board, and a few members could rotate based on the unique needs of each project. By creating a formal board and process for managing changes, better overall change control should result.

However, CCBs can have some drawbacks. One drawback is the time it takes to make decisions on proposed changes. CCBs often meet only once a week or once a month and may not make decisions in one meeting. Some organizations have streamlined processes for making quick decisions on smaller project changes. One company created a "48-hour policy," in which task leaders on a large information technology project would reach agreements on key decisions or changes within their expertise and authority. The person in the area most affected by this decision or change then had 48 hours to go to his or her top management to seek approval. If for some reason the project team's decision could not be implemented, the top manager consulted would have 48 hours to reverse a decision; otherwise, the project team's decision was approved. This type of process is a great way to deal with the many time-sensitive decisions or changes that project teams must make on many information technology projects.

Configuration management is another important part of integrated change control. **Configuration management** ensures that the descriptions of the project's products are correct and complete. It involves identifying and controlling the functional and physical design characteristics of products and their support documentation. Members of the project team, frequently called configuration management specialists, are often assigned to perform configuration management for large projects. Their job is to identify and document the functional and physical characteristics of the project's products, control any changes to such characteristics, record and report the changes, and audit the products to verify conformance to requirements. Visit the Institute of Configuration Management's Web site (*www.icmhq.com*) for more information on this topic.

Another critical factor in change control is communication. Project managers should use written and oral performance reports to help identify and manage project changes. For example, on software development projects, most programmers must make their edits to one master file in a database that requires the programmers to "check out" the file to edit it. If two programmers check out the same file, they must coordinate their work before they can check the file back in to the database. In addition to written or formal communication methods, oral and informal communications are also important. Some project managers have stand-up meetings once a week or even every morning, depending on the nature of the project. The goal of a stand-up meeting is to communicate what is most important on the project quickly. For example, the project manager might have an early morning stand-up meeting every day with all of his or her team leaders. There might be a weekly stand-up meeting every Monday morning with all interested stakeholders. Requiring participants to stand keeps meetings short and forces everyone to focus on the most important project events.

Why is good communication so critical to success? One of the most frustrating aspects of project change is not having everyone coordinated and informed about the latest project information. Again, it is the project manager's responsibility to integrate all project changes so that the project stays on track. The project manager and his or her staff must develop a system for notifying everyone affected by a change in a timely manner. E-mail, real-time databases, cell phones, and the Web make it easier to disseminate the most current project information. You will learn more about good communication in Chapter 10, Project Communications Management.

Table 4-3 lists suggestions for performing integrated change control. As described earlier, project management is a process of constant communication and negotiation. Project managers should plan for changes and use appropriate tools and techniques such as a change control board, configuration management, and good communication. It is helpful to define procedures for making timely decisions on small changes, use written and oral performance reports to help identify and manage changes, and use software to assist in planning, updating, and controlling projects.

TABLE 4-3 Suggestions for performing integrated change control

View project management as a process of constant communication and negotiation
Plan for change
Establish a formal change control system, including a change control board (CCB)
Use effective configuration management
Define procedures for making timely decisions on smaller changes
Use written and oral performance reports to help identify and manage change
Use project management and other software to help manage and communicate changes
Focus on leading the project team and meeting overall project goals and expectations

Project managers must also provide strong leadership to steer the project to successful completion. They must not get too involved in managing project changes. Project managers should delegate much of the detailed work to project team members and focus on providing overall leadership for the project in general. Remember, project managers must focus on the big picture and perform project integration management well to lead their team and organization to success.

CLOSING PROJECTS OR PHASES

The last process in project integration management is closing the project or phase. In order to close a project or phase, you must finalize all activities and transfer the completed or cancelled work to the appropriate people. The main inputs to this process are the project management plan, accepted deliverables, and organizational process assets. The main tool and technique is again expert judgment. The outputs of closing projects are:

- *Final product, service, or result transition*: Project sponsors are usually most interested in making sure they receive delivery of the final products, services, or results they expected when they authorized the project. For items produced under contract, formal acceptance or handover includes a written statement that the terms of the contract were met. Internal projects can also include some type of project completion form.

- *Organizational process asset updates*: The project team should provide a list of project documentation, project closure documents, and historical information produced by the project in a useful format. This information is considered a process asset. Project teams normally produce a final project report, which often includes a transition plan describing work to be done as part of operations after the project is completed. They also often write a lessons-learned report at the end of a project, and this information can be a tremendous asset for future projects. (See Chapter 10, Project Communications Management for more information on creating project final reports, lessons-learned reports, and other project communications.) Several organizations also conduct a post-implementation review to analyze whether or not the project achieved what it set out to do. Information from this type of review also becomes an organizational process asset for future projects.

USING SOFTWARE TO ASSIST IN PROJECT INTEGRATION MANAGEMENT

As described throughout this chapter, project teams can use various types of software to assist in project integration management. Project teams can create documents with word processing software, give presentations with presentation software, track information with spreadsheets, databases, or customized software, and transmit information using various types of communication software.

Project management software is also an important tool for developing and integrating project planning documents, executing the project management plan and related project plans, monitoring and controlling project activities, and performing integrated change control. Small project teams can use low-end or midrange project management software products to coordinate their work. For large projects, however, such as managing the Olympic Games described in the Media Snapshot, organizations may benefit most from high-end tools that provide enterprise project management capabilities and integrate all aspects of project management. All projects can benefit from using some type of project management information system to coordinate and communicate project information.

Another category of software that can help align projects with business strategy, as described in this chapter, is called **business service management (BSM) tools**. "BSM tools track the execution of business process flows and expose how the state of supporting IT systems and resources is impacting end-to-end business process performance in real time. Consider, for example, the difference between IT working to increase network capacity and having IT able to demonstrate that because of their efforts, they increased the ability to process new customer orders by 15 percent."[12] BSM tools can help improve alignment between information technology projects, such as upgrading network capacity, and business goals, such as reducing costs by processing customer orders more quickly. In addition, BSM tools can help validate the projects' contributions to the success of the business. However, recent studies suggest that successfully implementing

BSM tools, like many other new tools, is far from easy. "Like those work-from-home, get-rich-quick schemes, you will hear from vendors claiming fast and easy business services management. Smaller upstart vendors will often oversimplify problems and oversell their products' capabilities, while most larger vendors still have work to do integrating disparate product portfolios. Both tend to understate the effort and cost to deploy and configure."[13]

As you can see, there is a lot of work involved in project integration management. Project managers and their teams must focus on pulling all the elements of a project together to successfully complete projects.

CASE WRAP-UP

Without consulting Nick Carson or his team, Nick's CEO hired a new person, Jim, to act as a middle manager between himself and the people in Nick's department. The CEO and other top managers really liked Jim, the new middle manager. He met with them often, shared ideas, and had a great sense of humor. He started developing standards the company could use to help manage projects in the future. For example, he developed templates for creating plans and progress reports and put them on the company's intranet. However, Jim and Nick did not get along. Jim accidentally sent an e-mail to Nick that was supposed to go to the CEO. In this e-mail, Jim said that Nick was hard to work with and preoccupied with the birth of his son.

Nick was furious when he read the e-mail and stormed into the CEO's office. The CEO suggested that Nick move to another department, but Nick did not like that option. Without considering the repercussions, the CEO offered Nick a severance package to leave the company. Because of the planned corporate buyout, the CEO knew they might have to let some people go anyway. Nick talked the CEO into giving him a two-month sabbatical he had not yet taken plus a higher percentage on his stock options. After discussing the situation with his wife and realizing that he would get over $70,000 if he resigned, Nick took the severance package. He had such a bad experience as a project manager that he decided to stick with being a technical expert. Jim, however, thrived in his position and helped the company improve their project management practices and ensure success in a highly competitive market.

Chapter Summary

Project integration management is usually the most important project management knowledge area, since it ties together all the other areas of project management. A project manager's primary focus should be on project integration management.

Before selecting projects to pursue, it is important for organizations to follow a strategic planning process. Many organizations perform a SWOT analysis to help identify potential projects based on their strengths, weaknesses, opportunities, and threats. Information technology projects should support the organization's overall business strategy. Common techniques for selecting projects include focusing on broad organizational needs, categorizing projects, performing financial analyses, developing weighted scoring models, and using balanced scorecards.

Project integration management includes the following processes:

- Developing the project charter involves working with stakeholders to create the document that formally authorizes a project. Project charters can have different formats, but they should include basic project information and signatures of key stakeholders.
- Developing the project management plan involves coordinating all planning efforts to create a consistent, coherent document—the project management plan. The main purpose of project plans is to facilitate action.
- Directing and managing project execution involves carrying out the project plans by performing the activities included in it. Project plan execution should require the majority of a project's budget.
- Monitoring and controlling project work is needed to meet the performance objectives of the project. The project team should continuously monitor project performance to assess the overall health of the project.
- Performing integrated change control involves identifying, evaluating, and managing changes throughout the project life cycle. A change control system often includes a change control board (CCB), configuration management, and a process for communicating changes.
- Closing the project or phase involves finalizing all project activities. It is important to follow good procedures to ensure that all project activities are completed and that the project sponsor accepts delivery of the final products, services, or results of the project.

There are several types of software products available to assist in project integration management. There are also several tools to assist in project selection and to ensure that projects align with business strategy.

Quick Quiz

1. Which of the following processes is not part of project integration management?
   a. develop the project business case
   b. develop the project charter
   c. develop the project management plan
   d. close the project or phase
2. What is the last step in the four-stage planning process for selecting information technology projects?
   a. information technology strategy planning
   b. business area analysis
   c. mind mapping
   d. resource allocation
3. Which of the following is not a best practice for new product development projects?
   a. align projects and resources with business strategy
   b. select projects that will take less than two years to provide payback
   c. focus on customer needs in identifying projects
   d. assign project managers to lead projects
4. A new government law requires an organization to report data in a new way. Under which category would a new information system project to provide this data fall?
   a. problem
   b. opportunity
   c. directive
   d. regulation
5. If estimates for total discounted benefits for a project are $120,000 and total discounted costs are $100,000, what is the estimated return on investment (ROI)?
   a. $20,000
   b. $120,000
   c. 20 percent
   d. 120 percent
6. A ____________ is a document that formally recognizes the existence of a project and provides direction on the project's objectives and management.
   a. project charter
   b. contract
   c. business case
   d. project management plan

7. Which of the following items is not normally included in a project charter?
   a. the name of the project manager
   b. budget information
   c. stakeholder signatures
   d. a Gantt chart

8. __________ ensures that the descriptions of the project's products are correct and complete.
   a. Configuration management
   b. Integrated change control
   c. Integration management
   d. A change control board
9. Which of the following is not a suggestion for performing integrated change control?
   a. use good configuration management
   b. minimize change
   c. establish a formal change control system
   d. view project management as a process of constant communication and negotiation
10. What tool and technique is used for all of the other project integration management processes?
    a. project management software
    b. templates
    c. expert judgment
    d. all of the above

Quick Quiz Answers

1. a; 2. d; 3. b; 4. c; 5. c; 6. a; 7. d; 8. a; 9. b; 10. c

Discussion Questions

1. Describe project integration management. How does project integration management relate to the project life cycle, stakeholders, and the other project management knowledge areas?
2. Briefly describe the strategic planning process, including a SWOT analysis. Which project selection method(s) do you think organizations use most often for justifying information technology projects?
3. Summarize key work involved in each of the six processes for project integration management.
4. Either from your own experience or by searching the Internet, describe a well-planned and executed project. Describe a disastrous project. What were some of the main differences between these projects?
5. Discuss the importance of following a well-integrated change control process on information technology projects. What do you think of the suggestions made in this chapter? Think of three additional suggestions for integrated change control on information technology projects.

Exercises

1. Write a two-page paper based on the opening case. Answer the following questions:
   a. What do you think the real problem was in this case?
   b. Does the case present a realistic scenario? Why or why not?
   c. Was Nick Carson a good project manager? Why or why not?
   d. What should top management have done to help Nick?
   e. What could Nick have done to be a better project manager?
2. Download a free trial of mind mapping software and create a mind map of a SWOT analysis for your organization or your personal life. Include at least two strengths, weaknesses, opportunities, and threats and ideas for at least three potential projects.
3. Use spreadsheet software to create Figure 4-4 through Figure 4-7 in this text. Make sure your formulas work correctly.
4. Perform a financial analysis for a project using the format provided in Figure 4-5. Assume the projected costs and benefits for this project are spread over four years as follows: Estimated costs are $200,000 in Year 1 and $30,000 each year in Years 2, 3, and 4. Estimated benefits are $0 in Year 1 and $100,000 each year in Years 2, 3, and 4. Use a 9 percent discount rate, and round the discount factors to two decimal places. Create a spreadsheet (or use the business case financials template provided on the companion Web site) to calculate and clearly display the NPV, ROI, and year in which payback occurs. In addition, write a paragraph explaining whether you would recommend investing in this project, based on your financial analysis.
5. Create a weighted scoring model to determine grades for a course. Final grades are based on three exams worth 20 percent, 15 percent, and 25 percent, respectively; homework is worth 15 percent; and a group project is worth 25 percent. Enter scores for three students. Assume Student 1 earns 100 percent (or 100) on every item. Assume Student 2 earns 70 percent on each of the exams, 80 percent on the homework, and 95 percent on the group project. Assume Student 3 earns 90 percent on Exam 1, 80 percent on Exam 2, 75 percent on Exam 3, 80 percent on the homework, and 70 percent on the group project. You can use the weighted scoring model template, create your own spreadsheet, or make the matrix by hand.
6. Develop an outline (major headings and subheadings only) for a project management plan to create a Web site for your class, and then fill in the details for the introduction or overview section. Assume that this Web site would include a home page with links to a syllabus for the class, lecture notes or other instructional information, links to the Web site for this textbook, links to other Web sites with project management information, and links to personal pages for each member of your class and future classes. Also, include a bulletin board and chat room feature where students and the instructor can exchange information. Assume your instructor is the project's sponsor, you are the project manager, your classmates are your project team, and you have three months to complete the project.
7. Research software mentioned in this chapter, such as software for assisting in project selection, enterprise project management software, BSM tools, etc. Find at least two references and summarize your findings in a two-page paper.

8. Read and critique two of the Suggested Readings provided on the companion Web site for this book, or find similar articles related to topics discussed in this chapter. Write a two-page paper summarizing your ideas.

Running Case

Note: Additional running cases are provided in Appendix C and on the companion Web site. Template files are also available on the companion Web site.

Manage Your Health, Inc. (MYH) is a Fortune 500 company that provides a variety of health care services across the globe. MYH has more than 20,000 full-time employees and more than 5,000 part-time employees. MYH recently updated its strategic plan, and key goals include reducing internal costs, increasing cross-selling of products, and exploiting new Web-based technologies to help employees, customers, and suppliers work together to improve the development and delivery of its health care products and services. Below are some ideas the Information Technology department has developed for supporting these strategic goals:

1. *Recreation and Wellness Intranet Project*: Provide an application on the current intranet to help employees improve their health. A recent study found that MYH, Inc. pays 20 percent more than the industry average for employee health care premiums, primarily due to the poor health of its employees. You believe that this application will help improve employee health within one year of its rollout so that you can negotiate lower health insurance premiums, providing net savings of at least $30/employee/year for full-time employees over the next four years. This application would include the following capabilities:
    - Allow employees to register for company-sponsored recreational programs, such as soccer, softball, bowling, jogging, walking, and other sports
    - Allow employees to register for company-sponsored classes and programs to help them manage their weight, reduce stress, stop smoking, and manage other health-related issues.
    - Track data on employee involvement in these recreational and health-management programs
    - Offer incentives for people to join the programs and do well in them (e.g., incentives for achieving weight goals, winning sports team competitions, etc.).
2. *Health Coverage Costs Business Model*: Develop an application to track employee health care expenses and company health care costs. Health care premiums continue to increase, and the company has changed insurance carriers several times in the past ten years. This application should allow business modeling of various scenarios as well as tracking and analyzing current and past employee health care expenses and company health care costs. This application must be secure and run on the current intranet so several managers and analysts could access it and download selective data for further analysis. The new application must also import data from the current systems that track employee expenses submitted to the company and the company's costs to the insurance provider. You believe that having this data will help you revise policies concerning employee contributions to health care premiums and help you negotiate for lower premiums with insurance companies. You estimate that this application would save your company about $20/employee/year for full-time employees over the next four years and cost about $100,000 to develop

3. *Cross-Selling System*: Develop an application to improve cross-selling to current customers. The current sales management system has separate sections for major product/service categories and different sales reps based on those products and services. You see great opportunities to increase sales to current customers by providing them discounts when they purchase multiple products/services. You estimate that this system would increase profits by $1 million each year for the next three years and cost about $800,000 each year for development and maintenance.
4. *Web-Enhanced Communications System*: Develop a Web-based application to improve development and delivery of products and services. There are currently several incompatible systems related to the development and delivery of products and services to customers. This application would allow customers and suppliers to provide suggestions, enter orders, view the status and history of orders, and use electronic commerce capabilities to purchase and sell their products. You estimate that this system would save your company about $2 million each year for three years after implementation. You estimate it will take one year and $3 million to develop and require 20 percent of development costs each year to maintain.

Tasks

1. Summarize each of the above-proposed projects in a simple table format suitable for presentation to top management. Include the name for each project, identify how each one supports business strategies, assess the potential financial benefits and other benefits of each project, and provide your initial assessment of the value of each project. Write your results in a one- to two-page memo to top management, including appropriate back-up information and calculations.
2. Prepare a weighted scoring model using the template provided on the companion Web site for this text to evaluate these four projects. Develop at least four criteria, assign weights to each criterion, assign scores, and then calculate the weighted scores. Print the spreadsheet and bar chart with the results. Also write a one-page paper describing this weighted scoring model and what the results show.
3. Prepare a business case for the Recreation and Wellness Intranet Project. Assume the project will take six months to complete and cost about $200,000. Use the business case template provided on the companion Web site for this text.
4. Prepare a project charter for the Recreation and Wellness Intranet Project. Assume the project will take six months to complete and cost about $200,000. Use the project charter template provided in this text and the sample project charter provided in Table 4-1 as a guide.
5. Prepare a change request for this project, using the template provided on the companion Web site for this text. Be creative in making up information.

Companion Web Site

Visit the companion Web site for this text at *www.cengage.com/mis/schwalbe* to access:

- References cited in the text and additional suggested readings for each chapter
- Template files
- Lecture notes
- Interactive quizzes
- Podcasts
- Links to general project management Web sites
- And more

See the Preface of this text for more information on accessing the companion Web site.

Key Terms

balanced scorecard — a methodology that converts an organization's value drivers to a series of defined metrics

baseline — the approved project management plan plus approved changes

business service management (BSM) tools — tools that help track the execution of business process flows and expose how the state of supporting IT systems and resources is impacting end-to-end business process performance in real time

capitalization rate — the rate used in discounting future cash flow; also called the discount rate or opportunity cost of capital

cash flow — benefits minus costs or income minus expenses

change control board (CCB) — a formal group of people responsible for approving or rejecting changes on a project

change control system — a formal, documented process that describes when and how official project documents may be changed

configuration management — a process that ensures that the descriptions of the project's products are correct and complete

cost of capital — the return available by investing the capital elsewhere

directives — new requirements imposed by management, government, or some external influence

discount factor — a multiplier for each year based on the discount rate and year

discount rate — the rate used in discounting future cash flow; also called the capitalization rate or opportunity cost of capital

integrated change control — identifying, evaluating, and managing changes throughout the project life cycle

interface management — identifying and managing the points of interaction between various elements of a project

internal rate of return (IRR) — the discount rate that results in an NPV of zero for a project

mind mapping — a technique that uses branches radiating out from a core idea to structure thoughts and ideas

net present value (NPV) analysis — a method of calculating the expected net monetary gain or loss from a project by discounting all expected future cash inflows and outflows to the present point in time

opportunities — chances to improve the organization

opportunity cost of capital — the rate used in discounting future cash flow; also called the capitalization rate or discount rate

organizational process assets — formal and informal plans, policies, procedures, guidelines, information systems, financial systems, management systems, lessons learned, and historical information that can be used to influence a project's success

payback period — the amount of time it will take to recoup, in the form of net cash inflows, the total dollars invested in a project

problems — undesirable situations that prevent the organization from achieving its goals

project charter — a document that formally recognizes the existence of a project and provides direction on the project's objectives and management

project integration management — processes that coordinate all project management knowledge areas throughout a project's life, including developing the project charter, developing the preliminary project scope statement, developing the project management plan, directing and managing the project, monitoring and controlling the project, providing integrated change control, and closing the project

project management plan — a document used to coordinate all project planning documents and guide project execution and control

required rate of return — the minimum acceptable rate of return on an investment

return on investment (ROI) — (benefits minus costs) divided by costs

strategic planning — determining long-term objectives by analyzing the strengths and weaknesses of an organization, studying opportunities and threats in the business environment, predicting future trends, and projecting the need for new products and services

SWOT analysis — analyzing **S**trengths, **W**eaknesses, **O**pportunities, and **T**hreats; used to aid in strategic planning

weighted scoring model — a technique that provides a systematic process for basing project selection on numerous criteria

End Notes

[1] Carol Matlack, "First, Blame the Software," *BusinessWeek* Online (October 5, 2006).

[2] James Bacon, "The Use of Decision Criteria in Selecting Information Systems/Technology Investments," *MIS Quarterly*, Vol. 16, No. 3 (September 1992).

[3] Robert G. Cooper, "Winning at New Products: Pathways to Profitable Intervention," PMI Research Conference Proceedings (July 2006).

[4] Dennis J. Cohen and Robert J. Graham, *The Project Manager's MBA*, San Francisco, Jossey-Bass (2001), p. 31.

[5] CIO View Corp., "White Papers: Business Benefits of Utilizing ROI Analysis," *Information Week* (2007).

[6] Jake Widman, "Big IT to small biz: Listen up, little dudes!" *ComputerWorld* (January 24, 2008).

[7] Eric Berkman, "How to Use the Balanced Scorecard," *CIO Magazine* (May 15, 2002).

[8] Fragan Milosevic and A. Ozbay. "Delivering Projects: What the Winners Do." Proceedings of the Project Management Institute Annual Seminars & Symposium (November 2001).

[9] Sarah Parkes, "Crosstown Traffic," *PM Network* (August 2004).

[10] Ross Foti, "The Best Winter Olympics, Period," *PM Network* (January 2004) p. 23.

[11] Ibid, 23.

[12] Mary Johnson Turner, Beyond ITIL: Process-Aware BSM Connects IT to Business Priorities, Summit Strategies, (July 2005).

[13] Michael Biddick, "Uncertain Future," *Information Week Research & Reports* (May 12, 2008), p. 47.

CHAPTER 5

PROJECT SCOPE MANAGEMENT

LEARNING OBJECTIVES

After reading this chapter, you will be able to:

- Understand the importance of good project scope management
- Discuss methods for collecting and documenting requirements in order to meet stakeholder needs and expectations
- Explain the scope definition process and describe the contents of a project scope statement
- Discuss the process for creating a work breakdown structure using the analogy, top-down, bottom-up, and mind-mapping approaches
- Explain the importance of verifying scope and how it relates to defining and controlling scope
- Understand the importance of controlling scope and approaches for preventing scope-related problems on information technology projects
- Describe how software can assist in project scope management

OPENING CASE

Kim Nguyen was leading a meeting to create the work breakdown structure (WBS) for the IT Upgrade Project. This project was necessary because of several high-priority, Internet-based applications the company was developing. The IT Upgrade Project involved creating and implementing a plan to get all employees' information technology assets to meet new corporate standards within nine months. These standards specified the minimum equipment required for each desktop or laptop computer, including the type of processor, amount of memory, hard disk size, type of network connection, and software. Kim knew that to perform the upgrades, they would first have to create a detailed inventory of all of the current hardware, networks, and software in the entire company of 2000 employees.

Kim had worked with other stakeholders to develop a project charter and initial scope statement. The project charter included rough cost and schedule estimates for the project and signatures of key stakeholders; the initial scope statement provided a start in defining the hardware, software, and network requirements as well as other information related to the project scope. Kim called a meeting with her project team and other stakeholders to further define the scope of the project. She wanted to get everyone's ideas on what the project involved, who would do what, and how they could avoid scope creep. The company's new CEO, Walter Schmidt, was known for keeping a close eye on major projects like this one. The company had started using a new project management information system that let everyone know the status of projects at a detailed and high level. Kim knew that a good WBS was the foundation for scope, time, and cost performance, but she had never led a team in creating one or allocating costs based on a WBS. Where should she begin?

WHAT IS PROJECT SCOPE MANAGEMENT?

Recall from Chapter 1 that several factors are associated with project success. Many of these factors, such as user involvement, clear business objectives, a minimized or clearly defined scope, and firm basic requirements, are elements of project scope management.

One of the most important and most difficult aspects of project management is defining the scope of a project. **Scope** refers to *all* the work involved in creating the products of the project and the processes used to create them. Recall from Chapter 2 that the term **deliverable** describes a product produced as part of a project. Deliverables can be product-related, such as a piece of hardware or software, or process-related, such as a planning document or meeting minutes. Project stakeholders must agree on what the products of the project are and, to some extent, how they should produce them to define all of the deliverables.

Project scope management includes the processes involved in defining and controlling what work is or is not included in a project. It ensures that the project team and stakeholders have the same understanding of what products the project will produce and what processes the project team will use to produce them. There are five main processes involved in project scope management:

1. *Collecting requirements* involves defining and documenting the features and functions of the products produced during the project as well as the processes used for creating them. The project team creates stakeholder requirements

documentation, a requirements management plan, and a requirements traceability matrix as outputs of the requirements collection process.

2. *Defining scope* involves reviewing the project charter, requirements documents, and organizational process assets to create a scope statement, adding more information as requirements are developed and change requests are approved. The main outputs of scope definition are the project scope statement and updates to project documents.
3. *Creating the WBS* involves subdividing the major project deliverables into smaller, more manageable components. The main outputs include a work breakdown structure, a WBS dictionary, a scope baseline, and updates to project documents.
4. *Verifying scope* involves formalizing acceptance of the project deliverables. Key project stakeholders, such as the customer and sponsor for the project, inspect and then formally accept the deliverables during this process. If the deliverables are not acceptable, the customer or sponsor usually requests changes. The main outputs of this process, therefore, are accepted deliverables and change requests.
5. *Controlling scope* involves controlling changes to project scope throughout the life of the project—a challenge on many information technology projects. Scope changes often influence the team's ability to meet project time and cost goals, so project managers must carefully weigh the costs and benefits of scope changes. The main outputs of this process are change requests, work performance measurements, and updates to organizational process assets, the project management plan, and project documents.

Figure 5 1 summarizes these processes and outputs and shows when they occur in a typical project.

COLLECTING REQUIREMENTS

The first step in project scope management is often the most difficult: collecting requirements. A major consequence of not defining requirements well is rework, which can consume up to half of project costs, especially for software development projects. As illustrated in Figure 5-2, it costs much more to correct a software defect that is found in later development phases than to fix it in the requirements phase.

Part of the difficulty is that people often don't have a consistent definition of what requirements are, how to collect them, and how to document them.

What Are Requirements?

The 1990 IEEE Standard Glossary of Software Engineering Terminology defines a requirement as follows:

> "1. A condition or capability needed by a user to solve a problem or achieve an objective.
> 2. A condition or capability that must be met or possessed by a system or system component to satisfy a contract, standard, specification, or other formally imposed document.
> 3. A documented representation of a condition or capability as in 1 or 2."[1]

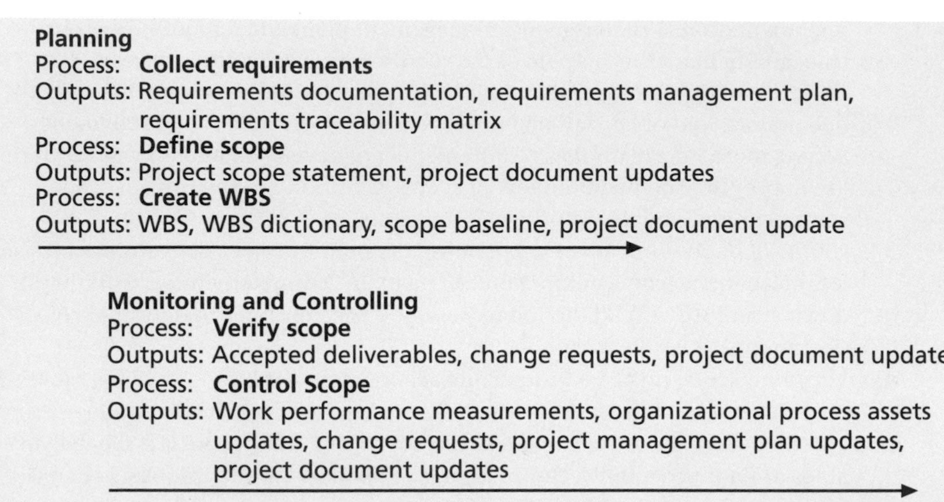

Planning
Process: Collect requirements
Outputs: Requirements documentation, requirements management plan, requirements traceability matrix
Process: Define scope
Outputs: Project scope statement, project document updates
Process: Create WBS
Outputs: WBS, WBS dictionary, scope baseline, project document update
Monitoring and Controlling
Process: Verify scope
Outputs: Accepted deliverables, change requests, project document updates
Process: Control Scope
Outputs: Work performance measurements, organizational process assets updates, change requests, project management plan updates, project document updates
Project Start
Project Finish

FIGURE 5-1 Project scope management summary

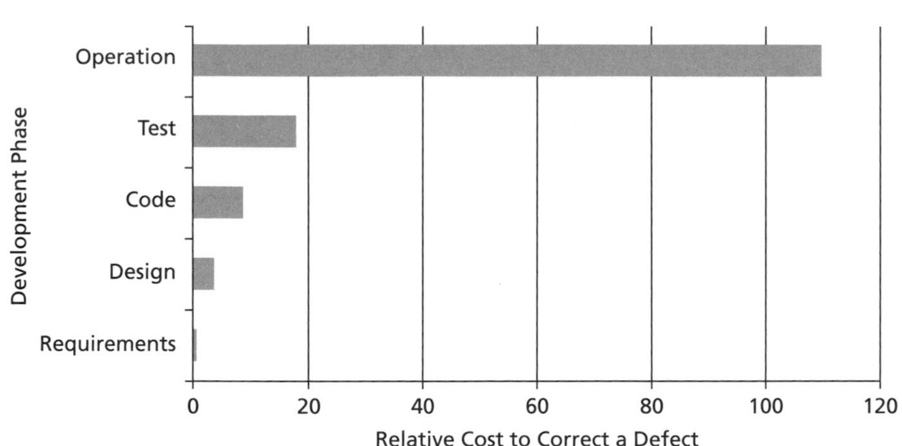

Source: Robert B. Grady, "An Economic Release Decision Model: Insights into Software Project Management." *Proceedings of the Applications of Software Measurement Conference* (Orange Park, FL: Software Quality Engineering, 1999), pp.227–239.

FIGURE 5-2 Relative cost to correct a software requirement defect

The *PMBOK® Guide, Fourth Edition*, defines a requirement almost identical to item 2 above: It says that a **requirement** is "a condition or capability that must be met or possessed by a system, product, service, result, or component to satisfy a contract, standard, specification, or other formal document." It is important to document requirements in enough detail so that they can be measured during project execution. After all, meeting scope goals is often based on meeting documented requirements.

For example, the opening case describes a project for upgrading IT assets to meet corporate standards. It says that these standards specify the minimum equipment required for each desktop or laptop computer, such as the type of processor, amount of memory, and hard disk size. The documented requirements for this project might include, therefore, that all computers include an Intel processor, 4GB of memory, and a 160GB hard drive.

For some IT projects, it is helpful to divide requirements development into categories called *elicitation*, *analysis*, *specification*, and *validation*. These categories include all the activities involved in gathering, evaluating, and documenting requirements for a software or software-containing product. It is also important to use an iterative approach to defining requirements since requirements are often unclear early in a project. (See the Suggested Readings on the companion Web site for further information.)

How Do You Collect Requirements?

There are several ways to collect requirements. Interviewing stakeholders one-on-one is often very effective, although it can be very expensive and time-consuming. Holding focus groups, facilitated workshops, and using group creativity and decision-making techniques to collect requirements are normally faster and less expensive than one-on-one interviews. Questionnaires and surveys can be very efficient ways to collect requirements as long as key stakeholders provide honest and thorough information. Observation can also be a good technique for collecting requirements, especially for projects that involve improving work processes and procedures. Prototyping is a commonly used technique for collecting requirements for software development projects. There are also several software tools available to assist in collecting and managing requirements, as described later in this chapter and in the following What Went Right? example.

WHAT WENT RIGHT?

With over 4,000 customers and 1,500 employees worldwide, Genesys Telecommunications Laboratories has a reputation for pioneering telephony solutions by developing software to manage customer interactions over the phone, via the Web, and with e-mail. However, as the company grows, it has to make changes to meet the challenges of maintaining its competitive edge in new product development. For example, Genesys now uses Accept software, a product planning and innovation management application and winner of the Excellence in Product Management Award from 2006–2008. Before implementing Accept, Genesys' product planning process was time-consuming and difficult to replicate from release to release. Paul Lang, Vice President of Product Management and Strategy, says that

continued

Accept provides them a single system that contains all of their planning data across multiple products for a multi-year, multi-phase program. With Accept, Lang says they can instill a consistent, repeatable, and predictable process for new product definition and development. They can define what information comprises a requirement and enforce discipline around that process. "Among other things, each requirement must show who requested that enhancement and why, and these must be linked back to the corporate strategy theme, product theme, and the release theme," Lang says.[2]

The project's size, complexity, importance, and other factors will affect how much effort is spent on collecting requirements. For example, a team working on a project to upgrade the entire corporate accounting system for a multibillion dollar company with more than 50 geographic locations should spend a fair amount of time collecting requirements. A project to upgrade the hardware and software for a small accounting firm with only five employees, on the other hand, would need a much smaller effort. In any case, it is important for a project team to decide how they will collect and manage requirements. It is crucial to gather inputs from key stakeholders and align the scope, a key aspect of the entire project, with business strategy, as described in Chapter 4.

How Do You Document Requirements?

Just as there are several ways to collect requirements, there are several ways to document them. Project teams should first review the project charter since it includes high-level requirements for the project and may refer to other documents that include requirements. They should also review the stakeholder register to ensure that all key stakeholders have a say in determining requirements. The format for documenting stakeholder requirements can range from a listing of all requirements on a single piece of paper to a room full of notebooks documenting requirements. People who have worked on complex projects, such as building a new airplane, know that the paper documenting requirements for a plane can weigh more than the plane itself! Requirements documents are often generated by software and include text, images, diagrams, videos, and other media. Requirements are also often broken down into different categories such as functional requirements, service requirements, performance requirements, quality requirements, training requirements, and so on.

In addition to preparing stakeholder requirements documentation as an output of the collecting requirements process, project teams often create a requirements management plan and a requirements traceability matrix. The **requirements management plan** describes how project requirements will be analyzed, documented, and managed. A **requirements traceability matrix (RTM)** is a table that lists requirements, various attributes of each requirement, and the status of the requirements to ensure that all requirements are addressed. Table 5-1 provides an example of an RTM entry for the IT Upgrade Project described in the opening case. There are many variations of what can be included in an RTM. For example, software requirements are often documented in an RTM that cross-references each requirement with related ones and lists specific tests to verify that they are met. Remember that the main purpose of an RTM is to maintain the linkage from the source of each requirement through its decomposition to implementation and verification.

TABLE 5-1 Sample requirements traceability matrix

Requirement No.	Name	Category	Source	Status
R32	Laptop memory	Hardware	Project charter and corporate laptop specifications	Complete. Laptops ordered meet requirement by having 4GB of memory.

DEFINING SCOPE

The next step in project scope management is to define in detail the scope or work required for the project. Good scope definition is very important to project success because it helps improve the accuracy of time, cost, and resource estimates, it defines a baseline for performance measurement and project control, and it aides in communicating clear work responsibilities. The main tools and techniques used in defining scope include expert judgment, product analysis, alternatives identification, and facilitated workshops. The main outputs of scope definition are the project scope statement and project document updates.

Key inputs for preparing the project scope statement include the project charter, requirements documentation, and organizational process assets such as policies and procedures related to scope statements as well as project files and lessons learned from previous, similar projects. Table 5-2 shows the project charter for the IT Upgrade Project described in the opening case. Notice how information from the project charter provides a basis for further defining the project scope. The charter describes the high-level scope, time, and cost goals for the project objectives and success criteria, a general approach to accomplishing the project's goals, and the main roles and responsibilities of important project stakeholders.

TABLE 5-2 Sample project charter

Project Title: Information Technology (IT) Upgrade Project

Project Start Date: March 4 **Projected Finish Date:** December 4

Key Schedule Milestones:

- Inventory update completed April 15
- Hardware and software acquired August 1
- Installation completed October 1
- Testing completed November 15

Budget Information: Budgeted $1,000,000 for hardware and software costs and $500,000 for labor costs.

Project Manager: Kim Nguyen, (310) 555–2784, knguyen@course.com

(continued)

Project Objectives: Upgrade hardware and software for all employees (approximately 2,000) within nine months based on new corporate standards. See attached sheet describing the new standards. Upgrades may affect servers, as well as associated network hardware and software.

Main Project Success Criteria: The hardware, software, and network upgrades must meet all written specifications, be thoroughly tested, and be completed in less than ten months. Employee work disruptions will be minimal.

Approach:

- Update the information technology inventory database to determine upgrade needs
- Develop detailed cost estimate for project and report to CIO
- Issue a request for quote to obtain hardware and software
- Use internal staff as much as possible for planning, analysis, and installation

ROLES AND RESPONSBILITES

Name	Role	Responsibility
Walter Schmidt	CEO	Project sponsor, monitor project
Mike Zwack	CIO	Monitor project, provide staff
Kim Nguyen	Project Manager	Plan and execute project
Jeff Johnson	Director of Information Technology Operations	Mentor Kim
Nancy Reynolds	VP, Human Resources	Provide staff, issue memo to all employees about project
Steve McCann	Director of Purchasing	Assist in purchasing hardware and software

Sign–off: (Signatures of all the above stakeholders)

Comments: (Handwritten or typed comments from above stakeholders, if applicable)

"This project must be done within ten months at the absolute latest." Mike Zwack, CIO

"We are assuming that adequate staff will be available and committed to supporting this project. Some work must be done after hours to avoid work disruptions, and overtime will be provided." Jeff Johnson and Kim Nguyen, Information Technology department.

Although contents vary, project scope statements should include, at a minimum, a product scope description, product user acceptance criteria, and detailed information on all project deliverables. It is also helpful to document other scope-related information, such as the project boundaries, constraints, and assumptions. The project scope statement should also reference supporting documents, such as product specifications that will affect what products are produced or purchased, or corporate policies, which might affect how products or services are produced. Many information technology projects also require detailed functional and design specifications for developing software, which also should be referenced in the detailed scope statement.

As time progresses, the scope of a project should become more clear and specific. For example, the project charter for the IT Upgrade Project shown in Table 5-2 includes a short statement about the servers and other computers and software that the IT Upgrade Project may affect. Table 5-3 provides an example of how the scope becomes progressively elaborated or more detailed in scope statements labeled Version 1 and Version 2.

TABLE 5-3 Further defining project scope

Project Charter:
Upgrades may affect servers . . . (listed under Project Objectives)
Project Scope Statement, Version 1:
Servers: If additional servers are required to support this project, they must be compatible with existing servers. If it is more economical to enhance existing servers, a detailed description of enhancements must be submitted to the CIO for approval. See current server specifications provided in Attachment 6. The CEO must approve a detailed plan describing the servers and their location at least two weeks before installation.
Project Scope Statement, Version 2:
Servers: This project will require purchasing ten new servers to support Web, network, database, application, and printing functions. Virtualization will be used to maximize efficiency. Detailed descriptions of the servers are provided in a product brochure in Appendix 8 along with a plan describing where they will be located.

Notice in Table 5-3 that the project scope statements often refer to related documents, which can be product specifications, product brochures, or other plans. As more information becomes available and decisions are made related to project scope, such as specific products that will be purchased or changes that have been approved, the project team should update the project scope statement. They might name different iterations of the scope statement Version 1, Version 2, and so on. These updates may also require changes to be made to other project documents. For example, if the company must purchase servers for the project from a supplier it has never worked with before, the procurement management plan should include information on working with that new supplier.

An up-to-date project scope statement is an important document for developing and confirming a common understanding of the project scope. It describes in detail the work to be accomplished on the project and is an important tool for ensuring customer satisfaction and preventing scope creep, as described later in this chapter.

Recall from Chapter 1 the importance of addressing the triple constraint of project management—meeting scope, time, and cost goals for a project. Time and cost goals are normally straightforward. For example, the time goal for the IT Upgrade Project is nine months, and the cost goal is $1.5 million. It is much more difficult to describe, agree upon, and meet the scope goal of many projects.

MEDIA SNAPSHOT

Many people enjoy watching television shows like *Trading Spaces*, where participants have two days and $1,000 to update a room in their neighbor's house. Since the time and cost are set, it's the scope that has the most flexibility. Examples of some of the work completed include new flooring, light fixtures, paint, new shelves, or artwork to brighten up a dull room.

Designers on these shows often have to change initial scope goals due to budget or time constraints. For example, designers often go back to local stores to exchange items, such as lights, artwork, or fabric, for less expensive items to meet budget constraints. Or they might describe a new piece of furniture they'd like the carpenter to build, but the carpenter changes the design or materials to meet time constraints. Occasionally designers can buy more expensive items or have more elaborate furniture built because they underestimated costs and schedules.

Another important issue related to project scope management is meeting customer expectations. Who wouldn't be happy with a professionally designed room at no cost to them? Although most homeowners are very happy with work done on the show, some are obviously disappointed. Unlike most projects where the project team works closely with the customer, homeowners have little say in what gets done and cannot inspect the work along the way. They walk into their newly decorated room with their eyes closed. Modernizing a room can mean something totally different to a homeowner and the interior designer. For example, one woman was obviously shocked when she saw her bright orange kitchen with black appliances. Another couple couldn't believe there was moss on their bedroom walls. What happens when the homeowners don't like the work that's been done? Part of agreeing to be on the show includes signing a release statement acknowledging that you will accept whatever work has been done. Too bad you can't get sponsors for most projects to sign a similar release statement. It would make project scope management much easier!

CREATING THE WORK BREAKDOWN STRUCTURE

After collecting requirements and defining scope, the next step in project scope management is to create a work breakdown structure. A **work breakdown structure (WBS)** is a deliverable-oriented grouping of the work involved in a project that defines the total scope of the project. Because most projects involve many people and many different deliverables, it is important to organize and divide the work into logical parts based on how the work will be performed. The WBS is a foundation document in project management because it provides the basis for planning and managing project schedules, costs, resources, and changes. Since the WBS defines the total scope of the project, some project management experts believe that work should not be done on a project if it is not included in the WBS. Therefore, it is crucial to develop a good WBS.

The project scope statement, stakeholder requirements documentation, and organizational process assets are the primary inputs for creating a WBS. The main tool or technique is **decomposition**, that is, subdividing project deliverables into smaller pieces. The outputs of the process of creating the WBS are the WBS itself, the WBS dictionary, a scope baseline, and project document updates.

What does a WBS look like? A WBS is often depicted as a task-oriented family tree of activities, similar to an organizational chart. A project team often organizes the WBS around project products, project phases, or using the project management process groups. Many people like to create a WBS in chart form first to help them visualize the whole project and all of its main parts. For example, Figure 5-3 shows a WBS for an intranet project. Notice that product areas provide the basis for its organization. In this case, there are main boxes or groupings on the WBS for developing the Web site design, the home page for the intranet, the marketing department's pages, and the sales department's pages.

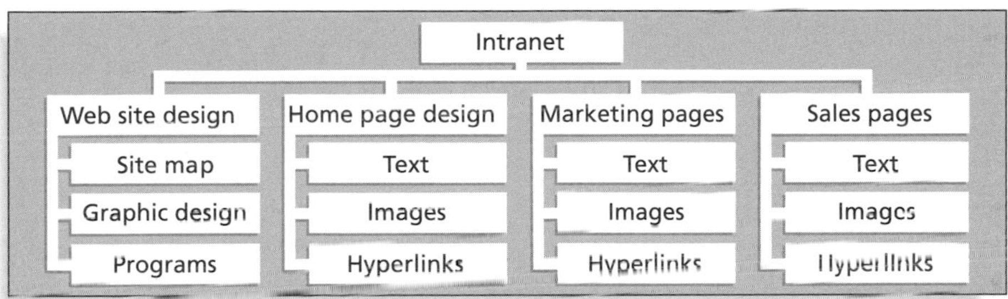

FIGURE 5-3 Sample intranet WBS organized by product

In contrast, a WBS for the same intranet project can be organized around project phases, as shown in Figure 5-4.[3] Notice that project phases of concept, Web site design, Web site development, roll out, and support provide the basis for its organization.

Also note the levels in Figure 5-4. The name of the entire project is the top box, called Level 1, and the main groupings for the work are listed in the second tier of boxes, called Level 2. This level numbering is based on PMI's *Practice Standard for Work Breakdown Structures, Second Edition* (2006). Each of those boxes can be broken down into subsequent tiers of boxes to show the hierarchy of the work. PMI uses the term "task" to describe each level of work in the WBS. For example, in Figure 5-4, the following items can be referred to as tasks: the Level 2 item called Concept, the Level 3 item called Define requirements, and the Level 4 item called Define user requirements. Tasks that are decomposed into smaller tasks are called summary tasks. Figure 5-4 shows a sample WBS in both chart and tabular form. Notice that both of these formats show the same information. Many documents, such as contracts, use the tabular format. Project management software also uses this format. The WBS becomes the contents of the Task Name column in Microsoft Project, and the hierarchy or level of tasks is shown by indenting and numbering tasks within the software. The numbering shown in the tabular form on the left in Figure 5-4 coincides with numbering in Microsoft

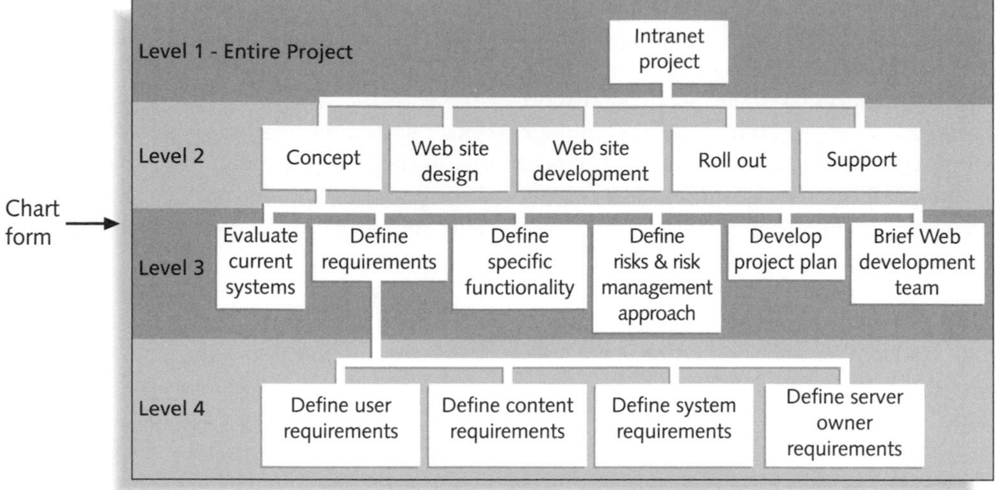

Tabular form with Microsoft Project numbering

1.0 Concept
    1.1 Evaluate current systems
    1.2 Define requirements
        1.2.1 Define user requirements
        1.2.2 Define content requirements
        1.2.3 Define system requirements
        1.2.4 Define server owner requirements
    1.3 Define specific functionality
    1.4 Define risks and risk management approach
    1.5 Develop project plan
    1.6 Brief Web development team
2.0 Web site design
3.0 Web site development
4.0 Roll out
5.0 Support

Tabular form with PMI numbering

1.1 Concept
    1.1.1 Evaluate current systems
    1.1.2 Define requirements
        1.1.2.1 Define user requirements
        1.1.2.2 Define content requirements
        1.1.2.3 Define system requirements
        1.1.2.4 Define server owner requirements
    1.1.3 Define specific functionality
    1.1.4 Define risks and risk management approach
    1.1.5 Develop project plan
    1.1.6 Brief Web development team
1.2 Web site design
1.3 Web site development
1.4 Roll out
1.5 Support

FIGURE 5-4 Sample intranet WBS organized by phase in chart and tabular form

Project and other sources. The numbering shown in the tabular form on the right in Figure 5-4 is based on PMI's *Practice Standard for Work Breakdown Structures, Second Edition*. Be sure to check with your organization to see what numbering scheme they prefer to use for work breakdown structures.

In Figure 5-4, the lowest level of the WBS is Level 4. A **work package** is a task at the lowest level of the WBS. In Figure 5-4, tasks 1.2.1, 1.2.2, 1.2.3, and 1.2.4 (based on the numbering on the left) are work packages. The other tasks would probably be broken down further. However, some tasks can remain at Level 2 or 3 in the WBS. Some might be broken down to Level 5 or 6, depending on the complexity of the work. A work package also represents the level of work that the project manager monitors and controls. You can think of work packages in terms of accountability and reporting. If a project has a relatively short time frame and requires weekly progress reports, a work package might represent work completed in one week or less. If a project has a very long time frame and requires quarterly progress reports, a work package might represent work completed in one month or more. A work package might also be the procurement of a specific product or products, such as an item or items purchased from an outside source.

Another way to think of work packages relates to entering data into project management software. *You can only enter duration estimates for work packages*. The rest of the WBS items are just groupings or summary tasks for the work packages. The software automatically calculates duration estimates for various WBS levels based on data entered for each work package and the WBS hierarchy. See Appendix A for detailed information on using Project 2007.

Figure 5-5 shows the phase-oriented intranet WBS, using the Microsoft Project numbering scheme from Figure 5-4, in the form of a Gantt chart created in Project 2007. You can see from this figure that the WBS is the basis for project schedules. Notice that the WBS is in the left part of the figure under the Task Name column. The resulting schedule is in the right part of the figure. You will learn more about Gantt charts in Chapter 6, Project Time Management.

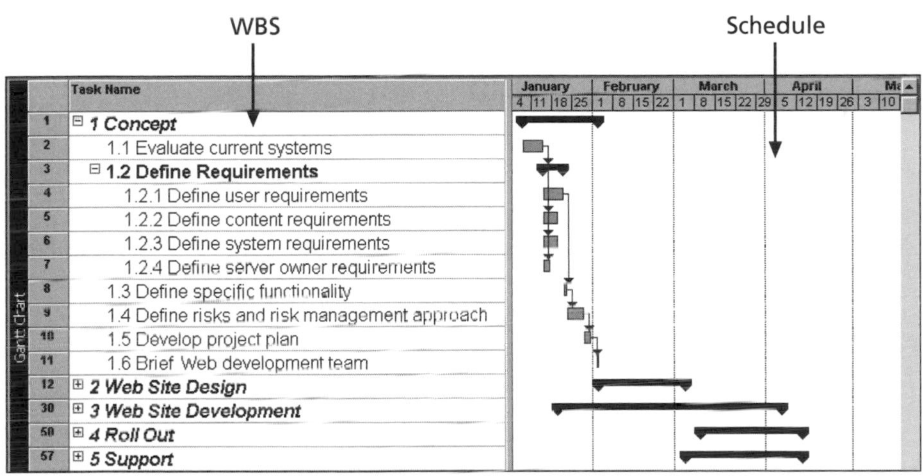

FIGURE 5-5 Intranet Gantt chart in Microsoft Project

The sample WBSs shown here seem somewhat easy to construct and understand. *Nevertheless, it is very difficult to create a good WBS*. To create a good WBS, you must understand the project and its scope and incorporate the needs and knowledge of the stakeholders. The project manager and the project team must decide as a group how to organize the work and how many levels to include in the WBS. Many project managers have found that it is better to focus on getting the top levels done well before getting too bogged down in more detailed levels.

Many people confuse tasks on a WBS with specifications. Tasks on a WBS represent work that needs to be done to complete the project. For example, if you are creating a WBS to redesign a kitchen, you might have Level 2 categories called design, purchasing, flooring, walls, cabinets, and appliances. Under flooring, you might have tasks to remove the old flooring, install the new flooring, and install the trim. You would not have tasks like "12 ft. by 14 ft. of light oak" or "flooring must be durable."

Another concern when creating a WBS is how to organize it so that it provides the basis for the project schedule. You should focus on what work needs to be done and how it will be done, not when it will be done. In other words, the tasks do not have to be developed as a sequential list of steps. If you do want some time-based flow for the work, you can create a WBS using the project management process groups of initiating, planning, executing, monitoring and controlling, and closing as Level 2 in the WBS. By doing this, not only does the project team follow good project management practice, but the WBS tasks can also be mapped more easily against time. For example, Figure 5-6 shows a WBS and Gantt chart for the intranet project, organized by the five project management process groups. Tasks under initiating include selecting a project manager, forming the project team, and developing the project charter. Tasks under planning include developing a scope statement, creating a WBS, and developing and refining other plans, which would be broken down in more detail for a real project. The tasks of concept, Web site design, Web site development, and roll out, which were WBS Level 2 items in Figure 5-4, now become WBS Level 3 items under executing. The executing tasks vary the most from project to project, but many of the tasks under the other project management process groups would be similar for all projects. If you do not use the project management process groups in the WBS, you can have a Level 2 category called project management to make sure that tasks related to managing the project are accounted for. Remember that all work should be included in the WBS, including project management.

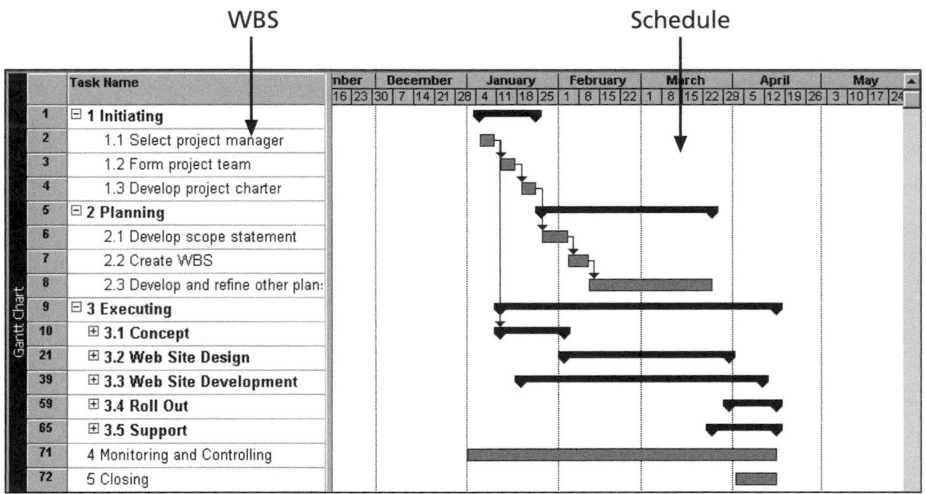

FIGURE 5-6 Intranet project Gantt chart organized by project management process groups

JWD Consulting used the project management process groups for the Level 2 items in its WBS for the Project Management Intranet Site Project in Chapter 3. The project team focused on the product deliverables they had to produce for the project in breaking down the executing task. Table 5-4 shows the categories they used for that part of the WBS. Some project teams like to list every deliverable they need to produce and then use those as the basis for creating all or part of their WBS. Recall that the scope statement should list and describe all of the deliverables required for the project. It is very important to ensure consistency between the project charter, scope statement, WBS, and Gantt chart to define the scope of the project accurately.

TABLE 5-4 Executing tasks for JWD Consulting's WBS

3.0 Executing
- 3.1 Survey
- 3.2 User inputs
- 3.3 Intranet site content
  - 3.3.1 Templates and tools
  - 3.3.2 Articles
  - 3.3.3 Links
  - 3.3.4 Ask the Expert
  - 3.3.5 User requests
- 3.4 Intranet site design
- 3.5 Intranet site construction
- 3.6 Site testing
- 3.7 Site promotion
- 3.8 Site roll out
- 3.9 Project benefits measurement

It is also very important to involve the entire project team and the customer in creating and reviewing the WBS. *People who will do the work should help to plan the work* by creating the WBS. Having group meetings to develop a WBS helps everyone understand *what* work must be done for the entire project and *how* it should be done, given the people involved. It also helps to identify where coordination between different work packages will be required.

Approaches to Developing Work Breakdown Structures

There are several approaches you can use to develop a work breakdown structure. These approaches include:

- Using guidelines
- The analogy approach
- The top-down approach
- The bottom-up approach
- The mind-mapping approach

Using Guidelines

If guidelines for developing a WBS exist, it is very important to follow them. Some organizations—the U.S. Department of Defense (DOD) for example—prescribe the form and content for WBSs for particular projects. Many DOD projects require contractors to prepare their proposals based on the DOD-provided WBS. These proposals must include cost estimates for each task in the WBS at a detailed and summary level. The cost for the entire project must be calculated by summing the costs of all of the lower level WBS tasks. When DOD personnel evaluate cost proposals, they must compare the contractors' costs with the DOD's estimates. A large variation in costs for a certain WBS task often indicates confusion as to what work must be done.

Consider a large automation project for the U.S. Air Force. In the mid-1980s, the Air Force developed a request for proposals for the Local On-Line Network System (LONS) to automate 15 Air Force Systems Command bases. This $250 million project involved providing the hardware and developing software for sharing documents such as contracts, specifications, requests for proposals, and so on. The Air Force proposal guidelines included a WBS that contractors were required to follow in preparing their cost proposals. Level 2 WBS items included hardware, software development, training, project management, and the like. The hardware item was composed of several Level 3 items, such as servers, workstations, printers, network hardware, and so on. Air Force personnel reviewed the contractors' cost proposals against their internal cost estimate, which was also based on this WBS. Having a prescribed WBS helped contractors to prepare their cost proposals and the Air Force to evaluate them.

Many organizations provide guidelines and templates for developing WBSs, as well as examples of WBSs from past projects. Microsoft Project 2007 comes with several templates, and more are available on Microsoft's Web site and other sites. At the request of many of its members, the Project Management Institute developed a WBS Practice Standard to provide guidance for developing and applying the WBS to project management (see the Suggested Readings for this chapter on the companion Web site). This document includes sample WBSs for a wide variety of projects in various industries, including projects for Web design, telecom, service industry outsourcing, and software implementation.

Project managers and their teams should review appropriate information to develop their unique project WBSs more efficiently. For example, Kim Nguyen and key team members from the opening case should review their company's WBS guidelines, templates, and other related information before and during the team meetings to create their WBS.

The Analogy Approach

Another approach for constructing a WBS is the analogy approach. In the **analogy approach**, you use a similar project's WBS as a starting point. For example, Kim Nguyen from the opening case might learn that one of her organization's suppliers did a similar information technology upgrade project last year. She could ask them to share their WBS for that project to provide a starting point for her own project.

McDonnell Aircraft Company, now part of Boeing, provides an example of using an analogy approach when creating WBSs. McDonnell Aircraft Company designed and manufactured several different fighter aircraft. When creating a WBS for a new aircraft design, it started by using 74 predefined subsystems for building a fighter aircraft based on past experience. There was a Level 2 WBS item for the airframe that was composed of Level 3 items such as a forward fuselage, center fuselage, aft fuselage, and wings. This generic product-oriented WBS provided a starting point for defining the scope of new aircraft projects and developing cost estimates for new aircraft designs.

Some organizations keep a repository of WBSs and other project documentation on file to assist people working on projects. Project 2007 and many other software tools include sample files to assist users in creating a WBS and Gantt chart. Viewing examples of other similar projects' WBSs allows you to understand different ways to create a WBS.

The Top-down and Bottom-up Approaches

Two other approaches for creating WBSs are the top-down and bottom-up approaches. Most project managers consider the top-down approach of WBS construction to be conventional.

To use the **top-down approach,** start with the largest items of the project and break them into their subordinate items. This process involves refining the work into greater and greater levels of detail. For example, Figure 5-4 shows how work was broken down to Level 4 for part of the intranet project. After finishing the process, all resources should be assigned at the work package level. The top-down approach is best suited to project managers who have vast technical insight and a big-picture perspective.

In the **bottom-up approach,** team members first identify as many specific tasks related to the project as possible. They then aggregate the specific tasks and organize them into summary activities, or higher levels in the WBS. For example, a group of people might be responsible for creating a WBS to create an e-commerce application. Instead of looking for guidelines on how to create a WBS or viewing similar projects' WBSs, they could begin by listing detailed tasks they think they would need to do in order to create the application. After listing these detailed tasks, they would group the tasks into categories. Then they would group these categories into higher-level categories. Some people have found that writing all possible tasks down on notes and then placing them on a wall helps them see all the work required for the project and develop logical groupings for performing the work. For example, a business analyst on the project team might know that they had to define user requirements and content requirements for the e-commerce application. These tasks might be part of the requirements documents they would have to create as one of the project deliverables. A hardware specialist might know they had to define system requirements and server requirements, which would also be part of a requirements document. As a group, they might decide to put all four of these tasks under a higher-level item called "define requirements" that would result in the delivery of a requirements document. Later, they might realize that defining requirements should fall under a broader category of concept design for the e-commerce application, along with other groups of tasks related to the concept design. The bottom-up approach can be very time-consuming, but it can also be a very effective way to create a WBS. Project managers often use the bottom-up approach for projects that represent entirely new systems or approaches to doing a job, or to help create buy-in and synergy with a project team.

Mind Mapping

Some project managers like to use mind mapping to help develop WBSs. As described in Chapter 4 when showing an example of performing a SWOT analysis, mind mapping is a technique that uses branches radiating out from a core idea to structure thoughts and ideas. Instead of writing tasks down in a list or immediately trying to create a structure for tasks, mind mapping allows people to write and even draw pictures of ideas in a nonlinear format. This more visual, less-structured approach to defining and then grouping tasks can unlock creativity among individuals and increase participation and morale among teams.[4]

Figure 5-7 shows a diagram that uses mind mapping to create a WBS for the IT Upgrade Project from Chapter 3. The figure was created using MindManager software by Mindjet (*www.mindjet.com*). The circle in the center represents the entire project. Each of the four main branches radiating out from the center represents the main tasks or Level 2 items for the WBS. Different people at the meeting creating this mind map might have different roles in the project, which could help in deciding the tasks and WBS structure. For example, Kim would want to focus on all of the project management tasks, and she might also know that they will be tracked in a separate budget category. People who are familiar with acquiring or installing hardware and software might focus on that work, and so on. Branching off from the main task called "Update inventory" are two subtasks, "Perform physical inventory" and "Update database." Branching off from the "Perform physical inventory" subtask are three further subdivisions, labeled Building A, Building B, and Building C, and so on. The team would continue to add branches and items until they have exhausted ideas on what work needs to be performed.

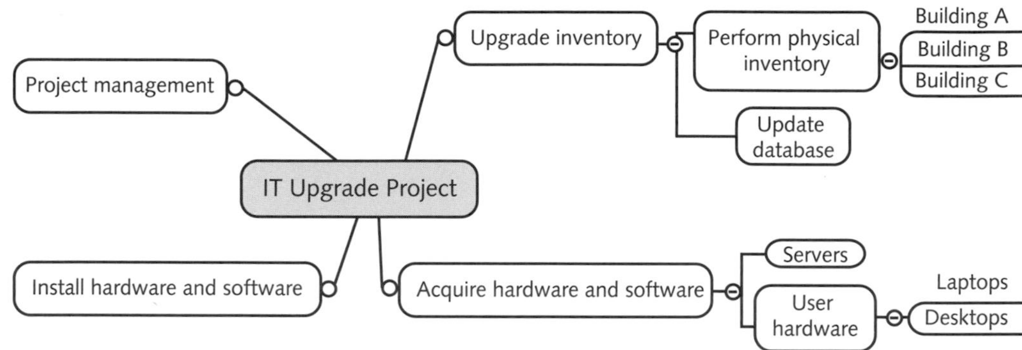

FIGURE 5-7 Sample mind-mapping technique for creating a WBS

After discovering WBS items and their structure using the mind-mapping technique, you could then translate the information into chart or tabular form, as described earlier. A feature of MindManager software is that you can export your map into Microsoft Project. The WBS is entered in the Task List column, with the structure automatically created based on the mind map. Figure 5-8 shows the resulting Project 2007 file for the IT Upgrade Project.

Mind mapping can be used for developing WBSs using the top-down or bottom-up approach. For example, you could conduct mind mapping for an entire project by listing the whole project in the center of a document, adding the main categories on branches radiating out from the center, and then adding branches for appropriate subcategories. You could also develop a separate mind-mapping diagram for each deliverable and then merge them to create one large diagram for the entire project. You can also add items anywhere on a mind-mapping document without following a strict top-down or bottom-up approach. After the mind-mapping documents are complete, you can convert them into a chart or tabular WBS form.

The WBS Dictionary and Scope Baseline

As you can see from these sample WBSs, many of the items listed on them are rather vague. What exactly does "Update database" mean, for example? The person responsible for this task might think that it does not need to be broken down any further, which could be fine. However, the task should be described in more detail so everyone has the same understanding of what it involves. What if someone else has to perform the task? What would you tell him/her to do? What will it cost to complete the task? Information that is more detailed is needed to answer these and other questions.

A **WBS dictionary** is a document that describes detailed information about each WBS item. The format of the WBS dictionary can vary based on project needs. It might be appropriate to have just a short paragraph describing each work package. For a more complex project, an entire page or more might be needed for the work package descriptions. Some

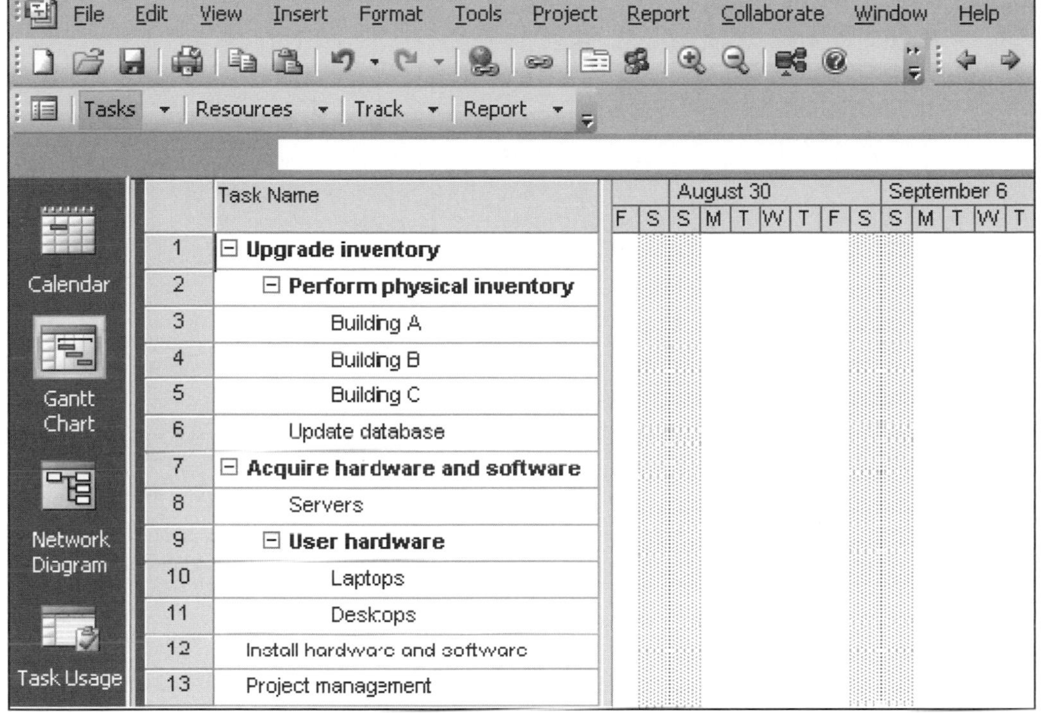

FIGURE 5-8 Project 2007 file with WBS generated from a mind map

projects might require that each WBS item describe the responsible organization, resource requirements, estimated costs, and other information.

Kim should work with her team and sponsor to determine the level of detail needed in the WBS dictionary. They should also decide where this information will be entered and how it will be updated. Project teams often review WBS dictionary entries from similar tasks to get a better idea of how to create these entries. For the IT Upgrade Project, Kim and her team decided to enter all of the WBS dictionary information into their enterprise project management system, following departmental guidelines. Table 5-5 is an example of one entry.

TABLE 5-5 Sample WBS dictionary entry

WBS Dictionary Entry March 20
Project Title: Information Technology (IT) Upgrade Project
WBS Item Number: 2.2
WBS Item Name: Update Database
Description: The IT department maintains an online database of hardware and software on the corporate Intranet. However, we need to make sure that we know exactly what

(continued)

hardware and software employees are currently using and if they have any unique needs before we decide what to order for the upgrade. This task will involve reviewing information from the current database, producing reports that list each department's employees and location, and updating the data after performing the physical inventory and receiving inputs from department managers. Our project sponsor will send out a notice to all department managers to communicate the importance of this project and this particular task. In addition to general hardware and software upgrades, the project sponsors will ask the department managers to provide information for any unique requirements they might have that could affect the upgrades. This task also includes updating the inventory data for network hardware and software. After updating the inventory database, we will send an e-mail to each department manager to verify the information and make changes online, as needed. Department managers will be responsible for ensuring that their people are available and cooperative during the physical inventory. Completing this task is dependent on WBS Item Number 2.1, Perform Physical Inventory and must precede WBS Item Number 3.0, Acquire Hardware and Software.

The approved project scope statement and its associated WBS and WBS dictionary form the **scope baseline**. Performance in meeting project scope goals is based on this scope baseline.

Advice for Creating a WBS and WBS Dictionary

As stated previously, creating a good WBS is no easy task and usually requires several iterations. Often, it is best to use a combination of approaches to create a project's WBS. There are some basic principles, however, that apply to creating any good WBS and its WBS dictionary.

- A unit of work should appear at only one place in the WBS.
- The work content of a WBS item is the sum of the WBS items below it.
- A WBS item is the responsibility of only one individual, even though many people may be working on it.
- The WBS must be consistent with the way in which work is actually going to be performed; it should serve the project team first, and other purposes only if practical.
- Project team members should be involved in developing the WBS to ensure consistency and buy-in.
- Each WBS item must be documented in a WBS dictionary to ensure accurate understanding of the scope of work included and not included in that item.
- The WBS must be a flexible tool to accommodate inevitable changes while properly maintaining control of the work content in the project according to the scope statement.[5]

VERIFYING SCOPE

It is difficult to create a good project scope statement and WBS for a project. It is even more difficult, especially on information technology projects, to verify the project scope and minimize scope changes. Some project teams know from the start that the scope is very unclear and that they must work closely with the project customer to design and produce various deliverables. In this case, the project team must develop a process for scope verification that meets unique project needs. Careful procedures must be developed to ensure the customer is getting what they want and the project team has enough time and money to produce the desired products and services.

Even when the project scope is fairly well defined, many information technology projects suffer from **scope creep**—the tendency for project scope to keep getting bigger and bigger. There are many horror stories about information technology projects failing due to scope problems such as scope creep, with a few classic examples in the following What Went Wrong? feature. For this reason, it is very important to verify the project scope with users throughout the life of the project and develop a process for controlling scope changes.

WHAT WENT WRONG?

A project scope that is too broad and grandiose can cause severe problems. Scope creep and an overemphasis on technology for technology's sake resulted in the bankruptcy of a large pharmaceutical firm, Texas-based FoxMeyer Drug. In 1994, the CIO was pushing for a $65 million system to manage the company's critical operations. He did not believe in keeping things simple, however. The company spent nearly $10 million on state-of-the-art hardware and software and contracted the management of the project to a prestigious (and expensive) consulting firm. The project included building an $18 million robotic warehouse, which looked like something out of a science fiction movie, according to insiders. The scope of the project kept getting bigger and more impractical. The elaborate warehouse was not ready on time, and the new system generated erroneous orders that cost FoxMeyer Drug more than $15 million in unrecovered excess shipments. In July 1996, the company took a $34 million charge for its fourth fiscal quarter, and by August of that year, FoxMeyer Drug filed for bankruptcy.[6] Another example of scope creep comes from McDonald's Restaurants. In 2001, the fast-food chain initiated a project to create an intranet that would connect its headquarters with all of its restaurants to provide detailed operational information in real time. For example, headquarters would know if sales were slowing or if the grill temperature was correct in every single store—all 30,000 of them in more than 120 countries. McDonald's would not divulge detailed information, but they admitted that the project was too large in scale and scope. After spending $170 million on consultants and initial implementation planning, McDonald's realized that the project was too much to handle and terminated it.[7]

Another major scope problem on information technology projects is a lack of user involvement. For example, in the late 1980s at Northrop Grumman, which specializes in defense electronics, information technology, advanced aircraft, shipbuilding, and space technology, an information technology project team became convinced that it could, and should, automate the review and approval process of government proposals. The team implemented a powerful workflow system to manage the whole process. Unfortunately, the end users for the system were aerospace engineers who preferred to work in a more casual, ad hoc fashion. They dubbed the system "Naziware" and refused to use it. This example illustrates an information technology project that wasted millions of dollars developing a system that was not in touch with the way end users did their work.[8]

continued

Failing to follow good project management processes and use off-the-shelf software also results in scope problems. 21st Century Insurance Group in Woodland Hills, California, paid Computer Sciences Corporation $100 million on a project to develop a system for managing business applications, including managing insurance policies, billing, claims, and customer service. After five years, the system was still in development and used to support less than 2 percent of the company's business. Joshua Greenbaum, an analyst at Enterprise Applications Consulting, called the project a "huge disaster" and questioned the insurance company's ability "to manage a process that is pretty well known these days . . . . I'm surprised that there wasn't some way to build what they needed using off-the-shelf components and lower their risk."[9]

Scope verification involves formal acceptance of the completed project scope by the stakeholders. This acceptance is often achieved by a customer inspection and then sign-off on key deliverables. To receive formal acceptance of the project scope, the project team must develop clear documentation of the project's products and procedures to evaluate if they were completed correctly and satisfactorily. Recall from Chapter 4 that configuration management specialists identify and document the functional and physical characteristics of the project's products, record and report the changes, and audit the products to verify conformance to requirements. To minimize scope changes, it is crucial to do a good job of configuration management and verifying project scope.

The project management plan, requirements documentation, the requirements traceability matrix, and validated deliverables are the main inputs for scope verification. The main tool for performing scope verification is inspection. The customer, sponsor, or user inspects the work after it is delivered. The main outputs of scope verification are accepted deliverables, change requests, and project document updates. For example, suppose Kim's team members deliver upgraded computers to users as part of the IT Upgrade Project. Several users might complain because the computers did not include special keyboards they need for medical reasons. Appropriate people would review this change request and take appropriate corrective action, such as getting sponsor approval for purchasing the special keyboards.

CONTROLLING SCOPE

As discussed in the section of Chapter 4 on integrated change control, change is inevitable on projects, especially changes to the scope of information technology projects. Scope control involves controlling changes to the project scope. Users often are not exactly sure how they want screens to look or what functionality they will really need to improve business performance. Developers are not exactly sure how to interpret user requirements, and they also have to deal with constantly changing technologies.

The goal of scope control is to influence the factors that cause scope changes, assure changes are processed according to procedures developed as part of integrated change control, and manage changes when they occur. You cannot do a good job of controlling scope if you do not first do a good job of collecting requirements, defining scope, and verifying scope. How can you prevent scope creep when you have not agreed on the work to be performed and your sponsor hasn't verified that the proposed work was acceptable? You also need to develop a process for soliciting and monitoring changes to project scope.

Stakeholders should be encouraged to suggest changes that will benefit the overall project and discouraged from suggesting unnecessary changes.

The project management plan, work performance data, requirements documentation, requirements traceability matrix, and organizational process assets are the main inputs to scope control. An important tool for performing scope control is variance analysis. **Variance** is the difference between planned and actual performance. For example, if a supplier was supposed to deliver five special keyboards and you received only four, the variance would be one keyboard. The outputs of scope control include work performance measurements, organizational process assets updates, change requests, project management plan updates, and project document updates.

Table 1-2 in Chapter 1 lists the top ten factors that help information technology projects succeed. Four of these ten factors are related to scope verification and control: user involvement, clear business objectives, minimized or clearly defined scope, and firm basic requirements. To avoid project failures, therefore, it is crucial for information technology project managers and their teams to work on improving user input and reducing incomplete and changing requirements and specifications.

BEST PRACTICE

As seen from the examples of What Went Wrong?, companies should follow these best practices to avoid major scope problems:

1. Keep the scope realistic. Don't make projects so large that they can't be completed. Break large projects down into a series of smaller ones.
2. Involve users in project scope management. Assign key users to the project team and give them ownership of requirements definition and scope verification.
3. Use off-the-shelf hardware and software whenever possible. Many IT people enjoy using the latest and greatest technology, but business needs, not technology trends, must take priority.
4. Follow good project management processes. As described in this chapter and others, there are well-defined processes for managing project scope and others aspects of projects.

Managing the scope of software development is often very difficult, but frameworks such as IBM's Rational Unified Process® (RUP) can help. For example, RUP describes a set of principles that characterize best practices in the creation, deployment, and evolution of software-intensive systems as follows:

- Adapt the process
- Balance competing stakeholder priorities
- Collaborate across teams
- Demonstrate value iteratively
- Elevate the level of abstraction
- Focus continuously on quality[10]

The following sections provide more suggestions for improving scope management on information technology projects.

Suggestions for Improving User Input

Lack of user input leads to problems with managing scope creep and controlling change. How can you manage this important issue? Following are suggestions for improving user input:

- Develop a good project selection process for information technology projects. Insist that all projects have a sponsor from the user organization. The sponsor should not be someone in the information technology department, nor should the sponsor be the project manager. Make project information, including the project charter, project management plan, project scope statement, WBS, and WBS dictionary, easily available in the organization. Making basic project information available will help avoid duplication of effort and ensure that the most important projects are the ones on which people are working.
- Have users on the project team. Some organizations require project managers to come from the business area of the project instead of the information technology group. Some organizations assign co-project managers to information technology projects, one from information technology and one from the main business group. Users should be assigned full-time to large information technology projects and part-time to smaller projects. A key success factor in Northwest Airline's ResNet project (see the companion Web site to read the entire case study for this project) was training reservation agents—the users—in how to write programming code for their new reservation system. Because the sales agents had intimate knowledge of the business, they provided excellent input and actually created most of the software.
- Have regular meetings with defined agendas. Meeting regularly sounds obvious, but many information technology projects fail because the project team members do not have regular interaction with users. They assume they understand what users need without getting direct feedback. To encourage this interaction, users should sign off on key deliverables presented at meetings.
- Deliver something to project users and sponsors on a regular basis. If it is some sort of hardware or software, make sure it works first.
- Do not promise to deliver what cannot be delivered in a particular time frame. Make sure the project schedule allows enough time to produce the deliverables.
- Co-locate users with the developers. People often get to know each other better by being in close proximity. If the users cannot be physically moved to be near developers during the entire project, they could set aside certain days for co-location.

Suggestions for Reducing Incomplete and Changing Requirements

Some requirement changes are expected on information technology projects, but many projects have too many changes to their requirements, especially during later stages of the project life cycle when it is more difficult to implement them. The following are suggestions for improving the requirements process:

- Develop and follow a requirements management process that includes procedures for initial requirements determination. (See the Suggested Readings on the companion Web site by Wiegers and Robertson for detailed information on managing requirements.)
- Employ techniques such as prototyping, use case modeling, and Joint Application Design to understand user requirements thoroughly. **Prototyping** involves developing a working replica of the system or some aspect of the system. These working replicas may be throwaways or an incremental component of the deliverable system. Prototyping is an effective tool for gaining an understanding of requirements, determining the feasibility of requirements, and resolving user interface uncertainties. **Use case modeling** is a process for identifying and modeling business events, who initiated them, and how the system should respond to them. It is an effective tool for understanding requirements for information systems. **Joint Application Design (JAD)** uses highly organized and intensive workshops to bring together project stakeholders—the sponsor, users, business analysts, programmers, and so on—to jointly define and design information systems. These techniques also help users become more active in defining system requirements.
- Put all requirements in writing and keep them current and readily available. Several tools are available to automate this function. For example, a type of software called a requirements management tool aids in capturing and maintaining requirements information, provides immediate access to the information, and assists in establishing necessary relationships between requirements and information created by other tools.
- Create a requirements management database for documenting and controlling requirements. Computer Aided Software Engineering (CASE) tools or other technologies can assist in maintaining a repository for project data. A CASE tool's database can also be used to document and control requirements.
- Provide adequate testing to verify that the project's products perform as expected. Conduct testing throughout the project life cycle. Chapter 8, Project Quality Management, includes more information on testing.
- Use a process for reviewing requested requirements changes from a systems perspective. For example, ensure that project scope changes include associated cost and schedule changes. Require approval by appropriate stakeholders. It is crucial for the project manager to lead the team in their focus on achieving approved scope goals and not get side-tracked into doing additional work. For example, in his book, *Alpha Project Managers*, Andy Crowe tried to uncover what the "best" or "alpha" project managers do differently from other project managers. One of these alpha project managers explained how he learned an important lesson about scope control:

> "Toward the end of some projects I've worked on, the managers made their teams work these really long hours. After the second or third time this happened, I just assumed that this was the way things worked. Then I got to work with a manager who planned

everything out really well and ran the team at a good pace the whole time, and we kept on schedule. When the customer found out that things were on schedule, he kept trying to increase the scope, but we had a good manager this time, and she wouldn't let him do it without adjusting the baselines. That was the first time I was on a project that finished everything on time and on budget, and I was amazed at how easy she made it look."[11]

- Emphasize completion dates. For example, a project manager at Farmland Industries, Inc. in Kansas City, Missouri, kept her 15-month, $7 million integrated supply-chain project on track by setting the project deadline. She says, "May 1 was the drop-dead date, and everything else was backed into it. Users would come to us and say they wanted something, and we'd ask them what they wanted to give up to get it. Sticking to the date is how we managed scope creep."[12]
- Allocate resources specifically for handling change requests. For example, Peeter Kivestu and his ResNet team at Northwest Airlines knew that users would request enhancements to the reservations system they were developing. They provided a special function key on the ResNet screen for users to submit their requests, and the project included three full-time programmers to handle these requests. Users made over 11,000 enhancement requests. The managers who sponsored the four main software applications had to prioritize the software enhancement requests and decide as a group what changes to approve. The three programmers then implemented as many items as they could, in priority order, given the time they had. Although they only implemented 38 percent of the requested enhancements, they were the most important ones, and the users were very satisfied with the system and process. (You can find a detailed description of the ResNet project on the companion Web site for this text.)

USING SOFTWARE TO ASSIST IN PROJECT SCOPE MANAGEMENT

Project managers and their teams can use several types of software to assist in project scope management. As shown in several of the figures and tables in this chapter, you can use word processing software to create scope-related documents, and most people use spreadsheet or presentation software to develop various charts, graphs, and matrixes related to scope management. Mind-mapping software can be useful in developing a WBS. Project stakeholders also transmit project scope management information using various types of communication software such as e-mail and assorted Web-based applications.

Project management software helps you develop a WBS, which serves as a basis for creating Gantt charts, assigning resources, allocating costs, and so on. You can also use the templates that come with various project management software products to help you create a WBS for your project. (See the section on project scope management in Appendix A for detailed information on using Project 2007 and the companion Web site for information on templates related to project scope management.)

You can also use many types of specialized software to assist in project scope management. Many information technology projects use special software for requirements management, prototyping, modeling, and other scope-related work. Because scope is such a crucial part of project management, there are many software products available to assist in managing project scope.

Project scope management is very important, especially on information technology projects. After selecting projects, organizations must collect the requirements and define the scope of the work, break down the work into manageable pieces, verify the scope with project stakeholders, and manage changes to project scope. Using the basic project management concepts, tools, and techniques discussed in this chapter can help you successfully manage project scope.

CASE WRAP-UP

Kim Nguyen reviewed guidelines for creating WBSs provided by her company and other sources. She had a meeting with the three team leaders for her project to get their input on how to proceed. They reviewed several sample documents and decided to have major groupings for their project based on updating the inventory database, acquiring the necessary hardware and software, installing the hardware and software, and performing project management. After they decided on a basic approach, Kim led a meeting with the entire project team of 12 people, with some attending virtually. She reviewed the project charter and stakeholder register, described the basic approach they would use to collect requirements and define the project scope, and reviewed sample WBSs. Kim opened the floor for questions, which she answered confidently. She then let each team leader work with his or her people to start writing the detailed scope statement and their sections of the WBS and WBS dictionary. Everyone participated in the meeting, sharing their individual expertise and openly asking questions. Kim could see that the project was off to a good start.

Chapter Summary

Project scope management includes the processes required to ensure that the project addresses all the work required, and only the work required, to complete the project successfully. The main processes include collecting requirements, defining scope, creating the WBS, verifying scope, and controlling scope.

The first step in project scope management is collecting requirements, a crucial part of many IT projects. It is important to review the project charter and meet with key stakeholders listed in the stakeholder register when collecting requirements. The main outputs of this process are requirements documentation, a requirements management plan, and a requirements traceability matrix.

A project scope statement is created in the scope definition process. This document often includes a product scope description, product user acceptance criteria, detailed information on all project deliverables, and information on project boundaries, constraints, and assumptions. There are often several versions of the project scope statement to keep scope information detailed and up-to-date.

A work breakdown structure (WBS) is a deliverable-oriented grouping of the work involved in a project that defines the total scope of the project. The WBS forms the basis for planning and managing project schedules, costs, resources, and changes. You cannot use project management software without first creating a good WBS. A WBS dictionary is a document that describes detailed information about each WBS item. A good WBS is often difficult to create because of the complexity of the project. There are several approaches for developing a WBS, including using guidelines, the analogy approach, the top-down approach, the bottom-up approach, and mind mapping.

Verifying scope involves formal acceptance of the project scope by the stakeholders. Controlling scope involves controlling changes to the project scope.

Poor project scope management is one of the key reasons projects fail. For information technology projects, it is important for good project scope management to have strong user involvement, a clear statement of requirements, and a process for managing scope changes.

There are many software products available to assist in project scope management. The WBS is a key concept in properly using project management software since it provides the basis for entering tasks.

Quick Quiz

1. ________________ refer(s) to all the work involved in creating the products of the project and the processes used to create them.
   a. Deliverables
   b. Milestones
   c. Scope
   d. Product development

2. Which tool or technique for collecting requirements is often the most expensive and time consuming?
   a. interviews
   b. focus groups
   c. surveys
   d. observation
3. A ___________ is a deliverable-oriented grouping of the work involved in a project that defines the total scope of the project.
   a. scope statement
   b. WBS
   c. WBS dictionary
   d. work package
4. What approach to developing a WBS involves writing down or drawing ideas in a nonlinear format?
   a. top-down
   b. bottom-up
   c. analogy
   d. mind mapping
5. Assume you have a project with major categories called planning, analysis, design, and testing. What level of the WBS would these items fall under?
   a. 0
   b. 1
   c. 2
   d. 3
6. Which of the following is not a best practice that can help in avoiding scope problems on information technology projects?
   a. Keep the scope realistic
   b. Use off-the-shelf hardware and software whenever possible
   c. Follow good project management processes
   d. Don't involve too many users in scope management
7. What major restaurant chain terminated a large project after spending $170 million on it, primarily because they realized the project scope was too much to handle?
   a. Burger King
   b. Pizza Hut
   c. McDonald's
   d. Taco Bell

8. Scope ____________ is often achieved by a customer inspection and then sign-off on key deliverables.
    a. verification
    b. validation
    c. completion
    d. close-out
9. Which of the following is not a suggestion for improving user input?
    a. Develop a good project selection process for information technology projects
    b. Have users on the project team
    c. Co-locate users with developers
    d. Only have meetings as needed, not on a regular basis
10. Project management software helps you develop a ___________, which serves as a basis for creating Gantt charts, assigning resources, and allocating costs.
    a. project plan
    b. schedule
    c. WBS
    d. deliverable

Quick Quiz Answers

1. c; 2. a; 3. b; 4. d; 5. c; 6. d; 7. c; 8. a; 9. d; 10. c

Discussion Questions

1. What is involved in project scope management, and why is good project scope management so important on information technology projects?
2. What is involved in collecting requirements for a project? Why is it often such a difficult thing to do?
3. Discuss the process of defining project scope in more detail as a project progresses, going from information in a project charter to a project scope statement, WBS, and WBS dictionary.
4. Describe different ways to develop a WBS and explain why it is often so difficult to do.
5. What is the main technique used for verifying scope? Give an example of scope verification on a project.
6. Using examples in this book or online, describe a project that suffered from scope creep. Could it have been avoided? How? Can scope creep be a good thing? When?
7. Why do you need a good WBS to use project management software? What other types of software can you use to assist in project scope management?

Exercises

1. You are working on a project to develop a new or enhanced system to help people at your college, university, or organization to find jobs. The system must be tailored to your student

or work population and be very easy to use. Write a two-page paper describing how you would collect requirements for this system and include at least five requirements in a requirements traceability matrix.

2. Use PowerPoint, Visio, or similar software to create a WBS in chart form (similar to an organizational chart—see the sample in the top of Figure 5-4). Assume the Level 2 categories are initiating, planning, executing, monitoring and controlling, and closing. Under the executing section, include Level 3 categories of analysis, design, prototyping, testing, implementation, and support. Assume the support category includes Level 4 items called training, documentation, user support, and enhancements.

3. Create the same WBS described in Exercise 2 using Project 2007, indenting categories appropriately. Use the outline numbering feature to display the outline numbers (click Tools on the menu bar, click Options, and then click Show outline number). For example, your WBS should start with 1.0 Initiating. Do not enter any durations or dependencies. See Appendix A or Project 2007's Help for instructions on creating a WBS. Print the resulting Gantt chart on one page, being sure to display the entire Task Name column.
4. Create a WBS for one of the following projects:
   - Introducing self-checkout registers at your school's bookstore
   - Updating 50 laptops from Project 2003 to Project 2007
   - Providing a new Internet Cafe onsite at your organization

   Decide on all of the Level 2 categories for the WBS. Draw a mind map (or use mind-mapping software, if desired) and break down the work to at least the fourth level for one of the WBS items. Enter the WBS into Project 2007 and print out the Gantt chart. Do not enter any durations or dependencies. Make notes of questions you had while completing this exercise.
5. Review a template file in the Microsoft Project 2007 templates folder, from Microsoft's "Project templates" link at *http://office.microsoft.com/project*, or from another source. What do you think about the WBS? Write a two-page paper summarizing your analysis, providing at least three suggestions for improving the WBS.
6. Read one of the suggested readings on the companion Web site or find an article related to project scope management. Write a two-page summary of the article, its key conclusions, and your opinion.

Running Case

Managers at Manage Your Health, Inc. (MYH) selected Tony Prince as the project manager for the Recreation and Wellness Intranet Project. The schedule goal is six months, and the budget is $200,000. Tony had previous project management and systems analysis experience within the company, and he was an avid sports enthusiast. Tony was starting to put the project team together. Tony knew he would have to develop a survey to solicit input from all employees about this new system and make sure it was very user-friendly.

Recall from Chapter 4 that this application would include the following capabilities:

- Allow employees to register for company-sponsored recreational programs, such as soccer, softball, bowling, jogging, walking, and other sports.

- Allow employees to register for company-sponsored classes and programs to help them manage their weight, reduce stress, stop smoking, and manage other health-related issues.
- Track data on employee involvement in these recreational and health-management programs.
- Offer incentives for people to join the programs and do well in them (e.g., incentives for achieving weight goals, winning sports team competitions, etc.).

Assume that MYH would not need to purchase any additional hardware or software for the project.

Tasks

1. Document your approach for collecting requirements for this project in a two-page paper, and include at least five requirements in a requirements traceability matrix.
2. Develop a first version of a project scope statement for the project. Use the template provided on the companion Web site for this text and the example in Chapter 3 as guides. Be as specific as possible in describing product characteristics and requirements, as well as all of the project's deliverables. Be sure to include testing and training as part of the project scope.
3. Develop a work breakdown structure for the project. Break down the work to Level 3 or Level 4, as appropriate. Use the template on the companion Web site and samples in this text as guides. Print the WBS in list form as a Word file. Be sure the WBS is based on the project charter (created in the Chapter 4 Running Case), the project scope statement created in Task 2 above, and other relevant information.
4. Use the WBS you developed in Task 3 above to begin creating a Gantt chart in Project 2007 for the project. Use the outline numbering feature to display the outline numbers (click Tools on the menu bar, click Options, and then click Show outline number). Do not enter any durations or dependencies. Print the resulting Gantt chart on one page, being sure to display the entire Task Name column.
5. Develop a strategy for scope verification and change control for this project. Write a two-page paper summarizing key points of the strategy.

Companion Web Site

Visit the companion Web site for this text (*www.cengage.com/mis/schwalbe*) to access:

- References cited in the text and additional suggested readings for each chapter
- Template files
- Lecture notes
- Interactive quizzes
- Podcasts
- Links to general project management Web sites
- And more

See the Preface of this text for additional information on accessing the companion Web site.

Key Terms

analogy approach — creating a WBS by using a similar project's WBS as a starting point

bottom-up approach — creating a WBS by having team members identify as many specific tasks related to the project as possible and then grouping them into higher level categories

decomposition — subdividing project deliverables into smaller pieces

deliverable — a product, such as a report or segment of software code, produced as part of a project

Joint Application Design (JAD) — using highly organized and intensive workshops to bring together project stakeholders—the sponsor, users, business analysts, programmers, and so on—to jointly define and design information systems

project scope management — the processes involved in defining and controlling what work is or is not included in a project

project scope statement — a document that includes, at a minimum, a description of the project, including its overall objectives and justification, detailed descriptions of all project deliverables, and the characteristics and requirements of products and services produced as part of the project

prototyping — developing a working replica of the system or some aspect of the system to help define user requirements

requirement — a condition or capability that must be met or possessed by a system, product, service, result, or component to satisfy a contract, standard, specification, or other formal document

requirements management plan — a plan that describes how project requirements will be analyzed, documented, and managed

requirements traceability matrix (RTM) — a table that lists requirements, various attributes of each requirement, and the status of the requirements to ensure that all requirements are addressed

scope — all the work involved in creating the products of the project and the processes used to create them

scope baseline — the approved project scope statement and its associated WBS and WBS dictionary

scope creep — the tendency for project scope to keep getting bigger

top-down approach — creating a WBS by starting with the largest items of the project and breaking them into their subordinate items

use case modeling — a process for identifying and modeling business events, who initiated them, and how the system should respond to them

variance — the difference between planned and actual performance

WBS dictionary — a document that describes detailed information about each WBS item

work breakdown structure (WBS) — a deliverable-oriented grouping of the work involved in a project that defines the total scope of the project

work package — a task at the lowest level of the WBS

End Notes

[1] Karl Weigers, *Software Requirements, Second Edition*, (Microsoft Press: Microsoft, 2003), p. 7.

[2] Accept Software, "Success Story: Genesys Connects with Accept to Maintain Competitive Edge, *AcceptSoftware.com* (accessed August 7, 2008).

[3] This particular structure is based on a sample Project 98 file. See *www.microsoft.com* for additional template files.

[4] Mindjet Visual Thinking, "About Mind Maps," *Mindjet.com* (2002).

[5] David I. Cleland, *Project Management: Strategic Design and Implementation*, 2nd ed. (New York: McGraw-Hill, 1994).

[6] Geoffrey James, "Information Technology fiascoes . . . and how to avoid them," *Datamation* (November 1997).

[7] Paul McDougall, "8 Expensive IT Blunders," *InformationWeek* (Oct. 16, 2006).

[8] Geoffrey James, "Information Technology fiascoes . . . and how to avoid them," *Datamation* (November 1997).

[9] Marc L. Songini, "21st Century Insurance apps in limbo despite $100M investment," *ComputerWorld* (December 6, 2002).

[10] Per Kroll and Walker Royce, "Key principles of business-driven development," IBM's DeveloperWorks Rational Library, (October 15, 2005).

[11] Andy Crowe, *Alpha Project Managers: What the Top 2% Know That Everyone Else Does Not*, (Kennesaw, GA: Velociteach Press), 2006, p. 46–47.

[12] Julia King, "IS reins in runaway projects," *ComputerWorld* (September 24, 1997).

CHAPTER 6

PROJECT TIME MANAGEMENT

LEARNING OBJECTIVES

After reading this chapter, you will be able to:

- Understand the importance of project schedules and good project time management
- Define activities as the basis for developing project schedules
- Describe how project managers use network diagrams and dependencies to assist in activity sequencing
- Understand the relationship between estimating resources and project schedules
- Explain how various tools and techniques help project managers perform activity duration estimating
- Use a Gantt chart for planning and tracking schedule information, find the critical path for a project, and describe how critical chain scheduling and the Program Evaluation and Review Technique (PERT) affect schedule development
- Discuss how reality checks and discipline are involved in controlling and managing changes to the project schedule
- Describe how project management software can assist in project time management and review words of caution before using this software

OPENING CASE

Sue Johnson was the project manager for a consulting company contracted to provide a new online registration system at a local college. This system absolutely had to be operational by May 1, so students could use it to register for the fall semester. Her company's contract had a stiff penalty clause if the system was not ready by then, and Sue and her team would get nice bonuses for doing a good job on this project and meeting the schedule. Sue knew that it was her responsibility to meet the schedule and manage scope, cost, and quality expectations. She and her team developed a detailed schedule and network diagram to help organize the project.

Developing the schedule turned out to be the easy part; keeping the project on track was more difficult. Managing people issues and resolving schedule conflicts were two of the bigger challenges. Many of the customers' employees took unplanned vacations and missed or rescheduled project review meetings. These changes made it difficult for the project team to follow their planned schedule for the system because they had to have customer sign-off at various stages of the systems development life cycle. One senior programmer on Sue's project team quit, and she knew it would take extra time for a new person to get up to speed. It was still early in the project, but Sue knew they were falling behind. What could she do to meet the operational date of May 1?

THE IMPORTANCE OF PROJECT SCHEDULES

Many information technology projects are failures in terms of meeting scope, time, and cost projections. Managers often cite delivering projects on time as one of their biggest challenges and the main cause of conflict.

Perhaps part of the reason schedule problems are so common is that time is easily and simply measured. You can debate scope and cost overruns and make actual numbers appear closer to estimates, but once a project schedule is set, anyone can quickly estimate schedule performance by subtracting the original time estimate from how long it really took to complete the project. People often compare planned and actual project completion times without taking into account approved changes in the project. Time is also the one variable that has the least amount of flexibility. Time passes no matter what happens on a project.

Individual work styles and cultural differences may also cause schedule conflicts. You will learn in Chapter 9, Project Human Resource Management, about the Myers Briggs Type Indicator. One dimension of this team-building tool deals with peoples' attitudes toward structure and deadlines. Some people prefer detailed schedules and emphasize task completion. Others prefer to keep things open and flexible. Different cultures and even entire countries have different attitudes about schedules. For example, some countries close businesses for several hours every afternoon to have siestas. Others countries may have different religious or secular holidays at certain times of the year when not much work will be done. Cultures may also have different perceptions of work ethic—some may value hard work and strict schedules while others may value the ability to remain relaxed and flexible.

In contrast to the 2002 Salt Lake City Winter Olympic Games (see Chapter 4's Media Snapshot) or the 2008 Beijing Summer Olympic Games, planning and scheduling was not well implemented for the 2004 Summer Olympic Games held in Athens, Greece. Many articles were written before the opening ceremonies predicting that the facilities would not be ready in time. "With just 162 days to go to the opening of the Athens Olympics, the Greek capital is still not ready for the expected onslaught. . . . By now 22 of the 30 Olympic projects were supposed to be finished. This week the Athens Olympic Committee proudly announced 19 venues would be finished by the end of next month. That's a long way off target."[1]

However, many people were pleasantly surprised by the amazing opening ceremonies, beautiful new buildings, and state-of-the-art security and transportation systems in Athens. For example, traffic flow, considered a major pre-Games hurdle, was superb. One spectator at the games commented on the prediction that the facilities would not be ready in time, "Athens proved them all wrong. . . . It has never looked better."[2] The Greeks even made fun of critics by having construction workers pretend to still be working as the ceremonies began. Athens Olympics chief Gianna Angelopoulos-Daskalaki deserves a gold medal for her performance in leading the many people involved in organizing the 2004 Olympic Games. Unfortunately, the Greek government suffered a huge financial deficit since the games cost more than twice the planned budget.

With all these possibilities for schedule conflicts, it's important to use good project time management so that project managers can help improve performance in this area. **Project time management**, simply defined, involves the processes required to ensure timely completion of a project. Achieving timely completion of a project, however, is by no means simple. There are six main processes involved in project time management:

1. *Defining activities* involves identifying the specific activities that the project team members and stakeholders must perform to produce the project deliverables. An **activity** or **task** is an element of work normally found on the work breakdown structure (WBS) that has an expected duration, a cost, and resource requirements. The main outputs of this process are an activity list, activity attributes, and milestone list.
2. *Sequencing activities* involves identifying and documenting the relationships between project activities. The main outputs of this process include project schedule network diagrams and project document updates.
3. *Estimating activity resources* involves estimating how many **resources**—people, equipment, and materials—a project team should use to perform project activities. The main outputs of this process are activity resource requirements, a resource breakdown structure, and project document updates.
4. *Estimating activity durations* involves estimating the number of work periods that are needed to complete individual activities. Outputs include activity duration estimates and project document updates.

5. *Developing the schedule* involves analyzing activity sequences, activity resource estimates, and activity duration estimates to create the project schedule. Outputs include a project schedule, a schedule baseline, schedule data, and project document updates.
6. *Controlling the schedule* involves controlling and managing changes to the project schedule. Outputs include work performance measurements, organizational process assets updates, change requests, project management plan updates, and project document updates.

Figure 6-1 summarizes these processes and outputs, showing when they occur in a typical project.

Planning
Process: **Define activities**
Outputs: Activity list, activity attributes, milestone list
Process: **Sequence activities**
Outputs: Project schedule network diagrams, project document updates
Process: **Estimate activity resources**
Outputs: Activity resource requirements, resource breakdown structure, project document updates
Process: **Estimate activity durations**
Outputs: Activity duration estimates, project document updates
Process: **Develop schedule**
Outputs: Project schedule, schedule baseline, schedule data, project document updates

Monitoring and Controlling
Process: **Control schedule**
Outputs: Work performance measurements, organizational process assets updates, change requests, project management plan updates, project document updates

Project Start → **Project Finish**

FIGURE 6-1 Project time management summary

You can improve project time management by performing these processes and by using some basic project management tools and techniques. Every manager is familiar with some form of scheduling, but most managers have not used several of the tools and techniques unique to project time management, such as Gantt charts, network diagrams, and critical path analysis.

DEFINING ACTIVITIES

Project schedules grow out of the basic documents that initiate a project. The project charter often mentions planned project start and end dates, which serve as the starting points for a more detailed schedule. The project manager starts with the project charter and develops a project scope statement and WBS, as discussed in Chapter 5, Project Scope Management. The project charter should also include some estimate of how much money will be allocated to the project. Using this information with the main inputs for defining activities—the scope baseline (the scope statement, WBS, and WBS dictionary), enterprise environmental factors, and organizational process assets—the project manager and project team begin developing a detailed list of activities, their attributes, and a milestone list.

The **activity list** is a tabulation of activities to be included on a project schedule. The list should include the activity name, an activity identifier or number, and a brief description of the activity. The **activity attributes** provide more schedule-related information about each activity, such as predecessors, successors, logical relationships, leads and lags, resource requirements, constraints, imposed dates, and assumptions related to the activity. The activity list and activity attributes should be in agreement with the WBS and WBS dictionary. Information is added to the activity attributes as it becomes available, such as logical relationships and resource requirements that are determined in later processes. Many project teams use an automated system to keep track of all of this activity-related information.

A **milestone** on a project is a significant event that normally has no duration. It often takes several activities and a lot of work to complete a milestone, but the milestone itself is like a marker to help in identifying necessary activities. Milestones are also useful tools for setting schedule goals and monitoring progress. For example, milestones on a project like the one in the opening case might include completion and customer sign-off of documents, such as design documents and test plans; completion of specific products, such as software modules or installation of new hardware; and completion of important process-related work, such as project review meetings, tests, and so on. Not every deliverable or output created for a project is really a milestone. Milestones are the most important and visible ones. For example, the term *milestone* is used in several contexts, such as in child development. Parents and doctors check for milestones, such as a child first rolling over, sitting, crawling, walking, talking, and so on. You will learn more about milestones later in this chapter.

Activity information is a required input to the other time management processes. You cannot determine activity sequencing, resources, or durations, develop the schedule, or control the schedule until you have a good understanding of project activities.

Recall the triple constraint of project management—balancing scope, time, and cost goals—and note the order of these items. Ideally, the project team and key stakeholders first define the project scope, then the time or schedule for the project, and then the project's cost. The order of these three items reflects the basic order of the first four processes in project time management: defining activities (further defining the scope), sequencing activities (further defining the time), and estimating activity resources and activity durations (further defining the time and cost). These four project time management processes are the basis for creating a project schedule.

The goal of the defining activities is to ensure that the project team has complete understanding of all the work they must do as part of the project scope so they can start scheduling the work. For example, a WBS item might be "Produce study report." The project team would have to understand what that means before they can make schedule-related decisions. How long should the report be? Does it require a survey or extensive research to produce it? What skill level does the report writer need to have? Further defining that task will help the project team determine how long it will take to do and who should do it.

The WBS is often dissected further as the project team members further define the activities required for performing the work. For example, the task "Produce study report" might be broken down into several subtasks describing the steps involved in producing the report, such as developing a survey, administering the survey, analyzing the survey results, performing research, writing a draft report, editing the report, and finally producing the report. This process of progressive elaboration, as mentioned as an attribute of a project in Chapter 1, is sometimes called "rolling wave planning."

As stated earlier, activities or tasks are elements of work performed during the course of a project; they have expected durations, costs, and resource requirements. Defining activities also results in supporting detail to document important product information as well as assumptions and constraints related to specific activities. The project team should review the activity list and activity attributes with project stakeholders before moving on to the next step in project time management. If they do not review these items, they could produce an unrealistic schedule and deliver unacceptable results. For example, if a project manager simply estimated that it would take one day for the "Produce study report" task and had an intern or trainee write a 10-page report to complete that task, the result could be a furious customer who expected extensive research, surveys, and a 100-page report. Clearly defining the work is crucial to all projects. If there are misunderstandings about activities, requested changes may be required.

In the opening case, Sue Johnson and her project team had a contract and detailed specifications for the college's new online registration system. They also had to focus on meeting the May 1 date for an operational system so the college could start using the new system for the new semester's registration. To develop a project schedule, Sue and her team had to review the contract, detailed specifications, and desired operational date, create an activity list, activity attributes, and milestone list. After developing more detailed definitions of project activities, Sue and her team would review them with their customers to ensure that they were on the right track.

WHAT WENT WRONG?

At the U.S. Federal Bureau of Investigation (FBI), poor time management was one of the reasons behind the failure of Trilogy, a "disastrous, unbelievably expensive piece of vaporware, which was more than four years in the (un)making. The system was supposed to enable FBI agents to integrate intelligence from isolated information silos within the Bureau."[3] In May 2006, the Government Accounting Agency said that the Trilogy project failed at its core mission of improving the FBI's investigative abilities and was plagued with missed milestones and escalating costs.

The FBI rushed to develop the new system, beginning in 2001, in response to the attacks on September 11. The need for new software was obvious to former FBI agent, David J. Williams, who recalls joining a roomful of agents shortly after 9/11 to help with intelligence. Agents were wearing out the casters on their chairs by sliding back and forth between 20 old computer terminals, many of which were attached to various databases containing different information.

continued

Congressional hearings revealed numerous problems with the project. The requirements for the project were very loosely defined, there were many leadership changes throughout the project, and several contracts had no scheduled milestones for completion or penalties if work was late. The new system was finally completed in 2006 and cost more than $537 million—more than a year late and $200 million over budget. The FBI replaced Trilogy with a new system called Sentinel and began training employees to use it in May 2007. Although that was about a month behind schedule, director Robert Mueller told a Senate panel that he was optimistic about the $425 million project's progress.[4]

SEQUENCING ACTIVITIES

After defining project activities, the next step in project time management is sequencing them or determining their dependencies. Inputs to the activity sequencing process include the activity list and attributes, project scope statement, milestone list, and organizational process assets. It involves evaluating the reasons for dependencies and the different types of dependencies.

Dependencies

A **dependency** or **relationship** relates to the sequencing of project activities or tasks. For example, does a certain activity have to be finished before another one can start? Can the project team do several activities in parallel? Can some overlap? Determining these relationships or dependencies between activities has a significant impact on developing and managing a project schedule.

There are three basic reasons for creating dependencies among project activities:

- **Mandatory dependencies** are inherent in the nature of the work being performed on a project. They are sometimes referred to as hard logic. For example, you cannot test code until after the code is written.
- **Discretionary dependencies** are defined by the project team. For example, a project team might follow good practice and not start the detailed design of a new information system until the users sign off on all of the analysis work. Discretionary dependencies are sometimes referred to as soft logic and should be used with care since they may limit later scheduling options.
- **External dependencies** involve relationships between project and non-project activities. The installation of a new operating system and other software may depend on delivery of new hardware from an external supplier. Even though the delivery of the new hardware may not be in the scope of the project, you should add an external dependency to it because late delivery will affect the project schedule.

As with activity definition, it is important that project stakeholders work together to define the activity dependencies that exist on their project. If you do not define the sequence of activities, you cannot use some of the most powerful schedule tools available to project managers: network diagrams and critical path analysis.

Network Diagrams

Network diagrams are the preferred technique for showing activity sequencing. A **network diagram** is a schematic display of the logical relationships among, or sequencing of, project activities. Some people refer to network diagrams as project schedule network diagrams or PERT charts. PERT is described later in this chapter. Figure 6-2 shows a sample network diagram for Project X, which uses the arrow diagramming method (ADM) or activity-on-arrow (AOA) approach.

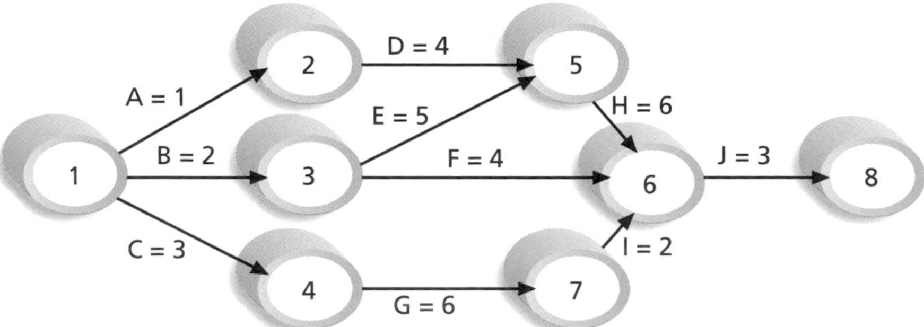

Note: Assume all durations are in days; A=1 means Activity A has a duration of 1 day.

FIGURE 6-2 Activity-on-arrow (AOA) network diagram for Project X

Note the main elements on this network diagram. The letters A through J represent activities with dependencies that are required to complete the project. These activities come from the WBS and activity definition process described earlier. The arrows represent the activity sequencing or relationships between tasks. For example, Activity A must be done before Activity D; Activity D must be done before Activity H, and so on.

The format of this network diagram uses the **activity-on-arrow (AOA)** approach or the **arrow diagramming method (ADM)**—a network diagramming technique in which activities are represented by arrows and connected at points called nodes to illustrate the sequence of activities. A **node** is simply the starting and ending point of an activity. The first node signifies the start of a project, and the last node represents the end of a project.

Keep in mind that the network diagram represents activities that must be done to complete the project. It is not a race to get from the first node to the last node. *Every* activity on the network diagram must be completed in order for the project to finish. It is also important to note that not every single item on the WBS needs to be on the network diagram; only activities with dependencies need to be shown on the network diagram. However, some people like to have start and end milestones and to list every activity. It is a matter of preference. For projects with hundreds of activities, it might be simpler to include only activities with dependencies on a network diagram, especially on large projects. Sometimes it is enough to put summary tasks on a network diagram or to break down the project into several smaller network diagrams.

Assuming you have a list of the project activities and their start and finish nodes, follow these steps to create an AOA network diagram:

1. Find all of the activities that start at Node 1. Draw their finish nodes, and draw arrows between Node 1 and each of those finish nodes. Put the activity letter or name on the associated arrow. If you have a duration estimate, write that next to the activity letter or name, as shown in Figure 6-2. For example, A = 1 means that the duration of Activity A is one day, week, or other standard unit of time. Also be sure to put arrowheads on all arrows to signify the direction of the relationships.
2. Continue drawing the network diagram, working from left to right. Look for bursts and merges. **Bursts** occur when two or more activities follow a single node. A **merge** occurs when two or more nodes precede a single node. For example, in Figure 6-2, Node 1 is a burst since it goes into Nodes 2, 3, and 4. Node 5 is a merge preceded by Nodes 2 and 3.
3. Continue drawing the AOA network diagram until all activities are included on the diagram.
4. As a rule of thumb, all arrowheads should face toward the right, and no arrows should cross on an AOA network diagram. You may need to redraw the diagram to make it look presentable.

Even though AOA or ADM network diagrams are generally easy to understand and create, a different method is more commonly used: the precedence diagramming method. The **precedence diagramming method (PDM)** is a network diagramming technique in which boxes represent activities. It is particularly useful for visualizing certain types of time relationships.

Figure 6-3 illustrates the types of dependencies that can occur among project activities. After you determine the reason for a dependency between activities (mandatory,

Task dependencies

The nature of the relationship between two linked tasks. You link tasks by defining a dependency between their finish and start dates. For example, the "Contact caterers" task must finish before the start of the "Determine menus" task. There are four kinds of task dependencies in Microsoft Project:

Task dependency	Example	Description
Finish-to-start (FS)	A → B	Task (B) cannot start until task (A) finishes.
Start-to-start (SS)	A → B	Task (B) cannot start until task (A) starts.
Finish-to-finish (FF)	A → B	Task (B) cannot finish until task (A) finishes.
Start-to-finish (SF)	A → B	Task (B) cannot finish until task (A) starts.

FIGURE 6-3 Task dependency types

discretionary, or external), you must determine the type of dependency. Note that the terms activity and task are used interchangeably, as are relationship and dependency. See Appendix A to learn how to create dependencies in Microsoft Project 2007. The four types of dependencies or relationships between activities include:

- **Finish-to-start dependency:** a relationship where the "from" activity or predecessor must finish before the "to" activity or successor can start. For example, you cannot provide user training until after software, or a new system, has been installed. Finish-to-start is the most common type of relationship, or dependency, and AOA network diagrams use only finish-to-start dependencies.
- **Start-to-start dependency:** a relationship in which the "from" activity cannot start until the "to" activity or successor is started. For example, on several information technology projects, a group of activities all start simultaneously, such as the many tasks that occur when a new system goes live.
- **Finish-to-finish dependency:** a relationship where the "from" activity must be finished before the "to" activity can be finished. One task cannot finish before another finishes. For example, quality control efforts cannot finish before production finishes, although the two activities can be performed at the same time.
- **Start-to-finish dependency:** a relationship where the "from" activity must start before the "to" activity can be finished. This type of relationship is rarely used, but it is appropriate in some cases. For example, an organization might strive to stock raw materials just in time for the manufacturing process to begin. A delay in the manufacturing process starting should delay completion of stocking the raw materials. Another example would be a babysitter who wants to finish watching a young child but is dependent on the parent arriving. The parent must show up or "start" before the babysitter can finish his or her oversight.

Figure 6-4 illustrates Project X using the precedence diagramming method. Notice that the activities are placed inside boxes, which represent the nodes on this diagram. Arrows show the relationships between activities. This figure was created using Microsoft Project, which automatically places additional information inside each node. Each task box includes the start and finish date, labeled Start and Finish, the task ID number, labeled ID, the task's duration, labeled Dur, and the names of resources, if any, assigned to the task, labeled Res. The border of the boxes for tasks on the critical path appears automatically in red in the Microsoft Project network diagram view. In Figure 6-4, the boxes for critical tasks have a thicker border.

The precedence diagramming method is used more often than AOA network diagrams and offers a number of advantages over the AOA technique. First, most project management software uses the precedence diagramming method. Second, the precedence diagramming method avoids the need to use dummy activities. **Dummy activities** have no duration and no resources but are occasionally needed on AOA network diagrams to show logical relationships between activities. They are represented with dashed arrow lines, and have zero for the duration estimate. Third, the precedence diagramming method shows different dependencies among tasks, whereas AOA network diagrams use only finish-to-start dependencies. You will learn more about activity sequencing using Project 2007 in Appendix A.

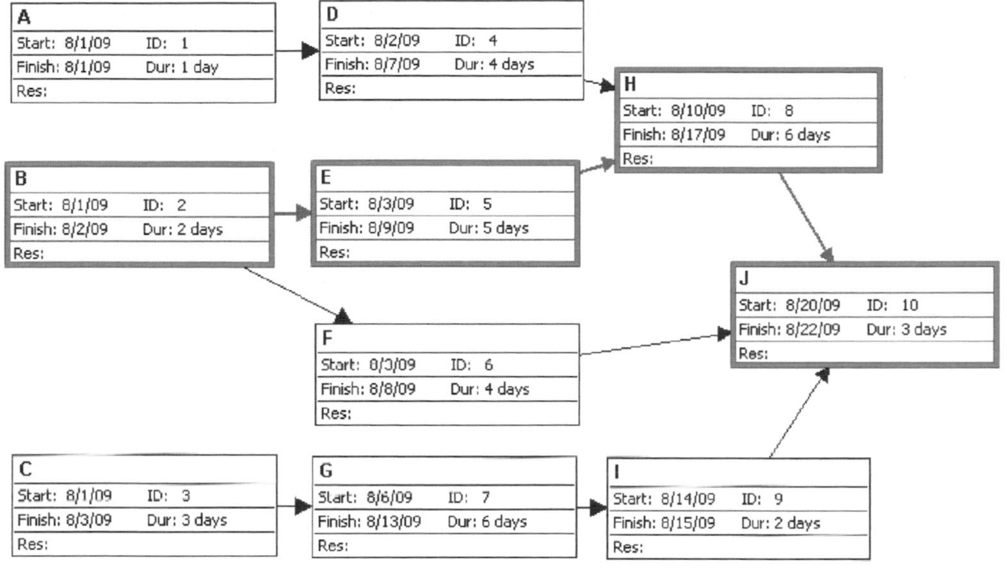

FIGURE 6-4 Precedence diagramming method (PDM) network diagram for Project X

ESTIMATING ACTIVITY RESOURCES

Before you can estimate the duration for each activity, you must have a good idea of the quantity and type of resources (people, equipment, and materials) that will be assigned to each activity. The nature of the project and the organization will affect resource estimating. Expert judgment, an analysis of alternatives, estimating data, and project management software are tools available to assist in resource estimating. It is important that the people who help determine what resources are necessary include people who have experience and expertise in similar projects and with the organization performing the project.

Important questions to answer in activity resource estimating include:

- How difficult will it be to do specific activities on this project?
- Is there anything unique in the project's scope statement that will affect resources?
- What is the organization's history in doing similar activities? Has the organization done similar tasks before? What level of personnel did the work?
- Does the organization have people, equipment, and materials that are capable and available for performing the work? Are there any organizational policies that might affect the availability of resources?
- Does the organization need to acquire more resources to accomplish the work? Would it make sense to outsource some of the work? Will outsourcing increase or decrease the amount of resources needed and when they'll be available?

A project's activity list, activity attributes, resource calendars or availability, enterprise environmental factors, and organizational process assets (such as policies regarding staffing and outsourcing) are all important inputs to answering these questions. During the early phases of a project, the project team may not know which specific people, equipment, and materials will be available. For example, they might know from past projects that there will be a mix of experienced and inexperienced programmers working on a project. They might also have information available that approximates the number of people or hours it normally takes to perform specific activities.

It is important to thoroughly brainstorm and evaluate alternatives related to resources, especially on projects that involve people from multiple disciplines and companies. Since most projects involve many human resources and the majority of costs are for salaries and benefits, it is often effective to solicit ideas from different people to help develop alternatives and address resource-related issues early in a project. The resource estimates should also be updated as more detailed information becomes available.

The main outputs of the resource estimating process include a list of activity resource requirements, a resource breakdown structure, and project document updates. For example, if junior employees will be assigned to many activities, the project manager might request that additional activities, time, and resources be approved to help train and mentor those employees. In addition to providing the basis for estimating activity durations, estimating activity resources provides vital information for project cost estimating (Chapter 7), project human resource management (Chapter 9), project communications management (Chapter 10), project risk management (Chapter 11), and project procurement management (Chapter 12). For example, a **resource breakdown structure** is a hierarchical structure that identifies the project's resources by category and type. Resource categories might include analysts, programmers, and testers. Under programmers, there might be types of programmers, such as Java programmers or COBOL programmers. This information would be helpful in determining resource costs, acquiring resources, and so on.

ESTIMATING ACTIVITY DURATIONS

After working with key stakeholders to define activities, determine their dependencies, and estimate their resources, the next process in project time management is to estimate the duration of activities. It is important to note that **duration** includes the actual amount of time worked on an activity *plus* elapsed time. For example, even though it might take one workweek or five workdays to do the actual work, the duration estimate might be two weeks to allow extra time needed to obtain outside information. The resources assigned to a task will also affect the task duration estimate.

Do not confuse duration with **effort**, which is the number of workdays or work hours required to complete a task. A duration estimate of one day could be based on eight hours of work or eighty hours of work. Duration relates to the time estimate, not the effort estimate. Of course, the two are related, so project team members must document their assumptions when creating duration estimates and update the estimates as the project progresses. The people who will actually do the work, in particular, should have a lot of say in these duration estimates, since they are the ones whose performance will be evaluated on meeting them. If scope changes occur on the project, the duration estimates should be updated to reflect those changes. It is also helpful to review similar projects and seek the advice of experts in estimating activity durations.

There are several inputs to activity duration estimating. The activity list, activity attributes, activity resource requirements, resource calendars, project scope statement, enterprise environmental factors, and organizational process assets all include information that affect duration estimates. In addition to reviewing past project information, the team should also review the accuracy of the duration estimates thus far on the project. For example, if they find that all of their estimates have been much too long or short, the team should update the estimates to reflect what they have learned. One of the most important considerations in making activity duration estimates is the availability of resources, especially human resources. What specific skills do people need to do the work? What are the skill levels of the people assigned to the project? How many people are expected to be available to work on the project at any one time?

The outputs of activity duration estimating include activity duration estimates and project document updates. Duration estimates are often provided as a discrete number, such as four weeks, or as a range, such as three to five weeks, or as a three-point estimate. A **three-point estimate** is an estimate that includes an optimistic, most likely, and pessimistic estimate, such as three weeks for the optimistic, four weeks for the most likely, and five weeks for the pessimistic estimate. The optimistic estimate is based on a best-case scenario, while the pessimistic estimate is based on a worst-case scenario. The most likely estimate, as it sounds, is an estimate based on a most likely or expected scenario. A three-point estimate is required for performing PERT estimates, as described later in this chapter, and for performing Monte Carlo simulations, described in Chapter 11, Project Risk Management. Other duration estimating techniques include analogous and parametric estimating and reserve analysis, as described in Chapter 7, Project Cost Management. Expert judgment is also an important tool for developing good activity duration estimates.

DEVELOPING THE SCHEDULE

Schedule development uses the results of all the preceding project time management processes to determine the start and end dates of the project. There are often several iterations of all the project time management processes before a project schedule is finalized. The ultimate goal of developing the schedule is to create a realistic project schedule that provides a basis for monitoring project progress for the time dimension of the project. The main outputs of this process are the project schedule, a schedule baseline, project document updates, and schedule data. Some project teams create a computerized model to create a network diagram, enter resource requirements and availability by time period, and adjust other information to quickly generate alternative schedules. See Appendix A for information on using Project 2007 to assist in schedule development.

Several tools and techniques assist in schedule development:

- A Gantt chart is a common tool for displaying project schedule information.
- Critical path analysis is a very important tool for developing and controlling project schedules.
- Critical chain scheduling is a technique that focuses on limited resources when creating a project schedule.
- PERT analysis is a means for considering schedule risk on projects.

The following sections provide samples of each of these tools and techniques and discuss their advantages and disadvantages. (See the *PMBOK® Guide, Fourth Edition* to learn how these main techniques and others are broken into additional categories.)

Gantt Charts

Gantt charts provide a standard format for displaying project schedule information by listing project activities and their corresponding start and finish dates in a calendar format. Gantt charts are sometimes referred to as bar charts since the activities' start and end dates are shown as horizontal bars. Figure 6-5 shows a simple Gantt chart for Project X created with Microsoft Project. Figure 6-6 shows a Gantt chart that is more sophisticated based on a software launch project from a template provided by Microsoft. Recall that the activities on the Gantt chart should coincide with the activities on the WBS, which should coincide with the activity list and milestone list. Notice that the software launch project's Gantt chart contains milestones, summary tasks, individual task durations, and arrows showing task dependencies.

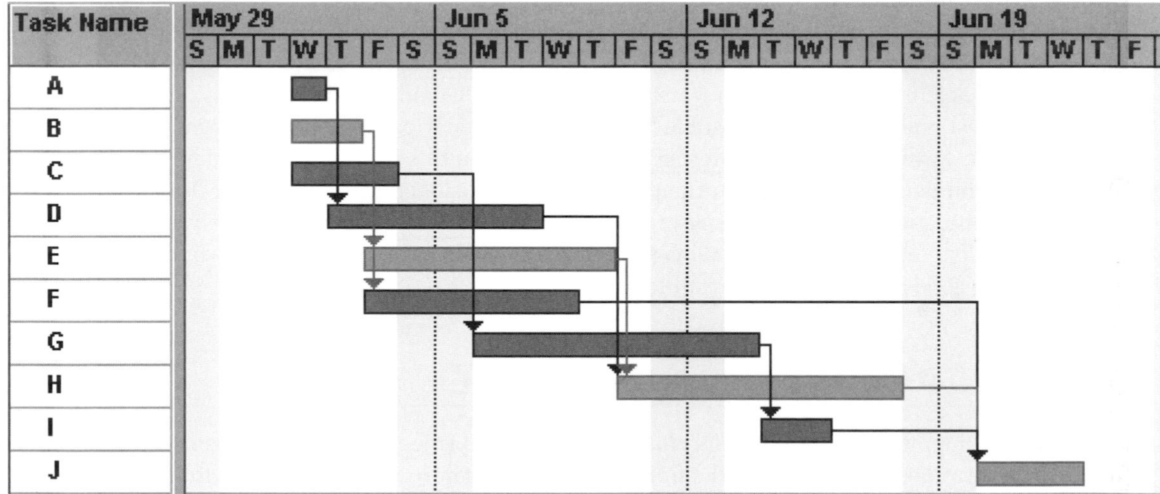

FIGURE 6-5 Gantt chart for Project X

Notice the different symbols on the software launch project's Gantt chart (Figure 6-6):

- The black diamond symbol represents a milestone. In Figure 6-6, Task 1, "Marketing Plan distributed," is a milestone that occurs on March 17. Tasks 3, 4, 8, 9, 14, 25, 27, 43, and 45 are also milestones. For very large projects, top managers might want to see only milestones on a Gantt chart. Microsoft Project allows you to filter information displayed on a Gantt chart so you can easily show specific tasks, such as milestones.
- The thick black bars with arrows at the beginning and end represent summary tasks. For example, Activities 12 through 15—"Develop creative briefs," "Develop concepts," "Creative concepts," and "Ad development"—are all subtasks of the summary task called "Advertising," Task 11. WBS activities are referred to as tasks and subtasks in most project management software.

- The light gray horizontal bars such as those found in Figure 6-6 for Tasks 5, 6, 7, 10, 12, 13, 15, 22, 24, 26, and 44, represent the duration of each individual task. For example, the light gray bar for Subtask 5, "Packaging," starts in mid-February and extends until early May.
- Arrows connecting these symbols show relationships or dependencies between tasks. Gantt charts often do not show dependencies, which is their major disadvantage. If dependencies have been established in Microsoft Project, they are automatically displayed on the Gantt chart.

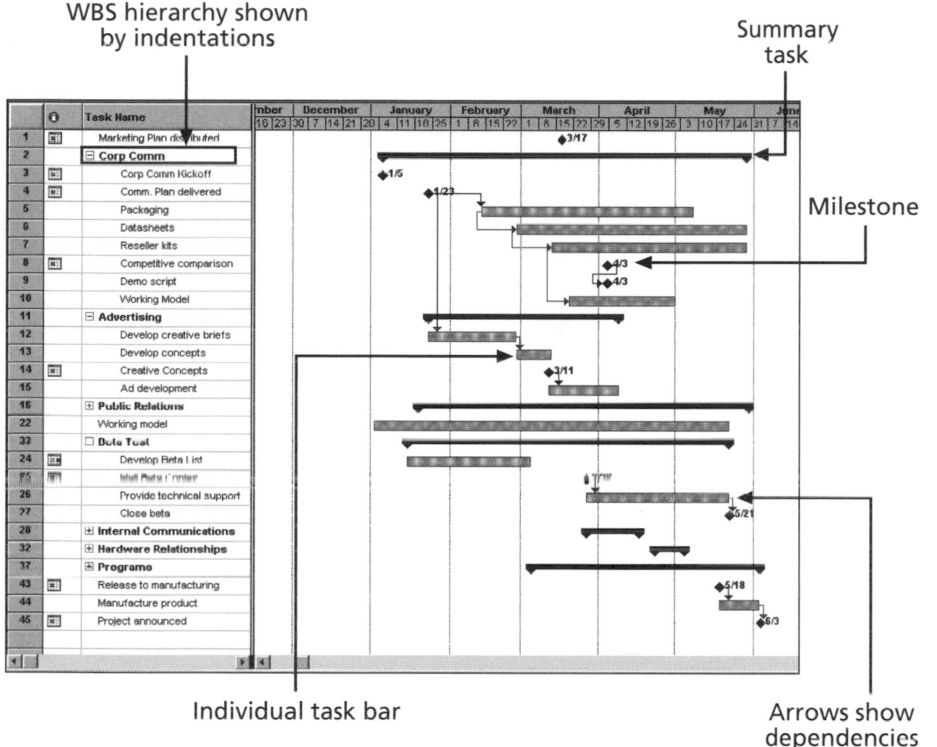

FIGURE 6-6 Gantt chart for software launch project

Adding Milestones to Gantt Charts

Milestones can be a particularly important part of schedules, especially for large projects. Many people like to focus on meeting milestones, so you can create milestones to emphasize important events or accomplishments on projects. Normally, you create milestones by entering tasks with zero duration. In Microsoft Project, you can also mark any task as a milestone by checking the appropriate box in the Advanced tab of the Task Information dialog box. The duration of the task will not change to zero, but the Gantt chart will show the milestone symbol to represent that task based on its start date. See Appendix A for more information.

To make milestones meaningful, some people use the SMART criteria to help define them. The **SMART criteria** are guidelines suggesting that milestones should be:

- Specific
- Measurable
- Assignable
- Realistic
- Time-framed

For example, distributing a marketing plan is specific, measurable, and assignable if everyone knows what should be in the marketing plan, how it should be distributed, how many copies should be distributed and to whom, and who is responsible for the actual delivery. Distributing the marketing plan is realistic and able to be time-framed if it is an achievable event and scheduled at an appropriate time.

BEST PRACTICE

Schedule risk is inherent in the development of complex systems. Luc Richard, the founder of *www.projectmangler.com*, suggests that project managers can reduce schedule risk through project milestones, a best practice that involves identifying and tracking significant points or achievements in the project. The five key points of using project milestones include the following:

1. Define milestones early in the project and include them in the Gantt chart to provide a visual guide.
2. Keep milestones small and frequent.
3. The set of milestones must be all-encompassing.
4. Each milestone must be binary, meaning it is either complete or incomplete.
5. Carefully monitor the critical path.

Additional best practices Richard recommends for software development projects include the following:

- Monitor the project's progress and revise the plan.
- Build on a solid base; that means developing a system with less than a .1 percent defect rate.
- Assign the right people to the right tasks. Put the best developers on the critical tasks.
- Start with high-risk tasks.
- "Don't boil the ocean." In other words, if the entire project consists of high-risk tasks, then the project itself is high-risk and bound for failure.
- Integrate early and often, and follow practices like the daily build process.[5] (A daily build involves compiling the latest version of a software program each day to ensure that all required dependencies are present and that the program is tested to avoid introducing new bugs.)

Using Tracking Gantt Charts to Compare Planned and Actual Dates

You can use a special form of a Gantt chart to evaluate progress on a project by showing actual schedule information. Figure 6-7 shows a **Tracking Gantt chart**—a Gantt chart that compares planned and actual project schedule information. The planned schedule dates for activities are called the **baseline dates**, and the entire approved planned schedule is called the **schedule baseline**. The Tracking Gantt chart includes columns (hidden in Figure 6-7) labeled "Start" and "Finish" to represent actual start and finish dates for each task, as well as columns labeled "Baseline Start" and "Baseline Finish" to represent planned start and finish dates for each task. In this example, the project is completed, but several tasks missed their planned start and finish dates.

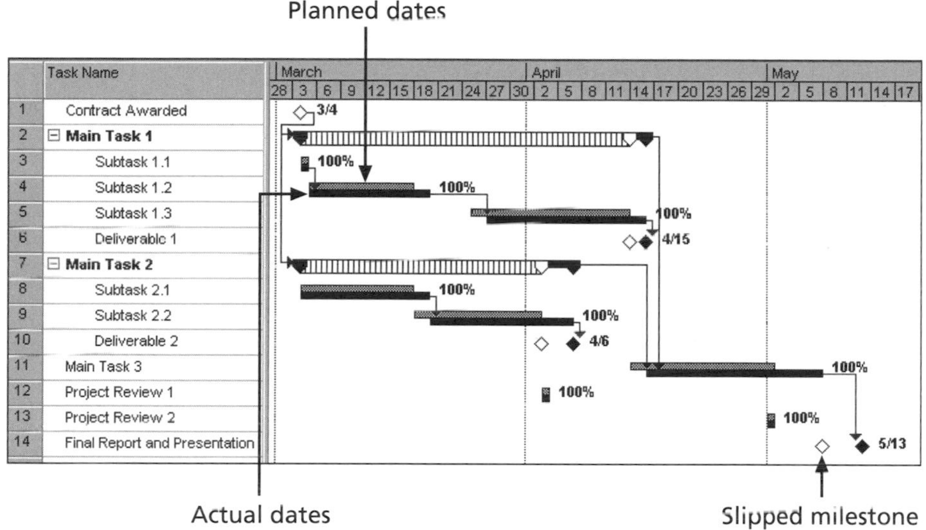

FIGURE 6-7 Sample Tracking Gantt chart

To serve as a progress evaluation tool, a Tracking Gantt chart uses a few additional symbols:

- Notice that the Gantt chart in Figure 6-7 often shows two horizontal bars for tasks. The top horizontal bar represents the planned or baseline duration for each task. The bar below it represents the actual duration. Subtasks 1.2 and 1.3 illustrate this type of display. If these two bars are the same length, and start and end on the same dates, then the actual schedule was the same as the planned schedule for that task. This scheduling occurred for Subtask 1.1, where the task started and ended as planned on March 4. If the bars do not start and end on the same dates, then the actual schedule differed from the planned or baseline schedule. If the top horizontal bar is shorter than the bottom one, the task took longer than planned, as you can see for Subtask 1.2. If the top horizontal bar is longer than the bottom one, the task took less time than planned. A striped horizontal bar, illustrated by Main Tasks 1 and 2, represents the planned duration for summary tasks. The black bar adjoining it shows progress for summary tasks. For example, Main Task 2 clearly shows the actual duration took longer than what was planned.
- A white diamond on the Tracking Gantt chart represents a **slipped milestone**. A slipped milestone means the milestone activity was actually completed later than originally planned. For example, the last task provides an example of a

slipped milestone since the final report and presentation were completed later than planned.

- Percentages to the right of the horizontal bars display the percentage of work completed for each task. For example, 100 percent means the task is finished, 50 percent means the task is still in progress and is 50 percent completed.

A Tracking Gantt chart is based on the percentage of work completed for project tasks or the actual start and finish dates. It allows the project manager to monitor schedule progress on individual tasks and the whole project. For example, Figure 6-7 shows that this project is completed. It started on time, but it finished a little late, on May 13 (5/13) versus May 8.

The main advantage of using Gantt charts is that they provide a standard format for displaying planned and actual project schedule information. In addition, they are easy to create and understand. The main disadvantage of Gantt charts is that they do not *usually* show relationships or dependencies between tasks. If Gantt charts are created using project management software and tasks are linked, then the dependencies *will* be displayed, but differently than they would be displayed on a network diagram. However, whether you prefer viewing dependencies on a Gantt chart or network diagram is a matter of personal preference.

Critical Path Method

Many projects fail to meet schedule expectations. **Critical path method (CPM)**—also called **critical path analysis**—is a network diagramming technique used to predict total project duration. This important tool will help you combat project schedule overruns. A **critical path** for a project is the series of activities that determine the *earliest* time by which the project can be completed. It is the *longest* path through the network diagram and has the least amount of slack or float. **Slack** or **float** is the amount of time an activity may be delayed without delaying a succeeding activity or the project finish date. There are normally several tasks done in parallel on projects, and most projects have multiple paths through a network diagram. The longest path or path containing the critical tasks is what is driving the completion date for the project. You are not finished with the project until you have finished *all* the tasks.

Calculating the Critical Path

To find the critical path for a project, you must first develop a good network diagram, which, in turn, requires a good activity list based on the WBS. Once you create a network diagram, you must also estimate the duration of each activity to determine the critical path. Calculating the critical path involves adding the durations for all activities on each path through the network diagram. The longest path is the critical path.

Figure 6-8 shows the AOA network diagram for Project X again. Note that you can use either the AOA or precedence diagramming method to determine the critical path on projects. Figure 6-8 shows all of the paths—a total of four—through the network diagram. Note that each path starts at the first node (1) and ends at the last node (8) on the AOA network diagram. This figure also shows the length or total duration of each path through the network diagram. These lengths are computed by adding the durations of each activity on the path. Since path B-E-H-J at 16 days has the longest duration, it is the critical path for the project.

What does the critical path really mean? The critical path shows the shortest time in which a project can be completed. Even though the critical path is the *longest* path, it

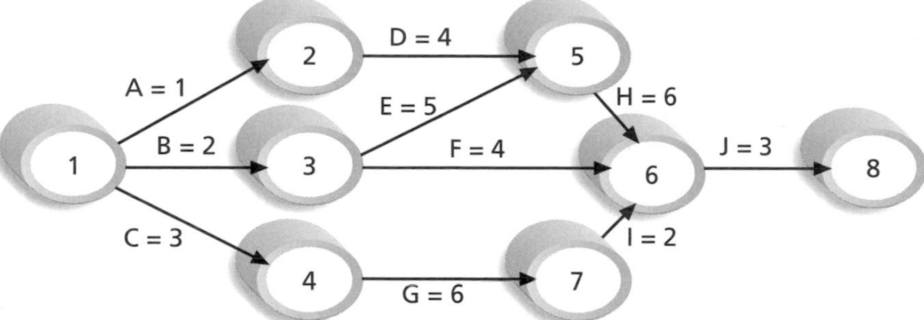

Note: Assume all durations are in days.

Path 1:	A-D-H-J	Length = 1+4+6+3 = 14 days
Path 2:	B-E-H-J	Length = 2+5+6+3 = 16 days
Path 3:	B-F-J	Length = 2+4+3 = 9 days
Path 4:	C-G-I-J	Length = 3+6+2+3 = 14 days

Since the critical path is the longest path through the network diagram, Path 2, B-E-H-J, is the critical path for Project X.

FIGURE 6-8 Determining the critical path for Project X

represents the *shortest* time it takes to complete a project. If one or more of the activities on the critical path takes longer than planned, the whole project schedule will slip *unless* the project manager takes corrective action.

Project teams can be creative in managing the critical path. For example, Joan Knutson, a well-known author and speaker in the project management field, often describes how a gorilla helped Apple computer complete a project on time. Team members worked in an area with cubicles, and whoever was in charge of a task currently on the critical path had a big, stuffed gorilla on top of his or her cubicle. Everyone knew that person was under the most time pressure, so they tried not to distract him or her. When a critical task was completed, the person in charge of the next critical task received the gorilla.

Growing Grass Can Be on the Critical Path

People are often confused about what the critical path is for a project or what it really means. Some people think the critical path includes the most critical activities. However, the critical path is concerned only with the time dimension of a project. The fact that its name includes the word *critical* does not mean that it includes all critical activities. For example, Frank Addeman, Executive Project Director at Walt Disney Imagineering, explained in a keynote address at a PMI-ISSIG Professional Development Seminar that growing grass was on the critical path for building Disney's Animal Kingdom theme park! This 500-acre park required special grass for its animal inhabitants, and some of the grass took years to grow. Another misconception is that the critical path is the shortest path through the network diagram. In some areas, such as transportation modeling, similar network diagrams are drawn in which identifying the shortest path is the goal. For a project, however, each task or activity must be done in order to complete the project. It is not a matter of choosing the shortest path.

Other aspects of critical path analysis may cause confusion. Can there be more than one critical path on a project? Does the critical path ever change? In the Project X example, suppose that Activity A has a duration estimate of three days instead of one day. This new duration estimate would make the length of Path 1 equal to 16 days. Now the project has two longest paths of equal duration, so there are two critical paths. Therefore, there *can* be more than one critical path on a project. Project managers should closely monitor performance of activities on the critical path to avoid late project completion. If there is more than one critical path, project managers must keep their eyes on all of them.

The critical path on a project can change as the project progresses. For example, suppose everything is going as planned at the beginning of the project. In this example, suppose Activities A, B, C, D, E, F, and G all start and finish as planned. Then suppose Activity I runs into problems. If Activity I takes more than four days, it will cause path C-G-I-J to be longer than the other paths, assuming they progress as planned. This change would cause path C-G-I-J to become the new critical path. Therefore, the critical path can change on a project.

Using Critical Path Analysis to Make Schedule Trade-Offs

It is important to know what the critical path is throughout the life of a project so the product manager *can* make trade-offs. If the project manager knows that one of the tasks on the critical path is behind schedule, he or she needs to decide what to do about it. Should the schedule be renegotiated with stakeholders? Should more resources be allocated to other items on the critical path to make up for that time? Is it okay if the project finishes behind schedule? By keeping track of the critical path, the project manager and his or her team take a proactive role in managing the project schedule.

A technique that can help project managers make schedule trade-offs is determining the free slack and total slack for each project activity. **Free slack** or **free float** is the amount of time an activity can be delayed without delaying the early start date of any immediately following activities. The **early start date** for an activity is the earliest possible time an activity can start based on the project network logic. **Total slack** or **total float** is the amount of time an activity can be delayed from its early start without delaying the planned project finish date.

Project managers calculate free slack and total slack by doing a forward and backward pass through a network diagram. A **forward pass** determines the early start and early finish dates for each activity. The **early finish date** for an activity is the earliest possible time an activity can finish based on the project network logic. The project start date is equal to the early start date for the first network diagram activity. Early start plus the duration of the first activity is equal to the early finish date of the first activity. It is also equal to the early start date of each subsequent activity unless an activity has multiple predecessors. When an activity has multiple predecessors, its early start date is the latest of the early finish datesof those predecessors. For example, Tasks D and E immediately precede Task H in Figure 6-8. The early start date for Task H, therefore, is the early finish date of Task E, since it occurs later than the early finish date of Task D. A **backward pass** through the network diagram determines the late start and late finish dates for each activity in a similar fashion. The **late start date** for an activity is the latest possible time an activity might begin without delaying the project finish date. The **late finish date** for an activity is the latest possible time an activity can be completed without delaying the project finish date.

Project managers can determine the early and late start and finish dates of each activity by hand. For example, Figure 6-9 shows a simple network diagram with three tasks, A, B, and C. Tasks A and B both precede Task C. Assume all duration estimates are in days. Task A has an estimated duration of 5 days, Task B has an estimated duration of 10 days, and Task C has an estimated duration of 7 days. There are only two paths through this small network diagram: path A-C has a duration of 12 days (5+7), and path B-C has a duration of 17 days (10+7). Since path B-C is longest, it is the critical path. There is no float or slack on this path, so the early and late start and finish dates are the same. However, Task A has 5 days of float or slack. Its early start date is day 0, and its late start date is day 5. Its early finish date is day 5, and its late finish date is day 10. Both the free and total float amounts for Task A are the same at 5 days.

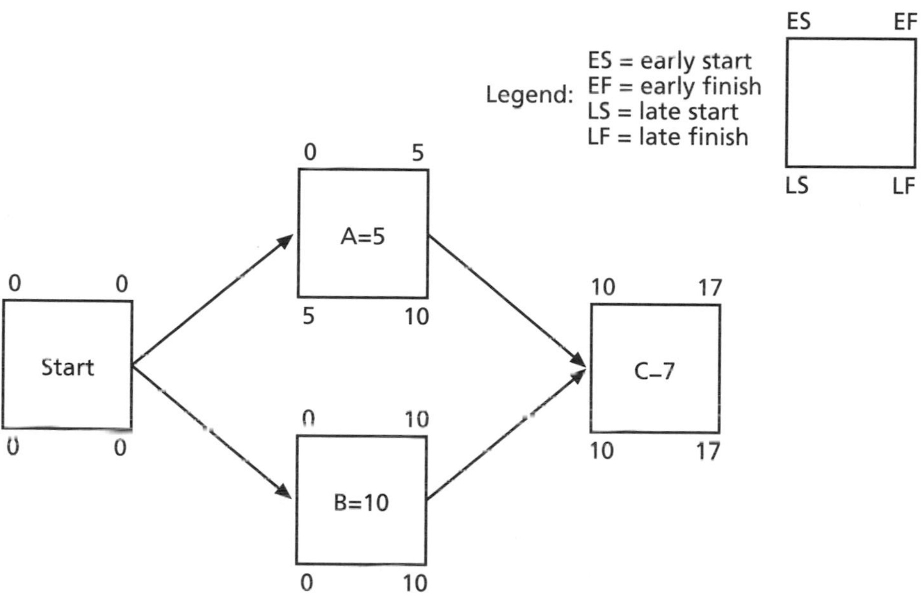

FIGURE 6-9 Calculating early and late start and finish dates

A much faster and easier way to determine early and late start and finish dates and free and total slack amounts for activities is by using project management software. Table 6-1 shows the free and total slack for all activities on the network diagram for Project X after entering the data from Figure 6-8 and assuming Tasks A, B, and C started on August 3, 2009. (The network diagram is shown in Figure 6-4.) The data in this table was created by selecting the Schedule Table view in Microsoft Project. Knowing the amount of float or slack allows project managers to know whether the schedule is flexible and how flexible it might be. For example, at 7 days (7d), Task F has the most free and total slack. The most slack on any other activity is only 2 days (2d). Understanding how to create and use slack information provides a basis for negotiating (or not negotiating) project schedules. See the Help information in Microsoft Project or research other resources for more detailed information on calculating slack.

TABLE 6-1 Free and total float or slack for Project X

Task Name	Start	Finish	Late Start	Late Finish	Free Slack	Total Slack
A	8/3/09	8/3/09	8/5/09	8/5/09	0d	2d
B	8/3/09	8/4/09	8/3/09	8/4/09	0d	0d
C	8/3/09	8/5/09	8/5/09	8/7/09	0d	2d
D	8/4/09	8/7/09	8/6/09	8/11/09	2d	2d
E	8/5/09	8/11/09	8/5/09	8/11/09	0d	0d
F	8/5/09	8/10/09	8/14/09	8/17/09	7d	7d
G	8/6/09	8/13/09	8/10/09	8/17/09	0d	2d
H	8/12/09	8/19/09	8/12/09	8/19/09	0d	0d
I	8/14/09	8/17/09	8/18/09	8/19/09	2d	2d
J	8/20/09	8/24/09	8/20/09	8/24/09	0d	0d

Using the Critical Path to Shorten a Project Schedule

It is common for stakeholders to want to shorten a project schedule estimate. A project team may have done their best to develop a project schedule by defining activities, determining sequencing, and estimating resources and durations for each activity. The results of this work may have shown that the project team needs ten months to complete the project. The sponsor might ask if the project can be done in eight or nine months. Rarely do people ask the project team to take longer than they suggested. By knowing the critical path, the project manager and his or her team can use several duration compression techniques to shorten the project schedule. One technique is to reduce the duration of activities on the critical path. The project manager can shorten the duration of critical path activities by allocating more resources to those activities or by changing their scope.

Recall that Sue Johnson in the opening case was having schedule problems with the online registration project because several users missed important project review meetings and one of the senior programmers quit. If Sue and her team created a realistic project schedule, produced accurate duration estimates, and established dependencies between tasks, they could analyze their status in terms of meeting the May 1 deadline. If some activities on the critical path had already slipped and they did not build in extra time at the end of the project, then they would have to take corrective actions to finish the project on time. Sue could request that her company or the college provide more people to work on the project in an effort to make up time. She could also request that the scope of activities be reduced to complete the project on time. Sue could also use project time management techniques, such as crashing or fast tracking, to shorten the project schedule.

Crashing is a technique for making cost and schedule trade-offs to obtain the greatest amount of schedule compression for the least incremental cost. For example, suppose one of the items on the critical path for the online registration project was entering course data for the new semester into the new system. If this task is yet to be done and was originally estimated to take two weeks based on the college providing one part-time data entry clerk, Sue could suggest that the college have the clerk work full time to finish the task in one week instead of two. This change would not cost Sue's company more money, and it could shorten the project end date by one week. If the college could not meet this request, Sue could consider hiring a temporary data entry person for one week to help get the task done faster. By focusing on tasks on the critical path that could be done more quickly for no extra cost or a small cost, the project schedule can be shortened.

The main advantage of crashing is shortening the time it takes to finish a project. The main disadvantage of crashing is that it often increases total project costs. You will learn more about project costs in Chapter 7, Project Cost Management.

Another technique for shortening a project schedule is fast tracking. **Fast tracking** involves doing activities in parallel that you would normally do in sequence. For example, Sue Johnson's project team may have planned not to start any of the coding for the online registration system until *all* of the analysis was done. Instead, they could consider starting some coding activity before the analysis is completed. The main advantage of fast tracking, like crashing, is that it can shorten the time it takes to finish a project. The main disadvantage of fast tracking is that it can end up lengthening the project schedule since starting some tasks too soon often increases project risk and results in rework.

Importance of Updating Critical Path Data

In addition to finding the critical path at the beginning of a project, it is important to update the schedule with actual data. After the project team completes activities, the project manager should document the actual durations of those activities. He or she should also document revised estimates for activities in progress or yet to be started. These revisions often cause a project's critical path to change, resulting in a new estimated completion date for the project. Again, proactive project managers and their teams stay on top of changes so they can make informed decisions and keep stakeholders informed of, and involved in, major project decisions.

Critical Chain Scheduling

Another technique that addresses the challenge of meeting or beating project finish dates is an application of the Theory of Constraints called critical chain scheduling. The **Theory of Constraints (TOC)** is a management philosophy developed by Eliyahu M. Goldratt and discussed in his books *The Goal* and *Critical Chain*. The Theory of Constraints is based on the fact that, like a chain with its weakest link, any complex system at any point in time often has only one aspect or constraint that limits its ability to achieve more of its goal. For the system to attain any significant improvements, that constraint must be identified, and the whole system must be managed with it in mind. **Critical chain scheduling** is a method of scheduling that considers limited resources when creating a project schedule and includes buffers to protect the project completion date.

An important concept in critical chain scheduling is the availability of scarce resources. Some projects cannot be done unless a particular resource is available to work on one or several tasks. For example, if a television station wants to produce a show centered around a particular celebrity, it must first check the availability of that celebrity. As another example, if a particular piece of equipment is needed full time to complete each of two tasks that were originally planned to occur simultaneously, critical chain scheduling acknowledges that you must either delay one of those tasks until the equipment is available or find another piece of equipment in order to meet the schedule. Other important concepts related to critical chain scheduling include multitasking and time buffers.

Multitasking occurs when a resource works on more than one task at a time. This situation occurs frequently on projects. People are assigned to multiple tasks within the same project or different tasks on multiple projects. For example, suppose someone is working on three different tasks, Task 1, Task 2, and Task 3, for three different projects, and each task takes 10 days to complete. If the person did not multitask, and instead completed each task sequentially, starting with Task 1, then Task 1 would be completed after day 10, Task 2 would be completed after day 20, and Task 3 would be completed after day 30, as shown in Figure 6-10a. However, because many people in this situation try to please all three people who need their tasks completed, they often work on the first task for some time, then the second, then the third, then go back to the first task, and so on, as shown in Figure 6-10b. In this example, the tasks were all half-done one at a time, then completed one at a time. Task 1 is now completed at the end of day 20 instead of day 10, Task 2 is completed at the end of day 25 instead of day 20, and Task 3 is still completed on day 30. This example illustrates how multitasking can delay task completions. Multitasking also often involves wasted setup time, which increases total duration.

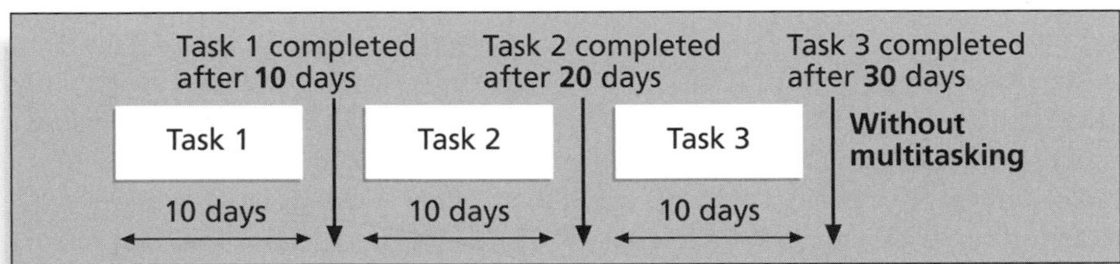

FIGURE 6-10a Three tasks without multitasking

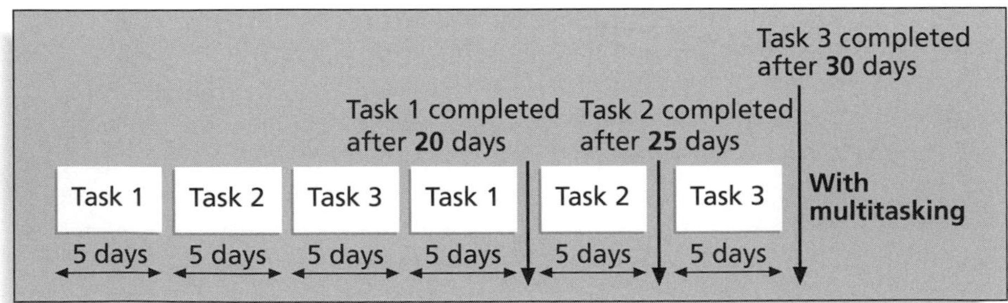

FIGURE 6-10b Three tasks with multitasking

Critical chain scheduling assumes that resources do not multitask or at least minimize multitasking. Someone should not be assigned to two tasks simultaneously on the same project when critical chain scheduling is in effect. Likewise, critical chain theory suggests that projects be prioritized so people working on more than one project at a time know which tasks take priority. Preventing multitasking avoids resource conflicts and wasted setup time caused by shifting between multiple tasks over time.

An essential concept to improving project finish dates with critical chain scheduling is to change the way people make task estimates. Many people add a safety or **buffer**, which is additional time to complete a task, to an estimate to account for various factors. These factors include the negative effects of multitasking, distractions and interruptions, fear that estimates will be reduced, Murphy's Law, and so on. **Murphy's Law** states that if something can go wrong, it will. Critical chain scheduling removes buffers from individual tasks and instead creates a **project buffer**, which is additional time added before the project's due date. Critical chain scheduling also protects tasks on the critical chain from being delayed by using **feeding buffers**, which consist of additional time added before tasks on the critical chain that are preceded by non-critical-path tasks.

Figure 6-11 provides an example of a network diagram constructed using critical chain scheduling. Note that the critical chain accounts for a limited resource, X, and the schedule includes use of feeding buffers and a project buffer in the network diagram. The tasks marked with an X are part of the critical chain, which can be interpreted as being the critical path using this technique. The task estimates in critical chain scheduling should be shorter than traditional estimates because they do not include their own buffers. Not having task buffers should mean less occurrence of **Parkinson's Law**, which states that work expands to fill the time allowed. The feeding and project buffers protect the date that really needs to be met—the project completion date.

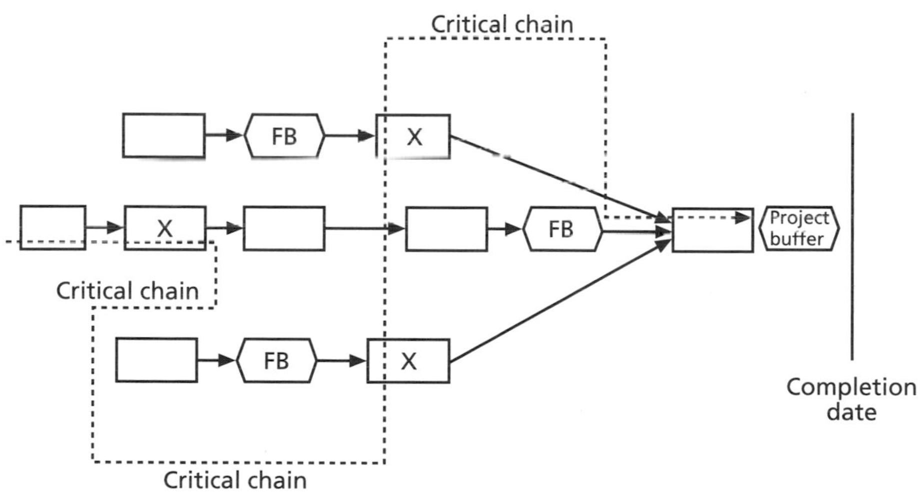

FIGURE 6-11 Example of critical chain scheduling[6]

Several organizations have reported successes with critical chain scheduling. For example, the U.S. health care industry is learning to think differently by using the Theory of Constraints.

> "Consider a relatively simple system of a physician's office or clinic. The steps in the process could be patients checking in, filling out forms, having vital signs taken by a nurse, seeing the physician, seeing the nurse for a prescribed procedure such as vaccination, and so forth. These steps could take place in a simple linear sequence or chain ... This process or chain only can produce an average of eight per hour. The chain is only as strong as its weakest link and the rate of the slowest resource in this example, the weakest link, is eight. This is true regardless of how fast each of the other resources can process individually, how much work is stuffed into the pipeline, or how complex the process or set of interconnected processes is to complete. Moreover, improving the performance of any link besides the constraint does nothing to improve the system as a whole."[7]

As you can see, critical chain scheduling is a fairly complicated yet powerful tool that involves critical path analysis, resource constraints, and changes in how task estimates are made in terms of buffers. Some consider critical chain scheduling one of the most important new concepts in the field of project management.

Program Evaluation and Review Technique (PERT)

Another project time management technique is the **Program Evaluation and Review Technique (PERT)**—a network analysis technique used to estimate project duration when there is a high degree of uncertainty about the individual activity duration estimates. PERT applies the critical path method (CPM) to a weighted average duration estimate. This approach was developed about the same time as CPM, in the late 1950s, and also uses network diagrams, which are still sometimes referred to as PERT charts.

PERT uses **probabilistic time estimates**—duration estimates based on using optimistic, most likely, and pessimistic estimates of activity durations—instead of one specific or discrete duration estimate, as CPM does. In other words, PERT uses a three-point estimate, as described earlier. To use PERT, you calculate a weighted average for the duration estimate of each project activity using the following formula:

$$\text{PERT weighted average} = \frac{\text{optimistic time} + 4 * \text{most likely time} + \text{pessimistic time}}{6}$$

By using the **PERT weighted average** for each activity duration estimate, the total project duration estimate takes into account the risk or uncertainty in the individual activity estimates.

Suppose Sue Johnson's project team in the opening case used PERT to determine the schedule for the online registration system project. They would have to collect numbers for the optimistic, most likely, and pessimistic duration estimates for each project activity. Suppose one of the activities was to design an input screen for the system. Someone might estimate that it would take about two weeks or 10 workdays to do this activity. Without using PERT, the duration estimate for that activity would be 10 workdays. Using PERT, the project team would also need to estimate the pessimistic and optimistic times for completing this activity. Suppose an optimistic estimate is that the input screen can be designed in eight workdays, and a pessimistic time estimate is 24 workdays. Applying the PERT formula, you get the following:

$$\text{PERT weighted average} = \frac{8 \text{ workdays } + 4 * 10 \text{ workdays} + 24 \text{ workdays}}{6}$$
$$= 12 \text{ work days}$$

Instead of using the most likely duration estimate of 10 workdays, the project team would use 12 workdays when doing critical path analysis. These additional two days could really help the project team in getting the work completed on time.

The main advantage of PERT is that it attempts to address the risk associated with duration estimates. Since many projects exceed schedule estimates, PERT may help in developing schedules that are more realistic. PERT's main disadvantages are that it involves more work than CPM since it requires several duration estimates, and there are better probabilistic methods for assessing schedule risk (see the information on Monte Carlo simulations in Chapter 11, Project Risk Management).

CONTROLLING THE SCHEDULE

The final process in project time management is controlling the schedule. Like scope control, schedule control is a portion of the integrated change control process under project integration management. The goal of schedule control is to know the status of the schedule, influence the factors that cause schedule changes, determine that the schedule has changed, and manage changes when they occur.

The main inputs to schedule control are the project management plan, project schedule, work performance data, and organizational process assets. Some of tools and techniques include:

- Progress reports
- A schedule change control system, operated as part of the integrated change control system described in Chapter 4, Project Integration Management
- A scheduling tool and/or project management software, such as Project 2007 or similar software
- Schedule comparison bar charts, such as the Tracking Gantt chart
- Variance analysis, such as analyzing float or slack
- What-if scenario analysis, which can be done manually or with the aid of software
- Adjusting leads and lags
- Schedule compression, such as crashing and fast-tracking described earlier in this chapter
- Performance measurement, such as earned value, described in Chapter 7, Project Cost Management
- Resource leveling, as described in Chapter 9, Project Human Resource Management

The main outputs of schedule control include work performance measurements, organizational process assets updates, such as lessons-learned reports related to schedule control, change requests, project management plan updates, and project document updates.

There are many issues involved in controlling changes to project schedules. It is important first to ensure that the project schedule is realistic. Many projects, especially in information technology, have very unrealistic schedule expectations. It is also important to use discipline and leadership to emphasize the importance of following and meeting project schedules. Although the various tools and techniques assist in developing and managing project schedules, project managers must handle several people-related issues to keep projects on track. "Most projects fail because of people issues, not from failure to draw a good PERT chart."[8] Project managers can perform a number of reality checks that will help them manage changes to project schedules. Several soft skills can help project managers to control schedule changes.

Reality Checks on Scheduling and the Need for Discipline

It is important for projects to have realistic schedule goals and for project managers to use discipline to help meet those goals. One of the first reality checks a project manager should make is to review the draft schedule usually included in the project charter. Although this draft schedule might include only a project start and end date, the project charter sets some initial schedule expectations for the project. Next, the project manager and his or her team should prepare a more detailed schedule and get stakeholders' approval. To establish the schedule, it is critical to get involvement and commitment from all project team members, top management, the customer, and other key stakeholders.

Several experts have written about the lack of realistic schedule estimates for information technology projects. Ed Yourdon, a well-known and respected software development expert, describes "death march" projects as projects doomed for failure from the start, due to unclear and/or unrealistic expectations, especially for meeting time constraints.[9] For example, in 2008, twenty months after a project was started to overhaul and integrate more than 300 key IT systems for the city of Portland, Oregon, the city changed IT consultants as the cost and schedule for the project continued to increase. Robert Stoll, a Portland attorney representing Ariston Consulting & Technologies, Inc. in the termination negotiations with the city, said Ariston did the best it could do with the information it was given by the city. From Ariston's point of view, he said, city officials who prepared the project requirements and put it out for bid weren't familiar enough with their overall IT systems and needs, making the goal for the work an impossible target to hit—a death march project. "It's sort of garbage in, garbage out, if you know what I mean," Stoll said. "I certainly don't think that Ariston made any mistakes."[10]

Experts in chaos theory suggest that project managers must account not only for project risks based upon their inaccuracies in estimation, but also for the complex behavior of the organization brought on by multiple independent project managers who also must estimate project risks. The interdependencies of such a complex system will typically result in a generally predictable inefficiency. They propose that this inefficiency can be addressed by arranging for additional resources to be committed to the project. Using an analogy related to the behavior of traffic systems, they suggest that project managers schedule resources on the project so that no single resource is utilized more than 75 percent. The actual inefficiency estimate can and should be assessed for each individual organization, but typically will vary between 70 and 80 percent.[11] It is very important, therefore, to set realistic project schedules and allow for contingencies throughout the life of a project.

Another type of reality check comes from progress meetings with stakeholders. The project manager is responsible for keeping the project on track, and key stakeholders like to stay informed, often through high-level periodic reviews. Managers like to see progress made on projects approximately each month. Project managers often illustrate progress with a Tracking Gantt chart showing key deliverables and activities. The project manager needs to understand the schedule, including why activities are or are not on track, and take a proactive approach to meeting stakeholder expectations. It is also important to verify schedule progress, as Sue Johnson from the opening case discovered (see the Case Wrap-Up). Just because a team member says a task was completed on time does not always mean that it was. Project managers must review the actual work and develop a good relationship with team members to ensure work is completed as planned or changes are reported as needed.

Top management hates surprises, so the project manager must be clear and honest in communicating project status. By no means should project managers create the illusion that the project is going fine when, in fact, it is having serious problems. When serious conflicts arise that could affect the project schedule, the project manager must alert top management and work with them to resolve the conflicts.

Project managers must also use discipline to control project schedules. Several information technology project managers have discovered that setting firm dates for key project milestones helps minimize schedule changes. It is very easy for scope creep to raise its ugly head on information technology projects. Insisting that important schedule dates be met and that proper planning and analysis be completed up front helps everyone focus on doing what is most important for the project. This discipline results in meeting project schedules.

WHAT WENT RIGHT?

A recent example of using discipline and strong user involvement to meet project schedules comes from a winner of Poland's Project Excellence Award in 2007. Mittal Steel Poland is part of ArcelorMittal which is the world's number one steel company, with 320,000 employees in more than 60 countries. The main goal of Mittal Steel Poland's Implementation of SAP System project was to unify IT systems with other Mittal branches in Europe and to improve business and financial processes.[12] Research by AMR found that 46 percent of ERP licenses are unused, leaving many users with unnecessary support and maintenance bills. Derek Prior, research director at AMR Research, identified three things the most successful SAP implementation projects do to deliver business benefits:

- "Form a global competence centre. You need a team, including IT professionals and business analysts, who understand the intricacies of how the software is set up in your company and the business processes it enables.
- Identify super-users for each location. These need to be business managers keen to use the software to its full capacity who also have the respect of their local business peers so they can spread the message on what the software offers.
- You need ongoing involvement of managers in business processes so they feel they own these processes."[13]

USING SOFTWARE TO ASSIST IN PROJECT TIME MANAGEMENT

Several types of software are available to assist in project time management. Software for facilitating communications helps project managers exchange schedule-related information with project stakeholders. Decision support models can help project managers analyze various trade-offs that can be made related to schedule issues. However, project management software, such as Microsoft Project 2007, was designed specifically for performing project management tasks. You can use project management software to draw network diagrams, determine the critical path for a project, create Gantt charts, and report, view, and filter specific project time management information.

Many projects involve hundreds of tasks with complicated dependencies. After you enter the necessary information, project management software automatically generates a network diagram and calculates the critical path(s) for the project. It also highlights the critical path in red on the network diagram. Project management software also calculates the free and total float or slack for all activities. For example, the data in Table 6-1 was created using Microsoft Project by selecting the schedule table view from the menu bar. Using project management software eliminates the need to perform cumbersome calculations manually and allows for "what if" analysis as activity duration estimates or dependencies change. Recall that knowing which activities have the most slack gives the project manager an opportunity to reallocate resources or make other changes to compress the schedule or help keep it on track.

Project 2007 easily creates Gantt charts and Tracking Gantt charts, which make tracking actual schedule performance versus the planned or baseline schedule much easier. It is important, however, to enter actual schedule information in a timely manner in order to benefit from using the Tracking Gantt chart feature. Some organizations use e-mail or other communications software to send up-to-date task and schedule information to the person responsible for updating the schedule. He or she can then quickly authorize these updates and enter them directly into the project management software. This process provides an accurate and up-to-date project schedule in Gantt chart form.

Project 2007 also includes many built-in reports, views, and filters to assist in project time management. For example, a project manager can quickly run a report to list all tasks that are to start soon. He or she could then send out a reminder to the people responsible for these tasks. If the project manager were presenting project schedule information to top management, he or she could create a Gantt chart showing only summary tasks or milestones. You can also create custom reports, views, tables, and filters. See Appendix A to learn how to use the project time management features of Project 2007.

Words of Caution on Using Project Management Software

Many people misuse project management software because they do not understand the concepts behind creating a network diagram, determining the critical path, or setting a schedule baseline. They might also rely too heavily on sample files or templates in developing their own project schedules. Understanding the underlying concepts (even being able to work with the tools manually) is critical to successful use of project management software, as is understanding the specific needs of your project.

Many top managers, including software professionals, have made blatant errors using various versions of Microsoft Project and similar tools. For example, one top manager did not know about establishing dependencies among project activities and entered every single start and end date for hundreds of activities. When asked what would happen if the project started a week or two late, she responded that she would have to reenter all of the dates.

This manager did not understand the importance of establishing relationships among the tasks. Establishing relationships among tasks allows the software to update formulas automatically when the inputs change. If the project start date slips by one week, the project management software will update all the other dates automatically, as long as they are not hard-coded into the software. (Hard-coding involves entering all activity dates manually instead of letting the software calculate them based on durations and relationships.) If one activity cannot start before another ends, and the first activity's actual start date is two days late, the start date for the succeeding activity will automatically be moved back two days. To achieve this type of functionality, tasks that have relationships must be linked in project management software.

Another top manager on a large information technology project did not know about setting a baseline in Microsoft Project. He spent almost one day every week copying and pasting information from Microsoft Project into a spreadsheet and using complicated "IF" statements to figure out what activities were behind schedule. He had never received any training on Microsoft Project and did not know about many of its capabilities. To use any software effectively, users must have adequate training in the software and an understanding of its underlying concepts.

Many project management software programs also come with templates or sample files. It is very easy to use these files without considering unique project needs. For example, a project manager for a software development project can use the Microsoft Project Software Development template file, the files containing information from similar projects done in the past, or sample files purchased from other companies. All of these files include suggested tasks, durations, and relationships. There are benefits to using templates or sample files, such as less setup time and a reality check if the project manager has never managed this type of project before. However, there are also drawbacks to this approach. There are many assumptions in these template files that may not apply to the project, such as a design phase that takes three months to complete or the performance of certain types of testing. Project managers and their teams may over-rely on templates or sample files and ignore unique concerns for their particular projects.

CASE WRAP-UP

It was now March 15, just a month and a half before the new online registration system was supposed to go live. The project was in total chaos. Sue Johnson thought she could handle all of the conflicts that kept appearing on the project, and she was too proud to admit to her top management or the college president that things were not going well. She spent a lot of time preparing a detailed schedule for the project, and she thought she was using their project management software well enough to keep up with project status. However, the five main programmers on the project all figured out a way to generate automatic updates for their tasks every week, saying that everything was completed as planned. They paid very little attention to the actual plan and hated filling out status information. Sue did not verify most of their work to check that it was actually completed. In addition, the head of the Registrar's Office was uninterested in the project and delegated sign-off responsibility to one of his clerks who really did not understand the entire registration process. When Sue and her team started testing the new system, she learned they were using last year's course data. Using last year's course data caused additional problems because the college was moving from quarters to semesters in the new semester. How could they have missed that requirement? Sue hung her head in shame as she walked into a meeting with her manager to ask for help. She learned the hard way how difficult it was to keep a project on track. She wished she had spent more time talking face-to-face with key project stakeholders, especially her programmers and the Registrar's Office representatives, to verify that the project was on schedule and that the schedule was updated accurately.

Chapter Summary

Project time management is often cited as the main source of conflict on projects. Most information technology projects exceed time estimates. The main processes involved in project time management include defining activities, sequencing activities, estimating activity resources, estimating activity durations, developing the schedule, and controlling the schedule.

Defining activities involves identifying the specific activities that must be done to produce the project deliverables. It usually results in a more detailed WBS.

Sequencing activities determines the relationships or dependencies between activities. Three reasons for creating relationships are that they are mandatory based on the nature of the work, discretionary based on the project team's experience, or external based on non-project activities. Activity sequencing must be done in order to use critical path analysis.

Network diagrams are the preferred technique for showing activity sequencing. The two methods used for creating these diagrams are the arrow diagramming method and the precedence diagramming method. There are four types of relationships between tasks: finish-to-start, finish-to-finish, start-to-start, and start-to-finish.

Estimating activity resources involves determining the quantity and type of resources (people, equipment, and materials) that will be assigned to each activity. The nature of the project and the organization will affect resource estimating.

Estimating activity durations creates estimates for the amount of time it will take to complete each activity. These time estimates include the actual amount of time worked plus elapsed time.

Developing the schedule uses results from all of the other project time management processes to determine the start and end dates for the project. Project managers often use Gantt charts to display the project schedule. Tracking Gantt charts show planned and actual schedule information.

The critical path method predicts total project duration. The critical path for a project is the series of activities that determines the earliest completion date for the project. It is the longest path through a network diagram. If any activity on the critical path slips, the whole project will slip unless the project manager takes corrective action.

Crashing and fast tracking are two techniques for shortening project schedules. Project managers and their team members must be careful about accepting unreasonable schedules, especially for information technology projects.

Critical chain scheduling is an application of the Theory of Constraints (TOC) that uses critical path analysis, resource constraints, and buffers to help meet project completion dates.

The Program Evaluation and Review Technique (PERT) is a network analysis technique used to estimate project duration when there is a high degree of uncertainty about the individual activity duration estimates. It uses optimistic, most likely, and pessimistic estimates of activity durations. PERT is seldom used today.

Controlling the schedule is the final process in project time management. Even though scheduling techniques are very important, most projects fail because of people issues, not from a poor network diagram. Project managers must involve all stakeholders in the schedule development process. It is critical to set realistic project schedules and use discipline to meet schedule goals.

Project management software can assist in project scheduling if used properly. With project management software, you can avoid the need to perform cumbersome calculations manually and perform "what if" analysis as activity duration estimates or dependencies change. Many people misuse project management software because they do not understand the concepts behind creating a network diagram, determining the critical path, or setting a schedule baseline. Project managers must also avoid over-relying on sample files or templates when creating their unique project schedules.

Quick Quiz

1. What is the first process in planning a project schedule?
   a. defining milestones
   b. defining activities
   c. estimating activity resources
   d. sequencing activity sequencing
2. Predecessors, successors, logical relationships, leads and lags, resource requirements, constraints, imposed dates, and assumptions are all examples of _______ .
   a. items in an activity list
   b. items on a Gantt chart
   c. milestone attributes
   d. activity attributes
3. As the project manager for a software development project, you are helping to develop the project schedule. You decide that writing code for a system should not start until users sign off on the analysis work. What type of dependency is this?
   a. technical
   b. mandatory
   c. discretionary
   d. external
4. You cannot start editing a technical report until someone else completes the first draft. What type of dependency does this represent?
   a. finish-to-start
   b. start-to-start
   c. finish-to-finish
   d. start-to-finish
5. Which of the following statements is false?
   a. A resource breakdown structure is a hierarchical structure that identifies the project's resources by category and type.
   b. Duration and effort are synonymous terms.
   c. A three-point estimate is an estimate that includes an optimistic, most likely, and pessimistic estimate.
   d. A Gantt chart is a common tool for displaying project schedule information.

6. What symbol on a Gantt chart represents a slipped milestone?
   a. a black arrow
   b. a white arrow
   c. a black diamond
   d. a white diamond
7. What type of diagram shows planned and actual project schedule information?
   a. a network diagram
   b. a Gantt chart
   c. a Tracking Gantt chart
   d. a milestone chart
8. ___________ is a network diagramming technique used to predict total project duration.
   a. PERT
   b. A Gantt chart
   c. Critical path method
   d. Crashing
9. Which of the following statements is false?
   a. "Growing grass" was on the critical path for a large theme park project.
   b. The critical path is the series of activities that determine the earliest time by which a project can be completed.
   c. A forward pass through a project network diagram determines the early start and early finish dates for each activity.
   d. Fast tracking is a technique for making cost and schedule trade-offs to obtain the greatest amount of schedule compression for the least incremental cost.
10. ___________ is a method of scheduling that considers limited resources when creating a project schedule and includes buffers to protect the project completion date.
   a. Parkinson's Law
   b. Murphy's Law
   c. Critical path analysis
   d. Critical chain scheduling

Quick Quiz Answers

1. b; 2. d; 3. c; 4. a; 5. b; 6. d; 7. c; 8. a; 9. d; 10. d

Discussion Questions

1. Why do you think schedule issues often cause the most conflicts on projects?
2. Why is defining activities the first process involved in project time management?
3. Why is it important to determine activity sequencing on projects? Discuss diagrams you have seen that are similar to network diagrams. Describe their similarities and differences.

4. How does activity resource estimating affect estimating activity durations?
5. Explain the difference between estimating activity durations and estimating the effort required to perform an activity.
6. Explain the following schedule development tools and concepts: Gantt charts, critical path method, PERT, and critical chain scheduling.
7. How can you minimize or control changes to project schedules?

8. List some of the reports you can generate with Project 2007 to assist in project time management.
9. Why is it difficult to use project management software well?

Exercises

1. Using Figure 6-2, enter the activities, their durations (in days), and their relationships in Project 2007. Use a project start date of August 1, 2009. View the network diagram. Does it look like Figure 6-4? Print the network diagram on one page. Return to the Gantt Chart view. Click View on the menu bar, select Table: Entry, and then click Schedule to re-create Table 6-1. You may need to move the split bar to the right to reveal all of the table columns. (See Appendix for detailed information on using Project 2007.) Write a few paragraphs explaining what the network diagram and schedule table show concerning Project X's schedule.
2. Consider Table 6-2, Network Diagram Data for a Small Project. All duration estimates or estimated times are in days; and the network proceeds from Node 1 to Node 9.

TABLE 6-2 Network diagram data for a small project

Activity	Initial Node	Final Node	Estimated Duration
A	1	2	2
B	2	3	2
C	2	4	3
D	2	5	4
E	3	6	2
F	4	6	3
G	5	7	6
H	6	8	2
I	6	7	5
J	7	8	1
K	8	9	2

a. Draw an AOA network diagram representing the project. Put the node numbers in circles and draw arrows from node to node, labeling each arrow with the activity letter and estimated time.

b. Identify all of the paths on the network diagram and note how long they are, using Figure 6-8 as a guide for how to represent each path.

c. What is the critical path for this project and how long is it?

d. What is the shortest possible time it will take to complete this project?

e. Review the online tutorials for Gantt and PERT charts by Mark Kelly, available on the companion Web site or directly at *www.mckinnonsc.vic.edu.au/vceit/ganttpert*. Write a one-page paper with your answers to the questions in the tutorials. Also include any questions you had in doing the tutorials.

3. Consider Table 6-3, Network Diagram Data for a Large Project. All duration estimates or estimated times are in weeks; and the network proceeds from Node 1 to Node 8.

TABLE 6-3 Network diagram data for a large project

Activity	Initial Node	Final Node	Estimated Duration
A	1	2	10
B	1	3	12
C	1	4	8
D	2	3	4
E	2	5	8
F	3	4	6
G	4	5	4
H	4	6	8
I	5	6	6
J	5	8	12
K	6	7	8
L	7	8	10

a. Draw an AOA network diagram representing the project. Put the node numbers in circles and draw arrows from node to node, labeling each arrow with the activity letter and estimated time.

b. Identify all of the paths on the network diagram and note how long they are, using Figure 6-8 as a guide for how to represent each path.

c. What is the critical path for this project and how long is it?

d. What is the shortest possible time it will take to complete this project?

4. Enter the information from Exercise 2 into Project 2007. View the network diagram and task schedule table to see the critical path and float or slack for each activity. Print the Gantt chart and network diagram views and the task schedule table. Write a short paper that interprets this information for someone unfamiliar with project time management.

5. Enter the information from Exercise 3 into Project 2007. View the network diagram and task schedule table to see the critical path and float or slack for each activity. Print the Gantt chart and network diagram views and the task schedule table. Write a short paper that interprets this information for someone unfamiliar with project time management.

6. You have been asked to determine a rough schedule for a nine-month Billing System Conversion project, as part of your job as a consultant to a Fortune 500 firm. The firm's old system was written in COBOL on a mainframe computer, and the maintenance costs are prohibitive. The new system will run on an off-the-shelf application. You have identified several high-level activities that must be done in order to initiate, plan, execute, control, and close the project. Table 6-4 shows your analysis of the project's tasks and schedule so far.

TABLE 6-4 COBOL conversion project schedule

Tasks	Mar	Apr	May	Jun	Jul	Aug	Sep	Oct	Nov
Initiating									
Develop project charter									
Meet with stakeholders									
Planning									
Create detailed WBS and schedule									
Estimate project costs									
Create project team									
Create communication plan									
Organize a comprehensive project plan									
Executing									
Award and manage contract for software conversion									
Install new software on servers									
Install new hardware and software on clients' machines									
Test new billing system									
Train users on new system									
Controlling									
Closing									

a. Using the information in Table 6-4, draw horizontal bars to illustrate when you think each task would logically start and end. Then use Project 2007 to create a Gantt chart and network diagram based on this information.

b. Identify at least two milestones that could be included under each of the process groups in Table 6-4. Then write a detailed description of each of these milestones that meets the SMART criteria.

7. Interview someone who uses some of the techniques discussed in this chapter. How does he or she feel about network diagrams, critical path analysis, Gantt charts, critical chain scheduling, using project management software, and managing the people issues involved in project time management? Write a two-page paper describing the responses.

8. Review two different articles about critical chain scheduling. Write a two-page paper describing how this technique can help improve project schedule management.

Running Case

Tony Prince is the project manager for the Recreation and Wellness Intranet Project, and team members include you, a programmer/analyst and aspiring project manager; Patrick, a network specialist; Nancy, a business analyst; and Bonnie, another programmer/analyst. Other people supporting the project from other departments are Yusaff from human resources, and Cassandra from finance. Assume these are the only people who can be assigned and charged to work on project activities. Recall that your schedule and cost goals are to complete the project in six months for under $200,000.

Tasks

1. Review the WBS and Gantt chart you created for Chapter 5, Task 3. Propose three to five additional activities you think should be added to help you estimate resources and durations. Write a one-page paper describing these new activities.
2. Identify at least eight milestones for this project. Write a one-page paper describing each milestone using the SMART criteria. Discuss how determining these milestones might add additional activities or tasks to the Gantt chart. Remember that milestones normally have no duration, so you must have tasks that will lead to completing the milestone.
3. Using the Gantt chart you created for Chapter 5, Task 3, and the new activities and milestones you proposed in Tasks 1 and 2 above, create a new Gantt chart using Project 2007. Estimate the task durations and enter dependencies, as appropriate. Remember that your schedule goal for the project is six months. Print the Gantt chart and network diagram, each on one page.
4. Write a one-page paper summarizing how you would assign people to each activity. Include a table or matrix listing how many hours each person would work on each task. These resource assignments should make sense given the duration estimates made in Task 3 above. Remember that duration estimates are not the same as effort estimates since they include elapsed time.

Key Terms

activity — an element of work, normally found on the WBS, that has an expected duration and cost, and expected resource requirements; also called a task

activity attributes — information about each activity, such as predecessors, successors, logical relationships, leads and lags, resource requirements, constraints, imposed dates, and assumptions related to the activity

activity list — a tabulation of activities to be included on a project schedule

activity-on-arrow (AOA) — a network diagramming technique in which activities are represented by arrows and connected at points called nodes to illustrate the sequence of activities; also called arrow diagramming method (ADM)

arrow diagramming method (ADM) — a network diagramming technique in which activities are represented by arrows and connected at points called nodes to illustrate the sequence of activities; also called activity-on-arrow (AOA)

backward pass — a project network diagramming technique that determines the late start and late finish dates for each activity in a similar fashion

baseline dates — the planned schedule dates for activities in a Tracking Gantt chart

buffer — additional time to complete a task, added to an estimate to account for various factors

burst — when a single node is followed by two or more activities on a network diagram

crashing — a technique for making cost and schedule trade-offs to obtain the greatest amount of schedule compression for the least incremental cost

critical chain scheduling — a method of scheduling that takes limited resources into account when creating a project schedule and includes buffers to protect the project completion date

critical path — the series of activities in a network diagram that determines the earliest completion of the project; it is the longest path through the network diagram and has the least amount of slack or float

critical path method (CPM) or **critical path analysis** — a project network analysis technique used to predict total project duration

dependency — the sequencing of project activities or tasks; also called a relationship

discretionary dependencies — sequencing of project activities or tasks defined by the project team and used with care since they may limit later scheduling options

dummy activities — activities with no duration and no resources used to show a logical relationship between two activities in the arrow diagramming method of project network diagrams

duration — the actual amount of time worked on an activity *plus* elapsed time

early finish date — the earliest possible time an activity can finish based on the project network logic

early start date — the earliest possible time an activity can start based on the project network logic

effort — the number of workdays or work hours required to complete a task

external dependencies — sequencing of project activities or tasks that involve relationships between project and non-project activities

fast tracking — a schedule compression technique in which you do activities in parallel that you would normally do in sequence

feeding buffers — additional time added before tasks on the critical path that are preceded by non-critical-path tasks

finish-to-finish dependency — a relationship on a project network diagram where the "from" activity must be finished before the "to" activity can be finished

finish-to-start dependency — a relationship on a project network diagram where the "from" activity must be finished before the "to" activity can be started

float — the amount of time a project activity may be delayed without delaying a succeeding activity or the project finish date; also called slack

forward pass — a network diagramming technique that determines the early start and early finish dates for each activity

free slack (free float) — the amount of time an activity can be delayed without delaying the early start of any immediately following activities

Gantt chart — a standard format for displaying project schedule information by listing project activities and their corresponding start and finish dates in a calendar format; sometimes referred to as bar charts

late finish date — the latest possible time an activity can be completed without delaying the project finish date

late start date — the latest possible time an activity may begin without delaying the project finish date

mandatory dependencies — sequencing of project activities or tasks that are inherent in the nature of the work being done on the project

merge — when two or more nodes precede a single node on a network diagram

milestone — a significant event that normally has no duration on a project; serves as a marker to help in identifying necessary activities, setting schedule goals, and monitoring progress

multitasking — when a resource works on more than one task at a time

Murphy's Law — principle that if something can go wrong, it will

network diagram — a schematic display of the logical relationships or sequencing of project activities

node — the starting and ending point of an activity on an activity-on-arrow diagram

Parkinson's Law — principle that work expands to fill the time allowed

PERT weighted average — $\frac{\text{optimistic time} + 4 * \text{most likely time} + \text{pessimistic time}}{6}$

Precedence Diagramming Method (PDM) — a network diagramming technique in which boxes represent activities

probabilistic time estimates — duration estimates based on using optimistic, most likely, and pessimistic estimates of activity durations instead of using one specific or discrete estimate

Program Evaluation and Review Technique (PERT) — a project network analysis technique used to estimate project duration when there is a high degree of uncertainty with the individual activity duration estimates

project buffer — additional time added before the project's due date

project time management — the processes required to ensure timely completion of a project

relationship — the sequencing of project activities or tasks; also called a dependency

resource breakdown structure — a hierarchical structure that identifies the project's resources by category and type

resources — people, equipment, and materials

schedule baseline — the approved planned schedule for the project

slack — the amount of time a project activity may be delayed without delaying a succeeding activity or the project finish date; also called float

slipped milestone — a milestone activity that is completed later than planned

SMART criteria — guidelines to help define milestones that are **s**pecific, **m**easurable, **a**ssignable, **r**ealistic, and **t**ime-framed

start-to-finish dependency — a relationship on a project network diagram where the "from" activity cannot start before the "to" activity is finished

start-to-start dependency — a relationship on a project network diagram in which the "from" activity cannot start until the "to" activity starts

task — an element of work, normally found on the WBS, that has an expected duration and cost, and expected resource requirements; also called an activity

Theory of Constraints (TOC) — a management philosophy that states that any complex system at any point in time often has only one aspect or constraint that is limiting its ability to achieve more of its goal

three-point estimate — an estimate that includes an optimistic, most likely, and pessimistic estimate

total slack (total float) — the amount of time an activity may be delayed from its early start without delaying the planned project finish date

Tracking Gantt chart — a Gantt chart that compares planned and actual project schedule information

End Notes

[1] Kelly, Fran, "The World Today – Olympic planning schedule behind time," *ABC Online* (March 4, 2004).

[2] Weiner, Jay and Rachel Blount, "Olympics are safe but crowds are sparse," *Minneapolis Star Tribune* (August 22, 2004), A9.

[3] Roberts, Paul, "Frustrated contractor sentenced for hacking FBI to speed deployment," *InfoWorld Tech Watch*, (July 6, 2006).

[4] Losey, Stephen, "FBI to begin training employees on Sentinel case management system," FederalTimes.com (April 26, 2007).

[5] Richard, Luc K. "Reducing Schedule Risk, Parts 1 and 2," Gantthead.com (November 10, 2003 and January 31, 2005).

[6] Goldratt, Eliyahu, *Critical Chain* (Great Barrington, MA: The North River Press), 1997, p. 218.

[7] Breen, Anne M., Tracey Burton-Houle, and David C. Aron, "Applying the Theory of Constraints in Health Care: Part 1 - The Philosophy," *Quality Management in Health Care*, Volume 10, Number 3 (Spring 2002) (*www.goldratt.com/for-cause/applyingtocinhcpt1fco.htm*).

[8] Bolton, Bart, "IS Leadership," *ComputerWorld* (May 19, 1997).

[9] Yourdon, Ed, *Death March, Second Edition*, Upper Saddle River, NJ: Prentice Hall (2003).

[10] Weiss, Todd, "Portland IT overhaul runs into delays, excessive costs," ComputerWorld (May 15, 2008).

[11] Monson, Robert, *Conquering Chaos*, Unpublished Manuscript, Saint Paul, Minnesota (2008).

[12] International Project Management Association, "The best managed projects in the world 2007 awarded," www.ipma.ch (2008).

[13] ComputerWeekly.com, " IT rises to the challenge of standardisation of ERP as Mittal goes on a buying spree," (November 29, 2005).

CHAPTER 7

PROJECT COST MANAGEMENT

LEARNING OBJECTIVES

After reading this chapter, you will be able to:

- Understand the importance of project cost management
- Explain basic project cost management principles, concepts, and terms
- Discuss different types of cost estimates and methods for preparing them
- Understand the processes involved in cost budgeting and preparing a cost estimate and budget for an information technology project
- Understand the benefits of earned value management and project portfolio management to assist in cost control
- Describe how project management software can assist in project cost management

OPENING CASE

Juan Gonzales was a systems analyst and network specialist for a major Mexican city's waterworks department. He enjoyed helping the city develop its infrastructure. His next career objective was to become a project manager so he could have even more influence. One of his colleagues invited him to attend an important project review meeting for large government projects, including the Surveyor Pro project, in which Juan was most interested. The Surveyor Pro project was a concept for developing a sophisticated information system that included expert systems, object-oriented databases, and wireless communications. The system would provide instant, graphical information to government surveyors to help them do their jobs. For example, after a surveyor touched a map on the screen of a handheld device, the system would prompt him or her for the type of information needed for that area. This system would help in planning and implementing many projects, from laying fiber-optic cable to installing water lines.

Juan was very surprised, however, when the majority of the meeting was spent discussing cost-related issues. The government officials were reviewing many existing projects to evaluate their performance to date and the potential impact on their budgets before discussing funding for any new projects. Juan did not understand many of the terms and charts the presenters were showing. What was this "earned value" term they kept referring to? How were they estimating what it would cost to complete projects or how long it would take? Juan thought he would learn more about the new technologies the Surveyor Pro project would use, but he discovered that the cost estimate and projected benefits were of most interest to the government officials at the meeting. It also seemed as if a lot of effort would go toward detailed financial studies before any technical work could even start. Juan wished he had taken some accounting and finance courses so he could understand the acronyms and concepts people were discussing. Although Juan had a degree in electrical engineering, he had no formal education and little experience in finance. If Juan could understand information systems and networks, he was confident that he could understand financial issues on projects, too. He jotted down questions to discuss with his colleagues after the meeting.

THE IMPORTANCE OF PROJECT COST MANAGEMENT

Information technology projects have a poor track record in meeting budget goals. The Standish Group's CHAOS studies reported an average cost **overrun**—the additional percentage or dollar amount by which actual costs exceed estimates—for unsuccessful IT projects ranged from 180 percent in 1994 to 56 percent in 2004. Although academic researchers question the validity of these numbers, more rigorous, scientifically reviewed studies acknowledge the problem of cost overruns for IT projects. For example, three separate surveys of software project cost overruns done by Jenkins, Phan, and Bergeron in 1984, 1988, and 1992, respectively, found that the average cost overrun for all of the projects in their survey samples (not just unsuccessful projects) was 33–34 percent.[1] Obviously, there is room for improvement in meeting cost goals for IT projects. This chapter describes important concepts in project cost management, particularly, creating good estimates and using earned value management (EVM) to assist in cost control.

WHAT WENT WRONG?

There is no shortage of examples of information technology projects that suffered from poor cost management. The U.S. Internal Revenue Service (IRS) and other government agencies continue to provide examples of how not to manage costs.

- The IRS managed a series of project failures in the 1990s that cost taxpayers more than $50 billion a year—roughly as much money as the annual net profit of the entire computer industry in those years.[2]
- In 2006, the IRS was again in the news for a botched upgrade to its fraud-detection software. The IRS planned to launch the system in January, in time for the 2006 tax season and one year *after* the original implementation date, but that did not happen. The U.S. government estimated that the lack of a functioning anti-fraud system cost $318 million in fraudulent refunds that didn't get caught.[3]
- A 2008 Government Accountability Office (GAO) report stated that more than 400 U.S. government agency IT projects, worth an estimated $25 billion, suffer from poor planning and underperformance. U.S. Senator Tom Carper of Delaware said the IT projects are redundant, lack clear goals, and are managed by unqualified individuals.[4]

Another example that shows the challenges of managing project costs was the United Kingdom's National Health Service (NHS) IT modernization program. Called "the greatest IT disaster in history" by one London columnist, this ten-year program, which started in 2002, was created to provide an electronic patient records system, appointment booking, and a prescription drug system in England and Wales. Britain's Labor government estimates that the program will eventually cost more than $55 billion, *a $26 billion overrun*. The program has been plagued by technical problems due to incompatible systems, resistance from physicians who say they were not adequately consulted about system features, and arguments among contractors about who's responsible for what.[5] A government audit in June 2006 found the program, one of the largest civilian IT projects undertaken worldwide, was progressing despite high-profile problems. In an effort to reduce cost overruns, the NHS program will no longer pay for products until delivery, shifting some financial responsibility to prime contractors, including BT Group, Accenture, and Fujitsu Services.[6]

What Is Cost?

A popular cost accounting textbook states, "Accountants usually define cost as a resource sacrificed or foregone to achieve a specific objective."[7] Webster's dictionary defines cost as "something given up in exchange." Costs are often measured in monetary amounts, such as dollars, that must be paid to acquire goods and services. (For convenience, the examples in this chapter use dollars for monetary amounts, but monetary amounts could be in any currency.) Because projects cost money and consume resources that could be used elsewhere, it is very important for project managers to understand project cost management.

Many information technology professionals, however, often react to cost overrun information with a smirk. They know that many of the original cost estimates for information technology projects are low to begin with or based on very unclear project requirements, so naturally there will be cost overruns. Not emphasizing the importance of realistic project cost estimates from the outset is only one part of the problem. In addition, many information technology professionals think preparing cost estimates is a job for accountants. On the contrary, preparing good cost estimates is a very demanding, important skill that many professionals need to acquire.

Another perceived reason for cost overruns is that many information technology projects involve new technology or business processes. Any new technology or business process is untested and has inherent risks. Thus, costs grow and failures are to be expected, right? Wrong. Using good project cost management can change this false perception.

What Is Project Cost Management?

Recall from Chapter 1 that the triple constraint of project management involves balancing scope, time, and cost goals. Chapters 5 and 6 discuss project scope and time management, and this chapter describes project cost management. **Project cost management** includes the processes required to ensure that a project team completes a project within an approved budget. Notice two crucial phrases in this definition: "a project" and "approved budget." Project managers must make sure *their* projects are well defined, have accurate time and cost estimates, and have a realistic budget that *they* were involved in approving. It is the project manager's job to satisfy project stakeholders while continuously striving to reduce and control costs. There are three project cost management processes:

1. *Estimating costs* involves developing an approximation or estimate of the costs of the resources needed to complete a project. The main outputs of the cost estimating process are activity cost estimates, basis of estimates, and project document updates. A cost management plan is created as part of integration management when creating the project management plan. It should include information related to the level of accuracy for estimates, variance thresholds for monitoring cost performance, reporting formats, and other related information.
2. *Determining the budget* involves allocating the overall cost estimate to individual work items to establish a baseline for measuring performance. The main outputs of the cost budgeting process are a cost performance baseline, project funding requirements, and project document updates.
3. *Controlling costs* involves controlling changes to the project budget. The main outputs of the cost control process are work performance measurements, budget forecasts, organizational process asset updates, change requests, project management plan updates, and project document updates.

Figure 7-1 summarizes these processes and outputs, showing when they occur in a typical project.

To understand each of the project cost management processes, you must first understand the basic principles of cost management. Many of these principles are not unique to project management; however, project managers need to understand how these principles relate to their specific projects.

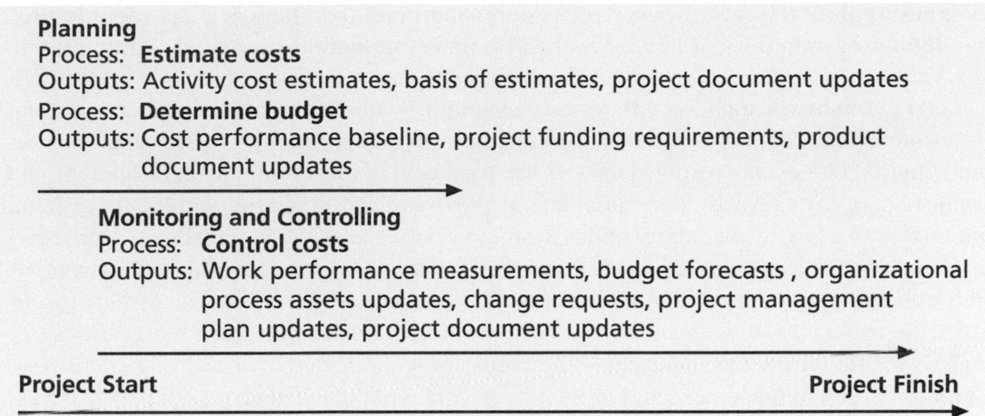

Planning
Process: Estimate costs
Outputs: Activity cost estimates, basis of estimates, project document updates
Process: Determine budget
Outputs: Cost performance baseline, project funding requirements, product document updates
Monitoring and Controlling
Process: Control costs
Outputs: Work performance measurements, budget forecasts , organizational process assets updates, change requests, project management plan updates, project document updates
Project Start
Project Finish

FIGURE 7-1 Project cost management summary

BASIC PRINCIPLES OF COST MANAGEMENT

Many information technology projects are never initiated because information technology professionals do not understand the importance of basic accounting and finance principles. Important concepts such as net present value analysis, return on investment, and payback analysis were discussed in Chapter 4, Project Integration Management. Likewise, many projects that are started never finish because of cost management problems. Most members of an executive board have a better understanding of and are more interested in financial terms than information technology terms. Therefore, information technology project managers need to be able to present and discuss project information in financial terms as well as in technical terms. In addition to net present value analysis, return on investment, and payback analysis, project managers must understand several other cost management principles, concepts, and terms. This section describes general topics such as profits, life cycle costing, cash flow analysis, tangible and intangible costs and benefits, direct costs, sunk costs, learning curve theory, and reserves. Another important topic and one of the key tools and techniques for controlling project costs—earned value management—is described in detail in the section on cost control.

Profits are revenues minus expenditures. To increase profits, a company can increase revenues, decrease expenses, or try to do both. Most executives are more concerned with profits than with other issues. When justifying investments in new information systems and technology, it is important to focus on the impact on profits, not just revenues or expenses. Consider an e-commerce application that you estimate will increase revenues for a $100 million company by 10 percent. You cannot measure the potential benefits of the e-commerce application without knowing the profit margin. **Profit margin** is the ratio of revenues to profits. If revenues of $100 generate $2 in profits, there is a 2 percent profit margin. If the company loses $2 for every $100 in revenue, there is a –2 percent profit margin.

Life cycle costing allows you to see a big-picture view of the cost of a project throughout its life cycle. This helps you develop an accurate projection of a project's financial costs and benefits. Life cycle costing considers the total cost of ownership, or development plus support costs, for a project. For example, a company might complete a project to develop and implement a new customer service system in one or two years, but the new system could be in place for ten years. Project managers, with assistance from financial experts in their organizations, should create estimates of the costs and benefits of the project for its entire life cycle, or ten years in the preceding example. Recall that the net present value analysis for the project would include the entire ten-year period of costs and benefits (see Chapter 4). Top management and project managers need to consider the life cycle costs of projects when they make financial decisions.

Organizations have a history of not spending enough money in the early phases of information technology projects, which impacts total cost of ownership. For example, it is much more cost-effective to spend money on defining user requirements and doing early testing on information technology projects than to wait for problems to appear after implementation. Recall from Chapter 5 that it can cost over 100 times more to correct a defect on a software project that is found late in the project than to fix it early.

Since organizations depend on reliable information technology, there are also huge costs associated with downtime. For example, Table 7-1 summarizes the average cost of a minute of downtime for different IT applications. Costs include the cost to bring the system back up, staff cost to make up for the lost work in production during the system downtime, and direct and indirect lost revenue.

TABLE 7-1 Costs of downtime for IT applications[8]

Type of IT Application	Cost/Minute
Securities trading	$73,000
Enterprise Requirements Planning (ERP)	$14,800
Order processing	$13,300
Electronic commerce	$12,600
Supply chain	$11,500
Point of sale (POS)	$ 4,700
Automatic teller machine (ATM)	$ 3,600
E-mail	$ 1,900

The Standish Group International, "Trends in IT Value," (www.standishgroup.com) (2008).

WHAT WENT RIGHT?

Many organizations use IT to reduce operational costs. For example, a recent study shows that technology has decreased the costs (adjusted for inflation) associated with processing an automated teller machine (ATM) transaction from a financial institution:

- In 1968, the average cost was $5.
- In 1978, the cost went down to $1.50
- In 1988, the cost was just a nickel.
- In 1998, it only cost a penny.
- In 2008, the cost was just half a penny![9]

Another cost-cutting strategy has been inspired by the global emphasis on improving the environment. Investing in green IT and other initiatives has helped both the environment and companies' bottom lines. Michael Dell, CEO of Dell, said he aimed to make his company "carbon neutral" in 2008. "The computer giant is looking to zero-out its carbon emissions through a number of initiatives, such as offering small businesses and consumers curbside recycling of their old computers, stuffing small recycling bags with free postage into new printer-ink cartridge boxes, and operating a 'Plant a Tree for Me' program."[10] (Dell did reach his goal. Visit *www.dell.com/earth* for more information.)

Cash flow analysis is a method for determining the estimated annual costs and benefits for a project and the resulting annual cash flow. Project managers must conduct cash flow analysis to determine net present value. Most consumers understand the basic concept of cash flow. If they do not have enough money in their wallets or checking/credit accounts, they cannot purchase something. Top management must consider cash flow concerns when selecting projects in which to invest. If top management selects too many projects that have high cash flow needs in the same year, the company will not be able to support all of its projects and maintain its profitability. It is also important to define clearly the year on which the company bases the dollar amounts. For example, if a company bases all costs on 2008 estimates, it would need to account for inflation and other factors when projecting costs and benefits in future-year dollars.

Tangible and intangible costs and benefits are categories for determining how definable the estimated costs and benefits are for a project. **Tangible costs or benefits** are those costs or benefits that an organization can easily measure in dollars. For example, suppose the Surveyor Pro project described in the opening case included a preliminary feasibility study. If a company completed this study for $100,000, the tangible cost of the study is $100,000. If Juan's government estimated that it would have cost $150,000 to do the study itself, the tangible benefits of the study would be $50,000 if it assigned the people who would have done the study to other projects. Conversely, **intangible costs or benefits** are costs or benefits that are difficult to measure in monetary terms. Suppose Juan and a few other people, out of personal interest, spent some time using government-owned computers, books, and other resources to research areas related to the study. Although their hours and the government-owned materials were not billed to the project, they could be considered intangible costs. Intangible benefits for projects often include items like goodwill, prestige, and general statements of improved productivity that an organization cannot easily translate into dollar amounts. Because intangible costs and benefits are difficult to quantify, they are often harder to justify.

Direct costs are costs that can be directly related to producing the products and services of the project. You can attribute direct costs directly to a certain project. For example, the salaries of people working full time on the project and the cost of hardware and software purchased specifically for the project are direct costs. Project managers should focus on direct costs, since they can control them.

Indirect costs are costs that are not directly related to the products or services of the project, but are indirectly related to performing the project. For example, the cost of electricity, paper towels, and so on in a large building housing a thousand employees who work on many projects would be indirect costs. Indirect costs are allocated to projects, and project managers have very little control over them.

Sunk cost is money that has been spent in the past. Consider it gone, like a sunken ship that can never be returned. When deciding what projects to invest in or continue, you should not include sunk costs. For example, in the opening case, suppose Juan's office had spent $1 million on a project over the past three years to create a geographic information system, but they never produced anything valuable. If his government were evaluating what projects to fund next year and someone suggested that they keep funding the geographic information system project because they had already spent $1 million on it, he or she would be incorrectly making sunk cost a key factor in the project selection decision. Many people fall into the trap of considering how much money has been spent on a failing project and, therefore, hate to stop spending money on it. This trap is similar to gamblers not wanting to stop gambling because they have already lost money. Sunk costs should be forgotten.

Learning curve theory states that when many items are produced repetitively, the unit cost of those items decreases in a regular pattern as more units are produced. For example, suppose the Surveyor Pro project would potentially produce 1,000 handheld devices that could run the new software and access information via satellite. The cost of the first handheld device or unit would be much higher than the cost of the thousandth unit. Learning curve theory should help estimate costs on projects involving the production of large quantities of items. Learning curve theory also applies to the amount of time it takes to complete some tasks. For example, the first time a new employee performs a specific task, it will probably take longer than the tenth time that employee performs a very similar task.

Reserves are dollars included in a cost estimate to mitigate cost risk by allowing for future situations that are difficult to predict. **Contingency reserves** allow for future situations that may be partially planned for (sometimes called **known unknowns**) and are included in the project cost baseline. For example, if an organization knows it has a 20 percent rate of turnover for information technology personnel, it should include contingency reserves to pay for recruiting and training costs for information technology personnel. **Management reserves** allow for future situations that are unpredictable (sometimes called **unknown unknowns**). For example, if a project manager gets sick for two weeks or an important supplier goes out of business, management reserve could be set aside to cover the resulting costs.

ESTIMATING COSTS

Project managers must take cost estimates seriously if they want to complete projects within budget constraints. After developing a good resource requirements list, project managers and their project teams must develop several estimates of the costs for these resources. Recall from Chapter 6 that an important process in project time management is estimating activity resources, which provides a list of activity resource requirements. For example, if an activity on a project is to perform a particular type of test, the list of activity resource requirements would describe the skill level of the people needed to perform the test, the number of people and hours suggested to perform the test, the need for special software or equipment, and so on. All of this information is required to develop a good cost estimate. This section describes various types of cost estimates, tools and techniques for estimating costs, typical problems associated with information technology cost estimates, and a detailed example of a cost estimate for an information technology project.

Types of Cost Estimates

One of the main outputs of project cost management is a cost estimate. Project managers normally prepare several types of cost estimates for most projects. Three basic types of estimates include the following:

- A **rough order of magnitude (ROM) estimate** provides an estimate of what a project will cost. ROM estimates can also be referred to as a ballpark estimate, a guesstimate, a swag, or a broad gauge. This type of estimate is done very early in a project or even before a project is officially started. Project managers and top management use this estimate to help make project selection decisions. The timeframe for this type of estimate is often three or more years prior to project completion. A ROM estimate's accuracy is typically −50 percent to +100 percent, meaning the project's actual costs could be 50 percent below the ROM estimate or 100 percent above. For example, the actual cost for a project with a ROM estimate of $100,000 could range between $50,000 to $200,000. For information technology project estimates, this accuracy range is often much wider. Many information technology professionals automatically double estimates for software development because of the history of cost overruns on information technology projects.
- A **budgetary estimate** is used to allocate money into an organization's budget. Many organizations develop budgets at least two years into the future. Budgetary estimates are made one to two years prior to project completion. The accuracy of budgetary estimates is typically −10 percent to +25 percent, meaning the actual costs could be 10 percent less or 25 percent more than the budgetary estimate. For example, the actual cost for a project with a budgetary estimate of $100,000 could range between $90,000 to $125,000.
- A **definitive estimate** provides an accurate estimate of project costs. Definitive estimates are used for making many purchasing decisions for which accurate estimates are required and for estimating final project costs. For example, if a project involves purchasing 1,000 personal computers from an outside supplier in the next three months, a definitive estimate would be required to aid in

evaluating supplier proposals and allocating the funds to pay the chosen supplier. Definitive estimates are made one year or less prior to project completion. A definitive estimate should be the most accurate of the three types of estimates. The accuracy of this type of estimate is normally –5 percent to +10 percent, meaning the actual costs could be 5 percent less or 10 percent more than the definitive estimate. For example, the actual cost for a project with a definitive estimate of $100,000 could range between $95,000 to $110,000. Table 7-2 summarizes the three basic types of cost estimates.

TABLE 7-2 Types of cost estimates

Type of Estimate	When Done	Why Done	How Accurate
Rough Order of Magnitude (ROM)	Very early in the project life cycle, often 3–5 years before project completion	Provides estimate of cost for selection decisions	–50% to +100%
Budgetary	Early, 1–2 years out	Puts dollars in the budget plans	–10% to +25%
Definitive	Later in the project, less than 1 year out	Provides details for purchases, estimates actual costs	–5% to +10%

The number and type of cost estimates vary by application area. For example, the Association for the Advancement of Cost Engineering (AACE) International identifies five types of cost estimates for construction projects: order of magnitude, conceptual, preliminary, definitive, and control. The main point is that estimates are usually done at various stages of a project and should become more accurate as time progresses.

In addition to creating cost estimates, it is also important to provide supporting details for the estimates. The supporting details include the ground rules and assumptions used in creating the estimate, a description of the project (scope statement, WBS, and so on) used as a basis for the estimate, and details on the cost estimation tools and techniques used to create the estimate. These supporting details should make it easier to prepare an updated estimate or similar estimate as needed.

A **cost management plan** is a document that describes how the organization will manage cost variances on the project. For example, if a definitive cost estimate provides the basis for evaluating supplier cost proposals for all or part of a project, the cost management plan describes how to respond to proposals that are higher or lower than the estimates. Some organizations assume that a cost proposal within 10 percent of the estimate is acceptable and only negotiate items that are more than 10 percent higher or 20 percent lower than the estimated costs. The cost management plan is part of the overall project management plan described in Chapter 4, Project Integration Management.

Another important consideration in preparing cost estimates is labor costs, because a large percentage of total project costs are often labor costs. Many organizations estimate the number of people or hours they need by department or skill over the life cycle of a project. For example, when Northwest Airlines developed initial cost estimates for its reservation system project, ResNet, it determined the maximum number of people it could assign to the project each year by department. Table 7-3 shows this information. (Figure 9-7 in Chapter 9, Project Human Resource Management, provides similar resource information in graphical form, where the number of resources are provided by job category, such as business analyst, programmer, and so on.) Note the small number of contractors Northwest Airlines planned to use. Labor costs are often much higher for contractors, so it is important to distinguish between internal and external resources. (See the companion Web site for this text to read the detailed case study on ResNet, including cost estimates.)

TABLE 7-3 Maximum departmental headcounts by year

Department	Year 1	Year 2	Year 3	Year 4	Year 5	Totals
Information systems	24	31	35	13	13	116
Marketing systems	3	3	3	3	3	15
Reservations	12	29	33	9	7	90
Contractors	2	3	1	0	0	6
Totals	41	66	72	25	23	227

Cost Estimation Tools and Techniques

As you can imagine, developing a good cost estimate is difficult. Fortunately, there are several tools and techniques available to assist in creating one. Commonly used tools and techniques include analogous cost estimating, bottom-up estimating, parametric modeling, the cost of quality, project management estimating software, vendor bid analysis, and reserve analysis.

Analogous estimates, also called **top-down estimates**, use the actual cost of a previous, similar project as the basis for estimating the cost of the current project. This technique requires a good deal of expert judgment and is generally less costly than others are, but it is also less accurate. Analogous estimates are most reliable when the previous projects are similar in fact, not just in appearance. In addition, the groups preparing cost estimates must have the needed expertise to determine whether certain parts of the project will be more or less expensive than analogous projects. For example, estimators often try to find a similar project and then customize/modify it for known differences. However, if the project to be estimated involves a new programming language or working with a new type of hardware or network, the analogous estimate technique could easily result in too low an estimate.

Bottom-up estimates involve estimating individual work items or activities and summing them to get a project total. It is sometimes referred to as activity-based costing. The size of the individual work items and the experience of the estimators drive the accuracy of the estimates. If a detailed WBS is available for a project, the project manager could have each person responsible for a work package develop his or her own cost estimate for that work package, or at least an estimate of the amount of resources required. Someone in the financial area of an organization often provides resource cost rates, such as labor rates or costs per pound of materials, which can be entered into project management software to calculate costs. The software automatically calculates information to create cost estimates for each level of the WBS and finally for the entire project. See Appendix A's section on project cost management for detailed information on entering resource costs and assigning resources to tasks to create a bottom-up estimate using Project 2007. Using smaller work items increases the accuracy of the cost estimate because the people assigned to do the work develop the cost estimate instead of someone unfamiliar with the work. The drawback with bottom-up estimates is that they are usually time-intensive and therefore expensive to develop.

Parametric modeling uses project characteristics (parameters) in a mathematical model to estimate project costs. A parametric model might provide an estimate of $50 per line of code for a software development project based on the programming language the project is using, the level of expertise of the programmers, the size and complexity of the data involved, and so on. Parametric models are most reliable when the historical information that was used to create the model is accurate, the parameters are readily quantifiable, and the model is flexible in terms of the size of the project. For example, in the 1980s, engineers at McDonnell Douglas Corporation (now part of Boeing) developed a parametric model for estimating aircraft costs based on a large historical database. The model included the following parameters: the type of aircraft (fighter aircraft, cargo aircraft, or passenger aircraft), how fast the plane would fly, the thrust-to-weight ratio of the engine, the estimated weights of various parts of the aircraft, the number of aircraft produced, the amount of time available to produce them, and so on. In contrast to this sophisticated model, some parametric models involve very simple heuristics or rules of thumb. For example, a large office automation project might use a ballpark figure of $10,000 per workstation based on a history of similar office automation projects developed during the same time period. Parametric models that are more complicated are usually computerized. See the Suggested Readings on the companion Web site for examples of parametric models, such as the COCOMO II model. In practice, many people find that using a combination or hybrid approach involving analogous, bottom up, and/or parametric modeling provides the best cost estimates.

Other considerations to make when preparing cost estimates are how much to include in reserves, as described earlier, the cost of quality, described in Chapter 8, Project Quality Management, and other cost estimating methods such as vendor bid analysis, as described in Chapter 12, Project Procurement Management. Using software to assist in cost estimating is described later in this chapter.

Typical Problems with Information Technology Cost Estimates

Although there are many tools and techniques to assist in creating project cost estimates, many information technology project cost estimates are still very inaccurate, especially those involving new technologies or software development. Tom DeMarco, a well-known author on software development, suggests four reasons for these inaccuracies and some ways to overcome them.[11]

- *Estimates are done too quickly*. Developing an estimate for a large software project is a complex task requiring a significant amount of effort. Many estimates must be done quickly and before clear system requirements have been produced. For example, the Surveyor Pro project described in the opening case involves a lot of complex software development. Before fully understanding what information surveyors really need in the system, someone would have to create a ROM estimate and budgetary estimates for this project. Rarely are the more precise, later estimates less than the earlier estimates for information technology projects. It is important to remember that estimates are done at various stages of the project, and project managers need to explain the rationale for each estimate.
- *Lack of estimating experience*. The people who develop software cost estimates often do not have much experience with cost estimation, especially for large projects. There is also not enough accurate, reliable project data available on which to base estimates. If an organization uses good project management techniques and develops a history of keeping reliable project information, including estimates, it should help improve the organization's estimates. Enabling information technology people to receive training and mentoring on cost estimating will also improve cost estimates.
- *Human beings are biased toward underestimation*. For example, senior information technology professionals or project managers might make estimates based on their own abilities and forget that many junior people will be working on a project. Estimators might also forget to allow for extra costs needed for integration and testing on large information technology projects. It is important for project managers and top management to review estimates and ask important questions to make sure the estimates are not biased.
- *Management desires accuracy*. Management might ask for an estimate, but really wants a more accurate number to help them create a bid to win a major contract or get internal funding. This problem is similar to the situation discussed in Chapter 6, Project Time Management, in which top managers or other stakeholders want project schedules to be shorter than the estimates. It is important for project managers to help develop good cost and schedule estimates and to use their leadership and negotiation skills to stand by those estimates.

It is also important to be cautious with initial estimates. Top management never forgets the first estimate and rarely, if ever, remembers how approved changes affect the estimate. It is a never-ending and crucial process to keep top management informed about revised cost estimates. It should be a formal process, albeit a possibly painful one.

Sample Cost Estimate

One of the best ways to learn how the cost estimating process works is by studying sample cost estimates. Every cost estimate is unique, just as every project is unique. You can see a short sample cost estimate in Chapter 3 for JWD Consulting's Project Management

Intranet Site project. You can also view the ResNet cost estimate on the companion Web site for this text.

This section includes a step-by-step approach for developing a cost estimate for the Surveyor Pro project described in the opening case. Of course, it is much shorter and simpler than a real cost estimate would be, but it illustrates a process to follow and uses several of the tools and techniques described earlier. For more detailed information on creating a cost estimate, see the NASA Cost Estimating Handbook and other references provided in the Suggested Readings on the companion Web site.

Before beginning any cost estimate, you must first gather as much information as possible about the project and ask how the organization plans to use the cost estimate. If the cost estimate will be the basis for contract awards and performance reporting, it should be a definitive estimate and as accurate as possible, as described earlier.

It is also important to clarify the ground rules and assumptions for the estimate. For the Surveyor Pro project cost estimate, these include the following:

- This project was preceded by a detailed study and proof of concept to show that it was possible to develop the hardware and software needed by surveyors and link the new devices to existing information systems. The proof of concept project produced a prototype handheld device and much of the software to provide basic functionality and link to the Global Positioning Systems (GPS) and other government databases used by surveyors. There is some data available to help estimate future labor costs, especially for the software development. There is also some data to help estimate the cost of the handheld devices.
- The main goal of this project is to produce 100 handheld devices, continue developing the software (especially the user interface), test the new system in the field, and train 100 surveyors in selected cities on how to use the new system. A follow-up contract is expected for a much larger number of devices based on the success of this project.
- There is a WBS for the project, as shown below:
  1. Project management
  2. Hardware
     - 2.1 Handheld devices
     - 2.2 Servers
  3. Software
     - 3.1 Licensed software
     - 3.2 Software development
  4. Testing
  5. Training and support
  6. Reserves
- Costs must be estimated by WBS and by month. The project manager will report progress on the project using earned value analysis, which requires this type of estimate.
- Costs will be provided in U.S. dollars. Since the project length is one year, inflation will not be included.
- The project will be managed by the government's project office. There will be a part-time project manager and four team members assigned to the project. The team members will help manage various parts of the project and provide

their expertise in the areas of software development, training, and support. Their total hours will be allocated as follows: 25 percent to project management, 25 percent to software development, 25 percent to training and support, and 25 percent to non-project work.

- The project involves purchasing the handheld devices from the same company that developed the prototype device. Based on producing 100 devices, the cost rate is estimated to be $600 per unit. The project will require four additional servers to run the software required for the devices and for managing the project.
- The project requires purchased software licenses for accessing the GPS and three other external systems. Software development includes developing a graphical user interface for the devices, an online help system, and a new module for tracking surveyor performance using the device.
- Testing costs should be low due to the success of the prototype project. An estimate based on 10 percent multiplied by the total hardware and software estimates should be sufficient.
- Training will include instructor-led classes in five different locations. The project team believes it will be best to outsource most of the training, including developing course materials, holding the sessions, and providing help desk support for three months as the surveyors start using their devices in the field.
- Because there are several risks related to this project, include 20 percent of the total estimate as reserves.
- You must develop a computer model for the estimate, making it easy to change several inputs, such as the number of labor hours for various activities or labor rates.

Fortunately, the project team can easily access cost estimates and actual information from similar projects. There is a great deal of information available from the proof of concept project, and the team can also talk to contractor personnel from the past project to help them develop the estimate. There are also some computer models available, such as a software-estimating tool based on function points.

Since the estimate must be provided by WBS and by month, the team first reviews a draft of the project schedule and makes further assumptions, as needed. They decide first to estimate the cost of each WBS item and then determine when the work will be performed, even though costs may be incurred at different times than the work is performed. Their budget expert has approved this approach for the estimate. Below are further assumptions and information for estimating the costs for each WBS category:

1. *Project management*: Estimate based on compensation for the part-time project manager and 25 percent of team members' time. The budget expert for this project suggested using a labor rate of $100/hour for the project manager and $75/hour for each team member, based on working an average of 160 hours per smonth, full time. Therefore, the total hours for the project manager under this category are 960 (160/2 * 12 = 960). Costs are also included for the four project team members working 25 percent of their time each, or, a total of 160 hours per month for all project personnel (160 * 12 = 1920). An additional amount will

be added for all contracted labor, estimated by multiplying 10 percent of their total estimates for software development and testing costs (10% * ($594,000 + $69,000)).

2. *Hardware*
   2.1 *Handheld devices*: 100 devices estimated by contractor at $600 per unit.
   2.2 *Servers*: Four servers estimated at $4,000 each, based on recent server purchases.

3. *Software*
   3.1 *Licensed software:* License costs will be negotiated with each supplier. Since there is a strong probability of large future contracts and great publicity if the system works well, costs are expected to be lower than usual. A cost of $200/handheld device will be used.
   3.2 *Software development:* This estimate will use two approaches: a labor estimate and a function point estimate. The higher estimate will be used. If the estimates are more than 20 percent apart, a third approach to providing the estimate will be required. The supplier who did the development on the proof of concept project will provide the labor estimate input, and local technical experts will make the function point estimates.
4. *Testing*: Based on similar projects, testing will be estimated as 10 percent of the total hardware and software cost.
5. *Training and support*: Based on similar projects, training will be estimated on a per-trainee basis, plus travel costs. The cost per trainee (100 total) will be $500, and travel will be $700/day/person for the instructors and project team members. It is estimated that there will be a total of 12 travel days. Labor costs for the project team members will be added to this estimate to assist in training and providing support after the training. The labor hours estimate for team members is 1,920 hours total.
6. *Reserves*: As directed, reserves will be estimated at 20 percent of the total estimate.

The project team then develops a cost model using the above information. Figure 7-2 shows a spreadsheet that summarizes the costs by WBS item based on the above information. Notice that the WBS items are listed in the first column, and sometimes the items are broken down into more detail based on how the costs are estimated. For example, the project management category includes three items to calculate costs for the project manager, the project team members, and the contractors, since all of these people will perform some project management activities. Also notice that there are columns for entering the number of units or hours and the cost per unit or hour. Several items are estimated using this approach. There are also some short comments within the estimate, such as reserves being 20 percent of the total estimate. Also notice that you can easily change several input variables, such as number of hours or cost per hour, to quickly change the estimate.

There is also an asterisk by the software development item in Figure 7-2, referring to another reference for detailed information on how this more complicated estimate was made. Recall that one of the assumptions was that software development must be estimated using two approaches, and that the higher estimate be used as long as both estimates were no more than 20 percent apart. The labor estimate in this case was slightly higher than the function

Surveyor Pro Project Cost Estimate Created October 5

	# Units/Hrs.	Cost/Unit/Hr.	Subtotals	WBS Level 2 Totals	% of Total
WBS Items					
1. Project Management				**$306,300**	**20%**
Project manager	960	$100	$96,000		
Project team members	1920	$75	$144,000		
Contractors (10% of software development and testing)			$66,300		
2. Hardware				**$76,000**	**5%**
2.1 Handheld devices	100	$600	$60,000		
2.2 Servers	4	$4,000	$16,000		
3. Software				**$614,000**	**40%**
3.1 Licensed software	100	$200	$20,000		
3.2 Software development*			$594,000		
4. Testing (10% of total hardware and software costs)			$69,000	**$69,000**	**5%**
5. Training and Support				**$202,400**	**13%**
Trainee cost	100	$500	$50,000		
Travel cost	12	$700	$8,400		
Project team members	1920	$75	$144,000		
6. Reserves (20% of total estimate)			$253,540	**$253,540**	**17%**
Total project cost estimate				**$1,521,240**	

* See software development estimate

FIGURE 7-2 Surveyor Pro project cost estimate

point estimate, so that number was used ($594,000 versus $562,158). Details are provided in Figure 7-3 on how the function point estimate was made. As you can see, there are many assumptions made in producing the function point estimate. Again, by putting the information into a cost model, you can easily change several inputs to adjust the estimate. See the referenced article and other sources for more information on function point estimates.

It is very important to have several people review the project cost estimate. It is also helpful to analyze the total dollar value as well as the percentage of the total amount for each major WBS category. For example, a senior executive could quickly look at the Surveyor Pro project cost estimate and decide if the numbers are reasonable and the assumptions are well documented. In this case, the government had budgeted $1.5 million for the project, so the estimate was right in line with that amount. The WBS Level 2 items (project management, hardware, software, testing, etc.) also seemed to be at appropriate percentages of the total cost based on similar past projects. In some cases, a project team might also be asked to provide a range estimate for each item instead of one discrete amount. For example, they might estimate that the testing costs will be between $60,000 and $80,000 and document their assumptions in determining those values. It is also import to update cost estimates, especially if any major changes occur on a project.

After the total cost estimate is approved, the team can then allocate costs for each month based on the project schedule and when costs will be incurred. Many organizations also require that the estimated costs be allocated into certain budget categories, as described in the next section.

Surveyor Pro Software Development Estimate Created October 5

1. Labor Estimate	# Units/Hrs.	Cost/Unit/Hr.	Subtotals	Calculations
Contractor labor estimate	3000	$150	$450,000	3000 * 150
Project team member estimate	1920	$75	$144,000	1920 * 75
Total labor estimate			**$594,000**	Sum above two values
2. Function point estimate**	Quantity	Conversion Factor	Function Points	**Calculations**
External inputs	10	4	40	10 * 4
External interface files	3	7	21	3 * 7
External outputs	4	5	20	4 * 5
External queries	6	4	24	6 * 4
Logical internal tables	7	10	70	7 * 10
Total function points			**175**	Sum above function point values
Java 2 languange equivalency value			46	Assumed value from reference
Source lines of code (SLOC) estimate			8,050	175 * 46
Productivity×KSLOC^Penalty (in months)			29.28	3.13 * 8.05^1.072 (see reference)
Total labor hours (160 hours/month)			4,684.65	29.28 * 160
Cost/labor hour ($120/hour)			$120	Assumed value from budget expert
Total function point estimate			**$562,158**	4684.65 * 120

**Approach based on paper by William Roetzheim, "Estimating Software Costs," Cost Xpert Group, Inc. (2003) using the COCOMO II default linear productivity factor (3.13) and penalty factor (1.072).

FIGURE 7-3 Surveyor Pro software development estimate

DETERMINING THE BUDGET

Determining the project budget involves allocating the project cost estimate to individual work items over time. These work items are based on the activities in the work breakdown structure for the project. The activity cost estimates, basis of estimates, scope baseline, project schedule, resource calendars, contracts, and organizational process assets are all inputs for determining the budget. The main goal of the cost budgeting process is to produce a cost baseline for measuring project performance and project funding requirements. It may also result in project document updates, such as items being added, removed, or modified to the scope statement or project schedule.

For example, the Surveyor Pro project team could use the cost estimate from Figure 7-2 along with the project schedule and other information to allocate costs for each month. Figure 7-4 provides an example of a cost baseline for this project. Again, it's important for the team to document assumptions they made when developing the cost baseline and have several experts review it.

Most organizations have a well-established process for preparing budgets. For example, many organizations require budget estimates to include the number of full-time equivalent (FTE) staff, often referred to as headcount, for each month of the project. This number provides the basis for estimating total compensation costs each year. Many organizations also want to know the amount of money projected to be paid to suppliers for their labor costs or other purchased goods and services. Other common budget categories include travel, depreciation, rents/leases, and other supplies and expenses. It is important to understand these budget categories before developing an estimate to make sure data is collected accordingly. Organizations use this information to track costs across projects and

Surveyor Pro Project Cost Baseline Created October 10*

WBS Items	1	2	3	4	5	6	7	8	9	10	11	12	Totals
1. Project Management													
1.1 Project manager	8,000	8,000	8,000	8,000	8,000	8,000	8,000	8,000	8,000	8,000	8,000	8,000	96,000
1.2 Project team members	12,000	12,000	12,000	12,000	12,000	12,000	12,000	12,000	12,000	12,000	12,000	12,000	144,000
1.3 Contractors		6,027	6,027	6,027	6,027	6,027	6,027	6,027	6,027	6,027	6,027	6,027	66,300
2. Hardware													
2.1 Handheld devices				30,000	30,000								60,000
2.2 Servers				8,000	8,000								16,000
3. Software													
3.1 Licensed software				10,000	10,000								20,000
3.2 Software development		60,000	60,000	80,000	127,000	127,000	90,000	50,000					594,000
4. Testing			6,000	8,000	12,000	15,000	15,000	13,000					69,000
5. Training and Support													
5.1 Trainee cost									50,000				50,000
5.2 Travel cost									8,400				8,400
5.3 Project team members							24,000	24,000	24,000	24,000	24,000	24,000	144,000
6. Reserves				10,000	10,000	30,000	30,000	60,000	40,000	40,000	30,000	3,540	253,540
Totals	20,000	86,027	92,027	172,027	223,027	198,027	185,027	173,027	148,427	90,027	80,027	53,567	1,521,240

*See the lecture slides for this chapter on the companion Web site for a larger view of this and other figures in this chapter. Numbers are rounded, so some totals appear to be off.

FIGURE 7-4 Surveyor Pro project cost baseline

non-project work and look for ways to reduce costs. They also use the information for legal and tax purposes.

In addition to providing input for budgetary estimates, cost budgeting provides a cost baseline. A **cost baseline** is a time-phased budget that project managers use to measure and monitor cost performance. Estimating costs for each major project activity over time provides project managers and top management with a foundation for project cost control, as described in the next section. See Appendix A for information on using Project 2007 for cost control.

Cost budgeting, as well as requested changes or clarifications, may result in updates to the cost management plan, a subsidiary part of the project management plan. Cost budgeting also provides information for project funding requirements. For example, some projects have all funds available when the project begins, but others must rely on periodic funding to avoid cash flow problems. If the cost baseline shows that more funds are required in certain months than are expected to be available, the organization must make adjustments to avoid financial problems.

MEDIA SNAPSHOT

Anyone who has run for a public office or worked on a political campaign knows how expensive they can be. Barack Obama and his campaign leaders understood the potential of today's news media and technology, especially for raising money and finding volunteers for his highly successful campaign to become the 44th President of the U.S.

- The Obama campaign used 16 different online social platforms, including Facebook, LinkedIn (business networkers), MySpace (youth), YouTube (video), Fickr (images), Digg (social bookmarking), Twitter (mobile), BlackPlanet (African-

continued

Americans), Eons (baby boomers), GLEE (gay and lesbians), and MiGente (Latinos) to interact with people from various backgrounds. Sources say 80 percent of all contributions originated from these social networks, and some say 90 percent of all contributions (which totaled over $600 million) were less than $100.[12]

- In a *60 Minutes* episode shortly after the election, campaign leaders discussed some of the details of the campaign. David Axelrod, Obama's chief strategist, recalled, "When we started the campaign, we met around a table like this. And there was just a handful of us. You know, we started with nothing. And Barack said to us, 'I want this to be a grassroots campaign. I wanna reinvigorate our democracy. First of all I think that's the only way we can win and secondly I want to rekindle some idealism that together we can get things done in this country."[13]
- The Web site My.BarackObama was created to develop an online community with over a million members. Users could get access to the tools they needed to effectively organize on a local level to help elect Obama. For example, the site helped users find local events and groups, contact undecided voters in their areas, and share their stories on blogs. Obama spread his message of change and invigorated millions of people to support him.

CONTROLLING COSTS

Controlling project costs includes monitoring cost performance, ensuring that only appropriate project changes are included in a revised cost baseline, and informing project stakeholders of authorized changes to the project that will affect costs. The project management plan, project funding requirements, work performance data, and organizational process assets are inputs for controlling costs. Outputs of this process are work performance measurements, budget forecasts, organizational process asset updates, change requests, project management plan updates, and product document updates.

Several tools and techniques assist in project cost control. As shown in Appendix A, Project 2007 has many cost management features to help you enter budgeted costs, set a baseline, enter actuals, calculate variances, and run various cost reports. In addition to using software, however, there must be some change control system to define procedures for changing the cost baseline. This cost control change system is part of the integrated change control system described in Chapter 4, Project Integration Management. Since many projects do not progress exactly as planned, new or revised cost estimates are often required, as are estimates to evaluate alternate courses of action. Performance review meetings can be a powerful tool for helping to control project costs. People often perform better when they know they must report on their progress. Another very important tool for cost control is performance measurement. Although many general accounting approaches are available for measuring cost performance, earned value management (EVM) is a very powerful cost control technique that is unique to the field of project management.

Earned Value Management

Earned value management (EVM) is a project performance measurement technique that integrates scope, time, and cost data. Given a cost performance baseline, project managers and their teams can determine how well the project is meeting scope, time, and cost goals by entering actual information and then comparing it to the baseline. A **baseline** is the original project plan plus approved changes. Actual information includes whether or not a WBS item was completed or approximately how much of the work was completed, when the work actually started and ended, and how much it actually cost to do the completed work.

In the past, earned value management was used primarily on large government projects. Today, however, more and more companies are realizing the value of using this tool to help control costs. In fact, a discussion by several academic experts in earned value management and a real practitioner revealed the need to clarify how to actually calculate earned value. Brenda Taylor, a senior project manager for P2 Project Management Solutions in Johannesburg, South Africa, questioned calculating earned value by simply multiplying the planned value to date by a percentage complete value. She suggested using the rate of performance instead, as described below.

Earned value management involves calculating three values for each activity or summary activity from a project's WBS.

1. The **planned value (PV)**, also called the budget, is that portion of the approved total cost estimate planned to be spent on an activity during a given period. Table 7-3 shows an example of earned value calculations. Suppose a project included a summary activity of purchasing and installing a new Web server. Suppose further that, according to the plan, it would take one week and cost a total of $10,000 for the labor hours, hardware, and software involved. The planned value (PV) for that activity that week is, therefore, $10,000.
2. The **actual cost (AC)** is the total direct and indirect costs incurred in accomplishing work on an activity during a given period. For example, suppose it actually took two weeks and cost $20,000 to purchase and install the new Web server. Assume that $15,000 of these actual costs were incurred during Week 1 and $5,000 was incurred during Week 2. These amounts are the actual cost (AC) for the activity each week.
3. The **earned value (EV)** is an estimate of the value of the physical work actually completed. It is based on the original planned costs for the project or activity and the rate at which the team is completing work on the project or activity to date. The **rate of performance (RP)** is the ratio of actual work completed to the percentage of work planned to have been completed at any given time during the life of the project or activity. For example, suppose the server installation was halfway completed by the end of Week 1. The rate of performance would be 50 percent (50/100) because by the end of Week 1, the planned schedule reflects that the task should be 100 percent complete and only 50 percent of that work has been completed. In Table 7-4, the earned value estimate after one week is therefore $5,000.[11]

TABLE 7-4 Earned value calculations for one activity after Week 1

Activity	Week 1
Earned Value (EV)	5,000
Planned Value (PV)	10,000
Actual cost (AC)	15,000
Cost variance (CV)	−10,000
Schedule variance (SV)	−5,000
Cost performance index (CPI)	33%
Schedule performance index (SPI)	50%

The earned value calculations in Table 7-4 are carried out as follows:

$$EV = 10,000 * 50\% = 5,000$$
$$CV = 5,000 - 15,000 = -10,000$$
$$SV = 5,000 - 10,000 = -5,000$$
$$CPI = 5,000/15,000 = 33\%$$
$$SPI = 5,000/10,000 = 50\%$$

Table 7-5 summarizes the formulas used in earned value management. Note that the formulas for variances and indexes start with EV, the earned value. Variances are calculated by subtracting the actual cost or planned value from EV, and indexes are calculated by

TABLE 7-5 Earned value formulas

Term	Formula
Earned value (EV)	EV = PV to date * RP
Cost variance (CV)	CV = EV – AC
Schedule variance (SV)	SV = EV – PV
Cost performance index (CPI)	CPI = EV/AC
Schedule performance index (SPI)	SPI = EV/PV
Estimate at completion (EAC)	EAC = BAC/CPI
Estimated time to complete	Original time estimate/SPI

dividing EV by the actual cost or planned value. After you total the EV, AC, and PV data for all activities on a project, you can use the CPI and SPI to project how much it will cost and how long it will take to finish the project based on performance to date. Given the budget at completion and original time estimate, you can divide by the appropriate index to calculate the estimate at completion (EAC) and estimated time to complete, assuming performance remains the same. There are no standard acronyms for the term estimated time to complete or original time estimate.

Cost variance (CV) is the earned value minus the actual cost. If cost variance is a negative number, it means that performing the work cost more than planned. If cost variance is a positive number, it means that performing the work cost less than planned.

Schedule variance (SV) is the earned value minus the planned value. A negative schedule variance means that it took longer than planned to perform the work, and a positive schedule variance means that it took less time than planned to perform the work.

The **cost performance index (CPI)** is the ratio of earned value to actual cost and can be used to estimate the projected cost of completing the project. If the cost performance index is equal to one, or 100 percent, then the planned and actual costs are equal—the costs are exactly as budgeted. If the cost performance index is less than one or less than 100 percent, the project is over budget. If the cost performance index is greater than one or more than 100 percent, the project is under budget.

The **schedule performance index (SPI)** is the ratio of earned value to planned value and can be used to estimate the projected time to complete the project. Similar to the cost performance index, a schedule performance index of one, or 100 percent, means the project is on schedule. If the schedule performance index is greater than one or 100 percent, then the project is ahead of schedule. If the schedule performance index is less than one or 100 percent, the project is behind schedule.

Note that in general, *negative numbers for cost and schedule variance indicate problems in those areas*. Negative numbers mean the project is costing more than planned or taking longer than planned. Likewise, *CPI and SPI less than one or less than 100 percent also indicate problems*.

The cost performance index can be used to calculate the **estimate at completion (EAC)**—an estimate of what it will cost to complete the project based on performance to date. Similarly, the schedule performance index can be used to calculate an estimated time to complete the project.

You can graph earned value information to track project performance. Figure 7-5 shows an earned value chart for a one-year project after five months. Note that the actual cost and earned value lines end at five months, since that is the point in time where the data is collected or estimated. The chart includes three lines and two points, as follows:

- Planned value (PV), the cumulative planned amounts for all activities by month. Note that the planned value line extends for the estimated length of the project and ends at the BAC point.
- Actual cost (AC), the cumulative actual amounts for all activities by month.
- Earned value (EV), the cumulative earned value amounts for all activities by month.
- **Budget at completion (BAC)**, the original total budget for the project, or $100,000 in this example. The BAC point is plotted on the chart at the original time estimate of 12 months.

- Estimate at completion (EAC), estimated to be $122,308, in this example. This number is calculated by taking the BAC, or $100,000 in this case, and dividing by the CPI, which, in this example, was 81.761 percent. This EAC point is plotted on the chart at the estimated time to complete of 12.74 months. This number is calculated by taking the original time estimate, or 12 months in this case, and dividing by the SPI, which in this example was 94.203 percent.

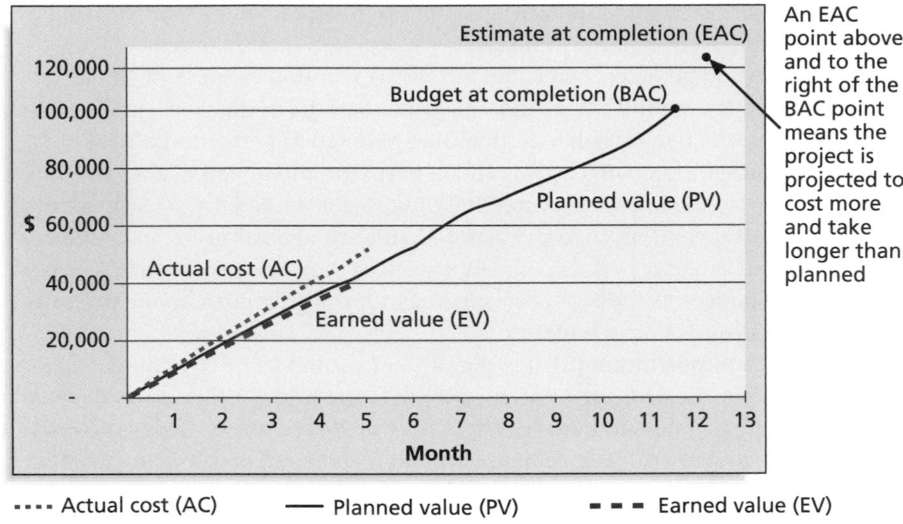

FIGURE 7-5 Earned value chart for project after five months

Viewing earned value information in chart form helps you visualize how the project is performing. For example, you can see the planned performance by looking at the planned value line. If the project goes as planned, it will finish in 12 months and cost $100,000. Notice in the example in Figure 7-5 that the actual cost line is always right on or above the earned value line. When the actual cost line is right on or above the earned value line, costs are equal to or more than planned. The planned value line is pretty close to the earned value line, just slightly higher in the last month. This relationship means that the project has been right on schedule until the last month, when the project fell behind schedule.

Top managers overseeing multiple projects often like to see performance information in a graphical form such as the earned value chart in Figure 7-5. For example, in the opening case, the government officials were reviewing earned value charts and estimates at completion for several different projects. Earned value charts allow you to see how projects are performing quickly. If there are serious cost and schedule performance problems, top management may decide to terminate projects or take other corrective action. The estimates at completion (EAC) are important inputs to budget decisions, especially if total funds are limited. Earned value management is an important technique because, when used effectively, it helps top management and project managers evaluate progress and make sound management decisions.

If earned value management is such a powerful cost control tool, then why doesn't every organization use it? Why do many government projects require it, but many commercial projects don't? Two reasons why organizations do not widely use earned value management are its focus on tracking actual performance versus planned performance and the importance of percentage completion data in making calculations. Many projects, particularly information technology projects, do not have good planning information, so tracking performance against a plan might produce misleading information. Several cost estimates are usually made on information technology projects, and keeping track of the most recent cost estimate and the actual costs associated with it could be cumbersome. In addition, estimating percentage completion of tasks might produce misleading information. What does it really mean to say that a task is actually 75 percent complete after three months? Such a statement is often not synonymous with saying the task will be finished in one more month or after spending an additional 25 percent of the planned budget.

To make earned value management simpler to use, organizations can modify the level of detail and still reap the benefits of the technique. For example, you can use percentage completion data such as 0 percent for items not yet started, 50 percent for items in progress, and 100 percent for completed tasks. As long as the project is defined in enough detail, this simplified percentage completion data should provide enough summary information to allow managers to see how well a project is doing overall. You can get very accurate total project performance information using these simple percentage complete amounts. For example, using simplified percentage complete amounts for a one-year project with weekly reporting and an average task size of one week, you can expect about a 1 percent error rate.[15]

You can also only enter and collect earned value data at summary levels of the WBS. Quentin Fleming, author of the book *Earned Value Project Management*,[16] often gives presentations about earned value management. Many people express their frustration in trying to collect such detailed information. Quentin explains that you do not have to collect information at the work package level to use earned value management. It is most important to have a deliverable-oriented WBS, and many WBS items can summarize several subdeliverables. For example, you might have a WBS for a house that includes items for each room in the house. Just collecting earned value data for each room would provide meaningful information instead of trying to collect the detailed information on each component of the room, such as flooring, furniture, lighting, and so on.

It is important to remember that the heart and soul of EVM are estimates. The entire EVM process begins with an estimate and when the estimate is off, all the calculations will be off. Before an organization attempts to use EVM, it must learn to develop good estimates. Earned value management is the primary method available for integrating performance, cost, and schedule data. It can be a powerful tool for project managers and top management to use in evaluating project performance. Project management software, such as Project 2007, includes tables for collecting earned value data and reports that calculate variance information. Project 2007 also allows you to easily produce the earned value chart, similar to the one in Figure 7-5, without importing the data into Microsoft Excel. See the project cost management section of Appendix A for an example of using earned value management and the Suggested Readings on the companion Web site for more information. Another approach to evaluating the performance of multiple projects is project portfolio management.

Project Portfolio Management

As mentioned in Chapter 1, many organizations now collect and control an entire suite of projects or investments as one set of interrelated activities in one place—a portfolio. Project managers need to understand how their projects fit into the bigger picture, and they need to help their organizations make wise investment decisions. Many project managers also want to move on to manage larger projects, become program managers, then vice presidents, and eventually CEOs. Understanding project portfolio management, therefore, is important for project and organizational success.

There can be a portfolio for information technology projects, for example, and portfolios for other types of projects. An organization can view project portfolio management as having five levels, from simplest to most complex, as follows:

1. Put all your projects in one database.
2. Prioritize the projects in your database.
3. Divide your projects into two or three budgets based on type of investment, such as utilities or required systems to keep things running, incremental upgrades, and strategic investments.
4. Automate the repository.
5. Apply modern portfolio theory, including risk-return tools that map project risk on a curve.

For example, Jane Walton, the project portfolio manager for information technology projects at Schlumberger, saved the company $3 million in one year by organizing the organization's 120 information technology projects into a portfolio. Manufacturing companies used project portfolio management in the 1960s, and Walton anticipated the need to justify investments in information technology projects just as managers have to justify capital investment projects. She found that 80 percent of the organization's projects overlapped, and 14 separate projects were trying to accomplish the same thing. Other managers, such as Douglas Hubbard, president of a consulting firm, see the need to use project portfolio management, especially for information technology projects. Hubbard suggests, "IT investments are huge, risky investments. It's time we do this."[17]

Project portfolio managers can start by using spreadsheet software to develop and manage project portfolios, or they can use sophisticated software designed to help manage project portfolios. Several software tools available today help project portfolio managers summarize earned value and project portfolio information, as described in the following section. Although many organizations have adopted project portfolio management tools and techniques (including portfolio management software) for information technology projects, they are not following best practices to truly reap the benefits, as described in the Best Practice feature below.

BEST PRACTICE

A global survey released by Borland Software in 2006 suggests that many organizations are still at a low-level of maturity in terms of how they define project goals, allocate resources, and measure overall success of their information technology portfolios. Approximately 54 percent of survey respondents were from the Americas, 32 percent were from Asia Pacific, and 14 percent were from Europe, the Middle East and Africa. Some of the findings include the following:

- Only 22 percent of survey respondents reported that their organization either effectively or very effectively uses a project plan for managing projects.
- Only 17 percent have either rigorous or very rigorous processes for project plans, which include developing a baseline and estimating schedule, cost, and business impact of projects.
- Only 20 percent agreed their organizations monitor portfolio progress and coordinate across inter-dependent projects.
- The majority of respondents agreed their organization has no business impact assessment for completed projects, and success is measured only at the project level, based on performance against schedule and budget.
- Just two percent of survey respondents felt their organization was very effective at measuring performance of the overall portfolio.

According to Branndon Stewart, director of Information Technology Management and Governance products at Borland, "The most successful organizations are taking a holistic view of focusing, managing, and measuring their IT efforts with an integrated combination of best practice processes, training and technology. Unfortunately, most organizations today still aren't taking this approach.... IT leaders understand the value of a balanced portfolio aligned with business objectives, but most lack a well-defined and consistent process for managing the origination, evaluation, and execution of IT investments." Stewart continued, "Portfolio management enables IT to make fact-based investment decisions in unison with business stakeholders, thus ensuring alignment, improving visibility, and shifting the burden of investment decisions from the CIO to all stakeholders."[18]

USING PROJECT MANAGEMENT SOFTWARE TO ASSIST IN PROJECT COST MANAGEMENT

Most organizations use software to assist in various activities related to project cost management. Spreadsheets are a common tool for cost estimating, cost budgeting, and cost control. Many companies also use more sophisticated and centralized financial applications software to provide important cost-related information to accounting and finance personnel. This section focuses specifically on how you can use project management software in cost management. Appendix A includes a section on using the cost management features in Project 2007.

Project management software can be a very helpful tool during each project cost management process. It can help you study overall project information or focus on tasks that are over a specified cost limit. You can use the software to assign costs to resources and tasks, prepare cost estimates, develop cost budgets, and monitor cost performance. Project 2007 has several standard cost reports: cash flow, budget, over budget tasks, over budget resources, and earned value reports. For several of these reports, you must enter percentage completion information and actual costs, just as you need this information when manually calculating earned value or other analyses.

Although Microsoft Project 2007 has a fair amount of cost management features, many information technology project managers use other tools to manage cost information; they do not know that they can use Project 2007 for cost management or they simply do not track costs based on a WBS, as most project management software does. As with most software packages, users need training to use the software effectively and understand the features available. Instead of using dedicated project management software for cost management, some information technology project managers use company accounting systems; others use spreadsheet software to achieve more flexibility. Project managers who use other software often do so because these other systems are more generally accepted in their organizations and more people know how to use them. In order to improve project cost management, several companies have developed methods to link data between their project management software and their main accounting software systems.

Many organizations are starting to use software to organize and analyze all types of project data into project portfolios and across the entire enterprise. Enterprise or project portfolio management tools integrate information from multiple projects to show the projects' status, or health. See Figure 1-5 in Chapter 1 for a sample. A 2008 study by the Gantry Group measured the return on investment of implementing portfolio management software by IT departments. They estimated savings of 6.5 percent of the average annual IT budget by the end of year one. They also found that using project portfolio management software had the following benefits:

- Improved the annual average project timeliness by 45.2 percent
- Reduced IT management time spent on project status reporting by 43 percent, reclaiming 3.8 hours of each manager's time per week
- Reduced IT management time spent on IT labor capitalization reporting by 55 percent, recouping 3.6 hours per report
- Decreased the time to achieve financial sign-off for new IT projects by 20.4 percent, or 8.4 days[19]

As with using any software, however, managers must make sure that the data is accurate and up-to-date and ask pertinent questions before making any major decisions.

CASE WRAP-UP

After talking to his colleagues about the meeting, Juan had a better idea of the importance of project cost management. He understood the value of doing detailed studies before making major expenditures on new projects, especially after learning about the high cost of correcting defects late in a project. He also learned how important it is to develop good cost estimates and keep costs on track. He really enjoyed seeing how the cost estimate for the Surveyor Pro project was developed and was eager to learn more about various estimating tools and techniques.

At the meeting, government officials cancelled several projects when the project managers showed how poorly the projects were performing and admitted that they did not do much planning and analysis early in the projects. Juan knew that he could not focus on just the technical aspects of projects if he wanted to move ahead in his career. He began to wonder whether several projects the city was considering were really worth the taxpayers' money. Issues of cost management added a new dimension to Juan's job.

Chapter Summary

Project cost management is a traditionally weak area of information technology projects. Information technology project managers must acknowledge the importance of cost management and take responsibility for understanding basic cost concepts, cost estimating, budgeting, and cost control.

Project managers must understand several basic principles of cost management in order to be effective in managing project costs. Important concepts include profits and profit margins, life cycle costing, cash flow analysis, sunk costs, and learning curve theory.

Estimating costs is a very important part of project cost management. There are several types of cost estimates, including rough order of magnitude (ROM), budgetary, and definitive. Each type of estimate is done during different stages of the project life cycle, and each has a different level of accuracy. There are several tools and techniques for developing cost estimates, including analogous estimating, bottom-up estimating, parametric modeling, and computerized tools. A detailed example of a project cost estimate is provided, illustrating how to apply several of these concepts.

Determining the budget involves allocating costs to individual work items over time. It is important to understand how particular organizations prepare budgets so estimates are made accordingly.

Controlling costs includes monitoring cost performance, reviewing changes, and notifying project stakeholders of changes related to costs. Many basic accounting and finance principles relate to project cost management. Earned value management is an important method used for measuring project performance. Earned value management integrates scope, cost, and schedule information. Project portfolio management allows organizations to collect and control an entire suite of projects or investments as one set of interrelated activities.

Several software products assist with project cost management. Project 2007 has many cost management features, including earned value management. Enterprise project management software and portfolio management software can help managers evaluate data on multiple projects.

Quick Quiz

1. ________________ is a resource sacrificed or foregone to achieve a specific objective or something given up in exchange.
   a. Money
   b. Liability
   c. Trade
   d. Cost
2. What is the main goal of project cost management?
   a. to complete a project for as little cost as possible
   b. to complete a project within an approved budget
   c. to provide truthful and accurate cost information on projects
   d. to ensure that an organization's money is used wisely

3. Which of the following is not a key output of project cost management?
   a. activity cost estimates
   b. a cost management plan
   c. updates to the project management plan
   d. a cost performance baseline

4. If a company loses $5 for every $100 in revenue for a certain product, what is the profit margin for that product?
   a. –5 percent
   b. 5 percent
   c. –$5
   d. $5

5. _______________ reserves allow for future situations that are unpredictable.
   a. Contingency
   b. Financial
   c. Management
   d. Baseline

6. You are preparing a cost estimate for a building based on its location, purpose, number of square feet, and other characteristics. What cost estimating technique are you using?
   a. parametric
   b. analogous
   c. bottom-up
   d. top-down

7. _______________ involves allocating the project cost estimate to individual work items over time.
   a. Reserve analysis
   b. Life cycle costing
   c. Project cost budgeting
   d. Earned value analysis

8. _______________ is a project performance measurement technique that integrates scope, time, and cost data.
   a. Reserve analysis
   b. Life cycle costing
   c. Project cost budgeting
   d. Earned value analysis

9. If the actual cost for a WBS item is $1500 and its earned value was $2000, what is its cost variance, and is it under or over budget?
   a. the cost variance is –$500, which is over budget
   b. the cost variance is –$500, which is under budget
   c. the cost variance is $500, which is over budget
   d. the cost variance is $500, which is under budget
10. If a project is halfway completed and its schedule performance index is 110 percent and its cost performance index is 95 percent, how is it progressing?
    a. it is ahead of schedule and under budget
    b. it is ahead of schedule and over budget
    c. it is behind schedule and under budget
    d. it is behind schedule and over budget

Quick Quiz Answers

1. d; 2. b; 3. b; 4. a; 5. c; 6. a; 7. c; 8. d; 9. d; 10. b

Discussion Questions

1. Discuss why many information technology professionals may overlook project cost management and how this might affect completing projects within budget.
2. Explain some of the basic principles of cost management, such as profits, life cycle costs, tangible and intangible costs and benefits, direct and indirect costs, reserves, and so on.
3. Give examples of when you would prepare rough order of magnitude (ROM), budgetary, and definitive cost estimates for an information technology project. Give an example of how you would use each of the following techniques for creating a cost estimate: analogous, parametric, and bottom-up.
4. Explain what happens during the process to determine the project budget.
5. Explain how earned value management (EVM) can be used to control costs and measure project performance and speculate as to why it is not used more often. What are some general rules of thumb for deciding if cost variance, schedule variance, cost performance index, and schedule performance index numbers are good or bad?
6. What is project portfolio management? Can project managers use it with earned value management?
7. Describe several types of software that project managers can use to support project cost management.

Exercises

1. Given the following information for a one-year project, answer the following questions. Recall that PV is the planned value, EV is the earned value, AC is the actual cost, and BAC is the budget at completion.

   PV = $ 23,000

   EV = $ 20,000

   AC = $ 25,000

   BAC = $ 120,000

   a. What is the cost variance, schedule variance, cost performance index (CPI), and schedule performance index (SPI) for the project?
   b. How is the project doing? Is it ahead of schedule or behind schedule? Is it under budget or over budget?
   c. Use the CPI to calculate the estimate at completion (EAC) for this project. Is the project performing better or worse than planned?
   d. Use the schedule performance index (SPI) to estimate how long it will take to finish this project.
   e. Sketch the earned value chart based for this project, using Figure 7-5 as a guide.

2. Create a cost estimate/model for building a new, state-of-the-art multimedia classroom for your organization within the next six months. The classroom should include 20 high-end personal computers with appropriate software for your organization, a network server, Internet access for all machines, an instructor station, and a projection system. Be sure to include personnel costs associated with the project management for this project. Document the assumptions you made in preparing the estimate and provide explanations for key numbers.
3. Research online information, textbooks, and local classes for using the cost management features of Project 2007 or other software tools, including project portfolio management software (e.g., CA Clarity PPM, Primavera, Daptiv PPM, etc.). Also review the project cost management section of Appendix A. Ask three people in different information technology organizations that use project management software if they use the cost management features of the software and in what ways they use them. Write a brief report of what you learned from your research.
4. Read the article by William Roetzheim on the companion Web site on estimating software costs. Find one or two other references on using SLOC and function points. In your own words, explain how to estimate software development costs using both of these approaches in a two-page paper.
5. Create a spreadsheet to calculate your projected total costs, total revenues, and total profits for giving a seminar on cost estimating. Below are some of your assumptions:
   - You will charge $600 per person for a two-day class.
   - You estimate that 30 people will register for and attend the class, but you want to change this input.
   - Your fixed costs include $500 total to rent a room for both days, setup fees of $400 for registration, and $300 for designing a postcard for advertising.

- You will not include any of your labor costs for this estimate, but you estimate that you will spend at least 150 hours developing materials, managing the project, and giving the actual class. You would like to know what your time is worth given different scenarios.
- You will order 5,000 postcards, mail 4,000, and distribute the rest to friends and colleagues.
- Your variable costs include the following:
  a. –$5 per person for registration plus four percent of the class fee per person to handle credit card processing; assume everyone pays by credit card.
  b. $.40 per postcard for printing if you order 5,000 or more.
  c. $.25 per postcard for mailing and postage.
  d. $25 per person for beverages and lunch.
  d. $30 per person for class handouts.

Be sure to have input cells for any variables that might change, such as the cost of postage, handouts, and so on. Calculate your profits based on the following number of people who attend: 10, 20, 30, 40, 50, and 60. In addition, calculate what your time would be worth per hour based on the number of students. Try to use the Excel data table feature showing the profits based on the number of students. If you are unfamiliar with data tables, just repeat the calculations for each possibility of 10, 20, 30, 40, 50, and 60 students. Print your results on one page, highlighting the profits for each scenario and what your time is worth.

Running Case

Tony Prince and his team working on the Recreation and Wellness Intranet Project have been asked to refine the existing cost estimate for the project so they can evaluate supplier bids and have a solid cost baseline for evaluating project performance. Recall that your schedule and cost goals are to complete the project in six months for under $200,000.

Tasks

1. Prepare and print a one-page cost model for the project, similar to the one provided in Figure 7-2. Use the following WBS, and be sure to document assumptions you make in preparing the cost model. Assume a labor rate of $100/hour for the project manager and $60/hour for other project team members. Assume that none of the work is outsourced, labor costs for users are not included, and there are no additional hardware costs. The total estimate should be $200,000.
   1. Project management
   2. Requirements definition
   3. Web site design
      3.1 Registration for recreational programs
      3.2 Registration for classes and programs
      3.3 Tracking system
      3.4 Incentive system

    4. Web site development
        4.1 Registration for recreational programs
        4.2 Registration for classes and programs
        4.3 Tracking system
        4.4 Incentive system
    5. Testing
    6. Training, roll out, and support

2. Using the cost model you created above, prepare a cost baseline by allocating the costs by WBS for each month of the project.
3. Assume you have completed three months of the project. The BAC was $200,000 for this six-month project. Also assume the following:

   PV = $ 120,000

   EV = $ 100,000

   AC = $ 90,000

   a. What is the cost variance, schedule variance, cost performance index (CPI), and schedule performance index (SPI) for the project?
   b. How is the project doing? Is it ahead of schedule or behind schedule? Is it under budget or over budget?
   c. Use the CPI to calculate the estimate at completion (EAC) for this project. Is the project performing better or worse than planned?
   d. Use the schedule performance index (SPI) to estimate how long it will take to finish this project.
   e. Sketch an earned value chart using the above information. See Figure 7-5 as a guide.

Companion Web Site

Visit the companion Web site for this text at *www.cengage.com/mis/schwalbe* to access:

- References cited in the text and additional suggested readings for each chapter
- Template files
- Lecture notes
- Interactive quizzes
- Podcasts
- Links to general project management Web sites
- And more

See the Preface of this text for additional information on accessing the companion Web site.

Key Terms

actual cost (AC) — the total of direct and indirect costs incurred in accomplishing work on an activity during a given period.

analogous estimates — a cost estimating technique that uses the actual cost of a previous, similar project as the basis for estimating the cost of the current project, also called top-down estimates.

baseline — the original project plan plus approved changes.

bottom-up estimates — a cost estimating technique based on estimating individual work items and summing them to get a project total.

budget at completion (BAC) — the original total budget for a project.

budgetary estimate — a cost estimate used to allocate money into an organization's budget.

cash flow analysis — a method for determining the estimated annual costs and benefits for a project.

contingency reserves — dollars included in a cost estimate to allow for future situations that may be partially planned for (sometimes called **known unknowns**) and are included in the project cost baseline.

controlling costs — controlling changes to the project budget.

cost baseline — a time-phased budget that project managers use to measure and monitor cost performance.

cost management plan — a document that describes how cost variances will be managed on the project.

cost performance index (CPI) — the ratio of earned value to actual cost; can be used to estimate the projected cost to complete the project.

cost variance (CV) — the earned value minus the actual cost.

definitive estimate — a cost estimate that provides an accurate estimate of project costs.

determining the budget — allocating the overall cost estimate to individual work items to establish a baseline for measuring performance.

direct costs — costs that can be directly related to producing the products and services of the project.

earned value (EV) — an estimate of the value of the physical work actually completed.

earned value management (EVM) — a project performance measurement technique that integrates scope, time, and cost data.

estimate at completion (EAC) — an estimate of what it will cost to complete the project based on performance to date.

estimating costs — developing an approximation or estimate of the costs of the resources needed to complete the project.

indirect costs — costs that are not directly related to the products or services of the project, but are indirectly related to performing the project.

intangible costs or benefits — costs or benefits that are difficult to measure in monetary terms.

known unknowns — dollars included in a cost estimate to allow for future situations that may be partially planned for (sometimes called **contingency reserves**) and are included in the project cost baseline.

learning curve theory — a theory that states that when many items are produced repetitively, the unit cost of those items normally decreases in a regular pattern as more units are produced.

life cycle costing — considers the total cost of ownership, or development plus support costs, for a project.

management reserves — dollars included in a cost estimate to allow for future situations that are unpredictable (sometimes called unknown unknowns).

overrun — the additional percentage or dollar amount by which actual costs exceed estimates.

parametric modeling — a cost-estimating technique that uses project characteristics (parameters) in a mathematical model to estimate project costs.

planned value (PV) — that portion of the approved total cost estimate planned to be spent on an activity during a given period.

profit margin — the ratio between revenues and profits.

profits — revenues minus expenses.

project cost management — the processes required to ensure that the project is completed within the approved budget.

rate of performance (RP) — the ratio of actual work completed to the percentage of work planned to have been completed at any given time during the life of the project or activity.

reserves — dollars included in a cost estimate to mitigate cost risk by allowing for future situations that are difficult to predict.

rough order of magnitude (ROM) estimate — a cost estimate prepared very early in the life of a project to provide a rough idea of what a project will cost.

schedule performance index (SPI) — the ratio of earned value to planned value; can be used to estimate the projected time to complete a project.

schedule variance (SV) — the earned value minus the planned value.

sunk cost — money that has been spent in the past.

tangible costs or benefits — costs or benefits that can be easily measured in dollars.

top-down estimates — a cost estimating technique that uses the actual cost of a previous, similar project as the basis for estimating the cost of the current project, also called analogous estimates.

unknown unknowns — dollars included in a cost estimate to allow for future situations that are unpredictable (sometimes called management reserves).

End Notes

1 Magne Jørgensen and Kjetil Moløkken, "How Large Are Software Cost Overruns? A Review of the 1994 CHAOS Report," Simula Research Laboratory (2006).

2 Geoffrey James, "IT Fiascoes ... and How to Avoid Them," *Datamation* (November 1997).

3 Paul McDougall, "8 Expensive IT Blunders," *InformationWeek* (October 16, 2006).

4 Roy Mark,"GAO: Billions Wasted on Federal IT Projects," eWeek.com (July 31, 2008).

5 Paul McDougall, "U.K. Health System IT Upgrade Called A 'Disaster'" *InformationWeek* (June 5, 2006).

6 Jeremy Kirk, "Datacenter failure pinches U.K. health service," IDG News Service (August 1, 2006).

[7] Charles T. Horngren, George Foster, and Srikanti M. Datar, *Cost Accounting*, 8th ed. Englewood Cliffs, NJ: Prentice-Hall, 1994.

[8] The Standish Group International, "Trends in IT Value," (www.standishgroup.com) (2008).

[9] Ibid.

[10] Dawn Kawamoto, "Dell's green goal for 2008," CNET (September 27, 2007).

[11] Tom DeMarco, *Controlling Software Projects*. New York: Yourdon Press, 1982.

[12] David Krejci, "Message received," StarTribune, Minneapolis, MN (November 5, 2008).

[13] Steve Kroft, "Obama's Inner Circle Shares Inside Story," CBS News (November 9, 2008).

[14] Brenda Taylor, P2 Senior Project Manager, P2 Project Management Solutions, Johannesburg, South Africa, E-mail, 2004.

[15] Daniel M. Brandon, Jr., "Implementing Earned Value Easily and Effectively," *Project Management Journal* (June 1998) 29 (2), p. 11–18.

[16] Quentin W. Fleming and Joel M. Koppelman, *Earned Value Project Management, Third Edition* (Project Management Institute, 2006).

[17] Scott Berinato, "Do the Math," *CIO Magazine* (October 1, 2001).

[18] Borland Software, "Organizations Making Progress with IT Management and Governance but Still Face Significant Challenges according to Borland Survey," Borland Press Release (August 28, 2006).

[19] Michael Kringsman, "ROI Study: Product Portfolio Management Yields Results," *ZDNet* (March 7, 2008).

PROJECT QUALITY MANAGEMENT

LEARNING OBJECTIVES

After reading this chapter, you will be able to:

- Understand the importance of project quality management for information technology products and services
- Define project quality management and understand how quality relates to various aspects of information technology projects
- Describe quality planning and its relationship to project scope management
- Discuss the importance of quality assurance
- Explain the main outputs of the quality control process
- Understand the tools and techniques for quality control, such as the Seven Basic Tools of Quality, statistical sampling, Six Sigma, and testing
- Summarize the contributions of noteworthy quality experts to modern quality management
- Describe how leadership, the cost of quality, organizational influences, expectations, cultural differences, and maturity models relate to improving quality in information technology projects
- Discuss how software can assist in project quality management

OPENING CASE

A large medical instruments company just hired Scott Daniels, a senior consultant from a large consulting firm, to lead a project to resolve the quality problems with the company's new Executive Information System (EIS). A team of internal programmers and analysts worked with several company executives to develop this new system. Many executives were hooked on the new, user-friendly EIS. They loved the way the system allowed them to track sales of various medical instruments quickly and easily by product, country, hospital, and sales representative. After successfully testing the new EIS with several executives, the company decided to make the system available to all levels of management.

Unfortunately, several quality problems developed with the new EIS after a few months of operation. People were complaining that they could not get into the Web-based system. The system started going down a couple of times a month, and the response time was reportedly getting slower. Users complained when they could not access information within a few seconds. Several people kept forgetting how to log in to the system, thus increasing the number of calls to the company's help desk. There were complaints that some of the reports in the system gave inconsistent information. How could a summary report show totals that were not consistent with a detailed report on the same information? The executive sponsor of the EIS wanted the problems fixed quickly and accurately, so he decided to hire an expert in quality from outside the company whom he knew from past projects. Scott Daniels' job was to lead a team of people from both the medical instruments company and his own firm to identify and resolve quality-related issues with the EIS and to develop a plan to help prevent quality problems from happening on future projects.

THE IMPORTANCE OF PROJECT QUALITY MANAGEMENT

Most people have heard jokes about what cars would be like if they followed a development history similar to that of computers. A well-known joke that has been traveling around the Internet goes as follows:

> At a recent computer exposition (COMDEX), Bill Gates, the founder and CEO of Microsoft Corporation, stated: "If General Motors had kept up with technology like the computer industry has, we would all be driving $25 cars that got 1,000 miles to the gallon." In response to Gates' comments, General Motors issued a press release stating: "If GM had developed technology like Microsoft, we would all be driving cars with the following characteristics:
>
> 1. For no reason whatsoever your car would crash twice a day.
> 2. Every time they repainted the lines on the road, you would have to buy a new car.
> 3. Occasionally, your car would die on the freeway for no reason, and you would just accept this, restart, and drive on.
> 4. Occasionally, executing a maneuver such as a left turn would cause your car to shut down and refuse to restart, in which case you would have to reinstall the engine.

5. Only one person at a time could use the car, unless you bought "Car95" or "CarNT." But then you would have to buy more seats.
6. Macintosh would make a car that was powered by the sun, reliable, five times as fast, and twice as easy to drive, but would run on only five percent of the roads.
7. The oil, water temperature, and alternator warning lights would be replaced by a single "general car default" warning light.
8. New seats would force everyone to have the same size hips.
9. The airbag system would say "Are you sure?" before going off.
10. Occasionally, for no reason whatsoever, your car would lock you out and refuse to let you in until you simultaneously lifted the door handle, turned the key, and grabbed hold of the radio antenna.
11. GM would require all car buyers to also purchase a deluxe set of Rand McNally road maps (now a GM subsidiary), even though they neither need them nor want them. Attempting to delete this option would immediately cause the car's performance to diminish by 50 percent or more. Moreover, GM would become a target for investigation by the Justice Department.
12. Every time GM introduced a new model car, buyers would have to learn how to drive all over again because none of the controls would operate in the same manner as the old car.
13. You would press the Start button to shut off the engine.[1]

Most people simply accept poor quality from many information technology products. So what if your computer crashes a couple of times a month? Just make sure you back up your data. So what if you cannot log in to the corporate intranet or the Internet right now? Just try a little later when it is less busy. So what if the latest version of your word-processing software was shipped with several known bugs? You like the software's new features, and all new software has bugs. Is quality a real problem with information technology projects?

Yes, it is! Information technology is not just a luxury available in some homes, schools, or offices. Companies throughout the world provide employees with access to computers. The majority of people in the United States use the Internet, and usage in other countries continues to grow rapidly. It took only five years for 50 million people to use the Internet compared to 25 years for 50 million people to use telephones. Many aspects of our daily lives depend on high-quality information technology products. Food is produced and distributed with the aid of computers; cars have computer chips to track performance; children use computers to help them learn in school; corporations depend on technology for many business functions; and millions of people rely on technology for entertainment and personal communications. Many information technology projects develop mission-critical systems that are used in life-and-death situations, such as navigation systems on aircraft and computer components built into medical equipment. Financial institutions and their customers also rely on high-quality information systems. Customers get very upset when systems provide inaccurate financial data or reveal information to unauthorized users that could lead to identity theft. When one of these systems does not function correctly, it is much more than a slight inconvenience, as described in the following What Went Wrong? examples.

WHAT WENT WRONG?

- In 1981, a small timing difference caused by a computer program change created a 1 in 67 chance that the space shuttle's five on-board computers would not synchronize. The error caused a launch abort.[2]
- In 1986, two hospital patients died after receiving fatal doses of radiation from a Therac 25 machine. A software problem caused the machine to ignore calibration data.[3]
- In one of the biggest software errors in banking history, Chemical Bank mistakenly deducted about $15 million from more than 100,000 customer accounts. The problem resulted from a single line of code in an updated computer program that caused the bank to process every withdrawal and transfer at its automated teller machines (ATMs) twice. For example, a person who withdrew $100 from an ATM had $200 deducted from his or her account, though the receipt indicated only a withdrawal of $100. The mistake affected 150,000 transactions.[4]
- In August 2008, the Privacy Rights Clearinghouse, a nonprofit consumer advocacy group in San Diego, stated on their Web site that more than 236 million data records of U.S. residents have been exposed due to security breaches since January 2005. For example, Bank of America Corp. lost computer data tapes containing personal information of 1.2 million federal employees, including some U.S. senators; Ameritrade lost a back-up computer tape containing the personal information of 200,000 online trading customers; and the U.S. Air Force confirmed that personal data of 33,000 officers and enlisted personnel were hacked from an online system.[5]

Before you can improve the quality of information technology projects, it is important to understand the basic concepts of project quality management.

WHAT IS PROJECT QUALITY MANAGEMENT?

Project quality management is a difficult knowledge area to define. The International Organization for Standardization (ISO) defines **quality** as "the totality of characteristics of an entity that bear on its ability to satisfy stated or implied needs" (ISO8042:1994) or "the degree to which a set of inherent characteristics fulfils requirements." (ISO9000:2000). Many people spent many hours coming up with these definitions, yet they are still very vague. Other experts define quality based on conformance to requirements and fitness for use. **Conformance to requirements** means the project's processes and products meet written specifications. For example, if the project scope statement requires delivery of 100 computers with specific processors, memory, and so on, you could easily check whether suitable computers had been delivered. **Fitness for use** means a product can be used as it was intended. If these computers were delivered without monitors or keyboards and were left in boxes on the customer's shipping dock, the customer might not be satisfied because the computers would not be fit for use. The customer may have assumed that the delivery included monitors and keyboards, unpacking the computers, and installation so they would be ready to use.

The purpose of **project quality management** is to ensure that the project will satisfy the needs for which it was undertaken. Recall that project management involves meeting or exceeding stakeholder needs and expectations. The project team must develop good relationships with key stakeholders, especially the main customer for the project, to understand what quality means to them. *After all, the customer ultimately decides if quality is acceptable*. Many technical projects fail because the project team focuses only on meeting the written requirements for the main products being produced and ignores other stakeholder needs and expectations for the project. For example, the project team should know what successfully delivering 100 computers means to the customer.

Quality, therefore, must be on an equal level with project scope, time, and cost. If a project's stakeholders are not satisfied with the quality of the project management or the resulting products of the project, the project team will need to adjust scope, time, and cost to satisfy the stakeholder. Meeting only written requirements for scope, time, and cost is not sufficient. To achieve stakeholder satisfaction, the project team must develop a good working relationship with all stakeholders and understand their stated or implied needs.

Project quality management involves three main processes:

1. *Planning quality* includes identifying which quality standards are relevant to the project and how to satisfy those standards. Incorporating quality standards into project design is a key part of quality planning. For an information technology project, quality standards might include allowing for system growth, planning a reasonable response time for a system, or ensuring that the system produces consistent and accurate information. Quality standards can also apply to information technology services. For example, you can set standards for how long it should take to get a reply from a help desk or how long it should take to ship a replacement part for a hardware item under warranty. The main outputs of quality planning are a quality management plan, quality metrics, quality checklists, a process improvement plan, and project document updates. A **metric** is a standard of measurement. Examples of common metrics include failure rates of products produced, availability of goods and services, and customer satisfaction ratings.
2. *Performing quality assurance* involves periodically evaluating overall project performance to ensure that the project will satisfy the relevant quality standards. The quality assurance process involves taking responsibility for quality throughout the project's life cycle. Top management must take the lead in emphasizing the roles all employees play in quality assurance, especially senior managers' roles. The main outputs of this process are organizational process asset updates, change requests, project management plan updates, and project document updates.
3. *Performing quality control* involves monitoring specific project results to ensure that they comply with the relevant quality standards while identifying ways to improve overall quality. This process is often associated with the technical tools and techniques of quality management, such as Pareto charts, quality control charts, and statistical sampling. You will learn more about these tools and

techniques later in this chapter. The main outputs of quality control include quality control measurements, validated changes, validated deliverables, organizational process asset updates, change requests, project management plan updates, and project document updates.

Figure 8-1 summarizes these processes and outputs, showing when they occur in a typical project.

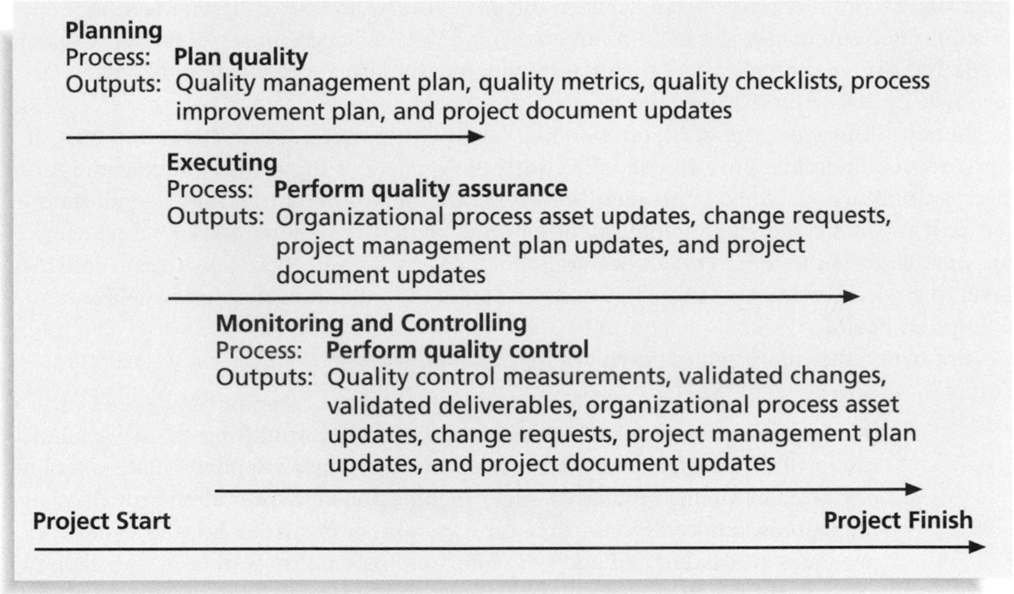

Planning
Process: **Plan quality**
Outputs: Quality management plan, quality metrics, quality checklists, process improvement plan, and project document updates

Executing
Process: **Perform quality assurance**
Outputs: Organizational process asset updates, change requests, project management plan updates, and project document updates

Monitoring and Controlling
Process: **Perform quality control**
Outputs: Quality control measurements, validated changes, validated deliverables, organizational process asset updates, change requests, project management plan updates, and project document updates

Project Start **Project Finish**

FIGURE 8-1 Project quality management summary

PLANNING QUALITY

Project managers today have a vast knowledge base of information related to quality, and the first step to ensuring project quality management is planning. **Quality planning** implies the ability to anticipate situations and prepare actions that bring about the desired outcome. The current thrust in modern quality management is the prevention of defects through a program of selecting the proper materials, training and indoctrinating people in quality, and planning a process that ensures the appropriate outcome. In project quality planning, it is important to identify relevant quality standards, such as ISO standards described later in this chapter, for each unique project and to design quality into the products of the project and the processes involved in managing the project.

Design of experiments is a quality planning technique that helps identify which variables have the most influence on the overall outcome of a process. Understanding which variables affect outcome is a very important part of quality planning. For example, computer chip designers might want to determine which combination of materials and equipment will produce the most reliable chips at a reasonable cost. You can also apply design of experiments to project management issues such as cost and schedule trade-offs. For example, junior programmers or consultants cost less than senior programmers or consultants, but you cannot expect them to complete the same level of work in the same amount of time. An appropriately designed experiment to compute project costs and durations for various combinations of junior and senior programmers or consultants can allow you to determine an optimal mix of personnel, given limited resources. Refer to the section on the Taguchi method later in this chapter for more information.

Quality planning also involves communicating the correct actions for ensuring quality in a format that is understandable and complete. In quality planning for projects, it is important to describe important factors that directly contribute to meeting the customer's requirements. Organizational policies related to quality, the particular project's scope statement and product descriptions, and related standards and regulations are all important input to the quality planning process.

As mentioned in the discussion of project scope management (see Chapter 5), it is often difficult to completely understand the performance dimension of information technology projects. Even if the development of hardware, software, and networking technology would stand still for a while, it is often difficult for customers to explain exactly what they want in an information technology project. Important scope aspects of information technology projects that affect quality include functionality and features, system outputs, performance, and reliability and maintainability.

- **Functionality** is the degree to which a system performs its intended function. **Features** are the system's special characteristics that appeal to users. It is important to clarify what functions and features the system *must* perform, and what functions and features are *optional*. In the EIS example in the opening case, the mandatory functionality of the system might be that it allows users to track sales of specific medical instruments by predetermined categories such as the product group, country, hospital, and sales representative. Mandatory features might be a graphical user interface with icons, menus, online help, and so on.
- **System outputs** are the screens and reports the system generates. It is important to define clearly what the screens and reports look like for a system. Can the users easily interpret these outputs? Can users get all of the reports they need in a suitable format?
- **Performance** addresses how well a product or service performs the customer's intended use. To design a system with high quality performance, project stakeholders must address many issues. What volumes of data and transactions should the system be capable of handling? How many simultaneous users should the system be designed to handle? What is the projected growth rate in the number of users? What type of equipment must the system run on? How fast must the response time be for different aspects of the system under different circumstances? For the EIS in the opening case, several of the quality problems appear to relate to performance issues. The system is failing a couple of times a month, and users are unsatisfied with the response time. The project team may not have had specific performance requirements or tested the system under the right conditions to deliver the expected performance. Buying faster hardware might address these performance issues. Another performance

problem that might be more difficult to fix is the fact that some of the reports are generating inconsistent results. This could be a software quality problem that may be difficult and costly to correct since the system is already in operation.

- **Reliability** is the ability of a product or service to perform as expected under normal conditions. In discussing reliability for information technology projects, many people use the term IT service management. See the Suggested Readings on the companion Web site, such as ISO/IEC 20000, which is based on the Information Technology Infrastructure Library (ITIL).
- **Maintainability** addresses the ease of performing maintenance on a product. Most information technology products cannot reach 100 percent reliability, but stakeholders must define what their expectations are. For the EIS, what are the normal conditions for operating the system? Should reliability tests be based on 100 people accessing the system at once and running simple queries? Maintenance for the EIS might include uploading new data into the system or performing maintenance procedures on the system hardware and software. Are the users willing to have the system be unavailable several hours a week for system maintenance? Providing help desk support could also be a maintenance function. How fast a response do users expect for help desk support? How often can users tolerate system failure? Are the stakeholders willing to pay more for higher reliability and fewer failures?

These aspects of project scope are just a few of the requirement issues related to quality planning. Project managers and their teams need to consider all of these project scope issues in determining quality goals for the project. The main customers for the project must also realize their role in defining the most critical quality needs for the project and constantly communicate these needs and expectations to the project team. Since most information technology projects involve requirements that are not set in stone, it is important for all project stakeholders to work together to balance the quality, scope, time, and cost dimensions of the project. *Project managers, however, are ultimately responsible for quality management on their projects*.

Project managers should be familiar with basic quality terms, standards, and resources. For example, the International Organization for Standardization (ISO) provides information based on inputs from 157 different countries. They have an extensive Web site (*www.iso.org*), which is the source of ISO 9000 and more than 17,000 international standards for business, government and society. If you're curious where the acronym came from, the word "iso" comes from the Greek, meaning "equal." IEEE also provides many standards related to quality and has detailed information on their Web site (*www.ieee.org*).

PERFORMING QUALITY ASSURANCE

It is one thing to develop a plan for ensuring quality on a project; it is another to ensure delivery of quality products and services. **Quality assurance** includes all of the activities related to satisfying the relevant quality standards for a project. Another goal of quality assurance is continuous quality improvement.

Many companies understand the importance of quality assurance and have entire departments dedicated to this area. They have detailed processes in place to make sure their products and services conform to various quality requirements. They also know they must produce those products and services at competitive prices. To be successful in today's competitive business environment, successful companies develop their own best practices and evaluate other organizations' best practices to continuously improve the way they do business.

Top management and project managers can have the greatest impact on the quality of projects by doing a good job of quality assurance. The importance of leadership in improving information technology project quality is discussed in more detail later in this chapter.

Several tools used in quality planning can also be used in quality assurance. Design of experiments, as described under quality planning, can also help ensure and improve product quality. **Benchmarking** generates ideas for quality improvements by comparing specific project practices or product characteristics to those of other projects or products within or outside the performing organization. For example, if a competitor has an EIS with an average down time of only one hour a week, that might be a benchmark for which to strive. Fishbone or Ishikawa diagrams, as described later in this chapter, can assist in ensuring and improving quality by finding the root causes of quality problems.

An important tool for quality assurance is a quality audit. A **quality audit** is a structured review of specific quality management activities that help identify lessons learned that could improve performance on current or future projects. In-house auditors or third parties with expertise in specific areas can perform quality audits, and quality audits can be scheduled or random. Industrial engineers often perform quality audits by helping to design specific quality metrics for a project and then applying and analyzing the metrics throughout the project. For example, the Northwest Airlines ResNet project (available on the companion Web site for this text) provides an excellent example of using quality audits to emphasize the main goals of a project and then track progress in reaching those goals. The main objective of the ResNet project was to develop a new reservation system to increase direct airline ticket sales and reduce the time it took for sales agents to handle customer calls. The measurement techniques for monitoring these goals helped ResNet's project manager and project team supervise various aspects of the project by focusing on meeting those goals. Measuring progress toward increasing direct sales and reducing call times also helped the project manager justify continued investments in ResNet.

PERFORMING QUALITY CONTROL

Many people only think of quality control when they think of quality management. Perhaps it is because there are many popular tools and techniques in this area. Before describing some of these tools and techniques, it is important to distinguish quality control from quality planning and quality assurance.

Although one of the main goals of **quality control** is to improve quality, the main outcomes of this process are acceptance decisions, rework, and process adjustments.

- **Acceptance decisions** determine if the products or services produced as part of the project will be accepted or rejected. If they are accepted, they are considered to be validated deliverables. If project stakeholders reject some of the products or services produced as part of the project, there must be rework. For example, the executive who sponsored development of the EIS in the opening case was obviously not satisfied with the system and hired an outside consultant, Scott Daniels, to lead a team to address and correct the quality problems.

- **Rework** is action taken to bring rejected items into compliance with product requirements or specifications or other stakeholder expectations. Rework often results in requested changes and validated defect repair, resulting from recommended defect repair or corrective or preventive actions. Rework can be very expensive, so the project manager must strive to do a good job of quality planning and quality assurance to avoid this need. Since the EIS did not meet all of the stakeholders' expectations for quality, the medical instruments company was spending additional money for rework.
- **Process adjustments** correct or prevent further quality problems based on quality control measurements. Process adjustments are often found by using quality control measurements, and they often result in updates to the quality baseline, organization process assets, and the project management plan. For example, Scott Daniels, the consultant in the opening case, might recommend that the medical instruments company purchase a faster server for the EIS to correct the response-time problems. This change would require changes to the project management plan since it would require more work to be done related to the project. The company also hired Scott to develop a plan to help prevent future information technology project quality problems.

TOOLS AND TECHNIQUES FOR QUALITY CONTROL

Quality control includes many general tools and techniques. This section describes the Seven Basic Tools of Quality, statistical sampling, and Six Sigma—and discusses how they can be applied to information technology projects. The section concludes with a discussion on testing, since information technology projects use testing extensively to ensure quality.

The following seven tools are known as the Seven Basic Tools of Quality:

1. *Cause-and-effect diagrams*: **Cause-and-effect diagrams** trace complaints about quality problems back to the responsible production operations. In other words, they help you find the root cause of a problem. They are also known as **fishbone** or **Ishikawa diagrams**, named after their creator, Kaoru Ishikawa. You can also use the technique known as the **5 whys**, where you repeatedly ask the question "Why?" (five is a good rule of thumb) to help peel away the layers of symptoms that can lead to the root cause of a problem. These symptoms can be branches on the cause-and-effect diagram.

   Figure 8-2 provides an example of a cause-and-effect diagram that Scott Daniels, the consultant in the opening case, might create to uncover the root cause of the problem of users not being able to log in to the EIS. Notice that it resembles the skeleton of a fish, hence the name fishbone diagram.
   This fishbone diagram lists the main areas that could be the cause of the problem: the EIS system's hardware, the user's hardware or software, or the user's

training. This figure describes two of these areas, the individual user's hardware and training, in more detail. For example, using the 5 whys, you could first ask why the users cannot get into the system, then why they keep forgetting their passwords, why they did not reset their passwords, why they did not check a box to save a password, and so on. The root cause of the problem would have a significant impact on the actions taken to solve the problem. If many users could not get into the system because their computers did not have enough memory, the solution might be to upgrade memory for those computers. If many users could not get into the system because they forgot their passwords, there might be a much quicker, less expensive solution.

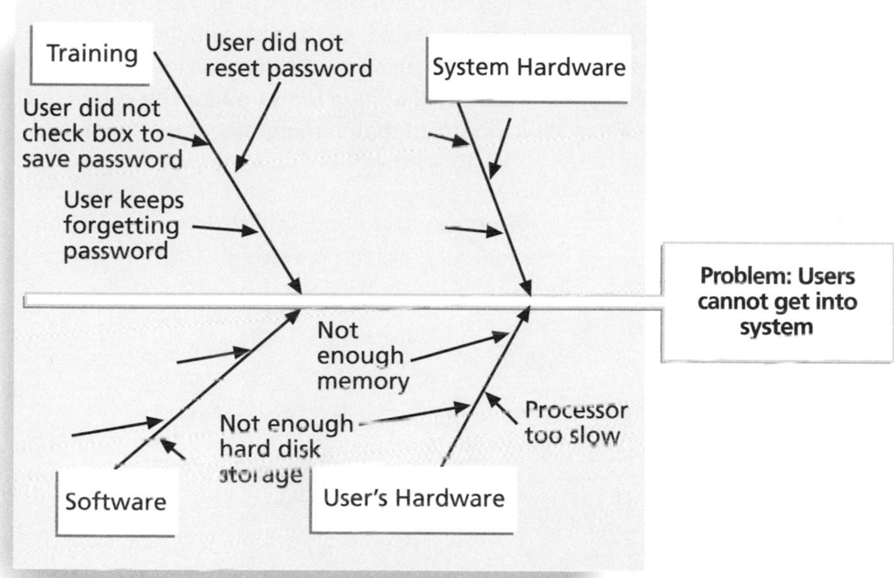

FIGURE 8-2 Sample cause-and-effect diagram

2. *Control charts*: A **control chart** is a graphic display of data that illustrates the results of a process over time. Control charts allow you to determine whether a process is in control or out of control. When a process is in control, any variations in the results of the process are created by random events. Processes that are in control do not need to be adjusted. When a process is out of control, variations in the results of the process are caused by nonrandom events. When a process is out of control, you need to identify the causes of those nonrandom events and adjust the process to correct or eliminate them. For example, Figure 8-3 provides an example of a control chart for a process that manufactures 12-inch rulers. Assume that these are wooden rulers created by machines on an assembly line. Each point on the chart represents a length measurement for a ruler that comes off the assembly line. The scale on the vertical axis goes from 11.90 to 12.10. These numbers represent the lower and upper

specification limits for the ruler. In this case, this would mean that the customer for the rulers has specified that all rulers purchased must be between 11.90 and 12.10 inches long, or 12 inches plus or minus 0.10 inches. The lower and upper control limits on the quality control chart are 11.91 and 12.09 inches, respectively. This means the manufacturing process is designed to produce rulers between 11.91 and 12.09 inches long. Looking for and analyzing patterns in process data is an important part of quality control. You can use quality control charts and the seven run rule to look for patterns in data. The **seven run rule** states that if seven data points in a row are all below the mean, above the mean, or are all increasing or decreasing, then the process needs to be examined for non-random problems. In Figure 8-3, data points that violate the seven run rule are starred. Note that you include the first point in a series of points that are all increasing or decreasing. In the ruler manufacturing process, these data points may indicate that a calibration device may need adjustment. For example, the machine that cuts the wood for the rulers might need to be adjusted or the blade on the machine might need to be replaced.

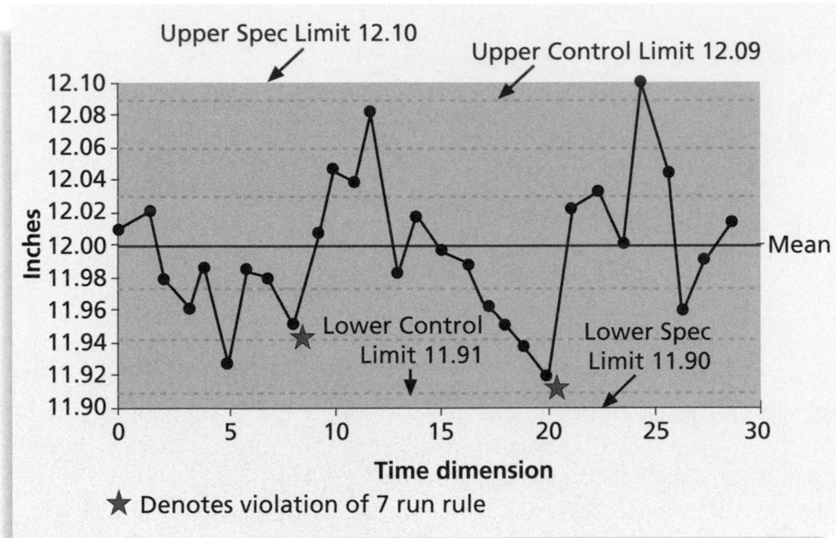

FIGURE 8-3 Sample control chart

3. *Run chart*: A **run chart** displays the history and pattern of variation of a process over time. It is a line chart that shows data points plotted in the order in which they occur. You can use run charts to perform trend analysis to forecast future outcomes based on historical results. For example, trend analysis can help you analyze how many defects have been identified over time and see if there are trends. Figure 8-4 shows a sample run chart, charting the number of defects each month for three different types of defects. Notice that you can easily see the patterns of Defect 1 continuing to increase over time, Defect 2 decreasing the first several months and then holding steady, and Defect 3 fluctuating each month.

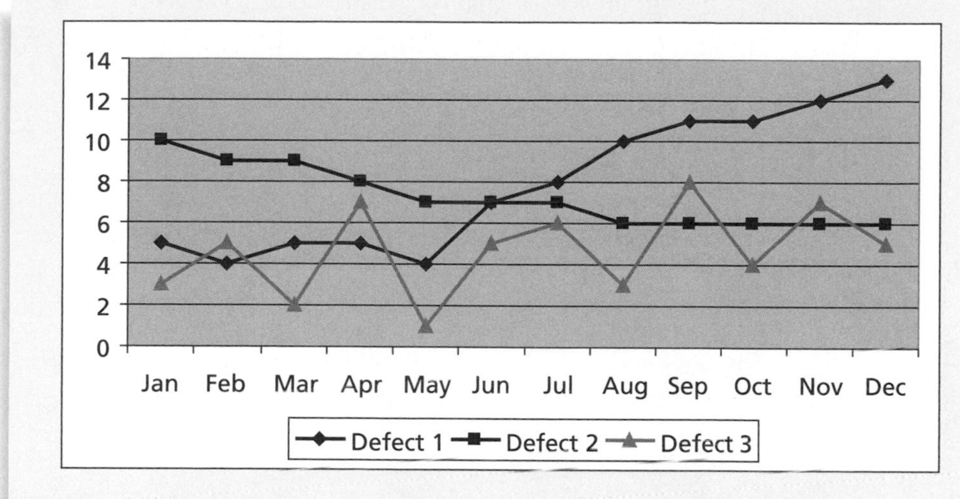

FIGURE 8-4 Sample run chart

4. *Scatter diagram*: A **scatter diagram** helps to show if there is a relationship between two variables. The closer data points are to a diagonal line, the more closely the two variables are related. For example, Figure 8-5 provides a sample scatter diagram that Scott Daniels might create to compare user satisfaction ratings of the EIS system to the age of respondents to see if there is a relationship. They might find that younger users are less satisfied with the system, for example, and make decisions based on that finding.

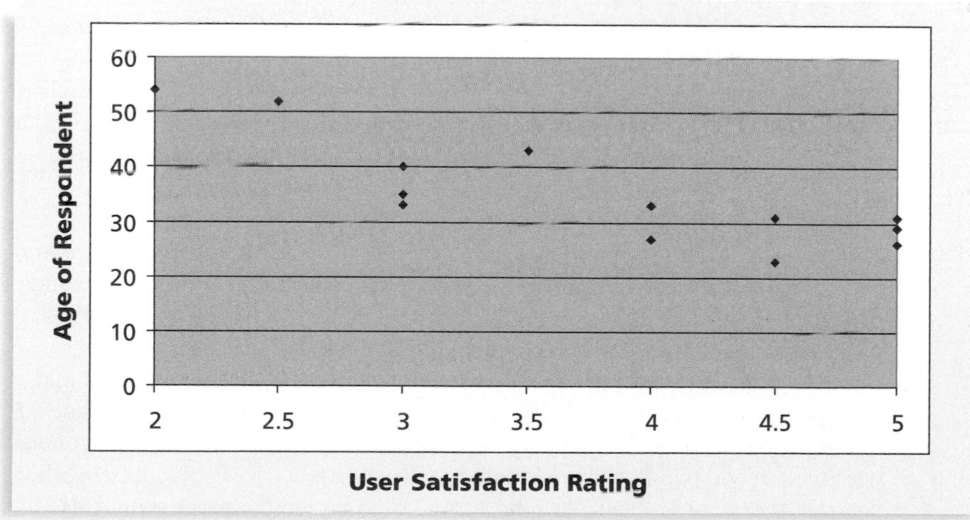

FIGURE 8-5 Sample scatter diagram

5. *Histograms*: A **histogram** is a bar graph of a distribution of variables. Each bar represents an attribute or characteristic of a problem or situation, and the height of the bar represents its frequency. For example, Scott Daniels might ask the Help Desk to create a histogram to show how many total complaints they received each week related to the EIS system. Figure 8-6 shows a sample histogram.

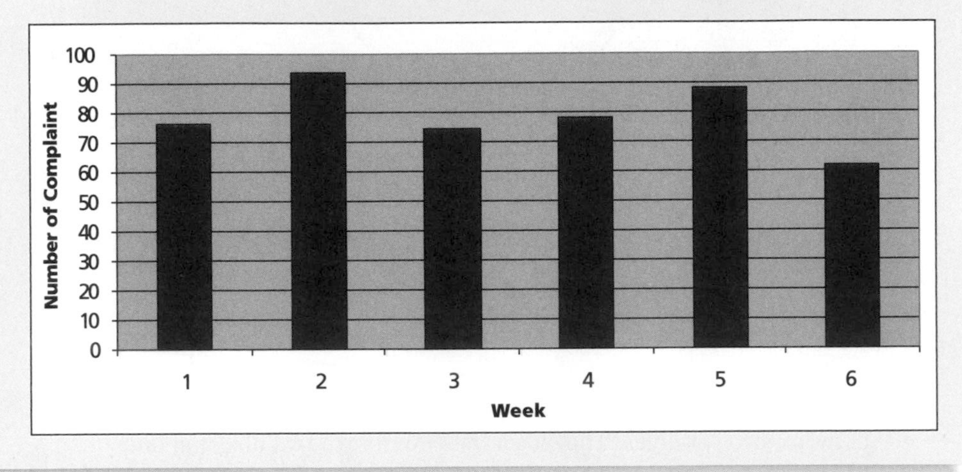

FIGURE 8-6 Sample histogram

6. *Pareto charts*: A **Pareto chart** is a histogram that can help you identify and prioritize problem areas. The variables described by the histogram are ordered by frequency of occurrence. Pareto charts help you identify the vital few contributors that account for most quality problems in a system. **Pareto analysis** is sometimes referred to as the 80-20 rule, meaning that 80 percent of problems are often due to 20 percent of the causes. For example, suppose there was a detailed history of user complaints about the EIS. The project team could create a Pareto chart based on that data, as shown in Figure 8-7. Notice that login problems are the most frequent user complaint, followed by the system locking up, the system being too slow, the system being hard to use, and the reports being inaccurate. The first complaint accounts for 55 percent of the total complaints. The first and second complaints have a cumulative percentage of almost 80 percent, meaning these two areas account for 80 percent of the complaints. Therefore, the company should focus on making it easier to log in to the system to improve quality, since the majority of complaints fall under that category. The company should also address why the system locks up. Because Figure 8-7 shows that inaccurate reports are a problem that is rarely mentioned, the project manager should investigate who made this complaint before spending a lot of effort on addressing that potentially critical problem with the system. The project manager should also find out if complaints about the system being too slow were actually due to the user not being able to log in or the system locking up.

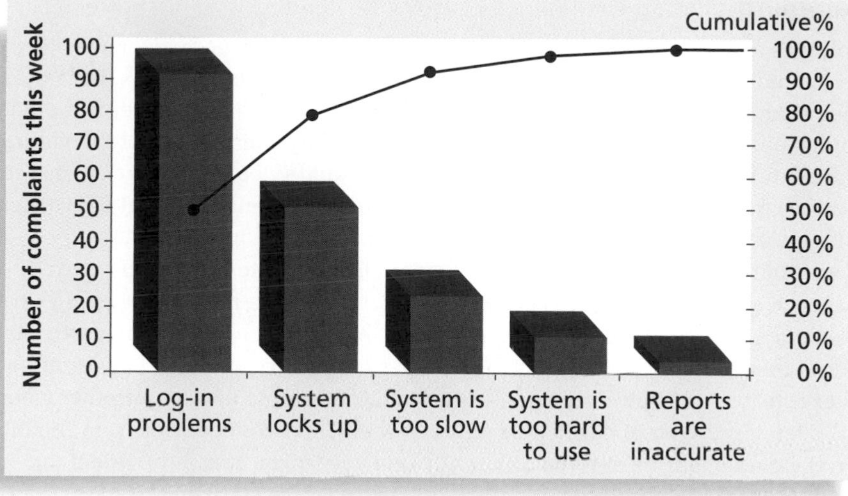

FIGURE 8-7 Sample Pareto chart

7. *Flowcharts*: **Flowcharts** are graphic displays of the logic and flow of processes that help you analyze how problems occur and how processes can be improved. They show activities, decision points, and the order of how information is processed. Figure 8-8 provides a simple example of a flowchart that shows the process a project team might use for accepting or rejecting deliverables.

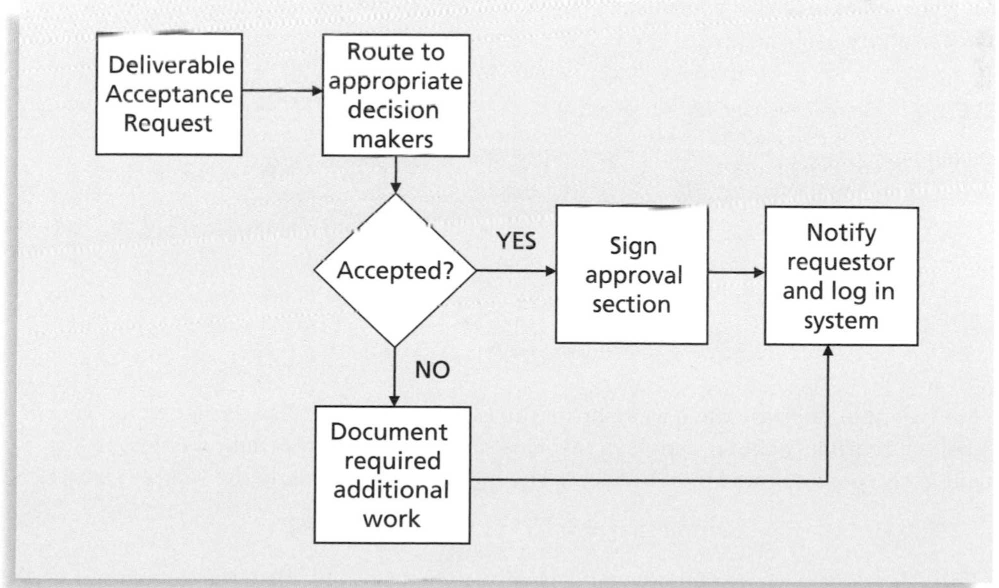

FIGURE 8-8 Sample flowchart

Statistical Sampling

Statistical sampling is a key concept in project quality management. Members of a project team who focus on quality control must have a strong understanding of statistics, but other project team members need to understand only the basic concepts. These concepts include statistical sampling, certainty factor, standard deviation, and variability. Standard deviation and variability are fundamental concepts for understanding quality control charts. This section briefly describes these concepts and describes how a project manager might apply them to information technology projects. Refer to statistics texts for additional details.

Statistical sampling involves choosing part of a population of interest for inspection. For example, suppose a company wants to develop an electronic data interchange (EDI) system for handling data on invoices from all of its suppliers. Assume also that in the past year, the total number of invoices was 50,000 from 200 different suppliers. It would be very time consuming and expensive to review every single invoice to determine data requirements for the new system. Even if the system developers did review all 200 invoice forms from the different suppliers, the data might be entered differently on every form. It is impractical to study every member of a population, such as all 50,000 invoices, so statisticians have developed techniques to help determine an appropriate sample size. If the system developers used statistical techniques, they might find that by studying only 100 invoices, they would have a good sample of the type of data they would need in designing the system.

The size of the sample depends on how representative you want the sample to be. A simple formula for determining sample size is:

$$\text{Sample size} = .25 * (\text{certainty factor} / \text{acceptable error})^2$$

The certainty factor denotes how certain you want to be that the data sampled will not include variations that do not naturally exist in the population. You calculate the certainty factor from tables available in statistics books. Table 8-1 shows some commonly used certainty factors.

TABLE 8-1 Commonly used certainty factors

Desired Certainty	Certainty Factor
95%	1.960
90%	1.645
80%	1.281

For example, suppose the developers of the EDI system described earlier would accept a 95 percent certainty that a sample of invoices would contain no variation unless it was present in the population of total invoices. They would then calculate the sample size as:

$$\text{Sample size} = 0.25 * (1.960 / .05)^2 = 384$$

If the developers wanted 90 percent certainty, they would calculate the sample size as:

$$\text{Sample size} = 0.25 * (1.645 / .10)^2 = 68$$

If the developers wanted 80 percent certainty, they would calculate the sample size as:

$$\text{Sample size} = 0.25 * (1.281 / .20)^2 = 10$$

Assume the developers decide on 90 percent for the certainty factor. Then they would need to examine 68 invoices to determine the type of data the EDI system would need to capture.

Six Sigma

The work of many project quality experts contributed to the development of today's Six Sigma principles. There has been some confusion in the past few years about the term Six Sigma. This section summarizes recent information about this important concept and explains how organizations worldwide use Six Sigma principles to improve quality, decrease costs, and better meet customer needs.

In their book, *The Six Sigma Way*, authors Peter Pande, Robert Neuman, and Roland Cavanagh define **Six Sigma** as "a comprehensive and flexible *system* for achieving, sustaining and maximizing business success. Six Sigma is uniquely driven by close understanding of customer needs, disciplined use of facts, data, and statistical analysis, and diligent attention to managing, improving, and reinventing business processes."[6]

Six Sigma's target for perfection is the achievement of no more than 3.4 defects, errors, or mistakes per million opportunities. This target number is explained in more detail later in this section. An organization can apply the Six Sigma principles to the design and production of a product, a help desk, or other customer-service process.

Projects that use Six Sigma principles for quality control normally follow a five-phase improvement process called **DMAIC** (pronounced de-MAY-ick), which stands for Define, Measure, Analyze, Improve, and Control. DMAIC is a systematic, closed-loop process for continued improvement that is scientific and fact based. The following are brief descriptions of each phase of the DMAIC improvement process:

1. *Define*: Define the problem/opportunity, process, and customer requirements. Important tools used in this phase include a project charter, a description of customer requirements, process maps, and Voice of the Customer (VOC) data. Examples of VOC data include complaints, surveys, comments, and market research that represent the views and needs of the organization's customers.
2. *Measure*: Define measures, then collect, compile, and display data. Measures are defined in terms of defects per opportunity, as defined later in this section.
3. *Analyze*: Scrutinize process details to find improvement opportunities. A project team working on a Six Sigma project, normally referred to as a Six Sigma team, investigates and verifies data to prove the suspected root causes of quality problems and substantiates the problem statement. An important tool in this phase is the fishbone or Ishikawa diagram, as described earlier in this chapter.
4. *Improve*: Generate solutions and ideas for improving the problem. A final solution is verified with the project sponsor, and the Six Sigma team develops a plan to pilot test the solution. The Six Sigma team reviews the results of the

pilot test to refine the solution, if needed, and then implements the solution where appropriate.

5. *Control*: Track and verify the stability of the improvements and the predictability of the solution. Control charts are one tool used in the control phase, as described later in this chapter.

How Is Six Sigma Quality Control Unique?

How does using Six Sigma principles differ from using previous quality control initiatives? Many people remember other quality initiatives from the past few decades such as Total Quality Management (TQM) and Business Process Reengineering (BPR), to name a few. The origins of many Six Sigma principles and tools are found in these previous initiatives; however, there are several new ideas included in Six Sigma principles that help organizations improve their competitiveness and bottom-line results. Below are a few of these principles:

- Using Six Sigma principles is an organization-wide commitment. CEOs, top managers, and all levels of employees in an organization that embraces Six Sigma principles (often referred to as a *Six Sigma organization*) have seen remarkable improvements due to its use. There are often huge training investments, but these investments pay off as employees practice Six Sigma principles and produce higher quality goods and services at lower costs.
- Six Sigma training normally follows the "belt" system, similar to a karate class in which students receive different color belts for each training level. In Six Sigma training, those in the Yellow Belt category receive the minimum level of training, which is normally two to three full days of Six Sigma training for project team members who work on Six Sigma projects on a part-time basis. Those in the Green Belt category usually participate in two to three full weeks of training. Those in the Black Belt category normally work on Six Sigma projects full-time and attend four to five full weeks of training. Project managers are often Black Belts. The Master Black Belt category describes experienced Black Belts who act as technical resources and mentors to people with lower-level belts.
- Organizations that successfully implement Six Sigma principles have the ability and willingness to adopt two seemingly contrary objectives at the same time. Authors James Collins and Jerry Porras describe this as the "We can do it all" or "Genius of the And" approach in their book, *Built to Last*.[7] For example, Six Sigma organizations believe that they can be creative *and* rational, focus on the big picture *and* minute details, reduce errors *and* get things done faster, and make customers happy *and* make a lot of money.
- Six Sigma is not just a program or a discipline to organizations that have benefited from it. Six Sigma is an operating philosophy that is customer-focused and strives to drive out waste, raise levels of quality, and improve financial performance at *breakthrough* levels. A Six Sigma organization sets high goals and uses the DMAIC improvement process to achieve extraordinary quality improvements.

Many organizations do some of what now fits under the definition of Six Sigma, and many Six Sigma principles are not brand-new. What *is* new is its ability to bring together many different themes, concepts, and tools into a coherent management process that can be used on an organization-wide basis.

WHAT WENT RIGHT?

Many organizations have reported dramatic improvements as a result of implementing Six Sigma principles.

- Motorola, Inc. pioneered the adoption of Six Sigma in the 1980s. Its reason for developing and implementing Six Sigma was clear: to stay in business. Japanese competitors were putting several U.S. and European companies out of business. Using Six Sigma provided Motorola with a simple, consistent way to track and compare performance to customer requirements and meet ambitious quality goals in terms of defect reduction. Chairman Bob Galvin set a goal of ten times improvement in defect reduction every two years, or 100 times improvement in four years. Motorola did stay in business, achieving excellent growth and profitability in the 1980s and 1990s. Motorola estimates the cumulative savings based on Six Sigma efforts to be about $14 billion.[8]
- Allied Signal/Honeywell, a technology and manufacturing company, began several quality improvement activities in the early 1990s. By 1999, the company reported saving more than $600 million a year, thanks to training in and application of Six Sigma principles. Six Sigma teams reduced the costs of reworking defects and applied the same principles to designing new products, like aircraft engines. They reduced the time it took from design to certification of engines from 42 to 33 months. Allied Signal/Honeywell credits Six Sigma with a 6 percent productivity increase in 1998 and record profit margins of 13 percent. As one of the company's directors said, "[Six Sigma] changed the way we think and the way we communicate. We never used to talk about the process or the customer; now they're part of our everyday conversation."[9]
- In an effort to improve the efficiency of the Specials Radiology Department, Baptist St. Anthony's Hospital in Amarillo, Texas initiated an improvement project in May 2006. Project goals included improving start times for cases, increasing throughput, implementing control mechanisms for continuous improvement, and providing feedback to other departments concerning performance. After implementing the solutions recommended by the project team and measuring results, the percent of delayed cases dropped from 79 percent to 33 percent, delays within the department decreased by 22 percent, and the number of orders missing or needing clarification dropped to zero from 11 percent. The hospital receives orders from more than 500 physicians at an average rate of 250 orders per day, so this one aspect of the project affects more than 90,000 orders per year.[10]

Six Sigma and Project Selection and Management

Joseph M. Juran stated, "All improvement takes place project by project, and in no other way."[11] Organizations implement Six Sigma by selecting and managing projects. An important part of project management is good project selection.

This statement is especially true for Six Sigma projects. Pande, Neuman, and Cavanagh conducted an informal poll to find out what the most critical and most commonly mishandled activity was in launching Six Sigma, and the unanimous answer was project selection. "It's a pretty simple equation, really: Well-selected and -defined improvement projects equal better, faster results. The converse equation is also simple: Poorly selected and defined projects equal delayed results and frustration."[12]

Organizations must also be careful to apply higher quality where it makes sense. An article in *Fortune* stated that companies that have implemented Six Sigma have not necessarily boosted their stock values. Although GE boasted savings of more than $2 billion in 1999 due to its use of Six Sigma, other companies, such as Whirlpool, could not clearly demonstrate the value of their investments. Why can't all companies benefit from Six Sigma? Because minimizing defects does not matter if an organization is making a product that no one wants to buy. As one of Six Sigma's biggest supporters, Mikel Harry, puts it, "I could genetically engineer a Six Sigma goat, but if a rodeo is the marketplace, people are still going to buy a Four Sigma horse."[13]

As described in Chapter 4, Project Integration Management, there are several methods for selecting projects. However, what makes a project a potential Six Sigma project? First, there must be a quality problem or gap between the current and desired performance. Many projects do not meet this first criterion, such as building a house, merging two corporations, or providing an information technology infrastructure for a new organization. Second, the project should not have a clearly understood problem. Third, the solution should not be predetermined, and an optimal solution should not be apparent.

Once a project is selected as a good candidate for Six Sigma, many project management concepts, tools, and techniques described in this text come into play. For example, Six Sigma projects usually have a business case, a project charter, requirements documents, a schedule, a budget, and so on. Six Sigma projects are done in teams and have sponsors called champions. There are also, of course, project managers, often called *team leaders* in Six Sigma organizations. In other words, Six Sigma projects are simply types of projects that focus on supporting the Six Sigma philosophy by being customer-focused and striving to drive out waste, raise levels of quality, and improve financial performance at breakthrough levels.

Six Sigma and Statistics

An important concept in Six Sigma is improving quality by reducing variation. The term *sigma* means standard deviation. **Standard deviation** measures how much variation exists in a distribution of data. A small standard deviation means that data clusters closely around the middle of a distribution and there is little variability among the data. A large standard deviation means that data is spread out around the middle of the distribution and there is relatively greater variability. Statisticians use the Greek symbol σ (sigma) to represent the standard deviation.

Figure 8-9 provides an example of a **normal distribution**—a bell-shaped curve that is symmetrical regarding the **mean** or average value of the population (the data being analyzed). In any normal distribution, 68.3 percent of the population is within one standard deviation (1σ) of the mean, 95.5 percent of the population is within two standard deviations (2σ), and 99.7 percent of the population is within three standard deviations (3σ) of the mean.

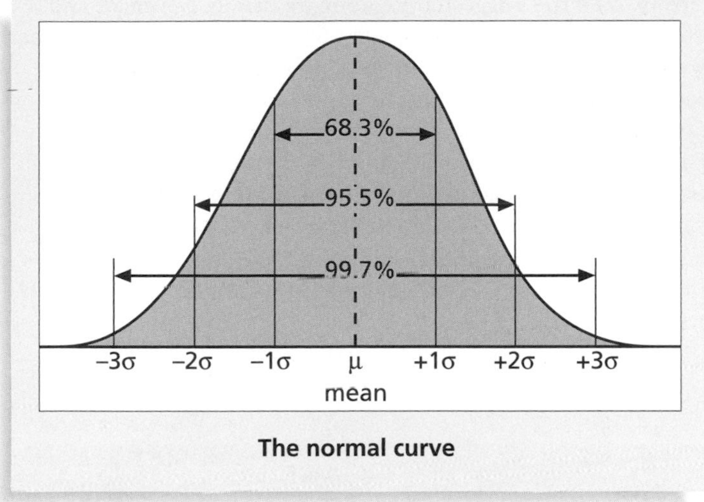

FIGURE 8-9 Normal distribution and standard deviation

Standard deviation is a key factor in determining the acceptable number of defective units found in a population. Table 8-2 illustrates the relationship between sigma, the percentage of the population within that sigma range, and the number of defective units per billion. Note that this table shows that being plus or minus six sigma in pure statistical terms means only *two* defective units per *billion*. Why, then, is the target for Six Sigma programs 3.4 defects per million opportunities, as stated earlier in this chapter?

TABLE 8-2 Sigma and defective units

Specification Range (in +/– Sigmas)	Percent of Population within Range	Defective Units per Billion
1	68.27	317,300,000
2	95.45	45,400,000
3	99.73	2,700,000
4	99.9937	63,000
5	99.999943	57
6	99.9999998	2

Based on Motorola's original work on Six Sigma in the 1980s, the convention used for Six Sigma is a scoring system that accounts for more variation in a process than you would typically find in a few weeks or months of data gathering. In other words, time is an important factor in determining process variations. Table 8-3 shows the Six Sigma conversion table applied to Six Sigma projects. (See the Suggested Reading by Pande, Neuman, and Cavanagh for a detailed description of Six Sigma scoring.) The **yield** represents the number of units handled correctly through the process steps. A **defect** is any instance where the product or service fails to meet customer requirements. Because most products or services have multiple customer requirements, there can be several opportunities to have a defect. For example, suppose a company is trying to reduce the number of errors on customer billing statements. There could be several errors on a billing statement due to a misspelled name, incorrect address, wrong date of service, calculation error, and so on. There might be 100 opportunities for a defect to occur on one billing statement. Instead of measuring the number of defects per unit or billing statement, Six Sigma measures the number of defects based on the number of opportunities.

TABLE 8-3 Sigma conversion table

Sigma	Yield	Defects per Million Opportunities (DPMO)
1	31.0%	690,000
2	69.2%	308,000
3	93.3%	66,800
4	99.4%	6,210
5	99.97%	230
6	99.99966%	3.4

As you can see, the Six Sigma conversion table shows that a process operating at six sigma means there are no more than 3.4 defects per million opportunities. However, most organizations today use the term *six sigma project* in a broad sense to describe projects that will help them in achieving, sustaining, and maximizing business success through better business processes.

Another term you may hear being used in the telecommunications industry is **six 9s of quality**. Six 9s of quality is a measure of quality control equal to 1 fault in 1 million opportunities. In the telecommunications industry, it means 99.9999 percent service availability or *30 seconds of down time a year*. This level of quality has also been stated as the target goal for the number of errors in a communications circuit, system failures, or errors in lines of code. To achieve six 9s of quality requires continual testing to find and eliminate errors or enough redundancy and back-up equipment in systems to reduce the overall system failure rate to that low a level.

Testing

Many information technology professionals think of testing as a stage that comes near the end of information technology product development. Instead of putting serious effort into proper planning, analysis, and design of information technology projects, some organizations rely on testing just before a product ships to ensure some degree of quality. In fact, testing needs to be done during almost every phase of the systems development life cycle, not just before the organization ships or hands over a product to the customer.

Figure 8-10 shows one way of portraying the systems development life cycle. This example includes 17 main tasks involved in a software development project and shows their relationship to each other. For example, every project should start by initiating the project, conducting a feasibility study, and then performing project planning. The figure then shows that the work involved in preparing detailed requirements and the detailed architecture for the system can be performed simultaneously. The oval-shaped phases represent actual tests or tasks, which will include test plans to help ensure quality on software development projects.[14]

Several of the phases in Figure 8-10 include specific work related to testing.

- A **unit test** is done to test each individual component (often a program) to ensure that it is as defect-free as possible. Unit tests are performed before moving onto the integration test.
- **Integration testing** occurs between unit and system testing to test functionally grouped components. It ensures a subset(s) of the entire system works together.
- **System testing** tests the entire system as one entity. It focuses on the big picture to ensure that the entire system is working properly.
- **User acceptance testing** is an independent test performed by end users prior to accepting the delivered system. It focuses on the business fit of the system to the organization, rather than technical issues.

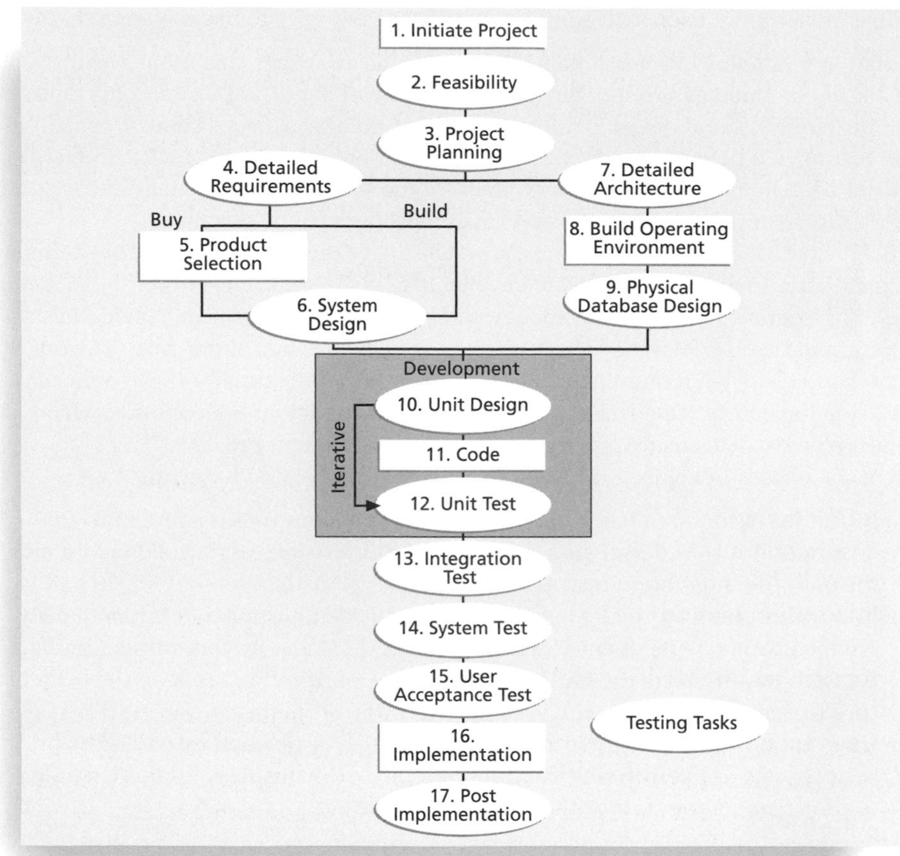

FIGURE 8-10 Testing tasks in the software development life cycle

To help improve the quality of software development projects, it is important for organizations to follow a thorough and disciplined testing methodology. System developers and testers must also establish a partnership with all project stakeholders to make sure the system meets their needs and expectations and the tests are done properly. As described in the next section, there are tremendous costs involved in failure to perform proper testing.

Testing alone, however, cannot always solve software defect problems, according to Watts S. Humphrey, a renowned expert on software quality and Fellow at Carnegie Mellon's Software Engineering Institute. He believes that the traditional code/test/fix cycle for software development is not enough. As code gets more complex, the number of defects missed by testing increases and becomes the problem not just of testers, but also of paying customers. Humphrey says that, on average, programmers introduce a defect for every nine or ten lines of code, and the finished software, after all testing, contains about five to six defects per thousand lines of code. Although there are many different definitions, Humphrey defines a **software defect** as anything that must be changed before delivery of the program. Testing does not sufficiently prevent software defects because the number of ways to test a complex system is huge. In addition, users will continue to invent new ways to use a system that its developers never considered, so certain functionalities may never have been tested or even included in the system requirements. Humphrey suggests that people rethink the software development process to provide *no* potential defects when you enter system testing. This means that developers must be responsible for providing error-free code at each stage of testing. Humphrey teaches a development process where programmers measure and track the kinds of errors they commit so they can use the data to improve their performance. He also acknowledges that top management must support developers by letting them self-direct their work. Programmers need to be motivated and excited to do high-quality work and have some control over how they do it.[15]

MODERN QUALITY MANAGEMENT

Modern quality management requires customer satisfaction, prefers prevention to inspection, and recognizes management responsibility for quality. Several noteworthy people helped develop the following theories, tools, and techniques that define modern quality management.[16] The suggestions from these quality experts led to many projects to improve quality and provided the foundation for today's Six Sigma projects. This section summarizes major contributions made by Deming, Juran, Crosby, Ishikawa, Taguchi, and Feigenbaum.

Deming and His 14 Points for Management

Dr. W. Edwards Deming is known primarily for his work on quality control in Japan. Dr. Deming went to Japan after World War II, at the request of the Japanese government, to assist them in improving productivity and quality. Deming, a statistician and former professor at New York University, taught Japanese manufacturers that higher quality meant greater productivity and lower cost. American industry did not recognize Deming's theories until Japanese manufacturers started producing products that seriously challenged American products, particularly in the auto industry. Ford Motor Company then adopted Deming's quality methods and experienced dramatic improvement in quality and sales thereafter. By the 1980s, after seeing the excellent work coming out of Japan, several U.S. corporations vied for Deming's expertise to help them establish quality improvement programs in their own factories. Many people are familiar with the Deming Prize, an award given to recognize high-quality organizations, and Deming's Cycle for Improvement: plan, do, check, and act. Most Six Sigma principles described earlier are based on the plan-do-check-act model created by Deming. Many are also familiar with Deming's 14 Points for Management, summarized below from Deming's text *Out of the Crisis*[17]:

1. Create constancy of purpose for improvement of product and service.
2. Adopt the new philosophy.
3. Cease dependence on inspection to achieve quality.
4. End the practice of awarding business based on price tag alone. Instead, minimize total cost by working with a single supplier.
5. Improve constantly and forever every process for planning, production, and service.
6. Institute training on the job.

7. Adopt and institute leadership.
8. Drive out fear.
9. Break down barriers between staff areas.
10. Eliminate slogans, exhortations, and targets for the workforce.
11. Eliminate numerical quotas for the workforce and numerical goals for management.
12. Remove barriers that rob people of workmanship. Eliminate the annual rating or merit system.
13. Institute a vigorous program of education and self-improvement for everyone.
14. Put everyone in the company to work to accomplish the transformation.

Juran and the Importance of Top Management Commitment to Quality

Joseph M. Juran, like Deming, taught Japanese manufacturers how to improve their productivity. U.S. companies later discovered him as well. He wrote the first edition of the *Quality Control Handbook* in 1974, stressing the importance of top management commitment to continuous product quality improvement. In 2000, at the age of 94, Juran published the fifth edition of this famous handbook.[18] He also developed the Juran Trilogy: quality improvement, quality planning, and quality control. Juran stressed the difference between the manufacturer's view of quality and the customer's view. Manufacturers often focus on conformance to requirements, but customers focus on fitness for use. Most definitions of quality now use fitness for use to stress the importance of satisfying stated or implied needs and not just meeting stated requirements or specifications. Juran developed ten steps to quality improvement:

1. Build awareness of the need and opportunity for improvement.
2. Set goals for improvement.
3. Organize to reach the goals (establish a quality council, identify problems, select projects, appoint teams, designate facilitators).
4. Provide training.
5. Carry out projects to solve problems.
6. Report progress.
7. Give recognition.
8. Communicate results.
9. Keep score.
10. Maintain momentum by making annual improvement part of the regular systems and processes of the company.

Crosby and Striving for Zero Defects

Philip B. Crosby wrote *Quality Is Free* in 1979 and is best known for suggesting that organizations strive for zero defects.[19] He stressed that the costs of poor quality should include all the costs of not doing the job right the first time, such as scrap, rework, lost labor hours and machine hours, customer ill will and lost sales, and warranty costs. Crosby suggested that the cost of poor quality is so understated that companies can profitably spend unlimited amounts of money on improving quality. Crosby developed the following 14 steps for quality improvement:

1. Make it clear that management is committed to quality.
2. Form quality improvement teams with representatives from each department.
3. Determine where current and potential quality problems lie.
4. Evaluate the cost of quality and explain its use as a management tool.
5. Raise the quality awareness and personal concern of all employees.
6. Take actions to correct problems identified through previous steps.
7. Establish a committee for the zero-defects program.
8. Train supervisors to actively carry out their part of the quality improvement program.
9. Hold a "zero-defects day" to let all employees realize that there has been a change.
10. Encourage individuals to establish improvement goals for themselves and their groups.
11. Encourage employees to communicate to management the obstacles they face in attaining their improvement goals.
12. Recognize and appreciate those who participate.
13. Establish quality councils to communicate on a regular basis.
14. Do it all over again to emphasize that the quality improvement program never ends.

Crosby also developed the Quality Management Process Maturity Grid in 1978. This grid can be applied to an organization's attitude toward product usability. For example, the first stage in the grid is ignorance, where people might think they don't have any problems with usability. The final stage is wisdom, where people have changed their attitude so that usability defect prevention is a routine part of their operation.

Ishikawa's Guide to Quality Control

Kaoru Ishikawa is best known for his 1972 book *Guide to Quality Control*.[20] He developed the concept of quality circles and pioneered the use of cause-and-effect diagrams, as described earlier in this chapter. **Quality circles** are groups of non-supervisors and work leaders in a single company department who volunteer to conduct group studies on how to improve the effectiveness of work in their department. Ishikawa suggested that Japanese managers and workers were totally committed to quality, but that most U.S. companies delegated the responsibility for quality to a few staff members.

Taguchi and Robust Design Methods

Genichi Taguchi is best known for developing the Taguchi methods for optimizing the process of engineering experimentation. Key concepts in the Taguchi methods are that quality should be designed into the product and not inspected into it and that quality is best achieved by minimizing deviation from the target value. For example, if the target response time for accessing the EIS described in the opening case is half a second, there should be little deviation from this time. By the late 1990s, Taguchi had become, in the words of *Fortune* magazine, "America's new quality hero."[21] Many companies, including Xerox, Ford, Hewlett-Packard, and Goodyear, have recently used Taguchi's Robust Design methods to design high-quality products. **Robust Design methods** focus on eliminating defects by substituting scientific inquiry for trial-and-error methods.

Feigenbaum and Workers' Responsibility for Quality

Armand V. Feigenbaum developed the concept of total quality control (TQC) in his 1983 book *Total Quality Control: Engineering and Management*.[22] He proposed that the responsibility for quality should rest with the people who do the work. In TQC, product quality is more important than production rates, and workers are allowed to stop production whenever a quality problem occurs.

Malcolm Baldrige National Quality Award

The **Malcolm Baldrige National Quality Award** originated in 1987 in the U.S. to recognize companies that have achieved a level of world-class competition through quality management. The award was started in honor of Malcolm Baldrige, who was the U.S. secretary of commerce from 1981 until his death in a rodeo accident in July 1987. Baldrige was a proponent of quality management as a key element in improving the prosperity and long-term strength of U.S. organizations. The Malcolm Baldrige National Quality Award is given by the president of the United States to U.S. businesses—manufacturing and service, small and large—and to education and health care organizations. Organizations must apply for the award, and they must be judged outstanding in seven areas: leadership, strategic planning, customer and market focus, information and analysis, human resource focus, process management, and business results. Three awards may be given annually in each of these categories: manufacturing, service, small business and, from 1999, education and health care. The awards recognize achievements in quality and performance and raise awareness about the importance of quality as a competitive edge; the award is not given for specific products or services.

ISO Standards

The International Organization for Standardization (ISO) is a network of national standards institutes that work in partnership with international organizations, governments, industries, businesses, and consumer representatives. **ISO 9000**, a quality system standard developed by the ISO, is a three-part, continuous cycle of planning, controlling, and documenting quality in an organization. ISO 9000 provides minimum requirements needed for an organization to meet its quality certification standards. The ISO 9000 family of international quality management standards and guidelines has earned a global reputation as the basis for establishing quality management systems. The ISO's Web site (*www.iso.org*) includes testimonials from many business leaders throughout the world explaining the benefits of following these standards.

- A government official in Malaysia believes that the universally accepted ISO 9000 standard can contribute significantly to improving quality and enhancing development of an excellent work culture. ISO 9000 leads to a more systematic management of quality and provides a means of consolidating quality management systems in public service.
- Managers in the United Kingdom say that ISO 9000 has become a firmly established cornerstone of their organizations' drive toward quality improvement. It leads to substantial cost savings and contributes strongly to customer satisfaction.

- A Brazilian newspaper reported that following ISO 9000 helped its home delivery service improve so much that the complaints dropped to a mere 0.06 percent of the total copies distributed.[23]

ISO continues to offer standards to provide a framework for the assessment of software processes. The overall goals of a standard are to encourage organizations interested in improving quality of software products to employ proven, consistent, and reliable methods for assessing the state of their software development processes. They can also use their assessment results as part of coherent improvement programs. One of the outcomes of assessment and consequent improvement programs is reliable, predictable, and continuously improving software processes.

The contributions of several quality experts, quality awards, and quality standards are important parts of project quality management. The Project Management Institute was proud to announce in 1999 that their certification department had become the first certification department in the world to earn ISO 9000 certification, and that the *PMBOK® Guide* had been recognized as an international standard. Emphasizing quality in project management helps ensure that projects produce products or services that meet customer needs and expectations.

IMPROVING INFORMATION TECHNOLOGY PROJECT QUALITY

In addition to some of the suggestions provided for using good quality planning, quality assurance, and quality control, there are several other important issues involved in improving the quality of information technology projects. Strong leadership, understanding the cost of quality, providing a good workplace to enhance quality, and working toward improving the organization's overall maturity level in software development and project management can all assist in improving quality.

Leadership

As Joseph M. Juran said in 1945, "It is most important that top management be quality-minded. In the absence of sincere manifestation of interest at the top, little will happen below."[24] Juran and many other quality experts argue that the main cause of quality problems is a lack of leadership.

As globalization continues to increase and customers become more and more demanding, creating quality products quickly at a reasonable price is essential for staying in business. Having good quality programs in place helps organizations remain competitive. To establish and implement effective quality programs, top management must lead the way. A large percentage of quality problems are associated with management, not technical issues. Therefore, top management must take responsibility for creating, supporting, and promoting quality programs.

Motorola provides an excellent example of a high-technology company that truly emphasizes quality. Leadership is one of the factors that helped Motorola achieve its great success in quality management and Six Sigma. Top management emphasized the need to improve quality and helped all employees take responsibility for customer satisfaction. Strategic objectives in Motorola's long-range plans included managing quality improvement in the same way that new products or technologies were managed. Top management stressed the need to develop and use quality standards and provided resources such as staff, training, and customer inputs to help improve quality.

Leadership provides an environment conducive to producing quality. Management must publicly declare the company's philosophy and commitment to quality, implement company-wide training programs in quality concepts and principles, implement measurement programs to establish and track quality levels, and actively demonstrate the importance of quality. When every employee understands and insists on producing high-quality products, then top management has done a good job of promoting the importance of quality.

The Cost of Quality

The **cost of quality** is the cost of conformance plus the cost of nonconformance. **Conformance** means delivering products that meet requirements and fitness for use. Examples of these costs include the costs associated with developing a quality plan, costs for analyzing and managing product requirements, and costs for testing. The **cost of nonconformance** means taking responsibility for failures or not meeting quality expectations.

A 2002 study by RTI International reported that software bugs cost the U.S. economy $59.6 billion each year, about 0.6 percent of gross domestic product. Most of the costs are borne by software users, and the rest by developers and vendors. RTI International also suggested that more than one third of these costs could be eliminated by an improved testing infrastructure to enable earlier and more effective identification and removal of software defects.[25]

Other studies estimate the costs per hour of down time for systems. For example, Gartner estimated that the hourly cost of downtime for computer networks is about $42,000. Therefore, a company that suffers from a worse-than-average downtime of 175 hours a year can lose more than $7 million per year.[26] The five major cost categories related to quality include:

1. **Prevention cost**: The cost of planning and executing a project so that it is error-free or within an acceptable error range. Preventive actions such as training, detailed studies related to quality, and quality surveys of suppliers and subcontractors fall under this category. Recall from the discussion of cost management (see Chapter 7) that detecting defects in information systems during the early phases of the systems development life cycle is much less expensive than during the later phases. One hundred dollars spent refining user requirements could save millions by finding a defect before implementing a large system. The Year 2000 (Y2K) issue provided a good example of these costs. If organizations had decided during the 1960s, 1970s, and 1980s that all dates would need four characters to represent the year instead of two characters, they would have saved billions of dollars.
2. **Appraisal cost**: The cost of evaluating processes and their outputs to ensure that a project is error-free or within an acceptable error range. Activities such as inspection and testing of products, maintenance of inspection and test equipment, and processing and reporting inspection data all contribute to appraisal costs of quality.

3. **Internal failure cost**: A cost incurred to correct an identified defect before the customer receives the product. Items such as scrap and rework, charges related to late payment of bills, inventory costs that are a direct result of defects, costs of engineering changes related to correcting a design error, premature failure of products, and correcting documentation all contribute to internal failure cost.
4. **External failure cost**: A cost that relates to all errors not detected and not corrected before delivery to the customer. Items such as warranty cost, field service personnel training cost, product liability suits, complaint handling, and future business losses are examples of external failure costs.
5. **Measurement and test equipment costs**: The capital cost of equipment used to perform prevention and appraisal activities.

Many industries tolerate a very low cost of nonconformance, but not the information technology industry. Tom DeMarco is famous for several studies he conducted on the cost of nonconformance in the information technology industry. In the early 1980s, DeMarco found that the average large company devoted more than 60 percent of its software development efforts to maintenance. Around 50 percent of development costs were typically spent on testing and debugging software.[27] Although these percentages may have improved some, they are still very high.

Top management is primarily responsible for the high cost of nonconformance in information technology. Top managers often rush their organizations to develop new systems and do not give project teams enough time or resources to do a project right the first time. To correct these quality problems, top management must create a culture that embraces quality.

MEDIA SNAPSHOT

What do Melissa, Anna Kournikova, Code Red, and Sobig have to do with quality and information technology? They are all names of computer viruses that have cost companies millions of dollars. A quality issue faced by computer users around the world is lost productivity due to computer viruses and spam—unsolicited e-mail sent to multiple mailing lists, individuals, or newsgroups. A 2007 study by Nucleus Research Inc. estimated that spam management costs U.S. businesses more than $71 billion annually in lost productivity or $712 per employee. One e-mail security firm estimated that spam accounts for 95 *percent* of total e-mail volume worldwide.[28]

Computer viruses are also getting more technically advanced and infectious as they flood systems across the globe. In 2008, Reuters reported that spyware (software installed on a computer without the owner's consent), viruses, and phishing (using e-mail to try to fraudulently get information such as passwords or credit card numbers) cost consumers $7.1 billion in 2007, up from $2 billion the previous year.[29]

Organizational Influences, Workplace Factors, and Quality

A study done by Tom DeMarco and Timothy Lister produced interesting results related to organizations and relative productivity. Starting in 1984, DeMarco and Lister conducted "Coding War Games" over several years, in which time more than 600 software developers from 92 organizations participated. The games were designed to examine programming quality and productivity over a wide range of organizations, technical environments, and programming languages. The study demonstrated that organizational issues had a much greater influence on productivity than the technical environment or programming languages.

For example, DeMarco and Lister found that productivity varied by a factor of about one to ten across all participants. That is, one team may have finished a coding project in one day while another team took ten days to finish the same project. In contrast, productivity varied by an average of only 21 percent between pairs of software developers from the same organization. If one team from a specific organization finished the coding project in one day, the longest time it took for another team from the same organization to finish the project was 1.21 days.

DeMarco and Lister also found *no correlation* between productivity and programming language, years of experience, or salary. Furthermore, the study showed that providing a dedicated workspace and a quiet work environment were key factors in improving productivity. The results of the study suggest that top managers must focus on workplace factors to improve productivity and quality.[30]

DeMarco and Lister wrote a book titled *Peopleware* in 1987, and the second edition was published in 1999.[31] Their underlying thesis is that major problems with work performance and project failures are not technological but sociological in nature. They suggest minimizing office politics and giving smart people physical space, intellectual responsibility, and strategic direction—and then just *letting* them work. The manager's function is not to *make* people work but to make it possible for people to work by removing political roadblocks.

Expectations and Cultural Differences in Quality

Many experienced project managers know that a crucial aspect of project quality management is managing expectations. Although many aspects of quality can be clearly defined and measured, many cannot. Different project sponsors, customers, users, and other stakeholders have different expectations about various aspects of projects. It's very important to understand these expectations and manage any conflicts that might occur due to differences in expectations. For example, in the opening case, several users were upset when they could not access information within a few seconds. In the past, it may have been acceptable to have to wait two or three seconds for a system to load, but many of today's computer users expect systems to run much faster. Project managers and their teams must consider quality-related expectations as they define the project scope.

Expectations can also vary based on an organization's culture or geographic region. Anyone who has traveled to different parts of an organization, a country, or the world understands that expectations are not the same everywhere. For example, one department in a company might expect workers to be in their work areas most of the work day and to dress a certain way. Another department in the same company might focus on whether or not workers produce expected results, no matter where they work or how they dress. People working in smaller towns expect little traffic driving to work, while people working in large cities expect traffic to be a problem or rely on mass transit systems.

People working in other countries for the first time are often amazed at different quality expectations. Visitors to other countries may complain about things they take for granted, such as easily making cell phone calls, using a train or subway instead of relying on a car for transportation, or getting up-to-date maps. It's important to realize that different countries are at different stages of development in terms of quality.

Maturity Models

Another approach to improving quality in software development projects and project management in general is the use of **maturity models**, which are frameworks for helping organizations improve their processes and systems. Maturity models describe an evolutionary path of increasingly organized and systematically more mature processes. Many maturity models have five levels, with the first level describing characteristics of the least organized or mature organizations, and level five describing the characteristics of the most organized and mature organizations. Three popular maturity models include the Software Quality Function Deployment (SQFD) model, the Capability Maturity Model Integration (CMMI), and the project management maturity model.

Software Quality Function Deployment Model

The **Software Quality Function Deployment (SQFD) model** is an adaptation of the quality function deployment model suggested in 1986 as an implementation vehicle for Total Quality Management (TQM). SQFD focuses on defining user requirements and planning software projects. The result of SQFD is a set of measurable technical product specifications and their priorities. Having clearer requirements can lead to fewer design changes, increased productivity, and, ultimately, software products that are more likely to satisfy stakeholder requirements. The idea of introducing quality early in the design stage was based on Taguchi's emphasis on robust design methods.[32]

Capability Maturity Model Integration

Another popular maturity model is in continuous development at the Software Engineering Institute at Carnegie Mellon University. The Software Engineering Institute (SEI) is a federally funded research and development center established in 1984 by the U.S. Department of Defense with a broad mandate to address the transition of software engineering technology. The **Capability Maturity Model Integration (CMMI)** is "a process improvement approach that provides organizations with the essential elements of effective processes. It can be used to guide process improvement across a project, a division, or an entire organization. CMMI helps integrate traditionally separate organizational functions, set process improvement goals and priorities, provide guidance for quality processes, and provide a point of reference for appraising current processes."

The capability levels of the CMMI are:

0. *Incomplete*: At this level, a process is either not performed or partially performed. No generic goals exist for this level, and one or more of the specific goals of the process area are not satisfied.
1. *Performed*: A performed process satisfies the specific goals of the process area and supports and enables the work needed to produce work products. Although this capability level can result in improvements, those improvements can be lost over time if they are not institutionalized.

2. *Managed*: At this level, a process has the basic infrastructure in place to support it. The process is planned and executed based on policies and employs skilled people who have adequate resources to produce controlled outputs. The process discipline reflected by this level ensures that existing practices are retained during times of stress.
3. *Defined*: At this maturity level, a process is rigorously defined and the standards, process descriptions, and procedures for a project are tailored from the organization's set of standard processes to suit that particular project.
4. *Quantitatively managed*: At this level, a process is controlled using statistical and other quantitative techniques. The organization establishes quantitative objectives for quality and process performance that are used as criteria in managing the process.[33]
5. *Optimizing*: An optimizing process is improved based on an understanding of the common causes of variation inherent in the process. The focus is on continually improving the range of process performance through incremental and innovative improvements.[34]

Many companies that want to work in the government market have realized that they will not get many opportunities even to bid on projects unless they have a CMMI Level 3. According to one manager, "CMMI is really the future. People who aren't on the bandwagon now are going to find themselves falling behind."[35]

Project Management Maturity Models

In the late 1990s, several organizations began developing project management maturity models based on the Capability Maturity Model. Just as organizations realized the need to improve their software development processes and systems, they also realized the need to enhance their project management processes and systems for all types of projects.

The PMI Standards Development Program published the Organizational Project Management Maturity Model (OPM3) in December 2003, and the second edition was released in late 2008. More than 200 volunteers from around the world were part of the initial OPM3 team. The model is based on market research surveys that had been sent to more than 30,000 project management professionals and incorporates 180 best practices and more than 2,400 capabilities, outcomes, and key performance indicators.[36] According to John Schlichter, the OPM3 program director, "The standard would help organizations to assess and improve their project management capabilities as well as the capabilities necessary to achieve organizational strategies through projects. The standard would be a project management maturity model, setting the standard for excellence in project, program, and portfolio management best practices, and explaining the capabilities necessary to achieve those best practices."[37]

OPM3 provides the following example to illustrate a best practice, capability, outcome, and key performance indicator:

- *Best practice*: Establish internal project management communities
- *Capability*: Facilitate project management activities
- *Outcome*: Local initiatives, meaning the organization develops pockets of consensus around areas of special interest
- *Key performance indicator*: Community addresses local issues

Best practices are organized into three levels: project, program, and portfolio. Within each of those categories, best practices are categorized by four stages of process improvement: standardize, measure, control, and improve. For example, the list that follows contains several best practices listed in OPM3:

- Project best practices:
  - Project Initiation Process Standardization
  - Project Plan Development Process Measurement
  - Project Scope Planning Process Control
  - Project Scope Definition Process Improvement
- Program best practices:
  - Program Activity Definition Process Standardization
  - Program Activity Sequencing Process Measurement
  - Program Activity Duration Estimating Process Control
  - Program Schedule Development Process Improvement
- Portfolio best practices:
  - Portfolio Resource Planning Process Standardization
  - Portfolio Cost Estimating Process Measurement
  - Portfolio Cost Budgeting Process Control
  - Portfolio Risk Management Planning Process Improvement

Several other companies provide similar project management maturity models. The International Institute for Learning, Inc. calls the five levels in its model common language, common processes, singular methodology, benchmarking, and continuous improvement. ESI International Inc.'s model's five levels are called ad hoc, consistent, integrated, comprehensive, and optimizing. Regardless of the names of each level, the goal is clear: organizations want to improve their ability to manage projects. Many organizations are assessing where they stand in terms of project management maturity, just as they did for software development maturity with the SQFD and CMMI maturity models. Organizations are recognizing that they must make a commitment to the discipline of project management to improve project quality.

USING SOFTWARE TO ASSIST IN PROJECT QUALITY MANAGEMENT

This chapter provides examples of several tools and techniques used in project quality management. Software can be used to assist with several of these tools and techniques. For example, you can create charts and diagrams from many of the Seven Basic Tools of Quality using spreadsheet and charting software. You can use statistical software packages to help you determine standard deviations and perform many types of statistical analyses. You can create Gantt charts using project management software to help you plan and track work related to project quality management. There are also several specialized software products to assist people with managing Six Sigma projects, creating quality control charts, and assessing maturity levels. Project teams need to decide what types of software will help them manage their particular projects.

As you can see, quality itself is a very broad topic, and it is only one of the nine project management knowledge areas. Project managers must focus on defining how quality relates to their specific projects and ensure that those projects will satisfy the needs for which they were undertaken.

CASE WRAP-UP

Scott Daniels assembled a team to identify and resolve quality-related issues with the EIS and to develop a plan to help the medical instruments company prevent future quality problems. The first thing Scott's team did was to research the problems with the EIS. They created a cause-and-effect diagram similar to the one in Figure 8-2. They also created a Pareto chart (Figure 8-7) to help analyze the many complaints the Help Desk received and documented about the EIS. After further investigation, Scott and his team found out that many of the managers using the system were very inexperienced in using computer systems beyond basic office automation systems. They also found out that most users received no training at all on how to properly access or use the new EIS. There did not appear to be any major problems with the hardware for the EIS or the users' individual computers. The complaints about reports not giving consistent information all came from one manager, who had actually misread the reports, so there were no problems with the way the software was designed. Scott was very impressed with the quality of the entire project, except for the training. Scott reported his team's findings to the project sponsor of the EIS, who was relieved to find out that the quality problems were not as serious as many people feared.

Chapter Summary

Many news headlines regarding the poor quality of information technology projects demonstrate that quality is a serious issue. Several mission-critical information technology systems have caused deaths, and quality problems in many business systems have resulted in major financial losses.

Customers are ultimately responsible for defining quality. Important quality concepts include satisfying stated or implied stakeholder needs, conforming to requirements, and delivering items that are fit for use.

Project quality management includes planning quality, performing quality assurance, and performing quality control. Quality planning identifies which quality standards are relevant to the project and how to satisfy them. Quality assurance involves evaluating overall project performance to ensure that the project will satisfy the relevant quality standards. Quality control includes monitoring specific project results to ensure that they comply with quality standards and identifying ways to improve overall quality.

There are many tools and techniques related to project quality management. The Seven Basic Tools of Quality include cause-and-effect diagrams, control charts, run charts, scatter diagrams, histograms, Pareto charts, and flowcharts. Statistical sampling helps define a realistic number of items to include in analyzing a population. Six Sigma helps companies improve quality by reducing defects. Standard deviation measures the variation in data. Testing is very important in developing and delivering high-quality information technology products.

Many people contributed to the development of modern quality management. Deming, Juran, Crosby, Ishikawa, Taguchi, and Feigenbaum all made significant contributions to the field. Many organizations today use their ideas, which also influenced Six Sigma principles. The Malcolm Baldrige National Quality Award and ISO 9000 have also helped organizations emphasize the importance of improving quality.

There is much room for improvement in information technology project quality. Strong leadership helps emphasize the importance of quality. Understanding the cost of quality provides an incentive for its improvement. Providing a good workplace can improve quality and productivity. Understanding stakeholders' expectations and cultural differences are also related to project quality management. Developing and following maturity models can help organizations systematically improve their project management processes to increase the quality and success rate of projects.

There are several types of software available to assist in project quality management. It is important for project teams to decide which software will be most helpful for their particular projects.

Quick Quiz

1. ____________ is the degree to which a set of inherent characteristics fulfils requirements.
    a. Quality
    b. Conformance to requirements
    c. Fitness for use
    d. Reliability
2. What is the purpose of project quality management?
    a. to produce the highest quality products and services possible
    b. to ensure that appropriate quality standards are met
    c. to ensure that the project will satisfy the needs for which it was undertaken
    d. All of the above
3. ____________ generates ideas for quality improvements by comparing specific project practices or product characteristics to those of other projects or products within or outside the performing organization.
    a. Quality audits
    b. Design of experiments
    c. Six Sigma
    d. Benchmarking
4. What tool could you use to see if there is a relationship between two variables?
    a. a cause-and-effect diagram
    b. a control chart
    c. a run chart
    d. a scatter diagram
5. What tool can you use to determine whether a process is in control or out of control?
    a. a cause-and-effect diagram
    b. a control chart
    c. a run chart
    d. a scatter diagram
6. Six Sigma's target for perfection is the achievement of no more than ________ defects, errors, or mistakes per million opportunities.
    a. 6
    b. 9
    c. 3.4
    d. 1

7. The seven run rule states that if seven data points in a row on a control chart are all below the mean, above the means, or all increasing or decreasing, then the process needs to be examined for ____________ problems.
   a. random
   b. non-random
   c. Six Sigma
   d. quality
8. What is the preferred order for performing testing on information technology projects?
   a. unit testing, integration testing, system testing, user acceptance testing
   b. unit testing, system testing, integration testing, user acceptance testing
   c. unit testing, system testing, user acceptance testing, integration testing
   d. unit testing, integration testing, user acceptance testing, system testing
9. ______________ is known for his work on quality control in Japan and developed the 14 Points for Management in his text *Out of the Crisis*.
   a. Juran
   b. Deming
   c. Crosby
   d. Ishikawa
10. PMI's OPM3 is an example of a model or framework for helping organizations improve their processes and systems.
    a. benchmarking
    b. Six Sigma
    c. maturity
    d. quality

Quick Quiz Answers

1. a; 2. c; 3. d; 4. d; 5. b; 6. c; 7. b; 8. a; 9. b; 10. c

Discussion Questions

1. Discuss some of the examples of poor quality in information technology projects presented in the "What Went Wrong?" section. Could most of these problems have been avoided? Why do you think there are so many examples of poor quality in information technology projects?
2. What are the main processes included in project quality management?
3. How do functionality, system outputs, performance, reliability, and maintainability requirements affect quality planning?
4. What are benchmarks, and how can they assist in performing quality assurance? Describe typical benchmarks associated with a college or university.
5. What are the three main categories of outputs for quality control?

6. Provide examples of when you would use the Seven Basic Tools of Quality on an information technology project.
7. Discuss the history of modern quality management. How have experts such as Deming, Juran, Crosby, and Taguchi affected the quality movement and today's use of Six Sigma?
8. Discuss three suggestions for improving information technology project quality that were not made in this chapter.
9. Describe three types of software that can assist in project quality management.

Exercises

1. Assume your organization wants to hire new instructors for your project management course. Develop a list of quality standards that you could use in making this hiring decision.
2. Create a Pareto chart based on the information in the following table. First, create a spreadsheet in Excel, using the data in the table. List the most frequent customer problems first. Use the Excel template called pareto_chart and check your entries so your resulting chart looks similar to the one in Figure 8-7. See the companion Web site for help in creating Pareto charts.

Customer Complaints	Frequency/Week
Customer is on hold too long	90
Customer gets transferred to wrong area or cut off	20
Service rep cannot answer customer's questions	120
Service rep does not follow through as promised	40

3. To illustrate a normal distribution, shake and roll a pair of dice 30 times and graph the results. It is more likely for someone to roll a 6, 7, or 8 than a 2 or 12, so these numbers should come up more often. To create the graph, use graph paper or draw a grid. Label the x-axis with the numbers 2 through 12. Label the y-axis with the numbers 1 through 10. Fill in the appropriate grid for each roll of the dice. Do your results resemble a normal distribution? Why or why not?
4. Research the criteria for the Malcolm Baldrige National Quality Award or a similar quality award provided by another organization. Investigate a company that has received this award. What steps did the company take to earn this quality award? What are the benefits of earning a quality award? Summarize your findings in a two-page paper.
5. Review the information in this chapter about Six Sigma principles and Six Sigma organizations. Brainstorm ideas for a potential Six Sigma project that could improve quality on your campus, at your workplace, or in your community. Write a two-page paper describing one project idea and explain why it would be a Six Sigma project. Review and discuss how you could use the DMAIC process on this project.
6. Review the concepts in this chapter related to improving the quality of software. Write a two-page paper describing how you could apply these concepts to software development projects.

Running Case

The Recreation and Wellness Intranet Project team is working hard to ensure that the new system they develop meets expectations. The team has a detailed scope statement, but the project manager, Tony Prince, wants to make sure they're not forgetting any requirements that might affect how different people view the quality of the project. He knows that the project's sponsor and other senior managers are most concerned with getting people to use the system, improve their health, and reduce healthcare costs. System users will want the system to be very user-friendly, informative, fun to use, and fast.

Tasks

1. Develop a list of quality standards or requirements related to meeting the stakeholder expectations described above. Also provide a brief description of each requirement. For example, a requirement might be that 90 percent of employees have logged into the system within two weeks after the system rolls out.
2. Based on the list created for Task 1, determine how you will measure progress on meeting the requirements. For example, you might have employees log into the system as part of the training program and track who attends the training. You could also build a feature into the system to track usage by user name, department, and so on.
3. After analyzing survey information, you decide to create a Pareto chart to easily see which types of recreational programs and company-sponsored classes most people were interested in. First, create a spreadsheet in Excel, using the data in the table below. List the most frequently requested programs or classes first. Use the Excel template called pareto_chart and check your entries so your resulting chart looks similar to the one in Figure 8-7. See the companion Web site for help in creating Pareto charts.

Requested Programs/Classes	# of Times Requested
Walking program	7,115
Volleyball program	2,054
Weight reduction class	8,875
Stop smoking class	4,889
Stress reduction class	1,894
Soccer program	3,297
Table tennis program	120
Softball program	976

Companion Web Site

Visit the companion Web site for this text at *www.cengage.com/mis/schwalbe* to access:

- References cited in the text and additional suggested readings for each chapter
- Template files
- Lecture notes
- Interactive quizzes
- Podcasts
- Links to general project management Web sites
- And more

See the Preface of this text for additional information on accessing the companion Web site.

Key Terms

5 whys — a technique where you repeatedly ask the question "Why?" (five is a good rule of thumb) to help peel away the layers of symptoms that can lead to the root cause of a problem

acceptance decisions — decisions that determine if the products or services produced as part of the project will be accepted or rejected

appraisal cost — the cost of evaluating processes and their outputs to ensure that a project is error-free or within an acceptable error range

benchmarking — a technique used to generate ideas for quality improvements by comparing specific project practices or product characteristics to those of other projects or products within or outside the performing organization

Capability Maturity Model Integration (CMMI) — a process improvement approach that provides organizations with the essential elements of effective processes

cause-and-effect diagram — diagram that traces complaints about quality problems back to the responsible production operations to help find the root cause. Also known as *fishbone diagram* or *Ishikawa diagram*

conformance — delivering products that meet requirements and fitness for use

conformance to requirements — the project processes and products meet written specifications

control chart — a graphic display of data that illustrates the results of a process over time

cost of nonconformance — taking responsibility for failures or not meeting quality expectations

cost of quality — the cost of conformance plus the cost of nonconformance

defect — any instance where the product or service fails to meet customer requirements

DMAIC (Define, Measure, Analyze, Improve, Control) — a systematic, closed-loop process for continued improvement that is scientific and fact based

design of experiments — a quality technique that helps identify which variables have the most influence on the overall outcome of a process

external failure cost — a cost related to all errors not detected and corrected before delivery to the customer

features — the special characteristics that appeal to users

fishbone diagram — diagram that traces complaints about quality problems back to the responsible production operations to help find the root cause. Also known as *cause-and-effect diagram* or *Ishikawa diagram*

flowchart — graphic display of the logic and flow of processes that helps you analyze how problems occur and how processes can be improved

fitness for use — a product can be used as it was intended

functionality — the degree to which a system performs its intended function

histogram — a bar graph of a distribution of variables

integration testing — testing that occurs between unit and system testing to test functionally grouped components to ensure a subset(s) of the entire system works together

internal failure cost — a cost incurred to correct an identified defect before the customer receives the product

Ishikawa diagram — diagram that traces complaints about quality problems back to the responsible production operations to help find the root cause. Also known as *cause-and-effect diagram* or *fishbone diagram*

ISO 9000 — a quality system standard developed by the International Organization for Standardization (ISO) that includes a three-part, continuous cycle of planning, controlling, and documenting quality in an organization

maintainability — the ease of performing maintenance on a product

Malcolm Baldrige National Quality Award — an award started in 1987 to recognize companies that have achieved a level of world-class competition through quality management

maturity model — a framework for helping organizations improve their processes and systems

mean — the average value of a population

measurement and test equipment costs — the capital cost of equipment used to perform prevention and appraisal activities

metric — a standard of measurement

normal distribution — a bell-shaped curve that is symmetrical about the mean of the population

Pareto analysis — identifying the vital few contributors that account for most quality problems in a system

Pareto chart — histogram that helps identify and prioritize problem areas

performance — how well a product or service performs the customer's intended use

prevention cost — the cost of planning and executing a project so that it is error-free or within an acceptable error range

process adjustments — adjustments made to correct or prevent further quality problems based on quality control measurements

project quality management — ensuring that a project will satisfy the needs for which it was undertaken

quality — the totality of characteristics of an entity that bear on its ability to satisfy stated or implied needs or the degree to which a set of inherent characteristics fulfill requirements

quality assurance — periodically evaluating overall project performance to ensure that the project will satisfy the relevant quality standards

quality audit — structured review of specific quality management activities that helps identify lessons learned and can improve performance on current or future projects

quality circles — groups of nonsupervisors and work leaders in a single company department who volunteer to conduct group studies on how to improve the effectiveness of work in their department

quality control — monitoring specific project results to ensure that they comply with the relevant quality standards and identifying ways to improve overall quality

quality planning — identifying which quality standards are relevant to the project and how to satisfy them

reliability — the ability of a product or service to perform as expected under normal conditions

rework — action taken to bring rejected items into compliance with product requirements or specifications or other stakeholder expectations

Robust Design methods — methods that focus on eliminating defects by substituting scientific inquiry for trial-and-error methods

run chart — chart that displays the history and pattern of variation of a process over time

scatter diagram — diagram that helps to show if there is a relationship between two variables; also called XY charts

seven run rule — if seven data points in a row on a quality control chart are all below the mean, above the mean, or are all increasing or decreasing, then the process needs to be examined for nonrandom problems

six 9s of quality — a measure of quality control equal to 1 fault in 1 million opportunities

Six Sigma — a comprehensive and flexible system for achieving, sustaining, and maximizing business success that is uniquely driven by close understanding of customer needs, disciplined use of facts, data, statistical analysis, and diligent attention to managing, improving, and reinventing business processes

software defect — anything that must be changed before delivery of the program

Software Quality Function Deployment (SQFD) model — a maturity model that focuses on defining user requirements and planning software projects

standard deviation — a measure of how much variation exists in a distribution of data

statistical sampling — choosing part of a population of interest for inspection

system outputs — the screens and reports the system generates

system testing — testing the entire system as one entity to ensure that it is working properly

unit test — a test of each individual component (often a program) to ensure that it is as defect-free as possible

user acceptance testing — an independent test performed by end users prior to accepting the delivered system

yield — the number of units handled correctly through the development process

End Notes

[1] This joke was found on hundreds of Web sites and printed in the *Consultants in Minnesota Newsletter*, Independent Computer Consultants Association, December 1998.

[2] *Design News* (February 1988).

[3] *Datamation* (May 1987).

[4] *New York Times* (February 18, 1994).

[5] Robert Gavin, "Subscriber credit data distributed by mistake," *Boston Globe* (February 1, 2006).

[6] Peter S. Pande, Robert P. Neuman, and Roland R. Cavanagh, *The Six Sigma Way* (New York: McGraw-Hill, 2000), p. xi.

[7] James C. Collins and Jerry I. Porras, *Built to Last: Successful Habits of Visionary Companies* (New York: HarperBusiness, 1994).

[8] Peter S. Pande, Robert P. Neuman, and Roland R. Cavanagh, *The Six Sigma Way* (New York: McGraw-Hill, 2000), p. 7.

[9] Ibid. p. 9.

[10] Lewis Brown and Denise Taylor, "Reducing Delayed Starts in Special Lab With Six Sigma," *iSixSigma Healthcare* 5, no. 2 (January 17, 2007).

[11] "What You Need to Know About Six Sigma," *Productivity Digest* (December 2001), p. 38.

[12] Peter S. Pande, Robert P. Neuman, and Roland R. Cavanagh, *The Six Sigma Way* (New York: McGraw-Hill, 2000), p. 137.

[13] Lee Clifford, "Why You Can Safely Ignore Six Sigma," *Fortune* (January 22, 2001), p. 140.

[14] Hollstadt & Associates, Inc., *Software Development Project Life Cycle Testing Methodology User's Manual* (Burnsville: MN, August 1998), p. 13.

[15] Bart Eisenberg, "Achieving Zero-Defects Software," *Pacific Connection* (January 2004).

[16] Harold Kerzner, *Project Management*, 6th ed. (New York: Van Nostrand Reinhold, 1998), p. 1048.

[17] W. Edwards Deming, *Out of the Crisis* (Boston: MIT Press, 1986).

[18] Joseph M. Juran and A. Blanton Godfrey, *Juran's Quality Handbook*, 5th ed. (New York: McGraw-Hill Professional, 2000).

[19] Philip B. Crosby, *Quality Is Free: The Art of Making Quality Certain* (New York: McGraw-Hill, 1979).

[20] Kaoru Ishikawa, *Guide to Quality Control*, 2nd ed. (Asian Productivity Organization, 1986).

[21] Bylinsky, Gene, "How to Bring Out Better Products Faster," *Fortune* (November 23, 1998) p. 238[B].

[22] Armand V. Feigenbaum, *Total Quality Control: Engineering and Management*, 3rd rev. ed. (New York: McGraw-Hill, 1991).

[23] International Organization for Standardization, (Market feedback) *ISO.org* (March 2003).

[24] American Society for Quality (ASQ), "About ASQ: Joseph M. Juran" *ASQ.com* (*www.asq.org/about-asq/who-we-are/bio_juran.html*).

[25] RTI International, "Software Bugs Cost U.S. Economy $59.6 Billion Annually, RTI Study Finds" (July 1, 2002).

[26] Tom Pisello and Bill Quirk, "How to Quantify Downtime," *Network World* (January 4, 2004).

[27] Tom DeMarco, *Quality Controlling Software Projects: Management, Measurement and Estimation* (New Jersey: Prentice Hall PTR Facsimile Edition, 1986).

[28] Thomas Claburn, "Spam Turns 30 and Never Looked Healthier," *Information Week* (May 2, 2008).

[29] Reuters, "Internet Fraud Ignored by Authorities, Study Charges," *PCWorld* (August 16, 2008).

[30] Tom DeMarco and Timothy Lister, *Peopleware: Productive Projects and Teams* (New York: Dorset House, 1987).

[31] Tom DeMarco and Timothy Lister, *Peopleware: Productive Projects and Teams*, 2nd ed. (New York: Dorset House, 1999).

[32] R. R. Yilmaz and Sangit Chatterjee, "Deming and the Quality of Software Development," *Business Horizons* [Foundation for the School of Business at Indiana University] 40, no. 6 (November–December 1997), pp. 51–58.

33 Software Engineering Institute, Carnegie Mellon, "What is CMMI," (January 2007) (*http://www.sei.cmu.edu/cmmi/general/index.html*).

34 CMMI Product Team, "CMMI® for Development, Version 1.2," CMU/SEI–2006–TR–008 ESC–TR–2006–008 (August 2006).

35 Michael Hardy, "Strength in numbers: New maturity ratings scheme wins support among systems integrators" *FCW.com* (March 28, 2004).

36 John Schlichter, "The Project Management Institute's Organizational Project Management Maturity Model: An Update on the PMI's OPM3 Program" *PMForum.com* (September 2002).

37 John Schlichter, "The History of OPM3," *Project Management World Today* (June 2003).

CHAPTER 9

PROJECT HUMAN RESOURCE MANAGEMENT

LEARNING OBJECTIVES

After reading this chapter, you will be able to:

- Explain the importance of good human resource management on projects, including the current state and future implications of the global IT workforce
- Define project human resource management and understand its processes
- Summarize key concepts for managing people by understanding the theories of Abraham Maslow, Frederick Herzberg, David McClelland, and Douglas McGregor on motivation, H. J. Thamhain and D. L. Wilemon on influencing workers, and Stephen Covey on how people and teams can become more effective
- Discuss human resource planning and be able to create a human resource plan, project organizational chart, responsibility assignment matrix, and resource histogram
- Understand important issues involved in project staff acquisition and explain the concepts of resource assignments, resource loading, and resource leveling
- Assist in team development with training, team-building activities, and reward systems
- Explain and apply several tools and techniques to help manage a project team and summarize general advice on managing teams
- Describe how project management software can assist in project human resource management

OPENING CASE

This was the third time someone from the Information Technology department tried to work with Ben, the head of the F-44 aircraft program. Ben, who had been with the company for almost 30 years, was known for being "rough around the edges" and very demanding. The company was losing money on the F-44 upgrade project because the upgrade kits were not being delivered on time. The Canadian government had written severe late-penalty fees into its contract, and other customers were threatening to take their business elsewhere. Ben blamed it all on the Information Technology department for not letting his staff access the F-44 upgrade project's information system directly so they could work with their customers and suppliers more effectively. The information system was based on very old technology that only a couple of people in the company knew how to use. It often took days or even weeks for Ben's group to get the information they needed.

Ed Davidson, a senior programmer, attended a meeting with Sarah Ellis, an internal information technology business consultant. Sarah was in her early thirties and had advanced quickly in her company, primarily due to her keen ability to work well with all types of people. Sarah's job was to uncover the real problems with the F-44 aircraft program's information technology support, and then develop a solution with Ben and his team. If she found it necessary to invest in more information technology hardware, software, or staff, Sarah would write a business case to justify these investments and then work with Ed, Ben, and his group to implement the suggested solution as quickly as possible. Ben and three of his staff entered the conference room. Ben threw his books on the table and started yelling at Ed and Sarah. Ed could not believe his eyes or ears when Sarah stood nose to nose with Ben and started yelling right back at him.

THE IMPORTANCE OF HUMAN RESOURCE MANAGEMENT

Many corporate executives have said, "People are our most important asset." People determine the success and failure of organizations and projects. Most project managers agree that managing human resources effectively is one of the toughest challenges they face. Project human resource management is a vital component of project management, especially in the information technology field—in which qualified people are often hard to find and keep. It is important to understand global IT workforce issues and their implications for the future.

The Global IT Workforce

Although there have been ups and downs in the information technology labor market, there will always be a need for people to develop and maintain hardware, software, networks, and applications of information technology. The global job market for information technology workers is expanding, and the demand for project managers continues to increase. Below are statistics from several recent studies.

The Digital Planet 2008 study estimated that the global marketplace for information and communications technology (ICT) would top $3.7 trillion in 2008 and reach almost $4 trillion by 2011. The marketplace posted a 10.8 percent average annual growth rate in 2007 and 2008. Additional findings from this report include the following:

- Communications products and services represented the largest single category of ICT spending (57 percent) in 2007 with $1.9 trillion;
- Consumers spent 29 percent of ICT dollars worldwide, while spending by business and government accounted for 71 percent;
- In spending by country, the top ten ICT spending countries are, in descending order: the United States, Japan, China, Germany, United Kingdom, France, Italy, Brazil, Canada, and Spain. In 2008, China jumped ahead of Germany, the United Kingdom, and France; and
- The Americas growth in ICT spending will be the slowest of the three broad regions charted in Digital Planet, at 4 percent between 2007 and 2011. The Asia-Pacific region and the Europe, Africa, and Middle East regions will grow annually at 10.5 percent and 5 percent, respectively.[1]

In the U.S. the size of the IT workforce topped 4 million workers for the first time in 2008. Unemployment rates in many information technology occupations are among the lowest in the labor force, at only 2.3 percent. Demand for talent is high, and several organizations cannot grow as desired due to difficulties in hiring and recruiting the people they need.[2] According to the Bureau of Labor Statistics, several IS-related occupations will be among the top 30 fastest-growing occupations in the United States between now and 2016, with network systems/data communications analysts and computer software engineers listed as numbers one and four, respectively.[3]

A 2007 Forrester survey found that project managers remain in high demand but short supply, with 26 percent of IT leaders planning to hire project managers and 59 percent planning to train their current staff in project management. Little had changed since their 2002 survey, when 55 percent of IT leaders identified project management as the missing skill set in their organization. "The reason for the continued emphasis on project management skills is because IT's value to business remains contingent on its ability to deliver projects which meet business requirements both on time and on budget. IT staff accustomed to more technical roles struggle to transition to project management, CIOs argue, and complain that educational institutions are not putting adequate focus on these skills through coursework."[4] Employers like to hire people with a solid record of accomplishment. It helps to have previous experience in a related field and a four-year college degree. Hiring managers say interpersonal skills are the most important soft skill for information technology workers.[5]

These studies highlight the continued need for skilled information technology workers and project managers to lead their projects. As the job market changes, however, people should upgrade their skills to remain marketable and flexible. Many highly qualified information technology workers lost their jobs in the past few years. Workers need to develop a support system and financial reserves to make it through difficult economic times. They also need to consider different types of jobs and industries where they can use their skills and earn a living. Negotiation and presentation skills also become crucial in finding and keeping a good job. Workers need to know how they personally contribute to an organization's bottom line.

Implications for the Future of IT Human Resource Management

It is crucial for organizations to practice what they preach about human resources. If people truly are their greatest asset, organizations must work to fulfill their human resource needs *and* the needs of individual people in their organizations, regardless of the job market. If organizations want to be successful at implementing information technology projects, they need to understand the importance of project human resource management and take actions to make effective use of people.

Proactive organizations are addressing current and future human resource needs by, for example, improving benefits, redefining work hours and incentives, and finding future workers. Many organizations have changed their benefits policies to meet worker needs. Most workers assume that their companies provide some perks, such as casual dress codes, flexible work hours, and tuition assistance. Other companies might provide on-site day care, fitness club discounts, or matching contributions to retirement savings. Google, the winner of Fortune's 100 Best Companies award in 2007 and 2008, provides employees with free gourmet meals and doctors on site, a swimming spa and corporate gym, beach volleyball, Foosball, videogames, pool tables, ping-pong, roller hockey, and weekly Thank Goodness It's Friday (TGIF) parties! Of course, employees are top-notch workers, and Google receives 1,300 resumes a day.

Other implications for the future of human resource management relate to the hours organizations expect many information technology professionals to work and how they reward performance. Today people brag about the fact that they can work *less* than 40 hours a week or work from home several days a week—not that they work a lot of overtime and haven't had a vacation in years. If companies plan their projects well, they can avoid the need for overtime, or they can make it clear that overtime is optional. Many companies also outsource more and more of their project work, as described in Chapter 12, Project Procurement Management, to manage the fluctuating demand for workers.

Companies can also provide incentives that use performance, not hours worked, as the basis of rewards. If performance can be objectively measured, as it can in many aspects of information technology jobs, then it should not matter where employees do their work or how long it takes them to do it. For example, if a technical writer can produce a high-quality publication at home in one week, the company and the writer are better off than if the company insisted that the writer come to the office and take two weeks to produce the publication. Objective measures of work performance and incentives based on meeting those criteria are important considerations.

MEDIA SNAPSHOT

People often brag about the productivity of American workers. An article in the *Minneapolis Star Tribune* by Joan Williams and Ariane Hegewisch, however, revealed some interesting facts:

> Here's the dirty little secret: U.S. productivity is No. 1 in the world when productivity is measured as gross domestic product per worker, but our lead vanishes when productivity is measured as GDP per hour worked, according to the Organization for Economic Cooperation and Development, whose members are the world's 30 most

continued

developed nations. Productivity per hour is higher in France, with the United States at about the same level as other advanced European economies. As it turns out, the U.S. "productivity advantage" is just another way of saying that we work more hours than workers in any other industrialized country except South Korea. Is that something to brag about? Europeans take an average of six to seven weeks of paid annual leave, compared with just 12 days in the United States. Twice as many American as European workers put in more than 48 hours per week. Particularly sobering is the fact that in two out of three American families with small children in which both parents work, the couples work more than 80 total hours per week, also more than double the European rate.[6]

Economists say that Americans prefer the higher income gained from working extra hours, while Europeans prefer more family time and leisure. However, sociologists have shown that many Americans, especially men, would like to have more family or leisure time. Recent surveys show that many Americans are willing to sacrifice up to a quarter of their salaries in return for more time off!

So why don't Americans work less? Some do need the money, but many others cannot find jobs where they can work fewer hours. Even more Americans fear losing their jobs, healthcare benefits, or promotion opportunities if they work fewer hours or even request the opportunity to do so. As a result, many families who would prefer both parents work less than 40 hours a week end up having one parent working 50 or more hours a week while the other parent is unemployed altogether. Williams and Hegewisch describe this situation as "a squandering of human capital that is typically overlooked in discussions of productivity and GDP. A new and more promising way to fuel economic growth would be to offer good jobs with working hours that enable fathers as well as mothers to maintain an active involvement with family life as well as an active career."[7]

The need to develop future talent in information technology also has important implications for everyone. Who will maintain the systems we have today when the last of the "baby boomer" generation retires? Who will continue to develop new products and services using new technologies that have not yet been developed? Some schools require all students to take computer literacy courses, although most teenagers today already know how to use computers, iPods, cell phones, and other technologies. But are today's children learning the skills they'll need to develop new technologies and work on global teams? As the workforce becomes more diverse, will more women and minorities be ready and willing to enter IT fields? Several colleges, government agencies, and private groups have programs to help recruit more women and minorities into technical fields. Some companies provide options for working parents to help them balance work and family. All of these efforts will help to develop the human resources needed for future information technology projects.

WHAT WENT WRONG?

A 2006 report by The Conference Board, Corporate Voices for Working Families, Partnership for 21st Century Skills, and the Society for Human Resource Management suggests that entry level workers in the U.S. are ill-prepared for the workplace. More than

continued

400 employers across the United States participated in the survey, describing what skills they believe are important for new job entrants and how well they think recently hired graduates exhibit these skills. Employers listed "very important" skills at all education levels and then rated entry level workers as being deficient, adequate, or excellent in each skill.

For high school graduates, respondents listed many deficiencies, as follows. The percentage next to each skill indicates the percentage of respondents who rated graduates as deficient.

- Written Communications—80.9%
- Professionalism/Work Ethic—70.3%
- Critical Thinking/Problem Solving—69.6%
- Oral Communications—52.7%
- Ethics/Social Responsibility—44.1%
- Reading Comprehension—38.4%
- Teamwork/Collaboration—34.6%
- Diversity—27.9%
- Information Technology Application—21.5%
- English Language—21.0%

Two-year college/technical school graduates were listed as deficient in the following seven skills:

- Written Communications—47.3%
- Writing in English—46.4%
- Lifelong Learning/Self Direction—27.9%
- Creativity/Innovation—27.6%
- Critical Thinking/Problem Solving—22.8%
- Oral Communications—21.3%
- Ethics/Social Responsibility—21.0%

Four-year college graduates were listed as deficient in the following three skills:

- Written Communications—27.8%
- Writing in English—26.2%
- Leadership—23.8%

An interesting finding was that 46.3 percent of respondents ranked graduates of four-year colleges as excellent in information technology application, but they were more concerned that college grads were deficient in written communications, writing in English, and leadership.[8]

WHAT IS PROJECT HUMAN RESOURCE MANAGEMENT?

Project human resource management includes the processes required to make the most effective use of the people involved with a project. Human resource management includes all project stakeholders: sponsors, customers, project team members, support staff, suppliers supporting the project, and so on. Human resource management includes the following four processes:

1. *Developing the human resource plan* involves identifying and documenting project roles, responsibilities, and reporting relationships. The main output of this process is a human resource plan.
2. *Acquiring the project team* involves getting the needed personnel assigned to and working on the project. Key outputs of this process are project staff assignments, resource calendars, and project management plan updates.
3. *Developing the project team* involves building individual and group skills to enhance project performance. Team-building skills are often a challenge for many project managers. The main outputs of this process are team performance assessments and enterprise environmental factors updates.
4. *Managing the project team* involves tracking team member performance, motivating team members, providing timely feedback, resolving issues and conflicts, and coordinating changes to help enhance project performance. Outputs of this process include enterprise environmental factors updates, organizational process assets updates, change requests, and project management plan updates.

Figure 9-1 summarizes these processes and outputs, showing when they occur in a typical project.

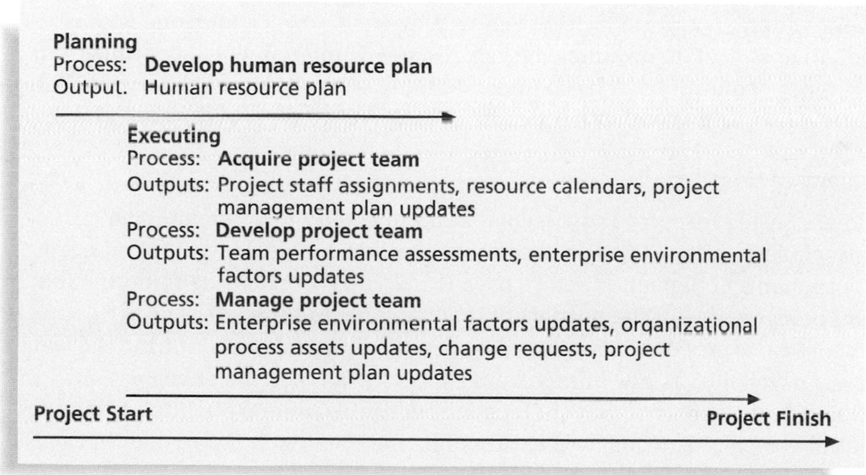

FIGURE 9-1 Project human resource management summary

Some topics related to human resource management (understanding organizations, stakeholders, and different organizational structures) were introduced in Chapter 2, The Project Management and Information Technology Context. This chapter will expand on some of those topics and introduce other important concepts in project human resource management, including theories about managing people, resource loading, and resource leveling. You will also learn how to use software to assist in project human resource management.

Industrial-organizational psychologists and management theorists have devoted much research and thought to the field of managing people at work. Psychosocial issues that affect how people work and how well they work include motivation, influence and power, and effectiveness. This section will review Abraham Maslow's, Frederick Herzberg's, David McClelland's, and Douglas McGregor's contributions to an understanding of motivation; H. J. Thamhain's and D. L. Wilemon's work on influencing workers and reducing conflict; the effect of power on project teams; and Stephen Covey's work on how people and teams can become more effective. Finally, you will look at some implications and recommendations for project managers.

Motivation Theories

Psychologists, managers, coworkers, teachers, parents, and most people in general still struggle to understand what motivates people, or, why they do what they do. **Intrinsic motivation** causes people to participate in an activity for their own enjoyment. For example, some people love to read, write, or play an instrument because it makes them feel good. **Extrinsic motivation** causes people to do something for a reward or to avoid a penalty. For example, some young children would prefer *not* to play an instrument, but they do because they receive a reward or avoid a punishment for doing so. Why do some people require no external motivation whatsoever to produce high-quality work while others require significant external motivation to perform routine tasks? Why can't you get someone who is extremely productive at work to do simple tasks at home? Humankind will continue to try to answer these types of questions. A basic understanding of motivational theory will help anyone who has to work or live with other people to understand themselves and others.

Maslow's Hierarchy of Needs

Abraham Maslow, a highly respected psychologist who rejected the dehumanizing negativism of psychology in the 1950s, is best known for developing a hierarchy of needs. In the 1950s, proponents of Sigmund Freud's psychoanalytic theory were promoting the idea that human beings were not the masters of their destiny and that all their actions were governed by unconscious processes dominated by primitive sexual urges. During the same period, behavioral psychologists saw human beings as controlled by the environment. Maslow argued that both schools of thought failed to recognize unique qualities of human behavior: love, self-esteem, belonging, self-expression, and creativity. He argued that these unique qualities enable people to make independent choices, which gives them full control of their destiny.

Figure 9-2 shows the basic pyramid structure of Maslow's **hierarchy of needs**, which states that people's behaviors are guided or motivated by a sequence of needs. At the bottom of the hierarchy are physiological needs. Once physiological needs are satisfied, safety needs guide behavior. Once safety needs are satisfied, social needs come to the forefront, and so on up the hierarchy. The order of these needs and their relative sizes in the pyramid are significant. Maslow suggests that each level of the hierarchy is a prerequisite for the levels above. For example, it is not possible for a person to consider self-actualization if he or she has not addressed basic needs concerning security and safety. People in an emergency situation, such as a flood or hurricane, are not going to worry about personal growth. Personal survival will be their main motivation. Once a particular need is satisfied, however, it no longer serves as a potent motivator of behavior.

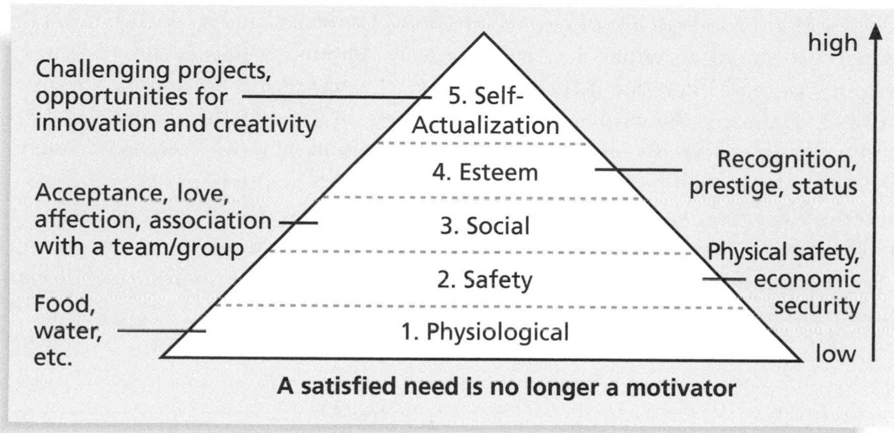

FIGURE 9-2 Maslow's hierarchy of needs

The bottom four needs in Maslow's hierarchy—physiological, safety, social, and esteem—are referred to as deficiency needs, and the highest level, self-actualization, is considered a growth need. Only after meeting deficiency needs can individuals act upon growth needs. Self-actualized people are problem-focused, have an appreciation for life, are concerned about personal growth, and have the ability to have peak experiences.

Most people working on an information technology project will probably have their basic physiological and safety needs met. If someone has a sudden medical emergency or is laid off from work, however, physiological and safety needs will move to the forefront. To motivate project team members, the project manager needs to understand each person's motivation, especially with regard to social, esteem, and self-actualization or growth needs. Team members new to a company and city might be motivated by social needs. To address social needs, some companies organize gatherings and social events for new workers. Other project members may find these events to be an invasion of personal time they would rather spend with their friends and family or working on an advanced degree.

Maslow's hierarchy conveys a message of hope and growth. People can work to control their own destinies and naturally strive to satisfy higher and higher needs. Successful project managers know they must focus on meeting project goals, but they also know that they must understand team members' personal goals and needs to provide appropriate motivation and maximize team performance.

Herzberg's Motivation-Hygiene Theory

Frederick Herzberg is best known for distinguishing between motivational factors and hygiene factors when considering motivation in work settings. He called factors that cause job satisfaction motivators and factors that cause dissatisfaction hygiene factors. The term "hygiene" is used in the sense that these factors are considered maintenance factors that are necessary to avoid dissatisfaction but, by themselves, they do not provide satisfaction.

Head of Case Western University's psychology department, Herzberg wrote the book *Work and the Nature of Man* in 1966 and a famous *Harvard Business Review* article, "One More Time: How Do You Motivate Employees?" in 1968.[9] Herzberg analyzed the factors that affected productivity among a sample of 1,685 employees. Popular beliefs at that time were that work output was most improved through larger salaries, more supervision, or a more attractive work environment. According to Herzberg, these hygiene factors would cause dissatisfaction if not present, but would not motivate workers to do more if present. Today, professionals might also expect employers to provide them with health benefits, training, and a computer or other equipment required to perform their jobs. Herzberg found that people were motivated to work mostly by feelings of personal achievement and recognition. Motivators, Herzberg concluded, included achievement, recognition, the work itself, responsibility, advancement, and growth, and are shown in Table 9-1.

TABLE 9-1 Examples of Herzberg's hygiene factors and motivators

Hygiene Factors	Motivators
Larger salaries	Achievement
More supervision	Recognition
More attractive work environment	Work itself
Computer or other required equipment	Responsibility
Health benefits	Advancement
Training	Growth

In his books and articles, Herzberg explained why attempts to use positive factors such as reducing time spent at work, upward spiraling wages, offering fringe benefits, providing human relations and sensitivity training, and so on did not instill motivation. He argued that people want to actualize themselves by being able to use their creativity and work on challenging projects. They need stimuli for their growth and advancement needs, in accordance with Maslow's hierarchy of needs. Factors such as achievement, recognition, responsibility, advancement, and growth produce job satisfaction and are work motivators.

McClelland's Acquired-Needs Theory

David McClelland proposed that an individual's specific needs are acquired or learned over time and shaped by life experiences. The main categories of acquired needs include achievement, affiliation, and power.[10] Normally one or two of these needs will be dominant in individuals.

- *Achievement*: People with a high need for achievement (nAch) seek to excel and tend to avoid both low-risk and high-risk situations to improve their chances for achieving something worthwhile. Achievers need regular feedback and often prefer to work alone or with other high achievers. Managers should give high achievers challenging projects with achievable goals. Achievers should receive frequent performance feedback, and although money is not an important motivator to them, it is an effective form of feedback.
- *Affiliation*: People with a high need for affiliation (nAff) desire harmonious relationships with other people and need to feel accepted by others. They tend to conform to the norms of their work group and prefer work that involves significant personal interaction. Managers should try to create a cooperative work environment to meet the needs of people with a high need for affiliation.
- *Power*: People with a need for power (nPow) desire either personal power or institutional power. People who need personal power want to direct others and can be seen as bossy. People who need institutional power or social power want to organize others to further the goals of the organization. Management should provide those seeking institutional or social power with the opportunity to manage others, emphasizing the importance of meeting organizational goals.

The Thematic Apperception Test (TAT) is a tool to measure the individual needs of different people using McClelland's categories. The TAT presents subjects with a series of ambiguous pictures and asks them to develop a spontaneous story for each picture, assuming they will project their own needs into the story.

McGregor's Theory X and Theory Y

Douglas McGregor was one of the great popularizers of a human relations approach to management, and he is best known for developing Theory X and Theory Y. In his research, documented in his 1960 book *The Human Side of Enterprise*, McGregor found that although many managers spouted the right ideas, they actually followed a set of assumptions about worker motivation that he called *Theory X* (sometimes referred to as classical systems theory).[11] People who believe in Theory X assume that workers dislike and avoid work if possible, so managers must use coercion, threats, and various control schemes to get workers to make adequate efforts to meet objectives. They assume that the average worker wants to be directed and prefers to avoid responsibility, has little ambition, and wants security above all else. Research seemed to demonstrate clearly that these assumptions were not valid. McGregor suggested a different series of assumptions about human behavior that he called *Theory Y* (sometimes referred to as human relations theory). Managers who believe in Theory Y assume that individuals do not inherently dislike work, but consider it as natural as play or rest. The most significant rewards are the satisfaction of esteem and self-actualization needs, as described by Maslow. McGregor urged managers to motivate people based on these more valid Theory Y notions.

In 1981, William Ouchi introduced another approach to management in his book *Theory Z: How American Business Can Meet the Japanese Challenge*.[12] Theory Z is based on the Japanese approach to motivating workers, which emphasizes trust, quality, collective decision making, and cultural values. Whereas Theory X and Theory Y emphasize how management views employees, Theory Z also describes how workers perceive management. Theory Z workers, it is assumed, can be trusted to do their jobs to their utmost ability, as long as management can be trusted to support them and look out for their well-being. Theory Z emphasizes things such as job rotation, broadening of skills, generalization versus specialization, and the need for continuous training of workers.

Thamhain and Wilemon's Influence and Power

Many people working on a project do not report directly to project managers, and project managers often do not have control over project staff who report to them. For example, people are free to change jobs. If they are given work assignments they do not like, many workers will simply quit or transfer to other departments or projects. H. J. Thamhain and D. L. Wilemon investigated the approaches project managers use to deal with workers and how those approaches relate to project success. They identified nine influence bases available to project managers:

1. *Authority*: the legitimate hierarchical right to issue orders
2. *Assignment*: the project manager's perceived ability to influence a worker's later work assignments
3. *Budget*: the project manager's perceived ability to authorize others' use of discretionary funds
4. *Promotion*: the ability to improve a worker's position
5. *Money*: the ability to increase a worker's pay and benefits
6. *Penalty*: the project manager's perceived ability to dispense or cause punishment
7. *Work challenge*: the ability to assign work that capitalizes on a worker's enjoyment of doing a particular task, which taps an intrinsic motivational factor
8. *Expertise*: the project manager's perceived special knowledge that others deem important
9. *Friendship*: the ability to establish friendly personal relationships between the project manager and others[13]

Top management grants authority to the project manager. Assignment, budget, promotion, money, and penalty influence bases may or may not be inherent in a project manager's position. Unlike authority, they are not automatically available to project managers as part of their position. Others' perceptions are important in establishing the usefulness of these influence bases. For example, any manager can influence workers by providing challenging work; the ability to provide challenging work (or take it away) is not a special ability of project managers. In addition, project managers must earn the ability to influence by using expertise and friendship.

Thamhain and Wilemon found that projects were more likely to fail when project managers relied too heavily on using authority, money, or penalty to influence people. *When project managers used work challenge and expertise to influence people, projects were more likely to succeed*. The effectiveness of work challenge in influencing people is consistent with Maslow's and Herzberg's research on motivation. The importance of expertise as a means of influencing people makes sense on projects that involve special knowledge, as in most information technology projects.

Influence is related to the topic of power. **Power** is the potential ability to influence behavior to get people to do things they would not otherwise do. Power has a much stronger connotation than influence, especially since it is often used to force people to change their behavior. There are five main types of power, based on French and Raven's classic study, "The Bases of Social Power."[14]

- **Coercive power** involves using punishment, threats, or other negative approaches to get people to do things they do not want to do. This type of power is similar to Thamhain's and Wilemon's influence category called *penalty*. For example, a project manager can threaten to fire workers or subcontractors to try to get them to change their behavior. If the project manager really has the power to fire people, he or she could follow through on the threat. Recall, however, that influencing using penalties is correlated with unsuccessful projects. Still, coercive power can be very effective in stopping negative behavior. For example, if students tend to hand in assignments late, an instructor can have a policy in his or her syllabus stating late penalties, such as a 20 percent grade reduction for each day an assignment is late.
- **Legitimate power** is getting people to do things based on a position of authority. This type of power is similar to the authority basis of influence. If top management gives project managers organizational authority, project managers can use legitimate power in several situations. They can make key decisions without involving the project team, for example. Overemphasis of legitimate power or authority also correlates with project failure.
- **Expert power** involves using personal knowledge and expertise to get people to change their behavior. If people perceive that project managers are experts in certain situations, they will follow their suggestions. For example, if a project manager has expertise in working with a particular information technology supplier and their products, the project team will be more likely to follow the project manager's suggestions on how to work with that vendor and its products.
- **Reward power** involves using incentives to induce people to do things. Rewards can include money, status, recognition, promotions, special work assignments, or other means of rewarding someone for desired behavior. Many motivation theorists suggest that only certain types of rewards, such as work challenge, achievement, and recognition, truly induce people to change their behavior or work hard.
- **Referent power** is based on an individual's personal charisma. People hold someone with referent power in very high regard and will do what they say based on their regard for the person. People such as Martin Luther King, Jr., John F. Kennedy, and Bill Clinton had referent power. Very few people possess the natural charisma that underlies referent power.

It is important for project managers to understand what types of influence and power they can use in different situations. New project managers often overemphasize their position—their legitimate power or authority influence—especially when dealing with project team members or support staff. They also neglect the importance of reward power or work challenge influence. People often respond much better to a project manager who motivates them with challenging work and provides positive reinforcement for doing a good job. It is important for project managers to understand the basic concepts of influence and power, and to practice using them to their own and their project team's advantage.

Covey and Improving Effectiveness

Stephen Covey, author of *The 7 Habits of Highly Effective People: Powerful Lessons in Personal Change*,[15] expanded on the work done by Maslow, Herzberg, and others to develop an approach for helping people and teams become more effective. Covey's first three habits of effective people—be proactive, begin with the end in mind, and put first things first—help people achieve a private victory by becoming independent. After achieving independence, people can then strive for interdependence by developing the next three habits—think win/win, seek first to understand then to be understood, and synergize. (**Synergy** is the concept that the whole is equal to more than the sum of its parts.) Finally, everyone can work on Covey's seventh habit—sharpen the saw—to develop and renew their physical, spiritual, mental, and social/emotional selves.

Project managers can apply Covey's seven habits to improve effectiveness on projects, as follows:

1. *Be proactive*. Covey, like Maslow, believes that people have the ability to be proactive and choose their responses to different situations. Project managers must be proactive, anticipate, and plan for problems and inevitable changes on projects. They can also encourage their team members to be proactive in working on their project activities.
2. *Begin with the end in mind*. Covey suggests that people focus on their values, what they really want to accomplish, and how they really want to be remembered in their lives. He suggests writing a mission statement to help achieve this habit. Many organizations and projects have mission statements that help them focus on their main purpose.
3. *Put first things first*. Covey developed a time management system and matrix to help people prioritize their time. He suggests that most people need to spend more time doing things that are important, but not urgent. Important but not urgent activities include planning, reading, and exercising. Project managers need to spend a lot of time working on important and not urgent activities, such as developing various project plans, building relationships with major project stakeholders, and mentoring project team members. They also need to avoid focusing only on important and urgent activities—putting out fires.
4. *Think win/win*. Covey presents several paradigms of interdependence, with think win/win being the best choice in most situations. When you use a win/win paradigm, parties in potential conflict work together to develop new solutions that benefit all parties. Project managers should strive to use a win/win approach in making decisions, but sometimes, especially in competitive situations, they must use a win/lose paradigm.
5. *Seek first to understand, then to be understood*. **Empathic listening** is listening with the intent to understand. It is even more powerful than active listening because you forget your personal interests and focus on truly understanding the other person. To really understand other people, you must learn to focus on others first. When you practice empathic listening, you can begin two-way communication. This habit is critical for project managers so they can really understand their stakeholders' needs and expectations.

6. *Synergize*. In projects, a project team can synergize by creating collaborative products that are much better than a collection of individual efforts. Covey also emphasizes the importance of valuing differences in others to achieve synergy. Synergy is essential to many highly technical projects; in fact, several major breakthroughs in information technology occurred because of synergy. For example, in his Pulitzer Prize–winning book, *The Soul of a New Machine*, Tracy Kidder documented the 1970s synergistic efforts of a team of Data General researchers to create a new 32-bit superminicomputer.[16]
7. *Sharpen the saw*. When you practice sharpening the saw, you take time to renew yourself physically, spiritually, mentally, and socially. The practice of self-renewal helps people avoid burnout. Project managers must make sure that they and their project team have time to retrain, reenergize, and occasionally even relax to avoid burnout.

Douglas Ross, author of *Applying Covey's Seven Habits to a Project Management Career*, related Covey's seven habits to project management. Ross suggests that Habit 5—Seek first to understand, then to be understood—differentiates good project managers from average or poor project managers. People have a tendency to focus on their own agendas instead of first trying to understand other people's points of view. Empathic listening can help project managers and team members find out what motivates different people. Understanding what motivates key stakeholders and customers can mean the difference between project success and project failure. Once project managers and team members begin to practice empathic listening, they can communicate and work together to tackle problems more effectively.[17]

Before you can practice empathic listening, you first have to get people to talk to you. In many cases, you must work on developing a rapport with the other person before he or she will really talk to you. **Rapport** is a relation of harmony, conformity, accord, or affinity. Without rapport, people cannot begin to communicate. For example, in the opening case, Ben was not ready to talk to anyone from the Information Technology department, even if Ed and Sarah were ready to listen. Ben was angry about the lack of support he received from the Information Technology department and bullied anyone who reminded him of that group. Before Sarah could begin to communicate with Ben, she had to establish rapport.

One technique for establishing rapport is mirroring. **Mirroring** is matching certain behaviors of the other person. People tend to like people who are like themselves, and mirroring helps you take on some of the other person's characteristics. It also helps them realize if they are behaving unreasonably, as in this case. You can mirror someone's voice tone and/or tempo, breathing, movements, or body postures. After Ben started yelling at her, Sarah quickly decided to mirror his voice tone, tempo, and body posture. She stood nose to nose with Ben and started yelling right back at him. This action made Ben realize what he was doing, and it also made him notice and respect this colleague from the Information Technology department. Once Ben overcame his anger, he could start communicating his needs. In most cases, such extreme measures are not needed, and mirroring must be used with caution. Done improperly or with the wrong person, it could result in very negative consequences. (This example is based on a true situation where the author was "Sarah.")

Recall the importance of getting users involved in information technology projects. For organizations to be truly effective in information technology project management, they must find ways to help users and developers of information systems work together. It is widely accepted that organizations make better project decisions when business professionals and information technology staff collaborate. It is also widely accepted that this task is easier said than done. Many companies have been very successful in integrating technology and business departments, but many other companies continue to struggle with this issue.

It is important to understand and pay attention to concepts of motivation, influence, power, and improving effectiveness in all project processes. It is likewise important to remember that projects operate within an organizational environment. The challenge comes from applying these theories to the many unique individuals involved in particular projects in particular organizations.

As you can see, there are many important topics related to motivation, influence, power, and effectiveness that are relevant to project management. Projects are done by and for people, so it is important for project managers and team members to understand and practice key concepts related to these topics. Remember that everyone prefers to work with people they like and respect, and it is important to treat others with respect, regardless of their title or position. This is especially true for people in support roles, such as administrative assistants, security guards, or members of the cleaning crew. You never know when you may need their help at some critical point in a project.

DEVELOPING THE HUMAN RESOURCE PLAN

In order to develop a human resource plan for a project, you must identify and document project roles, responsibilities, skills, and reporting relationships. The human resource plan often includes an organizational chart for the project, detailed information on roles and responsibilities, and a staffing management plan.

Before creating an organizational chart or any part of the human resource plan for a project, top management and the project manager must identify what types of people the project really needs to ensure project success. If the key to success lies in having the best Java programmers you can find, planning should reflect that need. If the real key to success is having a top-notch project manager and team leaders whom people respect in the company, that need should drive human resource planning.

Project Organizational Charts

Recall from Chapter 2 that the nature of information technology projects often means that project team members come from different backgrounds and possess a wide variety of skill sets. It can be very difficult to manage such a diverse group of people, so it is important to provide a clear organizational structure for a project. After identifying important skills and the types of people needed to staff a project, the project manager should work with top management and project team members to create an organizational chart for the project. Figure 9-3 provides a sample organizational chart for a large information technology project. Note that the project personnel include a deputy project manager, subproject managers, and teams. **Deputy project managers** fill in for project managers in their absence and assist them as needed, which is similar to the role of a vice president. **Subproject managers** are responsible for managing the subprojects into which a large project might be divided. There are often subproject managers that focus on managing various software (S/W) and hardware (H/W) components of large projects. This structure is typical for large projects. With many people working on a project, clearly defining and allocating project work is essential. (Visit the companion Web site for this text to see the project organization chart that Northwest Airlines used for their large ResNet project.) Smaller information technology projects usually do not have deputy project managers or subproject managers. On smaller projects, the project managers might have just team leaders reporting directly to them.

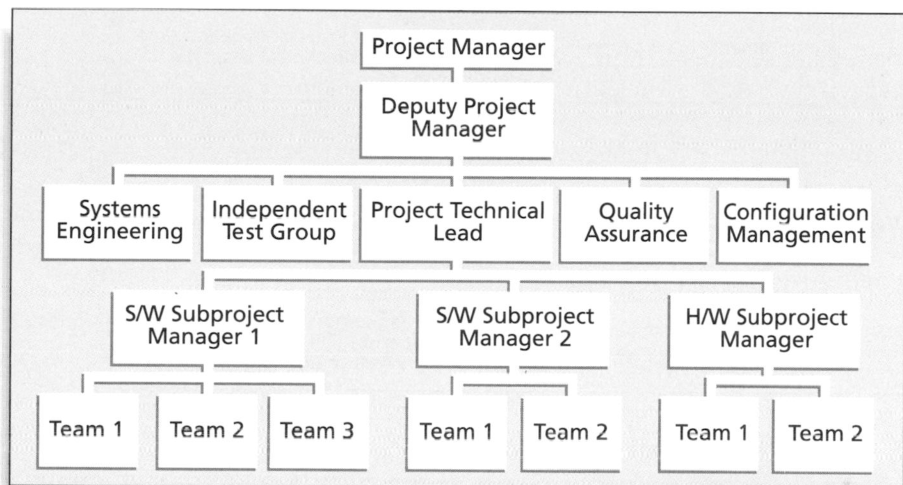

FIGURE 9-3 Sample organizational chart for a large information technology project

In addition to defining an organizational structure for a project, it is also important to follow a work definition and assignment process. Figure 9-4 provides a framework for defining and assigning work. This process consists of four steps:

1. Finalizing the project requirements
2. Defining how the work will be accomplished
3. Breaking down the work into manageable elements
4. Assigning work responsibilities

The work definition and assignment process is carried out during the proposal and startup phases of a project. Note that the process is iterative, meaning it often takes more than one pass to refine it. A Request for Proposal (RFP) or draft contract often provides the basis for defining and finalizing work requirements, which are then documented in a final contract and technical baseline. If there were not an RFP, then the internal project charter and scope statement would provide the basis for defining and finalizing work requirements, as described in Chapter 5, Project Scope Management. The project team leaders then decide on a technical approach for how to do the work. Should work be broken down using a product-oriented approach or a phased approach? Will the project team outsource some of the work or subcontract to other companies? Once the project team has decided on a technical approach, they develop a work breakdown structure (WBS) to establish manageable elements of work (see Chapter 5, Project Scope Management). They then develop activity definitions to define the work involved in each activity on the WBS further (see Chapter 6, Project Time Management). The last step is assigning the work.

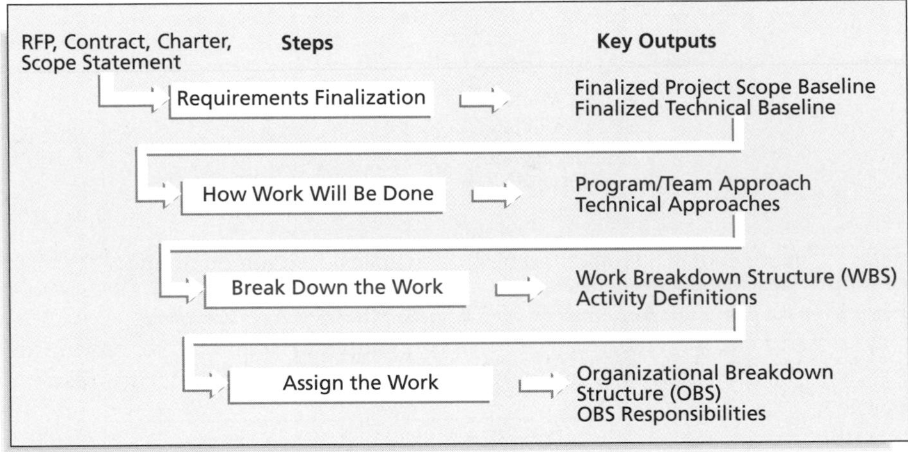

FIGURE 9-4 Work definition and assignment process

Once the project manager and project team have broken down the work into manageable elements, the project manager assigns work to organizational units. The project manager often bases these work assignments on where the work fits in the organization and uses an organizational breakdown structure to conceptualize the process. An **organizational breakdown structure (OBS)** is a specific type of organizational chart that shows which organizational units are responsible for which work items. The OBS can be based on a general organizational chart and then broken down into more detail, based on specific units within departments in the company or units in any subcontracted companies. For example, OBS categories might include software development, hardware development, training, and so on.

Responsibility Assignment Matrices

After developing an OBS, the project manager is in a position to develop a responsibility assignment matrix. A **responsibility assignment matrix (RAM)** is a matrix that maps the work of the project as described in the WBS to the people responsible for performing the work as described in the OBS. Figure 9-5 shows an example of a RAM. The RAM allocates work to responsible and performing organizations, teams, or individuals, depending on the desired level of detail. For smaller projects, it would be best to assign individual people to WBS activities. For very large projects, it is more effective to assign the work to organizational units or teams.

WBS activities → OBS units ↓	1.1.1	1.1.2	1.1.3	1.1.4	1.1.5	1.1.6	1.1.7	1.1.8
Systems Engineering	R	R P					R	
Software Development			R P					
Hardware Development				R P				
Test Engineering	P							
Quality Assurance					R P			
Configuration Management						R P		
Integrated Logistics Support							P	
Training								R P

R = Responsible organizational unit
P = Performing organizational unit

FIGURE 9-5 Sample responsibility assignment matrix (RAM)

In addition to using a RAM to assign detailed work activities, you can also use a RAM to define general roles and responsibilities on projects. This type of RAM can include the stakeholders in the project. Figure 9-6 provides a RAM that shows whether stakeholders are accountable or just participants in part of a project, and whether they are required to provide input, review, or sign off on parts of a project. This simple tool can be a very effective way for the project manager to communicate roles and expectations of important stakeholders on projects.

Items	Stakeholders A	B	C	D	E
Unit Test	S	A	I	I	R
Integration Test	S	P	A	I	R
System Test	S	P	A	I	R
User Acceptance Test	S	P	I	A	R

A = Accountable
P = Participant
R = Review Required
I = Input Required
S = Sign-off Required

FIGURE 9-6 RAM showing stakeholder roles

Some organizations use **RACI charts** to show Responsibility (who does the task), Accountability (who signs off on the task or has authority for it), Consultation (who has information necessary to complete the task), and Informed (who needs to be notified of task status/results) roles for project stakeholders. As shown in Table 9-2, a RACI chart lists tasks vertically, individuals or groups horizontally, and each intersecting cell contains an R, A, C, or I. Each task may have multiple R, C, or I entries, but there can be only one A entry to clarify which particular individual or group is accountable for each task. For example, a mechanic is responsible for repairing a car, but the shop owner is accountable for the repairs getting done properly. Note that some people reverse the definitions of responsible and accountable.

TABLE 9-2 Sample RACI Chart

	Group A	Group B	Group C	Group D	Group E
Test Plans	R	A	C	C	I
Unit Test	C	I	R	A	I
Integration Test	A	R	I	C	C
System Test	I	C	A	I	R
User Acceptance Test	R	I	C	R	A

Staffing Management Plans and Resource Histograms

A **staffing management plan** describes when and how people will be added to and taken off the project team. The level of detail may vary based on the type of project. For example, if an information technology project is projected to need 100 people on average over a year, the staffing management plan would describe the types of people needed to work on the project, such as Java programmers, business analysts, technical writers, and so on, and the number of each type of person needed each month. It would also describe how these resources would be acquired, trained, rewarded, reassigned after the project, and so on. All of these issues are important to meeting the needs of the project, the employees, and the organization.

WHAT WENT RIGHT?

Senior managers realize that they must invest in human resources to attract, hire, and retain qualified staff. In addition to providing technical training for IT personnel, several companies have made significant investments in project management training to provide career paths for project managers.

For example, Hewlett-Packard (HP) employed only six registered PMPs in 1997, but by August 2004, it employed more than 1,500 PMPs and was adding 500 more per year.[18] HP even paid for an ad in PMI's Project Network magazine stressing the importance they place on having certified project managers. "At HP, a PMP® [credential] is a stamp of approval. Our major reason for focusing on project management certification is customer-based: We want to make sure we've got the best project managers. Customers across countries and industries ask us, what kind of project managers do you have? What kind of certification do they have? We can tell them that the majority of our project managers are certified. HP values certification. We have four levels of project managers, and the top three require a PMP certification."[19]

IBM Global Business Services organization offers numerous paths to career success, with one dedicated to project management. While most consulting firms offer a single path

continued

to a leadership position, IBM has four to allow their people to succeed by focusing on their strengths and interests in one or more disciplines. Their four paths include:

- *Partner*: client management, practice development, engagement sales and delivery
- *Sales Executive*: client relationship and sales
- *Delivery Executive*: project management
- *Distinguished Engineer*: technical capabilities[20]

The staffing management plan often includes a **resource histogram**, which is a column chart that shows the number of resources assigned to a project over time. Figure 9-7 provides an example of a histogram that might be used for a six-month information technology project. Notice that the columns represent the number of people needed in each area—managers, business analysts, programmers, and technical writers. By stacking the columns, you can see the total number of people needed each month. After determining the project staffing needs, the next steps in project human resource management are to acquire the necessary staff and then develop the project team.

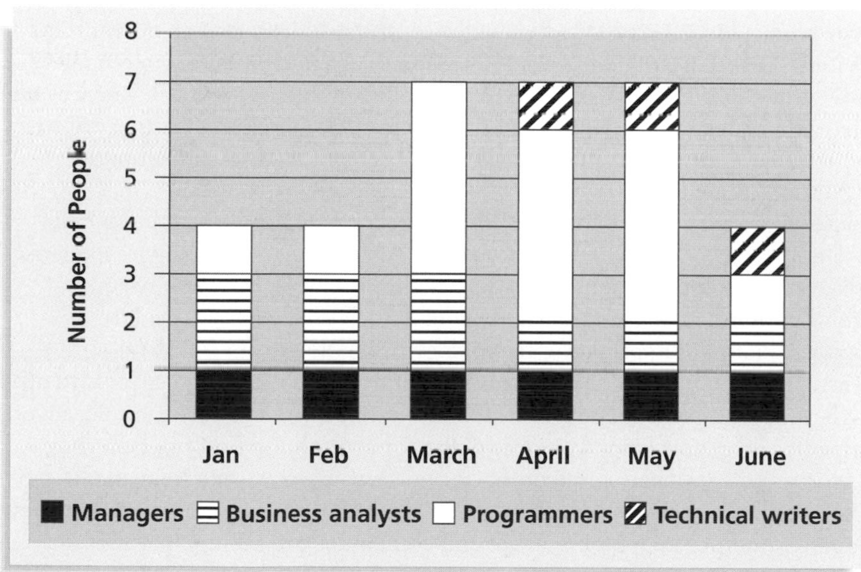

FIGURE 9-7 Sample resource histogram

ACQUIRING THE PROJECT TEAM

During the late 1990s, the information technology job market became extremely competitive. It was a seller's market with corporations competing fiercely for a shrinking pool of qualified, experienced information technology professionals. In the early 2000s, the market declined tremendously, so employers could be very selective in recruiting. Today, many organizations again face a shortage of IT staff. Regardless of the current job market, acquiring qualified information technology professionals is critical. There is a saying that the project manager who is the smartest person on the team has done a poor job of recruiting! In addition to recruiting team members, it is also important to assign the appropriate type and number of people to work on projects at the appropriate times. This section addresses important topics related to acquiring the project team: resource assignment, resource loading, and resource leveling.

Resource Assignment

After developing a staffing management plan, project managers must work with other people in their organizations to assign particular personnel to their projects or to acquire additional human resources needed to staff the project. Project managers with strong influencing and negotiating skills are often good at getting internal people to work on their projects. However, the organization must ensure that people are assigned to the projects that best fit their skills and the needs of the organization. The main outputs of this process are project staff assignments, resource availability information, and updates to the staffing management plan. Many project teams also find it useful to create a project team directory.

Organizations that do a good job of staff acquisition have good staffing plans. These plans describe the number and type of people who are currently in the organization and the number and type of people anticipated to be needed for the project based on current and upcoming activities. An important component of staffing plans is maintaining a complete and accurate inventory of employees' skills. If there is a mismatch between the current mix of people's skills and needs of the organization, it is the project manager's job to work with top management, human resource managers, and other people in the organization to address staffing and training needs.

It is also important to have good procedures in place for hiring subcontractors and recruiting new employees. Since the Human Resource department is normally responsible for hiring people, project managers must work with their human resource managers to address any problems in recruiting appropriate people. It is also a priority to address retention issues, especially for information technology professionals.

One innovative approach to hiring and retaining information technology staff is to offer existing employees incentives for helping recruit and retain personnel. For example, several consulting companies give their employees one dollar for every hour a new person they helped recruit works. This provides an incentive for current employees to help attract new people and to keep both the employees and the people they help to recruit working at their respective company. Another approach that several companies are taking to attract and retain information technology professionals is to provide benefits based on personal need. For example, some people might want to work only four days a week or have the option of working a couple of days a week from home. As it gets more difficult to find good information technology professionals, organizations must become more innovative and proactive in addressing this issue.

Several organizations, publications, and Web sites address the need for good staff acquisition and retention. Enrollment in U.S. computer science and engineering programs has dropped almost in half since 2000, and one-third of U.S. workers will be over the age of 50 by 2010. CIO's researchers suggest that organizations rethink hiring practices and incentives to hire and retain IT talent. For example, if it's important for IT employees to have strong business and communications skills, organizations shouldn't focus primarily on technical skills. A company could require candidates to give a presentation to see how well they communicate and understand the business. Also, organizations should focus on flexibility when negotiating perks. According to the "2006 Compensation and Benefits Report" by Hudson Highland Group, a third of IT workers said they value a flexible work schedule more than other nontraditional benefits. "Employees are more willing to forgo additional cash in order to have a more improved work-life balance," says Peg Buchenroth, Hudson Highland Group's managing director of compensation and benefits.[21]

It is very important to consider the needs of individuals and the organization when making recruiting and retention decisions and to study the best practices of leading companies in these areas. It is also important to address a growing trend in project team members—many of them work in a virtual environment. (See the section on managing the project team for suggestions on working with virtual team members.)

BEST PRACTICE

Best practices can also be applied to include the best places for people to work. For example, *Fortune* magazine lists the "100 Best Companies to Work For" in the United States every year, with Google taking the honors in 2007 and 2008. *Working Mothers* magazine lists the best companies in the U.S. for women based on benefits for working families. The *Timesonline* (*www.timesonline.co.uk*) provides the London *Sunday Times* list of the "100 Best Companies to Work For," a key benchmark against which U.K. companies can judge their performance as employers. The Great Place to Work Institute, which produces *Fortune* magazine's "100 Best Companies to Work For," uses the same selection methodology for more than 20 international lists, including "Best Companies to Work For" lists in all 15 countries of the European Union, Brazil, Korea, and a number of other countries throughout Latin America and Asia. Companies make these lists based on feedback from their best critics: their own employees. Quotes from employees often show why certain companies made the lists:

- "It is a friendly, courteous, caring hospital. We generally care about our co-workers and our patients. I can always get the help and support that I need to function in this hospital. This goes from the top all the way down to the cleaning people."
- "This is the best place I have ever worked. There's an open door policy. Everyone is allowed to voice their opinion."
- "I get information about everything—profits, losses, problems. Relationships with people are easier here. It's more direct and open."[22]

Resource Loading

Chapter 6, Project Time Management, described using network diagrams to help manage a project's schedule. One of the problems or dangers inherent in scheduling processes is that they often do not address the issues of resource utilization and availability. (Hence, the development of critical chain scheduling, as described in Chapter 6.) Schedules tend to focus primarily on time rather than on both time and resources, which includes people. An important measure of a project manager's success is how well he or she balances the trade-offs among performance, time, and cost. During a period of crisis, it is occasionally possible to add additional resources—such as additional staff—to a project at little or no cost. Most of the time, however, resolving performance, time, and cost trade-offs entails additional costs to the organization. The project manager's goal must be to achieve project success without increasing the costs or time required to complete the project. The key to accomplishing this goal is effectively managing human resources on the project.

Once people are assigned to projects, there are two techniques available to project managers that help them use project staff most effectively: resource loading and resource leveling. **Resource loading** refers to the amount of individual resources an existing schedule requires during specific time periods. Resource loading helps project managers develop a general understanding of the demands a project will make on the organization's resources, as well as on individual people's schedules. Project managers often use histograms, as described in Figure 9-7, to depict period-by-period variations in resource loading. A histogram can be very helpful in determining staffing needs or in identifying staffing problems.

A resource histogram can also show when work is being overallocated to a certain person or group. **Overallocation** means more resources than are available are assigned to perform work at a given time. For example, Figure 9-8 provides a sample resource histogram created in Microsoft Project. This histogram illustrates how much one individual, Joe Franklin, is assigned to work on the project each week. The percentage numbers on the vertical axis represent the percentage of Joe's available time that is allocated for him to work on the project. The top horizontal axis represents time in weeks. Note that Joe Franklin is overallocated most of the time. For example, for most of March and April and part of May, Joe's work allocation is 300 percent of his available time. If Joe is normally available eight hours per day, this means he would have to work 24 hours a day to meet this staffing projection! Many people don't use the resource assignment features of project management software properly. (See Appendix A for detailed information on using Microsoft Project 2007.)

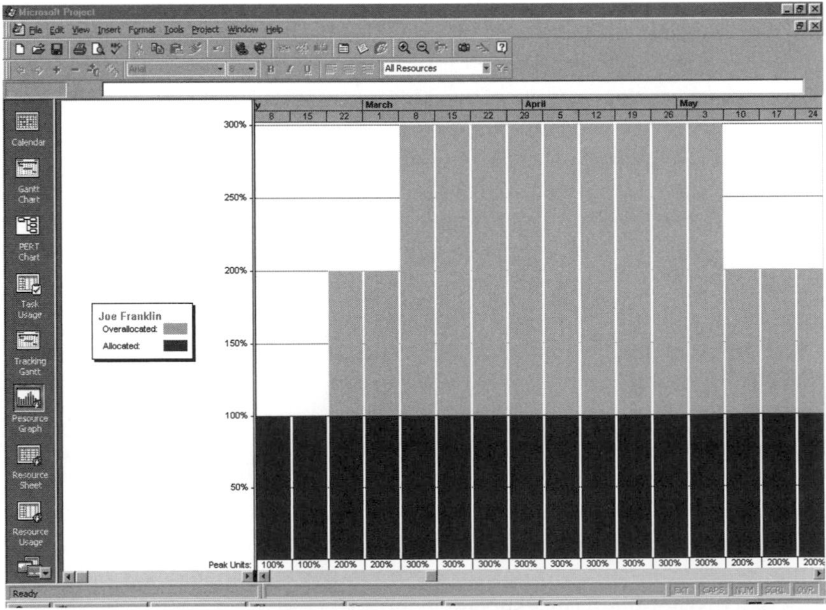

FIGURE 9-8 Sample histogram showing an overallocated individual

Resource Leveling

Resource leveling is a technique for resolving resource conflicts by delaying tasks. It is a form of network analysis in which resource management concerns drive scheduling decisions (start and finish dates). The main purpose of resource leveling is to create a smoother distribution of resource usage. Project managers examine the network diagram for areas of slack or float, and to identify resource conflicts. For example, you can sometimes remove overallocations by delaying noncritical tasks, which does not result in an overall schedule delay. Other times you will need to delay the project completion date to reduce or remove overallocations. Appendix A has information on using Microsoft Project 2007 to level resources using both of these approaches. You can also view resource leveling as addressing the resource constraints described in critical chain scheduling (see Chapter 6, Project Time Management).

Overallocation is one type of resource conflict. If a certain resource is overallocated, the project manager can change the schedule to remove resource overallocation. If a certain resource is underallocated, the project manager can change the schedule to try to improve the use of the resource. Resource leveling, therefore, aims to minimize period-by-period variations in resource loading by shifting tasks within their slack allowances.

Figure 9-9 illustrates a simple example of resource leveling. The network diagram at the top of this figure shows that Activities A, B, and C can all start at the same time. Activity A has a duration of two days and will take two people to complete; Activity B has a duration of five days and will take four people to complete; and Activity C has a duration of three

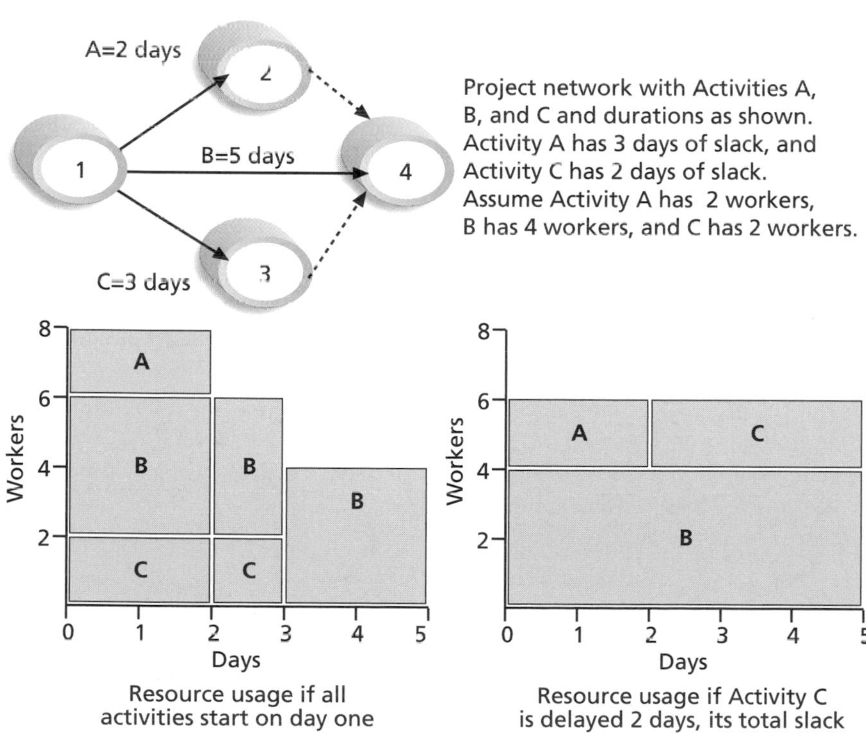

FIGURE 9-9 Resource leveling example

days and will take two people to complete. The histogram on the lower-left of this figure shows the resource usage if all activities start on day one. The histogram on the lower-right of Figure 9-9 shows the resource usage if Activity C is delayed two days, its total slack allowance. Notice that the lower-right histogram is flat or leveled; that is, its pieces (activities) are arranged to take up the least space (saving days and numbers of workers). You may recognize this strategy from the computer game Tetris, in which you earn points for keeping the falling shapes as level as possible. The player with the most points (most level shape allocation) wins. Resources are also used best when they are leveled.

Resource leveling has several benefits. First, when resources are used on a more constant basis, they require less management. For example, it is much easier to manage a part-time project member who is scheduled to work 20 hours per week on a project for the next three months than it is to manage the same person who is scheduled to work 10 hours one week, 40 the next, 5 the next, and so on.

Second, resource leveling may enable project managers to use a just-in-time inventory type of policy for using subcontractors or other expensive resources. For example, a project manager might want to level resources related to work that must be done by particular subcontractors such as testing consultants. This leveling might allow the project to use four outside consultants full-time to do testing for four months instead of spreading the work out over more time or needing to use more than four people. The latter approach is usually more expensive. Recall from Chapter 6 that crashing and fast-tracking can also be used along with resource concerns to improve a project schedule.

Third, resource leveling results in fewer problems for project personnel and accounting departments. Increasing and decreasing labor levels and particular human resources often produce additional work and confusion. For example, if a person with expertise in a particular area is only assigned to a project two days a week and another person they need to work with is not assigned to the project those same days, they cannot work well together. The Accounting department might complain when subcontractors charge a higher rate for billing less than 20 hours a week on a project. The accountants will remind project managers to strive for getting the lowest rates possible.

Finally, resource leveling often improves morale. People like to have some stability in their jobs. It is very stressful for people not to know from week to week or even day to day what projects they will be working on and with whom they will be working.

Project management software can automatically level resources. However, the project manager must be careful in using the results without making adjustments. Automatic leveling often pushes out the project's completion date. Resources may also be reallocated to work at times that are inappropriate with other constraints. A wise project manager would have one of his or her team members who is proficient in using the project management software ensure that the leveling is done appropriately.

DEVELOPING THE PROJECT TEAM

Even if a project manager has successfully recruited enough skilled people to work on a project, he or she must ensure that people can work together as a team to achieve project goals. Many information technology projects have had very talented individuals working on them. However, it takes teamwork to complete most projects successfully. The main goal of **team development** is to help people work together more effectively to improve project performance.

Dr. Bruce Tuckman published his four-stage model of team development in 1965 and modified it to include an additional stage in the 1970s. The **Tuckman model** describes five stages of team development:

1. *Forming* involves the introduction of team members, either at the initiation of the team, or as new members are introduced. This stage is necessary, but little work is actually achieved.
2. *Storming* occurs as team members have different opinions as to how the team should operate. People test each other, and there is often conflict within the team.
3. *Norming* is achieved when team members have developed a common working method, and cooperation and collaboration replace the conflict and mistrust of the previous phase.
4. *Performing* occurs when the emphasis is on reaching the team goals, rather than working on team process. Relationships are settled, and team members are likely to build loyalty towards each other. At this stage, the team is able to manage tasks that are more complex and cope with greater change.
5. *Adjourning* involves the break-up of the team after they successfully reach their goals and complete the work.[23]

There is an extensive body of literature on team development. This section will highlight a few important tools and techniques for team development, including training, team-building activities, and reward and recognition systems.

Training

Project managers often recommend that people take specific training courses to improve individual and team development. For example, Sarah from the opening case had gone through training in emotional intelligence and dealing with difficult people. She was familiar with the mirroring technique and felt comfortable using that approach with Ben. Many other people would not have reacted so quickly and effectively in the same situation. If Ben and Sarah did reach agreement on what actions they could take to resolve the F-44 aircraft program's information technology problems, it might result in a new project to develop and deliver a new system for Ben's group. If Sarah became the project manager for this new project, she would understand the need for special training in interpersonal skills for specific people in her and Ben's departments. Individuals could take special training classes to improve their personal skills. If Sarah thought the whole project team could benefit from taking training together to learn to work as a team, she could arrange for a special team-building session for the entire project team and key stakeholders.

It is very important to provide training in a just-in-time fashion. For example, if Sarah was preparing for a technical assignment where she would need to learn a new programming language, training to deal with difficult people would not help her much. However, the training was very timely for her new consulting position. Many organizations provide e-learning opportunities for their employees so they can learn specific skills at any time and any place. They have also found e-learning to sometimes be more cost-effective than traditional instructor-led training courses. It is important to make sure that the timing and delivery method for the training is appropriate for specific situations and individuals. Organizations have also found that it is often more economical to train current employees in particular areas than it is to hire new people who already possess those skills.

Several organizations that have successfully implemented Six Sigma principles have taken a unique and effective approach to training. They only let high-potential employees attend Six Sigma Black Belt training, which is a substantial investment in terms of time and money. In addition, they do not let employees into a particular Black Belt course until they have had a potential Six Sigma project approved that relates to their current job. Attendees can then apply the new concepts and techniques they learn in the classes to their work settings. High-potential employees feel rewarded by being picked to take this training, and the organization benefits by having these employees implement high-payoff projects because of the training.

Team-Building Activities

Many organizations provide in-house team-building training activities, and many also use specialized services provided by external companies that specialize in this area. Two common approaches to team-building activities include using physical challenges and psychological preference indicator tools. It is important to understand individual needs, including learning styles, past training, and physical limitations, when determining team-building training options.

Several organizations have teams of people go through certain physically challenging activities to help them develop as a team. Military basic training or boot camps provide one example. Men and women who wish to join the military must first make it through basic training, which often involves several strenuous physical activities such as rappelling off towers, running and marching in full military gear, going through obstacle courses, passing marksmanship training, and mastering survival training. Many organizations use a similar approach by sending teams of people to special locations where they work as a team to navigate white water rapids, climb mountains or rocks, participate in ropes courses, and so on. Research shows that physical challenges often help teams of strangers to work together more effectively, but it can cause already dysfunctional teams to have even more problems.

Even more organizations have teams participate in mental team-building activities in which they learn about themselves, each other, and how to work as a group most effectively. It is important for people to understand and value each other's differences in order to work effectively as a team. Three common exercises used in mental team building include the Myers-Briggs Type Indicator, Wilson Learning Social Styles Profile, and the DISC Profile.

The Meyers-Briggs Type Indicator

The **Myers-Briggs Type Indicator (MBTI)** is a popular tool for determining personality preferences. During World War II, Isabel B. Myers and Katherine C. Briggs developed the first version of the MBTI based on psychologist Carl Jung's theory of psychological type. The four dimensions of psychological type in the MBTI include:

- *Extrovert/Introvert (E/I)*: This first dimension determines if you are generally extroverted or introverted. The dimension also signifies whether people draw their energy from other people (extroverts) or from inside themselves (introverts).
- *Sensation/Intuition (S/N)*: This second dimension relates to the manner in which you gather information. Sensation (or Sensing) type people take in facts,

details, and reality and describe themselves as practical. Intuitive type people are imaginative, ingenious, and attentive to hunches or intuition. They describe themselves as innovative and conceptual.

- *Thinking/Feeling (T/F)*: This third dimension represents thinking judgment and feeling judgment. Thinking judgment is objective and logical, and feeling judgment is subjective and personal.
- *Judgment/Perception (J/P)*: This fourth dimension concerns people's attitude toward structure. Judgment type people like closure and task completion. They tend to establish deadlines and take them seriously, expecting others to do the same. Perceiving types prefer to keep things open and flexible. They regard deadlines more as a signal to start rather than complete a project and do not feel that work must be done before play or rest begins.[24]

There is much more involved in personality types, and many books are available on this topic. In 1998, David Keirsey published *Please Understand Me II: Temperament Character Intelligence*.[25] This book includes an easy-to-take and interpret test called the *Keirsey Temperament Sorter*, which is a personality type preference test based on the work done by Jung, Myers, and Briggs.

In 1985, an interesting study of the MBTI types of the general population in the United States and information systems (IS) developers revealed some significant contrasts.[26] Both groups of people were most similar in the judgment/perception dimension, with slightly more than half of each group preferring the judgment type (J). There were significant differences, however, in the other three dimensions. Most people would not be surprised to hear that most information systems developers are introverts. This study found that 75 percent of IS developers were introverts (I), and only 25 percent of the general population were introverts. This personality type difference might help explain some of the problems users have communicating with developers. Another sharp contrast found in the study was that almost 80 percent of IS developers were thinking types (T) compared to 50 percent of the general population. IS developers were also much more likely to be intuitive (N) (about 55 percent) than the general population (about 25 percent). These results fit with Keirsey's classification of NT (Intuitive/Thinking types) people as *rationals*. Educationally, they tend to study the sciences, enjoy technology as a hobby, and pursue systems work. Keirsey also suggests that no more than 7 percent of the general population are NTs. Would you be surprised to know that Bill Gates is classified as a rational?[27]

Project managers can often benefit from knowing their team members' MBTI profiles by adjusting their management styles for each individual. For example, if the project manager is a strong N and one of the team members is a strong S, the project manager should take the time to provide more concrete, detailed explanations when discussing that person's task assignments. Project managers may also want to make sure they have a variety of personality types on their teams. For example, if all team members are strong introverts, it may be difficult for them to work well with users and other important stakeholders who are often extroverts.

The MBTI, like any test, should be used with caution. A 2007 study argues that the lack of progress in improving software development teams is due in part to the inappropriate use of psychological tests and basic misunderstandings of personality theory by those who use them. "Software engineers often complain about those who, in the course of their work, do some programming in support of their professional activities: the claim being that such individuals are not professionals and do not understand the discipline. The same can be said of those who adopt psychological approaches without the relevant qualifications and background."[28]

The Social Styles Profile

Many organizations also use the Social Styles Profile in team-building activities. Psychologist David Merril, who helped develop the Wilson Learning Social Styles Profile, describes people as falling into four approximate behavioral profiles, or zones. People are perceived as behaving primarily in one of four zones, based on their assertiveness and responsiveness:

- *Drivers* are proactive and task-oriented. They are firmly rooted in the present, and they strive for action. Adjectives to describe drivers include pushy, severe, tough, dominating, harsh, strong-willed, independent, practical, decisive, and efficient.
- *Expressives* are proactive and people-oriented. They are future-oriented and use their intuition to look for fresh perspectives on the world around them. Adjectives to describe expressives include manipulating, excitable, undisciplined, reacting, egotistical, ambitious, stimulating, wacky, enthusiastic, dramatic, and friendly.
- *Analyticals* are reactive and task-oriented. They are past-oriented and strong thinkers. Adjectives to describe analyticals include critical, indecisive, stuffy, picky, moralistic, industrious, persistent, serious, expecting, and orderly.
- *Amiables* are reactive and people-oriented. Their time orientation varies depending on whom they are with at the time, and they strongly value relationships. Adjectives to describe amiables include conforming, unsure, ingratiating, dependent, awkward, supportive, respectful, willing, dependable, and agreeable.[29]

Figure 9-10 shows these four social styles and how they relate to assertiveness and responsiveness. Note that the main determinants of the social style are your levels of assertiveness—if you are more likely to tell people what to do or ask what should be done—and how you respond to tasks—by focusing on the task itself or on the people involved in performing the task.

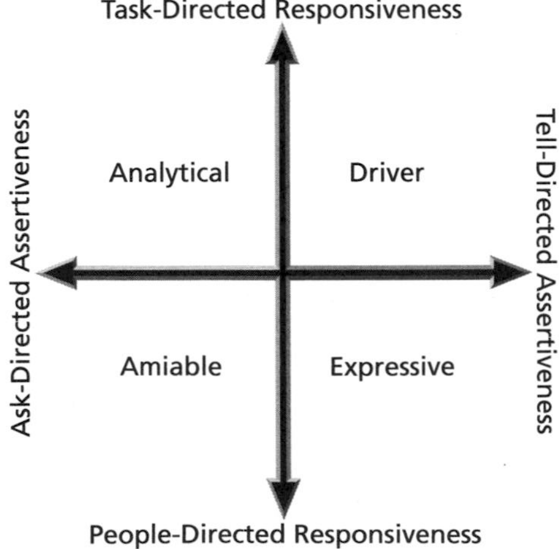

FIGURE 9-10 Social styles

Knowing the social styles of project stakeholders can help project managers understand why certain people may have problems working together. For example, drivers are often very impatient working with amiables, and analyticals often have difficulties understanding expressives.

DISC Profiles

Similar to the Social Styles Profile, the DISC Profile uses a four-dimensional model of normal behavior. The four dimensions—Dominance, Influence, Steadiness, and Compliance—provide the basis for the name, DISC. Note that similar terms are sometimes used for some of these letters, such as stability for steadiness or conscientiousness for compliance. The DISC Profile is based on the 1928 work of psychologist William Moulton Marston. The DISC Profile reveals people's behavioral tendencies under certain situations. For example, it reveals how you tend to behave under stress, in conflict, when communicating, when avoiding certain activities, and so on. According to *www.onlinediscprofile.com*, "over 5 million people have taken various forms of the DISC Profile throughout the world. Marston's original work continues to be enhanced by ongoing behavioral research and profiles can be found in more than 50 languages by various publishers of the disc assessment."[30]

Figure 9-11 shows the four dimensions of the DISC Profile model and describes key characteristics of each dimension. Notice that each dimension is also associated with a color and emphasis, such as I, We, You, or It:

- *Dominance*: Represented by red and emphasizes "I," dominance traits include being direct, decisive, assertive, outcome-oriented, competitive, self assured, controlling, and wanting to win

It **Compliance (Blue)** Data driven, risk averse, concerned, works well alone, prefers processes and procedures, not very communicative or social	*I* **Dominance (Red)** Direct, decisive, assertive, outcome oriented, competitive, self assured, takes control, has to win
You **Steadiness (Green)** Calm, sincere, sympathetic, cooperative, cautious, conflict averse, good listener, wants to maintain stability	*We* **Influence (Yellow)** Persuasive, optimistic , outgoing, verbal, enthusiastic, strives to win others over, leadership through acclimation

FIGURE 9-11 The DISC Profile

- *Influence*: Represented by yellow and emphasizes "We," influence traits include being persuasive, optimistic, outgoing, verbal, enthusiastic, striving to win others over, and practicing leadership through acclimation
- *Steadiness*: Represented by green and emphasizes "You," steadiness traits include being calm, sincere, cautious, conflict averse, a good listener, and wanting to maintain stability
- *Compliance*: Represented by blue and emphasizes "It," compliance traits include being data driven, risk averse, concerned, working well alone, preferring processes and procedures, and being not very communicative or social

Like the Social Styles Profile, people in opposite quadrants, such as Dominance and Steadiness or Influence and Compliance, can have problems understanding each other. There are many other team-building activities and tests available. For example, some people like to take Dr. Meredith Belbin's test to help determine which of nine team roles they might prefer. Again, any team-building or personality tool should be used by professionals with caution. In reality, most professionals must be flexible and do whatever work is needed for their teams to succeed. Project managers can use their leadership and coaching skills to help all types of people communicate better with each other and focus on meeting project goals.

Reward and Recognition Systems

Another important tool for promoting team development is the use of team-based reward and recognition systems. If management rewards teamwork, they will promote or reinforce people to work more effectively in teams. Some organizations offer bonuses, trips, or other rewards to workers that meet or exceed company or project goals. In a project setting, project managers can recognize and reward people who willingly work overtime to meet an aggressive schedule objective or go out of their way to help a teammate. Project managers should not reward people who work overtime just to get extra pay or because of their own poor work or planning.

Project managers must continually assess their team's performance. When they find areas where individuals or the entire team can improve, it's their job to find the best way to develop their people and improve performance.

MANAGING THE PROJECT TEAM

In addition to developing the project team, the project manager must lead them in performing various project activities. After assessing team performance and related information, the project manager must decide if changes should be requested to the project, or if updates are needed to enterprise environmental factors, organizational process assets, or the project management plan. Project managers must use their soft skills to find the best way to motivate and manage each team member.

Tools and Techniques for Managing Project Teams

There are several tools and techniques available to assist in managing project teams:

- *Observation and conversation*: It is hard to assess how your team members are performing or how they are feeling about their work if you never see or discuss these issues. Many project managers like to practice "management by walking around" to physically see and hear their team members at work. Informal or formal conversations about how a project is going can provide crucial information. For virtual workers, project managers can still observe and discuss work and personal issues via e-mail, telephone, or other communications media.

- *Project performance appraisals*: Just as general managers provide performance appraisals for their workers, so can project managers. The need for and type of project performance appraisals will vary depending on the length of the project, complexity of the project, organizational policies, contract requirements, and related communications. Even if a project manager does not provide official project performance appraisals for team members, it is still important to provide timely performance feedback. If a team member hands in sloppy or late work, the project manager should determine the reason for this behavior and take appropriate action. Perhaps the team member had a death in the family and could not concentrate. Perhaps the team member was planning to leave the project. The reasons for the behavior would have a strong impact on what action the project manager should take.
- *Conflict management*: Few projects are completed without any conflicts. Some types of conflict are actually desirable on projects, but many are not. As described in Chapter 10, Project Communications Management, there are several ways to handle conflicts. It's important for project managers to understand strategies for handling conflicts and to proactively manage conflict.
- *Issue logs*: Many project managers keep an **issue log** to document, monitor, and track issues that need to be resolved for the project team to work effectively. Issues could include items where people have differences of opinion, situations that need more clarification or investigation, or general concerns that need to be addressed. It is important to acknowledge issues that can hurt team performance and take action to resolve them. The project manager should assign someone to resolve each issue and assign a target date for resolution.
- *Interpersonal skills*: As mentioned in Chapter 1, project managers must possess several interpersonal skills. To effectively manage teams, it is especially important to focus on leadership, influencing, and decision-making skills.

General Advice on Managing Teams

According to Patrick Lencioni, a well-known author and consultant on teams, "Teamwork remains the one sustainable competitive advantage that has been largely untapped . . . teamwork is almost always lacking within organizations that fail, and often present within those that succeed."[31] The five dysfunctions of teams are:

1. Absence of trust
2. Fear of conflict
3. Lack of commitment
4. Avoidance of accountability
5. Inattention to results

Lencioni's books provide suggestions for overcoming each of these dysfunctions. For example, he suggests that team members take the Myers-Briggs Type Indicator, as described earlier in this chapter, to help people open up to each other and build trust. To master conflict, he suggests that teams practice having unfiltered, passionate debates about important issues. To achieve commitment, he stresses the importance of getting out all possible ideas, getting people to agree to disagree, but then having them commit to decisions. To embrace accountability, Lencioni stresses the importance of clarifying and focusing on everyone's top priorities. He also suggests that peer pressure and the distaste for letting down a colleague are often better motivators than authoritative intervention. Finally, using some type of scoreboard to focus on team results helps eliminate ambiguity so everyone knows what it means to achieve positive results.

Additional suggestions for ensuring that teams are productive include the following:

- Be patient and kind with your team. Assume the best about people; do not assume that your team members are lazy and careless.
- Fix the problem instead of blaming people. Help people work out problems by focusing on behaviors.
- Establish regular, effective meetings. Focus on meeting project objectives and producing positive results.
- Allow time for teams to go through the basic team-building stages of forming, storming, norming, performing, and adjourning. Don't expect teams to work at the highest performance level right away.
- Limit the size of work teams to three to seven members.
- Plan some social activities to help project team members and other stakeholders get to know each other better. Make the social events fun and not mandatory.
- Stress team identity. Create traditions that team members enjoy.
- Nurture team members and encourage them to help each other. Identify and provide training that will help individuals and the team as a whole become more effective.
- Acknowledge individual and group accomplishments.
- Take additional actions to work with virtual team members. If possible, have a face-to-face or phone meeting at the start of a virtual project or when introducing a virtual team member. Screen people carefully to make sure they can work effectively in a virtual environment. Clarify how virtual team members will communicate.

As you can imagine, team development and management are critical concerns on many information technology projects. Many information technology project managers must break out of their rational/NT preference and focus on empathically listening to other people to address their concerns and create an environment in which individuals and teams can grow and prosper.

USING SOFTWARE TO ASSIST IN HUMAN RESOURCE MANAGEMENT

Earlier in this chapter, you read that a simple responsibility assignment matrix (Figures 9-5 and 9-6) or histograms (Figures 9-7 and 9-8) are useful tools that can help you effectively manage human resources on projects. You can use several different software packages, including spreadsheets or project management software such as Microsoft Project 2007, to create matrixes and histograms. Many people do not realize that Project 2007 provides a variety of human resource management tools, some of which include assigning and tracking resources, resource leveling, resource usage reports, overallocated resource reports, and to-do lists. You can learn how to use many of these functions and features in Appendix A. (Collaborative software to help people communicate is described in Chapter 10, Project Communications Management.)

You can use Project 2007 to assign resources—including equipment, materials, facilities, or people—to tasks. Project 2007 enables you to allocate individual resources to individual projects or to pool resources and share them across multiple projects. By defining and assigning resources in Project 2007, you can:

- Keep track of the whereabouts of resources through stored information and reports on resource assignments.
- Identify potential resource shortages that could force a project to miss scheduled deadlines and possibly extend the duration of a project.
- Identify underutilized resources and reassign them, which may enable you to shorten a project's schedule and possibly reduce costs.
- Use automated leveling to make level resources easier to manage.

Just as many project management professionals are not aware of the powerful cost-management features of Project 2007, many are also unaware of its powerful human resource management features. The Microsoft Enterprise Project Management Solution provides additional human resource management capabilities. You can also purchase add-in software for Microsoft's products or purchase software from other companies to perform a variety of project human resource management functions. With the aid of this type of software, project managers can have more information available in useful formats to help them decide how to manage human resources most effectively.

Project resource management involves much more than using software to assess and track resource loading, level resources, and so on. People are the most important asset on most projects, and human resources are very different from other resources. You cannot simply replace people the same way that you would replace a piece of equipment. People need far more than a tune-up now and then to keep them performing well. It is essential to treat people with consideration and respect, to understand what motivates them, and to communicate carefully with them. What makes good project managers great is not their use of tools, but rather their ability to enable project team members to deliver the best work they possibly can on a project.

CASE WRAP-UP

After Sarah yelled right back at Ben, he said, "You're the first person who's had the guts to stand up to me." After that brief introduction, Sarah, Ben, and the other meeting participants had a good discussion about what was really happening on the F-44 upgrade project. Sarah was able to write a justification to get Ben's group special software and support to download key information from the old system so they could manage their project better. When Sarah stood nose to nose with Ben and yelled at him, she used a technique for establishing rapport called mirroring. Although Sarah was by no means a loud and obnoxious person, she saw that Ben was and decided to mirror his behavior and attitude. She put herself in his shoes for a while, and doing so helped break the ice so Sarah, Ben, and the other people at the meeting could really start communicating and working together as a team to solve their problems.

Chapter Summary

People are the most important assets in organizations and on projects. Therefore, it is essential for project managers to be good human resource managers.

The major processes involved in project human resource management include developing the human resource plan, acquiring the project team, developing the project team, and managing the project team.

Psychosocial issues that affect how people work and how well they work include motivation, influence and power, and effectiveness.

Maslow developed a hierarchy of needs that suggests physiological, safety, social, esteem, and self-actualization needs motivate behavior. Once a need is satisfied, it no longer serves as a motivator.

Herzberg distinguished between motivators and hygiene factors. Hygiene factors such as larger salaries or a more attractive work environment will cause dissatisfaction if not present, but do not motivate workers to do more if present. Achievement, recognition, the work itself, responsibility, and growth are factors that contribute to work satisfaction and motivate workers.

McClelland proposed the acquired-needs theory, suggesting that an individual's needs are acquired or learned over time and shaped by their life experiences. The three types of acquired needs are a need for achievement, a need for affiliation, and a need for power.

McGregor developed Theory X and Theory Y to describe different approaches to managing workers, based on assumptions of worker motivation. Research supports the use of Theory Y, which assumes that people see work as natural and indicates that the most significant rewards are the satisfaction of esteem and self-actualization needs that work can provide. According to Ouchi's Theory Z, workers can be trusted to do their jobs to their utmost ability, as long as management can be trusted to support them and look out for their well-being. Theory Z emphasizes things such as job rotation, broadening of skills, generalization versus specialization, and the need for continuous training of workers.

Thamhain and Wilemon identified nine influence bases available to project managers: authority, assignment, budget, promotion, money, penalty, work challenge, expertise, and friendship. Their research found that project success is associated with project managers who use work challenge and expertise to influence workers. Project failure is associated with using too much influence by authority, money, or penalty.

Power is the potential ability to influence behavior to get people to do things they would not otherwise do. The five main types of power are coercive power, legitimate power, expert power, reward power, and referent power.

Project managers can use Steven Covey's seven habits of highly effective people to help themselves and project teams become more effective. The seven habits include being proactive; beginning with the end in mind; putting first things first; thinking win/win; seeking first to understand, then to be understood; achieving synergy; and sharpening the saw. Using empathic listening is a key skill of good project managers.

Developing the human resource plan involves identifying, assigning, and documenting project roles, responsibilities, and reporting relationships. A responsibility assignment matrix (RAM), staffing management plans, resource histograms, and RACI charts are key tools for defining roles and responsibilities on projects. The main output is a human resource plan.

Acquiring the project team means getting the appropriate staff assigned to and working on the project. This is an important issue in today's competitive environment. Companies must use innovative approaches to find and retain good information technology staff.

Resource loading shows the amount of individual resources an existing schedule requires during specific time frames. Histograms show resource loading and identify overallocation of resources.

Resource leveling is a technique for resolving resource conflicts, such as overallocated resources, by delaying tasks. Leveled resources require less management, lower costs, produce fewer personnel and accounting problems, and often improve morale.

Two crucial skills of a good project manager are team development and team management. Teamwork helps people work more effectively to achieve project goals. Project managers can recommend individual training to improve skills related to teamwork, organize team-building activities for the entire project team and key stakeholders, and provide reward and recognition systems that encourage teamwork. Project managers can use several tools and techniques, including observation and conversation, project performance appraisals, conflict management, issue logs, and interpersonal skills to help them effectively manage their teams.

Spreadsheets and project management software such as Microsoft Project 2007 can help project managers in project human resource management. Software makes it easy to produce responsibility assignment matrixes, create resource histograms, identify overallocated resources, level resources, and provide various views and reports related to project human resource management.

Project human resource management involves much more than using software to facilitate organizational planning and assign resources. What makes good project managers great is their ability to enable project team members to deliver the best work they possibly can on a project.

Quick Quiz

1. Which of the following is not part of project human resource management?
   a. Resource estimating
   b. Acquiring the project team
   c. Developing the project team
   d. Managing the project team
2. ____________ causes people to participate in an activity for their own enjoyment.
   a. Intrinsic motivation
   b. Extrinsic motivation
   c. Self motivation
   d. Social motivation
3. At the bottom of Maslow's pyramid or hierarchy of needs are ____________ needs.
   a. self-actualization
   b. esteem
   c. safety
   d. physiological

4. According to McClelland's acquired needs theory, people who desire harmonious relations with other people and need to feel accepted have a high __________ need.
   a. social
   b. achievement
   c. affiliation
   d. extrinsic

5. __________ power is based on a person's individual charisma.
   a. Affiliation
   b. Referent
   c. Personality
   d. Legitimate

6. A __________ maps the work of a project as described in the WBS to the people responsible for performing the work.
   a. project organizational chart
   b. work definition and assignment process
   c. resource histogram
   d. responsibility assignment matrix

7. A staffing management plan often includes a resource __________, which is a column chart that shows the number of resources assigned to the project over time.
   a. chart
   b. graph
   c. histogram
   d. timeline

8. What technique can you use to resolve resource conflicts by delaying tasks?
   a. resource loading
   b. resource leveling
   c. critical path analysis
   d. overallocation

9. What are the five stages in Tuckman's model of team development, in chronological order?
   a. forming, storming, norming, performing, and adjourning
   b. storming, forming, norming, performing, and adjourning
   c. norming, forming, storming, performing, and adjourning
   d. forming, storming, performing, norming, and adjourning

10. Which of the following is not a tool or technique for managing project teams?
    a. observation and conversation
    b. project performance appraisals
    c. issue logs
    d. Social Styles Profile

Quick Quiz Answers

1. a; 2. a; 3. d; 4. c; 5. b; 6. d; 7. c; 8. b; 9. a; 10. d

Discussion Questions

1. Discuss the changes in the job market for information technology workers. How does the job market and current state of the economy affect human resource management?
2. Summarize the processes involved in project human resource management.
3. Briefly summarize the works of Maslow, Herzberg, McClelland, McGregor, Ouchi, Thamhain and Wilemon, and Covey. How do their theories relate to project management?
4. Describe situations where it would be appropriate to create a project organizational chart, a responsibility assignment matrix, a RACI chart, and a resource histogram. Describe what these charts or matrices look like.
5. Discuss the difference between resource loading and resource leveling, and provide an example of when you would use each technique.
6. Explain two types of team-building activities described in this chapter.
7. Summarize different tools and techniques project managers can use to help them manage project teams. What can they do to manage virtual team members?
8. How can you use Project 2007 to assist in project human resource management?

Exercises

1. Your company is planning to launch an important new project starting January 1, which will last one year. You estimate that you will need one full-time project manager, two full-time business analysts for the first six months, two full-time senior programmers for the whole year, four full-time junior programmers for the months of July, August, and September, and one full-time technical writer for the last three months. Use the resource_histogram template file from the companion Web site to create a stacked column chart showing a resource histogram for this project, similar to the one shown in Figure 9-6. Be sure to include a legend to label the types of resources needed. Use appropriate titles and axis labels.
2. Take the MBTI test and research information on this tool. There are several Web sites that have different versions of the test, such as *www.humanmetrics.com*, *www.personalitytype.com*, and *www.keirsey.com*. Write a two-page paper describing your MBTI type and your thoughts on this test as a team-building tool.

3. Summarize three of Covey's habits in your own words and give examples of how these habits would apply to project management. Document your ideas in a two-page paper, and include at least two references.
4. Research recruiting and retention strategies at three different companies. What distinguishes one company from another in this area? Are strategies such as signing bonuses, tuition reimbursement, and business casual dress codes standard for new information technology workers? What strategies appeal most to you? Summarize your ideas in a two-page paper, citing at least three references.
5. Write a two-page paper summarizing the main features of Microsoft Project 2007 that can assist project managers in human resource management. In addition, interview someone who uses Project 2007. Ask him or her if their organization uses any project human resource management features as described in this chapter and Appendix A, and document their reasons for using or not using certain features.
6. Developing good IT project managers is an important issue. Review several of the studies cited in this chapter related to the IT and project management job market and required skills. Also review requirements at your college or university for people entering these fields. Summarize your findings and opinions on this issue in a two- to three-page paper.

Running Case

Several people working on the Recreation and Wellness Intranet Project are confused about who needs to do what for the testing portion of the project. Recall that the team members include you, a programmer/analyst and aspiring project manager; Patrick, a network specialist; Nancy, a business analyst; and Bonnie, another programmer/analyst. Tony Prince is the project manager, and he has been working closely with managers in other departments to make sure everyone knows what's going on with the project.

1. Prepare a responsibility assignment matrix based on the following information: The main tasks that need to be done for testing include writing a test plan, unit testing, integration testing for each of the main system modules (registration, tracking, and incentives), system testing, and user acceptance testing. In addition to the project team members, there is a team of user representatives available to help with testing, and Tony has also hired an outside consulting firm to help as needed. Prepare a RACI chart to help clarify roles and responsibilities for these testing tasks. Document key assumptions you make in preparing the chart.
2. The people working for the outside consulting firm and user representatives have asked you to create a resource histogram to show how many people you think the project will need for the testing and when. Assume that the consulting firm has junior and senior testers and that the user group has workers and managers. You estimate that you'll need both groups involvement in testing over a period of six weeks. Assume you'll need one senior tester for all six weeks, two junior testers for the last four weeks, two user-group workers for the first week, four user-group workers for the last three weeks, and two user-group managers for the last two weeks. Create a resource histogram, similar to the one in Figure 9-6, based on this information.

3. One of the issues in Tony's issue log is working effectively with the user group during testing. Tony knows that several of his project team members are very introverted and strong thinking types, while several members of the user group are very extroverted and strong feeling types. Write a one-page paper describing options for resolving this issue.

Companion Web Site

Visit the companion Web site for this text (*www.cengage.com/mis/schwalbe*) to access:

- References cited in the text and additional suggested readings for each chapter
- Template files
- Lecture notes
- Interactive quizzes
- Podcasts
- Links to general project management Web sites
- And more

See the Preface of this text for additional information on accessing the companion Web site.

Key Terms

coercive power — using punishment, threats, or other negative approaches to get people to do things they do not want to do

deputy project managers — people who fill in for project managers in their absence and assist them as needed, similar to the role of a vice president

empathic listening — listening with the intent to understand

expert power — using one's personal knowledge and expertise to get people to change their behavior

extrinsic motivation — causes people to do something for a reward or to avoid a penalty

hierarchy of needs — a pyramid structure illustrating Maslow's theory that people's behaviors are guided or motivated by a sequence of needs

intrinsic motivation — causes people to participate in an activity for their own enjoyment

issue log — a tool for managing project teams where the project manager documents, monitors, and tracks issues that need to be resolved in order for the project to run smoothly

legitimate power — getting people to do things based on a position of authority

mirroring — matching certain behaviors of the other person

Myers-Briggs Type Indicator (MBTI) — a popular tool for determining personality preferences

organizational breakdown structure (OBS) — a specific type of organizational chart that shows which organizational units are responsible for which work items

overallocation — when more resources than are available are assigned to perform work at a given time

power — the potential ability to influence behavior to get people to do things they would not otherwise do

RACI charts — charts that show Responsibility, Accountability, Consultation, and Informed roles for project stakeholders

rapport — a relation of harmony, conformity, accord, or affinity

referent power — getting people to do things based on an individual's personal charisma

resource histogram — a column chart that shows the number of resources assigned to a project over time

resource leveling — a technique for resolving resource conflicts by delaying tasks

resource loading — the amount of individual resources an existing schedule requires during specific time periods

responsibility assignment matrix (RAM) — a matrix that maps the work of the project as described in the WBS to the people responsible for performing the work as described in the organizational breakdown structure (OBS)

reward power — using incentives to induce people to do things

staffing management plan — a document that describes when and how people will be added to and taken off a project team

subproject managers — people responsible for managing the subprojects that a large project might be broken into

synergy — an approach where the whole is greater than the sum of the parts

team development — building individual and group skills to enhance project performance

Tuckman model — describes five stages of team development: forming, storming, norming, performing, and adjourning

End Notes

[1] World Information Technology and Services Alliance, "Global ICT Spending Tops $3.5 Trillion," (May 4, 2008).

[2] Eric Chabrow, "Computer Jobs Hit Record High," *CIO Insight* (July 7, 2008).

[3] Bureau of Labor Statistics, "Economic and Employment Projections" (December 4, 2007).

[4] Deb Perelman, "Project Managers in High Demand, Short Supply," *eWeek.com* (March 12, 2007).

[5] Information Technology Association of America (ITAA), "Recovery Slight for IT Job Market in 2004," *ITAA.org* (September 8, 2004).

[6] Joan Williams and Ariane Hegewisch, "Confusing productivity with long workweek," *StarTribune.com* (Minneapolis–St. Paul, Minnesota) (September 6, 2004).

[7] Ibid.

[8] The Conference Board, Corporate Voices for Working Families, Partnership for 21st Century Skills, and Society for Human Resource Management, "*Are They Really Ready to Work? Employers' Perspectives on the Basic Knowledge and Applied Skills of New Entrants to the 21st Century U.S. Workforce*" (2006) (*www.conference-board.org/pdf_free/BED-06-Workforce.pdf*).

[9] Frederick Herzberg, "One More Time: How Do You Motivate Employees?" *Harvard Business Review* (February 1968) pp. 51–62.

[10] David C. McClelland, *The Achieving Society* (New York: Free Press, 1961).

[11] Douglas McGregor, *The Human Side of Enterprise* (New York: McGraw-Hill, 1960).

12 William Ouchi, *Theory Z: How American Business Can Meet the Japanese Challenge* (New York: Avon Books, 1981).

13 H. J. Thamhain and D. L. Wilemon, "Building Effective Teams for Complex Project Environments," *Technology Management* 5, no. 2 (May 1999).

14 John R. French and Bertram H. Raven, "The Bases of Social Power," in D. Cartwright (Ed.), *Studies in Social Power* (Ann Arbor: University of Michigan Press, 1959).

15 Stephen Covey, *The 7 Habits of Highly Effective People: Powerful Lessons in Personal Change* (New York: Simon & Schuster, 1990).

16 Kidder, Tracy, *The Soul of a New Machine*. (New York: Modern Library, 1997).

17 Douglas Ross, "Applying Covey's Seven Habits to a Project Management Career," *PM Network* (April 1996), pp. 26–30.

18 Rewi, Adrienne, "The Rise of PMP," *PM Network* (October 2004), p. 18.

19 Ronald L. Kempf, "The Most Universal Three Letters Since URL," *PM Network* (December 2006), p. 59.

20 IBM Global Business Services, "Career development" (*www-935.ibm.com/services/us/gbs/bus/html/bcs_careers_development.html*).

21 Stephanie Overby, "How to Hook the Talent You Need," *CIO Magazine* (September 1, 2006) (*www.cio.com/archive/090106/fea_talent.html*).

22 Great Place to Work Institute, "Best Companies Lists" *GreatPlaceToWork.com*.

23 Bruce Tuckman and Mary Ann Jensen, "Stages of Small-Group Development Revisited," Group Organization Management.1977; 2: 419 427.

24 Isabel Myers Briggs, with Peter Myers, *Gifts Differing: Understanding Personality Type* (Palo Alto, CA: Consulting Psychologists Press, 1995).

25 David Keirsey, *Please Understand Me II: Temperament, Character, Intelligence* (Del Mar, CA: Prometheus Nemesis Book Company, 1998).

26 Michael L. Lyons, "The DP Psyche," *Datamation* (August 15, 1985).

27 The information provided here about the Keirsey Temperament Sorter and Keirsey Temperament Theory was compiled from *Keirsey.com*.

28 Sharon McDonald and Helen M. Edwards, "Who Should Test Whom? Examining the use and abuse of personality tests in software engineering," *Communications of the ACM* 50, no. 1 (January 2007).

29 Harvey A. Robbins and Michael Finley, *The New Why Teams Don't Work: What Goes Wrong and How to Make It Right* (San Francisco, CA: Berrett-Koehler Publishers, 1999).

30 John C. Goodman, "DISC, What Is It? Who Created the DISC Model?" *OnlineDiscProfile.com* (2004–2008).

31 Patrick Lencioni, Overcoming the Five Dysfunctions of a Team: A Field Guide for Leaders, Managers, and Facilitators (San Francisco: Jossey-Bass, 2005), p. 3.

CHAPTER 10

PROJECT COMMUNICATIONS MANAGEMENT

LEARNING OBJECTIVES

After reading this chapter, you will be able to:

- Understand the importance of good communications on projects
- Discuss the process of identifying stakeholders and how to create a stakeholder register and stakeholder management strategy
- Explain the elements of project communications planning and how to create a communications management plan
- Describe various methods for distributing project information and the advantages and disadvantages of each, discuss the importance of addressing individual communication needs, and calculate the number of communications channels on a project
- Recognize the importance of managing stakeholder expectations
- Understand how reporting performance helps stakeholders stay informed about project progress
- List various methods for improving project communications, such as managing conflicts, running effective meetings, using e-mail and other technologies effectively, and using templates
- Describe how software can enhance project communications management

OPENING CASE

Peter Gumpert worked his way up the corporate ladder in a large telecommunications company. He was intelligent, competent, and a strong leader, but the new Fiber-optic Undersea Telecommunications program was much larger and more complicated than anything he had previously worked on, let alone managed. This program consisted of several distinct projects, and Peter was in charge of overseeing them all. The changing marketplace for undersea telecommunications systems and the large number of projects involved made communications and flexibility critical concerns for Peter. For missing milestone and completion dates, his company would suffer huge financial penalties ranging from thousands of dollars per day for smaller projects to more than $250,000 per day for larger projects. Many projects depended on the success of other projects, so Peter had to understand and actively manage those critical interfaces.

Peter held several informal and formal discussions with the project managers reporting to him on this program. He worked with them and his project executive assistant, Christine Braun, to develop a communications plan for the program. He was still unsure, however, of the best way to distribute information and manage all of the inevitable changes that would occur. He also wanted to develop consistent ways for all of the project managers to develop their plans and track performance without stifling their creativity and autonomy. Christine suggested that they consider using some new communications technologies to keep important project information up to date and synchronized. Although Peter knew a lot about telecommunications and laying fiber-optic lines, he was not an expert in using information technology to improve the communication process. In fact, that was part of the reason he asked Christine to be his assistant. Could they really develop a process for communicating that would be flexible and easy to use? Time was of the essence as more projects were being added to the Fiber-optics Undersea Telecommunications program every week.

THE IMPORTANCE OF PROJECT COMMUNICATIONS MANAGEMENT

Many experts agree that the greatest threat to the success of any project, especially information technology projects, is a failure to communicate. Many problems in other knowledge areas, such as an unclear scope or unrealistic schedules, indicate problems with communications. It is crucial for project managers and their teams to make good communications a priority, especially with key stakeholders, like top management.

The information technology field is constantly changing, and these changes bring with them a great deal of technical jargon. When computer professionals have to communicate with non–computer professionals, like most business professionals and senior managers, technical jargon can often complicate matters and confuse those who aren't technically savvy. Even though most people use computers today, the gap between users and developers increases as technology advances. Of course, not every computer professional is a poor communicator, but most people in any field can improve their communication skills.

In addition, most educational systems for information technology graduates promote strong technical skills over strong communication and social skills. Most IT–related degree programs have many technical requirements, but few require courses in communications (speaking, writing, listening), psychology, sociology, and the humanities. People often assume it is easy to pick up these soft skills, but they *are* important skills and, as such, people must learn and develop them.

Many studies have shown that information technology professionals need these soft skills just as much or even more than other skills. You cannot totally separate technical skills and soft skills when working on information technology projects. For projects to succeed, every project team member needs both types of skills and needs to develop them continuously through formal education and on-the-job training.

An article in the *Journal of Information Systems Education* on the importance of communications skills for information technology professionals presented the following conclusion:

> Based on the results of this research we can draw some general conclusions. First, it is evident that IS professionals engage in numerous verbal communication activities that are informal in nature, brief in duration, and with a small number of people at a time. Second, we can infer that most of the communication is indeed verbal in nature but sometimes it is supported by notes or graphs on a board or a handout and also by computer output. Third, it is clear that people expect their peers to listen carefully during a conversation and respond correctly to the issues at hand. Fourth, all IS professionals must be aware of the fact that they will have to engage in some form of informal public speaking. Fifth, it is evident that IS professionals must be able to communicate effectively in order to be successful in their current position, but they must also be able to do so in order to move to higher positions. Since our respondents, on average, seem to have moved throughout their IS career, from lower to higher positions, and they ranked verbal skills more important for their advancement than for their current job, the ability to communicate verbally seems to be a key factor in career advancement.[1]

In a recent study, respondents again stated that non-technical skills are most crucial for IT professionals, even at the entry level:

> The investigation confirms previous findings that non-technical skills are considered most important, especially those pertaining to Personal Attributes and Business Expertise. These soft skills are important as a foundation for all IT positions, and they enhance future learning and productivity as IT professionals advance in their careers. Nevertheless, technical skills are also important, though company dependent to a certain degree (different technical abilities are required for different jobs and organizations). Technical skills reduce the amount of training required of new employees and allow some entry-level personnel to be immediately productive.[2]

This chapter will highlight key aspects of project communications management, provide some suggestions for improving communications, and describe how software can assist in project communications management.

The goal of project communications management is to ensure timely and appropriate generation, collection, dissemination, storage, and disposition of project information. There are four main processes in project communications management:

1. *Identifying stakeholders* involves identifying everyone involved in or affected by the project and determining the best ways to manage relationships with them. The main outputs of this process are a stakeholder register and stakeholder management strategy.

2. *Planning communications* involves determining the information and communications needs of the stakeholders: who needs what information, when will they need it, and how will the information be given to them. The outputs of this process include a communications management plan and project document updates.
3. *Distributing information* involves making needed information available to project stakeholders in a timely manner. The main output of this process is organizational process assets updates. Recall from Chapter 4 that organizational process assets include formal and informal plans, policies, procedures, guidelines, information systems, financial systems, management systems, lessons learned, and historical information that help people understand, follow, and improve business processes in a specific organization.

4. *Managing stakeholder expectations* involves managing communications to satisfy the needs and expectations of project stakeholders and to resolve issues. The outputs of this process are organizational process assets updates, change requests, project management plan updates, and project document updates.
5. *Reporting performance* involves collecting and disseminating performance information, including status reports, progress measurements, and forecasts. The outputs of this process are performance reports, organizational process assets updates, and change requests.

Figure 10-1 summarizes these processes and outputs, showing when they occur in a typical project.

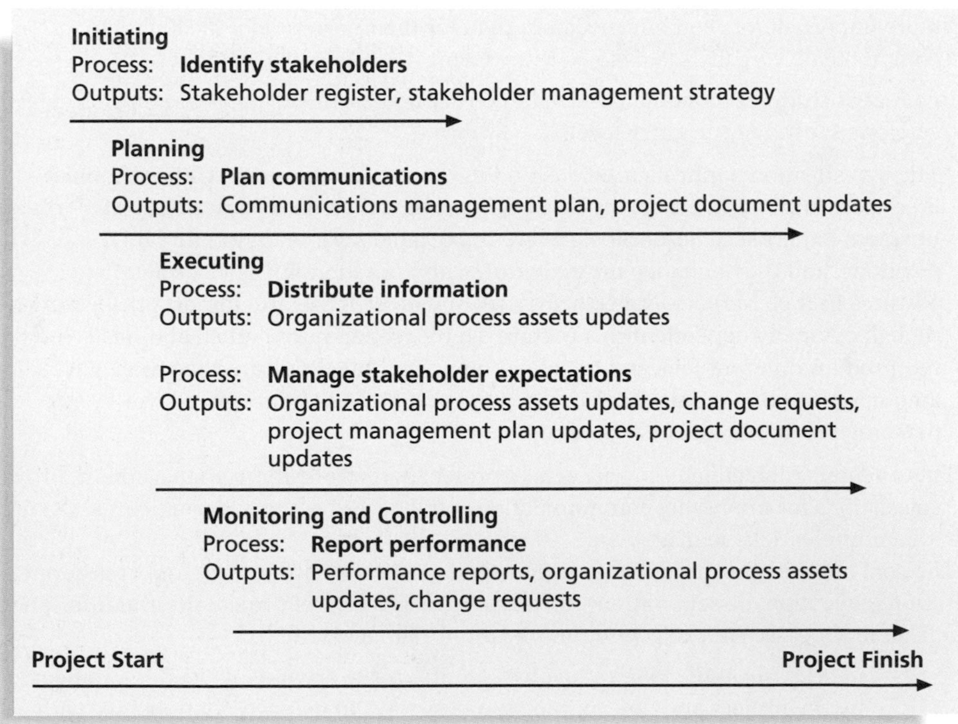

Initiating
Process: Identify stakeholders
Outputs: Stakeholder register, stakeholder management strategy
Planning
Process: Plan communications
Outputs: Communications management plan, project document updates
Executing
Process: Distribute information
Outputs: Organizational process assets updates
Process: Manage stakeholder expectations
Outputs: Organizational process assets updates, change requests, project management plan updates, project document updates
Monitoring and Controlling
Process: Report performance
Outputs: Performance reports, organizational process assets updates, change requests
Project Start
Project Finish

FIGURE 10-1 Project communications management summary

IDENTIFYING STAKEHOLDERS

Recall from Chapter 1 that stakeholders are people involved in or affected by project activities and include the project sponsor, project team, support staff, customers, users, suppliers, and even opponents to the project. Also recall that the ultimate goal of project management is to meet or exceed stakeholder needs and expectations from a project. In order to do that, you must first identify who your particular project stakeholders are. Identifying some stakeholders is obvious, but others might be more difficult. For example, there might be competitors outside the organization or even inside the organization who are opposed to the project without the project manager's knowledge. Stakeholders also might change during a project due to employee turnover, partnerships, and so on. It is important to use formal as well as informal communications networks to make sure that all key stakeholders are identified.

A simple way to document basic information on stakeholders is by creating a **stakeholder register**, a public document that includes details related to the identified project stakeholders. These details include the stakeholder's name, position, if he/she is internal or external to the organization, project role, and contact information. It might also include information on stakeholder requirements and expectations. Table 3-4 in Chapter 3 provides an example of a stakeholder register. Since this document is usually available to the public or people outside the project team, project managers should be careful not to include information that might be sensitive, such as how strongly the stakeholder supports the project. Sensitive information is often used in developing the stakeholder management strategy.

A **stakeholder management strategy** is an approach to help increase the support of stakeholders throughout the project. It includes basic information, such as stakeholder names, level of interest in the project, level of influence on the project, and potential management strategies for gaining support or reducing obstacles from that particular stakeholder. Since much of this information can be sensitive, it should be considered confidential. Some project managers do not even write down this information, but they do consider it since stakeholder management is a crucial part of their jobs.

For example, Peter Gumpert, the program manager from the opening case, worked with a few key colleagues to develop a stakeholder management strategy. Since Peter was in charge of several projects with many different stakeholders, it was crucial that he know who his most important stakeholders were and analyze how to work with them. Table 10-1 provides an example of part of Peter's stakeholder management strategy for the Fiber-optic Undersea Telecommunications program. This example also includes items from the stakeholder register, such as the stakeholder position and whether he or she is internal or external to the organization. Notice that the project managers working under Peter are also included in the stakeholder management strategy.

It is important to perform a stakeholder analysis during the initiating process group and to keep the stakeholder register and management strategy updated throughout the life of the project. As stakeholders and other information changes, it is important to update these documents. It is also important to use the stakeholder analysis information when planning communications.

TABLE 10-1 Sample stakeholder management strategy

Name	Position	Internal/ External	Level of interest	Level of influence	Potential management strategies
John Huntz	Project Manager for largest project under Peter	Internal	High	High	John does a great job, but he often upsets other PMs with his harsh approach. Keep him in line and remind him he is part of a bigger team.
Carolyn Morris	VP Telecommunications, Peter's boss	Internal	High	High	Carolyn is the first woman VP at our company and still likes to prove herself. Keep her informed of key issues and never surprise her!
Subbu Thangi	Dept. Head State of Oregon	External	Low	High	Subbu is in charge of a lot of state issues, like getting permits to install fiber-optic lines. He has a lot on his plate, but he doesn't seem concerned with our projects. Schedule a short, special meeting with him to increase visibility and discuss key issues.
Tom Morgan	CEO of major Telecomm. Customer	External	Medium	High	Tom is the sponsor of several of our projects. Give him the status on all of them at once to use his time efficiently.

PLANNING COMMUNICATIONS

Because communications is so important on projects, every project should include a **communications management plan**—a document that guides project communications. This plan should be part of the overall project management plan (described in Chapter 4, Project Integration Management). The communications management plan will vary with the needs of the project, but some type of written plan should always be prepared. For example, for small projects, such as the Project Management Intranet Site project described in Chapter 3, the communications management plan can be part of the team contract. For large projects, it should be a separate document. The communications management plan should address the following items:

1. Stakeholder communications requirements
2. Information to be communicated, including format, content, and level of detail
3. Who will receive the information and who will produce it
4. Suggested methods or technologies for conveying the information
5. Frequency of communication
6. Escalation procedures for resolving issues
7. Revision procedures for updating the communications management plan
8. A glossary of common terminology

It is important to know what kinds of information will be distributed to which stakeholders. By analyzing stakeholder communications needs, you can avoid wasting time or money on creating or disseminating unnecessary information.

Table 10-2 provides part of a sample stakeholder communications analysis that shows which stakeholders should get which written communications. Note that the stakeholder communications analysis includes information such as the contact person for the information, when the information is due, and the preferred format for the information. You can create a similar table to show which stakeholders should attend which project meetings. It is always a good idea to include comment sections with these types of tables to record special considerations or details related to each stakeholder, document, meeting, and so on.

TABLE 10-2 Sample stakeholder communications analysis

Stakeholders	Document Name	Document Format	Contact Person	Due
Customer management	Monthly status report	Hard copy and meeting	Tina Erndt, Tom Silva	First of month
Customer business staff	Monthly status report	Hard copy	Julie Grant, Sergey Cristobal	First of month
Customer technical staff	Monthly status report	E-mail	Li Chau, Nancy Michaels	First of month
Internal management	Monthly status report	Hard copy and meeting	Bob Thomson	First of month
Internal business and technical staff	Monthly status report	Intranet	Angie Liu	First of month
Training subcontractor	Training plan	Hard copy	Jonathan Kraus	November 1
Software subcontractor	Software implementation plan	E-mail	Najwa Gates	June 1

Comments: Put the titles and dates of documents in e-mail headings and have recipients acknowledge receipt.

Having stakeholders review and approve the stakeholder communications analysis will ensure that the information is correct and useful.

Many projects do not include enough initial information on communications. Project managers, top management, and project team members assume using existing communications channels to relay project information is sufficient. The problem with using existing communications channels is that each of these groups (as well as other stakeholders) has different communications needs. Creating some sort of communications management plan and reviewing it with project stakeholders early in a project helps prevent or reduce later communication problems. If organizations work on many projects, developing some consistency in handling project communications helps the organization run smoothly.

Consistent communication helps organizations improve project communications, especially for programs composed of multiple projects. For example, Peter Gumpert, the Fiber-optic Undersea Telecommunications Program manager in the opening case, would benefit greatly from having a communications management plan that all of the project managers who report to him help develop and follow. Since several of the projects have some of the same stakeholders, it is even more important to develop a coordinated communications management plan. For example, if customers receive status reports from Peter's company that have totally different formats and do not coordinate information from related projects within the same company, they will question the ability of Peter's company to manage large programs.

Information regarding the content of essential project communications comes from the work breakdown structure (WBS). In fact, many WBSs include a section for project communications to ensure that reporting key information is a project deliverable. If reporting essential information is an activity defined in the WBS, it becomes even more important to develop a clear understanding of what project information to report, when to report it, how to report it, who is responsible for generating the report, and so on.

DISTRIBUTING INFORMATION

Getting project information to the right people at the right time and in a useful format is just as important as developing the information in the first place. The stakeholder communications analysis serves as a good starting point for information distribution. Project managers and their teams must decide who receives what information, but they must also decide the best way to distribute the information. Is it sufficient to send written reports for project information? Are meetings alone effective in distributing project information? Are meetings and written communications both required for project information? What is the best way to distribute information to virtual team members?

During project execution, project teams must address important considerations for information distribution, and they often end up updating business processes through improved communications. For example, they might modify policies and procedures, information systems, or incorporate new technologies to improve information distribution. For example, Peter Gumpert, the program manager in the opening case, might decide that providing key people on his projects with handheld wireless devices, such as an iPhone or

BlackBerry, would enhance communications. He would need to request additional funds to provide these devices and training on how to use them.

After answering key questions related to project communications, project managers and their teams must decide the best way to distribute the information. Important considerations for information distribution include the use of technology, formal and informal communications, and the complexity of communications.

Using Technology to Enhance Information Distribution

Technology can facilitate the process of distributing information, when used properly. Most people and businesses rely on e-mail, instant messaging, Web sites, telephones, cell phones, and other technologies to communicate. Using an internal project management information system, you can organize project documents, meeting minutes, customer requests, and so on, and make them available in an electronic format. You can store this information in local software or make it available on an intranet, an extranet, or the Internet, if the information is not sensitive. Storing templates and samples of project documents electronically can make accessing standard forms easier, thus making the information distribution process easier. It is also important to have backup procedures in place in case something goes wrong with normal communications technologies, as described in the What Went Wrong? You will learn more about using software to assist in project communications management later in this chapter.

WHAT WENT WRONG?

Telecommunications throughout Asia were severely disrupted on December 26, 2006, after earthquakes off Taiwan damaged undersea cables, slowing Internet services and hindering financial transactions, particularly in the currency market. Property damage was minimal, but six of seven undersea cable systems, which accounted for 90 percent of telecommunications capacity of the region, broke in the quake and its aftershocks. International telephone traffic was restricted from some countries, and Internet access slowed to a crawl. The initial earthquake measured at a magnitude of 7.1 on the Richter scale by the U.S. Geological Survey. Philippine Long Distance Telephone Co. said its Internet service was intermittent, and international phone calls had been affected. Globe Telecom said, "the entire country's telecom services to the United States were disrupted."[3]

PCCW, the largest telephone company in Hong Kong, said on December 27 that it had lost half its Internet capacity because of the broken cables. PCCW reported "normal" voice services on December 29. On December 30, Singapore Telecommunications, the largest Southeast Asian phone operator, said that voice and Internet access was "back to normal." Chunghwa Telecom said that only 1 percent of major domestic customers' dedicated lines were damaged by December 30, compared with about 30 percent immediately after the quake. Operators were rerouting traffic to other lines and satellites. More than 80 percent of calls made through Chunghwa Telecom to the United States, Canada,

continued

Japan, Europe, and China could be connected as of December 31, rising from less than 30 percent after the quakes. However, *Bloomberg News* reported on December 31 that most Internet users would continue to experience slow access and suggested that customers minimize nonessential activities that demand large bandwidth over international connections.

"Phone calls and Internet connections are forecast to rise in time for the new year, but we have prepared contingency plans in case anything happens," said Kim Cheol Kee, a spokesman at KT, the biggest South Korean phone and Internet company. The financial impact of the cutoff was limited by the fact that many executives and traders were still away for the holidays. Luckily, markets were quiet and trading was light.[4]

Formal and Informal Methods for Distributing Information

It is not enough for project team members to submit status reports to their project managers and other stakeholders and assume that everyone who needs to know that information will read the reports. Some technical professionals might assume that submitting the appropriate status reports is sufficient because they are introverts and prefer communicating that way. Occasionally, that approach might work, but many people prefer informal communications. Recall from Chapter 9 that 75 percent of the general population are extroverts, so they enjoy talking to other people. Often, many non-technical professionals—from colleagues to managers—prefer to have a two-way conversation about project information, rather than reading detailed reports, e-mails, or Web pages to try to find pertinent information.

Instead of focusing on getting information by reading technical documents, many colleagues and managers want to know the people working on their projects and develop a trusting relationship with them. They use informal discussions about the project to develop these relationships. Therefore, project managers must be good at nurturing relationships through good communication. Many experts believe that the difference between good project managers and excellent project managers is their ability to nurture relationships and use empathic listening skills, as described in Chapter 9, Project Human Resource Management.

Effective distribution of information depends on project managers and project team members having good communication skills. Communicating includes many different dimensions such as writing, speaking, and listening, and project personnel need to use all of these dimensions in their daily routines. In addition, different people respond positively to different levels or types of communication. For example, a project sponsor may prefer to stay informed through informal discussions held once a week over coffee. The project manager needs to be aware and take advantage of this special communication need. The project sponsor will give better feedback about the project during these informal talks than he or she could give through some other form of communication. Informal conversations allow the project sponsor to exercise his or her role of leadership and provide insights and information that are critical to the success of the project and the organization as a whole. Short face-to-face meetings are often more effective than electronic communications, particularly for sensitive information.

Distributing Important Information in an Effective and Timely Manner

Many written reports neglect to provide the important information that good managers and technical people have a knack for asking about. For example, it is important to include detailed technical information that will affect critical performance features of products or services the company is producing as part of a project. It is even more important to document any changes in technical specifications that might affect product performance. For example, if the Fiber-Optic Undersea Telecommunications program included a project to purchase and provide special diving gear, and the supplier who provided the oxygen tanks enhanced the tanks so divers could stay under water longer, it would be very important to let other people know about this new capability. The information should not be buried in an attachment with the supplier's new product brochure.

People also have a tendency to not want to report bad news. If the oxygen tank vendor was behind on production, the person in charge of the project to purchase the tanks might wait until the last minute to report this critical information. Oral communication via meetings and informal talks helps bring important information—positive or negative—out into the open.

Oral communication also helps build stronger relationships among project personnel and project stakeholders. People make or break projects, and people like to interact with each other to get a true feeling for how a project is going. Many people cite research that says in a face-to-face interaction, 58 percent of communication is through body language, 35 percent through how the words are said, and a mere 7 percent through the content or words that are spoken. The author of this information (see *Silent Messages* by Albert Mehrabian[5]) was careful to note that these percentages were specific findings for a specific set of variables. Even if the actual percentages are different in verbal project communications today, it is safe to say that it is important to pay attention to more than just the actual words someone is saying. A person's tone of voice and body language say a lot about how they really feel.

Since information technology projects often require a lot of coordination, it is a good idea to have short, frequent meetings. For example, some information technology project managers require all project personnel to attend a "stand-up" meeting every week or even every morning, depending on the project needs. Stand-up meetings have no chairs, and the lack of chairs forces people to focus on what they really need to communicate. If people can't meet face to face, they are often in constant communications via cell phones, e-mail, instant messaging, or other technologies.

To encourage face-to-face, informal communications, some companies have instituted policies that workers cannot use e-mail between certain hours of the business day or even entire days of the week. For example, in the summer of 2004, Jeremy Burton, then vice president of marketing at a large Silicon Valley company, decreed that in his department, Fridays would be e-mail-free. The 240 people in his department had to use the phone or meet face-to-face with people, and violators who did use e-mail were fined.[6] Some companies are also taking advantage of social networking software to increase informal communications. In 2008, Jeremy Burton, now CEO of Serena Software, instituted Facebook Friday. "I told all the employees it's OK on a Friday for everybody to goof off and spend an hour or two on Facebook. . . . I said 'Go nuts! I dare you to participate, and I bet you'll find out something new about somebody in the company that you never knew before.'"[7] Burton wanted his people to get to know each other better, but he also wanted them to keep up with ever-changing technology so they could continue to develop useful software products. "The subversive message was 'Guys, the world is a different place and if we're going to stay relevant we're going to have to wake up,'" Burton said.[8]

Selecting the Appropriate Communications Medium

Table 10-3 provides guidelines from Practical Communications, Inc., a communications consulting firm, about how well different types of media, such as hard copy, phone calls,

TABLE 10-3 Media choice table

KEY: 1 = EXCELLENT	2 = ADEQUATE		3 = INAPPROPRIATE			
How Well Medium Is Suited to:	Hard Copy	Phone Call	Voice Mail	E-mail	Meeting	Web Site
Assessing commitment	3	2	3	3	1	3
Building consensus	3	2	3	3	1	3
Mediating a conflict	3	2	3	3	1	3
Resolving a misunderstanding	3	1	3	3	2	3
Addressing negative behavior	3	2	3	2	1	3
Expressing support/appreciation	1	2	2	1	2	3
Encouraging creative thinking	2	3	3	1	3	3
Making an ironic statement	3	2	2	3	1	3
Conveying a reference document	1	3	3	3	3	2
Reinforcing one's authority	1	2	3	3	1	1
Providing a permanent record	1	3	3	1	3	3
Maintaining confidentiality	2	1	2	3	1	3
Conveying simple information	3	1	1	1	2	3
Asking an informational question	3	1	1	1	3	3
Making a simple request	3	1	1	1	3	3
Giving complex instructions	3	3	2	2	1	2
Addressing many people	2	3 or 1*	2	2	3	1

*Depends on system functionality

See Tess Galati, *Email Composition and Communication (EmC2)*. Practical Communications, Inc. (*www.praccom.com*) (2001).

voice mail, e-mail, meetings, and Web sites, are suited to different communication needs. For example, if you were trying to assess commitment of project stakeholders, a meeting would be the most appropriate medium to use. (A face-to-face meeting would be preferable, but a Web conference, where participants can see and hear each other, would also qualify as a meeting.) A phone call would be adequate, but the other media would not be appropriate. Project managers must assess the needs of the organization, the project, and individuals in determining which communication medium to use, and when. They must also be aware of new technologies that can enhance communications and collaboration, as described in the What Went Right?

WHAT WENT RIGHT?

A 2006 Frost & Sullivan study sponsored by Verizon Business and Microsoft Corp. called "Meetings Around the World: The Impact of Collaboration on Business Performance" found that collaboration is a key driver of overall performance of companies around the world. The impact of collaboration is twice as significant as a company's aggressiveness in pursuing new market opportunities and five times as significant as the external market environment. The study defines collaboration as an interaction between culture and technology such as audio and Web conferencing, e-mail, and instant messaging. The researchers also created a method to specifically measure how collaboration affects business performance.

Of all the collaboration technologies that were studied, three were more commonly present in high-performing companies than in low-performing ones: Web conferencing, audio conferencing, and meeting-scheduler technologies. "This study reveals a powerful new metric business leaders can use to more successfully manage their companies and achieve competitive advantage," said Brian Cotton, a vice president at Frost & Sullivan. "Measuring the quality and capability of collaboration in a given organization presents an opportunity for management to prioritize technology investments, encourage adoption of new tools and open up communications lines for improved collaboration."[9]

The study also showed that there are regional differences in how people in various countries prefer to communicate with one another. These differences highlight an opportunity for greater cultural understanding to improve collaborative efforts around the world. For example,

- American professionals are more likely to enjoy working alone, and they prefer to send e-mail rather than calling a person or leaving a voice mail message. They are also more comfortable with audio, video, and Web conferencing technologies than people of other regions. In addition, they tend to multitask the most when on conference calls.
- Europeans thrive on teamwork more than their counterparts elsewhere and prefer to interact in real time with other people. They are more likely to feel it is irresponsible not to answer the phone, and they want people to call them back rather than leave a voice mail message.
- Professionals in the Asia-Pacific region, more than anywhere else, want to be in touch constantly during the workday. As a result, they find the phone to be an indispensable tool and prefer instant messaging to e-mail.

Understanding Group and Individual Communication Needs

Many top managers think they can just add more people to a project that is falling behind schedule. Unfortunately, this approach often causes more setbacks because of the increased complexity of communications. In his popular book, *The Mythical Man-Month*, Frederick Brooks illustrates this concept very clearly.[10] People are not interchangeable parts. You cannot assume that a task originally scheduled to take two months of one person's time can be done in one month by two people. A popular analogy is that you cannot take nine women and produce a baby in one month!

In addition to understanding that people are not interchangeable, it is also important to understand individuals' personal preferences for communications. As described in Chapter 9, people have different personality traits, which often affect their communication preferences. For example, if you want to praise a project team member for doing a good job, an introvert would be more comfortable receiving that praise in private while an extrovert would like everyone to hear about his or her good work. An intuitive person would want to understand how something fits into the big picture, while a sensing person would prefer to have more focused, step-by-step details. A strong thinker would want to know the logic behind information, while a feeling person would want to know how the information affects him or her personally as well as other people. Someone who is a judging person would be very driven to meet deadlines with few reminders while a perceiving person would need more assistance in developing and following plans.

Rarely does the receiver interpret a message exactly as the sender intended. Therefore, it is important to provide many methods of communication and an environment that promotes open dialogue. It is important for project managers and their teams to be aware of their own communication styles and preferences and those of other project stakeholders. As described in the previous chapter, many information technology professionals have different personality traits than the general population, such as being more introverted, intuitive, and oriented to thinking (as opposed to feeling). These personality differences can lead to miscommunication with people who are extroverted, sensation-oriented, and feeling types. For example, a user guide written by an information technology professional might not provide the detailed steps most users need. Many users also prefer face-to-face meetings to learn how to use a new system instead of trying to follow a cryptic user guide.

Geographic location and cultural background also affect the complexity of project communications. If project stakeholders are in different countries, it is often difficult or impossible to schedule times for two-way communication during normal working hours. Language barriers can also cause communication problems. The same word may have very different meanings in different languages. Times, dates, and other units of measure are also interpreted differently. People from some cultures also prefer to communicate in ways that may be uncomfortable to others. For example, managers in some countries still do not allow workers of lower ranks or women to give formal presentations. Some cultures also reserve written documents for binding commitments.

Setting the Stage for Communicating Bad News

It is also important to put information in context, especially if it's bad news. An amusing example of putting bad news in perspective is in the following letter from a college student to her parents. Variations of this letter can be found on numerous Web sites.

Dear Mom and Dad, or should I say Grandma & Grandpa,

Yes, I am pregnant. No, I'm not married yet since Larry, my boyfriend, is out of a job. Larry's employers just don't seem to appreciate the skills he has learned since he quit high school. Larry looks much younger than you, Dad, even though he is three years older. I'm quitting college and getting a job so we can get an apartment before the baby is born. I found a beautiful apartment above a 24-hour auto repair garage with good insulation so the exhaust fumes and noise won't bother us.

I'm very happy. I thought you would be too.

Love, Ashley

P.S. There is no Larry. I'm not pregnant. I'm not getting married. I'm not quitting school, but I am getting a "D" in Chemistry. I just wanted you to have some perspective.

Determining the Number of Communications Channels

Another important aspect of information distribution is the number of people involved in a project. As the number of people involved increases, the complexity of communications increases because there are more communications channels or pathways through which people can communicate. There is a simple formula for determining the number of communications channels as the number of people involved in a project increases. You can calculate the number of communications channels as follows:

$$\text{number of communications channels} = \frac{n(n-1)}{2}$$

where n is the number of people involved.

For example, two people have one communications channel: (2(2 – 1))/2 = 1. Three people have three channels: (3(3 – 1))/2 = 3. Four people have six channels, five people have 10, and so on. Figure 10-2 illustrates this concept. You can see that as the number of people communicating increases above three, the number of communications channels increases rapidly. Project managers should try to limit the size of teams or sub teams to avoid making communications too complex. For example, if three people are working together on one particular project task, they have three communications channels. If you add two more people to their team, you would have ten communications channels, an increase of seven. If you added three more people instead of two, you'd have 12 communication channels. You can see how quickly communications becomes more complex as you increase team size.

Good communicators consider many factors before deciding how to distribute information, including the size of the group, the type of information, and the appropriate communication medium. People tend to overuse e-mail because it is an easy, inexpensive way to send information to a lot of people. When asked why you cannot always send an e-mail to a team of 100 people, just as you would to a team of five, one CIO answered, "As a group increases in size, you have a whole slew of management challenges. Communicating badly exponentially increases the possibility of making fatal mistakes. A large-scale project has a

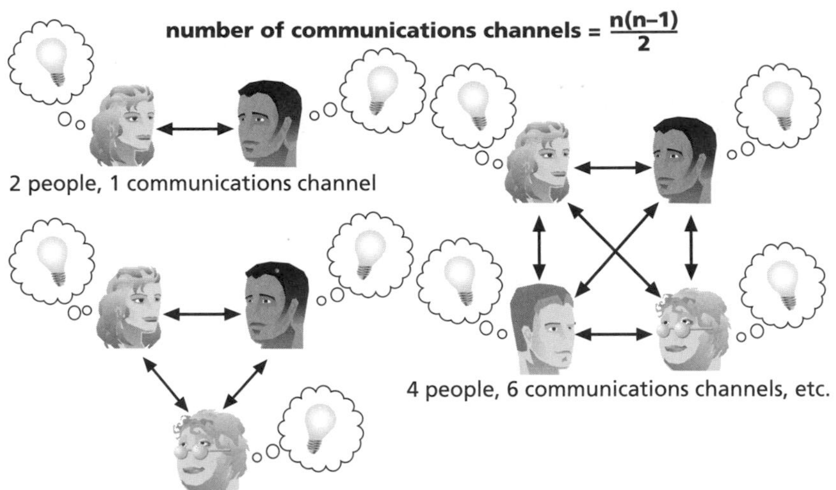

FIGURE 10-2 The impact of the number of people on communications channels

lot of moving parts, which makes it that much easier to break down. Communication is the oil that keeps everything working properly. It's much easier to address an atmosphere of distrust among a group of five team members than it is with a team of 500 members."[11]

However, there are situations in which you cannot have face-to-face meetings and must e-mail a large group of people. Many information technology professionals work on virtual projects where they never meet their project sponsors, other team members, or other project stakeholders. In a virtual project environment, it is crucial for project managers to develop clear communication procedures. They can and must use e-mail, Web conferencing, instant messaging, discussion threads, project Web sites, and other technologies to communicate most information. They might be able to use phone calls or other media occasionally, but in general, they must rely on good written communications.

As you can see, information distribution involves more than creating and sending status reports or holding periodic meetings. Many good project managers know their personal strengths and weaknesses in this area and surround themselves with people who complement their skills, just as Peter Gumpert in the opening case did in asking Christine to be his assistant. It is good practice to share the responsibility for project communications management with the entire project team.

MANAGING STAKEHOLDERS

Project managers must understand and work with various stakeholders; therefore, they should specifically address how they can use various communications methods as well as their interpersonal and management skills to satisfy the needs and expectations of project stakeholders. Recall that project success is often measured in different ways. Many studies define project success as meeting project scope, time, *and* cost goals. Many practitioners, however, define project success as satisfying the customer/sponsor, knowing that it's rare to meet scope, time, and cost goals without modifying at least one goal.

Project sponsors can usually rank scope, time, and cost goals in order of importance and provide guidelines on how to balance the triple constraint. This ranking is shown in an **expectations management matrix**, which can help clarify expectations. For example, Table 10-4 shows an expectations management matrix that Peter's project managers from the opening case could use to help manage their key stakeholders. The expectations management matrix includes a list of measures of success as well as priorities, expectations, and guidelines related to each measure. You could add additional measures of success, such as meeting quality expectations, achieving a certain customer satisfaction rating, meeting ROI projections after the project is completed, and so on to the matrix to meet individual project needs.

TABLE 10-4 Expectations management matrix

Measure of Success	Priority	Expectations	Guidelines
Scope	2	The scope statement clearly defines mandatory requirements and optional requirements.	Focus on meeting mandatory requirements before considering optional ones.
Time	1	There is no give in the project completion date. Every major deadline must be met, and the schedule is very realistic.	The project sponsor and program manager must be alerted if there are any issues that might affect meeting schedule goals.
Cost	3	This project is crucial to the organization. If you can clearly justify the need for more funds, they can be made available.	There are strict rules for project expenditures and escalation procedures. Cost is very important, but it takes a back seat to meeting schedule and then scope goals.
Quality	6	Quality is important, and the expectation is that we follow our well-established processes for testing this system.	All new personnel are required to complete several in-house courses to make sure they understand our quality processes. All corporate quality standards must be followed.
Customer Satisfaction	4	Our customer expects us to act professionally, answer questions in a timely manner, and work collaboratively with them to get the project done.	All presentations and formal documents provided to the customer must be edited by a tech writer. Everyone should reply to customer requests within 24 hours.

TABLE 10-4 Expectations management matrix (*continued*)

Measure of Success	Priority	Expectations	Guidelines
ROI Projections	5	The business case for this project projected an ROI of 40% within two years after implementation.	Our finance department will work with the customer to measure the ROI. Meeting/ exceeding this projection will help us bring in future business with this and other customers.
Etc.			

Understanding the stakeholders' expectations can help in managing issues. If the project manager knows that cost is not as high a priority as the schedule, he or she will know that it shouldn't be too difficult to ask the project sponsor for needed funds, as long as there is good logic behind the request. Unresolved issues can be a major source of conflict and result in not meeting stakeholder expectations.

REPORTING PERFORMANCE

Performance reporting keeps stakeholders informed about how resources are being used to achieve project objectives. Work performance information and measurements, forecasted completion dates, quality control measurements, the project management plan, approved change requests, and deliverables are all important inputs to performance reporting. Two key outputs of performance reporting are performance reports and forecasts. Performance reports are normally provided as status reports or progress reports. Many people use the two terms interchangeably, but some people distinguish between them as follows:

- **Status reports** describe where the project stands at a specific point in time. Recall the importance of the triple constraint. Status reports address where the project stands in terms of meeting scope, time, and cost goals. How much money has been spent to date? How long did it take to do certain tasks? Is work being accomplished as planned? Status reports can take various formats depending on the stakeholders' needs.
- **Progress reports** describe what the project team has accomplished during a certain period. Many projects have each team member prepare a monthly or sometimes weekly progress report. Team leaders often create consolidated progress reports based on the information received from team members. A sample template for a monthly progress report is provided later in this chapter.

Forecasts predict future project status and progress based on past information and trends. How long will it take to finish the project based on how things are going? How much more money will be needed to complete the project? Project managers can also use earned value management (see Chapter 7, Project Cost Management) to answer these questions by estimating the budget at completion and projected completion date based on how the project is progressing.

Another important technique for performance reporting is the status review meeting. Status review meetings, as described in Chapter 4, Project Integration Management, are a good way to highlight information provided in important project documents, empower people to be accountable for their work, and have face-to-face discussions about important project issues. Many program and project managers hold periodic status review meetings to exchange important project information and motivate people to make progress on their parts of the project. Likewise, many top managers hold monthly or quarterly status review meetings where program and project managers must report overall status information.

Status review meetings sometimes become battlegrounds where conflicts between different parties come to a head. Project managers or higher-level top managers should set ground rules for status review meetings to control the amount of conflict and should work to resolve any potential problems. It is important to remember that project stakeholders should work together to address performance problems.

SUGGESTIONS FOR IMPROVING PROJECT COMMUNICATIONS

You have seen that good communication is vital to the management and success of information technology projects; you have also learned that project communications management can ensure that essential information reaches the right people at the right time, that feedback and reports are appropriate and useful, and that there is a formalized process of stakeholder management. This section highlights a few areas that all project managers and project team members should consider in their quests to improve project communications. The following text provides guidelines for managing conflict, developing better communication skills, running effective meetings, using e-mail, instant messaging, and collaborative tools effectively, and using templates for project communications.

Using Communication Skills to Manage Conflict

Most large information technology projects are high-stake endeavors that are highly visible within organizations. They require tremendous effort from team members, are expensive, commandeer significant resources, and can have an extensive impact on the way work is done in an organization. When the stakes are high, conflict is never far away; when the potential for conflict is high, good communication is a necessity.

Chapter 6, Project Time Management, explained that schedule issues cause the most conflicts over the project life cycle and provided suggestions for improving project scheduling. Other conflicts occur over project priorities, staffing, technical issues, administrative procedures, personalities, and cost. It is crucial for project managers to develop and use their human resources and communication skills to help identify and manage conflict on projects. Project managers should lead their teams in developing norms for dealing with various types of conflicts that might arise on their projects. For example, team members should know that disrespectful behavior toward any project stakeholder is inappropriate, and that team members are expected to try to work out small conflicts themselves before elevating them to higher levels. As mentioned earlier in this chapter, escalation procedures should be documented in the communications management plan. Blake and Mouton (1964) delineated five basic modes for handling conflicts: confrontation, compromise, smoothing, forcing, and withdrawal.

1. *Confrontation*. When using the **confrontation mode**, project managers directly face a conflict using a problem-solving approach that allows affected parties to work through their disagreements. This approach is also called the problem-solving mode.
2. *Compromise*. With the **compromise mode**, project managers use a give-and-take approach to resolving conflicts. They bargain and search for solutions that bring some degree of satisfaction to all the parties in a dispute.
3. *Smoothing*. When using the **smoothing mode**, the project manager deemphasizes or avoids areas of differences and emphasizes areas of agreement. This approach is also called accommodating.
4. *Forcing*. The **forcing mode** can be viewed as the win-lose approach to conflict resolution. Project managers exert their viewpoint at the potential expense of another viewpoint. Managers who are very competitive or autocratic in their management style might favor this approach.
5. *Withdrawal*. When using the **withdrawal mode**, project managers retreat or withdraw from an actual or potential disagreement. This approach is also called avoiding and is the least desirable conflict-handling mode.

   More recent studies recognize a sixth conflict-handling mode:

6. *Collaborating*: Using the **collaborating mode**, decision makers incorporate different viewpoints and insights to develop consensus and commitment.

Research indicates that project managers favor using confrontation for conflict resolution over the other modes. The term confrontation may be misleading. This mode really focuses on addressing conflicts using a problem-solving approach. Using Stephen Covey's paradigms of interdependence, this mode focuses on a win-win approach. All parties work together to find the best way to solve the conflict. Other popular approaches to conflict resolution include collaboration and compromise. Successful project managers are less likely to use smoothing, forcing, or withdrawal if they want to make effective decisions.

Project managers must also realize that not all conflict is bad. In fact, conflict can often be good. Conflict often produces important results, such as new ideas, better alternatives, and motivation to work harder and more collaboratively. Project team members may become stagnant or develop **groupthink**—conformance to the values or ethical standards of a group—if there are no conflicting viewpoints on various aspects of a project. Research by Karen Jehn, Professor of Management at Wharton, suggests that task-related conflict, which is derived from differences over team objectives and how to achieve them, often improves team performance. Emotional conflict, however, which stems from personality clashes and misunderstandings, often depresses team performance.[12] Project managers should create an environment that encourages and maintains the positive and productive aspects of conflict.

Developing Better Communication Skills

Some people seem to be born with great communication skills. Others seem to have a knack for picking up technical skills. It is rare to find someone with a natural ability for both. Both communication and technical skills, however, can be developed. Most information technology professionals enter the field because of their technical skills. Most find, however, that communication skills are the key to advancing in their careers, especially if they want to become good project managers.

Most companies spend a lot of money on technical training for their employees, even when employees might benefit more from communications training. Individual employees are also more likely to enroll voluntarily in classes on the latest technology than those on developing their soft skills. Communication skills training usually includes role-playing activities in which participants learn concepts such as building rapport, as described in Chapter 9, Project Human Resource Management. Training sessions also give participants a chance to develop specific skills in small groups. Training sessions that focus on presentation skills usually use video to record the participants' presentations. Most people are surprised to see some of their mannerisms and enjoy the challenge of improving their skills. A minimal investment in communication and presentation training can have a tremendous payback to individuals, their projects, and their organizations. These skills also have a much longer shelf life than many of the skills learned in technical training courses.

As organizations become more global, they realize that they must also invest in ways to improve communication with people from different countries and cultures. For example, many Americans are raised to speak their minds, while in some other cultures people are offended by outspokenness. Not understanding how to communicate effectively with other cultures and people of diverse backgrounds hurts projects and businesses. Many training courses are available to educate people in cultural awareness, international business, and international team building.

It takes leadership to help improve communication. If top management lets employees give poor presentations, write sloppy reports, offend people from different cultures, or behave poorly at meetings, the employees will not want to improve their communication skills. Top management must set high expectations and lead by example. Some organizations send all information technology professionals to training that includes development of technical *and* communication skills. Successful organizations allocate time in project schedules for preparing drafts of important reports and presentations and incorporating feedback on the drafts. It is good practice to include time for informal meetings with customers to help develop relationships and provide staff to assist in relationship management. As with any other goal, improving communication can be achieved with proper planning, support, and leadership from top management.

MEDIA SNAPSHOT

Communications technology, such as using e-mail and searching the Web, should help improve project communications, but it can also cause conflict. How? Most people have heard the term "slackers" before, referring to people who avoid work. But have you heard the term "cyberslackers?" Cyberslackers are people who should be working, but instead spend their time online doing non-work-related activities, such as annoying friends or co-workers by sending unimportant e-mails. A recent study by Websense suggested that employees are using the Web more and more for personal reasons, and it is costing U.S.

continued

companies $178 billion annually, or $5,000 per employee.[13] Websense determined this number by surveying managers, who estimated that each employee was using the Internet for personal use for 5.9 hours a week on average, and then multiplying these numbers by the average American hourly salary. Cyberslacking is not a new phenomenon, nor is it restricted to people in certain countries. In 2000, Internet security company Surfcontrol estimated that every employee in Australia was taking the equivalent of a two-week "cyber-holiday" each year, costing the nation $22.5 billion annually.[14]

A two-year research project by postgraduate psychology student Kerryann Wyatt found that cyberslacking could be using as much as a quarter of the time employees spend online, and even more if they have outgoing personalities. Of the many Internet distractions tempting employees away from their work, e-mailing friends was the most popular, followed by general Internet searches, according to Wyatt's research. One of the goals of this study was to attempt to match personality types with Internet misuse at work. Wyatt said her findings indicated that, contrary to previous studies, introverted participants were not the key offenders. The report said: "People scoring highly in extroversion were significantly more likely to send higher numbers of both work and non work-related e-mails."[15]

A 2008 survey found that more than a quarter of U.S. employers have fired workers for misusing e-mail and one-third have fired workers for misusing the Internet on the job. Of the managers surveyed, 84 percent said employees were fired for accessing pornography or other inappropriate content on the Internet. Among managers who fired workers for e-mail misuse, 64 percent did so because the employee violated company policy, and 62 percent said the e-mail contained inappropriate or offensive language. Most employees who were fired knew that their computer usage was being monitored.[16]

Running Effective Meetings

A well-run meeting can be a vehicle for fostering team building and reinforcing expectations, roles, relationships, and commitment to the project. However, a poorly run meeting can have a detrimental effect on a project. For example, a terrible kick-off meeting may cause some important stakeholders to decide not to support the project further. Many people complain about the time they waste in unnecessary or poorly planned and poorly executed meetings. Following are some guidelines to help improve time spent at meetings:

- *Determine if a meeting can be avoided*. Do not have a meeting if there is a better way of achieving the objective at hand. For example, a project manager might know that he or she needs approval from a top manager to hire another person for the project team. It could take a week or longer to schedule even a ten-minute meeting on the top manager's calendar. Instead, an e-mail or phone call describing the situation and justifying the request is a faster, more effective approach than having a meeting. However, many times you do need a face-to-face meeting, and it would not be appropriate to try to use e-mail or a phone call. Consider which medium would be most effective, as described earlier.
- *Define the purpose and intended outcome of the meeting*. Be specific about what should happen as a result of the meeting. Is the purpose to brainstorm ideas, provide status information, or solve a problem? Make the purpose of a meeting very clear to all meeting planners and participants. For example, if a project manager calls a meeting of all project team members without knowing

the true purpose of the meeting, everyone will start focusing on their own agendas and very little will be accomplished. All meetings should have a purpose and intended outcome.

- *Determine who should attend the meeting*. Do certain stakeholders have to be at a meeting to make it effective? Should only the project team leaders attend a meeting, or should the entire project team be involved? Many meetings are most effective with the minimum number of participants possible, especially if decisions must be made. Other meetings require many attendees. It is important to determine who should attend a meeting based on the purpose and intended outcome of the meeting.
- *Provide an agenda to participants before the meeting*. Meetings are most effective when the participants come prepared. Did they read reports before the meeting? Did they collect necessary information? Some professionals refuse to attend meetings if they do not have an agenda ahead of time. Insisting on an agenda forces meeting organizers to plan the meeting and gives potential attendees the chance to decide whether they really need to attend the meeting.
- *Prepare handouts and visual aids, and make logistical arrangements ahead of time*. By creating handouts and visual aids, the meeting organizers must organize their thoughts and ideas. This usually helps the entire meeting run more effectively. It is also important to make logistical arrangements by booking an appropriate room, having necessary equipment available, and providing refreshments or entire meals, if appropriate. It takes time to plan for effective meetings. Project managers and their team members must take time to prepare for meetings, especially important ones with key stakeholders.
- *Run the meeting professionally*. Introduce people, restate the purpose of the meeting, and state any ground rules that attendees should follow. Have someone facilitate the meeting to make sure important items are discussed, watch the time, encourage participation, summarize key issues, and clarify decisions and action items. Designate someone to take minutes and send the minutes out soon after the meeting. Minutes should be short and focus on the crucial decisions and action items from the meeting.
- *Set the ground rules for the meeting*. State up front how the meeting will be run. For example, can people speak at will, or will the facilitator lead discussions? Can attendees use their laptops or other electronic devices during the meeting? Don't assume that all meetings are run in the same way. Do what works best in each specific case.
- *Build relationships*. Depending on the culture of the organization and project, it may help to build relationships by making meetings fun experiences. For example, it may be appropriate to use humor, refreshments, or prizes for good ideas to keep meeting participants actively involved. If used effectively, meetings are a good way to build relationships.

Using E-Mail, Instant Messaging, and Collaborative Tools Effectively

Since most people use e-mail and other electronic communications tools now, communications should improve, right? Not necessarily. In fact, few people have received any training or guidelines on when or how to use e-mail, instant messaging, or other collaborative tools, such as Microsoft SharePoint portals, Google Docs, or wikis. (A **SharePoint portal** allows users to create custom Web sites to access documents and applications stored on shared devices. **Google Docs** allow users to create, share, and edit documents, spreadsheets, and presentations online. A **wiki** is a Web site designed to enable anyone who accesses it to contribute or modify Web page content.) As discussed earlier in this chapter, e-mail is not an appropriate medium for several types of communications. The media choice table (Table 10-3) suggests that e-mail is not appropriate for assessing commitment, building consensus, mediating a conflict, resolving a misunderstanding, making an ironic statement, conveying a reference document, reinforcing one's authority, or maintaining confidentiality. The same is true for instant messaging and other electronic communications tools.

Even if people do know when to use e-mail or other tools for project communications, they also need to know how to use it. New features are added to e-mail, instant messaging, and collaborative software programs with every new release, but often users are unaware of these features and do not receive any training on how to use them. Do you know how to organize and file your e-mail messages, or do you have hundreds of e-mail messages sitting in your Inbox? Do you know how to use your address book or how to create distribution lists? Have you ever used sorting features to find e-mail messages by date, author, or key words? Do you use filtering software to prevent spam? Do you know how to share your desktop with instant messaging to teach someone how to use software on your computer? Do you know how to track and incorporate changes in Google Docs to create reports and spreadsheets as a collaborative effort? Does everyone on your project team know how to use important features of your SharePoint portal or wiki?

Even if you know how to use all the features of these communications systems, you will likely need to learn how to put ideas into words clearly. For example, the subject line for any e-mail messages you write should clearly state the intention of the e-mail. Folder and file names for collaborative projects should be clear and follow file naming conventions, if provided. A business professional who is not a very good writer may prefer to talk to people than to send an e-mail or instant message. Poor writing often leads to misunderstandings and confusion.

Project managers should do whatever they can to help their project stakeholders use e-mail, instant messaging, collaborative tools, or any other communications technologies effectively and not waste time with poor or unclear electronic communications.

The following guidelines will help you use several of these tools more effectively:

- Information sent via e-mail, instant messaging, or a collaborative tool should be appropriate for that medium, versus other media. If you can communicate the information better with a phone call or meeting, for example, then do so.
- Be sure to send the e-mail or instant message to the right people. Do not automatically "reply to all" on an e-mail, for example, if you do not need to.
- Use meaningful subject lines in e-mails so readers can quickly see what information the message will contain. If the entire message can be put in the subject line, put it there. For example, if a meeting is cancelled, just type that in the subject line. Also, do not continue replying to e-mail messages without changing the subject. The subject should always relate to the latest correspondence.

- Limit the content of the e-mail to one main subject. Send a second or third e-mail if it relates to a different subject.
- The body of the e-mail should be as clear and concise as possible and you should always reread your e-mail before you send it. Also, be sure to check your spelling using the spell check function. If you have three questions you need answered, number them as question 1, 2, and 3.
- Limit the number and size of e-mail attachments. If you can include a link to an online version of a document instead of attaching a file, do so.
- Delete e-mail that you do not need to save or respond to. Do not even open e-mail that you know is not important, such as spam. Use the e-mail blocking feature of the software, if available, to block unwanted junk mail.
- Make sure your virus protection software is up to date. Never open e-mail attachments if you do not trust the source.
- Respond to e-mail quickly, if possible. It will take you longer to open and read it again later. In addition, if you send an e-mail that does not require a response, make that clear as well.
- If you need to keep e-mail, file each message appropriately. Create folders with meaningful names to file the e-mail messages you want to keep. File them as soon as possible.
- Learn how to use important features of your e-mail, instant messaging, and collaborative software.
- Most people are comfortable with using e-mail, but some may not be familiar with using instant messaging. Develop a strategy for getting users up to date, and discuss when it's best to use instant messaging versus e-mail.
- Collaborative tools continue to advance. Make sure your team is using a good tool. Many, like Google Docs and several wikis, are available for free.
- Be sure to authorize the right people to share your collaborative documents. Also ensure that other security is in place. Confidential project documents should probably not be stored on Google Docs. Use more secure tools when needed. For example, Alaska Airlines uses an internally controlled wiki to improve project communications, as described in the following Best Practice feature.
- Make sure the right person can authorize changes to shared documents and that you back up files.
- Develop a logical structure for organizing and filing shared documents. Use good file-naming conventions for folder and document names.

BEST PRACTICE

At a 2008 conference, John Petroske shared successful practices Alaska Airlines follows in using wikis to facilitate project communications and collaboration. As Petroske explains, a wiki is a fully editable Web site. To prevent anyone on the Internet from seeing or

continued

modifying content, it is important to make the project wikis accessible only behind a protective corporate firewall. You can also enable tracking and authentication mechanisms to deter abuse and prevent non-project members from modifying a wiki.

The main benefits wikis bring to project management include:

- *Better documentation*: Data can be stored in different network locations, and a wiki can centrally organize this information. For example, after a meeting or hallway conversation, any authorized wiki user can document the information and make it available on the wiki. The wiki includes hyperlinks to related project documents, such as meeting notes, status reports, product specifications, use case definitions, lessons learned reports, and so on.
- *Improved trust and information sharing*: Project wikis encourage the project team to openly share information. By putting all information in one place and allowing users to edit information, team members develop a better working relationship. There can be problems with misuse if someone intentionally deletes or changes information in a negative way, but that has not occurred at Alaska Airlines because project teams are dedicated to project success and self-police content.
- *Sustained growth*: In order to ensure the sustainability of a wiki, it is important to train project users, keep the wiki organized, understand how people are using the wiki, lead by example by using the wiki often and appropriately, protect the wiki behind a corporate firewall and back it up often, and provide style guides. The Alaska Airlines IT department even created a "Mother of All Wikis" to serve as an index for all the known project wikis. Site visitors are encouraged to help maintain the site by adding related information or links.[17]

Using Templates for Project Communications

Many intelligent people have a hard time writing a performance report or preparing a ten-minute technical presentation for a customer review. Some people in these situations are too embarrassed to ask for help. To make preparing project communications easier, project managers need to provide examples and templates for common project communications items such as project descriptions, project charters, monthly performance reports, issue logs, and so on. Good documentation from past projects can be an ample source of examples. Samples and templates of both written and oral reports are particularly helpful for people who have never before had to write project documents or give project presentations. Finding, developing, and sharing relevant templates and sample documents are important tasks for many project managers. Several examples of project documentation such as a business case, project charter, scope statement, stakeholder analysis, WBS, Gantt chart, cost estimate, and so on are provided throughout this text. The companion Web site for this text includes the actual files used in creating the templates for these sample documents. A few of these templates and guidelines for preparing them are provided in this section.

Figure 10-3 shows a sample template for a one-page project description. This form could be used to show a "snapshot" of an entire project on one page. For example, top managers might require that all project managers provide a brief project description as part of a quarterly management review meeting. Peter Gumpert, the program manager in the opening case, might request this type of document from all of the project managers working for him to get an overall picture of what each project involves. According to Figure 10-3, a project description should include the project objective, scope, assumptions, cost information, and schedule information. This template suggests including information from the project's Gantt chart to highlight key deliverables and other milestones.

Project X Descripton

Objective: Describe the objective of the project in one or two sentences. Focus on the business benefits of doing the project.

Scope: Briefly describe the scope of the project. What business functions are involved, and what are the main products the project will produce?

Assumptions: Summarize the most critical assumptions for the project.

Cost: Provide the total estimated cost of the project. If desired, list the total cost each year.

Schedule: Provide summary information from the project's Gantt chart, as shown. Focus on summary tasks and milestones.

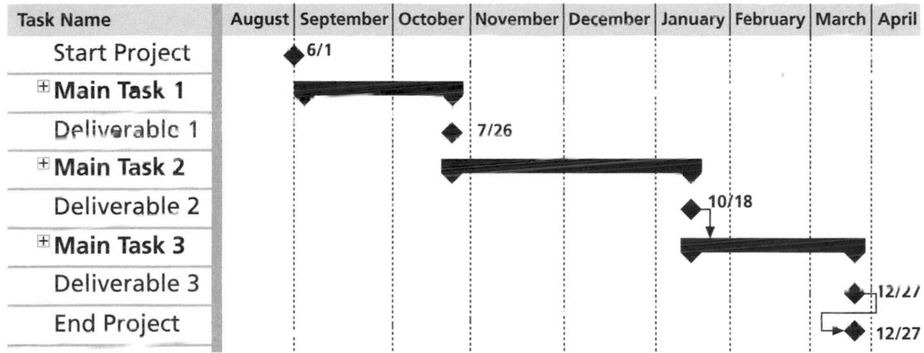

FIGURE 10-3 Sample template for a project description

Table 10-5 shows a template for a monthly progress report. Sections of the progress report include accomplishments from the current period, plans for the next period, issues, and project changes. Recall that progress reports focus on accomplishments during a specific time period while status reports focus on where the project stands at a certain point in time. Because progress and status reports are important ways to communicate project information, it is important for project teams to tailor them to meet their specific needs. Some organizations, such as JWD Consulting from Chapter 3, combine both progress and status information on the same template.

TABLE 10-5 Sample template for a monthly progress report

I.	Accomplishments for January (or appropriate month): • Describe most important accomplishments. Relate them to project's Gantt chart. • Describe other important accomplishments, one bullet for each. If any issues were resolved from the previous month, list them as accomplishments.
II.	Plans for February (or following month): • Describe most important items to accomplish in the next month. Again, relate them to project's Gantt chart. • Describe other important items to accomplish, one bullet for each.
III.	**Issues:** Briefly list important issues that surfaced or are still important. Managers hate surprises and want to help the project succeed, so be sure to list issues.
IV.	**Project Changes (Dates and Description):** List any approved or requested changes to the project. Include the date of the change and a brief description.

Table 10-6 provides an exhaustive list of all of the documentation that should be organized and filed at the end of a major project. From this list, you can see that a large project can generate a lot of documentation. In fact, some project professionals have observed that documentation for designing an airplane usually weighs more than the airplane itself. (Smaller projects usually generate much less documentation!)

TABLE 10-6 Final project documentation items

I.	Project description
II.	Project proposal and backup data (request for proposal, statement of work, proposal correspondence, and so on)
III.	Original and revised contract information and client acceptance documents
IV.	Original and revised project plans and schedules (WBS, Gantt charts and network diagrams, cost estimates, communications management plan, etc.)
V.	Design documents
VI.	Final project report
VII.	Deliverables, as appropriate
VIII.	Audit reports
IX.	Lessons-learned reports
X.	Copies of all status reports, meeting minutes, change notices, and other written and electronic communications

The project manager and project team members should all prepare a **lessons-learned report**—a reflective statement documenting important things they have learned from working on the project. The project manager often combines information from all of the lessons-learned reports into a project summary report. See Chapter 3 for an example of this type of lessons-learned report. Some items discussed in lessons-learned reports include reflections on whether project goals were met, whether the project was successful or not, the causes of variances on the project, the reasoning behind corrective actions chosen, the use of different project management tools and techniques, and personal words of wisdom based on team members' experiences. On some projects, all project members are required to write a brief lessons-learned report; on other projects, just the team leads or project manager writes the report. These reports provide valuable reflections by people who know what really worked or did not work on the project. Everyone learns in different ways and has different insights into a project, so it is helpful to have more than one person provide inputs on the lessons-learned reports. These reports can be an excellent resource and help future projects run more smoothly. To reinforce the benefits of lessons-learned reports, some companies require new project managers to read several past project managers' lessons-learned reports and discuss how they will incorporate some of their ideas into their own projects. It is also important to organize and prepare project archives. **Project archives** are a complete set of organized project records that provide an accurate history of the project. These archives can provide valuable information for future projects as well.

In the past few years, more and more project teams have started putting all or part of their project information, including various templates and lessons-learned reports, on project Web sites. Project Web sites provide a centralized way of delivering project documents and other communications. Project teams can develop project Web sites using wikis or Web-authoring tools, such as Adobe Dreamweaver or Microsoft Expression Web. The home page for the project Web site should include summary information about the project, such as the background and objectives of the project. The home page should also include contact information, such as names and e-mail addresses for the project manager, other team members, or the Webmaster. Links should be provided to items such as project documents, a team member list, meeting minutes, a discussions area, if applicable, and other materials related to the project. If the project involves creating research reports, software, design documents, or other items that can also be accessed via the Web site, links can be provided to those files as well. The project team should also address other issues in creating and using a project Web site, such as security, access, and type of content that should be included on the site.

For more sophisticated Web sites, project teams can also use one of the many software products created specifically to assist in project communications through the Web. These products vary considerably in price and functionality, as described in Chapter 1. For example, Figure 10-4 provides a sample screen from the Microsoft Office Enterprise Project Management (EPM) Solution for 2007. Notice the categories of information on the left side of the screen where users can access their individual work information (i.e., tasks, timesheets, and issues and risks), information on projects, resources, reporting, approvals, personal settings, and shared documents.

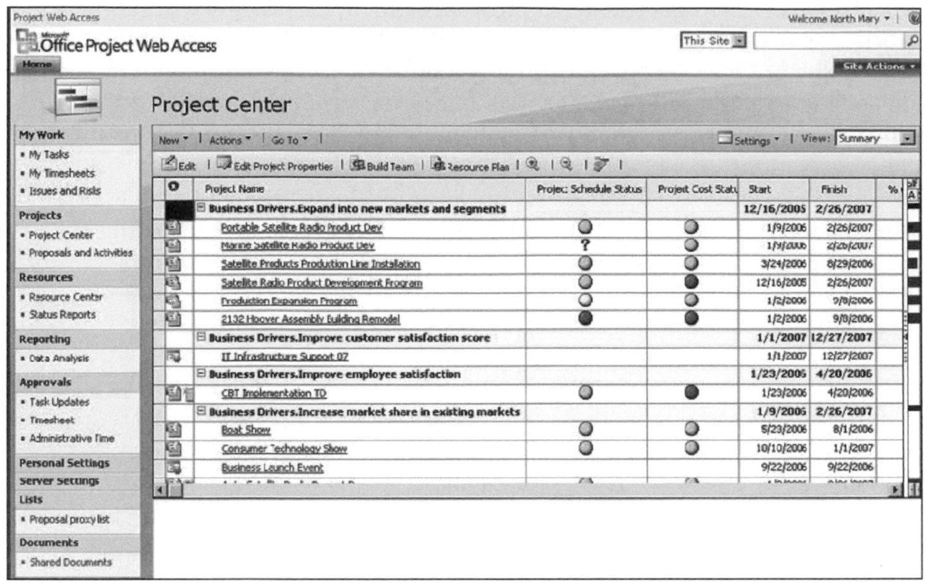

FIGURE 10-4 Microsoft Office Enterprise Project Management (EPM) Solution

When the project team develops their project communications management plan, they should also determine what templates to use for key documentation. To make it even more convenient to use templates, the organization should make project templates readily available online for all projects. The project team should also understand top management's and customers' documentation expectations for each particular project. For example, if a project sponsor or customer wants a one-page monthly progress report for a specific project, but the project team delivers a 20-page report, there are communication problems. In addition, if particular customers or top managers want specific items in all final project reports, they should make sure the project team is aware of those expectations and modifies any templates for those reports to take these requirements into account.

USING SOFTWARE TO ASSIST IN PROJECT COMMUNICATIONS

Many organizations are discovering how valuable project management software can be in communicating information about individual projects and multiple projects across the organization. Project management software can provide different views of information to help meet various communication needs. For example, senior managers might only need to see summary screens with colors indicating the overall health of all projects. Middle managers often want to see the status of milestones for all of the projects in their area. Project team members often need to see all project documentation. Often, one of the biggest communication problems on projects is providing the most recent project plans, Gantt charts, specifications, meeting information, change requests, and so on to all or selective stakeholders in a timely fashion. Most project management software allows users to insert hyperlinks to other project-related files. In Project 2007, you can insert a hyperlink from a task or milestone listed in a Gantt chart to another file that contains relevant information. For example, there might be a milestone that the project charter was signed. You can insert a hyperlink to the Word file containing the project charter from within the Gantt chart. You could also link appropriate tasks or milestones to Excel files that contain a staffing management plan or cost estimate or to Microsoft PowerPoint files with important presentations or other information. The Project 2007 file and all associated hyperlinked files could then be placed on a local area network server or Web server, allowing all project stakeholders easy access to important project information. (See Appendix A for more information on using Microsoft Project 2007 to assist in project communications management.)

Even though organizations routinely use many types of hardware and software to enhance communications, they need to take advantage of new technologies and adjust existing systems to serve the special communications needs of customers and project teams. In addition to diverse customer and project needs, they also have to address the changing expectations of consumers and the workforce. For example, several television shows have harnessed communications technology to engage their audiences by letting them vote online or via telephone for their favorite singers, e-mail celebrities, or access information on their Web sites. Many people, especially younger people, use instant messaging or cell phone text messages every day to communicate with friends. Some business and technical professionals also find instant messaging and text messaging to be a useful tool for quickly communicating with colleagues, customers, suppliers, and others. Web logs, or **blogs**, are easy-to-use journals on the Web that allow users to write entries, respond to another poster's comments, create links, upload pictures, and post comments to journal entries. Blogs have also become popular as a communication technology. If television shows and non-technical people can use advanced communications technologies, why can't project stakeholders?

Employers have made changes to meet changing expectations and needs in communications. The Telework Coalition reports that since 1990, the number of people telecommuting has grown from about 4 million to more than 45 million. At IBM, 40 percent of its 330,000 employees work from home, on the road, or at a client location on any given day.[18] On several IT projects, project managers have found that their team members can be more productive when they are allowed to work from home. Other project managers have no choice in the matter when some or all of their project team members work remotely. As described in Chapter 9, Project Human Resource Management, studies show that providing a quiet work environment and a dedicated workspace increases programmer productivity. Most people who work from home have well-equipped, comfortable home offices with fewer distractions and more space than corporate offices. Workers also appreciate the added bonus of avoiding traffic and having more flexible work schedules. However, it is important to make sure work is well defined and communications are in place to allow for remote workers to work effectively.

Several products are now available to assist individual consumers and organizations with communications. Many products were developed or enhanced in the early 2000s to address the issue of providing fast, convenient, consistent, and up-to-date project information. Webcasts are now a common tool for presenting video, graphics, sound, voice, and participant feedback live over the Web. Podcasts and YouTube videos have also become popular tools for providing various types of audio and video information, from exercise instructions to class lectures. Most working adults or college students have cell phones, and today it is common to see someone take and send a picture or send and receive text messages or e-mail with a cell phone. Many high school or college students are instant messaging or texting their friends to plan social activities or occasionally discuss academic topics.

These same technologies can enhance project communications. For even more powerful and integrated communications, enterprise project management software provides many workgroup functions that allow a team of people at different locations to work together on projects and share project information. Workgroup functions allow the exchange of messages through e-mail, an intranet, wireless devices, or the Web. For example, you can use Project 2007 to alert members about new or changed task assignments, and members can return status information and notify other workgroup members about changes in the schedule or other project parameters.

Microsoft Office Enterprise Project Management (EPM) Solution and similar products also provides the following tools to enhance communications:

- *Portfolio management*: By providing a centralized and consolidated view of programs and projects, the user can evaluate and prioritize activities across the organization. This feature makes it possible to maximize productivity, minimize costs, and keep activities aligned with strategic objectives.
- *Resource management*: Maximizing human resources is often the key to minimizing project costs. This feature enables the user to maximize resource use across the organization to help effectively plan and manage the workforce.
- *Project collaboration*: Sharing project information is often a haphazard endeavor. Project collaboration enables an organization to share knowledge immediately and consistently to improve communications and decision-making, eliminate redundancies, and take advantage of best practices for project management.

Communication is among the more important factors for success in project management. While technology can aid in the communications process and be the easiest aspect of the process to address, it is not the most important. Far more important is improving an organization's ability to communicate. Improving the ability to communicate often requires a cultural change in an organization that takes a lot of time, hard work, and patience. Information technology personnel, in particular, often need special coaching to improve their communications skills. The project manager's chief role in the communications process is that of facilitator. Project managers must educate all stakeholders—management, team members, and customers—on the importance of good project communications and ensure that the project has a communications management plan to help make good communication happen.

CASE WRAP-UP

Christine Braun worked closely with Peter Gumpert and his project managers to develop a communications management plan for all of the Fiber-optic Undersea Telecommunications projects. Peter was very skilled at running effective meetings, so everyone focused on meeting specific objectives. Peter stressed the importance of keeping himself, the project managers, and other major stakeholders informed about the status of all projects. He emphasized that the project managers were in charge of their projects, and that he did not intend to tell them how to do their jobs. He just wanted to have accurate and consistent information to help coordinate all of the projects and make everyone's jobs easier. When some of the project managers balked at the additional work of providing more project information in different formats, Peter openly discussed the issues with them in more detail. He then authorized each project manager to use additional staff to help develop and follow standards for all project communications.

Christine used her strong technical and communications skills to create a Web site that included samples of important project documents, presentations, and templates for other people to download and use on their own projects. After determining the need for more remote communications and collaboration between projects, Christine and other staff members researched the latest hardware and software products. Peter authorized funds for a new project led by Christine to evaluate and then purchase several wireless handheld devices and enterprise project management software with wiki capability that could be accessed via the Web. All managers and technical staff received their own devices, and any project stakeholder could check out one of these handheld devices and get one-on-one training on how to use it with the new Web-based software. Even Peter learned how to use one and doesn't know how he got along without it.

Chapter Summary

Failure to communicate is often the greatest threat to the success of any project, especially information technology projects. Communication is the oil that keeps a project running smoothly. Project communications management involves identifying stakeholders, planning communications, distributing information, managing stakeholder expectations, and reporting performance.

It is important to identify stakeholders and determine strategies for managing relationships with them in order to satisfy their needs and expectations. A stakeholder register and a stakeholder management strategy are key outputs of this process.

A communications management plan of some type should be created for all projects to help ensure good communications. Contents of this plan will vary based on the needs of the project.

The various methods for distributing project information include formal, informal, written, and verbal. It is important to determine the most appropriate means for distributing different types of project information. Project managers and their teams should focus on the importance of building relationships as they communicate project information. As the number of people that need to communicate increases, the number of communications channels also increases.

Reporting performance involves collecting and disseminating information about how well a project is moving toward meeting its goals. Project teams can use earned value charts and other forms of progress information to communicate and assess project performance. Status review meetings are an important part of communicating, monitoring, and controlling projects.

To improve project communications, project managers and their teams must develop good conflict management skills, as well as other communication skills. Conflict resolution is an important part of project communications management. The main causes of conflict during a project are schedules, priorities, staffing, technical opinions, procedures, cost, and personalities. A confrontational or problem-solving approach to managing conflict is often the best approach. Other suggestions for improving project communications include learning how to run more effective meetings, how to use e-mail, instant messaging, and collaborative software more effectively, and how to use templates for project communications.

New hardware and software continues to become available to help improve communications. As more people work remotely, it is important to make sure they have the necessary tools to be productive. Enterprise project management software provides many features to enhance communications across the organization.

Quick Quiz

1. What do many experts agree is the greatest threat to the success of any project?
   a. lack of proper funding
   b. a failure to communicate
   c. poor listening skills
   d. inadequate staffing

2. Which communication skill is most important for information technology professionals for career advancement?
   a. writing
   b. listening
   c. speaking
   d. using communication technologies
3. Which of the following is not a process in project communications management?
   a. information planning
   b. information distribution
   c. performance reporting
   d. managing stakeholders
4. What popular book illustrates the concept that people are not interchangeable parts and uses the analogy that you cannot take nine women and produce a baby in one month?
   a. Covey's *7 Habits of Highly Effective People*
   b. Goldratt's *Critical Chain*
   c. Gates's *Business @ the Speed of Thought*
   d. Brooks's *The Mythical Man-Month*
5. If you add three more people to a project team of five, how many more communications channels will you add?
   a. 2
   b. 12
   c. 15
   d. 18
6. A ________________ report describes where the project stands at a specific point in time.
   a. status
   b. performance
   c. forecast
   d. earned value
7. What tool can you use to help manage stakeholders by ranking scope, time, and cost goals in order of importance and provide guidelines on balancing these constraints?
   a. triple constraint matrix
   b. expectations matrix
   c. issue log
   d. priority log

8. You have two project stakeholders who do not get along at all. You know they both enjoy traveling, so you discuss great travel destinations when they are both in the room together to distract them from arguing with each other. What conflict-handling mode are you using?
   a. confrontation
   b. compromise
   c. smoothing
   d. withdrawal
9. Which of the following is not a guideline to help improve time spent at meetings?
   a. Determine if a meeting can be avoided.
   b. Invite extra people who support your project to make it run more smoothly.
   c. Define the purpose and intended outcome of the meeting.
   d. Build relationships.
10. A ________________ report is a reflective statement documenting important things that people learned from working on the project.
   a. final project
   b. lessons-learned
   c. project archive
   d. progress

Quick Quiz Answers

1. b; 2. c; 3. a; 4. d; 5. d; 6. a; 7. c; 8. c; 9. b; 10. b

Discussion Questions

1. Think of examples in the media that poke fun at the communications skills of technical professionals, such as Dilbert® cartoons. How does poking fun at technical professionals' communications skills influence the industry and educational programs?
2. Discuss the use of a stakeholder register and a stakeholder management strategy to assist in managing stakeholders.
3. What items should a communications management plan address? How can a stakeholder analysis assist in preparing and implementing parts of this plan?
4. Discuss the advantages and disadvantages of different ways of distributing project information.
5. What are some of the ways to create and distribute project performance information?
6. How can an expectations management matrix help a project manager in making important decisions?

7. Explain why you agree or disagree with some of the suggestions provided in this chapter for improving project communications, such as creating a communications management plan, stakeholder analysis, or performance reports, for example. What other suggestions do you have?
8. How can software assist in project communications? How can it hurt project communications?

Exercises

1. Create a stakeholder management strategy using Table 10-1 as a guide. Assume your organization has a project to determine employees' training needs and then provide in-house and external sources for courses in developing communications skills for employees. Stakeholders could be various levels and types of employees, suppliers, the Human Resources department in charge of the project, and so on. Determine at least five specific stakeholders for the project, and be creative in developing your potential management strategies
2. Create a stakeholder communications strategy using the information from Exercise 1. List at least one type of project communication for each stakeholder and the format for disseminating information to each. Use Table 10-2 as an example.
3. Review the following scenarios, and then write a paragraph for each one describing what media you think would be most appropriate to use and why. See Table 10-3 for suggestions.
   a. Many of the technical staff on the project come in from 9:30 a.m. to 10:00 a.m. while the business users always come in before 9:00 a.m. The business users have been making comments. The project manager wants to have the technical people come in by 9:00, although many of them leave late.
   b. Your company is bidding on a project for the entertainment industry. You know that you need new ideas on how to put together the proposal and communicate your approach in a way that will impress the customer.
   c. Your business has been growing successfully, but you are becoming inundated with phone calls and e-mails asking similar types of questions.
   d. You need to make a general announcement to a large group of people and want to make sure they get the information.
4. How many different communications channels does a project team with six people have? How many more communications channels would there be if the team grew to ten people?
5. Review the templates for various project documents provided in this chapter. Pick one of them and apply it to a project of your choice. Make suggestions for improving the template.
6. Write a lessons-learned report for a project of your choice using the template provided on the companion Web site and sample in Chapter 3 as guides. Do you think it is important for all project managers and team members to write lessons-learned reports? Would you take the time to read them if they were available in your organization? Why or why not?
7. Research new software products that assist in communications management for large projects. Write a two-page paper summarizing your findings. Include Web sites for software vendors and your opinion of some of the products.

Running Case

Several issues have arisen on the Recreation and Wellness Intranet Project. The person from the HR department supporting the project left the company, and the team really needs more support from that group. One of the members of the user group supporting the project is extremely vocal and hard to work with, and other users can hardly get a word in at meetings. The project manager, Tony, is getting weekly status reports from all of his team members, but many of them do not address challenges people are obviously facing. The team is having difficulties deciding how to communicate various project reports and documents and where to store all of the information being generated. Recall that the team members include you, a programmer/analyst and aspiring project manager; Patrick, a network specialist; Nancy, a business analyst; and Bonnie, another programmer/analyst.

1. Create a stakeholder management strategy for the project. Include at least four stakeholders. Be creative in developing potential management strategies.
2. Prepare a partial communications management plan to address some of the challenges mentioned in #1.
3. Prepare a template and sample of a good weekly progress report that could be used for this project. Include a list of tips to help team members provide information on these reports.
4. Write a one-page paper describing two suggested approaches to managing the conflict presented by the hard-to-work-with user.

Companion Web Site

Visit the companion Web site for this text (*www.cengage.com/mis/schwalbe*) to access:

- References cited in the text and additional suggested readings for each chapter
- Template files
- Lecture notes
- Interactive quizzes
- Podcasts
- Links to general project management Web sites
- And more

See the Preface of this text for additional information on accessing the companion Web site.

Key Terms

blogs — easy to use journals on the Web that allow users to write entries, create links, and upload pictures, while readers can post comments to journal entries

collaborating mode — a conflict-handling mode where decision makers incorporate different viewpoints and insights to develop consensus and commitment

communications management plan — a document that guides project communications

compromise mode — using a give-and-take approach to resolving conflicts; bargaining and searching for solutions that bring some degree of satisfaction to all the parties in a dispute

confrontation mode — directly facing a conflict using a problem-solving approach that allows affected parties to work through their disagreements

expectations management matrix — a tool to help understand unique measures of success for a particular project

forcing mode — using a win-lose approach to conflict resolution to get one's way

forecasts — used to predict future project status and progress based on past information and trends

Google Docs — online applications offered by Google that allow users to create, share, and edit documents, spreadsheets, and presentations online

groupthink — conformance to the values or ethical standards of a group

issue — a matter under question or dispute that could impede project success

issue log — a tool to document and monitor the resolution of project issues

lessons-learned report — reflective statements written by project managers and their team members to document important things they have learned from working on the project

progress reports — reports that describe what the project team has accomplished during a certain period of time

project archives — a complete set of organized project records that provide an accurate history of the project

SharePoint portal — allows users to create custom Web sites to access documents and applications stored on shared devices

smoothing mode — deemphasizing or avoiding areas of differences and emphasizing areas of agreements

stakeholder register — a public document that includes details related to the identified project stakeholders

stakeholder management strategy — an approach to help increase the support of stakeholders throughout the project

status reports — reports that describe where the project stands at a specific point in time

wiki — a Web site that has a page or pages designed to enable anyone who accesses it to contribute or modify content

withdrawal mode — retreating or withdrawing from an actual or potential disagreement

End Notes

1 Marcos P. Sivitanides, James R. Cook, Roy B. Martin, and Beverly A. Chiodo, "Verbal Communication Skills Requirements for Information Systems Professionals," *Journal of Information Systems Education* 7, no. 1 (Spring 1995), pp. 38–43.

2 Mark E. McMurtrey, James P. Downey, Steven M. Zeltmann, and William H. Friedman, "Critical Skill Sets of Entry-Level IT Professionals: An Empirical Examination of Perceptions from Field Personnel," *Journal of Information Technology Education* 7 (2008), p. 116.

3 *Reuters*, "Asia Quakes Damage Cables; Internet, Banks Affected," (December 27, 2006).

4 Ying Lou, "Initial repairs to quake-damaged cables pushed back by one week," *Bloomberg News* (December 31, 2006).

5 Albert Mehrabian, *Silent messages: Implicit communication of emotions and attitudes*, 2nd ed. (Belmont, CA: Wadsworth, 1981).

[6] Marion Walker, "E-mail is out at this office, at least on Fridays," *Minneapolis Star Tribune* (November 10, 2004).

[7] Kirkpatrick, David, "How one CEO Facebooked his company," *Fortune* (June 13, 2008).

[8] Ibid.

[9] "New Research Reveals Collaboration Is a Key Driver of Business Performance Around the World: Verizon Business, Microsoft sponsor international study; create first-of-its-kind collaboration index to measure impact of communications culture, technologies," *Microsoft PressPass* (June 5, 2006).

[10] Frederick P. Brooks, *The Mythical Man-Month*, 2nd ed. (Boston: Addison-Wesley, 1995).

[11] Carol Hildenbrand, "Loud and Clear," *CIO Magazine* (April 15, 1996).

[12] "Constructive Team Conflict" *Wharton Leadership Digest* 1, no. 6 (March 1997).

[13] Peter Saalfield, "Internet misuse costs businesses $178 billion annually," *IDG News Service* (July 19, 2005).

[14] Louisa Hearn, "Study probes web habits of office slackers," *Sydney Morning Herald* (January 17, 2006).

[15] Ibid.

[16] Nancy Gohring, "Over 50% of companies have fired workers for e-mail, Net abuse," *ComputerWorld Security* (February 28, 2008).

[17] John Petroske, "Promoting Project Communication Using Wikis," ProMAC 2008 Conference Proceedings (September 2008).

[18] Michael Cooney, "Telecommute. Kill a Career?" *Network World* (January 17, 2007).

CHAPTER 11

PROJECT RISK MANAGEMENT

LEARNING OBJECTIVES

After reading this chapter, you will be able to:

- Understand what risk is and the importance of good project risk management
- Discuss the elements involved in risk management planning and the contents of a risk management plan
- List common sources of risks on information technology projects
- Describe the process of identifying risks and be able to create a risk register
- Discuss the qualitative risk analysis process and explain how to calculate risk factors, create probability/impact matrixes, and apply the Top Ten Risk Item Tracking technique to rank risks
- Explain the quantitative risk analysis process and how to apply decision trees, simulation, and sensitivity analysis to quantify risks
- Provide examples of using different risk response planning strategies to address both negative and positive risks
- Discuss what is involved in monitoring and controlling risks
- Describe how software can assist in project risk management

OPENING CASE

Cliff Branch was the president of a small information technology consulting firm that specialized in developing Internet applications and providing full-service support. The staff consisted of programmers, business analysts, database specialists, Web designers, project managers, and so on. The firm had 50 full-time people and planned to hire at least ten more in the next year. It also planned to increase the number of part-time consultants they used. The company had done very well the past few years, but was recently having difficulty winning contracts. Spending time and resources to respond to various requests for proposals from prospective clients was becoming expensive. Many clients were starting to require presentations and even some prototype development before awarding a contract.

Cliff knew he had an aggressive approach to risk and liked to bid on the projects with the highest payoff. He did not use a systematic approach to evaluate the risks involved in various projects before bidding on them. He focused on the profit potentials and on how challenging the projects were. His strategy was now causing problems for the company because it was investing heavily in the preparation of proposals, yet winning few contracts. Several employees, who were not currently working on projects, were still on the payroll, and some of their part-time consultants were actively pursuing other opportunities since they were being underutilized. What could Cliff and his company do to get a better understanding of project risks? Should Cliff adjust his strategy for deciding what projects to pursue? How?

THE IMPORTANCE OF PROJECT RISK MANAGEMENT

Project risk management is the art and science of identifying, analyzing, and responding to risk throughout the life of a project and in the best interests of meeting project objectives. A frequently overlooked aspect of project management, risk management can often result in significant improvements in the ultimate success of projects. Risk management can have a positive impact on selecting projects, determining the scope of projects, and developing realistic schedules and cost estimates. It helps project stakeholders understand the nature of the project, involves team members in defining strengths and weaknesses, and helps to integrate the other project management knowledge areas.

Good project risk management often goes unnoticed, unlike crisis management. With crisis management, there is an obvious danger to the success of a project. The crisis, in turn, receives the intense interest of the entire project team. Resolving a crisis has much greater visibility, often accompanied by rewards from management, than successful risk management. In contrast, when risk management is effective, it results in fewer problems, and for the few problems that exist, it results in more expeditious resolutions. It may be difficult for outside observers to tell whether risk management or luck was responsible for the smooth development of a new system, but project teams will always know that their projects worked out better because of good risk management. Managing project risks takes dedicated, talented professionals. In response to this need, PMI introduced the PMI Risk Management Professional (PMI-RMP)^{SM} credential in 2008. (Consult PMI's Web site for further information.)

All industries, especially the software development industry, tend to underestimate the importance of project risk management. William Ibbs and Young H. Kwak performed a study to assess project management maturity. The 38 organizations participating in the study were divided into four industry groups: engineering and construction, telecommunications, information systems/software development, and high-tech manufacturing. Survey participants answered 148 multiple-choice questions to assess how mature their organization was in the project management knowledge areas of scope, time, cost, quality, human resources, communications, risk, and procurement. The rating scale ranged from 1 to 5, with 5 being the highest maturity rating. Table 11-1 shows the results of the survey. Notice that risk management was the only knowledge area for which all ratings were less than 3. This study shows that all organizations should put more effort into project risk management, especially the information systems/software development industry, which had the lowest rating of 2.75 (emphasized in bold in Table 11-1).[1]

TABLE 11-1 Project management maturity by industry group and knowledge area

KEY: 1 = Lowest Maturity Rating			5 = Highest Maturity Rating	
Knowledge Area	Engineering/ Construction	Tele-communications	Information Systems	Hi-Tech Manufacturing
Scope	3.52	3.45	3.25	3.37
Time	3.55	3.41	3.03	3.50
Cost	3.74	3.22	3.20	3.97
Quality	2.91	3.22	2.88	3.26
Human resources	3.18	3.20	2.93	3.18
Communications	3.53	3.53	3.21	3.48
Risk	**2.93**	**2.87**	**2.75**	**2.76**
Procurement	3.33	3.01	2.91	3.33

A similar survey was completed with software development companies in Mauritius, South Africa in 2003. The average maturity rating was only 2.29 for all knowledge areas, on a scale of 1-5, with 5 being the highest maturity rating. The lowest maturity rating in this study was also in the area of project risk management, with an average maturity rating of only 1.84. Cost management had the highest maturity rating of 2.5, and the authors of the survey noted that organizations in the study were often concerned with cost overruns and had metrics in place to help control costs. The authors also found that maturity rating was closely linked to the success rate of projects, and they noted the fact that the poor rating for risk management was a likely cause of project problems/failures.[2]

KLCI Research Group surveyed 260 software organizations worldwide in 2001 to study software risk management practices. Below are some of their findings:

- 97 percent of the participants said they had procedures in place to identify and assess risk.
- 80 percent identified anticipating and avoiding problems as the primary benefit of risk management.
- 70 percent of the organizations had defined software development processes.
- 64 percent had a Project Management Office.

Figure 11-1 shows the main benefits from software risk management practices cited by survey respondents. In addition to anticipating/avoiding problems, risk management practices helped software project managers prevent surprises, improve negotiations, meet customer commitments, and reduce schedule slips and cost overruns.[3]

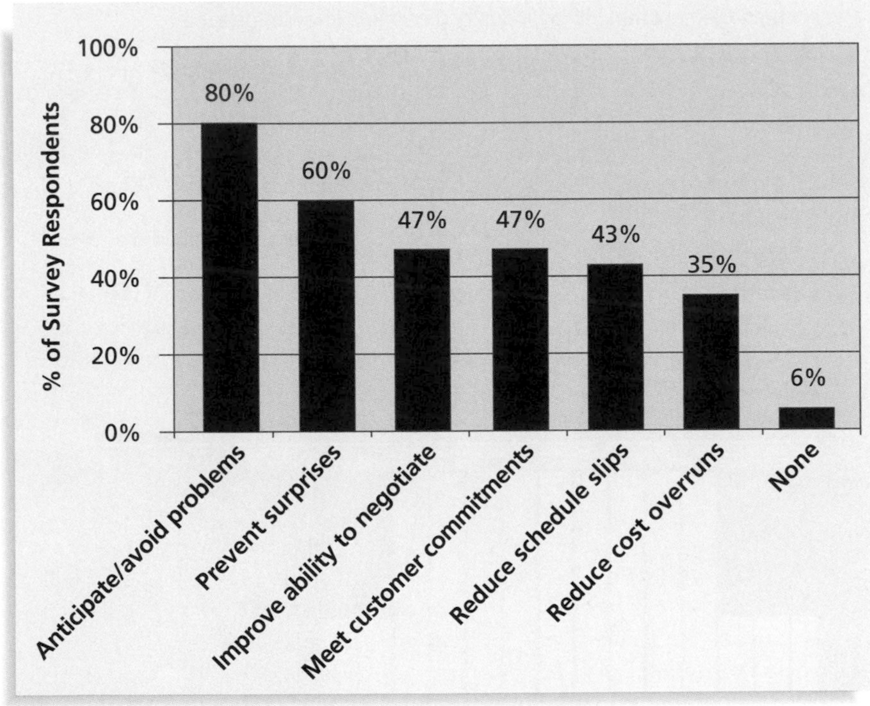

FIGURE 11-1 Benefits from software risk management practices

Although many organizations know that they do not do a good job of managing project risk, little progress seems to have been made in improving risk management on a project level or an enterprise level. Several books and articles have been written on the topic in recent years. For example, Dr David Hilson, PMP, wrote an article about the importance of project risk management shortly after the stock market declines in the fall of 2008. Hillson says,

> "There is no doubt that all sectors of industry and society are facing real challenges in coping with the current fallout from the credit crunch. But risk management should not be regarded as a nonessential cost to be cut in these difficult times. Instead, organisations should use the insights offered by the risk process to ensure that they can handle the inevitable uncertainties and emerge in the best possible position in [the] future. With high levels of volatility surrounding us on all sides, risk management is more needed now than ever, and cutting it would be a false economy. Rather than treating risk management as part of the problem, we should see it as a major part of the solution."[4]

MEDIA SNAPSHOT

Many people around the world suffered from financial losses as various financial markets dropped in the fall of 2008, even after the $700 billion bailout bill was passed by the U.S. Congress. According to a global survey of 316 financial services executives conducted in July 2008, over 70 percent of respondents believed that the losses stemming from the credit crisis were largely due to failures to address risk management issues. They identified several challenges in implementing risk management, including data and company culture issues. For example, access to relevant, timely and consistent data continues to be a major obstacle in many organizations. Many respondents also said that fostering a culture of risk management was a major challenge.

Executives and lawmakers finally started paying attention to risk management. Fifty-nine percent of survey respondents said the credit crisis prompted them to scrutinize their risk management practices in greater detail, and many institutions are revisiting their risk management practices. The Financial Stability Forum (FSF) and the Institute for International Finance (IIF) are now calling for closer scrutiny of the risk management process.

Rodney Nelsestuen, an analyst for TowerGroup, agrees. "Enterprise risk management has taken on new importance as stockholders, boards of directors and regulators demand better, more timely analysis of risk and a deeper understanding of how the institution is impacted by the dynamic risk environment of a global financial community."[5]

Before you can improve project risk management, you must understand what risk is. A basic dictionary definition says that risk is "the possibility of loss or injury." This definition highlights the negativity often associated with risk and suggests that uncertainty is involved. Project risk management involves understanding potential problems that might occur on the project and how they might impede project success. The *PMBOK® Guide, Fourth Edition* refers to this type of risk as a negative risk or threat. However, there are also positive risks or opportunities, which can result in good things happening on a project. A general definition of a project **risk**, therefore, is an uncertainty that can have a negative or positive effect on meeting project objectives.

In many respects, negative risk management is like a form of insurance. It is an activity undertaken to lessen the impact of potentially adverse events on a project. Positive risk management is like investing in opportunities. It is important to note that risk management *is* an investment—there are costs associated with it. The investment an organization is willing to make in risk management activities depends on the nature of the project, the experience of the project team, and the constraints imposed on both. In any case, the cost for risk management should not exceed the potential benefits.

If there is so much risk in information technology projects, why do organizations pursue them? Many companies are in business today because they took risks that created great opportunities. Organizations survive over the long term when they pursue opportunities. Information technology is often a key part of a business's strategy; without it, many businesses might not survive. Given that all projects involve uncertainties that can have negative or positive outcomes, the question is how to decide which projects to pursue and how to identify and manage project risk throughout a project's life cycle.

BEST PRACTICE

Some organizations make the mistake of only addressing tactical and negative risks when performing project risk management. David Hillson (*www.risk-doctor.com*) suggests overcoming this problem by widening the scope of risk management to encompass both *strategic risks* and *upside opportunities*, which he refers to as integrated risk management. Benefits of this approach include:

- Bridging the strategy and tactics gap to ensure that project delivery is tied to organizational needs and vision
- Focusing projects on the benefits they exist to support, rather than producing a set of deliverables
- Managing opportunities proactively as an integral part of business processes at both strategic and tactical levels
- Providing useful information to decision-makers at all levels when the environment is uncertain
- Allowing an appropriate level of risk to be taken intelligently with full awareness of the degree of uncertainty and its potential effects on objectives.[6]

Several risk experts suggest that organizations and individuals strive to find a balance between risks and opportunities in all aspects of projects and their personal lives. The idea of striving to balance risks and opportunities suggests that different organizations and people have different tolerances for risk. Some organizations or people have a neutral tolerance for risk, some have an aversion to risk, and others are risk-seeking. These three preferences for risk are part of the utility theory of risk.

Risk utility or **risk tolerance** is the amount of satisfaction or pleasure received from a potential payoff. Figure 11-2 shows the basic difference between risk-averse, risk-neutral, and risk-seeking preferences. The y-axis represents utility, or the amount of pleasure received from taking a risk. The x-axis shows the amount of potential payoff, opportunity, or dollar value of the opportunity at stake. Utility rises at a decreasing rate for a **risk-averse** person. In other words, when more payoff or money is at stake, a person or organization that is risk-averse gains less satisfaction from the risk, or has lower tolerance for the risk. Those who are **risk-seeking** have a higher tolerance for risk, and their satisfaction increases when more payoff is at stake. A risk-seeking person prefers outcomes that are more uncertain and is often willing to pay a penalty to take risks. A **risk-neutral** person achieves a balance between risk and payoff.

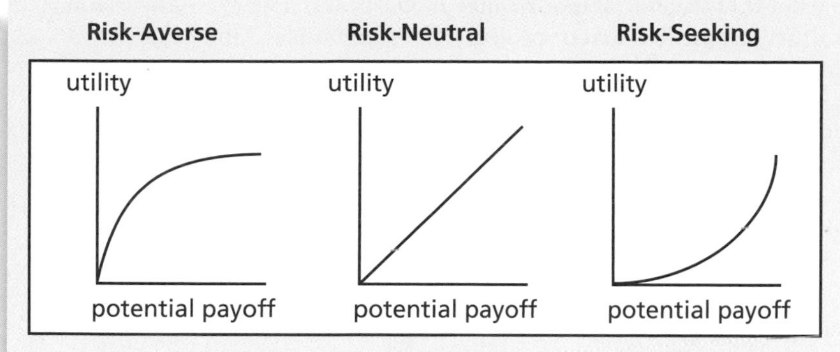

FIGURE 11-2 Risk utility function and risk preference

The goal of project risk management can be viewed as minimizing potential negative risks while maximizing potential positive risks. The term **known risks** is sometimes used to describe risks that the project team have identified and analyzed. Known risks can be managed proactively. However, **unknown risks**, or risks that have not been identified and analyzed, cannot be managed. As you can imagine, good project managers know it is good practice to take the time to identify and manage project risks. There are six major processes involved in risk management:

1. *Planning risk management* involves deciding how to approach and plan the risk management activities for the project. By reviewing the project scope statement; cost, schedule, and communications management plans; enterprise environmental factors; and organizational process assets, project teams can discuss and analyze risk management activities for their particular projects. The main output of this process is a risk management plan.
2. *Identifying risks* involves determining which risks are likely to affect a project and documenting the characteristics of each. The main output of this process is the start of a risk register, as described in more detail later in this chapter.
3. *Performing qualitative risk analysis* involves prioritizing risks based on their probability and impact of occurrence. After identifying risks, project teams can use various tools and techniques to rank risks and update information in the risk register. The main output is risk register updates.
4. *Performing quantitative risk analysis* involves numerically estimating the effects of risks on project objectives. The main output of this process is also risk register updates.
5. *Planning risk responses* involves taking steps to enhance opportunities and reduce threats to meeting project objectives. Using outputs from the preceding risk management processes, project teams can develop risk response strategies that often result in updates to the risk register, project management plan, and other project documents as well as risk-related contract decisions.
6. *Monitoring and controlling risk* involves monitoring identified and residual risks, identifying new risks, carrying out risk response plans, and evaluating the effectiveness of risk strategies throughout the life of the project. The main

outputs of this process include change requests and updates to the risk register, organizational process assets, project management plan, and project documents.

Figure 11-3 summarizes these processes and outputs, showing when they occur in a typical project.

Planning
Process: **Plan risk management**
Output: Risk management plan
Process: **Identify risks**
Output: Risk register
Process: **Perform qualitative risk analysis**
Output: Risk register updates
Process: **Perform quantitative risk analysis**
Output: Risk register updates
Process: **Plan risk responses**
Outputs: Risk register updates, risk-related contract decisions, project management plan updates, project document updates

Monitoring and Controlling
Process: **Monitor and control risks**
Outputs: Risk register updates, organizational process assets updates, change requests, project management plan updates, project document updates

Project Start **Project Finish**

FIGURE 11-3 Project risk management summary

The first step in project risk management is deciding how to address this knowledge area for a particular project by performing risk management planning.

PLANNING RISK MANAGEMENT

Planning risk management is the process of deciding how to approach and plan for risk management activities for a project, and the main output of this process is a risk management plan. A **risk management plan** documents the procedures for managing risk throughout the project. Project teams should hold several planning meetings early in the project's life cycle to help develop the risk management plan. The project team should review project documents as well as corporate risk management policies, risk categories, lessons-learned reports from past projects, and templates for creating a risk management plan. It is also important to review the risk tolerances of various stakeholders. For example, if the project sponsor is risk-averse, the project might require a different approach to risk management than if the project sponsor were a risk seeker.

A risk management plan summarizes how risk management will be performed on a particular project. Like other specific knowledge area plans, it becomes a subset of the project management plan. Table 11-2 lists the general topics that a risk management plan should address. It is important to clarify roles and responsibilities, prepare budget and schedule estimates for risk-related work, and identify risk categories for consideration. It is also important to describe how risk management will be done, including assessment of risk probabilities and impacts as well as the creation of risk related documentation. The level of detail included in the risk management plan can vary with the needs of the project.

TABLE 11-2 Topics addressed in a risk management plan

Topic	Questions to Answer
Methodology	How will risk management be performed on this project? What tools and data sources are available and applicable?
Roles and responsibilities	Who are the individuals responsible for implementing specific tasks and providing deliverables related to risk management?
Budget and schedule	What are the estimated costs and schedules for performing risk-related activities?
Risk categories	What are the main categories of risks that should be addressed on this project? Is there a risk breakdown structure for the project? (See the information on risk breakdown structures later in this section.)
Risk probability and impact	How will the probabilities and impacts of risk items be assessed? What scoring and interpretation methods will be used for the qualitative and quantitative analysis of risks? How will the probability and impact matrix be developed?
Revised stakeholders' tolerances	Have stakeholders' tolerances for risk changed? How will those changes affect the project?
Tracking	How will the team track risk management activities? How will lessons learned be documented and shared? How will risk management processes be audited?
Risk documentation	What reporting formats and processes will be used for risk management activities?

In addition to a risk management plan, many projects also include contingency plans, fallback plans, and contingency reserves.

- **Contingency plans** are predefined actions that the project team will take if an identified risk event occurs. For example, if the project team knows that a new release of a software package may not be available in time for them to use it for their project, they might have a contingency plan to use the existing, older version of the software.
- **Fallback plans** are developed for risks that have a high impact on meeting project objectives, and are put into effect if attempts to reduce the risk are not effective. For example, a new college graduate might have a main plan and

several contingency plans on where to live after graduation, but if none of those plans works out, a fallback plan might be to live at home for a while. Sometimes the terms contingency plan and fallback plan are used interchangeably.

- **Contingency reserves** or **contingency allowances** are provisions held by the project sponsor or organization to reduce the risk of cost or schedule overruns to an acceptable level. For example, if a project appears to be off course because the staff is inexperienced with some new technology and the team had not identified that as a risk, the project sponsor may provide additional funds from contingency reserves to hire an outside consultant to train and advise the project staff in using the new technology.

Before you can really understand and use the other project risk management processes on information technology projects, it is necessary to recognize and understand the common sources of risk.

COMMON SOURCES OF RISK ON INFORMATION TECHNOLOGY PROJECTS

Several studies have shown that information technology projects share some common sources of risk. For example, the Standish Group did a follow-up study to the CHAOS research, which they called Unfinished Voyages. This study brought together 60 information technology professionals to elaborate on how to evaluate a project's overall likelihood of being successful. Table 11-3 shows the Standish Group's success potential scoring sheet and the relative importance of the project success criteria factors. If a potential project does not

TABLE 11-3 Information technology success potential scoring sheet

Success Criterion	Relative Importance
User involvement	19
Executive management support	16
Clear statement of requirements	15
Proper planning	11
Realistic expectations	10
Smaller project milestones	9
Competent staff	8
Ownership	6
Clear visions and objectives	3
Hardworking, focused staff	3
Total	**100**

receive a minimum score, the organization might decide not to work on it or to take actions to reduce the risks before it invests too much time or money.[7]

The Standish Group provides specific questions for each success criterion to help decide the number of points to assign to a project. For example, the five questions related to user involvement include the following:

- Do I have the right user(s)?
- Did I involve the user(s) early and often?
- Do I have a quality relationship with the user(s)?
- Do I make involvement easy?
- Did I find out what the user(s) need(s)?

The number of questions corresponding to each success criterion determines the number of points each positive response is assigned. For example, in the case of user involvement there are five questions. For each positive reply, you would get 3.8 (19/5) points; 19 represents the weight of the criterion, and 5 represents the number of questions. Therefore, you would assign a value to the user involvement criterion by adding 3.8 points to the score for each question you can answer positively.

Many organizations develop their own risk questionnaires. Broad categories of risks described on these questionnaires might include:

- *Market risk*: If the information technology project is to produce a new product or service, will it be useful to the organization or marketable to others? Will users accept and use the product or service? Will someone else create a better product or service faster, making the project a waste of time and money?
- *Financial risk*: Can the organization afford to undertake the project? How confident are stakeholders in the financial projections? Will the project meet NPV, ROI, and payback estimates? If not, can the organization afford to continue the project? Is this project the best way to use the organization's financial resources?
- *Technology risk*: Is the project technically feasible? Will it use mature, leading edge, or bleeding edge technologies? When will decisions be made on which technology to use? Will hardware, software, and networks function properly? Will the technology be available in time to meet project objectives? Could the technology be obsolete before a useful product can be produced? You can also break down the technology risk category into hardware, software, and network technology, if desired.
- *People risk*: Does the organization have or can they find people with appropriate skills to complete the project successfully? Do people have the proper managerial and technical skills? Do they have enough experience? Does senior management support the project? Is there a project champion? Is the organization familiar with the sponsor/customer for the project? How good is the relationship with the sponsor/customer?
- *Structure/process risk*: What is the degree of change the new project will introduce into user areas and business procedures? How many distinct user groups does the project need to satisfy? With how many other systems does the new project/system need to interact? Does the organization have processes in place to complete the project successfully?

WHAT WENT WRONG?

KPMG, a large consulting firm, published a study in 1995 that found that 55 percent of **runaway projects** (i.e., projects with significant cost or schedule overruns) did *no* risk management at all, that 38 percent did some (but half did not use their risk findings after the project was underway), and that 7 percent did not know whether they did risk management or not.[8] This study suggests that performing risk management is important to improving the likelihood of project success and preventing runaway projects.

The timing of risk management is also an important consideration. For example, Cincinnati, Ohio–based Comair is a regional airline that operates in 117 cities and carries about 30,000 passengers on 1,130 flights a day. Comair's IT managers knew in the late 1990s that they had to address the replacement of an aging legacy system used to manage flight crews. The application was one of the oldest in the company (11 years old at the time), written in Fortran (code that no one at Comair was fluent in) and the only system left that ran on the airline's old IBM AIX platform. Although managers and crew addressed possible options for replacing the system, they kept putting it off as other priorities emerged. A replacement system was finally approved in 2004, but the switch didn't happen soon enough. "Over the holidays, the legacy system failed, bringing down the entire airline, canceling or delaying 3,900 flights, and stranding nearly 200,000 passengers. The network crash cost Comair and its parent company, Delta Air Lines, $20 million, damaged the airline's reputation and prompted an investigation by the Department of Transportation." Had Comair or Delta acted sooner, they could have taken steps to mitigate that risk to avoid the disaster.[9]

Reviewing a proposed project in terms of the Standish Group's success criteria, a risk questionnaire, or any other similar tool is a good method for understanding common sources of risk on information technology projects. It is also useful to review the work breakdown structure (WBS) for a project to see if there might be specific risks by WBS categories. For example, if one item on the WBS involves preparing a press release and no one on the project team has ever done that, it could be a negative risk if it is not handled professionally.

A risk breakdown structure is a useful tool to help project managers consider potential risks in different categories. Similar in structure to a work breakdown structure, a **risk breakdown structure** is a hierarchy of potential risk categories for a project. Figure 11-4 shows a sample risk breakdown structure that might apply to many information technology projects. The highest-level categories are business, technical, organizational, and project management. Competitors, suppliers, and cash flow are categories that fall under business risks. Under technical risks are the categories of hardware, software, and network. Notice how the risk breakdown structure provides a simple, one-page chart to help ensure a project team is considering important risk categories related to all information technology projects. For example, Cliff and his managers in the opening case could have benefited from considering several of the categories listed under project management—estimates, communication, and resources. They could have discussed these and other types of risks related to the projects their company bid on and developed appropriate strategies for optimizing positive risks and minimizing negative ones.

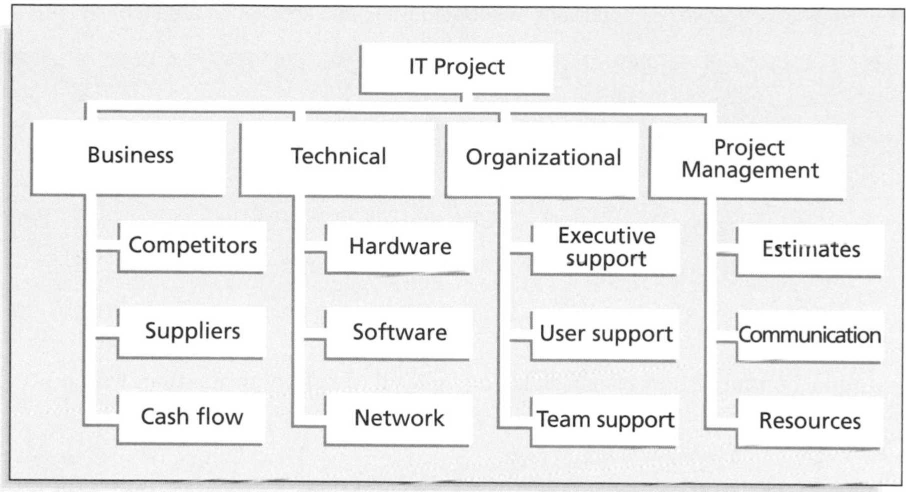

FIGURE 11-4 Sample risk breakdown structure

In addition to identifying risk based on the nature of the project or products produced, it is also important to identify potential risks according to project management knowledge areas, such as scope, time, cost, and quality. Notice that one of the major categories in the risk breakdown structure in Figure 11-4 is project management. Table 11-4 lists potential negative risk conditions that can exist within each knowledge area.[10]

TABLE 11-4 Potential negative risk conditions associated with each knowledge area

Knowledge Area	Risk Conditions
Integration	Inadequate planning; poor resource allocation; poor integration management; lack of post-project review
Scope	Poor definition of scope or work packages; incomplete definition
Time	Errors in estimating time or resource availability; errors in determining the critical path; poor allocation and management of float; early release of competitive products
Cost	Estimating errors; inadequate productivity, cost, change, or contingency
Quality	Poor attitude toward quality; substandard design/materials/workmanship; inadequate quality assurance program
Human resource	Poor conflict management; poor project organization and definition of responsibilities; absence of leadership

TABLE 11-4 Potential negative risk conditions associated with each knowledge area (continued)

Knowledge Area	Risk Conditions
Communications	Carelessness in planning or communicating; lack of consultation with key stakeholders
Risk	Ignoring risk; unclear analysis of risk; poor insurance management
Procurement	Unenforceable conditions or contract clauses; adversarial relations

Understanding common sources of risk is very helpful in risk identification, which is the next step in project risk management.

IDENTIFYING RISKS

Identifying risks is the process of understanding what potential events might hurt or enhance a particular project. It is important to identify potential risks early, but you must also continue to identify risks based on the changing project environment. Also remember that you cannot manage risks if you do not first identify them. By understanding common sources of risks and reviewing a project's planning documents (for risk, cost, schedule, and quality management), activity cost and duration estimates, the scope baseline, stakeholder register, other project documents, enterprise environmental factors, and organizational process assets, project managers and their teams can identify many potential risks.

Suggestions for Identifying Risks

There are several tools and techniques for identifying risks. Project teams often begin the risk identification process by reviewing project documentation, recent and historical information related to the organization, and assumptions that might affect the project. Project team members and outside experts often hold meetings to discuss this information and ask important questions about them as they relate to risk. After identifying potential risks at this initial meeting, the project team might then use different information-gathering techniques to further identify risks. Five common information-gathering techniques include brainstorming, the Delphi technique, interviewing, root cause analysis, and SWOT analysis.

Brainstorming is a technique by which a group attempts to generate ideas or find a solution for a specific problem by amassing ideas spontaneously and without judgment. This approach can help the group create a comprehensive list of risks to address later in the qualitative and quantitative risk analysis processes. An experienced facilitator should run the brainstorming session and introduce new categories of potential risks to keep the ideas flowing. After the ideas are collected, the facilitator can group and categorize the ideas to make them more manageable. Care must be taken, however, not to overuse or misuse brainstorming. Although businesses use brainstorming widely to generate new ideas, the psychology literature shows that individuals, working alone, produce a greater number of ideas than the same individuals produce through brainstorming in small, face-to-face groups. Group effects, such as fear of social disapproval, the effects of authority hierarchy, and domination of the session by one or two very vocal people often inhibit idea generation for many participants.[11]

An approach to gathering information that helps prevent some of the negative group affects found in brainstorming is the Delphi technique. The basic concept of the **Delphi technique** is to derive a consensus among a panel of experts who make predictions about future developments. Developed by the Rand Corporation for the U.S. Air Force in the late 1960s, the Delphi technique is a systematic, interactive forecasting procedure based on independent and *anonymous* input regarding future events. The Delphi technique uses repeated rounds of questioning and written responses, including feedback to earlier-round responses, to take advantage of group input, while avoiding the biasing effects possible in oral panel deliberations. To use the Delphi technique, you must select a panel of experts for the particular area in question. For example, Cliff Branch from the opening case could use the Delphi technique to help him understand why his company is no longer winning many contracts. Cliff could assemble a panel of people with knowledge in his business area. Each expert would answer questions related to Cliff's scenario, and then Cliff or a facilitator would evaluate their responses, together with opinions and justifications, and provide that feedback to each expert in the next iteration. Cliff would continue this process until the group responses converge to a specific solution. If the responses diverge, the facilitator of the Delphi technique needs to determine if there is a problem with the process.

Interviewing is a fact-finding technique for collecting information in face-to-face, phone, e-mail, or instant-messaging discussions. Interviewing people with similar project experience is an important tool for identifying potential risks. For example, if a new project involves using a particular type of hardware or software, someone with recent experience with that hardware or software could describe problems he or she had on a past project. If someone has worked with a particular customer, he or she might provide insight into potential risks involved in working for that group again. It is important to be well-prepared for leading interviews; it often helps to create a list of questions to use as a guide during the interview.

It is not uncommon for people to identify problems or opportunities without really understanding them. Before suggesting courses of action, it is important to identify the root cause of a problem or opportunity. Root cause analysis (discussed earlier in Chapter 8, Project Quality Management) often results in identifying even more potential risks for a project.

Another technique (described in Chapter 4, Project Integration Management) is a SWOT analysis of strengths, weaknesses, opportunities, and threats, which is often used in strategic planning. SWOT analysis can also be used during risk identification by having project teams focus on the broad perspectives of potential risks for particular projects. For example, before writing a particular proposal, Cliff Branch could have a group of his employees discuss in detail what their company's strengths are, what their weaknesses are related to that project, and what opportunities and threats exist. Do they know that several competing firms are much more likely to win a certain contract? Do they know that winning a particular contract will likely lead to future contracts and help expand their business? Applying SWOT to specific potential projects can help identify the broad risks and opportunities that apply in that scenario.

Three other techniques for risk identification include the use of checklists, analysis of assumptions, and creation of diagrams:

- Checklists, based on risks that have been encountered in previous projects, provide a meaningful template for understanding risks in a current project. You can use checklists similar to those developed by the Standish Group and other IT research consultants to help identify risks on information technology projects.
- It is important to analyze project assumptions to make sure they are valid. Incomplete, inaccurate, or inconsistent assumptions might lead to identifying more risks.
- Diagramming techniques include using cause-and-effect diagrams or fishbone diagrams, flow charts, and influence diagrams. Recall from Chapter 8, Project Quality Management, that fishbone diagrams help you trace problems back to their root cause. System or process **flowcharts** are diagrams that show how different parts of a system interrelate. For example, many programmers create flowcharts to show programming logic. (A sample flowchart is provided in Chapter 8.) Another type of diagram, an **influence diagram**, represents decision problems by displaying essential elements, including decisions, uncertainties, causality, and objectives, and how they influence each other. (See other references, such as *www.lumina.com/software/influencediagrams.html*, for detailed information on influence diagrams.)

The Risk Register

The main output of the risk identification process is a list of identified risks and other information needed to begin creating a risk register. A **risk register** is a document that contains results of various risk management processes, often displayed in a table or spreadsheet format. It is a tool for documenting potential risk events and related information. **Risk events** refer to specific, uncertain events that may occur to the detriment or enhancement of the project. For example, negative risk events might include the performance failure of a product produced as part of a project, delays in completing work as scheduled, increases in estimated costs, supply shortages, litigation against the company, strikes, and so on. Examples of positive risk events include completing work sooner or cheaper than planned, collaborating with suppliers to produce better products, good publicity resulting from the project, and so on.

Table 11-5 provides a sample of the format for a risk register that Cliff and his managers from the opening case might use on a new project. Actual data that might be entered for one of the risks is included below the table. Notice the main headings often included in the register. Many of these items are described in more detail later in this chapter.

- *An identification number for each risk event*: The project team may want to sort or quickly search for specific risk events, so they need to identify each risk with some type of unique descriptor, such as an identification number.
- *A rank for each risk event*: The rank is usually a number, with 1 being the highest ranked risk.
- *The name of the risk event*: For example, defective server, late completion of testing, reduced consulting costs, or good publicity.
- *A description of the risk event*: Because the name of a risk event is often abbreviated, it helps to provide a more detailed description. For example, reduced

consulting costs might be expanded in the description to say that the organization might be able to negotiate lower-than-average costs for a particular consultant because the consultant really enjoys working for that company in that particular location.

- *The category under which the risk event falls*: For example, defective server might fall under the broader category of technology or hardware technology.
- *The root cause of the risk*: The root cause of the defective server might be a defective power supply.
- *Triggers for each risk*: **Triggers** are indicators or symptoms of actual risk events. For example, cost overruns on early activities may be symptoms of poor cost estimates. Defective products may be symptoms of a low-quality supplier. Documenting potential risk symptoms for projects also helps the project team identify more potential risk events.
- *Potential responses to each risk*: A potential response to the risk event of a defective server might be the inclusion of a clause in a contract with the supplier to replace a defective server within a certain time period at a negotiated cost.
- *The* **risk owner** *or person who will own or take responsibility for the risk*: For example, a certain person might be in charge of any server-related risk events and managing response strategies.
- *The probability of the risk occurring*: There might be a high, medium, or low probability of a certain risk event occurring. For example, the risk might be low that the server would actually be defective.
- *The impact to the project if the risk occurs*: There might be a high, medium, or low impact to project success if the risk event actually occurs. A defective server might have a high impact on successfully completing a project on time.
- *The status of the risk*: Did the risk event occur? Was the response strategy completed? Is the risk no longer relevant to the project? For example, a contract clause may have been completed to address the risk of a defective server.

TABLE 11-5 Sample risk register

No.	Rank	Risk	Description	Category	Root Cause	Triggers	Potential Responses	Risk Owner	Probability	Impact	Status
R44	1										
R21	2										
R7	3										

For example, the following data might be entered for the first risk in the register as follows. Notice that Cliff's team is taking a very proactive approach in managing this risk.

- *No.*: R44
- *Rank*: 1
- *Risk*: New customer
- *Description*: We have never done a project for this organization before and don't know too much about them. One of our company's strengths is building

good customer relationships, which often leads to further projects with that customer. We might have trouble working with this customer since they are new to us.

- *Category*: People risk
- *Root cause*: We won a contract to work on a project without really getting to know the customer.
- *Triggers*: The project manager and other senior managers realize that we don't know much about this customer and could easily misunderstand their needs or expectations.
- *Risk responses*: Make sure the project manager is sensitive to the fact that this is a new customer and takes the time to understand them. Have the PM set up a meeting to get to know the customer and clarify their expectations. Have Cliff attend the meeting, too.
- *Risk owner*: Our project manager
- *Probability*: Medium
- *Impact*: High
- *Status*: PM will set up the meeting within the week.

After identifying risks, the next step is to understand which risks are most important by performing qualitative risk analysis.

PERFORMING QUALITATIVE RISK ANALYSIS

Qualitative risk analysis involves assessing the likelihood and impact of identified risks, to determine their magnitude and priority. This section describes examples of using a probability/impact matrix to produce a prioritized list of risks. It also provides examples of using the Top Ten Risk Item Tracking technique to produce an overall ranking for project risks and to track trends in qualitative risk analysis. Finally, it discusses the importance of expert judgment in performing risk analysis.

Using Probability/Impact Matrixes to Calculate Risk Factors

People often describe a risk probability or consequence as being high, medium or moderate, or low. For example, a meteorologist might predict that there is a high probability, or likelihood, of severe rain showers on a certain day. If that day happens to be your wedding day and you are planning a large outdoor wedding, the consequences or impact of severe showers might also be high.

A project manager can chart the probability and impact of risks on a **probability/impact matrix or chart**. A probability/impact matrix or chart lists the relative probability of a risk occurring on one side of a matrix or axis on a chart and the relative impact of the risk occurring on the other. Many project teams would benefit from using this simple technique to help them identify risks that they need to pay attention to. To use this approach, project stakeholders list the risks they think might occur on their projects. They then label each risk as being high, medium, or low in terms of its probability of occurrence and its impact if it did occur.

The project manager then summarizes the results in a probability/impact matrix or chart, as shown in Figure 11-5. For example, Cliff Branch and some of his project managers in the opening case could each identify three negative and positive potential risks for a particular project. They could then label each risk as being high, medium, or low in terms of probability and impact. For example, one project manager might list a severe market downturn as a negative risk that's low in probability but high in impact. Cliff may have listed the same risk as being medium in both probability and impact. The team could then plot all of the risks on a matrix or chart, combine any common risks, and decide where those risks should be on the matrix or chart. The team should then focus on any risks that fall in the high sections of the probability/impact matrix or chart. For example, Risks 1 and 4 are listed as high in both categories of probability and impact. Risk 6 is high in the probability category but low in the impact category. Risk 9 is high in the probability category and medium in the impact category, and so on. The team should then discuss how they plan to respond to those risks if they occur, as discussed later in this chapter in the section on risk response planning.

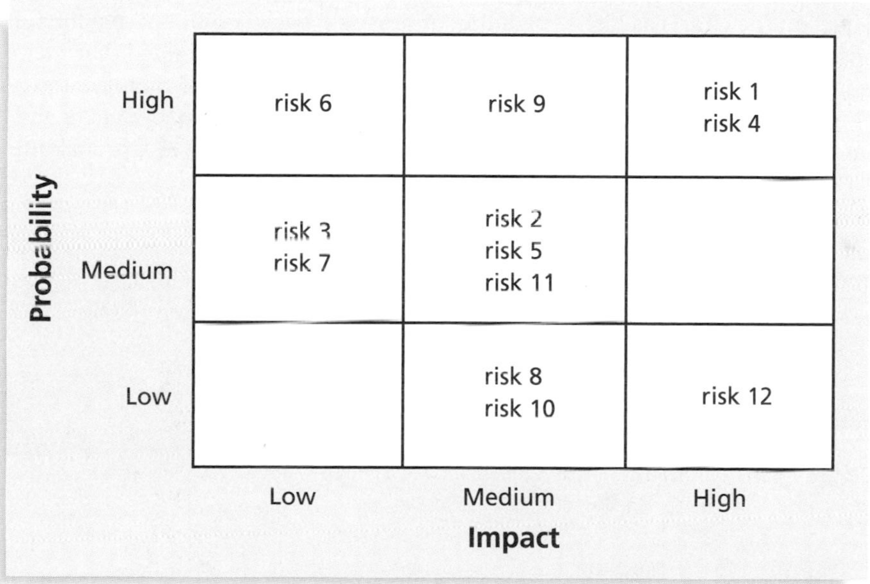

Probability	Low	Medium	High
High	risk 6	risk 9	risk 1 risk 4
Medium	risk 3 risk 7	risk 2 risk 5 risk 11	
Low		risk 8 risk 10	risk 12
	Impact		

FIGURE 11-5 Sample probability/impact matrix

It may be useful to create a separate probability/impact matrix or chart for negative risks and positive risks to make sure both types of risks are adequately addressed. Some project teams also collect data based on the probability and impact of risks in terms of negatively or positively affecting scope, time, and cost goals. Qualitative risk analysis is normally done quickly, so the project team has to decide what type of approach makes the most sense for their project.

Some project teams develop a single number for a risk score by simply multiplying a numeric score for probability by a numeric score for impact. A more sophisticated approach to using probability/impact information is to calculate risk factors. To quantify risk probability and consequence, the U.S. Defense Systems Management College (DSMC) developed a technique for calculating **risk factors**—numbers that represent the overall risk of specific events, based on their probability of occurring and the consequences to the project if they do occur. The technique makes use of a probability/impact matrix that shows the probability of risks occurring and the impact or consequences of the risks.

Probabilities of a risk occurring can be estimated based on several factors, as determined by the unique nature of each project. For example, factors evaluated for potential hardware or software technology risks could include the technology not being mature, the technology being too complex, and an inadequate support base for developing the technology. The impact of a risk occurring could include factors such as the availability of fallback solutions or the consequences of not meeting performance, cost, and schedule estimates.

Figure 11-6 provides an example of how risk factors were used to graph the probability of failure, and consequence of failure, for proposed technologies in a research study on which the author worked to design more reliable aircraft. The figure classifies potential technologies (dots on the chart) as high-, medium-, or low-risk, based on the probability of failure and consequences of failure. The study researchers highly recommended that the U.S. Air Force invest in the low- to medium-risk technologies and suggested that it not pursue the high-risk technologies.[12] The rigor behind using the probability/impact matrix and risk factors can provide a much stronger argument than simply stating that risk probabilities or consequences are high, medium, or low.

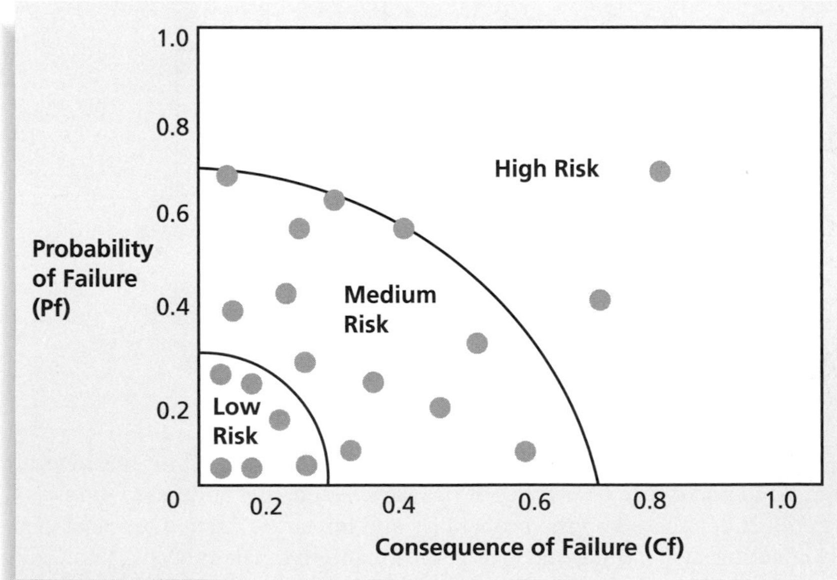

FIGURE 11-6 Chart showing high-, medium-, and low-risk technologies

Top Ten Risk Item Tracking

Top Ten Risk Item Tracking is a qualitative risk analysis tool, and in addition to identifying risks, it maintains an awareness of risks throughout the life of a project by also helping to monitor risks. It involves establishing a periodic review of the project's most significant risk items with management and, optionally, with the customer. The review begins with a summary of the status of the top-ten sources of risk on the project. The summary includes each item's current ranking, previous ranking, number of times it appears on the list over a period of time, and a summary of progress made in resolving the risk item since the previous review. The Microsoft Solution Framework (MSF) includes a risk management model that includes developing and monitoring a top-ten master list of risks. MSF is the methodology Microsoft uses for managing projects. It combines aspects of software design and development, and building and deploying infrastructure, into a single-project life cycle for guiding technology solutions of all kinds. (Consult Microsoft's Web site for more information on MSF.)

Table 11-6 provides an example of a Top Ten Risk Item Tracking chart that could be used at a management review meeting for a project. This particular example includes only the top five negative risk events. Notice that each risk event is ranked based on the current month, previous month, and how many months it has been in the top ten. The last column briefly describes the progress for resolving each particular risk item. You can have separate charts for negative and positive risks or combine them into one chart.

TABLE 11-6 Example of Top Ten Risk Item Tracking

	MONTHLY RANKING			
Risk Event	Rank This Month	Rank Last Month	Number of Months in Top Ten	Risk Resolution Progress
Inadequate planning	1	2	4	Working on revising the entire project management plan
Poor definition	2	3	3	Holding meetings with project customer and sponsor to clarify scope
Absence of leadership	3	1	2	After previous project manager quit, assigned a new one to lead the project
Poor cost estimates	4	4	3	Revising cost estimates
Poor time estimates	5	5	3	Revising schedule estimates

A risk management review accomplishes several objectives. First, it keeps management and the customer (if included) aware of the major influences that could prevent or enhance the project's success. Second, by involving the customer, the project team may be able to consider alternative strategies for addressing the risks. Third, it is a means of promoting confidence in the project team by demonstrating to management and the customer that the team is aware of the significant risks, has a strategy in place, and is effectively carrying out that strategy.

The main output of qualitative risk analysis is updating the risk register. The ranking column of the risk register should be filled in, along with a numeric value or high/medium/low rating for the probability and impact of the risk event. Additional information is often added for risk events, such as identification of risks that need more attention in the near term or those that can be placed on a watch list. A **watch list** is a list of risks that are low priority, but are still identified as potential risks. Qualitative analysis can also identify risks that should be evaluated on a quantitative basis, as described in the next section.

PERFORMING QUANTITATIVE RISK ANALYSIS

Quantitative risk analysis often follows qualitative risk analysis, yet both processes can be done together or separately. On some projects, the team may only perform qualitative risk analysis. The nature of the project and availability of time and money affect the type of risk analysis techniques used. Large, complex projects involving leading-edge technologies often require extensive quantitative risk analysis. The main techniques for quantitative risk analysis include data gathering, quantitative risk analysis and modeling techniques, and expert judgment. Data gathering often involves interviewing experts and collecting probability distribution information. This section focuses on using the quantitative risk analysis and modeling techniques of decision tree analysis, simulation, and sensitivity analysis.

Decision Trees and Expected Monetary Value

A **decision tree** is a diagramming analysis technique used to help select the best course of action in situations in which future outcomes are uncertain. A common application of decision tree analysis involves calculating expected monetary value. **Expected monetary value (EMV)** is the product of a risk event probability and the risk event's monetary value. Figure 11-7 uses the decision of which project(s) an organization might pursue to illustrate this concept. Suppose Cliff Branch's firm was trying to decide if it should submit a proposal for Project 1, Project 2, both projects, or neither project. The team could draw a decision tree with two branches, one for Project 1 and one for Project 2. The firm could then calculate the expected monetary value to help make this decision.

To create a decision tree, and to calculate expected monetary value specifically, you must estimate the probabilities, or chances, of certain events occurring. For example, in Figure 11-7 there is a 20 percent probability or chance ($P = .20$) that Cliff's firm will win the contract for Project 1, which is estimated to be worth $300,000 in profits—the outcome of the top branch in the figure. There is an 80 percent probability ($P = .80$) that it will not win the contract for Project 1, and the outcome is estimated to be –$40,000, meaning that the firm will have to invest $40,000 into Project 1 with

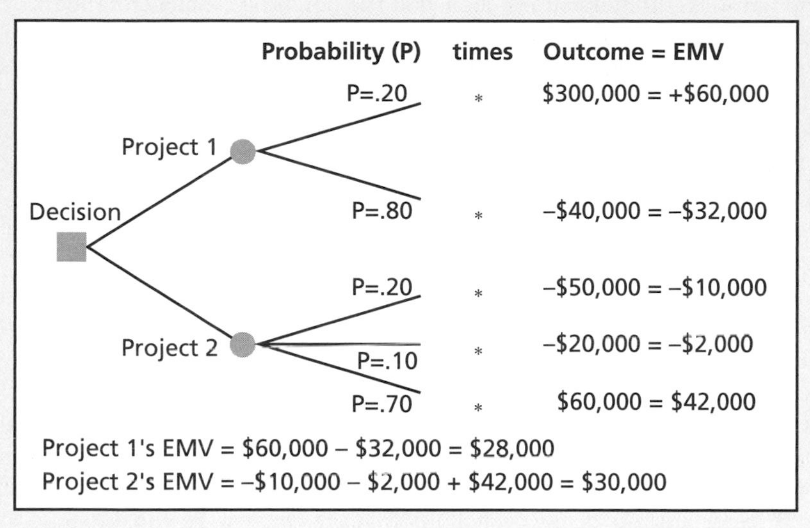

FIGURE 11-7 Expected monetary value (EMV) example

no reimbursement if it is not awarded the contract. The sum of the probabilities for outcomes for each project must equal one (for Project 1, 20 percent plus 80 percent). Probabilities are normally determined based on expert judgment. Cliff or other people in his firm should have some sense of their likelihood of winning certain projects.

Figure 11-7 also shows probabilities and outcomes for Project 2. Suppose there is a 20 percent probability that Cliff's firm will lose $50,000 on Project 2, a 10 percent probability that it will lose $20,000, and a 70 percent probability that it will earn $60,000. Again, experts would need to estimate these dollar amounts and probabilities.

To calculate the expected monetary value (EMV) for each project, multiply the probability by the outcome value for each potential outcome for each project and sum the results. To calculate expected monetary value for Project 1, going from left to right, multiply the probability by the outcome for each branch and sum the results. In this example, the EMV for Project 1 is $28,000.

$$.2(\$300{,}000) + .8(-\$40{,}000) = \$60{,}000 - \$32{,}000 = \$28{,}000$$

The EMV for Project 2 is $30,000.

$$.2(-\$50{,}000) + .1(-\$20{,}000) + .7(\$60{,}000) = -\$10{,}000 - \$2{,}000 + \$42{,}000 = \$30{,}000$$

Because the EMV provides an estimate for the total dollar value of a decision, you want to have a positive number; the higher the EMV, the better. Since the EMV is positive for both Projects 1 and 2, Cliff's firm would expect a positive outcome from each and could bid on both projects. If it had to choose between the two projects, perhaps because of limited resources, Cliff's firm should bid on Project 2 because it has a higher EMV.

Also notice in Figure 11-7 that if you just looked at the potential outcome of the two projects, Project 1 looks more appealing. You could earn $300,000 in profits from Project 1, but you can only earn $60,000 for Project 2. If Cliff were a risk seeker, he would naturally want to bid on Project 1. However, there is only a 20 percent chance of getting that $300,000 on Project 1, and there is a 70 percent chance of earning $60,000 on Project 2. Using EMV helps account for all possible outcomes and their probabilities of occurrence, thereby reducing the tendency to pursue overly aggressive or conservative risk strategies.

Simulation

A more sophisticated quantitative risk analysis technique is simulation. Simulation uses a representation or model of a system to analyze the expected behavior or performance of the system. Most simulations are based on some form of Monte Carlo analysis. **Monte Carlo analysis** simulates a model's outcome many times to provide a statistical distribution of the calculated results. Monte Carlo analysis can determine that a project will finish by a certain date only 10 percent of the time, and determine another date for which the project will finish 50 percent of the time. In another words, the Monte Carlo analysis can predict the probability of finishing by a certain date or the probability that the cost will be equal to or less than a certain value.

You can use several different types of distribution functions when performing a Monte Carlo analysis. The example below is a simplified approach.

The basic steps of a Monte Carlo analysis are:

1. Assess the range for the variables being considered. In other words, collect the most likely, optimistic, and pessimistic estimates for the variables in the model. For example, if you are trying to determine the likelihood of meeting project schedule goals, the project network diagram would be your model. You would collect the most likely, optimistic, and pessimistic time estimates for each task. Notice that this step is similar to collecting data for performing PERT estimates. However, instead of applying the same PERT weighted average formula, you go on to the following steps when performing a Monte Carlo simulation.
2. Determine the probability distribution of each variable. What is the likelihood of that variable falling between the optimistic and most likely estimates? For example, if an expert assigned to do a particular task provides a most likely estimate of ten weeks, an optimistic estimate of eight weeks, and a pessimistic estimate of 15 weeks, you then ask what the probability is of completing that task between 8 and 10 weeks. The expert might respond that there is a 20 percent probability.
3. For each variable, such as the time estimate for a task, select a random value based on the probability distribution for the occurrence of the variable. For example, using the above scenario, you would randomly pick a value between 8 weeks and 10 weeks 20 percent of the time and a value between 10 weeks and 15 weeks 80 percent of the time.
4. Run a deterministic analysis or one pass through the model using the combination of values selected for each one of the variables. For example, the one task described above might have a value of 12 on the first run. All of the other tasks would have one random value assigned to them on that first run, also, based on their estimates and probability distributions.

5. Repeat Steps 3 and 4 many times to obtain the probability distribution of the model's results. The number of iterations depends on the number of variables and the degree of confidence required in the results, but it typically lies between 100 and 1,000. Using the project schedule as an example, the final simulation results will show you the probability of completing the entire project within a certain time period.

Figure 11-8 illustrates the results from a Monte Carlo–based simulation of a project schedule. The simulation was done using Microsoft Project and Risk+ software. On the left side of Figure 11-8 is a chart displaying columns and an S-shaped curve. The height of each column, read by the scale on the left of the chart, indicates how many times the project was completed in a given time interval during the simulation run, which is the sample count. In this example, the time interval is two working days, and the simulation was run 250 times. The first column shows that the project was completed by 1/29 or January 29 (using month/day format) only two times during the simulation. The S-shaped curve, read from the scale on the right of the chart, shows the cumulative probability of completing the project on or before a given date. The right side of Figure 11-8 shows the information in tabular form. For example, there is a 10 percent probability that the project will be completed by 2/8, a 50 percent chance of completion by 2/17, and a 90 percent chance of completion by 2/25.

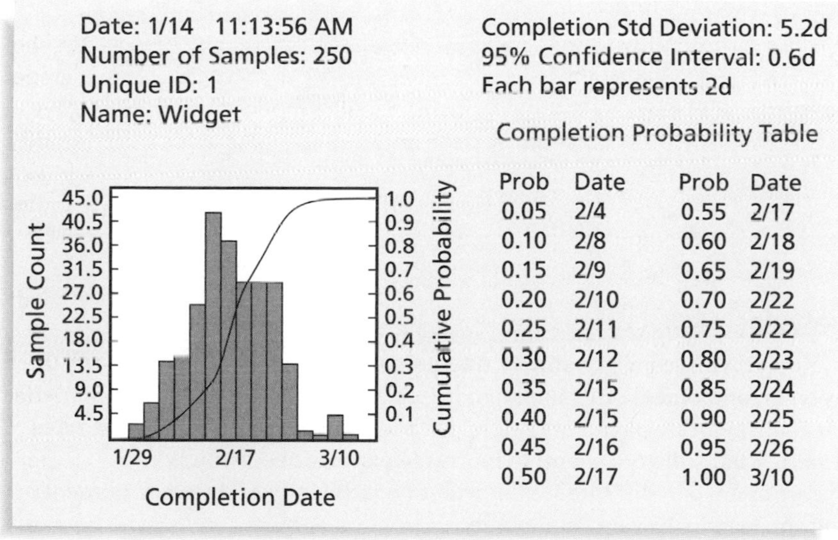

Prob	Date	Prob	Date
0.05	2/4	0.55	2/17
0.10	2/8	0.60	2/18
0.15	2/9	0.65	2/19
0.20	2/10	0.70	2/22
0.25	2/11	0.75	2/22
0.30	2/12	0.80	2/23
0.35	2/15	0.85	2/24
0.40	2/15	0.90	2/25
0.45	2/16	0.95	2/26
0.50	2/17	1.00	3/10

FIGURE 11-8 Sample Monte Carlo–based simulation results for project schedule

As you can imagine, people use software to perform the steps required for a Monte Carlo analysis. Several PC-based software packages are available that perform Monte Carlo simulations. Many products will show you what the major risk drivers are, based on the simulation results. For example, a wide range for a certain task estimate might be causing most of the uncertainty in the project schedule. You will learn more about using simulation and other software related to project risk management later in this chapter.

WHAT WENT RIGHT?

A large aerospace company used Monte Carlo analysis to help quantify risks on several advanced-design engineering projects. The U.S. National Aerospace Plane (NASP) project involved many risks. The purpose of this multibillion-dollar project was to design and develop a vehicle that could fly into space using a single-stage-to-orbit approach. A single-stage-to-orbit approach meant the vehicle would have to achieve a speed of Mach 25 (25 times the speed of sound) without a rocket booster. A team of engineers and business professionals worked together in the mid-1980s to develop a software model for estimating the time and cost of developing the NASP project. This model was then linked with simulation software to determine the sources of cost and schedule risk for the project. The company then used the results of the Monte Carlo analysis to determine how it would invest its internal research and development funds. Although the NASP project was terminated, the resulting research has helped develop more advanced materials and propulsion systems used on many modern aircraft.

Microsoft Excel is a common tool for performing quantitative risk analysis. Microsoft provides examples of how to use Excel to perform Monte Carlo simulation from its Web site, and explains how several companies use Monte Carlo simulation as an important tool for decision-making:

- General Motors uses simulation for forecasting net income for the corporation, predicting structural costs and purchasing costs of vehicles, and determining the company's susceptibility to different kinds of risk, such as interest rate changes and exchange rate fluctuations.
- Eli Lilly uses simulation to determine the optimal plant capacity that should be built for each drug.
- Procter & Gamble uses simulation to model and optimally hedge foreign exchange risk.[13]

Sensitivity Analysis

Many people are familiar with using **sensitivity analysis** to see the effects of changing one or more variables on an outcome. For example, many people perform a sensitivity analysis to determine what their monthly payments will be for a loan given different interest rates or periods of the loan. What will your monthly mortgage payment be if you borrow $100,000 for 30 years at a 6 percent rate? What will it be if the interest rate is 7 percent? What if you pay off the loan in 15 years at 5 percent?

Many professionals use sensitivity analysis to help make several common business decisions, such as determining break-even points based on different assumptions. People often use spreadsheet software like Microsoft Excel to perform sensitivity analysis. Figure 11-9 shows an example Excel file created to quickly show the break-even point for a product based on various inputs: the sales price per unit, the manufacturing cost per unit, and fixed monthly expenses. The current inputs result in a break-even point of 6,250 units sold. Users of this spreadsheet can change inputs and see the effects on the break-even point in chart format. Project teams often create similar models to determine the sensitivity of various project variables. For example, Cliff's team could develop sensitivity analysis models to estimate their profits on jobs by varying how many hours it would take them to do the job, costs per hour, and so on.

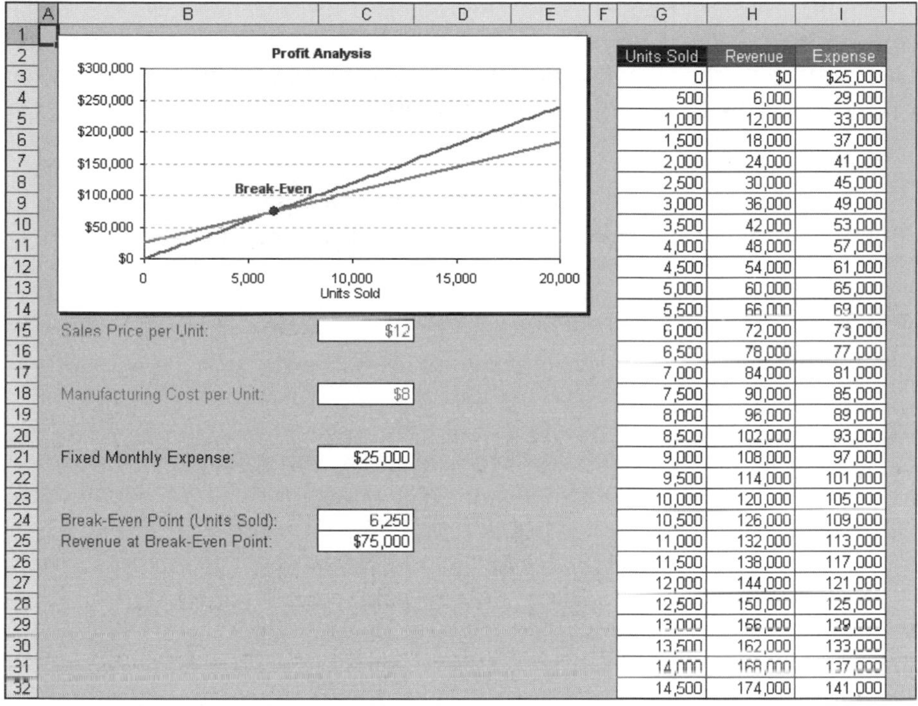

Units Sold	Revenue	Expense
0	$0	$25,000
500	6,000	29,000
1,000	12,000	33,000
1,500	18,000	37,000
2,000	24,000	41,000
2,500	30,000	45,000
3,000	36,000	49,000
3,500	42,000	53,000
4,000	48,000	57,000
4,500	54,000	61,000
5,000	60,000	65,000
5,500	66,000	69,000
6,000	72,000	73,000
6,500	78,000	77,000
7,000	84,000	81,000
7,500	90,000	85,000
8,000	96,000	89,000
8,500	102,000	93,000
9,000	108,000	97,000
9,500	114,000	101,000
10,000	120,000	105,000
10,500	126,000	109,000
11,000	132,000	113,000
11,500	138,000	117,000
12,000	144,000	121,000
12,500	150,000	125,000
13,000	156,000	129,000
13,500	162,000	133,000
14,000	168,000	137,000
14,500	174,000	141,000

FIGURE 11-9 Sample sensitivity analysis for determining break-even point

The main outputs of quantitative risk analysis are updates to the risk register, such as revised risk rankings or detailed information behind those rankings. The quantitative analysis also provides high-level information in terms of the probabilities of achieving certain project objectives. This information might cause the project manager to suggest changes in contingency reserves. In some cases, projects may be redirected or canceled based on the quantitative analysis, or they might cause the initiation of new projects to help the current one succeed, such as the NASP project described in the What Went Right example.

PLANNING RISK RESPONSES

After an organization identifies and quantifies risks, it must develop an appropriate response to them. Developing a response to risks involves developing options and defining strategies for reducing negative risks and enhancing positive risks.

The four basic response strategies for negative risks are:

1. **Risk avoidance** or eliminating a specific threat, usually by eliminating its causes. Of course, not all risks can be eliminated, but specific risk events can be. For example, a project team may decide to continue using a specific piece of hardware or software on a project because they know it works. Other products that could be used on the project may be available, but if the project

team is unfamiliar with them, they could cause significant risk. Using familiar hardware or software eliminates this risk.

2. **Risk acceptance** or accepting the consequences should a risk occur. For example, a project team planning a big project review meeting could take an active approach to risk by having a contingency or backup plan and contingency reserves if they cannot get approval for a specific site for the meeting. On the other hand, they could take a passive approach and accept whatever facility their organization provides them.
3. **Risk transference** or shifting the consequence of a risk and responsibility for its management to a third party. For example, risk transference is often used in dealing with financial risk exposure. A project team may purchase special insurance or warranty protection for specific hardware needed for a project. If the hardware fails, the insurer must replace it within an agreed-upon period of time.
4. **Risk mitigation** or reducing the impact of a risk event by reducing the probability of its occurrence. Suggestions for reducing common sources of risk on information technology projects were provided at the beginning of this chapter. Other examples of risk mitigation include using proven technology, having competent project personnel, using various analysis and validation techniques, and buying maintenance or service agreements from subcontractors.

Table 11-7 provides general mitigation strategies for technical, cost, and schedule risks on projects.[14] Note that increasing the frequency of project monitoring and using a work breakdown structure (WBS) and Critical Path Method (CPM) are strategies for all three areas. Increasing the project manager's authority is a strategy for mitigating technical and cost risks, and selecting the most experienced project manager is recommended for reducing schedule risks. Improving communication is also an effective strategy for mitigating risks.

TABLE 11-7 General risk mitigation strategies for technical, cost, and schedule risks

Technical Risks	Cost Risks	Schedule Risks
Emphasize team support and avoid stand-alone project structure	Increase the frequency of project monitoring	Increase the frequency of project monitoring
Increase project manager authority	Use WBS and CPM	Use WBS and CPM
Improve problem handling and communication	Improve communication, project goals understanding, and team support	Select the most experienced project manager
Increase the frequency of project monitoring	Increase project manager authority	
Use WBS and CPM		

The four basic response strategies for positive risks are:

- **Risk exploitation** or doing whatever you can to make sure the positive risk happens. For example, suppose Cliff's company funded a project to provide new computer classrooms for a nearby school in need. They might select one of their top project managers to organize news coverage of the project, write a press release, or hold some other public event to ensure the project produces good public relations for the company, which could lead to more business.
- **Risk sharing** or allocating ownership of the risk to another party. Using the same example of implementing new computer classrooms, the project manager could form a partnership with the school's principal, school board, or parent-teacher organization to share responsibility for achieving good public relations for the project. Or the company might partner with a local training firm that agrees to provide free training for all of the teachers on how to use the new computer classrooms.
- **Risk enhancement** or changing the size of the opportunity by identifying and maximizing key drivers of the positive risk. For example, an important driver of getting good public relations for the computer classrooms project might be getting the students, parents, and teachers aware of and excited about the project. They could then do their own formal or informal advertising of the project and Cliff's company, which in turn might interest other groups and could generate more business.
- **Risk acceptance** also applies to positive risks when the project team cannot or chooses not to take any actions toward a risk. For example, the computer classrooms project manager might just assume the project will result in good public relations for their company without doing anything extra.

The main outputs of risk response planning include risk-related contractual agreements, updates to the project management plan and other project documents, and updates to the risk register. For example, if Cliff's company decided to partner with a local training firm on the computer classrooms project to share the opportunity of achieving good public relations, it could write a contract with that firm. The project management plan and its related plans might need to be updated if the risk response strategies require additional tasks, resources, or time to accomplish them. Risk response strategies often result in changes to the WBS and project schedule, so plans with that information must be updated. The risk response strategies also provide updated information for the risk register by describing the risk responses, risk owners, and status information.

Risk response strategies often include identification of residual and secondary risks as well as contingency plans and reserves, as described earlier. **Residual risks** are risks that remain after all of the response strategies have been implemented. For example, even though a more stable hardware product may have been used on a project, there may still be some risk of it failing to function properly. **Secondary risks** are a direct result of implementing a risk response. For example, using the more stable hardware may have caused a risk of peripheral devices failing to function properly.

MONITORING AND CONTROLLING RISKS

Monitoring and controlling risks involves executing the risk management processes to respond to risk events. Executing the risk management processes means ensuring that risk awareness is an ongoing activity performed by the entire project team throughout the entire project. Project risk management does not stop with the initial risk analysis. Identified risks may not materialize, or their probabilities of occurrence or loss may diminish. Previously identified risks may be determined to have a greater probability of occurrence or a higher estimated loss value. Similarly, new risks will be identified as the project progresses. Newly identified risks need to go through the same process as those identified during the initial risk assessment. A redistribution of resources devoted to risk management may be necessary because of relative changes in risk exposure.

Carrying out individual risk management plans involves monitoring risks based on defined milestones and making decisions regarding risks and their response strategies. It may be necessary to alter a strategy if it becomes ineffective, implement a planned contingency activity, or eliminate a risk from the list of potential risks when it no longer exists. Project teams sometimes use **workarounds**—unplanned responses to risk events—when they do not have contingency plans in place.

Risk reassessment, risk audits, variance and trend analysis, technical performance measurements, reserve analysis, and status meetings or periodic risk reviews such as the Top Ten Risk Item Tracking method are all tools and techniques for performing risk monitoring and control. Outputs of this process are risk register updates, organizational process assets updates (such as lessons-learned information that might help future projects), change requests, and updates to the project management plan and other project documents.

USING SOFTWARE TO ASSIST IN PROJECT RISK MANAGEMENT

As demonstrated in several parts of this chapter, you can use a variety of software tools to enhance various risk management processes. Most organizations use software to create, update, and distribute information in their risk registers. The risk register is often a simple Microsoft Word or Excel file, but it can also be part of a more sophisticated database. Spreadsheets can aid in tracking and quantifying risks, preparing charts and graphs, and performing sensitivity analysis. Software can be used to create decision trees and estimate expected monetary value.

More sophisticated risk management software, such as Monte Carlo simulation software, can help you develop models and use simulations to analyze and respond to various risks. Several high-end project management tools include simulation capabilities. You can also purchase add-on software to perform Monte Carlo simulations using Excel (such as Decisioneering Crystal Ball or Palisade @Risk for Excel) or Project 2007 (such as CS Solutions Risk+ or Palisade @Risk for Project). Several software packages have also been specifically created for project risk management. Although it has become easier to do sophisticated risk analysis with new software tools, project teams must be careful not to over-rely on using software when performing project risk management. If a risk is not identified, it cannot be managed, and it takes intelligent, experienced people to do a good job of identifying risks. It also takes hard work to develop and implement good risk response strategies. Software should be used as a tool to help make good decisions in project risk management, not as a scapegoat for when things go wrong.

Well-run projects, like a master violinist's performance, an Olympic athlete's gold medal win, or a Pulitzer Prize–winning book, appear to be almost effortless. Those on the outside—whether audiences, customers, or managers—cannot observe the effort that goes into a superb performance. They cannot see the hours of practice, the edited drafts, or the planning, management, and foresight that create the appearance of ease. To improve information technology project management, project managers should strive to make their jobs look easy—it reflects the results of a well-run project.

CASE WRAP-UP

Cliff Branch and two of his senior people attended a seminar on project risk management where the speaker discussed several techniques, such as estimating the expected monetary value of projects, Monte Carlo simulations, and so on. Cliff asked the speaker how these techniques could be used to help his company decide which projects to bid on, since bidding on projects often required up-front investments with the possibility of no payback. The speaker walked through an example of EMV and then ran a quick Monte Carlo simulation. Cliff did not have a strong math background and had a hard time understanding the EMV calculations. He thought the simulation was much too confusing to have any practical use for him. He believed in his gut instincts much more than any math calculation or computer output.

The speaker finally sensed that Cliff was not impressed, so she explained the importance of looking at the odds of winning project awards and not just at the potential profits. She suggested using a risk-neutral strategy by bidding on projects that the company had a good chance of winning (50 percent or so) and that had a good profit potential, instead of focusing on projects that they had a small chance of winning and that had a larger profit potential. Cliff disagreed with this advice, and he continued to bid on high-risk projects. The two other managers who attended the seminar now understood why the firm was having problems—their leader loved taking risks, even if it hurt the company. They soon found jobs with competing companies, as did several other employees.

Chapter Summary

Risk is an uncertainty that can have a negative or positive effect on meeting project objectives. Projects, by virtue of their unique nature, involve risk. Many organizations do a poor job of project risk management, if they do any at all. Successful organizations realize the value of good project risk management.

Risk management is an investment; that is, there are costs associated with identifying risks, analyzing those risks, and establishing plans to address those risks. Those costs must be included in cost, schedule, and resource planning.

Risk utility or risk tolerance is the amount of satisfaction or pleasure received from a potential payoff. Risk seekers enjoy high risks, risk-averse people do not like to take risks, and risk-neutral people seek to balance risks and potential payoff.

Project risk management is a process in which the project team continually assesses what may negatively or positively impact the project, determines the probability of such events occurring, and determines the impact should such events occur. It also involves analyzing and determining alternate strategies to deal with risks. The six main processes involved in risk management are planning risk management, identifying risks, performing qualitative risk analysis, performing quantitative risk analysis, planning risk responses, and monitoring and controlling risks.

Planning risk management is the process of deciding how to approach and plan for risk management activities for a particular project. A risk management plan is a key output of the risk management planning process, and a risk register is a key output of the other risk management processes. Contingency plans are predefined actions that a project team will take if an identified risk event occurs. Fallback plans are developed for risks that have a high impact on meeting project objectives, and are implemented if attempts to reduce the risk are not effective. Contingency reserves or contingency allowances are provisions held by the project sponsor or organization to reduce the risk of cost or schedule overruns to an acceptable level.

Information technology projects often involve several risks: lack of user involvement, lack of executive management support, unclear requirements, poor planning, and so on. Lists developed by the Standish Group and other organizations can help you identify potential risks on information technology projects. A risk breakdown structure is a useful tool that can help project managers consider potential risks in different categories. Lists of common risk conditions in project management knowledge areas can also be helpful in identifying risks, as can information-gathering techniques such as brainstorming, the Delphi technique, interviewing, and SWOT analysis. A risk register is a document that contains results of various risk management processes, often displayed in a table or spreadsheet format. It is a tool for documenting potential risk events and related information. Risk events refer to specific, uncertain events that may occur to the detriment or enhancement of the project.

Risks can be assessed qualitatively and quantitatively. Tools for qualitative risk analysis include a probability/impact matrix and the Top Ten Risk Item Tracking technique. Tools for quantitative risk analysis include decision trees and Monte Carlo simulation. Expected monetary value (EMV) uses decision trees to evaluate potential projects based on their expected value. Simulations are a more sophisticated method for creating estimates to help you determine the likelihood of meeting specific project schedule or cost goals. Sensitivity analysis is used to show the effects of changing one or more variables on an outcome.

The four basic responses to risk are avoidance, acceptance, transference, and mitigation. Risk avoidance involves eliminating a specific threat or risk. Risk acceptance means accepting the consequences of a risk, should it occur. Risk transference is shifting the consequence of a risk and responsibility for its management to a third party. Risk mitigation is reducing the impact of a risk event by reducing the probability of its occurrence. The four basic response strategies for positive risks are risk exploitation, risk sharing, risk enhancement, and risk acceptance.

Monitoring and controlling risks involves executing the risk management processes and the risk management plan to respond to risks. Outputs of this process include risk register updates, organizational process assets updates, change requests, and updates to the project management plan and other project documents.

Several types of software can assist in project risk management. Monte Carlo–based simulation software is a particularly useful tool for helping get a better idea of project risks and top sources of risk or risk drivers.

Quick Quiz

1. _____________ is an uncertainty that can have a negative or positive effect on meeting project objectives.
   a. Risk utility
   b. Risk tolerance
   c. Risk management
   d. Risk
2. A person who is risk-_____________ receives greater satisfaction when more payoff is at stake and is willing to pay a penalty to take risks.
   a. averse
   b. seeking
   c. neutral
   d. aware
3. Which risk management process involves prioritizing risks based on their probability and impact of occurrence?
   a. planning risk management
   b. identifying risks
   c. performing qualitative risk analysis
   d. performing quantitative risk analysis
4. Your project involves using a new release of a common software application, but if that release is not available, your team has _____________ plans to use the current release.
   a. contingency
   b. fallback
   c. reserve
   d. mitigation

5. Which risk identification tool involves deriving a consensus among a panel of experts by using anonymous input regarding future events?
   a. risk breakdown structure
   b. brainstorming
   c. interviewing
   d. Delphi technique
6. A risk _____________ is a document that contains results of various risk management processes, often displayed in a table or spreadsheet format.
   a. management plan
   b. register
   c. breakdown structure
   d. probability/impact matrix

7. _____________ are indicators or symptoms of actual risk events, such as a cost overrun on early activities being a symptom of poor cost estimates.
   a. Probabilities
   b. Impacts
   c. Watch list items
   d. Triggers
8. Suppose there is a 30 percent chance that you will lose $10,000 and a 70 percent chance that you will earn $100,000 on a particular project. What is the project's estimated monetary value?
   a. –$30,000
   b. $70,000
   c. $67,000
   d. –$67,000
9. _____________ is a quantitative risk analysis tool that uses a model of a system to analyze the expected behavior or performance of the system.
   a. Simulation
   b. Sensitivity analysis
   c. Monte Carlo analysis
   d. EMV
10. Your project team has decided not to use an upcoming release of software because it might cause your schedule to slip. Which negative risk response strategy are you using?
    a. avoidance
    b. acceptance
    c. transference
    d. mitigation

Quick Quiz Answers

1. d; 2. b; 3. c; 4. a; 5. d; 6. b; 7. d; 8. c; 9. a; 10. a

Discussion Questions

1. Discuss the risk utility function and risk preference chart in Figure 11-2. Would you rate yourself as being risk-averse, risk-neutral, or risk-seeking? Give examples of each approach from different aspects of your life, such as your current job, your personal finances, romances, and eating habits.
2. What are some questions that should be addressed in a risk management plan?
3. Discuss the common sources of risk on information technology projects and suggestions for managing them. Which suggestions do you find most useful? Which do you feel would not work in your organization? Why?
4. What is the difference between using brainstorming and the Delphi technique for risk identification? What are some of the advantages and disadvantages of each approach? Describe the contents of a risk register and how the risk register is used in several risk management processes.
5. Describe how to use a probability/impact matrix and the Top Ten Risk Item Tracking approaches for performing qualitative risk analysis. How could you use each technique on a project?
6. Explain how to use decision trees and Monte Carlo analysis for quantifying risk. Give an example of how you could use each technique on an information technology project.
7. Provide realistic examples of each of the risk response strategies for both negative and positive risks.
8. List the tools and techniques for performing risk monitoring and control.
9. How can you use Excel to assist in project risk management? What other software can help project teams make better risk management decisions?

Exercises

1. Suppose your college or organization is considering a new project that would involve developing an information system that would allow all employees and students/customers to access and maintain their own human resources–related information, such as address, marital status, tax information, and so on. The main benefits of the system would be a reduction in human resources personnel and more accurate information. For example, if an employee, student, or customer had a new telephone number or e-mail address, he or she would be responsible for entering the new data in the new system. The new system would also allow employees to change their tax withholdings or pension plan contributions. Identify five potential risks for this new project, being sure to list some negative and positive risks. Provide a detailed description of each risk and propose strategies for addressing each risk. Document your results in a two-page paper.

2. Review a document related to risk management, such as Microsoft's Security Risk Management Guide available from the companion Web site for this text. Does this guide address most of the topics related to risk management planning as described in this text? Document your analysis in a two-page paper.
3. Research risk management software. Are many products available? What are the main advantages of using them in managing projects? What are the main disadvantages? Write a two-page paper discussing your findings, and include at least three references.
4. Suppose your organization is deciding which of four projects to bid on. Information on each is in the table below. Assume that all up-front investments are not recovered, so they are shown as negative profits. Draw a diagram and calculate the EMV for each project. Write a few paragraphs explaining which projects you would bid on. Be sure to use the EMV information and your personal risk tolerance to justify your answer.

Project	Chance of Outcome	Estimated Profits
Project 1	50 percent 50 percent	$120,000 –$50,000
Project 2	30 percent 40 percent 30 percent	$100,000 $ 50,000 –$60,000
Project 3	70 percent 30 percent	$ 20,000 –$ 5,000
Project 4	30 percent 30 percent 20 percent 20 percent	$ 40,000 $ 30,000 $ 20,000 –$50,000

5. Find an example of a company that took a big risk on an information technology project and succeeded. In addition, find an example of a company that took a big risk and failed. Summarize each project and situation in a two-page paper where you should also discuss whether you believe that anything besides luck makes a difference between success and failure.

Running Case

Tony and his team identified some risks during the first month of the Recreation and Wellness Intranet Project. However, all they did was document them in a list. They never ranked them or developed any response strategies. Since several problems have been occurring on the project, such as key team members leaving the company, users being uncooperative, and team members not providing good status information, Tony has decided to be more proactive in managing risks. He also wants to address positive as well as negative risks.

1. Create a risk register for the project, using Table 11-5 and the data below it as a guide. Identify six potential risks, including risks related to the problems described above. Include negative and positive risks.

2. Plot the six risks on a probability/impact matrix, using Figure 11-7. Also assign a numeric value for the probability and impact of each risk on meeting the main project objective. Use a scale of 1 to 10 in assigning the values, with 1 being low and 10 being high. For a simple risk factor calculation, multiply these two values (the probability score and the impact score). Add a column to your risk register to the right of the impact column called Risk Score. Enter the new data in the risk register. Write your rationale for how you determined the scores for one of the negative risks and one of the positive risks.
3. Develop a response strategy for one of the negative risks and one of the positive risks. Enter the information in the risk register. Also write a separate paragraph describing what specific tasks would need to be done to implement the strategy. Include time and cost estimates for each strategy, as well.

Companion Web Site

Visit the companion Web site for this text (*www.cengage.com/mis/schwalbe*) to access:

- References cited in the text and additional suggested readings for each chapter
- Template files
- Lecture notes
- Interactive quizzes
- Podcasts
- Links to general project management Web sites
- And more

See the Preface of this text for additional information on accessing the companion Web site.

Key Terms

brainstorming — a technique by which a group attempts to generate ideas or find a solution for a specific problem by amassing ideas spontaneously and without judgment

contingency allowances — provisions held by the project sponsor or organization to reduce the risk of cost or schedule overruns to an acceptable level; also called *contingency reserves*

contingency plans — predefined actions that the project team will take if an identified risk event occurs

contingency reserves — provisions held by the project sponsor or organization to reduce the risk of cost or schedule overruns to an acceptable level; also called *contingency allowances*

decision tree — a diagramming analysis technique used to help select the best course of action in situations in which future outcomes are uncertain

Delphi technique — an approach used to derive a consensus among a panel of experts, to make predictions about future developments

expected monetary value (EMV) — the product of the risk event probability and the risk event's monetary value

fallback plans — plans developed for risks that have a high impact on meeting project objectives, to be implemented if attempts to reduce the risk are not effective

flowcharts — diagrams that show how various elements of a system relate to each other

influence diagram — diagram that represents decision problems by displaying essential elements, including decisions, uncertainties, and objectives, and how they influence each other

interviewing — a fact-finding technique that is normally done face-to-face, but can also occur through phone calls, e-mail, or instant messaging

known risks — risks that the project team have identified and analyzed and can be managed proactively

Monte Carlo analysis — a risk quantification technique that simulates a model's outcome many times, to provide a statistical distribution of the calculated results

probability/impact matrix or chart — a matrix or chart that lists the relative probability of a risk occurring on one side of a matrix or axis on a chart and the relative impact of the risk occurring on the other

residual risks — risks that remain after all of the response strategies have been implemented

risk — an uncertainty that can have a negative or positive effect on meeting project objectives

risk acceptance — accepting the consequences should a risk occur

risk-averse — having a low tolerance for risk

risk avoidance — eliminating a specific threat or risk, usually by eliminating its causes

risk breakdown structure — a hierarchy of potential risk categories for a project

risk enhancement — changing the size of an opportunity by identifying and maximizing key drivers of the positive risk

risk events — specific uncertain events that may occur to the detriment or enhancement of the project

risk exploitation — doing whatever you can to make sure the positive risk happens

risk factors — numbers that represent overall risk of specific events, given their probability of occurring and the consequence to the project if they do occur

risk management plan — a plan that documents the procedures for managing risk throughout a project

risk mitigation — reducing the impact of a risk event by reducing the probability of its occurrence

risk-neutral — a balance between risk and payoff

risk owner — the person who will take responsibility for a risk and its associated response strategies and tasks

risk register — a document that contains results of various risk management processes, often displayed in a table or spreadsheet format

risk-seeking — having a high tolerance for risk

risk sharing — allocating ownership of the risk to another party

risk tolerance — the amount of satisfaction or pleasure received from a potential payoff; also called *risk utility*

risk transference — shifting the consequence of a risk and responsibility for its management to a third party

risk utility — the amount of satisfaction or pleasure received from a potential payoff; also called *risk tolerance*

runaway projects — projects that have significant cost or schedule overruns

secondary risks — risks that are a direct result of implementing a risk response

sensitivity analysis — a technique used to show the effects of changing one or more variables on an outcome

Top Ten Risk Item Tracking — a qualitative risk analysis tool for identifying risks and maintaining an awareness of risks throughout the life of a project

triggers — indications for actual risk events

unknown risks — risks that have not been identified and analyzed so they cannot be managed proactively

watch list — a list of risks that are low priority, but are still identified as potential risks

workarounds — unplanned responses to risk events when there are no contingency plans in place

End Notes

[1] C. William Ibbs and Young Hoon Kwak, "Assessing Project Management Maturity," *Project Management Journal* 31, no. 1 (March 2000), pp. 32–43.

[2] Aneerav Sukhoo, Andries Barnard, Mariki M. Eloff, and John A. Van der Poll, "An Assessment of Software Project Management Maturity in Mauritius," *Issues in Informing Science and Information Technology* 2 (May 2003), pp. 671–690.

[3] Peter Kulik and Catherine Weber, "Software Risk Management Practices—2001," KLCI Research Group (August 2001).

[4] David Hillson, "Boom, bust, and risk management," *Project Manager Today* (September 2008).

[5] SAS, "Survey: Better risk management would have lessened credit crisis," SAS Press Release (September 18, 2008).

[6] David Hillson, "Integrated Risk Management as a Framework for Organisational Success," PMI Global Congress Proceedings (2006).

[7] The Standish Group, "Unfinished Voyages" StandishGroup.com (1996).

[8] Andy Cole, "Runaway Projects—Cause and Effects," *Software World* 26, no. 3, (1995), pp. 3–5.

[9] Stephanie Overby, "Bound to Fail," CIO Magazine (May 1, 2005).

[10] R. Max Wideman, "Project and Program Risk Management: A Guide to Managing Project Risks and Opportunities," Upper Darby, PA, II–4 (1992).

[11] J. Daniel Couger, *Creative Problem Solving and Opportunity Finding*, Boyd & Fraser Publishing Company (1995).

[12] McDonnell Douglas Corporation, "Hi-Rel Fighter Concept," Report MDC B0642 (1988).

[13] Microsoft Corporation, "Introduction to Monte Carlo simulation" (*http://office.microsoft.com/en-us/excel/HA011118931033.aspx*) (accessed December 18, 2008).

[14] Jean Couillard, "The Role of Project Risk in Determining Project Management Approach," *Project Management Journal* 25, no. 4 (December 1995), pp. 3–15.

CHAPTER **12**

PROJECT PROCUREMENT MANAGEMENT

LEARNING OBJECTIVES

After reading this chapter, you will be able to:

- Understand the importance of project procurement management and the increasing use of outsourcing for information technology projects
- Describe the work involved in planning procurements for projects, including determining the proper type of contract to use and preparing a procurement management plan, statement of work, source selection criteria, and make-or-buy analysis
- Discuss what is involved in conducting procurements and strategies for obtaining seller responses, selecting sellers, and awarding contracts
- Understand the process of administering procurements by managing procurement relationships and monitoring contract performance
- Describe the process of closing procurements
- Discuss types of software available to assist in project procurement management

OPENING CASE

Marie McBride could not believe how much money her company was paying for outside consultants to help the company finish an important operating system conversion project. The consulting company's proposal said it would provide experienced professionals who had completed similar conversions, and that the job would be finished in six months or less with four consultants working full time. Nine months later her company was still paying high consulting fees, and half of the original consultants on the project had been replaced with new people. One new consultant had graduated from college only two months before and had extremely poor communications skills. Marie's internal staff complained that they were wasting time training some of these "experienced professionals." Marie talked to her company's purchasing manager about the contract, fees, and special clauses that might be relevant to the problems they were experiencing.

Marie was dismayed at how difficult it was to interpret the contract. It was very long and obviously written by someone with a legal background. When she asked what her company could do since the consulting firm was not following its proposal, the purchasing manager stated that the proposal was not part of the official contract. Marie's company was paying for time and materials, not specific deliverables. There was no clause stating the minimum experience level required for the consultants, nor were there penalty clauses for not completing the work on time. There was a termination clause, however, meaning the company could terminate the contract. Marie wondered why her company had signed such a poor contract. Was there a better way to deal with procuring services from outside the company?

THE IMPORTANCE OF PROJECT PROCUREMENT MANAGEMENT

Procurement means acquiring goods and/or services from an outside source. The term procurement is widely used in government; many private companies use the terms *purchasing* and *outsourcing*. Organizations or individuals who provide procurement services are referred to as suppliers, vendors, contractors, subcontractors, or sellers, with suppliers being the most widely used term. Many information technology projects involve the use of goods and services from outside the organization.

As described in Chapter 2, outsourcing has become a hot topic for research and debate, especially the implication of outsourcing to other countries, referred to as offshoring. The outsourcing statistics below are from an Information Technology Association of America (ITAA)–sponsored report:

- Spending for global sources of computer software and services is expected to grow at a compound annual rate of about 20 percent, increasing from about $15 billion in 2005 to $38 billion in 2010.
- Total savings from offshore resources during the same time period are estimated to grow from $8.7 billion to $20.4 billion. The cost savings and use of offshore resources lower inflation, increase productivity, and lower interest rates, which boosts business and consumer spending and increases economic activity.

- Although global outsourcing displaces some IT workers, total employment in the United States increases, according to ITAA, as the benefits ripple through the economy. "The incremental economic activity that follows offshore IT outsourcing creates over 257,000 net new jobs in 2005 and is expected to create over 337,000 net new jobs by 2010."[1]

Politicians debate on whether offshore outsourcing helps their own country or not. Andy Bork, chief operating officer of a computer network support service provider, describes outsourcing as an essential part of a healthy business diet. He describes good vs. bad outsourcing as something like good vs. bad cholesterol. He says that most people view offshore outsourcing as being bad because it takes jobs away from domestic workers. However, many companies are realizing that they can use offshore outsourcing *and* create more jobs at home. For example, Atlanta-based Delta Air Lines created 1,000 call-center jobs in India in 2003, saving $25 million, which enabled it to add 1,200 job positions for reservations and sales agents in the United States.[2] Other companies, like Wal-Mart, successfully manage the majority of their information technology projects in-house with very little commercial software and no outsourcing at all. (See the Suggested Reading on the companion Web site on "Wal-Mart's Way.")

Deciding whether to outsource, what to outsource, and how to outsource are important topics for many organizations throughout the world. In a 2008 survey, 74 percent of 600 global procurement executives believed that procurement issues are a high priority for their companies. About half of respondents also said that their companies focus too much on cost reduction instead of value creation. They also believe they are missing opportunities by not focusing on using technology to improve procurement processes. For example, 72 percent of respondents "have less than 10 percent of their spend channeled through eProcurement and eSourcing applications."[3]

Most organizations use some form of outsourcing to meet their information technology needs, spending most money within their own country. A 2008 report on IT outsourcing trends in the U.S. and Canada revealed the following:

- Application development is the most popular form of IT outsourcing and was used by 53 percent of organizations surveyed. Of the surveyed organizations, 44 percent outsourced application maintenance, 40 percent outsourced Web site or e-commerce systems, and 37 percent outsourced disaster recovery services.
- The IT function with the largest percentage of work outsourced is disaster recovery services, accounting for 50 percent of total IT outsourcing. Many organizations see the benefit in having an outside party perform offsite storage or maintenance of a recovery facility. Desktop support is the second most outsourced IT function (48 percent), followed closely by data center operations and help desk (47 percent each) and Web site or e-commerce systems (46 percent). IT security is at the bottom of the list, with only 29 percent of the work being outsourced.
- Even though application development and maintenance are frequently outsourced, they are a low percentage of the amount of total IT work outsourced. Application development and maintenance are often outsourced selectively since most organizations choose to do many projects in-house.[4]

Because outsourcing is a growing area, it is important for project managers to understand project procurement management. Many organizations are turning to outsourcing to:

- *Reduce both fixed and recurrent costs*. Outsourcing suppliers are often able to use economies of scale that may not be available to the client alone, especially for hardware and software. It can also be less expensive to outsource some labor costs to other organizations in the same country or offshore. Companies can also use outsourcing to reduce labor costs on projects by avoiding the costs of hiring, firing, and reassigning people to projects or paying their salaries when they are between projects.
- *Allow the client organization to focus on its core business*. Most organizations are not in business to provide information technology services, yet many have spent valuable time and resources on information technology functions when they should have focused on core competencies such as marketing, customer service, and new product design. By outsourcing many information technology functions, employees can focus on jobs that are critical to the success of the organization.
- *Access skills and technologies*. Organizations can gain access to specific skills and technologies when they are required by using outside resources. For example, a project may require an expert in a particular field or require the use of expensive hardware or software for one particular month on a project. Planning for this procurement ensure that the needed skills or technology will be available for the project.
- *Provide flexibility*. Outsourcing to provide extra staff during periods of peak workloads can be much more economical than trying to staff entire projects with internal resources. Many companies cite quicker flexibility in staffing as a key reason for outsourcing.
- *Increase accountability*. A well-written **contract**—a mutually binding agreement that obligates the seller to provide the specified products or services and obligates the buyer to pay for them—can clarify responsibilities and sharpen focus on key deliverables of a project. Because contracts are legally binding, there is more accountability for delivering the work as stated in the contract.

Organizations must also consider reasons they might *not* want to outsource. When an organization outsources work, it often does not have as much control over those aspects of projects that suppliers carry out. In addition, an organization could become too dependent on particular suppliers. If those suppliers went out of business or lost key personnel, it could cause great damage to a project. Organizations must also be careful to protect strategic information that could become vulnerable in the hands of suppliers. According to Scott McNeally, CEO of Sun Microsystems, Inc., "What you want to handle in-house is the stuff that gives you an edge over your competition—your core competencies. I call it your 'secret sauce.' If you're on Wall Street and you have your own program for tracking and analyzing the market, you'll hang onto that. At Sun, we have a complex program for testing microprocessor designs, and we'll keep it."[5] Project teams must think carefully about procurement issues and make wise decisions based on the unique needs of their projects and organizations. They can also change their minds on outsourcing as business conditions change.

In December 2002, when the financial services company JPMorgan Chase announced a seven-year, $5 billion deal to outsource much of its data processing to IBM, both companies bragged that the contract was the largest of its kind. It seemed like a win-win situation—IBM would make money and reduce costs, and JPMorgan Chase could push for innovation. However, in September 2004, JPMorgan Chase revoked the contract less than two years into its existence because the procurement plan no longer fit with JPMorgan Chase's business strategy. According to Austin Adams, chief information officer at JPMorgan Chase, "We believe managing our own technology infrastructure is best for the long-term growth and success of our company as well as our shareholders." However, IBM said the canceled contract was simply a result of JPMorgan Chase's merger earlier that year with Bank One. It tried to shrug off the loss of a large business deal. "The combined firm found itself with an abundance of IT assets," IBM spokesperson James Sciales said. "This decision was like other business decisions related to the merger."[6]

Outsourcing can also cause problems in other areas for companies and nations as a whole. For example, many people in Australia are concerned about outsourcing software development. "The Australian Computer Society says sending work offshore may lower the number of students entering IT courses, deplete the number of skilled IT professionals, and diminish the nation's strategic technology capability. Another issue is security, which encompasses the protection of intellectual property, integrity of data, and the reliability of infrastructure in offshore locations."[7]

The success of many information technology projects that use outside resources is often due to good project procurement management. **Project procurement management** includes the processes required to acquire goods and services for a project from outside the performing organization. Organizations can be either the buyer or the seller of products or services under a contract.

There are four main processes in project procurement management:

1. *Planning procurements* involves determining what to procure, when, and how. In procurement planning, one must decide what to outsource, determine the type of contract, and describe the work for potential sellers. **Sellers** are contractors, suppliers, or providers who provide goods and services to other organizations. Outputs of this process include a procurement management plan, statements of work, make-or-buy decisions, procurement documents, source selection criteria, and change requests.
2. *Conducting procurements* involves obtaining seller responses, selecting sellers, and awarding contracts. Outputs include selected sellers, procurement contract awards, resource calendars, change requests, and updates to the project management plan and other project documents.
3. *Administering procurements* involves managing relationships with sellers, monitoring contract performance, and making changes as needed. The main outputs of this process include procurement documentation, organizational

process asset updates, change requests, and project management plan updates.

4. *Closing procurements* involves completion and settlement of each contract, including resolution of any open items. Outputs include closed procurements and organizational process asset updates.

Figure 12-1 summarizes these processes and outputs, showing when they occur in a typical project.

Planning
Process: **Plan procurements**
Outputs: Procurement management plan, procurement statements of work, make-or-buy decisions, procurement documents, source selection criteria, and change requests

Executing
Process: **Conduct procurements**
Outputs: Selected sellers, procurement contract award, resource calendars, change requests, project management plan updates, project document updates

Monitoring and Controlling
Process: **Administer procurements**
Outputs: Procurement documentation, organizational process asset updates, change requests, project management plan updates

Closing
Process: **Close procurements**
Outputs: Closed procurements, organizational process asset updates

Project Start **Project Finish**

FIGURE 12-1 Project procurement management summary

PLANNING PROCUREMENTS

Planning procurements involves identifying which project needs can best be met by using products or services outside the organization. It involves deciding whether to procure, how to procure, what to procure, how much to procure, and when to procure. An important output of this process is the make-or-buy decision. A **make-or-buy decision** is one in which an organization decides if it is in its best interests to make certain products or perform certain services inside the organization, or if it is better to buy them from an outside organization. If there is no need to buy any products or services from outside the organization, then there is no need to perform any of the other procurement management processes.

For many projects, properly outsourcing some information technology functions can be a great investment, as shown in the following examples of What Went Right.

WHAT WENT RIGHT?

The Boots Company PLC, a pharmacy and health care company in Nottingham, England, outsourced its information technology systems to IBM in October 2002. The Boots Company signed a ten-year contract worth about $1.1 billion and expected to save $203.9 million over that period compared with the cost of running the systems itself. IBM managed and developed The Boots Company's systems infrastructure "from the mainframes to the tills in our 1,400 stores, to the computer on my desk," said spokesperson Francis Thomas. More than 400 Boots employees were transferred to IBM's payroll but continued to work at Boots' head office, with extra IBM staff brought in as needed. Thomas added, "The great thing about this is that if IBM has an expert in Singapore and [if] we need that expertise, we can tap into it for three months. It keeps our costs on an even keel."[8] It is not uncommon for long contracts to be renegotiated, becoming either shorter or longer in length. In May 2006, Boots and IBM began discussing amendments to their contract because much of Boots' IT infrastructure renewal program (including a new pharmacy system and an SAP rollout) was complete. A Boots spokesman said that the company achieved its goal much quicker than planned. In contrast, in 2005 Boots renegotiated its £90 million, seven-year IT contract it initially signed in 2002 with Xansa, extending it for another two years to 2011 in a £26 million deal.[9] It is also not uncommon to take advantage of competition and the changing marketplace for major procurements. In 2008, Boots announced that it would have up to six different suppliers competing to supply its IT products and services over the next year. "The company is keeping its business system management team and service management in-house, including helpdesk and project management."[10]

Properly planning purchases and acquisitions and writing good contracts can also save organizations millions of dollars. Many companies centralize purchasing for products, such as personal computers, software, and printers, to earn special pricing discounts. For example, in the mid-1980s the U.S. Air Force awarded a five-year, multimillion-dollar contract to automate 13 Air Force Systems Command bases. The project manager and contracting officer decided to allow for a unit pricing strategy for some items required in the contract, such as the workstations and printers. By not requiring everything to be negotiated at a fixed cost, the winning supplier lowered its final bid by more than $40 million.[11]

Inputs needed for planning procurements include the scope baseline, requirements documentation, teaming agreements, the risk register, risk-related contract decisions, activity resource requirements, the project schedule, activity cost estimates, the cost performance baseline, enterprise environmental factors, and organizational process assets. For example, a large clothing company might consider outsourcing the delivery of, maintenance of, and basic user training and support for laptops supplied to its international sales and marketing force. If there were suppliers who could provide this service well at a reasonable price, it would make sense to outsource, because this could reduce fixed and recurring costs for the clothing company and let them focus on their core business of selling clothes.

It is important to understand why a company would want to procure goods or services and what inputs are needed to plan purchases and acquisitions. In the opening case, Marie's company hired outside consultants to help complete an operating system conversion project because it needed people with specialized skills for a short period of time. This is a common occurrence in many information technology projects. It can be more effective to hire skilled consultants to perform specific tasks for a short period of time than to hire or keep employees on staff full time.

However, it is also important to define clearly the scope of the project, the products, services, or results required, market conditions, and constraints and assumptions. In Marie's case, the scope of the project and services required were relatively clear, but her company may not have adequately discussed or documented the market conditions or constraints and assumptions involved in using the outside consultants. Were there many companies that provided consultants to do operating conversion projects similar to theirs? Did the project team investigate the background of the company that provided the consultants? Did they list important constraints and assumptions for using the consultants, such as limiting the time that the consultants had to complete the conversion project or the minimum years of experience for any consultant assigned to the project? It is very important to answer these types of questions before going into an outsourcing agreement.

Tools and Techniques for Planning Procurements

There are several tools and techniques to help project managers and their teams in planning procurements, including make-or-buy analysis, expert judgment, and contract types.

Make-or-Buy Analysis

Make-or-buy analysis is a general management technique used to determine whether an organization should make or perform a particular product or service inside the organization or buy from someone else. This form of analysis involves estimating the internal costs of providing a product or service and comparing that estimate to the cost of outsourcing. Consider a company that has 1,000 international salespeople with laptops. Using make-or-buy analysis, the company would compare the cost of providing those services using internal resources to the cost of buying those services from an outside source. If supplier quotes were less than its internal estimates, the company should definitely consider outsourcing the training and user support services. Another common make-or-buy decision, though more complex, is whether a company should develop an application itself or purchase software from an outside source and customize it to the company's needs.

Many organizations also use make-or-buy analysis to decide if they should either purchase or lease items for a particular project. For example, suppose you need a piece of equipment for a project that has a purchase price of \$12,000. Assume it also had a daily operational cost of \$400. Suppose you could lease the same piece of equipment for \$800 per day, including the operational costs. You can set up an equation in which the purchase cost equals the lease cost to determine when it makes sense financially to lease or buy the equipment. In this example, d = the number of days you need the piece of equipment. The equation would then be:

$$\$800d = \$12{,}000 + \$400d$$

Subtracting \$400d from both sides, you get:

$$\$400d = \$12{,}000$$

Dividing both sides by $400, you get:

$$d = 30$$

which means that the purchase cost equals the lease cost in 30 days. So, if you need the equipment for less than 30 days, it would be more economical to lease it. If you need the equipment for more than 30 days, you should purchase it. In general, leasing is often cheaper for meeting short-term needs, but more expensive for long-term needs.

Expert Judgment

Experts inside an organization and outside an organization could provide excellent advice in planning purchases and acquisitions. Project teams often need to consult experts within their organization as part of good business practice. Internal experts might suggest that the company in the above example could not provide quality training and user support for the 1,000 laptop users since the service involves so many people with different skill levels in so many different locations. Experts in the company might also know that most of their competitors outsource this type of work and know who the qualified outside suppliers are. It is also important to consult legal experts since contracts for outsourced work are legal agreements.

Experts outside the company, including potential suppliers themselves, can also provide expert judgment. For example, suppliers might suggest an option for salespeople to purchase the laptops themselves at a reduced cost. This option would solve problems during employee turnover— exiting employees would own their laptops and new employees would purchase a laptop through the program. An internal expert might then suggest that employees receive a technology bonus to help offset what they might view as an added expense. Expert judgment, both internal and external, is an asset in making many procurement decisions.

Types of Contracts

Contract type is an important consideration. Different types of contracts can be used in different situations. Three broad categories of contracts are fixed price or lump sum, cost reimbursable, and time and material. A single contract can actually include all three of these categories, if it makes sense for that particular procurement. For example, you could have a contract with a seller that includes purchasing specific hardware for a fixed price or lump sum, some services that are provided on a cost reimbursable basis, and other services that are provided on a time and material basis. Project managers and their teams must understand and decide which approaches to use to meet their particular project needs. It is also important to understand when and how you can take advantage of unit pricing in contracts.

Fixed-price or **lump-sum contracts** involve a fixed total price for a well-defined product or service. The buyer incurs little risk in this situation since the price is predetermined. The sellers often pad their estimate somewhat to reduce their risk, realizing their price must still be competitive. For example, a company could award a fixed-price contract to purchase 100 laser printers with a certain print resolution and print speed to be delivered to one location within two months. In this example, the product and delivery date are well defined. Several sellers could create fixed price estimates for completing the job. Fixed-price contracts may also include incentives for meeting or exceeding selected project objectives. For example, the contract could include an incentive fee paid if the laser printers are delivered within one month. A firm-fixed-price (FFP) contract has the least amount of risk for the buyer, followed by a fixed-price incentive (FPI) contract.

Contracts can also include incentives to prevent or reduce cost overruns. For example, according to the U.S. Federal Acquisition Regulation (FAR) 16.4, fixed-price incentive fee contracts can include a **Point of Total Assumption (PTA)**, which is the cost at which the contractor assumes total responsibility for each additional dollar of contract cost. Contractors do not want to reach the point of total assumption because it hurts them financially, so they have an incentive to prevent cost overruns. The PTA is calculated with the following formula:

$$\text{PTA} = (\text{ceiling price} - \text{target price})/\text{government share} + \text{target cost}$$

For example, given the following information, assuming all dollars are in millions:

Ceiling price = \$1,250

Target price = \$1,100

Target cost = \$1,000

Share: 75%

$\text{PTA} = (\$1,250 - \$1,100)/.75 + \$1,000 = \$1,200$[12]

Cost-reimbursable contracts involve payment to the supplier for direct and indirect actual costs. Recall from Chapter 7 that direct costs are costs that can be directly related to producing the products and services of the project. They normally can be traced back to a project in a cost-effective way. Indirect costs are costs that are not directly related to the products or services of the project, but are indirectly related to performing the project. They normally cannot be traced back in a cost-effective way. For example, the salaries for people working directly on a project and hardware or software purchased for a specific project are direct costs, while the cost of providing a work space with electricity, a cafeteria, and so on are indirect costs. Indirect costs are often calculated as a percentage of direct costs. Cost-reimbursable contracts often include fees, such as a profit percentage or incentives for meeting or exceeding selected project objectives. These contracts are often used for projects that include providing goods and services that involve new technologies. The buyer absorbs more of the risk with cost-reimbursable contracts than they do with fixed-price contracts. Three types of cost-reimbursable contracts, in order of lowest to highest risk to the buyer, include cost plus incentive fee, cost plus fixed fee, and cost plus percentage of costs.

- With a **cost plus incentive fee (CPIF) contract**, the buyer pays the supplier for allowable performance costs along with a predetermined fee and an incentive bonus. See the Media Snapshot for an example of providing financial incentives to complete an important construction project ahead of schedule. Incentives are also often provided to suppliers to reducing contract costs. If the final cost is less than the expected cost, both the buyer and the supplier benefit from the cost savings, according to a pre-negotiated share formula. For example, suppose the expected cost of a project is \$100,000, the fee to the supplier is \$10,000, and the share formula is 85/15, meaning that the buyer absorbs 85 percent of the uncertainty and the supplier absorbs 15 percent. If the final price is \$80,000, the cost savings are \$20,000. The supplier would be paid the final cost and the fee plus an incentive of \$3,000 (15 percent of \$20,000), for a total reimbursement of \$93,000.

Contract incentives can be extremely effective. On August 1, 2007, tragedy struck Minneapolis, Minnesota, when a bridge on I-35W crossing the Mississippi River suddenly collapsed, killing 13 motorists, injuring 150 people, and leaving a mass of concrete and steel in the river and on its banks. The Minnesota Department of Transportation (MnDOT) acted quickly to find a contractor to rebuild the bridge. They also provided a strong incentive to finish the bridge as quickly as possible, ensuring quality and safety along the way.

Peter Sanderson, project manager for the joint venture of Flatiron-Manson, hired to build the bridge, led his team in completing the project three months ahead of schedule, and the new bridge opened on September 18, 2008. The contractors earned $25 million in incentive fees on top of their $234 million contract for completing the bridge ahead of schedule.

Why did MnDOT offer such a large incentive fee for finishing the project early? "I-35W in Minneapolis is a major transportation artery for the Twin Cities and entire state. Each day this bridge has been closed, it has cost road users more than $400,000," MnDOT Commissioner Tom Sorel remarked. "Area residents, business owners, motorists, workers and others have been affected by this corridor's closure. The opening of this bridge reconnects our community."[13]

- With a **cost plus fixed fee (CPFF) contract**, the buyer pays the supplier for allowable performance costs plus a fixed fee payment usually based on a percentage of estimated costs. This fee does not vary, however, unless the scope of the contract changes. For example, suppose the expected cost of a project is $100,000 and the fixed fee is $10,000. If the actual cost of the contract rises to $120,000 and the scope of the contract remains the same, the contractor will still receive the fee of $10,000.
- With a **cost plus award fee (CPAF) contract**, the buyer pays the supplier for allowable performance costs plus an award fee based on the satisfaction of subjective performance criteria. For example, you could consider the tip or gratuity you would give a server in a restaurant as a simple example, as long as there is no set gratuity percentage. You still have to pay for the cost of your meal, but you can decide on the tip amount based on your satisfaction with the food, drinks, and services provided. This type of contract is not usually subject to appeals.
- With a **cost plus percentage of costs (CPPC) contract**, the buyer pays the supplier for allowable performance costs along with a predetermined percentage based on total costs. From the buyer's perspective, this is the least desirable type of contract because the supplier has no incentive to decrease costs. In fact, the supplier may be motivated to increase costs, since doing so will automatically increase profits based on the percentage of costs. This type of contract is prohibited for U.S. federal government use, but it is sometimes used in private industry, particularly in the construction industry. All of the risk is borne by the buyer.

Time and material (T&M) contracts are a hybrid of both fixed-price and cost-reimbursable contracts. For example, an independent computer consultant might have a contract with a company based on a fee of $80 per hour for his or her services plus a fixed price of $10,000 for providing specific materials for the project. The materials fee might also be based on approved receipts for purchasing items, with a ceiling of $10,000. The consultant would send an invoice to the company each week or month, listing the materials fee, the number of hours worked, and a description of the work produced. This type of contract is often used for services that are needed when the work cannot be clearly specified and total costs cannot be estimated in a contract. Many contract programmers and consultants, such as those Marie's company hired in the opening case, prefer time and material contracts.

Unit pricing can also be used in various types of contracts to require the buyer to pay the supplier a predetermined amount per unit of product or service. The total value of the contract is a function of the quantities needed to complete the work. Consider an information technology department that might have a unit price contract for purchasing computer hardware. If the company purchases only one unit, the cost might be $1,000. If it purchases 10 units, the cost would be $10,000. This type of pricing often involves volume discounts. For example, if the company purchases between 10 and 50 units, the contracted cost might be $900 per unit. If it purchases over 50 units, the cost might go down to $800 per unit. This flexible pricing strategy is often advantageous to both the buyer and the seller. (See the second example in the What Went Right earlier in this chapter.)

Any type of contract should include specific clauses that take into account issues unique to the project. For example, if a company uses a time and material contract for consulting services, the contract should stipulate different hourly rates based on the level of experience of each individual contractor. The services of a junior programmer with no Bachelor's degree and less than three years' experience might be billed at $40 per hour, whereas the services of a senior programmer with at least a Bachelor's degree and more than ten years of experience might be billed at $80 per hour.

Figure 12-2 summarizes the spectrum of risk to the buyer and supplier for different types of contracts. Buyers have the lowest risk with firm-fixed price contracts, because they know exactly what they will need to pay the supplier. Buyers have the most risk with cost plus percentage of costs (CPPC) contracts because they do not know what the supplier's costs will be in advance, and the suppliers may be motivated to keep increasing costs. From the supplier's perspective, there is the least risk with a CPPC contract and the most risk with the firm-fixed price contract.

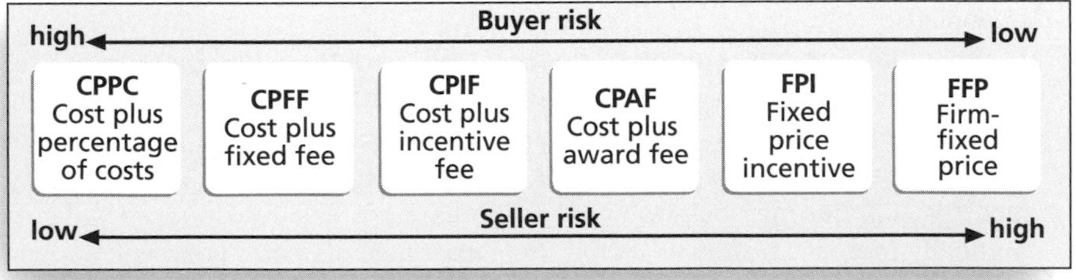

FIGURE 12-2 Contract types versus risk

Time and material contracts and unit-price contracts can be high- or low-risk, depending on the nature of the project and other contract clauses. For example, if an organization is unclear on what work needs to be done, it cannot expect a supplier to sign a firm-fixed price contract. However, the buyer could find a consultant or group of consultants to work on specific tasks based on a predetermined hourly rate. The buying organization could evaluate the work produced every day or week to decide if it wants to continue using the consultants. In this case the contract would include a **termination clause**—a contract clause that allows the buyer or supplier to end the contract. Some termination clauses state that the buyer can terminate a contract for any reason and give the supplier only 24 hours' notice. Suppliers must often give a one-week notice to terminate a contract and must have sufficient reasons for the termination. The buyer could also include a contract clause specifying hourly rates that are based on education and experience of consultants. These contract clauses reduce the risk incurred by the buyer while providing flexibility for accomplishing the work.

In addition to make-or-buy decisions and change requests based on the procurement decision, important outputs of planning procurements are a procurement management plan, statement of work, procurement documents (i.e., requests for proposals or quotes), and source selection criteria.

Procurement Management Plan

As stated earlier, every project management knowledge area includes some planning. The procurement management plan is a document that describes how the procurement processes will be managed, from developing documentation for making outside purchases or acquisitions to contract closure. Like other project plans, contents of the procurement management plan will vary with project needs. Some of the topics that can be included in a procurement management plan include:

- Guidelines on types of contracts to be used in different situations
- Standard procurement documents or templates to be used, if applicable
- Guidelines for creating contract work breakdown structures, statements of work, and other procurement documents
- Roles and responsibilities of the project team and related departments, such as the purchasing or legal department
- Guidelines on using independent estimates for evaluating sellers
- Suggestions on managing multiple providers
- Processes for coordinating procurement decisions, such as make-or-buy decisions, with other project areas, such as scheduling and performance reporting
- Constraints and assumptions related to purchases and acquisitions
- Lead times for purchases and acquisitions
- Risk mitigation strategies for purchases and acquisitions, such as insurance contracts and bonds
- Guidelines for identifying prequalified sellers and organizational lists of preferred sellers
- Procurement metrics to assist in evaluating sellers and managing contracts

Statement of Work

The **statement of work (SOW)** is a description of the work required for the procurement. Some organizations use the term statement of work to describe a document for describing internal work, as well. If a SOW is used as part of a contract to describe only the work required for that particular contract, it is called a *contract statement of work*. The contract SOW is a type of scope statement that describes the work in sufficient detail to allow prospective suppliers to determine if they are capable of providing the goods and services required and to determine an appropriate price. A contract SOW should be clear, concise, and as complete as possible. It should describe all services required and include performance reporting. It is important to use appropriate words in a contract SOW, such as *must* instead of *may*. For example, *must* implies that something has to be done; *may* implies that there is a choice involved in doing something or not. The contract SOW should specify the products and services required for the project, use industry terms, and refer to industry standards.

Many organizations use samples and templates to generate SOWs. Figure 12-3 provides a basic outline or template for a contract SOW that Marie's organization could use when they hire outside consultants or purchase other goods or services. For example, for the operating

Statement of Work (SOW)

I. **Scope of Work:** Describe the work to be done in detail. Specify the hardware and software involved and the exact nature of the work.

II. **Location of Work:** Describe where the work must be performed. Specify the location of hardware and software and where the people must perform the work.

III. **Period of Performance:** Specify when the work is expected to start and end, working hours, number of hours that can be billed per week, where the work must be performed, and related schedule information.

IV. **Deliverables Schedule:** List specific deliverables, describe them in detail, and specify when they are due.

V. **Applicable Standards:** Specify any company or industry-specific standards that are relevant to performing the work.

VI. **Acceptance Criteria:** Describe how the buyer organization will determine if the work is acceptable.

VII. **Special Requirements:** Specify any special requirements such as hardware or software certifications, minimum degree or experience level of personnel, travel requirements, and so on.

FIGURE 12-3 Statement of Work (SOW) template

system conversion project, Marie's company should specify the specific manufacturer and model number for the hardware involved, the former operating systems and new ones for the conversion, the number of pieces of each type of hardware involved (mainframes, midrange computers, or PCs), and so on. The contract SOW should also specify the location of the work, the expected period of performance, specific deliverables and when they are due, applicable standards, acceptance criteria, and special requirements. A good contract SOW gives bidders a better understanding of the buyer's expectations. A contract SOW should become part of the official contract to ensure that the buyer gets what the supplier bid on.

Procurement Documents

Planning procurements also involves preparing the documents needed for potential sellers to prepare their responses and determining the evaluation criteria for the contract award. The project team often uses standard forms and expert judgment as tools to help them create relevant procurement documents and evaluation criteria.

Two common examples of procurement documents include a Request for Proposal (RFP) and a Request for Quote (RFQ). A **Request for Proposal (RFP)** is a document used to solicit proposals from prospective suppliers. A **proposal** is a document prepared by a seller when there are different approaches for meeting buyer needs. For example, if an organization wants to automate its work practices or find a solution to a business problem, it can write and issue an RFP so suppliers can respond with proposals. Suppliers might propose various hardware, software, and networking solutions to meet the organization's need. Selections of winning sellers are often made on a variety of criteria, not just the lowest price. Developing an RFP is often a very time-consuming process. Organizations must do proper planning to ensure they adequately describe what they want to procure, what sellers should include in their proposals, and how they will evaluate proposals.

A **Request for Quote (RFQ)** is a document used to solicit quotes or bids from prospective suppliers. A **bid**, also called a *tender* or *quote* (short for quotation), is a document prepared by sellers providing pricing for standard items that have been clearly defined by the buyer. Organizations often use an RFQ for solicitations that involve specific items. For example, if a company wanted to purchase 100 personal computers with specific features, it might issue an RFQ to potential suppliers. RFQs usually do not take nearly as long to prepare as RFPs, nor do responses to them. Selections are often made based on the lowest price bid.

Writing a good RFP is a critical part of project procurement management. Many people have never had to write or respond to an RFP. To generate a good RFP, expertise is invaluable. Many examples of RFPs are available within different companies, from potential contractors, and from government agencies. There are often legal requirements involved in issuing RFPs and reviewing proposals, especially for government projects. It is important to consult with experts familiar with the contract planning process for particular organizations. To make sure the RFP has enough information to provide the basis for a good proposal, the buying organization should try to put itself in the suppliers' shoes. Could you develop a good proposal based on the information in the RFP? Could you determine detailed pricing and schedule information based on the RFP? Developing a good RFP is difficult, as is writing a good proposal.

Figure 12-4 provides a basic outline or template for an RFP. The main sections of an RFP usually include a statement of the purpose of the RFP, background information on the organization issuing the RFP, the basic requirements for the products and services being proposed, the hardware and software environment (usually important information for information technology related proposals), a description of the RFP process, the statement of work and schedule information, and possible appendices. A simple RFP might be three to five pages long, while an RFP for a larger, more complicated procurement might be hundreds of pages long.

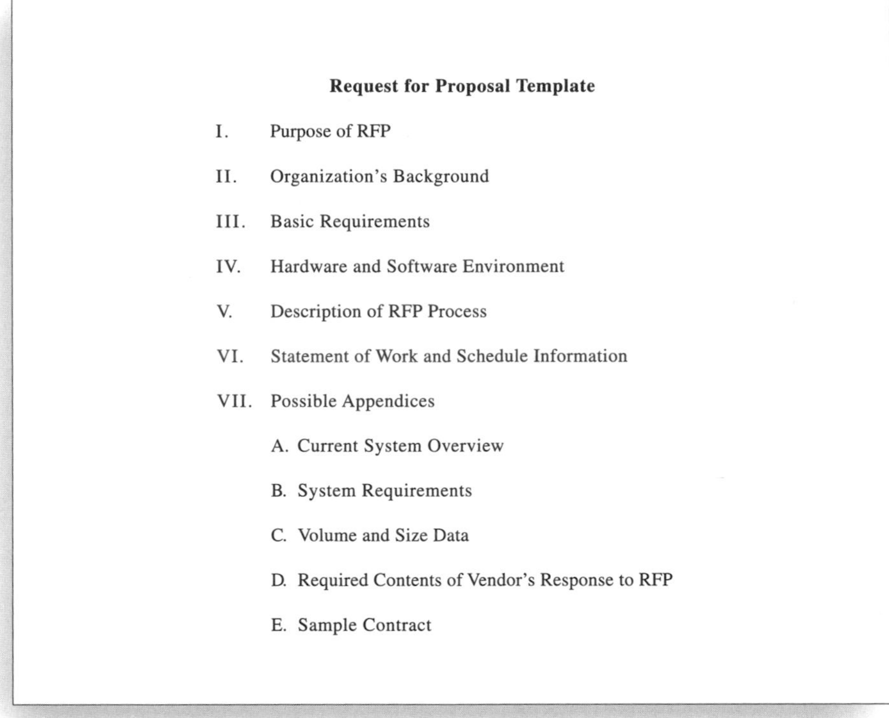

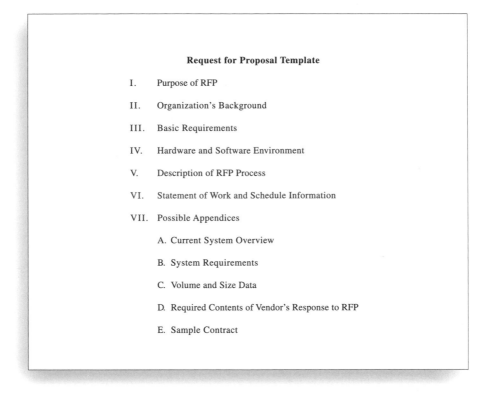

Request for Proposal Template

I. Purpose of RFP

II. Organization's Background

III. Basic Requirements

IV. Hardware and Software Environment

V. Description of RFP Process

VI. Statement of Work and Schedule Information

VII. Possible Appendices

A. Current System Overview

B. System Requirements

C. Volume and Size Data

D. Required Contents of Vendor's Response to RFP

E. Sample Contract

FIGURE 12-4 Request for Proposal (RFP) template

Other terms used for RFQs and RFPs include *invitations for bid*, *invitations for negotiation*, and *initial contractor responses*. Regardless of what they are called, all procurement documents should be written to facilitate accurate and complete responses from prospective sellers. They should include background information on the organization and project, the relevant statement of work, a schedule, a description of the desired form of response, evaluation criteria, pricing forms, and any required contractual provisions. They should also be rigorous enough to ensure consistent, comparable responses, but flexible enough to allow consideration of seller suggestions for better ways to satisfy the requirements.

Source Selection Criteria

It is very important for organizations to prepare some form of source selection evaluation criteria, preferably before they issue a formal RFP. Organizations use criteria to rate or score proposals, and they often assign a weight to each criterion to indicate how important it is. Some examples of criteria include the technical approach (30 percent weight), management approach (30 percent weight), past performance (20 percent weight), and price (20 percent weight). The criteria should be specific and objective. For example, if the buyer wants the supplier's project manager to be a certified Project Management Professional (PMP), the procurement documents should state that requirement clearly and follow it during the award process. Losing bidders may pursue legal recourse if the buyer does not follow a fair and consistent evaluation process.

Organizations should heed the saying, "Let the buyer beware." It is critical to evaluate proposals based on more than the appearance of the paperwork submitted. A key factor in evaluating bids, particularly for projects involving information technology, is the past performance record of the bidder. The RFP should require bidders to list other similar projects they have worked on and provide customer references for those projects. Reviewing performance records and references helps to reduce the risk of selecting a supplier with a poor track record. Suppliers should also demonstrate their understanding of the buyer's need, their technical and financial capabilities, their management approach to the project, and their price for delivering the desired goods and services. It is also crucial to write the contract to protect the buyer's interests.

Some information technology projects also require potential sellers to deliver a technical presentation as part of their proposal. The proposed project manager should lead the potential seller's presentation team. When the outside project manager leads the proposal presentation, the organization can begin building a relationship with the potential seller from the beginning. Visits to contractor sites can also help the buyer get a better feeling for the seller's capabilities and management style.

CONDUCTING PROCUREMENTS

After planning for procurements, the next procurement management process involves deciding whom to ask to do the work, sending appropriate documentation to potential sellers, obtaining proposals or bids, selecting a seller, and awarding a contract. Prospective sellers do some of the work in this process, normally at no cost to the buyer or project. The buying organization is responsible for advertising the work, and for large procurements, they often hold some sort of bidders' conference to answer questions about the job. Two of the main outputs of this process are a selected seller and procurement contract award.

Organizations can advertise to procure outside goods and services in many different ways. Sometimes a specific supplier might be the number-one choice for the buyer. In this case, the buyer gives procurement information to just that company. If the preferred supplier responds favorably, both organizations proceed to work together. Many organizations have formed good working relationships with certain suppliers, so they want to continue working with them.

In many cases, however, there may be more than one supplier qualified to provide the goods and services. Providing information and receiving bids from multiple sources often takes advantage of the competitive business environment. Offshore outsourcing, as described earlier, has increased tremendously as organizations find suitable sellers around the globe. As a result of pursuing a competitive bidding strategy, the buyer can receive better goods and services than expected at a lower price.

A bidders' conference, also called a *supplier conference* or *pre-bid conference*, is a meeting with prospective sellers prior to preparation of their proposals or bids. These conferences help ensure that everyone has a clear, common understanding of the buyer's desired products or services. In some cases, the bidders' conference might be held online via a Webcast or using other communications technology. Buyers will also post procurement information on a Web site and post answers to frequently asked questions. Before, during, or after the bidders' conference, the buyer may incorporate responses to questions into the procurement documents as amendments.

Once buyers receive proposals or bids, they can select a supplier or decide to cancel the procurement. Selecting suppliers or sellers, often called *source selection*, involves evaluating proposals or bids from sellers, choosing the best one, negotiating the contract, and awarding the contract. It can be a long, tedious process, especially for large procurements. Several stakeholders in the procurement process should be involved in selecting the best supplier for the project. Often teams of people are responsible for evaluating various sections of the proposals. There might be a technical team, a management team, and a cost team to focus on each of those major areas. Buyers typically develop a short list of the top three to five suppliers to reduce the work involved in selecting a source.

Experts in source selection highly recommend that buyers use formal proposal evaluation sheets during source selection. Figure 12-5 provides a sample proposal evaluation sheet that the project team might use to help create a short list of the best three to five proposals. Notice that this example is a form of a weighted scoring model as described in Chapter 4, Project Integration Management. The score for a criterion would be calculated by multiplying the weight of that criterion by the rating for that proposal. Adding up the scores would provide the total weighted score for each proposal. The proposals with the highest weighted scores should be included in the short list of possible sellers. Experts also recommend that technical criteria should not be given more weight than management or cost criteria. Many organizations have suffered the consequences of paying too much attention to the technical aspects of proposals. For example, the project might cost much more than expected or take longer to complete because the source selection team focused only on technical aspects of proposals. Paying too much attention to technical aspects of proposals is especially likely to occur on information technology projects. However, it is often the supplier's management team—not the technical team—that makes procurement successful.

		Proposal 1		Proposal 2		Proposal 3, etc.	
Criteria	**Weight**	**Rating**	**Score**	**Rating**	**Score**	**Rating**	**Score**
Technical approach	30%						
Management approach	30%						
Past performance	20%						
Price	20%						
Total score	100%						

FIGURE 12-5 Sample proposal evaluation sheet

After developing a short list of possible sellers, organizations often follow a more detailed proposal evaluation process. For example, they might list more detailed criteria for important categories, such as the management approach. They might assign points for the potential project manager's educational background and PMP certification, his or her presentation (meaning the sellers had to give a formal presentation as part of the evaluation process), top management support for the project, and the organization's project management methodologies. If the criteria and evaluation are done well, the seller with the most points based on all of the criteria should be offered the contract.

It is customary to have contract negotiations during the source selection process. Sellers on the short list are often asked to prepare a best and final offer (BAFO). People who negotiate contracts for a living often conduct these negotiations for contracts that involve large amounts of money. In addition, top managers from both the buying and selling organizations usually meet before making final decisions. The final output is a contract that obligates the seller to provide the specified products or services and obligates the buyer to pay for them. It is also appropriate on some projects to prepare a contract management plan to describe details about how the contract will be managed.

ADMINISTERING PROCUREMENTS

Administering procurements ensures that the seller's performance meets contractual requirements. The contractual relationship is a legal relationship and as such is subject to state and federal contract laws. It is very important that appropriate legal and contracting professionals be involved in writing and administering contracts.

Ideally, the project manager, a project team member, or an active user involved in the project should be actively involved in writing and administering the contract, so that everyone understands the importance of good procurement management. The project team should also seek expert advice in working with contractual issues. Project team members must be aware of potential legal problems they might cause by not understanding a contract. For example, most projects involve changes, and these changes must be handled properly for items under contract. Without understanding the provisions of the contract, a project manager may not realize he or she is authorizing the contractor to do additional work at additional costs. Therefore, change control is an important part of the contract administration process.

It is critical that project managers and team members watch for constructive change orders. **Constructive change orders** are oral or written acts or omissions by someone with actual or apparent authority that can be construed to have the same effect as a written change order. For example, if a member of the buyer's project team has met with the contractor on a weekly basis for three months to provide guidelines for performing work, he or she can be viewed as an apparent authority. If he or she tells the contractor to redo part of a report that has already been delivered and accepted by the project manager, that action can be viewed as a constructive change order and the contractor can legally bill the buyer for the additional work. Likewise, if this apparent authority tells the contractor to skip parts of a critical review meeting in the interests of time, the omission of that information is not the contractor's fault.

The following suggestions help ensure adequate change control and good contract administration:

- Changes to any part of the project need to be reviewed, approved, and documented by the same people in the same way that the original part of the plan was approved.
- Evaluation of any change should include an impact analysis. How will the change affect the scope, time, cost, and quality of the goods or services being provided? There must also be a baseline to understand and analyze changes.
- Changes must be documented in writing. Project team members should document all important meetings and telephone calls.
- When procuring complex information systems, project managers and their teams must stay closely involved to make sure the new system will meet business needs and work in an operational environment. Do not assume everything will go fine because you hired a reputable supplier. The buying organization needs to provide expertise as well.
- Have backup plans in case the new system does not work as planned when it is put into operation.
- Several tools and techniques can help in contract administration, such as a formal contract change control system, buyer-conducted procurement performance reviews, inspections and audits, performance reporting, payment systems, claims administration, and records management systems.

BEST PRACTICE

Accenture, one of the leading IT outsourcing firms, summarized survey responses from 565 executives from several countries to develop a list of best practices from experienced outsourcers throughout the world. Its seven suggestions include the following:

1. *Build in Broad Business Outcomes Early and Often*: Incorporate business outcomes as a performance measure from the outset of the arrangement.
2. *Hire a Partner, Not Just a Provider*: Look for an outsourcing provider that brings a wide set of skills and strengths, and a long-term track record of delivering results, in addition to competitive pricing.
3. *It's More Than a Contract, It's a Business Relationship*: Give as much attention to performance measurement and the quality of your relationship with your provider as you do to the contract.
4. *Leverage Gain-Sharing*: Use risk/reward provisions as incentives for higher-performance outsourcing.
5. *Use Active Governance*: Use active governance to manage the outsourcing relationship for maximum performance.
6. *Assign a Dedicated Executive*: Task your talented executives with the mission of optimizing your outsourcing arrangements
7. *Focus Relentlessly on Primary Objectives*: Be clear about objectives—cost, process improvement and the ability to focus on the core business are the most common among outsourcing veterans.[14]

CLOSING PROCUREMENTS

The final process in project procurement management is closing procurements, sometimes referred to as contract closure. Contract closure involves completion and settlement of contracts and resolution of any open items. The project team should determine if all work required in each contract was completed correctly and satisfactorily. They should also update records to reflect final results and archive information for future use.

Tools to assist in contract closure include procurement audits, negotiated settlements, and a records management system. Procurement audits are often done during contract closure to identify lessons learned in the entire procurement process. Organizations should strive to improve all of their business processes, including procurement management. Ideally, all procurements should end in a negotiated settlement between the buyer and seller. If negotiation is not possible, then some type of alternate disputes resolution such as mediation or arbitration can be used, and if all else fails, litigation in courts can be used to settle contracts. A records management system provides the ability to easily organize, find, and archive procurement-related documents. It is often an automated system, or at least partially automated, since there can be a large amount of information related to project procurement.

Outputs from contract closure include closed procurements and updates to organizational process assets. The buying organization often provides the seller with formal written notice that the contract has been completed. The contract itself should include requirements for formal acceptance and closure.

USING SOFTWARE TO ASSIST IN PROJECT PROCUREMENT MANAGEMENT

Over the years, organizations have used various types of productivity software to assist in project procurement management. For example, most organizations use word-processing software to write proposals or contracts, spreadsheet software to create proposal evaluation worksheets, databases to track suppliers, and presentation software to present procurement-related information.

Many companies are now using more advanced software to assist in procurement management. In fact, the term "e-procurement" often describes various procurement functions that are now done electronically. A 2008 Wikipedia entry for e-procurement described seven types of e-procurement:[15]

- *Web-based ERP (Electronic Resource Planning)*: Creating and approving purchasing requisitions, placing purchase orders and receiving goods and services by using a software system based on Internet technology.
- *e-MRO (Maintenance, Repair and Overhaul)*: The same as web-based ERP except that the goods and services ordered are non-product related MRO supplies.
- *e-sourcing*: Identifying new suppliers for a specific category of purchasing requirements using Internet technology.
- *e-tendering*: Sending requests for information and prices to suppliers and receiving the responses of suppliers using Internet technology.

- *e-reverse auctioning*: Using Internet technology to buy goods and services from a number of known or unknown suppliers.
- *e-informing*: Gathering and distributing purchasing information both from and to internal and external parties using Internet technology.
- *e-marketsites*: Expands on Web-based ERP to open up value chains. Buying communities can access preferred suppliers' products and services, add to shopping carts, create requisition, seek approval, receipt purchase orders and process electronic invoices with integration to suppliers' supply chains and buyers' financial systems.

Many different Web sites and software tools can assist in procurement functions. For example, most business travelers use the Web to purchase airline tickets and to reserve rental cars and hotel rooms for business trips. With the rise of applications for smartphones such as the Apple iPhone and T-Mobile G1, shoppers can even take a picture of a barcode on all types of products and compare prices with competing stores in the area so that they know they are getting the best deal. Likewise, many organizations can purchase numerous items online, or they can buy specialized software to help streamline their procurement activities. Companies such as Perfect Commerce, Ariba, and others started providing corporate procurement services over the Internet. Other established companies, such as Oracle, SAS, and Baan, have developed new software products to assist in procurement management. Traditional procurement methods were very inefficient and costly, and e-procurement services have proved to be very effective in reducing the costs and burdens of procurement.

Organizations can also take advantage of information available on the Web, in industry publications, or in various discussion groups offering advice on selecting suppliers. For example, many organizations invest millions of dollars in enterprise project management software. Before deciding which seller's software to use, organizations use the Internet to find information describing specific products provided by various suppliers, prices, case studies, and current customer information to assist in making procurement decisions. Buyers can also use the Internet to hold bidders' conferences, as described earlier in this chapter, or to communicate procurement-related information.

As with any information or software tool, organizations must focus on using the information and tools to meet project and organizational needs. Many nontechnical issues are often involved in getting the most value out of new technologies, especially new e-procurement software. For example, organizations must often develop partnerships and strategic alliances with other organizations to take advantage of potential cost savings. Organizations should practice good procurement management in selecting new software tools and managing relationships with the chosen suppliers.

The processes involved in project procurement management follow a clear, logical sequence. However, many project managers are not familiar with the many issues involved in purchasing goods and services from other organizations. If projects will benefit by procuring goods or services, then project managers and their teams must follow good project procurement management. As outsourcing for information technology projects increases, it is important for all project managers to have a fundamental understanding of this knowledge area.

CASE WRAP-UP

After reading the contract for her company's consultants carefully, Marie McBride found a clause giving her company the right to terminate the contract with a one-week notice. She met with her project team to get their suggestions. They still needed help completing the operating system conversion project. One team member had a friend who worked for a competing consulting firm. The competing consulting firm had experienced people available, and their fees were lower than the fees in the current contract. Marie asked this team member to help her research other consulting firms in the area that could work on the operating system conversion project. Marie then requested bids from these companies. She personally interviewed people from the top three suppliers' management teams and checked their references for similar projects.

Marie worked with the purchasing department to terminate the original contract and issue a new one with a new consulting firm that had a much better reputation and lower hourly rates. This time, she made certain the contract included a statement of work, specific deliverables, and requirements stating the minimum experience level of consultants provided. The contract also included incentive fees for completing the conversion work within a certain time period. Marie learned the importance of good project procurement management.

Chapter Summary

Procurement, purchasing, or outsourcing is acquiring goods and/or services from an outside source. Information technology outsourcing continues to grow, both within an organization's own country and offshore. Organizations outsource to reduce costs, focus on their core business, access skills and technologies, provide flexibility, and increase accountability. It is becoming increasingly important for information technology professionals to understand project procurement management.

Project procurement management processes include planning procurements, conducting procurements, administering procurements, and closing procurements.

Planning procurements involves deciding what to procure or outsource, what type of contract to use, and how to describe the effort in a statement of work. Make-or-buy analysis helps an organization determine whether it can cost-effectively procure a product or service. Project managers should consult internal and external experts to assist them with procurement planning because many legal, organizational, and financial issues are often involved.

The basic types of contracts are fixed price, cost reimbursable, and time and material. Fixed-price contracts involve a fixed total price for a well-defined product and entail the least risk to buyers. Cost-reimbursable contracts involve payments to suppliers for direct and indirect actual costs and require buyers to absorb some of the risk. Time and material contracts are a hybrid of fixed-price and cost-reimbursable contracts and are commonly used by consultants. Unit pricing involves paying suppliers a predetermined amount per unit of service and imposes different levels of risk on buyers, depending on how the contract is written. It is important to decide which contract type is most appropriate for a particular procurement. All contracts should include specific clauses that address unique aspects of a project and that describe termination requirements.

A statement of work (SOW) describes the work required for the procurement in enough detail to allow prospective suppliers to determine if they are capable of providing the goods and services and to determine an appropriate price.

Conducting procurements involves obtaining seller responses, selecting sellers, and awarding contracts. Organizations should use a formal proposal evaluation form when evaluating suppliers. Technical criteria should not be given more weight than management or cost criteria during evaluation.

Administering procurements involves managing relationships with sellers, monitoring contract performance, and making changes as needed. The project manager and key team members should be involved in writing and administering the contract. Project managers must be aware of potential legal problems they might cause when they do not understand a contract. Project managers and teams should use change control procedures when working with outside contracts and should be especially careful about constructive change orders.

Closing procurements involves completion and settlement of each contract, including resolution of any open items. Procurement audits, negotiated settlements, and records management systems are tools and techniques for closing procurements.

Several types of software can assist in project procurement management. E-procurement software helps organizations save money in procuring various goods and services. Organizations can also use the Web, industry publications, and discussion groups to research and compare various suppliers.

Quick Quiz

1. What IT function has the largest percentage of work outsourced?
   a. application development
   b. disaster recovery
   c. application maintenance
   d. help desk support
2. Your organization hired a specialist in a certain field to provide training for a short period of time. Which reason for outsourcing would this fall under?
   a. reducing costs
   b. allowing the client organization to focus on its core business
   c. accessing skills and technologies
   d. providing flexibility
3. In which project procurement management process is an RFP often written?
   a. planning procurements
   b. conducting procurements
   c. administering procurements
   d. selecting sellers
4. An item you need for a project has a daily lease cost of $200. To purchase the item, there is an investment cost of $6,000 and a daily cost of $100. Calculate the number of days when the lease cost would be the same as the purchase cost.
   a. 30
   b. 40
   c. 50
   d. 60
5. Which type of contract has the least amount of risk for the buyer?
   a. fixed-price
   b. cost plus incentive fee (CPIF)
   c. time and material
   d. cost plus fixed fee (CPFF)
6. The ______________ is the point at which the contractor assumes total responsibility for each additional dollar of contract cost.
   a. breakeven point
   b. Share Ratio Point
   c. Point of Reconciliation
   d. Point of Total Assumption

7. If your college or university wanted to get information from potential sellers for providing a new sports stadium, what type of document would they require of the potential sellers?
   a. RFP
   b. RFQ
   c. proposal
   d. quote
8. Buyers often prepare a ____________ list when selecting a seller to make this process more manageable.
   a. preferred
   b. short
   c. qualified suppliers
   d. BAFO
9. A proposal evaluation sheet is an example of a(n) ____________.
   a. RFP
   b. NPV analysis
   c. earned value analysis
   d. weighted scoring model
10. ____________ is a term used to describe various procurement functions that are now done electronically.
   a. E-procurement
   b. eBay
   c. E-commerce
   d. EMV

Quick Quiz Answers

1. b; 2. c; 3. a; 4. d; 5. a; 6. d; 7. c; 8. b; 9. d; 10. a

Discussion Questions

1. List five reasons why organizations outsource. Why is there a growing trend in outsourcing, especially offshore?
2. Explain the make-or-buy decision process and describe how to perform the financial calculations involved in the simple lease-or-buy example provided in this chapter. What are the main types of contracts if you decide to outsource? What are the advantages and disadvantages of each?
3. Do you think many information technology professionals have experience writing RFPs and evaluating proposals for information technology projects? What skills would be useful for these tasks?
4. How do organizations decide whom to send RFPs or RFQs?

5. How can organizations use a weighted decision matrix to evaluate proposals as part of seller selection?
6. List two suggestions for ensuring adequate change control on projects that involve outside contracts.
7. What is the main purpose of a procurement audit?
8. How can software assist in procuring goods and services? What is e-procurement software? Do you see any ethical issues with e-procurement? For example, should stores be able to block people with smartphones from taking pictures of barcodes in their stores to do comparison shopping?

Exercises

1. Search the Internet for the term "IT outsourcing." Find at least two articles that discuss outsourcing, whether beneficial or controversial. Summarize the articles and answer the following questions in a two-page paper:
   - What are the main types of goods and services being outsourced?
   - Why are the organizations in the articles choosing to outsource?
   - Have the organizations in your articles benefited from outsourcing? Why or why not?
2. Interview someone who was involved in an information technology procurement process, such as a manager in your organization's IT department, and have him or her explain the process that was followed. Alternatively, find an article describing an IT procurement in an organization. Write a two-page paper describing the procurement and any lessons learned by the organization.
3. Suppose your company is trying to decide whether it should buy special equipment to prepare some of its high-quality publications itself or lease the equipment from another company. Suppose leasing the equipment costs $240 per day. If you decide to purchase the equipment, the initial investment is $6,800, and operations will cost $70 per day. After how many days will the lease cost be the same as the purchase cost for the equipment? Assume your company would only use this equipment for 30 days. Should your company buy the equipment or lease it?
4. Search online for samples of IT contracts. Use search phrases like "IT contract" or "sample contract." Analyze the key features of the contract. What type of contract was used and why? Review the language and clauses in the contract. What are some of the key clauses? List questions you have about the contract and try to get answers from someone familiar with contracts.
5. Review the SUNY Library Automation Migration RFP (available on the companion Web site under Chapter 12) or another RFP for an IT project. Write a two-page paper summarizing the purpose of the RFP and how well you think it describes the work required.
6. Draft the source selection criteria that might be used for evaluating proposals for providing laptops for all students, faculty, and staff at your college or university or all business professionals in your organization. Use Figure 12-5 as a guide. Include at least five criteria, and make the total weights add up to 100. Write a two-page paper explaining and justifying the criteria and their weights.

Running Case

Senior management at Manage Your Health, Inc. (MYH) decided that it would be best to outsource the work involved in training employees on the soon to be rolled-out Recreation and Wellness system and provide incentives for employees to use the system and improve their health. MYH feels that the right outside company could get people excited about the system and provide a good incentive program. As part of the seller selection process, MYH will require interviews and samples of similar work to be physically presented to a review team. Recall that MYH has more than 20,000 full-time employees and more than 5,000 part-time employees. Assume the work would involve holding several instructor-led training sessions, developing a training video that could be viewed from the company's Intranet site, developing a training manual for the courses and for anyone to download from the Intranet site, developing an incentive program for using the system and improving health, creating surveys to assess the training and incentive programs, and developing monthly presentations and reports on the work completed. The initial contract would last one year, with annual renewal options.

1. Suppose that your team has discussed management's request. You agree that it makes sense to have another organization manage the incentive program for this new application, but you do not think it makes sense to outsource the training. Your company has a lot of experience doing internal training. You also know that your staff will have to support the system, so you want to develop the training to minimize future support calls. Write a one-page memo to senior management stating why you think the training should be done in-house.
2. Assume the source selection criteria for evaluating proposals is as follows:
    - Management approach, 15%
    - Technical approach, 15%
    - Past performance, 20%
    - Price, 20%
    - Interview results and samples, 30%

    Using Figure 12-5 as a guide and the weighted scoring model template, if desired, create a spreadsheet that could be used to enter ratings and calculate scores for each criterion and total weighted scores for three proposals. Enter scores for Proposal 1 as 80, 90, 70, 90, and 80, respectively. Enter scores for Proposal 2 as 90, 50, 95, 80, and 95. Enter scores for Proposal 3 as 60, 90, 90, 80, and 65. Add a paragraph summarizing the results and your recommendation on the spreadsheet. Print your results on one page.
3. Draft potential clauses you could include in the contract to provide incentives to the seller based on MYH achieving its main goal of improving employee health and lowering health care premiums as a result of this project. Be creative in your response, and document your ideas in a one-page paper.

Companion Web Site

Visit the companion Web site for this text (*www.cengage.com/mis/schwalbe*) to access:

- References cited in the text and additional suggested readings for each chapter
- Template files

- Lecture notes
- Interactive quizzes
- Podcasts
- Links to general project management Web sites
- And more

See the Preface of this text for additional information on accessing the companion Web site.

Key Terms

bid — also called a *tender* or *quote* (short for quotation), a document prepared by sellers providing pricing for standard items that have been clearly defined by the buyer

constructive change orders — oral or written acts or omissions by someone with actual or apparent authority that can be construed to have the same effect as a written change order

contract — a mutually binding agreement that obligates the seller to provide the specified products or services, and obligates the buyer to pay for them

cost plus award fee (CPAF) contract — a contract in which the buyer pays the supplier for allowable performance costs plus an award fee based on the satisfaction of subjective performance criteria

cost plus fixed fee (CPFF) contract — a contract in which the buyer pays the supplier for allowable performance costs plus a fixed fee payment usually based on a percentage of estimated costs

cost plus incentive fee (CPIF) contract — a contract in which the buyer pays the supplier for allowable performance costs along with a predetermined fee and an incentive bonus

cost plus percentage of costs (CPPC) contract — a contract in which the buyer pays the supplier for allowable performance costs along with a predetermined percentage based on total costs

cost-reimbursable contracts — contracts involving payment to the supplier for direct and indirect actual costs

fixed-price contract — contract with a fixed total price for a well-defined product or service; also called a *lump-sum contract*

lump-sum contract — contract with a fixed total price for a well-defined product or service; also called a *fixed-price contract*

make-or-buy decision — when an organization decides if it is in its best interests to make certain products or perform certain services inside the organization, or if it is better to buy them from an outside organization

Point of Total Assumption (PTA) — the cost at which the contractor assumes total responsibility for each additional dollar of contract cost in a fixed price incentive fee contract

procurement — acquiring goods and/or services from an outside source

project procurement management — the processes required to acquire goods and services for a project from outside the performing organization

proposal — a document prepared by sellers when there are different approaches for meeting buyer needs

Request for Proposal (RFP) — a document used to solicit proposals from prospective suppliers

Request for Quote (RFQ) — a document used to solicit quotes or bids from prospective suppliers

sellers — contractors, suppliers, or providers who provide goods and services to other organizations

statement of work (SOW) — a description of the work required for the procurement

termination clause — a contract clause that allows the buyer or supplier to end the contract

time and material (T&M) contracts — a hybrid of both fixed-price and cost-reimbursable contracts

unit pricing — an approach in which the buyer pays the supplier a predetermined amount per unit of service, and the total value of the contract is a function of the quantities needed to complete the work

End Notes

[1] Global Insight, "Executive Summary: The Comprehensive Impact of Offshore IT Software and Services Outsourcing on the U.S. Economy and the IT Industry," Information Technology Association of America, *ITAA.org* (October 2005).

[2] Andy Bork, "Soft skills needed in a hard world," *Minneapolis Star Tribune* (May 24, 2004).

[3] KPMG, "KPMG Survey finds procurement a high priority at most companies, yet many are failing to implement cost, operational improvements," *PR Newswire* (September 10, 2008).

[4] Computer Economics, Inc. *IT Spending, Staffing, and Technology Trends: 2008/2009* (2008).

[5] Scott McNeally, "The Future of the Net: Why We Don't Want You to Buy Our Software," *Sun Executive Perspectives* (*www.sun.com/dot-com/perspectives/stop.html*) (Sun Microsystems, Inc., 1999): 1.

[6] Gretchen Morgenson, "IBM Shrugs Off Loss of Big Contract," *TechNewsWorld* (September 17, 2004).

[7] Stan Beer, "Is going offshore good for Australia?" *The Age* (September 21, 2004).

[8] Gillian Law, "IBM wins $1.1B outsourcing deal in England," *ComputerWorld* (October 1, 2002).

[9] Computer Business Review Online, "Boots scales back $1.3 billion IBM deal," CBRonline.com (May 15, 2006),

[10] Karl Finders, "Boots' multi-sourcing will use up to six suppliers," ComputerWeekly.com (June 2008).

[11] Kathy Schwalbe, Air Force Commendation Medal Citation (1986).

[12] Robert Antonio, "The Fixed-Price Incentive Firm Target Contract: Not As Firm As the Name Suggests," *WIFCON.com* (November 2003).

[13] Dick Rohland, "I-35W Bridge Completion Brings Closure to Minneapolis," ConstructionEquipmentGuide.com (October 4, 2008).

[14] Accenture, "Driving High-Performance Outsourcing: Best Practices from the Masters," (2004).

[15] Wikipedia, "E-procurement," *http://en.wikipedia.org/wiki/E-procurement* (accessed December 2008).

GUIDE TO USING MICROSOFT PROJECT 2007

Introduction	A.2
New Features of Project 2007	A.3
Backward Compatibility	A.4
Before You Begin	A.4
Overview of Project 2007	A.5
Starting Project 2007 and Using the Getting Started and Project Guide Features	A.5
Main Screen Elements	A.8
Project 2007 Views	A.14
Project 2007 Filters	A.18
Project Scope Management	A.19
Creating a New Project File	A.20
Developing a Work Breakdown Structure	A.22
Saving Project Files with or without a Baseline	A.25
Project Time Management	A.26
Entering Task Durations	A.27
Establishing Task Dependencies	A.32
Changing Task Dependency Types and Adding Lead or Lag Time	A.35
Gantt Charts	A.38
Network Diagrams	A.40
Critical Path Analysis	A.42

Project Cost Management	A.44
Fixed and Variable Cost Estimates	A.44
Assigning Resources to Tasks	A.48
Baseline Plan, Actual Costs, and Actual Times	A.54
Earned Value Management	A.59
Project Human Resource Management	A.62
Resource Calendars	A.62
Resource Histograms	A.64
Resource Leveling	A.67
Project Communications Management	A.70
Common Reports and Views	A.70
Using Templates and Inserting Hyperlinks and Comments	A.71
Using the Copy Picture Feature	A.75
Discussion Questions	A.77
Exercises	A.77
Exercise A-1: Homework Assignments	A.77
Exercise A-2: Web Site Development	A.78
Exercise A-3: Software Training Program	A.80
Exercise A-4: Project Tracking Database	A.81
Exercise A-5: Real Project Application	A.84

INTRODUCTION

This appendix provides a concise guide to using Microsoft Office Project Professional 2007 (often referred to as Project 2007) to assist in performing project management functions. The Office Project 2007 family includes several different products:

- Project Standard 2007, a non-Web-based, stand-alone program for individuals who manage projects independently, similar to earlier versions of Project Standard.
- Project Professional 2007, which is basically Project Standard 2007 plus Project Web Access and allows you to connect to Project Server 2007, if available. (Note: This guide does not include information on connecting to Project Server 2007.)

- The Microsoft Office Enterprise Project Management (EPM) Solution, which combines Project Server 2007, Project Professional 2007, Project Web Access, Project Portfolio Server 2007, and Project Portfolio Web Access to form a business solution for organizations, departments, and teams. As its name suggests, this version is designed for use across an enterprise and provides project portfolio management capabilities. Organizations should develop and apply many standards, templates, codes, and procedures before using the enterprise version of Project 2007 to make the best use of its capabilities.

Each version of Project 2007 can help users manage different aspects of all nine project management knowledge areas. (Consult Microsoft's Web site for more details on all of the versions of Project 2007.) Most users, however, focus on using Project 2007 to assist with scope, time, cost, human resource, and communications management. This guide uses these project management knowledge areas as the context for learning how to use Project 2007. The basic order of steps in this appendix follows best practices in project management. That is, you should first determine the scope of a project, then the time, and then the resource and cost information. You can then set a baseline and enter actuals to track and communicate performance information.

Hundreds of project management software products are available today, but Microsoft Project is the clear market leader among midrange applications. Before you can use Project 2007 or any project management software effectively, you must understand the fundamental concepts of project management, such as creating work breakdown structures, linking tasks, entering duration estimates, and so on. See the Suggested Readings on the companion Web site (*www.cengage.com/mis/schwalbe*) for recommendations on other resources to help you gain an even deeper understanding of Project 2007.

New Features of Project 2007

Because there have been several previous versions of Microsoft Project, it is useful to understand some of the new capabilities of Project 2007, especially if you are working with people who are upgrading from a previous version. Several new or improved features are available in Project 2007, such as the following:

- The Review Tasks Drivers feature lets you show prerequisites and resource constraints that drive the start date of the selected task. Simply click these drivers to link to relevant information.
- The Visual Change Highlights feature allows you to determine the impact of each change you make on all other dependent tasks.
- The Multiple Level Undo feature allows you to reverse the most recent series of changes: undo and redo changes to views, data, and options. This function also lets you undo actions or sets of actions from macros or third-party applications.
- You can now apply predefined financial fields, such as cost codes, and improve mapping to the financial fields tracked in your organization's project accounting systems.
- The Budget Tracking feature lets you define a budget at a high level so you can allocate funds and track costs against the budget.
- The Cost Resources feature, which also supports integration of Project 2007 with accounting systems, allows you to assign planned and actual costs to a task, not just work or materials.

- You can now use Microsoft Excel and Visio Professional to produce charts, graphs, and diagrams based on Project 2007 data by means of the Visual Reports feature. For example, you can now create earned value charts using Visual Reports.
- You can now define and share custom report templates with other Project 2007 users. These reports include a data cube for drill downs and pivot tables.
- The Background Cell Highlighting feature lets you shade cells, similar to Excel, to add emphasis to cells.
- Enhancements to the Calendar Interface and the addition of 3-D Gantt bars allow you to create even more visually effective reports.

Backward Compatibility

Project 2007 can open files created in previous versions of Project, such as Project 98, 2000, 2002, or 2003. Any features that do not map to prior file formats will be discarded when a project is saved in the older file format. Project 2007 also saves to file formats including XML (extensible markup language), CSV (comma-separated values), text (tab-delimited), Excel workbook, Excel PivotTable, Web page, Project 2003, and Project 2002. Project 2007 no longer supports OLEDB (object linking and embedding, database).

Before You Begin

This appendix assumes you are using Project 2007 with Windows XP or Vista and are familiar with other Windows-based applications. You can download a free trial of Project 2007 from Microsoft's Web site, and you can launch the trial application for a total of 25 times before having to enter the Product Key and Activating the product. Additionally, students and faculty can purchase software at deep discounts from several sources, including *www.journeyed.com*. Check your work by reviewing the many screen shots included in the steps, or by using the solution files that are available for download from the companion Web site for this text or from your instructor.

HELP

You need to be running Windows XP or Vista as your operating system to use Project 2007. If you have any technical difficulties, contact Microsoft's Support Services at *www.microsoft.com*. To complete the hands-on activities in the appendix, you will need to copy a set of files from the companion Web site for this text (*www.cengage.com/mis/schwalbe*) to your computer. You can also download the files from the author's Web site (*www.kathyschwalbe.com*) under Book FAQs.

This appendix uses a fictitious information technology project—the Project Tracking Database project—to illustrate how to use the software. The goal of this project is to create a database to keep track of all the projects a company is working on. Each section of the appendix includes hands-on activities for you to perform. When you begin each set of steps, make sure you are using the correct file. Before you begin your work you should have the finance.mpp, resource.mpp, and kickoffmeeting.doc files.

In addition, you will create the following files from scratch as you work through the steps:

- scope.mpp
- time.mpp

- tracking.mpp
- baseline.mpp
- level.mpp

Now that you understand project management concepts and the basic project management terminology, you will learn how to start Project 2007, review the Help facility and a template file, and begin to plan the Project Tracking Database project.

OVERVIEW OF PROJECT 2007

The first step to mastering Project 2007 is to become familiar with the Help facility, online tutorials, major screen elements, views, and filters. This section describes each of these features.

Starting Project 2007 and Using the Getting Started and Project Guide Features

To start Project 2007:

1. *Open Project 2007.* Click the **Start** button on the taskbar, point to **All Programs** in Windows XP or **Programs** in Vista, point to or click **Microsoft Office**, and then click **Microsoft Office Project 2007.** Alternatively, a shortcut or icon might be available on the desktop; in this case, double-click the icon to start the software.
2. *Maximize Project 2007.* If the Project 2007 window does not fill the entire screen as shown in Figure A-1, click the **Maximize** button in the upper-right corner of the window.

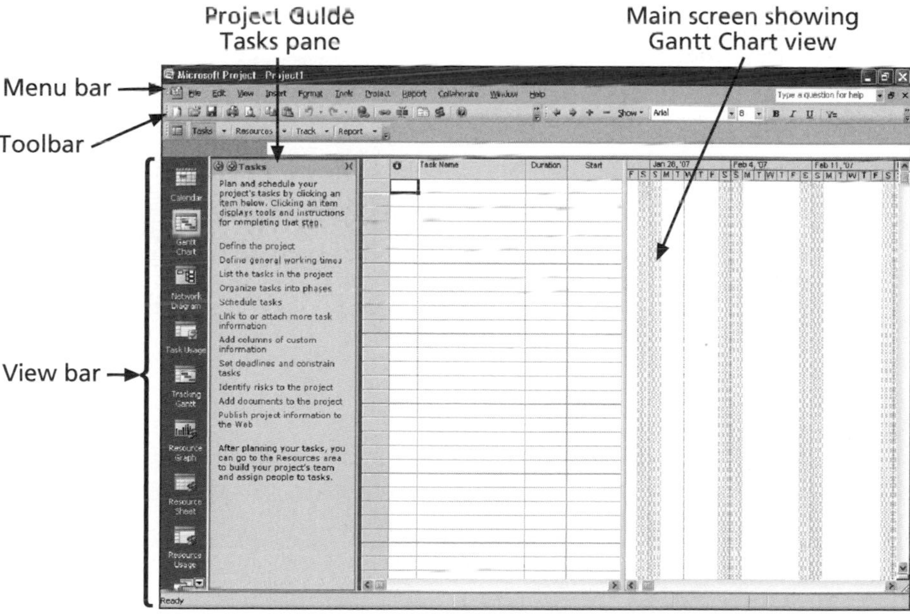

FIGURE A-1 Project Guide Tasks pane and Project 2007 main screen

HELP

If the View bar is not open, click View on the Menu bar, and then click View Bar. If the Project Guide pane is not open, click View on the Menu bar, and then click Turn On Project Guide. Also, your toolbars, date formats, or other screen elements may look slightly different from Figure A-1. All screen shots were taken using Windows XP. Focus on the Project 2007 main screen and the Project Guide Tasks pane.

Project 2007 is now running and ready to use. Look at some of the elements of the Project 2007 screen. The default view is the Gantt Chart view, which shows tasks and other information in the Entry table as well as a calendar display. You can access other views by clicking each button in the View bar on the left side of the screen. Notice that when Project 2007 starts, it opens a new file named Project1, as shown in the title bar. If you open a second file, the name will be Project2, and so on, until you save and rename the file.

When you start Project 2007, the Project Guide Tasks pane automatically opens, as shown in Figure A-1. The Project Guide helps you learn Project 2007 by providing instructions for completing various steps in building a Project 2007 file.

To use the Project Guide:

1. *Open the Project Guide*. Click the **Tasks** list arrow on the Project Guide toolbar, as shown in Figure A-2. Notice the various options listed. The Resources, Track, and Report buttons on the Project Guide toolbar list additional options. You will use some of these options later in this appendix.

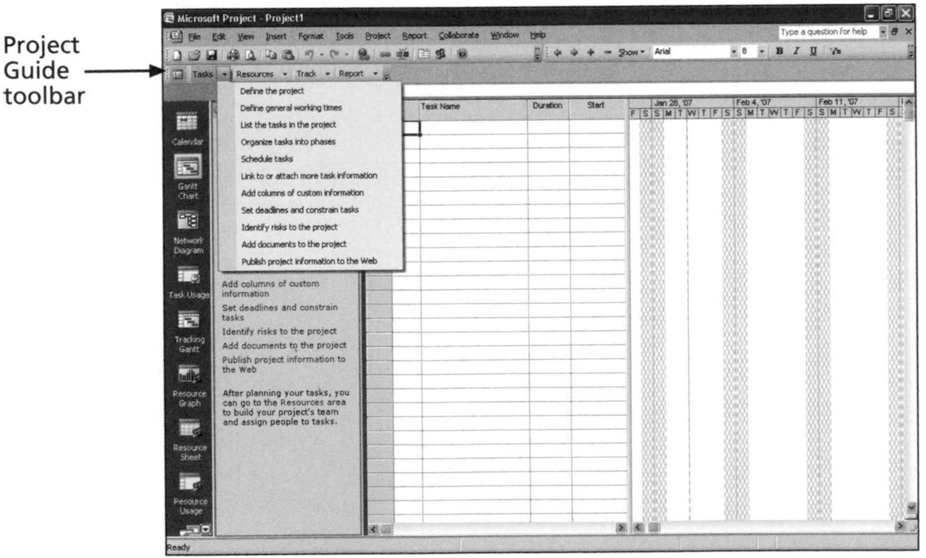

FIGURE A-2 Using the Project Guide

2. *Set the project start date*. Click the first option in the Tasks list, **Define the project.**
3. *Review the Project Guide instructions*. Review the information that displays in the pane on the left side of the screen. As you select different options in the Project Guide, the Task pane displays specific information related to that option. Notice that the default project start date is set at the current date. Click the **Date** list arrow on the pop-up calendar to select a date. Select the last day of the month that displays.
4. *Close the Project Guide*. Click the **Close** button ✕ in the upper-right corner of the Project Guide window, and click Yes to exit the wizard.

HELP

If the Project Guide toolbar is not visible, click View on the Menu bar, select Toolbars, and then click Project Guide.

In addition to using the Project Guide window, you can access other information to help you learn how to use Project 2007 under the Help menu. Figure A-3 shows the Help menu options available by clicking Help on the Menu bar or by pressing F1. Figure A-4 shows the detailed list of topics available from the first Help option, Microsoft Office Project Help.

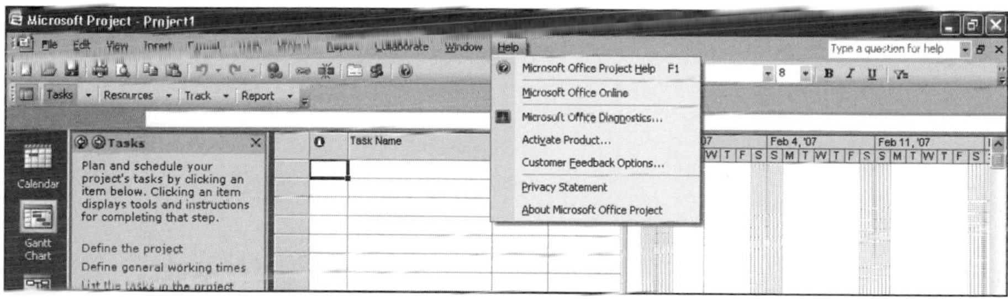

FIGURE A-3 Project 2007 Help menu options

Microsoft realizes that Project 2007 can take some time to learn and provides a number of resources on its Web site. Select Microsoft Office Online from the Project 2007 Help menu to go to Microsoft's Web site for Office products. Microsoft's Web site for Project 2007 (*www.microsoft.com/project*) provides files for users to download, case studies, articles, and other useful materials. Also see the Suggested Readings under Appendix A on the companion Web site for this text.

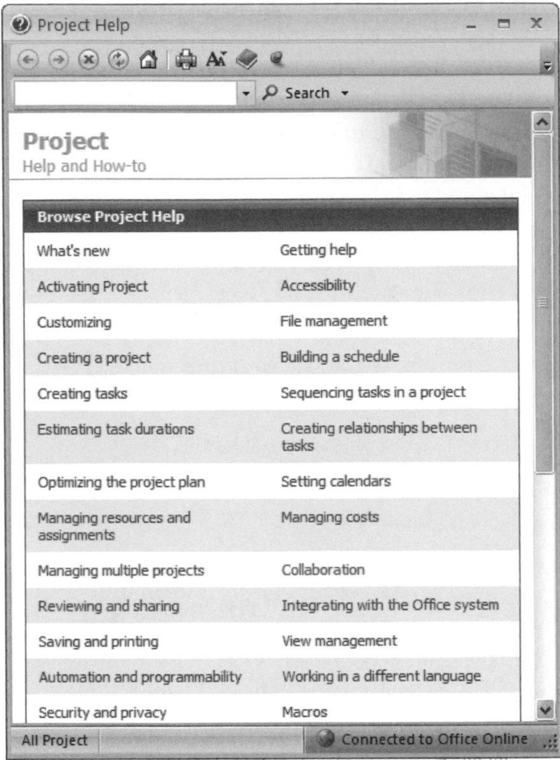

FIGURE A-4 Topics under Microsoft Office Project Help

Main Screen Elements

The Project 2007 default main screen is called the Gantt Chart view. At the top of the main screen, the Menu bar and Standard toolbar are similar to those in *Microsoft Windows 2003* programs. Project 2007 does *not* have the new ribbons. which replaced the toolbar feature, found in other Office 2007 applications. The order and appearance of buttons on the Standard toolbar may vary, depending on the features you are using and how the Standard toolbar is customized. When you use a button, it automatically becomes visible on the toolbar it is associated with. You can display the Standard toolbar in one row or two, or you can set it to always show full menus so that all buttons are visible all the time. Additional toolbars in Project 2007 include the Formatting toolbar, the Custom Forms toolbar, and the Tracking toolbar, among others.

To customize the Standard toolbar:

1. *Open the Customize dialog box*. Click **Tools** on the Menu bar, point to **Customize,** and then click **Toolbars** to display the Customize dialog box. Click the **Options** tab.
2. *Show full menus*. Click the option to **Always show full menus,** as shown in Figure A-5, and then click the **Close** button to close the dialog box.

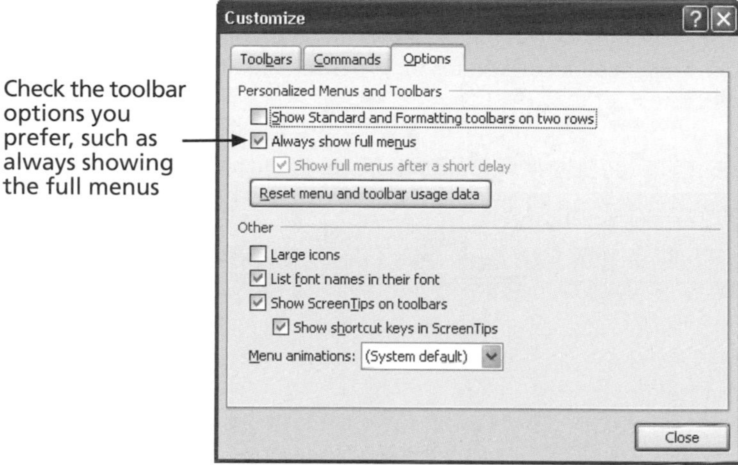

FIGURE A-5 Customizing toolbars

3. *If needed, add the Zoom In and Zoom Out buttons to the toolbar.* Click the **Toolbar Options** button on the toolbar, and then click the **Zoom In** button. Click the **Toolbar Options** button again, and then click the **Zoom Out** button, as shown in Figure A-6.

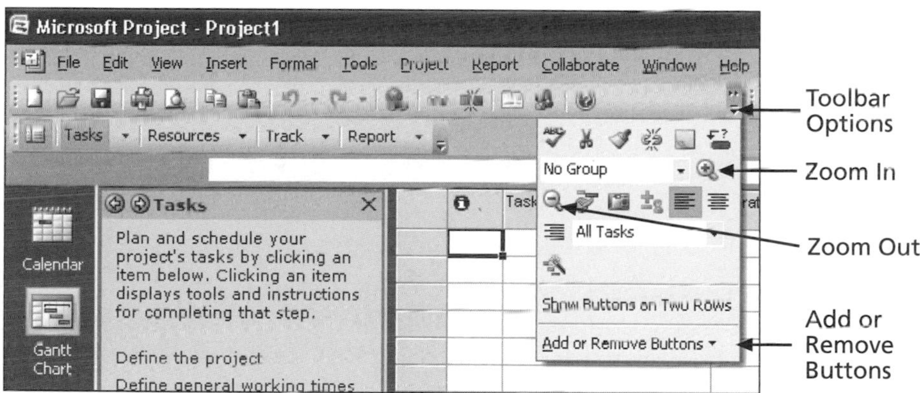

FIGURE A-6 Adding the Zoom In and Zoom Out buttons to the toolbar

TIP

You can select the Add or Remove Buttons option to add or remove several toolbar buttons at once.

Figure A-7 shows the main screen elements of Project 2007. Below the Standard toolbar is the Entry bar, which displays entries you make in the Entry table, located right below the Entry bar. The Gantt chart calendar display appears on the right of the split bar, which separates the Entry table and the Gantt chart. The column to the left of the Task Name column is the Indicators column. The Indicators column displays indicators or symbols related to items associated with each task, such as task notes or hyperlinks to other files.

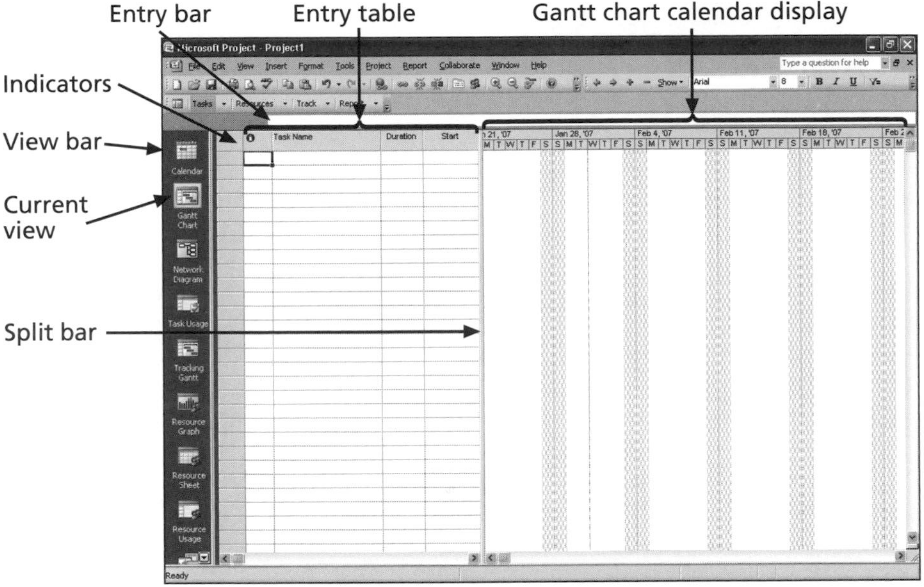

FIGURE A-7 Project 2007 main screen elements

TIP

Many features in Project 2007 are similar to ones in other Windows programs. For example, to collapse or expand tasks, click the appropriate symbols to the left of the task name. To access shortcut items, right-click in either the Entry table area or the Gantt chart. Many of the Entry table operations in Project 2007 are very similar to operations in Excel. For example, to adjust a column width, click and drag or double-click between the column heading titles.

If you select another view and want to return to the Gantt Chart view, click the Gantt Chart button on the View bar on the left of the screen, or select View from the Menu bar, and click Gantt Chart, as shown in Figure A-8. If the Entry table on the left appears to be different, select View from the Menu bar, point to Table: Entry, and then click Entry to return to the default Entry table view. If the View bar does not display, select View Bar from the View menu.

Notice the split bar that separates the Entry table from the Gantt chart. When you move the mouse over the split bar, your cursor changes to the resize pointer. Clicking and dragging the split bar to the right reveals other task information in the Entry table, including the Duration, Start date, Finish date, Predecessors, and Resource Names columns.

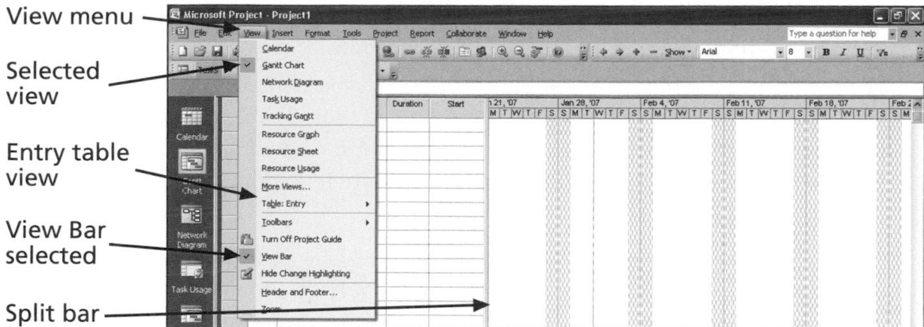

FIGURE A-8 Project 2007 View menu options

Next, you will open a template file to explore more screen elements. Project 2007 comes with several template files, and you can also access templates from Microsoft Office Online or other Web sites. To open template files on your computer, click File on the Menu bar, and then click New. In the New Project task pane, click the On computer option under Templates, as shown in Figure A-9.

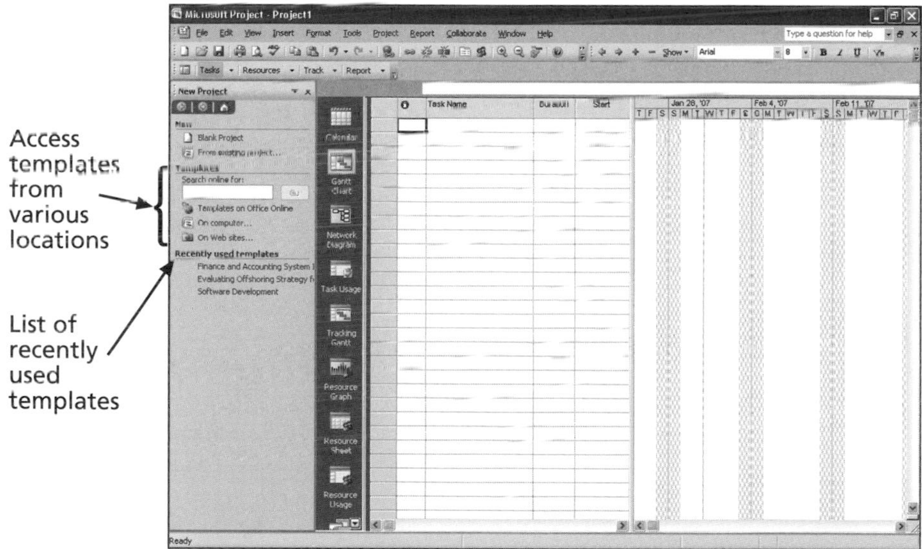

FIGURE A-9 Opening a template file

HELP

To access template files on your computer, you must do a full or custom install of Project 2007.

To open a template file and adjust Project 2007 screen elements:

1. *Open a template file*. Click the **Open button** on the Standard toolbar, browse to find the file named **finance.mpp** that you copied from the companion Web site, or author's Web site for this text, and then double-click the filename to open the file. This file provides a template for a project to implement a new finance and accounting system in a corporate environment.

TIP

The finance.mpp file is identical to the template named "Finance and Accounting System Implementation" that comes with Project 2007, which you can also access from the Templates, On computer . . . option shown in Figure A-9.

2. *View the Note*. Move your mouse over the **Notes icon** in the Indicators column and read its contents. It is a good idea to provide a short note describing the purpose of project files. (You'll learn how to add notes in the Communications section of this guide.) Your screen should resemble Figure A-10.

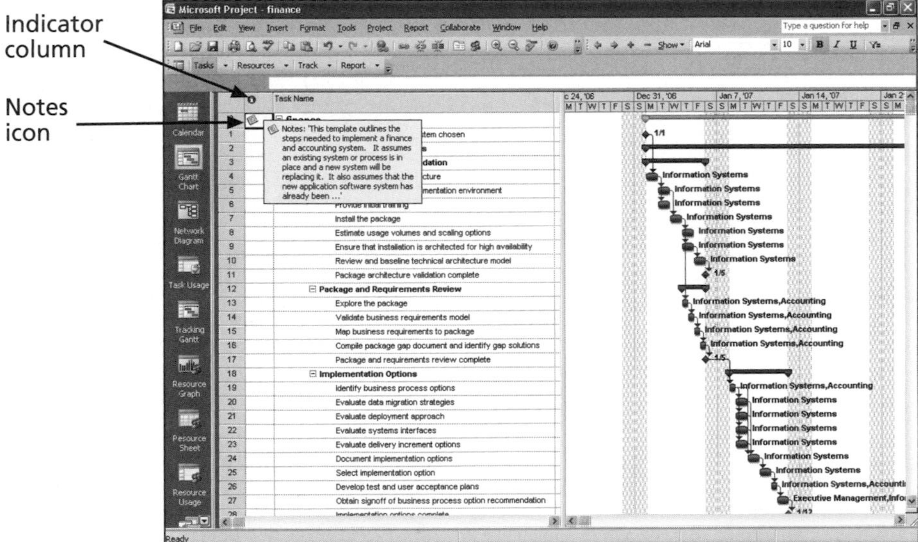

FIGURE A-10 The finance.mpp file

3. *Adjust the timescale*. Click the **Zoom Out** button on the toolbar *twice* to display the timescale in months and then weeks. If you cannot find the Zoom Out button, you can add it to the Standard toolbar by clicking the **Toolbar**

Options button, as described earlier. Notice that this project started on January 1, 2007, and ended in early April 2007. The first line in the Entry bar displays the filename, and the bar in the Gantt chart next to that line shows the time line for the entire project.

4. *Select Outline Level 1 to display WBS level 2 tasks*. On the Standard toolbar, click the **Show** button's list arrow Show ▾, and then click **Outline Level 1,** as shown in Figure A-11. Notice that only the outline level 1 items or WBS level 2 items display in the Entry table after you select Outline Level 1, and the timescale shows months. The black bars on the Gantt chart represent the summary tasks. Note that according to the Project Management Institute (PMI), the entire project is normally referred to as WBS level 1, and the next highest level is called level 2. This view of the file also shows two milestone tasks in rows 1 and 137 indicating when a new Accounting and Finance system was chosen and when the project was completed. Recall that the black diamond symbol on a Gantt chart shows milestones.

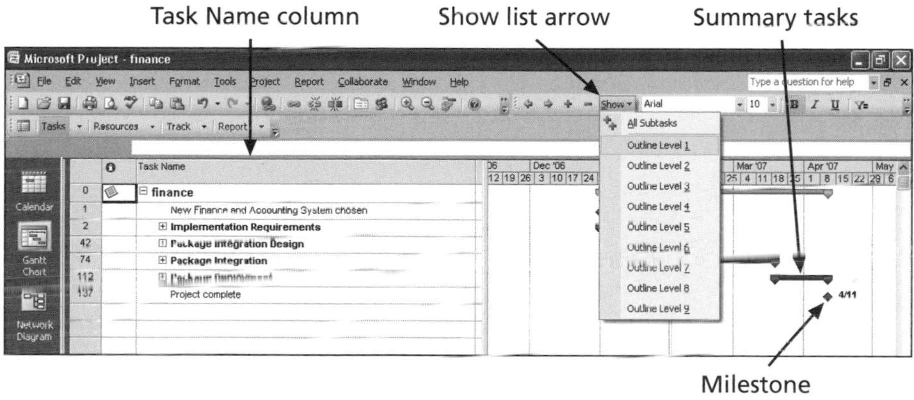

FIGURE A-11 Viewing summary tasks using the Show button

5. *Adjust the Task Name column*. Move the cursor over the right-column gridline in the Task Name column heading until you see the resize pointer, and then double-click the **left mouse** button to resize the column width automatically.
6. *Move the split bar to reveal more Entry table columns*. Move the split bar to the right to reveal the Resource Names column. Your screen should resemble Figure A-12.
7. *Expand a task*. Click the **expand symbol** [+] to the left of Task 112, Package Deployment, to see its subtasks. Click the **collapse symbol** [–] to hide its subtasks.

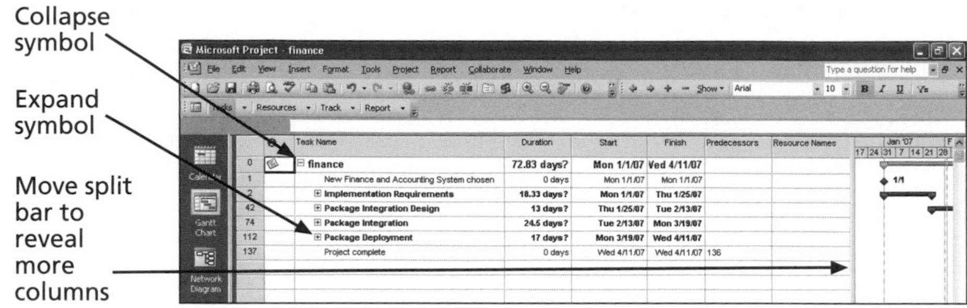

FIGURE A-12 Adjusting screen elements

Project 2007 Views

Project 2007 provides many ways to display project information. These displays are called views. To the left of the Entry table is the View bar. Instead of using commands on the View menu to change views, you can click buttons on the View bar. Several views discussed in the main text are on the default View bar: Gantt Chart, Network Diagram, Tracking Gantt, and Resource Graph. Other views include Calendar, Task Usage, Resource Sheet, Resource Usage, and an option to display More Views. These different views allow you to examine project information in different ways, which helps you analyze and understand what is happening on your project.

To save screen space, you can hide the View bar by selecting View from the Menu bar and deselecting View Bar. When the View bar is not visible, a blue bar with the name of the current view appears to the far left of the main screen. When you right-click this blue bar, a shortcut menu appears, which gives you quick access to the other views.

The View menu also provides access to different tables that display information in a variety of ways. Some tables that you can access from the View menu include Schedule, Cost, Tracking, and Earned Value. Some Project 2007 views, such as the Gantt Chart view, present a broad look at the entire project, whereas others, such as the Form views, focus on specific pieces of information about each task. Three main categories of views are available:

- *Graphical*: A chart or graphical representation of data using bars, boxes, lines, and images.
- *Task Sheet or Table*: A spreadsheet-like representation of data in which each task appears as a new row and each piece of information about the task is represented by a column. Different tables are applied to a task sheet to display different kinds of information.
- *Form*: A specific view of information for one task. Forms are used to focus on the details of one task.

Table A-1 describes some of the predesigned views within each category that Project 2007 provides to help you display the project or task information that you need.

TABLE A-1 Common Project 2007 views

Category of View	View Name	Description of View
Graphical	Gantt Chart	Standard format for displaying project schedule information that lists project tasks and their corresponding start and finish dates in a calendar format. Shows each task as a horizontal bar with the length and position corresponding to the timescale at the top of the Gantt chart.
	Network Diagram	Schematic display of the logical relationships or sequencing of project activities. Presents each task as a box with linking lines between tasks to show sequencing. Critical tasks appear in red.
Task Sheet or Table	Entry Table	Default table view showing columns for Task Name and Duration. By revealing more of the Entry table, you can enter start and end dates, predecessors, and resource names.
	Schedule Table	Displays columns for Task Name, Start, Finish, Late Start, Late Finish, Free Slack, and Total Slack.
	Cost Table	Displays columns for Task Name, Fixed Cost, Fixed Cost Accrual, Total Cost, Baseline, Variance, Actual, and Remaining.
	Tracking Table	Displays columns for Task Name, Actual Start, Actual Finish, % Complete, Physical % Complete, Actual Duration, Remaining Duration, Actual Cost, and Actual Work.
	Earned Value	Displays columns for Task Name, PV, EV, AC, SV, CV, EAC, BAC, and VAC. See the earned value section of this text for descriptions of these acronyms.
Form	Task Details Form	Displays detailed information about a single task in one window.
	Task Name Form	Displays columns for Task Name, Resources, and Predecessors for a single task.

Next, you will use the same file (finance.mpp) to access and explore some of the views available in Project 2007.

To access and explore different views:

1. *Show all subtasks*. Click the **Show** button Show ▾ on the toolbar, and then click **All Subtasks.** Click the Task Name for Task 0, finance.
2. *Explore the Network Diagram view*. Click the **Network Diagram** button on the View Bar, and then click the **Zoom Out** button on the toolbar *three times*. Your screen should resemble Figure A-13.

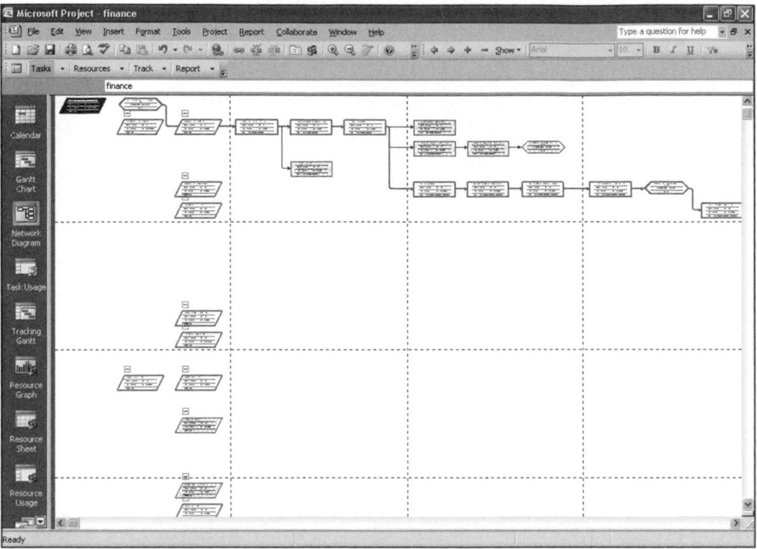

FIGURE A-13 Network Diagram view of Project 2007 finance file

3. *Explore the Calendar view*. Click the **Calendar** button on the View bar. Your screen should resemble Figure A-14.

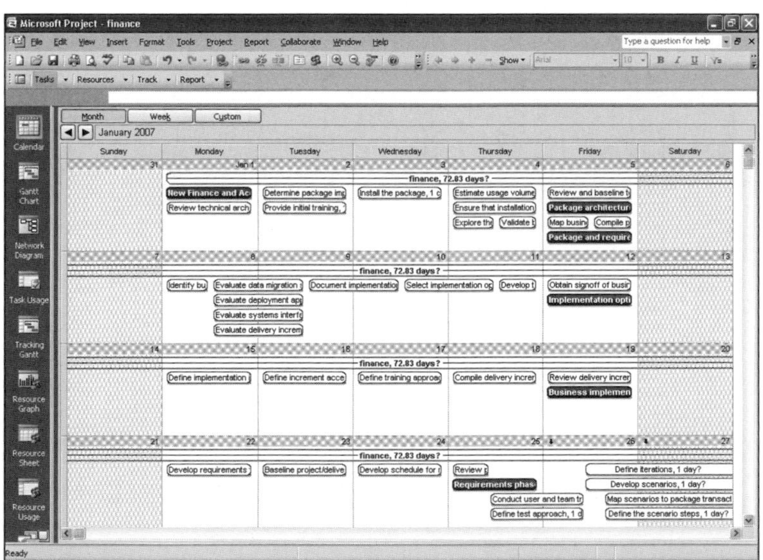

FIGURE A-14 Calendar view of Project 2007 finance file

4. *Examine columns in the Entry table*. Click the **Gantt Chart** button on the View bar, and observe the information provided in each column of the Entry table.

5. *Examine the Table: Schedule view*. Click **View** on the Menu bar, move your mouse to **Table: Entry**, and then click **Schedule** in the cascading menu to the right. Notice that the columns to the left of the Gantt chart now display more detailed schedule information. Also notice that all of the text in the Task Name column is not visible. You can widen the column by moving the mouse to the right of the Task Name column and double-clicking the resize pointer ✣. You can also move the split bar to the right to reveal more columns.
6. *Right-click the Select All button to access different table views*. Move your mouse to the **Select All** button to the left of the Task Name column symbol, and then right-click with your mouse. A shortcut menu to different table views displays, as shown in Figure A-15. Experiment with other table views, then return to the Table: Entry view.

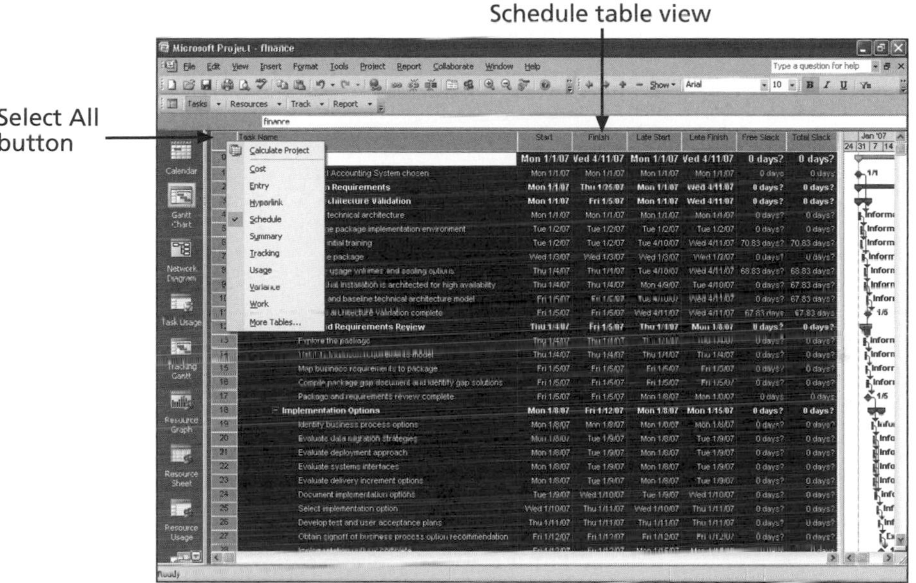

FIGURE A-15 Changing table views

7. *Explore the Reports feature*. Click **Report** on the Menu bar, and then click Reports. The **Reports** dialog box displays, as shown in Figure A-16.
8. *View the Project Summary report*. Double-click **Overview** from the Reports dialog box, and then double-click **Project Summary** in the Overview Reports dialog box. Notice that the insertion point now resembles a magnifying glass. Click inside the report to zoom in or zoom out. Click the **Close** button to close this report, and then experiment with viewing other reports. You will use several reports and other views throughout this appendix.
9. *Close the Reports feature*. Click **Close** to close the Reports dialog box and return to the Gantt Chart view.

FIGURE A-16 Reports dialog box

Project 2007 Filters

Project 2007 uses an underlying relational database to filter, sort, store, and display information. Filtering project information is very useful. For example, if a project includes hundreds of tasks, you might want to view only summary or milestone tasks to get an overview of the project. To get this type of overview of a project, select the Milestones or Summary Tasks filter from the Filter list. If you are concerned about the schedule, you can select a filter that shows only tasks on the critical path. Other filters include Completed Tasks, Late/Overbudget Tasks, and Date Range, which displays tasks based on dates you provide. As shown earlier, you can also click the Show button on the toolbar to display different levels in the WBS quickly. For example, Outline Level 1 shows the highest-level items in the WBS, Outline Level 2 shows the next level of detail in the WBS, and so on.

To explore Project 2007 filters:

1. *Apply a filter to see only milestone tasks*. From the Table: Entry view in the finance.mpp file, click the **Toolbar Options** button on the toolbar, and then click the Filter list arrow, as shown in Figure A-17.

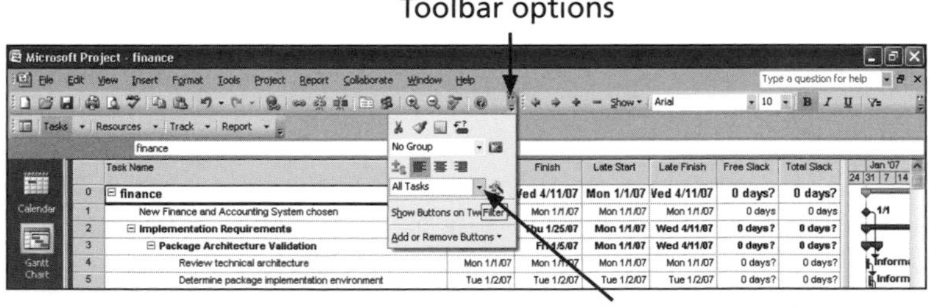

FIGURE A-17 Using a filter

2. *Filter to show specific tasks*. Click **Milestones** in the list of filters, and move the split bar to the left to see all the milestones on the Gantt chart. Your screen

should resemble Figure A-18. The black diamond symbol represents a milestone, a significant event on a project.

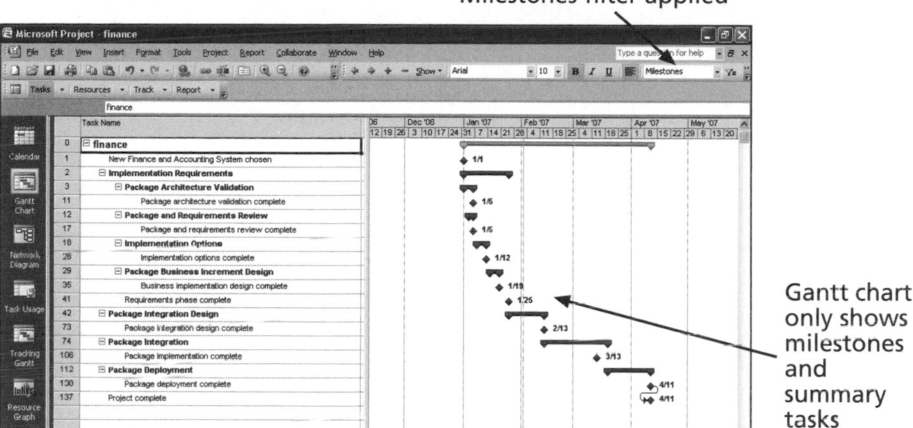

FIGURE A-18 Milestone tasks filter for Project 2007 finance file

3. *Show summary tasks*. Select **All Tasks** from the Filter list box to reveal all the tasks in the WBS again. Click the **Filter** list arrow, scroll down until you see Summary Tasks, and then click **Summary Tasks.** Now only the summary tasks appear in the WBS. Experiment with other outline levels and filters.
4. *Close the file*. When you are finished reviewing the finance.mpp file, click **Close** from the File menu or click the **Close** button. A dialog box appears asking if you want to save changes. Click **No.**
5. *Exit Project 2007*. Select **Exit** from the File menu or click the **Close** button for Project 2007.

Now that you are familiar with the Project 2007 main screen elements, views, and filters, you will learn how to use Project 2007 to assist in project scope management by creating a new project file, developing a WBS, and setting a baseline.

PROJECT SCOPE MANAGEMENT

Project scope management involves defining the work to perform to carry out the project. To use Project 2007, you must first determine the scope of the project. To begin determining the project's scope, create a new file with the project name and start date. Develop a list of tasks that need to be done to carry out the project. This list of tasks becomes the work breakdown structure (WBS). If you intend to track actual project information against the initial plan, you must set a baseline. In this section, you will learn how to create a new project file, develop a WBS, and set a baseline to help plan and manage the Project Tracking Database project. To start, you will enter the scope-related information.

TIP

In this section, you will go through several steps to create the scope.mpp Project 2007 file. If you want to download the completed file to check your work or continue to the next section, a copy of scope.mpp is available on the companion Web site for this text, from the author's Web site, or from your instructor. Try to complete an entire section of this appendix (project scope management, project time management, and so on) in one sitting to create the complete file. Also, be sure to save the scope.mpp file you create in a different folder than the one you download, and then compare the two files.

Creating a New Project File

To create a new project file:

1. *Create a blank project*. Open Project 2007, and close the Project Guide Tasks pane. A blank project file automatically opens when you start Project 2007. The default filenames are Project1, Project2, and so on. If Project 2007 is already open and you want to open a new file, click the **New** button on the toolbar or select File and then New from the Menu bar.
2. *Open the Project Information dialog box*. Click **Project** on the Menu bar, and then click **Project Information** to display the Project Information dialog box, as shown in Figure A-19. The Project Information dialog box enables you to set dates for the project, select the calendar to use, and view project statistics. The project start date will default to today's date.

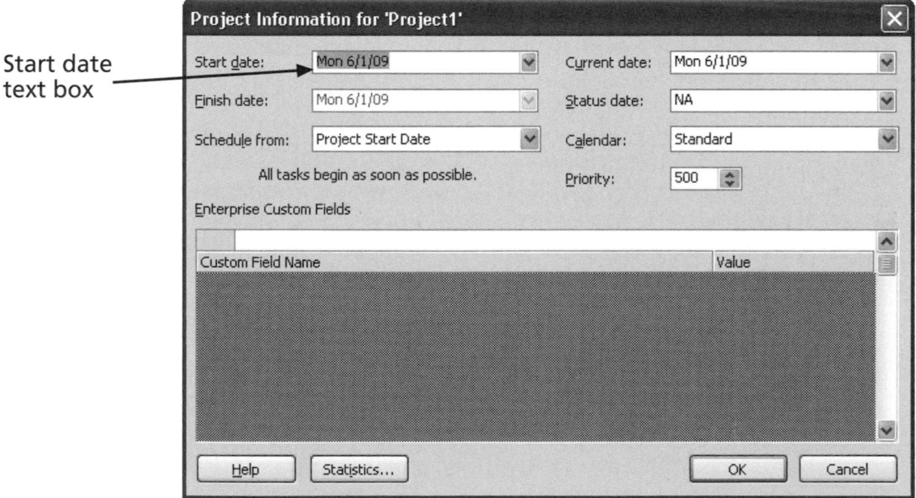

FIGURE A-19 Project Information dialog box

3. *Enter the project start date*. In the Start date text box, enter **6/01/09.** Setting your project start date to 6/01/09 will ensure that your work matches the results that appear in this appendix. Leave the Finish date, Current date, and other information at the default settings. Click **OK.**

HELP

This appendix uses American date formats. For example, 6/01/09 represents June 1, 2009. Be sure to enter dates in this format for these steps. However, you can change the date format by selecting Tools from the Menu bar, clicking Options, and then selecting the View tab. In the Date Format box, click the date format you want to use.

4. *Enter project properties*. Click **File** on the Menu bar, and then click **Properties.**

TIP

Any command that you click in the expanded menu is added immediately to the personalized (short) version of the menu. If you stop using a command for a while, Project 2007 stops showing it on the short version of the menu.

5. *Enter project information*. Type **Project Tracking Database** in the Title text box, type **Terry Dunlay** in the Author text box, as shown in Figure A-20, and then click **OK.** You may have some default information entered in the Project Properties dialog box, such as your company's name. Keep this file open for the next set of steps.

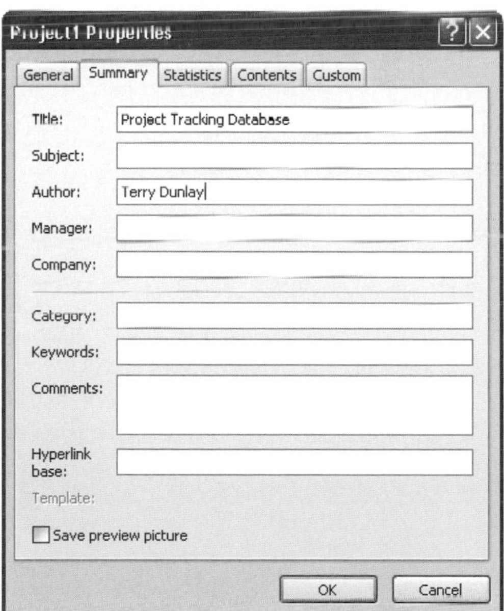

FIGURE A-20 Project Properties dialog box

Developing a Work Breakdown Structure

Before using Project 2007, you must develop a work breakdown structure (WBS) for your project. Developing a good WBS takes time, and it will make entering tasks into the Entry table easier if you develop the WBS first. It is also a good idea to establish milestones before entering tasks in Project 2007. You will use the information in Table A-2 to enter tasks for the Project Tracking Database project. Be aware that this example is much shorter and simpler than most WBSs.

To develop a WBS and enter milestones for the Project Tracking Database project:

1. *Enter task names*. Enter the 20 tasks in Table A-2 into the Task Name column in the order shown. Do not worry about durations or any other information at this time. Type the name of each task into the Task Name column of the Entry table, beginning with the first row. Press **Enter** or the **down arrow** key on your keyboard to move to the next row.

HELP

If you accidentally skip a task, highlight the task row and select **Insert** from the Menu bar, and then select **New Task** to insert a blank row. To edit a task entry, click the text for that task, click the Entry bar under the Formatting toolbar, and either type over the old text or edit the existing text.

TABLE A-2 Project Tracking Database tasks

Order	Task Name
1	Initiating
2	Kickoff meeting
3	Develop project charter
4	Charter signed
5	Planning
6	Develop project plans
7	Review project plans
8	Project plans approved
9	Executing
10	Analysis
11	Design
12	Implementation
13	System implemented
14	Controlling

TABLE A-2 Project Tracking Database tasks (*continued*)

Order	Task Name
15	Report performance
16	Control changes
17	Closing
18	Prepare final project report
19	Present final project
20	Project completed

TIP

Entering tasks into Project 2007 and editing the information is similar to entering and editing data in an Excel spreadsheet. Project 2007, like earlier versions, includes a feature called a SmartTag, which appears, for example, when you delete a row. The SmartTag clarifies whether you want to delete the entire task or only clear the contents of a cell.

2. *Move the split bar to reveal more columns*. If necessary, move the split bar to the right to reveal the entire Task Name and Duration columns.
3. *Adjust the Task Name column width as needed*. To make all the text display in the Task Name column, move the mouse over the right-column gridline in the Task Name column heading until you see the resize pointer ✛, and then click the **left mouse** button and drag the line to the right to make the column wider, or double-click to adjust the column width automatically.

This WBS separates tasks according to the project management process groups of initiating, planning, executing, controlling, and closing. These tasks will be the level 2 items in the WBS for this project. Remember that the whole project is considered level 1. It is a good idea to include all of these process groups because there are important tasks that must be done under each of them. Recall that the WBS should include *all* of the work required for the project. In the Project Tracking Database WBS, the tasks will be purposefully left at a high WBS level (level 3). You will create these levels, or the WBS hierarchy, next when you create summary tasks. For a real project, you would usually break the WBS into even more levels to provide more details to describe all the work involved in the project. For example, analysis tasks for a database project might be broken down further to include preparing entity relationship diagrams for the database and developing guidelines for the user interface. Design tasks might be broken down to include preparing prototypes, incorporating user feedback, entering data, and testing the database. Implementation tasks might include more levels, such as installing new hardware or software, training the users, fully documenting the system, and so on.

Creating Summary Tasks

After entering the WBS tasks listed in Table A-2 into the Entry table, the next step is to show the WBS levels by creating summary tasks. The summary tasks in this example are Tasks 1 (initiating), 5 (planning), 9 (executing), 14 (controlling), and 17 (closing). You create summary tasks by highlighting and indenting their respective subtasks.

To create the summary tasks:

1. *Select lower level or subtasks*. Highlight **Tasks 2** through **4** by clicking the cell for Task 2 and dragging the mouse through the cells to Task 4.
2. *Indent subtasks*. Click the **Indent** button on the Formatting toolbar so your screen resembles Figure A-21. After the subtasks (Tasks 2 through 4) are indented, notice that Task 1 automatically becomes boldface, which indicates that it is a summary task. A collapse symbol ⊟ appears to the left of the new summary task name. Clicking the collapse symbol will collapse the summary task and hide the subtasks beneath it. When subtasks are hidden, an expand symbol ⊞ appears to the left of the summary task name. Clicking the expand symbol will expand the summary task. Also, notice that the symbol for the summary task on the Gantt chart has changed from a blue to a black line with arrows indicating the start and end dates.

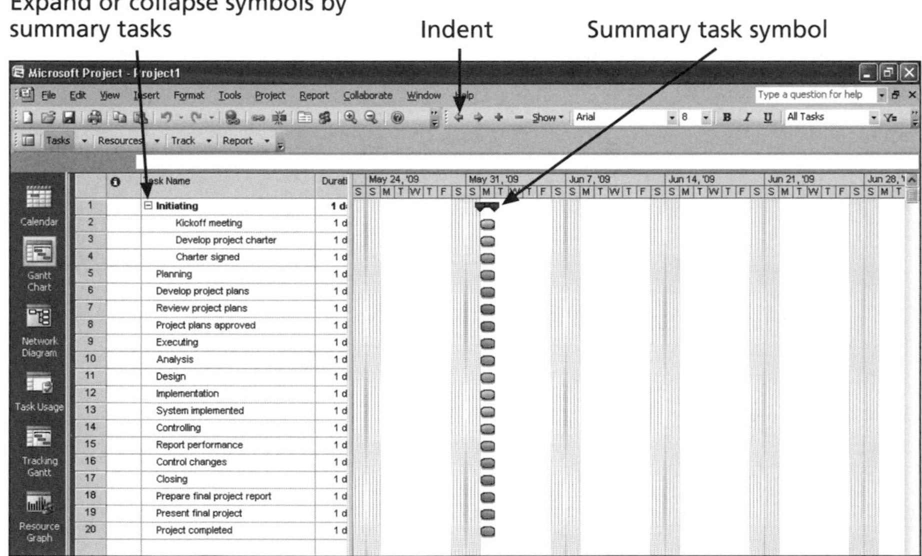

FIGURE A-21 Indenting tasks to create the WBS hierarchy

3. *Create other summary tasks and subtasks*. Create subtasks and summary tasks for Tasks 5, 9, 14, and 17 by following the same steps. Indent **Tasks 6** through **8** to make Task 5 a summary task. Indent **Tasks 10** through **13** to make Task 9 a summary task. Indent **Tasks 15** through **16** to make Task 14 a summary task. Indent **Tasks 18** through **20** to make Task 17 a summary task. Widen the Task Name column to see all of your text, as needed.

> **TIP**
>
> To change a task from a summary task to a subtask or to change its level up one in the WBS, you can "outdent" the task instead of indenting it. To outdent the task, click the cell of the task or tasks you want to change, and then click the Outdent button on the Formatting toolbar. Remember, the tasks in Project 2007 should be entered in an appropriate WBS format with several levels in the hierarchy.

Numbering Tasks

Depending on how Project 2007 is set up on your computer, you may or may not see numbers associated with tasks as you enter and indent them.

To display automatic numbering of tasks using the standard tabular numbering system for a WBS:

1. *Display the Options dialog box*. Click **Tools** on the Menu bar, and then click **Options.** The Options dialog box opens.
2. *Show outline numbers*. Click the **View** tab, if necessary. Check **Show** outline number in the "Outline options for Project1" section of the View tab. Click **OK** to close the dialog box. Figure A-22 shows the Options dialog box and resulting outline numbers applied to the WBS tasks.

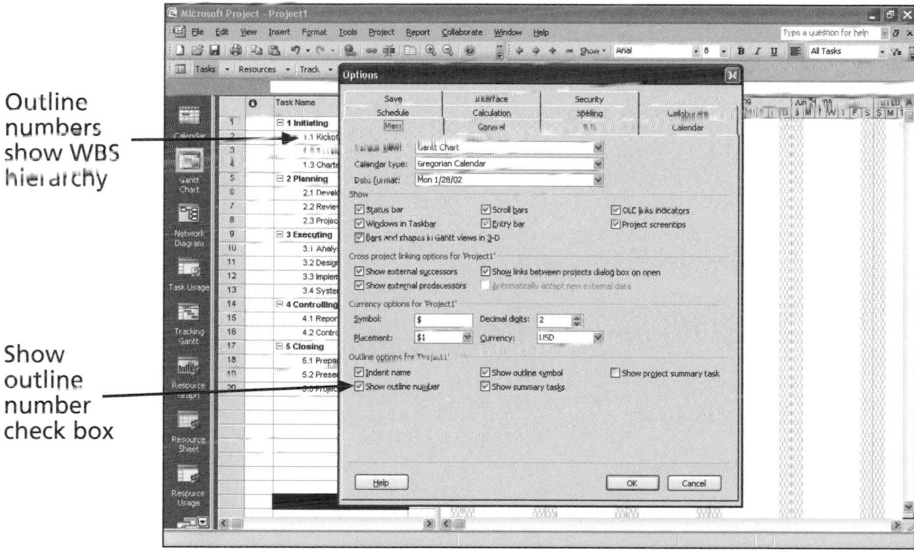

FIGURE A-22 Adding outline numbers

Saving Project Files with or without a Baseline

An important part of project management is tracking performance against a baseline, or approved plan. Project 2007 does not prompt you to save a file with or without a baseline each time you save it, as some previous versions did. The default is to save without a baseline. It is important to wait until you are ready to save your file with a baseline because

Project 2007 will show changes against a baseline. Since you are still developing your project file for the Project Tracking Database project, you want to save the file without a baseline. Later in this appendix, you will save the file with a baseline by selecting Tools, Tracking, and then Set Baseline. You will then enter actual information to compare planned and actual performance data.

To save a file without a baseline:

1. *Save your file*. Click **File** on the Menu bar and then click **Save**, or click the **Save** button on the Standard toolbar.
2. *Enter a filename*. In the Save As dialog box, type **scope** in the File name text box. Browse to the location in which you want to save the file, and then click **Save.** Your Project 2007 file should look like Figure A-23. (You can adjust the timescale to show months by clicking Zoom In or Zoom Out.)

HELP

If you want to download the Project 2007 file scope.mpp to check your work or continue to the next section, a copy is available on the companion Web site for this text, the author's Web site, or from your instructor. If you downloaded the scope.mpp file that comes with this text, you can save your file with a different name or in a different location to avoid overwriting that file. Keep this in mind for other files you save as well.

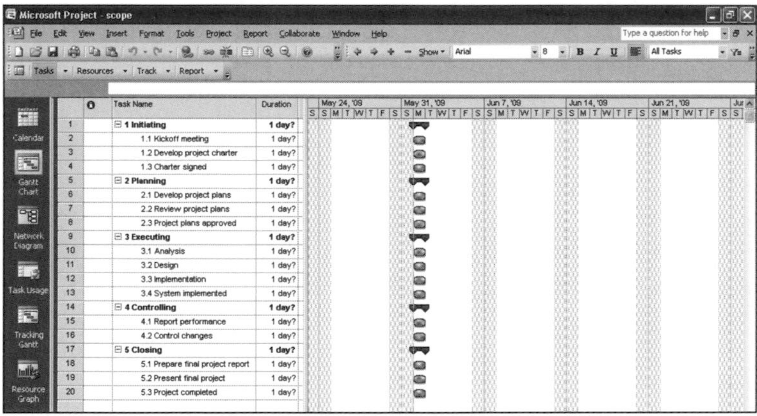

FIGURE A-23 Project 2007 scope file

Now that you have finished entering all 20 tasks, created the summary tasks and subtasks, set the options to show the standard WBS tabular numbering system, and saved your file, you will learn how to use the Project 2007 time management features.

PROJECT TIME MANAGEMENT

Many people use Project 2007 for its time management features. The first step in using these features, after inputting the WBS for the project, is to enter durations for tasks or specific dates when tasks will occur. Inserting durations or specific dates will automatically update the Gantt chart. To use Project 2007 to adjust schedules automatically and to do critical path analysis, you must also enter task dependencies. After entering durations and task dependencies, you can view the network diagram and critical path information. This section describes how to use each of these time management features.

Entering Task Durations

When you enter a task, Project 2007 automatically assigns to it a default duration of one day, followed by a question mark. To change the default duration, type a task's estimated duration in the Duration column. If you are unsure of an estimate and want to review it again later, enter a question mark after it. For example, you could enter 5d? for a task with an estimated duration of five days that you want to review later. You can then use the Tasks With Estimated Durations filter to see quickly the tasks for which you need to review duration estimates.

To indicate the length of a task's duration, you must type both a number and an appropriate duration symbol. If you type only a number, Project 2007 automatically enters days as the duration unit. Duration unit symbols include:

- d = days (default)
- w = weeks
- m = minutes
- h = hours
- mo or mon = months
- ed = elapsed days
- ew = elapsed weeks

For example, to enter one week for a task duration, type 1w in the Duration column. (You can also type wk, wks, week, or weeks, instead of just w.) To enter two days for a task duration, type 2d in the Duration column. The default unit is days, so if you enter 2 for the duration, it will be entered as 2 days. You can also enter elapsed times in the Duration column. For example, 2ed means two elapsed days, and 2ew means two elapsed weeks. You would use an elapsed duration for a task like "Allow paint to dry." The paint will dry in exactly the same amount of time regardless of whether it is a workday, a weekend, or a holiday.

TIP

If the Duration column is not visible, drag the split bar to the right until the Duration column is in view.

Entering time estimates or durations might seem like a straightforward process. However, you must follow a few important procedures:

- As you saw in the previous section, when you enter a task in the Task Name column, 1 day? appears in the Duration column. The question mark means that you are unsure of the duration or want to go back to it. Be sure to enter the durations you want to appear.

- Do not enter durations for summary tasks. Summary task durations are calculated automatically based on the subtasks. If you enter a duration for a task and then make it a summary task, its duration will automatically change to match the durations of its subtasks. Project 2007 will not allow you to enter or change the duration of a summary task. Think of it as entering durations for work packages, the lowest-level items in your WBS. The other items are really the WBS hierarchy. Let Project 2007 do the duration calculations for you.
- To mark a task as a milestone, enter 0 for the duration. You can also mark tasks that have a non-zero duration as milestones by checking the "Mark task as milestone" option in the Task Information dialog box on the Advanced tab. The milestone symbol for those tasks will appear at their start date. Double-click a task to access the Task Information dialog box.
- To enter recurring tasks, such as weekly meetings or monthly status reports, select Recurring Task from the Insert menu. Enter the task name, the duration, and when the task occurs. Project 2007 will automatically insert appropriate subtasks based on the length of the project and the number of tasks required for the recurring task. For example, if you enter a recurring task for monthly review meetings that occur on the first day of every month for a 12-month project, Project 2007 will enter a summary task for monthly review meetings and 12 subtasks—one meeting for each month.
- You can enter the exact start and finish dates for activities instead of entering durations. To enter start and finish dates, move the split bar to the right to reveal the Start and Finish columns. Enter start and finish dates only when those dates are certain. If you want task dates to adjust according to any other task dates, do not enter exact start and finish dates. Instead, enter a duration and then establish a dependency to related tasks. *The real scheduling power of Project 2007 comes from setting up dependencies or relationships among tasks, as described in the next section*.
- Project 2007 uses a default calendar with standard workdays and hours. Duration estimates will vary according to the calendar you use. For example, entering 5d in the standard calendar may result in more than five days on the Gantt chart if the time period includes Saturday or Sunday. You can change specific working and nonworking days, or the entire project calendar, by selecting Change Working Time from the Tools menu.
- You often need to adjust the timescale on the Gantt chart to see your project's schedule in different time frames, such as weeks, months, quarters, or years. You expand the timescale by clicking the Zoom Out button. The Zoom In button collapses the timescale. You can also change the format of the timescale by having three tiers instead of two or by formatting dates differently by double-clicking the timescale section of the Gantt chart.

Next, you will set task durations in the Project Tracking Database file (scope.mpp) that you created and saved in the previous section. If you did not create the file named scope.mpp, you can download it from the companion Web site for this text. You will create a new recurring task and enter its duration, and then you will enter other task durations. First, create a new recurring task called Status Reports above Task 15, Report performance.

To create a new recurring task:

1. *Insert a recurring task above Task 15, Report performance*. Open scope.mpp, if necessary, and then click **Report performance** (Task 15) in the Task Name column to select that task. Click **Insert** on the Menu bar, and then click **Recurring Task.** The Recurring Task Information dialog box opens.
2. *Enter task and duration information for the recurring task*. Type **Status Reports** as the task title in the Task Name text box. Type **1h** in the Duration text box. Select the **Weekly** radio button under Recurrence pattern. Make sure that 1 is entered in the **Recur every** list box. Select the **Wednesday** check box. In the Range of recurrence section, type **6/10/09** in the Start text box, click the **End by** radio button, and then type **10/28/09** in the End by text box. Click the **End by** list arrow to see the calendar, as shown in Figure A-24. You can use the calendar to enter the Start and End by dates. The new recurring task will appear above Task 15, Report performance, when you are finished.

TIP

You can also enter a number of occurrences instead of an End by for a recurring task. You might need to adjust the End by date after you enter all of your task durations and dependencies. Remember, the date on your computer determines the date listed as Today in the calendar.

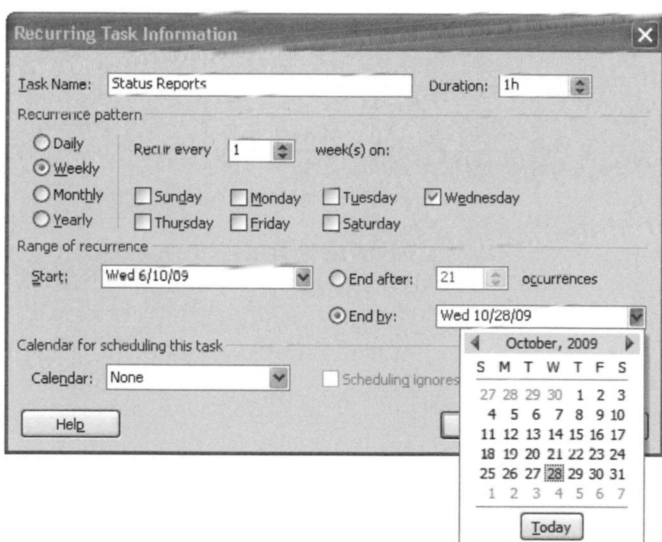

FIGURE A-24 Recurring Task Information dialog box

3. *View the new summary task and its subtasks*. Click **OK.** Project 2007 inserts a new Status Reports subtask in the Task Name column. Expand the new subtask by clicking the **expand symbol** [+] to the left of Status Reports. To collapse the recurring task, click the **collapse symbol** [−].
4. *Adjust the Duration column width and Gantt chart timescale*. Notice the # signs that appear in the Duration column for the Status Reports task. Like Excel, Project 2007 uses these symbols to denote that the column width needs to be increased. Increase the Duration column's width by moving your mouse to the right of the Duration column heading until you see a resize pointer. Double-click to adjust the column width and display the information. Click the **Zoom Out** button on the toolbar twice to display the Gantt chart in months. Move your mouse over the Recurring Task symbol in the Indicator column for row 15. Your screen should resemble Figure A-25. Notice that the recurring task appears on the appropriate dates on the Gantt chart.

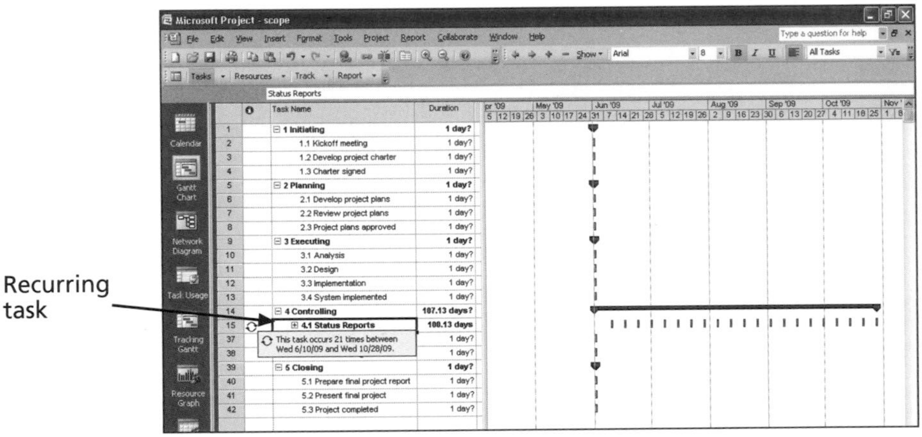

FIGURE A-25 A recurring task

Use the information in Table A-3 to enter durations for the other tasks for the Project Tracking Database project. The Project 2007 row number is shown to the left of each task name in the table. Remember, you already entered a duration for the recurring task. Also, remember that you should *not* enter durations for summary tasks. Durations for summary tasks are automatically calculated to match the durations and dependencies of subtasks, as described further in the next section, Establishing Task Dependencies.

To enter task durations for the other tasks:

1. *Enter the duration for Task 2*. Click the **Duration** column for row 2, Kickoff meeting, type **2h,** and then press **Enter.**
2. *Enter the duration for Task 3*. In the **Duration** column for row 3, Develop project charter, type **10d,** then press **Enter.** You can also just type 10, since d or days is the default duration.

3. *Enter remaining task durations*. Continue to enter the durations using the information in Table A-3.

TABLE A-3 Durations for Project Tracking Database tasks

Task Number/Row	Task Name	Duration
2	Kickoff meeting	2h
3	Develop project charter	10d
4	Charter signed	0
6	Develop project plans	3w
7	Review project plans	4mo
8	Project plans approved	0
10	Analysis	1mo
11	Design	2mo
12	Implementation	1mo
13	System implemented	0
37	Report performance	5mo
38	Control changes	5mo
40	Prepare final project report	2w
41	Present final project	1w
42	Project completed	0

4. Save your file and name it. Click **File** on the Menu bar, and then click **Save As.** Enter **time** as the filename, and then save the file to the desired location on your computer or network. Your file should resemble Figure A-26. Notice that all of the tasks still begin on June 1. This will change in the next section when we add task dependencies. Keep this file open for the next set of steps.

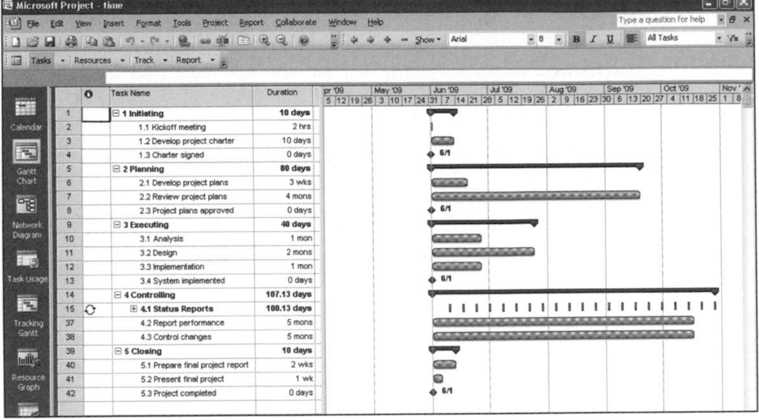

FIGURE A-26 Time file with durations entered

Establishing Task Dependencies

To use Project 2007 to adjust schedules automatically and to do critical path analysis, you *must* determine the dependencies or relationships among tasks. Project 2007 provides three methods for creating task dependencies: using the Link Tasks button, using the Predecessors column of the Entry table or the Predecessors tab in the Task Information dialog box, or clicking and dragging the Gantt chart symbols for tasks with dependencies.

To create dependencies using the Link Tasks button, highlight tasks that are related and then click the Link Tasks button on the toolbar. For example, to create a finish-to-start dependency between Task 1 and Task 2, click any cell in row 1, drag down to row 2, and then click the Link Tasks button. The default type of link is finish-to-start. In the Project Tracking Database example, all the tasks use this default relationship. You will learn about other types of dependencies later in this appendix.

> **TIP**
>
> Selecting tasks is similar to selecting cells in Excel. To select adjacent tasks, click and drag the mouse. You can also click the first task, hold down the Shift key, and then click the last task. To select nonadjacent tasks, hold down the Control (Ctrl) key as you click tasks in order of their dependencies.

When you use the Predecessors column of the Entry table to create dependencies, you must manually enter the information. To create dependencies manually, type the task row number of the preceding task in the Predecessors column of the Entry table. For example, Task 3 in Table A-3 has Task 2 as a predecessor, which can be entered in the Predecessors column, meaning that Task 3 cannot start until Task 2 is finished. To see the Predecessors column of the Entry table, move the split bar to the right. You can also double-click on the task, click the Predecessors tab in the Task Information dialog box, and enter the predecessors there. (This is more work than just typing it in the Predecessor column.)

You can also create task dependencies by clicking the Gantt chart symbol for a task and then dragging to the Gantt chart symbol for a task that succeeds it. For example, you could click the Milestone symbol ◆ for Task 4, hold down the left mouse button, and drag to the Task Bar symbol for Task 6 to create a dependency, as shown in the Gantt chart in Figure A-27. Note the Finish-to-Start Link dialog box that appears when you use this method.

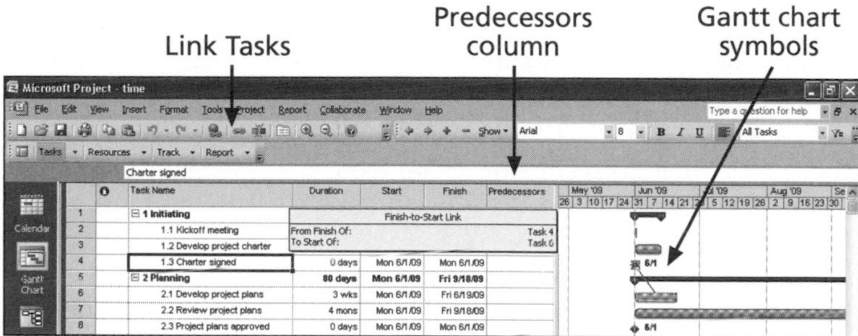

FIGURE A-27 Creating task dependencies

Next, you will use information from Figure A-28 to enter the predecessors for tasks as indicated. You will create some dependencies by manually typing the predecessors in the Predecessors column, some by using the Link Tasks button, some by using the Gantt chart symbols, and the remaining dependencies by using whichever method you prefer.

To link tasks or establish dependencies for the Project Tracking Database project:

1. *Display the Predecessors column in the Entry table*. Move the split bar to the right to reveal the full Predecessors column in the time.mpp file. Widen the Task Name or other columns, if needed.
2. *Highlight the cell where you want to enter a predecessor, and then type the task number for the preceding task*. Click the **Predecessors cell** for Task 3, type **2**, and press **Enter**. Notice that as you enter task dependencies, the Gantt chart changes to reflect the new schedule. Also notice that several cells become highlighted. In this case, the Duration and Finish cells for Task 1, and the Start and Finish cells for Task 3, are highlighted in light blue. *This is the new Visual Change Highlights feature of Project 2007*.
3. *Enter predecessors for Task 4*. Click the **Predecessors cell** for Task 4, type **3**, and press **Enter**.
4. *Establish dependencies using the Link Tasks button*. To link Tasks 10 through 13, click the task name for Task 10 in the Task Name column and drag down through Task 13. Then, click the **Link Tasks** button on the toolbar. Alternately, you can click **Edit** on the Menu bar, and then click **Link Tasks**.
5. *Create a dependency using Gantt chart symbols*. Click the **Milestone** symbol ◆ for Task 4 on the Gantt chart, hold down the **left mouse** button, and drag to the **Task Bar** symbol for Task 6. (See Figure A-27 to see this step in progress.)
6. *Enter remaining dependencies*. Link the other tasks by either manually entering the predecessors into the Predecessors column, by using the Link Tasks button, or by clicking and dragging the Gantt chart symbols. Note the visual change highlighting feature that displays as you enter dependencies. You can

view the dependencies in Figure A-28. For example, Task 8 has Task 6 as a predecessor, Task 10 has Task 8 as a predecessor, Task 11 has 10, Task 12 has 11, Task 13 has 12, Task 40 has 13, Task 41 has 40, and Task 42 has 41 as a predecessor. If you have entered all data correctly, the project should end on 11/16/09, or November 16, 2009.

7. *Adjust screen elements*. Click **View** from the Menu bar, and select **View Bar** to collapse the View bar. Drag the resize line between the Indicator column and the Task Name column to the left to remove the Indicator column. Click **View** on the Menu bar, point to **Toolbars,** and then click **Project Guide** to hide the Project Guide toolbar. When you finish, your screen should resemble Figure A-28. If needed, click the Zoom Out button to view the Gantt chart timescale in quarters. Double-check your screen to make sure you entered the dependencies correctly.

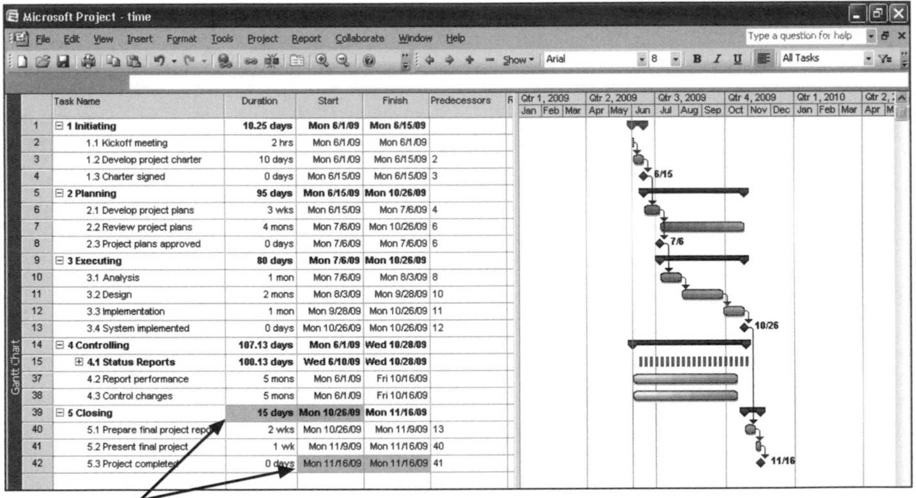

FIGURE A-28 Project Tracking Database file with durations and dependencies entered

8. *Preview and save your file*. Click **File** on the Menu bar, and then select **Print Preview,** or click the **Print Preview** button on the Standard toolbar. When you are finished, close the Print Preview and save your file again by clicking the **Save** button on the Standard toolbar. If you desire, print your file by clicking the **Print** button on the Standard toolbar, or by selecting Print from the File menu. Keep the file open for the next set of steps.

HELP

If your previewed file does not resemble Figure A-28, you may need to adjust the location of the split bar between the Entry table and the Gantt chart. The entire Predecessors column must be visible in the Gantt Chart view for it to show up in the Print Preview. Part of the next column may be showing, but it will not print. Close the Print Preview and move the split bar to reveal the column fully, and then select Print Preview again. Also, check your timescale to make sure you are not wasting paper by having a timescale too detailed. You should not print your file until the Print Preview displays the desired information.

Changing Task Dependency Types and Adding Lead or Lag Time

A task dependency or relationship describes how a task is related to the start or finish of another task. Project 2007 allows for four task dependencies: finish-to-start (FS), start-to-start (SS), finish-to-finish (FF), and start-to-finish (SF). By using these dependencies effectively, you can modify the critical path and shorten your project schedule. The most common type of dependency is finish-to-start (FS). All of the dependencies in the Project Tracking Database example are FS dependencies. However, sometimes you need to establish other types of dependencies. This section describes how to change task dependency types. It also explains how to add lead or lag times between tasks. You will shorten the duration of the Project Tracking Database project by adding lead time between some tasks.

To change a dependency type, open the Task Information dialog box for that task by double-clicking the task name. On the Predecessors tab of the Task Information dialog box, select a new dependency type from the Type column list arrow.

The Predecessors tab also allows you to add lead or lag time to a dependency. You can enter both lead and lag time using the Lag column on the Predecessors tab. Lead time reflects an overlap between tasks that have a dependency. For example, if Task B can start when its predecessor, Task A, is half-finished, you can specify a finish-to-start dependency with a lead time of 50% for the successor task. Enter lead times as negative numbers. In this example, enter –50% in the first cell of the Lag column. Adding lead times is also called fast tracking and is one way to compress a project's schedule.

Lag time is the opposite of lead time; it is a time gap or delay between tasks that have a dependency. If you need a two-day delay between the finish of Task C and the start of Task D, establish a finish-to-start dependency between Tasks C and D and specify a two-day lag time. Enter lag time as a positive value. In this example, type 2d in the Lag column.

In the Project Tracking Database example, notice that work on design tasks does not begin until all the work on the analysis tasks has been completed (see Rows 10 and 11), and work on implementation tasks does not begin until all the work on the design tasks has been completed (see Rows 11 and 12). In reality, it is rare to wait until all of the analysis work is complete before starting any design work, or to wait until all of the design work is finished before starting any implementation work. It is also a good idea to add some additional time, or a buffer, before crucial milestones, such as a system being implemented. To create a more realistic schedule, add lead times to the design and implementation tasks and lag time before the system implemented milestone.

To add lead and lag times:

1. *Open the Task Information dialog box for Task 11, Design*. In the Task Name column, double-click the text for Task 11, **Design.** The Task Information dialog box opens. Click the **Predecessors** tab.
2. *Enter lead time for Task 11*. Type **–10%** in the Lag column, as shown in Figure A-29. Click **OK.** You could also type a value such as –5d to indicate a five-day overlap. In the resulting Gantt chart, notice that the bar for this task has moved slightly to the left. Also, notice that the project completion date has moved from 11/16 to 11/12.

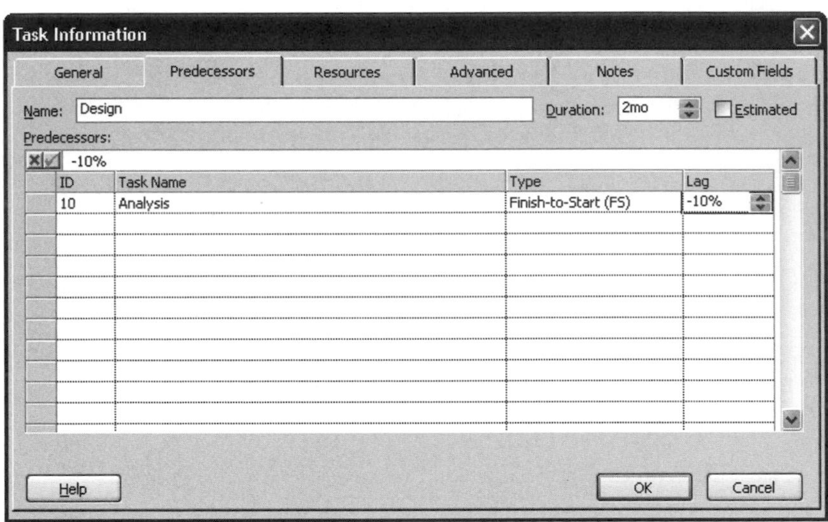

FIGURE A-29 Adding lead or lag time to task dependencies

3. *Enter lead time for Task 12*. Double-click the text for Task 12, **Implementation,** type **–3d** in the Lag column, and click **OK.** Notice that the project now ends on 11/9.
4. *Enter lag time for Task 13*. Double-click the text for Task 13, **System Implemented,** type **5d** in the Lag column for this task, and click **OK.** Move the split bar to the right, if necessary, to reveal the Predecessors column. Also double-click the Zoom In button to see the Gantt chart bars more clearly. When you are finished, your screen should resemble Figure A-30. Notice the slight overlap in the taskbars for Tasks 10 and 11 and the short gap between the taskbars for Tasks 12 and 13. Also notice the changes in the Predecessors column for tasks 11, 12, and 13. Double-click the Zoom Out button to see all of the Gantt chart symbols and the main time line in quarters. The project completion date should be 11/16.

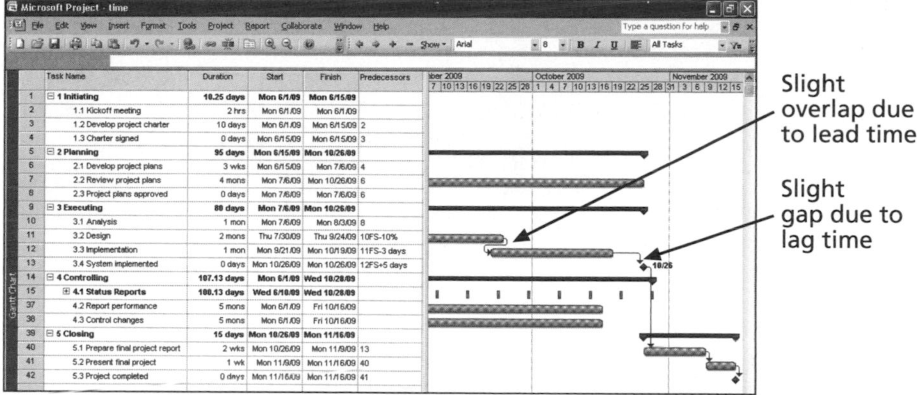

FIGURE A-30 Schedule for Project Tracking Database file with lead and lag times

5. *Review the Task Drivers pane.* Project 2007 includes a new feature to help you clearly identify how tasks affect each other. Click Task 13, **System Implemented,** click **Project** on the Menu bar, and then click **Task Drivers.** The Task Drivers pane appears on the left, as shown in Figure A-31. The Task Drivers pane describes what other tasks or factors are affecting the start date for this task.

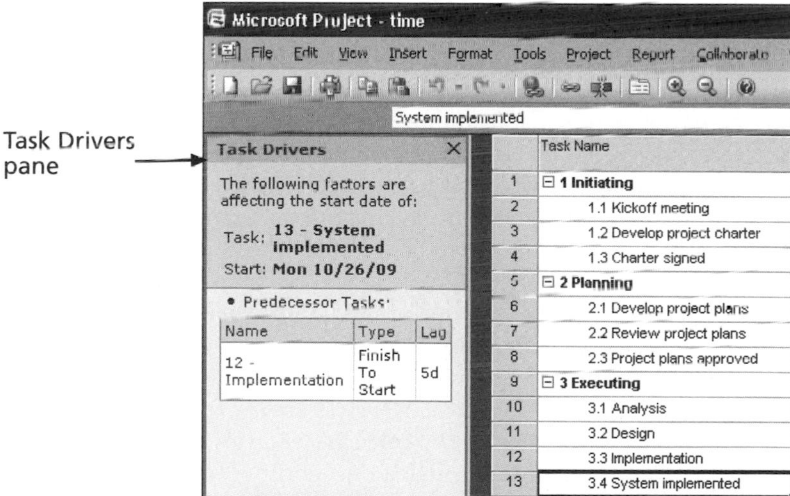

FIGURE A-31 Task Drivers pane

6. *Save your file.* Click the **Close** button to close the Task Drivers pane. Click **File** on the Menu bar, and then click **Save.** Or, click the **Save** button on the Standard toolbar. Keep this file open for the next set of steps.

TIP

You can enter or modify lead or lag times directly in the Predecessors column of the Entry table. Notice how the predecessors appear for Tasks 11, 12, and 13. For example, the Predecessors column for Task 11 shows 10FS-10%. This notation means that Task 11 has a finish-to-start (FS) dependency with Task 10 and a 10% lead. You can enter lead or lag times to task dependencies directly into the Predecessors column of the Entry table by using this same format: task row number, followed by type of dependency, followed by the amount of lead or lag.

Gantt Charts

Project 2007 shows a Gantt chart as the default view to the right of the Entry table. Gantt charts show the timescale for a project and all of its activities. In Project 2007, dependencies between tasks are shown on the Gantt chart by the arrows between tasks. Many Gantt charts, however, do not show any dependencies. Instead, as you might recall, network diagrams or PERT charts are used to show task dependencies. This section explains important information about Gantt charts and describes how to make critical path information more visible in the Gantt Chart view.

You must follow a few important procedures when working with Gantt charts:

- To adjust the timescale, click the Zoom Out button or the Zoom In button. Clicking these buttons automatically makes the dates on the Gantt chart show more or less information. For example, if the timescale for the Gantt chart is showing months and you click the Zoom Out button, the timescale will adjust to show quarters. Clicking Zoom Out again will display the timescale in years. Similarly, each time you click the Zoom In button, the timescale changes to display more detailed time information—from years to quarters, quarters to months, and months to weeks.
- You can also adjust the timescale and access more formatting options by selecting Timescale from the Format menu. Adjusting the timescale enables you to see the entire Gantt chart on one screen and in the time increments that you desire.
- A Gantt Chart Wizard is available on the Format menu. This wizard helps you adjust the format of the Gantt chart. For example, you can select an option to display critical path information on the Gantt chart, and those items on the critical path will automatically display using a red bar.
- You can view a tracking Gantt chart by setting a baseline for your entire project or for selected tasks and then entering actual durations for tasks. The Tracking Gantt view displays two taskbars, one above the other, for each task. One taskbar shows planned or baseline start and finish dates, and the other taskbar shows actual start and finish dates. You will find a sample Tracking Gantt chart later in this appendix, after you enter actual information for the Project Tracking Database project.

Because you have already created task dependencies, you can now find the critical path for the Project Tracking Database project. You can view the critical tasks by changing the color of those items on the critical path in the Task Name column. You can also change the color of the bars on the Gantt chart. Tasks on the critical path will automatically be red in the Network Diagram view, as described in the following section.

To make the text for the critical path tasks appear in red in the Entry table and on the Gantt chart:

1. *Open the Text Styles dialog box*. Click **Format** on the Menu bar, and then click **Text Styles.** The Text Styles dialog box opens.
2. *Change the critical tasks color option to red*. Click the **Item to Change** list arrow, and then select **Critical Tasks.** Click the **Color** list arrow, and then select **Red,** as shown in Figure A-32. Click **OK** to accept the changes to the text styles.

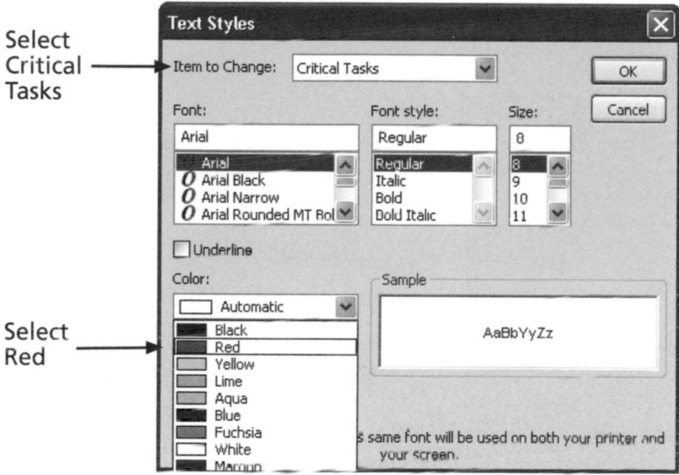

FIGURE A-32 Text Styles dialog box settings to display critical tasks in red

3. *Open the Gantt Chart Wizard*. Click **Format** on the Menu bar and then select **Gantt Chart Wizard.** Alternately, you can click the Gantt Chart Wizard button on the Formatting toolbar. The Gantt Chart Wizard opens. Click **Next**, and the next step of the wizard appears.
4. *Select the Critical path* option. Click the **Critical path** radio button, as shown in Figure A-33. Notice that the sample Gantt chart in the Gantt Chart Wizard displays some bars in red, representing tasks on the critical path. Click **Finish** to proceed to the next step in the Gantt Chart Wizard.
5. *Format the Gantt chart*. Click **Format It,** and then click **Exit Wizard.** Critical taskbars on the Gantt chart will now be red. Your screen should resemble Figure A-34, with task information and bars for all the critical tasks displayed in red on your computer screen.
6. *Save your file without a baseline*. Click **File** on the Menu bar, and then click **Save.** Or, click the **Save** button on the Standard toolbar to save your file. Keep this file open for the next set of steps.

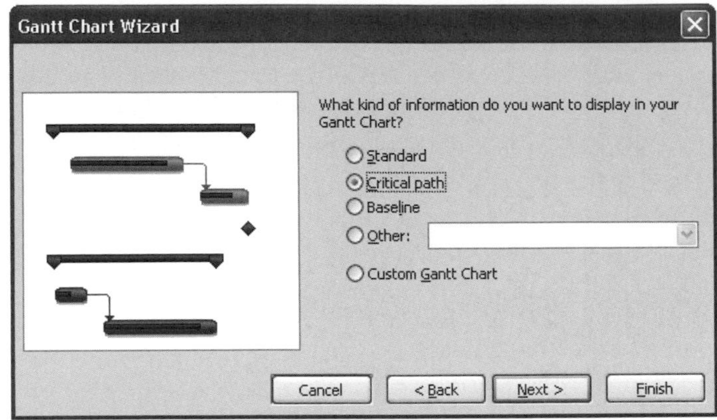

FIGURE A-33 Gantt Chart Wizard showing critical path format

Test and Gantt chart symbols for critical tasks should display in red on your computer

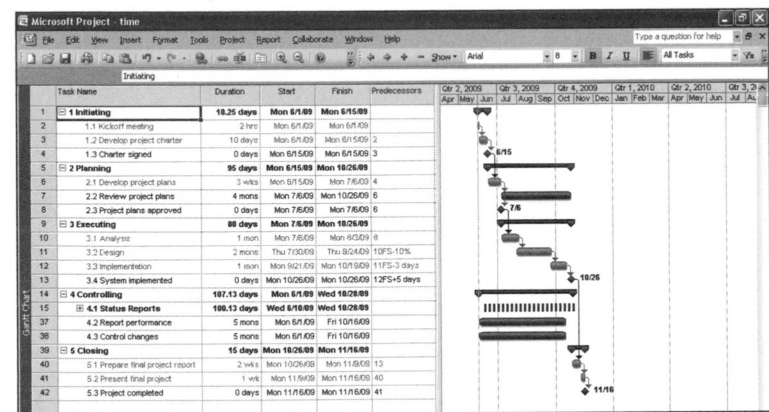

FIGURE A-34 Formatted Gantt chart

Network Diagrams

The network diagrams in Project 2007 use the precedence diagramming method, with tasks displayed in rectangular boxes and relationships shown by lines connecting the boxes. In the Network Diagram view, tasks on the critical path are automatically shown in red.

To view the network diagram for the Project Tracking Database project:

1. *View the network diagram*. Click **View** on the Menu bar, and then click **View Bar.** Click the **Network Diagram** button on the View bar or select **Network Diagram** from the View menu.
2. *Adjust the Network Diagram view*. To see more tasks in the Network Diagram view, double-click the **Zoom Out** button. You can also use the scroll bars to see different parts of the network diagram. Figure A-35 shows several of the tasks in the Project Tracking Database network diagram. Note that milestone tasks, such as Charter signed, appear as pointed rectangular boxes, while other

tasks appear as rectangles. Tasks on the critical path automatically appear in red, while noncritical tasks appear in blue. Each task in the network diagram also shows information such as the start and finish dates, task ID, and duration. Move your mouse over the Charter signed box to see it in a larger view. A dashed line on a network diagram represents a page break. You often need to change some of the default settings for the Network Diagram view before printing it.

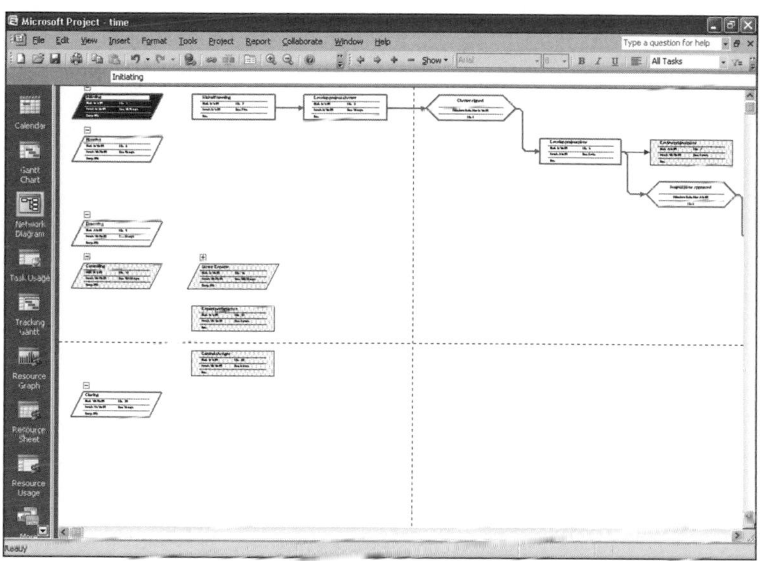

FIGURE A-35 Network Diagram view

3. *View the Help topic on rearranging network diagram boxes*. Click the **Microsoft Project Help** button on the Standard toolbar or press **F1** to display the Project Help. Type **Network diagram layout** in the text box and then press **Enter.** Click the resulting Help topic called **Move Network Diagram boxes manually.** Note that you can change several layout options for the network diagram, hide fields, and manually position boxes. Close the Help window, and then close the Search Results window.
4. *View the Layout menu*. Click **Format** on the Menu bar and then click **Layout.** Review the various options for changing the Network diagram layout, as shown in Figure A-36, and then click **OK** to close the Layout dialog box.
5. *Return to Gantt Chart view*. Click the **Gantt Chart** button on the View bar to return to **Gantt Chart** view. Alternately, you can select Gantt Chart from the View menu on the Menu bar. Keep this file open for the next set of steps.

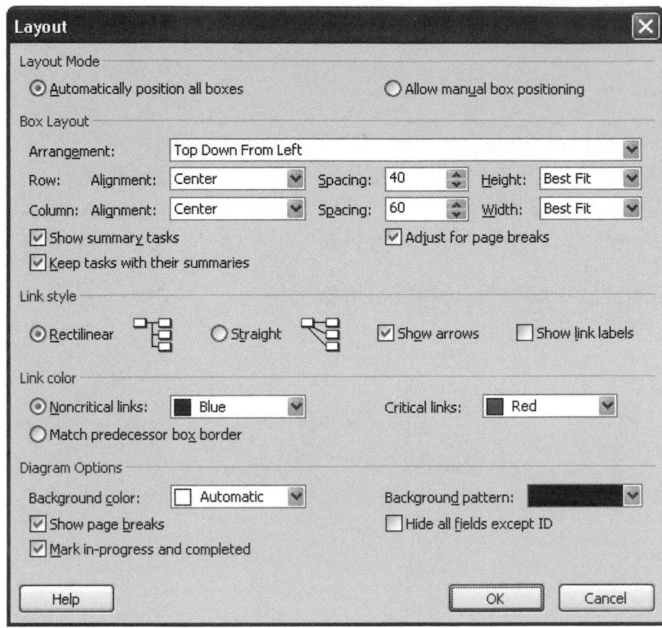

FIGURE A-36 Changing the network diagram layout

> **TIP**
>
> Some users prefer to create or modify files in Network Diagram view instead of Gantt Chart view. To add a new task or node in Network Diagram view, select New Task from the Insert menu, or press the Insert key on your keyboard. Double-click the new node to add a task name and other information. Create finish-to-start dependencies between tasks in Network Diagram view by clicking the preceding node and dragging to the succeeding node. To modify the type of dependency and add lead or lag time, double-click the arrow between the dependent nodes.

Critical Path Analysis

The critical path is the path through the network diagram with the least amount of slack; it represents the shortest possible time to complete the project. If a task on the critical path takes longer than planned, the project schedule will slip unless time is reduced on a task later on the critical path. Sometimes you can shift resources between tasks to help keep a project on schedule. Project 2007 has several views and reports to help analyze critical path information.

Two particularly useful features are the Schedule table view and the Critical Tasks report. The Schedule table view shows the early and late start dates for each task, the early and late finish dates for each task, and the free and total slack for each task. This information shows how flexible the schedule is and helps in making schedule compression decisions. The Critical Tasks report lists only tasks that are on the critical path for the project. If meeting schedule deadlines is essential for a project, project managers will want to monitor tasks on the critical path closely.

To access the Schedule table view and view the Critical Tasks report for a file:

1. *View the Schedule table.* Right-click the **Select All** button to the left of the Task Name column heading and select **Schedule.** Alternatively, you can click **View** on the Menu bar, point to **Table: Entry,** and then click Schedule. The **Schedule** table replaces the Entry table to the left of the Gantt chart.
2. *Reveal all columns in the Schedule table.* Move the split bar to the right until you see the entire Schedule table. Your screen should resemble Figure A-37. This view shows the start and finish (meaning the early start and early finish) and late start and late finish dates for each task, as well as free and total slack. Right-click the **Select All** button and select **Entry** to return to the Entry table view.

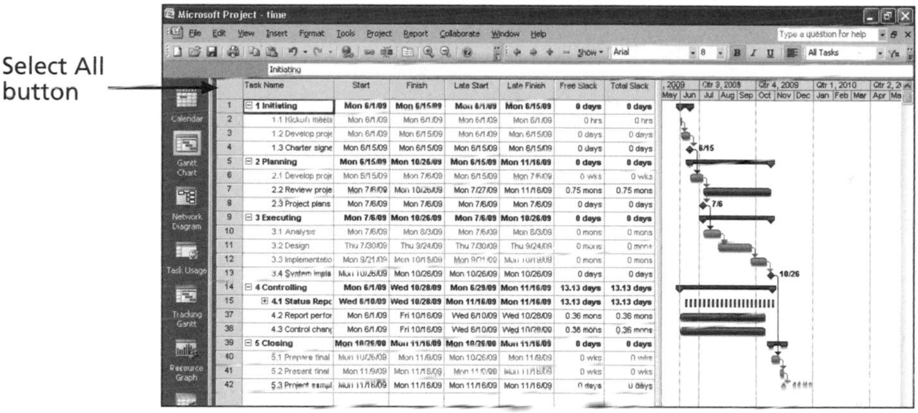

Select All button

FIGURE A-37 Schedule table view

3. *Open the Reports dialog box.* Click **Report** on the Menu bar, and then click **Reports.** Double-click Overview to open the **Overview** Reports dialog box. Your screen should resemble Figure A-38.

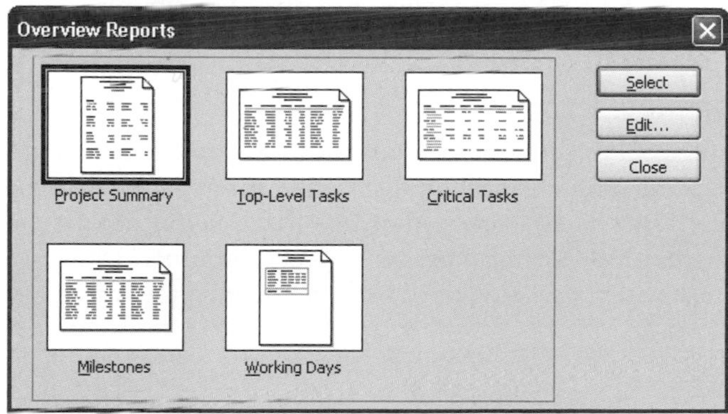

FIGURE A-38 Accessing the Critical Tasks report

4. *Display the Critical Tasks report*. Double-click **Critical Tasks.** A Critical Tasks report as of today's date is displayed.
5. *Close the report and save your file*. When you are finished examining the Critical Tasks report, click **Close.** Click **Close** on the Reports dialog box. Click the **Save** button on the Standard toolbar to save your file. Close Project 2007 if you are not continuing to the next section.

HELP

If you want to download the Project 2007 file time.mpp to check your work or continue to the next section, a copy is available on the companion Web site for this text, the author's Web site, or from your instructor.

Now that you have entered task durations, established task dependencies, and reviewed the network diagram and critical path information, you are ready to explore some of the Project 2007 cost management features.

PROJECT COST MANAGEMENT

Many people do not use Project 2007 for cost management. Most organizations have more established cost management software products and procedures in place, and many people simply do not know how to use the cost features of Project 2007. However, the cost features of Project 2007 make it possible to integrate total project information more easily. This section offers brief instructions for entering fixed and variable cost estimates and actual cost and time information after establishing a baseline plan. It also explains how to use Project 2007 for earned value management. More details on these features are available in Project 2007 Help, online tutorials, or other texts.

TIP

To complete the steps in this section, you need to use the Project 2007 file resource.mpp mentioned earlier. You can download it from the companion Web site for this text or from the author's Web site under Book FAQs.

Fixed and Variable Cost Estimates

The first step to using the cost features of Project 2007 is entering cost-related information. You enter costs as fixed or variable based on per-use material costs, or variable based on the type and amount of resources used. Costs related to personnel are often a significant part of project costs. A new feature of Project 2007 is the addition of a "cost resource," which allows you to add a fixed cost to a task without making the cost dependent on the work performed.

Entering Fixed Costs in the Cost Table

The Cost table allows you to enter fixed costs related to each task. To access the Cost table, right-click the Select All button in the Entry table and select Cost or select Table: Cost from the View menu. Figure A-39 shows the resulting view for the Project Tracking Database project using time.mpp. You can also assign a per-use cost to a resource that represents materials or supplies and use it as a base for calculating the total materials or supplies cost of a task. See Project 2007 Help for details on this feature.

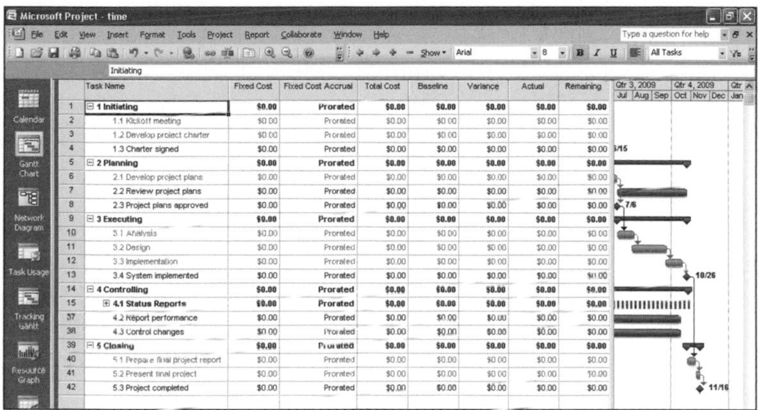

FIGURE A-39 Cost table view

Entering Human Resource Costs

Human resources represent a major part of the costs on many projects. By defining and then assigning human resources and their related costs to tasks in Project 2007, you can calculate human resource costs, track how people are used, identify potential resource shortages that could force you to miss deadlines, and identify underutilized resources. It is often possible to shorten a project's schedule by reassigning underutilized resources. This section focuses on entering human resource costs and assigning resources to tasks. The following section describes other features of Project 2007 related to human resource management.

Several methods are available for entering resource information in Project 2007. One of the easiest is to enter basic resource information in the Resource Sheet. Access the Resource Sheet from the View bar, or by selecting Resource Sheet from the View menu. The Resource Sheet allows you to enter the resource name, initials, resource group, maximum units, standard rate, overtime rate, cost/use, accrual method, base calendar, and code. Entering data into the Resource Sheet is similar to entering data into an Excel spreadsheet, and you can easily sort items by selecting Sort from the Project menu. In addition, you can use the Filter list on the Formatting toolbar to filter resources. Once you have established resources in the Resource Sheet, you can assign those resources to tasks in the Entry table with the list arrow that appears when you click a cell in the Resource Names column. The Resource Names column is the last column of the Entry table. You can also use other methods for assigning resources, as described below.

Next, you will use the Project 2007 file time.mpp, which you saved in the preceding section, to assign resources to tasks. (If you did not save your file, download it from the companion Web site or from the author's Web site.) Assume that there are four people working on the Project Tracking database project, and that the only costs for this project are for these human resources. Kathy is the project manager; John is the business analyst; Mary is the database analyst; and Chris is an intern or trainee.

To enter basic information about each person into the Resource Sheet:

1. *Display the Resource Sheet view*. Open your Project 2007 file time.mpp, if necessary. Click the **Resource Sheet** button on the View bar (you may need to scroll to see it), or click **View** on the Menu bar, and then click **Resource Sheet.**
2. *Enter resource information*. Enter the information from Table A-4 into the Resource Sheet. Type the information as shown and press the **Tab** key to move to the next field. Notice that you are putting abbreviated job titles in the Initials column: PM stands for project manager; BA, business analyst; DA, database analyst; and IN, intern. When you type the standard and overtime rates, you can just type 50, and Project 2007 will automatically enter $50.00/hr. The standard and overtime rates entered are based on hourly rates. You can also enter annual salaries by typing the annual salary number followed by /y for "per year." Leave the default values for the other columns in the Resource Sheet as they are. Your screen should resemble Figure A-40 when you are finished entering the resource data.

TABLE A-4 Project Tracking Database resource data

Resource Name	Initials	Group	Stand. Rate	Ovt. Rate
Kathy	PM	1	$50.00/h	$60.00/h
John	BA	1	$40.00/h	$50.00/h
Mary	DA	1	$40.00/h	$50.00/h
Chris	IN	1	$20.00/h	$25.00/h

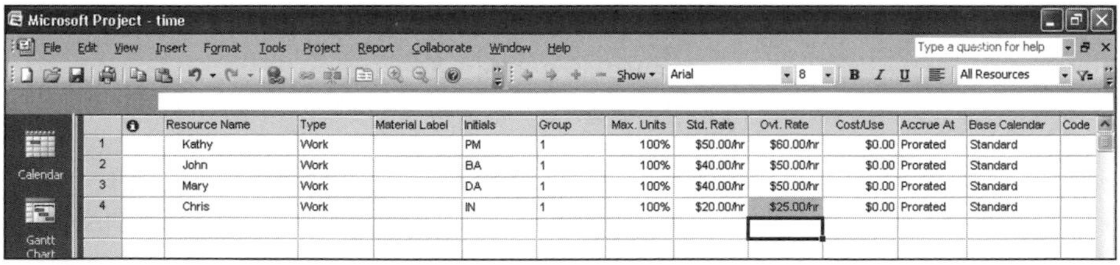

FIGURE A-40 Resource Sheet view with resource data entered

TIP

If you know that some people will be available for a project only part time, enter their percentage of availability in the Max Units column of the Resource Sheet. Project 2007 will then automatically assign those people based on their maximum units. For example, if someone can work only 25% of their time on a project throughout most of the project, enter 25% in the Max Units column for that person. When you enter that person as a resource for a task, his or her default number of hours will be 25% of a standard eight-hour workday, or two hours per day.

Adjusting Resource Costs

To make a resource cost adjustment, such as a raise, double-click the person's name in the Resource Name column, select the Costs tab in the Resource Information dialog box, and then enter the effective date and raise percentage. You can also adjust other resource cost information, such as standard and overtime rates.

To give the project manager a 10% raise starting 9/1/09:

1. *Open the Resource Information dialog box*. In Resource Sheet view, double-click **Kathy** in the Resource Name column. The Resource Information dialog box opens.
2. *Enter an effective date for a raise*. Select the **Costs** tab, and then select **tab A**, if needed. Type **9/1/09** in the second cell in the Effective Date column and press **Enter.** Alternately, click the **list arrow** in the second cell and use the calendar that appears to enter the effective date, September 1, 2009.
3. *Enter the raise percentage*. Type **10%** in the second cell for the Standard Rate column, and then press **Enter.** The Resource Information screen should resemble Figure A-41. Notice that Project 2007 calculated the 10% raise to be $55.00 per hour. Click **OK.**

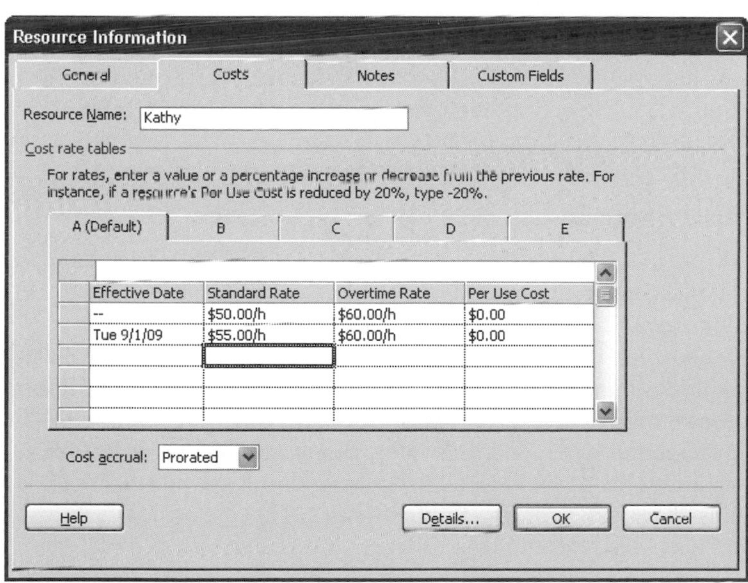

FIGURE A-41 Adjusting resource costs

Assigning Resources to Tasks

For Project 2007 to calculate resource costs, you must assign the appropriate resources to tasks in your WBS. There are several methods for assigning resources. The Resources column in the Entry table allows you to select a resource using a list. However, you can use this method to assign only one resource to a task full time, unless you know that you can enter a comma between each resource name. You can use other methods to assign resources, such as the Assign Resources button on the Resource Management toolbar or the Resource Cost window, to ensure that Project 2007 captures resource assignments as you intend them. Next, you will use these three methods for assigning resources to the Project Tracking Database project.

Assigning Resources Using the Entry Table

To assign resources using the Entry table:

1. *Select the task to which you want to assign resources*. Click the **Gantt Chart** button on the View bar. Click **View** on the Menu bar, and then point to **Table:** Cost, and then click **Entry,** to return to the Entry table.
2. *Reveal the Resource Names column of the Entry table*. Move the split bar to the right to reveal the entire Resource Names column in the Entry table.
3. *Select a resource from the Resource Names column*. In the Resource Names column, click the cell associated with Task 2, **Kickoff meeting.** Click the cell's **list arrow,** and then click **Kathy** to assign her to Task 2. Notice that the resource choices are based on information that you entered in the Resource Sheet. If you had not entered any resources, you would not have a list arrow or any choices to select.
4. *Try to select another resource for Task 2*. Again, click the cell's **list arrow** in the Resource Names column for Task 2, click **John,** and then press **Enter.** Notice that only John's name appears in the Resource Names column. You can assign only one resource to a task using this method.
5. *Clear the resource assignment*. Right-click the **Resource Names** column for Task 2, and then select **Clear Contents** to remove the resource assignments.

Assigning Resources Using the Toolbar

To assign resources using the Resource Management toolbar:

1. *Select the task to which you want to assign resources*. Click the task name for Task 2, **Kickoff meeting,** in the second row of the Task Name column.
2. *Open the Assign Resources dialog box*. Click View on the menu bar, select Toolbars, and then click Resource Management to display that toolbar. Click the **Assign Resources** button on the Resource Management toolbar. (If the Assign Resources button is not visible, click the **Toolbar Options** button on the Resource Management toolbar, and then click the **Assign Resources** button.) The Assign Resources dialog box, which lists the names of the people assigned to the project, is displayed, as shown in Figure A-42. This dialog box remains open while you move from task to task to assign resources.

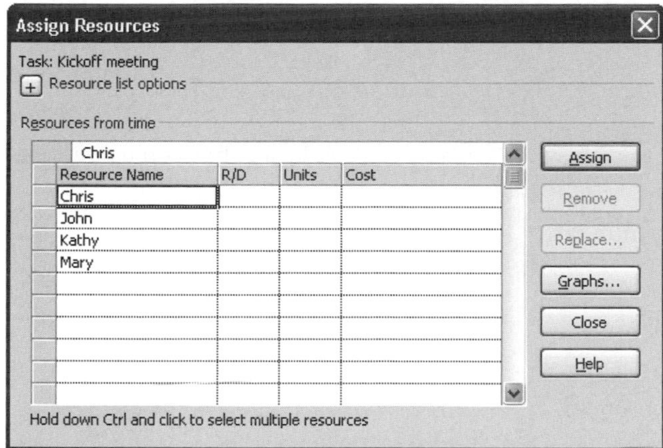

FIGURE A-42 Assign Resources dialog box

3. *Assign Kathy to Task 2*. Click **Kathy** in the Resource Name column of the Assign Resources dialog box, and then click **Assign.** Notice that the duration estimate for Task 2 remains at 2 hours, and Kathy's name appears on the Gantt chart by the bar for Task 2.
4. *Assign John to Task 2*. Click **John** in the Resource Name column of the Assign Resources dialog box, and then click **Assign.** The duration for Task 2 changes to 1 hour, *but you do not want this change to occur*. Click **Close** in the Assign Resources dialog box.
5. *Clear the resource assignments*. Right-click the **Resource Names** column for Task 2, and then select **Clear Contents** to remove the resource assignments.
6. *Reenter the duration for Task 2*. Type **2h** in the Duration column for Task 2 and press **Enter.**

TIP

Project 2007 includes a multiple-level undo feature, so you can click the Undo button on the standard toolbar several times to undo several steps in your file.

Assigning Resources Using the Split Window and Resource Cost View

Even though using the Assign Resources button seems simple, it is often better to use a split window and the Resource Cost view when assigning resources. When you assign resources using the split view, the durations of tasks will not automatically change when you assign more resources, and you have more control over how you enter information. Project 2007 Help offers more information on different options for resource assignment.

To assign both Kathy and John to attend the two-hour kickoff meeting:

1. *Split the window to reveal more information*. Click **Window** on the Menu bar, and then click **Split.** The Gantt Chart view is displayed at the top of the screen and a resource information table is displayed at the bottom of the screen.

2. *Open the Resource Cost window*. Right-click anywhere in the bottom window and select **Resource Cost.**
3. *Assign Kathy to Task 2*. Select Task 2, **Kickoff meeting** in the top window, and then click the first cell in the **Resource Name** column in the Resource Cost window. Click the cell's **list arrow** and select **Kathy.** Press **Enter.**
4. *Assign John to Task 2*. Click the cell's **list arrow** and select **John.** Press **Enter.**
5. *Enter the resource assignment and review the Gantt chart*. Click **OK** in the Resource Cost window. Your screen should resemble Figure A-43. Notice that the duration for Task 2 is still two hours, and both Kathy and John are assigned to that task 100%. You can also enter a different percentage under the Units column if resources will not work 100% of their available time on a task. Note that the default settings are tasks that are effort driven and that the Task type is Fixed Units. You will learn more about these settings later.

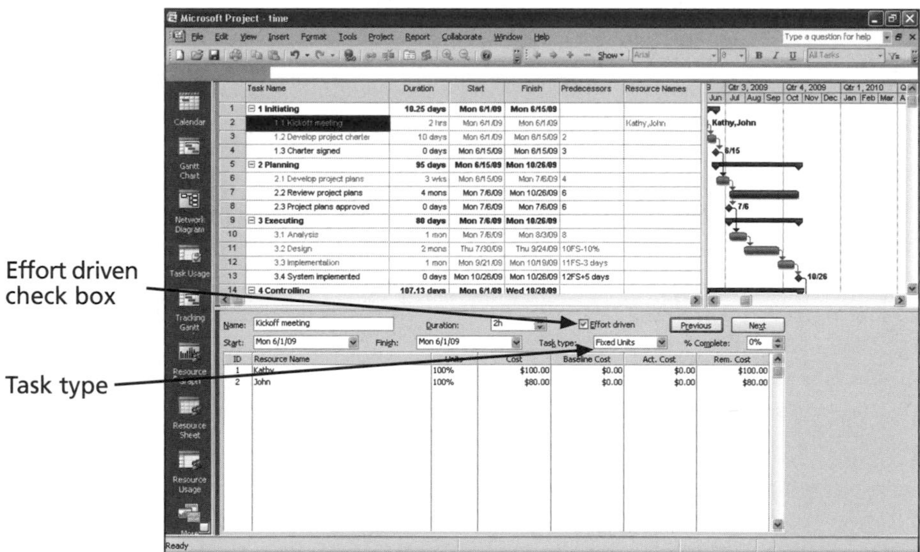

FIGURE A-43 Split screen view for entering resource information

6. *Open the Resource Schedule window*. Right-click anywhere in the lower window and select **Resource Schedule.** Notice that Kathy and John are assigned to Task 2 for two hours, as you intended. You can also enter resource information using the Resource Schedule option.
7. *Close the file and do not save it*. Close the file, but do not save the changes you made. Other resource information has been entered for you in the Project 2007 file named resource.mpp.

HELP

A copy of the Project 2007 file resource.mpp is available on the companion Web site for this text, from the author's Web site under Book FAQs, or from your instructor. You must use this file to continue the steps in the next section.

As you can see, you must be careful when assigning resources. Project 2007 assumes that the durations of tasks are not fixed, but are effort driven, and this assumption can create some problems when you are assigning resources. Figure A-44 shows the results of adding resources with different settings. The first four task entries assume the task, Design, is effort driven. When you assign one resource, John, to the Design task, the duration is one month. If you later assign two resources, John and Mary, to that same task without changing any settings, Project 2007 automatically adjusts the duration of that task to half its original duration, or 0.5 months. If you change the task type to be Fixed Duration and assign two resources, the duration remains at one month and each resource is assigned 50% to the task. If you change the type to Fixed Work and assign two resources, the duration is cut in half and the resources are assigned full time. The bottom part of Figure A-44 shows the results when a task is not effort driven or when you assign the Fixed Work task type. You must be very careful when entering resource information to make sure the task duration and work hours reflect what you want.

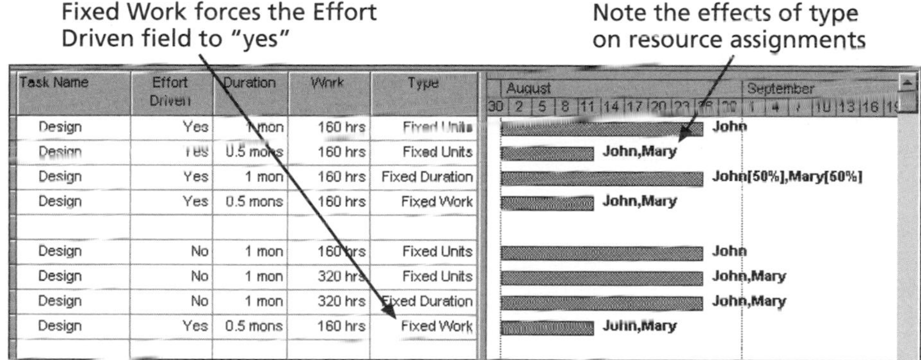

Task Name	Effort Driven	Duration	Work	Type	Resources
Design	Yes	1 mon	160 hrs	Fixed Units	John
Design	Yes	0.5 mons	160 hrs	Fixed Units	John,Mary
Design	Yes	1 mon	160 hrs	Fixed Duration	John[50%],Mary[50%]
Design	Yes	0.5 mons	160 hrs	Fixed Work	John,Mary
Design	No	1 mon	160 hrs	Fixed Units	John
Design	No	1 mon	320 hrs	Fixed Units	John,Mary
Design	No	1 mon	320 hrs	Fixed Duration	John,Mary
Design	Yes	0.5 mons	160 hrs	Fixed Work	John,Mary

FIGURE A-44 Results of adding resources with various task types

Viewing Project Cost Information

Once you enter resource information, Project 2007 automatically calculates resource costs for the project. There are several ways to view project cost information. You can view the Cost table to see cost information, or you can run various cost reports. Next, you will view cost information for the Project Tracking Database project.

To view cost information:

1. *Open resource.mpp*. Download **resource.mpp** from the companion Web site or the author's site. Open the file.
2. *Open the Cost table*. Right-click the **Select All** button in the Entry table and click **Cost,** or click **View** on the Menu bar, point to **Table: Entry,** and then click

Cost. The Cost table displays cost information and the Gantt chart. Move the split bar to the right to reveal all of the columns. Your screen should resemble Figure A-45. Note that by assigning resources, costs have been automatically calculated for tasks. You could also enter fixed costs for tasks in the cost table, but there are no fixed costs associated with this project.

	Task Name	Fixed Cost	Fixed Cost Accrual	Total Cost	Baseline	Variance	Actual	Remaining
1	**1 Initiating**	**$0.00**	**Prorated**	**$2,710.00**	**$0.00**	**$2,710.00**	**$0.00**	**$2,710.00**
2	1.1 Kickoff meeting	$0.00	Prorated	$190.00	$0.00	$190.00	$0.00	$190.00
3	1.2 Develop project charter	$0.00	Prorated	$2,520.00	$0.00	$2,520.00	$0.00	$2,520.00
4	1.3 Charter signed	$0.00	Prorated	$0.00	$0.00	$0.00	$0.00	$0.00
5	**2 Planning**	**$0.00**	**Prorated**	**$7,460.00**	**$0.00**	**$7,460.00**	**$0.00**	**$7,460.00**
6	2.1 Develop project plans	$0.00	Prorated	$5,700.00	$0.00	$5,700.00	$0.00	$5,700.00
7	2.2 Review project plans	$0.00	Prorated	$1,760.00	$0.00	$1,760.00	$0.00	$1,760.00
8	2.3 Project plans approved	$0.00	Prorated	$0.00	$0.00	$0.00	$0.00	$0.00
9	**3 Executing**	**$0.00**	**Prorated**	**$30,400.00**	**$0.00**	**$30,400.00**	**$0.00**	**$30,400.00**
10	3.1 Analysis	$0.00	Prorated	$7,920.00	$0.00	$7,920.00	$0.00	$7,920.00
11	3.2 Design	$0.00	Prorated	$12,000.00	$0.00	$12,000.00	$0.00	$12,000.00
12	3.3 Implementation	$0.00	Prorated	$10,480.00	$0.00	$10,480.00	$0.00	$10,480.00
13	3.4 System implemented	$0.00	Prorated	$0.00	$0.00	$0.00	$0.00	$0.00
14	**4 Controlling**	**$0.00**	**Prorated**	**$6,564.35**	**$0.00**	**$6,564.35**	**$0.00**	**$6,564.35**
15	**4.1 Status Reports**	**$0.00**	**Prorated**	**$3,484.35**	**$0.00**	**$3,484.35**	**$0.00**	**$3,484.35**
37	4.2 Report performance	$0.00	Prorated	$880.00	$0.00	$880.00	$0.00	$880.00
38	4.3 Control changes	$0.00	Prorated	$2,200.00	$0.00	$2,200.00	$0.00	$2,200.00
39	**5 Closing**	**$0.00**	**Prorated**	**$2,640.00**	**$0.00**	**$2,640.00**	**$0.00**	**$2,640.00**
40	5.1 Prepare final project report	$0.00	Prorated	$2,200.00	$0.00	$2,200.00	$0.00	$2,200.00
41	5.2 Present final project	$0.00	Prorated	$440.00	$0.00	$440.00	$0.00	$440.00
42	5.3 Project completed	$0.00	Prorated	$0.00	$0.00	$0.00	$0.00	$0.00

FIGURE A-45 Cost table for the resource file

3. *Open the Cost Reports dialog box*. Click **Report** on the Menu bar, and then click **Reports.** Double-click **Costs** to display the Cost Reports dialog box.
4. *Set the time units for the report*. Click **Cash Flow,** if necessary, and then click **Edit.** The Crosstab Report dialog box is displayed. Click the **Column** list arrow and select **Months,** as shown in Figure A-46, to change the report's display from Weeks to Months. Click **OK.**

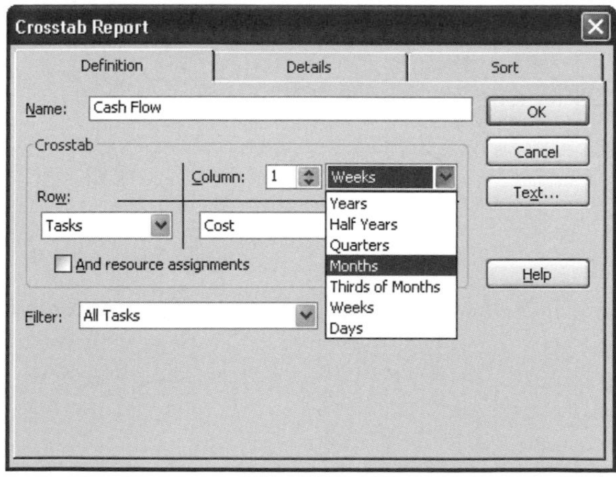

FIGURE A-46 Crosstab Report dialog box

5. *View the Cash Flow report*. Click **Select** in the Cost Reports dialog box. A Cash Flow report for the Project Tracking Database project appears, as shown in Figure A-47. Notice how it displays by WBS by month. Click **Close.**

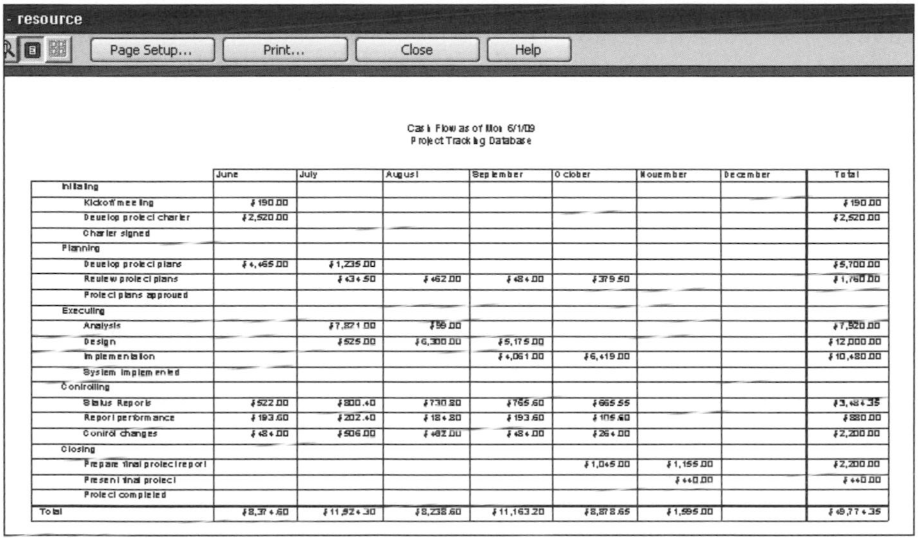

- resource

Page Setup... Print... Close Help

Cash Flow as of Mon 6/1/09
Project Tracking Database

	June	July	August	September	October	November	December	Total
Initiating								
Kickoff meeting	$190.00							$190.00
Develop project charter	$2,520.00							$2,520.00
Charter signed								
Planning								
Develop project plans	$4,465.00	$1,235.00						$5,700.00
Review project plans		$434.50	$462.00	$484.00	$379.50			$1,760.00
Project plans approved								
Executing								
Analysis		$7,871.00	$49.00					$7,920.00
Design		$525.00	$6,300.00	$5,175.00				$12,000.00
Implementation				$4,061.00	$6,419.00			$10,480.00
System implemented								
Controlling								
Status Reports	$522.00	$800.40	$730.80	$765.60	$665.55			$3,484.35
Report performance	$193.60	$202.40	$184.80	$193.60	$105.60			$880.00
Control changes	$484.00	$506.00	$482.00	$484.00	$264.00			$2,200.00
Closing								
Prepare final project report					$1,045.00	$1,155.00		$2,200.00
Present final project						$440.00		$440.00
Project completed								
Total	$8,374.60	$11,924.30	$8,238.60	$11,163.20	$8,878.65	$1,595.00		$49,774.35

FIGURE A-47 Cash Flow report

6. *View the Project Summary report*. In the Reports dialog box, double-click **Overview,** and then double-click **Project Summary.** A Project Summary report for the Project Tracking Database project is displayed, listing information such as project baseline start and finish dates; actual start and finish dates; summaries of duration, work hours, and costs; as well as variance information. Since you have not yet saved the file as a baseline, much of this information is blank in the report. The Project Summary report provides a high-level overview of a project. Click **Close** to close the report after reviewing it. Click **Close** on the Reports dialog box. Keep this file open for the next set of steps.

TIP

You can edit many of the report formats in Project 2007. Instead of double-clicking the report, select the desired report, and then click **Edit.**

The total estimated cost for this project, based on the information entered, should be $49,774.35, as shown in the Cash Flow and Project Summary reports. In the next section, you will save this data as a baseline plan and enter actual information.

Baseline Plan, Actual Costs, and Actual Times

Once you complete the initial process of creating a plan—entering tasks, establishing dependencies, assigning costs, and so on—you are ready to set a baseline plan. By comparing the information in your baseline plan to an updated plan during the course of the project, you can identify and solve problems. After the project ends, you can use the baseline and actual information to plan similar, future projects more accurately. To use Project 2007 to help control projects, you must establish a baseline plan, enter actual costs, and enter actual durations.

Establishing a Baseline Plan

An important part of project management is setting a baseline plan. If you plan to compare actual information such as durations and costs, you must first save the Project 2007 file as a baseline. Select Tools from the Menu bar, point to Tracking, and then click Set Baseline. Before setting a baseline, you must complete the baseline plan by entering time, cost, and human resources information. Be careful not to set a baseline until you have completed the baseline plan. If you do save a baseline before completing the baseline plan, Project 2007 allows you to save up to ten baselines. You can then clear unwanted baseline plans.

Even though you can clear a baseline plan or save multiple baselines, it is a good idea to save a separate, backup file of the original baseline for your project. Enter actuals and save that information in the main file, but always keep a backup baseline file without actuals. Keeping separate baseline and actual files will allow you to return to the original file in case you ever need to use it again.

To rename resource.mpp and then save it as a baseline plan in Project 2007:

1. *Save resource.mpp as a new file named baseline.mpp*. Click **File** on the Menu bar, and then click **Save As.** Type **baseline** as the filename, and then click **Save.**
2. *Open the Save Baseline dialog box*. Click **Tools** on the Menu bar, point to **Tracking,** and then click **Set Baseline.** The Set Baseline dialog box is displayed. Click the **Baseline** list arrow to reveal multiple baselines, as shown in Figure A-48.

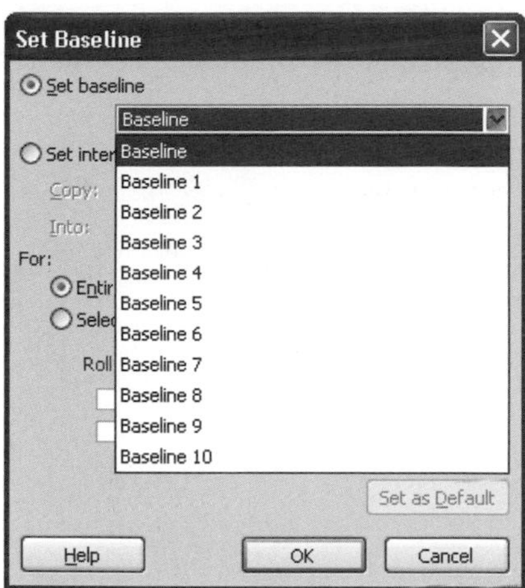

FIGURE A-48 Set Baseline dialog box showing ability to set multiple baselines

3. *Review the Set Baseline options, and save the entire project as a baseline*. If necessary, click the **Set baseline** radio button and the **Entire project** radio button. Use the default option of the first Set baseline name, Baseline. These options should be the default settings in Project 2007. Click **OK.**

TIP

There are several options in the Save Baseline dialog box, as shown in Figure A-48. You can save the file as an interim plan if you anticipate several versions of the plan. You can also select the entire project or selected tasks when saving a baseline or interim plan. As mentioned above, you can save up to ten baselines with Project 2007.

Entering Actual Costs and Times

After you set the baseline plan, you can track information on each of the tasks as the project progresses. You can also adjust planned task information for tasks still in the future. The Tracking table displays tracking information, and the Tracking toolbar helps you enter this information. Figure A-49 describes each button on the Tracking toolbar. The 100% button and the Update as Scheduled button are the most commonly used buttons for entering actual information.

Button	Name	Description
	Project Statistics	Provides summary information about the project baseline, the actual project start and finish dates, and overall project duration, costs, and work
	Update as Scheduled	Updates the selected tasks to indicate that actual dates, costs, and work match the scheduled dates, costs, and work
	Reschedule Work	Schedules the remaining duration for a task that is behind schedule so that it will continue from the status date
	Add Progress Line	Displays a progress line on the Gantt chart from a date that you select on the time scale
	0% Complete	Marks the selected tasks as 0% complete as of the status date (Actual date, work, and duration data is updated)
	25% Complete	Marks the selected tasks as 25% complete as of the status date (Actual date, work, and duration data is updated)
	50% Complete	Marks the selected tasks as 50% complete as of the status date (Actual date, work, and duration data is updated)
	75% Complete	Marks the selected tasks as 75% complete as of the status date (Actual date, work, and duration data is updated)
	100% Complete	Marks the selected tasks as 100% complete as of the status date (Actual date, work, and duration data is updated)
	Update Tasks	Displays the Update Tasks dialog box for the selected tasks so that you can enter their percentages completed, actual durations, remaining durations, or actual start or finish dates
	Set Reminder	Allows you to set a reminder for a specified time at the start or finish of a specific task
	Collaborate Toolbar	Turns the collaborate toolbar on and off

FIGURE A-49 Buttons on the Tracking toolbar

To practice entering actual information, enter just a few changes to the baseline. Assume that Tasks 1 through 8 were completed as planned, but that Task 10 took longer than planned.

To enter actual information for tasks that were completed as planned:

1. *Display the Tracking toolbar*. Click **View** on the Menu bar, point to **Toolbars,** and then click **Tracking.** Move the toolbar as desired.
2. *Display the Tracking table*. Right-click the **Select All** button in the Entry table, and then click **Tracking** to see more information as you enter actual data.

Widen the Task Name column to see all of the text, and then move the split bar to reveal all the columns in the Tracking table.

3. *Mark Tasks 1 though 8 as 100% complete.* Click the Task Name for Task 1, **Initiating,** and drag down through Task 8 to highlight the first eight tasks. Click the **100% Complete** button on the Tracking toolbar. The columns with dates, durations, and cost information should now contain data instead of the default values, such as NA or 0. The % Comp column should display 100%. Adjust column widths if needed. Your screen should resemble Figure A-50.

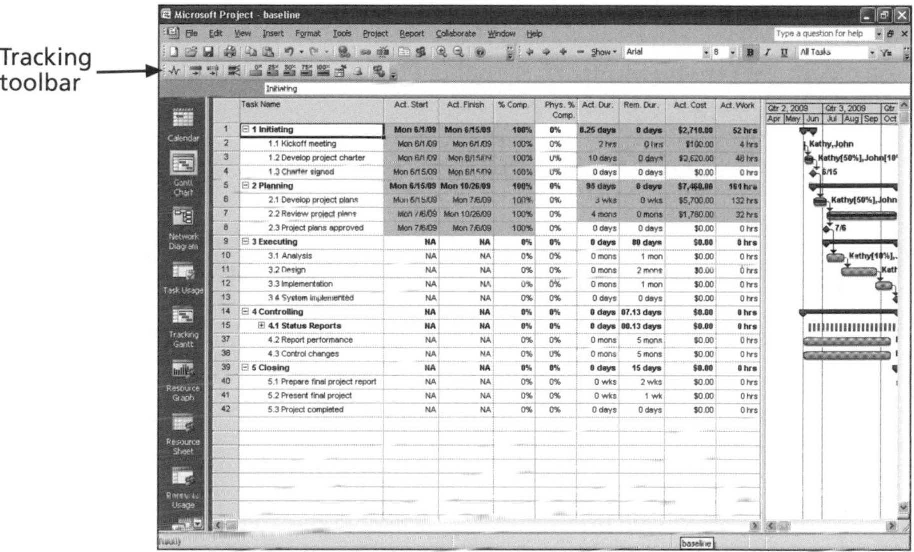

FIGURE A-50 Tracking table information

4. *Enter actual completion dates for Task 10.* Click the Task Name for Task 10, **Analysis,** and then click the **Update Tasks** button on the far right side of the Tracking toolbar. The Update Tasks dialog box opens. For Task 10, enter the Actual Start date as **7/08/09** and the Actual Finish date as **8/13/09**, as shown in Figure A-51. Click **OK.** Notice how the information in the tracking sheet has changed.

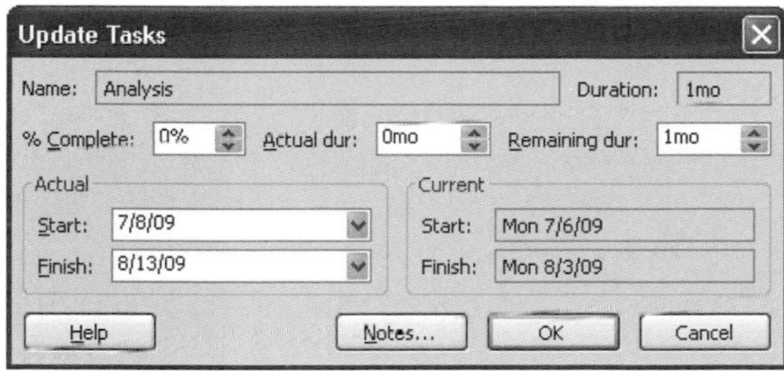

FIGURE A-51 Update Tasks dialog box

5. *Display the Indicators column*. Click **Insert** on the Menu bar, and then click **Column.** The Column Definition dialog box opens. Click the **Field name** list arrow, select **Indicators,** and then click **OK.** The Indicators column is displayed, showing a check mark by completed tasks.
6. *Display a project summary task bar*. Click **Tools** on the Menu bar, and then click **Options.** The Options dialog box opens. Click the **Show project summary task** option in the lower right side of the dialog box, and then click **OK.** The name of the file is now displayed in Row 0.
7. *Review changes in the Gantt chart*. Move the split bar to the left to reveal more of the Gantt chart. Notice that the Gantt chart bars for completed tasks have changed. Gantt chart bars for completed tasks appear with a black line drawn through the middle. You can also see the project summary task bar as the first bar displayed.

TIP

You can hide the Indicators column by dragging the right border of the column heading to the left.

You can also view actual and baseline schedule information more clearly with the Tracking Gantt view. See the main text or use the Help facility for descriptions of the symbols on a Tracking Gantt chart.

To display the Tracking Gantt chart:

1. *View the Tracking Gantt chart*. Click **View** on the Menu bar, and then click **Tracking Gantt.** Alternatively, you can click the **Tracking Gantt** button on the View Bar, if it is displayed. Use the horizontal scroll bar in the Gantt chart window, if necessary, to see symbols on the Tracking Gantt chart.
2. *Display Gantt chart information in months*. Double-click the **Zoom Out** button to display information in months. Your screen should resemble Figure A-52. Notice that the delay in this one task on the critical path has caused the planned completion date for the entire project to slip. Because the Analysis task preceded others on the critical path, such as Design, Implementation, and so on, they were delayed in starting. A good project manager would take corrective action to make up for this lost time or renegotiate the completion date.

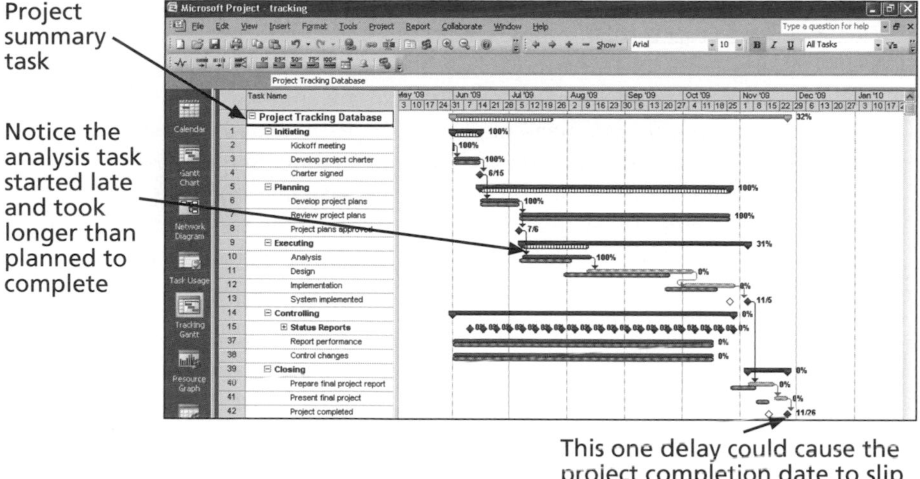
Project summary task
Notice the analysis task started late and took longer than planned to complete
This one delay could cause the project completion date to slip unless corrective action is taken

FIGURE A-52 Tracking Gantt Chart view

3. *Save your file as a new file named tracking.mpp*. Click **File** on the Menu bar, and then click **Save As.** Name the file **tracking,** and then click **Save.**

Notice the additional information available on the Tracking Gantt chart. Completed tasks have 100% by their symbols on the Tracking Gantt chart. Tasks that have not started yet display 0%. Tasks in progress, such as Task 9, show the percentage of the work completed (31% in this example). The project summary task bar indicates that the entire project is 32% complete. Also, note that the project completion date has moved to 11/26 since several tasks depended on the completion of Task 10, which took longer than planned. Recall from the main text that a white diamond represents a slipped milestone. Viewing the Tracking Gantt chart allows you to easily see your schedule progress against the baseline plan.

After you have entered some actuals, you can review earned value information for the initiating tasks of this project.

Earned Value Management

Earned value management is an important project management technique for measuring project performance. Because you have entered actual information for the initiating tasks in the Project Tracking Database project, you can now view earned value information in Project 2007. You can also view an earned value report using the new visual reports feature in Project 2007.

To view earned value information:

1. *View the Earned Value table*. Click **View** on the Menu bar, point to **Table: Entry,** and then select **More Tables.** The More Tables dialog box opens. Double-click **Earned Value.**
2. *Display all the Earned Value table columns*. Move the split bar to the right to reveal all of the columns, as shown in Figure A-53. Note that the Earned Value

table includes columns for each earned value acronym, such as SV, CV, etc., as explained in this text. Also note that the EAC (Estimate at Completion) is higher than the BAC (Budget at Completion) starting with Task 9, where the task took longer than planned to complete. Task 9 shows a VAC (Variance at Completion) of $2,772.00, meaning the project is projected to cost $2,772 more than planned at completion at that point in time. Remember that not all of the actual information has been entered yet. Also note that the date on your computer must be set later than the date of a completed task for the data to calculate properly.

	Task Name	BCWS	BCWP	ACWP	SV	CV	EAC	BAC	VAC
0	⊟ **Project Tracking Database**	**$49,774.35**	**$18,090.00**	**$20,862.00**	**($31,684.35)**	**($2,772.00)**	**$52,546.35**	**$49,774.35**	**($7,627.11)**
1	⊟ **Initiating**	**$2,710.00**	**$2,710.00**	**$2,710.00**	**$0.00**	**$0.00**	**$2,710.00**	**$2,710.00**	**$0.00**
2	Kickoff meeting	$190.00	$190.00	$190.00	$0.00	$0.00	$190.00	$190.00	$0.00
3	Develop project charter	$2,520.00	$2,520.00	$2,520.00	$0.00	$0.00	$2,520.00	$2,520.00	$0.00
4	Charter signed	$0.00	$0.00	$0.00	$0.00	$0.00	$0.00	$0.00	$0.00
5	⊟ **Planning**	**$7,460.00**	**$7,460.00**	**$7,460.00**	**$0.00**	**$0.00**	**$7,460.00**	**$7,460.00**	**$0.00**
6	Develop project plans	$5,700.00	$5,700.00	$5,700.00	$0.00	$0.00	$5,700.00	$5,700.00	$0.00
7	Review project plans	$1,760.00	$1,760.00	$1,760.00	$0.00	$0.00	$1,760.00	$1,760.00	$0.00
8	Project plans approved	$0.00	$0.00	$0.00	$0.00	$0.00	$0.00	$0.00	$0.00
9	⊟ **Executing**	**$30,400.00**	**$7,920.00**	**$10,692.00**	**($22,480.00)**	**($2,772.00)**	**$33,172.00**	**$30,400.00**	**($10,640.00)**
10	Analysis	$7,920.00	$7,920.00	$10,692.00	$0.00	($2,772.00)	$10,692.00	$7,920.00	($2,772.00)
11	Design	$12,000.00	$0.00	$0.00	($12,000.00)	$0.00	$12,000.00	$12,000.00	$0.00
12	Implementation	$10,480.00	$0.00	$0.00	($10,480.00)	$0.00	$10,480.00	$10,480.00	$0.00
13	System implemented	$0.00	$0.00	$0.00	$0.00	$0.00	$0.00	$0.00	$0.00
14	⊟ **Controlling**	**$6,564.35**	**$0.00**	**$0.00**	**($6,564.35)**	**$0.00**	**$6,564.35**	**$6,564.35**	**$0.00**
15	⊞ **Status Reports**	**$3,484.35**	**$0.00**	**$0.00**	**($3,484.35)**	**$0.00**	**$3,484.35**	**$3,484.35**	**$0.00**
37	Report performance	$880.00	$0.00	$0.00	($880.00)	$0.00	$880.00	$880.00	$0.00
38	Control changes	$2,200.00	$0.00	$0.00	($2,200.00)	$0.00	$2,200.00	$2,200.00	$0.00
39	⊟ **Closing**	**$2,640.00**	**$0.00**	**$0.00**	**($2,640.00)**	**$0.00**	**$2,640.00**	**$2,640.00**	**$0.00**
40	Prepare final project report	$2,200.00	$0.00	$0.00	($2,200.00)	$0.00	$2,200.00	$2,200.00	$0.00
41	Present final project	$440.00	$0.00	$0.00	($440.00)	$0.00	$440.00	$440.00	$0.00
42	Project completed	$0.00	$0.00	$0.00	$0.00	$0.00	$0.00	$0.00	$0.00

FIGURE A-53 Earned Value table

HELP

The Earned Value table in Figure A-53 uses earned value terms from the first edition of the *PMBOK® Guide*, which was published in 1996. BCWS is the same as PV or planned value, BCWP is the same as EV or earned vale, and ACWP is the same as AC or actual cost. See the earned value section of this text for explanations of all the earned value terms.

3. *View the earned value chart.* Click **Report** on the Menu bar, and then click **Visual Reports** to open the Visual Reports dialog box. Click **Earned Value Over Time Report,** as shown in Figure A-54. Notice the sample of the selected report on the right side of the dialog box. If you have Excel, click **View** to see the resulting report as Project 2007 automatically creates Excel data and a chart based on your current file. Close Excel without saving the file, and then click the **Close** button of the Visual Reports dialog box.

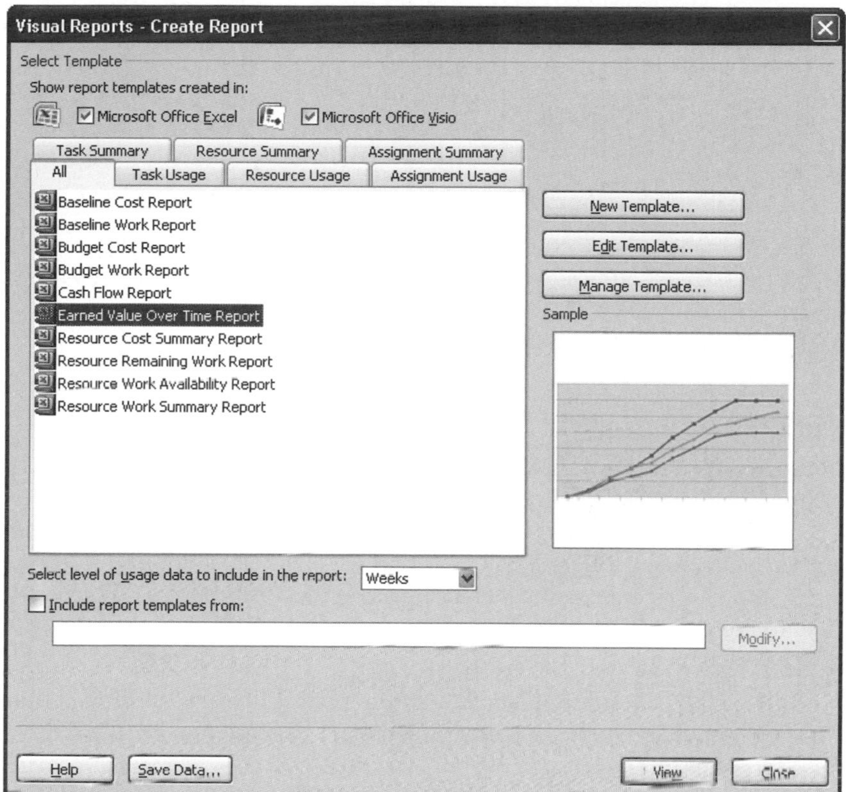

FIGURE A-54 Visual Reports dialog box

HELP

To take full advantage of the visual reports features, you must have .Net Framework 2.0, Excel 2007, and Visio 2007 installed on your computer. You may also need to adjust data, such as displaying weeks or months versus quarters, to get the reports to display as desired.

4. *Save and close the file*. Click the **Save** button on the Standard toolbar, and then close the tracking.mpp file. You can also exit Project 2007 and take a break, if desired.

HELP

If you want to download the Project 2007 files baseline.mpp and tracking.mpp to check your work or continue to the next section, a copy is available on the companion Web site, the author's Web site, or from your instructor.

Now that you have entered and analyzed various project cost information, you will examine some of the human resource management features of Project 2007.

PROJECT HUMAN RESOURCE MANAGEMENT

In the project cost management section, you learned how to enter resource information into Project 2007 and how to assign resources to tasks. Two other helpful human resource features include resource calendars and histograms. In addition, it is important to know how to use Project 2007 to assist in resource leveling.

Resource Calendars

When you created the Project Tracking Database file, you used the standard Project 2007 calendar. This calendar assumes that standard working hours are Monday through Friday, from 8:00 a.m. to 5:00 p.m., with an hour for lunch starting at noon. Rather than using this standard calendar, you can create a different calendar that takes into account each project's unique requirements. You can create a new calendar by using the Tasks pane or by changing the working time under the Tools menu.

To create a new base calendar:

1. *Open Project 2007, and open a new file*. After opening Project 2007, click the **New** button on the Standard toolbar to open a new Project 2007 file. The Tasks pane opens on the left side of your screen.
2. *Use the Tasks pane to create a new calendar*. Click **Define general working times** in the Tasks pane. A calendar wizard appears, as shown in Figure A-55.

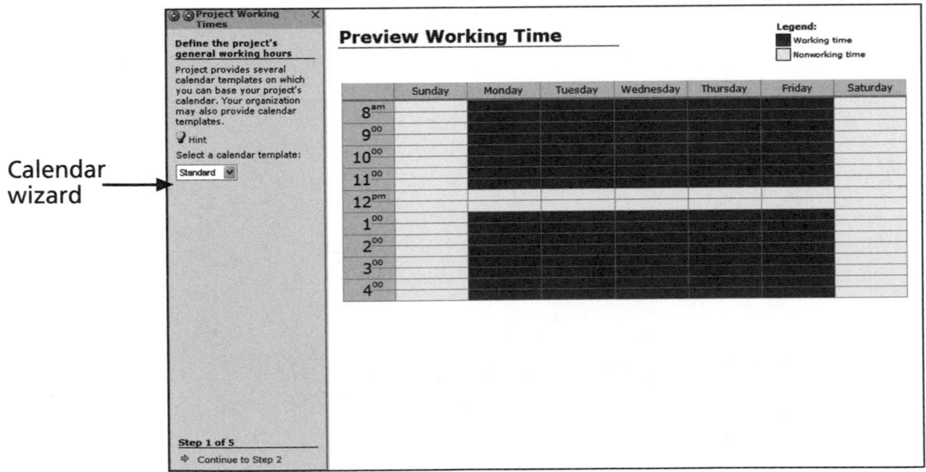

FIGURE A-55 Using the Tasks pane to change working time

HELP

If the Tasks pane does not appear on your screen, click **View** on the Menu bar, and then click **Turn On Project Guide** to see the Project Guide Task pane. Then click **Define general working times.**

3. *Make changes to the calendar using the wizard*. Click **Continue to Step 2** at the lower part of the Project Working Times pane, select the check box for **Saturday** to make it a working day, and then click the **I want to adjust the working hours shown for one or more days of the week** radio button. Scroll down to read the instructions for adjusting working hours, and make changes as desired. Click through the remaining steps to close the wizard.
4. *Create a new base calendar*. Click **Tools** on the Menu bar, and then click **Change Working Time.** The Change Working Time dialog box opens.
5. *Name the new base calendar*. In the Change Working Time dialog box, click **Create New Calendar.** The Create New Base Calendar dialog box opens. Click the **Create new base calendar** radio button, type **Mine** as the name of the new calendar in the **Name** text box, and then click **OK.** Click **OK** to close the Change Working Time dialog box.

You can use this new calendar for the whole project, or you can assign it to specific resources on the project.

To assign the new calendar to the whole project:

1. *Open the Project Information dialog box*. Click **Project** on the Menu bar, and then click **Project Information.** The Project Information dialog box opens.
2. *Select a new calendar*. Click the **Calendar** list arrow to display a list of available calendars. Select your new calendar named **Mine** from this list, and then click **OK.**

To assign a specific calendar to a specific resource:

1. *Assign a new calendar*. Click **View** on the Menu bar, and then click **Resource Sheet.** Type **Me** in the Resource Name column, press **Enter,** and then select the word **Me.**
2. *Select the calendar*. Click the **Base Calendar** cell for that resource name. If the Base Calendar column is not visible, click the horizontal scroll bar to view more columns. Click the **Base Calendar** list arrow to display the options, and then select **Mine,** if needed.
3. *Block off vacation time*. Double-click the resource name **Me** to display the Resource Information dialog box, and then click the **Change Working Time** button, located on the General tab in the Resource Information dialog box. You can block off vacation time for people by selecting the appropriate days on the calendar and marking them as nonworking days, as shown in Figure A-56. Click **OK** to accept your changes, and then click **OK** to close the Resource Information dialog box.
4. *Close the file without saving it*. Click **File** on the Menu bar, and then click **Close.** Click **No** when you are prompted to save the file.

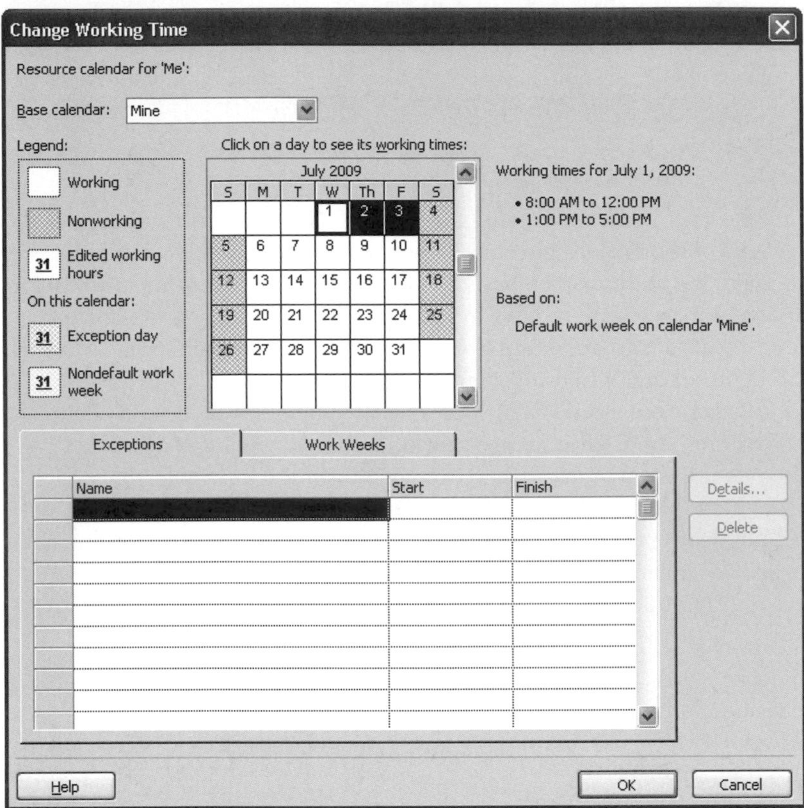

FIGURE A-56 Blocking off vacation time

Resource Histograms

A resource histogram is a type of chart that shows the number of resources assigned to a project over time. A histogram by individual shows whether a person is over- or underallocated during certain periods. To view histograms in Project 2007, select Resource Graph from the View bar or select Resource Graph from the View menu. The Resource Graph helps you see which resources are overallocated, by how much, and when. It also shows you the percentage of capacity each resource is scheduled to work, so you can reallocate resources, if necessary, to meet the needs of the project.

To view resource histograms for the Project Tracking Database project:

1. *View the Resource Graph*. Open the **baseline.mpp** file, and open the View bar, if necessary. Click the **Resource Graph** button on the View bar. If you cannot see the Resource Graph button, you may need to click the up or down arrows on the View bar. Alternatively, you can click **View** on the Menu bar, and then click **Resource Graph.** A histogram for Kathy appears, as shown in Figure A-57. The screen is divided into two sections: the left pane displays a person's name and the right pane displays a resource histogram for that person. You may need to click the right scroll bar to get the histogram to appear on

your screen. Notice that Kathy is overallocated slightly in the month of June, since the column for that month goes above the 100% line.

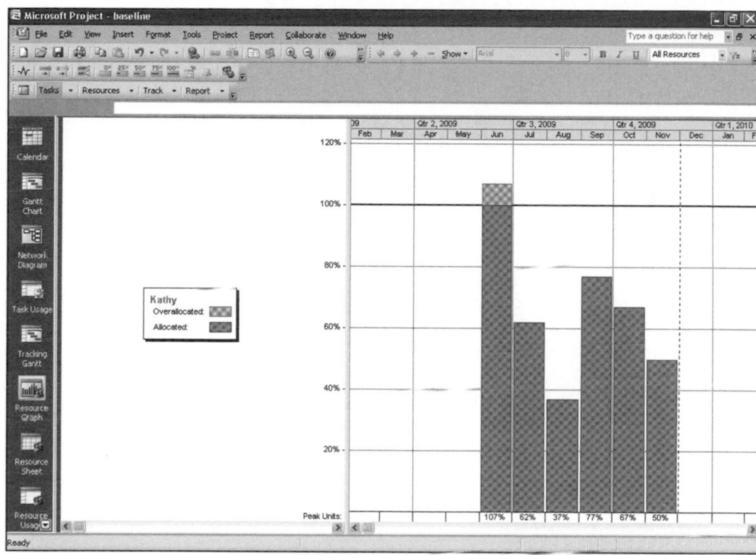

FIGURE A-57 Resource histogram view

2. *Adjust the histogram's timescale*. Click **Zoom Out** or **Zoom In**, if necessary, to adjust the timescale for the histogram so that it appears in quarters and then months, as shown in Figure A-57.
3. *View the next resource's histogram*. Click the **right scroll arrow** at the bottom of the resource name pane on the left side of the screen. The resource histogram for the next person appears. View the resource histograms for all four people, and then go back to the first one for Kathy.

Notice that Kathy's histogram has a partially red bar in June 2007. This red portion of the bar means that she has been overallocated during that month. The percentages at the bottom of each bar show the percentage each resource is assigned to work. For example, Kathy is scheduled to work 107% of her available time in June, 62% of her available time in July, and so on. Project 2007 has two tools that enable you to see more details about resource overallocation: the Resource Usage view and the Resource Management toolbar.

To see more details about an overallocated resource using the Resource Usage view:

1. *Display the Resource Usage view*. Click the **Resource Usage** button from the View bar or click **View** on the Menu bar, and then click **Resource Usage.**
2. *Adjust the information displayed*. On the right side of the screen, click the right scroll arrow to display the hours Kathy is assigned to work each day, starting on June 1, 2009. You may also need to click the scroll down arrow to see all of Kathy's hours. If you need to adjust the timescale to display weeks, click **Zoom Out** or **Zoom In.** When you are finished, your screen should resemble Figure A-58.

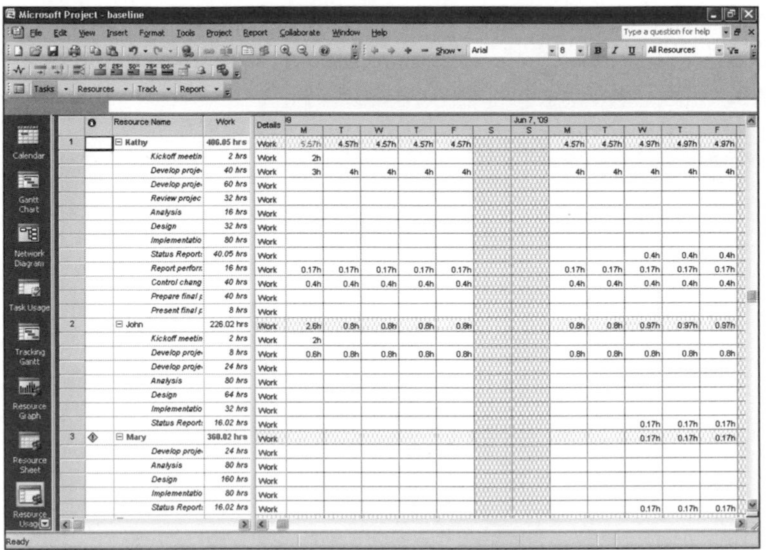

FIGURE A-58 Resource Usage view

3. *Examine overallocation information*. Notice in the Resource Usage view (Figure A-58) that Kathy's name appears in red, as does the value 5.57h in the column for Monday, June 1, 2009. Although Kathy is not scheduled to work more than eight hours on Monday, some of the tasks were entered as hours, and Project 2007 assumes those hours start as soon as possible, thus causing the scheduling conflict. You will remove the conflict using hour-by-hour leveling later in this section.

To learn more about an overallocated resource, you can also use the Resource Management toolbar for resource allocation.

To see more resource allocation information:

1. *View the Resource Management toolbar*. If the Resource Management toolbar is not already displayed, click **View** on the Menu bar, point to **Toolbars,** and then click **Resource Management.** The Resource Management toolbar displays below the Formatting toolbar.
2. *Select the Resource Allocation view*. Click the **Resource Allocation View** button, the first one on the left on the Resource Management toolbar. The Resource Allocation view appears, showing the Resource Usage view at the top of the screen and the Gantt Chart view at the bottom of the screen. Figure A-59 shows this view with Kathy's information highlighted.

HELP

If you are running Project 2007 Standard instead of Professional, you may have slightly different options on your screen.

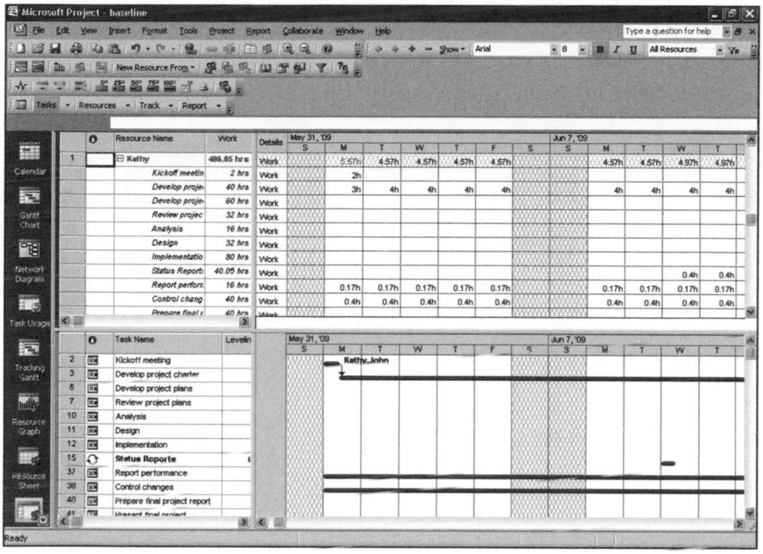

FIGURE A-59 Resource Allocation view

3. *Close the file, but do not save any changes.* Click **File** on the Menu bar, and then click **Close.** Click **No** when you are prompted to save changes.

The Resource Allocation view can help you identify the source of a resource overallocation. It is not obvious that Kathy has an overallocation the first day of the project because she is only assigned to work a total of 5.57 hours. The problem in this case is that she is assigned to several tasks that day that were entered with durations of hours, and Project 2007 assumes each of those tasks starts as soon as possible, thus resulting in the overallocation on an hourly basis. You could ignore this problem or fix it with resource leveling, as shown in the next section. By using the scroll bar, you can view information for other resources. If you scroll down to look at Mary's resource allocation information and scroll to the right to reveal August and September, you can see that overlapping the design and implementation tasks may have caused another overallocation problem. To fix the problem, you can have Mary work overtime, assign another resource to help, or reschedule the implementation task to reduce the overlap. You can also determine if resource leveling, as described in the next section, will help solve the problem.

Resource Leveling

Resource leveling is a technique for resolving resource conflicts by delaying tasks. Resource leveling also creates a smoother distribution of resource usage. You can find detailed information on resource leveling in the Help facility.

To use resource leveling:

1. *Reopen the baseline file.* Click **File** on the Menu bar, and then click the filename **baseline.mpp,** to open it. Notice by the last milestone on the Gantt chart that the project is projected to be completed on 11/16/09.

2. *Open the Resource Leveling dialog box*. Click **Tools** on the Menu bar, and then click **Level Resources.** The Resource Leveling dialog box opens, as shown in Figure A-60. Uncheck the **Level only within available slack** option, if necessary.

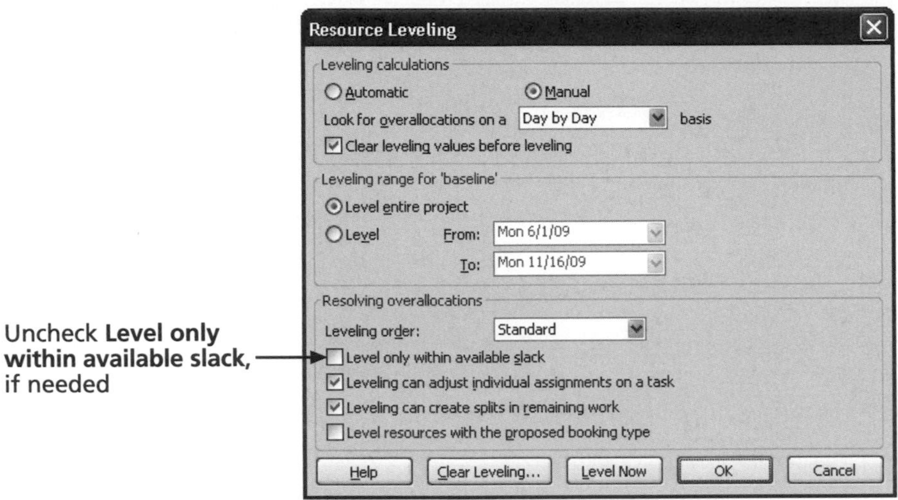

FIGURE A-60 Resource Leveling dialog box

3. *Level the file and review the date changes*. Click the **Level Now** button. In this example, resource leveling moved the project completion date from 11/16 to 11/19, as shown on the Gantt chart milestone symbol for Task 42, Project completed. Also notice that Project 2007 automatically highlighted the cells that were affected by this change.
4. *View Kathy's Resource Graph again*. Click the **Resource Graph** button on the View bar. If necessary, use the scroll bar in the resource histogram pane to display June 2009. Notice that Kathy is still overallocated in June 2009.
5. *Level using the Hour by Hour option*. Click **Tools** on the Menu bar, and then click **Level Resources.** Change the basis for leveling from Day by Day to **Hour by Hour,** click the **Level Now** button, keep the default option of Entire pool in the Level Now dialog box, and then click **OK.** Notice that Kathy's overallocation disappears. Double-click the right scroll arrow in the resource name pane to reveal information about Mary. Remember that the left pane displays different resources, and the right pane reveals the resource histogram over time. Mary's overallocations are also gone because of this resource leveling.
6. *View the Gantt chart again*. Click the **Gantt Chart** button on the View bar and move the split bar to review the Gantt chart, if necessary. The project completion date has been moved back to 11/23 because of the resource leveling.
7. *View the Leveling Gantt chart*. Click **View** on the Menu bar, click **More Views,** and then double-click **Leveling Gantt.** Click the **Zoom Out** button to adjust the timescale to show months and weeks, and scroll to the right in the Gantt

chart to reach June 2009, as needed. Also reveal all of the contents in the Task Name column. Your screen should resemble Figure A-61. Notice that Project 2007 adds a green bar to the Gantt chart to show leveled tasks.

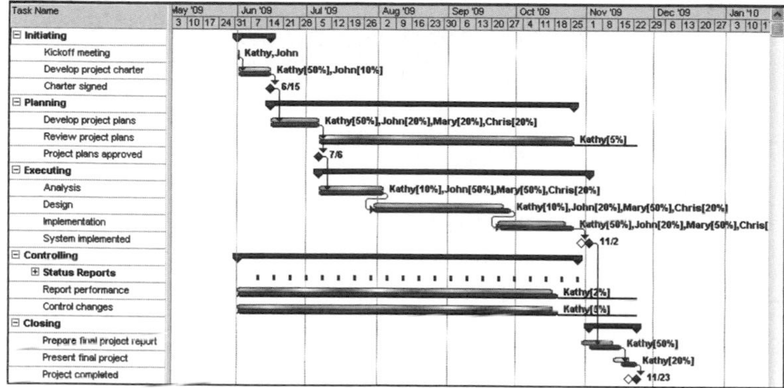

FIGURE A-61 Leveling Gantt Chart view

8. *Save the file as level.mpp.* Click **File** on the Menu bar, click **Save As**, type **level** as the filename, and then click **Save.** Close the file.

TIP

If you want to undo the leveling, immediately click the Undo button on the Standard toolbar. Alternatively, you can return to the Resource Leveling dialog box, and click the Clear Leveling button.

HELP

If you want to download the Project 2007 file level.mpp to check your work or continue to the next section, a copy is available on the companion Web site, the author's Web site, or from your instructor.

Consult the Project 2007 Help feature and use the keyword "level" for more information on resource leveling. Also, when setting options for this feature, be careful that the software adjusts resources only when it should. For example, the end date for the Project Tracking Database project was pushed back because you set the leveling options to allow the dates to slip. In this case, the project manager might prefer to ask her team to work a little overtime to remain on schedule.

Now that you have learned how to change resource calendars, view resource histograms, and level resources, you are ready to learn how to use Project 2007 to assist in project communications management.

PROJECT COMMUNICATIONS MANAGEMENT

Project 2007 can help you generate, collect, disseminate, store, and report project information. There are many different tables, views, reports, and formatting features to aid in project communications, as you have seen in the previous sections. This section highlights some common reports and views. It also describes how to use templates and insert hyperlinks from Project 2007 into other project documents, and how to use Project 2007 in a workgroup setting.

Common Reports and Views

To use Project 2007 to enhance project communications, it is important to know when to use the many different ways to collect, view, and display project information. Table A-5 provides a brief summary of Project 2007 features and their functions, which will help you understand when to use which feature. Examples of most of these features are provided as figures in this appendix.

You can see from Table A-5 that many different reports are available in Project 2007. The overview reports provide summary information that top management might want to see, such as a project summary or a report of milestone tasks. Current activities reports help project managers stay abreast of and control project activities. The reports of unstarted tasks and slipping tasks alert project managers to problem areas. Cost reports provide information related to the cash flow for the project, budget information, overbudget items, and earned value management.

Assignment reports help the entire project team by providing different views of who is doing what on a project. You can see who is overallocated by running the Overallocated Resources report or by viewing the two workload reports. You can also create custom reports based on any project information you have entered into Project 2007.

TABLE A-5 Functions of Project 2007 Features

Feature	Function
Gantt Chart view, Entry table	Enter basic task information
Network Diagram view	View task dependencies and critical path graphically
Schedule table	View schedule information in a tabular form
Cost table	Enter fixed costs or view cost information
Resource Sheet view	Enter resource information
Resource Information and Gantt Chart split view	Assign resources to tasks
Set Baseline	Save project baseline plan
Tracking toolbar	Enter actual information
Earned Value table	View earned value information

TABLE A-5 Functions of Project 2007 Features (*continued*)

Feature	Function
Resource Graph	View resource allocation
Resource Usage	View detailed resource usage
Resource Management	View resource usage and Gantt chart to find toolbar overallocation problems
Resource Leveling	Level resources
Overview Reports	View project summary, top-level tasks, critical tasks, milestones, working days
Current Activities Reports	View unstarted tasks, tasks starting soon, tasks in progress, completed tasks, should-have-started tasks, slipping tasks
Cost Reports	View cash flow, budget, overbudget tasks, overbudget resources, earned value
Assignment Reports	View who does what, who does what when, to-do list, overallocated resources
Workload Reports	View task usage, resource usage
Custom Reports	Allow customization of each type of report
Insert Hyperlink	Insert hyperlinks to other files or Web sites

Using Templates and Inserting Hyperlinks and Comments

This text provides examples of many templates that you can use to improve project communications. Because it is often difficult to create good project files, many organizations keep a repository of template or sample files. As shown earlier in this appendix, Project 2007 includes several template files, and you can also access several templates online. You must load the template files when installing Project 2007 or access templates via the Internet.

To access the Project 2007 templates:

1. *Open the New Project task pane*. Start Project 2007, if necessary, click **File** on the Menu bar, and then click **New** to display the New Project task pane, as shown in Figure A-62.

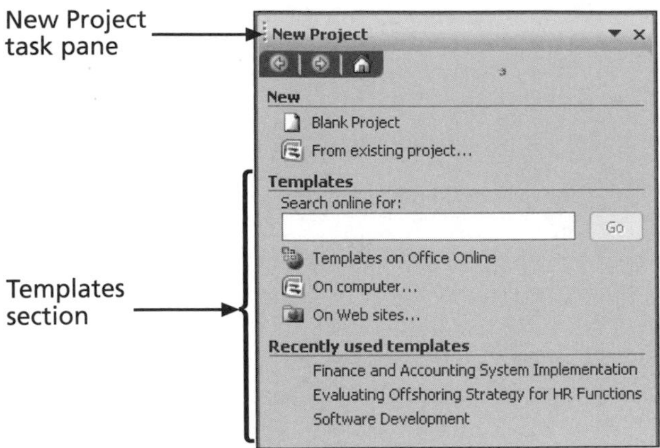

FIGURE A-62 Opening templates

2. *Open the Templates dialog box*. Click the **On computer** link in the **Templates** section of the New Project task pane. The Templates dialog box is displayed. Click the **Project Templates** tab, as shown in Figure A-63. As you can see, many templates are available. You can also access additional templates from the **Templates on Office Online** link from the New Project task pane, from other Web sites, or from your own organization.

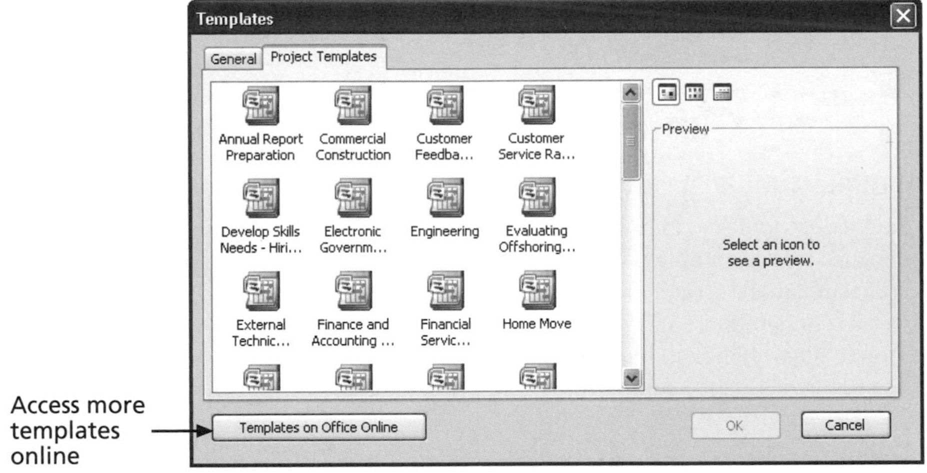

FIGURE A-63 Project templates on computer

HELP

If you do not have any templates loaded on your computer, you will not see the files displayed in Figure A-63. You must load the template files when installing Project 2007.

3. *Open the Microsoft Office Templates Gallery*. Click the **Templates on Office Online** button on the lower left section of the Templates dialog box. The resulting screen should resemble Figure A-64. Experiment with searching for various template files.

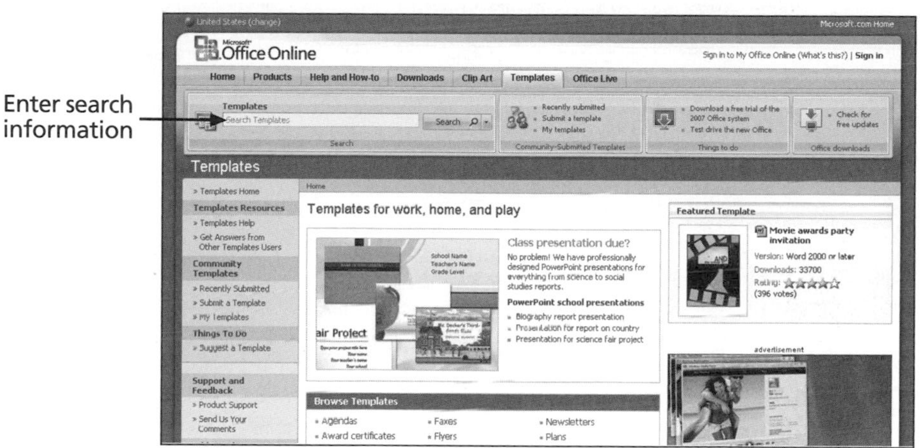

FIGURE A-64 Microsoft Office Online Web site

4. *Close your browser and the open Project file*. Click the **Close** button on your browser and then **close** the file in Project 2007.

Using templates can help you prepare your project files, but be careful to address the unique needs of your project and organization. For example, even though the Home Move template file can provide guidance in preparing a Project 2007 file for a specific home move project, you need to tailor the file for your particular situation and schedule. You can also create your own Project 2007 templates by saving your file as a template using the Save As option from the File menu. Simply change the Save As Type option to Template. Project 2007 then gives the file an .mpt extension (Microsoft Project Template) to identify the file as a template.

In addition to using templates for Project 2007 files, it is helpful to use templates for other project documents and insert hyperlinks to them from Project 2007. For example, your organization might have templates for meeting agendas, project charters, status reports, and project management plans. See the companion Web site for examples of other template files. Next, you will create hyperlinks to some template files created in other applications.

To insert a hyperlink within a Project 2007 file:

1. *Display the Entry table*. Open the **baseline.mpp** file. The Entry table and Gantt Chart view should display.
2. *Select the task in which you want to insert a hyperlink*. Click the Task Name for Task 2, **Kickoff meeting.**
3. *Open the Insert Hyperlink dialog box*. Click **Insert** on the Menu bar, and then click **Hyperlink.** Alternatively, you can right-click the task name and select

Hyperlink. The Insert Hyperlink dialog box opens, as shown in Figure A-65. You may have different folders visible based on your computer's directory structure.

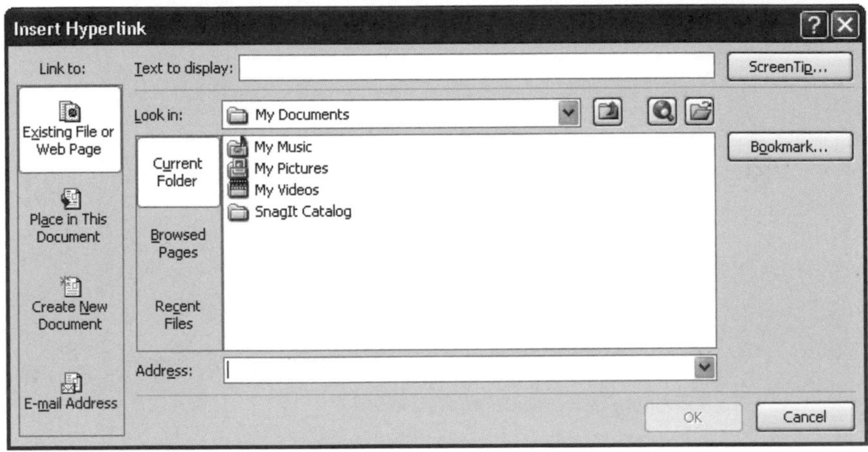

FIGURE A-65 Insert Hyperlink dialog box

4. *Enter the filename of the hyperlink file*. Click the **Browse for File** button to browse for the kickoffmeeting.doc file you downloaded earlier. Double-click **kickoffmeeting.doc,** and then click **OK.**
5. *Reveal the Indicators column*. Click **Insert** on the Menu bar, and then click **Column.** Click the **Field Name** list arrow select **Indicators,** and then click **OK.** A Hyperlink button appears in the Indicators column to the left of the Task Name for Task 2. Move your mouse over the hyperlink button until the mouse pointer changes to the Hand symbol to reveal the name of the hyperlinked file.

Clicking the Hyperlink button in the Indicators column or right-clicking, pointing to Hyperlink, and selecting Open will automatically open the hyperlinked file. Using hyperlinks is a good way to keep all project documents organized.

It is also a good idea to insert notes or comments into Project 2007 files to provide more information on specific tasks.

To insert a note for Task 4:

1. *Open the Task Information dialog box for Task 4*. Double-click the Task Name for Task 4, **Charter signed.** Click the **Notes** tab.
2. *Enter your note text*. Type **The charter was developed as a joint effort.** in the Notes text box, as shown in Figure A-66.

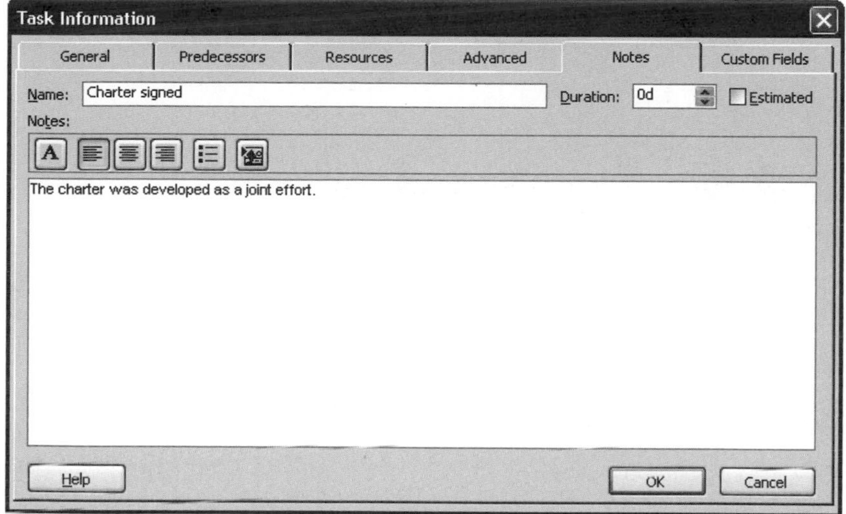

FIGURE A-66 Task Information dialog box Notes tab

3. *See the resulting Notes icon.* Click **OK** to enter the note. The Notes icon appears in the Indicators column next to Task 4.
4. *Open the note.* Double-click the **Notes** icon in the Indicators column for Task 4 to view the note, and then click **OK.**
5. *Close the file without saving it.* Click **File** on the Menu bar, and then click **Close.** Click **No** when you are prompted to save the file.

Using the Copy Picture Feature

The Copy Picture feature is now under the Report menu in Project 2007. This feature helps you easily create and copy graphical images into other applications. After answering a few questions in the wizard, you can quickly display project data as a static picture in Office applications, including PowerPoint, Word, and Visio. You can access this wizard on the Analysis toolbar.

To use the Copy Picture feature:

1. *Prepare the file you want to copy.* Open **tracking.mpp.** Drag the split bar to the left so that only the entire Task Name column is showing. You should be able to see the entire Gantt chart on your screen.
2. *Open the Copy Picture dialog box.* Click **Report** on the Menu bar, and then click **Copy Picture** to display the Copy Picture dialog box, as shown in Figure A-67.
3. *Copy a Picture.* After reviewing and adjusting the settings in the Copy Picture dialog box (you can accept the defaults for now), click **OK.**

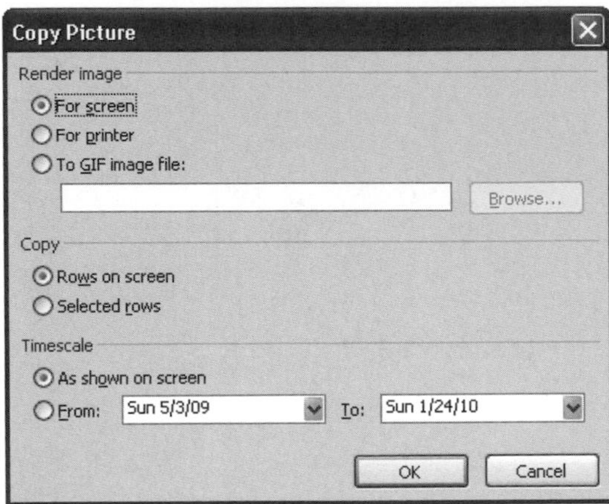

FIGURE A-67 Copy Picture dialog box

4. *Open the application where you want to copy the picture and paste it in.* Open PowerPoint, Word, or another application, if desired. Copy the picture of your Project 2007 file by pressing **Ctrl+V** or using another method to paste the picture. Figure A-68 shows the resulting picture in a PowerPoint file.

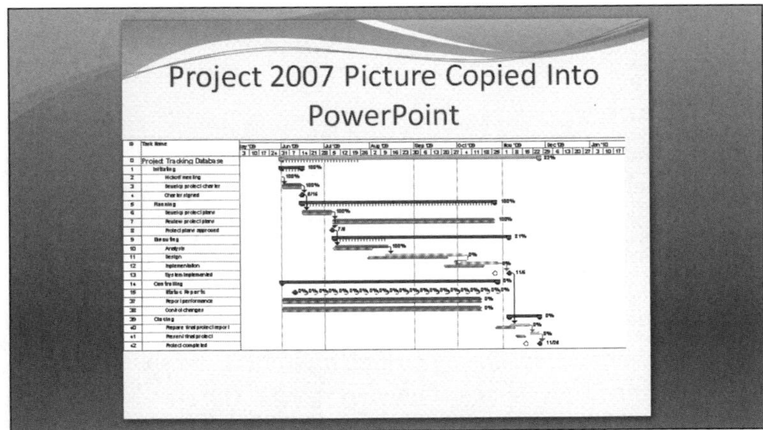

FIGURE A-68 Project 2007 picture copied into PowerPoint

5. *Close all open windows.* Click the **Close** button on any open windows. You do not need to save any of the open files.

As you can see, Project 2007 is a very powerful tool. If used properly, it can greatly help users successfully manage projects.

Discussion Questions

1. What are some new features of Project 2007 and how do they differ from previous versions of Microsoft Project?
2. How do you use Project 2007 to create a WBS hierarchy?
3. Summarize how you use Project 2007 to assist in time management. How do you enter durations, link tasks, and view critical path information?
4. How can Project 2007 assist you in project cost management? What table view would you use to enter fixed costs? How do you enter resources and assign them to tasks? How can you view earned value information?
5. Briefly describe how to change resource calendars, view resource histograms, and level resources.
6. Summarize ways to communicate information with Project 2007. How do you link to other files from within your Project 2007 file? How can you find and use templates? How can you copy pictures from Project 2007 into other applications?

Exercises

The more you practice using the features of Project 2007, the more quickly you will master the application and use it to manage projects. This section includes an exercise that you can do as a series of two homework assignments to make sure you understand the steps and concepts in this appendix. There are also exercises based on three examples of information technology projects that could benefit from using Project 2007 to assist in project scope, time, cost, human resource, and communications management. This section also includes an exercise you can use to apply Project 2007 on a real project. Simpler exercises that use Project 2007 are at the end of several chapters in this text.

Exercise A-1: Homework Assignments

You can go through this appendix as a series of homework assignments. The following two assignments are used by the author of this text in her classes. Instructors can easily change which items to print out or modify instructions to make this assignment more unique.

HW1: Project 2007, Part 1 (100 points, 25 points for each item)

See points for each item listed below. *Note*: You can download a free trial of Project 2007 from *www.microsoft.com* or use the PCs at school. Remember that you must be running Windows XP or Vista. Read and follow the hands-on instructions in this *Guide to Using Project 2007*. Read the first several pages of the appendix, and do all the steps starting under the Overview of Project 2007 heading (p. A.5) and stop after you finish the steps right before the heading called Baseline Plan, Actual Costs, and Actual Times (p. A.54). The files mentioned are on the companion Web site and the author's site (*www.kathyschwalbe.com* under Book FAQs on the left). In the section on Project Scope Management, Table A-2 lists the first task as Initiating. After the word Initiating, enter your first and last name (e.g., Initiating – Kathy Schwalbe). Continue doing all of the steps, and print out only the items described below.

1. Your formatted Gantt chart, Figure A-34 (50 points). Be sure it fits on one page before printing and that all the columns shown are visible.
2. The schedule table view, Figure A-37.
3. The Split Screen View for Entering Resource Information, Figure A-43. *Note*: Press the print screen button (PrtScrn [or PrtScrn and Fn] on your keyboard) and paste it into Word to print because it does not print out as shown from within Project 2007 (50 points).
4. Create a new Project file that shows the WBS for a generic project. Make the main categories project management, concept, development, implementation, and close-out. Include at least four tasks and one milestone under each of these main categories. Enter 0 for the duration of the milestones, but do not enter any durations for the other tasks. Be sure to indent tasks and show the outline numbers before printing out the Gantt chart view on one page.

HW2: Project 2007, Part 2 (100 points, 25 points for each item)

Do all the steps starting under the Baseline Plan, Actual Costs, and Actual Times heading (p. A.54) through the end of the appendix. Remember to type your first and last name after the first task, Initiating.

1. Print out the Tracking Gantt Chart View, Figure A-52.
2. Print out the Resource Histogram View, Figure A-57.
3. Use the Copy Picture feature (p. A.75) to copy the Leveling Gantt chart, Figure A-61, created with the level.mpp file, into PowerPoint and print out that one PowerPoint slide from within PowerPoint.
4. Write a one- to two-page, single-spaced paper summarizing what you think about Microsoft Project. What do you like and dislike about it. Do you think it would be useful for managing all projects, or just some? Which ones?

Exercise A-2: Web Site Development

A nonprofit organization would like you to lead a Web site development project. The organization has Internet access that includes space on a Web server, but no experience developing Web sites. In addition to creating its Web site, the organization would like you to train two people on its staff to do simple Web page updates. The Web site should include the following information, as a minimum: description of the organization (mission, history, and recent events), list of services, and contact information. The organization wants the Web site to include graphics (photographs and other images) and have an attractive, easy-to-use layout.

1. Project Scope Management
   Create a WBS for this project and enter the tasks in Project 2007. Create milestones and summary tasks. Assume that some of the project management tasks are similar to tasks from the Project Tracking Database project. Some of the specific analysis, design, and implementation tasks will be to:
   a. Collect information on the organization in hardcopy and digital form (brochures, reports, organization charts, photographs, and so on).
   b. Research Web sites of similar organizations.

   c. Collect detailed information about the customer's design preferences and access to space on a Web server.
   d. Develop a template for the customer to review (background color for all pages, position of navigation buttons, layout of text and images, typography, including basic text font and display type, and so on).
   e. Create a site map or hierarchy chart showing the flow of Web pages.
   f. Digitize the photographs and find other images for the Web pages; digitize hardcopy text.
   g. Create the individual Web pages for the site.
   h. Test the pages and the site.
   i. Implement the Web site on the customer's Web server.
   j. Get customer feedback.
   k. Incorporate changes.
   l. Create training materials for the customer on how to update the Web pages.
   m. Train the customer's staff on updating the Web pages.
2. Project Time Management
   a. Enter realistic durations for each task, and then link the tasks as appropriate. Be sure that all tasks are linked (in some fashion) to the start and end of the project. Assume that you have four months to complete the entire project. (*Hint*: Use the Project Tracking Database as an example.)
   b. Print the Gantt Chart view and Network Diagram view for the project.
   c. Print the Schedule table to see key dates and slack times for each task.
3. Project Cost Management
   a. Assume that you have three people working on the project, and each of them would charge $20 per hour. Enter this information in the Resource Sheet.
   b. Estimate that each person will spend an average of about five hours per week for the four-month period. Assign resources to the tasks, and try to make the final cost in line with this estimate.
   c. Print the budget report for your project.
4. Project Human Resource Management
   a. Assume that one project team member will be unavailable (due to vacation) for two weeks in the middle of the project. Make adjustments to accommodate this vacation so that the schedule does not slip and the costs do not change. Document the changes from the original plan and the new plan.
   b. Use the Resource Usage view to see each person's work each month. Print a copy of the Resource Usage view.
5. Project Communications Management
   a. Print a Gantt chart for this project. Use a timescale that enables the chart to fit on one page. Then paste a copy of the Gantt chart in PowerPoint and print out the slide.
   b. Print a "To-do List" report for each team member.
   c. Create a "Who Does What Report" and print it out.

Exercise A-3: Software Training Program

ABC Company has 50,000 employees and wants to increase employee productivity by setting up an internal software applications training program. The training program will teach employees how to use Microsoft software programs such as Vista, Word 2007, Excel 2007, PowerPoint 2007, Access 2007, and Project 2007. Courses will be offered in the evenings and on Saturdays and taught by qualified volunteer employees. Instructors will be paid $40 per hour. In the past, employees were sent to courses offered by local vendors during company time. In contrast, this internal training program should save the company money on training as well as make people more productive. The Human Resources department will manage the program, and any employee can take the courses. Employees will receive a certificate for completing courses, and a copy will be put in their personnel files. The company is not sure which vendor's off-the-shelf training materials to use. The company needs to set up a training classroom, survey employees on desired courses, find qualified volunteer instructors, and start offering courses. The company wants to offer the first courses within six months. One person from Human Resources is assigned full time to manage this project, and top management has pledged its support.

1. Project Scope Management
   Create a WBS for this project and enter the tasks in Project 2007. Create milestones and summary tasks. Assume that some of the project management tasks you need to do are similar to tasks from the Project Tracking Database example. Some of the tasks specific to this project will be to:

   a. Review off-the-shelf training materials from three major vendors and decide which materials to use.
   b. Negotiate a contract with the selected vendor for its materials.
   c. Develop communications information about this new training program. Disseminate the information via department meetings, e-mail, the company's intranet, and flyers to all employees.
   d. Create a survey to determine the number and type of courses needed and employees' preferred times for taking courses.
   e. Administer the survey.
   f. Solicit qualified volunteers to teach the courses.
   g. Review resumes, interview candidates for teaching the courses, and develop a list of preferred instructors.
   h. Coordinate with the Facilities department to build two classrooms with 20 personal computers each, a teacher station, and an overhead projection system (assume that Facilities will manage this part of the project).
   i. Schedule courses.
   j. Develop a fair system for signing up for classes.
   k. Develop a course evaluation form to assess the usefulness of each course and the instructor's teaching ability.
   l. Offer classes.

2. Project Time Management
   a. Enter realistic durations for each task and then link appropriate tasks. Be sure that all tasks are linked in some fashion to the start and end of the project. Use the Project Tracking Database as an example. Assume that you have six months to complete the entire project.
   b. Print the Gantt Chart view and Network Diagram view for the project.
   c. Print the Schedule table to see key dates and slack times for each task.
3. Project Cost Management
   a. Assume that you have four people from various departments available part time to support the full-time Human Resources person, Terry, on the project. Assume that Terry's hourly rate is $40. Two people from the Information Technology department will each spend up to 25% of their time supporting the project. Their hourly rate is $50. One person from the Marketing department is available 25% of the time at $40 per hour, and one person from Corporate is available 30% of the time at $35 per hour. Enter this information about time and hourly wages into the Resource Sheet. Assume that the cost to build the two classrooms will be $100,000, and enter it as a fixed cost.
   b. Using your best judgment, assign resources to the tasks.
   c. View the Resource Graphs for each person. If anyone is overallocated, make adjustments.
   d. Print the budget report for the project.
4. Project Human Resource Management
   a. Assume that the Marketing person will be unavailable for one week, two months into the project, and for another week, four months into the project. Make adjustments to accommodate this unavailability, so the schedule does not slip and costs do not change. Document the changes from the original plan and the new plan.
   b. Add to each resource a 5% raise that starts three months into the project. Print a new budget report.
   c. Use the Resource Usage view to see each person's work each month. Print a copy.
5. Project Communications Management
   a. Print a Gantt chart for this project. Use a timescale that enables the chart to fit on one page. Then copy a picture of the same Gantt chart in PowerPoint and print out the slide.
   b. Print a "To-do List" report for each team member.
   c. Review some of the other reports and print out one that you think would help in managing the project.

Exercise A-4: Project Tracking Database

Expand the Project Tracking Database example. Assume that XYZ Company wants to create a history of project information, and the Project Tracking Database example is the best format for this type of history. The company wants to track information on 20 past and current projects and wants the database to be able to handle 100 projects total. The company wants to track the following project information:

- Project name
- Sponsor name
- Sponsor department
- Type of project
- Project description
- Project manager
- Team members
- Date project was proposed
- Date project was approved or denied
- Initial cost estimate
- Initial time estimate
- Dates of milestones (e.g., project approval, funding approval, project completion)
- Actual cost
- Actual time
- Location of project files

1. Project Scope Management
   Open scope.mpp and add more detail to Executing tasks, using the information in Table A-6.

TABLE A-6 Company XYZ Project Tracking Database executing tasks

Analysis Tasks	Design Tasks	Implementation Tasks
Collect list of 20 projects	Gather detailed requirements for desired outputs from the database	Enter project data
Gather information on projects	Create fully attributed, normalized data model	Test database
Define draft requirements	Create list of edit rules for fields, determine default values, develop queries, and determine formats for reports	Make adjustments, as needed
Create entity relationship diagram for database	Develop list of queries required for database	Conduct user testing
Create sample entry screen	Review design information with customer	Make adjustments based on user testing
Create sample report	Make adjustments to design based on customer feedback	Create online Help, user manual, and other documentation

TABLE A-6 Company XYZ Project Tracking Database executing tasks (*continued*)

Analysis Tasks	Design Tasks	Implementation Tasks
Develop simple prototype of database	Create full table structure in database prototype	Train users on the system
Review prototype with customer	Create data input screens	
Make adjustments based on customer feedback	Write queries	
	Create reports	
	Create main screen	
	Review new prototype with customer	

2. Project Time Management
   a. Enter realistic durations for each task, and then link appropriate tasks. Make the additional tasks fit the time estimate: 20 days for analysis tasks, 30 days for design tasks, and 20 days for implementation tasks. Assume that all of the executing tasks have a total duration of 70 days. Do not overlap analysis, design, and implementation tasks.
   b. Print the Gantt Chart view and Network Diagram view for the project.
   c. Print the Schedule table to see key dates and slack times for each task.
3. Project Cost Management
   a. Use the resource and cost information provided in resource.mpp.
   b. Assign resources to the new tasks. Try to make the final cost about the same as that shown in the Project Tracking Database example: about $50,000.
   c. Print the budget report for the project.
4. Project Human Resources Management
   a. Two months after the project begins, give everyone on the team a 10% raise. Document the increase in costs that these raises cause.
   b. Use the Resource Usage view to see each person's work each month. Print a copy of the Resource Usage view.
5. Project Communications Management
   a. Print a Gantt chart for this project. Use a timescale that enables the chart to fit on one page. Then copy a picture of the Gantt chart in PowerPoint and print out the slide.
   b. Print a "Top-Level Tasks" report.
   c. Review some of the other reports and print out one that you think would help in managing the project.

Exercise A-5: Real Project Application

If you are doing a group project as part of your class or for a project at work, use Project 2007 to create a detailed file describing the work you plan to do. Enter a sufficient WBS, estimate task durations, link tasks, enter resources and costs, assign resources, and so on. Save your file as a baseline and track your progress. View earned value information when you are halfway through the project or course. Continue tracking your progress until the project or course is finished. Print your Gantt chart, Resource Sheet, Project Summary report, and relevant information. Write a two- to three-page report describing your experience. What did you learn about Project 2007 from this exercise? What did you learn about managing a project? How do you think Project 2007 helps in managing a project? You may also want to interview people who use Project 2007 for their experiences and suggestions.

ADVICE FOR THE PROJECT MANAGEMENT PROFESSIONAL (PMP) EXAM AND RELATED CERTIFICATIONS

INTRODUCTION TO PROJECT MANAGEMENT CERTIFICATION PROGRAMS

This appendix provides information on project management certification programs and offers advice for earning certifications. It briefly describes various certification programs and provides detailed information on PMI's PMP and CompTIA's Project+ certifications, the structure and content of these exams, suggestions on preparing for the exams, tips for taking the exams, sample questions, and information on related certifications.

WHAT IS PMP CERTIFICATION?

The Project Management Institute (PMI) offers certification as a Project Management Professional (PMP). As mentioned in Chapter 1, the number of people earning PMP certification grew rapidly in the past ten years. There are PMPs in more than 120 countries throughout the world. Detailed information about PMP certification, the PMP Certification Handbook, and an online application is available from PMI's Web site (*www.pmi.org*) under Career Development. The following information is quoted from PMI's Web site:

> "The Project Management Institute (PMI®) is the world's leading association for the project management profession. It administers a globally recognized, rigorous, education, and/or professional experience and examination-based professional credentialing program that maintains an ISO 9001 certification in Quality Management Systems. To get the latest information, please visit the breaking news section.

Earning a professional credential through PMI means that one has:

- Demonstrated the appropriate education and/or professional experience;
- Passed a rigorous examination;
- Agreed to abide by a professional code of conduct;
- Committed to maintaining their active credential through meeting continuing certification requirements.

PMI professional credentials—available to members of the Institute and non-members alike—are widely recognized and accepted throughout the world as evidence of a proven level of education, knowledge and experience in project management."[1]

Many companies and organizations are recommending or even requiring PMP certification for their project managers. A February 2003 newsletter reported that Microsoft chose PMI's PMP Certification Program as the certification of choice for its Microsoft Services Operation. Microsoft chose the PMP certification because of its global recognition and proven record in professional development for project managers.[2] *CertCities.com* ranked the PMP as No. 4 in their ten hottest certifications for 2006. It "made a strong showing this year, rising from its debut stop at No. 10 last year, thanks in part to even stronger buzz for this industry-neutral title within the IT community."[3]

Certification Magazine published its annual review of how certification affects salaries of information technology professionals. This industry-wide study uses real-world numbers to show how education and experience affect a person's bottom-line salary. During a down market, people might ask why they should seek additional technical certifications. According to Gary Gabelhouse of *Certification Magazine*, "Perhaps it is best expressed in two words: job security. In boom times, one constantly reviews the rate of growth in salary as a key personal-success measurement. However, in down times, job security is paramount."[4]

The October 2004 issue of *PM Network* included an article entitled "The Rise of PMP," which provided several examples of companies and countries that have made concerted efforts to increase their number of PMPs. Hewlett-Packard had only six registered PMPs in 1997, but by August 2004, it had more than 1,500 and was adding 500 per year. Although most PMPs are in the United States (51,498) and Canada (7,444), the PMP credential is growing in popularity in several countries, such as Japan (6,001), China (4,472), and India (2,281). Thomas Walenta, PMP, a senior project manager for IBM Germany, said, "The PMP credential lends portability to a career plan. It has significantly shaped careers in the IT industry, with global companies creating career models for project managers based on PMI certification requirements."[5]

As of January 2009, PMI also offers certifications as a Certified Associate in Project Management (CAPM), a PMI-Scheduling Professional (PMI-SP), a PMI-Risk Management Professional (PMI-RMP), and a Program Management Professional (PgMP). PMI developed the CAPM certification as a stepping-stone to PMP certification. Candidates for the CAPM certification must also meet specific education and experience requirements and pass an exam. As you can imagine, the requirements are not as rigorous as they are for the PMP exam. You might want to consider getting the CAPM, or just wait until you have enough experience to earn the more popular PMP certification. PMI reported only 6,729 active CAPMs by the end of December 2008 and 318,289 active PMPs.[6] As described on the following page, you need 4,500 hours of project experience or a minimum of three years if you have a bachelor's degree to qualify for PMP certification.

What Are the Requirements for Earning and Maintaining PMP Certification?

You can now apply to take the PMP exam online. You can also fill out the application forms and mail them in with a check, if desired. *Before* you apply to take the exam, you must meet the following four requirements:

1. Have experience working in the field of project management. When you apply to take the exam, you enter the role you played in leading and directing project tasks on one or several projects and how many hours you worked in each of the five project management process groups for each project. Roles include:

   - Project contributor
   - Supervisor
   - Manager
   - Project leader
   - Project manager
   - Educator
   - Consultant
   - Administrator
   - Other

   Note that you do not have to have experience as a project manager to take the PMP exam—any of these roles will suffice. PMP certification requires all applicants with a bachelor's degree to have a minimum of three years of unique, nonoverlapping project management experience where at least 4,500 hours are spent leading and directing project tasks. Applicants without a bachelor's degree are required to have a minimum of five years of unique, non-overlapping project management experience where at least 7,500 hours were spent leading and directing project tasks. In both cases, the experience must be accrued within eight years of the date of application. You must fill out a simple form online (or by paper, if you choose not to apply online) listing the title of a project or projects you worked on; the start and end date for when you worked on the project(s); your role on the project; the number of hours you spent in leading and directing tasks related to the initiating, planning, executing, controlling, and closing processes; and a summary of the project tasks that you led and directed on the project. You must list some hours in each of the five process groups, but not for each project, if you worked on multiple projects. PMI staff will review your qualifications and let you know if you are qualified to take the PMP exam. *You cannot take the exam without this experience qualification.*
2. Document at least 35 contact hours of project management education. A contact hour is defined as one hour of participation in an educational activity. There is no time frame for this requirement. A university or college, a training company or independent consultant, a PMI chapter, a PMI Registered Education Provider (REP), a company-sponsored program, or a distance-learning company can provide the education. The hours must include content on project quality, scope, time, cost, human resources, communications, risk, procurement, and integration management. You must list the course title, institution, date, and number of hours for each course. For example, if you took

a "principles of management" course at a university 20 years ago, you could list that on the education form along with a one- or two-day PMP exam preparation class.

3. Agree to the PMP certificant and candidate agreement and release statement. This form certifies that application information is accurate and complete and that candidates will conduct themselves in accordance with the Code of Ethics and Professional Conduct, professional development requirements, and other PMI certification program policies and procedures. You can simply check a box saying you agree to this information when applying online. Note that PMI randomly audits 10–15 percent of applications, so be prepared to provide more detailed information as requested if audited, such as college transcripts, signatures of supervisors or managers to verify experience, etc.
4. Pay the appropriate exam fee. As of January 2009, the PMP certification fee was $405 for PMI members and $555 for non-members. The re-examination fee (if you don't pass the exam) is $275 for PMI members and $375 for non-members. The annual individual PMI membership fee is $129 (including the $10 application fee). Note that students, or anyone enrolled in a degree-granting program at an accredited, or globally equivalent, college or university, can join PMI at the student member rate of only $40 (including the $10 application fee). If you want to earn your PMP certification, it makes sense to join PMI, not only for the financial savings, but also for other benefits. Consult PMI's Web site for membership information.

The last step in earning PMP certification is passing the exam! After PMI sends you an eligibility letter to take the PMP exam, you can sign up to take it at several different testing sites. You must take the exam within one year of receiving your eligibility letter. The eligibility letter will include complete details for scheduling your exam. As of January 2009, the PMP exam consisted of 200 four-option multiple-choice questions, and 25 of those questions are considered pretest questions that do not affect your score. The pretest questions are randomly placed throughout the exam and are used to test the validity of future examination questions. Although you cannot use any study aids during the exam, you can bring a nonprogrammable calculator to assist in performing calculations required to answer some of the questions. You are also given two blank pieces of paper, so you can write down formulas or other information when you enter the exam room, but you cannot bring in any notes or other materials. The questions on each test are randomly selected from a large test bank, so each person taking the exam receives different questions. The exam is preceded by a 15-minute computer tutorial to familiarize you with the mechanics of taking the exam. Test takers have four hours to take this computerized exam, and a passing score is 60.5 percent, or at least 106 correct answers out of the 175 scored questions, as of January 2009. PMI reviews and revises the exam annually. *Be sure you consult PMI's Web site for any notices about changes to the PMP exam*. For example, the passing percentage was changed several times to achieve PMI's goal of having around 75 percent of people pass the exam. PMI uses the Modified Angoff Technique, a certification industry practice standard, to determine the passing score.

PMI offers a professional development program for maintaining the PMP certification. To maintain your PMP status, you must earn at least 60 Professional Development Units within three years, pay a recertification fee every three years when you renew your certification ($60 as of January 2009), and agree to continue to adhere to PMI's Code of Ethics and Professional Conduct. The Continuing Certification Requirements Handbook, available from PMI's Web site, provides more details on maintaining your PMP status.

What Is the Structure and Content of the PMP Exam?

The PMP exam is based on information from the entire project management body of knowledge as well as the area of professional responsibility. Essentially, the exam reviews concepts and terminology in PMI's *PMBOK® Guide*, and texts such as this one will help to reinforce your understanding of key topics in project management. Table B-1 shows the approximate breakdown of questions on the PMP exam by process group as of January 2009. Candidates should review updated exam information on PMI's Web site to make sure they are using the latest information. Remember that this text is based on the *PMBOK® Guide, Fourth Edition*. The PMP exam will be based on the fourth edition starting July 1, 2009. There were not that many changes from the Third Edition, but make sure you study the correct edition for your exam. PMI also provides sample exam questions from their site as well. See a link to this site and other sites with free sample questions on the companion Web site.

TABLE B-1 Breakdown of questions on the PMP exam by process groups

Process Group	Percent of Questions on PMP Exam	Number of Questions on PMP Exam (out of 200)
Initiating	11	22
Planning	23	46
Executing	27	54
Monitoring and Controlling	21	42
Closing	9	18
Professional Responsibility	9	18

Study Table 3-1 from Chapter 3 of this text to understand the relationships among project management process groups, activities, and knowledge areas. Table 3-1 briefly outlines which activities are performed during each of the project management process groups and what is involved in each of the knowledge areas. It is also important to understand what each of the project management activities includes. Several questions on the certification exam require an understanding of this framework for project management, and many questions require an understanding of the various tools and techniques described in the *PMBOK® Guide, Fourth Edition* and this text.

The PMP exam includes three basic types of questions:

1. *Conceptual questions* test your understanding of key terms and concepts in project management. For example, you should know basic definitions such as what a project is, what project management is, and what key activities are included in project scope management.

2. *Application questions* test your ability to apply techniques to specific problems. For example, a question might provide information for constructing a network diagram and ask you to find the critical path or determine how much slack is available on another path. You might be given cost and schedule information and be asked to find the schedule or cost performance index by applying earned value formulas.
3. *Evaluative questions* provide situations or scenarios for you to analyze, and your response will indicate how you would handle them. For example, a project might have many problems. A question might ask what you would do in that situation, given the information provided. Remember that all questions are multiple-choice, so you must select the best answer from the options provided.

How Should You Prepare for the PMP Exam?

To prepare for the PMP exam, it is important to understand *your* learning and testing style, and to use whatever resources and study techniques work best for *you*. Below are some important questions to consider:

- *Are you a good test taker?* Some people are very good at studying and do well on multiple-choice exams, but others are not. If you have not taken a long multiple-choice test in a while, it may take you longer to prepare for the exam than others.
- *How confident do you need to be before taking the exam?* To pass the exam, you need to answer only 60.5 percent of the questions correctly. Your PMP certificate will not display your final score, so it does not matter if you get 61, 70, 80, 90, or even 100 percent correct.
- *How much information do you need to review before taking the exam?* The *PMBOK® Guide, Fourth Edition* and this text should be enough content information, but many people want to review even more information before taking the PMP exam. Several companies sell books, sample tests, CD-ROMs, and audiotapes, or provide courses designed to help people pass the PMP exam. There's even a *PMP Certification for Dummies* book available with a CD-ROM of sample questions. See the Suggested Readings section of the companion Web site for a list of suggested resources, many at no cost at all, such as *www.pmstudy.com* and *www.bestsamplequestions.com*.
- *How much time and money do you want to spend studying for the PMP exam?* Some people with little free time or money to spend on extra courses or materials would rather just take the PMP exam with little preparation; this will tell them what they need to study further if they don't pass on their first attempt. Even though there is a reexamination fee of $275 (for PMI members), this cost is generally less than what you would have to pay for most exam preparation courses. Spend the time and money you need to feel confident enough to pass the exam, but don't overextend yourself.
- *Do you know PMI's language?* Even if you think you know about project management, studying the material in the *PMBOK® Guide, Fourth Edition* before taking the exam will help you. Volunteer PMPs created the exam, and they often refer to information from the *PMBOK® Guide, Fourth Edition* when

writing questions. Many outstanding project managers might fail the exam if they don't use PMI's terminology or processes in their jobs.

- *Do you really understand the triple constraint of project management?* Many questions on the PMP exam are based on the scope, time, and cost knowledge areas. You should be familiar with project charters, WBSs, network diagrams, critical path analysis, cost estimates, earned value, and so on before you take the exam.
- *Do you want to meet other people in the field of project management as you study for your PMP exam?* Several chapters of PMI offer PMP exam review courses. These courses are often a good way to network with other local project managers or soon to be project managers. Many other organizations provide online and instructor-led courses in PMP preparation where you can also meet people in the field. Several organizations also provide their own in-house study groups as a means to network as well as pass the PMP exam.
- *Do you need extra support, peer pressure, or incentives to pass the PMP exam?* Having some support and positive peer pressure might help to ensure that you actually take and pass the exam in a timely manner. If you don't want to be part of a study group, even just telling a friend, colleague, or loved one that you have set a goal to pass the PMP exam by a certain date might provide motivation to actually do it. You could also reward yourself after you pass the exam.
- *How much are you willing to invest in getting PMP certification?* If you have the time and money, you could take one of the immersion courses several companies offer, like Cheetah Learning, Velociteach, Project Management Training Institute, or mScholar. These courses generally last four to five days and cost from $2,000 to $3,000. The company offering the course will have you come to class with your qualification to take the PMP exam already completed, and you actually take the PMP exam on the fourth or fifth day of the class. If you don't pass, many training companies will let you take the class again at no additional cost. If you don't have any extra money to spend, you can find several free resources (see the companion Web site) and join or form your own study group, or just go take the exam and see how you do. However, try not to over study for the exam; if you know the material well and are passing practice exams, trust yourself and your skills. If you need to take it a second time to pass, just do so.

Ten Tips for Taking the PMP Exam

1. The PMP exam is computer based and begins with a short tutorial on how to use the testing software. The software makes it easy to mark questions you want to review later, so learning how to mark questions is helpful. Using this feature can give you a feel for how well you are doing on the test. It is a good idea to go through every question somewhat quickly and mark those questions on which you want to spend more time. If you mark 79 questions or less (the total number you can miss to get 60.5 percent on all 200 questions), you should

pass the exam. Remember that 25 of the questions are not scored, and you need 60.5 percent correct on the 175 scored questions.

2. The time allotted for the exam is four hours, and each multiple-choice question has four answer choices. You should have plenty of time to complete the exam. Use the first two to three hours to go through all of the questions. Do not spend too much time on any one question. As you work, mark each question that you would like to return to for further consideration. Then use the remaining time to check the questions you are not sure of. If you're a morning person, schedule your exam in the morning. If you work better after lunch, schedule an afternoon exam. Make sure you are alert and well rested when you go in to take the exam.
3. Some people believe it is better to change answers you are unsure about. If you think that a different answer is better, after reading the question again, then change your answer. Don't get hung up on any questions. Move on and focus on answering the questions you can answer correctly.
4. Do not try to read more into the questions than what is stated. There are no trick questions, but some may be poorly worded or just bad questions. Remember that they were written by volunteers and are part of a huge test bank. Most of the questions are relatively short, and there are only four options from which to choose the answer.
5. To increase your chances of getting the right answer, first eliminate obviously wrong options, and then choose among the remaining options. Take the time to read all of the options before selecting an answer. Remember, you have to pick the *best* answer available.
6. Some questions require doing calculations such as earned value management. It is worthwhile to memorize the earned value formulas to make answering these questions easier. You may use a nonprogrammable calculator while taking the exam, so be sure to bring one to make performing calculations easier.
7. You should be given two pieces of blank paper to use during the exam. You might want to bring the paper yourself to make sure it is available. Before starting the test, you should write down important equations so that you do not have to rely on your memory. When you come to a question involving calculations, write the calculations down so you can check your work for errors. See Table B-2 for a summary of formulas you should know for the PMP exam.
8. Read all questions carefully. A few sections of the test require that you answer three to four questions about a scenario. These questions can be difficult; it can seem as if two of the choices could be correct, although you can choose only one. Read the directions for these types of questions several times to be sure you know exactly what you are supposed to do. Also, remember important concepts such as the importance of using a WBS, emphasizing teamwork, and practicing professional integrity. You might want to skip the longer or more difficult questions and answer the shorter or easier ones first.
9. If you do not know an answer and need to guess, be wary of choices that include words such as always, never, only, must, and completely. These extreme words usually indicate incorrect answers because there are many exceptions to rules.

10. After an hour or two, take a short break to clear your mind. You might want to bring a snack to have during your break. You might also consider bringing earplugs if you're easily distracted by noises in the room.

TABLE B-2 Formulas to know for the PMP exam

Time-Related Formulas
Assume o = 6, m = 21, and p = 36 for the following examples, where o = optimistic, m = most likely, and p = pessimistic estimate
PERT weighted average = (o + 4m + p)/6 Example: PERT weighted average = (36 + 4(21) + 6)/6 = 21
PERT standard deviation = (p – o)/6 Example: PERT standard deviation = (36 – 6)/6 = 5
Range of outcomes using 1 std. dev. = 21 – 5 = 16 days and 21 + 5 = 26 days. Range of outcomes using 2 std. dev. = 21 – 10 = 11 days and 21 + 10 = 31 days. Range of outcomes using 3 std. dev. = 21 – 15 = 6 days and 21 + 15 = 36 days. 1 std dev. = **68.3%** of the population 2 std dev. = **95.5%** of the population 3 std dev. = **99.7%** of the population
Cost/Earned Value Formulas
Earned Value = EV
Actual Cost = AC
Planned Value = PV
Cost Variance = CV = EV – AC
Schedule Variance = SV = EV – PV
Cost Performance Index = CPI = EV/AC
Schedule Performance Index = SPI = EV/PV
BAC = Budget At Completion or the planned total budget for the project EAC = Estimate At Completion = BAC/CPI
Estimated time at completion = estimated time/SPI
Estimate To Complete (ETC) = EAC – AC

(continued)

TABLE B-2 Formulas to know for the PMP exam (*continued*)

Variance At Completion (VAC) = BAC – EAC
Remember, a negative value for a variance or equivalently an index less than 100 percent means over budget/behind schedule.

Communications Formulas

Number of communications channels = (n(n – 1))/2
Example: Assume n = 5, where n = number of people
Number of communications channels = (5(5 – 1))/2 = (5 * 4)/2 = 10

Procurement Formulas

Point of Total Assumption (PTA) = (Ceiling Price – Target Price)/Government Share + Target Cost

Make or Buy Analysis: Create a formula so the "make" option equals the "buy" or "lease" option, and then solve for the number of days.
Example: Assume you can purchase equipment for $3,000 and it costs $100/day to operate OR you can lease the equipment for $400/day. In how many days is the lease price equal to the purchase price? Set up an equation where the cost to lease or buy the item is equal to the cost to purchase or make the item.
1. Let d = the number of days you'll use the equipment: $400d = $3,000 + $100d
2. Then solve for d. Subtract $100d from both sides to get $300d = $3,000
3. Then divide each side by $300 to get d = 10
Therefore, if you need the equipment for more than 10 days, it would be cheaper to buy it.

Sample PMP Exam Questions

A few sample questions similar to those you will find on the PMP exam are provided on the following pages. You can check your answers at the end of this appendix. If you miss seven or less out of these 20 questions, you are probably ready to take the PMP exam. You can find additional sample questions and their answers on the companion Web site, as well as links to other free sample tests from various Web sites.

1. A document that formally recognizes the existence of a project is a ________
    a. Gantt chart
    b. WBS
    c. project charter
    d. scope statement
2. Decomposition is used in developing ________.
    a. the management plan
    b. the communications plan
    c. the earned value
    d. the WBS

3. The critical path on a project represents ________.
   a. the shortest path through a network diagram
   b. the longest path through a network diagram
   c. the most important tasks on a project
   d. the highest-risk tasks on a project
4. If the earned value (EV) for a project is $30,000, the actual cost (AC) is $33,000, and the planned value (PV) is $25,000, what is the cost variance?
   a. $3,000
   b. –$3,000
   c. $5,000
   d. –$5,000
5. If the earned value (EV) for a project is $30,000, the actual cost (AC) is $33,000, and the planned value (PV) is $25,000, how is the project performing?
   a. The project is over budget and ahead of schedule.
   b. The project is over budget and behind schedule.
   c. The project is under budget and ahead of schedule.
   d. The project is under budget and behind schedule.
6. What is the target goal for defects per million opportunities using Six Sigma?
   a. 1
   b. 3.4
   c. 34
   d. 100
7. Project human resource management does not include which of the following processes?
   a. acquiring the project team
   b. developing the project team
   c. managing the project team
   d. estimating activity resources
8. If a project team goes from three to five people, how many more communications channels are there?
   a. 7
   b. 6
   c. 5
   d. 4
9. Your project team has identified several risks related to your project. You decide to take actions to reduce the impact of a particular risk event by reducing the probability of its occurrence. What risk response strategy are you using?
   a. risk avoidance
   b. risk acceptance
   c. risk mitigation
   d. contingency planning
10. Which type of contract provides the least amount of risk for the buyer?
   a. firm fixed price
   b. fixed price incentive
   c. cost plus incentive fee
   d. cost plus fixed fee

11. Suppose you have a project with four tasks as follows:
    - Task 1 can start immediately and has an estimated duration of 1.
    - Task 2 can start after Task 1 is completed and has an estimated duration of 4.
    - Task 3 can start after Task 2 is completed and has an estimated duration of 5.
    - Task 4 can start after Task 1 is completed and must be completed when Task 3 is completed. Its estimated duration is 8.

    What is the length of the critical path for this project?

    a. 9
    b. 10
    c. 11
    d. 12
12. In which project management process group is the most time and money typically spent?
    a. initiating
    b. planning
    c. executing
    d. monitoring and controlling
13. Creating a probability/impact matrix is part of which risk management process?
    a. plan risk management
    b. identify risks
    c. perform qualitative risk analysis
    d. perform quantitative risk analysis
14. It is crucial that your project team finish your project on time. Your team is using a technique to account for limited resources. You have also added a project buffer before the end date and feeding buffers before each critical task. What technique are you using?
    a. critical path analysis
    b. PERT
    c. critical chain scheduling
    d. earned value management
15. One of your senior technical specialists informs you that a major design flaw exists in a systems development project you are managing. You are already testing the system and planned to roll it out to more than 5,000 users in a month. You know that changing the design now will cause several cost and schedule overruns. As project manager, what should you do first?
    a. Issue a stop work order until you understand the extent of the flaw.
    b. Notify your project sponsor immediately to see if there are additional funds available to work on this problem.
    c. Notify your senior management and let them decide what to do.
    d. Hold a meeting as soon as possible with key members of your project team to discuss possible solutions to the problem.

16. You are a member of a large government project. You know that the contract insists that all equipment be manufactured in the United States. You see a senior member of your team replacing a company etching on a piece of equipment that was made in a foreign country. You confront this person, and he says he is following the project manager's orders. What should you do?
    a. Nothing; the project manager made the decision.
    b. Immediately report the violation to the government.
    c. Update your resume and look for another job.
    d. Talk to the project manager about the situation, and then decide what to do.
17. Which of the following is not an output of the integrated change control process?
    a. project management plan updates
    b. change request status updates
    c. forecasts
    d. project document updates
18. The ceiling price for a contract is $1.25 million, the target price is $1.1 million, the target cost is $1 million, and the government share is 75%. What is the point of total assumption?
    a. $1.2 million
    b. $1 million
    c. $1.1 million
    d. there is not enough information
19. Obtaining quotes, bids, offers, or proposals is part of which project procurement management process?
    a. plan procurements
    b. conduct procurements
    c. administer procurements
    d. close procurements
20. Your boss believes that all of your project team members avoid work as much as possible. He or she often uses threats and various control schemes to make sure people are doing their jobs. Which approach to managing people does your boss follow?
    a. Maslow's hierarchy of needs
    b. Theory X
    c. Theory Y
    d. Herzberg's motivation and hygiene factors

WHAT IS PROJECT+ CERTIFICATION?

The Computing Technology Industry Association (CompTIA) is the world's largest developer of vendor-neutral IT certification exams. By January 2009, more than one million people worldwide have earned CompTIA certifications in topics such as PC service, networking, security, and Radio Frequency Identification (RFID). In April 2001, CompTIA started offering its IT Project+ certification, which was purchased from Prometric-Thomson Learning, and recognized as the Gartner Institute Certification Program. The certification was renamed Project+ in August 2004. According to CompTIA's manager of public relations, there are more than 11,000 people with CompTIA's Project+ certification by the end of 2008. Detailed information about Project+ certification is available from CompTIA's Web site (*www.comptia.org*) under certification. The following information is quoted from CompTIA's Web site in January 2009:

> CompTIA Project+ is a globally recognized project management certification that provides validation of fundamental project management skills. It covers the entire project life cycle from initiation and planning through execution, acceptance, support and closure. Unlike some project management certifications, CompTIA Project+ can be acquired in a quick and cost-effective manner. There are no prerequisites, and candidates are not required to submit an application or complete additional hours of continuing education. CompTIA Project+ gives project managers the skills necessary to complete projects on time and within budget, and creates a common project management language among project team members.[7]

What Are the Requirements for Earning and Maintaining Project+ Certification?

You can register to take the Project+ exam online from CompTIA's Web site. Testing sites include Thomson Prometric and Pearson VUE. Unlike the PMP exam, there are very few requirements you need to meet to take the Project+ exam. CompTIA does not require that you have any work experience or formal education in project management before you can take the Project+ exam, but they do recommend 2,000 hours of work experience. The main requirements include paying a fee and passing the exam. Important information is summarized below:

1. As of January 2009, the cost for taking the Project+ exam is $239 for non-members in the United States.
2. To pass this 90-minute, 80-question exam, you must score at least 63 percent.
3. You do not need to renew your Project+ certification.
4. Project+ certification is one of the prerequisites or equivalents to Novell's Certified Novell Engineer (CNE), Certified Novell Administrator (CNA), and Certified Novell Instructor (CNI) certifications. CompTIA's Project+ certification is also a Continuing Certification Requirement (CCR) to maintaining a Master CNE certification.
5. You can earn college credit with the Project+ certification. For example, CompTIA's Web site says that Capella University will provide six credit hours to someone with the Project+ certification. Many colleges and universities will grant credit based on your experience or other certifications. There is usually some fee involved, but it's often much less than the cost of taking the courses.

Additional Information on the Project+ Exam

Because there are no experience or education requirements for taking the Project+ exam, you might want to take it very early in your career. Once you have enough experience and education to take the PMP exam, you might want to earn and maintain PMP certification.

As stated already, the Project+ exam consists of 80 questions. Table B-3 shows the approximate breakdown of questions on the Project+ exam by four domain areas. Candidates should review updated exam information on CompTIA's Web site to make sure they are prepared for the exams. For example, CompTIA provides a detailed list of objectives you should understand before taking the Project+ exam. Studying information in this book will also help you prepare for the Project+ exam. You might also want to purchase an exam guide to get specific information and access to more sample questions.

TABLE B-3 Breakdown of questions on the Project+ exam by domain areas

Domain Area	Percent of Questions on Project+ Exam
Project Initiation and Scope Definition	20
Project Planning	30
Project Execution, Control, and, Coordination	43
Project Closure, Acceptance, and Support	7

Much of the advice for taking the PMP exam also applies to taking the Project+ exam. Many people find the questions to be similar on both exams, although the PMP exam is longer and more comprehensive. Below are some of the main differences between the content and types of questions you will find on the Project+ exam:

- The Project+ exam includes some scenarios and content specific to the information technology industry. For example, you should understand the various systems development life cycles and issues that often occur on information technology projects.
- You should understand the various roles of people on information technology projects, such as business analysts, database analysts, programmers, and so on.
- Although many of the questions are multiple-choice like the PMP exam questions, several questions involve choosing two or more correct answers. Several questions also involve matching or putting items in order, called drag-and-drop questions.
- The Project+ exam is not based on the *PMBOK® Guide*, so you do not need to know the processes involved in the various knowledge areas. However, much of the terminology, concepts, tools, and techniques are the same on both exams.

Sample Project+ Exam Questions

A few sample questions similar to those you will find on the Project+ exam are provided below. CompTIA also provides sample questions on their Web site at *http://certification.comptia.org/resources/practice_test.aspx*. You can check your answers at the end of this appendix.

1. Two software developers on your project disagree on how to design an important part of a system. There are several technologies and methodologies they could use. What should be the primary driver in deciding how to proceed?
   a. following corporate standards
   b. following industry standards
   c. meeting business needs
   d. using the lowest-cost approach
2. Match the following items to their descriptions:

Stakeholder	a. Acts as a liaison between the business area and developers
Project manager	b. Writes software code
Business analyst	c. Person involved in or affected by project activities
Programmer	d. Responsible for managing project activities

3. For a project to be successful, the project manager should strive to understand and meet certain goals. What are the three main project goals to meet? Select three answers.
   a. scope or performance goals
   b. time goals
   c. political goals
   d. cost goals
   e. stock price goals
4. You have received an incomplete project scope definition. Put the following actions in order of how you should proceed to complete them.
   a. Incorporate additional changes to the scope definition document.
   b. Review the draft scope definition document with your project team.
   c. Get signatures on the completed scope definition document.
   d. Rewrite the draft scope definition document with your users and project team.
5. What term is used to describe the process of reaching agreement on a collective decision?
   a. collaboration
   b. cooperation
   c. coordination
   d. consensus
6. What is a variance?
   a. a buffer in a duration estimate
   b. a small amount of money set aside for contingencies
   c. a form of risk management
   d. a deviation from the project plan

7. Which of the following would be legitimate reasons for a vendor to request a delay in delivering a product? Select two answers.
   a. The vendor may have underestimated the amount of time required to produce and deliver the product.
   b. The project contact from the vendor's organization may be going on vacation.
   c. The vendor might be able to provide a better product by delivering the product late.
   d. The vendor might lose money by delivering the product late.
8. When should you involve stakeholders in the change control process on information technology projects?
   a. before a change is submitted
   b. after a change is submitted
   c. when a change is submitted
   d. throughout the life of a project
9. Which of the following techniques can be used to help manage requirements? Select three answers.
   a. prototyping
   b. use case modeling
   c. JAD
   d. worst case modeling
10. Match the following items to their descriptions:

Lessons learned	a. Leave a clear and complete history of a project
Project audits	b. Review project progress and results
Project archives	c. Document what went right or wrong on a project

WHAT OTHER EXAMS OR CERTIFICATIONS RELATED TO PROJECT MANAGEMENT ARE AVAILABLE?

In recent years, several organizations have been developing more certifications related to project management and information technology project management, in particular. Some involve taking exams while others require coursework or attendance at workshops. Below are brief descriptions of other existing exams or certifications related to project management:

- Microsoft provides certification as a Microsoft Office Specialist (MOS) to recognize proficiency in using its software products. In October 2006, Microsoft Learning launched a new Microsoft Office Project 2007 Certification program. You can become a Microsoft Certified Technology Specialist (MCTS) in either Managing Projects with Microsoft Office Project 2007 or Enterprise Project Management with Microsoft Office Project Server 2007. You can also earn a Microsoft Certified IT Professional (MCITP) in enterprise Project Management with Microsoft Office Project Server 2007. Its purpose is "to help advance project management as a profession and maximize value for its customer base of nearly 20 million Microsoft Office Project user licenses."[8] Microsoft is using the PMI's *PMBOK® Guide* as a foundation for supporting specific Project 2007 competencies. See Microsoft's Web site (*www.microsoft.com*) for more details.

- The International Project Management Association (IPMA) offers a four-level certification program. The main requirements for each level are derived from typical activities, responsibilities, and requirements from practice. The IPMA four-level certification system, in descending order, includes the Certified Project Director, Certified Senior Project Manager, Certified Project Manager, and Certified Project Management Associate. More than 50,000 people worldwide had earned IPMA certifications, according to IPMA's Web site in January 2007. See *www.ipma.ch* for more details.
- Certified IT Project Manager (CITPM): In 1998, the Singapore Computer Society collaborated with the Infocomm Development Authority of Singapore to establish an Information Technology Project Management Certification Program. PMI signed a Memorandum of Understanding with the Singapore Computer Society to support and advance the global credentialing of project management and information technology expertise. In January 2007, the Singapore Computer Society's Web site listed three levels of the CITPM Certification: CITPM (Senior), CITPM, and CITPM (Associate). For more details consult their Web site (*www.scs.org.sg/about_certprog.php*).
- PMI's additional certifications. As mentioned earlier, as of January 2009, PMI also offers certification as a Certified Associate in Project Management (CAPM), a PMI-Scheduling Professional (PMI-SP), a PMI-Risk Management Professional (PMI-RMP), and a Program Management Professional (PgMP). Check PMI's Web site for updated information on their certification programs.
- Many colleges, universities, and corporate training companies now provide their own certificate programs or entire degrees in project management. Typing "project management certificate" into *www.google.com* in January 2009 resulted in 58,400 hits. Some of the certificate courses apply toward bachelor's or advanced degrees, while many do not. Like any other educational program, it is important to research the quality of the program and find one that will meet your specific needs. The December 2006 issue of the Project Management Institute's PMI Today included a supplement that said they had identified over 284 project management degree programs at 235 institutions worldwide. See the author's Web site for a summary of more than 120 U.S. graduate programs created as part of a class project in 2006 (*www.kathyschwalbe.com*, under Project Management Info). Also see sites like *www.gradschools.com* to find more information on graduate programs in project management throughout the world.

Discussion Questions

1. What is PMP certification, and why do you think the number of people earning it has grown so much in the past 10 years?
2. What do you need to do before you can take the PMP exam? What is the exam itself like? What do you need to do to maintain PMP certification? What do you need to do to take the Project+ exam? How does the Project+ exam differ from the PMP exam? Do you need to renew Project+ certification?
3. What is the difference between conceptual, application, and evaluative questions? Which project management process groups have the most questions on the PMP exam? What are the four domain areas tested on the Project+ exam?
4. Which tips for taking the PMP exam do you think would be most helpful for you?
5. If you plan to take the Project+ or PMP exam soon, what should you do to prepare?
6. Briefly describe project management certification programs other than the PMP or Project+ certifications.

Exercises

1. Go to PMI's Web site and review the information about taking the PMP exam. Write a two-page paper summarizing what you found.
2. Go to CompTIA's Web site and review the information about taking the Project+ exam. Write a two-page paper summarizing what you found.
3. Answer the 20 sample PMP questions in this text or take another sample test, and then score your results. Summarize how you did and areas you would need to study before you could take the PMP exam.
4. Interview someone who has PMP or Project+ certification. Ask him or her why he or she earned the certification and how it has affected his or her career. Write your findings in a two-page paper.
5. Do an Internet search on earning PMP or Project+ certification. Be sure to search for Yahoo! groups or similar sites related to these topics. What are some of the options you found to help people prepare for either exam? If you were to take one of the exams, what do you think you would do to help study for it? Do you think you would need additional information beyond what is in this text to help you pass? Write a two-page paper describing your findings and opinions.
6. Read a recent issue of PMI's *PM Network* magazine. You can access a free sample copy from PMI's Web site. Summarize all of the ads you find in the magazine related to earning PMP or other project management related certification in a two-page paper. Also, include your opinion on which ad, course, book, CD-ROM, or other media appeals to you the most.

Answers to Sample PMP Exam Questions

1. c
2. d
3. b
4. b
5. a
6. b
7. d
8. a
9. c
10. a
11. b
12. c
13. c
14. c
15. d
16. d
17. c
18. a
19. b
20. b

Answers to Sample Project+ Exam Questions

1. c
2. c, d, a, b
3. a, b, d
4. b, d, a, c
5. d
6. d
7. a, c
8. d
9. a, b, c
10. c, b, a

End Notes

[1] Project Management Institute, "PMI® Certification Programs," (*www.pmi.org/*) (January 2007).

[2] Project Management Institute Information Systems Specific Interest Group (ISSIG), *ISSIG Bits* (*www.pmi-issig.org*) (February 2003).

[3] Becky Nagel, "CertCities.com's 10 Hottest Certifications for 2006," *CertCities.com*, (December 14, 2005).

[4] Global Knowledge, "2003 Certification Salary by Certmag," *Global Knowledge E-Newsletter*, Issue #56 (March 2003).

[5] Adrienne Rewi, "The Rise of PMP," *PM Network*, (October 2004), p. 18.

[6] The Project Management Institute, "PMI Today," (February 2009).

[7] CompTIA Web site (*http://certification.comptia.org/project*) (January 2009).

[8] Microsoft, "Microsoft Advances Its Project Management Technology and the Project Management Profession," Microsoft PressPass (October 20, 2006).

ADDITIONAL RUNNING CASES AND SIMULATION SOFTWARE

INTRODUCTION

This appendix provides two additional running cases as well as information about using simulation software. The first case includes tasks ordered by each of the nine knowledge areas discussed in Chapters 4 through 12 of this text. The second case includes tasks based on the five project management process groups. There is also information about using Fissure's project management simulation software. Additional running cases, including the Video Game Delivery Project case that was in the fifth edition of this text, and suggestions for finding more cases or having students do real projects are available on the companion Web site.

The purpose of these cases is to help you practice and develop the project management skills learned from this text. Several of the tasks involve using templates provided on the companion Web site (*www.cengage.com/mis/*schwalbe) and the author's personal Web site (*www.kathyschwalbe.com*). Instructors can download the suggested solutions for these cases from the password-protected section on Course Technology's Web site. Contact a sales rep at *www.cengage.com/coursetechnology*.

ADDITIONAL CASE 1: GREEN COMPUTING RESEARCH PROJECT

Part 1: Project Integration Management

You are working for We Are Big, Inc., an international firm with over 100, 000 employees located in several different countries. A strategic goal is to help improve the environment while increasing revenues and reducing costs. The Environmental Technologies Program just started, and the VP of Operations, Natalie, is the program sponsor. Ito is the program manager, and there is a steering committee made up of ten senior executives, including

Natalie, overseeing the program. There are several projects underneath this program, one being the Green Computing Research Project. The CIO and project sponsor, Ben, has given this project high priority and plans to hold special interviews to hand-pick the project manager and team. Ben is also a member of the program steering committee. Before coming to We Are Big, Inc., Ben sponsored a project at a large computer firm to improve data center efficiency. This project, however, is much broader than that one was. The main purpose of the Green Computing Research Project is to research possible applications of green computing including:

- Data center and overall energy efficiency
- The disposal of electronic waste and recycling
- Telecommuting
- Virtualization of server resources
- Thin client solutions
- Use of open source software, and
- Development of new software to address green computing for internal use and potential sale to other organizations

The budget for the project was $500, 000, and the goal was to provide an extensive report, including detailed financial analysis and recommendations on what green computing technologies to implement. Official project request forms for the recommended solutions would also be created as part of the project.

Ben decided to have a small group of people, five to be exact, dedicated to working on this six-month project full-time and to call on people in other areas on an as-needed basis. He wanted to personally be involved in selecting the project manager and have that person help him to select the rest of the project team. Ben wanted to find people already working inside the company, but he was also open to reviewing applications for potential new employees to work specifically on this project as long as they could start quickly. Since many good people were located in different parts of the world, Ben thought it made sense to select the best people he could find and allow them to work virtually on the project. Ben also wanted the project manager to do more than just manage the project. He or she would also do some of the research, writing, editing, and the like required to produce the desired results. He was also open to paying expert consultants for their advice and purchasing books and related articles, as needed.

Tasks

1. Research green computing and projects that have been done or are being done by large organizations such as IBM, Dell, HP, and Google. See *www.greener-computing.com* and similar sites provided on the companion Web site or that you find yourself. Include your definition of green computing to include all of the topics listed in the background scenario. Describe each of these areas of green computing, including a detailed example of how at least one organization has implemented each one, and investigate the return on investment. Summarize your results in a two- to three-page paper, citing at least three references.
2. Prepare a weighted decision matrix using the template from the companion Web site (wtd_decision_matrix.xls) for Ben to use to evaluate people applying to be the project manager for this important project. Develop at least five

criteria, assign weights to each criterion, assign scores, and then calculate the weighted scores for four fictitious people. Print the spreadsheet and bar chart with the results. Write a one-page paper describing this weighted decision matrix and summarize the results.

3. Prepare the financial section of a business case for the Green Computing Research Project. Assume this project will take six months to complete (done in Year 0) and cost $500,000, and costs to implement some of the technologies would be $2,000,000 for year one and $600,000 for years two and three. Estimated benefits are $500,000 the first year after implementation and $2.5 million the following two years. Use the business case spreadsheet template from the companion Web site (business_case_financials.xls) to help calculate the NPV, ROI, and the year in which payback occurs. Assume a 7 percent discount rate, but make sure it is an input that is easy to change.
4. Prepare a project charter for the Green Computing Research Project. Assume the project will take six months to complete and the budget is $500,000. Use the project charter template (charter.doc) and examples of project charters in Chapters 3 and 4 as guidelines. Assume that part of the approach is to select the project team as quickly as possible.
5. Since people will request changes to the project, you want to make sure you have a good integrated change control process in place. You will also want to address change requests as quickly as possible. Review the template for a change request form provided on the companion Web site (change_request.doc). Write a two-page paper describing how you plan to manage changes on this project in a timely manner. Address who will be involved in making change control decisions, what paperwork or electronic systems will be used to collect and respond to changes, and other related issues.

Part 2: Project Scope Management

Congratulations! You have been selected as the project manager for the Green Computing Research Project. The company's CIO, Ben, is the project sponsor, and Ito is the program manager for the larger Environmental Technologies Program that this project is part of. Now you need to put together your project team and get to work on this high-visibility project. You will work with Ben to hand-pick your team. Ben had already worked with the HR department to advertise these openings internally as well as outside the company. Ben had also used his personal contacts to let people know about this important project. In addition, you are encouraged to use outside consultants and other resources, as appropriate. Initial estimates suggest that about $300,000 budgeted for this project will go to internal staffing and the rest to outside sources. The main products you'll produce will be a series of research reports—one for each green computing technology listed earlier plus one final report including all data—plus formal project proposals for at least four recommendations for implementing some of these technologies. Ben also suggested that the team come up with at least 20 different project ideas and then recommend the top four based on extensive analysis. Ben thought some type of decision support model would make sense to help collect and analyze the project ideas. You are expected to tap into resources available from the Environmental Technologies Program, but you will need to include some of those resources in your project budget. Ben mentioned that he knew there had already been some research done on increasing the use of telecommuting. Ben also showed you examples of what he considered to be good research reports. You notice that his examples are very professional, with a lot of charts and references, and most are 20–30 pages long, single-spaced. Ben has also shown you examples of good formal project proposals for We Are Big, Inc., and you are surprised to see how detailed they are, as well. They often reference other research and include a detailed business case.

Tasks

1. Document requirements for your project so far, including a requirements traceability matrix. Use the template provided (reqs_matrix.xls). Also include a list of questions you would like to ask the sponsor about the scope.
2. Develop a scope statement for the project using the template provided (scope_statement.doc). Be as specific as possible in describing product characteristics and deliverables. Make assumptions as needed, assuming you got answers to the questions you had in Task 1.
3. Develop a work breakdown structure (WBS) for the project. Break down the work to level 3 or level 4, as appropriate. Use the template on the companion Web site (wbs.doc) and samples in the text as guides. Print the WBS in list form as a Word file. Be sure to base your WBS on the project scope statement, stakeholder requirements, and other relevant information. Remember to include the work involved in selecting the rest of your project team and outside resources as well as coordinating with the Environmental Technologies Program. Use the project management process groups as level 2 WBS items or include project management as a level 2 WBS item to make sure you include work related to managing the project.
4. Use the WBS you developed in Task 3 above to create a Gantt chart for the project in Microsoft Project 2007. Use the outline numbering feature to display the outline numbers (click Tools on the menu bar, click Options, and then click Show outline number). Do not enter any durations or dependencies. Print the resulting Gantt chart on one page, being sure to display the entire Task Name column.

Part 3: Project Time Management

As project manager, you are actively leading the Green Computing Research Project team in developing a schedule. You and Ben found three internal people and one new hire to fill the positions on the project team as follows:

- Matt was a senior technical specialist in the corporate IT department located in the building next to yours and Ben's. He is an expert in collaboration technologies and volunteers in his community helping to organize ways for residents to dispose of computers, printers, and cell phones.
- Teresa was a senior systems analyst in the IT department in a city 500 miles away from your office. She just finished an analysis of virtualization of server resources for her office, which has responsibility for the company's data center.

- James was a senior consultant in the strategic research department in a city 1,000 miles away from your office. He has a great reputation as being a font of knowledge and excellent presenter. Although he is over 60, he has a lot of energy.
- Le was a new hire and former colleague of Ben's. She was working in Malaysia, but she planned to move to your location, starting work about four weeks after the project started. Le has a lot of theoretical knowledge in green computing, and her doctoral thesis was on that topic.

While waiting for everyone to start working on your project, you talked to several people working on other projects under the Environmental Technologies Program and did some research on green computing. You can use a fair amount of the work already done on telecommuting, and you have the name of a consulting firm to help with that part of your project, if needed. Ito and Ben both suggested that you get up to speed on available collaboration tools since much of your project work will be done virtually. They knew that Matt would be a tremendous asset for your team in that area. You have also contacted other IT staff to get detailed information on your company's needs and plans in other areas of green computing. You also found out that there is a big program meeting in England next month that you and one or two of your team members should attend. It is a three-day meeting, plus travel. Recall that the Green Computing Research Project is expected to be completed in six months, and you and your four team members are assigned full-time to this project. Your project sponsor, Ben, has made it clear that delivering a good product is most important, but he also thinks you should have no problem meeting your schedule goal. He can authorize additional funds, if needed. You have decided to hire a part-time editor/consultant, Deb, whom you know from a past job to help your team produce the final reports and project proposals. Your team has agreed to add a one-week buffer at the end of the project to ensure that you finish on time or early.

Tasks

1. Review the WBS and Gantt chart you created for Tasks 3 and 4 in Part 2. Propose three to five additional activities you think should be added to help you estimate resources and durations. Write a one-page paper describing these new activities.
2. Identify at least four milestones for this project. Write a one-page paper describing each milestone using the SMART criteria.
3. Using the Gantt chart created for Task 4 in Part 2, and the new activities and milestones you proposed in Tasks 1 and 2 above, estimate the task durations and enter dependencies as appropriate. Remember that your schedule goal for the project is six months. Print the Gantt chart and network diagram.
4. Write a one-page paper summarizing how you would assign people to each activity. Include a table or matrix listing how many hours each person would work on each task. These resource assignments should make sense given the duration estimates made in Task 3 above.
5. Assume that your project team starts falling behind schedule. In several cases, it is difficult to find detailed information on some of the green computing technologies, especially financial data. You know that it is important to meet

or beat the six-month schedule goal, but quality is most important. Describe contingency strategies for making up lost time and avoiding schedule slips in the future.

C.6

Part 4: Project Cost Management

Your project sponsor has asked you and your team to refine the existing cost estimate for the project so that there is a solid cost baseline for evaluating project performance. Recall that your schedule and cost goals are to complete the project in six months or less for under $500, 000. Initial estimates suggested that about $300,000 for this project would go toward internal labor. You mistakenly thought that travel costs would be included in that $300,000, but now you realize that it is a separate cost item. The one trip to England early in the project cost $6,000, which you had not expected.

Tasks

1. Prepare and print a one-page cost estimate for the project, similar to the one provided in Chapter 7. Use the WBS categories you created earlier, and be sure to document assumptions you make in preparing the cost estimate. Assume a burdened labor rate of $100/hour for the project manager, $90 for Teresa, James, and Le, and $80/hour for Matt. Assume about $200/hour for outsourced labor.
2. Using the cost estimate you created in task 1, prepare a cost baseline by allocating the costs by WBS for each month of the project.
3. Assume you have completed three months of the project and have actual data. The BAC was $500,000 for this six-month project. Also assume the following:

   PV= $160,000
   EV= $150,000
   AC= $180,000

   Using this information, write a short report that answers the following questions.

   a. What is the cost variance, schedule variance, cost performance index (CPI), and schedule performance index (SPI) for the project?
   b. Use the CPI to calculate the estimate at completion (EAC) for this project. Use the SPI to estimate how long it will take to finish this project. Sketch an earned value chart using the above information, including the EAC point. See Figure 7-6 as a guide. Write a paragraph explaining what this chart shows.
   c. How is the project doing? Is it ahead of schedule or behind schedule? Is it under budget or over budget? Should you alert your sponsor or other senior management and ask for assistance?
4. You notice that several of the tasks that involve getting inputs from consultants outside of your own company have cost more and taken longer to complete than planned. You have talked to the consultants several times, but they say they are doing the best they can. You also underestimated travel costs for this project. Write a one-page paper describing corrective action you could take to address these problems.

Part 5: Project Quality Management

The Green Computing Research Project team is working hard to ensure their work meets expectations. The team has a detailed project scope statement, schedule, and so on, but as the project manager, you want to make sure you'll satisfy key stakeholders, especially Ben, the project sponsor, and Ito, the program manager. You have seen how tough Ito can be on project managers after listening to his critiques of other project managers at the monthly program review meeting. He was adamant on having solid research and financial analysis and liked to see people use technology to make quick what-if projections. You were impressed to see that several other project teams had developed computer models to help them perform sensitivity analysis and make important decisions. Most of the models were done using Excel, which Ito preferred, and you were glad that you were an expert with Excel, as was Matt. Ito was pretty easy on you at your first monthly review because things were just getting started, but he did give you a list of items to report on next month. You had Ben there to help answer some of the tough questions, but you wanted to be able to hold your own at future monthly meetings.

Tasks

1. Develop a list of at least five quality standards or requirements related to meeting the stakeholder expectations especially for Ben and Ito. Also provide a brief description of each standard or requirement. For example, a requirement might be related to the computer model (that the computer model you create to analyze the 20 or more technologies be done in Excel 2007). Other standards or requirements might be related to the quality of the financial analysis and research you use.
2. Review the Seven Basic Tools of Quality. Pick one and make up a scenario related to this project where it would be useful. Document the scenario and tool in a one-to-two page paper.
3. Find a high quality research report related to the green computing. Summarize the report and why you think it is of high quality in a one-to-two page paper.

Part 6: Project Human Resource Management

You are five weeks into the Green Computing Research Project, and all of the full-time team members are together face-to-face for the first time. Recall that you, Ben, Matt, and Le all work in the same location, but Teresa and James are based out of town and will do most of their work virtually. Le is also new to the company and just moved to the U.S. She is currently staying in a hotel and looking for a place to live. She'd like to buy her first home, but she wants to make sure it's a good investment and somewhere she'd like to stay for at least five years. You get along very well with your project sponsor, Ben, and Matt is a great resource, even though he is extremely reserved. Le is also very quiet, and you quickly discover that she is an excellent researcher and writer, but she is not comfortable speaking in public. Teresa and James are much more talkative and are excited to be working on this project. However, James seems to be reluctant to use much technology to share ideas and really enjoys face-to-face meetings and discussions. You have made preliminary agreements with two outside consultants to assist you with editing and the teleconferencing topic for your research. You have to prepare a monthly progress report and presentation for Ito, the program manager. You also have short meetings as needed with Ben, your sponsor, and send him a weekly progress report.

C.8

Tasks

1. Before this first face-to-face meeting, you asked everyone to send a brief introductory e-mail, including links to their personal Web sites, LinkedIn site, etc. You also asked everyone to take a short version of the Meyers-Briggs Type Indicator (MBTI) online and share their results with everyone else. Take this test yourself from *www.humanmetrics.com* and research how different MBTI types respond to work environments, especially for research projects and virtual teams. Summarize your findings in a one-to-two page paper. Also document what you would write in an e-mail to introduce yourself, assuming you are the project manager for this project. Be creative in your response.
2. Prepare a responsibility assignment matrix in RACI chart format based on the WBS you created earlier and the information you have on project team members and other stakeholders. Use the template (ram.xls) and samples in the text. Document key assumptions you made in preparing the chart.
3. Since everyone will be in town for most of the week, you want to make sure they develop good working relationships. You also want everyone to work together efficiently. You asked Matt to review collaboration tools he recommends the team use for this project. As Matt starts demonstrating some of these tools, including webcams and wikis, you notice that a couple of team members seem uncomfortable, especially James. He thought that he would be in charge of certain aspects of the research reports and didn't know how he'd feel about any team member being able to change what he wrote in a wiki. Le did not like the idea of using a Webcam. She'd rather not have her face on video when communicating virtually. Discuss these human resource-related concerns and others that you think would be common in this situation. Include strategies for addressing them as well.

Part 7: Project Communications Management

Several communications issues have arisen on the Green Computing Research Project. Three months have passed since the project started. Your team had agreed to post all of their work on a shared site, but a couple of team members don't seem to like using that site and prefer to use e-mails and attachments. When they do that, other team members cannot easily see what work is done in one place or provide feedback using the wiki tools. It is also clear that some team members are better researchers and writers than others. When you have weekly conference calls with the Webcams, at least a couple of people don't have the Webcam working and just use the audio. You also find that these meetings rarely end on time as some team members get very talkative. You also got grilled by Ito at the last monthly program review meeting. He thought you'd be much further along in the project than you are and expects you to have one recommendation on a green computing project that looks very promising by next month. You haven't seen any great ideas yet. You want to start having face-to-face meetings at least twice a month, but you know it will make your project go over budget even more. At least the Excel model is going well. You and Matt have put a good deal of time into developing it. If only you had enough good data to put into it.

Tasks

1. Create an issue log for the project using the template provided (issue_log.doc). List at least four issues and related information based on the scenario presented.
2. Research the use of wikis and address the concerns several team members have about using them, especially their fear of having others "mess up" their work. Document your findings in a one- to two-page paper.
3. Write a two-page paper describing how you might approach two of the conflicts described above.

Part 8: Project Risk Management

Since several problems have been occurring on the Green Computing Research Project (see the case information in Part 7), you decide to be more proactive in managing risks. You also want to address positive and negative risks.

Tasks

1. Create a risk register for the project, using the template (risk_register.xls). Identify six potential risks, including at least two positive risks.
2. Plot the six risks on a probability/impact matrix, using the template (prob_impact_matrix.ppt) and print it out. Assign a numeric value for the probability of each risk, and its impact on meeting the main project objectives. Use a scale of 1 to 10 to assign the values, with 1 being lowest and 10 being highest. For a simple risk factor calculation, multiply these two values (the probability score and the impact score). Document the results in a one-page paper, including your rationale for how you determined the scores for one of the negative risks and one of the positive risks.
3. Develop a response strategy for one of the negative risks and one of the positive risks. Enter the information in the risk register and print out your complete risk register. Also write a one-page paper describing what specific tasks would need to be done to implement these two strategies. Include time and cost estimates for each strategy.

Part 9: Project Procurement Management

After a monthly program management review meeting four months into your project, Ito and Ben approved adding $100,000 and one additional month to the project. You provided strong rationale for the need for additional travel funds and more money for outside consultants to help you in finding good research information. You decided to have James go back to his old job since he didn't seem open to sharing ideas with others. It would be best to have a consulting firm, one you were already using, pick up the work he was supposed to do, even though it would cost a lot more. The lead consultant, Anne, had done a great analysis of improving overall energy efficiency for the company that would save millions of dollars each year. Ben, your project sponsor, was disappointed that you couldn't meet the original time and cost goals, but he wanted to make sure the final results were of high quality.

Tasks

1. Draft a contract to have Anne's consulting firm perform the work that James was supposed to do for this project. Assume that the contract would last for three months and that Anne herself would be working about half-time, earning $200/hour. She would also have some other consultants do up to 100 hours of work at $150/hour. They would do most of the work virtually, but Anne would come in town at least once a month for face-to-face meetings. Limit the contract to two or three pages, and be sure to address specific personnel and travel requirements. Also make sure that all work produced would be owned and copyrighted by your company exclusively.
2. Deb, the editor you hired for this project, has asked for your assistance in organizing the final comprehensive research report. Draft a one-page executive summary and a table of contents for this report.
3. Although this is not really a procurement task, it is provided here for convenience purposes. Prepare a lessons-learned report for what you may have learned so far as project manager for this project. Use the template provided on the companion Web site (lessons_learned_report.doc) and be creative in your response.

ADDITIONAL CASE 2: PROJECT MANAGEMENT VIDEOS PROJECT

Part 1: Initiating

You and several of your classmates are taking a project management class, and your instructor suggested a project to find or create good video clips to illustrate various concepts related to the class. For example, the *Oceans 11*, *12*, and *13* movies all include great planning and execution clips. *Apollo 13* provides a great example of scope management and creative problem solving when the team has to figure out how to keep the astronauts alive. *The Office* television show includes many examples of poor motivation techniques. In addition to providing the clips on DVD, you will write a summary of them, including the length and source of the clip, introductions for each clip, discussion questions that you can pose before and after each clip, and suggested answers to those questions. Your instructor has suggested that teams find or create at least two good clips per team member. If several teams in your class work on this project, you will have to coordinate with them to avoid duplicating clips and to share resources. Everything your team creates for the project should fit on one DVD that will run on your instructor's computer. The DVD will be for educational use only, so there should not be any copyright issues.

Tasks

1. To become more familiar with finding short video clips, do some preliminary research. Go to sites like *youtube.com* and search for videos related to project management concepts. Also search for articles related to project management in the movies, and visit sites such as *imdb.com* to see movie trailers. Find other

sites that have legitimate movie and television clips. Also discuss movies or television shows that you and your teammates are familiar with that could be used for this project. Write a two- to three-page paper with your findings, citing all references.

2. To become familiar with creating or editing short video clips, research how to take short segments of an existing DVD and put it on a computer. Also research the devices and software needed to create, edit, and post your own videos (such as *theFlip.com* and *youtube.com*). Summarize at least three options, including price information. Write a two- to three-page paper with your findings, citing all references.
3. Prepare a team contract for this project. Use the team_contract.doc template provided on the companion Web site, and review the sample in the text.
4. Prepare a draft project charter for the Project Management Videos Project. Assume the project will be completed by the last day of class, and costs will include an estimate of hours (unpaid) your team will work on this project plus the cost of any necessary hardware/software you would like for the project (such as DVDs, a camcorder, video editing software, etc.). Use the charter.doc template provided on the companion Web site, and review the sample in the text.
5. Prepare a draft schedule for completing all of the tasks for this project. Include columns that list each task by process group; estimated start and end dates for each task; who has the main responsibility for each task; estimated hours for each task by person; and actual hours for each task by person that you'll complete as you have the information.
6. Write a brief summary of your team's MBTI types and how they might affect your team dynamics. You can take a version of the test from *www.humanmetrics.com*.
7. Prepare a 10-minute presentation that summarizes results from the above initiating tasks. Assume the presentation is for a review with your class and instructor. Be sure to document notes of any feedback received during the presentation and hand in hard copies of everything you produced.

Part 2: Planning

Work with your teammates and instructor to perform several planning activities for this project.

Tasks

1. Develop a scope statement for the project. Use the scope_statement.doc template provided on the companion Web site, and review the sample in the text. Be as specific as possible in describing product characteristics and requirements, as well as key deliverables. Determine which video clips your team will provide and what resources you think you will need (DVDs, camcorders, etc.). Be sure to coordinate the clips with your instructor and other teams and get feedback before handing in your scope statement.
2. Develop a WBS for the project. Use the wbs.doc template provided on the companion Web site, and review the samples in the text. Print the WBS in list form

as a Word file. Be sure the WBS is based on the project charter, scope statement, draft schedule, and other relevant information.

3. Create a milestone list for this project, and include at least ten milestones and estimated completion dates for them. Note that your instructor should have input for several of these milestones and completion dates. Use the milestone_report.doc template.
4. Develop a cost estimate for the project. Estimate hours needed to complete each task (including those already completed) and the costs of any items you would like to purchase for the project. Assume a rate of $10 per hour for all labor. Use the cost_estimate.xls template.
5. Use the WBS and milestone list you developed in numbers 2 and 3 above and the draft schedule you created earlier to create a Gantt chart and network diagram in Project 2007 for the project. Estimate task durations and enter dependencies, as appropriate. Print the Gantt chart and network diagram. Also update the draft schedule you created under Initiating, Task 5.
6. Create a quality checklist for ensuring that the project is completed successfully. Also define at least two quality metrics for the project.
7. Create a RACI chart for the main tasks and deliverables for the project.
8. Develop a communications management plan for the project. Use the comm_plan.doc template and sample provided.
9. Create a probability/impact matrix and list of prioritized risks for the project. Include at least ten risks. Use the prob_impact_matrix.ppt template and sample provided.
10. Prepare a ten-minute presentation that you would give to summarize results from the above planning tasks. Assume the presentation is for a review with your class and instructor. Be sure to document notes of any feedback received during the presentation and hand in hard copies of everything you produced. Plan to show one video clip along with the discussion questions to get feedback.

Part 3: Executing

Work with your teammates and instructor to perform several executing activities for this project.

Tasks

1. Find or create your video clips and put them on one DVD. Be sure it runs on your instructor's computer.
2. Write the clip summaries, introductions, discussion questions, and suggested answers to those questions.
3. Document any change requests you have during project execution and get sponsor approval, if needed.

Part 4: Monitoring and Controlling

Work with your teammates and instructor to perform several monitoring and controlling activities for this project.

Tasks

1. Review the Seven Basic Tools of Quality. Pick one of these tools and create a chart or diagram to help you solve problems you are facing. Use the available templates and samples provided. Note: There is only a template for the Pareto chart called pareto_chart.xls.
2. Create and update, as required, an issue log. Use the issue_log.doc template and sample provided.
3. As described in the last task for the initiating and planning sections, be ready to show progress you have made as part of a project review. Also be sure to document actual hours on each task in the draft schedule you first created for Task 5 under Initiating and updated for Task 5 under Planning.

Part 5: Closing

Work with your teammates and instructor to perform several closing activities for this project.

Tasks

1. Prepare a 20-minute final project presentation to summarize the results of the project. Describe the initial project goals, planned versus actual scope, time, and cost information, challenges faced, lessons-learned, and key products produced. Be sure to list all of the clips your team found and show at least two of them along with the discussion questions.
2. Prepare a final project report. Include a cover page and detailed table of contents, getting feedback from your instructor on information required. Be sure to include all of the documents and products you have prepared as appendices.
3. Get feedback from your sponsor in the form of a customer acceptance/project completion form (see the template called client_acceptance.doc) or in some other fashion. Also get feedback from your classmates.
4. If you are comfortable doing so, send a copy of your final project report and feedback on this case to the author of this text at *schwalbe@augsburg.edu*.

FISSURE SIMULATION SOFTWARE

Introduction

Another way to practice your project management skills is by using simulation software. This text can be purchased so that it is bundled with Fissure's project management simulation software, or you can buy it separately at *www.ichapters.com* for about $12. Search for Fissure from the site. The version provided is the correct one.

Fissure's project management simulation software is based on the SimProject Alliance Prototype project. The demo version of the simulation software includes a fairly simple, 11-week project consisting of only seven tasks and ten potential team members. Fissure estimates that it takes about three to four hours to run the demo simulation. To participate in this simulated project, you are expected to read about the company, project, and people available to work on this project. You plan your project and make typical project decisions each week, such as when to assign staff, when to hold meetings, and when to send staff to various training opportunities. You run your project a week at a time, analyzing your results each week, referring to your weekly reports, and making your decisions for the next week. As you run the simulation each week, you are presented with communications from people within the company, team members, or other stakeholders related to the project. You choose how to respond to these communications, and all the decisions you make impact how your project progresses. You can close the simulation at any time and save your work, if desired. You can also run the simulation as many times as you like, and the results vary based on your decisions. You can use the software for 120 days.

Instructions

NOTE

It often works best if students can do this assignment as a small team or in pairs, if possible.

Run the Fissure simulation software at least two different times. Summarize key decisions and results from each week for each run, and print out the final earned value chart as well as any other information you think is valuable. Write a two- to three-page single-spaced report summarizing what you thought about using this simulation software. Be honest, specific, and thorough in your report.

GLOSSARY

5 whys — A technique where you repeatedly ask the question "Why?" (five is a good rule of thumb) to help peel away the layers of symptoms that can lead to the root cause of a problem.

acceptance decisions — Decisions that determine if the products or services produced as part of the project will be accepted or rejected.

activity — An element of work, normally found on the WBS, that has an expected duration and cost, and expected resource requirements; also called a task.

activity attributes — Information about each activity, such as predecessors, successors, logical relationships, leads and lags, resource requirements, constraints, imposed dates, and assumptions related to the activity.

activity list — A tabulation of activities to be included on a project schedule.

activity-on-arrow (AOA) — A network diagramming technique in which activities are represented by arrows and connected at points called nodes to illustrate the sequence of activities; also called arrow diagramming method (ADM).

actual cost (AC) — The total of direct and indirect costs incurred in accomplishing work on an activity during a given period.

adaptive software development (ASD) — A software development approach used when requirements cannot be clearly expressed early in the life cycle.

agile software development — A method for software development that uses new approaches, focusing on close collaboration between programming teams and business experts.

analogous estimates — A cost estimating technique that uses the actual cost of a previous, similar project as the basis for estimating the cost of the current project, also called top-down estimates.

analogy approach — Creating a WBS by using a similar project's WBS as a starting point.

appraisal cost — The cost of evaluating processes and their outputs to ensure that a project is error-free or within an acceptable error range.

arrow diagramming method (ADM) — A network diagramming technique in which activities are represented by arrows and connected at points called nodes to illustrate the sequence of activities; also called activity-on-arrow (AOA).

backward pass — A project network diagramming technique that determines the late start and late finish dates for each activity in a similar fashion.

balanced scorecard — A methodology that converts an organization's value drivers to a series of defined metrics.

baseline — The original project plan plus approved changes.

baseline dates — The planned schedule dates for activities in a Tracking Gantt chart.

benchmarking — A technique used to generate ideas for quality improvements by comparing specific project practices or product characteristics to those of other projects or products within or outside the performing organization.

best practice — An optimal way recognized by industry to achieve a stated goal or objective.

bid — Also called a tender or quote (short for quotation), a document prepared by sellers providing pricing for standard items that have been clearly defined by the buyer.

blogs — Easy to use journals on the Web that allow users to write entries, create links, and upload pictures, while readers can post comments to journal entries.

bottom-up approach — Creating a WBS by having team members identify as many specific tasks related to the project as possible and then grouping them into higher level categories.

bottom-up estimates — A cost estimating technique based on estimating individual work items and summing them to get a project total.

brainstorming — A technique by which a group attempts to generate ideas or find a solution for a specific problem by amassing ideas spontaneously and without judgment.

budget at completion (BAC) — The original total budget for a project.

budgetary estimate — A cost estimate used to allocate money into an organization's budget.

buffer — Additional time to complete a task, added to an estimate to account for various factors.

burst — When a single node is followed by two or more activities on a network diagram.

business service management (BSM) tools — Tools that help track the execution of business process flows and expose how the state of supporting IT systems and resources is impacting end-to-end business process performance in real time.

Capability Maturity Model Integration (CMMI) — A process improvement approach that provides organizations with the essential elements of effective processes.

capitalization rate — The rate used in discounting future cash flow; also called the discount rate or opportunity cost of capital.

cash flow — Benefits minus costs or income minus expenses.

cash flow analysis — A method for determining the estimated annual costs and benefits for a project.

cause-and-effect diagram — A diagram that traces complaints about quality problems back to the responsible production operations to help find the root cause. Also known as fishbone diagram or Ishikawa diagram.

champion — A senior manager who acts as a key proponent for a project.

change control board (CCB) — A formal group of people responsible for approving or rejecting changes on a project.

change control system — A formal, documented process that describes when and how official project documents may be changed.

closing processes — Formalizing acceptance of the project or project phase and ending it efficiently.

coercive power — Using punishment, threats, or other negative approaches to get people to do things they do not want to do.

collaborating mode — A conflict-handling mode where decision makers incorporate different viewpoints and insights to develop consensus and commitment.

communications management plan — A document that guides project communications.

compromise mode — Using a give-and-take approach to resolving conflicts; bargaining and searching for solutions that bring some degree of satisfaction to all the parties in a dispute.

configuration management — A process that ensures that the descriptions of the project's products are correct and complete.

conformance — Delivering products that meet requirements and fitness for use.

conformance to requirements — The project processes and products meet written specifications.

confrontation mode — Directly facing a conflict using a problem-solving approach that allows affected parties to work through their disagreements.

constructive change orders — Oral or written acts or omissions by someone with actual or apparent authority that can be construed to have the same effect as a written change order.

contingency allowances — Provisions held by the project sponsor or organization to reduce the risk of cost or schedule overruns to an acceptable level; also called contingency reserves.

contingency plans — Predefined actions that the project team will take if an identified risk event occurs.

contingency reserves — Provisions held by the project sponsor or organization to reduce the risk of cost or schedule overruns to an acceptable level; also called contingency allowances.

contract — A mutually binding agreement that obligates the seller to provide the specified products or services, and obligates the buyer to pay for them.

control chart — A graphic display of data that illustrates the results of a process over time.

controlling costs — Controlling changes to the project budget.

cost management plan — A document that describes how cost variances will be managed on the project.

cost baseline — A time-phased budget that project managers use to measure and monitor cost performance.

cost of capital — The return available by investing the capital elsewhere.

cost of nonconformance — Taking responsibility for failures or not meeting quality expectations.

cost of quality — The cost of conformance plus the cost of nonconformance.

cost performance index (CPI) — The ratio of earned value to actual cost; can be used to estimate the projected cost to complete the project.

cost variance (CV) — The earned value minus the actual cost.

cost plus award fee (CPAF) contract — A contract in which the buyer pays the supplier for allowable performance costs plus an award fee based on the satisfaction of subjective performance criteria.

cost plus fixed fee (CPFF) contract — A contract in which the buyer pays the supplier for allowable performance costs plus a fixed fee payment usually based on a percentage of estimated costs.

cost plus incentive fee (CPIF) contract — A contract in which the buyer pays the supplier for allowable performance costs along with a predetermined fee and an incentive bonus.

cost plus percentage of costs (CPPC) contract — A contract in which the buyer pays the supplier for allowable performance costs along with a predetermined percentage based on total costs.

cost-reimbursable contracts — Contracts involving payment to the supplier for direct and indirect actual costs.

crashing — A technique for making cost and schedule trade-offs to obtain the greatest amount of schedule compression for the least incremental cost.

critical chain scheduling — A method of scheduling that takes limited resources into account when creating a project schedule and includes buffers to protect the project completion date.

critical path — The series of activities in a network diagram that determines the earliest completion of the project; it is the longest path through the network diagram and has the least amount of slack or float.

critical path method (CPM) or critical path analysis — A project network analysis technique used to predict total project duration.

decision tree — A diagramming analysis technique used to help select the best course of action in situations in which future outcomes are uncertain.

decomposition — Subdividing project deliverables into smaller pieces.

defect — Any instance where the product or service fails to meet customer requirements.

DMAIC (Define, Measure, Analyze, Improve, Control) — A systematic, closed-loop process for continued improvement that is scientific and fact based.

definitive estimate — A cost estimate that provides an accurate estimate of project costs.

deliverable — A product or service, such as a technical report, a training session, a piece of hardware, or a segment of software code, produced or provided as part of a project.

Delphi technique — An approach used to derive a consensus among a panel of experts, to make predictions about future developments.

dependency — The sequencing of project activities or tasks; also called a relationship.

deputy project managers — People who fill in for project managers in their absence and assist them as needed, similar to the role of a vice president.

design of experiments — A quality technique that helps identify which variables have the most influence on the overall outcome of a process.

determining the budget — Allocating the overall cost estimate to individual work items to establish a baseline for measuring performance.

direct costs — Costs that can be directly related to producing the products and services of the project.

directives — New requirements imposed by management, government, or some external influence.

discretionary dependencies — Sequencing of project activities or tasks defined by the project team and used with care since they may limit later scheduling options.

discount factor — A multiplier for each year based on the discount rate and year.

discount rate — The rate used in discounting future cash flow; also called the capitalization rate or opportunity cost of capital.

dummy activities — Activities with no duration and no resources used to show a logical relationship between two activities in the arrow diagramming method of project network diagrams.

duration — The actual amount of time worked on an activity *plus* elapsed time.

early finish date — The earliest possible time an activity can finish based on the project network logic.

early start date — The earliest possible time an activity can start based on the project network logic.

earned value (EV) — An estimate of the value of the physical work actually completed.

earned value management (EVM) — A project performance measurement technique that integrates scope, time, and cost data.

effort — The number of workdays or work hours required to complete a task.

empathic listening — Listening with the intent to understand.

enterprise or portfolio project management software — Software that integrates information from multiple projects to show the status of active, approved, and future projects across an entire organization.

estimate at completion (EAC) — An estimate of what it will cost to complete the project based on performance to date.

estimating costs — Developing an approximation or estimate of the costs of the resources needed to complete the project.

ethics — A set of principles that guide our decision making based on personal values of what is "right" and "wrong."

executing processes — Coordinating people and other resources to carry out the project plans and produce the products, services, or results of the project or project phase.

executive steering committee — A group of senior executives from various parts of the organization who regularly review important corporate projects and issues.

expectations management matrix — A tool to help understand unique measures of success for a particular project.

expected monetary value (EMV) — The product of the risk event probability and the risk event's monetary value.

expert power — Using one's personal knowledge and expertise to get people to change their behavior.

extrinsic motivation — Causes people to do something for a reward or to avoid a penalty.

external dependencies — Sequencing of project activities or tasks that involve relationships between project and non-project activities.

external failure cost — A cost related to all errors not detected and corrected before delivery to the customer.

fallback plans — Plans developed for risks that have a high impact on meeting project objectives, to be implemented if attempts to reduce the risk are not effective.

fast tracking — A schedule compression technique in which you do activities in parallel that you would normally do in sequence.

features — The special characteristics that appeal to users.

feeding buffers — Additional time added before tasks on the critical path that are preceded by non-critical-path tasks.

fishbone diagram — Diagram that traces complaints about quality problems back to the responsible production operations to help find the root cause. Also known as cause-and-effect diagram or Ishikawa diagram.

fitness for use — A product can be used as it was intended.

finish-to-start dependency — A relationship on a project network diagram where the "from" activity must be finished before the "to" activity can be started.

fixed-price contract — Contract with a fixed total price for a well-defined product or service; also called a lump-sum contract.

float — The amount of time a project activity may be delayed without delaying a succeeding activity or the project finish date; also called slack.

flowchart — Graphic display of the logic and flow of processes that helps you analyze how problems occur and how processes can be improved.

forecasts — Used to predict future project status and progress based on past information and trends.

forcing mode — Using a win-lose approach to conflict resolution to get one's way.

forward pass — A network diagramming technique that determines the early start and early finish dates for each activity.

free slack (free float) — The amount of time an activity can be delayed without delaying the early start of any immediately following activities.

functionality — The degree to which a system performs its intended function.

functional organizational structure — An organizational structure that groups people by functional areas such as information technology, manufacturing, engineering, and human resources.

Gantt chart — A standard format for displaying project schedule information by listing project activities and their corresponding start and finish dates in a calendar format; sometimes referred to as bar chart.

Google Docs — Online applications offered by Google that allow users to create, share, and edit documents, spreadsheets, and presentations online.

green IT or green computing — Developing and using computer resources in an efficient way to improve economic viability, social responsibility, and environmental impact.

groupthink — Conformance to the values or ethical standards of a group.

hierarchy of needs — A pyramid structure illustrating Maslow's theory that people's behaviors are guided or motivated by a sequence of needs.

histogram — A bar graph of a distribution of variables.

human resources frame — Focuses on producing harmony between the needs of the organization and the needs of people.

indirect costs — Costs that are not directly related to the products or services of the project, but are indirectly related to performing the project.

influence diagram — Diagram that represents decision problems by displaying essential elements, including decisions, uncertainties, and objectives, and how they influence each other.

initiating processes — Defining and authorizing a project or project phase.

intangible costs or benefits — Costs or benefits that are difficult to measure in monetary terms.

integrated change control — Identifying, evaluating, and managing changes throughout the project life cycle.

integration testing — Testing that occurs between unit and system testing to test functionally grouped components to ensure a subset(s) of the entire system works together.

interface management — Identifying and managing the points of interaction between various elements of a project.

internal failure cost — A cost incurred to correct an identified defect before the customer receives the product.

internal rate of return (IRR) — The discount rate that results in an NPV of zero for a project.

interviewing — A fact-finding technique that is normally done face-to-face, but can also occur through phone calls, e-mail, or instant messaging.

intrinsic motivation — Causes people to participate in an activity for their own enjoyment.

Ishikawa diagram — Diagram that traces complaints about quality problems back to the responsible production operations to help find the root cause. Also known as cause-and-effect diagram or fishbone diagram.

ISO 9000 — A quality system standard developed by the International Organization for Standardization (ISO) that includes a three-part, continuous cycle of planning, controlling, and documenting quality in an organization.

issue — A matter under question or dispute that could impede project success.

issue log — A tool to document and monitor the resolution of project issues.

IT governance — Addresses the authority and control for key IT activities in organizations, including IT infrastructure, IT use, and project management.

Joint Application Design (JAD) — Using highly organized and intensive workshops to bring together project stakeholders—the sponsor, users, business analysts, programmers, and so on—to jointly define and design information systems.

kick-off meeting — A meeting held at the beginning of a project so that stakeholders can meet each other, review the goals of the project, and discuss future plans.

known risks — Risks that the project team have identified and analyzed and can be managed proactively.

known unknowns — Dollars included in a cost estimate to allow for future situations that may be partially planned for (sometimes called contingency reserves) and are included in the project cost baseline.

late finish date — The latest possible time an activity can be completed without delaying the project finish date.

late start date — The latest possible time an activity may begin without delaying the project finish date.

leader — A person who focuses on long-term goals and big-picture objectives, while inspiring people to reach those goals.

learning curve theory — A theory that states that when many items are produced repetitively, the unit cost of those items normally decreases in a regular pattern as more units are produced.

legitimate power — Getting people to do things based on a position of authority.

lessons-learned report — Reflective statements written by project managers and their team members to document important things they have learned from working on the project.

life cycle costing — Considers the total cost of ownership, or development plus support costs, for a project.

lump-sum contract — Contract with a fixed total price for a well-defined product or service; also called a fixed-price contract.

maintainability — The ease of performing maintenance on a product.

make-or-buy decision — When an organization decides if it is in its best interests to make certain products or perform certain services inside the organization, or if it is better to buy them from an outside organization.

Malcolm Baldrige National Quality Award — An award started in 1987 to recognize companies that have achieved a level of world-class competition through quality management.

management reserves — Dollars included in a cost estimate to allow for future situations that are unpredictable (sometimes called unknown unknowns).

manager — A person who deals with the day to day details of meeting specific goals.

mandatory dependencies — Sequencing of project activities or tasks that are inherent in the nature of the work being done on the project.

matrix organizational structure — An organizational structure in which employees are assigned to both functional and project managers.

maturity model — A framework for helping organizations improve their processes and systems.

mean — The average value of a population.

measurement and test equipment costs — The capital cost of equipment used to perform prevention and appraisal activities.

merge — When two or more nodes precede a single node on a network diagram.

methodology — Describes *how* things should be done.

metric — A standard of measurement.

milestone — A significant event that normally has no duration on a project; serves as a marker to help in identifying necessary activities, setting schedule goals, and monitoring progress.

mind mapping — A technique that uses branches radiating out from a core idea to structure thoughts and ideas.

mirroring — Matching certain behaviors of the other person.

Monte Carlo analysis — A risk quantification technique that simulates a model's outcome many times, to provide a statistical distribution of the calculated results.

monitoring and controlling processes — Regularly measuring and monitoring progress to ensure that the project team meets the project objectives.

multitasking — When a resource works on more than one task at a time.

Murphy's Law — Principle that if something can go wrong, it will.

Myers-Briggs Type Indicator (MBTI) — A popular tool for determining personality preferences.

net present value (NPV) analysis — A method of calculating the expected net monetary gain or loss from a project by discounting all expected future cash inflows and outflows to the present point in time.

network diagram — A schematic display of the logical relationships or sequencing of project activities.

node — The starting and ending point of an activity on an activity-on-arrow diagram.

normal distribution — A bell-shaped curve that is symmetrical about the mean of the population.

offshoring — Outsourcing from another country.

organizational breakdown structure (OBS) — A specific type of organizational chart that shows which organizational units are responsible for which work items.

organizational culture — A set of shared assumptions, values, and behaviors that characterize the functioning of an organization.

organizational process assets — Formal and informal plans, policies, procedures, guidelines, information systems, financial systems, management systems, lessons learned, and historical information that can be used to influence a project's success.

opportunities — Chances to improve the organization.

opportunity cost of capital — The rate used in discounting future cash flow; also called the capitalization rate or discount rate.

outsourcing — When an organization acquires goods and/or sources from an outside source.

overallocation — When more resources than are available are assigned to perform work at a given time.

overrun — The additional percentage or dollar amount by which actual costs exceed estimates.

parametric modeling — A cost-estimating technique that uses project characteristics (parameters) in a mathematical model to estimate project costs.

Pareto analysis — Identifying the vital few contributors that account for most quality problems in a system.

Pareto chart — Histogram that helps identify and prioritize problem areas.

Parkinson's Law — Principle that work expands to fill the time allowed.

payback period — The amount of time it will take to recoup, in the form of net cash inflows, the total dollars invested in a project.

performance — How well a product or service performs the customer's intended use.

PERT weighted average — optimistic time + 4 * most likely time + pessimistic time

planned value (PV) — That portion of the approved total cost estimate planned to be spent on an activity during a given period.

planning processes — Devising and maintaining a workable scheme to ensure that the project addresses the organization's needs.

phase exit or kill point — Management review that should occur after each project phase to determine if projects should be continued, redirected, or terminated.

Point of Total Assumption (PTA) — The cost at which the contractor assumes total responsibility for each additional dollar of contract cost in a fixed price incentive fee contract.

political frame — Addresses organizational and personal politics.

politics — Competition between groups or individuals for power and leadership.

power — The potential ability to influence behavior to get people to do things they would not otherwise do.

Precedence Diagramming Method (PDM) — A network diagramming technique in which boxes represent activities.

predictive life cycle — A software development approach used when the scope of the project can be clearly articulated and the schedule and cost can be accurately predicted.

prevention cost — The cost of planning and executing a project so that it is error-free or within an acceptable error range.

probability/impact matrix or chart — A matrix or chart that lists the relative probability of a risk occurring on one side of a matrix or axis on a chart and the relative impact of the risk occurring on the other.

probabilistic time estimates — Duration estimates based on using optimistic, most likely, and pessimistic estimates of activity durations instead of using one specific or discrete estimate.

problems — Undesirable situations that prevent the organization from achieving its goals.

process — A series of actions directed toward a particular result.

process adjustments — Adjustments made to correct or prevent further quality problems based on quality control measurements.

procurement — Acquiring goods and/or services from an outside source.

profit margin — The ratio between revenues and profits.

profits — Revenues minus expenses.

program — A group of projects managed in a coordinated way to obtain benefits and control not available from managing them individually.

Program Evaluation and Review Technique (PERT) — A project network analysis technique used to estimate project duration when there is a high degree of uncertainty with the individual activity duration estimates.

program manager — A person who provides leadership and direction for the project managers heading the projects within a program.

progress reports — Reports that describe what the project team has accomplished during a certain period of time.

project — A temporary endeavor undertaken to create a unique product, service, or result.

project acquisition — The last two phases in a project (implementation and close-out) that focus on delivering the actual work.

project archives — A complete set of organized project records that provide an accurate history of the project.

project buffer — Additional time added before the project's due date.

project charter — A document that formally recognizes the existence of a project and provides direction on the project's objectives and management.

project cost management — The processes required to ensure that the project is completed within the approved budget.

project feasibility — The first two phases in a project (concept and development) that focus on planning.

project integration management — Processes that coordinate all project management knowledge areas throughout a project's life, including developing the project charter, developing the preliminary project scope statement, developing the project management plan, directing and managing the project, monitoring and controlling the project, providing integrated change control, and closing the project.

project life cycle — A collection of project phases, such as concept, development, implementation, and close-out.

project management — The application of knowledge, skills, tools, and techniques to project activities to meet project requirements.

Project Management Institute (PMI) — An international professional society for project managers.

project management knowledge areas — Project integration management, scope, time, cost, quality, human resource, communications, risk, and procurement management.

Project Management Office (PMO) — An organizational group responsible for coordinating the project management functions throughout an organization.

project management plan — A document used to coordinate all project planning documents and guide project execution and control.

project management process groups — The progression of project activities from initiation to planning, executing, monitoring and controlling, and closing.

Project Management Professional (PMP) — Certification provided by PMI that requires documenting project experience and education, agreeing to follow the PMI code of ethics, and passing a comprehensive exam.

project management tools and techniques — Methods available to assist project managers and their teams; some popular tools in the time management knowledge area include Gantt charts, network diagrams, and critical path analysis.

project manager — The person responsible for working with the project sponsor, the project team, and the other people involved in a project to meet project goals.

project organizational structure — An organizational structure that groups people by major projects, such as specific aircraft programs.

project procurement management — The processes required to acquire goods and services for a project from outside the performing organization.

project portfolio management (portfolio management) — When organizations group and manage projects as a portfolio of investments that contribute to the entire enterprise's success.

project quality management — Ensuring that a project will satisfy the needs for which it was undertaken.

project scope management — The processes involved in defining and controlling what work is or is not included in a project.

project scope statement — A document that includes, at a minimum, a description of the project, including its overall objectives and justification, detailed descriptions of all project deliverables, and the characteristics and requirements of products and services produced as part of the project.

PRojects IN Controlled Environments (PRINCE2) — A project management methodology developed in the U.K. that defines 45 separate sub-processes and organizes these into eight process groups.

project sponsor — The person who provides the direction and funding for a project.

project time management — The processes required to ensure timely completion of a project.

proposal — A document prepared by sellers when there are different approaches for meeting buyer needs.

prototyping — Developing a working replica of the system or some aspect of the system to help define user requirements.

quality — The totality of characteristics of an entity that bear on its ability to satisfy stated or implied needs or the degree to which a set of inherent characteristics fulfill requirements.

quality assurance — Periodically evaluating overall project performance to ensure that the project will satisfy the relevant quality standards.

quality audit — Structured review of specific quality management activities that helps identify lessons learned and can improve performance on current or future projects.

quality circles — Groups of nonsupervisors and work leaders in a single company department who volunteer to conduct group studies on how to improve the effectiveness of work in their department.

quality control — Monitoring specific project results to ensure that they comply with the relevant quality standards and identifying ways to improve overall quality.

quality planning — Identifying which quality standards are relevant to the project and how to satisfy them.

RACI charts — Charts that show Responsibility, Accountability, Consultation, and Informed roles for project stakeholders.

rapport — A relation of harmony, conformity, accord, or affinity.

rate of performance (RP) — The ratio of actual work completed to the percentage of work planned to have been completed at any given time during the life of the project or activity.

Rational Unified Process (RUP) — An iterative software development process that focuses on team productivity and delivers software best practices to all team members.

referent power — Getting people to do things based on an individual's personal charisma.

reliability — The ability of a product or service to perform as expected under normal conditions.

Request for Proposal (RFP) — A document used to solicit proposals from prospective suppliers.

Request for Quote (RFQ) — A document used to solicit quotes or bids from prospective suppliers.

required rate of return — The minimum acceptable rate of return on an investment.

requirement — A condition or capability that must be met or possessed by a system, product, service, result, or component to satisfy a contract, standard, specification, or other formal document.

requirements management plan — A plan that describes how project requirements will be analyzed, documented, and managed.

requirements traceability matrix — A table that lists requirements, various attributes of each requirement, and the status of the requirements to ensure that all requirements are addressed.

reserves — Dollars included in a cost estimate to mitigate cost risk by allowing for future situations that are difficult to predict.

residual risks — Risks that remain after all of the response strategies have been implemented.

resource breakdown structure — A hierarchical structure that identifies the project's resources by category and type.

resource histogram — A column chart that shows the number of resources assigned to a project over time.

resource leveling — A technique for resolving resource conflicts by delaying tasks.

resource loading — The amount of individual resources an existing schedule requires during specific time periods.

resources — People, equipment, and materials.

responsibility assignment matrix (RAM) — A matrix that maps the work of the project as described in the WBS to the people responsible for performing the work as described in the organizational breakdown structure (OBS).

return on investment (ROI) — (Benefits minus costs) divided by costs.

reward power — Using incentives to induce people to do things.

rework — Action taken to bring rejected items into compliance with product requirements or specifications or other stakeholder expectations.

risk — An uncertainty that can have a negative or positive effect on meeting project objectives.

risk acceptance — Accepting the consequences should a risk occur.

risk-averse — Having a low tolerance for risk.

risk avoidance — Eliminating a specific threat or risk, usually by eliminating its causes.

risk breakdown structure — A hierarchy of potential risk categories for a project.

risk enhancement — Changing the size of an opportunity by identifying and maximizing key drivers of the positive risk.

risk events — Specific uncertain events that may occur to the detriment or enhancement of the project.

risk exploitation — Doing whatever you can to make sure the positive risk happens.

risk factors — Numbers that represent overall risk of specific events, given their probability of occurring and the consequence to the project if they do occur.

risk management plan — A plan that documents the procedures for managing risk throughout a project.

risk mitigation — Reducing the impact of a risk event by reducing the probability of its occurrence.

risk-neutral — A balance between risk and payoff.

risk owner — The person who will take responsibility for a risk and its associated response strategies and tasks.

risk register — A document that contains results of various risk management processes, often displayed in a table or spreadsheet format.

risk-seeking — Having a high tolerance for risk.

risk sharing — Allocating ownership of the risk to another party.

risk tolerance — The amount of satisfaction or pleasure received from a potential payoff; also called risk utility.

risk transference — Shifting the consequence of a risk and responsibility for its management to a third party.

risk utility — The amount of satisfaction or pleasure received from a potential payoff; also called risk tolerance.

Robust Design methods — Methods that focus on eliminating defects by substituting scientific inquiry for trial-and-error methods.

rough order of magnitude (ROM) estimate — A cost estimate prepared very early in the life of a project to provide a rough idea of what a project will cost.

runaway projects — Projects that have significant cost or schedule overruns.

run chart — Chart that displays the history and pattern of variation of a process over time.

scatter diagram — Diagram that helps to show if there is a relationship between two variables; also called XY charts.

schedule baseline — The approved planned schedule for the project.

schedule performance index (SPI) — The ratio of earned value to planned value; can be used to estimate the projected time to complete a project.

schedule variance (SV) — The earned value minus the planned value.

scope — All the work involved in creating the products of the project and the processes used to create them.

scope baseline — The approved project scope statement and its associated WBS and WBS dictionary.

scope creep — The tendency for project scope to keep getting bigger.

secondary risks — Risks that are a direct result of implementing a risk response.

sellers — Contractors, suppliers, or providers who provide goods and services to other organizations.

sensitivity analysis — A technique used to show the effects of changing one or more variables on an outcome.

seven run rule — If seven data points in a row on a quality control chart are all below the mean, above the mean, or are all increasing or decreasing, then the process needs to be examined for nonrandom problems.

SharePoint portal — Allows users to create custom Web sites to access documents and applications stored on shared devices.

six 9s of quality — A measure of quality control equal to 1 fault in 1 million opportunities.

Six Sigma — A comprehensive and flexible system for achieving, sustaining, and maximizing business success that is uniquely driven by close understanding of customer needs, disciplined use of facts, data, statistical analysis, and diligent attention to managing, improving, and reinventing business processes.

Six Sigma methodologies — DMAIC (Define, Measure, Analyze, Improve, and Control) is used to improve an existing business process and DMADV (Define, Measure, Analyze, Design, and Verify) is used to create new product or process designs.

slack — The amount of time a project activity may be delayed without delaying a succeeding activity or the project finish date; also called float.

slipped milestone — A milestone activity that is completed later than planned.

SMART criteria — Guidelines to help define milestones that are specific, measurable, assignable, realistic, and time-framed.

smoothing mode — Deemphasizing or avoiding areas of differences and emphasizing areas of agreements.

software defect — Anything that must be changed before delivery of the program.

Software Quality Function Deployment (SQFD) model — A maturity model that focuses on defining user requirements and planning software projects.

staffing management plan — A document that describes when and how people will be added to and taken off a project team.

stakeholder management strategy — An approach to help increase the support of stakeholders throughout the project.

stakeholder register — A document that includes details related to the identified project stakeholders.

stakeholders — People involved in or affected by project activities.

standard — Describes best practices for *what* should be done.

standard deviation — A measure of how much variation exists in a distribution of data.

start-to-finish dependency — A relationship on a project network diagram where the "from" activity cannot start before the "to" activity is finished.

start-to-start dependency — A relationship on a project network diagram in which the "from" activity cannot start.

statement of work (SOW) — A description of the work required for the procurement.

statistical sampling — Choosing part of a population of interest for inspection until the "to" activity starts.

status reports — Reports that describe where the project stands at a specific point in time.

strategic planning — Determining long-term objectives by analyzing the strengths and weaknesses of an organization, studying opportunities and threats in the business environment, predicting future trends, and projecting the need for new products and services.

structural frame — Deals with how the organization is structured (usually depicted in an organizational chart) and focuses on different groups' roles and responsibilities to meet the goals and policies set by top management.

subproject managers — People responsible for managing the subprojects that a large project might be broken into.

sunk cost — Money that has been spent in the past.

SWOT analysis — Analyzing Strengths, Weaknesses, Opportunities, and Threats; used to aid in strategic planning.

symbolic frame — Focuses on the symbols, meanings, and culture of an organization.

synergy — An approach where the whole is greater than the sum of the parts.

system outputs — The screens and reports the system generates.

systems — Sets of interacting components working within an environment to fulfill some purpose.

systems analysis — A problem-solving approach that requires defining the scope of the system to be studied, and then dividing it into its component parts for identifying and evaluating its problems, opportunities, constraints, and needs.

systems approach — A holistic and analytical approach to solving complex problems that includes using a systems philosophy, systems analysis, and systems management.

systems development life cycle (SDLC) — A framework for describing the phases involved in developing and maintaining information systems.

systems management — Addressing the business, technological, and organizational issues associated with creating, maintaining, and making changes to a system.

systems philosophy — An overall model for thinking about things as systems.

system stakeholder register — A public document that includes details related to the identified project stakeholders.

systems thinking — Taking a holistic view of an organization to effectively handle complex situations.

tangible costs or benefits — Costs or benefits that can be easily measured in dollars.

task — An element of work, normally found on the WBS, that has an expected duration and cost, and expected resource requirements; also called an activity.

team development — Building individual and group skills to enhance project performance.

termination clause — A contract clause that allows the buyer or supplier to end the contract.

testing — Testing the entire system as one entity to ensure that it is working properly.

Theory of Constraints (TOC) — A management philosophy that states that any complex system at any point in time often has only one aspect or constraint that is limiting its ability to achieve more of its goal.

three-point estimate — An estimate that includes an optimistic, most likely, and pessimistic estimate.

time and material (T&M) contracts — A hybrid of both fixed-price and cost-reimbursable contracts.

top-down approach — Creating a WBS by starting with the largest items of the project and breaking them into their subordinate items.

top-down estimates — A cost estimating technique that uses the actual cost of a previous, similar project as the basis for estimating the cost of the current project, also called analogous estimates.

Top Ten Risk Item Tracking — A qualitative risk analysis tool for identifying risks and maintaining an awareness of risks throughout the life of a project.

total slack (total float) — The amount of time an activity may be delayed from its early start without delaying the planned project finish date.

Tracking Gantt chart — A Gantt chart that compares planned and actual project schedule information.

triggers — Indications for actual risk events.

triple constraint — Balancing scope, time, and cost goals.

Tuckman model — Describes five stages of team development: forming, storming, norming, performing, and adjourning.

unit pricing — An approach in which the buyer pays the supplier a predetermined amount per unit of service, and the total value of the contract is a function of the quantities needed to complete the work.

unit test — A test of each individual component (often a program) to ensure that it is as defect-free as possible.

unknown risks — Risks that have not been identified and analyzed so they cannot be managed proactively.

unknown unknowns — Dollars included in a cost estimate to allow for future situations that are unpredictable (sometimes called management reserves).

use case modeling — A process for identifying and modeling business events, who initiated them, and how the system should respond to them.

user acceptance testing — An independent test performed by end users prior to accepting the delivered system.

variance — The difference between planned and actual performance.

virtualization — Hiding the physical characteristics of computing resources from their users, such as making a single server, operating system, application, or storage device appear to function as multiple virtual resources.

virtual team — A group of individuals who work across time and space using communication technologies.

watch list — A list of risks that are low priority, but are still identified as potential risks.

WBS dictionary — A document that describes detailed information about each WBS item.

weighted scoring model — A technique that provides a systematic process for basing project selection on numerous criteria.

wiki — A Web site that has a page or pages designed to enable anyone who accesses it to contribute or modify content.

withdrawal mode — Retreating or withdrawing from an actual or potential disagreement.

workarounds — Unplanned responses to risk events when there are no contingency plans in place.

work breakdown structure (WBS) — A deliverable-oriented grouping of the work involved in a project that defines the total scope of the project.

work package — A task at the lowest level of the WBS.

yield — The number of units handled correctly through the development process.

INDEX

Note: Page numbers in **boldface** type indicate key terms and their definitions.

A

Accept software, 181–182
achievement, as motivator, 346–347
acquired-needs theory, 346–347
ACs. *See* actual costs (ACs)
activity attributes, **215**, 215–216
activity duration, estimating, 213–214, 223, 236
activity list, 213, **215**, 216
activity-on-arrow approach (AOA), **218**, 218–219
  sample, 218
activity resources, estimating 213, 222
activity sequencing, 217–220
actual costs (ACs), **273**
  Microsoft Project 2007, A.55
actual times, Microsoft Project 2007, A.55–A.59
Adaptive Software Development (ASD) life cycle, **60**, 60–61
Addeman, Frank, 229
ADM. *See* arrow-diagramming method (ADM)
affiliation, as motivator, 346–347
AgênciaClick, 86
agile methodologies, 85
Allied Signal/Honeywell, 309
Alpha Project Managers: What the Top 2% Know That Everyone Else Does Not (Crowe), 80
Ameritrade, 294
analogous estimates, 263
AOA. *See* activity-on arrow approach (AOA)
analogy approach, WBD development, 192
arrow-diagramming method (ADM), **218**, 218–219
ASD. *See* Adaptive Software Development (ASD) life cycle
Athens Olympic Games, 213
Axelrod, David, 272

B

BAC. *See* budget at completion (BAC)
BAFO. *See* best and final offer
balanced scorecard, **146**, 146–147
Balanced Scorecard Institute, 146
Bank of America, 294
Basecamp, 33
baseline, 159, 159–160
  saving files with or without in Microsoft Project 2007, A.25
  scope, 194–195
baseline plans, Microsoft Project 2007, A.54–A.55
"The Bases of Social Power" (French and Raven), 349
basic productivity software, 32
Belbin, Meredith, 368
benchmarking, **299**
benefits
  intangible, 270
  tangible, 270
best and final offer (BAFO), 479
"Best Companies to Work For," 359
best practices, **19**
bids, **475**, 477–478
blogs, **411**
Boots Company PLC, 467
bottom-up approach, WBD development, 192–193
bottom-up estimates, **264**
Briggs, Katherine C., 364–365
broad organizational needs, as method for selecting projects, 138

Brooks, Frederick, 394
BSM tools. *See* business service management (BSM) tools
budget at completion (BAC), 275, 275–276
buffers, 235
Bullock, Fraser, 160
bursts, in AOA diagrams, 219
business cases, 83, 88–91
  contents, 88
  sample, 89–91
Business Process Reengineering (BPR), 308
business service management (BSM) tools, 165–166
Butrick, Robert, 19

C

Calendar view, Microsoft Project 2007, A.16
Capability Maturity Model Integration (CMMI), 323
capital, opportunity cost of, 141
CAPM. *See* Certified Associate in Project Management (CAPM) certification
Carlyle, Thomas, 12
Carr, Nicholas, 6
cash flow analysis, 259
cause-and-effect diagrams, 300, 300–301
  sample, 301
Cavanaugh, Roland, 307, 309, 312
CCB. *See* change control board (CCB)
certifications, 29–32
  CAPM, B.2, B.18
  CITPM, B.18
  CNE, B.14
  CNI, B.14
  CompTIA, B.13
  IPMA, B.18
  MCITP, B.17
  MCTS, B.17
  MOS, B.17
  PgMP, B.2, B.18
  PMP, 30, 56, 356, 477, 479, B.1–B.10
Certified Associate in Project Management (CAPM) certification, B.2, B.18
Certified IT Project Manager (CTPM) certification, B.18
Certified Project Manager, B.18
Certified Project Management Associate, B.18
Certified Novell Engineer (CNE) certification, B.14
Certified Novell Instructor (CNI) certification, B.14
Certified Senior Project Manager, B.18
champions, 54
change control board (CCB), 162, 162–163
change control system, 162, 162–163
change requests, 14, 160–161
CHAOS Report, 3–4, 16
checklists, 295, 436
Chemical Bank, 294
CITPM. *See* Certified IT Project Manager (CITPM) certification
close-out phase of projects, 59, 164
closing processes, 79, 82, 114
CNE. *See* Certified Novell Engineer (CNE) certification
CNI. *See* Certified Novell Instructor (CNI) certification
code of ethics, 31–32
Cohen, Dennis, 139
collaborating mode, 400
collecting requirements, 179–182
Comair, 432
commitment of top management, 54–55, 62
communications
  formal versus informal, 390
  group communication needs, 394–396
  individual communication needs, 394–396
  team size, 395–396
communications management, 12, 13, 382–412
  appropriate medium, 390–394, 403–405
  best practices, 405–406
  channels, 395–396
  improving, 399–400
  information distribution, 388–396
  managing stakeholders, 385–386, 396–398
  mapping process groups to, 84
  Microsoft Project 2007, A.70–A.76
  performance reporting, 398–399
  updating business procedures, 388–389
communications management plans, 386, 386–388

communications management planning,
386–388
plans, 386–388
communications media, 392–393
compromise mode, 400
computer viruses, 321
Computing Technology Industry Association
(CompTIA) certification, B.13
concept stage of project(s), 57–58
configuration management, 163
conflict management, 399–400
conformance to requirements, 294
confrontation mode, 400
constructive change orders, 479, 479–480
contingency plans, 429
contingency reserves (allowances), 430
contracts, 464, 469–473
administration, 479–480
cost-reimbursable, 470–473
fixed price (lump-sum), 469–470
procurement, 477–479
risk-related, 472–473
time-and-material, 472
contract statements of work (SOWs), 474,
474–475
control charts, 301, 301–302
sample, 302
Cooper, Robert, 137
Copper, 33
Copy Picture feature, Microsoft Project 2007,
A.75–A.76
core projects, 20
corrective actions, 159–161
cost, 255
direct, 260
estimating, 261–270
indirect, 260
intangible, 259
tangible, 259
sunk, 260
cost, viewing in Microsoft Project 2007,
A.44–A.47, A.51–A.53
cost baselines, 271
cost budgeting, 270–271
cost estimates, 261–270
analogous estimates, 263
bottom-up estimates, 264
budgetary estimate, 261
definitive estimate, 261
parametric modeling, 264
problems, 264–265
rough order of magnitude (ROM), 261
sample, 265–270
cost estimates, Microsoft Project 2007,
A.44–A.47
cost management, 12, 13, 257–280
best practices, 279
controlling, 272–278
cost baseline, 271
cost budgeting, 270–272
mapping process groups to, 84
Microsoft Project 2007, 280, A.44–A.62
cost management planning, 256–257, 262
cost performance index (CPI), 275
cost-reimbursable contract, 470–473
cost table, Microsoft Project 2007, A.15,
A.44–A.47, A.51–A.52
cost table view, Microsoft Project
2007, A.45
cost variance, (CV), 275
Cottrell, Bill, 85
Covey, Steven, 350–351, 400
CPI. *See* cost performance index (CPI)
CPM. *See* critical path method (CPM)
crashing, 233
critical chain scheduling, 233,
233–236
critical path, 27, 228–229, 236
critical path calculation, 228–233
importance of updating data, 233
Microsoft Project 2007, 231, A.42–A.44
schedule trade-offs, 230–233
understanding, 229–230
critical path method (CPM), 228,
228–233
Crosby, Philip B., 316–317
Crosstab Report dialog box, Microsoft Project
2007, A.52
Crowe, Andy, 80
Cruise Control, 66
cultural differences, 212, 322–323
Customer Relationship Management (CRM)
Excellence Awards, 56
customer satisfaction, 9–10, 15
CV. *See* cost variance
cyberslackers, 401–402

D

D'Agostinho, Fabiano, 86
decision tree, 442, 442–444
deliverables, 57
  accepted and unaccepted, 179
Dell, Michael, 259
Delphi technique, 435
Demers, Clement, 111
Deming, W. Edwards, 315–316
dependencies, 217, 217–220
development phase of projects, 58
DFAS. *See* U.S. Defense Finance and Accounting Services (DFAS)
Digital Supply Chain, 6
directives, 139
DISC Profile, 367–368
discount factor, 142
discount rate, 141
discretionary dependencies, 217
DMADV (Define, Measure, Analyze, Design, Verify) methodology, 86
DMAIC (Define, Measure, Analyze, Improve, Control) methodology, 307–308
DOD. *See* U.S. Department of Defense (DOD)
Does IT Matter? Information Technology and the Corrosion of Competitive Advantage (Carr), 6
duration, 222
  estimating, 222–223

E

EAC. *See* estimate at completion
earned value (EV), 273
earned value management (EVM), 273, 273–278, 398–399
  actual cost, 273
  cost performance index, 275
  cost variance, 275
  estimate at completion, 275
  Microsoft Project 2007, 277–278, A.59–A.62
  planned value, 273
  schedule performance index, 275
  schedule variance, 275
Earned Value view, Microsoft Project 2007, A.14, A.15, A.59–A.60
effort, 222
e-mail, 403–406
empathic listening, 350, 350–351, 390
enterprise resource planning (ERP), 48
Entry table, assigning resources in Microsoft Project 2007, A.45, A.48
Entry Table view, Microsoft Project 2007, A.6, A.9–A.10
ERP. *See* enterprise resource planning (ERP)
estimate at completion (EAC), 275
ethics, 31, 31–32
EV. *See* earned value (EV)
EVM. *See* earned value management (EVM)
exams
  PMP certification, B.4–B.13
  Project+ certification, B.14–B.17
executing processes, 79, 81–82, 106–110
  communications management, 388–398
  human resource management, 357–368
  integration management, 156–158
  procurement management, 477–479
  project quality management, 298–299
  summary of tasks and outputs, 158–159
executing projects, 156–159
executive steering committee, 62
expectations management matrix, 397, 397–398
  sample, 398
expected monetary value, 442, 442–444
  sample, 443
external dependencies, 217
extreme programming, 85
extrinsic motivation, 344
Extrovert/Introvert (E/I) psychological type, 364

F

fallback plans, 429
fast tracking, 233
Federal Bureau of Investigation (FBI), 216–217

feeding buffers, 235
Feigenbaum, Armand V., 318
firm-fixed price (FFP) contracts, 470
fishbone diagrams. *See* cause-and-effect diagrams
fitness for use, 294
fixed costs, entering in Microsoft Project 2007, A.44–A.45
fixed-price contracts, 469, 469–470
float, 228, 230
flowcharts, 305
  sample, 305
forcing mode, 400
forecasts, 398, 398–399
Form views, Microsoft Project 2007, A.14
formal communications, 390
FoxMeyer Drug, 197
frames of organizations, 47–48
Freud, Sigmund, 344
functional organizational structure, 48–49, 50–51

G

Gantt charts, 14, 27, 224–228
  Microsoft Project 2007, 27, 224–225, 240, A.38–A.40
  sample, 28, 189, 224, 227
  tracking, 226–228
Gantt Chart view, Microsoft Project 2007, A.5–A.7, A.10, A.14, A.18, A.38, A.41
Gartner, Inc., 56
Genesys Telecommunications Laboratories, 181
Gertner Institute Certification Program, B.13–B.14
globalization, effect on IT projects, 65–68
Global Positioning Systems, 6
Goldratt, Eliyah M., 233
Google, 359
Google Docs, 404, 404–405
Gottron, Joe, 62–63
Government Accountability Office (GAO), 81, 255
Graham, Robert, 139
Graphical views, Microsoft Project 2007, A.14, A.15
Greenbaum, Joshua, 198
Ground Zero, 53–54
groupthink, 400
Groves, Leslie R., 27
guidelines, WBD development, 191–192

H

Harley-Davidson, 63
Herzberg, Frederick, 345–346
  motivation-hygiene theory, 345–346
Hewlett Packard, 137, 356
hierarchy of needs, 344–345
Hillson, David, 424–425
histograms, 304
  sample, 304
holistic thinking. *See* systems thinking
human resource costs, entering in Microsoft Project 2007, A.45–A.46
human resource management, 12, 13, 342–370
  effectiveness research, 344–352
  influence bases, 348
  mapping process groups to, 84
  Microsoft Project 2007, 370, A.62–A.69
  motivation, 344–352
  resource loading and leveling, 359–362
  reward and recognition systems, 368
  team acquisition, 357–359
  team development, 362–368
  team management tools and techniques, 368–370
  team performance assessment, 368
human resource management planning, 352–357
  organizational charts, 352–353
  RAMs, 354–354
  resource histograms, 357
  staffing management plans, 356–357
  work definition and assignment, 353–354
Human Side of Enterprise, The (McGregor), 347
hyperlinks, inserting with Microsoft Project 2007, A.71–A.74

I

Ibbs, William, 423
IBM Global Business Services, 356–357, 467
identifying risk, 434–438
implementation phase of projects, 58–59
influence bases, 348
informal communication, 351
information distribution, 388–396
information technologies, 4–6, 56–57, 338–339
  business strategy, 136–137
  communication, 389–390, 403–405
  IT governance, 55
  projects, 63–68
initiating processes, 79, 81, 87, 89–96
  example, 89–91
  pre-initiation, 87–88
Insert Hyperlink dialog box, Microsoft Project 2007, A.73–A.74
integrated change control, 161, 161–164
integration management. *See* project integration management
integration management planning, 151–155
  project management plans, 151–155
  team contracts, 147–148
interface management, 131–132
internal rate of return (IRR), 143
Internal Revenue Service (IRS), 80–81, 255
International Organization for Standardization (ISO), 294, 298, 318–319
International Project Management Association (IPMA) certification program, B.18
intrinsic motivation, 344
IPMA. *See* International Project Management Association (IPMA) certification program
IRR. *See* internal rate of return (IRR)
Ishikawa diagrams. *See* cause-and-effect diagrams
Ishikawa, Kaoru, 317
issues, 369
issue logs, 369
IT governance, 55
IT Governance: How Top Performers Manage Decision Rights for Superior Results (Weill and Ross), 55

J

Jackson, Peter, 82
JAD. *See* joint application design
Jehn, Karen, 400
Johnson, Jim, 62
joint application design (JAD), 60
JPMorgan Chase, 465
Judgment/Perception (J/P) psychological type, 365
Juran, Joseph M., 316

K

Kanter, Rosabeth Moss, 19
Kaplan, Robert, 146
kick-off meetings, 14, 95
  purpose, 95–06
  sample, 96
kill points. *See* management reviews
knowledge areas, mapping process groups to, 83–84
known unknowns, 260
Kwak, Young H., 423

L

lag time, Microsoft Project 2007, A.35–A.38
Lang, Paul, 181
lead time, Microsoft Project 2007, A.35–A.37
leadership, 24, 157, 319–320
  contrasted with management, 24
  skills, 24–25
learning curve theory, 260
Lehman, Matthew, 160
Lencioni, Patrick, 369–370
lessons-learned report, 409
Liew, Lawrence, 159
lump-sum contracts, 469, 469–470

M

make-or-buy analysis, 468, 468–470
  sample, 469–470

Malcolm Baldridge National Quality Award, 318
management, 24
  compared with leadership, 24
  skills, 22–24
management by walking around, 369
management reserves, 260
management reviews, 61–62
mandatory dependencies, 217
Manhattan Project, 27
Marche, Sunny, 48
Marston, William, Moulton, 367
Maslow, Abraham, 344–345
  hierarchy of needs, 344–345
matrix organized structure, 50–51
maturity models, 323, 323–325
  Capability Maturity Model Integration, 323–324
  Software Function Deployment Model, 323
MBTI. *See* Myers-Briggs Type Indicator (MBTI)
MBWA. *See* management by walking around (MBWA)
McClelland, David, 346–347
  acquired-needs theory, 346–347
McDonald's, 197
McGregor, Douglas, 347
  Theory X and Theory Y, 347
MCITP. *See* Microsoft Certified IT Professional (MCITP) certification
McNeally, Scott, 464
MCTS. *See* Microsoft Certified Technology Specialist (MCTS) certification
meetings, 14, 95, 96, 402–403
merges in AOA diagrams, 219
Merril, David, 366
methodology, 85
  development, 85–86
metrics, 295, 299
  quality, 295, 299
Microsoft Certified IT Professional (MCITP) certification, B.17
Microsoft Certified Technology Specialist (MCTS) certification, B.17
Microsoft Excel, 32–33, 446–447, A.4, A.60
Microsoft Office Enterprise Project Management (EPM) Solution, 409–410, 412, A.3
Microsoft Office Project Portfolio Server 2007, 33
Microsoft Office Project Professional 2007. *See* Microsoft Project 2007
Microsoft Office Project Server 2007, A.2–A.3
Microsoft Office Specialist (MOS) certification, B.17–B.18
Microsoft Project 2007
  actual costs and times, A.55
  assigning resources to tasks, A.48–A.53
  backward compatibility, A.4
  baseline plans, A.54
  communications management, A.70–A.76
  Copy Picture feature, A.75–A.76
  cost estimates, A.44–A.48
  cost management, 280, A.44–A.62
  creating new project file, A.20–A.22
  critical path analysis, A.42–A.44
  customizing standard toolbar, A.8–A.9
  earned value management, A.59–A.62
  entering task durations, 114, A.27–A.32
  evaluation copy, 33
  filters, A.18–A.19
  functions of features, A.70–A.71
  Gantt charts, 240, A.38–A.40
  human resource management, 370, A.62–A.69
  main screen elements, A.7–A.13
  network diagrams, A.40–A.42
  new features, A.3–A.4
  Project Guide feature, A.6–A.7
  reports, A.70–A.71
  resource calendars, A.62–A.64
  resource histograms, 360, A.64–A.67
  resource leveling, 361, A.67–A.69
  saving files, A.25–A.26
  scope management, A.19–A.26
  starting, A.5
  task dependencies, 220, A.32–A.40
  template files, A.11–A.14
  templates, A.71–A.76
  time management, 240, A.26–A.44
  views, A.14–A.18
  WBSs, 192, A.13, A.22–A.25
Microsoft Solution Framework, 441
Microsoft Word, 32, 102

milestones, 33, 215, 225–226
list, 213–217
milestone reports, 107–110
MindManager, 135
mind mapping, 134, 134–135
sample, 135, 194
WBD development, 193–194
Minuteman, 33
mirroring, 351
Mittal Steel Poland, 239
monitoring and controlling processes, 79, 82
monitoring and controlling projects, 111–114
communications management, 398–399
cost management, 272–279
human resource management, 368–370
integration management, 159–164
procurement management, 479–480
quality management, 299–315
risk management, 450
scope management, 196–202
summary of outputs, 111–112
time management, 237–239
Monte Carlo analysis, 444, 444–445, 450
sample, 445
MOS. *See* Microsoft Office Specialist (MOS) certification
motivation, 344–352
acquired-needs theory, 346–347
influences bases, 348
intrinsic versus extrinsic, 344
Maslow's hierarchy of needs, 344
motivation-hygiene theory, 345–346
Theory X and Theory Y, 347
Motorola, 309
Mueller, Robert, 217
multitasking, 234, 234–235
Murphy's Law, 235
Myers, Isabel B., 364
Myers-Briggs Type Indicator (MBTI), 364, 364–366

N

NASP. *See* U.S. National Aerospace Plane (NASP) project, 446
needs
achievement, 346–347
affiliation, 346–347
Maslow's hierarchy, 344
McClelland's acquired-needs theory, 346–347
McGregor's Theory X and Theory Y, 347
power, 346–349
Nelsestuen, Rodney, 425
net present value analysis, 139, 139–142
network diagrams, 27–28, 218, 218–220
Microsoft Project 2007, A.40–A.42
sample, 28
Network Diagram view, Microsoft Project 2007, A15, A16, A.40–A.42
Neuman, Robert, 307, 309, 312
New Line Cinema, 82
new product development (NPD), 137
NHS. *See* U. K. National Health Service.
nodes, in AOA diagrams, 218
Northrop Grumman, 197
Northwest Airlines, 263
Norton, David, 146
notes, inserting with Microsoft Project 2007, A.74–A.75
NPD. *See* new product development (NPD)
NPV. *See* net present value analysis

O

Obama, Barack, 271–272
Obermiller, Elizabeth, 56
OBS. *See* organizational breakdown structure (OBS)
Olympic Games, 160, 213
"One More Time: How Do You Motivate Employees?" (Herzberg), 346
OPM3. *See* Organizational Project Management Maturity Model (OPM3)
Oppenheimer, Robert, 27
opportunities, 139
opportunity cost of capital, 141
oral communication, 390–392, 394–396
organizations
four frames of, 467, 52–53
standards, 56–57
structures, 49–51
organizational breakdown structure (OBS), 354

organizational charts, 49, 152, 352–357
sample, 353
organizational culture, 51–52, 157
organizational needs, project selection based on, 138–139
Organizational Project Management Maturity Model (OPM3), 19, 324–325
organizational standards, 56–57
Ouchi, William, 347–348
outsourcing, 66–68, 462–465
overallocation of resources, 360
overrun, 254, 254–256

P

Pande, Peter, 307, 309, 312
parametric modeling, 264
Pareto charts, 305, 305–306
sample, 305
Parkinson's Law, 235
payback analysis, 143–144
payback period, 143, 143–144
PDM. *See* precedence diagramming method (PDM)
Pell, Philip, 80–81
people skills. *See* soft skills
performance assessment, 368–369
performance reporting, 398–399
PERT. *See* Program Evaluation and Review Technique (PERT)
Petroske, John, 405
PgMP. *See* Program Management Professional (PgMP) certification
phase exits. *See* management reviews
phases, 57–58, 61–62
planned value (PV), 273
planning. *See also* project planning
for project selection, 135
strategic, 133–134
summary of tasks and outputs, 79, 81
planning processes, 79, 81, 96–106
PMBOK Guide, 83–84, 85, 148, 425
mapping process groups to knowledge areas, 83–84
PMOs. *See* project management offices
PMP Certification. *See* Project Management Professional (PMP) certification
point of total assumption (PTA), 470
portfolio management, 18, 18–21, 278–278
categories, 19–20
contrasted with project management, 18
power, as factor in motivation, 346–349
precedence diagramming method (PDM), 219, 219–220
predictive life cycle, 60
Pricewaterhouse Coopers, 4
Primavera, 160
PRINCE2. *See* PRojects IN Controlled Environments
Prior, Derek, 239
priority, project selection based on, 138–139
probabilistic time estimates, 236
probability/impact matrices, 438–439
sample, 439
problems, 138, 138–139
processes, 79, 79–82
procurement documents, 475–477
procurement management, 12, 13, 462–483
best practices, 480
contract administration, 479–481
contracts, 469–473
mapping process groups to, 84
procurement documents, 475–477
requesting seller lists, 465
source selection, 478–479
procurement management plans, 473–477
checklist, 473
procurement management planning, 466–477
contracts, 469–473
make-or-buy analyses, 468–469
plans, 473–477
requests for proposal or quote, 475–476
statements of work, 474–475
supplier evaluation, 478–479
product life cycles, 59–61
programs, 17
Program Evaluation and Review Technique (PERT), 236, 236–237
program managers, 17, 17–18
Program Management Professional (PgMP) certification, B.2, B.18
progress reports, 14, 398
sample, 113, 408
progressive elaboration, 7, 215–216

projects, 4, 4–10
attributes, 7–8
examples, 4–5
phases, 57–62
Project 2007. *See* Microsoft Project 2007
project buffers, 235
Project+ certification
exam, B.15
requirements for earning and maintaining, B.14
sample exam questions, B.16–B.17
project charters, 94, 147, 147–150
checklist, 148–149
PMBOK Guide information, 148
sample, 149–150, 183
project communications management. *See* communications management
project cost management. *See* cost management
project files, creating with Microsoft Project 2007, A.71–A.73
project human resource management. *See* human resource management
Project Information dialog box, Microsoft Project 2007, A.20–A.21, A.63
project integration management, 12, 13, 130, 130–133
best practices, 137
change requests, 162–163
deliverables, 130
integrated change control, 161–164
mapping process groups to, 83
monitoring and controlling project work, 159–161
software, 165–166
Project Kickstart, 33
project management, 10, 10–14, 21–34
history of, 27–31
project portfolio management compared, 18
skills, 22–27
value, 2–4
Project Management Center (website), 32
Project Management Institute (PMI), 19, 23, 29–31
code of ethics, 31–32
Guide to the Project Management Body of Knowledge, 22–23
OPM3, 19
PMP certification, 30–31
Practice Standard for Work Breakdown Structure, Second Edition, 187, 188
website, 23, 30
project management knowledge areas, 12, 13, 83
project management offices, (PMOs), 29
project management plans, 151, 151–156
contents, 151–154
sample, 155
project management process groups, 79, 79–84
mapping to knowledge areas, 83–84
organizational standards, 85–85
methodology, 85–86
Project Management Professional (PMP) certification, 30, 30–32
exam structure and content, B.5–B.6
overview, B.1–B.2
preparing for exam, B.6–B.7
requirements for earning and maintaining, B.3–B.5
sample exam questions, B.10–B.13
tips for taking exam, B.7–B.10
useful formulas for exam, B.9–B.10 B.9–B.10
project management tools and techniques, 12–14
project organizational charts. *See* organizational charts
project organizational structure, 49, 50–51
project planning, 96–98
communications management, 261–272
cost management, 261–272
human resource management, 352–357
integration management, 151–156
procurement management, 466–477
purpose, 79
quality management, 296–298
risk management, 428–449
scope management, 181–196
summary of planning tasks and outputs, 81
time management, 214–237
project portfolios
creating, sample approach, 19–20

project portfolio management. *See* portfolio management
Project Properties dialog box, Microsoft Project 2007, A.21
project quality management. *See* quality management
project risk management. *See* risk management
project scope management. *See* scope management
project selection, 135–147
  balanced scorecard, 146–147
  financial projection methods, 139–144
  focusing on competitive strategy and broad organizational needs, 138
  four-stage planning process, 135
  problems, opportunities and directives method, 138–139
  project priority, 138–139
  weighted scoring model, 144–146
project selection methods, 138–147
project sponsors, 7–8
project teams
  acquisition, 357–359
  development, 362–368
  performance assessment, 369
  team management tools and techniques, 367–370
  team-building activities, 364
  training, 363–364
  virtual teams, 67–68
project time management. *See* time management
project web sites, 409–410
PRojects IN Controlled Environments (PRINCE2), 85
proposals, 475
proposal evaluation, 478
  sample, 478–479
PV. *See* planned value

Q

qualitative risk analysis, 438–447
quality, definition, 294
quality assurance, 295, 298, 299
quality audits, 299
quality control, 299–306
  acceptance decisions, 299–300
  measurement samples, 306–307
  process adjustments, 300
  rework, 300
  Seven Basic Tools of Quality, 300–306
Quality Is Free (Crosby), 316
quality management, 12, 13, 295–325
  best practices, 325
  improving project quality, 319–325
  mapping process groups to, 84
  metrics, 295
  quality checklists, 295
  quality-control measurement samples, 306–307
  quality planning and, 296–298
  scope aspects and, 297–298
  testing, 313–315
  zero defects, 316–317
quality management plans, 296–298
quality planning, 295, 296

R

RACI charts, 355
  sample, 356
RAD. *See* Rapid Application Development (RAD)
RAM. *See* responsibility assignment matrices (RAM)
Rapid Application Development (RAD), 60
rapport, 351
rate of performance (RP), 273
Rational Unified Process (RUP) framework, 85, 199
recognition systems, 368
recurring tasks, Microsoft Project 2007, A.28
recruiting teams. *See* project teams, acquisition
Reinke, Josh, 56
reports, Microsoft Project 2007, A.18, A.70–A.71
request for proposal (RFP), 475, 475–476
  sample, 476
request for quote (RFQ), 475
required rate of return, 142, 142–143

requirements, 179–192, 200–202
requirements traceability matrix, 182
 sample, 183
reserves, 260
 contingency, 260
 management, 260
resources(s), assigning to tasks with Microsoft Project 2007, A.48–A.53
resource calendars, Microsoft Project 2007, A.62–A.64
resource cost(s), adjusting in Microsoft Project 2007, A.47
Resource Cost view, in Microsoft Project 2007, A.49–A.51
resource histograms, 357
 Microsoft Project 2007, A.64–A.67
 sample, 357, 360
resource lending, 360
resource leveling, 361, 361–362
 Microsoft Project 2007, A.67–A.69
responsibility assignment matrices (RAM), 152, 354, 355
 sample, 355
return on investment (ROI), 142, 142–143
reward systems, 368
RFP. *See* request for proposal
RFQ. *See* request for quote
Richard, Luc, 226
risk, 425, 425–428, 430–447
risk breakdown structure, 432, 432–434
 sample, 433
risk events, 436
risk management, 12, 13, 422–450
 mapping process groups to, 84
risk management planning, 428–450
 analyzing risk, 438–447
 best practices, 426
 contracts, 449
 identifying risk, 434–438
 probability/impact matrices, 438–439
 risk responses, 447–449
risk management plans, 428, 428–430
risk registers, 436, 436–438
 sample, 437
risk register update samples, 442
risk tolerance, 426
ROI. *See* return on investment (ROI)
rolling wave planning. *See* progressive elaboration
Ross, Jeanne, 55
RP. *See* rate of performance (RP)
runaway projects, 432
run chart, 302, 302–303
 sample, 303
RUP. *See* Rational Unified Process (RUP) framework

S

Salt Lake Organizing Committee, 160
Sanderson, Peter, 471
Sarbanes-Oxley, 63
saving files, Microsoft Project 2007, A.4, A.25–A.26
scatter diagrams, 303
 sample, 303
schedule control, 237–239
schedule development, 223–237
schedule performance index (SPI), 275
Schedule Table view, Microsoft Project 2007, A.17, A.42–A.43, A.70
schedule variance (SV), 275
scheduling, 213–214
 critical chain, 233–236
Schlumberger, 278
scope, 8, 12, 13
 defining, 183
scope baseline, 196
scope control, 198–199
scope creep, 197
scope management, 12, 13, 178–204
 best practices, 199
 mapping process groups to, 83
 Microsoft Project 2007, A.19–A.26
scope management planning 179–196
 scope definition, 183–186
 work breakdown structure. *See* work breakdown structures (WBS)
scope statements, 202, 183–186
 contents, 101
 sample sections, 101–103
scope verification, 196–198, 198
SDLC. *See* systems development life cycle (SDLC)

sellers, selecting, 477–479
Sensation/Intuition (S/N) psychological type, 364–365
sensitivity analysis, 446–447
  sample, 447
Set Baseline dialog box, Microsoft Project 2007, A.54–A.55
7 Habits of Highly Effective People, The (Covey), 350–351
SharePoint portal, 404
simulation. *See* Monte Carlo analysis
Six Sigma, 86, 307–312, 364
slack, 228, 230
slipped milestones, 227, 227–228
SMART criteria, 226
smoothing mode, 400
Sobey's, 48
Social Styles Profile, 366–367
soft skills, 23–25, 382–383, 390, 400–401
software, 28–29, 32–34. *See also* specific software packages
  business service management (BSM) tools, 165–166
  communications management, 410–412
  cost management, 279–280
  human resource management, 370–371
  procurement management, 481–482
  project integration management, 165–166
  quality management, 326
  risk management, 450–451
  scope management, 202–203
  time management, 240–241
Software Quality Function Deployment model (SQFD), 323
Sorel, Tom, 471
SOWs. *See* statements of work (SOWs)
SPI. *See* schedule performance index (SPI)
split window, assigning resources in Microsoft Project 2007, A.49–A.51
staffing management plans, 356, 356–358
stakeholders, 10, 10–12
  analysis, 385–388
  identifying and understanding, 92–93
  managing, 23–25, 52–53, 93, 368–370, 385–386, 396–398
  register, 385
  sample communication analysis, 387
  sample management strategy, 386
standards, 85
Standish Group, 3–4, 14, 62, 254, 430–432
statements of work (SOWs), 474, 474–475
status reports, 398
Stewart, Branndon, 279
strategic planning, 133, 133–135
Students of Project Management Specific Interest Group (SIG) web site, 30
success, 3, 14–17
summary tasks, Microsoft Project 2007, A.24–A.26
suppliers
  qualified sellers list, 478–479
  requesting responses, 475
SV. *See* schedule variance (SV)
SWOT analysis, 134, 435
synergy, 350, 350–351
systems, 45
systems development life cycle (SDLC), 60, 60–61
systems management, 45, 45–46

T

Taguchi, Genichi, 317–318
task(s)
  assigning resources in Microsoft Project 2007, A.48–A.53
  numbering using Microsoft Project 2007, A.25
task dependencies, Microsoft Project 2007, A.32–A.37
Task Details Form view, Microsoft Project 2007, A.15
task durations
  entering in Microsoft Project 2007, A.27–A.31
Task Name Form view, Microsoft Project 2007, A.15
TAT. *See* Thematic Apperception Test (TAT)
teams. *See* project teams
team contracts, 99
  sample, 100
templates, 118–121, 406–410

testing and quality control, 313–315
Text Styles dialog box, Microsoft Project 2007, A.39
Thamhain, H. J., 348. *See also* influence bases
Thematic Apperception Test (TAT), 347
Theory of Constraints (TOC), 233, 236
Theory X, 347
Theory Y, 347
Theory Z, 347–348
Thinking/Feeling (T/F) psychological type, 365
three-point estimates, 223, 236
time-and-material contracts, 472
time management, 12, 13, 213–242
  mapping process groups to, 83–84
  Microsoft Project 2007, A.26–A.44
time management plans
  activity definition, 214–217
  activity duration estimation, 222–223
  activity list and attributes, 215
  activity resource estimation, 221–222
  activity sequencing, 217–220
  best practices, 226
  critical chain scheduling, 233–236
  critical path analysis, 228–233
  milestone list, 225–226
  network diagrams, 218–220, 228
  schedule development, 223–237
TOC. *See* Theory of Constraints (TOC)
toolbar, assigning resources in Microsoft Project 2007, A.48–A.49
top-down approach to WBD development, 192–193
top-down estimates, 263
Top Ten Risk Item Tracking, 441–442
Total Quality Management (TQM), 308, 323
TRAC, 66
tracking Gantt charts, 226–228
  Microsoft Project 2007, 27, 224–225, 240
Tracking Table view, Microsoft Project 2007, A.55–A.57
Tracking toolbar, Microsoft Project 2007, A.8, A.55–A.57
training project teams, 363–364
triggers, 437
Trilogy project, 216
triple constraint, 8, 8–10
Tuckman model, 363

U

U.K. National Health Service, 255
U.S. Air Force, 294, 467
U.S. Defense Finance and Accounting Services (DFAS), 146–147
U.S. Department of Defense (DOD), 191
U.S. National Aerospace Plane (NASP) project, 446
uncertainty, 8, 9
unit pricing, 472
unknown unknowns, 260
Update Tasks dialog box, Microsoft Project 2007, A.57
updating critical path data, 233
user input, 200

V

VCS web site, 32
Venue Integrated Planning Schedule, 160
Visual Reports dialog box, Microsoft Project 2007, A.60
VoIP, 6
VPMi Express, 32, 33

W

Wal-Mart, 463
Walt Disney Imagineering, 229
Walton, Jane, 278
WBS. *See* work breakdown structures
WBS dictionary, 194, 194–196
WebEx, 66
web sites
  communications management planning, 389–396
weighted scoring model, 144, 144–146
  sample, 144
Weill, Peter, 55

wikis, 404, 404–406
Wilemon, D. L., 348. *See also* influence bases
Williams, David J., 216
Wilson Learning Social Styles Profile, 364, 366
withdrawal mode, 400
Work and the Nature of Man (Herzberg), 346
work breakdown structures (WBS), 57, 8, 104, 153, 186–196, 202, 353–354, 388, 432
  developing, 191–196
  sample, 105, 188–189
  WBS dictionary, 194–196
work packages, 153, 188, 188–189
workarounds, 450
World Trade Center, 53–54
Wyatt, Kerryann, 402

X

XPlanner, 65

Z

zero defects, 316–317